TAKE A PEAK—
AND SEE HOW MUCH FUN IT CAN BE TO EXPLORE
AND EXPERIENCE PSYCHOLOGICAL PHENOMENA

Complete integration with this text
As you read this text, icons throughout every chapter direct you to specific topics on **PsykTrek** that reinforce and clarify what you have just read. Each icon is listed with the appropriate **PsykTrek** module number, so you reach the online activities in a snap.

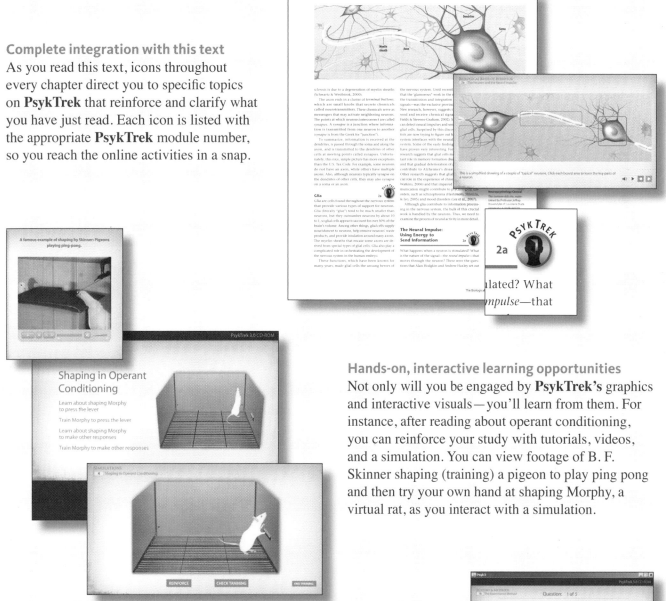

Hands-on, interactive learning opportunities
Not only will you be engaged by **PsykTrek's** graphics and interactive visuals—you'll learn from them. For instance, after reading about operant conditioning, you can reinforce your study with tutorials, videos, and a simulation. You can view footage of B. F. Skinner shaping (training) a pigeon to play ping pong and then try your own hand at shaping Morphy, a virtual rat, as you interact with a simulation.

Exercises to help you gear up for tests
Concept Checks, quizzes, and multiple-choice tests in every module reinforce learning, and provide immediate feedback. By taking them, and taking another look at material you didn't quite "get," you'll be better prepared for your in-class exams.

PSYCHOLOGY
Themes and Variations

8TH Edition

Wayne Weiten
University of Nevada, Las Vegas

WADSWORTH
CENGAGE Learning™

Australia • Brazil • Japan • Korea • Mexico • Singapore • Spain • United Kingdom • United States

Psychology: Themes and Variations, Eighth Edition
Wayne Weiten

Senior Publisher: Linda Schreiber

Executive Editor, Psychology: Jon-David Hague

Senior Development Editor: Kristin Makarewycz

Assistant Editor: Trina Tom

Technology Project Manager: Lauren Keyes

Marketing Managers: Liz Rhoden, Kim Russell

Marketing Assistant: Molly Felz

Marketing Communications Manager: Talia Wise

Project Manager, Editorial Production: Jennie Redwitz

Creative Director: Rob Hugel

Art Director: Vernon Boes

Print Buyer: Judy Inouye

Permissions Editors: Bob Kauser, Linda L Rill

Production Service: Tom Dorsaneo

Text Designer: Tani Hasegawa

Photo Researcher: Linda L Rill

Copy Editor: Jackie Estrada

Illustrator: Carol Zuber-Mallison and Thompson Type

Cover Designer: Irene Morris

Cover Image: Silhouettes of people walking across the iconic U Bein bridge over the Ayerwaddy River in Amarapura, Myanmar. © Blaine Harrington III/Alamy.

Compositor: Thompson Type

For product information and technology assistance, contact us at
Cengage Learning Customer & Sales Support, 1-800-354-9706.

For permission to use material from this text or product, submit all requests online at **www.cengage.com/permissions.**
Further permissions questions can be e-mailed to **permissionrequest@cengage.com.**

Library of Congress Control Number: 2008925748
Student Edition:
ISBN-13: 978-0-495-60197-5
ISBN-10: 0-495-60197-7

Loose-leaf Edition:
ISBN-13: 978-0-495-60413-6
ISBN-10: 0-495-60413-5

Wadsworth
10 Davis Drive
Belmont, CA 94002-3098
USA

Cengage Learning is a leading provider of customized learning solutions with office locations around the globe, including Singapore, the United Kingdom, Australia, Mexico, Brazil, and Japan. Locate your local office at **www.cengage.com/international.**

Cengage Learning products are represented in Canada by Nelson Education, Ltd.

To learn more about Wadsworth, visit **www.cengage.com/wadsworth**
Purchase any of our products at your local college store or at our preferred online store **www.ichapters.com.**

Printed in Canada
1 2 3 4 5 6 7 12 11 10 09 08

Beth, this one is for you

ABOUT THE AUTHOR

Wayne Weiten is a graduate of Bradley University and received his Ph.D. in social psychology from the University of Illinois, Chicago, in 1981. He currently teaches at the University of Nevada, Las Vegas. He has received distinguished teaching awards from Division Two of the American Psychological Association (APA) and from the College of DuPage, where he taught until 1991. He is a Fellow of Divisions 1 and 2 of the American Psychological Association. In 1991, he helped chair the APA National Conference on Enhancing the Quality of Undergraduate Education in Psychology and in 1996–1997 he served as President of the Society for the Teaching of Psychology. Weiten has conducted research on a wide range of topics, including educational measurement, jury decision making, attribution theory, stress, and cerebral specialization. His recent interests have included pressure as a form of stress and the technology of textbooks. He is also the co-author of *Psychology Applied to Modern Life* (Wadsworth, 2006) and the creator of an educational CD-ROM titled *PsykTrek: A Multimedia Introduction to Psychology.*

TO THE INSTRUCTOR

If I had to sum up in a single sentence what I hope will distinguish this text, that sentence would be this: I have set out to create a *paradox* instead of a *compromise*.

Let me elaborate. An introductory psychology text must satisfy two disparate audiences: professors and students. Because of the tension between the divergent needs and preferences of these audiences, textbook authors usually indicate that they have attempted to strike a compromise between being theoretical versus practical, comprehensive versus comprehensible, research oriented versus applied, rigorous versus accessible, and so forth. However, I believe that many of these dichotomies are false. As Kurt Lewin once remarked, "What could be more practical than a good theory?" Similarly, is rigorous really the opposite of accessible? Not in my dictionary. I maintain that many of the antagonistic goals that we strive for in our textbooks only *seem* incompatible and that we may not need to make compromises as often as we assume.

In my estimation, a good introductory textbook is a paradox in that it integrates characteristics and goals that appear contradictory. With this in mind, I have endeavored to write a text that is paradoxical in three ways. First, in surveying psychology's broad range of content, I have tried to show that its interests are characterized by both diversity *and* unity. Second, I have emphasized both research *and* application and how they work in harmony. Finally, I have aspired to write a book that is challenging to think about *and* easy to learn from. Let's take a closer look at these goals.

Goals

1. *To show both the unity and the diversity of psychology's subject matter.* Students entering an introductory psychology course are often unaware of the immense diversity of subjects studied by psychologists. I find this diversity to be part of psychology's charm, and throughout the book I highlight the enormous range of questions and issues addressed by psychology. Of course, psychology's diversity proves disconcerting for some students who see little continuity between such disparate areas of research as physiology, motivation, cognition, and abnormal behavior. Indeed, in this era of specialization, even some psychologists express concern about the fragmentation of the field.

However, I believe that the subfields of psychology overlap considerably and that we should emphasize their common core by accenting their connections and similarities. Consequently, I portray psychology as an integrated whole rather than as a mosaic of loosely related parts. A principal goal of this text, then, is to highlight the unity in psychology's intellectual heritage (the themes), as well as the diversity of psychology's interests and uses (the variations).

2. *To illuminate the process of research and its intimate link to application.* For me, a research-oriented book is not one that bulges with summaries of many studies but one that enhances students' appreciation of the logic and excitement of empirical inquiry. I want students to appreciate the strengths of the empirical approach and to see scientific psychology as a creative effort to solve intriguing behavioral puzzles. For this reason, the text emphasizes not only *what* psychologists know (and don't know) but *how* they attempt to find out. The book examines methods in some detail and encourages students to adopt the skeptical attitude of a scientist and to think critically about claims regarding behavior.

Learning the virtues of research should not mean that students cannot also satisfy their desire for concrete, personally useful information about the challenges of everyday life. Most researchers believe that psychology has a great deal to offer those outside the field and that we should share the practical implications of our work. In this text, practical insights are carefully qualified and closely tied to data, so that students can see the interdependence of research and application. I find that students come to appreciate the science of psychology more when they see that worthwhile practical applications are derived from careful research and sound theory.

3. *To make the text challenging to think about and easy to learn from.* Perhaps most of all, I have sought to create a *book of ideas* rather than a compendium of studies. I consistently emphasize concepts and theories over facts, and I focus on major issues and tough questions that cut across the subfields of psychology (for example, the extent to which behavior is governed by nature, nurture, and their interaction), as opposed to parochial debates (such as the merits of averaging versus adding in impression formation). Challenging students to think also means urging them to confront the complexity and ambiguity of psychological knowledge. Hence, the text doesn't

skirt around gray areas, unresolved questions, and theoretical controversies. Instead, it encourages readers to contemplate open-ended questions, to examine their assumptions about behavior, and to apply psychological concepts to their own lives. My goal is not simply to describe psychology but to stimulate students' intellectual growth.

However, students can grapple with "the big issues and tough questions" only if they first master the basic concepts and principles of psychology—ideally, with as little struggle as possible. I never let myself forget that a textbook is a teaching tool. Accordingly, great care has been taken to ensure that the book's content, organization, writing, illustrations, and pedagogical aids work in harmony to facilitate instruction and learning.

Admittedly, these goals are ambitious. If you're skeptical, you have every right to be. Let me explain how I have tried to realize the objectives I have outlined.

Special Features

A variety of unusual features each contributes in its own way to the book's paradoxical nature. These special elements include unifying themes, Featured Studies, Personal Application sections, Critical Thinking Application sections, a didactic illustration program, Web Links and other Internet-related features, an integrated running glossary, Concept Checks, Key Learning Goals, interim Reviews of Key Learning Goals, and Practice Tests.

Unifying Themes
Chapter 1 introduces seven key ideas that serve as unifying themes throughout the text. The themes serve several purposes. First, they provide threads of continuity across chapters that help students see the connections among various areas of research in psychology. Second, as the themes evolve over the course of the book, they provide a forum for a relatively sophisticated discussion of enduring issues in psychology, thus helping to make this a "book of ideas." Third, the themes focus a spotlight on a number of basic insights about psychology and its subject matter that should leave lasting impressions on your students. In selecting the themes, the question I asked myself (and other professors) was "What do I really want students to remember five years from now?" The resulting themes are grouped into two sets.

THEMES RELATED TO PSYCHOLOGY AS A FIELD OF STUDY
Theme 1: Psychology is empirical. This theme is used to enhance the student's appreciation of psychology's scientific nature and to demonstrate the advantages of empiricism over uncritical common sense and speculation. I also use this theme to encourage the reader to adopt a scientist's skeptical attitude and to engage in more critical thinking about information of all kinds.

Theme 2: Psychology is theoretically diverse. Students are often confused by psychology's theoretical pluralism and view it as a weakness. I don't downplay or apologize for the field's theoretical diversity, because I honestly believe that it is one of psychology's greatest strengths. Throughout the book, I provide concrete examples of how clashing theories have stimulated productive research, how converging on a question from several perspectives can yield increased understanding, and how competing theories are sometimes reconciled in the end.

Theme 3: Psychology evolves in a sociohistorical context. This theme emphasizes that psychology is embedded in the ebb and flow of everyday life. The text shows how the spirit of the times has often shaped psychology's evolution and how progress in psychology leaves its mark on our society.

THEMES RELATED TO PSYCHOLOGY'S SUBJECT MATTER
Theme 4: Behavior is determined by multiple causes. Throughout the book, I emphasize, and repeatedly illustrate, that behavioral processes are complex and that multifactorial causation is the rule. This theme is used to discourage simplistic, single-cause thinking and to encourage more critical reasoning.

Theme 5: Behavior is shaped by cultural heritage. This theme is intended to enhance students' appreciation of how cultural factors moderate psychological processes and how the viewpoint of one's own culture can distort one's interpretation of the behavior of people from other cultures. The discussions that elaborate on this theme do not simply celebrate diversity. They strike a careful balance—that accurately reflects the research in this area—highlighting both cultural variations *and* similarities in behavior.

Theme 6: Heredity and environment jointly influence behavior. Repeatedly discussing this theme permits me to air out the nature versus nurture issue in all its complexity. Over a series of chapters, students gradually learn how biology shapes behavior, how experience shapes behavior, and how scientists estimate the relative importance of each. Along the way, students will gain an in-depth appreciation of what we mean when we say that heredity and environment interact.

Theme 7: People's experience of the world is highly subjective.

All of us tend to forget the extent to which people view the world through their own personal lenses. This theme is used to explain the principles that underlie the subjectivity of human experience, to clarify its implications, and to repeatedly remind the readers that their view of the world is not the only legitimate one.

After introducing all seven themes in Chapter 1, I discuss different sets of themes in each chapter, as they are relevant to the subject matter. The connections between a chapter's content and the unifying themes are highlighted in a standard section near the end of the chapter, in which I reflect on the "lessons to be learned" from the chapter. The discussions of the unifying themes are largely confined to these sections, titled "Reflecting on the Chapter's Themes." I have not tried to make every chapter illustrate a certain number of themes. Rather, the themes were allowed to emerge naturally, and I found that two to five surfaced in any given chapter. The chart below shows which themes are highlighted in each chapter. Color-coded icons near the beginning of each "Reflecting on the Chapter's Themes" section indicate the specific themes featured in each chapter.

Unifying Themes Highlighted in Each Chapter

Chapter	THEME						
	1 Empiricism	2 Theoretical Diversity	3 Sociohistorical Context	4 Multifactorial Causation	5 Cultural Heritage	6 Heredity and Environment	7 Subjectivity of Experience
1. The Evolution of Psychology	●	●	●	●	●	●	●
2. The Research Enterprise in Psychology	●						●
3. The Biological Bases of Behavior	●			●		●	
4. Sensation and Perception		●			●		●
5. Variations in Consciousness		●	●	●	●		●
6. Learning			●			●	
7. Human Memory		●		●			●
8. Language and Thought	●				●	●	●
9. Intelligence and Psychological Testing			●		●	●	
10. Motivation and Emotion		●	●	●	●	●	
11. Human Development Across the Life Span		●	●	●	●	●	
12. Personality: Theory, Research, and Assessment		●	●		●		
13. Stress, Coping, and Health				●			●
14. Psychological Disorders			●	●	●	●	
15. Treatment of Psychological Disorders		●			●		
16. Social Behavior	●				●		●

Featured Studies

Each chapter except the first includes a Featured Study that provides a relatively detailed but succinct summary of a particular piece of research. Each Featured Study is presented in the conventional purpose-method-results-discussion format seen in journal articles, followed by a comment in which I discuss why the study is featured (to illustrate a specific method, raise ethical issues, and so forth). By showing research methods in action, I hope to improve students' understanding of how research is done while also giving them a painless introduction to the basic format of journal articles. Additionally, the Featured Studies show how complicated research can be, so students can better appreciate why scientists may disagree about the meaning of a study. The Featured Studies are fully incorporated into the flow of discourse in the text and are *not* presented as optional boxes.

In selecting the Featured Studies, I assembled a mixture of classic and recent studies that illustrate a wide variety of methods. To make them enticing, I tilted my selections in favor of those that students find interesting. Thus, readers will encounter explorations of the effects of sleep deprivation, the neuroanatomy of sexual arousal, and Milgram's legendary study of obedience.

Personal Applications

To reinforce the pragmatic implications of theory and research stressed throughout the text, each chapter closes with a Personal Application section that highlights the practical side of psychology. Each Personal Application devotes two to five *pages* of text (rather than the usual box) to a single issue that should be of special interest to many of your students. Although most of the Personal Application sections have a "how to" character, they continue to review studies and summarize data in much the same way as the main body of each chapter. Thus, they portray research and application not as incompatible polarities but as two sides of the same coin. Many of the Personal Applications—such as those on finding and reading journal articles, understanding art and illusion, and improving stress management—provide topical coverage unusual for an introductory text.

Critical Thinking Applications

A great deal of unusual coverage can also be found in the Critical Thinking Applications that follow the Personal Applications. Conceived by Diane Halpern (Claremont McKenna College), a leading authority on critical thinking, these applications are based on the assumption that critical thinking skills can be taught. They do not simply review research critically, as is typically the case in other introductory texts.

Instead, they introduce and model a host of critical thinking *skills*, such as looking for contradictory evidence or alternative explanations; recognizing anecdotal evidence, circular reasoning, hindsight bias, reification, weak analogies, and false dichotomies; evaluating arguments systematically; and working with cumulative and conjunctive probabilities.

The specific skills discussed in the Critical Thinking Applications are listed in the accompanying table on page ix, where they are organized into five categories using a taxonomy developed by Halpern (1994). In each chapter, some of these skills are applied to topics and issues related to the chapter's content. For instance, in the chapter that covers drug abuse (Chapter 5), the concept of alcoholism is used to highlight the immense power of definitions and to illustrate how circular reasoning can seem so seductive. Skills that are particularly important may surface in more than one chapter, so students see them applied in a variety of contexts. For example, in Chapter 7 students learn how hindsight bias can contaminate memory, while in Chapter 12 they see how hindsight can distort analyses of personality. Repeated practice across chapters should help students spontaneously recognize the relevance of specific critical thinking skills when they encounter certain types of information.

A Didactic Illustration Program

When I first outlined my plans for this text, I indicated that I wanted every aspect of the illustration program to have a genuine didactic purpose and that I wanted to be deeply involved in its development. In retrospect, I had no idea what I was getting myself into, but it has been a rewarding learning experience. In any event, I have been intimately involved in planning every detail of the illustration program. I have endeavored to create a program of figures, diagrams, photos, and tables that work hand in hand with the prose to strengthen and clarify the main points in the text.

The most obvious results of this didactic approach to illustration are the eight Illustrated Overviews that combine tabular information, photos, diagrams, and sketches to provide well-organized reviews of key ideas in the areas of history, research methods, sensation and perception, learning, development, personality theory, psychopathology, and psychotherapy. But I hope you will also notice the subtleties of the illustration program. For instance, diagrams of important concepts (conditioning, synaptic transmission, experimental design, and so forth) are often repeated in several chapters (with variations) to highlight connections among research areas and to enhance students' mastery of key ideas. Numerous easy-

Taxonomy of Skills Covered in the Critical Thinking Applications

Verbal Reasoning Skills

Understanding the way definitions shape how people think about issues	Chapter 5
Identifying the source of definitions	Chapter 5
Avoiding the nominal fallacy in working with definitions and labels	Chapter 5
Understanding the way language can influence thought	Chapter 8
Recognizing semantic slanting	Chapter 8
Recognizing name calling and anticipatory name calling	Chapter 8
Recognizing and avoiding reification	Chapter 9

Argument/Persuasion Analysis Skills

Understanding the elements of an argument	Chapter 10
Recognizing and avoiding common fallacies, such as irrelevant reasons, circular reasoning, slippery slope reasoning, weak analogies, and false dichotomies	Chapters 10 and 11
Evaluating arguments systematically	Chapter 10
Recognizing and avoiding appeals to ignorance	Chapter 9
Understanding how Pavlovian conditioning can be used to manipulate emotions	Chapter 6
Developing the ability to detect conditioning procedures used in the media	Chapter 6
Recognizing social influence strategies	Chapter 16
Judging the credibility of an information source	Chapter 16

Skills in Thinking as Hypothesis Testing

Looking for alternative explanations for findings and events	Chapters 1, 9, and 11
Looking for contradictory evidence	Chapters 1, 3, and 9
Recognizing the limitations of anecdotal evidence	Chapters 2 and 15
Understanding the need to seek disconfirming evidence	Chapter 7
Understanding the limitations of correlational evidence	Chapters 11 and 13
Understanding the limitations of statistical significance	Chapter 13
Recognizing situations in which placebo effects might occur	Chapter 15

Skills in Working with Likelihood and Uncertainty

Utilizing base rates in making predictions and evaluating probabilities	Chapter 13
Understanding cumulative probabilities	Chapter 14
Understanding conjunctive probabilities	Chapter 14
Understanding the limitations of the representativeness heuristic	Chapter 14
Understanding the limitations of the availability heuristic	Chapter 14
Recognizing situations in which regression toward the mean may occur	Chapter 15
Understanding the limits of extrapolation	Chapter 3

Decision-Making and Problem-Solving Skills

Using evidence-based decision making	Chapter 2
Recognizing the bias in hindsight analysis	Chapters 7 and 12
Seeking information to reduce uncertainty	Chapter 13
Making risk-benefit assessments	Chapter 13
Generating and evaluating alternative courses of action	Chapter 13
Recognizing overconfidence in human cognition	Chapter 7
Understanding the limitations and fallibility of human memory	Chapter 7
Understanding how contrast effects can influence judgments and decisions	Chapter 4
Recognizing when extreme comparitors are being used	Chapter 4

to-understand graphs of research results underscore psychology's foundation in research, and photos and diagrams often bolster each other (for example, see the treatment of classical conditioning in Chapter 6). Color is used carefully as an organizational device, and visual schematics are used to simplify hard-to-visualize concepts (for example, see the figure explaining reaction range for intelligence in Chapter 9). And we have strived to enhance the realism and pedagogical value of our drawings of the brain and other physiology. All of these efforts have gone toward the service of one master: the desire to make this an inviting book that is easy to learn from.

Internet-Related Features

The Internet is rapidly altering the landscape of modern life, and students clearly need help dealing with the information explosion in cyberspace. To assist them, this text has two features. First, I recruited web expert Vincent Hevern (Le Moyne College), formerly the Internet Editor for the Society for the Teaching of Psychology, to write an essay on how to critically evaluate websites and online resource materials. His highly informative essay is found in the back of the book in Appendix E. Given the highly variable quality and frequently questionable validity of much of the information on the web, I think this will be a valuable resource for students. Second, I also asked Professor Hevern to evaluate hundreds of psychology-related sites on the web and come up with some recommended sites that appear to provide reasonably accurate, balanced, and empirically sound information. Short descriptions of these recommended websites (called Web Links) are dispersed throughout the chapters, adjacent to related topical coverage. Because URLs change frequently, we have not placed the URLs for these Web Links in the book itself. Insofar as students are interested in visiting these sites, we recommend that they do so through the *Psychology: Themes & Variations* home page at the Wadsworth Cengage Learning website (www.cengage.com/psychology/weiten). Links to all the recommended sites are maintained there, and the webmaster periodically updates the URLs. Of course, students can also use a search engine, such as Google, to locate recommended websites that interest them.

Integrated Running Glossary

An introductory text should place great emphasis on acquainting students with psychology's technical language—not for the sake of jargon, but because a great many of the key terms are also cornerstone concepts (for example, *independent variable, reliability,* and *cognitive dissonance*). This text handles terminology with a running glossary embedded in the prose itself.

The terms are set off in *blue boldface italics,* and the definitions follow in **blue boldface roman** type. This approach retains the two advantages of a conventional running glossary: vocabulary items are made salient, and their definitions are readily accessible. However, the approach does so without interrupting the flow of discourse, while eliminating redundancy between text matter and marginal entries.

Concept Checks

To help students assess their mastery of important ideas, Concept Checks are sprinkled throughout the book (two to four per chapter). In keeping with my goal of making this a book of ideas, the Concept Checks challenge students to apply ideas instead of testing rote memory. For example, in Chapter 6 the reader is asked to analyze realistic examples of conditioning and identify conditioned stimuli and responses, reinforcers, and schedules of reinforcement. Many of the Concept Checks require the reader to put together ideas introduced in different sections of the chapter. For instance, in Chapter 2 students are asked to look for various types of deficiencies in hypothetical studies, and in Chapter 4 students are asked to identify parallels between vision and hearing. Some of the Concept Checks are quite challenging, but students find them engaging, and they report that the answers (available in Appendix A) are often illuminating.

Key Learning Goals and Reviews of Key Learning Goals

To help students organize, assimilate, and remember important ideas, each major section of every chapter begins with a succinct, numbered set of Key Learning Goals and ends with a detailed, numbered Review of Key Learning Goals. The Key Learning Goals are found adjacent to the level-one headings that begin each major section; the Reviews of Key Learning Goals are found at the end of each major section, just before the next level-one heading. The Key Learning Goals are thought-provoking learning objectives that should help students focus on the key issues in each section. Each Review of Key Learning Goals is an interim summary that addresses the issues posed in the preceding Learning Goals. Interspersing these reviews throughout the chapters permits students to check their understanding of each section's main ideas immediately after finishing the section instead of waiting until the end of the chapter. This approach also allows students to work with more modest-sized chunks of information.

Practice Tests

Each chapter ends with a 15-item multiple-choice Practice Test that should give students a realistic assessment of their mastery of that chapter and valuable practice in taking the type of test that many of them will face in the classroom (if the instructor uses the Test Bank). This feature grew out of some research that I conducted on students' use of textbook pedagogical devices (see Weiten, Guadagno, & Beck, 1996). This research indicated that students pay scant attention to some standard pedagogical devices. When I grilled my students to gain a better undertstanding of this finding, it quickly became apparent that students are very pragmatic about pedagogy. Essentially, their refrain was "We want study aids that will help us pass the next test." With this mandate in mind, I devised the Practice Tests. They should be very realistic, as I took most of the items from previous editions of the Test Bank (these items do not appear in the Test Bank for this edition).

In addition to the special features just described, the text includes a variety of more conventional, "tried and true" features. The back of the book contains a standard *alphabetical glossary*. Opening *outlines* preview each chapter, and a thorough *Recap of Key Ideas* appears at the end of each chapter, along with lists of *Key Terms* (with page numbers indicating where the terms were introduced) and *Key People* (important theorists and researchers). I make frequent use of *italics for emphasis,* and I depend on *frequent headings* to maximize organizational clarity. The preface for students describes these pedagogical devices in more detail.

Writing Style

I strive for a down-to-earth, conversational writing style; effective communication is always the paramount goal. My intent is to talk *with* the reader rather than throw information *at* the reader. To clarify concepts and maintain students' interest, I frequently provide concrete examples that students can relate to. As much as possible, I avoid using technical jargon when ordinary language serves just as well.

Making learning easier depends, above all else, on clear, well-organized writing. For this reason, I've worked hard to ensure that chapters, sections, and paragraphs are organized in a logical manner, so that key ideas stand out in sharp relief against supportive information.

Content

The text is divided into 16 chapters, which follow a traditional ordering. The chapters are not grouped into sections or parts, primarily because such groupings can limit your options if you want to reorganize the order of topics. The chapters are written in a way that facilitates organizational flexibility, as I always assumed that some chapters might be omitted or presented in a different order.

The topical coverage in the text is relatively conventional, but there are some subtle departures from the norm. For instance, Chapter 1 presents a relatively "meaty" discussion of the evolution of ideas in psychology. This coverage of history lays the foundation for many of the crucial ideas emphasized in subsequent chapters. The historical perspective is also my way of reaching out to the students who find that psychology isn't what they expected it to be. If we want students to contemplate the mysteries of behavior, we must begin by clearing up the biggest mysteries of them all: "Where did these rats, statistics, synapses, and JNDs come from, what could they possibly have in common, and why doesn't this course bear any resemblance to what I anticipated?" I use history as a vehicle to explain how psychology evolved into its modern form and why misconceptions about its nature are so common.

I also devote an entire chapter (Chapter 2) to the scientific enterprise—not just the mechanics of research methods but the logic behind them. I believe that an appreciation of the nature of empirical evidence can contribute greatly to improving students' critical thinking skills. Ten years from now, many of the "facts" reported in this book will have changed, but an understanding of the methods of science will remain invaluable. An introductory psychology course, by itself, isn't going to make a student think like a scientist, but I can't imagine a better place to start the process. Essential statistical concepts are introduced in Chapter 2, but no effort is made to teach actual calculations. For those who emphasize statistics, Appendix B expands on statistical concepts.

Overall, I trust you'll find the coverage up to date, although I do not believe in the common practice of piling up gratuitous references to recent studies to create an impression of currency. I think that an obsession with this year's references derogates our intellectual heritage and suggests to students that the studies we cite today will be written off tomorrow. I often chose to cite an older source over a newer one to give students an accurate feel for when an idea first surfaced or when an issue generated heated debate.

Changes in the Eighth Edition

A good textbook must evolve with the field of inquiry it covers. Although the professors and students who used the first seven editions of this book did not clamor for alterations, there are some changes. Perhaps the most noticeable is the replacement of the Preview Questions from previous editions with the numbered Key Learning Goals. The new learning goals are more precise and more thorough than the Preview Questions, which functioned more like "teasers" than learning objectives. Moreover, numbering both the Key Learning Goals and the material in the Review of Key Learning Goals makes it easier for students to see the relation between these companion features. The greater precision in this framework also led me to make the Reviews of Key Learning Goals longer and more detailed than their predecessors, which should prove helpful to students.

You will also find a variety of other changes in this edition, including two new Illustrated Overviews (in Chapters 2 and 4), and three new Featured Studies (in Chapters 5, 8, and 10). The graphic design of the text has been improved in a variety of ways. For instance, the beginning of each chapter features much more dramatic illustrations, and the level-one headings have been reworked in a refreshing way. We have also revised our thematic and *PsykTrek* icons and our treatment of theorist photos in the margins. And we have strived to make the photo program more engaging. One of the major changes in the back of the book is a new Appendix C, on industrial and organizational psychology, written by Kathy A. Hanisch of Iowa State University. Yet another change is the expansion of the appendix on careers in psychology (Appendix D). I have come to the conclusion that this is an overlooked topic that we should try to address in introductory courses. The expanded version of this appendix now provides brief profiles of the various areas in psychology. Students can read about nine major research areas in psychology, as well as six applied specialties. The other major changes for this edition involve two ancillaries that I will describe momentarily. We have released a completely revised version of *PsykTrek* and developed a new book that profiles a host of videos available on YouTube that can be used to facilitate teaching and discussion in class.

Of course, the book has been thoroughly updated to reflect recent advances in the field. One of the exciting things about psychology is that it is not a stagnant discipline. It continues to move forward at what seems a faster and faster pace. This progress has necessitated a number of specific content changes that you'll find sprinkled throughout the chapters. Of the more than 4600 references cited in the text, over 1300 are new to this edition.

Following is a partial list of specific changes to each chapter of the eighth edition.

Chapter 1: The Evolution of Psychology
- New introduction to the chapter focusing on the perplexing problem of pathological gambling

- Elaborated coverage of William James's ideas and contributions
- New data on rankings of the most important contributors to psychology
- Thoroughly revised and redesigned Illustrated Overview of psychology's history
- Revised coverage of areas of specialization in psychology featuring several areas not mentioned previously, including health psychology, clinical neuropsychology, and forensic psychology
- Expanded discussion of the concept of culture
- New discussion in the Personal Application of how effective text marking can enhance students' reading
- Additional advice on improving note taking in lectures

Chapter 2: The Research Enterprise in Psychology
- New introduction to the chapter focusing on more engaging empirical questions about behavior
- Greatly expanded coverage of the peer-review process for journal submissions
- Terms *between-subjects design* and *within-subjects design* added to the discussion of experimental method
- In coverage of naturalistic observation, new emphasis on its importance to studies of animal behavior and new discussion of reactivity
- New discussion of the recent decline in response rates to surveys
- New example of placebo effects in studies of the effects of alcohol
- New Illustrated Overview comparing major research methods in psychology
- Added section on how research is increasingly conducted via the Internet
- New discussion of the advantages of Internet-mediated research
- New discussion of the problems of sampling bias and poor experimental control in Internet-mediated research
- Elaboration on the nature of technical journals in the Personal Application on library research

Chapter 3: The Biological Bases of Behavior
- Expanded coverage of glial cells' functions and significance
- Added discussion of acetylcholine depletion in Alzheimer's disease
- New coverage of glutamate as neurotransmitter and its role in long-term potentiation
- Expanded and revised table summarizing various neurotransmitters' functions and characteristics
- Expanded discussion of the limitations of functional brain-imaging technologies

- New coverage of the discovery of mirror neurons and their possible significance
- More elaborated discussion of the plasticity of the brain
- Updated and expanded discussion of neurogenesis
- New discussion of fMRI research on hemispheric specialization
- Coverage of new research on how elevated stress hormones undermine immune response and neurogenesis in the hippocampus
- New coverage of variations in testosterone levels and individual differences in aggression
- New coverage of testosterone levels as related to cognitive functioning

Chapter 4: Sensation and Perception
- Coverage of new research on subliminal perception
- New discussion of recent research related to the concept of a "grandmother cell"
- New findings on how "face-detector" neurons can learn from experience
- Expanded discussion of inattentional blindness and its practical implications
- New discussion of how perception of forms can be influenced by motivational forces
- Added coverage of how judgments of distance can be skewed by people's goals and physical states
- New discussion of how supertasters and nontasters exhibit different consumption habits that affect their health
- Reporting of new research on the effects of subliminal odors on behavior
- Six new figures
- New Illustrated Overview comparing the five major senses

Chapter 5: Variations in Consciousness
- New data quantifying how often people's minds wander from the task at hand
- New discussion of the 17-year cycle in cicadas as an example of an extremely influential and unusual biological rhythm
- Coverage of new findings on individual differences in sleep architecture
- New Featured Study on the effects of sleep deprivation
- New discussion of sleep loss as related to physical health
- Reporting of new research suggesting a curvilinear relationship between typical sleep duration and mortality
- Revised coverage of the treatment of insomnia
- Expanded discussion of sleep apnea

- Expanded discussion of sleepwalking
- Revised discussion of hypnotic susceptibility
- New discussion of Kihlstrom's reconciliation of the role-playing and altered-state views of hypnosis
- New coverage of the OxyContin epidemic
- More detail on how marijuana affects neurotransmitter activity
- Coverage of new research linking cannabis use to vulnerability to psychotic disorders
- New emphasis on additional text theme (multifactorial causation)

Chapter 6: Learning
- Revised take on the degree to which a conditioned response tends to be similar to the unconditioned response it is based on
- New discussion of why fear conditioning is not automatic in the wake of traumatic conditioning experiences
- New coverage of compensatory conditioned responses that attempt to maintain homeostasis
- Added section on how classical conditioning can contribute to drug tolerance, drug addiction, and drug overdoses
- New discussion of the renewal effect and its contribution to the difficulty inherent in extinguishing conditioned fears
- New discussion questioning the value of the distinction between positive and negative reinforcement
- Reinstated section on preparedness and phobias
- New discussion of Öhman & Mineka's concept of an evolved module for fear learning
- Expanded discussion of the effects of violent video games and why they may be more problematic than violent movies or TV shows
- New data on the strength of the association between exposure to media violence and aggression

Chapter 7: Human Memory
- Discussion of proposed new resolution of the debate about early versus late selection in attention
- Expanded discussion of the costs of divided attention in relation to the controversy about cell phones and driving performance
- Expanded coverage of individual differences in working memory capacity
- Updated analysis of whether flashbulb memories are special
- Reporting of new research on how the goal-directed retelling of stories introduces errors into memory
- New discussion of how forgetting can be adaptive, including recent brain-imaging research on the issue

- Updated discussion of recovered memories that includes studies using doctored photos to create false memories
- New research on how neurogenesis may contribute to sculpting neural circuits that underlie memories
- Expanded coverage of prospective memory
- New research on the testing effect, the finding that testing on material enhances retention
- New data on the effects of spaced practice as a function of retention interval

Chapter 8: Language and Thought

- New discussion of why early research linking bilingualism to cognitive deficits was flawed
- Coverage of new research on whether chimps have a language-ready brain
- New analysis of the difficulties inherent in problems requiring insight
- New coverage of the hill-climbing heuristic in problem solving
- Recent research on the extent to which people depend on analogies in everyday problem solving efforts
- Added discussion of the theory that people in modern society are overwhelmed by decision overload
- New research on how judgments of the quality of products are swayed by prices
- New Featured Study on the benefits of intuition or "deliberation-without-awareness" in decision making
- Coverage of new research on individual differences in decision-making competence
- New coverage of predecisional distortion of decision-relevant information
- Added coverage of loss aversion in decision making

Chapter 9: Intelligence and Psychological Testing

- Spearman, Thurstone, and *g* added to section on history of testing
- Coverage of new findings reporting a strong relationship between intelligence and educational achievement
- New research on the association between students' self-discipline and academic performance
- New findings on the modest relationship between IQ and income
- Discussion of mental retardation incorporates new terminology suggested by the American Association on Intellectual and Developmental Disabilities
- New coverage of longitudinal research on mathematically precocious youth

- New meta-analytic findings on IQ increments following adoption
- New findings from molecular genetics studies of intelligence
- Coverage of new data on narrowing of cultural disparities in IQ scores
- Reports new research on possible cultural bias in IQ tests
- Revised evaluation of the concept of emotional intelligence
- New data on the relationship between creativity and intelligence

Chapter 10:, Motivation and Emotion

- New discussion of the role of the arcuate nucleus of the hypothalamus in the regulation of hunger
- Revised coverage of neurotransmitters and hunger, with new discussion of the importance of ghrelin
- Revised discussion of hormonal regulation of hunger, incorporating findings on ghrelin, CCK, and leptin resistance
- Reports new findings that being moderately overweight may not lead to increased mortality risk
- New discussion of whether the obesity "epidemic/crisis" has been exaggerated
- New findings relating to gender differences in orgasmic consistency
- New cross-cultural data on gender disparities in mating priorities and preferences
- Coverage of new research on the degree to which males and females pay attention to potential partners' willingness to invest in children
- New Featured Study on how women's judgments of men's faces are sensitive to the men's testosterone level and affinity for children
- New data supporting the idea that sexual orientation should be viewed as a continuum
- New findings on cultural disparities in the experience of socially engaging versus disengaging emotions
- New data on cultural variations in the categorization of emotions
- New discussion of the modest association between actual wealth and subjective perceptions of finances, and other new research on income and happiness
- New coverage of the heritability of subjective well-being
- New discussion of Gilbert's work on how people are surprisingly bad at predicting what will make them happy
- New research on the degree to which the hedonic treadmill makes it difficult for people to enhance their happiness

Chapter 11: Human Development Across the Life Span

• Expanded coverage of the effects of normal drinking during pregnancy on subsequent development

• New discussion of cohort effects in cross-sectional research

• New coverage of the link between infant temperament and adult personality

• New discussion of the stability of individual differences in patterns of attachment

• Added section profiling recent research on day care

• New discussion of the constricted focus of Kohlberg's theory

• New take on generational decreases in the age of onset of puberty

• New discussion of adolescent risk taking in relation to susceptibility to peer influence

• Streamlined discussion of whether adolescence is a time of turmoil

• Condensed coverage of identity development in adolescence

• New discussion of emerging adulthood as a distinct stage of development

• Expanded discussion of Roberts's work on personality trends in the adult years

• Revised discussion of male menopause

• Distinction between fluid and crystallized intelligence now included in coverage of age trends in intelligence

• New discussion of the "use it or lose it hypothesis" as related to aging and cognitive decline

Chapter 12: Personality: Theory, Research, and Assessment

• New introduction to the chapter focusing on the fascinating life of Richard Branson

• Revised figure providing more detailed information on the five-factor model of personality traits

• New discussion of how the Big Five traits are predictive of important life outcomes, such as occupational attainment and mortality

• Expanded discussion of the relations between self-efficacy and specific aspects of behavior

• New discussion of the dilution of the behavioral approach included in critique of behavioral theories

• New discussion of Nettle's evolutionary analysis of the adaptive implications of the Big Five traits

• In coverage of terror management theory, new discussion of how mortality salience can increase ambivalence about sexuality

• Coverage of new research on cross-cultural variations in scores on the Big Five traits

• New research on the inaccuracy of national character stereotypes

• New section on personality testing over the Internet

Chapter 13: Stress, Coping, and Health

• New discussion of how pressure is often self-imposed

• New coverage of Fredrickson's broaden-and-build theory of positive emotions

• Reports new findings on the effects of positive emotions on mental and physical health

• Profiles recent study linking positive emotional style to enhanced immune response

• New discussion of how stress can suppress the process of neurogenesis in the hippocampus

• New discussion of the importance of flexibility in coping style

• Coverage of new research on the adaptive value of giving up the pursuit of unattainable goals

• Addition of new findings that resilience in the face of traumatic stress is not as rare as assumed

• Discussion of new findings on how transient mental stress can trigger inflammatory responses

• New coverage of how stress can lead to immune system dysregulation that promotes chronic inflammation

• New research on the relationship between social support and reduced mortality

• Covers new research on how negative social interactions can undermine health

• New research on how exercise can reduce chronic inflammation and promote neurogenesis

• New study of how often HIV-positive individuals are unaware of their HIV status

Chapter 14: Psychological Disorders

• New discussion of the process being used to develop DSM-V

• New coverage of the socioeconomic costs of mental illness

• Reports new data relating inhibited temperament to vulnerability to anxiety disorders

• Coverage of new information on the prevalence of PTSD and concerns about PTSD in veterans of the Iraq war

• New discussion of Öhman and Mineka's notion of an evolved module for fear learning in relation to the acquisition of phobias

• Revised estimates of the prevalence of depressive disorders

• Expanded discussion of gender differences in depression

• New section on the association between mood disorders and suicide

- New figure presenting advice on suicide prevention
- Revised discussion of the course and outcome of schizophrenic disorders
- Reports new data linking marijuana use to increased vulnerability to schizophrenia
- Updated coverage of the prevalence of eating disorders among college students and males
- Description of binge-eating disorder now included in coverage of eating disorders

Chapter 15: Treatment of Psychological Disorders

- Coverage of new findings on the efficacy of psychodynamic therapies
- Added section on innovative insight therapies inspired by the positive psychology movement
- New discussion of the cost effectiveness of atypical antipsychotics in comparison to conventional antipsychotics
- Includes discussion of how antidepressant medications are not as effective for bipolar patients (in comparison to patients with unipolar depression)
- New coverage of serotonin-norepinephrine reuptake inhibitors
- Updated coverage of whether antidepressants elevate suicide risk in adolescents
- Added coverage of transcranial magnetic stimulation as a psychiatric treatment
- New coverage of direct brain stimulation as a psychiatric treatment
- Reports new data on the distribution of psychologists' theoretical approach to therapy
- New discussion on the impact of poverty on psychotherapy
- New information provided on the importance of a strong therapeutic alliance and the value of adapting treatments for ethnic minority clients

Chapter 16: Social Behavior

- New findings reported on how perceptions of facial appearance predict election results
- New research on how social perceptions based on facial features are formed in the blink of an eye
- New study of how familiarity with a situation reduces observers' tendency to make the fundamental attribution error
- New research on culture and attributional tendencies
- Discussion of new brain-imaging research suggesting that passionate love activates the same dopamine circuits activated by addictive drugs
- Updated discussion of attachment patterns and love, introducing attachment anxiety and ambivalence as continuous dimensions
- Expanded discussion of attachment style and patterns of sexual interaction
- New coverage of how the Internet can contribute to the development of close relationships
- New discussion of the differences between online and face-to-face relationships
- Coverage of new evolutionary research on women's mating preferences
- New evolutionary research relating women's menstrual cycles to their mate preferences and men's reactions to these changes
- New data on attitude-behavior consistency and how it is reduced by situational pressures
- New findings on moderators of the social loafing effect
- Added discussion of how groups can be superior to individuals in some decision-making processes

Concept Charts for Study and Review

To help your students organize and assimilate the main ideas contained in the text, I have created a unique supplement—a booklet of Concept Charts. This booklet contains a two-page Concept Chart for each chapter. Each Concept Chart provides a detailed visual map of the key ideas found in the main body of that chapter. These color-coded, hierarchically organized charts create snapshots of the chapters that should allow your students to quickly see the relationships among ideas and sections.

PsykTrek: A Multimedia Introduction to Psychology

PsykTrek is a multimedia supplement that will provide students with new opportunities for active learning and reach out to "visual learners" with greatly increased efficacy. *PsykTrek* is intended to give students a second pathway to learning much of the content of introductory psychology. Although it does not cover all of the content of the introductory course, I think you will see that a great many key concepts and principles can be explicated *more effectively* in an interactive audiovisual medium than in a textbook.

PsykTrek consists of four components. The main component is a set of 65 *Interactive Learning Modules* that present the core content of psychology in a whole new way. These tutorials include thousands of graphics, hundred of photos, hundreds of animations, approximately four hours of narration, 40 carefully selected videos, and about 160 uniquely visual concept checks and quizzes. The ten *Simulations* allow students to explore complex psychological phenomena in depth. They are highly interactive, experiential demonstrations that will enhance students' appreciation of research methods. The *Multimedia Glossary* allows students to look up over 800 psychological terms, access hundreds of pronunciations of obscure words, and pull up hundreds of related diagrams, photos, and videos. The *Video Selector* permits students (or faculty) to directly access the video segments that are otherwise embedded in the Interactive Learning Modules.

The key strength of *PsykTrek* is its ability to give students new opportunities for active learning outside of the classroom. For example, students can run through re-creations of classic experiments to see the complexities of data collection in action. Or they can play with visual illusions on screen in ways that will make them doubt their own eyes. Or they can stack color filters on screen to demonstrate the nature of subtractive color mixing. *PsykTrek* is intended to supplement and complement *Psychology: Themes & Variations*. For instance, after reading about operant conditioning in the text, a student could work through three interactive tutorials on operant principles, watch four videos (including historic footage of B. F. Skinner shaping a rat), and then try to shape Morphy, the virtual rat, in one of the simulations.

This edition of the text is accompanied by a brand new version (3.0) of *PsykTrek*. The new version has been re-created from the bottom up. It has a more modern look and has been designed to run more effectively on today's personal computers. Moreover, for the first time *PsykTrek* is available in an online format that can make student access easier than ever. *PsykTrek* 3.0 includes three new Interactive Learning Modules: Attachment, Forgetting, and Conformity and Obedience. All of the modules now include a multiple-choice test, as well as an interactive quiz. We have also incorporated unit-level multiple-choice exams to permit students to better assess their mastery of content. And each unit includes a critical thinking exercise, written by Jeffry Ricker (Scottsdale Community College). Finally, the new version of *PsykTrek* contains additional videos, including historically noteworthy segments showing B. F. Skinner's shaping of pigeons to play Ping-Pong, Albert Bandura's Bobo doll study, and Stanley Milgram's legendary study of obedience.

Other Supplementary Materials

The teaching/learning package that has been developed to supplement *Psychology: Themes & Variations* includes many other useful tools. The development of all its parts was carefully coordinated so that they are mutually supportive. Moreover, the materials have been created and written by highly experienced, top-flight professors I have worked hard to recruit.

Study Guide (by Richard Stalling and Ronald Wasden)

An exceptionally thorough *Study Guide* is available to help your students master the information in the text. It is written by two of my former professors, Richard Stalling and Ronald Wasden of Bradley University. They have over 40 years of experience as a team writing study guides for introductory psychology texts, and their experience is readily apparent in the high-quality materials that they have developed.

The review of key ideas for each chapter is made up of an engaging mixture of matching exercises, fill-in-the-blank items, free-response questions, and programmed learning. Each review is organized around the Key Learning Goals written by me. The *Study Guide* is closely coordinated with the *Test Bank,* as the same Key Learning Goals guided the construction of the questions in the *Test Bank*. The *Study Guide* also includes a review of key terms, a review of key people, and a self-test for each chapter in the text.

Instructor's Resource Manual (coordinated by Randolph Smith)

A talented roster of professors have contributed to the *Instructor's Resource Manual (IRM)* in their respective areas of expertise. The *IRM* was developed under the guidance of Randolph Smith, the editor of the journal *Teaching of Psychology*. It contains a diverse array of materials designed to facilitate efforts to teach the introductory course and includes the following sections:

- The *Instructor's Manual,* by Randolph Smith (Lamar University), contains a wealth of detailed suggestions for lecture topics, class demonstrations, exercises, discussion questions, and suggested readings, organized around the content of each chapter in the text. It also highlights the connections between the text coverage and *PsykTrek* content and features an expanded collection of masters for class handouts.

- *Strategies for Effective Teaching,* by Joseph Lowman (University of North Carolina), discusses practical issues such as what to put in a course syllabus, how to handle the first class meeting, how to cope with large classes, and how to train and organize teaching assistants.

- *AV Media for Introductory Psychology,* by Russ Watson (College of DuPage), provides a comprehensive, up-to-date, critical overview of educational films relevant to the introductory course.

- *The Use of Computers in Teaching Introductory Psychology,* by Susan J. Shapiro (Indiana University–East), offers a thorough listing of computer materials germane to the introductory course and analyzes their strengths and weaknesses.

• *Introducing Writing in Introductory Psychology,* by Dana Dunn (Moravian College), discusses how to work toward enhancing students' writing skills in the context of the introductory course and provides suggestions and materials for specific writing assignments chapter by chapter.

• *Crossing Borders/Contrasting Behaviors: Using Cross-Cultural Comparisons to Enrich the Introductory Psychology Course,* by Ginny Zahn, Bill Hill, and Michael Reiner (Kennesaw State University), discusses the movement toward "internationalizing" the curriculum and provides suggestions for lectures, exercises, and assignments that can add a cross-cultural flavor to the introductory course.

• *Teaching Introductory Psychology with the World Wide Web,* by Michael R. Snyder (University of Alberta), discusses how to work Internet assignments into the introductory course and provides a guide to many psychology-related sites on the World Wide Web.

• *Using InfoTrac College Edition in Introductory Psychology,* by Randolph Smith, discusses how to make effective use of the *InfoTrac College Edition* subscription that is made available to students with this text. *InfoTrac College Edition* is an online database of recent, full-text articles from hundreds of scholarly and popular periodicals.

Test Bank (by S. A. Hensch and Albert Bugaj)

S. A. Hensch (University of Wisconsin College-Online) and Albert Bugaj (University of Wisconsin-Marinette) have revised our large, diversified, and carefully constructed *Test Bank*. The questions are closely tied to each chapter's Key Learning Goals and to the lists of key terms and key people found in both the text and the *Study Guide*. The items are categorized as (a) factual, (b) conceptual/applied, (c) integrative, or (d) critical thinking questions. The *Test Bank* also includes a separate section that contains about 600 multiple-choice questions based on the content of *PsykTrek's* Interactive Learning Modules. Data on item difficulty are included for many questions.

Computerized Test Items

Electronic versions of the *Test Bank* are available for a variety of computer configurations. The *ExamView* software is user-friendly and allows teachers to insert their own questions and to customize those provided.

Using YouTube in Psychology (by Jeremy Houska)

An entirely new ancillary has been developed to help instructors make use of the ever-growing collection of psychology-related videos available online at the popular YouTube website. As is often the case with my books, this new idea emerged from my classroom experience. Each year I teach a seminar for graduate students in psychology who are teaching for the first time. Among other things, the seminar requires each graduate student to develop extensive teaching materials for a specific topic in the field, including audio-visual materials that he or she thinks would be worthwhile for classroom use. About two years ago, I noticed an unexpected trend, as the students started incorporating more and more videos from YouTube in their recommended audio-visual materials. I was surprised to learn that YouTube contains an amazing diversity of videos that can be relevant to a variety of psychological topics. These include educational videos posted by psychology teachers, interviews with prominent psychologists, TV clips profiling recent research, historically important footage from classic studies, and all sorts of creative, sometimes wacky, videos that can be used to stimulate discussion of an endless variety of topics. After developing a new appreciation for the treasure trove of valuable videos available via YouTube, I recruited one of my graduate students to compile a catalog of videos that would be potentially useful to introductory psychology instructors. Jeremy Houska (University of Nevada, Las Vegas and Nevada State College) has done an outstanding job in researching and creating this compilation. It is organized by chapter, and by specific topics within each chapter. Each entry identifies the video's title, posting, length, and URL. This information is followed by a list of psychological concepts covered, a brief description of the video, and suggestions for discussion questions. I think many instructors will be surprised by the educational potential of YouTube (I know I was).

Challenging Your Preconceptions: Thinking Critically About Psychology (by Randolph Smith)

This brief paperback book is a wonderful introduction to critical thinking as it applies to psychological issues. Written by Randolph Smith (Lamar University), this book helps students apply their critical thinking skills to a variety of topics, including hypnosis, advertising, misleading statistics, IQ testing, gender differences, and memory bias. Each chapter ends with critical thinking challenges that give students opportunities to practice their critical thinking skills.

ACKNOWLEDGMENTS

Creating an introductory psychology text is a complicated challenge, and a small army of people have contributed to the evolution of this book. Foremost among them are the psychology editors I have worked with—Claire Verduin, C. Deborah Laughton, Phil Curson, Eileen Murphy, Edith Beard Brady, Michele Sordi, and Jon-David Hague—and the developmental editor for the first edition of this book, John Bergez. They have helped me immeasurably, and each has become a treasured friend along the way. I am especially indebted to Claire, who educated me in the intricacies of textbook publishing, and to John, who has left an enduring imprint on my writing.

The challenge of meeting a difficult schedule in producing this book was undertaken by a talented team of people coordinated by Tom Dorsaneo, who did a superb job of pulling it all together. Credit for the text design goes to Tani Hasegawa, who was very creative in building on the previous design. Linda Rill handled permissions and photo research with enthusiasm and extraordinary efficiency, and Jackie Estrada did an outstanding job once again in copyediting the manuscript. Fred Harwin and Carol Zuber-Mallison made stellar contributions to the artwork, and the team at Thompson Type efficiently oversaw the composition process.

A number of psychologists deserve thanks for the contributions they made to this book. I am grateful to Diane Halpern for her work on the Critical Thinking Applications; to Vinny Hevern for contributing the Web Links and Internet essay; to Marky Lloyd for writing the appendix on careers in psychology; to Kathy Hanisch for writing the appendix on I/O psychology; to Rick Stalling and Ron Wasden for their work on the *Study Guide;* to Shirley Hensch and Albert Bugaj for their work on the *Test Bank;* to Randy Smith, Joseph Lowman, Russ Watson, Dana Dunn, Ginny Zahn, Bill Hill, Michael Reiner, Susan Shapiro, and Michael Snyder for their contributions to the *Instructor's Resource Manual;* to Jeffry Ricker for devising *PsykTrek's* critical thinking exercises; to Randy Smith, David Matsumoto, and Jeremy Houska for contributing ancillary books; to Jim Calhoun for providing item analysis data for the test items; to Harry Upshaw, Larry Wrightsman, Shari Diamond, Rick Stalling, and Claire Etaugh for their help and guidance over the years; and to the chapter consultants listed on page xx and the reviewers listed on pages xxi and xxii, who provided insightful and constructive critiques of various portions of the manuscript.

Many other people have also contributed to this project, and I am grateful to all of them for their efforts. Bill Roberts, Craig Barth, Nancy Sjoberg, John Odam, Fiorella Ljunggren, Jim Brace-Thompson, Susan Badger, Sean Wakely, Eve Howard, Joanne Terhaar, Marjorie Sanders, Kathryn Stewart, Lori Grebe, Dory Schaeffer, and Margaret Parks helped with varied aspects of previous editions. Vernon Boes, Jennie Redwitz, Kristin Makarewycz, Kim Russell, Lauren Keyes, and Ileana Shevlin made valuable contributions to the current edition. At the College of DuPage, where I taught until 1991, all of my colleagues in psychology provided support and information at one time or another, but I am especially indebted to Barb Lemme, Alan Lanning, Pat Puccio, and Don Green. I also want to thank my former colleagues at Santa Clara University (especially Tracey Kahan, Tom Plante, and Jerry Burger), and my current colleagues at UNLV who have been fertile sources of new ideas. And I am indebted to the many graduate students that I have worked with at UNLV, and to Melissa Lanctot who helped complete the reference entries.

My greatest debt is to my wife, Beth Traylor, who has been a steady source of emotional sustenance while enduring the rigors of her medical career, and to my son T. J., for making dad laugh all the time.

Wayne Weiten

Chapter Consultants

Chapter 1
David Baker
University of Akron
Charles L. Brewer
Furman University
C. James Goodwin
Wheeling Jesuit University
David Hothersall
Ohio State University
E. R. Hilgard
Stanford University
Michael G. Livingston
St. John's University

Chapter 2
Larry Christensen
Texas A & M University
Francis Durso
University of Oklahoma
Donald H. McBurney
University of Pittsburgh
Wendy Schweigert
Bradley University

Chapter 3
Nelson Freedman
Queen's University at Kingston
Michael W. Levine
University of Illinois, Chicago
Corinne L. McNamara
Kennesaw State University
James M. Murphy
Indiana University–Purdue University at Indianapolis
Paul Wellman
Texas A & M University

Chapter 4
Stephen Blessing
University of Tampa
Nelson Freedman
Queen's University at Kingston
Kevin Jordan
San Jose State University
Michael W. Levine
University of Illinois, Chicago
John Pittenger
University of Arkansas, Little Rock

Lawrence Ward
University of British Columbia
Chrislyn E. Randell
Metropolitan State College of Denver

Chapter 5
Frank Etscorn
New Mexico Institute of Mining and Technology
Tracey L. Kahan
Santa Clara University
Charles F. Levinthal
Hofstra University
Wilse Webb
University of Florida

Chapter 6
A. Charles Catania
University of Maryland
Michael Domjan
University of Texas, Austin
William C. Gordon
University of New Mexico
Russell A. Powell
Grant MacEwan College
Barry Schwartz
Swarthmore College
Deborah L. Stote
University of Texas, Austin

Chapter 7
Tracey L. Kahan
Santa Clara University
Ian Neath
Purdue University
Tom Pusateri
Loras College
Stephen K. Reed
San Diego State University
Patricia Tenpenny
Loyola University, Chicago

Chapter 8
John Best
Eastern Illinois University
David Carroll
University of Wisconsin, Superior

Tom Pusateri
Loras College
Stephen K. Reed
San Diego State University

Chapter 9
Charles Davidshofer
Colorado State University
Shalynn Ford
Teikyo Marycrest University
Richrd J. Haier
University of California, Irvine
Timothy Rogers
University of Calgary
Dennis Saccuzzo
San Diego State University

Chapter 10
Robert Franken
University of Calgary
Russell G. Geen
University of Missouri
Douglas Mook
University of Virginia
D. Louis Wood
University of Arkansas, Little Rock

Chapter 11
Ruth L. Ault
Davidson College
John C. Cavanaugh
University of Delaware
Claire Etaugh
Bradley University
Doug Friedrich
University of West Florida
Barbara Hansen Lemme
College of DuPage

Chapter 12
Susan Cloninger
Russel Sage College
Caroline Collins
University of Victoria
Howard S. Friedman
University of California, Riverside

Christopher F. Monte
Manhattanville College
Ken Olson
Fort Hays State University

Chapter 13
Robin M. DiMatteo
University of California, Riverside
Jess Feist
McNeese State University
Regan A. R. Gurung
University of Wisconsin, Green Bay
Chris Kleinke
University of Alaska, Anchorage

Chapter 14
David A. F. Haaga
American University
Richard Halgin
University of Massachusetts, Amherst
Chris L. Kleinke
University of Alaska, Anchorage
Elliot A. Weiner
Pacific University

Chapter 15
Gerald Corey
California State University, Fullerton
Herbert Goldenberg
California State University, Los Angeles
Jane S. Halonen
Alverno College
Thomas G. Plante
Santa Clara University

Chapter 16
Jerry M. Burger
Santa Clara University
Stephen L. Franzoi
Marquette University
Donelson R. Forsyth
Virginia Commonwealth University
Cheryl Kaiser
Michigan State University

Reviewers

Lyn Y. Abramson
University of Wisconsin

Bill Adler
Collin County Community College

James R. M. Alexander
University of Tasmania

Gordon A. Allen
Miami University of Ohio

Elise L. Amel
University of St. Thomas

Ruth L. Ault
Davidson College

Jeff D. Baker
Southeastern Louisiana University

Mark Basham
Regis University

Gina J. Bates
Southern Arkansas University

Scott C. Bates
Utah State University

Derryl K. Beale
Cerritos Community College

Ashleah Bectal
U.S. Military Academy

Robert P. Beitz
Pima County Community College

Daniel R. Bellack
Trident Technical College

Stephen Blessing
University of Tampa

Robert Bornstein
Miami University

Bette L. Bottoms
University of Illinois, Chicago

Lyn Boulter
Catawba College

Amy Badura Brack
Creighton University

Nicole Bragg
Mount Hood Community College

Allen Branum
South Dakota State University

Robert G. Bringle
Indiana University–Purdue University at Indianapolis

Michael Brislawn
Bellevue Community College

David R. Brodbeck
Sir Wilfred Grenfall College, Memorial University of Newfoundland

Dan W. Brunworth
Kishwaukee College

David M. Buss
University of Texas, Austin

James Butler
James Madison University

Mary M. Cail
University of Virginia

James F. Calhoun
University of Georgia

William Calhoun
University of Tennessee

Janet L. Chapman
U.S. Military Academy

Kevin Chun
University of San Francisco

Michael Clayton
Youngstown State University

Francis B. Colavita
University of Pittsburgh

Thomas B. Collins
Mankato State University

Stan Coren
University of British Columbia

Verne C. Cox
University of Texas at Arlington

Kenneth Cramer
University of Windsor

Dianne Crisp
Kwantlen University College

Norman Culbertson
Yakima Valley College

Betty M. Davenport
Campbell University

Stephen F. Davis
Emporia State University

Kenneth Deffenbacher
University of Nebraska

Kathy Denton
Douglas College

Marcus Dickson
Wayne State University

Deanna L. Dodson
Lebanon Valley College

Roger Dominowski
University of Illinois, Chicago

Dale V. Doty
Monroe Community College

Robert J. Douglas
University of Washington

Jim Duffy
Sir Wilfred Grenfall College, Memorial University of Newfoundland

James Eison
Southeast Missouri State University

Pamela G. Ely
St. Andrews Presbyterian College

M. Jeffrey Farrar
University of Florida

Donald Fields
University of New Brunswick

Thomas P. Fitzpatrick
Rockland Community College

Karen E. Ford
Mesa State College

Donelson R. Forsyth
Virginia Commonwealth University

Leslie D. Frazier
Florida International University

William J. Froming
University of Florida

Mary Ellen Fromuth
Middle Tennessee State University

Dean E. Frost
Portland State University

Judy Gentry
Columbus State Community College

Doba Goodman
York University

Jeffrey D. Green
Soka University

Richard Griggs
University of Florida

Arthur Gutman
Florida Institute of Technology

Jane S. Halonen
Alverno College

Roger Harnish
Rochester Institute of Technology

Philip L. Hartley
Chaffey College

Brad M. Hastings
Mount Aloysius College

Glenn R. Hawkes
Virginia Commonwealth University

Myra D. Heinrich
Mesa State College

George Hertl
Northwest Mississippi Community College

Lyllian B. Hix
Houston Community College

Mark A. Hopper
Loras College

John P. Hostetler
Albion College

Bruce Hunsberger
Wilfrid Laurier University

Mir Rabiul Islam
Charles Sturt University

Heide Island
University of Montana

Robert A. Johnston
College of William and Mary

Robert Kaleta
University of Wisconsin, Milwaukee

Alan R. King
University of North Dakota

Melvyn B. King
State University of New York, Cortland

James Knight
Humboldt State University

Mike Knight
Central State University

Ronald Kopcho
Mercer Community College

Barry J. Krikstone
Saint Michael's College

Jerry N. Lackey
Stephen F. Austin State University

Robin L. Lashley
Kent State University, Tuscarawas

Peter Leppman
University of Guelph

Charles F. Levinthal
Hofstra University

Wolfgang Linden
University of British Columbia

John Lindsay
Georgia College & State University

Diane Martichuski
University of Colorado, Boulder

Donald McBurney
University of Pittsburgh

Siobhan McEnaney-Hayes
Chestnut Hill College

Kathleen McCormick
Ocean County College

David G. McDonald
University of Missouri

Ronald K. McLaughlin
Juniata College

Steven E. Meier
University of Idaho

Sheryll Mennicke
University of Minnesota

Mitchell Metzger
Pennsylvania State University, Shenango

Richard Miller
Western Kentucky University

Mary Morris
Northern Territory University

Dan Mossler
Hampden-Sydney College

Darwin Muir
Queen's University at Kingston

Eric S. Murphy
University of Alaska, Anchorage

James M. Murphy
Indiana University–Purdue University at Indianapolis

Michael Murphy
Henderson State University

Carnot E. Nelson
University of South Florida

John Nezlek
College of William and Mary

Rachel Nitzberg
University of California, Davis

David L. Novak
Lansing Community College

Richard Page
Wright State University

Joseph J. Palladino
University of Southern Indiana

John N. Park
Mankato State University

Phil Pegg
Western Kentucky University

Gayle Pitman
Sacramento City College

Bobby J. Poe
Belleville Area College

Gary Poole
Simon Fraser University

Russell Powell
Grant MacEwan College

Maureen K. Powers
Vanderbilt University

Janet Proctor
Purdue University

Robin Raygor
Anoka-Ramsey Community College

Celia Reaves
Monroe Community College

Gary T. Reker
Trent University

Daniel W. Richards
Houston Community College

Kenneth M. Rosenberg
State University of New York, Oswego

Patricia Ross
Laurentian University

Angela Sadowski
Chaffey College

Sabato D. Sagaria
Capital University

Roger Sambrook
University of Colorado, Colorado Springs

Fred Shima
California State University Dominguez Hills

Susan A. Shodahl
San Bernardino Valley College

Steven M. Smith
Texas A & M University

Paul Stager
York University

Susan Snycerski
San Jose State University

Steven St. John
Rollins College

Marjorie Taylor
University of Oregon

Frank R. Terrant, Jr.
Appalachian State University

Donald Tyrrell
Franklin and Marshall College

Frank J. Vattano
Colorado State University

Wayne Viney
Colorado State University

Paul Wellman
Texas A & M University

Keith D. White
University of Florida

Randall D. Wight
Ouachita Baptist University

Daniel E. Wivagg
Baylor University

D. Louis Wood
University of Arkansas, Little Rock

John W. Wright
Washington State University

Cecilia Yoder
Oklahoma City Community College

BRIEF CONTENTS

Chapter 1 The Evolution of Psychology 1
PERSONAL APPLICATION Improving Academic Performance 28
CRITICAL THINKING APPLICATION Developing Critical Thinking Skills:
An Introduction 34

Chapter 2 The Research Enterprise in Psychology 38
PERSONAL APPLICATION Finding and Reading Journal Articles 70
CRITICAL THINKING APPLICATION The Perils of Anecdotal Evidence:
"I Have A Friend Who . . ." 74

Chapter 3 The Biological Bases of Behavior 78
PERSONAL APPLICATION Evaluating the Concept of
"Two Minds in One" 120
CRITICAL THINKING APPLICATION Building Better Brains:
The Perils of Extrapolation 124

Chapter 4 Sensation and Perception 128
PERSONAL APPLICATION Appreciating Art and Illusion 175
CRITICAL THINKING APPLICATION Recognizing Contrast Effects:
It's All Relative 180

Chapter 5 Variations in Consciousness 184
PERSONAL APPLICATION Addressing Practical Questions About Sleep
and Dreams 222
CRITICAL THINKING APPLICATION Is Alcoholism a Disease? The Power
of Definitions 226

Chapter 6 Learning 230
PERSONAL APPLICATION Achieving Self-Control Through Behavior
Modification 267
CRITICAL THINKING APPLICATION Manipulating Emotions:
Pavlov and Persuasion 270

Chapter 7 Human Memory 274
PERSONAL APPLICATION Improving Everyday Memory 308
CRITICAL THINKING APPLICATION Understanding the Fallibility of
Eyewitness Accounts 312

Chapter 8 Language and Thought 316
PERSONAL APPLICATION Understanding Pitfalls in Reasoning About
Decisions 346
CRITICAL THINKING APPLICATION Shaping Thought with Language:
"Only a Naive Moron Would Believe That" 350

Chapter 9 Intelligence and Psychological Testing 354
PERSONAL APPLICATION Understanding Creativity 387
CRITICAL THINKING APPLICATION The Intelligence Debate, Appeals
to Ignorance, and Reification 390

Chapter 10 Motivation and Emotion 394
PERSONAL APPLICATION Exploring the Ingredients of
Happiness 429

CRITICAL THINKING APPLICATION Analyzing Arguments:
Making Sense out of Controversy 434

**Chapter 11 Human Development Across the Life
Span** 438
PERSONAL APPLICATION Understanding Gender Differences 475
CRITICAL THINKING APPLICATION Are Fathers Essential to Children's
Well-Being? 484

**Chapter 12 Personality: Theory, Research, and
Assessment** 488
PERSONAL APPLICATION Understanding Personality
Assessment 524
CRITICAL THINKING APPLICATION Hindsight in Everyday Analyses of
Personality 528

Chapter 13 Stress, Coping, and Health 532
PERSONAL APPLICATION Improving Coping and Stress
Management 565
CRITICAL THINKING APPLICATION Thinking Rationally About Health
Statistics and Decisions 570

Chapter 14 Psychological Disorders 574
PERSONAL APPLICATION Understanding Eating Disorders 613
CRITICAL THINKING APPLICATION Working with Probabilities in
Thinking About Mental Illness 616

Chapter 15 Treatment of Psychological Disorders 620
PERSONAL APPLICATION Looking for a Therapist 654
CRITICAL THINKING APPLICATION From Crisis to Wellness—But Was
It the Therapy? 658

Chapter 16 Social Behavior 662
PERSONAL APPLICATION Understanding Prejudice 699
CRITICAL THINKING APPLICATION Whom Can You Trust? Analyzing
Credibility and Influence Tactics 704

Appendix A Answers to Concept Checks **A-1**
Appendix B Statistical Methods **A-7**
Appendix C Industrial/Organizational Psychology **A-15**
Appendix D Careers in Psychology **A-30**
Appendix E Critical Thinking About Internet Research Sources:
What Students Need to Know **A-35**

Glossary G-1
References R-1
Name Index I-1
Subject Index I-18
Credits C-1

1

THE EVOLUTION OF PSYCHOLOGY 1

Prague, Czech Republic (one of which is) Charles Bridge © ML Sinibaldil/Corbis

Psychology's Early History   3
A New Science Is Born: The Contributions of Wundt and Hall
The Battle of the "Schools" Begins: Structuralism Versus Functionalism
Freud Brings the Unconscious into the Picture
Watson Alters Psychology's Course as Behaviorism Makes Its Debut
Skinner Questions Free Will as Behaviorism Flourishes
The Humanists Revolt

Psychology's Modern History   12
Psychology Comes of Age as a Profession
Psychology Returns to Its Roots: Renewed Interest in Cognition and
    Physiology
Psychology Broadens Its Horizons: Increased Interest in Cultural Diversity
Psychology Adapts: The Emergence of Evolutionary Psychology
Psychology Moves in a Positive Direction

Psychology Today: Vigorous and Diversified   17
Research Areas in Psychology
Professional Specialties in Psychology

Illustrated Overview of Psychology's History   20

Seven Unifying Themes   23
Themes Related to Psychology as a Field of Study
Themes Related to Psychology's Subject Matter

**PERSONAL APPLICATION ▮ Improving Academic
Performance   28**
Developing Sound Study Habits
Improving Your Reading
Getting More Out of Lectures
Improving Test-Taking Strategies

**CRITICAL THINKING APPLICATION ▮ Developing Critical
Thinking Skills: An Introduction   34**
The Need to Teach Critical Thinking
An Example

Recap   36
Practice Test   37

2

THE RESEARCH ENTERPRISE IN PSYCHOLOGY 38

Vancouver, British Columbia, Capilano Suspension Bridge © Fred Derwal/Hemis/Corbis

Looking for Laws: The Scientific Approach to Behavior 40
Goals of the Scientific Enterprise
Steps in a Scientific Investigation
Advantages of the Scientific Approach

Looking for Causes: Experimental Research 45
Independent and Dependent Variables
Experimental and Control Groups
Extraneous Variables
Variations in Designing Experiments

FEATURED STUDY ▌ The Emotional Fallout of Expected and Unexpected Outcomes 49
Advantages and Disadvantages of Experimental Research

Looking for Links: Descriptive/Correlational Research 51
Naturalistic Observation
Case Studies
Surveys
Advantages and Disadvantages of Descriptive/Correlational Research

Looking for Conclusions: Statistics and Research 55
Descriptive Statistics
Inferential Statistics

Looking for Flaws: Evaluating Research 59
Sampling Bias
Placebo Effects

Distortions in Self-Report Data
Experimenter Bias

Illustrated Overview of Key Research Methods in Psychology 62

Looking into the Future: The Internet and Psychological Research 64

Looking at Ethics: Do the Ends Justify the Means? 66
The Question of Deception
The Question of Animal Research
Ethical Principles in Research

Reflecting on the Chapter's Themes 69

PERSONAL APPLICATION ▌ Finding and Reading Journal Articles 70
The Nature of Technical Journals
Finding Journal Articles
Reading Journal Articles

CRITICAL THINKING APPLICATION ▌ The Perils of Anecdotal Evidence: "I Have A Friend Who..." 74

Recap 76

Practice Test 77

3

THE BIOLOGICAL BASES OF BEHAVIOR 78

Austin, Texas, Austin's Congress St. Bridge © Patrick Byrd/Science Faction/Getty Images

Communication in the Nervous System   80
Nervous Tissue: The Basic Hardware
The Neural Impulse: Using Energy to Send Information
The Synapse: Where Neurons Meet
Neurotransmitters and Behavior

Organization of the Nervous System   89
The Peripheral Nervous System
The Central Nervous System

Looking Inside the Brain: Research Methods   92
Electrical Recordings
Lesioning
Electrical Stimulation of the Brain
Transcranial Magnetic Stimulation
Brain-Imaging Procedures

FEATURED STUDY ▌ Probing the Anatomy of Sexual Arousal   96

The Brain and Behavior   97
The Hindbrain
The Midbrain
The Forebrain
The Plasticity of the Brain

Right Brain/Left Brain: Cerebral Laterality   105
Bisecting the Brain: Split-Brain Research
Hemispheric Specialization in the Intact Brain

The Endocrine System: Another Way to Communicate   108

Heredity and Behavior: Is It All in the Genes?   110
Basic Principles of Genetics
Investigating Hereditary Influence: Research Methods
The Interplay of Heredity and Environment

The Evolutionary Bases of Behavior   116
Darwin's Insights
Subsequent Refinements to Evolutionary Theory
Behaviors as Adaptive Traits

Reflecting on the Chapter's Themes   120

PERSONAL APPLICATION ▌ Evaluating the Concept of "Two Minds in One"   120
Cerebral Specialization and Cognitive Processes
Complexities and Qualifications

CRITICAL THINKING APPLICATION ▌ Building Better Brains: The Perils of Extrapolation   124
The Key Findings on Neural Development
The Tendency to Overextrapolate

Recap   126

Practice Test   127

4

SENSATION AND PERCEPTION 128

Okinawa prefecture, Japan Ikema Bridge © DAJ/Getty Images

Psychophysics: Basic Concepts and Issues   130
Thresholds: Looking for Limits
Signal-Detection Theory
Perception Without Awareness
Sensory Adaptation

The Visual System: Essentials of Sight   134
The Stimulus: Light
The Eye: A Living Optical Instrument
The Retina: The Brain's Envoy in the Eye
Vision and the Brain
Viewing the World in Color

The Visual System: Perceptual Processes   146
Perceiving Forms, Patterns, and Objects
Perceiving Depth or Distance
Perceiving Geographical Slant

FEATURED STUDY ▌ **Why Hills Look Steeper Than They Are   155**
Perceptual Constancies in Vision
The Power of Misleading Cues: Visual Illusions

The Auditory System: Hearing   160
The Stimulus: Sound
Human Hearing Capacities
Sensory Processing in the Ear
Auditory Perception: Theories of Hearing
Auditory Localization: Perceiving Sources of Sound

The Chemical Senses: Taste and Smell   165
The Gustatory System: Taste
The Olfactory System: Smell

The Sense of Touch   169
Feeling Pressure
Feeling Pain

Illustrated Overview of Five Major Senses   172

Reflecting on the Chapter's Themes   175

PERSONAL APPLICATION ▌ **Appreciating Art and Illusion   175**

CRITICAL THINKING APPLICATION ▌ **Recognizing Contrast Effects: It's All Relative   180**

Recap   182

Practice Test   183

5

VARIATIONS IN CONSCIOUSNESS

184

Lanquedoc-Roussillon, France, Millau Viaduct © Jean PierreLascourmet/Corbis

On the Nature of Consciousness   186
Variations in Levels of Awareness
The Evolutionary Roots of Consciousness
Consciousness and Brain Activity

Biological Rhythms and Sleep   188
The Role of Circadian Rhythms
Ignoring Circadian Rhythms
Realigning Circadian Rhythms

The Sleep and Waking Cycle   191
Cycling Through the Stages of Sleep
Age Trends in Sleep
Culture and Sleep
The Neural Bases of Sleep
The Evolutionary Bases of Sleep
Doing Without: Sleep Deprivation

FEATURED STUDY ▌ The Surprising Costs of Sleep
Deprivation   197
Problems in the Night: Sleep Disorders

The World of Dreams   204
The Contents of Dreams
Links Between Dreams and Waking Life
Culture and Dreams
Theories of Dreaming

Hypnosis: Altered Consciousness or Role Playing?   208
Hypnotic Induction and Susceptibility
Hypnotic Phenomena
Theories of Hypnosis

Meditation: Pure Consciousness or Relaxation?   212
Physiological Correlates
Long-Term Benefits

Altering Consciousness with Drugs   214
Principal Abused Drugs and Their Effects
Factors Influencing Drug Effects
Mechanisms of Drug Action
Drug Dependence
Drugs and Health

Reflecting on the Chapter's Themes   222

PERSONAL APPLICATION ▌ Addressing Practical Questions
About Sleep and Dreams   222
Common Questions About Sleep
Common Questions About Dreams

CRITICAL THINKING APPLICATION ▌ Is Alcoholism a
Disease? The Power of Definitions   226
The Power to Make Definitions
Definitions, Labels, and Circular Reasoning

Recap   228

Practice Test   229

6

LEARNING 230

Cotonou, Benin Republic, bridge near Grand Market of Dantokpa © Massimo Borchi/Atlantide Phototravel/Corbis

Classical Conditioning 232
Pavlov's Demonstration: "Psychic Reflexes"
Terminology and Procedures
Classical Conditioning in Everyday Life
Basic Processes in Classical Conditioning

Operant Conditioning 241
Thorndike's Law of Effect
Skinner's Demonstration: It's All a Matter of Consequences
Terminology and Procedures
Basic Processes in Operant Conditioning
Schedules of Reinforcement
Positive Reinforcement Versus Negative Reinforcement
Punishment: Consequences That Weaken Responses

Changing Directions in the Study of Conditioning 254
Recognizing Biological Constraints on Conditioning
Recognizing Cognitive Processes in Conditioning

Observational Learning 259
Basic Processes
Acquisition Versus Performance
Observational Learning and the Media Violence Controversy

FEATURED STUDY ▌ The Power of Modeling: What They See Is What You Get 261

Illustrated Overview of Three Types of Learning 264

Reflecting on the Chapter's Themes 266

PERSONAL APPLICATION ▌ Achieving Self-Control Through Behavior Modification 267
Specifying Your Target Behavior
Gathering Baseline Data
Designing Your Program
Executing and Evaluating Your Program

CRITICAL THINKING APPLICATION ▌ Manipulating Emotions: Pavlov and Persuasion 270
Classical Conditioning in Advertising
Classical Conditioning in Business Negotiations
Classical Conditioning in the World of Politics
Becoming More Aware of Classical Conditioning Processes

Recap 272

Practice Test 273

7

HUMAN MEMORY 274

Taishun, Zheijang Province, China, Lixing Bridge © Keren Su/Corbis

Encoding: Getting Information into Memory 277
The Role of Attention
Levels of Processing
Enriching Encoding

Storage: Maintaining Information in Memory 280
Sensory Memory
Short-Term Memory
Long-Term Memory

FEATURED STUDY ▌ **How Accurate Are Flashbulb Memories?** 285

Are Short-Term Memory and Long-Term Memory Really Separate?
How Is Knowledge Represented and Organized in Memory?

Retrieval: Getting Information Out of Memory 290
Using Cues to Aid Retrieval
Reinstating the Context of an Event
Reconstructing Memories and the Misinformation Effect
Source Monitoring and Reality Monitoring

Forgetting: When Memory Lapses 294
How Quickly We Forget: Ebbinghaus's Forgetting Curve
Measures of Forgetting
Why We Forget
The Recovered Memories Controversy

In Search of the Memory Trace: The Physiology of Memory 302
The Neural Circuitry of Memory
The Anatomy of Memory

Systems and Types of Memory 305
Declarative Versus Procedural Memory
Semantic Versus Episodic Memory
Prospective Versus Retrospective Memory

Reflecting on the Chapter's Themes 307

PERSONAL APPLICATION ▌ **Improving Everyday Memory** 308
Engage in Adequate Rehearsal
Schedule Distributed Practice and Minimize Interference
Engage in Deep Processing and Organize Information
Enrich Encoding with Mnemonic Devices

CRITICAL THINKING APPLICATION ▌ **Understanding the Fallibility of Eyewitness Accounts** 312
The Contribution of Hindsight Bias
The Contribution of Overconfidence

Recap 314

Practice Test 315

8

LANGUAGE AND THOUGHT 316

Taiwan Republic of China, Sanhsientai, Three Immortals Terrace © Joe Viesti/Viesti Associates

Language: Turning Thoughts into Words 318
What Is Language?
The Structure of Language
Milestones in Language Development
Learning More Than One Language: Bilingualism
Can Animals Develop Language?
Language in Evolutionary Context
Theories of Language Acquisition
Culture, Language, and Thought

Problem Solving: In Search of Solutions 328
Types of Problems
Barriers to Effective Problem Solving
Approaches to Problem Solving
Culture, Cognitive Style, and Problem Solving

Decision Making: Choices and Chances 337
Making Choices About Preferences: Basic Strategies
Making Choices About Preferences: Quirks and Complexities

FEATURED STUDY ▌ Intuitive Decisions Versus Careful Deliberation: Which Leads to Better Decisions? 339
Taking Chances: Factors Weighed in Risky Decisions
Heuristics in Judging Probabilities
The Tendency to Ignore Base Rates
The Conjunction Fallacy
Evolutionary Analyses of Flaws in Human Decision Making
Fast and Frugal Heuristics

Reflecting on the Chapter's Themes 345

PERSONAL APPLICATION ▌ Understanding Pitfalls in Reasoning About Decisions 346
The Gambler's Fallacy
Overestimating the Improbable
Confirmation Bias
The Overconfidence Effect
The Effects of Framing
The Specter of Regret and Loss Aversion

CRITICAL THINKING APPLICATION ▌ Shaping Thought with Language: "Only a Naive Moron Would Believe That" 350
Semantic Slanting
Name Calling

Recap 352

Practice Test 353

9

INTELLIGENCE AND PSYCHOLOGICAL TESTING 354

Brooklyn, NY, Brooklyn Bridge © Richard Berenholtz/Corbis

Key Concepts in Psychological Testing 356
Principal Types of Tests
Standardization and Norms
Reliability
Validity

The Evolution of Intelligence Testing 361
Galton's Studies of Hereditary Genius
Binet's Breakthrough
Terman and the Stanford-Binet
Wechsler's Innovations
The Debate About the Structure of Intelligence
Intelligence Testing Today

Basic Questions About Intelligence Testing 364
What Kinds of Questions Are on Intelligence Tests?
What Do Modern IQ Scores Mean?
Do Intelligence Tests Have Adequate Reliability?
Do Intelligence Tests Have Adequate Validity?
Do Intelligence Tests Predict Vocational Success?
Are IQ Tests Widely Used in Other Cultures?

Extremes of Intelligence 369
Mental Retardation/Intellectual Disability
Giftedness

Heredity and Environment as Determinants of Intelligence 373
Evidence for Hereditary Influence
Evidence for Environmental Influence
The Interaction of Heredity and Environment
Cultural Differences in IQ Scores

FEATURED STUDY ‖ **Racial Stereotypes and Test Performance** 380

New Directions in the Assessment and Study of Intelligence 382
Exploring Biological Indexes and Correlates of Intelligence
Investigating Cognitive Processes in Intelligent Behavior
Expanding the Concept of Intelligence
Measuring Emotional Intelligence

Reflecting on the Chapter's Themes 387

PERSONAL APPLICATION ‖ **Understanding Creativity** 387
The Nature of Creativity
Measuring Creativity
Correlates of Creativity

CRITICAL THINKING APPLICATION ‖ **The Intelligence Debate, Appeals to Ignorance, and Reification** 390
Appeal to Ignorance
Reification

Recap 392

Practice Test 393

10

MOTIVATION AND EMOTION 394

New York, Verrazano-Narrows Bridge on Staten Island © Adam Woolfitt/Robert Harding Picture Library Ltd/Alamy

Motivational Theories and Concepts   396
Drive Theories
Incentive Theories
Evolutionary Theories
The Range and Diversity of Human Motives

The Motivation of Hunger and Eating   399
Biological Factors in the Regulation of Hunger
Environmental Factors in the Regulation of Hunger
Eating and Weight: The Roots of Obesity

Sexual Motivation and Behavior   406
The Human Sexual Response
Evolutionary Analyses of Human Sexual Behavior

FEATURED STUDY ▌ Can Women Judge Men's Mate Potential in Just One Glance?   411

The Controversial Issue of Pornography
The Mystery of Sexual Orientation

Achievement: In Search of Excellence   417
Individual Differences in the Need for Achievement
Situational Determinants of Achievement Behavior

The Elements of Emotional Experience   419
The Cognitive Component: Subjective Feelings
The Physiological Component: Diffuse and Multifaceted
The Behavioral Component: Nonverbal Expressiveness
Culture and the Elements of Emotion

Theories of Emotion   426
James-Lange Theory
Cannon-Bard Theory
Schachter's Two-Factor Theory
Evolutionary Theories of Emotion

Reflecting on the Chapter's Themes   429

PERSONAL APPLICATION ▌ Exploring the Ingredients of Happiness   429

Factors That Do Not Predict Happiness
Moderately Good Predictors of Happiness
Strong Predictors of Happiness
Conclusions About Subjective Well-Being

CRITICAL THINKING APPLICATION ▌ Analyzing Arguments: Making Sense out of Controversy   434

The Anatomy of an Argument
Common Fallacies
Evaluating the Strength of Arguments

Recap   436

Practice Test   437

11

HUMAN DEVELOPMENT ACROSS THE LIFE SPAN 438

Vietnam, Lao Cai Province, Sa Pa © Royalty Free/Masterfile

Progress Before Birth: Prenatal Development 440
The Course of Prenatal Development
Environmental Factors and Prenatal Development

The Wondrous Years of Childhood 445
Exploring the World: Motor Development
Easy and Difficult Babies: Differences in Temperament
Early Emotional Development: Attachment
Becoming Unique: Personality Development
The Growth of Thought: Cognitive Development

FEATURED STUDY ▌ **Can Infants Do Arithmetic?** 458
The Development of Moral Reasoning

The Transition of Adolescence 463
Physiological Changes
Neural Development
Time of Turmoil?
The Search for Identity
Emerging Adulthood as a New Developmental Stage

The Expanse of Adulthood 468
Personality Development
Transitions in Family Life
Aging and Physiological Changes
Aging and Neural Changes
Aging and Cognitive Changes

Reflecting on the Chapter's Themes 475

PERSONAL APPLICATION ▌ **Understanding Gender Differences** 475

Illustrated Overview of Human Development 476
How Do the Sexes Differ in Behavior?
Biological Origins of Gender Differences
Environmental Origins of Gender Differences
Conclusion

CRITICAL THINKING APPLICATION ▌ **Are Fathers Essential to Children's Well-Being?** 484
The Basic Argument
Evaluating the Argument

Recap 486

Practice Test 487

12

PERSONALITY: THEORY, RESEARCH, AND ASSESSMENT 488

Columbia River Gorge, Oregon, bridge at Multnomah Falls © Rich Reid/National Geographic Image Collection

The Nature of Personality   490
Defining Personality: Consistency and Distinctiveness
Personality Traits: Dispositions and Dimensions
The Five-Factor Model of Personality Traits

Psychodynamic Perspectives   493
Freud's Psychoanalytic Theory
Jung's Analytical Psychology
Adler's Individual Psychology
Evaluating Psychodynamic Perspectives

Behavioral Perspectives   502
Skinner's Ideas Applied to Personality
Bandura's Social Cognitive Theory

FEATURED STUDY ▌ Can Rooms Really Have Personality?   505
Mischel and the Person-Situation Controversy
Evaluating Behavioral Perspectives

Humanistic Perspectives   508
Rogers's Person-Centered Theory
Maslow's Theory of Self-Actualization
Evaluating Humanistic Perspectives

Biological Perspectives   513
Eysenck's Theory
Behavioral Genetics and Personality
The Evolutionary Approach to Personality
Evaluating Biological Perspectives

**A Contemporary Empirical Approach:
Terror Management Theory   517**
Essentials of Terror Management Theory
Applications of Terror Management Theory

Culture and Personality   519

Illustrated Overview of Major Theories of Personality   520

Reflecting on the Chapter's Themes   523

PERSONAL APPLICATION ▌ Understanding Personality Assessment   524
Self-Report Inventories
Projective Tests
Personality Testing on the Internet

CRITICAL THINKING APPLICATION ▌ Hindsight in Everyday Analyses of Personality   528
The Prevalence of Hindsight Bias
Hindsight and Personality
Other Implications of "20/20 Hindsight"

Recap   530

Practice Test   531

13

STRESS, COPING, AND HEALTH   532

San Francisco, CA, Golden Gate Bridge © Roger Ressmeyer/Corbis

The Nature of Stress   534
Stress as an Everyday Event
Appraisal: Stress Lies in the Eye of the Beholder
Major Types of Stress

Responding to Stress   540
Emotional Responses
Physiological Responses
Behavioral Responses

The Effects of Stress on Psychological Functioning   548
Impaired Task Performance
Burnout
Psychological Problems and Disorders
Positive Effects

The Effects of Stress on Physical Health   551
Personality, Hostility, and Heart Disease
Emotional Reactions, Depression, and Heart Disease

FEATURED STUDY ▌ **Is Depression a Risk Factor for Heart Disease?   553**

Stress, Other Diseases, and Immune Functioning
Sizing Up the Link Between Stress and Illness

Factors Moderating the Impact of Stress   556
Social Support
Optimism and Conscientiousness

Health-Impairing Behavior   558
Smoking
Poor Nutritional Habits
Lack of Exercise
Alcohol and Drug Use
Behavior and AIDS
How Does Health-Impairing Behavior Develop?

Reactions to Illness   562
Deciding to Seek Treatment
Communicating with Health Providers
Adhering to Medical Advice

Reflecting on the Chapter's Themes   564

PERSONAL APPLICATION ▌ **Improving Coping and Stress Management   565**
Reappraisal: Ellis's Rational Thinking
Using Humor as a Stress Reducer
Releasing Pent-Up Emotions and Forgiving Others
Learning to Relax
Minimizing Physiological Vulnerability

CRITICAL THINKING APPLICATION ▌ **Thinking Rationally About Health Statistics and Decisions   570**
Evaluating Statistics on Health Risks
Thinking Systematically About Health Decisions

Recap   572

Practice Test   573

14

PSYCHOLOGICAL DISORDERS 574

Brazil, Sao Paulo, Curitiba motorway under construction © Jens Lucking/Stone/Getty Images

Abnormal Behavior: Myths, Realities, and Controversies 576
The Medical Model Applied to Abnormal Behavior
Criteria of Abnormal Behavior
Stereotypes of Psychological Disorders
Psychodiagnosis: The Classification of Disorders
The Prevalence of Psychological Disorders

Anxiety Disorders 582
Generalized Anxiety Disorder
Phobic Disorder
Panic Disorder and Agoraphobia
Obsessive-Compulsive Disorder
Posttraumatic Stress Disorder
Etiology of Anxiety Disorders

Somatoform Disorders 586
Subtypes and Symptoms
Etiology of Somatoform Disorders

Dissociative Disorders 589
Dissociative Amnesia and Fugue
Dissociative Identity Disorder
Etiology of Dissociative Disorders

Mood Disorders 590
Major Depressive Disorder
Bipolar Disorder
Mood Disorders and Suicide
Etiology of Mood Disorders

FEATURED STUDY ▌ Does Negative Thinking Cause Depression? 595

Schizophrenic Disorders 598
General Symptoms
Subtypes, Course, and Outcome
Etiology of Schizophrenia

Personality Disorders 604
Diagnostic Problems
Antisocial Personality Disorder

Psychological Disorders and the Law 607

Illustrated Overview of Three Categories of Psychological Disorders 608

Insanity
Involuntary Commitment

Culture and Pathology 610
Are Equivalent Disorders Found Around the World?
Are Symptom Patterns Culturally Invariant?

Reflecting on the Chapter's Themes 612

PERSONAL APPLICATION ▌ Understanding Eating Disorders 613

Description
History and Prevalence
Etiology of Eating Disorders

CRITICAL THINKING APPLICATION ▌ Working with Probabilities in Thinking About Mental Illness 616

Recap 618

Practice Test 619

15

TREATMENT OF PSYCHOLOGICAL DISORDERS 620

location and name unknown © Richard T. Nowitz/National Geographic/Getty Images

The Elements of the Treatment Process　622
Treatments: How Many Types Are There?
Clients: Who Seeks Therapy?
Therapists: Who Provides Professional Treatment?

Insight Therapies　626
Psychoanalysis
Client-Centered Therapy
Therapies Inspired by Positive Psychology
Group Therapy
How Effective Are Insight Therapies?
How Do Insight Therapies Work?

Behavior Therapies　633
Systematic Desensitization
Aversion Therapy
Social Skills Training
Cognitive-Behavioral Treatments
How Effective Are Behavior Therapies?

Biomedical Therapies　638
Treatment with Drugs
Electroconvulsive Therapy (ECT)
New Brain Stimulation Techniques

Current Trends and Issues in Treatment　645
Grappling with the Constraints of Managed Care
Blending Approaches to Treatment

Illustrated Overview of Five Major Approaches to Treatment　646

FEATURED STUDY ▌ **Combining Insight Therapy and Medication**　648
Increasing Multicultural Sensitivity in Treatment

Institutional Treatment in Transition　650
Disenchantment with Mental Hospitals
Deinstitutionalization
Mental Illness, the Revolving Door, and Homelessness

Reflecting on the Chapter's Themes　653

PERSONAL APPLICATION ▌ **Looking for a Therapist**　654
Where Do You Find Therapeutic Services?
Is the Therapist's Profession or Sex Important?
Is Treatment Always Expensive?
Is the Therapist's Theoretical Approach Important?
What Should You Look for in a Prospective Therapist?
What Is Therapy Like?

CRITICAL THINKING APPLICATION ▌ **From Crisis to Wellness—But Was It the Therapy?**　658

Recap　660

Practice Test　661

16

SOCIAL BEHAVIOR 662

Shanghai, China, (Zigzag) Footbridge at Yu Yuan Gardens © Jose Fuste Raga/Corbis

Person Perception: Forming Impressions of Others 664
Effects of Physical Appearance
Stereotypes
Subjectivity in Person Perception
An Evolutionary Perspective on Bias in Person Perception

Attribution Processes: Explaining Behavior 667
Internal Versus External Attributions
Attributions for Success and Failure
Bias in Attribution
Culture and Attributional Tendencies

Close Relationships: Liking and Loving 672
Key Factors in Attraction
Perspectives on the Mystery of Love
Culture and Close Relationships
The Internet and Close Relationships
An Evolutionary Perspective on Attraction

Attitudes: Making Social Judgments 681
Components and Dimensions of Attitudes
Attitudes and Behavior
Trying to Change Attitudes: Factors in Persuasion
Theories of Attitude Formation and Change

Conformity and Obedience: Yielding to Others 688
Conformity
Obedience

FEATURED STUDY ❚ **"I Was Just Following Orders"** 689
Cultural Variations in Conformity and Obedience
The Power of the Situation: The Stanford Prison Simulation

Behavior in Groups: Joining with Others 694
Behavior Alone and in Groups: The Case of the Bystander Effect
Group Productivity and Social Loafing
Decision Making in Groups

Reflecting on the Chapter's Themes 699

PERSONAL APPLICATION UNDERSTANDING PREJUDICE 699
Stereotyping and Subjectivity in Person Perception
Biases in Attribution
Forming and Preserving Prejudicial Attitudes
Competition Between Groups
Dividing the World into Ingroups and Outgroups
Threats to Social Identity

CRITICAL THINKING APPLICATION ❚ **Whom Can You Trust? Analyzing Credibility and Influence Tactics** 704
Evaluating Credibility
Recognizing Social Influence Strategies

Recap 706

Practice Test 707

Appendix A Answers to Concept Checks **A-1**

Appendix B Statistical Methods **A-7**

Appendix C Industrial/Organizational Psychology **A-15**

Appendix D Careers in Psychology **A-30**

Appendix E Critical Thinking About Internet Research Sources: What Students Need to Know **A-35**

Glossary G-1

References R-1

Name Index I-1

Subject Index I-18

Credits C-1

TO THE STUDENT

Welcome to your introductory psychology textbook. In most college courses, students spend more time with their textbooks than with their professors, so it helps if students *like* their textbooks. Making textbooks likable, however, is a tricky proposition. By its very nature, a textbook must introduce students to many complicated concepts, ideas, and theories. If it doesn't, it isn't much of a textbook, and instructors won't choose to use it. Nevertheless, in writing this book I've tried to make it as likable as possible without compromising the academic content that your instructor demands. I've especially tried to keep in mind your need for a clear, well-organized presentation that makes the important material stand out and yet is interesting to read. Above all else, I hope you find this book challenging to think about and easy to learn from. Before you plunge into your first chapter, let me introduce you to the book's key features. Becoming familiar with how the book works will help you to get more out of it.

Key Features

You're about to embark on a journey into a new domain of ideas. Your text includes some important features that are intended to highlight certain aspects of psychology's landscape.

Unifying Themes

To help you make sense of a complex and diverse field of study, I introduce seven themes in Chapter 1 that reappear in a number of variations as we move from chapter to chapter. These unifying themes are meant to provoke thought about important issues and to highlight the connections between chapters. They are discussed near the end of the main body of each chapter in a section called "Reflecting on the Chapter's Themes."

Personal Applications

Toward the end of each chapter you'll find a Personal Application section that shows how psychology is relevant to everyday life. Some of these sections provide concrete, practical advice that could be helpful to you in your educational endeavors, such as those on improving academic performance, improving everyday memory, and achieving self-control. So, you may want to jump ahead and read some of these Personal Applications early.

Critical Thinking Applications

Each Personal Application is followed by a two-page Critical Thinking Application that teaches and models basic critical thinking skills. I think you will find these sections refreshing and interesting. Like the Personal Applications, they are part of the text's basic content and should be read unless you are told otherwise by your instructor. Although the "facts" of psychology will gradually change after you take this course (thanks to scientific progress), the critical thinking skills modeled in these sections should prove valuable for many years to come.

Web Links and Internet Essay

To help make this book a rich resource guide, we have included dozens of Web Links, which are recommended websites that can provide you with additional information on many topics. The recommended sites were selected by Professor Vincent Hevern, a web expert who sought out resources that are interesting and that provide accurate, empirically sound information. The Web Links are dispersed throughout the chapters, adjacent to related topical coverage. Because web addresses change frequently, we have not placed the URLs for our Web Links in the book. If you are interested in visiting these sites, we recommend that you do so through the *Psychology: Themes & Variations* home page at the Wadsworth Cengage Learning website (www.cengage.com/psychology/weiten). Links to all the recommended websites are maintained there, and the webmaster periodically updates the URLs. Of course, you can also track down the recommended sites by using a search engine, such as Google. The inclusion of the Web Links in this text illustrates that the Internet has become an enormously important source of information on psychology (and most topics). Cognizant of this reality, I asked Professor Hevern to write a brief essay on how to evaluate the quality and credibility of web-based resources. I urge you to read his essay in Appendix E.

Appendix on Careers in Psychology

Many students who take the introductory psychology course are intrigued by the possibility of pursuing a career in psychology. If you think you might be interested in a psychology-related career, you should consider reading Appendix D, which provides a succinct overview of career options in the field, written by Professor Marky Lloyd.

Learning Aids

This text contains a great deal of information. A number of learning aids have been incorporated into the book to help you digest it all.

An *outline* at the beginning of each chapter provides you with an overview of the topics covered in that chapter. Think of the outlines as road maps, and bear in mind that it's easier to reach a destination if you know where you're going.

Headings serve as road signs in your journey through each chapter. Four levels of headings are used to make it easy to see the organization of each chapter.

Key Learning Goals, found at the beginning of major sections, can help you focus on the important issues in the material you are about to read.

Reviews of Key Learning Goals, found at the ends of major sections, are interim summaries that permit you to check your understanding of a section's main ideas immediately after finishing the section. The numbered paragraphs in these reviews address the learning objectives outlined in the Key Learning Goals.

Italics (without boldface) are used liberally throughout the text to emphasize crucial points.

Key terms are identified with ***italicized blue boldface*** type to alert you that these are important vocabulary items that are part of psychology's technical language. The key terms are also listed at the end of the chapter.

An *integrated running glossary* provides an on-the-spot definition of each key term as it's introduced in the text. These formal definitions are printed in **blue boldface** type. Becoming familiar with psychology's terminology is an essential part of learning about the field. The integrated running glossary should make this learning process easier.

Concept Checks are sprinkled throughout the chapters to let you test your mastery of important ideas. Generally, they ask you to integrate or organize a number of key ideas, or to apply ideas to real-world situations. Although they're meant to be engaging and fun, they do check conceptual *understanding,* and some are challenging. But if you get stuck, don't worry; the answers (and explanations, where they're needed) are in the back of the book in Appendix A.

Illustrations in the text are important elements in your complete learning package. Some illustrations provide enlightening diagrams of complicated concepts; others furnish examples that help flesh out ideas or provide concise overviews of research results. Careful attention to the tables and figures in the book will help you understand the material discussed in the text.

A *Chapter Recap* at the end of each chapter provides a summary of the chapter's *Key Ideas,* a list of *Key Terms,* and a list of *Key People* (important theorists and researchers). It's wise to read over these review materials to make sure you've digested the information in the chapter. To aid your study efforts, the lists of key terms and key people show the page numbers where the terms or individuals were first introduced.

Each chapter ends with a 15-item *Practice Test* that should give you a realistic assessment of your mastery of that chapter and valuable practice in taking multiple-choice tests.

An *alphabetical glossary* is provided in the back of the book. Most key terms are formally defined in the integrated running glossary only when they are first introduced. So if you run into a technical term in a later chapter and can't remember its meaning, it may be easier to look it up in the alphabetical glossary than to try to find the location where the term was originally introduced.

A Few Footnotes

Psychology textbooks customarily identify the studies, theoretical treatises, books, and articles that information comes from. These *citations* occur (1) when names are followed by a date in parentheses, as in "Smith (1993) found that . . ." or (2) when names and dates are provided together within parentheses, as in "In one study (Smith, Miller, & Jones, 2001), the researchers attempted to . . ." All of the cited publications are listed by author in the alphabetized *References* section in the back of the book. The citations and references are a necessary part of a book's scholarly and scientific foundation. Practically speaking, however, you'll probably want to glide right over them as you read. You definitely don't need to memorize the names and dates. The only names you may need to know are the handful listed under Key People in each Chapter Recap (unless your instructor mentions a personal favorite that you should know).

Concept Charts for Study and Review

Your text should be accompanied by a booklet of Concept Charts that are designed to help you organize and master the main ideas contained in each chapter. Each Concept Chart provides a detailed visual map of the key ideas found in the main body of that chapter. Seeing how it all fits together should help you to better understand each chapter. You can use these charts to preview chapters, to get a handle on how ideas are interconnected, to double-check your mastery of the chapters, and to memorize the crucial principles in chapters.

PsykTrek: A Multimedia Introduction to Psychology

PsykTrek is a multimedia supplement developed to accompany this textbook. It is an enormously powerful learning tool that can enhance your understanding of many complex processes and theories, provide you with an alternative way to assimilate many crucial concepts, and add a little more fun to your journey through introductory psychology. *PsykTrek* has been designed to supplement and complement your textbook. I strongly encourage you to use it. The icons that you will see in many of the headings in the upcoming chapters refer to the content of *PsykTrek*. An icon indicates that the textbook topic referred to in the heading is covered in the Interactive Learning Modules or Simulations found on *PsykTrek*. The relevant simulations (Sim1, Sim2, and so forth) and the relevant Interactive Learning Modules (1a, 1b, 1c, and so forth) are listed adjacent to the icons.

A Word About the Study Guide

A *Study Guide* is available to accompany this text. It is written by two of my former professors, who introduced me to psychology years ago. They have done a great job of organizing review materials to help you master the information in the book. I suggest that you seriously consider using it to help you study.

A Final Word

I'm pleased to be a part of your first journey into the world of psychology, and I sincerely hope that you'll find the book as thought provoking and as easy to learn from as I've tried to make it. If you have any comments or advice on the book, please write to me in care of the publisher (Wadsworth/Cengage Learning, 10 Davis Drive, Belmont, CA 94002). You can be sure I'll pay careful attention to your feedback. Finally, let me wish you good luck. I hope you enjoy your course and learn a great deal.

Wayne Weiten

THE EVOLUTION OF PSYCHOLOGY

Psychology's Early History
A New Science Is Born: The Contributions of Wundt and Hall
The Battle of the "Schools" Begins: Structuralism Versus Functionalism
Freud Brings the Unconscious into the Picture
Watson Alters Psychology's Course as Behaviorism Makes Its Debut
Skinner Questions Free Will as Behaviorism Flourishes
The Humanists Revolt

Psychology's Modern History
Psychology Comes of Age as a Profession
Psychology Returns to Its Roots: Renewed Interest in Cognition
    and Physiology
Psychology Broadens Its Horizons: Increased Interest in Cultural Diversity
Psychology Adapts: The Emergence of Evolutionary Psychology
Psychology Moves in a Positive Direction

Illustrated Overview of Psychology's History

Psychology Today: Vigorous and Diversified
Research Areas in Psychology
Professional Specialties in Psychology

Seven Unifying Themes
Themes Related to Psychology as a Field of Study
Themes Related to Psychology's Subject Matter

PERSONAL APPLICATION ▮ Improving Academic
Performance
Developing Sound Study Habits
Improving Your Reading
Getting More Out of Lectures
Improving Test-Taking Strategies

CRITICAL THINKING APPLICATION ▮ Developing Critical
Thinking Skills: An Introduction
The Need to Teach Critical Thinking
An Example

Recap

Practice Test

What is psychology, and why is it worth your time to study? Let me approach these questions by sharing a couple of stories with you.

In 2005, Greg Hogan, a college sophomore, briefly achieved national notoriety when he was arrested for a crime. Greg wasn't anybody's idea of a likely criminal. He was the son of a Baptist minister and the president of his class. He played the cello in the university orchestra. He even worked part-time in the chaplain's office. So it shocked everybody who knew Greg when police arrested him at his fraternity house for bank robbery.

Earlier that day, Greg had faked having a gun and made away with over $2800 from a local bank. His reason? Over a period of months he had lost $5000 playing poker on the Internet. His lawyer said Greg's gambling habit had become "an addiction" (Dissell, 2005; McLoughlin & Paquet, 2005).

Greg eventually entered a clinic for treatment of his gambling problem. In a way, he was lucky—at least he got help. Moshe Pergament, a 19-year-old community college student in Long Island, New York, wasn't so fortunate. Moshe was shot to death after brandishing a gun at a police officer. The gun turned out to be plastic. On the front seat of his car was a note that began, "Officer, it was a plan. I'm sorry to get you involved. I just needed to die." Moshe had just lost $6000 betting on the World Series. His death was what people in law enforcement call "suicide by cop" (Lindsay & Lester, 2004).

These stories are at the extreme edge of a trend that concerns many public officials and mental health professionals: The popularity of gambling—from lotteries to sports betting to online poker—is booming, especially among the young (Jacobs, 2004). College students seem to be leading the way. To some observers, gambling on college campuses has become an "epidemic." Student bookies on some campuses make tens of thousands of dollars a year taking sports bets from other students. Television shows like *The World Series of Poker* are marketed squarely at college-student audiences. Poker sites on the web invite students to win their tuition by gambling online.

For most people, gambling is a relatively harmless—if sometimes expensive—pastime. However, estimates suggest that 5%–6% of teens and young adults develop serious problems with gambling—two to four times the rate for older adults (Jacobs, 2004; Petry, 2005; Winters et al., 2004). The enormous growth of pathological gambling among young people raises a host of questions. Is gambling dangerous? Can it really be addictive? What is an addiction, anyway? If pathological gamblers abuse drugs or commit crimes, is gambling the cause of their troubles, or is it a symptom of a deeper problem? Perhaps most critically of all, why do some people become pathological gamblers while the great majority do not? Every day millions of people in the United States play the lottery, bet on sports, or visit casinos without apparent harm. Yet others can't seem to stop gambling until they have lost everything—their savings, their jobs, their homes, and their self-respect. Why? What causes such perplexing, self-destructive behavior?

Psychology is about questions like these. More generally, psychology is about understanding *all* the things we do. All of us wonder sometimes about the reasons underlying people's behavior—why it's hard to diet, why we procrastinate about studying, why we fall in love with one person rather than another. We wonder why some people are outgoing while others are shy. We wonder why we sometimes do things that we know will bring us pain and anguish, whether it's clinging to a destructive relationship or losing our tuition money in a game of Texas Hold 'Em. The study of psychology is about all these things, and infinitely more.

Many of psychology's questions have implications for our everyday lives. For me, this is one of the field's major attractions—*psychology is practical*. Consider the case of gambling. Pathological gamblers suffer all kinds of misery, yet they can't seem to stop. Listen to the anguish of a gambler named Steve: "Over the past 2 years I have lost literally thousands . . . I have attempted to give up time after time after time, but failed every time. . . . I have debts around my neck which are destroying mine and my family's life. . . . I just want a massive light to be turned on with a message saying, 'This way to your old life, Steve'" (SJB, 2006).

What is the best way to help someone like Steve? Should he join a group like Gamblers Anonymous? Does counseling work? Are there drugs that can help? By probing the why's and how's of human behavior, psychology can help us find answers to pressing questions like these, as well as issues that affect each of us every day. You will see the practical side of psychology throughout this book, especially in the Personal Applications at the ends of chapters. These Applications focus on everyday problems, such as coping more effectively with stress, improving self-control, and dealing with sleep difficulties.

Beyond its practical value, psychology is worth studying because it provides a powerful *way of think-*

The perplexing problem of pathological gambling, which has increased dramatically among college students in recent years, raises a variety of complicated questions. As you will see throughout this text, psychologists investigate an infinite variety of fascinating questions.

ing. All of us make judgments every day about why people do the things they do. For example, we might think that pathological gamblers are weak willed, or irrational, or just too dumb to understand that the odds are stacked against them. Or we might believe they are in the grip of an addiction that simply overpowers them. How do we decide which of these judgments—if any—are right?

Psychologists are committed to investigating questions about human behavior in a scientific way. This means that they seek to formulate precise questions about behavior and then test possible answers through systematic observation. This commitment to testing ideas means that psychology provides a means of building knowledge that is relatively accurate and dependable. It also provides a model for assessing the assertions we hear every day about behavior, as you'll see in upcoming chapters' Critical Thinking Applications.

In the case of gambling, for example, researchers have designed careful studies to probe the relationship of gambling problems to any number of possible influences, from childhood experiences to membership in a college fraternity. They have compared the way slot machines are set to reward players with frequent small payoffs to the way rats and pigeons learn to earn food rewards in the laboratory. They have used state-of-the-art scanners to image the brains of people performing tasks similar to placing bets. They have even looked at whether some people are predisposed by their genes to develop problems with gambling (Petry, 2005; Rockey et al., 2005, Szegedy-Maszak, 2005).

If there is one clear conclusion that emerges from these studies, it is that there is no simple answer to the mystery of pathological gambling. Instead, it is likely that a full explanation of gambling problems will involve many influences that interact in complex ways (Derevensky & Gupta, 2004; Petry, 2005). As you'll see throughout this course, the same is true of most aspects of behavior. In my opinion, this is yet another reason to study psychology: it teaches us a healthy respect for the *complexity* of behavior. In a world that could use more understanding—and compassion—this can be an invaluable lesson.

As you go through this course, I hope you'll come to share my enthusiasm for psychology as a fascinating and immensely practical field of study. Let's begin our exploration by seeing how psychology has evolved from early speculations about behavior to a modern science. By looking at this evolution, you'll better understand psychology as it is today, a sprawling, multifaceted science and profession. We'll conclude our introduction with a look at seven unifying themes that will serve as connecting threads in the chapters to come. The chapter's Personal Application will review research that provides insights into how to be an effective student. Finally, the Critical Thinking Application will discuss how critical thinking skills can be enhanced.

Psychology's Early History

Psychology's story is one of people groping toward a better understanding of themselves. As psychology has evolved, its focus, methods, and explanatory models have changed. In this section we'll look at psychology's early years, as the discipline developed from philosophical speculations about the mind into a research-based science.

The term *psychology* comes from two Greek words, *psyche,* meaning the soul, and *logos,* referring to the study of a subject. These two Greek roots were first put together to define a topic of study in the 16th century, when *psyche* was used to refer to the soul, spirit, or mind, as distinguished from the body (Boring, 1966). Not until the early 18th century did the term *psychology* gain more than rare usage among scholars. By that time it had acquired its literal meaning, "the study of the mind."

Of course, people have always wondered about the mysteries of the mind. In that sense, psychology is as old as the human race. But it was only about 130 years ago that psychology emerged as a scientific discipline.

A New Science Is Born: The Contributions of Wundt and Hall   1a

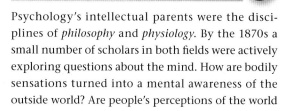

Psychology's intellectual parents were the disciplines of *philosophy* and *physiology.* By the 1870s a small number of scholars in both fields were actively exploring questions about the mind. How are bodily sensations turned into a mental awareness of the outside world? Are people's perceptions of the world

Key Learning Goals

1.1 Summarize Wundt's and Hall's accomplishments and contributions to psychology.

1.2 Describe the chief tenets of structuralism and functionalism and their impact on the development of psychology.

1.3 Articulate Freud's principal ideas and why they inspired controversy.

1.4 Trace the development of behaviorism and assess Watson's impact on the evolution of psychology.

1.5 Summarize Skinner's key insights and why they were controversial.

1.6 Explain the impetus for the emergence of humanism and its underlying philosophy.

**Wilhelm Wundt
1832–1920**

"Physiology informs us about those life phenomena that we perceive by our external senses. In psychology, the person looks upon himself as from within and tries to explain the interrelations of those processes that this internal observation discloses."

accurate reflections of reality? How do mind and body interact? The philosophers and physiologists who were interested in the mind viewed such questions as fascinating issues *within* their respective fields. It was a German professor, Wilhelm Wundt (1832–1920), who eventually changed this view. Wundt mounted a campaign to make psychology an independent discipline rather than a stepchild of philosophy or physiology.

The time and place were right for Wundt's appeal. German universities were in a healthy period of expansion, so resources were available for new disciplines. Furthermore, the intellectual climate favored the scientific approach that Wundt advocated. Hence, his proposals were well received by the academic community. In 1879 Wundt succeeded in establishing the first formal laboratory for research in psychology at the University of Leipzig. In deference to this landmark event, historians have christened 1879 as psychology's "date of birth." Soon afterward, in 1881, Wundt established the first journal devoted to publishing research on psychology. All in all, Wundt's campaign was so successful that today he is widely characterized as the founder of psychology.

Wundt's conception of psychology was influential for decades. Borrowing from his training in physiology, Wundt (1874) declared that the new psychology should be a *science* modeled after fields such as physics and chemistry. What was the subject matter of the new science? According to Wundt, psychology's primary focus was *consciousness*—the awareness of immediate experience. *Thus, psychology became the scientific study of conscious experience.* This orientation kept psychology focused on the mind and mental processes. But it demanded that the methods psychologists used to investigate the mind be as scientific as those of chemists or physicists.

Wundt was a tireless, dedicated scholar who generated an estimated 54,000 pages of books and articles in his career (Bringmann & Balk, 1992). Studies in his laboratory focused on attention, memory, sensory processes, and reaction-time experiments that provided estimates of the duration of various mental processes (Fuchs & Milar, 2003). Outstanding young scholars, including many Americans, came to Leipzig to study under Wundt. Many of his students then fanned out across Germany and America, establishing the research laboratories that formed the basis for the new, independent science of psychology. Indeed, it was in North America that Wundt's new science grew by leaps and bounds. Between 1883 and 1893, some 23 new psychological research laboratories sprang up in the United States and Canada, at the schools shown in Figure 1.1 (Benjamin, 2000). Many of the laboratories were started by Wundt's students, or by his students' students.

G. Stanley Hall (1846–1924), who studied briefly with Wundt, was a particularly important contributor to the rapid growth of psychology in America. Toward the end of the 19th century, Hall reeled off a series of "firsts" for American psychology. To begin with, he established America's first research laboratory in psychology at Johns Hopkins University in 1883. Four years later he launched America's first psychology journal. Furthermore, in 1892 he was the driving force behind the establishment of the Ameri-

Figure 1.1

Early research laboratories in North America. This map highlights the location and year of founding for the first 23 psychological research labs established in North American colleges and universities. As the color coding shows, a great many of these labs were founded by the students of Wilhelm Wundt, G. Stanley Hall, and William James. (Based on Benjamin, 2000)

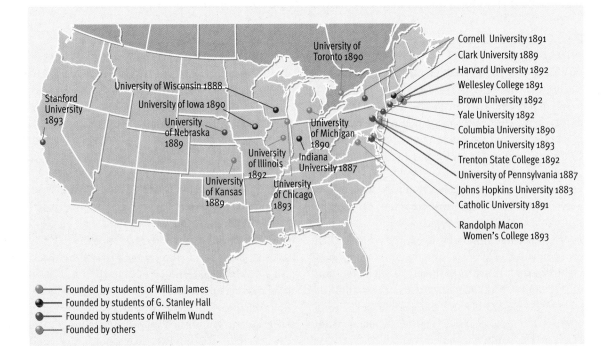

can Psychological Association (APA) and was elected its first president. Today the APA is the world's largest organization devoted to the advancement of psychology, with over 150,000 members and affiliates. Hall never envisioned such a vast membership when he and 26 others set up their new organization.

Exactly why Americans took to psychology so quickly is hard to say. Perhaps it was because America's relatively young universities were more open to new disciplines than the older, more tradition-bound universities in Europe. In any case, although psychology was born in Germany, it blossomed into adolescence in America. Like many adolescents, however, the young science was about to enter a period of turbulence and turmoil.

The Battle of the "Schools" Begins: Structuralism Versus Functionalism

1a

While reading about how psychology became a science, you might have imagined that psychologists became a unified group of scholars who busily added new discoveries to an uncontested store of "facts." In reality, no science works that way. Competing schools of thought exist in most scientific disciplines. Sometimes the disagreements among these schools are sharp. Such diversity in thought is natural and often stimulates enlightening debate. In psychology, the first two major schools of thought, *structuralism* and *functionalism,* were entangled in the field's first great intellectual battle.

Structuralism emerged through the leadership of Edward Titchener, an Englishman who emigrated to the United States in 1892 and taught for decades at Cornell University. Although Titchener earned his degree in Wundt's Leipzig laboratory and expressed great admiration for Wundt's work, he brought his own version of Wundt's psychology to America (Hilgard, 1987; Thorne & Henley, 1997). **Structuralism was based on the notion that the task of psychology is to analyze consciousness into its basic elements and investigate how these elements are related.** Just as physicists were studying how matter is made up of basic particles, the structuralists wanted to identify and examine the fundamental components of conscious experience, such as sensations, feelings, and images.

Although the structuralists explored many questions, most of their work concerned sensation and perception in vision, hearing, and touch. To examine the contents of consciousness, the structuralists depended on the method of **introspection, or the careful, systematic self-observation of one's own conscious experience.** As practiced by the structur-

alists, introspection required training to make the *subject*—the person being studied—more objective and more aware. Once trained, participants were typically exposed to auditory tones, optical illusions, and visual stimuli under carefully controlled and systematically varied conditions and were asked to analyze what they experienced.

The functionalists took a different view of psychology's task. **Functionalism was based on the belief that psychology should investigate the function or purpose of consciousness, rather than its structure.** The chief impetus for the emergence of functionalism was the work of William James (1842–1910), a brilliant American scholar (and brother of novelist Henry James). James's formal training was in medicine. However, he did not find medicine to be intellectually challenging and felt he was too sickly to pursue a medical practice (Ross, 1991), so when an opportunity arose in 1872, he joined the faculty of Harvard University to pursue a less arduous career in academia. Medicine's loss proved to be psychology's gain, as James quickly became an intellectual giant in the field. James's landmark book, *Principles of Psychology* (1890), became standard reading for generations of psychologists and is perhaps the most influential text in the history of psychology (Weiten & Wight, 1992).

James's thinking illustrates how psychology, like any field, is deeply embedded in a network of cultural and intellectual influences. James had been impressed with Charles Darwin's (1859, 1871) concept of *natural selection.* According to the principle of *natural selection*, **heritable characteristics that provide a survival or reproductive advantage are more likely than alternative characteristics to be**

The establishment of the first research laboratory in psychology by Wilhelm Wundt (far right) marked the birth of psychology as a modern science.

William James 1842–1910

"It is just this free water of consciousness that psychologists resolutely overlook."

Mind and Body: René Descartes to William James

Designed originally to celebrate psychology's first century as an independent discipline, this online exhibition traces three historical themes: the mind-body problem posed in the 17th century by philosopher René Descartes, the rise of experimental psychology, and the beginnings of psychology in America. **Note:** The URLs (addresses) for the Web Links can be found on the website for this text (academic.cengage.com/psychology/weiten), or you can find them using a search engine such as Google.

passed on to subsequent generations and thus come to be "selected" over time. This cornerstone notion of Darwin's evolutionary theory suggested that the typical characteristics of a species must serve some purpose. Applying this idea to humans, James (1890) noted that consciousness obviously is an important characteristic of our species. Hence, he contended that psychology should investigate the *functions* rather than the *structure* of consciousness.

James also argued that the structuralists' approach missed the real nature of conscious experience. Consciousness, he argued, consists of a continuous *flow* of thoughts. In analyzing consciousness into its *elements,* the structuralists were looking at static points in that flow. James wanted to understand the flow itself, which he called the *stream of consciousness.* Today, people take this metaphorical description of mental life for granted, but at the time it was a revolutionary insight. As Leary (2003) puts it, "No longer was consciousness depicted as some kind of encompassing mental container more or less full of such 'contents' as sensations, images, ideas, thoughts, feel-

ings, and the like; rather it was now portrayed as a continually ongoing, wholistic experience or process" (p. 25). James went on to provide enormously influential analyses of many crucial issues in the emerging field of psychology. Among other things, his discussions of how people acquired *habits* laid the groundwork for progress in the study of learning, and his conception of the *self* provided the foundation for subsequent theories of personality (Leary, 2003).

Whereas structuralists naturally gravitated to the laboratory, functionalists were more interested in how people adapt their behavior to the demands of the real world around them. This practical slant led them to introduce new subjects into psychology. Instead of focusing on sensation and perception, functionalists such as James McKeen Cattell and John Dewey began to investigate mental testing, patterns of development in children, the effectiveness of educational practices, and behavioral differences between the sexes. These new topics may have played a role in attracting the first women into the field of psychology (see **Figure 1.2**).

Figure 1.2

Women pioneers in the history of psychology. Women have long made major contributions to the development of psychology (Milar, 2000; Russo & Denmark, 1987), and today nearly half of all psychologists are female. As in other fields, however, women have often been overlooked in histories of psychology (Furumoto & Scarborough, 1986). The three psychologists profiled here demonstrate that women have been making significant contributions to psychology almost from its beginning—despite formidable barriers to pursuing their academic careers.

Mary Whiton Calkins (1863–1930)	Margaret Floy Washburn (1871–1939)	Leta Stetter Hollingworth (1886–1939)

Mary Calkins, who studied under William James, founded one of the first dozen psychology laboratories in America at Wellesley College in 1891, invented a widely used technique for studying memory, and became the first woman to serve as president of the American Psychological Association in 1905. Ironically, however, she never received her Ph.D. in psychology. Because she was a woman, Harvard University only reluctantly allowed her to take graduate classes as a "guest student." When she completed the requirements for her Ph.D., Harvard would only offer her a doctorate from its undergraduate sister school, Radcliffe. Calkins felt that this decision perpetuated unequal treatment of the sexes, so she refused the Radcliffe degree.

Margaret Washburn was the first woman to receive a Ph.D. in psychology. She wrote an influential book, *The Animal Mind* (1908), which served as an impetus to the subsequent emergence of behaviorism and was standard reading for several generations of psychologists. In 1921 she became the second woman to serve as president of the American Psychological Association. Washburn studied under James McKeen Cattell at Columbia University, but like Mary Calkins, she was only permitted to take graduate classes unofficially, as a "hearer." Hence, she transferred to Cornell University, which was more hospitable toward women, and completed her doctorate in 1894. Like Calkins, Washburn spent most of her career at a college for women (Vassar).

Leta Hollingworth did pioneering work on adolescent development, mental retardation, and gifted children. Indeed, she was the first person to use the term *gifted* to refer to youngsters who scored exceptionally high on intelligence tests. Hollingworth (1914, 1916) also played a major role in debunking popular theories of her era that purported to explain why women were "inferior" to men. For instance, she conducted a study refuting the myth that phases of the menstrual cycle are reliably associated with performance decrements in women. Her careful collection of objective data on gender differences forced other scientists to subject popular, untested beliefs about the sexes to skeptical, empirical inquiry.

The impassioned advocates of structuralism and functionalism saw themselves as fighting for high stakes: the definition and future direction of the new science of psychology. Their war of ideas continued energetically for many years. Who won? Most historians give the edge to functionalism. Although both schools of thought gradually faded away, functionalism fostered the development of two important descendants—behaviorism and applied psychology—that we will discuss momentarily.

Freud Brings the Unconscious into the Picture   1a, 10a

Sigmund Freud (1856–1939) was an Austrian physician who early in his career dreamed of achieving fame by making an important discovery. His determination was such that in medical school he dissected 400 male eels to prove for the first time that they had testes. His work with eels did not make him famous, but his subsequent work with people did. Indeed, his theories made him one of the most controversial intellectual figures of modern times.

Freud's (1900, 1933) approach to psychology grew out of his efforts to treat mental disorders. In his medical practice, Freud treated people troubled by psychological problems such as irrational fears, obsessions, and anxieties with an innovative procedure he called *psychoanalysis* (described in detail in Chapter 15). Decades of experience probing into his patients' lives provided much of the inspiration for Freud's theory. He also gathered material by looking inward and examining his own anxieties, conflicts, and desires.

His work with patients and his own self-exploration persuaded Freud of the existence of what he called the unconscious. According to Freud, **the *unconscious* contains thoughts, memories, and desires that are well below the surface of conscious awareness but that nonetheless exert great influence on behavior.** Freud based his concept of the unconscious on a variety of observations. For instance, he noticed that seemingly meaningless slips of the tongue (such as "I decided to take a summer school curse") often appeared to reveal a person's true feelings. He also noted that his patients' dreams often seemed to express important feelings they were unaware of. Knitting these and other observations together, Freud eventually concluded that psychological disturbances are largely caused by personal conflicts existing at an unconscious level. More generally, his *psychoanalytic theory* attempts **to explain personality, motivation, and mental disorders by focusing on unconscious determinants of behavior.**

Freud's concept of the unconscious was not entirely new (Rieber, 1998). However, it was a major departure from the prevailing belief that people are fully aware of the forces affecting their behavior. In arguing that behavior is governed by unconscious forces, Freud made the disconcerting suggestion that people are not masters of their own minds. Other aspects of Freud's theory also stirred up debate. For instance, he proposed that behavior is greatly influenced by how people cope with their sexual urges. At a time when people were far less comfortable discussing sexual issues than they are today, even scientists were offended and scandalized by Freud's emphasis on sex. Small wonder, then, that Freud was soon engulfed in controversy.

In part because of its controversial nature, Freud's theory was slow to gain influence. However, he was a superb and prolific writer who campaigned vigorously for his psychoanalytic movement (Messer & McWilliams, 2003). As a result, his approach gradually won acceptance within medicine, attracting prominent followers such as Carl Jung and Alfred Adler. Important public recognition from psychology came in 1909, when G. Stanley Hall invited Freud to give a series of lectures at Clark University in Massachusetts (see the photo below).

By 1920 psychoanalytic theory was widely known around the world, but it continued to meet with considerable resistance in psychology (Fancher, 2000). Most psychologists contemptuously viewed psychoanalytic theory as unscientific speculation that would eventually fade away (Hornstein, 1992). However, they turned out to be wrong. Psychoanalytic ideas steadily gained credence in the culture at large, influencing thought in medicine, the arts, and literature (Rieber, 1998). According to Hornstein (1992), by the 1940s, "Psychoanalysis was becoming

**Sigmund Freud
1856–1939**

"The unconscious is the true psychical reality; in its innermost nature it is as much unknown to us as the reality of the external world."

A portrait taken at the famous Clark University psychology conference, September 1909. Pictured are Freud, G. Stanley Hall, and four of Freud's students and associates. Seated, left to right: Freud, Hall, and Carl Jung; standing: Abraham Brill, Ernest Jones, and Sandor Ferenczi.

John B. Watson
1878–1958

"The time seems to have come when psychology must discard all references to consciousness."

so popular that it threatened to eclipse psychology entirely" (p. 258). Thus, the widespread popular acceptance of psychoanalytic theory essentially forced psychologists to apply their scientific methods to the topics Freud had studied: personality, motivation, and abnormal behavior. As they turned to these topics, many of them saw merit in some of Freud's notions (Rosenzweig, 1985). Although psychoanalytic theory continued to generate heated debate, it survived to become an influential theoretical perspective. Today, many psychoanalytic concepts have filtered into the mainstream of psychology (Luborsky & Barrett, 2006; Westen, 1998).

Watson Alters Psychology's Course as Behaviorism Makes Its Debut   1a, 5b

One reason psychoanalysis struggled to gain acceptance within psychology was that it conflicted in many basic ways with the tenets of *behaviorism*, a new school of thought that gradually became dominant within psychology between 1913 and the late 1920s. Founded by John B. Watson (1878–1958), *behaviorism* **is a theoretical orientation based on the premise that scientific psychology should study only observable behavior.** It is important to understand what a radical change this definition represents. Watson (1913, 1919) proposed that psychologists *abandon the study of consciousness altogether* and

focus exclusively on behaviors that they could observe directly. In essence, he was trying to redefine what scientific psychology should be about.

Why did Watson argue for such a fundamental shift in direction? Because to him, the power of the scientific method rested on the idea of *verifiability*. In principle, scientific claims can always be verified (or disproved) by anyone who is able and willing to make the required observations. However, this power depends on studying things that can be observed objectively. Otherwise, the advantage of using the scientific approach—replacing vague speculation and personal opinion with reliable, exact knowledge—is lost. In Watson's view, mental processes are not a proper subject for scientific study because they are ultimately private events. After all, no one can see or touch another's thoughts. Consequently, if psychology was to be a science, it would have to give up consciousness as its subject matter and become instead the *science of behavior*.

Behavior refers to any overt (observable) response or activity by an organism. Watson asserted that psychologists could study anything that people do or say—shopping, playing chess, eating, complimenting a friend—but they could *not* study scientifically the thoughts, wishes, and feelings that might accompany these observable behaviors. Obviously, psychology's shift away from the study of consciousness was fundamentally incompatible with psychoanalytic theory. Given that many psychologists were becoming uncomfortable with the study of *conscious* experience, you can imagine how they felt about trying to study *unconscious* mental processes. By the 1920s Watson had become an outspoken critic of Freud's views (Rilling, 2000b). Proponents of behaviorism and psychoanalysis engaged in many heated theoretical debates in the ensuing decades.

Watson's radical reorientation of psychology did not end with his redefinition of its subject matter. He also staked out a rather extreme position on one of psychology's oldest and most fundamental questions: the issue of *nature versus nurture*. This age-old debate is concerned with whether behavior is determined mainly by genetic inheritance ("nature") or by environment and experience ("nurture"). To oversimplify, the question is this: Is a great concert pianist or a master criminal born, or made? Watson argued that each is made, not born. In other words, he downplayed the importance of heredity, maintaining that behavior is governed primarily by the environment. Indeed, he boldly claimed:

Give me a dozen healthy infants, well-formed, and my own special world to bring them up in and I'll guarantee

---

concept check 1.1

Understanding the Implications of Major Theories: Wundt, James, and Freud

Check your understanding of the implications of some of the major theories reviewed in this chapter by indicating who is likely to have made each of the statements quoted below. Choose from the following theorists: (a) Wilhelm Wundt, (b) William James, and (c) Sigmund Freud. You'll find the answers in Appendix A in the back of the book.

_____ 1. "He that has eyes to see and ears to hear may convince himself that no mortal can keep a secret. If the lips are silent, he chatters with his fingertips; betrayal oozes out of him at every pore. And thus the task of making conscious the most hidden recesses of the mind is one which it is quite possible to accomplish."

_____ 2. "The book which I present to the public is an attempt to mark out a new domain of science. . . . The new discipline rests upon anatomical and physiological foundations. . . . The experimental treatment of psychological problems must be pronounced from every point of view to be in its first beginnings."

_____ 3. "Consciousness, then, does not appear to itself chopped up in bits. Such words as 'chain' or 'train' do not describe it fitly. . . . It is nothing jointed; it flows. A 'river' or 'stream' are the metaphors by which it is most naturally described."

to take any one at random and train him to become any type of specialist I might select—doctor, lawyer, artist, merchant-chief, and yes, even beggar-man and thief, regardless of his talents, penchants, tendencies, abilities, vocations and race of his ancestors. I am going beyond my facts and I admit it, but so have the advocates of the contrary and they have been doing it for many thousands of years. (1924, p. 82)

For obvious reasons, Watson's tongue-in-cheek challenge was never put to a test. Although this widely cited quote oversimplified Watson's views on the nature-nurture issue (Todd & Morris, 1992), his writings contributed to the strong environmental slant that became associated with behaviorism (Horowitz, 1992).

The gradual emergence of behaviorism was partly attributable to an important discovery made around the turn of the century by Ivan Pavlov, a Russian physiologist. As you'll learn in Chapter 6, Pavlov (1906) showed that dogs could be trained to salivate in response to an auditory stimulus such as a tone. This deceptively simple demonstration of the *conditioned reflex* provided insight into how stimulus-response bonds are formed. Such bonds were exactly what behaviorists wanted to investigate, so Pavlov's discovery paved the way for their work. Watson (1925), for instance, embraced Pavlov's model as a new way of thinking about learning (Rilling, 2000a), and the behaviorists eventually came to view psychology's mission as an attempt to relate overt behaviors (responses) to observable events in the environment (stimuli). Because the behaviorists investigated stimulus-response relationships, the behavioral approach is often referred to as *stimulus-response (S-R) psychology.*

Behaviorism's stimulus-response approach contributed to the rise of animal research in psychology. Having deleted consciousness from their scope of concern, behaviorists no longer needed to study human participants who could report on their mental processes. Many psychologists thought that animals would make better research subjects anyway. One key reason was that experimental research is often more productive if experimenters can exert considerable *control* over their subjects. Otherwise, too many complicating factors enter into the picture and contaminate the experiment. Obviously, a researcher can have much more control over a laboratory rat or pigeon than over a human participant, who arrives at a lab with years of uncontrolled experience and who will probably insist on going home at night. Thus, the discipline that had begun its life a few decades earlier as the study of the mind now

found itself heavily involved in the study of simple responses made by laboratory animals.

Skinner Questions Free Will as Behaviorism Flourishes 1a, 10b

The advocates of behaviorism and psychoanalysis tangled frequently during the 1920s, 1930s, and 1940s. As psychoanalytic thought slowly gained a foothold within psychology, many psychologists softened their stance on the acceptability of studying internal mental events. However, this movement toward the consideration of internal states was vigorously opposed by B. F. Skinner (1904–1990), an American psychologist whose thinking was influenced by the work of Ivan Pavlov and John B. Watson (Dinsmoor, 2004; Moore, 2005). Skinner set out to be a writer, but he gave up his dream after a few unproductive years. "I had," he wrote later, "nothing important to say" (1967, p. 395). However, he had many important things to say about psychology, and his ideas became highly influential starting in the 1940s and 1950s.

In response to the softening that had occurred in the behaviorist position, Skinner (1953) championed a return to Watson's strict focus on observable behavior. Skinner did not deny the existence of internal mental events. However, he insisted that they could not be studied scientifically. Moreover, there was no need to study them. According to Skinner, if the stimulus of food is followed by the response of eating, we can fully describe what is happening without making any guesses about whether the animal is experiencing hunger. Like Watson, Skinner also emphasized how environmental factors mold behavior.

The fundamental principle of behavior documented by Skinner is deceptively simple: *Organisms tend to repeat responses that lead to positive outcomes, and they tend not to repeat responses that lead to neutral or negative outcomes.* Despite its simplicity, this principle turns out to be quite powerful. Working primarily with laboratory rats and pigeons, Skinner showed that he could exert remarkable control over the behavior of animals by manipulating the outcomes of their responses. He was even able to train animals to perform unnatural behaviors. For example, he once trained some pigeons to play a credible version of Ping-Pong (see the video found within *PsykTrek*). Skinner's followers eventually showed that the principles uncovered in their animal research could be applied to complex human behaviors as

B. F. Skinner 1904–1990

"I submit that what we call the behavior of the human organism is no more free than its digestion."

well. Behavioral principles are now widely used in factories, schools, prisons, mental hospitals, and a variety of other settings (see Chapter 6).

Skinner's ideas had repercussions that went far beyond the debate among psychologists about what they should study. Skinner spelled out the full implications of his findings in his book *Beyond Freedom and Dignity* (1971). There he asserted that all behavior is fully governed by external stimuli. In other words, your behavior is determined in predictable ways by lawful principles, just as the flight of an arrow is governed by the laws of physics. Thus, if you believe that your actions are the result of conscious decisions, you're wrong. According to Skinner, people are controlled by their environment, not by themselves. In short, Skinner arrived at the conclusion that *free will is an illusion.*

As you can readily imagine, such a disconcerting view of human nature was not universally acclaimed. Like Freud, Skinner was the target of harsh criticism. Much of this criticism stemmed from misinterpretations of his ideas that were disseminated in the popular press (Rutherford, 2000). For example, his analysis of free will was often misconstrued as an attack on the concept of a free society—which it was not—and he was often mistakenly condemned for advocating an undemocratic "scientific police state" (Dinsmoor, 1992). Despite all the controversy, however, behaviorism flourished as the dominant school of thought in psychology during the 1950s

and 1960s (Gilgen, 1982). And even today, when experts are asked to nominate psychology's most important contributors, Skinner's name is typically found at the top of the list (see Figure 1.3).

The Humanists Revolt 1a, 10c

By the 1950s, behaviorism and psychoanalytic theory had become the most influential schools of thought in psychology. However, many psychologists found these theoretical orientations unappealing. The principal charge hurled at both schools was that they were "dehumanizing." Psychoanalytic theory was attacked for its belief that behavior is dominated by primitive, sexual urges. Behaviorism was criticized for its preoccupation with the study of simple animal behavior. Both theories were criticized because they suggested that people are not masters of their

B. F. Skinner created considerable controversy when he asserted that free will is an illusion.

Two Rankings of Important Figures in the History of Psychology

Estes et al. (1990)		Haggbloom et al. (2002)	
Rank	Name	Rank	Name
1	B. F. Skinner	1	B. F. Skinner
2	Sigmund Freud	2	Jean Piaget
3	William James	3	Sigmund Freud
4	Jean Piaget	4	John B. Watson
5	G. Stanley Hall	5	Albert Bandura
6	Wilhelm Wundt	6	William James
7	Carl Rogers	6	Ivan Pavlov
8	John B. Watson	8	Kurt Lewin
9	Ivan Pavlov	9	Carl Rogers
10	E. L. Thorndike	9	E. L. Thorndike

Figure 1.3

Influential contributors in the history of psychology. The results of two surveys regarding the most important people in the history of psychology are shown here. In the 1990 survey, 93 chairpersons of psychology departments ranked psychology's most influential contributors (Estes, Coston, & Fournet, 1990, as cited in Korn et al., 1991). In the 2002 survey, a sample of APS members was asked to identify the greatest psychologists of the 20th century (Haggbloom et al., 2002). As you can see, B. F. Skinner earned the top ranking in both surveys. Although these ratings of scholarly eminence are open to debate, these data should give you some idea of the relative impact of various figures discussed in this chapter.

SOURCES: List on left adapted from Korn, J. H., Davis, R., & Davis, S. F. (1991). Historians' and chairpersons' judgments of eminence among psychologists. *American Psychologist, 46,* 789–792. Copyright © 1991 by the American Psychological Association. List on right adapted from Haggbloom, S. J., et al. (2002). The 100 most eminent psychologists of the 20th century. *Review of General Psychology, 6,* 139–152. Copyright © 2002 by the Educational Publishing Foundation.

Copyright © 1971 Time Inc. Reprinted by permission via Getty Images.

Table 1.1 Overview of Six Contemporary Theoretical Perspectives in Psychology

Perspective and Its Influential Period	Principal Contributors	Subject Matter	Basic Premise
Behavioral (1913–present)	John B. Watson Ivan Pavlov B. F. Skinner	Effects of environment on the overt behavior of humans and animals	Only observable events (stimulus-response relations) can be studied scientifically.
Psychoanalytic (1900–present)	Sigmund Freud Carl Jung Alfred Adler	Unconscious determinants of behavior	Unconscious motives and experiences in early childhood govern personality and mental disorders.
Humanistic (1950s–present)	Carl Rogers Abraham Maslow	Unique aspects of human experience	Humans are free, rational beings with the potential for personal growth, and they are fundamentally different from animals.
Cognitive (1950s–present)	Jean Piaget Noam Chomsky Herbert Simon	Thoughts; mental processes	Human behavior cannot be fully understood without examining how people acquire, store, and process information.
Biological (1950s–present)	James Olds Roger Sperry David Hubel Torsten Wiesel	Physiological bases of behavior in humans and animals	An organism's functioning can be explained in terms of the bodily structures and biochemical processes that underlie behavior.
Evolutionary (1980s–present)	David Buss Martin Daly Margo Wilson Leda Cosmides John Tooby	Evolutionary bases of behavior in humans and animals	Behavior patterns have evolved to solve adaptive problems; natural selection favors behaviors that enhance reproductive success.

own destinies. Above all, many people argued, both schools of thought failed to recognize the unique qualities of *human* behavior.

Beginning in the 1950s, the diverse opposition to behaviorism and psychoanalytic theory blended into a loose alliance that eventually became a new school of thought called "humanism" (Bühler & Allen, 1972). In psychology, *humanism* is a theoretical orientation that emphasizes the unique qualities of humans, especially their freedom and their potential for personal growth. Some of the key differences among the humanistic, psychoanalytic, and behavioral viewpoints are summarized in Table 1.1, which compares six influential contemporary theoretical perspectives in psychology.

Humanists take an *optimistic* view of human nature. They maintain that people are not pawns of either their animal heritage or their environmental circumstances. Furthermore, these theorists say, because humans are fundamentally different from other animals, research on animals has little relevance to the understanding of human behavior (Davidson, 2000). The most prominent architects of the humanistic movement have been Carl Rogers (1902–1987) and Abraham Maslow (1908–1970). Rogers (1951) argued that human behavior is governed primarily by each individual's sense of self, or "self-concept"—which animals presumably lack. Both he and Maslow (1954) maintained that to fully understand people's behavior, psychologists must take into

account the fundamental human drive toward personal growth. They asserted that people have a basic need to continue to evolve as human beings and to fulfill their potentials. In fact, the humanists argued that many psychological disturbances are the result of thwarting these uniquely human needs.

concept check 1.2

Understanding the Implications of Major Theories: Watson, Skinner, and Rogers

Check your understanding of the implications of some of the major theories reviewed in this chapter by indicating who is likely to have made each of the statements quoted below. Choose from the following: (a) John B. Watson, (b) B. F. Skinner, and (c) Carl Rogers. You'll find the answers in Appendix A at the back of the book.

_____ 1. "In the traditional view, a person is free. . . . He can therefore be held responsible for what he does and justly punished if he offends. That view, together with its associated practices, must be reexamined when a scientific analysis reveals unsuspected controlling relations between behavior and environment."

_____ 2. "I do not have a Pollyanna view of human nature. . . . Yet one of the most refreshing and invigorating parts of my experience is to work with [my clients] and to discover the strongly positive directional tendencies which exist in them, as in all of us, at the deepest levels."

_____ 3. "Our conclusion is that we have no real evidence of the inheritance of traits. I would feel perfectly confident in the ultimately favorable outcome of careful upbringing of a healthy, well-formed baby born of a long line of crooks, murderers and thieves, and prostitutes."

Carl Rogers
1902–1987

"It seems to me that at bottom each person is asking, 'Who am I, really? How can I get in touch with this real self, underlying all my surface behavior? How can I become myself?'"

Fragmentation and dissent have reduced the influence of humanism in recent decades, although some advocates have predicted a renaissance for the humanistic movement (Taylor, 1999). To date, the humanists' greatest contribution to psychology has probably been their innovative treatments for psychological problems and disorders. For example, Carl Rogers pioneered a new approach to psychotherapy—called *person-centered therapy*—that remains extremely influential today (Kirschenbaum & Jourdan, 2005). More generally, the humanists have argued eloquently for a different picture of human nature than those implied by psychoanalysis and behaviorism (Wertz, 1998).

REVIEW of Key Learning Goals

1.1 Psychology became an independent discipline when Wilhelm Wundt established the first psychological research laboratory in 1879 at Leipzig, Germany. Wundt, who is widely characterized as the founder of psychology, viewed psychology as the scientific study of consciousness. The new discipline grew rapidly in North America in the late 19th century, as illustrated by G. Stanley Hall's career. Hall established America's first research lab in psychology and founded the American Psychological Association.

1.2 The structuralists, led by Edward Titchener, believed that psychology should use introspection to analyze consciousness into its basic elements. The functionalists, inspired by the ideas of William James, believed that psychology should focus on the purpose and adaptive functions of consciousness. Functionalism paved the way for behaviorism and applied psychology and had more of a lasting impact than structuralism.

1.3 Sigmund Freud was an Austrian physician who invented psychoanalysis. His psychoanalytic theory emphasized the unconscious determinants of behavior and the importance of sexuality. Freud's ideas were controversial, and they met with resistance in academic psychology. However, as more psychologists developed an interest in personality, motivation, and abnormal behavior, psychoanalytic concepts were incorporated into mainstream psychology.

1.4 Behaviorists, led by John B. Watson, argued that psychology should study only observable behavior. Thus, they campaigned to redefine psychology as the science of behavior. Emphasizing the importance of the environment over heredity, the behaviorists began to explore stimulus-response relationships, often using laboratory animals as subjects.

1.5 Working with laboratory rats and pigeons, American behaviorist B. F. Skinner demonstrated that organisms tend to repeat responses that lead to positive consequences and not to repeat responses that lead to neutral or negative consequences. Based on the belief that all behavior is fully governed by external stimuli, Skinner argued that free will is an illusion. His ideas were controversial and often misunderstood.

1.6 Finding both behaviorism and psychoanalysis unsatisfactory, advocates of a new theoretical orientation called humanism became influential in the 1950s. Humanism, led by Abraham Maslow and Carl Rogers, emphasized the unique qualities of human behavior and humans' freedom and potential for personal growth.

Key Learning Goals

1.7 Discuss how historical events contributed to the emergence of psychology as a profession.

1.8 Describe two trends emerging in the 1950s–1960s that represented a return to psychology's intellectual roots.

1.9 Explain why Western psychology has shown an increased interest in cultural variables in recent decades.

1.10 Discuss the emergence and basic ideas of evolutionary psychology.

1.11 Explain the development and principal tenets of the positive psychology movement.

Psychology's Modern History

The principal storyline of psychology's early history was its gradual maturation into a research-based science. The seminal work of Wundt, Hall, James, Watson, Skinner, and a host of other pioneers served to establish psychology as a respected scientific discipline in the halls of academia. As you will learn momentarily, the principal storyline of psychology's modern history has been its remarkable growth into a multifaceted scientific and professional enterprise. In more recent decades psychology's story has been marked by expanding boundaries and broader interests.

Psychology Comes of Age as a Profession

1a

As you probably know, psychology is not all pure science. It has a highly practical side. Many psychologists provide a variety of professional services to the public. Their work falls within the domain of *applied psychology,* **the branch of psychology concerned with everyday, practical problems.** This branch of psychology, so prominent today, was actually slow to develop. Although a small number of early psychologists dabbled in various areas of applied psychology, it remained on the fringes of mainstream psychology until World War II (Benjamin et al., 2003). It was only in the 1950s that psychology really started to come of age as a profession.

The first applied arm of psychology to achieve any prominence was *clinical psychology.* As practiced today, *clinical psychology* is **the branch of psychology concerned with the diagnosis and treatment of psychological problems and disorders.** In the early days, however, the emphasis was almost exclusively on psychological testing and adjustment problems in school children. Although the first psychological clinic was established as early as 1896, by 1937 only about one in five members of the American Psychological Association reported an interest in clinical psychology (Goldenberg, 1983). Clinicians were a small minority in a field devoted primarily to research.

That picture was about to change with dramatic swiftness. During World War II (1939–1945), many academic psychologists were pressed into service as clinicians. They were needed to screen military recruits and to treat soldiers suffering from trauma. Many of these psychologists (often to their surprise) found the clinical work to be challenging and rewarding, and a substantial portion continued to do clinical work after the war. More significant, some 40,000 American veterans returned to seek postwar treatment in Veterans Administration (VA) hospitals for their psychological scars. With the demand for clinicians far greater than the supply, the VA stepped in to finance many new training programs in clinical psychology. These programs, emphasizing training in the treatment of psychological disorders as well as psychological testing, proved attractive. Within a few years, about half the new Ph.D.'s in psychology were specializing in clinical psychology, and most went on to offer professional services to the public (Goldenberg, 1983). Assessing the impact of World War II, Routh and Reisman (2003) characterize it as "a watershed in the history of clinical psychology. In its aftermath, clinical psychology received something it had not received before: enormous institutional support" (p. 345). Thus, during the 1940s and 1950s the prewar orphan of applied/professional psychology started to mature into a robust, powerful adult.

In the academic world, many traditional research psychologists were alarmed by the professionalization of the field. They argued that the energy and resources previously devoted to research would be diluted. Because of conflicting priorities, tensions between the research and professional arms of psychology have continued to grow. Although the American Psychological Association has worked diligently to represent both the scientific and professional branches of psychology, many researchers complained that the APA had come to be dominated by clinicians. In 1988 this rift stimulated some research psychologists to form a new organization, now called the Association for Psychological Science (APS), to serve exclusively as an advocate for the science of psychology.

Despite the conflicts, the professionalization of psychology has continued at a steady pace. In fact, the trend has spread into additional areas of psychology. Today the broad umbrella of applied psychology covers a variety of professional specialties, including school psychology, industrial/organizational psychology, counseling psychology, and emerging new areas, such as forensic psychology (Benjamin & Baker, 2004). Whereas psychologists were once almost exclusively academics, the vast majority of today's psychologists devote some of their time to providing professional services.

Archives of the History of American Psychology, University of Akron, Akron, Ohio.

World War I and World War II played a major role in the growth of applied psychology, as psychologists were forced to apply their expertise to practical problems, such as ability testing and training. The top photo shows military personnel working on one of a series of tests devised to aid in the selection of air crew trainees during World War II. The bottom photo shows a booklet sold to help recruits prepare for the Army General Classification Test and other related tests. Its popularity illustrates the importance attached to the military's mental testing progam.

Psychology Returns to Its Roots: Renewed Interest in Cognition and Physiology 1a

While applied psychology started to blossom in the 1950s, research in psychology continued to evolve. Ironically, two trends that emerged in the 1950s and picked up momentum in the 1960s represented a return to psychology's 19th century roots, when psychologists were principally interested in consciousness and physiology. Since the 1950s and 1960s, psychologists have shown a renewed interest in consciousness (now called "cognition") and the physiological bases of behavior.

Cognition refers to the mental processes involved in acquiring knowledge. In other words, cognition involves thinking or conscious experience. For many decades, the dominance of behaviorism discouraged investigation of "unobservable" mental processes, and most psychologists showed little interest in cognition (Mandler, 2002). During the 1950s and 1960s, however, research on cognition slowly began to emerge (Miller, 2003). The research of Swiss psychologist Jean Piaget (1954) focused increased attention on the study of children's cognitive development, while the work of Noam Chomsky (1957) elicited new interest in the psychological underpinnings of language. Around the same time, Herbert Simon and his colleagues (Newell, Shaw, & Simon, 1958) began influential, groundbreaking research on problem solving that eventually led to a Nobel prize for Simon (in 1978). These advances sparked a surge of interest in cognitive processes.

Since then, cognitive theorists have argued that psychology must include the study of internal mental events to fully understand behavior (Gardner, 1985; Neisser, 1967). Advocates of the *cognitive perspective* point out that the ways people think about events surely influence how they behave. Consequently, focusing exclusively on overt behavior yields an incomplete picture of why individuals behave as they do. Equally important, psychologists investigating decision making, reasoning, and problem solving have shown that methods *can* be devised to study cognitive processes scientifically. Although the methods are different from those used in psychology's early days, modern research on the

inner workings of the mind has put the *psyche* back in psychology. In fact, many observers maintain that the cognitive perspective has become the dominant perspective in contemporary psychology—and some interesting data support this assertion, as can be seen in **Figure 1.4** (Robins, Gosling, & Craik, 1999).

The 1950s and 1960s also saw many important discoveries that highlighted the interrelations among mind, body, and behavior (Thompson & Zola, 2003). For example, Canadian psychologist James Olds (1956) demonstrated that electrical stimulation of the brain could evoke emotional responses such as pleasure and rage in animals. Other work, which eventually earned a Nobel prize for Roger Sperry (in 1981), showed that the right and left halves of the brain are specialized to handle different types of mental tasks (Gazzaniga, Bogen, & Sperry, 1965). The 1960s also brought the publication of David Hubel and Torsten Wiesel's (1962, 1963) Nobel prize–winning work on how visual signals are processed in the brain.

These and many other findings stimulated an increase in research on the biological bases of behavior. Advocates of the *biological perspective* maintain that much of human and animal behavior can be explained in terms of the bodily structures and biochemical processes that allow organisms to behave. In the 19th century the young science of psychology had a heavy physiological emphasis. Thus, increased interest in the biological bases of behavior represents another return to psychology's heritage.

Although adherents of the cognitive and biological perspectives haven't done as much organized campaigning for their viewpoints as the proponents of the older schools of thought, these newer perspectives have become important theoretical orientations in modern psychology. They are increasingly influential regarding what psychology should study and how. The cognitive and biological perspectives are compared to other contemporary theoretical perspectives in **Table 1.1**.

web link 1.4

The Archives of the History of American Psychology (AHAP)

The Archives of the History of American Psychology (AHAP) at the University of Akron is a huge repository of information and materials on the history of psychology. Its website provides a well-organized overview of the archive's holdings and access to numerous photos of instruments and equipment used in psychological research.

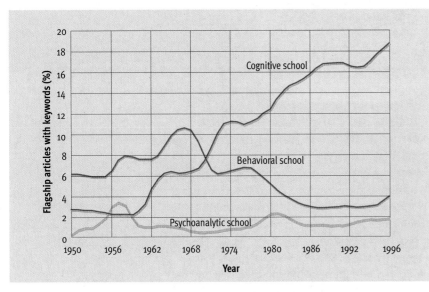

Figure 1.4

The relative prominence of three major schools of thought in psychology. To estimate the relative influence of various theoretical orientations in recent decades, Robins, Gosling, and Craik (1999) analyzed the subject matter of four prestigious general publications in psychology, measuring the percentage of articles relevant to each school of thought. Obviously, their approach is just one of many ways one might gauge the prominence of various theoretical orientations in psychology. Nonetheless, the data are thought provoking. Their findings suggest that the cognitive perspective surpassed the behavioral perspective in influence sometime around 1970. As you can see, the psychoanalytic perspective has always had a modest impact on the mainstream of psychology.

SOURCE: Adapted from Robins, R. W., Gosling, S. D., & Craik, K. H. (1999). An empirical analysis of trends in psychology. *American Psychologist, 54*, 117–128. Copyright © 1999 by the American Psychological Association. Reprinted by permission of the author.

Psychology Broadens Its Horizons: Increased Interest in Cultural Diversity 1a

Throughout psychology's history, most researchers have worked under the assumption that they were seeking to identify general principles of behavior that would be applicable to all of humanity (Smith, Spillane, & Annus, 2006). In reality, however, psychology has largely been a Western (North American and European) enterprise with a remarkably provincial slant (Gergen et al., 1996; Norenzayan & Heine,

2005). The vast preponderance of psychology's research has been conducted in the United States by middle- and upper-class white psychologists who have used mostly middle- and upper-class white males as participants (Hall, 1997; Norenzayan & Heine, 2005). Traditionally, Western psychologists have paid scant attention to how well their theories and research might apply to non-Western cultures, to ethnic minorities in Western societies, or even to women as opposed to men.

Why has the focus of Western psychology been so narrow? A number of factors have probably contributed (Heine & Norenzayan, 2006; Markus & Hamedani, 2007; Segall, Lonner, & Berry, 1998). First, cross-cultural research is costly, difficult, and time consuming. It has always been cheaper, easier, and more convenient for academic psychologists to study the middle-class white students enrolled in their schools. Second, some psychologists worry that cultural comparisons may inadvertently foster stereotypes of various cultural groups, many of whom already have a long history of being victimized by prejudice. Third, *ethnocentrism*—the tendency to view one's own group as superior to others and as the standard for judging the worth of foreign ways—may have contributed to Western psychologists' lack of interest in other cultures.

Despite these considerations, in recent decades Western psychologists have begun to recognize that their neglect of cultural variables has diminished the value of their work, and they are devoting increased attention to culture as a determinant of behavior. What brought about this shift? Some of the impetus probably came from the sociopolitical upheavals of the 1960s and 1970s (Bronstein & Quina, 1988). The civil rights movement, the women's movement, and the gay rights movement all raised doubts about whether psychology had dealt adequately with human diversity. Above all else, however, the new interest in culture appears attributable to two recent trends: (1) Advances in communication, travel, and international trade have "shrunk" the world and increased global interdependence, bringing more and more Americans and Europeans into contact with people from non-Western cultures, and (2) the ethnic makeup of the Western world has become an increasingly diverse multicultural mosaic (Brislin, 2000; Hermans & Kempen, 1998; Mays et al., 1996). These trends and other factors led to a dramatic surge in research on cultural factors that began in the 1980s and continues through today.

Today, more and more Western psychologists are broadening their horizons and incorporating cultural factors into their theories and research (Adamopoulos & Lonner, 2001; Matsumoto & Yoo, 2006).

These psychologists are striving to study previously underrepresented groups of subjects to test the generality of earlier findings and to catalog both the differences and similarities among cultural groups. They are working to increase knowledge of how culture is transmitted through socialization practices and how culture colors a person's view of the world. They are seeking to learn how people cope with cultural change and to find ways to reduce misunderstandings and conflicts in intercultural interactions. In addition, they are trying to enhance understanding of how cultural groups are affected by prejudice, discrimination, and racism. In all these efforts, they are striving to understand the unique experiences of culturally diverse people *from the point of view of those people*. These efforts to ask new questions, study new groups, and apply new perspectives promise to enrich the discipline of psychology in the 21st century (Fowers & Davidov, 2006; Lehman, Chiu, & Schaller, 2004; Matsumoto, 2003; Sue, 2003).

Psychology Adapts: The Emergence of Evolutionary Psychology 1a

Another relatively recent development in psychology has been the emergence of *evolutionary psychology* as an influential theoretical perspective. Evolutionary psychologists assert that the patterns of behavior seen in a species are products of evolution in the same way that anatomical characteristics are. **Evolutionary psychology examines behavioral processes in terms of their adaptive value for members of a species over the course of many generations.** The basic premise of evolutionary psychology is that natural selection favors behaviors that enhance organisms' reproductive success—that is, passing on genes to the next generation. Thus, if a species is highly aggressive, evolutionary psychologists argue that it's because aggressiveness conveys a survival or reproductive advantage for members of that species, so genes that promote aggressiveness are more likely to be passed on to the next generation. Although evolutionary psychologists have a natural interest in animal behavior, they have not been bashful about analyzing the evolutionary bases of human behavior. As La Cerra and Kurzban (1995) put it, "The human mind was sculpted by natural selection, and it is this evolved organ that constitutes the subject matter of psychology" (p. 63).

Looking at behavioral patterns in terms of their evolutionary significance is not an entirely new idea (Graziano, 1995). As noted earlier, William James and other functionalists were influenced by Darwin's

The praying mantis has an astonishing ability to blend in with its environment, along with remarkably acute hearing and vision that permit it to detect prey up to 60 feet away and powerful jaws that allow it to devour its prey. They are so deadly they will eat each other, which makes sex quite a challenge, but males have evolved a reflex module that allows them to copulate successfully while being eaten (even after decapitation)! These physical characteristics obviously represent adaptations that have been crafted by natural selection over the course of millions of generations. Evolutionary psychologists maintain that many patterns of behavior seen in various species are also adaptations that have been shaped by natural selection.

concept of natural selection over a century ago. Until the 1990s, however, applications of evolutionary concepts to *psychological* processes were piecemeal, halfhearted, and not particularly well received. The 1960s and 1970s brought major breakthroughs in the field of evolutionary *biology* (Hamilton, 1964; Trivers, 1971, 1972; Williams, 1966), but these advances had little immediate impact in psychology. The situation began to change in the 1980s. A growing cadre of evolutionary psychologists, led by David Buss (1985, 1988, 1989), Martin Daly and Margo Wilson (1985, 1988), and Leda Cosmides and John Tooby (Cosmides & Tooby, 1989; Tooby & Cosmides, 1989), published widely cited studies on a broad range of topics, including mating preferences, jealousy, aggression, sexual behavior, language, decision making, personality, and development. By the mid-1990s, it became clear that psychology was witnessing the birth of its first major, new theoretical perspective since the cognitive revolution in the 1950s and 1960s.

As with all prominent theoretical perspectives in psychology, evolutionary theory has its critics (Gould, 1993; Lickliter & Honeycutt, 2003; Plotkin, 2004; Rose & Rose, 2000). They argue that many evolutionary hypotheses are untestable and that evolutionary explanations are post hoc, speculative accounts for obvious behavioral phenomena (see the Critical Thinking Application for this chapter). However, evolutionary psychologists have articulated persuasive rebuttals to these and other criticisms (Buss & Reeve, 2003; Conway & Schaller, 2002; Hagen, 2005), and the evolutionary perspective has become increasingly influential.

Psychology Moves in a Positive Direction

 1a

Shortly after Martin Seligman was elected president of the American Psychological Association in 1997, he experienced a profound insight that he character-

ized as an "epiphany." This pivotal insight came from an unusual source—Seligman's 5-year-old daughter, Nikki. She scolded her overachieving, task-oriented father for being "grumpy" far too much of the time. Provoked by his daughter's criticism, Seligman suddenly realized that his approach to life *was* overly and unnecessarily negative. More important, he recognized that the same assessment could be made of the field of psychology—that, it too, was excessively and needlessly negative in its approach (Seligman, 2003). This revelation inspired Seligman to launch a new initiative within psychology that came to be known as the *positive psychology movement.*

Seligman went on to argue convincingly that the field of psychology had historically devoted too much attention to pathology, weakness, damage, and ways to heal suffering. He acknowledged that this approach had yielded valuable insights and progress, but he argued that it also resulted in an unfortunate neglect of the forces that make life worth living. Seligman convened a series of informal meetings with influential psychologists and then more formal conferences to gradually outline the philosophy and goals of positive psychology. Other major architects of the positive psychology movement have included Mihaly Csikszentmihalyi (2000), Christopher Peterson (2000, 2006), and Barbara Fredrickson (2002, 2005). Like humanism before it, positive psychology seeks to shift the field's focus away from negative experiences. As Seligman and Csikszentmihalyi (2000) put it, "The aim of positive psychology is to begin to catalyze a change in the focus of psychology from preoccupation with only repairing the worst things in life to also building positive qualities" (p. 5). Thus, **positive psychology uses theory and research to better understand the positive, adaptive, creative, and fulfilling aspects of human existence.**

The emerging field of positive psychology has three areas of interest (Seligman, 2003). The first is the study of *positive subjective experiences,* or positive emotions, such as happiness, love, gratitude, contentment, and hope. The second focus is on *positive individual traits*—that is, personal strengths and virtues. Theorists are working to identify, classify, and analyze the origins of such positive traits as courage, perseverance, nurturance, tolerance, creativity, integrity, and kindness. The third area of interest is in *positive institutions and communities.* Here the focus is on how societies can foster civil discourse, strong families, healthful work environments, and supportive neighborhood communities.

Although it has proven far less controversial than evolutionary psychology, positive psychology has its critics (La Torre, 2007; Sugarman, 2007). For example, Richard Lazarus (2003) has argued that dividing human experience into positive and negative domains is an oversimplification and that the line between them is not as clear and obvious as most have assumed. Lazarus expresses concern that positive psychology may be little more than "one of the many fads that come and go in our field" (p. 93). Only time will tell, as positive psychology is still in its infancy. It will be fascinating to see whether and how this new movement reshapes psychology's research priorities and theoretical interests in the years to come.

Our review of psychology's past has shown the field's evolution (an Illustrated Overview of the highlights of psychology's history can be found on pages 20–21). We have seen psychology develop from philosophical speculation into a rigorous science committed to research. We have seen how a highly visible professional arm involved in mental health services emerged from this science. We have seen how psychology's focus on physiology is rooted in its 19th-century origins. We have seen how and why psychologists began conducting research on lower animals. We have seen how psychology has evolved from the study of mind and body to the study of behavior. And we have seen how the investigation of mind and body has been welcomed back into the mainstream of modern psychology. We have seen how various theoretical schools have defined the scope and mission of psychology in different ways. We have seen how psychology's boundaries have expanded and how its interests have become increasingly diverse. Above all else, we have seen that psychology is a growing, evolving intellectual enterprise.

Psychology's history is already rich, but its story has barely begun. The century or so that has elapsed since Wilhelm Wundt put psychology on a scientific footing is only an eyeblink of time in human history. What has been discovered during those years, and what remains unknown, is the subject of the rest of this book.

REVIEW of Key Learning Goals

1.7 Stimulated by the demands of World War II, clinical psychology grew rapidly in the 1950s. Thus, psychology became a profession as well as a science. This movement toward professionalization eventually spread to other areas in psychology, such as counseling psychology, industrial/organizational psychology, and school psychology.

1.8 During the 1950s and 1960s advances in the study of cognition led to renewed interest in mental processes, as psychology returned to its roots. Advocates of the cognitive perspective argue that human behavior cannot be fully understood without considering how people think. The 1950s and 1960s also saw advances in research on the physiological bases of behavior. Advocates of the biological perspective assert that human and animal behavior can be explained in terms of the bodily structures and biochemical processes that allow organisms to behave.

1.9 In the 1980s, Western psychologists, who had previously been rather provincial, developed a greater interest in how cultural factors influence behavior. This trend was sparked in large part by growing global interdependence and by increased cultural diversity in Western societies.

1.10 The 1990s witnessed the emergence of a new theoretical perspective called evolutionary psychology. The central premise of this new school of thought is that the patterns of behavior seen in a species are products of evolution in the same way that anatomical characteristics are and that the human mind has been sculpted by natural selection.

1.11 Around the beginning of the 21st century, the positive psychology movement became an influential force. Advocates of positive psychology argue that the field has historically devoted too much attention to pathology, weakness, and ways to heal suffering. Positive psychology seeks to better understand the adaptive, creative, and fulfilling aspects of human existence.

Psychology Today: Vigorous and Diversified

We began this chapter with an informal description of what psychology is about. Now that you have a feel for how psychology has developed, you can better appreciate a definition that does justice to the field's modern diversity: *Psychology* **is the science that studies behavior and the physiological and cognitive processes that underlie it, and it is the profession that applies the accumulated knowledge of this science to practical problems.**

Contemporary psychology is a thriving science and profession. Its growth has been remarkable. One simple index of this growth is the dramatic rise in membership in the American Psychological Association. **Figure 1.5** on the next page shows that APA membership has increased ninefold since 1950. In the United States, psychology is the second most popular undergraduate major (see **Figure 1.6**), and the field accounts for almost 10% of all doctoral degrees awarded in the sciences and humanities. The comparable figure in 1945 was only 4% (Howard et al., 1986). Of course, psychology is an international enterprise. Today, over 2100 technical journals from all over the world publish research articles on psychology. Thus, by any standard of measurement—

Key Learning Goals

1.12 Discuss the growth of psychology, and identify the most common work settings for contemporary psychologists.

1.13 List and describe nine major research areas in psychology.

1.14 List and describe six professional specialties in psychology, and distinguish between clinical psychology and psychiatry.

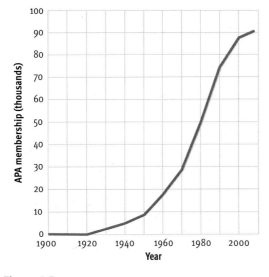

Figure 1.5

Membership in the American Psychological Association, 1900–2007. The steep rise in the number of psychologists in the APA since 1950 testifies to psychology's remarkable growth as a science and a profession. If graduate student members are also counted, the APA has over 155,000 members. (Adapted from data published by the American Psychological Association by permission.)

the number of people involved, the number of degrees granted, the number of journals published—psychology is a healthy, growing field.

Psychology's vigorous presence in modern society is also demonstrated by the great variety of settings in which psychologists work. They were once found almost exclusively in academia. Today, however, colleges and universities are the primary work set-

ting for fewer than 30% of American psychologists. The remaining 70% work in hospitals, clinics, police departments, research institutes, government agencies, business and industry, schools, nursing homes, counseling centers, and private practice. Figure 1.7 shows the distribution of psychologists employed in various categories of settings.

Clearly, contemporary psychology is a multifaceted field, a fact that is especially apparent when we consider the many areas of specialization in both the science and the profession of psychology.

Research Areas in Psychology

Although most psychologists receive broad training that provides them with knowledge about many areas of psychology, they usually specialize when it comes to doing research. Such specialization is necessary because the subject matter of psychology has become so vast over the years. Today it is virtually impossible for anyone to stay abreast of the new research in all specialties. Specialization is also necessary because specific skills and training are required to do research in some areas.

The nine major research areas in modern psychology are (1) developmental psychology, (2) social psychology, (3) experimental psychology, (4) physiological psychology, (5) cognitive psychology, (6) personality, (7) psychometrics, (8) educational psychology, and (9) health psychology. Figure 1.8 describes these areas briefly and shows the percentage of research psychologists in the APA who identify each

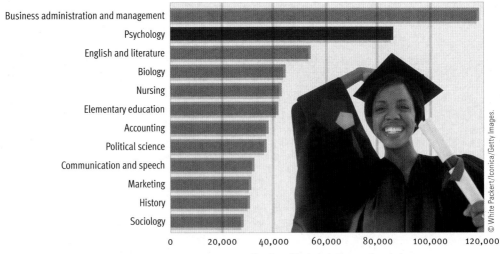

Figure 1.6

Psychology's place among leading college majors. This graphic lists the 12 most popular undergraduate majors in the United States, based on the number of bachelor's degrees awarded in 2004–2005. As you can see, psychology ranked second only to business administration and management in the number of degrees awarded. (Data from U.S. Department of Education, National Center for Education Statistics, *Digest of Education Statistics: 2006*)

area as their primary interest. As you can see, social psychology and developmental psychology have become especially active areas of research.

Professional Specialties in Psychology

Applied psychology consists of four well-established areas of specialization and a couple of new, emerging specialties. The four established professional specialties are (1) clinical psychology, (2) counseling psychology, (3) school psychology, and (4) industrial/organizational psychology. The two emerging specialties are clinical neuropsychology and forensic psychology. Descriptions of all six of these specialties can be found in **Figure 1.9** (on page 22) along with the percentage of professional psychologists in the APA who cite each area as their chief interest. As the graphic indicates, clinical psychology is the most prominent and widely practiced professional specialty in the field.

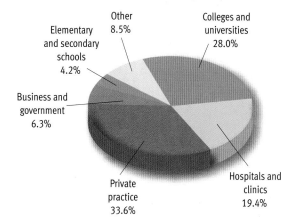

Figure 1.7

Employment of psychologists by setting. The work settings in which psychologists are employed have become very diverse. Survey data on the primary employment setting of APA members indicates that one-third are in private practice (compared to 12% in 1976), while only 28% work in colleges and universities (compared to 47% in 1976). These data may slightly underestimate the percentage of psychologists in academia, given the competition between APA and APS to represent research psychologists. (Based on *2000 APA Directory Survey*)

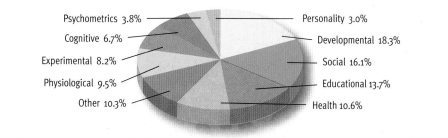

Figure 1.8

Major research areas in contemporary psychology. Most research psychologists specialize in one of the nine broad areas described here. The figures in the pie chart reflect the percentage of academic and research psychologists belonging to APA who identify each area as their primary interest. (Based on data published by the American Psychological Association)

Area	Focus of research
Developmental psychology	Looks at human development across the life span. Developmental psychology once focused primarily on child development, but today devotes a great deal of research to adolescence, adulthood, and old age.
Social psychology	Focuses on interpersonal behavior and the role of social forces in governing behavior. Typical topics include attitude formation, attitude change, prejudice, conformity, attraction, aggression, intimate relationships, and behavior in groups.
Educational psychology	Studies how people learn and the best ways to teach them. Examines curriculum design, teacher training, achievement testing, student motivation, classroom diversity, and other aspects of the educational process.
Health psychology	Focuses on how psychological factors relate to the promotion and maintenance of physical health and the causation, prevention, and treatment of illness.
Physiological psychology	Examines the influence of genetic factors on behavior and the role of the brain, nervous system, endocrine system, and bodily chemicals in the regulation of behavior.
Experimental psychology	Encompasses the traditional core of topics that psychology focused on heavily in its first half-century as a science: sensation, perception, learning, conditioning, motivation, and emotion. The name experimental psychology is somewhat misleading, as this is not the only area in which experiments are done. Psychologists working in all the areas listed here conduct experiments.
Cognitive psychology	Focuses on "higher" mental processes, such as memory, reasoning, information processing, language, problem solving, decision making, and creativity.
Psychometrics	Is concerned with the measurement of behavior and capacities, usually through the development of psychological tests. Psychometrics is involved with the design of tests to assess personality, intelligence, and a wide range of abilities. It is also concerned with the development of new techniques for statistical analysis.
Personality	Is interested in describing and understanding individuals' consistency in behavior, which represents their personality. This area of interest is also concerned with the factors that shape personality and with personality assessment.

ILLUSTRATED OVERVIEW OF PSYCHOLOGY'S HISTORY

1870 1880 1890 1900 1910 1920 1930

1875
First demonstration laboratories are set up independently by **William James** (at Harvard) and Wilhelm Wundt (at the University of Leipzig).

1905
Alfred Binet develops first successful intelligence test in France.

1914–1918
Widespread intelligence testing is begun by military during World War I.

1879
Wilhelm Wundt establishes first research laboratory in psychology at Leipzig, Germany.

1908
Margaret Washburn publishes *The Animal Mind*, which serves as an impetus for behaviorism.

1916
Lewis Terman publishes Stanford-Binet Intelligence Scale, which becomes the world's foremost intelligence test.

1920s
Gestalt pychology nears its peak influence.

1909
Sigmund Freud's increasing influence receives formal recognition as G. S. Hall invites Freud to give lectures at Clark University.

1933
Sigmund Freud's influence continues to build as he publishes *New Introductory Lectures on Psychoanalysis*.

1881
Wilhelm Wundt establishes first journal devoted to research in psychology.

1890
William James publishes his seminal work, *The Principles of Psychology*.

1913
John B. Watson writes classic behaviorism manifesto, arguing that psychology should study only observable behavior.

1883
G. Stanley Hall establishes America's first research laboratory in psychology at Johns Hopkins University.

1892
G. Stanley Hall founds American Psychological Association.

1904
Ivan Pavlov shows how conditioned responses are created, paving the way for stimulus-response psychology.

1914
Leta Hollingworth publishes pioneering work on the psychology of women.

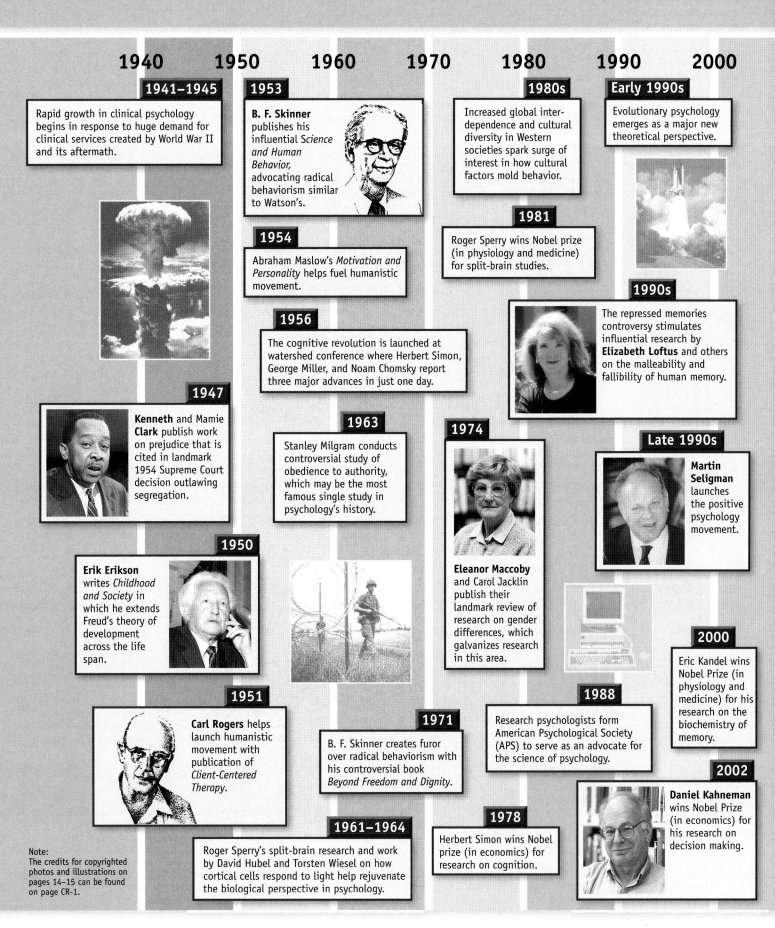

1940   **1950**   **1960**   **1970**   **1980**   **1990**   **2000**

1941–1945

Rapid growth in clinical psychology begins in response to huge demand for clinical services created by World War II and its aftermath.

1953

B. F. Skinner publishes his influential *Science and Human Behavior,* advocating radical behaviorism similar to Watson's.

1954

Abraham Maslow's *Motivation and Personality* helps fuel humanistic movement.

1956

The cognitive revolution is launched at watershed conference where Herbert Simon, George Miller, and Noam Chomsky report three major advances in just one day.

1947

Kenneth and Mamie **Clark** publish work on prejudice that is cited in landmark 1954 Supreme Court decision outlawing segregation.

1963

Stanley Milgram conducts controversial study of obedience to authority, which may be the most famous single study in psychology's history.

1950

Erik Erikson writes *Childhood and Society* in which he extends Freud's theory of development across the life span.

1951

Carl Rogers helps launch humanistic movement with publication of *Client-Centered Therapy.*

1961–1964

Roger Sperry's split-brain research and work by David Hubel and Torsten Wiesel on how cortical cells respond to light help rejuvenate the biological perspective in psychology.

1971

B. F. Skinner creates furor over radical behaviorism with his controversial book *Beyond Freedom and Dignity.*

1974

Eleanor Maccoby and Carol Jacklin publish their landmark review of research on gender differences, which galvanizes research in this area.

1978

Herbert Simon wins Nobel prize (in economics) for research on cognition.

1980s

Increased global inter-dependence and cultural diversity in Western societies spark surge of interest in how cultural factors mold behavior.

1981

Roger Sperry wins Nobel prize (in physiology and medicine) for split-brain studies.

1988

Research psychologists form American Psychological Society (APS) to serve as an advocate for the science of psychology.

Early 1990s

Evolutionary psychology emerges as a major new theoretical perspective.

1990s

The repressed memories controversy stimulates influential research by **Elizabeth Loftus** and others on the malleability and fallibility of human memory.

Late 1990s

Martin Seligman launches the positive psychology movement.

2000

Eric Kandel wins Nobel Prize (in physiology and medicine) for his research on the biochemistry of memory.

2002

Daniel Kahneman wins Nobel Prize (in economics) for his research on decision making.

Note:
The credits for copyrighted photos and illustrations on pages 14–15 can be found on page CR-1.

Figure 1.9
Principal professional specialties in contemporary psychology. Most psychologists who deliver professional services to the public specialize in one of the six areas described here. The figures in the pie chart reflect the percentage of APA members delivering professional services who identify each area as their chief specialty. (Based on *2000 APA Directory Survey*)

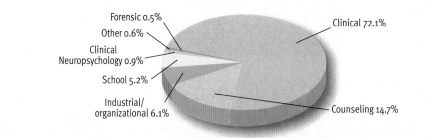

Specialty	Focus of professional practice
Clinical psychology	Clinical psychologists are concerned with the evaluation, diagnosis, and treatment of individuals with psychological disorders, as well as treatment of less severe behavioral and emotional problems. Principal activities include interviewing clients, psychological testing, and providing group or individual psychotherapy.
Counseling psychology	Counseling psychology overlaps with clinical psychology in that specialists in both areas engage in similar activities—interviewing, testing, and providing therapy. However, counseling psychologists usually work with a somewhat different clientele, providing assistance to people struggling with everyday problems of moderate severity. Thus, they often specialize in family, marital, or career counseling.
Industrial and organizational psychology	Psychologists in this area perform a wide variety of tasks in the world of business and industry. These tasks include running human resources departments, working to improve staff morale and attitudes, striving to increase job satisfaction and productivity, examining organizational structures and procedures, and making recommendations for improvements.
School psychology	School psychologists strive to promote the cognitive, emotional, and social development of children in schools. They usually work in elementary or secondary schools, where they test and counsel children having difficulties in school and aid parents and teachers in solving school-related problems.
Clinical neuropsychology	Clinical neuropsychologists are involved in the assessment and treatment of people who suffer from central nervous system dysfunctions due to head trauma, dementia, stroke, seizure disorders, and so forth.
Forensic psychology	Forensic psychologists apply psychological principles to issues arising in the legal system, such as child custody decisions, hearings on competency to stand trial, violence risk assessments, involuntary commitment proceedings, and so forth.

web link 1.7

Marky Lloyd's Career Page

For those who think they might want to find a job or career in psychology or a related field, Marky Lloyd of Georgia Southern University has put together a fine set of resources to help in both planning and making choices.

The data in Figures 1.8 and 1.9 are based on APA members' reports of their single, principal area of specialization. However, many psychologists work on both research and application. Some academic psychologists work as consultants, therapists, and counselors on a part-time basis. Similarly, some applied psychologists conduct basic research on issues related to their specialty. For example, many clinical psychologists are involved in research on the nature and causes of abnormal behavior.

Some people are confused about the difference between clinical psychology and psychiatry. The confusion is understandable, as both clinical psychologists and psychiatrists are involved in analyzing and treating psychological disorders. Although some overlap exists between the two professions, the training and educational requirements for the two are quite different. Clinical psychologists go to graduate school to earn one of several doctoral degrees (Ph.D., Ed.D., or Psy.D.) in order to enjoy full status in their profession. Psychiatrists go to medical school for their postgraduate education, where they receive general training in medicine and earn an M.D. degree. They then specialize by completing residency training in psychiatry at a hospital. Clinical psychologists and psychiatrists also differ in the way they

tend to approach the treatment of mental disorders, as we will see in Chapter 15. To summarize, *psychiatry is a branch of medicine concerned with the diagnosis and treatment of psychological problems and disorders.* In contrast, clinical psychology takes a nonmedical approach to such problems.

REVIEW of Key Learning Goals

1.12 Contemporary psychology is a diversified science and profession that has grown rapidly in recent decades, as evidenced by the fact that APA membership has grown ninefold since 1950. The main work settings for contemporary psychologists are (1) private practice, (2) colleges and universities, (3) hospitals and clinics, and (4) business and government.

1.13 Major areas of research in modern psychology include developmental psychology, social psychology, experimental psychology, physiological psychology, cognitive psychology, personality, psychometrics, educational psychology, and health psychology.

1.14 Applied psychology encompasses six professional specialties: clinical psychology, counseling psychology, school psychology, industrial/organizational psychology, clinical neuropsychology, and forensic psychology. Although clinical psychology and psychiatry share some of the same interests, they are different professions with different types of training. Psychiatrists are physicians who specialize in the diagnosis and treatment of mental disorders, whereas clinical psychologists take a nonmedical approach to psychological problems.

Key Learning Goals
1.15 Clarify the text's three unifying themes relating to psychology as a field of study.
1.16 Clarify the text's four unifying themes relating to psychology's subject matter.

Seven Unifying Themes

The enormous breadth and diversity of psychology make it a challenging subject for the beginning student. In the pages ahead you will be introduced to many areas of research and a multitude of ideas, concepts, and principles. Fortunately, ideas are not all created equal. Some are far more important than others. In this section, I will highlight seven fundamental themes that will reappear in a number of variations as we move from one area of psychology to another in this text. You have already met some of these key ideas in our review of psychology's past and present. Now we will isolate them and highlight their significance. In the remainder of the book these ideas serve as organizing themes to provide threads of continuity across chapters and to help you see the connections among the various areas of research in psychology.

In studying psychology, you are learning about both behavior and the scientific discipline that investigates it. Accordingly, our seven themes come in two sets. The first set consists of statements highlighting crucial aspects of psychology as a way of thinking and as a field of study. The second set consists of broad generalizations about psychology's subject matter: behavior and the cognitive and physiological processes that underlie it.

Themes Related to Psychology as a Field of Study

Looking at psychology as a field of study, we see three crucial ideas: (1) psychology is empirical, (2) psychology is theoretically diverse, and (3) psychology evolves in a sociohistorical context. Let's look at each of these ideas in more detail.

Theme 1: Psychology Is Empirical

Everyone tries to understand behavior. Most of us have our own personal answers to questions such as why some people are hard workers, why some are overweight, and why others stay in demeaning relationships. If all of us are amateur psychologists, what makes scientific psychology different? The critical difference is that psychology is *empirical*. This aspect of psychology is fundamental, and virtually every page of this book reflects it.

What do we mean by empirical? *Empiricism* **is the premise that knowledge should be acquired through observation.** This premise is crucial to the scientific method that psychology embraced in the late 19th century. To say that psychology is empirical means that its conclusions are based on direct observation rather than on reasoning, speculation, traditional beliefs, or common sense. Psychologists are not content with having ideas that sound plausible. They conduct research to *test* their ideas. Is intelligence higher, on average, in some social classes than in others? Are men more aggressive than women? Psychologists find a way to make direct, objective, and precise observations to answer such questions.

The empirical approach requires a certain attitude—a healthy brand of *skepticism*. Empiricism is a tough taskmaster. It demands data and documentation. Psychologists' commitment to empiricism means that they must learn to think critically about generalizations concerning behavior. If someone asserts that people tend to get depressed around Christmas, a psychologist is likely to ask, "How many people get depressed? In what population? In comparison to what baseline rate of depression? How is depression defined?" Their skeptical attitude means that psychologists are trained to ask, "Where's the evidence? How do you know?" If psychology's empirical orientation rubs off on you (and I hope it does), you will be asking similar questions by the time you finish this book.

Theme 2: Psychology Is Theoretically Diverse

Although psychology is based on observation, a string of unrelated observations would not be terribly enlightening. Psychologists do not set out to just collect isolated facts; they seek to explain and understand what they observe. To achieve these goals they must construct theories. **A** *theory* **is a system of interrelated ideas used to explain a set of observations.** In other words, a theory links apparently unrelated observations and tries to explain them. As an example, consider Sigmund Freud's observations about slips of the tongue, dreams, and psychological disturbances. On the surface, these observations appear unrelated. By devising the concept of the *unconscious,* Freud created a theory that links and explains these seemingly unrelated aspects of behavior.

Our review of psychology's past should have made one thing abundantly clear: Psychology is marked by theoretical diversity. Why do we have so many competing points of view? One reason is that no single theory can adequately explain everything that is known about behavior. Sometimes different theories focus on different aspects of behavior—that is, different collections of observations. Sometimes there is simply more than one way to look at something. Is the glass half empty or half full? Obviously, it is both. To take an example from another science, physicists wrestled for years with the nature of light. Is it a wave, or is it a particle? In the end, scientists found it useful to think of light sometimes as a wave and sometimes as a particle. Similarly, if a business executive lashes out at her employees with stinging criticism, is she releasing pent-up aggressive urges (a psychoanalytic view)? Is she making a habitual response to the stimulus of incompetent work (a behavioral view)? Or is she scheming to motivate her employees by using "mind games" (a cognitive view)? In some cases, all three of these explanations might have some validity. In short, it is an oversimplification to expect that one view has to be right while all others are wrong. Life is rarely that simple.

Students are often troubled by psychology's many conflicting theories, which they view as a weakness. However, many psychologists argue that theoretical diversity is a strength rather than a weakness (Hilgard, 1987). As we proceed through this text, you will see how differing theoretical perspectives often provide a more complete understanding of behavior than could be achieved by any one perspective alone.

Theme 3: Psychology Evolves in a Sociohistorical Context

Science is often seen as an "ivory tower" undertaking, isolated from the ebb and flow of everyday life. In reality, however, psychology and other sciences do not exist in a cultural vacuum. Dense interconnections exist between what happens in psychology and what happens in society at large (Altman, 1990; Danziger, 1990; Runyan, 2006). Trends, events, issues, and values in society influence psychology's evolution. Similarly, progress in psychology affects trends, events, issues, and values in society. To put it briefly, psychology develops in a *sociohistorical* (social and historical) context.

Our review of psychology's past is filled with examples of how social trends have left their imprint on psychology. In the late 19th century, psychology's rapid growth as a laboratory science was due, in part, to its fascination with physics as the model discipline. Thus, the spirit of the times fostered a scientific approach rather than a philosophical approach to the investigation of the mind. Similarly, Freud's groundbreaking ideas emerged out of a specific sociohistorical context. Cultural values in Freud's era encouraged the suppression of sexuality. As a result, people tended to feel guilty about their sexual urges

to a much greater extent than is common today. This situation clearly contributed to Freud's emphasis on unconscious sexual conflicts. For another example, consider the impact of World War II on the development of psychology as a profession. The rapid growth of professional psychology was largely attributable to the war-related surge in the demand for clinical services. Hence, World War II reshaped the landscape of psychology in a remarkably short time. Finally, in recent years we have seen how growing global interdependence and increased cultural diversity have prompted psychologists to focus new attention on cultural factors as determinants of behavior.

If we reverse our viewpoint, we can see that psychology has in turn left its mark on society. Consider, for instance, the pervasive role of mental testing in modern society. Your own career success may depend in part on how well you weave your way through a complex maze of intelligence and achievement tests made possible (to the regret of some) by research in psychology. As another example of psychology's impact on society, consider the influence that various theorists have had on parenting styles. Trends in childrearing practices have been shaped by the ideas of John B. Watson, Sigmund Freud, B. F. Skinner, and Carl Rogers—not to mention many more psychologists yet to be discussed. In short, society and psychology influence each other in complex ways. In the chapters to come, we will frequently have occasion to notice this dynamic relationship.

Themes Related to Psychology's Subject Matter

Looking at psychology's subject matter, we see four additional crucial ideas: (4) behavior is determined by multiple causes, (5) behavior is shaped by cultural heritage, (6) heredity and environment jointly influence behavior, and (7) people's experience of the world is highly subjective.

Theme 4: Behavior Is Determined by Multiple Causes

As psychology has matured, it has provided more and more information about the forces that govern behavior. This growing knowledge has led to a deeper appreciation of a simple but important fact: Behavior is exceedingly complex, and most aspects of behavior are determined by multiple causes.

Although the complexity of behavior may seem self-evident, people usually think in terms of single causes. Thus, they offer explanations such as "Andrea flunked out of school because she is lazy." Or they assert that "teenage pregnancies are increasing because of all the sex in the media." Single-cause explanations are sometimes accurate as far as they go, but they usually are incomplete. In general, psychologists find that behavior is governed by a complex network of interacting factors, an idea referred to as the *multifactorial causation of behavior.*

As a simple illustration, consider the multiple factors that might influence your performance in your introductory psychology course. Relevant personal factors might include your overall intelligence, your reading ability, your memory skills, your motivation, and your study skills. In addition, your grade could be affected by numerous situational factors, including whether you like your psychology professor, whether you like your assigned text, whether the class meets at a good time for you, whether your work schedule is light or heavy, and whether you're having any personal problems.

As you proceed through this book, you will learn that complexity of causation is the rule rather than the exception. If we expect to understand behavior, we usually have to take into account multiple determinants.

Theme 5: Behavior Is Shaped by Cultural Heritage

Among the multiple determinants of human behavior, cultural factors are particularly prominent. Just as psychology evolves in a sociohistorical context, so, too, do individuals. People's cultural backgrounds exert considerable influence over their behavior. As Markus and Hamedani (2007) put it, "The option of being *a*social or *a*cultural—that is, living as a neutral being who is not bound to particular practices and socioculturally structured ways of behaving—is not available. People eat, sleep, work, and relate to one another in culture-specific ways" (p. 5). What is *culture?* Theorists have argued about the exact details of how to define culture for over a century, and the precise boundaries of the concept remain a little fuzzy (Matsumoto & Yoo, 2006). Broadly speaking, *culture* **refers to the widely shared customs, beliefs, values, norms, institutions, and other products of a community that are transmitted socially across generations.** Culture is a far-reaching construct, encompassing everything from a society's legal system to its assumptions about family roles, from its dietary habits to its political ideals, from its technology to its attitudes about time, from its modes of dress to its spiritual beliefs, and from its art and music to its unspoken rules about sexual liaisons. We tend to think of culture as belonging to entire societies or broad ethnic groups within societies—which it does—but the concept can also be applied to small groups (a tiny Aboriginal tribe

in Australia, for example) and to nonethnic groups (gay culture, for instance).

Triandis (2007) emphasizes that culture has a dual nature, existing both outside and inside people. Culture lies outside of people in that one can identify various customs, practices, and institutions that mold people's behavior. Culture lies inside people in that everything that happens to them is viewed through a cultural lens—a way of thinking—that cannot be set aside. The fact that culture lies within people means that much of a person's cultural heritage is invisible (Brislin, 2000). Assumptions, ideals, attitudes, beliefs, and unspoken rules exist in people's minds and may not be readily apparent to outsiders. Moreover, because a cultural background is widely shared, members feel little need to discuss it with others and often take it for granted. For example, you probably don't spend much time thinking about the importance of living in rectangular rooms, trying to minimize body odor, limiting yourself to one spouse at a time, or using credit cards to obtain material goods and services.

Even though we generally fail to appreciate its influence, our cultural heritage has a pervasive impact on our thoughts, feelings, and behavior (Matsumoto & Juang, 2008; Triandis, 2007). For example, in North America, when people are invited to dinner in someone's home, they generally show their

Cultural background has an enormous influence on people's behavior, shaping everything from modes of dress to sexual values and norms. Increased global interdependence brings more and more people into contact with cultures other than their own. This increased exposure to diverse cultures only serves to underscore the importance of cultural factors.

Nature or nurture? Serial killer Ted Bundy bludgeoned, raped, and murdered dozens of young women in the 1970s. A number of the victims' bodies were dumped at a rural mountain site, where he would visit them and have sex with their decomposing corpses. What could explain such depraved, grotesque, evil behavior? Heredity? Environment? Or some combination of the two? One detective who interviewed Bundy extensively blamed heredity, asserting that he was "born to kill." But Bundy was raised by an abusive, violent grandfather who tortured animals, so one could just as easily indict his upbringing. In any event, the nature versus nurture question comes up endlessly in efforts to understand behavior.

appreciation of their host's cooking efforts by eating all of the food they are served. In India, this behavior would be insulting to the host, as guests are expected to leave some food on their plates. The leftover food acknowledges the generosity of the host, implying that he or she provided so much food the guest could not eat it all (Moghaddam, Taylor, & Wright, 1993). Cultures also vary in their emphasis on punctuality. In North America, we expect people to show up for meetings on time; if someone is more than 10 to 15 minutes late we begin to get upset. We generally strive to be on time, and many of us are quite proud of our precise and dependable punctuality. However, in many Asian and Latin American countries, social obligations that arise at the last minute are given just as much priority as scheduled commitments. Hence, people often show up for important meetings an hour or two late with little remorse, and they may be quite puzzled by the consternation of their Western visitors (Brislin, 2000). These examples may seem trivial, but as you will see in upcoming chapters, culture can also influence crucial matters, such as educational success, mental health, and vulnerability to physical illnesses.

Although the influence of culture is everywhere, generalizations about cultural groups must always be tempered by the realization that great diversity also exists within any society or ethnic group (Markus & Hamedani, 2007). Researchers may be able to pinpoint genuinely useful insights about Ethiopian, Korean American, or Ukrainian culture, for example, but it would be foolish to assume that all Ethiopians, Korean Americans, or Ukrainians exhibit identical behavior. It is also important to realize that both differences and similarities in behavior occur across cultures. As we will see repeatedly, psychological processes are characterized by both cultural

variance and invariance. Caveats aside, if we hope to achieve a sound understanding of human behavior, we need to consider cultural determinants.

Theme 6: Heredity and Environment Jointly Influence Behavior

Are individuals who they are—athletic or artistic, quick tempered or calm, shy or outgoing, energetic or laid back—because of their genetic inheritance or because of their upbringing? This question about the importance of nature versus nurture, or heredity versus environment, has been asked in one form or another since ancient times. Historically, the nature-versus-nurture question was framed as an all-or-none proposition. In other words, theorists argued that personal traits and abilities are governed either entirely by heredity or entirely by environment. John B. Watson, for instance, asserted that personality and ability depend almost exclusively on an individual's environment. In contrast, Sir Francis Galton, a 19th-century pioneer in mental testing (see Chapter 9), maintained that personality and ability depend almost entirely on genetic inheritance.

Today, most psychologists agree that heredity and environment are both important. A century of research has shown that genetics and experience jointly influence an individual's intelligence, temperament, personality, and susceptibility to many psychological disorders (Grigerenko & Sternberg, 2003; Plomin, 2004). If we ask whether individuals are born or made, psychology's answer is "Both." This does not mean that nature versus nurture is a dead issue. Lively debate about the *relative influence* of genetics and experience continues unabated. Furthermore, psychologists are actively seeking to understand the complex ways in which genetic inheritance and experience interact to mold behavior.

Theme 7: People's Experience of the World Is Highly Subjective

Even elementary perception—for example, of sights and sounds—is not a passive process. People actively process incoming stimulation, selectively focusing on some aspects of that stimulation while ignoring others. Moreover, they impose organization on the stimuli that they pay attention to. These tendencies combine to make perception personalized and subjective.

The subjectivity of perception was demonstrated nicely in a classic study by Hastorf and Cantril (1954). They showed students at Princeton and Dartmouth universities a film of a recent football game between the two schools. The students were told to watch for rules infractions. Both groups saw the same film, but the Princeton students "saw" the

Dartmouth players engage in twice as many infractions as the Dartmouth students "saw." The investigators concluded that the game "actually was many different games and that each version of the events that transpired was just as 'real' to a particular person as other versions were to other people" (Hastorf & Cantril, 1954). In this study, the subjects' perceptions were swayed by their motives. It shows how people sometimes see what they *want* to see.

Other studies reveal that people also tend to see what they *expect* to see. For example, Harold Kelley (1950) showed how perceptions of people are influenced by their reputation. Kelley told students that their class would be taken over by a new lecturer, whom they would be asked to evaluate later. Before the class, the students were given a short description of the incoming instructor, with one important variation. Half the students were led to expect a "warm" person, while the other half were led to expect a "cold" one (see **Figure 1.10**). All the subjects were exposed to the same 20 minutes of lecture and interaction with the new instructor. However, the group of subjects who *expected* a warm person rated the instructor as more considerate, sociable, humorous, good natured, informal, and humane than the subjects in the group who had expected a cold person.

Thus, it is clear that motives and expectations color people's experiences. To some extent, individuals see what they want to see or what they expect to see. This subjective bias in perception turns out

to explain a variety of behavioral tendencies that would otherwise be perplexing (Pronin, Lin, & Ross, 2002; Pronin, Gilovich, & Ross, 2004).

Human subjectivity is precisely what the scientific method is designed to counteract. In using the scientific approach, psychologists strive to make their observations as objective as possible. In some respects, overcoming subjectivity is what science is all about. Left to their own subjective experience, people might still believe that the earth is flat and that the sun revolves around it. Thus, psychologists are committed to the scientific approach because they believe it is the most reliable route to accurate knowledge.

Now that you have been introduced to the text's organizing themes, let's turn to an example of how psychological research can be applied to the challenges of everyday life. In our first Personal Application, we'll focus on a subject that should be highly relevant to you: how to be a successful student. In the Critical Thinking Application that follows it, we discuss the nature and importance of critical thinking skills.

Figure 1.10

Manipulating person perception. Read the accompanying description of Mr. Blank carefully. If you were about to hear him give a lecture, would this description bias your perceptions of him? You probably think not, but when Kelley (1950) altered one adjective in this description (replacing the word *warm* with *cold*), the change had a dramatic impact on subjects' ratings of the guest lecturer.

Mr. Blank is a graduate student in the Department of Economics and Social Science here at M.I.T. He has had three semesters of teaching experience in psychology at another college. This is his first semester teaching Ec. 70. He is 26 years old, a veteran, and married. People who know him consider him to be a very *warm* person, industrious, critical, practical, and determined.

SOURCE: Description from Kelley, H. H. (1950). The warm-cold variable in first impressions of persons. *Journal of Personality, 8,* 431–439. Copyright © 1950 by the Ecological Society of America. Reprinted by permission.

concept check 1.3

Understanding the Seven Key Themes

Check your understanding of the seven key themes introduced in the chapter by matching the vignettes with the themes they exemplify. You'll find the answers in Appendix A.

Themes

1. Psychology is empirical.

2. Psychology is theoretically diverse.

3. Psychology evolves in a sociohistorical context.

4. Behavior is determined by multiple causes.

5. Behavior is shaped by cultural heritage.

6. Heredity and environment jointly influence behavior.

7. People's experience of the world is highly subjective.

Vignettes

_____ a. Several or more theoretical models of emotion have contributed to our overall understanding of the dynamics of emotion.

_____ b. According to the stress-vulnerability model, some people are at greater risk for developing certain psychological disorders for genetic reasons. Whether these people actually develop the disorders depends on how much stress they experience in their work, families, or other areas of their lives.

_____ c. Physical health and illness seem to be influenced by a complex constellation of psychological, biological, and social system variables.

_____ d. One of the difficulties in investigating the effects of drugs on consciousness is that individuals tend to have different experiences with a given drug because of their different expectations.

REVIEW of Key Learning Goals

1.15 Psychology is empirical because psychologists base their conclusions on observation through research rather than reasoning or common sense. Psychology is theoretically diverse, as there are many competing schools of thought in the field. This diversity has fueled progress and is a strength rather than a weakness. Psychology also evolves in a sociohistorical context, as trends, issues, and values in society influence what goes on in psychology, and vice versa.

1.16 Behavior is determined by multiple causes, as most aspects of behavior are influenced by complex networks of interacting factors. Although cultural heritage is often taken for granted, it has a pervasive impact on people's thoughts, feelings, and behavior. Lively debate about the relative importance of nature versus nurture continues, but it is clear that heredity and environment jointly influence behavior. People's experience of the world is highly subjective, as they sometimes see what they want to see or what they expect to see.

PERSONAL

APPLICATION

Improving Academic Performance

Key Learning Goals

1.17 Review three important considerations in designing a program to promote adequate studying.

1.18 Describe the SQ3R method, and discuss text-marking strategies.

1.19 Summarize advice provided on how to get more out of lectures.

1.20 Summarize advice provided on improving test-taking strategies.

Answer the following "true" or "false."

_____ **1** It's a good idea to study in as many different locations (your bedroom or kitchen, the library, lounges around school, and so forth) as possible.

_____ **2** If you have a professor who delivers chaotic, hard-to-follow lectures, there is little point in attending class.

_____ **3** Cramming the night before an exam is an effective method of study.

_____ **4** In taking lecture notes, you should try to be a "human tape recorder" (that is, write down everything your professor says).

_____ **5** You should never change your answers to multiple-choice questions, because your first hunch is your best hunch.

All of the above statements are false. If you answered them all correctly, you may have already acquired the kinds of skills and habits that facilitate academic success. If so, however, you are *not* typical. Today, many students enter college with poor study skills and habits—and it's not entirely their fault. The American educational system generally provides minimal instruction on good study techniques. In this first Application,

we will try to remedy this situation to some extent by reviewing some insights that psychology offers on how to improve academic performance. We will discuss how to promote better study habits, how to enhance reading efforts, how to get more out of lectures, and how to improve test-taking strategies. You may also want to jump ahead and read the Personal Application for Chapter 7, which focuses on how to improve everyday memory.

Developing Sound Study Habits

Effective study is crucial to success in college. Although you may run into a few classmates who boast about getting good grades without studying, you can be sure that if they perform well on exams, they *do* study. Students who claim otherwise simply want to be viewed as extremely bright rather than as studious.

Learning can be immensely gratifying, but studying usually involves hard work. The first step toward effective study habits is to face up to this reality. You don't have to feel guilty if you don't look forward to studying. Most students don't. Once you accept the premise that studying doesn't come naturally, it should be apparent that you need to set up an organized program to promote adequate study. According to Siebert and Karr (2003), such a program should include the following considerations:

1. *Set up a schedule for studying.* If you wait until the urge to study strikes you, you

may still be waiting when the exam rolls around. Thus, it is important to allocate definite times to studying. Review your various time obligations (work, chores, and so on) and figure out in advance when you can study. When allotting certain times to studying, keep in mind that you need to be wide awake and alert. Be realistic about how long you can study at one time before you wear down from fatigue. Allow time for study breaks—they can revive sagging concentration.

It's important to write down your study schedule. A written schedule serves as a reminder and increases your commitment to following it. You should begin by setting up a general schedule for the quarter or semester, like the one in Figure 1.11. Then, at the beginning of each week, plan the specific assignments that you intend to work on during each study session. This approach to scheduling should help you avoid cramming for exams at the last minute. Cramming is an ineffective study strategy for most students (Underwood, 1961; Wong, 2006; Zechmeister & Nyberg, 1982). It will strain your memorization capabilities, can tax your energy level, and may stoke the fires of test anxiety.

In planning your weekly schedule, try to avoid the tendency to put off working on major tasks such as term papers and reports. Time-management experts such as Alan Lakein (1996) point out that many people tend to tackle simple, routine tasks first, saving larger tasks for later when they supposedly will have more time. This common tendency leads many individuals to repeatedly delay working on major assignments

Figure 1.11

One student's general activity schedule for a semester. Each week the student fills in the specific assignments to work on during each study period.

Weekly Activity Schedule							
	Monday	Tuesday	Wednesday	Thursday	Friday	Saturday	Sunday
8 A.M.						Work	
9 A.M.	History	Study	History	Study	History		
10 A.M.	Psychology	French	Psychology	French	Psychology		
11 A.M.	Study	↓	Study	↓	Study		
Noon	Math	Study	Math	Study	Math	↓	Study
1 P.M.							
2 P.M.	Study	English	Study	English	Study		
3 P.M.	↓	↓	↓	↓	↓		↓
4 P.M.							
5 P.M.							
6 P.M.	Work	Study	Study	Work			Study
7 P.M.							
8 P.M.							
9 P.M.	↓	↓	↓				↓
10 P.M.	↓			↓			

until it's too late to do a good job. A good way to avoid this trap is to break major assignments down into smaller component tasks that can be scheduled individually.

Research on the differences between successful and unsuccessful college students suggests that successful students monitor and regulate their use of time more effectively (Allgood et al., 2000). You can assess various aspects of your time-management practices by responding to the questionnaire in **Figure 1.12** on the next page.

2. *Find a place to study where you can concentrate.* Where you study is also important. The key is to find a place where distractions are likely to be minimal. Most people cannot study effectively while the TV or stereo is on or while other people are talking. Don't depend on willpower to carry you through such distractions. It's much easier to plan ahead and avoid the distractions altogether. In fact, you would be wise to set up one or two specific places to use solely for study (Hettich, 1998).

3. *Reward your studying.* One reason that it is so difficult to be motivated to study regularly is that the payoffs often lie in the distant future. The ultimate reward, a degree, may be years away. Even short-term rewards, such as an A in the course, may be weeks or months away. To combat this

problem, it helps to give yourself immediate, tangible rewards for studying, such as a snack, TV show, or phone call to a friend. Thus, you should set realistic study goals for yourself, then reward yourself when you meet them. The systematic manipulation of rewards involves harnessing the principles of *behavior modification* described by B. F. Skinner and other behavioral psychologists. These principles are covered in the Chapter 6 Personal Application.

Improving Your Reading

Much of your study time is spent reading and absorbing information. *These efforts must be active.* You can use a number of methods to actively attack your reading assignments. One of the more widely taught strategies is Robinson's (1970) SQ3R method. **SQ3R is a study system designed to promote effective reading, which includes five steps: survey, question, read, recite, and review.**

Some locations are far more conducive to successful studying than others.

Listed below are ten statements that reflect generally accepted principles of good time management. Answer these items by circling the response most characteristic of how you perform. Please be honest. No one will know your answers except you.

1 Each day I set aside a small amount of time for planning and thinking about my responsibilities.
0. Almost never 1. Sometimes 2. Often 3. Almost always

2 I set specific, written goals and put deadlines on them.
0. Almost never 1. Sometimes 2. Often 3. Almost always

3 I make a daily "to do" list, arrange items in order of importance, and try to get the important items done as soon as possible.
0. Almost never 1. Sometimes 2. Often 3. Almost always

4 I am aware of the 80/20 rule and use it. (The 80/20 rule states that 80% of your effectiveness will generally come from achieving only 20% of your goals.)
0. Almost never 1. Sometimes 2. Often 3. Almost always

5 I keep a loose schedule to allow for crises and the unexpected.
0. Almost never 1. Sometimes 2. Often 3. Almost always

6 I delegate everything I can to others.
0. Almost never 1. Sometimes 2. Often 3. Almost always

7 I try to handle each piece of paper only once.
0. Almost never 1. Sometimes 2. Often 3. Almost always

8 I eat a light lunch so I don't get sleepy in the afternoon.
0. Almost never 1. Sometimes 2. Often 3. Almost always

9 I make an active effort to keep common interruptions (visitors, meetings, telephone calls) from continually disrupting my work day.
0. Almost never 1. Sometimes 2. Often 3. Almost always

10 I am able to say no to others' requests for my time that would prevent my completing important tasks.
0. Almost never 1. Sometimes 2. Often 3. Almost always

To get your score, give yourself	If you scored	
3 points for each "almost always"	0–15	Better give some thought to managing your time.
2 points for each "often"		
1 point for each "sometimes"	16–20	You're doing OK, but there's room for improvement.
0 points for each "almost never"		
	21–25	Very good.
Add up your points to get your total score.	26–30	You cheated!

Figure 1.12

Assessing your time management. This brief questionnaire (from LeBoeuf, 1980) is designed to evaluate the quality of one's time management. It should allow you to get a rough handle on how well you manage your time.

SOURCE: Le Boeuf, M. (1980, February). Managing time means managing yourself. *Business Horizons Magazine*, p. 45. Copyright © by the Foundation for the School of Business at Indiana University. Used with permission.

Its name is an acronym for the five steps in the procedure:

Step 1: Survey. Before you plunge into the reading itself, glance over the topic headings in the chapter. If you know where the chapter is going, you can better appreciate and organize the information you are about to read.

Step 2: Question. Once you have an overview of your reading assignment, you should proceed through it one section at a time. Take a look at the heading of the first section and convert it into a question. Doing so is usually quite simple. If the heading is "Prenatal Risk Factors," your question should be "What are sources of risk during prenatal development?" If the heading is "Stereotyping," your question should be "What is stereotyping?" Asking these questions gets you actively involved in your reading and helps you identify the main ideas.

Step 3: Read. Only now, in the third step, are you ready to sink your teeth into the reading. Read only the specific section that you have decided to tackle. Read it with an eye toward answering the question you have just formulated. If necessary, reread the section until you can answer that question. Decide whether the segment addresses any other important questions and answer them as well.

Step 4: Recite. Now that you can answer the key question for the section, recite the answer out loud to yourself in your own words. Don't move on to the next section until you understand the main ideas of the current section. You may want to write down these ideas for review later. When you have fully digested the first section, you may go on to the next. Repeat steps 2 through 4 with the next section. Once you have mastered the crucial points there, you can go on again.

Step 5: Review. When you have read the entire chapter, refresh your memory by going back over the key points. Repeat your questions and try to answer them without consulting your book or notes. This review should fortify your retention of the main ideas. It should also help you see how the main ideas are related.

The SQ3R method should probably be applied to many texts on a paragraph-by-paragraph basis. Obviously, doing so will require you to formulate some questions without the benefit of topic headings. If you don't have enough headings, you can simply reverse the order of steps 2 and 3. Read the paragraph first and then formulate a question that addresses the basic idea of the paragraph. Then work at answering the question in your own words. The point is that you can be flexible in your use of the SQ3R technique.

Using the SQ3R method does not automatically lead to improved mastery of textbook reading assignments. It won't be effective unless it is applied diligently and skillfully, and it tends to be most helpful to students with low to medium reading ability (Caverly, Orlando, & Mullen, 2000). Any strategy that facilitates active processing of text material, the identification of key ideas, and effective review of these ideas should enhance your reading.

Modern textbooks often contain a variety of learning aids that you can use to improve your reading. If a book provides a chapter outline, chapter summary, or learning objectives, don't ignore them. They can help you recognize the important points in the chapter. Graphic organizers (such as the

Concept Charts available for this text) can also enhance understanding of text material (Nist & Holschuh, 2000). A lot of effort and thought go into formulating these and other textbook learning aids. It is wise to take advantage of them.

Another important issue related to textbook reading is whether and how to mark up reading assignments. Many students deceive themselves into thinking that they are studying by running a marker through a few sentences here and there in their text. If they do so without thoughtful selectivity, they are simply turning a textbook into a coloring book. This situation probably explains why some professors are skeptical about the value of highlighting textbooks. Nonetheless, research suggests that highlighting textbook material *is* a useful strategy—if students are reasonably effective in focusing on the main ideas in the material and if they subsequently review what they have highlighted (Caverly, Orlando, & Mullen, 2000).

When executed effectively, highlighting can foster active reading, improve reading comprehension, and reduce the amount of material that must be reviewed later (Van Blerkom, 2006). The key to effective text marking is to identify (and highlight) only the main ideas, key supporting details, and technical terms (Daiek & Anter, 2004). Most textbooks are carefully crafted such that every paragraph has a purpose for being there. Try to find the sentence or two that best captures the purpose of each paragraph. Text marking is a delicate balancing act. If you highlight too little of the content, you are not identifying enough of the key ideas. But if you highlight too much of the content, you are not going to succeed in condensing what you have to review to a manageable size.

Getting More Out of Lectures

Although lectures are sometimes boring and tedious, it is a simple fact that poor class attendance is associated with poor grades. For example, in one study, Lindgren (1969) found that absences from class were much more common among "unsuccessful" students (grade average C– or below) than among "successful" students (grade average B or above), as shown in **Figure**

1.13. Even when you have an instructor who delivers hard-to-follow lectures, it is still important to go to class. If nothing else, you can get a feel for how the instructor thinks, which can help you anticipate the content of exams and respond in the manner expected by your professor.

Fortunately, most lectures are reasonably coherent. Studies indicate that attentive, accurate note taking *is* associated with enhanced learning and performance in college classes (Titsworth & Kiewra, 2004; Williams & Eggert, 2002). However, research also shows that many students' lecture notes are surprisingly incomplete, with the average student often recording less than 40% of the crucial ideas in a lecture (Armbruster, 2000). Thus, the key to getting more out of lectures is to stay motivated, stay attentive, and expend the effort to make your notes as complete as possible. Books on study skills (Longman & Atkinson, 2005; McWhorter, 2007) offer a number of suggestions on how to take good-quality lecture notes, some of which are summarized here:

• Extracting information from lectures requires *active listening*. Focus full attention on the speaker. Try to anticipate what's coming and search for deeper meanings.
• When course material is especially complex, it is a good idea to prepare for the lec-

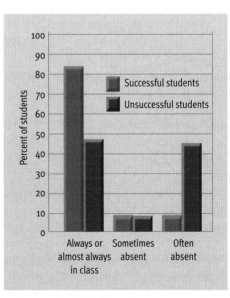

Figure 1.13

Attendance and grades. When Lindgren (1969) compared the class attendance of successful students (B average or above) and unsuccessful students (C– average or below), he found a clear association between poor attendance and poor grades.

ture by *reading ahead* on the scheduled subject in your text. Then you have less new information to digest.
• You are not supposed to be a human tape recorder. Insofar as possible, try to write down the lecturer's thoughts *in your own words*. Doing so forces you to organize the ideas in a way that makes sense to you.
• In taking notes, pay attention to clues about what is most important. These clues may range from subtle hints, such as an instructor repeating a point, to not-so-subtle hints, such as an instructor saying "You'll run into this again."
• In delivering their lectures most professors follow an organized outline, which they may or may not share with the class (on the blackboard or via a presentation tool, such as PowerPoint). Insofar as you can decipher the outline of a lecture, try to organize your notes accordingly. When you go back to review your notes later, they will make more sense and it should be easier to identify the most important ideas.
• *Asking questions* during lectures can be helpful. Doing so keeps you actively involved in the lecture and allows you to clarify points that you may have misunderstood. Many students are more bashful about asking questions than they should be. They don't realize that most professors welcome questions.

Improving Test-Taking Strategies

Let's face it—some students are better than others at taking tests. *Testwiseness* is the ability to use the characteristics and format of a cognitive test to maximize one's score. Students clearly vary in testwiseness, and such variations are reflected in performance on exams (Geiger, 1997; Rogers & Yang, 1996). Testwiseness is *not* a substitute for knowledge of the subject matter. However, skill in taking tests can help you show what you know when it is critical to do so (Flippo, Becker & Wark, 2000).

A number of myths exist about the best way to take tests. For instance, it is widely believed that students shouldn't go back and change their answers to multiple-choice questions. Benjamin, Cavell, and Shallenberger (1984) found this to be the dominant belief among college *faculty* as

well as students (see **Figure 1.14**). However, the old adage that "your first hunch is your best hunch" on tests has been shown to be wrong. Empirical studies clearly and consistently indicate that, over the long run, changing answers pays off. Benjamin and his colleagues reviewed 20 studies on this issue; their findings are presented in **Figure 1.15**. As you can see, answer changes that go from a wrong answer to a right answer outnumber changes that go from a right answer to a wrong one by a sizable margin. The popular belief that answer changing is harmful is probably attributable to painful memories of right-to-wrong changes. In any case, you can see how it pays to be familiar with sound test-taking strategies.

General Tips

The principles of testwiseness were first described by Millman, Bishop, and Ebel (1965). Here are a few of their general ideas:

• If efficient time use appears crucial, set up a mental schedule for progressing through the test. Make a mental note to check whether you're one-third finished when a third of your time is gone.

• Don't waste time pondering difficult-to-answer questions excessively. If you have no idea at all, just guess and go on. If you need to devote a good deal of time to the question, skip it and mark it so you can return to it later if time permits.

• Adopt the appropriate level of sophistication for the test. Don't read things into questions. Sometimes students make things more complex than they were intended to be. Often, simple-looking questions are just what they appear to be.

• If you complete all of the questions and still have some time remaining, review the test. Make sure that you have recorded your answers correctly. If you were unsure of some answers, go back and reconsider them.

Tips for Multiple-Choice Exams

Sound test-taking strategies are especially important with multiple-choice (and true-false) questions. These types of questions often include clues that may help you converge on the correct answer (Mentzer, 1982; Weiten, 1984). You may be able to improve your performance on such tests by considering the following points (Flippo, 2000; Millman et al., 1965; Smith, 2005; Van Blerkom, 2006):

• As you read the stem of each multiple-choice question, *anticipate* the answer if you can, before looking at the options. If the answer you anticipated is among the options, it is likely to be the correct one.

• Always read each question completely. Continue reading even if you find your anticipated answer among the options. A more complete option may be farther down the list.

• Learn how to quickly eliminate options that are highly implausible. Many questions have only two plausible options, accompanied by "throwaway" options for filler. You should work at spotting these implausible options so that you can quickly discard them and narrow your task.

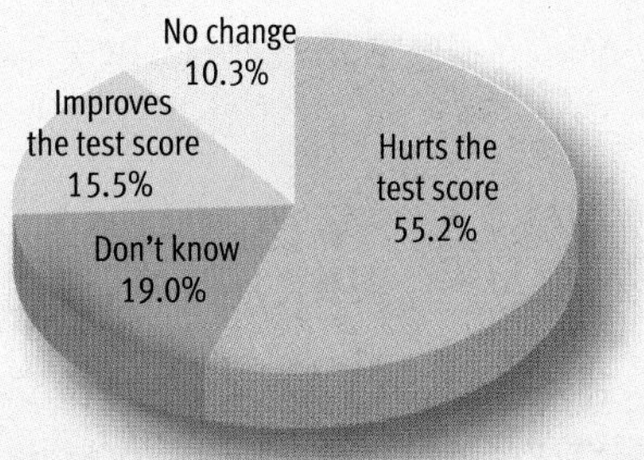

Figure 1.14

Beliefs about the effects of answer changing on tests. Ludy Benjamin and his colleagues (1984) asked 58 college faculty whether changing answers on tests is a good idea. Like most students, the majority of the faculty felt that answer changing usually hurts a student's test score, even though the research evidence contradicts this belief (see **Figure 1.15**).

Pie chart labels: No change 10.3%; Improves the test score 15.5%; Don't know 19.0%; Hurts the test score 55.2%

Figure 1.15

Actual effects of changing answers on multiple-choice tests. When the data from all the relevant studies were combined by Benjamin et al. (1984), they indicated that answer changing on tests generally increased rather than reduced students' test scores. It is interesting to note the contrast between beliefs about answer changing (see **Figure 1.14**) and the actual results of this practice.

Pie chart labels: Right to wrong 20.2%; Wrong to wrong 22%; Wrong to right 57.8%

© Rob Gage/Taxi/Getty Images

• Be alert to the fact that information relevant to one question is sometimes given away in another test item.

• On items that have "all of the above" as an option, if you know that just two of the options are correct, you should choose "all of the above." If you are confident that one of the options is incorrect, you should eliminate this option and "all of the above" and choose from the remaining options.

• Options that represent broad, sweeping generalizations tend to be incorrect. You should be vigilant for words such as *always, never, necessarily, only, must, completely, totally,* and so forth that create these improbable assertions.

• In contrast, options that represent carefully qualified statements tend to be correct. Words such as *often, sometimes, perhaps, may,* and *generally* tend to show up in these well-qualified statements.

Tips for Essay Exams

Little research has been done on testwiseness as it applies to essay exams. That's because relatively few clues are available in the essay format. Nonetheless, various books (Flippo, 2000; Pauk, 1990; Wong, 2006) offer tips based on expert advice, including the following:

• Time is usually a crucial factor on essay tests. Therefore, you should begin by looking over the questions and making time allocations on the basis of (1) your knowledge, (2) the time required to answer each question, and (3) the points awarded for answering each question. It's usually a good idea to answer the questions that you know best first.

• Many students fail to appreciate the importance of good organization in their essay responses. If your instructor can't follow where you are going with your answers, you won't get many points. Essay answers are often poorly organized because students feel pressured for time and plunge into writing without any planning. It will pay off in the long run if you spend a minute getting organized first. Also, many examiners appreciate it if you make your organization quite explicit by using headings or by numbering the points you're making.

• In many courses you'll learn a great deal of jargon or technical terminology. Demonstrate your learning by using this technical vocabulary in your essay answers.

In summary, sound study skills and habits are crucial to academic success. Intelligence alone won't do the job (although it certainly helps). Good academic skills do not develop overnight. They are acquired gradually, so be patient with yourself. Fortunately, tasks such as reading textbooks, writing papers, and taking tests get easier

with practice. Ultimately, I think you'll find that the rewards—knowledge, a sense of accomplishment, and progress toward a degree—are worth the effort.

REVIEW of Key Learning Goals

1.17 To foster sound study habits, you should devise a written study schedule and reward yourself for following it. Try to avoid the tendency to put off working on major tasks. You should also try to find one or two specific places for studying that are relatively free of distractions.

1.18 You should use active reading techniques to select the most important ideas from the material you read. SQ3R is one helpful approach to active reading. It involves five steps: survey, question, read, recite, and review. Highlighting textbook material *is* a useful strategy—if you are reasonably effective in focusing on the main ideas in the material and if you subsequently review what you have highlighted.

1.19 The key to good note taking is to strive to make lecture notes as complete as possible. It's important to use active listening techniques and to record lecturers' ideas in your own words. It also helps if you read ahead to prepare for lectures and ask questions as needed.

1.20 In taking tests, it's a good idea to devise a schedule for progressing through an exam, to adopt the appropriate level of sophistication, to avoid wasting time on troublesome questions, and to review your answers. On multiple-choice tests it is wise to anticipate answers, to read questions completely, and to quickly eliminate implausible options. On essay tests, it is wise to start with questions you know, to emphasize good organization, and to use technical vocabulary when appropriate.

Key Learning Goals

1.21 Explain the nature of critical thinking skills.

1.22 Evaluate some weaknesses in evolutionary explanations for gender differences in spatial abilities.

Developing Critical Thinking Skills: An Introduction

If you ask any group of professors, parents, employers, or politicians, "What is the most important outcome of an education?" The most popular answer is likely to be "the development of the ability to think critically." *Critical thinking* is purposeful, reasoned, goal-directed thinking that involves solving problems, formulating inferences, working with probabilities, and making carefully thought-out decisions. Critical thinking is the use of cognitive skills and strategies that increase the probability of a desirable outcome. Such outcomes would include good career choices, effective decisions in the workplace, wise investments, and so forth. In the long run, critical thinkers should have more desirable outcomes than people who are not skilled in critical thinking (Halpern, 1998, 2003). Here are some of the skills exhibited by critical thinkers:

• They understand and use the principles of scientific investigation. (How can the effectiveness of punishment as a disciplinary procedure be determined?)
• They apply the rules of formal and informal logic. (If most people disapprove of sex sites on the Internet, why are these sites so popular?)
• They carefully evaluate the quality of information. (Can I trust the claims made by this politician?)
• They analyze arguments for the soundness of the conclusions. (Does the rise in drug use mean that a stricter drug policy is needed?)

The topic of thinking has a long history in psychology, dating back to Wilhelm Wundt in the 19th century. Modern cognitive psychologists have found that a useful model of critical thinking has at least two components: (1) knowledge of the skills of critical thinking—the *cognitive component,* and (2) the attitude or disposition of a criti-

cal thinker—the *emotional or affective component.* Both are needed for effective critical thinking.

Instruction in critical thinking is based on two assumptions: (1) a set of skills or strategies exists that students can learn to recognize and apply in appropriate contexts; (2) if the skills are applied appropriately, students will become more effective thinkers (Halpern, 2007). Critical thinking skills that would be useful in any context might include understanding how reasons and evidence support or refute conclusions; distinguishing among facts, opinions, and reasoned judgments; using principles of likelihood and uncertainty when thinking about probabilistic events; generating multiple solutions to problems and working systematically toward a desired goal; and understanding how causation is determined. This list provides some typical examples of what is meant by the term *critical thinking skills.* Because these skills are useful in a wide variety of contexts, they are sometimes called *transcontextual skills.*

It is of little use to know the skills of critical thinking if you are unwilling to exert the hard mental work to use them or if you have a sloppy or careless attitude toward thinking. A critical thinker is willing to plan, flexible in thinking, persistent, able to admit mistakes and make corrections, and mindful of the thinking process. The use of the word *critical* represents the notion of a critique or evaluation of thinking processes and outcomes. It is not meant to be negative (as in a "critical person") but rather to con-

vey that critical thinkers are vigilant about their thinking (Riggio & Halpern, 2006).

The Need to Teach Critical Thinking

Decades of research on instruction in critical thinking have shown that the skills and attitudes of critical thinking need to be deliberately and consciously taught, because they often do not develop by themselves with standard instruction in a content area (Nisbett, 1993). For this reason, each chapter in this text ends with a Critical Thinking Application. The material presented in each of these Critical Thinking Applications relates to the chapter topics, but the focus is on how to think about a particular issue, line of research, or controversy. Because the emphasis is on the thinking process, you may be asked to consider conflicting interpretations of data, judge the credibility of information sources, or generate your own testable hypotheses. The specific critical thinking skills highlighted in each lesson are summarized in a table so that they are easily identified. Some of the skills will show up in multiple chapters because the goal is to help you spontaneously select the appropriate critical thinking skills when you encounter new information. Repeated practice with selected skills across chapters should help you develop this ability.

An Example

As explained in the main body of the chapter, *evolutionary psychology* is emerging as an

NON SEQUITUR

influential school of thought. To show you how critical thinking skills can be applied to psychological issues, let's examine the evolutionary explanation of gender differences in spatial talents and then use some critical thinking strategies to evaluate this explanation.

On the average, males tend to perform slightly better than females on most visual-spatial tasks, especially tasks involving mental rotation of images and navigation in space (Halpern, 2000; Silverman & Choi, 2005; see Figure 1.16). Irwin Silverman and his colleagues maintain that these gender differences originated in human evolution as a result of the sex-based division of labor in ancient hunting-and-gathering societies (Silverman & Phillips, 1998; Silverman et al., 2000). According to this analysis, males' superiority in mental rotation and navigation developed because the chore of *hunting* was largely assigned to men over the course of human history, and these skills would have facilitated success on hunting trips (by helping men to traverse long distances, aim projectiles at prey, and so forth) and thus been favored by natural selection. In contrast, women in ancient societies generally had responsibility for *gathering* food rather than hunting it. This was an efficient division of labor because women spent much of their adult lives pregnant, nursing, or caring for the young and, therefore, could not travel long distances. Silverman and Eals (1992) thus hypothesized that females ought to be superior to males on spatial skills that would have facilitated gathering, such as memory for locations, which is exactly what they found in a series of four studies. Thus, evolutionary psychologists explain gender differences in spatial ability—like other aspects of human behavior—in terms of how such abilities evolved to meet the adaptive pressures faced by our ancestors.

How can you critically evaluate these claims? If your first thought was that you

Figure 1.16
An example of a spatial task involving mental rotation. Spatial reasoning tasks can be divided into a variety of subtypes. Studies indicate that males perform slightly better than females on most, but not all, spatial tasks. The tasks on which males are superior often involve mentally rotating objects, such as in the problem shown here. In this problem, the person has to figure out which object on the right (A through E) could be a rotation of the object at the left. The answer is B.

SOURCE: Stafford, R. E., & Gullikson, H. (1962). *Identical Blocks,* Form AA.

need more information, good for you, because you are already showing an aptitude for critical thinking. Some additional information about gender differences in cognitive abilities is presented in Chapter 11 of this text. You also need to develop the habit of asking good questions, such as, "Are there alternative explanations for these results? Are there contradictory data?" Let's briefly consider each of these questions.

Are there alternative explanations for gender differences in spatial skills? Well, there certainly are other explanations for males' superiority on most spatial tasks. For example, one could attribute this finding to the gender-typed activities that males are encouraged to engage in more than females, such as playing with building blocks, Lego sets, Lincoln Logs, and various types of construction sets, as well as a variety of spatially oriented video games. These gender-typed activities appear to provide boys with more practice than girls on most types of spatial tasks (Voyer, Nolan, & Voyer, 2000), and experience with spatial activities appears to enhance spatial skills (Lizarraga & Ganuza, 2003). If we can explain gender differences in spatial abilities in terms of disparities

in the everyday activities of contemporary males and females, we may have no need to appeal to natural selection.

Are there data that run counter to the evolutionary explanation for modern gender differences in spatial skills? Again, the answer is yes. Some scholars who have studied hunting-and-gathering societies suggest that women often traveled long distances to gather food and that women were often involved in hunting (Adler, 1993). In addition, women wove baskets and clothing and worked on other tasks that required spatial thinking (Halpern, 1997). Moreover—think about it—men on long hunting trips obviously needed to develop a good memory for locations or they might never have returned home. So, there is room for some argument about exactly what kinds of adaptive pressures males and females faced in ancient hunting-and-gathering societies.

Thus, you can see how considering alternative explanations and contradictory evidence weakens the evolutionary explanation of gender differences in spatial abilities. The questions we raised about alternative explanations and contradictory data are two generic critical thinking questions that can be asked in a wide variety of contexts. The answers to these questions do *not* prove that evolutionary psychologists are wrong in their explanation of gender differences in visual-spatial skills, but they do *weaken* the evolutionary explanation. In thinking critically about psychological issues, you will see that it makes more sense to talk about the *relative strength of an argument* as opposed to whether an argument is right or wrong, because we will be dealing with complex issues that rarely lend themselves to being correct or incorrect.

REVIEW of Key Learning Goals

1.21 Critical thinking is the use of cognitive skills and strategies that increase the probability of a desirable outcome. A critical thinker is flexible, vigilant, able to admit mistakes, and mindful of the thinking process.

1.22 Evolutionary psychologists attribute gender differences in spatial abilities to the sex-based division of labor in hunting-and-gathering societies. However, alternative explanations have been offered for these differences, focusing on the gender-typed activities that modern males and females engage in. There also are contradictory data regarding the adaptive pressures faced by females and males in hunting-and-gathering societies.

Table 1.2 Critical Thinking Skills Discussed in This Application

Skill	Description
Looking for alternative explanations for findings and events	In evaluating explanations, the critical thinker explores whether there are other explanations that could also account for the findings or events under scrutiny.
Looking for contradictory evidence	In evaluating the evidence presented on an issue, the critical thinker attempts to look for contradictory evidence that may have been left out of the debate.

Key Ideas

Psychology's Early History

❚ Psychology's intellectual parents were 19th-century philosophy and physiology, which shared an interest in the mysteries of the mind. Psychology was born as an independent discipline when Wilhelm Wundt established the first psychological research laboratory in 1879 at Leipzig, Germany. He argued that psychology should be the scientific study of consciousness.

❚ The structuralists believed that psychology should use introspection to analyze consciousness into its basic elements. The functionalists, inspired by William James, believed that psychology should focus on the purpose and adaptive functions of consciousness.

❚ Sigmund Freud's psychoanalytic theory emphasized the unconscious determinants of behavior and the importance of sexuality. Freud's ideas were controversial, and they met with resistance in academic psychology.

❚ Behaviorists, led by John B. Watson, argued that psychology should study only observable behavior. Thus, they campaigned to redefine psychology as the science of behavior. Emphasizing the importance of the environment over heredity, they began to explore stimulus-response relationships, often using laboratory animals as subjects.

❚ The influence of behaviorism was boosted greatly by B. F. Skinner's research. Like Watson before him, Skinner asserted that psychology should study only observable behavior, and he generated controversy by arguing that free will is an illusion.

❚ Finding both behaviorism and psychoanalysis unsatisfactory, advocates of a new theoretical orientation called humanism became influential in the 1950s. Humanism, led by Abraham Maslow and Carl Rogers, emphasized humans' freedom and potential for personal growth.

Psychology's Modern History

❚ Stimulated by the demands of World War II, clinical psychology grew rapidly in the 1950s. Thus, psychology became a profession as well as a science. This movement toward professionalization eventually spread to other areas in psychology.

❚ During the 1950s and 1960s advances in the study of mental processes and the biological bases of behavior led to renewed interest in cognition and physiology, as psychology returned to its original roots.

❚ In the 1980s, Western psychologists, who had previously been rather provincial, developed a greater interest in how cultural factors influence thoughts, feelings, and behavior. This trend was sparked in large part by growing global interdependence and by increased cultural diversity in Western societies.

❚ The 1990s witnessed the emergence of a new theoretical perspective called evolutionary psychology. The central premise of this new school of thought is that patterns of behavior are the product of evolutionary forces, just as anatomical characteristics are shaped by natural selection.

❚ The turn of the 21st century saw the emergence of the positive psychology movement, which argues that psychology has historically devoted too much attention to pathology and problems, ignoring the fulfilling aspects of human existence.

Psychology Today: Vigorous and Diversified

❚ Contemporary psychology is a diversified science and profession that has grown rapidly in recent decades. Major areas of research in modern psychology include developmental psychology, social psychology, experimental psychology, physiological psychology, cognitive psychology, personality, psychometrics, educational psychology, and health psychology.

❚ Applied psychology encompasses four established professional specialties: clinical psychology, counseling psychology, school psychology, and industrial/organizational psychology. Two emerging professional specialties are clinical neuropsychology and forensic psychology.

Seven Unifying Themes

❚ As we examine psychology in all its many variations, we will emphasize seven key ideas as unifying themes. Looking at psychology as a field of study, our three key themes are (1) psychology is empirical, (2) psychology is theoretically diverse, and (3) psychology evolves in a sociohistorical context.

❚ Looking at psychology's subject matter, the remaining four themes are (4) behavior is determined by multiple causes, (5) behavior is shaped by cultural heritage, (6) heredity and environment jointly influence behavior, and (7) people's experience of the world is highly subjective.

PERSONAL APPLICATION Improving Academic Performance

❚ To foster sound study habits, you should devise a written study schedule and reward yourself for following it. You should also try to find one or two specific places for studying that are relatively free of distractions.

❚ You should use active reading techniques to select the most important ideas from the material you read. SQ3R, one approach to active reading, breaks a reading assignment into manageable segments and requires that you understand each segment before you move on. Judicious text marking can also facilitate the mastery of reading assignments.

❚ Good note taking can help you get more out of lectures. It's important to use active listening techniques and to record lecturers' ideas in your own words.

❚ Being an effective student also requires sound test-taking skills. In general, it's a good idea to devise a schedule for progressing through an exam, to adopt the appropriate level of sophistication, to avoid wasting time on troublesome questions, and to review your answers whenever time permits.

CRITICAL THINKING APPLICATION Developing Critical Thinking Skills: An Introduction

❚ Critical thinking is the use of cognitive skills and strategies that increase the probability of a desirable outcome. Critical thinking is purposeful, reasoned thinking. A critical thinker is flexible, persistent, able to admit mistakes, and mindful of the thinking process.

❚ Evolutionary psychologists have attributed contemporary gender differences in spatial abilities to the sex-based division of labor in hunting-and-gathering societies. However, alternative explanations have been offered for these differences, focusing on the gender-typed activities that modern males and females engage in. There also are contradictory data regarding the adaptive pressures faced by females and males in hunting-and-gathering societies.

Key Terms

Applied psychology (p. 12)
Behavior (p. 8)
Behaviorism (p. 8)
Clinical psychology (p. 12)
Cognition (p. 13)
Critical thinking (p. 34)
Culture (p. 25)
Empiricism (p. 23)
Ethnocentrism (p. 15)
Evolutionary psychology (p. 15)
Functionalism (p. 5)
Humanism (p. 11)
Introspection (p. 5)
Natural selection (pp. 5–6)
Positive psychology (p. 16)
Psychiatry (p. 22)
Psychoanalytic theory (p. 7)
Psychology (p. 17)
SQ3R (p. 29)
Structuralism (p. 5)
Testwiseness (p. 31)
Theory (p. 23)
Unconscious (p. 7)

Key People

Mary Whiton Calkins (p. 6)
Sigmund Freud (pp. 7–8)
G. Stanley Hall (pp. 4–5)
Leta Stetter Hollingworth (p. 6)
William James (pp. 5–6)
Carl Rogers (pp. 11–12)
Martin Seligman (p. 16)
B. F. Skinner (pp. 9–10)
Margaret Floy Washburn (p. 6)
John B. Watson (pp. 8–9)
Wilhelm Wundt (p. 4)

1. For which of the following is Wilhelm Wundt primarily known?
   A. the establishment of the first formal laboratory for research in psychology
   B. the distinction between mind and body as two separate entities
   C. the discovery of how signals are conducted along nerves in the body
   D. the development of the first formal program for training in psychotherapy

2. G. Stanley Hall is noteworthy in the history of psychology because he:
   A. established the first American research laboratory in psychology.
   B. launched America's first psychological journal.
   C. was the driving force behind the establishment of the American Psychological Association.
   D. did all of the above.

3. Which of the following approaches might William James criticize for examining a movie frame by frame instead of seeing the motion in the motion picture?
   A. structuralism
   B. functionalism
   C. dualism
   D. humanism

4. Which of the following approaches might suggest that forgetting to pick his mother up at the airport was Henry's unconscious way of saying that he did not welcome her visit?
   A. psychoanalytic
   B. behavioral
   C. humanistic
   D. cognitive

5. Fred, a tennis coach, insists that he can make any reasonably healthy individual into an internationally competitive tennis player. Fred is echoing the thoughts of:
   A. Sigmund Freud.
   B. John B. Watson.
   C. Abraham Maslow.
   D. William James.

6. Which of the following is a statement with which Skinner's followers would agree?
   A. Most behavior is controlled by unconscious forces.
   B. The goal of behavior is self-actualization.
   C. Nature is more influential than nurture.
   D. Free will is an illusion.

7. Which of the following approaches has the most optimistic view of human nature?
   A. humanism
   B. behaviorism
   C. psychoanalysis
   D. structuralism

8. Which of the following historical events created a demand for clinicians that was far greater than the supply?
   A. World War I
   B. the Depression
   C. World War II
   D. the Korean War

9. The tendency to view one's own group as superior to others and as the standard for judging the worth of foreign ways is known as:
   A. behaviorism.
   B. ethnocentrism.
   C. humanism.
   D. functionalism.

10. The study of the endocrine system and genetic mechanisms would most likely be undertaken by a:
    A. clinical psychologist.
    B. physiological psychologist.
    C. social psychologist.
    D. educational psychologist.

11. The fact that psychologists do not all agree about the nature and development of personality demonstrates:
    A. that there are many ways of looking at the same phenomenon.
    B. the fundamental inability of psychologists to work together in developing a single theory.
    C. the failure of psychologists to communicate with one another.
    D. the possibility that personality may simply be incomprehensible.

12. A multifactorial causation approach to behavior suggests that:
    A. most behaviors can be explained best by single-cause explanations.
    B. most behavior is governed by a complex network of interrelated factors.
    C. data must be subjected to rigorous statistical analysis in order to make sense.
    D. explanations of behavior tend to build up from the simple to the complex in a hierarchical manner.

13. Psychology's answer to the question of whether we are born or made tends to be:
    A. we are born.
    B. we are made.
    C. we are both born and made.
    D. neither.

14. In regard to changing answers on multiple-choice tests, research indicates that _____ changes tend to be more common than other types of changes.
    A. wrong to right
    B. right to wrong
    C. wrong to wrong

15. Critical thinking skills:
    A. are abstract abilities that cannot be identified.
    B. usually develop spontaneously through normal content instruction.
    C. usually develop spontaneously without any instruction.
    D. need to be deliberately taught, because they often do not develop by themselves with standard content instruction.

Answers

1 A p. 4
2 D pp. 4–5
3 A p. 6
4 A p. 7
5 B pp. 8–9
6 D pp. 9–10
7 A p. 11
8 C pp. 12–13
9 B p. 15
10 B p. 19
11 A pp. 23–24
12 B pp. 24–25
13 C p. 26
14 A pp. 32–33
15 D p. 34

PsykTrek

To view a demo: www.cengage.com/psychology/psyktrek
To order: www.cengage.com/psychology/weiten
Go to the PsykTrek website or CD-ROM for further study of the concepts in this chapter. Both online and on the CD-ROM, PsykTrek includes dozens of learning modules with videos, animations, and quizzes, as well as simulations of psychological phenomena and a multimedia glossary that includes word pronunciations.

CengageNOW
www.cengage.com/tlc

Go to this site for the link to CengageNOW, your one-stop study shop. Take a Pretest for this chapter, and CengageNOW will generate a personalized Study Plan based on your test results. The Study Plan will identify the topics you need to review and direct you to online resources to help you master those topics. You can then take a Posttest to help you determine the concepts you have mastered and what you still need to work on.

Companion Website
www.cengage.com/psychology/weiten

Go to this site to find online resources directly linked to your book, including a glossary, flash cards, drag-and-drop exercises, quizzes, and more!

THE RESEARCH ENTERPRISE IN PSYCHOLOGY

© Fred Derwal/Hemis/Corbis

Looking for Laws: The Scientific Approach to Behavior
Goals of the Scientific Enterprise
Steps in a Scientific Investigation
Advantages of the Scientific Approach

Looking for Causes: Experimental Research
Independent and Dependent Variables
Experimental and Control Groups
Extraneous Variables
Variations in Designing Experiments

FEATURED STUDY ▮ The Emotional Fallout of Expected and Unexpected Outcomes

Advantages and Disadvantages of Experimental Research

Looking for Links: Descriptive/Correlational Research
Naturalistic Observation
Case Studies
Surveys
Advantages and Disadvantages of Descriptive/Correlational Research

Looking for Conclusions: Statistics and Research
Descriptive Statistics
Inferential Statistics

Looking for Flaws: Evaluating Research
Sampling Bias
Placebo Effects
Distortions in Self-Report Data
Experimenter Bias

Illustrated Overview of Key Research Methods in Psychology

Looking into the Future: The Internet and Psychological Research

Looking at Ethics: Do the Ends Justify the Means?
The Question of Deception
The Question of Animal Research
Ethical Principles in Research

Reflecting on the Chapter's Themes

PERSONAL APPLICATION ▮ Finding and Reading Journal Articles

The Nature of Technical Journals
Finding Journal Articles
Reading Journal Articles

CRITICAL THINKING APPLICATION ▮ The Perils of Anecdotal Evidence: "I Have A Friend Who . . ."

Recap

Practice Test

• Does sleeping less than seven hours a day reduce how long you will live?

• Do violent video games make people more aggressive?

• Can you make better decisions by not deliberating about them?

• Can women judge men's testosterone level in just one glance?

• Do IQ scores predict how long people will live?

Questions, questions, questions—everyone has questions about behavior. Investigating these questions is what psychology is all about.

Some of these questions pop up in everyday life. Many a parent, for example, has wondered whether violent video games might be having a harmful effect on their children's behavior. Other questions explored by psychologists might not occur to most people. For example, you may never have wondered about what effects your IQ or sleeping habits could have on your life expectancy, or whether women can judge men's testosterone levels. Of course, now that you've been exposed to these questions, you may be curious about the answers!

In the course of this book, you'll find out what psychologists have learned about the five questions asked above. Right now I want to call your attention to the most basic question of all—namely, how should we go about investigating questions like these? How do we find answers to our questions about behavior that are accurate and trustworthy?

As noted in Chapter 1, *psychology is empirical.* Psychologists are committed to addressing questions about behavior through formal, systematic observation. This commitment to the empirical method is what makes psychology a scientific endeavor. Many people may have beliefs about the effects of playing violent video games based on personal opinion, a feeling of aversion toward violence, a generally permissive attitude toward children's games, anecdotal reports from parents, or other sources. As scientists, however, psychologists withhold judgment on questions like these until they have objective evidence based on valid, reproducible studies. Even then, their judgments are likely to be carefully qualified so that they do not go beyond what the evidence actually shows.

Gathering and evaluating that empirical evidence is an exercise in creative problem solving. As scientists, psychologists have to figure out how to make observations that will shed light on the puzzles they want to solve—and stand up to the critical scrutiny of their peers. In this endeavor psychologists rely on a large toolkit of research methods because different kinds of questions call for different strategies of investigation. In this chapter, you'll learn about some of the principal methods used by psychologists in their research.

Why should you care about psychologists' research methods? There are at least two good reasons. First, having a good grasp of these methods will enhance your ability to understand the information you will be reading in the rest of this book, all of which is based on research. Second, becoming familiar with the logic of the empirical approach will improve your ability to think critically about claims concerning behavior. This ability is important because you are exposed to such claims—in conversa-

tions with friends, in advertising, in the news media—nearly every day. Learning how to evaluate the basis of these claims can make you a more skilled consumer of psychological information.

We'll begin our introduction to the research enterprise in psychology by examining the scientific approach to the study of behavior. From there we'll move to the specific research methods that psychologists use most frequently. We'll also see how and why psychologists use statistics in their research.

Scientific methods have stood the test of time, but individual scientists are human and fallible. For this reason we'll conclude our discussion with a look at some common flaws in research. This section alone can make you a more skilled evaluator of claims that are said to be based on psychological studies. Then, in the Personal Application, you'll learn how to find and read journal articles that report on research. Finally, in the Critical Thinking Application, we'll examine the perils of a type of evidence people are exposed to all the time—anecdotal evidence.

Looking for Laws: The Scientific Approach to Behavior

Key Learning Goals

2.1 Explain science's main assumption, and describe the goals of the scientific enterprise.

2.2 Clarify the relations among theory, hypotheses, and research.

2.3 Outline the steps in a scientific investigation.

2.4 Identify the advantages of the scientific approach.

Whether the object of study is gravitational forces or people's behavior under stress, *the scientific approach assumes that events are governed by some lawful order.* As scientists, psychologists assume that behavior is governed by discernible laws or principles, just as the movement of the earth around the sun is governed by the laws of gravity. The behavior of living creatures may not seem as lawful and predictable as the "behavior" of planets. However, the scientific enterprise is based on the belief that there *are* consistencies or laws that can be uncovered. Fortunately, the plausibility of applying this fundamental assumption to psychology has been supported by the discovery of a great many such consistencies in behavior, some of which provide the subject matter for this text.

Goals of the Scientific Enterprise

Psychologists and other scientists share three sets of interrelated goals: measurement and description, understanding and prediction, and application and control.

1. *Measurement and description.* Science's commitment to observation requires that an investigator figure out a way to measure the phenomenon under study. For example, a psychologist could not investigate whether men are more or less sociable than women without first developing some means of measuring sociability. Thus, the first goal of psychology is to develop measurement techniques that make it possible to describe behavior clearly and precisely.

2. *Understanding and prediction.* A higher-level goal of science is understanding. Scientists believe that they understand events when they can explain the reasons for the occurrence of the events. To evaluate their understanding, scientists make and test predictions called hypotheses. A *hypothesis* is a tentative statement about the relationship between two or more variables. *Variables* are any measurable conditions, events, characteristics, or behaviors that are controlled or observed in a study. If we hypothesized, for example, that putting people under time pressure would lower the accuracy of their time perception, the variables in our study would be time pressure and accuracy of time perception.

3. *Application and control.* Ultimately, many scientists hope that the information they gather will be of some practical value in helping to solve everyday problems. Once people understand a phenomenon, they often can exert more control over it. Today, the profession of psychology attempts to apply research findings to practical problems in schools, busi-

nesses, factories, and mental hospitals. For example, a school psychologist might use findings about the causes of math anxiety to devise a program to help students control their math phobias.

How do theories help scientists achieve their goals? As noted in Chapter 1, psychologists do not set out just to collect isolated facts about relationships between variables. To build toward a better understanding of behavior, they construct theories. A *theory* is a system of interrelated ideas used to explain a set of observations. For example, using a handful of concepts, such as natural selection and reproductive fitness, evolutionary theorists in psychology attempt to explain a diverse array of known facts about mating preferences, jealousy, aggression, sexual behavior, and so forth (see Chapter 1). Thus, by integrating apparently unrelated facts and principles into a coherent whole, theories permit psychologists to make the leap from the *description* of behavior to the *understanding* of behavior. Moreover, the enhanced understanding afforded by theories guides future research by generating new predictions and suggesting new lines of inquiry (Fiske, 2004; Higgins, 2004).

A scientific theory must be testable, as the cornerstone of science is its commitment to putting ideas to an empirical test. Most theories are too complex to be tested all at once. For example, it would be impossible to devise a single study that could test all the many facets of evolutionary theory. Rather, in a typical study, investigators test one or two specific hypotheses derived from a theory. If their findings support the hypotheses, confidence in the theory that the hypotheses were derived from grows. If their findings fail to support the hypotheses, confidence in the theory diminishes, and the theory may be revised or discarded (see **Figure 2.1**). Thus, theory construction is a gradual, iterative process that is always subject to revision.

Steps in a Scientific Investigation

Curiosity about a question provides the point of departure for any kind of investigation, scientific or otherwise. Scientific investigations, however, are *systematic*. They follow an orderly pattern, which is outlined in **Figure 2.2** on the next page. Let's look at how this standard series of steps was followed in a study of *naive realism* conducted by David Sherman, Leif Nelson, and Lee Ross (2003). Sherman and his colleagues wanted to investigate whether adversaries in political debates overestimate the gap between their views.

Step 1: Formulate a Testable Hypothesis
The first step in a scientific investigation is to translate a theory or an intuitive idea into a testable hypothesis. Sherman et al. (2003) noted that in heated disputes people seem to assume that they see matters as they really are—that their perceptions are objective and accurate—whereas their opponents' views must be distorted by self-interest, ideology, or some other source of bias. The researchers call this belief in one's own objectivity and opponents'

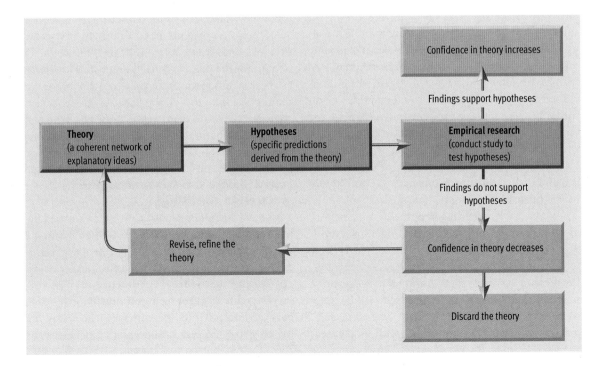

Figure 2.1
Theory construction. A good theory will generate a number of testable hypotheses. In a typical study, only one or a few of these hypotheses can be evaluated. If the evidence supports the hypotheses, confidence in the theory they were derived from generally grows. If the hypotheses are not supported, confidence in the theory decreases, and revisions to the theory may be made to accommodate the new findings. If the hypotheses generated by a theory consistently fail to garner empirical support, the theory may be discarded altogether. Thus, theory construction and testing is a gradual process.

Figure 2.2

Flowchart of steps in a scientific investigation. As illustrated in the study by Sherman, Nelson, and Ross (2003), a scientific investigation consists of a sequence of carefully planned steps, beginning with the formulation of a testable hypothesis and ending with the publication of the study, if its results are worthy of examination by other researchers.

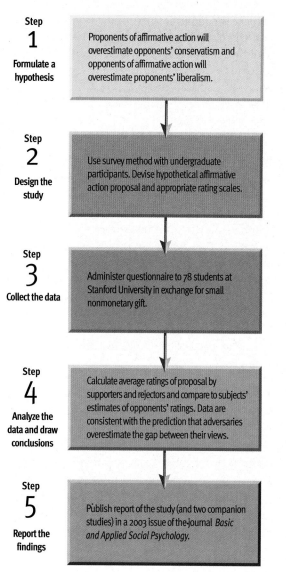

Step 1 — Formulate a hypothesis
> Proponents of affirmative action will overestimate opponents' conservatism and opponents of affirmative action will overestimate proponents' liberalism.

Step 2 — Design the study
> Use survey method with undergraduate participants. Devise hypothetical affirmative action proposal and appropriate rating scales.

Step 3 — Collect the data
> Administer questionnaire to 78 students at Stanford University in exchange for small nonmonetary gift.

Step 4 — Analyze the data and draw conclusions
> Calculate average ratings of proposal by supporters and rejectors and compare to subjects' estimates of opponents' ratings. Data are consistent with the prediction that adversaries overestimate the gap between their views.

Step 5 — Report the findings
> Publish report of the study (and two companion studies) in a 2003 issue of the journal *Basic and Applied Social Psychology*.

"IT MAY VERY WELL BRING ABOUT IMMORTALITY, BUT IT WILL TAKE FOREVER TO TEST IT."

subjectivity "naive realism." Sherman and his colleagues speculated that in political debates people on both sides would tend to characterize their opponents as extremists and to overestimate the extent of their mutual disagreement. To explore this line of thinking, they chose to examine individuals' views on the contentious issue of affirmative action. Thus, they hypothesized that proponents of affirmative action would overestimate opponents' conservativism and that opponents of affirmative action would overestimate proponents' liberalism.

To be testable, scientific hypotheses must be formulated precisely, and the variables under study must be clearly defined. Researchers achieve these clear formulations by providing operational definitions of the relevant variables. An *operational definition* describes the actions or operations that will be used to measure or control a variable. Operational definitions—which may be quite different from dictionary definitions—establish precisely what is meant by each variable in the context of a study.

To illustrate, let's see how Sherman and his colleagues operationalized their variables. They decided that the issue of affirmative action is too complex and multifaceted to ask people about their views of affirmative action *in general*. Each person would be judging something different, based on his or her highly varied exposure to affirmative action initiatives. To circumvent this problem they asked students to respond to a specific affirmative action program that supposedly had been proposed for their university. To get a precise measurement of participants' views, they asked the students to indicate their degree of support for the proposal on a 9-point scale anchored by the descriptions *definitely adopt* and *definitely reject*. Those checking 1 to 4 on the scale were designated as *supporters* of the proposal, while those checking 6 to 9 on the scale were designated as *rejecters* (those who checked the midpoint of 5 were classified as *neutral*).

Step 2: Select the Research Method and Design the Study

The second step in a scientific investigation is to figure out how to put the hypothesis to an empirical test. The research method chosen depends to a large degree on the nature of the question under study. The various methods—experiments, case studies, surveys, naturalistic observation, and so forth—each have advantages and disadvantages. The researcher has to ponder the pros and cons, then select the

Table 2.1 Key Data Collection Techniques in Psychology

Technique	Description
Direct observation	Observers are trained to watch and record behavior as objectively and precisely as possible. They may use some instrumentation, such as a stopwatch or video recorder.
Questionnaire	Subjects are administered a series of written questions designed to obtain information about attitudes, opinions, and specific aspects of their behavior.
Interview	A face-to-face dialogue is conducted to obtain information about specific aspects of a subject's behavior.
Psychological test	Participants are administered a standardized measure to obtain a sample of their behavior. Tests are usually used to assess mental abilities or personality traits.
Physiological recording	An instrument is used to monitor and record a specific physiological process in a subject. Examples include measures of blood pressure, heart rate, muscle tension, and brain activity.
Examination of archival records	The researcher analyzes existing institutional records (the archives), such as census, economic, medical, legal, educational, and business records.

strategy that appears to be the most appropriate and practical. In this case, Sherman and colleagues decided that their question called for *survey* research, which involves administering questionnaires or interviews to people.

Once researchers have chosen a general method, they must make detailed plans for executing their study. Thus, Sherman and associates had to decide how many people they needed to survey and where they would get their participants. *Participants,* or *subjects,* are the persons or animals whose behavior is systematically observed in a study. For their first study, the researchers chose to use 78 undergraduates (45 women and 29 men) at Stanford University. They also had to devise a plausible-sounding affirmative action proposal that students could evaluate, and they had to craft rating scales that would permit the assessment of subjects' political ideology and their perceptions of their opponents' political ideology.

Step 3: Collect the Data

The third step in a research endeavor is to collect the data. Researchers use a variety of *data collection techniques,* which are procedures for making empirical observations and measurements. Commonly used techniques include direct observation, questionnaires, interviews, psychological tests, physiological recordings, and examination of archival records (see Table 2.1). The data collection techniques used in a study depend largely on what is being investigated. For example, questionnaires are well suited for studying attitudes, psychological tests for studying personality, and physiological recordings for studying the biological bases of behavior. Depending on the nature and complexity of the study, data collection can often take months, and it sometimes requires years of work. One advantage of the survey method, however, is that data can often be collected quickly and easily, which was true in this case. Sherman and his colleagues simply had their subjects complete a carefully designed questionnaire in exchange for a small nonmonetary gift.

Step 4: Analyze the Data and Draw Conclusions

The observations made in a study are usually converted into numbers, which constitute the raw data of the study. Researchers use *statistics* to analyze their data and to decide whether their hypotheses have been supported. Thus, statistics play an essential role in the scientific enterprise. Based on their statistical analyses, Sherman et al. (2003) concluded that their data supported their hypothesis. As predicted, they found that supporters of the affirmative action proposal greatly overestimated the conservatism of the rejectors and that the rejectors of the proposal greatly overestimated the liberalism of the supporters (see Figure 2.3). The data indicated that

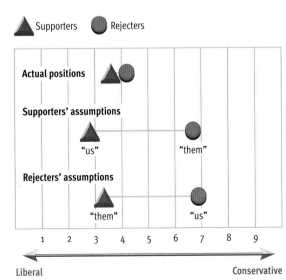

Figure 2.3

Results of the Sherman et al. (2003) study. As you can see, the actual liberal-conservative positions of the supporters and rejectors of the affirmative action proposal were not all that far apart (top row). However, when supporters of the proposal were asked to estimate the average rating given by other supporters as well as those who rejected the proposal, they assumed that there was a huge gap between the two groups (middle row). Similarly, when those who were against the proposal were asked to make the same estimates (bottom row), they also overestimated the disparity between the two groups.

SOURCE: Sherman, D. K., Nelson, L. D., & Ross, L. D. (2003). Naive realism and affirmative action: Adversaries are more similar than they think. *Basic and Applied Social Psychology, 25,* 275–289. Copyright © 2003 Lawrence Erlbaum Associates, Inc. Reprinted by permission.

the actual (average) attitudes of the two groups were not all that far apart, but each group *assumed* that their opponents held very dissimilar views. Obviously, insofar as this may be true of political debates in general, it sheds light on (1) why it is often so difficult for opposing sides to bridge the (perceived) gap between them, and (2) why people often have such pervasively negative views of their adversaries.

Peer Review of Scientific Articles

Researcher or research team authors manuscript that describes the methods, findings, and implications of an empirical study or series of related studies.

Manuscript is submitted to the editor of a professional journal (such as *Journal of Abnormal Psychology* or *Psychological Science*) that seems appropriate given the topic of the research. A manuscript can be submitted to only one journal at a time.

The journal editor sends the manuscript to two to four experts in the relevant area of research who are asked to serve as reviewers. The reviewers provide their input anonymously and are not paid for their work.

The reviewers carefully critique the strengths, weaknesses, and theoretical significance of the research and make a recommendation as to whether it is worthy of publication in that specific journal. If the research has merit, the reviewers usually offer numerous suggestions for improving the clarity of the manuscript.

The editor reads the manuscript and expert reviews and decides whether the submission deserves publication. Most journals reject a substantial majority of submissions. The editorial decision, the reasoning behind it, and the expert reviews are sent to the author.

If the manuscript is accepted, the author may incorporate suggestions for improvement from the reviews, make final revisions, and resubmit the article to the journal editor.

If the manuscript is rejected, the author may (a) abandon the publication effort, or (b) use reviewers' suggestions to make revisions and then submit the article to another journal.

The article is published in a professional journal usually three to six months after final acceptance.

Following rejection, researchers sometimes give up on a line of research, but often they go back to the drawing board and attempt to design a better study.

Figure 2.4

The peer review process for journal submissions. Scientists use an elaborate peer review process to determine whether studies merit publication in a technical journal. The goal of this process is to maximize the quality and reliability of published scientific findings.

Step 5: Report the Findings

Scientific progress can be achieved only if researchers share their findings with one another and with the general public. Therefore, the final step in a scientific investigation is to write up a concise summary of the study and its findings. Typically, researchers prepare a report that is delivered at a scientific meeting and submitted to a journal for publication. **A *journal* is a periodical that publishes technical and scholarly material, usually in a narrowly defined area of inquiry.** The study by Sherman and his colleagues was published, along with two companion studies, in a journal called *Basic and Applied Social Psychology*.

The process of publishing scientific studies allows other experts to evaluate and critique new research findings. When articles are submitted to scientific journals they go through a demanding *peer review process* that is summarized in Figure 2.4. Experts thoroughly scrutinize each submission. They carefully evaluate each study's methods, statistical analyses, and conclusions, as well as its contribution to knowledge and theory. The peer review process is so demanding, many top journals reject over 90% of submitted articles! The purpose of the peer review process is to ensure that journals publish reliable findings based on high-quality research. The peer review process is a major strength of the scientific approach because it greatly reduces the likelihood of publishing erroneous findings.

Advantages of the Scientific Approach

Science is certainly not the only method that can be used to draw conclusions about behavior. Everyone uses logic, casual observation, and good old-fashioned common sense. Because the scientific method often requires painstaking effort, it seems reasonable to ask what advantages make it worth the trouble.

Basically, the scientific approach offers two major advantages. The first is its clarity and precision. Commonsense notions about behavior tend to be vague and ambiguous. Consider the old adage "Spare the rod and spoil the child." What exactly does this generalization about childrearing amount to? How severely should children be punished if parents are not to "spare the rod"? How do we assess whether a child qualifies as "spoiled"? A fundamental problem is that such statements have different meanings, depending on the person. When people disagree about this assertion, it may be because they are talking about entirely different things. In contrast, the scientific approach requires that people specify *exactly* what they are talking about when they formulate hypotheses. This clarity and precision enhance communication about important ideas.

The second and perhaps greatest advantage offered by the scientific approach is its relative intolerance of error. Scientists are trained to be skeptical. They subject their ideas to empirical tests. They also scrutinize one another's findings with a critical eye. They demand objective data and thorough documentation before they accept ideas. When the findings of two studies conflict, the scientist tries to figure out why, usually by conducting additional research. In contrast, common sense and casual observation often tolerate contradictory generalizations, such as "Opposites attract" and "Birds of a feather flock together." Furthermore, commonsense analyses involve little effort to verify ideas or detect errors. Thus, many "truisms" about behavior that come to be widely believed are simply myths.

All this is not to say that science has an exclusive copyright on truth. However, the scientific approach does tend to yield more accurate and dependable information than casual analyses and armchair speculation do. Knowledge of scientific data can thus provide a useful benchmark against which to judge claims and information from other kinds of sources.

Now that we have had an overview of how the scientific enterprise works, we can focus on how specific research methods are used. *Research methods* consist of various approaches to the observation, measurement, manipulation, and control of variables in empirical studies. In other words, they are general strategies for conducting studies. No single research method is ideal for all purposes and situations. Much of the ingenuity in research involves selecting and tailoring the method to the question at hand. The next two sections of this chapter discuss the two basic types of methods used in psychology: *experimental research methods* and *descriptive/correlational research methods*.

web link 2.1

PubMed

Few commercial databases of journal articles or abstracts in the health sciences are available online for no charge. However, the National Library of Medicine has opened the millions of items in MEDLINE's database to anyone wanting to search within the scientific literature of medical journals, including some important psychology publications.

REVIEW of Key Learning Goals

2.1 The scientific approach assumes that there are laws of behavior that can be discovered through empirical research. The goals of the science of psychology include (1) the measurement and description of behavior, (2) the understanding and prediction of behavior, and (3) the application of this knowledge to the task of controlling behavior.

2.2 By integrating apparently unrelated facts into a coherent whole, theories permit psychologists to make the leap from the description of behavior to the understanding of behavior. Confidence in a theory increases when hypotheses derived from it are supported by research.

2.3 A scientific investigation follows a systematic pattern that includes five steps: (1) formulate a testable hypothesis, (2) select the research method and design the study, (3) collect the data, (4) analyze the data and draw conclusions, and (5) report the findings.

2.4 One major advantage of the scientific approach is its clarity in communication, which is promoted by its use of operational definitions. Another key advantage is its relative intolerance of error, which is promoted by scientists' constant testing of hypotheses and skeptical scrutiny of research findings.

Looking for Causes: Experimental Research

Does misery love company? This question intrigued social psychologist Stanley Schachter. When people feel anxious, he wondered, do they want to be left alone, or do they prefer to have others around? Schachter's review of relevant theories suggested that in times of anxiety people would want others around to help them sort out their feelings. Thus, his hypothesis was that increases in anxiety would cause increases in the desire to be with others, which psychologists call the *need for affiliation*. To test this hypothesis, Schachter (1959) designed a clever experiment.

The *experiment* is a research method in which the investigator manipulates a variable under carefully controlled conditions and observes whether any changes occur in a second variable as a result. The experiment is a relatively powerful procedure that allows researchers to detect cause-and-effect relationships. Psychologists depend on this method more than any other.

Although its basic strategy is straightforward, in practice the experiment is a fairly complicated technique. A well-designed experiment must take into account a number of factors that could affect the clarity of the results. To see how an experiment is designed, let's use Schachter's study as an example.

Independent and Dependent Variables
SIM1,1b

The purpose of an experiment is to find out whether changes in one variable (let's call it X) cause changes in another variable (let's call it Y). To put it more

Key Learning Goals

2.5 Describe the experimental method, independent and dependent variables, and experimental and control groups.

2.6 Explain how experiments can vary in format and design.

2.7 Describe the Featured Study on how expectations influence reactions to positive and negative outcomes.

2.8 Evaluate the major advantages and disadvantages of the experimental method.

concisely, we want to find out *how X affects Y.* In this formulation, we refer to *X* as the *independent variable* and to *Y* as the *dependent variable.*

An *independent variable* **is a condition or event that an experimenter varies in order to see its impact on another variable.** The independent variable is the variable that the experimenter controls or manipulates. It is hypothesized to have some effect on the dependent variable, and the experiment is conducted to verify this effect. **The *dependent variable* is the variable that is thought to be affected by manipulation of the independent variable.** In psychology studies, the dependent variable is usually a measurement of some aspect of the participants' behavior. The independent variable is called *independent* because it is *free* to be varied by the experimenter. The dependent variable is called *dependent* because it is thought to *depend* (at least in part) on manipulations of the independent variable.

In Schachter's experiment, *the independent variable was the subjects' anxiety level.* He manipulated anxiety level in a clever way. Participants assembled in his laboratory were told by a "Dr. Zilstein" that they would be participating in a study on the physiological effects of electric shock. They were further informed that during the experiment they would receive a series of electric shocks while their pulse and blood pressure were being monitored. Half of the subjects were warned that the shocks would be very painful. They made up the *high-anxiety* group. The other half of the participants (the *low-anxiety* group) were told that the shocks would be mild and painless. In reality, there was no plan to shock anyone at any time. These orientation procedures were simply intended to evoke different levels of anxiety. After the orientation, the experimenter indicated that there would be a delay while he prepared the shock apparatus for use. The participants were asked whether they would prefer to wait alone or in the company of others. *The participants' desire to affiliate with others was the dependent variable.*

Experimental and Control Groups

SIM1, 1b

In an experiment the investigator typically assembles two groups of subjects who are treated differently with regard to the independent variable. These two groups are referred to as the experimental group and the control group. **The *experimental group* consists of the subjects who receive some special treatment in regard to the independent variable. The *control group* consists of similar subjects who do *not* receive the special treatment given to the experimental group.**

In the Schachter study, the participants in the high-anxiety condition constituted the experimental group. They received a special treatment designed to create an unusually high level of anxiety. The participants in the low-anxiety condition served as the control group. They were not exposed to the special anxiety-arousing procedure.

It is crucial that the experimental and control groups in a study be alike, except for the different treatment that they receive in regard to the independent variable. This stipulation brings us to the logic that underlies the experimental method. If the two groups are alike in all respects *except for the variation created by the manipulation of the independent variable,* any differences between the two groups on the dependent variable *must be due to the manipulation of the independent variable.* In this way researchers isolate the effect of the independent variable on the dependent variable. Schachter, for example, isolated the impact of anxiety on the need for affiliation. As predicted, he found that increased anxiety led to increased affiliation. As **Figure 2.5** indicates, the percentage of participants in the high-anxiety group who wanted to wait with others was nearly twice that of the low-anxiety group.

---

concept check 2.1

Recognizing Independent and Dependent Variables

Check your understanding of the experimental method by identifying the independent variable (IV) and dependent variable (DV) in the following investigations. Note that one study has two IVs and another has two DVs. You'll find the answers in Appendix A in the back of the book.

1. A researcher is interested in how heart rate and blood pressure are affected by viewing a violent film sequence as opposed to a nonviolent film sequence.
   IV _____
   DV _____

2. An organizational psychologist develops a new training program to improve clerks' courtesy to customers in a large chain of retail stores. She conducts an experiment to see whether the training program leads to a reduction in the number of customer complaints.
   IV _____
   DV _____

3. A researcher wants to find out how stimulus complexity and stimulus contrast (light/dark variation) affect infants' attention to stimuli. He manipulates stimulus complexity and stimulus contrast and measures how long infants stare at various stimuli.
   IV _____
   DV _____

4. A social psychologist investigates the impact of group size on subjects' conformity in response to group pressure.
   IV _____
   DV _____

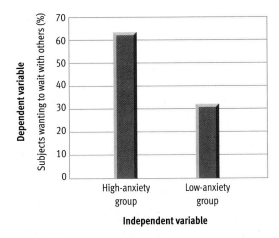

Figure 2.5

Results of Schachter's study of affiliation. The percentage of people wanting to wait with others was higher in the high-anxiety (experimental) group than in the low-anxiety (control) group, consistent with Schachter's (1959) hypothesis that anxiety would increase the desire for affiliation. The graphic portrayal of these results allows us to see at a glance the effects of the experimental manipulation on the dependent variable.

Extraneous Variables   SIM1,1b

As we have seen, the logic of the experimental method rests on the assumption that the experimental and control groups are alike except for their treatment in regard to the independent variable. Any other differences between the two groups can cloud the situation and make it impossible to draw conclusions about how the independent variable affects the dependent variable.

In practical terms, of course, it is impossible to ensure that two groups of participants are exactly alike in *every* respect. In reality, the experimental and control groups have to be alike only on dimensions relevant to the dependent variable. Thus, Schachter did not need to worry about whether his two groups were similar in hair color, height, or interest in ballet, as these variables were unlikely to influence the dependent variable of affiliation behavior.

Instead, experimenters concentrate on ensuring that the experimental and control groups are alike on a limited number of variables that could have a bearing on the results of the study. These variables are called extraneous, secondary, or nuisance variables. *Extraneous variables* are any variables other than the independent variable that seem likely to influence the dependent variable in a specific study.

In Schachter's study, one extraneous variable would have been the subjects' tendency to be sociable. Why? Because participants' sociability could affect their desire to be with others (the dependent

variable). If the participants in one group had happened to be more sociable (on the average) than those in the other group, the variables of anxiety and sociability would have been confounded. A *confounding of variables* occurs when two variables are linked together in a way that makes it difficult to sort out their specific effects. When an extraneous variable is confounded with an independent variable, a researcher cannot tell which is having what effect on the dependent variable.

Unanticipated confoundings of variables have wrecked innumerable experiments. That is why so much care, planning, and forethought must go into designing an experiment. One of the key qualities that separates a talented experimenter from a mediocre one is the ability to foresee troublesome extraneous variables and control them to avoid confoundings.

Experimenters use a variety of safeguards to control for extraneous variables. For instance, subjects are usually assigned to the experimental and control groups randomly. *Random assignment* of subjects occurs when all subjects have an equal chance of being assigned to any group or condition in the study. When experimenters distribute subjects into groups through some random procedure, they can be reasonably confident that the groups will be similar in most ways. Figure 2.6 on the next page provides an overview of the elements in an experiment, using Schachter's study as an example.

Variations in Designing Experiments   SIM1,1b

We have discussed the experiment in only its simplest format, with just one independent variable and one dependent variable. Actually, many variations are possible in conducting experiments. Because you'll be learning about experiments with more complicated designs, these variations merit a brief mention.

First, it is sometimes advantageous to use only one group of subjects who serve as their own control group. The effects of the independent variable are evaluated by exposing this single group to two different conditions—an *experimental condition* and a *control condition*. For example, imagine that you wanted to study the effects of loud music on typing performance. You could have a group of participants work on a typing task while loud music was played (experimental condition) and in the absence of music (control condition). This approach would ensure that the participants in the experimental and control conditions would be alike on any extraneous variables involving their personal characteristics, such as motivation or typing skill. After all, the same people would be studied in both conditions.

web link 2.3

Psychological Research on the Net

This site, sponsored by the American Psychological Society, is a jumping-off point for people interested in participating in ongoing research projects that are collecting data over the Internet. Visitors will find a variety of opportunities for taking part in genuine research.

Figure 2.6
Figure 2.6
The basic elements of an experiment. As illustrated by the Schachter (1959) study, the logic of experimental design rests on treating the experimental and control groups exactly alike (to control for extraneous variables) except for the manipulation of the independent variable. In this way, the experimenter attempts to isolate the effects of the independent variable on the dependent variable.

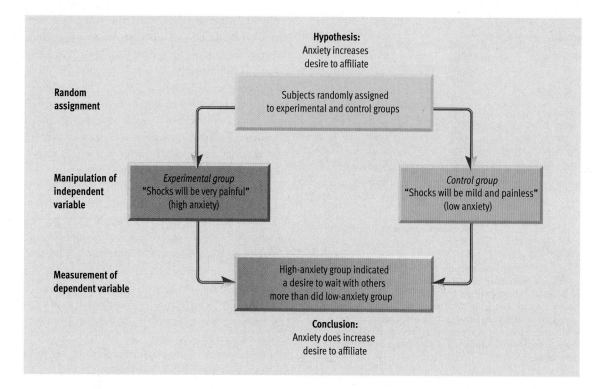

Hypothesis:
Anxiety increases
desire to affiliate

Random assignment
Subjects randomly assigned
to experimental and control groups

Manipulation of independent variable
Experimental group
"Shocks will be very painful"
(high anxiety)

Control group
"Shocks will be mild and painless"
(low anxiety)

Measurement of dependent variable
High-anxiety group indicated
a desire to wait with others
more than did low-anxiety group

Conclusion:
Anxiety does increase
desire to affiliate

When subjects serve as their own control group, the experiment is said to use a *within-subjects design* because comparisons are made within the same group of participants. In contrast, when two or more independent groups of subjects are exposed to a manipulation of an independent variable, the experiment is said to use a *between-subjects design* because comparisons are made between two different groups of participants. Although within-subjects designs are not used as frequently as between-subjects designs, they are advantageous for certain types of investigations and they play a major role in experimental research.

Second, it is possible to manipulate more than one independent variable in a single experiment. Researchers often manipulate two or three independent variables to examine their joint effects on the dependent variable. For example, in another study of typing performance, you could vary both room temperature and the presence of distracting music (see **Figure 2.7**). The main advantage of this approach is that it permits the experimenter to see whether two variables interact. An *interaction* means that the effect of one variable depends on the effect of another. For instance, if we found that distracting music impaired typing performance only when room temperature was high, we would be detecting an interaction.

Third, it is also possible to use more than one dependent variable in a single study. Researchers frequently use a number of dependent variables to get a more complete picture of how experimental manipulations affect subjects' behavior. For example, in your studies of typing performance, you would probably measure two dependent variables: speed (words per minute) and accuracy (number of errors).

Now that you're familiar with the logic of the experiment, let's turn to our Featured Study for Chapter 2. You will find a Featured Study in each chapter from this point onward. These studies are provided to give you in-depth examples of how psychologists conduct empirical research. Each is described in

Figure 2.7
Manipulation of two independent variables in an experiment. As this example shows, when two independent variables are manipulated in a single experiment, the researcher has to compare four groups of subjects (or conditions) instead of the usual two. The main advantage of this procedure is that it allows an experimenter to see whether two variables interact.

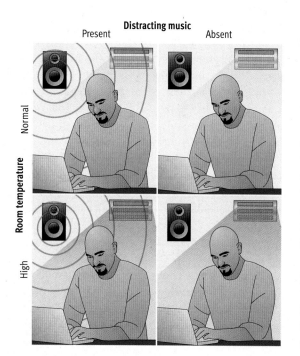

Distracting music
Present   Absent

Normal

Room temperature

High

a way that resembles a journal article, thereby acquainting you with the format of scientific reports (see the Personal Application at the end of the chapter for more information on this format). The Featured Study for this chapter gives you another example of an experiment in action.

The Emotional Fallout of Expected and Unexpected Outcomes

SOURCE: Shepperd, J. A., & McNulty, J. K. (2002). The affective consequences of expected and unexpected outcomes. *Psychological Science, 13*, 85–88.

Common sense suggests that people feel good when they experience positive outcomes and that they are disappointed when they experience setbacks, but Shepperd and McNulty theorize that people's reactions to events aren't that simple—that outcomes are judged relative to expectations. According to decision affect theory (Mellers et al., 1997), people's feelings about events are determined in part by comparing what actually happened with what might have been. Thus, two outcomes that are objectively the same can produce very different emotional reactions depending on the participant's expectations. Specifically, they hypothesized that bad outcomes feel worse when unexpected than when expected and that positive outcomes feel better when unexpected than when expected.

Their first test of this hypothesis consisted of a small survey in which students rated how happy they would feel in response to four scenarios: (1) they expected to earn an A in a course and they received an A, (2) they expected an A and got a C, (3) they expected a C and got an A, and (4) they expected a C and got a C. Subjects' ratings of how they would feel about each of these scenarios, which can be seen in **Figure 2.8**, supported the hypothesis that events are judged relative to expectations. After obtaining these encouraging findings, Shepperd and McNulty then put their hypothesis to an experimental test.

Method

Participants. Ninety introductory psychology students (25 males, 65 females) served as subjects. They earned credit toward a course requirement mandating participation in research. They participated in groups of 1 to 3 people.

Procedure. Subjects met an experimenter wearing a lab coat who appeared to be affiliated with the university hospital. They were told that the study was concerned with their attitudes about a new home medical test that was designed to detect a plausible-sounding but fictitious medical condition (an enzyme deficiency). They were given the (bogus) medical test, which required them to hold a strip under their tongue for 30 seconds. The strips were collected and taken away for analysis. In a few minutes the experimenter returned and gave each participant a sealed envelope containing his or her test results. Using a between-subjects design, participants' expectations were manipulated as follows. Half the subjects were told that the enzyme deficiency was uncommon among college students, so they expected good news, whereas the other half were told that the enzyme deficiency was quite prevalent among college students, so they expected bad news. After getting their test results, participants were asked to rate their emotions. After their ratings were turned in, they were thoroughly debriefed about the true nature of the study.

Results

The data are summarized in **Figure 2.9**, which shows the mean emotion ratings for each condition. As predicted, subjects who were informed that they tested positive for the enzyme deficiency felt worse when this news was unexpected than when it was expected. And those who were told that they did not have the enzyme deficiency felt better when this result was unexpected than when it was expected.

Discussion

The authors conclude that their results provide strong support for their hypothesis that people's expectations color their evaluation of events. As they put it, "People feel bad

Figure 2.8

Effects of expectations on reactions to grades. Shepperd and McNulty (2002) asked subjects to rate how happy they would feel if they experienced each of the grading scenarios described on the left. As predicted, a positive outcome (receiving an A) resulted in greater happiness when it was unexpected, and a negative outcome (receiving a C) generated more disappointment when it was unexpected.

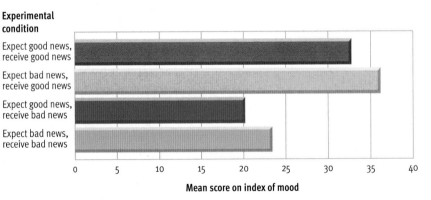

Figure 2.9

Effects of expectations on reactions to positive and negative outcomes. In their experiment, Shepperd and McNulty (2002) manipulated subjects' expectations about the likely result of an apparent medical test. After receiving either good or bad test results, participants filled out ratings of their emotions that were summed into the mood scores graphed here. As you can see, people felt better about good news when it was unexpected, and they felt better about bad news when it was expected.

when their outcomes fall short of their expectations and feel elated when their outcomes exceed their expectations" (p. 87). They note that their findings are consistent with the folk wisdom contained in the advice "Expect the worst and you will never be disappointed."

Comment
This study was featured because it addresses an interesting question using a reasonably straightforward experimental design. It also provides a nice demonstration of one of this text's unifying themes—that people's experience of the world is highly subjective. It shows how two individuals can experience the same event—for example, getting a grade of C in a course—but react to it very differently. The study also highlights the enormous power of expectations, which is a phenomenon that we will see repeatedly as we proceed through this book.

Advantages and Disadvantages of Experimental Research

The experiment is a powerful research method. Its principal advantage is that it permits conclusions about cause-and-effect relationships between variables. Researchers are able to draw these conclusions about causation because the precise control available in the experiment allows them to isolate the relationship between the independent variable and the dependent variable while neutralizing the effects of extraneous variables. No other research method can duplicate this strength of the experiment. This advantage is why psychologists usually prefer to use the experimental method whenever possible.

For all its power, however, the experiment has limitations. One problem is that experiments are often artificial. Because experiments require great control over proceedings, researchers must often construct simple, contrived situations to test their hypotheses experimentally. For example, to investigate decision making in juries, psychologists have conducted many experiments in which subjects read a brief summary of a trial and then record their individual "verdicts" of innocence or guilt. This approach allows the experimenter to manipulate a variable, such as the race of the defendant, to see whether it affects the participants' verdicts. However, critics have pointed out that having a participant read a short case summary and make an individual decision cannot really compare to the complexities of real trials (Weiten & Diamond, 1979). In actual court cases, jurors may spend weeks listening to confusing testimony while making subtle judgments about the credibility of witnesses. They then retire for hours of debate to arrive at a group verdict, which is quite different from rendering an individual decision. Many researchers have failed to do justice to this complex process in their laboratory experiments. When experiments are highly artificial, doubts arise about the applicability of findings to everyday behavior outside the experimental laboratory.

Another disadvantage is that the experimental method can't be used to explore some research questions. Psychologists are frequently interested in the effects of factors that cannot be manipulated as independent variables because of ethical concerns or practical realities. For instance, you might be interested in whether a nutritionally poor diet during pregnancy increases the likelihood of birth defects. This clearly is a significant issue. However, you obviously cannot select 100 pregnant women and assign 50 of them to a condition in which they consume an inadequate diet. The potential risk to the health of the women and their unborn children would make this research strategy unethical.

In other cases, manipulations of variables are difficult or impossible. For example, you might want to know whether being brought up in an urban as opposed to a rural area affects people's values. An experiment would require you to randomly assign similar families to live in urban and rural areas, which obviously is impossible to do. To explore this question, you would have to use descriptive/correlational research methods, which we turn to next.

Looking for Links: Descriptive/Correlational Research

Key Learning Goals

2.9 Explain the role of naturalistic observation, case studies, and surveys in psychological research.

2.10 Evaluate the major advantages and disadvantages of descriptive/correlational research.

As we just noted, in some situations psychologists cannot exert experimental control over the variables they want to study. In such situations, investigators must rely on *descriptive/correlational research methods.* These methods include naturalistic observation, case studies, and surveys. What distinguishes these methods is that the researcher cannot manipulate the variables under study. This lack of control means that these methods cannot be used to demonstrate cause-and-effect relationships between variables. *Descriptive/correlational methods permit investigators to only describe patterns of behavior and discover links or associations between variables.* That is not to suggest that associations are unimportant. You'll see in this section that information on associations between variables can be extremely valuable in our efforts to understand behavior.

Naturalistic Observation

Does the pace of everyday life vary substantially from one culture to the next? Do people operate at a different speed in say, Germany, as opposed to Canada or Brazil? Are factors such as economic vitality and climate related to differences in the pace of life? These are the kinds of questions that intrigued Robert V. Levine and Ara Norenzayan (1999), who compared the pace of life in more than two dozen countries around the world. Perhaps they could have devised an experiment to examine this question, but they wanted to focus on the pace of life in the real world rather than in the laboratory.

To study the pace of life, Levine and Norenzayan (1999) had to come up with concrete ways to measure it—their operational definition of the concept. The measures they chose depended on *naturalistic observation.* In **naturalistic observation** a researcher engages in careful observation of behavior without intervening directly with the subjects. In this instance, the researchers observed (1) the average walking speed in downtown locations, (2) the accuracy of public clocks, and (3) the speed with which postal clerks completed a simple request. Their collection of data on walking speed illustrates the careful planning required to execute naturalistic observation effectively. In the main downtown area of each city, they had to find two flat, unobstructed, uncrowded 60-foot walkways where they could unobtrusively time pedestrians during normal business hours. Only adult pedestrians walking alone and not window shopping were timed. In most cities, the observations continued until 35 men and 35 women had been timed.

Levine and Norenzayan conducted their naturalistic observations in 31 countries, typically using the largest city in each country as the locale for their research. Their findings, based on all three measures, are summarized in Table 2.2, which ranks the pace of life in the countries studied. Their data suggest that the pace of life is fastest in the countries of Western Europe and in Japan. Using archival data, they also conducted correlational analyses to see whether variations in the pace of life were associated with factors such as climate, economic

Table 2.2 Levine and Norenzayan's (1999) Ranking of the Pace of Life in 31 Cultures

Rank	Country	Rank	Country	Rank	Country
1	Switzerland	11	France	21	Greece
2	Ireland	12	Poland	22	Kenya
3	Germany	13	Costa Rica	23	China
4	Japan	14	Taiwan	24	Bulgaria
5	Italy	15	Singapore	25	Romania
6	England	16	United States	26	Jordan
7	Sweden	17	Canada	27	Syria
8	Austria	18	S. Korea	28	El Salvador
9	Netherlands	19	Hungary	29	Brazil
10	Hong Kong	20	Czech Republic	30	Indonesia
				31	Mexico

Source: Adapted from Levine, R. V., & Norenzayan, A. (1999). The pace of life in 31 countries. *Journal of Cross-Cultural Psychology, 30* (2), 178–205. Copyright © 1999 by Sage Publications. Reprinted by permission.

The method of naturalistic observation can be particularly useful in studying animals in their natural habitats. For example, Jane Goodall conducted ground-breaking research on the social lives of chimpanzees through years of painstaking naturalistic observation.

vitality, or population size. Among other things, they found that the pace of life was faster in colder climates and in countries that were more economically productive.

This type of research is called *naturalistic* because behavior is allowed to unfold naturally (without interference) in its natural environment—that is, the setting in which it would normally occur. The major strength of naturalistic observation is that it allows researchers to study behavior under conditions that are less artificial than in experiments. Another plus is that engaging in naturalistic observation can represent a good starting point when little is known about the behavior under study. And, unlike case studies and surveys, naturalistic observation can be used to study animal behavior. Many landmark studies of animal behavior, such as Jane Goodall's (1986, 1990) work on the social and family life of chimpanzees, have depended on naturalistic observation. A major problem with this method is that researchers often have trouble making their observations unobtrusively so they don't affect their participants' behavior. *Reactivity* occurs when a subject's behavior is altered by the presence of an observer. Both animals and humans may exhibit reactivity if observational efforts are too obvious. Another disadvantage is that it often is difficult to translate naturalistic observations into numerical data that permit precise statistical analyses.

Case Studies

What portion of people who commit suicide suffer from psychological disorders? Which disorders are most common among victims of suicide? In health care visits during the final month of their lives, do people who commit suicide communicate their intent to do so? A research team in Finland wanted to investigate the psychological characteristics of people who take their own lives (Henriksson et al., 1993; Isometsa et al., 1995). Other researchers had explored these questions, but the Finnish team planned a comprehensive, national study of unprecedented scope. Their initial sample consisted of all the known suicides in Finland for an entire year.

The research team decided that their question called for a case study approach. A *case study* is an in-depth investigation of an individual subject. When this method is applied to victims of suicide the case studies are called *psychological autopsies*. A variety of data collection techniques can be used in case studies. In normal circumstances, when the participants are not deceased, typical techniques include interviewing the subjects, interviewing people who are close to the subjects, direct observation of the participants, examination of records, and psychological testing. In this study, the investigators conducted thorough interviews with the families of the suicide victims and with the health care professionals who had treated them. The researchers also examined the suicide victims' medical, psychiatric, and social agency records, as well as relevant police investigations and forensic reports. Comprehensive case reports were then assembled for each person who committed suicide.

These case studies revealed that in 93% of the suicides the victim suffered from a significant psychological disorder (Henriksson et al., 1993). The most common diagnoses, by a large margin, were depression and alcohol dependence. In 571 cases, victims had a health care appointment during the last four weeks of their lives, but only 22% of these people discussed the possibility of suicide during their final visit (Isometsa et al., 1995). Even more surprising, the sample included 100 people who saw a health professional on the same day they killed themselves, yet only 21% of these individuals raised the issue of suicide. The investigators concluded that mental illness is a contributing factor in virtually all completed suicides and that the vast majority of suicidal people do not spontaneously reveal their intentions to health care professionals.

Clinical psychologists, who diagnose and treat psychological problems, routinely do case studies of their clients (see Figure 2.10). When clinicians assemble a case study for diagnostic purposes, they generally are *not* conducting empirical research. Case study *research* typically involves investigators analyzing a collection or consecutive series of case studies to look for patterns that permit general conclusions. That said, clinicians sometimes publish individual case studies that seem to yield useful insights about a particular disorder or approach to treatment (Edwards, 2007).

Case studies are particularly well suited for investigating certain phenomena, especially the roots of psychological disorders and the efficacy of selected therapeutic practices (Fishman, 2007). They can also provide compelling, real-life illustrations that bolster a hypothesis or theory. However, the main problem with case studies is that they are highly subjective. Information from several sources must be knit together to capture one's impressions of the subject. In this process, clinicians and researchers often focus selectively on information that fits with their expectations, which usually reflect their theoretical slant. Thus, it is relatively easy for investigators to see what they expect to see in case study research. Another worrisome issue is that the clinical samples typically used in case study research are often unrepresentative of the general population.

Surveys

Are taller people more successful in life? That would hardly seem fair, but folk wisdom suggests that height is associated with success. Some empirical studies of this issue have been conducted over the years, but many of them are extremely old and hobbled by a variety of methodological weaknesses. Hence, Timothy Judge and Daniel Cable (2004) set out to conduct a thorough investigation of the relationship between height and income. Their study depended on survey data. **In a** *survey* **researchers use questionnaires or interviews to gather information about specific aspects of participants' background, attitudes, beliefs, or behavior.** In this case, Judge and Cable examined already-existing data that had been collected in four large-scale surveys that were concerned with other issues. Information on height and income was available for over 8000 participants from these studies.

What did the survey data reveal? In all four studies a modest association was found between height and income, with taller people earning more money. The association was not particularly strong, but it was not negligible. For example, based on their data, Judge and Cable estimated that someone 6 feet tall would earn $166,000 more during a 30-year career than someone 5 feet 5 inches tall. The relationship between greater height and greater income held for

Case Study   Page 2

    Jennie is a 21-year-old single college student with no prior psychiatric history. She was admitted to a short-term psychiatric ward from a hospital emergency room with a chief complaint of "I think I was psychotic." For several months prior to her admission she reported a series of "strange experiences." These included religious experiences, increased anxiety, a conviction that other students were conspiring against her, visual distortions, auditory hallucinations, and grandiose delusions. During the week prior to admission, the symptoms gradually worsened, and eventually she became agitated and disorganized.
    A number of stressful events preceded this decompensation. A maternal aunt, a strong and central figure in her family, had died four months previously. As a college senior, she was struggling with decisions about her career choices following graduation. She was considering applying to graduate programs but was unable to decide which course of study she preferred. She was very much involved with her boyfriend, also a college senior. He, too, was struggling with anxiety about graduation, and it was not clear that their relationship would continue. The patient also reported feeling pressured and overextended.
    The patient's older sister had suffered two psychotic episodes. This sister had slowly deteriorated, particularly after

Figure 2.10
An example of a case study report. As this example illustrates, case studies are particularly appropriate for clinical situations in which efforts are made to diagnose and treat psychological problems. Usually, one case study does not provide much basis for deriving general laws of behavior. However, if you examine a series of case studies involving similar problems, you can look for threads of consistency that may yield general conclusions.

SOURCE: Greenfield, D. (1985). *The psychotic patient: Medication and psychotherapy.* New York: The Free Press. Copyright © 1985 by David Greenfield. Reprinted by permission of the author.

both men and women. The strength of the association varied somewhat across occupational areas. The height-income link was strongest for people in sales or management. The authors conclude that "our analyses revealed that height clearly matters in the context of workplace success" (p. 437). They discuss a variety of possible explanations for the association between height and earnings. Among other things, they note that taller people may develop higher self-esteem, which could foster better performance. Another possibility is that people just assume that taller individuals are more capable and competent and hence are more likely to buy products from them, hire them for good jobs, and promote them into even better positions. The exact mechanisms underlying the correlation between height and income are yet to be determined.

Surveys are often used to obtain information on aspects of behavior that are difficult to observe directly. Surveys also make it relatively easy to collect data on attitudes and opinions from large samples of participants. However, potential participants' tendency to cooperate with surveys appears to have declined noticeably in recent decades (Tourangeau,

"CONTRARY TO THE POPULAR VIEW, OUR STUDIES SHOW THAT IT IS REAL LIFE THAT CONTRIBUTES TO VIOLENCE ON TELEVISION."

© 2004 by Sidney Harris/Science Cartoons Plus.com

2004). The growing resentment of intrusive telemarketing and heightened concerns about privacy and identity theft seem to be the culprits underlying the reduced response rates for research surveys. This problem may be partially offset by new technology, as survey studies are increasingly being conducted over the Internet (Skitka & Sargis, 2006). The major weakness of surveys is that they depend on *self-report data*. As we'll discuss later, intentional deception, wishful thinking, memory lapses, and poorly worded questions can distort participants' verbal reports about their behavior (Krosnick, 1999).

Advantages and Disadvantages of Descriptive/Correlational Research

Descriptive/correlational research methods have advantages and disadvantages, which are compared with the strengths and weaknesses of experimental research in an Illustrated Overview of research methods that appears on pages 62–63. As a whole, the foremost advantage of these methods is that they give researchers a way to explore questions that could not be examined with experimental procedures. For example, after-the-fact analyses would be the only ethical way to investigate the possible link between poor maternal nutrition and birth defects in humans. In a similar vein, if researchers hope to learn how urban and rural upbringing relate to people's values, they have to depend on descriptive methods, since they can't control where subjects grow up. Thus, *descriptive/correlational research broadens the scope of phenomena that psychologists are able to study.*

Unfortunately, descriptive methods have one significant disadvantage: Investigators cannot control events to isolate cause and effect. *Consequently, correlational research cannot demonstrate conclusively that two variables are causally related.* As an example, consider the cross-cultural investigation of the pace of life that we discussed earlier. Although Levine and Norenzayan (1999) found an association between colder climates and a faster pace of life, their data do not permit us to conclude that a cold climate *causes* a culture to move at a faster pace. Too many factors were left uncontrolled in the study. For example, we do not know how similar the cold and warm cities were. Climate could co-vary with some other factors, such as modernization or economic vitality, that might have led to the observed differences in the pace of life.

REVIEW of Key Learning Goals

2.9 Naturalistic observation involves careful, prolonged observation of behavior in its natural setting without any intervention. Clinical research depends heavily on case studies, which involve in-depth investigations of individuals. In a survey, researchers interview participants or administer questionnaires to gather information on specific aspects of attitudes or behavior. Each approach has its unique strengths and weaknesses.

2.10 Descriptive/correlational research methods allow psychologists to explore issues that might not be open to experimental investigation because the variables of interest cannot be manipulated. However, these research methods cannot demonstrate cause-effect relationships.

Looking for Conclusions: Statistics and Research

Whether researchers use experimental or correlational methods, they need some way to make sense of their data. *Statistics is the use of mathematics to organize, summarize, and interpret numerical data.* Statistical analyses permit researchers to draw conclusions based on their observations. Many students find statistics intimidating, but statistics are an integral part of modern life. Although you may not realize it, you are bombarded with statistics nearly every day. When you read about economists' projections for inflation, when you check a baseball player's batting average, when you see the popularity ratings of television shows, you are dealing with statistics. In this section, we will examine a few basic statistical concepts that will help you understand the research discussed throughout this book. For the most part, we won't concern ourselves with the details of statistical *computations*. These details and some additional statistical concepts are discussed in Appendix B at the back of the book. At this juncture, we will discuss only the purpose, logic, and value of the two basic types of statistics: descriptive statistics and inferential statistics.

Descriptive Statistics 1c, 1d

Descriptive statistics are used to organize and summarize data. They provide an overview of numerical data. Key descriptive statistics include measures of central tendency, measures of variability, and the coefficient of correlation. Let's take a brief look at each of these.

Central Tendency 1c

In summarizing numerical data, researchers often want to know what constitutes a typical or average score. To answer this question, they use three measures of central tendency: the median, the mean, and the mode. *The median is the score that falls exactly in the center of a distribution of scores.* Half of the scores fall above the median and half fall below it. *The mean is the arithmetic average of the scores in a distribution.* It is obtained by adding up all the scores and dividing by the total number of scores. Finally, *the mode is the most frequent score in a distribution.*

In general, the mean is the most useful measure of central tendency because additional statistical

manipulations can be performed on it that are not possible with the median or mode. However, the mean is sensitive to extreme scores in a distribution, which can sometimes make the mean misleading. To illustrate, imagine that you're interviewing for a sales position at a company. Unbeknownst to you, the company's five salespeople earned the following incomes in the previous year: $20,000, $20,000, $25,000, $35,000, and $200,000. You ask how much the typical salesperson earns in a year. The sales director proudly announces that her five salespeople earned a *mean* income of $60,000 last year (the calculations are shown in Figure 2.11). However, before you order that new sports car, you had better inquire about the *median* and *modal* income for the sales staff. In this case, one extreme score ($200,000) has inflated the mean, making it unrepresentative of the sales staff's earnings. In this instance, the median ($25,000) and the mode ($20,000) both provide better estimates of what you are likely to earn.

Variability 1c

In describing a set of data, it is often useful to have some estimate of the variability among the scores. *Variability refers to how much the scores in a data set vary from each other and from the mean.* The *standard deviation* is an index of the amount of variability in a set of data. When variability is great, the standard deviation will be relatively large. When variability is low, the standard deviation will be smaller. This relationship is apparent if you examine the two sets of data in Figure 2.12 on the next page. The mean is the same for both sets of scores, but variability clearly is greater in set B than in set A. This greater variability yields a higher stan-

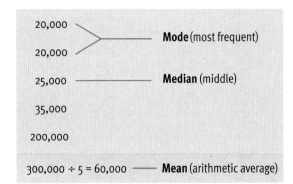

Figure 2.11

Measures of central tendency. The three measures of central tendency usually converge, but that is not always the case, as these data illustrate. Which measure is most useful depends on the nature of the data. Generally, the mean is the best index of central tendency, but in this instance the median is more informative.

Figure 2.12

Variability and the standard deviation. Although these two sets of data produce the same mean, or average, an observer on Wild Street would see much more variability in the speeds of individual cars than an observer on Perfection Boulevard would. As you can see, the standard deviation for set B is higher than that for set A because of the greater variability in set B.

Speed (miles per hour)		
Set A **Perfection Boulevard**		**Set B** **Wild Street**
35		21
34		37
33		50
37		28
38		42
40		37
36		39
33		25
34		23
30		48
35	Mean	35
2.87	Standard deviation	10.39

dard deviation for set B than for set A. Estimates of variability play a crucial role when researchers use statistics to decide whether the results of their studies support their hypotheses.

Correlation

A *correlation* exists when two variables are related to each other. Investigators often want to quantify the strength of an association between two variables, such as between class attendance and course grades, or between cigarette smoking and physical disease. In this effort, they depend extensively on a useful descriptive statistic: the correlation coefficient. **The correlation coefficient is a numerical index of the degree of relationship between two variables.** A correlation coefficient indicates (1) the direction (positive or negative) of the relationship and (2) how strongly the two variables are related.

Positive Versus Negative Correlation. A *positive correlation* indicates that two variables co-vary in the *same* direction. This means that high scores on variable *X* are associated with high scores on variable *Y* and that low scores on variable *X* are associated with low scores on variable *Y*. For example, a positive correlation exists between high school grade point average (GPA) and subsequent college GPA. That is, people who do well in high school tend to do well in college, and those who perform poorly in high school tend to perform poorly in college (see Figure 2.13).

In contrast, a *negative* correlation indicates that two variables co-vary in the *opposite* direction. This means that people who score high on variable *X* tend to score low on variable *Y*, whereas those who score low on *X* tend to score high on *Y*. For example, in most college courses a negative correlation exists between how frequently students are absent and how well they perform on exams. Students who have a high number of absences tend to get low exam scores, while students who have a low number of absences tend to earn higher exam scores (see Figure 2.13).

If a correlation is negative, a minus sign (–) is always placed in front of the coefficient. If a correlation is positive, a plus sign (+) may be placed in front of the coefficient, or the coefficient may be shown with no sign. Thus, if there's no sign, the correlation is positive.

Strength of the Correlation. Whereas the positive or negative sign indicates the direction of an association, the *size of the coefficient* indicates the *strength* of an association between two variables. The coefficient can vary between 0 and +1.00 (if

Figure 2.13

Positive and negative correlation. Notice that the terms *positive* and *negative* refer to the direction of the relationship between two variables, not to its strength. Variables are positively correlated if they tend to increase and decrease together; they are negatively correlated if one tends to increase when the other decreases.

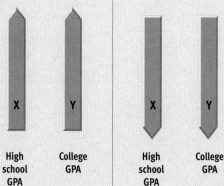
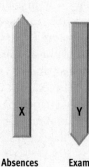
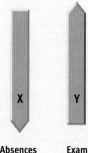

Positive correlation

High scores on *X* are associated with high scores on *Y*, and low scores on *X* are associated with low scores on *Y*.

X Y   X Y

High school GPA   College GPA   High school GPA   College GPA

Negative correlation

High scores on *X* are associated with low scores on *Y*, and low scores on *X* are associated with high scores on *Y*.

X Y   X Y

Absences from class   Exam scores   Absences from class   Exam scores

positive) or between 0 and –1.00 (if negative). A coefficient near 0 indicates no relationship between the variables; that is, high or low scores on variable *X* show no consistent relationship to high or low scores on variable *Y*. A coefficient of +1.00 or –1.00 indicates a perfect, one-to-one correspondence between the two variables. Most correlations fall between these extremes.

The closer the correlation is to either –1.00 or +1.00, the stronger the relationship (see **Figure 2.14**). Thus, a correlation of .90 represents a stronger tendency for variables to be associated than a correlation of .40 does. Likewise, a correlation of –.75 represents a stronger relationship than a correlation of –.45. Keep in mind that the *strength* of a correlation depends only on the *size* of the coefficient. The positive or negative sign simply indicates the *direction* of the relationship. Therefore, a correlation of –.60 reflects a stronger relationship than a correlation of +.30.

To give you some concrete examples of correlation coefficients of different strengths, let's revisit some of the studies we discussed in the previous section. In our earlier example of naturalistic observation, Levine and Norenzayan (1999) found a robust correlation of +.74 between a measure of economic vitality (gross domestic product per capita) and the overall pace of life in various cultures, but they found a negligible correlation (–.07) between population size and the pace of life. In our earlier example of survey research, Judge and Cable (2004) found an average correlation of .29 between height and income. Thus, the computation of correlation coefficients permits researchers to precisely quantify the strength of the associations between variables.

Correlation and Prediction. You may recall that one of the key goals of scientific research is accurate *prediction*. A close link exists between the magnitude of a correlation and the power it gives scientists to make predictions. *As a correlation increases in strength (gets closer to either –1.00 or +1.00), the ability to predict one variable based on knowledge of the other variable increases.*

To illustrate, consider how college admissions tests (such as the SAT or ACT) are used to predict college performance. When students' admissions test scores and first-year college GPA are correlated, researchers generally find moderate positive correlations in the .40s and .50s (Gregory, 1996). Because of this relationship, college admissions committees can predict with modest accuracy how well prospective students will do in college. Admittedly, the predictive power of these admissions tests is *far* from perfect. But it's substantial enough to justify the use of the tests as one factor in making admissions decisions. However, if this correlation were much higher, say .90, admissions tests could predict with superb accuracy how students would perform. In contrast, if this correlation were much lower, say .20, the tests' prediction of college performance would be so poor that it would be unreasonable to consider the test scores in admissions decisions.

Correlation and Causation. Although a high correlation allows us to predict one variable from another, it does not tell us whether a cause-effect relationship exists between the two variables. The problem is that variables can be highly correlated even though they are not causally related. For example, there is a substantial positive correlation between the size of young children's feet and the size of their vocabulary. That is, larger feet are associated with a larger vocabulary. Obviously, increases in foot size do not *cause* increases in vocabulary size. Nor do increases in vocabulary size cause increases in foot size. Instead, both are caused by a third variable: an increase in the children's age.

When we find that variables *X* and *Y* are correlated, we can safely conclude only that *X* and *Y* are related. We do not know *how* *X* and *Y* are related. We do not know whether *X* causes *Y* or *Y* causes *X* or whether both are caused by a third variable. For example, survey studies have found a positive correla-

web link 2.4

HyperStat Online

For psychology researchers who find they've temporarily misplaced their statistics textbook, here's one written in hypertext by Professor David M. Lane of Rice University, and it's always available free online. He also includes links to excellent resources involving statistics, the analysis of experimental data, and even some statistical humor.

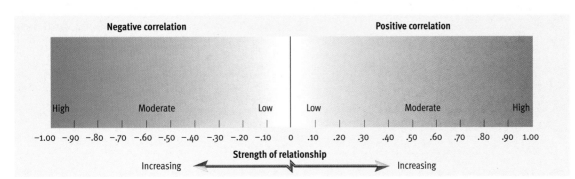

Figure 2.14

Interpreting correlation coefficients. The magnitude of a correlation coefficient indicates the strength of the relationship between two variables. The sign (plus or minus) indicates whether the correlation is positive or negative. The closer the coefficient comes to +1.00 or –1.00, the stronger the relationship between the variables.

Understanding Correlation

Check your understanding of correlation by interpreting the meaning of the correlation in item 1 and by guessing the direction (positive or negative) of the correlations in item 2. You'll find the answers in Appendix A.

1. Researchers have found a substantial positive correlation between youngsters' self-esteem and their academic achievement (measured by grades in school). Check any acceptable conclusions based on this correlation.

   _____ **a.** Low grades cause low self-esteem.

   _____ **b.** There is an association between self-esteem and academic achievement.

   _____ **c.** High self-esteem causes high academic achievement.

   _____ **d.** High ability causes both high self-esteem and high academic achievement.

   _____ **e.** Youngsters who score low in self-esteem tend to get low grades, and those who score high in self-esteem tend to get high grades.

2. Indicate whether you would expect the following correlations to be positive or negative.

   _____ **a.** The correlation between age and visual acuity (among adults).

   _____ **b.** The correlation between years of education and income.

   _____ **c.** The correlation between shyness and the number of friends one has.

tion between smoking and the risk of experiencing a major depressive disorder (Johnson & Breslau, 2006; Kinnunen et al., 2006). Although it's clear that an association exists between smoking and depression, it's hard to tell what's causing what. The investigators acknowledge that they don't know whether smoking makes people more vulnerable to depression or whether depression increases the tendency to smoke. Moreover, they note that they can't rule out the possibility that both are caused by a third variable (*Z*). Perhaps anxiety and neuroticism increase the likelihood of both taking up smoking and becoming depressed. The plausible causal relationships in this case are diagrammed in **Figure 2.15**, which illustrates the "third variable problem" in interpreting correlations. This is a common problem in research, and you'll see this type of diagram again when we discuss other correlations. Thus, it is important to remember that *correlation is not equivalent to causation.*

Figure 2.15

Three possible causal relations between correlated variables. If variables *X* and *Y* are correlated, does *X* cause *Y*, does *Y* cause *X*, or does some hidden third variable, *Z*, account for the changes in both *X* and *Y*? As the relationship between smoking and depression illustrates, a correlation alone does not provide the answer. We will encounter this problem of interpreting the meaning of correlations frequently in our discussions of behavioral research.

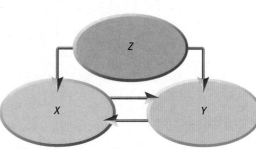

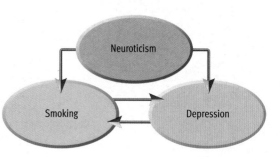

Inferential Statistics

After researchers have summarized their data with descriptive statistics, they still need to decide whether their data support their hypotheses. *Inferential statistics* are used to interpret data and draw conclusions. Working with the laws of probability, researchers use inferential statistics to evaluate the possibility that their results might be due to the fluctuations of chance.

To illustrate this process, envision a hypothetical experiment. A computerized tutoring program (the independent variable) is designed to increase sixth-graders' reading achievement (the dependent variable). Our hypothesis is that program participants (the experimental group) will score higher than non-participants (the control group) on a standardized reading test given near the end of the school year. Let's assume that we compare 60 subjects in each group. We obtain the following results, reported in terms of participants' grade-level scores for reading:

Control group		Experimental group
6.3	Mean	6.8
1.4	Standard deviation	2.4

We hypothesized that the training program would produce higher reading scores in the experimental group than in the control group. Sure enough, that is indeed the case. However, we have to ask ourselves a critical question: Is this observed difference between the two groups large enough to support our hypothesis? That is, do the higher scores in the experimental group reflect the effect of the training program? Or could a difference of this size have occurred by chance? If our results could easily have occurred by chance, they don't provide meaningful support for our hypothesis.

When statistical calculations indicate that research results are not likely to be due to chance, the results are said to be *statistically significant.* You will probably hear your psychology professor use this phrase quite frequently. In discussing research, it is routine to note that "statistically significant differences were found." In statistics, the word *significant* has a precise and special meaning. *Statistical significance* is said to exist when the probability that the observed findings are due to chance is very low. "Very low" is usually defined as less than 5 chances in 100, which is referred to as the *.05 level of significance.*

Notice that in this special usage, *significant* does not mean "important," or even "interesting." Statistically significant findings may or may not be theoretically significant or practically significant. They simply are research results that are unlikely to be due to chance.

You don't need to be concerned here with the details of how statistical significance is calculated. However, it is worth noting that a key consideration is the amount of variability in the data. That is why the standard deviation, which measures variability, is such an important statistic. When the necessary computations are made for our hypothetical experiment, the difference between the two groups does *not* turn out to be statistically significant. Thus, our results would not be adequate to demonstrate that our tutoring program leads to improved reading achievement. Psychologists have to do this kind of

statistical analysis as part of virtually every study. Thus, inferential statistics are an integral element in the research enterprise.

Looking for Flaws: Evaluating Research

Scientific research is a more reliable source of information than casual observation or popular belief. However, it would be wrong to conclude that all published research is free of errors. As we just saw, when researchers report statistically significant differences at the .05 level, there are 5 chances in 100 that the results really are a misleading by-product of chance fluctuation. This probability is pretty low, but it's not zero. Moreover, scientists' effort to minimize the probability of obtaining significant differences when none really exist increases the likelihood of the opposite mistake—failing to find significant differences when the groups really are different. Thus, even when research is conducted in a sound fashion, there's still a small chance of erroneous conclusions. Above and beyond this problem, we need to recognize that scientists are fallible human beings who do not conduct flawless research. Their personal biases in designing and interpreting studies can also distort research results (MacCoun, 1998).

For these reasons, researchers are reluctant to settle scientific questions on the basis of just one empirical study. Instead, important questions usually generate a flurry of studies to see whether key findings will stand the test of replication. *Replica-*

tion is the repetition of a study to see whether the earlier results are duplicated. The replication process helps science identify and purge erroneous findings. Of course, the replication process sometimes leads to contradictory results. You'll see some examples in later chapters. Inconsistent findings on a research question can be frustrating and confusing for students. However, some inconsistency in results is to be expected, given science's commitment to replication.

As you will see in upcoming chapters, scientific advances often emerge out of efforts to double-check perplexing findings or to explain contradictory research results. Thus, like all sources of information, scientific studies need to be examined with a critical eye. This section describes a number of common methodological problems that often spoil studies. Being aware of these pitfalls will make you more skilled in evaluating research.

Sampling Bias

A *sample* is the collection of subjects selected for observation in an empirical study. In contrast, the *population* is the much larger collection of ani-

Key Learning Goals

2.15 Articulate the importance of replication in research.

2.16 Recognize sampling bias and placebo effects in research.

2.17 Recognize problems with self-report data and experimenter bias in research.

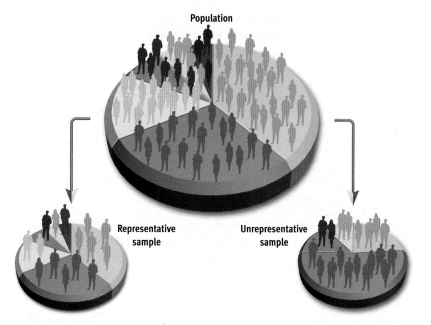

Population

Representative sample

Unrepresentative sample

Figure 2.16
The relationship between the population and the sample. The process of drawing inferences about a population based on a sample works only if the sample is reasonably representative of the population. A sample is representative if its demographic makeup is similar to that of the population, as shown on the left. If some groups in the population are overrepresented or underrepresented in the sample, as shown on the right, inferences about the population may be skewed or inaccurate.

mals or people (from which the sample is drawn) that researchers want to generalize about (see Figure 2.16). For example, when political pollsters attempt to predict elections, all the voters in a jurisdiction represent the population, and the voters who are actually surveyed constitute the sample. If a researcher was interested in the ability of 6-year-old children to form concepts, those 6-year-olds actually studied would be the sample, and all similar 6-year-old children (perhaps those in modern, Western cultures) would be the population.

The strategy of observing a limited sample in order to generalize about a much larger population rests on the assumption that the sample is reasonably *representative* of the population. A sample is representative if its composition is similar to the composition of the population. *Sampling bias* exists

Before accepting the results of a survey poll, one should know something about how the poll was conducted. A polling could, for instance, contain sampling bias. Opinions collected solely from middle-class people but generalized to the voting public as a whole would be an example of such bias.

when a sample is not representative of the population from which it was drawn. When a sample is not representative, generalizations about the population may be inaccurate. For instance, if a political pollster were to survey only people in posh shopping areas frequented by the wealthy, the pollster's generalizations about the voting public as a whole would be off the mark.

As we discussed in Chapter 1, psychologists have historically tended to undersample women, ethnic minorities, and people from non-Western cultures. They have also tended to neglect older adults, while depending much too heavily on white middle- and upper-class college students. This excessive reliance on college students may not be all that problematic for some research questions, but it certainly seems likely to distort results in many research areas (Sears, 1986). In general, then, when you have doubts about the results of a study, the first thing to examine is the composition of the sample.

Placebo Effects

In pharmacology, a *placebo* is a substance that resembles a drug but has no actual pharmacological effect. In studies that assess the effectiveness of medications, placebos are given to some subjects to control for the effects of a treacherous extraneous variable: participants' expectations. Placebos are used because researchers know that participants' expectations can influence their feelings, reactions, and behavior (Stewart-Williams, 2004). Thus, *placebo effects* occur when participants' expectations lead them to experience some change even though they receive empty, fake, or ineffectual treatment. In medicine, placebo effects are well documented (Quitkin, 1999). Many physicians tell of patients being "cured" by prescriptions of sugar pills. Placebo effects have also been seen in laboratory experiments on the effects of alcohol. In these studies, some of the participants are led to believe that they are drinking alcoholic beverages when in reality the drinks only appear to contain alcohol. Many of the subjects show effects of intoxication even though they haven't really consumed any alcohol (Assefi & Garry, 2003). If you know someone who shows signs of intoxication as soon as they start drinking, before their alcohol intake could take effect physiologically, you have seen placebo effects in action.

In the realm of research the problem is that psychologists have found that participants' expectations can be powerful determinants of their perceptions and behavior when they are under the microscope in an empirical study. For example, placebo effects have been seen in research on meditation. A number of studies have found that meditation can improve people's energy level, mental and physical health, and happiness (Alexander et al., 1990; Reibel et al., 2001). However, in many of the early studies of meditation, researchers assembled their experimental groups with volunteer subjects eager to learn meditation. Most of these subjects *wanted* and *expected* meditation to have beneficial effects. Their positive expectations may have colored their subsequent ratings of their energy level, happiness, and so on. Better-designed studies have shown that meditation can be beneficial (see Chapter 5). However, placebo effects have probably exaggerated these benefits in some studies (Canter, 2003; Shapiro, 1987).

Researchers should guard against placebo effects whenever subjects are likely to have expectations that a treatment will affect them in a certain way. The possible role of placebo effects can be assessed by including a fake version of the experimental treatment (a placebo condition) in a study.

Distortions in Self-Report Data

Research psychologists often work with *self-report data,* consisting of subjects' verbal accounts of their behavior. This is the case whenever questionnaires, interviews, or personality inventories are used to measure variables. Self-report methods can be quite useful, taking advantage of the fact that people have a unique opportunity to observe themselves fulltime (Baldwin, 2000). However, self-reports can be plagued by several kinds of distortion.

One of the most problematic of these distortions is the *social desirability bias,* which is a tendency to give socially approved answers to questions about oneself. Participants who are influenced by this bias try hard to create a favorable impression, especially when they are asked about sensitive issues (Tourangeau & Yan, 2007). For example, many survey respondents will report that they voted in an election, gave to a charity, or attend church regularly when in fact it is possible to determine that these assertions are untrue (Granberg & Holmberg, 1991; Hadaway, Marler, & Chaves, 1993). Respondents influenced by social desirability bias also tend to report that they are healthier, happier, and less prejudiced than other types of evidence would suggest. People who answer questions in socially desirable ways take slightly longer to respond to the questions, suggesting that they are carefully "editing" their responses (Holtgraves, 2004).

Other problems can also produce distortions in self-report data (Krosnick, 1999; Schuman & Kalton, 1985). Respondents misunderstand questionnaire items surprisingly often, and the way questions

are worded can shape subjects' responses (Schwarz, 1999). Memory errors can undermine the accuracy of verbal reports. Response sets are yet another problem. A *response set* is a tendency to respond to questions in a particular way that is unrelated to the content of the questions. For example, some people tend to agree with nearly everything on a questionnaire (Krosnick & Fabrigar, 1998). Obviously, distortions like these can produce inaccurate results. Although researchers have devised ways to neutralize these problems—such as carefully pretesting survey instruments—we should be cautious in drawing conclusions from self-report data (Schaeffer, 2000).

Experimenter Bias

As scientists, psychologists try to conduct their studies in an objective, unbiased way so that their own views will not influence the results. However, objectivity is a *goal* that scientists strive for, not an accomplished fact that can be taken for granted (MacCoun, 1998). In reality, most researchers have an emotional investment in the outcome of their research. Often they are testing hypotheses that they have developed themselves and that they would like to see supported by the data. It is understandable, then, that *experimenter bias* is a possible source of error in research.

Experimenter bias occurs when a researcher's expectations or preferences about the outcome of a study influence the results obtained. Experimenter bias can slip through to influence studies in many subtle ways. One problem is that researchers, like others, sometimes *see what they want to see.* For instance, when experimenters make apparently honest mistakes in recording subjects' responses, the mistakes tend to be heavily slanted in favor of supporting the hypothesis (O'Leary, Kent, & Kanowitz, 1975).

Research by Robert Rosenthal (1976) suggests that experimenter bias may lead researchers to unintentionally influence the behavior of their subjects. In a classic study, Rosenthal and Fode (1963) recruited undergraduate psychology students to serve as the "experimenters." The students were told that they would be collecting data for a study of how participants rated the success of people portrayed in photographs. In a pilot study, photos were selected that generated (on the average) neutral ratings on a scale extending from –10 (extreme failure) to +10 (extreme success). Rosenthal and Fode then manipulated the expectancies of their experimenters. Half of them were told that, based on pilot data, they would probably obtain average ratings of –5. The other half were led to expect average ratings of +5. The experimenters were forbidden from conversing with their sub-

Robert Rosenthal

"Quite unconsciously, a psychologist interacts in subtle ways with the people he is studying so that he may get the response he expects to get."

ILLUSTRATED OVERVIEW OF KEY RESEARCH METHODS IN PSYCHOLOGY

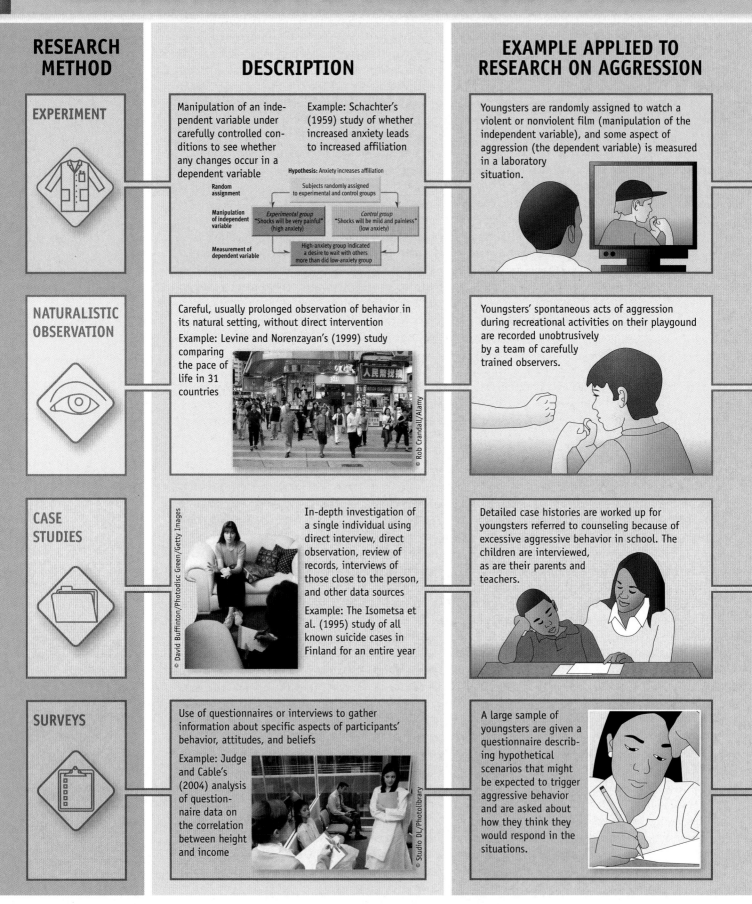

RESEARCH METHOD

DESCRIPTION

EXAMPLE APPLIED TO RESEARCH ON AGGRESSION

EXPERIMENT

Manipulation of an independent variable under carefully controlled conditions to see whether any changes occur in a dependent variable

Example: Schachter's (1959) study of whether increased anxiety leads to increased affiliation

Hypothesis: Anxiety increases affiliation

Random assignment — Subjects randomly assigned to experimental and control groups

Manipulation of independent variable — *Experimental group* "Shocks will be very painful" (high anxiety) | *Control group* "Shocks will be mild and painless" (low anxiety)

Measurement of dependent variable — High-anxiety group indicated a desire to wait with others more than did low-anxiety group

Youngsters are randomly assigned to watch a violent or nonviolent film (manipulation of the independent variable), and some aspect of aggression (the dependent variable) is measured in a laboratory situation.

NATURALISTIC OBSERVATION

Careful, usually prolonged observation of behavior in its natural setting, without direct intervention

Example: Levine and Norenzayan's (1999) study comparing the pace of life in 31 countries

© Rob Crandall/Alamy

Youngsters' spontaneous acts of aggression during recreational activities on their playgound are recorded unobtrusively by a team of carefully trained observers.

CASE STUDIES

© David Buffinton/Photodisc Green/Getty Images

In-depth investigation of a single individual using direct interview, direct observation, review of records, interviews of those close to the person, and other data sources

Example: The Isometsa et al. (1995) study of all known suicide cases in Finland for an entire year

Detailed case histories are worked up for youngsters referred to counseling because of excessive aggressive behavior in school. The children are interviewed, as are their parents and teachers.

SURVEYS

Use of questionnaires or interviews to gather information about specific aspects of participants' behavior, attitudes, and beliefs

Example: Judge and Cable's (2004) analysis of questionnaire data on the correlation between height and income

© Studio DL/Photolibrary

A large sample of youngsters are given a questionnaire describing hypothetical scenarios that might be expected to trigger aggressive behavior and are asked about how they think they would respond in the situations.

ADVANTAGES

DISADVANTAGES

Precise control over variables can eliminate alternative explanations for findings.

Researchers are able to draw conclusions about cause-and-effect relationships between variables.

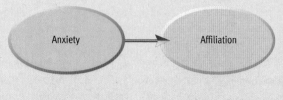

Confounding of variables must be avoided.

Contrived laboratory situations are often artificial, making it risky to generalize findings to the real world.

Ethical concerns and practical realities preclude experiments on many important questions.

Artificiality that can be a problem in laboratory studies is minimized.

It can be good place to start when little is known about the phenomena under study.

Unlike other descriptive/correlational methods, it can be used to study animal as well as human behavior.

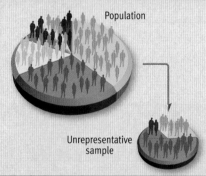

© Michael Nichols/National Geographic Image Collection

It can be difficult to remain unobtrusive; even animal behavior may be altererd by the observation process.

Researchers are unable to draw causal conclusions.

Observational data are often difficult to quantify for statistical analyses.

Case studies are well suited for study of psychological disorders and therapeutic practices.

Individual cases can provide compelling illustrations to support or undermine a theory.

Population

Unrepresentative sample

Subjectivity makes it easy to see what one expects to see based on one's theoretical slant.

Researchers are unable to draw causal conclusions.

Clinical samples are often unrepresentative and suffer from sampling bias.

Data collection can be relatively easy, saving time and money.

Researchers can gather data on difficult-to-observe aspects of behavior.

Questionnaires are well suited for gathering data on attitudes, values, and beliefs from large samples.

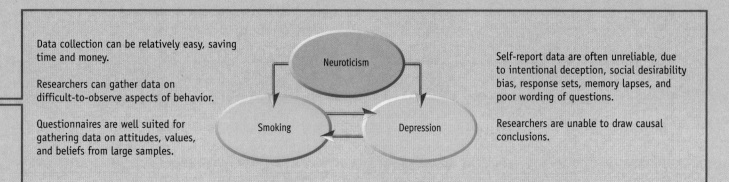

Neuroticism

Smoking

Depression

Self-report data are often unreliable, due to intentional deception, social desirability bias, response sets, memory lapses, and poor wording of questions.

Researchers are unable to draw causal conclusions.

concept check 2.4

Detecting Flaws in Research

Check your understanding of how to conduct sound research by looking for methodological flaws in the following studies. You'll find the answers in Appendix A.

Study 1. A researcher announces that he will be conducting an experiment to investigate the detrimental effects of sensory deprivation on perceptual-motor coordination. The first 40 students who sign up for the study are assigned to the experimental group, and the next 40 who sign up serve in the control group. The researcher supervises all aspects of the study's execution. Experimental subjects spend two hours in a sensory deprivation chamber, where sensory stimulation is minimal. Control subjects spend two hours in a waiting room that contains magazines and a TV. All subjects then perform ten 1-minute trials on a pursuit-rotor task that requires them to try to keep a stylus on a tiny rotating target. The dependent variable is their average score on the pursuit-rotor task.

Study 2. A researcher wants to know whether there is a relationship between age and racial prejudice. She designs a survey in which respondents are asked to rate their prejudice against six different ethnic groups. She distributes the survey to over 500 people of various ages who are approached at a shopping mall in a low-income, inner-city neighborhood.

Check the flaws that are apparent in each study.

Methodological flaw	Study 1	Study 2
Sampling bias	_____	_____
Placebo effects	_____	_____
Distortions in self-reports	_____	_____
Confounding of variables	_____	_____
Experimenter bias	_____	_____

jects except for reading some standardized instructions. Even though the photographs were exactly the same for both groups, the experimenters who *expected* positive ratings *obtained* significantly higher ratings than those who expected negative ratings.

How could the experimenters have swayed the participants' ratings? According to Rosenthal, the experimenters may have unintentionally influenced their subjects by sending subtle nonverbal signals as the experiment progressed. Without realizing it, they may have smiled, nodded, or sent other positive cues when participants made ratings that were in line with the experimenters' expectations. Thus, experimenter bias may influence both researchers' observations and their subjects' behavior (Rosenthal, 1994, 2002).

The problems associated with experimenter bias can be neutralized by using a double-blind procedure. The *double-blind procedure* is a research strategy in which neither participants nor experimenters know which subjects are in the experimental or control groups. It's not particularly unusual for participants to be "blind" about their treatment condition. However, the double-blind procedure keeps the experimenter in the dark as well. Of course, a member of the research team who isn't directly involved with subjects keeps track of who is in which group.

Key Learning Goals

2.18 Discuss the growth and the strengths and weaknesses of Internet-mediated research.

Looking into the Future: The Internet and Psychological Research

The Internet is revolutionizing many aspects of modern life. Some experts compare the emergence of the World Wide Web to the shift from speech to writing, the invention of the printing press, and the widespread distribution of electricity (Weiten, 2002). As Lenert and Skoczen (2002) note, "The Internet has profoundly changed how Americans communicate, obtain information, and conduct commerce" (p. 251). Small wonder then, that the Internet is gradually altering the ways in which psychological research is conducted.

Internet-mediated research refers to studies in which data collection occurs over the web. All of the methods we have discussed in this chapter can be used in Internet-mediated research. Mostly, investigators have conducted online experiments and distributed online surveys. An example of a web experiment is a study by Goritz (2006) that compared various cash lottery incentives to see which would yield the highest response rates in online studies. An example of a web survey is a study by Tower and Krasner (2006), in which over 1100 online participants responded to measures of marital closeness and depressive symptoms to explore the correlation between marital adjustment and depression. Although experiments and surveys have dominated Internet-mediated research, the web has also afforded psychologists enlightening opportunities to engage in naturalistic observation of social interaction in online communities, such as chatrooms and newsgroups (Glaser & Kahn, 2005; McKenna & Bargh, 2000; McKenna & Seidman, 2005).

Why have researchers been drawn to the web? Because the Internet offers some enticing advantages in the data collection process. For example, studies conducted via the Internet can often obtain samples that are much larger and much more diverse than the samples typically used in laboratory research (Buchanan, 2000; Reips, 2007). If a researcher is interested in some special population, whether it be gamblers, steroid users, atheists, dentists, elderly marathon runners, or lesbians living in rural areas, creative recruitment via the Internet can yield sizable samples that would be difficult or impossible to obtain through traditional research procedures (Mathy et al., 2002; Skitka & Sargis, 2005). Moreover, once an online survey or experiment is set up, data can be collected effortlessly 24 hours a day, 7 days a week. Research assistants do not need to spend endless hours testing subjects in a lab, and participants' responses can be saved automatically into data files for statistical analyses. Thus, Internet-mediated research can reduce costs and save time (Goritz, 2007; Skitka & Sargis, 2006). Studies that might require six months or a year of data collection in the laboratory can sometimes be completed in a few weeks online.

As you can see, Internet-mediated research offers many attractive benefits, but this approach also has some weaknesses that concern researchers. One major concern is the potential for sampling bias. Although the population of web users grows daily, not everyone has access to the Internet. Web users tend to be younger, brighter, and more affluent than nonusers (Lenert & Skoczen, 2002). A related issue is that web studies tend to have lower participation rates than conventional studies (Skitka & Sargis, 2005). In laboratory studies, although subjects can always elect to not participate, the vast majority generally tend to go along with whatever study they are assigned to. In most web studies, broad invitations to participate are issued via e-mail or posted announcements, and only a small minority of potential subjects typically choose to volunteer their time. Researchers worry that their self-selected volunteers might be systematically different from the majority of people who, for one reason or another, chose not to participate. Sampling bias resulting from self-selection can also occur in lab research, but it appears to be a much more troublesome issue in Internet-mediated research. Web studies also tend to have higher dropout rates than laboratory studies, which provides another possible source of sampling bias (Birnbaum, 2004).

Another issue in Internet-mediated research is that data are collected under far less controlled conditions than in traditional studies (Buchanan, 2007; Hewson, 2003). Laboratory studies are conducted under carefully controlled conditions that are held constant for all participants. Researchers routinely obsess over details such as room temperature, lighting, and the gender of the research assistant who interacts with subjects. In contrast, subjects in web studies usually participate from home, where environmental conditions are uncontrolled and unknown. Some participants may be distracted by TV, some may sit around and discuss their data input with friends, some may provide data while intoxicated, and some may ignore crucial instructions. Similar problems can crop up in traditional approaches to research, such as when subjects fill out paper-and-pencil surveys at home. But lack of control appears to be a more serious problem for Internet-mediated research than conventional research.

So, given problems such as these, will Internet-mediated research turn out to be a temporary fad? Or will it become the wave of the future? It seems likely that Internet-mediated research will continue to grow. Although web studies have created some new complexities related to sampling bias, they appear to have the *potential* to yield more diverse and representative samples than traditional approaches to research (Hewson, 2003). The control problem seems more worrisome, but when investigators have run identical studies over the web and through traditional methods, the results have generally turned out to be highly similar (Birnbaum, 2004; McGraw, Tew, & Williams, 2000). These findings suggest that the control issue may be less problematic than feared. And while some researchers have expressed concern about the greater anonymity of participants in web studies, this increased anonymity actually may reduce the impact of social desirability bias (Hewson, 2007; Skitka & Sargis, 2006). In sum, it appears that the Internet will gradually alter the landscape of psychological research, just as it has altered the landscape of communication, shopping, politics, real estate, entertainment, and many other aspects of modern life.

REVIEW of Key Learning Goals

2.18 Internet-mediated research has grown in recent years because it offers access to larger and more diverse samples and to specialized samples while reducing costs and saving time.

However, Internet-mediated research raises its own concerns about sampling bias and uncontrolled conditions during data collection.

Looking at Ethics: Do the Ends Justify the Means?

Key Learning Goals

2.19 Contrast the pros and cons of deception in research with human subjects.

2.20 Discuss the controversy about the use of animals as research subjects.

2.21 Summarize the major ethical principles governing psychological research.

Think back to Stanley Schachter's (1959) study on anxiety and affiliation. Imagine how you would have felt if you had been one of the subjects in Schachter's high-anxiety group. You show up at a research laboratory, expecting to participate in a harmless experiment. The room you are sent to is full of unusual electronic equipment. An official-looking man in a lab coat announces that this equipment will be used to give you a series of painful electric shocks. His statement that the shocks will leave "no permanent tissue damage" is hardly reassuring. Surely, you think, there must be a mistake. All of a sudden, your venture into research has turned into a nightmare! Your stomach knots up in anxiety. The researcher explains that there will be a delay while he prepares his apparatus. He asks you to fill out a short questionnaire about whether you would prefer to wait alone or with others. Still reeling in dismay at the prospect of being shocked, you fill out the questionnaire. He takes it and then announces that you won't be shocked after all—it was all a hoax! Feelings of relief wash over you, but they're mixed with feelings of anger. You feel as though the experimenter has just made a fool out of you, and you're embarrassed and resentful.

Should researchers be allowed to play with your feelings in this way? Should they be permitted to deceive subjects in such a manner? Is this the cost that must be paid to advance scientific knowledge? As these questions indicate, the research enterprise sometimes presents scientists with difficult ethical dilemmas. *These dilemmas reflect concern about the possibility for inflicting harm on participants.* In psychological research, the major ethical dilemmas center on the use of deception and the use of animals.

The Question of Deception

Elaborate deception, such as that seen in Schachter's study, has been fairly common in psychological research since the 1960s, especially in the area of social psychology (Epley & Huff, 1998; Korn, 1997). Over the years, psychologists have faked fights, thefts, muggings, faintings, epileptic seizures, rapes, and automobile breakdowns to explore a host of issues. They have led participants to believe that they were hurting others with electrical shocks, that they had homosexual tendencies, and that they were over-hearing negative comments about themselves. Why have psychologists used so much deception in their research? Quite simply, they are trying to deal with the methodological problems discussed earlier. They often misinform participants about the purpose of a study to reduce problems resulting from placebo effects, the unreliability of self-reports, and the like that can undermine the scientific value and validity of research (Berghmans, 2007).

Critics argue against the use of deception on several grounds (Baumrind, 1985; Kelman, 1982; Ortmann & Hertwig, 1997). First, they assert that deception is only a nice word for lying, which they see as inherently immoral. Second, they argue that by deceiving unsuspecting participants, psychologists may undermine many individuals' trust in others. Third, they point out that many deceptive studies produce distress for participants who were not forewarned about that possibility. Specifically, subjects may experience great stress during a study or be made to feel foolish when the true nature of a study is explained.

Those who defend the use of deception in research maintain that many important issues could not be investigated if experimenters were not permitted to mislead participants (Bröder, 1998). They argue that most research deceptions involve "white lies" that are not likely to harm participants. Moreover, they point out that critics have *assumed* that deception studies are harmful to subjects, without collecting empirical data to document these detrimental effects. In reality, the relevant research suggests that deception studies are *not* harmful to participants (Christensen, 1988). Indeed, most subjects who participate in experiments involving deception report that they enjoyed the experience and that they didn't mind being misled. Moreover, the empirical evidence does not support the notions that deceptive research undermines subjects' trust in others or their respect for psychology or scientific re-

web link 2.5

Bad Blood: The Tuskegee Syphilis Study

The enduring damage of unethical scientific and medical research—here seen in the infamous 1932–1972 Tuskegee Syphilis Study among 399 poor African-American men in Alabama—is detailed in several government reports and a rare presidential apology to the victims.

search (Kimmel, 1996; Sharpe, Adair, & Roese, 1992). Curiously, the weight of the evidence suggests that researchers are more concerned about the negative effects of deception on participants than the participants themselves are (Fisher & Fyrberg, 1994; Korn, 1987). Finally, researchers who defend deception argue that the benefits—advances in knowledge that often improve human welfare—are worth the costs. They assert that it would be unethical *not* to conduct effective research on conformity, obedience, aggression, and other important social issues.

The issue of deception creates a difficult dilemma for scientists, pitting honesty against the desire to advance knowledge. Today, institutions that conduct research have committees that evaluate the ethics of research proposals before studies are allowed to proceed. These committees have often blocked studies requiring substantial deception. Many psychologists believe that this conservativism has obstructed important lines of research and slowed progress in the field. Although this belief may be true, it is not easy to write off the points made by the critics of deception. Warwick (1975) states the issue eloquently: "If it is all right to use deceit to advance knowledge, then why not for reasons of national security, for maintaining the Presidency, or to save one's own hide?" (p. 105). That's a tough question regarding a tough dilemma that will probably generate heated debate for a long time to come.

The Question of Animal Research

Psychology's other major ethics controversy concerns the use of animals in research. Psychologists use animals as research subjects for several reasons. Sometimes they simply want to know more about the behavior of a specific type of animal. In other instances, they want to see whether certain laws of behavior apply to both humans and animals. Finally, in some cases psychologists use animals because they can expose them to treatments that clearly would be unacceptable with human subjects. For example, most of the research on the relationship between deficient maternal nutrition during pregnancy and the incidence of birth defects has been done with animals.

It's this third reason for using animals that has generated most of the controversy. Some people maintain that it is wrong to subject animals to harm or pain for research purposes. Essentially, they argue that animals are entitled to the same rights as humans (Regan, 1997; Ryder, 2006). They accuse researchers of violating these rights by subjecting animals to unnecessary cruelty in many "trivial" studies (Bowd & Shapiro, 1993; Hollands, 1989). They also assert that most animal studies are a waste of time because the results may not even apply to humans (Millstone, 1989; Norton, 2005). For example, Ulrich (1991) argues that "pigeons kept confined at 80% body weight in home cages that don't allow them ever to spread their wings, take a bath, or relate socially to other birds provide questionable models for humans" (pp. 200–201).

Although some animal rights activists simply advocate more humane treatment of research animals, a survey of 402 activists questioned at a Washington, D.C. rally found that 85% wanted to eliminate *all* research with animals (Plous, 1991). Some of the more militant animal rights activists have broken into

web link 2.6

Animal Welfare Information Center

This site, maintained by the U.S. Department of Agriculture, is an excellent source for information relating to all aspects of how animals are (and should be) cared for in research, laboratory, and other settings.

Best Supporting Role in a Medical Drama.

Perhaps you didn't know that rats and mice are the foundation for all medical research and that they have played a vital role in virtually every major medical discovery in history. Learn more about the essential need for animal research.

FOUNDATION FOR BIOMEDICAL RESEARCH
www.fbresearch.org

© 2005 Foundation for Biomedical Research

© William West/AFP/Getty Images

Many important scientific discoveries have been achieved through animal research, as the advertisement on the left notes. But many people remain vigorously opposed to animal research. The animal liberation activist shown here was covered in fake blood and strapped to a giant vivisection board as part of a protest against animal research in Melbourne, Australia. Clearly, the ethics of animal research is a highly charged controversy.

laboratories, destroyed scientists' equipment and research records, and stolen experimental animals. The animal rights movement has enjoyed considerable success. For example, membership in People for the Ethical Treatment of Animals (PETA) grew from 8,000 in 1984 to 750,000 in 2003 (Herzog, 2005). David Johnson (1990) noted that "the single issue citizens write about most often to their congresspersons and the president is not homelessness, not the drug problem, not crime. It is animal welfare" (p. 214).

In spite of the great furor, only 7%–8% of all psychological studies involve animals (mostly rodents and birds). Relatively few of these studies require subjecting the animals to painful or harmful manipulations (American Psychological Association, 1984). Psychologists who defend animal research point to the major advances attributable to psychological research on animals, which many people are unaware of (Baldwin, 1993; Compton, Dietrich, & Smith, 1995; Paul & Paul, 2001). Among them are advances in the treatment of mental disorders, neuromuscular disorders, strokes, brain injuries, visual defects, headaches, memory defects, high blood pressure, and problems with pain (Carroll & Overmier, 2001; Domjan & Purdy, 1995). To put the problem in context, Neal Miller (1985), a prominent psychologist who has done pioneering work in several areas, noted the following:

At least 20 million dogs and cats are abandoned each year in the United States; half of them are killed in pounds and shelters, and the rest are hit by cars or die of neglect. Less than 1/10,000 as many dogs and cats were used in psychological laboratories. . . . Is it worth sacrificing the lives of our children in order to stop experiments, most of which involve no pain, on a vastly smaller number of mice, rats, dogs, and cats? (p. 427)

Far more compelling than Miller are the advocates for disabled people who have entered the fray to campaign against the animal rights movement in recent years. For example, Dennis Feeney (1987), a psychologist disabled by paraplegia, quotes a newsletter from an organization called The Incurably Ill for Animal Research:

No one has stopped to think about those of us who are incurably ill and are desperately waiting for new research results that can only be obtained through the use of animals. We have seen successful advances toward other diseases, such as polio, diphtheria, mumps, measles, and hepatitis through animal research. We want the same chance for a cure, but animal rights groups would deny us this chance. (p. 595)

As you can see, the manner in which animals can ethically be used for research is a highly charged controversy. Psychologists are becoming increasingly sensitive to this issue. Although animals continue to be used in research, strict regulations have been imposed that govern nearly every detail of how laboratory animals can be used for research purposes (Ator, 2005; Garnett, 2005).

Ethical Principles in Research

The ethics issues that we have discussed in this section have led the APA to develop a set of ethical standards for researchers (American Psychological Association, 2002; see Figure 2.17). Although most psychological studies are fairly benign, these ethical principles are intended to ensure that both human and animal subjects are treated with dignity. Some of the most important guidelines for research with human participants include the following: (1) people's participation in research should always be voluntary and they should be allowed to withdraw from a study at any time; (2) participants should not be subjected to harmful or dangerous treatments; (3) if a study requires deception, participants should be debriefed (informed of the true nature and purpose of the research) as soon as possible; and (4) particpants' right to privacy should never be compromised. Crucial guidelines for research with animals include (1) harmful or painful procedures cannot be justified unless the potential benefits of the research are substantial, and (2) research animals are entitled to decent living conditions.

In regard to research ethics, the newest source of concern and debate centers on social scientists' increased use of the Internet as a tool for collecting data (Ess, 2007; Keller & Lee, 2003; Pittenger, 2003). As we have discussed, the emergence of the Internet has created a variety of new opportunities for behavioral researchers. For instance, chatrooms and other types of virtual communities provide remarkable opportunities for naturalistic observation of group processes in action. Psychologists are moving quickly to take advantage of these opportunities, but this new venue for research sometimes raises complicated questions about how the APA's ethical guidelines should be applied. Is interaction on the Internet similar to interaction in a public location like a park or sidewalk, open to observation? Or is it more like interaction on a phone line where one would expect some privacy? Is it acceptable for researchers to lurk in chat rooms and systematically record interactions? What if they pose as group members and provoke discussion of specific issues? If an Internet

web link 2.7

Office of Research Integrity

Anyone who needs a comprehensive, up-to-date overview of ethical concerns in research from the perspective of the U.S. government should consider visiting this site. Although the Office of Research Integrity (ORI) deals with research sponsored by the U.S. Public Health Service, it also offers links to parallel offices and resources in many other agencies.

Courtesy of Neal Miller

Neal Miller

"Who are the cruel and inhumane ones, the behavioral scientists whose research on animals led to the cures of the anorexic girl and the vomiting child, or those leaders of the radical animal activists who are making an exciting career of trying to stop all such research and are misinforming people by repeatedly asserting that it is without any value?"

Figure 2.17
Ethics in research. Key ethical principles in psychological research, as set forth by the American Psychological Association (2002), are summarized here. These principles are meant to ensure the welfare of both human and animal subjects.

APA Ethical Guidelines for Research

1 A subject's participation in research should be voluntary and based on informed consent. Subjects should never be coerced into participating in research. They should be informed in advance about any aspects of the study that might be expected to influence their willingness to cooperate. Furthermore, they should be permitted to withdraw from a study at any time if they so desire.

2 Participants should not be exposed to harmful or dangerous research procedures. This guideline is intended to protect subjects from psychological as well as physical harm. Thus, even stressful procedures that might cause emotional discomfort are largely prohibited. However, procedures that carry a modest risk of moderate mental discomfort may be acceptable.

3 If an investigation requires some deception of participants (about matters that do not involve risks), the researcher is required to explain and correct any misunderstandings as soon as possible. The deception must be disclosed to subjects in "debriefing" sessions as soon as it is practical to do so without compromising the goals of the study.

4 Subjects' rights to privacy should never be violated. Information about a subject that might be acquired during a study must be treated as highly confidential and should never be made available to others without the consent of the participant.

5 Harmful or painful procedures imposed upon animals must be thoroughly justified in terms of the knowledge to be gained from the study. Furthermore, laboratory animals are entitled to decent living conditions that are spelled out in detailed rules that relate to their housing, cleaning, feeding, and so forth.

6 Prior to conducting studies, approval should be obtained from host institutions and their research review committees. Research results should be reported fully and accurately, and raw data should be promptly shared with other professionals who seek to verify substantive claims. Retractions should be made if significant errors are found in a study subsequent to its publication.

study includes deception, then participants must be debriefed. But given the anonymity of the Internet, how can researchers debrief subjects who abandon their study midway and cannot be located? As you can see, Internet-mediated research poses complex new ethical dilemmas for researchers.

REVIEW of Key Learning Goals

2.19 Critics argue that deception in research is unethical because it is inherently immoral, may undermine participants' trust in others, and may expose them to high levels of stress. Those who defend deception in research argue that many important issues could not be investigated without misleading subjects and that the negative effects of deception on participants have been overestimated.

2.20 Critics of animal research argue that it violates animals' rights and that the findings of animal studies may not general-ize to humans. Psychologists who defend animal research argue that it has brought major advances that are worth the costs.

2.21 The APA has formulated ethical principles to serve as guidelines for researchers. Human subjects' participation should be voluntary, they should not be exposed to harmful treatments, they should be debriefed about deception, and their privacy should be respected. Animal subjects are entitled to decent living conditions and should not be exposed to dangerous procedures unless the potential benefits of the research are substantial.

Reflecting on the Chapter's Themes

Two of our seven unifying themes emerged strongly in this chapter. First, the entire chapter is a testimonial to the idea that psychology is empirical. Second, we saw numerous examples of how people's experience of the world can be highly subjective. Let's examine each of these points in more detail.

As explained in Chapter 1, the empirical approach entails testing ideas, basing conclusions on systematic observation, and relying on a healthy brand of skepticism. All those features of the empirical approach have been apparent in our review of the research enterprise in psychology.

As you have seen, psychologists test their ideas by formulating clear hypotheses that involve predictions about relations between variables. They then use a variety of research methods to collect data so they can see whether their predictions are supported. The data collection methods are designed to make researchers' observations systematic and precise. The entire venture is saturated with skepticism. Psychologists are impressed only by research results that are highly unlikely to have occurred by chance. In planning and executing their research, they are constantly on the lookout for methodologi-

Key Learning Goals
2.22 Identify the two unifying themes highlighted in this chapter.

Empiricism

Subjectivity of Experience

cal flaws. They submit their articles to a demanding peer review process so that other experts can subject their methods and conclusions to critical scrutiny. Collectively, these procedures represent the essence of the empirical approach.

The subjectivity of personal experience was apparent in our discussion of how adversaries overestimate the gap between their views, and in our Featured Study, which showed that two people experiencing the same event can have different feelings about it because of differing expectations. Subjective perception was also prominent in our coverage of methodological problems, especially placebo effects and experimenter bias. When subjects report beneficial effects from a fake treatment (the placebo), it's because they expected to see these effects. As pointed out in Chapter 1, psychologists and other scientists are not immune to the effects of subjective experience. Although they are trained to be objective, even scientists may see what they expect to see or what they want to see. This is one reason that

the empirical approach emphasizes precise measurement and a skeptical attitude. The highly subjective nature of experience is exactly what the empirical approach attempts to neutralize.

The publication of empirical studies allows us to apply a critical eye to the research enterprise. However, you cannot critically analyze studies unless you know where and how to find them. In the upcoming Personal Application, we will discuss where studies are published, how to find studies on specific topics, and how to read research reports. In the subsequent Critical Thinking Application, we'll analyze the shortcomings of anecdotal evidence, which should help you to appreciate the value of empirical evidence.

> **REVIEW of Key Learning Goals**
>
> **2.22** The empirical nature of psychology was elucidated throughout this chapter. Empiricism involves testing hypotheses, basing conclusions on systematic observation, and taking a skeptical approach. The chapter also showed repeatedly that our experience of the world is highly subjective.

Key Learning Goals

2.23 Characterize the nature of technical journals.
2.24 Explain how to use PsycINFO to search for research literature in psychology.
2.25 Describe the standard organization of journal articles reporting on empirical research.

Answer the following "yes" or "no."

____ **1** I have read about scientific studies in newspapers and magazines and sometimes wondered, "How did they come to those conclusions?"

____ **2** When I go to the library, I often have difficulty figuring out how to find information based on research.

____ **3** I have tried to read scientific reports and found them to be too technical and difficult to understand.

If you responded "yes" to any of the above statements, you have struggled with the information explosion in the sciences. We live in a research-oriented society. The number of studies conducted in most sciences is growing at a dizzying pace. This expansion has been particularly spectacular in psy-

Finding and Reading Journal Articles

chology. Moreover, psychological research increasingly commands attention from the popular press because it is often relevant to people's personal concerns.

This Personal Application is intended to help you cope with the information explosion in psychology. It assumes that there may come a time when you need to examine original psychological research. Perhaps it will be in your role as a student (working on a term paper, for instance), in another role (parent, teacher, nurse, administrator), or merely out of curiosity. In any case, this Application explains the nature of technical journals and discusses how to find and read articles in them. You can learn more about how to use library resources in psychology from an excellent little book titled *Library Use: A Handbook for Psychology* (Reed & Baxter, 2003).

The Nature of Technical Journals

As you will recall from earlier in the chapter, a *journal* is a periodical that publishes technical and scholarly material, usually in a narrowly defined area of inquiry. Scholars in most fields—whether economics, chemistry, education, or psychology—publish the bulk of their work in these journals. Journal articles represent the core of intellectual activity in any academic discipline. Although they are periodicals, you generally will not find technical journals at your local newsstand. Even public libraries carry relatively few professional journals. Academic libraries and professors account for the vast majority of subscriptions to technical journals. Individual professors typically subscribe to five to ten journals that publish articles in their area of expertise, whereas large college libraries subscribe to thousands of professional journals.

In general, journal articles are written for other professionals in the field. Hence, authors assume that their readers are other interested economists or chemists or psychologists. Because journal articles are written in the special language unique to a particular discipline, they are often difficult for nonprofessionals to understand. You will be learning a great deal of psychology's special language in this course, which will improve your ability to understand articles in psychology journals.

In psychology, most journal articles are reports that describe original empirical studies. These reports permit researchers to disseminate their findings to the scientific community. Another common type of article is the review article. *Review articles* summarize and reconcile the findings of a large number of studies on a specific issue. Some psychology journals also publish comments or critiques of previously published research, book reviews, theoretical treatises, and descriptions of methodological innovations.

Finding Journal Articles

 1e

Reports of psychological research are commonly mentioned in newspapers and popular magazines. These summaries can be helpful to readers, but they often embrace the most sensational conclusions that might be drawn from the research. They also tend to include many oversimplifications and factual errors. Thus, if a study mentioned in the press is of interest to you, you may want to track down the original article to ensure that you get accurate information.

Most discussions of research in the popular press do not mention where you can find the original technical article. However, there is a way to find out. A computerized database called PsycINFO makes it possible to locate journal articles by specific researchers or scholarly work on specific topics. This huge online database, which is updated constantly, contains brief summaries, or *abstracts*, of journal articles, books, and chapters in edited books, reporting, reviewing, or theorizing about psychological research. Over 2100 journals are checked regularly to select items for inclusion. The abstracts are concise—about 75 to 175 words. They briefly describe the hypotheses, methods, results, and conclusions of the studies. Each abstract should allow you to determine whether an article is relevant to your interests. If it is, you should be able to find the article in your library (or to order it) because a complete bibliographic reference is provided.

PsycINFO: Search Results

Your query: ((timothy judge):author) AND (2004<=Year<=2004)
Results: 12 documents

1. **Intelligence and Leadership: A Quantitative Review and Test of Theoretical Propositions.**
   By Judge, Timothy A.; Colbert, Amy E.; Ilies, Remus
   Journal of Applied Psychology. 89(3), Jun 2004, 542–552.
   Citation and Abstract | Expanded Record | Expanded Record with References | View Article (HTML) | View Article (PDF)

2. **The Effect of Physical Height on Workplace Success and Income: Preliminary Test of a Theoretical Model.**
   By Judge, Timothy A.; Cable, Daniel M.
   Journal of Applied Psychology. 89(3), Jun 2004, 428–441.
   Citation and Abstract | Expanded Record | Expanded Record with References | View Article (HTML) | View Article (PDF)

3. **Organizational Justice and Stress: The Mediating Role of Work-Family Conflict.**
   By Judge, Timothy A.; Colquitt, Jason A.
   Journal of Applied Psychology. 89(3) Jun 2004, 395–404.
   Citation and Abstract | Expanded Record | Expanded Record with References | View Article (HTML) | View Article (PDF)

4. **Employee attitudes and job satisfaction.**
   By Saari, Lise M.; Judge, Timothy A.
   Human Resource Management. 43(4), Win 2004, 395–407.
   Citation and Abstract | Expanded Record | Expanded Record with References

5. **Personality and Transformational and Transactional Leadership: A Meta-Analysis.**
   By Bono, Joyce E.; Judge, Timothy A.
   Journal of Applied Psychology. 89(5) Oct 2004, 901–910.
   Citation and Abstract | Expanded Record | Expanded Record with References | View Article (HTML) | View Article (PDF)

6. **Transformational and Transactional Leadership: A Meta-Analytic Test of Their Relative Validity.**
   By Judge, Timothy A.; Piccolo, Ronald F.
   Journal of Applied Psychology. 89(5) Oct 2004, 755–768.
   Citation and Abstract | Expanded Record | Expanded Record with References | View Article (HTML) | View Article (PDF)

Figure 2.18

Searching PsycINFO. If you searched PsycINFO for journal articles published by Timothy Judge during 2004, the database would return 12 listings, of which the first 6 are shown here. For each article, you can click to see its abstract or its full PsycINFO record (the abstract plus subject descriptors and other details). In some cases (depending on the version of PsycINFO that your library has ordered) you can click to see the full PsycINFO record plus references, or the *full text* of some articles.

Although news accounts of research rarely mention where a study was published, they often mention the name of the researcher. If you have this information, the easiest way to find a specific article is to search PsycINFO for materials published by that researcher. For example, let's say you read a news report that summarized the survey study that we described earlier on the correlation between height and income (Judge & Cable, 2004; see p. 53). Let's assume that the news report mentioned the name of Timothy Judge as the lead author and indicated that the article was published in 2004. To track down the original article, you would search for journal articles published by Timothy Judge in 2004. If you conducted this search, you would turn up a list of 12 articles. The information for the first six articles in this list is shown in **Figure 2.18**. The second item in the list appears to be the article you are interested in. **Figure 2.19** on the next page shows what you would see if you clicked to obtain the Citation and Abstract for this article. As you can see, the abstract shows that the original report was published in the June 2004 issue of the *Journal of Applied Psychology*. Armed with this information, you could obtain the article easily.

PsycINFO: Citation and Abstract

Title	The Effect of Physical Height on Workplace Success and Income: Preliminary Test of a Theoretical Model.
Abstract	In this article, the authors propose a theoretical model of the relationship between physical height and career success. We then test several linkages in the model based on a meta-analysis of the literature, with results indicating that physical height is significantly related to measures of social esteem (p = .41), leader emergence (p = .24), and performance (p = .18). Height was somewhat more strongly related to success for men (p = .29) than for women (p = .21), although this difference was not significant. Finally, given that almost no research has examined the relationship between individuals' physical height and their incomes, we present four large-sample studies (total N = 8,590) showing that height is positively related to income (b = .26) after controlling for sex, age, and weight. Overall, this article presents the most comprehensive analysis of the relationship of height to workplace success to date, and the results suggest that tall individuals have advantages in several important aspects of their careers and organizational lives (PsycINFO Database Record © 2004 APA, all rights reserved)
Authors	Judge, Timothy A.; Cable, Daniel N.
Affiliations	Judge, Timothy A.: Department of Management, Warrington College of Business, University of Florida, FL, US Cable, Daniel M.: Kenan-Flagler Business School, University of North Carolina, NC, US
Source	Journal of Applied Psychology. 89(3), Jun 2004, 428–441.

Figure 2.19

Example of a PsycINFO abstract. This information is what you would see if you clicked to see the abstract of item 2 in the list shown in Figure 2.18. It is a typical abstract from the online PsycINFO database. Each abstract in PsycINFO provides a summary of a specific journal article, book, or chapter in an edited book, and complete bibliographical information.

SOURCE: Sample record reprinted with permission of the American Psychological Association, publisher of the PsycINFO® database. Copyright © 1887–present, American Psychological Association. All rights reserved. For more information contact psycinfo.apa.org.

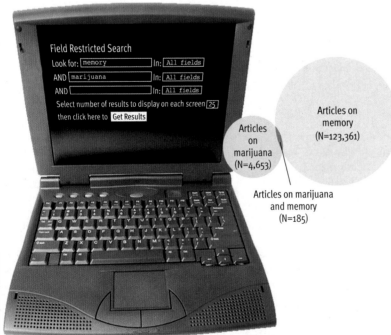

Figure 2.20

Combining topics in a PsycINFO search. A computerized literature search can be a highly efficient way to locate the specific research that you need. For example, if you had set out in November of 2007 to find all the journal articles on marijuana and memory using PsycINFO, you would have obtained the results summarized here. At that time, the database contained 123,361 articles related to memory and 4,653 articles related to marijuana. The search depicted on the left yielded 185 abstracts that relate to both marijuana and memory. Thus, in a matter of moments, the computer can sift through over 2 million abstracts to find those that are most germane to a specific question, such as: Does marijuana affect memory?

You can also search PsycINFO for research literature on particular topics, such as achievement motivation, aggressive behavior, alcoholism, appetite disorders, or artistic ability. These computerized literature searches can be much more powerful, precise, and thorough than traditional, manual searches in a library. PsycINFO can sift through several million articles in a matter of seconds to identify *all* the articles on a subject, such as alcoholism. Obviously, there is no way you can match this efficiency stumbling around in the stacks at your library. Moreover, the computer allows you to pair up topics to swiftly narrow your search to exactly those issues that interest you. For example, Figure 2.20 shows a PsycINFO search that identified all the articles on marijuana *and* memory. If you were preparing a term paper on whether marijuana affects memory, this precision would be invaluable.

The PsycINFO database can be accessed online through many libraries or via the Internet (see Web Link 2.2 for a description of PsycINFO Direct). The summaries contained in PsycINFO formerly were also found in a monthly print journal called *Psychological Abstracts.* However, the publication of this journal was discontinued in 2006 after 80 years of service as it became an antiquated source of information in comparison to the PsycINFO database (Benjamin & Vanden-Bos, 2006).

Reading Journal Articles

Once you find the journal articles you want to examine, you need to know how to decipher them. You can process the in-

formation in such articles more efficiently if you understand how they are organized. Depending on your needs and purpose, you may want to simply skim through some of the sections. Journal articles follow a fairly standard organization, which includes the following sections and features.

Abstract

Most journals print a concise summary at the beginning of each article. This abstract allows readers scanning the journal to quickly decide whether articles are relevant to their interests.

Introduction

The introduction presents an overview of the problem studied in the research. It mentions relevant theories and quickly reviews previous research that bears on the problem, usually citing shortcomings in previous research that necessitate the present study. This review of the current state of knowledge on the topic usually progresses to a specific and precise statement regarding the hypotheses under investigation.

Method

The method section provides a thorough description of the research methods used in the study. Information is provided on the subjects used, the procedures followed, and the data collection techniques employed. This description is made detailed enough to permit another researcher to attempt to replicate the study.

Results

The data obtained in the study are reported in the results section. This section often creates problems for novice readers because it includes complex statistical analyses, figures, tables, and graphs. This section does *not* include any inferences based on the data, as such conclusions are supposed to follow in the next section. Instead, it simply contains a concise summary of the raw data and the statistical analyses.

Discussion

In the discussion section you will find the conclusions drawn by the author(s). In contrast to the results section, which is a straightforward summary of empirical observations, the discussion section allows for interpretation and evaluation of the data. Implications for theory and factual knowledge in the discipline are discussed. Conclusions are usually qualified carefully, and any limitations in the study may be ac-knowledged. This section may also include suggestions for future research on the issue.

References

At the end of each article you will find a list of bibliographic references for any studies cited. This list permits you to examine first-hand other relevant studies mentioned in the article. The references list is often a rich source of leads about other articles that are germane to the topic that you are looking into.

REVIEW of Key Learning Goals

2.23 Journals publish technical and scholarly material. Usually they are written for other professionals in a narrow area of inquiry. In psychology, most journal articles are reports of original research. Subscriptions to journals are mostly held at academic libraries.

2.24 PsycINFO is a computerized database that contains brief summaries of newly published journal articles, books, and chapters in edited books. Works on specific topics and publications by specific authors can be found by using the search mechanisms built into the database. Computerized literature searches can be much more powerful and precise than manual searches.

2.25 Journal articles are easier to understand if one is familiar with the standard format. Most articles include six elements: abstract, introduction, method, results, discussion, and references.

Key Learning Goals

2.26 Recognize anecdotal evidence and understand why it is unreliable.

The Perils of Anecdotal Evidence: "I Have a Friend Who . . ."

Here's a tough problem. Suppose you are the judge in a family law court. As you look over the cases that will come before you today, you see that one divorcing couple have managed to settle almost all of the important decisions with minimal conflict—such as who gets the house, who gets the car and the dog, and who pays which bills. However, there is one crucial issue left: Each parent wants custody of the children, and because they could not reach an agreement on their own, the case is now in your court. You will need the wisdom of the legendary King Solomon for this decision. How can you determine what is in the best interests of the children?

Child custody decisions have major consequences for all of the parties involved. As you review the case records, you see that both parents are loving and competent, so there are no obvious reasons for selecting one parent over the other as the primary caretaker. In considering various alternatives, you mull over the possibility of awarding *joint custody,* an arrangement in which the children spend half their time with each parent, instead of the more usual arrangement where one parent has primary custody and the other has visitation rights.

Joint custody seems to have some obvious benefits, but you are not sure how well these arrangements actually work. Will the children feel more attached to both parents if the parents share custody equally? Or will the children feel hassled by always moving around, perhaps spending half the week at one parent's home and half at the other parent's home? Can parents who are already feuding over child custody issues make these complicated arrangements work? Or is joint custody just too disruptive to everyone's life? You really don't know the answer to any of these vexing questions.

One of the lawyers involved in the case knows that you are thinking about the possibility of joint custody. She also understands that you want more information about how well joint custody tends to work before you render a decision. To help you make up your mind, she tells you about a divorced couple that has had a joint custody arrangement for many years and offers to have them appear in court to describe their experiences "firsthand." They and their children can answer any questions you might have about the pros and cons of joint custody. They should be in the best position to know how well joint custody works because they are living it. Sounds like a reasonable plan. What do you think?

I hope you said, "No, no, no!" What's wrong with asking someone who's been there how well joint custody works? The

crux of the problem is that the evidence a single family brings to the question of joint custody is *anecdotal evidence,* which consists of personal stories about specific incidents and experiences. Anecdotal evidence can be seductive. For example, one study found that psychology majors' choices of future courses to enroll in were influenced more by a couple of students' brief anecdotes than by extensive statistics on many other students' ratings of the courses from the previous term (Borgida & Nisbett, 1977). Anecdotes readily sway people because they are often concrete, vivid, and memorable. Indeed, people tend to be influenced by anecdotal information even when they are explicitly forewarned that the information is *not* representative (Hammill, Wilson, & Nisbett, 1980). Many politicians are keenly aware of the power of anecdotes and frequently rely on a single vivid story rather than solid data to sway voters' views. However, anecdotal evidence is fundamentally flawed (Ruscio, 2006; Stanovich, 2004).

What, exactly, is wrong with anecdotal evidence? Let's use some of the concepts introduced in the main body of the chapter to analyze its shortcomings. First, in the language of research designs, the anecdotal experiences of one family resemble a single *case study.* The story they tell about their experiences with joint custody may be quite interesting, but their experiences—

DILBERT

WHAT CAN I DO TO AVOID GETTING COMPUTER VIRUSES?

GIVE YOUR POWER CORD A SPINAL ADJUSTMENT ONCE A WEEK TO PREVENT DISEASE.

I WAS SKEPTICAL UNTIL HE SAID THERE'S ANECDOTAL EVIDENCE THAT IT WORKS!

scottadams@aol.com www.dilbert.com © 2002 United Feature Syndicate, Inc.

© Scott Adams/Distributed by United Feature Syndicate, Inc.

An abundance of anecdotal reports suggest that there is an association between the full moon and strange, erratic behavior. These reports often sound compelling, but as the text explains, anecdotal evidence is flawed in many ways. When researchers have examined the issue systematically, they have consistently found no association between lunar phases and the incidence of psychiatric emergencies, domestic violence, suicide, and so forth. (Biermann et al., 2005; Chudler, 2007; Dowling, 2005; Kung & Mrazek, 2005; McLay, Daylo, & Hammer, 2006).

dency to give socially approved information about themselves (the *social desirability bias*). When researchers use tests and surveys to gather self-report data, they can take steps to reduce or assess the impact of distortions in their data, but there are no comparable safeguards with anecdotal evidence. Thus, the family that appears in your courtroom may be eager to make a good impression and unknowingly slant their story accordingly.

Anecdotes are often inaccurate and riddled with embellishments. We will see in Chapter 7 that memories of personal experiences are far more malleable and far less reliable than widely assumed (Loftus, 2004; Schacter, 2001). And, although it would not be an issue in this case, in other situations *anecdotal evidence often consists of stories that people have heard about others' experiences*. Hearsay evidence is not accepted in courtrooms for good reason. As stories are passed on from one person to another, they often become increasingly distorted and inaccurate.

good or bad—cannot be used to generalize to other couples. Why not? Because they are only one family, and they may be unusual in some way that affects how well they manage joint custody. To draw general conclusions based on the case study approach, you need a systematic series of case studies, so you can look for threads of consistency. A single family is a sample size of one, which surely is not large enough to derive broad principles that would apply to other families.

Second, anecdotal evidence is similar to *self-report data,* which can be distorted for a variety of reasons, such as people's ten-

Can you think of any other reasons for being wary of anecdotal evidence? After reading the chapter, perhaps you thought about the possibility of *sampling bias*. Do you think that the lawyer will pick a couple at random from all those who have been awarded joint custody? It seems highly unlikely. If she wants you to award joint custody, she will find a couple for whom this arrangement worked very well, while if she wants you to award sole custody to her client, she will find a couple whose inability to make joint custody work had dire consequences for their children. One reason peo-

ple love to work with anecdotal evidence is that it is so readily manipulated; they can usually find an anecdote or two to support their position, whether or not these anecdotes are representative of most people's experiences.

If the testimony of one family cannot be used in making this critical custody decision, what sort of evidence should you be looking for? One goal of effective critical thinking is to make decisions based on solid evidence. This process is called *evidence-based decision making.* In this case, you would need to consider the overall experiences of a large sample of families who have tried joint custody arrangements. In general, across many different families, did the children in joint custody develop well? Was there a disproportionately high rate of emotional problems or other signs of stress for the children or the parents? Was the percentage of families who returned to court at a later date to change their joint custody arrangements higher than for other types of custody arrangements? You can probably think of additional information that you would want to collect regarding the outcomes of various custody arrangements.

In examining research reports, many people recognize the need to evaluate the evidence by looking for the types of flaws described in the main body of the chapter (sampling bias, experimenter bias, and so forth). Curiously, though, many of the same people then fail to apply the same principles of good evidence to their personal decisions in everyday life. The tendency to rely on the anecdotal experiences of a small number of people is sometimes called the *"I have a friend who" syndrome,* because no matter what the topic is, it seems that someone will provide a personal story about a friend as evidence for his or her particular point of view. In short, when you hear people support their assertions with personal stories, a little skepticism is in order.

Table 2.3 Critical Thinking Skills Discussed in This Application

Skill	Description
Recognizing the limitations of anecdotal evidence	The critical thinker is wary of anecdotal evidence, which consists of personal stories used to support one's assertions. Anecdotal evidence tends to be unrepresentative, inaccurate, and unreliable.
Using evidence-based decision making	The critical thinker understands the need to seek sound evidence to guide decisions in everyday life.

REVIEW of Key Learning Goals

2.26 Anecdotal evidence consists of personal stories about specific incidents and experiences. However, anecdotal evidence is usually based on the equivalent of a single case study, which is not an adequate sample, and there are no safeguards to reduce the distortions often found in self-report data. Many anecdotes are inaccurate, second-hand reports of others' experiences.

Key Ideas

Looking for Laws: The Scientific Approach to Behavior

▌ The scientific approach assumes that there are laws of behavior that can be discovered through empirical research. The goals of the science of psychology include (1) the measurement and description of behavior, (2) the understanding and prediction of behavior, and (3) the application of this knowledge to the task of controlling behavior.

▌ By integrating apparently unrelated facts into a coherent whole, theories permit psychologists to make the leap from describing behavior to understanding behavior.

▌ A scientific investigation follows a systematic pattern that includes five steps: (1) formulate a testable hypothesis, (2) select the research method and design the study, (3) collect the data, (4) analyze the data and draw conclusions, and (5) report the findings. The two major advantages of the scientific approach are its clarity in communication and its relative intolerance of error.

Looking for Causes: Experimental Research

▌ Experimental research involves the manipulation of an independent variable to determine its effect on a dependent variable. This research is usually done by comparing experimental and control groups, which must be alike in regard to important extraneous variables.

▌ Experimental designs may vary. For example, sometimes an experimental group serves as its own control group. And many experiments have more than one independent variable or more than one dependent variable. In the Featured Study, Shepperd and McNulty (2002) used the experimental method to demonstrate that emotional reactions to events depend on people's expectations.

▌ The experiment is a powerful research method that permits conclusions about cause-effect relationships between variables. However, the experimental method is in many cases not usable for a specific problem, and many experiments tend to be artificial.

Looking for Links: Descriptive/Correlational Research

▌ Psychologists rely on descriptive/correlational research when they are unable to manipulate the variables they want to study. Key descriptive methods include naturalistic observation, case studies, and surveys.

▌ Naturalistic observation involves careful, prolonged observation of behavior in its natural setting without any intervention. Clinical research depends heavily on case studies, which involve in-depth investigations of individuals. In a survey, researchers interview participants or administer questionnaires to gather information on specific aspects of attitudes or behavior

▌ Descriptive/correlational research methods allow psychologists to explore issues that might not be open to experimental investigation. However, these research methods cannot demonstrate cause-effect relationships.

Looking for Conclusions: Statistics and Research

▌ Psychologists use descriptive statistics, such as measures of central tendency and variability, to organize and summarize their numerical data. The mean, median, and mode are widely used measures of central tendency. Variability is usually measured with the standard deviation.

▌ Correlations may be either positive (when two variables co-vary in the same direction) or negative (when two variables co-vary in the opposite direction). The closer a correlation is to either +1.00 or −1.00, the stronger the association. Higher correlations yield greater predictability. However, a correlation is no assurance of causation.

▌ Hypothesis testing involves deciding whether observed findings support the researcher's hypothesis. Findings are statistically significant only when they are unlikely to be due to chance.

Looking for Flaws: Evaluating Research

▌ Scientists often try to replicate research findings to double-check their validity. Sampling bias occurs when a sample is not representative of the population of interest. Placebo effects occur when subjects' expectations cause them to change their behavior in response to a fake treatment.

▌ Distortions in self-reports are a source of concern whenever questionnaires and personality inventories are used to collect data. Experimenter bias occurs when researchers' expectations and desires distort their observations or unintentionally influence their subjects' behavior.

Looking into the Future: The Internet and Psychological Research

▌ Internet-mediated research has grown in recent years because it offers access to larger and more diverse samples, as well as specialized samples, while reducing costs and saving time. However, Internet-mediated research raises its own concerns about sampling bias and uncontrolled conditions during data collection.

Looking at Ethics: Do the Ends Justify the Means?

▌ Research sometimes raises complex ethical issues. In psychology, the key questions concern the use of deception with human subjects and the use of harmful or painful manipulations with animal subjects. The APA has formulated ethical principles to serve as guidelines for researchers.

Reflecting on the Chapter's Themes

▌ The empirical nature of psychology was elucidated throughout this chapter. Empiricism involves testing hypotheses, basing conclusions on systematic observation, and taking a skeptical approach. The chapter also showed repeatedly that our experience of the world is highly subjective.

PERSONAL APPLICATION Finding and Reading Journal Articles

▌ Journals publish technical and scholarly material. Usually they are written for other professionals in a narrow area of inquiry. Technical journals are mostly available in academic libraries.

▌ PsycINFO is a computerized database that contains brief summaries of published journal articles, books, and chapters in edited books. Works on specific topics and publications by specific authors can be found by using the search mechanisms built into the database.

▌ Journal articles are easier to understand if one is familiar with the standard format. Most articles include six elements: abstract, introduction, method, results, discussion, and references.

CRITICAL THINKING APPLICATION The Perils of Anecdotal Evidence: "I Have a Friend Who . . ."

▌ Anecdotal evidence consists of personal stories about specific incidents and experiences. Anecdotes often influence people because they tend to be concrete, vivid, and memorable.

▌ However, anecdotal evidence is usually based on the equivalent of a single case study, which is not an adequate sample, and there are no safeguards to reduce the distortion often found in self-report data. Many anecdotes are inaccurate, second-hand reports of others' experiences. Effective critical thinking depends on evidence-based decision making.

Key Terms

Anecdotal evidence (p. 74)
Case study (p. 52)
Confounding of variables (p. 47)
Control group (p. 46)
Correlation (p. 56)
Correlation coefficient (p. 56)
Data collection techniques (p. 43)
Dependent variable (p. 46)
Descriptive statistics (p. 55)
Double-blind procedure (p. 64)
Experiment (p. 45)
Experimental group (p. 46)
Experimenter bias (p. 61)
Extraneous variables (p. 47)
Hypothesis (p. 40)
Independent variable (p. 46)
Inferential statistics (p. 58)
Internet-mediated research (p. 64)
Journal (p. 44)
Mean (p. 55)
Median (p. 55)
Mode (p. 55)
Naturalistic observation (p. 51)
Operational definition (p. 42)

Participants (p. 43)
Placebo effects (p. 60)
Population (pp. 59–60)
Random assignment (p. 47)
Reactivity (p. 52)
Replication (p. 59)
Research methods (p. 45)
Response set (p. 61)
Sample (p. 59)
Sampling bias (p. 60)
Social desirability bias (p. 61)
Standard deviation (p. 55)
Statistical significance (pp. 58–59)
Statistics (p. 55)
Subjects (p. 43)
Survey (p. 53)
Theory (p. 41)
Variability (p. 55)
Variables (p. 40)

Key People

Neal Miller (p. 68)
Robert Rosenthal (pp. 61, 64)
Stanley Schachter (pp. 45–47)

1. A tentative prediction about the relationship between two variables is:
   A. a confounding of variables.
   C. a theory.
   B. an operational definition.
   D. a hypothesis.

2. Researchers must describe the actions that will be taken to measure or control each variable in their studies. In other words, they must:
   A. provide operational definitions of their variables.
   B. decide if their studies will be experimental or correlational.
   C. use statistics to summarize their findings.
   D. decide how many subjects should participate in their studies.

3. A researcher found that clients who were randomly assigned to same-sex groups participated more in group therapy sessions than clients who were randomly assigned to coed groups. In this experiment, the independent variable was:
   A. the amount of participation in the group therapy sessions.
   B. whether or not the group was coed.
   C. the clients' attitudes toward group therapy.
   D. how much the clients' mental health improved.

4. A researcher wants to see whether a protein-enriched diet will enhance the maze-running performance of rats. One group of rats are fed the high-protein diet for the duration of the study; the other group continues to receive ordinary rat chow. In this experiment, the diet fed to the two groups of rats is the _____ variable.
   A. correlated
   C. dependent
   B. control
   D. independent

5. In a study of the effect of a new teaching technique on students' achievement test scores, an important extraneous variable would be the students':
   A. hair color.
   C. IQ scores.
   B. athletic skills.
   D. sociability.

6. Whenever you have a cold, you rest in bed, take aspirin, and drink plenty of fluids. You can't determine which remedy is most effective because of which of the following problems?
   A. sampling bias
   C. confounding of variables
   B. distorted self-report data
   D. experimenter bias

7. A psychologist monitors a group of nursery-school children, recording each instance of helping behavior as it occurs. The psychologist is using:
   A. the experimental method.
   B. naturalistic observation.
   C. case studies.
   D. the survey method.

8. Among the advantages of descriptive/correlational research is (are):
   A. it allows investigators to isolate cause and effect.
   B. it permits researchers to study variables that would be impossible to manipulate.
   C. it can demonstrate conclusively that two variables are causally related.
   D. both a and b.

9. Which of the following correlation coefficients would indicate the strongest relationship between two variables?
   A. .58
   C. −.97
   B. .19
   D. −.05

10. When psychologists say that their results are statistically significant, they mean that the results:
    A. have important practical applications.
    B. have important implications for scientific theory.
    C. are unlikely to be due to the fluctuations of chance.
    D. are all of the above.

11. Sampling bias exists when:
    A. the sample is representative of the population.
    B. the sample is not representative of the population.
    C. two variables are confounded.
    D. the effect of the independent variable can't be isolated.

12. The problem of experimenter bias can be avoided by:
    A. not informing participants of the hypothesis of the experiment.
    B. telling the subjects that there are no "right" or "wrong" answers.
    C. using a research strategy in which neither subjects nor experimenter know which participants are in the experimental and control groups.
    D. having the experimenter use only nonverbal signals when communicating with the participants.

13. Critics of deception in research have assumed that deceptive studies are harmful to participants. The empirical data on this issue suggest that:
    A. many deceptive studies do produce significant distress for subjects who were not forewarned about the possibility of deception.
    B. most participants in deceptive studies report that they enjoyed the experience and didn't mind being misled.
    C. deceptive research seriously undermines subjects' trust in others.
    D. both a and c are the case.

14. PsycINFO is:
    A. a new journal that recently replaced *Psychological Abstracts*.
    B. a computerized database containing abstracts of articles, chapters, and books reporting psychological research.
    C. a reference book that explains the format and techniques for writing journal articles.
    D. a computerized database containing information about studies that have not yet been published.

15. Anecdotal evidence:
    A. is often concrete, vivid, and memorable.
    B. tends to influence people.
    C. is fundamentally flawed and unreliable.
    D. is all of the above.

Answers

1 D p. 40	6 C p. 47	11 B pp. 59–60
2 A p. 42	7 B pp. 51–52	12 C p. 64
3 B p. 46	8 B p. 54	13 B p. 66
4 D p. 46	9 C p. 57	14 B p. 71
5 C p. 47	10 C pp. 58–59	15 D pp. 74–75

PsykTrek

To view a demo: www.cengage.com/psychology/psyktrek
To order: www.cengage.com/psychology/weiten
Go to the PsykTrek website or CD-ROM for further study of the concepts in this chapter. Both online and on the CD-ROM, PsykTrek includes dozens of learning modules with videos, animations, and quizzes, as well as simulations of psychological phenomena and a multimedia glossary that includes word pronunciations.

CengageNow

www.cengage.com/tlc

CENGAGENOW™

Go to this site for the link to CengageNOW, your one-stop study shop. Take a Pretest for this chapter, and CengageNOW will generate a personalized Study Plan based on your test results. The Study Plan will identify the topics you need to review and direct you to online resources to help you master those topics. You can then take a Posttest to help you determine the concepts you have mastered and what you still need to work on.

Companion Website

www.cengage.com/psychology/weiten

Go to this site to find online resources directly linked to your book, including a glossary, flash cards, drag-and-drop exercises, quizzes, and more!

3

THE BIOLOGICAL
BASES OF BEHAVIOR

Communication in the Nervous System
Nervous Tissue: The Basic Hardware
The Neural Impulse: Using Energy to Send Information
The Synapse: Where Neurons Meet
Neurotransmitters and Behavior

Organization of the Nervous System
The Peripheral Nervous System
The Central Nervous System

Looking Inside the Brain: Research Methods
Electrical Recordings
Lesioning
Electrical Stimulation of the Brain
Transcranial Magnetic Stimulation
Brain-Imaging Procedures

FEATURED STUDY ▌ Probing the Anatomy of Sexual Arousal

The Brain and Behavior
The Hindbrain
The Midbrain
The Forebrain
The Plasticity of the Brain

Right Brain/Left Brain: Cerebral Laterality
Bisecting the Brain: Split-Brain Research
Hemispheric Specialization in the Intact Brain

The Endocrine System: Another Way to Communicate

Heredity and Behavior: Is It All in the Genes?
Basic Principles of Genetics
Investigating Hereditary Influence: Research Methods
The Interplay of Heredity and Environment

The Evolutionary Bases of Behavior
Darwin's Insights
Subsequent Refinements to Evolutionary Theory
Behaviors as Adaptive Traits

Reflecting on the Chapter's Themes

PERSONAL APPLICATION ▌ Evaluating the Concept of "Two Minds in One"
Cerebral Specialization and Cognitive Processes
Complexities and Qualifications

CRITICAL THINKING APPLICATION ▌ Building Better Brains: The Perils of Extrapolation
The Key Findings on Neural Development
The Tendency to Overextrapolate

Recap

Practice Test

If you have ever visited an aquarium, you may have encountered one of nature's more captivating animals: the octopus. Although this jellylike mass of arms and head appears to be a relatively simple creature, it is capable of a number of interesting behaviors. The octopus has highly developed eyes that enable it to respond to stimuli in the darkness of the ocean. When threatened, it can release an inky cloud to befuddle enemies while it makes good its escape by a kind of rocket propulsion. If that doesn't work, it can camouflage itself by changing color and texture to blend into its surroundings. Furthermore, the animal is surprisingly intelligent. In captivity, an octopus can learn, for example, to twist the lid off a jar with one of its tentacles to get at a treat inside.

Despite its talents, there are many things an octopus cannot do. An octopus cannot study psychology, plan a weekend, dream about its future, or discover the Pythagorean theorem. Yet the biological processes that underlie these uniquely human behaviors are much the same as the biological processes that enable an octopus to escape from a preda-tor or forage for food. Indeed, some of science's most important insights about how the nervous system works came from studies of a relative of the octopus, the squid.

Organisms as diverse as humans and squid share many biological processes. However, the unique behavioral capacities of various organisms depend on the differences in their physiological makeup. You and I have a larger repertoire of behaviors than the octopus in large part because we come equipped with a more complex brain and nervous system. The activity of the human brain is so complex that no computer has ever come close to duplicating it. Your nervous system contains as many cells busily integrating and relaying information as there are stars in our galaxy. Whether you are scratching your nose or composing an essay, the activity of those cells underlies what you do. It is little wonder, then, that many psychologists have dedicated themselves to exploring the biological bases of behavior.

How do mood-altering drugs work? Are the two halves of the brain specialized to perform different functions? What happens inside the body when you feel a strong emotion? Are some mental illnesses the result of chemical imbalances in the brain? To what extent is intelligence determined by biological inheritance? These questions only begin to suggest the countless ways in which biology is fundamental to the study of behavior.

Communication in the Nervous System

Imagine that you are watching a scary movie. As the tension mounts, your palms sweat and your heart beats faster. You begin shoveling popcorn into your mouth, carelessly spilling some in your lap. If someone were to ask you what you are doing at this moment, you would probably say, "Nothing—just watching the movie." Yet some highly complex processes are occurring without your thinking about them. A stimulus (the light from the screen) is striking your eye. Almost instantaneously, your brain is interpreting the light stimulus and signals are flashing to other parts of your body, leading to a flurry of activity. Your sweat glands are releasing perspiration, your heartbeat is quickening, and muscular movements are enabling your hand to find the popcorn and, more or less successfully, lift it to your mouth.

Even in this simple example, you can see that behavior depends on rapid information processing. Information travels immediately from your eye to your brain, from your brain to the muscles of your arm and hand, and from your palms back to your brain. In essence, your nervous system is a complex communication network in which signals are constantly being transmitted, received, and integrated. The nervous system handles information, just as the circulatory system handles blood. In this section, we take a look at how communication occurs in the nervous system.

Nervous Tissue: The Basic Hardware

2a

Your nervous system is living tissue composed of cells. The cells in the nervous system fall into two major categories: *neurons* and *glia*.

Neurons

2a

Neurons are individual cells in the nervous system **that receive, integrate, and transmit information. They are the basic links that permit communica**tion within the nervous system. The vast majority of them communicate only with other neurons. However, a small minority receive signals from outside the nervous system (from sensory organs) or carry messages from the nervous system to the muscles that move the body.

A highly simplified drawing of a "typical" neuron is shown in **Figure 3.1**. Actually, neurons come in such a tremendous variety of types and shapes that no single drawing can adequately represent them. Trying to draw the "typical" neuron is like trying to draw the "typical" tree. In spite of this diversity, the drawing in **Figure 3.1** highlights some common features of neurons.

The *soma*, or cell body, **contains the cell nucleus and much of the chemical machinery common to most cells** (*soma* is Greek for "body"). The rest of the neuron is devoted exclusively to handling information. The neurons in **Figure 3.1** have a number of branched, feelerlike structures called *dendritic trees* (*dendrite* is a Greek word for "tree"). Each individual branch is a *dendrite*. **Dendrites are the parts of a neuron that are specialized to receive information.** Most neurons receive information from many other cells—sometimes thousands of others—and so have extensive dendritic trees.

From the many dendrites, information flows into the cell body and then travels away from the soma along the *axon* (from the Greek for "axle"). The *axon* **is a long, thin fiber that transmits signals away from the soma to other neurons or to muscles or glands.** Axons may be quite long (sometimes several feet), and they may branch off to communicate with a number of other cells.

In humans, many axons are wrapped in cells with a high concentration of a white, fatty substance called *myelin*. The *myelin sheath* **is insulating material that encases some axons and that acts to speed up the transmission of signals that move along axons.** If an axon's myelin sheath deteriorates, its signals may not be transmitted effectively. The loss of muscle control seen with the disease *multiple*

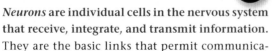

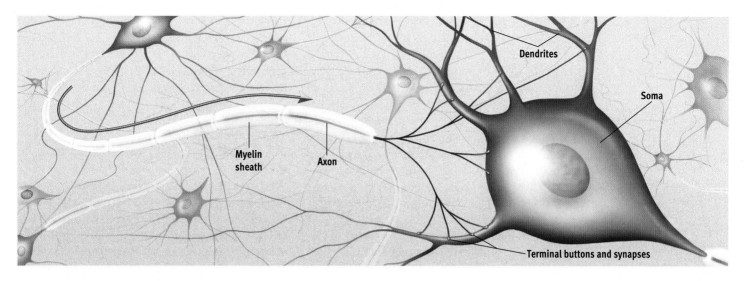

Myelin sheath

Axon

Dendrites

Soma

Terminal buttons and synapses

sclerosis is due to a degeneration of myelin sheaths (Schwartz & Westbrook, 2000).

The axon ends in a cluster of **terminal buttons,** **which are small knobs that secrete chemicals** **called neurotransmitters.** These chemicals serve as messengers that may activate neighboring neurons. The points at which neurons interconnect are called *synapses.* A *synapse* is a junction where information is transmitted from one neuron to another (*synapse* is from the Greek for "junction").

To summarize, information is received at the dendrites, is passed through the soma and along the axon, and is transmitted to the dendrites of other cells at meeting points called synapses. Unfortunately, this nice, simple picture has more exceptions than the U.S. Tax Code. For example, some neurons do not have an axon, while others have multiple axons. Also, although neurons typically synapse on the dendrites of other cells, they may also synapse on a soma or an axon.

Glia

2a

Glia **are cells found throughout the nervous system** **that provide various types of support for neurons.** Glia (literally "glue") tend to be much smaller than neurons, but they outnumber neurons by about 10 to 1, so glial cells appear to account for over 50% of the brain's volume. Among other things, glial cells supply nourishment to neurons, help remove neurons' waste products, and provide insulation around many axons. The myelin sheaths that encase some axons are derived from special types of glial cells. Glia also play a complicated role in orchestrating the development of the nervous system in the human embryo.

These functions, which have been known for many years, made glial cells the unsung heroes of the nervous system. Until recently, it was thought that the "glamorous" work in the nervous system—the transmission and integration of informational signals—was the exclusive province of the neurons. New research, however, suggests that glia may also send and receive chemical signals (Fields, 2004; Fields & Stevens-Graham, 2002). Some types of glia can detect neural impulses and send signals to other glial cells. Surprised by this discovery, neuroscientists are now trying to figure out how this signaling system interfaces with the neural communication system. Some of the early findings and theorizing have proven very interesting. For example, recent research suggests that glial cells may play an important role in memory formation (Bains & Oliet, 2007) and that gradual deterioration of glial tissue might contribute to Alzheimer's disease (Streit, 2005). Other research suggests that glial cells play a crucial role in the experience of chronic pain (Banks & Watkins, 2006) and that impaired neural-glial communication might contribute to psychological disorders, such as schizophrenia (Hashimoto, Shimizu, & Iyo, 2005) and mood disorders (Lee et al., 2007).

Although glia contribute to information processing in the nervous system, the bulk of this crucial work is handled by the neurons. Thus, we need to examine the process of neural activity in more detail.

The Neural Impulse: Using Energy to Send Information

2a

What happens when a neuron is stimulated? What is the nature of the signal—the *neural impulse*—that moves through the neuron? These were the questions that Alan Hodgkin and Andrew Huxley set out

Figure 3.1
Structure of the neuron. Neurons are the communication links of the nervous system. This diagram highlights the key parts of a neuron, including specialized receptor areas (dendrites), the cell body (soma), the axon fiber along which impulses are transmitted, and the terminal buttons, which release chemical messengers that carry signals to other neurons. Neurons vary considerably in size and shape and are usually densely interconnected.

web link 3.1

Neuropsychology Central
This content-rich site, maintained by Professor Jeffrey Browndyke of Louisiana State University, is dedicated to all aspects of human neuropsychology, from the perspectives of the experimental research laboratory as well as the applied clinical setting of the hospital and professional office.

to answer in their groundbreaking experiments with axons removed from squid. Why did they choose to work with squid axons? Because the squid has a pair of "giant" axons that are about a hundred times larger than those in humans (which still makes them only about as thick as a human hair). This large size permitted Hodgkin and Huxley to insert fine wires called *microelectrodes* into the axons. By using the microelectrodes to record the electrical activity in individual neurons, Hodgkin and Huxley unraveled the mystery of the neural impulse.

The Neuron at Rest: A Tiny Battery

Hodgkin and Huxley (1952) learned that the neural impulse is a complex electrochemical reaction. Both inside and outside the neuron are fluids containing electrically charged atoms and molecules called *ions*. Positively charged sodium and potassium ions and negatively charged chloride ions flow back and forth across the cell membrane, but they do not cross at the same rate. The difference in flow rates leads to a slightly higher concentration of negatively charged ions inside the cell. The resulting voltage means that the neuron at rest is a tiny battery, a store of poten-tial energy. The *resting potential* of a neuron is its stable, negative charge when the cell is inactive. As shown in **Figure 3.2(a)**, this charge is about –70 millivolts, roughly one-twentieth of the voltage of a flashlight battery.

The Action Potential

As long as the voltage of a neuron remains constant, the cell is quiet, and no messages are being sent. When the neuron is stimulated, channels in its cell membrane open, briefly allowing positively charged sodium ions to rush in. For an instant, the neuron's charge is less negative, or even positive, creating an action potential (Koester & Siegelbaum, 2000). An *action potential* is a very brief shift in a neuron's electrical charge that travels along an axon. The firing of an action potential is reflected in the volt-age spike shown in **Figure 3.2(b)**. Like a spark travel-ing along a trail of gunpowder, the voltage change races down the axon.

After the firing of an action potential, the chan-nels in the cell membrane that opened to let in so-dium close up. Some time is needed before they are ready to open again, and until that time the neuron cannot fire. The *absolute refractory period* is the minimum length of time after an action potential during which another action potential cannot begin. This "down time" isn't very long, only 1 or 2 milliseconds. It is followed by a brief *relative refrac-tory period*, during which the neuron can fire, but its threshold for firing is elevated, so more intense stim-ulation is required to initiate an action potential.

The All-or-None Law

The neural impulse is an all-or-none proposition, like firing a gun. You can't half-fire a gun. The same is true of the neuron's firing of action potentials. Either the neuron fires or it doesn't, and its action potentials are all the same size (Kandel, 2000). That is, weaker stimuli do not produce smaller action potentials.

Even though the action potential is an all-or-nothing event, neurons *can* convey information about the strength of a stimulus. They do so by varying the *rate* at which they fire action potentials. In general, a stronger stimulus will cause a cell to fire a more rapid volley of neural impulses than a weaker stimulus will.

Various neurons transmit neural impulses at dif-ferent speeds. For example, thicker axons transmit

Figure 3.2

The neural impulse. The electrochemical properties of the neuron allow it to transmit signals. The electric charge of a neuron can be measured with a pair of electrodes connected to an oscil-loscope, as Hodgkin and Huxley showed with a squid axon. Because of its exceptionally thick axons, the squid has frequently been used by scientists studying the neural impulse. (a) At rest, the neu-ron's voltage hovers around –70 millivolts. (b) When a neuron is stimulated, a brief jump occurs in a neuron's voltage, resulting in a spike on the oscilloscope recording of the neuron's electrical activ-ity. This change in voltage, called an action potential, travels along the axon like a spark traveling along a trail of gunpowder.

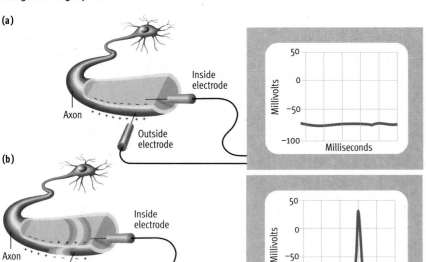

neural impulses more rapidly than thinner ones do. Although neural impulses do not travel as fast as electricity along a wire, they *are* very fast, moving at up to 100 meters per second, which is equivalent to more than 200 miles per hour. The entire, complicated process of neural transmission takes only a few thousandths of a second. In the time it has taken you to read this description of the neural impulse, billions of such impulses have been transmitted in your nervous system!

The Synapse: Where Neurons Meet

2b

In the nervous system, the neural impulse functions as a signal. For that signal to have any meaning for the system as a whole, it must be transmitted from the neuron to other cells. As noted earlier, this transmission takes place at special junctions called *synapses,* which depend on *chemical* messengers.

Sending Signals: Chemicals as Couriers
2b

A "typical" synapse is shown in Figure 3.3. The first thing that you should notice is that the two neurons don't actually touch. They are separated by the *synaptic cleft,* a microscopic gap between the terminal button of one neuron and the cell membrane of another neuron. Signals have to jump this gap to permit neurons to communicate. In this situation,

PSYK TREK

Figure 3.3

The synapse. When a neural impulse reaches an axon's terminal buttons, it triggers the release of chemical messengers called neurotransmitters. The neurotransmitter molecules diffuse across the synaptic cleft and bind to receptor sites on the postsynaptic neuron. A specific neurotransmitter can bind only to receptor sites that its molecular structure will fit into, much like a key must fit a lock.

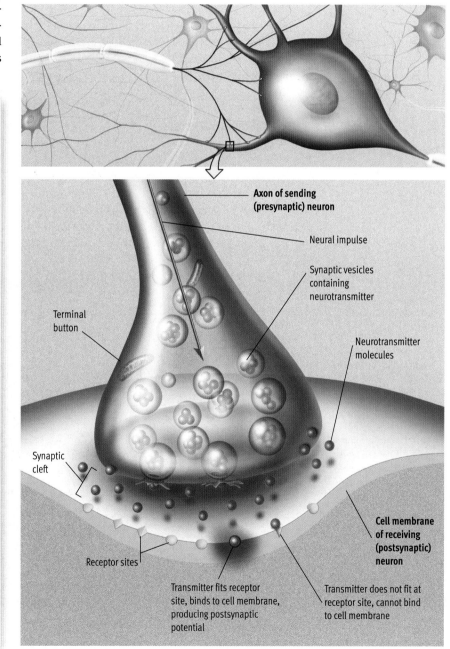

Axon of sending (presynaptic) neuron

Neural impulse

Synaptic vesicles containing neurotransmitter

Terminal button

Neurotransmitter molecules

Synaptic cleft

Receptor sites

Cell membrane of receiving (postsynaptic) neuron

Transmitter fits receptor site, binds to cell membrane, producing postsynaptic potential

Transmitter does not fit at receptor site, cannot bind to cell membrane

---

concept check 3.1

Understanding Nervous System Hardware Using Similes

A useful way to learn about the structures and functions of parts of the nervous system is through similes. Check your understanding of the basic components of the nervous system by matching the simile descriptions below with the correct terms in the following list: (a) glia, (b) neuron, (c) soma, (d) dendrite, (e) axon, (f) myelin, (g) terminal button, (h) synapse. You'll find the answers in Appendix A.

_____ 1. Like a tree. Also, each branch is a telephone wire that carries incoming messages to you.

_____ 2. Like the insulation that covers electrical wires.

_____ 3. Like a silicon chip in a computer that receives and transmits information between input and output devices as well as between other chips.

_____ 4. Like an electrical cable that carries information.

_____ 5. Like the maintenance personnel who keep things clean and in working order so the operations of the enterprise can proceed.

_____ 6. Like the nozzle at the end of a hose, from which water is squirted.

_____ 7. Like a railroad junction, where two trains may meet.

the neuron that sends a signal across the gap is called the *presynaptic neuron,* and the neuron that receives the signal is called the *postsynaptic neuron.*

How do messages travel across the gaps between neurons? The arrival of an action potential at an axon's terminal buttons triggers the release of **neurotransmitters**—chemicals that transmit information from one neuron to another. Within the buttons, most of these chemicals are stored in small sacs, called *synaptic vesicles.* The neurotransmitters are released when a vesicle fuses with the membrane of the presynaptic cell and its contents spill into the synaptic cleft. After their release, neurotransmitters diffuse across the synaptic cleft to the membrane of the receiving cell. There they may bind with special molecules in the postsynaptic cell membrane at various *receptor sites.* These sites are specifically "tuned" to recognize and respond to some neurotransmitters but not to others.

Receiving Signals: Postsynaptic Potentials   2b

When a neurotransmitter and a receptor molecule combine, reactions in the cell membrane cause a *postsynaptic potential (PSP),* a voltage change at a receptor site on a postsynaptic cell membrane. Postsynaptic potentials do *not* follow the all-or-none law as action potentials do. Instead, postsynaptic potentials are *graded.* That is, they vary in size and

they increase or decrease the *probability* of a neural impulse in the receiving cell in proportion to the amount of voltage change.

Two types of messages can be sent from cell to cell: excitatory and inhibitory. An *excitatory PSP* is a positive voltage shift that increases the likelihood that the postsynaptic neuron will fire action potentials. An *inhibitory PSP* is a negative voltage shift that decreases the likelihood that the postsynaptic neuron will fire action potentials. The direction of the voltage shift, and thus the nature of the PSP (excitatory or inhibitory), depends on which receptor sites are activated in the postsynaptic neuron (Kandel, 2000).

The excitatory or inhibitory effects produced at a synapse last only a fraction of a second. Then neurotransmitters drift away from receptor sites or are inactivated by enzymes that metabolize (convert) them into inactive forms. Most are reabsorbed into the presynaptic neuron through *reuptake,* a process in which neurotransmitters are sponged up from the synaptic cleft by the presynaptic membrane. Reuptake allows synapses to recycle their materials. Reuptake and the other key processes in synaptic transmission are summarized in Figure 3.4.

Integrating Signals: Neural Networks   2b

A neuron may receive a symphony of signals from *thousands* of other neurons. The same neuron may

Figure 3.4

Overview of synaptic transmission. The main elements in synaptic transmission are summarized here, superimposed on a blowup of the synapse seen in Figure 3.3. The five key processes involved in communication at synapses are (1) synthesis and storage, (2) release, (3) binding, (4) inactivation or removal, and (5) reuptake of neurotransmitters. As you'll see in this chapter and the remainder of the book, the effects of many phenomena—such as pain, drug use, and some diseases—can be explained in terms of how they alter one or more of these processes (usually at synapses releasing a specific neurotransmitter).

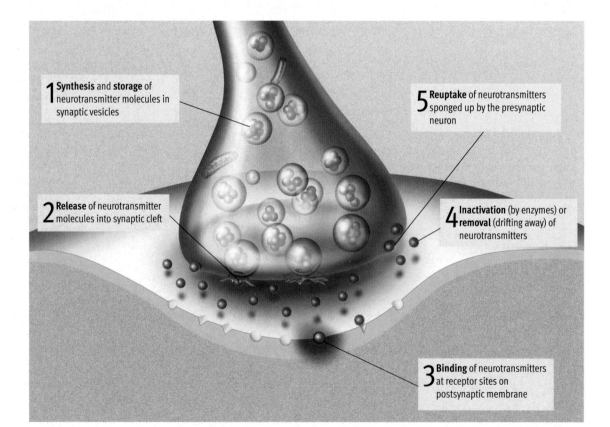

1 **Synthesis** and **storage** of neurotransmitter molecules in synaptic vesicles

2 **Release** of neurotransmitter molecules into synaptic cleft

3 **Binding** of neurotransmitters at receptor sites on postsynaptic membrane

4 **Inactivation** (by enzymes) or **removal** (drifting away) of neurotransmitters

5 **Reuptake** of neurotransmitters sponged up by the presynaptic neuron

pass its messages along to thousands of neurons as well. Thus, a neuron must do a great deal more than simply relay messages it receives. It must *integrate* signals arriving at many synapses before it "decides" whether to fire a neural impulse. If enough excitatory PSPs occur in a neuron, the electrical currents can add up, causing the cell's voltage to reach the threshold at which an action potential will be fired. However, if many inhibitory PSPs also occur, they will tend to cancel the effects of excitatory PSPs. Thus, the state of the neuron is a weighted balance between excitatory and inhibitory influences (Kandel & Siegelbaum, 2000).

As Rita Carter (1998) has pointed out in *Mapping the Mind,* "The firing of a single neuron is not enough to create the twitch of an eyelid in sleep, let alone a conscious impression. . . . Millions of neurons must fire in unison to produce the most trifling thought" (p. 19). Most neurons are interlinked in complex chains, pathways, circuits, and networks. Our perceptions, thoughts, and actions depend on *patterns* of neural activity in elaborate neural networks. These networks consist of interconnected neurons that frequently fire together or sequentially to perform certain functions (Song et al., 2005). The links in these networks are fluid, as new synaptic connections may be made while some old connections whither away (Hua & Smith, 2004).

Ironically, the *elimination of old synapses* appears to play a larger role in the sculpting of neural networks than the *creation of new synapses.* The nervous system normally forms more synapses than needed and then gradually eliminates the less-active synapses. For example, the number of synapses in the human visual cortex peaks at around age one and then declines, as diagrammed in **Figure 3.5** (Huttenlocher, 1994). Thus, *synaptic pruning* is a key process in the formation of the neural networks that are crucial to communication in the nervous system.

Neurotransmitters and Behavior

2b, 4d

As we have seen, the nervous system relies on chemical couriers to communicate information between neurons. These *neurotransmitters* are fundamental to behavior, playing a key role in everything from muscle movements to moods and mental health.

You might guess that the nervous system would require only two neurotransmitters—one for excitatory potentials and one for inhibitory potentials. In reality, there are nine well-established, classic (small-molecule) transmitters, about 40 additional neuropeptide chemicals that function, at least part-

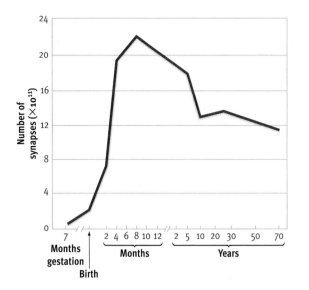

Figure 3.5
Synaptic pruning. This graph summarizes data on the estimated number of synapses in the human visual cortex as a function of age (Huttenlocher, 1994). As you can see, the number of synapses in this area of the brain peaks at around age 1 and then mostly declines over the course of the life span. This decline reflects the process of *synaptic pruning,* which involves the gradual elimination of less active synapses.

SOURCE: Data based on Huttenlocher, P. R. (1994). Synaptogenesis in human cerebral cortex. In G. Dawson & K. W. Fischer (Eds.), *Human behavior and the developing brain.* New York: Guilford Press. Graphic adapted from Kolb, B. & Whishaw, I. Q. (2001). *An introduction to brain and behavior.* New York: Worth Publishers.

time, as neurotransmitters, and a variety of recently recognized "novel" neurotransmitters (Schwartz, 2000; Snyder, 2002). As scientists continue to discover new and increasingly diverse transmitter substances, they are being forced to reevaluate their criteria regarding what qualifies as a neurotransmitter (Snyder & Ferris, 2000).

Specific neurotransmitters work at specific kinds of synapses. You may recall that transmitters deliver their messages by binding to receptor sites on the postsynaptic membrane. However, a transmitter cannot bind to just any site. The binding process operates much like a lock and key, as was shown in **Figure 3.3.** Just as a key has to fit a lock to work, a transmitter has to fit into a receptor site for binding to occur. As a result, specific transmitters can deliver signals at only certain locations on cell membranes.

Why are there many neurotransmitters, each of which works only at certain synapses? This variety and specificity reduces crosstalk between densely packed neurons, making the nervous system's communication more precise. Let's briefly review some of the most interesting findings about how specific neurotransmitters regulate behavior, as summarized in **Table 3.1** on page 87.

Acetylcholine

2b

The discovery that cells communicate by releasing chemicals was first made in connection with the transmitter *acetylcholine* (ACh). ACh has been found throughout the nervous system. It is the only transmitter between motor neurons and voluntary muscles. Every move you make—typing, walking, talking, breathing—depends on ACh released to your muscles by motor neurons (Kandel & Siegelbaum, 2000). ACh also appears to contribute to attention, arousal, and memory. An inadequate supply of ACh in certain areas of the brain is associated with the memory losses seen in Alzheimer's disease (Bourgeois, Seaman, & Servis, 2003). Although ACh depletion does *not* appear to be the crucial causal factor underlying Alzheimer's disease, the drug treatments currently available, which can slow the progress of the disease (slightly), work by amplifying ACh activity (Neugroschl et al., 2005).

The activity of ACh (and other neurotransmitters) may be influenced by other chemicals in the brain. Although synaptic receptor sites are sensitive to specific neurotransmitters, sometimes they can be "fooled" by other chemical substances. For example, if you smoke tobacco, some of your ACh synapses will be stimulated by the nicotine that arrives in your brain. At these synapses, the nicotine acts like ACh itself. It binds to receptor sites for ACh, causing postsynaptic potentials (PSPs). In technical language, nicotine is an ACh agonist. **An *agonist* is a chemical that mimics the action of a neurotransmitter.**

Not all chemicals that fool synaptic receptors are agonists. Some chemicals bind to receptors but fail to produce a PSP (the key slides into the lock, but it doesn't work). In effect, they temporarily *block* the action of the natural transmitter by occupying its receptor sites, rendering them unusable. Thus, they act as antagonists. **An *antagonist* is a chemical that opposes the action of a neurotransmitter.** For example, the drug *curare* is an ACh antagonist. It blocks action at the same ACh synapses that are fooled by nicotine. As a result, muscles are unable to move. Some South American natives put a form of curare on arrow tips. If they wound an animal, the curare blocks the synapses from nerve to muscle, causing paralysis.

Monoamines

2b, 4d

The *monoamines* include three neurotransmitters: dopamine, norepinephrine, and serotonin. Neurons using these transmitters regulate many aspects of everyday behavior. Dopamine (DA), for example, is used by neurons that control voluntary movements. The degeneration of such neurons in a specific area of the brain causes *Parkinsonism,* a disease marked by tremors, muscular rigidity, and reduced control over voluntary movements (DeLong, 2000). The drug that is used to treat Parkinsonism (L-dopa) is converted to dopamine in the brain to partially compensate for diminished dopamine activity.

Although other neurotransmitters are also involved, serotonin-releasing neurons appear to play a prominent role in the regulation of sleep and wakefulness (Jones, 2005) and of eating behavior (Klump & Culbert, 2007; Steiger et al., 2005). Considerable evidence also suggests that neural circuits using serotonin modulate aggressive behavior in animals, and some preliminary evidence relates serotonin activity to aggression and impulsive behavior in humans (Dolan, Anderson, & Deakin, 2001; Douzenis et al., 2004).

Abnormal levels of monoamines in the brain have been related to the development of certain psychological disorders. For example, people who suffer from depressive disorders appear to have lowered levels of activation at norepinephrine (NE) and serotonin synapses. Although other biochemical changes may also contribute to depression, abnormalities at NE and serotonin synapses seem to play a central role, as most antidepressant drugs exert their main effects at these synapses (Delgado & Moreno, 2006). Dysregulation in serotonin circuits has also been implicated as a factor in eating disorders, such as anorexia and bulimia (Kaye et al., 2005), and in obsessive-compulsive disorders (Sullivan & Coplan, 2000).

In a similar fashion, the *dopamine hypothesis* asserts that abnormalities in activity at dopamine synapses play a crucial role in the development of *schizophrenia*. This severe mental illness is marked by irrational thought, hallucinations, poor contact with reality, and deterioration of routine adaptive behavior. Afflicting roughly 1% of the population, schizophrenia

Cosmetic botox treatments temporarily reduce wrinkles by blocking ACh receptors at synapses between motor neurons and voluntary muscles (in the vicinity of the injection). This action basically paralyzes muscles to prevent wrinkles from forming. The cosmetic effects only last about three to five months, however, because the synapse adapts and new ACh receptors are gradually generated.

Muhammed Ali and Michael J. Fox are two well-known victims of Parkinson's disease. Roughly one million Americans suffer from Parkinson's disease, which is caused by a decline in the synthesis of the neurotransmitter dopamine. The reduction in dopamine synthesis occurs because of the deterioration of a structure located in the midbrain.

requires hospitalization more often than any other psychological disorder (see Chapter 14). Studies suggest, albeit with many complications, that overactivity in dopamine circuits constitutes the neurochemical basis for schizophrenia (Javitt & Laruelle, 2006). Why? Primarily because the therapeutic drugs that tame schizophrenic symptoms are known to be DA antagonists that reduce the neurotransmitter's activity (Tamminga & Carlsson, 2003).

Temporary alterations at monoamine synapses also appear to account for the powerful effects of amphetamines and cocaine. These stimulants seem to exert most of their effects by creating a storm of increased activity at dopamine and norepinephrine synapses (King & Ellinwood, 2005; Repetto & Gold, 2005). Some theorists believe that the rewarding effects of most abused drugs depend on increased activity in a particular dopamine pathway (Wise, 2002; see Chapter 5). Furthermore, dysregulation in this dopamine pathway appears to be the chief factor underlying drug craving and addiction (Nestler & Malenka, 2004).

GABA and Glutamate   2b

Another group of transmitters consists of *amino acids.* One of these, *gamma-aminobutyric acid* (GABA) is notable in that it seems to produce only *inhibitory* postsynaptic potentials. Some transmitters, such as ACh and NE, are versatile. They can produce either excitatory or inhibitory PSPs, depending on the synaptic receptors they bind to. However, GABA appears to have inhibitory effects at virtually all synapses where it is present. GABA receptors are widely distributed in the brain and may be present at 40% of all synapses. GABA appears to be responsible for much of the inhibition in the central nervous system. Studies suggest that GABA is involved in the regulation of anxiety in humans and that disturbances in GABA circuits may contribute to some types of anxiety disorders (Skolnick, 2003). GABA circuits also play a central role in the expression of some types of seizures (Shank, Smith-Swintosky, & Twyman, 2000), and they contribute to the modulation of sleep (Siegel, 2004).

web link 3.3

Neurosciences on the Internet

Dr. Neil Busis has gathered what appears to be the largest collection of neuroscience links currently on the web, along with a search engine to help visitors.

Table 3.1 Common Neurotransmitters and Some of Their Relations to Behavior

Neurotransmitter	Characteristics and Relations to Behavior	Disorders Associated with Dysregulation
Acetylcholine (ACh)	Released by motor neurons controlling skeletal muscles Contributes to the regulation of attention, arousal, and memory Some ACh receptors stimulated by nicotine	Alzheimer's disease
Dopamine (DA)	Contributes to control of voluntary movement Cocaine and amphetamines elevate activity at DA synapses Dopamine circuits in medial forebrain bundle characterized as "reward pathway"	Parkinsonism Schizophrenic disorders Addictive disorders
Norepinephrine (NE)	Contributes to modulation of mood and arousal Cocaine and amphetamines elevate activity at NE synapses	Depressive disorders
Serotonin	Involved in regulation of sleep and wakefulness, eating, aggression Prozac and similar antidepressant drugs affect serotonin circuits	Depressive disorders Obsessive-compulsive disorders Eating disorders
GABA	Serves as widely distributed inhibitory transmitter, contributing to regulation of anxiety and sleep/arousal Valium and similar antianxiety drugs work at GABA synapses	Anxiety disorders
Glutamate	Serves as widely distributed excitatory transmitter Involved in learning and memory	Schizophrenia
Endorphins	Resemble opiate drugs in structure and effects Play role in pain relief and response to stress Contribute to regulation of eating behavior	

Candace Pert

"When human beings engage in various activities, it seems that neuro-juices are released that are associated with either pain or pleasure."

Solomon Snyder

"Brain research of the past decade, especially the study of neurotransmitters, has proceeded at a furious pace, achieving progress equal in scope to all the accomplishments of the preceding 50 years—and the pace of discovery continues to accelerate."

Glutamate is another amino acid neurotransmitter that is widely distributed in the brain. Whereas GABA has only inhibitory effects, glutamate always has excitatory effects. Glutamate is best known for its contribution to learning and memory. A subset of glutamate circuits appears to play a key role in a complicated process called *long-term potentiation* (LTP), which involves durable increases in excitability at synapses along a specific neural pathway (Baudry & Lynch, 2001). Many theorists view LTP as one of the basic building blocks of memory formation (see Chapter 7). In recent decades, disturbances in glutamate circuits have been implicated as factors that might contribute to certain features of schizophrenic disorders that are not easily explained by the dopamine hypothesis (Javitt & Laruelle, 2006). More research is needed on this relatively new line of thinking about the neurochemical bases for schizophrenia.

Endorphins
2b, 4d

In 1970, after a horseback-riding accident, Candace Pert, a graduate student in neuroscience, lay in a hospital bed receiving frequent shots of *morphine,* a pain-killing drug derived from the opium plant. This experience left her with a driving curiosity about how morphine works. A few years later, she and Solomon Snyder rocked the scientific world by showing that *morphine exerts its effects by binding to specialized receptors in the brain* (Pert & Snyder, 1973).

This discovery raised a perplexing question: Why would the brain be equipped with receptors for morphine, a powerful, addictive opioid drug not normally found in the body? It occurred to Pert and others that the nervous system must have its own,

endogenous (internally produced) morphinelike substances. Investigators dubbed these as-yet undiscovered substances *endorphins*—**internally produced chemicals that resemble opiates in structure and effects.** A search for the body's natural opiate ensued. In short order, a number of endogenous opioids were identified (Hughes et al., 1975). Subsequent studies revealed that endorphins and their receptors are widely distributed in the human body and that they clearly contribute to the modulation of pain (Apkarian et al., 2005; Basbaum & Jessell, 2000), as we will discuss in Chapter 4. Subsequent research has suggested that the endogenous opioids also contribute to the modulation of eating behavior and the body's response to stress (Adam & Epel, 2007).

In this section we have highlighted just a few of the more interesting connections between neurotransmitters and behavior. These highlights barely begin to convey the rich complexity of biochemical processes in the nervous system. Most aspects of behavior are probably regulated by several types of transmitters. To further complicate matters, researchers are finding fascinating *interactions* between various neurotransmitter systems (Frazer et al., 2003). Although scientists have learned a great deal about neurotransmitters and behavior, much still remains to be discovered.

REVIEW of Key Learning Goals

3.1 Neurons receive, integrate, and transmit signals. Information is received at the dendrites, is passed through the soma and along the axon, and is transmitted to the dendrites of other cells at meeting points called synapses, where neurotransmitters are released from terminal buttons. Glial cells provide various types of support for neurons and may contribute to signal transmission in the nervous system.

3.2 The neural impulse is a brief change in a neuron's electrical charge that moves along an axon. An action potential is an all-or-none event. Neurons convey information about the strength of a stimulus by variations in their rate of firing.

3.3 Action potentials trigger the release of chemicals called neurotransmitters that diffuse across a synapse to communicate with other neurons. Transmitters bind with receptors in the postsynaptic cell membrane, causing excitatory or inhibitory PSPs. Whether the postsynaptic neuron fires a neural impulse depends on the balance of excitatory and inhibitory PSPs. Our thoughts and actions depend on patterns of activity in neural circuits and networks.

3.4 The transmitter ACh plays a key role in muscular movement. Serotonin circuits may contribute to the regulation of sleep, eating, and aggression. Depression is associated with reduced activation at norepinephrine and serotonin synapses. Schizophrenia has been linked to overactivity at dopamine synapses. Cocaine and amphetamines appear to exert their main effects by altering activity at DA and NE synapses.

3.5 GABA is an important amino acid transmitter whose inhibitory effects appear to regulate anxiety and sleep. Glutamate is another amino acid transmitter, best known for its role in memory. Endorphins, which resemble opiates, contribute to pain relief and may modulate eating and stress reactions.

---

concept check 3.2

Linking Brain Chemistry to Behavior

Check your understanding of relations between brain chemistry and behavior by indicating which neurotransmitters have been linked to the phenomena listed below. Choose your answers from the following list: (a) acetylcholine, (b) norepinephrine, (c) dopamine, (d) serotonin, (e) endorphins. Indicate your choice (by letter) in the spaces on the left. You'll find the answers in Appendix A.

_____ 1. A transmitter involved in the regulation of sleep, eating, and aggression.

_____ 2. The two monoamines that have been linked to depression.

_____ 3. Chemicals that resemble opiate drugs in structure and that are involved in pain relief.

_____ 4. A neurotransmitter for which abnormal levels have been implicated in schizophrenia.

_____ 5. The only neurotransmitter between motor neurons and voluntary muscles.

Organization of the Nervous System

Clearly, communication in the nervous system is fundamental to behavior. So far we have looked at how individual cells communicate with one another. In this section, we examine the organization of the nervous system as a whole.

Experts believe that there are roughly *100 billion* neurons in the human brain (Kandel, 2000). Obviously, this is only an *estimate*. If you counted them nonstop at the rate of one per second, you'd be counting for over 3000 years! And, remember, most neurons have synaptic connections to many other neurons, so there may be *100 trillion* synapses in a human brain!

The fact that our neurons and synapses are so abundant as to be uncountable is probably why it is widely believed that "we only use 10% of our brains." This curious tidbit of folk wisdom is utter nonsense (McBurney, 1996). There is no way to quantify the percentage of the brain that is "in use" at any specific time. And think about it, if 90% of the human brain consisted of unused "excess baggage," localized brain damage would not be a problem much of the time. In reality, damage in even very tiny areas of the brain usually has severe, disruptive effects (Zillmer, Spiers, & Culbertson, 2008). The 10% myth appeals to people because it suggests that they have a huge reservoir of untapped potential. Hucksters selling self-improvement programs often disseminate the 10% myth because it makes their claims and promises seem more plausible ("Unleash your potential!").

In any event, the multitudes of neurons in your nervous system have to work together to keep information flowing effectively. To see how the nervous system is organized to accomplish this end, we will divide it into parts. In many instances, the parts will be divided once again. Figure 3.6 presents an organizational chart that shows the relationships of the major parts of the nervous system.

The Peripheral Nervous System

2b, 8c

The first and most important division separates the *central nervous system* (the brain and spinal cord) from the *peripheral nervous system* (see Figure 3.7 on the next page). The *peripheral nervous system* is made up of all those nerves that lie outside the brain and spinal cord. *Nerves* are bundles of neuron fibers (axons) that are routed together in

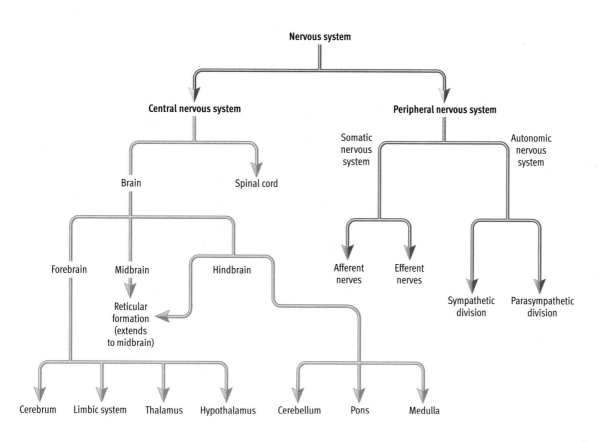

Figure 3.6

Organization of the human nervous system. This overview of the human nervous system shows the relationships of its various parts and systems. The brain is traditionally divided into three regions: the hindbrain, midbrain, and forebrain. The reticular formation runs through both the midbrain and the hindbrain on its way up and down the brainstem. These and other parts of the brain are discussed in detail later in the chapter. The peripheral nervous system is made up of the somatic nervous system, which controls voluntary muscles and sensory receptors, and the autonomic nervous system, which controls the involuntary activities of smooth muscles, blood vessels, and glands.

the peripheral nervous system. This portion of the nervous system is just what it sounds like: the part that extends outside the central nervous system. The peripheral nervous system can be subdivided into the *somatic nervous system* and the *autonomic nervous system.*

The Somatic Nervous System 2a

The *somatic nervous system* is made up of nerves that connect to voluntary skeletal muscles and to sensory receptors. These nerves are the cables that carry information from receptors in the skin, muscles, and joints to the central nervous system (CNS) and that carry commands from the CNS to the muscles. These functions require two kinds of nerve fibers. *Afferent nerve fibers* are axons that carry information inward to the central nervous system from the periphery of the body. *Efferent nerve fibers* are axons that carry information outward from the central nervous system to the periphery of the body. Each body nerve contains many axons of each type. Thus, somatic nerves are "two-way streets" with incoming (afferent) and outgoing (efferent) lanes. The somatic nervous system lets you feel the world and move around in it.

The Autonomic Nervous System 2a, 8c

The *autonomic nervous system (ANS)* is made up of nerves that connect to the heart, blood vessels, smooth muscles, and glands. As its name hints, the autonomic system is a separate (autonomous) system, although it is ultimately governed by the central nervous system. The autonomic nervous system controls automatic, involuntary, visceral functions that people don't normally think about, such as heart rate, digestion, and perspiration (see Figure 3.8).

The autonomic nervous system mediates much of the physiological arousal that occurs when people experience emotions. For example, imagine that you are walking home alone one night when a seedy-looking character falls in behind you and begins to follow you. If you feel threatened, your heart rate and breathing will speed up. Your blood pressure may surge, you may get goosebumps, and your palms may begin to sweat. These difficult-to-control reactions are aspects of autonomic arousal.

Walter Cannon (1932), one of the first psychologists to study this reaction, called it the *fight-or-flight response.* Cannon carefully monitored this response in cats—after confronting them with dogs. He concluded that organisms generally respond to threat by preparing physiologically for attacking (fight) or fleeing from (flight) the enemy. Unfortunately, as you will see in Chapter 13, this fight-or-flight response can backfire if stress leaves a person in a chronic state of autonomic arousal. Prolonged autonomic arousal can eventually contribute to the development of physical diseases (Selye, 1974).

The autonomic nervous system can be subdivided into two branches: the sympathetic division and the parasympathetic division (see Figure 3.8). The *sympathetic division* is the branch of the autonomic nervous system that mobilizes the body's resources for emergencies. It creates the fight-or-flight response. Activation of the sympathetic division slows digestive processes and drains blood from the periphery, lessening bleeding in the case of an injury. Key sympathetic nerves send signals to the adrenal glands, triggering the release of hormones that ready the body for exertion. In contrast, the *parasympathetic division* is the branch of the autonomic nervous system that generally conserves bodily resources. It activates processes that allow the body to save and store energy. For example, actions by parasympathetic nerves slow heart rate, reduce blood pressure, and promote digestion.

The Central Nervous System 2a

The central nervous system is the portion of the nervous system that lies within the skull and spinal column (see Figure 3.7). Thus, the *central nervous system (CNS)* consists of the brain and the spinal cord. It is protected by enclosing sheaths called the *meninges* (hence *meningitis,* the name for the disease in which the meninges become inflamed). In addition, the central nervous system is bathed in its own special nutritive "soup," the cerebrospinal fluid. The *cerebrospinal fluid (CSF)* nourishes the brain and provides a protective cushion for it. The hollow cavities in the brain that are filled with CSF are called *ventricles* (see Figure 3.9).

The Spinal Cord

The *spinal cord* connects the brain to the rest of the body through the peripheral nervous system. Although the spinal cord looks like a cable from which the somatic nerves branch, it is part of the central nervous system. Like the brain, it is enclosed by the meninges and bathed in CSF. In short, the spinal cord is an extension of the brain.

The spinal cord runs from the base of the brain to just below the level of the waist. It houses bundles of axons that carry the brain's commands to peripheral

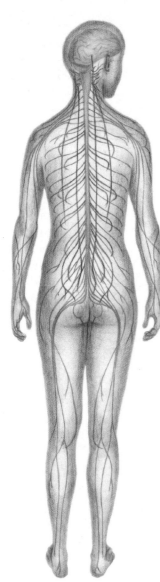

Figure 3.7
The central and peripheral nervous systems. The central nervous system (CNS) consists of the brain and the spinal cord. The peripheral nervous system consists of the remaining nerves that fan out throughout the body. The peripheral nervous system is further divided into the somatic nervous system, which is shown in blue, and the autonomic nervous system, which is shown in green.

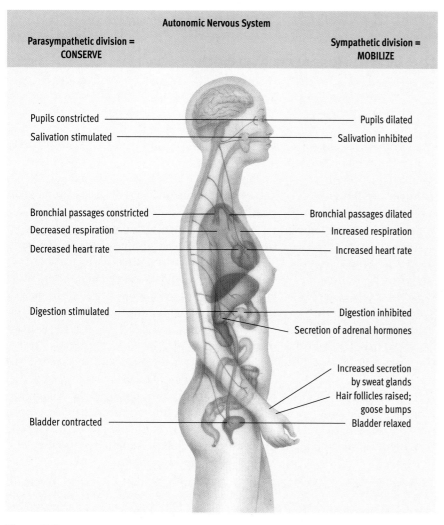

Autonomic Nervous System

Parasympathetic division = CONSERVE		Sympathetic division = MOBILIZE
Pupils constricted		Pupils dilated
Salivation stimulated		Salivation inhibited
Bronchial passages constricted		Bronchial passages dilated
Decreased respiration		Increased respiration
Decreased heart rate		Increased heart rate
Digestion stimulated		Digestion inhibited
		Secretion of adrenal hormones
		Increased secretion by sweat glands
		Hair follicles raised; goose bumps
Bladder contracted		Bladder relaxed

Figure 3.8

The autonomic nervous system (ANS). The ANS is composed of the nerves that connect to the heart, blood vessels, smooth muscles, and glands. The ANS is divided into the sympathetic division, which mobilizes bodily resources in times of need, and the parasympathetic division, which conserves bodily resources. Some of the key functions controlled by each division of the ANS are summarized in the diagram.

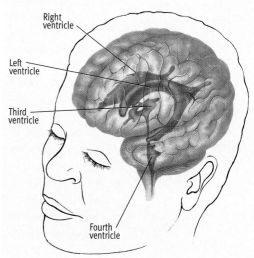

Figure 3.9

The ventricles of the brain. Cerebrospinal fluid (CSF) circulates around the brain and the spinal cord. The hollow cavities in the brain filled with CSF are called ventricles. The four ventricles in the human brain are depicted here.

Right ventricle
Left ventricle
Third ventricle
Fourth ventricle

nerves and that relay sensations from the periphery of the body to the brain. Many forms of paralysis result from spinal cord damage, a fact that underscores the critical role the spinal cord plays in transmitting signals from the brain to the motor neurons that move the body's muscles.

The Brain

The crowning glory of the central nervous system is, of course, the *brain*. Anatomically, the brain is the part of the central nervous system that fills the upper portion of the skull. Although it weighs only about three pounds and could be held in one hand, the brain contains billions of interacting cells that integrate information from inside and outside the body, coordinate the body's actions, and enable human beings to talk, think, remember, plan, create, and dream.

Because of its central importance for behavior, the brain is the subject of the next three sections of the chapter. We begin by looking at the remarkable methods that have enabled researchers to unlock some of the brain's secrets.

REVIEW of Key Learning Goals

3.6 The peripheral nervous system consists of the nerves that lie outside the brain and spinal cord. It can be subdivided into the somatic nervous system, which connects to muscles and sensory receptors, and the autonomic nervous system, which connects to blood vessels, smooth muscles, and glands. The autonomic nervous system mediates the largely automatic arousal that accompanies emotion and is divided into the sympathetic and the parasympathetic divisions.

3.7 The central nervous system consists of the brain and spinal cord. Hollow cavities in the brain called ventricles contain cerebrospinal fluid. The spinal cord connects the brain to the rest of the body through the peripheral nervous system.

Key Learning Goals

3.8 Explain how the EEG, lesioning, and electrical stimulation of the brain are used to investigate brain function.

3.9 Describe transcranial magnetic stimulation and various brain-imaging procedures.

3.10 Describe the Featured Study, which illustrates fMRI research and some limitations of functional imaging technology.

Looking Inside the Brain: Research Methods

Scientists who want to find out how parts of the brain are related to behavior are faced with a formidable task. The geography, or *structure,* of the brain can be mapped out relatively easily by examining and dissecting brains removed from animals or from deceased humans who have donated their bodies to science. Mapping of brain *function,* however, requires a working brain. Thus, special research methods are needed to discover relations between brain activity and behavior.

Investigators who conduct research on the brain or other parts of the nervous system are called *neuroscientists.* Often, brain research involves collaboration by neuroscientists from several disciplines, including anatomy, physiology, biology, pharmacology, neurology, neurosurgery, psychiatry, and psychology. Neuroscientists use many specialized techniques to investigate connections between the brain and behavior. Among the methods they have depended on most heavily are electrical recordings, lesioning, and electrical stimulation. More recently, transcranial magnetic stimulation and such brain-imaging techniques as CT and MRI scans have enhanced neuroscientists' ability to observe brain structure and function.

Electrical Recordings

The electrical activity of the brain can be recorded, much as Hodgkin and Huxley recorded the electrical activity of individual neurons. Recordings of single cells in the brain have proven valuable, but scientists also need ways to record the simultaneous activity of many of the billions of neurons in the brain. Fortunately, in 1929 a German psychiatrist

named Hans Berger invented a machine that could record broad patterns of brain electrical activity. **The *electroencephalograph (EEG)* is a device that monitors the electrical activity of the brain over time by means of recording electrodes attached to the surface of the scalp** (see Figure 3.10). An EEG electrode sums and amplifies electric potentials occurring in many thousands of brain cells.

Usually, six to ten recording electrodes are attached (with paste) at various places on the skull. The resulting EEG recordings are translated into line tracings, commonly called *brain waves.* These brain-wave recordings provide a useful overview of the electrical activity in the brain. Different brain-wave patterns are associated with different states of mental activity (Martin, 1991; Westbrook, 2000), as shown in Figure 3.10. The EEG is often used in the clinical diagnosis of brain damage, epilepsy, and other neurological disorders. In research applications, the EEG can be used to identify patterns of brain activity that occur when participants engage in specific behaviors or experience specific emotions. For example, in one study, researchers used EEG recordings to investigate how meditation affects brain activity (Takahashi et al., 2005). Overall, EEG technology has contributed greatly to our understanding of brain-behavior relations (Eastman, 2004; Rosler, 2005), and as you'll see in Chapter 5, the EEG has been particularly valuable to researchers exploring the neural bases of sleep.

Lesioning

Brain tumors, strokes, head injuries, and other misfortunes often produce brain damage in people.

Figure 3.10

The electroencephalograph (EEG). Recording electrodes attached to the surface of the scalp permit the EEG to record electrical activity in the cortex over time. The EEG provides output in the form of line tracings called brain waves. Brain waves vary in frequency (cycles per second) and amplitude (measured in voltage). Various states of consciousness are associated with different brain waves. Characteristic EEG patterns for alert wakefulness, drowsiness, and deep, dreamless sleep are shown here. The use of the EEG in research is discussed in more detail in Chapter 5.

SOURCE: Brain wave graphic adapted from Hauri, P. (1982). *Current concepts: The sleep disorders.* Kalamazoo, MI: The Upjohn Company. Reprinted by permission.

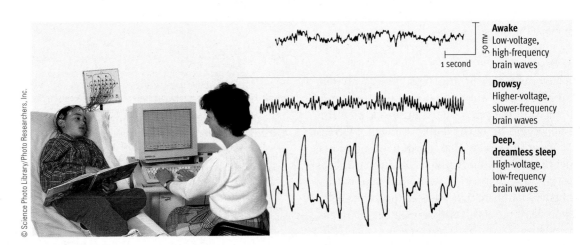

Awake
Low-voltage, high-frequency brain waves

50 µV

1 second

Drowsy
Higher-voltage, slower-frequency brain waves

Deep, dreamless sleep
High-voltage, low-frequency brain waves

© Science Photo Library/Photo Researchers, Inc.

Many major insights about brain-behavior relations have resulted from observations of behavioral changes in people who have suffered damage in specific brain areas (Rorden & Karnath, 2004). However, this type of research has its limitations. Subjects are not plentiful, and it is often difficult to determine the exact location and the severity of subjects' brain damage. Furthermore, variations in the participants' histories create a variety of extraneous variables that make it difficult to isolate cause-and-effect relationships between brain damage and behavior. The modern brain-imaging methods that we will discuss momentarily have improved neuroscientists' ability to pinpoint the location of subjects' brain damage (Rorden, Karnath, & Bonhila, 2007), but this approach remains an inexact science.

To study the relations between brain and behavior more precisely, scientists sometimes observe what happens when specific brain structures in animals are purposely disabled. *Lesioning involves destroying a piece of the brain.* It is typically done by inserting an electrode into a brain structure and passing a high-frequency electric current through it to burn the tissue and disable the structure.

Lesioning requires researchers to get an electrode to a particular place buried deep inside the brain. They do so with a *stereotaxic instrument,* a device used to implant electrodes at precise brain locations. The use of this surgical device is described in Figure 3.11. Of course, appropriate anesthetics are used to minimize pain and discomfort for the animals. The lesioning of brain structures in animals has proven invaluable in neuroscientists' research on brain functioning. For example, major advances in understanding how the brain regulates hunger were achieved using the lesion method.

Electrical Stimulation of the Brain

2c

Electrical stimulation of the brain (ESB) involves sending a weak electric current into a brain structure to stimulate (activate) it. The current is delivered through an electrode, but the current is different from that used in lesioning. This sort of electrical stimulation does not exactly duplicate normal signals in the brain. However, it is usually a close enough approximation to activate the brain structures in which the electrodes are lodged. If areas deep within the brain are to be stimulated, the electrodes are implanted with the same stereotaxic techniques used in lesioning procedures.

Most ESB research is conducted with animals. However, ESB is occasionally used on humans in the

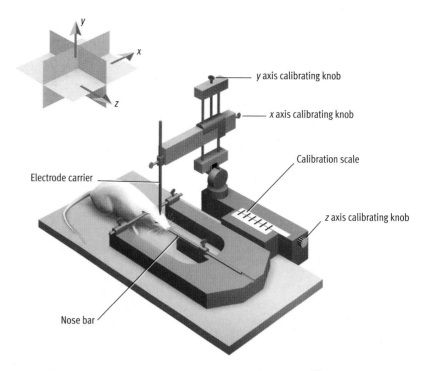

Electrode carrier

Nose bar

y axis calibrating knob

x axis calibrating knob

Calibration scale

z axis calibrating knob

Figure 3.11

An anesthetized rat in a stereotaxic instrument. This rat is undergoing brain surgery. After consulting a detailed map of the rat brain, researchers use the control knobs on the apparatus to position an electrode along the three axes (*x, y,* and *z*) shown in the upper left corner. This precise positioning allows researchers to implant the electrode in an exact location in the rat's brain.

context of brain surgery required for medical purposes (see Moriarty et al., 2001 for an example). After a patient's skull is opened, the surgeons may stimulate areas to map the individual patient's brain (to some extent, each of us is unique), so that they don't slice through critical areas. ESB research has led to advances in the understanding of many aspects of brain-behavior relations (Berman, 1991; Yudofsky, 1999).

Transcranial Magnetic Stimulation

Transcranial magnetic stimulation (TMS) is a new technique that permits scientists to temporarily enhance or depress activity in a specific area of the brain. In TMS, a magnetic coil mounted on a small paddle is held over a specific area of a subject's head (see Figure 3.12 on the next page). The coil creates a magnetic field that penetrates to a depth of 2 centimeters (Sack & Linden, 2003). By varying the timing and duration of the magnetic pulses, a researcher can either increase or decrease the excitability of neurons in the local tissue (George et al., 2007; Nahas et al., 2007). Thus far, researchers have mostly been interested in temporarily deactivating discrete areas of the brain to learn more about their functions. In essence, this technology allows scientists to create "virtual lesions" in human subjects for short periods of time, using a painless, noninvasive method. Moreover, this approach circumvents the numerous uncontrolled variables that plague the study of natural lesions in humans who have experienced brain damage (Rafal, 2001).

web link 3.4

The Visible Human Project

This site from the National Library of Medicine provides a rich collection of online resources related to the highly detailed visual analysis of two human cadavers—a male and female—that has been carried out over the last decade. This site is a good place to explore advanced techniques in the imaging of the human body, including the central nervous system.

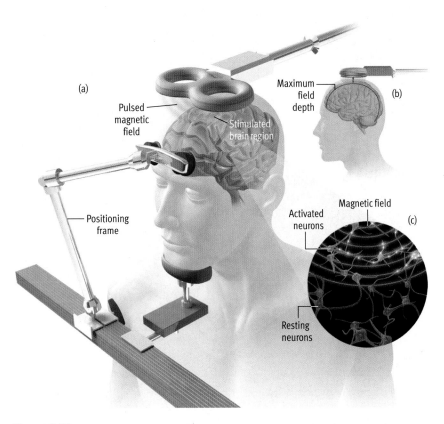

(a)

Pulsed
magnetic
field

Stimulated
brain region

Maximum
field
depth

(b)

Positioning
frame

Activated
neurons

Magnetic field

(c)

Resting
neurons

Figure 3.12

Transcranial magnetic stimulation (TMS). In TMS, magnetic pulses are delivered to a localized area of the brain from a magnet mounted on a small paddle (a). The magnetic field penetrates to a depth of only 2 centimeters (b). This technique can be used to either increase or decrease the excitability of the affected neurons. The inset at bottom right depicts neurons near the surface of the brain being temporarily activated by TMS (c).

Adapted from Bremner, J. D. (2005). *Brain imaging handbook*. New York: W. W. Norton, p. 34. © Bryan Christie Design. Adapted by permission.

In using TMS to investigate brain function, researchers typically suppress activity in a discrete area of the brain and then put subjects to work on a specific type of perceptual or cognitive task to see whether the virtual lesion interferes with performance of the task. For example, this approach has been used to explore whether specific areas of the brain are involved in visual-spatial processing (Sack et al., 2002), memory for objects (Oliveri et al., 2001), and language (Knecht et al., 2002). The chief limitation of TMS is that it cannot be used to study areas deep within the brain. Still, its potential as a research tool is enormous (Hilgetag, 2004), and scientists are studying whether it might have potential as a therapeutic treatment for anxiety disorders (Greenberg, 2007), depression (Mantovani & Liasanby, 2007), and schizophrenia (Hoffman, 2007).

Brain-Imaging Procedures   2c

In recent decades, the invention of new brain-imaging devices has led to spectacular advances in science's ability to look into the brain (Raichle, 2006). The *CT (computerized tomography) scan* is a computer-enhanced X-ray of brain structure. Multiple X-rays are shot from many angles, and the computer combines the readings to create a vivid image of a horizontal slice of the brain (see Figure 3.13). The entire brain can be visualized by assembling a series of images representing successive slices. Of the modern brain-imaging techniques, the CT scan is

Figure 3.13

CT technology. CT scans can be used in research to examine aspects of brain structure. They provide computer-enhanced X-rays of horizontal slices of the brain. (a) The patient's head is positioned in a large cylinder, as shown here. (b) An X-ray beam and X-ray detector rotate around the patient's head, taking multiple X-rays of a horizontal slice of the patient's brain. (c) A computer combines X-rays to create an image of a horizontal slice of the brain. This scan shows a tumor (in red) on the right.

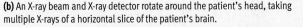

(a) The patient's head is positioned in a large cylinder.

(b) An X-ray beam and X-ray detector rotate around the patient's head, taking multiple X-rays of a horizontal slice of the patient's brain.

(c) A computer combines X-rays to create an image of a horizontal slice of the brain. This scan shows a tumor (in red) on the right.

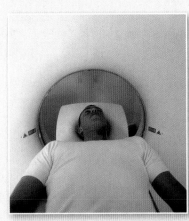

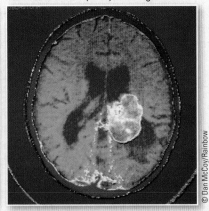

X-ray source

Fan-shaped beam

X-ray detectors

© Henrik Sørensen/Photonica/Getty Images

© Dan McCoy/Rainbow

the least expensive, and it has been widely used in research. For example, many researchers have used CT scans to look for abnormalities in brain structure among people suffering from specific types of mental illness, especially schizophrenia. This research has uncovered an interesting association between schizophrenic disturbance and enlargement of the brain's ventricles (Andreasen, 2001). Scientists are currently trying to determine whether this ventricular enlargement is a cause or a consequence of schizophrenia (see Chapter 14).

In research on how brain and behavior are related, *PET (positron emission tomography) scanning* is proving especially valuable. Whereas CT scans can portray only brain *structure,* PET scans can examine brain *function,* mapping actual *activity* in the brain over time. In PET scans, radioactively tagged chemicals are introduced into the brain. They serve as markers of blood flow or metabolic activity in the brain, which can be monitored with X-rays. Thus, a PET scan can provide a color-coded map indicating which areas of the brain become active when subjects clench their fist, sing, or contemplate the mysteries of the universe (see **Figure 3.14**). In this way, neuroscientists are using PET scans to better pinpoint the brain areas that handle various types of mental activities (Gronholm et al., 2005; Perrin et al., 2005). Because PET scans monitor chemical processes, they can also be used to study the activity of specific neurotransmitters. For example, PET scans have helped researchers determine how amphetamines affect activity in dopamine circuits in the human brain (Oswald et al., 2005).

The *MRI (magnetic resonance imaging) scan* uses magnetic fields, radio waves, and computerized enhancement to map out brain structure. MRI scans provide much better images of brain structure than

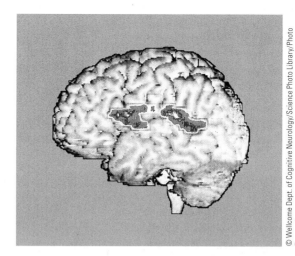

Figure 3.14
PET scans. PET scans are used to map brain activity rather than brain structure. They provide color-coded maps that show areas of high activity in the brain over time. The PET scan shown here pinpointed two areas of high activity (indicated by the red and green colors) when a research participant worked on a verbal short-term memory task.

CT scans (Vythilingam et al., 2005), producing three-dimensional pictures of the brain that have remarkably high resolution (see **Figure 3.15a**). *Functional magnetic resonance imaging (fMRI)* is a new variation on MRI technology that monitors blood flow and oxygen consumption in the brain to identify areas of high activity (Song, Huettel, & McCarthy, 2006). This technology is exciting because, like PET scans, it can map actual *activity* in the brain over time, but with vastly greater precision (see **Figure 3.15b**). For example, using fMRI scans, researchers have identified patterns of brain activity associated with cocaine craving in cocaine addicts (Wexler et al., 2001), the learning of specific motor skills (Poldrack & Willingham, 2006), the recognition and comprehension of verbal stimuli (Wise & Price, 2006), and the contemplation of risky gambles (Tom et al., 2007).

Research with fMRI scans has given neuroscientists a new appreciation of the complexity and interdependence of brain organization. The opportunity to look at ongoing brain function has revealed that

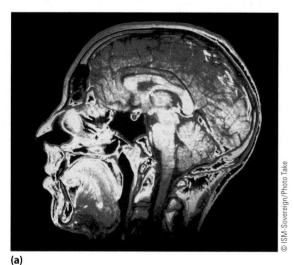

(a)

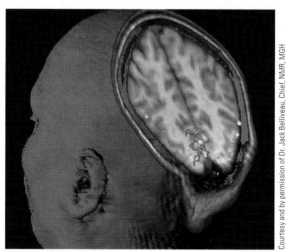

(b)

Figure 3.15
MRI and fMRI scans.
(a) MRI scans can be used to produce remarkably high-resolution pictures of brain structure. A vertical view of a brain from the left side is shown here. (b) Like PET scans, functional MRIs can monitor chemical activity in the brain. This image shows regions of the brain that were activated by the visual stimulus of a flashing light.

even simple, routine mental operations depend on coordinated activation of several or more areas in the brain (Raichle, 2006). Both types of MRI technology have proven extremely valuable in behavioral research in the last decade. Our Featured Study for this chapter is a functional MRI study that investigated whether males' and females' brains may be wired somewhat differently.

FEATURED STUDY

SOURCE: Hamann, S., Herman, R. A., Nolan, C. L., & Wallen, K. (2004). Men and women differ in amygdala response to visual sexual stimuli. *Nature Neuroscience, 7*, 411–416.

Probing the Anatomy of Sexual Arousal

Many interesting differences exist between males and females in typical patterns of sexual behavior, as you will learn in upcoming chapters (see Chapter 10 in particular). One well-known disparity between the sexes is that men tend to be more interested than women in visually depicted sexual stimuli. Many theorists believe that men's fondness for visual sexual stimuli has been hardwired into the male brain by evolutionary forces, but other theorists argue that this gender gap could be a product of learning and socialization. The present study was a pioneering effort to harness fMRI technology to shed some new light on this complicated question. Stephan Hamann and his colleagues at Emory University set out to see if they could find a neuroanatomical basis for gender differences in responsiveness to visual sexual stimuli. Based on existing knowledge of brain function, they hypothesized that males might show greater activation than females in the amygdala and hypothalamus, areas of the brain thought to be implicated in the modulation of emotion and sexual motivation (consult **Figure 3.16**).

Method

Participants. Potential subjects were prescreened to verify that they were heterosexual and that they found visual erotica sexually arousing (people who found such material to be offensive would not make good subjects). The nature of the study was described to them in advance so they could provide informed consent. The final subject pool consisted of 14 females (mean age 25.0 years) and 14 males (mean age 25.9 years).

Materials. Four types of visual stimuli were presented: (1) pictures of heterosexual couples engaged in explicit sexual activity, (2) pictures of attractive, opposite-sex nudes in modeling poses, (3) pictures of clothed males and females in nonsexual interactions, and (4) a plain cross that subjects were asked to fixate on. The sexual stimuli were carefully screened in a pilot study to ensure that female subects would find them arousing (pornographic images are generally geared toward men, which would have biased the results).

Procedure. Stimuli were presented on viewing screens inside special goggles to accommodate the fMRI recording equipment. Subjects were instructed to view each stimulus attentively. A brain scan was completed for each stimulus presentation, and subjects rated the stimuli on various dimensions.

Results

Males and females returned similar ratings of how attractive and how arousing both types of sexual stimuli were. For the most part, the sexual stimuli evoked similar patterns of brain activation in the male and female subjects. Both sexes showed roughly equal activation of areas associated with visual processing, attention, and reward. Against this backdrop of similarities, however, some important disparities were found. As predicted, in response to sexual stimuli males exhibited greater activation than females in the hypothalamus and the right and left amygdala.

Discussion

The authors assert that "the current findings suggest a possible neural basis for the greater role of visual stimuli in human male sexual behavior" (p. 415). In other words, they conclude that their findings provide some preliminary support for the notion that males' and females' brains may be wired somewhat differently. However, they are quick to note that this sex difference could be attributable to either genetics (nature) or experience (nurture).

Comment

This study was featured because it is a particularly interesting example of how new brain-imaging techniques are being used to investigate brain-behavior relations. Science depends on observation. Improvements in scientists' ability to observe the brain have resulted in new opportunities to explore how brain structure and function are related to psychological phenomena. It is an exciting time for the neurosciences, and great advances in our understanding of the brain may be on the horizon.

That said, I hasten to add that brain-imaging techniques suffer from more technical and interpretive problems than is widely appreciated. The stunning images yielded by these incredibly sophisticated devices suggest that their measurements of brain structure and function are more precise, reliable, and unambiguous than they actually are. In reality, brain-imaging procedures, especially those that map brain function, provide only a rough approximation of what is going on inside a subject's brain. PET and fMRI scans do not measure neural activity directly. They only show areas of increased metabolic activity in relation to some baseline condition (in this case, viewing the fixation cross). The areas that "light up" depend to some extent on what was chosen as a baseline for comparison (Uttal, 2001, 2002). The chain of inference underlying this technology is illustrated by the fact that fMRI experts are not sure whether this increased metabolic activity reflects neurons' output (the firing action potentials), incoming signals (postsynaptic potentials), or some combination of neural input and output (Gusnard & Raichle, 2004).

More important, increased metabolic activity in an area does not prove that the area plays a crucial role in a particular psychological function (Sack et al., 2002). The crucial role could be fulfilled by a more efficient neural circuit that draws less blood flow and shows up as minor activity (Rorden & Karnath, 2004). Brain scans also require numerous arcane technical decisions that can influence the results obtained (Culham, 2006; Hardcastle & Stewart, 2002). For example, the thresholds for what will be accepted as various levels of "activation" are somewhat arbitrary and vary from one study to the next, leading to "mushy" measurement. These problems and a number of other complications probably explain why the results of brain scan studies have turned out to be less consistent than scientists originally expected (Cabeza & Nyberg, 2000; Dobbs,

2005). Another problem is that some researchers have been rather cavalier in overinterpreting their data (Dobbs, 2005). For instance, a researcher might collect fMRI data while participants perform a very specific linguistic task (such as thinking of antonyms), then draw broad conclusions about language processing in general, when the results might apply only to the specific task studied.

Caveats aside, brain-imaging procedures have greatly enhanced our ability to look inside the brain. These remarkable techniques are permitting scientists to explore questions that would otherwise be impossible to investigate—such as whether males' and females' brains are wired differently. But the results of such studies should be scrutinized with a critical eye, just like any other research.

REVIEW of Key Learning Goals

3.8 Neuroscientists use a variety of methods to investigate brain-behavior relations. The EEG can record broad patterns of electrical activity in the brain. Different EEG brain waves are associated with different states of consciousness. Lesioning involves destroying a piece of the brain to see the effect on behavior. Another technique is electrical stimulation of areas in the brain in order to activate them.

3.9 Transcranial magnetic stimulation is a new, noninvasive technique that permits scientists to create temporary virtual lesions in human subjects. In recent decades, new brain-

imaging procedures have been developed. CT scans and MRI scans provide images of brain structure. PET scans and fMRI scans can track brain activity.

3.10 The Featured Study used fMRI technology to explore whether males' and females' brains may be wired differently. Brain-imaging techniques have enormous potential as research tools. However, brain scans are not as precise and unambiguous as they appear to be. And increased metabolic activity in an area does not prove that it is crucial to a particular psychological function.

The Brain and Behavior

Now that we have examined selected techniques of brain research, let's look at what researchers have discovered about the functions of various parts of the brain.

The brain can be divided into three major regions: the hindbrain, the midbrain, and the forebrain. The principal structures found in each of these regions are listed in the organizational chart of the nervous system in **Figure 3.6**. You can see where these regions are located in the brain by looking at **Figure 3.16** on the next page. They can be found easily in relation to the *brainstem*. The brainstem looks like its name—it appears to be a stem from which the rest of the brain "flowers," like a head of cauliflower. At its lower end it is contiguous with the spinal cord. At its higher end it lies deep within the brain.

We'll begin at the brain's lower end, where the spinal cord joins the brainstem. As we proceed upward, notice how the functions of brain structures

go from the regulation of basic bodily processes to the control of "higher" mental processes.

The Hindbrain

The *hindbrain* includes the cerebellum and two structures found in the lower part of the brainstem: the medulla and the pons. The *medulla*, which attaches to the spinal cord, controls largely unconscious but vital functions, including circulating blood, breathing, maintaining muscle tone, and regulating reflexes such as sneezing, coughing, and salivating. The *pons* (literally "bridge") includes a bridge of fibers that connects the brainstem with the cerebellum. The pons also contains several clusters of cell bodies involved with sleep and arousal.

The *cerebellum* (literally "little brain") is a relatively large and deeply folded structure located adjacent to

Key Learning Goals

3.11 Review the key functions of the medulla, pons, cerebellum, and midbrain.

3.12 Summarize the key functions of the thalamus and hypothalamus.

3.13 Identify the key structures in the limbic system and some of their functions.

3.14 Locate the four lobes in the cerebral cortex, and state some of their key functions.

3.15 Summarize evidence on the brain's plasticity.

Figure 3.16

Structures and areas in the human brain. (Top left) This photo of a human brain shows many of the structures discussed in this chapter. (Top right) The brain is divided into three major areas: the hindbrain, midbrain, and forebrain. These subdivisions actually make more sense for the brains of other animals than for the human brain. In humans, the forebrain has become so large it makes the other two divisions look trivial. However, the hindbrain and midbrain aren't trivial; they control such vital functions as breathing, waking, and maintaining balance. (Bottom) This cross section of the brain highlights key structures and some of their principal functions. As you read about the functions of a brain structure, such as the corpus callosum, you may find it helpful to visualize it.

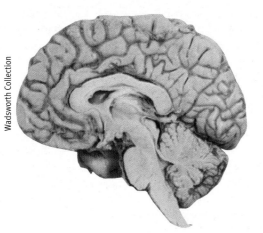

Wadsworth Collection

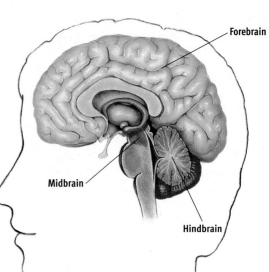

Forebrain

Midbrain

Hindbrain

Cerebrum
Responsible for sensing, thinking, learning, emotion, consciousness, and voluntary movement

Amygdala
Part of limbic system involved in emotion and aggression

Corpus callosum
Bridge of fibers passing information between the two cerebral hemispheres

Thalamus
Relay center for cortex; handles incoming and outgoing signals

Hypothalamus
Responsible for regulating basic biological needs: hunger, thirst, temperature control

Cerebellum
Structure that coordinates fine muscle movement, balance

Pituitary gland
"Master" gland that regulates other endocrine glands

Reticular formation
Group of fibers that carry stimulation related to sleep and arousal through brainstem

Pons
Involved in sleep and arousal

Hippocampus
Part of limbic system involved in learning and memory

Medulla
Responsible for regulating largely unconscious functions such as breathing and circulation

Spinal cord
Responsible for transmitting information between brain and rest of body; handles simple reflexes

the back surface of the brainstem. The cerebellum is critical to the coordination of movement and to the sense of equilibrium, or physical balance (Ghez & Thach, 2000). Although the actual commands for muscular movements come from higher brain centers, the cerebellum plays a key role in organizing the sensory information that guides these movements. It is your cerebellum that allows you to hold your hand out to the side and then smoothly bring your finger to a stop on your nose. This exercise is a useful roadside test for drunken driving because the cerebellum is one of the structures first depressed by alcohol. Damage to the cerebellum disrupts fine motor skills, such as those involved in writing, typing, or playing a musical instrument.

The Midbrain

The *midbrain* is the segment of the brainstem that lies between the hindbrain and the forebrain. The midbrain contains an area that is concerned with integrating sensory processes, such as vision and hearing (Stein, Wallace, & Stanford, 2000). An important system of dopamine-releasing neurons that projects into various higher brain centers originates in the midbrain. Among other things, this dopamine system is involved in the performance of voluntary movements. The decline in dopamine synthesis that causes Parkinsonism is due to degeneration of a structure located in the midbrain (DeLong, 2000).

Running through both the hindbrain and the midbrain is the *reticular formation* (see Figure 3.16). Located at the central core of the brainstem, the reticular formation contributes to the modulation of muscle reflexes, breathing, and pain perception (Saper, 2000). It is best known, however, for its role in the regulation of sleep and arousal. Activity in the ascending fibers of the reticular formation contributes to arousal (Coenen, 1998).

The Forebrain

The *forebrain* is the largest and most complex region of the brain, encompassing a variety of structures, including the thalamus, hypothalamus, limbic system, and cerebrum (consult Figure 3.16 once again). The thalamus, hypothalamus, and limbic system form the core of the forebrain. All three structures are located near the top of the brainstem. Above them is the *cerebrum*—the seat of complex thought. The wrinkled surface of the cerebrum is the *cerebral cortex*—the outer layer of the brain, which looks like a cauliflower.

The Thalamus: A Way Station

The *thalamus* is a structure in the forebrain through which all sensory information (except smell) must pass to get to the cerebral cortex. This way station is made up of clusters of cell bodies, or somas. Each cluster is concerned with relaying sensory information to a particular part of the cortex. However, it would be a mistake to characterize the thalamus as nothing more than a passive relay station. The thalamus also appears to play an active role in integrating information from various senses.

The Hypothalamus: A Regulator of Biological Needs

The *hypothalamus* is a structure found near the base of the forebrain that is involved in the regulation of basic biological needs. The hypothalamus lies beneath the thalamus (*hypo* means "under," making the hypothalamus the area under the thalamus). Although no larger than a kidney bean, the hypothalamus contains various clusters of cells that have many key functions. One such function is to control the autonomic nervous system (Iversen, Iversen, & Saper, 2000). In addition, the hypothalamus serves as a vital link between the brain and the *endocrine system* (a network of hormone-producing glands, discussed later in this chapter).

The hypothalamus plays a major role in the regulation of basic biological drives related to survival, including the so-called "four F's": fighting, fleeing, feeding, and mating. For example, when researchers lesion the lateral areas (the sides) of the hypothalamus, animals lose interest in eating. The animals must be fed intravenously or they starve, even in the presence of abundant food. In contrast, when electrical stimulation (ESB) is used to *activate* the lateral hypothalamus, animals eat constantly and gain weight rapidly (Grossman et al., 1978; Keesey & Powley, 1975). Does this mean that the lateral hypothalamus is the "hunger center" in the brain? Not necessarily. The regulation of hunger turns out to be complex and multifaceted, as you'll see in Chapter 10. Nonetheless, the hypothalamus clearly contributes to the control of hunger and other basic biological processes, including thirst, sexual motivation, and temperature regulation (Kupfermann, Kandel, & Iversen, 2000).

The Limbic System: The Seat of Emotion

The *limbic system* is a loosely connected network of structures located roughly along the border between the cerebral cortex and deeper subcortical areas (hence the term *limbic,* which means "border"). First described by Paul MacLean (1954), the limbic system is *not* a well-defined anatomical system with clear boundaries. Indeed, scientists disagree about which structures it includes (Van Hoesen, Morecraft, & Semendeferi, 1996). Broadly defined, the limbic system includes the hypothalamus, the hippocampus, the amygdala, the olfactory bulb, and the cingulate gyrus. The limbic system is involved in the regulation of emotion, memory, and motivation.

The *hippocampus* and adjacent structures clearly play a role in memory processes, although the exact nature of that role is the subject of debate (Squire, Clark, & Bayley, 2004). Some theorists believe that the hippocampal region is responsible for the *consolidation* of memories for factual information (Dudai, 2004). Consolidation involves the conversion of information into a durable memory code. In any event, many other brain structures contribute to memory processes, so the hippocampus is only one element in a complex system (see Chapter 7).

Similarly, there is ample evidence linking the limbic system to the experience of emotion, but the exact mechanisms of control are not yet well understood. Recent evidence suggests that the *amygdala* may play a central role in the learning of fear responses and the processing of other basic emotional responses (Phelps, 2006; Schafe & LeDoux, 2004). The limbic system is also one of the areas in the

The amygdala appears to play a key role in learned fear reactions in animals—such as this owl—and in humans as well. The amygdala lies at the core of a complex set of neural circuits that process emotion.

brain that appears to be rich in emotion-tinged "pleasure centers." This intriguing possibility first surfaced, quite by chance, in brain stimulation research with rats. James Olds and Peter Milner (1954)

Figure 3.17

Electrical stimulation of the brain (ESB) in the rat. Olds and Milner (1954) were using an apparatus like that depicted here when they discovered self-stimulation centers, or "pleasure centers," in the brain of a rat. In this setup, the rat's lever pressing earns brief electrical stimulation that is sent to a specific spot in the rat's brain where an electrode has been implanted.

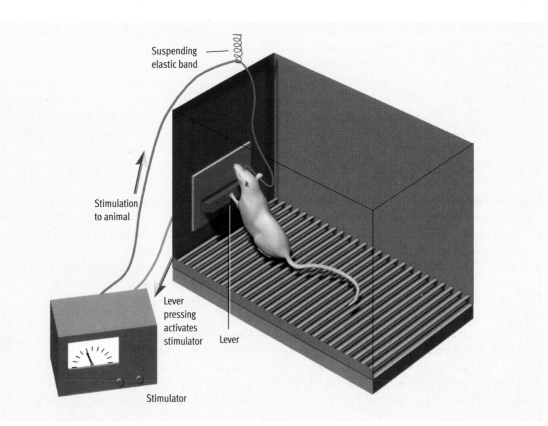

Suspending elastic band

Stimulation to animal

Lever pressing activates stimulator

Lever

Stimulator

discovered that a rat would press a lever repeatedly to send brief bursts of electrical stimulation to a specific spot in its brain where an electrode was accidentally implanted (see Figure 3.17). Much to their surprise, the rat kept coming back for more self-stimulation in this area. Subsequent studies showed that rats and monkeys would press a lever *thousands of times per hour,* until they sometimes collapsed from exhaustion, to stimulate certain brain sites. Although the experimenters obviously couldn't ask the animals about it, they *inferred* that the animals were experiencing some sort of pleasure.

Where are the self-stimulation centers located in the brain? Many of them have been found in the limbic system (Olds & Fobes, 1981). The heaviest concentration appears to be where the *medial forebrain bundle* (a bundle of axons) passes through the hypothalamus. The medial forebrain bundle is rich in dopamine-releasing neurons. The rewarding effects of ESB at self-stimulation sites may be largely mediated by the activation of these dopamine circuits (Nakajima & Patterson, 1997). The rewarding, pleasurable effects of opiate and stimulant drugs (cocaine and amphetamines) also appear to depend on excitation of this dopamine system (Wise, 1999, 2002). Although it seems to play a central role in many forms of reinforcement, this dopamine system is *not* the ultimate biological basis for *all* reward (Koob & Le Moal, 2006). That is not surprising, as the brain is never that simple. Nonetheless, recent evidence suggests that the so-called "pleasure centers" in the brain may not be anatomical centers so much as neural circuits releasing dopamine.

The Cerebrum: The Seat of Complex Thought

The *cerebrum* is the largest and most complex part of the human brain. It includes the brain areas that are responsible for the most complex mental activities, including learning, remembering, thinking, and consciousness itself. **The *cerebral cortex* is the convoluted outer layer of the cerebrum.** The cortex is folded and bent, so that its large surface area—about 1.5 square feet—can be packed into the limited volume of the skull (Hubel & Wiesel, 1979).

The cerebrum is divided into two halves called hemispheres. Hence, **the *cerebral hemispheres* are the right and left halves of the cerebrum** (see Figure 3.18). The hemispheres are separated in the center of the brain by a longitudinal fissure that runs from the front to the back of the brain. This fissure descends to a thick band of fibers called the *corpus callosum* (also shown in Figure 3.18). **The *corpus callosum* is the structure that connects the two cerebral hemispheres.** We'll discuss the functional specialization of the cerebral hemispheres in the next section of this chapter. Each cerebral hemisphere is divided into four parts called *lobes.* To some extent, each of these lobes is dedicated to specific purposes. The location of these lobes can be seen in Figure 3.19 on the next page.

The *occipital lobe,* at the back of the head, includes the cortical area where most visual signals are sent

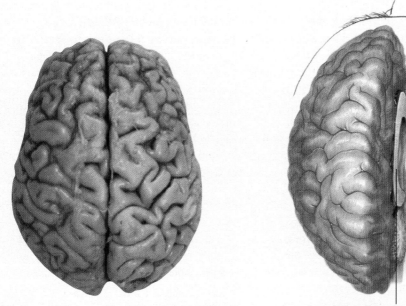

Corpus callosum

Figure 3.18

The cerebral hemispheres and the corpus callosum. (Left) As this photo shows, the longitudinal fissure running down the middle of the brain (viewed from above) separates the left and right halves of the cerebral cortex. **(Right)** In this drawing the cerebral hemispheres have been "pulled apart" to reveal the corpus callosum. This band of fibers is the communication bridge between the right and left halves of the human brain.

Wadsworth collection

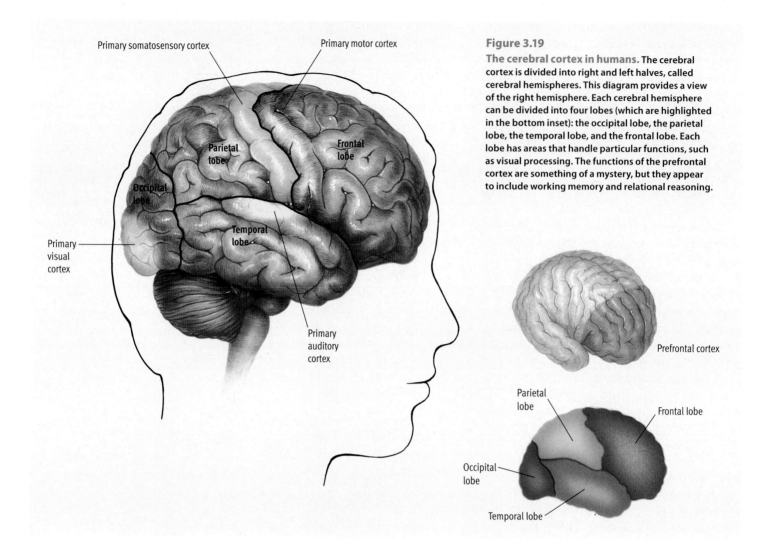

Figure 3.19

The cerebral cortex in humans. The cerebral cortex is divided into right and left halves, called cerebral hemispheres. This diagram provides a view of the right hemisphere. Each cerebral hemisphere can be divided into four lobes (which are highlighted in the bottom inset): the occipital lobe, the parietal lobe, the temporal lobe, and the frontal lobe. Each lobe has areas that handle particular functions, such as visual processing. The functions of the prefrontal cortex are something of a mystery, but they appear to include working memory and relational reasoning.

and visual processing is begun. This area is called the *primary visual cortex*. We will discuss how it is organized in Chapter 4.

The *parietal lobe* is forward of the occipital lobe. It includes the area that registers the sense of touch, called the *primary somatosensory cortex*. Various sections of this area receive signals from different regions of the body. When ESB is delivered in these parietal lobe areas, people report physical sensations—as if someone actually touched them on the arm or cheek, for example. The parietal lobe is also involved in integrating visual input and in monitoring the body's position in space.

The *temporal lobe* (meaning "near the temples") lies below the parietal lobe. Near its top, the temporal lobe contains an area devoted to auditory processing, called the *primary auditory cortex*. As we will see momentarily, damage to an area in the temporal lobe on the left side of the brain can impair the comprehension of speech and language.

Continuing forward, we find the *frontal lobe*, the largest lobe in the human brain. It contains the

principal areas that control the movement of muscles, called the *primary motor cortex*. ESB applied in these areas can cause actual muscle contractions. The amount of motor cortex allocated to the control of a body part depends not on the part's size but on the diversity and precision of its movements. Thus, more of the cortex is given to parts we have fine control over, such as fingers, lips, and the tongue. Less of the cortex is devoted to larger parts that make crude movements, such as the thighs and shoulders (see **Figure 3.20**).

An area just forward of the primary motor cortex is where "mirror neurons" were first discovered accidentally in the mid-1990s. An Italian research team (Gallese et al., 1996) was recording activity in individual neurons as monkeys reached for various objects. A member of the research team happened to reach out and pick up one of the designated objects and much to his amazement the monkey's neuron fired just as it had previously when the monkey picked up the object itself. The researchers went on to find many such neurons in the frontal lobe, which

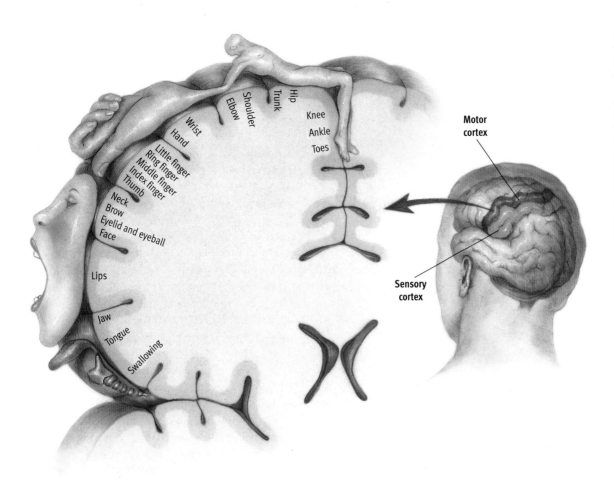

Figure 3.20
The primary motor cortex. This diagram shows the amount of motor cortex devoted to the control of various muscles and limbs. The anatomical features in the drawing are distorted because their size is proportional to the amount of cortex devoted to their control. As you can see, more of the cortex is allocated to controlling muscle groups that must make relatively precise movements.

Motor cortex

Sensory cortex

they christened *mirror neurons*—neurons that are activated by performing an action or by seeing another monkey or person perform the same action.

A search for mirror neurons in humans quickly ensued. In human subjects, it is difficult to record from individual neurons, but researchers have used fMRI scans to demonstrate that humans also have mirror neuron circuits, which have been found in both the frontal and parietal lobes (Rizzolatti & Craighero, 2004; Iacoboni & Dapretto, 2006). It is hard to convey just how much excitement this discovery has generated among neuroscientists. As UCLA researcher Marco Iacoboni puts it, "This completely changes the way we think about how the brain works" (Dobbs, 2006, p. 23). His comment may be a tad melodramatic, but mirror neurons do appear to provide a new model for understanding complex social cognition at a neural level. Recent research has suggested that mirror neurons may play a fundamental role in the acquisition of new motor skills (Buccino & Riggio, 2006); the imitation of others, which is crucial to much of human development (Rizzolatti, 2005); the understanding of others' intentions and the ability to feel empathy for others (Kaplan & Iacoboni, 2006); and the evolution of humans' unique capacity for language

(Fogassi & Ferrari, 2007). Research also suggests that dysfunctions in mirror neuron circuits may underlie the severe social deficits seen in autistic disorders (Dapretto et al., 2006). Thus, the accidental discovery of mirror neurons may have a dramatic impact on brain-behavior research in the years to come.

The portion of the frontal lobe to the front of the motor cortex, which is called the *prefrontal cortex* (see the inset in Figure 3.19), is something of a mystery. This area is disproportionately large in humans, accounting for about one-third of the cerebral cortex (Huey, Krueger, & Grafman, 2006). In light of this fact, it was once assumed to house the highest, most abstract intellectual functions, but this view was eventually dismissed as an oversimplification. Still, recent studies suggest that the prefrontal cortex *does* contribute to an impressive variety of higher-order functions, such as memory for sequences of events (Kesner, 1998); working memory, which is a temporary buffer that processes current information (Sala & Courtney, 2007); reasoning about relations between objects and events (Huettel et al., 2002); and some types of decision making (Walton, Devlin, & Rushworth, 2004). Its contribution to working memory and relational reasoning has led some theorists to suggest that the prefrontal cortex houses some

web link 3.6

The Society for Neuroscience

The largest scientific association devoted solely to the study of the nervous system and its functioning has gathered a host of materials that will introduce visitors to the latest research on a full spectrum of brain-related topics.

sort of "executive control system," which is thought to monitor, organize, integrate, and direct thought processes (Beer, Shimamura, & Knight, 2004; Kane & Engle, 2002; Miller & Cohen, 2001). Much remains to be learned, however, as the prefrontal cortex constitutes a huge chunk of the brain with many sub-areas whose specific functions are still being worked out (Huey et al., 2006).

The Plasticity of the Brain

It was once believed that significant changes in the anatomy and organization of the brain were limited to early periods of development in both humans and animals. However, research has gradually demonstrated that the anatomical structure and functional organization of the brain is more "plastic" or malleable than widely assumed (Kolb, Gibb, & Robinson, 2003; Steven & Blakemore, 2004). This conclusion is based on several lines of research.

First, studies have shown that aspects of experience can sculpt features of brain structure. For example, brain-imaging studies have shown that an area in the somatosensory cortex that receives input from the fingers of the left hand is enlarged in string musicians who constantly use the left hand to finger the strings of their instruments (Elbert et al., 1995). In a similar vein, subjects given three months to practice and master a juggling routine show structural changes in brain areas known to handle the processing of visual and motor tasks (Draganski et al., 2004). Researchers have also found greater dendritic branching and synaptic density in the brains of rats raised in a stimulating, enriched environment, as opposed to a dull, barren environment (Van Praag, Zhao, & Gage, 2004; see the Critical Thinking Application for this chapter).

Second, research has shown that damage to incoming sensory pathways or the destruction of brain tissue can lead to neural reorganization. For example, when scientists amputated the third finger in an owl monkey, the part of its cortex that formerly responded to the third finger gradually became responsive to the second and fourth fingers (Kaas, 2000). And in blind people, areas in the occipital lobe that are normally dedicated to visual processing are "recruited" to help with verbal processing (Amedi et al., 2004). Neural reorganization has also been seen in response to brain damage as healthy neurons attempt to compensate for the loss of nearby neurons (Cao et al., 1994; Lipert et al., 2000).

Third, studies indicate that the adult brain can generate new neurons. Until relatively recently it was believed that *neurogenesis*—**the formation of new neurons**—did not occur in adult humans. It was thought that the brain formed all its neurons by infancy at the latest. This doctrine was so strongly held that initial reports to the contrary were ignored or dismissed (Gross, 2000). However, research eventually demonstrated convincingly that adult humans can form new neurons in the olfactory bulb and the hippocampus (Van Praag et al., 2004). Furthermore, Elizabeth Gould (2004) and her colleagues have found that adult monkeys form *thousands* of new brain cells each day in the dentate gyrus of the hippocampus. These new neurons then migrate to areas in the cortex where they sprout axons and form new synapses with existing neurons, becoming fully integrated into the brain's communication networks. Neuroscientists are now scrambling to figure out the functional significance of neurogenesis. It does not appear to be a simple restorative process that compensates for the normal dying off of brain cells (Lledo, Alonso, & Grubb, 2006). But some theorists believe that neurogenesis might contribute to the natural repair processes that occur after brain damage (Kozorovitskiy & Gould, 2007). Given the important role of the hippocampus in memory, it has been suggested that neurogenesis might contribute to learning, (Leuner, Gould, & Shors, 2006; see Chapter 7).

In sum, research suggests that the brain is not "hard wired" the way a computer is. It appears that the neural wiring of the brain is flexible and constantly evolving. That said, this plasticity is not unlimited. Rehabilitation efforts with people who have suffered severe brain damage clearly demonstrate that there are limits on the extent to which the brain can rewire itself (Zillmer et al., 2008). And the evidence suggests that the brain's plasticity declines with age (Rains, 2002). Younger brains are more malleable than older brains. Still, the neural circuits of the brain show substantial plasticity, which certainly helps organisms adapt to their environments.

REVIEW of Key Learning Goals

3.11 Structures in the hindbrain include the medulla, pons, and cerebellum. The medulla regulates functions such as breathing and circulation, the cerebellum is involved in movement and balance, and the pons contributes to sleep and arousal. The midbrain plays a role in the coordination of sensory processes.

3.12 In the forebrain, the thalamus is a relay station through which all sensory information (except smell) must pass to get to the cortex. The hypothalamus is involved in the regulation of basic biological drives such as hunger and sex. It plays a major role in the regulation of the autonomic nervous system and the endocrine system.

3.13 The limbic system is a network of loosely connected structures located along the border between the cortex and deeper subcortical areas. It includes the hippocampus, which appears to play a role in memory; the amygdala, which is involved in the regulation of emotion; and areas rich in self-stimulation sites.

3.14 The cerebrum is the brain area implicated in the most complex mental activities. The cortex is the cerebrum's convoluted outer layer, which is subdivided into four lobes. These lobes and their primary known functions are the occipital lobe (vision), the parietal lobe (touch), the temporal lobe (hearing), and the frontal lobe (movement of the body). Although the prefrontal cortex is something of a mystery, it is known to be involved in some memory, reasoning, and decision-making functions.

3.15 Studies show that experience can affect brain structure, that brain damage can lead to neural reorganization, and that neurogenesis (formation of new neurons) can occur in some areas of the adult brain. Hence, the structure and function of the brain appears to be more plastic than widely appreciated.

Right Brain/Left Brain: Cerebral Laterality

As we saw in the previous section, the cerebrum—the seat of complex thought—is divided into two separate hemispheres (see **Figure 3.18**). Recent decades have seen an exciting flurry of research on the specialized abilities of the right and left cerebral hemispheres. Some theorists have gone so far as to suggest that we really have two brains in one!

Hints of this hemispheric specialization have been available for many years, from cases in which one side of a person's brain has been damaged. The left hemisphere was implicated in the control of language as early as 1861, by Paul Broca, a French surgeon. Broca was treating a patient who had been unable to speak for 30 years. After the patient died, Broca showed that the probable cause of his speech deficit was a localized lesion on the left side of the frontal lobe. Since then, many similar cases have shown that this area of the brain—known as *Broca's area*—plays an important role in the *production* of speech (see **Figure 3.21**). Another major language center—*Wernicke's area*—was identified in the temporal lobe of the left hemisphere in 1874. Damage in Wernicke's area (see **Figure 3.21**) usually leads to problems with the *comprehension* of language.

Key Learning Goals

3.16 Explain how split-brain research changed our understanding of the brain's hemispheric organization.

3.17 Describe research on cerebral specialization in normal subjects and what this research has revealed.

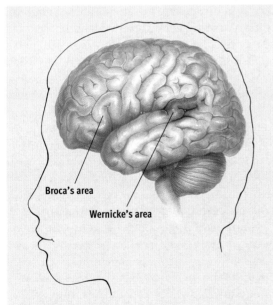

Figure 3.21

Language processing in the brain. This view of the left hemisphere highlights the location of two centers for language processing in the brain: *Broca's area,* **which is involved in speech production, and** *Wernicke's area,* **which is involved in language comprehension.**

Broca's area
Wernicke's area

concept check 3.3

Relating Disorders to the Nervous System

Imagine that you are working as a neuropsychologist at a clinic. You are involved in the diagnosis of the cases described below. You are asked to identify the probable cause(s) of the disorders in terms of nervous system malfunctions. Based on the information in this chapter, indicate the probable location of any brain damage or the probable disturbance of neurotransmitter activity. The answers can be found in the back of the book in Appendix A.

Case 1. Miriam is exhibiting language deficits. In particular, she does not seem to comprehend the meaning of words.

_____

_____

Case 2. Camille displays tremors and muscular rigidity and is diagnosed as having Parkinsonism.

_____

_____

Case 3. Ricardo, a 28-year-old computer executive, has gradually seen his strength and motor coordination deteriorate badly. He is diagnosed as having multiple sclerosis.

_____

_____

Case 4. Wendy is highly irrational, has poor contact with reality, and reports hallucinations. She is given a diagnosis of schizophrenic disorder.

_____

_____

Evidence that the left hemisphere usually processes language led scientists to characterize it as the "dominant" hemisphere. Because thoughts are usually coded in terms of language, the left hemisphere was given the lion's share of credit for handling the "higher" mental processes, such as reasoning, remembering, planning, and problem solving. Meanwhile, the right hemisphere came to be viewed as the "nondominant," or "dumb," hemisphere, lacking any special functions or abilities.

This characterization of the left and right hemispheres as major and minor partners in the brain's work began to change in the 1960s. It all started with landmark research by Roger Sperry, Michael

Gazzaniga, and their colleagues who studied "split-brain" patients: individuals whose cerebral hemispheres had been surgically disconnected (Gazzaniga, 1970; Gazzaniga, Bogen, & Sperry, 1965; Levy, Trevarthen, & Sperry, 1972; Sperry, 1982). In 1981 Sperry received a Nobel prize in physiology/medicine for this work.

Bisecting the Brain: Split-Brain Research

2f, SIM2

In *split-brain surgery* the bundle of fibers that connects the cerebral hemispheres (the corpus callosum) is cut to reduce the severity of epileptic seizures. It is a radical procedure that is chosen only as a last resort in exceptional cases that have not responded to other forms of treatment (Wolford, Miller, & Gazzaniga, 2004). But the surgery provides scientists with an unusual opportunity to study people who have had their brain literally split in two.

To appreciate the logic of split-brain research, you need to understand how sensory and motor information is routed to and from the two hemispheres. *Each hemisphere's primary connections are to the opposite side of the body.* Thus, the left hemisphere controls, and communicates with, the right hand, right arm, right leg, right eyebrow, and so on. In contrast, the right hemisphere controls, and communicates with, the left side of the body.

Vision and hearing are more complex. Both eyes deliver information to both hemispheres, but there still is a separation of input. Stimuli in the right half of the *visual field* are registered by receptors on the left side of each eye, which send signals to the left hemisphere. Stimuli in the left half of the visual field are transmitted by both eyes to the right hemisphere (see Figure 3.22). Auditory inputs to each ear also go to both hemispheres. However, connections to the opposite hemisphere are stronger or more immediate. That is, sounds presented exclusively to the right ear (through headphones) are registered in the left hemisphere first, while sounds presented to the left ear are registered more quickly in the right hemisphere.

For the most part, people don't notice this asymmetric, "crisscrossed" organization because the two hemispheres are in close communication with each other. Information received by one hemisphere is readily shared with the other via the corpus callosum. However, when the two hemispheres are surgically disconnected, the functional specialization of the brain becomes apparent.

In their classic study of split-brain patients, Gazzaniga, Bogen, and Sperry (1965) presented visual stimuli such as pictures, symbols, and words in a

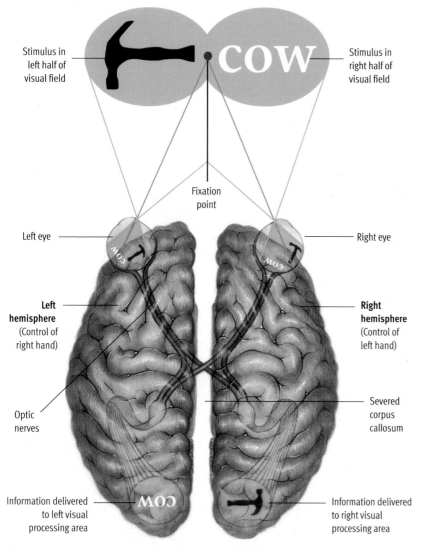

Figure 3.22

Visual input in the split brain. If a participant stares at a fixation point, the point divides the subject's visual field into right and left halves. Input from the right visual field (the word COW in this example) strikes the left side of each eye and is transmitted to the left hemisphere. Input from the left visual field (a picture of a hammer in this example) strikes the right side of each eye and is transmitted to the right hemisphere. Normally, the hemispheres share the information from the two halves of the visual field, but in split-brain patients, the corpus callosum is severed, and the two hemispheres cannot communicate. Hence, the experimenter can present a visual stimulus to just one hemisphere at a time.

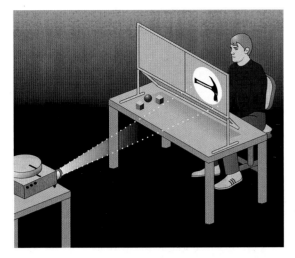

Figure 3.23

Experimental apparatus in split-brain research. On the left is a special slide projector that can present images very briefly, before the subject's eyes can move and thus change the visual field. Images are projected on one side of the screen to present stimuli to just one hemisphere. The portion of the apparatus beneath the screen is constructed to prevent participants from seeing objects that they may be asked to handle with their right or left hand, another procedure that can be used to send information to just one hemisphere.

single visual field (the left or the right), so that the stimuli would be sent to only one hemisphere. The stimuli were projected onto a screen in front of the participants, who stared at a fixation point (a spot) in the center of the screen (see Figure 3.23). The images were flashed to the right or the left of the fixation point for only a split second. Thus, the subjects did not have a chance to move their eyes, and the stimuli were only glimpsed in one visual field.

When pictures were flashed in the right visual field and thus sent to the left hemisphere, the split-brain subjects were able to name and describe the objects depicted (such as a cup or spoon). However, the subjects were *not* able to name and describe the same objects when they were flashed in the left vi-

sual field and sent to the right hemisphere. In a similar fashion, an object placed out of view in the right hand (communicating with the left hemisphere) could be named. However, the same object placed in the left hand (right hemisphere) could not be. These findings supported the notion that language is housed in the left hemisphere.

Although the split-brain subjects' right hemisphere was not able to speak up for itself, further tests revealed that it *was* processing the information presented. If subjects were given an opportunity to *point out a picture* of an object they had held in their left hand, they were able to do so. They were also able to point out pictures that had been flashed to the left visual field. Furthermore, the right hemisphere (left hand) turned out to be *superior* to the left hemisphere (right hand) in assembling little puzzles and copying drawings, even though the subjects were right-handed. These findings provided the first compelling demonstration that the right hemisphere has its own special talents. Subsequent studies of additional split-brain patients showed the right hemisphere to be better than the left on a variety of visual-spatial tasks, including discriminating colors, arranging blocks, and recognizing faces.

Hemispheric Specialization in the Intact Brain   2f, SIM2

The problem with the split-brain operation, of course, is that it creates an abnormal situation. The vast majority of us remain "neurologically intact." Moreover, the surgery is done only with people who suffer from prolonged, severe cases of epilepsy. These people may have had somewhat atypical brain organization even before the operation. Thus, theorists couldn't help wondering whether it was safe to generalize broadly from the split-brain studies. For this reason, researchers developed methods that allowed them to study cerebral specialization in the intact brain.

Roger Sperry

"Both the left and right hemispheres of the brain have been found to have their own specialized forms of intellect."

SPLIT-BRAIN

Michael Gazzaniga

"Nothing can possibly replace a singular memory of mine: that of the moment when I discovered that case W.J. could no longer verbally describe (from his left hemisphere) stimuli presented to his freshly disconnected right hemisphere."

One method involves looking at *perceptual asymmetries—left-right imbalances between the cerebral hemispheres in the speed of visual or auditory processing.* As just discussed, it is possible to present visual stimuli to just one visual field at a time. In normal individuals, the input sent to one hemisphere is quickly shared with the other. However, subtle differences in the "abilities" of the two hemispheres can be detected by precisely measuring how long it takes participants to recognize different types of stimuli.

For instance, when *verbal* stimuli are presented to the right visual field (and thus sent to the *left hemisphere* first), they are identified more quickly and more accurately than when they are presented to the left visual field (and sent to the right hemisphere first). The faster reactions in the left hemisphere presumably occur because it can recognize verbal stimuli on its own, while the right hemisphere has to take extra time to "consult" the left hemisphere. In contrast, the *right hemisphere* is faster than the left on *visual-spatial* tasks, such as locating a dot or recognizing a face (Bradshaw, 1989; Bryden, 1982).

Researchers have also used a variety of other approaches to explore hemispheric specialization in normal people. For the most part, their findings have converged nicely with the results of the split-brain studies (Reuter-Lorenz & Miller, 1998). Overall, the findings suggest that the two hemispheres are specialized, with each handling certain types of cognitive tasks better than the other (Corballis, 2003; Gazzaniga, 2005; Springer & Deutsch, 1998). *The left hemisphere usually is better on tasks involving verbal processing, such as language, speech, reading, and writing. The right hemisphere exhibits superiority on many tasks involving nonverbal processing, such as most visual-spatial and musical tasks, and tasks involving the perception of others' emotions.*

In recent years, research on hemispheric specialization has been increasingly conducted with modern brain-imaging technology, especially fMRI scans (Friston, 2003; Pizzagalli, Shackman, & Davidson, 2003). These scans can provide a more direct and precise view of hemispheric activation on various types of tasks than the study of perceptual asymmetries. For the most part, this new approach has painted a picture that is consistent with previous findings, but more nuanced and detailed. Using fMRI scans, investigators can identify the specific areas and neural circuits within the right or left hemisphere that appear to handle various cognitive tasks (Gazzaniga, 2005). They can also use brain-imaging techniques to gain insights into how the two hemispheres communicate and collaborate on more complicated tasks (Banich, 2003). This research promises to enhance our understanding of cerebral lateralization.

Hemispheric specialization is a fascinating area of research that has broad implications, which we will discuss further in the Personal Application. For now, however, let's leave the brain and turn our attention to the endocrine system.

REVIEW of Key Learning Goals

3.16 The cerebrum is divided into right and left hemispheres connected by the corpus callosum. Evidence that the left cerebral hemisphere usually processes language led scientists to view it as the dominant hemisphere. However, studies of split-brain patients revealed that the right and left halves of the brain each have unique talents, with the right hemisphere being specialized to handle visual-spatial functions.

3.17 Studies of perceptual asymmetries in normal subjects also showed that the left hemisphere is better equipped to handle verbal processing, whereas the right hemisphere is more adept at nonverbal processing, including visual-spatial tasks, musical tasks, and the perception of emotion. In recent years, research on hemispheric specialization has been increasingly conducted with modern brain-imaging technology, especially fMRI scans.

The Endocrine System: Another Way to Communicate

Key Learning Goals

3.18 Describe the key elements of the endocrine system.

3.19 Discuss some ways in which hormones regulate behavior.

The major way the brain communicates with the rest of the body is through the nervous system. However, the body has a second communication system that is also important to behavior. **The *endocrine system* consists of glands that secrete chemicals into the bloodstream that help control bodily functioning.** The messengers in this communication network are called hormones. **Hormones are the chemical substances released by the endocrine glands.** In a way, hormones are like neurotransmitters in the ner-

vous system. They are stored for subsequent release as chemical messengers, and once released, they diffuse through the bloodstream and bind to special receptors on target cells. In fact, some chemical substances do double duty, functioning as hormones when they're released in the endocrine system and as neurotransmitters in the nervous system (norepinephrine, for example). However, there are some important differences between hormones and neurotransmitters. Neural messages generally are transmitted short distances with lightning speed (measured in milliseconds) along very specific pathways, whereas hormonal messages often travel to distant cells at a much slower speed (measured in seconds and minutes) and tend to be less specific, as they can act on many target cells throughout the body.

The major endocrine glands are shown in Figure 3.24. Some hormones are released in response to changing conditions in the body and act to regulate those conditions. For example, hormones released by the stomach and intestines help control digestion. Kidney hormones play a part in regulating blood pressure. And pancreatic hormone (insulin) is essential for cells to use sugar from the blood. Hormone release tends to be *pulsatile*. That is, hormones tend to be released several times per day in brief bursts or pulses that last only a few minutes. The levels of many hormones increase and decrease in a rhythmic pattern throughout the day.

Much of the endocrine system is controlled by the nervous system through the *hypothalamus*. This structure at the base of the forebrain has intimate connections with the pea-sized *pituitary gland*. The **pituitary gland releases a great variety of hormones that fan out around the body, stimulating actions in the other endocrine glands.** In this sense, the pituitary is the "master gland" of the endocrine system, although the hypothalamus is the real power behind the throne.

The intermeshing of the nervous system and the endocrine system can be seen in the fight-or-flight response described earlier. In times of stress, the hypothalamus sends signals along two pathways—through the autonomic nervous system and through the pituitary gland—to the adrenal glands (Clow, 2001). In response, the adrenal glands secrete so-called "stress hormones" that radiate throughout the body, preparing it to cope with an emergency. Unfortunately, chronic elevations of stress hormones can suppress people's immune response and make them more vulnerable to various diseases (Segerstrom & Miller, 2004), as we will discuss in Chapter 13. Moreover, recent research suggests that stress hormones may also suppress the recently discovered process of *neurogenesis* in the hippocampus, which may have important ramifications (McEwen, 2004).

A topic of current research interest is whether circulating levels of certain hormones are related to individual differences in behavior. In particular, researchers have been exploring whether variations in testosterone levels are predictive of variations in aggression, sexual motivation, and cognitive functioning. **Testosterone is a male sex hormone produced by the testes; women secrete smaller amounts of testosterone from the adrenal cortex and ovary.**

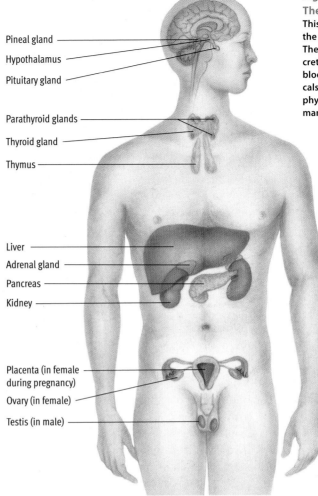

Figure 3.24
The endocrine system. This graphic depicts most of the major endocrine glands. The endocrine glands secrete hormones into the bloodstream. These chemicals regulate a variety of physical functions and affect many aspects of behavior.

Pineal gland
Hypothalamus
Pituitary gland
Parathyroid glands
Thyroid gland
Thymus
Liver
Adrenal gland
Pancreas
Kidney
Placenta (in female during pregnancy)
Ovary (in female)
Testis (in male)

Researchers *have* uncovered links between testosterone levels and aspects of behavior, but the findings have been complicated. Consider, for example, the research on testosterone and aggression. Overall, studies tend to find a positive correlation between testosterone levels and aggression in both males and females, but the association is weak, and there is far more evidence on males (Archer, 2005).

Moreover, one cannot conclude that higher testosterone *causes* higher aggressiveness, because studies show that situational contexts that call for aggressiveness, such as sports competitions, can temporarily elevate testosterone (Filaire et al., 2001; Gonzalez-Bono et al., 1999). So, we cannot rule out the possibility that aggressive behavior leads to increased testosterone levels. Further complicating matters, some theorists believe that testosterone is mainly linked to dominance needs rather than to aggression, but efforts to dominate others often lead to aggressive behavior as a by-product (Schultheiss et al., 2005). Different sorts of complexities are seen in research on testosterone and cognitive functioning. Among samples of young adults with normal testosterone levels, researchers

© Kevin Mazur/WireImage/Getty Images

Professional wrestler Chris Benoit killed his wife, his 7-year-old son, and himself in 2007, prompting rumors that steroid abuse caused an episode of "roid rage." Severe steroid abuse can lead to extreme elevations in testosterone levels that are associated with incidents of uncontrollable rage. However, subsequent investigation indicated that "roid rage" probably was not the cause of the Benoit tragedy.

nal sexual organs in the developing fetus (Gorski, 2000). Thus, your sexual identity as a male or female was shaped during prenatal development by the actions of hormones. At puberty, increased levels of sexual hormones are responsible for the emergence of secondary sexual characteristics, such as male facial hair and female breasts (Susman, Dorn, & Schiefelbein, 2003). The actions of other hormones are responsible for the spurt in physical growth that occurs around puberty (see Chapter 11).

These developmental effects of hormones illustrate how genetic programming has a hand in behavior. Obviously, the hormonal actions that shaped your sex were determined by your genetic makeup. Similarly, the hormonal changes in early adolescence that launched your growth spurt and aroused your interest in sexuality were preprogrammed over a decade earlier by your genetic inheritance, which brings us to the role of heredity in shaping behavior.

generally do not find any reliable correlations between testosterone and cognitive abilities (Janowsky, 2006). However, among samples of older adults, higher testosterone levels are predictive of higher scores on measures of memory, information processing speed, and spatial abilities, although most of the data are based on male samples (Cherrier et al., 2007; Muller et al., 2005). The limited information available linking hormone levels to behavior is thought provoking, but a great deal of additional research will be needed to sort out all the complexities.

Vastly more is known about how hormones help to modulate human physiological development. For example, among the more interesting hormones released by the pituitary are the *gonadotropins,* which affect the *gonads,* or sexual glands. Prior to birth, these hormones direct the formation of the exter-

Heredity and Behavior: Is It All in the Genes?

Key Learning Goals

3.20 Describe the structures and processes involved in genetic transmission.

3.21 Distinguish between genotype and phenotype and explain polygenic inheritance.

3.22 Compare the special methods used to investigate the influence of heredity on behavior.

As you have learned throughout this chapter, your biological makeup is intimately related to your behavior. That is why your genetic inheritance, which shapes your biological makeup, may have much to do with your behavior. Most people realize that physical characteristics such as height, hair color, blood type, and eye color are largely shaped by heredity. But what about psychological characteristics, such as intelligence, moodiness, impulsiveness, and shyness? To what extent are people's behavioral qualities molded by their genes? These questions are the central focus of *behavioral genetics*—an interdisciplinary field that studies the influence of genetic factors on behavioral traits.

As we saw in Chapter 1, questions about the relative importance of heredity versus environment are very old ones in psychology. However, research in behavioral genetics has grown by leaps and bounds since the 1970s, and this research has shed new light on the age-old nature versus nurture debate. Ironically, although behavioral geneticists have mainly sought to demonstrate the influence of heredity on behavior, their recent work has also highlighted the importance of the environment, as we shall see in this section.

Basic Principles of Genetics

Every cell in your body contains enduring messages from your mother and father. These messages are found on the *chromosomes* that lie within the nucleus of each cell.

Chromosomes and Genes

Chromosomes are strands of DNA (deoxyribonucleic acid) molecules that carry genetic information (see Figure 3.25). Every cell in humans, except the sex cells (sperm and eggs), contains 46 chromosomes. These chromosomes operate in 23 pairs, with one chromosome of each pair being contributed by each parent. Parents make this contribution when fertilization creates a *zygote,* a single cell formed by the union of a sperm and an egg. The sex cells that form a zygote each have 23 chromosomes; together they contribute the 46 chromosomes that appear in the zygote and in all the body cells that develop from it. Each chromosome in turn contains thousands of biochemical messengers called genes. *Genes* are DNA segments that serve as the key functional units in hereditary transmission.

If all offspring are formed by a union of the parents' sex cells, why aren't family members identical clones? The reason is that a single pair of parents can produce an extraordinary variety of combinations of chromosomes. When sex cells form in each parent, it is a matter of chance as to which member of each chromosome pair ends up in the sperm or egg. Each parent's 23 chromosome pairs can be scrambled in over 8 million (2^{23}) different ways, yielding roughly 70 trillion possible configurations (2^{46}) when sperm and egg unite. Actually, this is a conservative estimate. It doesn't take into account complexities such as *mutations* (changes in the genetic code) or *crossing over* during sex-cell formation (an interchange of material between chromosomes). Thus, genetic transmission is a complicated process, and everything is a matter of probability. Except for identical twins, each person ends up with a unique genetic blueprint.

Like chromosomes, genes operate in pairs, with one gene of each pair coming from each parent. In the *homozygous condition,* the two genes in a specific pair are the same. In the *heterozygous* condition, the two genes in a specific pair are different (see Figure 3.26). In the simplest scenario, a single pair of genes determines a trait. Attached versus detached earlobes provide a nice example. When both parents contribute a gene for the same type of earlobe (the *homozygous* condition), the child will have an earlobe of that type. When the parents contribute genes for different types of earlobes (the *heterozygous*

Figure 3.25
Genetic material. This series of enlargements shows the main components of genetic material. (Top) In the nucleus of every cell are chromosomes, which carry the information needed to construct new human beings. (Center) Chromosomes are threadlike strands of DNA that carry thousands of genes, the functional units of hereditary transmission. (Bottom) DNA is a spiraled double chain of molecules that can copy itself to reproduce.

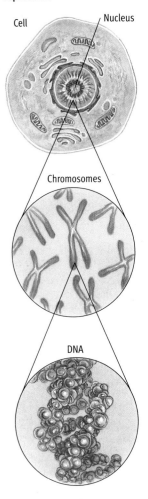

Cell   Nucleus

Chromosomes

DNA

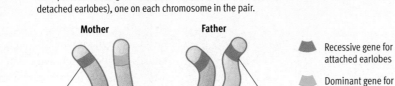

Each parent has two genes for each trait (such as attached versus detached earlobes), one on each chromosome in the pair.

Mother   **Father**

Recessive gene for attached earlobes

Dominant gene for detached earlobes

Their offspring receive one chromosome of the pair from each parent.

If the gene for a trait is identical on each chromosome of a pair, the pair is called **homozygous.**

In this case, two recessive genes for attached earlobes (left) leads to attached earlobes while one gene of each type (right) leads to detached earlobes because detached earlobes are dominant.

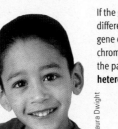

If the gene for a trait is different from that gene on the other chromosome of a pair, the pair is called **heterozygous.**

© Laura Dwight

© Laura Dwight

Figure 3.26

Homozygous and heterozygous genotypes. Like chromosomes, genes operate in pairs, with one gene in each pair coming from each parent. When paired genes are the same, they are said to be *homozygous.* When paired genes are different, they are said to be *heterozygous.* Whether people have attached or detached earlobes is determined by a single pair of genes. In the heterozygous condition, genes for detached earlobes are dominant over genes for attached earlobes.

condition), one gene in the pair—called the *dominant gene*—overrides or masks the other, called the *recessive gene.* Thus, **a *dominant gene* is one that is expressed when paired genes are different. A *recessive gene* is one that is masked when paired genes are different.** In the case of earlobes, genes for detached earlobes are dominant over genes for attached earlobes.

Because genes operate in pairs, a child has a 50% probability of inheriting a specific gene in a particular gene pair from each parent. Thus, the *genetic relatedness* of parents and children is said to be 50%. The genetic relatedness of other types of relatives can be calculated in the same way; the results are shown in **Figure 3.27.** As you can see, genetic relatedness ranges from 100% for identical twins down to 6.25% for second cousins. The numbers in **Figure 3.27** are purely theoretical, and for a variety of complicated reasons they underestimate the actual genetic overlap among people. But the key to the concept of genetic relatedness is that members of a family share more of the same genes than nonmembers, and closer relatives share a larger proportion of genes than more distant relatives. These realities explain why family members tend to resemble one another and why this resemblance tends to be greater among closer relatives.

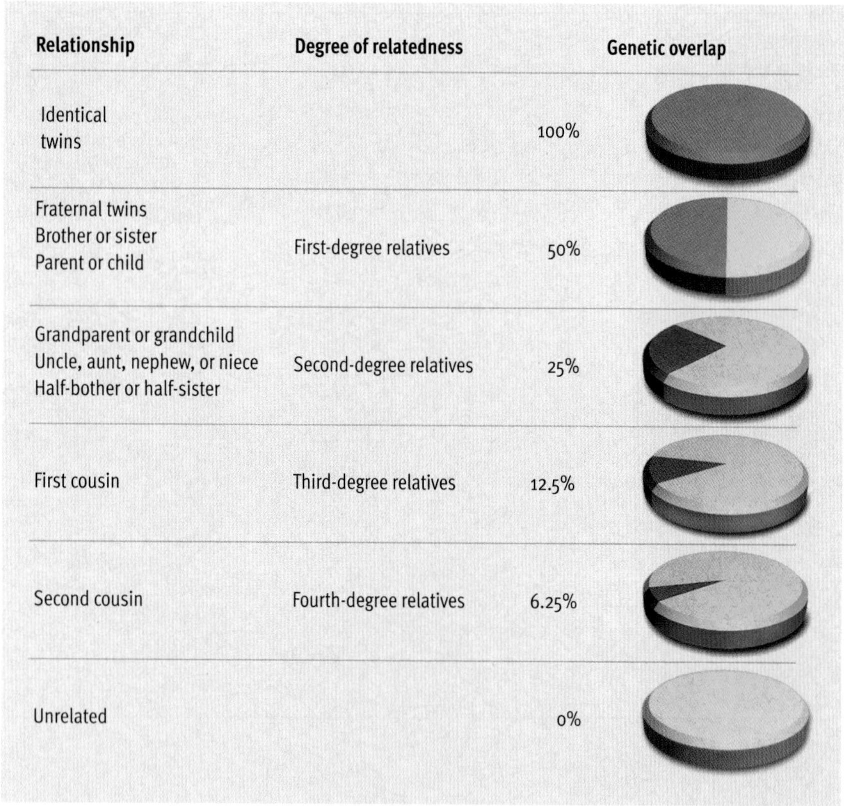

Genotype Versus Phenotype

It might seem that two parents with the same manifest trait, such as detached earlobes, should always produce offspring with that trait. However, that isn't always the case. For instance, two parents with detached earlobes can produce a child with attached earlobes. This happens because there are unexpressed recessive genes in the family's gene pool—in this case, genes for attached earlobes.

This point brings us to the distinction between genotype and phenotype. ***Genotype* refers to a person's genetic makeup. *Phenotype* refers to the ways in which a person's genotype is manifested in observable characteristics.** Different genotypes (such as two genes for detached earlobes as opposed to one gene for detached and one for attached) can yield the same phenotype (detached earlobes). Genotype is determined at conception and is fixed forever. In contrast, phenotypic characteristics (hair color, for instance) may change over time. They may also be modified by environmental factors.

Genotypes translate into phenotypic characteristics in a variety of ways. Not all gene pairs operate according to the principles of dominance. In some instances, when paired genes are different, they produce a blend, an "averaged out" phenotype. In other cases, paired genes that are different strike another type of compromise, and both characteristics show up phenotypically. In the case of type AB blood, for example, one gene is for type A and the other is for type B.

Polygenic Inheritance

Most human characteristics appear to be *polygenic traits,* or characteristics that are influenced by more than one pair of genes. For example, three to five gene pairs are thought to interactively determine skin color. Complex physical abilities, such as motor coordination, may be influenced by tangled interactions among a great many pairs of genes. Most psychological characteristics that appear to be affected by heredity seem to involve complex polygenic inheritance (Kendler & Greenspan, 2006).

Investigating Hereditary Influence: Research Methods

7d

Relationship	Degree of relatedness	Genetic overlap
Identical twins		100%
Fraternal twins Brother or sister Parent or child	First-degree relatives	50%
Grandparent or grandchild Uncle, aunt, nephew, or niece Half-bother or half-sister	Second-degree relatives	25%
First cousin	Third-degree relatives	12.5%
Second cousin	Fourth-degree relatives	6.25%
Unrelated		0%

Figure 3.27

Genetic relatedness. Research on the genetic bases of behavior takes advantage of the different degrees of genetic relatedness between various types of relatives. If heredity influences a trait, relatives who share more genes should be more similar with regard to that trait than are more distant relatives, who share fewer genes. Comparisons involving various degrees of biological relationships will come up frequently in later chapters.

How do behavioral geneticists and other scientists disentangle the effects of genetics and experience to determine whether heredity affects behavioral traits? Researchers have designed special types of studies to assess the impact of heredity. Of course, with humans they are limited to correlational rather than experimental methods, as they cannot manipulate genetic variables by assigning subjects to mate with each other (this approach, called *selective breeding*, is used in animal studies). The three most important methods in human research are family studies, twin studies, and adoption studies. After examining these classic methods of research, we'll discuss the impact of new developments in genetic mapping.

Family Studies

7d

In *family studies* researchers assess hereditary influence by examining blood relatives to see how much they resemble one another on a specific trait. If heredity affects the trait under scrutiny, researchers should find phenotypic similarity among relatives. Furthermore, they should find more similarity among relatives who share more genes. For instance, siblings should exhibit more similarity than cousins.

Illustrative of this method are the numerous family studies conducted to assess the contribution of heredity to the development of schizophrenic disorders. These disorders strike approximately 1% of the population, yet as Figure 3.28 reveals, 9% of the siblings of schizophrenic patients exhibit schizophrenia themselves (Gottesman, 1991). Thus, these first-degree relatives of schizophrenic patients show a risk for the disorder that is nine times higher than normal. This risk is greater than that observed for more distantly related, second-degree relatives, such as nieces and nephews (4%), who, in turn, are at greater risk than third-degree relatives, such as second cousins (2%). This pattern of results is consistent with the hypothesis that genetic inheritance influences the development of schizophrenic disorders (Gottesman & Moldin, 1998; Ho, Black, & Andreasen, 2003).

Family studies can indicate whether a trait runs in families. However, this correlation does not provide conclusive evidence that the trait is influenced by heredity. Why not? Because family members generally share not only genes but also similar environments. Furthermore, closer relatives are more likely to live together than more distant relatives. Thus, genetic similarity and environmental similarity *both* tend to be greater for closer relatives. Either of these confounded variables could be responsible when greater phenotypic similarity is found in closer relatives. Family studies can offer useful insights about the possible impact of heredity, but they cannot provide definitive evidence.

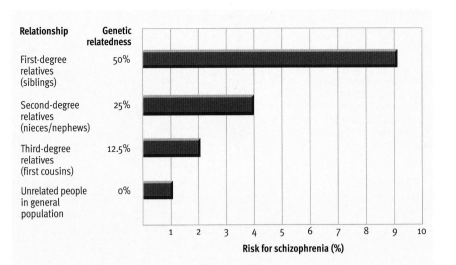

Twin Studies

7d

Twin studies can yield better evidence about the possible role of genetic factors. In *twin studies* researchers assess hereditary influence by comparing the resemblance of identical twins and fraternal twins with respect to a trait. The logic of twin studies hinges on the genetic relatedness of identical and fraternal twins (see Figure 3.29 on the next page). *Identical (monozygotic) twins* emerge from one zygote that splits for unknown reasons. Thus, they have exactly the same genotype; their genetic relatedness is 100%. *Fraternal (dizygotic) twins* result when two eggs are fertilized simultaneously by different sperm cells, forming two separate zygotes. Fraternal twins are no more alike in genetic makeup than any two siblings born to a pair of parents at different times. Their genetic relatedness is only 50%.

Fraternal twins provide a useful comparison to identical twins because in both cases the twins usually grow up in the same home, at the same time, exposed to the same configuration of relatives,

Figure 3.28
Family studies of risk for schizophrenic disorders. First-degree relatives of schizophrenic patients have an elevated risk of developing a schizophrenic disorder (Gottesman, 1991). For instance, the risk for siblings of schizophrenic patients is about 9% instead of the baseline 1% for unrelated people. Second- and third-degree relatives have progressively smaller elevations in risk for this disorder. Although these patterns of risk do not prove that schizophrenia is partly inherited, they are consistent with this hypothesis.

Figure 3.29
**Identical versus fra-
ternal twins.** Identical
(monozygotic) twins emerge
from one zygote that splits,
so their genetic relatedness
is 100%. Fraternal (dizy-
gotic) twins emerge from
two separate zygotes, so
their genetic relatedness is
only 50%.

SOURCE: Adapted from Kalat, J.
(1996). *Introduction to psychology.*
Belmont, CA: Wadsworth. Reprinted
by permission.

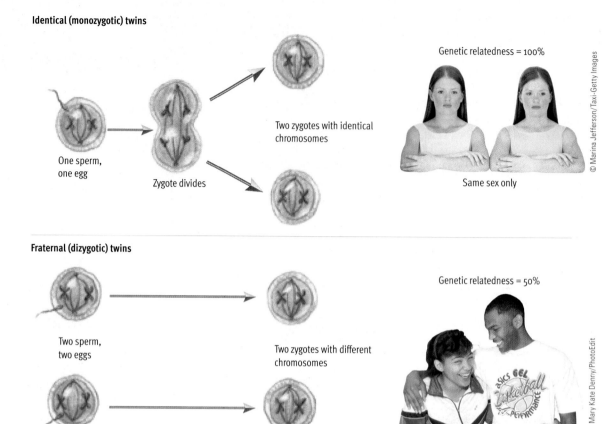

Figure 3.30
**Twin studies of intel-
ligence and personality.**
Identical twins tend to be
more similar than fraternal
twins (as reflected in higher
correlations) with regard
to intelligence and specific
personality traits, such as
extraversion. These findings
suggest that intelligence and
personality are influenced
by heredity. (Data from
Plomin et al., 2001)

neighbors, peers, teachers, events, and so forth.
Thus, both kinds of twins normally develop under
equally similar environmental conditions. However,
identical twins share more genetic kinship than fraternal twins. Consequently, if sets of identical twins
tend to exhibit more similarity on a trait than sets of
fraternal twins do, it is reasonable to infer that this
greater similarity is *probably* due to heredity rather
than environment.

Twin studies have been conducted to assess the
impact of heredity on a variety of traits. Some representative results are summarized in Figure 3.30. The
higher correlations found for identical twins indicate
that they tend to be more similar to each other than
fraternal twins on measures of general intelligence
and measures of specific personality traits, such as extraversion (Plomin et al., 2001). These results support
the notion that intelligence and personality are influenced to some degree by genetic makeup. However,
the fact that identical twins are far from identical in
intelligence and personality also shows that environment influences these characteristics.

Adoption Studies   7d

Adoption studies assess hereditary influence by
examining the resemblance between adopted
children and both their biological and their
adoptive parents. Generally, adoptees are used as
subjects in this type of study only if they were given
up for adoption in early infancy and were raised
without having contact with their biological parents. The logic underlying the adoption study approach is quite simple. If adopted children resemble
their biological parents on a trait, even though they
were not raised by them, genetic factors probably
influence that trait. In contrast, if adopted children
resemble their adoptive parents, even though they
inherited no genes from them, environmental factors probably influence the trait.

In recent years, adoption studies have contributed to science's understanding of how genetics and the environment influence intelligence. The research shows modest similarity between adopted children and their biological parents, as indicated by an average correlation of about .22 (Grigerenko, 2000). Interestingly, adopted children resemble their adoptive parents to roughly the same degree (an average correlation of about .20). These findings suggest that both heredity and environment have an influence on intelligence.

The Cutting Edge: Genetic Mapping

While behavioral geneticists have recently made great progress in documenting the influence of heredity on behavior, *molecular geneticists,* who study the biochemical bases of genetic inheritance, have made even more spectacular advances in their efforts to unravel the genetic code. *Genetic mapping* is the process of determining the location and chemical sequence of specific genes on specific chromosomes. New methods of manipulating DNA are now allowing scientists to create detailed physical maps of the genetic material on chromosomes in plants, animals, and humans. The Human Genome Project, a huge international enterprise, has produced a working draft of the sequence of all 3 billion letters of DNA in the human genome, and the chromosomal location of almost all human genes has been identified (Collins et al., 2006; Kelsoe, 2004). Gene maps, by themselves, do not reveal which genes govern which traits. However, the compilation of a precise genetic atlas may fuel a quantum leap in the ability of scientists to pinpoint links between specific genes and specific traits and disorders. For example, medical researchers have already identified the genes responsible for cystic fibrosis, Huntington's chorea, and muscular dystrophy. Many medical researchers predict that genetic mapping will ultimately lead to revolutionary advances in the diagnosis and treatment of physical diseases.

Will genetic mapping permit researchers to discover the genetic basis for intelligence, extraversion, schizophrenia, musical ability, and other *behavioral* traits? Perhaps someday, but progress is likely to be painstakingly slow (Caspi & Moffitt, 2006; Plomin & McGuffin, 2003). Thus far, the major medical breakthroughs from genetic mapping have involved dichotomous traits (you either do or do not have the trait, such as muscular dystrophy) governed by a single gene pair. However, most behavioral traits do not involve a dichotomy, as everyone has varying amounts of intelligence, musical ability, and so forth. Moreover, virtually all behavioral traits appear to be *polygenic* and are shaped by many genes rather than a single gene. Because of these and many other complexities, scientists are not likely to find a single gene that controls intelligence, extraversion, or musical talent (Plomin, Kennedy, & Craig, 2006). The challenge will be to identify specific constellations of genes that each exert modest influence over particular aspects of behavior. What's exciting is that until recently, behavioral geneticists were largely limited to investigating *how much* heredity influences various traits. Genetic mapping will allow them to begin investigating *how* heredity influences specific aspects of behavior (Plomin, 2004).

concept check 3.4

Recognizing Hereditary Influence

Check your understanding of the methods scientists use to explore hereditary influences on specific behavioral traits by filling in the blanks in the descriptive statements below. The answers can be found in the back of the book in Appendix A.

1. The findings from family studies indicate that heredity may influence a trait if _____ show more trait similarity than _____ .

2. The findings from twin studies suggest that heredity influences a trait if _____ show more trait similarity than _____ .

3. The findings from adoption studies suggest that heredity influences a trait if children adopted at a young age share more trait similarity with their _____ than their _____ .

4. The findings from family studies, twin studies, or adoption studies suggest that heredity does not influence a trait when _____ is not related to _____ .

web link 3.7

Human Genome Project Information

This site provides a rich array of educational resources related to the ongoing Human Genome Project, which was originally launched in 1990. Visitors can learn about the goals and history of this massive project and get updates on recent progress.

The Interplay of Heredity and Environment

We began this section by asking, is it all in the genes? When it comes to behavioral traits, the answer clearly is no. According to Robert Plomin (1993, 2004), perhaps the leading behavioral genetics researcher in recent decades, what scientists find again and again is that heredity and experience jointly influence most aspects of behavior. Moreover, their effects are interactive—genetics and experience play off each other (Gottesman & Hanson, 2005; Rutter, 2006, 2007).

For example, consider what researchers have learned about the development of schizophrenic disorders. Although the evidence indicates that genetic factors influence the development of schizophrenia, it does *not* appear that anyone directly inherits the disorder itself. Rather, what people appear to inherit is a certain degree of *vulnerability* to the disorder (McDonald & Murphy, 2003; Paris, 1999). Whether

Courtesy of Tara McKearney

Robert Plomin

"The transformation of the social and behavioral sciences from environmentalism to biological determinism is happening so fast that I find I more often have to say, 'Yes, genetic influences are substantial, but environmental influences are important, too.'"

this vulnerability is ever converted into an actual disorder depends on each person's experiences in life. As we will discuss in Chapter 14, certain types of stressful experience seem to evoke the disorder in people who are more vulnerable to it. Thus, as Danielle Dick and Richard Rose (2002) put it in a review of behavioral genetics research, "Genes confer dispositions, not destinies" (p 73).

The Evolutionary Bases of Behavior

To round out our look at the biological bases of behavior, we need to discuss how evolutionary forces have shaped many aspects of human and animal behavior. As you may recall from Chapter 1, *evolutionary psychology* is a major new theoretical perspective in the field that analyzes behavioral processes in terms of their adaptive significance. In this section, we will outline some basic principles of evolutionary theory and relate them to animal behavior. These ideas will create a foundation for forthcoming chapters, where we'll see how these principles can enhance our understanding of many aspects of human behavior.

Darwin's Insights

Charles Darwin, the legendary British naturalist, was *not* the first person to describe the process of evolution. Well before Darwin's time, other biologists who had studied the earth's fossil record noted that various species appeared to have undergone gradual changes over the course of a great many generations. What Darwin (1859) contributed in his landmark book, *The Origin of Species,* was a creative, new explanation for *how and why* evolutionary changes unfold over time. He identified *natural selection* as the mechanism that orchestrates the process of evolution.

The mystery that Darwin set out to solve was complicated. He wanted to explain how the characteristics of a species might change over generations and why these changes tended to be surprisingly adaptive. In other words, he wanted to shed light on why organisms tend to have characteristics that serve them well in the context of their environments. How did giraffes acquire their long necks that allow them to reach high into acacia trees to secure their main source of food? How did woodpeckers develop their sharp, chisel-shaped beaks that permit them to probe trees for insects so effectively? How did frogs develop their long and powerful hindlimbs that enable them to catapult through the air on land and move swiftly through water? Darwin's explanation for the seemingly purposive nature of evolution centered on four crucial insights.

First, he noted that organisms vary in endless ways, such as size, speed, strength, aspects of appearance, visual abilities, hearing capacities, digestive processes, cell structure, and so forth. Second, he noted that some of these characteristics are heritable—that is, they are passed down from one generation to the next. Although genes and chromosomes had not yet been discovered, the concept of heredity was well established. In Darwin's theory, variations in hereditary traits provide the crude materials for evolution. Third, borrowing from the work of Thomas Malthus, he noted that organisms tend to produce offspring at a pace that outstrips the local availability of food supplies, living space, and other crucial resources. As a population increases and resources dwindle, the competition for precious resources intensifies. Thus, it occurred to Darwin—and this was his grand insight—that variations in hereditary traits might affect organisms' ability to obtain the resources necessary for survival and reproduction. Fourth, building on this insight, Darwin argued that if a specific heritable trait con-

Charles Darwin

"Can we doubt (remembering that many more individuals are born than can possibly survive) that individuals having any advantage, however slight, over others, would have the best chance of surviving and procreating their kind? . . . This preservation of favourable variations and the rejection of injurious variations, I call Natural Selection."

The behavior that helps this grasshopper hide from predators is a product of evolution, just like the physical characteristics that help it blend in with its surroundings.

Table 3.2 Female Mate Choices Based on Differences in Males' Morphological and Behavioral Attributes

Species	Favored attribute
Scorpionfly	More symmetrical wings
Barn swallow	More symmetrical and larger tail ornaments
Wild turkey	Larger beak ornaments
House finch	Redder feathers
Satin bowerbird	Bowers with more ornaments
Cichlid fish	Taller display "bower"
Field cricket	Longer calling bouts
Woodhouse's toad	More frequent calls

Source: Adapted from Alcock, J. (1998). *Animal behavior* (p. 463). Sunderland, MA: Sinauer Associates. Copyright © 1998 John Alcock. Reprinted by permission of Sinauer Associates and the author.

much a product of evolution as the grasshopper's remarkable camouflage.

Many behavioral adaptations are designed to improve organisms' chances of reproductive success. Consider, for instance, the wide variety of species in which females actively choose which male to mate with. In many such species, females demand material goods and services from males in return for copulation opportunities. For example, in one type of moth, males have to spend hours extracting sodium from mud puddles, which they then transfer to prospective mates, who use it to supply their larvae with an important nutritional element (Smedley & Eisner, 1996). In the black-tipped hangingfly, females insist on a nuptial gift of food before they mate. They reject suitors bringing unpalatable food, and they tie the length of subsequent copulation to the size of the nuptial gift (Thornhill, 1976).

The adaptive value of trading sex for material goods that can aid the survival of an organism and its offspring is obvious, but the evolutionary significance of other mating strategies is more perplexing. In some species characterized by female choice, the choices hinge on males' appearance and courtship behavior. Females usually prefer males sporting larger or more brightly colored ornaments, or those capable of more extreme acoustical displays. For ex-

ample, female house finches are swayed by redder feathers, whereas female wild turkeys are enticed by larger beak ornaments (see Table 3.2 for additional examples). What do females gain by selecting males with redder feathers, larger beaks, and other arbitrary characteristics? This is one of the more difficult questions in evolutionary biology, and addressing all the complexities that may be involved would take us far beyond the scope of this discussion. But, caveats aside, favored attributes generally seem to be indicators of males' relatively good genes, sound health, low parasite load, or superior ability to provide future services, such as protection or food gathering, all of which may serve to make their offspring more viable (Alcock, 2005). For example, the quality of peacocks' plumage appears to be associated with their parasite load (Hamilton & Zuk, 1982) and their genetic quality (as indexed by their subsequent survival) (Petrie, 1994). So, even mating preferences for seemingly nonadaptive aspects of appearance may often have adaptive significance.

REVIEW of Key Learning Goals

3.23 Darwin argued that if a heritable trait contributes to an organism's survival or reproductive success, organisms with that trait should produce more offspring than those without the trait and that the prevalence of that trait should gradually increase over generations—thanks to natural selection.

3.24 Because of the gradual, incremental nature of evolution, adaptations sometimes linger in a population even though they no longer provide a survival or reproductive advantage. Hamilton proposed the theory of inclusive fitness to explain the paradox of self-sacrifice.

3.25 Theorists have focused primarily on the evolution of physical characteristics in the animal kingdom, but from the very beginning Darwin recognized that natural selection was applicable to behavioral traits as well. Examples of behaviors sculpted by evolution include eating behavior, the avoidance of predators, and mating strategies.

Key Learning Goals

3.26 Identify the three unifying themes that were highlighted in this chapter.

Heredity and Environment

Multifactorial Causation

Empiricism

Three of our seven themes stood out in this chapter: (1) heredity and environment jointly influence behavior, (2) behavior is determined by multiple causes, and (3) psychology is empirical. Let's look at each of these points.

In Chapter 1, when it was first emphasized that heredity and environment jointly shape behavior, you may have been a little perplexed about how your genes could be responsible for your sarcastic wit or your interest in art. In fact, there are no genes for behavior per se. Experts do not expect to find genes for sarcasm or artistic interest, for example. Insofar as your hereditary endowment plays a role in your behavior, it does so *indirectly,* by molding the physiological machine that you work with. Thus, your genes influence your physiological makeup, which in turn influences your personality, temperament, intelligence, interests, and other traits. Bear in mind, however, that genetic factors do not operate in a vacuum. Genes exert their effects in an environmental context. The impact of genetic makeup depends on environment, and the impact of environment depends on genetic makeup.

It was evident throughout the chapter that behavior is determined by multiple causes, but this fact was particularly apparent in the discussions of schizophrenia. At various points in the chapter we saw that schizophrenia may be a function of (1) abnormalities in neurotransmitter activity (especially dopamine and perhaps glutamate), (2) structural defects in the brain (enlarged ventricles), and (3) genetic vulnerability to the illness. These findings do not contradict one another. Rather, they demonstrate that a complex array of biological factors are involved in the development of schizophrenia. In Chapter 14, we'll see that a variety of environmental factors also play a role in the multifactorial causation of schizophrenia.

The empirical nature of psychology was apparent in the numerous discussions of the specialized research methods used to study the physiological bases of behavior. As you know, the empirical approach depends on precise observation. Throughout this chapter, you've seen how investigators have come up with innovative methods to observe and measure elusive phenomena such as electrical activity in the brain, neural impulses, brain function, cerebral specialization, and the impact of heredity on behavior. The point is that empirical methods are the lifeblood of the scientific enterprise. When researchers figure out how to better observe something, their new methods usually facilitate major advances in our scientific knowledge. That is why brain-imaging techniques and genetic mapping hold such exciting promise.

The importance of empiricism will also be apparent in the upcoming Personal Application and Critical Thinking Application that follow. In both you'll see that it is important to learn to distinguish between scientific findings and conjecture based on those findings.

REVIEW of Key Learning Goals

3.26 The interactive influence of heredity and environment was highlighted in this chapter, as was the multifactorial causation of behavior. The special research techniques used to study the biological bases of behavior show that empirical methods are the lifeblood of the scientific enterprise.

PERSONAL APPLICATION

Evaluating the Concept of "Two Minds in One"

Key Learning Goals

3.27 Describe five popular beliefs regarding the specialization of the cerebral hemispheres.

3.28 Critically evaluate popular ideas on cerebral specialization and cognitive processes.

Answer the following "true" or "false."

____ **1** The right and left brains give people two minds in one.

____ **2** Each half of the brain has its own special mode of thinking.

____ **3** Some people are left-brained while others are right-brained.

____ **4** Schools should devote more effort to teaching the overlooked right side of the brain.

Do people have two minds in one that think differently? Do some people depend on one side of the brain more than the other? Is the right side of the brain neglected? These questions are too complex to resolve with a simple true or false, but in this Application we'll take a closer look at the issues involved in these proposed applications of the findings on cerebral specialization. You'll learn that some of these ideas are plausible, but in many cases the hype has outstripped the evidence.

Earlier, we described Roger Sperry's Nobel prize–winning research with split-brain patients, whose right and left hemispheres were disconnected (to reduce epileptic seizures). The split-brain studies showed that the previously underrated right hemisphere has some special talents of its own. This discovery detonated an explosion of research on cerebral laterality.

Cerebral Specialization and Cognitive Processes

2f, SIM2

Using a variety of methods, scientists have compiled mountains of data on the specialized abilities of the right and left hemispheres. These findings have led to extensive theorizing about how the right and left brains might be related to cognitive processes. Some of the more intriguing ideas include the following:

1. *The two hemispheres are specialized to process different types of cognitive tasks* (Corballis, 1991; Ornstein, 1977). The findings of many researchers have been widely interpreted as showing that the left hemisphere handles verbal tasks, including language, speech, writing, math, and logic, while the right hemisphere handles nonverbal tasks, including spatial problems, music, art, fantasy, and creativity. These conclusions have attracted a great deal of public interest and media attention. For example, Figure 3.31 shows a *Newsweek* artist's depiction of how the brain divides its work.

2. *Each hemisphere has its own independent stream of consciousness* (Bogen, 1985, 2000; Pucetti, 1981). For instance, Joseph Bogen has asserted, "Pending further evidence, I believe that each of us has two minds in one person" (Hooper & Teresi, 1986, p. 221). Supposedly, this duality of consciousness goes largely unnoticed because of the considerable overlap between the experiences of each independent mind. Ultimately, though, the apparent unity of consciousness is but an illusion.

3. *The two hemispheres have different modes of thinking* (Banich & Heller, 1998; Davis & Dean, 2005). According to this notion, the documented differences between the hemispheres in dealing with verbal and non-

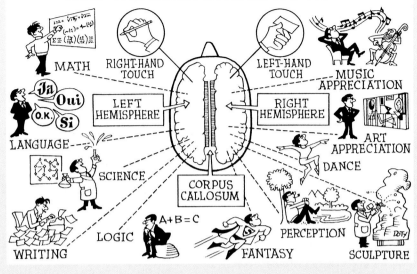

HOW THE BRAIN DIVIDES ITS WORK

Figure 3.31

Popular conceptions of hemispheric specialization. As this *Newsweek* diagram illustrates, depictions of hemispheric specialization in the popular press have often been oversimplified.

SOURCE: Cartoon courtesy of Roy Doty.

verbal materials are caused by more basic differences in *how* the hemispheres process information. The standard version of this theory holds that the reason the left hemisphere handles verbal material well is that it is analytic, abstract, rational, logical, and linear. In contrast, the right hemisphere is thought to be better equipped to handle spatial and musical material because it is synthetic, concrete, nonrational, intuitive, and holistic.

4. *People vary in their reliance on one hemisphere as opposed to the other* (Pink, 2005; Zenhausen, 1978). Allegedly, some people are "left-brained." Their greater dependence on their left hemisphere supposedly makes them analytic, rational, and logical. Other people are "right-brained." Their greater use of their right hemisphere supposedly makes them intuitive, holistic, and irrational. Being right-brained or left-brained is thought to explain many personal characteristics, such as whether an individual likes to read, is good with maps, or enjoys music. This notion of "brainedness" has even been used to explain occupational choice. Supposedly, right-brained people are more likely to become artists or musicians, while left-brained people are more likely to become writers or scientists.

Does artistic ability depend on being "right-brained"? The popular press has certainly suggested that this is the case, but as your text explains, there is no solid empirical evidence to support this assertion.

5. *Schools should place more emphasis on teaching the right side of the brain* (Kitchens, 1991; Wonder, 1992). "A real reform of the educational system will not occur until individual teachers learn to understand the true duality of their students' minds," says Thomas Blakeslee (1980, p. 59). Those sympathetic to his view assert that American schools overemphasize logical, analytical left-hemisphere thinking (required for English, math, and science) while short-changing intuitive, holistic right-hemisphere thinking (required for art and music). These educators have concluded that modern schools turn out an excess of left-brained graduates. They advocate curriculum reform to strengthen the right side of the brain in their students. This line of thinking has also spawned quite a collection of popular self-help books, such as *Unleashing the Right Side of the Brain* (Williams & Stockmyer, 1987), *Right-Brained Children in a Left-Brained World* (Freed & Parsons, 1998), and *Workout for a Balanced Brain* (Carter & Russell, 2001).

Complexities and Qualifications

The ideas just outlined are the source of considerable debate among psychologists and neuroscientists. These ideas are intriguing and have clearly captured the imagination of the general public. However, the research on cerebral specialization is complex, and doubts have been raised about many of these ideas (Efron, 1990; Springer & Deutsch, 1998). Let's examine each point.

1. There *is* ample evidence that the right and left hemispheres are specialized to handle different types of cognitive tasks, *but only to a degree* (Brown & Kosslyn, 1993; Corballis, 2003). Doreen Kimura (1973) compared the abilities of the right and left hemispheres to quickly recognize letters, words, faces, and melodies in a series of perceptual asymmetry studies, like those described earlier in the chapter. She found that the superiority of one hemisphere over the other was usually quite modest, as you can see in **Figure 3.32**, which shows superiority ratios for four cognitive tasks.

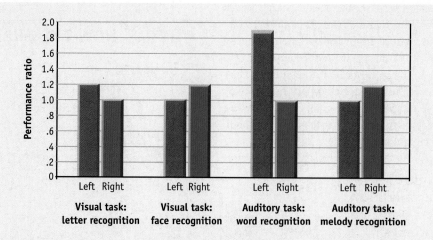

Figure 3.32

Relative superiority of one brain hemisphere over the other in studies of perceptual asymmetry. These performance ratios from a study by Doreen Kimura (1973) show the degree to which one hemisphere was "superior" to the other on each type of task in one study of normal participants. For example, the right hemisphere was 20% better than the left hemisphere in quickly recognizing melodic patterns (ratio 1.2 to 1). Most differences in the performance of the two hemispheres are quite small.

Furthermore, in normal individuals, the hemispheres don't work alone. As Hellige (1993a) notes, "In the intact brain, it is unlikely that either hemisphere is ever completely uninvolved in ongoing processing" (p. 23). Most tasks probably engage *both* hemispheres, albeit to different degrees (Beeman & Chiarello, 1998; Ornstein, 1997). For instance, imagine that you are asked the following question: "In what direction are you headed if you start north and make two right turns and a left turn?" In answering this question, you're confronted with a *spatial* task that should engage the right hemisphere. However, first you have to process the wording of the question, a *language* task that should engage the left hemisphere. Research suggests that as cognitive tasks become more complex and difficult, the more likely it is that *both* hemispheres will be involved (Weissman & Banich, 2000).

Furthermore, people differ in their patterns of cerebral specialization (Springer & Deutsch, 1998). Some people display little specialization—that is, their hemispheres seem to have equal abilities on various types of tasks. Others even reverse the usual specialization, so that verbal processing might be housed in the right hemisphere. These unusual patterns are especially common among left-handed people (Josse & Tzourio-Mazoyer, 2004). For example, when Rasmussen and Milner (1977) tested subjects for the localization of speech, they found bilateral representation in 15% of the left-handers. They found a reversal of the usual specialization (speech handled by the right hemisphere) in another 15% of the left-handed subjects (see **Figure 3.33**). These variations in cerebral specialization are not well understood. However, they clearly indicate that the functional specialization of the cerebral hemispheres is not set in concrete.

2. The evidence for the idea that people have a separate stream of consciousness in each hemisphere is weak. There *are* clear signs of such duality among *split-brain patients* (Bogen, 1990; Mark, 1996). But this duality is probably a unique by-product of the radical procedure that they have undergone—the surgical disconnection of their hemispheres (Bradshaw, 1981). In fact, many theorists have been impressed by the degree to which even split-brain patients mostly experience *unity* of consciousness (Wolford et al., 2004). There is little empirical basis for the idea that people have two independent streams of awareness neatly housed in the right and left halves of the brain.

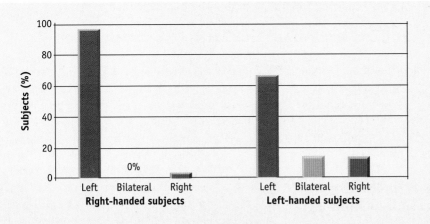

Figure 3.33

Handedness and patterns of speech localization. Left-handed people tend to show more variety in cerebral specialization and more bilateral representation than right-handers. For example, speech processing is almost always localized in the left hemisphere of right-handed subjects. However, Rasmussen and Milner (1977) found the usual pattern of speech localization in only 70% of their left-handed subjects.

3. Similarly, there is little direct evidence to support the notion that each hemisphere has its own mode of thinking, or *cognitive style* (Bradshaw, 1989; Corballis, 1999). This notion is plausible and there *is* some supportive evidence, but the evidence is inconsistent and more research is needed (Gordon, 1990; Reuter-Lorenz & Miller, 1998). One key problem with this idea is that aspects of cognitive style have proven difficult to define and measure. For instance, there is debate about the meaning of analytic versus synthetic thinking, or linear versus holistic thinking.

4. The evidence on the assertion that some people are left-brained while others are right-brained is inconclusive at best (Hellige, 1990). This notion has some plausibility—*if* it means only that some people consistently display more activation of one hemisphere than the other. However, researchers have yet to develop reliable measures of these possible "preferences" in cerebral activation. As a result, there are no convincing data linking brainedness to musical ability, occupational choice, or the like (Knecht et al., 2001; Springer & Deutsch, 1998).

5. The idea that schools should be reformed to better exercise the right side of the brain represents intriguing but wild speculation. In neurologically intact people it is impossible to teach just one hemisphere at a time (Levy, 1985). Many sound arguments exist for reforming American schools to encourage more holistic, intuitive thinking, but these arguments have nothing to do with cerebral specialization.

In summary, the theories linking cerebral specialization to cognitive processes are highly speculative. There's nothing wrong with theoretical speculation. Unfortunately, the tentative, conjectural nature of these ideas about cerebral specialization has got-

ten lost in the popular book descriptions of research on the right and left hemispheres (Coren, 1992). Popular writers continue to churn out allegedly scientific books, applying brain lateralization concepts to a variety of new topics on which there often is little or no real evidence. Thus, one can find books on how to have right-brain sex (Wells, 1991), develop right-brain social skills (Snyder, 1989), lose weight with a right-brain diet (Sommer, 1987), and become better organized by relying on the right hemisphere (Silber, 2004). Commenting on this popularization, Hooper and Teresi (1986) noted, "A widespread cult of the right brain ensued, and the duplex house that Sperry built grew into the K-Mart of brain science. Today our hairdresser lectures us about the 'Two Hemispheres of the Brain'" (p. 223). Cerebral specialization is an important and intriguing area of research. However, it is unrealistic to expect that the hemispheric divisions in the brain will provide a biological explanation for every dichotomy or polarity in modes of thinking.

REVIEW of Key Learning Goals

3.27 It is widely believed that each cerebral hemisphere has its own stream of consciousness and mode of thinking, which are applied to specific types of cognitive tasks. It has also been suggested that people vary in their reliance on the right and left halves of the brain and that schools should work more to exercise the right half of the brain.

3.28 The cerebral hemispheres are specialized for handling different cognitive tasks, but only to a degree, as most tasks engage both hemispheres. Moreover, people vary in their patterns of hemispheric specialization. Evidence for duality in consciousness divided along hemispheric lines is weak. Evidence on whether people vary in brainedness and whether the two hemispheres vary in cognitive style is inconclusive. There is no way to teach only one hemisphere of the brain, so a "right-brain curriculum" is pointless. Popular ideas about the right and left brain have gone far beyond the actual research findings.

Key Learning Goals

3.29 Explain how neuroscience research has been overextrapolated to educational issues.

Building Better Brains: The Perils of Extrapolation

Summarizing the implications of research in neuroscience, science writer Ronald Kotulak (1996) concluded, "The first three years of a child's life are critically important to brain development" (pp. ix–x). Echoing this sentiment, the president of a U.S. educational commission asserted that "research in brain development suggests it is time to rethink many educational policies" (Bruer, 1999, p. 16). Based on findings in neuroscience, many states launched expensive programs in the 1990s intended to foster better neural development in infants. For example, the governor of Georgia at the time, Zell Miller, sought funding to distribute classical music tapes to the state's infants, saying, "No one doubts that listening to music, especially at a very early age, affects the spatial-temporal reasoning that underlies math, engineering, and chess" (Bruer, 1999, p. 62). Well-intended educational groups and Hollywood celebrities have argued for the creation of schools for infants on the grounds that enriched educational experiences during infancy will lead to enhanced neural development.

What are these practical, new discoveries about the brain that will permit parents and educators to optimize infants' brain development? Well, we will discuss the pertinent research momentarily, but it is not as new or as practical as suggested in many quarters. Unfortunately, as we saw in our discussion of research on hemispheric specialization, the hype in the media has greatly outstripped the realities of what scientists have learned in the laboratory (Chance, 2001).

In recent years, many child-care advocates and educational reformers have used research in neuroscience as the rationale for the policies they have sought to promote. This strategy has led to the publication of numerous books on "brain-based learning" (see Jensen, 2000, 2006; Sousa, 2000; Sprenger, 2001; Zull, 2002), and the development of curricular programs that have

been adopted at many schools (Goswami, 2006). The people advocating these ideas have good intentions, but the neuroscience rationale has been stretched to the breaking point. The result? An enlightening case study in overextrapolation.

The Key Findings on Neural Development

The education and child-care reformers who have used brain science as the basis for their campaigns have primarily cited two key findings: the discovery of critical periods in neural development and the demonstration that rats raised in "enriched environments" have more synapses than rats raised in "impoverished environments." Let's look at each of these findings.

A *critical period* is a limited time span in the development of an organism when it is optimal for certain capacities to emerge because the organism is especially responsive to certain experiences. The seminal research on critical periods in neural development was conducted by Torsten Wiesel and David Hubel (1963, 1965) in the 1960s. They showed that if an eye of a newborn kitten is sutured shut early in its development (typically the first 4 to 6 weeks), the kitten will become permanently blind in that eye, but if the eye is covered for the same amount of time at later ages (after 4 months) blindness does not result. Such studies show that certain types of visual input are necessary during a critical period of development or neural pathways between the eye and brain will not form properly. Basically, what happens is that the inactive synapses from the closed eye are displaced by the active synapses from the open eye. Critical periods have been found for other aspects of neural development and in other species, but a great deal remains to be learned. Based on this type of research, some educational and child-care reformers have argued that the first three years of life are a critical period for human neural development.

The pioneering work on environment and brain development was begun in the

1960s by Mark Rosenzweig and his colleagues (1961, 1962). They raised some rats in an impoverished environment, (housed individually in small, barren cages) and other rats in an enriched environment (housed in groups of 10 to 12 in larger cages, with a variety of objects available for exploration), as shown in Figure 3.34. They found that the rats raised in the enriched environment performed better on problem-solving tasks than the impoverished rats and had slightly heavier brains and a thicker cerebral cortex in some areas of the brain. Subsequent research by William Greenough demonstrated that enriched environments resulted in heavier and thicker cortical areas by virtue of producing denser dendritic branching, more synaptic contacts, and richer neural networks (Greenough, 1975; Greenough & Volkmar, 1973). More recently, scientists have learned that enriched environments also promote the newly discovered process of *neurogenesis* in the brain (Nithianantharajah & Hannan, 2006). Based on this type of research, some child-care reformers have argued that human infants need to be brought up in enriched environments during the critical period before age 3, to promote synapse formation and to optimize the development of their emerging neural circuits.

The findings on critical periods and the effects of enriched environments were genuine breakthroughs in neuroscience, but except for the recent research on neurogenesis, they certainly aren't *new* findings, as suggested by various political action groups. Moreover, one can raise many doubts about whether this research can serve as a meaningful guide for decisions about parenting practices, day-care programs, educational policies, and welfare reform (Goswami, 2006; Thompson & Nelson, 2001).

The Tendency to Overextrapolate

Extrapolation occurs when an effect is estimated by extending beyond some known values or conditions. Extrapolation is a normal process, but some extrapolations are

Figure 3.34

Enriched environments in the study of rats' neural development. In the studies by Rosenzweig and colleagues (1961, 1962), rats raised in an impoverished environment were housed alone in small cages, whereas rats raised in enriched environments were housed in groups and were given playthings that were changed daily. Although the enriched conditions provided more stimulating environments than what laboratory rats normally experience, they may not be any more stimulating than rats' natural habitats. Thus, the "enriched" condition may reveal more about the importance of normal stimulation than about the benefits of extra stimulation (Gopnik, Meltzoff, & Kuhl, 1999).

conservative, plausible projections drawn from directly relevant data, whereas others are wild leaps of speculation based on loosely related data. The extrapolations made regarding the educational implications of critical periods and environmental effects on synapse formation are highly conjectural *overextrapolations*. The studies that highlighted the possible importance of early experience in animals have all used extreme conditions to make their comparisons, such as depriving an animal of all visual input or raising it in stark isolation. So-called "enriched" environments probably resemble normal conditions in the real world, whereas the standard laboratory environment may reflect extreme environmental deprivation (Gould, 2004). In light of the findings, it seems plausible to speculate that children probably need normal stimulation to experience normal brain development. However, great difficulty arises when these findings are extended to con-

clude that adding *more* stimulation to a normal environment will be beneficial to brain development (Shatz, 1992).

The ease with which people fall into the trap of overextrapolating has been particularly apparent in recent recommendations that infants listen to classical music to enhance their brain development. These recommendations have been derived from two studies that showed that college students' performance on spatial reasoning tasks was enhanced slightly for about 10–15 minutes after listening to a brief Mozart recording (Rauscher, Shaw, & Ky, 1993, 1995). This peculiar finding, dubbed the "Mozart effect," has proven difficult to replicate (McKelvie & Low, 2002; Steele, 2003), but the pertinent point here is that there was no research on how classical music affects *infants,* no research relating classical music to *brain development,* and no research on anyone showing *lasting effects.* Nonetheless, many people (including the governor of Georgia) were quick

to extrapolate the shaky findings on the Mozart effect to infants' brain development.

As discussed in Chapter 1, thinking critically about issues often involves asking questions such as: What is missing from this debate? Is there any contradictory evidence? In this case, there is some contradictory evidence that is worthy of consideration. The basis for advocating infant educational programs is the belief that the brain is malleable during the hypothesized critical period of birth to age 3 but not at later ages. However, Greenough's work on synaptic formation and other lines of research suggest that the brain remains somewhat malleable throughout life, responding to stimulation into old age (Thompson & Nelson, 2001). Thus, advocates for the aged could just as readily argue for new educational initiatives for the elderly to help them maximize their intellectual potential. Another problem is the implicit assumption that greater synaptic density is associated with greater intelligence. As noted in the main body of the chapter, there is evidence that infant animals and humans begin life with an overabundance of synaptic connections and that learning involves selective *pruning* of inactive synapses (Huttenlocher, 2003; Rakic, Bourgeois, & Goldman-Rakic, 1994). Thus, in the realm of synapses, more may *not* be better.

In conclusion, there may be many valid reasons for increasing educational programs for infants, but research in neuroscience does not appear to provide a clear rationale for much in the way of specific infant care policies (Bruer, 2002; Bruer & Greenough, 2001). One problem in evaluating these proposals is that few people want to argue against high-quality child care or education. But modern societies need to allocate their limited resources to the programs that appear most likely to have beneficial effects, so even intuitively appealing ideas need to be subjected to critical scrutiny.

Table 3.3 Critical Thinking Skills Discussed in This Application

Skill	Description
Understanding the limits of extrapolation	The critical thinker appreciates that extrapolations are based on certain assumptions, vary in plausibility, and ultimately involve speculation.
Looking for contradictory evidence	In evaluating the evidence presented on an issue, the critical thinker attempts to look for contradictory evidence that may have been left out of the debate.

REVIEW of Key Learning Goals

3.29 Some education and child-care reformers have used research in neuroscience as the basis for their campaigns. However, research has not demonstrated that birth to 3 is a critical period for human neural development or that specific enrichment programs can enhance brain development. These assertions are highly conjectural overextrapolations from existing data.

Key Ideas

Communication in the Nervous System

▮ The nervous system is made up of neurons and glial cells. Neurons are the basic communication links in the nervous system. Glial cells provide support for neurons and contribute to communication. Neurons normally transmit a neural impulse (an electric current) along an axon to a synapse with another neuron. The neural impulse is a brief change in a neuron's electrical charge that moves along an axon. It is an all-or-none event.

▮ Action potentials trigger the release of chemicals called neurotransmitters that diffuse across a synapse to communicate with other neurons. Transmitters bind with receptors in the postsynaptic cell membrane, causing excitatory or inhibitory PSPs. Most neurons are linked in neural pathways, circuits, and networks.

▮ ACh plays a key role in muscular movement. Disturbances in the activity of the monoamine transmitters have been related to the development of depression and schizophrenia. GABA and glutamate are widely distributed amino acid transmitters. Endorphins contribute to the relief of pain.

Organization of the Nervous System

▮ The nervous system can be divided into the central nervous system and the peripheral nervous system. The central nervous system consists of the brain and spinal cord.

▮ The peripheral nervous system can be subdivided into the somatic nervous system, which connects to muscles and sensory receptors, and the autonomic nervous system, which connects to blood vessels, smooth muscles, and glands.

Looking Inside the Brain: Research Methods

▮ The EEG can record broad patterns of electrical activity in the brain. Lesioning involves destroying a piece of the brain. Another technique is electrical stimulation of areas in the brain in order to activate them.

▮ Transcranial magnetic stimulation is a new method of virtual lesioning. CT scans and MRI scans can provide excellent depictions of brain structure. PET scans and fMRI scans can show brain functioning in action.

The Brain and Behavior

▮ The brain has three major regions: the hindbrain, midbrain, and forebrain. Structures in the hindbrain and midbrain handle essential functions. The thalamus is primarily a relay station. The hypothalamus is involved in the regulation of basic biological drives such as hunger and sex.

▮ The limbic system is involved in emotion and memory. The hippocampus contributes to memory, whereas the amygdala plays a role in learned fears. The cortex is the cerebrum's convoluted outer layer, which is subdivided into occipital, parietal, temporal, and frontal lobes. The brain's organization is somewhat malleable, thanks in part to the process of neurogenesis.

Right Brain/Left Brain: Cerebral Laterality

▮ The cerebrum is divided into right and left hemispheres connected by the corpus callosum. Studies of split-brain patients and perceptual asymmetries have revealed that the right and left halves of the brain each have unique talents.

The Endocrine System: Another Way to Communicate

▮ The endocrine system consists of glands that secrete hormones, which are chemicals involved in the regulation of basic bodily processes. The control centers for the endocrine system are the hypothalamus and the pituitary gland.

Heredity and Behavior: Is It All in the Genes?

▮ The basic units of genetic transmission are genes housed on chromosomes. Most behavioral qualities appear to involve polygenic inheritance. Researchers assess hereditary influence through a variety of methods, including family studies, twin studies, adoption studies, and genetic mapping.

The Evolutionary Bases of Behavior

▮ Darwin argued that if a heritable trait contributes to an organism's survival or reproductive success, organisms with that trait should produce more offspring than those without the trait and the prevalence of that trait should gradually increase over generations—thanks to natural selection.

▮ Darwin recognized from the beginning that natural selection was applicable to behavioral traits, as well as physical traits. Adaptations sometimes linger in a population even though they no longer provide a survival or reproductive advantage.

Reflecting on the Chapter's Themes

▮ The interactive influence of heredity and environment was highlighted in this chapter, as was the multifactorial causation of behavior. The special research techniques used to study the biological bases of behavior show that empirical methods are the lifeblood of the scientific enterprise.

PERSONAL APPLICATION Evaluating the Concept of "Two Minds in One"

▮ The cerebral hemispheres are specialized for handling different cognitive tasks, but only to a degree, and people vary in their patterns of hemispheric specialization. Evidence on whether people vary in brainedness and whether the two hemispheres vary in cognitive style is inconclusive.

CRITICAL THINKING APPLICATION Building Better Brains: The Perils of Extrapolation

▮ Although some education and child-care reformers have used findings in neuroscience as the basis for their campaigns, research has not demonstrated that birth to 3 is a critical period for human neural development or that specific enrichment programs can enhance brain development. These assertions are highly conjectural overextrapolations from existing data.

Key Terms

Absolute refractory period (p. 82)
Action potential (p. 82)
Adaptation (p. 118)
Adoption studies (p. 114)
Afferent nerve fibers (p. 90)
Agonist (p. 86)
Antagonist (p. 86)
Autonomic nervous system (ANS) (p. 90)
Axon (p. 80)
Central nervous system (CNS) (p. 90)
Cerebral cortex (p. 101)
Cerebral hemispheres (p. 101)
Cerebrospinal fluid (CSF) (p. 90)
Chromosomes (p. 111)
Corpus callosum (p. 101)
Critical period (p. 124)
Dendrites (p. 80)
Dominant gene (p. 112)
Efferent nerve fibers (p. 90)
Electrical stimulation of the brain (ESB) (p. 93)
Electroencephalograph (EEG) (p. 92)
Endocrine system (p. 108)
Endorphins (p. 88)
Family studies (p. 113)
Fitness (p. 117)
Forebrain (p. 99)
Fraternal (dizygotic) twins (p. 113)
Genes (p. 111)
Genetic mapping (p. 115)
Genotype (p. 112)
Glia (p. 81)
Heterozygous condition (p. 111)
Hindbrain (p. 97)
Homozygous condition (p. 111)
Hormones (p. 108)
Identical (monozygotic) twins (p. 113)
Inclusive fitness (p. 118)
Lesioning (p. 93)
Limbic system (pp. 99–100)

Midbrain (p. 99)
Mirror neurons (p. 103)
Natural selection (p. 117)
Nerves (pp. 89–90)
Neurogenesis (p. 104)
Neurons (p. 80)
Neurotransmitters (p. 84)
Parasympathetic division (p. 90)
Perceptual asymmetries (p. 108)
Peripheral nervous system (p. 89)
Phenotype (p. 112)
Pituitary gland (p. 109)
Polygenic traits (p. 112)
Postsynaptic potential (PSP) (p. 84)
Recessive gene (p. 112)
Resting potential (p. 82)
Reuptake (p. 84)
Soma (p. 80)
Somatic nervous system (p. 90)
Split-brain surgery (p. 106)
Sympathetic division (p. 90)
Synapse (p. 81)
Synaptic cleft (p. 83)
Terminal buttons (p. 81)
Testosterone (p. 109)
Transcranial magnetic stimulation (TMS) (p. 93)
Twin studies (p. 113)
Zygote (p. 111)

Key People

Charles Darwin (pp. 116–117)
Elizabeth Gould (pp. 104–105)
Alan Hodgkin and Andrew Huxley (pp. 81–82)
James Olds and Peter Milner (pp. 100–101)
Candace Pert and Solomon Snyder (p. 88)
Robert Plomin (p. 115)
Roger Sperry and Michael Gazzaniga (pp. 106–108)

1. A neural impulse is initiated when a neuron's charge momentarily becomes less negative, or even positive. This event is called:
   A. an action potential.
   B. a resting potential.
   C. impulse facilitation.
   D. inhibitory.

2. Neurons convey information about the strength of stimuli by varying:
   A. the size of their action potentials.
   B. the velocity of their action potentials.
   C. the rate at which they fire action potentials.
   D. all of the above.

3. Alterations in activity at dopamine synapses have been implicated in the development of:
   A. anxiety.
   B. schizophrenia.
   C. Alzheimer's disease.
   D. nicotine addiction.

4. Jim just barely avoided a head-on collision on a narrow road. With heart pounding, hands shaking, and body perspiring, Jim recognizes that these are signs of the body's fight-or-flight response, which is controlled by the:
   A. empathetic division of the peripheral nervous system.
   B. parasympathetic division of the autonomic nervous system.
   C. somatic division of the peripheral nervous system.
   D. sympathetic division of the autonomic nervous system.

5. The hindbrain consists of the:
   A. endocrine system and the limbic system.
   B. reticular formation.
   C. thalamus, hypothalamus, and cerebrum.
   D. cerebellum, medulla, and pons.

6. Juan is watching a basketball game. The neural impulses from his eyes will ultimately travel to his primary visual cortex, but first they must pass through the:
   A. amygdala.
   B. hypothalamus.
   C. thalamus.
   D. pons.

7. The _____ lobe is to hearing as the occipital lobe is to vision.
   A. frontal
   B. temporal
   C. parietal
   D. cerebellar

8. Paul has profound difficulty producing spoken language. If his problem is attributable to brain damage, the damage would probably be found in:
   A. the cerebellum.
   B. Sperry's area.
   C. Broca's area.
   D. Wernicke's area.

9. Sounds presented to the right ear are registered:
   A. only in the right hemisphere.
   B. only in the left hemisphere.
   C. more quickly in the right hemisphere.
   D. more quickly in the left hemisphere.

10. In people whose corpus callosums have not been severed, verbal stimuli are identified more quickly and more accurately:
    A. when sent to the right hemisphere first.
    B. when sent to the left hemisphere first.
    C. when presented to the left visual field.
    D. when presented auditorally rather than visually.

11. Hormones are to the endocrine system as _____ are to the nervous system.
    A. nerves
    B. synapses
    C. neurotransmitters
    D. action potentials

12. Jenny has brown hair and blue eyes and is 5'8" tall. What is being described is Jenny's:
    A. genotype.
    B. phenotype.
    C. somatotype.
    D. physique.

13. Adopted children's similarity to their biological parents is generally attributed to _____ ; adopted children's similarity to their adoptive parents is generally attributed to _____ .
    A. heredity; the environment
    B. the environment; heredity
    C. the environment; the environment
    D. heredity; heredity

14. In evolutionary theory, _____ refers to the reproductive success of an individual organism relative to the average reproductive success in the population.
    A. natural selection
    B. gene flow
    C. adaptation
    D. fitness

15. For which of the following assertions is the empirical evidence strongest?
    A. The two cerebral hemispheres are specialized to handle different types of cognitive tasks.
    B. People have a separate stream of consciousness in each hemisphere.
    C. Each hemisphere has its own cognitive style.
    D. Some people are right-brained, while others are left-brained.

Answers

1 A p. 82
2 C p. 82
3 B pp. 86–87
4 D p. 90
5 D pp. 89, 97
6 C p. 99
7 B pp. 101–102
8 C p. 105
9 D p. 106
10 B p. 108
11 C pp. 108–109
12 B p. 112
13 A p. 114
14 D p. 117
15 B pp. 122–123

PsykTrek

To view a demo: www.cengage.com/psychology/psyktrek
To order: www.cengage.com/psychology/weiten
Go to the PsykTrek website or CD-ROM for further study of the concepts in this chapter. Both online and on the CD-ROM, PsykTrek includes dozens of learning modules with videos, animations, and quizzes, as well as simulations of psychological phenomena and a multimedia glossary that includes word pronunciations.

CengageNow

www.cengage.com/tlc

Go to this site for the link to CengageNOW, your one-stop study shop. Take a Pretest for this chapter, and CengageNOW will generate a personalized Study Plan based on your test results. The Study Plan will identify the topics you need to review and direct you to online resources to help you master those topics. You can then take a Posttest to help you determine the concepts you have mastered and what you still need to work on.

Companion Website
www.cengage.com/psychology/weiten

Go to this site to find online resources directly linked to your book, including a glossary, flash cards, drag-and-drop exercises, quizzes, and more!

4

SENSATION
AND PERCEPTION

Psychophysics: Basic Concepts and Issues
Thresholds: Looking for Limits
Signal-Detection Theory
Perception Without Awareness
Sensory Adaptation

The Visual System: Essentials of Sight
The Stimulus: Light
The Eye: A Living Optical Instrument
The Retina: The Brain's Envoy in the Eye
Vision and the Brain
Viewing the World in Color

The Visual System: Perceptual Processes
Perceiving Forms, Patterns, and Objects
Perceiving Depth or Distance
Perceiving Geographical Slant
FEATURED STUDY ▌ Why Hills Look Steeper Than They Are
Perceptual Constancies in Vision
The Power of Misleading Cues: Visual Illusions

The Auditory System: Hearing
The Stimulus: Sound
Human Hearing Capacities
Sensory Processing in the Ear
Auditory Perception: Theories of Hearing
Auditory Localization: Perceiving Sources of Sound

The Chemical Senses: Taste and Smell
The Gustatory System: Taste
The Olfactory System: Smell

The Sense of Touch
Feeling Pressure
Feeling Pain

Illustrated Overview of Five Major Senses

Reflecting on the Chapter's Themes

PERSONAL APPLICATION ▌ **Appreciating Art and Illusion**

CRITICAL THINKING APPLICATION ▌ **Recognizing Contrast Effects: It's All Relative**

Recap

Practice Test

© Steve Cole/Photodisc Green/Getty Images

Take a look at the adjacent photo. What do you see? You probably answered, "a rose" or "a flower." But is that what you really see? No, this isn't a trick question. Let's examine the odd case of "Dr. P." It shows that there's more to seeing than meets the eye.

Dr. P was an intelligent and distinguished music professor who began to exhibit some worrisome behaviors that seemed to be related to his vision. Sometimes he failed to recognize familiar students by sight, although he knew them instantly by the sound of their voices. Sometimes he acted as if he saw faces in inanimate objects, cordially greeting fire hydrants and parking meters as if they were children. On one occasion, reaching for what he thought was his hat, he took hold of his wife's head and tried to put it on! Except for these kinds of visual mistakes, Dr. P was a normal, talented man.

Ultimately Dr. P was referred to Oliver Sacks, a neurologist, for an examination. During one visit, Sacks handed Dr. P a fresh red rose to see whether he would recognize it. Dr. P took the rose as if he were being given a model of a geometric solid rather than a flower. "About six inches in length," Dr. P observed, "a convoluted red form with a linear green attachment."

"Yes," Sacks persisted, "and what do you think it is, Dr. P?"

"Not easy to say," the patient replied. "It lacks the simple symmetry of the Platonic solids . . ."

"Smell it," the neurologist suggested. Dr. P looked perplexed, as if being asked to smell symmetry, but he complied and brought the flower to his nose. Suddenly, his confusion cleared up. "Beautiful. An early rose. What a heavenly smell" (Sacks, 1987, pp. 13–14).

What accounted for Dr. P's strange inability to recognize faces and familiar objects by sight? There was nothing wrong with his eyes. He could readily spot a pin on the floor. If you're thinking that he must have had something wrong with his vision, look again at the photo of the rose. What you see *is* "a convoluted red form with a linear green attachment." It doesn't occur to you to describe it that way only because, without thinking about it, you instantly perceive that combination of form and color as a flower. This is precisely what Dr. P was unable to do. He could see perfectly well, but he was losing the ability to assemble what he saw into a meaningful

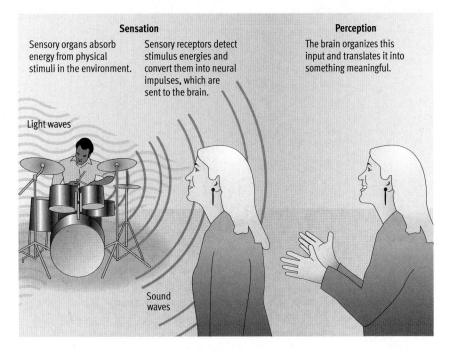

Sensation

Sensory organs absorb energy from physical stimuli in the environment.

Sensory receptors detect stimulus energies and convert them into neural impulses, which are sent to the brain.

Perception

The brain organizes this input and translates it into something meaningful.

Light waves

Sound waves

Figure 4.1

The distinction between sensation and perception. Sensation involves the stimulation of sensory organs, whereas perception involves the interpretation of sensory input. The two processes merge at the point where sensory receptors convert physical energy into neural impulses.

Sensation involves the absorption of energy, such as light or sound waves, by sensory organs, such as the eyes and ears. Perception involves organizing and translating sensory input into something meaningful (see **Figure 4.1**). For example, when you look at the photo of the rose, your eyes are *sensing* the light reflected from the page, including areas of low reflectance where ink has been deposited in an irregular shape. What you *perceive,* however, is a picture of a rose.

The distinction between sensation and perception stands out in Dr. P's case of visual agnosia. His eyes were doing their job of registering sensory input and transmitting signals to the brain. However, damage in his brain interfered with his ability to put these signals together into organized wholes. Thus, Dr. P's process of visual *sensation* was intact, but his process of visual *perception* was severely impaired.

Dr. P's case is unusual, of course. Normally, the processes of sensation and perception are difficult to separate because people automatically start organizing incoming sensory stimulation the moment it arrives. Although the distinction between sensation and perception has been useful in organizing theory and research, in operation the two processes merge.

We'll begin our discussion of sensation and perception by examining some general concepts that are relevant to all the senses. Next, we'll examine individual senses, in each case beginning with the sensory aspects and working our way through to the perceptual aspects. The chapter's Personal Application explores how principles of visual perception come into play in art and illusion. The Critical Thinking Application discusses how perceptual contrasts can be used in efforts to persuade us.

picture of the world. Technically, he suffered from a condition called *visual agnosia,* an inability to recognize objects through sight. As Sacks (1987) put it, "Visually, he was lost in a world of lifeless abstractions" (p. 15).

As Dr. P's case illustrates, without effective processing of sensory input, our familiar world can become a chaos of bewildering sensations. To acknowledge the need to both take in and process sensory information, psychologists distinguish between sensation and perception. *Sensation is the stimulation of sense organs. Perception is the selection, organization, and interpretation of sensory input.*

Psychophysics: Basic Concepts and Issues

Key Learning Goals

4.1 Explain how stimulus intensity is related to absolute thresholds and JNDs.

4.2 Articulate the basic thrust of signal-detection theory.

4.3 Summarize evidence on perception without awareness, and discuss its practical implications.

4.4 Clarify the meaning and significance of sensory adaptation.

As you may recall from Chapter 1, the first experimental psychologists were interested mainly in sensation and perception. They called their area of interest *psychophysics—the study of how physical stimuli are translated into psychological experience.* A particularly important contributor to psychophysics was Gustav Fechner, who published pioneering work on the subject in 1860. Fechner was a German scientist working at the University of Leipzig, where Wilhelm Wundt later founded the first formal laboratory and journal devoted to psychological research. Unlike Wundt, Fechner was not a "campaigner" interested in establishing psy-

chology as an independent discipline. However, his groundbreaking research laid the foundation that Wundt built upon.

Thresholds: Looking for Limits

Sensation begins with a *stimulus,* any detectable input from the environment. What counts as detectable, though, depends on who or what is doing the detecting. For instance, you might not be able to detect a weak odor that is readily apparent to your dog. Thus, Fechner wanted to know: For any given sense, what is the weakest detectable stimulus? For example, what is the minimum amount of light needed for a person to see that there is light?

Implicit in Fechner's question is a concept central to psychophysics: the threshold. A *threshold* is a dividing point between energy levels that do and do not have a detectable effect. For example, hardware stores sell a gadget with a photocell that automatically turns a lamp on when a room gets dark. The level of light intensity at which the gadget clicks on is its threshold.

An *absolute threshold* for a specific type of sensory input is the minimum stimulus intensity that an organism can detect. Absolute thresholds define the boundaries of an organism's sensory capabilities. Fechner and his contemporaries used a variety of methods to determine humans' absolute threshold for detecting light. They discovered that absolute thresholds are anything but absolute. When lights of varying intensity are flashed at a subject, there is no single stimulus intensity at which the subject jumps from no detection to completely accurate detection. Instead, as stimulus intensity increases, subjects' probability of responding to stimuli *gradually* increases, as shown in red in Figure 4.2. Thus, researchers had to arbitrarily define the absolute threshold as the stimulus intensity *detected 50% of the time*.

Using this definition, investigators found that under ideal conditions, human abilities to detect weak stimuli are greater than appreciated. Some concrete examples of the absolute thresholds for various senses can be seen in Table 4.1. For example, on a clear, dark night, in the absence of other distracting lights, you could see the light of a candle burning

Table 4.1 Examples of Absolute Thresholds

Sense	Absolute Threshold
Vision	A candle flame seen at 30 miles on a dark clear night
Hearing	The tick of a watch under quiet conditions at 20 feet
Taste	One teaspoon of sugar in two gallons of water
Smell	One drop of perfume diffused into entire volume of a six-room apartment
Touch	The wing of a fly falling on your cheek from a distance of 1 centimeter

Source: Galanter, E. (1962). Contemporary psychophysics. In R. Brown (Ed.), *New directions in psychology.* New York: Holt, Rinehart & Winston. © 1962 Eugene Galanter. Reprinted by permission.

30 miles in the distance! Of course, we're talking about ideal conditions—you would have to go out to the middle of nowhere to find the darkness required to put this assertion to a suitable test.

Fechner was also interested in people's sensitivity to differences between stimuli. A *just noticeable difference (JND)* is the smallest difference in stimulus intensity that a specific sense can detect. JNDs are close cousins of absolute thresholds. In fact, an absolute threshold is simply the just noticeable difference from nothing (no stimulus input) to something. In general, as stimuli increase in magnitude, the JND between them becomes larger. However, the size of a just noticeable difference in a specific sense tends to be a constant proportion of the size of the initial stimulus.

Signal-Detection Theory

Modern psychophysics has a more complicated view of how stimuli are detected. *Signal-detection theory* **proposes that the detection of stimuli involves decision processes as well as sensory processes, which are both influenced by a variety of factors besides stimulus intensity** (Egan, 1975; Swets, Tanner, & Birdsall, 1961).

Imagine that you are monitoring a radar screen, looking for signs of possible enemy aircraft. Your mission is to detect signals that represent approaching airplanes as quickly and as accurately as possible. In this situation, there are four possible outcomes, which are outlined in Figure 4.3 (on the next page): *hits* (detecting signals when they are present), *misses* (failing to detect signals when they are present), *false alarms* (detecting signals when they are not present), and *correct rejections* (not detecting signals when they are absent). Given these possibilities, signal-detection theory attempts to account for the influence of decision-making processes on stimulus detection.

Gustav Fechner

"The method of just noticeable differences consists in determining how much the weights have to differ so that they can just be discriminated."

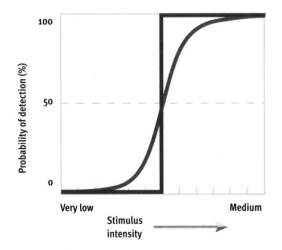

Figure 4.2

The absolute threshold. If absolute thresholds were truly absolute, then at threshold intensity the probability of detecting a stimulus would jump from 0 to 100%, as graphed here in blue. In reality, the chances of detecting a stimulus increase gradually with stimulus intensity, as shown in red. Accordingly, an "absolute" threshold is defined as the intensity level at which the probability of detection is 50%.

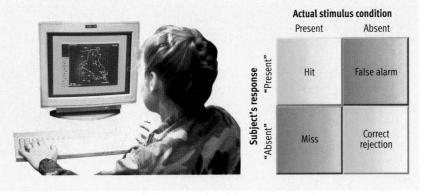

Actual stimulus condition

	Present	Absent
Subject's response "Present"	Hit	False alarm
Subject's response "Absent"	Miss	Correct rejection

Figure 4.3

Signal-detection theory. Signal-detection theory emerged from pragmatic efforts to improve the monitoring of modern equipment, such as the radar screen shown in the photo on the left. This diagram shows the four outcomes that are possible in attempting to detect the presence of weak signals. The criterion you set for how confident you want to feel before reporting a signal will affect your responding. For example, if you require high confidence before reporting a signal, you will minimize false alarms, but you'll be more likely to miss some signals.

In detecting weak signals on the radar screen, you will often have to decide whether a faint signal represents an airplane or you're just imagining that it does. Your responses will depend in part on the *criterion* you set for how sure you must feel before you react. Setting this criterion involves higher mental processes rather than raw sensation and depends on your expectations and on the consequences of missing a signal or of reporting a false alarm.

A major innovation of signal-detection theory was its assertion that your performance will also depend on the level of "noise" in the system (Kubovy, Epstein, & Gepshtein, 2003). Noise comes from all the irrelevant stimuli in the environment and the neural activity they elicit. Noise is analogous to the background static on a radio station. The more noise in the system, the harder it will be for you to pick up a weak signal. Variations in noise provide another reason that sensory thresholds depend on more than just the intensity of stimuli.

The key point is that signal-detection theory replaces Fechner's sharp threshold with the concept of "detectability." Detectability is measured in terms of probability and depends on decision-making processes as well as sensory processes. In comparison to classical models of psychophysics, signal-detection theory is better equipped to explain some of the complexities of perceived experience in the real world.

Perception Without Awareness

The concepts of thresholds and detectability lie at the core of an interesting debate: Can sensory stimuli that fall beneath the threshold of awareness still influence behavior? This issue centers on the concept of *subliminal perception*—the registration of sensory input without conscious awareness (*limen* is another term for threshold, so *subliminal* means below threshold). This question might be just another technical issue in the normally staid world of psychophysics, except that subliminal perception has become tied up in highly charged controversies relating to money, sex, religion, and rock music.

The controversy began in 1957 when an executive named James Vicary placed hidden messages such as "Eat popcorn" in a film showing at a theater in New Jersey. The messages were superimposed on only a few frames of the film, so that they flashed by quickly and imperceptibly. Nonetheless, Vicary claimed in the press that popcorn sales increased by 58%, and a public outcry ensued (McConnell, Cutler, & McNeil, 1958; Merikle, 2000). Since then, Wilson Brian Key, a former advertising executive, has written several books claiming that sexual words and drawings are embedded subliminally in magazine advertisements to elicit favorable unconscious reactions from consumers (Key, 1973, 1976, 1980, 1992). Taking the sexual manipulation theme a step further, entrepreneurs are now marketing music audiotapes containing subliminal messages that are supposed to help seduce unsuspecting listeners. Furthermore, subliminal self-help tapes intended to facilitate weight loss, sleep, memory, self-esteem, and the like have become a $50 million industry. Religious overtones were added to this controversy in the 1980s when subliminal messages encouraging devil worship were allegedly found in rock music played *backward* (Vokey & Read, 1985).

Can listening to Led Zeppelin's "Stairway to Heaven" promote Satanic rituals? Can your sexual urges be manipulated by messages hidden under music? Can advertisers influence your product preferences with subliminal stimuli? Those who are concerned about subliminal messages assert that such messages are likely to be persuasive because people supposedly are defenseless against appeals operating below their threshold of awareness. How justified are these fears? Research on subliminal perception was sporadic in the 1960s and 1970s because scientists initially dismissed the entire idea as preposterous. However, empirical studies have begun to accumulate since the 1980s.

Quite a number of studies have found support for the existence of subliminal perception (De Houwer, 2001; Greenwald, 1992; Snodgrass, Bernat, & Shevrin, 2004). Using diverse methodological and conceptual approaches, researchers have examined a variety of phenomena, such as unconscious semantic priming (Abrams, Klinger, & Greenwald, 2002), subliminal affective conditioning (Dijksterhuis, 2004), subliminal mere exposure effects (Monahan, Murphy, & Zajonc, 2000), subliminal visual priming (Haneda et al., 2003), and subliminal psychodynamic activation (Sohlberg & Birgegard, 2003), and they have found evidence that perception without awareness *can* take place.

© Fernado Serna/Corbis

ZITS

For example, in one recent study, Karremans, Stroebe, and Claus (2006) set out to determine whether participants' inclination to consume a particular drink (Lipton iced tea) could be influenced without their awareness. Subjects were asked to work on a visual detection task that was supposedly designed to determine whether people could spot small deviations in visual stimuli. Specifically, they were asked to view brief presentations of letter strings containing mostly capital letters (BBBBBBBBBB) and identify any that included a lower-case letter (such as BBBBBBBbBB). For half of the participants, subliminal presentations (23/1000 of a second) of the words LIPTON ICE were interspersed among these visual stimuli. Control subjects were given subliminal presentations of neutral words. After the visual detection task, subjects participated in a study of "consumer behavior" and their inclination to drink Lipton iced tea was assessed with a variety of comparative ratings. As predicted, participants exposed subliminally to LIPTON ICE were significantly more interested in consuming Lipton iced tea, especially among those who indicated that they were thirsty (see Figure 4.4). In a somewhat similar study, Cooper and Cooper (2002) demonstrated that subliminal presentations of pictures of Coca Cola cans and the word THIRSTY increased participants' ratings of their thirst. Thus, subliminal inputs can produce measurable, although small, effects in subjects who subsequently report that they did not consciously register the stimuli. As a result, the dominant view today is that subliminal perception is a genuine phenomenon worthy of experimental investigation. Indeed, researchers have recently begun to use brain imaging technology to study how the brain processes subliminal stimuli (Dehaene et al., 2006; Ortigue et al., 2007)

So, should we be worried about the threat of subliminal persuasion? The research to date suggests that there is little reason for concern. The effects of subliminal stimuli turn out to be nearly as subliminal as the stimuli themselves. Subliminal stimula-

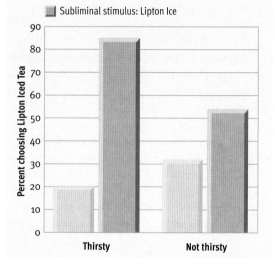

Figure 4.4

Results of Karremans et al. (2006) study of subliminal perception. One measure of whether the subliminal presentation of LIPTON ICE affected participants' drink preferences was to ask them to choose between Lipton Iced Tea and another popular drink. As you can see, the experimental group subjects showed a decided preference for Lipton Iced Tea in comparison to the control group subjects, especially among subjects who indicated that they were thirsty.

SOURCE: Adapted from Karremans, J. C., Stroebe, W., & Claus, J. (2006). Beyond Vicary's fantasies: The impact of subliminal priming and brand choice. *Journal of Experimental Psychology, 42,* 792–798 (Figure 2 from Study 2). Reprinted by permission of Elsevier.

tion generally produces weak effects (De Houwer, Hendrickx, & Baeyens, 1997; Kihlstrom, Barnhardt, & Tataryn, 1992). These effects can be detected only by very precise measurement, under carefully controlled laboratory conditions, in which subjects are asked to focus their undivided attention on visual or auditory materials that contain the subliminal stimuli. Although these effects are theoretically interesting, they appear unlikely to have much practical importance (Merikle, 2000). More research on the manipulative potential of subliminal persuasion is needed, but so far there is no cause for alarm.

Sensory Adaptation

The process of sensory adaptation is yet another factor that influences the registration of sensory input. *Sensory adaptation* is a gradual decline in sensitivity to prolonged stimulation. For example, suppose the garbage in your kitchen has started to smell. If you stay in the kitchen without removing the garbage, the stench will soon start to fade. In reality, the stimulus intensity of the odor is stable, but with

Because of sensory adaptation, people who live near foul-smelling industrial plants tend to grow accustomed to the stench in the air, whereas visitors may initially be overwhelmed by the same odors.

continued exposure, your *sensitivity* to it decreases. Meanwhile, someone new walking into the room is likely to remark on the foul odor. Sensory adaptation is a pervasive aspect of everyday life. When you put on your clothes in the morning, you feel them initially, but the sensation quickly fades. Similarly, if you jump reluctantly into a pool of cold water, you'll probably find that the water temperature feels fine in a few moments after you *adapt* to it.

Sensory adaptation is an automatic, built-in process that keeps people tuned in to the *changes* rather than the *constants* in their sensory input. It allows people to ignore the obvious. After all, you don't need constant confirmation that your clothes are still on. But, like most organisms, people are interested in changes in their environment that may signal threats to safety. Thus, as its name suggests, sensory adaptation probably is a behavioral adaptation that has been sculpted by natural selection. Sensory adaptation also shows once again that there is no one-to-one correspondence between sensory input and sensory experience.

The general points we've reviewed so far begin to suggest the complexity of the relationships between the world outside and people's perceived experience of it. As we review each of the principal sensory systems in detail, we'll see repeatedly that people's experience of the world depends on both the physical stimuli they encounter and their active processing of stimulus inputs. We begin our exploration of the senses with vision—the sense that most people think of as nearly synonymous with a direct perception of reality. The case is actually quite different, as you'll see.

REVIEW of Key Learning Goals

4.1 Psychophysicists use a variety of methods to relate sensory inputs to subjective perception. They have found that absolute thresholds are not really absolute. The size of a just noticeable difference tends to be a constant proportion of the size of the initial stimulus.

4.2 According to signal-detection theory, the detection of sensory inputs is influenced by noise in the system and by decision-making strategies. Signal-detection theory replaces Fechner's sharp threshold with the concept of detectability and emphasizes that factors besides stimulus intensity influence detectability.

4.3 In recent years, a number of researchers, using very different conceptual approaches, have demonstrated that perception can occur without awareness. However, research indicates that the effects of subliminal perception are relatively weak and of little or no practical concern.

4.4 Prolonged stimulation may lead to sensory adaptation, which involves a reduction in sensitivity to constant stimulation. Sensory adaptation keeps people tuned in to the changes rather than the constants in their sensory input.

The Visual System: Essentials of Sight

Key Learning Goals

4.5 List the three properties of light and the aspects of visual perception that they influence.

4.6 Describe the role of the lens and pupil in the functioning of the eye.

4.7 Explain how the retina contributes to visual information processing.

4.8 Trace the routing of signals from the eye to the brain, and explain the brain's role in visual information processing.

4.9 Distinguish two types of color mixing, and compare the trichromatic and opponent process theories of color vision.

"Seeing is believing." Good ideas are "bright," and a good explanation is "illuminating." This section is an "overview." Do you see the point? As these common expressions show, humans are visual animals. People rely heavily on their sense of sight, and they virtually equate it with what is trustworthy (seeing is believing). Although it is taken for granted, you'll see (there it is again) that the human visual system is amazingly complex. Furthermore, as in all sensory domains, what people "sense" and what they "perceive" may be quite different. In this section, we will focus on basic sensory processes in the visual system; in the following section we will look at higher-level perceptual processes in vision.

The Stimulus: Light

3a

For people to see, there must be light. *Light* is a form of electromagnetic radiation that travels as a wave, moving, naturally enough, at the speed of light. As **Figure 4.5(a)** shows, light waves vary in *amplitude* (height) and in *wavelength* (the distance between peaks). Amplitude affects mainly the perception of brightness, while wavelength affects mainly the perception of color. The lights humans normally see are mixtures of several wavelengths. Thus, light can also vary in its *purity* (how varied the mix is). Purity influences perception of the saturation, or richness, of colors. *Saturation* refers to the relative amount of whiteness in a color. The less whiteness seen in a color, the more saturated it is (see **Figure 4.6**). Of course, most objects do not emit light, they reflect it (the sun, lamps, and fireflies being some exceptions).

What most people call light includes only the wavelengths that humans can see. But as **Figure 4.5(c)** shows, the visible spectrum is only a slim portion of the total range of wavelengths. Vision is a filter that permits people to sense but a fraction of the

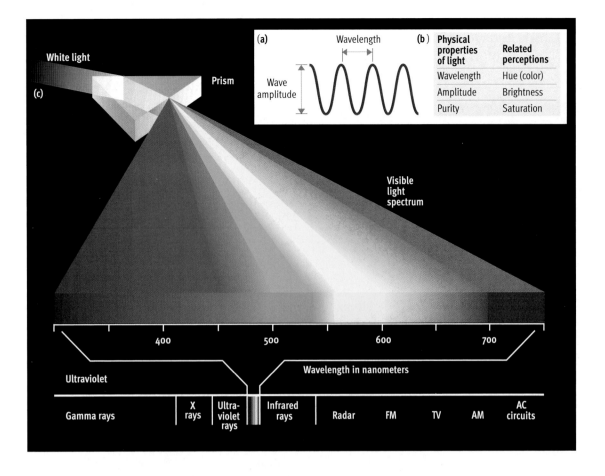

(a)
Wavelength
Wave amplitude

(b) Physical properties of light	Related perceptions
Wavelength	Hue (color)
Amplitude	Brightness
Purity	Saturation

White light

Prism

(c)

Visible light spectrum

Wavelength in nanometers

400   500   600   700

Ultraviolet

Gamma rays	X rays	Ultra-violet rays	Infrared rays	Radar	FM	TV	AM	AC circuits

Figure 4.5

Light, the physical stimulus for vision. (a) Light waves vary in amplitude and wavelength. (b) Within the spectrum of visible light, amplitude (corresponding to physical intensity) affects mainly the experience of brightness. Wavelength affects mainly the experience of color, and purity is the key determinant of saturation. (c) If white light (such as sunlight) passes through a prism, the prism separates the light into its component wavelengths, creating a rainbow of colors. However, visible light is only the narrow band of wavelengths to which human eyes happen to be sensitive.

Saturation: intensity of color

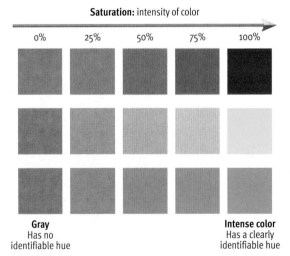

0%   25%   50%   75%   100%

Gray Has no identifiable hue

Intense color Has a clearly identifiable hue

Figure 4.6

Saturation. Saturation refers to the amount of whiteness in a color. As you can see in these examples, as the amount of whiteness declines (moving to the right), the saturation or richness of a color increases.

real world. Other animals have different capabilities and so live in a quite different visual world. For example, many insects can see shorter wavelengths than humans, in the *ultraviolet* spectrum, whereas many fish and reptiles can see longer wavelengths,

in the *infrared* spectrum. Although the sense of sight depends on light waves, for people to *see,* incoming visual input must be converted into neural impulses that are sent to the brain. Let's investigate how this transformation is accomplished.

The Eye: A Living Optical Instrument

PSYK TREK 3a

The eyes serve two main purposes: They channel light to the neural tissue that receives it, called the *retina,* and they house that tissue. The structure of the eye is shown in **Figure 4.7** (on the next page). Each eye is a living optical instrument that creates an image of the visual world on the light-sensitive retina lining its inside back surface.

Light enters the eye through a transparent "window" at the front, the *cornea.* The cornea and the crystalline *lens,* located behind it, form an upside-down image of objects on the retina. It might seem disturbing that the image is upside down, but the brain knows the rule for relating positions on the retina to the corresponding positions in the world.

The *lens* is the transparent eye structure that focuses the light rays falling on the retina. The lens is made up of relatively soft tissue, capable of adjustments that facilitate a process called accommodation.

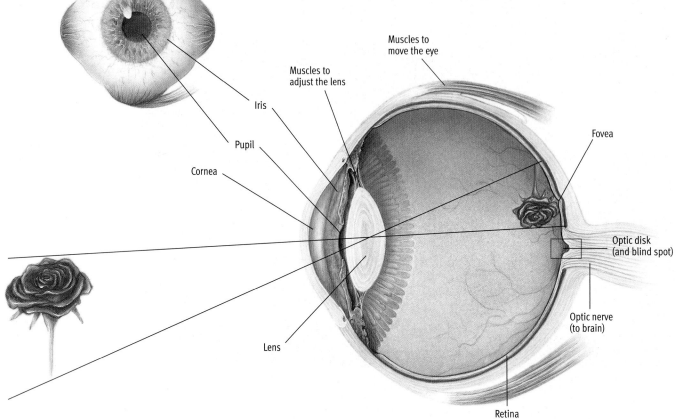

Figure 4.7

The human eye. Light passes through the cornea, pupil, and lens and falls on the light-sensitive surface of the retina, where images of objects are reflected upside down. The lens adjusts its curvature to focus the images falling on the retina. The iris and pupil regulate the amount of light passing into the rear chamber of the eye.

Muscles to move the eye

Muscles to adjust the lens

Fovea

Iris

Pupil

Cornea

Optic disk (and blind spot)

Optic nerve (to brain)

Lens

Retina

Figure 4.8

Nearsightedness and farsightedness. The pictures shown here simulate how a scene might look to nearsighted and farsighted people. Nearsightedness occurs because light from distant objects focuses in front of the retina. Farsightedness is due to the opposite situation—light from close objects focuses behind the retina.

Nearsightedness

Normal eye shape

Retina

Focus point falls in front of retina

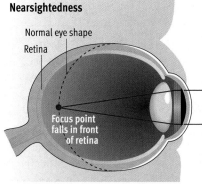

Farsightedness

Normal eye shape

Retina

Focus point falls behind retina

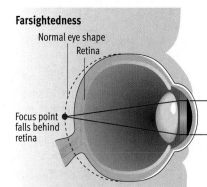

Craig McClain

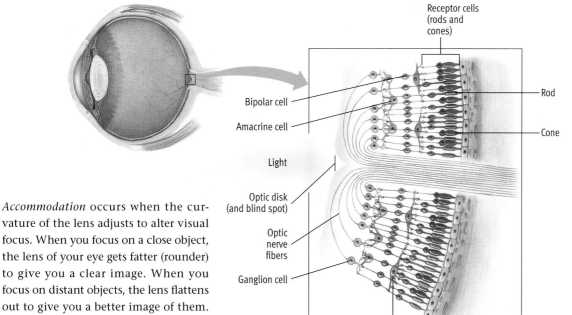

Receptor cells
(rods and
cones)

Bipolar cell

Amacrine cell

Light

Optic disk
(and blind spot)

Optic
nerve
fibers

Ganglion cell

Rod

Cone

Horizontal cell

Figure 4.9
The retina. The closeup shows the several layers of cells in the retina. The cells closest to the back of the eye (the rods and cones) are the receptor cells that actually detect light. The intervening layers of cells receive signals from the rods and cones and form circuits that begin the process of analyzing incoming information. The visual signals eventually converge into *ganglion cells,* whose axons form the optic fibers that make up the optic nerve. These optic fibers all head toward the "hole" in the retina where the optic nerve leaves the eye—the point known as the optic disk (which corresponds to the blind spot).

Accommodation occurs when the curvature of the lens adjusts to alter visual focus. When you focus on a close object, the lens of your eye gets fatter (rounder) to give you a clear image. When you focus on distant objects, the lens flattens out to give you a better image of them.

Some common visual deficiencies are attributable to light not being focused clearly on the retina (Oyster, 1999). For example, in *nearsightedness,* close objects are seen clearly but distant objects appear blurry because the focus of light from distant objects falls a little short of the retina (see Figure 4.8). This problem occurs when the cornea or lens bends light too much, or when the eyeball is too long. In *farsightedness,* distant objects are seen clearly but close objects appear blurry because the focus of light from close objects falls behind the retina (see Figure 4.8). This problem typically occurs when the eyeball is too short.

The eye can make adjustments to alter the amount of light reaching the retina. The *iris* is the colored ring of muscle surrounding the *pupil,* or black center of the eye. The iris regulates the amount of light entering the eye because it controls the size of the pupil. The *pupil* is the opening in the center of the iris that permits light to pass into the rear chamber of the eye. When the pupils are constricted, they let less light into the eye, but they sharpen the image falling on the retina. When the pupils are dilated (opened more), they let more light in, but the image is less sharp. In bright light, the pupils constrict to take advantage of the sharpened image. But in dim light, the pupils dilate; image sharpness is sacrificed to allow more light to fall on the retina so that more remains visible.

The Retina: The Brain's Envoy in the Eye

3b

The *retina* is the neural tissue lining the inside back surface of the eye; it absorbs light, processes images, and sends visual information to the brain. You may be surprised to learn that the retina *processes* images. But it's a piece of the central nervous system that happens to be located in the eyeball. Much as the spinal cord is a complicated extension of the brain, the retina is the brain's envoy in the eye. About half as thick as a credit card, this thin sheet of neural tissue contains a complex network of specialized cells arranged in layers (Rodieck, 1998), as shown in Figure 4.9.

The axons that run from the retina to the brain converge at the *optic disk,* a hole in the retina where the optic nerve fibers exit the eye. Because the optic disk is a *hole* in the retina, you cannot see the part of an image that falls on it. It is therefore known as the *blind spot.* You may not be aware that you have a blind spot in each eye, as each normally compensates for the blind spot of the other.

Visual Receptors: Rods and Cones

3b

The retina contains millions of receptor cells that are sensitive to light. Surprisingly, these receptors are located in the innermost layer of the retina. Hence, light must pass through several layers of cells before it gets to the receptors that actually detect it. Interestingly, only about 10% of the light arriving at the cornea reaches these receptors (Leibovic, 1990). The retina contains two types of receptors, *rods* and *cones.* Their names are based on their shapes, as rods are elongated and cones are stubbier. Rods outnumber cones by a huge margin, as humans have

100–125 million rods, but only 5–6.4 million cones (Frishman, 2001).

Cones are specialized visual receptors that play a key role in daylight vision and color vision. The cones handle most of people's daytime vision, because bright lights dazzle the rods. The special sensitivities of cones also allow them to play a major role in the perception of color. However, cones do not respond well to dim light, which is why you don't see color very well in low illumination. Nonetheless, cones provide better *visual acuity*—that is, sharpness and precise detail—than rods. Cones are concentrated most heavily in the center of the retina and quickly fall off in density toward its periphery. The *fovea is a tiny spot in the center of the retina that contains only cones; visual acuity is greatest at this spot.* When you want to see something sharply, you usually move your eyes so the object is centered in the fovea.

Rods are specialized visual receptors that play a key role in night vision and peripheral vision. Rods handle night vision because they are more sensitive than cones to dim light. They handle the lion's share of peripheral vision because they greatly outnumber cones in the periphery of the retina. The density of the rods is greatest just outside the fovea and gradually decreases toward the periphery of the retina. Because of the distribution of rods, when you want to see a faintly illuminated object in the dark, it's best to look slightly above or below the place it should be. Averting your gaze this way moves the image from the cone-filled fovea, which requires more light, to the rod-dominated area just outside the fovea, which requires less light. This trick of averted vision is well known to astronomers, who use it to study dim objects viewed through the eyepiece of a telescope.

Dark and Light Adaptation

 3b

You've probably noticed that when you enter a dark theater on a bright day, you stumble around almost blindly. But within minutes you can make your way about quite well in the dim light. This adjustment is called *dark adaptation—the process in which the eyes become more sensitive to light in low illumination.* Figure 4.10 maps out the course of this process. The declining absolute thresholds over time indicate that you require less and less light to see. Dark adaptation is virtually complete in about 30 minutes, with considerable progress occurring in the first 10 minutes. The curve (in Figure 4.10) that charts this progress consists of two segments because cones adapt more rapidly than rods (Walraven et al., 1990).

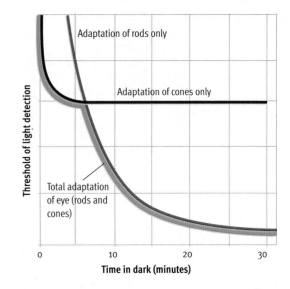

Figure 4.10

The process of dark adaptation. The declining thresholds over time indicate that your visual sensitivity is improving, as less and less light is required to see. Visual sensitivity improves markedly during the first 5 to 10 minutes after entering a dark room, as the eye's bright-light receptors (the cones) rapidly adapt to low light levels. However, the cones' adaptation, which is plotted in purple, soon reaches its limit, and further improvement comes from the rods' adaptation, which is plotted in red. The rods adapt more slowly than the cones, but they are capable of far greater visual sensitivity in low levels of light.

When you emerge from a dark theater on a sunny day, you need to squint to ward off the overwhelming brightness, and the reverse of dark adaptation occurs. *Light adaptation is the process whereby the eyes become less sensitive to light in high illumination.* As with dark adaptation, light adaptation improves your visual acuity under the prevailing circumstances. Both types of adaptation are due in large part to chemical changes in the rods and cones, but neural changes in the receptors and elsewhere in the retina also contribute (Frumkes, 1990).

Information Processing in the Retina

 3b

In processing visual input, the retina transforms a pattern of light falling onto it into a very different representation of the visual scene. Light striking the retina's receptors (rods and cones) triggers the firing of neural signals that pass into the intricate network of cells in the retina, which in turn send impulses along the *optic nerve*—a collection of axons from *ganglion cells* that connect the eye with the brain (see Figure 4.9). These axons, which depart from the eye through the optic disk, carry visual information, encoded as a stream of neural impulses, to the brain.

A great deal of complex information processing goes on in the retina itself before visual signals are sent

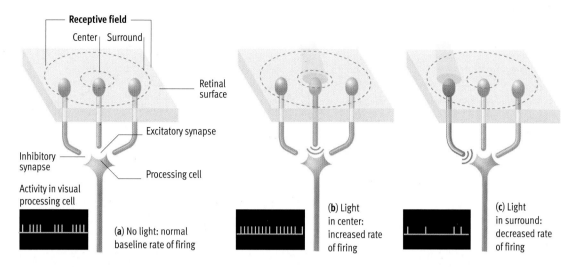

Figure 4.11

Receptive fields in the retina. Visual cells' receptive fields—made up of rods and cones in the retina—are often circular with a center-surround arrangement (a), so that light striking the center of the field produces the opposite result of light striking the surround. In the receptive field depicted here, light in the center produces excitatory effects (symbolized by green at the synapse) and increased firing in the visual cell (b), whereas light in the surround produces inhibitory effects (symbolized by red at the synapse) and decreased firing (c). Interestingly, no light in the receptive field and light in both center and surround produce similar baseline rates of firing. This arrangement makes the visual cell particularly sensitive to *contrast,* which facilitates the extremely important task of recognizing the *edges* of objects.

to the brain. Ultimately, the information from over 100 million rods and cones converges to travel along "only" 1 million axons in the optic nerve (Slaughter, 1990). The collection of rod and cone receptors that funnel signals to a particular visual cell in the retina (or ultimately in the brain) make up that cell's *receptive field*. Thus, **the *receptive field of a visual cell* is the retinal area that, when stimulated, affects the firing of that cell.**

Receptive fields in the retina come in a variety of shapes and sizes. Particularly common are circular fields with a center-surround arrangement (Tessier-Lavigne, 2000). In these receptive fields, light falling in the center has the opposite effect of light falling in the surrounding area (see **Figure 4.11**). For example, the rate of firing of a visual cell might be *increased* by light in the *center* of its receptive field and *decreased* by light in the *surrounding area,* as **Figure 4.11** shows. Other visual cells may work in just the opposite way. Either way, when receptive fields are stimulated, retinal cells send signals both toward the brain and *laterally* (sideways) toward nearby visual cells. These lateral signals allow visual cells in the retina to have interactive effects on each other.

Lateral antagonism (also known as lateral inhibition) is the most basic of these interactive effects. *Lateral antagonism* occurs when neural activity in a cell opposes activity in surrounding cells. Lateral antagonism is responsible for the opposite effects that occur when light falls on the inner versus outer portions of center-surround receptive fields.

Lateral antagonism allows the retina to compare the light falling in a specific area against general lighting. This means that the visual system can compute the *relative* amount of light at a point instead of reacting to *absolute* levels of light. This attention to *contrast* is exactly what is needed, because most of the crucial information required to recognize objects in a visual scene is contained in the pattern of contrasts, which reveal the *edges* of the objects (Tessier-Lavigne, 2000). If you look at **Figure 4.12**, you will experience a perplexing illusion attributable to lateral antagonism in the ganglion cells of the retina.

Figure 4.12
The Hermann grid. If you look at this grid, you will see dark spots at the intersections of the white bars, except in the intersection you're staring at directly. This illusion is due to lateral antagonism.

Understanding Sensory Processes in the Retina

Check your understanding of sensory receptors in the retina by completing the following exercises. Consult Appendix A for the answers.

The receptors for vision are rods and cones in the retina. These two types of receptors have many important differences, which are compared systematically in the chart below. Fill in the missing information to finish the chart.

Dimension	Rods	Cones
Physical shape	Elongated	
Number in the retina		5–6.4 million
Area of the retina in which they are dominant receptor	Periphery	
Critical to color vision		
Critical to peripheral vision		No
Sensitivity to dim light	Strong	
Speed of dark adaptation		Rapid

Vision and the Brain

3c

Light falls on the eye, but you see with your brain. Although the retina does an unusual amount of information processing for a sensory organ, visual input is meaningless until it is processed in the brain.

Visual Pathways to the Brain

3c

How does visual information get to the brain? Axons from ganglion cells leaving the back of each eye form the optic nerves, which travel to the *optic chiasm—* **the point at which the optic nerves from the inside half of each eye cross over and then project to the opposite half of the brain.** This arrangement ensures that signals from both eyes go to both hemispheres of the brain. Thus, as **Figure 4.13** shows, axons from the left half of each retina carry signals to the left side of the brain, and axons from the right half of each retina carry information to the right side of the brain.

After reaching the optic chiasm, the optic nerve fibers diverge along two pathways. The main pathway projects into the thalamus, the brain's major relay station. Here, about 90% of the axons from the retinas synapse in the *lateral geniculate nucleus* (LGN) (Pasternak, Bisley, & Calkins, 2003). Visual signals are processed in the LGN and then distributed to areas in the occipital lobe that make up the *primary visual cortex* (see **Figure 4.13**). The second visual pathway leaving the optic chiasm branches off to an area in the midbrain called the *superior col-liculus* before traveling through the thalamus and on to the occipital lobe. The principal function of the second pathway appears to be the perception of motion and the coordination of visual input with other sensory input (Casanova et al., 2001; Stein & Meredith, 1993).

The main visual pathway is subdivided into two more specialized pathways called the *magnocellular* and *parvocellular* channels (based on the layers of the LGN they synapse in). These channels engage in *parallel processing,* **which involves simultaneously extracting different kinds of information from the same input.** For example, the parvocellular channel handles the perception of color, while the magnocellular channel processes information regarding brightness (Wurtz & Kandel, 2000). Of course, this brief description hardly does justice to the immense complexity of visual processing in the brain.

Information Processing in the Visual Cortex

3c

Most visual input eventually arrives in the primary visual cortex, located in the occipital lobe. Explaining how the cortical cells in this area respond to light used to pose a perplexing problem. Researchers investigating the question placed microelectrodes in the primary visual cortex of animals to record action potentials from individual cells. They would flash spots of light in the retinal receptive fields that the cells were thought to monitor, but there was rarely any response.

Figure 4.13

Visual pathways through the brain. (a) Input from the right half of the visual field strikes the left side of each retina and is transmitted to the left hemisphere (shown in blue). Input from the left half of the visual field strikes the right side of each retina and is transmitted to the right hemisphere (shown in red). The nerve fibers from each eye meet at the optic chiasm, where fibers from the inside half of each retina cross over to the opposite side of the brain. After reaching the optic chiasm, the major visual pathway projects through the lateral geniculate nucleus (LGN) in the thalamus and onto the primary visual cortex (shown with solid lines). A second pathway detours through the superior colliculus and then projects through the thalamus and onto the primary visual cortex (shown with dotted lines). (b) This inset shows a vertical view of how the optic pathways project through the thalamus and onto the visual cortex in the back of the brain [the two pathways mapped out in diagram (a) are virtually indistinguishable from this angle].

(a)

Left visual field   Right visual field

Retinas

Left eye   Right eye

Optic nerves

Optic chiasm

Superior colliculus

Visual cortex (occipital lobe)

(b)

Optic nerve   Thalamus

Retina

Lateral geniculate nucleus of the thalamus

Visual cortex

According to David Hubel and Torsten Wiesel (1962, 1963), they discovered the solution to this mystery quite by accident. One of the projector slides they used to present a spot to a cat had a crack in it. The spot elicited no response, but when they removed the slide, the crack moved through the cell's receptive field, and the cell fired like crazy in response to the moving dark line. It turns out that individual cells in the primary visual cortex don't really respond much to little spots—they are much more sensitive to lines, edges, and other more complicated stimuli. Armed with new slides, Hubel and Wiesel embarked on years of painstaking study of the visual cortex (see Figure 4.14 on the next page). Their work eventually earned them a Nobel prize in 1981.

Hubel and Wiesel (1979, 1998) identified various types of specialized cells in the primary visual cortex that respond to different stimuli. For example, *simple cells* respond best to a line of the correct width, oriented at the correct angle, and located in the correct position in its receptive field. *Complex cells* also care about width and orientation, but they respond to any position in their receptive fields. Some complex cells are most responsive if a line sweeps across their receptive field—but only if it's moving in the "right" direction. The key point of all this is that the cells in the visual cortex seem to be highly specialized. They have been characterized as *feature detectors,* **neurons that respond selectively to very specific features of more complex stimuli.** According to

David Hubel

"One can now begin to grasp the significance of the great number of cells in the visual cortex. Each cell seems to have its own specific duties."

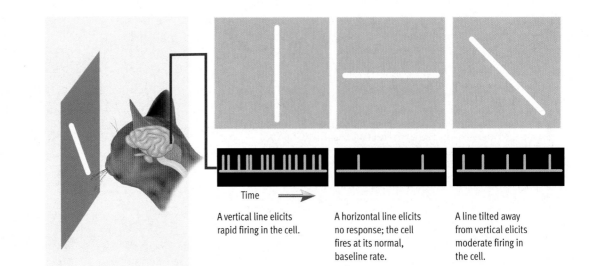

Figure 4.14
Hubel and Wiesel's procedure for studying the activity of neurons in the visual cortex. As the cat is shown various stimuli, a microelectrode records the firing of a neuron in the cat's visual cortex. The figure shows the electrical responses of a visual cell apparently "programmed" to respond to lines oriented vertically.

Time

A vertical line elicits rapid firing in the cell.

A horizontal line elicits no response; the cell fires at its normal, baseline rate.

A line tilted away from vertical elicits moderate firing in the cell.

some theorists, most visual stimuli could ultimately be represented by combinations of lines such as those registered by these feature detectors (Maguire, Weisstein, & Klymenko, 1990).

After visual input is processed in the primary visual cortex, it is often routed to other cortical areas for additional processing. These signals travel through two streams that have sometimes been characterized as the *what* and *where pathways* (see Figure 4.15). The *ventral stream* processes the details of *what* objects are out there (the perception of form and color), while the *dorsal stream* processes *where* the objects are (the perception of motion and depth) (Pasternak et al., 2003; Ungerleider & Haxby, 1994).

As signals move farther along in the visual processing system, neurons become even more specialized or fussy about what turns them on, and the stimuli that activate them become more and more complex. For example, researchers have identified

cells in the temporal lobe (along the *what* pathway) of monkeys and humans that are especially sensitive to pictures of faces (Levine, 2001; Rolls & Tovee, 1995). These neurons respond even to pictures that merely *suggest* the form of a face (Cox, Meyers, & Sinha, 2004). Scientists have also found neurons in a nearby region that respond to body parts and another group of neurons that respond to indoor and outdoor scenes (Downing et al., 2006).

This incredible specificity led researchers to joke that they might eventually find a neuron that only recognizes one's grandmother (Cowey, 1994). Although the concept of a "grandmother cell" was meant to be humorous, researchers recently have discovered the equivalent, albeit in areas of the brain that handle memory rather than vision (Gaschler, 2006). Using pictures of famous people as stimuli, Quiroga et al. (2005) found individual neurons in the hippocampal area that would respond only to Bill Clinton, others that would respond only to Halle Berry, and still others that were activated only by Jennifer Aniston. Interestingly, these cells would also respond to the words BILL CLINTON or HALLE BERRY (see Figure 4.16), so it appears that they are activated by *concepts* rather than *visual forms*. Hence, these ultraspecific cells probably have more to do with memory than vision. Nonetheless, it is fascinating that the frequently mocked concept of a "grandmother cell" is not as preposterous as once assumed.

Another dramatic finding in this area of research is that the neurons in the what pathway that are involved in perceiving faces can learn from experience (Gauthier & Curby, 2005; Palmeri & Gauthier, 2004). In one eye-opening study, participants were given extensive training in discriminating among similar artificial objects called Greebles (see Figure 4.17). After this training, neurons that

Figure 4.15
The *what* and *where* pathways from the primary visual cortex. Cortical processing of visual input is begun in the primary visual cortex. From there, signals are shuttled onward to a variety of other areas in the cortex along a number of pathways. Two prominent pathways are highlighted here. The *dorsal stream,* or *where pathway,* which processes information about motion and depth, moves on to areas of the parietal lobe. The *ventral stream,* or *what pathway,* which processes information about color and form, moves on to areas of the temporal lobe.

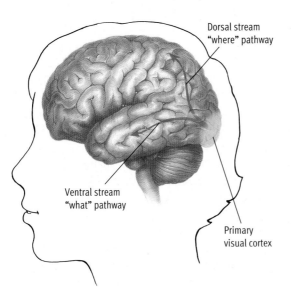

Dorsal stream "where" pathway

Ventral stream "what" pathway

Primary visual cortex

are normally sensitive to faces were found to be almost as sensitive to Greebles as to faces (Gauthier et al., 1999). In other words, neurons that usually serve as face detectors were "retooled" to be responsive to other visual forms. Like many findings discussed in Chapter 3 (see pp. 104–105), these results demonstrate that the functional organization of the brain is somewhat "plastic" and that the brain can be rewired by experience.

Viewing the World in Color

So far, we've considered only how the visual system deals with light and dark. Let's journey now into the world of color. On the one hand, you can see perfectly well without seeing in color. Many animals get by with little or no color vision, and no one seemed to suffer back when all photographs, movies, or TV shows were in black and white. On the other hand, color clearly adds rich information to our perception of the world. The ability to identify objects is enhanced by the addition of color (Tanaka, Weiskopf, & Williams, 2001). Thus, some theorists have suggested that color vision evolved in humans and monkeys because it improved their abilities to find food through foraging, to spot prey, and to quickly recognize predators (Spence et al., 2006). Although the purpose of color vision remains elusive, scientists have learned a great deal about the mechanisms underlying the perception of color.

The Stimulus for Color

Figure 4.16

Examples of stimuli used by Quiroga et al. (2005). Quiroga and colleagues exposed participants to varied views of specific objects, buildings, animals, faces, and random photos while monitoring activity in selected brain cells. They discovered neurons in the hippocampal area that were uniquely responsive to certain famous people, such as Halle Berry. These cells apparently were responding to the *concept* of Halle Berry rather than to her *face* because they responded not only to facial photos but also to pictures of the actress in a Catwoman costume and to the words HALLE BERRY. Similar results were observed for diverse stimuli related to other famous people.

As noted earlier, the lights people see are mixtures of various wavelengths. Perceived color is primarily a function of the dominant wavelength in these mixtures. In the visible spectrum, lights with the longest wavelengths appear red, whereas those with the shortest appear violet. Notice the word *appear*. Color is a psychological interpretation. It's not a physical property of light itself.

Although wavelength wields the greatest influence, perception of color depends on complex blends of all three properties of light. *Wavelength* is most closely related to hue, *amplitude* to brightness, and *purity* to saturation. These three dimensions of color are illustrated in the *color solid* shown in Figure 4.18 on the next page.

As a color solid demonstrates systematically, people can perceive many different colors. Indeed, experts estimate that humans can discriminate among roughly a million colors (Boynton, 1990). Most of these diverse variations are the result of mixing a few basic colors. There are two kinds of color mixture:

Figure 4.17

Distinguishing Greebles. Gauthier et al. (1999) gave subjects seven hours of training in the recognition of novel stimuli called Greebles, four of which are shown here. As the text explains, this training was conducted to explore whether neurons that normally respond to faces could be retuned by experience.

SOURCE: Reproduced by permission of Gauthier, I., (2008). Copyright © by Isabel Gauthier.

subtractive and additive. *Subtractive color mixing works by removing some wavelengths of light, leaving less light than was originally there.* You probably became familiar with subtractive mixing as a child when you mixed yellow and blue paints to make green. Paints yield subtractive mixing because pigments *absorb* most wavelengths, selectively reflecting specific wavelengths that give rise to particular colors. Subtractive color mixing can also be demonstrated by stacking color filters. If you look through a sandwich of yellow and blue cellophane filters, they will block out certain wavelengths. The middle wavelengths that are left will look green.

Additive color mixing works by superimposing lights, putting more light in the mixture than exists in any one light by itself. If you shine red, green, and blue spotlights on a white surface, you'll

Figure 4.18
The color solid. The color solid shows how color varies along three perceptual dimensions: brightness (increasing from the bottom to the top of the solid), hue (changing around the solid's perimeter), and saturation (increasing toward the periphery of the solid).

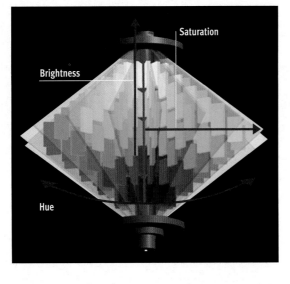

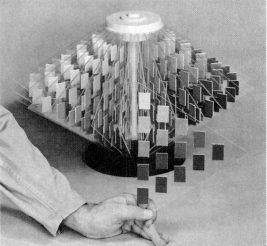

Courtesy of BASF

have an additive mixture. As Figure 4.19 shows, additive and subtractive mixtures of the same colors produce different results. Human processes of color perception parallel additive color mixing much more closely than subtractive mixing, as you'll see in the following discussion of theories of color vision.

Trichromatic Theory of Color Vision

3d

The *trichromatic theory* of color vision (*tri* for "three," *chroma* for "color") was first stated by Thomas Young and modified later by Hermann von Helmholtz (1852). The *trichromatic theory* of color vision holds that the human eye has three types of receptors with differing sensitivities to different light wavelengths. Helmholtz theorized that the eye contains specialized receptors sensitive to the specific wavelengths associated with red, green, and blue. According to this model, people can see all the colors of the rainbow because the eye does its own "color mixing" by varying the ratio of neural activity among these three types of receptors.

The impetus for the trichromatic theory was the demonstration that a light of any color can be matched by the additive mixture of three *primary colors*. Any three colors that are appropriately spaced out in the visible spectrum can serve as primary colors, although red, green, and blue are usually used. Does it sound implausible that three colors should be adequate for creating all other colors? If so, consider that this is exactly what happens on your color TV screen. Additive mixtures of red, green, and blue fool you into seeing all the colors of a natural scene.

Most of the known facts about color blindness also meshed well with trichromatic theory. *Color blindness* encompasses a variety of deficiencies in the ability to distinguish among colors. Color blindness occurs much more frequently in males than in females. Actually, the term color *blindness* is somewhat misleading, since complete blindness to differences in colors is quite rare. Most people who are color blind are *dichromats;* that is, they make do with only two types of color receptors. There are

Figure 4.19
Additive versus subtractive color mixing. Lights mix additively because all the wavelengths contained in each light reach the eye. If red, blue, and green lights are projected onto a white screen, they produce the colors shown on the left, with white at the intersection of all three lights. If paints of the same three colors were combined in the same way, the subtractive mixture would produce the colors shown on the right, with black at the intersection of all three colors. As you can see, additive and subtractive color mixing produce different results.

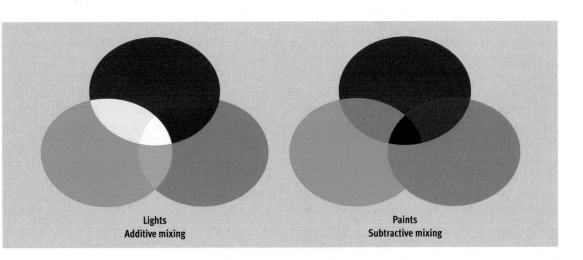

Lights
Additive mixing

Paints
Subtractive mixing

three types of dichromats, and each type is insensitive to a different color (red, green, or blue, although the latter is rare) (Gouras, 1991). The three deficiencies seen among dichromats support the notion that there are three sets of receptors for color vision, as proposed by trichromatic theory.

Opponent Process Theory of Color Vision

Although trichromatic theory explained some facets of color vision well, it ran aground in other areas. Consider complementary afterimages, for instance. *Complementary colors* are pairs of colors that produce gray tones when mixed together. The various pairs of complementary colors can be arranged in a *color circle,* such as the one in Figure 4.20. If you stare at a strong color and then look at a white background, you'll see an *afterimage*—a visual image that persists after a stimulus is removed. The color of the afterimage will be the *complement* of the color you originally stared at. Trichromatic theory cannot account for the appearance of complementary afterimages.

Here's another peculiarity to consider. If you ask people to describe colors but restrict them to using three names, they run into difficulty. For example, using only red, green, and blue, they simply don't feel comfortable describing yellow as "reddish green." However, if you let them have just one more name, they usually choose yellow; they can then describe any color quite well (Gordon & Abramov, 2001). If colors can be reduced to three primaries, why are four color names required to describe the full range of possible colors?

In an effort to answer questions such as these, Ewald Hering proposed the *opponent process theory* in 1878. The **opponent process theory** of color vision holds that color perception depends on receptors that make antagonistic responses to three pairs of colors. The three pairs of opponent colors he posited were red versus green, yellow versus blue, and black versus white. The antagonistic processes in this theory provide plausible explanations for complementary afterimages and the need for four names (red, green, blue, and yellow) to describe colors. Opponent process theory also explains some aspects of color blindness. For instance, it can explain why dichromats typically find it hard to distinguish either green from red or yellow from blue.

Reconciling Theories of Color Vision

Advocates of trichromatic theory and opponent process theory argued about the relative merits of their models for almost a century. Most researchers assumed that one theory must be wrong and the other

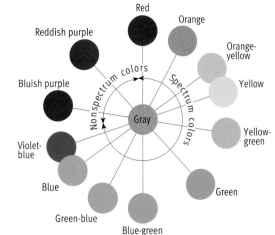

Figure 4.20

The color circle and complementary colors. Colors opposite each other on this color circle are complements, or "opposites." Additively mixing complementary colors produces gray. Opponent process principles help explain this effect as well as the other peculiarities of complementary colors noted in the text.

must be right. In recent decades, however, it has become clear that *it takes both theories to explain color vision.* Eventually a physiological basis for both theories was found. Research that earned George Wald a Nobel prize demonstrated that *the eye has three types of cones,* with each type being most sensitive to a different band of wavelengths, as shown in Figure 4.21 (Lennie, 2000; Wald, 1964). The three types of cones represent the three different color receptors predicted by trichromatic theory. Interestingly, the three types of cones are distributed in a seemingly random fashion in the central area of the retina where cones predominate (Solomon & Lennie, 2007).

Researchers also discovered a biological basis for opponent processes. They found cells in the retina,

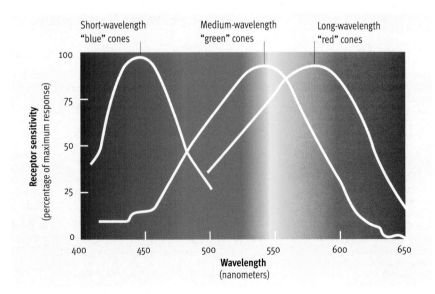

Figure 4.21

Three types of cones. Research has identified three types of cones that show varied sensitivity to different wavelengths of light. As the graph shows, these three types of cones correspond only roughly to the red, green, and blue receptors predicted by trichromatic theory, so it is more accurate to refer to them as cones sensitive to short, medium, and long wavelengths.

SOURCE: Wald, G., & Brown, P. K. (1965). Human color vision and color blindness. *Symposium Cold Spring Harbor Laboratory of Quantitative Biology, 30,* 345–359 (p. 351). Copyright © 1965. Reprinted by permission of the author.

LGN, and visual cortex *that respond in opposite ways to red versus green and blue versus yellow* (DeValois & Jacobs, 1984; Zrenner et al., 1990). For example, specific ganglion cells in the retina are excited by green and inhibited by red. Other retinal ganglion cells work in just the opposite way, as predicted in opponent process theory.

In summary, the perception of color appears to involve sequential stages of information processing (Hurvich, 1981). The receptors that do the first stage of processing (the cones) seem to follow the principles outlined in trichromatic theory. In later stages of processing, at least some cells in the retina, the LGN, and the visual cortex seem to follow the principles outlined in opponent process theory. As you can see, vigorous theoretical debate about color vision produced a solution that went beyond the contributions of either theory alone.

REVIEW of Key Learning Goals

4.5 Light varies in terms of wavelength, amplitude, and purity. Perceptions of color (hue) are primarily a function of light wavelength, while amplitude mainly affects brightness and purity mainly affects saturation.

4.6 Light enters the eye through the cornea and pupil and is focused upside down on the retina by the lens. Distant objects appear blurry to nearsighted people and close objects appear blurry to farsighted people. The pupils control the amount of light entering the eye.

4.7 The retina is the neural tissue in the eye that absorbs light, processes images, and sends visual signals to the brain. Cones, which are concentrated in the fovea, play a key role in daylight vision and color perception. Rods, which have their greatest density just outside the fovea, are critical to night vision and peripheral vision. Dark adaptation and light adaptation both involve changes in the retina's sensitivity to light. Receptive fields are areas in the retina that affect the firing of visual cells.

4.8 The optic nerves from the inside half of each eye cross at the optic chiasm and then project to the opposite half of the brain. Two visual pathways engage in parallel processing and send signals to different areas of the primary visual cortex. The main pathway is routed through the LGN in the thalamus. After processing in the primary visual cortex, visual information is shuttled along the *what* and *where* pathways to other cortical areas. Research suggests that the visual cortex contains cells that function as feature detectors. The *what pathway* has neurons inside it that are especially sensitive to faces and other highly specific stimuli.

4.9 There are two types of color mixing: additive and subtractive. Human color perception depends on processes that resemble additive color mixing. The trichromatic theory holds that people have three types of receptors that are sensitive to wavelengths associated with red, green, and blue. The opponent process theory holds that color perception depends on receptors that make antagonistic responses to red versus green, blue versus yellow, and black versus white. The evidence now suggests that both theories are necessary to account for color vision.

The Visual System: Perceptual Processes

Key Learning Goals

4.10 Discuss the subjectivity of form perception, the phenomenon of inattentional blindness, and the concept of feature analysis.

4.11 State the basic premise of Gestalt psychology, and describe Gestalt principles of visual perception.

4.12 Clarify how form perception can be a matter of formulating perceptual hypotheses.

4.13 Describe the monocular and binocular cues used in depth perception, and discuss cultural variations in depth perception.

4.14 Summarize the Featured Study on the perception of geographical slant.

4.15 Describe perceptual constancies and illusions in vision, and discuss cultural variations in susceptibility to certain illusions.

We have seen how sensory receptors in the eye transform light into neural impulses that are sent to the brain. We focus next on how the brain makes sense of it all—how does it convert streams of neural impulses into perceptions of chairs, doors, friends, automobiles, and buildings? In this section we explore *perceptual processes* in vision, such as the perception of forms, objects, depth, and so forth.

Perceiving Forms, Patterns, and Objects

3c, 3e

The drawing in **Figure 4.22** is a poster for a circus act involving a trained seal. Take a good look at it. What do you see?

No doubt you see a seal balancing a ball on its nose and a trainer holding a fish and a whip. But suppose you had been told that the drawing is actually a poster for a costume ball. Would you have perceived it differently?

If you focus on the idea of a costume ball (stay with it a minute if you still see the seal and trainer), you will probably see a costumed man and woman in **Figure 4.22**. She's handing him a hat, and he has a sword in his right hand. This tricky little sketch was made ambiguous quite intentionally. It's a *reversible figure,* **a drawing that is compatible with two interpretations that can shift back and forth.** Another classic reversible figure is shown in **Figure 4.23**. What do you see? A rabbit or a duck? It all depends on how you look at the drawing.

The key point is simply this: *The same visual input can result in radically different perceptions.* No one-to-one correspondence exists between sensory input and what you perceive. *This is a principal reason that people's experience of the world is subjective.* Perception involves much more than passively receiving signals from the outside world. It involves the *interpretation* of sensory input. To some extent, this interpretive process can be influenced by manipulating people's

Figure 4.22

A poster for a trained seal act. Or is it? The picture is an ambiguous figure, which can be interpreted as either of two scenes, as explained in the text.

Figure 4.23

Another ambiguous figure. What animal do you see here? As the text explains, two very different perceptions are possible. This ambiguous figure was devised around 1900 by Joseph Jastrow, a prominent psychologist at the turn of the 20th century (Block & Yuker, 1992).

expectations. For example, information given to you about the drawing of the "circus act involving a trained seal" created a *perceptual set*—a readiness to perceive a stimulus in a particular way. A perceptual set creates a certain slant in how someone interprets sensory input.

Like expectations, motivational forces can foster perceptual sets, as demonstrated in one recent study (Balcetis & Dunning, 2006) using reversible figures as stimuli. Participants were told that a computer would flash a *number* or a *letter* to indicate whether they were assigned to a pleasant or unpleasant experimental task (trying some orange juice or a nasty looking health food drink). Each of the subjects briefly saw the same ambiguous stimulus (see Figure 4.24), which could be viewed as either a number (13) or a letter (B), and then the computer appeared to crash. Participants were then asked what they had seen before the computer crashed. Subjects hoping for a letter were much more likely to interpret the stimulus as a B, and those hoping for a number were much more likely to view the stimulus as a 13. Thus, we see once again, that people have a tendency to see what they want to see.

Form perception also depends on the *selection* of sensory input—that is, what people focus their attention on (Chun & Wolfe, 2001). A visual scene

may include many objects and forms. Some of them may capture viewers' attention, while others may not. This fact has been demonstrated in dramatic fashion in studies of *inattentional blindness*, which involves the failure to see visible objects or events because one's attention is focused elsewhere. In one such study (Simons & Chabris, 1999), participants watched a video of a group of people in white shirts passing a basketball that was laid over another video of people in black shirts passing a basketball (the two videos were partially transparent). The observers were instructed to focus on one of the two teams and press a key whenever that team passed the ball. Thirty seconds into the task, a woman carrying an umbrella clearly walked through the scene for four seconds. You might guess that this bizarre development would be noticed by virtually all the observers, but 44% of the participants failed to see the woman. Moreover, when someone in a gorilla suit strolled through the same scene, even more subjects (73%) missed the unexpected event!

Additional studies using other types of stimulus materials have demonstrated that people routinely overlook obvious forms that are unexpected (Most et al., 2005). Inattentional blindness has been attributed to a perceptual set that leads people to focus most of their attention on a specific feature in a scene (such as the basketball passes) while neglecting other facets of the scene (Most et al., 2001). Consistent with this analysis, recent research has shown that the likelihood of inattentional blindness increases when people work on tasks that require a lot of attention or create a heavy perceptual load (Cartwright-Finch & Lavie, 2007). Inattentional blindness may account for many automobile accidents, as accident reports frequently include the statement "I looked right there, but I never saw them" (Shermer, 2004). Although this phenomenon can happen to an attentive and unimpaired driver, research shows that inattentional blindness increases when people talk on a cell phone or are even slightly intoxicated (Clifasefi, Takarangi, & Bergman, 2006; Strayer & Drews, 2007).

The idea that we see much less of the world than we think we do surprises many people, but an auditory parallel exists that people take for granted (Mack, 2003). Think of how often you have had someone clearly say something to you, but you did not hear a word of what was said because you were "not listening." Inattentional blindness is essentially the same thing in the visual domain.

An understanding of how people perceive forms and objects also requires knowledge of how people *organize* their visual inputs. Several influential approaches to this issue emphasize *feature analysis.*

Figure 4.24

Ambiguous stimulus used by Balcetis and Dunning (2006). Participants saw brief presentations of this stimulus, which could be viewed as a letter (B) or as a number (13). The study demonstrated that motivational factors influence what people tend to see.

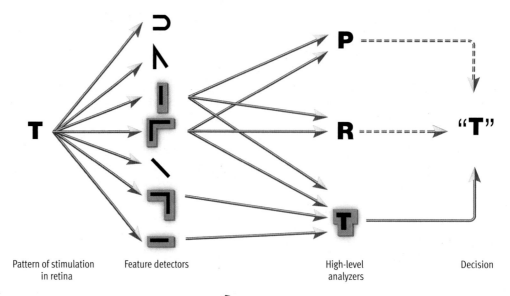

Figure 4.25

Feature analysis in form perception. One vigorously debated theory of form perception is that the brain has cells that respond to specific aspects or features of stimuli, such as lines and angles. Neurons functioning as higher-level analyzers then respond to input from these "feature detectors." The more input each analyzer receives, the more active it becomes. Finally, other neurons weigh signals from these analyzers and make a "decision" about the stimulus. In this way perception of a form is arrived at by assembling elements from the bottom up.

Pattern of stimulation in retina   Feature detectors   High-level analyzers   Decision

Feature Analysis: Assembling Forms

3c

The information received by your eyes would do you little good if you couldn't recognize objects and forms—ranging from words on a page to mice in your cellar and friends in the distance. According to some theories, perceptions of form and pattern entail *feature analysis* (Lindsay & Norman, 1977; Maguire et al., 1990). **Feature analysis is the process of detecting specific elements in visual input and assembling them into a more complex form.** In other words, you start with the components of a form, such as lines, edges, and corners, and build them into perceptions of squares, triangles, stop signs, bicycles, ice cream cones, and telephones. An application of this model of form perception is diagrammed in Figure 4.25.

Feature analysis assumes that form perception involves *bottom-up processing,* **a progression from individual elements to the whole** (see Figure 4.26). The plausibility of this model was bolstered greatly when Hubel and Wiesel showed that cells in the visual cortex operate as highly specialized feature detectors. Indeed, their findings strongly suggested that at least some aspects of form perception involve feature analysis.

Can feature analysis provide a complete account of how people perceive forms? Clearly not. A crucial problem for the theory is that form perception often does not involve bottom-up processing. In fact, there is ample evidence that perceptions of form frequently involve *top-down processing,* **a progression from the whole to the elements** (see Figure 4.26). For example, there is evidence that people can perceive a word before its individual letters, a phenomenon that has to reflect top-down processing (Johnston & McClelland, 1974). If readers depended exclusively on bottom-up processing, they would have to analyze the features of letters in words to recognize them and then assemble the letters into words. This task would be terribly time-consuming and would slow down reading speed to a snail's pace.

Subjective contours is another phenomenon traditionally attributed to top-down processing, although that view is changing (Gunn et al., 2000; Murray et al., 2004). **Subjective contours involves the perception of contours where none actually exist.** Consider, for instance, the triangle shown in Figure 4.27. We see the contours of the triangle easily, even though no physical edges or lines are present. It is hard to envision how feature detectors could detect edges that are not really there, so most theorists have argued that bottom-up models of form perception are unlikely to account for subjec-

Figure 4.26

Bottom-up versus top-down processing. As explained in these diagrams, bottom-up processing progresses from individual elements to whole elements, whereas top-down processing progresses from the whole to the individual elements.

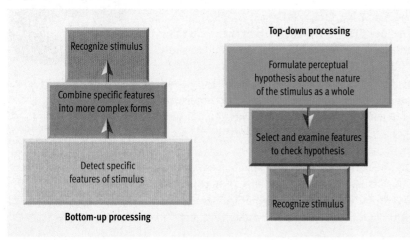

Recognize stimulus

Combine specific features into more complex forms

Detect specific features of stimulus

Bottom-up processing

Top-down processing

Formulate perceptual hypothesis about the nature of the stimulus as a whole

Select and examine features to check hypothesis

Recognize stimulus

Figure 4.27

Subjective contours. Your perception of the triangle on the right and the circle on the left results from subjective contours that are not really there. The effect is so powerful, the triangle and circle appear lighter than the background, which they are not. To demonstrate the illusory nature of these contours for yourself, cover the red circles that mark off the triangle. You'll see that the triangle disappears.

tive contours. In any event, it appears that both top-down and bottom-up processing have their niches in form perception.

Looking at the Whole Picture: Gestalt Principles

Top-down processing is clearly at work in the principles of form perception described by the Gestalt psychologists. As mentioned in Chapter 1, *Gestalt psychology* was an influential school of thought that emerged out of Germany during the first half of the 20th century. (*Gestalt* is a German word for "form" or "shape.") Gestalt psychologists repeatedly demonstrated that *the whole can be greater than the sum of its parts.*

A simple example of this principle is the *phi phenomenon*, first described by Max Wertheimer in 1912. The *phi phenomenon* is the illusion of movement created by presenting visual stimuli in rapid succession. You encounter examples of the phi phenomenon nearly every day. For example, movies and TV consist of separate still pictures projected rapidly one after the other. You see smooth motion, but in reality the "moving" objects merely take slightly different positions in successive frames. Viewed as a whole, a movie has a property (motion) that isn't evident in any of its parts (the individual frames). The Gestalt psychologists formulated a series of principles that describe how the visual system organizes a scene into discrete forms. Let's examine some of these principles.

Figure and Ground. Take a look at Figure 4.28. Do you see the figure as two silhouetted faces against a white background, or as a white vase against a black background? This reversible figure illustrates the Gestalt principle of *figure and ground.* Dividing visual displays into figure and ground is a fundamental way in which people organize visual perceptions (Baylis & Driver, 1995). The *figure* is the thing being looked at, and the *ground* is the background against which it stands. Figures seem to have more substance and shape, appear to be closer to the viewer, and seem to stand out in front of the ground. Other things being equal, an object is more likely to be viewed as a figure when it is smaller in size, higher in contrast, or greater in symmetry (Palmer, 2003), and especially when it is lower in one's frame of view (Vecera & Palmer, 2006). More often than not, your visual field may contain many figures sharing a background. The following Gestalt principles relate to how these elements are grouped into higher-order figures (Palmer, 2003).

Proximity. Things that are near one another seem to belong together. The black dots in the upper left panel of Figure 4.29(a) on the next page could be grouped into vertical columns or horizontal rows.

Max Wertheimer

"The fundamental 'formula' of Gestalt theory might be expressed in this way: There are wholes, the behaviour of which is not determined by that of their individual elements."

The illusion of movement in a highway construction sign is an instance of the phi phenomenon, which is also at work in motion pictures and television. The phenomenon illustrates the Gestalt principle that the whole can have properties that are not found in any of its parts.

Figure 4.28

The principle of figure and ground. Whether you see two faces or a vase depends on which part of this drawing you see as figure and which as background. Although this reversible drawing allows you to switch back and forth between two ways of organizing your perception, you can't perceive the drawing both ways at once.

Figure 4.29
Gestalt principles of perceptual organization.
Gestalt principles help explain some of the factors that influence form perception. (a) Proximity: These dots might well be organized in vertical columns rather than horizontal rows, but because of proximity (the dots are closer together horizontally), they tend to be perceived in rows. (b) Closure: Even though the figures are incomplete, you fill in the blanks and see a circle and a dog. (c) Similarity: Because of similarity of color, you see dots organized into the number 2 instead of a random array. If you did not group similar elements, you wouldn't see the number 2 here. (d) Simplicity: You could view this as a complicated 11-sided figure, but given the preference for simplicity, you are more likely to see it as an overlapping rectangle and triangle. (e) Continuity: You tend to group these dots in a way that produces a smooth path rather than an abrupt shift in direction.

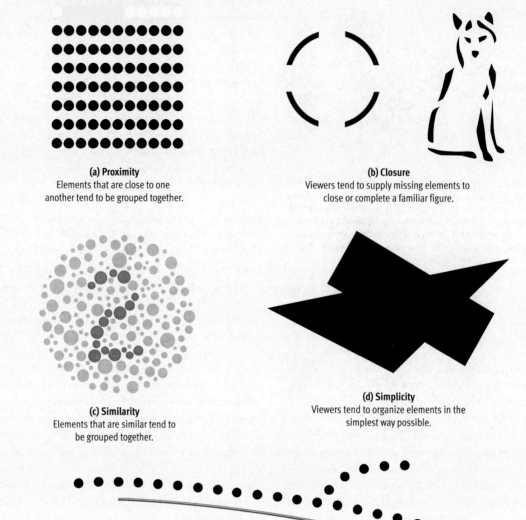

(a) Proximity
Elements that are close to one another tend to be grouped together.

(b) Closure
Viewers tend to supply missing elements to close or complete a familiar figure.

(c) Similarity
Elements that are similar tend to be grouped together.

(d) Simplicity
Viewers tend to organize elements in the simplest way possible.

(e) Continuity
Viewers tend to see elements in ways that produce smooth continuation.

web link 4.3

Sensation and Perception Tutorials

John Krantz of Hanover College has assembled a collection of quality tutorials on sensation and perception. Topics covered include receptive fields, depth perception, Gestalt laws, and the use of perceptual principles in art.

However, people tend to perceive rows because of the effect of proximity (the dots are closer together horizontally).

Closure.   People often group elements to create a sense of *closure*, or completeness. Thus, you may "complete" figures that actually have gaps in them. This principle is demonstrated in the upper right panel of **Figure 4.29(b)**.

Similarity.   People also tend to group stimuli that are similar. This principle is apparent in **Figure 4.29(c)**, where viewers group elements of similar lightness into the number two.

Simplicity.   The Gestaltists' most general principle was the law of *Pragnanz*, which translates from German as "good form." The idea is that people tend to group elements that combine to form a good figure.

This principle is somewhat vague in that it's often difficult to spell out what makes a figure "good" (Biederman, Hilton, & Hummel, 1991). Some theorists maintain that goodness is largely a matter of simplicity, asserting that people tend to organize forms in the simplest way possible (see **Figure 4.29d**).

Continuity.   The principle of continuity reflects people's tendency to follow in whatever direction they've been led. Thus, people tend to connect points that result in straight or gently curved lines that create "smooth" paths, as shown in the bottom panel of **Figure 4.29(e)**.

Although Gestalt psychology is no longer an active theoretical orientation in modern psychology, its influence is still felt in the study of perception (Banks & Krajicek, 1991). The Gestalt psychologists raised many important questions that still occupy

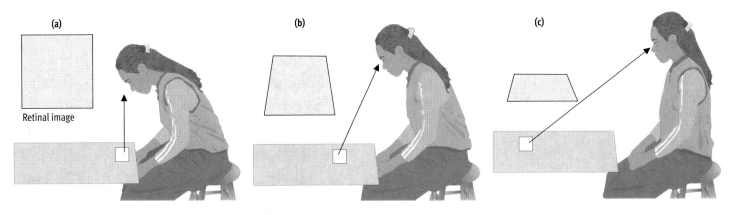

Figure 4.30

Distal and proximal stimuli. Proximal stimuli are often distorted, shifting representations of distal stimuli in the real world. If you look directly down at a small, square piece of paper on a desk (a), the distal stimulus (the paper) and the proximal stimulus (the image projected on your retina) will both be square. But as you move the paper away on the desktop, as shown in (b) and (c), the square distal stimulus projects an increasingly trapezoidal image on your retina, making the proximal stimulus more and more distorted. Nevertheless, you continue to perceive a square.

researchers, and they left a legacy of many useful insights about form perception that have stood the test of time (Sharps & Wertheimer, 2000).

Formulating Perceptual Hypotheses

The Gestalt principles provide some indications of how people organize visual input. However, scientists are still one step away from understanding how these organized perceptions result in a representation of the real world. Understanding the problem requires distinguishing between two kinds of stimuli: distal and proximal (Hochberg, 1988). *Distal stimuli* are stimuli that lie in the distance (that is, in the world outside the body). In vision, these are the objects that you're looking at. They are "distant" in that your eyes don't touch them. What your eyes do "touch" are the images formed by patterns of light falling on your retinas. These images are the *proximal stimuli,* the stimulus energies that impinge directly on sensory receptors. The distinction is important, because there are great differences between the objects you perceive and the stimulus energies that represent them.

In visual perception, the proximal stimuli are distorted, two-dimensional versions of their actual, three-dimensional counterparts. For example, consider the distal stimulus of a square such as the one in Figure 4.30. If the square is lying on a desk in front of you, it is actually projecting a trapezoid (the proximal stimulus) onto your retinas, because the top of the square is farther from your eyes than the bottom. Obviously, the trapezoid is a distorted representation of the square. If what people have to work with is so distorted a picture, how do they get an accurate view of the world out there?

One explanation is that people bridge the gap between distal and proximal stimuli by constantly making and testing *hypotheses* about what's out there in the real world (Gregory, 1973). Thus, a *perceptual hypothesis* is an inference about which distal stimuli could be responsible for the proximal stimuli sensed. In effect, people make educated guesses about what form could be responsible for a pattern of sensory stimulation. The square in Figure 4.30 may project a trapezoidal image on your retinas, but your perceptual system "guesses" correctly that it's a square—and that's what you see.

Let's look at another ambiguous drawing to further demonstrate the process of making a perceptual hypothesis. Figure 4.31 is a famous reversible figure, first published as a cartoon in a humor magazine. Perhaps you see a drawing of a young woman looking back over her right shoulder. Alternatively, you might see an old woman with her chin down on her chest.

Figure 4.31
A famous reversible figure. What do you see? Consult the text to learn the two possible interpretations of this figure.

The ambiguity exists because there isn't enough information to force your perceptual system to accept only one of these hypotheses. Incidentally, studies show that people who are led to *expect* the young woman or the old woman generally see the one they expect (Leeper, 1935). This is another example of how perceptual sets influence what people see.

Psychologists have used a variety of reversible figures to study how people formulate perceptual hypotheses. Another example can be seen in Figure 4.32, which shows the *Necker cube*. The shaded surface can appear as either the front or the rear of the transparent cube. When people stare at the cube continuously, their perception tends to involuntarily alternate between these possibilities (Leopold et al., 2002).

The *context* in which something appears often guides people's perceptual hypotheses. To illustrate, take a look at Figure 4.33. What do you see? You probably saw the words "THE CAT." But look again; the middle characters in both words are identical. You identified an "H" in the first word and an "A" in the second because of the surrounding letters, which created an expectation—another example of top-down processing in visual perception. The power of expectations explains why typographocal errors like those in this sentence often pass unoberved (Lachman, 1996).

Our perceptual hypotheses clearly are guided by our experience-based expectations. For example, subjects recognize everyday objects more quickly when they are presented from familiar viewpoints as opposed to unfamiliar viewpoints (Enns, 2004;

see Figure 4.34). We also realize that certain objects and settings generally go together. We expect to see a sofa sitting in a living room, but not on a beach. When subjects are given brief glimpses of objects in typical versus unusual settings, the objects that appear in typical settings are identified more accurately (Davenport & Potter, 2004; see Figure 4.35). This finding illustrates the importance of both context and experience.

Perceiving Depth or Distance 3f

More often than not, forms and figures are objects in space. Spatial considerations add a third dimension to visual perception. *Depth perception* involves interpretation of visual cues that indicate how near or far away objects are. To make judgments of distance, people rely on a variety of cues, which can be classified into two types: binocular and monocular (Hochberg, 1988; Proffitt & Caudek, 2003).

Binocular Cues 3f

Because they are set apart, the eyes each have a slightly different view of the world. *Binocular depth cues* are clues about distance based on the differing views of the two eyes. "Stereo" viewers like the Viewmaster toy you may have had as a child make use of this principle by presenting slightly different flat images of the same scene to each eye. The brain

Figure 4.32
The Necker cube. The tinted surface of this reversible figure can become either the front or the back of the cube.

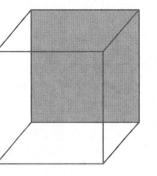

Figure 4.34
Effect of viewpoint on form perception. Research on object recognition shows that the time needed to recognize an object depends on the perspective from which it is viewed (Enns, 2004). Subjects recognize familiar, prototypical views of everyday objects (such as the tricycle on the left) more quickly than atypical views of the same objects (such as the tricycle on the right) (Palmer, Rosch, & Chase, 1981). This finding shows that our perceptual hypotheses are guided by our experience.

SOURCE: Enns, J. T. (2004). *The thinking eye, the seeing brain: Explorations in visual cognition.* New York: W. W. Norton, p. 204. Copyright © 2004 by W. W. Norton & Company. Used by permission of W. W. Norton & Company.

Figure 4.33
Context effects. You probably read these letters as "THE CAT" even though the middle letter of each word is the same. This simple demonstration shows that the context in which a stimulus is seen can affect your perceptual hypotheses.

Figure 4.35

Effect of object and background consistency on object recognition. In a study by Davenport and Potter (2004), participants were given brief glimpses of objects that were presented in a typical setting consistent with expectations, such as a football player on a football field or a priest in a church (top), or in an unusual, unexpected setting, as seen in the bottom photos, where the priest is on a football field and the football player is in a church. The findings showed that when objects are consistent with their background, they are recognized more accurately. Thus, context and experience affect form perception.

SOURCE: Davenport, J. L., & Potter, M. C. (2004). Scene consistency in object and background perception. *Psychological Science, 15,* 559–564. Reprinted by permission of Blackwell Publishers and the author.

then supplies the "depth," and you perceive a three-dimensional scene.

The principal binocular depth cue is *retinal disparity,* which refers to the fact that objects within 25 feet project images to slightly different locations on the right and left retinas, so the right and left eyes see slightly different views of the object. The closer an object gets, the greater the disparity between the images seen by each eye. Thus, retinal disparity increases as objects come closer, providing information about distance. Another binocular cue is *convergence,* which involves sensing the eyes converging toward each other as they focus on closer objects.

BIZARRO

I HAVE NO SENSE OF DEPTH PERCEPTION. COULD YOU TELL ME—IS THAT SOMEONE STANDING WAY UP THERE ON THE CORNER, OR IS THERE A LITTLE MAN IN YOUR HAIR?

Bizarro © 1991 by Dan Piraro. Reprinted by permission of King Features Syndicate

Monocular Cues

3f

Monocular depth cues are clues about distance based on the image in either eye alone. There are two kinds of monocular cues to depth. One kind is the result of active use of the eye in viewing the world. For example, as an object comes closer, you may sense the accommodation (the change in the curvature of the lens) that must occur for the eye to adjust its focus. Furthermore, if you cover one eye and move your head from side to side, closer objects appear to move more than distant objects. In a similar vein, you may notice when driving along a highway that nearby objects (such as fenceposts along the road) appear to move by more rapidly than objects that are farther away (such as trees in the distance). Thus, you get cues about depth from *motion parallax,* which involves images of objects at different distances moving across the retina at different rates.

The other kind of monocular cues are *pictorial depth cues*—clues about distance that can be given in a flat picture. There are many pictorial cues to depth, which is why some paintings and photographs seem so realistic that you feel you can climb right into them. Six prominent pictorial depth cues are described and illustrated in Figure 4.36 on the next page. *Linear perspective* is a depth cue reflecting the fact that lines converge in the distance. Because details are too small to see when they are far away, *texture gradients* can provide information about depth. If an object comes between you and another object, it must be closer to you, a cue called *interposition. Relative size* is a cue because closer objects appear larger. *Height in plane* reflects the fact that distant objects appear higher in a picture. Finally, the familiar effects of shadowing make *light and shadow* useful in judging distance.

Linear perspective Parallel lines that run away from the viewer seem to get closer together.

Texture gradient As distance increases, a texture gradually becomes denser and less distinct.

Interposition The shapes of near objects overlap or mask those of more distant ones.

Relative size If separate objects are expected to be of the same size, the larger ones are seen as closer.

Height in plane Near objects are low in the visual field; more distant ones are higher up.

Light and shadow Patterns of light and dark suggest shadows that can create an impression of three-dimensional forms.

Figure 4.36
Pictorial cues to depth.
Six pictorial depth cues are explained and illustrated here. Although one cue stands out in each photo, in most visual scenes several pictorial cues are present. Try looking at the light-and-shadow picture upside down. The change in shadowing reverses what you see.

There appear to be some cultural differences in the ability to take advantage of pictorial depth cues in two-dimensional drawings. These differences were first investigated by Hudson (1960, 1967), who presented pictures like that shown in **Figure 4.37** to various cultural groups in South Africa. Hudson's approach was based on the assumption that subjects who indicate that the hunter is trying to spear the elephant instead of the antelope don't understand the depth cues (interposition, relative size, height in plane) in the picture, which place the elephant in the distance. Hudson found that subjects from a rural South African tribe (the Bantu), who had little exposure at that time to pictures and photos, frequently misinterpreted the depth cues in his pictures. Similar difficulties with depth cues in pictures have been documented for other cultural groups who have little experience with two-dimensional representations of three-dimensional space (Berry et al., 1992). Thus, the application of pictorial depth cues to pictures varies to some degree across cultures.

Figure 4.37
Testing understanding of pictorial depth cues. In his cross-cultural research, Hudson (1960) asked subjects to indicate whether the hunter is trying to spear the antelope or the elephant. He found cultural disparities in subjects' ability to make effective use of the pictorial depth cues, which place the elephant in the distance and make it an unlikely target.

SOURCE: Adapted by permission from an illustration by Ilil Arbel, in Deregowski, J. B. (1972, November). Pictorial perception and culture. *Scientific American, 227* (5), p. 83. Copyright © 1972 by Scientific American, Inc. All rights reserved.

Recent studies have shown that estimates of distance can be skewed by transient changes in people's goals and their physical and emotional states (Proffitt, 2006a). For example, the effort required to walk to a target destination influences how far away the target appears to be. Participants wearing a heavy backpack estimate that target destinations are farther away than do subjects not burdened with the backpack (Proffitt et al., 2003). Similarly, when participants are asked to throw a ball at targets, subjects throwing a heavy ball estimate that the targets are farther away than do subjects throwing a light ball (Witt, Proffitt, & Epstein, 2004). And when they are standing on a high balcony, the more anxious subjects are about heights, the more they tend to overestimate the distance to the ground (Proffitt, 2006b). Thus, like other perceptual experiences, judgments of distance can be highly subjective. We will draw similar conclusions in our discussion of the perception of geographical slant.

Perceiving Geographical Slant

The perception of *geographical slant* involves making judgments about how steep hills and other inclines are in relation to the norm of a flat, horizontal surface. As with depth perception, the perception of geographical slant involves juggling spatial considerations. However, unlike with depth perception, which has a rich tradition of empirical inquiry, the perception of geographical slant has largely been neglected by researchers. Nevertheless, a clever series of studies have turned up some thought-provoking findings and raised some interesting questions. We will look at this work in our Featured Study for Chapter 4.

FEATURED

STUDY

SOURCE: Proffitt, D. R., Bhalla, M., Gossweiler, R., & Midgett, J. (1995). Perceiving geographical slant. *Psychonomic Bulletin and Review, 2,* 409–428.

Why Hills Look Steeper Than They Are

Accurate perceptions of geographical slant have obvious practical significance for people walking up hills, skiing down mountain slopes, working on pitched roofs, and so forth. Yet anecdotal accounts suggest that people tend to overestimate geographical slant. Thus, Proffitt and his colleagues set out to collect the first systematic data on everyday geographical pitch perception. They ended up conducting a series of five studies. We'll focus on their first study.

Method

Participants. Three hundred students at the University of Virginia agreed to participate in the study when asked by an experimenter stationed near the bottom of various hills around campus. Each participant made estimates for only one hill.

Stimuli. Nine hills on the University of Virginia campus were used as stimuli. The experimenters chose hills with

A participant works with the tilt board to provide a haptic estimate of the pitch of a hill.

lots of foot traffic, unobstructed views, and wide variation in geographical slant. The inclinations of the nine hills were 2, 4, 5, 6, 10, 21, 31, 33, and 34 degrees. To put these figures in perspective, the authors note that 9 degrees is the steepest incline allowed for roads in Virginia and that a 30-degree hill is about the limit of what most people can walk up (the very steep hills on campus had stairs nearby).

Measures and apparatus. The participants were asked to estimate geographical slant in three ways. They provided a *verbal measure* by estimating the slope of the hill they were viewing in degrees. They provided a *visual measure* by adjusting the incline on the disk shown in **Figure 4.38(a)** to match the slope of the hill they were viewing. Finally, they provided a *haptic measure* (one based on touch) by adjusting the tilt board shown in **Figure 4.38(b)** to match the slope of the stimulus hill. To keep the latter measure exclusively haptic and not visual, participants were not allowed to look at their hand while they adjusted the tilt board.

Results

The mean slant estimates for all three measures and all nine hills are summarized graphically in **Figure 4.39**. As you can see, the participants' verbal and visual judgments resulted in large overestimates of all nine hills' geographic slant. For example, participants' verbal estimates for the 5-degree hill in the study averaged 20 degrees. Similarly, their visual estimates for the 10-degree hill averaged 25 degrees. In contrast, the subjects' haptic judgments were much more accurate.

Discussion

Why do hills appear substantially steeper than they are? Why are haptic judgments relatively immune to this peculiar perceptual bias? The authors argue that the data for all three measures make sense from an adaptive point of view. Subjects' verbal and visual estimates reflect their conscious awareness of how challenging hills will be to climb. Overestimates of slant are functional in that they should prevent people from undertaking climbs they are not equipped to handle, and they should lead people to pace themselves and conserve energy on the steep hills they do attempt to traverse. Although overestimates of slant may be functional when people make conscious decisions about climbing hills, they would be dysfunctional if they distorted people's locomotion on hills. If people walking up a 5-degree hill raised their feet to accommodate a 20-degree slope, they would stumble. Accurate tactile perceptions are thus crucial to people's motor responses when they walk up a hill, so it is functional for haptic perceptions to be largely unaffected by the misperception of slant. Thus, learning, or evolution, or some combination has equipped people with perceptual responses that are adaptive.

Comment

The study of sensation and perception is one of the oldest areas of scientific research in psychology. Yet this study shows that there are still fascinating areas of inquiry that remain unexplored. It just takes some creativity and insight to recognize them. This research also illustrates the importance of using more than a single measure of the

Figure 4.38

Apparatus used to measure visual and haptic estimates of geographical slant. (a) Visual estimates of pitch were made by adjusting the incline on a disk to match the incline of the hill. **(b)** Haptic estimates of pitch were made by adjusting a tilt board by hand without looking at it.

SOURCE: Adapted from Proffitt, D. R., Bhalla, M., Gossweiler, R., & Midgett, J. (1995). Perceiving geographical slant. *Psychonomic Bulletin & Review, 214,* 409–428. Copyright © 1995 by Psychonomic Society Publications. Reprinted by permission.

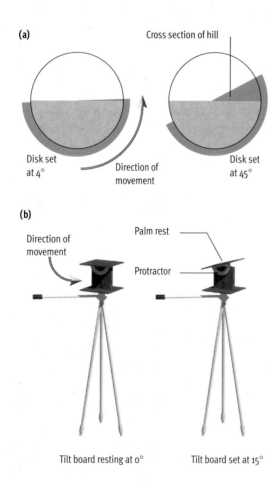

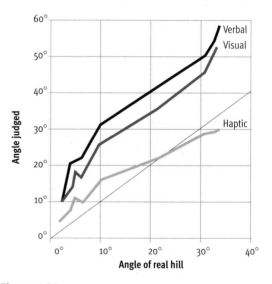

Figure 4.39

Mean slant estimates. The average pitch estimates for all three types of measures are plotted here. The red line shows where accurate estimates would fall. As you can see, verbal and visual measures yielded substantial overestimates, but haptic measures were reasonably accurate.

SOURCE: Adapted from Proffitt, D. R., Bhalla, M., Gossweiler, R., & Midgett, J. (1995). Perceiving geographical slant. *Psychonomic Bulletin & Review, 214,* 409–428. Copyright © 1995 by Psychonomic Society Publications. Reprinted by permission.

phenomenon that one is interested in. The investigators chose to assess the dependent variable of slant perception in several ways, leading to a much richer understanding of slant perception than if only one of the three measures had been used. Finally, the highly exaggerated estimates of slant show once again that human perceptions are not simple reflections of reality, although most people tend to assume that they are. The authors note that many of their subjects were "incredulous" during their postexperimental briefings: "To look at a 10-degree hill—typically judged to be about 30 degrees by verbal reports and visual matching—and to be told that it is actually 10 degrees is an astonishing experience for anyone unfamiliar with the facts of geographical slant overestimation" (p. 425).

Perceptual Constancies in Vision

When a person approaches you from a distance, his or her image on your retinas gradually changes in size. Do you perceive that the person is growing right before your eyes? Of course not. Your perceptual system constantly makes allowances for this variation in visual input. The task of the perceptual system is to provide an accurate rendition of distal stimuli based on distorted, ever-changing proximal stimuli. In doing so, it relies in part on perceptual constancies. A *perceptual constancy* is a tendency to experience a stable perception in the face of continually changing sensory input. Among other things, people tend to view objects as having a stable size, shape, brightness, hue, and location in space.

The Power of Misleading Cues: Visual Illusions   SIM3, 3g

In general, perceptual constancies, depth cues, and principles of visual organization (such as the Gestalt laws) help people perceive the world accurately. Sometimes, however, perceptions are based on inappropriate assumptions, and *visual illusions* can result. A *visual illusion* involves an apparently inexplicable discrepancy between the appearance of a visual stimulus and its physical reality.

One famous visual illusion is the *Müller-Lyer illusion*, shown in Figure 4.40. The two vertical lines in this figure are equally long, but they certainly don't look that way. Why not? Several mechanisms probably play a role (Day, 1965; Gregory, 1978). The figure

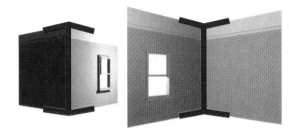

on the left looks like the outside of a building, thrust toward the viewer, while the one on the right looks like an inside corner, thrust away (see Figure 4.41). The vertical line in the left figure therefore seems closer. If two lines cast equally long retinal images but one seems closer, the closer one is assumed to be shorter. Thus, the Müller-Lyer illusion may result from a combination of size constancy processes and misperception of depth.

The geometric illusions shown in Figure 4.42 also demonstrate that visual stimuli can be highly

Figure 4.41
Explaining the Müller-Lyer illusion. The figure on the left seems to be closer, since it looks like an outside corner thrust toward you, whereas the figure on the right looks like an inside corner thrust away from you. Given retinal images of the same length, you assume that the "closer" line is shorter.

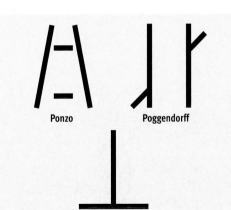
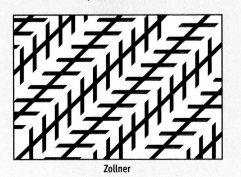

Figure 4.42
Four geometric illusions. Ponzo: The horizontal lines are the same length. Poggendorff: The two diagonal segments lie on the same straight line. Upside-down T: The vertical and horizontal lines are the same length. Zollner: The long diagonals are all parallel (try covering up some of the short diagonal lines if you don't believe it).

Ponzo   Poggendorff

Upside-down T

Zollner

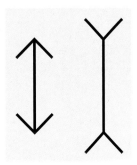

Figure 4.40
The Müller-Lyer illusion. The vertical lines in this classic illusion are very deceptive. Although they do not appear to be the same length, they are. Go ahead, measure them.

web link 4.4

Eyetricks

Eyetricks houses a comprehensive collection of optical and sensory illusions. The illusions are not accompanied by explanations, but they are entertaining.

web link 4.5

Visual Illusions Gallery

This site contains a smaller collection of illusions than the Eyetricks site, but here the illusions are accompanied by brief explanations that elucidate key principles of perception. The site is maintained by psychology professor David Landrigan of the University of Massachusetts (Lowell).

deceptive. The *Ponzo illusion*, which is shown at the top of Figure 4.42, appears to result from the same factors at work in the Müller-Lyer illusion (Coren & Girgus, 1978). The upper and lower horizontal lines are the same length, but the upper one appears longer. This illusion probably occurs because the converging lines convey linear perspective, a key depth cue suggesting that the upper line lies farther away. Figure 4.43 shows a drawing by Stanford University psychologist Roger Shepard (1990) that creates a similar illusion. The second monster appears much larger than the first, even though they are really identical in size.

Adelbert Ames designed a striking illusion that makes use of misperception of distance. It's called, appropriately enough, the *Ames room*. It's a specially contrived room built with a trapezoidal rear wall and a sloping floor and ceiling. When viewed from the correct point, as in the picture, it looks like an ordinary rectangular room (see Figure 4.44). But in reality, the left corner is much taller and much farther from the viewer than the right corner. Hence, bizarre illusions unfold in the Ames room. People standing in the right corner appear to be giants, while those standing in the left corner appear to be midgets. Even more disconcerting, a person who walks across the room from right to left appears to shrink before your eyes! The Ames room creates these misperceptions by toying with the perfectly reasonable assumption that the room is vertically and horizontally rectangular.

Impossible figures create another form of illusion. **Impossible figures are objects that can be represented in two-dimensional pictures but cannot exist in three-dimensional space.** These figures may look fine at first glance, but a closer look reveals

that they are geometrically inconsistent or impossible. Three widely studied impossible figures are shown in Figure 4.45, and a more recent impossible figure created by Roger Shepard (1990) can be seen

Figure 4.43

A monster of an illusion. The principles underlying the Ponzo illusion also explain the striking illusion seen here, in which two identical monsters appear to be quite different in size, although they really are equal in size.

SOURCE: Shepard, R. N. (1990). *Mind sights.* New York: W. H. Freeman. Copyright © 1990 by Roger N. Shepard. Used by permission of Henry Holt & Company, LLC.

Figure 4.44

The Ames room. The diagram on the right shows the room as it is actually constructed. However, the viewer assumes that the room is rectangular, and the image cast on the retina is consistent with this hypothesis. Because of this reasonable perceptual hypothesis, the normal perceptual adjustments made to preserve size constancy lead to the illusions described in the text. For example, naive viewers "conclude" that the boy on the right is much larger than the other, when in fact he is merely closer.

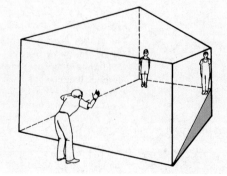

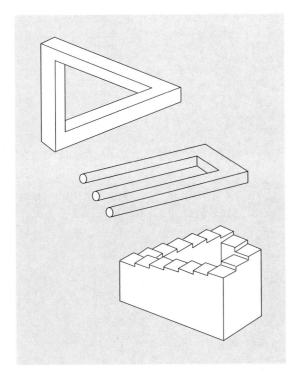

Figure 4.45

Three classic impossible figures. These figures are impossible, yet they clearly exist—on the page. What makes them impossible is that they appear to be three-dimensional representations yet are drawn in a way that frustrates mental attempts to "assemble" their features into possible objects. It's difficult to see the drawings simply as lines lying in a plane—even though this perceptual hypothesis is the only one that resolves the contradiction.

A puzzling perceptual illusion common in everyday life is the moon illusion: the moon looks larger when at the horizon than when overhead.

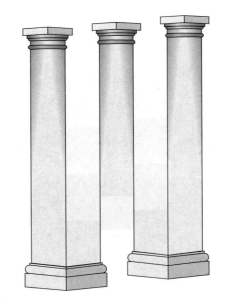

Figure 4.46
Another impossible figure. This impossible figure, drawn by Stanford University psychologist Roger Shepard (1990), seems even more perplexing than the classic impossible figure that it is based on (the one seen in the middle of **Figure 4.45**).

SOURCE: Shepard, R. N. (1990). *Mind sights.* New York: W. H. Freeman. Copyright © 1990 by Roger N. Shepard. Used by permission of Henry Holt & Company, LLC.

in **Figure 4.46**. Notice that specific portions of these figures are reasonable, but they don't add up to a sensible whole. The parts don't interface properly. The initial illusion that the figures make sense is probably a result of bottom-up processing. You perceive specific features of the figure as acceptable but are baffled as they are built into a whole.

Obviously, illusions such as impossible figures and their real-life relative, the Ames room, involve a conspiracy of cues intended to deceive the viewer. Many visual illusions, however, occur quite naturally. A well-known example is the *moon illusion.* The full moon appears to be much smaller when overhead than when looming on the horizon (see the adjacent photo). As with many of the other illusions we have discussed, the moon illusion appears to be due mainly to size constancy effects coupled with the misperception of distance (Coren & Aks, 1990; Kaufman & Rock, 1962), although other factors may also play a role (Suzuki, 2007). The moon illusion shows that optical illusions are part of everyday life. Indeed, many people are virtually addicted to an optical illusion called television (an illusion of movement created by a series of still images presented in quick succession).

Cross-cultural studies have uncovered some interesting differences among cultural groups in their propensity to see certain illusions. For example, Segall, Campbell, and Herskovits (1966) found that people from a variety of non-Western cultures are less susceptible to the Müller-Lyer illusion than Western samples. What could account for this difference? The most plausible explanation is that in the West, we live in a "carpentered world" dominated by straight lines, right angles, and rectangular rooms, buildings, and furniture. Thus, our experience prepares us to readily view the Müller-Lyer figures as

© N. R. Rowan/The Image Works

web link 4.6

The Moon Illusion Explained

Don McCready, professor emeritus at the University of Wisconsin (Whitewater), addresses the age-old puzzle of why the moon appears much larger at the horizon than overhead. He uses a helpful collection of illustrations in a comprehensive review of alternative theories.

Unlike people in Western nations, the Zulus live in a culture where straight lines and right angles are scarce. Thus, they are not affected by such phenomena as the Müller-Lyer illusion nearly as much as people raised in environments that abound with rectangular structures.

inside and outside corners of buildings—inferences that help foster the illusion (Segall et al., 1990). In contrast, people in many non-Western cultures, such as the Zulu (see the above photo) who were tested by Segall and associates (1966), live in a less carpentered world, making them less prone to see the Müller-Lyer figures as building corners.

What do illusions reveal about visual perception? They drive home the point that people go through life formulating perceptual hypotheses about what lies out there in the real world. The fact that these are only hypotheses becomes especially striking when the hypotheses are wrong, as they are with illusions. Finally, like ambiguous figures, illusions clearly demonstrate that human perceptions are not simple reflections of objective reality. Once again, we see that perception of the world is subjective. These insights do not apply to visual perception only. We will encounter these lessons again as we examine other sensory systems, such as hearing, which we turn to next.

REVIEW of Key Learning Goals

4.10 Reversible figures and perceptual sets demonstrate that the same visual input can result in very different perceptions. Form perception depends on both the selection and interpretation of sensory inputs. Inattentional blindness involves the failure to see readily visible objects. According to feature analysis theories, people detect specific elements in stimuli and build them into recognizable forms through bottom-up processing, but form perception also involves top-down processing.

4.11 Gestalt psychology emphasized that the whole may be greater than the sum of its parts (features), as illustrated by the phi phenomenon. Objects are more likely to be viewed as figure rather than ground when they are smaller, higher in contrast or symmetry, and lower in one's frame of view. Gestalt principles of form perception include proximity, similarity, continuity, closure, and simplicity.

4.12 Other approaches to form perception emphasize that people develop perceptual hypotheses about the distal stimuli that could be responsible for the proximal stimuli that are sensed. These perceptual hypotheses are influenced by context and guided by experience-based expectations.

4.13 Binocular cues such as retinal disparity and convergence can contribute to depth perception. Depth perception depends primarily on monocular cues, including pictorial cues such as texture gradient, linear perspective, light and shadow, interposition, relative size, and height in plane. People from pictureless societies have some difficulty in applying pictorial depth cues to two-dimensional pictures.

4.14 The Featured Study showed that conscious perceptions of geographical slant, as reflected by visual and verbal estimates of pitch angles, tend to be greatly exaggerated, but haptic (tactile) judgments seem largely immune to this perceptual bias. Overestimates of slant can be adaptive and may reflect the influence of evolution.

4.15 Perceptual constancies in vision help viewers deal with the ever-shifting nature of proximal stimuli. Visual illusions demonstrate that perceptual hypotheses can be inaccurate and that perceptions are not simple reflections of objective reality. Researchers have found some interesting cultural differences in susceptibility to the Müller-Lyer and Ponzo illusions.

The Auditory System: Hearing

Key Learning Goals

4.16 List the three properties of sound and the aspects of auditory perception that they influence.

4.17 Summarize information on human hearing capacities, and describe how sensory processing occurs in the ear.

4.18 Compare the place and frequency theories of pitch perception, and discuss the resolution of the debate.

4.19 Identify the cues used in auditory localization.

Stop reading for a moment, close your eyes, and listen carefully. What do you hear?

Chances are, you'll discover that you're immersed in sounds: street noises, a high-pitched laugh from the next room, the buzzing of a fluorescent lamp, perhaps some background music you put on a while ago but forgot about. As this little demonstration shows, physical stimuli producing sound are present almost constantly, but you're not necessarily aware of these sounds.

Like vision, the auditory (hearing) system provides input about the world "out there," but not until incoming information is processed by the brain. A distal stimulus—a screech of tires, someone laughing, the hum of the refrigerator—produces a proximal stimulus in the form of sound waves reaching the ears. The perceptual system must somehow transform this stimulation into the psychological experience of hearing. We'll begin our discussion of hearing by looking at the stimulus for auditory experience: sound.

The Stimulus: Sound

3h

Sound waves are vibrations of molecules, which means that they must travel through some physical medium, such as air. They move at a fraction of the speed of light. Sound waves are usually generated by vibrating objects, such as a guitar string, a loudspeaker cone, or your vocal cords. However, sound waves can also be generated by forcing air past a chamber (as in a pipe organ), or by suddenly releasing a burst of air (as when you clap).

Like light waves, sound waves are characterized by their *amplitude*, their *wavelength*, and their *purity* (see Figure 4.47). The physical properties of amplitude, wavelength, and purity affect mainly the perceived (psychological) qualities of *loudness, pitch,* and *timbre*, respectively. However, the physical properties of sound interact in complex ways to produce perceptions of these sound qualities (Hirsh & Watson, 1996).

Human Hearing Capacities 3h

Wavelengths of sound are described in terms of their *frequency*, which is measured in cycles per second, or *hertz (Hz)*. For the most part, higher frequencies are perceived as having higher pitch. That is, if you strike the key for high C on a piano, it will produce higher-frequency sound waves than the key for low C. Although the perception of pitch depends mainly on frequency, the amplitude of the sound waves also influences it.

Just as the visible spectrum is only a portion of the total spectrum of light, so, too, what people can hear is only a portion of the available range of sounds. Humans can hear sounds ranging from a low of 20 Hz up to a high of about 20,000 Hz. Sounds at either end of this range are harder to hear, and sensitivity to high-frequency tones declines as adults grow older. Other organisms have different capabilities. Low-frequency sounds under 10 Hz are audible to homing pigeons, for example. At the other extreme, bats and porpoises can hear frequencies well above 20,000 Hz.

In general, the greater the amplitude of sound waves, the louder the sound perceived. Whereas frequency is measured in hertz, amplitude is measured in *decibels (dB)*. The relationship between decibels (which measure a physical property of sound) and loudness (a psychological quality) is complex. A rough rule of thumb is that perceived loudness doubles about every 10 decibels (Stevens, 1955). Very loud sounds can jeopardize the quality of your hearing. Even brief exposure to sounds over 120 decibels can be painful and may cause damage to your auditory system (Henry, 1984).

As shown in Figure 4.48, the absolute thresholds for the weakest sounds people can hear differ for sounds of various frequencies. The human ear is most sensitive to sounds at frequencies near 2000 Hz. That is, these frequencies yield the lowest absolute thresholds. To summarize, amplitude is the principal determinant of loudness, but loudness ultimately depends on an interaction between amplitude and frequency.

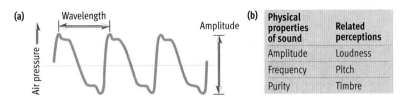

Figure 4.47

Sound, the physical stimulus for hearing. (a) Like light, sound travels in waves—in this case, waves of air pressure. A smooth curve would represent a pure tone, such as that produced by a tuning fork. Most sounds, however, are complex. For example, the wave shown here is for middle C played on a piano. The sound wave for the same note played on a violin would have the same wavelength (or frequency) as this one, but the "wrinkles" in the wave would be different, corresponding to the differences in timbre between the two sounds. (b) The table shows the main relations between objective aspects of sound and subjective perceptions.

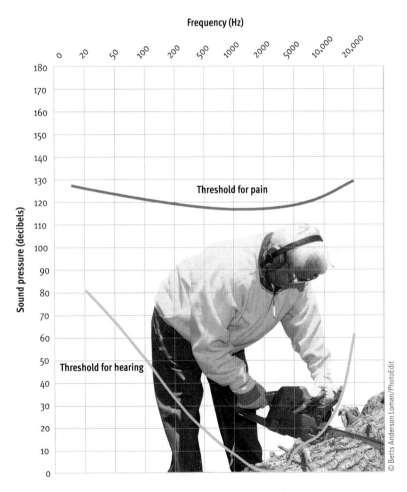

Figure 4.48

Sound pressure and auditory experience. The threshold for human hearing (graphed in green) is a function of both sound pressure (decibel level) and frequency. Human hearing is keenest for sounds at a frequency of about 2000 Hz; at other frequencies, higher decibel levels are needed to produce sounds people can detect. On the other hand, the human threshold for pain (graphed in red) is almost purely a function of decibel level.

People are also sensitive to variations in the purity of sounds. The purest sound is one that has only a single frequency of vibration, such as that produced by a tuning fork. Most everyday sounds are complex mixtures of many frequencies. The purity or complexity of a sound influences how *timbre* is perceived. To understand timbre, think of a note with precisely the same loudness and pitch played on a French horn and then on a violin. The difference you perceive in the sounds is a difference in timbre.

Sensory Processing in the Ear

3h

Like your eyes, your ears channel energy to the neural tissue that receives it. Figure 4.49 shows that the human ear can be divided into three sections: the external ear, the middle ear, and the inner ear. Sound is conducted differently in each section. The external ear depends on the *vibration of air molecules.* The middle ear depends on the *vibration of movable bones.* And the inner ear depends on *waves in a fluid,* which are finally converted into a stream of neural signals sent to the brain (Moore, 2001).

The *external ear* consists mainly of the *pinna,* a sound-collecting cone. When you cup your hand behind your ear to try to hear better, you are augmenting that cone. Many animals have large external ears that they can aim directly toward a sound source. However, humans can adjust their aim only crudely, by turning their heads. Sound waves collected by the pinna are funneled along the auditory canal toward the *eardrum,* a taut membrane that vibrates in response.

In the *middle ear,* the vibrations of the eardrum are transmitted inward by a mechanical chain made up of the three tiniest bones in your body (the hammer, anvil, and stirrup), known collectively as the *ossicles.* The ossicles form a three-stage lever system that converts relatively large movements with little force into smaller motions with greater force. The ossicles serve to amplify tiny changes in air pressure.

The *inner ear* consists largely of the *cochlea,* a **fluid-filled, coiled tunnel that contains the receptors for hearing.** The term *cochlea* comes from the Greek word for a spiral-shelled snail, which this chamber resembles (see Figure 4.49). Sound enters the cochlea through the *oval window,* which is vibrated by the ossicles. The ear's neural tissue, analogous to the retina in the eye, lies within the cochlea. This tissue sits on the basilar membrane that divides the cochlea into upper and lower chambers. **The *basilar membrane,* which runs the length of the spiraled cochlea, holds the auditory receptors.** The auditory receptors are called *hair cells* because of

Figure 4.49

The human ear. Converting sound pressure to information processed by the nervous system involves a complex relay of stimuli. Waves of air pressure create vibrations in the eardrum, which in turn cause oscillations in the tiny bones in the inner ear (the hammer, anvil, and stirrup). As they are relayed from one bone to the next, the oscillations are magnified and then transformed into pressure waves moving through a liquid medium in the cochlea. These waves cause the basilar membrane to oscillate, stimulating the hair cells that are the actual auditory receptors (see Figure 4.50).

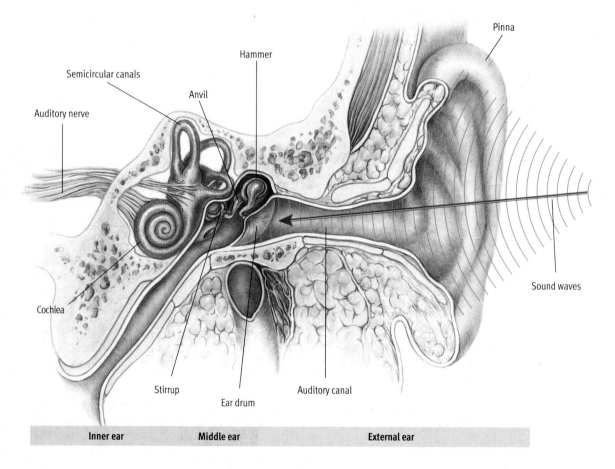

Inner ear   Middle ear   External ear

the tiny bundles of hairs that protrude from them. Waves in the fluid of the inner ear stimulate the hair cells. Like the rods and cones in the eye, the hair cells convert this physical stimulation into neural impulses that are sent to the brain (Hudspeth, 2000).

These signals are routed through the thalamus to the auditory cortex, which is located mostly in the temporal lobes of the brain. Studies demonstrate that the auditory cortex has specialized cells—similar to the feature detectors found in the visual cortex—that have special sensitivity to certain features of sound (Pickles, 1988). Evidence also suggests that the parallel processing of input seen in the visual system also occurs in the auditory pathways (Rouiller, 1997).

Auditory Perception: Theories of Hearing

Theories of hearing need to account for how sound waves are physiologically translated into the perceptions of pitch, loudness, and timbre. To date, most of the theorizing about hearing has focused on the perception of pitch, which is reasonably well understood. Researchers' understanding of loudness and timbre perception is primitive by comparison. Consequently, we'll limit our coverage to theories of pitch perception.

Two theories have dominated the debate on pitch perception: *place theory* and *frequency theory.* You'll be able to follow the development of these theories more easily if you can imagine the spiraled cochlea unraveled, so that the basilar membrane becomes a long, thin sheet, lined with about 25,000 individual hair cells (see **Figure 4.50**).

Place Theory
Long ago, Hermann von Helmholtz (1863) proposed that specific sound frequencies vibrate specific portions of the basilar membrane, producing distinct pitches, just as plucking specific strings on a harp produces sounds of varied pitch. This model, called *place theory,* **holds that perception of pitch corresponds to the vibration of different portions, or places, along the basilar membrane.** Place theory assumes that hair cells at various locations respond independently and that different sets of hair cells are vibrated by different sound frequencies. The brain then detects the frequency of a tone according to which area along the basilar membrane is most active.

Frequency Theory
Other theorists in the 19th century proposed an alternative theory of pitch perception, called frequency theory (Rutherford, 1886). *Frequency theory* **holds that perception of pitch corresponds to the rate, or**

frequency, at which the entire basilar membrane vibrates. This theory views the basilar membrane as more like a drumhead than a harp. According to frequency theory, the whole membrane vibrates in unison in response to sounds. However, a particular sound frequency, say 3000 Hz, causes the basilar membrane to vibrate at a corresponding rate of 3000 times per second. The brain detects the frequency of a tone by the rate at which the auditory nerve fibers fire.

Reconciling Place and Frequency Theories
The competition between these two theories is reminiscent of the dispute between the trichromatic and opponent process theories of color vision. As with that argument, the debate between place and frequency theories generated roughly a century of research. Although both theories proved to have some flaws, *both turned out to be valid in part.*

Helmholtz's place theory was basically on the mark except for one detail. The hair cells along the basilar membrane are not independent. They vibrate together, as suggested by frequency theory. The actual pattern of vibration, described in Nobel prize–winning research by Georg von Békésy (1947), is a traveling wave that moves along the basilar membrane. Place theory is correct, however, in that the wave peaks at a particular place, depending on the frequency of the sound wave.

Frequency theory was also found to be flawed when investigators learned that neurons fire at a maximum

Figure 4.50

The basilar membrane. This graphic shows how the cochlea might look if it were unwound and cut open to reveal the basilar membrane, which is covered with thousands of hair cells (the auditory receptors). Pressure waves in the fluid filling the cochlea cause oscillations to travel in waves down the basilar membrane, stimulating the hair cells to fire. Although the entire membrane vibrates, as predicted by frequency theory, the point along the membrane where the wave peaks depends on the frequency of the sound stimulus, as suggested by place theory.

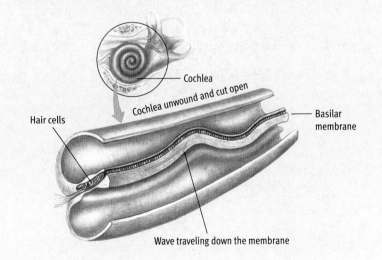

Cochlea

Cochlea unwound and cut open

Hair cells

Basilar membrane

Wave traveling down the membrane

Hermann von Helmholtz

"The psychic activities, by which we arrive at the judgment that a certain object of a certain character exists before us at a certain place, are generally not conscious activities but unconscious ones.... It may be permissible to designate the psychic acts of ordinary perception as unconscious inferences."

rate of about 1000 impulses per second. How, then, can frequency theory account for the translation of 4000 Hz sound waves, which would require 4000 impulses per second? The answer, suggested by Wever and Bray (1937), is that groups of hair cells operate according to the volley principle. The *volley principle* holds that groups of auditory nerve fibers fire neural impulses in rapid succession, creating volleys of impulses. These volleys exceed the 1000-per-second limit. Studies suggest that auditory nerves can team up like this to generate volleys of up to 5000 impulses per second (Zwislocki, 1981).

Although the original theories had to be revised, the current thinking is that pitch perception depends on both place and frequency coding of vibrations along the basilar membrane (Goldstein, 1996). Sounds under 1000 Hz appear to be translated into pitch through frequency coding. For sounds between 1000 and 5000 Hz, pitch perception seems to depend on a combination of frequency and place coding. Sounds over 5000 Hz seem to be handled through place coding only. Again we find that theories that were pitted against each other for decades are complementary rather than contradictory.

Auditory Localization: Perceiving Sources of Sound

You're driving down a street when suddenly you hear a siren wailing in the distance. As the wail grows louder, you glance around, cocking your ear to the sound. Where is it coming from? Behind you? In front of you? From one side? This example illustrates a common perceptual task called *auditory localization*—locating the source of a sound in space. The process of recognizing where a sound is coming from is analogous to recognizing depth or distance in vision. Both processes involve spatial aspects of sensory input. The fact that human ears are set *apart* contributes to auditory localization, just as the separation of the eyes contributes to depth perception.

Many features of sounds can contribute to auditory localization, but two cues are particularly important: the intensity (loudness) and the timing of sounds arriving at each ear (Yost, 2001). For example, a sound source to one side of the head produces a greater intensity at the ear nearer to the sound. This difference is due partly to the loss of sound intensity with distance. Another factor at work is the "shadow," or partial sound barrier, cast by the head itself (see **Figure 4.51**). The intensity difference between the two ears is greatest when the sound source is well to one side. The human perceptual system uses this difference as a clue in localizing sounds. Because the path to the farther ear is longer, a sound takes longer to reach that ear. This fact means that sounds can be localized by comparing the timing of their arrival at each ear. Such comparison of the timing of sounds is remarkably sensitive. People can detect timing differences as small as $1/100{,}000$ of a second

---

concept check 4.3

Comparing Vision and Hearing

Check your understanding of both vision and hearing by comparing key aspects of sensation and perception in these senses. The dimensions of comparison are listed in the first column below. The second column lists the answers for the sense of vision. Fill in the answers for the sense of hearing in the third column. The answers can be found in Appendix A in the back of the book.

Dimension	Vision	Hearing
1. Stimulus	Light waves	
2. Elements of stimulus and related perceptions	Wavelength/hue	
	Amplitude/brightness	
	Purity/saturation	
3. Receptors	Rods and cones	
4. Location of receptors	Retina	
5. Main location of processing in brain	Occipital lobe	
	Visual Cortex	
6. Spatial aspect of perception	Depth perception	

(Durlach & Colburn, 1978). Evidence suggests that people depend primarily on timing differences to localize low-frequency sounds and intensity differences to localize high-frequency sounds (Yost, 2003).

REVIEW of Key Learning Goals

4.16 Sound varies in terms of wavelength (frequency), amplitude, and purity. Wavelength mainly affects perceptions of pitch, amplitude mainly influences perceptions of loudness, and purity is the key determinant of timbre.

4.17 The human ear can detect sounds between 20 and 20,000 Hz, but it is most sensitive to sounds around 2000 Hz. Even brief exposure to sounds over 120 decibels can be painful and damaging. Sound is transmitted through the external ear via air conduction to the middle ear, where sound waves are translated into the vibration of tiny bones called ossicles. In the inner ear, fluid conduction vibrates hair cells along the basilar membrane in the cochlea. These hair cells are the receptors for hearing.

4.18 Place theory proposed that pitch perception depends on where vibrations occur along the basilar membrane. Frequency theory countered with the idea that pitch perception depends on the rate at which the basilar membrane vibrates. Modern evidence suggests that these theories are complementary rather than incompatible.

4.19 Auditory localization involves locating the source of a sound in space. People pinpoint where sounds have come from by comparing interear differences in the intensity and timing of sounds.

Figure 4.51

Cues in auditory localization. A sound coming from the left reaches the left ear sooner than the right. When the sound reaches the right ear, it is also less intense because it has traveled a greater distance and because it is in the sound shadow produced by the listener's head. These cues are used to localize the sources of sound in space.

Sound shadow

Signal to left ear stronger, earlier

Extra distance sound must travel to reach right ear

Path of sound to near (left) ear

Path of sound to far (right) ear

Sound source

The Chemical Senses: Taste and Smell

Psychologists have devoted most of their attention to the visual and auditory systems. Although less is known about the chemical senses, taste and smell also play a critical role in people's experience of the world. Let's take a brief look at what psychologists have learned about the *gustatory system*—the sensory system for taste—and its close cousin, the *olfactory system*—the sensory system for smell.

The Gustatory System: Taste

True wine lovers go through an elaborate series of steps when they are served a good bottle of wine. Typically, they begin by drinking a little water to cleanse their palate. Then they sniff the cork from the wine bottle, swirl a small amount of the wine around in a glass, and sniff the odor emerging from the glass. Finally, they take a sip of the wine, rolling it around in their mouth for a short time before swallowing it. At last they are ready to confer their approval or disapproval. Is all this activity really a meaningful way to put the wine to a sensitive test?

Or is it just a harmless ritual passed on through tradition? You'll find out in this section.

The physical stimuli for the sense of taste are chemical substances that are soluble (dissolvable in

© Commercial Eye/Stone/Getty Images

Are the elaborate wine-tasting rituals of wine lovers just a pretentious tradition, or do they make sense in light of what science has revealed about the gustatory system? Your text answers this question in this section.

Key Learning Goals

4.20 Describe the stimulus and receptors for taste, and discuss some determinants of taste preferences.

4.21 Review research on individual differences in taste sensitivity, and explain what is meant by the perception of flavor.

4.22 Describe the stimulus and receptors for smell, discuss odor identification, and explain how odors can influence behavior.

Figure 4.52

The tongue and taste. Taste buds are clustered around tiny bumps on the tongue called papillae. The three types of papillae are distributed on the tongue as shown here. The taste buds found in each type of papillae show slightly different sensitivities to the four basic tastes, as mapped out in the graph at the top. Thus, sensitivity to the primary tastes varies across the tongue, but these variations are small, and all four primary tastes can be detected wherever there are taste receptors.

SOURCE: Adapted from Bartoshuk, L. M. (1993). Genetic and pathological taste variation: What can we learn from animal models and human disease? In D. Chadwick, J. Marsh, & J. Goode (Eds.), *The molecular basis of smell and taste transduction* (pp. 251–267). New York: Wiley.

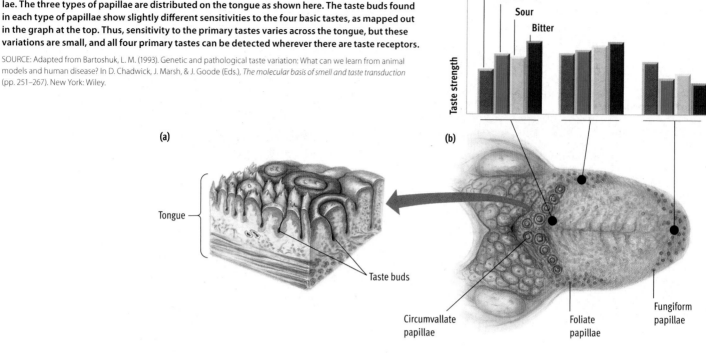

water). The gustatory receptors are clusters of taste cells found in the *taste buds* that line the trenches around tiny bumps on the tongue (see **Figure 4.52**). When these cells absorb chemicals dissolved in saliva, they trigger neural impulses that are routed through the thalamus to the cortex. Interestingly, taste cells have a short life, spanning only about ten days, and they are constantly being replaced (Cowart, 2005). New cells are born at the edge of the taste bud and migrate inward to die at the center.

It's generally (but not universally) agreed that there are four *primary tastes:* sweet, sour, bitter, and salty (Buck, 2000). Sensitivity to these tastes is distributed somewhat unevenly across the tongue, but the variations in sensitivity are quite small and highly complicated (Bartoshuk, 1993b; see **Figure 4.52**). Although taste cells respond to more than one of the primary tastes, they typically respond best to a specific taste (Di Lorenzo & Youngentob, 2003). Perceptions of taste quality appear to depend on complex *patterns* of neural activity initiated by taste receptors (Erickson, DiLorenzo, & Woodbury, 1994). Taste signals are routed through the thalamus and onto the *insular cortex* in the frontal lobe, where the initial cortical processing takes place.

Some basic taste preferences appear to be inborn and to be automatically regulated by physiological mechanisms. In humans, for instance, newborn infants react positively to sweet tastes and negatively to strong concentrations of bitter or sour tastes

(Cowart, 2005). To some extent, these innate taste preferences are flexible, changing to accommodate the body's nutritional needs (Scott, 1990).

Although some basic aspects of taste perception may be innate, taste preferences are largely learned and heavily influenced by social processes (Rozin, 1990). Most parents are aware of this fact and intentionally try—with varied success—to mold their children's taste preferences early in life (Patrick et al., 2005). This extensive social influence contributes greatly to the striking ethnic and cultural disparities found in taste preferences (Kittler & Sucher, 2008). Foods that are a source of disgust in Western cultures—such as worms, fish eyes, and blood—may be delicacies in other cultures (see **Figure 4.53**). Indeed, Rozin (1990) asserts that feces may be the only universal source of taste-related disgust in humans. To a large degree, variations in taste preferences depend on what one has been exposed to (Capaldi & VandenBos, 1991; Zellner, 1991). Exposure to particular foods varies along ethnic lines because different cultures have different traditions in food preparation, different agricultural resources, different climates to work with, and so forth.

Research by Linda Bartoshuk and others reveals that people vary considerably in their sensitivity to certain tastes. These individual differences depend in part on the density of taste buds on the tongue, which appears to be a matter of genetic inheritance (Bartoshuk, 1993a). People characterized as *non-*

web link 4.8

The ChemoReception Web

This site is devoted to the sensory and biological aspects of the chemical senses of taste and smell. It includes abstracts of relevant research, book reviews, and links to many other useful websites.

Grubs. For most North Americans, the thought of eating a worm would be totally unthinkable. For the Asmat of New Guinea, however, a favorite delicacy is the plump, white, 2-inch larva or beetle grub.

Fish eyes. For some Eskimo children, raw fish eyes are like candy. Here you see a young girl using the Eskimo's all-purpose knife to gouge out the eye of an already-filleted Artic fish.

Blood. Several tribes in East Africa supplement their diet with fresh blood that is sometimes mixed with milk. They obtain the blood by puncturing a cow's jugular vein with a sharp arrow. The blood-milk drink provides a rich source of protein and iron.

Figure 4.53
Culture and taste preferences. Taste preferences are heavily influenced by learning and vary dramatically from one society to the next, as these examples demonstrate.

tasters, as determined by their insensitivity to PTC (phenythiocarbamide), or its close relative, PROP (propylthiouracil), tend to have about one-quarter as many taste buds per square centimeter as people at the other end of the spectrum, who are called *supertasters* (Miller & Reedy, 1990). Supertasters also have specialized taste receptors that are not found in nontasters (Bufe et al., 2005). In the United States, roughly 25% of people are nontasters, another 25% are supertasters, and the remaining 50% fall between these extremes and are characterized as *medium tasters* (Di Lorenzo & Youngentob, 2003). Supertasters and nontasters respond similarly to many foods, but supertasters are much more sensitive to certain sweet and bitter substances. For example, supertasters react far more strongly to the chemical (capsaicin) in hot peppers (Tepper & Nurse, 1997). Supertasters also respond more intensely to many fatty substances (Bartoshuk, 2000).

These differences in taste sensitivity influence people's eating habits in ways that can have important repercussions for their physical health. For example, supertasters are less likely to be fond of sweets (Yeomans et al., 2007) and tend to consume fewer high-fat foods, both of which are likely to reduce their risk for cardiovascular disease (Duffy, Lucchina, & Bartoshuk, 2004). Supertasters also tend to react more negatively to alcohol and smoking, thereby reducing their likelihood of developing drinking problems or nicotine addiction (Duffy, Peterson, & Bartoshuk, 2004; Snedecor et al., 2006). The only health disadvantage identified for supertasters thus far is that they respond more negatively to many vegetables, which seems to hold down their vegetable intake (Basson et al., 2005; Dinehart et al., 2006). Overall, however, supertasters tend to have better health habits than nontasters, thanks to their strong reactions to certain tastes (Duffy, 2004).

Women are somewhat more likely to be supertasters than men (Bartoshuk, Duffy, & Miller, 1994). Some psychologists speculate that the gender gap in this trait may have evolutionary significance. Over the course of evolution, women have generally been more involved than men in feeding children. Increased reactivity to sweet and bitter tastes would have been adaptive in that it would have made women more sensitive to the relatively scarce high-caloric foods (which often taste sweet) needed for survival and to the toxic substances (which often taste bitter) that hunters and gatherers needed to avoid.

So far, we've been discussing taste, but what we are really interested in is the *perception of flavor.* Flavor is a combination of taste, smell, and the tactile sensation of food in one's mouth (Smith & Margolskee, 2006). Odors make a surprisingly great contribution to the perception of flavor (Lawless, 2001). Although taste and smell are distinct sensory systems, they interact extensively. The ability to identify flavors declines noticeably when odor cues are absent. You might have noticed this interaction when you ate a favorite meal while enduring a severe head cold. The food probably tasted bland, because your stuffy nose impaired your sense of smell.

Linda Bartoshuk
"Good and bad are so intimately associated with taste and smell that we have special words for the experiences (e.g., repugnant, foul). The immediacy of the pleasure makes it seem absolute and thus inborn. This turns out to be true for taste but not for smell."

Now that we've explored the dynamics of taste, we can return to our question about the value of the wine-tasting ritual. This elaborate ritual is indeed an authentic way to put wine to a sensitive test. The aftereffects associated with sensory adaptation make it wise to cleanse one's palate before tasting the wine. Sniffing the cork, and the wine in the glass, is important because odor is a major determinant of flavor. Swirling the wine in the glass helps release the wine's odor. And rolling the wine around in your mouth is especially critical, because it distributes the wine over the full diversity of taste cells. It also forces the wine's odor up into the nasal passages. Thus, each action in this age-old ritual makes a meaningful contribution to the tasting.

The Olfactory System: Smell

In many ways, the sense of smell is much like the sense of taste. The physical stimuli are chemical substances—volatile ones that can evaporate and be carried in the air. These chemical stimuli are dissolved in fluid—specifically, the mucus in the nose. The receptors for smell are *olfactory cilia,* hairlike structures in the upper portion of the nasal passages (see **Figure 4.54**). They resemble taste cells in that they have a short life (30–60 days) and are constantly being replaced (Buck, 2000). Olfactory receptors have axons that synapse with cells in the *olfactory bulb* and then are routed directly to the olfactory cortex in the temporal lobe and other areas in the cortex. This arrangement is unique. *Smell is the only sensory system in which incoming information is not routed through the thalamus before it projects to the cortex.*

Odors cannot be classified as neatly as tastes, since efforts to identify primary odors have proven unsatisfactory (Doty, 1991). If primary odors exist, there must be a fairly large number of them. Perhaps that is why humans have about 350 different types of olfactory receptors (Buck, 2004). Most olfactory receptors respond to a wide range of odors (Doty, 2001). Specific odors trigger responses in different *combinations* of receptors (Malnic et al., 1999). Like the other senses, the sense of smell shows sensory adaptation. The perceived strength of an odor usually fades to less than half its original strength within about 4 minutes (Cain, 1988).

Humans can distinguish a great many odors, with estimates of the number of distinct odors ranging from 10,000 (Axel, 1995) to 100,000 (Firestein, 2001). However, when people are asked to identify the sources of specific odors (such as smoke or soap), their performance is rather mediocre. For some un-

known reason, people have a hard time attaching names to odors (Cowart & Rawson, 2001). Gender differences have been found in the ability to identify odors, as females tend to be somewhat more accurate than males on odor-recognition tasks (de Wijk, Schab, & Cain, 1995).

Although smell is often viewed as an unimportant sense in humans, ample evidence demonstrates that odors can have profound effects on people's mood and cognition (Herz & Schooler, 2002; Jacob et al., 2002). The $4 billion spent on perfumes annually in the United States shows how motivated people are to enjoy pleasant fragrances. Interestingly, recent research indicates that subtle background odors that people are unaware of can influence their behavior. In one study, subliminal exposure to a citrus-scented cleaning solution led participants to keep their immediate environment cleaner (Holland, Hendriks, & Aarts, 2005). In another study, subjects' ratings of the likability of a series of faces were swayed by the subliminal introduction of pleasant versus unpleasant odors (Li et al., 2007). Small wonder, given these results, that "environmental fragrancing" is a growing industry (Gilbert & Firestein, 2002; Peltier, 1999).

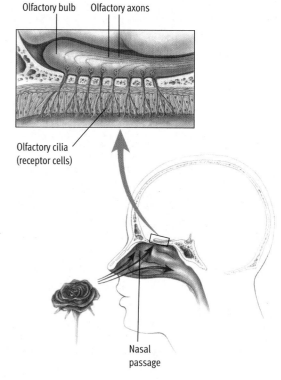

Figure 4.54

The olfactory system. Odor molecules travel through the nasal passages and stimulate olfactory cilia. An enlargement of these hairlike olfactory receptors is shown in the inset. The olfactory nerves transmit neural impulses through the olfactory bulb to the brain.

REVIEW of Key Learning Goals

4.20 The taste buds are sensitive to four basic tastes: sweet, sour, bitter, and salty. Sensitivity to these tastes is distributed unevenly across the tongue, but the variations are small. Some basic taste preferences appear to be innate, but taste preferences are largely learned as a function of what one is exposed to. Taste preferences are also heavily influenced by cultural background.

4.21 Supertasters are much more sensitive to some tastes than nontasters, with medium tasters falling in between these extremes. Nontasters tend to be more susceptible to the lure of sweets, high-fat foods, alcohol, and smoking, which means their consumption habits tend to be less healthy than those of supertasters. The perception of flavor involves a mixture of taste, smell, and the tactile sensation of food in one's mouth.

4.22 Like taste, smell is a chemical sense. Chemical stimuli activate receptors, called olfactory cilia, that line the nasal passages. Most of these receptors respond to more than one odor. Smell is the only sense that is not routed through the thalamus. Humans can distinguish many odors, but their performance on odor identification tasks tends to be surprisingly mediocre. Ambient odors can influence mood and cognition—even when they are subliminal.

The Sense of Touch

If there is any sense that people trust almost as much as sight, it is the sense of touch. Yet, like all the senses, touch involves converting the sensation of physical stimuli into a psychological experience—and it can be fooled.

The physical stimuli for touch are mechanical, thermal, and chemical energy that impinges on the skin. These stimuli can produce perceptions of tactile stimulation (the pressure of touch against the skin), warmth, cold, and pain. The human skin is saturated with at least six types of sensory receptors, four of which are depicted in Figure 4.55. To some degree, these different types of receptors are specialized for different functions, such as the registration of pressure, heat, cold, and so forth. However, these distinctions are not as clear as researchers had originally expected (Sinclair, 1981).

Feeling Pressure

If you've been to a mosquito-infested picnic lately, you'll appreciate the need to quickly know where

Key Learning Goals

4.23 Describe the processes involved in the perception of pressure on the skin.

4.24 Trace the two pathways along which pain signals travel, and discuss evidence that the perception of pain is subjective.

4.25 Explain the gate-control theory of pain perception and recent findings related to it.

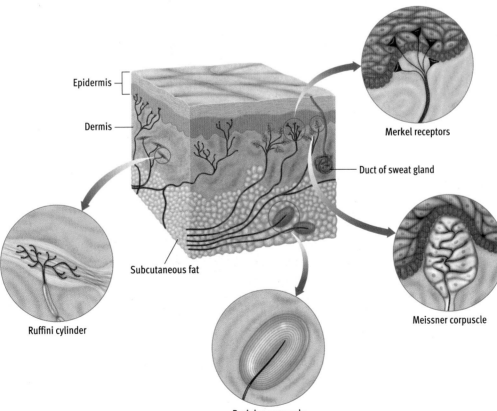

Figure 4.55

Receptors in the skin. Human skin houses quite a variety of receptors in a series of layers. The four types of receptors shown in this diagram all respond to various aspects of pressure, stretching, and vibration. In addition to these receptors, free nerve endings in the skin respond to pain, warmth, and cold, and hair-follicle receptors register the movement of hairs.

Source: Goldstein, E. B. (2007). *Sensation and perception*. Belmont, CA: Wadsworth.

Epidermis

Dermis

Subcutaneous fat

Ruffini cylinder

Pacinian corpuscle

Merkel receptors

Duct of sweat gland

Meissner corpuscle

tactile stimulation is coming from. The sense of touch is set up to meet this need for tactile localization with admirable precision and efficiency. Cells in the nervous system that respond to touch are sensitive to specific patches of skin. These skin patches, which vary considerably in size, are the functional equivalents of *receptive fields* in vision. Like visual receptive fields, they often involve a center-surround arrangement. Thus, stimuli falling in the center produce the opposite effect of stimuli falling in the surrounding area (Kandel & Jessell, 1991).

If a stimulus, such as a finger or the top of a pen, is applied continuously to a specific spot on the skin, the perception of pressure gradually fades. Thus, sensory adaptation occurs in the perception of touch, as it does in other sensory systems.

The nerve fibers that carry incoming information about tactile stimulation are routed through the spinal cord to the brainstem. There, the fibers from each side of the body cross over mostly to the opposite side of the brain. The tactile pathway then projects through the thalamus and onto the *somatosensory cortex* in the brain's parietal lobe. Some cells in the somatosensory cortex function like the *feature detectors* discovered in vision (Gardner & Kandel, 2000). They respond to specific features of touch, such as a movement across the skin in a particular direction.

Feeling Pain

As unpleasant as it is, the sensation of pain is crucial to survival. Pain is a marvelous warning system. It tells people when they should stop shoveling snow or remove their hand from a hot oven. Although a life without pain may sound appealing, people born with a rare, congenital insensitivity to pain would testify otherwise, as they routinely harm themselves (Coderre, Mogil, & Bushnell, 2003). However, chronic pain is a frustrating, demoralizing affliction that affects roughly 75 million people in American society (Gallagher & Rosenthal, 2007). Although scientists have learned a great deal about the neural bases for the experience of pain, clinical treatment of pain remains only moderately effective (Scholz & Woolf, 2002). Thus, there are pressing practical reasons for psychologists' keen interest in the perception of pain.

Pathways to the Brain

The receptors for pain are mostly free nerve endings in the skin. Pain messages are transmitted to the brain via two types of pathways that pass through different areas in the thalamus (Willis, 1985). One is a *fast pathway* that registers localized pain and relays it to the cortex in a fraction of a second. This is the system that hits you with sharp pain when you first cut your finger. The second system uses a *slow pathway* that lags a second or two behind the fast system. This pathway (which also carries information about temperature) conveys the less localized, longer-lasting, aching or burning pain that comes after the initial injury. The slow pathway depends on thin, unmyelinated neurons called *C fibers,* whereas the fast pathway is mediated by thicker, myelinated neurons called *A-delta fibers* (see Figure 4.56). Pain signals may be sent to many areas in the cortex, as well as to subcortical centers associated with emotion (such as the hypothalamus and amygdala), depending in part on the nature of the pain (Hunt & Mantyh, 2001).

Puzzles in Pain Perception

As with other perceptions, pain is not an automatic result of certain types of stimulation. Some people with severe injuries report little pain, whereas other people with much more modest injuries report agonizing pain (Coderre et al., 2003). The perception of pain can be influenced greatly by beliefs, expectations, personality, mood, and other factors involving higher mental processes (Turk & Okifuji, 2003). The subjective nature of pain is illustrated by placebo effects. As we saw in Chapter 2, many people suffering from pain report relief when given a placebo—such as an inert "sugar pill" that is presented to them as if it were a painkilling drug (Stewart-Williams, 2004; Vase, Riley, & Price, 2002).

Further evidence regarding the subjective quality of pain has come from studies that have found ethnic and cultural differences in pain tolerance (Ondeck, 2003). According to Melzack and Wall (1982), culture does not affect the process of pain perception so much as the willingness to tolerate certain types of pain, a conclusion echoed by Zatzick and Dimsdale (1990).

The psychological element in pain perception becomes clear when something distracts your attention from pain and the hurting temporarily disappears. For example, imagine that you've just hit your thumb with a hammer and it's throbbing with pain. Suddenly, your child cries out that there's a fire in the laundry room. As you race to deal with this emergency, you forget all about the pain in your thumb.

As you can see, then, tissue damage that sends pain impulses on their way to the brain doesn't necessarily result in the experience of pain. Cognitive and emotional processes that unfold in higher brain centers can somehow block pain signals coming from peripheral receptors. Thus, any useful explanation of pain perception must be able to answer a critical question: How does the central nervous system block incoming pain signals?

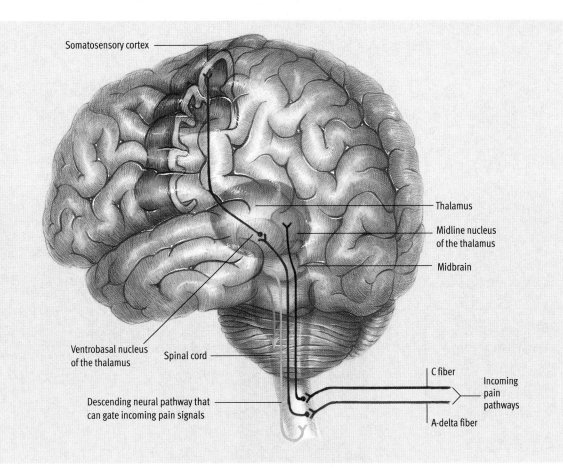

Figure 4.56

Pathways for pain signals. Pain signals are sent inward from receptors to the brain along the two ascending pathways depicted here in red and black. The fast pathway (red) and the slow pathway (black) depend on different types of nerve fibers and are routed through different parts of the thalamus. The gate-control mechanism hypothesized by Melzack and Wall (1965) apparently depends on signals in a descending pathway (shown in green) that originates in an area of the midbrain.

Somatosensory cortex

Thalamus

Midline nucleus of the thalamus

Midbrain

Ventrobasal nucleus of the thalamus

Spinal cord

C fiber

Incoming pain pathways

A-delta fiber

Descending neural pathway that can gate incoming pain signals

In an influential effort to answer this question, Ronald Melzack and Patrick Wall (1965) devised the gate-control theory of pain. *Gate-control theory* holds that incoming pain sensations must pass through a "gate" in the spinal cord that can be closed, thus blocking ascending pain signals. The gate in this model is not an anatomical structure but a pattern of neural activity that inhibits incoming pain signals. Melzack and Wall suggested that this imaginary gate can be closed by signals from peripheral receptors or by signals from the brain. They theorized that the latter mechanism can help explain how factors such

concept check 4.4

Comparing Taste, Smell, and Touch

Check your understanding of taste, smell, and touch by comparing these sensory systems on the dimensions listed in the first column below. A few answers are supplied; see whether you can fill in the rest. The answers can be found in Appendix A.

Dimension	Taste	Smell	Touch
1. Stimulus		*Volatile chemicals in the air*	
2. Receptors			*Many (at least six types)*
3. Location of receptors		*Upper area of nasal passage*	
4. Basic elements of perception	*Sweet, sour, salty, bitter*		

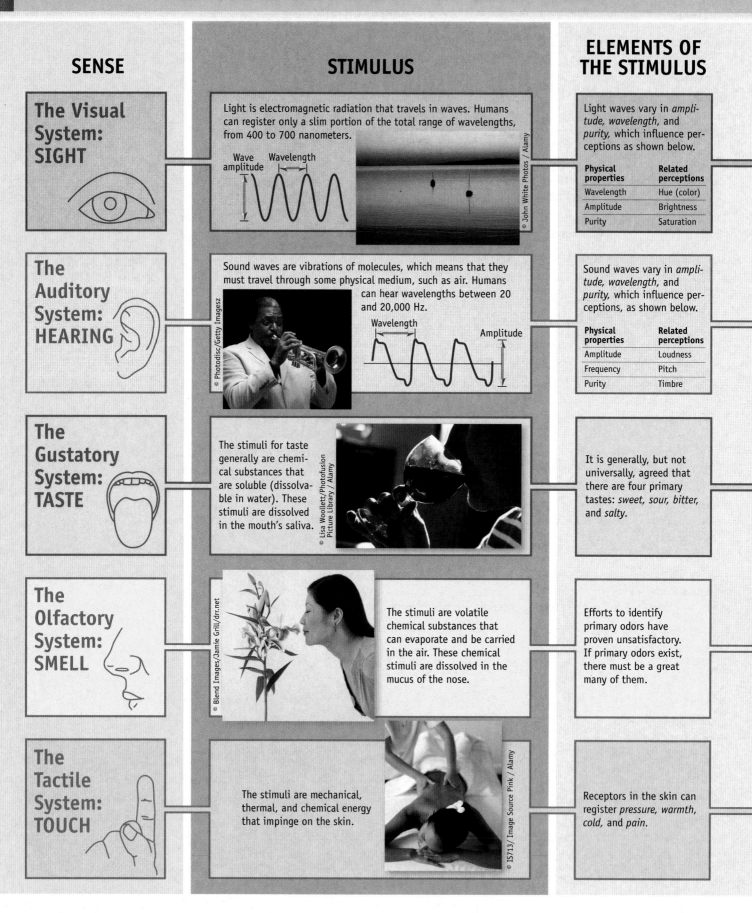

SENSE	STIMULUS	ELEMENTS OF THE STIMULUS
The Visual System: SIGHT	Light is electromagnetic radiation that travels in waves. Humans can register only a slim portion of the total range of wavelengths, from 400 to 700 nanometers. *Wave amplitude / Wavelength* (© John White Photos / Alamy)	Light waves vary in *amplitude, wavelength,* and *purity,* which influence perceptions as shown below.
The Auditory System: HEARING	Sound waves are vibrations of molecules, which means that they must travel through some physical medium, such as air. Humans can hear wavelengths between 20 and 20,000 Hz. *Wavelength / Amplitude* (© Photodisc/Getty Imagesz)	Sound waves vary in *amplitude, wavelength,* and *purity,* which influence perceptions, as shown below.
The Gustatory System: TASTE	The stimuli for taste generally are chemical substances that are soluble (dissolvable in water). These stimuli are dissolved in the mouth's saliva. (© Lisa Woollett/Photofusion Picture Library / Alamy)	It is generally, but not universally, agreed that there are four primary tastes: *sweet, sour, bitter,* and *salty.*
The Olfactory System: SMELL	The stimuli are volatile chemical substances that can evaporate and be carried in the air. These chemical stimuli are dissolved in the mucus of the nose. (© Blend Images/Jamie Grill/drr.net)	Efforts to identify primary odors have proven unsatisfactory. If primary odors exist, there must be a great many of them.
The Tactile System: TOUCH	The stimuli are mechanical, thermal, and chemical energy that impinge on the skin. (© IS713/ Image Source Pink / Alamy)	Receptors in the skin can register *pressure, warmth, cold,* and *pain.*

Light waves (SIGHT):

Physical properties	Related perceptions
Wavelength	Hue (color)
Amplitude	Brightness
Purity	Saturation

Sound waves (HEARING):

Physical properties	Related perceptions
Amplitude	Loudness
Frequency	Pitch
Purity	Timbre

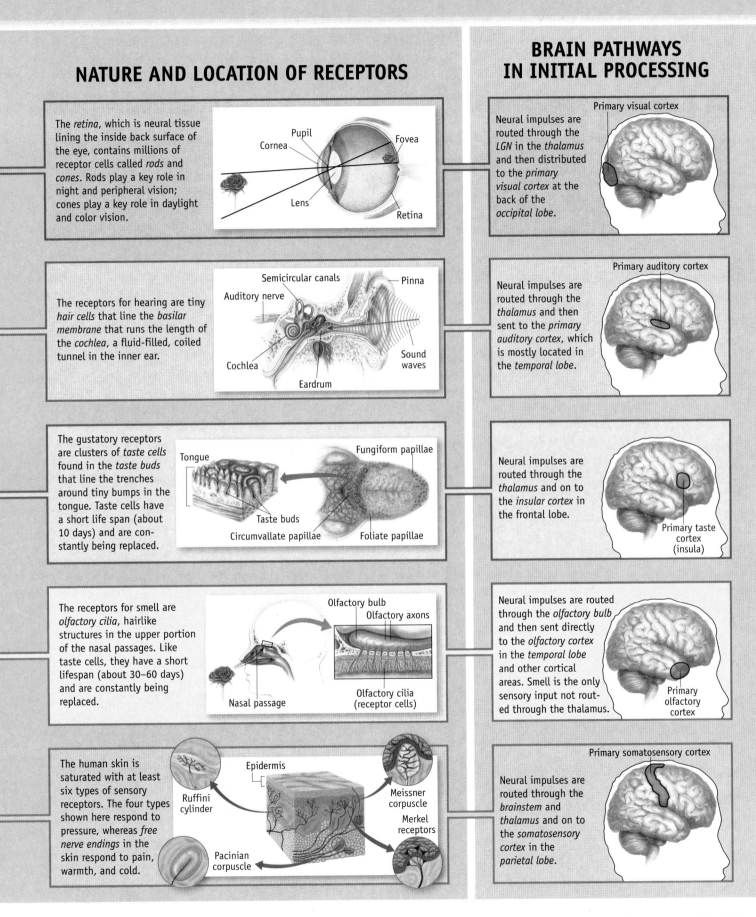

NATURE AND LOCATION OF RECEPTORS

The *retina*, which is neural tissue lining the inside back surface of the eye, contains millions of receptor cells called *rods* and *cones*. Rods play a key role in night and peripheral vision; cones play a key role in daylight and color vision.

Cornea
Pupil
Fovea
Lens
Retina

The receptors for hearing are tiny *hair cells* that line the *basilar membrane* that runs the length of the *cochlea*, a fluid-filled, coiled tunnel in the inner ear.

Semicircular canals
Pinna
Auditory nerve
Cochlea
Sound waves
Eardrum

The gustatory receptors are clusters of *taste cells* found in the *taste buds* that line the trenches around tiny bumps in the tongue. Taste cells have a short life span (about 10 days) and are constantly being replaced.

Tongue
Fungiform papillae
Taste buds
Circumvallate papillae
Foliate papillae

The receptors for smell are *olfactory cilia*, hairlike structures in the upper portion of the nasal passages. Like taste cells, they have a short lifespan (about 30–60 days) and are constantly being replaced.

Olfactory bulb
Olfactory axons
Nasal passage
Olfactory cilia (receptor cells)

The human skin is saturated with at least six types of sensory receptors. The four types shown here respond to pressure, whereas *free nerve endings* in the skin respond to pain, warmth, and cold.

Ruffini cylinder
Epidermis
Meissner corpuscle
Merkel receptors
Pacinian corpuscle

BRAIN PATHWAYS IN INITIAL PROCESSING

Neural impulses are routed through the *LGN* in the *thalamus* and then distributed to the *primary visual cortex* at the back of the *occipital lobe*.

Primary visual cortex

Neural impulses are routed through the *thalamus* and then sent to the *primary auditory cortex*, which is mostly located in the *temporal lobe*.

Primary auditory cortex

Neural impulses are routed through the *thalamus* and on to the *insular cortex* in the frontal lobe.

Primary taste cortex (insula)

Neural impulses are routed through the *olfactory bulb* and then sent directly to the *olfactory cortex* in the *temporal lobe* and other cortical areas. Smell is the only sensory input not routed through the thalamus.

Primary olfactory cortex

Neural impulses are routed through the *brainstem* and *thalamus* and on to the *somatosensory cortex* in the *parietal lobe*.

Primary somatosensory cortex

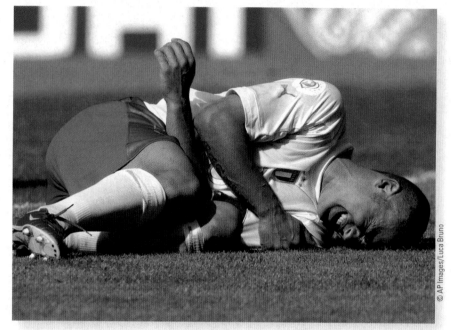

People tend to assume that the perception of pain is an automatic result of bodily injuries, but the process of pain perception is much more subjective than widely appreciated. For example, in athletic endeavors an injury is often a major competitive setback, which may intensify one's pain.

as attention and expectations can shut off pain signals. As a whole, research suggests that the concept of a gating mechanism for pain has merit (Craig & Rollman, 1999; Sufka & Price, 2002). However, relatively little support has been found for the neural circuitry originally hypothesized by Melzack and Wall in the 1960s. Other neural mechanisms, discovered after gate-control theory was proposed, appear to be responsible for blocking the perception of pain.

One of these discoveries was the identification of endorphins. As discussed in Chapter 3, *endorphins* are the body's own natural morphinelike painkillers. Studies suggest that the endorphins play an important role in the modulation of pain (Pert, 2002). For example, the analgesic effects that can be achieved through the ancient Chinese art of acupuncture appear to involve endorphins (Cabyoglu, Ergene, & Tan, 2006). Endorphins are widely distributed in the central nervous system. Scientists are still working out the details of how they suppress pain (Zubieta et al., 2001).

The other discovery involved the identification of a descending neural pathway that mediates the suppression of pain (Basbaum & Jessell, 2000). This pathway appears to originate in an area of the midbrain called the *periaqueductal gray (PAG)*. Neural activity in this pathway is probably initiated by endorphins acting on PAG neurons, which eventually trigger impulses sent down neural circuits that mostly release serotonin. These circuits synapse in the spinal cord, where they appear to release more endorphins, thus inhibiting the activity of neurons that would normally transmit incoming pain impulses to the brain (see **Figure 4.56**). The painkilling effects of morphine appear to be at least partly attributable to activity in this descending pathway, as cutting the fibers in this pathway reduces the analgesic effects of morphine (Jessell & Kelly, 1991). In contrast, activation of this pathway by electrical stimulation of the brain can produce an analgesic effect. Clearly, this pathway plays a central role in gating incoming pain signals.

Our understanding of the experience of pain continues to evolve. The newest discovery is that certain types of *glial cells* may contribute to the modulation of pain (Watkins, 2007). As noted in Chapter 3, only recently have neuroscientists realized that glial cells contribute to signal transmission in the nervous system (Fields, 2004). At least two types of glia in the spinal cord (astrocytes and microglia) appear to play an important role in *chronic pain* (Watkins & Maier, 2002). These glia are activated by immune system responses to infection or by signals from neurons in pain pathways. Once activated, these glial cells appear to "egg on neurons in the pain pathway," thus amplifying the experience of chronic pain (Watkins & Maier, 2003; Watkins et al., 2007). The discovery that glia play a role in the human pain system may eventually open up new avenues for treating chronic pain.

One final point merits emphasis as we close our tour of the human sensory systems. Although we have discussed the various sensory domains separately, it's important to remember that all the senses send signals to the same brain, where the information is pooled. We have already encountered examples of sensory integration. For example, it's at work when the sight and smell of food influence taste. *Sensory integration is the norm in perceptual experience.* For instance, when you sit around a campfire, you *see* it blazing, you *hear* it crackling, you *smell* it burning, and you feel the *touch* of its warmth. If you cook something over it, you may even *taste* it. Thus, perception involves building a unified model of the world out of integrated input from all the senses (Kayser, 2007; Stein, Wallace, & Stanford, 2001).

REVIEW of Key Learning Goals

4.23 The skin houses many types of sensory receptors. They respond to pressure, temperature, and pain. Tactile localization depends on receptive fields similar to those seen for vision. Some cells in the somatosensory cortex appear to function like feature detectors.

4.24 Pain signals are sent to the brain along two pathways that are characterized as fast and slow. The perception of pain is highly subjective and may be influenced by mood and distractions. Placebo effects in pain treatment and cultural variations in pain tolerance also highlight the subjective nature of pain perception.

4.25 Gate-control theory holds that incoming pain signals can be blocked in the spinal cord. Endorphins and a descending neural pathway appear responsible for the suppression of pain by the central nervous system. Recent studies indicate that glial cells contribute to the modulation of chronic pain.

Reflecting on the Chapter's Themes

In this chapter, three of our unifying themes stood out in sharp relief. Let's discuss the value of theoretical diversity first. Contradictory theories about behavior can be disconcerting and frustrating for theorists, researchers, teachers, and students alike. Yet this chapter provided two dramatic demonstrations of how theoretical diversity can lead to progress in the long run. For decades, the trichromatic and opponent process theories of color vision and the place and frequency theories of pitch perception were viewed as fundamentally incompatible. As you know, in each case the evidence eventually revealed that both theories were needed to fully explain the sensory processes that each sought to explain individually. If it hadn't been for these theoretical debates, current understanding of color vision and pitch perception might be far more primitive.

Our coverage of sensation and perception should also have enhanced your appreciation of why human experience of the world is highly subjective. As ambiguous figures and optical illusions clearly show, there is no one-to-one correspondence between sensory input and perceived experience of the world. Perception is an active process in which people organize and interpret the information received by the senses. These interpretations are shaped by a number of factors, including the environmental context and perceptual sets. Small wonder, then,

that people often perceive the same event in very different ways.

Finally, this chapter provided numerous examples of how cultural factors can shape behavior—in an area of research where one might expect to find little cultural influence. Most people are not surprised to learn that there are cultural differences in attitudes, values, social behavior, and development. But perception is widely viewed as a basic, universal process that should be invariant across cultures. In most respects it is, as the similarities among cultural groups in perception far outweigh the differences. Nonetheless, we saw cultural variations in depth perception, susceptibility to illusions, taste preferences, and pain tolerance. Thus, even a fundamental, heavily physiological process such as perception can be modified to some degree by one's cultural background.

The following Personal Application demonstrates the subjectivity of perception once again. It focuses on how painters have learned to use the principles of visual perception to achieve a variety of artistic goals.

Key Learning Goals

4.26 Identify the three unifying themes that were highlighted in this chapter.

Theoretical Diversity

Subjectivity of Experience

Cultural Heritage

REVIEW of Key Learning Goals

4.26 This chapter provided two dramatic demonstrations of the value of theoretical diversity. It also provided numerous examples of how and why people's experience of the world is highly subjective. Finally, it highlighted the importance of cultural background.

Appreciating Art and Illusion

Answer the following multiple-choice question:

Artistic works such as paintings:

____ **1** render an accurate picture of reality.

____ **2** create an illusion of reality.

____ **3** provide an interpretation of reality.

____ **4** make us think about the nature of reality.

____ **5** do all of the above.

The answer to this question is (5), "all of the above." Historically, artists have had many and varied purposes, including each

of those listed in the question (Goldstein, 2001). To realize their goals, artists have had to use a number of principles of perception—sometimes quite deliberately, and sometimes not. Here we'll use the example of painting to explore the role of perceptual principles in art and illusion.

The goal of most early painters was to produce a believable picture of reality. This goal immediately created a problem familiar to most of us who have attempted to draw realistic pictures: The real world is three-dimensional, but a canvas or a sheet

Key Learning Goals

4.27 Discuss how the Impressionists, Cubists, and Surrealists used various principles of visual perception.

4.28 Discuss how Escher, Vasarely, and Magritte used various principles of visual perception.

of paper is flat. Paradoxically, then, painters who set out to re-create reality had to do so by creating an illusion of three-dimensional reality.

Prior to the Renaissance, these efforts to create a convincing illusion of reality were awkward by modern standards. Why? Because artists did not understand how to use depth cues. This fact is apparent in **Figure 4.57**, a religious scene painted around 1300. The painting clearly lacks a sense of depth. The people seem paper-thin. They have no real position in space.

Although earlier artists made some use of depth cues, Renaissance artists manipulated the full range of pictorial depth cues and really harnessed the crucial cue of linear perspective (Solso, 1994). **Figure 4.58** dramatizes the resulting transition in art. This scene, painted by Italian Renaissance artists Gentile and Giovanni Bellini, seems much more realistic and lifelike than the painting in **Figure 4.57** because it uses a number of pictorial depth cues. Notice how the buildings on the sides converge to make use of linear perspective. Additionally, distant objects are smaller than nearby ones, an application of relative size. This painting also uses height in plane, as well as interposition. By taking advantage of pictorial depth cues, an artist can enhance a painting's illusion of reality.

In the centuries since the Renaissance, painters have adopted a number of viewpoints about the portrayal of reality. For instance, the French Impressionists of the 19th century did not want to re-create the photographic "reality" of a scene. They set out to interpret a viewer's fleeting perception or impression of reality. To accomplish this end, they worked with color in unprecedented ways.

Consider, for instance, the work of Georges Seurat, a French artist who used a technique called pointillism. Seurat carefully studied what scientists knew about the composition of color in the 1880s, then applied this knowledge in a calculated, laboratory-like manner. Indeed, critics in his era dubbed him the "little chemist." Seurat constructed his paintings out of tiny dots of pure, intense colors. He used additive color mixing, a departure from the norm in painting, which usually depends on subtractive mixing of pigments. A famous result of Seurat's "scientific" approach to painting was *Sunday Afternoon on the Island of La Grande Jatte* (see **Figure 4.59**). As the work of Seurat illustrates, modernist paint-

ers were moving away from attempts to re-create the world as it is literally seen.

If 19th-century painters liberated color, their successors at the turn of the 20th century liberated form. This was particularly true of the Cubists. Cubism was begun in 1909 by Pablo Picasso, a Spanish artist who went on to experiment with other styles in his prolific career. The Cubists didn't try to portray reality so much as to reassemble it. They attempted to reduce everything to combinations of geometric forms (lines, circles, triangles, rectangles, and such) laid out in a flat space, lacking depth. In a sense, they applied the theory of feature analysis to canvas, as they built their figures out of simple features.

The resulting paintings were decidedly unrealistic, but the painters would leave realistic fragments that provided clues about the subject. Picasso liked to challenge his viewers to decipher the subject of his paintings. Take a look at the painting in **Figure 4.60** and see whether you can figure out what Picasso was portraying.

The work in **Figure 4.60** is titled *Violin and Grapes*. Note how Gestalt principles of perceptual organization are at work to create these forms. Proximity and similarity serve to bring the grapes together in the bottom right corner. Closure accounts for your being able to see the essence of the violin.

Figure 4.57
Master of the Arrest of Christ (detail, central part) by S. Francesco, Assisi, Italy (circa 1300). Notice how the absence of depth cues makes the painting seem flat and unrealistic.

Scala/Art Resource, New York

Figure 4.58
Brera Predica di S. Marco Pinacoteca by Gentile and Giovanni Bellini (circa 1480). In this painting, the Italian Renaissance artists use a number of depth cues—including linear perspective, relative size, height in plane, light and shadow, and interposition—to enhance the illusion of three-dimensional reality.

Scala/Art Resource, New York

Other Gestalt principles are the key to the effect achieved in the painting in Figure 4.61 on the next page. This painting, by Marcel Duchamp, a French artist who blended Cubism and a style called Futurism, is titled *Nude Descending a Staircase*. The effect clearly depends on the Gestalt principle of continuity.

The Surrealists toyed with reality in a different way. Influenced by Sigmund Freud's writings on the unconscious, the Surrealists explored the world of dreams and fantasy. Specific elements in their paintings are often depicted realistically, but the strange combination of elements yields a disconcerting irrationality reminiscent of dreams. A prominent example of this style is Salvador Dali's *Slave Market with the Disappearing Bust of Voltaire*, shown in Figure 4.62. Notice the reversible figure near the center of the painting. The "bust of Voltaire" is made up of human figures in the distance, standing in front of an arch. Dali often used reversible figures to enhance the ambiguity of his bizarre visions.

Perhaps no one has been more creative in manipulating perceptual ambiguity than M. C. Escher, a modern Dutch artist. Escher closely followed the work of the Gestalt psychologists, and he readily acknowledged his debt to psychology as a source of inspiration (Teuber, 1974). *Waterfall,* a 1961

lithograph by Escher, is an impossible figure that appears to defy the law of gravity (see Figure 4.63). The puzzling problem here is that a level channel of water terminates in a waterfall that "falls" into the same channel two levels "below." This drawing is made

Figure 4.60

***Violin and Grapes* by Pablo Picasso (1912). This painting makes use of the Gestalt principles of proximity, similarity, and closure.**

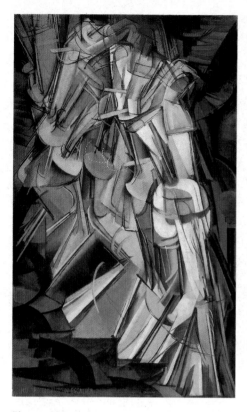

Figure 4.61

Marcel Duchamp's *Nude Descending a Staircase, No 2* (1912). **This painting uses the Gestalt principle of continuity and another Gestalt principle not discussed in the text, called common fate (elements that appear to move together tend to be grouped together).**

Duchamp, Marcel, 1912, *Nude Descending a Staircase, No. 2*, oil on canvas, 58" x 35". Philadelphia Museum of Art: Louise and Walter Arensburg Collection, #1950-134-69. Reproduced by permission. © 2009 Artists Rights Society.

Figure 4.62

Salvador Dali's *Slave Market with the Disappearing Bust of Voltaire* (1940). **This painting playfully includes a reversible figure (in the center of the painting, two nuns form the bust of Voltaire, a philosopher known for his stringent criticisms of the Catholic church).**

Salvador Dali, *The Slave Market with the Disappearing Bust of Voltaire*, (1940), Oil on canvas, 18-1/4 × 25-3/8 inches. Collection of The Salvador Dali Museum, St. Petersburg, FL. Copyright © 2006 The Salvador Dali Museum, Inc. © 2009 Salvador Dali, Gala-Salvador Dali Foundation/Artists Rights Socity (ARS), New York.

up of two of the impossible triangles shown earlier, in **Figure 4.45**. In case you need help seeing them, the waterfall itself forms one side of each triangle.

The Necker cube, a reversible figure mentioned earlier in the chapter, was the inspiration for Escher's 1958 lithograph *Belvedere*, shown in **Figure 4.64**. You have to look carefully to realize that this is another impossible figure. Note that the top story runs at a right angle from the first story. Note also how the pillars are twisted around. The pillars that start on one side of the building end up supporting the second story on the other side! Escher's debt to the Necker cube is manifested in several

places. Notice, for instance, the drawing of a Necker cube on the floor next to the seated boy (on the lower left).

Like Escher, Hungarian artist Victor Vasarely, who pioneered Kinetic Art, challenged viewers to think about the process of perception. His paintings are based on illusions, as squares seem to advance and recede, or spheres seem to inflate and deflate. For example, note how Vasareley used the depth cues of texture gradient and linear perspective to convey the look of great depth in his painting *Tukoer-Ter-Ur*, shown in **Figure 4.65**.

While Escher and Vasarely challenged viewers to think about perception, Belgian artist René Magritte challenged people to think about the conventions of painting. Many of his works depict paintings on an easel, with the "real" scene continuing unbroken at the edges. The painting in **Figure 4.66** is such a picture within a picture. Ultimately, Magritte's painting blurs the line between the real world and the illusory world created by the artist, suggesting that there is no line—that everything is an illusion. In this way, Magritte "framed" the ageless, unanswerable question: What is reality?

REVIEW of Key Learning Goals

4.27 After the Renaissance, painters began to routinely use pictorial depth cues to make their scenes more lifelike. Nineteenth-century painters, such as the Impressionists, manipulated color mixing in creative, new ways. The Cubists were innovative in manipulating form, as they applied the theory of feature analysis to canvas. The Surrealists toyed with reality, exploring the world of fantasy and dreams.

4.28 Inspired by Gestalt psychology, Escher tried to stimulate viewers to think about the process of perception. Among other things, Escher worked with the Necker cube and the impossible triangle. Vasarely manipulated depth cues to create illusions, whereas Magritte challenged people to think about the conventions of painting and their relation to reality.

Figure 4.63
Escher's lithograph *Waterfall* (1961).
Escher's use of depth cues and impossible triangles deceives the brain into seeing water flow uphill.

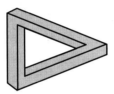

Figure 4.64
Escher's *Belvedere* (1958). This lithograph depicts an impossible figure inspired by the Necker cube. The cube appears in the architecture of the building, in the model held by the boy on the bench, and in the drawing lying at his feet.

Figure 4.66
René Magritte's *Les Promenades d'Euclide* (1955).
Notice how the pair of nearly identical triangles look quite different in different contexts.

Magritte, Rene, *Les Promenades d'Euclide*, The Minneapolis Institute of Arts, The William Hood Dunwoody Fund. Copyright © 2009 Charly Herscovic, Brussels/Artists Rights Society (ARS) New York.

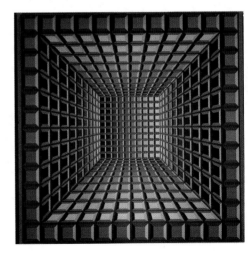

Figure 4.65
Victor Vasarely's *Tukoer-Ter-Ur* (1989). In this painting, Vasarely manipulates texture gradients and linear perspective to create a remarkable illusion of depth.

Vasarely, Victor (1908–1997) *Tukoer-Ter-Ur*, 1989. Acrylic on canvas, 220 × 220 cm. Private Collection, Monaco. © Erich Lessing / Art Resource, NY. Copyright © 2009 Artists Rights Society (ARS), New York/ADAGP, Paris

Recognizing Contrast Effects: It's All Relative

Key Learning Goals

4.29 Understand how contrast effects can be manipulated to influence or distort judgments.

You're sitting at home one night, when the phone rings. It's Simone, an acquaintance from school who needs help with a recreational program for youngsters that she runs for the local park district. She tries to persuade you to volunteer four hours of your time every Friday night throughout the school year to supervise the volleyball program. The thought of giving up your Friday nights and adding this sizable obligation to your already busy schedule makes you cringe with horror. You politely explain to Simone that you can't possibly afford to give up that much time and you won't be able to help her. She accepts your rebuff graciously, but the next night she calls again. This time she wants to know whether you would be willing to supervise volleyball every third Friday. You still feel like it's a big obligation that you really don't want to take on, but the new request seems much more reasonable than the original one. So, with a sigh of resignation, you agree to Simone's request.

What's wrong with this picture? Well, there's nothing wrong with volunteering your time for a good cause, but you just succumbed to a social influence strategy called the "door-in-the face technique." *The door-in-the-face technique involves making a large request that is likely to be turned down as a way*

to increase the chances that people will agree to a smaller request later (see **Figure 4.67**). The name for this strategy is derived from the expectation that the initial request will be quickly rejected (the "door" is slammed in the "salesperson's" face). Although they may not be familiar with the strategy's name, many people use this manipulative tactic. For example, a husband who wants to coax his frugal wife into agreeing to buy a $30,000 SUV might begin by proposing that they purchase a $50,000 sports car. By the time the wife talks her husband out of the $50,000 car, the $30,000 price tag may look quite reasonable to her—which is what the husband wanted all along.

Research has demonstrated that the door-in-the-face technique is a highly effective persuasive strategy (Cialdini, 2001). One of the reasons it works so well is that it depends on a simple and pervasive perceptual principle. As noted throughout the chapter, in the domain of perceptual experience, *everything is relative*. This relativity means that people are easily swayed by *contrast effects*. For example, lighting a match or a small candle in a dark room will produce a burst of light that seems quite bright, but if you light the same match or candle in a well-lit room, you may not even detect the additional illumination. The relativity of perception is apparent in the painting by Josef Albers shown in **Figure 4.68**. The two Xs are exactly the same color, but the X in the top half looks yellow, whereas the X in the

bottom half looks brown. These varied perceptions occur because of contrast effects—the two X's are contrasted against different background colors. Another example of how contrast effects can influence perception can be seen in **Figure 4.69**. The middle disk in each panel is exactly the same size, but the one in the top panel looks larger because it is surrounded by much smaller disks.

The same principles of relativity and contrast that operate when we are making judgments about the intensity, color, or size of visual stimuli also affect the way we make judgments in a wide variety of domains. For example, a 6'3" basketball player, who is really quite tall, can look downright small when surrounded by teammates who are all over 6'8". And a salary of $42,000 per year for your first full-time job may seem like a princely sum, until a close friend gets an offer of $75,000 a year. The assertion that everything is relative raises the issue of *relative to what? Comparitors* are people, objects, events, and other standards used as a baseline for comparison in making judgments. It is fairly easy to manipulate many types of judgments by selecting *extreme* comparitors that may be unrepresentative.

The influence of extreme comparitors was demonstrated in some interesting studies of judgments of physical attractiveness. In one study, undergraduate males were asked to rate the attractiveness of an average-looking female (who was described

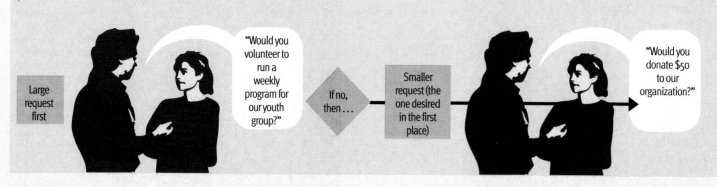

Figure 4.67

The door-in-the-face technique. The door-in-the-face technique is a frequently used compliance strategy in which you begin with a large request and work down to the smaller request you are really after. It depends in part on contrast effects.

Figure 4.68

Contrast effects in color perception. This composition by Joseph Albers shows how one color can be perceived differently when contrasted against different backgrounds. The top X looks yellow and the bottom X looks brown, but they're really the same color.

SOURCE: Albers, Joseph. *Interaction of Color.* Copyright © 1963 and reprinted by permission of the publisher, Yale University Press.

as a potential date for another male in the dorm) presented in a photo either just before or just after the participants watched a TV show dominated by strikingly beautiful women (Kenrick & Gutierres, 1980). The female was viewed as less attractive when the ratings were obtained just after the men had seen gorgeous women cavorting on TV as opposed to when they hadn't. In other studies, both male and female participants have rated *themselves* as less attractive after being exposed to many pictures of extremely attractive models (Little & Mannion, 2006; Thornton & Moore, 1993; Thornton & Maurice, 1999). Thus, contrast effects can influence important social judgments that are likely to affect how people feel about themselves and others.

Anyone who understands how easily judgments can be manipulated by a careful choice of comparitors could influence your thinking. For example, a politician who is caught in some illegal or immoral act could sway public opinion by bringing to mind (perhaps subtly) the fact that many other politicians have committed acts that were much worse. When considered against a backdrop of more extreme comparitors, the politician's transgression will probably seem less offensive. A defense attorney could use a similar strategy in an attempt to obtain a lighter sentence for a client by comparing the client's offense to much more serious crimes. And a realtor who wants to sell you an expensive house that will require huge mortgage payments will be quick to mention other homeowners who have taken on even larger mortgages.

In summary, critical thinking is facilitated by conscious awareness of the way

Figure 4.69

Contrast effects in size perception. The middle disk in the top panel looks larger than the middle disk in the bottom panel, but they really are exactly the same size. This illusion occurs because of contrast effects created by the surrounding disks.

comparitors can influence and perhaps distort a wide range of judgments. In particular, it pays to be vigilant about the possibility that others may manipulate contrast effects in their persuasive efforts. One way to reduce the influence of contrast effects is to consciously consider comparitors that are both worse and better than the event you are judging, as a way of balancing the effects of the two extremes.

Table 4.2 Critical Thinking Skills Discussed in This Application

Skill	Description
Understanding how contrast effects can influence judgments and decisions	The critical thinker appreciates how striking contrasts can be manipulated to influence many types of judgments.
Recognizing when extreme comparitors are being used	The critical thinker is on the lookout for extreme comparitors that distort judgments.

REVIEW of Key Learning Goals

4.29 The study of perception often highlights the relativity of experience. This relativity can be manipulated by arranging for contrast effects. Critical thinking is enhanced by an awareness of how extreme comparitors can distort many judgments.

Key Ideas

Psychophysics: Basic Concepts and Issues

▌ Absolute thresholds, which indicate the minimum stimulus intensity that is detectable in a sensory system, are not really absolute. The size of a just noticeable difference tends to be a constant proportion of the size of the initial stimulus.

▌ According to signal-detection theory, the detection of sensory inputs is influenced by noise in the system and by decision-making strategies. In recent decades, it has become apparent that perception can occur without awareness. However, subliminal persuasion does not appear to be a serious problem. Prolonged stimulation may lead to sensory adaptation.

The Visual System: Essentials of Sight

▌ Light varies in terms of wavelength, amplitude, and purity. Light enters the eye through the cornea and pupil and is focused on the retina by the lens. Rods and cones are the visual receptors found in the retina. Cones play a key role in daylight vision and color perception, and rods are critical to night vision and peripheral vision. Dark and light adaptation both involve changes in the retina's sensitivity to light.

▌ The retina transforms light into neural impulses that are sent to the brain via the optic nerve. Receptive fields are areas in the retina that affect the firing of visual cells. Two visual pathways, which engage in parallel processing, send signals through the thalamus to the primary visual cortex. From there, visual signals are shuttled along pathways that have been characterized as the *what* and *where* pathways. Some neurons appear to be uniquely responsive to faces and other highly specific stimuli.

▌ Perceptions of color (hue) are primarily a function of light wavelength, while amplitude affects brightness and purity affects saturation. Perceptions of many varied colors depend on processes that resemble additive color mixing. The evidence now suggests that both the trichromatic and opponent process theories are necessary to account for color vision.

The Visual System: Perceptual Processes

▌ Form perception depends on the selection and interpretation of visual inputs, as illustrated by inattentional blindness and perceptual sets. According to feature analysis theories, people detect specific elements in stimuli and build them into forms through bottom-up processing. However, evidence suggests that form perception also involves top-down processing.

▌ Gestalt psychology emphasized that the whole may be greater than the sum of its parts (features), as illustrated by Gestalt principles of form perception. Other approaches to form perception emphasize that people develop perceptual hypotheses about the distal stimuli that could be responsible for the proximal stimuli that are sensed.

▌ Depth perception depends primarily on monocular cues. Binocular cues such as retinal disparity and convergence can also contribute to depth perception. Conscious perceptions of geographical slant tend to be greatly exaggerated, but haptic judgments seem largely immune to this perceptual bias.

▌ Perceptual constancies help viewers deal with the ever-shifting nature of proximal stimuli. Visual illusions demonstrate that perceptual hypotheses can be inaccurate and that perceptions are not simple reflections of objective reality.

The Auditory System: Hearing

▌ Sound varies in terms of wavelength (frequency), amplitude, and purity. These properties affect mainly perceptions of pitch, loudness, and timbre, respectively. Auditory signals are transmitted through the thalamus to the auditory cortex in the temporal lobe.

▌ Modern evidence suggests that place theory and frequency theory are complementary rather than incompatible explanations of pitch perception. People pinpoint the source of sounds by comparing interear differences in the intensity and timing of sounds.

The Chemical Senses: Taste and Smell

▌ The taste buds are sensitive to four basic tastes: sweet, sour, bitter, and salty. Taste preferences are largely learned and are heavily influenced by one's cultural background. Supertasters are more sensitive to bitter and sweet tastes than others are, which leads them to have relatively healthy consumption habits.

▌ Like taste, smell is a chemical sense. Chemical stimuli activate olfactory receptors lining the nasal passages. Most of these receptors respond to more than one odor. Humans exhibit surprising difficulty attaching names to odors.

The Sense of Touch

▌ Sensory receptors in the skin respond to pressure, temperature, and pain. Pain signals are sent to the brain along two pathways characterized as fast and slow. The perception of pain is highly subjective and may be influenced by mood, attention, personality, and culture.

▌ Gate-control theory holds that incoming pain signals can be blocked in the spinal cord. Endorphins and a descending neural pathway appear responsible for the suppression of pain by the central nervous system.

Reflecting on the Chapter's Themes

▌ This chapter provided two dramatic demonstrations of the value of theoretical diversity. It also provided numerous examples of how and why our experience of the world is highly subjective. Finally, it highlighted the importance of cultural background.

PERSONAL APPLICATION   Appreciating Art and Illusion

▌ The principles of visual perception are often applied to artistic endeavors. Painters routinely use pictorial depth cues to make their scenes more lifelike. Color mixing, feature analysis, Gestalt principles, reversible figures, and impossible figures have also been used in influential paintings.

CRITICAL THINKING APPLICATION   Recognizing Contrast Effects: It's All Relative

▌ The study of perception often highlights the relativity of experience. This relativity can be manipulated by arranging for contrast effects. Critical thinking is enhanced by an awareness of how comparitors can distort many judgments.

Key Terms

Absolute threshold (p. 131)
Additive color mixing (p. 143)
Afterimage (p. 145)
Auditory localization (p. 164)
Basilar membrane (p. 162)
Binocular depth cues (p. 152)
Bottom-up processing (p. 148)
Cochlea (p. 162)
Color blindness (p. 144)
Complementary colors (p. 145)
Cones (p. 138)
Convergence (p. 153)
Dark adaptation (p. 138)
Depth perception (p. 152)
Distal stimuli (p. 151)
Farsightedness (p. 137)
Feature analysis (p. 148)
Feature detectors (p. 141)
Fovea (p. 138)
Frequency theory (p. 163)
Gate-control theory (p. 171)
Gustatory system (p. 165)
Impossible figures (p. 158)
Inattentional blindness (p. 147)
Just noticeable difference (JND) (p. 131)
Lateral antagonism (p. 139)
Lens (p. 135)
Light adaptation (p. 138)
Monocular depth cues (p. 153)
Motion parallax (p. 153)
Nearsightedness (p. 137)
Olfactory system (p. 165)
Opponent process theory (p. 145)
Optic chiasm (p. 140)
Optic disk (p. 137)

Parallel processing (p. 140)
Perception (p. 130)
Perceptual constancy (p. 157)
Perceptual hypothesis (p. 151)
Perceptual set (p. 147)
Phi phenomenon (p. 149)
Pictorial depth cues (p. 153)
Place theory (p. 163)
Proximal stimuli (p. 151)
Psychophysics (p. 130)
Pupil (p. 137)
Receptive field of a visual cell (p. 139)
Retina (p. 137)
Retinal disparity (p. 153)
Reversible figure (p. 146)
Rods (p. 138)
Sensation (p. 130)
Sensory adaptation (p. 133)
Signal-detection theory (p. 131)
Subjective contours (p. 148)
Subliminal perception (p. 132)
Subtractive color mixing (p. 143)
Top-down processing (p. 148)
Trichromatic theory (p. 144)
Visual illusion (p. 157)

Key People

Linda Bartoshuk (pp. 166–167)
Gustav Fechner (pp. 130–131)
Hermann von Helmholtz (pp. 144, 163)
David Hubel and Torsten Wiesel (pp. 141–142)
Ronald Melzack and Patrick Wall (pp. 171, 174)
Max Wertheimer (p. 149)

1. In psychophysical research, the absolute threshold has been arbitrarily defined as:
   A. the stimulus intensity that can be detected 100% of the time.
   B. the stimulus intensity that can be detected 50% of the time.
   C. the minimum amount of difference in intensity needed to tell two stimuli apart.
   D. a constant proportion of the size of the initial stimulus.

2. A tone-deaf person would probably not be able to tell two musical notes apart unless they were very different. We could say that this person has a relatively large:
   A. just noticeable difference.
   B. relative threshold.
   C. absolute threshold.
   D. detection threshold.

3. In their study of the influence of subliminal perception, Karremans and his colleagues (2006) found:
   A. absolutely no evidence of such influence.
   B. evidence that subliminal stimuli influenced subjects' drink preferences.
   C. that subliminal stimuli do not really exist.
   D. that it is nearly impossible to measure subliminal effects.

4. In farsightedness:
   A. close objects are seen clearly but distant objects appear blurry.
   B. the focus of light from close objects falls behind the retina.
   C. the focus of light from distant objects falls a little short of the retina.
   D. A and B.
   E. A and C.

5. The collection of rod and cone receptors that funnel signals to a particular visual cell in the retina make up that cell's:
   A. blind spot.   C. opponent process field.
   B. optic disk.   D. receptive field.

6. The visual pathway that has been characterized as _____ travels through the dorsal stream to the parietal lobes, whereas the pathway that has been labeled the _____ travels through the ventral stream to the temporal lobes.
   A. the *what* pathway; the *where* pathway
   B. the *where* pathway; the *what* pathway
   C. the *opponent process* pathway; the *trichromatic* pathway
   D. the *trichromatic* pathway; the *opponent process* pathway

7. Which theory would predict that the American flag would have a green, black, and yellow afterimage?
   A. subtractive color mixing
   B. opponent process theory
   C. additive color mixing
   D. trichromatic theory

8. The illusion of movement created by presenting visual stimuli in rapid succession is called:
   A. convergence.   C. motion parallax.
   B. retinal disparity.   D. the phi phenomenon.

9. In a painting, train tracks may look as if they go off into the distance because the artist draws the tracks as converging lines, a pictorial cue to depth known as:
   A. interposition.   C. convergence.
   B. texture gradient.   D. linear perspective.

10. Sarah has just finished a long, exhausting 6-mile run. She and her friend Jamal are gazing at a hill they need to climb to get back to their car. Jamal asks Sarah, "Gee, how steep do you think that hill is?" Based on research by Proffitt and his colleagues, Sarah is likely to:
    A. make a reasonably accurate estimate of the hill's slant, as most people do.
    B. underestimate the hill's slant, as most people do.
    C. overestimate the hill's slant, but to a lesser degree than she would have before her exhausting run.
    D. overestimate the hill's slant to an even greater degree than she would have before her exhausting run.

11. The fact that cultural groups with less exposure to carpentered buildings are less susceptible to the Müller-Lyer illusion suggests that:
    A. not all cultures test perceptual hypotheses.
    B. people in technologically advanced cultures are more gullible.
    C. illusions can be experienced only by cultures that have been exposed to the concept of illusions.
    D. perceptual inferences can be shaped by experience.

12. Perception of pitch can best be explained by:
    A. place theory.
    B. frequency theory.
    C. both place theory and frequency theory.
    D. neither theory.

13. In what way(s) is the sense of taste like the sense of smell?
    A. There are four primary stimulus groups for both senses.
    B. Both systems are routed through the thalamus on the way to the cortex.
    C. The physical stimuli for both senses are chemical substances dissolved in fluid.
    D. All of the above.
    E. None of the above.

14. Which school of painting applied the theory of feature analysis to canvas by building figures out of simple features?
    A. Kineticism   C. Surrealism
    B. Impressionism   D. Cubism

15. In the study by Kenrick and Gutierres (1980), exposing male subjects to a TV show dominated by extremely beautiful women:
    A. had no effect on their ratings of the attractiveness of a prospective date.
    B. increased their ratings of the attractiveness of a prospective date.
    C. decreased their ratings of the attractiveness of a prospective date.
    D. increased their ratings of their own attractiveness.

Answers
1 B p. 131   6 B p. 142   11 D pp. 159–160
2 A p. 131   7 B p. 145   12 C pp. 163–164
3 B p. 133   8 D p. 149   13 C pp. 165, 168
4 B pp. 136–137 9 D pp. 153–154 14 D p. 176
5 D p. 139   10 D p. 156   15 C pp. 180–181

5 VARIATIONS IN CONSCIOUSNESS

On the Nature of Consciousness
Variations in Levels of Awareness
The Evolutionary Roots of Consciousness
Consciousness and Brain Activity

Biological Rhythms and Sleep
The Role of Circadian Rhythms
Ignoring Circadian Rhythms
Realigning Circadian Rhythms

The Sleep and Waking Cycle
Cycling Through the Stages of Sleep
Age Trends in Sleep
Culture and Sleep
The Neural Bases of Sleep
The Evolutionary Bases of Sleep
Doing Without: Sleep Deprivation

FEATURED STUDY ▍ The Surprising Costs of Sleep Deprivation
Problems in the Night: Sleep Disorders

The World of Dreams
The Contents of Dreams
Links Between Dreams and Waking Life
Culture and Dreams
Theories of Dreaming

Hypnosis: Altered Consciousness or Role Playing?
Hypnotic Induction and Susceptibility
Hypnotic Phenomena
Theories of Hypnosis

Meditation: Pure Consciousness or Relaxation?
Physiological Correlates
Long-Term Benefits

Altering Consciousness with Drugs
Principal Abused Drugs and Their Effects
Factors Influencing Drug Effects
Mechanisms of Drug Action
Drug Dependence
Drugs and Health

Reflecting on the Chapter's Themes

PERSONAL APPLICATION ▍ Addressing Practical Questions About Sleep and Dreams
Common Questions About Sleep
Common Questions About Dreams

CRITICAL THINKING APPLICATION ▍ Is Alcoholism a Disease? The Power of Definitions
The Power to Make Definitions
Definitions, Labels, and Circular Reasoning

Recap

Practice Test

Nathaniel Kleitman and Eugene Aserinsky couldn't believe their eyes—or their subjects' eyes, either. It was the spring of 1952, and Kleitman, a physiologist and prominent sleep researcher, was investigating the slow, rolling eye movements displayed by subjects at the onset of sleep. Kleitman had begun to wonder whether these slow eye movements would show up during later phases of sleep. The trouble was that watching a subject's closed eyelids all night long was a surefire way to put the *researcher* to sleep. Cleverly, Kleitman and Aserinsky, a graduate student, came up with a better way to document eye movements. They hooked participants up to an apparatus that was connected to electrodes pasted near the eyes. The electrodes picked up the small electrical signals generated by moving eyeballs. In turn, these signals moved a pen on a chart recorder, much like an electroencephalograph (EEG) traces brain waves (see Chapter 3). The result was an objective record of subjects' eye movements during sleep that could be studied at leisure (Dement, 1992).

One night, while one of their participants was asleep, the researchers were astonished to see a tracing in the recording that suggested a different, much more rapid eye movement. This result was so unexpected that they at first thought the recording device was defective. "It was a rickety old thing, anyway," a technician in Kleitman's lab recalled (Coren, 1996, p. 21). Only when they decided to walk in and personally observe sleeping subjects were they convinced that the eye movements were real. The subjects were deeply asleep, yet the bulges in their closed eyelids showed that their eyeballs were moving laterally in sharp jerks, first in one direction and then in the other. It was almost as if the sleeping subjects were watching a chaotic movie. The researchers wondered—what in the world was going on?

In retrospect, it's amazing that no one had discovered these rapid eye movements before. It turns out that periods of rapid eye movement are a routine characteristic of sleep in humans and many animals. In fact, you can observe them for yourself in your pet dog or cat. The phenomenon had been there for everyone to see for eons, but those who noticed must not have attached any significance to it.

Kleitman and Aserinsky's discovery might have remained something of an oddity, but then they had a brainstorm. Could the rapid eye movements be related to dreaming? With the help of William Dement, a medical student who was interested in dreams, they soon found the answer. When Dement woke up subjects during periods of rapid eye movement, about 80 percent reported that they had just been having a vivid dream. By contrast, only a small minority of subjects awakened during other phases of sleep reported that they had been dreaming. Dement knew that he was on to something. "I was overwhelmed with excitement," he wrote later (Dement, 1992, pp. 24–25). Subsequently, EEG recordings showed that periods of rapid eye movement were also associated with marked changes in brainwave patterns. What Kleitman and his graduate students had stumbled on was considerably more than an oddity: It was a window into the most private aspect of consciousness imaginable—the experience of dreaming.

As you will learn in this chapter, the discovery of rapid eye movement (REM) sleep blossomed into a number of other fascinating insights about what goes on in the brain during sleep. This research is just one example of how contemporary psychologists have tried to come to grips with the slippery topic of consciousness. Over time, consciousness has represented something of a paradox for psychology.

On the one hand, people's conscious experience—their awareness of themselves and the world around them, their thoughts, and even their dreams—would seem to be an obvious and central concern for psychologists. On the other hand, psychology is committed to the empirical approach, which requires having objective, replicable ways of studying a given phenomenon. And consciousness is the ultimate in subjective experience. No one can directly observe another person's consciousness. Individuals have a hard enough time even describing their own conscious experience to someone else (Schooler & Fiore, 1997). Yet in recent decades researchers have been finding inventive ways to shed some objective light on the mysteries of consciousness.

We'll begin our tour of variations in consciousness with a few general points about the nature of consciousness. After that, much of the chapter will be a "bedtime story," as we take a long look at sleep and dreaming. We'll continue our discussion of consciousness by examining hypnosis, meditation, and the effects of mind-altering drugs. The Personal Application will address a number of practical questions about sleep and dreams. Finally, the Critical Thinking Application looks at the concept of alcoholism to highlight the power of definitions.

On the Nature of Consciousness

Consciousness is the awareness of internal and external stimuli. Your consciousness includes (1) your awareness of external events ("The professor just asked me a difficult question about medieval history"), (2) your awareness of your internal sensations ("My heart is racing and I'm beginning to sweat"), (3) your awareness of your self as the unique being having these experiences ("Why me?"), and (4) your awareness of your thoughts about these experiences ("I'm going to make a fool of myself!"). To put it more concisely, consciousness is personal awareness.

The contents of your consciousness are continually changing. Rarely does consciousness come to a standstill. It moves, it flows, it fluctuates, it wanders (Wegner, 1997). For example, in one recent study college students were prompted eight times a day to record whether their thoughts were wandering from what they were doing (Kane et al., 2007). On average, the participants reported that their minds were wandering from the task at hand about one-third of the time. Mind wandering was more likely when subjects were bored, anxious, tired, or stressed.

Recognizing that consciousness fluctuates continuously, William James (1902) long ago christened this flow the *stream of consciousness*. If you could tape-record your thoughts, you would find an endless flow of ideas that zigzag in all directions. As you will soon learn, even when you sleep your consciousness moves through a series of transitions. Constant shifting and changing seem to be part of the essential nature of consciousness.

Variations in Levels of Awareness

Whereas William James emphasized the stream of consciousness, Sigmund Freud (1900) wanted to examine what went on beneath the surface of this stream. As explained in Chapter 1, Freud argued that people's feelings and behavior are influenced by *unconscious* needs, wishes, and conflicts that lie below the surface of conscious awareness. According to Freud, the stream of consciousness has depth. Conscious and unconscious processes are different *levels of awareness*. Thus, Freud was one of the first theorists to recognize that consciousness is not an all-or-none phenomenon.

Since Freud's time, research has shown that people continue to maintain some awareness during sleep and sometimes even when they are put under anesthesia for surgery. How do we know? Because some stimuli can still penetrate awareness. For example, people under surgical anesthesia occasionally hear comments made during their surgery, which they later repeat to their surprised surgeons (Merikle, 2007). Such incidents occur infrequently (in about 0.2% of surgeries), but they do happen (Kihlstrom & Cork, 2007). Other research indicates that while people are asleep they remain aware of external events to some degree (K. B. Campbell, 2000; Evans, 1990). A good example is the new parent who can sleep through a loud thunderstorm or a buzzing alarm clock but who immediately hears the muffled sound of the baby crying down the hall. The parent's selective sensitivity to sounds means that some mental processing must be going on even during sleep.

The Evolutionary Roots of Consciousness

Why do humans experience consciousness? Like other aspects of human nature, consciousness must have evolved because it helped our ancient ancestors survive and reproduce (Ornstein & Dewan, 1991). That said, there is plenty of debate about exactly how consciousness proved adaptive (Guzeldere, Flanagan, & Hardcastle, 2000). One line of thinking is that consciousness allowed our ancestors to think through courses of action and their consequences—and attempt to choose the best course—without actually executing ill-advised actions (by trial and error) that may have led to disastrous consequences (Plotkin, 1998). In other words, a little forethought and planning may have proved valuable in efforts to obtain food, avoid predators, and find mates. Although this analysis seems plausible, a number of alternative explanations focus on other adaptive benefits of personal awareness, and relatively little empirical evidence exists to judge their merits (Polger, 2007). Thus, the evolutionary bases of consciousness remain elusive.

Consciousness and Brain Activity

4b

Consciousness does not arise from any distinct structure in the brain but rather from activity in distributed networks of neural pathways (Kinsbourne, 1997; Singer, 2007). Scientists are increasingly using brain-

imaging methods to explore the link between brain activity and consciousness (Cahn & Polich, 2006; Ray & Oathes, 2003), but historically, the most commonly used indicator of variations in consciousness has been the EEG, which records activity from broad swaths of the cortex. **The *electroencephalograph* (EEG) is a device that monitors the electrical activity of the brain over time by means of recording electrodes attached to the surface of the scalp.** Ultimately, the EEG summarizes the rhythm of cortical activity in the brain in terms of line tracings called *brain waves*. These brain-wave tracings vary in *amplitude* (height) and *frequency* (cycles per second, abbreviated *cps*). You can see what brain waves look like if you glance ahead to Figure 5.4 (on page 192). Human brain-wave activity is usually divided into four principal bands based on the frequency of the brain waves. These bands, named after letters in the Greek alphabet, are *beta* (13–24 cps), *alpha* (8–12 cps), *theta* (4–7 cps), and *delta* (under 4 cps).

Different patterns of EEG activity are associated with different states of consciousness, as summarized in Table 5.1. For instance, when you are alertly engaged in problem solving, beta waves tend to dominate. When you are relaxed and resting, alpha waves increase. When you slip into deep, dreamless sleep, delta waves become more prevalent. Although these correlations are far from perfect, changes in EEG activity are closely related to variations in consciousness (Wallace & Fisher, 1999).

As is often the case with correlations, researchers are faced with a chicken-or-egg puzzle when it comes to the relationship between mental states and the brain's electrical activity. If you become drowsy while you are reading this passage, your brain-wave activity will probably change. But are these changes causing your drowsiness, or is your drowsiness causing the changes in brain-wave activity? Or are the drowsiness and the shifts in brain-wave activity both caused by a *third* factor—perhaps signals coming from a subcortical area in the brain? (See Figure 5.1 on the next page.) Frankly, no one knows. All that is known for sure is that variations in consciousness are correlated with variations in brain activity.

Table 5.1 EEG Patterns Associated with States of Consciousness

EEG pattern	Frequency (cps)	Typical States of Consciousness
Beta (β)	13–24	Normal waking thought, alert problem solving
Alpha (α)	8–12	Deep relaxation, blank mind, meditation
Theta (θ)	4–7	Light sleep
Delta (Δ)	less than 4	Deep sleep

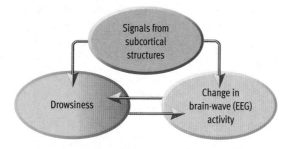

Figure 5.1

The correlation between mental states and cortical activity. As discussed in Chapter 2, because of the "third-variable problem," correlations alone do not establish causation. For example, there are strong correlations between drowsiness and a particular pattern of cortical activity, as reflected by EEG brain waves. But does drowsiness cause a change in cortical activity, or do changes in cortical activity cause drowsiness? Or does some third variable—such as signals from the brainstem or other subcortical structures—account for the changes in both brain waves and drowsiness?

EEG measures of brain-wave activity have provided investigators with a method for mapping out the mysterious state of consciousness called sleep. As we will see in the next two sections of the chapter, this state turns out to be far more complex and varied than you might expect.

REVIEW of Key Learning Goals

5.1 William James emphasized that consciousness is a continually changing stream of mental activity. Consciousness varies along a continuum of levels of awareness. Consciousness may have evolved because it allowed humans to think through the possible consequences of their actions and avoid some negative outcomes.

5.2 People maintain some degree of awareness during sleep and sometimes while under anesthesia. Brain waves vary in amplitude and frequency (cps) and are divided into four bands: beta, alpha, theta, and delta. Domination by each type of brain wave is associated with a different state of consciousness.

Biological Rhythms and Sleep

Key Learning Goals

5.3 Summarize what is known about human biological clocks and their relationship to sleep.

5.4 Explain how people get out of sync with their circadian rhythms and how these rhythms can be realigned.

Cicadas provide a fascinating example of how biological rhythms can regulate organisms' behavior. In North America most cicadas have a 17-year life cycle (although it is 13 years for some). After 17 years underground millions of cicada emerge together for two to four weeks and then the cycle begins again.

Variations in consciousness are shaped in part by biological rhythms. Rhythms pervade the world around us. The daily alternation of light and darkness, the annual pattern of the seasons, and the phases of the moon all reflect this rhythmic quality of repeating cycles. Humans, many other animals, and even plants display biological rhythms that are tied to these planetary rhythms (Foster, 2004). *Biological rhythms* are periodic fluctuations in physiological functioning. The existence of these rhythms means that organisms have internal "biological clocks" that somehow monitor the passage of time. The performance of these internal clocks can border on amazing. Consider the humble cicada, an insect that, after hatching, burrows 6–18 inches into the ground and spends the next 17 years there. After counting off 17 years with remarkable precision (within a few days), millions of cicada emerge together for a 2- to 4-week orgy of reproduction, after which they die and the cycle begins again. How does this simple insect monitor the passage of 17 years? No one knows, but cicadas provide a dramatic demonstration of the precision and potential power of biological rhythms (Foster & Kreitzman, 2004).

The Role of Circadian Rhythms

PSYK TREK

4a

Circadian rhythms are the 24-hour biological cycles found in humans and many other species. In humans, circadian rhythms are particularly influential in the regulation of sleep (Moore, 2006). However, daily cycles also produce rhythmic variations in blood pressure, urine production, hormonal secretions, and other physical functions (see **Figure 5.2**), as well as alertness, short-term

© Gary Meszaros/Photo Researchers, Inc.

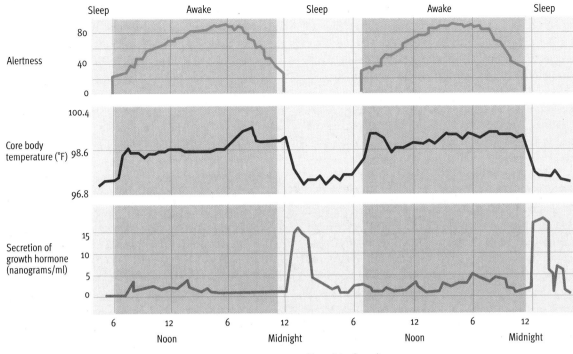

Figure 5.2

Examples of circadian rhythms. These graphs show how alertness, core body temperature, and the secretion of growth hormone typically fluctuate in a 24-hour rhythm. Note how body temperature declines when people fall asleep.

SOURCE: Adapted from Coleman, R. (1986). *Wide awake at 3:00 A.M.* New York: W. H. Freeman. Copyright © 1986 by Richard M. Coleman. Reprinted by permission of Henry Holt & Co., LLC.

memory, and other aspects of cognitive performance (Refinetti, 2006; Van Dongen & Dinges, 2005). For instance, body temperature varies rhythmically in a daily cycle, usually peaking in the afternoon and reaching its low point in the depths of the night.

Research indicates that people generally fall asleep as their body temperature begins to drop and awaken as it begins to ascend once again (Kumar, 2004). Investigators have concluded that circadian rhythms can leave individuals physiologically primed to fall asleep most easily at a particular time of day (Richardson, 1993). This optimal time varies from person to person, depending on their schedules, but it's interesting to learn that each individual may have an "ideal" time for going to bed. This ideal bedtime may also promote better-quality sleep during the night (Akerstedt et al., 1997).

To study biological clocks, researchers have monitored physiological processes while subjects are cut off from exposure to the cycle of day and night and all other external time cues. These studies have demonstrated that circadian rhythms generally persist even when external time cues are eliminated. However, when people are isolated in this way, their cycles run a little longer than normal, about 24.2 hours on the average (Czeisler, Buxton, & Khalsa, 2005). Investigators aren't sure why this slight drift toward a longer cycle occurs, but it is not apparent under normal circumstances because daily exposure to light *readjusts* people's biological clocks.

In fact, researchers have worked out many of the details regarding how the day-night cycle resets bio-

logical clocks. When exposed to light, some receptors in the retina send direct inputs to a small structure in the hypothalamus called the *suprachiasmatic nucleus (SCN)* (Gooley & Saper, 2005). The SCN sends signals to the nearby *pineal gland,* whose secretion of the hormone *melatonin* plays a key role in adjusting biological clocks (Harrington & Mistlberger, 2000). Circadian rhythms in humans actually appear to be regulated by *multiple* internal clocks, but the central pacemaker clearly is located in the SCN (Foster, 2004).

Ignoring Circadian Rhythms

4a

What happens when you ignore your biological clock and go to sleep at an unusual time? Typically, the quality of your sleep suffers. Getting out of sync with your circadian rhythms also causes *jet lag.* When you fly across several time zones, your biological clock keeps time as usual, even though official clock time changes. You then go to sleep at the "wrong" time and are likely to experience difficulty falling asleep and poor quality sleep. This inferior sleep, which can continue to occur for several days, can make you feel fatigued, sluggish, and irritable during the daytime (Arendt, Stone, & Skene, 2005).

People differ in how quickly they can reset their biological clocks to compensate for jet lag, and the speed of readjustment depends on the direction traveled. Generally, it's easier to fly westward and lengthen your day than it is to fly eastward and shorten it (Arendt et al., 2005). This east-west disparity in jet lag is sizable enough to have an impact on the performance of sports teams. Studies have found that teams flying westward perform significantly better than teams flying eastward in professional baseball (Recht, Lew, & Schwartz, 1995; see **Figure 5.3**) and college football (Worthen & Wade, 1999). A rough rule of thumb for jet lag is that the readjustment process takes about a day for each time zone crossed when you fly eastward, and about two-thirds of a day per time zone when you fly westward (Monk, 2006).

Rotating work shifts and late night shifts that are endured by many nurses, firefighters, and industrial workers also play havoc with biological rhythms. About 17% of the United States workforce works nights or rotating shifts (Richardson, 2006). Shift rotation tends to have far more detrimental effects than jet lag (Monk, 2000). People suffering from jet lag get their circadian rhythms realigned within a matter of days, but workers on night or rotating shifts are constantly at odds with local time cues and normal rhythms. Studies show that such workers get less total sleep and poorer quality sleep. These work schedules can also have a negative impact on employees' productivity and accident proneness at work, the quality of their social relations at home, and their physical and mental health (Cruz, della Rocco, & Hackworth, 2000; Hossain & Shapiro, 1999). For example, one study found a 40% increase in rotating-shift workers' risk for cardiovascular disease (Boggild & Knutsson, 1999). Other studies have found that shift rotation for women is associated with irregular menstrual cycles, reduced fertility, and an increased risk of premature births (Rogers & Dinges, 2002).

Realigning Circadian Rhythms

As scientists have come to appreciate the importance of circadian rhythms, they have begun to look for new ways to help people realign their daily rhythms. One promising line of research has focused on giving people small doses of the hormone melatonin, which appears to regulate the human biological clock. The evidence from a number of studies suggests that melatonin *can* reduce the effects of jet lag by helping travelers resynchronize their biological clocks, but the research results are inconsistent (Arendt & Skene, 2005; Monk, 2006). One reason for the inconsistent findings is that when melatonin is used to combat jet lag, the timing of the dose is crucial; because calculating the optimal timing is rather complicated, it is easy to get it wrong (Czeisler, Cajochen, & Turek, 2000).

Researchers have also tried carefully timed exposure to bright light as a treatment to realign circadian rhythms in rotating shift workers in industrial settings. Positive effects have been seen in some studies (Lowden, Akerstedt, & Wibom, 2004). This treatment can accelerate workers' adaptation to a new sleep-wake schedule, leading to improvements in sleep quality and alertness during work hours. How-

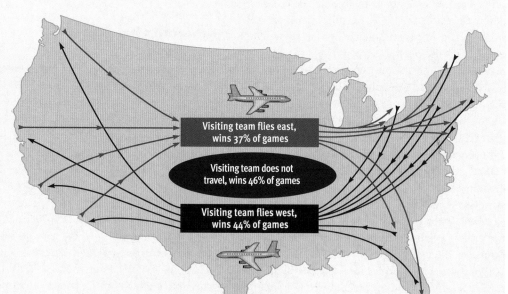

Figure 5.3

Effects of direction traveled on the performance of professional baseball teams. To gain some insight into the determinants of jet lag, Recht, Lew, and Schwartz (1995) analyzed the performance of visiting teams in major league baseball over a three-year period. In baseball, visiting teams usually play three or four games in each destination city, so there are plenty of games in which the visiting team has not traveled the day before. These games, which served as a baseline for comparison, were won by the visiting team 46% of the time. Consistent with the observation that flying west creates less jet lag than flying east, visiting teams that flew westward the day (or night) before performed only slightly worse, winning 44% of the time. In contrast, visiting teams that flew eastward the day before won only 37% of their games, presumably because flying east and shortening one's day creates greater jet lag.

SOURCE: Adapted from Kalat, J. W. (2001). *Biological psychology.* Belmont, CA: Wadsworth. Reprinted by permission.

ever, the effects of bright-light administration have been modest and somewhat inconsistent (Rogers & Dinges, 2002), and it isn't a realistic option in many work settings. Another strategy to help rotating shift workers involves carefully planning their rotation schedules to reduce the severity of their circadian disruption. The negative effects of shift rotation can be reduced somewhat if workers move through progressively later starting times (instead of progressively earlier starting times) and if they have longer periods between shift changes (Kostreva, McNelis, & Clemens, 2002). Although enlightened scheduling practices can help, the unfortunate reality is that most people find rotating shift work very difficult.

The Sleep and Waking Cycle

Although it is a familiar state of consciousness, sleep is widely misunderstood. Historically, people have thought of sleep as a single, uniform state of physical and mental inactivity, during which the brain is "shut down" (Dement, 2003). In reality, sleepers experience quite a bit of physical and mental activity throughout the night. Scientists have learned a great deal about sleep since the landmark discovery of REM sleep in the 1950s.

The advances in psychology's understanding of sleep are the result of hard work by researchers who have spent countless nighttime hours watching other people sleep. This work is done in sleep laboratories, where volunteer subjects come to spend the night. Sleep labs have one or more "bedrooms" in which the subjects retire, usually after being hooked up to a variety of physiological recording devices. In addition to an EEG, the other two crucial devices are an *electromyograph (EMG)*, which records muscular activity and tension, and an *electrooculograph (EOG)*, which records eye movements (Carskadon & Rechtschaffen, 2005; Collop, 2006). Typically, other instruments are also used to monitor heart rate, breathing, pulse rate, and body temperature. The researchers observe the sleeping subject through a window (or with a video camera) from an adjacent room, where they also monitor elaborate physiological recording equipment (see the adjacent photo). For most people, it takes just one night to adapt to the strange bedroom and the recording devices and return to their normal mode of sleeping (Carskadon & Dement, 1994).

Cycling Through the Stages of Sleep

PSYK TREK 4b

Not only does sleep occur in a context of daily rhythms, but subtler rhythms are evident within the experience of sleep itself. During sleep, people cycle through a series of five stages. Let's take a look at what researchers have learned about the changes that occur during each of these stages (Carskadon & Dement, 2005; Rosenthal, 2006).

Stages 1–4

PSYK TREK 4b

Although it may only take a few minutes, the onset of sleep is gradual, with no obvious transition point

Researchers in a sleep laboratory can observe subjects while using elaborate equipment to record physiological changes during sleep. This kind of research has disclosed that sleep is a complex series of physical and mental states.

© Christian Voulagaropoulos/ISM/PhotoTake

between wakefulness and sleep (Rechtschaffen, 1994). The length of time it takes people to fall asleep varies considerably, but the *average* in a recent study of over 35,000 people from 10 countries was 25 minutes (Soldatos et al., 2005). The time required to fall asleep depends on quite an array of factors, including how long it has been since the person has slept, where the person is in his or her circadian cycle, the amount of noise or light in the sleep environment, and the person's age, desire to fall asleep, boredom level, recent caffeine or drug intake, and stress level, among other things (Broughton, 1994). In any event, stage 1 is a brief transitional stage of light sleep that usually lasts only 10–12 minutes (Rama, Cho, & Kushida, 2006). Breathing and heart rate slow as muscle tension and body temperature decline. The alpha waves that probably dominated EEG activity just before falling asleep give way to lower-frequency EEG activity in which theta waves are prominent (see Figure 5.4). *Hypnic jerks,* those brief muscular contractions that occur as people fall asleep, generally occur during stage 1 drowsiness (Broughton, 1994).

As the sleeper descends through stages 2, 3, and 4 of the cycle, respiration rate, heart rate, muscle ten-

sion, and body temperature continue to decline. During stage 2, which typically lasts about 10–25 minutes, brief bursts of higher-frequency brain waves, called *sleep spindles,* appear against a background of mixed EEG activity (refer to Figure 5.4 once again). Gradually, brain waves become higher in amplitude and slower in frequency, as the body moves into a deeper form of sleep, called slow-wave sleep. *Slow-wave sleep (SWS) consists of sleep stages 3 and 4, during which high-amplitude, low-frequency delta waves become prominent in EEG recordings.* Typically, individuals reach slow-wave sleep in about a half-hour and stay there for roughly 30 minutes. Then the cycle reverses itself and the sleeper gradually moves back upward through the lighter stages. That's when things start to get especially interesting.

REM Sleep
4b

When sleepers reach what should be stage 1 once again, they usually go into the *fifth* stage of sleep, which is most widely known as *REM sleep*. As we have seen, REM is an abbreviation for the *rapid eye movements* prominent during this stage. In a sleep lab, researchers use an electrooculograph to monitor these lateral (side-to-side) movements that occur beneath the sleeping person's closed eyelids. However, these movements can be seen with the naked eye if you closely watch someone in the REM stage of sleep (little ripples move back and forth across his or her closed eyelids). Decades of research have shown that virtually all mammals and birds exhibit REM sleep (see the photo on the next page for a notable exception).

In humans, the REM stage tends to be a "deep" stage of sleep in the sense that people are relatively hard to awaken from it (although arousal thresholds vary during REM). The REM stage is also marked by irregular breathing and pulse rate. Muscle tone is extremely relaxed—so much so that bodily movements are minimal and the sleeper is virtually paralyzed. *Although REM is a relatively deep stage of sleep, EEG activity is dominated by high-frequency beta waves that resemble those observed when people are alert and awake* (see Figure 5.4 again).

This paradox is probably related to the association between REM sleep and dreaming. As noted earlier, when subjects are awakened during various stages of sleep and asked whether they are dreaming, most dream reports come from the REM stage (Dement, 1978; McCarley, 1994). Although decades of research have revealed that some dreaming also occurs in the non-REM stages, dreaming is most frequent, vivid, and memorable during REM sleep (Pace-Schott, 2005).

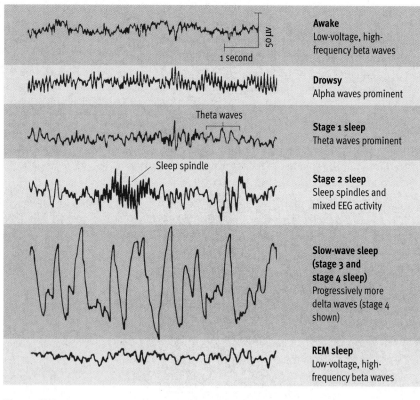

Awake
Low-voltage, high-frequency beta waves

50 μV
1 second

Drowsy
Alpha waves prominent

Theta waves

Stage 1 sleep
Theta waves prominent

Sleep spindle

Stage 2 sleep
Sleep spindles and mixed EEG activity

Slow-wave sleep (stage 3 and stage 4 sleep)
Progressively more delta waves (stage 4 shown)

REM sleep
Low-voltage, high-frequency beta waves

Figure 5.4

EEG patterns in sleep and wakefulness. Characteristic brain waves vary depending on one's state of consciousness. Generally, as people move from an awake state through deeper stages of sleep, their brain waves decrease in frequency (cycles per second) and increase in amplitude (height). However, brain waves during REM sleep resemble "wide-awake" brain waves.

SOURCE: Adapted from Hauri, P. (1982). *Current concepts: The sleep disorders.* Kalamazoo, MI: The Upjohn Company. Reprinted by permission.

To summarize, *REM sleep* is a relatively deep stage of sleep marked by rapid eye movements, high-frequency, low-amplitude brain waves, and vivid dreaming. It is such a special stage of sleep that the other four stages are often characterized simply as "non-REM sleep." *Non-REM (NREM) sleep* consists of sleep stages 1 through 4, which are marked by an absence of rapid eye movements, relatively little dreaming, and varied EEG activity.

Repeating the Cycle 4b

During the course of a night, people usually repeat the sleep cycle about four times. As the night wears on, the cycle changes gradually. The first REM period is relatively short, lasting only a few minutes. Subsequent REM periods get progressively longer, peaking at around 40–60 minutes. Additionally, NREM intervals tend to get shorter, and descents into NREM stages usually become more shallow. These trends can be seen in **Figure 5.5** on pages 194–195, which provides an overview of a typical night's sleep cycle. These trends mean that most slow-wave sleep occurs early in the sleep cycle and that REM sleep tends to pile up in the second half of the sleep cycle. Summing across the entire cycle, young adults typically spend about 15%–20% of their sleep time in slow-wave sleep and another 20%–25% in REM sleep (Rama et al., 2006).

What we have described thus far is the big picture—the typical structure of sleep averaged over many people. However, recent research by Tucker, Dinges, and Van Dongen (2007) has shown that the "architecture" of sleep—how quickly one falls asleep, how long one sleeps, how one cycles through the various stages—varies from one person to the next more than sleep researchers initially realized. And these personal variations are pretty stable from one night to the next, meaning that each of us has a signature sleep pattern. Tucker et al. (2007) believe that these signature patterns are mostly shaped by biological factors rather than personal habits, although much more research is needed on this issue.

Age Trends in Sleep 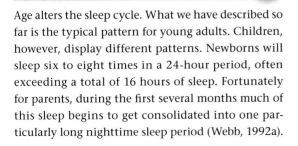 4b

Age alters the sleep cycle. What we have described so far is the typical pattern for young adults. Children, however, display different patterns. Newborns will sleep six to eight times in a 24-hour period, often exceeding a total of 16 hours of sleep. Fortunately for parents, during the first several months much of this sleep begins to get consolidated into one particularly long nighttime sleep period (Webb, 1992a).

REM sleep is not unique to humans. Nearly all mammals and birds exhibit REM sleep. The only known exceptions among warm-blooded vertebrates are dolphins and some whales (Morrison, 2003). Dolphins are particularly interesting, as they sleep while swimming, resting one hemisphere of the brain while the other hemisphere remains alert.

Interestingly, infants spend much more of their sleep time in the REM stage than adults do. In the first few months, REM accounts for about 50% of babies' sleep, as compared to 20% of adults' sleep. During the remainder of the first year, the REM portion of infants' sleep declines to roughly 30% (Ohayon et al., 2004). The REM portion of sleep continues to decrease gradually until it levels off at about 20% (see **Figure 5.6** on the next page).

During adulthood, gradual, age-related changes in sleep continue. Although the proportion of REM sleep remains fairly stable (Floyd et al., 2007), the percentage of slow-wave sleep declines and the percentage of time spent in stage 1 increases slightly, with these trends stronger in men than women (Bliwise, 2005). These shifts toward lighter sleep *may* contribute to the increased frequency of nighttime awakenings seen among the elderly (Klerman et al., 2004). As **Figure 5.6** shows, the average amount of total sleep time also declines with advancing age. However, these averages mask important variability, as total sleep *increases* with age in a substantial minority of older people (Webb, 1992a).

Culture and Sleep

Although age clearly affects the nature and structure of sleep itself, the psychological and physiological experience of sleep does not appear to vary much across cultures. For example, a recent cross-cultural survey (Soldatos et al., 2005) found relatively modest differences in the average amount of time that

web link 5.2

SleepQuest

Leading sleep researcher William Dement of Stanford University—the founder of sleep medicine—is the chief scientific advisor at this site. Visitors can access an archive of columns written by Dr. Dement and a diverse array of resources on sleep disorders.

Figure 5.5

An overview of the cycle of sleep. The white line charts how a typical, healthy, young adult moves through the various stages of sleep during the course of a night. This diagram also shows how dreams and rapid eye movements tend to coincide with REM sleep, whereas posture changes occur between REM periods (because the body is nearly paralyzed during REM sleep). Notice how the person cycles into REM four times, as descents into NREM sleep get shallower and REM periods get longer. Thus, slow-wave sleep is prominent early in the night, while REM sleep dominates the second half of a night's sleep. Although these patterns are typical, keep in mind that sleep patterns vary from one person to another and that they change with age.

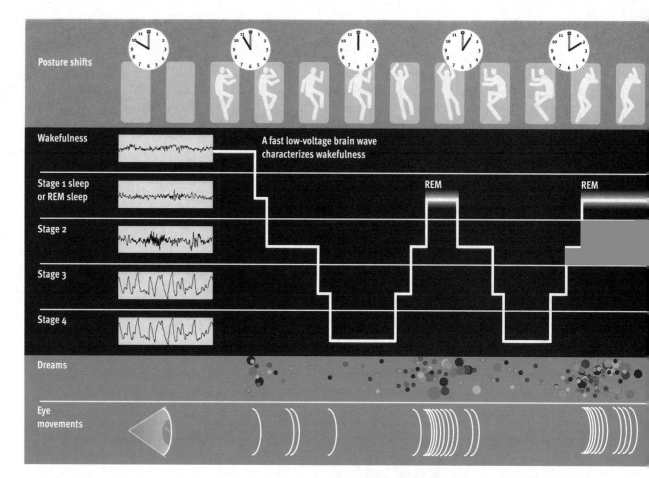

Figure 5.6

Changes in sleep patterns over the life span. Both the total amount of sleep per night and the portion of sleep that is REM sleep change with age. Sleep patterns change most dramatically during infancy, with total sleep time and amount of REM sleep declining sharply in the first two years of life. After a noticeable drop in the average amount of sleep in adolescence, sleep patterns remain relatively stable, although total sleep and slow-wave sleep continue to decline gradually with age.

SOURCE: Adapted from an updated revision of a figure in Roffwarg, H. P., Muzio, J. N., & Dement, W. C. (1966). Ontogenetic development of human sleep-dream cycle. *Science*, *152*, 604–609. Copyright © 1966 by the American Association for the Advancement of Science. Adapted and revised by permission of the authors.

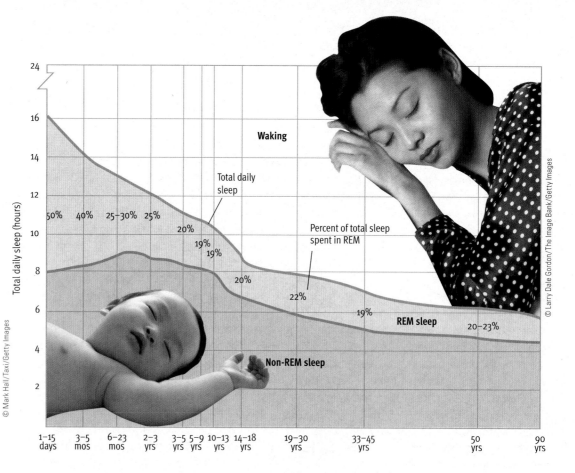

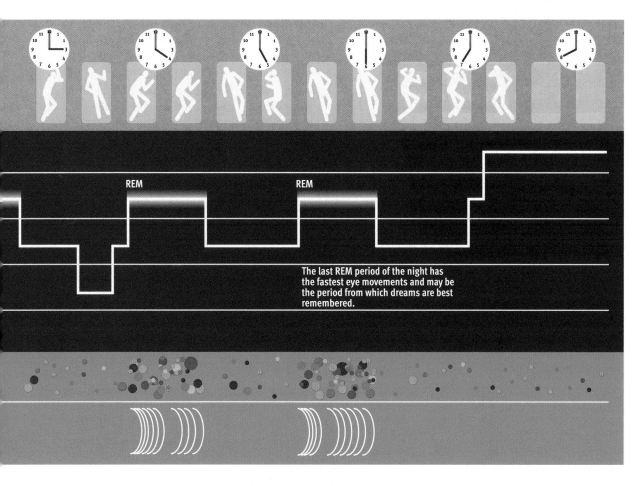

The last REM period of the night has the fastest eye movements and may be the period from which dreams are best remembered.

people sleep and in the time it takes for them to fall asleep (see Figure 5.7 on page 196). Cultural disparities in sleep are limited to more peripheral matters, such as sleeping arrangements and napping customs. For instance, there are cultural differences in *co-sleeping,* the practice of children and parents sleeping together (McKenna, 1993). In modern Western societies, co-sleeping tends to be discouraged in most homes. As part of their effort to foster self-reliance, American parents teach their children to sleep alone.

concept check 5.1

Comparing REM and NREM Sleep

A table here could have provided you with a systematic comparison of REM sleep and NREM sleep, but that would have deprived you of the opportunity to check your understanding of these sleep phases by creating your own table. Fill in each of the blanks below with a word or phrase highlighting the differences between REM and NREM sleep with regard to the various characteristics specified. You can find the answers in the back of the book in Appendix A.

Characteristic	REM sleep	NREM sleep
1. Type of EEG activity		
2. Eye movements		
3. Dreaming		
4. Depth (difficulty in awakening)		
5. Percentage of total sleep (in adults)		
6. Increases or decreases (as percentage of sleep) during childhood		
7. Timing in sleep cycle (dominates early or late)		

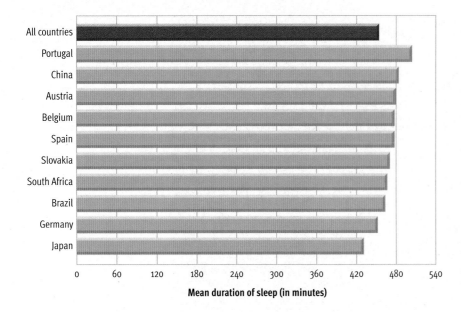

Figure 5.7
Cultural variations in how long people tend to sleep. A recent study (Soldatos et al., 2005) surveyed over 35,000 people in ten countries about various aspects of their sleep habits. This graph shows the average duration of nighttime sleep reported by the respondents in each country. Although Japan was a bit of an "outlier," the cultural differences are rather modest. Cultural variability in the average time required to fall asleep was also modest. Consistent with previous findings, the results of this study suggest that the basic architecture of sleep does not vary much across cultures.

In contrast, co-sleeping is more widely accepted in Japanese culture, which emphasizes interdependence and group harmony (Latz, Wolf, & Lozoff, 1999). Around the world as a whole, co-sleeping is normative (Ball, Hooker, & Kelly, 2000). Discomfort with co-sleeping appears to be largely an urban, Western phenomenon.

Napping practices also vary along cultural lines. In many societies, shops close and activities are curtailed in the afternoon to permit people to enjoy a 1- to 2-hour midday nap. These "siesta cultures" are found mostly in tropical regions of the world (Webb & Dinges, 1989). There, this practice is adaptive in that it allows people to avoid working during the hottest part of the day. The siesta is not a fixture in all tropical societies, however. It is infrequent among nomadic groups and those that depend on irregular food supplies. As a rule, the siesta tradition is not found in industrialized societies, where it conflicts with the emphasis on productivity and the philosophy that "time is money." Moreover, when industrialization comes to a siesta culture, it undermines the practice. For instance, modernization in Spain has led to a decline in midday napping there (Kribbs, 1993).

The Neural Bases of Sleep

The rhythm of sleep and waking appears to be regulated primarily by subcortical structures that lie deep within the brain. One brain structure that is important to sleep and wakefulness is the *reticular formation* in the core of the brainstem (Steriade, 2005). The *ascending reticular activating system (ARAS)* consists of the afferent (incoming) nerve fibers running through the reticular formation that

influence physiological arousal. As you can see in Figure 5.8, the ARAS projects diffusely into many areas of the cortex. When these ascending fibers are cut in the brainstem of a cat, the result is continuous sleep (Moruzzi, 1964). Electrical stimulation along the same pathways produces arousal and alertness.

Although the ARAS contributes to the neural regulation of sleep and waking, many other brain structures are also involved (Marks, 2006). For example, activity in the *pons* and adjacent areas in the *midbrain* seems to be critical to the generation of REM sleep (Siegel, 2005). Recent research has focused on the importance of various areas in the *hypothalamus* for the regulation of sleep and wakefulness (Saper, Scammell, & Lu, 2005). Specific areas in the medulla, thalamus, and basal forebrain have also been implicated in the control of sleep (see Figure 5.8). Thus, the ebb and flow of sleep and waking is regulated through activity in a *constellation* of interacting brain centers.

Efforts to identify the neurotransmitters involved in the regulation of sleep and waking have uncovered similar diffusion of responsibility. Serotonin and GABA appear to play especially important roles in sleep (Siegel, 2004; Ursin, 2002). However, a variety of other neurotransmitters—norepinephrine, dopamine, and acetylcholine—clearly influence the

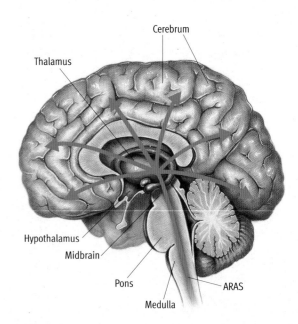

Figure 5.8
The ascending reticular activating system (ARAS) and other areas involved in sleep. A number of brain areas and structures interact to regulate sleep and waking, including all those highlighted in this graphic. Particularly important are the pons and the ARAS (represented by the green arrows), which conveys neural stimulation to many areas of the cortex. Recent research has focused on the role of the hypothalamus. But the bottom line is that sleep depends on an interacting constellation of brain structures.

course of sleep and arousal, and several other chemicals play contributing roles (Jones, 2005; Mendelson, 2001). In summary, no single structure in the brain serves as a "sleep center," nor does any one neurotransmitter serve as a "sleep chemical." Instead, sleep depends on the interplay of many neural centers and neurotransmitters.

The Evolutionary Bases of Sleep

What is the evolutionary significance of sleep? The fact that sleep is seen in a highly diverse array of organisms and that it appears to have evolved independently in birds and mammals suggests that it has considerable adaptive value. But theorists disagree about *how* exactly sleep is adaptive. One hypothesis is that sleep evolved to conserve organisms' energy. According to this notion, sleep evolved millions of years ago in service of warmbloodedness, which requires the maintenance of a constant, high body temperature by metabolic means. An alternative hypothesis is that the immobilization associated with sleep is adaptive because it reduces exposure to predators and other sources of danger. A third hypothesis is that sleep is adaptive because it helps animals restore bodily resources depleted by waking activities. But what, exactly, sleep restores is not readily apparent (Frank, 2006). Overall, the evidence seems strongest for the energy conservation hypothesis, but there is room for extensive debate about the evolutionary bases of sleep (Zepelin, Siegel, & Tobler, 2005). Complicating the picture more, many theorists believe that the function and evolutionary roots of REM sleep and NREM sleep may be quite different (Siegel, 2005).

Doing Without: Sleep Deprivation

Do people really need eight hours of sleep per night? A great many people, including countless college students, try to get by on less sleep than that. Many sleep experts believe that much of American society chronically suffers from sleep deprivation (Walsh, Dement, & Dinges, 2005). It appears that more and more people are trying to squeeze additional waking hours out of their days as they attempt to juggle work, family, household, and school responsibilities. Let's look at the research on the effects of sleep deprivation.

Sleep Restriction

Research has mostly focused on *partial sleep deprivation*, or *sleep restriction*, which occurs when people make do with substantially less sleep than normal over a period of time. Research findings and expert opinions on this matter have varied over recent decades. One reason for this variability is that the effects of sleep restriction vary depending on the amount of sleep lost, on where subjects are in their circadian cycles when tested, and on the nature of the task (Bonnet, 2000; Dorrian & Dinges, 2006). Moreover, recent research has also found variability among individuals in how sensitive they are to sleep restriction. Over a series of three carefully controlled sleep-deprivation episodes, Van Dongen et al. (2004) found that some subjects were more vulnerable to the negative effects of sleep deprivation than others. Caveats aside, the emerging consensus is that sleep restriction has far more negative effects than most people assume, as will be apparent in our Featured Study for this chapter.

William Dement

"Sleep deprivation is a major epidemic in our society.... Americans spend so much time and energy chasing the American dream, that they don't have much time left for actual dreaming."

The Surprising Costs of Sleep Deprivation

Numerous studies of sleep deprivation have been conducted in recent decades, but given the inherent challenges in conducting research in this area, most of them have suffered from methodological weaknesses. For example, many studies have failed to keep participants under supervision to make sure they do not consume stimulants or get more sleep than they are supposed to. Even carefully controlled studies have generally been too brief (typically a few days) to effectively assess the cumulative impact of sleep deprivation. The present study attempted to correct these shortcomings in a highly controlled and exceptionally precise effort to compare and quantify the effects of sleep restriction and total sleep deprivation.

Method

Participants and design. The subjects were 48 healthy, young adults (ages 21–38) who were carefully screened to ensure that they were drug-free and had no medical, psychological, or sleep-related disorders. They agreed to not use any alcohol, tobacco, or caffeine for two weeks prior to the study. The participants were randomly assigned to one of four groups: a control group that slept 8 hours per night, a sleep-restriction group that was allowed 6 hours of sleep per night, a sleep-restriction group that was allowed 4 hours of sleep per night, and a total-deprivation group that was not permitted any sleep. The total-deprivation group went without any sleep for 3 days; the other three groups followed their sleep schedules for 14 days.

Procedure. The volunteers reported to the lab for one day of adaptation (to sleeping with recording devices hooked up) and two days of baseline recordings before the sleep manipulations were begun. Participants stayed in the laboratory throughout the study. When scheduled to be awake, they were given batteries of cognitive tests

FEATURED

STUDY

SOURCE: Van Dongen, H. P. A., Maislin, G., Mullington, J. M., & Dinges, D. F. (2003). The cumulative cost of additional wakefulness: Dose-response effects on neurobehavioral functions and sleep physiology from chronic sleep restriction and total sleep deprivation. *Sleep, 26,* 117–126.

every 2 hours. Between test sessions they were allowed to read, watch movies, and interact. During scheduled sleep times they were hooked up to standard sleep lab recording devices and retired with the lights off.

Measures. The repeated tests of participants' mental functioning included (a) a series of psychomotor vigilance tasks that assessed alertness, (b) a series of digit-symbol matching tasks that assessed short-term memory, and (c) a series of arithmetic tasks that assessed complex problem solving. In each testing session subjects also responded to a self-report scale that assessed their subjective feelings of sleepiness.

Results

As anticipated, the control group who were not deprived of sleep showed no cognitive deficits over the course of 14 days, while the total-deprivation group showed rapid and steep deterioration on all measures. These baselines provided useful comparisons to assess the impact of the two sleep restriction conditions. Participants restricted to 4 or 6 hours of sleep showed a gradual decline in performance on the cognitive measures over the course of the 14 days. These decrements in performance were substantial. By the end of the study, the group limited to 6 hours sleep showed cognitive impairments that were equivalent to those seen after one day of total sleep deprivation, and the group limited to 4 hours of sleep showed decrements comparable to those caused by two days of total sleep deprivation. Participants' ratings of their sleepiness soared rapidly in the total-deprivation group but grew gradually and moderately in the sleep-restriction groups.

Discussion

The authors conclude that "even relatively moderate sleep restriction—if sustained night after night—can seriously impair waking neurobehavioral functions in healthy young adults" (p. 124). They assert that their findings contradict the claim made in some quarters that humans gradually adapt to sleep restriction so that impairments become relatively modest after a while. And they note that participants' cognitive deficits were consistent over many repeated tests, thus undermining the notion that deprivation effects might be limited to a few points in the day because of waxing and waning performance. Finally, they point out that participants' ratings of their sleepiness were modest in relation to the steep decrements in performance that were observed, suggesting that people may not appreciate the extent to which sleep restriction undermines their mental functioning.

Comment

This study was selected because it exemplifies how carefully crafted controls can enhance the quality of empirical research and thus yield more compelling findings. Many previous studies of sleep restriction had observed less severe deterioration in participants' performance, but the exceptional control of extraneous variables in the present study lends greater credence to its findings. The disconnect between participants' ratings of their sleepiness and the size of the cognitive deficits observed also provides yet another demonstration that human experience is highly subjective.

A large number of traffic accidents occur because drivers get drowsy or fall asleep at the wheel. Although the effects of sleep deprivation seem innocuous, sleep loss can be deadly.

Our Featured Study is representative of a great deal of recent research suggesting that the effects of sleep deprivation are not as benign as widely believed. Studies indicate that sleep restriction can impair individuals' attention, reaction time, cognitive speed and accuracy, motor coordination, and decision making (Dinges, Rogers, & Baynard, 2005). Evidence suggests that sleep deprivation contributes to errors in medical treatment by physicians in training (medical residents), who often work 80 to 100 hours a week without adequate rest (Weinger & Ancoli-Israel, 2002). Sleep deprivation has also been blamed for a large proportion of transportation accidents and mishaps in the workplace (Walsh et al., 2005). For example, sleepiness appears to be a contributing factor in roughly 20% of motor vehicle accidents (Mac-Lean, Davies, & Thiele, 2003). Sleep deprivation seems to be particularly problematic among young drivers, truck drivers, and drivers who work late or rotating shifts (Durmer & Dinges, 2005).

Studies also suggest that nighttime workers in many industries frequently fall asleep on the job (Roehrs et al., 2005). Obviously, for a person running a punch press, driving a bus, or working as an air traffic controller, a momentary lapse in attention could be very costly. In recent decades, a number of major disasters, such as the nuclear accidents at Three

© Andy Sacks/Stone/Getty Images

Mile Island and Chernobyl, the running aground of the Exxon *Valdez* in Alaska, and the *Challenger* space shuttle tragedy, have been blamed in part on lapses in judgment and attention resulting from sleep deprivation (Doghramji, 2001). Experts have *estimated* that accidents attributed to drowsiness induced by sleep deprivation cost the U.S. economy as much as $56 billion annually (Durmer & Dinges, 2005).

Selective Deprivation

The unique quality of REM sleep led researchers to look into the effects of a special type of sleep deprivation: *selective deprivation.* In a number of laboratory studies, subjects were awakened over a period of nights whenever they began to go into the REM stage. These subjects usually got a decent amount of sleep in NREM stages, but they were selectively deprived of REM sleep.

What are the effects of REM deprivation? The evidence suggests that it has little discernable impact on daytime functioning, but it *does* have some interesting effects on subjects' patterns of sleeping (Bonnet, 2005). As the nights go by in REM-deprivation studies, it becomes necessary to awaken the subjects more and more often to deprive them of their REM sleep, because they spontaneously shift into REM more and more frequently. In one study, researchers had to awaken a subject 64 times by the third night of REM deprivation, as shown in **Figure 5.9** (Borbely, 1986). Furthermore, when a REM-deprivation experiment comes to an end and participants are allowed to sleep without interruption, they experience a "rebound effect." That is, they spend extra time in REM periods for one to three nights to make up for their REM deprivation (Bonnet, 2005).

Similar results have been observed when subjects have been selectively deprived of slow-wave sleep (Bonnet, 2005). As the nights go by, more awakenings are required to prevent SWS, and after deprivation of SWS, people experience a rebound effect

(Borbely & Achermann, 2005). What do theorists make of these spontaneous pursuits of REM and slow-wave sleep? They conclude that people must have specific *needs* for REM and slow-wave sleep—and rather strong needs, at that.

Why do we need REM and slow-wave sleep? Some recent studies suggest that REM and slow-wave sleep contribute to firming up learning that takes place during the day—a process called *memory consolidation* (Gais & Born, 2004; Stickgold, 2001). Efforts to explore this hypothesis have led to some interesting findings in recent years. For example, in one study participants were given training on a perceptual-motor task and then retested 12 hours later. Subjects who slept during the 12-hour interval showed substantial *improvement* in performance that was not apparent in subjects who did not sleep (Walker et al., 2002). A host of similar studies have shown that sleep seems to enhance subjects' memory of specific learning activities that occurred during the day and that depriving subjects of either REM sleep or slow-wave sleep reduces these increments in memory (Walker & Stickgold, 2004). These studies also find that the length of time spent in REM and SWS correlates with subjects' learning and memory performance (Walker & Stickgold, 2006). Some studies even suggest that sleep may foster creative insights the next morning related to the previous day's learning (Stickgold & Walker, 2004; Wagner et al., 2004). The theoretical meaning of these findings is still being debated, but the most widely accepted explanations center on how time spent in specific stages of sleep may stabilize or solidify memories formed during the day (Stickgold, 2005).

Sleep Loss and Health

In recent years, researchers have begun to investigate the notion that sleep deprivation might have serious health consequences. Accumulating evidence suggests that sleep loss can affect physiological processes

web link 5.3

National Sleep Foundation
This attractive, well-organized website houses a great deal of information on sleep. Highlights include an interactive test to assess your sleep habits; electronic pamphlets on practical sleep topics, such as strategies for shift workers, the dangers of drowsy driving, and ways to reduce jet lag; and extensive coverage of the full range of sleep disorders.

Figure 5.9
The effects of REM deprivation on sleep. This graph plots how often researchers had to awaken a subject over the course of three nights of REM deprivation. Notice how the awakenings rapidly became more frequent during the course of each night and from night to night. This pattern of awakenings illustrates how a REM-deprived subject tends to compensate by repeatedly slipping back into REM sleep.

SOURCE: Adapted from Borbely, A. (1986) *Secrets of sleep* (English translation). New York: Basic Books. Copyright © 1986 by Basic Books. Reprinted by permission of Basic Books, inc., a member of Perseus Books, LLC and Penguin UK.

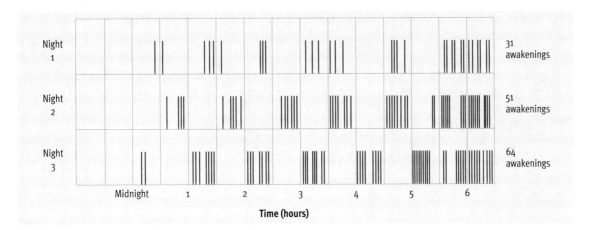

in ways that may undermine physical health. For example, sleep restriction appears to trigger hormonal changes that increase hunger (Spiegel et al., 2004). Consistent with this finding, studies have found a link between short sleep duration and increased obesity, which is a risk factor for a number of health problems (Kohatsu et al., 2006). Researchers have also found that sleep loss leads to impaired immune system functioning (Motivala & Irwin, 2007) and increased inflammatory responses (Irwin et al., 2006), which are likely to heighten vulnerability to a variety of diseases. Hence, it is not surprising that studies have uncovered links between short sleep duration and an increased risk for diabetes (Gottlieb et al., 2005), hypertension (Gangwisch et al., 2006), and coronary disease (Ayas et al., 2003).

These findings have motivated researchers to explore the correlation between habitual sleep time and overall mortality. The results of this research have provided a bit of a surprise. As expected, people who consistently sleep less than seven hours exhibit an elevated mortality risk, but so do those who routinely sleep *more* than eight hours, and mortality rates are especially high among those who sleep over 10 hours (see **Figure 5.10**; Patel et al., 2004; Tamakoshi et al., 2004). Researchers are now scrambling to figure out why long sleep duration is correlated with elevated mortality. It could be that prolonged sleep is a "marker" for other problems, such as depression or a sedentary lifestyle, that have negative effects on health (Patel et al., 2006). Bear in mind, also, that the studies linking typical sleep duration to mortality have depended on participants' *self-report esti-*

mates of how long they normally sleep, which could be inaccurate.

The evidence linking sleep duration to mortality has inspired new research intended to determine exactly how much people really sleep. Using a wristwatch-like device that can record sleep data around the clock, Lauderdale and colleagues (2006) monitored the sleep habits of 669 participants for three days. They found that while their subjects spent an average of 7.51 hours in bed each day, actual sleep time was only 6.06 hours. This finding suggests that self-estimates of sleep duration may be distorted, which will greatly complicate the effort to clarify the association between sleep patterns and mortality. In any event, the relationship between sleep and health is an emerging area of research that probably will yield some very interesting findings in the years to come.

Problems in the Night: Sleep Disorders

Not everyone is able to consistently enjoy the luxury of a good night's sleep. In this section we will briefly discuss what is currently known about a variety of sleep disorders.

Insomnia

Insomnia is the most common sleep disorder. *Insomnia refers to chronic problems in getting adequate sleep.* It occurs in three basic patterns: (1) difficulty in falling asleep initially, (2) difficulty in remaining asleep, and (3) persistent early-morning awakening. Difficulty falling asleep is the most common problem among young people, whereas trouble staying asleep and early-morning awakenings are the most common syndromes among middle-aged and elderly people (Hublin & Partinen, 2002). Insomnia may sound like a minor problem to those who haven't struggled with it, but it can be a very unpleasant malady. Insomniacs have to endure the agony of watching their precious sleep time tick away as they toss and turn in restless frustration. Moreover, insomnia is associated with daytime fatigue, impaired functioning, an elevated risk for accidents, reduced productivity, depression, anxiety, substance abuse, and increased health problems (see **Figure 5.11**; Benca, 2001; Breslau et al., 1996; Edinger & Means, 2005).

Prevalence. Estimates of the prevalence of insomnia vary considerably because surveys have to depend on respondents' highly subjective judgments of whether their sleep is adequate, and results vary depending on how survey questions are posed

Figure 5.10
Mortality rates as a function of typical sleep duration. In a study of over 100,000 subjects followed for 10 years, Tamakoshi et al. (2004) estimated mortality rates in relation to typical sleep duration. The lowest mortality rate was found among those who slept 7 hours, so that figure was arbitrarily set to 1.00 and the mortality rates for other sleep lengths were calculated relative to that baseline. The rates shown here are averaged for males and females. As you can see, higher mortality rates are associated with both shorter sleep durations and longer sleep durations. Mortality rates were especially elevated among those who reported that they slept 10 or more hours per night.

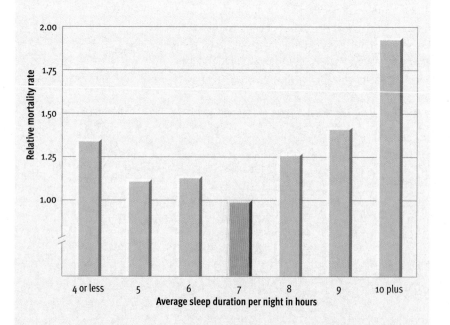

(Ohayon & Guilleminault, 2006). Another complicating consideration is that nearly everyone suffers *occasional* sleep difficulties because of stress, disruptions of biological rhythms, or other temporary circumstances. Fortunately, these problems clear up spontaneously for most people. Caveats aside, the best *estimates* suggest that about 30%–35% of adults report problems with insomnia and about half to two-thirds of these people suffer from severe or frequent insomnia (Brown, 2006; Zorick & Walsh, 2000). The prevalence of insomnia increases with age and is about 50% more common in women than in men (Partinen & Hublin, 2005).

Causes. Insomnia has many causes (Hauri, 2002; Roehrs, Zorick, & Roth, 2000; Roth & Drake, 2004). In some cases, excessive anxiety and tension prevent relaxation and keep people awake. Insomnia is frequently a side effect of emotional problems, such as depression, or of significant stress, such as pressures at work. Understandably, health problems such as back pain, ulcers, and asthma can lead to difficulties falling or staying asleep. Recent research suggests that some people are predisposed to insomnia because they have a higher level of physiological arousal than the average person (Stepanski, 2006). And it is clear that the use of certain recreational drugs (especially stimulants), and a variety of prescription medications may lead to problems in sleeping (Welsh & Fugit, 2006).

Treatment. A huge portion of people suffering from insomnia do not pursue professional treatment (Sivertsen et al., 2006). Many of them probably depend on over-the-counter sleep aids, which have questionable value (Mahowald & Schenck, 2005). The most common approach in the medical treatment of insomnia is the prescription of two classes of drugs: *benzodiazepine sedatives* (such as Dalmane, Halcion, and Restoril), which were originally developed to relieve anxiety, and newer *nonbenzodiazepine sedatives* (such as Ambien, Sonata, and Lunesta), which were designed primarily for sleep problems (Mendelson, 2005). Both types of sedative medications are fairly effective in helping people fall asleep more quickly, and they reduce nighttime awakenings and increase total sleep (Lee-Chiong & Sateia, 2006; Mendelson, 2005). Nonetheless, sedative drugs may be used to combat insomnia *too* frequently. Many sleep experts argue that in the past physicians prescribed sleeping pills far too readily. Nonetheless, about 5%–15% of adults still use sleep medication with some regularity (Hublin & Partinen, 2002).

Sedatives can be a poor long-term solution for insomnia for a number of reasons (Roehrs & Roth,

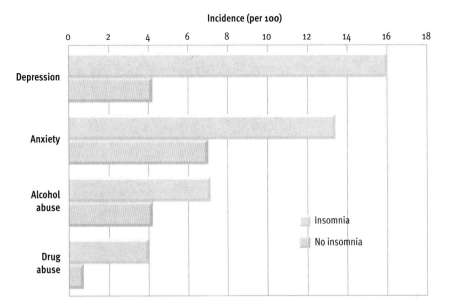

Figure 5.11

Psychiatric conditions associated with insomnia. Insomnia may sound like a trivial problem, but as the text notes, it is associated with an elevated vulnerability to a variety of problems. Data on the magnitude of this elevation are shown here for depression, anxiety, alcohol abuse, and drug abuse, based on research by Breslau et al. (1996). Of course, causation is probably bidirectional in these relationships. Depression, for instance, probably contributes to the causation of insomnia and is caused by insomnia. In any event, the elevations in the incidence of these psychiatric maladies are sizable.

SOURCE: Adapted from Breslau, N., Roth, T., Rosenthal, L., & Andreski, P. (1996). Sleep disturbance and psychiatric disorders: A longitudinal epidemiological study of young adults. *Biological Psychiatry, 39*(6), 411-418.

2000; Wesson et al., 2005). One problem is that sedatives have carryover effects that can make people drowsy and sluggish the next day and impair their functioning (Vermeeren, 2004). They can also cause an overdose in combination with alcohol or opiate drugs. Although the abuse of sleeping medications appears to be less common than widely assumed, there are legitimate concerns about people becoming physically dependent on sedatives (Ballenger, 2000). Moreover, with continued use most sedatives gradually become less effective, so some people increase their dose to higher levels, creating a vicious circle of escalating dependency and daytime sluggishness (Lader, 2002; see Figure 5.12 on the next page). Another problem is that when people abruptly discontinue their sleep medication, they can experience unpleasant withdrawal symptoms and increased insomnia (Lee-Chiong & Sateia, 2006). Fortunately, the newer generation of nonbenzodiazepine sedatives have reduced (but not eliminated) many of the problems associated with previous generations of sleeping pills (Sanger, 2004). People suffering from insomnia can also turn to melatonin, the hormone that has been used to treat jet lag (see p. 190), which is available over the counter in the United States. Research indicates that melatonin can function as

Figure 5.12
The vicious circle of dependence on sleeping pills. Because of the body's ability to develop tolerance to drugs, using sedatives routinely to "cure" insomnia can lead to a vicious circle of escalating dependency as larger and larger doses of the sedative are needed to produce the same effect.

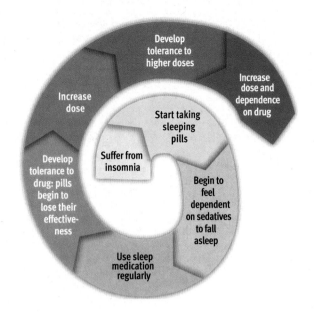

Develop tolerance to higher doses

Increase dose and dependence on drug

Increase dose

Start taking sleeping pills

Suffer from insomnia

Develop tolerance to drug: pills begin to lose their effectiveness

Begin to feel dependent on sedatives to fall asleep

Use sleep medication regularly

web link 5.4

Sleep Medicine Homepage

This site, assembled by sleep-wake specialist Michael J. Thorpy (Montefiore Medical Center), brings together a broad range of Internet links regarding sleep in all its aspects, along with information on clinical problems associated with disruptions in normal sleep and waking patterns.

a mild sedative and that it has some value in the treatment of insomnia (Turek & Gillete, 2004). In conclusion, sedatives *do* have an important place in the treatment of insomnia, but they need to be used cautiously and conservatively. They should be used primarily for short-term treatment (2–4 weeks) of sleep problems.

Aside from medications, it is difficult to generalize about how insomnia should be treated, because the many causes call for different solutions. Relaxation procedures and behavioral interventions can be helpful for many individuals (Morin, 2002, 2005). Recent studies suggest that cognitive-behavioral treatments are just as effective as medication in the short term and that these interventions produce more long-lasting benefits than drug therapies (Sivertsen et al., 2006; Smith et al., 2002). Some additional insights about how to combat insomnia are presented in the Personal Application at the end of this chapter.

Other Sleep Problems

Although insomnia is the most common difficulty associated with sleep, people are plagued by many other types of sleep problems as well. Here we'll look at the symptoms, causes, and prevalence of five additional sleep problems, as described by Kryger, Roth, and Dement (2005) and Bootzin et al. (2001).

Narcolepsy is a disease marked by sudden and irresistible onsets of sleep during normal waking periods. A person suffering from narcolepsy goes directly from wakefulness into REM sleep, usually for a short period of time (10–20 minutes). This is a potentially dangerous condition, since some victims fall asleep instantly, even while walking across a room or driving a car (Pelayo & Lopes, 2006). Narcolepsy is relatively uncommon, as it is seen in only

about 0.05% of the population (Partinen & Hublin, 2005). Its causes are not well understood, but some people appear to be genetically predisposed to the disease (Mignot, 2005). Stimulant drugs have been used to treat this condition with modest success (Guilleminault & Fromherz, 2005). But as you will see in our upcoming discussion of drugs, stimulants carry many problems of their own.

Sleep apnea involves frequent, reflexive gasping for air that awakens a person and disrupts sleep. Some victims are awakened from their sleep hundreds of times a night. Apnea occurs when a person literally stops breathing for a minimum of 10 seconds. This disorder, which is usually accompanied by loud snoring, is seen in about 2% of women and about 4% of men, with a higher incidence among older adults, postmenopausal women, and those who are obese (Sanders & Givelber, 2006). As you might expect, sleep apnea can have a very disruptive effect on sleep, leading to excessive daytime sleepiness. Sleep apnea is a more serious disorder than widely appreciated because it increases vulnerability to hypertension, coronary disease, and stroke (Hahn, Olson, & Somers, 2006). Apnea may be treated via lifestyle modifications (weight loss, reduced alcohol intake, improved sleep hygiene), drug therapy, special masks and oral devices that improve airflow, and upper airway and craniofacial surgery (Phillips & Kryger, 2005; Strollo, Atwood, & Sanders, 2005).

Nightmares are anxiety-arousing dreams that lead to awakening, usually from REM sleep (see Figure 5.13). Typically, a person who awakens from a nightmare recalls a vivid dream and may have difficulty getting back to sleep. Significant stress in one's life is associated with increased frequency and intensity of nightmares. In adults, nightmare distress is correlated with neuroticism and depression (Blagrove, Farmer, & Williams, 2004). Although about 10% of adults have occasional troubles with nightmares, these frightening episodes are mainly a problem among children. Most youngsters have sporadic nightmares, but *persistent* nightmares may reflect an emotional disturbance. If a child's nightmares are frequent and unpleasant, counseling may prove helpful. Otherwise, treatment is unnecessary, as most children outgrow the problem.

Night terrors (also called sleep terrors) are abrupt awakenings from NREM sleep accompanied by intense autonomic arousal and feelings of panic. Night terrors, which can produce remarkable accelerations of heart rate, usually occur during stage 4 sleep early in the night, as shown in Figure 5.13 (Nielsen & Zadra, 2000). Victims typically let out a piercing cry, bolt upright, and then stare into space. They do not usually recall a coherent dream, although they may remember a simple, frightening image. The panic normally fades quickly, and a return to sleep is fairly easy. Night terrors occur in adults, but they are especially common in children ages 3 to 8. Night terrors are *not* indicative of an emotional disturbance. Treatment may not be necessary, as night terrors are often a temporary problem.

Somnambulism, or sleepwalking, occurs when a person arises and wanders about while remaining asleep. About 15% of children and 3% of adults exhibit repetitive sleepwalking (Cartwright, 2006). Sleepwalking tends to occur during the first 3 hours of sleep, when individuals are in slow-wave sleep (see **Figure 5.13**). Episodes may last from 15 seconds to 30 minutes (Aldrich, 2000). Sleepwalkers may awaken during their journey, or they may return to bed without any recollection of their excursion. The causes of this unusual disorder are unknown, although it appears to have a genetic predisposition (Keefauver & Guilleminault, 1994), and episodes may be more likely in people who use nonbenzodiazepine sedatives, especially Ambien (Gunn & Gunn, 2006). Sleepwalking does not appear to be a manifestation of underlying emotional or psychological problems (Mahowald, 1993). However, while sleepwalking, some people have engaged in inappropriate aggressive or sexual behavior (Cartwright, 2006). Sleepwalkers *are* prone to accidents, including life-threatening incidents (Gunn & Gunn, 2006). In this regard, contrary to popular myth, it is best to awaken people (gently) from a sleepwalking episode—awakening them is much safer than letting them wander about.

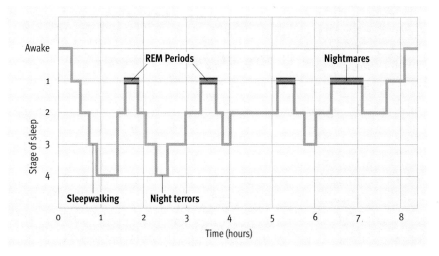

Figure 5.13

Sleep problems and the cycle of sleep. Different sleep problems tend to occur at different points in the sleep cycle. Whereas sleepwalking and night terrors are associated with slow-wave sleep, nightmares are associated with the heightened dream activity of REM sleep.

"Wait! Don't! It can be dangerous to wake them!"

REVIEW of Key Learning Goals

5.5 When people fall asleep, they pass through a series of stages in cycles of approximately 90 minutes. Slow-wave sleep consists of stages 3 and 4, during which delta waves are prominent. During the REM stage, sleepers experience rapid eye movements, brain waves that are characteristic of waking thought, and vivid dreaming. The sleep cycle tends to be repeated about four times a night, as REM sleep gradually becomes more predominant and NREM sleep dwindles. People vary somewhat in their signature sleep architecture.

5.6 The REM portion of sleep declines during childhood, leveling off at around 20%. During adulthood, slow-wave sleep tends to decline. Total sleep time decreases for most elderly people. Culture appears to have little impact on the physiological experience of sleep, but it does influence napping patterns and sleeping arrangements, such as co-sleeping.

5.7 The neural bases of sleep are complex. Arousal depends on activity in the ascending reticular activating system, but a constellation of brain structures and neurotransmitters contribute to the regulation of the sleep and waking cycle. Hypotheses about the evolutionary bases of sleep focus on energy conservation, reduced exposure to predators, and restoration of resources depleted by waking activity.

5.8 The effects of sleep restriction depend on a variety of factors. The Featured Study showed that sleep restriction produces a gradual decline in cognitive performance that is substantial. Increased sleepiness can be a significant problem that appears to contribute to many transportation accidents and mishaps at work.

5.9 Research on selective sleep deprivation suggests that people need REM sleep and slow-wave sleep. These stages of sleep may contribute to memory consolidation. Short sleep duration is associated with a variety of health problems. People who sleep 7–8 hours per day have lower mortality rates than individuals who are long or short sleepers.

5.10 Roughly 30%–35% of people suffer from insomnia, which is associated with impaired functioning, depression, and health problems. Insomnia has a variety of causes. Sleeping pills generally are a poor solution for insomnia, although they can be helpful in the short term. The optimal treatment for insomnia depends on its apparent cause.

5.11 Narcolepsy is a disease marked by sudden, irresistible onsets of sleep during normal waking periods. Sleep apnea involves frequent gasping for air, which occurs when people stop breathing. Night terrors are abrupt awakenings from NREM sleep accompanied by panic, whereas nightmares are anxiety-arousing dreams that typically awaken one from REM sleep. Somnambulism (sleepwalking) typically occurs during slow-wave sleep.

The World of Dreams

Key Learning Goals

5.12 Discuss the nature of dreams and findings on dream content.

5.13 Describe cultural variations in beliefs about the nature and importance of dreams.

5.14 Explain three theories of dreaming.

For the most part, dreams are not taken very seriously in Western societies. Paradoxically, though, Robert Van de Castle (1994) points out that dreams have sometimes changed the world. For example, Van de Castle describes how René Descartes's philosophy of dualism, Frederick Banting's discovery of insulin, Elias Howe's refinement of the sewing machine, Mohandas Gandhi's strategy of nonviolent protest, and Lyndon Johnson's withdrawal from the 1968 presidential race were all inspired by dreams. He also explains how Mary Shelley's *Frankenstein* and Robert Louis Stevenson's *The Strange Case of Dr. Jekyll and Mr. Hyde* emerged out of their dream experiences. In his wide-ranging discussion, Van de Castle also relates how the Surrealist painter Salvador Dali characterized his works as "dream photographs" and how legendary filmmakers Ingmar Bergman, Orson Welles, and Federico Fellini all drew on their dreams in making their films. Thus, Van de Castle concludes that "dreams have had a dramatic influence on almost every important aspect of our culture and history" (p. 10).

What exactly is a dream? This question is more complex and controversial than you might guess (Pagel et al., 2001). The conventional view is that dreams are mental experiences during REM sleep that have a storylike quality, include vivid visual imagery, are often bizarre, and are regarded as perceptually real by the dreamer (Antrobus, 1993). However, theorists have begun to question virtually every aspect of this characterization. Decades of research on the contents of dreams, which we will discuss momentarily, have shown that dreams are not as bizarre as widely assumed (Domhoff, 2007). Recent years have seen renewed interest in the fact that dreams are not the exclusive property of REM sleep (Antrobus, 2000). Moreover, studies that have focused on dream reports from non-REM stages of sleep have found that these dreams appear to be less vivid, visual, emotional, and storylike than REM dreams (McNamara et al., 2007; Verdone, 1993). And research suggests that dreamers realize they are dreaming more often than previously thought and that mental processes during sleep are more similar to waking thought processes than is widely assumed (Kahan, 2001; Kahan & LaBerge, 1994, 1996). Thus, the concept of dreaming is undergoing some revision in scientific circles.

The Contents of Dreams

What do people dream about? Overall, dreams are not as exciting as advertised. Perhaps dreams are seen as exotic because people are more likely to remember their more bizarre nighttime dramas (De Koninck, 2000). After analyzing the contents of more than 10,000 dreams, Calvin Hall (1966) concluded that most dreams are relatively mundane. They tend to unfold in familiar settings with a cast of characters dominated by family, friends, and colleagues. We *are* more tolerant of logical discrepancies and implausible scenarios in our dreams than our waking thought (Kahn, 2007), but in our dreams we generally move through coherent virtual worlds with a coherent sense of self (Nielsen & Stenstrom, 2005).

Certain themes tend to be more common than others in dreams. **Figure 5.14** lists the most common dream themes reported by 1181 college students in a recent study of typical dream content (Nielsen et al., 2003). If you glance through this list, you will see that people dream quite a bit about sex, aggression, and misfortune. According to Hall, dreams tend to center on classic sources of internal conflict, such as the conflict between taking chances and playing it safe. Hall was struck by how rarely people dream about public affairs and current events. Typically, dreams are self-centered; people dream mostly about themselves.

Researchers have found some modest gender differences in dream patterns, starting with the fact that women are more likely to remember their dreams than men (Schredl & Piel, 2003). Studies have also found gender disparities in dream content, as men dream more than women about both aggression and sexuality (Schredl, 2007). Strangers show up more often in men's dreams, while women are more likely to dream of children. Men are more likely to dream about acting aggressively; women are more likely to dream about being the target of aggression. In their sexual dreams, men tend to have liaisons with attractive female strangers, whereas women are more likely to dream about sex with their boyfriends and husbands (Van de Castle, 1993).

Links Between Dreams and Waking Life

Though dreams seem to belong in a world of their own, what people dream about is affected by what is

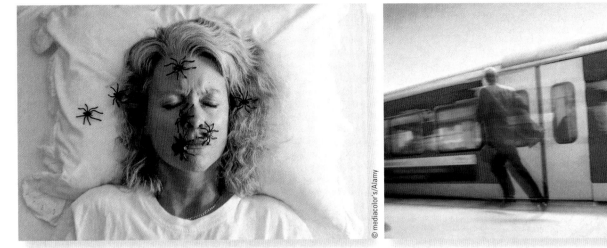

Rank	Dream content	Total prevalence
1	Chased or pursued, not physically injured	81.5
2	Sexual experiences	76.5
3	Falling	73.8
4	School, teachers, studying	67.1
5	Arriving too late, e.g., missing a train	59.5
6	Being on the verge of falling	57.7
7	Trying again and again to do something	53.5
8	A person now alive as dead	54.1
9	Flying or soaring through the air	48.3
10	Vividly sensing . . . a presence in the room	48.3
11	Failing an examination	45.0
12	Physically attacked (beaten, stabbed, raped)	42.4
13	Being frozen with fright	40.7
14	A person now dead as alive	38.4
15	Being a child again	36.7
16	Being killed	34.5
17	Swimming	34.3
18	Insects or spiders	33.8
19	Being nude	32.6
20	Being inappropriately dressed	32.5
21	Discovering a new room at home	32.3
22	Losing control of a vehicle	32.0
23	Eating delicious foods	30.7
24	Being half awake and paralyzed in bed	27.2
25	Finding money	25.7

Figure 5.14

Common themes in dreams. Studies of dream content find that certain themes are particularly common. The data shown here are from a recent study of 1181 college students in Canada (Nielsen et al., 2003). This list shows the 25 dreams most frequently reported by the students. Total prevalence refers to the percentage of students reporting each dream.

SOURCE: Nielsen, T. A., Zadra, A. L., Simard, V., Saucier, S., Stenstrom, P., Smith, C., & Kuiken, D. (2003). The typical dreams of Canadian university students. *Dreaming, 13,* 211–235. Copyright © 2003 Association for the Study of Dreams. [from Table 1, p. 217]. Reprinted by permission.

going on in their lives (Kramer, 1994). If you're struggling with financial problems, worried about an upcoming exam, or sexually attracted to a classmate, these themes may very well show up in your dreams. As Domhoff (2001) puts it, "Dream content in general is continuous with waking conceptions and emotional preoccupations" (p. 13). Freud noticed

long ago that the contents of waking life tend to spill into dreams; he labeled this spillover the *day residue.*

On occasion, the content of dreams can also be affected by stimuli experienced while one is dreaming (De Koninck, 2000). For example, William Dement sprayed water on one hand of sleeping subjects while they were in the REM stage (Dement & Wolpert,

SLEEP DISORDER RESEARCH

© 2004 by Sidney Harris. ScienceCartoonPlus.com

1958). Subjects who weren't awakened by the water were awakened by the experimenter a short time later and asked what they had been dreaming about. Dement found that 42% of the subjects had incorporated the water into their dreams. They said that they had dreamt that they were in rainfalls, floods, baths, swimming pools, and the like. Some people report that they occasionally experience the same sort of phenomenon at home when the sound of their alarm clock fails to awaken them. The alarm is incorporated into their dream as a loud engine or a siren, for instance. As with day residue, the incorporation of external stimuli into dreams shows that people's dream world is not entirely separate from their real world.

Culture and Dreams

Striking cross-cultural variations occur in beliefs about the nature of dreams and the importance attributed to them (Lohmann, 2007). In modern Western society, people typically make a distinction between the "real" world they experience while awake and the "imaginary" world they experience while dreaming. Some people realize that events in the real world can affect their dreams, but few believe that events in their dreams hold any significance for their waking life. Although a small minority of individuals take their dreams seriously, in Western cultures dreams are largely written off as insignificant, meaningless meanderings of the unconscious (Tart, 1988).

In many non-Western cultures, however, dreams are viewed as important sources of information about oneself, about the future, or about the spiritual world (Kracke, 1991). Although no culture confuses dreams with waking reality, many view events in dreams as another type of reality that may be just as important as events experienced while awake. Among Australian aborigines, for example,

Sigmund Freud

"[Dreams are] the royal road to the unconscious."

© National Library of Medicine

"Dreaming is the focal point of traditional aboriginal existence and simultaneously determines their way of life, their culture, and their relationship to the physical and spiritual environment" (Dawson, 1993, p. 1). In some instances, people are even held responsible for their dream actions. Among the New Guinea Arapesh, for example, an erotic dream about someone may be viewed as the equivalent of an adulterous act. People in some cultures believe that dreams provide information about the future—good or bad omens about upcoming battles, hunts, births, and so forth (Tedlock, 1992).

In regard to dream content, both similarities and differences occur across cultures in the types of dreams that people report (Domhoff, 2005b; Hunt, 1989). Some basic dream themes appear to be nearly universal (falling, being pursued, having sex). However, the contents of dreams vary some from one culture to another because people in different societies deal with different worlds while awake. For example, in a 1950 study of the Siriono, a hunting-and-gathering people of the Amazon who were almost always hungry and spent most of their time in a grim search for food, *half* of the reported dreams focused on hunting, gathering, and eating food (D'Andrade, 1961).

Theories of Dreaming

Many theories have been proposed to explain why people dream. Sigmund Freud (1900), who analyzed clients' dreams in therapy, believed that the principal purpose of dreams is *wish fulfillment*. He thought that people fulfill unconscious urges and ungratified needs through wishful thinking in dreams. For example, if you were feeling unconscious guilt about being rude to a friend, you might dream about the incident in a way that renders you blameless. Freud asserted that the wish-fulfilling quality of many dreams may not be readily apparent because the unconscious attempts to censor and disguise the true meaning of dreams. Freud distinguished between the *manifest content* and the *latent content* of a dream. The *manifest content* consists of the plot of a dream at a surface level. The *latent content* refers to the hidden or disguised meaning of the events in the plot. According to Freud, deciphering the latent content of a dream is a complicated matter of interpretation that requires intimate knowledge of the dreamer's current issues and childhood conflicts. Freud's influential theory sounded plausible when it was proposed over 100 years ago, but research has not provided much support for Freud's conception of dreaming (Fisher & Greenberg, 1996). That said, efforts are under way to modernize and rehabilitate the Freudian view of dreams (Solms, 2000b, 2004). Whether these efforts will prove to be influential remains to be seen.

Other theorists, such as Rosalind Cartwright (1977; Cartwright & Lamberg, 1992), have proposed that dreams provide an opportunity to work through everyday problems and emotional issues in one's life. According to her *cognitive, problem-solving view,* considerable continuity exists between waking and sleeping thought. Proponents of this view believe that dreams allow people to engage in creative thinking about pressing personal issues because dreams are not restrained by logic or realism. Consistent with this view, Cartwright (1991) has found that women going through divorce frequently dream about divorce-related problems. Cartwright's analysis is thought provoking, but critics point out that just because people dream about problems from their waking life doesn't mean they are dreaming up solutions (Blagrove, 1992, 1996). Nonetheless, recent research showing that sleep can enhance learning (Walker & Stickgold, 2004; see p. 199) adds new credibility to the problem-solving view of dreams (Cartwright, 2004).

J. Allan Hobson and colleagues argue that dreams are simply the by-product of bursts of activity emanating from subcortical areas in the brain. Their *activation-synthesis model* (Hobson & McCarley, 1977;

McCarley, 1994) and its more recent revisions (Hobson, 2007; Hobson, Pace-Schott, & Stickgold, 2000;) propose that dreams are *side effects* of the neural activation that produces the beta brain waves during REM sleep that are associated with wakefulness. According to this model, neurons firing periodically in lower brain centers (especially the pons) send random signals to the cortex (the seat of complex thought). The cortex supposedly synthesizes (constructs) a dream to make sense out of these signals. The activation-synthesis model does *not* assume that dreams are meaningless. As Hobson (1988) puts it, "Dreams are as meaningful as they can be under the adverse working conditions of the brain in REM sleep" (p. 214). In contrast to the theories of Freud and Cartwright, this theory obviously downplays the role of emotional factors as determinants of dreams. Like other theories of dreams, the activation-synthesis model has its share of critics. They point out that the model has a hard time accommodating the fact that dreaming occurs outside of REM sleep, that damage to the pons does not eliminate dreaming, and that the contents of dreams are considerably more meaningful than the model would predict (Domhoff, 2005a; Foulkes, 1996; Solms, 2000a).

These approaches, summarized in Figure 5.15, are only three out of many theories about the functions of dreams. All theories of dreaming include a great

Rosalind Cartwright

"One function of dreams may be to restore our sense of competence.... It is also probable that in times of stress, dreams have more work to do in resolving our problems and are thus more salient and memorable."

J. Allan Hobson

"Activation-synthesis ascribes dreaming to brain activation in sleep. The principal engine of this activation is the reticular formation of the brainstem."

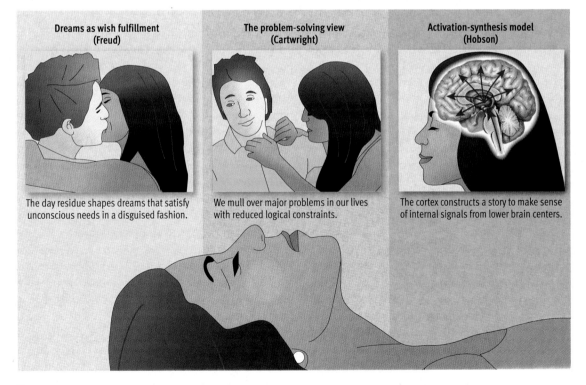

Dreams as wish fulfillment (Freud)	The problem-solving view (Cartwright)	Activation-synthesis model (Hobson)
The day residue shapes dreams that satisfy unconscious needs in a disguised fashion.	We mull over major problems in our lives with reduced logical constraints.	The cortex constructs a story to make sense of internal signals from lower brain centers.

Figure 5.15

Three theories of dreaming. Dreams can be explained in a variety of ways. Freud stressed the wish-fulfilling function of dreams. Cartwright emphasizes the problem-solving function of dreams. Hobson asserts that dreams are merely a by-product of periodic neural activation. All three theories are speculative and have their critics.

deal of conjecture and some liberal extrapolations from research. In the final analysis, the purpose of dreaming remains a mystery.

We'll encounter more unsolved mysteries in the next two sections of this chapter as we discuss hypnosis and meditation. Whereas sleep and dreams are familiar to everyone, most people have little familiarity with hypnosis and meditation, which both involve deliberate efforts to temporarily alter consciousness.

REVIEW of Key Learning Goals

5.12 The conventional view is that dreams are mental experiences during REM sleep that have a storylike quality, include vivid imagery, are often bizarre, and are regarded as real by the dreamer, but theorists have begun to question many aspects of this view. Dreams are not as bizarre as widely assumed. Researchers have found modest differences between men and women in dream content. The content of one's dreams may be affected by what is going on in one's life and by external stimuli that are experienced during the dream.

5.13 In many non-Western cultures, dreams are viewed as important sources of information. Cultures vary in beliefs about the nature of dreams, dream recall, dream content, and dream interpretation.

5.14 Freud argued that the principal purpose of dreams is wish fulfillment, and he distinguished between the manifest and latent content of dreams. Cartwright has articulated a problem-solving view, whereas Hobson and colleagues assert that dreams are side effects of the neural activation seen during REM sleep.

Hypnosis: Altered Consciousness or Role Playing?

Key Learning Goals

5.15 Discuss hypnotic susceptibility, and list some prominent effects of hypnosis.

5.16 Compare the role-playing and altered-state theories of hypnosis.

Hypnosis has a long and checkered history. It all began with a flamboyant 18th-century Austrian physician by the name of Franz Anton Mesmer. Working in Paris, Mesmer claimed to cure people of illnesses through an elaborate routine involving a "laying on of hands." Mesmer had some complicated theories about how he had harnessed "animal magnetism." However, we know today that he had simply stumbled onto the power of suggestion. It was rumored that the French government offered him a princely amount of money to disclose how he effected his cures. He refused, probably because he didn't really know. Eventually he was dismissed as a charlatan and run out of town by the local authorities. Although officially discredited, Mesmer inspired followers—practitioners of "mesmerism"—who continued to ply their trade. To this day, our language preserves the memory of Franz Mesmer: When we are under the spell of an event or a story, we are "mesmerized."

Eventually, a Scottish physician, James Braid, became interested in the trancelike state that could be induced by the mesmerists. It was Braid who popularized the term *hypnotism* in 1843, borrowing it from the Greek word for sleep. Braid thought that hypnotism could be used to produce anesthesia for surgeries. However, just as hypnosis was catching on as a general anesthetic, more powerful and reliable chemical anesthetics were discovered, and interest in hypnotism dwindled.

Since then, hypnotism has led a curious dual existence. On the one hand, it has been the subject of numerous scientific studies. Furthermore, it has enjoyed considerable use as a clinical tool by physicians, dentists, and psychologists for over a century and has empirically supported value in the treatment of a variety of psychological and physical maladies (Lynn et al., 2000; Maldonado & Spiegel, 2003b). On the other hand, however, an assortment of entertainers and quacks have continued in the less respectable tradition of mesmerism, using hypnotism for parlor tricks and gimmickry. It is little wonder, then, that many myths about hypnosis have come to be widely accepted (see Figure 5.16). In this section, we'll work on clearing up some of the confusion surrounding hypnosis.

Hypnotic Induction and Susceptibility

Hypnosis is a systematic procedure that typically produces a heightened state of suggestibility. It may also lead to passive relaxation, narrowed attention, and enhanced fantasy. If only in popular films, virtually everyone has seen a *hypnotic induction* enacted with a swinging pendulum. Actually many techniques can be used for inducing hypnosis (Meyer, 1992). Usually, the hypnotist will suggest to the subject that he or she is relaxing. Repetitively, softly, subjects are told that they are getting tired, drowsy, or sleepy. Often, the hypnotist vividly describes bodily sensations that should be occurring. Subjects are told that their arms are going limp, their feet are getting warm, their eyelids are getting heavy. Gradually, most subjects succumb and become hypnotized.

People differ in how well they respond to hypnotic induction. Ernest and Josephine Hilgard have done extensive research on this variability in *hypnotic susceptibility*. Responsiveness to hypnosis is a stable, measurable trait. It can be estimated with the Stanford Hypnotic Susceptibility Scale (SHSS) or its derivative, the Harvard Group Scale of Hypnotic Susceptibility (Perry, Nadon, & Button, 1992). The distribution of scores on the SHSS is graphed in Figure 5.17. Not everyone can be hypnotized. About 10%–20% of the population doesn't respond well at all. At the other end of the continuum, about 10%-15% of people are exceptionally good hypnotic subjects (Hilgard, 1965). As Kihlstrom (2007) notes, "the most dramatic phenomena of hypnosis—the ones that really count as reflecting alterations in consciousness—are generally observed in those 'hypnotic virtuosos' who comprise the upper 10 to 15% of the distribution of hypnotizability" (p. 446). People who are highly hypnotizable may even slip in and out of hypnotic-like states spontaneously without being aware of it (Spiegel, 2007).

What makes some people highly susceptible to hypnosis? Variations in hypnotic susceptibility were originally assumed to depend on differences in personality traits, but decades of research on the personality correlates of hypnotizability have turned up relatively little (Kihlstrom, 2007). According to Spiegel, Greenleaf, and Spiegel (2005), high hypnotizability is made up of three components: absorption, dissociation, suggestibility. *Absorption* involves the capacity to reduce or block peripheral awareness and narrow the focus of one's attention. *Dissociation* involves the ability to separate aspects of perception, memory, or identity, from the mainstream

Hypnosis: Myth and Reality	
If you think . . .	**The reality is . . .**
Relaxation is an important feature of hypnosis.	It's not. Hypnosis has been induced during vigorous exercise.
It's mostly just compliance.	Many highly motivated subjects fail to experience hypnosis.
It's a matter of willful faking.	Physiological responses indicate that hypnotized subjects generally are not lying.
It has something to do with a sleeplike state.	It does not. Hypnotized subjects are fully awake.
Responding to hypnosis is like responding to a placebo.	Placebo responsiveness and hypnotizability are not correlated.
People who are hypnotized lose control of themselves.	Subjects are perfectly capable of saying no or terminating hypnosis.
Hypnosis can enable people to "relive" the past.	Age-regressed adults behave like adults play-acting as children.
When hypnotized, people can remember more accurately.	Hypnosis may actually muddle the distinction between memory and fantasy and may artificially inflate confidence.
Hypnotized people do not remember what happened during the session.	Posthypnotic amnesia does not occur spontaneously.
Hypnosis can enable people to perform otherwise impossible feats of strength, endurance, learning, and sensory acuity.	Performance following hypnotic suggestions for increased muscle strength, learning and sensory acuity does not exceed what can be accomplished by motivated subjects outside hypnosis.

Figure 5.16

Misconceptions regarding hypnosis. Mistaken ideas about the nature of hypnosis are common. Some widely believed myths about hypnosis are summarized here along with more accurate information on each point, based on an article by Michael Nash (2001), a prominent hypnosis researcher. Many of these myths and realities are discussed in more detail in the text.

SOURCE: Adapted from Nash, M. R. (2001, July). The truth and the hype of hypnosis. *Scientific American, 285*, 36–43. Copyright © 2001 by Scientific American, Inc.

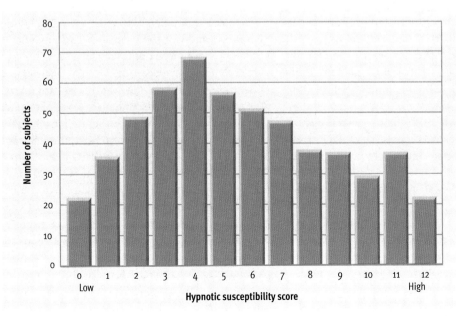

Figure 5.17

Variation in hypnotic susceptibility. This graph shows the distribution of scores of more than 500 subjects on the Stanford Hypnotic Susceptibility Scale. As you can see, responsiveness to hypnotism varies widely, and many people are not very susceptible to hypnotic induction.

SOURCE: Adapted from Hilgard, E. (1965). *Hypnotic susceptibility*. San Diego: Harcourt Brace Jovanovich. Copyright © 1965 by Ernest R. Hilgard. Reprinted by permission of Ernest R. Hilgard.

of conscious awareness. *Suggestibility* involves the tendency to accept directions and information relatively uncritically.

Hypnotic Phenomena

Many interesting effects can be produced through hypnosis. Some of the more prominent include:

1. *Analgesia.* Under the influence of hypnosis, some participants can withstand treatments that would normally cause considerable pain (Patterson, 2004). As a result, some physicians and dentists have used hypnosis as a substitute for anesthetic drugs. Admittedly, drugs are far more reliable pain relievers, making hypnosis something of a scientific curiosity as a solo treatment for acute pain. Nonetheless, hypnosis can be surprisingly effective in the treatment of both acute and chronic pain (Boly et al., 2007; Patterson & Jensen, 2003). Hypnotic analgesia exceeds placebo effects, does not appear to be mediated by simple relaxation, and does not appear to depend on the action of endorphins (Kihlstrom, 2007).

2. *Sensory distortions and hallucinations.* Hypnotized participants may be led to experience auditory or visual hallucinations (Spiegel, 2003b). They may hear sounds or see things that are not there, or fail to hear or see stimuli that are present. In one study, for instance, hypnotized participants were induced to "see" a cardboard box that blocked their view of a television (Spiegel et al., 1985). Subjects may also have their sensations distorted so that something sweet tastes sour or an unpleasant odor smells fragrant.

3. *Disinhibition.* Generally, it is difficult to get hypnotized participants to do things that they would normally consider unacceptable. Nonetheless, hypnosis *can* sometimes reduce inhibitions that would normally prevent subjects from acting in ways that they would see as socially undesirable. In experiments, hypnotized participants have been induced to throw what they believed to be a toxic substance into the face of a research assistant. Similarly, stage hypnotists are sometimes successful in getting people to disrobe in public. One lay hypnotist even coaxed a man into robbing a bank (Deyoub, 1984). This disinhibition effect may occur simply because hypnotized people feel that they cannot be held responsible for their actions while they are hypnotized.

4. *Posthypnotic suggestions and amnesia.* Suggestions made during hypnosis may influence a subject's later behavior (Barnier, 2002). The most common posthypnotic suggestion is the creation of posthypnotic amnesia. That is, participants are told

that they will remember nothing that happened while they were hypnotized. Such subjects usually claim to remember nothing, as ordered. However, when pressed, many of these subjects acknowledge that they have not really forgotten the information (Kirsch & Lynn, 1998).

Theories of Hypnosis

Although a number of theories have been developed to explain hypnosis, it is still not well understood. One popular view is that hypnotic effects occur because participants are put into a special, altered state of consciousness, called a *hypnotic trance* (Christensen, 2005). Although hypnotized subjects may feel as though they are in an altered state, they do not seem to show reliable alterations in brain activity that are unique to hypnosis (Burgess, 2007; Lynn et al., 2007). The failure to find special changes in brain activity that are consistently associated with hypnosis has led some theorists to conclude that hypnosis is a normal state of consciousness that is characterized by dramatic role playing.

Hypnosis as Role Playing

One influential view of hypnosis is that it produces a normal mental state in which suggestible people act out the role of a hypnotic subject and behave as they think hypnotized people are supposed to. Theodore Barber (1969, 1979), Nicholas Spanos (1986, 1991), and Irving Kirsch (2000; Kirsch & Lynn, 1998) have been the leading advocates of this view, which emphasizes the social context of hypnosis. According to this notion, it is subjects' *role expectations* that produce hypnotic effects, rather than a special trance-like state of consciousness.

Two lines of evidence support the role-playing view. First, many of the seemingly amazing effects of hypnosis have been duplicated by nonhypnotized participants or have been shown to be exaggerated (Kirsch, 1997; Kirsch, Mazzoni, & Montgomery, 2007). For example, much has been made of the fact that hypnotized subjects can be used as "human planks," but it turns out that nonhypnotized subjects can easily match this feat (Barber, 1986). In a similar vein, anecdotal reports that hypnosis can enhance memory have not stood up well to empirical testing. Although hypnosis may occasionally facilitate recall in some people, experimental studies have tended to find that hypnotized participants make more memory errors than nonhypnotized participants, even though they often feel more con-

© Courtesy of X. Ted Barber

Theodore Barber

"Thousands of books, movies, and professional articles have woven the concept of 'hypnotic trance' into the common knowledge. And yet there is almost no scientific support for it."

Some feats performed under hypnosis can be performed equally well by nonhypnotized subjects. Here "the Amazing Kreskin" demonstrates that proper positioning is the only requirement for the famous human plank feat.

fident about their recollections (McConkey, 1992; Scoboria et al., 2002). These findings suggest that no special state of consciousness is required to explain hypnotic feats.

The second line of evidence involves demonstrations that hypnotized participants are often acting out a role. For example, Martin Orne (1951) regressed hypnotized subjects back to their sixth birthday and asked them to describe it. They responded with detailed descriptions that appeared to represent great feats of hypnosis-enhanced memory. However, instead of accepting this information at face value, Orne compared it with information that he had obtained from the subjects' parents. It turned out that many of the participants' memories were inaccurate and invented! Many other studies have also found that age-regressed subjects' recall of the distant past tends to be more fanciful than factual (Green, 1999; Perry, Kusel, & Perry, 1988). Thus, the role-playing explanation of hypnosis suggests that situational factors lead some subjects to act out a certain role in a highly cooperative manner.

Hypnosis as an Altered State of Consciousness

Despite the doubts raised by role-playing explanations, many prominent theorists still maintain that hypnotic effects are attributable to a special, altered state of consciousness (Fromm, 1979, 1992; Hilgard, 1986; Naish, 2006; Spiegel, 1995, 2003a). These

theorists argue that it is doubtful that role playing can explain all hypnotic phenomena. For instance, they assert that even the most cooperative subjects are unlikely to endure surgery without a drug anesthetic just to please their physician and live up to their expected role. They also cite studies in which hypnotized participants have continued to display hypnotic responses when they thought they were alone and not being observed (Perugini et al., 1998). If hypnotized participants were merely acting, they would drop the act when alone. The most impressive research undermining the role-playing view has come from recent brain-imaging studies, which suggest that hypnotized participants experience changes in brain activity that appear consistent with their reports of hypnosis-induced hallucinations (Spiegel, 2003b) or pain suppression (Hofbauer et al., 2001).

The most influential explanation of hypnosis as an altered state of awareness has been offered by Ernest Hilgard (1986, 1992). According to Hilgard, hypnosis creates a *dissociation* in consciousness. **Dissociation is a splitting off of mental processes into two separate, simultaneous streams of awareness.** In other words, Hilgard theorizes that hypnosis splits consciousness into two streams. One stream is in communication with the hypnotist and the external world, while the other is a difficult-to-detect "hidden observer." Hilgard believes that many hypnotic effects are a product of this divided consciousness. For instance, he suggests that a hypnotized person might appear unresponsive to pain because the pain isn't registered in the portion of consciousness that communicates with other people.

One appealing aspect of Hilgard's theory is that *divided consciousness* is a common, normal experience. For example, people will often drive a car a great distance, responding to traffic signals and other cars, with no recollection of having consciously done so. In such cases, consciousness is clearly divided between driving and the person's thoughts about other matters. Interestingly, this common experience has long been known as *highway hypnosis*. In this condition, there is even an "amnesia" for the component of consciousness that drove the car, similar to posthypnotic amnesia. In summary, Hilgard presents hypnosis as a plausible variation in consciousness that has continuity with everyday experience.

John Kihlstrom (2007) takes the position that the role-playing and altered-state views of hypnosis are not entirely incompatible. He maintains that hypnotic phenomena involve *both* alterations in consciousness and complex social interactions that

Ernest Hilgard

"Many psychologists argue that the hypnotic trance is a mirage. It would be unfortunate if this skeptical view were to gain such popularity that the benefits of hypnosis are denied to the numbers of those who could be helped."

are shaped by role expectations. Kihlstrom (2005a) also argues that the role-playing versus altered-state debate has been a "distraction." Although his view seems to have some merit, it appears likely that the grand debate of hypnosis will continue for the foreseeable future (Kirsch, 2004). As you will see momentarily, a similar debate has dominated the scientific discussion of meditation.

REVIEW of Key Learning Goals

5.15 Hypnosis has had a long and curious history since the era of Mesmerism in the 18th century. Hypnotic susceptibility is a stable trait made up of three components: absorption, dissociation, and suggestibility. It is only weakly correlated with personality. Hypnosis can produce anesthesia, sensory distortions, disinhibition, and posthypnotic amnesia.

5.16 One approach to hypnosis is to view it as a normal state of consciousness in which subjects play the role of being hypnotized. Another approach asserts that hypnosis leads to an altered state in which consciousness is split into two streams of awareness.

Meditation: Pure Consciousness or Relaxation?

Key Learning Goals

5.17 Explain the nature of meditation and describe its physiological correlates.

5.18 Assess the evidence on the long-term benefits of meditation.

Recent years have seen growing interest in the ancient discipline of meditation. *Meditation* refers **to a family of practices that train attention to heighten awareness and bring mental processes under greater voluntary control.** There are many approaches to meditation. In North America, the most widely practiced approaches are those associated with yoga, Zen, and transcendental meditation (TM). All three of these approaches are rooted in Eastern religions (Hinduism, Buddhism, and Taoism). However, meditation has been practiced throughout history as an element of all religious and spiritual traditions, including Judaism and Christianity (Walsh & Shapiro, 2006). Moreover, the practice of meditation can be largely divorced from religious beliefs. In fact, most Americans who meditate have only vague ideas regarding its religious significance. Of interest to psychology is the fact that meditation involves a deliberate effort to alter consciousness.

Most meditative techniques are deceptively simple. For example, in TM a person is supposed to sit in a comfortable position with eyes closed and silently focus attention on a *mantra*. A mantra is a specially assigned Sanskrit word that is personalized to each meditator. This exercise in mental self-discipline is to be practiced twice daily for about 20 minutes. The technique has been described as "diving from the active surface of the mind to its quiet depths" (Bloomfield & Kory, 1976, p. 49). Most proponents of TM believe it involves an altered state of "pure consciousness" that has many unique benefits. Many skeptics counter that meditation is merely an effective relaxation technique. Let's look at the evidence.

Physiological Correlates

What happens when an experienced meditator goes into the meditative state? One intriguing finding is that alpha waves and theta waves become more prominent in EEG recordings (Cahn & Polich, 2006). Many studies also find that subjects' heart rate, skin conductance, respiration rate, oxygen consumption, and carbon dioxide elimination decline (see **Figure 5.18**; Dillbeck & Orme-Johnson, 1987; Fenwick, 1987; Travis, 2001). Taken together, these changes suggest that meditation leads to a potentially beneficial physiological state characterized by suppression of bodily arousal. However, some researchers have argued that a variety of systematic relaxation training procedures can produce similar results (Holmes, 1987; Shapiro, 1984). Mere relaxation hardly seems like an adequate explanation for the transcendent experiences reported by many meditators. Hence, debate continues about whether unique physiological changes are associated with meditation (Shear & Jevning, 1999; Travis & Pearson, 2000). The most promising leads are currently coming from studies using new brain-imaging techniques, such as PET and fMRI scans (see Chapter 3). The results of this research are extremely complicated, in part because different approaches to meditation appear to produce different patterns of change in brain activity, but the changes observed seem unlikely to be due to simple relaxation effects (Lutz, Dunne, & Davidson, 2007).

Long-Term Benefits

What about the long-term benefits that have been claimed for meditation? Research suggests that

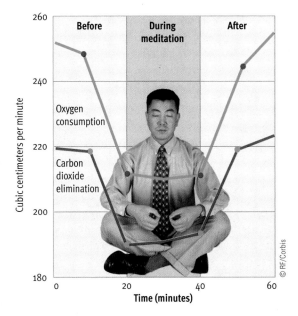

Figure 5.18

The suppression of physiological arousal during transcendental meditation. The physiological changes shown in the graph are evidence of physical relaxation during the meditative state. However, critics argue that similar changes may also be produced by systematic relaxation procedures.

SOURCE: Adapted from Wallace, R. K., & Benson, H. (1972, February). The physiology of meditation. *Scientific American, 226,* 85–90. Graphic redrawn from illustration on p. 86 by Lorelle A. Raboni. Copyright © 1972 by Scientific American, Inc.

meditation may have some value in reducing the effects of stress (Grossman et al., 2004; Salmon et al., 2004). In particular, regular meditation is associated with lower levels of some "stress hormones" (Infante et al., 2001) and enhanced immune response (Davidson et al., 2003a). Research also suggests that meditation can improve mental health while reducing anxiety and drug abuse (Alexander et al., 1994). Other studies report that meditation may have beneficial effects on self-esteem (Emavardhana & Tori, 1997), mood and one's sense of control (Easterlin & Cardena, 1999), depression (Kabat-Zinn, 2003), eating disorders (Kristeller, Baer, & Quillian-Wolever, 2006), and overall well-being (Reibel et al., 2001). In the physiological domain, research has suggested that meditation may help to control blood pressure (Barnes, Treiber, & Davis, 2001), improve cardiovascular health (Walton et al., 2004), and reduce chronic pain (Orme-Johnson et al., 2006). Finally, although more difficult to measure, some theorists assert that meditation can enhance human potential by improving concentration, heightening awareness, building emotional resilience, and fostering moral maturity (Walsh & Shapiro, 2006).

At first glance these results are profoundly impressive, but they need to be viewed with caution.

concept check 5.2

Relating EEG Activity to Variations in Consciousness

Early in the chapter we emphasized the intimate relationship between brain activity and variations in consciousness. Check your understanding of this relationship by indicating the kind of EEG activity (alpha, beta, theta, or delta) that would probably be dominant in each of the following situations. The answers are in Appendix A.

_____ 1. You are playing a video game.

_____ 2. You are deep in meditation.

_____ 3. You have just fallen asleep.

_____ 4. You are sleepwalking across the lawn.

_____ 5. You are in the midst of a terrible nightmare.

At least *some* of these effects may be just as attainable through systematic relaxation or other mental focusing procedures (Shapiro, 1984; Smith, 1975). Critics also wonder whether placebo effects, sampling bias, inability to use double-blind procedures, and other methodological problems may contribute to some of the reported benefits of meditation (Baer, 2003; Bishop, 2002; Canter, 2003; Caspi & Burleson, 2005). In a relatively enthusiastic review of meditation research, the authors acknowledge that many meditation studies "do not use rigorous research design (including lack of randomization, lack of follow-up, and imprecise measurement of constructs) and sometimes are based on small samples" (Shapiro, Schwartz, & Santerre, 2002).

In summary, it seems safe to conclude that meditation is a potentially worthwhile relaxation strategy. And it's entirely possible that meditation involves much more than mere relaxation, as meditation advocates insist. Certainly, it is hard to envision mere relaxation providing such a diverse constellation of benefits. At present, however, there is great debate about the notion that meditation produces a unique state of "pure consciousness" and healthy skepticism about some of its alleged long-term benefits.

REVIEW of Key Learning Goals

5.17 Meditation refers to a family of practices that train attention to heighten awareness and bring mental processes under greater voluntary control. Studies suggest that meditation leads to a potentially beneficial physiological state characterized by suppression of bodily arousal.

5.18 Evidence suggests that meditation may reduce stress hormones, enhance self-esteem and well-being, and reduce vulnerability to a variety of diseases. However, some critics suggest that the benefits of meditation are not unique to meditation and are a product of any effective relaxation procedure.

Key Learning Goals

5.19 Identify the major types of abused drugs, and explain why their effects vary.

5.20 Understand how psychoactive drugs exert their effects in the brain.

5.21 Contrast psychological and physical dependence.

5.22 Summarize evidence on the major health risks associated with drug abuse.

5.23 Evaluate controversies related to marijuana and the risks of ecstasy (MDMA).

Altering Consciousness with Drugs

Like hypnosis and meditation, drugs are commonly used in deliberate efforts to alter consciousness. In this section, we focus on the use of drugs for nonmedical purposes, commonly referred to as "drug abuse" or "recreational drug use." Drug abuse reaches into every corner of modern society. Although small declines occurred in the overall abuse of drugs in the 1980s, survey data show that illicit drug use has mostly been increasing since the 1960s (Compton et al., 2005). In spite of extraordinary efforts to reduce drug abuse, it seems reasonable to conclude that widespread recreational drug use is here to stay for the foreseeable future (Winick & Norman, 2005).

As with other controversial social problems, recreational drug use often inspires more rhetoric than reason. For instance, a former president of the American Medical Association made headlines when he declared that marijuana "makes a man of 35 sexually like a man of 70." In reality, the research findings do not support this assertion. This influential physician later retracted his statement, admitting that he had made it simply to campaign against marijuana use (Leavitt, 1995). Unfortunately, such scare tactics can backfire by undermining the credibility of drug education efforts.

Recreational drug use involves personal, moral, political, and legal issues that are not matters for science to resolve. However, the more knowledgeable you are about drugs, the more informed your decisions and opinions about them will be. Accordingly, this section describes the types of drugs that are most commonly used for recreational purposes and summarizes their effects on consciousness, behavior, and health.

Principal Abused Drugs and Their Effects

The drugs that people use recreationally are *psychoactive*. *Psychoactive drugs* are chemical substances that modify mental, emotional, or behavioral functioning. Not all psychoactive drugs produce effects that lead to recreational use. Generally, people prefer drugs that elevate their mood or produce other pleasurable alterations in consciousness.

The principal types of recreational drugs are described in Table 5.2. The table lists representative drugs in each of six categories. It also summarizes how the drugs are taken, their medical uses, their effects on consciousness, and their common side effects (based on Julien, Advokat, & Comaty, 2008; Levinthal, 2008; Lowinson et al., 2005). The six categories of psychoactive drugs that we will focus on are narcotics, sedatives, stimulants, hallucinogens, cannabis, and alcohol. We will also discuss one specific drug that is not listed in the table (because it does not fit into traditional drug categories) but that cannot be ignored in light of its escalating popularity: MDMA, better known as "ecstasy."

Narcotics, or opiates, are drugs derived from opium that are capable of relieving pain. The main drugs in this category are heroin and morphine, although less potent opiates such as codeine, Demerol, and methadone are also abused. The emerging problem in this category is a new drug called oxycodone (trade name: OxyContin). Its time-release format was supposed to make it an effective analgesic with less potential for abuse than the other opiates (Cicero, Inciardi, & Munoz, 2005). But people quickly learned that they could grind it up and gain a powerful high, leading to a new epidemic of serious drug abuse, especially in rural areas of the United States (Tunnell, 2005). In sufficient dosages the opiate drugs can produce an overwhelming sense of euphoria or well-being. This euphoric effect has a relaxing, "Who cares?" quality that makes the high an attractive escape from reality. Common side effects include lethargy, nausea, and impaired mental and motor functioning.

Sedatives are sleep-inducing drugs that tend to decrease central nervous system (CNS) activation and behavioral activity. People abusing sedatives, or "downers," generally consume larger doses than are prescribed for medical purposes. The desired effect is a euphoria similar to that produced by drinking large amounts of alcohol. Feelings of tension or dejection are replaced by a relaxed, pleasant state of intoxication, accompanied by loosened inhibitions. Prominent side effects include drowsiness, unpredictable emotional swings, and severe impairments in motor coordination and mental functioning.

Stimulants are drugs that tend to increase CNS activation and behavioral activity. Stimulants range from mild, widely available drugs, such as caffeine and nicotine, to stronger, carefully regulated ones, such as cocaine. Our focus here is on cocaine and amphetamines. Cocaine is a natural substance that comes from the coca shrub. In contrast, amphet-

Table 5.2 Psychoactive Drugs: Methods of Ingestion, Medical Uses, and Effects

Drugs	Methods of Ingestion	Principal Medical Uses	Desired Effects	Potential Short-Term Side Effects
Narcotics (opiates) Morphine Heroin Oxycodone	Injected, smoked, oral	Pain relief	Euphoria, relaxation, anxiety reduction, pain relief	Lethargy, drowsiness, nausea, impaired coordination, impaired mental functioning, constipation
Sedatives Barbiturates (e.g., Seconal) Nonbarbiturates (e.g., Quaalude)	Oral, injected	Sleeping pill, anticonvulsant	Euphoria, relaxation, anxiety reduction, reduced inhibitions	Lethargy, drowsiness, severely impaired coordination, impaired mental functioning, emotional swings, dejection
Stimulants Amphetamines Cocaine	Oral, sniffed, injected, freebased, smoked	Treatment of hyperactivity and narcolepsy, local anesthetic (cocaine only)	Elation, excitement, increased alertness, increased energy, reduced fatigue	Increased blood pressure and heart rate, increased talkativeness, restlessness, irritability, insomnia, reduced appetite, increased sweating and urination, anxiety, paranoia, increased aggressiveness, panic
Hallucinogens LSD Mescaline Psilocybin	Oral	None	Increased sensory awareness, euphoria, altered perceptions, hallucinations, insightful experiences	Dilated pupils, nausea, emotional swings, paranoia, jumbled thought processes, impaired judgment, anxiety, panic reaction
Cannabis Marijuana Hashish THC	Smoked, oral	Treatment of glaucoma and chemotherapy—induced nausea and vomiting; other uses under study	Mild euphoria, relaxation, altered perceptions, enhanced awareness	Elevated heart rate, bloodshot eyes, dry mouth, reduced short-term memory, sluggish motor coordination, sluggish mental functioning, anxiety
Alcohol	Drinking	None	Mild euphoria, relaxation, anxiety reduction, reduced inhibitions	Severely impaired coordination, impaired mental functioning, increased urination, emotional swings, depression, quarrelsomeness, hangover

amines are synthesized in a pharmaceutical laboratory. Cocaine and amphetamines have fairly similar effects, except that cocaine produces a briefer high. Stimulants produce a euphoria very different from that created by narcotics or sedatives. They produce a buoyant, elated, energetic "I can conquer the world!" feeling accompanied by increased alertness. In recent years, cocaine and amphetamines have become available in much more potent (and dangerous) forms than before. "Freebasing" is a chemical treatment used to extract nearly pure cocaine from ordinary street cocaine. "Crack" is the most widely distributed by-product of this process, consisting of chips of pure cocaine that are usually smoked. Amphetamines are increasingly sold as a crystalline powder, called "crank," or "crystal meth" (short for "methamphetamine"), that may be snorted or injected intravenously. Side effects of stimulants vary with dosage and potency but may include restlessness, anxiety, paranoia, and insomnia.

Hallucinogens are a diverse group of drugs that have powerful effects on mental and emotional functioning, marked most prominently by distortions in sensory and perceptual experience. The principal hallucinogens are LSD, mescaline, and psilocybin. These drugs have similar effects, although they vary in potency. Hallucinogens produce euphoria, increased sensory awareness, and a distorted sense of time. In some users, they lead to profound, dreamlike, "mystical" feelings that are difficult to describe. This effect is why they have been used in religious ceremonies for centuries in some cultures. Unfortunately, at the other end of the emotional spectrum hallucinogens can also produce nightmarish feelings of anxiety and paranoia, commonly called a "bad trip." Other side effects include impaired judgment and jumbled thought processes.

Cannabis is the hemp plant from which marijuana, hashish, and THC are derived. Marijuana is a mixture of dried leaves, flowers, stems, and seeds taken from the plant. Hashish comes from the plant's resin. Smoking is the usual route of ingestion for both marijuana and hashish. THC, the active chemical ingredient in cannabis, can be synthesized for research purposes (for example, to give to animals, who can't very well smoke marijuana). When smoked, cannabis has an immediate impact that may last several hours. The desired effects of the drug are a mild, relaxed euphoria and enhanced sensory awareness. Unintended effects may include increased heart rate, anxiety, sluggish mental functioning, and impaired memory.

violent crime on campus. Alcohol can also contribute to reckless sexual behavior. In the Harvard survey, 21% of students who drank reported that they had unplanned sex as a result of drinking, and 10% indicated that their drinking had led to unprotected sex.

MDMA is a compound drug related to both amphetamines and hallucinogens, especially mescaline. MDMA was originally formulated in 1912 but was not widely used in the United States until the 1990s, when "ecstasy" became popular in the context of raves and dance clubs. MDMA produces a high that typically lasts a few hours or more. Users report that they feel warm, friendly, euphoric, sensual, insightful, and empathetic, but alert and energetic. Problematic side effects include increased blood pressure, muscle tension, sweating, blurred vision, insomnia, and transient anxiety.

Factors Influencing Drug Effects

The drug effects summarized in Table 5.2 are the *typical* ones. Drug effects can vary from person to person and even for the same person in different situations. The impact of any drug depends in part on the user's age, mood, motivation, personality, previous experience with the drug, body weight, and physiology. The dose and potency of a drug, the method of administration, and the setting in which a drug is taken also influence its effects (Leavitt, 1995). Our theme of *multifactorial causation* clearly applies to the effects of drugs.

So, too, does our theme emphasizing the *subjectivity of experience*. Expectations are potentially powerful factors that can influence the user's perceptions of a drug's effects. You may recall from the discussion of placebo effects in Chapter 2 that some people who are misled to *think* that they are drinking alcohol show signs of intoxication (Assefi & Garry, 2003). If people *expect* a drug to make them feel giddy, serene, or profound, their expectation may contribute to the feelings they experience.

A drug's effects can also change as the person's body develops a tolerance for the chemical as a result of continued use. **Tolerance refers to a progressive decrease in a person's responsiveness to a drug.** Tolerance usually leads people to consume larger and larger doses of a drug to attain the effects they desire. Most drugs produce tolerance effects, but some do so more rapidly than others. For example, tolerance to alcohol usually builds slowly, while tolerance to heroin increases much more quickly. Table 5.3 indicates whether various categories of drugs tend to produce tolerance rapidly or gradually.

"JUST TELL ME WHERE YOU KIDS GET THE IDEA TO TAKE SO MANY DRUGS."

web link 5.7

Web of Addictions

From the earliest days of the World Wide Web, this page at The Well has been regularly recognized as a primary source for accurate and responsible information about alcohol and other drugs.

Alcohol **encompasses a variety of beverages containing ethyl alcohol,** such as beers, wines, and distilled liquors (whiskey, vodka, rum, and so forth). The concentration of ethyl alcohol varies from about 4% in most beers to 40% in 80-proof liquor—and occasionally more in higher-proof liquors. When people drink heavily, the central effect is a relaxed euphoria that temporarily boosts self-esteem, as problems seem to melt away and inhibitions diminish. Common side effects include severe impairments in mental and motor functioning, mood swings, and quarrelsomeness. Alcohol is the most widely used recreational drug in our society. Because alcohol is legal, many people use it casually without even thinking of it as a drug.

Excessive drinking is a particularly prevalent problem on college campuses. Researchers from the Harvard School of Public Health (Wechsler et al., 2002) surveyed nearly 11,000 undergraduates at 119 schools and found that 81% of the students drank. Moreover, 49% of the men and 41% of the women reported that they engage in binge drinking with the intention of getting drunk. With their inhibitions released, some drinkers become argumentative and prone to aggression. In the Harvard survey, 29% of the students who did *not* engage in binge drinking reported that they had been insulted or humiliated by a drunken student, 19% had experienced serious arguments, 9% had been pushed, hit, or assaulted, and 19.5% had been the target of unwanted sexual advances (Wechsler et al., 2002). Worse yet, alcohol appears to contribute to about 90% of student rapes and 95% of

Table 5.3 Psychoactive Drugs: Tolerance, Dependence, Potential for Fatal Overdose, and Health Risks

Drugs	Tolerance	Risk of Physical Dependence	Risk of Psychological Dependence	Fatal Overdose Potential	Health Risks
Narcotics (opiates)	Rapid	High	High	High	Infectious diseases, accidents, immune suppression
Sedatives	Rapid	High	High	High	Accidents
Stimulants	Rapid	Moderate	High	Moderate to high	Sleep problems, malnutrition, nasal damage, hypertension, respiratory disease, stroke, liver disease, heart attack
Hallucinogens	Gradual	None	Very low	Very low	Accidents, acute panic
Cannabis	Gradual	None	Low to moderate	Very low	Accidents, lung cancer, respiratory disease, pulmonary disease, increased vulnerability to psychosis
Alcohol	Gradual	Moderate	Moderate	Low to high	Accidents, liver disease, malnutrition, brain damage, neurological disorders, heart disease, stroke, hypertension, ulcers, cancer, birth defects

Mechanisms of Drug Action

4d

Most drugs have effects that reverberate throughout the body. However, psychoactive drugs work primarily by altering neurotransmitter activity in the brain. As discussed in Chapter 3, neurotransmitters are chemicals that transmit information between neurons at junctions called *synapses*.

The actions of amphetamines and cocaine illustrate how drugs have selective, multiple effects on neurotransmitter activity (see **Figure 5.19**). Amphetamines exert their main effects on two of the monoamine neurotransmitters: norepinephrine (NE) and dopamine (DA). Indeed, the name *amphetamines* reflects the kinship between these drugs and the *monoamines*. Amphetamines mainly increase the release of DA and NE by presynaptic neurons. They also interfere with the reuptake of DA and NE from

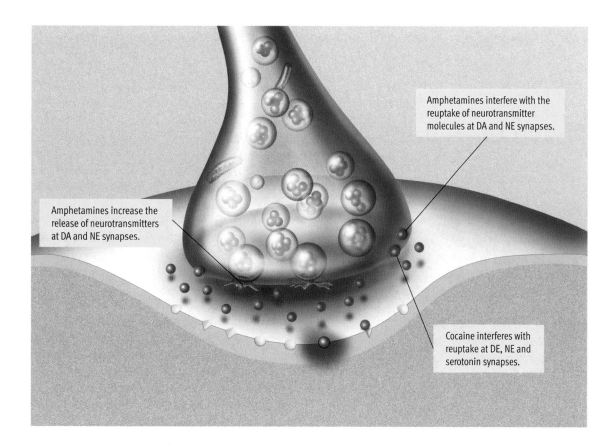

Amphetamines interfere with the reuptake of neurotransmitter molecules at DA and NE synapses.

Amphetamines increase the release of neurotransmitters at DA and NE synapses.

Cocaine interferes with reuptake at DE, NE and serotonin synapses.

Figure 5.19

Stimulant drugs and neurotransmitter activity. Like other psychoactive drugs, amphetamines and cocaine alter neurotransmitter activity at specific synapses. Amphetamines primarily increase the release of dopamine (DA) and norepinephrine (NE) and secondarily inhibit the reuptake of these neurotransmitters. Cocaine slows the reuptake process at DA, NE, and serotonin synapses. The psychological and behavioral effects of the drugs have largely been attributed to their impact on dopamine circuits.

synaptic clefts (Koob & Le Moal, 2006). These actions serve to increase the levels of dopamine and norepinephrine at the affected synapses. Cocaine shares some of these actions, which is why cocaine and amphetamines produce similar stimulant effects. Cocaine mainly blocks reuptake at DA, NE, and serotonin synapses. For both amphetamines and cocaine, elevated activity in certain *dopamine circuits* is believed to be crucial to the drugs' pleasurable, rewarding effects (Volkow, Fowler, & Wang, 2004).

The discovery of endorphins (the body's internally produced opiatelike chemicals) has led to new insights about the actions of opiate drugs (see Chapter 3). These drugs apparently bind to specific subtypes of endorphin receptors, and their actions at these receptor sites indirectly elevate activity in the dopamine pathways that modulate reward (Cami & Farre, 2003). In the 1990s scientists discovered two types of receptors in the brain for THC, the active chemical ingredient in marijuana, which are called *cannabinoid receptors* (Stephens, 1999). Soon after, they found two internally produced chemicals similar to THC—christened *endocannabinoids*—that activate these receptors and thereby influence activity at GABA and glutamate synapses (Julien et al., 2008). It appears that THC from marijuana "hijacks" the brain's cannabinoid receptors (Piomelli, 2004), eventually leading to increased release of endorphins and activation of the dopamine circuits associated with reward (Solinas et al., 2003, 2006).

Although specific drugs exert their initial effects in the brain on a wide variety of neurotransmitter systems, many theorists believe that virtually all abused drugs eventually increase activity in a particular neural pathway, called the *mesolimbic dopamine pathway* (Nestler & Malenka, 2004). This neural circuit, which runs from an area in the midbrain through the *nucleus accumbens* and on to the prefrontal cortex (see **Figure 5.20**), has been characterized as a "reward pathway" (Pierce & Kumaresan, 2006). Large and rapid increases in the release of dopamine along this pathway are thought to be the neural basis of the reinforcing effects of most abused drugs (Volkow et al., 2004).

Drug Dependence

People can become either physically or psychologically dependent on a drug. Physical dependence is a common problem with narcotics, sedatives, alcohol, and stimulants. **Physical dependence** exists **when a person must continue to take a drug to avoid withdrawal illness.** The symptoms of withdrawal illness depend on the specific drug. Withdrawal from heroin, barbiturates, and alcohol can produce fever, chills, tremors, convulsions, vomiting, cramps, diarrhea, and severe aches and pains. Withdrawal from stimulants can lead to a more subtle syndrome, marked by fatigue, apathy, irritability, and disorientation. Withdrawal also triggers a cascade of negative emotions and powerful urges for drug pursuit, which often lead people to relapse and reinstate their drug use (Baker et al., 2006).

Psychological dependence exists when a person **must continue to take a drug to satisfy intense mental and emotional craving for the drug.** Psychological dependence is more subtle than physical dependence, but the need it creates can be powerful. Cocaine, for instance, can produce an overwhelming psychological need for continued use. Psychological dependence is possible with all recreational drugs, although it seems rare for hallucinogens.

Both types of dependence are established gradually with repeated use of a drug. It was originally assumed that only physical dependence has a physiological basis, but theorists now believe that both types of dependence reflect alterations in synaptic transmission (Di Chara, 1999; Self, 1997). Dysregulation in the mesolimbic dopamine pathway appears to be a major factor underlying addiction (Nestler & Malenka, 2004), but long-term changes in other neural circuits running through the amygdala and prefrontal cortex may also contribute to drug craving (Kalivas & Volkow, 2005). Drugs vary in their potential for creating either physical or psychologi-

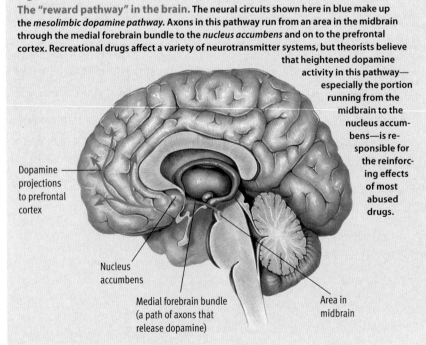

Figure 5.20

The "reward pathway" in the brain. The neural circuits shown here in blue make up the *mesolimbic dopamine pathway*. Axons in this pathway run from an area in the midbrain through the medial forebrain bundle to the *nucleus accumbens* and on to the prefrontal cortex. Recreational drugs affect a variety of neurotransmitter systems, but theorists believe that heightened dopamine activity in this pathway—especially the portion running from the midbrain to the nucleus accumbens—is responsible for the reinforcing effects of most abused drugs.

Dopamine projections to prefrontal cortex

Nucleus accumbens

Medial forebrain bundle (a path of axons that release dopamine)

Area in midbrain

cal dependence. Table 5.3 provides estimates of the risk of each kind of dependence for the six categories of recreational drugs covered in our discussion.

Drugs and Health

Recreational drug use can affect health in a variety of ways. The three principal ways are by triggering an overdose, by producing various types of physiological damage (direct effects), and by causing health-impairing behavior (indirect effects).

Overdose

Any drug can be fatal if a person takes enough of it, but some drugs are much more dangerous than others. Table 5.3 shows estimates of the risk of accidentally consuming a lethal overdose of each listed drug. Drugs that are CNS depressants—sedatives, narcotics, and alcohol—carry the greatest risk of overdose. It's important to note that these drugs are additive with each other, so many overdoses involve lethal *combinations* of CNS depressants. What happens when a person overdoses on these drugs? The

In 2008, actor Heath Ledger died from an accidental overdose of prescription drugs. Subsequent investigation revealed that he had overmedicated himself in an effort to deal with chronic sleep problems. The toxicology report found traces of two narcotic painkillers, two antianxiety agents, and two sedative medications. His tragic death illustrates how dangerous combinations of CNS depressants can be.

respiratory system grinds to a halt, producing coma, brain damage, and death within a brief period. Fatal overdoses with CNS stimulants usually involve a heart attack, stroke, or cortical seizure. Deaths attributable to overdoses of stimulant drugs used to be *relatively* infrequent, but overdoses have increased sharply as more people have experimented with free-basing, smoking crack, and using other, more dangerous modes of ingestion (Repetto & Gold, 2005).

Direct Effects

In some cases, drugs cause tissue damage directly. For example, chronic snorting of cocaine can damage nasal membranes. Cocaine use can also foster cardiovascular disease, and crack smoking is associated with several respiratory problems (Gold & Jacobs, 2005; Gourevitch & Arnsten, 2005). Long-term, excessive alcohol consumption is associated with an elevated risk for a wide range of serious health problems, including liver damage, ulcers, hypertension, stroke, heart disease, neurological disorders, and some types of cancer (Johnson & Ait-Daoud, 2005; Mack, Franklin, & Frances, 2003).

Indirect Effects

The negative effects of drugs on physical health are often indirect results of the drugs' impact on behavior. For instance, people using stimulants tend not to eat or sleep properly. Sedatives increase the risk of accidental injuries because they severely impair motor coordination. People who abuse downers often trip down stairs, fall off stools, and suffer other mishaps. Many drugs impair driving ability, increasing the risk of automobile accidents. Alcohol, for instance, may contribute to roughly 40% of all automobile fatalities (Hingson & Sleet, 2006). Intravenous drug users risk contracting infectious diseases that can be spread by unsterilized needles. In recent years, acquired immune deficiency syndrome (AIDS) has been transmitted at an alarming rate through the population of intravenous drug users (Des Jarlais, Hagan, & Friedman, 2005).

The major health risks (other than overdose) of various recreational drugs are listed in the sixth column of Table 5.3. As you can see, alcohol appears to have the most diverse negative effects on physical health. The irony, of course, is that alcohol is the only recreational drug listed that is legal.

Controversies Concerning Marijuana

The possible health risks associated with marijuana use have generated considerable debate in recent years. The available evidence suggests that chronic

web link 5.8

National Institute on Alcohol Abuse and Alcoholism (NIAAA)

Just two of the many research sources here include the entire collection of the bulletin *Alcohol Alert*, issued since 1988 on specific topics related to alcoholism, and the ETOH Database, a searchable repository of more than 100,000 records on alcoholism and alcohol abuse.

web link 5.9

National Institute on Drug Abuse (NIDA)

This government-sponsored site houses a great deal of information on the medical consequences of abusing various drugs. It is also an excellent resource for statistics on trends in drug abuse.

marijuana use increases the risk for respiratory and pulmonary disease (Aldington et al., 2007; Tashkin et al., 2002). Some studies have also found a link between long-term marijuana use and the risk for lung cancer, although the data are surprisingly inconsistent (Aldington et al., 2008; Mehra et al., 2006). There is convincing evidence that smoking marijuana increases the risk of automobile accidents if users drive while high (Ramaekers et al., 2004). Finally, a rash of recent studies have reported an unexpected link between cannabis use and severe psychotic disorders, including schizophrenia (Degenhardt & Hall, 2006; DiForti et al., 2007). Obviously, the vast majority of marijuana users do not develop psychoses, but it appears that cannabis may trigger psychotic illness in individuals who have a genetic vulnerability to such disorders (D'Souza, 2007; Murray et al., 2007). These dangers are listed in Table 5.3, but some other widely publicized dangers are omitted because the findings on these other risks have been exaggerated or remain debatable. Here is a brief overview of the evidence on some of these controversies:

• *Does marijuana reduce one's immune response?* Research with animals clearly demonstrates that cannabis can suppress various aspects of immune system responding (Cabral & Pettit, 1998). However, infectious diseases do not appear to be more common among marijuana smokers than among nonsmokers. Thus, it is unclear whether marijuana increases susceptibility to infectious diseases in humans (Bredt et al., 2002; Klein, Friedman, & Specter, 1998).

• *Does marijuana lead to impotence and sterility in men?* In animal research, cannabis temporarily decreases testosterone levels and sperm production (Brown & Dobs, 2002). Citing these findings, the popular media have frequently implied that marijuana is likely to make men sterile and impotent. However, research with humans has yielded weak, inconsistent, and reversible effects on testosterone and sperm levels (Brown & Dobs, 2002). At present, the evidence suggests that marijuana has little lasting impact on male smokers' fertility or sexual functioning (Grinspoon, Bakalar, & Russo, 2005).

• *Does marijuana have long-term negative effects on cognitive functioning?* It has long been known that marijuana has a negative impact on attention and memory while users are high (Ranganathan & D'Souza, 2006), but until recently studies had failed to find any permanent cognitive deficits attributable to cannabis use. However, a flood of recent studies using more elaborate and precise assessments of cognitive functioning *have* found an association between chronic, heavy marijuana use and measurable impairments in attention and memory (see Figure 5.21) that

show up when users are not high (Bolla et al., 2002; Solowij et al., 2002). That said, the cognitive deficits that have been observed are modest and certainly not disabling, and one study found that the deficits vanished after a month of marijuana abstinence (Pope, Gruber, & Yurgelun-Todd, 2001; Pope et al., 2001). Although more research is needed, the recent studies in this area provide some cause for concern.

New Findings Regarding Ecstasy

Like marijuana, ecstasy is viewed as a harmless drug in some quarters, but accumulating empirical evidence is beginning to alter that perception.

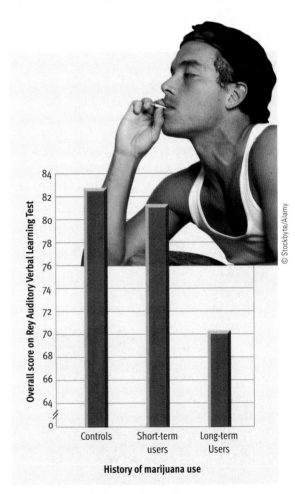

Figure 5.21

Chronic cannabis use and cognitive performance. Solowij and associates (2002) administered a battery of neuropsychological tests to 51 long-term cannabis users who had smoked marijuana regularly for an average of 24 years, 51 short-term cannabis users who had smoked marijuana regularly for an average of 10 years, and 33 control subjects who had little or no history of cannabis use. The cannabis users were required to abstain from smoking marijuana for a minimum of 12 hours prior to their testing. The study found evidence suggestive of subtle cognitive impairments among the long-term cannabis users on many of the tests. The graph depicts the results observed for overall performance on the Rey Auditory Verbal Learning Test, which measures several aspects of memory functioning.

Research on MDMA is in its infancy, so conclusions about its risks must be tentative. MDMA does not appear to be especially addictive, but psychological dependence clearly can become a problem for some people. MDMA has been implicated in cases of stroke and heart attack, seizures, heat stroke, and liver damage, but its exact contribution is hard to gauge because MDMA users typically consume quite a variety of drugs, and ecstasy often contains contaminants (Grob & Poland, 2005; Scholey et al., 2004). Chronic, heavy use of ecstasy appears to be associated with sleep disorders, depression, and elevated anxiety and hostility (Morgan, 2000). Moreover, studies of former MDMA users suggest that ecstasy may have subtle, long-term effects on cognitive functioning (Parrott, 2000). Quite a few studies have found memory deficits in former users (Jager et al, 2008; Schilt et al., 2007). Other studies have found decreased performance on laboratory tasks requiring attention and learning (Gouzoulis-Mayfrank et al., 2000). In short, the preliminary evidence suggests that MDMA may be more harmful than widely assumed.

MDMA, better known as "ecstasy," surged in popularity in the 1990s in the context of "raves" and dance clubs. Although many people view MDMA as a relatively harmless drug, recent research suggests otherwise.

---

concept check 5.3

Recognizing the Unique Characteristics of Commonly Abused Drugs

From our discussion of the principal psychoactive drugs, it is clear that considerable overlap exists among the categories of drugs in terms of their methods of ingestion, medical uses, desired effects, and short-term side effects. Each type of drug, however, has at least one or two characteristics that make it different from the other types. Check your understanding of the unique characteristics of each type of drug by indicating which of them has the characteristics listed below. Choose from the following: (a) narcotics/opiates, (b) sedatives, (c) stimulants, (d) hallucinogens, (e) cannabis, and (f) alcohol. You'll find the answers in Appendix A.

_____ **1.** Increases alertness and energy, reduces fatigue.

_____ **2.** No recognized medical use. May lead to insightful or "mystical" experiences.

_____ **3.** Used as a "sleeping pill" because it reduces CNS activity.

_____ **4.** Contributes to 40% of all traffic fatalities.

_____ **5.** Derived from opium; used for pain relief.

_____ **6.** Health risks of concern include respiratory and pulmonary disease and lung cancer.

REVIEW of Key Learning Goals

5.19 The principal categories of abused drugs are narcotics, sedatives, stimulants, hallucinogens, cannabis, and alcohol. Although it's possible to describe the typical effects of various drugs, the actual effects on any individual depend on a host of factors, including subjective expectations and tolerance to the drug.

5.20 Psychoactive drugs exert their main effects in the brain, where they alter neurotransmitter activity at synaptic sites in a variety of ways. For example, amphetamines increase the release of DA and NE, and like cocaine, they slow reuptake at DA and NE synapses. The mesolimbic dopamine pathway may mediate the reinforcing effects of most abused drugs.

5.21 Physical dependence exists when people must continue drug use to avoid withdrawal. Psychological dependence involves intense mental and emotional craving for a drug. Both types of dependence reflect alterations in synaptic transmission.

5.22 Recreational drug use can prove harmful to health by producing an overdose, by causing tissue damage, or by increasing health-impairing behavior. The chances of accidentally consuming a lethal overdose are greatest for the CNS depressants and cocaine. Direct tissue damage occurs most frequently with alcohol and cocaine.

5.23 Cannabis may increase risk for respiratory disease, lung cancer, accidents, psychotic disorders, and subtle cognitive impairments. Concerns about immune response and reproductive health appear to be exaggerated. Preliminary evidence suggests that MDMA may be more dangerous than widely assumed.

Reflecting on the Chapter's Themes

Sociohistorical Context

Subjectivity of Experience

Cultural Heritage

Multifactorial Causation

Theoretical Diversity

This chapter highlights five of our unifying themes. First, we saw how psychology evolves in a sociohistorical context. Psychology began as the science of consciousness in the 19th century, but consciousness proved difficult to study empirically. Research on consciousness dwindled after John B. Watson and others redefined psychology as the science of behavior. However, in the 1960s people began to turn inward, showing a new interest in altering consciousness through drug use, meditation, hypnosis, and biofeedback. Psychologists responded to these social trends by beginning to study variations in consciousness in earnest. This renewed interest in consciousness shows how social forces can have an impact on psychology's evolution.

A second theme that predominates in this chapter is the idea that people's experience of the world is highly subjective. We encountered this theme when we learned that people often misjudge the quality and quantity of their sleep and that the alterations of consciousness produced by drugs depend significantly on personal expectations.

Third, we saw once again how culture molds some aspects of behavior. Although the basic physiological process of sleep appears largely invariant from one society to another, culture influences certain aspects of sleep habits and has a dramatic impact on whether people remember their dreams and how they interpret and feel about their dreams.

Fourth, we learned once again that behavior is governed by multifactorial causation. For example, we discussed how the effects of jet lag, sleep deprivation, and psychoactive drugs depend on a number of interacting factors. Likewise, we saw that insomnia is rooted in a constellation of causal factors.

Finally, the chapter illustrated psychology's theoretical diversity. We discussed conflicting theories about dreams, hypnosis, and meditation. For the most part, we did not see these opposing theories converging toward reconciliation, as we did in the areas of sensation and perception. However, it's important to emphasize that rival theories do not always merge neatly into tidy models of behavior. Many theoretical controversies go on indefinitely. This fact does not negate the value of theoretical diversity. While it's always nice to resolve a theoretical debate, the debate itself can advance knowledge by stimulating and guiding empirical research.

Indeed, our upcoming Personal Application demonstrates that theoretical debates need not be resolved in order to advance knowledge. Many theoretical controversies and enduring mysteries remain in the study of sleep and dreams. Nonetheless, researchers have accumulated a great deal of practical information on these topics, which we'll discuss in the next few pages.

PERSONAL

APPLICATION

Addressing Practical Questions About Sleep and Dreams

Indicate whether the following statements are "true" or "false."

____ **1** Naps rarely have a refreshing effect.

____ **2** Some people never dream.

____ **3** When people cannot recall their dreams, it's because they are trying to repress them.

____ **4** Only an expert in symbolism, such as a psychoanalytic therapist, can interpret the real meaning of dreams.

These assertions were all drawn from the Sleep and Dreams Information Questionnaire (Palladino & Carducci, 1984), which measures practical knowledge about sleep and dreams. Are they true or false? You'll see in this Application.

Common Questions About Sleep

How much sleep do people need? The average amount of daily sleep for young adults is 7.5 hours. However, there is considerable

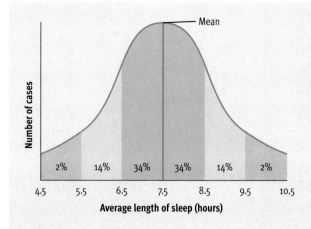

Figure 5.22

Variation in sleep length. Based on data from a variety of sources, Webb (1992b) estimates that average sleep length among young adults is distributed normally, as shown here. Although most young adults sleep an average of 6.5 to 8.5 hours per night, some people sleep less and some sleep more.

SOURCE: Adapted from Webb, W. B. (1992). *Sleep, the gentle tyrant* (2nd Ed.). Bolton, MA: Anker Publishing Co. Copyright © 1992 by Anker Publishing Co. Adapted by permission.

variability in how long people sleep. Based on a synthesis of data from many studies, Webb (1992b) estimates that sleep time is normally distributed as shown in Figure 5.22. Sleep needs vary some from person to person. That said, many sleep experts believe that most people would function more effectively if they increased their amount of sleep (Banks & Dinges, 2007). Bear in mind, too, that research suggests that people who sleep 7–8 hours per night have the lowest mortality rates (Patel et al., 2004; Tamakoshi et al., 2004).

Can short naps be refreshing? Some naps are beneficial and some are not. The effectiveness of napping varies from person to person. Also, the benefits of any specific nap depend on the time of day and the amount of sleep one has had recently (Dinges, 1993). On the negative side, naps are not very *efficient* ways to sleep because you're often just getting into the deeper stages of sleep when your nap time is up. Another potential problem is that overly long naps or naps that occur too close to bedtime can disrupt nighttime sleep (Thorpy & Yager, 2001).

Nonetheless, many highly productive people (including Thomas Edison, Winston Churchill, and John F. Kennedy) have made effective use of naps. Naps can enhance subsequent alertness and task performance and reduce sleepiness (Takahashi & Kaida, 2006). In conclusion, naps can be refreshing for most people (so the first statement opening this Application is false), and they can pay off in the long run if they don't interfere with nighttime sleep.

How do alcohol and drugs affect sleep? Obviously, stimulants such as cocaine and amphetamines make it difficult to sleep. More

surprising is the finding that most of the CNS depressants that facilitate sleep (such as alcohol, analgesics, sedatives, and tranquilizers) actually disrupt the normal sleep cycle (Carskadon & Dement, 2005). The principal problem is that many drugs reduce the time spent in REM sleep and slow-wave sleep (Hyde, Roehrs, & Roth, 2006). Unfortunately, these are the sleep stages that appear to be most important to a refreshing night's sleep.

What is the significance of yawning and snoring? Yawning is a universal phenomenon seen in all cultural groups—not to mention other mammals, birds, fish, and reptiles (Baenninger, 1997). Contrary to popular belief, yawning is not a response to a buildup of carbon dioxide or a shortage of oxygen (Provine, 2005). However, as reputed, yawning *is* correlated with sleepiness and boredom (Provine, 2005). According to one theory, the principal function of yawning is to cool the brain down (Gallup & Gallup, 2007). The most fascinating and perplexing facet of yawning is that it is contagious—seeing others yawn creates a powerful urge to follow suit (Platek, Mohamed, & Gallup, 2005).

Snoring is a common phenomenon seen in roughly 30%–40% of adults (Hoffstein, 2005). Snoring increases after age 35, occurs in men more than women, and is more common among people who are overweight (Kryger, 1993; Stoohs et al., 1998). Many factors, including colds, allergies, smoking, and some drugs, can contribute to snoring, mainly by forcing people to breathe through their mouths while sleeping. Some people who snore loudly disrupt their own sleep as well as that of their bed partners. It can be difficult to prevent snoring in some people,

whereas others are able to reduce their snoring by simply losing weight or by sleeping on their side instead of their back (Lugaresi et al., 1994). Snoring may seem like a trivial problem, but it is associated with sleep apnea and cardiovascular disease, and it may have considerably more medical significance than most people realize (Dement & Vaughn, 1999; Olson & Park, 2006).

What can be done to avoid sleep problems? There are many ways to improve your chances of getting satisfactory sleep (see Figure 5.23). Most of them involve developing sensible daytime habits that won't interfere with sleep (see Foldvary-Schaefer, 2006; Maas, 1998; Stepanski & Wyatt, 2003; Thorpy & Yager, 2001; Zarcone, 2000). For example, if you've been having trouble sleeping at night, it's wise to avoid daytime naps, so you will be *tired* when bedtime arrives. Some people find that daytime exercise helps them fall asleep more readily at bedtime (King et al., 1997). Of course, the exercise should be part of a regular regimen that doesn't leave one sore or aching.

Figure 5.23

Improving the quality of one's sleep. In his book *Power Sleep,* James Maas (1998) offers this advice for people concerned about enhancing their sleep. Maas argues convincingly that good daytime habits can make all the difference in the world to the quality of one's sleep.

SOURCE: Adapted from Maas, J. B. (1998). *Power sleep.* New York: Random House. Copyright © 1998 by James B. Mass, Ph. D. Reprinted by permission of Villard Books, a division of Random House, Inc.

Suggestions for Better Sleep

1. Reduce stress as much as possible.
2. Exercise to stay fit.
3. Keep mentally stimulated during the day.
4. Eat a proper diet.
5. Stop smoking.
6. Reduce caffeine intake.
7. Avoid alcohol near bedtime.
8. Take a warm bath before bed.
9. Maintain a relaxing atmosphere in the bedroom.
10. Establish a bedtime ritual.
11. Have pleasurable sexual activity.
12. Clear your mind at bedtime.
13. Try some bedtime relaxation techniques.
14. Avoid trying too hard to get to sleep.
15. Learn to value sleep.

It's also a good idea to minimize consumption of stimulants such as caffeine or nicotine. Because coffee and cigarettes aren't prescription drugs, people don't appreciate how much the stimulants they contain can heighten physical arousal. Many foods (such as chocolate) and beverages (such as cola drinks) contain more caffeine than people realize. Also, bear in mind that ill-advised eating habits can interfere with sleep. Try to avoid going to bed hungry, uncomfortably stuffed, or soon after eating foods that disagree with you.

In addition to these prudent habits, two other preventive measures are worth mentioning. First, try to establish a reasonably regular bedtime. This habit will allow you to take advantage of your circadian rhythm, so you'll be trying to fall asleep when your body is primed to cooperate. Second, create a favorable environment for sleep. This advice belabors what should be obvious, but many people fail to heed it. Make sure you have a good bed that is comfortable for you. Take steps to ensure that your bedroom is quiet enough and that the humidity and temperature are to your liking.

What can be done about insomnia? First, don't panic if you run into a little trouble sleeping. An overreaction to sleep problems can begin a vicious circle of escalating problems, like that depicted in Figure 5.24. If you jump to the conclusion that you are becoming an insomniac, you

People typically get very upset when they have difficulty falling asleep. Unfortunately, the emotional distress tends to make it even harder for people to get to sleep.

may approach sleep with anxiety that will aggravate the problem. The harder you work at falling asleep, the less success you're likely to have. As noted earlier, temporary sleep problems are common and generally clear up on their own.

One sleep expert, Dianne Hales (1987), lists 101 suggestions for combating insomnia in her book *How to Sleep Like a Baby*. Many involve "boring yourself to sleep" by playing alphabet games, reciting poems, or listening to your clock. Another recommended strategy is to engage in some not-so-engaging activity. For instance, you might try reading your dullest textbook. It could turn out to be a superb sedative. Whatever you think about, try to avoid ruminating about the current stresses and problems in your life. Research has shown that the tendency to ruminate is one of the key factors contributing to insomnia (Kales et al., 1984), as the data in Figure 5.25 show.

Anything that relaxes you—whether it's music, meditation, prayer, or a warm bath—can aid you in falling asleep. Experts have also devised systematic relaxation procedures that can make these efforts more effective. You may want to learn about techniques such as *progressive relaxation* (Jacobson, 1938), *autogenic training* (Schultz &

Luthe, 1959), or the *relaxation response* (Benson & Klipper, 1988).

Common Questions About Dreams

Does everyone dream? Yes. Some people just don't *remember* their dreams. However, when these people are brought into a sleep lab and awakened from REM sleep, they report having been dreaming—much to their surprise (statement 2 at the start of this Application is false). Scientists have studied a small number of people who have sustained brain damage in the area of the *pons* that has wiped out their REM sleep, but even these people report dreams (Klosch & Kraft, 2005).

Why don't some people remember their dreams? The evaporation of dreams appears to be quite normal. Given the lowered level of awareness during sleep, it's understandable that memory of dreams is mediocre. Dream recall is best when people are awakened during or very soon after a dream (Goodenough, 1991). Most of the time, people who *do* recall dreams upon waking are remembering either their *last* dream from their final REM period or a dream that awakened them earlier in the night. Hobson's (1989) educated guess is that people probably forget 95%–

Figure 5.24
The vicious circle of anxiety and sleep difficulty. Anxiety about sleep difficulties leads to poorer sleep, which increases anxiety further, which in turn leads to even greater difficulties in sleeping.

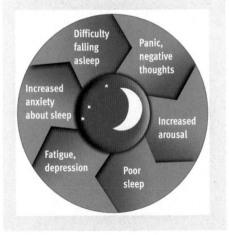

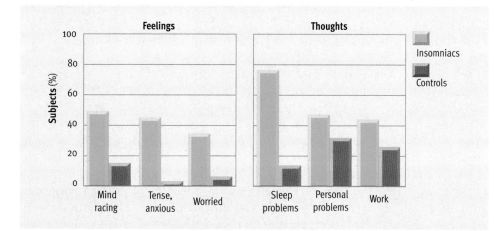

Feelings

Thoughts

Insomniacs

Controls

Figure 5.25

Thoughts and emotions associated with insomnia. This graph depicts the percentage of insomniacs and control subjects reporting various presleep feelings and thoughts. Insomniacs' tendency to ruminate about their problems contributes to their sleep difficulties.

SOURCE: Data from Kales, A., & Kales, J. D. (1984). *Evaluation and treatment of insomnia.* New York: Oxford University Press. Copyright © 1984 by Oxford University Press.

99% of their dreams. This forgetting is natural and is not due to repression, so statement 3 is also false. People who never remember their dreams probably have a sleep pattern that puts too much time between their last REM/dream period and awakening, so even their last dream is forgotten.

Are dreams instantaneous? No. It has long been speculated that dreams flash through consciousness almost instantaneously. According to this notion, complicated plots that would require 20 minutes to think through in waking life could bolt through the dreaming mind in a second or two. However, modern research suggests that this isn't the case (LaBerge, 2007; Weinstein, Schwartz, & Arkin, 1991).

Do dreams require interpretation? Most theorists would say yes, but interpretation may not be as difficult as generally assumed. People have long believed that dreams are symbolic and that it is necessary to interpret the symbols to understand the meaning of dreams. We saw earlier in the chapter that Freud, for instance, believed that dreams have a hidden ("latent") content that represented their true meaning. Thus, a Freudian therapist might equate such dream events as walking into a tunnel or riding a horse with sexual intercourse.

Freudian theorists assert that dream interpretation is a complicated task requiring considerable knowledge of symbolism. However, many dream theorists argue that symbolism in dreams is less deceptive and mysterious than Freud thought (Faraday, 1974; Foulkes, 1985; Hall, 1979). Calvin Hall makes the point that dreams require some interpretation simply because they are more visual than verbal. That is, pictures need to be translated into ideas. According to Hall, dream symbolism is highly personal, and the dreamer may be the person best equipped to decipher a dream (statement 4 is also false). Thus, it is not unreasonable for you to try to interpret your own dreams. Unfortunately, you'll never know whether you're "correct," because there is no definitive way to judge the validity of different dream interpretations.

What is lucid dreaming? Generally, when people dream, they are not aware that they are dreaming. Occasionally, however, some people experience "lucid" dreams in which they recognize that they are dreaming (LaBerge, 2007). Typically, normal dreams become lucid when people puzzle over some-thing bizarre in a dream and recognize that they must be dreaming. **In *lucid dreams* people can think clearly about the circumstances of waking life and the fact that they are dreaming, yet they remain asleep in the midst of a vivid dream.** Perhaps the most intriguing aspect of this dual consciousness is that people can often exert some control over the events unfolding in their lucid dreams (LaBerge, 1990).

Could a shocking dream be fatal? According to folklore, if you fall from a height in a dream, you'd better wake up on the plunge downward, for if you hit the bottom the shock to your system will be so great that you will actually die in your sleep. Think about this one for a moment. *If* it were a genuine problem, who would have reported it? You can be sure that no one has ever testified to experiencing a fatal dream. This myth presumably exists because many people do awaken during the downward plunge, thinking that they've averted a close call. A study by Barrett (1988–1989) suggests that dreams of one's own death are relatively infrequent. However, people do have such dreams—and live to tell about them.

REVIEW of Key Learning Goals

5.25 Naps can prove helpful, but alcohol and many other widely used drugs have a negative effect on sleep. Yawning appears to be associated with boredom and sleepiness but is not well understood. Snoring may have more medical significance than most people realize. People can do many things to avoid or reduce sleep problems. Individuals troubled by transient insomnia should avoid panic, pursue effective relaxation, and try distracting themselves so they don't work too hard at falling asleep.

5.26 Everyone dreams, but some people don't remember their dreams. Freud asserted that dreams require interpretation, but modern theorists assert that this process may not be as complicated as Freud assumed. In lucid dreams, people consciously recognize that they are dreaming and exert some control over the events in their dreams.

FRANK AND ERNEST

Is Alcoholism a Disease? The Power of Definitions

Key Learning Goals

5.27 Recognize the influence of definitions, and understand the nominal fallacy.

Alcoholism is a major problem in most, perhaps all, societies. As we saw in the main body of the chapter, alcohol is a dangerous drug. Alcoholism destroys countless lives, tears families apart, and is associated with an elevated risk for a variety of physical maladies (Johnson & Ait-Daoud, 2005). With roughly 15 million problem drinkers in the United States (Mack et al., 2003), it seems likely that alcoholism has touched the lives of a majority of Americans.

In almost every discussion about alcoholism someone will ask, "Is alcoholism a disease?" If alcoholism is a disease, it is a strange one, because the alcoholic is the most direct cause of his or her own sickness. If alcoholism is *not* a disease, then what else might it be? Over the course of history, alcoholism has been categorized under many labels, from a personal weakness to a crime, a sin, a mental disorder, and a physical illness (Meyer, 1996). Each of these definitions carries important personal, social, political, and economic implications.

Consider, for instance, the consequences of characterizing alcoholism as a disease. If that is the case, alcoholics should be treated like diabetics, heart patients, or victims of other physical illnesses. That is, they should be viewed with sympathy and should be given appropriate medical and therapeutic interventions to foster recovery from their illness. These treatments should be covered by medical insurance and delivered by health care professionals. Just as important, if alcoholism is defined as a disease, it should lose much of its stigma. After all, we don't blame people with diabetes or heart disease for their illnesses. Yes, alcoholics admittedly contribute to their own disease (by drinking too much), but so do many victims of diabetes and heart disease, who eat the wrong foods, fail to control their weight, and so forth (McLellan et al., 2000). And, as is the case with many physical illnesses, one can inherit a genetic vulnerability to alcoholism (Lin & Anthenelli, 2005), so it is difficult to argue that alcoholism is caused solely by one's behavior.

Conversely, if alcoholism is defined as a personal failure or a moral weakness, alcoholics are less likely to be viewed with sympathy and compassion. They might be admonished to quit drinking, be put in prison, or be punished in some other way. These responses to their alcoholism would be administered primarily by the legal system rather than the health care system, as medical interventions are not designed to remedy moral failings. Obviously, the interventions that would be available would not be covered by health insurance, which would have enormous financial repercussions (for both health care providers and alcoholics).

The key point here is that definitions lie at the center of many complex debates, and they can have profound and far-reaching implications. People tend to think of definitions as insignificant, arbitrary, abstruse sets of words found buried in the obscurity of thick dictionaries compiled by ivory tower intellectuals. Much of this characterization may be accurate, but definitions are *not* insignificant. They are vested with enormous power to shape how people think about important issues. And an endless array of issues boil down to matters of definition. For example, the next time you hear people arguing over whether a particular movie is pornographic, whether the death penalty is cruel and unusual punishment, or whether spanking is child abuse, you'll find it helps to focus the debate on clarifying the definitions of the crucial concepts.

The Power to Make Definitions

So, how can we resolve the debate about whether alcoholism is a disease? Scientists generally try to resolve their debates by conducting research to achieve a better understanding of the phenomena under scrutiny. You may have noticed already that the assertion "We need more research on this issue . . ." is a frequent refrain in this text. Is more research the answer in this case? For once, the answer is "no." There is no conclusive way to determine whether alcoholism is a disease. It is not as though there is a "right" answer to this question that we can discover through more and better research.

The question of whether alcoholism is a disease is a *matter of definition:* Does alcoholism fit the currently accepted definition of what constitutes a disease? If you consult medical texts or dictionaries, you will find that *disease is typically defined as an impairment in the normal functioning of an organism that alters its vital functions.* Given that alcoholism clearly impairs people's normal functioning and disrupts a variety of vital functions (see **Figure 5.26**), it seems reasonable to characterize it as a disease, and this has been the dominant view in the United States since the middle of the 20th century (Maltzman, 1994; Meyer, 1996). This view has only been strengthened by recent evidence that addiction to alcohol (and other drugs) is the result of dysregulation in key neural circuits in the brain (Cami & Farre, 2003). Still, many critics express vigorous doubts about the wisdom of defining alcoholism as a disease (Peele, 1989, 2000). They often raise a question that comes up frequently in arguments about definitions: Who should have the power to make the definition? In this case, the power lies in the hands of the medical community, which seems sensible, given that disease is a medical concept. But some critics argue that the medical community has a strong bias in favor of defining conditions as diseases because doing so creates new markets and fuels economic growth for the health industry (Nikelly, 1994). Thus, debate about whether alcoholism is a disease seems likely to continue for the indefinite future.

To summarize, definitions generally do not emerge out of research. They are typically crafted by experts or authorities in a specific field who try to reach a consensus about how to best define a particular concept. Thus, in analyzing the validity of a definition, you need to look not only at the definition itself but at where it came from. Who decided what the definition should be? Does the source of the definition seem

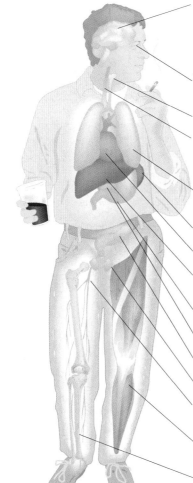

Brain Wernicke's syndrome, an acute condition characterized by mental confusion and ocular abnormalities; Korsakoff's syndrome, a psychotic condition characterized by impairment of memory and learning, apathy, and degeneration of the white brain matter

Eyes Tobacco-alcohol blindness; Wernicke's ophthalmoplegia, a reversible paralysis of the muscles of the eye

Pharynx Cancer of the pharynx

Esophagus Esophageal varices, an irreversible condition in which the person can die by drowning in his own blood when the varices open

Lungs Lowered resistance thought to lead to greater incidence of tuberculosis, pneumonia, and emphysema

Spleen Hypersplenism

Heart Alcoholic cardiomyopathy, a heart condition

Liver Acute enlargement of liver, which is reversible, as well as irreversible alcoholic's liver (cirrhosis)

Stomach Gastritis and ulcers

Pancreas Acute and chronic pancreatitis

Rectum Hemorrhoids

Testes Atrophy of the testes

Nerves Polyneuritis, a condition characterized by loss of sensation

Muscles Alcoholic myopathy, a condition resulting in painful muscle contractions

Blood and bone marrow Coagulation defects and anemia

Figure 5.26

Physiological malfunctions associated with alcoholism. This chart amply demonstrates that alcoholism is associated with a diverse array of physiological maladies. In and of itself, however, this information does not settle the argument about whether alcoholism should be regarded as a disease. It all depends on one's definition of what constitutes a disease.

SOURCE: Edlin, G., & Golanty, E. (1992). *Health and wellness: A holistic approach*. Boston: Jones & Bartlett. Copyright © 1992 by Jones & Bartlett Publishers, Inc. www.jbpub.com.

Table 5.4 Critical Thinking Skills Discussed in This Application

Skill	Description
Understanding the way definitions shape how people think about issues	The critical thinker appreciates the enormous power of definitions and the need to clarify definitions in efforts to resolve disagreements.
Identifying the source of definitions	The critical thinker recognizes the need to determine who has the power to make specific definitions and to evaluate their credibility.
Avoiding the nominal fallacy in working with definitions and labels	The critical thinker understands that labels do not have explanatory value.

legitimate and appropriate? Did the authorities who formulated the definition have any biases that should be considered?

Definitions, Labels, and Circular Reasoning

One additional point about definitions is worth discussing. Perhaps because definitions are imbued with so much power, people have an interesting tendency to incorrectly use them as *explanations* for the phenomena they describe. This logical error, which equates *naming* something with *explaining* it, is sometime called the *nominal fallacy*. Names and labels that are used as explanations may sound reasonable at first glance, but definitions do not really have any explanatory value; they simply specify what certain terms mean. Consider an example. Let's say your friend Frank has a severe drinking problem. You are sitting around with some other friends discussing why Frank drinks so much. Rest assured, at least one of these friends will assert that "Frank drinks too much because he is an alcoholic." This is circular reasoning, which is just as useless as explaining that Frank is an alcoholic because he drinks too much. It tells us nothing about *why* Frank has a drinking problem. The diagnostic labels that are used in the classification of mental disorders—labels such as schizophrenia, depression, autism, and obsessive-compulsive disorder—seem to invite this type of circular reasoning. For example, people often say things like "That person is delusional because she is schizophrenic," or "He is afraid of small, enclosed places because he is claustrophobic." These statements are just as logical as saying "She is a redhead because she has red hair." The logical fallacy of mistaking a label for an explanation will get us as far in our understanding as a dog gets in chasing its own tail.

Key Ideas

On the Nature of Consciousness

❚ Consciousness is the continually changing stream of mental activity. People have some degree of awareness during sleep and sometimes even when they are under anesthesia.

❚ Consciousness clearly is adaptive, but the question of exactly why it evolved is open to debate. Variations in consciousness are related to brain activity, as measured by the EEG.

Biological Rhythms and Sleep

❚ The cycle of sleep and wakefulness is influenced by circadian rhythms. Exposure to light resets biological clocks by affecting the activity of the suprachiasmatic nucleus and the pineal gland, which secretes melatonin.

❚ Being out of sync with circadian rhythms is one reason for jet lag and for the unpleasant nature of rotating shift work. Melatonin may have some value in treating jet lag. The negative effects of rotating shifts may be reduced by bright-light administration or circadian-friendly scheduling.

The Sleep and Waking Cycle

❚ During the night, sleepers go through a series of stages in cycles of approximately 90 minutes. During the REM stage they experience rapid eye movements, brain waves characteristic of waking thought, and vivid dreaming. The sleep cycle tends to be repeated four times in a night, as REM sleep gradually becomes more predominant and NREM sleep dwindles, although the architecture of sleep varies somewhat among people.

❚ The REM portion of sleep declines during childhood, leveling off at around 20%. During adulthood, total sleep tends to decline gradually. Culture appears to have little impact on the physiological experience of sleep, but it does influence sleeping arrangements and napping patterns.

❚ The modulation of sleep and arousal depends on a constellation of brain structures and a variety of neurotransmitters. Hypotheses about the evolutionary bases of sleep focus on energy conservation, reduced exposure to predators, and restoration of depleted resources.

❚ People often underestimate the impact of sleep deprivation. Going without sleep appears to contribute to many transportation accidents and mishaps at work. Research on selective sleep deprivation suggests that people need REM sleep and slow-wave sleep. These stages of sleep may contribute to the process of memory consolidation. Sleep loss may have negative ramifications for health and mortality.

❚ Many people are troubled by sleep disorders. Foremost among these disorders is insomnia, which has a variety of causes. Other common sleep problems include narcolepsy, sleep apnea, night terrors, nightmares, and somnambulism.

The World of Dreams

❚ The conventional view is that dreams are mental experiences during REM sleep that have a storylike quality, include vivid imagery, are often bizarre, and are regarded as real by the dreamer, but theorists have begun to question many aspects of this view.

❚ The content of one's dreams may be affected by one's gender, events in one's life, and external stimuli experienced during the dream. There are variations across cultures in dream recall, content, and interpretation.

❚ Freud argued that the purpose of dreams is wish fulfillment. Cartwright has articulated a problem-solving view, whereas Hobson asserts that dreams are side effects of the neural activation seen during REM sleep.

Hypnosis: Altered Consciousness or Role Playing?

❚ Hypnosis has a long and curious history. People vary in their susceptibility to hypnosis. Among other things, hypnosis can produce anesthesia, sensory distortions, disinhibition, and posthypnotic amnesia.

❚ The two major theoretical approaches to hypnosis view it either as an altered state of consciousness or as a normal state of consciousness in which subjects assume a hypnotic role.

Meditation: Pure Consciousness or Relaxation?

❚ Evidence suggests that meditation leads to a potentially beneficial physiological state characterized by suppression of bodily arousal. However, the long-term benefits of meditation may not be unique to meditation, and critics are worried about methodological flaws in meditation research.

Altering Consciousness with Drugs

❚ Recreational drug use involves an effort to alter consciousness with psychoactive drugs. Such drugs exert their main effects in the brain, where they alter neurotransmitter activity in a variety of ways. The mesolimbic dopamine pathway may mediate the reinforcing effects of most abused drugs.

❚ Drugs vary in their potential for psychological and physical dependence. Likewise, the dangers to health vary depending on the drug. Recreational drug use can prove harmful to health by producing an overdose, by causing tissue damage, or by increasing health-impairing behavior.

Reflecting on the Chapter's Themes

❚ Five of our unifying themes were highlighted in this chapter. We saw that psychology evolves in a sociohistorical context, that experience is highly subjective, that culture influences many aspects of behavior, that behavior is governed by multiple factors, and that psychology is characterized by theoretical diversity.

PERSONAL APPLICATION Addressing Practical Questions About Sleep and Dreams

❚ People's sleep needs vary, although many could benefit from more sleep. The value of short naps depends on many factors, but they can be beneficial. Snoring has more medical significance than most people realize.

❚ People can do many things to avoid or reduce sleep problems. Mostly, it's a matter of developing good daytime habits that do not interfere with sleep. Individuals troubled by transient insomnia should avoid panic, pursue relaxation, and try distracting themselves.

❚ Everyone dreams, but some people cannot remember their dreams, probably because of the nature of their sleep cycle. In lucid dreams, people consciously recognize that they are dreaming and exert some control over the events in their dreams. Most theorists believe that dreams require some interpretation, but doing so may not be as complicated as once assumed.

CRITICAL THINKING APPLICATION Is Alcoholism a Disease? The Power of Definitions

❚ Like many questions, the issue of whether alcoholism should be regarded as a disease is a matter of definition. In evaluating the validity of a definition, one should look not only at the definition but also at where it came from. People have a tendency to use definitions as explanations for the phenomena they describe, but doing so involves circular reasoning.

Key Terms

Alcohol (p. 216)
Ascending reticular activating system (ARAS) (p. 196)
Biological rhythms (p. 188)
Cannabis (p. 215)
Circadian rhythms (p. 188)
Dissociation (p. 211)
Electroencephalograph (EEG) (p. 187)
Electromyograph (EMG) (p. 191)
Electrooculograph (EOG) (p. 191)
Hallucinogens (p. 215)
Hypnosis (p. 208)
Insomnia (p. 200)
Latent content (p. 206)
Lucid dreams (p. 225)
Manifest content (p. 206)
MDMA (p. 216)
Meditation (p. 212)
Narcolepsy (p. 202)
Narcotics (p. 214)
Night terrors (p. 202)
Nightmares (p. 202)
Non-REM (NREM) sleep (p. 193)
Opiates (p. 214)
Physical dependence (p. 218)
Psychoactive drugs (p. 214)
Psychological dependence (p. 218)
REM sleep (p. 193)
Sedatives (p. 214)
Sleep apnea (p. 202)
Slow-wave sleep (SWS) (p. 192)
Somnambulism (p. 203)
Stimulants (p. 214)
Tolerance (p. 216)

Key People

Rosalind Cartwright (p. 207)
William Dement (pp. 186, 197, 205–206)
Sigmund Freud (pp. 186–87, 206)
Calvin Hall (p. 204)
Ernest Hilgard (p. 211)
J. Allan Hobson (p. 207)
William James (p. 186)

1. An EEG would indicate primarily _____ activity while you take this test.
   A. alpha
   B. beta
   C. delta
   D. theta

2. Other things being equal, which of the following flights would lead to the greatest difficulty with jet lag?
   A. northward
   B. southward
   C. eastward
   D. westward

3. Slow-wave sleep consists of stages _____ of sleep and is dominated by _____ waves.
   A. 1 and 2; beta
   B. 2 and 3; alpha
   C. 3 and 4; delta
   D. 1 and 2; delta

4. As the sleep cycle evolves through the night, people tend to:
   A. spend more time in REM sleep and less time in NREM sleep.
   B. spend more time in NREM sleep and less time in REM sleep.
   C. spend a more or less equal amount of time in REM sleep and NREM sleep.
   D. spend more time in stage 4 sleep and less time in REM sleep.

5. Newborn infants spend about _____% of their sleep time in REM, while adults spend about _____% of their sleep time in REM.
   A. 20; 50
   B. 50; 20
   C. 20; 20
   D. 50; 50

6. Tamara has taken part in a three-day study in which she was awakened every time she went in to REM sleep. Now that she is home sleeping without interference, it is likely that she will:
   A. exhibit psychotic symptoms for a few nights.
   B. experience severe insomnia for about a week.
   C. spend extra time in REM sleep for a few nights.
   D. spend less time in REM sleep for a few nights.

7. Which of the following is associated with REM sleep?
   A. sleep apnea
   B. somnambulism
   C. night terrors
   D. nightmares

8. Which of the following is *not* true of cultural influences on dream experiences?
   A. The ability to recall dreams is fairly consistent across cultures.
   B. In some cultures, people are held responsible for their dream actions.
   C. In Western cultures, dreams are not taken very seriously.
   D. People in some cultures believe that dreams provide information about the future.

9. The activation-synthesis theory of dreaming contends that:
   A. dreams are simply the by-product of bursts of activity in the brain.
   B. dreams provide an outlet for energy invested in socially undesirable impulses.
   C. dreams represent the person's attempt to fulfill unconscious wishes.
   D. dreams are an attempt to restore a neurotransmitter balance within the brain.

10. A common driving experience is "highway hypnosis," in which one's consciousness seems to be divided between the driving itself and one's conscious train of thought. This phenomenon is consistent with the idea that hypnosis is:
    A. an exercise in role playing.
    B. a dissociated state of consciousness.
    C. a goal-directed fantasy.
    D. not an altered state of consciousness.

11. Stimulant is to depressant as:
    A. cocaine is to alcohol.
    B. mescaline is to barbiturates.
    C. caffeine is to amphetamines.
    D. alcohol is to barbiturates.

12. Amphetamines work by increasing the levels of _____ in a variety of ways.
    A. GABA and glycine
    B. melatonin
    C. acetylcholine
    D. norepinephrine and dopamine

13. Which of the following drugs would be most likely to result in a fatal overdose?
    A. LSD
    B. mescaline
    C. marijuana
    D. sedatives

14. Which of the following is a true statement about naps?
    A. Daytime naps invariably lead to insomnia.
    B. Daytime naps are invariably refreshing and an efficient way to rest.
    C. Daytime naps are not very efficient ways to sleep, but their effects are sometimes beneficial.
    D. Taking many naps during the day can substitute for a full night's sleep.

15. Definitions:
    A. generally emerge out of research.
    B. often have great explanatory value.
    C. generally exert little influence over how people think.
    D. are usually constructed by experts or authorities in a specific field.

Answers

1 B p. 187	6 C p. 199	11 A pp. 214–216
2 C pp. 189–190	7 D pp. 202–203	12 D pp. 217–218
3 C p. 192	8 A p. 206	13 D pp. 217, 219
4 A pp. 193–194	9 A p. 207	14 C p. 223
5 B pp. 193–194	10 B p. 211	15 D pp. 226–227

PsykTrek

To view a demo: www.cengage.com/psychology/psyktrek
To order: www.cengage.com/psychology/weiten
Go to the PsykTrek website or CD-ROM for further study of the concepts in this chapter. Both online and on the CD-ROM, PsykTrek includes dozens of learning modules with videos, animations, and quizzes, as well as simulations of psychological phenomena and a multimedia glossary that includes word pronunciations.

CengageNow

www.cengage.com/tlc
Go to this site for the link to CengageNOW, your one-stop study shop. Take a Pretest for this chapter, and CengageNOW will generate a personalized Study Plan based on your test results. The Study Plan will identify the topics you need to review and direct you to online resources to help you master those topics. You can then take a Posttest to help you determine the concepts you have mastered and what you still need to work on.

Companion Website

www.cengage.com/psychology/weiten
Go to this site to find online resources directly linked to your book, including a glossary, flash cards, drag-and-drop exercises, quizzes, and more!

6 LEARNING

Classical Conditioning
Pavlov's Demonstration: "Psychic Reflexes"
Terminology and Procedures
Classical Conditioning in Everyday Life
Basic Processes in Classical Conditioning

Operant Conditioning
Thorndike's Law of Effect
Skinner's Demonstration: It's All a Matter of Consequences
Terminology and Procedures
Basic Processes in Operant Conditioning
Schedules of Reinforcement
Positive Reinforcement Versus Negative Reinforcement
Punishment: Consequences That Weaken Responses

Changing Directions in the Study of Conditioning
Recognizing Biological Constraints on Conditioning
Recognizing Cognitive Processes in Conditioning

Observational Learning
Basic Processes
Acquisition Versus Performance
Observational Learning and the Media Violence Controversy

FEATURED STUDY ‖ The Power of Modeling: What They See Is What You Get

Illustrated Overview of Three Types of Learning

Reflecting on the Chapter's Themes

PERSONAL APPLICATION ‖ Achieving Self-Control Through Behavior Modification
Specifying Your Target Behavior
Gathering Baseline Data
Designing Your Program
Executing and Evaluating Your Program

CRITICAL THINKING APPLICATION ‖ Manipulating Emotions: Pavlov and Persuasion
Classical Conditioning in Advertising
Classical Conditioning in Business Negotiations
Classical Conditioning in the World of Politics
Becoming More Aware of Classical Conditioning Processes

Recap

Practice Test

Let's see if you can guess the answer to a riddle. What do the following scenarios have in common?

• In 1953 a Japanese researcher observed a young macaque (a type of monkey) on the island of Koshima washing a sweet potato in a stream before eating it. No one had ever seen a macaque do this before. Soon, other members of the monkey's troop were showing the same behavior. Several generations later, macaques on Koshima still wash their potatoes before eating them (De Waal, 2001).
• In 2005 Wade Boggs was elected to baseball's Hall of Fame. Boggs was as renowned for his superstitions as he was for his great hitting. For 20 years Boggs ate chicken every day of the year. Before games he followed a rigorous set of rituals that included stepping on the bases in reverse order, running wind sprints at precisely 17 minutes past the hour, and tossing exactly three pebbles off the field. Every time he stepped up to hit during a game, he drew the Hebrew letter *chai* in the dirt with his bat. For Boggs, the slightest deviation in this routine was profoundly upsetting (Gaddis, 1999; Vyse, 2000).

• Barn swallows in Minnesota have built nests inside a Home Depot warehouse store, safe from the weather and from predators. So how do they get in and out to bring food to their chicks when the doors are closed? They flutter near the motion sensors that operate the doors until they open!
• A firefighter in Georgia routinely braves life-threatening situations to rescue people in distress. Yet the firefighter is paralyzed with fear whenever he sees someone dressed as a clown. He has been terrified of clowns ever since the third grade (Ryckeley, 2005).

What common thread runs through these diverse situations? What connects a superstitious ballplayer or a clown-phobic firefighter to potato-washing monkeys and door-opening swallows?

The answer is *learning*. That may surprise you. When most people think of learning, they picture students reading textbooks or novices gaining proficiency in a skill, such as skiing or playing the guitar. To a psychologist, however, **learning** is any relatively durable change in behavior or knowledge that is due to experience. Macaques aren't born with the habit of washing their sweet potatoes, nor do swallows begin life knowing how to operate motion sensors. Wade Boggs adopted his superstitious rituals because they seemed to be associated with his successfully hitting a baseball. The firefighter in Georgia wasn't born with a fear of clowns, since he only began to be frightened of them in the third grade. In short, all these behaviors are the product of experience—that is, they represent learning.

When you think about it, it would be hard to name a lasting change in behavior that *isn't* the result of experience. That is why learning is one of the most fundamental concepts in all of psychology. Learning shapes personal habits, such as nailbiting; personality traits, such as shyness; personal preferences, such as a distaste for formal clothes; and emotional responses, such as reactions to favorite songs. If all your learned responses could somehow be stripped away, little of your behavior would be left. You would not be able to talk, read a book, or cook yourself a hamburger. You would be about as complex and interesting as a turnip.

As the examples at the start of this discussion show, learning is not an exclusively human process. Learning is pervasive in the animal world as well, a fact that won't amaze anyone who has ever owned a dog or seen a trained seal in action. Another insight, however, is considerably more startling: *The principles that explain learned responses in animals explain much of human learning, too.* Thus, the same mechanisms that explain how barn swallows learn to operate an automated door can account for a professional athlete's bizarre superstitions. Indeed, many of the most fascinating discoveries in the study of learning originated in studies of animals.

In this chapter, you will see how fruitful the research into learning has been and how wide ranging its applications are. We will focus most of our attention on a specific kind of learning: conditioning. *Conditioning* involves learning associations between events that occur in an organism's environment (eating chicken and having success hitting a baseball is one example). In investigating conditioning, psychologists study learning at a fundamental level. This strategy has paid off with insights that have laid the foundation for the study of more complex forms of learning, such as learning by observation (the kind of learning that may account for the Koshima macaques picking up one monkey's habit of washing her sweet potatoes). In the Personal Application, you'll see how you can harness the principles of conditioning to improve your self-control. The Critical Thinking Application shows how conditioning procedures can be used to manipulate emotions.

Key Learning Goals

6.1 Describe Pavlov's demonstration of classical conditioning and the key elements in this form of learning.

6.2 Clarify how classical conditioning may shape emotions and physiological processes, including drug effects.

6.3 Describe acquisition, extinction, and spontaneous recovery in classical conditioning.

6.4 Compare the processes of generalization and discrimination, and review the classic study of Little Albert.

6.5 Explain what happens in higher-order conditioning.

Classical Conditioning

Do you go weak in the knees at the thought of standing on the roof of a tall building? Does your heart race when you imagine encountering a harmless garter snake? If so, you can understand, at least to some degree, what it's like to have a phobia. *Phobias* are irrational fears of specific objects or situations. Mild phobias are commonplace. Over the years, students in my classes have described their phobic responses to a diverse array of stimuli, including bridges, elevators, tunnels, heights, dogs, cats, bugs, snakes, professors, doctors, strangers, thunderstorms, and germs. If you have a phobia, you may have wondered how you managed to acquire such a perplexing fear. Chances are, it was through classical conditioning (Antony & McCabe, 2003).

Classical conditioning is a type of learning in which a stimulus acquires the capacity to evoke a response that was originally evoked by another stimulus. The process was first described around 1900 by Ivan Pavlov, and it is sometimes called *Pavlovian conditioning* in tribute to him. The term *conditioning* came from Pavlov's determination to discover the "conditions" that produce this kind of learning. The learning process described by Pavlov was characterized as "classical" conditioning decades later (starting in the 1940s) to distinguish it from other types of conditioning that attracted research interest around then (Clark, 2004).

Pavlov's Demonstration: "Psychic Reflexes"

Ivan Pavlov was a prominent Russian physiologist who did Nobel prize–winning research on digestion. Something of a "classic" himself, he was an absent-minded but brilliant professor obsessed with his research. Legend has it that Pavlov once reprimanded an assistant who arrived late for an experiment because of trying to avoid street fighting in the midst of the Russian Revolution. The assistant defended his tardiness, saying, "But Professor, there's a revolution going on with shooting in the streets!" Pavlov supposedly replied, "What the hell difference does a revolution make when you've work to do in the laboratory? Next time there's a revolution, get up earlier!" Apparently, dodging bullets wasn't an adequate excuse for delaying the march of scientific progress (Fancher, 1979; Gantt, 1975).

Pavlov was studying the role of saliva in the digestive processes of dogs when he stumbled onto what he called "psychic reflexes" (Pavlov, 1906). Like many great discoveries, Pavlov's was partly acciden-

Ivan Pavlov
"Next time there's a revolution, get up earlier!"

Surrounded by his research staff, the great Russian physiologist Ivan Pavlov (center, white beard) demonstrates his famous classical conditioning experiment with dogs.

tal, although he had the insight to recognize its significance. His subjects were dogs restrained in harnesses in an experimental chamber (see Figure 6.1). Their saliva was collected by means of a surgically implanted tube in the salivary gland. Pavlov would present meat powder to a dog and then collect the resulting saliva. As his research progressed, he noticed that dogs accustomed to the procedure would start salivating *before* the meat powder was presented. For instance, they would salivate in response to a clicking sound made by the device that was used to present the meat powder.

Intrigued by this unexpected finding, Pavlov decided to investigate further. To clarify what was happening, he paired the presentation of the meat powder with various stimuli that would stand out in the laboratory situation. For instance, in some experiments he used a simple auditory stimulus—the presentation of a tone. After the tone and the meat powder had been presented together a number of times, the tone was presented alone. What happened? The dogs responded by salivating to the sound of the tone alone.

What was so significant about a dog salivating when a tone was presented? The key is that the tone started out as a *neutral* stimulus. That is, it did not originally produce the response of salivation. However, Pavlov managed to change that by pair-

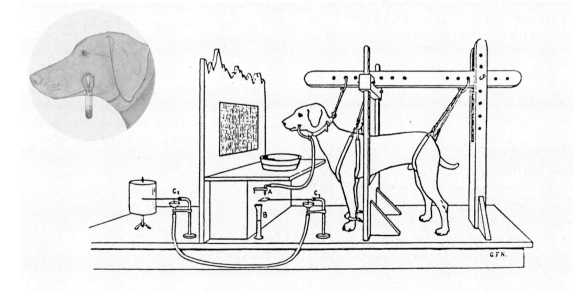

Figure 6.1

Classical conditioning apparatus. An experimental arrangement similar to the one depicted here (taken from Yerkes & Morgulis, 1909) has typically been used in demonstrations of classical conditioning, although Pavlov's original setup (see inset) was quite a bit simpler. The dog is restrained in a harness. A tone is used as the conditioned stimulus (CS), and the presentation of meat powder is used as the unconditioned stimulus (US). The tube inserted into the dog's salivary gland allows precise measurement of its salivation response. The pen and rotating drum of paper on the left are used to maintain a continuous record of salivary flow. (Inset) The less elaborate setup that Pavlov originally used to collect saliva on each trial is shown here (Goodwin, 1991).

"HE SALIVATES."

© 2004 by Sidney Harris. ScienceCartoonPlus.com

ing the tone with a stimulus (meat powder) that did produce the salivation response. Through this process, the tone acquired the capacity to trigger the response of salivation. What Pavlov had demonstrated was how learned associations—which were viewed as the basic building blocks of the entire learning process—were formed by events in an organism's environment. Based on this insight, he built a broad theory of learning that attempted to explain aspects of emotion, temperament, neuroses, and language (Windholz, 1997). His research and theory proved enormously influential around the world and remains so today (Boakes, 2003; Marks, 2004).

Terminology and Procedures

5a

Classical conditioning has its own special vocabulary. Although it may seem intimidating to the uninitiated, this terminology is not all that mysterious. The bond Pavlov noted between the meat powder and salivation was a natural, unlearned association. It did not have to be created through conditioning. It is therefore called an *unconditioned* association. Thus, **the *unconditioned stimulus (US)* is a stimulus that evokes an unconditioned response without previous conditioning. The *unconditioned response (UR)* is an unlearned reaction to an unconditioned stimulus that occurs without previous conditioning.**

In contrast, the link between the tone and salivation was established through conditioning. It is therefore called a *conditioned* association. Thus, **the *conditioned stimulus (CS)* is a previously neutral stimulus that has, through conditioning, acquired the capacity to evoke a conditioned response. The *conditioned response (CR)* is a learned reaction to a conditioned stimulus that occurs because of previous conditioning.** In Pavlov's initial demonstration, the UR and CR were both salivation. When evoked by the US (meat powder), salivation was an unconditioned response. When evoked by the CS (the tone), salivation was a conditioned response. Although the unconditioned response and conditioned response sometimes consist of the same behavior, there usually are subtle differences between them, as conditioned responses often are weaker or less intense. And in some cases the UR and CR may be quite different, albeit intimately related. For example, if an animal is given a brief shock as a US, the unconditioned response is *pain,* whereas the conditioned response is *fear* of imminent pain. In any event, the procedures involved in classical conditioning are outlined in Figure 6.2.

Pavlov's "psychic reflex" came to be called the *conditioned reflex.* Classically conditioned responses have traditionally been characterized as reflexes and are said to be *elicited* (drawn forth) because most of them are relatively automatic or involuntary. However, research in recent decades has demonstrated that classical conditioning is involved in a wider range of human and animal behavior than previously appreciated, including some types of non-reflexive responding (Allan, 1998). Finally, **a *trial* in classical conditioning consists of any presentation of a stimulus or pair of stimuli.** Psychologists are interested in how many trials are required to establish a particular conditioned bond. The number of trials needed to form an association varies considerably. Although classical conditioning generally proceeds gradually, it *can* occur quite rapidly, sometimes in just one pairing of the CS and US.

Classical Conditioning in Everyday Life

5a

In laboratory experiments on classical conditioning, researchers have generally worked with extremely simple responses. Besides salivation, frequently studied favorites include eyelid closure, knee jerks, and the flexing of various limbs. The study of such simple responses has proven both practical and productive. However, these responses do not even begin to convey the rich diversity of everyday behaviors regulated by classical conditioning. Let's look at some examples of classical conditioning taken from everyday life.

Conditioned Fears

Classical conditioning often plays a key role in shaping emotional responses such as fears. Phobias are a good example of such responses. Case studies of patients suffering from phobias suggest that many irrational fears can be traced back to experiences that involve classical conditioning (Antony & McCabe, 2003; Muris & Mercklebach, 2001). It is easy to imagine how such conditioning can occur outside of the laboratory. For example, a student of mine troubled by a severe bridge phobia was able to pinpoint childhood conditioning experiences as the source of her phobia (see **Figure 6.3**). Whenever her family drove to visit her grandmother, they had to cross a rickety, dilapidated bridge in the countryside. Her father, in a misguided attempt at humor, would stop short of the bridge and carry on about the enormous danger. The naive young girl was terrified by her father's scare tactics. Hence, the bridge became a conditioned stimulus eliciting great fear. Unfortunately, the fear spilled over to *all* bridges and 40 years later she was still troubled by this phobia.

Everyday fear responses that are less severe than phobias may also be products of classical conditioning. For instance, if you cringe when you hear the sound of a dentist's drill, this response is a result of classical conditioning. In this case, pain has been paired with the sound of the drill, which became a CS eliciting your cringe.

That is *not* to say that traumatic experiences associated with stimuli *automatically* lead to conditioned fears or phobias. Whether fear conditioning takes place depends on a constellation of factors. Some people acquire conditioned fears less readily than others, probably because of differences in their genetic makeup (Hettema et al., 2003). Conditioned fears are less likely to develop when events seem escapable and controllable and when people have a history of nontraumatic encounters in similar situations (for example, with dentists) (Mineka & Zinbarg, 2006).

Other Conditioned Emotional Responses

Classical conditioning is not limited to producing unpleasant emotions such as fear. Many pleasant emotional responses are also acquired through classical conditioning. Consider the following example, described by a woman who wrote a letter to a newspaper columnist about the news that a company was

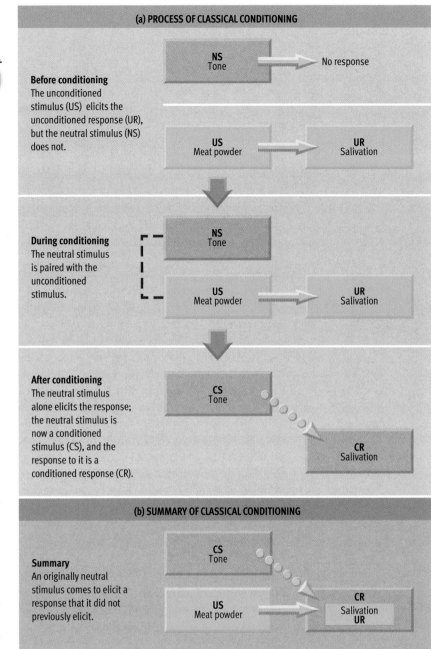

Figure 6.2

The sequence of events in classical conditioning. (a) Moving downward, this series of three panels outlines the sequence of events in classical conditioning, using Pavlov's original demonstration as an example. **(b)** As you encounter other examples of classical conditioning throughout the book, you will see many diagrams like the one in this panel, which will provide snapshots of specific instances of classical conditioning.

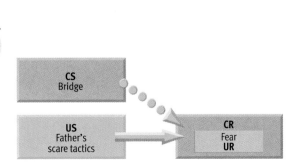

Figure 6.3

Classical conditioning of a fear response. Many emotional responses that would otherwise be puzzling can be explained by classical conditioning. In the case of one woman's bridge phobia, the fear originally elicited by her father's scare tactics became a conditioned response to the stimulus of bridges.

bringing back a discontinued product—Beemans gum. She wrote:

That was the year I met Charlie. I guess first love is always the same. . . . Charlie and I went out a lot. He chewed Beemans gum and he smoked. . . . We would go to all the passion pits—the drive-in movies and the places to park. We did a lot of necking. . . [but] Charlie and I drifted apart. We both ended up getting married to different people.

And the funny thing is . . . for years the combined smell of cigarette smoke and Beemans gum made my knees weak. Those two smells were Charlie to me. When I would smell the Beemans and the cigarette smoke, I could feel the butterflies dancing all over my stomach.

The writer clearly had a unique and long-lasting emotional response to the smell of Beemans gum and cigarettes. The credit for this *pleasant* response goes to classical conditioning (see **Figure 6.4**).

Advertising campaigns often try to take advantage of classical conditioning (see the Personal Application for this chapter). Advertisers often pair their products with USs that elicit pleasant emotions (Till & Priluck, 2000). The most common strategy is to present a product in association with an attractive person or enjoyable surroundings. Advertisers hope that these pairings will make their products conditioned stimuli that evoke good feelings. For example, automobile manufacturers like to show their sports-utility vehicles in stunningly beautiful outdoor vistas that evoke pleasant feelings and nostalgic thoughts of past vacations.

Conditioning and Physiological Responses

5a

Classical conditioning affects not only overt behaviors but physiological processes as well. Consider, for example, your body's immune functioning. When an infectious agent invades your body, your immune system attempts to repel the invasion by producing specialized proteins called *antibodies*. The critical importance of the immune response becomes evident when the immune system is disabled, as occurs with the disease AIDS (acquired immune deficiency syndrome).

Research has revealed that the functioning of the immune system can be influenced by psychological factors, including conditioning (Ader, 2001, 2003). Robert Ader and Nicholas Cohen (1984, 1993) have shown that classical conditioning procedures can lead to *immunosuppression*—a decrease in the production of antibodies. In a typical study, animals are injected with a drug (the US) that *chemically* causes immunosuppression while they are simultaneously given an unusual-tasting liquid to drink (the CS). Days later, after the chemical immunosuppression has ended, some of the animals are reexposed to the CS by giving them the unusual-tasting solution. Measurements of antibody production indicate that animals exposed to the CS show a reduced immune response (see **Figure 6.5**).

Studies have also demonstrated that classical conditioning can influence *sexual arousal* (Pfaus, Kippin, & Centeno, 2001). For example, research has shown that quail can be conditioned to become sexually aroused by a neutral, nonsexual stimulus—such as a red light—that has been paired with opportunities to copulate (Domjan, 1992, 1994). Conditioned stimuli can even elicit *increased sperm release* in male quail—a conditioned response that would convey an obvious evolutionary advantage (Domjan, Blesbois, & Williams, 1998). This line of research bolsters the idea that stimuli routinely paired with human sexual interactions, such as seductive nightgowns, mood music, lit candles, and the like, probably become conditioned stimuli that elicit arousal (as you might guess, this hypothesis has been difficult to investigate with human subjects). Classical conditioning may also underlie the development of *fetishes* for inanimate objects. If quail can be conditioned to find a red light arousing, it seems likely that humans may be conditioned to be aroused by objects such as shoes, boots, leather, and undergarments that may be paired with events eliciting sexual arousal.

Conditioning and Drug Effects

As we discussed in Chapter 5, *drug tolerance* involves a gradual decline in responsiveness to a drug with repeated use, so that larger and larger doses are required to attain the user's customary effect. Most theories assert that drug tolerance is largely attributable to physiological changes in the user. However, research by Shepard Siegel (2005) demonstrates that classical conditioning also contributes to drug tolerance—sometimes in unexpected ways.

Figure 6.4
Classical conditioning and romance. Pleasant emotional responses can be acquired through classical conditioning, as illustrated by one person's unusual conditioned response to the aroma of Beemans gum and cigarette smoke.

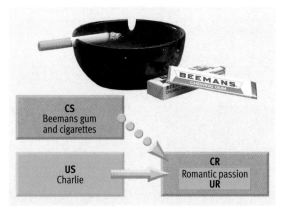

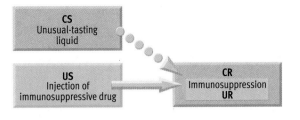

CS
Unusual-tasting liquid

US
Injection of immunosuppressive drug

CR
Immunosuppression
UR

Figure 6.5

Classical conditioning of immunosuppression. When a neutral stimulus is paired with a drug that chemically causes immunosuppression, it can become a CS that elicits immunosuppression on its own. Thus, even the immune response can be influenced by classical conditioning.

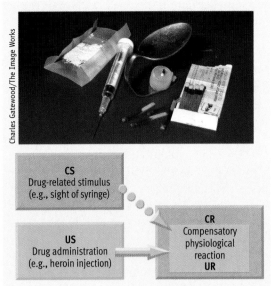

Charles Gatewood/The Image Works

CS
Drug-related stimulus (e.g., sight of syringe)

US
Drug administration (e.g., heroin injection)

CR
Compensatory physiological reaction
UR

Figure 6.6

The contribution of classical conditioning to drug tolerance. According to Siegel (2005), stimuli that are paired with drug administration often come to elicit compensatory CRs that partially offset some of the physiological effects of the drugs. The growth of these compensatory CRs contributes to users' tolerance of these drugs.

Stimuli that are consistently paired with administration of drugs can acquire the capacity to elicit conditioned responses in both humans and laboratory animals. There is a special wrinkle, however, when drug administration serves as a US. In many instances, the conditioned responses are physiological reactions that are just the *opposite* of the normal effects of the drugs (Siegel et al., 2000). These opponent responses, which have been seen as the result of conditioning with narcotics, stimulants, and alcohol, are called *compensatory CRs* because they partially compensate for some drug effects. These compensatory CRs help maintain homeostasis (internal balance) in physiological processes. They are adaptive in the short term, as they counterbalance some of the potentially dangerous effects of various drugs.

What role do these compensatory CRs play in drug tolerance? Most drug users have routines that lead to the consistent pairing of drug administration and certain stimuli, such as syringes, cocaine bottles, and specific settings and rituals. Even the drug administration process itself can become a CS associated with drug effects (Weise-Kelly & Siegel, 2001). According to Siegel (2005), these environmental cues eventually begin to elicit compensatory CRs that partially cancel out some of the anticipated effects of abused drugs (see **Figure 6.6**). As these compensatory CRs strengthen, they neutralize more and more of a drug's pleasureable effects, producing a gradual decline in the user's responsiveness to the drug (in other words, tolerance).

Things can go awry, however, when drug users depart from their normal drug routines. If drugs are taken in new ways or in new settings, the usual compensatory CRs may not occur. With their counterbalancing effects eliminated, the drugs may have a much stronger impact than usual, thus increasing the risk of an overdose (Siegel, 2001). This model may explain why heroin addicts seem more prone to overdose when they shoot up in unfamiliar settings.

Another problem is that when people try to quit drugs, exposure to drug-related cues—in the absence of actual drug administration—may trigger compensatory CRs that increase drug cravings and fuel drug addiction and relapse (McDonald & Siegel, 2004). Thus, complicated conditioning processes appear to play a role in drug tolerance, drug craving, and drug overdoses, which need to be factored into the treatment of drug addiction (Siegel & Ramos, 2002).

Basic Processes in Classical Conditioning

5b

Classical conditioning is often portrayed as a mechanical process that inevitably leads to a certain result. This view reflects the fact that most conditioned responses are reflexive and difficult to control—Pavlov's dogs would have been hard pressed to withhold their salivation. Similarly, most people with phobias have great difficulty suppressing their fear. However, this vision of classical conditioning as an "irresistible force" is misleading, because it fails to consider the many factors involved in classical conditioning (Kehoe & Macrae, 1998). In this section, we'll look at basic processes in classical conditioning to expand on the rich complexity of this form of learning.

Acquisition: Forming New Responses

5b

We have already discussed *acquisition* without attaching a formal name to the process. *Acquisition* **refers to the initial stage of learning something.** Pavlov theorized that the acquisition of a conditioned response depends on *stimulus contiguity,* or the occurrence of stimuli together in time and space.

Stimulus contiguity is important, but learning theorists now realize that contiguity alone doesn't automatically produce conditioning (Miller & Grace, 2003). People are bombarded daily by countless stimuli that could be perceived as being paired, yet only some of these pairings produce classical conditioning. Consider the woman who developed a conditioned emotional reaction to the smell of Beemans gum and cigarettes. There were no doubt other stimuli that shared contiguity with her boyfriend, Charlie. He smoked, so ashtrays were probably present, but she doesn't get weak in the knees at the sight of an ashtray.

If conditioning does not occur to all the stimuli present in a situation, what determines its occurrence? Evidence suggests that stimuli that are novel, unusual, or especially intense have more potential to become CSs than routine stimuli, probably because they are more likely to stand out among other stimuli (Hearst, 1988).

concept check 6.1

Identifying Elements in Classical Conditioning

Check your understanding of classical conditioning by trying to identify the unconditioned stimulus (US), unconditioned response (UR), conditioned stimulus (CS), and conditioned response (CR) in each of the examples below. Fill in the diagram next to each example. You'll find the answers in Appendix A in the back of the book.

1. Sam is 3 years old. One night his parents build a roaring fire in the family room fireplace. The fire spits out a large ember that hits Sam in the arm, giving him a nasty burn that hurts a great deal for several hours. A week later, when Sam's parents light another fire in the fireplace, Sam becomes upset and fearful, crying and running from the room.

2. Melanie is driving to work on a rainy highway when she notices that the brake lights of all the cars just ahead of her have come on. She hits her brakes but watches in horror as her car glides into a four-car pileup. She's badly shaken up in the accident. A month later she's driving in the rain again and notices that she tenses up every time she sees brake lights come on ahead of her.

3. At the age of 24, Tyrone has recently developed an allergy to cats. When he's in the same room with a cat for more than 30 minutes, he starts wheezing. After a few such allergic reactions, he starts wheezing as soon as he sees a cat in a room.

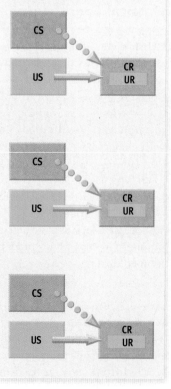

Extinction: Weakening Conditioned Responses

Fortunately, a newly formed stimulus-response bond does not necessarily last indefinitely. If it did, learning would be inflexible, and organisms would have difficulty adapting to new situations. Instead, the right circumstances produce *extinction,* **the gradual weakening and disappearance of a conditioned response tendency.**

What leads to extinction in classical conditioning? The consistent presentation of the conditioned stimulus *alone,* without the unconditioned stimulus. For example, when Pavlov consistently presented *only* the tone to a previously conditioned dog, the tone gradually lost its capacity to elicit the response of salivation. Such a sequence of events is depicted in the tan portion of **Figure 6.7,** which graphs the amount of salivation by a dog over a series of conditioning trials. Note how the salivation response declines during extinction.

For an example of extinction from outside the laboratory, let's assume that you cringe at the sound of a dentist's drill, which has been paired with pain in the past. You take a job as a dental assistant and you start hearing the drill (the CS) day in and day out without experiencing any pain (the US). Your cringing response will gradually diminish and extinguish altogether.

How long does it take to extinguish a conditioned response? That depends on many factors, but particularly important is the strength of the conditioned bond when extinction begins. Some conditioned responses extinguish quickly, while others are difficult to weaken. Conditioned *fears* tend to be relatively hard to extinguish.

Spontaneous Recovery: Resurrecting Responses

Some conditioned responses display the ultimate in tenacity by "reappearing from the dead" after having been extinguished. Learning theorists use the term *spontaneous recovery* to describe such a resurrection from the graveyard of conditioned associations. **Spontaneous recovery is the reappearance of an extinguished response after a period of nonexposure to the conditioned stimulus.**

Pavlov (1927) observed this phenomenon in some of his pioneering studies. He fully extinguished a dog's CR of salivation to a tone and then returned the dog to its home cage for a "rest interval" (a period of nonexposure to the CS). On a subsequent day, when the dog was brought back to the experimental chamber for retesting, the tone was sounded and the salivation response reappeared. Although it had returned, the rejuvenated response was weak. The amount of salivation was less than when the response was at its peak strength. If Pavlov consistently presented the CS by itself again, the response reextinguished quickly. However, in some of the dogs the response made still another spontaneous recovery (typically even weaker than the first) after they had spent another period in their cages (consult Figure 6.7 once again).

Recent studies have uncovered a related phenomenon called the *renewal effect*—if a response is extinguished in a different environment than it was acquired, the extinguished response will reappear if the animal is returned to the original environment where acquisition took place. This phenomenon, along with the evidence on spontaneous recovery, suggests that extinction somehow *suppresses* a conditioned response rather than *erasing* a learned association. In other words, *extinction does not appear to lead to unlearning* (Bouton, 2002, 2004). The theoretical meaning of spontaneous recovery and the renewal effect is complex and the subject of some debate. However, their practical meaning is quite simple. Even if you manage to rid yourself of an unwanted conditioned response (such as cringing when you hear a dental drill), there is an excellent chance that it may make a surprise reappearance later. This reality may also help explain why people who manage to give up cigarettes, drugs, or poor eating habits for a while often relapse and return to their unhealthy habits (Bouton, 2000, 2002). The renewal effect is also one of the reasons why conditioned fears and phobias are difficult to extinguish permanently (Hermans et al., 2006).

Stimulus Generalization and the Case of Little Albert

5b

After conditioning has occurred, organisms often show a tendency to respond not only to the exact CS used but also to other, similar stimuli. For example, Pavlov's dogs might have salivated in response to a different-sounding tone, or you might cringe at the sound of a jeweler's as well as a dentist's drill. These are examples of stimulus generalization. *Stimulus generalization* occurs when an organism that has learned a response to a specific stimulus responds in the same way to new stimuli that are similar to the original stimulus. Generalization is adaptive given that organisms rarely encounter the exact same stimulus more than once (Thomas, 1992). Stimulus generalization is also commonplace. We have already discussed a real-life example: the woman who acquired a bridge phobia during her childhood because her father scared her whenever

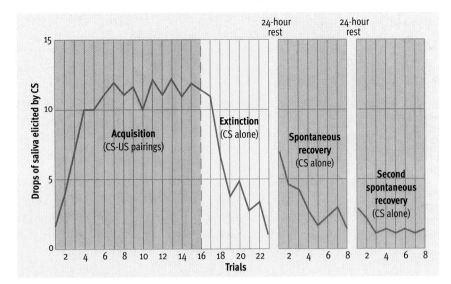

they went over a particular old bridge. The original CS for her fear was that specific bridge, but her fear was ultimately *generalized* to all bridges.

John B. Watson, the founder of behaviorism (see Chapter 1), conducted an influential early study of generalization. Watson and a colleague, Rosalie Rayner, examined the generalization of conditioned fear in an 11-month-old boy, known in the annals of psychology as "Little Albert." Like many babies, Albert was initially unafraid of a live white rat. Then Watson and Rayner (1920) paired the presentation of the rat with a loud, startling sound (made by striking a steel gong with a hammer). Albert *did* show fear in response to the loud noise. After seven pairings of the rat and the gong, the rat was established as a CS eliciting a fear response (see Figure 6.8). Five days later, Watson and Rayner exposed the youngster to other stimuli that resembled the rat in being white and furry. They found that Albert's fear response generalized to a

Figure 6.7
Acquisition, extinction, and spontaneous recovery. During acquisition, the strength of the dog's conditioned response (measured by the amount of salivation) increases rapidly, then levels off near its maximum. During extinction, the CR declines erratically until it's extinguished. After a "rest" period in which the dog is not exposed to the CS, a spontaneous recovery occurs, and the CS once again elicits a (weakened) CR. Repeated presentations of the CS alone reextinguish the CR, but after another "rest" interval, a weaker spontaneous recovery occurs.

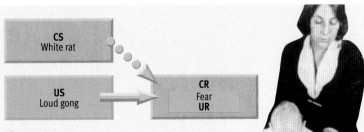

Figure 6.8
The conditioning of Little Albert. The diagram shows how Little Albert's fear response to a white rat was established. Albert's fear response to other white, furry objects illustrates generalization. In the photo, made from a 1919 film, John B. Watson's collaborator, Rosalie Rayner, is shown with Little Albert before he was conditioned to fear the rat.

John B. Watson

"Surely this proof of the conditioned origin of a fear response puts us on natural science grounds in our study of emotional behavior."

variety of stimuli, including a rabbit, a dog, a fur coat, a Santa Claus mask, and Watson's hair.

The likelihood and amount of generalization to a new stimulus depend on the similarity between the new stimulus and the original CS (Balsam, 1988). The basic law governing generalization is this: *The more similar new stimuli are to the original CS, the greater the generalization.* This principle can be quantified in graphs called *generalization gradients,* such as those shown in Figure 6.9. These generalization gradients map out how a dog conditioned to salivate to a tone of 1200 hertz might respond to other tones. As you can see, the strength of the generalization response declines as the similarity between the new stimuli and the original CS decreases.

Stimulus Discrimination 5b

Stimulus discrimination is just the opposite of stimulus generalization. *Stimulus discrimination* **occurs when an organism that has learned a response to a specific stimulus does** *not* **respond in the same way to new stimuli that are similar to the original stimulus.** Like generalization, discrimination is adaptive in that an animal's survival may hinge on its being able to distinguish friend from foe, or edible from poisonous food (Thomas, 1992). Organisms can gradually learn to discriminate between an original CS and similar stimuli if they have adequate experience with

both. For instance, let's say your pet dog runs around, excitedly wagging its tail, whenever it hears your car pull up in the driveway. Initially it will probably respond to *all* cars that pull into the driveway (stimulus generalization). However, if there is anything distinctive about the sound of your car, your dog may gradually respond with excitement to only your car and not to other cars (stimulus discrimination).

The development of stimulus discrimination usually requires that the original CS (your car) continue to be paired with the US (your arrival) while similar stimuli (the other cars) not be paired with the US. As with generalization, a basic law governs discrimination: *The less similar new stimuli are to the original CS, the greater the likelihood (and ease) of discrimination.* Conversely, if a new stimulus is quite similar to the original CS, discrimination will be relatively difficult to learn. What happens to a generalization gradient when an organism learns a discrimination? The generalization gradient gradually narrows around the original CS, which means that the organism is generalizing to a smaller and smaller range of similar stimuli (consult Figure 6.9 again).

Higher-Order Conditioning 5b

Imagine that you were to conduct the following experiment. First, you condition a dog to salivate in response to the sound of a tone by pairing the tone with meat powder. Once the tone is firmly established as a CS, you pair the tone with a new stimulus, let's say a red light, for 15 trials. You then present the red light alone, without the tone. Will the dog salivate in response to the red light?

The answer is "yes." Even though the red light has never been paired with the meat powder, the light will acquire the capacity to elicit salivation by virtue of being paired with the tone (see Figure 6.10). This is a demonstration of *higher-order conditioning,* **in which a conditioned stimulus functions as if it were an unconditioned stimulus.** Higher-order conditioning shows that classical conditioning does not depend on the presence of a genuine, natural US. An already established CS can do just fine. In higher-order conditioning, new conditioned responses are built on the foundation of already established conditioned responses. Many human conditioned responses are the product of higher-order conditioning (Rescorla, 1980). For example, while driving, many people react to the sight of a police car with a surge of anxiety, even if they are under the speed limit. This reflexive response is an example of higher-order conditioning (the visual stimulus of a police car has probably been paired with a traffic ticket in the past, which is a previously established CS).

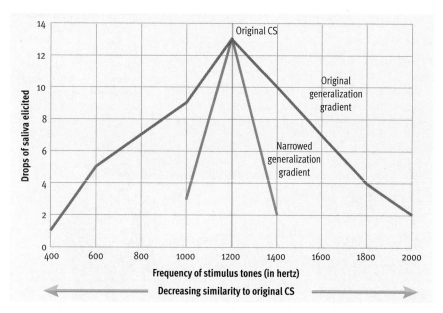

Figure 6.9

Generalization gradients. In a study of stimulus generalization, an organism is typically conditioned to respond to a specific CS, such as a 1200-hertz tone, and then is tested with similar stimuli, such as other tones between 400 and 2000 hertz. Graphs of the organism's responding are called *generalization gradients.* The graphs normally show, as depicted here, that generalization declines as the similarity between the original CS and the new stimuli decreases. When an organism gradually learns to *discriminate* between a CS and similar stimuli, the generalization gradient tends to narrow around the original CS (as shown in orange).

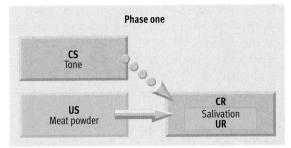

Phase one

CS
Tone

US
Meat powder

CR
Salivation
UR

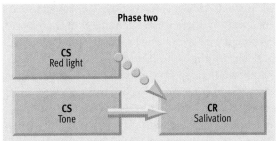

Phase two

CS
Red light

CS
Tone

CR
Salivation

Figure 6.10
Higher-order conditioning. Higher-order conditioning involves a two-phase process. In the first phase, a neutral stimulus (such as a tone) is paired with an unconditioned stimulus (such as meat powder) until it becomes a conditioned stimulus that elicits the response originally evoked by the US (such as salivation). In the second phase, another neutral stimulus (such as a red light) is paired with the previously established CS, so that it also acquires the capacity to elicit the response originally evoked by the US.

REVIEW of Key Learning Goals

6.1 Classical conditioning explains how a neutral stimulus can acquire the capacity to elicit a response originally elicited by another stimulus. This kind of conditioning was originally described by Ivan Pavlov, who conditioned dogs to salivate in response to the sound of a tone. The key elements in classical conditioning are the unconditioned stimulus (US), the unconditioned response (UR), the conditioned stimulus (CS), and the conditioned response (CR). Classically conditioned responses are said to be elicited.

6.2 Many kinds of everyday responses are regulated through classical conditioning, including phobias, mild fears, and pleasant emotional responses. Even subtle physiological responses such as immune system functioning and sexual arousal respond to classical conditioning. Compensatory CRs contribute to drug tolerance and may explain why overdoses are more likely to occur when drugs are used in new settings.

6.3 Stimulus contiguity plays a key role in the acquisition of new conditioned responses, but it does not produce conditioning automatically. A conditioned response may be weakened and extinguished when the CS is no longer paired with the US. In some cases, spontaneous recovery occurs and an extinguished response reappears after a period of nonexposure to the CS.

6.4 Conditioning may generalize to additional stimuli that are similar to the original CS. Watson and Rayner conducted an influential early study of generalization with a subject known as Little Albert, whose fear response to a rat generalized to a variety of other white, furry objects. The opposite of generalization is discrimination, which involves not responding to stimuli that resemble the original CS.

6.5 Classical conditioning does not require a genuine unconditioned stimulus, as an already established CS can serve the same role. Higher-order conditioning occurs when a CS functions as if it were a US.

Operant Conditioning

Even Pavlov recognized that classical conditioning is not the only form of conditioning. Classical conditioning best explains reflexive responding that is largely controlled by stimuli that *precede* the response. However, humans and other animals make a great many responses that don't fit this description. Consider the response that you are engaging in right now: studying. It is definitely not a reflex (life might be easier if it were). The stimuli that govern it (exams and grades) do not precede it. Instead, your studying is mainly influenced by stimulus events that *follow* the response—specifically, its *consequences*.

In the 1930s, this kind of learning was christened *operant conditioning* by B. F. Skinner. The term was derived from his belief that in this type of responding, an organism "operates" on the environment instead of simply reacting to stimuli. Learning occurs because responses come to be influenced by the outcomes that follow them. Thus, *operant conditioning is a form of learning in which responses come to be controlled by their consequences.* Learning theorists originally distinguished between classical and operant conditioning on the grounds that

classical conditioning regulated reflexive, involuntary responses, whereas operant conditioning governed voluntary responses. This distinction holds up much of the time, but it is not absolute. Research in recent decades has shown that classical conditioning sometimes contributes to the regulation of voluntary behavior, that operant conditioning can influence involuntary, autonomic responses, and that the two types of conditioning jointly and interactively govern some aspects of behavior (Allan, 1998; Turkkan, 1989). Indeed, some theorists have argued that classical and operant conditioning should be viewed as just two different aspects of a single learning process (Donahoe & Vegas, 2004).

Thorndike's Law of Effect

Pioneering work by Edward L. Thorndike on what he called *instrumental learning* provided the foundation for some of the ideas proposed later by Skinner (Chance, 1999). Thorndike (1913) began studying animal learning around the turn of the century. Setting out to determine whether animals could think,

Key Learning Goals

6.6 Contrast operant and classical conditioning, and articulate Thorndike's law of effect.

6.7 Explain Skinner's principle of reinforcement, and describe the terminology and procedures in operant research.

6.8 Describe acquisition, shaping, and extinction in operant conditioning.

6.9 Explain how stimuli govern operant behavior through generalization and discrimination.

6.10 Identify various types of schedules of reinforcement, and discuss their typical effects.

6.11 Distinguish between positive and negative reinforcement.

6.12 Compare escape learning and avoidance learning.

6.13 Describe punishment, and assess issues related to punishment as a disciplinary procedure.

Edward L. Thorndike

"We may, subject to similar limitations, get any response of which a learner is capable associated with any situation to which he is sensitive."

B. F. Skinner

"Operant conditioning shapes behavior as a sculptor shapes a lump of clay."

he conducted some classic studies of problem solving in cats. In these studies, a hungry cat was placed in a small cage or "puzzle box" with food available just outside. The cat could escape to obtain the food by performing a specific response, such as pulling a wire or depressing a lever (see **Figure 6.11**). After each escape, the cat was rewarded with a small amount of food and then returned to the cage for another trial. Thorndike monitored how long it took the cat to get out of the box over a series of trials. If the cat could think, Thorndike reasoned, a sudden drop would be seen in the time required to escape when the cat recognized the solution to the problem.

Instead of a sudden drop, Thorndike observed a gradual, uneven decline in the time it took cats to escape from his puzzle boxes (see the graph in **Figure 6.11**). The decline in solution time showed that the cats *were learning.* But the gradual nature of this decline suggested that this learning did *not* depend on thinking and understanding. Instead, Thorndike attributed this learning to a principle he called the *law of effect.* According to the **law of effect, if a response in the presence of a stimulus leads to satisfying effects, the association between the stimulus and the response is strengthened.** Thorndike viewed instrumental learning as a mechanical process in which successful responses are gradually "stamped in" by their favorable effects. His law of effect became the cornerstone of Skinner's theory of operant conditioning, although Skinner used different terminology.

Skinner's Demonstration: It's All a Matter of Consequences

5c

B. F. Skinner had great admiration for Pavlov's work (Catania & Laties, 1999) and used it as the founda-

tion for his own theory, even borrowing some of Pavlov's terminology (Dinsmoor, 2004). And, like Pavlov, Skinner (1953, 1969, 1984) conducted some deceptively simple research that became enormously influential (Lattal, 1992). Ironically, he got off to an inauspicious start. His first book, *The Behavior of Organisms* (1938), sold only 80 copies in its first four years in print. Nonetheless, he went on to become, in the words of historian Albert Gilgen (1982), "without question the most famous American psychologist in the world" (p. 97).

The fundamental principle of operant conditioning is uncommonly simple and was anticipated by Thorndike's law of effect. Skinner demonstrated that *organisms tend to repeat those responses that are followed by favorable consequences.* This fundamental principle is embodied in Skinner's concept of reinforcement. **Reinforcement occurs when an event following a response increases an organism's tendency to make that response.** In other words, a response is strengthened because it leads to rewarding consequences (see **Figure 6.12**).

The principle of reinforcement may be simple, but it is immensely powerful. Skinner and his followers have shown that much of everyday behavior is regulated by reinforcement. For example, you put money in a soda vending machine and you get a soft drink back as a result. You go to work because this behavior leads to your receiving paychecks. Perhaps you work extra hard because promotions and raises tend to follow such behavior. You tell jokes, and your friends laugh—so you tell some more. The principle of reinforcement clearly governs complex aspects of human behavior.

Please note, reinforcement is defined *after the fact,* in terms of its *effect* on behavior (strengthening a response). Something that is clearly reinforc-

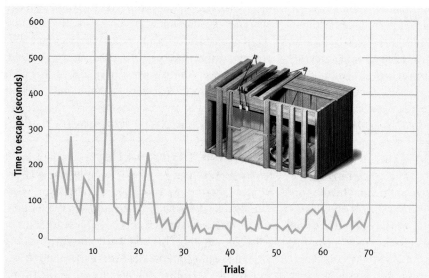

Figure 6.11

The learning curve of one of Thorndike's cats. The inset shows one of Thorndike's puzzle boxes. The cat had to perform three separate acts to escape the box, including pressing the pedal on the right. The learning curve shows how the cat's escape time declined gradually over a number of trials. Thorndike concluded that successful responses are gradually "stamped in" by their favorable consequences; he called this principle the *law of effect.*

"Mommy, we keep saying 'go home, kitty-cat' -- but she just keeps hanging around here!"

© The Family Circus—BIL KEANE, Inc. King Features Syndicate

Figure 6.12

Reinforcement in operant conditioning. According to Skinner, reinforcement occurs when a response is followed by rewarding consequences and the organism's tendency to make the response increases. The two examples diagrammed here illustrate the basic premise of operant conditioning—that voluntary behavior is controlled by its consequences. These examples involve positive reinforcement (for a comparison of positive and negative reinforcement, see Figure 6.18).

ing for an organism at one time may not function as a reinforcer later (Catania, 1992). For example, food may not be reinforcing if an organism is not hungry. Similarly, something that serves as a reinforcer for one person may not function as a reinforcer for another person. For example, parental approval is a potent reinforcer for most children, but not all. To know whether an event is reinforcing, researchers must make it contingent on a response and observe whether the rate of this response increases.

Terminology and Procedures

5c

Like Pavlov, Skinner created a prototype experimental procedure that has been repeated (with variations) thousands of times. In this procedure, an animal, typically a rat or a pigeon, is placed in an *operant chamber* that has come to be better known as a "Skinner box" (much to Skinner's chagrin). **An *operant chamber*, or *Skinner box*, is a small enclosure in which an animal can make a specific response that is recorded while the consequences of the response are systematically controlled.** In the boxes designed for rats, the main response made available is pressing a small lever mounted on one side wall (see Figure 6.13 on the next page). In the boxes made for pigeons, the designated response is pecking a small disk mounted on a side wall. Because operant responses tend to be voluntary, they are said to be *emitted* rather than *elicited*. To *emit* means to send forth.

The Skinner box permits the experimenter to control the reinforcement contingencies that are in effect for the animal. *Reinforcement contingencies* are the circumstances or rules that determine

whether responses lead to the presentation of reinforcers. Typically, the experimenter manipulates whether positive consequences occur when the animal makes the designated response. The main positive consequence is usually delivery of a small bit of food into a food cup mounted in the chamber. Because the animals are deprived of food for a while prior to the experimental session, their hunger virtually ensures that the food serves as a reinforcer.

The key dependent variable in most research on operant conditioning is the subjects' *response rate* over time. An animal's rate of lever pressing or disk pecking in the Skinner box is monitored continuously by a device known as a cumulative recorder (see Figure 6.13). **The *cumulative recorder* creates a graphic record of responding and reinforcement in a Skinner box as a function of time.** The recorder works by means of a roll of paper that moves at a steady rate underneath a movable pen. When there is no responding, the pen stays still and draws a straight horizontal line, reflecting the passage of time. Whenever the designated response occurs, however, the pen moves upward a notch. The pen's movements produce a graphic summary of the animal's responding over time. The pen also makes slash marks to record the delivery of each reinforcer.

The results of operant-conditioning studies are usually portrayed in graphs. In these graphs, the horizontal axis is used to mark the passage of time, while the vertical axis is used to plot the

Figure 6.13

Skinner box and cumulative recorder. (a) This diagram highlights some of the key features of an operant chamber, or Skinner box. In this apparatus designed for rats, the response under study is lever pressing. Food pellets, which may serve as reinforcers, are delivered into the food cup on the right. The speaker and light permit manipulations of auditory and visual stimuli, and the electric grid gives the experimenter control over aversive consequences (shock) in the box. **(b)** A cumulative recorder connected to the box keeps a continuous record of responses and reinforcements. A small segment of a cumulative record is shown here. The entire process is automatic as the paper moves with the passage of time; each lever press moves the pen up a step, and each reinforcement is marked with a slash. **(c)** This photo shows the real thing—a rat being conditioned in a Skinner box. Note the food dispenser on the right, which was omitted from the diagram.

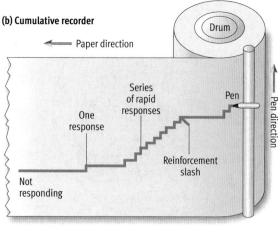

(b) Cumulative recorder

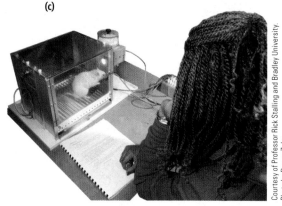

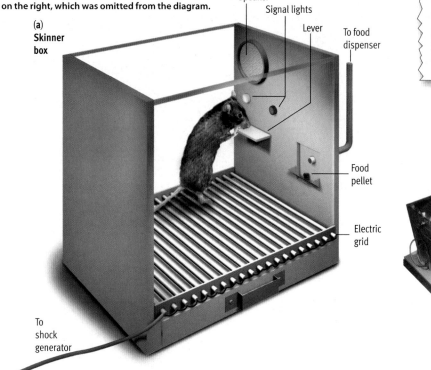

(a) Skinner box

Courtesy of Professor Rick Stalling and Bradley University. Photo by Duane Zehr.

accumulation of responses, as shown in Figure 6.14. In interpreting these graphs, the key consideration is the *slope* of the line that represents the record of responding. *A rapid response rate produces a steep slope, whereas a slow response rate produces a shallow slope.* Because the response record is cumulative, the line never goes down. It can only go up as more responses are made or flatten out if the response rate slows to zero. The magnifications shown in Figure 6.14 show how slope and response rate are related.

Operant theorists make a distinction between unlearned, or primary, reinforcers as opposed to conditioned, or secondary, reinforcers. *Primary reinforcers are events that are inherently reinforcing because they satisfy biological needs.* A given species has a limited number of primary reinforcers because they are closely tied to physiological needs. In humans, primary reinforcers include food, water, warmth, sex, and perhaps affection expressed through hugging and close bodily contact. *Secondary, or conditioned, reinforcers are events that ac-*

quire reinforcing qualities by being associated with primary reinforcers. The events that function as secondary reinforcers vary among members of a species because they depend on learning. Examples of common secondary reinforcers in humans include money, good grades, attention, flattery, praise, and applause. Similarly, people *learn* to find stylish clothes, sports cars, fine jewelry, exotic vacations, and state-of-the-art stereos reinforcing.

Basic Processes in Operant Conditioning

PSYK TREK SIM4, 5c

Although the principle of reinforcement is strikingly simple, many other processes involved in operant conditioning make this form of learning just as complex as classical conditioning. In fact, some of the *same* processes are involved in both types of conditioning. In this section, we'll discuss how the processes of acquisition, extinction, generalization, and discrimination occur in operant conditioning.

Acquisition and Shaping   SIM4, 5c

As in classical conditioning, *acquisition* in operant conditioning refers to the initial stage of learning some new pattern of responding. However, the procedures used to establish an operant response are different from those used to create the typical conditioned response. Operant responses are usually established through a gradual process called *shaping*, **which consists of the reinforcement of closer and closer approximations of a desired response.**

Shaping is necessary when an organism does not, on its own, emit the desired response. For example, when a rat is first placed in a Skinner box, it may not press the lever at all. In this case an experimenter begins shaping by releasing food pellets whenever the rat moves toward the lever. As this response becomes more frequent, the experimenter starts requiring a closer approximation of the desired response, possibly releasing food only when the rat actually touches the lever. As reinforcement increases the rat's tendency to touch the lever, the rat will spontaneously press the lever on occasion, finally providing the experimenter with an opportunity to reinforce the designated response. These reinforcements will gradually increase the rate of lever pressing.

The mechanism of shaping is the key to training animals to perform impressive tricks. When you go to a zoo, circus, or marine park and see bears riding bicycles, monkeys playing the piano, and whales leaping through hoops, you are witnessing the results of shaping. To demonstrate the power of shaping techniques, Skinner once trained some pigeons so that they appeared to play a crude version of Ping-Pong. They would run about at opposite ends

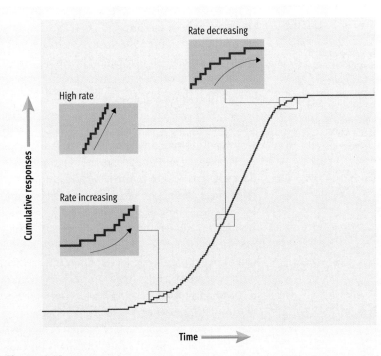

Figure 6.14

A graphic portrayal of operant responding. The results of operant conditioning are often summarized in a graph of cumulative responses over time. The insets magnify small segments of the curve to show how an increasing response rate yields a progressively steeper slope (bottom); a high, steady response rate yields a steep, stable slope (middle); and a decreasing response rate yields a progressively flatter slope (top).

of a tiny Ping-Pong table and peck the ball back and forth. Keller and Marian Breland, a couple of psychologists influenced by Skinner, went into the business of training animals for advertising and entertainment purposes. One of their better-known feats was shaping "Priscilla, the Fastidious Pig" to turn on a

Shaping—an operant technique in which an organism is rewarded for closer and closer approximations of the desired response—is used in teaching both animals and humans. It is the main means of training animals to perform unnatural tricks. Breland and Breland's (1961) famous subject, "Priscilla, the Fastidious Pig," is shown in the center.

web link 6.3

Animal Training at Sea World and Busch Gardens

The practical applications of shaping and other principles of operant conditioning are demonstrated at this interesting site, which explains how animal training is accomplished at these well-known parks.

radio, eat at a kitchen table, put dirty clothes in a hamper, run a vacuum, and then "go shopping" with a shopping cart. Of course, Priscilla picked the sponsor's product off the shelf in her shopping expedition (Breland & Breland, 1961).

Extinction SIM4, 5c

In operant conditioning, *extinction* refers to the gradual weakening and disappearance of a response tendency because the response is no longer followed by reinforcers. Extinction begins in operant conditioning whenever previously available reinforcement is stopped. In laboratory studies with rats, this usually means that the experimenter stops delivering food when the rat presses the lever. When the extinction process is begun, a brief surge often occurs in the rat's responding, followed by a gradual decline in response rate until it approaches zero. The same effects are generally seen in the extinction of human behaviors.

A key issue in operant conditioning is how much *resistance to extinction* an organism will display when reinforcement is halted. ***Resistance to extinction occurs when an organism continues to make a response after delivery of the reinforcer has been terminated.*** The greater the resistance to extinction, the longer the responding will continue. Resistance to extinction may sound like a matter of purely theoretical interest, but it's actually quite practical. People often want to strengthen a response in such a way that it will be relatively resistant to extinction. For instance, most parents want to see their child's studying response survive even if the child hits a rocky stretch when studying doesn't lead to reinforcement (good grades). In a similar fashion, a casino wants to see patrons continue to gamble, even if they encounter a lengthy losing streak. Thus, a high degree of resistance to extinction can be desirable in many situations. Resistance to extinction depends on a variety of factors. Chief among them is the *schedule of reinforcement* used during acquisition, a matter that we will discuss a little later in this chapter.

Stimulus Control: Generalization and Discrimination

Operant responding is ultimately controlled by its consequences, as organisms learn response-outcome (R-O) associations (Colwill, 1993). However, stimuli that *precede* a response can also exert considerable influence over operant behavior. When a response is consistently followed by a reinforcer *in the presence of a particular stimulus,* that stimulus comes to serve as a "signal" indicating that the response is likely to lead to a reinforcer. Once an organism

learns the signal, it tends to respond accordingly (Honig & Alsop, 1992). For example, a pigeon's disk pecking may be reinforced only when a small light behind the disk is lit. When the light is out, pecking does not lead to the reward. Pigeons quickly learn to peck the disk only when it is lit. The light that signals the availability of reinforcement is called a *discriminative stimulus. **Discriminative stimuli are cues that influence operant behavior by indicating the probable consequences (reinforcement or nonreinforcement) of a response.***

Discriminative stimuli play a key role in the regulation of operant behavior. For example, birds learn that hunting for worms is likely to be reinforced after a rain. Children learn to ask for sweets when their parents are in a good mood. Drivers learn to slow down when the highway is wet. Human social behavior is also regulated extensively by discriminative stimuli. Consider the behavior of asking someone out for a date. Many people emit this response only cautiously, after receiving many signals (such as eye contact, smiles, encouraging conversational exchanges) that reinforcement (a favorable answer) is fairly likely. The potential power of discriminative stimuli to govern behavior has recently been demonstrated in dramatic fashion by research (Talwar et al., 2002) showing that it is possible to use operant procedures to train what *Time* magazine called "roborats," radio-controlled rodents that can be precisely directed through complex environments (see Figure 6.15).

Reactions to a discriminative stimulus are governed by the processes of *stimulus generalization* and *stimulus discrimination,* just like reactions to a CS in classical conditioning. For instance, envision a cat that comes running into the kitchen whenever it hears the sound of a can opener because that sound has become a discriminative stimulus signaling a good chance of its getting fed. If the cat also responded to the sound of a new kitchen appliance (say a blender), this response would represent *generalization*—responding to a new stimulus as if it were the original. *Discrimination* would occur if the cat learned to respond only to the can opener and not to the blender.

As you have learned in this section, the processes of acquisition, extinction, generalization, and discrimination in operant conditioning parallel these same processes in classical conditioning. Table 6.1 compares these processes in the two kinds of conditioning.

Schedules of Reinforcement 5d

Organisms make innumerable responses that do not lead to favorable consequences. It would be nice

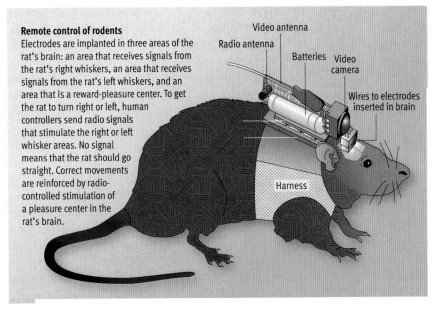

Remote control of rodents
Electrodes are implanted in three areas of the rat's brain: an area that receives signals from the rat's right whiskers, an area that receives signals from the rat's left whiskers, and an area that is a reward-pleasure center. To get the rat to turn right or left, human controllers send radio signals that stimulate the right or left whisker areas. No signal means that the rat should go straight. Correct movements are reinforced by radio-controlled stimulation of a pleasure center in the rat's brain.

Video antenna
Radio antenna
Batteries
Video camera
Wires to electrodes inserted in brain
Harness

Figure 6.15

Remote-controlled rodents: An example of operant conditioning in action. In a study that almost reads like science fiction, Sanjiv Talwar and colleagues (2002) used operant conditioning procedures to train radio-controlled "roborats" that could have a variety of valuable applications, such as searching for survivors in a collapsed building. As this graphic shows, radio signals can be used to direct the rat to go forward or turn right or left, while a video feed is sent back to a control center. The *reinforcer* in this setup is brief electrical stimulation of a pleasure center in the rat's brain (see Chapter 3), which can be delivered by remote control. The brief signals sent to the right or left whisker areas are *discriminative stimuli* that indicate which types of responses will be reinforced. The entire procedure depended on extensive *shaping.*

if people were reinforced every time they took an exam, watched a movie, hit a golf shot, asked for a date, or made a sales call. However, in the real world most responses are reinforced only some of the time. How does this fact affect the potency of reinforcers? To find out, operant psychologists have devoted an enormous amount of attention to how *intermittent schedules of reinforcement* influence operant behavior (Ferster & Skinner, 1957; Skinner, 1938, 1953).

A *schedule of reinforcement* determines which occurrences of a specific response result in the presentation of a reinforcer. The simplest pattern is continuous reinforcement. *Continuous reinforcement* occurs when every instance of a designated

response is reinforced. In the laboratory, experimenters often use continuous reinforcement to shape and establish a new response before moving on to more realistic schedules involving intermittent reinforcement. *Intermittent, or partial, reinforcement* occurs when a designated response is reinforced only some of the time.

Which do you suppose leads to longer-lasting effects—being reinforced every time you emit a response, or being reinforced only some of the time? Studies show that, given an equal number of reinforcements, *intermittent* reinforcement makes a response more resistant to extinction than continuous reinforcement does (Falls, 1998). In other words,

Table 6.1 Comparison of Basic Processes in Classical and Operant Conditioning

Process and Definition	Description in Classical Conditioning	Description in Operant Conditioning
Acquisition: The initial stage of learning	CS and US are paired, gradually resulting in CR.	Responding gradually increases because of reinforcement, possibly through shaping.
Extinction: The gradual weakening and disappearance of a conditioned response tendency	CS is presented alone until it no longer elicits CR.	Responding gradually slows and stops after reinforcement is terminated.
Stimulus generalization: An organism's responding to stimuli other than the original stimulus used in conditioning	CR is elicited by new stimulus that resembles original CS.	Responding increases in the presence of new stimulus that resembles original discriminative stimulus.
Stimulus discrimination: An organism's lack of response to stimuli that are similar to the original stimulus used in conditioning	CR is not elicited by new stimulus that resembles original CS	Responding does not increase in the presence of new stimulus that resembles original discriminative stimulus.

organisms continue responding longer after removal of reinforcers when a response has been reinforced only *some* of the time. In fact, schedules of reinforcement that provide only sporadic delivery of reinforcers can yield great resistance to extinction. This finding explains why behaviors that are reinforced only occasionally—such as youngsters' temper tantrums—can be very durable and difficult to eliminate.

Reinforcement schedules come in many varieties, but four particular types of intermittent schedules have attracted the most interest. These schedules are described here along with examples drawn from the laboratory and everyday life (see Figure 6.16 for additional examples).

Ratio schedules require the organism to make the designated response a certain number of times to gain each reinforcer. **With a *fixed-ratio (FR) schedule*, the reinforcer is given after a fixed number of nonreinforced responses.** *Examples:* (1) A rat is reinforced for every tenth lever press. (2) A salesperson receives a bonus for every fourth set of encyclopedias sold. **With a *variable-ratio (VR) schedule*, the reinforcer is given after a variable number of non-reinforced responses.** The number of nonreinforced responses varies around a predetermined average. *Examples:* (1) A rat is reinforced for every tenth lever press on the average. The exact number of responses required for reinforcement varies from one time to the next. (2) A slot machine in a casino pays off once every six tries on the average. The number of nonwinning responses between payoffs varies greatly from one time to the next.

Interval schedules require a time period to pass between the presentation of reinforcers. **With a *fixed-interval (FI) schedule*, the reinforcer is given for the first response that occurs after a fixed time interval has elapsed.** *Examples:* (1) A rat is reinforced for the first lever press after a 2-minute interval has elapsed and then must wait 2 minutes before being able to earn the next reinforcement. (2) A man washing his clothes periodically checks to see whether each load is finished. The reward (clean clothes) is available only after a fixed time interval (corresponding to how long the washer takes to complete a cycle) has elapsed, and checking responses during the interval are not reinforced. **With a *variable-interval (VI) schedule*, the reinforcer is given for the first response after a variable time interval has elapsed.** The interval length varies around a predetermined average. *Examples:* (1) A rat is reinforced for the first lever press after a 1-minute interval has elapsed, but the following intervals are 3 minutes, 2 minutes, 4 minutes, and so on—with an average length of 2 minutes. (2) A person repeatedly dials a busy phone number (getting through is the reinforcer).

More than 50 years of research has yielded an enormous volume of data on how these schedules of reinforcement are related to patterns of responding (Williams, 1988; Zeiler, 1977). Some of the more prominent findings are summarized in Figure 6.17, which depicts typical response patterns generated by each schedule. For example, with fixed-interval schedules, a pause in responding usually occurs after each reinforcer is delivered, and then responding gradually increases to a rapid rate at the end of the interval. This pattern of behavior yields a "scalloped" response curve. In general, ratio schedules tend to produce more rapid responding than interval schedules. Why? Because faster responding leads to reinforcement sooner when a ratio schedule is in effect. Variable schedules tend to generate steadier

concept check 6.2

Recognizing Schedules of Reinforcement

Check your understanding of schedules of reinforcement in operant conditioning by indicating the type of schedule that would be in effect in each of the examples below. In the spaces on the left, fill in CR for continuous reinforcement, FR for fixed-ratio, VR for variable-ratio, FI for fixed-interval, and VI for variable-interval. The answers can be found in Appendix A in the back of the book.

_____ 1. Sarah is paid on a commission basis for selling computer systems. She gets a bonus for every third sale.

_____ 2. Juan's parents let him earn some pocket money by doing yard work approximately (on average) once a week.

_____ 3. Martha is fly-fishing. Think of each time that she casts her line as the response that may be rewarded.

_____ 4. Jamal, who is in the fourth grade, gets a gold star from his teacher for every book he reads.

_____ 5. Skip, a professional baseball player, signs an agreement that his salary increases will be renegotiated every third year.

response rates and greater resistance to extinction than their fixed counterparts.

Most of the research on reinforcement schedules was conducted on rats and pigeons in Skinner boxes. However, the available evidence suggests that humans react to schedules of reinforcement in much the same way as animals (De Villiers, 1977; Perone, Galizio, & Baron, 1988). For example, when animals are placed on ratio schedules, shifting to a higher ratio (that is, requiring more responses per reinforcement) tends to generate faster responding. Managers of factories that pay on a piecework basis (a fixed-ratio schedule) have seen the same reaction in humans. Shifting to a higher ratio (more pieces for the same pay) usually stimulates harder work and greater productivity (although workers often complain). There are many other parallels between animals' and humans' reactions to various schedules of reinforcement. For instance, with rats and pigeons, variable-ratio schedules yield steady responding and great resistance to extinction. Similar effects are routinely observed among people who gamble. Most gambling is reinforced according to variable-ratio schedules, which tend to produce rapid, steady responding and great resistance to extinction—exactly what casino operators want.

Positive Reinforcement Versus Negative Reinforcement
5e, 5f

According to Skinner, reinforcement can take two forms, which he called *positive reinforcement* and *negative reinforcement* (see **Figure 6.18** on the next page). *Positive reinforcement* occurs when a response is strengthened because it is followed by the presentation of a rewarding stimulus. Thus far, for purposes of simplicity, our examples of reinforcement have involved positive reinforcement. Good grades, tasty meals, paychecks, scholarships, promotions, nice clothes, nifty cars, attention, and flattery are all positive reinforcers.

In contrast, *negative reinforcement* occurs when a response is strengthened because it is followed by the removal of an aversive (unpleasant) stimulus. Don't let the word "negative" confuse you. Negative reinforcement *is* reinforcement. Like all reinforcement it involves a favorable outcome that *strengthens* a response tendency. However, this strengthening takes place because a response leads to the *removal of an aversive stimulus* rather than the arrival of a pleasant stimulus (see **Figure 6.18** on the next page).

In laboratory studies, negative reinforcement is usually accomplished as follows: While a rat is

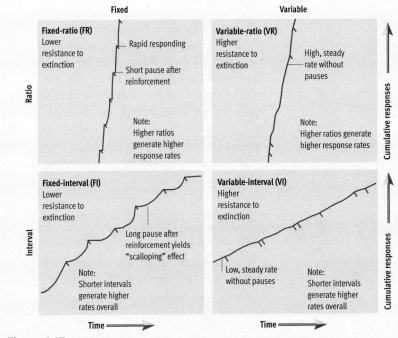

Figure 6.16

Reinforcement schedules in everyday life. Complex human behaviors are regulated by schedules of reinforcement. Piecework in factories is reinforced on a fixed-ratio schedule. Playing slot machines is based on variable-ratio reinforcement. Watching the clock at work is rewarded on a fixed-interval basis (the arrival of quitting time is the reinforcer). Surfers waiting for a big wave are rewarded on a variable-interval basis.

Figure 6.17

Schedules of reinforcement and patterns of response. In graphs of operant responding, such as these, a steeper slope indicates a faster rate of response and the slash marks reflect the delivery of reinforcers. Each type of reinforcement schedule tends to generate a characteristic pattern of responding. In general, ratio schedules tend to produce more rapid responding than interval schedules (note the steep slopes of the FR and VR curves). In comparison to fixed schedules, variable schedules tend to yield steadier responding (note the smoother lines for the VR and VI schedules on the right) and greater resistance to extinction.

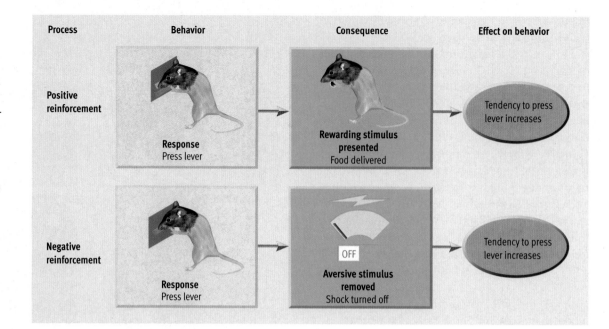

Process	Behavior	Consequence	Effect on behavior
Positive reinforcement	**Response** Press lever	**Rewarding stimulus presented** Food delivered	Tendency to press lever increases
Negative reinforcement	**Response** Press lever	OFF **Aversive stimulus removed** Shock turned off	Tendency to press lever increases

in a Skinner box, a moderate electric shock is delivered to the animal through the floor of the box. When the rat presses the lever, the shock is turned off for a period of time. Thus, lever pressing leads to removal of an aversive stimulus (shock), which reliably strengthens the rat's lever-pressing response. Everyday human behavior appears to be regulated extensively by negative reinforcement. Consider a handful of examples: You rush home in the winter to get out of the cold. You clean house to get rid of a mess. You give in to a roommate or spouse to bring an unpleasant argument to an end.

Although the distinction between positive and negative reinforcement has been a fundamental feature of operant models since the beginning, some theorists have recently questioned its value (Baron & Galizio, 2005; Iwata, 2006). They argue that the distinction is ambiguous and unnecessary. For example, the behavior of rushing home to get out of the cold (negative reinforcement) could also be viewed as rushing home to enjoy the warmth (positive reinforcement). According to the critics, positive and negative reinforcement are just two sides of the same coin. Although they clearly are correct in noting that the distinction is troubled by ambiguity, for the present the distinction continues to guide thinking about operant consequences. For example, a recent theory of drug addiction centers on the thesis that addicts use drugs to reduce and ward off unpleasant emotions, which results in negative reinforcement (Baker et al., 2004).

Likewise, most theorists continue to believe that negative reinforcement plays a key role in escape learning and avoidance learning. In *escape learning,* an organism acquires a response that decreases or ends some aversive stimulation. Psychologists often study escape learning in the laboratory with rats that are conditioned in a *shuttle box.* The shuttle box has two compartments connected by a doorway, which can be opened and closed by the experimenter, as depicted in **Figure 6.19(a)**. In a typical study, an animal is placed in one compartment and the shock in the floor of that chamber is turned on, with the doorway open. The animal learns to escape the shock by running to the other compartment. This escape response leads to the removal of an aversive stimulus (shock), so it is conceptualized as being strengthened through negative reinforcement. If you were to leave a party where you were getting picked on by peers, you would be engaging in an escape response.

Escape learning often leads to avoidance learning. In *avoidance learning* an organism acquires a response that prevents some aversive stimulation from occurring. In shuttle box studies of avoidance learning, the experimenter simply gives the animal a signal that shock is forthcoming. The typical signal is a light that goes on a few seconds prior to the shock. At first the rat runs only when shocked (escape learning). Gradually, however, the animal learns to run to the safe compartment as soon as the light comes on, showing avoidance learning. Similarly, if you were to quit going to parties because of your concern about being picked on, you would be demonstrating avoidance learning.

Avoidance learning presents an interesting example of how classical conditioning and operant condi-

(a)

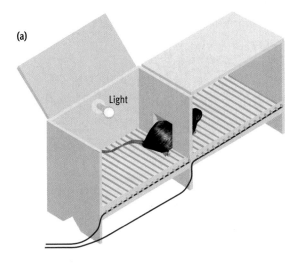

Light

(b)

1. Classical conditioning

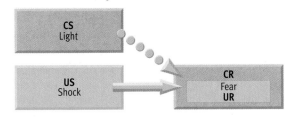

CS Light	
US Shock	CR Fear UR

2. Operant conditioning

(negative reinforceme

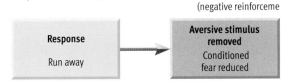

Response Run away	Aversive stimulus removed Conditioned fear reduced

Figure 6.19

Escape and avoidance learning. (a) Escape and avoidance learning are often studied with a shuttle box like that shown here. Warning signals, shock, and the animal's ability to flee from one compartment to another can be controlled by the experimenter. (b) Avoidance begins because classical conditioning creates a conditioned fear that is elicited by the warning signal (panel 1). Avoidance continues because it is maintained by operant conditioning (panel 2). Specifically, the avoidance response is strengthened through negative reinforcement, since it leads to removal of the conditioned fear.

tioning can work together to regulate behavior (Levis, 1989; Mowrer, 1947). In avoidance learning, the warning light that goes on before the shock becomes a CS (through classical conditioning) eliciting reflexive, conditioned fear in the animal. However, the response of fleeing to the other side of the box is operant behavior. This response is presumably strengthened through *negative reinforcement* because it reduces the animal's conditioned fear (see Figure 6.19b). Thus, in avoidance learning a fear response is acquired

through classical conditioning and an avoidance response is maintained by operant conditioning.

The principles of avoidance learning shed some light on why phobias are so resistant to extinction (Levis, 1989; Levis & Brewer, 2001). Suppose you have a phobia of elevators. Chances are, you acquired your phobia through classical conditioning. At some point in your past, elevators became paired with a frightening event. Now whenever you need to use an elevator, you experience conditioned fear. If your phobia is severe, you probably take the stairs instead. Taking the stairs is an avoidance response that should lead to consistent reinforcement by relieving your conditioned fear. Thus, it's hard to get rid of phobias for two reasons. First, responses that allow you to avoid a phobic stimulus earn reinforcement each time they are made—so the avoidance behavior is strengthened and continues. Second, these avoidance responses prevent any opportunity to extinguish the phobic conditioned response because you're never exposed to the conditioned stimulus (in this case, riding in an elevator).

Punishment: Consequences That Weaken Responses

Reinforcement is defined in terms of its consequences. It *increases* an organism's tendency to make a certain response. Are there also consequences that *decrease* an organism's tendency to make a particular response? Yes. In Skinner's model of operant behavior, such consequences are called *punishment.*

Punishment occurs when an event following a response weakens the tendency to make that response. In a Skinner box, the administration of punishment is very simple. When a rat presses the lever or a pigeon pecks the disk, it receives a brief shock. This procedure usually leads to a rapid decline in the animal's response rate (Dinsmoor, 1998). Punishment typically involves presentation of an aversive stimulus (for instance, spanking a child). However, punishment may also involve the removal of a rewarding stimulus (for instance, taking away a child's TV-watching privileges).

The concept of punishment in operant conditioning is confusing to many students on two counts. First, they often confuse it with negative reinforcement, which is entirely different. Negative reinforcement involves the *removal* of an aversive stimulus, thereby *strengthening* a response. Punishment, on the other hand, involves the *presentation* of an aversive stimulus, thereby *weakening* a response. Thus, punishment and negative reinforcement are oppo-

Figure 6.20

Comparison of negative reinforcement and punishment. Although punishment can occur when a response leads to the removal of a rewarding stimulus, it more typically involves the presentation of an aversive stimulus. Students often confuse punishment with negative reinforcement because they associate both with aversive stimuli. However, as this diagram shows, punishment and negative reinforcement represent opposite procedures that have opposite effects on behavior.

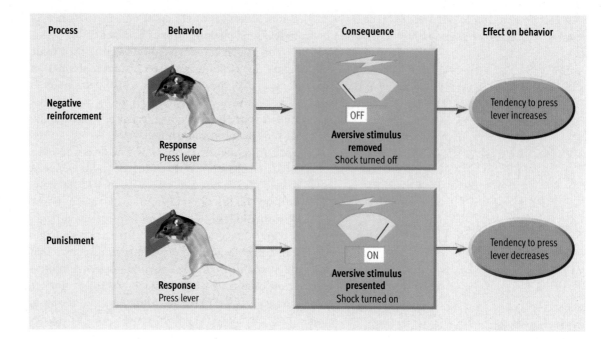

Process	Behavior	Consequence	Effect on behavior

Negative reinforcement — **Response** Press lever — **OFF** **Aversive stimulus removed** Shock turned off — Tendency to press lever increases

Punishment — **Response** Press lever — **ON** **Aversive stimulus presented** Shock turned on — Tendency to press lever decreases

site procedures that yield opposite effects on behavior (see **Figure 6.20**).

The second source of confusion involves the tendency to equate punishment with *disciplinary procedures* used by parents, teachers, and other authority figures. In the operant model, punishment occurs any time undesirable consequences weaken a response tendency. Defined in this way, the concept of punishment goes far beyond things like parents spanking children and teachers handing out detentions. For example, if you wear a new outfit and your classmates make fun of it, your behavior will have been punished and your tendency to emit this response (wear the same clothing) will probably decline. Similarly, if you go to a restaurant and have a horrible meal, your response will have been punished, and your tendency to go to that restaurant will probably decline. Although punishment in operant conditioning encompasses far more than disciplinary acts, it *is* used frequently for disciplinary purposes. In light of this reality, it is worth looking at the research on punishment as a disciplinary measure.

Side Effects of Physical Punishment

About three-quarters of parents report that they sometimes spank their children (Straus & Stewart, 1999), but quite a bit of controversy exists about the wisdom of using spanking or other physical punishment. Opponents of corporal punishment argue that it produces many unintended and undesirable side effects (Lytton, 1997; McCord, 2005; Straus, 2000). For example, they worry that physical punishment may trigger strong emotional responses, including anxiety, anger, and resentment, and that it can generate hostility toward the source of the punishment, such as a parent. Some theorists also argue that children who are subjected to a lot of physical punishment tend to become more aggressive than average. These views were bolstered by a comprehensive review of the empirical research on physical punishment with children. Summarizing the results of 88 studies, Elizabeth Thompson Gershoff (2002) concluded that physical punishment is associated with poor-quality parent-child relations; elevated aggression, delinquency, and behavioral problems in youngsters; and an increased likelihood

---

concept check 6.3

Recognizing Outcomes in Operant Conditioning

Check your understanding of the various types of consequences that can occur in operant conditioning by indicating whether the examples below involve positive reinforcement (PR), negative reinforcement (NR), punishment (P), or extinction (E) (assume that each of these procedures is effective in changing the frequency of the behavior in the expected direction). The answers can be found in Appendix A.

_____ 1. Antonio gets a speeding ticket.

_____ 2. Diane's supervisor compliments her on her hard work.

_____ 3. Leon goes to the health club for a rare workout and pushes himself so hard that his entire body aches and he throws up.

_____ 4. Audrey lets her dog out so she won't have to listen to its whimpering.

_____ 5. Richard shoots up heroin to ward off tremors and chills associated with heroin withdrawal.

_____ 6. Sharma constantly complains about minor aches and pains to obtain sympathy from colleagues at work. Three co-workers who share an office with her decide to ignore her complaints instead of responding with sympathy.

---

of children being abused. Moreover, she concluded that these effects can carry over into adulthood, as studies find increased aggression, criminal behavior, mental health problems, and child abuse among adults who were physically punished as children. These conclusions about the negative effects of corporal punishment have been echoed in more recent studies (Aucoin, Frick, & Bodin, 2006; Lynch et al., 2006; Mulvaney & Mebert, 2007).

However, in the wake of Gershoff's (2002) stinging indictment of physical punishment, critics have raised some doubts about her conclusions. They argue that her review failed to distinguish between the effects of frequent, harsh, heavy-handed physical punishment and the effects of occasional, mild spankings, used as a backup when other disciplinary strategies fail (Baumrind, Larzelere, & Cowan, 2002). Critics also point out that the evidence linking spanking to negative effects is correlational, and correlation is no assurance of causation (Kazdin & Benjet, 2003). Perhaps spanking causes children to be more aggressive, but it is also plausible that aggressive children cause their parents to rely more on physical punishment (see Figure 6.21). Based on objections such as these, Baumrind et al. (2002) assert that the empirical evidence "does not justify a blanket injunction against mild to moderate disciplinary spanking" (p. 586).

So, what can we conclude about the corporal punishment controversy? It is important to note that the critics of Gershoff's conclusions are not exactly *advocates* of physical punishment. As Holden (2002) notes, "There is unanimous accord among experts that harsh, abusive punishment is detrimental for children" (p. 590). The critics think, however, that it is premature to condemn the judicious use of mild spankings, especially when children are too young to understand a verbal reprimand or the withdrawal of privileges. But even the critics would mostly agree that parents should minimize their dependence on physical punishment.

Making Punishment More Effective

Although many experts believe that punishment is overused in disciplinary efforts, it does have a role to play. The following guidelines summarize evidence on how to make punishment more effective while reducing its side effects.

1. *Apply punishment swiftly.* A delay in delivering punishment tends to undermine its impact (Abramowitz & O'Leary, 1990). When a mother says, "Wait until your father gets home . . ." she is making a fundamental mistake in the use of punishment. This problem with delayed punishment also explains the

ineffectiveness of punishing a pet hours after it has misbehaved, when the owner finally returns home. For instance, it won't do any good to shove your dog's face close to the feces it previously left on your carpet. This common punishment doesn't teach a dog to stop defecating on the carpet—it teaches the dog to keep its face out of its feces.

2. *Use punishment just severe enough to be effective.* The intensity of punishment is a two-edged sword. Severe punishments usually are more effective in weakening unwanted responses. However, they also increase the likelihood of undesirable side effects. Thus, it's best to use the least severe punishment that seems likely to have the necessary impact (Powell, Symbaluk, & MacDonald, 2002).

3. *Make punishment consistent.* If you want to eliminate a response, you should punish the response every time it occurs. When parents are inconsistent about punishing a particular behavior, they create more confusion than learning (Acker & O'Leary, 1996).

4. *Explain the punishment.* When children are punished, the reason for their punishment should be explained as fully as possible, given the constraints of their age. Punishment combined with reasoning is more effective than either alone (Larzelere et al., 1996; Parke, 2002). The more that children understand why they were punished, the more effective the punishment tends to be.

5. *Use noncorporal punishments, such as withdrawal of privileges.* Given the concerns about physical punishment, many experts argue that noncorporal punishments are a more prudent means to achieve disciplinary goals. For example, Kazdin and Benjet (2003) assert that "mild noncorporal punishments such as a brief time out from reinforcement or short-term loss of privileges in the context of praise and rewards can accomplish the goals for which spanking is usually employed" (p. 103). Although more research is needed, physical punishment in many cases may not be as effective as most people assume (Holden, 2002). Even a vigorous spanking isn't felt by a child an hour later. In contrast, withdrawing valued privileges can give children hours to contemplate the behavior that got them in trouble.

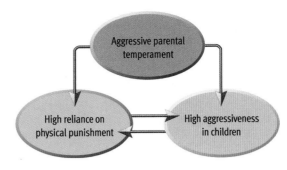

Figure 6.21
The correlation between physical punishment and aggressiveness. As we have discussed before, a correlation does not establish causation. It seems plausible that extensive reliance on physical punishment causes children to be more aggressive, as many experts suspect. However, it is also possible that highly aggressive children cause their parents to depend heavily on physical punishment. Or, perhaps parents with an aggressive, hostile temperament pass on genes for aggressiveness to their children, rely on heavy use of physical punishment, and model aggressive behavior.

Changing Directions in the Study of Conditioning

Key Learning Goals

6.14 Articulate the theoretical significance of conditioned taste aversion and preparedness.

6.15 Explain the importance of ecologically relevant conditioned stimuli and discuss whether the laws of learning are universal.

6.16 Describe Tolman's research on latent learning and its theoretical importance.

6.17 Understand the theoretical implications of research on signal relations and response-outcome relations.

As you learned in Chapter 1, science is constantly evolving and changing in response to new research and new thinking. Such change has certainly occurred in the study of conditioning. In this section, we will examine two major changes in thinking about conditioning. First, we'll consider the recent recognition that an organism's biological heritage can limit or channel conditioning. Second, we'll discuss the increased appreciation of the role of cognitive processes in conditioning.

Recognizing Biological Constraints on Conditioning

Learning theorists have traditionally assumed that the fundamental laws of conditioning have great generality—that they apply to a wide range of species. Although no one ever suggested that hamsters could learn physics, until the 1960s most psychologists assumed that associations could be conditioned between any stimulus an organism could register and any response it could make. However, findings in recent decades have demonstrated that there are limits to the generality of conditioning principles—limits imposed by an organism's biological heritage.

Conditioned Taste Aversion

A number of years ago, a prominent psychologist, Martin Seligman, dined out with his wife and enjoyed a steak with sauce béarnaise. About 6 hours afterward, he developed a wicked case of stomach flu and endured severe nausea. Subsequently, when he ordered sauce béarnaise, he was chagrined to discover that its aroma alone nearly made him throw up.

Seligman's experience was not unique. Many people develop aversions to food that has been followed by nausea from illness, alcohol intoxication, or food poisoning. However, Seligman was puzzled by his aversion to béarnaise sauce (Seligman & Hager, 1972). On the one hand, it appeared to be the straightforward result of classical conditioning, as diagrammed in **Figure 6.22**. On the other hand, Seligman recognized that his aversion to béarnaise sauce seemed to violate certain basic principles of conditioning. First, the lengthy delay of 6 hours between the CS (the sauce) and the US (the flu) should have prevented conditioning from occurring. Second, why was it that *only* the béarnaise sauce became a CS eliciting nausea? Why not other stimuli that were present in the restaurant? Shouldn't plates, knives, tablecloths, or his wife, for example, also trigger Seligman's nausea?

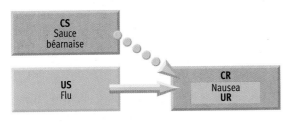

CS
Sauce
béarnaise

US
Flu

CR
Nausea
UR

Figure 6.22

Conditioned taste aversion. Martin Seligman's aversion to sauce béarnaise was clearly the product of classical conditioning. However, as the text explains, his acquisition of this response *appeared* to violate basic principles of classical conditioning. This paradox was resolved by John Garcia's work on conditioned taste aversions (see the text).

The riddle of Seligman's sauce béarnaise syndrome was solved by John Garcia (1989) and his colleagues. They conducted a series of studies on *conditioned taste aversion* (Garcia, Clarke, & Hankins, 1973; Garcia & Koelling, 1966; Garcia & Rusiniak, 1980). In these studies, they manipulated the kinds of stimuli preceding the onset of nausea and other noxious experiences in rats, using radiation to artificially induce the nausea. They found that when taste cues were followed by nausea, rats quickly acquired conditioned taste aversions. However, when taste cues were followed by other types of noxious stimuli (such as shock), rats did *not* develop conditioned taste aversions. Furthermore, visual and auditory stimuli followed by nausea also failed to produce conditioned aversions. In short, Garcia and his co-workers found that it was almost impossible to create certain associations, whereas taste-nausea associations (and odor-nausea associations) were almost impossible to prevent.

What is the theoretical significance of this unique readiness to make connections between taste and nausea? Garcia argues that it is a by-product of the evolutionary history of mammals. Animals that consume poisonous foods and survive must learn not to repeat their mistakes. Natural selection will favor organisms that quickly learn what *not* to eat. Thus, evolution may have biologically programmed some organisms to learn certain types of associations more easily than others.

Preparedness and Phobias

According to Martin Seligman (1971) and other theorists (Öhman, 1979; Öhman, Dimberg, & Öst, 1985), evolution has also programmed organisms to acquire certain fears more readily than others, because of a phenomenon called preparedness. *Preparedness* involves species-specific predispositions to be conditioned in certain ways and not others. Seligman believes that preparedness can explain why certain phobias are vastly more common than others. People tend to develop phobias to snakes, spiders, heights, and darkness relatively easily. However, even after painful experiences with hammers, knives, hot stoves, and electrical outlets, phobic fears of these stimuli are rare. What characteristics do common phobic stimuli share? Most were once genuine threats to our ancient ancestors. Consequently, a fear response to such stimuli may have survival value for our species. According to Seligman, evolutionary forces gradually wired the human brain to acquire conditioned fears of these stimuli easily and rapidly.

Laboratory simulations of phobic conditioning have provided some support for the concept of preparedness (Mineka & Öhman, 2002). For example, slides of "prepared" phobic stimuli (snakes, spiders) and neutral or modern fear-relevant stimuli

John Garcia

"Taste aversions do not fit comfortably within the present framework of classical or instrumental conditioning: These aversions selectively seek flavors to the exclusion of other stimuli. Interstimulus intervals are a thousandfold too long."

Taking advantage of the ease with which conditioned taste aversions can be established, sheep ranchers have reduced coyotes' attacks on their livestock by spreading tainted sheep carcasses around their ranches. The coyotes develop a conditioned response of nausea brought on by the sight of sheep.

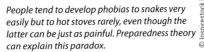

People tend to develop phobias to snakes very easily but to hot stoves rarely, even though the latter can be just as painful. Preparedness theory can explain this paradox.

(flowers, mushrooms, guns, knives) have been paired with shock. Consistent with the concept of preparedness, physiological monitoring of the participants indicates that the prepared phobic stimuli tend to produce more rapid conditioning, stronger fear responses, and greater resistance to extinction. Arne Öhman and Susan Mineka (2001) have elaborated on the theory of preparedness, outlining the key elements of what they call an *evolved module for fear learning*. They assert that this evolved module is (1) preferentially activated by stimuli related to survival threats in evolutionary history, (2) automatically activated by these stimuli, (3) relatively resistant to conscious efforts to suppress the resulting fears, and (4) dependent on neural circuitry running through the amygdala.

Arbitrary Versus Ecological Conditioned Stimuli

Michael Domjan (2005) argues that the rapid learning seen in conditioned taste aversions and conditioned fears is not all that unique. They are just two examples of what happens when *ecologically relevant conditioned stimuli* are studied, as opposed to *arbitrary, neutral stimuli*. Domjan points out that laboratory studies of classical conditioning have traditionally paired a US with a neutral stimulus that is unrelated to the US (such as a bell, tone, or light). This strategy ensured that the association created through conditioning was a newly acquired association rather than the product of previous learning. This approach yielded decades of useful insights about the laws governing classical conditioning, but Domjan argues that a gap exists between this paradigm and the way learning takes place in the real world.

According to Domjan (2005), in natural settings conditioned stimuli generally are not arbitrary cues that are unrelated to the US. In the real world, conditioned stimuli tend to have natural relations to the unconditioned stimuli they predict. For example, a rattlesnake bite is typically preceded by the snake's distinctive rattling sound; copulation among animals is typically preceded by specific mating signals; the consumption of toxic food is normally preceded by a specific taste. Hence, Domjan concludes that the heavy focus on arbitrary cues has probably given investigators a somewhat distorted picture of the principles of conditioning. If taste aversion learning appears to "violate" the normal laws of conditioning, it's because these laws have been compiled in unrealistic situations that are not representative of how conditioning unfolds in natural settings. Thus, Domjan maintains that researchers should shift their focus to ecologically relevant con-

ditioned stimuli, which may yield somewhat different patterns of learning (such as more rapid acquisition, greater resistance to extinction, and so forth).

Domjan (2005) stresses that conditioning is an adaptive process that routinely occurs under natural circumstances in service of reproductive fitness. Over the course of evolution, organisms have developed distinct response systems to deal with crucial tasks, such as finding food and avoiding predators. When a learning task in the laboratory happens to mesh with an animal's evolutionary history, learning is likely to proceed more quickly and easily than when arbitrary stimuli are used (Domjan, Cusato, & Krause, 2004). Thus, biological constraints on learning are not really "constraints" on the general laws of learning. These species-specific predispositions are the norm—an insight that eluded researchers for decades because they mostly worked with neutral conditioned stimuli.

Evolutionary Perspectives on Learning

So, what is the current thinking on the idea that the laws of learning are *universal* across various species? The predominant view among learning theorists seems to be that the basic mechanisms of learning are *similar* across species but that these mechanisms have sometimes been modified in the course of evolution as species have adapted to the specialized demands of their environments (Shettleworth, 1998). According to this view, learning is a very general process because the biological bases of learning and the basic problems confronted by various organisms are much the same across species. For example, developing the ability to recognize stimuli that signal important events (such as lurking predators) is probably adaptive for virtually any organism. However, given that different organisms confront different adaptive problems to survive and reproduce, it makes sense that learning has evolved along somewhat different paths in different species (Hollis, 1997; Sherry, 1992).

Recognizing Cognitive Processes in Conditioning

Pavlov, Watson, Thorndike, and their followers traditionally viewed conditioning as a mechanical process in which stimulus-response associations are "stamped in" by experience. Learning theorists asserted that because creatures such as flatworms and sea slugs can be conditioned, conditioning can't depend on higher mental processes. This viewpoint did not go entirely unchallenged, as we will discuss momentarily, but mainstream theories of conditioning did not allocate any role to cognitive processes. In recent decades, however, research findings have led theorists to shift toward more cognitive explanations of conditioning. Let's review how this transition gradually occurred.

Latent Learning and Cognitive Maps

The first major "renegade" to chip away at the conventional view of learning was an American psychologist named Edward C. Tolman (1932, 1938). Tolman and his colleagues conducted a series of studies that posed some difficult questions for the prevailing views of conditioning. In one landmark study (Tolman & Honzik, 1930), three groups of food-deprived rats learned to run a complicated maze over a series of once-a-day trials (see Figure 6.23a). The rats in Group A received a food reward when they got to the end of the maze each day. Because of this reinforcement, their performance in running the maze (measured by how many "wrong turns" they made) gradually improved over the course of 17 days (see Figure 6.23b). The rats in Group B did not receive any food reward. Lacking reinforcement for getting to the goal box swiftly, this group made many "errors" and showed only modest improvement in performance. Group C was the critical group; they did not get any reward for their first 10 trials in the maze, but they were rewarded from the 11th trial onward. The rats in this group showed little improvement in performance over the first 10 trials (just like Group B), but after finding food in the goal box on the 11th trial, they showed sharp improvement on subsequent trials. In fact, their performance was even

a little better than that of the Group A rats who had been rewarded after every trial (see Figure 6.23b).

Tolman concluded that the rats in Group C had been learning about the maze all along, just as much as the rats in group A, but they had no motivation to demonstrate this learning until a reward was introduced. Tolman called this phenomenon *latent learning*—learning that is not apparent from behavior when it first occurs. *Why did these findings present a challenge for the prevailing view of learning?* First, they suggested that learning can take place in the absence of reinforcement—at a time when learned responses were thought to be stamped in by reinforcement. Second, they suggested that the rats who displayed latent learning had formed a *cognitive map* of the maze (a mental representation of the spatial layout) at a time when cognitive processes were thought to be irrelevant to understanding conditioning even in humans.

Tolman (1948) went on to conduct other studies that suggested cognitive processes play a role in conditioning. But his ideas mostly attracted rebuttals and criticism from the influential learning theorists of his era (Hilgard, 1987). In the long run, however, Tolman's ideas prevailed, as models of conditioning eventually started to incorporate cognitive factors.

Signal Relations

One theorist who has been especially influential in highlighting the potential importance of cognitive factors in conditioning is Robert Rescorla (1978, 1980; Rescorla & Wagner, 1972). Rescorla asserts that environmental stimuli serve as signals and that some stimuli are better, or more dependable, signals

Edward C. Tolman

"Learning consists not in stimulus-response connections but in the building up in the nervous system of sets which function like cognitive maps."

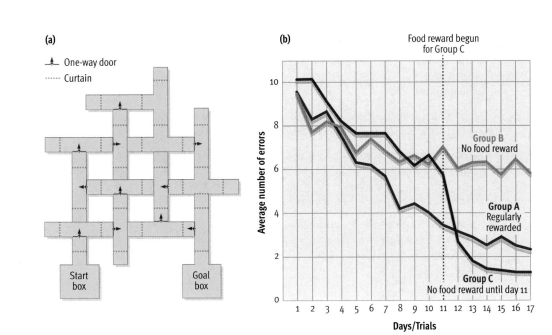

(a)

⊥ One-way door
...... Curtain

Start box

Goal box

(b)

Food reward begun for Group C

Average number of errors

Group B
No food reward

Group A
Regularly rewarded

Group C
No food reward until day 11

Days/Trials

Figure 6.23

Latent learning. (a) In the study by Tolman and Honzik (1930), rats learned to run the complicated maze shown here. **(b) The results** obtained by Tolman and Honzik (1930) are summarized in this graph. The rats in Group C showed a sudden improvement in performance when a food reward was introduced on Trial 11. Tolman concluded that the rats in this group were learning about the maze all along but that their learning remained "latent" until reinforcement was made available.

Source: Adapted from Tolman, E. C., & Honzik, C. H. (1930). Introduction and removal of reward and maze performance in rats. *University of California Publications in Psychology, 4, 257–275.*

than others. Hence, he has manipulated *signal relations* in classical conditioning—that is, CS-US relations that influence whether a CS is a good signal. A "good" signal is one that allows accurate prediction of the US.

In essence, Rescorla manipulates the *predictive value* of a conditioned stimulus. How does he do so? He varies the proportion of trials in which the CS and US are paired. Consider the following example. A tone and shock are paired 20 times for one group of rats. Otherwise, these rats are never shocked. For these rats the CS (tone) and US (shock) are paired in 100% of the experimental trials. Another group of rats also receive 20 pairings of the tone and shock. However, the rats in this group are also exposed to the shock on 20 other trials when the tone does *not* precede it. For this group, the CS and US are paired in only 50% of the trials. Thus, the two groups of rats have had an equal number of CS-US pairings, but the CS is a better signal or predictor of shock for the 100% CS-US group than for the 50% CS-US group.

What did Rescorla find when he tested the two groups of rats for conditioned fear? He found that the CS elicits a much stronger response in the 100% CS-US group than in the 50% CS-US group. Given that the two groups have received an equal number of CS-US pairings, this difference must be due to the greater predictive power of the CS for the 100% group. Numerous studies of signal relations have shown that the predictive value of a CS is an influential factor governing classical conditioning (Rescorla, 1978).

Response-Outcome Relations and Reinforcement

Studies of response-outcome relations and reinforcement also highlight the role of cognitive processes in conditioning. Imagine that on the night before an important exam you study hard while repeatedly playing a Coldplay song. The next morning you earn an A on your exam. Does this result strengthen your tendency to play Coldplay's music before exams? Probably not. Chances are, you will recognize the logical relation between the response of studying hard and the reinforcement of a good grade, and only the response of studying will be strengthened (Killeen, 1981).

Thus, reinforcement is *not* automatic when favorable consequences follow a response. People actively reason out the relations between responses and the outcomes that follow. When a response is followed by a desirable outcome, the response is more likely to be strengthened if the person thinks that the response *caused* the outcome. You might guess that only humans would engage in this causal reasoning. However, evidence suggests that under the right circumstances even pigeons can learn to recognize causal relations between responses and outcomes (Killeen, 1981).

In sum, modern, reformulated models of conditioning view it as a matter of detecting the *con-*

Robert Rescorla

"Pavlovian conditioning is a sophisticated and sensible mechanism by which organisms represent the world. . . . I encourage students to think of animals as behaving like little statisticians. . . . They really are very finely attuned to small changes in the likelihood of events."

---

concept check 6.4

Distinguishing Between Classical Conditioning and Operant Conditioning

Check your understanding of the usual differences between classical conditioning and operant conditioning by indicating the type of conditioning process involved in each of the following examples. In the space on the left, place a C if the example involves classical conditioning, an O if it involves operant conditioning, or a B if it involves both. The answers can be found in Appendix A.

_____ 1. Whenever Midori takes her dog out for a walk, she wears the same old blue windbreaker. Eventually, she notices that her dog becomes excited whenever she puts on this windbreaker.

_____ 2. The Creatures are a successful rock band with three hit albums to their credit. They begin their U.S. tour featuring many new, unreleased songs, all of which draw silence from their concert fans. The same fans cheer wildly when the Creatures play any of their old hits. Gradually, the band reduces the number of new songs it plays and starts playing more of the old standbys.

_____ 3. When Cindy and Mel first fell in love, they listened constantly to the Creatures' hit song "Transatlantic Obsession." Although several years have passed, whenever they hear this song they experience a warm, romantic feeling.

_____ 4. For nearly 20 years Ralph has worked as a machinist in the same factory. His new foreman is never satisfied with Ralph's work and criticizes him constantly. After a few weeks of heavy criticism, Ralph experiences anxiety whenever he arrives at work. He starts calling in sick more and more often to evade this anxiety.

tingencies among environmental events (Beckers et al., 2006; Penn & Povinelli, 2007). According to these theories, organisms actively try to figure out what leads to what (the contingencies) in the world around them. Stimuli are viewed as signals that help organisms minimize their aversive experiences and maximize their pleasant experiences. The new, cognitively oriented theories of conditioning are quite a departure from older theories that depicted conditioning as a mindless, mechanical process. We can also see this new emphasis on cognitive processes in our next topic, observational learning.

REVIEW of Key Learning Goals

6.14 Conditioned taste aversions can be readily acquired even when a lengthy delay occurs between the CS and US. Preparedness, or an evolved module for fear learning, appears to explain why people acquire phobias of ancient sources of threat much more readily than modern sources of threat. The findings on conditioned taste aversion and preparedness led to the conclusion that there are biological constraints on conditioning.

6.15 Domjan argues that researchers' focus on arbitrary conditioned stimuli has led to a distorted picture of the principles of conditioning. Evolutionary psychologists argue that learning processes vary somewhat across species because different species have to grapple with very different adaptive problems.

6.16 Tolman's studies suggested that learning can take place in the absence of reinforcement, which he called latent learning. His findings suggested that cognitive processes contribute to conditioning, but his work was not influential at the time.

6.17 Rescorla's work on signal relations showed that the predictive value of a CS is an influential factor governing classical conditioning. When a response is followed by a desirable outcome, the response is more likely to be strengthened if the response appears to have caused the outcome. Studies of signal relations and response-outcome relations suggest that cognitive processes play a larger role in conditioning than originally believed.

Observational Learning

Key Learning Goals

6.18 Explain the nature and importance of observational learning.

6.19 List the basic processes in observational learning, and discuss Bandura's distinction between acquisition and performance.

6.20 Describe the Featured Study profiling Bandura's classic research on TV models and aggression.

6.21 Discuss modern research on the effects of media violence.

Can classical and operant conditioning account for all learning? Absolutely not. Consider how people learn a fairly basic skill such as driving a car. They do not hop naively into an automobile and start emitting random responses until one leads to favorable consequences. On the contrary, most people learning to drive know exactly where to place the key and how to get started. How are these responses acquired? Through *observation*. Most new drivers have years of experience observing others drive, and they put those observations to work. Learning through observation accounts for a great deal of learning in both animals and humans.

Observational learning **occurs when an organism's responding is influenced by the observation of others, who are called models.** This process has been investigated extensively by Albert Bandura (1977, 1986). Bandura does not see observational learning as entirely separate from classical and operant conditioning. Instead, he asserts that it greatly extends the reach of these conditioning processes. Whereas previous conditioning theorists emphasized the organism's direct experience, Bandura has demonstrated that both classical and operant conditioning can take place "vicariously" through observational learning.

Essentially, observational learning involves being conditioned indirectly by virtue of observing another's conditioning (see Figure 6.24 on the next page). To illustrate, suppose you observe a friend behaving assertively with a car salesperson. You see your friend's assertive behavior reinforced by the exceptionally good buy she gets on the car. Your own tendency to behave assertively with salespeople might well be strengthened as a result. Notice that the reinforcement is experienced by your friend, not you. The good buy should strengthen your friend's tendency to bargain assertively, but your tendency to do so may also be strengthened indirectly.

Bandura's theory of observational learning can help explain why physical punishment tends to increase aggressive behavior in children, even when it is intended to do just the opposite. Parents who depend on physical punishment often punish a child for hitting other children—by hitting the child. The parents may sincerely intend to reduce the child's aggressive behavior, but they are unwittingly serving as *models* of such behavior. Although they may tell the child that "hitting people won't accomplish anything," they are in the midst of hitting the child in order to accomplish something. Because parents usually accomplish their immediate goal of stopping the child's hitting, the child witnesses the reinforcement of aggressive behavior. In this situation, actions speak louder than words—because of observational learning.

Albert Bandura

"Most human behavior is learned by observation through modeling."

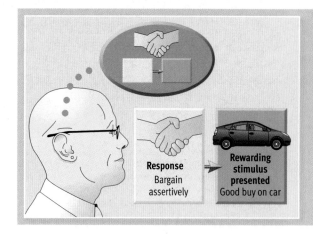

Figure 6.24

Observational learning. In observational learning, an observer attends to and stores a mental representation of a model's behavior (example: assertive bargaining) and its consequences (example: a good buy on a car). If the observer sees the modeled response lead to a favorable outcome, the observer's tendency to emit the modeled response will be strengthened.

Response
Bargain
assertively

Rewarding stimulus presented
Good buy on car

Basic Processes

Bandura has identified four key processes that are crucial in observational learning. The first two—attention and retention—highlight the importance of cognition in this type of learning.

• *Attention.* To learn through observation, you must pay attention to another person's behavior and its consequences.

• *Retention.* You may not have occasion to use an observed response for weeks, months, or even years. Thus, you must store a mental representation of what you have witnessed in your memory.

• *Reproduction.* Enacting a modeled response depends on your ability to reproduce the response by converting your stored mental images into overt behavior. This may not be easy for some responses. For example, most people cannot execute a breathtaking windmill dunk after watching Kobe Bryant do it in a basketball game.

• *Motivation.* Finally, you are unlikely to reproduce an observed response unless you are motivated to do so. Your motivation depends on whether you encounter a situation in which you believe that the response is likely to pay off for you.

Observational learning has proven especially valuable in explaining complex human behaviors, but animals can also learn through observation (Öhman & Mineka, 2001; Zentall, 2003). A simple example is the thieving behavior of the English tit-mouse, a

Observational learning occurs in both humans and animals. For example, no one trained this dog to "pray" with its owner; the chihuahua just picked up the response through observation. In a similar vein, children acquire a diverse array of responses from role models through observational learning.

small bird renowned for its early-morning raids on its human neighbors. The titmouse has learned how to open cardboard caps on bottles of milk delivered to the porches of many homes in England. Having opened the bottle, the titmouse skims the cream from the top of the milk. This clever learned behavior has been passed down from one generation of titmouse to the next through observational learning.

Acquisition Versus Performance

Like Edward C. Tolman (1932) many decades before, Bandura points out that organisms can store cognitive representations of learned responses that they may or may not perform, depending on the reinforcement contingencies. Thus, he distinguishes between the *acquisition* of a learned response and the *performance* of that response. He maintains that *reinforcement affects which responses are actually performed more than which responses are acquired.* People emit those responses that they think are likely to be reinforced. For instance, you may study hard for a course in which the professor gives fair exams, because you expect studying to lead to reinforcement in the form of a good grade. In contrast, you may hardly open the text for a course in which the professor gives arbitrary, unpredictable exams, because

you do not expect studying to be reinforced. Your performance is different in the two situations because you think the reinforcement contingencies are different. Thus, like Skinner, Bandura asserts that reinforcement is a critical determinant of behavior. However, Bandura maintains that reinforcement influences performance rather than learning per se.

Observational Learning and the Media Violence Controversy

The power of observational learning has been at the center of a long-running controversy about the effects of media violence. Children spend an average of about 40 hours per week with various types of entertainment media, and more than half of that time is devoted to watching television, videos, and DVDs (Bushman & Anderson, 2001). Children are very impressionable, and extensive evidence indicates that they pick up many responses from viewing models on TV (Huston et al., 1992). Social critics have expressed concern about the amount of violence on television ever since TV became popular in the 1950s. In the 1960s, Bandura and his colleagues conducted landmark research on the issue that remains widely cited and influential. One of those classic studies serves as the Featured Study for Chapter 6.

The English titmouse has learned how to break into milk bottles to swipe cream from its human neighbors. This behavior has been passed across generations through observational learning.

The Power of Modeling: What They See Is What You Get

FEATURED STUDY

SOURCE: Bandura, A., Ross, D. & Ross, S. (1963b). Vicarious reinforcement and imitative learning. *Journal of Abnormal & Social Psychology, 67,* 601–607.

This study was designed to explore the influence of observing the consequences of another's behavior on the learning of aggressive behavior in children. In a previous study, the same researchers had shown that children exposed to an aggressive adult model displayed more aggression than children exposed to a similar but nonaggressive model (Bandura, Ross, & Ross, 1961). The first study used live (in-person) adult models who did or did not play very roughly with a 5-foot-tall "Bobo doll" while in the same room with the children. A second study by the same research team investigated whether filmed models were as influential as in-person models (Bandura, Ross, & Ross, 1963a). The researchers found that a TV depiction of an adult model roughing up the Bobo doll led to increased aggression just as exposure to a live model had. In this third study of the series, the investigators used filmed models and manipulated the consequences experienced by the aggressive models. The hypothesis was that children who saw the models rewarded for their aggression would become more aggressive than children who saw the models punished for their aggression.

Method

Subjects. The subjects were 40 girls and 40 boys drawn from a nursery school. The average age for the 80 children was 4 years, 3 months.

Procedure. While at the nursery school, each child was invited to play in a toy room. On the way to the toy room an adult escort indicated that she needed to stop in her office for a few minutes. The child was told to watch a TV in the office during this brief delay. On the TV, the child was exposed to one of three 5-minute film sequences. In the *aggressive-model-rewarded* condition, Rocky and Johnny are playing and Rocky attacks Johnny, striking him with a baton, throwing a ball at him repeatedly, and dragging him off to a far corner of the room. The final scene shows Rocky having a great time with the toys while helping himself to soda and cookies. In the *aggressive-model-punished* condition, Rocky engages in the same pattern of aggression, but the outcome is different. Johnny rises to the challenge and thrashes Rocky, who is shown cowering in a corner in the final scene. In the *nonaggressive-model-control* condition, Rocky and Johnny are simply shown engaged in vigorous play without any aggression. In a fourth condition, the *no-model-control* condition, the child did not watch TV while in the office.

After the brief detour to the adult's office, the child was taken to the toy room, as promised, where he or she was allowed to play alone with a diverse array of toys that allowed for either aggressive or nonaggressive play. Among the toys were two Bobo dolls that served as convenient targets

The Bobo doll from Albert Bandura's legendary series of studies on observational learning of aggression can be seen here. The photo on the left shows a filmed depiction of an adult role model exhibiting aggressive behavior toward the Bobo doll. The photo on the right shows how one of the young subjects in the study imitated this aggressive behavior later by attacking the Bobo doll with a hammer.

for aggressive responses. The child's play was observed through a one-way mirror from an adjoining room. The key dependent variable was the number of aggressive acts displayed by the child during the 20-minute play period.

Results

Children in the *aggressive-model-rewarded* condition displayed significantly more total aggression and imitative aggression (specific aggressive acts similar to Rocky's) than children in the *aggressive-model-punished* condition. The amount of imitative aggression exhibited by children in each of the four conditions is summarized in **Figure 6.25**. A clear elevation of imitative aggression was observed only among the children who saw aggression pay off with reinforcement for the model.

Discussion

The results supported a basic premise of Bandura's theory—that observers are more likely to imitate another's behavior when that behavior leads to positive consequences than when it leads to negative consequences. Of particular interest was the fact that filmed models were shown to influence the likelihood of aggressive behavior in children.

Comment

This classic series of studies by Bandura, Ross, and Ross played a prominent role in the early stages of the vigorous debate about the impact of televised violence. People concerned about media violence noted that aggression on TV shows usually leads to rewards and admiration for heroic TV characters. The findings of this study suggested that youngsters watching aggressive models on TV are likely to learn that aggressive behavior pays off. Critics argued

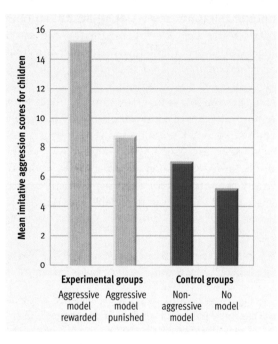

Figure 6.25

Filmed models and aggression. Bandura, Ross, and Ross (1963b) found that acts of imitative aggression were most frequent among children exposed to an aggressive role model on TV whose aggression was rewarded, as predicted by Bandura's theory of observational learning.

that Bandura's Bobo doll studies were too artificial to be conclusive. This criticism led to hundreds of more realistic experiments and correlational studies on the possible link between TV violence and aggressiveness.

Subsequent research demonstrated that youngsters are exposed to an astonishing amount of violence when they watch TV. The National Television Violence Study, a large-scale review of the content of network and cable television shows, revealed that 61% of programs contained violence; 44% of violent actors were enticing role models (i.e., the "good guys"); 75% of violent actions occurred without punishment or condemnation; and 51% of violent actions were "sanitized," as they featured no apparent pain (Anderson et al., 2003).

Does this steady diet of media violence foster increased aggression? Decades of research since Bandura's pioneering work indicate that the answer is "yes" (Bushman & Huesmann, 2001). The short-term effects of media violence have been investigated in hundreds of experimental studies. These studies consistently demonstrate that exposure to TV and movie violence increases the likelihood of physical aggression, verbal aggression, aggressive thoughts, and aggressive emotions in both children and adults (C. A. Anderson et al., 2003).

Research indicates that exposure to aggressive content in video games produces similar results (Carnagey, Anderson, & Bartholow, 2007). Experimental studies find that violent video games increase physiological arousal, aggressive thoughts and emotions, and aggressive behavior, while decreasing helping behavior and desensitizing players to violence (Anderson, 2004; Carnagey, Anderson, & Bushman, 2007). Moreover, theorists are concerned that violence in video games may have even more detrimental effects than violence in other media. Why? Because video games require a higher level of attention and more active involvement than movies or TV; players clearly identify with the characters that they control; and they are routinely reinforced (within the context of the games) for their violent actions (Carnagey & Anderson, 2004). Unfortunately, the amount of violence in popular games is escalating at an alarming rate and their depictions of grotesque violence are becoming increasingly realistic (Gentile & Anderson, 2006).

The real-world and long-term effects of media violence have been investigated through correlational research. The findings of these studies show that the more violence children watch on TV, the more aggressive they tend to be at home and at school (Huesmann & Miller, 1994). Of course, critics point out that this correlation could reflect a variety of causal relationships (see **Figure 6.26**). Perhaps high aggressiveness in children causes an increased interest in violent television shows. However, a handful of long-term studies that have followed the same subjects since the 1960s and 1970s have clarified the causal relations underlying the link between media violence and elevated aggression. These studies show

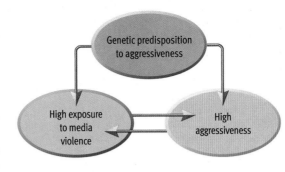

that the extent of youngsters' exposure to media violence in childhood predicts their aggressiveness in adolescence and early adulthood, but not vice versa (Huesman, 1986; Huesman et al., 2003). In other words, high exposure to media violence precedes, and presumably causes, high aggressiveness.

The empirical evidence linking media violence to aggression is clear, convincing, and unequivocal. In fact, the strength of the association between media violence and aggression is nearly as great as the correlation between smoking and cancer (Bushman & Anderson, 2001; see **Figure 6.27** on page 266). Nonetheless, the general public remains uncertain, perhaps even skeptical. One reason is that everyone knows individuals (perhaps themselves) who were raised on a robust diet of media violence but who do not appear to be particularly aggressive. If media violence is so horrible, why aren't we all axe murderers? The answer is that aggressive behavior is influenced by a number of factors besides media violence, which only has a "modest" effect on people's aggressiveness. The problem, experts say, is that TV and movies reach millions upon millions of people, so even a small effect can have big repercussions (Bushman & Anderson, 2001). Suppose that 25 million people watch an extremely violent program. Even if only 1 in 100 viewers become a little more prone to aggression, that is 250,000 people who are a bit more likely to wreak havoc in someone's life.

In any event, the heated debate about media violence shows that observational learning plays an

Figure 6.26

The correlation between exposure to media violence and aggression. The more violence children watch on TV, the more aggressive they tend to be, but this correlation could reflect a variety of underlying causal relationships. Although watching violent shows probably causes increased aggressiveness, it is also possible that aggressive children are drawn to violent shows. Or perhaps a third variable (such as a genetic predisposition to aggressiveness) leads to both a preference for violent shows and high aggressiveness.

web link 6.6

Media Violence

Maintained by a Canadian nonprofit organization called the Media Awareness Network, which develops media literacy programs, this site permits visitors to access a great deal of background information and dialogue on the debate about the effects of violence in the media.

CALVIN AND HOBBES

TYPE OF LEARNING	PROCEDURE	DIAGRAM	RESULT

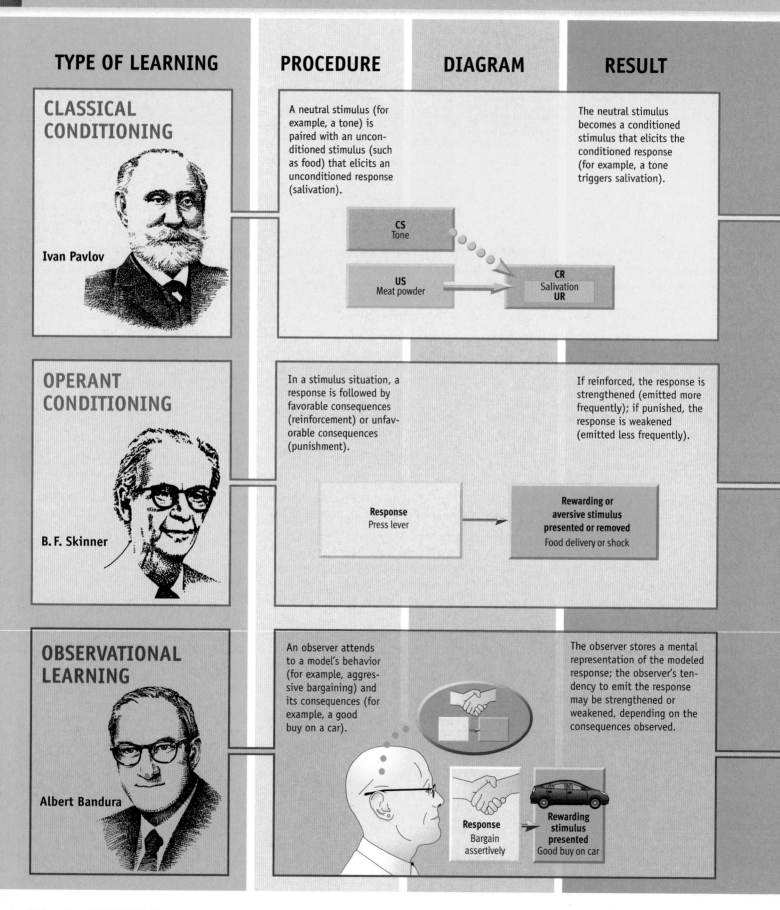

CLASSICAL CONDITIONING

Ivan Pavlov

A neutral stimulus (for example, a tone) is paired with an unconditioned stimulus (such as food) that elicits an unconditioned response (salivation).

CS
Tone

US
Meat powder

CR
Salivation
UR

The neutral stimulus becomes a conditioned stimulus that elicits the conditioned response (for example, a tone triggers salivation).

OPERANT CONDITIONING

B. F. Skinner

In a stimulus situation, a response is followed by favorable consequences (reinforcement) or unfavorable consequences (punishment).

Response
Press lever

Rewarding or aversive stimulus presented or removed
Food delivery or shock

If reinforced, the response is strengthened (emitted more frequently); if punished, the response is weakened (emitted less frequently).

OBSERVATIONAL LEARNING

Albert Bandura

An observer attends to a model's behavior (for example, aggressive bargaining) and its consequences (for example, a good buy on a car).

Response
Bargain assertively

Rewarding stimulus presented
Good buy on car

The observer stores a mental representation of the modeled response; the observer's tendency to emit the response may be strengthened or weakened, depending on the consequences observed.

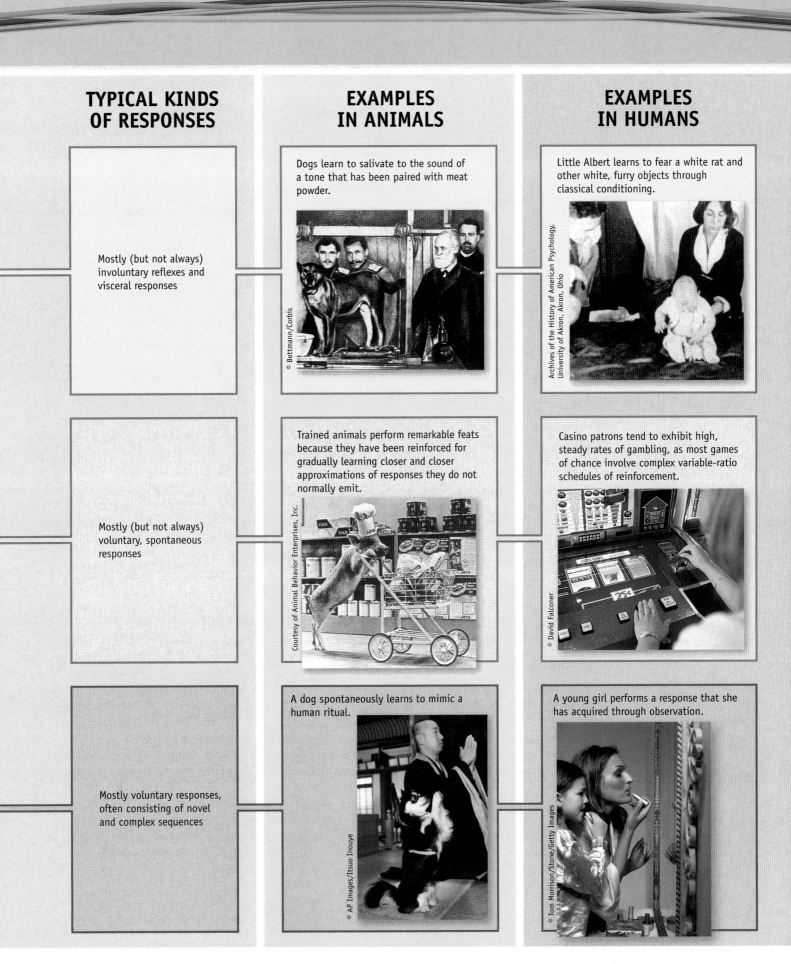

TYPICAL KINDS OF RESPONSES

Mostly (but not always) involuntary reflexes and visceral responses

Mostly (but not always) voluntary, spontaneous responses

Mostly voluntary responses, often consisting of novel and complex sequences

EXAMPLES IN ANIMALS

Dogs learn to salivate to the sound of a tone that has been paired with meat powder.

© Bettmann/Corbis

Trained animals perform remarkable feats because they have been reinforced for gradually learning closer and closer approximations of responses they do not normally emit.

Courtesy of Animal Behavior Enterprises, Inc.

A dog spontaneously learns to mimic a human ritual.

© AP Images/Itsuo Inouye

EXAMPLES IN HUMANS

Little Albert learns to fear a white rat and other white, furry objects through classical conditioning.

Archives of the History of American Psychology, University of Akron, Akron, Ohio

Casino patrons tend to exhibit high, steady rates of gambling, as most games of chance involve complex variable-ratio schedules of reinforcement.

© David Falconer

A young girl performs a response that she has acquired through observation.

© Tom Morrison/Stone/Getty Images

Figure 6.27

Comparison of the relationship between media violence and aggression to other correlations. Many studies have found a correlation between exposure to media violence and aggression. However, some critics have argued that the correlation is too weak to have any practical significance in the real world. In a rebuttal of this criticism, Bushman and Anderson (2001) note that the average correlation in studies of media violence and aggression is .31. They argue that this association is almost as strong as the correlation between smoking and the probability of developing lung cancer, which is viewed as very relevant to real-world issues and is notably stronger than a variety of other correlations shown here that are assumed to have practical importance.

Adapted from Bushman, B. J., & Anderson, C. A. (2001). Media violence and the American public. *American Psychologist, 56*(6-7), 477–489. (Figure 2). Copyright © 2001 American Psychological Association.

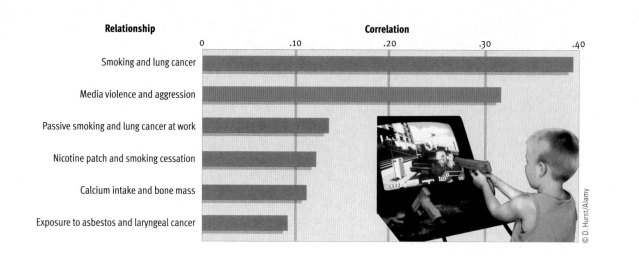

Relationship | **Correlation**

- Smoking and lung cancer
- Media violence and aggression
- Passive smoking and lung cancer at work
- Nicotine patch and smoking cessation
- Calcium intake and bone mass
- Exposure to asbestos and laryngeal cancer

© D. Hurst/Alamy

important role in regulating behavior. It represents a third major type of learning that builds on the first two types—classical conditioning and operant conditioning. These three basic types of learning are summarized and compared in an Illustrated Overview on pages 264–265.

REVIEW of Key Learning Goals

6.18 In observational learning, an organism is conditioned vicariously by watching a model's conditioning. Both classical and operant conditioning can occur through observational learning, which extends their influence. The principles of observational learning have been used to explain why physical punishment increases aggressive behavior.

6.19 Observational learning depends on the processes of attention, retention, reproduction, and motivation. According to Bandura, reinforcement influences which responses one

will perform more than it influences the acquisition of new responses.

6.20 In a landmark study, Bandura and colleagues demonstrated that exposure to aggressive TV models led to increased aggression in children, especially when the TV models were reinforced for their aggression.

6.21 Research on observational learning has played a central role in the debate about the effects of media violence for many decades. Both experimental and correlational studies suggest that violent TV shows, movies, and video games contribute to increased aggression among children and adults.

Key Learning Goals

6.22 Identify the two unifying themes highlighted in this chapter.

Heredity and Environment

Sociohistorical Context

Reflecting on the Chapter's Themes

Two of our seven unifying themes stand out in this chapter. First, you can see how nature and nurture interactively govern behavior. Second, looking at psychology in its sociohistorical context, you can see how progress in psychology spills over to affect trends and values in society at large. Let's examine each of these points in more detail.

In regard to nature versus nurture, research on learning clearly demonstrates the enormous power of the environment in shaping behavior. Pavlov's model of classical conditioning shows how experiences can account for everyday fears and other emotional responses. Skinner's model of operant conditioning shows how reinforcement and punishment can mold everything from a child's bedtime whimpering to an adult's restaurant preferences. Indeed, many learning theorists once believed that *all* aspects of behavior could be explained in terms

of environmental determinants. In recent decades, however, studies of conditioned taste aversion and preparedness have shown that there are biological constraints on conditioning. Thus, even in explanations of learning—an area once dominated by nurture theories—we see once again that biology and experience jointly influence behavior.

The history of research on conditioning also shows how progress in psychology can seep into every corner of society. For example, the behaviorists' ideas about reinforcement and punishment have influenced patterns of discipline in our society. Research on operant conditioning has also affected management styles in the business world, leading to an increased emphasis on positive reinforcement. In the educational arena, the concept of individualized, programmed learning is a spinoff from behavioral research. The fact that the principles of conditioning are routinely applied in homes, businesses, schools, and factories clearly shows that psychology is not an ivory tower endeavor.

In the upcoming Personal Application, you will see how you can apply the principles of conditioning to improve your self-control, as we discuss the technology of behavior modification.

Achieving Self-Control Through Behavior Modification

Answer the following "yes" or "no."

___ **1** Do you have a hard time passing up food, even when you're not hungry?

___ **2** Do you wish you studied more often?

___ **3** Would you like to cut down on your smoking or drinking?

___ **4** Do you experience difficulty in getting yourself to exercise regularly?

If you answered "yes" to any of these questions, you have struggled with the challenge of self-control. This Application discusses how you can use the principles and techniques of behavior modification to improve your self-control. *Behavior modification* **is a systematic approach to changing behavior through the application of the principles of conditioning.** Advocates of behavior modification assume that behavior is mainly a product of learning, conditioning, and environmental control. They further assume that *what is learned can be unlearned.* Thus, they set out to "recondition" people to produce more desirable and effective patterns of behavior.

The technology of behavior modification has been applied with great success in schools, businesses, hospitals, factories, child-care facilities, prisons, and mental health centers (Kazdin, 2001; O'Donohue, 1998; Rachman, 1992). Moreover, behavior modification techniques have proven particularly valuable in efforts to improve self-control. Our discussion will borrow liberally from an excellent book on self-modification by David Watson and Roland Tharp (2007). We will discuss five steps in the process of self-modification, which are outlined in Figure 6.28.

Specifying Your Target Behavior

The first step in a self-modification program is to specify the target behavior(s) that you

want to change. Behavior modification can only be applied to a clearly defined, overt response, yet many people have difficulty pinpointing the behavior they hope to alter. They tend to describe their problems in terms of unobservable personality *traits* rather than overt *behaviors*. For example, asked what behavior he would like to change, a man might say, "I'm too irritable." That may be true, but it is of little help in designing a self-modification program. To use a behavioral approach, vague statements about traits need to be translated into precise descriptions of specific target behaviors.

To identify target responses, you need to ponder past behavior or closely observe future behavior and list specific *examples* of responses that lead to the trait description. For instance, the man who regards himself as "too irritable" might identify two overly frequent responses, such as arguing with his wife and snapping at his children. These are specific behaviors for which he could design a self-modification program.

Gathering Baseline Data

The second step in behavior modification is to gather baseline data. You need to systematically observe your target behavior for a period of time (usually a week or two) before you work out the details of your program. In gathering your baseline data, you need to monitor three things.

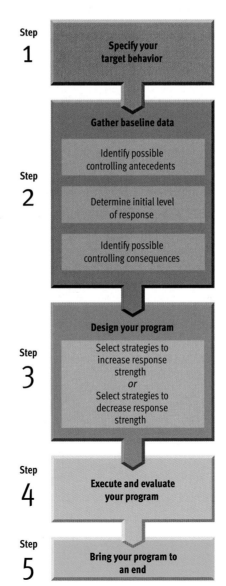

Figure 6.28

Steps in a self-modification program. This flowchart provides an overview of the five steps necessary to execute a self-modification program. Many people are tempted to plunge into their program and skip the first two steps, but these steps are critical to success.

Overeating is just one of the many types of maladaptive habits that can be reduced or eliminated through self-modification techniques.

First, you need to determine the initial response level of your target behavior. After all, you can't tell whether your program is working effectively unless you have a baseline for comparison. In most cases, you would simply keep track of how often the target response occurs in a certain time interval. Thus, you might count the daily frequency of snapping at your children, smoking cigarettes, or biting your fingernails. *It is crucial to gather accurate data.* You should record the behavior as soon as possible after it occurs, and it is usually best to portray these records graphically (see Figure 6.29).

Second, you need to monitor the *antecedents* of your target behavior. Antecedents are events that typically precede the target response. Often these events play a major role in evoking your target behavior. For example, if your target is overeating, you might discover that the bulk of your overeating occurs late in the evening while you watch TV. If you can pinpoint this kind of antecedent-response connection, you may be able to design your program to circumvent or break the link.

Third, you need to monitor the typical consequences of your target behavior. Try to identify the reinforcers that are maintaining an undesirable target behavior or the unfavorable outcomes that are suppressing a desirable target behavior. In trying to identify reinforcers, remember that avoidance behavior is usually maintained by negative reinforcement. That is, the payoff for avoidance is usually the removal of something aversive, such as anxiety or a threat to self-esteem. You should also take into account the fact that a response may not be reinforced every time, as most behavior is maintained by intermittent reinforcement.

Designing Your Program

Once you have selected a target behavior and gathered adequate baseline data, it is time to plan your intervention program. Generally speaking, your program will be designed either to increase or to decrease the frequency of a target response.

Increasing Response Strength

Efforts to increase the frequency of a target response depend largely on the use of positive reinforcement. In other words, you reward yourself for behaving properly. Although the basic strategy is quite simple, doing it skillfully involves a number of considerations.

Selecting a Reinforcer To use positive reinforcement, you need to find a reward that will be effective for you. Reinforcement is subjective. What is reinforcing for one person may not be reinforcing for another. To determine your personal reinforcers you need to ask yourself questions such as (see Figure 6.30): What do I like to do for fun? What makes me feel good? What would be a nice present? What would I hate to lose?

You don't have to come up with spectacular new reinforcers that you've never experienced before. *You can use reinforcers that you are already getting.* However, you have to restructure the contingencies so that you get them only if you behave appropriately. For example, if you normally buy two music CDs per week, you might make these purchases contingent on studying a certain number of hours during the week.

Arranging the Contingencies Once you have chosen your reinforcer, you have to set up reinforcement contingencies. These contingencies will describe the exact behavioral goals that must be met and the reinforcement that may then be awarded. For example, in a program to increase exercise, you might make spending $40 on clothes (the reinforcer) contingent on having jogged 15 miles during the week (the target behavior).

Figure 6.29

Example of record-keeping in a self-modification program. Graphic records are ideal for tracking progress in behavior modification efforts. The records shown here illustrate what people would be likely to track in a behavior modification program for weight loss.

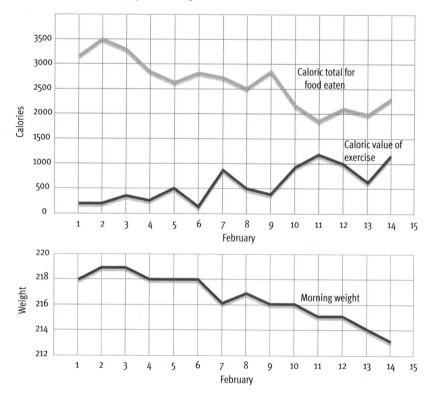

1. What will be the rewards of achieving your goal?
2. What kind of praise do you like to receive, from yourself and others?
3. What kinds of things do you like to have?
4. What are your major interests?
5. What are your hobbies?
6. What people do you like to be with?
7. What do you like to do with those people?
8. What do you do for fun?
9. What do you do to relax?
10. What do you do to get away from it all?
11. What makes you feel good?
12. What would be a nice present to receive?
13. What kinds of things are important to you?
14. What would you buy if you had an extra $20? $50? $100?
15. On what do you spend your money each week?
16. What behaviors do you perform every day? (Don't overlook the obvious or commonplace.)
17. Are there any behaviors you usually perform instead of the target behavior?
18. What would you hate to lose?
19. Of the things you do every day, which would you hate to give up?
20. What are your favorite daydreams and fantasies?
21. What are the most relaxing scenes you can imagine?

Figure 6.30

Choosing a reinforcer for a self-modification program. Finding a good reinforcer to use in a behavior modification program can require a lot of thought. The questions listed here can help people identify their personal reinforcers.

Source: Adapted from Watson, D. L., & Tharp, R. G. (1997). *Self-directed behavior: Self-modification for personal adjustment.* Belmont, CA: Wadsworth. Reprinted by permission.

Try to set behavioral goals that are both challenging and realistic. You want your goals to be challenging so that they lead to improvement in your behavior. However, setting unrealistically high goals—a common mistake in self-modification—often leads to unnecessary discouragement.

Decreasing Response Strength

Let's turn now to the challenge of reducing the frequency of an undesirable response. You can go about this task in a number of ways. Your principal options include reinforcement, control of antecedents, and punishment.

Reinforcement Reinforcers can be used in an indirect way to decrease the frequency of a response. This may sound paradoxical, since you have learned that reinforcement strengthens a response. The trick lies in how you define the target behavior. For example, in the case of overeating you might define your target behavior as eating more than 1600 calories a day (an excess response that you want to decrease) or eating less than 1600 calories a day (a deficit response that you want to increase). You can choose the latter definition and reinforce yourself whenever you eat less than 1600 calories in a day. Thus, you can reinforce yourself for not emitting a response, or for emitting it less, and thereby decrease a response through reinforcement.

Control of Antecedents A worthwhile strategy for decreasing the occurrence of an undesirable response may be to identify its antecedents and avoid exposure to them. This strategy is especially useful when you are trying to decrease the frequency of a consummatory response, such as smoking or eating. In the case of overeating, for instance, the easiest way to resist temptation is to avoid having to face it. Thus, you might stay away from favorite restaurants, minimize time spent in your kitchen, shop for groceries just after eating (when willpower is higher), and avoid purchasing favorite foods.

Punishment The strategy of decreasing unwanted behavior by punishing yourself for that behavior is an obvious option that people tend to overuse. The biggest problem with punishment in a self-modification effort is that it is difficult to follow through and punish yourself. Nonetheless, there may be situations in which your manipulations of reinforcers need to be bolstered by the threat of punishment.

If you're going to use punishment, keep two guidelines in mind. First, do not use punishment alone. Use it in conjunction with positive reinforcement. If you set up a program in which you can earn only negative consequences, you probably won't stick to it. Second, use a relatively mild punishment so that you will actually be able to administer it to yourself.

Executing and Evaluating Your Program

Once you have designed your program, the next step is to put it to work by enforcing the contingencies that you have carefully planned. During this period, you need to continue to accurately record the frequency of your target behavior so you can evaluate your progress. The success of your program depends on your not "cheating." The most common form of cheating is to reward yourself when you have not actually earned it.

You can do two things to increase the likelihood that you will comply with your program. One is to make up a *behavioral contract*—a written agreement outlining a promise to adhere to the contingencies of a behavior modification program. The formality of signing such a contract in front of friends or family seems to make many people take their program more seriously. You can further reduce the likelihood of cheating by having someone other than yourself dole out the reinforcers and punishments.

Generally, when you design your program you should spell out the conditions under which you will bring it to an end. Doing so involves setting terminal goals such as reaching a certain weight, studying with a certain regularity, or going without cigarettes for a certain length of time. Often, it is a good idea to phase out your program by planning a gradual reduction in the frequency or potency of your reinforcement for appropriate behavior.

REVIEW of Key Learning Goals

6.23 Behavior modification techniques can be used to increase one's self-control. The first step in self-modification involves explicitly specifying the overt, measurable target behavior to be increased or decreased. The second step involves gathering data about the initial rate of the target response and identifying any typical antecedents and consequences associated with the behavior.

6.24 In designing a program, if you are trying to increase the strength of a response, you'll depend on positive reinforcement contingencies that should be spelled out exactly. A number of strategies can be used to decrease the strength of a response, including reinforcement, control of antecedents, and punishment. In executing and evaluating your program you should use a behavioral contract, monitor your behavior carefully, and decide how and when you will phase out your program.

Manipulating Emotions: Pavlov and Persuasion

Key Learning Goals

6.25 Recognize how classical conditioning is used to manipulate emotions.

With all due respect to the great Ivan Pavlov, when we focus on his demonstration that dogs can be trained to slobber in response to a tone, it is easy to lose sight of the importance of classical conditioning. At first glance, most people do not see a relationship between Pavlov's slobbering dogs and anything that they are even remotely interested in. However, in the main body of the chapter, we saw that classical conditioning actually contributes to the regulation of many important aspects of behavior, including fears, phobias, and other emotional reactions; immune function and other physiological processes; food preferences; and even sexual arousal. In this Application you will learn that classical conditioning is routinely used to manipulate emotions in persuasive efforts. If you watch TV, you have been subjected to Pavlovian techniques. An understanding of these techniques can help you recognize when your emotions are being manipulated by advertisers, politicians, and the media.

Manipulation efforts harnessing Pavlovian conditioning generally involve a special subtype of classical conditioning that theorists have recently christened *evaluative conditioning*. **Evaluative conditioning consists of efforts to transfer the emotion attached to a US to a new CS.** In other words, evaluative conditioning involves the acquisition of emotion-laden likes and dislikes, or preferences, through classical conditioning. Of interest here is that research shows that attitudes can be shaped through evaluative conditioning without participants' conscious awareness (Olson & Fazio, 2001) and that evaluative conditioning is remarkably resistant to extinction (Walther, Nagengast, & Trasselli, 2005). Thus, an especially interesting aspect of evaluative conditioning is that people often are unaware of the origin of their attitudes or of the fact that they even feel the way they do. The key to this process is simply to manipulate the automatic, subconscious associations that people make in response to various stimuli. Let's look at how this manipulation is done in advertising, business negotiations, and the world of politics.

Classical Conditioning in Advertising

The art of manipulating people's associations has been perfected by the advertising industry, leading Till and Priluck (2000) to comment, "conditioning of attitudes towards products and brands has become generally accepted and has developed into a unique research stream" (p. 57). Advertisers consistently endeavor to pair the products they are peddling with stimuli that seem likely to elicit positive emotional responses (see **Figure 6.31**). An extensive variety of stimuli are used for this purpose. Products are paired with well-liked celebrity spokespersons; depictions of warm, loving families; beautiful pastoral scenery; cute, cuddly pets; enchanting, rosy-cheeked children; upbeat, pleasant music; and opulent surroundings that reek of wealth. Advertisers also like to pair their products with exciting events, such as the NBA Finals, and cherished symbols, such as flags and the Olympic rings insignia. But, above all else, advertisers like to link their products with sexual imagery and extremely attractive models—especially, glamorous, alluring women (Reichert, 2003; Reichert & Lambiase, 2003).

Advertisers mostly seek to associate their products with stimuli that evoke pleasurable feelings of a general sort, but in some cases they try to create more specific associations. For example, cigarette brands sold mainly to men are frequently paired with tough-looking men in rugged settings to create an association between the cigarettes and masculinity. In contrast, cigarette brands that are mainly marketed to women are paired with images that evoke feelings of femininity. In a similar vein, manufacturers of designer jeans typically seek to forge associations between their products and things that are young, urban, and hip. Advertisers marketing expensive automobiles or platinum credit cards pair their products with symbols of affluence, luxury, and privilege, such as mansions, butlers, and dazzling jewelry.

Figure 6.31

Classical conditioning in advertising. Many advertisers attempt to make their products conditioned stimuli that elicit pleasant emotional responses by pairing their products with attractive or popular people or sexual imagery.

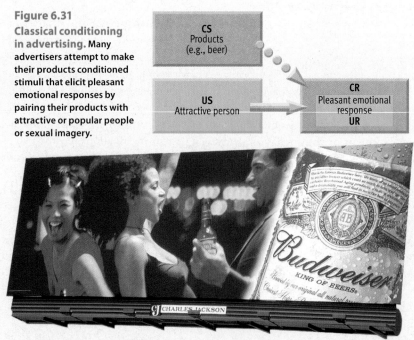

© Bill Aron/PhotoEdit

Classical Conditioning in Business Negotiations

In the world of business interactions, two standard practices are designed to get customers to make an association between one's company and pleasurable feelings. The first is to take customers out to dinner at fine restaurants. The provision of delicious food and fine wine in a luxurious environment is a powerful unconditioned stimulus that reliably elicits pleasant feelings that are likely to be associated with the host. The second practice is the strategy of entertaining customers at major events, such as concerts and football games. Over the last couple of decades, America's sports arenas have largely been rebuilt with vastly more "luxury skyboxes" to accommodate this business tactic. It reaches its zenith every year at the Super Bowl, where most of the seats go to the guests of Fortune 500 corporations. This practice pairs the host with both pleasant feelings and the excitement of a big event.

It is worth noting that these strategies take advantage of other processes besides classical conditioning. They also make use of the *reciprocity norm*—the social rule that one should pay back in kind what one receives from others (Cialdini, 2001). Thus, wining and dining clients creates a sense of obligation that they should reciprocate their host's generosity—presumably in their business dealings.

Classical Conditioning in the World of Politics

Like advertisers, candidates running for election need to influence the attitudes of many people quickly, subtly, and effectively—and they depend on evaluative conditioning to help them do so. For example, have you noticed how politicians show up at an endless variety of pleasant public events (such as the opening of a new mall) that often have nothing to do with their public service? When a sports team wins some sort of championship, local politicians are drawn like flies to the subsequent celebrations. They want to pair themselves with these positive events, so that they are associated with pleasant emotions.

Election campaign ads use the same techniques as commercial ads (except they don't rely much on sexual appeals). Candidates are paired with popular celebrities, wholesome families, pleasant music, and symbols of patriotism. Cognizant of the power of classical conditioning, politicians also exercise great care to ensure that they are not paired with people or events that might trigger negative feelings. For example, in 1999, when the U.S. government finally turned control of the Panama Canal over to Panama, President Bill Clinton and Vice-President Al Gore chose to not attend the ceremonies because this event was viewed negatively in some quarters.

The ultimate political perversion of the principles of classical conditioning probably occurred in Nazi Germany. The Nazis used many propaganda techniques to create prejudice toward Jews and members of other targeted groups (such as Gypsies). One such strategy was the repeated pairing of disgusting, repulsive images with stereotypical pictures of Jews. For example, the Nazis would show alternating pictures of rats or roaches crawling over filthy garbage and stereotypical Jewish faces, so that the two images would become associated in the minds of the viewers. Thus, the German population was conditioned to have negative emotional reactions to Jews and to associate them with vermin subject to extermination. The Nazis reasoned that if people would not hesitate to exterminate rats and roaches, then why not human beings associated with these vermin?

Becoming More Aware of Classical Conditioning Processes

How effective are the efforts to manipulate people's emotions through classical conditioning? It's hard to say. In the real world, these strategies are always used in combination with other persuasive tactics, which creates multiple confounds that make it difficult to assess the impact of the Pavlovian techniques (Walther et al., 2005). Laboratory research can eliminate these confounds, but surprisingly little research on these strategies has been published, and virtually all of it has dealt with advertising. The advertising studies suggest that classical conditioning can be effective and leave enduring imprints on consumers' attitudes (Grossman & Till, 1998; Shimp, Stuart, & Engle, 1991; Walther & Grigoriadis, 2003). And research indicates that sexual appeals in advertising are attention getting, likable, and persuasive (Reichert, Heckler, & Jackson, 2001). But a great deal of additional research is needed. Given the monumental sums that advertisers spend using these techniques, it seems reasonable to speculate that individual companies have data on their specific practices to demonstrate their efficacy, but these data are not made available to the public.

What can you do to reduce the extent to which your emotions are manipulated through Pavlovian procedures? Well, you could turn off your radio and TV, close up your magazines, stop your newspaper, disconnect your modem, and withdraw into a media-shielded shell, but that hardly seems realistic for most people. Realistically, the best defense is to make a conscious effort to become more aware of the pervasive attempts to condition your emotions and attitudes. Some research on persuasion suggests that *to be forewarned is to be forearmed* (Pfau et al., 1990). In other words, if you know how media sources try to manipulate you, you should be more resistant to their strategies.

Table 6.2 Critical Thinking Skills Discussed in This Application

Skill	Description
Understanding how Pavlovian conditioning can be used to manipulate emotions	The critical thinker understands how stimuli can be paired together to create automatic associations that people may not be aware of.
Developing the ability to detect conditioning procedures used in the media	The critical thinker can recognize Pavlovian conditioning tactics in commercial and political advertisements.

REVIEW of Key Learning Goals

6.25 Advertisers routinely pair their products with stimuli that seem likely to elicit positive emotions or other specific feelings. The business practice of taking customers out to dinner or to major events also takes advantage of Pavlovian conditioning. Politicians also work to pair themselves with positive events. The best defense against these tactics is to become more aware of efforts to manipulate your emotions.

Key Ideas

Classical Conditioning

▌ Classical conditioning explains how a neutral stimulus can acquire the capacity to elicit a response originally evoked by another stimulus. This kind of conditioning was originally described by Ivan Pavlov.

▌ Many kinds of everyday responses are regulated through classical conditioning, including phobias, fears, and pleasant emotional responses. Even physiological responses such as immune and sexual functioning and drug tolerance can be influenced by classical conditioning.

▌ A conditioned response may be weakened and extinguished entirely when the CS is no longer paired with the US. In some cases, spontaneous recovery occurs, and an extinguished response reappears after a period of nonexposure to the CS.

▌ Conditioning may generalize to additional stimuli that are similar to the original CS. The opposite of generalization is discrimination, which involves not responding to stimuli that resemble the original CS. Higher-order conditioning occurs when a CS functions as if it were a US, to establish new conditioning.

Operant Conditioning

▌ Operant conditioning involves largely voluntary responses that are governed by their consequences. Following the lead of E. L. Thorndike, B. F. Skinner investigated this form of conditioning, working mainly with rats and pigeons in Skinner boxes.

▌ The key dependent variable in operant conditioning is the rate of response over time. When this responding is shown graphically, steep slopes indicate rapid responding. Primary reinforcers are unlearned; secondary reinforcers acquire their reinforcing quality through conditioning.

▌ New operant responses can be shaped by gradually reinforcing closer and closer approximations of the desired response. In operant conditioning, extinction occurs when reinforcement for a response is terminated and the rate of that response declines.

▌ Operant responses are regulated by discriminative stimuli that are cues regarding the likelihood of obtaining reinforcers. These stimuli are subject to the same processes of generalization and discrimination that occur in classical conditioning.

▌ Intermittent schedules of reinforcement produce greater resistance to extinction than similar continuous schedules. Ratio schedules tend to yield higher rates of response than interval schedules. Shorter intervals and higher ratios are associated with faster responding.

▌ Responses can be strengthened through either the presentation of positive reinforcers or the removal of negative reinforcers. Negative reinforcement regulates escape and avoidance learning. The process of avoidance learning may shed light on why phobias are so difficult to eliminate.

▌ With punishment, unfavorable consequences lead to a decline in response strength. Some of the problems associated with physical punishment as a disciplinary procedure are emotional side effects and increased aggressive behavior.

Changing Directions in the Study of Conditioning

▌ The findings on conditioned taste aversion and preparedness in the acquisition of phobias have led to the recognition that there are species-specific biological constraints on conditioning. Domjan argues that researchers' focus on arbitrary conditioned stimuli has led to a distorted picture of the principles of conditioning. Some psychologists argue that learning processes vary somewhat across species, because of evolutionary pressures.

▌ Tolman's studies of latent learning suggested that cognitive processes contribute to conditioning, but his work was not influential at the time. Studies of signal relations in classical conditioning and response-outcome relations in operant conditioning suggest that cognitive processes play a larger role in conditioning than originally believed.

Observational Learning

▌ In observational learning, an organism is conditioned by watching a model's conditioning. Both classical and operant conditioning can occur through observational learning, which depends on the processes of attention, retention, reproduction, and motivation.

▌ According to Bandura, reinforcement influences which responses one will perform more than it influences the acquisition of new responses. Research on observational learning has played a central role in the debate about the effects of media violence for many decades. This research suggests that media violence contributes to increased aggression among children and adults.

Reflecting on the Chapter's Themes

▌ Two of our key themes were especially apparent in our coverage of learning and conditioning. One theme involves the interaction of biology and experience in learning. The other involves the way progress in psychology affects society at large.

PERSONAL APPLICATION Achieving Self-Control Through Behavior Modification

▌ The first step in self-modification is specifying the target behavior to be increased or decreased. The second step is gathering baseline data on the initial rate of the target response.

▌ The third step is to design a program, using procedures such as reinforcement, control of antecedents, and punishment. The fourth step is executing and evaluating your program.

CRITICAL THINKING APPLICATION Manipulating Emotions: Pavlov and Persuasion

▌ Advertisers routinely pair their products with stimuli that seem likely to elicit positive emotions or other specific feelings. Politicians also work to pair themselves with positive events. The best defense against these tactics is to become more aware of efforts to manipulate your emotions.

Key Terms

Acquisition (p. 237)
Avoidance learning (p. 250)
Behavior modification (p. 267)
Behavioral contract (p. 269)
Classical conditioning (p. 232)
Conditioned reinforcers (p. 244)
Conditioned response (CR) (p. 234)
Conditioned stimulus (CS) (p. 234)
Continuous reinforcement (p. 247)
Cumulative recorder (p. 243)
Discriminative stimuli (p. 246)
Elicit (p. 234)
Emit (p. 243)
Escape learning (p. 250)
Evaluative conditioning (p. 270)
Extinction (p. 238)
Fixed-interval (FI) schedule (p. 248)
Fixed-ratio (FR) schedule (p. 248)
Higher-order conditioning (p. 240)
Intermittent reinforcement (p. 247)
Latent learning (p. 257)
Law of effect (p. 242)
Learning (pp. 231–232)
Negative reinforcement (p. 249)
Observational learning (p. 259)
Operant chamber (p. 243)
Operant conditioning (p. 241)
Partial reinforcement (p. 247)
Pavlovian conditioning (p. 232)
Phobias (p. 232)
Positive reinforcement (p. 249)
Preparedness (p. 255)

Primary reinforcers (p. 244)
Punishment (p. 251)
Reinforcement (p. 242)
Reinforcement contingencies (p. 243)
Renewal effect (p. 239)
Resistance to extinction (p. 246)
Schedule of reinforcement (p. 247)
Secondary reinforcers (p. 244)
Shaping (p. 245)
Skinner box (p. 243)
Spontaneous recovery (p. 238)
Stimulus discrimination (p. 240)
Stimulus generalization (p. 239)
Trial (p. 234)
Unconditioned response (UR) (p. 234)
Unconditioned stimulus (US) (p. 234)
Variable-interval (VI) schedule (p. 248)
Variable-ratio (VR) schedule (p. 248)

Key People

Albert Bandura (pp. 259–262)
John Garcia (p. 255)
Ivan Pavlov (pp. 232–234)
Robert Rescorla (pp. 257–258)
Martin Seligman (pp. 254–255)
B. F. Skinner (pp. 241–245)
E. L. Thorndike (pp. 241–242)
Edward C. Tolman (p. 257)
John B. Watson (pp. 239–240)

1. After repeatedly pairing a tone with meat powder, Pavlov found that a dog will salivate when the tone is presented. Salivation to the tone is a(n):
   A. unconditioned stimulus.
   B. unconditioned response.
   C. conditioned stimulus.
   D. conditioned response.

2. Sam's wife always wears the same black nightgown whenever she is "in the mood" for sexual relations. Sam becomes sexually aroused as soon as he sees his wife in the nightgown. For Sam, the nightgown is a(n):
   A. unconditioned stimulus.
   B. unconditioned response.
   C. conditioned stimulus.
   D. conditioned response.

3. Watson and Rayner (1920) conditioned "Little Albert" to fear white rats by banging a hammer on a steel bar as the child played with a white rat. Later, it was discovered that Albert feared not only white rats but white stuffed toys and Santa's beard as well. Albert's fear of these other objects can be attributed to:
   A. the law of effect.
   B. stimulus generalization.
   C. stimulus discrimination.
   D. an overactive imagination.

4. The phenomenon of higher-order conditioning shows that:
   A. only a genuine, natural US can be used to establish a CR.
   B. auditory stimuli are easier to condition than visual stimuli.
   C. visual stimuli are easier to condition than auditory stimuli.
   D. an already established CS can be used in the place of a natural US.

5. Which of the following statements is (are) true?
   A. Classical conditioning regulates reflexive, involuntary responses exclusively.
   B. Operant conditioning regulates voluntary responses exclusively.
   C. The distinction between the two types of conditioning is not absolute, with both types jointly and interactively governing some aspects of behavior.
   D. Both a and b.

6. A pigeon in a Skinner box is pecking the disk at a high, steady rate. The graph portraying this pigeon's responding will have:
   A. a steep, unchanging slope.
   B. a shallow, unchanging slope.
   C. a progressively steeper slope
   D. a progressively shallower slope.

7. A primary reinforcer has _____ reinforcing properties; a secondary reinforcer has _____ reinforcing properties.
   A. biological; acquired
   B. conditioned; unconditioned
   C. weak; potent
   D. immediate; delayed

8. The steady, rapid responding of a person playing a slot machine is an example of the pattern of responding typically generated on a _____ schedule.
   A. fixed-ratio
   B. variable-ratio
   C. fixed-interval
   D. variable-interval

9. Positive reinforcement _____ the rate of responding; negative reinforcement _____ the rate of responding.
   A. increases; decreases
   B. decreases; increases
   C. increases; increases
   D. decreases; decreases

10. Research on avoidance learning suggests that a fear response is acquired through _____ conditioning; the avoidance response is maintained as a result of _____ conditioning.
    A. classical; operant
    B. operant; classical
    C. classical; classical
    D. operant; operant

11. Nolan used to love tequila. However, a few weeks ago he drank way too much tequila and became very, very sick. His tendency to drink tequila has since declined dramatically. In operant terms, this sequence of events represents:
    A. generalization
    B. negative reinforcement.
    C. higher-order conditioning.
    D. punishment.

12. According to Rescorla, the strength of a conditioned response depends on:
    A. the number of trials in which the CS and US are paired.
    B. the number of trials in which the CS is presented alone.
    C. the percentage of trials in which the CS and US are paired.
    D. resistance to extinction.

13. Bandura maintains that reinforcement mainly determines the _____ of a response.
    A. acquisition
    B. development
    C. performance
    D. generalization

14. The link between physical punishment and subsequent aggressive behavior is probably best explained by:
    A. observational learning.
    B. noncontingent reinforcement.
    C. resistance to extinction.
    D. classical conditioning.

15. The *second* step in a self-modification program is to:
    A. specify the target behavior.
    B. design your program.
    C. gather baseline data.
    D. set up a behavioral contact.

Answers

1 D pp. 234–235	6 A p. 245	11 D pp. 251–252
2 C pp. 234–235	7 A p. 244	12 C pp. 257–258
3 B pp. 234–235	8 B pp. 248–249	13 C p. 261
4 D pp. 239–240	9 C pp. 249–250	14 A p. 259
5 C p. 241	10 A pp. 250–251	15 C p. 267

PsykTrek

To view a demo: www.cengage.com/psychology/psyktrek
To order: www.cengage.com/psychology/weiten
Go to the PsykTrek website or CD-ROM for further study of the concepts in this chapter. Both online and on the CD-ROM, PsykTrek includes dozens of learning modules with videos, animations, and quizzes, as well as simulations of psychological phenomena and a multimedia glossary that includes word pronunciations.

CengageNow
www.cengage.com/tlc

Go to this site for the link to CengageNOW, your one-stop study shop. Take a Pretest for this chapter, and CengageNOW will generate a personalized Study Plan based on your test results. The Study Plan will identify the topics you need to review and direct you to online resources to help you master those topics. You can then take a Posttest to help you determine the concepts you have mastered and what you still need to work on.

Companion Website
www.cengage.com/psychology/weiten

Go to this site to find online resources directly linked to your book, including a glossary, flash cards, drag-and-drop exercises, quizzes, and more!

7 HUMAN MEMORY

Encoding: Getting Information into Memory
The Role of Attention
Levels of Processing
Enriching Encoding

Storage: Maintaining Information in Memory
Sensory Memory
Short-Term Memory
Long-Term Memory

FEATURED STUDY ▮ How Accurate Are Flashbulb Memories?

Are Short-Term Memory and Long-Term Memory Really Separate?
How Is Knowledge Represented and Organized in Memory?

Retrieval: Getting Information Out of Memory
Using Cues to Aid Retrieval
Reinstating the Context of an Event
Reconstructing Memories and the Misinformation Effect
Source Monitoring and Reality Monitoring

Forgetting: When Memory Lapses
How Quickly We Forget: Ebbinghaus's Forgetting Curve
Measures of Forgetting
Why We Forget
The Recovered Memories Controversy

In Search of the Memory Trace: The Physiology of Memory
The Neural Circuitry of Memory
The Anatomy of Memory

Systems and Types of Memory
Declarative Versus Procedural Memory
Semantic Versus Episodic Memory
Prospective Versus Retrospective Memory

Reflecting on the Chapter's Themes

PERSONAL APPLICATION ▮ Improving Everyday Memory
Engage in Adequate Rehearsal
Schedule Distributed Practice and Minimize Interference
Engage in Deep Processing and Organize Information
Enrich Encoding with Mnemonic Devices

CRITICAL THINKING APPLICATION ▮ Understanding the Fallibility of Eyewitness Accounts
The Contribution of Hindsight Bias
The Contribution of Overconfidence

Recap

Practice Test

If you live in the United States, you've undoubtedly handled thousands upon thousands of American pennies. Surely, then, you remember what a penny looks like—or do you? Take a look at Figure 7.1. Which drawing corresponds to a real penny? Did you have a hard time selecting the real one? If so, you're not alone. Nickerson and Adams (1979) found that most people can't recognize the real penny in this collection of drawings. And their surprising finding was not a fluke. Undergraduates in England showed even worse memory for British coins (Jones, 1990). How can that be? Why do most of us have so poor a memory for an object we see every day?

Let's try another exercise. A definition of a word follows. It's not a particularly common word, but there's a good chance that you're familiar with it. Try to think of the word.

Definition: Favoritism shown or patronage granted by persons in high office to relatives or close friends.

If you can't think of the word, perhaps you can remember the letter of the alphabet it begins with, or what it sounds like. If so, you're experiencing the

Figure 7.1

A simple memory test. Nickerson and Adams (1979) presented these 15 versions of an object most people have seen hundreds or thousands of times and asked, "Which one is correct?" Can you identify the real penny shown here?

SOURCE: Nickerson, R. S., & Adams, M. J. (1979). Long-term memory for a common object. *Cognitive Psychology, 11,* 287–307. Copyright © 1979 Elsevier Science USA, reproduced with permission from the publisher.

tip-of-the-tongue phenomenon, in which forgotten information feels like it's just out of reach. In this case, the word you may be reaching for is *nepotism.*

You've probably endured the tip-of-the-tongue phenomenon while taking exams. You blank out on a term that you're sure you know. You may feel as if you're on the verge of remembering the term, but you can't quite come up with it. Later, perhaps while you're driving home, the term suddenly comes to you. "Of course," you may say to yourself, "how could I forget that?" That's an interesting question. Clearly, the term was stored in your memory.

As these examples suggest, memory involves more than taking information in and storing it in some mental compartment. In fact, psychologists probing the workings of memory have had to grapple with three enduring questions: (1) How does information get *into* memory? (2) How is information *maintained* in memory? and (3) How is information pulled *back out* of memory? These three questions correspond to the three key processes involved in memory (see Figure 7.2): *encoding* (getting information in), *storage* (maintaining it), and *retrieval* (getting it out).

***Encoding* involves forming a memory code.** For example, when you form a memory code for a word, you might emphasize how it looks, how it sounds, or what it means. Encoding usually requires attention, which is why you may not be able to recall exactly what a penny looks like—most people don't pay much attention to the appearance of a penny. ***Storage* involves maintaining encoded information in memory over time.** Psychologists have focused much of their memory research on trying to identify just what factors help or hinder memory storage. But, as the tip-of-the-tongue phenomenon shows, information storage isn't enough to guarantee that you'll remember something. You need to be able to get information out of storage. ***Retrieval* involves recovering information from memory stores.** Research issues concerned with retrieval include the study of how people search memory and why some retrieval strategies are more effective than others.

Most of this chapter is devoted to an examination of memory encoding, storage, and retrieval. As you'll see, these basic processes help explain the ultimate puzzle in the study of memory: why people forget. Just as memory involves more than storage, forgetting involves more than "losing" something from the memory store. Forgetting may be due to deficiencies in any of the three key processes in memory—encoding, storage, or retrieval. After our discussion of forgetting, we will take a brief look at the physiological bases of memory. Finally, we will describe distinctions between different types of memory. The chapter's Personal Application provides some practical advice on how to improve your memory. The Critical Thinking Application discusses some reasons that memory is less reliable than people assume it to be.

Figure 7.2

Three key processes in memory. Memory depends on three sequential processes: encoding, storage, and retrieval. Some theorists have drawn an analogy between these processes and elements of information processing by computers, as depicted here. The analogies for encoding and retrieval work pretty well, but the storage analogy is somewhat misleading. When information is stored on a hard drive, it remains unchanged indefinitely and you can retrieve an exact copy. As you will learn in this chapter, memory storage is a much more dynamic process. People's memories change over time and are rough reconstructions rather than exact copies of past events.

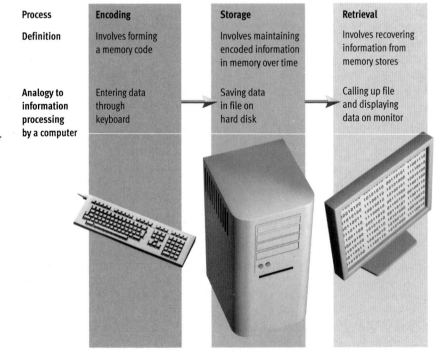

Process	Encoding	Storage	Retrieval
Definition	Involves forming a memory code	Involves maintaining encoded information in memory over time	Involves recovering information from memory stores
Analogy to information processing by a computer	Entering data through keyboard	Saving data in file on hard disk	Calling up file and displaying data on monitor

Encoding: Getting Information into Memory

Have you ever been introduced to someone and then realized only 30 seconds into your interaction that you had already "forgotten" his or her name? More often than not, this familiar kind of forgetting results from a failure to form a memory code for the name. When you're introduced to people, you're often busy sizing them up and thinking about what you're going to say. With your attention diverted in this way, names go in one ear and out the other. You don't remember them because they aren't encoded for storage into memory. This common problem illustrates that active encoding is a crucial process in memory. In this section, we discuss the role of attention in encoding, various types of encoding, and ways to enrich the encoding process.

The Role of Attention

Although there are some fascinating exceptions, you generally need to pay attention to information if you intend to remember it (Lachter, Forster, & Ruthruff, 2004; Mulligan, 1998). For example, if you sit through a class lecture but pay little attention to it, you're unlikely to remember much of what the professor had to say. **Attention involves focusing awareness on a narrowed range of stimuli or events.** If you pause to devote a little attention to the matter, you'll realize that selective attention is critical to everyday functioning. If your attention were distributed equally among all stimulus inputs, life would be utter chaos. If you weren't able to filter out most of the potential stimulation around you, you wouldn't be able to read a book, converse with a friend, or even carry on a coherent train of thought.

Attention is often likened to a *filter* that screens out most potential stimuli while allowing a select few to pass through into conscious awareness. However, a great deal of debate has been devoted to *where* the filter is located in the information-processing system. The key issue in this debate is whether stimuli are screened out *early,* during sensory input, or *late,* after the brain has processed the meaning or significance of the input (see **Figure 7.3**).

Evidence on the "cocktail party phenomenon" suggests the latter. For example, imagine a young woman named Claudia at a crowded party where many conversations are taking place. Claudia is paying attention to her conversation with a friend and filtering out the other conversations. However, if someone in another conversation mentions her name, Claudia may notice it, even though she has been ignoring that conversation. In experimental simulations of this situation, about 35% of participants report hearing their own name (Wood & Cowan, 1995). If selection is early, how can these people register input they've been blocking out? This cocktail party phenomenon suggests that attention involves *late* selection, based on the *meaning* of input.

Which view is supported by the weight of scientific evidence—early selection or late selection? Studies have found ample evidence for *both* as well as for intermediate selection (Cowan, 1988; Posner & DiGirolamo, 2000). These findings have led some theorists to conclude that the location of the attention filter may be flexible rather than fixed. According to Lavie (2005, 2007), the location of the attention filter depends on the "cognitive load" of current information processing. When one is attending to complicated,

Key Learning Goals

7.1 Clarify the role of attention in memory, and discuss the effects of divided attention.

7.2 Describe the three types of encoding discussed by Craik and Lockhart, and explain how depth of processing relates to memory.

7.3 Identify three techniques for enriching encoding.

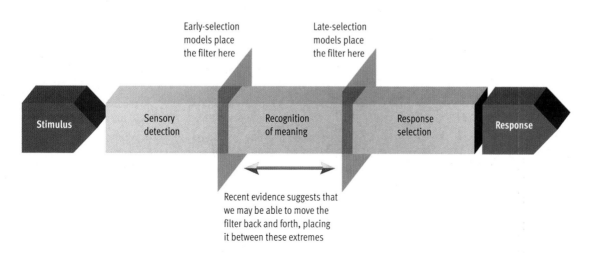

Early-selection models place the filter here

Late-selection models place the filter here

Stimulus | Sensory detection | Recognition of meaning | Response selection | Response

Recent evidence suggests that we may be able to move the filter back and forth, placing it between these extremes

Figure 7.3

Models of selective attention. Early-selection models propose that input is filtered before meaning is processed. Late-selection models hold that filtering occurs after the processing of meaning. There is evidence to support early, late, and intermediate selection, suggesting that the location of the attentional filter may not be fixed.

high-load tasks that consume much of one's attentional capacity, selection tends to occur early. However, when one is involved in simpler, low-load tasks, more attentional capacity is left over to process the meaning of distractions, allowing for later selection.

Wherever filtering occurs, it is clear that people have difficulty if they attempt to focus their attention on two or more inputs simultaneously. For example, if Claudia tried to continue her original conversation while also monitoring the other conversation in which she was mentioned, she would struggle in her efforts to attend to both conversations and would remember less of her original conversation. Studies indicate that when participants are forced to divide their attention between memory encoding and some other task, large reductions in memory performance are seen (Craik, 2001; Craik & Kester, 2000).

Moreover, the negative effects of divided attention are not limited to memory. Divided attention can have a negative impact on the performance of quite a variety of tasks, especially when the tasks are complex or unfamiliar (Pashler, Johnston, & Ruthruff, 2001). Although people tend to think that they can multitask with no deterioration in performance, research suggests that the human brain can effectively handle only one attention-consuming task at a time (Lien, Ruthruff, & Johnston, 2006). When people multitask, they really are switching their attention back and forth among tasks, rather than processing them simultaneously. That may be fine in many circumstances, but the cost of divided attention does have profound implications for the controversy about the advisability of driving while conversing on a cell phone. Carefully controlled research clearly demonstrates that cell phone conversations undermine people's driving performance, even when hands-free phones are used (Horrey & Wickens, 2006; Kass, Cole, & Stanny, 2007; Strayer, Drews,

& Crouch, 2006). For example, one study of a simulated driving task found that cellular conversations increased the chances of missing traffic signals and slowed down reactions to signals that were detected, as shown in **Figure 7.4** (Strayer & Johnston, 2001).

Levels of Processing   SIM5, 6a

Attention is critical to the encoding of memories, but not all attention is created equal. You can attend to things in different ways, focusing on different aspects of the stimulus input. According to some theorists, these qualitative differences in *how* people attend to information are important factors influencing how much they remember. In an influential theoretical treatise, Fergus Craik and Robert Lockhart (1972) proposed that incoming information can be processed at different levels. For instance, they maintained that in dealing with verbal information, people engage in three progressively deeper levels of processing: structural, phonemic, and semantic encoding (see **Figure 7.5**). *Structural encoding* is relatively shallow processing that emphasizes the physical structure of the stimulus. For example, if words are flashed on a screen, structural encoding registers such things as how they were printed (capital, lowercase, and so on) or the length of the words (how many letters). Further analysis may result in *phonemic encoding,* which emphasizes what a word sounds like. Phonemic encoding involves naming or saying (perhaps silently) the words. Finally, *semantic encoding* emphasizes the meaning of verbal input; it involves thinking about the objects and actions the words represent. **Levels-of-processing theory proposes that deeper levels of processing result in longer-lasting memory codes.**

In one experimental test of levels-of-processing theory, Craik and Tulving (1975) compared the durability of structural, phonemic, and semantic encoding. They directed participants' attention to particular aspects of briefly presented stimulus words by asking them questions about characteristics of the words (see **Figure 7.5**). The questions were designed to engage the subjects in different levels of processing. After responding to 60 words, the participants received an unexpected test of their memory for the words. As predicted, the subjects' recall was low after structural encoding, notably better after phonemic encoding, and highest after semantic encoding (see **Figure 7.6**).

The hypothesis that deeper processing leads to enhanced memory has been replicated in many studies (Craik, 2002; Lockhart & Craik, 1990). Nonetheless, the levels-of-processing model is not without its weaknesses (Roediger & Gallo, 2001; Watkins,

Figure 7.4
Divided attention and driving performance.
Working on a simulated driving task, subjects in a study by Strayer and Johnston (2001) were supposed to brake as promptly as possible when they saw red lights, while participating or not participating in a phone conversation. (a) The data on the left show that participants missed the red lights more than twice as often when engaged in a cell phone conversation. (b) The data on the right show that participants' reaction time to red lights was slower with the cell phone.

SOURCE: Adapted from Strayer, D. L., & Johnston, W. A. (2001). Driven to distraction: Dual task studies of simulated driving and conversing on a cellular phone. *Psychological Science 12*, 462–465. Copyright © 2001 Association for Psychological Science. Reprinted by permission of Blackwell Publishing.

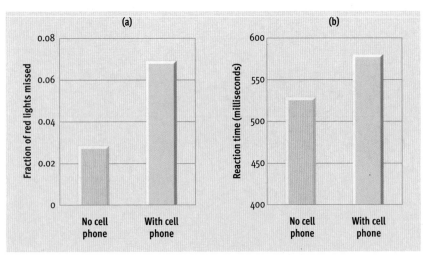

2002). Among other things, critics ask, what exactly is a "level" of processing? And how do we determine whether one level is deeper than another? Efforts to find an objective index of processing depth have failed, leaving the levels in levels-of-processing theory vaguely defined (Craik, 2002). Still, the theory has been enormously influential; it has shown that memory involves more than just storage and has inspired a great deal of research on how processing considerations influence memory (Roediger, Gallo, & Geraci, 2002).

Enriching Encoding 6a

Structural, phonemic, and semantic encoding do not exhaust the options when it comes to forming memory codes. There are other dimensions to encoding, dimensions that can enrich the encoding process and thereby improve memory.

Elaboration

Semantic encoding can often be enhanced through a process called elaboration. *Elaboration* **is linking a stimulus to other information at the time of encoding.** For example, let's say you read that phobias are often caused by classical conditioning, and you apply this idea to your own fear of spiders. In doing so, you are engaging in elaboration. The additional associations created by elaboration usually help people remember information. Differences in elaboration can help explain why different approaches to semantic processing result in varied amounts of retention (Toyota & Kikuchi, 2004, 2005; Willoughby, Motz, & Wood, 1997).

Visual Imagery 6a

Imagery—the creation of visual images to represent the words to be remembered—can also be used to enrich encoding. Of course, some words are easier to create images for than others. If you were asked to remember the word *juggler,* you could readily form an image of someone juggling balls. However, if you were asked to remember the word *truth,* you would probably have more difficulty forming a suitable image. The difference is that *juggler* refers to a concrete object, whereas *truth* refers to an abstract concept. Allan Paivio (1969) points out that it is easier to form images of concrete objects than of abstract concepts. He believes that this ease of image formation affects memory.

The beneficial effect of imagery on memory was demonstrated in a study by Paivio, Smythe, and Yuille (1968). They asked subjects to learn a list of 16 pairs of words. They manipulated whether the

Level of processing	Type of encoding	Example of questions used to elicit appropriate encoding
Shallow processing	*Structural encoding:* emphasizes the physical structure of the stimulus	Is the word written in capital letters?
Intermediate processing	*Phonemic encoding:* emphasizes what a word sounds like	Does the word rhyme with weight?
Deep processing	*Semantic encoding:* emphasizes the meaning of verbal input	Would the word fit in the sentence: "He met a _____ on the street"?

Depth of processing

Figure 7.5
Levels-of-processing theory. According to Craik and Lockhart (1972), structural, phonemic, and semantic encoding—which can be elicited by questions such as those shown on the right—involve progressively deeper levels of processing, which should result in more durable memories.

words were concrete, high-imagery words or abstract, low-imagery words. In terms of imagery potential, the list contained four types of pairings: high-high (*juggler-dress*), high-low (*letter-effort*), low-high (*duty-hotel*), and low-low (*quality-necessity*). The results showed that high-imagery words are easier to remember than low-imagery words (see **Figure 7.7** on the next page). Similar results were observed in a more recent study that controlled for additional confounding factors (Paivio, Khan, & Begg, 2000).

According to Paivio (1986, 2007), imagery facilitates memory because it provides a second kind of memory code, and two codes are better than one. His *dual-coding theory* **holds that memory is enhanced by forming semantic and visual codes, since either can lead to recall.** Although some aspects of dual-coding theory have been questioned, it's clear that the use of mental imagery can enhance memory in many situations (Marschark, 1992; McCauley, Eskes, & Moscovitch, 1996).

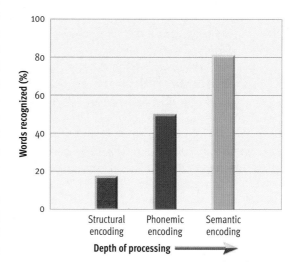

Figure 7.6
Retention at three levels of processing. In accordance with levels-of-processing theory, Craik and Tulving (1975) found that structural, phonemic, and semantic encoding, which involve progressively deeper levels of processing, led to progressively better retention.

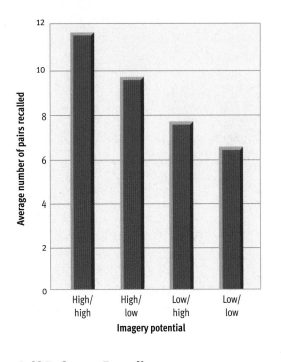

Figure showing a bar graph. Y-axis: "Average number of pairs recalled" (0 to 12). X-axis: "Imagery potential" with categories High/high, High/low, Low/high, Low/low.

coding was compared to structural, phonemic, and semantic encoding in a study by Rogers, Kuiper, and Kirker (1977). To induce self-referent encoding, subjects were asked to decide whether adjectives flashed on a screen applied to them personally. The results showed that self-referent encoding led to improved recall of the adjectives. Self-referent encoding appears to enhance recall by promoting additional elaboration and better organization of information (Symons & Johnson, 1997).

Self-Referent Encoding

Making material *personally* meaningful can also enrich encoding. People's recall of information tends to be slanted in favor of material that is personally relevant (Kahan & Johnson, 1992). *Self-referent encoding* involves deciding how or whether information is personally relevant. This approach to en-

REVIEW of Key Learning Goals

7.1 Attention, which facilitates encoding, is inherently selective and has been compared to a filter. The cocktail party phenomenon suggests that input is screened late in mental processing. Evidence indicates that the location of the attention filter may be flexible, depending on the cognitive load of current processing. Divided attention undermines encoding and performance on other tasks, including driving.

7.2 According to levels-of-processing theory, structural, phonemic, and semantic encoding represent progressively deeper levels of processing. Deeper processing generally results in better recall of information, but processing depth is difficult to measure.

7.3 Elaboration enriches encoding by linking a stimulus to other information. The creation of visual images to represent words can enrich encoding. Visual imagery may help by creating two memory codes rather than just one. Encoding that emphasizes personal self-reference may be especially useful in facilitating retention.

Storage: Maintaining Information in Memory

Key Learning Goals

7.4 Describe the role of the sensory store in memory.

7.5 Evaluate evidence on the durability and capacity of short-term memory.

7.6 Describe Baddeley's model of working memory.

7.7 Review findings on the notion that all memories are stored permanently, including the Featured Study on flashbulb memories.

7.8 Articulate the debate about whether short-term and long-term memory are really distinct.

7.9 Describe conceptual hierarchies, schemas, and semantic networks, and their role in long-term memory.

7.10 Explain how parallel distributed processing (PDP) models view the representation of information in memory.

In their efforts to understand memory storage, theorists have historically related it to the technologies of their age (Roediger, 1980). One of the earliest models used to explain memory storage was the wax tablet. Both Aristotle and Plato compared memory to a block of wax that differed in size and hardness for various individuals. Remembering, according to this analogy, was like stamping an impression into the wax. As long as the image remained in the wax, the memory would remain intact.

Modern theories of memory reflect the technological advances of the 20th century. For example, many theories formulated at the dawn of the computer age drew an analogy between information storage by computers and information storage in human memory (Atkinson & Shiffrin, 1968, 1971; Broadbent, 1958; Waugh & Norman, 1965). The main contribution of these *information-processing theories* was to subdivide memory into three separate memory stores (Estes, 1999; Pashler & Carrier, 1996). The names

for these stores and their exact characteristics varied some from one theory to the next. For purposes of simplicity, we'll organize our discussion around the model devised by Atkinson and Shiffrin, which proved to be the most influential of the information-processing theories. According to their model, incoming information passes through two temporary storage buffers—the sensory store and short-term store—before it is transferred into a long-term store (see **Figure 7.8**). Like the wax tablet before it, the information-processing model of memory serves as a metaphor; the three memory stores are not viewed as anatomical structures in the brain, but rather as functionally distinct types of memory.

Sensory Memory

Sensory memory preserves information in its original sensory form for a brief time, usually only a fraction of a second. Sensory memory allows the

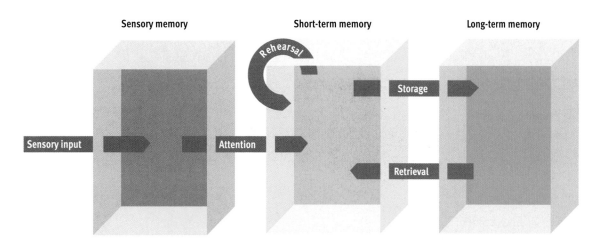

Figure 7.8

The Atkinson and Shiffrin model of memory storage. Atkinson and Shiffrin (1971) proposed that memory is made up of three information stores. *Sensory memory* can hold a large amount of information just long enough (a fraction of a second) for a small portion of it to be selected for longer storage. *Short-term memory* has a limited capacity, and unless aided by rehearsal, its storage duration is brief. *Long-term memory* can store an apparently unlimited amount of information for indeterminate periods.

sensation of a visual pattern, sound, or touch to linger for a brief moment after the sensory stimulation is over. In the case of vision, people really perceive an *afterimage* rather than the actual stimulus. You can demonstrate the existence of afterimages for yourself by rapidly moving a lighted sparkler or flashlight in circles in the dark. If you move a sparkler fast enough, you should see a complete circle even though the light source is only a single point (see the photo below). Sensory memory preserves the sensory image long enough for you to perceive a continuous circle rather than separate points of light.

The brief preservation of sensations in sensory memory is adaptive in that it gives you additional time to try to recognize stimuli. However, you'd better take advantage of this stimulus persistence immediately, because it doesn't last long. This brevity was demonstrated in a classic experiment by George Sperling (1960). His subjects saw three rows of letters flashed on a screen for just $1/20$ of a second. A tone following the exposure signaled which row of letters

Because the image of the sparkler persists briefly in sensory memory, when the sparkler is moved fast enough, the blending of afterimages causes people to see a continuous stream of light instead of a succession of individual points.

the subject should report to the experimenter (see **Figure 7.9** on the next page). Subjects were fairly accurate when the signal occurred immediately. However, their accuracy steadily declined as the delay of the tone increased to one second. Why? Because memory traces in the sensory store decay in about $1/4$ of a second (Massaro & Loftus, 1996). There is some debate about whether stimulus persistence really involves *memory storage* (Nairne, 2003). Some theorists view it as an artifact of perceptual processing caused by excitatory feedback in neural circuits (Francis, 1999). In other words, the brief persistence of stimuli may be more like an echo than a memory.

Short-Term Memory   6b

Short-term memory (STM) is a limited-capacity store that can maintain unrehearsed information for about 10–20 seconds. In contrast, information stored in long-term memory may last weeks, months, or years. However, there is a way that you can maintain information in your short-term store indefinitely. How? Primarily, by engaging in *rehearsal*—the process of repetitively verbalizing or thinking about the information. For instance, when you look up a phone number, you probably recite it over and over until you can dial it. Rehearsal keeps recycling the information through your short-term memory. In theory, this recycling could go on forever, but in reality something eventually distracts you and breaks the rehearsal loop. In any event, this reliance on recitation illustrates that short-term memory has been thought to depend primarily on *phonemic encoding.*

Durability of Storage   6b

Without rehearsal, information in short-term memory is lost in 10 to 20 seconds (Nairne, 2003). This rapid loss was demonstrated in a study by Peterson

Figure 7.9

Sperling's (1960) study of sensory memory. After the participants had fixated on the cross, the letters were flashed on the screen just long enough to create a visual afterimage. High, medium, and low tones signaled which row of letters to report. Because subjects had to rely on the afterimage to report the letters, Sperling (1960) was able to measure how rapidly the afterimage disappeared by varying the delay between the display and the signal to report.

Fixation

Display
1/20 second

G T F B
Q Z C R
K P S N

Tone
Tone occurs either before the display goes off or at a delay of .15, .30, .50, or 1 second

High

Medium

Low

Pitch of tone signals which row to report

Report

"G, T, F, B"

Time (fractions of seconds)

and Peterson (1959). They measured how long undergraduates could remember three consonants if they couldn't rehearse them. To prevent rehearsal, the Petersons required the students to count backward by threes from the time the consonants were presented until they saw a light that signaled the recall test (see **Figure 7.10**). Their results showed that subjects' recall accuracy was pretty dismal (about 10%) after only 15 seconds. Theorists originally believed that the loss of information from short-term memory was

Figure 7.10

Peterson and Peterson's (1959) study of short-term memory. After a warning light was flashed, the participants were given three consonants to remember. The researchers prevented rehearsal by giving the subjects a three-digit number at the same time and telling them to count backward by three from that number until given the signal to recall the letters. By varying the amount of time between stimulus presentation and recall, Peterson and Peterson (1959) were able to measure how quickly information was lost from short-term memory.

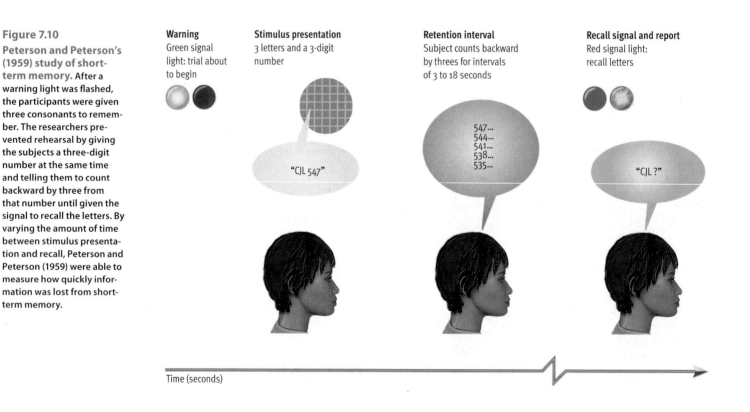

Warning
Green signal light: trial about to begin

Stimulus presentation
3 letters and a 3-digit number

"CJL 547"

Retention interval
Subject counts backward by threes for intervals of 3 to 18 seconds

547...
544...
541...
538...
535...

Recall signal and report
Red signal light: recall letters

"CJL ?"

Time (seconds)

due purely to time-related *decay* of memory traces, but follow-up research showed that *interference* from competing material also contributes (Lewandowsky, Duncan, & Brown, 2004; Nairne, 2002).

Capacity of Storage

6b

Short-term memory is also limited in the number of items it can hold. The small capacity of STM was pointed out by George Miller (1956) in a famous paper called "The Magical Number Seven, Plus or Minus Two: Some Limits on Our Capacity for Processing Information." Miller noticed that people could recall only about seven items in tasks that required the use of STM. When short-term memory is filled to capacity, the insertion of new information "bumps out" some of the information currently in STM. The limited capacity of STM constrains people's ability to perform tasks in which they need to mentally juggle various pieces of information (Baddeley & Hitch, 1974). Some approaches to this issue suggest that the capacity of short-term memory may even be less than widely assumed. Nelson Cowan (2001, 2005) cites evidence indicating that the capacity of STM is *four* plus or minus *one*. According to Cowan, the capacity of STM has been overestimated because researchers have often failed to control for covert *chunking* by participants.

It has long been known that people can increase the capacity of their short-term memory by combining stimuli into larger, possibly higher-order units, called *chunks* (Simon, 1974). **A *chunk* is a group of familiar stimuli stored as a single unit.** You can demonstrate the effect of chunking by asking someone to recall a sequence of 12 letters grouped in the following way:

FB - INB - CC - IAIB - M

As you read the letters aloud, pause at the hyphens. Your subject will probably attempt to remember each letter separately because there are no obvious groups or chunks. But a string of 12 letters is too long for STM, so errors are likely. Now present the same string of letters to another person, but place the pauses in the following locations:

FBI - NBC - CIA - IBM

The letters now form four familiar chunks that should occupy only four slots in STM, resulting in successful recall (Bower & Springston, 1970). To successfully chunk the letters I B M, a subject must first recognize these letters as a familiar unit. This familiarity has to be stored somewhere in long-term memory. Thus, in this case information was transferred from long-term into short-term memory. This situation is not unusual. People routinely draw information out of their long-term memory banks to evaluate and understand information that they are working with in short-term memory.

Short-Term Memory as "Working Memory"

6b

Research eventually uncovered a number of problems with the original model of short-term memory (Bower, 2000). Among other things, studies showed that short-term memory is *not* limited to phonemic encoding as originally thought and that decay is *not* the only process responsible for the loss of information from STM. These and other findings suggested that short-term memory involves more than a simple rehearsal buffer, as originally envisioned. To make sense of such findings, Alan Baddeley (1986, 1992, 2001, 2007) proposed a more complex, modular model of short-term memory that characterizes it as "working memory."

Baddeley's model of working memory consists of four components (see **Figure 7.11**). The first component is the *phonological loop* that represented all of short-term memory in earlier models. This component is at work when you use recitation to temporarily hold on to a phone number. Baddeley (2003)

Figure 7.11

Baddeley's model of working memory. This diagram depicts the revised model of the short-term store proposed by Alan Baddeley. According to Baddeley (2001), working memory includes four components: a phonological loop, a visuospatial sketchpad, a central executive system, and an episodic buffer. The elements shown in tan are memory stores, whereas the central executive is not.

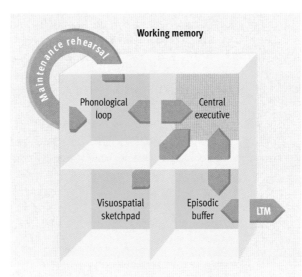

George Miller

"The Magical Number Seven, Plus or Minus Two."

web link 7.1

The Magical Number Seven Plus or Minus Two

In 1956, Princeton psychology professor George A. Miller published one of the most famous papers in the history of psychology: "The Magical Number Seven Plus or Minus Two: Some Limits on Our Capacity for Processing Information." At this site, you'll find a copy of the original text with tables so you can see why this is such an important research milestone in psychology.

believes that the phonological loop evolved to facilitate the acquisition of language. The second component in working memory is a *visuospatial sketchpad* that permits people to temporarily hold and manipulate visual images. This element is at work when you try to mentally rearrange the furniture in your bedroom or map out a complicated route that you need to follow to travel somewhere. Researchers investigate this module of working memory by showing subjects visual sequences and spatial arrays, which they are asked to re-create. The third component is a *central executive* system. This component, which is not a storage system, controls the deployment of attention, switching the focus of attention and dividing attention as needed (for example, dividing attention between a conversation with your mother and a TV show you are trying to watch). The central executive also coordinates the actions of the other modules. The fourth component is the *episodic buffer,* a temporary, limited-capacity store that allows the various components of working memory to integrate information and that serves as an interface between working memory and long-term memory. The two key characteristics that originally defined short-term memory—limited capacity and storage duration—are still present in the concept of working memory, but Baddeley's model accounts for evidence that STM handles a greater variety of functions than previously thought.

Baddeley's model of working memory has generated an enormous volume of research. For example, research has shown that people vary in how well they can juggle information in their working memory while fending off distractions (Engle, 2001). Interestingly, these variations in *working memory capacity* seem to influence people's ability to control the focus of their attention. People with greater working memory capacity exhibit greater selectivity and flexibility in their deployment of attention (Colflesh & Conway, 2007). Greater working memory capacity also correlates positively with measures of high-level cognitive abilities, such as reading comprehension, complex reasoning, and even intelligence (Conway, Kane, & Engle, 2003; Oberauer et al., 2007). This finding has led some theorists to conclude that working memory capacity is critical to complex cognitive processes and intelligence (Lepine, Barrouillet, & Camos, 2005). Unfortunately, working memory capacity tends to decline gradually during late adulthood (Otsuka & Osaka, 2005; Zacks, Hasher, & Li, 2000). This erosion may play a critical role in age-related decreases in performance on a variety of cognitive tasks.

Alan Baddeley

"The concept of working memory proposes that a dedicated system maintains and stores information in the short term, and that this system underlies human thought processes."

Long-Term Memory   6b

Long-term memory (LTM) is an unlimited capacity store that can hold information over lengthy periods of time. Unlike sensory memory and short-term memory, which have very brief storage durations, LTM can store information indefinitely. In fact, one point of view is that all information stored in long-term memory is stored there *permanently*. According to this view, forgetting occurs only because people sometimes cannot *retrieve* needed information from LTM.

The notion that LTM storage may be permanent is certainly intriguing. A couple of interesting lines of research seemed to provide compelling evidence of permanent storage, but each turned out to be less convincing than appeared at first glance. The first line of research consisted of some landmark studies conducted by Canadian neuroscientist Wilder Penfield in the 1960s. He reported triggering long-lost memories through electrical stimulation of the brain (ESB) during brain surgeries (Penfield & Perot, 1963). When Penfield used ESB (see Chapter 3) to map brain function in patients undergoing surgery for epilepsy, he found that stimulation of the temporal lobe sometimes elicited vivid descriptions of events long past. Patients would describe events that apparently came from their childhood—such as "being in a lumberyard" or "watching Mom make a phone call"—as if they were there once again. Penfield and others inferred that these descriptions were

Wilder Penfield and his associates conducted a series of studies with human subjects undergoing brain surgery for medical reasons. In these studies they used electrical stimulation of the brain to map out brain function in the cortex. In the course of these studies they thought they triggered long-lost memories when they stimulated areas in the temporal lobe (seen near the bottom of the photo). However, as your text explains, subsequent evidence led to a reinterpretation of their findings.

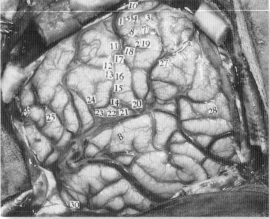

"The matters about which I'm being questioned, Your Honor, are all things I should have included in my long-term memory but which I mistakenly inserted in my short-term memory."

exact playbacks of long-lost memories unearthed by electrical stimulation of the brain.

The second line of research has centered on the phenomenon of *flashbulb memories,* **which are unusually vivid and detailed recollections of momentous events.** For instance, many older adults in the United States can remember exactly where they were, what they were doing, and how they felt when they learned that President John F. Kennedy had been shot. You may have a similar recollection related to the terrorist attacks that took place in New York and Washington, DC, on September 11, 2001. The vivid detail of people's memories of President Kennedy's assassination decades ago would seem to provide a striking example of permanent storage.

So, why don't these findings demonstrate that LTM storage is permanent? Let's look at each. Closer scrutiny eventually showed that the remarkable "memories" activated by ESB in Penfield's studies often included major distortions or factual impossibilities. For instance, the person who recalled being in a lumberyard had never actually been to one. The ESB-induced recollections of Penfield's subjects apparently were hallucinations, dreams, or loose reconstructions of events rather than exact replays of the past (Squire, 1987). In a similar vein, subsequent research has undermined the notion that flashbulb memories represent an instance of permanent storage. Although flashbulb memories tend to be strong, vivid, and detailed, studies suggest they are neither as accurate nor as special as once believed (Neisser & Harsch, 1992; Schmolck, Buffalo, & Squire, 2000). Like other memories, they become less detailed and complete with time and are often inaccurate (Pezdek, 2003; Weaver & Krug, 2004). This observation brings us to our Featured Study for this chapter, which examined the accuracy of students' flashbulb memories of the 9/11 terrorist attacks on the World Trade Center in New York and the Pentagon in Washington, DC.

How Accurate Are Flashbulb Memories?

Overall, research on flashbulb memories has suggested that they are not any more accurate than other memories, but the findings have been somewhat inconsistent, probably because the studies have focused on different notable events, used different types of samples, and varied methods of measuring memory accuracy. Another problem is that events capable of generating flashbulb memories—such as the 9/11 terrorist attacks in this case—occur infrequently and unexpectedly, so many studies have been launched weeks or months after the focal event, which makes it hard to determine exactly what subjects experienced at the time. The chief advantages of the present study were that it was launched immediately (the day after the 9/11 terrorist attacks) and that it compared recall of this event to an everyday event (of each subject's choice) that had occurred in the same time frame. Thus, the investigators were able to collect better data on questions such as: How do people feel about their flashbulb memories? Are flashbulb memo-

ries exceptionally vivid? And, most critically, are flashbulb memories more accurate than other memories?

Method

Participants. Students at Duke University were contacted and tested on September 12 for their memory of hearing about the 9/11 terrorist attacks. The 54 students (14 males, 40 females) were randomly assigned to three groups. The first group was retested one week after 9/11; the second group was retested six weeks after the attacks; the third group was retested 32 weeks after the incident.

Procedure. For purposes of comparison, each participant was asked to identify and describe a recent (last three days) memorable event in their lives. They then filled out similar questionnaires and rating scales inquiring about this event and their experiences on 9/11. When subjects returned for their retesting, they responded to the same questionnaires and rating scales. Accuracy of recall was gauged by

FEATURED

STUDY

SOURCE: Talarico, J. M., & Rubin, D. G. (2003). Confidence, not consistency, characterizes flashbulb memories. *Psychological Science, 14,* 455–461.

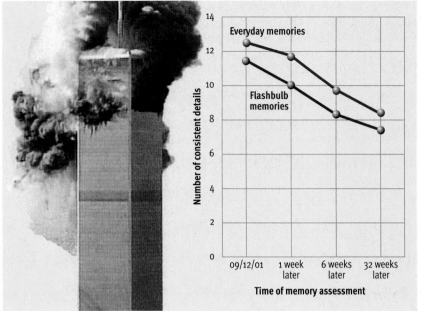

Figure 7.12
Accuracy of flashbulb memories. Talarico and Rubin (2003) estimated the accuracy of participants' flashbulb memories of the 9/11 terrorist attacks (and their selected everyday memories) by comparing the details of their original memories against their memories reported 1, 6, or 32 weeks later. This graph shows that the number of consistent details in subjects' flashbulb memories and everyday memories declined at the same pace, suggesting that flashbulb memories are not more accurate or longer lasting than other memories.

measuring how consistent the retest reports were with the original reports collected on September 12.

Materials. The questionnaire administered on September 12 and in the retest sessions asked participants open-ended questions about their experiences when they learned of the terrorist attacks, such as: When did you first hear the news? Where were you when you first heard the news? Who or what first told you the information? Similar questions were also posed regarding the everyday event chosen by the subject, such as: When did this event occur? Where were you, physically? Participants were also asked to respond to various 7-point rating scales that measured their perceptions about the vividness of their memories and their confidence in the accuracy of their recollections.

Results

The principal finding was that there was no appreciable difference in consistency between participants' flashbulb memories of the terrorist attacks and their everyday memories over time. The consistency between participants' original reports and their retest reports declined over time at about the same rate for both types of memories (see **Figure 7.12**). In contrast, after six weeks, participants viewed their flashbulb memories as being more vivid than their everyday memories, and they had more confidence in the accuracy of their flashbulb memories.

Discussion

The authors conclude that flashbulb memories fade gradually over time, even though people subjectively feel that these memories are especially vivid and accurate. They interpret their findings as undermining the notion that flashbulb memories have special characteristics that make them less vulnerable to forgetting than ordinary memories. They further suggest that the "true mystery" for future research is to explain "why people are so confident for so long in the accuracy of their flashbulb memories."

Comment

This research was featured because it examined a timely question and because it demonstrated that human memory is not as reliable as we assume it to be, a conclusion that will be echoed throughout this chapter. When it comes to the fallibility of human memory, no one is immune. When asked to recall his reactions to the 9/11 attacks, even President George W. Bush showed quite a bit of inconsistency across three separate interviews—and he had TV recordings to remind him of how he reacted (Greenberg, 2004). And, like many people, President Bush reported recollections that could not possibly be accurate. For instance, he has said that on the morning of 9/11 he saw video footage of the first plane hitting the World Trade Center, when, in reality, this video did not surface until later (Greenberg, 2004). Although some of the President's critics have made a big deal out of these inconsistencies and mistakes, they are not the least bit unusual. As you will see in the upcoming pages, research has shown repeatedly that human memory is more malleable and less accurate that generally appreciated.

In a followup study, Talarico and Rubin tested the same participants one year after the 9/11 terrorist attacks. Once again, they found that flashbulb memories fade much the same as everyday memories but that people's gut feelings about them are different. They concluded that it is not extraordinary accuracy or longevity that distinguishes flashbulb memories. Rather, what makes them special is that people subjectively feel that these memories are exceptionally vivid, people have exceptional confidence (albeit misplaced) in their accuracy, and more emotional intensity is attached (Talarico & Rubin, 2007). So, perhaps flashbulb memories are "special," but not in the way originally envisioned.

Returning to the question at hand, the research findings on flashbulb memories clearly conflict with the hypothesis that memory storage is permanent. Although the possibility cannot be ruled out completely, there is no convincing evidence that memories are stored away permanently and that forgetting is all a matter of retrieval failure (Payne & Blackwell, 1998; Schacter, 1996).

Are Short-Term Memory and Long-Term Memory Really Separate?

The partitioning of memory into the sensory, short-term, and long-term stores has dominated thinking about memory for many decades, but over the years some theorists have expressed doubts about whether there really are separate memory stores. A handful of theorists have questioned the concept of sensory memory on the grounds that it may be nothing more than perceptual processes at work, rather than memory. A larger number of theorists have questioned the concept of short-term memory on the grounds that it really isn't all that different from long-term memory (Crowder, 1993; Nairne, 1996; Ranganath & Blumenfeld, 2005). The view of short-term memory and long-term memory as independent systems was originally based, in part, on the belief that they depended on different types of encoding and were subject to different mechanisms of forgetting. STM was thought to depend on *phonemic* encoding (based on sound), whereas LTM encoding was thought to be largely *semantic* (based on meaning). Information loss from STM was believed to be caused by time-related *decay,* whereas *interference* was viewed as the principal mechanism of LTM forgetting. However, decades of research have shown that these distinctions are not absolute, as both semantic encoding and interference effects have been found in research on short-term memory (Meiser & Klauer, 1999; Walker & Hulme, 1999).

How do theorists who doubt the existence of separate memory stores view the structure of memory? Their views vary considerably (Nairne, 2002). One perspective is to view short-term memory as a tiny and constantly changing portion of long-term memory that happens to be in a heightened state of activation (Cowan, 1999; Jonides et al., 2008). Other, more radical views assert that there is a single, unitary, "generic" memory store that is governed by one set of rules and processes (Nairne, 2001). The outcome of the debate about whether there are separate memory stores is difficult to predict. At present, the multiple stores viewpoint remains dominant, but alternative approaches are becoming increasingly influential.

How Is Knowledge Represented and Organized in Memory?

6b

Over the years, memory researchers have wrestled endlessly with another major question relating to memory storage: How is knowledge represented and organized in memory? In other words, what forms do mental representations of information take? Most theorists seem to agree that they probably take a variety of forms, depending on the nature of the material that needs to be tucked away in memory. For example, memories of visual scenes, of how to perform actions (such as typing or hitting a backhand stroke in tennis), and of factual information (such as definitions or dates in history) are probably represented and organized in very different ways. Most of the theorizing to date has focused on how factual knowledge may be represented in memory. In this section, we'll look at a small sample of the organizational structures that have been proposed for semantic information.

Clustering and Conceptual Hierarchies

6b

People spontaneously organize information into categories for storage in memory. This fact was apparent in a study by Bousfield (1953), who asked subjects to memorize a list of 60 words. Although presented in a scrambled order, each of the words in the list fit into one of four categories: animals, men's names, vegetables, or professions. Bousfield showed that subjects recalling this list engage in *clustering*—the tendency to remember similar or related items in groups. Even though the words were not presented in organized groups, participants tended to remember them in bunches that belonged in the same category. Thus, when applicable, factual information is routinely organized into simple categories.

Similarly, when possible, factual information may be organized into conceptual hierarchies.

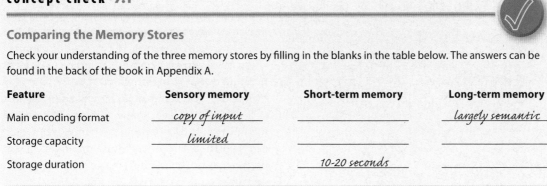

concept check 7.1

Comparing the Memory Stores

Check your understanding of the three memory stores by filling in the blanks in the table below. The answers can be found in the back of the book in Appendix A.

Feature	Sensory memory	Short-term memory	Long-term memory
Main encoding format	*copy of input*		*largely semantic*
Storage capacity	*limited*		
Storage duration		*10-20 seconds*	

Figure 7.13
Conceptual hierarchies and long-term memory. Some types of information can be organized into a multilevel hierarchy of concepts, like the one shown here, which was studied by Bower and others (1969). They found that subjects remember more information when they organize it into a conceptual hierarchy.

SOURCE: Adapted from Bower, G. (1970). Organizational factors in memory. *Cognitive Psychology, 1* (1), 18–46. Copyright © 1970 Elsevier Science USA, reproduced with permission from the publisher.

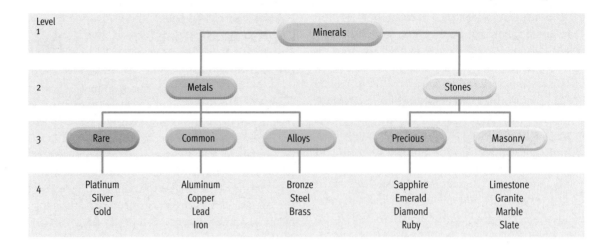

Level 1 — Minerals

Level 2 — Metals | Stones

Level 3 — Rare | Common | Alloys | Precious | Masonry

Level 4 —
Platinum / Silver / Gold
Aluminum / Copper / Lead / Iron
Bronze / Steel / Brass
Sapphire / Emerald / Diamond / Ruby
Limestone / Granite / Marble / Slate

A *conceptual hierarchy* is a multilevel classification system based on common properties among items. A conceptual hierarchy that a person might construct for minerals can be found in Figure 7.13. According to Gordon Bower (1970), organizing information into a conceptual hierarchy can improve recall dramatically.

Schemas

6b

Imagine that you've just visited Professor Smith's office, which is shown in the photo below. Take a brief look at the photo and then cover it up. Now pretend that you want to describe Professor Smith's office to a friend. Write down what you saw in the office (the picture).

After you finish, compare your description with the picture. Chances are, your description will include elements—books or filing cabinets, for instance—that were *not* in the office. This common phenomenon demonstrates how *schemas* can influence memory.

A *schema* is an organized cluster of knowledge about a particular object or event abstracted from previous experience with the object or event. For example, college students have schemas for what professors' offices are like. When Brewer and Treyens (1981) tested the recall of 30 subjects who had briefly visited the office shown in the photo, most subjects recalled the desks and chairs, but few recalled the wine bottle or the picnic basket, which aren't part of a typical office schema. Moreover, nine subjects in the Brewer and Treyens study falsely recalled that the office contained books. Perhaps you made the same mistake.

These results and other studies (Tuckey & Brewer, 2003) suggest that *people are more likely to remember things that are consistent with their schemas than things that are not.* Although this principle seems applicable much of the time, the inverse is also true: *People sometimes exhibit better recall of things that violate their schema-based expectations* (Koriat, Goldsmith, & Pansky, 2000; Neuschatz et al., 2002). If information really clashes with a schema, it may attract extra attention and deeper processing and thus become more memorable. For example, if you saw a slot machine in a professor's office, you would probably remember it. In short, the impact of schemas on memory can be difficult to predict, but either way it is apparent that information stored in memory is often organized around schemas (Brewer, 2000).

Professor Smith's office is shown in this photo. Follow the instructions in the text to learn how Brewer and Treyens (1981) used it in a study of memory.

© Courtesy of W. F. Brewer

Semantic Networks

6b

Of course, not all information fits neatly into conceptual hierarchies or schemas. Much knowledge seems to be organized into less systematic frameworks, called semantic networks (Collins & Loftus, 1975). A *semantic network* **consists of nodes representing concepts, joined together by pathways that link related concepts.** A small semantic network is shown in **Figure 7.14.** The ovals are the nodes, and the words inside the ovals are the interlinked concepts. The lines connecting the nodes are the pathways. The length of each pathway represents the degree of association between two concepts. Shorter pathways imply stronger associations.

Semantic networks have proven useful in explaining why thinking about one word (such as *butter*) can make a closely related word (such as *bread*) easier to remember (Meyer & Schvaneveldt, 1976). According to Collins and Loftus (1975), when people think about a word, their thoughts naturally go to related words. These theorists call this process *spreading activation* within a semantic network. They assume that activation spreads out along the pathways of the semantic network surrounding the word. They also theorize that the strength of this activation decreases as it travels outward, much as ripples decrease in size as they radiate outward from a rock tossed into a pond. Consider again the semantic network shown in **Figure 7.14.** If subjects see the word *red*, words that are closely linked to it (such as *orange*) should be easier to recall than words that have longer links (such as *sunrises*).

Connectionist Networks and Parallel Distributed Processing (PDP) Models

Instead of taking their cue from how computers process information, *connectionist models* of memory take their inspiration from how neural networks appear to handle information. As we noted in our discussion of visual perception in Chapter 4, the human brain appears to depend extensively on *parallel distributed processing*—that is, simultaneous processing of the same information that is spread across networks of neurons. Based on this insight and basic findings about how neurons operate, *connectionist* **or** *parallel distributed processing (PDP) models* **assume that cognitive processes depend on patterns of activation in highly interconnected computational networks that resemble neural networks** (McClelland, 2000; McClelland & Rogers, 2003; McClelland & Rumelhart, 1985). A PDP system consists of a large network of interconnected computing units, or *nodes,* that operate much like neurons. These nodes may be inactive or they may send either excitatory or inhibitory signals to other units. Like an individual neuron, a specific node's level of activation reflects the weighted balance of excitatory and inhibitory inputs from many other units. Given this framework, *PDP models assert that specific memories correspond to particular patterns of activation*

web link 7.2

Memory Principles

This brief overview of practical guidelines for improving recall of academic material is maintained by Carolyn Hopper at Middle Tennessee State University. Ten basic principles are outlined succinctly. Elsewhere at this site you will find other worthwhile materials intended to help students improve their study techniques.

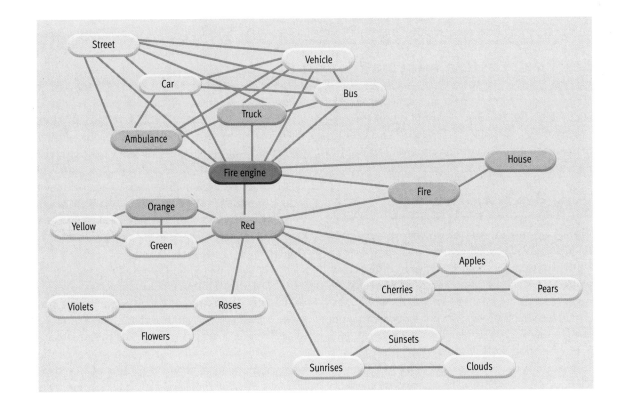

Figure 7.14
A semantic network. **Much of the organization of long-term memory depends on networks of associations among concepts. In this highly simplified depiction of a fragment of a semantic network, the shorter the line linking any two concepts, the stronger the association between them. The coloration of the concept boxes represents activation of the concepts. This is how the network might look just after a person hears the words** *fire engine.*

SOURCE: Adapted from Collins, A. M., & Loftus, E. F. (1975). A spreading activation theory of semantic processing. *Psychological Review, 82,* 407–428. Copyright © 1975 by the American Psychological Association. Adapted by permission of the authors.

in these networks (McClelland, 1992). Connectionist networks bear some superficial resemblance to semantic networks, but there is a crucial difference. In semantic networks, specific nodes represent specific concepts or pieces of knowledge. In connectionist networks, a piece of knowledge is represented by a particular *pattern* of activation across an entire network. Thus, the information lies in the strengths of the *connections,* which is why the PDP approach is called "connectionism."

What are the strengths of the PDP approach? For one thing, connectionist models provide a highly plausible account for how mental structures may be derived from neural structures. In other words, they make sense in light of what research has revealed about neurophysiology. Another strength is that the emphasis on parallel processing seems to explain the blazing speed of humans' cognitive functioning more persuasively than alternative models do. You may not always *feel* like your mental processes are blazingly fast, but the reality is that a routine act like recognizing a complex visual stimulus typically takes a scant 300 milliseconds. Most other models implicitly assume that thinking involves *serial processing,* which requires executing operations in a single sequence. However, serial processing seems much too slow to account for how the brain fires millions of neural impulses to accomplish simple actions.

REVIEW of Key Learning Goals

7.4 The sensory store preserves information in its original form, probably for only a fraction of a second. Some theorists view stimulus persistence as more like an echo than a memory.

7.5 Short-term memory can maintain unrehearsed information for about 10–20 seconds. Short-term memory has a limited capacity that is widely assumed to be about seven chunks of information, although one recent estimate suggests that the capacity of STM is four items plus or minus one.

7.6 Short-term memory appears to involve more than a simple rehearsal loop and has been reconceptualized by Baddeley as working memory. Working memory includes the phonological loop, the visuospatial sketchpad, a central executive system, and an episodic buffer. Individual differences in working memory capacity correlate with measures of many cognitive abilities.

7.7 Long-term memory is an unlimited capacity store that may hold information indefinitely. Penfield's ESB research and

the existence of flashbulb memories suggest that LTM storage may be permanent, but the evidence is not convincing. The Featured Study showed that flashbulb memories are not as durable or accurate as claimed.

7.8 Some theorists have questioned the distinction between short-term and long-term memory. Most of these theorists view STM as a tiny, shifting portion of LTM that happens to be in a heightened state of activation.

7.9 Information in long-term memory can be organized in simple categories or multilevel classification systems called conceptual hierarchies. A schema is an organized cluster of knowledge about a particular object or event. Semantic networks consist of concepts joined by pathways. Research suggests that activation spreads along the paths of semantic networks to activate closely associated words.

7.10 Parallel distributed processing models of memory assert that specific memories correspond to particular patterns of activation in connectionist networks. Parallel processing may explain the remarkable speed of human information processing.

Retrieval: Getting Information Out of Memory

Key Learning Goals

7.11 Explain the tip-of-the-tongue phenomenon and how retrieval cues and context cues influence retrieval.

7.12 Understand the reconstructive nature of memory, and summarize research on the misinformation effect.

7.13 Apply the concepts of source monitoring and reality monitoring to everyday memory errors.

Storing information in long-term memory is a worthy goal, but it's insufficient if you can't get the information back out again when you need it. Some theorists maintain that understanding retrieval is the key to understanding human memory (Roediger, 2000).

Using Cues to Aid Retrieval

At the beginning of this chapter we discussed the *tip-of-the-tongue phenomenon*—**the temporary inability to remember something you know, accompanied by a feeling that it's just out of reach.** The tip-of-the-tongue phenomenon is a common experience that is typically triggered by a name that one can't quite recall. Most people experience this temporary frustration about once a week, although its occurrence increases with age (A. Brown, 1991; Burke & Shafto, 2004). It appears to be a universal experience

found in widely diverse cultures (Brennen, Vikan, & Dybdahl, 2007; Schwartz, 1999). Stronger tip-of-the-tongue experiences in which people feel like recall is particularly imminent are more likely to be resolved than weaker ones (B. L. Schwartz et al., 2000) The tip-of-the-tongue phenomenon clearly constitutes a failure in retrieval. However, the exact mechanisms underlying this failure are the subject of debate, as a variety of explanations have been proposed for this phenomenon (Schwartz, 1999, 2002).

Fortunately, memories can often be jogged with *retrieval cues*—stimuli that help gain access to memories. This was apparent when Roger Brown and David McNeill (1966) studied the tip-of-the-tongue phenomenon. They gave subjects definitions of obscure words and asked them to come up with the words. Our example at the beginning of the chapter (the definition for *nepotism*) was taken from their study. Brown and McNeill found that subjects groping for obscure words were correct in guessing the first letter of the missing word 57% of the time. This figure far exceeds chance and shows that partial recollections are often headed in the right direction.

Reinstating the Context of an Event

Let's test your memory: What did you have for breakfast two days ago? If you can't immediately answer, you might begin by imagining yourself sitting at the breakfast table. Trying to recall an event by putting yourself back in the context in which it occurred involves working with *context cues* to aid retrieval.

Context cues often facilitate the retrieval of information (Smith, 1988). Most people have experienced the effects of context cues on many occasions. For instance, when people return after a number of years to a place where they used to live, they are typically flooded with long-forgotten memories. Or consider how often you have gone from one room to another to get something (scissors, perhaps), only to discover that you can't remember what you were after. However, when you return to the first room (the original context), you suddenly recall what it was ("Of course, the scissors!"). These examples illustrate the potentially powerful effects of context cues on memory.

The technique of reinstating the context of an event has been used effectively in legal investigations to enhance eyewitness recall (Chandler & Fisher, 1996). The eyewitness may be encouraged to retrieve information about a crime by mentally replaying the sequence of events. The value of reinstating the context of an event may account for how hypnosis *occasionally* stimulates eyewitness recall (Meyer, 1992). The hypnotist usually attempts to reinstate the context of the event by telling the witness to imagine being at the scene of the crime once again. Unfortunately, research suggests that hypnosis often increases individuals' tendency to report *incorrect* information while making them feel overconfident about the accuracy of their recall (Lynn, Neuschatz, & Fite, 2002; Mazzoni & Lynn, 2007). Concerns about the accuracy of hypnosis-aided recall have led courts to be extremely cautious about allowing hypnosis-aided recollections as admissible testimony.

Reconstructing Memories and the Misinformation Effect

When you retrieve information from long-term memory, you're not able to pull up a "mental videotape" that provides an exact replay of the past. To some extent, your memories are sketchy *reconstructions* of the past that may be distorted and may include details that

did not actually occur (Roediger, Wheeler, & Rajaram, 1993). The reconstructive nature of memory was first highlighted many years ago by Sir Frederic Bartlett, a prominent English psychologist. Bartlett (1932) had his subjects read the tale "War of the Ghosts," reproduced in **Figure 7.15**. Subjects read the story twice and waited 15 minutes. Then they were asked to write down the tale as best they could recall it.

What did Bartlett find? As you might expect, subjects condensed the story, leaving out boring details. Of greater interest was Bartlett's discovery that subjects often *changed* the tale to some extent. The canoe became a boat or the two young men were hunting beavers instead of seals. Subjects often introduced entirely *new elements* and twists. For instance, in one case, the death at the end was attributed to fever and the character was described as "foaming at the mouth" (instead of "something black came out of his mouth"). Bartlett concluded that the distortions in recall occurred because subjects reconstructed the tale to fit with their established schemas. Modern schema theories also emphasize the reconstructive nature of memory (Hirt, McDonald, & Markman, 1998). These theories propose that part of what people recall about an event is the details of that particular event and part is a reconstruction of the event based on their schemas.

Research by Elizabeth Loftus (1979, 1992, 2005) and others on the *misinformation effect* has shown that reconstructive distortions show up frequently

web link 7.3

Mind Tools—Tools for Improving Your Memory

The Mind Tools site details practical techniques to help people improve their cognitive efficiency in many areas. The subpage dedicated to memory functioning offers an excellent collection of suggestions for ways to enhance memory.

Figure 7.15

A story used in a study of reconstructive memory by Bartlett (1932). As explained in the text, subjects recalling the story shown here tended to change details and to "remember" elements not in the original at all.

SOURCE: Excerpt from Bartlett, F. C. (1932). *Remembering: A study in experimental and social psychology.* New York: Cambridge University Press, p. 65. Copyright © 1932.

WAR OF THE GHOSTS

One night two young men from Egulac went down to the river to hunt seals, and while they were there it became foggy and calm. Then they heard war cries, and they thought: "Maybe this is a war party." They escaped to the shore, and hid behind a log. Now canoes came up, and they heard the noise of paddles, and saw one canoe coming up to them. There were five men in the canoe, and they said:

"What do you think? We wish to take you along. We are going up the river to make war on the people."

One of the young men said: "I have no arrows."

"Arrows are in the canoe," they said.

"I will not go along. I might be killed. My relatives do not know where I have gone. But you," he said, turning to the other, "may go with them."

So one of the young men went, but the others returned home.

And the warriors went up to the river to a town on the other side of Kalama. The people came down to the water, and they began to fight, and many were killed. But presently the young man heard one of the warriors say: "Quick, let us go home: that Indian has been hit." Now he thought: "Oh, they are ghosts." He did not feel sick, but they said he had been shot.

So the canoes went back to Egulac, and the young man went ashore to his house, and made a fire. And he told everybody and said: "Behold I accompanied the ghosts, and we went to fight. Many of our fellows were killed, and many of those who attacked us were killed. They said I was hit, and I did not feel sick."

He told it all, and then he became quiet. When the sun rose he fell down. Something black came out of his mouth. His face became contorted. The people jumped up and cried.

He was dead.

Elizabeth Loftus

"One reason most of us, as jurors, place so much faith in eyewitness testimony is that we are unaware of how many factors influence its accuracy."

Figure 7.16

The misinformation effect. In an experiment by Loftus and Palmer (1974), participants who were asked leading questions in which cars were described as *hitting* or *smashing* each other were prone to recall the same accident differently one week later, demonstrating the reconstructive nature of memory.

in eyewitness testimony. **The *misinformation effect* occurs when participants' recall of an event they witnessed is altered by introducing misleading postevent information.** For example, in one study Loftus and Palmer (1974) showed subjects a videotape of an automobile accident. Participants were then "grilled" as if they were providing eyewitness testimony, and biasing information was introduced. Some subjects were asked, "How fast were the cars going when they *hit* each other?" Other subjects were asked, "How fast were the cars going when they *smashed into* each other?" A week later, subjects' recall of the accident was tested and they were asked whether they remembered seeing any broken glass in the accident (there was none). Participants who had earlier been asked about the cars *smashing into* each other were more likely to "recall" broken glass. Why would they add this detail to their reconstructions of the accident? Probably because broken glass is consistent with their schema for cars *smashing* together (see **Figure 7.16**). The misinformation effect, which has been replicated in "countless studies," is a remarkably reliable phenomenon that has "challenged prevailing views about the validity of memory" (Zaragoza, Belli, & Payment, 2007, p. 37). Indeed, the effect is difficult to escape, as even subjects who have been forewarned can be swayed by postevent misinformation (Loftus, 2005).

In a related line of research, Loftus and colleagues showed that simple print advertisements can distort some people's recollections of their personal past (Braun, Ellis, & Loftus, 2002). Exposing subjects to a nostalgic ad for Disney World—which presumably led the subjects to imagine being there in the past—increased their confidence that they had once shaken hands with Mickey Mouse as a child visiting a Disney park. Of course, the ad could have revived a genuine memory in some of the participants. To rule out this possibility, the researchers demonstrated that a similar ad featuring Bugs Bunny increased subjects' belief that they had once met Bugs at a Disney Park—an event that would be impossible, since Bugs is a Warner Bros. character who would never be encountered at a Disney park.

Research demonstrating the misinformation effect involves clever manipulations that produce surprising memory distortions, but similar distortions routinely occur without any crafty manipulations. Recent research has demonstrated that the simple act of retelling a story can introduce inaccuracies into memory (Marsh, 2007). When people retell stories, they tend to make a number of "adjustments" that depend on their goals, their audience, and the social context. Think about it: People tell stories to entertain others, to inform others, to impress others, to gain sympathy from their friends, and so forth. Depending on one's goals, one may streamline a story, embellish the facts, exaggerate one's role, omit important situational considerations, and so forth. Not surprisingly, when participants in one study were asked to evaluate the accuracy of recent retellings, they admitted that 42% were "inaccurate" and that another one-third contained "distortions" (Marsh & Tversky, 2004). When retelling their stories, people may be aware that they are being a little loose with the facts, but what is interesting is that their intentional distortions can reshape their subsequent recollections of the same events. Somehow, the "real" story and the storyteller's "spin" on it probably begin to blend imperceptibly. So, even routine retellings of events can contribute to the malleability of memory.

Source Monitoring and Reality Monitoring

The misinformation effect and similar memory distortions appear to be due, *in part,* to the unreliability of a retrieval process called *source monitoring* (Mitchell & Johnson, 2000). **Source monitoring involves making attributions about the origins of memories.** Marcia Johnson and her colleagues maintain that source monitoring is a crucial facet of memory retrieval that contributes to many of the mistakes that people make in reconstructing their experiences (Johnson, 1996, 2006; Johnson, Hashtroudi, & Lindsay, 1993). According to Johnson, memories are not tagged with labels that specify their sources. Thus, when people pull up specific memory records, they have to make decisions *at the time of retrieval* about where the memories came from (example: "Did I read that in the *New York Times* or *Rolling Stone*?"). Much of the time, these decisions are so easy and automatic, people make them without

Leading question asked during witness testimony

Possible schemas activated

Response of subjects asked one week later, "Did you see any broken glass?" (There was none.)

"About how fast were the cars going when they hit each other?"

"About how fast were the cars going when they smashed into each other?"

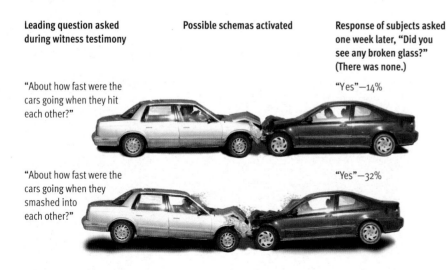

"Yes"—14%

"Yes"—32%

being consciously aware of the source-monitoring process. In other instances, however, they may consciously struggle to pinpoint the source of a memory. A *source-monitoring error* occurs when a memory derived from one source is misattributed to another source. For example, you might attribute your roommate's remark to your psychology professor, or something you heard on *Oprah* to your psychology textbook. Inaccurate memories that reflect source-monitoring errors may seem quite compelling, and people often feel extremely confident about their authenticity even though the recollections really are inaccurate (Lampinen, Neuschatz, & Payne, 1999).

Source-monitoring errors appear to be commonplace and may shed light on many interesting memory phenomena. For instance, in studies of eyewitness suggestibility, some subjects have gone so far as to insist that they "remember" seeing something that was only verbally suggested to them. Most theories have a hard time explaining how people can have memories of events that they never actually saw or experienced, but this paradox doesn't seem all that perplexing when it is explained as a source-monitoring error (Lindsay et al., 2004). The source-monitoring approach can also make sense of *cryptomnesia*—inadvertent plagiarism that occurs when people come up with an idea that they think is original when they were actually exposed to it earlier (Bredart, Lampinen, & Defeldre, 2003). Source-monitoring errors also appear to underlie the common tendency for people to mix up fictional information from novels and movies with factual information from news reports and personal experiences (Marsh, Meade, & Roediger, 2003).

Marcia Johnson's source-monitoring theory has built and expanded on an earlier concept that she called *reality monitoring,* which she now views as a subtype of source monitoring. **Reality monitoring refers to the process of deciding whether memories are based on external sources (one's perceptions of actual events) or internal sources (one's thoughts and imaginations).** People engage in reality monitoring when they reflect on whether something actually happened or they only thought about it happen-

ing. This dilemma may sound like an odd problem that would arise only infrequently, but it isn't. People routinely ponder questions like "Did I pack the umbrella or only think about packing it?" "Did I take my morning pill or only intend to do so?" Studies indicate that people focus on several types of clues in making their reality-monitoring decisions (Johnson, 2006; Johnson, Kahan, & Raye, 1984; Kahan et al., 1999). When memories are rich in sensory information (you can recall the feel of shoving the umbrella into your suitcase) or contextual information (you can clearly see yourself in the hallway packing your umbrella), or when memories can be retrieved with little effort, one is more likely to infer that the event really happened. In contrast, one is more likely to infer that an event did *not* actually occur when memories of it lack sensory or contextual details or are difficult to retrieve.

George Harrison of the Beatles is one of several prominent musicians who have been accused of plagiarizing the work of others. Harrison was successfully sued for picking up the melody for one of his hits (My Sweet Lord) from another song that was recorded eight years earlier. We can only speculate, but this incident may have involved cryptomnesia—inadvertent plagiarism that occurs when people come up with an idea that they think is original, when they really were exposed to it earlier. Cryptomnesia may occur beceause of source-monitoring errors in retrieval.

Marcia Johnson

"Our long-term goal is to develop ways of determining which aspects of mental experience create one's sense of a personal past and one's conviction (accurate or not) that memories, knowledge, beliefs, attitudes, and feelings are tied to reality in a veridical fashion."

REVIEW of Key Learning Goals

7.11 The tip-of-the-tongue phenomenon is the temporary inability to remember something you know, which feels just out of reach. It clearly represents a failure in retrieval. Memories can be jogged by retrieval cues. Reinstating the context of an event can also facilitate recall. This factor may account for cases in which hypnosis appears to aid recall of previously forgotten information. However, hypnosis seems to increase people's tendency to report incorrect information.

7.12 Memories are not exact replicas of past experiences. As Bartlett showed many years ago, memory is partially re-

constructive. Research by Loftus on the misinformation effect shows that information learned after an event can alter one's memory of the event. Even the simple act of retelling a story can introduce inaccuracies into memory.

7.13 Source monitoring is the process of making attributions about the origins of memories. According to Johnson, source-monitoring errors appear to be common and may explain why people sometimes "recall" something that was only suggested to them or confuse their own ideas with others' ideas. Reality monitoring involves deciding whether memories are based on perceptions of actual events or on just thinking about the events.

Key Learning Goals

7.14 Describe Ebbinghaus's forgetting curve and three measures of retention.

7.15 Assess ineffective encoding and decay as potential causes of forgetting.

7.16 Evaluate interference and factors in the retrieval process as potential causes of forgetting.

7.17 Summarize evidence for the view that most recovered memories of childhood sexual abuse are genuine.

7.18 Summarize evidence for the view that most recovered memories of childhood sexual abuse are inaccurate.

Forgetting: When Memory Lapses

Forgetting gets a "bad press" that it may not deserve. People tend to view forgetting as a failure, weakness, or deficiency in cognitive processing. Although forgetting important information *can* be frustrating, some memory theorists argue that forgetting is actually adaptive. How so? Imagine how cluttered your memory would be if you never forgot anything. According to Daniel Schacter (1999), you need to forget information that is no longer relevant, such as out-of-date phone numbers, discarded passwords, lines that were memorized for a tenth-grade play, and where you kept your important papers three apartments ago. Forgetting can reduce competition among memories that can cause confusion. In a recent exploration of this hypothesis, scientists used brain-imaging technology to track neural markers of cognitive effort in a series of tasks in which participants memorized pairs of words (Kuhl et al., 2007). They found that the forgetting of word pairs deemed "irrelevant" made it easier to remember the "relevant" word pairs and reduced the "demands" placed on crucial neural circuits. In a nutshell, they found that forgetting helped subjects remember the information they needed to remember.

Although forgetting may be adaptive in the long run, the fundamental question of memory research remains: Why do people forget information that they would like to remember? There isn't one simple answer to this question. Research has shown that forgetting can be caused by defects in encoding, storage, retrieval, or some combination of these processes.

How Quickly We Forget: Ebbinghaus's Forgetting Curve

6d

The first person to conduct scientific studies of forgetting was Hermann Ebbinghaus. He published a series of insightful memory studies way back in 1885. Ebbinghaus studied only one subject—himself. To give himself lots of new material to memorize, he invented *nonsense syllables*—**consonant-vowel-consonant arrangements that do not correspond to words** (such as BAF, XOF, VIR, and MEQ). He wanted to work with meaningless materials that would be uncontaminated by his previous learning.

Ebbinghaus was a remarkably dedicated researcher. For instance, in one study he went through over 14,000 practice repetitions, as he tirelessly memorized 420 lists of nonsense syllables (Slamecka, 1985).

He tested his memory of these lists after various time intervals. **Figure 7.17** shows what he found. This diagram, called a *forgetting curve,* **graphs retention and forgetting over time.** Ebbinghaus's forgetting curve showed a precipitous drop in retention during the first few hours after the nonsense syllables were memorized. Thus, he concluded that most forgetting occurs very rapidly after learning something.

That's a depressing conclusion. What is the point of memorizing information if you're going to forget it all right away? Fortunately, subsequent research showed that Ebbinghaus's forgetting curve was unusually steep (Postman, 1985). Forgetting isn't usually quite as swift or as extensive as Ebbinghaus thought. One problem was that he was working with such meaningless material. When subjects memorize more meaningful material, such as prose or poetry, forgetting curves aren't nearly as steep. Studies of how well people recall their high school classmates suggest that forgetting curves for autobiographical information are even shallower (Bahrick, 2000). Also, different methods of measuring forgetting yield varied estimates of how quickly people forget. This variation underscores the importance of the methods used to measure forgetting, the matter we turn to next.

Measures of Forgetting

SIM5, SIM6, 6d

To study forgetting empirically, psychologists need to be able to measure it precisely. Measures of forgetting inevitably measure retention as well. *Retention* **refers to the proportion of material retained (remembered).** In studies of forgetting, the results may be reported in terms of the amount forgotten or the amount retained. In these studies, the *retention interval* is the length of time between the presentation of materials to be remembered and the measurement of forgetting. The three principal methods used to measure forgetting are recall, recognition, and relearning (Lockhart, 1992).

Who is the current U.S. secretary of state? What movie won the Academy Award for best picture last year? These questions involve recall measures of retention. A *recall* measure of retention requires subjects to reproduce information on their own without any cues. If you were to take a recall test on a list of 25 words you had memorized, you would simply be told to write down as many of the words as you could remember.

Hermann Ebbinghaus

"Left to itself every mental content gradually loses its capacity for being revived.... Facts crammed at examination time soon vanish."

© Bettmann/Corbis

In contrast, in a recognition test you might be shown a list of 100 words and asked to choose the 25 words that you had memorized. **A *recognition* measure of retention requires subjects to select previously learned information from an array of options.** Subjects not only have cues to work with, they have the answers right in front of them. In educational testing, essay questions and fill-in-the-blanks questions are recall measures of retention. Multiple-choice, true-false, and matching questions are recognition measures.

If you're like most students, you probably prefer multiple-choice tests over essay tests. This preference is understandable, because evidence shows that recognition measures tend to yield higher scores than recall measures of memory for the same information (Lockhart, 2000). This situation was demonstrated many decades ago by Luh (1922), who measured subjects' retention of nonsense syllables with both a recognition test and a recall test. As **Figure 7.18** shows, subjects' performance on the recognition measure was far superior to their performance on the recall measure. There are two ways to look at this disparity between recall and recognition tests. One is to see recognition tests as especially *sensitive* measures of retention. The other is to see recognition tests as excessively *easy* measures of retention.

Actually, there is no guarantee that a recognition test will be easier than a recall test. This tends to be the case, but the difficulty of a recognition test can vary greatly, depending on the number, similarity, and plausibility of the options provided as possible answers. To illustrate, see whether you know the answer to the following multiple-choice question:

The capital of Washington is:
   a.   *Seattle*
   b.   *Spokane*
   c.   *Tacoma*
   d.   *Olympia*

Most students who aren't from Washington find this a fairly difficult question. The answer is Olympia. Now take a look at the next question:

The capital of Washington is:
   a.   *London*
   b.   *New York*
   c.   *Tokyo*
   d.   *Olympia*

Virtually anyone can answer this question because the incorrect options are readily dismissed. Although this illustration is a bit extreme, it shows that two recognition measures of the same information can vary dramatically in difficulty.

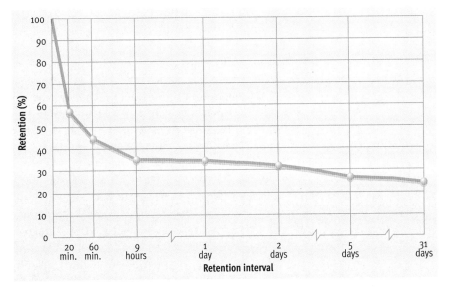

Figure 7.17
Ebbinghaus's forgetting curve for nonsense syllables. From his experiments on himself, Ebbinghaus (1885) concluded that forgetting is extremely rapid immediately after the original learning and then levels off. Although this generalization remains true, subsequent research has shown that forgetting curves for nonsense syllables are unusually steep.

The third method of measuring forgetting is relearning. **A *relearning* measure of retention requires a subject to memorize information a second time to determine how much time or how many practice trials are saved by having learned it before.** Subjects' *savings scores* provide an estimate of their retention. Relearning measures can detect retention that is overlooked by recognition tests (Crowder & Greene, 2000).

Why We Forget

6d

Measuring forgetting is only the first step in the long journey toward explaining why forgetting occurs. In this section, we explore the possible causes of forgetting, looking at factors that may affect encoding, storage, and retrieval processes.

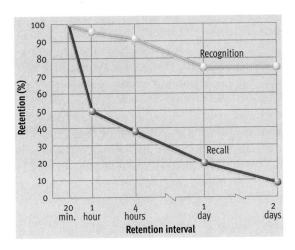

Figure 7.18
Recognition versus recall in the measurement of retention. Luh (1922) had participants memorize lists of nonsense syllables and then measured their retention with either a recognition test or a recall test at various intervals up to two days. As you can see, the forgetting curve for the recall test was quite steep, whereas the recognition test yielded much higher estimates of subjects' retention.

Ineffective Encoding 6d

A great deal of forgetting may only *appear* to be forgetting. The information in question may never have been inserted into memory in the first place. Since you can't really forget something you never learned, this phenomenon is sometimes called *pseudoforgetting*. We opened the chapter with an example of pseudoforgetting. People usually assume that they know what a penny looks like, but most have actually failed to encode this information. Pseudoforgetting is usually attributable to *lack of attention*.

Even when memory codes *are* formed for new information, subsequent forgetting may be the result of ineffective or inappropriate encoding (Brown & Craik, 2000). The research on levels of processing shows that some approaches to encoding lead to more forgetting than others (Craik & Tulving, 1975). For example, if you're distracted while you read your textbooks, you may be doing little more than saying the words to yourself. This is *phonemic encoding*, which is inferior to *semantic encoding* for retention of verbal material. When you can't remember the information that you've read, your forgetting may be due to ineffective encoding.

Decay 6d

Instead of focusing on encoding, decay theory attributes forgetting to the impermanence of memory *storage*. **Decay theory proposes that forgetting occurs because memory traces fade with time.** The implicit assumption is that decay occurs in the physiological mechanisms responsible for memories. According to decay theory, the mere passage of time produces forgetting. This notion meshes nicely with commonsense views of forgetting.

As we noted earlier, evidence suggests that decay *does* contribute to the loss of information from the sensory and short-term memory stores. However, the critical task for theories of forgetting is to explain the loss of information from long-term memory. Researchers have *not* been able to reliably demonstrate that decay causes LTM forgetting (Slamecka, 1992).

If decay theory is correct, the principal cause of forgetting should be the passage of time. In studies of long-term memory, however, researchers have repeatedly found that time passage is not as influential as what happens during the time interval. Research has shown that forgetting depends not on the amount of time that has passed since learning but on the amount, complexity, and type of information that subjects have had to assimilate *during* the retention interval. The negative impact of competing information on retention is called *interference*. Although theorists have not given up entirely on the intuitively plausible principle of decay (Altmann & Gray, 2002), research on LTM forgetting has been dominated by the concept of interference.

Interference 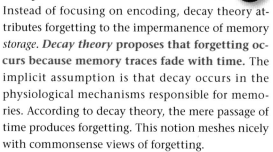 6d

Interference theory **proposes that people forget information because of competition from other material.** Although demonstrations of decay in long-term memory have remained elusive, hundreds of studies have shown that interference influences forgetting (Anderson & Neely, 1996; Bower, 2000). In many of these studies, researchers have controlled interference by varying the *similarity* between the original material given to subjects (the test material) and the material studied in the intervening period. Interference is assumed to be greatest when intervening material is most similar to the test material. Decreasing the similarity should reduce interference and cause less forgetting. This is exactly what McGeoch and McDonald (1931) found in an influential study. They had subjects memorize test material that consisted of a list of two-syllable adjectives. They varied the similarity of intervening learning by having subjects then memorize one of five lists. In order of decreasing similarity to the test material, the lists contained synonyms of the test words, antonyms of the test words, unrelated adjectives, nonsense syllables, and numbers. Later, subjects' recall of the test material was measured. **Figure 7.19** shows that as the similarity of the intervening material decreased, the amount of forgetting also decreased—because of reduced interference.

There are two kinds of interference: *retroactive* and *proactive* (Jacoby, Hessels, & Bopp, 2001). **Retroactive interference occurs when new information impairs the retention of previously learned information.** Retroactive interference occurs between the original learning and the retest on that learning, during the retention interval (see **Figure 7.20**). For example, the interference manipulated by McGeoch and McDonald (1931) was retroactive interference. In contrast, **proactive interference occurs when previously learned information interferes with the retention of new information.** Proactive interference is rooted in learning that comes *before* exposure to the test material.

Retrieval Failure 6d

People often remember things that they were unable to recall at an earlier time. This phenomenon may be obvious only during struggles with the tip-of-the-tongue phenomenon, but it happens frequently. In fact, a great deal of forgetting may be due to breakdowns in the process of retrieval.

Why does an effort to retrieve something fail on one occasion and succeed on another? That's a tough question. One theory is that retrieval failures may be more likely when a mismatch occurs between retrieval cues and the encoding of the information you're searching for. According to the *encoding specificity principle*, **the value of a retrieval cue depends on how well it corresponds to the memory code.** This principle provides one explanation for the inconsistent success of retrieval efforts (Tulving & Thomson, 1973).

A related line of research indicates that memory is influenced by the "fit" between the processing during encoding and retrieval. *Transfer-appropriate processing* **occurs when the initial processing of information is similar to the type of processing required by the subsequent measure of retention.** For example, Morris, Bransford, and Franks (1977) gave subjects a list of words and a task that required either semantic or phonemic processing. Retention was measured with recognition tests that emphasized either the meaning or the sound of the words. Semantic processing yielded higher retention when the testing emphasized semantic factors, while phonemic processing yielded higher retention when the testing emphasized phonemic factors. Thus, retrieval failures are more likely when a poor fit occurs between the processing done during encoding and the processing invoked by the measure of retention (Lockhart, 2002; Roediger & Guynn, 1996).

Motivated Forgetting

Many years ago, Sigmund Freud (1901) came up with an entirely different explanation for retrieval failures. As we noted in Chapter 1, Freud asserted that people often keep embarrassing, unpleasant, or painful memories buried in their unconscious. For example, a person who was deeply wounded by perceived slights at a childhood birthday party might suppress all recollection of that party. In his therapeutic work with patients, Freud recovered many such buried memories. He theorized that the memories were there all along, but their retrieval was blocked by unconscious avoidance tendencies.

The tendency to forget things one doesn't want to think about is called *motivated forgetting,* or to use Freud's terminology, *repression.* In Freudian theory, **repression refers to keeping distressing thoughts**

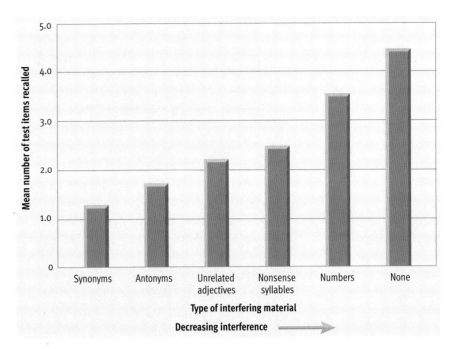

Figure 7.19

Effects of interference. According to interference theory, more interference from competing information should produce more forgetting. McGeoch and McDonald (1931) controlled the amount of interference with a learning task by varying the similarity of an intervening task. The results were consistent with interference theory. The amount of interference is greatest at the left of the graph, as is the amount of forgetting. As interference decreases (moving to the right on the graph), retention improves.

Figure 7.20

Retroactive and proactive interference. Retroactive interference occurs when learning produces a "backward" effect, reducing recall of previously learned material. Proactive interference occurs when learning produces a "forward" effect, reducing recall of subsequently learned material. For example, if you were to prepare for an economics test and then study psychology, the interference from the psychology study would be retroactive interference. However, if you studied psychology first and then economics, the interference from the psychology study would be proactive interference.

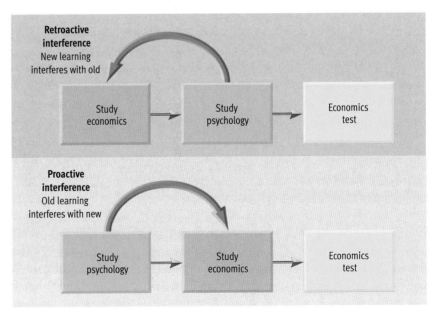

and feelings buried in the unconscious (see Chapter 12). Although it is difficult to demonstrate the operation of repression in laboratory studies (Holmes, 1995; Kihlstrom, 2002), a number of experiments suggest that people don't remember anxiety-laden material as readily as emotionally neutral material, just as Freud proposed (Guenther, 1988; Reisner, 1998). Thus, when you forget unpleasant things such as a dental appointment, a promise to help a friend move, or a term paper deadline, motivated forgetting *may* be at work.

The Recovered Memories Controversy

SIM6

Although the concept of repression has been around for a century, interest in this phenomenon has surged in recent years, thanks to a rash of prominent reports involving the return of individuals' long-lost memories of sexual abuse and other traumas during childhood. The media have been flooded with reports of adults accusing their parents, teachers, and neighbors of horrific child abuse decades earlier, based on previously repressed memories of these travesties. For

the most part, these parents, teachers, and neighbors have denied the allegations. Many of them have seemed genuinely baffled by the accusations, which have torn some previously happy families apart (Gudjonsson, 2001; McHugh et al., 2004). In an effort to make sense of the charges, some accused parents have argued that their children's recollections are false memories created inadvertently by well-intentioned therapists through the power of suggestion.

The controversy surrounding recovered memories of abuse is complex and difficult to sort out. The crux of the problem is that child abuse usually takes place behind closed doors. In the absence of corroborative evidence, there is no way to reliably distinguish genuine recovered memories from false ones. A handful of recovered memory incidents have been substantiated by independent witnesses or belated admissions of guilt from the accused (Brewin, 2003, 2007; Bull, 1999; Shobe & Schooler, 2001). But in the vast majority of cases, the allegations of abuse have been vehemently denied, and independent corroboration has not been available. What do psychologists and psychiatrists have to say about the authenticity of repressed memories? They are sharply divided on the issue.

Support for Recovered Memories

Many psychologists and psychiatrists, especially clinicians involved in the treatment of psychological disorders, largely accept recovered memories of abuse at face value (Banyard & Williams, 1999; Briere & Conte, 1993; Legault & Laurence, 2007; Skinner, 2001; Terr, 1994; Whitfield, 1995). For example, in a survey of British clinicians, 44% reported that they believed that recovered memories are always or usually genuine (Andrews, 2001). Clinicians who believe in recovered memories assert that sexual abuse in childhood is far more widespread than most people realize. For example, one large-scale Canadian survey (MacMillan et al., 1997), using a random sample of 9953 residents of Ontario, found that 12.8% of the females and 4.3% of the males reported that they had been victims of sexual abuse during childhood (see Figure 7.21). Supporters further assert that there is ample evidence that it is common for people to repress traumatic incidents in their unconscious (DelMonte, 2000; Wilsnack et al., 2002). For instance, in one widely cited study, L. M. Williams (1994) followed up on 129 female children who had been brought to a hospital emergency room for treatment of sexual abuse. When interviewed approximately 17 years later about a variety of things, including their history of sexual abuse, 38% of the women failed to report the original incident, which Williams largely attributed to amnesia for the incident. According to Freyd (1996, 2001;

Freyd, DePrince, & Gleaves, 2007), sexual abuse by a parent evokes coping efforts that attempt to block awareness of the abuse because that awareness would interfere with normal attachment processes. The clinicians who accept the authenticity of recovered memories of abuse attribute the recent upsurge in recovered memories to therapists' and clients' increased sensitivity to an issue that people used to be reluctant to discuss.

Skepticism Regarding Recovered Memories

In contrast, many other psychologists, especially memory researchers, have expressed skepticism about the upsurge of recovered memories that began in the 1990s (Kihlstrom, 2004; Laney & Loftus, 2005; Loftus, 1998, 2003; McNally, 2003, 2007). They point out that the women in the Williams (1994) study may have failed to report their earlier sexual abuse for a variety of reasons besides amnesia, including embarrassment, poor rapport with the interviewer, normal forgetfulness, or a conscious preference not to revisit painful experiences from the past (Loftus, Garry & Feldman, 1998; Pope & Hudson, 1998). As McNally (2004) notes, "Not thinking about one's abuse is not the same thing as being unable to remember it" (p. 99).

The skeptics do *not* say that people are lying about their previously repressed memories. Rather, they maintain that some suggestible people wrestling with emotional problems have been convinced by persuasive therapists that their emotional problems must be the result of abuse that occurred years before. Critics blame a minority of therapists who presumably have good intentions but who operate under the dubious assumption that virtually all psychological problems are attributable to childhood sexual abuse (Lindsay & Read, 1994; Loftus & Davis, 2006; Spanos, 1994). Using hypnosis, guided imagery, dream interpretation, and leading questions, they apparently prod and probe patients until they inadvertently create the memories of abuse that they are searching for (Lynn et al., 2003; Thayer & Lynn, 2006).

Psychologists who doubt the authenticity of repressed memories support their analysis by pointing to discredited cases of recovered memories (Brown, Goldstein, & Bjorklund, 2000). For example, with the help of a church counselor, one woman recovered memories of how her minister father had repeatedly raped her, got her pregnant, and then aborted the pregnancy with a coat-hanger; however, subsequent evidence revealed that the woman was still a virgin and that her father had had a vasectomy years before (Brainerd & Reyna, 2005). The skeptics also point to published case histories that clearly involved sugges-

tive questioning and to cases in which patients have recanted recovered memories of sexual abuse after realizing that these memories were created by their therapists (Loftus, 1994; Shobe & Schooler, 2001). Indeed, quite a number of malpractice lawsuits have been filed against therapists for allegedly implanting false memories in patients (Brainerd & Reyna, 2005; Ost, 2006).

Those who question the accuracy of repressed memories also point to findings on the misinformation effect, the tendency to confuse real and imagined memories (reality-monitoring errors), and other demonstrations of the relative ease of creating "memories" of events that never happened (Lindsay et al., 2004; Loftus & Cahill, 2007; Strange, Clifasefi, & Garry, 2007). For example, working with college students, Ira Hyman and his colleagues have managed to implant recollections of fairly substantial events (such as spilling a punch bowl at a wedding, being in a grocery store when the fire sprinkler system went off, being hospitalized for an earache) in about 25% of their subjects, just by asking them to elaborate on events supposedly reported by their

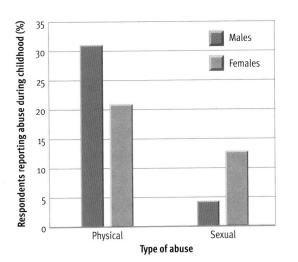

Figure 7.21

Estimates of the prevalence of childhood physical and sexual abuse. In one of the better efforts to estimate the prevalence of child abuse, MacMillan and her colleagues (1997) questioned a random sample of almost 10,000 adults living in the province of Ontario, Canada, about whether they were abused during childhood. As you can see, males were more likely to have experienced physical abuse and females were more likely to have suffered sexual abuse. The data support the assertion that millions of people have been victimized by childhood sexual abuse, which is far from rare.

web link 7.4

False Memory Syndrome Foundation (FMSF) Online

This site marshals evidence that recovered memories of childhood abuse are often false, therapist induced, and grounded in shoddy and nonscientific claims. Dealing with perhaps the most bitterly contested topic in current psychology, the FMSF has elicited fierce opposition.

Tom Rutherford (shown here with his wife, Joyce) received a $1 million settlement in a suit against a church therapist and a Springfield, Missouri, church in a false memory case. Under the church counselor's guidance, the Rutherfords' daughter, Beth, had "recalled" childhood memories of having been raped repeatedly by her minister father, gotten pregnant, and undergone a painful coathanger abortion. Her father lost his job and was ostracized. After he later revealed he'd had a vasectomy when Beth was age 4, and a physical exam revealed that at age 23 she was still a virgin, the memories were shown to be false.

parents (Hyman, Husband, & Billings, 1995; Hyman & Kleinknecht, 1999). Other studies have succeeded in implanting false memories of nearly drowning (Heaps & Nash, 2001) and of being attacked by a vicious animal (Porter, Yuille, & Lehman, 1999) in many participants. Moreover, subjects in these studies often feel very confident about their false memories, which frequently generate strong emotional reactions and richly detailed "recollections" (Loftus & Bernstein, 2005). The newest wrinkle in this line of research involves using Photoshop to doctor photographs to show participants taking a childhood ride in a hot air balloon. Even with no supportive information supplied, exposing subjects to these bogus photos led 50% of the participants to develop "memories" of their balloon experience (Garry & Gerrie, 2005).

In a similar vein, building on much earlier work by James Deese (1959), Henry Roediger and Kathleen McDermott (1995, 2000) have devised a simple laboratory paradigm involving the learning of word lists that is remarkably reliable at producing memory illusions. In this procedure, now known as the *Deese-Roediger-McDermott (DRM) paradigm,* a series of lists of 15 words are presented to participants, who are asked to recall the words immediately after each list is presented and are given a recognition measure of their retention at the end of the session. The trick

is that each list consists of a set of words (such as *bed, rest, awake, tired*) that are strongly associated with another target word that is not on the list (in this case, *sleep*). When subjects *recall* the words on each list, they remember the nonpresented target word over 50% of the time, and when they are given the final *recognition* test, they typically indicate that about 80% of the nonstudied target words were presented in the lists (see **Figure 7.22**).

The trivial memory illusions created in this experiment may seem a far cry from the vivid, detailed recollections of previously forgotten sexual abuse that have generated the recovered memories controversy. But these false memories can be reliably created in normal, healthy participants in a matter of minutes, with little effort and no pressure or misleading information. Thus, this line of research provides a dramatic demonstration of how easy it is to get people to remember that they saw something they really didn't see (McDermott, 2007; Neuschatz et al., 2007).

Skepticism about the validity of recovered memories of abuse has also been fueled by the following observations and research findings:

• Many repressed memories of abuse have been recovered under the influence of hypnosis. However, an extensive body of research indicates that hypnosis tends to increase memory distortions while para-

DOONESBURY

doxically making people feel more confident about their recollections (Mazzoni & Lynn, 2007).

• Many repressed memories of abuse have been recovered through therapists' dream interpretations. But as you learned in Chapter 5, dream interpretation depends on highly subjective guesswork that cannot be verified. Moreover, research shows that bogus dream interpretations can lead normal subjects to believe that they actually experienced the events suggested in the dream analyses (Loftus, 2000; Loftus & Mazzoni, 1998).

• Some recovered memories have described incidents of abuse that occurred before the victim reached age 3 and even when the victim was still in the womb (Taylor, 2004). However, when adults are asked to recall their earliest memories, their oldest recollections typically don't go back to earlier than age 2 or 3 (Bruce, Dolan, & Phillips-Grant, 2000; Hayne, 2007).

Rebuttals to the Skeptics

Of course, those who believe in recovered memories have mounted rebuttals to the numerous arguments raised by the skeptics. For example, Kluft (1999) argues that a recantation of a recovered memory of abuse does not prove that the memory was false. Gleaves (1994) points out that individuals with a history of sexual abuse often vacillate between denying and accepting that the abuse occurred. Harvey (1999) argues that laboratory demonstrations that it is easy to create false memories have involved insignificant memory distortions that do not resemble the emotionally wrenching recollections of sexual abuse that have been recovered in therapy. Olio (1994) concluded, "The possibility of implanting entire multiple scenarios of horror that differ markedly from the individual's experience, such as memories of childhood abuse in an individual who does not have a trauma history, remains an unsubstantiated hypothesis" (p. 442). Moreover, even if one accepts the assertion that therapists *can* create false memories of abuse in their patients, some critics have noted that there is virtually no direct evidence on how often this occurs and no empirical basis for the claim that there has been an *epidemic* of such cases (Berliner & Briere, 1999; Leavitt, 2001; Wilsnack et al., 2002). Other rebuttals have focused on the sociopolitical repercussions of denying the existence of recovered memories, arguing that this position is intended to undermine the credibility of abused women and silence their accusations (Raitt & Zeedyk, 2003). Finally, many critics argue that contrived, artificial laboratory studies of memory and hypnosis may have limited relevance to the com-

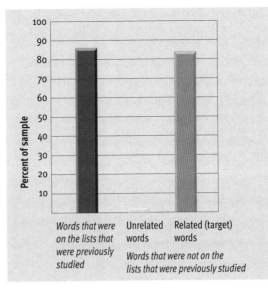

plexities of recovered memories in the real world (Brown, Scheflin, & Hammond, 1998; Gleaves et al., 2004; Pezdek & Lam, 2007).

Conclusions

Although both sides seem genuinely concerned about the welfare of the people involved, the debate about recovered memories of sexual abuse has grown increasingly bitter and emotionally charged. So, what can we conclude about the recovered memories controversy? It seems pretty clear that therapists can unknowingly create false memories in their patients and that a significant portion of recovered memories of abuse are the product of suggestion. But it also seems likely that some cases of recovered memories are authentic (Brewin, 2007; Smith & Gleaves, 2007). At this point, we don't have adequate data to estimate what proportion of recovered memories of abuse fall in each category (Lindsay & Read, 2001). Thus, the matter needs to be addressed with great caution. On the one hand, people should be extremely careful about accepting recovered memories of abuse in the absence of some corroboration. On the other hand, recovered memories of abuse cannot be summarily dismissed, and it would be tragic if the repressed memories controversy made people overly skeptical about the all-too-real problem of childhood sexual abuse.

The repressed memories controversy deserves one last comment regarding its impact on memory research and scientific conceptions of memory. The controversy has helped inspire a great deal of research that has increased our understanding of just how fragile, fallible, malleable, and subjective human memory is. It is presumptuous to trust

Figure 7.22

The prevalence of false memories observed by Roediger and McDermott (1995). The graph shown here summarizes the recognition test results in Study 1 conducted by Roediger and McDermott (1995). Participants correctly identified words that had been on the lists that they had studied 86% of the time and only misidentified unrelated words that had not been on the lists 2% of the time, indicating that they were paying careful attention to the task. Nonetheless, they mistakenly reported that they "remembered" related target words that were *not* on the lists 84% of the time— a remarkably high prevalence of false memories.

web link 7.5

The Recovered Memory Project

Directed by Professor Russ Cheit (Brown University), this site takes issue with the point of view that most recovered memories of abuse are false memories. It provides descriptions of "corroborated" cases of recovered memories and links to scientists and research articles that are sympathetic to those who believe in repressed memories.

memory—whether recovered or not—to provide accurate recollections of the past. Moreover, the implicit dichotomy underlying the repressed memories debate—that some memories are true, whereas others are false—is misleading and oversimplified. Research demonstrates that all human memories are imperfect reconstructions of the past that are subject to many types of distortion.

REVIEW of Key Learning Goals

7.14 Ebbinghaus's early studies of nonsense syllables suggested that people forget very rapidly. Subsequent research showed that Ebbinghaus's forgetting curve was exceptionally steep. Forgetting can be measured by asking people to recall, recognize, or relearn information. Different methods of measuring retention often produce different estimates of forgetting. Recognition measures tend to yield higher estimates of retention than recall measures.

7.15 Some forgetting, including pseudoforgetting, is caused by ineffective encoding of information, which is usually due to lack of attention. Decay theory proposes that forgetting occurs spontaneously with the passage of time. It has proven difficult to show that decay occurs in long-term memory.

7.16 Interference theory proposes that people forget information because of competition from other material. Proactive interference occurs when old learning interferes with new information. Retroactive interference occurs when new learning interferes with old information. Forgetting may also be a matter of retrieval failure. According to the encoding specificity principle, the effectiveness of a retrieval cue depends on how well it corresponds to the memory code that represents the stored item.

7.17 Recent years have seen a controversial surge of reports of recovered memories of sexual abuse in childhood. Those who tend to accept recovered memories of abuse note that child abuse is quite common and argue that repression is a normal response to it. They tend to dismiss laboratory demonstrations of how easy it is to implant false memories as artificial and irrelevant.

7.18 Memory researchers who tend to be skeptical about recovered memories argue that a minority of therapists prod their patients until they inadvertently create the memories of abuse that they are searching for. They point out that countless studies have demonstrated that it is not all that difficult to create false memories and that memory is more malleable and less reliable than assumed.

In Search of the Memory Trace: The Physiology of Memory

Key Learning Goals

7.19 Describe evidence on neural circuits and memory, including work on long-term potentiation and neurogenesis.

7.20 Distinguish between two types of amnesia, and identify the anatomical structures implicated in memory.

Eric Kandel

"Learning results from changes in the strength of the synaptic connections between precisely interconnected cells."

For decades, neuroscientists have ventured forth in search of the physiological basis for memory, often referred to as the "memory trace." On several occasions scientists have been excited by new leads, only to be led down blind alleys. For example, as we noted earlier, Wilder Penfield's work with electrical stimulation of the brain during surgery suggested that the cortex houses exact tape recordings of past experiences (Penfield & Perot, 1963). At the time, scientists believed that this was a major advance. Ultimately, it was not.

Similarly, James McConnell rocked the world of science when he reported that he had chemically transferred a specific memory from one flatworm to another. McConnell (1962) created a conditioned reflex (contraction in response to light) in flatworms and then transferred RNA (a basic molecular constituent of all living cells) from trained worms to untrained worms. The untrained worms showed evidence of "remembering" the conditioned reflex. McConnell boldly speculated that in the future, chemists might be able to formulate pills containing the information for Physics 201 or History 101! Unfortunately, the RNA transfer studies proved difficult to replicate (Rilling, 1996). Today, decades after McConnell's "breakthrough," we are still a long way from breaking the chemical code for memory.

Investigators continue to explore a variety of leads about the physiological bases for memory. In light of past failures, these lines of research should probably be viewed with guarded optimism, but we'll look at some of the more promising approaches. You may want to consult Chapter 3 if you need to refresh your memory about the physiological processes and structures discussed in this section.

The Neural Circuitry of Memory

PSYK TREK
6c

One line of research suggests that memory formation results in *alterations in synaptic transmission* at specific sites. According to this view, specific memories depend on biochemical changes that occur at specific synapses. Like McConnell, Eric Kandel (2001) and his colleagues have studied conditioned reflexes in a simple organism—a sea slug. In research that earned a Nobel prize for Kandel, they showed that reflex learning in the sea slug produces changes in the strength of specific synaptic connections by enhancing the availability and release of neurotransmitters at these synapses (Bailey & Kandel, 2004; Kennedy, Hawkins, & Kandel, 1992). Kandel believes that durable changes in synaptic transmission may be the neural building blocks of more complex memories as well.

Richard F. Thompson (1989, 1992, 2005) and his colleagues have shown that specific memories may depend on *localized neural circuits* in the brain. In other words, memories may create unique, reusable pathways in the brain along which signals flow. Thompson has traced the pathway that accounts for a rabbit's memory of a conditioned eyeblink response. The key link in this circuit is a microscopic spot in the *cerebellum*, a structure in the hindbrain (see **Figure 7.23**). When this spot is destroyed, the conditioned stimulus no longer elicits the eyeblink response, even though the unconditioned stimulus still does (Steinmetz, 1998). This finding does *not* mean that the cerebellum is the key to all memory. Other memories presumably create entirely different pathways in other areas of the brain. The key implication of this work is that it may be possible to map out specific neural circuits that correspond to at least some types of specific memories.

Evidence on *long-term potentiation* also supports the idea that memory traces consist of specific neural circuits. **Long-term potentiation (LTP) is a long-lasting increase in neural excitability at synapses along a specific neural pathway.** Researchers produce LTP artificially by sending a burst of high-frequency electrical stimulation along a neural pathway, but theorists suspect that natural events produce the same sort of potentiated neural circuit when a memory is formed (Abraham, 2006; Lynch, 2004). LTP appears to involve changes in both presynaptic (sending) and postsynaptic (receiving) neurons in neural circuits in the hippocampus (refer to **Figure 7.23**) (Bi & Poo, 2001). The evidence on LTP has inspired promising work on the development of drugs that might enhance memory in humans (Lynch & Gall, 2006). The opposite of LTP, a durable *decrease* in synaptic excitability along a neural pathway, has also been observed and is called *long-term depression (LTD)*. This process may shed light on how forgetting occurs at the level of the synapse (Rosenzweig, Barnes, & Nc-Naughton, 2002; Villarreal et al., 2002).

Recent research suggests that the process of *neurogenesis*—the formation of new neurons—may contribute to the sculpting of neural circuits that underlie memory. As we noted in Chapter 3, scientists have recently discovered that new brain cells are formed constantly in the *dentate gyrus* of the *hippocampus* (Gould, 2004). Animal studies show that manipulations that suppress neurogenesis lead to memory impairments on many types of learning tasks and that conditions that increase neurogenesis are associated with enhanced learning on many tasks (Leuner, Gould, & Shors, 2006). According to Becker and Woj-

towicz (2007), newly formed neurons are initially more excitable than mature neurons, so they may be more readily recruited into new neural circuits corresponding to memories. Moreover, neurogenesis provides the brain with a supply of neurons that vary in age and these variations may somehow allow the brain to "time stamp" some memories. The theorizing about how neurogenesis contributes to memory encoding is highly speculative, but research on neurogenesis is an exciting new line of investigation.

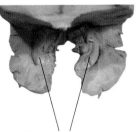

The Anatomy of Memory

Cases of *organic amnesia*—extensive memory loss due to head injury—are another source of clues about the physiological bases of memory. There are two basic types of amnesia: retrograde and anterograde (see **Figure 7.24**). **Retrograde amnesia** involves the

Prefrontal cortex
Contains areas important in working memory

Cerebral cortex
After consolidation in hippocampal area, stores memories in widely distributed areas

Hippocampus
Crucial to the consolidation of memories (along with adjacent structures in the medial temporal lobe)

Cerebellum
Contains an area crucial to neural circuits for conditioned eyeblink responses

Amygdala
Plays major role in learned fears and other emotional memories

Figure 7.23
The anatomy of memory. All the brain structures identified here have been implicated in efforts to discover the anatomical structures involved in memory. The hippocampus is the hub of the medial temporal lobe memory system, which is thought to play a critical role in the consolidation of long-term memories.

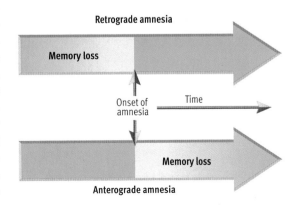

Figure 7.24
Retrograde versus anterograde amnesia. In retrograde amnesia, memory for events that occurred prior to the onset of amnesia is lost. In anterograde amnesia, memory for events that occur subsequent to the onset of amnesia suffers.

Brenda Milner

"Some effects of temporal lobe lesions in man are hard to reconcile with any unitary-process theory of memory."

loss of memories for events that occurred prior to the onset of amnesia. For example, a 25-year-old gymnast who sustains a head trauma might find the prior three years, or seven years, or her entire lifetime erased. *Anterograde amnesia* involves the loss of memories for events that occur after the onset of amnesia. For instance, after her accident, the injured gymnast might suffer impaired ability to remember people she meets, where she has parked her car, and so on.

The study of anterograde amnesia has proven to be an especially rich source of information about the brain and memory. One well-known case, that of a man referred to as H. M., has been followed by Brenda Milner and her colleagues since 1953 (Corkin, 1984, 2002; Milner, Corkin, & Teuber, 1968; Scoville & Milner, 1957). H. M. had surgery to relieve debilitating epileptic seizures. Unfortunately, the surgery inadvertently wiped out most of his ability to form long-term memories. H. M.'s short-term memory is fine, but he has no recollection of anything that has happened since 1953 (other than about the most recent 20–30 seconds of his life). He doesn't recognize the doctors treating him, and he can't remember routes to and from places. He can read a magazine story over and over, thinking he is reading it for the first time each time. He can't remember what he did yesterday, let alone what he has done for the last 50 years. He doesn't even recognize a current photo of himself, as aging has changed his appearance considerably.

H. M.'s memory losses were originally attributed to the removal of his *hippocampus* (see Figure 7.23), although theorists eventually realized that other nearby structures that were removed also contributed to H. M.'s dramatic memory deficits (Delis & Lucas, 1996). Based on decades of additional research, scientists now believe that the entire *hippocampal region* (including the hippocampus, dentate gyrus, subiculum, and entorhinal cortex) and adjacent areas in the cortex are critical for many types of long-term memory (Zola & Squire, 2000). Many scientists now refer to this broader memory complex as the *medial temporal lobe memory system* (Squire, Clark, & Bayley, 2004). Given its apparent role in long-term memory, it is interesting to note that the

hippocampal region is one of the first areas of the brain to sustain significant damage in the course of Alzheimer's disease, which produces severe memory impairment in many people, typically after age 65 (Albert & Moss, 2002).

Do these findings mean that memories are stored in the hippocampal region and adjacent areas? Probably not. Many theorists believe that the medial temporal lobe memory system plays a key role in the *consolidation* of memories (Dudai, 2004). *Consolidation* is a hypothetical process involving the gradual conversion of information into durable memory codes stored in long-term memory. According to this view, memories are consolidated in the hippocampal region and then stored in diverse and widely distributed areas of the cortex (Eichenbaum, 2004; Markowitsch, 2000). This setup allows new memories to become independent of the hippocampal region and to gradually be integrated with other memories already stored in various areas of the cortex (Frankland & Bontempi, 2005). Interestingly, recent research suggests that much of the consolidation process may unfold while people sleep (Stickgold & Walker, 2005).

Neuroscientists continue to forge ahead in their efforts to identify the anatomical bases of memory. One recent advance has been the demonstration that the *amygdala seems to be critical to the formation of memories for learned fears* (Phelps, 2006; Schafe, Doyere, & LeDoux, 2005). This subcortical structure, which is a close neighbor of the hippocampus (see Figure 7.23), may also contribute to the consolidation of other emotional memories (McGaugh, 2004).

Researchers exploring the anatomy of memory have traditionally focused on the anatomical bases of *long-term memory*. However, recent years have brought progress in understanding the neural correlates of *working memory*. Various lines of research suggest that areas in the prefrontal cortex contribute to working memory (Runyan & Dash, 2005; E. Smith, 2000).

As you can see, a variety of neural circuits and anatomical structures have been implicated as playing a role in memory. Looking for the physiological basis for memory is only slightly less daunting than looking for the physiological basis for thought itself.

web link 7.6

The Skeptic's Dictionary: Memory

This site provides a brief but accurate introduction to a variety of issues related to memory, with many useful hyperlinks. Topics covered include forgetting, source-monitoring errors, amnesia, and the reliability of memory.

REVIEW of Key Learning Goals

7.19 According to Kandel, memory traces reflect alterations in neurotransmitter release at specific synapses. Thompson's research suggests that memory traces may consist of localized neural circuits. Memories may also depend on long-term potentiation, which is a durable increase in neural excitability at synapses along a specific neural pathway. Neurogenesis may contribute to the sculpting of neural circuits for memories.

7.20 In retrograde amnesia, a person loses memory for events prior to the amnesia. In anterograde amnesia, a person shows memory deficits for events subsequent to the onset of the amnesia. Studies of amnesia and other research suggest that the hippocampus and broader medial temporal lobe system play a major role in memory. These areas may be crucial to the consolidation of memories.

Systems and Types of Memory

Some theorists believe that evidence on the physiology of memory is complicated because investigators are probing into several distinct memory systems that may have different physiological bases. The various memory systems are distinguished primarily by the types of information they handle.

Declarative Versus Procedural Memory

6c

The most basic division of memory into distinct systems contrasts *declarative memory* with *nondeclarative* or *procedural memory* (Squire, 2004; see Figure 7.25). The *declarative memory system* handles factual information. It contains recollections of words, definitions, names, dates, faces, events, concepts, and ideas. The *nondeclarative memory system* houses memory for actions, skills, conditioned responses, and emotional responses. It contains *procedural memories* of how to execute perceptual-motor skills, such as riding a bike, typing, and tying one's shoes. To illustrate the distinction, if you know the rules of tennis (the number of games in a set, scoring, and such), this factual information is stored in declarative memory. If you remember how to hit a serve and swing through a backhand, these are procedural memories that are part of the nondeclarative system. The nondeclarative system also includes the memory base for conditioned reflexes and emotional reactions based on previous learning, such as a person's tensing up in response to the sound of a dental drill.

Support for the distinction between declarative and nondeclarative memory comes from evidence that the two systems seem to operate somewhat differently (Squire, Knowlton, & Musen, 1993). For example, the recall of factual information generally depends on conscious, effortful processes, whereas memory for conditioned reflexes is largely automatic, and memories for skills often require little effort and attention (Johnson, 2003). People execute perceptual-motor tasks such as playing the piano or typing with little conscious awareness of what they're doing. In fact, performance on such tasks sometimes deteriorates if people think too much about what they're doing. Another disparity is that the memory for skills (such as typing and bike riding) doesn't decline much over long retention intervals, while declarative memory appears more vulnerable to forgetting.

Although much remains to be learned, researchers have made some progress toward identifying the

Key Learning Goals

7.21 Compare and contrast declarative and nondeclarative (procedural) memory.

7.22 Distinguish between episodic and semantic memory.

7.23 Summarize factors that influence prospective memory.

neural bases of declarative versus nondeclarative memory. Declarative memory appears to be handled by the *medial temporal lobe* memory system and the far-flung areas of the cortex with which it communicates (Eichenbaum, 2003). Pinpointing the neural bases of nondeclarative memory has proven more difficult because it consists of more of a hodgepodge of memory functions; however, structures such as the cerebellum and amygdala appear to contribute (Delis & Lucas, 1996; Squire, 2004).

Semantic Versus Episodic Memory

Endel Tulving (1986, 1993, 2002) has further subdivided declarative memory into episodic and semantic memory (see Figure 7.25). Both contain factual information, but episodic memory contains *personal facts* and semantic memory contains *general facts*. The *episodic memory system* is made up of chronological, or temporally dated, recollections of personal experiences. Episodic memory is a record of things

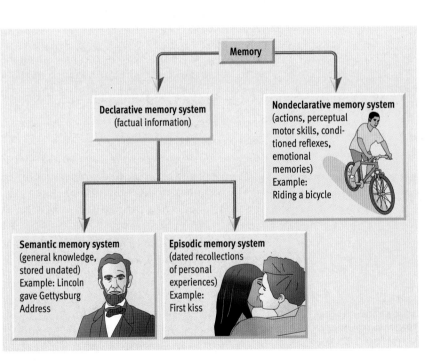

Figure 7.25

Theories of independent memory systems. Theorists have distinguished between declarative memory, which handles facts and information, and nondeclarative memory, which handles motor skills, conditioned responses, and emotional memories. Declarative memory is further subdivided into semantic memory (general knowledge) and episodic memory (dated recollections of personal experiences). The extent to which nondeclarative memory can be usefully subdivided remains the subject of debate, although many theorists view procedural memory, which handles actions and perceptual-motor skills, as an independent subsystem. (Adapted from Squire, 1987; Tulving, 1985, 1987)

Endel Tulving

"Memory systems constitute the major subdivisions of the overall organization of the memory complex.... An operating component of a system consists of a neural substrate and its behavioral or cognitive correlates."

you've done, seen, and heard. It includes information about *when* you did these things, saw them, or heard them. It contains recollections about being in a ninth-grade play, visiting the Grand Canyon, attending a Norah Jones concert, or going to a movie last weekend. Tulving (2001) emphasizes that the function of episodic memory is "time travel"—that is, to allow one to reexperience the past. He also speculates that episodic memory may be unique to humans.

The *semantic memory system* **contains general knowledge that is not tied to the time when the information was learned.** Semantic memory contains information such as Christmas is December 25, dogs have four legs, and Phoenix is located in Arizona. You probably don't remember when you learned these facts. Such information is usually stored undated. The distinction between episodic and semantic memory can be better appreciated by drawing an analogy to books: Episodic memory is like an autobiography, while semantic memory is like an encyclopedia.

Some studies suggest that episodic and semantic memory may have distinct neural bases (Schacter, Wagner, & Buckner, 2000, Tulving, 2002). For instance, some amnesiacs forget mostly personal facts, while their recall of general facts is largely unaffected (Wood, Ebert, & Kinsbourne, 1982). Brain-imaging studies suggest that the retrieval of episodic and semantic memories produces different—but overlapping—patterns of activation (Levine et al., 2004; Nyberg et al., 2002). However, debate continues about the neural substrates of episodic and semantic memory (Barba et al., 1998; Wiggs, Weisberg, & Martin, 1999).

Prospective Versus Retrospective Memory

A 1984 paper with a clever title, "Remembering to Do Things: A Forgotten Topic" (Harris, 1984), introduced yet another distinction between types of memory: *prospective memory* versus *retrospective memory* (see **Figure 7.26**). This distinction does not refer to independent *memory systems,* but rather to

fundamentally different types of *memory tasks.* **Prospective memory involves remembering to perform actions in the future.** Examples of prospective memory tasks include remembering to walk the dog, to call someone, to grab the tickets for the big game, and to turn off your lawn sprinkler. In contrast, *retrospective memory* **involves remembering events from the past or previously learned information.** Retrospective memory is at work when you try to recall who won the Super Bowl last year, when you reminisce about your high school days, or when you try to remember what your professor said in a lecture last week. Prospective memory has been a "forgotten" topic in that it has been the subject of relatively little study. But that has begun to change, as research on prospective memory has increased in recent years (McDaniel & Einstein, 2007).

Researchers interested in prospective memory argue that the topic merits far more study because it plays such a pervasive role in everyday life (Graf & Uttl, 2001). Think about it—a brief trip to attend class at school can be saturated with prospective memory tasks. You may need to remember to pack your notebook, take your cell phone, turn off the coffeemaker, and grab your parking card before you even get out the door. Unfortunately, experiments demonstrate that it is easy to forget these kinds of intentions, especially when confronted by interruptions and distractions (Einstein et al., 2003). The recollection of intentions to undertake actions are often spontaneous—the intentions "pop" into people's minds unexpectedly (Einstein & McDaniel, 2005) People vary somewhat in their ability to successfully carry out prospective memory tasks (Searleman, 1996). Individuals who appear deficient in prospective memory are often characterized as "absent-minded."

Much remains to be learned about the factors that influence prospective memory. One key factor appears to be whether a prospective memory task is tied to some sort of cue. *Event-based tasks* involve future actions that should be triggered by a specific cue. For example, remembering to give a message to

Figure 7.26
Retrospective versus prospective memory. Most memory research has explored the dynamics of *retrospective memory,* which focuses on recollections from the past. However, *prospective memory,* which requires people to remember to perform actions in the future, also plays an important role in everyday life.

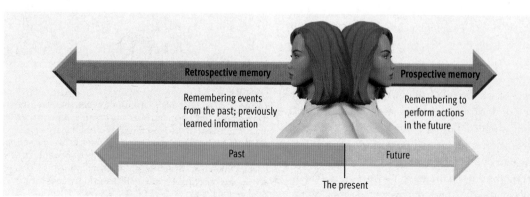

Retrospective memory — Remembering events from the past; previously learned information

Prospective memory — Remembering to perform actions in the future

Past | The present | Future

a friend is cued by seeing the friend, or remembering to take medication with one's meal is cued by the meal. *Time-based tasks* require that an action be performed at a certain time or after a certain length of time has elapsed. For example, you might want to record a TV show at a specific time, or you might need to remember to turn off the oven after an hour of baking. Evidence suggests that the cues available in event-based prospective memory tasks make these tasks easier to remember than time-based tasks (Einstein & McDaniel, 1996). Age appears to be another factor that influences the functioning of prospective memory. Older adults seem to be somewhat more vulnerable to problems with prospective memory than younger people are (McDaniel et al., 2003). However, age trends are not entirely consistent. It appears that older adults handle event-based prospective memory tasks pretty well, with age-related declines seen mostly on the more difficult time-based tasks (Hicks, Marsh, & Cook, 2005). As you might guess, researchers have sought to identify the neural bases of prospective memory. Two areas in the frontal lobes appear to be particularly important for hatching plans to remember intentions, but prospective memory also draws on the medial temporal lobe memory system (McDaniel & Einstein, 2007).

concept check 7.3

Recognizing Various Types of Memory

Check your understanding of the various types of memory discussed in this chapter by matching the definitions below with the following: (a) sensory memory, (b) short-term memory, (c) long-term memory, (d) declarative memory, (e) nondeclarative memory, (f) episodic memory, (g) semantic memory, (h) retrospective memory, and (i) prospective memory. The answers can be found in Appendix A.

_____ 1. Memory for factual information.

_____ 2. An unlimited capacity store that can hold information over lengthy periods of time.

_____ 3. The preservation of information in its original sensory form for a brief time, usually only a fraction of a second.

_____ 4. Chronological, or temporally dated, recollections of personal experiences.

_____ 5. The repository of memories for actions, skills, operations, and conditioned responses.

_____ 6. General knowledge that is not tied to the time when the information was learned.

_____ 7. Remembering to perform future actions.

_____ 8. A limited-capacity store that can maintain unrehearsed information for about 10-20 seconds.

REVIEW of Key Learning Goals

7.21 Declarative memory is memory for facts, whereas nondeclarative memory is memory for actions, skills, and conditioned responses. Declarative memory depends more on conscious attention and is more vulnerable to forgetting.

7.22 Tulving subdivided declarative memory into episodic and semantic memory. Episodic memory is made up of temporally dated recollections of personal experiences, much like an autobiography. Semantic memory contains general facts, much like an encyclopedia.

7.23 Theorists have also distinguished between retrospective memory (remembering past events) and prospective memory (remembering to do things in the future). In regard to prospective memory, event-based tasks are easier to remember than time-based tasks. Aging affects prospective memory, especially on time-based tasks.

Reflecting on the Chapter's Themes

One of our integrative themes—the idea that people's experience of the world is subjective—stood head and shoulders above the rest in this chapter. Let's briefly review how the study of memory has illuminated this idea and then examine two other themes that are relevant.

First, our discussion of attention as inherently selective should have shed light on why people's experience of the world is subjective. To a great degree, what you see in the world around you depends on where you focus your attention. This is one of the main reasons that two people can be exposed to the "same" events and walk away with entirely different perceptions. Second, the reconstructive nature of memory should further explain people's tendency to view the world with a subjective slant. When you observe an event, you don't store an exact copy of the event in your memory. Instead, you store a rough, "bare bones" approximation of the event that may be reshaped as time goes by.

A second theme that was apparent in our discussion of memory is psychology's theoretical diversity. We saw illuminating theoretical debates about the nature of memory storage, the causes of forgetting,

Key Learning Goals

7.24 Identify the three unifying themes highlighted in this chapter.

 Subjectivity of Experience

 Theoretical Diversity

 Multifactorial Causation

and the existence of multiple memory systems. Finally, the multifaceted nature of memory demonstrated once again that behavior is governed by multiple causes. For instance, your memory of a specific event may be influenced by your attention to it, your level of processing, your elaboration, your exposure to interference, how you search your memory store, how you reconstruct the event, and so forth. Given the multifaceted nature of memory, it should come as no surprise that there are many ways to improve memory. We discuss a variety of strategies in the Personal Application section.

REVIEW of Key Learning Goals

7.24 Our discussion of attention and memory enhances understanding of why people's experience of the world is highly subjective. Work on memory also highlights the field's theoretical diversity and shows that behavior is governed by multiple causes.

Improving Everyday Memory

Key Learning Goals

7.25 Discuss the importance of rehearsal, distributed practice, and interference in efforts to improve everyday memory.

7.26 Discuss the value of deep processing, good organization, and mnemonic devices in efforts to improve everyday memory.

Answer the following "true" or "false."

_____ **1** Memory strategies were recently invented by psychologists.

_____ **2** Overlearning of information leads to poor retention.

_____ **3** Outlining what you read is not likely to affect retention.

_____ **4** Massing practice in one long study session is better than distributing practice across several shorter sessions.

Mnemonic devices are strategies for enhancing memory. They have a long and honorable history. In fact, one of the mnemonic devices covered in this Application—the method of loci—was described in Greece as early as 86–82 B.C. (Yates, 1966). Actually, mnemonic devices were even more crucial in ancient times than they are today. In ancient Greece and Rome, for instance, writing instruments were not readily available for people to jot down things they needed to remember, so they had to depend heavily on mnemonic devices.

Are mnemonic devices the key to improving one's everyday memory? No. Mnemonic devices can clearly be helpful in some situations (Wilding & Valentine, 1996), but they are not a cure-all. They can be hard to use and hard to apply to many everyday situations. Most books and training programs designed to improve memory probably overemphasize mnemonic techniques (Searleman & Herrmann, 1994). Although less exotic strategies such as increasing rehearsal, engaging in deeper processing, and organizing material are more crucial to everyday memory, we will discuss some popular mnemonics as we proceed through this Application. Along the way, you'll learn that all of our opening true-false statements are false.

In this Application, we will focus primarily (although not exclusively) on how to use memory principles to *enhance performance in academic pursuits*. Obviously, this is only one aspect of everyday memory. You may also want to improve your memory of phone numbers, passwords, addresses, others' names and faces, errands that you need to run, where you filed things, what you said to certain people, and so forth. For more advice on these diverse everyday memory tasks you may want to consult a couple of very practical books: *Memory Fitness* by Einstein and McDaniel (2004) and *Improving Memory and Study Skills* by Hermann, Raybeck, and Gruneberg (2002) (which has *much* broader coverage than its title suggests).

Engage in Adequate Rehearsal

SIM5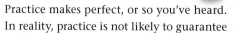

Practice makes perfect, or so you've heard. In reality, practice is not likely to guarantee perfection, but it usually leads to improved retention. Studies show that retention improves with increased rehearsal (Greene, 1992). This improvement presumably occurs because rehearsal helps to transfer information into long-term memory.

Although the benefits of practice are well known, people have a curious tendency to overestimate their knowledge of a topic and how well they will perform on a subsequent memory test of this knowledge (Koriat & Bjork, 2005). That's why it is a good idea to informally test yourself on information that you think you have mastered before confronting a real test. In addition to checking your mastery, recent research suggests that testing actually enhances retention, a phenomenon dubbed the *testing effect* (Roediger & Karpicke, 2006a). Studies have shown that taking a test on material increases performance on a subsequent test even more than studying for an equal amount of time (see Figure 7.27). Why is testing so beneficial? Theorists are not sure yet, but the key may be that testing forces students to engage in deep processing of the material, as well as transfer-appropriate processing (Roediger & Karpicke, 2006b). In any event, self-testing appears to be an excellent memory tool, which suggests that it would be prudent to take the Practice Tests in this text or additional tests available on the website for the book.

Another possible remedy for overconfidence is trying to overlearn material (Driskell, Willis, & Copper, 1992). **Overlearning refers to continued rehearsal of material after you first appear to have mastered it.**

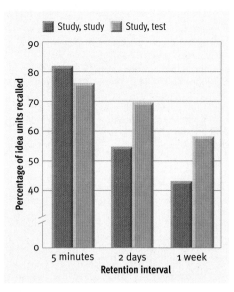

Figure 7.27

The testing effect. In one study by Roediger and Karpicke (2006b), participants studied a brief prose passage for 7 minutes. Then some of them studied it again for 7 minutes while others took a 7-minute test on the material. In the second phase of the study, subjects took another test on the material after either 5 minutes, 2 days, or 1 week. There wasn't much of a performance gap when subjects were tested over a 5-minute retention interval, but the testing group showed a significant advantage in recall when the retention interval was extended to 2 days or 1 week.

SOURCE: Roediger, III H. L., & Karpicke, J. D. (2006). Test-enhanced learning: Taking memory tests improves long-term retention. *Psychological Science, 17,* 3, 249–255. Copyright 2006 Blackwell Publishing. Reprinted by permission.

In one study, after subjects had mastered a list of nouns (they recited the list without error), Krueger (1929) required them to continue rehearsing for 50% or 100% more trials. Measuring retention at intervals up to 28 days, Krueger found that greater overlearning was related to better recall of the list. Modern studies have also shown that overlearning can enhance performance on an exam that occurs within a week, although the evidence on its long-term benefits (months later) is inconsistent (Peladeau, Forget, & Gagne, 2003; Rohrer et al., 2005).

One other point related to rehearsal is also worth mentioning. If you are memorizing some type of list, be aware of the serial-position effect, which is often observed when subjects are tested on their memory of lists (Murdock, 2001). The **serial-position effect** occurs when subjects show better recall for items at the beginning and end of a list than for items in the middle (see **Figure 7.28**). The reasons

for the serial-position effect are complex and need not concern us, but its pragmatic implications are clear: If you need to memorize a list of say, cranial nerves or past presidents, devote extra practice trials to items in the middle of the list and check your memorization of those items very carefully.

Schedule Distributed Practice and Minimize Interference

Let's assume that you need to study 9 hours for an exam. Should you "cram" all your studying into one 9-hour period (massed practice)? Or would it be better to distribute your study among, say, three 3-hour periods on successive days (distributed practice)? The evidence indicates that retention tends to be greater after distributed practice than after massed practice (Rohrer & Taylor, 2006; Seabrook, Brown, & Solity, 2005). Moreover, a recent review of over 300 experiments (Cepeda et al., 2006) showed that the longer the retention interval between studying and testing, the bigger the advantage for massed practice, as shown in **Figure 7.29** (on the next page). The same review concluded that the longer the retention interval, the longer the

optimal "break" between practice trials. When an upcoming test is more than two days away, the optimal interval between practice periods appears to be around 24 hours. The superiority of distributed practice over massed practice suggests that cramming is an ill-advised approach to studying for exams (Dempster, 1996).

Because interference is a major cause of forgetting, you'll probably want to think about how you can minimize it. This issue is especially important for students, because memorizing information for one course can interfere with the retention of information for another course. Thus, the day before an exam in a course, you should study for that course only—if possible. If demands in other courses make that plan impossible, you should study the test material last.

Engage in Deep Processing and Organize Information

Research on levels of processing suggests that how *often* you go over material is less critical than the *depth* of processing that you engage in (Craik & Tulving, 1975). If you expect to remember what you read, you

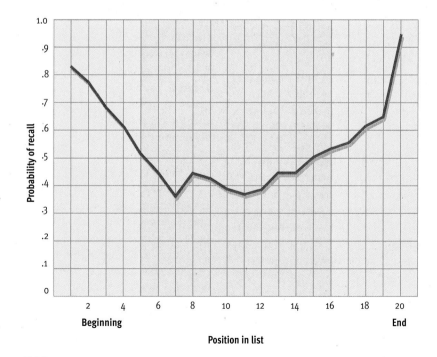

Figure 7.28

The serial-position effect. After learning a list of items to remember, people tend to recall more of the items from the beginning and the end of the list than from the middle, producing the characteristic U-shaped curve shown here. This phenomenon is called the serial-position effect.

SOURCE: Adapted from Rundus, D. (1971). Analysis of rehearsal processes in free recall. *Journal of Experimental Psychology, 89,* 63–77. Copyright © 1971 by the American Psychological Association. Adapted by permission of the author.

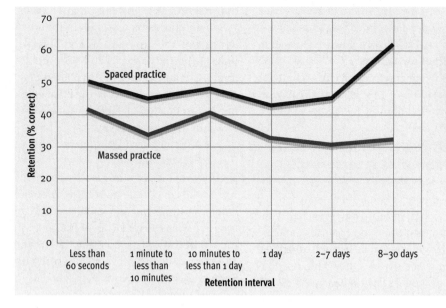

Figure 7.29

Effects of massed versus distributed practice on retention. In a review of over 300 experiments on massed versus distributed or spaced practice, Cepeda et al. (2006) examined the importance of the retention interval. As you can see, spaced practice was superior to massed practice at all retention intervals, but the gap widened at longer intervals. These findings suggest that distributed practice is especially advantageous when you need or want to remember material over the long haul.

have to fully comprehend its meaning (Einstein & McDaniel, 2004). Many students could probably benefit if they spent less time on rote repetition and devoted more effort to actually paying attention to and analyzing the meaning of their reading assignments. In particular, it is useful to make material *personally* meaningful. When you read your textbooks, try to relate information to your own life and experience. For example, when you read about classical conditioning, try to think of your own responses that are attributable to classical conditioning.

It is also important to understand that retention tends to be greater when information is well organized (Einstein & McDaniel, 2004). Gordon Bower (1970) has shown that hierarchical organization is particularly helpful when it is applicable. Thus, it may be a good idea to *outline* reading assignments for school, since outlining forces you to organize material hierarchically. Consistent with this reasoning, there is some empirical evidence that outlining material from textbooks can enhance retention of the material (McDaniel, Waddill, & Shakesby, 1996).

Enrich Encoding with Mnemonic Devices 6a

Although it's often helpful to make information personally meaningful, it's not always easy to do so. For instance, when you study chemistry you may have a hard time relating to polymers at a personal level. Thus, many mnemonic devices—such as acrostics, acronyms, and narrative methods—are designed to make abstract material more meaningful. Other mnemonic devices depend on visual imagery. As you may recall, Allan Paivio (1986, 2007) believes that visual images create a second memory code and that two codes are better than one.

Acrostics and Acronyms

Acrostics are phrases (or poems) in which the first letter of each word (or line) functions as a cue to help you recall information to be remembered. For instance, you may remember the order of musical notes with the saying "Every good boy does fine." A slight variation on acrostics is the *acronym*—a word formed out of the first letters of a series of words. Students memorizing the order of colors in the light spectrum often store the name "Roy G. Biv" to remember red, orange, yellow, green, blue, indigo, and violet. Notice that this acronym also takes advantage of the principle of chunking. Acrostics and acronyms that individuals create for themselves can be effective memory tools (Hermann et al., 2002).

Narrative Methods

Another useful way to remember a list of words is to create a story that includes the words in the appropriate order. The narrative both increases the meaningfulness of the words and links them in a specific order. Examples of this technique can be seen in **Figure 7.30**. Bower and Clark (1969) found that this procedure greatly enhanced subjects' recall of lists of unrelated words.

Rhymes

Another verbal mnemonic that people often rely on is rhyming. You've probably repeated, "I before E except after C . . ." thousands of times. Perhaps you also remember the number of days in each month with the old standby, "Thirty days hath September . . ." Rhyming something to remember it is an old and useful trick.

Link Method 6a

The link method is a mnemonic that relies on the power of imagery. The *link method* involves forming a mental image of items to be remembered in a way that links them together. For instance, suppose that you need to remember some items to pick up at the drugstore: a news magazine, shaving cream, film, and pens. To remember these items, you might visualize a public figure on the magazine cover shaving with a pen while being photographed. The more bizarre you make your image, the more helpful it is likely to be (McDaniel & Einstein, 1986).

Word lists	Stories
Bird Costume Mailbox Head River Nurse Theater Wax Eyelid Furnace	A man dressed in a *Bird Costume* and wearing a *Mailbox* on his *Head* was seen leaping into the *River*. A *Nurse* ran out of a nearby *Theater* and applied *Wax* to his *Eyelids*, but her efforts were in vain. He died and was tossed into the *Furnace*.
Rustler Penthouse Mountain Sloth Tavern Fuzz Gland Antler Pencil Vitamin	A *Rustler* lived in a *Penthouse* on top of a *Mountain*. His specialty was the three-toed *Sloth*. He would take his captive animals to a *Tavern* where he would remove *Fuzz* from their *Glands*. Unfortunately, all this exposure to sloth fuzz caused him to grow *Antlers*. So he gave up his profession and went to work in a *Pencil* factory. As a precaution he also took a lot of *Vitamin* E.

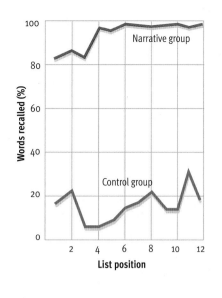

Method of Loci

Another visual mnemonic is the ***method of loci,*** which involves taking an imaginary walk along a familiar path where images of items to be remembered are associated with certain locations. The first step is to commit to memory a series of loci, or places along a path. Usually these loci are specific locations in your home or neighborhood. Then envision each thing you want to re- member in one of these locations. Try to form distinctive, vivid images. When you need to remember the items, imagine your- self walking along the path. The various loci on your path should serve as cues for the retrieval of the images that you formed (see **Figure 7.31**). Evidence suggests that the method of loci can be effective in increas- ing retention (Moe & De Beni, 2004; Mas- sen & Vterrodt-Plunnecke, 2006). Moreover, this method ensures that items are remem- bered in their *correct order* because the order is determined by the sequence of locations along the pathway.

Understanding the Fallibility of Eyewitness Accounts

Key Learning Goals

7.27 Understand how hindsight bias and over-confidence contribute to the frequent inaccuracy of eyewitness memory.

A number of years ago, the Wilmington, Delaware, area was plagued by a series of armed robberies committed by a perpetrator who was dubbed the "gentleman bandit" by the press because he was an unusually polite and well-groomed thief. The local media published a sketch of the gentleman bandit, and eventually an alert resident turned in a suspect who resembled the sketch. Much to everyone's surprise, the accused thief was a Catholic priest named Father Bernard Pagano—who vigorously denied the charges. Unfortunately for Father Pagano, his denials and alibis were unconvincing and he was charged with the crimes. At the trial, *seven* eyewitnesses confidently identified Father Pagano as the gentleman bandit. The prosecution was well on its way to a conviction when there was a stunning turn of events—another man, Ronald Clouser, confessed to the police that he was the culprit. The authorities dropped the charges against Father Pagano, and the relieved priest was able to return to his normal existence (Rodgers, 1982).

This bizarre tale of mistaken identity—which sounds like it was lifted from a movie script—raises some interesting questions about memory. How could seven people "remember" seeing Father Pagnano commit armed robberies that he had nothing to do with? How could they mistake him for Ronald Clouser, when the two really didn't look very similar (see the adjacent photos)? How could they be so confident when they were so wrong? Perhaps you're thinking that this is just one case and it must be unrepresentative (which would be sound critical thinking). Well, yes, it *is* a rather extreme example of eyewitness fallibility, but researchers have compiled mountains of evidence that eyewitness testimony is not nearly as reliable or as accurate as widely assumed (Kassin et al., 2001; Wells, Memon, & Penrod, 2006). This finding is ironic in that people are most confident about their assertions when they can say, "I saw it with my own eyes." Television news shows like to use the title "Eyewitness News" to create the impression that they chronicle events with great clarity and accuracy. And our legal system accords special status to eyewitness testimony because it is considered much more dependable than hearsay or circumstantial evidence.

So, why are eyewitness accounts surprisingly inaccurate? Well, many factors and processes contribute to this inaccuracy. We'll briefly review some of the relevant processes that were introduced in the main body of the chapter; then we'll focus on two common errors in thinking that also contribute.

Can you think of any memory phenomena described in the chapter that seem likely to undermine eyewitness accuracy? You could point to the fact that *memory is a reconstructive process,* and eyewitness recall is likely to be distorted by the schemas that people have for various events. A second consideration is that *witnesses sometimes make source-monitoring errors* and get confused about where they saw a face. For example, one rape victim mixed up her assailant with a guest on a TV show that she was watching when she was attacked. Fortunately, the falsely accused suspect had an airtight alibi, as he could demonstrate that he was on live television when the rape occurred (Schacter, 1996). Perhaps the most pervasive factor is the misinformation effect (Davis & Loftus, 2007). *Witnesses' recall of events is routinely distorted by information introduced after the event* by police officers, attorneys, news reports, and so forth. In addition to these factors, eyewitness inaccuracy is fueled by the *hindsight bias* and *overconfidence effects.*

The Contribution of Hindsight Bias

The *hindsight bias* is the tendency to mold one's interpretation of the past to fit how events actually turned out. When you know the outcome of an event, this knowledge slants your recall of how the event unfolded and what your thinking was at the time. With the luxury of hindsight, people have a curious tendency to say, "I knew it all along" when explaining events that objectively would have been difficult to foresee. The tendency to exhibit the hindsight bias is normal, pervasive, and surprisingly strong (Guilbault et al., 2004). With regard to eyewitnesses, their recollections may often be distorted by knowing that a particular person has been arrested and accused of the crime in question. For

Although he doesn't look that much like the real "gentleman bandit," who is shown on the left, seven eyewitnesses identified Father Pagano (right) as the gentleman bandit, showing just how unreliable eyewitness accounts can be.

example, Wells and Bradfield (1998) had simulated eyewitnesses select a perpetrator from a photo lineup. The eyewitnesses' confidence in their identifications tended to be quite modest, which made sense given that the actual perpetrator was not even in the lineup. But when some subjects were told, "Good, you identified the actual suspect," they became highly confident about their identifications, which obviously were incorrect. In another study, participants read identical scenarios about a couple's first date that either had no ending or ended in a rape (described in one additional sentence). The subjects who received the rape ending reconstructed the story to be more consistent with their stereotypes of how rapes occur (Carli, 1999).

The Contribution of Overconfidence

Another flaw in thinking that contributes to inaccuracy in eyewitness accounts is people's tendency to be overconfident about the reliability of their memory. When tested for their memory of information, people tend to overestimate their accuracy (Koriat & Bjork, 2005; Lichtenstein, Fischhoff, & Phillips, 1982). In studies of eyewitness recall, participants also tend to be overconfident about their recollections. Although jurors are likely to be more convinced by eyewitnesses who appear confident, the evidence indicates that only a modest correlation is found between eyewitness confidence and eyewitness accuracy (Shaw, McClure, & Dykstra, 2007). Thus, many convictions of innocent people have been attributed to the impact of testimony from highly confident

but mistaken eyewitnesses (Wells, Olson, & Charman, 2002).

Can you learn to make better judgments of the accuracy of your recall of everyday events? Yes, with effort you can get better at making accurate estimates of how likely you are to be correct in the recall of some fact or event. One reason that people tend to be overconfident is that if they can't think of any reasons that they might be wrong, they assume they must be right. Thus, overconfidence is fueled by yet another common error in thinking—*the failure to seek disconfirming evidence.* Even veteran scientists fall prey to this weakness, as most people don't seriously consider reasons that they might be wrong about something (Mynatt, Doherty, & Tweney, 1978).

Thus, to make more accurate assessments of what you know and don't know, it helps to engage in a deliberate process of considering why you might be wrong. Here is an example. Based on your reading of Chapter 1, write down the schools of thought associated with the following major theorists: William James, John B. Watson, and Carl Rogers. After you provide your answers, rate your confidence that the information you just provided is correct. Now, write three reasons that your answers might be wrong and three reasons they might be right. Most people will balk at this exercise, arguing that they cannot think of any reasons why they might be wrong, but after some resistance, they can come up with several. Such reasons might include "I was half asleep when I read that part of the chapter" or "I might be confusing Watson and James." Reasons that you think you're right could include "I distinctly recall discussing this with my friend" or "I really worked on

Although courts give special credence to eyewitness testimony, scientific evidence indicates that eyewitness accounts are less reliable than widely assumed.

those names in Chapter 1." After listing reasons that you might be right and reasons that you might be wrong, rate your confidence in your accuracy once again. Guess what? Most people are less confident after going through such an exercise than they were before (depending, of course, on the nature of the topic).

The new confidence ratings tend to be more realistic than the original ratings (Koriat, Lichtenstein, & Fischhoff, 1980). Why? Because this exercise forces you to think more deeply about your answers and to search your memory for related information. Most people stop searching their memory as soon as they generate an answer they believe to be correct. Thus, the process of considering reasons that you might be wrong about something—a process that people rarely engage in—is a useful critical thinking skill that can reduce overconfidence effects. Better assessment of what you know and don't know can be an important determinant of the quality of the decisions you make and the way you solve problems and reason from evidence.

Table 7.1 Critical Thinking Skills Discussed in This Application

Skill	Description
Understanding the limitations and fallibility of human memory	The critical thinker appreciates that memory is reconstructive and that even eyewitness accounts may be distorted or inaccurate.
Recognizing the bias in hindsight analysis	The critical thinker understands that knowing the outcome of events biases our recall and interpretation of the events.
Recognizing overconfidence in human cognition	The critical thinker understands that people are frequently overconfident about the accuracy of their projections for the future and their recollections of the past.
Understanding the need to seek disconfirming evidence	The critical thinker understands the value of thinking about how or why one might be wrong about something.

REVIEW of Key Learning Goals

7.27 Research indicates that eyewitness memory is not nearly as reliable or as accurate as widely believed. The hindsight bias, which is the tendency to reshape one's interpretation of the past to fit with known outcomes, often distorts eyewitness memory. People tend to be overconfident about their eyewitness recollections.

Key Ideas

Encoding: Getting Information into Memory

▌ The multifaceted process of memory begins with encoding. Attention, which facilitates encoding, is inherently selective and has been compared to a filter. Divided attention undermines memory and performance on many tasks.

▌ According to levels-of-processing theory, the kinds of memory codes people create depend on which aspects of a stimulus are emphasized; deeper processing results in better recall of information. Structural, phonemic, and semantic encoding represent progressively deeper and more effective levels of processing.

▌ Elaboration enriches encoding by linking a stimulus to other information. Visual imagery may work in much the same way, creating two memory codes rather than just one. Encoding that emphasizes personal self-reference may be especially useful in facilitating retention.

Storage: Maintaining Information in Memory

▌ Sensory memory preserves information in its original form, for only a fraction of a second. Short-term memory has a limited capacity and can maintain unrehearsed information for about 10–20 seconds. Baddeley has reconceptualized short-term memory as working memory, which consists of four modules: the phonological loop, visuospatial sketchpad, central executive, and episodic buffer.

▌ Long-term memory is an unlimited capacity store that may hold information indefinitely. Certain lines of evidence, such as the existence of flashbulb memories, suggest that LTM storage may be permanent, but the evidence is not convincing. Some theorists have raised doubts about whether short-term and long-term memory are really separate.

▌ Information in LTM can be organized in simple categories, conceptual hierarchies, or semantic networks. A schema is an organized cluster of knowledge about a particular object or event. Parallel distributed processing (PDP) models of memory assert that specific memories correspond to particular patterns of activation in connectionist networks.

Retrieval: Getting Information out of Memory

▌ The tip-of-the-tongue phenomenon demonstrates retrieval failure. Reinstating the context of an event can facilitate recall. This factor may account for cases in which hypnosis appears to aid recall, although hypnosis can distort memory. Memories are not exact replicas of past experiences. Bartlett showed long ago that memory is partially reconstructive.

▌ Research by Loftus on the misinformation effect shows that information learned after an event can alter one's memory of it. In fact, simply retelling a story can alter one's memory of it. Source-monitoring and reality-monitoring errors may explain why people sometimes "recall" something that was only suggested to them or something they only imagined.

Forgetting: When Memory Lapses

▌ Ebbinghaus's early studies of nonsense syllables suggested that people forget very rapidly. Subsequent research showed that Ebbinghaus's forgetting curve was exceptionally steep. Forgetting can be measured by asking people to recall, recognize, or relearn information.

▌ Some forgetting is due to ineffective encoding. Decay theory proposes that forgetting occurs spontaneously with the passage of time. It has proven difficult to show that decay occurs in long-term memory. Interference theory proposes that people forget information because of competition from other material.

▌ Repression involves the motivated forgetting of painful or unpleasant memories. Recent years have seen a surge of reports of repressed memories of sexual abuse in childhood. The authenticity of these recovered memories is the subject of enormous controversy. Skeptics argue that in many cases therapists have inadvertently created false memories of abuse in their patients. The recovered memories debate has demonstrated that memory is more fallible and malleable than widely realized.

In Search of the Memory Trace: The Physiology of Memory

▌ Kandel's research suggests that memory traces may reflect alterations in the strength of synaptic connections at specific locations. Memory traces may also consist of localized neural circuits that undergo long-term potentiation.

▌ The study of amnesia and other research has implicated the hippocampal region as a key player in memory processes. The medial temporal lobe memory system may be responsible for the consolidation of memories.

Systems and Types of Memory

▌ Declarative memory is memory for facts and information, whereas nondeclarative memory is memory for actions, skills, and conditioned responses. Declarative memory can be subdivided into episodic memory, for temporally dated personal facts, and semantic memory, for general facts. Theorists have also distinguished between retrospective and prospective memory.

Reflecting on the Chapter's Themes

▌ Our discussion of attention and memory enhances understanding of why people's experience of the world is highly subjective. Work in this area also highlights the field's theoretical diversity and shows that behavior is governed by multiple causes.

PERSONAL APPLICATION Improving Everyday Memory

▌ Rehearsal, even when it involves overlearning, facilitates retention, although one should be wary of the serial-position effect. Testing can enhance retention. Distributed practice tends to be more efficient than massed practice. It is wise to plan study sessions so as to minimize interference. Processing during rehearsal should be deep.

▌ Meaningfulness can be enhanced with mnemonic devices such as acrostics, acronyms, and narrative methods. The link method and the method of loci are mnemonic devices that depend on visual imagery.

CRITICAL THINKING APPLICATION Understanding the Fallibility of Eyewitness Accounts

▌ Research indicates that eyewitness memory is not nearly as reliable or as accurate as widely believed. Two common errors in thinking that contribute to this situation are the hindsight bias and overconfidence effects. The hindsight bias is the tendency to reshape one's interpretation of the past to fit with known outcomes.

Key Terms

Anterograde amnesia (p. 304)
Attention (p. 277)
Chunk (p. 283)
Conceptual hierarchy (p. 288)
Connectionist models (p. 289)
Consolidation (p. 304)
Decay theory (p. 296)
Declarative memory system (p. 305)
Dual-coding theory (p. 279)
Elaboration (p. 279)
Encoding (p. 276)
Encoding specificity principle
    (p. 297)
Episodic memory system (p. 305)
Flashbulb memories (p. 285)
Forgetting curve (p. 294)
Hindsight bias (p. 312)
Interference theory (p. 296)
Levels-of-processing theory (p. 278)
Link method (p. 310)
Long-term memory (LTM) (p. 284)
Long-term potentiation (LTP)
    (p. 303)
Method of loci (p. 311)
Misinformation effect (p. 292)
Mnemonic devices (p. 308)
Nondeclarative memory system
    (p. 305)
Nonsense syllables (p. 294)
Overlearning (p. 308)
Parallel distributed processing (PDP)
    models (p. 289)
Proactive interference (p. 296)
Prospective memory (p. 306)
Reality monitoring (p. 293)
Recall (p. 294)
Recognition (p. 295)

Rehearsal (p. 281)
Relearning (p. 295)
Repression (pp. 297–298)
Retention (p. 294)
Retrieval (p. 276)
Retroactive interference (p. 296)
Retrograde amnesia (pp. 303–304)
Retrospective memory (p. 306)
Schema (p. 288)
Self-referent encoding (p. 280)
Semantic memory system (p. 306)
Semantic network (p. 289)
Sensory memory (p. 280)
Serial-position effect (p. 309)
Short-term memory (STM) (p. 281)
Source monitoring (p. 292)
Source-monitoring error (p. 293)
Storage (p. 276)
Tip-of-the-tongue phenomenon
    (p. 290)
Transfer-appropriate processing
    (p. 297)

Key People

Alan Baddeley (pp. 283–284)
Frederic Bartlett (p. 291)
Fergus Craik and Robert Lockhart
    (pp. 278–279)
Hermann Ebbinghaus (pp. 294–295)
Marcia Johnson (pp. 292–293)
Eric Kandel (p. 302)
Elizabeth Loftus (pp. 291–292)
George Miller (p. 283)
Brenda Milner (p. 304)
Richard Thompson (p. 303)
Endel Tulving (pp. 305–306)

1. Getting information into memory is called _____; getting information out of memory is called _____.
   A. storage; retrieval
   B. encoding; storage
   C. encoding; retrieval
   D. storage; encoding

2. The word *big* is flashed on a screen. A mental picture of the word *big* represents a _____ code; the definition "large in size" represents a _____ code; "sounds like pig" represents a _____ code.
   A. structural; phonemic; semantic
   B. phonemic; semantic; structural
   C. structural; semantic; phonemic
   D. phonemic; structural; semantic

3. Miles is listening as his mother rattles through a list of 15 or so things that he needs to remember to pack for an upcoming trip. According to George Miller, if Miles doesn't write the items down as he hears them, he will probably remember:
   A. fewer than 5 items from the list.
   B. about 10 to 12 items from the list.
   C. all the items from the list.
   D. 5 to 9 items from the list.

4. Which statement best represents current evidence on the durability of long-term storage?
   A. All forgetting involves breakdowns in retrieval.
   B. LTM is like a barrel of marbles in which none of the marbles ever leak out.
   C. There is no convincing evidence that all one's memories are stored away permanently.
   D. All long-term memories gradually decay at a constant rate.

5. An organized cluster of knowledge about a particular object or event is called a:
   A. semantic network.
   B. conceptual hierarchy.
   C. schema.
   D. retrieval cue.

6. The tip-of-the-tongue phenomenon:
   A. is a temporary inability to remember something you know, accompanied by a feeling that it's just out of reach.
   B. is clearly due to a failure in retrieval.
   C. reflects a permanent loss of information from LTM.
   D. is both a and b.

7. Roberto is telling Rachel about some juicy gossip when she stops him and informs him that she is the one who passed this gossip on to him about a week ago. In this example, Roberto has:
   A. been fooled by the misinformation effect.
   B. made a reality-monitoring error.
   C. made a source-monitoring error.
   D. made a prospective memory error.

8. If decay theory is correct:
   A. information can never be permanently lost from long-term memory.
   B. forgetting is simply a case of retrieval failure.
   C. the principal cause of forgetting should be the passage of time.
   D. all of the above.

9. Bulldog McRae was recently traded to a new football team. He is struggling to remember the plays for his new team because he keeps mixing them up with the plays from his previous team. Bulldog's problem illustrates the operation of:
   A. retroactive interference.
   B. proactive interference.
   C. transfer-inappropriate processing.
   D. parallel distributed processing.

10. Research suggests that the *consolidation* of memories depends on activity in the:
    A. cerebellum.
    B. prefrontal cortex.
    C. medial temporal lobe.
    D. corpus callosum.

11. Your memory of how to ride a bicycle is contained in your _____ memory.
    A. declarative
    B. nondeclarative (procedural)
    C. structural
    D. episodic

12. Your knowledge that birds fly, that the sun rises in the east, and that 2 + 2 = 4 is contained in your _____ memory.
    A. structural
    B. procedural
    C. implicit
    D. semantic

13. Dorothy memorized her shopping list. When she got to the store, however, she found she had forgotten many of the items from the middle of the list. This is an example of:
    A. inappropriate encoding.
    B. retrograde amnesia.
    C. proactive interference.
    D. the serial-position effect.

14. Overlearning:
    A. refers to continued rehearsal of material after the point of apparent mastery.
    B. promotes improved recall.
    C. should not be done, since it leads to increased interference.
    D. does both a and b.

15. The tendency to mold one's interpretation of the past to fit how events actually turned out is called:
    A. the overconfidence effect.
    B. selective amnesia.
    C. retroactive interference.
    D. the hindsight bias.

Answers
1 C p. 276
2 C pp. 278–279
3 D p. 283
4 C pp. 284–286
5 C p. 288
6 D p. 290
7 C pp. 292–293
8 C p. 296
9 B p. 296
10 C p. 304
11 B p. 305
12 D pp. 305–306
13 D p. 309
14 D pp. 308–309
15 D p. 312

PsykTrek

To view a demo: www.cengage.com/psychology/psyktrek
To order: www.cengage.com/psychology/weiten
Go to the PsykTrek website or CD-ROM for further study of the concepts in this chapter. Both online and on the CD-ROM, PsykTrek includes dozens of learning modules with videos, animations, and quizzes, as well as simulations of psychological phenomena and a multimedia glossary that includes word pronunciations.

CengageNow

www.cengage.com/tlc

Go to this site for the link to CengageNOW, your one-stop study shop. Take a Pretest for this chapter, and CengageNOW will generate a personalized Study Plan based on your test results. The Study Plan will identify the topics you need to review and direct you to online resources to help you master those topics. You can then take a Posttest to help you determine the concepts you have mastered and what you still need to work on.

Companion Website

www.cengage.com/psychology/weiten

Go to this site to find online resources directly linked to your book, including a glossary, flash cards, drag-and-drop exercises, quizzes, and more!

LANGUAGE AND THOUGHT

© Joe Viesti/Viesti Associates

Language: Turning Thoughts into Words

What Is Language?
The Structure of Language
Milestones in Language Development
Learning More Than One Language: Bilingualism
Can Animals Develop Language?
Language in Evolutionary Context
Theories of Language Acquisition
Culture, Language, and Thought

Problem Solving: In Search of Solutions

Types of Problems
Barriers to Effective Problem Solving
Approaches to Problem Solving
Culture, Cognitive Style, and Problem Solving

Decision Making: Choices and Chances

Making Choices About Preferences: Basic Strategies
Making Choices About Preferences: Quirks and Complexities

FEATURED STUDY ▮ Intuitive Decisions Versus Careful Deliberation: Which Leads to Better Decisions?

Taking Chances: Factors Weighed in Risky Decisions
Heuristics in Judging Probabilities
The Tendency to Ignore Base Rates
The Conjunction Fallacy
Evolutionary Analyses of Flaws in Human Decision Making
Fast and Frugal Heuristics

Reflecting on the Chapter's Themes

PERSONAL APPLICATION ▮ Understanding Pitfalls in Reasoning About Decisions

The Gambler's Fallacy
Overestimating the Improbable
Confirmation Bias
The Overconfidence Effect
The Effects of Framing
The Specter of Regret and Loss Aversion

CRITICAL THINKING APPLICATION ▮ Shaping Thought with Language: "Only a Naive Moron Would Believe That"

Semantic Slanting
Name Calling

Recap

Practice Test

"Mr. Watson—Mr. Sherlock Holmes," said Stamford, introducing us.

"How are you?" he said, cordially, gripping my hand with a strength for which I should hardly have given him credit. "You have been in Afghanistan, I perceive."

"How on earth did you know that?" I asked, in astonishment.

(From A Study in Scarlet by Arthur Conan Doyle)

If you've ever read any Sherlock Holmes stories, you know that the great detective constantly astonished his stalwart companion, Dr. Watson, with his extraordinary deductions. Obviously, Holmes could not arrive at his conclusions without a chain of reasoning. Yet to him even an elaborate reasoning process was a simple, everyday act. Consider his feat of knowing at once, on first meeting Watson, that the doctor had been in Afghanistan. When asked, Holmes explained his reasoning as follows:

"I knew you came from Afghanistan. From long habit the train of thought ran so swiftly through my mind that I arrived at the conclusion without being conscious of the intermediate steps. There were such steps, however. The train of reasoning ran: 'Here is a gentleman of a medical type, but with the air of a military man. Clearly an army doctor, then. He has just come from the tropics, for his face is dark, and that is not the natural tint of his skin, for his wrists are fair. He has undergone hardship and sickness, as his haggard face says clearly. His left arm has been injured. He holds it in a stiff and unnatural manner. Where in the tropics could an English army doctor have seen much hardship and got his arm wounded? Clearly in Afghanistan.' The whole train of thought did not occupy a second."

Admittedly, Sherlock Holmes's deductive feats are fictional. But even to read about them appreciatively—let alone imagine them, as Sir Arthur Conan Doyle did—is a remarkably complex mental act. Our everyday thought processes seem ordinary to us only because we take them for granted, just as Holmes saw nothing extraordinary in what to him was a simple deduction.

In reality, everyone is a Sherlock Holmes, continually performing magical feats of thought. Even elementary perception—for instance, watching a football game or a ballet—involves elaborate cognitive processes. People must sort through distorted, constantly shifting perceptual inputs and deduce what they see out there in the real world. Imagine, then, the complexity of thought required to read a book, fix an automobile, or balance a checkbook. Of course, all this is not to say that human thought processes are flawless or unequaled. You probably own a $10 calculator that can run circles around you when it comes to computing square roots. As we'll see, some of the most interesting research in this chapter focuses on ways in which people's thinking can be limited, simplistic, or illogical.

In any event, as we have noted before, in psychology, *cognition* **refers broadly to mental processes or thinking.** When psychology first emerged as an independent science in the 19th century, it focused on the mind. Mental processes were explored through *introspection*—analysis of one's own conscious experience (see Chapter 1). Unfortunately, early psychologists' study of mental processes ran aground, as the method of introspection yielded unreliable results. Psychology's empirical approach depends on observation, and private mental events proved difficult to observe. Furthermore, during the first half of the 20th century, the study of cognition was actively discouraged by the theoretical dominance of behaviorism. Herbert Simon, a pioneer of

cognitive psychology, recalls that "you couldn't use a word like *mind* in a psychology journal—you'd get your mouth washed out with soap" (Holden, 1986).

Although it wasn't fully recognized until much later, the 1950s brought a "cognitive revolution" in psychology (Baars, 1986). Renegade theorists, such as Herbert Simon, began to argue that behaviorists' exclusive focus on overt responses was doomed to yield an incomplete understanding of human functioning. More important, creative new approaches to research on cognitive processes led to exciting progress. For example, in his book on the cognitive revolution, Howard Gardner (1985) notes that three major advances were reported at a watershed 1956 conference—in just one day! First, Herbert Simon and Allen Newell described the first computer program to successfully simulate human problem solving. Second, Noam Chomsky outlined a new model that changed the way psychologists studied language. Third, George Miller delivered the legendary paper that we discussed in Chapter 7, arguing that the capacity of short-term memory is seven (plus or minus two) items. Since then, cognitive science has grown into a robust, interdisciplinary enterprise (Simon, 1992). Besides memory (which we covered in Chapter 7), cognitive psychologists investigate the complexities of language, problem solving, decision making, and reasoning. We'll look at all these topics in this chapter, beginning with language.

Herbet Simon

"You couldn't use a word like mind in a psychology journal—you'd get your mouth washed out with soap."

© Carnegie-Mellon University

Key Learning Goals

8.1 Outline the key properties of language, and describe its structure.

8.2 Trace the development of human language during childhood.

8.3 Summarize the effects of bilingualism on language and cognitive development.

8.4 Evaluate the controversy regarding language acquisition in animals.

8.5 Discuss the possible evolutionary bases of language.

8.6 Compare the behaviorist, nativist, and interactionist perspectives on language acquisition.

8.7 Discuss culture and language and the status of the linguistic relativity hypothesis.

Language: Turning Thoughts into Words

Language obviously plays a fundamental role in human behavior. Indeed, if you were to ask people, "What characteristic most distinguishes humans from other living creatures?" a great many would reply, "Language." In this section, we'll discuss the nature, structure, and development of language and related topics, such as bilingualism and whether animals can learn language.

What Is Language?

A *language* consists of symbols that convey meaning, plus rules for combining those symbols, that can be used to generate an infinite variety of messages. Language systems include a number of critical properties.

First, language is symbolic. People use spoken sounds and written words to represent objects, actions, events, and ideas. The word *lamp,* for instance, refers to a class of objects that have certain properties. The symbolic nature of language greatly expands what people can communicate about. Symbols allow one to refer to objects that may be in another place and to events that happened at another time (for example, a lamp broken at work yesterday). The symbols used in a language are *arbitrary* in that no built-in relationship exists between the look or sound of words and the objects they stand for. *Lamps* could have been called *books,* for instance, and vice versa.

Second, language is generative. A limited number of symbols can be combined in an infinite variety of ways to *generate* an endless array of novel messages. Everyone has some "stock sayings," but every day

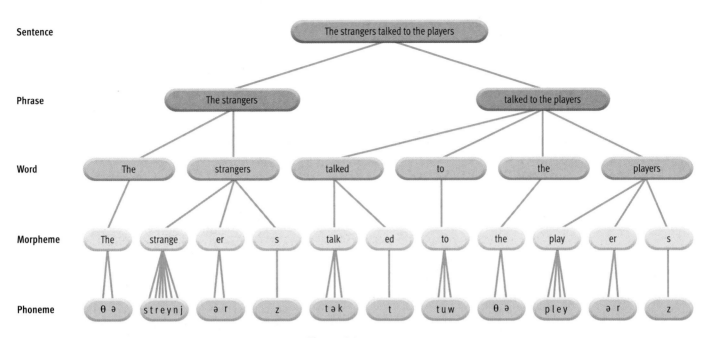

Figure 8.1

An analysis of a simple English sentence. As this example shows, verbal language has a hierarchical structure. At the base of the hierarchy are the *phonemes,* which are units of vocal sound that do not, in themselves, have meaning. The smallest units of meaning in a language are *morphemes,* which include not only root words but such meaning-carrying units as the past-tense suffix *ed* and the plural *s.* Complex rules of syntax govern how the words constructed from morphemes may be combined into phrases, and phrases into meaningful statements, or sentences.

SOURCE: Clarke-Stewart, A., Friedman, S., & Koch, J. (1985). *Child development: A topical approach* (p. 417). New York: Wiley. Reprinted by permission of John Wiley & Sons, Inc.

you create sentences that you have never spoken before. You also comprehend many sentences that you have never encountered before (like this one).

Third, language is structured. Although people can generate an infinite variety of sentences, these sentences must be structured in a limited number of ways. Rules govern the arrangement of words into phrases and sentences; some arrangements are acceptable and some are not. For example, you might say, "The swimmer jumped into the pool," but you would never recombine the same words to say, "Pool the into the jumped swimmer." The structure of language allows people to be inventive with words and still understand each other. Let's take a closer look at the structural properties of language.

The Structure of Language

Human languages have a hierarchical structure (Ratner, Gleason, & Narasimhan, 1998). As **Figure 8.1** shows, basic sounds are combined into units with meaning, which are combined into words. Words are combined into phrases, which are combined into sentences.

Phonemes

At the base of the language hierarchy are *phonemes,* **the smallest speech units in a language that can be distinguished perceptually.** Considering that an unabridged English dictionary contains more than 450,000 words, you might imagine that there must be a huge number of phonemes. In fact, linguists estimate that humans are capable of recognizing only about 100 such basic sounds. Moreover, no one language uses all of these phonemes. Different languages use different groups of about 20 to 80 phonemes.

For all its rich vocabulary, the English language is composed of about 40 phonemes, corresponding roughly to the 26 letters of the alphabet plus several variations (see **Table 8.1**). A letter in the alphabet can represent more than one phoneme if it has more than one pronunciation. For example, the letter *a* is pronounced differently in the words *father, had, call,*

Table 8.1 Phonemic Symbols for the Sounds of American English

Consonants									Vowels			
/p/	pill	/t/	toe	/g/	gill				/i/	beet	/ɪ/	bit
/b/	bill	/d/	doe	/ŋ/	ring				/e/	bait	/ɛ/	bet
/m/	mill	/n/	no	/h/	hot				/u/	boot	/ʊ/	foot
/f/	fine	/s/	sink	/ʔ/	uh-oh				/o/	boat	/ɔ/	caught
/v/	vine	/z/	zinc	/l/	low				/æ/	bat	/a/	pot
/θ/	thigh	/č/	choke	/r/	row				/ʌ/	but	/ə/	sofa
/ð/	thy	/j/	joke	/y/	you				/aɪ/	bite	/au/	out
/š/	shoe	/k/	kill	/w/	win				/ɔɪ/	boy		
/ž/	treasure											

Source: Hoff, E. (2001). *Language development.* Belmont, CA: Wadsworth. Reprinted by permission.

and *take*. Each of these pronunciations corresponds to a different phoneme. In addition, some phonemes are represented by combinations of letters, such as *ch* and *th*. Working with this handful of basic sounds, people can understand and generate all the words in the English language—and invent new ones besides.

Morphemes and Semantics

Morphemes **are the smallest units of meaning in a language.** There are approximately 50,000 English morphemes, which include root words as well as prefixes and suffixes. Many words, such as *fire, guard,* and *friend,* consist of a single morpheme. Many others represent combinations of morphemes. For example, the word *unfriendly* consists of three morphemes: the root word *friend,* the prefix *un,* and the suffix *ly.* Each of the morphemes contributes to the meaning of the entire word. *Semantics* **is the area of language concerned with understanding the meaning of words and word combinations.** Learning about semantics entails learning about the infinite variety of objects and actions that words refer to. A word's meaning may consist of both its *denotation,* which is its dictionary definition, and its *connotation,* which includes its emotional overtones and secondary implications.

Syntax

Of course, most utterances consist of more than a single word. As we've already noted, people don't combine words randomly. *Syntax* **is a system of rules that specify how words can be arranged into sentences.** A simple rule of syntax is that a sentence must have both a *noun phrase* and a *verb phrase.* Thus, "The sound of cars is annoying" is a sentence. However, "The sound of cars" is not a sentence, because it lacks a verb phrase.

Rules of syntax underlie all language use, even though you may not be aware of them. Thus, although they may not be able to verbalize the rule, virtually all English speakers know that an *article* (such as *the*) comes before the word it modifies. For example, you would never say *swimmer the* instead of *the swimmer.* How children learn the complicated rules of syntax is one of the major puzzles investigated by psychologists interested in language. Like other aspects of language development, children's acquisition of syntax seems to progress at an amazingly rapid pace. Let's look at how this remarkable development unfolds.

Milestones in Language Development

Learning to use language requires learning a number of skills that become important at various points in a child's development (Siegler & Alibali, 2005). We'll examine this developmental sequence by looking first at how children learn to pronounce words, then at their use of single words, and finally at their ability to combine words to form sentences (see Table 8.2).

Moving Toward Producing Words

Three-month-old infants display a surprising language-related talent: They can distinguish phonemes from all the world's languages, including phonemes that they do not hear in their environment. In contrast, adults cannot readily discriminate phonemes that are not used in their native language. Actually, neither can 1-year-old children, as this curious ability disappears by the time children reach 12 months of age (Bates, Devescovi, & Wulfeck, 2001; Werker & Tees, 1999). The exact mechanisms responsible for this transition are not understood, but it is clear that long before infants utter their first words, they are making remarkable progress in learning the sound structure of their native language. Progress toward understanding words also occurs during the first year. By 7.5 months, infants begin to recognize common word forms (Houston, Santelmann, & Jusczyk, 2004), and by 8 months many show the

Table 8.2 Overview of Typical Language Development

Age	General Characteristics
Months	
1–5	*Reflexive communication:* Vocalizes randomly, coos, laughs, cries, engages in vocal play, discriminates language from nonlanguage sounds
6–18	*Babbling:* Verbalizes in response to speech of others; responses increasingly approximate human speech patterns
10–13	*First words:* Uses words; typically to refer to objects
12–18	*One-word sentence stage:* Vocabulary grows slowly; uses nouns primarily; overextensions begin
18–24	*Vocabulary spurt:* Fast-mapping facilitates rapid acquisition of new words
Years	
2	*Two-word sentence stage:* Uses telegraphic speech; uses more pronouns and verbs
2.5	*Three-word sentence stage:* Modifies speech to take listener into account; over-regularizations begin
3	Uses complete simple active sentence structure; uses sentences to tell stories that are understood by others; uses plurals
3.5	*Expanded grammatical forms:* Expresses concepts with words; uses four-word sentences
4	Uses imaginary speech; uses five-word sentences
5	*Well-developed and complex syntax:* Uses more complex syntax; uses more complex forms to tell stories
6	Displays metalinguistic awareness

Note: Children often show individual differences in the exact ages at which they display the various developmental achievements outlined here.

primitive first signs of understanding the meanings of familiar words (Bates et al., 2001).

During the first six months of life, a baby's vocalizations are dominated by crying, cooing, and laughter, which have limited value as a means of communication. Soon, infants are *babbling,* producing a wide variety of sounds that correspond to phonemes and, eventually, many repetitive consonant-vowel combinations, such as "lalalalalala." Babbling gradually becomes more complex and increasingly resembles the language spoken by parents and others in the child's environment (Hoff, 2005). Babbling lasts until around 18 months, continuing even after children utter their first words.

At around 10 to 13 months of age, most children begin to utter sounds that correspond to words. Most infants' first words are similar in phonetic form and meaning—even in different languages (Waxman, 2002). The initial words resemble the syllables that infants most often babble spontaneously. For example, words such as *dada, mama,* and *papa* are names for parents in many languages because they consist of sounds that are easy to produce.

Using Words

After children utter their first words, their vocabulary grows slowly for the next few months (Dapretto & Bjork, 2000). Toddlers typically can say between 3 and 50 words by 18 months. However, their *receptive vocabulary* is larger than their *productive vocabulary.* That is, they can comprehend more words spoken by others than they can actually produce to express themselves (Dan & Gleason, 2001). Thus, toddlers can *understand* 50 words months before they can *say* 50 words. Toddlers' early words tend to refer most often to *objects* and secondarily to *social actions,* such as *hello* and *goodbye* (Camaioni, 2001). Children probably acquire nouns before verbs, because the meanings of nouns, which often refer to distinct, concrete objects, tend to be easier to encode than the meanings of verbs, which often refer to more abstract relationships (Poulin-Dubois & Graham, 2007). However, this generalization may not apply to all languages (Bates et al., 2001).

Youngsters' vocabularies soon begin to grow at a dizzying pace, as a *vocabulary spurt* or *naming explosion* begins at around 18 months when toddlers realize that everything has a name (Camaioni, 2001) (see **Figure 8.2**). By the first grade, the average child has a vocabulary of approximately 10,000 words, which builds to an astonishing 40,000 words by the fifth grade (Anglin, 1993) (see **Figure 8.3**). In building these impressive vocabularies, some 2-year-olds learn as many as 20 new words every week. *Fast mapping* appears to be one factor underlying this rapid growth

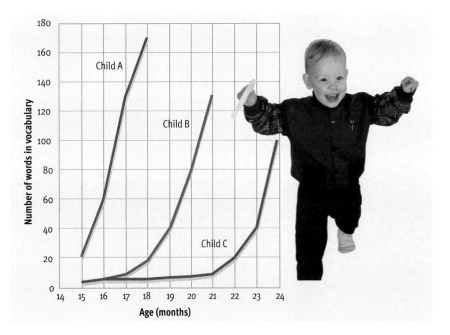

Figure 8.2

The vocabulary spurt. Children typically acquire their first 10–15 words very slowly, but they soon go through a *vocabulary spurt*—a period during which they rapidly acquire many new words. The vocabulary spurt usually begins at around 18 months, but children vary, as these graphs of three toddlers' vocabulary growth show.

SOURCE: Adapted from Goldfield, B. A., & Resnick, J. S. (1990). Early lexical acquisition: Rate, content, and the vocabulary spurt. *Journal of Child Language, 17,* 171–183. Copyright © 1990 by Cambridge University Press. Photo: Courtesy of Wayne Weiten

of vocabulary (Gershkoff-Stowe & Hahn, 2007; Markman, Wasow, & Hansen, 2003). **Fast mapping is the process by which children map a word onto an underlying concept after only one exposure.** Thus, children often add words like *tank, board,* and *tape* to their vocabularies after their first encounter with objects that illustrate these concepts. The vocabulary spurt may be attributable to children's improved articulation skills, improved understanding of syntax, underlying cognitive development, or some combination of these factors (MacWhinney, 1998).

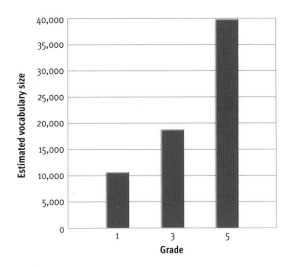

Figure 8.3

The growth of school children's vocabulary. Vocabulary growth is rapid during the early years of grade school. Youngsters' estimated vocabulary doubles about every two years between first grade and fifth grade.

SOURCE: Anglin, J. M. (1993). Vocabulary development: A morphological analysis. *Child Development, 58,* Serial 238. Copyright © 1993 The Society for Research in Child Development. Reprinted by permission.

Of course, these efforts to learn new words are not flawless. Toddlers often make errors, such as overextensions and underextensions (Harley, 2008). **An *overextension* occurs when a child incorrectly uses a word to describe a wider set of objects or actions than it is meant to.** For example, a child might use the word *ball* for anything round—oranges, apples, even the moon. Overextensions usually appear in children's speech between ages 1 and 2½. Specific overextensions typically last up to several months. Toddlers also tend to be guilty of **underextensions, which occur when a child incorrectly uses a word to describe a narrower set of objects or actions than it is meant to.** For example, a child might use the word *doll* to refer only to a single, favorite doll. Overextensions and underextensions show that toddlers are actively trying to learn the rules of language—albeit with mixed success.

Combining Words

Children typically begin to combine words into sentences near the end of their second year. Early sentences are characterized as "telegraphic" because they resemble old-fashioned telegrams, which omitted nonessential words because senders were charged by the word (Bochner & Jones, 2003). **Telegraphic speech consists mainly of content words; articles, prepositions, and other less critical words are omitted.** Thus, a child might say, "Give doll" rather than "Please give me the doll." Although not unique to the English language, telegraphic speech is not cross-culturally universal, as once thought (de Villiers & de Villiers, 1999).

Researchers sometimes track language development by keeping tabs on subjects' **mean length of utterance (MLU)—the average length of youngsters' spoken statements (measured in morphemes).** As children grow and begin to combine words, their vocal expressions gradually become longer (Hoff, 2005).

By the end of their third year, most children can express complex ideas such as plurals or past tense. However, their efforts to learn the rules of language continue to result in revealing mistakes. **Overregularizations occur when grammatical rules are incorrectly generalized to irregular cases where they do not apply.** For example, children will say things like "The girl goed home" or "I hitted the ball." Cross-cultural research suggests that these overregularizations occur in all languages (Slobin, 1985). Most theorists believe that overregularizations demonstrate that children are working actively to master the *rules* of language (Marcus, 1996). These efforts pay off gradually, however, as specific overregularizations often linger in a child's speech even though the child has heard the correct constructions many

times (Maslen et al., 2004). Children don't learn the fine points of grammar and usage in a single leap but gradually acquire them in small steps.

Refining Language Skills

Youngsters make their largest strides in language development in their first 4 to 5 years. However, they continue to refine their language skills during their school-age years. They generate longer and more complicated sentences as they receive formal training in written language.

As their language skills develop, school-age children begin to appreciate ambiguities in language. They can, for instance, recognize two possible meanings in sentences such as "Visiting relatives can be bothersome." This interest in ambiguities indicates that they're developing **metalinguistic awareness—the ability to reflect on the use of language.** As metalinguistic awareness grows, children begin to recognize that statements may have a *literal meaning* and an *implied meaning.* They begin to make more frequent and sophisticated use of metaphors, such as "We were packed in the room like sardines" (Gentner, 1988).

Between the ages of 6 and 8 most children begin to appreciate irony and sarcasm (Creusere, 1999). *Irony* involves conveying an implied meaning that is the opposite of a statement's literal meaning (on learning that he got a D on an exam, a student says, "Oh, that's just great"). *Sarcasm* is a variation on irony in which there is a caustic element directed at a particular person (commenting on a blunder by her husband a woman says, "My husband, the genius"). Understanding sarcasm requires appreciating the subtleties of an utterance's social and

---

concept check 8.1

Tracking Language Development

Check your understanding of how language skills progress in youngsters. Number the utterances below to indicate the developmental sequence in which they would probably occur. The answers can be found in Appendix A in the back of the book.

_____ 1. "Doggie," while pointing to a cow.

_____ 2. "The dogs runned away."

_____ 3. "Doggie run."

_____ 4. "The dogs ran away."

_____ 5. "Doggie," while pointing to a dog.

_____ 6. "Tommy thinks like his head is full of mashed potatoes."

cultural context (Katz, Blasko, & Kazmerski, 2004). Interestingly, although language processing is generally handled by the left hemisphere of the brain (see Chapter 3), the right hemisphere appears to play a key role in the understanding of sarcasm (Shamay-Tsoory, Tomer, & Aharon-Peretz, 2005).

Learning More Than One Language: Bilingualism

Given the complexities involved in acquiring one language, you may be wondering about the ramifications of being asked to learn *two* languages. *Bilingualism is the acquisition of two languages that use different speech sounds, vocabulary, and grammatical rules.* Although not the norm in the United States, bilingualism is quite common in Europe and many other regions, and nearly half of the world's population grows up bilingual (Hakuta, 1986; Snow, 1998). Moreover, bilingualism is far from rare even in the English-dominated United States, where roughly 6–7 million children speak a language other than English at home. Bilingualism has sparked considerable controversy in the United States, as a number of new laws and court rulings have reduced the availability of bilingual educational programs in many school systems (Wiese & Garcia, 2007). These laws are based on the implicit assumption that bilingualism hampers language development and has a negative impact on youngsters' educational progress. But does the empirical evidence support this assumption? Let's take a look at the research on bilingualism.

Does Learning Two Languages in Childhood Slow Down Language Development?

If youngsters are learning two languages simultaneously, does one language interfere with the other so that the acquisition of both is impeded? Given the far-reaching sociopolitical implications of this question, you might guess that many relevant studies have been conducted, but in reality there is only a modest body of research. Some studies *have* found that bilingual children have smaller vocabularies in each of their languages than monolingual children have in their one language (Umbel et al., 1992). But when their two overlapping vocabularies are added, their total vocabulary is similar or slightly superior to that of children learning a single language (Oller & Pearson, 2002). Taken as a whole, the available evidence suggests that bilingual and monolingual children are largely similar in the course and rate of their language development (de Houwer, 1995; Nicoladis & Genesee, 1997). Learning two languages simultaneously may not be as easy as learning just one, but there is little empirical support for the belief that bilingualism has serious negative effects on language development (Hoff, 2005).

Does Bilingualism Affect Cognitive Processes and Skills?

Does learning two languages slow down cognitive development or have a negative impact on intellectual skills? Some early studies of this question suggested that the answer is "yes," but the studies suffered from fundamental flaws (Hakuta, 1986). Typically, immigrant bilingual children and native English-speaking children were given IQ tests *in English,* with the results favoring the English speakers. But these results were misleading, because the bilingual students tended to come from more impoverished backgrounds and because they were handicapped by having to take the IQ test in their second language (Hakuta, 2000). Imagine if you had to take an IQ test in French after a couple years of French instruction. When studies use proper controls, the evidence is mixed, depending on the variables measured—and sometimes the results *favor* the bilinguals. For example, when middle-class bilingual subjects who are fluent in both languages are studied, they tend to score somewhat *higher* than monolingual subjects on measures of cognitive flexibility, analytical

The utility of bilingual education programs has been a hotly debated local issue across the United States and Canada. Critics argue that bilingualism has a negative effect on children's language and cognitive development, but there is relatively little empirical support for this assertion.

Sue Savage-Rumbaugh

"What Kanzi tells us is that humans are not the only species that can acquire language if exposed to it at an early age."

Kanzi, a pygmy chimpanzee, has learned to communicate with his caretakers in surprisingly sophisticated ways via computer-controlled symbol boards, thus raising some doubt about whether language is unique to humans.

reasoning, selective attention, and metalinguistic awareness (Bialystok, 2001, 2005, 2007; Campbell & Sais, 1995). However, on some types of tasks, bilinguals may have a slight disadvantage in terms of raw language-processing *speed* (Taylor & Taylor, 1990). Nonetheless, when researchers control for the effects of social class, they do not find significant cognitive deficits in bilingual youngsters.

Can Animals Develop Language?

Can other species besides humans develop language? Although this issue does not have the practical, sociopolitical repercussions of the debate about bilingualism, it has intrigued researchers for many decades and has led to some fascinating research. Scientists have taught some language-like skills to a number of species, including dolphins (Herman, Kuczaj, & Holder, 1993), sea lions (Schusterman & Gisiner, 1988), and an African gray parrot (Pepperberg, 1993, 2002), but their greatest success has come with the chimpanzee, an intelligent primate widely regarded as humans' closest cousin.

In early studies, researchers tried training chimps to use a nonoral human language: American Sign Language (ASL). ASL is a complex language of hand gestures and facial expressions used by thousands of deaf people in the United States. With extensive training, a chimp named Washoe acquired a sign vocabulary of roughly 160 words and learned to combine these words into simple sentences, such as "Gimme flower" (Gardner & Gardner, 1969). Although these accomplishments were impressive, critics expressed doubts about whether Washoe and other chimps that learned ASL had really acquired

rules of language. According to Terrace (1986), the chimps' sentences were the products of imitation and operant conditioning, rather than *generative* creations based on linguistic rules.

In more recent years, Sue Savage-Rumbaugh and her colleagues have reported some striking advances with *bonobo pygmy chimpanzees* that have fueled additional debate (Savage-Rumbaugh, 1991; Savage-Rumbaugh, Shanker, & Taylor, 1998; Savage-Rumbaugh, Rumbaugh, & Fields, 2006). In this line of research, the bonobos have been trained to communicate with their caretakers by touching geometric symbols representing words on a computer-monitored keyboard. Savage-Rumbaugh's star pupil has been a chimp named Kanzi, although many of his feats have been duplicated by his younger sister, Panbanisha. Kanzi has acquired hundreds of words and has used them in thousands of combinations. Many of these combinations have been spontaneous and seem to follow rules of language. For example, to specify whether he wanted to chase or be chased, Kanzi had to differentiate between symbol combinations in a way that appeared to involve the use of grammatical rules. As the years went by, Kanzi's trainers noticed that he often seemed to understand the normal utterances that they exchanged with each other. Subseqently, they began to systematically evaluate his comprehension of spoken English and found that he could understand hundreds of sentences that directed him to execute simple actions, such as "Put the collar in the water."

How have the linguistics experts reacted to Kanzi's surprising progress in language development? Many remain skeptical. Wynne (2004) has raised questions about the scoring system used to determine whether Kanzi "understood" oral requests, arguing that it was extremely "generous." Wynne and other critics (Budiansky, 2004; Kako, 1999; Wallman, 1992) have also questioned whether Kanzi's communications demonstrate all the basic properties of a language.

The newest evidence in the debate about whether language is unique to humans is a recent study of chimpanzees using brain-imaging technology. As you may recall from Chapter 3, in humans *Broca's area* is a small region in the left hemisphere of the brain that is crucial to language production (consult **Figure 3.21**). Taglialatela and colleagues (2008) set out to determine whether chimps have a comparable brain area in roughly the same location. Using PET scans to map brain activity while chimps engaged in communication, they determined that chimps do have an analogous area in the left hemisphere. The investigators conclude that the neurological substrates underlying language may also be present in chimpanzees.

FRANK & ERNEST

PRIMATE SPEECH LAB

HE'S JUST FILLING IN WHILE THE RECEPTIONIST IS ON A BREAK.

10-9 THAVES

© 2007 Bob Thaves. Distributed by Newspaper Enterprise Association, Inc.

So, what can we conclude? Overall, it seems reasonable to assert that the ability to use language—in a basic, primitive way—may not be entirely unique to humans, as has been widely assumed.

However, make no mistake, there is no comparison between human linguistic abilities and those of apes or other animals. As remarkable as the language studies with apes are, they should make us marvel even more at the fluency, flexibility, and complexity of human language. A normal human toddler quickly surpasses even the most successfully trained chimps. In mastering language, children outstrip chimps the way jet airplanes outrace horse-drawn buggies. Why are humans so well suited for learning language? According to some theorists, this talent for language is a product of evolution. Let's look at their thinking.

Language in Evolutionary Context

All human societies depend on complex language systems. Even primitive cultures use languages that are just as complicated as those used in modern societies. The universal nature of language suggests that it is an innate human characteristic. Consistent with this view, Steven Pinker argues that humans' special talent for language is a species-specific trait that is the product of natural selection (Pinker, 1994, 2004; Pinker & Jackendoff, 2005). According to Pinker, language is a valuable means of communication that has enormous adaptive value. As Pinker and Bloom (1992) point out, "There is an obvious advantage in being able to acquire information about the world second-hand . . . one can avoid having to duplicate the possibly time-consuming and dangerous trial-and-error process that won that knowledge" (p. 460). Dunbar (1996) argues that language evolved as a device to build and maintain social coalitions in increasingly larger groups. Although the impetus for the evolution of language remains a matter of speculation and debate (Kirby, 2007), it does not take much imagination to envision how more-effective communication among our ancient ancestors could have aided hunt-

ing, gathering, fighting, and mating and the avoidance of poisons, predators, and other dangers.

Although the adaptive value of language seems obvious, some scholars take issue with the assertion that human language is the product of evolution. For example, David Premack (1985) has expressed skepticism that small differences in language skill would influence reproductive fitness in primitive societies where all one had to communicate about was the location of the closest mastadon herd. In an effort to refute this argument, Pinker and Bloom (1992) point out that very small adaptive disparities are sufficient to fuel evolutionary change. For example, they cite an estimate that a 1% difference in mortality rates among overlapping Neanderthal and human populations could have led to the extinction of Neanderthals in just 30 generations. They also note that a trait variation that produces on average just 1% more offspring than its alternative genetic expression would increase in prevalence from 0.1% to 99.9% of the population in 4000 generations. That many generations may seem like an eternity, but in the context of evolution, it is a modest amount of time.

Whether or not evolution gets the credit, language acquisition in humans seems remarkably rapid. As you will see in the next section, this fact looms large in theories of language acquisition.

Theories of Language Acquisition

Since the 1950s, a great debate has raged about the key processes involved in language acquisition. As with arguments we have seen in other areas of psychology, this one centers on the *nature versus nurture* issue. The debate was stimulated by the influential behaviorist B. F. Skinner (1957), who argued that environmental factors govern language development. His provocative analysis brought a rejoinder from Noam Chomsky (1959), who emphasized biological determinism. Let's examine their views and subsequent theories that stake out a middle ground.

© Rebecca Goldstein, courtesy of Steven Pinker

Steven Pinker

"If human language is unique in the modern animal kingdom, as it appears to be, the implications for a Darwinian account of its evolution would be as follows: none. A language instinct unique to modern humans poses no more of a paradox than a trunk unique to modern elephants."

Behaviorist Theories

The behaviorist approach to language was first outlined by Skinner in his book *Verbal Behavior* (1957). He argued that children learn language the same way they learn everything else: through imitation, reinforcement, and other established principles of conditioning. According to Skinner, vocalizations that are not reinforced gradually decline in frequency. The remaining vocalizations are shaped with reinforcers until they are correct. Behaviorists assert that by controlling reinforcement, parents encourage their children to learn the correct meaning and pronunciation of words (Staats & Staats, 1963). For example, as children grow older, parents may insist on closer and closer approximations of the word *water* before supplying the requested drink.

Behavioral theorists also use the principles of imitation and reinforcement to explain how children learn syntax. According to the behaviorists' view, children learn how to construct sentences by imitating the sentences of adults and older children. If children's imitative statements are understood, parents are able to answer their questions or respond to their requests, thus reinforcing their verbal behavior.

Nativist Theories

Skinner's explanation of language acquisition soon inspired a critique and rival explanation from Noam Chomsky (1959, 1965). Chomsky pointed out that there are an infinite number of sentences in a language. It's therefore unreasonable to expect that children learn language by imitation. For example, in English, we add *ed* to the end of a verb to construct past tense. Children routinely overregularize this rule, producing incorrect verbs such as *goed,* *eated,* and *thinked.* Mistakes such as these are inconsistent with Skinner's emphasis on imitation, because most adult speakers don't use ungrammatical words like *goed.* Children can't imitate things they don't hear. According to Chomsky, children learn *the rules of language,* not specific verbal responses, as Skinner proposed.

An alternative theory favored by Chomsky (1975, 1986, 2006) is that humans have an inborn or "native" propensity to develop language. (Here *native* is a variation on the word *nature* as it's used in the nature versus nurture debate.) *Nativist theory* proposes that humans are equipped with a **language acquisition device (LAD)—an innate mechanism or process that facilitates the learning of language.** According to this view, humans learn language for the same reason that birds learn to fly—because they're biologically equipped for it. The exact nature of the LAD has not been spelled out in nativist theories. It presumably consists of brain structures and neural wiring that leave humans well prepared to discriminate among phonemes, to fast-map morphemes, to acquire rules of syntax, and so on.

Why does Chomsky believe that children have an innate capacity for learning language? One reason is that children seem to acquire language quickly and effortlessly. How could they develop so complex a skill in such a short time unless they have a built-in capacity for it? Another reason is that language development tends to unfold at roughly the same pace for most children, even though children obviously are reared in diverse home environments. This finding suggests that language development is determined by biological maturation more than personal experience. The nativists also cite evidence that the early course of language development is similar across very different cultures (Gleitman & Newport, 1996; Slobin, 1992). They interpret this to mean that children all over the world are guided by the same innate capabilities.

Interactionist Theories

Like Skinner, Chomsky has his critics (Bohannon & Bonvillian, 2001). They ask: What exactly is a language acquisition device? How does the LAD work? What are the neural mechanisms involved? They argue that the LAD concept is awfully vague. Other critics question whether the rapidity of early language development is as exceptional as nativists assume. They assert that it isn't fair to compare the rapid progress of toddlers, who are immersed in their native language, against the struggles of older students, who may devote only a few hours per week to their foreign language course.

The problems apparent in Skinner's and Chomsky's explanations of language development have led some researchers to outline *interactionist theories* of language acquisition. These theories assert that biology and experience *both* make important contributions to the development of language. For example, *emergentist theories* argue that the neural circuits supporting language are not prewired but *emerge* gradually in response to language learning experiences (Bates, 1999; MacWhinney, 2001, 2004). These theories tend to assume that incremental changes in connectionist networks (see Chapter 7) underlie children's gradual acquisition of various language skills (Elman, 1999).

Like the nativists, interactionists believe that the human organism is biologically well equipped for learning language. They also agree that much of this learning involves the acquisition of rules. However, like the behaviorists, they believe that social exchanges with parents and others play a critical role in molding language skills. Thus, interaction-

Noam Chomsky

"Even at low levels of intelligence, at pathological levels, we find a command of language that is totally unattainable by an ape."

ist theories maintain that a biological predisposition *and* a supportive environment both contribute to language development (see Figure 8.4).

Culture, Language, and Thought

Another long-running controversy in the study of language concerns the relations between culture, language, and thought. Obviously, people from different cultures generally speak different languages. But does your training in English lead you to think about certain things differently than someone who was raised to speak Chinese or French? In other words, does a cultural group's language determine their thought? Or does thought determine language?

Benjamin Lee Whorf (1956) has been the most prominent advocate of *linguistic relativity,* **the hypothesis that one's language determines the nature of one's thought.** Whorf speculated that different languages lead people to view the world differently. His classic example compared English and Eskimo views of snow. He asserted that the English language has just one word for snow, whereas the Eskimo language has many words that distinguish among falling snow, wet snow, and so on. Because of this language gap, Whorf argued that Eskimos perceive snow differently than English-speaking people do. However, Whorf's conclusion about these perceptual differences was based on casual observation rather than systematic cross-cultural comparisons of perceptual processes. Moreover, critics subsequently noted that advocates of the linguistic relativity hypothesis had carelessly overestimated the number of Eskimo words for snow, while conveniently ignoring the variety of English words that refer to snow, such as slush and blizzard (Martin, 1986; Pullum, 1991).

In any event, Whorf's hypothesis has been the subject of considerable research and continues to generate spirited debate (Chiu, Leung, & Kwan, 2007; Gleitman & Papafragou, 2005). Many studies have focused on cross-cultural comparisons of how people perceive colors, because substantial variations exist among cultures in how colors are categorized with names. For example, some languages have a single color name that includes both blue and green, whereas other languages view light blue and dark blue as fundamentally different colors (Davies, 1998). If a language doesn't distinguish between blue and green, do people who speak that language think about colors differently than people in other cultures do?

Early efforts to answer this question suggested that the color categories in a language have relatively little influence on how people perceive and

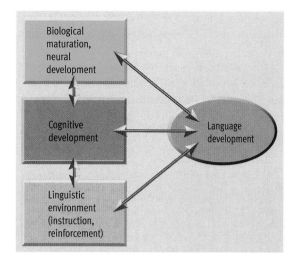

Figure 8.4
Interactionist theories of language acquisition. The interactionist view is that nature and nurture are both important to language acquisition. Maturation is thought to drive language development directly and to influence it indirectly by fostering cognitive development. Meanwhile, verbal exchanges with parents and others are also thought to play a critical role in molding language skills. The complex bidirectional relations depicted here shed some light on why there is room for extensive debate about the crucial factors in language acquisition.

think about colors (Berlin & Kay, 1969; Rosch, 1973). However, a flurry of recent studies have provided new evidence favoring the linguistic relativity hypothesis (Davidoff, 2001, 2004; Roberson et al., 2005). For example, studies of subjects who speak African languages that do not have a boundary between blue and green have found that language affects their color perception, as they have more trouble making quick discriminations between blue and green colors than English-speaking subjects do (Ozgen, 2004). Additional studies using a variety of methods have found that a culture's color categories shape subjects' similarity judgments and groupings of colors (Pilling & Davies, 2004; Roberson, Davies, & Davidoff, 2000). These findings have led Ozgen (2004) to conclude that "it is just possible that what you see when you look at the rainbow depends on the language you speak" (p. 98). Moreover, the new support for linguistic relativity is not limited to the study of color perception. Other studies have found that language also has some impact on how people

Does the language you speak determine how you think? Yes, said Benjamin Lee Whorf, who argued that the Eskimo language, which has numerous words for snow, leads Eskimos to perceive snow differently than English speakers. Whorf's hypothesis has been the subject of spirited debate.

© Peter Arnold, Inc./Alamy

think about motion (Gennari et al., 2002), time (Boroditsky, 2001), and shapes (Roberson, Davidoff, & Shapiro, 2002).

So, what is the status of the linguistic relativity hypothesis? At present, the debate seems to center on whether the new data are sufficient to support the original, "strong" version of the hypothesis—that a given language makes certain ways of thinking obligatory or impossible—or a "weaker" version of the hypothesis—that a language makes certain ways of thinking easier or more difficult. Either way, empirical support for the linguistic relativity hypothesis has increased dramatically in recent years.

REVIEW of Key Learning Goals

8.1 The key properties of language include being symbolic, generative, and structured. Human languages are structured hierarchically. At the bottom of the hierarchy are the basic sound units, called phonemes. At the next level are morphemes, the smallest units of meaning. Rules of syntax specify how words can be combined into sentences.

8.2 The initial vocalizations by infants are similar across languages, but their babbling gradually begins to resemble the sounds from their surrounding language. Children typically utter their first words around their first birthday. A vocabulary spurt often begins around 18 months. Most children begin to combine words by the end of their second year. Their early sentences are telegraphic. Over the next several years, children gradually learn the complexities of syntax and develop metalinguistic awareness.

8.3 Research does not support the assumption that bilingualism has a negative effect on language development. Early research on bilingualism and cognitive development was flawed. When appropriate controls are used, researchers do not find significant cognitive deficits in bilingual youngsters.

8.4 Efforts to teach chimpanzees American Sign Language were impressive, but doubts were raised about whether the chimps learned rules of language. Sue Savage-Rumbaugh's work with Kanzi suggests that chimps are capable of some very basic language acquisition, but there is no comparison between the linguistic abilities of humans and other animals.

8.5 Many theorists, such as Steven Pinker, believe that humans' special talent for language is the product of natural selection because more effective communication would confer a variety of adaptive benefits. However, this assertion has been challenged.

8.6 According to Skinner and other behaviorists, children acquire a language through imitation and reinforcement. Nativist theories assert that humans have an innate capacity to learn language rules. Today, theorists are moving toward interactionist perspectives, which emphasize the role of both biology and experience.

8.7 The theory of linguistic relativity asserts that language determines thought, thus suggesting that people from different cultures may think about the world somewhat differently. Recent studies have provided new support for the linguistic relativity hypothesis.

Key Learning Goals

8.8 List the three types of problems proposed by Greeno.

8.9 Identify and describe four common barriers to effective problem solving.

8.10 Review a variety of general problem-solving strategies and heuristics.

8.11 Discuss cultural variations in cognitive style as they relate to problem solving.

Problem Solving: In Search of Solutions

Look at the two problems below. Can you solve them?

In the Thompson family there are five brothers, and each brother has one sister. If you count Mrs. Thompson, how many females are there in the Thompson family?

Fifteen percent of the people in Topeka have unlisted telephone numbers. You select 200 names at random from the Topeka phone book. How many of these people can be expected to have unlisted phone numbers?

These problems, borrowed from Sternberg (1986, p. 214), are exceptionally simple, but many people fail to solve them. The answer to the first problem is *two:* The only females in the family are Mrs. Thompson and her one daughter, who is a sister to each of her brothers. The answer to the second problem is *none*—you won't find any people with *unlisted* phone numbers in the phone book.

Why do many people fail to solve these simple problems? You'll learn why in a moment, when we discuss barriers to effective problem solving. But first, let's examine a scheme for classifying problems into a few basic types.

Types of Problems

SIM7, 7e

***Problem solving* refers to active efforts to discover what must be done to achieve a goal that is not readily attainable.** Obviously, if a goal is readily attainable, there isn't a problem. But in problem-solving situations, one must go beyond the information given to overcome obstacles and reach a goal. Jim Greeno (1978) has proposed that problems can be categorized into three basic classes:

1. *Problems of inducing structure* require people to discover the relations among numbers, words, symbols, or ideas. The *series completion problems* and the *analogy problems* in **Figure 8.5** are examples of problems of inducing structure.

2. *Problems of arrangement* require people to arrange the parts of a problem in a way that satisfies some criterion. The parts can usually be arranged in many

A. Analogy

What word completes the analogy?

Merchant : Sell : : Customer : _____

Lawyer : Client : : Doctor : _____

B. String problem

Two strings hang from the ceiling but are too far apart to allow a person to hold one and walk to the other. On the table are a book of matches, a screwdriver, and a few pieces of cotton. How could the strings be tied together?

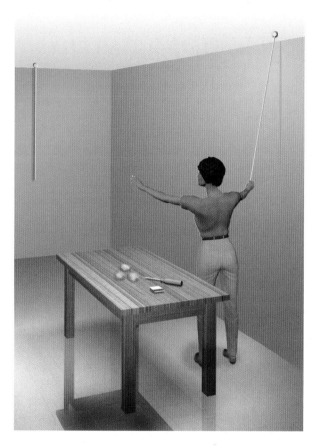

C. Hobbits and orcs problem

Three hobbits and three orcs arrive at a river bank, and they all wish to cross onto the other side. Fortunately, there is a boat, but unfortunately, the boat can hold only two creatures at one time. Also, there is another problem. Orcs are vicious creatures, and whenever there are more orcs than hobbits on one side of the river, the orcs will immediately attack the hobbits and eat them up. Consequently, you should be certain that you never leave more orcs than hobbits on either river bank. How should the problem be solved? It must be added that the orcs, though vicious, can be trusted to bring the boat back! (From Matlin, 1989, p. 319)

D. Water jar problem

Suppose that you have a 21-cup jar, a 127-cup jar, and a 3-cup jar. Drawing and discarding as much water as you like, you need to measure out exactly 100 cups of water. How can this be done?

E. Anagram

Rearrange the letters in each row to make an English word.

RWAET

KEROJ

F. Series completion

What number or letter completes each series?

1 2 8 3 4 6 5 6 _____

A B M C D M _____

Figure 8.5

Six standard problems used in studies of problem solving. Try solving the problems and identifying which class each belongs to before reading further. The problems can be classified as follows. The *analogy problems* and *series completion problems* are problems of inducing structure. The solutions for the analogy problems are *Buy* and *Patient*. The solutions for the series completion problems are *4* and *E*. The *string problem* and the *anagram problems* are problems of arrangement. To solve the string problem, attach the screwdriver to one string and set it swinging as a pendulum. Hold the other string and catch the swinging screwdriver. Then you need only untie the screwdriver and tie the strings together. The solutions for the anagram problems are *WATER* and *JOKER*. The *hobbits and orcs problem* and the *water jar problem* are problems of transformation. The solutions for these problems are outlined in **Figure 8.6** and **Figure 8.7**.

ways, but only one or a few of the arrangements form a solution. The *string problem* and the *anagrams* in **Figure 8.5** fit in this category.

3. *Problems of transformation* require people to carry out a sequence of transformations in order to reach a specific goal. The *hobbits and orcs problem* and the *water jar problem* in **Figure 8.5** are examples of transformation problems. Transformation problems can be challenging. Even though you know exactly what

the goal is, it's often not obvious how the goal can be achieved.

Greeno's list is not an exhaustive scheme for classifying problems, but it provides a useful system for understanding some of the variety seen in problems. Although researchers have recently shown an increased interest in how people solve real-world problems in science, medicine, or law, research in this area has

Figure 8.6
Solution to the hobbits and orcs problem. This problem is difficult because it is necessary to temporarily work "away" from the goal.

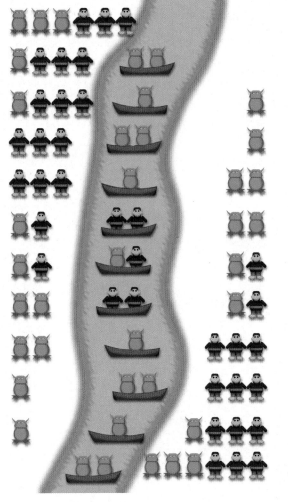

traditionally focused on "generic" problems like those in **Figure 8.5**, which are largely uncontaminated by variations in subjects' knowledge or expertise.

Barriers to Effective Problem Solving

On the basis of their studies of problem solving, psychologists have identified a number of barriers that frequently impede subjects' efforts to arrive at solutions. Common obstacles to effective problem solving include a focus on irrelevant information, functional fixedness, mental set, and the imposition of unnecessary constraints.

Irrelevant Information

We began our discussion of problem solving with two simple problems that people routinely fail to solve (see page 328). The catch is that these problems contain *irrelevant information* that leads people astray. In the first problem, the number of brothers is irrelevant in determining the number of females in the Thompson family. In the second problem, subjects tend to focus on the figures of 15% and 200 names. But this numerical information is irrelevant, since all the names came out of the phone book.

Sternberg (1986) points out that people often incorrectly assume that all the numerical information in a problem is necessary to solve it. They therefore try to figure out how to use quantitative information before they even consider whether it's relevant. Focusing on irrelevant information can have adverse effects on reasoning and problem solving (Gaeth & Shanteau, 2000). Thus, effective problem solving requires that you attempt to figure out what information is relevant and what is irrelevant before proceeding.

Functional Fixedness

Another common barrier to successful problem solving, identified by Gestalt psychologists, is *functional fixedness*—the tendency to perceive an item only in terms of its most common use. Functional fixedness has been seen in the difficulties that people have with the string problem in Figure 8.5 (Maier, 1931). Solving this problem requires finding a novel use for one of the objects: the screwdriver. Subjects tend to think of the screwdriver in terms of its usual functions—turning screws and perhaps prying things open. They have a hard time viewing the screwdriver as a weight. Their rigid way of thinking about the screwdriver illustrates functional fixedness (Dominowski & Bourne, 1994). Ironically, young children appear to be less vulnerable to functional fixedness than older children or adults because they have less knowledge about the conventional uses of various objects (Defeyter & German, 2003).

Mental Set

7e

Rigid thinking is also at work when a mental set interferes with effective problem solving. A *mental set* exists when people persist in using problem-solving strategies that have worked in the past. The effects of mental set were seen in a classic study by Gestalt psychologist Abraham Luchins (1942). He asked subjects to work a series of water jar problems,

Figure 8.7
The method for solving the water jar problem. As explained in the text, the correct formula is B – A – 2C.

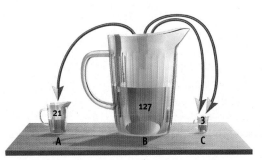

DILBERT

I ASK ALL PROSPECTIVE EMPLOYEES THIS QUESTION TO TEST THEIR REASONING.

YOU HAVE ONE FOX AND TWO CHICKENS THAT YOU NEED TO GET ACROSS A RIVER. YOU CAN ONLY TAKE ONE AT A TIME IN THE ROW-BOAT. THE FOX WILL EAT THE CHICKENS IF LEFT ALONE.

I'D BUY LIVESTOCK INSURANCE, THEN BARBECUE THE CHICKENS AND BLAME THE FOX.

CAN YOU START TODAY?

DILBERT: © 2003 Scott Adams/Dist. by United Feature Syndication, Inc.

like the one introduced earlier. Six such problems are outlined in **Figure 8.8**, which shows the capacities of the three jars and the amounts of water to be measured out. Try solving these problems.

Were you able to develop a formula for solving these problems? The first four all require the same strategy, which was described in **Figure 8.7**. You have to fill jar B, draw off the amount that jar A holds once, and draw off the amount that jar C holds twice. Thus, the formula for your solution is B – A – 2C. Although there is an obvious and much simpler solution (A – C) for the fifth problem (see **Figure 8.13** on page 334), Luchins found that most subjects stuck with the more cumbersome strategy that they had used in problems 1–4. Moreover, most subjects couldn't solve the sixth problem in the allotted time, because they kept trying to use their proven strategy, which does *not* work for this problem. The subjects' reliance on their "tried and true" strategy is an illustration of mental set in problem solving. This tendency to let one's thinking get into a rut is a common barrier to successful problem solving (Smith, 1995). Mental set may explain why having expertise in an area sometimes backfires and in

fact hampers problem-solving efforts (Leighton & Sternberg, 2003).

Unnecessary Constraints 7e

Effective problem solving requires specifying all the constraints governing a problem *without assuming any constraints that don't exist.* An example of a problem in which people place an unnecessary constraint on the solution is the nine-dot problem shown in **Figure 8.9** (Maier, 1930). Without lifting your pencil from the paper, try to draw four straight lines that will cross through all nine dots. If you struggle with this one, don't feel bad. When a time limit of a few minutes is imposed on this problem, the typical solution rate is 0% (MacGregor et al., 2001). The key factor that makes this a difficult problem is that most people will not draw lines outside the imaginary boundary that surrounds the dots. Notice that this constraint is not part of the problem statement. It's imposed only by the problem solver (Adams, 1980). Correct solutions, two of which are shown in **Figure 8.14** on page 334, extend outside the imaginary boundary. To solve this problem you literally need

Figure 8.8

Additional water jar problems. Using jars A, B, and C, with the capacities indicated in each row, figure out how to measure out the desired amount of water specified on the far right. The solutions are shown in **Figure 8.13**. (Based on Luchins, 1942)

Problem	Capacity of empty jars			Desired amount of water
	A	B	C	
1	14	163	25	99
2	18	43	10	5
3	9	42	6	21
4	20	59	4	31
5	23	49	3	20
6	28	76	3	25

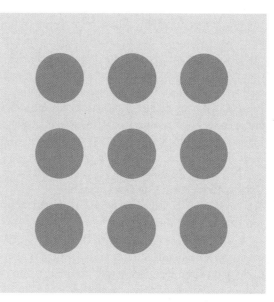

Figure 8.9

The nine-dot problem. Without lifting your pencil from the paper, draw no more than four lines that will cross through all nine dots. For possible solutions, see **Figure 8.14**.

SOURCE: Adams, J. L. (1980). *Conceptual block-busting: A guide to better ideas.* New York: W. H. Freeman. Copyright © 1980 by James L. Adams. Reprinted by permission of W. H. Freeman & Co.

to "think outside the box." This popular slogan, spawned by the nine-dot problem, reflects the fact that people often make assumptions that impose unnecessary constraints on problem-solving efforts.

The nine-dot problem is often solved with a burst of insight. *Insight occurs when people suddenly discover the correct solution to a problem after struggling with it for a while.* Problems requiring insight tend to be difficult for a variety of reasons. Difficulties may emerge from (1) how people structure the problem, (2) how they apply prior knowledge, or (3) how much they need to juggle information in working memory (Kershaw & Ohlsson, 2004). For example, in the nine-dot problem, the main barrier to a solution is that people tend to structure the problem poorly by imposing unnecessary boundaries. But people also struggle because their prior knowledge suggests that the "turns" in their lines should occur on the dots (rather than in the white space) and because envisioning all the options strains working memory. Although insight feels like a sudden, "aha" experience to problem solvers, some researchers have questioned whether insight solutions emerge full blown or are preceded by incremental movement toward a solution (Chronicle, MacGregor, & Ormerod, 2004). Recent studies suggest the latter—that insight breakthroughs are often preceded by gradual movement toward a solution that occurs outside of the problem solver's awareness (Novick & Bassok, 2005).

Approaches to Problem Solving

In their classic treatise on problem solving, Allen Newell and Herbert Simon (1972) used a spatial metaphor to describe the process of problem solving. They used the term *problem space* **to refer to the set of possible pathways to a solution considered by the problem solver.** Thus, they see problem solving as a search in space. The problem solver's task is to find a solution path among the potential pathways that could lead from the problem's initial state to its goal state. The problem space metaphor highlights the fact that people must choose from among a variety of conceivable pathways or strategies in attempting to solve problems (Hunt, 1994). In this section, we'll examine some of these general strategies.

Using Algorithms and Heuristics

Trial and error is a common approach to solving problems. *Trial and error involves trying possible solutions and discarding those that are in error until one works.* Trial and error is often applied haphazardly, but people sometimes try to be systematic. **An** *algorithm* **is a methodical, step-by-**

step procedure for trying all possible alternatives in searching for a solution to a problem (Dietrich, 1999). For instance, to solve the anagram IHCRA, you could write out all the possible arrangements of these letters until you eventually reached an answer (CHAIR). If an algorithm is available for a problem, it guarantees that one can eventually find a solution.

Algorithms can be effective when there are relatively few possible solutions to be tried out. However, algorithms do not exist for many problems, and they can become impractical when the problem space is large. Consider, for instance, the problem shown in Figure 8.10. The challenge is to move just two matches to create a pattern containing four equal squares. Sure, you could follow an algorithm in moving pairs of matches about. But you'd better allocate plenty of time to this effort, as there are over 60,000 possible rearrangements to check out (see Figure 8.15 on page 334 for the solution).

Because algorithms are inefficient, people often use shortcuts called *heuristics* in problem solving. A *heuristic* **is a guiding principle or "rule of thumb" used in solving problems or making decisions.** In solving problems, a heuristic allows you to discard some alternatives while pursuing selected alternatives that appear more likely to lead to a solution (Holyoak, 1995). Heuristics can be useful because they selectively narrow the problem space, but they don't guarantee success (Fischhoff, 1999; Hertwig & Todd, 2002). Helpful heuristics in problem solving include forming subgoals, hill climbing, working backward, searching for analogies, and changing the representation of a problem.

Forming Subgoals

A useful strategy for many problems is to formulate *subgoals,* intermediate steps toward a solution (Catrambone, 1998). When you reach a subgoal, you've solved part of the problem. Some problems have fairly obvious subgoals, and research has shown that people take advantage of them. For instance, in analogy problems, the first subgoal is usually to figure out the possible relations between the first two parts of the analogy. In a study by Simon and Reed (1976), subjects working on complex problems were given subgoals that weren't obvious. Providing subgoals helped the subjects solve the problems much more quickly.

The wisdom of formulating subgoals can be seen in the *tower of Hanoi problem,* depicted in Figure 8.11. The terminal goal for this problem is to move all three rings on peg A to peg C, while abiding by two restrictions: only the top ring on a peg can be moved, and a ring must never be placed above a smaller ring. See whether you can solve the problem before continuing.

Figure 8.10
The matchstick problem.
Move two matches to form four equal squares. A solution can be found in Figure 8.15.

SOURCE: Kendler, H. H. (1974). *Basic psychology.* Menlo Park, CA: Benjamin-Cummings. Copyright © 1974 The Benjamin-Cummings Publishing Co. Adapted by permission of Howard H. Kendler.

CALVIN & HOBBES

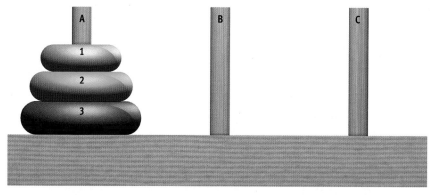

Figure 8.11

The tower of Hanoi problem. Your mission is to move the rings from peg A to peg C. You can move only the top ring on a peg and can't place a larger ring above a smaller one. The solution is explained in the text.

Dividing this problem into subgoals facilitates a solution (Kotovsky, Hayes, & Simon, 1985). If you think in terms of subgoals, your first task is to get ring 3 to the bottom of peg C. Breaking this task into sub-subgoals, subjects can figure out that they should move ring 1 to peg C, ring 2 to peg B, and ring 1 from peg C to peg B. These maneuvers allow you to place ring 3 at the bottom of peg C, thus meeting your first subgoal. Your next subgoal—getting ring 2 over to peg C—can be accomplished in just two steps: move ring 1 to peg A and ring 2 to peg C. It should then be obvious how to achieve your final subgoal—getting ring 1 over to peg C.

Hill Climbing

Try the six-coin problem shown in Figure 8.12. Some people find it easy, while others struggle with the 7,426 possible sequences of moves (one solution is shown in Figure 8.16 on page 334). In one recent study, only 32% of participants solved it within 10 minutes (Chronicle et al., 2004). In any event, this problem tends to be approached with the *hill-climbing heuristic,* **which entails selecting the alternative at each choice point that appears to lead most directly to one's goal.** The name for this heuristic derives from the notion that if you need to climb a hill with many choice points along the pathway (and limited ability to see ahead), one simple strategy would be to always choose the path with

the steepest upward slope. The hill-climbing heuristic is a logical strategy that works much of the time, but it can also backfire. Sometimes the optimal solution to a problem involves an indirect pathway or even moving backward, away from one's goal. However, people tend to be reluctant to make moves that seem to take them away from their goal-state (Robertson, 2001).

Working Backward

Try to work the *lily pond problem* described below:

The water lilies on the surface of a small pond double in area every 24 hours. From the time the first water lily appears until the pond is completely covered takes 60 days. On what day is half of the pond covered with lilies?

If you're working on a problem that has a well-specified end point, you may find the solution more readily if you begin at the end and work backward. This strategy is the key to solving the lily pond problem (Davidson, 2003). If the entire pond is covered on the 60th day, and the area covered doubles every day, how much is covered on the 59th day? One-half of the pond will be covered, and that happens to be the exact point you were trying to reach. The lily pond problem is remarkably simple when you work backward. In contrast, if you move forward from the starting point, you wrestle with questions about the area of the pond and the size of the lilies, and you find the problem riddled with ambiguities.

Searching for Analogies

Searching for analogies is another of the major heuristics for solving problems (Holyoak, 2005). If you can spot an analogy between problems, you may be able to use the solution to a previous problem to solve a current one. Of course, using this strategy depends on recognizing the similarity between two problems, which may itself be a challenging problem. Nevertheless, recent studies of real-world problem

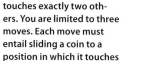

Figure 8.12

The six-coin problem. Your mission is to rearrange the coins so that each coin touches exactly two others. You are limited to three moves. Each move must entail sliding a coin to a position in which it touches exactly two others, without disturbing any coins. A solution is shown in Figure 8.16.

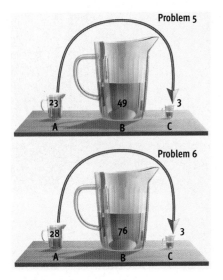

Problem 5

23 | A 49 | B 3 | C

Problem 6

28 | A 76 | B 3 | C

Figure 8.13
Solutions to the additional water jar problems. The solution for problems 1–4 is the same (B – A – 2C) as the solution shown in **Figure 8.8**. This method will work for problem 5, but there also is a simpler solution (A – C), which is the only solution for problem 6. Many subjects exhibit a mental set on these problems, as they fail to notice the simpler solution for problem 5.

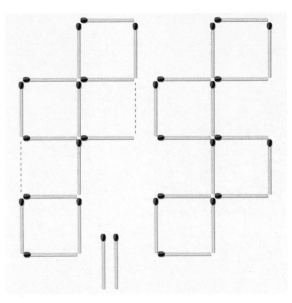

Figure 8.14
Two solutions to the nine-dot problem. The key to solving the problem is to recognize that nothing in the problem statement forbids going outside the imaginary boundary surrounding the dots.

SOURCE: Adams, J. L. (1980). *Conceptual blockbusting: A guide to better ideas.* New York: W. H. Freeman. Copyright © 1980 by James L. Adams. Reprinted by permission of W. H. Freeman & Co.

Figure 8.15
Solution to the matchstick problem. The key to solving this problem is to "open up" the figure, something many subjects are reluctant to do because they impose unnecessary constraints on the problem.

SOURCE: Kendler, H. H. (1974). *Basic psychology.* Menlo Park, CA: Benjamin-Cummings. Copyright © 1974 The Benjamin-Cummings Publishing Co. Adapted by permission of Howard H. Kendler.

solving efforts show that we depend on analogies far more than most people appreciate. For example, one study of biologists' problem solving recorded during their lab meetings found that they threw out 3-15 analogies per hour (Dunbar & Blanchette, 2001). Another study of design engineers recorded during their product development meetings found that they came up with an average of 11 analogies per hour of deliberation (Christensen & Schunn, 2007).

Unfortunately, people often are unable to recognize that two problems are similar and that an analogy might lead to a solution (Kurtz & Lowenstein, 2007). One reason that people have difficulty recognizing analogies between problems is that they often focus on superficial, surface features of problems rather than their underlying structure (Bassok, 2003). Nonetheless, analogies can be a powerful tool in efforts to solve problems. Try to make use of analogies to solve the following two problems:

A teacher had 23 pupils in his class. All but 7 of them went on a museum trip and thus were away for the day. How many students remained in class that day?

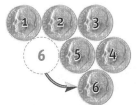

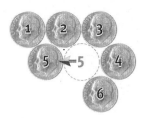

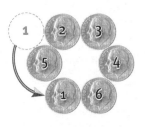

Figure 8.16
A solution to the six-coin problem. One of the two 3-move sequences that will solve this problem is shown here. According to Chronicle et al. (2004), participants tend to use the hill-climbing heuristic when working on this problem.

Susan gets in her car in Boston and drives toward New York City, averaging 50 miles per hour. Twenty minutes later, Ellen gets in her car in New York City and starts driving toward Boston, averaging 60 miles per hour. Both women take the same route, which extends a total of 220 miles between the two cities. Which car is nearer to Boston when they meet?

These problems, taken from Sternberg (1986, pp. 213 and 215), resemble the ones that opened our discussion of problem solving. Each has an obvious solution that's hidden in irrelevant quantitative information. If you recognized this similarity, you probably solved the problems easily. If not, take another look now that you know what the analogy is. Neither problem requires any calculation whatsoever. The answer to the first problem is *7*. As for the second problem, when the two cars meet they're in the same place. Obviously, they have to be the same distance from Boston.

Changing the Representation of the Problem

Whether you solve a problem often hinges on how you envision it—your *representation of the problem.* Many problems can be represented in a variety of ways, such as verbally, mathematically, or spatially. You might represent a problem with a list, a table, an equation, a graph, a matrix of facts or numbers, a hierarchical tree diagram, or a sequential flowchart (Halpern, 2003). There isn't one ideal way to represent problems. However, when researchers compare experts and novices in a particular area of problem solving, they find that the experts strip away irrelevant details and represent problems much more efficiently (Pretz, Naples, & Sternberg, 2003). This finding highlights the importance of how problems are represented. Thus, when you fail to make progress on a problem with your initial representation, changing your representation is often a good strategy (Novick & Bassok, 2005). As an illustration, see whether you can solve the *bird and train problem* (from Bransford & Stein, 1993, p. 11):

Two train stations are 50 miles apart. At 1 P.M. on Sunday a train pulls out from each of the stations and the trains start toward each other. Just as the trains pull out from the stations, a hawk flies into the air in front of the first train and flies ahead to the front of the second train. When the hawk reaches the second train, it turns around and flies toward the first train. The hawk continues in this way until the trains meet. Assume that both trains travel at the speed of 25 miles per hour and the hawk flies at a constant speed of 100 miles per hour. How many miles will the hawk have flown when the trains meet?

This problem asks about the *distance* the bird will fly, so people tend to represent the problem spatially, as shown in **Figure 8.17** on the next page. Represented this way, the problem can be solved, but the steps are tedious and difficult. But consider another angle. The problem asks how far the bird will fly in the time it takes the trains to meet. Since we know how fast the bird flies, all we really need to know is how much *time* it takes for the trains to meet. Changing the representation of the problem from a question of *distance* to a question of *time* makes for an easier solution, as follows: The train stations are 50 miles apart. Since the trains are traveling toward each other at the same speed, they will meet midway and each will have traveled 25 miles. The trains are moving at 25 miles per hour. Hence, the time it takes them to meet 25 miles from each station is 1 hour. Since the bird flies at 100 miles per hour, it will fly 100 miles in the hour it takes the trains to meet.

concept check 8.2

Thinking About Problem Solving

Check your understanding of problem solving by answering some questions about the following problem. Begin by trying to solve the problem.

The candle problem. Using the objects shown—candles, a box of matches, string, and some tacks—figure out how you could mount a candle on a wall so that it could be used as a light. Work on the problem for a while, then turn to page 336 to see the solution. After you've seen the solution, respond to the following questions. The answers are in Appendix A.

Craig McClain

1. If it didn't occur to you that the matchbox could be converted from a container to a platform, this illustrates _____ _____ .

2. While working on the problem, if you thought to yourself, "How can I create a platform attached to the wall?" you used the heuristic of _____ _____ .

3. If it occurred to you suddenly that the matchbox could be used as a platform, this realization would be an example of _____ .

4. If you had a hunch that there might be some similarity between this problem and the string problem in **Figure 8.5** (the similarity is the novel use of an object), your hunch would illustrate the heuristic of _____ _____ _____ .

5. In terms of Greeno's three types of problems, the candle problem is a(n) _____ problem.

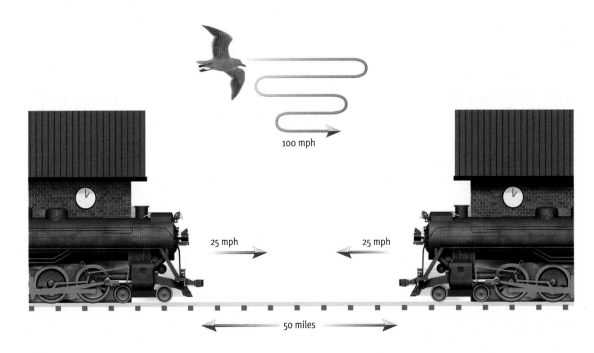

Figure 8.17
Representing the bird and train problem. The typical inclination is to envision this problem spatially, as shown here. However, as the text explains, this representation makes the problem much more difficult than it really is.

100 mph

25 mph   25 mph

50 miles

The solution to the candle problem in Concept Check 8.2.

Craig McClain

Culture, Cognitive Style, and Problem Solving

Do the varied experiences of people from different cultures lead to cross-cultural variations in problem solving? Yes, at least to some degree, as researchers have found cultural differences in the cognitive style that people exhibit in solving problems.

Richard Nisbett and his colleagues (Nisbett et al., 2001; Nisbett & Miyamoto, 2005) have argued that people from East Asian cultures (such as China, Japan, and Korea) display a *holistic cognitive style* that focuses on context and relationships among elements in a field, whereas people from Western cultures (America and Europe) exhibit an *analytic cogni-*

tive style that focuses on objects and their properties rather than context. To put it simply, *Easterners see wholes where Westerners see parts.*

In one test of this hypothesis, Masuda and Nisbett (2001) presented computer-animated scenes of fish and other underwater objects to Japanese and American participants and asked them to report what they had seen. The initial comments of American subjects typically referred to the focal fish, whereas the initial comments of Japanese subjects usually referred to background elements (see **Figure 8.18**). Furthermore, compared to the Americans, the Japanese participants made about 70% more statements about context or background and about twice as many statements about relationships between elements in the scenes. Other studies have also found that people from Asian cultures pay more attention to contextual information than people from North American cultures do (Kitayama et al., 2003).

Cultural variations in analytic versus holistic thinking appear to influence subjects' patterns of logical reasoning, their vulnerability to hindsight bias (see Chapter 7), and their tolerance of contradictions (Nisbett, 2003). Based on these and many other findings, Nisbett et al. (2001) conclude that cultural disparities in cognitive style are substantial and that "literally different cognitive processes are often invoked by East Asians and Westerners dealing with the same problem" (p. 305).

Problems are not the only kind of cognitive challenge that people grapple with on a regular basis. Life also seems to constantly demand decisions. As you might expect, cognitive psychologists have shown great interest in the process of decision making, which is our next subject.

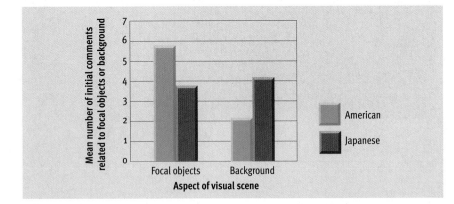

Figure 8.18
Cultural disparities in cognitive style. In one of the studies conducted by Masuda and Nisbett (2001), the participants were asked to describe computer-animated visual scenes. As you can see, the initial comments made by American subjects referred more to focal objects in the scenes, whereas the initial comments made by Japanese subjects referred more to background elements in the scenes. These findings are consistent with the hypothesis that Easterners see wholes (a holistic cognitive style) where Westerners see parts (an analytic cognitive style).

Decision Making: Choices and Chances

Decisions, decisions. Life is full of them. You decided to read this book today. Earlier today you decided when to get up, whether to eat breakfast, and if so, what to eat. Usually you make routine decisions like these with little effort. But on occasion you need to make important decisions that require more thought. Big decisions—such as selecting a car, a home, or a job—tend to be difficult. The alternatives usually have a number of attributes that need to be weighed. For instance, in choosing among several cars, you may want to compare their costs, roominess, fuel economy, handling, acceleration, stylishness, reliability, safety features, and warranties.

Decision making involves evaluating alternatives and making choices among them. Most people try to be systematic and rational in their decision making. However, the work that earned Herbert Simon the 1978 Nobel prize in economics showed that people don't always live up to these goals. Before Simon's work, most traditional theories in economics assumed that people make rational choices to maximize their economic gains. Simon (1957) demonstrated that people have a limited ability to process and evaluate information on numerous facets of possible alternatives. Thus, Simon's *theory of bounded rationality* asserts that people tend to use simple strategies in decision making that focus on only a few facets of available options and often result in "irrational" decisions that are less than optimal.

Spurred by Simon's analysis, psychologists have devoted several decades to the study of how cognitive biases distort people's decision making. This focus on *biases and mistakes* in making decisions may seem a little peculiar, but as Kahneman (1991) has pointed out, the study of people's misguided decisions has illuminated the process of decision making, just as the study of illusions and forgetting has enhanced our understanding of visual perception and memory, respectively.

Making Choices About Preferences: Basic Strategies

Many decisions involve choices about *preferences,* which can be made using a variety of strategies (Goldstein & Hogarth, 1997). In a fascinating recent analysis, Barry Schwartz (2004) has argued that people in modern societies are overwhelmed by an overabundance of such choices about preferences. For example, Schwartz describes how a simple visit to a local supermarket can require a consumer to choose from 285 varieties of cookies, 61 suntan lotions, 150 lipsticks, and 175 salad dressings. Although increased choice is most tangible in the realm of consumer goods, Schwartz argues that it also extends into more significant domains of life. Today, people tend to have unprecedented opportunities to make choices about how they will be educated, how and where they will work, how their intimate relationships will unfold, and even how they will look (because of advances in plastic surgery). Although enormous freedom of choice sounds attractive, Schwartz (2004) argues that the overabundance of choices in modern life has unexpected costs. He argues that people routinely make errors even when choosing among a handful of alternatives and that errors become much more likely when decisions become more complex. And he explains how having more alternatives increases the potential for rumination and postdecision regret. Ultimately, he argues, the malaise associated with choice overload undermines individuals' happiness and contributes to depression. It is hard

People often have to decide between alternative products, such as computers, cars, refrigerators, and so forth, that are not all that different. They often struggle with the abundant choices and delay making a decision. However, as the text explains, extra deliberation does not necessarily lead to better decisions.

web link 8.3

Society for Judgment and Decision Making

The Society for Judgment and Decision Making is an interdisciplinary academic organization dedicated to the study of decision processes. The main attraction for students will be the news section, which profiles recent developments in decision research.

to say whether choice overload is as detrimental to well-being as Schwartz believes, but it is clear that people wrestle with countless choices about preferences, and their reasoning about these decisions is often far from optimal. Let's look at some strategies that people use in making these types of decisions.

Imagine that your friend Boris has found two reasonably attractive apartments and is trying to decide between them. How should he go about selecting between his alternatives? If Boris wanted to use an *additive strategy,* he would list the attributes that influence his decision. Then he would rate the desirability of each apartment on each attribute. For example, let's say that Boris wants to consider four attributes: rent, noise level, distance to campus, and cleanliness. He might make ratings from –3 to +3, like those shown in Table 8.3, add up the ratings for each alternative, and select the one with the largest total. Given the ratings in Table 8.3, Boris should select apartment B. To make an additive strategy more useful, you can *weight* attributes differently, based on their importance (Shafir & LeBoeuf, 2004). For example, if Boris considers distance to campus to be

twice as important as the other considerations, he could multiply his ratings of this attribute by 2. The distance rating would then be +6 for apartment A and –2 for apartment B, and apartment A would become the preferred choice.

People also make choices by gradually eliminating less attractive alternatives (Slovic, 1990; Tversky, 1972). This strategy is called *elimination by aspects* because it assumes that alternatives are eliminated by evaluating them on each attribute or aspect in turn. Whenever any alternative fails to satisfy some minimum criterion for an attribute, it is eliminated from further consideration. To illustrate, suppose Juanita is looking for a new car. She may begin by eliminating all cars that cost over $24,000. Then she may eliminate cars that don't average at least 20 miles per gallon of gas. By continuing to reject choices that don't satisfy some minimum criterion on selected attributes, she can gradually eliminate alternatives until only a single car remains. The final choice in elimination by aspects depends on the order in which attributes are evaluated. For example, if cost was the last attribute Juanita evaluated, she could have previously eliminated all cars that cost under $24,000. If she has only $24,000 to spend, her decision-making strategy would not have brought her very far. Thus, when using elimination by aspects, it's best to evaluate attributes in the order of their importance.

Both the additive and the elimination-by-aspects strategies have advantages, but which strategy do people actually tend to use? Research suggests that people adapt their approach to the demands of the task. When their choices are fairly simple they use additive strategies, but as choices become very complex, they shift toward simpler strategies, such as elimination by aspects (Payne & Bettman, 2004).

Making Choices About Preferences: Quirks and Complexities

Beyond the basics we've been discussing, research has turned up a number of quirks and complexities that people exhibit in making decisions about preferences. Some of the more interesting findings include the following:

• When people decide between various options (let's say two job opportunities), their evaluations of the options' specific attributes (such as salary, commute, and work hours) fluctuate more than most models of decision making anticipated (Shafir & LeBoeuf, 2004). Models of "rational" choice assumed that people know what they like and don't like and that these evaluations would be stable, but research

Table 8.3 Application of the Additive Model to Choosing an Apartment

Attribute	Apartment	
	A	B
Rent	+1	+2
Noise level	–2	+3
Distance to campus	+3	–1
Cleanliness	+2	+2
Total	**+4**	**+6**

suggests otherwise. One reason that these judgments tend to be unstable is that they are swayed by incidental emotional fluctuations (Lerner, Small, & Loewenstein, 2004).

• Another reason these evaluations tend to be inconsistent is that *comparative* evaluations of options tend to yield different results than *separate* evaluations (assessing an option on its own, in isolation) (Hsee, Zhang, & Chen, 2004). For example, when participants directly compare a job with an $80,000 salary at a firm where one's co-workers tend to earn $100,000 against a job with a $70,000 salary at a company where peers earn only $50,000, they rate the $80,000 job as more desirable. However, when two sets of subjects evaluate the same job options in isolation, the $70,000 job is rated as more desirable (LeBoeuf & Shafir, 2005). Thus, the dynamics and implications of comparative and separate evaluations can be quite different.

• A chronic problem faced by decision makers is that although they commonly make choices based on comparative evaluations, the chosen product, activity, or event is actually experienced in isolation (Hsee & Zhang, 2004). This mismatch can lead to decisions that people regret. For example, a shopper may make precise head-to-head comparisons of several speaker systems at an audio store and decide to spend an extra $1500 on the best speakers, but at home the selected speakers will be experienced in isolation. This person may have been delighted with a much less expensive set of speakers if they

had been brought to his or her home and evaluated in isolation.

• Judgments about the quality of various alternatives, such as consumer products, can be swayed by extraneous factors such as brand familiarity and price. In one recent demonstration of this phenomenon, participants tasted wines and rated their quality (Plassmann et al., 2008). In some cases, they thought they were tasting two different wines, but it was the same wine presented at two very different prices (such as $10 and $90). As you might guess, the more "expensive" wines garnered higher ratings. Moreover, brain imaging (fMRI scans) during the wine tasting showed higher activity in a brain region thought to register the actual experienced pleasantness of stimuli when subjects consumed the more "expensive" wine. These findings suggest that people really do get what they pay for in terms of subjective pleasure. And they show that decisions about preferences can be distorted by considerations that should be irrelevant.

Another line of research has looked at whether decisions about preferences work out better when people engage in conscious deliberation or go with intuitive, unconscious feelings based on minimal deliberation. Ap Dijksterhuis and colleagues argue that the answer to this question depends on the complexity of the decision, but probably not in the way you might guess, as you will see in our Featured Study for this chapter.

web link 8.4

Online Decision Research Center Experiments

Michael Birnbaum (California State University, Fullerton) presents a range of continuing and completed experiments conducted online that illustrate how people make decisions.

Intuitive Decisions Versus Careful Deliberation: Which Leads to Better Decisions?

FEATURED STUDY

"Look before you leap," we are told. Conventional wisdom suggests that important, complicated choices require thoughtful deliberation, which is more likely to lead to decisions that prove satisfying. Scientific research on decision making has tended to echo conventional wisdom in touting the benefits of thorough deliberation. But Dijksterhuis and his colleagues (Dijksterhuis, 2004; Dijksterhuis & Nordgren, 2006; Dijksterhuis & van Olden, 2006) have argued that unconscious, intuitive thought processes sometimes lead to better decisions. Why? Primarily, he indicts the limited capacity of conscious thought. As first noted by Herbert Simon and demonstrated in countless studies, people have a surprisingly finite capacity for juggling information on numerous facets of possible options. Although one might guess that careful deliberation ought to be more valuable when choices are complicated, Dijksterhuis and his colleagues hypothesized just the opposite. They predicted that deliberate decisions would be superior to intuitive decisions when choices were simple but that intuitive, unconscious decisions would be superior when choices were complex. We'll examine two of the four studies they conducted to test this proposition.

Study A
Method. Eighty undergraduate participants read information about four hypothetical cars and were asked to choose their favorite. In the simple decision, only 4 attributes of each car were described. In the complex version of the same decision, subjects were given information on 12 attributes of the cars. The desirability of the cars was manipulated by making 75% of the attributes positive for one car, 50% positive for two cars, and 25% positive for one car. So, in both versions of the choice, one of the cars should have stood out as the optimal alternative. In the conscious thought condition, participants were told to mull over their options for 4 minutes and report their choice. In the unconscious thought condition, subjects were distracted from thinking about the decision for 4 minutes (they were

SOURCE: Dijksterhuis, A., Bos, M. W., Nordgren, L. F., & van Baaren, R. B. (2006). On making the right choice: The deliberation-without-attention effect. *Science, 311*(5763), 1005–1007.

Figure 8.19
Conscious versus unconscious decision making in Study A. The percentage of participants who selected the optimal car in each condition is shown here. When the choice was simple (only 4 aspects of the car were described), conscious deliberation proved superior. However, when the choice was more complex (12 aspects to consider), unconscious, intuitive thinking proved superior.

SOURCE: Dijksterhuis, A., Bos, M. W., Nordgren, L. F., & van Baaren, R. B. (2006). On making the right choice: The deliberation-without-attention effect. *Science, 311*(5763), 1005–1007. Copyright © 2006 the American Society for the Study of Science. Reprinted by permission from the AAAS.

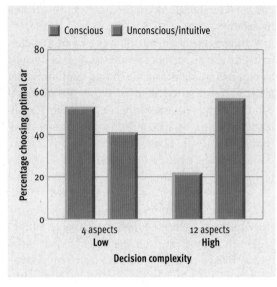

kept busy solving anagrams) and then asked for their choice of the best car.

Results. As you can see in **Figure 8.19**, when the car choice was relatively simple, conscious thought was superior to unconscious thought in selecting the optimal auto. But when the choice was more complicated, unconscious thought was notably superior to conscious deliberation in selecting the best car.

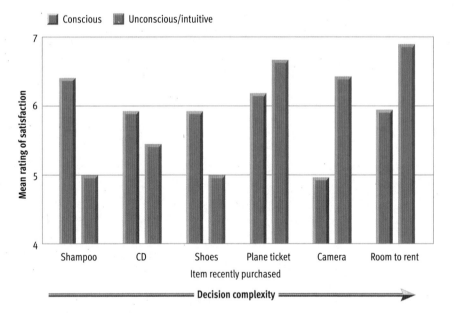

Figure 8.20
Postchoice satisfaction as a function of decision complexity in Study B. Mean ratings of postchoice satisfaction for the six products chosen most often are shown here. The products are arranged, from left to right, in order of increasing decision complexity. For each product, participants' ratings of how much they deliberated about their purchase were split at the median, dividing them into conscious versus unconscious decision makers. When decision complexity was low, conscious deliberation was associated with greater satisfaction, but when decision complexity was high, conscious deliberation was associated with less satisfaction.

SOURCE: Dijksterhuis, A., Bos, M. W., Nordgren, L. F., & van Baaren, R. B. (2006). On making the right choice: The deliberation-without-attention effect. *Science, 311*(5763), 1005–1007. Copyright © 2006 the American Society for the Study of Science. Reprinted by permission from the AAAS.

Study B

Method. Sixty-one student participants indicated how many facets they would evaluate in deciding to purchase 40 consumer products, such as shampoos, shoes, and cameras, yielding a *decision complexity* score for each product. Subsequently, another group of 93 undergraduates picked a product from a list of items that they recently bought and were asked about how much conscious thought they put into the decision and how satisfied they were with their choice.

Results. **Figure 8.20** depicts participants' postchoice satisfaction for the six products that were chosen from the list most frequently, with the products listed in order of decision complexity (from left to right). As predicted, conscious deliberation promoted greater satisfaction when decisions were simple, but just the opposite occurred for complex decisions.

Discussion

The results of these two studies demonstrate what Dijksterhuis calls the *deliberation-without-attention effect*—when people are faced with complex choices, they tend to make better decisions if they don't devote careful attention to the matter. Dijksterhuis believes that deliberations are taking place—but outside of conscious awareness. Thus, like studies of subliminal perception (see Chapter 4) and studies showing that sleep can enhance memory and problem solving (see Chapter 5), this study suggests that unconscious mental processes are more influential than widely assumed. The authors conclude that "there is no *a priori* reason to assume that the deliberation-without-attention effect does not generalize to other types of choices—political, managerial, or otherwise" (p. 1007).

Comment

This research was featured because it provided an elegant test of an interesting hypothesis that seems to defy common sense. It also illustrates the value of approaching an issue with different methodologies. Standing alone, the experimental study (A) on car choices might not be convincing. Four minutes of conscious thought is not much time for testing the efficacy of "careful deliberation," and one could quibble about whether the optimal car was really optimal for all subjects. But, when the carefully controlled experimental study is combined with the more realistic correlational study (B), the converging evidence provides impressive support for the authors' theory.

That said, critics note that it may be premature to broadly generalize these findings to diverse kinds of decision making in the real world (Haslam, 2007). In the studies thus far, even the "complex" choices have involved relatively simple decisions about product preferences. It is quite a leap to assume that physicians, corporate managers, and government leaders, who confront choices of profound complexity and importance, would make better decisions if they avoided careful deliberation. Although other lines of research also suggest that intuition can sometimes be superior to logic and reflection (Gladwell, 2005; Myers, 2002), the boundary conditions of this phenomenon need to be determined.

Taking Chances: Factors Weighed in Risky Decisions

Suppose you have the chance to play a dice game in which you might win some money. You must decide whether it would be to your advantage to play. You're going to roll a fair die. If the number 6 appears, you win $5. If one of the other five numbers appears, you win nothing. It costs you $1 every time you play. Should you participate?

This problem calls for a type of decision making that is somewhat different from making choices about preferences. In selecting alternatives that reflect preferences, people generally weigh known outcomes (apartment A will require a long commute to campus, car B will get 30 miles per gallon, and so forth). In contrast, *risky decision making* involves making choices under conditions of uncertainty. Uncertainty exists when people don't know what will happen. At best, they know the probability that a particular event will occur.

One way to decide whether to play the dice game would be to figure out the *expected value* of participation in the game. To do so, you would need to calculate the average amount of money you could expect to win or lose each time you play. The value of a win is $4 ($5 minus the $1 entry fee). The value of a loss is –$1. To calculate expected value, you also need to know the probability of a win or loss. Since a die has six faces, the probability of a win is 1 out of 6, and the probability of a loss is 5 out of 6. Thus, on five out of every six trials, you lose $1. On one out of six, you win $4. The game is beginning to sound unattractive, isn't it? We can figure out the precise expected value as follows:

$$\text{Expected value} = (\tfrac{1}{6} \times 4) + (\tfrac{5}{6} \times -1)$$
$$= \tfrac{4}{6} + (-\tfrac{5}{6}) = -\tfrac{1}{6}$$

The expected value of this game is $-\tfrac{1}{6}$ of a dollar, which means that you lose an average of about 17 cents per turn. Now that you know the expected value, surely you won't agree to play. Or will you?

If we want to understand why people make the decisions they do, the concept of expected value is not enough. People frequently behave in ways that are inconsistent with expected value (Slovic, Lichtenstein, & Fischhoff, 1988). Anytime the expected value is negative, a gambler should expect to lose money. Yet a great many people gamble at racetracks and casinos and buy lottery tickets. Although they realize that the odds are against them, they continue to gamble. Even people who don't gamble buy homeowner's insurance, which has a negative expected value. After all, when you buy insurance,

your expectation (and hope!) is that you will lose money on the deal.

To explain decisions that violate expected value, some theories replace the objective value of an outcome with its *subjective utility* (Fischhoff, 1988). Subjective utility represents what an outcome is personally worth to an individual. For example, buying a few lottery tickets may allow you to dream about becoming wealthy. Buying insurance may give you a sense of security. Subjective utilities like these vary from one person to another. Interestingly, however, studies show that people often make inaccurate predictions about how much subjective utility or enjoyment various experiences will yield (Loewenstein & Schkade, 1999).

Heuristics in Judging Probabilities

 7f

- What are your chances of passing your next psychology test if you study only 3 hours?
- How likely is a major downturn in the stock market during the upcoming year?
- What are the odds of your getting into graduate school in the field of your choice?

These questions ask you to make probability estimates. Amos Tversky and Daniel Kahneman (1974, 1982; Kahneman & Tversky, 2000) have conducted extensive research on the *heuristics,* or mental shortcuts, that people use in grappling with probabilities. This research on heuristics earned Kahneman the Nobel prize in economics in 2002 (unfortunately, his collaborator, Amos Tversky, died in 1996).

Availability is one such heuristic. The *availability heuristic* involves basing the estimated probability of an event on the ease with which relevant instances come to mind. For example, you may estimate the divorce rate by recalling the number of divorces among your friends' parents. Recalling specific instances of an event is a reasonable strategy to use in estimating the event's probability. However, if instances occur frequently but you have difficulty retrieving them from memory, your estimate will be biased. For instance, it's easier to think of words that begin with a certain letter than words that contain that letter at some other position. Hence, people should tend to respond that there are more words starting with the letter *K* than words having a *K* in the third position. To test this hypothesis, Tversky and Kahneman (1973) selected five consonants (*K, L, N, R, V*) that occur more frequently in the third position of a word than in the first. Subjects were asked whether each of the letters appears more often in the first or third position. Most of the subjects

Daniel Kahneman

"The human mind suppresses uncertainty. We're not only convinced that we know more about our politics, our businesses, and our spouses than we really do, but also that what we don't know must be unimportant."

Amos Tversky

"People treat their own cases as if they were unique, rather than part of a huge lottery. You hear this silly argument that 'The odds don't apply to me.' Why should God, or whoever runs this lottery, give you special treatment?"

erroneously believed that all five letters were much more frequent in the first than in the third position, confirming the hypothesis.

Representativeness is another guide in estimating probabilities identified by Kahneman and Tversky (1982). **The *representativeness heuristic* involves basing the estimated probability of an event on how similar it is to the typical prototype of that event.** To illustrate, imagine that you flip a coin six times and keep track of how often the result is heads (H) or tails (T). Which of the following sequences is more likely?

1. T T T T T T
2. H T T H T H

People generally believe that the second sequence is more likely. After all, coin tossing is a random affair, and the second sequence looks much more representative of a random process than the first. In reality, the probability of each exact *sequence* is precisely the same ($\frac{1}{2} \times \frac{1}{2} \times \frac{1}{2} \times \frac{1}{2} \times \frac{1}{2} \times \frac{1}{2} = \frac{1}{64}$). Overdependence on the representativeness heuristic has been used to explain quite a variety of decision-making tendencies (Teigen, 2004), as you will see in the upcoming pages.

The Tendency to Ignore Base Rates

Steve is very shy and withdrawn, invariably helpful, but with little interest in people or in the world of real-

ity. A meek and tidy soul, he has a need for order and structure and a passion for detail. Do you think Steve is a salesperson or a librarian? (Adapted from Tversky & Kahneman, 1974, p. 1124)

Using the *representativeness heuristic,* subjects tend to guess that Steve is a librarian because he resembles their prototype of a librarian (Tversky & Kahneman, 1982). In reality, this is not a wise guess, because it *ignores the base rates* of librarians and salespeople in the population. Virtually everyone knows that salespeople outnumber librarians by a wide margin (roughly 75 to 1 in the United States). This fact makes it much more likely that Steve is in sales. But in estimating probabilities, people often ignore information on base rates.

Researchers are still debating how common it is for people to neglect base rate information (Birnbaum, 2004; Koehler, 1996), but it does not appear to be a rare event. Indeed, evidence indicates that people are particularly bad about applying base rates to themselves. For instance, Weinstein (1984; Weinstein & Klein, 1995) has found that people underestimate the risks of their own health-impairing habits while viewing others' risks much more accurately. Thus, smokers are realistic in estimating the degree to which smoking increases someone else's risk of heart attack but underestimate the risk for themselves. Similarly, people starting new companies ignore the high failure rate for new businesses, and burglars underestimate the likelihood that they

---

concept check 8.3

Recognizing Heuristics in Decision Making

Check your understanding of heuristics in decision making by trying to identify the heuristics used in the following example. Each numbered element in the anecdote below illustrates a problem-solving heuristic. Write the relevant heuristic in the space on the left. You can find the answers in Appendix A.

_____ 1. Marsha can't decide on a college major. She evaluates all the majors available at her college on the attributes of how much she would enjoy them (likability), how challenging they are (difficulty), and how good the job opportunities are in the field (employability). She drops from consideration any major that she regards as "poor" on any of these three attributes.

_____ 2. When she considers history as a major, she thinks to herself, "Gee, I know four history graduates who are still looking for work," and concludes that the probability of getting a job using a history degree is very low.

_____ 3. She finds that every major gets a "poor" rating on at least one attribute, so she eliminates everything. Because this is unacceptable, she decides she has to switch to another strategy. Marsha finally focuses her consideration on five majors that received just one "poor" rating. She uses a 4-point scale to rate each of these majors on each of the three attributes she values. She adds up the ratings and selects the major with the highest total as her leading candidate.

will end up in jail. Thus, in risky decision making, people often think that they can beat the odds. As Amos Tversky puts it, "People treat their own cases as if they were unique, rather than part of a huge lottery. You hear this silly argument that 'The odds don't apply to me.' Why should God, or whoever runs this lottery, give you special treatment?" (McKean, 1985, p. 27).

The Conjunction Fallacy

Imagine that you're going to meet a man who is an articulate, ambitious, power-hungry wheeler-dealer. Do you think it's more likely that he's a college teacher or a college teacher who's also a politician?

People tend to guess that the man is a "college teacher who's a politician" because the description fits with the typical prototype of politicians. But stop and think for a moment. The broader category of college teachers completely includes the smaller subcategory of college teachers who are politicians (see Figure 8.21). The probability of being in the subcategory cannot be higher than the probability of being in the broader category. It's a logical impossibility!

Tversky and Kahneman (1983) call this error the *conjunction fallacy.* The *conjunction fallacy* occurs when people estimate that the odds of two uncertain events happening together are greater than the odds of either event happening alone. The conjunction fallacy has been observed in a number of studies and has generally been attributed to the influence of the representativeness heuristic (Epstein, Donovan, & Denes-Raj, 1999), although some doubts have been raised about this interpretation (Fisk, 2004).

Evolutionary Analyses of Flaws in Human Decision Making

A central conclusion of the last 30 years of research on decision making has been that human decision-making strategies are riddled with errors and biases

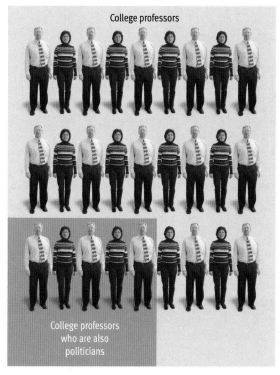

College professors

College professors who are also politicians

Figure 8.21
The conjunction fallacy. Subjects often fall victim to the conjunction fallacy, but as this diagram makes obvious, the probability of being in a subcategory (college teachers who are politicians) cannot be higher than the probability of being in the broader category (college teachers). As this case illustrates, it often helps to represent a problem in a diagram.

that yield surprisingly irrational results (Goldstein & Hogarth, 1997; Risen & Gilovich, 2007; Shafir & LeBoeuf, 2002). Theorists have discovered that people have "mental limitations" and have concluded that people are not as bright and rational as they think they are. This broad conclusion has led some evolutionary psychologists to reconsider the work on human decision making, and their take on the matter is quite interesting. First, they argue that traditional decision research has imposed an invalid and unrealistic standard of rationality, which assumes that people should be impeccable in applying the laws of deductive logic and statistical probability while objectively and precisely weighing multiple factors in arriving at decisions (Gigerenzer, 2000). Second, they argue that humans only *seem* irrational because cognitive psychologists have been asking the wrong questions and formulating problems in the wrong ways—ways that have nothing to do

**John Tooby and
Leda Cosmides**

*"The problems our cognitive
devices are designed to solve
do not reflect the problems our
modern life experiences lead
us to see as normal...Instead,
they are the ancient and seemingly esoteric problems that
our hunter-gatherer ancestors encountered generation
after generation over hominid
evolution."*

web link 8.5

**Has Natural Selection
Shaped How Humans
Reason?**

This link will take you to a presentation by Leda Cosmides
and John Tooby (University
of California, Santa Barbara)
in which they discuss their
evolutionary perspective on
human decision making.

with the adaptive problems that the human mind
has evolved to solve (Cosmides & Tooby, 1996).

According to Leda Cosmides and John Tooby
(1994, 1996), the human mind consists of a large
number of specialized cognitive mechanisms that
have emerged over the course of evolution to solve
specific adaptive problems, such as finding food,
shelter, and mates and dealing with allies and enemies. Thus, human decision and problem-solving
strategies have been tailored to handle real-world
adaptive problems. Participants perform poorly in
cognitive research, say Cosmides and Tooby, because
it confronts them with contrived, artificial problems
that do not involve natural categories and have no
adaptive significance.

For example, evolutionary psychologists argue
that the human mind is wired to think in terms of
raw frequencies rather than *base rates and probabilities* (Gigerenzer, 1997, 2000). Asking about the probability of a single event is routine in today's world,
where we are inundated with statistical data ranging
from batting averages to weather predictions. But
our ancient ancestors had access to little data other
than their own observations, which were accumulating counts of natural frequencies, such as "we had
a good hunt three out of the last five times we went
to the north plains." Thus, evolutionary theorists
assert that many errors in human reasoning, such
as neglect of base rates and the conjunction fallacy,
should vanish if classic laboratory problems are reformulated in terms of raw frequencies rather than
probabilities and base rates.

Consistent with this analysis, evolutionary psychologists have shown that some errors in reasoning
that are seen in laboratory studies disappear or are
decreased when problems are presented in ways that
resemble the type of input humans would have processed in ancestral times (Brase, Cosmides & Tooby,
1998; Gigerenzer & Hoffrage, 1999; Hertwig & Gigerenzer, 1999). Although there is plenty of room for
debate (Mellers, Hertwig & Kahneman, 2001; Shafir
& LeBoeuf, 2002), this evidence and a couple of
other lines of research are gradually reducing cognitive psychologists' tendency to characterize human
reasoning as "irrational."

Fast and Frugal Heuristics

To further expand on the evolutionary point of view,
Gerd Gigerenzer has argued that humans' reasoning
largely depends on "fast and frugal heuristics" that
are quite a bit simpler than the complicated mental
processes studied in traditional cognitive research
(Gigerenzer, 2000, 2004, 2008; Todd & Gigerenzer,

2000, 2007). According to Gigerenzer, organisms
from toads to stockbrokers have to make fast decisions under demanding circumstances with limited
information. In most instances organisms (including humans) do not have the time, resources, or cognitive capacities to gather all the relevant information, consider all the possible options, calculate all
the probabilities and risks, and then make the statistically optimal decision. Instead, they use quick and
dirty heuristics that are less than perfect but that
work well enough most of the time to be adaptive in
the real world.

To explore these fast and frugal heuristics, Gigerenzer and his colleagues have typically studied inferences from *memory,* which challenge participants
to search some portion of their general knowledge,
rather than inferences from *givens,* which challenge
participants to draw logical conclusions from information provided by the experimenter. What has
this research revealed? It has demonstrated that fast
and frugal heuristics can be surprisingly effective.
One heuristic that is often used in selecting between
alternatives based on some quantitative dimension
is the *recognition heuristic,* which works as follows: If
one of two alternatives is recognized and the other
is not, infer that the recognized alternative has the
higher value. Consider the following questions—
Which city has more inhabitants: San Diego or San
Antonio? Hamburg or Munich? In choosing between
U.S. cities, American college students weighed a lifetime of facts useful for inferring population and
made the correct choice 71% of the time; in choosing between German cities about which they knew
very little, the same students depended on the recognition heuristic and chose correctly 73% of the
time (Goldstein & Gigerenzer, 2002). Thus, the recognition heuristic allowed students to perform just
as well with very limited knowledge as they did with
extensive knowledge.

Gigerenzer and his colleagues have studied a variety of other quick, one-reason decision-making
strategies and demonstrated that they can yield inferences that are just as accurate as much more elaborate and time-consuming strategies that carefully
weigh many factors. And they have demonstrated
that people actually use these fast and frugal heuristics in a diverse array of situations (Gigerenzer &
Todd, 1999; Rieskamp & Hoffrage, 1999). Thus, the
study of fast and frugal heuristics promises to be
an intriguing new line of research in the study of
human decision making.

How have traditional decision-making theorists
responded to the challenge presented by Gigerenzer
and other evolutionary theorists? They acknowledge
that people often rely on fast and frugal heuristics,

but they argue that this finding does not make decades of research on carefully reasoned approaches to decision making meaningless. Rather, they propose *dual-process theories,* which posit that people depend on two very different modes or systems of thinking when making decisions (De Neys, 2006; Kahneman, 2003; Kahneman & Frederick, 2005; Stanovich & West, 2002). One system consists of quick, simple, effortless, automatic judgments, like Gigerenzer's fast and frugal heuristics, which traditional theorists prefer to characterize as "intuitive

thinking." The second system consists of slower, more elaborate, effortful, controlled judgments, like those studied in traditional decision research. According to this view, the second system monitors and corrects the intuitive system as needed and takes over when complicated or important decisions loom. Thus, traditional theorists maintain that fast and frugal heuristics and reasoned, rule-governed decision strategies exist side-by-side and that both need to be studied to fully understand decision making.

Gerd Gigerenzer

"These 'fast and frugal' heuristics operate with simple psychological principles that satisfy the constraints of limited time, knowledge, and computational might, rather than those of classical rationality."

REVIEW of Key Learning Goals

8.12 Simon's theory of bounded rationality suggests that human decision strategies are simplistic and often yield irrational results. Schwartz argues that in modern societies people suffer from choice overload, which leads to rumination, regret, and diminished well-being.

8.13 An additive decision model is used when people make decisions by rating the attributes of each alternative and selecting the alternative that has the highest sum of ratings. When elimination by aspects is used, people gradually eliminate alternatives whose attributes fail to satisfy some minimum criterion. To some extent, people adapt their decision-making strategy to the situation, moving toward simpler strategies when choices become complex.

8.14 In making decisions, evaluations of options fluctuate more than expected. Comparative evaluations of options often yield different results than separate evaluations. Judgments of products may be influenced by their prices. Our Featured Study on the deliberation-without-attention effect showed that intuitive, unconscious decisions may be more satisfying than those based on conscious deliberation, especially when choices are complex.

8.15 Risky decision making involves making choices under conditions of uncertainty. Models of how people make risky

decisions focus on the expected value or subjective utility of various outcomes.

8.16 The availability heuristic involves basing probability estimates on the ease with which relevant examples come to mind. The representativeness heuristic involves basing the estimated probability of an event on how similar it is to the prototype of that event.

8.17 In estimating probabilities, people often ignore information on base rates due to the influence of the representativeness heuristic. The conjunction fallacy occurs when people estimate that the odds of two uncertain events happening together are greater than the odds of either event happening alone.

8.18 Evolutionary psychologists maintain that many errors and biases in human reasoning are greatly reduced when problems are presented in ways that resemble the type of input humans would have processed in ancestral times.

8.19 Gigerenzer argues that people largely depend on fast and frugal decision heuristics that are adaptive in the real world. Research shows that these simple heuristics can be surprisingly effective. Dual-process theories propose that people depend on two different modes of thinking in making decisions: fast and frugal heuristics and effortful, controlled deliberation.

web link 8.6

Simple Minds—Smart Choices

This link leads to an article from *Science News* on Gerd Gigerenzer's research, which suggests that decisions can be made quickly and accurately with remarkably simple strategies.

Reflecting on the Chapter's Themes

Four of our unifying themes have been especially prominent in this chapter. The first is the continuing question about the relative influence of heredity and environment. The controversy about how children acquire language skills replays the nature versus nurture debate. The behaviorist theory, that children learn language through imitation and reinforcement, emphasizes the importance of the environment. The nativist theory, that children come equipped with an innate language acquisition device, argues for the importance of biology. The debate is far from settled, but the accumulating evidence suggests that language development depends on both nature and nurture, as more recent interactionist theories have proposed.

The second pertinent theme is the empirical nature of psychology. For many decades, psychologists

paid little attention to cognitive processes, because most of them assumed that thinking is too private to be studied scientifically. During the 1950s and 1960s, however, psychologists began to devise creative new ways to measure mental processes. These innovations fueled the cognitive revolution that put the *psyche* (the mind) back in psychology. Thus, once again, we see how empirical methods are the lifeblood of the scientific enterprise.

Third, the study of cognitive processes shows how there are both similarities and differences across cultures in behavior. On the one hand, we saw that language development unfolds in much the same way in widely disparate cultures. On the other hand, we learned that there are interesting cultural variations in cognitive style.

Key Learning Goals

8.20 Identify the four unifying themes highlighted in this chapter.

Heredity and Environment

Empiricism

Cultural Heritage

Subjectivity of Experience

The fourth theme is the subjective nature of human experience. We have seen that decision making is a highly subjective process. The subjectivity of decision processes will continue to be prominent in the upcoming Personal Application, which discusses some more common pitfalls in reasoning about decisions.

PERSONAL

APPLICATION

Understanding Pitfalls in Reasoning About Decisions

Key Learning Goals

8.21 Explain what is meant by the gambler's fallacy and the tendency to overestimate the improbable.

8.22 Describe the propensity to seek confirming information and the overconfidence effect.

8.23 Analyze the effects of framing and loss aversion on decisions.

Consider the following scenario:

Laura is in a casino watching people play roulette. The 38 slots in the roulette wheel include 18 black numbers, 18 red numbers, and 2 green numbers. Hence, on any one spin, the probability of red or black is slightly less than 50-50 (.474 to be exact). Although Laura hasn't been betting, she has been following the pattern of results in the game very carefully. The ball has landed in red seven times in a row. Laura concludes that black is long overdue and she jumps into the game, betting heavily on black.

Has Laura made a good bet? Do you agree with Laura's reasoning? Or do you think that Laura misunderstands the laws of probability? You'll find out momentarily, as we discuss how people reason their way to decisions—and how their reasoning can go awry.

The pioneering work of Amos Tversky and Daniel Kahneman (1974, 1982) led to an explosion of research on risky decision making. In their efforts to identify the heuristics that people use in decision making, investigators stumbled onto quite a few misconceptions, oversights, and biases. It turns out that people deviate in predictable ways from optimal decision strategies—with surprising regularity (Goldstein & Hogarth, 1997). As explained in the chapter, recent evolutionary research on decision making has offered a new explanation for *why* our decision making appears to be muddled. And evolutionary theorists argue that our decision strategies actually are rational—when viewed as evolved mechanisms designed to solve the adaptive problems faced in ancestral times (Cosmides & Tooby, 1996).

But, while the evolutionary explanations for our foibles in reasoning *may* be on target, the fact remains that *we do not live in ancestral times*. We live in the information age and we have to deal with base rates, probabilities, and percentages on a routine basis. In our modern world, reproductive fitness surely depends more on SAT scores than on counting berries. So, mainstream cognitive research on flaws in human reasoning about decisions remains relevant (Stanovich, 2003).

Moreover, recent research suggests that people exhibit consistent differences in the ability to reason effectively about decisions. Parker and Fischoff (2005) developed a scale to measure seven skills required for competent decision making. Their initial study indicated that people vary considerably in their talent for making sound decisions. In a follow-up study, they found that people who score relatively high on their scale tend to report fewer negative life events indicative of poor decision making than people who score relatively low (de Bruin, Parker, & Fischoff, 2007). Fortunately, research indicates that increased awareness of common shortcomings in reasoning about decisions can lead to improved decision making (Agnoli & Krantz, 1989; Fischhoff, 1982; Keren, 1990). With this goal in mind, let's look at some common pitfalls in decision making.

The Gambler's Fallacy

7f

As you may have guessed by now, Laura's reasoning in our opening scenario is flawed. A great many people tend to believe that Laura has made a good bet (Stanovich, 2003; Tversky & Kahneman, 1982). However, they're wrong. Laura's behavior illustrates the *gambler's fallacy*—the belief that the odds of a chance event increase if the event hasn't occurred recently. People believe that the laws of probability should yield fair results. If they believe that a process is random, they expect the process to be self-correcting (Burns & Corpus, 2004). These aren't bad assumptions in the long run. However, they don't apply to individual, independent events.

The roulette wheel does not remember its recent results and make adjustments for them. Each spin of the wheel is an independent event. The probability of black on each spin remains at .474, even if red comes up 100 times in a row! The gambler's fallacy reflects the pervasive influence of the *representativeness heuristic*. In betting on black, Laura is predicting that future results will be more representative of a random process. This logic can be used to estimate the probability of black across a *string of spins*. But it doesn't apply to a *specific spin* of the roulette wheel.

Overestimating the Improbable

7f

Various causes of death are paired up below. In each pairing, which is the more likely cause of death?

> *Asthma or tornadoes?*
> *Accidental falls or shooting accidents?*
> *Tuberculosis or floods?*
> *Suicide or murder?*

Table 8.4 shows the actual mortality rates for each of the causes of death just listed. As you can see, the first choice in each pair is the more common cause of death. If you guessed wrong for several pairings, don't feel bad. Like many other people, you may be a victim of the tendency to *overestimate the improbable*. People tend to greatly overestimate the likelihood of dramatic, vivid—but infrequent—events that receive heavy media coverage. Thus, the number of fatalities due to tornadoes, shooting accidents, floods, and murders is usually overestimated (Slovic, Fischhoff, & Lichtenstein, 1982). Fatalities due to asthma and other common diseases, which receive less media coverage, tend to be underestimated. For instance, a majority of subjects estimate that tornadoes kill more people than asthma, even though asthma fatalities outnumber tornado fatalities by a ratio of 80 to 1. This tendency to exaggerate the improbable has generally been attributed to operation of the *availability heuristic* (Reber, 2004). Instances of floods, tornadoes, and such are readily available in memory because people are exposed to a great deal of media coverage of such events.

Table 8.4 Actual Mortality Rates for Selected Causes of Death

Cause of Death	Rate	Cause of Death	Rate
Asthma	2,000	Tornadoes	25
Accidental falls	6,021	Firearms accidents	320
Tuberculosis	400	Floods	44
Suicide	11,300	Homicide	6,800

Note: Mortality rates are per 100 million people and are based on the Statistical Abstract of the United States, 2001.

As a general rule, people's beliefs about what they should fear tend to be surprisingly inconsistent with actual probabilities (Glassner, 1999). This propensity has been especially prominent in the aftermath of 9/11, which left countless people extremely worried about the possibility of being harmed in a terrorist attack (as the terrorists intended). To date, one's chances of being hurt in a terrorist attack are utterly microscopic in comparison to one's chances of *perishing* in an automobile accident, yet people worry about the former and not the latter (Myers, 2001). People tend to overestimate the likelihood of rare events when their estimates are based on descriptive information (such as media coverage) as opposed to when their estimates are based on personal experiences (Hertwig et al., 2004).

Confirmation Bias

Imagine a young physician examining a sick patient. The patient is complaining of a high fever and a sore throat. The physician must decide on a diagnosis from among a myriad possible diseases. The physician thinks that it may be the flu. She asks the patient if he feels "achey all over." The answer is "yes." The physician asks if the symptoms began a few days ago. Again, the response is "yes." The physician concludes that the patient has the flu. (Adapted from Halpern, 1984, pp. 215–216)

Do you see any flaws in the physician's reasoning? Has she probed into the causes of the patient's malady effectively? No, she has asked about symptoms that would be

The availability heuristic can be dramatized by juxtaposing the unrelated phenomena of floods and tuberculosis (TB). Many people are killed by floods, but far more die from tuberculosis (see **Table 8.4**). However, since the news media report flood fatalities frequently and prominently, but rarely focus on deaths from tuberculosis, people tend to assume that flood-related deaths are more common.

consistent with her preliminary diagnosis, but she has not inquired about symptoms that could rule it out. Her questioning of the patient illustrates *confirmation bias*— **the tendency to only seek information that is likely to support one's decisions and beliefs.** This bias is common in medical diagnosis and other forms of decision making (Nickerson, 1998). There's nothing wrong with searching for confirming evidence to support one's decisions. However, people should also seek disconfirming evidence—which they often neglect to do. A closely related problem is *predecisional distortion* of information (Carlson, Meloy, & Russo, 2006). When people confront a choice, they often have an initial inclination to lean one way or the other. This slant often leads to biased evaluations of incoming information that bolster one's initial choice. Recent research demonstrates that predecisional distortion can induce participants to choose inferior alternatives (Russo, Carlson, & Meloy, 2006).

The Overconfidence Effect 7f

Make high and low estimates of the total U.S. Defense Department budget in the year 2007. Choose estimates far enough apart to be 98% confident that the actual figure lies between them. In other words, you should feel that there is only a 2% chance that the correct figure is lower than your low estimate or higher than your high estimate. Write your estimates in the spaces provided, before reading further.

    High estimate: _____

    Low estimate: _____

When working on problems like this one, people reason their way to their best estimate and then create a confidence interval around it. For instance, let's say that you arrived at $300 billion as your best estimate of the defense budget. You would then expand a range around that estimate—say $250 billion to $350 billion—that you're sure will contain the correct figure. The answer in this case is $439 billion. If the answer falls outside your estimated range, you are not unusual. In making this type of estimate, people consistently tend to make their confidence intervals too narrow (Epley &

Gilovich, 2006; Lichtenstein, Fischhoff, & Phillips, 1982; Soll & Klayman, 2004). For example, subjects' 98% confidence intervals should include the correct answer 98% of the time, but they actually do so only about 60% of the time.

The crux of the problem is that people tend to put too much faith in their estimates, beliefs, and decisions, even when they should know better, a principle called the *overconfidence effect.* People vary considerably in their tendency to be overconfident (Stanovich, 1999), but overconfidence effects are very frequent (West & Stanovich, 1997). Studies have shown that physicians, weather forecasters, military leaders, gamblers, investors, and scientists tend to be overconfident about their predictions. As Daniel Kahneman puts it, "The human mind suppresses uncertainty. We're not only convinced that we know more about our politics, our businesses, and our spouses than we really do, but also that what we don't know must be unimportant" (McKean, 1985, p. 27). Thus, the overconfidence effect sometimes leads people to ignore useful sources of information that might well improve their predictions (Sieck & Arkes, 2005).

The Effects of Framing 7f

Another consideration in making decisions involving risks is the framing of questions (Tversky & Kahneman, 1988, 1991). *Framing* **refers to how decision issues are posed or how choices are structured.** People often allow a decision to be shaped by the language or context in which it's presented, rather than explore it from different perspectives. Consider the following scenario, which is adapted from Kahneman and Tversky (1984, p. 343):

Imagine that the U.S. is preparing for the outbreak of a dangerous disease, which is expected to kill 600 people. Two alternative programs to combat the disease have been proposed. Assume that the exact scientific estimates of the consequences of the programs are as follows.

    • *If Program A is adopted, 200 people will be saved.*

    • *If Program B is adopted, there is a one-third probability that all 600 people will be saved and a two-thirds probability that no people will be saved.*

Kahneman and Tversky found that 72% of their subjects chose the "sure thing" (Program A) over the "risky gamble" (Program B). However, they obtained different results when the alternatives were reframed as follows:

    • *If Program C is adopted, 400 people will die.*

    • *If Program D is adopted, there is a one-third probability that nobody will die and a two-thirds probability that all 600 people will die.*

Although framed differently, Programs A and B represent exactly the same probability situation as Programs C and D (see **Figure 8.22**). In spite of this equivalence, 78% of the subjects chose Program D. Thus, sub-

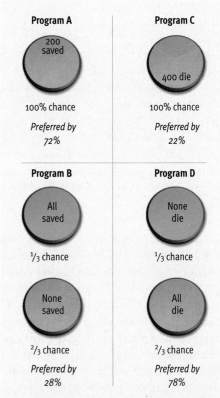

Figure 8.22

The framing of questions. This chart shows that Programs A and B are parallel in probability to Programs C and D, but these parallel pairs of alternatives lead subjects to make different choices. Studies show that when choices are framed in terms of possible gains, people prefer the safer plan. However, when choices are framed in terms of losses, people are more willing to take a gamble.

jects chose the sure thing when the decision was framed in terms of lives saved, but they went with the risky gamble when the decision was framed in terms of lives lost. Obviously, sound decision making should yield consistent decisions that are not altered dramatically by superficial changes in how options are presented, so framing effects once again highlight the foibles of human decision making.

The Specter of Regret and Loss Aversion

A surprisingly influential factor in decision making is the need to avoid regret about making a bad decision. People routinely think about how much regret they are likely to experience if the selection of a particular option backfires (Connolly & Zeelenberg, 2002). These estimates of anticipated regret are weighed heavily and often lead people to make overly cautious decisions. Interestingly, research suggests that people tend to overestimate how much regret they will experience as a result of poor decisions (Gilbert et al., 2004).

A related phenomenon is *loss aversion*—in general, losses loom larger than gains of equal size (Kahneman & Tversky, 1979; Novemsky & Kahneman, 2005). Thus, most people expect that the negative impact of losing $1000 will be greater than the positive impact of wining $1000. Loss aversion can lead people to pass up excellent opportunities. For instance, subjects tend to decline a theoretical gamble in which they are given an 85% chance of doubling their life savings versus a 15% chance of losing their life savings, which mathematically is vastly more attractive than any bet one could place in a casino (Gilbert, 2006). Loss aversion can influence decisions in many areas of life, including choices of consumer goods, investments, business negotiations, and approaches to health care (Camerer, 2005; Klapper, Ebling, & Temme, 2005). The problem with loss aversion is that, as Daniel Gilbert and his colleagues have shown, people generally overestimate the intensity and duration of the negative emotions they will experience after all sorts of losses, ranging from losing a job or romantic partner to botching an interview or watching one's

team lose in a big game (Gilbert, Driver-Linn, & Wilson, 2002; Kermer et al., 2006) (see Chapter 10). Interestingly, people overestimate the emotional impact of losses because they do not appreciate how good most of us are at rationalizing, discounting, and distorting negative events in our lives. In any event, well-informed decision makers should be aware of how the specter of regret and loss aversion can sway their everyday decisions.

REVIEW of Key Learning Goals

8.21 The gambler's fallacy is the belief that the odds of a chance event increase if the event hasn't occurred recently. People tend to inflate estimates of improbable events that garner heavy coverage in the media, because of the availability heuristic.

8.22 People often exhibit confirmation bias— the tendency to only seek information that supports one's view. In making predictions and estimates people tend to be overly confident about their forecasts.

8.23 Framing refers to how decision issues are posed or how choices are structured. Decisions can be influenced by the language in which they are framed. Most people expect that the negative impact of a loss will be greater than the positive impact of a similar gain, but research shows that people overestimate the impact of losses.

Key Learning Goals

8.24 Recognize key language manipulation strategies that people use to shape others' thought.

Shaping Thought with Language: "Only a Naïve Moron Would Believe That"

As explained in the chapter, the *linguistic relativity hypothesis* asserts that different languages may lead people to think about things differently. Given the power of language, it should come as no surprise that carefully chosen words and labels (within a specific language) can exert subtle influence on people's feelings about various issues (Calvert, 1997; Johnson & Dowling-Guyer, 1996; Pohl, 2004; Weatherall, 1992). In everyday life, many people clearly recognize that language can tilt thought along certain lines. This possibility is the basis for some of the concerns that have been expressed about sexist language. Women who object to being called "girls," "chicks," and "babes" believe that these terms influence the way people think about and interact with women. In a similar vein, used car dealers that sell "preowned cars" and airlines that outline precautions for "water landings" are manipulating language to influence thought. Indeed, bureaucrats,

politicians, advertisers, and big business have refined the art of shaping thought by tinkering with language, and to a lesser degree the same techniques are used by many people in everyday interactions. Let's look at two of these techniques: semantic slanting and name calling.

Semantic Slanting

Semantic slanting refers to deliberately choosing words to create specific emotional responses. For example, consider the crafty word choices made in the incendiary debate about abortion (Halpern, 1996). The anti-abortion movement recognized that it is better to be *for* something than to be *against* something and then decided to characterize its stance as "pro-life" rather than "anti-choice." Likewise, the faction that favored abortion did not like the connotation of an "anti-life" or "pro-abortion" campaign, so they characterized their position as "pro-choice." The position advocated is exactly the same either way, but the label clearly influences how people respond. Thinking

along similar lines, some "pro-life" advocates have asserted that the best way to win the debate about abortion is to frequently use the words *kill* and *baby* in the same sentence (Kahane, 1992). Obviously, these are words that push people's buttons and trigger powerful emotional responses.

In his fascinating book *Doublespeak,* William Lutz (1989) describes an endless series of examples of how government, business, and advertisers manipulate language to bias people's thoughts and feelings. For example, in the language of the military, an invasion is a "preemptive counterattack," bombing the enemy is providing "air support," a retreat is a "backloading of augmentation personnel," civilians accidentally killed or wounded by military strikes are "collateral damage," and troops killed by their own troops are "friendly casualties." In the world of business, layoffs and firings become "headcount reductions," "workforce adjustments," or "career alternative enhancement programs," whereas bad debts become "nonperforming assets." And in the language of bureaucrats, hospital deaths become "negative patient care outcomes" and tax increases become "revenue enhancement initiatives," leading Lutz to quip that "Nothing in life is certain except negative patient care outcome and revenue enhancement." You can't really appreciate how absurd this process can become until you go shopping for "genuine imitation leather" or "real counterfeit diamonds."

Of course, you don't have to be a bureaucrat or military spokesperson to use semantic slanting. For example, if a friend of yours is annoyed at her 60-year-old professor for giving a tough exam and describes him as an "old geezer," she would be using semantic slanting. She would have communicated that the professor's age is a negative factor—one that is associated with a host of unflattering stereotypes about older people. And she would have implied that he gave an inappropriate exam because of his antiquated expectations or senile incompetence—all with a couple of well-chosen words. We are

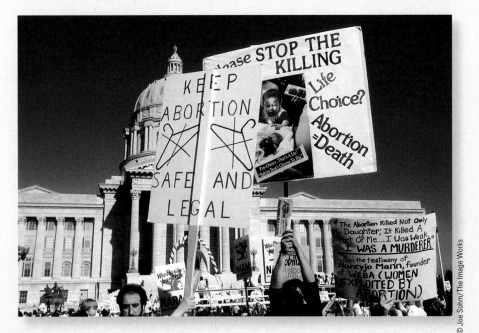

Semantic slanting, which consists of carefully choosing words to create specific emotional reactions, has been used extensively by both sides in the debate about abortion.

© Joe Sohm/The Image Works

Briefings on the status of miliary actions are renowned for their creative but unintelligible manipulation of language, which is often necessary to obscure the unpleasant realities of war.

all the recipients of many such messages containing emotionally laden words and content. An important critical thinking skill is to recognize when semantic slanting is being used to influence how you think so you can resist this subtle technique.

In becoming sensitive to semantic slanting, notice how the people around you and those whom you see on television and read about in the newspapers refer to people from other racial and ethnic groups. You can probably determine a politician's attitudes toward immigration, for example, by considering the words he or she uses when speaking about people from other countries. Are the students on your campus who come from other countries referred to as "international students" or "foreign students"? The term "international" seems to convey a more positive image, with associations of being cosmopolitan and worldly. On the other hand, the term "foreign" suggests someone who is strange. Clearly, it pays to be careful when selecting the words you use in your own communication.

Name Calling

Another way that word choice influences thinking is in the way people tend to label and categorize others through the strategy of *name calling*. People often attempt to neutralize or combat views they don't like by attributing such views to "radical feminists," "knee-jerk liberals," "right-wingers," "religious zealots," or "extremists." In everyday interactions, someone who inspires our wrath may be labeled as a "bitch," a "moron," or a "cheapskate." In these examples, the name calling is not subtle and is easy to recognize. But name calling can also be used with more cunning and finesse. Sometimes, there is an *implied threat* that if you make an unpopular decision or arrive at a conclusion that is not favored, a negative label will be applied to you. For example, someone might say, "Only a naive moron would believe that" to influence your attitude on an issue. This strategy of *anticipatory name calling* makes it difficult for you to declare that you favor the negatively valued belief because it means that you make yourself look like a "naive moron." Anticipatory name calling can also invoke positive group memberships, such as asserting that "all good Americans will agree . . ." or "people in the know think that . . ." Anticipatory name calling is a shrewd tactic that can be effective in shaping people's thinking.

Regardless of your position on these issues, how would you respond to someone who says, "Only a knee-jerk liberal would support racial quotas or affirmative action programs that give unfair advantages to minorities." Or "Only a stupid bigot would oppose affirmative action programs that rectify the unfair discrimination that minorities face." Can you identify the anticipatory name calling and the attempts at semantic slanting in each of these examples? More important, can you resist attempts like these to influence how you think about complex social issues?

Table 8.5 Critical Thinking Skills Discussed in This Application

Skill	Description
Understanding the way language can influence thought	The critical thinker appreciates that when you want to influence how people think, you should choose your words carefully.
Recognizing semantic slanting	The critical thinker is vigilant about how people deliberately choose certain words to elicit specific emotional responses.
Recognizing name calling and anticipatory name calling	The critical thinker is on the lookout for name calling and the implied threats used in anticipatory name calling.

REVIEW of Key Learning Goals

8.24 Language can exert subtle influence over how people feel about various issues. Semantic slanting refers to the deliberate choice of words to create specific emotional responses, as has been apparent in the debate about abortion. In anticipatory name calling, there is an implied threat that a negative label will apply to you if you express certain views.

Key Ideas

Language: Turning Thoughts into Words

❚ Languages are symbolic, generative, and structured. Human languages are structured hierarchically. At the bottom of the hierarchy are the basic sound units, called phonemes. At the next level are morphemes, the smallest units of meaning.

❚ Children typically utter their first words around their first birthday. Vocabulary growth is slow at first, but a vocabulary spurt often begins at around 18 months. Children begin to combine words by the end of their second year. Their early sentences are telegraphic, in that they omit many nonessential words.

❚ Over the next several years, children gradually learn the complexities of syntax and develop metalinguistic awareness. Research does not support the assumption that bilingualism has a negative effect on language development or on cognitive development.

❚ Sue Savage-Rumbaugh's work with Kanzi suggests that some animals are capable of some basic language acquisition, although some skeptics disagree. Many theorists believe that humans' special talent for language is the product of natural selection.

❚ According to Skinner and other behaviorists, children acquire a language through imitation and reinforcement. Nativist theories assert that humans have an innate capacity to learn language rules. Today, theorists are moving toward interactionist perspectives, which emphasize the role of both biology and experience.

❚ The linguistic relativity hypothesis suggests that language determines the nature of people's thinking to some degree. Recent research has bolstered the plausibility of this notion.

Problem Solving: In Search of Solutions

❚ Psychologists have differentiated among several types of problems, including problems of inducing structure, problems of transformation, and problems of arrangement. Common barriers to problem solving include functional fixedness, mental set, attending to irrelevant information, and placement of unnecessary constraints on one's solutions.

❚ A variety of strategies, or heuristics, are used for solving problems, including using trial and error, forming subgoals, hill-climbing, working backward, searching for analogies, and changing the representation of a problem.

❚ Cultural disparities in problem solving style have been observed. According to Nisbett, Eastern cultures exhibit a more holistic cognitive style, whereas Western cultures display a more analytic cognitive style.

Decision Making: Choices and Chances

❚ Simon's theory of bounded rationality suggests that human decision strategies are simplistic and often yield irrational results. Schwartz argues that people in modern societies suffer from choice overload, which undermines their well-being.

❚ An additive decision model is used when people make decisions by rating the attributes of each alternative and selecting the alternative that has the highest sum of ratings. When elimination by aspects is used, people gradually eliminate alternatives if their attributes fail to satisfy some minimum criterion.

❚ In making decisions, evaluations of options' pros and cons tend to fluctuate more than expected. Comparative evaluations of options often yield different results than separate evaluations. Research suggests that intuitive, unconscious choices may be superior to conscious deliberation in making some decisions.

❚ Models of how people make risky decisions focus on the expected value or subjective utility of various outcomes. People use the representativeness and availability heuristics in estimating probabilities. These heuristics can lead people to ignore base rates and to fall for the conjunction fallacy.

❚ Evolutionary psychologists maintain that many errors and biases in human reasoning are greatly reduced when problems are presented in ways that resemble the type of input humans would have processed in ancestral times. Gigerenzer argues that people largely depend on fast and frugal decision heuristics that are adaptive in the real world.

Reflecting on the Chapter's Themes

❚ Four of our unifying themes surfaced in the chapter. Our discussion of language acquisition revealed once again that all aspects of behavior are shaped by both nature and nurture. The recent progress in the study of cognitive processes showed how science depends on empirical methods. Research on decision making illustrated the importance of subjective perceptions. We also saw that cognitive processes are moderated—to a limited degree—by cultural factors.

PERSONAL APPLICATION Understanding Pitfalls in Reasoning About Decisions

❚ The heuristics that people use in decision making lead to various flaws in reasoning. For instance, the use of the representativeness heuristic contributes to the gambler's fallacy. The availability heuristic underlies the tendency to overestimate the improbable. People sometimes exhibit confirmation bias—the tendency to seek only information that supports one's view.

❚ People generally fail to appreciate these shortcomings, which leads to the overconfidence effect. In evaluating choices, it is wise to understand that decisions can be influenced by the language in which they are framed. Loss aversion may also distort decision making processes.

CRITICAL THINKING APPLICATION Shaping Thought with Language: "Only a Naive Moron Would Believe That"

❚ Language can exert subtle influence over how people feel about various issues. Semantic slanting refers to the deliberate choice of words to create specific emotional responses, as has been apparent in the debate about abortion. In anticipatory name calling, there is an implied threat that a negative label will apply to you if you express certain views.

Key Terms

Algorithm (p. 332)
Availability heuristic (p. 341)
Bilingualism (p. 323)
Cognition (p. 318)
Confirmation bias (p. 348)
Conjunction fallacy (p. 343)
Decision making (p. 337)
Fast mapping (p. 321)
Framing (p. 348)
Functional fixedness (p. 330)
Gambler's fallacy (p. 346)
Heuristic (p. 332)
Hill-climbing heuristic (p. 333)
Insight (p. 332)
Language (p. 318)
Language acquisition device (LAD) (p. 326)
Linguistic relativity (p. 327)
Mean length of utterance (MLU) (p. 322)
Mental set (p. 330)
Metalinguistic awareness (p. 322)
Morphemes (p. 320)
Overextensions (p. 322)
Overregularization (p. 322)

Phonemes (p. 319)
Problem solving (p. 328)
Problem space (p. 332)
Representativeness heuristic (p. 342)
Risky decision making (p. 341)
Semantics (p. 320)
Syntax (p. 320)
Telegraphic speech (p. 322)
Theory of bounded rationality (p. 337)
Trial and error (p. 332)
Underextensions (p. 322)

Key People

Noam Chomsky (p. 326)
Leda Cosmides & John Tooby (p. 344)
Gerd Gigerenzer (pp. 344–345)
Daniel Kahneman (pp. 341–343)
Steven Pinker (p. 325)
Sue Savage-Rumbaugh (p. 324)
Herbert Simon (p. 318, 337)
B. F. Skinner (p. 326)
Amos Tversky (pp. 341–343)

1. The 2-year-old child who refers to every four-legged animal as "doggie" is making which of the following errors?
   A. underextension
   B. overextension
   C. overregularization
   D. underregularization

2. Research suggests that bilingualism has a negative effect on:
   A. language development.
   B. cognitive development.
   C. metalinguistic awareness.
   D. none of the above.

3. Based on the work with Kanzi, which statement best summarizes the current status of the research on whether chimps can learn language?
   A. Chimps can acquire the use of symbols but cannot combine them into sentences or learn rules of language.
   B. Chimps are nearly as well suited for learning and using language as humans.
   C. Chimps are incapable even of learning the symbols of a language.
   D. Chimps can learn some basic language skills, but the linguistic capacities of humans are far superior.

4. Chomsky proposed that children learn language swiftly:
   A. because they possess an innate language acquisition device.
   B. through imitation, reinforcement, and shaping.
   C. as the quality of their thought improves with age.
   D. because they need to in order to get their increasingly complex needs met.

5. The linguistic relativity hypothesis is the notion that:
   A. one's language determines the nature of one's thought.
   B. one's thought determines the nature of one's language.
   C. language and thought are separate and independent processes.
   D. language and thought interact, with each influencing the other.

6. The nine-dot problem is:
   A. often solved suddenly with a burst of insight.
   B. difficult because people assume constraints that are not part of the problem.
   C. solved through fast mapping.
   D. both a and b.

7. Problems that require a common object to be used in an unusual way may be difficult to solve because of:
   A. mental set.
   B. irrelevant information.
   C. unnecessary constraints.
   D. functional fixedness.

8. A heuristic is:
   A. a flash of insight.
   B. a guiding principle or "rule of thumb" used in problem solving.
   C. a methodical procedure for trying all possible solutions to a problem.
   D. a way of making a compensatory decision.

9. Which of the following is *not* a heuristic used in solving problems?
   A. Hill climbing
   B. Fast-mapping
   C. Forming subgoals
   D. Searching for analogies

10. According to Nisbett, Eastern cultures tend to favor a(n) _____ cognitive style, whereas Western cultures tend to display a(n) _____ cognitive style.
    A. analytic; holistic
    B. holistic; analytic
    C. heuristic; algorythmic
    D. algorhythmic; heuristic

11. The theory of bounded rationality was originally developed by:
    A. Herbert Simon.
    B. Noam Chomsky.
    C. Steven Pinker.
    D. Gerd Gigerenzer.

12. When you estimate the probability of an event by judging the ease with which relevant instances come to mind, you are relying on:
    A. an additive decision-making model.
    B. the representativeness heuristic.
    C. the availability heuristic.
    D. a noncompensatory model.

13. The belief that the probability of heads is higher after a long string of tails:
    A. is rational and accurate.
    B. is an example of the "gambler's fallacy."
    C. reflects the influence of the representativeness heuristic.
    D. b and c.

14. The tendency to overestimate the probability of events that get heavy media coverage reflects the operation of:
    A. framing effects.
    B. the representativeness heuristic.
    C. the availability heuristic.
    D. mental set.

15. If someone says, "Only a congenital pinhead would make that choice," this use of language would represent:
    A. confirmation bias.
    B. syntactic slanting.
    C. anticipatory name calling.
    D. telegraphic speech.

Answers

1 B p. 322
2 D pp. 323–324
3 D pp. 324–325
4 A p. 326
5 A pp. 327–328
6 D pp. 331–332
7 D p. 330
8 B p. 332
9 B pp. 332–333
10 B p. 336
11 A p. 337
12 C p. 341
13 D pp. 346–347
14 C p. 347
15 C p. 351

PsykTrek

To view a demo: www.cengage.com/psychology/psyktrek
To order: www.cengage.com/psychology/weiten
Go to the PsykTrek website or CD-ROM for further study of the concepts in this chapter. Both online and on the CD-ROM, PsykTrek includes dozens of learning modules with videos, animations, and quizzes, as well as simulations of psychological phenomena and a multimedia glossary that includes word pronunciations.

CengageNow
www.cengage.com/tlc

Go to this site for the link to CengageNOW, your one-stop study shop. Take a Pretest for this chapter, and CengageNOW will generate a personalized Study Plan based on your test results. The Study Plan will identify the topics you need to review and direct you to online resources to help you master those topics. You can then take a Posttest to help you determine the concepts you have mastered and what you still need to work on.

Companion Website
www.cengage.com/psychology/weiten

Go to this site to find online resources directly linked to your book, including a glossary, flash cards, drag-and-drop exercises, quizzes, and more!

9 INTELLIGENCE AND PSYCHOLOGICAL TESTING

Key Concepts in Psychological Testing
Principal Types of Tests
Standardization and Norms
Reliability
Validity

The Evolution of Intelligence Testing
Galton's Studies of Hereditary Genius
Binet's Breakthrough
Terman and the Stanford-Binet
Wechsler's Innovations
The Debate About the Structure of Intelligence
Intelligence Testing Today

Basic Questions About Intelligence Testing
What Kinds of Questions Are on Intelligence Tests?
What Do Modern IQ Scores Mean?
Do Intelligence Tests Have Adequate Reliability?
Do Intelligence Tests Have Adequate Validity?
Do Intelligence Tests Predict Vocational Success?
Are IQ Tests Widely Used in Other Cultures?

Extremes of Intelligence
Mental Retardation/Intellectual Disability
Giftedness

Heredity and Environment as Determinants of Intelligence
Evidence for Hereditary Influence
Evidence for Environmental Influence

The Interaction of Heredity and Environment
Cultural Differences in IQ Scores

FEATURED STUDY ‖ Racial Stereotypes and Test Performance

New Directions in the Assessment and Study of Intelligence
Exploring Biological Indexes and Correlates of Intelligence
Investigating Cognitive Processes in Intelligent Behavior
Expanding the Concept of Intelligence
Measuring Emotional Intelligence

Reflecting on the Chapter's Themes

PERSONAL APPLICATION ‖ Understanding Creativity
The Nature of Creativity
Measuring Creativity
Correlates of Creativity

CRITICAL THINKING APPLICATION ‖ The Intelligence Debate, Appeals to Ignorance, and Reification
Appeal to Ignorance
Reification

Recap

Practice Test

Have you ever thought about the role that psychological testing has played in your life? In all likelihood, your years in grade school and high school were punctuated with a variety of intelligence tests, achievement tests, creativity tests, aptitude tests, and occupational interest tests. In the lower grades, you were probably given standardized achievement tests once or twice a year. For instance, you may have taken the Iowa Tests of Basic Skills, which measured your progress in reading, language, vocabulary, mathematics, and study skills. Perhaps you still have vivid memories of the serious atmosphere in the classroom, the very formal instructions ("Do not break the seal on this test until your examiner tells you to do so"), and the heavy pressure to work fast (I can still see Sister Dominic marching back and forth with her intense gaze riveted on her stopwatch).

Where you're sitting at this very moment may have been influenced by your performance on standardized tests. That is, the college you chose to attend may have hinged on your SAT or ACT scores. Moreover, your interactions with standardized tests may be far from finished. Even at this point in your life, you may be selecting your courses to gear up for the Graduate Record Exam (GRE), the Law School Admission Test (LSAT), the Medical College Admission Test (MCAT), or certification tests in fields such as accounting or nursing. After graduation, when you go job hunting, you may find that prospective employers expect you to take still more batteries of psychological tests as they attempt to assess your personality, your motivation, and your talents.

The vast enterprise of modern testing evolved from psychologists' pioneering efforts to measure *general intelligence*. The first useful intelligence tests, which were created soon after the turn of the 20th century, left a great many "descendants." Today, over 2600 published psychological tests measure a diverse array of mental abilities and other behavioral traits. Indeed, psychological testing has become a big business that annually generates hundreds of millions of dollars in revenues (Koocher & Rey-Casserly, 2003).

Clearly, American society has embraced psychological testing (Giordano, 2005). Each year in the United States alone, people take *hundreds of millions* of intelligence and achievement tests. Scholarships, degrees, jobs, and self-concepts are on the line as Americans attempt to hurdle a seemingly endless

Most children become familiar with standardized psychological tests—intelligence, achievement, and aptitude tests—in school settings.

In this chapter we'll explore many questions about testing, including the following:

- How did psychological testing become so prevalent in modern society?
- How do psychologists judge the validity of their tests?
- What exactly do intelligence tests measure?
- Is intelligence inherited? If so, to what extent?
- How do psychological tests measure creativity?

We'll begin by introducing some basic concepts in psychological testing. Then we'll explore the history of intelligence tests, because they provided the model for subsequent psychological tests. Next we'll address practical questions about how intelligence tests work. After examining the nature versus nurture debate as it relates to intelligence, we'll explore some new directions in the study of intelligence. In the Personal Application, we'll discuss efforts to measure and understand another type of mental ability: creativity. In the Critical Thinking Application, we will critique some of the reasoning used in the vigorous debate about the roots of intelligence.

succession of tests. Because your life is so strongly affected by how you perform on psychological tests, it pays to be aware of their strengths and limitations.

Key Concepts in Psychological Testing

Key Learning Goals

9.1 List and describe the principal categories of psychological tests.

9.2 Clarify the concepts of standardization and test norms.

9.3 Explain the meaning of test reliability and how it is estimated.

9.4 Distinguish among three types of validity.

A *psychological test* is a standardized measure of a sample of a person's behavior. Psychological tests are measurement instruments. They're used to measure the *individual differences* among people in their abilities, aptitudes, interests, and aspects of personality.

Your responses to a psychological test represent a *sample* of your behavior. The word *sample* should alert you to one of the key limitations of psychological tests: A particular behavior sample may not be representative of your characteristic behavior. Everyone has bad days. A stomachache, a fight with a friend, a problem with your car—all might affect your responses to a particular test on a particular day.

This sampling problem is not unique to psychological testing. It's an unavoidable problem for any measurement technique that relies on sampling. For example, a physician taking your blood pressure might get an unrepresentative reading. Likewise, a football scout clocking a prospect's 40-yard sprint time might get a misleading figure. Because of the limitations of the sampling process, test scores should always be interpreted *cautiously*.

Principal Types of Tests

 7a

Psychological tests are used extensively in research, but most of them were developed to serve a practical purpose outside of the laboratory. Most tests can be placed in one of two broad categories: mental ability tests and personality tests.

Mental Ability Tests

 7a

Psychological testing originated with efforts to measure general mental ability. Today, tests of mental abilities remain the most common kind of psychological test. This broad class of tests includes three principal subcategories: intelligence tests, aptitude tests, and achievement tests.

Intelligence tests measure general mental ability. They're intended to assess intellectual potential rather than previous learning or accumulated knowledge. *Aptitude tests* are also designed to measure potential more than knowledge, but they break mental ability into separate components. Thus, *aptitude tests* assess specific types of mental abilities. For example, the Differential Aptitude Tests assess verbal reasoning, numerical ability, abstract reasoning, perceptual speed and accuracy, mechanical reasoning, space relations, spelling, and language usage. Like aptitude tests, *achievement tests* have a specific focus, but they're supposed to measure previous learning instead of potential. Thus, *achievement tests* gauge a person's mastery and knowledge of various subjects (such as reading, English, or history).

Personality Tests

 7a

If you had to describe yourself in a few words, what words would you use? Are you introverted? Independent? Ambitious? Enterprising? Conventional? Assertive? Domineering? Words such as these refer to personality traits. These *traits* can be assessed systematically with personality tests, of which there are more than 500. *Personality tests* measure various aspects of personality, including motives, interests, values, and attitudes. Many psychologists prefer to call these tests personality *scales* because, unlike tests of mental abilities, the questions do not have right or wrong answers. We'll look at the various types of personality scales in our upcoming chapter on personality (Chapter 12).

Standardization and Norms

SIM8, 7b

Both personality scales and tests of mental abilities are *standardized* measures of behavior. *Standardization* refers to the uniform procedures used in the administration and scoring of a test. All subjects get the same instructions, the same questions, and the same time limits so that their scores can be compared meaningfully. This means, for instance, that a person taking the Differential Aptitude Tests (DAT) in 1989 in San Diego, another taking the DAT in 1999 in Baltimore, and another taking it in 2009 in Peoria all confront the same test-taking task.

The standardization of a test's scoring system includes the development of test norms. *Test norms* provide information about where a score on a psychological test ranks in relation to other scores on that test. Why are test norms needed? Because in psychological testing, everything is relative. Psychological tests tell you how you score *relative to other people*. They tell you, for instance, that you are average in creativity or slightly above average in clerical ability. These interpretations are derived from the test norms that help you understand what your test score means.

Usually, test norms allow you to convert your "raw score" on a test into a *percentile*. A *percentile score* indicates the percentage of people who score at or below the score one has obtained. For example, imagine that you take a 40-item assertiveness scale and obtain a raw score of 26. In other words, you indicate a preference for the assertive option on 26 of the questions. Your score of 26 has little meaning until you consult the test norms and find out that it places you at the 82nd percentile. This normative information would indicate that you appear to be as assertive as or more assertive than 82% of the sample of people who provided the basis for the test norms.

The sample of people that the norms are based on is called a test's *standardization group* or *norm group*. Ideally, test norms are based on a large sample of people who were carefully selected to be representative of the broader population. For example, the norms for most intelligence tests are based on samples of 2000–6000 people whose demographic characteristics closely match the overall demographics of the United States (Woodcock, 1994). Although intelligence tests have been standardized carefully, the representativeness of standardization groups for other types of tests varies considerably. Another issue is that the norms for psychological tests need to be updated periodically with contemporary samples, as test norms may gradually grow old and out-of-date (Wasserman & Bracken, 2003).

Reliability

SIM8, 7b

Any kind of measuring device, whether it's a tire gauge, a stopwatch, or a psychological test, should be reasonably consistent. That is, repeated measurements should yield reasonably similar results. Psychologists call this quality *reliability*. To better appreciate the importance of reliability, think about how you would react if a tire pressure gauge were to give you several very different readings for the same tire. You would probably conclude that the gauge is broken and toss it into the trash. Consistency in measurement is essential to accuracy in measurement.

Reliability refers to the measurement consistency of a test (or of other kinds of measurement techniques). Like most other types of measuring devices, psychological tests are not perfectly reliable. A test's reliability can be estimated in several ways (Hempel, 2005). One widely used approach is to check *test-retest reliability*, which is estimated by comparing subjects' scores on two administrations of a test. If we wanted to check the test-retest reliability of a newly developed test of assertiveness, we would ask a group of subjects to take the test on two occasions, probably a few weeks apart (see **Figure 9.1** on the next page). The underlying assumption is

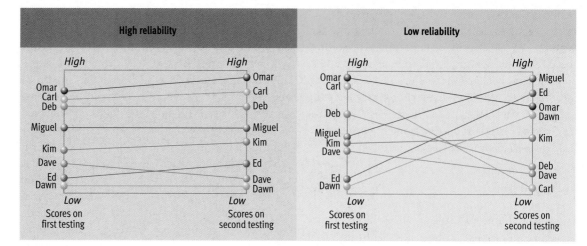

Figure 9.1

Test-retest reliability. In each panel, subjects' scores on the first administration of an assertiveness test are represented on the left, and their scores on a second administration of the same test a few weeks later are shown on the right. If participants obtain similar scores on both administrations, as in the left panel, the test measures assertiveness consistently and has high test-retest reliability. If they get very different scores on the second administration, as in the right panel, the test has low reliability.

web link 9.1

Finding Information About Psychological Tests

Maintained by the American Psychological Association, this FAQ site answers all sorts of questions about the availability of various kinds of tests. It explains how to find specific tests, describes how to get information on tests, and outlines information on the proper use of tests.

Figure 9.2

Correlation and reliability. As explained in Chapter 2, a positive correlation means that two variables co-vary in the *same* direction; a negative correlation means that two variables co-vary in the *opposite* direction. The closer the correlation coefficient gets to either −1.00 or +1.00, the stronger the relationship. At a minimum, reliability estimates for psychological tests must be fairly high positive correlations. Most reliability coefficients fall between .70 and .95. Tests used in "high stakes" testing should have reliability coefficients above .90.

that assertiveness is a fairly stable aspect of personality that won't change in a matter of a few weeks. Thus, changes in participants' scores across the two administrations of the test would presumably reflect inconsistency in measurement.

Reliability estimates require the computation of correlation coefficients, which we introduced in Chapter 2 (see **Figure 9.2** for a brief review). A *correlation coefficient* is a numerical index of the degree of relationship between two variables. In estimating test-retest reliability, the two variables that must be correlated are the two sets of scores from the two administrations of the test. If people get fairly similar scores on the two administrations of our hypothetical assertiveness test, this consistency yields a substantial positive correlation. The magnitude of the correlation gives us a precise indication of the test's consistency. The closer the correlation comes to +1.00, the more reliable the test is.

There are no absolute guidelines about acceptable levels of reliability. What's acceptable depends to some extent on the nature and purpose of the test

(Fekken, 2000). The reliability estimates for most psychological tests range from the .70s through the .90s. The higher the reliability coefficient, the more consistent the test is. As reliability goes down, concern about measurement error increases. Tests that are used to make important decisions about people's lives should have reliability coefficients in the .90s (Nunnally & Bernstein, 1994).

Validity

SIM8, 7b

Even if a test is quite reliable, we still need to be concerned about its validity. *Validity* **refers to the ability of a test to measure what it was designed to measure.** If we develop a new test of assertiveness, we have to provide some evidence that it really measures assertiveness. Increasingly, the term *validity* is also used to refer to the accuracy or usefulness of the *inferences* or *decisions* based on a test (Haladyna, 2006). This broader conception of validity highlights the fact that a specific test might be valid for one purpose, such as placing students in school,

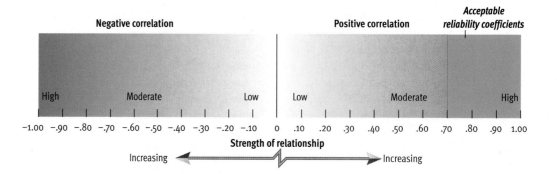

and invalid for another purpose, such as making employment decisions for a particular occupation. Validity can be estimated in several ways, depending on the nature and purpose of a test (Krueger & Kling, 2000; Wasserman & Bracken, 2003).

Content Validity 7b

Achievement tests and educational tests such as classroom exams should have adequate content validity. *Content validity* refers to the degree to which the content of a test is representative of the domain it's supposed to cover. Imagine a poorly prepared physics exam that includes questions on material that was not covered in class or in assigned reading. The professor has compromised the content validity of the exam. Achieving content validity depends on being able to clearly specify the content domain of interest (Kane, 2006).

Criterion-Related Validity 7b

Psychological tests are often used to make predictions about specific aspects of individuals' behavior. They are used to predict performance in college, job capability, and suitability for training programs, as just a few examples. Criterion-related validity is a central concern in such cases. *Criterion-related validity* **is estimated by correlating subjects' scores on a test with their scores on an independent criterion (another measure) of the trait assessed by the test.** For example, let's say you developed a test to measure aptitude for becoming an airplane pilot. You could check its validity by correlating subjects' scores on your aptitude test with subsequent ratings of their performance in their pilot training (see **Figure 9.3**). The performance ratings would be the independent criterion of pilot aptitude. If your test has reasonable validity, there ought to be a fairly strong positive correlation between the test and the crite-

rion measure. Such a correlation would help validate your test's predictive ability.

Construct Validity 7b

Many psychological tests attempt to measure abstract personal qualities, such as creativity, intelligence, extraversion, or independence. No obvious criterion measures exist for these abstract qualities, which are called *hypothetical constructs*. In measuring abstract qualities, psychologists are concerned about *construct validity*—the extent to which evidence shows that a test measures a particular hypothetical construct.

The process of demonstrating construct validity can be complicated. It depends on starting with a clear conceptualization of the hypothetical construct to be measured (Clark & Watson, 2003). Then it usually requires a series of studies that examine the correlations between the test and various measures *related* to the trait in question. A thorough demonstration of construct validity requires looking at the relations between a test and many other measures (Han, 2000). For example, some of the evidence on the construct validity of a measure of extraversion (the Expression scale from the Psychological Screening Inventory) is summarized in **Figure 9.4** (on the next page). This network of correlation coefficients shows that the Expression scale correlates negatively, positively, or not at all with various measures, much as one would expect if the scale is really assessing extraversion. Ultimately, the overall pattern of correlations is what provides convincing (or unconvincing) evidence of a test's construct validity.

The complexities involved in demonstrating construct validity will be apparent in our upcoming discussion of intelligence testing. The ongoing debate about the construct validity of intelligence tests is one of the oldest debates in psychology. We'll look first at the origins of intelligence tests; this historical review will help you appreciate the current controversies about intelligence testing.

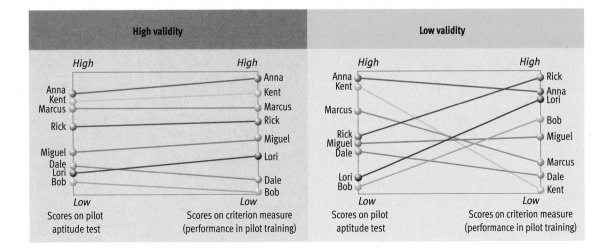

Figure 9.3
Criterion-related validity. To evaluate the criterion-related validity of a pilot aptitude test, a psychologist would correlate subjects' test scores with a criterion measure of their aptitude, such as ratings of their performance in a pilot training program. The validity of the test is supported if the people who score high on the test also score high on the criterion measure (as shown in the left panel), yielding a substantial correlation between the two measures. If little or no relationship exists between the two sets of scores (as shown in the right panel), the data do not provide support for the validity of the test.

Figure 9.4

Construct validity. Some of the evidence on the construct validity of the Expression Scale from the Psychological Screening Inventory is summarized here. This scale is supposed to measure the personality trait of *extraversion*. As you can see on the left side of this network of correlations, the scale correlates negatively with measures of social introversion, social discomfort, and neuroticism, just as one would expect if the scale is really tapping extraversion. On the right, you can see that the scale is correlated positively with measures of sociability and self-acceptance and another index of extraversion, as one would anticipate. At the bottom, you can see that the scale does not correlate with several traits that should be unrelated to extraversion. Thus, the network of correlations depicted here supports the idea that the Expression Scale measures the construct of extraversion.

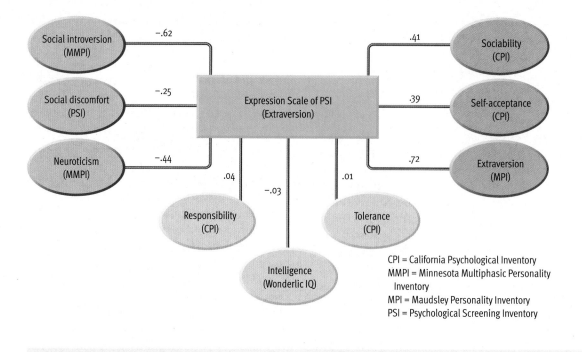

CPI = California Psychological Inventory
MMPI = Minnesota Multiphasic Personality
    Inventory
MPI = Maudsley Personality Inventory
PSI = Psychological Screening Inventory

REVIEW of Key Learning Goals

9.1 Psychological tests are standardized measures of behavior. Mental ability tests can be divided into intelligence tests, aptitude tests, and achievement tests. Personality tests measure behavioral traits, motives, and interests.

9.2 Standardization refers to the uniform procedures used in the administration and scoring of a test. Test scores are interpreted by consulting test norms to find out what represents a high or low score.

9.3 As measuring devices, psychological tests should produce consistent results, a quality called reliability. Test-retest

reliability is estimated by comparing subjects' scores on two administrations of a test. Reliability estimates should yield fairly high positive correlations.

9.4 Validity refers to the degree to which there is evidence that a test measures what it was designed to measure. Content validity is crucial on classroom tests. Criterion-related validity is critical when tests are used to predict performance. Construct validity is critical when a test is designed to measure a hypothetical construct.

---

concept check 9.1

Recognizing Basic Concepts in Testing

Check your understanding of basic concepts in psychological testing by answering the questions below. Select your responses from the following concepts. The answers are in Appendix A.

Test norms   Criterion-related validity

Test-retest reliability   Construct validity

Split-half reliability   Content validity

1. At the request of the HiTechnoLand computer store chain, Professor Charlz develops a test to measure aptitude for selling computers. Two hundred applicants for sales jobs at HiTechnoLand stores are asked to take the test on two occasions, a few weeks apart. A correlation of +.82 is found between applicants' scores on the two administrations of the test. Thus, the test appears to possess reasonable _____.

2. All 200 of these applicants are hired and put to work selling computers. After six months Professor Charlz correlates the new workers' aptitude test scores with the dollar value of the computers that each sold during the first six months on the job. This correlation turns out to be −.21. This finding suggests that the test may lack _____.

3. Back at the university, Professor Charlz is teaching a course in theories of personality. He decides to use the same midterm exam that he gave last year, even though the exam includes questions about theorists that he did not cover or assign reading on this year. There are reasons to doubt the _____ of Professor Charlz's midterm exam.

The Evolution of Intelligence Testing

Psychological tests may play a prominent role in contemporary society, but this wasn't always so. The first psychological tests were invented only a little over a hundred years ago. Since then, reliance on psychological tests has grown gradually. In this section, we discuss the pioneers who launched psychological testing with their efforts to measure general intelligence.

Galton's Studies of Hereditary Genius

It all began with the work of a British scholar, Sir Francis Galton, in the later part of the 19th century. Galton studied family trees and found that success and eminence appeared consistently in some families over generations. For the most part, these families were much like Galton's: well-bred, upper-class families with access to superior schooling and social connections that pave the way to success. Yet Galton discounted the advantages of such an upbringing (Fancher, 2005). In his book *Hereditary Genius*, Galton (1869) concluded that success runs in families because great intelligence is passed from generation to generation through genetic inheritance.

To better demonstrate that intelligence is governed by heredity, Galton needed an objective measure of intelligence. His approach to this problem was guided by the theoretical views of his day. Thus, he assumed that the contents of the mind are built out of elementary *sensations,* and he hypothesized that exceptionally bright people should exhibit exceptional sensory acuity. Working from this premise, he tried to assess innate mental ability by measuring simple sensory processes. Among other things, he measured sensitivity to high-pitched sounds, color perception, and reaction time (the speed of one's response to a stimulus). His efforts met with little success. Research eventually showed that the sensory processes that he measured were largely unrelated to the criteria of mental ability that he was trying to predict, such as success in school or in professional life (Kaufman, 2000).

In pursuing this line of investigation, Galton coined the phrase *nature versus nurture* to refer to the heredity-environment issue (Hilgard, 1989), and he pioneered the idea that the bell curve could be applied to psychological characteristics (Simonton, 2003). Along the way, he also invented the concepts of *correlation* and *percentile test scores* (Roberts et al., 2005). Although Galton's mental tests were a failure, his work created an interest in the measurement of mental ability, setting the stage for a subsequent breakthrough by Alfred Binet, a prominent French psychologist.

Binet's Breakthrough

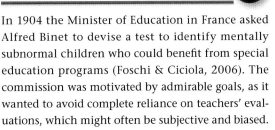

In 1904 the Minister of Education in France asked Alfred Binet to devise a test to identify mentally subnormal children who could benefit from special education programs (Foschi & Ciciola, 2006). The commission was motivated by admirable goals, as it wanted to avoid complete reliance on teachers' evaluations, which might often be subjective and biased.

In response to this need, Binet and a colleague, Theodore Simon, published the first useful test of general mental ability in 1905. They had the insight to load it with items that required abstract reasoning skills, rather than the sensory skills Galton had measured (Brody, 2000; Sternberg & Jarvin, 2003). Their scale was a success because it was inexpensive, easy to administer, objective, and capable of predicting children's performance in school fairly well (Siegler, 1992). Thanks to these qualities, its use spread across Europe and America.

The Binet-Simon scale expressed a child's score in terms of "mental level" or "mental age." A child's *mental age* indicated that he or she displayed the mental performance typical of a child of that chronological (actual) age. Thus, a child with a mental age of 6 performed like an average 6-year-old on the test at that point in time. Binet realized that his scale was a somewhat crude initial effort at measuring mental ability. He revised it in 1908 and again in 1911. Unfortunately, his revising came to an abrupt end with his death in 1911. However, other psychologists continued to build on Binet's work.

Terman and the Stanford-Binet

In America, Lewis Terman and his colleagues at Stanford University soon went to work on a major expansion and revision of Binet's test. Their work led to the 1916 publication of the Stanford-Binet Intelligence Scale (Terman, 1916). Although this revision was quite loyal to Binet's original conceptions, it incorporated a new scoring scheme based on William Stern's (1914) "intelligence quotient" (Minton, 2000). An *intelligence quotient (IQ)* is a child's

Key Learning Goals
9.5 Identify the contributions of Galton and Binet to the evolution of intelligence testing.

9.6 Summarize the contributions of Terman and Wechsler to the evolution of intelligence testing.

9.7 Outline the debate between Spearman and Thurstone about the structure of intelligence.

Sir Francis Galton

"There is no escape from the conclusion that nature prevails enormously over nurture when the differences in nurture do not exceed what is commonly to be found among persons of the same rank of society and in the same country."

Alfred Binet

"The intelligence of anyone is susceptible of development. With practice, enthusiasm, and especially with method one can succeed in increasing one's attention, memory, judgment, and in becoming literally more intelligent than one was before."

mental age divided by chronological age, multiplied by 100. As you can see, IQ scores originally involved actual quotients:

$$IQ = \frac{\text{Mental age}}{\text{Chronological age}} \times 100$$

The ratio of mental age to chronological age made it possible to compare children of different ages. In Binet's system, such comparisons had been awkward. Using the IQ ratio, all children (regardless of age) were placed on the same scale, which was centered at 100 if their mental age corresponded to their chronological age (see Table 9.1 for examples of IQ calculations).

Terman's technical and theoretical contributions to psychological testing were modest, but he made an articulate case for the potential educational benefits of testing and became the key force behind American schools' widespread adoption of IQ tests (Chapman, 1988). As a result of his efforts, the Stanford-Binet quickly became the world's foremost intelligence test and the standard of comparison for virtually all intelligence tests that followed (White, 2000). Since its publication in 1916, the Stanford-Binet has been updated periodically—in 1937, 1960, 1973, 1986, and 2003. Although the 1986 revision introduced some major changes in the organizational structure of the test, the modern Stanford-Binet remains loyal to the conception of intelligence originally formulated by Binet and Terman.

Wechsler's Innovations   7c

As chief psychologist at New York's massive Bellevue Hospital, David Wechsler was charged with overseeing the psychological assessment of thousands of adult patients. He found the Stanford-Binet somewhat unsatisfactory for this purpose. Thus, Wechsler set out to improve on the measurement of intelligence *in adults*. In 1939 he published the first high-quality IQ test designed specifically for adults, which came to be known as the Wechsler Adult Intelligence Scale (WAIS) (Wechsler, 1955, 1981, 1997). Ironically, Wechsler (1949, 1967, 1991, 2003) eventually devised downward extensions of his scale for children.

The Wechsler scales were characterized by at least two major innovations (Prifitera, 1994). First,

"YOU DID VERY WELL ON YOUR I.Q. TEST. YOU'RE A MAN OF 49 WITH THE INTELLIGENCE OF A MAN OF 53."

Wechsler made his scales less dependent on subjects' verbal ability than the Stanford-Binet. He included many items that required nonverbal reasoning. To highlight the distinction between verbal and nonverbal ability, he formalized the computation of separate scores for verbal IQ, performance (nonverbal) IQ, and full-scale (total) IQ.

Second, Wechsler discarded the intelligence quotient in favor of a new scoring scheme based on the *normal distribution*. This scoring system has since been adopted by most other IQ tests, including the Stanford-Binet. Although the term *intelligence quotient* lingers on in our vocabulary, scores on intelligence tests are no longer based on an actual quotient. We'll take a close look at the modern scoring system for IQ tests a little later.

The Debate About the Structure of Intelligence

The first half of the 20th century also witnessed a long-running debate about the structure of intellect. The debate was launched by Charles Spearman, a British psychologist who invented a complicated statistical procedure called factor analysis. In *factor analysis*, correlations among many variables are analyzed to identify closely related clusters of variables. If a number of variables correlate highly

Lewis Terman

"It is the method of tests that has brought psychology down from the clouds and made it useful to men; that has transformed the 'science of trivialities' into the 'science of human engineering.'"

David Wechsleer

"The subtests [of the WAIS] are different measures of intelligence, not measures of different kinds of intelligence."

Table 9.1 Calculating the Intelligence Quotient

Measure	Child 1	Child 2	Child 3	Child 4
Mental age (MA)	6 years	6 years	9 years	12 years
Chronological age (CA)	6 years	9 years	12 years	9 years
$IQ = \frac{MA}{CA} \times 100$	$\frac{6}{6} \times 100 = 100$	$\frac{6}{9} \times 100 = 67$	$\frac{9}{12} \times 100 = 75$	$\frac{12}{9} \times 100 = 133$

with one another, the assumption is that a single factor is influencing all of them. Factor analysis attempts to identify these hidden factors.

Spearman (1904, 1927) used factor analysis to examine the correlations among tests of many specific mental abilities. He concluded that all cognitive abilities share an important core factor, which he labeled *g* for *general* mental ability. Spearman recognized that people also have "special" abilities (such as numerical reasoning or spatial ability). However, he thought that individuals' ability in these specific areas is largely determined by their general mental ability (see **Figure 9.5**).

A very different view of the structure of intellect was soon proposed by L. L. Thurstone, an American psychologist who developed the test that evolved into the SAT (L. V. Jones, 2000). Using a somewhat different approach to factor analysis, Thurstone (1931, 1938, 1955) concluded that intelligence involves multiple abilities. Thurstone argued that Spearman and his followers placed far too much emphasis on *g*. In contrast, Thurstone carved intelligence into seven distinct factors called *primary mental abilities:* word fluency, verbal comprehension, spatial ability, perceptual speed, numerical ability, inductive reasoning, and memory. Thurstone found no evidence for a general factor in intelligence, and he believed that the primary mental abilities are independent of each other.

The debate about the structure of intelligence continued for many decades and in some respects the issue lingers in the background even today (Brody, 2000). That said, in retrospect it is clear that Spearman's view prevailed. Armed with computers, researchers using enhanced approaches to factor analysis have shown again and again that batteries of cognitive tests are highly intercorrelated, as Spearman had suggested (Brand, Constales, & Kane, 2003; Brody, 2005; Carroll, 1993, 1996; Jensen, 1998). Hence, the architects of intelligence tests gradually came to see *g* as the Holy Grail in their quest to measure mental ability. Today, the vast majority of intelligence tests are designed to tap as much of *g* as possible. Some influential modern theorists lament the obsession with *g* (Gardner, 1993, Sternberg, 2003b), but this emphasis seems unlikely to change in the foreseeable future.

Intelligence Testing Today

Today, psychologists and educators have many IQ tests available for their use. Basically, these tests fall into two categories: *individual tests* and *group tests*. Individual IQ tests are administered only by psycholo-

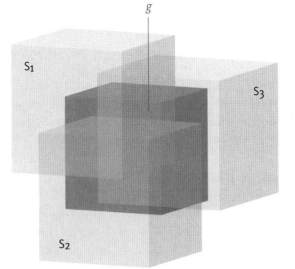

Figure 9.5
Spearman's *g*. In his analysis of the structure of intellect, Charles Spearman found that *specific* mental talents (S₁, S₂, S₃, and so on) were highly intercorrelated. Thus, he concluded that all cognitive abilities share a common core, which he labeled *g* for general mental ability.

gists who have special training for this purpose. A psychologist works face to face with a single examinee at a time. The Stanford-Binet and the Wechsler scales are both individual IQ tests.

The problem with individual IQ tests is that they're expensive and time-consuming to administer. Therefore, researchers have developed a number of IQ tests that can be administered to large groups of people at once, such as the Otis-Lennon School Ability Test and the Cognitive Abilities Test (Kaufman, 2000). Group IQ tests are a little different in character from individual tests (much more time pressure, for instance), but their widespread usage is a testimonial to their much greater efficiency and cost-effectiveness (Cianciolo & Sternberg, 2004). Indeed, if you've taken an IQ test, chances are that it was a group test.

REVIEW of Key Learning Goals

9.5 The first crude efforts to devise intelligence tests were made by Sir Francis Galton, who wanted to show that intelligence is inherited. Galton is also known for his pioneering work on correlation, percentiles, and the bell curve. Modern intelligence testing began with the work of Alfred Binet, a French psychologist who published the first useful intelligence test in 1905. Binet's scale measured a child's mental age.

9.6 Lewis Terman revised the original Binet scale to produce the Stanford-Binet in 1916. It introduced the intelligence quotient and became the standard of comparison for subsequent intelligence tests. David Wechsler devised an improved measure of intelligence for adults and a series of IQ tests that reduced the emphasis on verbal ability. He also introduced a new scoring system based on the normal distribution.

9.7 Spearman argued that all cognitive tests share a core, which he called *g*, whereas Thurstone asserted that intelligence is made up of several independent abilities. Today, there are many individual and group intelligence tests. An individual IQ test is administered to a single examinee by a psychologist who has special training for this purpose. Group IQ tests can be administered to many people simultaneously.

Basic Questions About Intelligence Testing

Key Learning Goals

9.8 Clarify the meaning of deviation IQ scores on modern intelligence tests.

9.9 Summarize evidence on the reliability and validity of modern IQ test scores.

9.10 Analyze how well intelligence tests predict vocational success.

9.11 Discuss the use of IQ tests in non-Western cultures.

Misconceptions abound when it comes to intelligence tests. In this section we'll use a question-and-answer format to explain the basic principles underlying intelligence testing.

What Kinds of Questions Are on Intelligence Tests?

The nature of the questions found on IQ tests varies somewhat from test to test. These variations depend on whether the test is intended for children or adults (or both) and whether the test is designed for individuals or groups. Overall, the questions are fairly diverse in format. The Wechsler scales, with their numerous subtests, provide a representative example of the kinds of items that appear on most IQ tests. As you can see in Figure 9.6, the items in the Wechsler subtests require subjects to furnish information, recognize vocabulary, figure out patterns, and demonstrate basic memory. Generally speaking, examinees are required to manipulate words, numbers, and images through abstract reasoning.

What Do Modern IQ Scores Mean?

7c

As we've discussed, scores on intelligence tests once represented a ratio of mental age to chronological age. However, this system has given way to one based on the normal distribution and the standard deviation (see Chapter 2). The *normal distribution* **is a symmetric, bell-shaped curve that represents the pattern in which many characteristics are dispersed in the population.** When a trait is normally distributed, most cases fall near the center of the distribution (an average score), and the number of cases gradually declines as one moves away from the center in either direction (see Figure 9.7 on page 366).

The normal distribution was first discovered by 18th-century astronomers. They found that their measurement errors were distributed in a predictable way that resembled a bell-shaped curve. Since then, research has shown that many human traits, ranging from height to running speed to spatial ability, also follow a normal distribution. Psychologists eventually recognized that intelligence scores also fall into a normal distribution. This insight permit-

ted David Wechsler to devise a more sophisticated scoring system for his tests that has been adopted by virtually all subsequent IQ tests. In this system, raw scores are translated into *deviation IQ scores* **that locate subjects precisely within the normal distribution, using the standard deviation as the unit of measurement.**

For most IQ tests, the mean of the distribution is set at 100 and the standard deviation (SD) is set at 15. These choices were made to provide continuity with the original IQ ratio (mental age to chronological age) that was centered at 100. In this system, which is depicted in Figure 9.7, a score of 115 means that a person scored exactly one SD (15 points) above the mean. A score of 85 means that a person scored one SD below the mean. A score of 100 means that a person showed average performance. You don't really need to know how to work with standard deviations to understand this system (but if you're interested, consult Appendix B). *The key point is that modern IQ scores indicate exactly where you fall in the normal distribution of intelligence.* Thus, a score of 120 does not indicate that you answered 120 questions correctly. Nor does it mean that you have 120 "units" of intelligence. A deviation IQ score places you at a specific point in the normal distribution of intelligence.

Deviation IQ scores can be converted into percentile scores (see Figure 9.7). In fact, a major advantage of this scoring system is that a specific score on a specific test always translates into the same percentile score, regardless of the person's age group. The old system of IQ ratio scores lacked this consistency.

Do Intelligence Tests Have Adequate Reliability?

Do IQ tests produce consistent results when people are retested? Yes. Most IQ tests report commendable reliability estimates. The correlations generally range into the .90s (Kaufman, 2000). In comparison to most other types of psychological tests, IQ tests are exceptionally reliable. However, like other tests, they *sample* behavior, and a specific testing may yield an unrepresentative score.

Variations in examinees' motivation to take an IQ test or in their anxiety about the test can sometimes produce misleading scores (Hopko et al., 2005;

Wechsler Adult Intelligence Scale (WAIS)		
Test	**Description**	**Example**
Verbal scale		
Information	Taps general range of information	On what continent is France?
Comprehension	Tests understanding of social conventions and ability to evaluate past experience	Why are children required to go to school?
Arithmetic	Tests arithmetic reasoning through verbal problems	How many hours will it take to drive 150 miles at 50 miles per hour?
Similarities	Asks in what way certain objects or concepts are similar; measures abstract thinking	How are a calculator and a typewriter alike?
Digit span	Tests attention and rote memory by orally presenting series of digits to be repeated forward or backward	Repeat the following numbers backward: 2 4 3 5 1 8 6
Vocabulary	Tests ability to define increasingly difficult words	What does audacity mean?
Performance scale		
Digit symbol	Tests speed of learning through timed coding tasks in which numbers must be associated with marks of various shapes	Shown: 1 2 3 4 Fill in: 1 4 3 2
Picture completion	Tests visual alertness and visual memory through presentation of an incompletely drawn figure; the missing part must be discovered and named	Tell me what is missing: 
Block design	Tests ability to perceive and analyze patterns by presenting designs that must be copied with blocks	Assemble blocks to match this design: 
Picture arrangement	Tests understanding of social situations through a series of comic-strip-type pictures that must be arranged in the right sequence to tell a story	Put the pictures in the right order:  1 2 3
Object assembly	Tests ability to deal with part/whole relationships by presenting puzzle pieces that must be assembled to form a complete object	Assemble the pieces into a complete object: 

Figure 9.6

Subtests on the Wechsler Adult Intelligence Scale (WAIS). The WAIS is divided into scales that yield separate verbal and performance (nonverbal) IQ scores. The verbal scale consists of six subtests and the performance scale is made up of five subtests. Examples of low-level (easy) test items that closely resemble those on the WAIS are shown on the right.

Zimmerman & Woo-Sam, 1984). The most common problem is that low motivation or high anxiety may drag a person's score down on a particular occasion. For instance, a fourth-grader who is made to feel that the test is really important may get jittery and be unable to concentrate. The same child might score much higher on a subsequent testing by another examiner who creates a more comfortable atmosphere. Although the reliability of IQ tests is excellent, caution is always in order in interpreting test scores.

Figure 9.7

The normal distribution. Many characteristics are distributed in a pattern represented by this bell-shaped curve. The horizontal axis shows how far above or below the mean a score is (measured in plus or minus standard deviations). The vertical axis is used to graph the number of cases obtaining each score. In a normal distribution, the cases are distributed in a fixed pattern. For instance, 68.26% of the cases fall between +1 and –1 standard deviation. Modern IQ scores indicate where a person's measured intelligence falls in the normal distribution. On most IQ tests, the mean is set at an IQ of 100 and the standard deviation at 15. Any deviation IQ score can be converted into a percentile score. The mental classifications at the bottom of the figure are descriptive labels that roughly correspond to ranges of IQ scores.

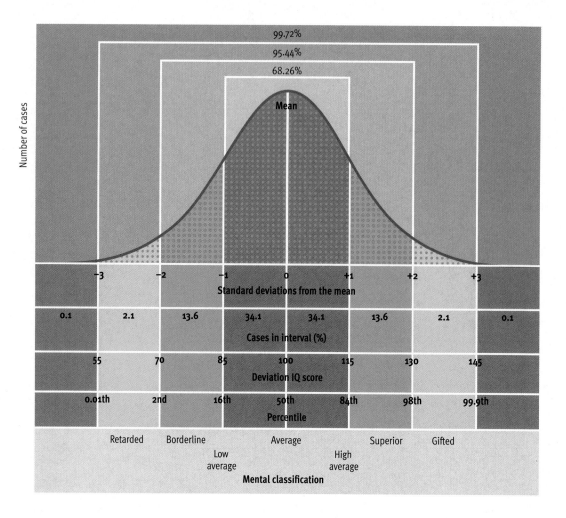

web link 9.3

Educational Psychology Interactive: Intelligence

This site, maintained by Bill Huitt of Valdosta State University, leads to a helpful review of psychological approaches to intelligence and is an excellent resource for other topics in educational psychology.

Do Intelligence Tests Have Adequate Validity?

Do intelligence tests measure what they're supposed to measure? Yes, but this answer has to be qualified very carefully. IQ tests are valid measures of the kind of intelligence that's necessary to do well in academic work. But if the purpose is to assess intelligence in a broader sense, the validity of IQ tests is debatable.

As you may recall, intelligence tests were originally designed with a relatively limited purpose in mind: to predict school performance. This has continued to be the principal purpose of IQ testing. As a result, efforts to document the validity of IQ tests have usually concentrated on their relationship to grades in school. Typically, positive correlations in the .40s and .50s are found between IQ scores and school grades (Kline, 1991; Mackintosh, 1998). Moreover, a recent, huge study of over 70,000 children in England found an even stronger relationship between intelligence and educational achievement. When Deary and colleagues (2007) used a composite measure of *g* (based on several tests) to predict a composite estimate of educational progress (based

on 25 achievement tests) five years later, they found correlations in the vicinity of .70.

These correlations are about as high as one could expect, given that many factors besides a person's intelligence are likely to affect grades and school progress. For example, school grades may be influenced by a student's motivation or personality, not to mention teachers' subjective biases. Indeed, a recent study reported that measures of students' *self-discipline* are surprisingly strong predictors of students' performance. In two studies of eighth-graders, Duckworth and Seligman (2005) found correlations of .55 and .67 between an elaborate index of self-discipline and students' final GPA. Thus, given all the other factors likely to influence performance in school, IQ tests appear to be reasonably valid indexes of school-related intellectual ability, or academic intelligence.

However, over the years people have mistakenly come to believe that IQ tests measure mental ability in a truly general sense. In reality, IQ tests have always focused on the abstract reasoning and verbal fluency that are essential to academic success. The tests do not tap social competence, practical problem solving, creativity, mechanical ingenuity, or artistic talent.

When Robert Sternberg and his colleagues (1981) asked people to list examples of intelligent behavior, they found that the examples fell into three categories: (1) *verbal intelligence,* (2) *practical intelligence,* and (3) *social intelligence* (see **Figure 9.8**). Thus, people generally recognize three basic components of intelligence. For the most part, IQ tests assess only the first of these three components. Although IQ tests are billed as measures of *general* mental ability, they actually focus somewhat narrowly on a specific type of intelligence: academic/verbal intelligence (Sternberg, 1998, 2003b).

Do Intelligence Tests Predict Vocational Success?

Vocational success is a vague, value-laden concept that's difficult to quantify. Nonetheless, researchers have attacked this question by examining correlations between IQ scores and specific indicators of vocational success, such as income, the prestige of subjects' occupations, or ratings of subjects' job performance. The data relating IQ to occupational attainment are pretty clear. *People who score high on IQ tests are more likely than those who score low to end up in high-status jobs* (Gottfredson, 2003b; Herrnstein & Murray, 1994; Schmidt & Hunter, 2004). Because IQ tests measure school ability fairly well and because school performance is important in reaching certain occupations, this link between IQ scores and job status makes sense. Of course, the correlation between IQ and occupational attainment is moder-

ate. For example, in a meta-analysis of many studies of the issue, Strenze (2007) found a correlation of .37 between IQ and occupational status. That figure means that there are plenty of exceptions to the general trend. Some people probably outperform brighter colleagues through bulldog determination and hard work. The relationship between IQ and income appears to be somewhat weaker. The meta-analysis by Strenze (2007) reported a correlation of .21 between IQ and income based on 31 studies. In one recent, large-scale study of American baby boomers, the correlation between intelligence and income was .30 (Zagorsky, 2007). These findings suggest that intelligence fosters vocational success, but the strength of the relationship is modest.

The association between intelligence and vocational success is modest for a variety of reasons, including people's motivational idiosyncrasies. Shown here is electronic genius Mark Antman, who prefers to apply his extraordinary intelligence to private projects in his basement workshop rather than have it "exploited" by employment in a technical occupation.

Figure 9.8
Laypersons' conceptions of intelligence.
Robert Sternberg and his colleagues (1981) asked participants to list examples of behaviors characteristic of intelligence. The examples tended to sort into three groups that represent the three types of intelligence recognized by the average person: verbal intelligence, practical intelligence, and social intelligence. The three well-known individuals shown here are prototype examples of verbal intelligence (Meryl Streep), practical intelligence (Steve Jobs), and social intelligence (The Dalai Lama).

SOURCE: Adapted from Sternberg, R. J., Conway, B. E., Keton, J. L., & Bernstein, M. (1981). People's conceptions of intelligence. *Journal of Personality and Social Psychology, 41* (1), 37–55. Copyright © 1981 by the American Psychological Association. Adapted by permission of the publisher and author.

Verbal intelligence

Speaks clearly and articulately

Is verbally fluent

Is knowledgeable about a particular field

Reads with high comprehension

Practical intelligence

Sees all aspects of a problem

Sizes up situations well

Makes good decisions

Poses problems in an optimal way

Social intelligence

Accepts others for what they are

Has social conscience

Thinks before speaking and doing

Is sensitive to other people's needs and desires

There is far more debate about whether IQ scores are effective predictors of performance *within* a particular occupation. On the one hand, research suggests that (a) there is a substantial correlation (about .50) between IQ scores and job performance, (b) this correlation varies somewhat depending on the complexity of a job's requirements but does not disappear even for low-level jobs (see **Figure 9.9**), (c) this association holds up even when workers have more experience at their jobs, and (d) measures of specific mental abilities and personality traits are much less predictive of job performance than measures of intelligence (Gottfredson, 2002; Ones, Viswesvaran, & Dilchert, 2005; Schmidt, 2002). On the other hand, critics argue that a correlation of .50 provides only modest accuracy in prediction (accounting for about 25% of the variation in job performance) (Goldstein, Zedeck, & Goldstein, 2002; Sternberg & Hedlund, 2002). Critics have also questioned the validity of the supervisory ratings that have typically been used as an index of job performance (Tenopyr, 2002). Concerns have also been raised that when IQ tests are used for job selection, they can have an adverse impact on employment opportunities for many minority groups that tend to score somewhat lower (on average) on such tests (Murphy, 2002; Outtz, 2002). In the final analysis, there is no question that intelligence is associated with vocational success, but there is room for argument about whether this association is strong enough to justify reliance on IQ testing in hiring employees.

Are IQ Tests Widely Used in Other Cultures?

In other Western cultures with European roots, the answer to this question is yes. In most non-Western cultures, the answer is not really. IQ testing has a

The skills and knowledge that are crucial to success vary from one culture to the next. IQ tests were designed to assess the skills and knowledge valued in modern, Western cultures. They have proven useful in some non-Western cultures that value similar sets of skills, but they have also proven irrelevant in many cultures.

long history and continues to be a major enterprise in many Western countries, such as Britain, France, Norway, Canada, and Australia (Irvine & Berry, 1988). However, efforts to export IQ tests to non-Western societies have met with mixed results. The tests have been well received in some non-Western cultures, such as Japan, where the Binet-Simon scales were introduced as early as 1908 (Iwawaki & Vernon, 1988), but they have been met with indifference or resistance in other cultures, such as China and India (Chan & Vernon, 1988; Sinha, 1983).

The bottom line is that Western IQ tests do not translate well into the language and cognitive frameworks of many non-Western cultures (Berry, 1994; Sternberg, 2004). Using an intelligence test with a cultural group other than the one for which it was originally designed can be problematic. The entire

Figure 9.9
Intelligence as a predictor of job performance. Based on a review of 425 studies, Schmidt and Hunter (2004) report that the correlation between general mental ability and job performance depends on the complexity of the job. As jobs become more complicated, intelligence becomes a better predictor of performance. Schmidt and Hunter conclude that these correlations show that IQ tests can be valuable in hiring decisions. However, as the text explains, some other experts have reservations about using intelligence tests in employee selection.

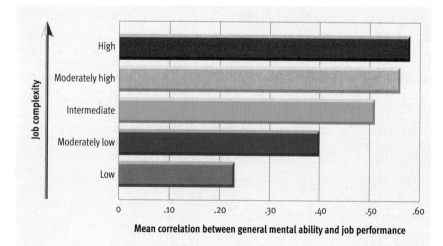

"YOU CAN'T BUILD A HUT, YOU DON'T KNOW HOW TO FIND EDIBLE ROOTS AND YOU KNOW NOTHING ABOUT PREDICTING THE WEATHER. IN OTHER WORDS, YOU DO TERRIBLY ON OUR I.Q. TEST."

process of test administration, with its emphasis on rapid information processing, decisive responding, and the notion that ability can be quantified, is foreign to some cultures (Serpell, 2000). Moreover, different cultures have different conceptions of what intelligence is and value different mental skills (Baral & Das, 2004; Sato et al., 2004; Sternberg, 2007).

REVIEW of Key Learning Goals

9.8 In the modern scoring system, deviation IQ scores indicate where people fall in the normal distribution of intelligence for their age group. On most tests, the mean is set at 100 and the standard deviation is set at 15.

9.9 IQ tests are exceptionally reliable, with reliability coefficients typically ranging into the .90s. IQ tests are reasonably valid measures of academic intelligence in that they predict school grades and the number of years of school that people complete. However, they do not measure intelligence in a truly general sense.

9.10 IQ scores are associated with occupational attainment and income, but the correlations are modest. There is active debate about whether IQ scores predict performance within an occupation well enough to be used in hiring decisions.

9.11 Intelligence testing is largely a Western enterprise, and IQ tests are not widely used in most non-Western cultures. One reason is that different cultures have different conceptions of intelligence.

Extremes of Intelligence

What are the cutoff scores for extremes in intelligence that lead children to be designated as mentally retarded or as gifted? On the low end, IQ scores roughly two standard deviations or more below the mean are regarded as subnormal. On the high end, children who score more than two or three standard deviations above the mean are regarded as gifted. However, designations of mental retardation and giftedness should not be based exclusively on IQ test results. Let's look more closely at the evolving concepts of mental retardation and intellectual giftedness.

Mental Retardation/ Intellectual Disability

The terminology used to refer to those who exhibit subnormal intelligence is undergoing a transition. For decades many authorities have expressed concerns about the term *retardation* because they see it as demeaning, stigmatizing, and powerful, in that people diagnosed with retardation seem to be totally defined by it (Bersani, 2007). These concerns finally led the American Association on Mental Retardation (AAMR) to change its name in 2006 to the American Association on Intellectual and Developmental Disabilities (AAIDD) (Schalock et al., 2007). The next edition of its classification manual, due in 2009 or 2010, will use the term *intellectual disability* as a substitute for *mental retardation*. In this period of transition, I will use the two terms interchangeably here. One can only hope that the new terminology will eventually reduce the stigma associated with retardation, although such change is far from a certainty.

In any event, *mental retardation or intellectual disability* refers to subnormal general mental ability accompanied by deficiencies in adaptive skills, originating before age 18. Adaptive skills consist of everyday living skills in ten domains, including communication (example: writing a letter), self-care (dressing oneself), home living (preparing meals), social interaction (coping with others' demands), community use (shopping), and health/safety (recognizing illness).

There are two noteworthy aspects to this definition. First, the IQ criterion of subnormality is arbitrary. In the 1992 release of its classification manual, the AAMR (as it was then known) set a flexible cutoff line, which was an IQ score of 70 to 75 or below. This cutoff line could be drawn elsewhere. Indeed the AAMR made the cutoff 70 (with caveats) in its 2002 edition. These periodic changes in the scoring norms for IQ tests have had erratic effects on the percentage of children falling below the cutoffs (Flynn, 2000; Kanaya, Scullin, & Ceci, 2003). Five IQ points may not sound like much, but if the line is drawn exactly at 75 instead of 70 the number of people qualifying for special education programs doubles (King, Hodapp, & Dykens, 2005). Second, the requirement of deficits in everyday living skills is included because experts feel that high-stakes decisions should not be based on just a test score (Lichten & Simon, 2007). This requirement acknowledges that "school learning" is not the only important kind of learning. Unfortunately, the methods available for measuring everyday living skills have tended to be vague, imprecise, and subjective, although efforts to improve

Key Learning Goals

9.12 Describe how mental retardation is defined and divided into various levels.

9.13 Review what is known about the causes of intellectual disability.

9.14 Discuss the identification of gifted children and evidence on their personal qualities.

9.15 Articulate the drudge theory of exceptional achievement and alternative views.

web link 9.4

The ARC

The ARC is a "national organization of and for people with mental retardation and related developmental disabilities and their families." Materials available here include overviews of the causes of intellectual disability, education and employment of the mentally retarded, and the rights of mentally retarded individuals, among many other issues.

Table 9.2 Categories of Mental Retardation/Intellectual Disability

Category	IQ Range	Education Possible	Life Adaptation Possible
Mild	55–70	Sixth grade (maximum) by late teens; special education helpful	Can be self-supporting in nearly normal fashion if environment is stable and supportive; may need help with stress
Moderate	40–55	Second to fourth grade by late teens; special education necessary	Can be semi-independent in sheltered environment; needs help with even mild stress
Severe	25–40	Limited speech, toilet habits, and so forth with systematic training	Can help contribute to self-support under total supervision
Profound	below 25	Little or no speech; not toilet-trained; relatively unresponsive to training	Requires total care

Note: As explained in the text, diagnoses of retardation should not be made on the basis of IQ scores alone.

these assessments are under way (Detterman, Gabriel, & Ruthsatz, 2000; Lichten & Simon, 2007).

Levels

Historically, estimates of the prevalence of mental retardation have varied between 1% and 3%. Recent evidence suggests that the prevalence of intellectual disability probably is closer to the 1% end of this range (Szymanski & Wilska, 2003). Mental retardation has traditionally been classified into four levels characterized as mild, moderate, severe, or profound. Table 9.2 lists the IQ range for each level and the typical behavioral and educational characteristics of individuals at each level.

As Figure 9.10 shows, the vast majority of people diagnosed with intellectual disability fall in the *mild* category. Only about 15% of people diagnosed with intellectual disability exhibit the obvious mental deficiencies that most people envision when they think of retardation. Many individuals with mild retardation are not all that easily distinguished from the rest of the population. The mental deficiency of children in the mild disability category often is not noticed until they have been in school a few years. Outside of school, many are considered normal. Fur-

thermore, as many as two-thirds of these children manage to shed the label of retardation when they reach adulthood and leave the educational system (Popper et al., 2003). A significant portion of them become self-supporting and are integrated into the community. Some are even able to attend college (Getzel & Wehman, 2005).

Origins

Many organic conditions can cause mental retardation (Szymanski & Wilska, 2003). For example, *Down syndrome* is a condition marked by distinctive physical characteristics (such as slanted eyes, stubby limbs, and thin hair) that is associated with mild to severe retardation. Most children exhibiting this syndrome carry an extra chromosome. *Phenylketonuria* is a metabolic disorder (due to an inherited enzyme deficiency) that can lead to intellectual disability if it is not caught and treated in infancy. In *hydrocephaly,* an excessive accumulation of cerebrospinal fluid in the skull destroys brain tissue and causes retardation. Although about 1000 such organic syndromes are known to cause retardation, with more being identified every year (Popper et al., 2003), diagnosticians are unable to pin down an organic cause for as many as 50% of cases (King et al., 2005).

The cases of unknown origin tend to involve milder forms of retardation. A number of theories have attempted to identify the factors that underlie intellectual disability in the absence of a known organic pathology (Hodapp, 1994). Some theorists believe that subtle, difficult-to-detect physiological defects contribute to many of these cases. However, others believe the majority of cases are caused by a variety of unfavorable environmental factors. Consistent with this hypothesis, the vast majority of children with mild disability come from the lower socioeconomic classes (see Figure 9.11), where a number of factors—such as greater marital instabil-

Figure 9.10

The prevalence of various levels of mental retardation. When people think of mental retardation they tend to imagine people who suffer from severe intellectual disability. However, in reality, the vast majority (85%) of individuals diagnosed with retardation fall in the mild category (IQ: 55–70). Only about 15% of people with intellectual disability fall into the subcategories of moderate, severe, or profound retardation.

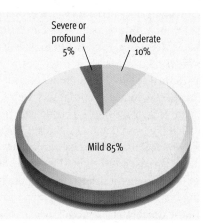

Severe or profound 5%
Moderate 10%
Mild 85%

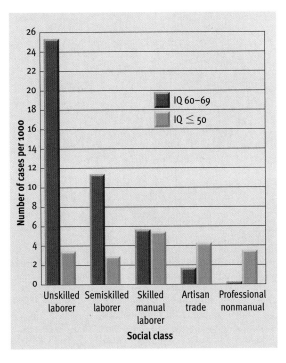

Figure 9.11

Social class and mental retardation. This graph charts the prevalence of mild retardation (defined as an IQ between 60 and 69 in this study) and more severe forms of retardation (defined as an IQ below 50) in relation to social class. Severe forms of retardation are distributed pretty evenly across the social classes, a finding that is consistent with the notion that they are the product of biological aberrations that are equally likely to strike anyone. In contrast, the prevalence of mild retardation is greatly elevated in the lower social classes, a finding that meshes with the notion that mild retardation is largely a product of unfavorable environmental factors. (Data from Popper and Steingard, 1994)

ity and parental neglect, inadequate nutrition and medical care, and lower-quality schooling—may contribute to children's poor intellectual development (Popper et al., 2003).

Giftedness

Like mental retardation, giftedness is widely misunderstood. This misunderstanding is a result, in part, of television and movies inaccurately portraying gifted children as social misfits and "nerds."

Identifying Gifted Children

Definitions of giftedness vary considerably (Cramond, 2004; Freeman, 2005), and some curious discrepancies exist between ideals and practice in how gifted children are identified. The experts consistently assert that giftedness should not be equated with high intelligence, and they recommend that schools not rely too heavily on IQ tests to select gifted children

(von Karolyi & Winner, 2005; Robinson & Clinkenbeard, 1998; Sternberg, 2005c). In practice, however, efforts to identify gifted children focus almost exclusively on IQ scores and rarely consider qualities such as creativity, leadership, or special talent (Callahan, 2000). Most school districts consider children who fall in the upper 2%–3% of the IQ distribution to be gifted. Thus, the minimum IQ score for gifted programs usually falls somewhere around 130. The types of school programs and services available to gifted students vary enormously from one school district to the next (Olszewski-Kubilius, 2003).

Personal Qualities of the Gifted

Gifted children have long been stereotyped as weak, sickly, socially inept "bookworms" who are often emotionally troubled. The empirical evidence *largely* contradicts this view. The best evidence comes from a major longitudinal study of gifted children begun by Lewis Terman in 1921 (Terman, 1925; Terman & Oden, 1959). Other investigators have continued to study Terman's subjects through the present (Cronbach, 1992; Holahan & Sears, 1995; Lippa, Martin, & Friedman, 2000). This project represents psychology's longest-running study.

Terman's original subject pool consisted of around 1500 youngsters who had an average IQ of 150. In comparison to normal subjects, Terman's gifted children were found to be above average in height, weight, strength, physical health, emotional adjustment, mental health, and social maturity. As a group, Terman's subjects continued to exhibit better-than-average physical health, emotional stability, and social satisfaction throughout their adult years. A variety of other studies have also found that samples of high-IQ children are either average or above average in social and emotional development (Garland & Zigler, 1999; Robinson & Clinkenbeard, 1998).

However, some other lines of research raise some questions about this conclusion. For instance, Ellen Winner (1997, 1998) asserts that profoundly gifted children (those with an IQ above 180) are very different from moderately gifted children (those with an IQ of 130–150). She asserts that profoundly gifted children are often introverted and socially isolated. She also estimates that the incidence of interpersonal and emotional problems in this group is about twice as high as in other children. Another line of research, which is discussed in more detail in the Personal Application, has focused on samples of people who have displayed truly exceptional creative achievement. Contrary to the findings of the Terman study, investigators have found elevated

Ellen Winner

"Moderately gifted children are very different from profoundly gifted children.... Most gifted children do not grow into eminent adults."

rates of mental illness in these samples (Andreasen, 2005; Ludwig, 1998). Thus, the psychosocial adjustment of gifted individuals may depend in part on their level of giftedness.

Giftedness and Achievement in Life

Terman's gifted children grew up to be very successful by conventional standards. By midlife they had produced 92 books, 235 patents, and nearly 2200 scientific articles. Although Terman's gifted children accomplished a great deal, no one in the group achieved recognition for genius-level contributions. In retrospect, this finding may not be surprising. The concept of giftedness is applied to two very different groups. One consists of high-IQ children who are the cream of the crop in school. The other consists of eminent adults who make enduring contributions in their fields. According to Ellen Winner (2000), a sizable gap exists between these two groups. Joseph Renzulli (1986, 1999, 2005) theorizes that this rarer form of eminent giftedness depends on the intersection of three factors: high intelligence, high creativity, and high motivation (see **Figure 9.12**). He emphasizes that high intelligence alone does not usually foster genuine greatness. Thus, the vast majority of children selected for gifted school programs do not achieve eminence as adults or make genius-like contributions to society (Callahan, 2000; Richert, 1997; Winner, 2003).

Another hot issue in the study of giftedness concerns the degree to which extraordinary achievement depends on innate talent as opposed to intensive training and hard work. In recent years, the emphasis has been on what Simonton (2001) calls the "drudge theory" of exceptional achievement. Ac-

Ten-year-old Moshe Kai Cavalin is a sophomore in college who has maintained an A+ average in his classes. Moshe clearly is a highly gifted child. Nonetheless, it is hard to say whether Moshe will go on to achieve eminence, which typically requires a combination of exceptional intelligence, extraordinary motivation, and high creativity.

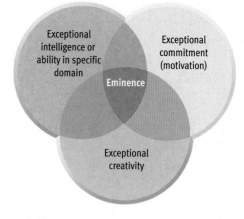

Figure 9.12

A three-ring conception of eminent giftedness. According to Renzulli (1986), high intelligence is only one of three requirements for achieving eminence. He proposes that a combination of exceptional ability, creativity, and motivation leads some people to make enduring contributions in their fields.

SOURCE: Adapted from Renzulli, J. S. (1986). The three-ring conception of giftedness: A developmental model for creative productivity. In R. J. Sternberg & J. E. Davidson (Eds.), *Conceptions of Giftedness* (pp. 53–92). New York: Cambridge University Press. Copyright © 1986 Cambridge University Press. Adapted by permission.

cording to this view, eminence primarily or entirely depends on dogged determination; endless, tedious practice; and outstanding mentoring and training (Bloom, 1985; Ericsson, Roring, & Nandagopal, 2007; Howe, 1999). This conclusion is based on studies of eminent scientists, artists, writers, musicians, and athletes, which show that they push themselves much harder and engage in far more deliberate practice than their less successful counterparts. The essence of the drudge theory is captured by the reaction of one violin virtuoso after a critic hailed him as a genius: "A genius! For 37 years I've practiced 14 hours a day, and now they call me a genius!" (quoted in Simonton, 1999b).

Although the evidence linking strenuous training and prodigious effort to world-class achievement is convincing, Winner (2000) points out that obsessive hard work and inborn ability may be confounded in retrospective analyses of eminent individuals. The youngsters who work the hardest may be those with the greatest innate talent, who are likely to find their efforts more rewarding than others. In other words, innate ability may be the key factor fostering the single-minded commitment that seems to be crucial to greatness. Simonton (1999b, 2005) has devised an elaborate theory of talent development that allocates a significant role to both innate ability and a host of supportive environmental factors.

Additional evidence that supports the importance of both innate talent and educational and other opportunities comes from a long-running study of

mathematically precocious youth begun by Julian Stanley back in 1971 (Benbow & Stanley, 1983, 1996; Keating & Stanley, 1972). Most of the youngsters followed in this study were identified in seventh or eighth grade, based on their excellent performance on the SAT Math subtest, intended for high school juniors and seniors. All of these students fell in the upper 1% of math ability, but the clever use of the above-their-level SAT found highly varied test scores that differentiated the bright students from the extraordinary students. These data provided a sensitive test of the widely believed notion that beyond a certain high level of talent, more ability might not matter. The long-term findings did not support this

notion. The data showed that the career accomplishments (earning PhDs, securing patents, and so on) of the top one-quarter of the top 1% were notably superior to the bottom quarter of the top 1% (Lubinski & Benbow, 2006). Although this finding highlights the importance of variations in innate ability, the study also gathered extensive data showing that acceleration programs in high school enhance gifted students' achievements.

In sum, recent research has clearly demonstrated that quality training, monumental effort, and perseverance are crucial factors in greatness, but many experts on giftedness maintain that extraordinary achievement also requires rare, innate talent.

REVIEW of Key Learning Goals

9.12 Mental retardation, which has been reconceptualized as intellectual disability, refers to subnormal general mental ability accompanied by deficits in adaptive skills. IQ scores below 70 are usually diagnostic of mental retardation, but such diagnoses should not be based solely on test results. Four levels of retardation have been distinguished: mild, moderate, severe, and profound.

9.13 Although about 1000 organic conditions can cause retardation, diagnosticians are unable to pinpoint a biological cause in as many as 50% of cases. Research suggests that cases of unknown origin are mostly caused by unfavorable environmental factors, such as poverty, neglect, and poor nutrition.

9.14 Children who obtain IQ scores above 130 may be viewed as gifted, but cutoffs for accelerated programs vary, and schools

rely too much on IQ scores. Research by Terman showed that gifted children tend to be socially mature and well adjusted. However, Winner has expressed some concerns about the adjustment of profoundly gifted individuals.

9.15 Gifted youngsters typically become very successful, but most do not make genius-level contributions because such achievements depend on a combination of high intelligence, creativity, and motivation. The drudge theory suggests that determination, hard work, and intensive training are the key to achieving eminence, but many theorists are reluctant to dismiss the importance of innate talent. A long-running study of mathematically precocious youth suggests that both innate talent and quality training are important.

Heredity and Environment as Determinants of Intelligence

Most early pioneers of intelligence testing maintained that intelligence is inherited (Cravens, 1992). Small wonder, then, that this view lingers among many people. Gradually, however, it has become clear that both heredity and environment influence intelligence (Bartels et al., 2002; Davis, Arden, & Plomin, 2008; Plomin, 2003). Does this mean that the nature versus nurture debate has been settled with respect to intelligence? Absolutely not. Theorists and researchers continue to argue *vigorously* about which of the two is more important, in part because the issue has such far-reaching sociopolitical implications.

Theorists who believe that intelligence is largely inherited downplay the value of special educational programs for underprivileged groups (Herrnstein & Murray, 1994; Kanazawa, 2006; Rushton & Jensen, 2005). They assert that a child's intelligence cannot be increased noticeably, because a child's genetic

destiny cannot be altered. Other theorists take issue with this argument, pointing out that traits with a strong genetic component are not necessarily unchangeable (Flynn, 2007; Sternberg, Grigorenko, & Kidd, 2005). The people in this camp tend to maintain that even more funds should be allocated for remedial education programs, improved schooling in lower-class neighborhoods, and college financial aid for the underprivileged. Because the debate over the role of heredity in intelligence has direct relevance to important social issues and political decisions, we'll take a detailed look at this complex controversy.

Evidence for Hereditary Influence

7d

Galton's observation that intelligence runs in families was quite accurate. However, *family studies* can determine only whether genetic influence on a trait

Key Learning Goals

9.16 Summarize evidence that heredity affects intelligence, and discuss the concept of heritability.

9.17 Describe various lines of research that indicate that environment affects intelligence.

9.18 Explain the concept of reaction range, and discuss recent work on the molecular genetics of intelligence.

9.19 Evaluate heredity and socioeconomic disadvantage as explanations for cultural differences in IQ.

9.20 Assess stereotype threat and cultural bias as explanations for cultural differences in IQ.

is *plausible,* not whether it is certain (see Chapter 3). Family members share not just genes, but similar environments. If high intelligence (or low intelligence) appears in a family over several generations, this consistency could reflect the influence of either shared genes or shared environment. Because of this problem, researchers must turn to *twin studies* and *adoption studies* to obtain more definitive evidence on whether heredity affects intelligence.

Twin Studies

7d

The best evidence regarding the role of genetic factors in intelligence comes from studies that compare identical and fraternal twins. The rationale for twin studies is that both identical and fraternal twins normally develop under similar environmental conditions. However, identical twins share more genetic kinship than fraternal twins. Hence, if pairs of identical twins are more similar in intelligence than pairs of fraternal twins, it's presumably because of their greater genetic similarity. (See Chapter 3 for a more detailed explanation of the logic underlying twin studies.)

What are the findings of twin studies regarding intelligence? The data from over 100 studies of intellectual similarity for various kinds of kinship relations and childrearing arrangements are summarized in **Figure 9.13**. This figure plots the average correlation observed for various types of relationships. As you can see, the average correlation reported for identical twins (.86) is very high, indicating that identical twins tend to be quite similar in intelligence. The average correlation for fraternal twins (.60) is significantly lower. This correlation indicates that fraternal twins also tend to be similar in intelligence, but noticeably less so than identical twins. These results support the notion that IQ is inherited to a considerable degree (Bouchard, 1998; Plomin & Spinath, 2004).

Of course, critics have tried to poke holes in this reasoning. They argue that identical twins are more alike in IQ because parents and others treat them more similarly than they treat fraternal twins. This environmental explanation of the findings has some merit. After all, identical twins are always the same sex, and gender influences how a child is raised. However, this explanation seems unlikely in light of the evidence on identical twins reared apart because of family breakups or adoption (Bouchard, 1997; Bouchard et al., 1990). *Although reared in different environments, these identical twins still display greater similarity in IQ (average correlation: .72) than fraternal twins reared together (average correlation: .60).* Moreover, the gap in IQ similarity between identical and fraternal twins appears to widen in adulthood, suggesting paradoxically that the influence of heredity increases with age (Plomin & Spinath, 2004).

Adoption Studies

7d

Research on adopted children also provides evidence about the effects of heredity (and of environ-

Figure 9.13
Studies of IQ similarity. The graph shows the mean correlations of IQ scores for people of various types of relationships, as obtained in studies of IQ similarity. Higher correlations indicate greater similarity. The results show that greater genetic similarity is associated with greater similarity in IQ, suggesting that intelligence is partly inherited (compare, for example, the correlations for identical and fraternal twins). However, the results also show that living together is associated with greater IQ similarity, suggesting that intelligence is partly governed by environment (compare, for example, the scores of siblings reared together and reared apart). (Data from McGue et al., 1993; Plomin & Spinath, 2004; Plomin et al., 2008)

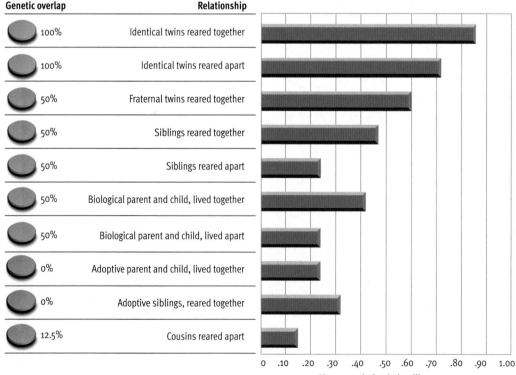

ment, as we shall see). If adopted children resemble their biological parents in intelligence even though they were not reared by these parents, this finding supports the genetic hypothesis. The relevant studies indicate that there is indeed more than chance similarity between adopted children and their biological parents (Plomin et al., 2008; refer again to Figure 9.13).

Heritability Estimates

Various experts have sifted through mountains of correlational evidence to estimate the *heritability* of intelligence. A *heritability ratio* is an estimate of the proportion of trait variability in a population that is determined by variations in genetic inheritance. Heritability can be estimated for any trait. For example, the heritability of height is estimated to be around 90% and the heritability of weight is estimated to be around 85% (Bouchard, 2004). Heritability can be estimated in a variety of ways that appear logically and mathematically defensible (Grigerenko, 2000; Loehlin, 1994). Given the variety of methods available and the strong views that experts bring to the IQ debate, it should come as no surprise that heritability estimates for intelligence vary considerably (see Figure 9.14).

At the high end, some theorists estimate that the heritability of IQ ranges as high as 80% (Bouchard, 2004; Jensen, 1980, 1998). That is, they believe that only about 20% of the variation in intelligence is attributable to environmental factors. Estimates at the low end of the spectrum suggest that the heritability of intelligence is around 40% (Plomin, 2003). *In recent years, the consensus estimates of the experts tend to hover around 50%* (Petrill, 2005; Plomin & Spinath, 2004).

However, it's important to understand that heritability estimates have certain limitations (Ceci et al., 1997; Grigorenko, 2000; Reeve & Hakel, 2002). First, a heritability estimate is a *group statistic* based on studies of trait variability within a specific group. A heritability estimate cannot be applied meaningfully to *individuals*. In other words, even if the heritability of intelligence were 70%, it would *not* mean that each individual's intelligence was 70% inherited. Second, a specific trait's *heritability may vary from one group to another* depending on a variety of factors. For instance, in a group with a given gene pool, heritability will decrease if a shift occurs toward rearing youngsters in more diverse circumstances. Why? Because environmental variability will be increased. Third, it is crucial to understand that "there really is no single fixed value that represents any true, constant value for the heritability of IQ or anything

else" (Sternberg et al., 2005, p. 53). Heritability ratios are merely sample-specific estimates.

Evidence for Environmental Influence

Heredity unquestionably influences intelligence, but a great deal of evidence indicates that upbringing also affects mental ability. In this section, we'll examine various approaches to research that show how life experiences shape intelligence.

Adoption Studies

Research with adopted children provides useful evidence about the impact of experience as well as heredity (Dickens & Flynn, 2001; Locurto, 1990; Loehlin, Horn, & Willerman, 1997). Many of the correlations in Figure 9.13 reflect the influence of the environment. For example, adopted children show some resemblance to their foster parents in IQ. This similarity is usually attributed to the fact that their foster parents shape their environment. Adoption studies also indicate that siblings reared together are more similar in IQ than siblings reared apart. This is true even for identical twins who have the same genetic endowment. Moreover, entirely unrelated children who are raised in the same home also show a significant resemblance in IQ. All of these findings indicate that environment influences intelligence.

Environmental Deprivation and Enrichment

If environment affects intelligence, children who are raised in substandard circumstances should experience a gradual decline in IQ as they grow older (since other children will be progressing more rapidly). This *cumulative deprivation hypothesis* was tested decades ago. Researchers studied children consigned to understaffed orphanages and children raised in the poverty and isolation of the back hills of Appalachia

Figure 9.14

The concept of heritability. A heritability ratio is an estimate of the portion of trait variation in a population determined by heredity—with the remainder presumably determined by environment—as these pie charts illustrate. Typical heritability estimates for intelligence range between a high of 80% and a low of 40%. In recent years, the consensus of the experts seems to hover around 50%. Bear in mind that heritability ratios are *estimates* and have certain limitations that are discussed in the text.

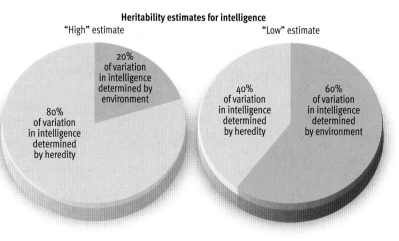

Heritability estimates for intelligence

"High" estimate

80% of variation in intelligence determined by heredity

20% of variation in intelligence determined by environment

"Low" estimate

40% of variation in intelligence determined by heredity

60% of variation in intelligence determined by environment

(Sherman & Key, 1932; Stoddard, 1943). Generally, investigators *did* find that environmental deprivation led to the predicted erosion in IQ scores.

Conversely, children who are removed from a deprived environment and placed in circumstances more conducive to learning should benefit from their environmental enrichment. Their IQ scores should gradually increase. This hypothesis has been tested by studying children who have been moved from disadvantaged homes or institutional settings into middle- and upper-class adoptive homes (Scarr & Weinberg, 1977, 1983; Schiff & Lewontin, 1986). A recent meta-analysis of relevant studies found that adopted children scored notably higher on IQ tests than siblings or peers "left behind" in institutions or disadvantaged homes (van IJzendoorn & Juffer, 2005). These gains are sometimes reduced if children suffer from severe, lengthy deprivation prior to their adoptive placement. But the overall trends clearly show that improved environments lead to increased IQ scores for most adoptees. These findings show that IQ scores are not unchangeable and that they are sensitive to environmental influences.

Generational Changes: The Flynn Effect

The most interesting, albeit perplexing, evidence showcasing the importance of the environment is the finding that performance on IQ tests has steadily increased over generations. This trend was not widely appreciated until relatively recently, because the tests are renormed periodically with new standardization groups so that the mean IQ always remains at 100. However, in a study of the IQ tests used by the U.S. military, James Flynn noticed that the level of performance required to earn a score of 100 jumped upward every time the tests were renormed. Curious about this unexpected finding, he eventually gathered extensive data from 20 nations and demonstrated that IQ performance has been rising steadily all over the industrialized world since the 1930s (Flynn, 1987, 1999, 2003, 2007). Thus, the performance that today would earn you an average score of 100 would have earned you an IQ score of about 120 back in the 1930s (see Figure 9.15). Researchers who study intelligence are now scrambling to explain this trend, which has been dubbed the "Flynn effect." About the only thing they mostly agree on is that the Flynn effect has to be attributed to environmental factors, as the modern world's gene pool could not have changed overnight (in evolutionary terms, 70 years is more like a fraction of a second) (Dickens & Flynn, 2001; Neisser, 1998; Sternberg et al., 2005)

The Interaction of Heredity and Environment 7d

Clearly, heredity and environment both influence intelligence to a significant degree. And their effects involve intricate, dynamic, reciprocal interactions (Dickens & Flynn, 2001; Grigerenko, 2000; Petrill, 2005). Genetic endowments influence the experiences that people are exposed to, and environments influence the degree to which genetic predispositions are realized. Indeed, many theorists now assert that the question of whether heredity or environment is more important ought to take a back seat to the question of *how they interact* to govern IQ.

One influential model of this interaction, perhaps championed most prominently by Sandra Scarr (1991), is that heredity may set certain limits on intelligence and that environmental factors determine where individuals fall within these limits (Bouchard, 1997; Weinberg, 1989). According to this idea, genetic makeup places an upper limit on a person's IQ that can't be exceeded even when environment is ideal. Heredity is also thought to place a lower limit on an individual's IQ, although extreme circumstances (for example, being locked in an attic until age 10) could drag a person's IQ beneath this boundary. Theorists use the term **reaction range** to refer to these genetically determined limits on IQ (or other traits).

According to the reaction-range model, children reared in high-quality environments that promote

Sandra Scarr

"My research has been aimed at asking in what kind of environments genetic differences shine through and when do they remain hidden."

Figure 9.15

Generational increases in measured IQ. IQ tests are renormed periodically so that the mean score remains at 100. However, research by James Flynn has demonstrated that performance on IQ tests around the world has been increasing throughout most of the century. This graph traces the estimated increases in IQ in the United States from 1918 to 1995. In relation to the axis on the right, the graph shows how average IQ would have increased if IQ tests continued to use 1918 norms. In relation to the axis on the left, the graph shows how much lower the average IQ score would have been in earlier years if 1995 norms were used. The causes of the "Flynn effect" are unknown, but they have to involve environmental factors.

SOURCE: Adapted from Flynn, J. R. (1998). IQ gains over time: Toward finding the causes. In U. Neisser (Ed.), *The rising curve: Long-term gains in IQ and related measures* (p. 37). Washington, DC: American Psychological Association. Copyright © by the American Psychological Association. Reprinted by permission of the author.

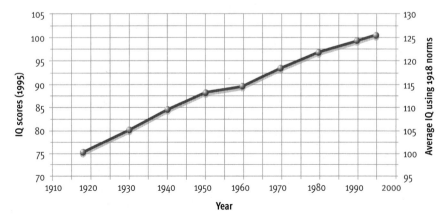

the development of intelligence should score near the top of their potential IQ range (see Figure 9.16). Children reared under less ideal circumstances should score lower in their reaction range. The concept of a reaction range can explain why high-IQ children sometimes come from poor environments. It can also explain why low-IQ children sometimes come from very good environments. Moreover, it can explain these apparent paradoxes without discounting the role that environment undeniably plays.

Scientists hope to achieve a more precise understanding of how heredity and environment interactively govern intelligence by identifying the specific genes that influence general mental ability. Advances in molecular genetics, including the mapping of the human genome, are allowing researchers to search for individual genes that are associated with measures of intelligence (Plomin, 2003). For example, recent studies have identified specific areas on chromosomes 2, 6, and 7 that appear to be associated with variations in intelligence (Posthuma et al., 2005). However, these associations have proven difficult to replicate in different samples and a great deal of additional research is needed (Posthuma & de Geus, 2006).

This new line of research is promising, but progress has been *much* slower than expected (Plomin, Kennedy, & Craig, 2006). The problem is that intelligence may be influenced by hundreds of specific genes, each of which may have a small effect that is extremely difficult to detect with current technologies (Petrill, 2005). In recent research, the *strongest* links found between genes and intelligence each were associated with less than ½ of 1% of the variation in

Carolyn Barnes grappled with an exceptionally difficult childhood which included bouts of homelessness and being abandoned by her mentally ill father. Yet she managed to graduate from Virginia Tech in just three years and was recognized as the top student in the College of Liberal Arts and Human Sciences. She currently is enrolled in a doctoral program at the University of Michigan. The reaction range model can explain how high-IQ individuals can emerge from deprived, impoverished environments.

intelligence (Plomin et al., 2006). However, researchers in this area hope to achieve breakthroughs as the technology of molecular genetics gradually becomes more powerful (Butcher et al., 2005).

Cultural Differences in IQ Scores

The age-old nature versus nurture debate lies at the core of the long-running controversy about ethnic differences in average IQ. Although the full range of IQ scores is seen in all ethnic groups, the average IQ for many of the larger minority groups in the United States (such as African Americans, Native Americans, and Hispanics) is somewhat lower than the average for whites. The typical disparity is around

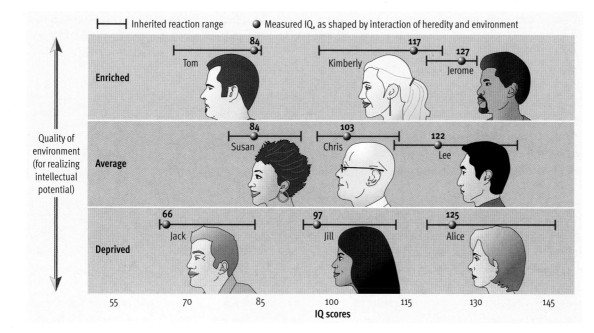

Figure 9.16

Reaction range. The concept of reaction range posits that heredity sets limits on one's intellectual potential (represented by the horizontal bars), while the quality of one's environment influences where one scores within this range (represented by the dots on the bars). People raised in enriched environments should score near the top of their reaction range, whereas people raised in poor-quality environments should score near the bottom of their range. Genetic limits on IQ can be inferred only indirectly, so theorists aren't sure whether reaction ranges are narrow (like Ted's) or wide (like Chris's). The concept of reaction range can explain how two people with similar genetic potential can be quite different in intelligence (compare Tom and Jack) and how two people reared in environments of similar quality can score quite differently (compare Alice and Jack).

10 to 15 points, depending on the group tested and the IQ scale used (Loehlin, 2000; Nisbett, 2005; Rushton & Jensen, 2005). However, data from the standardization samples for the Stanford-Binet and Wechsler scales suggests that the gap between blacks and whites has shrunk by about 4–7 points since the 1970s (Dickens & Flynn, 2006). There is relatively little argument about the existence of these group differences, variously referred to as racial, ethnic, or cultural differences in intelligence. The controversy concerns *why* the differences are found. A vigorous debate continues as to whether cultural differences in intelligence are attributable mainly to the influence of heredity or of environment.

Heritability as an Explanation

In 1969 Arthur Jensen sparked a heated war of words by arguing that racial differences in average IQ are largely the result of heredity. The cornerstone for Jensen's argument was his analysis suggesting that the heritability of intelligence is about 80%. Essentially, he asserted that (1) intelligence is largely genetic in origin, and (2) therefore, genetic factors are "strongly implicated" as the cause of ethnic differences in intelligence. Jensen's article triggered outrage and bitter criticism in many quarters, as well as a great deal of additional research on the determinants of intelligence. Twenty-five years later, Richard Herrnstein and Charles Murray (1994) reignited the same controversy with the publication of their widely discussed book *The Bell Curve*. They argued that ethnic differences in average intelligence are substantial, not easily reduced, and at least partly genetic in origin. The implicit message throughout *The Bell Curve* was that disadvantaged groups cannot

avoid their fate because it is their genetic destiny. And as recently as 2005, based on an extensive review of statistical evidence, J. Phillipe Rushton and Arthur Jensen argued that genetic factors account for the bulk of the gap between races in average IQ.

As you might guess, these analyses and conclusions have elicited many lengthy and elaborate rebuttals. Critics argue that heritability explanations for ethnic differences in IQ have a variety of flaws and weaknesses (Brody, 2003; Devlin et al., 2002; Horn, 2002; Nisbett, 2005; Sternberg, 2003b, 2005a). For example, recent research suggests that the heritability of intelligence may be notably lower in samples drawn from the lower socioeconomic classes as opposed to higher socioeconomic classes (Turkheimer et al., 2003). However, heritability estimates for intelligence have largely been based on samples drawn from white, middle-class, North American and European populations (Grigerenko, 2000). Hence, there is

Arthur Jensen

"Despite more than half a century of repeated efforts by psychologists to improve the intelligence of children, particularly those in the lower quarter of the IQ distribution relative to those in the upper half of the distribution, strong evidence is still lacking as to whether or not it can be done."

"I don't know anything about the bell curve, but I say heredity is everything."

doubt about the validity of applying these heritability estimates to other cultural groups.

Moreover, even if one accepts the assumption that the heritability of IQ is very high, it does not follow logically that differences *between groups* must be due largely to heredity. Leon Kamin has presented a compelling analogy that highlights the logical fallacy in this reasoning (see **Figure 9.17**):

We fill a white sack and a black sack with a mixture of different genetic varieties of corn seed. We make certain that the proportions of each variety of seed are identical in each sack. We then plant the seed from the white sack in fertile Field A, while that from the black sack is planted in barren Field B. We will observe that within Field A, as within Field B, there is considerable variation in the height of individual corn plants. This variation will be due largely to genetic factors (seed differences). We will also observe, however, that the average height of plants in Field A is greater than that in Field B. That difference will be entirely due to environmental factors (the soil). The same is true of IQs: differences in the average IQ of various human populations could be entirely due to environmental differences, even if within each population all variation were due to genetic differences! (Eysenck & Kamin, 1981, p. 97)

This analogy shows that even if *within-group differences* in IQ are highly heritable, *between-groups differences* in average IQ could still be caused *entirely* by environmental factors (Block, 2002). For decades,

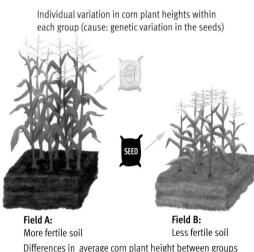

Individual variation in corn plant heights within each group (cause: genetic variation in the seeds)

Field A:
More fertile soil

Field B:
Less fertile soil

Differences in average corn plant height between groups (cause: the soils in which the plants were grown)

Figure 9.17
Genetics and between-group differences on a trait. Leon Kamin's analogy (see text) shows how between-group differences on a trait (the average height of corn plants) could be due to environment, even if the trait is largely inherited. The same reasoning can be applied to ethnic group differences in average intelligence.

critics of Jensen's thesis have relied on this analogy rather than actual data to make the point that between-groups differences in IQ do not necessarily reflect genetic differences. They depended on the analogy because no relevant data were available. However, the recent discovery of the Flynn effect has provided compelling new data that are directly relevant (Dickens & Flynn, 2001; Flynn, 2003). Generational gains in IQ scores show that a between-groups disparity in average IQ (in this case the gap is between generations rather than ethnic groups) can be environmental in origin, even though intelligence is highly heritable.

The available evidence certainly does not allow us to rule out the possibility that ethnic and cultural disparities in average intelligence are partly genetic. And the hypothesis should not be dismissed without study simply because many people find it offensive or distasteful. However, there are several alternative explanations for the culture gap in intelligence that seem more plausible. Let's look at them.

Socioeconomic Disadvantage as an Explanation

Some theorists have approached the issue by trying to show that socioeconomic disadvantages are the main cause of ethnic differences in average IQ. Many social scientists argue that minority students' IQ scores are depressed because these children tend to grow up in deprived environments that create a disadvantage—both in school and on IQ tests. Obviously, living circumstances vary greatly within ethnic groups, but there is no question that, on the average, whites and minorities tend to be raised in different circumstances. Most minority groups have endured a long history of economic discrimination and are greatly overrepresented in the lower social classes. A lower-class upbringing tends to carry a number of disadvantages that work against the development of a youngster's full intellectual potential (Evans, 2004; Lareau, 2003; Lott, 2002; McLoyd, 1998; Noble, McCandliss, & Farah, 2007; Seifer, 2001). In comparison to the middle and upper classes, lower-class children are more likely to come from large families and from single-parent homes, factors that may often limit the parental attention they receive. Lower-class children also tend to be exposed to fewer books, to have fewer learning supplies, to have less privacy for concentrated study, and to get less parental assistance in learning. Typically, they also have poorer role models for language development, experience less pressure to work hard on intellectual pursuits, and attend poorer-quality schools that are underfunded and understaffed. Many of these children grow up in crime-, drug-,

web link 9.5

Upstream-Issues:
The Bell Curve

The editors of *Upstream,* champions of "politically incorrect" conversation, have assembled perhaps the broadest collection of commentaries on the web regarding Herrnstein and Murray's *The Bell Curve.* Despite the marked political conservatism of this site, it contains a full range of opinion and analyses of the book.

and gang-infested neighborhoods where it is far more important to develop street intelligence than school intelligence. Some theorists also argue that children in the lower classes are more likely to suffer from malnutrition or to be exposed to environmental toxins (Brody, 1992). Either of these circumstances could interfere with youngsters' intellectual development (Bellinger & Adams, 2001; Grantham-McGregor, Ani, & Fernald, 2001).

In light of these disadvantages, it's not surprising that average IQ scores among children from lower social classes tend to run about 15 points below the average scores obtained by children from middle- and upper-class homes (Seifer, 2001; Williams & Ceci, 1997). This is the case even if race is factored out of the picture by studying whites exclusively. Admittedly, there is room for argument about the direction of the causal relationships underlying this association between social class and intelligence (Turkheimer, 1994). Nonetheless, given the overrepresentation of minorities in the lower classes, many researchers argue that ethnic differences in intelligence are really social class differences in disguise.

Stereotype Vulnerability as an Explanation

Socioeconomic disadvantages probably are a major factor in various minority groups' poor performance on IQ tests, but some theorists maintain that other factors and processes are also at work. For example, Claude Steele (1992, 1997), a social psychologist at Stanford University, has argued that derogatory stereotypes of stigmatized groups' intellectual capabilities create unique feelings of vulnerability in the educational arena. These feelings of *stereotype vulnerability* can undermine group members' performance on tests, as well as other measures of academic achievement.

Steele points out that demeaning stereotypes of stigmatized groups are widely disseminated. He further notes that members of minority groups are keenly aware of any negative stereotypes that exist regarding their intellect. Hence, when an African American or Hispanic American does poorly on a test, he or she must confront a disturbing possibility: *that others will attribute the failure to racial inferiority.* Steele maintains that females face the same problem when they venture into academic domains where stereotypes suggest that they are inferior to males, such as mathematics, engineering, and the physical sciences. That is, *they worry about people blaming their failures on their gender.*

Steele maintains that stigmatized groups' apprehension about "confirming" people's negative stereotypes can contribute to academic underachievement in at least two ways. First, it can undermine their emotional investment in academic work, leading many students to "disidentify" with school and write off academic pursuits as a source of self-worth. Their academic motivation declines and their performance suffers as a result. Second, standardized tests such as IQ tests may be especially anxiety arousing for members of stigmatized groups because the importance attributed to the tests makes one's stereotype vulnerability particularly salient. This anxiety may impair students' test performance by temporarily disrupting their cognitive functioning. How Steele tested his theory is the topic of our Featured Study.

© Courtesy of Claude Steele

Claude Steele

"I believe that in significant part the crisis in black Americans' education stems from the power of this vulnerability to undercut identification with schooling."

FEATURED

STUDY

SOURCE: Steele, C. M., & Aronson, J. (1995). Stereotype threat and the intellectual test performance of African Americans. *Journal of Personality and Social Psychology, 69,* 797–811.

Racial Stereotypes and Test Performance

In this article, Steele and Aronson report on a series of four studies that tested various aspects of Steele's theory about the ramifications of stereotype vulnerability. We will examine their first study in some detail and then discuss the remaining studies more briefly. The purpose of the first study was to test the hypothesis that raising the threat of stereotype vulnerability would have a negative impact on African American students' performance on a mental ability test.

Method

Participants. The participants were 114 black and white undergraduates attending Stanford University who were recruited through campus advertisements. As expected, given Stanford's highly selective admissions, both groups of students were well above average in academic ability, as evidenced by their mean scores on the verbal subtest of the SAT. The study compared black and white students with high and roughly equal ability and preparation (based on their SAT scores) to rule out cultural disadvantage as a factor.

Procedure. The participants were asked to take a challenging, 30-minute test of verbal ability composed of items from the verbal subtest of the Graduate Record Exam (GRE). In one condition, the issue of stereotype vulnerability was not made salient, as the test was presented to subjects as a device to permit the researchers to analyze problem-solving strategies (rather than as a measure of ability). In another condition, the specter of stereotype vulnerability was raised, as the test was presented as an excellent index of a person's general verbal ability. The principal dependent variable was subjects' performance on the verbal test.

Results

When the African American students' stereotype vulnerability was not made obvious, the performance of the black and white students did not differ, as you can see in **Figure 9.18**. However, when the same test was presented in a way that increased blacks' stereotype vulnerability, the African American students scored significantly lower than their white counterparts (see **Figure 9.18**).

Discussion

Based on their initial study, the authors inferred that stereotype vulnerability does appear to impair minority group members' test performance. They went on to replicate their finding in a second study of 40 black and white female students. In a third study, they demonstrated that their manipulations of stereotype vulnerability were indeed activating thoughts about negative stereotypes, ability-related self-doubts, and performance apprehension in their African American participants. Their fourth study showed that stereotype vulnerability can be activated even when a test is not explicitly presented as an index of individual ability.

Comment

The potential negative effects of stereotype vulnerability have been replicated in numerous studies (Cadinu et al., 2005; Croizet et al., 2004; Shapiro & Neuberg, 2007). The concept of stereotype vulnerability has the potential to clear up some of the confusion surrounding the controversial issue of racial disparities in IQ scores. It seems likely that socioeconomic disadvantage makes a substantial contribution to cultural differences in average IQ, but various lines of evidence suggest that this factor cannot account

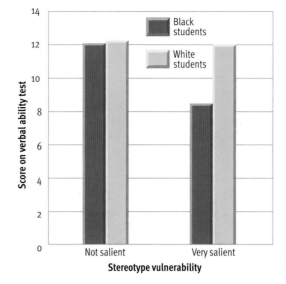

Figure 9.18

Stereotype vulnerability and test performance. Steele and Aronson (1995) compared the performance of African American and white students of equal ability on a 30-item verbal ability test constructed from difficult GRE questions. When the black students' stereotype vulnerability was not obvious, their performance did not differ from that of the white students; but when the specter of stereotype vulnerability was raised, the African American students performed significantly worse than the white students.

SOURCE: Adapted from Steele, C. M., & Aronson, J. (1995). Stereotype threat and the intellectual test performance of African Americans. *Journal of Personality and Social Psychology, 69,* 797–811. Copyright © 1995 by the American Psychological Association. Reprinted by permission of the author.

for the culture gap by itself (Neisser et al., 1996). Thus, Steele's groundbreaking research gives scientists an entirely new explanatory tool for understanding the vexing cultural disparities in average IQ.

Cultural Bias on IQ Tests as an Explanation

Some critics of IQ tests have argued that cultural differences in IQ scores are partly due to a cultural bias built into IQ tests. They argue that because IQ tests are constructed by white, middle-class psychologists, they naturally draw on experience and knowledge typical of white, middle-class lifestyles and use language and vocabulary that reflect the white, middle-class origins of their developers (Cohen, 2002; Helms, 1992, 2006; Hilliard, 1984). Fagan and Holland (2002, 2007) have collected data suggesting that the IQ gap between whites and African Americans is a result of cultural differences in knowledge caused by disparities in *exposure to information*. Most theorists acknowledge that IQ tests measure a combination of ability and knowledge (Ackerman & Beier, 2005; Cianciolo & Sternberg, 2004). Test de-

velopers try to tilt the balance toward the assessment of ability as much as possible, but factual knowledge clearly has an impact on IQ scores. According to Fagan and Holland (2002, 2007) cultural disparities in IQ reflect differences in *knowledge* rather than differences in *ability*. That said, other approaches to this issue, which have focused on whether there are cultural disparities in the predictive validity of IQ tests, suggest that the cultural slant on IQ tests is modest. Many experts assert that the evidence indicates that cultural bias produces only weak and inconsistent effects on the IQ scores of minority examinees (Hunter & Schmidt, 2000; Reynolds, 2000; Reynolds & Ramsay, 2003). Thus, debate continues about the degree to which IQ tests may contain a cultural slant.

Taken as a whole, the various alternative explanations for cultural and ethnic disparities in average IQ provide serious challenges to genetic explanations, which appear weak at best—and suspiciously racist at worst. Unfortunately, since the earliest days of IQ testing some people have used IQ tests to further elitist goals. The current controversy about ethnic differences in IQ is just another replay of a record that has been heard before. For instance, begin- ning in 1913, Henry Goddard tested a great many immigrants to the United States at Ellis Island in New York. Goddard reported that the vast majority of Italian, Hungarian, and Jewish immigrants tested out as *feeble-minded* (Kamin, 1974). As you can see, claims about ethnic deficits in intelligence are noth- ing new—only the victims have changed.

REVIEW of Key Learning Goals

9.16 Twin studies show that identical twins, even when raised apart, are more similar in IQ than fraternal twins, sug- gesting that intelligence is inherited. Adoption studies reveal that people resemble their parents in intelligence even when not raised by them. Estimates of the heritability of intelligence range from 40% to 80% with the consensus estimate hovering around 50%, but heritability ratios have certain limitations.

9.17 Studies show that adopted children resemble their parents and adoptive siblings in intelligence. The effects of environmental deprivation and enrichment also indicate that IQ is shaped by experience. And generational changes in IQ (the Flynn effect) can only be due to environmental factors.

9.18 The concept of reaction range posits that heredity places limits on one's intellectual potential while the environment determines where one falls within these limits. Scientists are

striving to identify the specific genes that influence intelligence, but progress has been slow thus far. Intelligence may be shaped by hundreds of genes that each have tiny effects.

9.19 Arthur Jensen and the authors of *The Bell Curve* sparked controversy by arguing that cultural differences in average IQ are partly due to heredity. Even if the heritability of IQ is great, group differences in average intelligence may not be due to heredity. Many theorists note that ethnicity co-varies with social class, so socioeconomic disadvantage may contribute to low IQ scores among minority students.

9.20 Claude Steele has suggested that stereotype vulnerabil- ity contributes to the culture gap in average IQ. The Featured Study showed how the specter of negative stereotypes can impair test performance. Cultural bias on IQ tests may also fac- tor into ethnic differences in IQ.

New Directions in the Assessment and Study of Intelligence

Key Learning Goals

9.21 Summarize evidence on biological indicators and correlates of intelligence.

9.22 Contrast Sternberg's triarchic theory with Gard- ner's theory of multiple intelligences.

9.23 Explain the notion of emotional intelligence, and outline recent criticism of the concept.

Intelligence testing has been through a period of turmoil, and changes are on the horizon. In fact, many changes have occurred already. Let's look at some of the major new trends and projections for the future.

Exploring Biological Indexes and Correlates of Intelligence

The controversy about cultural disparities in IQ scores has led to increased interest in biological indexes of IQ that ought to provide "culture-free" measures of intelligence (Eysenck, 1989; Jensen, 1993, 1998). Arthur Jensen's (1982, 1987, 1992) stud- ies of mental speed are representative of this line of inquiry. In his studies, Jensen measures *reaction time* (RT), using a panel of paired buttons and lights. On each trial, the subject rests a hand on a "home but- ton." When one of the lights is activated, the sub- ject is supposed to push the button for that light as quickly as possible. RT is typically averaged over a number of trials involving varied numbers of lights. Modest correlations (.20s to .30s) have been found between faster RTs and higher scores on conven- tional IQ tests (Deary, 2003).

Jensen's findings suggest an association between raw mental speed and intelligence, as Galton origi- nally suggested. However, the correlation between RT and IQ appears to be too weak to give RT any practical value as an index of intelligence. However, another approach to measuring mental speed may have more practical potential. Measures of *inspection time* assess how long it takes participants to make simple perceptual discriminations that meet a cer- tain criterion of accuracy (Deary & Stough, 1996). For example, in a series of trials, participants may be asked repeatedly to indicate which of two lines is shorter. The pairs of lines are presented for very brief exposures and participants are told to concentrate on making *accurate* judgments. A person's inspec- tion time is the exposure duration required for that person to achieve a specific level of accuracy, such as 85% correct judgments (see **Figure 9.19**). Correla- tions in the .30s and .40s have been found between participants' inspection time scores and their scores on measures of intelligence (Deary, 2000; McCrory & Cooper, 2007; Nettelbeck, 2003). These correla- tions are closing in on being high enough to have some practical value, although a great deal of work remains to be done to standardize inspection time

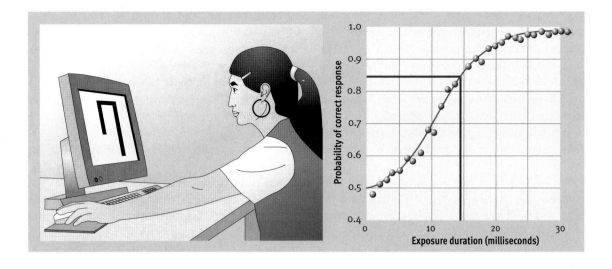

Figure 9.19
Research on inspection time as a biological index of intelligence.
(Left) In studies of inspection time, participants are shown stimuli for very brief durations and are asked to make accurate judgments about them (such as whether the longer line is on the right or the left). (Right) Each participant's accuracy in making these perceptual discriminations is graphed as a function of exposure duration. A subject's inspection time for a particular task is the exposure duration required to achieve a certain level of accuracy. In this case, 85% accuracy is the criterion and the participant's inspection time for the task is 14 milliseconds.

SOURCE: Graph adapted from Deary, I. J., Caryl, P. G., & Gibson, G. J. (1993). Nonstationarity and the measurement of psychophysical response in a visual inspection time task. *Perception, 22,* 1245–1256. Copyright © 1993 by Pion Ltd. Adapted by permission.

measures and to figure out why they are associated with intelligence.

Some researchers have also begun to explore the relations between brain size and intelligence. The early studies in this area used various measures of head size as an indicator of brain size. These studies generally found positive, but very small correlations (average = .15) between head size and IQ (Vernon et al., 2000), leading researchers to speculate that head size is probably a very crude index of brain size. This line of research might have languished, but the invention of sophisticated brain-imaging technologies gave it a huge shot in the arm. Since the 1990s, quite a few studies have examined the correlation between IQ scores and measures of brain volume based on MRI scans (see Chapter 3), yielding an average correlation of about .35 (Anderson, 2003; McDaniel, 2005; Rushton & Ankney, 2007). One obvious implication of these findings, eagerly embraced by those who tout the influence of heredity on intelligence, is that genetic inheritance gives some people larger brains than others and that larger brain size promotes greater intelligence (Rushton, 2003). However, as always, we must be cautious about interpreting correlational data. As discussed in Chapter 3, research has demonstrated that an enriched environment can produce denser neural networks and heavier brains in laboratory rats (Rosenzweig & Bennett, 1996). Hence, it is also possible that causation runs in the opposite direction—that developing greater intelligence promotes larger brain size, much like weightlifting can promote larger muscles.

Research on the biological correlates of intelligence has turned up another interesting finding that seems likely to occupy researchers for some time to come. IQ scores measured in childhood correlate with longevity decades later. For example, one study has followed a large cohort of people in Scotland who were given IQ tests in 1932 when they were 11 years old (Deary et al., 2004). People who scored one standard deviation (15 points) below average on the IQ test in 1932 were only 79% as likely as those who scored average or above to be alive in 1997. A handful of other studies have yielded the same conclusion: Smarter people live longer (Gottfredson & Deary, 2004). Based on these findings, Linda Gottfredson (2004) argues that health self-care is a complicated, mentally challenging lifelong mission, for which brighter people are better prepared. One huge complication is that higher socioeconomic class is correlated with both higher IQ and better health outcomes. Thus, it is hard to rule out the possibility that affluence promotes longevity and that higher intelligence is merely an incidental correlate of both.

Investigating Cognitive Processes in Intelligent Behavior

As noted in Chapters 1 and 8, psychologists are increasingly taking a cognitive perspective in their efforts to study many topics. For over a century, the investigation of intelligence has been approached primarily from a *testing perspective*. This perspective emphasizes measuring the *amount* of intelligence people have and figuring out why some have more than others. In contrast, the *cognitive perspective* focuses on how people *use* their intelligence. The interest is in process rather than amount. In particular, cognitive psychologists focus on the information-processing strategies that underlie intelligence. The application of the cognitive perspective to intelligence has been spearheaded by Robert Sternberg (1985, 1988b, 1991).

Robert Sternberg

"To understand intelligent behavior, we need to move beyond the fairly restrictive tasks that have been used both in experimental laboratories and in psychometric tests of intelligence."

Sternberg's *triarchic theory of human intelligence* consists of three parts: the contextual, experiential, and componential subtheories. In his *contextual subtheory,* Sternberg argues that intelligence is a culturally defined concept. He asserts that different manifestations of intelligent behavior are valued in different contexts. In his *experiential subtheory,* Sternberg explores the relationships between experience and intelligence. He emphasizes two factors as the hallmarks of intelligent behavior. The first is the ability to deal effectively with novelty—new tasks, demands, and situations. The second factor is the ability to learn how to handle familiar tasks automatically and effortlessly. Sternberg's *componential subtheory* describes three types of mental processes that intelligent thought depends on: metacomponents, performance components, and knowledge-acquisition components (see **Figure 9.20**).

In more recent extensions of his theory, Sternberg (1999, 2000b, 2003a, 2005b) has asserted that three aspects or facets characterize what he calls "successful intelligence": analytical intelligence, creative intelligence, and practical intelligence. *Analytical intelligence* involves abstract reasoning, evaluation, and judgment. It is the type of intelligence that is crucial to most schoolwork and that is assessed by conventional IQ tests. *Creative intelligence* involves the ability to generate new ideas and to be inventive in dealing with novel problems. *Practical intelligence* involves the ability to deal effectively with the kinds of problems that people encounter in everyday life, such as on the job or at home. A big part of practical intelligence involves acquiring *tacit knowledge*— what one needs to know to work efficiently in an environment that is not explicitly taught and that often is not even verbalized.

In a series of studies, Sternberg and his colleagues have gathered data suggesting that (1) all three facets of intelligence can be measured reliably, (2) the three facets of intelligence are relatively independent (uncorrelated), and (3) the assessment of all three aspects of intelligence can improve the prediction of intelligent behavior in the real world (Grigorenko & Sternberg, 2001; Henry, Sternberg, & Grigorenko, 2005; Sternberg et al., 1999, 2001). Recent findings suggest that measurements based on Sternberg's model can be used as supplements to traditional tests (such as the SAT) to enhance the prediction of academic achievement (Stemler et al., 2006; Sternberg et al., 2006). Some critics doubt that Sternberg's measures will facilitate better prediction of meaningful outcomes than traditional IQ tests (Gottfredson, 2003a), but that is an empirical question that should be resolved by future research. In any event, Sternberg certainly has been an articulate voice arguing for a broader, expanded concept of intelligence, which is a theme that has been echoed by others.

Figure 9.20

Sternberg's triarchic theory of intelligence. Sternberg's model of intelligence consists of three parts: the contextual subtheory, the experiential subtheory, and the componential subtheory. Much of Sternberg's research has been devoted to the componential subtheory, as he has attempted to identify the cognitive processes that contribute to intelligence. He believes that these processes fall into three groups: metacomponents, performance components, and knowledge-acquisition components. All three component processes contribute to each of three aspects or types of intelligence: analytical intelligence, practical intelligence, and creative intelligence.

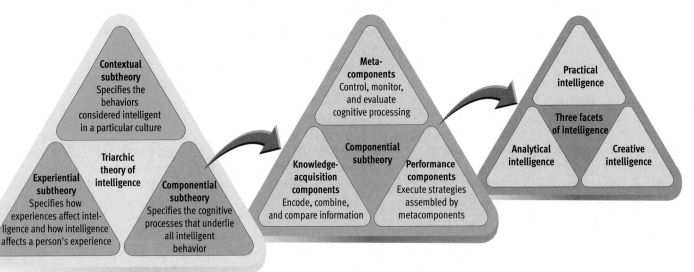

Expanding the Concept of Intelligence

In recent years, a number of theorists besides Sternberg have concluded that the focus of traditional IQ tests is too narrow. The most prominent proponent of this view has been Howard Gardner (1983, 1993, 1999, 2004, 2006). According to Gardner, IQ tests have generally emphasized verbal and mathematical skills, to the exclusion of other important skills. He suggests the existence of a number of relatively autonomous human intelligences, which are listed in Table 9.3. To build his list of *multiple intelligences,* Gardner reviewed the evidence on cognitive capacities in normal individuals, people suffering from brain damage, and special populations, such as prodigies and idiot savants. He concluded that humans exhibit eight intelligences: logical-mathematical, linguistic, musical, spatial, bodily-kinesthetic, interpersonal, intrapersonal, and naturalist. These intelligences obviously include quite a variety of talents that are not assessed by conventional IQ tests. Gardner is investigating the extent to which these intelligences are largely independent, as his theory asserts. For the most part, he has found that people tend to display a mixture of strong, intermediate, and weak abilities, which is consistent with the idea that the various types of intelligence are independent.

Gardner's books have been popular, and his theory clearly resonates with many people (Shearer, 2004). His ideas have had an enormous impact on educators' attitudes and beliefs around the world (Cuban, 2004; Kornhaber, 2004). He has done a superb job of synthesizing research from neuropsychology, developmental psychology, cognitive psychology, and other areas to arrive at fascinating speculations about the structure of human abilities. He has raised thought-provoking questions about what abilities should be included under the rubric of intelligence (Eisner, 2004). However, he has his critics (Hunt, 2001; Klein, 1997; Morgan, 1996; Waterhouse, 2006). Some argue that his use of the term *intelligence* is so broad, encompassing virtually any valued human ability, as to make the term almost meaningless. These critics wonder whether there is any advantage to relabeling tal-

ents such as musical ability and motor coordination as forms of intelligence. Critics also note that Gardner's theory has not generated much research on the predictive value of measuring individual differences in the eight intelligences he has described. This research would require the development of tests to measure the eight intelligences, but Gardner is not particularly interested in the matter of assessment and he loathes conventional testing. This situation makes it difficult to predict where Gardner's theory will lead, as research is crucial to the evolution of a theory.

Measuring Emotional Intelligence

In yet another highly publicized effort to expand the concept of intelligence, a variety of theorists have argued that the measurement of *emotional intelligence* can enhance the prediction of success at school, at work, and in interpersonal relationships. The concept of emotional intelligence was originally developed by Peter Salovey and John Mayer (1990). Their concept languished in relative obscurity until Daniel Goleman (1995) wrote a compelling book titled *Emotional Intelligence,* which made the best-seller lists. Since then, empirical research on the measurement of emotional intelligence has increased dramatically.

Emotional intelligence (EI) consists of the ability to perceive and express emotion, assimilate emotion in thought, understand and reason with emotion, and regulate emotion. Emotional intel-

Howard Gardner

"It is high time that the view of intelligence be widened to incorporate a range of human computational capacities.... But where is it written that intelligence needs to be determined on the basis of tests?"

web link 9.6

HowardGardner.com

You can find a wealth of resources on Gardner's theory of multiple intelligences at this site, including biographical information on Gardner, seminal and recent papers on his multiple intelligence perspective, and links to other relevant sites.

Table 9.3 Gardner's Eight Intelligences

Intelligence	End-States	Core Components
Logical-mathematical	Scientist Mathematician	Sensitivity to, and capacity to discern, logical or numerical patterns; ability to handle long chains of reasoning
Linguistic	Poet Journalist	Sensitivity to the sounds, rhythms, and meanings of words; sensitivity to the different functions of language
Musical	Composer Violinist	Abilities to produce and appreciate rhythm, pitch, and timbre; appreciation of the forms of musical expressiveness
Spatial	Navigator Sculptor	Capacities to perceive the visual-spatial world accurately and to perform transformations on one's initial perceptions
Bodily-kinesthetic	Dancer Athlete	Abilities to control one's body movements and to handle objects skillfully
Interpersonal	Therapist Salesperson	Capacities to discern and respond appropriately to the moods, temperaments, motivations, and desires of other people
Intrapersonal	Person with detailed, accurate self-knowledge	Access to one's own feelings and the ability to discriminate among them and draw upon them to guide behavior; knowledge of one's own strengths, weaknesses, desires, and intelligences
Naturalist	Biologist Naturalist	Abilities to recognize and categorize objects and processes in nature

Source: Adapted from Gardner, H., & Hatch, T. (1989). Multiple intelligences go to school: Educational implications of the theory of multiple intelligences. *Educational Researcher, 18* (8), 4–10. American Educational Research Association. Additional information from Gardner (1998).

ligence includes four essential components (Salovey, Mayer, & Caruso, 2002; Salovey & Grewal, 2005). First, people need to be able to accurately perceive emotions in themselves and others and have the ability to express their own emotions effectively. Second, people need to be aware of how their emotions shape their thinking, decisions, and coping mechanisms. Third, people need to be able to understand and analyze their emotions, which may often be complex and contradictory. Fourth, people need to be able to regulate their emotions so that they can dampen negative emotions and make effective use of positive emotions.

Several tests have been developed to measure the relatively new concept of emotional intelligence. The test that has the strongest empirical founda-tion is the Mayer-Salovey-Caruso Emotional Intelligence Test (2002). The authors have strived to make this test a performance-based measure of the ability to deal effectively with emotions rather than a measure of personality or temperament. Preliminary results suggest that they have made considerable progress toward this goal, as evidenced by the scale's ability to predict intelligent management of emotions in real-world situations (Ciarrochi, Dean & Anderson, 2002; Lam & Kirby, 2002; Mayer et al., 2001). Illustrating the practical importance of emotional intelligence, scores on the scale also predict the quality of subjects' social interactions (Lopes et al., 2004). Yet another study of college-age couples found that the happiest couples were those in which both individuals scored relatively high in emotional intelligence (Salovey & Grewal, 2005).

Skeptics have questioned whether sophistication about emotion should be viewed as a form of intelligence, and they have noted that definitions of EI vary and tend to be fuzzy (Matthews et al., 2006; Murphy & Sideman, 2006b). Critics also assert that claims about the practical utility of EI in the business world have been exaggerated and that a great deal of additional research will be needed to fully validate measures of emotional intelligence (Conte & Dean, 2006; Jordan, Ashton-James, & Ashkanasy, 2006). In spite of these concerns, the concept of emotional intelligence has been accepted with great enthusiasm in the realm of business management, and hundreds of consultants provide a plethora of intervention programs to enhance leadership, teamwork, and productivity (Schmit, 2006). Skeptics characterize these programs as little more than a "fad" in the business world, but many of these critics acknowledge that the EI concept may have some explanatory value if buttressed by more research (Hogan & Stokes, 2006; Murphy & Sideman, 2006a). Thus, the concept of emotional intelligence seems to have reached a crossroads. It will be interesting to see what unfolds over the next decade.

REVIEW of Key Learning Goals

9.21 Although reaction time indexes of intelligence are being explored, they seem to have little practical utility. Measures of inspection time may prove more useful, although additional research is needed. Recent research has uncovered a moderate positive correlation between IQ and brain volume estimated from MRI scans. Studies have also found that IQ measured in childhood correlates with longevity decades later.

9.22 Robert Sternberg's triarchic theory uses a cognitive perspective, which emphasizes the need to understand how people use their intelligence. According to Sternberg, the three facets of successful intelligence are analytical, creative, and practical intelligence. Howard Gardner argues that the concept of intelligence should be expanded to encompass a diverse set of eight types of abilities.

9.23 Researchers have made some progress in efforts to measure emotional intelligence and they have shown that it is predictive of effective management of emotions in real-world situations. However, skeptics question whether being savvy about emotions should be viewed as a form of intelligence and they assert that EI is a fuzzy concept that is difficult to measure.

Reflecting on the Chapter's Themes

As you probably noticed, three of our integrative themes surfaced in this chapter. Our discussions illustrated that cultural factors shape behavior, that psychology evolves in a sociohistorical context, and that heredity and environment jointly influence behavior.

Pervasive psychological testing is largely a Western phenomenon. The concept of general intelligence also has a special, Western flavor to it. Many non-Western cultures have very different ideas about the nature of intelligence. Within Western societies, the observed ethnic differences in average intelligence also illustrate the importance of cultural factors, as these disparities appear to be due in large part to cultural disadvantage and other culture-related considerations. Thus, we see once again that if we hope to achieve a sound understanding of behavior, we need to appreciate the cultural contexts in which behavior unfolds.

Human intelligence is shaped by a complex interaction of hereditary and environmental factors. We've drawn similar conclusions before in other chapters where we examined other aspects of behavior. However, this chapter should have enhanced your appreciation of this idea in at least two ways. First, we examined more of the details of how scientists arrive at the conclusion that heredity and environment jointly shape behavior. Second, we encountered dramatic illustrations of the immense importance attached to the nature versus nurture debate. For example, Arthur Jensen has been the target of savage criticism. After his controversial 1969 article, he was widely characterized as a racist. When he gave speeches, he was often greeted by protestors carrying signs, such as "Kill Jensen" and "Jensen Must Perish." As you can

see, the debate about the inheritance of intelligence inspires passionate feelings in many people. In part, this is because the debate has far-reaching social and political implications, which brings us to another prominent theme in the chapter.

There may be no other area in psychology where the connections between psychology and society at large are so obvious. Prevailing social attitudes have always exerted some influence on testing practices and the interpretation of test results. In the first half of the 20th century, a strong current of racial and class prejudice was apparent in the United States and Britain. This prejudice supported the idea that IQ tests measured innate ability and that "undesirable" groups scored poorly because of their genetic inferiority. Although these beliefs did not go unchallenged within psychology, their widespread acceptance in the field reflected the social values of the time. It's ironic that IQ tests have sometimes been associated with social prejudice. When used properly, intelligence tests provide relatively objective measures of mental ability that are less prone to bias than the subjective judgments of teachers or employers.

Today, psychological tests serve many diverse purposes. In the upcoming Personal Application, we focus on creativity tests and on the nature of creative thinking and creative people.

 Cultural Heritage

 Heredity and Environment

 Sociohistorical Context

REVIEW of Key Learning Goals
9.24 Our discussions of intelligence showed how heredity and environment interact to shape behavior, how psychology evolves in a sociohistorical context, and how one has to consider cultural contexts to fully understand behavior.

PERSONAL

Understanding Creativity

APPLICATION

Answer the following "true" or "false."

____ 1 Creative ideas often come out of nowhere.

____ 2 Creativity usually occurs in a burst of insight.

____ 3 Creativity depends on divergent thinking.

Intelligence is not the only type of mental ability that psychologists have studied. They have devised tests to explore a variety of mental abilities. Creativity is certainly one of the most interesting among them. People tend to view creativity as an essential trait for artists, musicians, and writers,

Key Learning Goals
9.25 Evaluate the role of insight and divergent thinking in creativity.
9.26 Describe creativity tests, and summarize how well they predict creative achievement.
9.27 Clarify the associations between creativity and personality, intelligence, and mental illness.

but it is important in *many* walks of life. In this Application, we'll discuss psychologists' efforts to measure and understand creativity. As we progress, you'll learn that all of the above statements are false.

The Nature of Creativity

What makes thought creative? *Creativity* involves the generation of ideas that are original, novel, and useful. Creative thinking is fresh, innovative, and inventive. But novelty by itself is not enough. In addition to being unusual, creative thinking must be adaptive. It must be appropriate to the situation and problem.

Does Creativity Occur in a Burst of Insight?

It is widely believed that creativity usually involves sudden flashes of insight and great leaps of imagination. Robert Weisberg (1986) calls this belief the "aha! myth." Undeniably, creative bursts of insight do occur (Feldman, 1988). However, the evidence suggests that major creative achievements generally are logical extensions of existing ideas, involving long, hard work and many small, faltering steps forward (Weisberg, 1993). Creative ideas do not come out of nowhere. Creative ideas come from a deep well of experience and training in a specific area, whether it's music, painting, business, or science (Weisberg, 1999, 2006). As Snow (1986) put it, "Creativity is not a light bulb in the mind, as most cartoons depict it. It is an accomplishment born of intensive study, long reflection, persistence, and interest" (p. 1033).

Does Creativity Depend on Divergent Thinking?

According to many theorists, the key to creativity lies in *divergent thinking*—thinking "that goes off in different directions," as J. P. Guilford (1959) put it. Guilford distinguished between convergent thinking and divergent thinking. In *convergent thinking* one tries to narrow down a list of alternatives to converge on a single correct answer. For example, when you take a multiple-choice exam, you try to eliminate incorrect options until you hit on the correct response. Most training in school encourages convergent thinking. In *divergent*

thinking one tries to expand the range of alternatives by generating many possible solutions. Imagine that you work for an advertising agency. To come up with as many slogans as possible for a client's product, you must use divergent thinking. Some of your slogans may be clear losers, and eventually you will have to engage in convergent thinking to pick the best, but coming up with the range of new possibilities depends on divergent thinking.

Thirty years of research on divergent thinking has yielded mixed results. As a whole, the evidence suggests that divergent thinking can contribute to creativity (Runco, 2004), but it clearly does not represent the essence of creativity, as originally proposed (Brown, 1989; Plucker & Renzulli, 1999; Weisberg, 2006). In retrospect, it was probably unrealistic to expect creativity to depend on a single cognitive skill.

Measuring Creativity   SIM8

Although its nature may be elusive, creativity clearly is important in today's world. Creative masterpieces in the arts and literature enrich human existence. Creative insights in the sciences illuminate people's understanding of the world. Creative inventions fuel technological progress. Thus, it is understandable that psychologists have been interested in measuring creativity with psychological tests.

How Do Psychological Tests Measure Creativity?   SIM8

A diverse array of psychological tests have been devised to measure individuals' creativity (Cooper, 1991). Usually, the items on creativity tests assess divergent thinking by giving respondents a specific starting point and then requiring them to generate as many possibilities as they can in a short period of time. Typical items on a creativity test might include the following: (1) List as many uses as you can for a newspaper. (2) Think of as many fluids that burn as you can. (3) Imagine that people no longer need sleep and think of as many consequences as you can. Subjects' scores on these tests depend on the *number* of alternatives they

generate and on the *originality* and *usefulness* of the alternatives.

How Well Do Tests Predict Creative Productivity?

In general, studies indicate that creativity tests are mediocre predictors of creative achievement in the real world (Hocevar & Bachelor, 1989; Plucker & Renzulli, 1999). Why? One reason is that these tests measure creativity in the abstract, as a *general trait*. However, the accumulation of evidence suggests that *creativity is specific to particular domains* (Amabile, 1996; Feist, 2004; Kaufman & Baer, 2002, 2004). Despite some rare exceptions, creative people usually excel in a single field, in which they typically have considerable training and expertise (Policastro & Gardner, 1999). A remarkably innovative physicist might have no potential to be a creative poet or an inventive advertising executive. Measuring this person's creativity outside of physics may be meaningless. Thus, creativity tests may have limited value because they measure creativity out of context.

Even if better tests of creativity were devised, predicting creative achievement would probably still prove difficult. Why? Because creative achievement depends on many factors besides creativity (Cropley, 2000). Creative productivity over the course of an individual's career will depend on his or her motivation, personality, and intelligence, as well as situational factors, including training, mentoring, and good fortune (Amabile, 2001; Feldman, 1999; Simonton, 1999a, 2004).

Correlates of Creativity

What are creative people like? Are they brighter, or more open minded, or less well adjusted than average? A great deal of research has been conducted on the correlates of creativity.

Is There a Creative Personality?

Creative people exhibit the full range of personality traits, but investigators have found modest correlations between certain personality characteristics and creativity (Ochse, 1990). Based on a meta-analysis of over 80 studies, Feist (1998) concludes that highly creative people tend to be "more autonomous, introverted, open to new experiences, norm-doubting, self-confident, self-accepting, driven, ambitious, dominant, hostile, and impulsive" (p. 299). At the core of this set of personality characteristics are the related traits of independence and non-conformity. Creative people tend to think for themselves and are less easily influenced by the opinions of others than the average person is. That said, there is no single personality profile that accounts for creativity (Weisberg, 2006).

Are Creativity and Intelligence Related?

Are creative people exceptionally smart? Conceptually, creativity and intelligence represent different types of mental ability. Thus, it's not surprising that correlations between measures of creativity and measures of intelligence are generally weak (Sternberg & O'Hara, 1999). For example, a recent meta-analysis of many studies reported a correlation of only .17 (Kim, 2005). However, some findings suggest that the association between creativity and intelligence is somewhat stronger than that. When Silvia (2008) administered several intelligence scales and calculated estimates of *g* for subjects, this higher-order measure of intelligence correlated over .40 with creativity. One widely-cited model of the relationship between creativity and intelligence is the *threshold hypothesis* proposed decades ago by pioneering creativity researchers (Barron, 1963; Torrance, 1962). According to this hypothesis, creative achievements

require a minimum level of intelligence, so most highly creative people are probably well above average in intelligence. An IQ of 120 has been proposed as the minimum threshold for creative achievement (Lubart, 2003). One assumption of this model is that the correlation between IQ and creativity should be weaker among people above this IQ threshold than for those below it, but recent research has failed to support this assumption (Preckel, Holling, & Wiese, 2006; Sligh, Conners, & Roskos-Ewoldsen, 2005). At this point, all one can conclude is that there appears to be a weak to modest association between IQ and creativity.

Is There a Connection Between Creativity and Mental Illness?

Some connection may exist between truly exceptional creativity and mental illness. The list of creative geniuses who suffered from psychological disorders is endless (Prentky, 1989). Kafka, Hemingway, Rembrandt, Van Gogh, Chopin, Tchaikovsky, Descartes, and Newton are but a few examples. Of course, a statistical association cannot be demonstrated by citing a handful of examples.

In this case, however, some statistical data are available. And these data *do* suggest a correlation between creative genius and maladjustment—in particular, mood disorders such as depression. When Nancy Andreasen studied 30 accomplished writers who had been invited as visiting faculty to the prestigious Iowa Writers Workshop, she found that 80% of her sample had suffered

a mood disorder at some point in their lives (Andreasen, 1987, 2005). In a similar study of 59 female writers from another writers' conference, Ludwig (1994) found that 56% had experienced depression. These figures are far above the base rate (roughly 15%) for mood disorders in the general population. Other studies have also found an association between creativity and mood disorders, as well as other kinds of psychological disorders (Jamison, 1988; Nettle, 2001; Post, 1996). Perhaps the most ambitious examination of the issue has been Arnold Ludwig's (1995) analyses of the biographies of 1004 people who achieved eminence in 18 fields. He found greatly elevated rates of depression and other disorders among eminent writers, artists, and composers (see **Figure 9.21**). Recent studies suggest that mental illness may be especially elevated among poets (Kaufman, 2001, 2005).

Thus, accumulating empirical data tentatively suggest that a correlation may exist between major creative achievement and vulnerability to mood disorders. According to Andreasen (1996, 2005), creativity and maladjustment probably are *not* causally related. Instead, she speculates that certain personality traits and cognitive styles may both foster creativity and predispose people to psychological disorders. Another, more mundane possibility is that creative individuals' elevated pathology may simply reflect all the difficulty and frustration they experience as they struggle to get their ideas or works accepted in artistic fields that enjoy relatively little public support (Csikszentmihalyi, 1994, 1999).

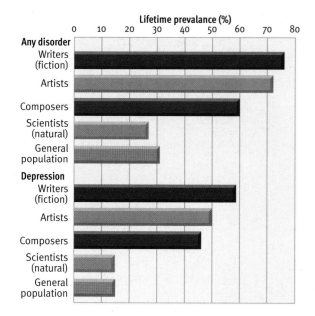

Figure 9.21

Estimated prevalence of psychological disorders among people who achieved creative eminence. Ludwig (1995) sudied biographies of 1004 people who had clearly achieved eminence in one of 18 fields and tried to determine whether each person suffered from any specific mental disorders in their lifetimes. The data summarized here show the prevalence rates for depression and for a mental disorder of any kind for four fields where creativity is often the key to achieving eminence. As you can see, the estimated prevalence of mental illness was extremely elevated among eminent writers, artists, and composers (but not natural scientists) in comparison to the general population, with depression accounting for much of this elevation.

Key Learning Goals

9.28 Understand how appeals to ignorance and reification have cropped up in debates about intelligence.

The Intelligence Debate, Appeals to Ignorance, and Reification

A *fallacy* is a mistake or error in the process of reasoning. Cognitive scientists who study how people think have developed long lists of common errors that people make in their reasoning processes. One of these fallacies has a curious name, which is the *appeal to ignorance*. It involves misusing the general lack of knowledge or information on an issue (a lack of knowledge is a kind of ignorance) to support an argument. This fallacy often surfaces in the debate about the relative influence of heredity and environment on intelligence. But before we tackle the more difficult issue of how this fallacy shows up in the debate about intelligence, let's start with a simpler example.

Appeal to Ignorance

Do ghosts exist? This is probably not the kind of question you expected to find in your psychology textbook, but it can clarify the appeal to ignorance. Those who assert that ghosts *do* exist will often support their conclusion by arguing that no one can prove that ghosts do *not* exist; therefore ghosts must exist. The lack of evidence or inability to show that ghosts do not exist is used to conclude the opposite. Conversely, those who assert that ghosts *do not* exist often rely on the same logic. They argue that no one can prove that ghosts exist; therefore, they must not exist. Can you see what is wrong with these appeals to ignorance? The lack of information on an issue cannot be used to support any conclusion—other than the conclusion that we are too ignorant to draw a conclusion.

One interesting aspect of the appeal to ignorance is that the same appeal can be used to support two conclusions that are diametrically opposed to each other. This paradox is a telltale clue that appeals to ignorance involve flawed reasoning. It is easy to see what is wrong with appeals to ignorance when the opposite arguments (ghosts exist—ghosts do

not exist) are presented together and the lack of evidence on the issue under discussion is obvious. However, when the same fallacy surfaces in more complex debates and the appeal to ignorance is not as blatant, the strategy can be more difficult to recognize. Now let's see how the appeal to ignorance has surfaced in the debate about intelligence.

As noted in the main body of the chapter, the debate about the relative contributions of nature and nurture to intelligence is one of psychology's longest-running controversies. This complex and multifaceted debate is exceptionally bitter and acrimonious because it has far-reaching sociopolitical repercussions. In this exchange, one frequently made argument is that we have little or no evidence that intelligence can be increased by environmental (educational) interventions; therefore, intelligence must be mostly inherited. In other words, the argument runs: No one has demonstrated that intelligence is largely shaped by environment, so it must be largely inherited. This argument was part of Jensen's (1969) landmark treatise that greatly intensified the debate about intelligence, and it was one of the arguments made by Herrnstein and Murray (1994) in

their controversial book *The Bell Curve*. What the argument refers to is the evidence that educational enrichment programs such as Head Start, which have been designed to enhance the cognitive development of underprivileged children, generally have not produced substantial, long-term gains in IQ (Neisser et al., 1996). The programs produce other benefits, including enduring improvements in school achievement, but short-term gains in IQ scores typically have faded by the middle grades (Barnett, 2004). These findings may have some implications for government policy in the educational arena, but the way in which they have been applied to the nature-nurture debate regarding intelligence has resulted in an appeal to ignorance. In its simplest form, the absence of evidence showing that environmental changes can increase intelligence is used to support the conclusion that intelligence is mostly determined by genetic inheritance. But the absence of evidence (ignorance) cannot be used to argue for or against a position.

By the way, if you have assimilated some of the critical thinking skills discussed in earlier chapters, you may be thinking, "Wait

Do ghosts exist? Littledean Hall, shown here, is said to be the home of 11 ghosts and is reputed to be the most haunted house in Great Britain. Those who believe in ghosts often support their view by arguing that no one can prove that ghosts do not exist. But as the text explains, this appeal to ignorance is logically flawed. This fallacy has also surfaced in some of the debates about the nature of intelligence.

© Simon Marsden, marsdenarchive.com

a minute. Aren't there alternative explanations for the failure of educational enrichment programs to increase IQ scores?" Yes, one could argue that the programs failed to yield improvements in IQ scores because they often were poorly executed, too brief, or underfunded (Ramey, 1999; Sigel, 2004). Moreover, Head Start programs are not really designed to increase IQ scores, but rather to enhance deprived students' readiness for school (Schrag, Styfco, & Zigler, 2004). The inability of the enrichment programs to produce enduring increases in IQ does not necessarily imply that intelligence is unchangeable because it is largely a product of heredity.

You may also be wondering, "Aren't there contradictory data?" Once again, the answer is yes. Barnett (2004) argues that failures to find enduring gains in intelligence from Head Start programs can often be attributed to flaws and shortcomings in the research design of the studies. Furthermore, studies of some lesser-known educational enrichment programs attempted with smaller groups of children *have* yielded durable gains in IQ and other standardized test scores (Ramey & Ramey, 2004; Reynolds et al., 2001; Woodhead, 2004).

But we're supposed to be discussing appeals to ignorance, and there was another notable example of this fallacy in the chapter. Can you identify where this slippery logic was used? It surfaced in the discussion of the causes of mental retardation. As you may recall, roughly 50% of the time diagnosticians can pinpoint a biological cause for retardation. The remaining 50% of the cases are of unknown origin, but they are typically assumed to be due to environmental factors. In other words, the reasoning goes, *we don't have any evidence that these cases are due to biological anomalies, so*

they must be environmental in origin. This is an appeal to ignorance and the assertion is open to questioning.

Reification

The dialogue on intelligence has also been marred by the tendency to engage in reification. *Reification* **occurs when a hypothetical, abstract concept is given a name and then treated as though it were a concrete, tangible object.** Some hypothetical constructs just become so familiar and so taken for granted that we begin to think about them as if they were real. People often fall into this trap with the Freudian personality concepts of id, ego, and superego (see Chapter 12). They begin to think of the *ego*, for instance, as a genuine entity that can be strengthened or controlled, when the ego is really nothing more than a hypothetical abstraction. The concept of intelligence has also been reified in many quarters. Like the ego, intelligence is nothing more than a useful abstraction—a hypothetical construct that is estimated, rather arbitrarily, by a collection of paper-and-pencil measures called IQ tests. Yet people routinely act as if intelligence is a tangible commodity, fighting vitriolic battles over whether it can be measured precisely, whether it can be changed, and whether it can ensure job success. This reification clearly contributes to the tendency for people to attribute excessive importance to the concept of intelligence. It would be wise to remember that intelligence is no more real than the concept of "environment," or "cyberspace," or "the American dream."

Reification has also occurred in the debate about the *degree* to which intelligence is inherited. Arguments about the heritability coefficient for intelligence often imply

Reification occurs when we think of hypothetical constructs as if they were real. Like intelligence, the concept of cyberspace has been subject to reification. The fact that cyberspace is merely an abstraction becomes readily apparent when artists are asked to "draw" cyberspace for conference posters or book covers.

that a single, true number lurks somewhere "out there" waiting to be discovered. In reality, heritability is a hypothetical construct that can be legitimately estimated in several ways that can lead to somewhat different results. Moreover, heritability ratios will vary from one population to the next, depending on the amount of genetic variability and the extent of environmental variability in the populations. No exactly accurate number that corresponds to "true heritability" awaits discovery. Thus, it is important to understand that hypothetical constructs have great heuristic value in the study of complex phenomena such as human thought and behavior, but they do not actually exist in the world—at least not in the same way that a table or a person exists.

Table 9.4 Critical Thinking Skills Discussed in This Application

Skill	Description
Recognizing and avoiding appeals to ignorance	The critical thinker understands that the lack of information on an issue cannot be used to support an argument.
Recognizing and avoiding reification	The critical thinker is vigilant about the tendency to treat hypothetical constructs as if they were concrete things.
Looking for alternative explanations for findings and events	In evaluating explanations, the critical thinker explores whether there are other explanations that could also account for the findings or events under scrutiny.
Looking for contradictory evidence	In evaluating the evidence presented on an issue, the critical thinker attempts to look for contradictory evidence that may have been left out of the debate.

REVIEW of Key Learning Goals

9.28 The appeal to ignorance involves misusing the general lack of knowledge or information on an issue to support an argument. This fallacy has surfaced in the debate about intelligence, wherein it has been argued that because we have little or no evidence that intelligence can be increased by environmental interventions, intelligence must be mostly inherited. Reification occurs when a hypothetical construct, such as intelligence, is treated as though it were a tangible object.

Key Ideas

Key Concepts in Psychological Testing

▌ Psychological tests are standardized measures of behavior—usually mental abilities or aspects of personality. Test scores are interpreted by consulting test norms to find out what represents a high or low score. Psychological tests should produce consistent results, a quality called reliability.

▌ Validity refers to the degree to which there is evidence that a test measures what it was designed to measure. Content validity is crucial on classroom tests. Criterion-related validity is critical when tests are used to predict performance. Construct validity is critical when a test is designed to measure a hypothetical construct.

The Evolution of Intelligence Testing

▌ The first crude efforts to devise intelligence tests were made by Sir Francis Galton, who wanted to show that intelligence is inherited. Modern intelligence testing began with the work of Alfred Binet, who devised a scale to measure a child's mental age.

▌ Lewis Terman revised the original Binet scale to produce the Stanford-Binet in 1916. It introduced the intelligence quotient and became the standard of comparison for subsequent tests. David Wechsler devised an improved measure of intelligence for adults and a new scoring system based on the normal distribution. Charles Spearman argued that all cognitive abilities share a common core, which he called *g* for general mental ability.

Basic Questions About Intelligence Testing

▌ In the modern scoring system, deviation IQ scores indicate where people fall in the normal distribution of intelligence for their age group. IQ tests are exceptionally reliable. They are reasonably valid measures of academic intelligence, but they do not tap social or practical intelligence.

▌ IQ scores are correlated with occupational attainment and income, but their ability to predict performance within occupations is the subject of debate. Intelligence testing is largely a Western enterprise; IQ tests are not widely used in most non-Western cultures.

Extremes of Intelligence

▌ IQ scores below 70 are usually diagnostic of mental retardation, but these diagnoses should not be based solely on test results. Four levels of intellectual disability have been distinguished. Most of the people diagnosed with retardation fall in the mild category. Although many biological conditions can cause retardation, biological causes can be pinpointed in only about 50% of cases.

▌ Children who obtain IQ scores above 130 may be viewed as gifted, but cutoffs for accelerated programs vary. Research by Terman showed that gifted children tend to be socially mature and well adjusted, although Winner has raised concerns about the adjustment of profoundly gifted individuals. According to the drudge theory, extraordinary achievement depends on intensive training and hard work, but many theorists argue that innate talent is also a crucial factor.

Heredity and Environment as Determinants of Intelligence

▌ Twin studies show that identical twins are more similar in IQ than fraternal twins, suggesting that intelligence is inherited, at least in part. Estimates of the heritability of intelligence range from 40% to 80% but converge around 50%. However, heritability ratios have certain limitations.

▌ Many lines of evidence indicate that environment is also an important determinant of intelligence. Of particular interest are studies of environmental deprivation and enrichment and the recent discovery of generational increases in measured IQ, dubbed the Flynn effect.

▌ The concept of reaction range posits that heredity places limits on one's intellectual potential while the environment determines where one falls within these limits. Genetic mapping efforts to pinpoint the genes responsible for intelligence have met with little success thus far.

▌ Genetic explanations for cultural differences in IQ have been challenged on a variety of grounds. Even if the heritability of IQ is great, group differences in average intelligence may not be due to heredity. Moreover, race varies with social class, so socioeconomic disadvantage may account for low IQ scores among minority students. Some researchers have suggested that stereotype vulnerability and cultural bias on IQ tests may also contribute to ethnic differences in average IQ.

New Directions in the Assessment and Study of Intelligence

▌ Biological indexes of intelligence are being explored; however, they seem to have little practical utility, although the inspection time measure appears to have potential. IQ scores appear to correlate modestly with brain size and longevity.

▌ Robert Sternberg's triarchic theory takes a cognitive perspective, which emphasizes the need to understand how people use their intelligence. Howard Gardner argues that the concept of intelligence should be expanded to encompass a greater variety of skills. Some theorists argue that emotional intelligence is as important as general mental ability.

Reflecting on the Chapter's Themes

▌ Three of our integrative themes stood out in the chapter. Our discussions of intelligence showed how heredity and environment interact to shape behavior, how psychology evolves in a sociohistorical context, and how one has to consider cultural contexts to fully understand behavior.

PERSONAL APPLICATION Understanding Creativity

▌ Creativity involves the generation of original, novel, and useful ideas. Creativity does not usually involve sudden insight, and it consists of more than divergent thinking. Creativity tests are mediocre predictors of creative productivity in the real world.

▌ The association between creativity and intelligence is weak to moderate. The correlations are modest, but some personality traits are associated with creativity. Recent evidence suggests that creative geniuses may exhibit heightened vulnerability to psychological disorders, especially mood disorders.

CRITICAL THINKING APPLICATION The Intelligence Debate, Appeals to Ignorance, and Reification

▌ The appeal to ignorance involves misusing the general lack of knowledge or information on an issue to support an argument. This fallacy has surfaced in the debate about intelligence, wherein it has been argued that because we have little or no evidence that intelligence can be increased by environmental interventions, intelligence must be mostly inherited.

▌ Reification occurs when a hypothetical construct is treated as though it were a tangible object. The concepts of intelligence and heritability have both been subject to reification.

Key Terms

Achievement tests (p. 357)
Aptitude tests (p. 356)
Construct validity (p. 359)
Content validity (p. 359)
Convergent thinking (p. 388)
Correlation coefficient (p. 358)
Creativity (p. 388)
Criterion-related validity (p. 359)
Deviation IQ scores (p. 364)
Divergent thinking (p. 388)
Emotional intelligence (EI) (p. 385)
Factor analysis (p. 362)
Heritability ratio (p. 375)
Intellectual disability (p. 369)
Intelligence quotient (IQ)
  (pp. 361–362)
Intelligence tests (p. 356)
Mental age (p. 361)
Mental retardation (p. 369)
Normal distribution (p. 364)
Percentile score (p. 357)

Personality tests (p. 357)
Psychological test (p. 356)
Reaction range (p. 376)
Reification (p. 391)
Reliability (p. 357)
Standardization (p. 357)
Test norms (p. 357)
Validity (p. 358)

Key People

Alfred Binet (p. 361)
Francis Galton (p. 361)
Howard Gardner (p. 385)
Arthur Jensen (p. 378)
Sandra Scarr (pp. 376–377)
Charles Spearman (pp. 362–363)
Claude Steele (pp. 380–381)
Robert Sternberg (pp. 383–384)
Lewis Terman (pp. 361–362)
David Wechsler (p. 362)
Ellen Winner (p. 371)

1. Which of the following does not belong with the others?
   A. aptitude tests
   B. personality tests
   C. intelligence tests
   D. achievement tests

2. If you score at the 75th percentile on a standardized test, it means that:
   A. 75% of those who took the test scored better than you did.
   B. 25% of those who took the test scored less than you did.
   C. 75% of those who took the test scored the same or less than you did.
   D. you answered 75% of the questions correctly.

3. If a test has good test-retest reliability:
   A. there is a strong correlation between items on the test.
   B. it accurately measures what it says it measures.
   C. it can be used to predict future performance.
   D. the test yields similar scores if taken at two different times.

4. Which of the following is a true statement regarding Francis Galton?
   A. He took the position that intelligence is largely determined by heredity.
   B. He advocated the development of special programs to tap the intellectual potential of the culturally disadvantaged.
   C. He developed tests that identified those children who were unable to profit from a normal education.
   D. He took the position that intelligence is more a matter of environment than heredity.

5. On most modern IQ tests, a score of 115 would be:
   A. about normal.
   B. about 15% higher than the average of one's agemates.
   C. an indication of genius.
   D. one standard deviation above the mean.

6. IQ tests have proven to be good predictors of:
   A. social intelligence.
   B. practical problem-solving intelligence.
   C. school performance.
   D. all of the above.

7. Mr. and Mrs. Proudparent are beaming because their son, little Newton, has been selected for a gifted children program at school. They think Newton is a genius. What sort of advice do they need to hear?
   A. Youngsters with a 130–140 IQ tend to be very maladjusted.
   B. Most gifted children do not go on to make genius-level, major contributions to society that earn them eminence.
   C. They should prepare to be famous, based on their parentage of Newton.
   D. They should be warned that gifted children often have deficits in practical intelligence.

8. Which of the following is a true statement about mental retardation/intellectual disability?
   A. Most people with retardation are unable to live normal lives because of their mental deficiencies.
   B. With special tutoring, a mentally retarded person can attain average intelligence.
   C. The majority of people who exhibit intellectual disability fall in the mild category.
   D. Diagnoses of mental retardation should be based exclusively on IQ scores.

9. Most school districts consider children who _____ to be gifted.
   A. have IQ scores above 115
   B. score in the upper 2%–3% of the IQ distribution
   C. have parents in professional careers
   D. demonstrate high levels of leadership and creativity

10. In which of the following cases would you expect to find the greatest similarity in IQ?
    A. between fraternal twins
    B. between identical twins
    C. between nontwin siblings
    D. between parent and child

11. Evidence indicating that upbringing affects one's mental ability is provided by which of the following findings?
    A. Identical twins are more similar in IQ than fraternal twins.
    B. There is more than a chance similarity between adopted children and their biological parents.
    C. Siblings reared together are more similar in IQ than siblings reared apart.
    D. Identical twins reared apart are more similar in IQ than siblings reared together.

12. Which of the following is a likely consequence of stereotype vulnerability for members of minority groups?
    A. Academic motivation declines.
    B. Academic performance often suffers.
    C. Standardized tests may be especially anxiety arousing.
    D. All of the above are likely consequences.

13. The triarchic theory of intelligence, which emphasizes a cognitive perspective, was developed by:
    A. Howard Gardner.
    B. Arthur Jensen.
    C. Claude Steele.
    D. Robert Sternberg.

14. When you try to narrow down a list of alternatives to arrive at a single correct answer, you engage in:
    A. convergent thinking.
    B. divergent thinking.
    C. creativity.
    D. insight.

15. Nora has a blind date with Nick, who, she's been told, is considered a true genius by the faculty in the art department. Now she's having second thoughts, because she's always heard that geniuses are a little off their rocker. Does she have reason to be concerned?
    A. Yes. It's been well documented that the stress of creative achievement often leads to schizophrenic symptoms.
    B. No. Extensive research on creativity and psychological disorders shows no evidence for any connection.
    C. Perhaps. There is evidence of a correlation between major creative achievement and vulnerability to mood disorders.
    D. Of course not. The stereotype of the genius who's mentally ill is purely a product of the jealousy of untalented people.

Answers

1 B pp. 356–357	6 C p. 366	11 C pp. 374–375
2 C p. 357	7 B pp. 371–372	12 D pp. 380–381
3 D pp. 357–358	8 C p. 370	13 D pp. 383–384
4 A p. 361	9 B p. 371	14 A p. 388
5 D pp. 364, 366	10 B p. 374	15 C p. 389

PsykTrek

To view a demo: www.cengage.com/psychology/psyktrek
To order: www.cengage.com/psychology/weiten
Go to the PsykTrek website or CD-ROM for further study of the concepts in this chapter. Both online and on the CD-ROM, PsykTrek includes dozens of learning modules with videos, animations, and quizzes, as well as simulations of psychological phenomena and a multimedia glossary that includes word pronunciations.

CengageNOW

www.cengage.com/tlc

Go to this site for the link to CengageNOW, your one-stop study shop. Take a Pretest for this chapter, and CengageNOW will generate a personalized Study Plan based on your test results. The Study Plan will identify the topics you need to review and direct you to online resources to help you master those topics. You can then take a Posttest to help you determine the concepts you have mastered and what you still need to work on.

Companion Website

www.cengage.com/psychology/weiten

Go to this site to find online resources directly linked to your book, including a glossary, flash cards, drag-and-drop exercises, quizzes, and more!

10 MOTIVATION AND EMOTION

Motivational Theories and Concepts
Drive Theories
Incentive Theories
Evolutionary Theories
The Range and Diversity of Human Motives

The Motivation of Hunger and Eating
Biological Factors in the Regulation of Hunger
Environmental Factors in the Regulation of Hunger
Eating and Weight: The Roots of Obesity

Sexual Motivation and Behavior
The Human Sexual Response
Evolutionary Analyses of Human Sexual Behavior

FEATURED STUDY ▌ Can Women Judge Men's Mate Potential
in Just One Glance?

The Controversial Issue of Pornography
The Mystery of Sexual Orientation

Achievement: In Search of Excellence
Individual Differences in the Need for Achievement
Situational Determinants of Achievement Behavior

The Elements of Emotional Experience
The Cognitive Component: Subjective Feelings
The Physiological Component: Diffuse and Multifaceted
The Behavioral Component: Nonverbal Expressiveness
Culture and the Elements of Emotion

Theories of Emotion
James-Lange Theory
Cannon-Bard Theory
Schachter's Two-Factor Theory
Evolutionary Theories of Emotion

Reflecting on the Chapter's Themes

PERSONAL APPLICATION ▌ Exploring the Ingredients
of Happiness

Factors That Do Not Predict Happiness
Moderately Good Predictors of Happiness
Strong Predictors of Happiness
Conclusions About Subjective Well-Being

CRITICAL THINKING APPLICATION ▌ Analyzing
Arguments: Making Sense out of Controversy

The Anatomy of an Argument
Common Fallacies
Evaluating the Strength of Arguments

Recap

Practice Test

It was a bright afternoon in May 1996, and 41-year-old Jon Krakauer was on top of the world—literally. Krakauer had just fulfilled a boyhood dream by climbing Mount Everest, the tallest peak on Earth. Clearing the ice from his oxygen mask, he looked down on a sweeping vista of ice, snow, and majestic mountains. His triumph should have brought him intense joy, but he felt strangely detached. "I'd been fantasizing about this moment, and the release of emotion that would accompany it, for many years," he wrote later. "But now that I was finally here, standing on the summit of Mount Everest, I just couldn't summon the energy to care" (Krakauer, 1998, p. 6).

Why were Krakauer's emotions so subdued? A major reason was that he was physically spent. Climbing Mount Everest is an incredibly grueling experience. At just over 29,000 feet, the mountain's peak is at the altitude flown by jumbo jets. Because such high altitudes wreak havoc on the human body, Krakauer and his fellow climbers couldn't even approach the summit until they had spent six weeks acclimating at Base Camp, 17,600 feet above sea level. Even getting that far would test the limits of most

Jon Krakauer (the third person) and other climbers are seen here during their ascent of Mount Everest at an elevation of about 28,200 feet.

395

people's endurance. At Base Camp, Krakauer found that ordinary bodily functions became painfully difficult. On most nights, he awoke three or four times, gasping for breath and feeling like he was suffocating. His appetite vanished, and his oxygen-starved digestive system failed to metabolize food normally. "My body began consuming itself for sustenance. My arms and legs gradually began to wither to sticklike proportions" (Krakauer, 1998, p. 87).

At this point you may be wondering why anyone would willingly undergo such extreme discomfort, but Base Camp was just the beginning. From Base Camp it is another two vertical miles through the aptly named Death Zone to the summit. Even for a fully acclimated climber, the final leg of the ascent is excruciating. By the time Krakauer reached the summit, every step was labored, every gasping breath hurt. He hadn't slept in 57 hours, and he had two separated ribs from weeks of violent coughing. He was bitterly cold and utterly exhausted. Instead of elation, he felt only apprehension. Even though his oxygen-starved brain was barely functioning, he understood that getting down from the summit would be fully as dangerous as getting up.

Tragically, events proved just how dangerous an assault on Everest can be. During Krakauer's descent, a sudden, howling storm hit the mountain. Winds exceeding 100 miles per hour whipped the snow into a blinding white blur and sent the temperature plummeting. While Krakauer barely escaped with his life, 12 men and women died on the mountain, including several in Krakauer's own party. Some of them perished needlessly because they had fallen victim to "summit fever." Once they got close to the top, they refused to turn back despite extreme exhaustion and the obvious threat posed by the storm.

The saga of Jon Krakauer and the other climbers is packed with motivation riddles. Why would people push on toward a goal even at the risk of their lives? Why would they choose to endure such a punishing and hazardous ordeal in the first place? In the case of Mount Everest, perhaps the most obvious motive is simply the satisfaction of conquering the world's tallest peak. When British climber George Leigh Mallory was asked why he wanted to climb Everest in the 1920s, his famous reply was, "Because it is there." Some people seem to have an intense desire to take on the toughest challenges imaginable, to achieve something incredibly difficult. Yet—as is usually the case with human behavior—things are not quite so simple. Krakauer observed that a wide variety of motives drove the climbers and professional expedition leaders he met on Everest, including desires for "minor celebrity, career advancement, ego massage, ordinary bragging rights, filthy lucre," and even a quest for "a state of grace" (Krakauer, 1998, p. 177).

Krakauer's story is also filled with strong emotions. He anticipated that he would experience a transcendent emotional high when he reached the summit of Mount Everest. As it turned out, his triumph was accompanied more by anxiety than by ecstasy. And though the harrowing events that followed left him emotionally numb at first, he was soon flooded with intense feelings of despair, grief, and guilt over the deaths of his companions. His tale illustrates the intimate connection between motivation and emotion—the topics we'll examine in this chapter.

Motivational Theories and Concepts

Key Learning Goals

10.1 Compare drive, incentive, and evolutionary approaches to understanding motivation.

10.2 Distinguish between the two major categories of motives found in humans.

Motives are the needs, wants, interests, and desires that propel people in certain directions. In short, *motivation* involves goal-directed behavior. Psychologists have developed a number of theoretical approaches to motivation. Let's look at some of these theories and the concepts they include.

Drive Theories

Many theories view motivational forces in terms of *drives*. The drive concept appears in a diverse array of theories that otherwise have little in common, such as psychoanalytic (Freud, 1915) and behaviorist formulations (Hull, 1943). This approach to understanding motivation was explored most fully by Clark Hull in the 1940s and 1950s.

Hull's concept of drive was derived from Walter Cannon's (1932) observation that organisms seek to maintain *homeostasis,* a state of physiological equilibrium or stability. The body maintains homeostasis in various ways. For example, human body temperature normally fluctuates around 98.6 degrees Fahrenheit (see **Figure 10.1**). If your body temperature rises or drops noticeably, automatic responses occur: If your temperature goes up, you'll perspire; if your temperature goes down, you'll shiver. These re-

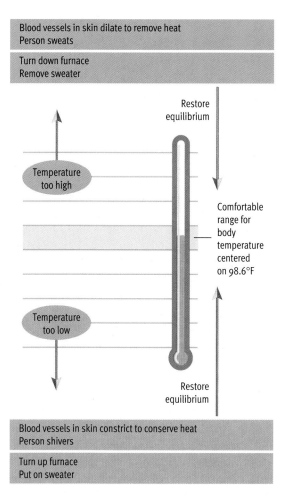

Blood vessels in skin dilate to remove heat
Person sweats

Turn down furnace
Remove sweater

Restore
equilibrium

Temperature
too high

Comfortable
range for
body
temperature
centered
on 98.6°F

Temperature
too low

Restore
equilibrium

Blood vessels in skin constrict to conserve heat
Person shivers

Turn up furnace
Put on sweater

Figure 10.1

Temperature regulation as an example of homeostasis. The regulation of body temperature provides a simple example of how organisms often seek to maintain homeostasis, or a state of physiological equilibrium. When your temperature moves out of an acceptable range, automatic bodily reactions (such as sweating or shivering) occur that help restore equilibrium. Of course, these automatic reactions may not be sufficient by themselves, so you may have to take other actions (such as turning a furnace up or down) to bring your body temperature back into its comfort zone.

actions are designed to move your temperature back toward 98.6 degrees. Thus, your body reacts to many disturbances in physiological stability by trying to restore equilibrium.

Drive theories apply the concept of homeostasis to behavior. A *drive* **is an internal state of tension that motivates an organism to engage in activities that should reduce this tension.** These unpleasant states of tension are viewed as disruptions of the preferred equilibrium. According to drive theories, when individuals experience a drive, they're motivated to pursue actions that will lead to *drive reduction*. For example, the hunger motive has usually been conceptualized as a drive system. If you go without food for a while, you begin to experience

some discomfort. This internal tension (the drive) motivates you to obtain food. Eating reduces the drive and restores physiological equilibrium.

Drive theories have been very influential, and the drive concept continues to be widely used in modern psychology. *However, drive theories were not able to explain all motivation* (Berridge, 2004). Homeostasis appears irrelevant to some human motives, such as a "thirst for knowledge." Also, motivation may exist without drive arousal. This point is easy to illustrate. Think of all the times that you've eaten when you weren't the least bit hungry. You're walking home from class, amply filled by a solid lunch, when an ice cream parlor beckons seductively. You stop in and have a couple of scoops of your favorite flavor. Not only are you motivated to eat in the absence of internal tension, you may cause yourself some internal tension—from overeating. Because drive theories assume that people always try to reduce internal tension, they can't explain this behavior very well. Incentive theories, which represent a different approach to motivation, can account for this behavior more readily.

Incentive Theories

Incentive theories propose that external stimuli regulate motivational states (Bolles, 1975; McClelland, 1975; Skinner, 1953). **An *incentive* is an external goal that has the capacity to motivate behavior.** Ice cream, a juicy steak, a monetary prize, approval from friends, an A on an exam, and a promotion at work are all incentives. Some of these incentives may reduce drives, but others may not.

Drive and incentive models of motivation are often contrasted as *push versus pull* theories. Drive theories emphasize how *internal* states of tension *push* people in certain directions. Incentive theories emphasize how *external* stimuli *pull* people in certain directions. According to drive theories, the source of motivation lies *within* the organism. According to incentive theories, the source of motivation lies *outside* the organism, in the environment. This means that incentive models don't operate according to the principle of homeostasis, which hinges on internal changes in the organism. Rather, incentive theories emphasize environmental factors and downplay the biological bases of human motivation.

Evolutionary Theories

Psychologists who take an evolutionary perspective assert that human motives and those of other species are the products of natural selection, just as anatomical characteristics are (Durrant & Ellis, 2003).

They argue that natural selection favors behaviors that maximize reproductive success—that is, passing on genes to the next generation. Thus, they explain motives such as affiliation, achievement, dominance, aggression, and sex drive in terms of their adaptive value. If dominance is a crucial motive for a species, they say, it's because dominance provides a reproductive or survival advantage.

Evolutionary analyses of motivation are based on the premise that motives can best be understood in terms of the adaptive problems they solved for our hunter-gatherer ancestors (Tooby & Cosmides, 2005). For example, the need for dominance is thought to be greater in men than in women because it could facilitate males' reproductive success in a variety of ways: (1) females may prefer mating with dominant males, (2) dominant males may poach females from subordinate males, (3) dominant males may intimidate male rivals in competition for sexual access, and (4) dominant males may acquire more material resources, which may increase mating opportunities (Buss, 1999). Consider, also, the *affiliation motive,* or need for belongingness. The adaptive benefits of affiliation for our ancient ancestors probably included help with rearing offspring, collaboration in hunting or defense, opportunities for sexual interaction, and so forth (Baumeister & Leary, 1995). David Buss (1995) points out that it is no accident that achievement, power (dominance), and intimacy are among the most heavily studied social motives, as the satisfaction of each of these motives is likely to affect one's reproductive success.

The Range and Diversity of Human Motives

Motivational theorists of all persuasions agree on one point: Humans display an enormous diversity of motives. Most theories (evolutionary theories being a notable exception) distinguish between *biological motives* that originate in bodily needs, such as hunger, and *social motives* that originate in social experiences, such as the need for achievement.

People have a limited number of biological needs. According to K. B. Madsen (1968, 1973), most theories identify 10 to 15 such needs, some of which are listed on the left side of Figure 10.2. As you can see, most biological motives reflect needs that are essential to survival, such as the needs for food, water, and maintenance of body temperature within an acceptable range.

People all share the same biological motives, but their social motives vary depending on their experiences. For example, we all need to eat, but not everyone acquires a need for orderliness. Although people have a limited number of biological motives, they can acquire an unlimited number of social motives through learning and socialization. Some examples of social motives—from an influential list compiled by Henry Murray (1938)—are shown on the right side of Figure 10.2. He theorized that most people have needs for achievement, autonomy, affiliation, dominance, exhibition, and order, among other things. Of course, the strength of these motives varies from person to person, depending on personal history.

Given the range and diversity of human motives, we can examine only a handful in depth. To a large degree, our choices reflect the motives psychologists have studied the most: hunger, sex, and achievement. After discussing these motivational systems, we will explore the elements of emotional experience and examine various theories of emotion.

Examples of Biological Motives in Humans	Examples of Social Motives in Humans
Hunger motive	Achievement motive (need to excel)
Thirst motive	Affiliation motive (need for social bonds)
Sex motive	Autonomy motive (need for independence)
Temperature motive (need for appropriate body temperature)	Nurturance motive (need to nourish and protect others)
Excretory motive (need to eliminate bodily wastes)	Dominance motive (need to influence or control others)
Sleep and rest motive	Exhibition motive (need to make an impression on others)
Activity motive (need for optimal level of stimulation and arousal)	Order motive (need for orderliness, tidiness, organization)
Aggression motive	Play motive (need for fun, relaxation, amusement)

Figure 10.2

The diversity of human motives. People are motivated by a wide range of needs, which can be divided into two broad classes: biological motives and social motives. The list on the left (adapted from Madsen, 1973) shows some important biological motives in humans. The list on the right (adapted from Murray, 1938) provides examples of prominent social motives in humans. The distinction between biological and social motives is not absolute.

> **REVIEW of Key Learning Goals**
>
> **10.1** Drive theories apply a homeostatic model to motivation. They assume that organisms seek to reduce unpleasant states of tension called drives. In contrast, incentive theories emphasize how external goals energize behavior. Evolutionary theorists explain motives in terms of their adaptive value.
>
> **10.2** Humans display an enormous diversity of motives, which can be divided into biological motives and social motives. Madsen's list of biological needs includes motives such as hunger, thirst and sex, whereas Murray's list of social needs includes motives such as achievement, affiliation, and dominance.

The Motivation of Hunger and Eating

Why do people eat? Because they're hungry. What makes them hungry? A lack of food. Any grade-school child can explain these basic facts. So hunger is a simple motivational system, right? Wrong! Hunger is deceptive. It only looks simple. Actually, it's a puzzling and complex motivational system. Despite extensive studies, scientists are still struggling to understand the factors that regulate hunger and eating behavior. Let's examine a few of these factors.

Biological Factors in the Regulation of Hunger

2e, 8a

You have probably had embarrassing occasions when your stomach growled loudly at an inopportune moment. Someone may have commented, "You must be starving!" Most people equate a rumbling stomach with hunger, and, in fact, the first scientific theories of hunger were based on this simple equation. In an elaborate 1912 study, Walter Cannon and A. L. Washburn verified what most people have noticed based on casual observation: There is an association between stomach contractions and the experience of hunger.

Based on this correlation, Cannon theorized that stomach contractions *cause* hunger. However, as we've seen before, correlation is no assurance of causation, and his theory was eventually discredited. Stomach contractions sometimes accompany hunger (the association is actually rather weak), but they don't cause it. How do we know? Because later research showed that people continue to experience hunger even after their stomachs have been removed out of medical necessity (Wangensteen & Carlson, 1931). If hunger can occur without a stomach, then stomach contractions can't be the cause of hunger. This realization led to more complex theories of hunger that focus on (1) the role of the brain, (2) blood sugar level, and (3) hormones.

Brain Regulation

2e, 8a

Research with laboratory animals eventually suggested that the experience of hunger is controlled in the brain—specifically, in two centers in the hypothalamus. As we have noted before, the *hypothalamus* is a tiny structure involved in the regulation of a variety of biological needs related to survival (see

Figure 10.3 on the next page). Investigators found that when they lesioned animals' *lateral hypothalamus (LH)*, the animals showed little or no interest in eating, as if their hunger center had been destroyed (Anand & Brobeck, 1951). In contrast, when researchers lesioned animals' *ventromedial nucleus of the hypothalamus (VMH)*, the animals ate excessively and gained weight rapidly, as if their ability to recognize satiety (fullness) had been destroyed (Brobeck, Tepperman, & Long, 1943). Given these results, investigators concluded that the LH and VMH were the brain's on-off switches for the control of hunger (Stellar, 1954). However, over the course of several decades, a variety of empirical findings complicated this simple picture and undermined the dual-centers model of hunger (Valenstein, 1973; Winn, 1995). The current thinking is that the lateral and ventromedial areas of the hypothalamus are elements in the neural circuitry that regulates hunger but are not the key elements and are not simple on-off centers (King, 2006; Meister, 2007). Today, scientists believe that two other areas of the hypothalamus—the *arcuate nucleus* and the *paraventricular nucleus*—play a larger role in the modulation of hunger (Scott, McDade, & Luckman, 2007) (see Figure 10.3). In recent years the arcuate nucleus has been singled out as especially important (Becskei, Lutz, & Riediger, 2008; Grill, 2006). This area in the hypothalamus appears to contain a group of neurons that are sensitive to incoming hunger signals and another group of neurons that respond to satiety signals.

Contemporary theories of hunger focus more on *neural circuits* that pass through areas of the hypothalamus rather than on *anatomical centers* in the brain. These circuits depend on a remarkable variety of neurotransmitters. *Neuropeptide Y* and *serotonin* play prominent roles (Halford & Blundell, 2000; Seeley & Schwartz, 1997), as do *GABA, ghrelin,* and *orexins* (Meister, 2007; Naslund & Hellstrom, 2007),

The rat on the left has had its ventromedial hypothalamus lesioned, resulting in a dramatic increase in weight.

Figure 10.3

The hypothalamus. This small structure at the base of the forebrain plays a role in regulating a variety of human biological needs, including hunger. The detailed blowup shows that the hypothalamus is made up of a variety of discrete areas. Scientists used to believe that the lateral and ventromedial areas were the brain's on-off centers for eating. However, more recent research suggests that the arcuate and paraventricular areas may be more crucial to the regulation of hunger and that thinking in terms of neural circuits rather than anatomical centers makes more sense.

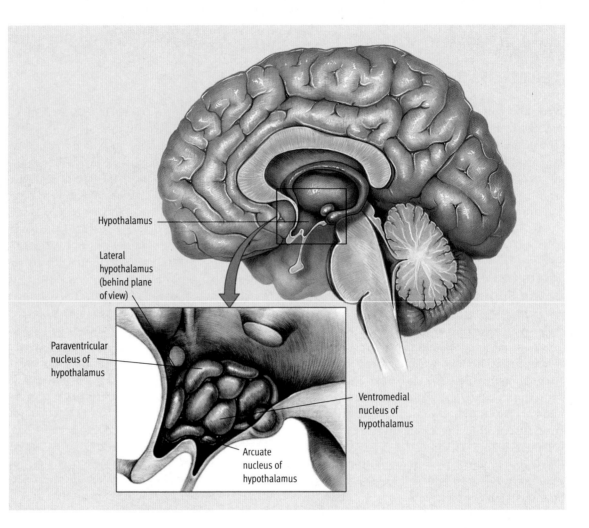

not to mention the endogenous cannabinoids that resemble the active ingredient in marijuana (see Chapter 5; Di Marzo & Matias, 2005). In recent years scientists have realized that increased levels of ghrelin play a particularly crucial role in stimulating hunger (Scott et al., 2007). Ghrelin performs double duty as a neurotransmitter in the nervous system and as a hormone in the endocrine system. In both systems, elevated ghrelin levels are associated with increased food intake.

Accumulating evidence suggests that the hypothalamus contains a confluence of interacting systems that regulate eating by monitoring a diverse array of physiological processes. Let's examine some other physiological processes that appear to provide input to these systems.

Glucose and Digestive Regulation

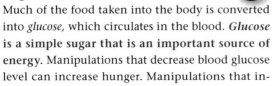

Much of the food taken into the body is converted into *glucose,* which circulates in the blood. *Glucose is a simple sugar that is an important source of energy.* Manipulations that decrease blood glucose level can increase hunger. Manipulations that in-

crease glucose level can make people feel satiated. Based on these findings, Jean Mayer (1955, 1968) proposed that hunger is regulated by the rise and fall of blood glucose levels. *Glucostatic theory* proposed that fluctuations in blood glucose level are monitored in the brain by *glucostats—neurons sensitive to glucose in the surrounding fluid.* Like the dual-centers theory, the glucostatic theory of hunger gradually ran into a number of complications, not the least of which was that glucose levels in the blood really don't fluctuate all that much or all that fast (LeMagnen, 1981). Nonetheless, some researchers continue to believe that glucostatic mechanisms *contribute* to the modulation of eating (Smith & Campfield, 1993).

The digestive system also includes a variety of other mechanisms that influence hunger (Ritter, 2004). It turns out that Walter Cannon was not entirely wrong in hypothesizing that the stomach regulates hunger. After you have consumed food, cells in the stomach can send signals to the brain that inhibit further eating (Deutsch, 1990). For example, the vagus nerve carries information about the stretching of the stomach walls that indicates when the stomach is full. Other nerves carry satiety messages that depend on how rich in nutrients the contents of the stomach are.

Hormonal Regulation

A variety of hormones circulating in the bloodstream also appear to contribute to the regulation of hunger. *Insulin* is a hormone secreted by the pancreas. It must be present for cells to extract glucose from the blood. Indeed, an inadequate supply of insulin is what causes diabetes. Insulin levels increase when people eat. Moreover, insulin levels appear to be sensitive to fluctuations in the body's fat stores (Schwartz et al., 2000). These findings suggest that insulin secretions play a role in the fluctuation of hunger.

At least two other hormones play a key role in the short-term regulation of hunger. After going without food for a while, the stomach secretes ghrelin, which causes stomach contractions and promotes hunger (Cummings, 2006). In contrast, after food is consumed, the upper intestine releases a hormone called CCK that delivers satiety signals to the brain, thus reducing hunger (Moran, 2004; Schwartz & Azzara, 2004)

Finally, evidence indicates that a hormone called *leptin* contributes to the long-term regulation of hunger, as well as the modulation of numerous other bodily functions (Ahima & Osei, 2004). Leptin is produced by fat cells throughout the body and released into the bloodstream. Higher levels of fat generate higher levels of leptin (Schwartz et al., 1996). Leptin circulates through the bloodstream and ultimately provides the hypothalamus with information about the body's fat stores (Campfield, 2002). When leptin levels are high, the propensity to feel hungry diminishes. One theory of obesity suggests that many overweight people develop *leptin resistance*—reduced responsiveness to the hunger-suppressing effects of leptin (Munzberg & Myers, 2005). The hormonal signals that influence hunger (the fluctuations of insulin, ghrelin, CCK, and leptin) all seem to converge in the hypothalamus, especially the arcuate and paraventricular nuclei of the hypothalamus (Kuo et al., 2007; Naslund & Hellstrom, 2007).

If all this sounds confusing, it is, and we haven't even mentioned *all* the physiological processes involved in the regulation of hunger and eating. Frankly, researchers are still struggling to figure out exactly how all these processes work together, as hunger depends on complex interactions between neural circuits, neurotransmitter systems, digestive processes, and hormonal fluctuations (Berthoud & Morrison, 2008).

Environmental Factors in the Regulation of Hunger

Hunger clearly is a biological need, but eating is not regulated by biological factors alone. Studies show that social and environmental factors govern eating to a considerable extent. Three key environmental factors are (1) the availability and palatability of food, (2) learned preferences and habits, and (3) stress.

Food Availability and Related Cues

Most of the research on the physiological regulation of hunger has been based on the assumption that hunger operates as a drive system in which homeostatic mechanisms are at work. However, some theorists emphasize the incentive value of food and argue that humans and other animals are often motivated to eat not by the need to compensate for energy deficits but by the anticipated pleasure of eating (Hetherington & Rolls, 1996; Ramsay et al., 1996). This perspective has been bolstered by evidence that the following variables exert significant influence over food consumption:

- *Palatability.* As you might expect, the better food tastes, the more of it people consume (de Castro et al., 2000; Pliner & Mann, 2004). This principle is not limited to humans, as the eating behavior of rats and other animals is also influenced by palatability.
- *Quantity available.* A powerful determinant of the amount eaten is the amount available. People tend to consume what is put in front of them. The more people are served, the more they eat (Mrdjenovic & Levitsky, 2005; Rozin et al., 2003). Thus, the large portions served in modern American restaurants probably foster increased consumption (Geier, Rozin, & Doros, 2006).
- *Variety.* Humans and animals increase their consumption when a greater variety of foods is available (Raynor & Epstein, 2001; Temple et al., 2008). As you eat a specific food, its incentive value declines. This phenomenon is called *sensory-specific satiety* (Hollis & Henry, 2007; Raynor, Niemeier, & Wing, 2006). If only a few foods are available, the appeal of all of them can decline quickly. But if many foods are available, people can keep shifting to new foods and end up eating more overall. This principle explains why people are especially likely to overeat at buffets where many foods are available.

Eating can also be triggered by exposure to environmental cues that have been associated with food. You have no doubt had your hunger aroused by

According to incentive models of hunger, the availability and palatability of food are key factors regulating hunger. An abundance of diverse foods tends to lead to increased eating.

television commercials for delicious-looking meals or by seductive odors coming from the kitchen. Consistent with this observation, studies have shown that hunger can be increased by exposure to pictures, written descriptions, and video depictions of attractive foods (Halford et al., 2004; Marcelino et al., 2001; Oakes & Slotterback, 2000). Thus, it's clear that hunger and eating are governed in part by the incentive qualities of food.

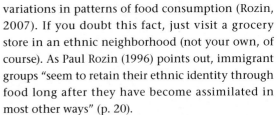

Learned Preferences and Habits   8a

Are you fond of eating calves' brains? How about eels or snakes? Could I interest you in a grasshopper or some dog meat? Probably not, but these are delicacies in some regions of the world. Arctic Eskimos like to eat maggots! You probably prefer chicken, apples, eggs, lettuce, potato chips, pizza, cornflakes, or ice cream. These preferences are acquired through learning. People from different cultures display enormous

variations in patterns of food consumption (Rozin, 2007). If you doubt this fact, just visit a grocery store in an ethnic neighborhood (not your own, of course). As Paul Rozin (1996) points out, immigrant groups "seem to retain their ethnic identity through food long after they have become assimilated in most other ways" (p. 20).

Humans do have some innate taste preferences of a general sort. For example, a preference for sweet tastes is present at birth (Menella & Beauchamp, 1996), and humans' preference for high-fat foods appears to be at least partly genetic in origin (Schiffman et al., 1998). Evidence also suggests that an unlearned preference for salt emerges at around four months of age in humans (Birch & Fisher, 1996). Nonetheless, learning wields a great deal of influence over what people prefer to eat (Rozin, 2007). Taste preferences are partly a function of learned associations formed through classical conditioning (Appleton, Gentry, & Shepherd, 2006). For example, youngsters can be conditioned to prefer flavors paired with pleasant events. Of course, as we learned in Chapter 6, taste aversions can also be acquired through conditioning when foods are followed by nausea (Schafe & Bernstein, 1996).

Eating habits are also shaped by observational learning (see Chapter 6). To a large degree, food preferences are a matter of exposure (Cooke, 2007). People generally prefer familiar foods. But geographical, cultural, religious, and ethnic factors limit people's exposure to certain foods. Young children are more likely to taste an unfamiliar food if an adult tries it first. Repeated exposures to a new food usually lead to increased liking. However, as many parents have learned the hard way, forcing a child to eat a specific food can backfire—coercion tends to have a negative effect on a youngster's preference for the mandated food (Benton, 2004). Learned habits and social considerations also influence *when* and *how much* people eat. For example, a key determinant of when people eat is their memory of how much time has passed since they ate their last meal and what they consumed (Rozin et al., 1998). These expecta-

CATHY

Food preferences are influenced greatly by culture. For example, the fried sparrow shown here would not be a popular treat for most Americans, but it is a delicacy in some cultures.

tions about how often and how much one should eat are the product of years of learning.

Stress and Eating

8a

Studies have shown that stress leads to increased eating in a substantial percentage of people (Greeno & Wing, 1994; Laitinen, Ek, & Sovio, 2002). Some studies suggest that stress-induced eating may be especially common among chronic dieters (Heatherton, Striepe, & Wittenberg, 1998). Theorists have suggested that the *negative emotions* often evoked by stress are what promotes additional eating (Macht & Simons, 2000). Some people respond to emotional distress by eating tasty foods because they expect the enjoyable treats to make them feel better (Tice, Bratslavsky, & Baumeister, 2001). Unfortunately, this strategy of emotional regulation does not appear to be very effective, as eating does not usually lead to lasting mood changes (Thayer, 1996). In any event, stress is another environmental factor that can influence hunger, although it's not clear whether the effects are direct or indirect.

Eating and Weight: The Roots of Obesity

As we've seen, hunger is regulated by a complex interaction of biological and psychological factors. The same kinds of complexities emerge when inves-

tigators explore the roots of *obesity,* the condition of being overweight. Most experts assess obesity in terms of *body mass index (BMI)*—weight (in kilograms) divided by height (in meters) squared (kg/m^2). This index of weight controls for variations in height. A BMI of 25–29.9 is typically regarded as moderately overweight and a BMI of over 30 as obese (Bjorntorp, 2002). Although American culture seems to be obsessed with slimness, recent surveys show surprisingly sharp increases in the incidence of obesity (Corsica & Perri, 2003; Mokdad et al., 2003). If a BMI over 25 is used as the cutoff, almost two-thirds of American adults are struggling with weight problems, while the prevalence of obesity (BMI > 30) is estimated to be 32% (Ogden et al., 2006). Moreover, overweight adults have plenty of company from their children, as weight problems among children and adolescents have increased 15%–22% in recent decades (West et al., 2004).

If obesity merely affected people's vanity, there would be little cause for concern. Unfortunately, however, obesity is a significant health problem that elevates an individual's mortality risk (Flegal et al., 2005; Fontaine et al., 2003). Obese individuals are more vulnerable than others to cardiovascular diseases, diabetes, hypertension, respiratory problems, gallbladder disease, stroke, arthritis, muscle and skeletal pain, and some types of cancer (Manson, Skerrett, & Willet, 2002; Pi-Sunyer, 2002). For example, **Figure 10.4** shows how the prevalence of diabetes, hypertension, coronary disease, and musculoskeletal pain are elevated as BMI increases.

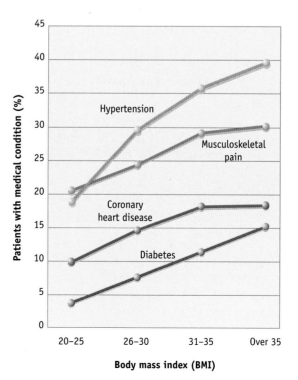

Figure 10.4

Weight and the prevalence of various diseases. This graph shows how obesity, as indexed by BMI, is related to the prevalence of four common types of illness. The prevalence of diabetes, heart disease, muscle pain, and hypertension increases as BMI goes up, suggesting that obesity is a significant health risk. (Based on data in Brownell & Wadden, 2000)

That said, recent research suggests that mortality rates among people who are *moderately overweight* (BMI 25–29.9) are *not* elevated in today's population (Flegal et al., 2005, 2007). One hypothesis to explain this surprising finding is that improvements in the treatment of cardiovascular diseases have neutralized much of the danger associated with being slightly overweight (Gibbs, 2005). These findings and other issues have led some critics (Campos, 2004; Oliver, 2006) to argue that the widely heralded obesity "epidemic/crisis" has been greatly exaggerated by a small community of scientists and physicians who have a vested interest in obesity research, weight-loss programs, and pharmaceutical treatments. These critics assert that BMIs in the 25–29 range are not particularly unhealthy and that the BMI cutoffs for weight problems are not realistic. They also argue that the correlation between genuine obesity and mortality may not reflect a causal relationship, since poor *fitness,* rather than *fatness,* could be the key determinant of health. Although these critics have raised some legitimate doubts about whether increased obesity should be portrayed as a national health care *crisis,* the fact remains that genuine obesity is associated with an elevated vulnerability to a host of diseases, and these risks should be taken seriously.

Evolutionary-oriented researchers have a plausible explanation for the dramatic increase in the prevalence of obesity (Pinel, Assanand & Lehman, 2000). They point out that over the course of history, most animals and humans lived in environments characterized by fierce competition for limited, unreliable food resources and in which starvation was a very real threat. Thus, warm-blooded, foraging animals evolved a propensity to consume more food than immediately necessary when the opportunity presented itself because food might not be available later. Excess calories were stored in the body (as fat) to prepare for future food shortages. This approach to eating remains adaptive for most species of (nondomesticated) animals that continue to struggle with the ebb and flow of unpredictable food supplies. However, in today's modern, industrialized societies, the vast majority of humans live in environments that provide an abundant, reliable supply of tasty, high-calorie food. In these environments, humans' evolved tendency to overeat when food is plentiful leads most people down a path of chronic, excessive food consumption. According to this line of thinking, most people in food-replete environments tend to overeat in relation to their physiological needs, but because of variations in genetics, metabolism, and other factors only some become overweight.

Given the health concerns associated with weight problems, scientists have devoted a great deal of attention to the causes of obesity. Let's look at some of the factors they have identified.

Genetic Predisposition

You may know some people who can eat constantly without gaining weight. You may also know less fortunate people who get chubby eating far less. Differences in physiological makeup must be the cause of this paradox. Research suggests that these differences have a genetic basis (Bouchard, 2002).

In one influential study, adults raised by foster parents were compared with their biological and foster parents in regard to body mass index (Stunkard et al., 1986). The investigators found that the adoptees resembled their biological parents much more than their adoptive parents. In a subsequent *twin study,* Stunkard and colleagues (1990) found that identical twins reared apart were far more similar in BMI than fraternal twins reared together (see **Figure 10.5**). In another study of over 4000 twins, Allison and colleagues (1994) estimated that genetic factors account for 61% of the variation in weight among men and 73% among women. Thus, it appears that some people inherit a genetic *vulnerability* to obesity (Cope, Fernandez, & Allison, 2004).

Excessive Eating and Inadequate Exercise

The bottom line for overweight people is that their energy intake from food consumption chronically exceeds their energy expenditure from physical activities and resting metabolic processes. In other words, they eat too much in relation to their level of exercise (Wing & Polley, 2001). In modern America,

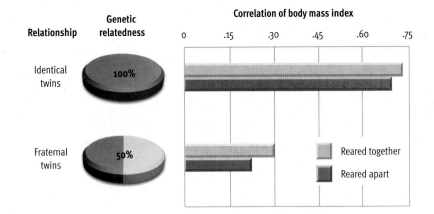

Figure 10.5

The heritability of weight. These data from a twin study by Stunkard et al. (1990) reveal that identical twins are much more similar in body mass index than fraternal twins, suggesting that genetic factors account for much of the variation among people in the propensity to become overweight.

CATHY

the tendency to overeat and exercise too little is easy to understand (Henderson & Brownell, 2004). Tasty, high-calorie, high-fat foods are heavily advertised and readily available nearly everywhere—not just in restaurants and grocery stores, but in shopping malls, airports, gas stations, schools, and workplaces. Nutritious foods can hardly compete with the convenience of highly caloric fast food. And when people eat out, they tend to eat larger meals and consume more high-fat food than they would have at home (French, Harnack, & Jeffery, 2000). Obesity expert Kelly Brownell (2002) argues that modern societies have created a "toxic environment" for eating. Unfortunately, this increasingly toxic environment has been paralleled by declining physical activity (Hill & Peters, 1998). Modern conveniences, such as cars and elevators, and changes in the world of work, such as the shift to more desk jobs, have conspired to make American lifestyles more sedentary then ever before.

The Concept of Set Point

People who lose weight on a diet have a rather strong (and depressing) tendency to gain back all the weight they lose (Mann et al., 2007). The reverse is also true. People who have to work to put weight on often have trouble keeping it on. According to Richard Keesey (1995), these observations suggest that your body may have a *set point,* or a natural point of stability in body weight. *Set-point theory* **proposes that the body monitors fat-cell levels to keep them (and weight) fairly stable.** When fat stores slip below a crucial set point, the body supposedly begins to compensate for this change (Keesey, 1993). This compensation apparently leads to increased hunger and decreased metabolism.

Studies have raised some doubts about various details of set-point theory, leading some researchers to propose an alternative called *settling-point theory* (Pinel et al., 2000). *Settling-point theory* **proposes that weight tends to drift around the level** at which the constellation of factors that determine food consumption and energy expenditure achieve an equilibrium. According to this view, weight tends to remain stable as long as there are no durable changes in any of the factors that influence it. Settling-point theory casts a much wider net than set-point theory, which attributes weight stability to specific physiological processes. Another difference is that set-point theory asserts that an obese person's body will initiate processes that actively defend an excessive weight, whereas settling-point theory suggests that if an obese person makes long-term changes in eating or exercise, his or her settling point will drift downward without active resistance. Thus, settling-point theory is a little more encouraging to those who hope to lose weight.

---

concept check 10.1

Understanding Factors in the Regulation of Hunger

Check your understanding of the effects of the various factors that influence hunger by indicating whether hunger would tend to increase or decrease in each of the situations described below. Indicate your choice by marking an I (increase), a D (decrease), or a ? (can't be determined without more information) next to each situation. You'll find the answers in Appendix A at the back of the book.

_____ 1. The ventromedial nucleus of a rat's brain is destroyed by lesioning.

_____ 2. The glucose level in Marlene's bloodstream decreases.

_____ 3. Norman just ate, but his roommate just brought home his favorite food—a pizza that smells great.

_____ 4. You're offered an exotic, strange-looking food from another culture and told that everyone in that culture loves it.

_____ 5. You are eating at a huge buffet where an enormous variety of foods are available.

_____ 6. Elton has been going crazy all day. It seems like everything's happening at once, and he feels totally stressed out. Finally he's been able to break away for a few minutes so he can catch a bite to eat.

REVIEW of Key Learning Goals

10.3 In the brain, the lateral and ventromedial areas of the hypothalamus were once viewed as on-off centers for the control of hunger, but that model proved to be an oversimplification, as the arcuate and paraventricular areas and neural circuits may be more important. Fluctuations in blood glucose also seem to play a role in hunger, but the exact location of the glucostats and their mode of functioning have yet to be determined. Hormonal regulation of hunger depends primarily on insulin, ghrelin, CCK, and leptin.

10.4 Organisms consume more food when it is palatable, when more is available, and when there is greater variety. Cultural traditions also shape food preferences, primarily through variations in exposure to various foods. Learning processes, such as classical conditioning and observational learning, exert

a great deal of influence over both what people eat and how much they eat. Stress can stimulate eating.

10.5 Surveys suggest that perhaps as many as two-thirds of people in the United States are struggling with weight problems. Obesity elevates one's risk for many diseases, but recent evidence suggests that being moderately overweight may not increase mortality. Some theorists argue that the obesity crisis has been exaggerated. Evolutionary theorists suggest that humans are wired to overeat because food supplies used to be so unreliable.

10.6 Evidence indicates that there is a genetic predisposition to obesity. Weight problems occur when people eat too much in relation to their exercise level. According to set-point theory, the body monitors fat stores to keep them fairly stable. Settling-point theory suggests that a multitude of factors contribute to weight stability.

Sexual Motivation and Behavior

Key Learning Goals

10.7 Outline the four phases of the human sexual response.

10.8 Discuss parental investment theory and findings on gender differences in sexual activity.

10.9 Describe gender differences in mating preferences, including the Featured Study on women's snap judgments of men's mate potential.

10.10 Evaluate evidence on the impact of erotic materials, including aggressive pornography, on human sexual behavior.

10.11 Clarify the nature of sexual orientation and discuss the prevalence of homosexuality.

10.12 Compare environmental and biological theories of sexual orientation.

How does sex resemble food? Sometimes it seems that people are obsessed with both. People joke and gossip about sex constantly. Magazines, novels, movies, and television shows are saturated with sexual activity and innuendo. The advertising industry uses sex to sell everything from mouthwash to designer jeans to automobiles. This intense interest in sex reflects the importance of sexual motivation. In this portion of the chapter, we will examine the physiology of the human sexual response, review evolutionary analyses of human sexual motivation, discuss some controversies surrounding pornography, and analyze the roots of sexual orientation.

The Human Sexual Response

Assuming people are motivated to engage in sexual activity, exactly what happens to them physically? This may sound like a simple question. But scientists really knew very little about the physiology of the human sexual response before William Masters and Virginia Johnson did groundbreaking research in the 1960s. Although our society seems obsessed with sex, until relatively recently (the 1980s) it did not encourage scientists to study sex. At first Masters and Johnson even had difficulty finding journals that were willing to publish their studies.

Masters and Johnson used physiological recording devices to monitor the bodily changes of volunteers engaging in sexual activities. They even equipped an artificial penile device with a camera to study physiological reactions inside the vagina. Their observations of and interviews with subjects yielded a detailed description of the human sexual response that eventually won them widespread acclaim.

Masters and Johnson (1966, 1970) divide the sexual response cycle into four stages: excitement, plateau, orgasm, and resolution. **Figure 10.6** shows how the intensity of sexual arousal changes as women and men progress through these stages. Let's take a closer look at these phases in the human sexual response.

Excitement Phase. During the initial phase of excitement, the level of physical arousal usually escalates rapidly. In both sexes, muscle tension, respiration rate, heart rate, and blood pressure increase quickly. *Vasocongestion*—**engorgement of blood vessels**—produces penile erection and swollen testes in males. In females, vasocongestion leads to a swelling and hardening of the clitoris, expansion of the vaginal lips, and vaginal lubrication.

Plateau Phase. During the plateau phase, physiological arousal usually continues to build, but at a much slower pace. In women, further vasocongestion produces a tightening of the vaginal entrance, as the clitoris withdraws under the clitoral hood. Many men secrete a bit of fluid at the tip of the penis. This is not ejaculate, but it may contain sperm. When foreplay is lengthy, fluctuation in arousal is normal for both sexes. This fluctuation is more apparent in men; erections may increase and decrease noticeably. In women, this fluctuation may be reflected in changes in vaginal lubrication.

Orgasm Phase. *Orgasm* occurs when sexual arousal reaches its peak intensity and is discharged in a series of muscular contractions that pulsate through the pelvic area. Heart rate, respiration rate, and blood pressure increase sharply during this exceedingly pleasant spasmodic response. In males, orgasm is ac-

Figure 10.6

The human sexual response cycle. There are similarities and differences between men and women in patterns of sexual arousal. Pattern A, which culminates in orgasm and resolution, is the ideal sequence for both sexes but not something one can count on. Pattern B, which involves sexual arousal without orgasm followed by a slow resolution, is seen in both sexes but is more common among women (see Figure 10.7). Pattern C, which involves multiple orgasms, is seen almost exclusively in women, as men go through a refractory period before they are capable of another orgasm.

SOURCE: Based on Masters, W. H., & Johnson, V. E. (1966). *Human sexual response.* Boston: Little, Brown. Copyright ©1966 Little, Brown and Company.

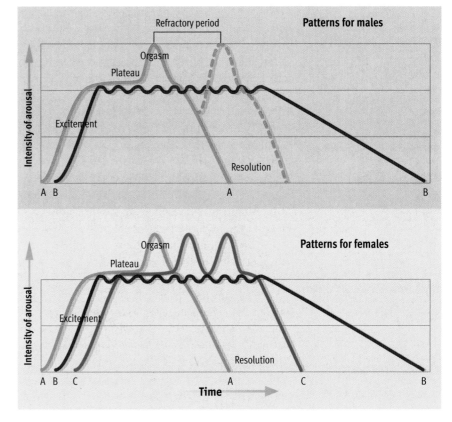

companied by ejaculation of the seminal fluid. The subjective experience of orgasm appears to be very similar for men and women. However, there *are* some interesting gender differences in the orgasm phase of the sexual response cycle. On the one hand, women are more likely than men to be *multiorgasmic*. A woman is said to be multiorgasmic if she experiences more than one climax in a time period (pattern C in Figure 10.6). On the other hand, women are more likely than men to engage in intercourse without experiencing an orgasm (see Figure 10.7; Laumann et al., 1994). Whether these differences reflect attitudes and sexual practices versus physiological processes is open to debate. On the one hand, it is easy to argue that males' greater orgasmic consistency must be a product of evolution, as it would have obvious adaptive significance for promoting men's reproductive fitness. On the other hand, over the years theorists have come up with a variety of plausible environmental explanations for this disparity, such as gender differences in the socialization of guilt feelings about sex, as well as sexual scripts and practices that are less than optimal for women (Lott, 1987). For example, some theorists argue that women are socialized to be sexually submissive, and some data suggest that this submissiveness undermines their sexual arousal (Sanchez, Kiefer, & Ybarra, 2006). Another consideration is that orgasm consistency seems to be influenced by relationship quality more in women than men. Consistent with this analysis, one recent study found a correlation of .43 between the intensity of heterosexual women's love for their partner and their ease in reaching orgasm (Ortigue, Grafton, & Bianchi-Demicheli, 2007). In other words, sex is more satisfying for women in love and presumably less satisfying for those who are not.

Resolution Phase. During the resolution phase, the physiological changes produced by sexual arousal subside. If orgasm has not occurred, the reduction in sexual tension may be relatively slow and sometimes unpleasant. After orgasm, men experience a *refractory period,* a time following orgasm during

which males are largely unresponsive to further stimulation. The length of the refractory period varies from a few minutes to a few hours and increases with age.

Evolutionary Analyses of Human Sexual Behavior

As you have already seen in previous chapters, the relatively new evolutionary perspective in psychology has generated intriguing hypotheses related to a

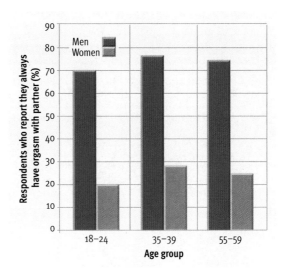

Figure 10.7

The gender gap in orgasm consistency. In their sexual interactions, men seem to reach orgasm more reliably than women. The data shown here suggest that the gender gap in orgasmic consistency is pretty sizable. Both biological and sociocultural factors may contribute to this gender gap. (Data from Laumann et al., 1994)

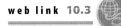
variety of topics, including perception, learning, language, and problem solving. However, evolutionary theorists' analyses of sexual behavior have drawn the most attention. Obviously, the task of explaining sexual behavior is crucial to the evolutionary perspective, given its fundamental thesis that natural selection is fueled by variations in reproductive success.

The thinking in this area has been guided by Robert Trivers's (1972) *parental investment theory.* **Parental investment refers to what each sex has to invest—in terms of time, energy, survival risk, and forgone opportunities—to produce and nurture offspring.** For example, the efforts required to guard eggs, build nests, or nourish offspring represent parental investments. In most species, striking disparities exist between males and females in their parental investment, and these discrepancies shape mating strategies. According to Trivers, *members of the sex that makes the smaller investment (males in most species) will pursue mating opportunities vigorously and compete with each other for these opportunities, whereas members of the sex that makes the larger investment (females in most species) will tend to be more conservative and discriminating about mating behavior.* This rule of thumb predicts mating patterns in many types of animals. But how does it apply to humans?

Like many mammalian species, human males are *required* to invest little in the production of offspring beyond the act of copulation, so their reproductive fitness is maximized by mating with as many females as possible. The situation for females is quite different. Females have to invest nine months in pregnancy, and our female ancestors typically had to devote at least several additional years to nourishing offspring through breastfeeding. These realities place a ceiling on the number of offspring women can produce, regardless of how many males they mate with. Hence, females have little or no incentive for mating with many males. Instead, females can optimize their reproductive potential by being selective in mating.

Thus, in humans, males are thought to compete with other males for the relatively scarce and valuable "commodity" of reproductive opportunities. Parental investment theory predicts that in compari-

son to women, men will show more interest in sexual activity, more desire for variety in sexual partners, and more willingness to engage in uncommitted sex (see **Figure 10.8**). In contrast, females are thought to be the conservative, discriminating sex that is more selective about mating. This selectivity supposedly entails seeking partners who have the greatest ability to contribute toward feeding and caring for offspring. Why? Because in the world of our ancient ancestors, males' greater strength and agility would have been crucial assets in the never-ending struggle to find food and shelter and defend one's territory. A female who chose a mate who was lazy or unreliable or who had no hunting, fighting, building, farming, or other useful economic skills would have suffered a substantial disadvantage in her efforts to raise her children and pass on her genes.

Does the empirical evidence mesh with these predictions from parental investment theory? Let's look at some of the evidence.

Gender Differences in Patterns of Sexual Activity

Consistent with evolutionary theory, males generally show a greater interest in sex than females do (Peplau, 2003). Men think about sex more often than women (see **Figure 10.9**), and they initiate sex more often (Morokoff et al., 1997). Males have more frequent and varied sexual fantasies (Okami & Shackelford, 2001), and their subjective ratings of their sex drive tend to be higher than females' (Ostovich & Sabini, 2004). Men also tend to overestimate women's sexual interest in them (a cognitive bias not shared by women), which seems designed to ensure that males do not overlook sexual opportunities (Buss, 2001; Levesque, Nave, & Lowe, 2006). When heterosexual couples are asked about their sex lives, male partners are more likely than their female counterparts to report that they would like to have sex more frequently, and men spend vastly more money than women on sexual entertainment (Baumeister, Catanese, & Vohs, 2001).

Men also are more motivated than women to pursue sex with a greater variety of partners (McBurney,

Figure 10.8

Parental investment theory and mating preferences. Parental investment theory suggests that basic differences between males and females in parental investment have great adaptive significance and lead to gender differences in mating propensities and preferences, as outlined here.

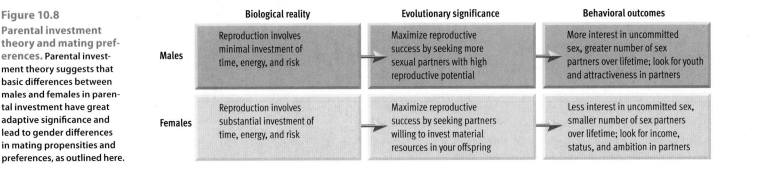

	Biological reality	Evolutionary significance	Behavioral outcomes
Males	Reproduction involves minimal investment of time, energy, and risk	Maximize reproductive success by seeking more sexual partners with high reproductive potential	More interest in uncommitted sex, greater number of sex partners over lifetime; look for youth and attractiveness in partners
Females	Reproduction involves substantial investment of time, energy, and risk	Maximize reproductive success by seeking partners willing to invest material resources in your offspring	Less interest in uncommitted sex, smaller number of sex partners over lifetime; look for income, status, and ambition in partners

Zapp, & Streeter, 2005). For example, Buss and Schmitt (1993) found that college men indicated that they would ideally like to have 18 sex partners across their lives, whereas college women reported that they would prefer only 5 partners. Similar findings were observed in a follow-up study that examined desire for sexual variety in over 16,000 subjects from 10 major regions of the world (Schmitt et al., 2003). As you can see in **Figure 10.10**, males expressed a desire for more partners than females in all 10 world regions, and in most cases the differences were substantial.

Clear gender disparities are also seen in regard to people's willingness to engage in casual or uncommitted sex. For example, Buss and Schmitt (1993) asked undergraduates about the likelihood that they would consent to sex with someone they found desirable whom they had known for one hour, one day, one week, one month, or longer periods. Men were much more likely than women to have sex with someone they had known for only a brief period. Moreover, a compelling field study, with no concerns about self-report issues, yielded similar results. Clark and Hatfield (1989) had average-looking men approach female (college-age) strangers and ask if they would go back to the man's apartment to have sex with him. None of the women agreed to this proposition. But when Clark and Hatfield had average-looking women approach males with the same proposition 75% of the men eagerly agreed!

In a definitive review of the empirical evidence, Roy Baumeister and colleagues (2001) concluded, "Across many different studies and measures, men have been shown to have more frequent and more intense sexual desires than women, as reflected in spontaneous thoughts about sex, frequency and variety of sexual fantasies, desired frequency of intercourse, desired number of partners, masturbation, liking for various sexual practices, . . . No contrary findings (indicating stronger sexual motivation among women) were found" (p. 242). That said, evidence suggests that the sexual disparities between males and females may be exaggerated a little by reliance on subjects' self-reports

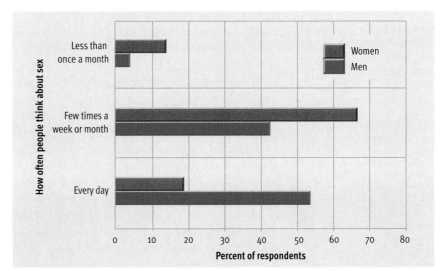

Figure 10.9

The gender gap in how much people think about sex. This graph summarizes data on how often males and females think about sex, based on a large-scale survey. As evolutionary theorists would predict, based on parental investment theory, males seem to manifest more interest in sexual activity than their female counterparts do. (Data from Laumann et al.,1994)

(Alexander & Fisher, 2003). Because of the double standard regarding sexuality, women worry more than men about being viewed as sexually permissive, which may lead them to underestimate or downplay their sexual motivation (Crawford & Popp, 2003).

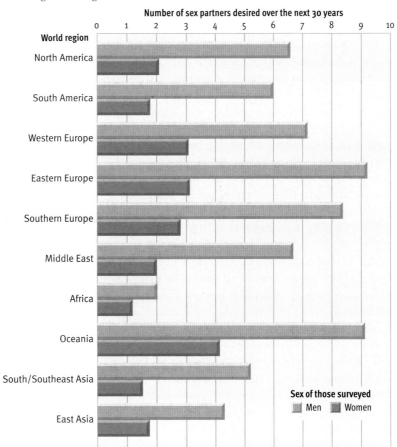

Figure 10.10

The gender gap in desire for a variety of sexual partners. Schmitt et al. (2003) gathered cross-cultural data on gender disparities in the number of sex partners desired by people. Respondents were asked about how many sexual partners they ideally would like to have in the next 30 years. As evolutionary theorists would predict, males reported that they would like to have more sexual partners in all ten world regions examined.

SOURCE: Schmitt, D. P., and 118 Members of the International Sexuality Description Project. (2003). Universal sex differences in the desire for sexual variety: Tests from 52 nations, 6 continents, and 13 islands. *Journal of Personality and Social Psychology, 85,* 85–104. Copyright © 2003 by the American Psychological Association. Reprinted by permission of the authors.

David Buss

*"Evolutionary psychologists
develop hypotheses about the
psychological mechanisms
that have evolved in humans to
solve particular adaptive problems that humans have faced
under ancestral conditions."*

Gender Differences in Mate Preferences

According to evolutionary theorists, if males were
left to their own devices over the course of history,
they probably would have shown relatively little
interest in long-term mating commitments, but females have generally demanded long-term commitments from males as part of consenting to sex (Buss,
1994a). As a result, long-term mating commitments
are a normal part of the social landscape in human
societies. However, parental investment theory suggests that there should be some glaring disparities
between men and women in what they look for in a
long-term mate (consult Figure 10.8 again).

The adaptive problem for our male ancestors was
to find a female with good reproductive potential who
would be sexually faithful and effective in nurturing
children. Given these needs, evolutionary theory
predicts that men should place more emphasis than
women on partner characteristics such as youthfulness (which allows for more reproductive years) and
attractiveness (which is assumed to be correlated
with health and fertility). In contrast, the adaptive
problem for our female ancestors was to find a male
who could provide material resources and protect his
family and who was dependable and willing to invest
his resources in his family. Given these needs, evolutionary theory predicts that women should place
more emphasis than men on partner characteristics
such as intelligence, ambition, income, and social
status (which are associated with the ability to provide more material resources). Evolutionary theorists
are quick to point out that these differing priorities
do not reflect conscious strategies. For the most part,
people do not think about sex in terms of maximizing their reproductive potential. Instead, these different priorities are viewed as subconscious preferences
that have been hardwired into the human brain by
evolutionary forces. In any event, if these evolutionary analyses of sexual motivation are on the mark,
gender differences in mating preferences should be
virtually universal and thus transcend culture.

To test this hypothesis, David Buss (1989) and
50 scientists from around the world surveyed more
than 10,000 people from 37 cultures about what
they looked for in a mate. As predicted by parental
investment theory, they found that women placed a
higher value than men on potential partners' status,
ambition, and financial prospects (see Figure 10.11).
These priorities were not limited to industrialized
or capitalist countries; they were apparent in third-
world cultures, socialist countries, and all varieties of
economic systems. In contrast, men around the world
consistently showed more interest than women in

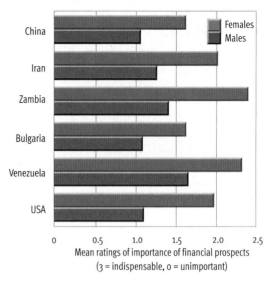

Figure 10.11
Gender and potential mates' financial prospects.
Consistent with evolutionary theory, Buss (1989) found that
females place more emphasis on potential partners' financial
prospects than males do. Moreover, he found that this trend
transcended culture. The specific results for 6 of the 37 cultures
studied by Buss are shown here.

potential partners' youthfulness and physical attractiveness (see Figure 10.12). A host of studies, using
diverse samples and a variety of research methods,
have replicated the disparities between males and
females in mating priorities and preferences (Shackelford, Schmitt, & Buss, 2005; Schmitt, 2005). For

BIZARRO

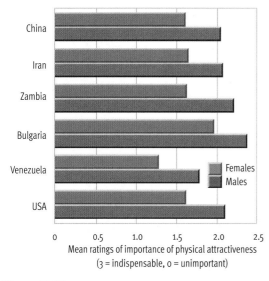

Mean ratings of importance of physical attractiveness
(3 = indispensable, 0 = unimportant)

Figure 10.12

Gender and potential mates' physical attractiveness. Consistent with evolutionary theory, Buss (1989) found that all over the world, males place more emphasis on potential partners' good looks than females do. The specific results for 6 of the 37 cultures studied by Buss are shown here.

Evolutionary theory posits that men can maximize their reproductive fitness by seeking youthful partners, whereas women can maximize their reproductive success by searching for mates that are rich in material resources that can be invested in children. Obviously, this theory can explain why attractive young women often become romantically involved with much older men who happen to be wealthy.

example, in a study of personal ads placed in newspapers and magazines, Wiederman (1993) found that female advertisers explicitly sought financial resources in potential partners eleven times as often as male advertisers did. And a recent study found that higher income in men was associated with a greater frequency of sex, yielding more reproductive opportunities for higher status men, as evolutionary theory would predict (Hopcroft, 2006). Recent research also supports the notion that women pay more attention than men to a potential partner's willingness to invest in children (Brase, 2006). The

gender gap on this dimension occurs because men appear to be largely indifferent to females' potential for parental investment. Moreover, the same study showed that men who were perceived to be favorably disposed to investing in children were judged to be more attractive by women. That brings us to another fascinating study of women's perceptions of men's mating potential that serves as our Featured Study for this chapter.

Can Women Judge Men's Mate Potential in Just One Glance?

According to evolutionary theories, human females can improve their reproductive fitness by seeking male partners who have access to material resources and who show a willingness to invest in children. And females can enhance their chances of passing on their genes by pursuing males who exhibit high masculinity, which is assumed to be a marker for genetic quality and reproductive potential. The present study looked at women's judgments of the latter two characteristics (parental investment potential and masculinity) based on nothing more than a snapshot and the impact of these judgments on women's ratings of males' mate potential. The investigators wanted to know whether women could draw meaningful inferences

about males' masculinity and parental potential from facial cues.

Method

Stimulus targets and characteristics. The male stimulus persons were 39 students from the University of Chicago, with a mean age of 21. They were instructed to assume a neutral facial expression while their facial photos were shot from a standard distance. To operationalize their masculinity, saliva samples were taken to measure each stimulus person's testosterone level. To assess their parental investment potential, they each took a test that measured their interest in infants.

SOURCE: Roney, J. R., Hanson, K. N., Durante, K. M., & Maestripieri, D. (2006). Reading men's faces: Women's mate attractiveness judgments track men's testosterone and interest in infants. *Proceedings of the Royal Society of London B, 273,* 2169–2175.

FEATURED

STUDY

Participants and procedure. The women who rated the men were 29 undergraduates from the University of California, Santa Barbara, with a mean age of 18. These women viewed the photos of the men in a standard order and were asked to rate each for "likes children," "masculine," "physically attractive," and "kind." After the first set of ratings, they were shown all the photos again and asked to rate each male's mate potential for a short-term and a long-term romantic relationship.

Results

The women's ratings of the male stimulus persons' masculinity correlated moderately well (.34) with the males' actual testosterone levels. Likewise, the women's ratings of the degree to which the male stimulus persons liked children correlated (.38) with the males' scores on the test of interest in infants. The data also showed that women's perceptions of masculinity and parental interest influenced their ratings of the male stimulus persons' mate potential. Higher ratings of masculinity fostered higher estimates of the males' short-term mate potential, whereas higher ratings of parental interest led to higher estimates of long-term mate potential.

Discussion

The authors conclude that "the present study provides the first direct evidence that women's attractiveness judgments specifically track both men's affinity for children and men's hormone concentrations" (p. 2173). They assert that their most interesting finding was the demonstration that women can draw meaningful inferences about males' parental interest based on a brief exposure to a single photograph.

Comment

A description of this study in the *Chicago Tribune* captured the essence of its remarkable findings: "Just from looking at a man's face, women can sense how much he likes children, gauge his testosterone level and decide whether he would be more suitable as a one-night stand or as a husband" (Gorner, 2006). Given the modest magnitude of the correlations observed that is a bit of an overstatement, but the study did provide fascinating new evidence that humans may subconsciously register subtle features of potential mates that are relevant to enhancing reproductive fitness, as predicted by evolutionary theory.

Criticism and Alternative Explanations

So, the findings on gender differences in sexual behavior mesh nicely with predictions derived from evolutionary theory. But, in the world of science, everyone is a critic—so you may be wondering: What types of criticism has this line of research generated? One set of concerns centers on the fact that the findings do not paint a very flattering picture of human nature. Men end up looking like sordid sexual predators; women come across as cynical, greedy materialists; and evolutionary theory appears to endorse these ideas as the inevitable outcome of natural selection. As Buss (1998) acknowledges, "Much of what I discovered about human mating is not nice" (p. 408). This controversy demonstrates once again that psychological theories can have far-reaching social and political ramifications, but the sociopolitical fallout has no bearing on evolutionary theory's scientific validity or utility.

However, some critics *have* expressed doubts about the validity of evolutionary explanations of gender differences in sexual behavior. They note that one can come up with alternative explanations for the findings. For example, women's emphasis on males' material resources could be a by-product of cultural and economic forces rather than the result of biological imperatives (Eagly & Wood, 1999). Women may have learned to value males' economic clout because their own economic potential has been severely limited in virtually all cultures by a long history of dis-crimination (Hrdy, 1997; Kasser & Sharma, 1999). In a similar vein, Roy Baumeister, who has convincingly documented that men have stronger sexual motivation than women (Baumeister et al., 2001), has argued that this disparity may be largely attributable to extensive cultural processes that serve to suppress female sexuality (Baumeister & Twenge, 2002). Evolutionary theorists counter these arguments by pointing out that the cultural and economic processes at work may themselves be products of evolution.

The Controversial Issue of Pornography

According to some social critics, we live in the golden age of pornography. As Strager (2003) puts it, "Following the proliferation of video and the dawn of the Internet, never has so much pornography been available to so many so easily" (p. 50). What effects do erotic photographs and films have on sexual desire? Laboratory studies show that erotic materials stimulate sexual desire in many people (Geer & Janssen, 2000). Generally speaking, men are more likely than women to report that they find erotic materials enjoyable and arousing (Gardos & Mosher, 1999; Koukounas & McCabe, 1997). However, this finding may partly reflect the fact that the vast majority of erotic materials are scripted to appeal to males and often portray women in degrading roles that elicit negative reactions from female viewers (Mosher & Mac-

Ian, 1994; Pearson & Pollack, 1997). Consistent with this perspective, one study found that when subjects viewed erotic films chosen by males, men rated the films as more arousing than women did, but when subjects viewed erotic films *chosen by females,* gender differences in participants' responsiveness were negligible (Janssen, Carpenter, & Graham, 2003).

How much impact does erotic material have on actual sexual behavior? The empirical data on this hotly debated question are inconsistent and are open to varied interpretations (Seto, Maric, & Barbaree, 2001). The balance of evidence suggests that exposure to erotic material elevates the likelihood of overt sexual activity for a period of hours immediately after the exposure (Both et al., 2004; Donnerstein, Linz, & Penrod, 1987). This relatively modest effect may explain why attempts to find a link between the availability of erotica and sex crime rates have largely yielded negative results. For the most part, researchers have not found correlations between greater availability of pornography and elevated rates of sex crimes (Kimmel & Linders, 1996; Kutchinsky, 1991; Nemes, 1992; Winick & Evans, 1996). Although most sex offenders admit to an extensive history of using pornographic materials, sex offenders typically do not have earlier or more extensive exposure to pornography in childhood or adolescence than other people (Bauserman, 1996), and pornography appears to play a minor role in the commission of sexual offenses (Langevin & Curnoe, 2004).

Although erotic materials don't appear to incite overpowering sexual urges, they may alter *attitudes* in ways that eventually influence sexual behavior. Zillmann and Bryant (1984) found that male and female undergraduates exposed to a large dose of pornography (three or six films per week for six weeks) developed more liberal attitudes about sexual practices. For example, they came to view premarital and extramarital sex as more acceptable. Another study by Zillmann and Bryant (1988) suggests that viewing sexually explicit films may make some people dissatisfied with their own sexual interactions. In comparison to control subjects, the subjects exposed to a steady diet of pornography reported less satisfaction with their partners' physical appearance, sexual curiosity, and sexual performance. Thus, pornography may create unrealistic expectations about sexual relations.

Moreover, research on *aggressive pornography* has raised some serious concerns about its effects. Aggressive pornography typically depicts violence against women. Many films show women who gradually give in to and enjoy rape and other sexually degrading acts after some initial resistance. Some studies indicate that this type of material increases male subjects' aggressive behavior toward women, at least in the context of the research laboratory (Donnerstein & Malamuth, 1997; Vega & Malamuth, 2007). In the typical study, male subjects work on a laboratory task and are led to believe (falsely) that they are delivering electric shocks to other subjects. In this situation, their aggression toward females tends to be elevated after exposure to aggressive pornography. Such exposure may also make sexual coercion seem less offensive and help perpetuate the myth that women enjoy being raped and ravaged (Allen et al., 1995). And these attitudes can influence actual behavior. Research suggests that males who believe that "women who are raped asked for it" are more likely than others to commit sexual assault (Bohner, Siebler, & Schmelcher, 2006; Chiroro et al., 2004).

The effects of aggressive pornography are especially worrisome in light of evidence about rape. It is difficult to obtain accurate information about the prevalence of rape because only a minority of victims make reports to authorities (Fisher et al., 2003) Despite extensive rape prevention efforts, the incidence of rape appears to be unchanged (Rozee & Koss, 2001). Estimates suggest that as many as one-quarter of young women in the United States may be victims of rape or attempted rape (Campbell & Wasco, 2005; Koss, 1993). Only a minority of reported rapes are committed by strangers (see Figure 10.13). Particularly common is *date rape,* which occurs when a woman is forced to have sex in the context of dating. Research suggests that date rape is a serious problem on college campuses (Banyard et al., 2005). In one survey of students at 32 colleges, 1 in 7 women reported that they had been victimized by date rape or an attempted date rape (Koss, Gidycz, & Wisniewski, 1987). Moreover, 1 in 12 men admitted either to having forced a date into sex or to having tried to do so. However, *none* of these men identified himself as a rapist. Although other factors are surely at work,

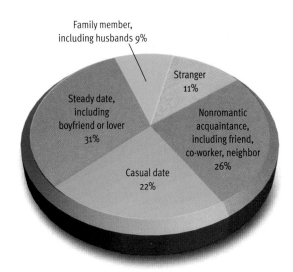

Family member,
including husbands 9%

Stranger
11%

Steady date,
including
boyfriend or lover
31%

Nonromantic
acquaintance,
including friend,
co-worker, neighbor
26%

Casual date
22%

Figure 10.13
Rape victim-offender relationships. Based on a national survey of 3187 college women, Mary Koss and her colleagues (1988) identified a sample of 468 women who indicated that they had been a victim of rape and who provided information on their relationship to the offender. Contrary to the prevailing stereotype, only a small minority (11%) of these women were raped by a stranger. As you can see, many of the women were raped by men they were dating.

0	1	2	3	4	5	6
Exclusively heterosexual	Predominantly heterosexual only incidentally homosexual	Predominantly heterosexual more than incidentally homosexual	Equally heterosexual and homosexual	Predominantly homosexual more than incidentally heterosexual	Predominantly homosexual only incidentally heterosexual	Exclusively homosexual

many theorists believe that aggressive pornography has contributed to this failure to see sexual coercion for what it is (Malamuth, Addison, & Koss, 2000).

The Mystery of Sexual Orientation

The controversy swirling around evolutionary explanations of gender differences in sexuality and the dangers of pornography is easily equaled by the controversy surrounding the determinants of *sexual orientation*. *Sexual orientation* refers to a person's preference for emotional and sexual relationships with individuals of the same sex, the other sex, or either sex. *Heterosexuals* seek emotional-sexual relationships with members of the other sex, *bi-*

sexuals with members of either sex, and *homosexuals* with members of the same sex. In recent years, the terms *gay* and *straight* have become widely used to refer to homosexuals and heterosexuals, respectively. Although *gay* can refer to homosexuals of either sex, most homosexual women prefer to call themselves *lesbians*.

People tend to view heterosexuality and homosexuality as an all-or-none distinction. However, in a pioneering study of sexual behavior, Alfred Kinsey and his colleagues (1948, 1953) discovered that many people who define themselves as heterosexuals have had homosexual experiences—and vice versa. Thus, Kinsey concluded that it is more accurate to view heterosexuality and homosexuality as end points on a continuum (Haslam, 1997). Indeed, Kinsey devised a seven-point scale, shown in Figure 10.14, that can be used to characterize individuals' sexual orientation. To reevaluate Kinsey's theory, Robert Epstein (2007) recently collected data via the Internet from over 18,000 people who characterized themselves as gay, straight, or bisexual and then responded to a questionnaire about their sexual desires and experiences. As you can see in Figure 10.15, Epstein's data are consistent with the notion that sexual orientation should be viewed as a continuum rather than a matter of discrete categories.

How common is homosexuality? No one knows for sure. Part of the problem is that this question is vastly more complex than it appears at first glance (LeVay, 1996; Savin-Williams, 2006). Given that sexual orientation is best represented as a continuum, where do you draw the lines between heterosexuality, bisexuality, and homosexuality? And how do you handle the distinction between overt behavior and desire? Where, for instance, do you put a person who is married and has never engaged in homosexual behavior but who reports homosexual fantasies and acknowledges being strongly drawn to members of the same sex? The other part of the problem is that many people have extremely prejudicial attitudes about homo-

Figure 10.15

New evidence that sexual orientation exists on a continuum. Robert Epstein (2007) conducted a large Internet survey in which 18,000 people characterized themselves as straight, bisexual, or gay and then responded to a questionnaire that placed them on a scale that indexed their sexual orientation. Epstein used a 14-point scale rather than Kinsey's 7-point scale. Given the self-selected nature of the sample, these data cannot tell us much about the exact percentage of people who are gay or bisexual, but the data provide dramatic evidence in support of the notion that sexual orientation exists on a continuum. If sexual orientation was an either-or proposition, people's scores would pile up at the two ends of the distribution with little overlap, which clearly is not the case.

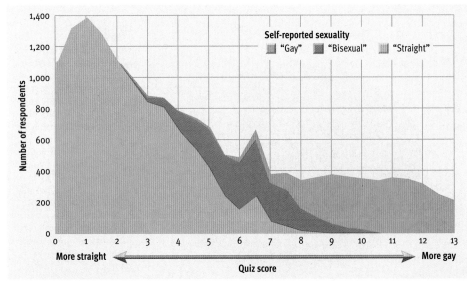

sexuality, which makes gays cautious and reluctant to give candid information about their sexuality (Herek, 1996, 2000). Small wonder, then, that estimates of the portion of the population that is homosexual vary widely. A frequently cited estimate of the number of people who are gay is 10%, but recent surveys suggest that this percentage may be an overestimate. Michaels (1996) combined data from two of the better large-scale surveys to arrive at the estimates seen in Figure 10.16. As you can see, the numbers are open to varying interpretations, but as a whole they suggest that about 5%–8% of the population could reasonably be characterized as homosexual.

Environmental Theories of Homosexuality

Over the years many environmental theories have been floated to explain the origins of homosexuality, but when tested empirically, these theories have garnered remarkably little support. For example, psychoanalytic and behavioral theorists, who usually agree on very little, both proposed environmental explanations for the development of homosexuality. The Freudian theorists argued that a male is likely to become gay when raised by a weak, detached, ineffectual father who is a poor heterosexual role model and by an overprotective, close-binding mother, with whom the boy identifies. Behavioral theorists argued that homosexuality is a learned preference acquired when same-sex stimuli have been paired with sexual arousal, perhaps through chance seductions by adult homosexuals. Extensive research on homosexuals' upbringing and childhood experiences has failed to support either of these theories (Bell, Weinberg, & Hammersmith, 1981).

However, efforts to research homosexuals' personal histories have yielded a number of interesting insights. Extremely feminine behavior in young boys or masculine behavior in young girls does predict the subsequent development of homosexuality (Bailey & Zucker, 1995; Bem, 2000). For example, 75%–90% of highly feminine young boys eventually turn out to be gay (Blanchard et al., 1995). Consistent with this finding, most gay men and women report that they can trace their homosexual leanings back to their early childhood, even before they understood what sex was really about (Bailey, 2003). Most also report that because of negative parental and societal attitudes about homosexuality, they initially struggled to deny their sexual orientation. Thus, they felt that their homosexuality was not a matter of choice and not something that they could readily change (Breedlove, 1994). These findings obviously suggest that the roots of homosexuality are more biological than environmental.

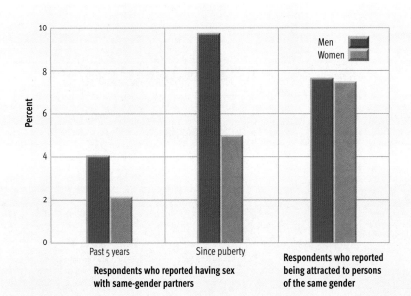

Figure 10.16

How common is homosexuality? The answer to this question is both complex and controversial. Michaels (1996) brought together data from two large-scale surveys to arrive at the estimates shown here. If you look at how many people have actually had a same-sex partner in the last five years, the figures are relatively low, but if you count those who have had a same-sex partner since puberty the figures more than double. Still another way to look at it is to ask people whether they are attracted to people of the same sex (regardless of their actual behavior). This approach suggests that about 8% of the population could be characterized as homosexual.

Biological Theories of Homosexuality

Nonetheless, initial efforts to find a biological basis for homosexuality met with little success. Most theorists originally assumed that hormonal differences between heterosexuals and homosexuals must underlie a person's sexual orientation (Doerr et al., 1976; Dorner, 1988). However, studies comparing circulating hormone levels in gays and straights found only small, inconsistent differences that could not be linked to sexual orientation in any convincing way (Bailey, 2003; Banks & Gartrell, 1995).

Thus, like environmental theorists, biological theorists were stymied for quite a while in their efforts to explain the roots of homosexuality. However, that picture changed in the 1990s when a pair of behavioral genetics studies reported findings suggesting that homosexuality has a hereditary basis. In the first study, conducted by Bailey and Pillard (1991), the subjects were gay men who had either a twin brother or an adopted brother. They found that 52% of the subjects' identical twins were gay, that 22% of their fraternal twins were gay, and that 11% of their adoptive brothers were gay. A companion study (Bailey et al., 1993) of lesbians yielded a similar pattern of results (see Figure 10.17 on the next page). Given that identical twins share more genetic overlap than fraternal twins, who share more genes than unre-

web link 10.5

Queer Resources Directory (QRD)

In its 1994 mission statement, the *Queer Resources Directory* described itself as "an electronic research library specifically dedicated to sexual minorities—groups that have traditionally been labeled as 'queer' and systematically discriminated against." Composed of more than 25,000 files and still growing, QRD offers a rich array of resources.

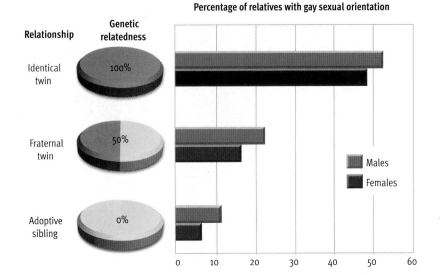

Percentage of relatives with gay sexual orientation

Identical twin — Genetic relatedness 100%
Fraternal twin — Genetic relatedness 50%
Adoptive sibling — Genetic relatedness 0%

Males
Females

0   10   20   30   40   50   60

Figure 10.17

Genetics and sexual orientation. If relatives who share more genetic relatedness show greater similarity on a trait than relatives who share less genetic overlap, this evidence suggests a genetic predisposition to the characteristic. Studies of both gay men and lesbian women have found a higher prevalence of homosexuality among their identical twins than their fraternal twins, who, in turn, are more likely to be homosexual than their adoptive siblings. These findings suggest that genetic factors influence sexual orientation. (Data from Bailey & Pillard, 1991; Bailey et. al., 1993)

lated adoptive siblings, these results suggest a genetic predisposition to homosexuality (Hyde, 2005b; see Chapter 3 for an explanation of the logic underlying twin and adoption studies). More recent twin studies, with larger and more representative samples, have provided further support for the conclusion that heredity influences sexual orientation (Bailey, Dunne, & Martin, 2000; Kendler et al., 2000). However, these newer studies have yielded smaller estimates of genetic influence, which have been attributed to improved sampling.

Many theorists suspect that the roots of homosexuality may lie in the organizing effects of prenatal hormones on neurological development (James, 2005). Several lines of research suggest that hormonal secretions during critical periods of prenatal development may shape sexual development, organize the brain in a lasting manner, and influence subsequent sexual orientation (Berenbaum & Snyder, 1995). For example, researchers have found elevated rates of homosexuality among women exposed to abnormally high androgen levels during prenatal development (because their mothers had an adrenal disorder or were given a synthetic hormone to reduce the risk of miscarriage) (Breedlove, 1994; Meyer-Bahlburg et al., 1995). Several other independent lines of research suggest that abnormalities in prenatal hormonal secretions may foster a predisposition to homosexuality (Mustanski, Chivers, & Bailey, 2002).

Despite the recent breakthroughs, much remains to be learned about the determinants of sexual orientation. The behavioral genetics data suggest that the hereditary predisposition to homosexuality is not overpowering. Environmental influences of some kind probably contribute to the development of homosexuality (Bem, 1996, 1998), but the nature of these environmental factors remains a mystery.

Another complication is that the pathways to homosexuality may be somewhat different for males than for females (Gladue, 1994). Females' sexuality appears to be characterized by more *plasticity* than males' sexuality (Baumeister, 2000, 2004). In other words, women's sexual behavior may be more easily shaped and modified by sociocultural factors. For example, although sexual orientation is assumed to be a stable characteristic, research shows that lesbian and bisexual women often change their sexual orientation over the course of their adult years (Diamond, 2003, 2007). And, in comparison to gay males, lesbians are less likely to trace their homosexuality back to their childhood and more likely to indicate that their attraction to the same sex emerged during adulthood (Tolman & Diamond, 2001). These findings suggest that sexual orientation may be more fluid and malleable in women than in men.

Once again, though, we can see that the nature versus nurture debate can have far-reaching social and political implications. Homosexuals have long been victims of extensive—and in many instances *legal*—discrimination. In most jurisdictions gays cannot legally formalize their unions in marriage, they are not allowed to openly join the U.S. military, and they are barred from some jobs (for example,

Some people are befuddled by the fact that actress Anne Heche (left) had a lengthy intimate relationship with comedian Ellen DeGeneres (right), but now has settled into a conventional heterosexual marriage. Although shifts in sexual orientation like this are uncommon among males, research has shown that females' sexual orientation tends to be characterized by more plasticity than that of males. These findings suggest that males' and females' pathways into homosexuality may be somewhat different.

many school districts will not hire gay teachers). However, if research were to show that being gay is largely a matter of biological destiny, much like being Hispanic or female or short, many of the arguments against equal rights for gays would disintegrate. Why ban gays from teaching, for instance, if their sexual preference cannot "rub off" on their students? Although one would hope that discrimination against gays would be brought to an end either way, many individuals' opinions about gay rights may be swayed by the outcome of the nature-nurture debate on the roots of homosexuality.

REVIEW of Key Learning Goals

10.7 The human sexual response cycle can be divided into four stages: excitement, plateau, orgasm, and resolution. The subjective experience of orgasm is fairly similar for both sexes. Intercourse leads to orgasm in women less consistently than in men, but women are much more likely to be multiorgasmic.

10.8 According to parental investment theory, males are thought to compete with other males for reproductive opportunities while females are assumed to be the discriminating sex that is selective in choosing partners. Consistent with evolutionary theory, males tend to think about and initiate sex more than females do, and they have more sexual partners and more interest in casual sex than females.

10.9 Gender differences in mating preferences appear to largely transcend cultural boundaries. Males emphasize potential partners' youthfulness and attractiveness, whereas females emphasize potential partners' status and financial prospects. As our Featured Study showed, women also pay attention to

males' willingness to invest in children and their masculinity, which is viewed as a marker for genetic quality.

10.10 People respond to a variety of erotic materials, which may elevate sexual desire for only a few hours but can have an enduring impact on attitudes about sex. Aggressive pornography may make sexual coercion seem less offensive to its consumers and may contribute to date rape.

10.11 Modern theorists view heterosexuality and homosexuality not as an all-or-none distinction but as endpoints on a continuum. Recent data on the prevalence of homosexuality suggest that 5%–8% of the population may be gay.

10.12 Although most gays can trace their homosexual leanings back to early childhood, research has not supported Freudian or behavioral theories of sexual orientation. Recent studies suggest that there is a genetic predisposition to homosexuality. Idiosyncrasies in prenatal hormonal secretions may also contribute to the development of homosexuality. The pathways into homosexuality may be somewhat different for males and females.

Achievement: In Search of Excellence

At the beginning of this chapter, we discussed Jon Krakauer's laborious, grueling effort to reach the summit of Mount Everest. He and the other climbers confronted incredible perils and endured extraordinary hardships to achieve their goal. What motivates people to push themselves so hard? In all likelihood, it's a strong need for achievement. The *achievement motive* **is the need to master difficult challenges, to outperform others, and to meet high standards of excellence.** Above all else, the need for achievement involves the desire to excel, especially in competition with others.

Research on achievement motivation was pioneered by David McClelland and his colleagues (McClelland, 1985; McClelland et al., 1953). McClelland argued that achievement motivation is of the utmost importance. He viewed the need for achievement as the spark that ignites economic growth, scientific progress, inspirational leadership, and masterpieces in the creative arts.

Individual Differences in the Need for Achievement

8b

You've no doubt heard the stories of Abraham Lincoln as a young boy, reading through the night by firelight. Find a biography of any high achiever, and you'll probably find a similar drive—throughout the person's life. The need for achievement is a fairly stable aspect of personality. Hence, research in this area has focused mostly on individual differences in achievement motivation. Subjects' need for achievement can be measured effectively with the Thematic Apperception Test (C. Smith, 1992; Spangler, 1992). The Thematic Apperception Test (TAT) is a *projective test,* one that requires subjects to respond to vague, ambiguous stimuli in ways that may reveal personal motives and traits (see Chapter 12). The stimulus materials for the TAT are pictures of people in ambiguous scenes open to interpretation. Examples include a man working at a desk and a woman seated in a chair staring off into space. Subjects are asked to write or tell stories about what's happening in the scenes and what the characters are feeling. The themes of these stories are then scored to measure the strength of various needs. Figure 10.18 (on the next page) shows examples of stories dominated by the themes of achievement and affiliation (the need for social bonds and belongingness).

The research on individual differences in achievement motivation has yielded interesting findings on the characteristics of people who score high in the need for achievement. They tend to work harder and

Key Learning Goals

10.13 Describe how the need for achievement is measured.

10.14 Articulate how variations in the need for achievement influence behavior.

10.15 Explain how situational factors influence achievement strivings.

David McClelland

"People with a high need for achievement are not gamblers; they are challenged to win by personal effort, not by luck."

Figure 10.18
Measuring motives with the Thematic Apperception Test (TAT). Subjects taking the TAT tell or write stories about what is happening in a scene, such as this one showing a man at work. The two stories shown here illustrate strong affiliation motivation and strong achievement motivation. The italicized parts of the stories are thematic ideas that would be identified by a TAT scorer.

SOURCE: Stories reprinted by permission of Dr. David McClelland.

Affiliation arousal
George is an engineer who is working late. He is *worried that his wife will be annoyed* with him for neglecting her. She has been *objecting* that he cares more about his work than his wife and family. He seems *unable to satisfy* both his boss and his wife, but he *loves her* very much and will do his best to *finish up* fast and get home to her.

Achievement arousal
George is an engineer who *wants to win* a competition in which the man with the *most practicable drawing* will be awarded the contract to build a bridge. He is taking a moment to think *how happy he will be* if he wins. He has been *baffled by how to make such a long span strong*, but he remembers to *specify a new steel alloy* of great strength, submits his entry, but does not win, and is *very unhappy*.

more persistently on tasks than people low in the need for achievement (Brown, 1974), and they handle negative feedback about task performance more effectively than others (Fodor & Carver, 2000). They also are more future oriented than others and more likely to delay gratification in order to pursue long-term goals (Mischel, 1961; Raynor & Entin, 1982). In terms of careers, they typically go into competitive, entrepreneurial occupations that provide them with an opportunity to excel (McClelland, 1987; Stewart & Roth, 2007). Apparently, their persistence and hard work often pay off. High achievement mo-

tivation correlates positively with measures of career success and with upward social mobility among lower-class men (Crockett, 1962; McClelland & Boyatzis, 1982).

Do people high in achievement need always tackle the biggest challenges available? Not necessarily. A curious finding has emerged in laboratory studies in which subjects have been asked to choose how difficult a task they want to work on. Subjects high in the need for achievement tend to select tasks of intermediate difficulty (McClelland & Koestner, 1992). For instance, in one study, subjects playing a ring-tossing game were allowed to stand as close to or far away from the target peg as they wanted; high achievers tended to prefer a moderate degree of challenge (Atkinson & Litwin, 1960).

Most people attribute Kobe Bryant's success in basketball to his remarkable ability, which is undeniably important. But the contribution of his extremely high need for achievement should not be underestimated. Bryant's competitive zeal is legendary, and he is widely regarded as one of the hardest working athletes in professional sports.

© AP Images/Eric Gay

Situational Determinants of Achievement Behavior

8b

Your achievement drive is not the only determinant of how hard you work. Situational factors can also influence achievement strivings. John Atkinson (1974, 1981, 1992) has elaborated extensively on McClelland's original theory of achievement motivation and has identified some important situational determinants of achievement behavior. Atkinson theorizes that the tendency to pursue achievement in a particular situation depends on the following factors:

- The strength of one's *motivation* to *achieve success*. This factor is viewed as a stable aspect of personality.
- One's estimate of the *probability of success* for the task at hand. This factor varies from task to task.
- The *incentive value of success*. This factor depends on the tangible and intangible rewards for success on the specific task.

The last two variables are situational determinants of achievement behavior. That is, they vary from one situation to another. According to Atkinson, the pursuit of achievement increases as the probability and incentive value of success go up (and decreases as they go down). Let's apply Atkinson's model to a simple example. Given a certain motivation to achieve success, you will pursue a good grade in calculus less vigorously if your professor gives impossible exams (thus lowering your expectancy of success) or if a good grade in calculus is not required for your major (lowering the incentive value of success).

The joint influence of these situational factors may explain why high achievers prefer tasks of intermediate difficulty. Atkinson notes that the probability of success and the incentive value of success on tasks are interdependent to some degree. As tasks get easier, success becomes less satisfying. As tasks get harder, success becomes more satisfying, but its likelihood obviously declines. When the probability and incentive value of success are weighed together, moderately challenging tasks seem to offer the best overall value in terms of maximizing one's sense of accomplishment.

Motivation and emotion are often intertwined (Zurbriggen & Sturman, 2002). On the one hand, *emotion can cause motivation*. For example, *anger* about your work schedule may motivate you to look for a new job. *Jealousy* of an ex-girlfriend may motivate you to ask out her roommate. On the other hand, *motivation can cause emotion*. For example, your motivation to win a photography contest may lead to great *anxiety* during the judging and either great *joy* if you win or great *gloom* if you don't. Although motivation and emotion are closely related, they're *not* the same thing. We'll analyze the nature of emotion in the next section.

Understanding the Determinants of Achievement Behavior

According to John Atkinson, one's pursuit of achievement in a particular situation depends on several factors. Check your understanding of these factors by identifying each of the following vignettes as an example of one of the following three determinants of achievement behavior: (a) need for achievement, (b) perceived probability of success, and (c) incentive value of success. The answers can be found in Appendix A.

_____ 1. Belinda is nervously awaiting the start of the finals of the 200-meter dash in the last meet of her high school career. "I've gotta win this race! This is the most important race of my life!"

_____ 2. Corey grins as he considers the easy time he's going to have this semester. "This class is supposed to be a snap. I hear the professor gives A's and B's to nearly everyone."

_____ 3. Diana's just as hard-charging as ever. She's gotten the highest grade on every test throughout the semester, yet she's still up all night studying for the final. "I know I've got an A in the bag, but I want to be the best student Dr. McClelland's ever had!"

REVIEW of Key Learning Goals

10.13 Achievement, which was first investigated by David McClelland, involves the need to excel, especially in competition with others. The need for achievement is usually measured with a projective test called the TAT.

10.14 People who are relatively high in the need for achievement work harder and more persistently than others. They delay gratification well and pursue competitive careers. However, in choosing challenges they often select tasks of intermediate difficulty.

10.15 Situational factors also influence achievement behavior. The pursuit of achievement tends to increase when the probability of success and the incentive value of success are high. The joint influence of these factors may explain why people high in achievement need tend to prefer challenges of intermediate difficulty.

The Elements of Emotional Experience

The most profound and important experiences in life are saturated with emotion. Think of the *joy* that people feel at weddings, the *grief* they feel at funerals, the *ecstasy* they feel when they fall in love. Emotions also color everyday experiences. For instance, you might experience *anger* when a professor treats you rudely, *dismay* when you learn that your car needs expensive repairs, and *happiness* when you see that you aced your economics exam. In some respects, emotions lie at the core of mental health. The two most common complaints that lead people to seek psychotherapy are *depression* and *anxiety*. Clearly, emotions play a pervasive role in people's lives. Reflecting this reality, modern psychologists have increased their research on emotion in recent decades (Barrett et al., 2007; Cacioppo & Gardner, 1999).

But exactly what is an emotion? Everyone has plenty of personal experience with emotion, but it's an elusive concept to define (Izard, 2007; LeDoux, 1995). Emotion includes cognitive, physiological, and behavioral components, which are summarized in the following definition: *Emotion* involves **(1) a subjective conscious experience (the cognitive component) accompanied by (2) bodily arousal (the physiological component) and by (3) characteristic overt expressions (the behavioral**

Key Learning Goals

10.16 Describe the cognitive component of emotion.

10.17 Understand the physiological and neural bases of emotions.

10.18 Explain how emotions are reflected in facial expressions, and describe the facial feedback hypothesis.

10.19 Review cross-cultural similarities and variations in emotional experience.

component). That's a pretty complex definition. Let's take a closer look at each of these three components of emotion.

The Cognitive Component: Subjective Feelings

8c

Over 550 words in the English language refer to emotions (Averill, 1980). Ironically, however, people often have difficulty describing their emotions to others (Zajonc, 1980). Emotion is a highly personal, subjective experience. In studying the cognitive component of emotions, psychologists generally rely on participants' verbal reports of what they're experiencing. Their reports indicate that emotions are potentially intense internal feelings that sometimes seem to have a life of their own. People can't click their emotions on and off like a bedroom light. If it were as simple as that, you could choose to be happy whenever you wanted. As Jeremy Gray (2004), puts it, "Some emotions are like fires, seemingly started by a motivational spark" (p. 47). In a similar vein, Joseph LeDoux (1996) notes, "Emotions are things that happen to us rather than things we will to occur" (p. 19). Actually, some degree of emotional control is possible (Thayer, 1996), but emotions tend to involve automatic reactions that are difficult to regulate (Öhman & Wiens, 2003). In some cases these emotional reactions may occur at an unconscious level of processing, outside of one's awareness (Winkielman & Berridge, 2004).

People's cognitive appraisals of events in their lives are key determinants of the emotions they experience (Ellsworth & Scherer, 2003; Lazarus, 1995). A specific event, such as giving a speech, may be highly threatening and thus anxiety arousing for one person but a "ho-hum," routine matter for another. The conscious experience of emotion includes an *evaluative* aspect. People characterize their emotions as pleasant or unpleasant (Barrett et al., 2007; Lang, 1995). These evaluative reactions can be automatic and subconscious (Ferguson & Bargh, 2004). Of course, individuals often experience "mixed emotions" that include both pleasant and unpleasant qualities (Cacioppo & Berntson, 1999). For example, an executive just given a promotion with challenging new responsibilities may experience both happiness and anxiety. The landscape of mixed emotions was explored in a recent study of people's reactions to good outcomes that could have been better and bad outcomes that could have been worse (Larsen et al., 2004). As predicted, these events elicited mixtures of positive and negative emotions. These contrasting

Emotions involve automatic reactions that can be difficult to control.

emotions tended to occur *simultaneously* rather than alternating back and forth sequentially.

For the most part, researchers have paid more attention to negative emotions than positive ones (Fredrickson, 1998). Why have positive emotions been neglected? For one thing, there appear to be fewer positive emotions than negative ones. In addition, positive emotions are less clearly differentiated from each other than negative emotions (Fredrickson & Branigan, 2001; Rozin, 2003). Another consideration is that negative emotions appear to have more powerful effects than positive ones (Baumeister, Bratslavsky, & Finkenauer, 2001; Rozin & Royzman, 2001). Although these factors probably have contributed, the neglect of positive emotions is symptomatic of a broad and deeply rooted bias in the field of psychology, which has historically focused on pathology, weaknesses, and suffering (and how to heal these conditions) rather than health, strengths, and resilience (Fredrickson, 2002). In recent years, the architects of the positive psychology movement (see Chapter 1) have set out to shift the field's focus away from negative experiences (Seligman, 2002; Seligman & Csikszentmihalyi, 2000). The advocates of *positive psychology* argue for increased research on contentment, well-being, human strengths, and positive emotions. One outgrowth of this movement has been increased interest in the dynamics of happiness. We will discuss this research in the upcoming Personal Application.

The Physiological Component: Diffuse and Multifaceted

8c

Emotional processes are closely tied to physiological processes, but the interconnections are enormously complex. The biological bases of emotions are diffuse, involving many areas in the brain and many neurotransmitter systems, as well as the autonomic nervous system and the endocrine system.

Autonomic Arousal

8c

Imagine your reaction as your car spins out of control on an icy highway. Your fear is accompanied by a variety of physiological changes. Your heart rate and breathing accelerate. Your blood pressure surges, and your pupils dilate. The hairs on your skin stand erect, giving you "goose bumps," and you start to perspire. Although the physical reactions may not always be as obvious as in this scenario, *emotions are generally accompanied by visceral arousal* (Cacioppo et al., 1993). Surely you've experienced a "knot in your stomach" or a "lump in your throat"—thanks to anxiety.

Much of the discernible physiological arousal associated with emotion occurs through the actions of the *autonomic nervous system* (Janig, 2003), which regulates the activity of glands, smooth muscles, and blood vessels (see Figure 10.19). As you may recall from Chapter 3, the autonomic nervous system is responsible for the highly emotional *fight-or-flight response,* which is largely modulated by the release of adrenal *hormones* that radiate throughout the body. Hormonal changes clearly play a crucial role in emotional responses to stress and may contribute to many other emotions as well.

One notable part of emotional arousal is **the *galvanic skin response (GSR)*, an increase in the electrical conductivity of the skin that occurs when sweat glands increase their activity.** GSR is a convenient and sensitive index of autonomic arousal that has been used as a measure of emotion in many laboratory studies.

The connection between emotion and autonomic arousal provides the basis for the *polygraph,* or *lie detector,* **a device that records autonomic fluctuations while a subject is questioned.** The polygraph was invented in 1915 by psychologist William Marston—who also dreamed up the comic book superhero Wonder Woman (Knight, 2004). A polygraph can't actually detect lies. It's really an emotion detector. It monitors key indicators of autonomic arousal, typically heart rate, blood pressure, respiration rate, and GSR. The assumption is that when subjects lie, they experience emotion (presumably anxiety) that produces noticeable changes in these physiological indicators (see Figure 10.20 on the next page). The polygraph examiner asks a subject a number of nonthreatening questions to establish the subject's baseline on these autonomic indicators. Then the examiner asks the critical questions (for example, "Where were you on the night of the burglary?") and observes whether the person's autonomic arousal changes.

The polygraph has been controversial since its invention (Grubin & Madsen, 2005). Polygraph advocates claim that lie detector tests are about 85%–90% accurate and that the validity of polygraph testing has been demonstrated in empirical studies, but these claims clearly are not supported by the evidence (Iacono & Lykken, 1997; Iacono & Patrick, 1999). Methodologically sound research on the

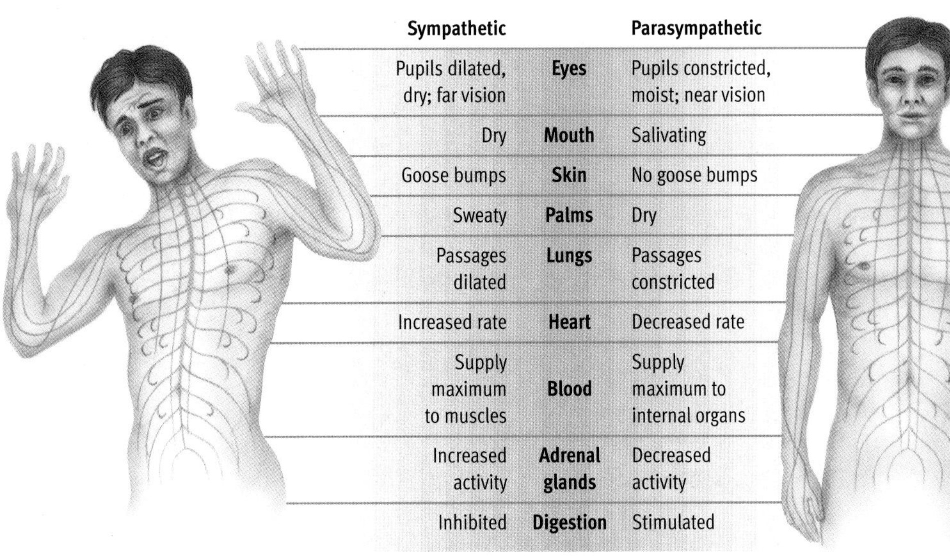

	Sympathetic		Parasympathetic
	Pupils dilated, dry; far vision	**Eyes**	Pupils constricted, moist; near vision
	Dry	**Mouth**	Salivating
	Goose bumps	**Skin**	No goose bumps
	Sweaty	**Palms**	Dry
	Passages dilated	**Lungs**	Passages constricted
	Increased rate	**Heart**	Decreased rate
	Supply maximum to muscles	**Blood**	Supply maximum to internal organs
	Increased activity	**Adrenal glands**	Decreased activity
	Inhibited	**Digestion**	Stimulated

Figure 10.19

Emotion and autonomic arousal. The autonomic nervous system (ANS) is composed of the nerves that connect to the heart, blood vessels, smooth muscles, and glands (consult Figure 3.8 for a more detailed view). The ANS is divided into the *sympathetic system,* which mobilizes bodily resources in response to stress, and the *parasympathetic system,* which conserves bodily resources. Emotions are frequently accompanied by sympathetic ANS activation, which leads to goose bumps, sweaty palms, and the other physical responses listed on the left side of the diagram.

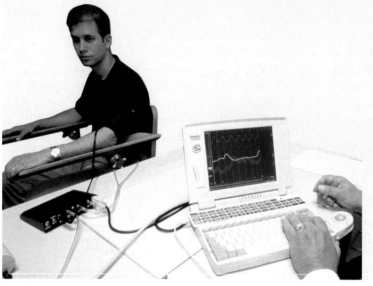

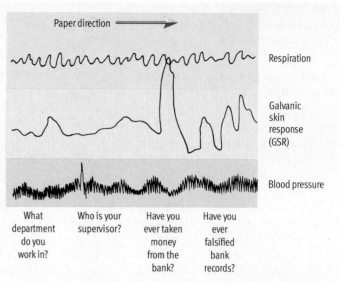

What department do you work in?	Who is your supervisor?	Have you ever taken money from the bank?	Have you ever falsified bank records?

Figure 10.20

Emotion and the polygraph. A lie detector measures the autonomic arousal that most people experience when they tell a lie. After using nonthreatening questions to establish a baseline, a polygraph examiner looks for signs of arousal (such as the sharp change in GSR shown here) on incriminating questions. Unfortunately, the polygraph is not a dependable index of whether people are lying.

Joseph LeDoux

"In situations of danger, it is very useful to be able to respond quickly. The time saved by the amygdala in acting on the thalamic information, rather than waiting for the cortical input, may be the difference between life and death."

validity of polygraph testing is surprisingly sparse (largely because it is difficult research to do), and the limited evidence is not very impressive (Branaman & Gallagher, 2005; Fiedler, Schmid, & Stahl, 2002; Lykken, 1998). Part of the problem is that people who are telling the truth may experience emotional arousal when they respond to incriminating questions. Thus, polygraph tests sometimes lead to accusations of lying against people who are innocent. Another problem is that some people can lie without experiencing anxiety or autonomic arousal. The crux of the problem, as Leonard Saxe (1994) notes, is that "there is no evidence of a unique physiological reaction to deceit" (p. 71). The polygraph *is* a potentially useful tool that can help police check out leads and alibis. However, polygraph results are not reliable enough to be submitted as evidence in most types of courtrooms.

Neural Circuits

8c

The autonomic responses that accompany emotions are ultimately controlled in the brain. The hypothalamus, amygdala, and adjacent structures in the *limbic system* have long been viewed as the seat of emotions in the brain (Izard & Saxton, 1988; MacLean, 1993). Although these structures do contribute to emotion, the limbic system is not a clearly defined anatomical system (see Chapter 3), and research has shown that a variety of brain structures that lie outside the limbic system influence the experience of emotion (Berridge, 2003).

Nonetheless, recent evidence suggests that the *amygdala* (see Figure 10.21) plays a central role in the acquisition and memory of conditioned fears

(LaBar & LeDoux, 2003; Phelps, 2006). According to Joseph LeDoux (1993, 1996, 2000), the amygdala lies at the core of a complex set of neural circuits that process emotion. He believes that sensory inputs capable of eliciting emotions arrive in the thalamus, which simultaneously routes the information along two separate pathways: a fast pathway to the nearby amygdala and a slower pathway to areas in the cortex (see Figure 10.21). The amygdala processes the information quickly, and if it detects a threat it almost instantly triggers neural activity that leads to the autonomic arousal and endocrine (hormonal) responses associated with emotion. The processing in this pathway is extremely fast, so that emotions may be triggered even before the brain has had a chance to really "think" about the input. Meanwhile, the information shuttled along the other pathway is subjected to a more "leisurely" cognitive appraisal in the cortex. LeDoux believes that the rapid-response pathway evolved because it is a highly adaptive warning system that can "be the difference between life and death." Consistent with LeDoux's theory, evidence indicates that the amygdala can process emotion independent of cognitive awareness (Phelps, 2005). Research linking the amygdala to emotion has mainly focused on fear, but recent evidence suggests that the amygdala may play a role in positive emotions as well (Murray, 2007).

What other areas of the brain are involved in the modulation of emotion? The list is extensive. Much like we saw with sleep and memory (see Chapters 5 and 7), the neural bases of emotion are widely distributed throughout the brain. For example, the *prefrontal cortex,* known for its role in planning and executive control, appears to contribute to efforts to voluntarily control emotional reactions (Davidson, Fox, & Kalin, 2007; Quirk, 2007). The front portion of the *cingulate cortex* has been implicated in the processing of pain-related emotional distress (Berridge, 2003). And as noted in Chapters 3 and 5, a neural circuit called the *mesolimbic dopamine pathway* plays a major role in the experience of pleasurable emotions associated with rewarding events (Nestler & Malenka, 2004). Quite a variety of other brain structures have been linked to specific facets of emotion, including the hippocampus, the lateral hypothalamus, the septum, and the brainstem (Berridge, 2003). Thus, it is clear that emotion depends on activity in a *constellation of interacting brain centers.*

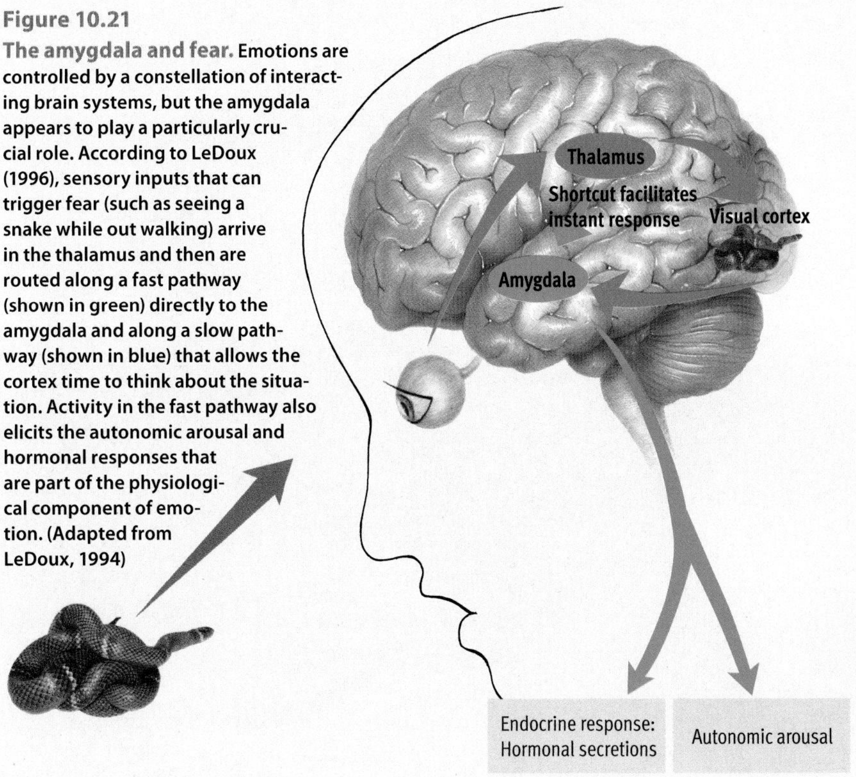

The Behavioral Component: Nonverbal Expressiveness

8c

At the behavioral level, people reveal their emotions through characteristic overt expressions such as smiles, frowns, furrowed brows, intense vocalizations, clenched fists, and slumped shoulders. In other words, *emotions are expressed in "body language," or nonverbal behavior.*

Facial expressions reveal a variety of basic emotions. In an extensive research project, Paul Ekman and Wallace Friesen have asked subjects to identify what emotion a person was experiencing on the basis of facial cues in photographs. They have found that subjects are generally successful in identifying *six fundamental emotions:* happiness, sadness, anger, fear, surprise, and disgust (Ekman & Friesen, 1975, 1984). People can also identify a number of other emotions from facial expressions, such as contempt, embarrassment, shame, amusement, and sympathy, but less reliably than the basic six emotions (Keltner et al., 2003). Furthermore, the identification of emotions from facial expressions tends to occur quickly and automatically (Tracy & Robins, 2008). These studies have been criticized on the grounds that they have used a rather small set of artificial, highly posed photographs that don't do justice to the variety of facial expressions that can accompany specific emotions (Carroll & Russell, 1997). Still, the overall evidence indicates that people are reasonably skilled at deciphering emotions from others' facial expressions (Galati, Scherer, & Ricci-Bitti, 1997).

Some theorists believe that muscular feedback from one's own facial expressions contributes to one's conscious experience of emotions (Izard, 1990; Tomkins, 1991). Proponents of the *facial feedback hypothesis* assert that facial muscles send signals to the brain and that these signals help the brain recognize the emotion that one is experiencing (see Fig-

Figure 10.21

The amygdala and fear. Emotions are controlled by a constellation of interacting brain systems, but the amygdala appears to play a particularly crucial role. According to LeDoux (1996), sensory inputs that can trigger fear (such as seeing a snake while out walking) arrive in the thalamus and then are routed along a fast pathway (shown in green) directly to the amygdala and along a slow pathway (shown in blue) that allows the cortex time to think about the situation. Activity in the fast pathway also elicits the autonomic arousal and hormonal responses that are part of the physiological component of emotion. (Adapted from LeDoux, 1994)

Thalamus

Shortcut facilitates instant response

Visual cortex

Amygdala

Endocrine response: Hormonal secretions

Autonomic arousal

ure 10.22 on the next page). According to this view, smiles, frowns, and furrowed brows help create the subjective experience of various emotions. Consistent with this idea, studies show that if subjects are instructed to contract their facial muscles to mimic facial expressions associated with certain emotions, they tend to report that they actually experience these emotions to some degree (Kleinke, Peterson, & Rutledge, 1998; Levenson, 1992).

Culture and the Elements of Emotion

Are emotions innate reactions that are universal across cultures? Or are they socially learned reactions that are culturally variable? The voluminous research on this lingering question has not yielded a simple answer. Investigators have found both remarkable similarities and dramatic differences among cultures in the experience of emotion.

Cross-Cultural Similarities in Emotional Experience

After demonstrating that Western subjects could discern specific emotions from facial expressions, Ekman and Friesen (1975) took their facial-cue photographs on the road to other societies to see whether nonverbal expressions of emotion transcend cultural boundaries. Testing subjects in Argentina, Spain, Japan, and other countries, they

web link 10.6

UCSC Perceptual Science Laboratory

Perceptions of other people, especially of speech and facial expression, serve as a primary focus for research at this laboratory at the University of California, Santa Cruz. The site offers a broad set of resources, including a comprehensive guide to nonverbal facial analysis research being conducted in laboratories worldwide.

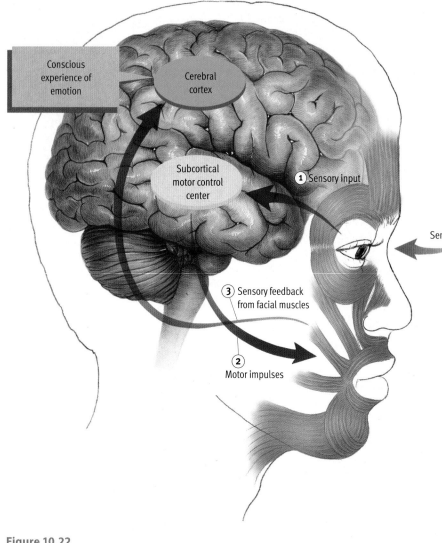

Figure 10.22

The facial feedback hypothesis. According to the facial feedback hypothesis, inputs to subcortical centers automatically evoke facial expressions associated with certain emotions, and the facial muscles then feed signals to the cortex that help it recognize the emotion that one is experiencing. In this view, facial expressions help create the subjective experience of various emotions.

found considerable cross-cultural agreement in the identification of happiness, sadness, anger, fear, surprise, and disgust based on facial expressions (see **Figure 10.23**). Still, Ekman and Friesen wondered whether this agreement might be the result of learning rather than biology, given that people in different cultures often share considerable exposure to Western mass media (magazines, newspapers, television, and so forth), which provide many visual depictions of people's emotional reactions. To rule out this possibility, they took their photos to a remote area in New Guinea and showed them to a group of natives (the Fore) who had had virtually no contact with Western culture. Even the people from this preliterate culture did a fair job of identifying the emotions portrayed in the pictures (see the data in the bottom row of **Figure 10.23**). Subsequent comparisons of many other societies have also shown considerable cross-cultural congruence in the judgment of facial expressions (Biehl et al., 1997; Ekman, 1992, 1993). Although some theorists disagree (J. A. Russell, 1994, 1995), there is reasonably convincing evidence that people in widely disparate cultures express their emotions and interpret those expressions in much the same way (Izard, 1994; Keltner et al., 2003; Matsumoto, 2001). That said, culture is *not* irrelevant to the expression and perception of emotion. Research shows that subjects are somewhat more accurate in recognizing emotions expressed by people from their own culture than they are when asked to identify emotions expressed by a different cultural group (Elfenbein & Ambady, 2002, 2003).

Cross-cultural similarities have also been found in the cognitive and physiological elements of emotional experience (Scherer & Wallbott, 1994). For ex-

Figure 10.23

Cross-cultural comparisons of people's ability to recognize emotions from facial expressions. Ekman and Friesen (1975) found that people in highly disparate cultures showed fair agreement on the emotions portrayed in these photos. This consensus across cultures suggests that facial expressions of emotions may be universal and that they have a strong biological basis.

SOURCE: Data from Ekman, P., & Friesen, W. V. (1975). *Unmasking the face.* Englewood Cliffs, NJ: Prentice-Hall. © 1975 by Paul Ekman, photographs courtesy of Paul Ekman.

Country	Fear	Disgust	Happiness	Anger
	Agreement in judging photos (%)			
United States	85	92	97	67
Brazil	67	97	95	90
Chile	68	92	95	94
Argentina	54	92	98	90
Japan	66	90	100	90
New Guinea	54	44	82	50

ample, in making cognitive appraisals of events that might elicit emotional reactions, people from different cultures broadly think along the same lines (Mauro, Sato, & Tucker, 1992; Matsumoto, Nezlek, & Koopmann, 2007). That is, they evaluate situations along the same dimensions (pleasant versus unpleasant, expected versus unexpected, fair versus unfair, and so on). Understandably, then, the types of events that trigger specific emotions are fairly similar across cultures (Frijda, 1999; Matsumoto & Willingham, 2006). Around the globe, achievements lead to joy, injustices lead to anger, and risky situations lead to fear. Finally, as one might expect, the physiological arousal that accompanies emotion also appears to be largely invariant across cultures (Breugelmans et al., 2005; Wallbott & Scherer, 1988). Thus, researchers have found a great deal of cross-cultural continuity and uniformity in the cognitive, physiological, and behavioral (expressive) elements of emotional experience.

Cross-Cultural Differences in Emotional Experience

The cross-cultural similarities in emotional experience are impressive, but researchers have also found many cultural disparities in how people perceive, think about, and express their emotions and in how often they experience specific emotions (Mesquita, 2003; Mesquita & Leu, 2007). For example, Japanese culture encourages the experience of *socially engaging emotions* (such as friendly feelings, sympathy, and guilt) more than North American culture, and Japanese participants report experiencing these types of emotion more (Kitayama, Mesquita, & Karasawa, 2006). In contrast, North American culture encourages *socially disengaging emotions* (such as pride, and anger) more than Japanese culture, and North American subjects report experiencing these kinds of emotion more.

Fascinating variations have also been observed in how cultures categorize emotions. Some basic categories of emotion that are universally understood in Western cultures appear to go unrecognized—or at least unnamed—in some non-Western cultures. James Russell (1991) has compiled numerous examples of English words for emotions that have no equivalent in other languages. For example, Tahitians have no word that corresponds to *sadness*. Many non-Western groups, including the Yoruba of Nigeria, the Kaluli of New Guinea, and the Chinese, lack a word for *depression*. The concept of *anxiety* seems to go unrecognized among Eskimos, and the Quichua of Ecuador lack a word for *remorse*. However, a lack of words for emotional concepts does not necessarily mean that those emotions are not recognized in a culture. The Raramuri Indians in Mexico use one word to refer to both *guilt* and *shame,* but they differentiate between guilt and shame feelings in ways that are similar to cultures that have distinct words for these emotions (Breugelmans & Poortinga, 2006). These findings suggest that cultural disparities in naming emotions may not reflect differences in emotional processing.

Cultural disparities have also been found in regard to nonverbal expressions of emotion. Although the natural facial expressions associated with basic emotions appear to transcend culture, people can and do learn to control and modify these expressions. *Display rules* are norms that regulate the appropriate expression of emotions. They prescribe when, how, and to whom people can show various emotions. These norms vary from one culture to another (Ekman, 1992), as do attitudes about specific emotions (Eid & Diener, 2001). For instance, the Ifaluk (a Pacific island culture) severely restrict expressions of happiness because they believe that this emotion often leads people to neglect their duties (Lutz, 1987). Japanese culture emphasizes the suppression of negative emotions in public. More so than in other cultures, the Japanese are socialized to mask emotions such as anger, sadness, and disgust with stoic facial expressions or polite smiling. Thus, nonverbal expressions of emotions vary somewhat across cultures because of culture-specific attitudes and display rules.

REVIEW of Key Learning Goals

10.16 Emotion is made up of cognitive, physiological, and behavioral components. The cognitive component involves subjective feelings that have an evaluative aspect. People's cognitive appraisals of events in their lives determine the emotions they experience. Generally, researchers have paid more attention to negative emotions than positive ones.

10.17 The most readily apparent aspect of the physiological component of emotion is autonomic arousal. This arousal is the basis for the lie detector, which is really an emotion detector. Polygraphs are not all that accurate in assessing individuals' veracity. The amygdala appears to be the hub of an emotion-processing system in the brain that modulates conditioned fears, but a variety of other areas in the brain contribute to the regulation of emotion.

10.18 At the behavioral level, emotions are expressed through body language, with facial expressions being particularly prominent. Ekman and Friesen have found considerable cross-cultural agreement in the identification of emotions based on facial expressions. Advocates of the facial-feedback hypothesis maintain that facial muscles send signals to the brain that help the brain recognize the emotion one is experiencing.

10.19 Cross-cultural similarities have been found in the facial expressions associated with specific emotions, the cognitive appraisals that provoke emotions, and physiological underpinnings of emotion. However, there are some striking cultural variations in how people categorize their emotions and in the display rules that govern how much people show their emotions.

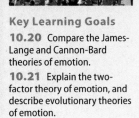

Key Learning Goals

10.20 Compare the James-Lange and Cannon-Bard theories of emotion.

10.21 Explain the two-factor theory of emotion, and describe evolutionary theories of emotion.

Theories of Emotion

How do psychologists explain the experience of emotion? A variety of theories and conflicting models exist. Some have been vigorously debated for over a century. As we describe these theories, you'll recognize a familiar bone of contention. Like so many other types of theories, theories of emotion differ in their emphasis on the innate biological basis of emotion versus the social, environmental basis.

James-Lange Theory   8d

As noted in Chapter 1, William James was a prominent early theorist who urged psychologists to explore the functions of consciousness. James (1884) developed a theory of emotion over 125 years ago that remains influential today. At about the same time, he and Carl Lange (1885) independently pro-

posed that *the conscious experience of emotion results from one's perception of autonomic arousal.* Their theory stood common sense on its head. Everyday logic suggests that when you stumble onto a rattlesnake in the woods, the conscious experience of fear leads to visceral arousal (the fight-or-flight response). The James-Lange theory of emotion asserts the opposite: that the perception of visceral arousal leads to the conscious experience of fear (see Figure 10.24). In other words, while you might assume that your pulse is racing because you're fearful, James and Lange argued that you're fearful because your pulse is racing.

The James-Lange theory emphasizes the physiological determinants of emotion. According to this view, *different patterns of autonomic activation lead to the experience of different emotions.* Hence, people supposedly distinguish emotions such as fear, joy,

Figure 10.24

Theories of emotion. Three influential theories of emotion are contrasted with one another and with the commonsense view. The James-Lange theory was the first to suggest that feelings of arousal cause emotion, rather than vice versa. Schachter built on this idea by adding a second factor—interpretation (appraisal and labeling) of arousal.

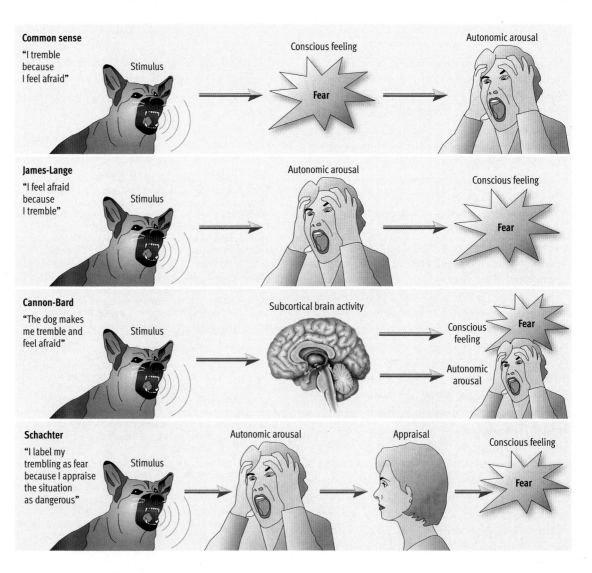

and anger on the basis of the exact configuration of autonomic reactions they experience. Decades of research have supported the concept of *autonomic specificity*—that different emotions are accompanied by somewhat different patterns of autonomic activation (Janig, 2003; Levenson, 2003). However, the question of whether people identify their emotions based on these varied patterns of autonomic activation remains unresolved.

Cannon-Bard Theory 8d

Walter Cannon (1927) found the James-Lange theory unconvincing. Cannon pointed out that physiological arousal may occur without the experience of emotion (if one exercises vigorously, for instance). He also argued that visceral changes are too slow to precede the conscious experience of emotion. Finally, he argued that people experiencing very different emotions, such as fear, joy, and anger, exhibit similar patterns of autonomic arousal that are not readily distinguishable.

Thus, Cannon espoused a different explanation of emotion. Later, Philip Bard (1934) elaborated on it. The resulting Cannon-Bard theory argues that emotion occurs when the thalamus sends signals *simultaneously* to the cortex (creating the conscious experience of emotion) and to the autonomic nervous system (creating visceral arousal). The Cannon-Bard model is compared to the James-Lange model in Figure 10.24. Cannon and Bard were off the mark a bit in pinpointing the thalamus as the neural center for emotion. However, *many modern theorists agree with the Cannon-Bard view that emotions originate in subcortical brain structures* (LeDoux, 1996; Panksepp, 1991; Rolls, 1990) and with the assertion that people do not discern their emotions from different patterns of autonomic activation (Frijda, 1999; Wagner, 1989).

Schachter's Two-Factor Theory 8d

In another influential analysis, Stanley Schachter asserted that people look at situational cues to differentiate between alternative emotions. According to Schachter (1964; Schachter & Singer, 1962, 1979), the experience of emotion depends on two factors: (1) autonomic arousal and (2) cognitive interpretation of that arousal. Schachter proposed that when you experience visceral arousal, you search your environment for an explanation (see Figure 10.24 again). If you're stuck in a traffic jam, you'll probably label your arousal as anger. If you're taking an important exam, you'll probably label it as anxiety. If you're celebrating your birthday, you'll probably label it as happiness.

Schachter agreed with the James-Lange view that emotion is inferred from arousal. However, he also agreed with the Cannon-Bard position that different emotions yield largely indistinguishable patterns of autonomic activity. He reconciled these views by arguing that people look to external rather than internal cues to differentiate and label their specific emotions. In essence, Schachter suggested that people think along the following lines: "If I'm aroused and you're obnoxious, I must be angry."

Although the two-factor theory has received support, studies have revealed some limitations as well (Leventhal & Tomarken, 1986). Situations can't mold emotions in just any way at any time. And in searching to explain arousal, subjects don't limit themselves to the immediate situation (Sinclair et al., 1994). Thus, emotions are not as pliable as the two-factor theory initially suggested.

Evolutionary Theories of Emotion 8d

When the limitations of the two-factor theory were exposed, theorists began returning to ideas espoused by Charles Darwin well over a century ago. Darwin (1872) believed that emotions developed because of their adaptive value. Fear, for instance, would help an organism avoid danger and thus would aid in survival. Hence, Darwin viewed emotions as a product of evolution. This premise serves as the foundation for several prominent theories of emotion developed independently by S. S. Tomkins (1980, 1991), Carroll Izard (1984, 1991), and Robert Plutchik (1984, 1993).

These *evolutionary theories* consider emotions to be largely innate reactions to certain stimuli. As such, emotions should be immediately recognizable under most conditions without much thought. After all, primitive animals that are incapable of complex thought seem to have little difficulty in recognizing their emotions. Evolutionary theorists believe that emotion evolved before thought. They assert that thought plays a relatively small role in emotion, although they admit that learning and cognition may have some influence on human emotions. Evolutionary theories generally assume that emotions originate in subcortical brain structures that evolved before the higher brain areas in the cortex associated with complex thought.

Evolutionary theories also assume that natural selection has equipped humans with a small number of innate emotions with proven adaptive value.

Stanley Schachter

"Cognitive factors play a major role in determining how a subject interprets his bodily feelings."

Figure 10.25

Primary emotions. Evolutionary theories of emotion attempt to identify primary emotions. Three leading theorists—Silvan Tomkins, Carroll Izard, and Robert Plutchik—have compiled different lists of primary emotions, but this chart shows great overlap among the basic emotions identified by these theorists. (Based on Mandler, 1984)

Silvan Tomkins	Carroll Izard	Robert Plutchik
Fear	Fear	Fear
Anger	Anger	Anger
Enjoyment	Joy	Joy
Disgust	Disgust	Disgust
Interest	Interest	Anticipation
Surprise	Surprise	Surprise
Contempt	Contempt	
Shame	Shame	
	Sadness	Sadness
Distress		
	Guilt	
		Acceptance

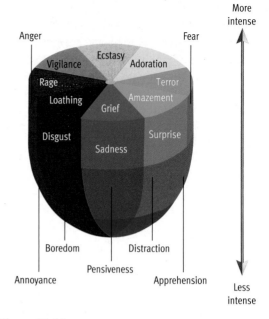

Figure 10.26

Emotional intensity in Plutchik's model. According to Plutchik, diversity in human emotion is a product of variations in emotional intensity, as well as blendings of primary emotions. Each vertical slice in the diagram is a primary emotion that can be subdivided into emotional expressions of varied intensity, ranging from most intense (top) to least intense (bottom).

SOURCE: Based on art in Plutchik, R. (1980). A language for emotions. *Psychology Today, 13* (9), 68–78. Reprinted with permission from Psychology Today Magazine. Copyright © 1980 by Sussex Publishers.

Thus, the principal question that evolutionary theories of emotion wrestle with is, *What are the fundamental emotions?* Figure 10.25 summarizes the conclusions of the leading theorists in this area. As you can see, Tomkins, Izard, and Plutchik have not come up with identical lists, but there is considerable agreement. All three conclude that people exhibit eight to ten primary emotions. Moreover, six of these emotions appear on all three lists: fear, anger, joy, disgust, interest, and surprise.

Of course, people experience more than just eight to ten emotions. How do evolutionary theories account for this variety? They propose that the many emotions that people experience are produced by blends of primary emotions and variations in intensity. For example, Robert Plutchik (1980, 1993) has devised an elegant model of how primary emotions such as fear and surprise may blend into secondary emotions such as awe. Plutchik's model also proposes that various emotions, such as apprehension, fear, and terror, involve one primary emotion experienced at different levels of intensity (see Figure 10.26).

concept check 10.3

Understanding Theories of Emotion

Check your understanding of theories of emotion by matching the theories we discussed with the statements below. Let's borrow William James's classic example: Assume that you just stumbled onto a bear in the woods. The first statement expresses the common-sense explanation of your fear. Each of the remaining statements expresses the essence of a different theory; indicate which theory in the spaces provided. The answers are provided in Appendix A.

1. You tremble because you're afraid.
   Common Sense

2. You're afraid because you're trembling.
   _____

3. You're afraid because situational cues (the bear) suggest that's why you're trembling.
   _____

4. You're afraid because the bear has elicited an innate primary emotion.
   _____

REVIEW of Key Learning Goals

10.20 Common sense suggests that emotions cause autonomic arousal, but the James-Lange theory asserted that emotion *results* from one's perception of autonomic arousal. The Cannon-Bard theory countered with the proposal that emotions originate in subcortical areas of the brain.

10.21 According to Schachter's two-factor theory, people infer emotion from arousal and then label the emotion in accordance with their cognitive explanation for the arousal. Evolutionary theories of emotion maintain that emotions are innate reactions that require little cognitive interpretation. Evolutionary theorists seek to identify a small number of innate, fundamental emotions.

Reflecting on the Chapter's Themes

Five of our organizing themes were particularly prominent in this chapter: the influence of cultural contexts, the dense connections between psychology and society at large, psychology's theoretical diversity, the interplay of heredity and environment, and the multiple causes of behavior.

Our discussion of motivation and emotion demonstrated once again that there are both similarities and differences across cultures in behavior. The neural, biochemical, genetic, and hormonal processes underlying hunger and eating, for instance, are universal. But cultural factors influence what people prefer to eat, how much they eat, and whether they worry about dieting. In a similar vein, researchers have found a great deal of cross-cultural congruence in the cognitive, physiological, and expressive elements of emotional experience, but they have also found cultural variations in how people think about and express their emotions. Thus, as we have seen in previous chapters, psychological processes are characterized by both cultural variance and invariance.

Our discussion of the controversies surrounding evolutionary theory, aggressive pornography, and the determinants of sexual orientation show once again that psychology is not an ivory tower enterprise. It evolves in a sociohistorical context that helps shape the debates in the field, and these debates often have far-reaching social and political ramifications for so-

ciety at large. We ended the chapter with a discussion of various theories of emotion, which showed once again that psychology is characterized by great theoretical diversity.

Finally, we repeatedly saw that biological and environmental factors jointly govern behavior. For example, we learned that eating behavior, sexual desire, and the experience of emotion all depend on complicated interactions between biological and environmental determinants. Indeed, complicated interactions permeated the entire chapter, demonstrating that if we want to fully understand behavior, we have to take multiple causes into account.

In the upcoming Personal Application, we will continue our discussion of emotion, looking at recent research on the correlates of happiness. In the Critical Thinking Application that follows, we discuss how to carefully analyze the types of arguments that permeated this chapter.

 Cultural Heritage

 Sociohistorical Context

Theoretical Diversity

 Heredity and Environment

Multifactorial Causation

REVIEW of Key Learning Goals

10.22 Our look at motivation and emotion showed once again that psychology is characterized by theoretical diversity, that biology and environment shape behavior interactively, that behavior is governed by multiple causes, that psychological processes are characterized by both cultural variance and invariance, and that psychology evolves in a sociohistorical context.

Exploring the Ingredients of Happiness

Answer the following "true" or "false."

_____ **1** The empirical evidence indicates that most people are relatively unhappy.

_____ **2** Although wealth doesn't *guarantee* happiness, wealthy people are much more likely to be happy than the rest of the population.

_____ **3** People who have children are happier than people without children.

_____ **4** Good health is an essential requirement for happiness.

_____ **5** Good-looking people are happier than those who are unattractive.

The answer to all these questions is "false." These assertions are all reasonable and widely believed hypotheses about the correlates of happiness, but they have *not* been supported by empirical research. Thanks in part to the positive psychology movement, recent years have brought a surge of interest in the correlates of *subjective well-being*—individuals' personal perceptions of their overall happiness and life satisfaction. The findings of these studies are quite interesting. As you have already seen from our true-false questions, many com-

Key Learning Goals

10.23 Identify factors that do not predict happiness.
10.24 Review information on factors that are moderately or strongly correlated with happiness.
10.25 Explain four conclusions that can be drawn about the dynamics of happiness.

monsense notions about happiness appear to be inaccurate.

One of these inaccuracies is the apparently widespread assumption that most people are relatively unhappy. Writers, social

Figure 10.27

Measuring happiness with a nonverbal scale. Researchers have used a variety of methods to estimate the distribution of happiness. For example, in one study in the United States, respondents were asked to examine the seven facial expressions shown and select the one that "comes closest to expressing how you feel about your life as a whole." As you can see, the vast majority of participants chose happy faces. (Data adapted from Myers, 1992)

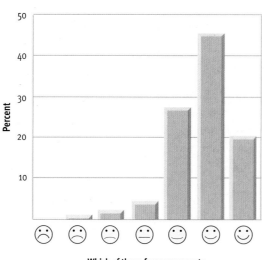

Which of these faces represents the way you feel about life as a whole?

scientists, and the general public seem to believe that people around the world are predominantly dissatisfied and unhappy, yet empirical surveys consistently find that the vast majority of respondents—even those who are poor or disabled—characterize themselves as fairly happy (Diener & Diener, 1996; Myers & Diener, 1995). When people are asked to rate their happiness, only a small minority place themselves below the neutral point on the various scales used (see Figure 10.27). When the average subjective well-being of entire nations is computed, the means cluster toward the positive end of the scale, as shown in Figure 10.28 (Tov & Diener, 2007). That's

not to say that everyone is equally happy. Researchers find substantial and thought-provoking disparities among people in subjective well-being, which we will analyze momentarily, but the overall picture seems rosier than anticipated.

Factors That Do Not Predict Happiness

Let us begin our discussion of individual differences in happiness by highlighting those things that turn out to be relatively unimportant determinants of subjective well-being. Quite a number of factors that you might expect to be influential appear

to bear little or no relationship to general happiness.

Money. There *is* a positive correlation between income and subjective feelings of happiness, but the association is surprisingly weak (Diener & Seligman, 2004). For example, one study found a correlation of just .13 between income and happiness in the United States (Diener et al., 1993) and another recent investigation yielded an almost identical correlation of .12 (Johnson & Krueger, 2006). Admittedly, being very poor can make people unhappy, but once people ascend above the poverty level, little relation is seen between income and happiness. On the average, wealthy people are only marginally happier than those in the middle classes. One reason for this weak association is that there seems to be a disconnect between actual income and how people feel about their financial situation. Recent research (Johnson & Krueger, 2006) suggests that the correlation between actual wealth and people's subjective perceptions of whether they have enough money to meet their needs is surprisingly modest (around .30).

Another problem with money is that pervasive advertising and rising income fuel escalating material desires (Frey & Stutzer, 2002; Kasser et al., 2004). When these growing material desires outstrip what people can afford, dissatisfaction is likely (Solberg et al., 2002). Thus, complaints about not having enough money are routine even among people who earn hefty six-figure incomes. Interestingly, there is some evidence that people who place an especially strong emphasis on the pursuit of wealth and materialistic goals tend to be somewhat less happy than others (Kasser, 2002; Van Boven, 2005), perhaps in large part because they are so focused on financial success that they don't derive much satisfaction from their family life (Nickerson et al., 2003). Consistent with this view, a recent study (Kahneman et al., 2006) found that higher income was associated with working longer hours and allocating fewer hours to leisure pursuits. Insofar as money does foster happiness, it appears to do so by reducing the negative impact of life's setbacks, allowing

Figure 10.28

The subjective well-being of nations. Veenhoven (1993) combined the results of almost 1000 surveys to calculate the average subjective well-being reported by representative samples from 43 nations. The mean happiness scores clearly pile up at the positive end of the distribution, with only two scores falling below the neutral point of 5. (Data adapted from Diener and Diener, 1996)

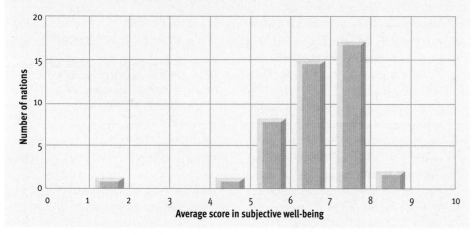

wealthier people to feel like they have a little more control over their lives (Johnson & Krueger, 2006; Smith et al., 2005).

Age. Age and happiness are consistently found to be unrelated. Age accounts for less than 1% of the variation in people's happiness (Lykken, 1999). The key factors influencing subjective well-being may shift some as people grow older—work becomes less important, health more so—but people's average level of happiness tends to remain remarkably stable over the life span.

Parenthood. Children can be a tremendous source of joy and fulfillment, but they can also be a tremendous source of headaches and hassles. Compared to childless couples, parents worry more and experience more marital problems (Argyle, 1987). Apparently, the good and bad aspects of parenthood balance each other out, because the evidence indicates that people who have children are neither more nor less happy than people without children (Argyle, 2001).

Intelligence and attractiveness. Intelligence and physical attractiveness are highly valued traits in modern society, but researchers have not found an association between either characteristic and happiness (Diener, 1984; Diener, Wolsic, & Fujita, 1995).

Moderately Good Predictors of Happiness

Research has identified three facets of life that appear to have a *moderate* association with subjective well-being: health, social activity, and religious belief.

Health. Good physical health would seem to be an essential requirement for happiness, but people adapt to health problems. Research reveals that individuals who develop serious, disabling health conditions aren't as unhappy as one might guess (Myers, 1992; Riis et al., 2005). Good health may not, by itself, produce happiness, because people tend to take good health for granted. Considerations such as these may help explain why researchers find only a moderate positive correlation (average =

"*Who can say? I suppose I'm as happy as my portfolio will allow me to be.*"

.32) between health status and subjective well-being (Argyle, 1999).

Social Activity. Humans are social animals, and interpersonal relations *do* appear to contribute to people's happiness. Those who are satisfied with their social support and friendship networks and those who are socially active report above-average levels of happiness (Diener & Seligman, 2004; Myers, 1999). Furthermore, people who are exceptionally happy tend to report greater satisfaction with their social relations than those who are average or low in subjective well-being (Diener & Seligman, 2002).

Religion. The link between religiosity and subjective well-being is modest, but a number of large-scale surveys suggest that people with heartfelt religious convictions are more likely to be happy than people who characterize themselves as nonreligious (Abdel-Khalek, 2006; Myers, 2008). Researchers aren't sure how religious faith fosters happiness, but Myers (1992) offers some interesting conjectures. Among other things, he discusses how religion can give people a sense of purpose and meaning in their lives, help them accept their setbacks gracefully, connect them to a car-

ing, supportive community, and comfort them by putting their ultimate mortality in perspective.

Strong Predictors of Happiness

The list of factors that turn out to have fairly strong associations with happiness is surprisingly short. The key ingredients of happiness appear to involve love, work, and genetic predisposition expressed through personality.

Love and Marriage. Romantic relationships can be stressful, but people consistently rate being in love as one of the most critical ingredients of happiness (Myers, 1999). Furthermore, although people complain a lot about their marriages, the evidence indicates that marital status is a key correlate of happiness. Among both men and women, married people are happier than people who are single or divorced (see Figure 10.29 on the next page; Myers & Diener, 1995), and this relationship holds around the world in widely different cultures (Diener et al., 2000). However, the causal relations underlying this correlation are unclear. It may be that happiness causes

Figure 10.29

Happiness and marital status. This graph shows the percentage of adults characterizing themselves as "very happy" as a function of marital status (Myers, 1999). Among both women and men, happiness shows up more in those who are married as opposed to those who are separated, are divorced, or have never married. These data and many others suggest that marital satisfaction is a key ingredient of happiness.

SOURCE: Myers, D. G. (1999). Close relationships and quality of life. In D. Kahneman, E. Diener, & N. Schwarz (Eds.), *Well-being: The foundations of hedonic psychology.* New York: Russell Sage Foundation. Copyright © 1999. Reprinted by permission of the Russell Sage Foundation.

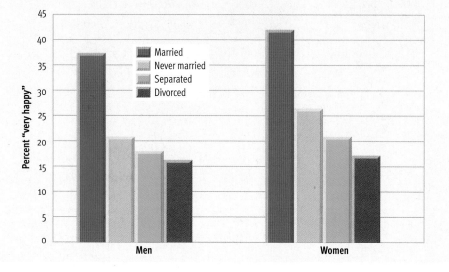

marital satisfaction more than marital satisfaction promotes happiness. Perhaps people who are happy tend to have better intimate relationships and more stable marriages, while people who are unhappy have more difficulty finding and keeping mates.

Work. Given the way people often complain about their jobs, one might not expect work to be a key source of happiness, but it is. Although less critical than love and marriage, job satisfaction has a substantial association with general happiness (Judge & Klinger, 2008; Warr, 1999). Studies also show that unemployment has strong negative effects on subjective well-being (Lucas et al., 2004). It is difficult to sort out whether job satisfaction causes happiness or vice versa, but evidence suggests that causation flows both ways (Argyle, 2001).

Genetics and Personality. The best predictor of individuals' future happiness is their past happiness (Diener & Lucas, 1999). Some people seem destined to be happy and others unhappy, regardless of their triumphs or setbacks. The limited influence of life events was apparent in a stunning study that found only marginal differences in

overall happiness between recent lottery winners and recent accident victims who became quadriplegics (Brickman, Coates, & Janoff-Bulman, 1978). Investigators were amazed that such extremely fortuitous and horrible events didn't have a dramatic impact on happiness. Actually, several lines of evidence suggest that happiness does not depend on external circumstances—buying a nice house, getting promoted—so much as internal factors, such as one's outlook on life (Lykken & Tellegen, 1996; Lyubomirsky, Sheldon, & Schkade, 2005).

With this reality in mind, researchers have investigated whether there might be a hereditary basis for variations in happiness. These studies suggest that people's genetic predispositions account for a substantial portion of the variance in happiness, perhaps as much as 50% (Lyubomirsky et al., 2005; Stubbe et al., 2005). How can one's genes influence one's happiness? Presumably, by shaping one's temperament and personality, which are known to be heritable (Weiss, Bates, & Luciano, 2008). Hence, research-

ers have begun to look for links between personality and subjective well-being, and they have found some interesting correlations. For example, *extraversion* (sometimes referred to as *positive emotionality*) is one of the better predictors of happiness. People who are outgoing, upbeat, and sociable tend to be happier than others (Fleeson, Malanos, & Achille, 2002). Additional personality correlates of happiness include conscientiousness, agreeableness, self-esteem, and optimism (Lucas, 2008; Lyubomirsky, Tkach, & DiMatteo, 2006).

Conclusions About Subjective Well-Being

We must be cautious in drawing inferences about the causes of happiness, because the available data are correlational (see **Figure 10.30**). Nonetheless, the empirical evidence suggests that many popular beliefs about the sources of happiness are unfounded. The data also demonstrate that happiness is shaped by a complex constellation of variables. In spite of this complexity, however, a number of worthwhile insights about the ingredients of happiness can be gleaned from the recent flurry of research.

First, research on happiness demonstrates that the determinants of subjective well-being are precisely that: subjective. *Objective realities are not as important as subjective feelings.* In other words, your health,

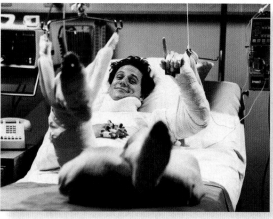

Research shows that happiness does not depend on people's positive and negative experiences as much as one would expect. Some people, presumably because of their personality, seem destined to be happy in spite of major setbacks, and others seem destined to cling to unhappiness even though their lives seem reasonably pleasant.

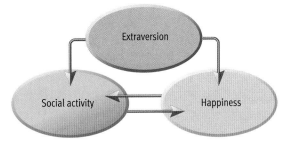

Figure 10.30

Possible causal relations among the correlates of happiness. Although we have considerable data on the correlates of happiness, it is difficult to untangle the possible causal relationships. For example, we know that a moderate positive correlation exists between social activity and happiness, but we can't say for sure whether high social activity causes happiness or whether happiness causes people to be more socially active. Moreover, in light of the research showing that a third variable—extraversion—correlates with both variables, we have to consider the possibility that extraversion causes both greater social activity and greater happiness.

your wealth, and your job are not as influential as how you *feel* about your health, wealth, and job (Schwarz & Strack, 1999). These feelings are likely to be influenced by what your *expectations* were. Research suggests that bad outcomes feel worse when unexpected than when expected and that good outcomes feel better when unexpected than when expected (Shepperd & McNulty, 2002). Thus, the same objective event, such as a pay raise of $2000 annually, may generate positive feelings in someone who wasn't expecting a raise and negative feelings in someone expecting a much larger increase in salary.

Second, *when it comes to happiness everything is relative* (Argyle, 1999; Hagerty, 2000). In other words, you evaluate what you have relative to what the people around you have. Generally, we compare ourselves with others who are similar to us. Thus, people who are wealthy assess what they have by comparing themselves with their wealthy friends and neighbors. This is one reason for the low correlation between wealth and happiness. You might have a lovely home, but if it sits next door to a neighbor's palatial mansion, it might be a source of more dissatisfaction than happiness.

Third, *research on happiness has shown that people are surprisingly bad at predicting what will make them happy.* We assume that we know what is best for us. But research on *affective forecasting*—efforts to predict one's emotional reactions to future events—suggests otherwise (Gilbert, 2006;

Hsee & Hastie, 2006; Wilson & Gilbert, 2005). People routinely overestimate the pleasure that they will derive from buying an expensive automobile, taking an exotic vacation, earning an important promotion, moving to a beautiful coastal city, or building their dream home. Likewise, people tend to overestimate the misery and regret that they will endure if they experience a romantic breakup, don't get into the college they want, fail to get a promotion, or develop a serious illness. In particular, people tend to make inaccurate predictions about the *intensity* and *duration* of the emotions that they will experience in the wake of both positive and negative events (Loewenstein, 2007). Thus, the roadmap to happiness is less clearly marked than widely assumed.

Fourth, *research on subjective well-being indicates that people often adapt to their circumstances.* This adaptation effect is one reason that increases in income don't necessarily bring increases in happiness. *Hedonic adaptation* occurs when the mental scale that people use to judge the pleasantness-unpleasantness of their experiences shifts so that their neutral point, or baseline for comparison, changes. Unfortunately, when people's experiences improve, hedonic adaptation may *sometimes* put them on a *hedonic treadmill*—their neutral point moves upward, so that the improvements yield no real benefits (Kahneman, 1999). However, when people have to grapple with major setbacks, hedonic adaptation proba-

bly helps protect their mental and physical health. For example, people who are sent to prison and people who develop debilitating diseases are not as unhappy as one might assume, because they adapt to their changed situations and evaluate events from a new perspective (Frederick & Loewenstein, 1999).

That's not to say that hedonic adaptation in the face of life's difficulties is inevitable or complete (Lucas, 2007). Evidence suggests that people adapt more slowly to negative events than to positive events (Larsen & Prizmic, 2008). Thus, even years later, people who suffer major setbacks, such as the death of a spouse or serious illness, often are not as happy as they were before the setback, but generally they are not nearly as unhappy as they or others would have predicted (Diener & Oishi, 2005). The downside to the concept of hedonic adaptation is that it suggests there is nothing people can do to increase their happiness. Fortunately, recent research on the upside of the hedonic treadmill is not as pessimistic as earlier research (Diener, Lucas, & Scollon, 2006). This research has shown that people vary considerably in the degree to which they experience hedonic adaptation and that enduring increases in individuals' set points for happiness can be achieved.

Key Learning Goals
10.26 Identify the key elements in arguments.
10.27 Recognize common fallacies that often show up in arguments.

Analyzing Arguments: Making Sense out of Controversy

Consider the following argument. "Dieting is harmful to your health because the tendency to be obese is largely inherited." What is your reaction to this reasoning? Do you find it convincing? We hope not, as this argument is seriously flawed. Can you see what's wrong? There is no relationship between the conclusion that "dieting is harmful to your health" and the reason given that "the tendency to be obese is largely inherited." The argument is initially seductive because you know from reading this chapter that obesity *is* largely inherited, so the reason provided represents a true statement. But the reason is unrelated to the conclusion advocated. This scenario may strike you as odd, but if you start listening carefully to discussions about controversial issues, you will probably notice that people often cite irrelevant considerations in support of their favored conclusions.

This chapter was loaded with controversial issues that sincere, well-meaning people could argue about for weeks. Does the availability of pornography increase the prevalence of sex crimes? Are gender differences in mating preferences a product of evolution or of modern economic realities? Is there a biological basis for homosexuality?

Unfortunately, arguments about issues such as these typically are unproductive in terms of moving toward resolution or agreement because most people know little about the rules of argumentation. In this application, we will explore what makes arguments sound or unsound in the hope of improving your ability to analyze and think critically about arguments.

The Anatomy of an Argument

In everyday usage, the word *argument* is used to refer to a dispute or disagreement between two or more people, but in the technical language of rhetoric, an *argument* consists of one or more premises that are used to provide support for a conclusion. *Premises* are the reasons that are presented to persuade someone that a conclusion is true or probably true. *Assumptions* are premises for which no proof or evidence is offered. Assumptions are often left unstated. For example, suppose that your doctor tells you that you should exercise regularly because regular exercise is good for your heart. In this simple argument, the conclusion is "You should exercise regularly." The premise that leads to this conclusion is the idea that "exercise is good for your heart." An unstated assumption is that everyone wants a healthy heart.

In the language of argument analysis, premises are said to support (or not support) conclusions. A conclusion may be supported by one reason or by many reasons. One way to visualize these possibilities is to draw an analogy between the reasons that support a conclusion and the legs that support a table (Halpern, 2003). As shown in Figure 10.31, a table top (conclusion) could be supported by one strong leg (a single strong reason) or many thin legs (lots of weaker reasons). Of course, the reasons provided for a conclusion may fail to support the conclusion. Returning to our table analogy, the table top might not be supported because the legs are too thin (very weak reasons) or because the legs are not attached (irrelevant reasons).

Arguments can get complicated, as they usually have more parts than just reasons and conclusions. In addition, there often are *counterarguments,* which are reasons that take support away from a conclusion. And sometimes the most important part of an argument is a part that is not there—reasons that have been omitted, either deliberately or not, that would lead to a different conclusion if they were supplied. Given all the complex variations that are possible in arguments, it is impossible to give you simple rules for judging arguments, but we can highlight some common fallacies and then provide some criteria that you can apply in thinking critically about arguments.

Figure 10.31

An analogy for understanding the strength of arguments. Halpern (2003) draws an analogy between the reasons that support a conclusion and the legs that support a table. She points out that a conclusion may be supported effectively by one strong premise or many weak premises. Of course, the reasons provided for a conclusion may also *fail* to provide adequate support.

SOURCE: Halpern, D. F. (2003). *Thought & knowledge: An introduction to critical thinking.* Mahwah, NJ: Erlbaum. Copyright © 2003 Lawrence Erlbaum Associates. Reprinted by permission.

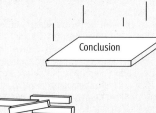

Premises unrelated to conclusion

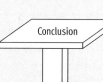

Single strong premise supports conclusion

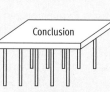

Many weak premises support conclusion

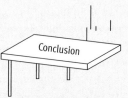

Few weak premises fail to support conclusion

Common Fallacies

As noted in previous chapters, cognitive scientists have compiled lengthy lists of fallacies that people frequently display in their reasoning. These fallacies often show up in arguments. In this section we will describe five common fallacies. To illustrate each one, we will assume the role of someone arguing that pornographic material on the Internet (cyberporn) should be banned or heavily regulated.

Irrelevant Reasons. Reasons cannot provide support for an argument unless they are relevant to the conclusion. Arguments that depend on irrelevant reasons—either intentionally or inadvertently—are quite common. You already saw one example at the beginning of this application. The Latin term for this fallacy is *non sequitur,* which literally translates to "it doesn't follow." In other words, the conclusion does not follow from the premise. For example, in the debate about Internet pornography, you might hear the following *non sequitur:* "We need to regulate cyberporn because research has shown that most date rapes go unreported."

Circular Reasoning. In *circular reasoning* the premise and conclusion are simply restatements of each other. People vary their wording a little so it isn't obvious, but when you look closely, the conclusion *is* the premise. For example, in arguments about Internet pornography you might hear someone assert, "We need to control cyberporn because it currently is unregulated."

Slippery Slope. The concept of *slippery slope* argumentation takes its name from the notion that if you are on a slippery slope and you don't dig your heels in, you will slide and slide until you reach bottom. A slippery slope argument typically asserts that if you allow X to happen, things will spin out of control and far worse events will follow. The trick is that there is no inherent connection between X and the events that are predicted to follow. For example, in the debate about medical marijuana, opponents have argued, "If you legalize medical marijuana, the next thing you know cocaine and heroin will be legal." In the debate about cyberporn, a slippery slope argument might go, "If we don't ban cyberporn, the next thing you know, grade-school children will be watching smut all day long in their school libraries."

Weak Analogies. An *analogy* asserts that two concepts or events are similar in some way. Hence, you can draw conclusions about event B because of its similarity to event A. Analogies are useful in thinking about complex issues, but some analogies are weak or inappropriate because the similarity between A and B is superficial, minimal, or irrelevant to the issue at hand. For example, in the debate about Internet erotica, someone might argue, "Cyberporn is morally offensive, just like child molestation. We wouldn't tolerate child molestation, so we shouldn't permit cyberporn."

False Dichotomy. A *false dichotomy* creates an either-or choice between two outcomes: the outcome advocated and some obviously horrible outcome that any sensible person would want to avoid. These outcomes are presented as the only two possibilities, when in reality there could be other outcomes, including ones that lie somewhere between the extremes depicted in the false dichotomy. In the debate about Internet pornography, someone might argue, "We can ban cyberporn, or we can hasten the moral decay of modern society."

Evaluating the Strength of Arguments

In everyday life, you may frequently need to assess the strength of arguments made by friends, family, co-workers, politicians, media pundits, and so forth. You may also want to evaluate your own arguments when you write papers or speeches for school or prepare presentations for your work. The following questions can help you make systematic evaluations of arguments (adapted from Halpern, 2003):

- What is the conclusion?
- What are the premises provided to support the conclusion? Are the premises valid?
- Does the conclusion follow from the premises? Are there any fallacies in the chain of reasoning?
- What assumptions have been made? Are they valid assumptions? Should they be stated explicitly?
- What are the counterarguments? Do they weaken the argument?
- Is there anything that has been omitted from the argument?

Table 10.1 Critical Thinking Skills Discussed in This Application

Skill	Description
Understanding the elements of an argument	The critical thinker understands that an argument consists of premises and assumptions that are used to support a conclusion.
Recognizing and avoiding common fallacies, such as irrelevant reasons, circular reasoning, slippery slope reasoning, weak analogies, and false dichotomies	The critical thinker is vigilant about conclusions based on unrelated premises, conclusions that are rewordings of premises, unwarranted predictions that things will spin out of control, superficial analogies, and contrived dichotomies.
Evaluating arguments systematically	The critical thinker carefully assesses the validity of the premises, assumptions, and conclusions in an argument, and considers counterarguments and missing elements.

Key Ideas

Motivational Theories and Concepts

▮ Drive theories apply a homeostatic model to motivation. They assume that organisms seek to reduce unpleasant states of tension called drives. In contrast, incentive theories emphasize how external goals energize behavior.

▮ Evolutionary theorists explain motives in terms of their adaptive value. Madsen's list of biological needs and Murray's list of social needs illustrate that a diverse array of motives govern human behavior.

The Motivation of Hunger and Eating

▮ Eating is regulated by a complex interaction of biological and environmental factors. In the brain, the lateral, ventromedial, arcuate, and paraventricular areas of the hypothalamus appear to be involved in the control of hunger.

▮ Fluctuations in blood glucose also seem to play a role in hunger. The stomach can send two types of satiety signals to the brain. Hormonal regulation of hunger depends primarily on insulin, ghrelin, CCK, and leptin secretions.

▮ Incentive-oriented models assert that eating is regulated by the availability and palatability of food. Learning processes, such as classical conditioning and observational learning, exert a great deal of influence over both what people eat and how much they eat. Cultural traditions also shape food preferences. Stress can stimulate eating.

▮ The prevalence of obesity appears to be increasing, but some theorists have questioned whether there is an obesity crisis. Evidence indicates that there is a genetic predisposition to obesity. According to set-point theory, the body monitors fat stores to keep them fairly stable. Settling-point theory suggests that a multitude of factors contribute to weight stability.

Sexual Motivation and Behavior

▮ The human sexual response cycle can be divided into four stages: excitement, plateau, orgasm, and resolution. Intercourse leads to orgasm less consistently in women than in men.

▮ Consistent with evolutionary theory, males tend to think about and initiate sex more than females do and to have more sexual partners and more interest in casual sex than females. Buss demonstrated that gender differences exist in mating preferences that largely transcend cultural boundaries. Males emphasize potential partners' youthfulness and attractiveness, whereas females emphasize potential partners' financial prospects. Females also pay attention to males' masculinity and their willingness to invest in children.

▮ People respond to a variety of erotic materials, which may elevate sexual desire for only a few hours but may have an enduring impact on attitudes about sex. Aggressive pornography may make sexual coercion seem less offensive and may contribute to date rape.

▮ Sexual orientation is best viewed as a continuum rather than as discrete categories. The determinants of sexual orientation are not well understood. Recent studies suggest that there may be a genetic predisposition to homosexuality and that idiosyncrasies in prenatal hormonal secretions may contribute, but much remains to be learned.

Achievement: In Search of Excellence

▮ McClelland pioneered the use of the TAT to measure achievement motivation. People who are high in the need for achievement work harder and more persistently than others, although they often choose to tackle challenges of intermediate difficulty. The pursuit of achievement tends to increase when the probability of success and the incentive value of success are high.

The Elements of Emotional Experience

▮ Emotion is made up of cognitive, physiological, and behavioral components. The cognitive component involves subjective feelings that have an evaluative aspect. In the peripheral nervous system, the physiological component is dominated by autonomic arousal. In the brain, the amygdala seems to be the hub of the neural circuits that process fear, but many other brain structures also contribute to emotion. At the behavioral level, emotions are expressed through body language, with facial expressions being particularly prominent.

▮ Ekman and Friesen have found considerable cross-cultural agreement in the identification of emotions based on facial expressions. Cross-cultural similarities have also been found in the cognitive and physiological components of emotion. However, there are cultural variations in how people categorize and display their emotions.

Theories of Emotion

▮ The James-Lange theory asserts that emotion results from one's perception of autonomic arousal. The Cannon-Bard theory counters with the proposal that emotions originate in subcortical areas of the brain. According to Schachter's two-factor theory, people infer emotion from arousal and then label the emotion in accordance with their cognitive explanation for the arousal. Evolutionary theories of emotion maintain that emotions are innate reactions that require little cognitive interpretation.

Reflecting on the Chapter's Themes

▮ Our look at motivation and emotion showed once again that psychology is characterized by theoretical diversity, that biology and environment shape behavior interactively, that behavior is governed by multiple causes, that psychological processes are characterized by both cultural variance and invariance, and that psychology evolves in a sociohistorical context.

PERSONAL APPLICATION Exploring the Ingredients of Happiness

▮ Factors such as income, age, parenthood, intelligence, and attractiveness are largely uncorrelated with subjective well-being. Physical health, good social relationships, and religious faith appear to have a modest impact on feelings of happiness.

▮ Strong predictors of happiness include love and marriage, work satisfaction, and personality and genetic predisposition. Research on happiness indicates that objective realities are not that important, that happiness is relative, that people are mediocre at affective forecasting, and that people adapt to their circumstances.

CRITICAL THINKING APPLICATION Analyzing Arguments: Making Sense out of Controversy

▮ An argument consists of one or more premises used to provide support for a conclusion. Arguments are often marred by logical fallacies, such as irrelevant reasons, circular reasoning, slippery slope scenarios, weak analogies, and false dichotomies. Arguments can be evaluated more effectively by applying systematic criteria.

Key Terms

Achievement motive (p. 417)
Affective forecasting (p. 433)
Argument (p. 434)
Assumptions (p. 434)
Bisexuals (p. 414)
Body mass index (BMI) (p. 403)
Display rules (p. 425)
Drive (p. 397)
Emotion (p. 419)
Galvanic skin response
  (GSR) (p. 421)
Glucose (p. 400)
Glucostats (p. 400)
Hedonic adaptation (p. 433)
Heterosexuals (p. 414)
Homeostasis (p. 396)
Homosexuals (p. 414)
Incentive (p. 397)
Lie detector (p. 421)
Motivation (p. 396)
Obesity (p. 403)

Parental investment (p. 408)
Polygraph (p. 421)
Premises (p. 434)
Refractory period (p. 407)
Set-point theory (p. 405)
Settling-point theory (p. 405)
Sexual orientation (p. 414)
Subjective well-being (p. 429)
Vasocongestion (p. 406)

Key People

David Buss (p. 410)
Walter Cannon (pp. 396, 399, 427)
Paul Ekman and
  Wallace Friesen (pp. 423–424)
William James (pp. 426–427)
Joseph LeDoux (pp. 422–423)
William Masters and
  Virginia Johnson (pp. 406–407)
David McClelland (pp. 417–418)
Stanley Schachter (p. 427)

1. Jackson had a huge breakfast this morning and is still feeling stuffed when he arrives at work. However, one of his colleagues has brought some delicious-looking donuts to the morning staff meeting and Jackson just can't resist. Although he feels full, he eats three donuts. His behavior is inconsistent with:
   A. incentive theories of motivation.
   B. drive theories of motivation.
   C. evolutionary theories of motivation.
   D. the Cannon-Bard theory of motivation.

2. Which of the following tends to promote increased eating?
   A. increased palatability
   B. having a greater quantity of food available
   C. having a greater variety of food available
   D. all of the above

3. The heritability of weight appears to be:
   A. virtually impossible to demonstrate.
   B. very low.
   C. in the range of 60%–70%.
   D. irrelevant to the understanding of obesity.

4. Which of the following has *not* been found in research on gender differences in sexual interest?
   A. Men think about sex more than women.
   B. Men initiate sex more frequently than women.
   C. Women are more interested in having many partners than men are.
   D. Women are less interested in uncommitted sex.

5. Some recent studies suggest that exposure to aggressive pornography:
   A. may increase males' aggressive behavior toward women.
   B. may perpetuate the myth that women enjoy being raped.
   C. does both a and b.
   D. does neither a nor b.

6. Kinsey maintained that sexual orientation:
   A. depends on early classical conditioning experiences.
   B. should be viewed as a continuum.
   C. depends on normalities and abnormalities in the amygdala.
   D. should be viewed as an either-or distinction.

7. In research on the need for achievement, individual differences are usually measured:
   A. by observing subjects' actual behavior in competitive situations.
   B. by interviewing subjects about their achievement needs.
   C. with the Thematic Apperception Test.
   D. with the Minnesota Multiphasic Personality Inventory.

8. The determinant of achievement behavior that increases when a college student enrolls in a class that is *required* for graduation is:
   A. the probability of success.
   B. the need to avoid failure.
   C. the incentive value of success.
   D. the fear of success.

9. A polygraph (lie detector) works by:
   A. monitoring physiological indices of autonomic arousal.
   B. directly assessing the truthfulness of a person's statements.
   C. monitoring the person's facial expressions.
   D. all of the above.

10. Which of the following statements about cross-cultural comparisons of emotional experience is *not* true?
    A. The facial expressions that accompany specific emotions are fairly similar across cultures.
    B. The physiological reactions that accompany emotions tend to be similar across cultures.
    C. People of different cultures tend to categorize emotions somewhat differently.
    D. Display rules do not vary from one culture to another.

11. According to the James-Lange theory of emotion:
    A. the experience of emotion depends on autonomic arousal and on one's cognitive interpretation of that arousal.
    B. different patterns of autonomic activation lead to the experience of different emotions.
    C. emotion occurs when the thalamus sends signals simultaneously to the cortex and to the autonomic nervous system.
    D. emotions develop because of their adaptive value.

12. Which theory of emotion implies that people can change their emotions simply by changing the way they label their arousal?
    A. the James-Lange theory
    B. the Cannon-Bard theory
    C. Schachter's two-factor theory
    D. opponent-process theory.

13. The fact that eating behavior, sexual desire, and the experience of emotion all depend on interactions between biological and environmental determinants lends evidence to which of this text's organizing themes?
    A. psychology's theoretical diversity
    B. psychology's empiricism
    C. people's experience of the world is subjective
    D. the joint influence of heredity and experience

14. Which of the following statements is (are) true?
    A. For the most part, people are pretty happy.
    B. Age is unrelated to happiness.
    C. Income is largely unrelated to happiness.
    D. All of the above.

15. The sales pitch "We're the best dealership in town because the other dealerships just don't stack up against us" is an example of:
    A. a false dichotomy.   C. circular reasoning.
    B. semantic slanting.   D. slippery slope.

Answers

1 B pp. 396–397
2 D p. 401
3 C p. 404
4 C pp. 408–409
5 C pp. 413–414

6 B p. 414
7 C pp. 417–418
8 C p. 418
9 A p. 421
10 D pp. 423–425

11 B pp. 426–427
12 C p. 427
13 D p. 429
14 D pp. 430–431
15 C p. 435

PsykTrek

To view a demo: www.cengage.com/psychology/psyktrek
To order: www.cengage.com/psychology/weiten
Go to the PsykTrek website or CD-ROM for further study of the concepts in this chapter. Both online and on the CD-ROM, PsykTrek includes dozens of learning modules with videos, animations, and quizzes, as well as simulations of psychological phenomena and a multimedia glossary that includes word pronunciations.

CengageNow

www.cengage.com/tlc

Go to this site for the link to CengageNOW, your one-stop study shop. Take a Pretest for this chapter, and CengageNOW will generate a personalized Study Plan based on your test results. The Study Plan will identify the topics you need to review and direct you to online resources to help you master those topics. You can then take a Posttest to help you determine the concepts you have mastered and what you still need to work on.

Companion Website

www.cengage.com/psychology/weiten

Go to this site to find online resources directly linked to your book, including a glossary, flash cards, drag-and-drop exercises, quizzes, and more!

HUMAN DEVELOPMENT ACROSS THE LIFESPAN

Progress Before Birth: Prenatal Development
The Course of Prenatal Development
Environmental Factors and Prenatal Development

The Wondrous Years of Childhood
Exploring the World: Motor Development
Easy and Difficult Babies: Differences in Temperament
Early Emotional Development: Attachment
Becoming Unique: Personality Development
The Growth of Thought: Cognitive Development

FEATURED STUDY ▮ Can Infants Do Arithmetic?

The Development of Moral Reasoning

The Transition of Adolescence
Physiological Changes
Neural Development
Time of Turmoil?
The Search for Identity
Emerging Adulthood as a New Developmental Stage

The Expanse of Adulthood
Personality Development
Transitions in Family Life
Aging and Physiological Changes
Aging and Neural Changes
Aging and Cognitive Changes

Reflecting on the Chapter's Themes

PERSONAL APPLICATION ▮ Understanding Gender Differences

Illustrated Overview of Human Development

How Do the Sexes Differ in Behavior?
Biological Origins of Gender Differences
Environmental Origins of Gender Differences
Conclusion

CRITICAL THINKING APPLICATION ▮ Are Fathers Essential to Children's Well-Being?

The Basic Argument
Evaluating the Argument

Recap

Practice Test

On July 29, 1981, 20-year-old Diana Spencer stood before more than 2,000 guests at St. Paul's Cathedral in London and fumbled through an exchange of wedding vows, nervously transposing two of her husband's middle names. Diana could hardly believe what was happening. Just a few months before, she had been a giggly teenager with a playful sign on her bedroom door that read "Chief Chick." Dubbed "Shy Di" by the hordes of photographers who followed her every move, she had never even had a boyfriend (Morton, 1998). Now she was marrying Charles, Prince of Wales, the heir to the British throne, in an ostentatious wedding ceremony that was televised around the world.

Marriage—let alone to a future king—is a major transition for most people, but for Diana it was only the beginning of an extraordinary series of changes. When Diana became engaged, she was a pretty if slightly pudgy 19-year-old who was just on the threshold of adulthood. A high school dropout, she had few serious interests or ambitions. Her most obvious talent was her rapport with young children, who adored her. Far from a fashion plate, she owned "one long dress, one silk skirt, one smart pair of shoes, and that was it" (Morton, 1998, p. 66).

Yet, like Cinderella, the "fairy tale princess" soon blossomed. "It happened before our very eyes," said one photographer, "the transformation from this shy teenager who hid beneath big hats, and hung her head, into the self-assured woman and mother, confident in her beauty" (Clayton & Craig, 2001, p. 113). The Shy Di who sometimes burst into tears at the sight of crowds became Disco Di, a svelte beauty celebrated for her stylish clothes and hairstyles. Then came Dynasty Di, the doting mother of Princes William and Harry. Finally, as her marriage to Charles crumbled and she sought a new and more fulfilling role for herself, still another Diana emerged. Now she was Dedicated Di, a poised and effective spokesperson for important causes, such as AIDS and the removal of land mines from war-torn areas. No longer a frightened young princess or her husband's beautiful accessory, by her 30s Diana was a seemingly confident and independent woman who could publicly rebuke the royal family for their treatment of her and declare that she would rather be the "Queen of people's hearts" than the Queen of England (Edwards, 1999, p. 342).

Diana's transformations were startling, yet there was also a strong element of continuity in her life. As

The story of Princess Diana's metamorphosis from an awkward teenager into an elegant, self-assured public figure provides a dramatic demonstration of how human development is marked by both continuity and transition.

an adult, Diana continued to display qualities she had shown as a child, including her mischievous sense of humor, her love of swimming and dancing, and even her attachment to stuffed animals (S. B. Smith, 2000). Her childhood feeling of destiny ultimately blossomed into a deep sense of mission that took her to homeless shelters, clinics for lepers, and the bedsides of AIDS patients. Although cynics doubted the genuineness of her empathy for society's "outcasts," she had displayed a similar caring and naturalness as a young teenager dancing with patients in wheelchairs at a hospital for the mentally and physically handicapped (Clayton & Craig, 2001).

Other, more troubling, continuities also marked Diana's turbulent passage through life. Despite her growing mastery of her public roles, privately she remained vulnerable, moody, and insecure. Diana's parents had divorced when she was 6, and fears of abandonment never left her. As a young girl being taken to boarding school, she had begged her father, "If you love me, don't leave me here"—a plea she later echoed in tearful arguments with Prince Charles (Smith, 2000, p. 53). Her childhood feelings of intellectual inferiority continued to plague her as an adult. "A brain the size of a pea I've got," she would say (Clayton & Craig, 2001, p. 22). Throughout her marriage, she suffered bouts of bulimia (an eating disorder) and depression. While she projected a new confidence and maturity after her separation from Prince Charles, some observers felt that she was as needy and insecure as ever. A succession of relationships with men, before and after her divorce, seemed to bring her no closer to the love and security she craved. One biographer argues that in fundamental ways she had changed little, if at all (Smith, 2000). Others, however, believed that a new chapter in her life was just beginning and that many more changes were undoubtedly in store when Diana was tragically killed in an auto accident at the age of 36.

What does Princess Diana have to do with developmental psychology? Although her story is obviously unique in many ways, it provides an interesting illustration of the two themes that permeate the study of human development: *transition* and *continuity*. In investigating human development, psychologists study how people evolve through transitions over time. In looking at these transitions, developmental psychologists inevitably find continuity with the past. This continuity may be the most fascinating element in Diana's story. The metamorphosis of the shy, awkward teenager into an elegant, self-assured public figure was a more radical transformation than most people go through. Nonetheless, the threads of continuity connecting Diana's childhood to the development of her adult personality were quite obvious.

Development is the sequence of age-related changes that occur as a person progresses from conception to death. It is a reasonably orderly, cumulative process that includes both the biological and behavioral changes that take place as people grow older. An infant's newfound ability to grasp objects, a child's gradual mastery of grammar, an adolescent's spurt in physical growth, a young adult's increasing commitment to a vocation, and an older adult's transition into the role of grandparent all represent development. These transitions are predictable changes that are related to age.

Traditionally, psychologists have been most interested in development during childhood. Our coverage reflects this emphasis. However, decades of research have clearly demonstrated that development is a lifelong process. In this chapter we divide the life span into four broad periods—(1) the prenatal period, between conception and birth, (2) childhood, (3) adolescence, and (4) adulthood—and examine aspects of development that are especially dynamic during each period. Let's begin by looking at events that occur before birth, during prenatal development.

Key Learning Goals
11.1 Outline the major events of the three stages of prenatal development.
11.2 Summarize the impact of environmental factors on prenatal development.

Progress Before Birth: Prenatal Development

Development begins with conception. Conception occurs when fertilization creates a *zygote*, **a one-celled organism formed by the union of a sperm and an egg.** All the other cells in your body developed from this single cell. Each of your cells contains enduring messages from your parents carried on the *chromosomes* that lie within its nucleus. Each chromosome houses many *genes*, the functional

units in hereditary transmission. Genes carry the details of your hereditary blueprints, which are revealed gradually throughout life (see Chapter 3 for more information on genetic transmission).

The *prenatal period* extends from conception to birth, usually encompassing nine months of pregnancy. A great deal of important development occurs before birth. In fact, development during the prenatal period is remarkably rapid. If you were an average-sized newborn and your physical growth had continued during the first year of your life at a prenatal pace, by your first birthday you would have weighed 200 pounds! Fortunately, you didn't grow at that rate—and no human does—because in the final weeks before birth the frenzied pace of prenatal development tapers off dramatically. In this section, we'll examine the usual course of prenatal development and discuss how environmental events can leave their mark on development even before birth exposes the newborn to the outside world.

The Course of Prenatal Development

9a

The prenatal period is divided into three phases: (1) the germinal stage (the first two weeks), (2) the embryonic stage (two weeks to two months), and (3) the fetal stage (two months to birth). Some key developments in these phases are outlined here.

Germinal Stage

9a

The *germinal stage* is the first phase of prenatal development, encompassing the first two weeks after conception. This brief stage begins when a zygote is created through fertilization. Within 36 hours, rapid cell division begins, and the zygote becomes a microscopic mass of multiplying cells. This mass of cells slowly migrates along the mother's fallopian tube to the uterine cavity. On about the seventh day, the cell mass begins to implant itself in the uterine wall. This process takes about a week and is far from automatic. Many zygotes are rejected at this point. As many as one in five pregnancies end with the woman never being aware that conception has occurred (Simpson, 2002).

During the implantation process, the placenta begins to form (Buster & Carson, 2002). The *placenta* is a structure that allows oxygen and nutrients to pass into the fetus from the mother's bloodstream and bodily wastes to pass out to the mother. This critical exchange takes place across thin membranes that block the passage of blood cells, keeping the fetal and maternal bloodstreams separate.

Embryonic Stage

9a

The *embryonic stage* is the second stage of prenatal development, lasting from two weeks until the end of the second month. During this stage, most of the

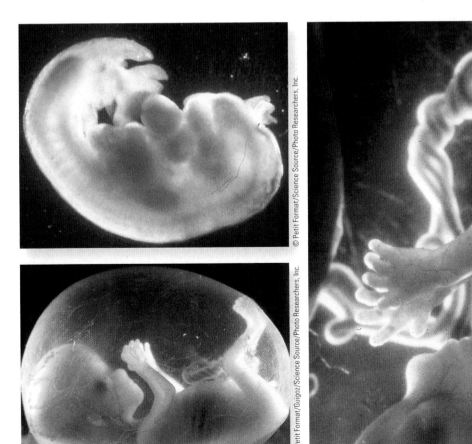

Prenatal development is remarkably rapid. Top left: This 30-day-old embryo is just 6 millimeters in length. Bottom left: At 14 weeks, the fetus is approximately 2 inches long. Note the well-developed fingers. The fetus can already move its legs, feet, hands, and head and displays a variety of basic reflexes. Right: After 4 months of prenatal development, facial features are beginning to emerge.

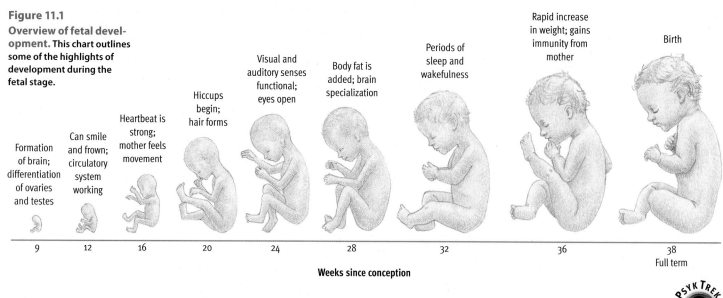

Formation of brain; differentiation of ovaries and testes

Can smile and frown; circulatory system working

Heartbeat is strong; mother feels movement

Hiccups begin; hair forms

Visual and auditory senses functional; eyes open

Body fat is added; brain specialization

Periods of sleep and wakefulness

Rapid increase in weight; gains immunity from mother

Birth

9   12   16   20   24   28   32   36   38
Full term

Weeks since conception

vital organs and bodily systems begin to form in the developing organism, which is now called an *embryo*. Structures such as the heart, spine, and brain emerge gradually as cell division becomes more specialized. Although the embryo is typically only about an inch long at the end of this stage, it's already beginning to look human. Arms, legs, hands, feet, fingers, toes, eyes, and ears are already discernible.

The embryonic stage is a period of great vulnerability because virtually all the basic physiological structures are being formed. If anything interferes with normal development during the embryonic phase, the effects can be devastating. Most miscarriages occur during this period (Simpson, 2002). Most major structural birth defects are also due to problems that occur during the embryonic stage (Simpson & Niebyl, 2002).

Fetal Stage   9a

The *fetal stage* is the third stage of prenatal development, lasting from two months through birth. Some highlights of fetal development are summarized in **Figure 11.1**. The first two months of the fetal stage bring rapid bodily growth, as muscles and bones begin to form (Moore & Persaud, 2003). The developing organism, now called a *fetus*, becomes capable of physical movements as skeletal structures harden. Organs formed in the embryonic stage continue to grow and gradually begin to function. The sense of hearing, for example, is functional by around 20–24 weeks (Hepper, 2003).

During the final three months of the prenatal period, brain cells multiply at a brisk pace. A layer of fat is deposited under the skin to provide insulation, and the respiratory and digestive systems ma-

concept check 11.1

Understanding the Stages of Prenatal Development

Check your understanding of the stages of prenatal development by filling in the blanks in the chart below. The first column contains descriptions of a main event from each of the three stages. In the second column, write the name of the stage; in the third column, write the term used to refer to the developing organism during that stage; and in the fourth column, write the time span (in terms of weeks or months) covered by the stage. The answers are in Appendix A at the back of the book.

	Stage	Term for organism	Time span
1. Uterine implantation	_____	_____	_____
2. Muscle and bone begin to form	_____	_____	_____
3. Vital organs and body systems begin to form	_____	_____	_____

ture (Adolph & Berger, 2005). All of these changes ready the fetus for life outside the cozy, supportive environment of its mother's womb. Sometime between 22 weeks and 26 weeks the fetus reaches the *age of viability*—the age at which a baby can survive in the event of a premature birth. Thanks to advances in medical technology, the age of viability has declined in recent decades in modern societies. At 22–23 weeks the probability of survival is still slim (14%–26%), but it climbs steadily over the next month to an 80%–83% survival rate at 26 weeks (Iams, 2002).

Environmental Factors and Prenatal Development

Although the fetus develops in the protective buffer of the womb, events in the external environment can affect it indirectly through the mother. Because the developing organism and its mother are linked through the placenta, a mother's eating habits, drug use, and physical health, among other things, can affect prenatal development and have long-term health consequences (Hampton, 2004). Figure 11.2 shows the periods of prenatal development during which various structures are most vulnerable to damage.

Maternal Nutrition

The developing fetus needs a variety of essential nutrients. Thus, it's not surprising that severe maternal malnutrition increases the risk of birth complications and neurological defects for the newborn (Coutts, 2000; Fifer, Monk, & Grose-Fifer, 2001). The effects of severe malnutrition are a major problem in underdeveloped nations where food shortages are common. The impact of moderate malnutrition, which is more common in modern, developed countries, is more difficult to gauge, in part because maternal malnutrition is often confounded with other risk factors associated with poverty, such as drug abuse and limited access to health care (Guerrini, Thomson, & Gurling, 2007). Recent research suggests that prenatal malnutrition may have negative effects decades after a child's birth. For example, prenatal malnutrition has been linked to vulnerability to schizophrenia and other psychiatric disorders in adolescence and early adulthood (Susser, Brown, & Matte, 1999). And low birth weight is associated with an increased risk of heart disease, diabetes, and obesity in middle adulthood (Forsén et al., 2000; Roseboom, de Rooij, & Painter, 2006). Although low

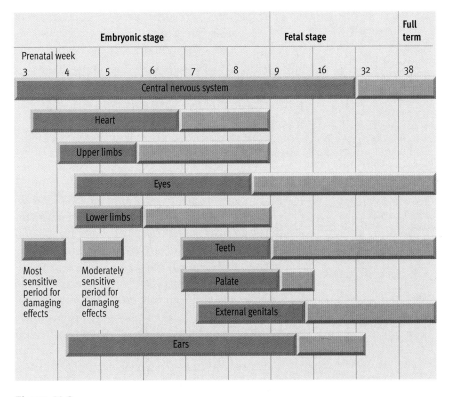

Figure 11.2

Periods of vulnerability in prenatal development. Generally, structures are most susceptible to damage when they are undergoing rapid development. The red regions of the bars indicate the most sensitive periods for various organs and structures, while the purple regions indicate periods of continued, but lessened, vulnerability. As a whole, sensitivity is greatest in the embryonic stage, but some structures remain vulnerable throughout prenatal development.

SOURCE: Adapted from Moore, K. L., & Persaud, T. V. N. (2008). *Before we are born: Essentials of embryology and birth defects.* Philadelphia: W. B. Saunders/ Elsevier. Copyright © 2008 Elsevier Science (USA). All rights reserved. Reprinted by permission.

birth weight can be attributable to factors besides maternal malnutrition (Osrin & del Costello, 2000), these findings are alarming.

Maternal Drug Use

A major source of concern about fetal and infant well-being is the mother's consumption of drugs, including such widely used substances as tobacco and alcohol, as well as prescription and recreational drugs. Unfortunately, most drugs consumed by a pregnant woman can pass through the membranes of the placenta.

Virtually all "recreational" drugs (see Chapter 5) can be harmful, with sedatives, narcotics, and cocaine being particularly dangerous. Babies of heroin users are born addicted to narcotics and have an increased risk of early death due to prematurity, birth defects, respiratory difficulties, and problems associated with their addiction (Finnegan & Kandall, 2005). Prenatal exposure to cocaine is associated with increased risk of birth complications

(Sokol et al., 2007) and a variety of cognitive deficits that are apparent in childhood (Accornero et al., 2007; Singer et al., 2004). Problems can also be caused by a great variety of drugs prescribed for legitimate medical reasons, and even by some over-the-counter drugs (Niebyl, 2002). The impact of drugs on the embryo or fetus varies greatly depending on the drug, the dose, and the phase of prenatal development.

Alcohol consumption during pregnancy also carries risks. It has long been clear that heavy drinking by a mother can be hazardous to a fetus. *Fetal alcohol syndrome is a collection of congenital (inborn) problems associated with excessive alcohol use during pregnancy.* Typical problems include microcephaly (a small head), heart defects, irritability, hyperactivity, and delayed mental and motor development (Hannigan & Armant, 2000; Pellegrino & Pellegrino, 2008). Fetal alcohol syndrome is the most common known cause of mental retardation (Niccols, 2007), and it is related to an increased incidence of difficulties in school, depression, suicide, drug problems, and criminal behavior in adolescence and adulthood (Kelly, Day, & Streissguth, 2000; Streissguth et al., 2004).

Furthermore, many children fall short of the criteria for fetal alcohol syndrome but still show serious impairments attributable to their mothers' drinking during pregnancy (Willford, Leech, & Day, 2006). The best evidence on this issue comes from a long-running study begun in 1974 in Seattle, which was recently summarized by Ann Streissguth (2007). This study has followed roughly 500 offspring of mothers who engaged in varied amounts of drinking during their pregnancy. When the youngsters were 14, higher prenatal alcohol intake was found to be associated with deficits in IQ, reaction time, motor skills, attention span, and math skills and with increased impulsive, antisocial, and delinquent behavior. At ages 21 and 25, prenatal alcohol intake was found to predict an increased incidence of alcohol problems and psychiatric disorders. Clearly, even normal drinking during pregnancy can have enduring and substantial negative effects.

Tobacco use during pregnancy is also hazardous to prenatal development. Smoking produces a number of subtle physiological changes in the mother that seem to reduce the flow of oxygen and nutrients to the fetus. Smoking appears to increase a mother's risk for miscarriage, stillbirth, and prematurity, and newborns' risk for sudden infant death syndrome (Shea & Steiner, 2008). Maternal smoking may also contribute to slower than average cognitive development (Trasti, Jacobson, & Bakketeig, 1999), as well as attention deficits, hyperactivity, and conduct problems (Button, Maughan, & McGuffin, 2007).

Maternal Illness

The fetus is largely defenseless against infections because its immune system matures relatively late in the prenatal period. The placenta screens out quite a number of infectious agents, but not all. Thus, many maternal illnesses can interfere with prenatal development. Diseases such as measles, rubella (German measles), syphilis, and chicken pox can be hazardous to the fetus (Duff, 2002), with the nature of any damage depending, in part, on when the mother contracts the illness. The HIV virus that causes AIDS can also be transmitted by pregnant women to their offspring. The transmission of AIDS may occur prenatally through the placenta, during delivery, or through breastfeeding. Up through the mid-1990s, about 20%–30% of HIV-positive pregnant women passed the virus on to their babies, but improved antiretroviral drugs (given to the mother) and more cautious obstetrical care have reduced this figure to about 2% in the United States (Cotter & Potter, 2006). Yet another risk is that a variety of genital infections, such as gonorrhea, chlamydia, and herpes, can be transmitted to newborns during delivery (Duff, 2002). These common diseases can be quite dangerous to the newborn.

Science has a long way to go before it uncovers all the factors that shape development before birth. For example, scientists are showing renewed interest in how prenatal maternal stress might have repercussions for children's development, but the effects of fluctuations in maternal emotions are not well understood at present (DiPietro, 2004). Nonetheless, it's clear that critical developments unfold quickly during the prenatal period. In the next section, you'll learn that development continues at a fast pace during the early years of childhood.

REVIEW of Key Learning Goals

11.1 Prenatal development proceeds through the germinal (first 2 weeks), embryonic (2 weeks to 2 months), and fetal stages (2 months to birth) as the zygote is differentiated into a human organism. The embryonic stage is a period of great vulnerability, as most physiological structures are being formed. The fetal stage brings rapid growth as physiological systems mature.

11.2 Maternal malnutrition during the prenatal period has been linked to birth complications and other subsequent problems. Maternal use of illicit drugs can be dangerous to the unborn child. Even normal social drinking and routine tobacco use can be very hazardous during prenatal development. A variety of maternal illnesses can interfere with prenatal development.

The Wondrous Years of Childhood

A certain magic is associated with childhood. Young children have an extraordinary ability to captivate adults' attention, especially their parents'. Legions of parents apologize repeatedly to friends and strangers alike as they talk on and on about the cute things their kids do. Most wondrous of all are the rapid and momentous developmental changes of the childhood years. Helpless infants become curious toddlers almost overnight. Before parents can catch their breath, these toddlers are schoolchildren engaged in spirited play with young friends. Then, suddenly, they're insecure adolescents, worrying about dates, part-time jobs, cars, and college. The whirlwind transitions of childhood often seem miraculous.

Of course, the transformations that occur in childhood only *seem* magical. In reality, they reflect an orderly, predictable, gradual progression. In this section you'll see what psychologists have learned about this progression. We'll examine various aspects of development that are especially dynamic during childhood. Language development is omitted from this section because we covered it in the chapter on language and thought (Chapter 8). Let's begin by looking at motor development.

Exploring the World: Motor Development

One of the earliest topics studied by developmental psychologists was motor development. *Motor development* refers to the progression of muscular coordination required for physical activities. Basic motor skills include grasping and reaching for objects, manipulating objects, sitting up, crawling, walking, and running.

Basic Principles

A number of principles are apparent in motor development (Adolph & Berger, 2005). One is the *cephalocaudal trend*—the head-to-foot direction of motor development. Children tend to gain control over the upper part of their bodies before the lower part. You've seen this trend in action if you've seen an infant learn to crawl. Infants gradually shift from using their arms for propelling themselves to using their legs. The *proximodistal trend* is the center-outward direction of motor development. Children gain control over their torso before their extremities. Thus, infants initially reach for things by

twisting their entire body, but gradually they learn to extend just their arms.

Early motor development depends in part on physical growth, which is not only rapid during infancy but also more uneven than previously appreciated. In a study of infants from birth to 21 months, Lampl, Veldhuis, and Johnson (1992) found that lengthy periods of no growth were punctuated by sudden bursts of growth. These growth spurts tended to be accompanied by restlessness and irritability. Thus, parents who sometimes feel that their children are changing overnight may not be imagining it!

Early progress in motor skills has traditionally been attributed almost entirely to the process of maturation. *Maturation* is development that reflects the gradual unfolding of one's genetic blueprint. It is a product of genetically programmed physical changes that come with age—as opposed to experience and learning. However, research that has taken a closer look at the *process* of motor development suggests that infants are active agents rather than passive organisms waiting for their brain and limbs to mature (Thelen, 1995). According to this newer view, the driving force behind motor development is infants' ongoing exploration of their world and their need to master specific tasks (such as grasping a larger toy or looking out a window). Progress in motor development is attributed to infants' experimentation and their learning the consequences of their activities. Although modern researchers acknowledge that maturation facilitates motor development, they argue that its contribution has been oversimplified and overestimated (Bertenthal & Clifton, 1998).

Understanding Developmental Norms

Parents often pay close attention to early motor development, comparing their child's progress with developmental norms. *Developmental norms* indicate the typical (median) age at which individuals display various behaviors and abilities. Developmental norms are useful benchmarks as long as parents don't expect their children to progress exactly at the pace specified in the norms. Some parents get unnecessarily alarmed when their children fall behind developmental norms. What these parents overlook is that developmental norms are group *averages*. Variations from the average are entirely normal. This normal variation stands out in **Figure 11.3**, which indicates the age at which 25%, 50%, and 90% of

Key Learning Goals

11.3 Understand general principles and cultural variations in motor development.

11.4 Review Thomas and Chess's longitudinal study of infant temperament and other work on temperament.

11.5 Describe Harlow's and Bowlby's views on attachment, and discuss research on patterns of attachment.

11.6 Discuss day care in relation to attachment, and describe cultural variations in attachment.

11.7 Describe the basic tenets of Erikson's theory and his stages of childhood personality development.

11.8 Outline Piaget's stages of cognitive development, and discuss the strengths and weaknesses of Piaget's theory.

11.9 Describe Vygotsky's sociocultural theory, and evaluate the notion that some cognitive abilities may be innate.

11.10 Outline Kohlberg's stages of moral development, and discuss the strengths and weaknesses of Kohlberg's theory.

Figure 11.3

Landmarks in motor development. The left edge, interior mark, and right edge of each bar indicate the age at which 25%, 50%, and 90% of infants (in North America) have mastered each motor skill shown. Developmental norms typically report only the median age of mastery (the interior mark), which can be misleading in light of the variability in age of mastery apparent in this chart.

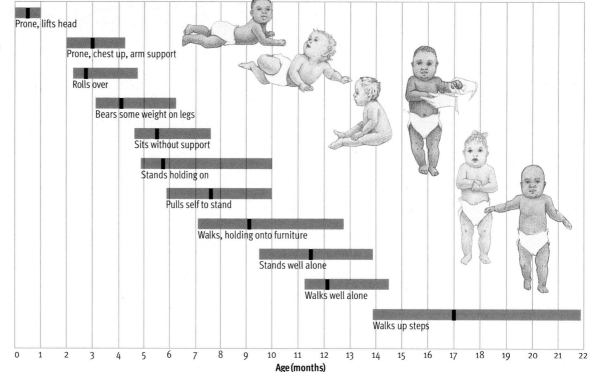

Prone, lifts head

Prone, chest up, arm support

Rolls over

Bears some weight on legs

Sits without support

Stands holding on

Pulls self to stand

Walks, holding onto furniture

Stands well alone

Walks well alone

Walks up steps

Age (months)

youngsters can demonstrate various motor skills. As Figure 11.3 shows, a substantial portion of children often don't achieve a particular milestone until long after the average time cited in norms.

Cultural Variations and Their Significance

Cross-cultural research has highlighted the dynamic interplay between experience and maturation in motor development. Relatively rapid motor development has been observed in some cultures that provide special practice in basic motor skills. For example, soon after birth the Kipsigis people of Kenya begin active efforts to train their infants to sit up, stand, and walk. Thanks to this training, Kipsi-

Cultures across the world use a variety of methods to foster rapid development of motor abilities in their children. The Kung San of the Kalahari, Botswana, teach their young to dance quite early, using poles to develop the kinesthetic sense of balance.

gis children achieve these developmental milestones (but not others) about a month earlier than babies in the United States (Super, 1976). In contrast, relatively slow motor development has been found in some cultures that discourage motor exploration. For example, among the Ache, a nomadic people living in the rain forests of Paraguay, safety concerns dictate that children under age 3 rarely venture more than 3 feet from their mothers, who carry them virtually everywhere. As a result of these constraints, Ache children are delayed in acquiring a variety of motor skills and typically begin walking about a year later than other children (Kaplan & Dove, 1987). Cultural variations in the emergence of basic motor skills demonstrate that environmental factors can accelerate or slow early motor development.

Easy and Difficult Babies: Differences in Temperament

Infants show considerable variability in temperament. *Temperament* refers to characteristic mood, activity level, and emotional reactivity. From the very beginning, some babies seem animated and cheerful while others seem sluggish and ornery. Infants show consistent differences in emotional tone, tempo of activity, and sensitivity to environmental stimuli very early in life (Martin & Fox, 2006).

Alexander Thomas and Stella Chess conducted a landmark *longitudinal* study of the development of temperament (Thomas & Chess, 1977, 1989; Thomas,

Chess, & Birch, 1970). **In a *longitudinal design* investigators observe one group of participants repeatedly over a period of time.** This approach to the study of development is usually contrasted with the *cross-sectional* approach (the logic of both approaches is diagrammed in Figure 11.4). **In a *cross-sectional design* investigators compare groups of participants of differing age at a single point in time.** For example, in a cross-sectional study an investigator tracing the growth of children's vocabulary might compare fifty 6-year-olds, fifty 8-year-olds, and fifty 10-year-olds. In contrast, an investigator using the longitudinal method would assemble one group of fifty 6-year-olds and measure their vocabulary at age 6, again at age 8, and once more at age 10.

Each method has its advantages and disadvantages. Cross-sectional studies can be completed more quickly, easily, and cheaply than longitudinal studies, which often extend over many years. However, in cross-sectional studies changes that appear to reflect development may really be cohort effects. ***Cohort effects* occur when differences between age groups are due to the groups growing up in different time periods.** For example, if you used the cross-sectional method to examine gender roles in groups aged 20, 40, and 60 years, you would be comparing people who grew up before, during, and after

the women's movement, which would probably lead to major differences as a result of historical context rather than development. Unfortunately, longitudinal designs have weaknesses too. When a longitudinal study takes years to complete, participants often drop out because they move away or lose interest. The changing composition of the sample may produce misleading developmental trends. That said, longitudinal designs tend to be more sensitive to developmental changes than cross-sectional designs (Magnusson & Stattin, 1998). To some extent, the choice of a research design to investigate development depends on what the investigators want to learn about. Thomas and Chess wanted to learn about the long-term stability of children's temperaments. Given this goal, they needed to follow the same children in a longitudinal study to assess their temperamental stability over time.

Thomas and Chess identified three basic styles of temperament that were apparent in most of the children. About 40% of the youngsters were *easy children* who tended to be happy, regular in sleep and eating, adaptable, and not readily upset. Another 15% were *slow-to-warm-up children* who tended to be less cheery, less regular in their sleep and eating, and slower in adapting to change. These children were wary of new experiences, and their emotional

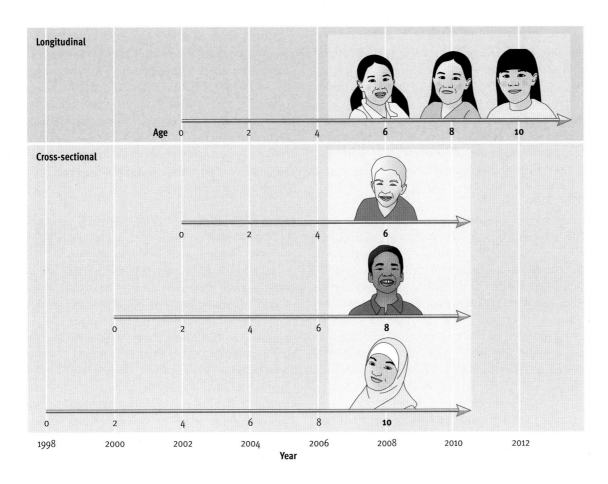

Figure 11.4
Longitudinal versus cross-sectional research. In a longitudinal study of development between ages 6 and 10, the same children would be observed at 6, again at 8, and again at 10. In a cross-sectional study of the same age span, a group of 6-year-olds, a group of 8-year-olds, and a group of 10-year-olds would be compared simultaneously. Note that data collection could be completed immediately in the cross-sectional study, whereas the longitudinal study would require 4 years to complete.

reactivity was moderate. *Difficult children* constituted 10% of the group. They tended to be glum, erratic in sleep and eating, resistant to change, and relatively irritable. The remaining 35% of the children showed mixtures of these three temperaments.

A child's temperament at 3 months was a fair predictor of the child's temperament at age 10. Infants categorized as "difficult" developed more emotional problems requiring counseling than other children did. Although basic changes in temperament were seen in some children, temperament was generally stable over time (Chess & Thomas, 1996).

Some critics have expressed concern because Thomas and Chess's data were based on parents' highly subjective ratings of their children's temperament (Martin & Fox, 2006). But other investigators, using a variety of methods to assess infant temperament, have also found it to be fairly stable (Rothbart & Bates, 2006; Sanson, Hemphill, & Smart, 2002). However, the evidence indicates that temperament tends to stabilize a little later (around age 1 or 2) than Thomas and Chess suggested (Thompson & Goodvin, 2005).

One prominent example of contemporary research on temperament is the work of Jerome Kagan and his colleagues, who have relied on direct observations of children in their studies (Kagan & Snidman, 1991; Kagan, Snidman, & Arcus, 1992). They have found that about 15%–20% of infants display an *inhibited temperament* characterized by shyness, timidity, and wariness of unfamiliar people, objects, and events. In contrast, about 25%–30% of infants exhibit an *uninhibited temperament* (the remainder fall in between these extremes). These children are less restrained, approaching unfamiliar people, objects, and events with little trepidation. Evidence suggests that these temperamental styles have a genetic basis and are reasonably stable into young adulthood (Kagan, 2004; Kagan, Reznick, & Snidman, 1999).

Moreover, recent research suggests that infant temperament lays the foundation for personality traits in adulthood (Rothbart, 2007). For example, a large-scale, longitudinal study that began with 1037 3-year-old children in 1972–1973 conducted personality assessments of the participants many years later when they reached the age of 26 (Caspi et al., 2003). The 3-year-olds had been classified into five temperament types: inhibited, undercontrolled, confident, reserved, and well-adjusted. At age 26, these temperaments had significant predictive effects on all three higher-order personality traits examined. These data provide the "longest and strongest evidence to date" that early temperamental characteristics can foretell the contours of adult personality.

Jerome Kagan

"Every psychological quality in an adult can be likened to a pale gray fabric woven from thin black threads representing biology and white threads representing experience, neither visible in the homogeneously gray cloth."

web link 11.2

Early Childhood Care and Development

This site's subtitle, International Resources for Early Childhood Development, emphasizes the focus of resources provided: the worldwide (not just North American) challenge of caring for children from birth through age 6 and fulfilling the needs of their families.

A child's temperament can influence parental reactions, which can have some effect on the child's temperament. For example, parents tend to play more vigorously with children who are temperamentally active, which may help to make them more active.

Although temperament is heavily influenced by heredity and tends to be fairly stable over time, theorists emphasize that temperament is not unchangeable (Thompson, Easterbrooks, & Padilla-Walker, 2003). Parental reactions and other social experiences can gradually massage a child's temperamental characteristics. As Kagan (2004) puts it, "There is no fixed determinism between an infant temperament and what that child will become 20 years later. Temperament is not destiny" (p. 65).

Early Emotional Development: Attachment

Do mothers and infants forge lasting emotional bonds in the first few hours after birth? Do early emotional bonds affect later development? These are just two of the questions investigated by psychologists interested in attachment. *Attachment* refers to the close, emotional bonds of affection that develop between infants and their caregivers. Researchers have shown a keen interest in how infant-mother attachments are formed early in life. Children eventually may form attachments to many people, including their fathers, grandparents, and others (Cassidy, 1999). However, a child's first important attachment usually occurs with his or her mother because in most cultures she is the principal caregiver, especially in the early years of life (Lamb et al., 1999).

Contrary to popular belief, infants' attachment to their mothers is *not* instantaneous. Initially, babies show relatively little in the way of a special preference for their mothers. At 2–3 months of age, infants may smile and laugh more when they interact with their mother, but they generally can be handed over to strangers such as babysitters with little difficulty. This situation gradually changes, and by about 6–8 months, infants begin to show a pronounced preference for their mother's company and often protest when separated from her (Lamb, Ketterlinus, & Fracasso, 1992). This is the first manifestation of *separation anxiety*—emotional distress seen in many infants when they are separated from people with whom they have formed an attachment. Separation anxiety, which may occur with fathers and other familiar caregivers as well as with mothers, typically peaks at around 14–18 months and then begins to decline.

Theories of Attachment

Why do children gradually develop a special attachment to their mothers? This question sounds simple enough, but it has been the subject of a lively theoretical dialogue. Behaviorists have argued that the infant-mother attachment develops because mothers are associated with the powerful, reinforcing event of being fed. Thus, the mother becomes a conditioned reinforcer. This reinforcement theory of attachment came into question as a result of Harry Harlow's famous studies of attachment in infant rhesus monkeys (Harlow, 1958, 1959).

Harlow removed monkeys from their mothers at birth and raised them in the laboratory with two types of artificial "substitute mothers." One type of artificial mother was made of terrycloth and could provide "contact comfort" (see the photo above). The other type of artificial mother was made of wire. Half of the monkeys were fed from a bottle attached to a wire mother and the other half were fed by a cloth mother. The young monkeys' attachment to their substitute mothers was tested by introducing a frightening stimulus, such as a strange toy. If reinforcement through feeding were the key to attachment, the frightened monkeys should have scampered off to the mother that had fed them. This was not the case. The young monkeys scrambled for their cloth mothers, who had provided contact comfort, even if they were *not* fed by them.

Harlow's work seriously undermined the behaviorists' reinforcement explanation of attachment. Attention then turned to an alternative explanation

Even if fed by a wire surrogate mother, the Harlows' infant monkeys cuddled up with a terry cloth surrogate that provided contact comfort. When threatened by a frightening toy, the monkeys sought security from their terry cloth mothers.

of attachment proposed by John Bowlby (1969, 1973, 1980). Bowlby was impressed by the importance of contact comfort to Harlow's monkeys and by the apparently unlearned nature of this preference. Influenced by evolutionary theories, Bowlby argued that there must be a biological basis for attachment. According to his view, infants are biologically programmed to emit behavior (smiling, cooing, clinging, and so on) that triggers an affectionate, protective response from adults. Bowlby also asserted that adults are programmed by evolutionary forces to be captivated by this behavior and to respond with warmth, love, and protection. Obviously, these characteristics would be adaptive in terms of promoting children's survival. Bowlby's theory has guided most of the research on attachment over the last several decades, including Mary Ainsworth's influential work on patterns of attachment.

Patterns of Attachment

Research by Mary Ainsworth and her colleagues (Ainsworth, 1979; Ainsworth et al., 1978) demonstrated that infant-mother attachments vary in quality. Ainsworth found that attachments fall into three categories (see **Figure 11.5** on the next page). Fortunately, most infants develop a *secure attachment*. These infants use their mother as a secure base from which to venture out and explore the world. They play comfortably with their mother present, become visibly upset when she leaves, and are quickly calmed by her return. However, some children display a pattern called *anxious-ambivalent attachment* (also

Harry Harlow

"The little we know about love does not transcend simple observation, and the little we write about it has been written better by poets and novelists."

John Bowlby

"The only relevant criterion by which to consider the natural adaptedness of any particular part of present-day man's behavioural equipment is the degree to which and the way in which it might contribute to population survival in man's primeval environment."

Figure 11.5

Overview of the attachment process. The unfolding of attachment depends on the interaction between a mother (or other caregiver) and an infant. Research by Mary Ainsworth suggested that attachment relations fall into three categories—secure, avoidant, and anxious-ambivalent—which depend in part on how sensitive and responsive caregivers are to their children's needs. The feedback loops shown in the diagram reflect the fact that babies are not passive bystanders in the attachment drama; their reactions to caregivers can affect the caregivers' behavior. Ainsworth's model did not include the fourth attachment pattern (disorganized-disoriented), which was recognized later.

SOURCE: Adapted from Shaver, P. R., & Hazan, C. (1994). Attachment. In A. Weber & J. H. Harvey (Eds.), *Perspectives on close relationships.* Boston: Allyn & Bacon. Copyright © 1994 by Allyn and Bacon. Reprinted by permission.

Mary Salter Ainsworth

"Where familial security is lacking, the individual is handicapped by the lack of what might be called a secure base from which to work."

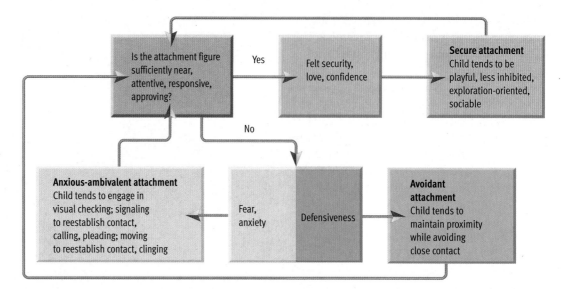

called *resistant* attachment). They appear anxious even when their mothers are near and protest excessively when she leaves, but they are not particularly comforted when she returns. Children in the third category seek little contact with their mothers and often are not distressed when she leaves, a condition labeled *avoidant attachment.* Years later, other researchers added a fourth category called *disorganized-disoriented* attachment (Main & Solomon, 1986, 1990). These children appear confused about whether they should approach or avoid their mother and are especially insecure (Lyons-Ruth & Jacobvitz, 1999).

Maternal behaviors appear to have considerable influence over the type of attachment that emerges between an infant and mother (Ainsworth et al., 1978; Posada et al., 2007). Mothers who are sensitive and responsive to their children's needs are more likely to promote secure attachments than mothers who are relatively insensitive or inconsistent in their responding (Nievar & Becker, 2008; van den Boom, 2001). However, infants are not passive bystanders as this process unfolds. They are active participants who influence the process with their crying, smiling, fussing, and babbling. Temperamentally difficult infants who spit up most of their food, make bathing a major battle, and rarely smile may sometimes slow the process of attachment (van IJzendoorn & Bakermans-Kranenburg, 2004). Thus, the type of attachment that emerges between an infant and mother may depend on the nature of the infant's temperament as well as the mother's sensitivity (Kagan & Fox, 2006).

How stable are the various patterns of attachment over time? The results of research on attachment stability vary considerably, depending on the way attachment is measured, the nature of the sample, and the time interval examined (Thompson, 1998, 2000). Overall, attachment types tend to be moder-

ately stable through childhood and into adulthood (Ammaniti, Speranza, & Fedele, 2005; Fraley, 2002). When changes in attachment type are seen, they often reflect changed circumstances in youngsters' lives, such as increases in family stress or alterations in parental support.

Evidence suggests that the quality of the attachment relationship can have important consequences for children's subsequent development. Based on their attachment experiences, children develop *internal working models* of the dynamics of close relationships that influence their future interactions with a wide range of people (Bretherton & Munholland, 1999). Infants with a relatively secure attachment *tend* to become resilient, sociable, competent toddlers with high self-esteem (Ranson & Urichuk, 2006; Thompson, 1999a). In their preschool years, they display more persistence, curiosity, self-reliance, and leadership and have better peer relations (Weinfield et al., 1999) while experiencing fewer negative emotions and more positive emotions (Kochanska, 2001). In middle childhood, those who had secure attachments in infancy exhibit higher levels of positive moods, healthier strategies for coping with stress, and better regulation of their emotions (Kerns et al., 2007). Studies have also found a relationship between secure attachment and more advanced cognitive development during childhood and adolescence (Ranson & Urichuk, 2006). However, it is worth noting that all the relevant data on attachment effects are correlational (experimenters cannot manipulate caregiver-infant attachments), so we cannot assume that secure attachment *causes* all these favorable outcomes. Secure attachment could co-vary with other important factors that contribute to high self-esteem, self-reliance, and so forth.

The repercussions of attachment patterns in infancy appear to even reach into adulthood. In Chapter 16 we'll discuss thought-provoking evidence that infant attachment patterns set the tone for people's romantic relationships in adulthood, not to mention their gender roles, religious beliefs, and patterns of self-disclosure (Kirkpatrick, 2005; Mikulincer, 2006; Mikulincer & Shaver, 2007; Schwartz, Waldo, & Higgins, 2004; Shaver & Hazan, 1993, 1994).

Day Care and Attachment

The impact of day care on attachment has been the subject of considerable debate. Some theorists have argued that frequent infant-mother separations might disrupt the attachment process (Belsky, 1988, 1992). The issue is an important one, given that the vast majority of the children under age 5 in the United States receive some nonmaternal care, and by age 2, 43% are in *full-time* (more than 35 hours per week) day care (Phillips, McCartney, & Sussman, 2006). To explore this question and other issues related to day care, a major, long-term study was launched in the United States in the 1990s by the National Institute of Child Health and Human Development (NICHD). Some of the early findings from this 10-site study of over 1300 children lent credence to concerns about day care and attachment. For example, infants were found to be more likely to develop insecure attachments when low-quality day care was paired with low levels of maternal sensitivity (NICHD, 1997). And more time in nonmaternal care was found to be associated with elevated levels of aggression and disobedience in preschoolers (NICHD, 2003).

That said, the magnitude of these effects tended to be small, and some of the effects had diminished further by the time the children reached the sixth grade (Belsky et al., 2007). Although some researchers have expressed concern about children who spend long hours in day care (Belsky, 2006), the overall evidence suggests that nonmaternal care is not harmful to children's social and emotional development (NICHD, 2006). In fact, research has uncovered some *favorable* outcomes associated with day care. Children exposed to *high-quality* day care tend to show more advanced cognitive development, language skills, and school readiness (NICHD, 2006). Once again, the effects are relatively small in magnitude, but they do suggest that it is prudent for parents to seek high-quality day care for their children (Belsky, 2006).

Culture and Attachment

Separation anxiety emerges in children at about 6–8 months and peaks at about 14–18 months in cultures around the world (Grossmann & Grossmann, 1990). These findings, which have been replicated in quite a variety of non-Western cultures, suggest that

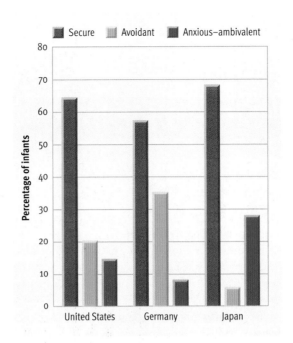

Figure 11.6
Cultural variations in attachment patterns. This graph shows the distribution of the three original attachment patterns found in specific studies in Germany, Japan, and the United States. As you can see, secure attachment is the most common pattern in all three societies, as it is around the world. However, there are some modest cultural differences in the prevalence of each pattern of attachment, which are probably attributable to cultural variations in childrearing practices. (Data from van IJzendoorn & Kroonenberg, 1988)

attachment is a universal feature of human development. However, studies have found some modest cultural variations in the proportion of infants who fall into the three attachment categories described by Ainsworth. Working mostly with white, middle-class subjects in the United States, researchers have found that 67% of infants display a secure attachment, 21% an avoidant attachment, and 12% an anxious-ambivalent attachment (the fourth attachment pattern mentioned earlier is not included here because it has only been tracked in a minority of cross-cultural studies) (van IJzendoorn & Sagi, 1999). Interestingly, studies in Japan and Germany have yielded somewhat different estimates of the prevalence of various types of attachment, as shown in Figure 11.6. Nonetheless, the differences are small and secure attachment appears to be the predominant type of attachment around the world.

Becoming Unique: Personality Development

How do individuals develop their unique constellations of personality traits over time? Many theories have addressed this question. The first major theory of personality development was constructed by Sigmund Freud back around 1900. As we'll discuss in Chapter 12, he claimed that the basic foundation of an individual's personality is firmly laid down by age 5. Half a century later, Erik Erikson (1963) proposed a sweeping revision of Freud's theory that has proven influential. Like Freud, Erikson concluded that events in early childhood leave a permanent stamp on adult personality. However, unlike Freud,

Erik Erikson

"Human personality in principle develops according to steps predetermined in the growing person's readiness to be driven toward, to be aware of, and to interact with a widening social radius."

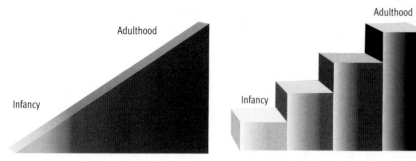

Adulthood

Infancy

Continuous development

Adulthood

Infancy

Discontinuous development (stages)

Figure 11.7

Stage theories of development. Some theories view development as a relatively continuous process, albeit not as smooth and perfectly linear as depicted on the left. In contrast, stage theories assume that development is marked by major discontinuities (as shown on the right) that bring fundamental, qualitative changes in capabilities or characteristic behavior.

Erikson theorized that personality continues to evolve over the entire life span.

Building on Freud's earlier work, Erikson devised a stage theory of personality development. As you'll see in reading this chapter, many theories describe development in terms of stages. **A *stage* is a developmental period during which characteristic patterns of behavior are exhibited and certain capacities become established.** Stage theories assume that (1) individuals must progress through specified stages in a particular order because each stage builds on the previous stage, (2) progress through these stages is strongly related to age, and (3) development is marked by major discontinuities that usher in dramatic transitions in behavior (see Figure 11.7).

Erikson's Stage Theory

9b

Erikson partitioned the life span into eight stages, each of which brings a *psychosocial crisis* involving transitions in important social relationships. According to Erikson, personality is shaped by how individuals deal with these psychosocial crises. Each crisis involves a struggle between two opposing tendencies, such as trust versus mistrust or initiative versus guilt, both of which are experienced by the person. Erikson described the stages in terms of these antagonistic tendencies, which represent personality traits that people display in varying degrees over the remainder of their lives. Although the names for Erikson's stages suggest either-or outcomes, he viewed each stage as a tug of war that determined the subsequent *balance* between opposing polarities in personality. All eight stages in Erikson's theory are charted in Figure 11.8. We describe the first four childhood stages here and discuss the remaining stages in the upcoming sections on adolescence and adulthood.

Trust Versus Mistrust. Erikson's first stage encompasses the first year of life, when an infant has to depend completely on adults to take care of its basic needs for such necessities as food, a warm blanket, and changed diapers. If an infant's basic biological needs are adequately met by his or her caregivers and sound attachments are formed, the child should develop an optimistic, trusting attitude toward the world. However, if the infant's basic needs are taken care of poorly, a more distrusting, pessimistic personality may result.

Autonomy Versus Shame and Doubt. Erikson's second stage unfolds during the second and third years of life, when parents begin toilet training and other efforts to regulate the child's behavior. The child must begin to take some personal responsibility for feeding, dressing, and bathing. If all goes well, he or she acquires a sense of self-sufficiency. But, if parents are never satisfied with the child's efforts and there are constant parent-child conflicts, the child may develop a sense of personal shame and self-doubt.

Figure 11.8

Erikson's stage theory. Erikson's theory of personality development posits that people evolve through eight stages over the life span. Each stage is marked by a *psychosocial crisis* that involves confronting a fundamental question, such as "Who am I and where am I going?" The stages are described in terms of alternative traits that are potential outcomes from the crises. Development is enhanced when a crisis is resolved in favor of the healthier alternative (which is listed first for each stage).

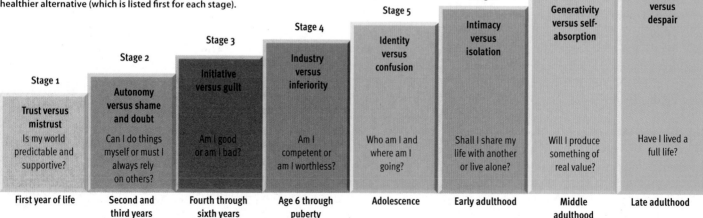

Stage 1	Stage 2	Stage 3	Stage 4	Stage 5	Stage 6	Stage 7	Stage 8
Trust versus mistrust	**Autonomy versus shame and doubt**	**Initiative versus guilt**	**Industry versus inferiority**	**Identity versus confusion**	**Intimacy versus isolation**	**Generativity versus self-absorption**	**Integrity versus despair**
Is my world predictable and supportive?	Can I do things myself or must I always rely on others?	Am I good or am I bad?	Am I competent or am I worthless?	Who am I and where am I going?	Shall I share my life with another or live alone?	Will I produce something of real value?	Have I lived a full life?
First year of life	Second and third years	Fourth through sixth years	Age 6 through puberty	Adolescence	Early adulthood	Middle adulthood	Late adulthood

Initiative Versus Guilt. In Erikson's third stage, lasting roughly from ages 3 to 6, children experiment and take initiatives that may sometimes conflict with their parents' rules. Overcontrolling parents may begin to instill feelings of guilt, and self-esteem may suffer. Parents need to support their children's emerging independence while maintaining appropriate controls. In the ideal situation, children will retain their sense of initiative while learning to respect the rights and privileges of other family members.

Industry Versus Inferiority. In the fourth stage (age 6 through puberty), the challenge of learning to function socially is extended beyond the family to the broader social realm of the neighborhood and school. Children who are able to function effectively in this less nurturant social sphere where productivity is highly valued should learn to value achievement and to take pride in accomplishment, resulting in a sense of competence. Or, if things don't go well in this broader social domain, they may develop a sense of inferiority.

Evaluating Erikson's Theory

The strength of Erikson's theory is that it accounts for both continuity and transition in personality development. It accounts for transition by showing how new challenges in social relations stimulate personality development throughout life. It accounts for continuity by drawing connections between early childhood experiences and aspects of adult personality. One measure of a theory's value is how much research it generates, and Erikson's theory continues to guide a fair amount of research (Thomas, 2005).

On the negative side of the ledger, Erikson's theory has depended heavily on illustrative case studies, which are open to varied interpretations (Thomas, 2005). Another weakness is that the theory provides an "idealized" description of "typical" developmental patterns. Thus, it's not well suited for explaining the enormous personality differences that exist among people. Inadequate explanation of individual differences is a common problem with stage theories of development. This shortcoming surfaces again in the next section, where we'll examine Jean Piaget's stage theory of cognitive development.

The Growth of Thought: Cognitive Development

 9c

Cognitive development refers to transitions in youngsters' patterns of thinking, including reasoning, remembering, and problem solving. The

investigation of cognitive development was dominated in most of the second half of the 20th century by the theory of Jean Piaget (Kessen, 1996). Much of our discussion of cognitive development is devoted to Piaget's theory and the research it generated, although we'll also delve into other approaches.

Overview of Piaget's Stage Theory

9c

Jean Piaget (1929, 1952, 1983) was an interdisciplinary scholar whose own cognitive development was exceptionally rapid. In his early 20s, after he had earned a doctorate in natural science and published a novel, Piaget turned his focus to psychology. He soon found himself administering intelligence tests to children to develop better test norms. In doing this testing, Piaget became intrigued by the reasoning underlying the children's *wrong* answers. He decided that measuring children's intelligence was less interesting than studying how children *use* their intelligence. He spent the rest of his life studying cognitive development. Many of his ideas were based on insights gleaned from careful observations of his own three children during their infancy.

Like Erikson's theory, Piaget's model is a *stage theory* of development. Piaget proposed that youngsters progress through four major stages of cognitive development, which are characterized by fundamentally different thought processes: (1) the *sensorimotor period* (birth to age 2), (2) the *preoperational period* (ages 2 to 7), (3) the *concrete operational period* (ages 7 to 11), and (4) the *formal operational period* (age 11 onward). Figure 11.9 on the next page provides an overview of each of these periods. Piaget regarded his age norms as approximations and acknowledged that transitional ages may vary, but he was convinced that all children progress through the stages of cognitive development in the same order.

According to Erik Erikson, school-age children face the challenge of learning how to function in social situations outside of their family, especially with peers and at school. If they succeed, they will develop a sense of competence; if they fail, they may feel inferior.

Jean Piaget

"It is virtually impossible to draw a clear line between innate and acquired behavior patterns."

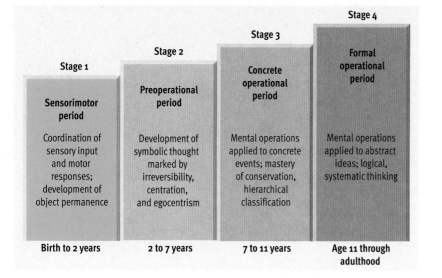

Figure 11.9

Piaget's stage theory. Piaget's theory of cognitive development identifies four stages marked by fundamentally different modes of thinking through which youngsters evolve. The approximate age norms and some key characteristics of thought at each stage are summarized here.

Sensorimotor Period. One of Piaget's foremost contributions was to greatly enhance our understanding of mental development in the earliest months of life. The first stage in his theory is the *sensorimotor period,* which lasts from birth to about age 2. Piaget called this stage *sensorimotor* because infants are developing the ability to coordinate their sensory input with their motor actions. The major development during the sensorimotor stage is the gradual appearance of symbolic thought. At the beginning of this stage, a child's behavior is dominated by innate reflexes. But by the end of the stage, the child can use mental symbols to represent objects (for example, a mental image of a favorite toy). The key to this transition is the acquisition of the concept of object permanence.

Object permanence develops when a child recognizes that objects continue to exist even when they are no longer visible. Although you surely take the permanence of objects for granted, infants aren't aware of this permanence at first. If you show a 4-month-old an eye-catching toy and then cover the toy with a pillow, the child will not attempt to search for the toy. Piaget inferred from this observation that the child does not understand that the toy continues to exist under the pillow. The notion of object permanence does not dawn on children overnight. According to Piaget, the first signs of this insight usually appear between 4 and 8 months of age, when children will often pursue an object that is *partially* covered in their presence. Progress is gradual, and Piaget believed that children typically don't master the concept of object permanence until they're about 18 months old.

Preoperational Period. During the *preoperational period,* which extends roughly from age 2 to age 7, children gradually improve in their use of mental images. Although progress in symbolic thought continues, Piaget emphasized the *shortcomings* in preoperational thought.

Consider a simple problem that Piaget presented to youngsters. He would take two identical beakers and fill each with the same amount of water. After a child had agreed that the two beakers contained the same amount of water, he would pour the water from one of the beakers into a much taller and thinner beaker (see **Figure 11.10**). He would then ask the child whether the two differently shaped beakers still contained the same amount of water. Confronted with a problem like this, children in the preoperational period generally said no. They typically focused on the higher water line in the taller beaker and insisted that there was more water in the slender beaker. They had not yet mastered the principle of conservation. *Conservation* **is Piaget's term for the awareness that physical quantities remain constant in spite of changes in their shape or appearance.**

Why are preoperational children unable to solve conservation problems? According to Piaget, their inability to understand conservation is caused by some basic flaws in preoperational thinking. These flaws include centration, irreversibility, and egocentrism.

Centration **is the tendency to focus on just one feature of a problem, neglecting other important aspects.** When working on the conservation problem with water, preoperational children tend to concentrate on the height of the water while ignoring the width. They have difficulty focusing on several aspects of a problem at once.

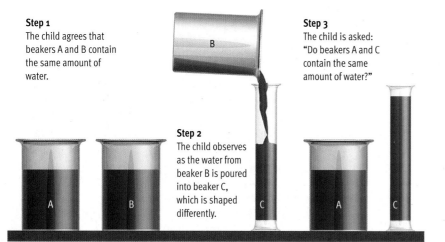

Step 1
The child agrees that beakers A and B contain the same amount of water.

Step 2
The child observes as the water from beaker B is poured into beaker C, which is shaped differently.

Step 3
The child is asked: "Do beakers A and C contain the same amount of water?"

Figure 11.10

Piaget's conservation task for liquid. After watching the transformation shown, a preoperational child will usually answer that the taller beaker contains more water. In contrast, a child in the concrete operational period tends to respond correctly, recognizing that the amount of water in beaker C remains the same as the amount in beaker A.

Irreversibility is the inability to envision reversing an action. Preoperational children can't mentally "undo" something. For instance, in grappling with the conservation of water, they don't think about what would happen if the water were poured back from the tall beaker into the original beaker.

Egocentrism in thinking is characterized by a limited ability to share another person's viewpoint. Indeed, Piaget felt that preoperational children fail to appreciate that there are points of view other than their own. For instance, if you ask a preoperational girl whether her sister has a sister, she'll probably say no if they are the only two girls in the family. She's unable to view sisterhood from her sister's perspective.

A notable feature of egocentrism is *animism*—the belief that all things are living, just like oneself. Thus, youngsters attribute lifelike, human qualities to inanimate objects, asking questions such as, "When does the ocean stop to rest?" or "Why does the wind get so mad?"

As you can see, Piaget emphasized the weaknesses apparent in preoperational thought. Indeed, that is why he called this stage *pre*operational. The ability to perform *operations*—internal transformations, manipulations, and reorganizations of mental structures—emerges in the next stage.

Concrete Operational Period.   The development of mental operations marks the beginning of the *concrete operational period,* which usually lasts from about age 7 to age 11. Piaget called this stage *concrete* operations because children can perform operations only on images of tangible objects and actual events.

Among the operations that children master during this stage are reversibility and decentration. *Reversibility* permits a child to mentally undo an action. *Decentration* allows the child to focus on more than one feature of a problem simultaneously. The newfound ability to coordinate several aspects of a problem helps the child appreciate that there are several ways to look at things. This ability in turn leads to a *decline in egocentrism* and *gradual mastery of conservation* as it applies to liquid, mass, number, volume, area, and length (see Figure 11.11).

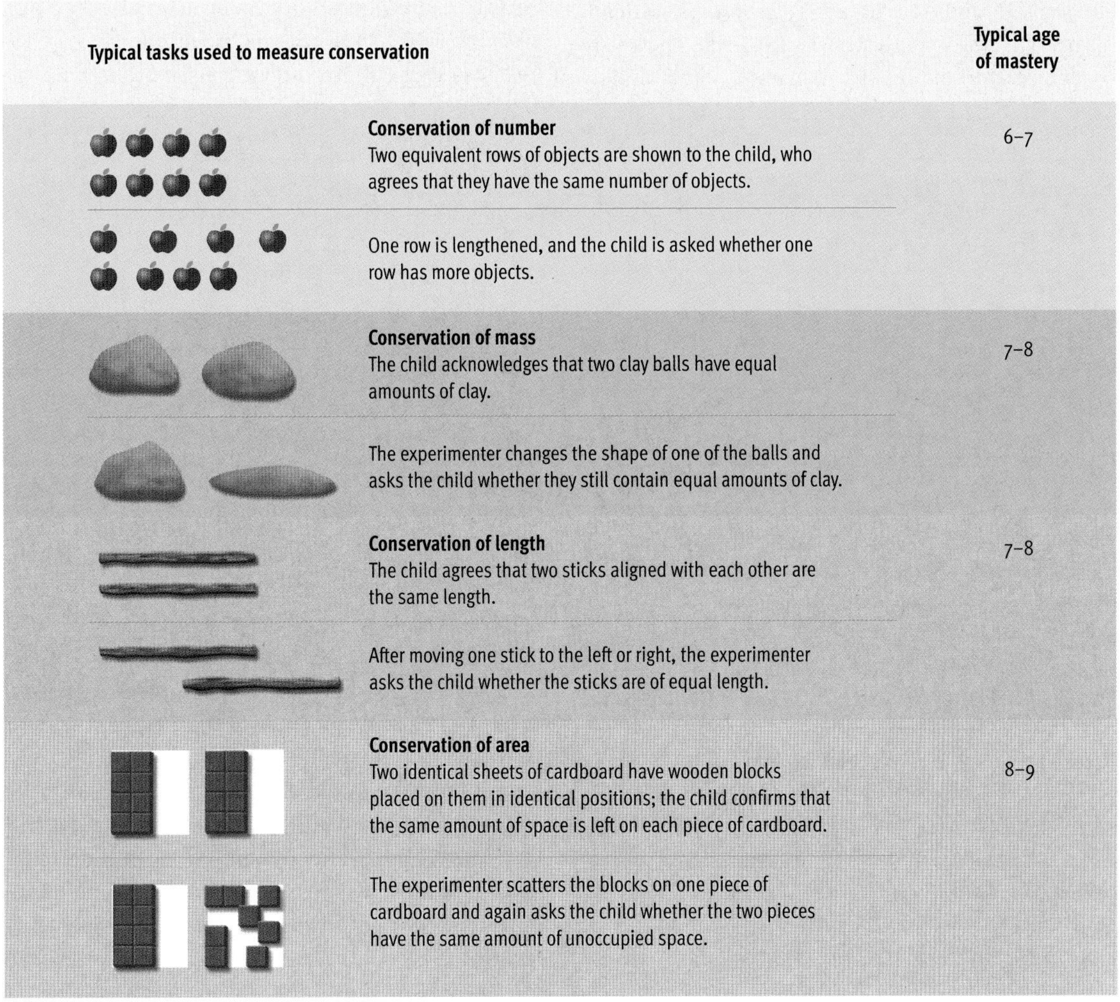

Typical tasks used to measure conservation	Typical age of mastery
Conservation of number Two equivalent rows of objects are shown to the child, who agrees that they have the same number of objects.	6–7
One row is lengthened, and the child is asked whether one row has more objects.	
Conservation of mass The child acknowledges that two clay balls have equal amounts of clay.	7–8
The experimenter changes the shape of one of the balls and asks the child whether they still contain equal amounts of clay.	
Conservation of length The child agrees that two sticks aligned with each other are the same length.	7–8
After moving one stick to the left or right, the experimenter asks the child whether the sticks are of equal length.	
Conservation of area Two identical sheets of cardboard have wooden blocks placed on them in identical positions; the child confirms that the same amount of space is left on each piece of cardboard.	8–9
The experimenter scatters the blocks on one piece of cardboard and again asks the child whether the two pieces have the same amount of unoccupied space.	

Figure 11.11
The gradual mastery of conservation. Children master conservation during the concrete operational period, but their mastery is gradual. As outlined here, children usually master the conservation of number at age 6 or 7, but they may not understand the conservation of area until age 8 or 9.

As children master concrete operations, they develop a variety of new problem-solving capacities. Let's examine another problem studied by Piaget. Give a preoperational child seven carnations and three daisies. Tell the child the names for the two types of flowers and ask the child to sort them into carnations and daisies. That should be no problem. Now ask the child whether there are more carnations or more daisies. Most children will correctly respond that there are more carnations. Now ask the child whether there are more carnations or more flowers. At this point, most preoperational children will stumble and respond incorrectly that there are more carnations than flowers. Generally, preoperational children can't handle *hierarchical classification* problems that require them to focus simultaneously on two levels of classification. However, the child who has advanced to the concrete operational stage is not as limited by centration and can work successfully with hierarchical classification problems.

Formal Operational Period. The final stage in Piaget's theory is the *formal operational period,* which typically begins around 11 years of age. In this stage, children begin to apply their operations to *abstract* concepts in addition to concrete objects. Indeed, during this stage, youngsters come to *enjoy* the heady contemplation of abstract concepts. Many adolescents spend hours mulling over hypothetical possibilities related to abstractions such as justice, love, and free will.

According to Piaget, youngsters graduate to relatively adult modes of thinking in the formal operations stage. He did *not* mean to suggest that no further cognitive development occurs once children reach this stage. However, he believed that after

children achieve formal operations, further developments in thinking are changes in *degree* rather than fundamental changes in the *nature* of thinking.

Adolescents in the formal operational period become more *systematic* in their problem-solving efforts. Children in earlier developmental stages tend to attack problems quickly, with a trial-and-error approach. In contrast, children who have achieved formal operations are more likely to think things through. They envision possible courses of action and try to use logic to reason out the likely consequences of each possible solution before they act. Thus, thought processes in the formal operational period can be characterized as abstract, systematic, logical, and reflective.

Evaluating Piaget's Theory

Jean Piaget made a landmark contribution to psychology's understanding of children in general and their cognitive development in particular (Beilin, 1992). He founded the field of cognitive development and fostered a new view of children that saw them as active agents constructing their own worlds (Fischer & Hencke, 1996). Above all else, he sought answers to new questions. As he acknowledged in a 1970 interview, "It's just that no adult ever had the idea of asking children about conservation. It was so obvious that if you change the shape of an object, the quantity will be conserved. Why ask a child? The novelty lay in asking the question" (Hall, 1987, p. 56). Piaget's theory guided an enormous volume of productive research that continues through today (Brainerd, 1996; Feldman, 2003). This research has supported many of Piaget's central propositions (Flavell, 1996). In such a far-reaching theory, however, there are bound to be some weak spots. Here are some of the criticisms of Piaget's theory:

1. In many areas, Piaget appears to have underestimated young children's cognitive development (Birney et al., 2005). For example, researchers have found evidence that children begin to develop object permanence much earlier than Piaget thought, perhaps as early as 3 to 4 months of age (Baillargeon, 2002; Wang, Baillargeon, & Paterson, 2005). Others have marshaled evidence that preoperational children exhibit less egocentrism than Piaget believed (Newcombe & Huttenlocher, 1992).

2. Piaget's model suffers from problems that plague most stage theories. Like Erikson, Piaget had little to say about individual differences in development (Siegler, 1994). Also, people often simultaneously display patterns of thinking that are characteristic of several stages. This "mixing" of stages and the fact that the transitions between stages are grad-

ual rather than abrupt call into question the value of organizing development in terms of stages (Courage & Howe, 2002; Krojgaard, 2005).

3. Piaget believed that his theory described universal processes that should lead children everywhere to progress through uniform stages of thinking at roughly the same ages. Subsequent research has shown that the *sequence* of stages is largely invariant, but the *timetable* that children follow in passing through these stages varies considerably across cultures (Dasen, 1994; Rogoff, 2003). Thus, Piaget underestimated the influence of cultural factors on cognitive development. Indeed, it is probably fair to say that Piaget underestimated the importance of environmental factors in general while focusing too heavily on the role of maturation (Birney et al., 2005; Maratsos, 2007).

Vygotsky's Sociocultural Theory

In recent decades, as the limitations and weaknesses of Piaget's ideas have become more apparent, some developmental researchers have looked elsewhere for theoretical guidance. Ironically, the theory that has recently inspired the greatest interest—Lev Vygotsky's *sociocultural theory*—dates back to around the same time that Piaget began formulating his theory (1920s–1930s). Vygotsky was a prominent Russian psychologist whose research ended prematurely in 1934 when he died of tuberculosis at the age of 37. Western scientists had little exposure to his ideas until the 1960s, and it was only in 1986 that a complete version of his principal book (Vygotsky, 1934) was published in English. Working in a perilous political climate in the post-Revolution Soviet Union, Vygotsky had to devise a theory that would not be incompatible with the Marxist social philosophy that ruled communist thinking (Thomas, 2005). Given the constraints placed on his theorizing, one might expect that 70 years later his ideas would not resonate with contemporary psychologists in capitalist societies, but the reality is just the opposite, as his theory has become very influential (Daniels, 2005; Feldman, 2003).

Vygotsky's and Piaget's perspectives on cognitive development have much in common, but they also differ in several important respects (DeVries, 2000; Matusov & Hayes, 2000; Rowe & Wertsch, 2002). First, in Piaget's theory, cognitive development is primarily fueled by individual children's active exploration of the world around them. The child is viewed as the agent of change. In contrast, Vygotsky places enormous emphasis on how children's cognitive development is fueled by social interactions with parents, teachers, and older children who can provide invaluable guidance (Hedegaard, 2005). Second,

© Richard Hutchings/Photo Researchers, Inc.

Piaget viewed cognitive development as a universal process that should unfold in largely the same way across widely disparate cultures. Vygotsky, on the other hand, asserted that culture exerts great influence over how cognitive growth unfolds (Wertsch & Tulviste, 2005). For example, the cognitive skills acquired in literate cultures that rely on schools for training will differ from those acquired in tribal societies where there may be no formal schooling. Third, Piaget viewed children's gradual mastery of language as just another aspect of cognitive development, whereas Vygotsky argued that language acquisition plays a crucial, central role in fostering cognitive development (Kozulin, 2005).

According to Vygotsky, children acquire most of their culture's cognitive skills and problem-solving strategies through collaborative dialogues with more experienced members of their society. He saw cognitive development as more like an *apprenticeship* than a journey of individual discovery. His emphasis on the social origins of cognitive development is apparent in his concept of the *zone of proximal development*. The *zone of proximal development (ZPD)* is **the gap between what a learner can accomplish alone and what he or she can achieve with guidance from more skilled partners.** For example, a young child learning to run a personal computer, working solo, will be stymied in many ways and may

Vygotsky and Piaget differ about the importance of private speech, young children's tendency to talk to themselves as they go about their business. Piaget viewed private speech as insignificant, whereas Vygotsky asserted that children use private speech to regulate their actions and plan their strategies.

Archives of the History of American Psychology, University of Akron, Akron, Ohio

Lev Vygotsky

"In the process of development the child not only masters the items of cultural experience but the habits and forms of cultural behaviour, the cultural methods of reasoning."

web link 11.3

Theories of Development

Maintained by the Psychology Department at George Mason University, this site is an excellent resource, providing links to many other sites that focus on influential theories of human development. Starting here, a visitor can learn a great deal about the ideas of Erik Erikson, Jean Piaget, Lev Vygotsky, and Lawrence Kohlberg.

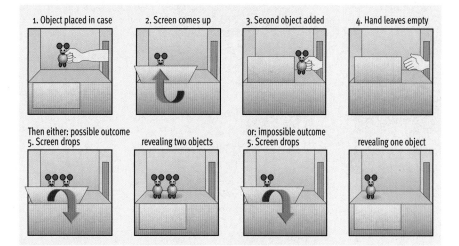

1. Object placed in case   2. Screen comes up   3. Second object added   4. Hand leaves empty

Then either: possible outcome
5. Screen drops   revealing two objects   or: impossible outcome
5. Screen drops   revealing one object

Figure 11.12

The procedure used to test infants' understanding of number. To see if 5-month-old infants have some appreciation of addition and subtraction, Wynn (1992, 1996) showed them sequences of events like those depicted here. If children express surprise (primarily assessed by time spent looking) when the screen drops and they see only one object, this result suggests that they understand that 1 + 1 = 2. Wynn and others have found that infants seem to have some primitive grasp of simple addition and subtraction.

SOURCE: Adapted from Wynn, K. (1992). Addition and subtraction by human infants. *Nature, 358,* 749–750. Copyright © 1992 Macmillan Magazines, Ltd. Reprinted with permission.

ment (Feldman, 2003). This research has provided empirical support for many of Vygotsky's ideas (Rogoff, 1998; Winsler, 2003). Like Piaget's theory, Vygotsky's perspective promises to enrich our understanding of how children's thinking develops and matures.

Are Some Cognitive Abilities Innate?

The frequent finding that Piaget underestimated infants' cognitive abilities has led to a rash of studies suggesting that infants have a surprising grasp of many complex concepts. Studies have demonstrated that infants understand basic properties of objects and some of the rules that govern them (Baillargeon, 2004). At 3 to 4 months of age, infants understand that objects are distinct entities with boundaries, that objects move in continuous paths, that one solid object cannot pass through another, that an object cannot pass through an opening that is smaller than the object, and that objects on slopes roll down rather than up (Baillargeon, 2008; Spelke & Newport, 1998).

In this line of research, perhaps the most stunning discovery has been the finding that *infants seem to exhibit surprisingly sophisticated numerical abilities* (Lipton & Spelke, 2004; Wood & Spelke, 2005). For example, Karen Wynn (1992, 1996) has conducted some groundbreaking studies of infants' numerical capabilities. She demonstrated that if 5-month-old infants are shown a sequence of events in which one object is added to another behind a screen, they expect to see two objects when the screen is removed (see Figure 11.12). And they exhibit surprise—in the form of longer looking—when their expectation is violated. This finding suggested that the infants understood that 1 + 1 = 2. Similar manipulations in subsequent studies suggested that infants also understand that 2 – 1 = 1, that 2 + 1 = 3, and that 3 – 1 = 2 (Hauser & Carey, 1998; Wynn, 1998). Thus, Wynn concluded that infants have a primitive "number sense." However, skeptics raised some questions about the interpretation of these surprising findings, which brings us to our Featured Study for this chapter.

quickly reach a point at which progress is stalled. But the same child may progress much further with a judicious hint here or there from an experienced computer user. The ZPD for a task is the area in which new cognitive growth is likely. Vygotsky's emphasis on the primacy of language is reflected in his discussion of *private speech.* Preschool children talk aloud to themselves a lot as they go about their activities. Piaget viewed this speech as egocentric and insignificant. Vygotsky argued that children use this private speech to plan their strategies, regulate their actions, and accomplish their goals. As children grow older, this private speech is internalized and becomes the normal verbal dialogue that people have with themselves as they go about their business. Thus, language increasingly serves as the *foundation* for youngsters' cognitive processes.

Vygotsky's sociocultural theory is guiding a great deal of contemporary research on cognitive develop-

SOURCE: McCrink, K., & Wynn, K. (2004). Large-number addition and subtraction by 9-month-old infants. *Psychological Science, 15,* 776–781.

FEATURED STUDY

Can Infants Do Arithmetic?

Critics of Wynn's previous research argued that alternative explanations could account for her findings. Specifically, they suggested that infants' surprise in response to incorrect numerical outcomes could reflect the operation of a simple object-tracking system rather than a capacity to work with numbers (Simon, 1997; Trick & Pylyshyn, 1994). According to this view, infants attempt to keep track of ob-

jects in their view; they look longer at incorrect outcomes because these outcomes produce a mismatch between the "object files" they stored in memory and the objects presented visually. In other words, their surprise does not mean that they are doing arithmetic. In the present study, McCrink and Wynn set out to conduct an experiment that might rule out this potentially plausible explanation for earlier findings. They note that research on infants' object-tracking capabilities indicates that they are able to track only a maximum of four objects simultaneously. So, the object-tracking explanation is plausible when problems involve four or fewer elements, as in previous research, but it would not be a viable alternative explanation if earlier findings could be replicated with larger numbers. Thus, the present study tested the hypothesis that infants would look longer at wrong outcomes for the arithmetic operations of 5 + 5 and 10 − 5.

Method

Participants. The final sample consisted of twenty-six 9-month-old infants (13 males and 13 females) whose parents responded to recruitment efforts in the southeastern Connecticut area. Some additional infants were tested but had to be excluded because they were too fussy or uncooperative to complete the experiment. Half of the subjects were presented with an addition problem (5 + 5) and the other half were presented with a subtraction problem (10 − 5).

Procedure. The infants sat in a carseat in front of a computer monitor with a parent present, but the parent was facing away from the computer. The numerical scenarios were presented on the computer screen. A small curtain was lowered to block the infant's view of the computer at the end of each trial and raised to begin the next trial. A hidden observer monitored how long the infants looked when the final outcomes in the numerical sequences were revealed.

Materials. In the addition scenario, five rectangles were dropped into view and then moved to the right side of the screen where they were covered by a panel that rose up from the bottom. Then five more rectangles dropped into view and migrated behind the panel. Finally, the panel moved downward to reveal either 10 rectangles (the correct outcome) or only 5 rectangles (the incorrect outcome). In the subtraction scenario, 10 rectangles dropped into view and moved behind the panel. Then 5 rectangles moved out from behind the panel and migrated off the screen. Finally, the panel moved downward to reveal either 10 rectangles (the incorrect outcome) or 5 rectangles (the correct outcome).

Results

The infants who saw the addition operation looked longer at the wrong outcome (mean = 10.28 seconds) than right outcome (mean = 7.35 seconds). Likewise, the subjects who viewed the subtraction sequence looked at the

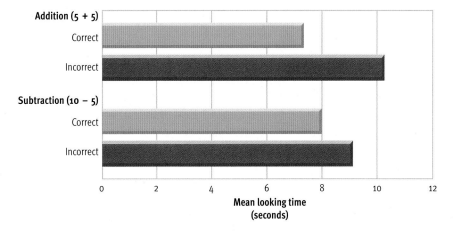

Figure 11.13

Mean looking time for correct and incorrect numerical operations. As predicted, 9-month-old infants shown correct and incorrect numerical operations looked longer at incorrect outcomes, suggesting that they were surprised by the wrong outcomes. (Data from McCrink & Wynn, 2004)

wrong outcome longer than the right outcome, although the difference was not as large as in the addition scenario (see **Figure 11.13**).

Discussion

The results suggest that 9-month-old infants have some understanding that 5 + 5 = 10 and that 10 − 5 = 5. Given the larger size of these numbers (in comparison to previous research), these results cannot be attributed to the operation of infants' object-tracking system. Hence, the authors conclude that the infants "were performing numerical computations." They also note that their findings support the idea that the human brain may have an innate ability to work with numbers.

Comment

This study was featured primarily because the results border on amazing. Prior to Wynn's breakthrough research in the 1990s, few scientists would have given any credence to the hypothesis that infants could understand mathematical operations that would make a kindergartner proud. The study also illustrates the typical ebb and flow of scientific progress, which often involves someone reporting an interesting finding, only to have its meaning challenged by a skeptic who suggests an alternative explanation, which leads to further research that pits the competing explanations against each other.

Karen Wynn

"Human infants are able to represent and reason about number. . . . humans possess a mental 'number mechanism,' designed through natural selection."

Again and again in recent years, research has shown that infants appear to understand surprisingly complex concepts that they have had virtually no opportunity to learn about. These findings have led some theorists to conclude that certain basic cognitive abilities are biologically built into humans'

neural architecture. The theorists who have reached this conclusion tend to fall into two camps: nativists and evolutionary theorists. The *nativists* simply assert that humans are prewired to readily understand certain concepts without making any assumptions about *why* humans are prewired in these ways

(Spelke & Kinzler, 2007; Spelke & Newport, 1998). Their principal interest is to sort out the complex matter of what is prewired and what isn't.

Evolutionary theorists agree with the nativists that humans are prewired for certain cognitive abilities, but they are keenly interested in *why*. As you might expect, they maintain that this wiring is a product of natural selection, and they strive to understand its adaptive significance (Hauser & Carey, 1998; Wynn, 1998). For example, evolutionary theorists are interested in how basic addition-subtraction abilities may have enhanced our hominid ancestors' success in hunting, foraging, and social bargaining. The evolutionary theorists also argue that the findings on infants' surprising abilities support their view that *the human mind is modular*—that it is made up of domain-specific modules that have been crafted by natural selection to solve specific adaptive problems, such as recognizing faces, discriminating simple speech sounds, and understanding basic properties of objects (Gelman & Williams, 1998; Leslie, 1994).

The Development of Moral Reasoning

In Europe, a woman was near death from cancer. One drug might save her, a form of radium that a druggist in the same town had recently discovered. The druggist was charging $2,000, ten times what the drug cost him to make. The sick woman's husband, Heinz, went to everyone he knew to borrow the money, but he could only get together about half of what it cost. He told the druggist that his wife was dying and asked him to sell it cheaper or let him pay later. But the druggist said, "No." The husband got desperate and broke into the man's store to steal the drug for his wife. Should the husband have done that? Why? (Kohlberg, 1969, p. 379)

What's your answer to Heinz's dilemma? Would you have answered the same way three years ago? Can you guess what you might have said at age 6? By presenting similar dilemmas to participants and studying their responses, Lawrence Kohlberg (1976, 1984; Colby & Kohlberg, 1987) developed a model of *moral development.* What is morality? That's a complicated question that philosophers have debated for centuries. For our purposes, it will suffice to say that *morality* involves the ability to distinguish right from wrong and to behave accordingly.

Kohlberg's Stage Theory

Kohlberg's model is the most influential of a number of competing theories that attempt to explain how youngsters develop a sense of right and wrong. His work was derived from much earlier work by Piaget (1932). Piaget theorized that moral development is determined by cognitive development. By this he meant that the way individuals think out moral issues depends on their level of cognitive development. This assumption provided the springboard for Kohlberg's research.

Kohlberg's theory focuses on moral *reasoning* rather than overt *behavior*. This point is best illustrated by describing Kohlberg's method of investigation. He presented his participants with thorny moral questions such as Heinz's dilemma, then asked the subjects what the actor in the dilemma should do, and more important, why. It was the *why* that interested Kohlberg. He examined the nature and progression of subjects' moral reasoning.

The result of this work is the stage theory of moral reasoning outlined in Figure 11.14. Kohlberg found that individuals progress through a series of three levels of moral development, each of which can be broken into two sublevels, yielding a total of six stages. Each stage represents a different approach to thinking about right and wrong.

Younger children at the *preconventional level* think in terms of external authority. Acts are wrong be-

Figure 11.14

Kohlberg's stage theory. Kohlberg's model posits three levels of moral reasoning, each of which can be divided into two stages. This chart summarizes some of the key facets in how individuals think about right and wrong at each stage.

Stage 1	Stage 2	Stage 3	Stage 4	Stage 5	Stage 6
Punishment orientation	**Naive reward orientation**	**Good boy/good girl orientation**	**Authority orientation**	**Social contract orientation**	**Individual principles and conscience orientation**
Right and wrong is determined by what is punished.	Right and wrong is determined by what is rewarded.	Right and wrong is determined by close others' approval or disapproval.	Right and wrong is determined by society's rules, and laws, which should be obeyed rigidly.	Right and wrong is determined by society's rules, which are viewed as fallible rather than absolute.	Right and wrong is determined by abstract ethical principles that emphasize equity and justice.
Preconventional level		**Conventional level**		**Postconventional level**	

cause they are punished, or right because they lead to positive consequences. Older children who have reached the *conventional level* of moral reasoning see rules as necessary for maintaining social order. They therefore accept these rules as their own. They "internalize" these rules not to avoid punishment but to be virtuous and win approval from others. Moral thinking at this stage is relatively inflexible. Rules are viewed as absolute guidelines that should be enforced rigidly.

During adolescence, some youngsters move on to the *postconventional level,* which involves working out a personal code of ethics. Acceptance of rules is less rigid, and moral thinking shows some flexibility. Subjects at the postconventional level allow for the possibility that someone might not comply with some of society's rules if they conflict with personal ethics. For example, participants at this level might applaud a newspaper reporter who goes to jail rather than reveal a source of information who was promised anonymity.

Evaluating Kohlberg's Theory

How has Kohlberg's theory fared in research? The central ideas have received reasonable support. Progress in moral reasoning is indeed closely tied to cognitive development (Walker, 1988). Studies also show that youngsters generally do progress through Kohlberg's stages of moral reasoning in the order that he proposed (Walker, 1989). Furthermore, relations between age and level of moral reasoning are in the predicted directions (Rest, 1986). Repre-

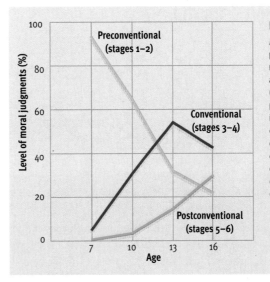

Figure 11.15

Age and moral reasoning. The percentages of different types of moral judgments made by subjects at various ages are graphed here (based on Kohlberg, 1963, 1969). As predicted, preconventional reasoning declines as children mature, conventional reasoning increases during middle childhood, and postconventional reasoning begins to emerge during adolescence. But at each age, children display a mixture of various levels of moral reasoning.

sentative age trends are shown in Figure 11.15: As children get older, stage 1 and stage 2 reasoning declines, while stage 3 and stage 4 reasoning increases. However, there is great variation in the age at which individuals reach specific stages, and very few people reach stage 6, which raises doubts about its validity (Lapsley, 2006). Finally, evidence suggests that moral *reasoning* is predictive of moral *behavior,* although the association is disappointingly modest (Bruggerman & Hart, 1996). That is, youngsters who are at higher stages of moral development are somewhat more likely to be altruistic, conscientious, and honest than youngsters at lower stages (Fabes et al., 1999; Taylor & Walker, 1997). Although these

web link 11.4

Parenthood.com

Parents are faced with all sorts of questions about development; this site provides a variety of useful resources for answering some of those questions. Topics tend to be practical, ranging from potty training to how much back talk parents should tolerate.

concept check 11.3

Analyzing Moral Reasoning

Check your understanding of Kohlberg's theory of moral development by analyzing hypothetical responses to the following moral dilemma.

A midwest biologist has conducted numerous studies demonstrating that simple organisms such as worms and paramecia can learn through conditioning. It occurs to her that perhaps she could condition fertilized human ova, to provide a dramatic demonstration that abortions destroy adaptable, living human organisms. This possibility appeals to her, as she is ardently opposed to abortion. However, there is no way to conduct the necessary research on human ova without sacrificing the lives of potential human beings. She desperately wants to conduct the research, but obviously, the sacrifice of human ova is fundamentally incompatible with her belief in the sanctity of human life. What should she do? Why? [Submitted by a student (age 13) to Professor Barbara Banas at Monroe Community College]

In the spaces on the left of each numbered response, indicate the level of moral reasoning shown, choosing from the following: (a) preconventional level, (b) conventional level, or (c) postconventional level. The answers are in Appendix A.

_____ 1. She should do the research. Although it's wrong to kill, there's a greater good that can be realized through the research.

_____ 2. She shouldn't do the research because people will think that she's a hypocrite and condemn her.

_____ 3. She should do the research because she may become rich and famous as a result.

NON SEQUITUR

findings support the utility of Kohlberg's model, like all influential theorists, he has his critics. They have raised the following issues:

1. It's not unusual to find that a person shows signs of several adjacent levels of moral reasoning at a particular point in development (Walker & Taylor, 1991). As we noted in the critique of Piaget, this mixing of stages is a problem for virtually all stage theories.

2. Evidence is mounting that Kohlberg's dilemmas may not be valid indicators of moral development in some cultures (Nucci, 2002). Some critics believe that the value judgments built into Kohlberg's theory reflect a liberal, individualistic ideology characteristic of modern Western nations that is much more culture-specific than Kohlberg appreciated (Miller, 2006).

3. A consensus is building that Kohlberg's theory led to a constricted focus on reasoning about interpersonal conflicts while ignoring many other important aspects of moral development (Walker, 2007). Thus, contemporary researchers are increasingly turning their attention to other dimensions of moral development, including the development of empathy (Eisenberg, Spinrad, & Sadovsky, 2006), the emergence of conscience (Grusec, 2006), the development of prosocial (helping, sharing) behavior (Carlo, 2006), and the significance of moral emotions (such as shame and guilt) (Tangney, Stuewig, & Mashek, 2007).

REVIEW of Key Learning Goals

11.3 Motor development follows cephalocaudal (head-to-foot) and proximodistal (center-outward) trends. Early motor development depends on both maturation and learning. Developmental norms for motor skills and other types of development are only group averages. Cultural variations in the pacing of motor development demonstrate the importance of learning.

11.4 In a longitudinal study, Thomas and Chess found that most infants could be classified as easy, slow-to-warm-up, or difficult children during the first few months of life. Kagan's research suggests that variations in inhibited-uninhibited temperament are fairly stable and have a genetic basis. Infant temperament may lay the foundation for adult personality.

11.5 Harlow's work with monkeys undermined the reinforcement explanation of attachment. Bowlby proposed an evolutionary explanation that has been very influential. Infant-mother attachments fall into four categories: secure, anxious-ambivalent, avoidant, and disorganized-disoriented. Research shows that attachment emerges out of an interplay between infant and mother. A secure attachment fosters self-esteem, persistence, curiosity, and self-reliance, among other desirable traits.

11.6 Some studies suggest that extensive dependence on day care might disrupt the attachment process. But the negative effects of day care appear to be small and inconsistent, while high-quality day care is associated with some positive effects. Cultural variations in childrearing can affect the patterns of attachment seen in a society, but secure attachment is predominant around the world.

11.7 Like other stage theories, Erikson's theory of personality development proposes that individuals evolve through a series of stages over the life span. In each of the eight stages the person wrestles with two opposing tendencies evoked by that stage's psychosocial crisis.

11.8 According to Piaget's theory of cognitive development, the key advance during the sensorimotor period is the child's gradual recognition of the permanence of objects. The preoperational period is marked by certain deficiencies in thinking—notably, centration, irreversibility, and egocentrism. During the concrete operations period, children develop the ability to perform operations on mental representations. The stage of formal operations ushers in more abstract, systematic, and logical thought. Piaget may have underestimated some aspects of children's cognitive development, and his theory, like other stage theories, does not explain individual differences very well.

11.9 Vygotsky's sociocultural theory maintains that children's cognitive development is fueled by social interactions with parents and others and that culture influences how cognitive growth unfolds. Recent research has shown that infants appear to understand surprisingly complex concepts that they have had virtually no opportunity to learn about. For example, the Featured Study showed that infants can add and subtract small numbers. Findings such as these have led some theorists to conclude that basic cognitive abilities are biologically built into humans' neural architecture.

11.10 According to Kohlberg, moral reasoning progresses through six stages that are related to age and determined by cognitive development. Age-related progress in moral reasoning has been found in research, although a great deal of overlap occurs between adjacent stages, and Kohlberg's theory is more culture-specific than he realized.

The Transition of Adolescence

Adolescence is a transitional period between childhood and adulthood. Its age boundaries are not exact, but in our society adolescence is thought to begin around age 13 and end at about age 21–22. Although most contemporary societies have at least a brief period of adolescence, it has *not* been universal historically or across cultures (Larson & Wilson, 2004; Schlegel & Barry, 1991). In some societies, young people used to move directly from childhood to adulthood. A protracted period of adolescence emerged in conjunction with industrialization. In modern societies, rapid technological progress made lengthy education, and therefore prolonged economic dependence, the norm. Thus, in our own culture, middle school, high school, and college students often have a "marginal" status. They become physiologically mature and capable of reproduction. Yet they have not achieved the emotional and economic independence from their parents that are the hallmarks of adulthood. Let's begin our discussion of adolescent development with its most visible aspect: the physical changes that transform the body of a child into that of an adult.

Physiological Changes

Recall for a moment your junior high school days. Didn't it seem that your body grew so fast about this time that your clothes just couldn't "keep up"? This phase of rapid growth in height and weight is called the *adolescent growth spurt*. Brought on by hormonal changes, it typically starts at about 10 years of age in girls and about two years later in boys (Archibald, Graber, & Brooks-Dunn, 2003). Scientists are not sure about what triggers the hormonal changes that underlie the adolescent growth spurt, but evidence suggests that rising levels of *leptin,* the recently discovered hormone that reflects the body's fat cell storage (see Chapter 10), may play a role (Shalitin & Phillip, 2003).

The term *pubescence* **is used to describe the two-year span preceding puberty during which the changes leading to physical and sexual maturity take place.** In addition to growing taller and heavier during pubescence, children begin to develop the physical features that characterize adults of their respective sexes. These features are termed *secondary sex characteristics*—**physical features that distinguish one sex from the other but that are not essential for reproduction.** For example, males go through a voice change, develop facial hair, and experience greater skeletal and muscle growth in the upper torso, leading to broader shoulders (see Figure 11.16). Females experience breast growth and a widening of the pelvic bones plus increased fat deposits in this area, resulting in wider hips (Susman & Rogol, 2004).

Note, however, that the capacity to reproduce is not attained in pubescence. This comes later.

Key Learning Goals

11.11 Review the physiological changes of puberty, and discuss the ramifications of early versus late maturation.

11.12 Summarize research on neural development in adolescence.

11.13 Assess the claim that adolescence is a time of turmoil.

11.14 Discuss some common patterns of identity formation in adolescence.

11.15 Articulate the chief characteristics of emerging adulthood as described by Arnett.

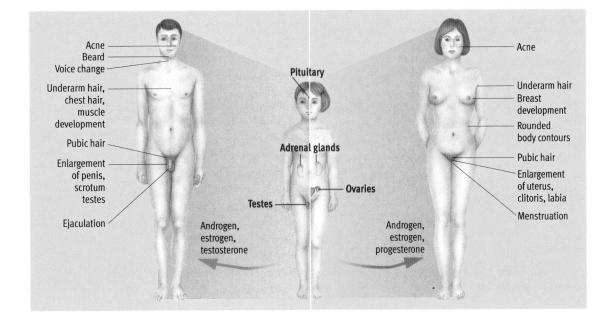

Figure 11.16

Physical development at puberty. Hormonal changes during puberty lead not only to a growth spurt but also to the development of secondary sex characteristics. The pituitary gland sends signals to the adrenal glands and gonads (ovaries and testes), which secrete hormones responsible for various physical changes that differentiate males and females.

Puberty is the stage during which sexual functions reach maturity, which marks the beginning of adolescence. It is during puberty that the *primary sex characteristics*—the structures necessary for reproduction—develop fully. In the male these include the testes, penis, and related internal structures. In the female they include the ovaries, vagina, uterus, and other internal structures.

In females, the onset of puberty is typically signaled by *menarche*—the first occurrence of menstruation, which reflects the culmination of a series of hormonal changes (Pinyerd & Zipf, 2005). American girls typically reach menarche at ages 12–13, with further sexual maturation continuing until approximately age 16 (Susman, Dorn, & Schiefelbein, 2003). American boys typically experience *spermarche—the first occurrence of ejaculation*, at ages 13–14, with further sexual maturation continuing until approximately 18 (Archibald et al., 2003).

Interestingly, *generational* changes have occurred in the timing of puberty over the last 150 years. Today's adolescents begin puberty at a younger age, and complete it more rapidly, than their counterparts in earlier generations (Bellis, Downing, & Ashton, 2006). This trend appears to be occurring in both sexes, although more precise data are available for females, as the marker for puberty (menarche) is more readily apparent in females (Herman-Giddens, 2006). The reasons for this trend are the subject of debate, but it seems likely that a multiplicity of factors have contributed (Archibald et al., 2003; Bellis et al. 2006). The most obvious potential causes are widespread improvements in nutrition and medical care, which would probably explain why the trend toward younger puberty has been limited to modern, "developed" countries. The earlier onset of puberty may also be attributable to increases in family-related stress. Evolutionary theorists have hypothesized that humans have been programmed by natural selection to respond to insensitive parenting (rejection, family discord, father absence) with accelerated sexual maturation (Belsky, 1999; Ellis, 2004). Research on individual variations in the onset of puberty has supported this hypothesis for females (Belsky, 2007). So, increases in family stress and instability over the last century may be a contributing factor to generational changes in the onset of puberty.

The timing of puberty varies from one adolescent to the next over a range of about 5 years (ages 10–15 for girls, 11–16 for boys). Generally, *girls who mature early and boys who mature late seem to experience more subjective distress and emotional difficulty with the transition to adolescence* (Susman et al., 2003). However, in both males and females, early maturation is associated with greater use of alcohol and drugs, more

The timing of sexual maturation can have important implications for adolescents. Youngsters who mature unusually early or unusually late often feel uneasy about this transition.

high-risk behavior, greater aggression, and more delinquency (Lynne et al., 2007; Steinberg & Morris, 2001). Among females, early maturation is also correlated with earlier experience of intercourse, more unwanted pregnancies, a greater risk for eating problems, and a variety of psychological disorders (Archibald et al., 2003). Thus, we might speculate that early maturation often thrusts both sexes (but especially females) toward the adult world too soon.

Neural Development

Recent years have brought significant advances in the study of adolescents' neural development (Geidd, 2008; McAnarney, 2008). The size of the human brain does not increase significantly after age 5 (Durston et al., 2001). Given this fact, it was widely assumed until recently that the brain did not undergo much development after middle childhood. However, the increased availability of MRI scans, which can provide exquisitely detailed images of the brain, has permitted neuroscientists to conduct entirely new investigations of whether there are age-related changes in brain structure. These studies have uncovered some interesting developmental trends during adolescence. For example, the volume of white matter in the brain grows throughout adolescence (Schmithorst et al., 2002). This means that *neurons are becoming more myelinated* (see Chapter 3), which presumably leads to enhanced conductivity and connectivity in the brain. In contrast, gray mat-

ZITS

ZITS by Scott and Borgman. © 2008 by ZITS Partnership, King Features Syndicate, Inc. Reprinted by permission.

ter decreases in volume (Toga, Thompson, & Sowell, 2006). This finding is thought to reflect the process of *synaptic pruning*—the elimination of less-active synapses—which plays a key role in the formation of neural networks (see Chapter 3).

Perhaps the most interesting discovery about the adolescent brain has been that increased myelinization and synaptic pruning are most pronounced in the *prefrontal cortex* (see **Figure 11.17**; Keating, 2004). Thus, *the prefrontal cortex appears to be the last area of the brain to fully mature,* and this maturation may not be complete until one's mid-20s (Gogtay et al., 2004). Much has been made of this finding, because the prefrontal cortex has been characterized as an "executive control center" that is crucial to high-level cognitive functions, such as planning, organizing, emotional regulation, and response inhibition (Nelson et al., 2002). Theorists have suggested that the immaturity of the prefrontal cortex may explain why risky behavior (such as reckless driving, experimentation with drugs, dangerous stunts, binge drinking, unprotected sex, and so forth) peaks during adolescence (Compas, 2004; Dahl, 2003).

That said, Kuhn (2006) notes that media pundits have gotten carried away, blaming the immaturity of the adolescent prefrontal cortex for "just about everything about teens that adults have found perplexing" (p. 59). Other factors also contribute to risky behavior during adolescence. One of these factors is susceptibility to peer influence (Steinberg, 2007). Adolescents spend a great deal of time with their peers. One elegant laboratory study found that the presence of peers more than doubled the number of risks taken by teenagers in a video game involving in-the-moment decisions about crash risks (Gardner & Steinberg, 2005). In contrast, older adults' risk taking was not elevated by the presence of peers (see **Figure 11.18**).

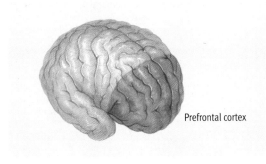

Figure 11.17

The prefrontal cortex. Recent research suggests that neural development continues throughout adolescence. Moreover, the chief site for much of this development is the prefrontal cortex, which appears to be the last area of the brain to mature fully. This discovery may have fascinating implications for understanding the adolescent brain, as the prefrontal cortex appears to play a key role in emotional regulation and self-control.

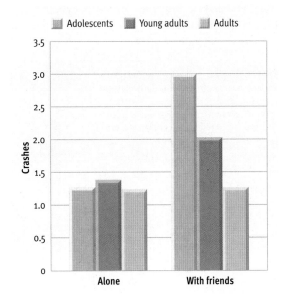

Figure 11.18

Peer influence on risk taking. Gardner and Steinberg (2005) had adolescents, young adults, and adults play a video game involving simulated driving in which participants had to make quick decisions about crash risks. The dependent variable, which indexed subjects' risk taking, was the number of crashes experienced. Some participants played the video game alone, whereas others played in the presence of peers. The data showed that the presence of peers increased risk taking by young adults moderately and by adolescents considerably, but adults' risk taking was unaffected. These findings suggest that susceptibility to peer influence may increase risky behavior among adolescents and young adults.

SOURCE: Adapted from Steinberg, L. (2007). Risk taking in adolescence: New perspectives from brain and behavioral science. *Current Directions in Psychological Science,* 16, 55–59. Copyright © 2007 Blackwell Publishing.

Time of Turmoil?

Back around the beginning of the 20th century, G. Stanley Hall (1904), one of psychology's great pioneers (see Chapter 1), proposed that the adolescent years are characterized by convulsive instability and disturbing inner turmoil. Hall attributed this turmoil to adolescents' erratic physical changes and resultant confusion about self-image. Over the decades, many theorists have agreed with Hall's characterization of adolescence as a stormy period.

Statistics on *adolescent suicide* would seem to support the idea that adolescence is a time marked by turmoil, but the figures can be interpreted in various ways. On the one hand, suicide rates among adolescents have risen alarmingly in recent decades. On the other hand, even with this steep increase, suicide rates for adolescents are a little lower than those for older age groups (Sudak, 2005; see **Figure 11.19**). Actually, the suicide crisis among teenagers involves *attempted* suicide more than *completed* suicide. It is difficult to compile accurate data on suicide attempts (which are often covered up), but experts estimate that when all age groups are lumped together, suicide attempts outnumber actual suicidal deaths by as much as 20 to 1 (Sudak, 2005). However, this ratio of attempted to completed suicides is much higher for adolescents and is estimated to range anywhere from 100:1 to 200:1 (Maris, Berman, & Silverman, 2000). Thus, attempted suicide is a major issue during adolescence. About 2% of adolescent males and about 5% of adolescent females attempt suicide each year in the United States (Blum & Rinehart, 2000). Although adolescent girls *attempt* suicide more often than adolescent boys, completed suicide rates are almost six times higher for boys (Serocynski, Jacquez, & Cole, 2003).

Returning to our original question, does the weight of evidence support the idea that adolescence is usually a period of turmoil and turbulence? Overall, the consensus of the experts seems to be that adolescence is *not* an exceptionally difficult period (Petersen et al., 1993; Steinberg & Levine, 1997). However, in an influential reanalysis of the evidence, Jeffrey Arnett (1999) has argued convincingly that "not all adolescents experience storm and stress, but storm and stress is more likely during adolescence than at other ages" (p. 317). Arnett supports his intermediate position by summarizing research on adolescents' moods, risky behaviors, and conflicts with their parents. Research shows that adolescents do experience more volatile and more negative emotions than their parents or younger children do (Rosenblum & Lewis, 2003). Studies also show that various types of risky behavior, such as substance abuse, careless sexual practices, and dangerous driving, peak during late adolescence (Perkins & Borden, 2003). Finally, adolescence *does* bring an increase in parent-child conflicts (Granic, Dishion, & Hollenstein, 2003). Arnett is quick to emphasize that turmoil in adolescence is far from universal, but he maintains that, on the average, adolescence is somewhat more stressful than other developmental periods.

Although turbulence and turmoil are not *universal* features of adolescence, challenging adaptations *do* have to be made during this period. In particular, most adolescents struggle to some extent in their effort to achieve a sound sense of identity.

The Search for Identity

Erik Erikson was especially interested in personality development during adolescence, which is the fifth of the eight major life stages he described (consult **Figure 11.8** on page 452). According to Erikson (1968), the premier challenge of adolescence is the struggle to form a clear sense of identity. This struggle involves working out a stable concept of oneself as a unique individual and embracing an ideology

Figure 11.19

Suicide rates by age. Although suicide rates for adolescents have increased dramatically in recent decades, the suicide rates for this age group remain lower than the suicide rates for all older age groups.

Source: Centers for Disease Control and Prevention, *Health United States*, 2005.

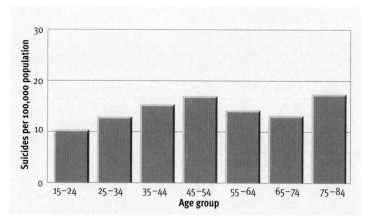

or system of values that provides a sense of direction. In Erikson's view, adolescents grapple with questions such as "Who am I, and where am I going in life?"

Erikson recognized that the process of identity formation often extends beyond adolescence, as his own life illustrates (Coles, 1970; Roazen, 1976). During adolescence Erikson began to resist family pressures to study medicine. Instead, he wandered about Europe until he was 25, trying to "find himself" as an artist. His interest in psychoanalysis was sparked by an introduction to Sigmund Freud's youngest daughter, Anna, a pioneer of child psychoanalysis. After his psychoanalytic training, he moved to the United States. When he became a naturalized citizen in 1939, he changed his surname from Homburger to Erikson. Clearly, Erikson was struggling with the question of "Who am I?" well into adulthood. Small wonder, then, that he focused a great deal of attention on identity formation.

Although the struggle for a sense of identity can be a lifelong process, it does tend to be especially intense during adolescence. Adolescents deal with identity formation in a variety of ways. According to James Marcia (1966, 1980, 1994), the presence or absence of a sense of commitment (to life goals and values) and a sense of crisis (active questioning and exploration) can combine to produce four different *identity statuses* (see Figure 11.20). These are not stages that people pass through, but orientations that may occur at a particular time. In order of increasing maturity, Marcia's four identity statuses begin with *identity diffusion,* a state of rudderless apathy, with no commitment to an ideology. *Identity foreclosure* is a premature commitment to visions, values, and roles—typically those prescribed by one's parents. Foreclosure is associated with conformity and not being very open to new experiences (Kroger, 2003). An *identity moratorium* involves delaying commitment for a while to experiment with alternative ideologies and careers. *Identity achievement* involves arriving at a sense of self and direction after some consideration of alternative possibilities. Identity achievement is associated with higher self-esteem, conscientiousness, security, achievement motivation, and capacity for intimacy (Kroger, 2003).

Research has revealed that a sizable majority of adolescents shift back and forth among the four identity statuses (Berzonsky & Adams, 1999). Moreover, people tend to reach identity achievement at later ages than originally envisioned by Marcia. By late adolescence, only a small minority of individuals have reached identity achievement, so the struggle for a sense of identity routinely extends into young adulthood.

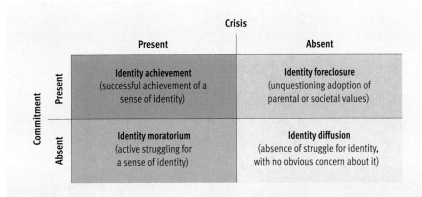

Emerging Adulthood as a New Developmental Stage

The finding that the search for identity routinely extends into adulthood is one of many considerations that have led Jeffrey Arnett to make the radical claim that we ought to recognize the existence of a new developmental stage in modern societies, which he has christened *emerging adulthood*. According to Arnett (2000, 2004, 2006), the years between age 18 and 25 (roughly) have become a distinct, new transitional stage of life. He attributes the rise of this new developmental period to a variety of demographic trends, such as more people delaying marriage and parenthood until their late 20s or early 30s, lengthier participation in higher education, increased barriers to financial independence, and so forth. "What is different today," he says, "is that experiencing the period from the late teens through the mid-20s as a time of exploration and instability is now the norm" (Arnett, 2006, p. 4).

Arnett (2000, 2006) maintains that emerging adulthood is characterized by a number of prominent features. A central feature is the subjective feeling that one is in between adolescence and adulthood. When 18–25-year-olds are asked "Do you feel like you have reached adulthood?" the modal response is "Yes and no" (see Figure 11.21 on the next page). They don't feel like adolescents, but most don't see themselves as adults either. Another feature of emerging adulthood is that it is an age of possibilities. It tends to be a time of great optimism about one's personal future. A third aspect of emerging adulthood is that it is a self-focused time of life. People in this period tend to be unfettered by duties, commitments, and social obligations, which gives them unusual autonomy and freedom to explore new options. Finally, Arnett has found that to a surprising degree emerging adulthood is a period of identity formation. Although the search for identity has traditionally been viewed as

Figure 11.20
Marcia's four identity statuses. According to Marcia (1980), the occurrence of identity crisis and exploration and the development of personal commitments can combine into four possible identity statuses, as shown in this diagram. The progressively darker shades of blue signify progressively more mature identity statuses.

SOURCE: Adapted from Marcia, J. E. (1980). Identity in adolescence. In J. Adelson (Ed.), *Handbook of adolescent psychology* (pp. 159–210). New York: John Wiley. Copyright © 1980 by John Wiley. Adapted by permission.

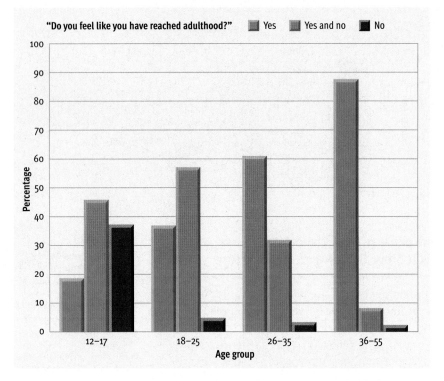

"Do you feel like you have reached adulthood?" ■ Yes ■ Yes and no ■ No

Figure 11.21

Emerging adulthood as a phase in between adolescence and adulthood. Arnett (2006) characterizes emerging adulthood as an "age of feeling in-between." This characterization comes from a study (2001) in which he asked participants of various ages "Do you feel like you have reached adulthood?" As you can see in the data shown here, the dominant response in the 18–25 age group was an ambivalent "Yes and no," but it shifted to predominantly "Yes" in the 26–35 age group.

SOURCE: Arnett, J. J. (2006). Emerging adulthood: Understanding the new way of coming of age. In J. J. Arnett & J. L. Tanner (Eds.), *Emerging adults in America: Coming of age in the 21st century* (p. 11). Washington, DC: American Psychological Association. Copyright © 2006 by the American Psychological Association. Reprinted by permission of the author.

an adolescent phenomenon, Arnett's research indicates that identity formation continues to be a crucial issue for most young adults. Arnett's provocative theory has already inspired a good deal of research on the dynamics and developmental significance of emerging adulthood (Acquilino, 2006; Cote, 2006; Labouvie-Vief, 2006; Tanner, 2006). This research needs to determine whether emerging adulthood really represents a new stage of development or a historical curiosity associated with recent decades.

REVIEW of Key Learning Goals

11.11 The growth spurt at puberty is a prominent event involving the development of reproductive maturity and secondary sex characteristics. Generational changes have been seen in the timing of puberty. Early sexual maturation is associated with a variety of problems, especially among females.

11.12 During adolescence neurons are becoming more myelinated, while synaptic pruning continues to sculpt neural networks. The prefrontal cortex, which has been characterized as an executive control center, appears to be the last area of the brain to mature fully. This reality may contribute to adolescent risk taking.

11.13 G. Stanley Hall believed that adolescence is a time of turmoil. Consistent with this view, attempted suicides among adolescents have climbed dramatically in recent decades. Nonetheless, most theorists do not view adolescence as a time of exceptional turmoil. However, Arnett argues that adolescence is slightly more stressful than other periods of life.

11.14 According to Erikson, the key challenge of adolescence is to make some progress toward a sense of identity. Marcia identified four patterns of identity formation: foreclosure, moratorium, identity diffusion, and identity achievement.

11.15 Arnett argues that we ought to recognize the existence of a new developmental stage in modern societies, which he has christened emerging adulthood. Central features of this stage include feeling in between adolescence and adulthood, optimism, self-focus, and continued identity formation.

The Expanse of Adulthood

Key Learning Goals

11.16 Discuss the stability of personality in adulthood, and outline Erikson's stages of adult development.

11.17 Trace typical transitions in family relations during the adult years.

11.18 Summarize the physical changes associated with aging.

11.19 Review information on the onset, symptoms, and causes of Alzheimer's disease.

11.20 Analyze how intelligence, memory, and mental speed change in later adulthood.

The concept of development was once associated almost exclusively with childhood and adolescence, but today development is widely recognized as a lifelong journey. Interestingly, patterns of development during the adult years are becoming increasingly diverse. The boundaries between young, middle, and late adulthood are becoming blurred as more and more people have children later than one is "supposed" to, retire earlier than one is "supposed" to, and so forth. In the upcoming pages we will look at some of the major developmental transitions in adult life, but you should bear in mind that in adulthood (even more so than childhood or adolescence) there are many divergent pathways and timetables.

Personality Development

In recent years, research on adult personality development has been dominated by one key question: How stable is personality over the life span? We'll look at this issue and Erikson's view of adulthood in our discussion of personality development in the adult years.

The Question of Stability

How common are significant personality changes in adulthood? Is a grouchy 20-year-old going to be a grouchy 40-year-old and a grouchy 65-year-old? Or can the grouchy young adult become a mel-low senior citizen? After tracking subjects through adulthood, many researchers have been impressed by the amount of change observed (Helson, Jones, & Kwan, 2002; Whitbourne et al., 2002). For example, Roger Gould (1975) concluded that "the evolution of a personality continues through the fifth decade of life." In contrast, many other researchers have concluded that personality tends to be quite stable over periods of 20 to 40 years (Caspi & Herbener, 1990; Costa & McCrae, 1994, 1997). A review of 150 relevant studies, involving almost 50,000 participants, concluded that personality in early adulthood is a good predictor of personality in late adulthood and that the stability of personality increases with age up to about age 50 (Roberts & DelVecchio, 2000).

Clearly, researchers assessing the stability of personality in adulthood have reached very different conclusions. How can these contradictory conclusions be reconciled? It appears that *both* conclusions are accurate—they just reflect different ways of looking at the data (Bertrand & Lachman, 2003). Recall from Chapter 9 that psychological test scores are *relative* measures—they show how one scores *relative to other people*. Raw scores are converted into *percentile scores* that indicate the precise degree to which one is above or below average on a particular trait. The data indicate that these percentile scores tend to be remarkably stable over lengthy spans of time—people's relative standing doesn't tend to change much.

However, if we examine participants' raw scores, we can see meaningful developmental trends. For example, adults' mean raw scores on extraversion, neuroticism, and openness to experience tend to decline moderately with increasing age, while measures of agreeableness and conscientiousness tend to increase (Bertrand & Lachman, 2003; Caspi, Roberts, & Shiner, 2005; see Figure 11.22).

A recent meta-analysis of 92 studies found statistically significant change over the course of the adult years in 75% of the personality traits studied (Roberts, Walton, & Viechtbauer, 2006). The bulk of this change appears to occur between the ages of 20 and 40, but substantial changes continue into old age on some traits (Roberts & Mroczek, 2008). The trends seen could be characterized as positive changes, in that aging seems to bring increased warmth, self-confidence, self-control, and emotional stability (Roberts & Wood, 2006). Moreover, the people who exhibit these trends at the youngest ages tend to lead healthier and longer lives (Roberts et al., 2007). In sum, it appears that personality in adulthood is characterized by *both* stability and change.

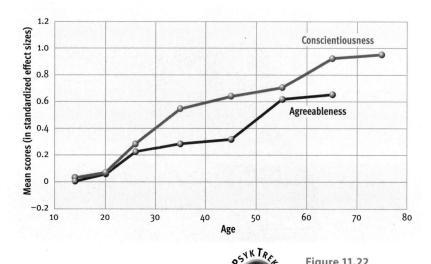

Erikson's View of Adulthood — 9b

Insofar as personality changes during the adult years, Erik Erikson's (1963) theory offers some clues about the nature of changes people can expect. In his eight-stage model of development over the life span, Erikson divided adulthood into three stages (see again **Figure 11.8**). In the *early adulthood* stage called *intimacy versus isolation,* the key concern is whether one can develop the capacity to share intimacy with others. Successful resolution of the challenges in this stage should promote empathy and openness. In *middle adulthood,* the psychosocial crisis pits *generativity versus self-absorption.* The key challenge is to acquire a genuine concern for the welfare of future generations, which results in providing unselfish guidance to younger people and concern with one's legacy. During the *late adulthood* stage called *integrity versus despair,* the challenge is to avoid the tendency to dwell on the mistakes of the past and on one's imminent death. People need to find meaning and satisfaction in their lives, rather than wallow in bitterness and resentment. Empirical research on the adult stages in Erikson's theory has been sparse, but generally supportive of the theory. For example, researchers have found that generativity increases between young adulthood and middle age, as Erikson's theory predicts (de St. Aubin, McAdams, & Kim, 2004; Stewart, Ostrove, & Helson, 2001).

Transitions in Family Life

Many of the important transitions in adulthood involve changes in family responsibilities and relationships. Nearly everyone emerges from a family, and most people go on to form their own families. However, the transitional period during which young adults are "between families" until they form a new family is being prolonged by more and more people.

Figure 11.22
Examples of personality trends in the adult years.
According to Brent Roberts and Daniel Mroczek (2008), when researchers examine participants' mean raw scores on personality measures, they find meaningful trends over the decades of adulthood. The trends for two specific traits—agreeableness and conscientiousness—are shown here as examples. Using subjects' test scores in adolescence as a baseline, you can see how measures of agreeableness and conscientiousness increase substantially over the decades.

SOURCE: Roberts, B. W., & Mroczek, D. (2008). Personality trait change in adulthood. *Current Directions in Psychological Science, 17,* 31–35. Copyright © 2008 Blackwell Publishing. Reprinted by permission.

Figure 11.23

Median age at first marriage. The median age at which people in the United States marry for the first time has been creeping up for both males and females since the mid-1960s. This trend indicates that more people are postponing marriage. (Data from the U.S. Bureau of the Census, 2007)

The percentage of young adults who are postponing marriage until their late twenties or early thirties has risen dramatically (see **Figure 11.23**). This trend is probably the result of a number of factors. Chief among them are the availability of new career options for women, increased educational requirements in the world of work, and increased emphasis on personal autonomy. Remaining single is a much more acceptable option today than it was a few decades ago (DeFrain & Olson, 1999). Nonetheless, over 90% of adults in the U.S. eventually marry.

Adjusting to Marriage

The newly married couple usually settle into their roles as husband and wife gradually. Difficulties with this transition are more likely when spouses come into a marriage with different expectations about marital roles. Unfortunately, substantial differences in role expectations seem particularly likely in this era of transition in gender roles (Brewster & Padavic, 2000). Most new couples are pretty happy, but 8%–14% of newlyweds score in the distressed range on measures of marital satisfaction, with the most commonly reported problems being difficulties balancing work and marriage and financial concerns (Schramm et al., 2005).

Women may be especially vulnerable to ambivalence about shifting marital roles. More and more women are aspiring to demanding careers, yet research shows that husbands' careers continue to take priority over their wives' vocational ambitions

(Haas, 1999). Moreover, many husbands maintain traditional role expectations about housework, child care, and decision making. Men's contribution to housework has increased noticeably since the 1960s, as you can see in **Figure 11.24**. However, studies indicate that wives are still doing the bulk of the household chores in America, even when they work outside the home (Bianchi et al., 2000; Sayer, 2005). Although married women perform about two-thirds of all housework, only about one-third of wives characterize their division of labor as unfair, because most women don't expect a 50-50 split (Coltrane, 2001). Women who have nontraditional attitudes about gender roles are more likely to perceive their share of housework as unfair than women with traditional attitudes (Coltrane, 2001). In contrast, couples in which the husband holds egalitarian attitudes have higher levels of martial happiness than those where the husband holds more traditional attitudes (Kaufman & Taniguchi, 2006).

The prechildren phase of the family life cycle used to be rather short for most newly married couples. Traditionally, couples just *assumed* that they would proceed to have children. In recent decades, however, ambivalence about the prospect of having children has clearly increased (Koropeckyj-Cox & Pendell, 2007), and the percentage of childless couples has doubled since 1960 (Bulcroft & Teachman, 2004). Hence, more and more couples are finding themselves struggling to decide *whether* to have children. Interestingly, in-

Figure 11.24

Housework trends since the 1960s. As these data show, the housework gap between husbands and wives has narrowed since the 1960s. Married men have more than doubled their housework, but it is the large reduction in wives' housework that has really shrunk the housework gap. (Data from Bianchi et al., 2000)

tentions about having children are not as stable over time as one might expect. In one study that followed adult participants over a span of six years, about one-quarter of the respondents changed their plans (Heaton, Jacobson, & Holland, 1999). These subjects were almost evenly split between those who planned to remain childless but subsequently decided they wanted to have children and those who intended to have children but subsequently expressed a preference for remaining child-free.

Adjusting to Parenthood

Although an increasing number of people are choosing to remain childless, the vast majority of married couples continue to have children. Most couples are happy with their decision to have children, but the arrival of the first child represents a major transition, and the disruption of routines can be emotionally draining (Bost et al., 2002). The transition to parenthood tends to have more impact on mothers than fathers (Nomaguchi & Milkie, 2003). New mothers, already physically exhausted by the birth process, are particularly prone to postpartum distress, and about 10%–13% experience depression within the first 12 weeks after birth (Dennis & Ross, 2005; Formichelli, 2001). The transition is more difficult when a wife's expectations regarding how much the father will be involved in child care are not met (Fox, Bruce, & Combs-Orme, 2000). A review of decades of research on parenthood and marital satisfaction, found that (1) parents exhibit lower marital satisfaction than comparable nonparents, (2) mothers of infants report the steepest decline in marital satisfaction, and (3) the more children couples have, the lower their marital satisfaction tends to be (Twenge, Campbell, & Foster, 2003).

Crisis during the transition to first parenthood is far from universal, however (Cox et al., 1999). Couples who have high levels of affection and commitment prior to the first child's birth are likely to maintain a stable level of satisfaction after the birth (Shapiro, Gottman, & Carrère, 2000). The key to making this transition less stressful may be to have *realistic expectations* about parental responsibilities (Belsky & Kelly, 1994). Studies find that stress is greatest in new parents who have overestimated the benefits and underestimated the costs of their new role. Interestingly, the nature of parenthood appears to be undergoing a cultural transition. Parents in more recent age cohorts tend to be more involved with and accessible to their children than previous generations (Parke, 2004).

As children grow up, parental influence over them tends to decline, and the early years of parenting—that once seemed so difficult—are often recalled with fondness. When youngsters reach adolescence and seek to establish their own identities, gradual realignments occur in parent-child relationships. On the one hand, these relations generally are not as bitter or contentious as widely assumed (Laursen, Coy, & Collins, 1998). On the other hand, adolescents do spend less time in family activities, and their closeness to their parents declines while conflicts become more frequent (Smetana, Campione-Barr, & Metzger, 2006). The conflicts tend to involve everyday matters (chores and appearance) more than substantive issues (sex and drugs) (Collins & Laursen, 2006). When conflicts occur, they seem to have more adverse effects on the parents than the children. Ironically, although research has shown that adolescence is not as turbulent or difficult for youngsters as once believed, their parents *are* stressed out (Steinberg, 2001).

Adjusting to the Empty Nest

When parents get all their children launched into the adult world, they find themselves faced with an "empty nest." This period was formerly thought to be a difficult transition for many parents, especially mothers who were familiar only with the maternal role. In recent decades, however, more women have experience with other roles outside the home. Hence, evidence suggests that most parents adjust effectively to the empty nest transition and are more likely to have problems if their children *return* to the once-empty nest (Blacker, 1999; Dennerstein, Dudley, & Guthrie, 2002). Interestingly, one study found that the empty nest transition was tougher for fathers than mothers because fathers were less prepared for the change (Hagen & DeVries, 2004).

Aging and Physiological Changes

People obviously experience many physical changes as they progress through adulthood. In both sexes, hair tends to thin out and become gray, and many males confront receding hairlines and baldness. To the dismay of many, the proportion of body fat tends to increase with age, while the amount of muscle tissue decreases. Overall, weight tends to increase in most adults through the mid-50s, when a gradual decline may begin. These changes have little functional significance, but in our youth-oriented society, they often have a negative impact on self-concept, leading many people to view themselves as less attractive (Aldwin & Gilmer, 2004).

In the sensory domain, the key developmental changes occur in vision and hearing. The proportion

web link 11.8

**USDHHS:
Administration on Aging**

The U.S. Department of Health and Human Services provides a content-rich site devoted to all aspects of aging; it includes one of the best available guides to on-line information about older Americans.

of people with 20/20 visual acuity declines with age, while farsightedness and difficulty seeing in low illumination become more common (Schieber, 2006). Sensitivity to color and contrast is also reduced (Fozard & Gordon-Salant, 2001). Hearing sensitivity begins declining gradually in early adulthood but usually isn't noticeable until after age 50. Hearing loss tends to be greater in men than in women and for high-frequency sounds more than low-frequency sounds (Yost, 2000). Even mild hearing loss can undermine speech perception and put an added burden on cognitive processing (Wingfield, Tun, & McCoy, 2005). These sensory losses would be more problematic, but in modern society they can usually be partially compensated for with eyeglasses, contacts, and hearing aids.

Age-related changes also occur in hormonal functioning during adulthood. Among women, these changes lead to *menopause*. This ending of menstrual periods, accompanied by a loss of fertility, typically occurs at around age 50 (Grady, 2006). Most women experience at least some unpleasant symptoms, such as hot flashes, headaches, night sweats, mood changes, sleep difficulties, and reduced sex drive, but the amount of discomfort varies considerably (Grady, 2006; Williams et al., 2007). Menopause is also accompanied by an elevated vulnerability to depression (Deecher et al., 2008). Not long ago, menopause was thought to be almost universally accompanied by severe emotional strain. However, it is now clear that most women experience relatively modest psychological distress (George, 2002; Walter, 2000).

Although people sometimes talk about "male menopause," men don't really go through an equivalent experience. Starting in middle age, testosterone levels *do* decline substantially (Bain, 2007; Morley & Perry, 2003), but these decreases are gradual rather than abrupt, and they are not associated with the onset of a constellation of symptoms comparable to what women experience (Jacobs, 2001; Wald, Miner, & Seftel, 2008). That said, the effects of declining testosterone levels in aging men *do* have functional significance (Hollander & Samons, 2003). Reduced testosterone is thought to contribute to age-related declines in muscle mass, sexual functioning, and mental sharpness (Bain, 2007). In light of such findings, physicians are increasingly providing testosterone supplementation to reduce these effects (Smith, 2003; Wald et al., 2008).

Aging and Neural Changes

The amount of brain tissue and the brain's weight decline gradually in late adulthood, mostly after age 60 (Victoroff, 2005). These trends appear to reflect both a decrease in the number of active neurons in some areas of the brain and shrinkage of still-active neurons, with neuron loss perhaps being less important than once believed (Albert & Killiany, 2001). Although this gradual loss of brain tissue sounds alarming, it is a normal part of the aging process. Its functional significance is the subject of some debate, but it doesn't appear to be a key factor in any of the age-related dementias. A *dementia* is an abnormal condition marked by multiple cognitive deficits that include memory impairment. Dementia can be caused by quite a variety of diseases, such as Alzheimer's disease, Parkinson's disease, Huntington's disease, and AIDS, to name just a few (Caine & Lyness, 2000). Because many of these diseases are more prevalent in older adults, dementia is seen in about 15%–20% of people over age 75 (Wise, Gray, & Seltzer, 1999). However, it is important to emphasize that dementia and "senility" are not part of the normal aging process. As Cavanaugh (1993) notes, "The term *senility* has no valid medical or psychological meaning, and its continued use simply perpetuates the myth that drastic mental decline is a product of normal aging" (p. 85).

Alzheimer's disease accounts for roughly 60% of all cases of dementia (Small, 2005). The estimated prevalence of Alzheimer's disease is 1% for ages 65–74, 8% for ages 80–85, and 20% for those over 90 (Hybels & Blazer, 2005). Alzheimer's disease is accompanied by major structural deterioration in the brain. Alzheimer's patients exhibit profound and widespread loss of neurons and brain tissue and the accumulation of characteristic neural abnormalities known as neuritic plaques and neurofibrillary tangles (Haroutunian & Davis, 2003). In the early stages of the disease, this damage is largely centered in the hippocampal region, which is known to play a crucial role in many facets of memory, but as the disease advances it spreads throughout much of the brain (Bourgeois, Seaman, & Servis, 2003).

Alzheimer's disease is a vicious affliction that can strike during middle age but usually emerges after age 65. The beginnings of Alzheimer's disease are so subtle they are often recognized only after the disease has progressed for a year or two. The hallmark early symptom is the forgetting of newly learned information after surprisingly brief periods of time (Albert & Killiany, 2001). The course of the disease is one of progressive deterioration, typically over a period of eight to ten years, ending in death (Neugroschl et al., 2005). In the beginning, victims simply lose the thread of conversations or forget to follow through on tasks they have started. Gradually, much more obvious problems begin to emerge, including difficulties in speaking, comprehending, and performing complicated tasks, as well as depression and sleep disturbance. Job performance deteriorates noticeably as victims forget important appointments and suffer indignities such as getting lost while driving and paying the same bill several times. From this point, profound memory loss develops. For example, patients may fail to recognize familiar people, something particularly devastating to family and friends. Many patients become restless and experience hallucinations, delusions, and paranoid thoughts. Eventually, victims become completely disoriented and are unable to care for themselves. There are some encouraging leads for treatments that might slow the progression of this horrific disease, but a cure does not appear to be on the horizon.

The causes that launch this debilitating neural meltdown are not well understood. Genetic factors clearly contribute, but their exact role remains unclear (Ashford & Mortimer, 2002). Some "protective" factors that reduce vulnerability to Alzheimer's disease have been identified, including regular exercise (Schuit et al., 2001) and frequent participation in stimulating cognitive activities (Wilson & Bennet, 2003). The importance of the latter factor emerged in a widely discussed longitudinal investigation called the Nun Study, which followed a group of elderly Catholic Nuns who agreed to donate their brains upon death. The findings of the Nun Study suggest that a high prevalence of positive emotions and strong engagement in mentally challenging work and recreation reduce one's risk for Alzheimer's disease (Danner, Snowdon, & Friesen, 2001; Snowdon, 2001).

Aging and Cognitive Changes

The evidence indicates that general intelligence is fairly stable throughout most of adulthood, with a small decline in *average* test scores often seen after age 60 (Schaie, 1990, 1994, 1996, 2005). However, this seemingly simple assertion masks many complexities and needs to be qualified carefully. First, group averages can be deceptive in that mean scores can be dragged down by a small minority of people who show a decline. For example, when Schaie (1990) calculated the percentage of people who maintain stable performance on various abilities (see Figure 11.25), he found that about 80% showed no decline by age 60 and that about two-thirds were still stable through age 81. Second, some forms of intelligence are more vulnerable to aging than oth-

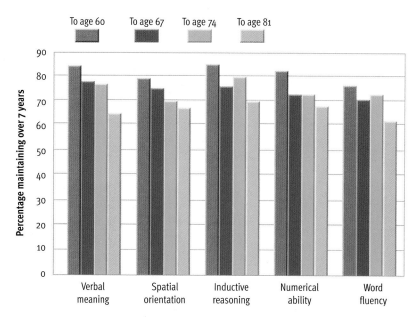

Figure 11.25

Age and the stability of primary mental abilities. In his longitudinal study of cognitive performance begun in 1956, Schaie (1983, 1993) has repeatedly assessed the five basic mental abilities listed along the bottom of this chart. The data graphed here show the percentage of subjects who maintained stable levels of performance on each ability through various ages up to age 81. As you can see, even through the age of 81, the majority of subjects show no significant decline on most abilities.

SOURCE: Adapted from Schaie, K. W. (1990). Intellectual development in adulthood. In J. E. Birren and K. W. Schaie (Eds.), *Handbook of the psychology of aging* (pp. 291–309). San Diego: Academic Press. Copyright © 1990 Elsevier Science (USA), reproduced with permission from the publisher.

ers. Many theorists distinguish between *fluid intelligence,* which involves basic reasoning ability, memory capacity, and speed of information processing, versus *crystallized intelligence,* which involves the ability to apply acquired knowledge and skills in problem solving. Research suggests that fluid intelligence is much more likely to decline with age, whereas crystallized intelligence tends to remain stable (Baltes, Staudinger, & Lindenberger, 1999; Horn & Hofer, 1992; Li et al., 2004).

What about memory? Numerous studies report decreases in older adults' memory capabilities (Hoyer & Verhaeghen, 2006). Most researchers maintain that the memory losses associated with normal aging tend to be moderate and are *not* experienced by everyone (Dixon & Cohen, 2003; Shimamura et al., 1995). However, Salthouse (2003, 2004) takes a much more pessimistic view, arguing that age-related decreases in memory are substantial in magnitude, that they begin in early adulthood, and that they affect everyone. One reason for these varied conclusions may be that a variety of memory types can be assessed (see Chapter 7 for a review of various systems of memory). The most reliable decrements are usually seen in *episodic memory* and *working memory,* with less consistent losses observed on tasks involving *procedural memory* and *semantic memory* (Dixon & Cohen, 2003; Hoyer & Verhaeghen, 2006).

In the cognitive domain, aging seems to take its toll on *speed* first. Many studies indicate that speed in learning, solving problems, and processing information tends to decline with age (Salthouse, 1996). The evidence suggests that the erosion of processing speed may be a gradual, lengthy trend beginning in middle adulthood (see Figure 11.26). The general nature of this trend (across differing tasks) suggests that it may be the result of age-related changes in neurological functioning (Salthouse, 2000). Some theorists believe that diminished mental speed is the key factor underlying the age-related declines seen on many, varied cognitive tasks (Salthouse, 2005), although doubts have been raised about this conclusion (Hartley, 2006). Even though mental speed declines with age, problem-solving ability remains largely unimpaired if older people are given adequate time to compensate for their reduced speed.

It should be emphasized that many people remain capable of great intellectual accomplishments well into their later years (Simonton, 1990, 1997). This fact was verified in a study of scholarly, scientific, and artistic productivity that examined lifelong patterns of work among 738 men who lived at least through the age of 79. Dennis (1966) found that the 40s decade was the most productive in most professions. However, productivity was remarkably stable through the 60s and even the 70s in many areas.

A hot issue in recent years has been whether high levels of mental activity in late adulthood can delay the typical age-related declines in cognitive functioning. This possibility is sometimes referred to as the "use it or lose it" hypothesis. Several lines of evidence seem to provide support for this notion. For example, people who continue to work further into old age, especially people who remain in mentally demanding jobs, tend to show smaller decrements in cognitive abilities than their age-mates (Bosma et al., 2002; Schooler, 2007). Other studies suggest that continuing to engage in intellectually challenging activities in late adulthood serves to buffer against cognitive declines (Hultsch et al., 1999; Kliegel, Zimprich, & Rott, 2004). The evidence is complex and there are skeptics (Salthouse, 2006), but it appears that keeping mentally active may help elderly people delay and diminish the negative effects of aging on cognitive functioning.

Figure 11.26

Age and mental speed. Many studies have found that mental speed decreases with age. The data shown here, from Salthouse (2000), are based on two perceptual speed tasks. The data points are means for large groups of subjects expressed in terms of how many standard deviations (see Chapter 2) they are above or below the mean for all ages (which is set at 0). Similar age-related declines are seen on many tasks that depend on mental speed.

SOURCE: Adapted from Salthouse, T. A. (2000). Aging and measures of processing speed. *Biological Psychology, 54,* 35–54. Copyright © 2000 Elsevier Science. Reproduced with permission from the publisher.

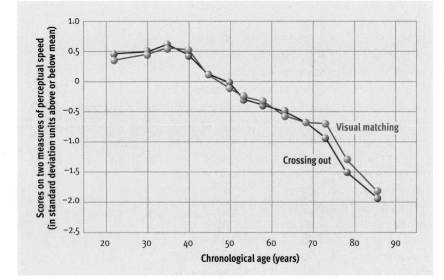

Reflecting on the Chapter's Themes

Key Learning Goals

11.21 Identify the five unifying themes highlighted in this chapter.

Many of our seven integrative themes surfaced to some degree in our coverage of human development. We saw theoretical diversity in the discussions of attachment, cognitive development, and personality development. We saw that psychology evolves in a sociohistorical context, investigating complex, real-world issues. We encountered multifactorial causation of behavior in the development of temperament and attachment, among other things. We saw cultural invariance and cultural diversity in our examination of attachment, motor development, cognitive development, and moral development.

But above all else, we saw how heredity and environment jointly mold behavior. We've encountered the dual influence of heredity and environment before, but this theme is rich in complexity, and each chapter draws out different aspects and implications. Our discussion of development amplified the point that genetics and experience work *interactively* to shape behavior. In the language of science, an interaction means that the effects of one variable depend on the effects of another. In other words, heredity and environment do not operate independently. Children with "difficult" temperaments will elicit different reactions from different parents, depending on the parents' personalities and expecta-

tions. Likewise, a particular pair of parents will affect children in different ways, depending on the inborn characteristics of the children. An interplay, or feedback loop, exists between biological and environmental factors. For instance, a temperamentally difficult child may elicit negative reactions from parents, which serve to make the child more difficult, which evokes more negative reactions. If this child develops into an ornery 11-year-old, which do we blame—genetics or experience? Clearly, this outcome is due to the reciprocal effects of both.

All aspects of development are shaped jointly by heredity and experience. We often estimate their relative weight or influence, as if we could cleanly divide behavior into genetic and environmental components. Although we can't really carve up behavior that neatly, such comparisons can be of great theoretical interest, as you'll see in our upcoming Personal Application, which discusses the nature and origins of gender differences in behavior.

 Theoretical Diversity

 Sociohistorical Context

 Multifactorial Causation

 Cultural Heritage

 Heredity and Environment

REVIEW of Key Learning Goals

11.21 This chapter showed that psychology is theoretically diverse, that psychology evolves in a sociohistorical context, that multifactorial causation is the norm, and that culture affects many aspects of behavior, but above all else, it demonstrated that heredity and environment jointly mold behavior.

Understanding Gender Differences

Answer the following "true" or "false."

_____ **1** Females are more socially oriented than males.

_____ **2** Males outperform females on most spatial tasks.

_____ **3** Females are more irrational than males.

_____ **4** Males are less sensitive to nonverbal cues than females.

_____ **5** Females are more emotional than males.

Are there genuine behavioral differences between the sexes similar to those mentioned

above? If so, why do these differences exist? How do they develop? These are the complex and controversial questions that we'll explore in this Personal Application.

Before proceeding further, we need to clarify how some key terms are used, as terminology in this area of research has been evolving and remains a source of confusion. *Sex* **usually refers to the biologically based categories of female and male.** In contrast, *gender* **usually refers to culturally constructed distinctions between femininity and masculinity.** Individuals are born female or male. However, they

Key Learning Goals

11.22 Summarize evidence on gender differences in behavior, and assess the significance of these differences.

11.23 Explain how biological factors are thought to contribute to gender differences.

11.24 Explain how environmental factors are thought to contribute to gender differences.

become feminine or masculine through complex developmental processes that take years to unfold.

The statements at the beginning of this Application reflect popular gender stereotypes in our society. *Gender stereotypes* **are**

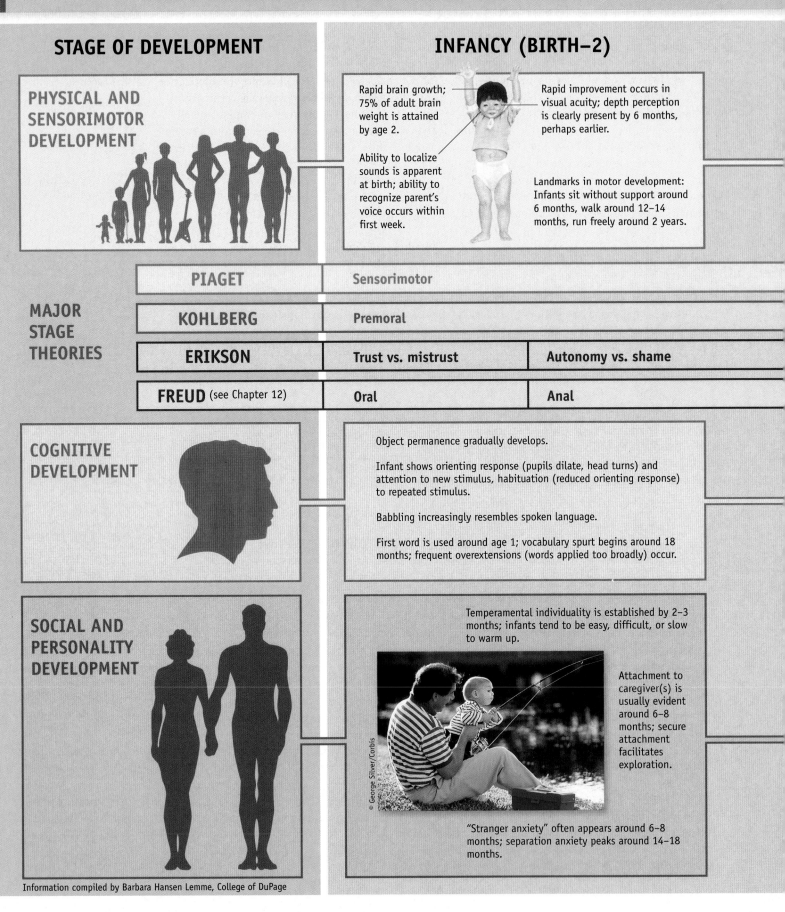

STAGE OF DEVELOPMENT

INFANCY (BIRTH–2)

PHYSICAL AND SENSORIMOTOR DEVELOPMENT

Rapid brain growth; 75% of adult brain weight is attained by age 2.

Ability to localize sounds is apparent at birth; ability to recognize parent's voice occurs within first week.

Rapid improvement occurs in visual acuity; depth perception is clearly present by 6 months, perhaps earlier.

Landmarks in motor development: Infants sit without support around 6 months, walk around 12–14 months, run freely around 2 years.

MAJOR STAGE THEORIES

PIAGET	Sensorimotor	
KOHLBERG	Premoral	
ERIKSON	Trust vs. mistrust	Autonomy vs. shame
FREUD (see Chapter 12)	Oral	Anal

COGNITIVE DEVELOPMENT

Object permanence gradually develops.

Infant shows orienting response (pupils dilate, head turns) and attention to new stimulus, habituation (reduced orienting response) to repeated stimulus.

Babbling increasingly resembles spoken language.

First word is used around age 1; vocabulary spurt begins around 18 months; frequent overextensions (words applied too broadly) occur.

SOCIAL AND PERSONALITY DEVELOPMENT

Temperamental individuality is established by 2–3 months; infants tend to be easy, difficult, or slow to warm up.

© George Silver/Corbis

Attachment to caregiver(s) is usually evident around 6–8 months; secure attachment facilitates exploration.

"Stranger anxiety" often appears around 6–8 months; separation anxiety peaks around 14–18 months.

Information compiled by Barbara Hansen Lemme, College of DuPage

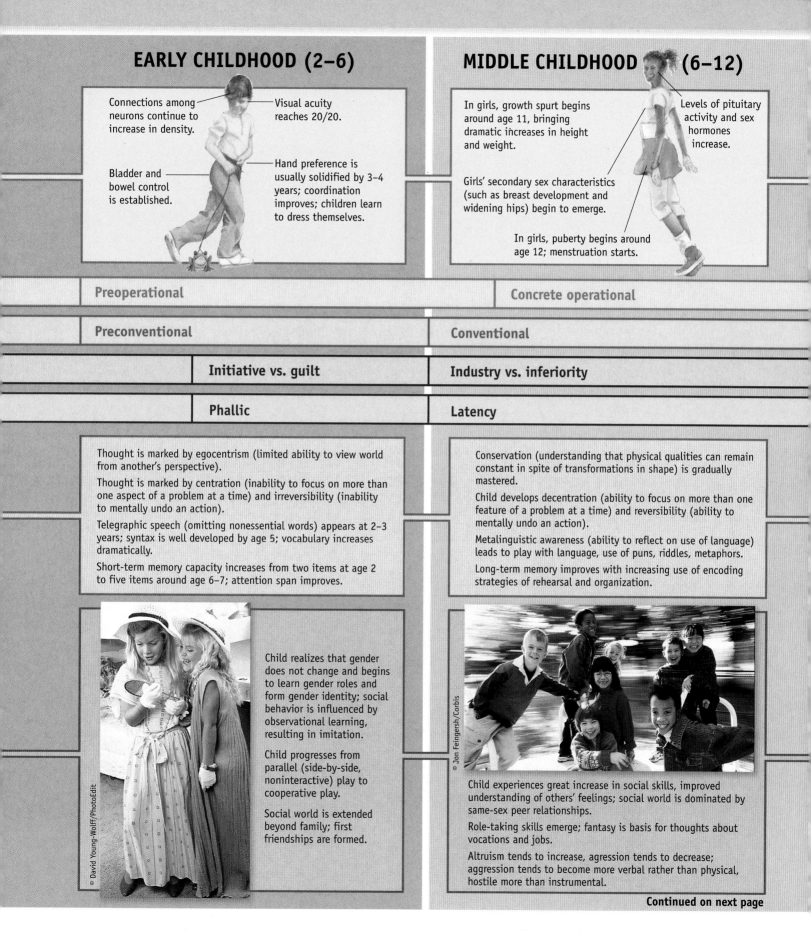

EARLY CHILDHOOD (2–6)

Connections among neurons continue to increase in density.

Visual acuity reaches 20/20.

Bladder and bowel control is established.

Hand preference is usually solidified by 3–4 years; coordination improves; children learn to dress themselves.

MIDDLE CHILDHOOD (6–12)

In girls, growth spurt begins around age 11, bringing dramatic increases in height and weight.

Levels of pituitary activity and sex hormones increase.

Girls' secondary sex characteristics (such as breast development and widening hips) begin to emerge.

In girls, puberty begins around age 12; menstruation starts.

Preoperational

Concrete operational

Preconventional

Conventional

Initiative vs. guilt

Industry vs. inferiority

Phallic

Latency

Thought is marked by egocentrism (limited ability to view world from another's perspective).

Thought is marked by centration (inability to focus on more than one aspect of a problem at a time) and irreversibility (inability to mentally undo an action).

Telegraphic speech (omitting nonessential words) appears at 2–3 years; syntax is well developed by age 5; vocabulary increases dramatically.

Short-term memory capacity increases from two items at age 2 to five items around age 6–7; attention span improves.

Conservation (understanding that physical qualities can remain constant in spite of transformations in shape) is gradually mastered.

Child develops decentration (ability to focus on more than one feature of a problem at a time) and reversibility (ability to mentally undo an action).

Metalinguistic awareness (ability to reflect on use of language) leads to play with language, use of puns, riddles, metaphors.

Long-term memory improves with increasing use of encoding strategies of rehearsal and organization.

Child realizes that gender does not change and begins to learn gender roles and form gender identity; social behavior is influenced by observational learning, resulting in imitation.

Child progresses from parallel (side-by-side, noninteractive) play to cooperative play.

Social world is extended beyond family; first friendships are formed.

© David Young-Wolff/PhotoEdit

© Jon Feingersh/Corbis

Child experiences great increase in social skills, improved understanding of others' feelings; social world is dominated by same-sex peer relationships.

Role-taking skills emerge; fantasy is basis for thoughts about vocations and jobs.

Altruism tends to increase, aggression tends to decrease; aggression tends to become more verbal rather than physical, hostile more than instrumental.

Continued on next page

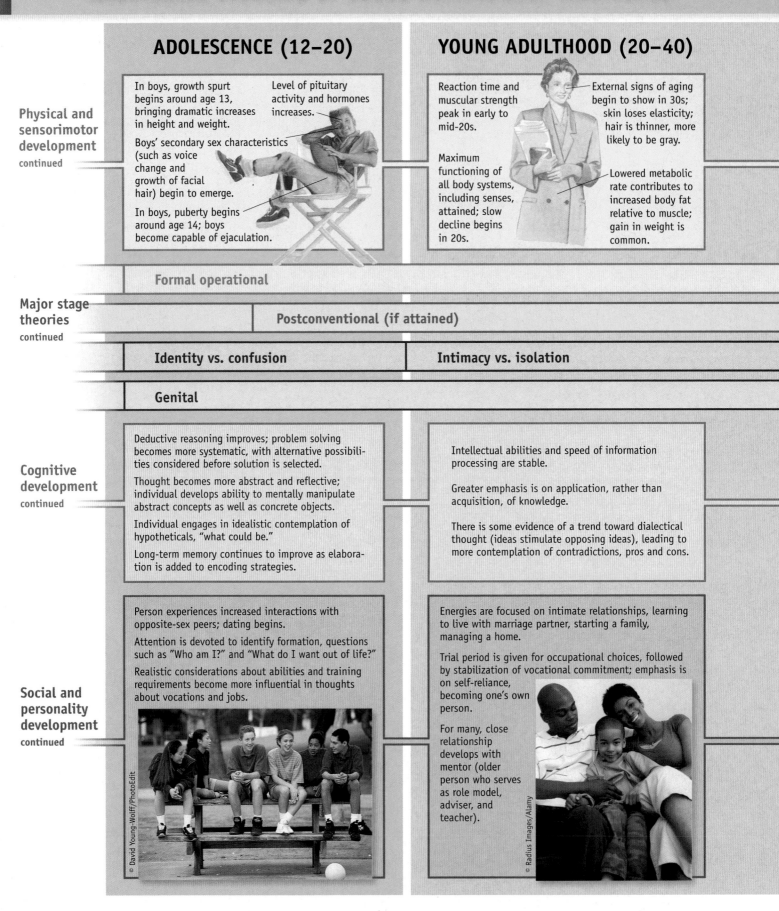

ADOLESCENCE (12–20)

YOUNG ADULTHOOD (20–40)

Physical and sensorimotor development continued

In boys, growth spurt begins around age 13, bringing dramatic increases in height and weight.

Boys' secondary sex characteristics (such as voice change and growth of facial hair) begin to emerge.

In boys, puberty begins around age 14; boys become capable of ejaculation.

Level of pituitary activity and hormones increases.

Reaction time and muscular strength peak in early to mid-20s.

Maximum functioning of all body systems, including senses, attained; slow decline begins in 20s.

External signs of aging begin to show in 30s; skin loses elasticity; hair is thinner, more likely to be gray.

Lowered metabolic rate contributes to increased body fat relative to muscle; gain in weight is common.

Major stage theories continued

Formal operational

Postconventional (if attained)

Identity vs. confusion

Intimacy vs. isolation

Genital

Cognitive development continued

Deductive reasoning improves; problem solving becomes more systematic, with alternative possibilities considered before solution is selected.

Thought becomes more abstract and reflective; individual develops ability to mentally manipulate abstract concepts as well as concrete objects.

Individual engages in idealistic contemplation of hypotheticals, "what could be."

Long-term memory continues to improve as elaboration is added to encoding strategies.

Intellectual abilities and speed of information processing are stable.

Greater emphasis is on application, rather than acquisition, of knowledge.

There is some evidence of a trend toward dialectical thought (ideas stimulate opposing ideas), leading to more contemplation of contradictions, pros and cons.

Social and personality development continued

Person experiences increased interactions with opposite-sex peers; dating begins.

Attention is devoted to identify formation, questions such as "Who am I?" and "What do I want out of life?"

Realistic considerations about abilities and training requirements become more influential in thoughts about vocations and jobs.

Energies are focused on intimate relationships, learning to live with marriage partner, starting a family, managing a home.

Trial period is given for occupational choices, followed by stabilization of vocational commitment; emphasis is on self-reliance, becoming one's own person.

For many, close relationship develops with mentor (older person who serves as role model, adviser, and teacher).

© David Young-Wolff/PhotoEdit

© Radius Images/Alamy

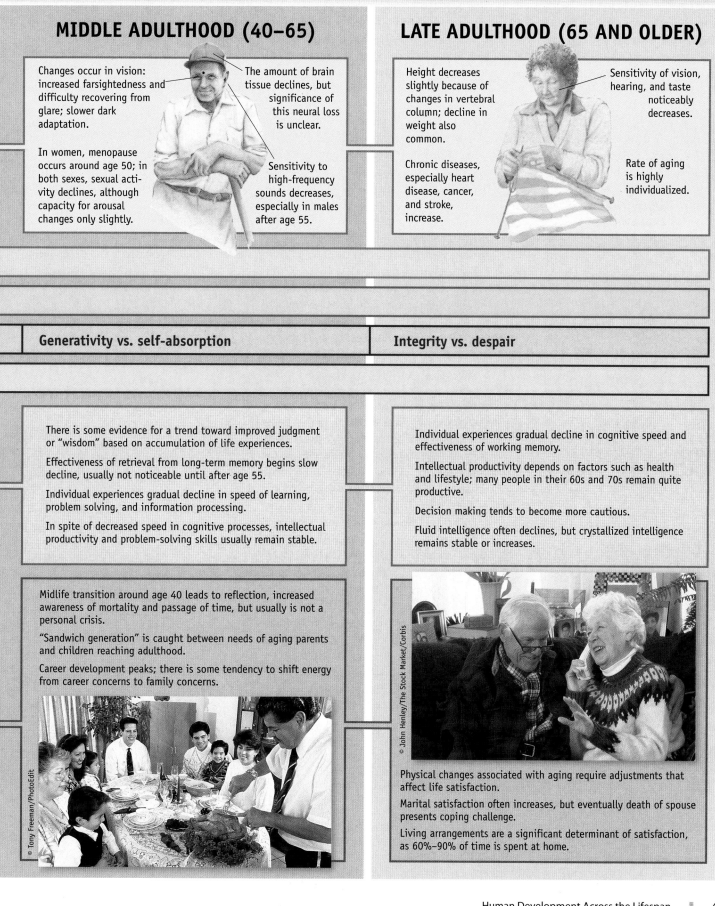

MIDDLE ADULTHOOD (40–65)

Changes occur in vision: increased farsightedness and difficulty recovering from glare; slower dark adaptation.

The amount of brain tissue declines, but significance of this neural loss is unclear.

In women, menopause occurs around age 50; in both sexes, sexual activity declines, although capacity for arousal changes only slightly.

Sensitivity to high-frequency sounds decreases, especially in males after age 55.

LATE ADULTHOOD (65 AND OLDER)

Height decreases slightly because of changes in vertebral column; decline in weight also common.

Sensitivity of vision, hearing, and taste noticeably decreases.

Chronic diseases, especially heart disease, cancer, and stroke, increase.

Rate of aging is highly individualized.

Generativity vs. self-absorption

Integrity vs. despair

There is some evidence for a trend toward improved judgment or "wisdom" based on accumulation of life experiences.

Effectiveness of retrieval from long-term memory begins slow decline, usually not noticeable until after age 55.

Individual experiences gradual decline in speed of learning, problem solving, and information processing.

In spite of decreased speed in cognitive processes, intellectual productivity and problem-solving skills usually remain stable.

Individual experiences gradual decline in cognitive speed and effectiveness of working memory.

Intellectual productivity depends on factors such as health and lifestyle; many people in their 60s and 70s remain quite productive.

Decision making tends to become more cautious.

Fluid intelligence often declines, but crystallized intelligence remains stable or increases.

Midlife transition around age 40 leads to reflection, increased awareness of mortality and passage of time, but usually is not a personal crisis.

"Sandwich generation" is caught between needs of aging parents and children reaching adulthood.

Career development peaks; there is some tendency to shift energy from career concerns to family concerns.

© Tony Freeman/PhotoEdit

© John Henley/The Stock Market/Corbis

Physical changes associated with aging require adjustments that affect life satisfaction.

Marital satisfaction often increases, but eventually death of spouse presents coping challenge.

Living arrangements are a significant determinant of satisfaction, as 60%–90% of time is spent at home.

widely held beliefs about females' and males' abilities, personality traits, and social behavior. Table 11.1 lists some characteristics that are part of the masculine and feminine stereotypes in North American society. The table shows something you may have already noticed on your own: The male stereotype is much more flattering, suggesting that men have virtually cornered the market on competence and rationality. After all, everyone knows that females are more dependent, emotional, irrational, submissive, and talkative than males. Right? Or is that not the case? Let's look at the research.

How Do the Sexes Differ in Behavior?

Gender differences are actual disparities between the sexes in typical behavior or

Table 11.1 Elements of Traditional Gender Sterotypes

Masculine	Feminine
Active	Aware of other's feelings
Adventurous	Considerate
Aggressive	Creative
Ambitious	Cries easily
Competitive	Devotes self to others
Dominant	Emotional
Independent	Enjoys art and music
Leadership qualities	Excitable in a crisis
Likes math and science	Expresses tender feelings
Makes decisions easily	Feelings hurt
Mechanical aptitude	Gentle
Not easily influenced	Home oriented
Outspoken	Kind
Persistent	Likes children
Self-confident	Neat
Skilled in business	Needs approval
Stands up under pressure	Tactful
Takes a stand	Understanding

Source: Adapted from Ruble, T. L. (1983). Sex stereotypes: Issues of change in the 70s. *Sex Roles, 9,* 397–402. Copyright © 1983 Plenum Publishing Group. Adapted with kind permission of Springer Science and Business Media.

average ability. Mountains of research, literally thousands of studies, exist on gender differences. What does this research show? Are the stereotypes of males and females accurate? Well, the findings are a mixed bag. The research indicates that genuine behavioral differences *do* exist between the sexes and that people's stereotypes are not entirely inaccurate (Eagly, 1995; Halpern, 2000). But the differences are fewer in number, smaller in size, and far more complex than stereotypes suggest. As you'll see, only two of the differences mentioned in our opening true-false questions (the even-numbered items) have been largely supported by the research.

Cognitive Abilities

In the cognitive domain, it appears that there are three genuine—albeit rather small—gender differences. First, on the average, females tend to exhibit slightly better *verbal skills* than males (Halpern et al., 2007). In particular, females seem stronger on tasks that require rapid access to semantic information in long-term memory and tasks that require the production or comprehension of complex prose (Halpern, 2004). Second, starting during high school, males show a slight advantage on tests of *mathematical ability.* When all students are compared, males' advantage is quite small (Hyde, 2005a). However, at the high end of the ability distribution, the gender gap is larger, as quite a few more males than females are found to have exceptional math skills (Halpern et al., 2007). Third, starting in the grade-school years, males tend to score higher than females on most measures of *visual-spatial ability* (Halpern et al., 2007). The size of these gender differences varies depending on the exact nature of the spatial task. Males appear to be strongest on tasks that require mental rotations or tracking the movement of objects through three-dimensional space (Halpern, 2004).

Social Behavior

In regard to social behavior, research findings support the existence of some additional gender differences. First, studies indicate that males tend to be much more *physically aggressive* than females (Archer, 2005). This disparity shows up early in childhood. Its continuation into adulthood

is supported by the fact that men account for a grossly disproportionate number of the violent crimes in our society (Kenrick, Trost, & Sundie, 2004). The findings on *verbal aggression* are more complex, as females appear to exhibit more relational aggression (snide remarks and so forth) (Archer, 2005). Second, there are gender differences in *nonverbal communication and interpersonal sensitivity.* The evidence indicates that females are more sensitive than males to subtle nonverbal cues (Hall, Carter, & Horgan, 2000; Hampson, van Anders, & Mullin, 2006) and that they pay more attention to interpersonal information (Hall & Mast, 2008). Third, males are more sexually active than females in a variety of ways, and they have more permissive attitudes about casual, premarital, and extramarital sex (Baumeister et al., 2001b; Hyde, 2005; see Chapter 10).

Some Qualifications

Although research has identified some genuine gender differences in behavior, bear in mind that these are group differences that indicate nothing about individuals. Essentially, research results compare the "average man" with the "average woman." However, you are—and every individual is—unique. The average female and male are ultimately figments of our imagination. Furthermore, the genuine group differences noted are relatively small (Hyde, 2005a). Figure 11.27 shows how scores on a trait, perhaps verbal ability, might be distributed for men and women. Although the group averages are detectably different, you can see the great variability within each group (sex) and the huge overlap between the two group distributions.

Biological Origins of Gender Differences

What accounts for the development of various gender differences? To what degree are they the product of learning or of biology? This question is yet another manifestation of the nature versus nurture issue. Investigations of the biological origins of gender differences have centered on the evolutionary bases of behavior, hormones, and brain organization.

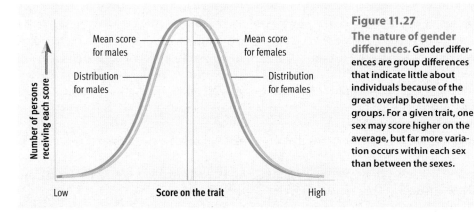

Figure 11.27
The nature of gender differences. Gender differences are group differences that indicate little about individuals because of the great overlap between the groups. For a given trait, one sex may score higher on the average, but far more variation occurs within each sex than between the sexes.

Evolutionary Explanations

Evolutionary analyses usually begin by arguing that gender differences in behavior are largely the same across divergent cultures because cultural invariance suggests that biological factors are at work. Although research has turned up some fascinating exceptions, the better-documented gender differences in cognitive abilities, aggression, and sexual behavior *are* found in virtually all cultures (Beller & Gafni, 1996; Kenrick et al., 2004). Evolutionary psychologists go on to argue that these universal gender differences reflect different natural selection pressures operating on males and females over the course of human history (Archer, 1996; Buss & Kenrick, 1998). For example, as we discussed in Chapter 10, males supposedly are more sexually active and permissive because they invest less than females in the process of procreation and can maximize their reproductive success by seeking many sexual partners (Buss, 1996; Schmitt, 2005). The gender gap in aggression is also explained in terms of reproductive fitness. Because females are more selective about mating than males, males have to engage in more competition for sexual partners than females do. Greater aggressiveness is thought to be adaptive for males in this competition for sexual access, as it should foster social dominance over other males and facilitate the acquisition of the material resources emphasized by females when they evaluate potential partners (Campbell, 2005; Cummins, 2005). Evolutionary theorists assert that gender differences in spatial ability reflect the division of labor in ancestral hunting-and-gathering societies in which males typically handled the hunting and females the gathering. Males' superior-

ity on most spatial tasks has been attributed to the adaptive demands of hunting (Silverman & Choi, 2005; see Chapter 1).

Evolutionary analyses of gender differences are interesting, but controversial. On the one hand, it seems eminently plausible that evolutionary forces could have led to some divergence between males and females in typical behavior. On the other hand, evolutionary hypotheses are highly speculative and difficult to test empirically (Eagly & Wood, 1999; Halpern, 2000). The crucial problem for some critics is that evolutionary analyses are so "flexible," they can be used to explain almost anything. For example, if the situation regarding spatial ability were reversed—if females scored higher than males—evolutionary theorists might attribute females' superiority to the adaptive demands of gathering food, weaving baskets, and making clothes—and it would be difficult to prove otherwise (Cornell, 1997).

The Role of Hormones

Disparities between males and females in hormone levels may contribute to gender differences in behavior (Hampson & Moffat, 2004). Hormones play a key role in sexual differentiation during prenatal development. The high level of androgens (the principal class of male hormones) in males and the low level of androgens in females lead to the differentiation of male and female genital organs. The critical role of prenatal hormones becomes apparent when something interferes with normal prenatal hormonal secretions. About a half-dozen endocrine disorders can cause overproduction or underproduction of specific gonadal hormones during prenatal development.

Scientists have also studied children born to mothers who were given an androgen-like drug to prevent miscarriage. The general trend in this research is that females exposed prenatally to abnormally high levels of androgens exhibit more male-typical behavior than other females do and that males exposed prenatally to abnormally low levels of androgens exhibit more female-typical behavior than other males (Hines, 2004).

These findings suggest that prenatal hormones contribute to the shaping of gender differences in humans. But there are some problems with this evidence (Basow, 1992; Fausto-Sterling, 1992). First, the evidence is much stronger for females than for males. Second, it's always dangerous to draw conclusions about the general population based on small samples of people who have abnormal conditions. Looking at the evidence as a whole, it does seem likely that hormones contribute to gender differences in behavior. However, a great deal remains to be learned.

Differences in Brain Organization

Many theorists believe that gender differences in behavior are rooted in male-female disparities in brain structure and organization (Cahill, 2006). For example, some theorists have tried to link gender differences to the specialization of the cerebral hemispheres in the brain (see **Figure 11.28** on the next page). As you may recall from Chapter 3, in most people the left hemisphere is more actively involved in verbal processing, whereas the right hemisphere is more active in visual-spatial processing (Springer & Deutsch, 1998). After these findings surfaced, theorists began to wonder whether this division of labor in the brain might be related to gender differences in verbal and spatial skills. Consequently, they began looking for sex-related disparities in brain organization.

Some thought-provoking findings *have* been reported. For instance, some studies have found that *males tend to exhibit more cerebral specialization than females* (Hellige, 1993b; Voyer, 1996). In other words, males tend to depend more heavily than females do on the left hemisphere in verbal processing and more heavily on the right hemisphere in spatial processing. Differences

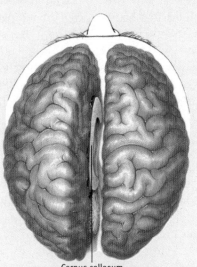

Figure 11.28
The cerebral hemispheres and the corpus callosum. In this drawing the cerebral hemispheres have been "pulled apart" to reveal the corpus callosum, the band of fibers that connects the right and left halves of the brain. Research has shown that the right and left hemispheres are specialized to handle different types of cognitive tasks (see Chapter 3), leading some theorists to speculate that patterns of hemispheric specialization might contribute to gender differences in verbal and spatial abilities.

between males and females have also been found in the size of the corpus callosum, the band of fibers that connects the two hemispheres of the brain. Some studies suggest that *females tend to have a larger corpus callosum* (Bigler et al., 1997), which might allow for better interhemispheric transfer of information, which, in turn, might underlie the less lateralized organization of females' brains (Innocenti, 1994). Thus, some theorists have concluded that differences between the sexes in brain organization are responsible for gender differences in verbal and spatial ability (Geschwind & Galaburda, 1987; Kimura & Hampson, 1993).

This idea is intriguing, but psychologists have a long way to go before they can explain gender differences in terms of right brain/left brain specialization. Studies have not been consistent in finding that males have more specialized brain organization than females (Halpern, 1992; Kinsbourne,

1980), and the finding of a larger corpus callosum in females has proven controversial (Halpern et al., 2007). Moreover, even if these findings were replicated consistently, no one is really sure just how they would account for the observed gender differences in cognitive abilities.

In summary, researchers have made some intriguing progress in their efforts to document the biological roots of gender differences in behavior. However, the idea that "anatomy is destiny" has proven difficult to demonstrate. Many theorists remain convinced that gender differences are largely shaped by experience. Let's examine their evidence.

Environmental Origins of Gender Differences

Socialization is the acquisition of the norms and behaviors expected of people in a particular society. In all cultures, the socialization process includes efforts to train children about gender roles. *Gender roles* are expectations about what is appropriate behavior for each sex. Although gender roles are in a period of transition in modern Western society, there are still many disparities in how males and females are brought up. Investigators have identified three key processes involved in the development of gender roles: operant conditioning, observational learning, and self-socialization. First we'll examine these processes. Then we'll look at the principal sources of gender-role socialization: families, schools, and the media.

Operant Conditioning

In part, gender roles are shaped by the power of reward and punishment—the key processes in *operant conditioning* (see Chapter 6). Parents, teachers, peers, and others often reinforce (usually with tacit approval) "gender-appropriate" behavior and respond negatively to "gender-inappropriate" behavior (Bussey & Bandura, 1999; Matlin, 2008). If you're a man, you might recall getting hurt as a young boy and being told that "big boys don't cry." If you succeeded in inhibiting your crying, you may have earned an approving smile or even something tan-

gible like an ice cream cone. The reinforcement probably strengthened your tendency to "act like a man" and suppress emotional displays. If you're a woman, chances are your crying wasn't discouraged as gender-inappropriate. Studies suggest that fathers encourage and reward gender-appropriate behavior in their youngsters more than mothers do and that boys experience more pressure to behave in gender-appropriate ways than girls do (Levy, Taylor, & Gelman, 1995).

Observational Learning

Observational learning (see Chapter 6) by children can lead to the imitation of adults' gender-appropriate behavior. Children imitate both males and females, but most children tend to imitate same-sex role models more than opposite-sex role models (Bussey & Bandura, 2004). Thus, imitation often leads young girls to play with dolls, dollhouses, and toy stoves. Young boys are more likely to tinker with toy trucks, miniature gas stations, or tool kits.

Self-Socialization

Children themselves are active agents in their own gender-role socialization. Several *cognitive theories* of gender-role development emphasize self-socialization (Bem, 1985; Cross & Markus, 1993; Martin & Ruble, 2004). Self-socialization entails three steps. First, children learn to classify themselves as male or female and to recognize their sex as a permanent quality (around ages 5 to 7). Second, this self-categorization motivates them to value those characteristics and behaviors associated with their sex. Third, they strive to bring their behavior in line with what is considered gender-appropriate in their culture. In other words, children get involved in their own socialization, working diligently to discover the rules that are supposed to govern their behavior.

Sources of Gender-Role Socialization

There are three main sources of influence in gender-role socialization: families, schools, and the media. Of course, we are now in an era of transition in gender roles, so the generalizations that follow may say more about

The socialization of gender roles begins very early, as parents dress their infants in gendered clothing, buy them gender-driven toys, and encourage them to participate in "gender-appropriate" activities.

how you were socialized than about how children will be socialized in the future.

Families.   A great deal of gender-role socialization takes place in the home (McHale, Crouter, & Whiteman, 2003; Pomerantz, Ng, & Wang, 2004). Fathers engage in more "rough-housing" play with their sons

than with their daughters, even in infancy (McBride-Chang & Jacklin, 1993). As children grow, boys and girls are encouraged to play with different types of toys (Wood, Desmarais, & Gugula, 2002). Generally, boys have less leeway to play with "feminine" toys than girls do with "masculine" toys. When children are old enough to help with household chores, the assignments tend to depend on sex (Cunningham, 2001). For example, girls wash dishes and boys mow the lawn. And parents are more likely to explain scientific concepts to boys than to girls (Crowley et al., 2001).

Schools.   Schools and teachers clearly contribute to the socialization of gender roles. The books that children use in learning to read can influence their ideas about what is suitable behavior for males and females (Diekman & Murnen, 2004). Traditionally, males have been more likely to be portrayed as clever, heroic, and adventurous in these books, while females have been more likely to be shown doing domestic chores. Preschool and grade-school teachers frequently reward sex-appropriate behavior in their pupils (Fagot et al., 1985; Ruble & Martin, 1998). Interestingly, teachers tend to pay greater attention to males, helping them, praising them, and scolding them more than females (Sadker & Sadker, 1994).

Media.   Television and other mass media are another source of gender-role socialization (Bussey & Bandura, 2004). Although some improvement has been made in recent years, television shows have traditionally depicted men and women in stereotypical ways (Galambos, 2004; Signorielli, 2001). Women are often portrayed as submissive, passive, and emotional. Men are more likely to be portrayed as independent, assertive, and competent. Even commercials contribute to the socialization of gender roles (Furnham & Mak, 1999; Signorielli, McLeod, & Healy, 1994). Women are routinely shown worrying about trivial matters such as the whiteness of their laundry or the shine of their dishes.

Conclusion

As you can see, the findings on gender and behavior are complex and confusing. Nonetheless, the evidence does permit one very general conclusion—a conclusion that you have seen before and will see again. Taken as a whole, the research in this area suggests that biological factors and environmental factors both contribute to gender differences in behavior—as they do to all other aspects of development.

Who is this teacher going to call on? Although girls tend to perform better in grade school, research suggests that grade-school teachers pay more attention to boys.

REVIEW of Key Learning Goals

11.22 Gender differences in behavior are fewer in number than gender stereotypes suggest. In the cognitive domain, research reviews suggest that there are genuine gender differences in verbal ability, mathematical ability, and spatial ability. In regard to social behavior, differences have been found in aggression, nonverbal communication, and sexual behavior. But most gender differences in behavior are very small in magnitude.

11.23 Evolutionary theorists maintain that gender differences transcend culture because males and females have confronted different adaptive demands over the course of human history. Extensive evidence suggests that prenatal hormones contribute to human gender differences, but the research is marred by interpretive problems. Research linking gender differences to cerebral specialization is intriguing, but much remains to be learned.

11.24 A vast research literature shows that gender differences are shaped by socialization processes. Operant conditioning, observational learning, and self-socialization contribute to the development of gender differences. Families, schools, and the media are among the main sources of gender-role socialization.

Key Learning Goals

11.25 Clarify and critique the argument that fathers are essential for healthy development.

Are Fathers Essential to Children's Well-Being?

Are fathers crucial to children's well-being? This seemingly simple question has sparked heated debate.

Are fathers essential for children to experience normal, healthy development? This question is currently the subject of heated debate. In recent years, a number of social scientists have mounted a thought-provoking argument that father absence due to divorce, abandonment, and so forth, is the chief factor underlying a host of modern social ills. For example, David Blankenhorn (1995) argues that "fatherlessness is the most harmful demographic trend of this generation. It is the leading cause of declining child well-being in our society" (p. 1). Expressing a similar view, David Popenoe (1996) maintains that "today's fatherlessness has led to social turmoil-damaged children, unhappy children, aimless children, children who strike back with pathological behavior and violence" (p.192).

The Basic Argument

What is the evidence for the proposition that fathers are essential to healthy development? Over the last 40 years, the proportion of children growing up without a father in the home has more than doubled. During the same time, we have seen dramatic increases in teenage pregnancy, juvenile delinquency, violent crime, drug abuse, eating disorders, teen suicide, and family dysfunction. Moreover, mountains of studies have demonstrated an association between father absence and an elevated risk for these problems. Summarizing this evidence, Popenoe (1996) asserts that "fatherless children have a risk factor two to three times that of fathered children for a wide range of negative outcomes, including dropping out of high school, giving birth as a teenager, and becoming a juvenile delinquent" (p. 192), which leads him to infer that "fathers have a unique and irreplaceable role to play in child development" (p. 197). Working from this premise, Popenoe concludes, "If present trends continue, our so-

ciety could be on the verge of committing social suicide" (p. 192). Echoing this dire conclusion, Blankenhorn (1995) comments that "to tolerate the trend of fatherlessness is to accept the inevitability of continued societal recession" (p. 222).

You might be thinking, "What's all the fuss about?" Surely, proclaiming the importance of fatherhood ought to be no more controversial than advocacy for motherhood or apple pie. But the assertion that a father is essential to a child's well-being has some interesting sociopolitical implications. It suggests that heterosexual marriage is the only appropriate context in which to raise children and that other family configurations are fundamentally deficient. Based on this line of reasoning, some people have argued for new laws that would make it more difficult to obtain a divorce and other policies and programs that would favor traditional families over families headed by single mothers, cohabiting parents, and gay and lesbian parents (Silverstein & Auerbach, 1999). Thus, the

question about the importance of fathers is creating a great deal of controversy, because it is really a question about alternatives to traditional family structure.

Evaluating the Argument

In light of the far-reaching implications of the view that fathers are essential to normal development, it makes sense to subject this view to critical scrutiny. How could you use critical thinking skills to evaluate this argument? At least three previously discussed ideas seem pertinent.

First, it is important to recognize that the position that fathers are essential for healthy development rests on a foundation of correlational evidence, and as we have seen repeatedly, *correlation is no assurance of causation*. Yes, there has been an increase in fatherlessness that has been paralleled by increases in teenage pregnancy, drug abuse, eating disorders, and other disturbing social problems. But think of all the other changes that have occurred in American culture over the last 40 years, such as the decline of organized religion, the growth of mass media, dramatic shifts in sexual mores, and so forth. Increased fatherlessness has co-varied with a host of other cultural trends. Hence, it is highly speculative to infer that father absence is the chief cause of most modern social maladies.

Second, it always pays to think about whether there are specific, *alternative explanations* for findings that you might have doubts about. What other factors might account for the association between father absence and children's maladjustment? Think for a moment: What is the most frequent cause of father absence? Obviously, it is divorce. Divorces tend to be highly stressful events that disrupt children's entire lives. Although the evidence suggests that a majority of children seem to survive divorce without lasting, detrimental effects, it is clear that divorce elevates youngsters' risk for a wide range of negative developmental outcomes (Amato, 2001, 2003; Hetherington, 1999, 2003). Given that father absence and divorce are inextricably intertwined, it is possible that the negative effects of divorce account for much of the association between father absence and social problems.

Are there any other alternative explanations for the correlation between fatherlessness and social maladies? Yes, critics point out that the prevalence of father absence co-varies with socioeconomic status. Father absence is much more common in low-income families (Anderson, Kohler, & Letiecq, 2002). Thus, the effects of father absence are entangled to some extent with the many powerful, malignant effects of poverty, which might account for much of the correlation between fatherlessness and negative outcomes (McLoyd, 1998).

A third possible strategy in thinking critically about the effects of father absence would be to look for some of the *fallacies in reasoning* introduced in Chapter 10 (irrelevant reasons, circular reasoning, slippery slope, weak analogies, and false dichotomy). A couple of the quotes from Popenoe and Blankenhorn were chosen to give you an opportunity to detect two of these fallacies in a new context. Take a look at the quotes once again and see whether you can spot the fallacies.

Popenoe's assertion that "if present trends continue, our society could be on the verge of social suicide" is an example of *slippery slope argumentation,* which involves predictions that if one allows X to happen, things will spin out of control and catastrophic events will follow. "Social suicide" is a little vague, but it sounds as if Popenoe is predicting that father absence will lead to the destruction of modern American culture. The other fallacy that you might have spotted was the *false dichotomy* apparent in Blankenhorn's assertion that "to tolerate the trend of fatherlessness is to accept the inevitability of continued societal recession." A false dichotomy creates an either-or choice between the position one wants to advocate (in this case, new social policies to reduce father absence) and some obviously horrible outcome that any sensible person would want to avoid (social decay), while ignoring other possible outcomes that might lie between these extremes.

In summary, we can find a number of flaws and weaknesses in the argument that fathers are *essential* to normal development. However, our critical evaluation of this argument *does not mean that fathers are unimportant.* Many types of evidence suggest that fathers generally make significant contributions to their children's development (Carlson, 2006; Lewis & Lamb, 2003; Rohner & Veneziano, 2001). We could argue with merit that fathers typically provide a substantial advantage for children that fatherless children do not have. But there is a crucial distinction between arguing that fathers *promote* normal, healthy development and arguing that fathers are *necessary* for normal, healthy development. If fathers are *necessary,* children who grow up without them could not achieve the same level of well-being as those who have fathers, yet it is clear that a great many children from single-parent homes turn out just fine.

Fathers surely are important, and it seems likely that father absence *contributes* to a variety of social maladies. So, why do Blankenhorn (1995) and Popenoe (1996) argue for the much stronger conclusion—that fathers are *essential?* They appear to prefer the stronger conclusion because it raises much more serious questions about the viability of nontraditional family forms. Thus, they seem to want to advance a *political agenda* that champions traditional family values. They are certainly entitled to do so, but when research findings are used to advance a political agenda—whether conservative or liberal—a special caution alert should go off in your head. When a political agenda is at stake, it pays to scrutinize arguments with extra care, because research findings are more likely to be presented in a slanted fashion. The field of psychology deals with a host of complex questions that have profound implications for a wide range of social issues. The skills and habits of critical thinking can help you find your way through the maze of reasons and evidence that hold up the many sides of these complicated issues.

Table 11.2 Critical Thinking Skills Discussed in This Application

Skill	Description
Understanding the limitations of correlational evidence	The critical thinker understands that a correlation between two variables does not demonstrate that there is a causal link between the variables.
Looking for alternative explanations for findings and events	In evaluating explanations, the critical thinker explores whether there are other explanations that could also account for the findings or events under scrutiny.
Recognizing and avoiding common fallacies, such as irrelevant reasons, circular reasoning, slippery slope reasoning, weak analogies, and false dichotomies	The critical thinker is vigilant about conclusions based on unrelated premises, conclusions that are rewordings of premises, unwarranted predictions that things will spin out of control, superficial analogies, and contrived dichotomies.

REVIEW of Key Learning Goals

11.25 Some social scientists have argued that father absence is the chief cause of a host of social problems and that fathers are essential for normal, healthy development. Critics note that all the relevant data are correlational, making causal inferences speculative, and they argue that there are alternative explanations for the association between father absence and negative developmental outcomes.

Key Ideas

Progress Before Birth: Prenatal Development

▌ Prenatal development proceeds through the germinal, embryonic, and fetal stages as the zygote is differentiated into a human organism. During this period, development may be affected by maternal malnutrition, maternal drug use, and some maternal illnesses.

The Wondrous Years of Childhood

▌ Motor development follows cephalocaudal and proximodistal trends. Early motor development depends on both maturation and learning. Developmental norms for motor skills and other types of development only reflect typical performance.

▌ Temperamental differences among children are apparent during the first few months of life. These differences are fairly stable and may influence adult personality. Harlow's work with monkeys undermined the reinforcement explanation of attachment. Bowlby proposed an evolutionary explanation that has been influential.

▌ Research shows that attachment emerges out of an interplay between infant and mother. Infant-mother attachments fall into four categories: secure, anxious-ambivalent, avoidant, and disorganized-disoriented. Attachment patterns may have lasting effects on individuals. Modest cultural variations in the prevalence of various patterns of attachment are seen, but secure attachment predominates in all cultures.

▌ Erikson's theory of personality development proposes that individuals evolve through eight stages over the life span. In each stage the person wrestles with changes (crises) in social relationships.

▌ According to Piaget's theory of cognitive development, the key advance during the sensorimotor period is the child's gradual recognition of the permanence of objects. The preoperational period is marked by certain deficiencies in thinking—notably, centration, irreversibility, and egocentrism.

▌ During the concrete operational period, children develop the ability to perform operations on mental representations, making them capable of conservation and hierarchical classification. The stage of formal operations ushers in more abstract, systematic, and logical thought.

▌ Vygotsky's sociocultural theory maintains that cognitive development is fueled by social interactions with parents and others. Vygotsky argued that language is central to cognitive development and that culture exerts great influence over how cognitive growth unfolds.

▌ Recent research has shown that infants appear to understand surprisingly complex concepts, including numerical operations that they have had virtually no opportunity to learn about, leading some theorists to conclude that basic cognitive abilities are innate.

▌ According to Kohlberg, moral reasoning progresses through three levels that are related to age and determined by cognitive development. Age-related progress in moral reasoning has been found in research, although a great deal of overlap occurs between adjacent stages.

The Transition of Adolescence

▌ The growth spurt at puberty is a prominent event involving the development of reproductive maturity and secondary sex characteristics. Neural development continues through adolescence and the prefrontal cortex appears to be the last area of the brain to fully mature. Adolescents' risk taking may be elevated by their susceptibility to peer influence.

▌ Recent decades have brought a surge in attempted suicide by adolescents. Nonetheless, the evidence suggests that adolescence is only slightly more stressful than other periods of life. According to Erikson, the key challenge of adolescence is to make some progress toward a sense of identity. Marcia identified four patterns of identity formation. Arnett has argued that emerging adulthood represents a new stage of development falling between adolescence and adulthood.

The Expanse of Adulthood

▌ During adulthood, personality is marked by both stability and change. Many landmarks in adult development involve transitions in family relationships, including adjusting to marriage, parenthood, and the empty nest. During adulthood, age-related physical transitions include changes in appearance, sensory losses, and hormonal changes.

▌ Research suggests that fluid intelligence declines in later adulthood, but crystallized intelligence tends to remain stable. Drastic mental decline is not a part of the normal aging process. However, many adults over age 75 suffer from some form of dementia. In late adulthood, mental speed declines and working memory suffers, but many people remain productive well into old age.

Reflecting on the Chapter's Themes

▌ Many of our seven integrative themes stood out in this chapter. But above all else, our discussion of development showed how heredity and environment interactively shape behavior.

PERSONAL APPLICATION Understanding Gender Differences

▌ Gender differences in behavior are fewer in number and smaller in magnitude than gender stereotypes suggest. Research reviews suggest that there are genuine (albeit small) gender differences in verbal ability, mathematical ability, spatial ability, aggression, nonverbal communication, and sexual behavior.

▌ Evolutionary theorists believe that gender differences reflect the influence of natural selection. Some research links gender differences in humans to prenatal hormones and brain organization, but the research is marred by interpretive problems. Operant conditioning, observational learning, and self-socialization contribute to the development of gender differences.

CRITICAL THINKING APPLICATION Are Fathers Essential to Children's Well-Being?

▌ Some social scientists have argued that father absence is the chief cause of a host of social problems and that fathers are essential for normal, healthy development. Critics have argued that there are alternative explanations for the association between father absence and negative developmental outcomes.

Key Terms

Age of viability (p. 443)
Animism (p. 455)
Attachment (p. 448)
Centration (p. 454)
Cephalocaudal trend (p. 445)
Cognitive development (p. 453)
Conservation (p. 454)
Cohort effects (p. 447)
Cross-sectional design (p. 447)
Crystallized intelligence (p. 473)
Dementia (p. 472)
Development (p. 440)
Developmental norms (p. 445)
Egocentrism (p. 455)
Embryonic stage (p. 441)
Fetal alcohol syndrome (p. 444)
Fetal stage (p. 442)
Fluid intelligence (p. 473)
Gender (p. 475)
Gender differences (p. 480)
Gender roles (p. 482)
Gender stereotypes (pp. 475–476)
Germinal stage (p. 441)
Irreversibility (p. 455)
Longitudinal design (p. 447)
Maturation (p. 445)
Menarche (p. 464)
Motor development (p. 445)
Object permanence (p. 454)

Placenta (p. 441)
Prenatal period (p. 440)
Primary sex characteristics (p. 464)
Proximodistal trend (p. 445)
Puberty (p. 464)
Pubescence (p. 463)
Secondary sex characteristics (p. 463)
Separation anxiety (p. 449)
Sex (p. 475)
Socialization (p. 482)
Spermarche (p. 464)
Stage (p. 452)
Temperament (p. 446)
Zone of proximal development (ZPD) (p. 457)
Zygote (p. 440)

Key People

Mary Ainsworth (pp. 449–450)
John Bowlby (p. 449)
Erik Erikson (pp. 451–453)
Harry Harlow (p. 449)
Jerome Kagan (p. 448)
Lawrence Kohlberg (pp. 460–462)
Jean Piaget (pp. 453–457)
Alexander Thomas and Stella Chess (pp. 446–448)
Lev Vygotsky (pp. 457–457)

1. The stage of prenatal development during which the developing organism is most vulnerable to injury is the:
   A. zygotic stage.
   B. germinal stage.
   C. embryonic stage.
   D. fetal stage.

2. The cephalocaudal trend in the motor development of children can be described simply as a:
   A. head-to-foot direction.
   B. center-outward direction.
   C. foot-to-head direction.
   D. body-appendages direction.

3. Developmental norms:
   A. can be used to make extremely precise predictions about the age at which an individual child will reach various developmental milestones.
   B. indicate the maximum age at which a child can reach a particular developmental milestone and still be considered "normal."
   C. indicate the average age at which individuals reach various developmental milestones.
   D. involve both a and b.

4. When the development of the same subjects is studied over a period of time, the study is called a:
   A. cross-sectional study.
   B. life history study.
   C. longitudinal study.
   D. sequential study.

5. The quality of infant-caregiver attachment depends:
   A. on the quality of bonding in the first few hours of life.
   B. exclusively on the infant's temperament.
   C. on the interaction between the infant's temperament and the caregiver's responsiveness.
   D. on how stranger anxiety is handled.

6. During the second year of life, toddlers begin to take some personal responsibility for feeding, dressing, and bathing themselves in an attempt to establish what Erikson calls a sense of:
   A. superiority.
   B. industry.
   C. generativity.
   D. autonomy.

7. Five-year-old David watches as you pour water from a short, wide glass into a tall, narrow one. He says there is now more water than before. This response demonstrates that:
   A. David understands the concept of conservation.
   B. David does not understand the concept of conservation.
   C. David's cognitive development is "behind" for his age.
   D. both b and c are the case.

8. Which of the following is *not* one of the criticisms of Piaget's theory of cognitive development?
   A. Piaget may have underestimated the cognitive skills of children in some areas.
   B. Piaget may have underestimated the influence of cultural factors on cognitive development.
   C. The theory does not clearly address the issue of individual differences in development.
   D. Evidence for the theory is based on children's answers to questions.

9. If a child's primary reason for not drawing pictures on the living room wall with crayons is to avoid the punishment that would inevitably follow this behavior, she would be said to be at which level of moral development?
   A. conventional
   B. postconventional
   C. preconventional
   D. unconventional

10. The portion of the brain that appears to be the last area to mature fully is the:
    A. hypothalamus.
    B. corpus callosum.
    C. prefrontal cortex.
    D. occipital lobe.

11. Girls who mature _____ and boys who mature _____ seem to experience more subjective distress and emotional difficulties with the transition to adolescence.
    A. early; early
    B. early; late
    C. late; early
    D. late; late

12. Sixteen-year-old Foster wants to spend a few years experimenting with different lifestyles and careers before he settles on who and what he wants to be. Foster's behavior illustrates the identity status of:
    A. identity moratorium.
    B. identity foreclosure.
    C. identity achievement.
    D. identity diffusion.

13. Although women perform about _____ of all housework, about _____ of wives characterize their household division of labor as unfair.
    A. one-half; one-half
    B. two-thirds; three-quarters
    C. two-thirds; one-third
    D. three-quarters; one-tenth

14. Males have been found to differ slightly from females in three well-documented areas of mental abilities. Which of the following is *not* one of these?
    A. verbal ability
    B. mathematical ability
    C. intelligence
    D. visual-spatial abilities

15. Research suggests that males exhibit _____ than females and that females have a _____ than males.
    A. less cerebral specialization; smaller corpus callosum
    B. less cerebral specialization; larger corpus callosum
    C. more cerebral specialization; smaller corpus callosum
    D. more cerebral specialization; larger corpus callosum

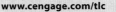

Answers
1 C p. 442
2 A p. 445
3 C pp. 445–446
4 C p. 447
5 C p. 450
6 D p. 452
7 B p. 454
8 D pp. 456–457
9 C pp. 460–461
10 C p. 465
11 B p. 464
12 A p. 467
13 C p. 470
14 C p. 480
15 D pp. 481–82

PsykTrek

To view a demo: www.cengage.com/psychology/psyktrek
To order: www.cengage.com/psychology/weiten

Go to the PsykTrek website or CD-ROM for further study of the concepts in this chapter. Both online and on the CD-ROM, PsykTrek includes dozens of learning modules with videos, animations, and quizzes, as well as simulations of psychological phenomena and a multimedia glossary that includes word pronunciations.

CengageNow

www.cengage.com/tlc

Go to this site for the link to CengageNOW, your one-stop study shop. Take a Pretest for this chapter, and CengageNOW will generate a personalized Study Plan based on your test results. The Study Plan will identify the topics you need to review and direct you to online resources to help you master those topics. You can then take a Posttest to help you determine the concepts you have mastered and what you still need to work on.

Companion Website

www.cengage.com/psychology/weiten

Go to this site to find online resources directly linked to your book, including a glossary, flash cards, drag-and-drop exercises, quizzes, and more!

12

PERSONALITY: THEORY, RESEARCH, AND ASSESSMENT

The Nature of Personality
Defining Personality: Consistency and Distinctiveness
Personality Traits: Dispositions and Dimensions
The Five-Factor Model of Personality Traits

Psychodynamic Perspectives
Freud's Psychoanalytic Theory
Jung's Analytical Psychology
Adler's Individual Psychology
Evaluating Psychodynamic Perspectives

Behavioral Perspectives
Skinner's Ideas Applied to Personality
Bandura's Social Cognitive Theory

FEATURED STUDY ▌ Can Rooms *Really* Have Personality?

Mischel and the Person-Situation Controversy
Evaluating Behavioral Perspectives

Humanistic Perspectives
Rogers's Person-Centered Theory
Maslow's Theory of Self-Actualization
Evaluating Humanistic Perspectives

Biological Perspectives
Eysenck's Theory
Behavioral Genetics and Personality
The Evolutionary Approach to Personality
Evaluating Biological Perspectives

A Contemporary Empirical Approach: Terror Management Theory
Essentials of Terror Management Theory
Applications of Terror Management Theory

Culture and Personality

Illustrated Overview of Major Theories of Personality

Reflecting on the Chapter's Themes

PERSONAL APPLICATION ▌ Understanding Personality Assessment
Self-Report Inventories
Projective Tests
Personality Testing on the Internet

CRITICAL THINKING APPLICATION ▌ Hindsight in Everyday Analyses of Personality
The Prevalence of Hindsight Bias
Hindsight and Personality
Other Implications of "20/20 Hindsight"

Recap

Practice Test

Richard Branson was sure that he was about to die. He was high above the Atlantic Ocean, alone in a capsule attached to the biggest balloon in the world. Per Lindstrand, the balloon's pilot, was somewhere in the icy waves far below. He and Branson had just become the first people ever to cross the Atlantic in a hot-air balloon, but when an emergency landing at sea failed, Lindstrand had leaped into the water. Before Branson could follow, the balloon had shot back up into the sky. Now Branson—who had never flown in a balloon before his all-too-brief training for the trip—was stranded in midair with no clear idea how to save himself.

Hastily Branson scribbled a note to his family: "I love you." Then he began trying to vent the huge balloon in a desperate attempt to guide it safely earthward. Much to his own surprise, he was able to get close enough to the sea to jump for it. A rescue helicopter plucked him out of the waves. (Lindstrand was saved by a passing fisherman.)

After this frightening brush with death, Branson swore that he would never risk his life so foolishly again. Yet three years later, he and Lindstrand were at it again, this time becoming the first to cross the Pacific in a hot-air balloon. The trip turned into another terrifying ordeal—at one point the balloon caught fire when they were thousands of feet above empty ocean—and once again they were nearly killed. But that didn't stop them from planning their next exploit—trying to become the first hot-air balloonists to fly completely around the world (Branson, 2005; Brown, 1998).

What kind of person has such an insatiable hunger for death-defying adventures? When people describe this side of Richard Branson, they are apt to use words such as *adventurous, brave, daring, impulsive,* and *reckless.* These are the kinds of words used to characterize what we call "personality." And Branson—a self-made billionaire and one of the richest people in the world—may be as famous for his exuberant personality as he is for his immense wealth.

A high school dropout, Branson is the founder of the Virgin group of companies. Among Virgin's 200 businesses are such varied enterprises as Virgin Megastores, the airline Virgin Atlantic, and Virgin Galactic, which aims to become the first company to fly tourists into space. Branson is a brash, shrewd, and relentless entrepreneur who loves cutting a deal. But he also loves parties, practical jokes, and flamboyant publicity stunts. Most of all, he relishes finding

Richard Branson, the founder of the Virgin group of companies, clearly manifests a powerful and unusual personality. But everyone has his or her own unique personality, which makes the study of personality a fascinating area of inquiry in psychology.

© Michael Buckner/Getty Images

new fields to conquer. It was typical of Branson—who made his first fortune with a music recording company—to decide that it would be "fun" to start an airline even though he had no knowledge of the business, let alone routes to fly or planes to fly them (Branson, 2005; Brown, 1998). His approach is nicely summed up in the title of his book of life lessons, *Screw It, Let's Do It* (Branson, 2006).

Most people would agree that Richard Branson has an unusual personality. But what exactly *is* personality? And why are personalities so different? Why is one person daring, while another is timid? Why is one person high-spirited and outgoing, while another is quiet and shy? Was Richard Branson born with the self-confidence and daring he is renowned for, or were environment and learning critical in shaping his personality? Consider that Branson's parents stressed the importance of being strong and independent, starting at an early age. When Branson was just 4 years old, he relates, his mother "stopped the car a few miles from our house and made me find my own way home across the fields" (Branson, 2005, p. 15). Branson believes that episodes like these nurtured his enduring appe-

tite for "huge, apparently unachievable challenges" (Branson, 2005, p. 219).

Yet can this be the whole explanation? After all, another 4-year-old might have simply sat down by the road and cried. Could part of the answer to the riddle of Branson's personality lie in biological inheritance? Branson (2005) describes his mother as a woman of dazzling energy and fierce determination who also has a taste for adventure. During World War II Eve Branson wanted to be a glider pilot even though the job was open only to males. Refusing to take no for an answer, she talked her way into pilot training on the condition that she disguise herself as a boy. Branson's father, Ted, is a quieter sort who nevertheless shares his wife's adventurousness. When Branson dreamed up the idea for Virgin Galactic, an airline offering suborbital spaceflights, Ted said that he intended to be one of the first passengers launched into space—at the age of 90! With parents like these, is being an "adrenaline junkie" wired into Branson's genetic makeup?

Psychologists have approached questions like these from a variety of perspectives. Traditionally, the study of personality has been dominated by "grand theories" that attempt to explain a great many facets of behavior. Our discussion will reflect this emphasis, as we'll devote most of our time to the sweeping theories of Freud, Skinner, Rogers, and several others. In recent decades, however, the study of personality has shifted toward narrower research programs that examine specific issues related to personality. This trend is reflected in our review of biological, cultural, and other contemporary approaches to personality in the last several sections of the chapter. In the Personal Application, we'll examine how psychological tests are used to measure aspects of personality. The Critical Thinking Application will explore how hindsight bias can taint people's analyses of personality.

The Nature of Personality

Key Learning Goals

12.1 Define the construct of personality in terms of consistency and distinctiveness.

12.2 Clarify what is meant by a personality trait, and describe the five-factor model of personality.

12.3 Summarize relations between the Big Five traits and aspects of behavior and life outcomes.

Personality is a complex hypothetical construct that has been defined in a variety of ways. Let's take a closer look at the concepts of personality and personality traits.

Defining Personality: Consistency and Distinctiveness

What does it mean to say that someone has an optimistic personality? This assertion indicates that the

person has a fairly *consistent tendency* to behave in a cheerful, hopeful, enthusiastic way, looking at the bright side of things, across a wide variety of situations. Although no one is entirely consistent in behavior, this quality of *consistency across situations* lies at the core of the concept of personality.

Distinctiveness is also central to the concept of personality. Personality is used to explain why not everyone acts the same way in similar situations. If you were stuck in an elevator with three people, each might react differently. One might crack jokes to relieve the tension. Another might make ominous predictions that "we'll never get out of here." The third might calmly think about how to escape. These varied reactions to the same situation occur because each person has a different personality. Each person has traits that are seen in other people, but each individual has his or her own distinctive *set* of personality traits.

In summary, the concept of personality is used to explain (1) the stability in a person's behavior over time and across situations (consistency) and (2) the behavioral differences among people reacting to the same situation (distinctiveness). We can combine these ideas into the following definition: **Personality refers to an individual's unique constellation of consistent behavioral traits.** Let's look more closely at the concept of *traits*.

Personality Traits: Dispositions and Dimensions

Everyone makes remarks like "Jan is very *conscientious*." Or you might assert that "Bill is too *timid* to succeed in that job." These descriptive statements refer to personality traits. **A *personality trait* is a durable disposition to behave in a particular way in a variety of situations.** Adjectives such as *honest, dependable, moody, impulsive, suspicious, anxious, excitable, domineering,* and *friendly* describe dispositions that represent personality traits.

Most approaches to personality assume that some traits are more basic than others. According to this notion, a small number of fundamental traits determine other, more superficial traits. For example, a person's tendency to be impulsive, restless, irritable, boisterous, and impatient might all be derived from a more basic tendency to be excitable.

A number of psychologists have taken on the challenge of identifying the basic traits that form the core of personality. For example, Raymond Cattell (1950, 1966, 1990) used the statistical procedure of *factor analysis* to reduce a list of 171 personality traits compiled by Gordon Allport (1937) to just 16 basic dimensions of personality. In ***factor analysis, correlations among many variables are analyzed to identify closely related clusters of variables*** (see Chapter 9). If the measurements of a number of variables (in this case, personality traits) correlate highly with one another, the assumption is that a single factor is influencing all of them. Factor analysis is used to identify these hidden factors. In factor analyses of personality traits, these hidden factors are viewed as basic, higher-order traits that determine less basic, more specific traits. Based on his factor analytic work, Cattell concluded that an individual's personality can be described completely by measuring just 16 traits. The 16 crucial traits are listed in Figure 12.20, which can be found in the Personal Application, where we discuss a personality test that Cattell designed to assess these traits.

The Five-Factor Model of Personality Traits

In recent years, Robert McCrae and Paul Costa (1987, 1997, 1999, 2003) have used factor analysis to arrive at an even simpler, *five-factor model of personality* (see Figure 12.1). McCrae and Costa maintain that most personality traits are derived from just five higher-order traits that have come to be known as the "Big Five":

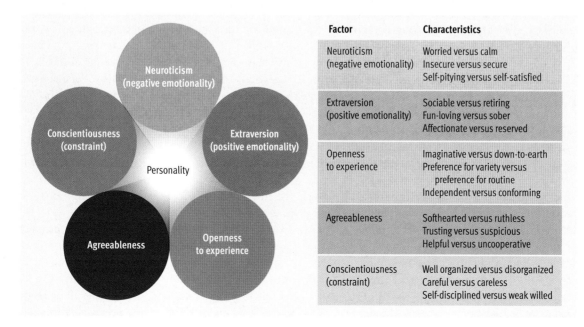

Factor	Characteristics
Neuroticism (negative emotionality)	Worried versus calm Insecure versus secure Self-pitying versus self-satisfied
Extraversion (positive emotionality)	Sociable versus retiring Fun-loving versus sober Affectionate versus reserved
Openness to experience	Imaginative versus down-to-earth Preference for variety versus preference for routine Independent versus conforming
Agreeableness	Softhearted versus ruthless Trusting versus suspicious Helpful versus uncooperative
Conscientiousness (constraint)	Well organized versus disorganized Careful versus careless Self-disciplined versus weak willed

Figure 12.1

The five-factor model of personality. Trait models attempt to analyze personality into its basic dimensions. In factor-analytic studies, the five traits shown here tend to emerge as higher-order factors that can account for other traits. McCrae and Costa (1985, 1987, 1997) maintain that personality can be described adequately by scores on the five traits identified here, which are widely referred to as the Big Five.

SOURCE: Trait descriptions from McCrae, R. R., & Costa, P. T. (1986). Clinical assessment can benefit from recent advances in personality psychology. *American Psychologist, 41,* 1001–1003.

1. *Extraversion.* People who score high in extraversion are characterized as outgoing, sociable, upbeat, friendly, assertive, and gregarious. Referred to as *positive emotionality* in some trait models, extraversion has been studied extensively for many decades (Watson & Clark, 1997). Extraverts tend to be happier than others (Fleeson, Malanos, & Achille, 2002).

2. *Neuroticism.* People who score high in neuroticism tend to be anxious, hostile, self-conscious, insecure, and vulnerable. Like extraversion, this trait has been the subject of thousands of studies. In some trait models it is called *negative emotionality.* Those who score high in neuroticism tend to overreact more than others in response to stress (Mroczek & Almeida, 2004).

3. *Openness to experience.* Openness is associated with curiosity, flexibility, vivid fantasy, imaginativeness, artistic sensitivity, and unconventional attitudes. McCrae (1996) maintains that its importance has been underestimated. Citing evidence that openness fosters liberalism, he argues that this trait is the key determinant of people's political attitudes and ideology. For example, evidence suggests that people high in openness tend to exhibit less prejudice against minorities than others (Flynn, 2005).

4. *Agreeableness.* Those who score high in agreeableness tend to be sympathetic, trusting, cooperative, modest, and straightforward. People who score at the opposite end of this personality dimension are characterized as suspicious, antagonistic, and aggressive. Agreeableness is associated with constructive approaches to conflict resolution, making agreeable people less quarrelsome than others (Jensen-Campbell & Graziano, 2001).

5. *Conscientiousness.* Conscientious people tend to be disciplined, well organized, punctual, and dependable. Referred to as *constraint* in some trait models, conscientiousness is associated with being highly diligent in the workplace (Lund et al., 2007).

Research shows that Big Five traits are predictive of specific aspects of behavior, as one would expect (Paunonen, 2003). For example, extraversion correlates positively with popularity and with dating a greater variety of people. Conscientiousness correlates with greater honesty, higher job performance ratings, and relatively low alcohol consumption. Openness to experience is associated with playing a musical instrument, whereas agreeableness correlates with honesty.

Correlations have also been found between the Big Five traits and quite a variety of important life outcomes (Ozer & Benet-Martinez, 2006). For instance, higher grades (GPA) in both high school and college are associated with higher conscientiousness, primarily because conscientious students work harder (Noftle & Robins, 2007). Several of the Big Five traits are associated with occupational attainment (career success). Extraversion and conscientiousness are positive predictors of occupational attainment, whereas neuroticism is a negative predictor (Roberts, Caspi, & Moffitt, 2003). The likelihood of divorce can also be predicted by personality traits, as neuroticism elevates the probability of divorce, whereas agreeableness and conscientiousness reduce it (Roberts et al., 2007). Finally, and perhaps most important, two of the Big Five traits are related to health and mortality over the course of the life span. Neuroticism is associated with an elevated prevalence of physical and mental disorders, whereas conscientiousness is correlated with the experience of less illness and with reduced mortality (Goodwin & Friedman, 2006; Martin, Friedman, & Schwartz, 2007). In other words, conscientious people live longer than others!

Like Cattell, McCrae and Costa maintain that personality can be described adequately by measuring the basic traits that they've identified. Their bold claim has been supported in many studies by other researchers, and the five-factor model has become the dominant conception of personality structure in contemporary psychology (John & Srivastava, 1999; McCrae, 2005). These five traits have been characterized as the "latitude and longitude" along which personality should be mapped (Ozer & Reise, 1994, p. 361).

However, some theorists have been critical of the model. Jack Block (1995) has questioned the generality of the model. He points out that the higher-order traits that emerge in factor analyses depend to some extent on the exact mix of the much larger set of lower-order traits that are measured in the first place. Thus, he asserts that the five-factor model is more arbitrary than widely appreciated. Other critics of the five-factor model maintain that more than five traits are necessary to account for most of the variation seen in human personality. For example, one recent article argued that honesty-humility ought to be recognized as a fundamental sixth factor in personality (Ashton, Lee, & Goldberg, 2004). And other theorists have argued that there are some important traits—such as being manipulative, frugal, conservative, humorous, and egotistical—that do not fit into the five-factor model (Paunonen & Jackson, 2000).

The debate about how many dimensions are necessary to describe personality is likely to continue for many years to come. As you'll see throughout the chapter, the study of personality is an area in psychology that has a long history of "dueling theories." We'll divide these diverse personality theories into four broad groups that share certain assumptions, emphases, and interests: (1) psychodynamic perspectives, (2) behavioral perspectives, (3) humanistic perspectives, and (4) biological perspectives. We'll begin our discussion of personality theories by examining the life and work of Sigmund Freud.

REVIEW of Key Learning Goals

12.1 The concept of personality focuses on consistency in people's behavior over time and across situations and on what traits make people distinctive from one another. Thus, personality refers to an individual's unique constellation of consistent behavioral traits.

12.2 A personality trait is a durable disposition to behave in a particular way. The five-factor model has become the dominant conception of personality structure. The Big Five personality traits are extraversion, neuroticism, openness to experience, agreeableness, and conscientiousness.

12.3 The Big Five traits are predictive of some kinds of behavior, such as honesty, job performance, and alcohol use. They also predict important life outcomes, such as grades, occupational attainment, divorce, health, and mortality.

Psychodynamic Perspectives

Psychodynamic theories include all the diverse theories descended from the work of Sigmund Freud, which focus on unconscious mental forces. Freud inspired many brilliant scholars who followed in his intellectual footsteps. Some of these followers simply refined and updated Freud's theory. Others veered off in new directions and established independent, albeit related, schools of thought. Today, the psychodynamic umbrella covers a large collection of loosely related theories that we can only sample from in this text. In this chapter, we'll examine the ideas of Sigmund Freud in some detail. Then we'll take a briefer look at the psychodynamic theories of Carl Jung and Alfred Adler.

Freud's Psychoanalytic Theory

10a

Born in 1856, Sigmund Freud grew up in a middle-class Jewish home in Vienna, Austria. He showed an early interest in intellectual pursuits and became an intense, hardworking young man, driven to achieve fame. He experienced his share of inner turmoil and engaged in regular self-analysis for over 40 years. Freud lived in the Victorian era, which was marked by sexual repression. His life was also affected by the first great World War, which devastated Europe, and by the growing anti-Semitism of the times. We'll see that the sexual repression and aggressive hostilities that Freud witnessed left their mark on his view of human nature.

Freud was a physician specializing in neurology when he began his medical practice in Vienna toward the end of the 19th century. Like other neurologists in his era, he often treated people troubled by nervous problems such as irrational fears, obses-sions, and anxieties. Eventually he devoted himself to the treatment of mental disorders using an innovative procedure he had developed, called *psychoanalysis,* that required lengthy verbal interactions with patients during which Freud probed deeply into their lives.

Freud's (1901, 1924, 1940) *psychoanalytic theory* grew out of his decades of interactions with his clients in psychoanalysis. Psychoanalytic theory attempts to explain personality, motivation, and psychological disorders by focusing on the influence of early childhood experiences, on unconscious motives and conflicts, and on the methods people use to cope with their sexual and aggressive urges.

Most of Freud's contemporaries were uncomfortable with his theory for at least three reasons. First, in arguing that people's behavior is governed by unconscious factors of which they are unaware, Freud made the disconcerting suggestion that individuals are not masters of their own minds. Second, in claiming that adult personalities are shaped by childhood experiences and other factors beyond one's control, he suggested that people are not masters of their own destinies. Third, by emphasizing the great importance of how people cope with their sexual urges, he offended those who held the conservative, Victorian values of his time. Let's examine the ideas that generated so much controversy.

Structure of Personality

10a

Freud divided personality structure into three components: the id, the ego, and the superego (see Figure 12.2 on the next page). He saw a person's behavior as the outcome of interactions among these three components.

Key Learning Goals

12.4 Distinguish among the three components of personality and the three levels of awareness in Freud's theory.

12.5 Explain the role of anxiety in Freud's theory, and discuss the operation of defense mechanisms.

12.6 Describe Freud's psychosexual stages of development and their importance.

12.7 Summarize the revisions of Freud's theory proposed by Jung and Adler.

12.8 Evaluate the strengths and weaknesses of the psychodynamic approach to personality.

Sigmund Freud

"No one who, like me, conjures up the most evil of those half-tamed demons that inhabit the human beast, and seeks to wrestle with them, can expect to come through the struggle unscathed."

© National Library of Medicine

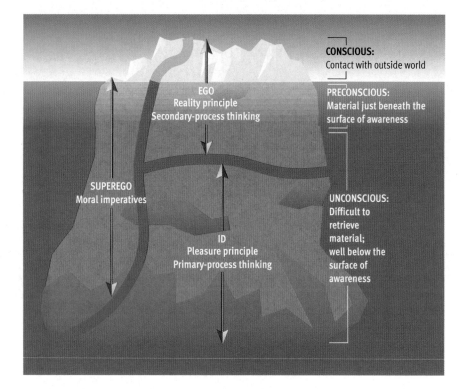

CONSCIOUS:
Contact with outside world

EGO
Reality principle
Secondary-process thinking

PRECONSCIOUS:
Material just beneath the surface of awareness

SUPEREGO
Moral imperatives

UNCONSCIOUS:
Difficult to retrieve material; well below the surface of awareness

ID
Pleasure principle
Primary-process thinking

Figure 12.2
Freud's model of personality structure. Freud theorized that people have three levels of awareness: the conscious, the preconscious, and the unconscious. The enormous size of the unconscious is often dramatized by comparing it to the portion of an iceberg that lies beneath the water's surface. Freud also divided personality structure into three components—id, ego, and superego—which operate according to different principles and exhibit different modes of thinking. In Freud's model, the id is entirely unconscious, but the ego and superego operate at all three levels of awareness.

The *id* is the primitive, instinctive component of personality that operates according to the pleasure principle. Freud referred to the id as the reservoir of psychic energy. By this he meant that the id houses the raw biological urges (to eat, sleep, defecate, copulate, and so on) that energize human behavior. The id operates according to the *pleasure principle,* which demands immediate gratification of its urges. The id engages in *primary-process thinking,* which is primitive, illogical, irrational, and fantasy oriented.

The *ego* is the decision-making component of personality that operates according to the reality principle. The ego mediates between the id, with its forceful desires for immediate satisfaction, and the external social world, with its expectations and norms regarding suitable behavior. The ego considers social realities—society's norms, etiquette, rules, and customs—in deciding how to behave. The ego is guided by the *reality principle,* which seeks to delay gratification of the id's urges until appropriate outlets and situations can be found. In short, to stay out of trouble, the ego often works to tame the unbridled desires of the id.

In the long run, the ego wants to maximize gratification, just as the id does. However, the ego engages in *secondary-process thinking,* which is relatively rational, realistic, and oriented toward problem solving. Thus, the ego strives to avoid negative consequences from society and its representatives (for example, punishment by parents or teachers)

by behaving "properly." It also attempts to achieve long-range goals that sometimes require putting off gratification.

While the ego concerns itself with practical realities, the *superego* is the moral component of personality that incorporates social standards about what represents right and wrong. Throughout their lives, but especially during childhood, people receive training about what constitutes good and bad behavior. Many social norms regarding morality are eventually internalized. The superego emerges out of the ego at around 3 to 5 years of age. In some people, the superego can become irrationally demanding in its striving for moral perfection. Such people are plagued by excessive feelings of guilt. According to Freud, the id, ego, and superego are distributed differently across three levels of awareness, which we'll describe next.

Levels of Awareness   10a

Perhaps Freud's most enduring insight was his recognition of how unconscious forces can influence behavior. He inferred the existence of the unconscious from a variety of observations that he made with his patients. For example, he noticed that "slips of the tongue" often revealed a person's true feelings. He also realized that his patients' dreams often expressed hidden desires. Most important, through psychoanalysis he often helped patients discover feelings and conflicts of which they had previously been unaware.

Freud contrasted the unconscious with the conscious and preconscious, creating three levels of awareness. The *conscious* consists of whatever one is aware of at a particular point in time. For example, at this moment your conscious may include the train of thought in this text and a dim awareness in the back of your mind that your eyes are getting tired and you're beginning to get hungry. The *preconscious* contains material just beneath the surface of awareness that can easily be retrieved. Examples might include your middle name, what you had for supper last night, or an argument you had with a friend yesterday. The *unconscious* contains thoughts, memories, and desires that are well below the surface of conscious awareness but that nonetheless exert great influence on behavior. Examples of material that might be found in your unconscious include a forgotten trauma from childhood, hidden feelings of hostility toward a parent, and repressed sexual desires.

Freud's conception of the mind is often compared to an iceberg that has most of its mass hidden beneath the water's surface (see **Figure 12.2**). He believed that the unconscious (the mass below the surface) is much larger than the conscious or preconscious. As you can see in **Figure 12.2**, he proposed that the ego and superego operate at all three levels of awareness. In contrast, the id is entirely unconscious, expressing its urges at a conscious level through the ego. Of course, the id's desires for immediate satisfaction often trigger internal conflicts with the ego and superego. These conflicts play a key role in Freud's theory.

Conflict and the Tyranny of Sex and Aggression

Freud assumed that behavior is the outcome of an ongoing series of internal conflicts. He saw internal battles between the id, ego, and superego as routine. Why? Because the id wants to gratify its urges immediately, but the norms of civilized society frequently dictate otherwise. For example, your id might feel an urge to clobber a co-worker who constantly irritates you. However, society frowns on such behavior, so your ego would try to hold this urge in check. Hence, you would find yourself in conflict. You may be experiencing conflict at this very moment. In Freudian terms, your id may be secretly urging you to abandon reading this chapter so that you can fix a snack and watch some television. Your ego may be weighing this appealing option against your society-induced need to excel in school.

Freud believed that people's lives are dominated by conflict. He asserted that individuals career from one conflict to another. The following scenario provides a concrete illustration of how the three components of personality interact to create constant conflicts:

Imagine lurching across your bed to shut off your alarm clock as it rings obnoxiously. It's 7 A.M. and time to get up for your history class. However, your id (operating according to the pleasure principle) urges you to return to the immediate gratification of additional sleep. Your ego (operating according to the reality principle) points out that you really must go to class since you haven't been able to decipher the textbook on your own. Your id (in its typical unrealistic fashion) smugly assures you that you will get the A grade that you need and suggests lying back to dream about how impressed your roommates will be. Just as you're relaxing, your superego jumps into the fray. It tries to make you feel guilty about all the money your parents paid in tuition for the class that you're about to skip. You haven't even gotten out of bed yet, but there's already a pitched battle in your psyche.

Not all conflicts are equal. Freud believed that conflicts centering on sexual and aggressive impulses are especially likely to have far-reaching con-

Freud's psychoanalytic theory was based on decades of clinical work. He treated a great many patients in the consulting room pictured here. The room contains numerous artifacts from other cultures—and the original psychoanalytic couch.

sequences. Why did he emphasize sex and aggression? Two reasons were prominent in his thinking. First, he thought that sex and aggression are subject to more complex and ambiguous social controls than other basic motives. The norms governing sexual and aggressive behavior are subtle, and people often get inconsistent messages about what's appropriate. Thus, Freud believed that these two drives are the source of much confusion. Second, he noted that the sexual and aggressive drives are thwarted more regularly than other basic biological urges. Think about it: If you get hungry or thirsty, you can simply head for a nearby vending machine or a drinking fountain. But if a department store clerk infuriates you, you aren't likely to reach across the counter and slug him or her. Likewise, when you see a person who inspires lustful urges, you don't normally walk up and propose a tryst in a nearby broom closet. There's nothing comparable to vending machines or drinking fountains for the satisfaction of sexual and aggressive urges. Freud ascribed great importance to these needs because social norms dictate that they be routinely frustrated.

Anxiety and Defense Mechanisms

Most internal conflicts are trivial and are quickly resolved one way or the other. Occasionally, however, a conflict will linger for days, months, or even years, creating internal tension. More often than not, such prolonged and troublesome conflicts involve sexual and aggressive impulses that society wants to tame. These conflicts are often played out entirely in the unconscious. Although you may not be aware of these unconscious battles, they can produce *anxiety*

web link 12.2

Sigmund Freud Museum, Vienna, Austria

This online museum, in both English and German versions, offers a detailed chronology of Freud's life and an explanation of the most important concepts of psychoanalysis. The highlights here, though, are the rich audiovisual resources, including photos, amateur movie clips, and voice recordings of Freud.

"ALL I WANT FROM THEM IS A SIMPLE MAJORITY ON THINGS."

© 2004 Sidney Harris/ScienceCartoonsPlus.com

that slips to the surface of conscious awareness. The anxiety can be attributed to your ego worrying about (1) the id getting out of control and doing something terrible that leads to severe negative consequences or (2) the superego getting out of control and making you feel guilty about a real or imagined transgression.

The arousal of anxiety is a crucial event in Freud's theory of personality functioning (see **Figure 12.3**). Anxiety is distressing, so people try to rid themselves of this unpleasant emotion any way they can. This effort to ward off anxiety often involves the use of defense mechanisms. *Defense mechanisms* **are largely unconscious reactions that protect a person from unpleasant emotions such as anxiety and guilt** (see Table 12.1). Typically, they're mental maneuvers that work through self-deception. Consider *rationalization,* **which is creating false but plausible excuses to justify unacceptable behavior.** For example, after cheating someone in a business transaction, you might reduce your guilt by rationalizing that "everyone does it."

Characterized as "the flagship in the psychoanalytic fleet of defense mechanisms" (Paulhus, Fridhandler, & Hayes, 1997), repression is the most basic and widely used defense mechanism. *Repression* **is keeping distressing thoughts and feelings buried in the unconscious.** People tend to repress desires that make them feel guilty, conflicts that make them anxious, and memories that are painful. Repression

has been called "motivated forgetting." If you forget a dental appointment or the name of someone you don't like, repression may be at work.

Self-deception can also be seen in projection and displacement. *Projection* **is attributing one's own thoughts, feelings, or motives to another.** Usually, the thoughts one projects onto others are thoughts that would make one feel guilty. For example, if lusting for a co-worker makes you feel guilty, you might attribute any latent sexual tension between the two of you to the *other person's* desire to seduce you. *Displacement* **is diverting emotional feelings (usually anger) from their original source to a substitute target.** If your boss gives you a hard time at work and you come home and slam the door, kick the couch, and scream at your spouse, you're displacing your anger onto irrelevant targets. Unfortunately, social constraints often force people to hold back their anger, and they end up lashing out at the people they love most.

Other prominent defense mechanisms include reaction formation, regression, and identification. *Reaction formation* **is behaving in a way that's exactly the opposite of one's true feelings.** Guilt about sexual desires often leads to reaction formation. For example, Freud theorized that many males who ridicule homosexuals are defending against their own latent homosexual impulses. The telltale sign of reaction formation is the exaggerated quality of the opposite behavior. *Regression* **is a reversion to immature patterns of behavior.** When anxious about their self-worth, some adults respond with childish boasting and bragging (as opposed to subtle efforts to impress others). For example, a fired executive having difficulty finding a new job might start making ridiculous statements about his incomparable talents and achievements. Such bragging is regressive when it's marked by massive exaggerations that virtually anyone can see through. *Identification* **is bolstering self-esteem by forming an imaginary or real alliance with some person or group.** Youngsters often shore up precarious feelings of self-worth by identifying with rock stars, movie stars, or famous athletes. Adults may join exclusive country clubs or civic organizations as a means of identification.

A great variety of theorists have made extensive additions to Freud's original list of defenses (Vaillant, 1992). We'll examine some of these additional defense mechanisms in the next chapter, when we discuss the role of defenses in coping with stress. For now, however, let's turn our attention to Freud's ideas about the development of personality.

Figure 12.3
Freud's model of personality dynamics. According to Freud, unconscious conflicts between the id, ego, and superego sometimes lead to anxiety. This discomfort may lead to the use of defense mechanisms, which may temporarily relieve anxiety.

Intrapsychic conflict (between id, ego, and superego) → Anxiety → Reliance on defense mechanisms

Table 12.1 Defense Mechanisms, with Examples

Defense Mechanism	Definition	Example
Repression	Keeping distressing thoughts and feelings buried in the unconscious	A traumatized soldier has no recollection of the details of a close brush with death.
Projection	Attributing one's own thoughts, feelings, or motives to another	A woman who dislikes her boss thinks she likes her boss but feels that the boss doesn't like her.
Displacement	Diverting emotional feelings (usually anger) from their original source to a substitute target	After parental scolding, a young girl takes her anger out on her little brother.
Reaction formation	Behaving in a way that is exactly the opposite of one's true feelings	A parent who unconsciously resents a child spoils the child with outlandish gifts.
Regression	A reversion to immature patterns of behavior	An adult has a temper tantrum when he doesn't get his way.
Rationalization	Creating false but plausible excuses to justify unacceptable behavior	A student watches TV instead of studying, saying that "additional study wouldn't do any good anyway."
Identification	Bolstering self-esteem by forming an imaginary or real alliance with some person or group	An insecure young man joins a fraternity to boost his self-esteem.

Note: See Table 13.2 for additional examples of defense mechanisms.

Development: Psychosexual Stages

10a

Freud believed that "the child is father to the man." In fact, he made the rather startling assertion that the basic foundation of an individual's personality has been laid down by the tender age of 5. To shed light on these crucial early years, Freud formulated a stage theory of development. He emphasized how young children deal with their immature but powerful sexual urges (he used the term *sexual* in a general way to refer to many urges for physical pleasure). According to Freud, these sexual urges shift in focus as children progress from one stage of development to another. Indeed, the names for the stages (oral, anal, genital, and so on) are based on where children are focusing their erotic energy during that

---

concept check 12.1

Identifying Defense Mechanisms

Check your understanding of defense mechanisms by identifying specific defenses in the story below. Each example of a defense mechanism is underlined, with a number beneath it. Write in the defense at work in each case in the numbered spaces after the story. The answers are in Appendix A.

My girlfriend recently broke up with me after we had dated seriously for several years. At first, I cried a great deal and locked myself in my room, where I pouted endlessly. I was sure that my former girlfriend felt as miserable as I did. I told several friends that she was probably lonely and depressed. Later, I decided that I hated her. I was happy about the breakup and talked about how much I was going to enjoy my newfound freedom. I went to parties and socialized a great deal and just forgot about her. It's funny—at one point I couldn't even remember her phone number! Then I started pining for her again. But eventually I began to look at the situation more objectively. I realized that she had many faults and that we were bound to break up sooner or later, so I was better off without her.

1. _____   4. _____

2. _____   5. _____

3. _____

period. Thus, *psychosexual stages* are developmental periods with a characteristic sexual focus that leave their mark on adult personality.

Freud theorized that each psychosexual stage has its own unique developmental challenges or tasks (see Table 12.2). The way these challenges are handled supposedly shapes personality. The process of *fixation* plays an important role in this process. **Fixation is a failure to move forward from one stage to another as expected.** Essentially, the child's development stalls for a while. Fixation can be caused by *excessive gratification* of needs at a particular stage or by *excessive frustration* of those needs. Either way, fixations left over from childhood affect adult personality. Generally, fixation leads to an overemphasis on the psychosexual needs prominent during the fixated stage. Freud described a series of five psychosexual stages. Let's examine some of the highlights in this sequence.

Oral Stage. This stage encompasses the first year of life. During this period, the main source of erotic stimulation is the mouth (in biting, sucking, chewing, and so on). In Freud's view, the way the child's feeding experiences is handled is crucial to subsequent development. He attributed considerable importance to the manner in which the child is weaned from the breast or the bottle. According to Freud, fixation at the oral stage could form the basis for obsessive eating or smoking later in life (among many other things).

Anal Stage. In their second year, children get their erotic pleasure from their bowel movements, through either the expulsion or retention of feces. The crucial event at this time is toilet training, which represents society's first systematic effort to regulate the child's biological urges. Severely punitive toilet training leads to a variety of possible outcomes. For example, excessive punishment might produce a latent feeling of hostility toward the "trainer," usually the mother. This hostility might generalize to women as a class. Another possibility is that heavy reliance on punitive measures could lead to an as-

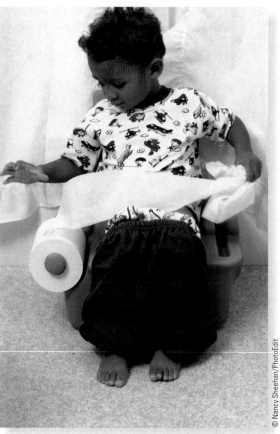

According to Freud, early childhood experiences such as toilet training (a parental attempt to regulate a child's biological urges) can influence an individual's personality, with consequences lasting throughout adulthood.

sociation between genital concerns and the anxiety that the punishment arouses. This genital anxiety derived from severe toilet training could evolve into anxiety about sexual activities later in life.

Phallic Stage. Around age 4, the genitals become the focus for the child's erotic energy, largely through self-stimulation. During this pivotal stage, the *Oedipal complex* emerges. That is, little boys develop an erotically tinged preference for their mother. They also feel hostility toward their father, whom they view as a competitor for mom's affection. Similarly, little girls develop a special attachment to their fa-

Table 12.2 Freud's Stages of Psychosexual Development

Stage	Approximate Ages	Erotic Focus	Key Tasks and Experiences
Oral	0–1	Mouth (sucking, biting)	Weaning (from breast or bottle)
Anal	2–3	Anus (expelling or retaining feces)	Toilet training
Phallic	4–5	Genitals (masturbating)	Identifying with adult role models; coping with Oedipal crisis
Latency	6–12	None (sexually repressed)	Expanding social contacts
Genital	Puberty onward	Genitals (being sexually intimate)	Establishing intimate relationships; contributing to society through working

ther. Around the same time, they learn that little boys have different genitals and supposedly develop *penis envy*. According to Freud, young girls feel hostile toward their mother because they blame her for their anatomical "deficiency."

To summarize, **in the *Oedipal complex* children manifest erotically tinged desires for their opposite-sex parent, accompanied by feelings of hostility toward their same-sex parent.** The name for this syndrome was taken from a tragic myth from ancient Greece. In this story, Oedipus was separated from his parents at birth. Not knowing the identity of his real parents, when he grew up he inadvertently killed his father and married his mother.

According to Freud, the way parents and children deal with the sexual and aggressive conflicts inherent in the Oedipal complex is of paramount importance. The child has to resolve the Oedipal dilemma by purging the sexual longings for the opposite-sex parent and by crushing the hostility felt toward the same-sex parent. In Freud's view, healthy psychosexual development hinges on the resolution of the Oedipal conflict. Why? Because continued hostility toward the same-sex parent may prevent the child from identifying adequately with that parent. Freudian theory predicts that without such identification, sex typing, conscience, and many other aspects of the child's development won't progress as they should.

Latency and Genital Stages. From around age 6 through puberty, the child's sexuality is largely suppressed—it becomes *latent*. Important events during this *latency stage* center on expanding social contacts beyond the immediate family. With puberty, the child progresses into the *genital stage*. Sexual urges reappear and focus on the genitals once again. At this point, sexual energy is normally channeled toward peers of the other sex, rather than toward oneself as in the phallic stage.

In arguing that the early years shape personality, Freud did not mean that personality development comes to an abrupt halt in middle childhood. However, he did believe that the foundation for adult personality has been solidly entrenched by this time. He maintained that future developments are rooted in early, formative experiences and that significant conflicts in later years are replays of crises from childhood.

In fact, Freud believed that unconscious sexual conflicts rooted in childhood experiences cause most personality disturbances. His steadfast belief in the psychosexual origins of psychological disorders eventually led to bitter theoretical disputes with two of his most brilliant colleagues: Carl Jung and Alfred Adler. Jung and Adler both argued that Freud over-emphasized sexuality. Freud rejected their ideas, and the other two theorists felt compelled to go their own way, developing their own theories of personality.

Jung's Analytical Psychology

Carl Jung was born to middle-class Swiss parents in 1875. The son of a Protestant pastor, he was a deeply introverted, lonely child, but an excellent student. Jung had earned his medical degree and was an established young psychiatrist in Zurich when he began to write to Freud in 1906. When the two men had their first meeting, they were so taken by each other's insights, they talked nonstop for 13 hours! They exchanged 359 letters before their friendship and theoretical alliance were torn apart. Their relationship was ruptured irreparably in 1913 by a variety of theoretical disagreements.

Jung called his new approach *analytical psychology* to differentiate it from Freud's psychoanalytic theory. Jung's analytical psychology eventually attracted many followers. Perhaps because of his conflicts with Freud, Jung claimed to deplore the way schools of thought often become dogmatic, discouraging new ideas. Although many theorists came to characterize themselves as "Jungians," Jung himself often remarked, "I am not a Jungian" and said, "I do not want anybody to be a Jungian. I want people above all to be themselves" (van der Post, 1975).

Like Freud, Jung (1921, 1933) emphasized the unconscious determinants of personality. However, he proposed that the unconscious consists of two layers. The first layer, called the *personal unconscious,* is essentially the same as Freud's version of the unconscious. The *personal unconscious* **houses material that is not within one's conscious awareness because it has been repressed or forgotten.** In addition, Jung theorized the existence of a deeper layer he called the collective unconscious. The *collective unconscious* **is a storehouse of latent memory traces inherited from people's ancestral past.** According to Jung, each person shares the collective unconscious with the entire human race (see Figure 12.4 on the next page). It contains the "whole spiritual heritage of mankind's evolution, born anew in the brain structure of every individual" (Jung, quoted in Campbell, 1971, p. 45).

Jung called these ancestral memories *archetypes.* They are not memories of actual, personal experiences. Instead, *archetypes* **are emotionally charged images and thought forms that have universal meaning.** These archetypal images and ideas show up frequently in dreams and are often manifested in a culture's use of symbols in art, literature, and religion. According to Jung, symbols from very different

Carl Jung

"I am not a Jungian . . . I do not want anybody to be a Jungian. I want people above all to be themselves."

web link 12.3

C. G. Jung, Analytical Psychology, & Culture

Synchronicity, archetypes, collective unconscious, introversion, extraversion—these and many other important concepts arising from analytical psychology and Jung's tremendously influential theorizing are examined at this comprehensive site.

Figure 12.4

Jung's vision of the collective unconscious. Much like Freud, Jung theorized that each person has conscious and unconscious levels of awareness. However, he also proposed that the entire human race shares a collective unconscious, which exists in the deepest reaches of everyone's awareness. He saw the collective unconscious as a storehouse of hidden ancestral memories, called archetypes. Jung believed that important cultural symbols emerge from these universal archetypes. Thus, he argued that remarkable resemblances among symbols from disparate cultures (such as the mandalas shown here) are evidence of the existence of the collective unconscious.

SOURCE: Images from C. G. Jung Bild Und Wort, © Walter-Verlag AG, Olten, Switzerland, 1977

Mandalas from various cultures

Russia

Navajo Indians

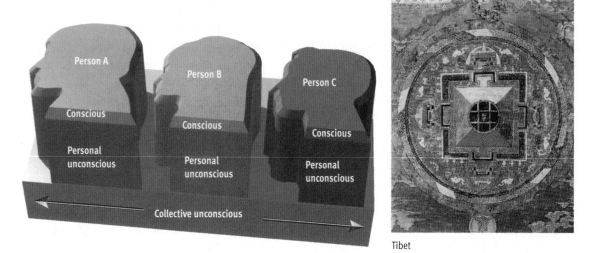
Collective unconscious

Tibet

cultures often show striking similarities because they emerge from archetypes that are shared by the whole human race. For instance, Jung found numerous cultures in which the *mandala,* or "magic circle," has served as a symbol of the unified wholeness of the self (see **Figure 12.4**). Jung felt that an understanding of archetypal symbols helped him make sense of his patients' dreams. This was of great concern to him, as he thought that dreams contain important messages from the unconscious. Like Freud, he depended extensively on dream analysis in his treatment of patients.

Adler's Individual Psychology

Like Freud, Alfred Adler grew up in Vienna in a middle-class Jewish home. He was a sickly child who struggled to overcome rickets (a vitamin-deficiency disease) and an almost fatal case of pneumonia. At home, he was overshadowed by an exceptionally bright and successful older brother. Nonetheless, he went on to earn his medical degree, and he practiced ophthalmology and general medicine before his interest turned to psychiatry. He was a charter member of Freud's inner circle—the Vienna Psychoanalytic Society. However, he soon began to develop his own theory of personality, perhaps because he didn't want

to be dominated once again by an "older brother" (Freud). His theorizing was denounced by Freud in 1911, and Adler was forced to resign from the Psychoanalytic Society. He took 9 of its 23 members with him to form his own organization. Adler's new approach to personality was christened *individual psychology.*

Like Jung, Adler (1917, 1927) argued that Freud had gone overboard in centering his theory on sexual conflicts. According to Adler, the foremost source of human motivation is a striving for superiority. In his view, this striving does not necessarily translate into the pursuit of dominance or high status. Adler saw *striving for superiority* as a universal drive to adapt, improve oneself, and master life's challenges. He noted that young children understandably feel weak and helpless in comparison with more competent older children and adults. These early inferiority feelings supposedly motivate them to acquire new skills and develop new talents. Thus, Adler maintained that striving for superiority is the prime goal of life, rather than physical gratification (as suggested by Freud).

Adler asserted that everyone has to work to overcome some feelings of inferiority—a process he called compensation. *Compensation* involves efforts to overcome imagined or real inferiorities by developing one's abilities. Adler believed that compen-

Alfred Adler

"The goal of the human soul is conquest, perfection, security, superiority."

sation is entirely normal. However, in some people inferiority feelings can become excessive, resulting in what is widely known today as an *inferiority complex*—exaggerated feelings of weakness and inadequacy. Adler thought that either parental pampering or parental neglect could cause an inferiority complex. Thus, he agreed with Freud on the importance of early childhood experiences, although he focused on different aspects of parent-child relations.

Adler explained personality disturbances by noting that excessive inferiority feelings can pervert the normal process of striving for superiority. He asserted that some people engage in *overcompensation* to conceal, even from themselves, their feelings of inferiority. Instead of working to master life's challenges, people with an inferiority complex work to achieve status, gain power over others, and acquire the trappings of success (fancy clothes, impressive cars, or whatever looks important to them). They tend to flaunt their success in an effort to cover up their underlying inferiority complex. However, the problem is that such people engage in unconscious self-deception, worrying more about *appearances* than *reality*.

Adler's theory stressed the social context of personality development (Hoffman, 1994). For instance, it was Adler who first focused attention on the possible importance of *birth order* as a factor governing personality. He noted that first-borns, second children, and later-born children enter varied home environments and are treated differently by parents and that these experiences are likely to affect their personality. For example, he hypothesized that only children are often spoiled by excessive attention from parents and that first-borns are often problem children because they become upset when they're "dethroned" by a second child. Adler's theory stimulated hundreds of studies on the effects of birth order, but these studies generally failed to support his hypotheses and did not uncover any reliable correlations between birth order and personality (Ernst & Angst, 1983; J. R. Harris, 2000).

In recent years, however, Frank Sulloway (1995, 1996, 2007) has argued persuasively that birth order *does* have an impact on personality. Sulloway's reformulated hypotheses focus on how the Big Five traits are shaped by competition among siblings as they struggle to find a "niche" in their family environments. For example, he hypothesizes that first-borns should be more conscientious but less agreeable and open to experience than later-borns. In light of these personality patterns, he further speculates that first-borns tend to be conventional and achievement oriented, whereas later-borns tend to be liberal and rebellious. To evaluate his hypotheses, Sulloway reexamined decades of research on birth

Adler's theory has been used to analyze the tragic life of the legendary actress Marilyn Monroe (Ansbacher, 1970). During her childhood, Monroe suffered from parental neglect that left her with acute feelings of inferiority. Her inferiority feelings led her to overcompensate by flaunting her beauty, marrying celebrities (Joe DiMaggio and Arthur Miller), keeping film crews waiting for hours, and seeking the adoration of her fans.

order. After eliminating many studies that failed to control for important confounding variables, such as social class and family size, he concluded that the results of the remaining, well-controlled studies provided impressive evidence in favor of his hypotheses. Some subsequent studies have provided additional support for Sulloway's analyses (Beck, Burnet, & Vosper, 2006; Healy & Ellis, 2007; Rohde et al., 2003), but others have not (Freese, Powell, & Steelman, 1999; J. R. Harris, 2000; Skinner, 2003). More studies will be needed, as research on birth order is enjoying a bit of a renaissance.

Evaluating Psychodynamic Perspectives

The psychodynamic approach has provided a number of far-reaching, truly "grand" theories of personality. These theories yielded some bold new insights when they were first presented. Although one might argue about exact details of interpretation, research has demonstrated that (1) unconscious forces can influence behavior, (2) internal conflict often plays a key role in generating psychological distress, (3) early childhood experiences can have powerful influences on adult personality, and (4) people do use defense mechanisms to reduce their experience of unpleasant emotions (Bornstein, 2003; Solms, 2004; Westen, 1998; Westen & Gabbard, 1999).

In addition to being praised, psychodynamic formulations have also been criticized on several grounds, including the following (Crews, 2006; Eysenck, 1990b; Kramer, 2006; Torrey, 1992):

1. *Poor testability.* Scientific investigations require testable hypotheses. Psychodynamic ideas have often been too vague and conjectural to permit a clear scientific test. For instance, how would you prove or disprove the assertion that the id is entirely unconscious?

2. *Inadequate evidence.* The empirical evidence on psychodynamic theories has often been characterized as "inadequate." Psychodynamic theories depend too heavily on clinical case studies in which it's much too easy for clinicians to see what they expect to see. Reexaminations of Freud's own clinical work suggest that he frequently distorted his patients' case histories to make them mesh with his theory (Esterson, 2001; Powell & Boer, 1995). Insofar as researchers have accumulated evidence on psychodynamic theories, the evidence has provided only modest support for many of the central hypotheses (Fisher & Greenberg, 1985, 1996; Westen & Gabbard, 1999; Wolitzky, 2006).

3. *Sexism.* Many critics have argued that psychodynamic theories are characterized by a sexist bias against women. Freud believed that females' penis envy made them feel inferior to males. He also thought that females tended to develop weaker superegos and to be more prone to neurosis than males. The sex bias in modern psychodynamic theories has been reduced considerably. Nonetheless, the psychodynamic approach has generally provided a rather male-centered point of view (Lerman, 1986; Person, 1990).

It's easy to ridicule Freud for concepts such as penis envy, and it's easy to point to Freudian ideas that have turned out to be wrong. However, you have to remember that Freud, Jung, and Adler began to fashion their theories over a century ago. It's not entirely fair to compare these theories to other models that are only a decade or two old. That's like asking the Wright brothers to race a modern military jet. Freud and his colleagues deserve great credit for breaking new ground with their speculations about psychodynamics. In psychology as a whole, no other school of thought has been as influential, with the exception of behaviorism, to which we turn next.

Behavioral Perspectives

Behaviorism is a theoretical orientation based on the premise that scientific psychology should study only observable behavior. As we saw in Chapter 1, behaviorism has been a major school of thought in psychology since 1913, when John B. Watson began campaigning for the behavioral point of view. Research in the behavioral tradition has focused largely on learning. For many decades behaviorists devoted relatively little attention to the study of personality. However, their interest in personality began to pick up after John Dollard and Neal Miller (1950) attempted to translate selected Freudian ideas into behavioral terminology. Dollard and Miller showed that behavioral concepts could provide enlightening insights about the complicated subject of personality.

In this section, we'll examine three behavioral views of personality, as we discuss the ideas of B. F. Skinner, Albert Bandura, and Walter Mischel. For the most part, you'll see that behaviorists explain personality the same way they explain everything else—in terms of learning.

Skinner's Ideas Applied to Personality

10b

As we noted in Chapters 1 and 6, modern behaviorism's most prominent theorist has been B. F. Skinner, an American psychologist who lived from 1904 to 1990. After earning his doctorate in 1931, Skinner spent most of his career at Harvard University. There he achieved renown for his research on the principles of learning, which were mostly discovered through the study of rats and pigeons. Skinner's (1953, 1957) concepts of *operant conditioning* were never meant to be a theory of personality. However, his ideas have affected thinking in all areas of psychology and have been applied to the explanation of personality. Here we'll examine Skinner's views as they relate to personality structure and development.

Personality Structure: A View from the Outside

Skinner made no provision for internal personality structures similar to Freud's id, ego, and superego because such structures can't be observed. Following in the tradition of Watson's radical behaviorism, Skinner showed little interest in what goes on "inside" people. He argued that it's useless to speculate about private, unobservable cognitive processes. Instead, he focused on how the external environment molds overt behavior. Indeed, he argued for a strong brand of *determinism,* asserting that behavior is fully determined by environmental stimuli. He claimed that free will is but an illusion, saying, "There is no place in the scientific position for a self as a true originator or initiator of action" (Skinner, 1974, p. 225).

How can Skinner's theory explain the consistency that can be seen in individuals' behavior? According to his view, people show some consistent patterns of behavior because they have some stable *response tendencies* that they have acquired through experience. These response tendencies may change in the future, as a result of new experience, but they're enduring enough to create a certain degree of consistency in a person's behavior. Implicitly, then, Skinner viewed an individual's personality as a *collection of response tendencies that are tied to various stimulus situations.* A specific situation may be associated with a number of response tendencies that vary in strength, depending on past conditioning (see Figure 12.5).

Personality Development as a Product of Conditioning

Skinner's theory accounts for personality development by explaining how various response tendencies are acquired through learning (Bolling, Terry, & Kohlenberg, 2006). He believed that most human responses are shaped by the type of conditioning that he described: operant conditioning. As discussed in Chapter 6, Skinner maintained that environmental consequences—reinforcement, punishment, and extinction—determine people's patterns of responding. On the one hand, when responses are followed by favorable consequences (reinforcement), they are strengthened. For example, if your joking at a party pays off with favorable attention, your tendency to joke at parties will increase (see Figure 12.6). On the

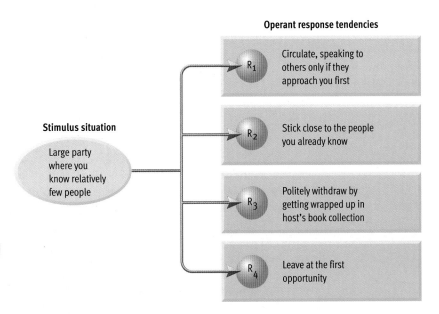

Operant response tendencies

Stimulus situation

Large party where you know relatively few people

R_1 Circulate, speaking to others only if they approach you first

R_2 Stick close to the people you already know

R_3 Politely withdraw by getting wrapped up in host's book collection

R_4 Leave at the first opportunity

Figure 12.5

A behavioral view of personality. Staunch behaviorists devote little attention to the structure of personality because it is unobservable, but they implicitly view personality as an individual's collection of response tendencies. A possible hierarchy of response tendencies for a particular person in a specific stimulus situation (a large party) is shown here.

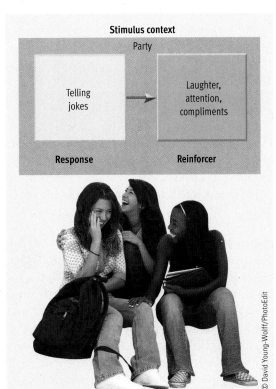

Stimulus context

Party

Telling jokes → Laughter, attention, compliments

Response **Reinforcer**

Figure 12.6

Personality development and operant conditioning. According to Skinner, people's characteristic response tendencies are shaped by reinforcers and other consequences that follow behavior. Thus, if your joking at a party leads to attention and compliments, your tendency to be witty and humorous will be strengthened.

B. F. Skinner

"The practice of looking inside the organism for an explanation of behavior has tended to obscure the variables which are immediately available for a scientific analysis. These variables lie outside the organism, in its immediate environment and in its environmental history.... The objection to inner states is not that they do not exist, but that they are not relevant."

other hand, when responses lead to negative consequences (punishment), they are weakened. Thus, if your impulsive decisions always backfire, your tendency to be impulsive will decline.

Because response tendencies are constantly being strengthened or weakened by new experiences, Skinner's theory views personality development as a continuous, lifelong journey. Unlike Freud and many other theorists, Skinner saw no reason to break the developmental process into stages. Nor did he attribute special importance to early childhood experiences.

Skinner believed that conditioning in humans operates much the same as it did in the rats and pigeons that he studied in his laboratory. Hence, he assumed that conditioning strengthens and weakens response tendencies "mechanically"—that is, without the person's conscious participation. Thus, Skinner was able to explain consistencies in behavior (personality) without being concerned about individuals' cognitive processes.

Skinner's ideas continue to be highly influential, but his mechanical, deterministic, noncognitive view of personality has not gone unchallenged by other behaviorists. In recent decades, several theorists have developed somewhat different behavioral models with a more cognitive emphasis.

Bandura's Social Cognitive Theory

 10b

Albert Bandura is a modern theorist who has helped reshape the theoretical landscape of behaviorism. Bandura grew up in Canada and earned his doctorate in psychology at the University of Iowa. He has spent his entire academic career at Stanford University, where he has conducted influential research on behavior therapy and the determinants of aggression.

Cognitive Processes and Reciprocal Determinism

 10b

Bandura is one of several theorists who have added a cognitive flavor to behaviorism since the 1960s. Bandura (1977), Walter Mischel (1973), and Julian Rotter (1982) take issue with Skinner's "pure" behaviorism. They point out that humans obviously are conscious, thinking, feeling beings. Moreover, these theorists argue that in neglecting cognitive processes, Skinner ignored the most distinctive and important feature of human behavior. Bandura and like-minded theorists originally called their modified brand of behaviorism *social learning theory*. Today, Bandura refers to his model as *social cognitive theory*.

Albert Bandura

"Most human behavior is learned by observation through modeling."

Bandura (1986, 1999b) agrees with the fundamental thrust of behaviorism in that he believes that personality is largely shaped through learning. However, he contends that conditioning is not a mechanical process in which people are passive participants. Instead, he maintains that "people are self-organizing, proactive, self-reflecting, and self-regulating, not just reactive organisms shaped and shepherded by external events" (Bandura, 1999b, p. 154). Bandura (2001, 2006) also emphasizes the important role of forward-directed planning, noting that "people set goals for themselves, anticipate the likely consequences of prospective actions, and select and create courses of action likely to produce desired outcomes and avoid detrimental ones" (Bandura, 2001, p. 7).

Comparing his theory to Skinner's highly deterministic view, Bandura advocates a position called *reciprocal determinism*. According to this notion, the environment does determine behavior (as Skinner would argue). However, behavior also determines the environment. In other words, people can select their environments and act to alter them (by changing the friends they hang around with, for instance). Moreover, personal factors (cognitive structures such as beliefs and expectancies) determine and are determined by both behavior and the environment (see **Figure 12.7**). Thus, *reciprocal determinism* **is the idea that internal mental events, external environmental events, and overt behavior all influence one another.** According to Bandura, humans are neither masters of their own destiny nor hapless victims buffeted about by the environment. To some extent, people shape their environments, an observation that brings us to our Featured Study, which looked at how individuals mold their physical environments—and the clues that these environments can provide about personality.

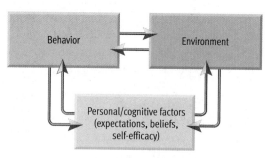

Figure 12.7

Bandura's reciprocal determinism. Bandura rejects Skinner's highly deterministic view that behavior is governed by environment and that freedom is an illusion. Bandura argues that internal mental events, external environmental contingencies, and overt behavior all influence one another.

Can Rooms *Really* Have Personality?

You may have heard someone comment that a particular house or specific room "has personality." This metaphor is usually intended to convey that the house or room is unusual or distinctive. But Bandura's point that people proactively choose and shape their environments raises the possibility that rooms could *literally* have personality—the personality of their occupants.

A variety of theories assert that individuals select and create their social and physical environments to match their dispositions and self-views. For example, people who choose formal or informal furniture or conventional versus unconventional decorating convey something about who they are, as do people who display an Amy Winehouse poster or photos of their travels. In places where they dwell, people also leave a *behavioral residue*—remnants of their activities, such as books, magazines, computer printouts, drawings, musical instruments, snacks, and discarded beer cans. Aware of these realities, Samuel Gosling and his colleagues set out to determine just how much observers can infer about an individual's personality based on visiting the person's office or bedroom. We will examine the study of offices in more detail and then summarize the results of the study of bedrooms.

Method

Occupants and observations. Ninety-four office occupants in five urban office buildings agreed to participate. Eight independent observers examined each participant's office and rated the occupant (who was not present) on a 44-item scale that assessed the Big Five personality traits. All photos of the occupants and references to their names were covered before the observers visited the offices. The intent was to see how ordinary people arrive at everyday impressions, so the observers had no special training or expertise.

Assessments of accuracy. To gauge the accuracy of the observers' personality inferences, the office occupants were asked to submit personality ratings of themselves and to suggest two peers who knew them well and who could also rate their personality (on the same 44-item scale used by the observers). The self-ratings and peer-ratings for each occupant were combined and then compared to the ratings made by the observers.

Results

Moderate positive correlations were found among the eight observers' personality ratings, indicating a reasonable consensus among them. Their combined ratings were then correlated with the self- and peer-ratings of the occupants. These correlations, which averaged .22, indicated that the observers were more accurate at judging some traits than others (see **Figure 12.8**). The assessments of the occupants' openness to experience were impressive, and

the judgments of the occupants' extraversion, conscientiousness, and emotional stability were substantial.

Follow-Up Study

A second study, focusing on individuals' bedrooms rather than offices, was conducted using identical methods. The occupants were 83 college students or recent graduates living near a university in apartments, houses, and dormitories. Once again, reasonable consensus was found among the observers' personality ratings. However, the accuracy of the ratings based on people's bedrooms was noticeably higher (average correlation of .37) than it was for offices. As in the first study, the inferences about some traits were more accurate than others (see **Figure 12.8**), with ratings of openness to experience yielding the greatest accuracy.

Discussion

The authors conclude that "much can be learned about persons from the spaces in which they dwell" (p. 397) and that personal dwellings yield more valid cues for certain traits than for others. To put their findings in context, they note that on some personality traits, the room-based ratings

SOURCE: Gosling, S. D., Ko, S. J., Mannarelli, T., & Morris, M. E. (2002). A room with a cue: Personality judgments based on offices and bedrooms. *Journal of Personality and Social Psychology, 82,* 379–398.

Figure 12.8

Accuracy of personality ratings based on people's rooms. To assess the accuracy of observers' personality ratings based on visiting people's offices or bedrooms, Gosling et al. (2002) correlated the observers' aggregated ratings with the combined self- and peer-ratings of the occupants of the rooms. Higher correlations are indicative of greater accuracy. If observers were not able to infer anything meaningful about occupants' personalities based on visiting their offices or bedrooms, these correlations would hover near zero, which was true in only one case (the ratings of agreeableness based on office visits). (Based on data from Gosling et al., 2002)

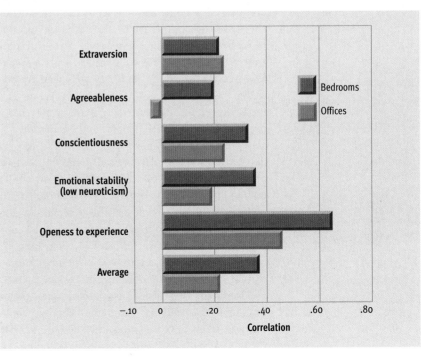

were more accurate than similar ratings from other studies that were based on long-term acquaintance! They speculate that bedrooms may be richer sources of information about their occupants than offices because people have more freedom to decorate bedrooms as they please and less need to project a professional image.

Comment

This study was featured because it took a creative approach to exploring an interesting phenomenon that has never before been subjected to scientific analysis. In retrospect, it seems readily apparent that people try to convey something about themselves in their dwellings and that visitors do form impressions based on these cues—but no one had previously thought to study these processes empirically. The creativity required to launch an entirely new line of research is apparent in one of its quirks: Who were the subjects? The occupants of the rooms? The observers who made the personality ratings? The participants in research are normally obvious—but in this case it is rather ambiguous. In any event, this study demonstrated that the relationship between personality and environment is a reciprocal one, as envisioned by Bandura.

Observational Learning 10b

Bandura's foremost theoretical contribution has been his description of observational learning, which we introduced in Chapter 6. *Observational learning* occurs when an organism's responding is influenced by the observation of others, who are called models. According to Bandura, both classical and operant conditioning can occur vicariously when one person observes another's conditioning. For example, watching your sister get cheated by someone giving her a bad check for her old stereo could strengthen your tendency to be suspicious of others. Although your sister would be the one actually experiencing the negative consequences, they might also influence you—through observational learning.

Bandura maintains that people's characteristic patterns of behavior are shaped by the *models* that they're exposed to. He isn't referring to the fashion models who dominate the mass media—although they do qualify. In observational learning, **a *model* is a person whose behavior is observed by another.** At one time or another, everyone serves as a model for others. Bandura's key point is that many response tendencies are the product of *imitation*.

As research has accumulated, it has become apparent that some models are more influential than others (Bandura, 1986). Both children and adults tend to imitate people they like or respect more than people they don't. People are also especially prone to imitate the behavior of people whom they consider attractive or powerful (such as rock stars). In addition, imitation is more likely when people see similarity between models and themselves. Thus, children tend to imitate same-sex role models somewhat more than opposite-sex models. Finally, people are more likely to copy a model if they observe that the model's behavior leads to positive outcomes.

Self-Efficacy

Bandura discusses how a variety of personal factors (aspects of personality) govern behavior. In recent years, the factor he has emphasized most is self-efficacy (Bandura, 1993, 1995, 2004). *Self-efficacy* **refers to one's belief about one's ability to perform behaviors that should lead to expected outcomes.** When self-efficacy is high, individuals feel confident that they can execute the responses necessary to earn reinforcers. When self-efficacy is low, individuals worry that the necessary responses may be beyond their abilities. Perceptions of self-efficacy are subjective and specific to certain kinds of tasks. For instance, you might feel extremely confident about your ability to handle difficult social situations but doubtful about your ability to handle academic challenges.

Perceptions of self-efficacy can influence which challenges people tackle and how well they perform. Studies have found that feelings of greater self-efficacy are associated with reduced procrastination (Steel, 2007); greater success in giving up smoking (Boudreaux et al., 1998); greater adherence to an exercise regimen (Rimal, 2001); more effective weight-loss efforts (Linde et al., 2006); better outcomes in substance abuse treatment (Bandura, 1999a); more success in coping with medical rehabilitation (Waldrop et al., 2001); reduced disability from problems with chronic pain (Hadjistavropoulos et al., 2007); greater persistence and effort in academic pursuits (Zimmerman, 1995); higher levels of academic performance (Chemers, Hu, & Garcia, 2001); reduced vulnerability to anxiety and depression in childhood (Muris, 2002); less jealousy in romantic relationships (Hu, Zhang, & Li, 2005); enhanced performance in athletic competition (Kane et al., 1996); greater receptiveness to technological training (Christoph, Schoenfeld, & Tansky, 1998); greater success in searching for a new job (Saks, 2006); higher work-related performance

Perceptions of self-efficacy can influence which challenges people pursue and how well they perform. For example, research has linked self-efficacy to job performance and success in adhering to an exercise regime.

(Stajkovic & Luthans, 1998); and reduced strain from occupational stress (Grau, Salanova, & Peiro, 2001), among many other things.

Mischel and the Person-Situation Controversy

Walter Mischel was born in Vienna, not far from Freud's home. His family immigrated to the United States in 1939, when he was 9. After earning his doctorate in psychology, he spent many years on the faculty at Stanford, as a colleague of Bandura's. He has since moved to Columbia University.

Like Bandura, Mischel (1973, 1984) is an advocate of social learning theory. Mischel's chief contribution to personality theory has been to focus attention on the extent to which situational factors govern behavior. According to social learning theory, people try to gauge the reinforcement contingencies and adjust their behavior to the circumstances. For example, if you believe that hard work in your job will pay off by leading to raises and promotions, you'll probably be diligent and industrious. But if you think that hard work in your job is unlikely to be rewarded, you may act lazy and irresponsible. Thus, social learning theory predicts that people will often behave differently in different situations.

Mischel (1968, 1973) reviewed decades of research and concluded that, indeed, people exhibit far less consistency across situations than had been widely assumed. For example, studies show that a person who is honest in one situation may be dishonest in another. That is, someone who wouldn't dream of being dishonest in a business deal might engage in wholesale cheating in filling out tax returns. Similarly, some people are quite shy in one situation and outgoing in another. In light of these realities,

Mischel maintains that behavior is characterized by more *situational specificity* than consistency.

Mischel's position has generated great controversy because it strikes at the heart of the concept of personality itself. As we discussed at the beginning of the chapter, the concept of personality is used to explain consistency in people's behavior over time and situations. If there isn't much consistency, there isn't much need for the concept of personality.

Mischel's views have generated many rebuttals that have defended the value of the personality concept. For instance, Epstein (1980, 1986) argued that the methods used in much of the research reviewed by Mischel led to an underestimate of cross-situational consistency. Critics also noted that it is unreasonable to expect complete cross-situational consistency, because specific traits are more easily expressed in some situations than others (Kenrick & Funder, 1991). For example, a person's fun-loving, humorous qualities aren't likely to be apparent at a funeral.

Thus, Mischel's provocative theories have sparked a robust debate about the relative importance of the *person* as opposed to the *situation* in determining behavior. This debate has led to a growing recognition that *both* the person and the situation are important determinants of behavior (Funder, 2001; Roberts & Pomerantz, 2004). As William Fleeson (2004) puts it, "The person-situation debate is coming to an end because both sides of the debate have turned out to

Walter Mischel

"It seems remarkable how each of us generally manages to reconcile his seemingly diverse behavior into one self-consistent whole."

be right" (p. 83). Fleeson reconciles the two opposing views by arguing that each prevails at a different level of analysis. When small chunks of behavior are examined on a moment-to-moment basis, situational factors dominate and most individuals' behavior tends to be highly variable. However, when larger chunks of typical behavior over time are examined, people tend to be reasonably consistent and personality traits prove to be more influential.

Evaluating Behavioral Perspectives

Behavioral theories are firmly rooted in extensive empirical research rather than clinical intuition. Skinner's ideas have shed light on how environmental consequences and conditioning mold people's characteristic behavior. Bandura's social cognitive theory has expanded the horizons of behaviorism and increased its relevance to the study of personality. Mischel deserves credit for increasing psychology's awareness of how situational factors shape behavior. Of course, each theoretical approach has its weaknesses and shortcomings, and the behavioral approach is no exception. Major lines of criticism include the following (Liebert & Liebert, 1998; Pervin & John, 2001):

1. *Dehumanizing nature of radical behaviorism.* Skinner and other radical behaviorists have been criticized heavily for denying the existence of free will and the importance of cognitive processes. The critics argue that the radical behaviorist viewpoint strips human behavior of its most uniquely human elements and that it therefore cannot provide an accurate model of human functioning.

2. *Dilution of the behavioral approach.* The behaviorists used to be criticized because they neglected cognitive processes, which clearly are important factors in human behavior. The rise of social cognitive theory blunted this criticism. However, social cognitive theory undermines the foundation on which behaviorism was built—the idea that psychologists should study only observable behavior. Thus, some critics complain that behavioral theories aren't very behavioral anymore.

3. *Fragmentation of personality.* Behaviorists have also been criticized for providing a fragmented view of personality. The behavioral approach carves personality up into stimulus-response associations. There are no unifying structural concepts (such as Freud's ego) that tie these pieces together. Humanistic theorists, whom we shall cover next, have been particularly vocal in criticizing this piecemeal analysis of personality.

REVIEW of Key Learning Goals

12.9 Skinner had little interest in unobservable cognitive processes and embraced a strong determinism. Skinner's followers view personality as a collection of response tendencies tied to specific stimulus situations. They assume that personality development is a lifelong process in which response tendencies are shaped and reshaped by learning, especially operant conditioning.

12.10 Social cognitive theory focuses on how cognitive factors such as expectancies regulate learned behavior. The Featured Study provided support for the assertion that people choose and shape their environments, consistent with Bandura's reciprocal determinism. High self-efficacy has been related to successful health regimens, academic success, and athletic performance, among many other things.

12.11 Mischel has questioned the degree to which people display cross-situational consistency in behavior. Mischel's arguments have increased psychologists' awareness of the situational determinants of behavior. According to Fleeson, situational factors dominate small chunks of behavior, whereas personality traits shape larger chunks of behavior.

12.12 Behavioral approaches to personality are based on rigorous research. They have provided ample insights into how environmental factors and learning mold personalities. This approach has been criticized for its fragmented analysis of personality, for radical behaviorism's dehumanizing view of human nature, and for the dilution of modern behavioral approaches.

Humanistic Perspectives

Key Learning Goals

12.13 Identify the impetus for, and assumptions of, humanism.

12.14 Articulate Rogers's views on self-concept, development, and defensive behavior.

12.15 Explain Maslow's hierarchy of needs, and summarize his findings on self-actualizing persons.

12.16 Evaluate the strengths and weaknesses of the humanistic approach to personality.

Humanistic theory emerged in the 1950s as something of a backlash against the behavioral and psychodynamic theories that we have just discussed (Cassel, 2000; DeCarvalho, 1991). The principal charge hurled at these two models was that they are dehumanizing. Freudian theory was criticized for its belief that behavior is dominated by primitive, animalistic drives. Behaviorism was criticized for its preoccupation with animal research and for its mechanistic, fragmented view of personality. Critics argued that both schools of thought are too deterministic and that both fail to recognize the unique qualities of human behavior.

Many of these critics blended into a loose alliance that came to be known as humanism, because of its exclusive focus on human behavior. *Humanism is a theoretical orientation that emphasizes the unique qualities of humans, especially their freedom and their potential for personal growth.* Humanistic psychologists don't believe that animal research can reveal anything of any significance about the human condition. In contrast to most psychodynamic and behavioral theorists, humanistic theorists take an optimistic view of human nature. They assume that (1) people can rise above their primitive animal heritage and control their biological urges, and (2) people are largely conscious and rational beings who are not dominated by unconscious, irrational needs and conflicts.

Humanistic theorists also maintain that a person's subjective view of the world is more important than objective reality (Wong, 2006). According to this notion, if you think that you're homely or bright or sociable, this belief will influence your behavior more than the realities of how homely, bright, or sociable you actually are. Therefore, the humanists embrace the *phenomenological approach,* **which assumes that one has to appreciate individuals' personal, subjective experiences to truly understand their behavior.** As Carl Rogers (1951) put it, "The best vantage point for understanding behavior is from the internal frame of reference of the individual himself" (p. 494). Let's look at Rogers's ideas.

Rogers's Person-Centered Theory

 10c

Carl Rogers (1951, 1961, 1980) was one of the founders of the human potential movement. This movement emphasizes self-realization through sensitivity training, encounter groups, and other exercises intended to foster personal growth. Rogers grew up in a religious, upper-middle-class home in the suburbs of Chicago. He was a bright student, but he had to rebel against his parents' wishes in order to pursue his graduate study in psychology. While he was working at the University of Chicago in the 1940s, Rogers devised a major new approach to psychotherapy. Like Freud, Rogers based his personality theory on his extensive therapeutic interactions with many clients. Because of its emphasis on a person's subjective point of view, Rogers's approach is called a *person-centered theory.*

The Self

 10c

Rogers viewed personality structure in terms of just one construct. He called this construct the *self,* although it's more widely known today as the *self-concept.* **A *self-concept* is a collection of beliefs about one's own nature, unique qualities, and typical behavior.** Your self-concept is your own mental picture of yourself. It's a collection of self-perceptions. For example, a self-concept might include beliefs such as "I'm easygoing" or "I'm sly

and crafty" or "I'm pretty" or "I'm hardworking." According to Rogers, individuals are aware of their self-concept. It's not buried in their unconscious.

Rogers stressed the subjective nature of the self-concept. Your self-concept may not be entirely consistent with your experiences. Most people tend to distort their experiences to some extent to promote a relatively favorable self-concept. For example, you may believe that you're quite bright, but your grade transcript might suggest otherwise. Rogers called the gap between self-concept and reality "incongruence." ***Incongruence* is the degree of disparity between one's self-concept and one's actual experience.** In contrast, if a person's self-concept is reasonably accurate, it's said to be *congruent* with reality (see **Figure 12.9**). Everyone experiences *some* incongruence. The crucial issue is how much. As we'll see, Rogers maintained that too much incongruence undermines one's psychological well-being.

Development of the Self

 10c

In terms of personality development, Rogers was concerned with how childhood experiences promote congruence or incongruence between one's self-concept and one's experience. According to Rogers, people have a strong need for affection, love, and acceptance from others. Early in life, parents provide most of this affection. Rogers maintained that some parents make their affection *conditional.* That is, it depends on the child's behaving well and living up to expectations. When parental love seems conditional, children often block out of their self-concept those experiences that make them feel unworthy of love. They do so because they're worried about parental acceptance, which appears precarious. At the other end of the spectrum, some parents make their affection *unconditional.* Their children

Carl Rogers

"I have little sympathy with the rather prevalent concept that man is basically irrational, and that his impulses, if not controlled, will lead to destruction of others and self. Man's behavior is exquisitely rational, moving with subtle and ordered complexity toward the goals his organism is endeavoring to achieve."

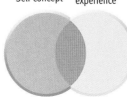

Self-concept — Actual experience

Congruence
Self-concept meshes well with actual experience (some incongruence is probably unavoidable)

Self-concept — Actual experience

Incongruence
Self-concept does not mesh well with actual experience

Figure 12.9
Rogers's view of personality structure. In Rogers's model, the self-concept is the only important structural construct. However, Rogers acknowledged that one's self-concept may not be consistent with the realities of one's actual experience—a condition called incongruence.

is a "self-centered, snotty brat." How might she react in order to protect her self-concept? She might ignore or block out those occasions when she behaves selfishly. She might attribute her girlfriends' negative comments to their jealousy of her good looks. Perhaps she would blame her boyfriends' negative remarks on their disappointment because she won't get more serious with them. As you can see, people will sometimes go to great lengths to defend their self-concept.

Maslow's Theory of Self-Actualization   10c

Abraham Maslow, who grew up in Brooklyn, described his childhood as "unhappy, lonely, [and] isolated." To follow through on his interest in psychology, he had to resist parental pressures to go into law. Maslow spent much of his career at Brandeis University, where he created an influential theory of motivation and provided crucial leadership for the fledgling humanistic movement. Like Rogers, Maslow (1968, 1970) argued that psychology should take an optimistic view of human nature instead of dwelling on the causes of disorders. "To oversimplify the matter somewhat," he said, "it's as if Freud supplied to us the sick half of psychology and we must now fill it out with the healthy half" (1968, p. 5). Maslow's key contributions were his analysis of how motives are organized hierarchically and his description of the healthy personality.

Hierarchy of Needs   10c

Maslow proposed that human motives are organized into a *hierarchy of needs*—a systematic arrangement of needs, according to priority, in which basic needs must be met before less basic needs are aroused. This hierarchical arrangement is usually portrayed as a pyramid (see Figure 12.11). The needs toward the bottom of the pyramid, such as physiological or security needs, are the most basic. Higher levels in the pyramid consist of progressively less basic needs. When a person manages to satisfy a

have less need to block out unworthy experiences because they've been assured that they're worthy of affection, no matter what they do.

Hence, Rogers believed that unconditional love from parents fosters congruence and that conditional love fosters incongruence. He further theorized that if individuals grow up believing that affection from others is highly conditional, they will go on to distort more and more of their experiences in order to feel worthy of acceptance from a wider and wider array of people (see Figure 12.10).

Anxiety and Defense   10c

According to Rogers, experiences that threaten people's personal views of themselves are the principal cause of anxiety. The more inaccurate your self-concept, the more likely you are to have experiences that clash with your self-perceptions. Thus, people with highly incongruent self-concepts are especially likely to be plagued by recurrent anxiety (see Figure 12.10).

To ward off this anxiety, individuals often behave defensively in an effort to reinterpret their experience so that it appears consistent with their self-concept. Thus, they ignore, deny, and twist reality to protect and perpetuate their self-concept. Consider a young woman who, like most people, considers herself a "nice person." Let's suppose that in reality she is rather conceited and selfish. She gets feedback from both boyfriends and girlfriends that she

Figure 12.10

Rogers's view of personality development and dynamics. Rogers's theory of development posits that conditional love leads to a need to distort experiences, which fosters an incongruent self-concept. Incongruence makes one prone to recurrent anxiety, which triggers defensive behavior, which fuels more incongruence.

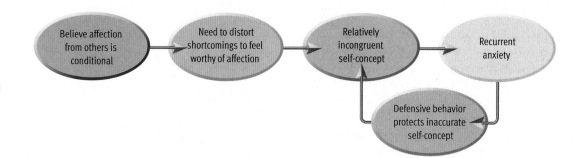

Figure 12.11

Maslow's hierarchy of needs. According to Maslow, human needs are arranged in a hierarchy, and people must satisfy their basic needs before they can satisfy higher needs. In the diagram, higher levels in the pyramid represent progressively less basic needs. Individuals progress upward in the hierarchy when lower needs are satisfied reasonably well, but they may regress back to lower levels if basic needs are no longer satisfied.

Progression if lower needs are satisfied

Need for self-actualization:
Realization of potential

Aesthetic needs:
Order and beauty

Cognitive needs:
Knowledge and understanding

Esteem needs:
Achievement and gaining of recognition

Belongingness and love needs:
Affiliation and acceptance

Safety and security needs:
Long-term survival and stability

Physiological needs:
Hunger, thirst, and so forth

Regression if lower needs are not being satisfied

---

level of needs reasonably well (complete satisfaction is not necessary), *this satisfaction activates needs at the next level.*

Like Rogers, Maslow argued that humans have an innate drive toward personal growth—that is, evolution toward a higher state of being. Thus, he described the needs in the uppermost reaches of his hierarchy as *growth needs*. These include the needs for knowledge and aesthetic beauty. Foremost among them is the *need for self-actualization,* **which is the need to fulfill one's potential; it is the highest need in Maslow's motivational hierarchy.** Maslow summarized this concept with a simple statement: "What a man *can* be, he *must* be." According to Maslow, people will be frustrated if they are unable to fully utilize their talents or pursue their true interests. For example, if you have great musical talent but must work as an accountant, or if you have scholarly interests but must work as a sales clerk, your need for self-actualization will be thwarted.

The Healthy Personality

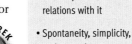 10c

Because of his interest in self-actualization, Maslow set out to discover the nature of the healthy personality. He tried to identify people of exceptional mental health so that he could investigate their characteristics. In one case, he used psychological tests and interviews to sort out the healthiest 1% of a sizable population of college students. He also studied admired historical figures (such as Thomas Jefferson and William James) and personal acquaintances characterized by superior adjustment. Over a period of years, he accumulated his case histories

and gradually sketched, in broad strokes, a picture of ideal psychological health.

According to Maslow, *self-actualizing persons* **are people with exceptionally healthy personalities, marked by continued personal growth.** Maslow identified various traits characteristic of self-actualizing people. Many of these traits are listed in Figure 12.12. In brief, Maslow found that self-actualizers are accurately tuned in to reality and that they're at peace with themselves. He found that they're open and spontaneous and that they retain a fresh appreciation of the world around them. Socially, they're sensitive to others' needs and enjoy

Abraham Maslow

"It is as if Freud supplied to us the sick half of psychology and we must now fill it out with the healthy half."

Characteristics of self-actualizing people	
• Clear, efficient perception of reality and comfortable relations with it	• Mystical and peak experiences
• Spontaneity, simplicity, and naturalness	• Feelings of kinship and identification with the human race
• Problem centering (having something outside themselves they "must" do as a mission)	• Strong friendships, but limited in number
• Detachment and need for privacy	• Democratic character structure
• Autonomy, independence of culture and environment	• Ethical discrimination between good and evil
• Continued freshness of appreciation	• Philosophical, unhostile sense of humor
	• Balance between polarities in personality

Figure 12.12

Maslow's view of the healthy personality. Humanistic theorists emphasize psychological health instead of maladjustment. Maslow's description of characteristics of self-actualizing people evokes a picture of the healthy personality.

rewarding interpersonal relations. However, they're not dependent on others for approval or uncomfortable with solitude. They thrive on their work, and they enjoy their sense of humor. Maslow also noted that they have "peak experiences" (profound emotional highs) more often than others. Finally, he found that they strike a nice balance between many polarities in personality. For instance, they can be both childlike and mature, both rational and intuitive, both conforming and rebellious.

Evaluating Humanistic Perspectives

The humanists added a refreshing new perspective to the study of personality. Their argument that a person's subjective views may be more important than objective reality has proven compelling. As we noted earlier, even behavioral theorists have begun to take into account subjective personal factors such as beliefs and expectations. The humanistic approach also deserves some of the credit for making the self-concept an important construct in psychol-

ogy. Finally, one could argue that the humanists' optimistic, growth- and health-oriented approach laid the foundation for the emergence of the positive psychology movement that is increasingly influential in contemporary psychology (Sheldon & Kasser, 2001; Taylor, 2001).

Of course, there's a negative side to the balance sheet as well. Critics have identified some weaknesses in the humanistic approach to personality, including the following (Burger, 2008; Wong, 2006):

1. *Poor testability.* Like psychodynamic theorists, the humanists have been criticized for generating hypotheses that are difficult to put to a scientific test. Humanistic concepts such as personal growth and self-actualization are difficult to define and measure.

2. *Unrealistic view of human nature.* Critics also charge that the humanists have been unrealistic in their assumptions about human nature and their descriptions of the healthy personality. For instance, Maslow's self-actualizing people sound nearly *perfect.* In reality, Maslow had a hard time finding such

---

concept check 12.2

Recognizing Key Concepts in Personality Theories

Check your understanding of psychodynamic, behavioral, and humanistic personality theories by identifying key concepts from these theories in the scenarios below. The answers can be found in Appendix A.

1. Thirteen-year-old Sarah watches a TV show in which the leading female character manipulates her boyfriend by acting helpless and purposely losing a tennis match against him. The female lead repeatedly expresses her slogan, "Never let them [men] know you can take care of yourself." Sarah becomes more passive and less competitive around boys her own age.

   Concept: _____

2. Yolanda has a secure, enjoyable, reasonably well-paid job as a tenured English professor at a state university. Her friends are dumbfounded when she announces that she's going to resign and give it all up to try writing a novel. She tries to explain, "I need a new challenge, a new mountain to climb. I've had this lid on my writing talents for years, and I've got to break free. It's something I have to try. I won't be happy until I do."

   Concept: _____

3. Vladimir, who is 4, seems to be emotionally distant from and inattentive to his father. He complains whenever he's left with his dad. In contrast, he often cuddles up in bed with his mother and tries very hard to please her by behaving properly.

   Concept: _____

people. When he searched among the living, the results were so disappointing that he turned to the study of historical figures. Thus, humanistic portraits of psychological health are perhaps a bit too optimistic.

3. *Inadequate evidence.* For the most part, humanistic psychologists haven't been particularly research oriented. Although Rogers and Maslow both conducted and encouraged empirical research, many of their followers have been scornful of efforts to quantify human experience to test hypotheses. Much more research is needed to catch up with the theorizing in the humanistic camp. This is precisely the opposite of the situation that we'll encounter in the next section, which examines biological approaches to personality.

Biological Perspectives

Like many identical twins reared apart, Jim Lewis and Jim Springer found they had been leading eerily similar lives. Separated four weeks after birth in 1940, the Jim twins grew up 45 miles apart in Ohio and were reunited in 1979. Eventually, they discovered that both drove the same model blue Chevrolet, chain-smoked Salems, chewed their fingernails, and owned dogs named Toy. Each had spent a good deal of time vacationing at the same three-block strip of beach in Florida. More important, when tested for such personality traits as flexibility, self-control, and sociability, the twins responded almost exactly alike. (Leo, 1987, p. 63)

So began a *Time* magazine summary of a major twin study conducted at the University of Minnesota Center for Twin and Adoption Research. Since 1979 the investigators at this center have been studying the personality resemblance of identical twins reared apart. Not all the twin pairs have been as similar as Jim Lewis and Jim Springer, but many of the parallels have been uncanny (Lykken et al., 1992). Identical twins Oskar Stohr and Jack Yufe were separated soon after birth. Oskar was sent to a Nazi-run school in Czechoslovakia while Jack was raised in a Jewish home on a Caribbean island. When they were reunited for the first time during middle age, they showed up wearing similar mustaches, hair-cuts, shirts, and wire-rimmed glasses! A pair of previously separated female twins both arrived at the Minneapolis airport wearing seven rings on their fingers. One had a son named Richard Andrew and the other had a son named Andrew Richard!

Could personality be largely inherited? These anecdotal reports of striking resemblances between identical twins reared apart certainly raise this possibility. In this section we'll discuss Hans Eysenck's theory, which emphasizes the influence of heredity, look at recent behavioral genetics research on the heritability of personality, and outline the evolutionary perspective on personality.

Eysenck's Theory 10d

Hans Eysenck was born in Germany but fled to London during the era of Nazi rule. He went on to become one of Britain's most prominent psychologists. Eysenck (1967, 1982, 1990a) viewed personality structure as a hierarchy of traits, in which many superficial traits are derived from a smaller number of more basic traits, which are derived from a handful of fundamental higher-order traits, as shown in Figure 12.13 on the next page. His studies suggested that all aspects of personality emerge from just three higher-order traits: extraversion, neuroticism,

Is personality largely inherited? The story of these identical twins would certainly suggest so. Although they were reared apart from 4 weeks after their birth, Jim Lewis (left) and Jim Springer (right) exhibit remarkable correspondence in personality. Some of the similarities in their lives—such as the benches built around trees in their yards—seem uncanny.

Hans Eysenck

"Personality is determined to a large extent by a person's genes."

and psychoticism, which involves being egocentric, impulsive, cold, and antisocial.

According to Eysenck, "Personality is determined to a large extent by a person's genes" (1967, p. 20). How is heredity linked to personality in Eysenck's model? In part, through conditioning concepts borrowed from behavioral theory. Eysenck theorized that some people can be conditioned more readily than others because of differences in their physiological functioning. These variations in "conditionability" are assumed to influence the personality traits that people acquire through conditioning processes.

Eysenck has shown a special interest in explaining variations in *extraversion-introversion*. He has proposed that introverts tend to have higher levels of physiological arousal, or perhaps higher "arousability," which make them more easily conditioned than extraverts. According to Eysenck, people who

condition easily acquire more conditioned inhibitions than others. These inhibitions make them more bashful, tentative, and uneasy in social situations. This social discomfort leads them to turn inward. Hence, they become introverted.

Behavioral Genetics and Personality

10d

Recent research in behavioral genetics has provided impressive support for the idea that many personality traits are largely inherited (Livesley, Jang, Vernon, 2003; Rowe & van den Oord, 2005). For instance, **Figure 12.14** shows the mean correlations observed for identical and fraternal twins in studies of the Big Five personality traits. Higher correlations are indicative of greater similarity on a trait. On all five traits, identical twins have been found to be much more similar than fraternal twins (Plomin et al., 2008). Based on these and many other findings, theorists conclude that genetic factors exert considerable influence over personality (see Chapter 3 for an explanation of the logic of twin studies).

Some skeptics wonder whether identical twins might exhibit more trait similarity than fraternal twins because they're treated more alike. In other words, they wonder whether environmental factors (rather than heredity) could be responsible for identical twins' greater personality resemblance. This nagging question can be answered only by studying identical twins reared apart, which is why the twin study at the University of Minnesota has been so important. The Minnesota study (Tellegen et al., 1988) was the first to administer the same personality test to identical and fraternal twins reared apart, as well as together. Most of the twins reared apart were separated quite early in life (median age of 2.5 months) and remained separated for a long time (median period of almost 34 years).

The results revealed that identical twins reared apart were substantially more similar in personality

Figure 12.13

Eysenck's model of personality structure. Eysenck described personality structure as a hierarchy of traits. In this scheme, a few higher-order traits, such as extraversion, determine a number of lower-order traits, which determine a person's habitual responses.

SOURCE: Eysenck, H. J. (1976). *The biological basis of personality.* Springfield, IL: Charles C. Thomas. Reprinted by permission of the publisher.

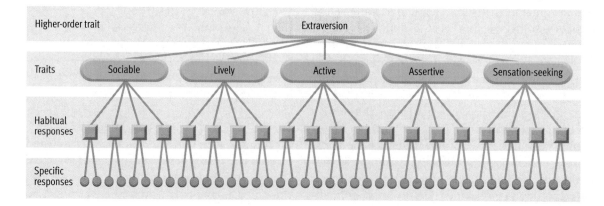

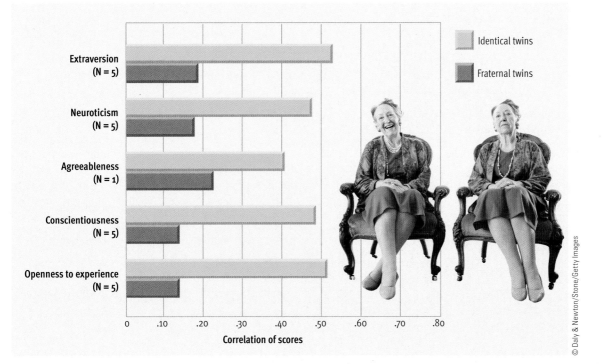

Figure 12.14

Twin studies of personality. Loehlin (1992) has summarized the results of twin studies that have examined the Big Five personality traits. The N under each trait indicates the number of twin studies that have examined that trait. The chart plots the average correlations obtained for identical and fraternal twins in these studies. As you can see, identical twins have shown greater resemblance in personality than fraternal twins have, suggesting that personality is partly inherited. (Based on data from Loehlin, 1992)

than fraternal twins reared together. The *heritability estimates* (see Chapter 9) for the traits examined ranged from 40% to 58%. The investigators concluded that their results support the hypothesis that genetic blueprints shape the contours of personality.

Research on the heritability of personality has inadvertently turned up an interesting discovery: *shared family environment* appears to have remarkably little impact on personality. This unexpected finding has been observed quite consistently in behavioral genetics research (Beer, Arnold, & Loehlin, 1998; Rowe & van den Oord, 2005). It is surprising in that social scientists have long assumed that the family environment shared by children growing up together led to some personality resemblance among them. *These findings have led some theorists to conclude that parents don't matter—that they wield very little influence over how their children develop* (Cohen, 1999; Harris, 1998; Rowe, 1994).

Critics of this conclusion have argued that the methods used in behavioral genetics studies have probably underestimated the impact of shared environment on personality (Collins et al., 2000; Stoolmiller, 1999). They also note that shared experiences—such as being raised with authoritarian discipline—may often have different effects on two siblings, which obscures the impact of environment

but is not the same result as having no effect (Turkheimer & Waldron, 2000). And the critics argue that decades of research in developmental psychology have clearly demonstrated that parents have significant influence on their children (Maccoby, 2000). Thus, the assertion that "parents don't matter" seems premature and overstated.

The Evolutionary Approach to Personality

In the realm of biological perspectives on personality, another recent development has been the emergence of evolutionary theory. Evolutionary theorists assert that personality has a biological basis because natural selection has favored certain traits over the course of human history (Figueredo et al., 2005). Thus, evolutionary analyses focus on how various personality traits—and the ability to recognize these traits in others—may have contributed to reproductive fitness in ancestral human populations.

For example, David Buss (1991, 1995, 1997) has argued that the Big Five personality traits stand out as important dimensions of personality because those traits have had significant adaptive implications. Buss points out that humans historically have depended heavily on groups, which afford protection

web link 12.7

Great Ideas in Personality

Personality psychologist G. Scott Acton (Rochester Institute of Technology) demonstrates that scientific research programs in personality generate broad and compelling ideas about what it is to be a human being. He charts the contours of 12 research perspectives, including behaviorism, behavioral genetics, and sociobiology, and backs them up with extensive links to published and online resources associated with each perspective.

concept check 12.3

Understanding the Implications of Major Theories: Who Said This?

Check your understanding of the implications of the personality theories we've discussed by indicating which theorist is likely to have made the statements below. The answers are in Appendix A.

Choose from the following theorists:

Alfred Adler

Albert Bandura

Hans Eysenck

Sigmund Freud

Abraham Maslow

Walter Mischel

Quotes:

1. _____ "If you deliberately plan to be less than you are capable of being, then I warn you that you'll be deeply unhappy for the rest of your life."

2. _____ "I feel that the major, most fundamental dimensions of personality are likely to be those on which [there is] strong genetic determination of individual differences."

3. _____ "People are in general not candid over sexual matters . . . they wear a heavy overcoat woven of a tissue of lies, as though the weather were bad in the world of sexuality."

Courtesy of David M. Buss

David Buss

"In sum, the five factors of personality, in this account, represent important dimensions of the social terrain that humans were selected to attend to and act upon."

from predators or enemies, opportunities for sharing food, and a diverse array of other benefits. In the context of these group interactions, people have had to make difficult but crucial judgments about the characteristics of others, asking such questions as: Who will make a good member of my coalition? Who can I depend on when in need? Who will share their resources? Thus, Buss (1995) argues, "those individuals able to accurately discern and act upon these individual differences likely enjoyed a considerable reproductive advantage" (p. 22).

According to Buss, the Big Five traits emerge as fundamental dimensions of personality because humans have evolved special sensitivity to variations in the ability to bond with others (extraversion), the willingness to cooperate and collaborate (agreeableness), the tendency to be reliable and ethical (conscientiousness), the capacity to be an innovative problem solver (openness to experience), and the ability to handle stress (low neuroticism). In a nutshell, Buss argues that the Big Five reflect the most salient features of others' adaptive behavior over the course of evolutionary history.

Daniel Nettle (2006) takes this line of thinking one step further, asserting that the traits themselves (as opposed to the ability to recognize them in others) are products of evolution that were adaptive in ancestral environments. For example, he discusses how extraversion could have promoted mating success, how neuroticism could have fueled competitiveness and avoidance of dangers, how agreeableness could have fostered the effective building of coalitions, and so forth. Nettle also discusses how

each of the Big Five traits may have had adaptive costs (extraversion, for example, is associated with risky behavior) as well as benefits. Thus, he argues that evolutionary analyses of personality need to weigh the *trade-offs* between the adaptive advantages and disadvantages of the Big Five traits.

Evaluating Biological Perspectives

Researchers have compiled convincing evidence that biological factors exert considerable influence over personality. Nonetheless, we must take note of some weaknesses in biological approaches to personality:

1. David Funder (2001) has observed that behavioral genetics researchers exhibit something of an "obsession with establishing the exact magnitude of heritability coefficients" (p. 207). As we discussed in Chapter 9, heritability ratios are ballpark estimates that will vary depending on sampling procedures and other considerations (Sternberg, Grigorenko, & Kidd, 2005). There is no one magic number awaiting discovery, so the inordinate focus on heritability does seem ill-advised.

2. At present there's no comprehensive biological theory of personality. Eysenck's model doesn't provide a systematic overview of how biological factors govern personality structure and development (and was never intended to). In regard to personality, evolutionary theory is even more limited in scope than Eysenck's theory. Additional theoretical work is needed to catch up with recent empirical findings on the biological basis for personality.

12.17 Eysenck views personality structure as a hierarchy of traits. He believes that heredity influences individual differences in physiological functioning that affect how easily people acquire conditioned inhibitions.

12.18 Twin studies of the Big Five personality traits find that identical twins are more similar in personality than fraternal twins, thus suggesting that personality is partly inherited. Estimates for the heritability of personality hover in the vicinity of 50%. Recent research in behavioral genetics has suggested that shared family environment has surprisingly little impact on personality, although a variety of theorists have been critical of this conclusion.

12.19 According to Buss, the ability to recognize and judge others' status on the Big Five traits may have contributed to reproductive fitness. Nettle argues that the Big Five traits themselves (rather than the ability to recognize them) are products of evolution that were adaptive in ancestral times.

12.20 Researchers have compiled convincing evidence that genetic factors exert considerable influence over personality. However, the biological approach has been criticized because of methodological problems with heritability ratios and because it offers no systematic model of how physiology shapes personality.

A Contemporary Empirical Approach: Terror Management Theory

So far, our coverage has been largely devoted to grand, panoramic theories of personality. In this section we'll examine a new approach to understanding personality functioning that has a narrower focus than the classic theories of personality. *Terror management theory* emerged as an influential perspective in the 1990s. Although the theory borrows from Freudian and evolutionary formulations, it provides its own unique analysis of the human condition. Developed by Sheldon Solomon, Jeff Greenberg, and Tom Pyszczynski (1991, 2004b), this fresh perspective is currently generating a huge volume of research.

Essentials of Terror Management Theory

One of the chief goals of terror management theory is to explain why people need self-esteem (Solomon, Greenberg, & Pyszczynski, 1991). The theory begins by noting that humans have evolved complex cognitive abilities that permit self-awareness and contemplation of the future. These cognitive capacities make humans keenly aware of the inevitability of death—they appreciate that life can be snuffed out unpredictably at any time. Humans' awareness of the inevitability of death creates the potential for experiencing anxiety, alarm, and terror when individuals think about their mortality (see Figure 12.15).

How do people deal with this potential for terror? According to terror management theory, "What saves us is culture. Cultures provide ways to view the world—worldviews—that 'solve' the existential crisis engendered by the awareness of death" (Pyszczynski, Solomon, & Greenberg, 2003, p. 16). Cultural world-views diminish anxiety by providing answers to such universal questions as: Why am I here? What is the meaning of life? Cultures create stories, traditions, and institutions that give their members a sense of being part of an enduring legacy through their contributions to their families, tribes, schools, churches, professions, and so forth. Thus, faith in a cultural worldview can give people a sense of order, meaning, and context that can soothe humans' fear of death.

Where does self-esteem fit into the picture? Self-esteem is viewed as a sense of personal worth that depends on one's confidence in the validity of one's cultural worldview and the belief that one is living up to the standards prescribed by that worldview. "It is the feeling that one is a valuable contributor to a meaningful universe" (Pyszczynski et al., 2004,

Key Learning Goals

12.21 Understand the chief concepts and hypotheses of terror management theory.

12.22 Describe how reminders of death influence people's behavior.

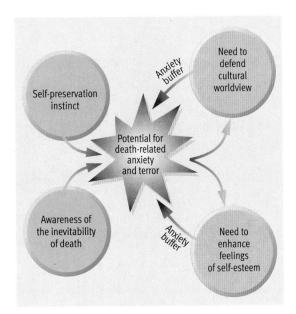

Figure 12.15

Overview of terror management theory. This graphic maps out the relations among the key concepts proposed by terror management theory. The theory asserts that humans' unique awareness of the inevitability of death fosters a need to defend one's cultural worldview and one's self-esteem, which serve to protect one from mortality-related anxiety.

p. 437). Hence, self-esteem buffers people from the profound anxiety associated with the awareness that we are transient animals destined to die. In other words, self-esteem serves a *terror management* function (refer to **Figure 12.15**).

The notion that self-esteem functions as an *anxiety buffer* has been supported by numerous studies (Pyszczynski et al., 2004). In many of these experiments, researchers have manipulated what they call *mortality salience* by asking subjects to briefly think about their own death. Consistent with the anxiety buffer hypothesis, reminding people of their mortality leads subjects to engage in a variety of behaviors that are likely to bolster their self-esteem, thus reducing anxiety.

Applications of Terror Management Theory

Increasing mortality salience also leads people to work harder at defending their cultural worldview (Arndt, Cook, & Routledge, 2004). For instance, after briefly pondering their mortality, research participants (1) hand out harsher penalties to moral transgressors, (2) respond more negatively to people who criticize their culture, and (3) show more respect for cultural icons, such as a flag (Greenberg et al., 1990; Rosenblatt et al., 1989). This need to defend one's cultural worldview may even fuel prejudice. Reminding subjects of their mortality leads to (1) more negative evaluations of people from different religious or ethnic backgrounds, and (2) more stereotypic thinking about minority group members (McGregor et al., 1998; Schimel et al., 1999).

Terror management theory asserts that much of people's behavior is motivated by the overlapping needs to defend their cultural worldview and preserve their self-esteem. This perspective yields novel hypotheses regarding many phenomena. For instance, Solomon, Greenberg, and Pyszczynski (2004a) explain excessive materialism in terms of the anxiety-buffering function of self-esteem. Specifically, they argue that "conspicuous possession and consumption are thinly veiled efforts to assert that one is special and therefore more than just an animal fated to die and decay" (p. 134). One recent study even applied terror management theory to the political process. Cohen et al. (2004) found that mortality salience increased participants' preference for "charismatic" candidates who articulate a grand vision that makes people feel like they are part of an important movement of lasting significance.

In another thought-provoking analysis, Goldenberg (2005) argues that bodily concerns remind people of their animal nature and hence their ultimate mortality. Based on this analysis, Goldenberg and colleages have predicted and found that mortality salience can increase individuals' ambivalence about the physical aspects of sexuality and lead to the suppression of some sexual urges (Goldenberg et al., 2002; Landau, Goldenberg et al., 2006). Mortality salience can also inhibit health-protective behaviors, such as breast self-exams by women, when these behaviors highlight the frailty of the human body.

As you can see, although terror management theory is narrower in scope than psychoanalytic, behavioral, and humanistic theories, it has wide-ranging implications. In particular, given its focus on death anxiety, it has much to say about people's reactions to the contemporary threat of terrorism. Pyszczynski, Solomon, and Greenberg (2003) point out that terrorist attacks are intended to produce a powerful, nationwide manipulation of mortality salience. When mortality salience is elevated, terror management theory predicts that people will embrace their cultural worldviews even more strongly than before. Consistent with this prediction, in the months following the September 11 terrorist attacks on New York and Washington, D.C., expressions of patriotism and religious faith increased dramatically. Research on terror management processes has also shown that when death anxiety is heightened, people become less tolerant of opposing views and more prejudiced against those who are different. Consistent with this analysis, in the aftermath of September 11, individuals who questioned government policies met more hostility than usual. The theory also predicts that reminders of mortality increase the tendency to admire those who uphold cultural standards. More than ever, people need heroes who personify cultural values. This need was

According to terror management theory, events that remind people of their mortality motivate them to defend their cultural worldview. One manifestation of this process is an increased interest in, and respect for, cultural icons, such as flags.

© Gilles Peress/Magnum Photos

apparent following September 11 in the way the media made firefighters into larger-than-life heroes.

At first glance, a theory that explains everything from prejudice to compulsive shopping in terms of death anxiety may seem highly implausible. After all, most people do not appear to walk around all day obsessing about the possibility of their death. The architects of terror management theory are well aware of this reality. They explain that the defensive reactions uncovered in their research generally occur when death anxiety surfaces on the fringes of conscious awareness and that these reactions are automatic and subconscious (Pyszczynski, Greenberg, & Solomon, 1999). They also assert that people experience far more reminders of their mortality than most of us appreciate. They point out that people may be reminded of their mortality by a variety of everyday events, such as driving by a cemetery or funeral home, reading about an auto accident, visiting a doctor's office, hearing about a celebrity's heart attack, learning about alarming medical research, and so forth. Thus, the processes discussed by terror management theory may be more commonplace that one might guess.

Culture and Personality

Are there connections between culture and personality? The investigation of this question dates back to the 1940s and 1950s, when researchers set out to describe various cultures' *modal personality* (Kardiner & Linton, 1945) or *national character* (Kluckhohn & Murray, 1948). These investigations sought to describe the *prototype* or *typical* personality in various cultures. For example, Ruth Benedict (1934) concluded that American Pueblo Indians were sober, orderly, conventional, and cooperative. Largely guided by Freud's psychoanalytic theory, this line of research generated interest for a couple decades, but ultimately met with little success (Bock, 2000; LeVine, 2001). Part of the problem may have been the rather culture-bound, Eurocentric nature of Freudian theory, but the crux of the problem was that it was unrealistic to expect to find a single, dominant personality profile in each culture. As we have seen repeatedly, given the realities of multifactorial causation, behavior is never that simple.

Studies of the links between culture and personality dwindled after the disappointments of the 1940s and 1950s. However, in recent years psychology's new interest in cultural factors has led to a renaissance of culture-personality research. This research has sought to determine whether Western personality constructs are relevant to other cultures and whether cultural differences can be seen in the prevalence of specific personality traits. As with cross-cultural research in other areas of psychology, these studies have found evidence of both continuity and variability across cultures.

For the most part, continuity has been apparent in cross-cultural comparisons of the *trait structure* of personality. When English language personality scales have been translated and administered in other cultures, the predicted dimensions of personality have emerged from the factor analyses (Paunonen & Ashton, 1998). For example, when scales that tap the Big Five personality traits have been administered and subjected to factor analysis in other cultures, the usual five traits have typically emerged (Katigbak et al., 2002; McCrae et al., 2005). Thus, research tentatively suggests that the basic dimensions of personality trait structure may be universal.

On the other hand, some cross-cultural variability is seen when researchers compare the average trait scores of samples from various cultural groups. For example, in a study comparing 51 cultures, McCrae et al. (2005) found that Brazilians scored relatively high in neuroticism, Australians in extraversion, Germans in openness to experience, Czechs in agreeableness, and Malaysians in conscientiousness, to give but a handful of examples. These findings should be viewed as preliminary, since more data are needed from larger and more carefully selected samples. Nonetheless, the findings suggest that there may be genuine cultural differences on some personality traits. That said, the cultural disparities in average trait scores that were observed were pretty modest in size.

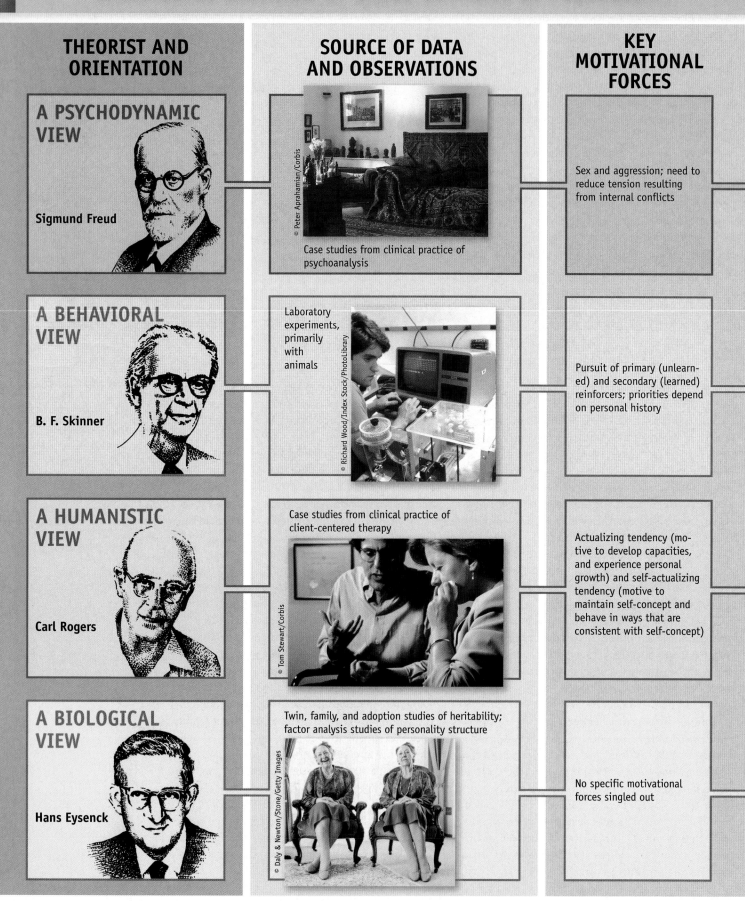

THEORIST AND ORIENTATION

A PSYCHODYNAMIC VIEW

Sigmund Freud

A BEHAVIORAL VIEW

B. F. Skinner

A HUMANISTIC VIEW

Carl Rogers

A BIOLOGICAL VIEW

Hans Eysenck

SOURCE OF DATA AND OBSERVATIONS

© Peter Aprahamian/Corbis

Case studies from clinical practice of psychoanalysis

Laboratory experiments, primarily with animals

© Richard Wood/Index Stock/PhotoLibrary

Case studies from clinical practice of client-centered therapy

© Tom Stewart/Corbis

Twin, family, and adoption studies of heritability; factor analysis studies of personality structure

© Daly & Newton/Stone/Getty Images

KEY MOTIVATIONAL FORCES

Sex and aggression; need to reduce tension resulting from internal conflicts

Pursuit of primary (unlearned) and secondary (learned) reinforcers; priorities depend on personal history

Actualizing tendency (motive to develop capacities, and experience personal growth) and self-actualizing tendency (motive to maintain self-concept and behave in ways that are consistent with self-concept)

No specific motivational forces singled out

MODEL OF PERSONALITY STRUCTURE

VIEW OF PERSONALITY DEVELOPMENT

ROOTS OF DISORDERS

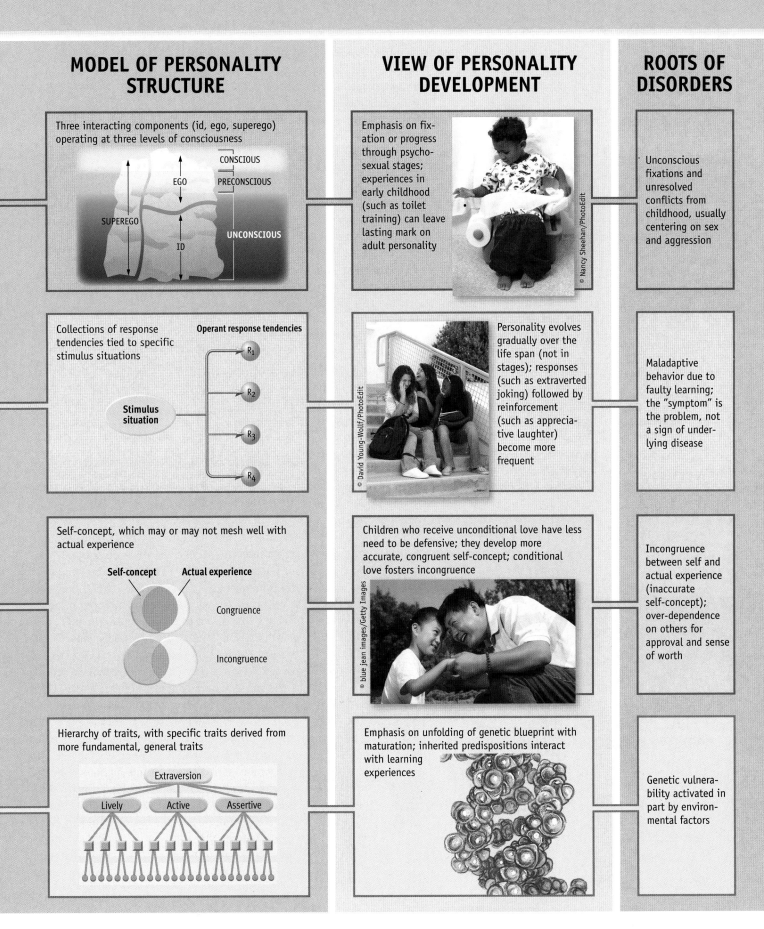

Three interacting components (id, ego, superego) operating at three levels of consciousness

CONSCIOUS
EGO
PRECONSCIOUS
SUPEREGO
ID
UNCONSCIOUS

Emphasis on fixation or progress through psychosexual stages; experiences in early childhood (such as toilet training) can leave lasting mark on adult personality

© Nancy Sheehan/PhotoEdit

Unconscious fixations and unresolved conflicts from childhood, usually centering on sex and aggression

Collections of response tendencies tied to specific stimulus situations

Operant response tendencies

Stimulus situation

R₁
R₂
R₃
R₄

Personality evolves gradually over the life span (not in stages); responses (such as extraverted joking) followed by reinforcement (such as appreciative laughter) become more frequent

© David Young-Wolff/PhotoEdit

Maladaptive behavior due to faulty learning; the "symptom" is the problem, not a sign of underlying disease

Self-concept, which may or may not mesh well with actual experience

Self-concept   Actual experience

Congruence

Incongruence

Children who receive unconditional love have less need to be defensive; they develop more accurate, congruent self-concept; conditional love fosters incongruence

© blue jean images/Getty Images

Incongruence between self and actual experience (inaccurate self-concept); over-dependence on others for approval and sense of worth

Hierarchy of traits, with specific traits derived from more fundamental, general traits

Extraversion

Lively   Active   Assertive

Emphasis on unfolding of genetic blueprint with maturation; inherited predispositions interact with learning experiences

Genetic vulnerability activated in part by environmental factors

Hazel Markus and Shinobu Kitayama

"Most of what psychologists currently know about human nature is based on one particular view—the so-called Western view of the individual as an independent, self-contained, autonomous entity."

Culture can shape personality. Children in Asian cultures, for example, grow up with a value system that allows them to view themselves as interconnected parts of larger social units. Hence, they tend to avoid positioning themselves so that they stand out from others.

The availability of the data from the McCrae et al. (2005) study allowed Terracciano et al. (2005) to revisit the concept of *national character*. Terracciano and his colleagues asked subjects from many cultures to describe the *typical* member of *their* culture on rating forms guided by the five-factor model. Generally, subjects displayed substantial agreement on these ratings of what was typical for their culture. The averaged ratings, which served as the measures of each culture's national character, were then correlated with the actual mean trait scores for various cultures compiled in the McCrae et al. (2005) study. The results were definitive—the vast majority of the correlations were extremely low and often even negative. In other words, there was little or no relationship between perceptions of national character and actual trait scores for various cultures (see **Figure 12.16**). People's beliefs about national character, which often fuel cultural prejudices, turned out to be profoundly inaccurate stereotypes (McCrae & Terracciano, 2006).

Perhaps the most interesting and influential work on culture and personality has been that of Hazel Markus and Shinobu Kitayama (1991, 1994, 2003) comparing American and Asian conceptions of the self. According to Markus and Kitayama, American parents teach their children to be self-reliant, to feel good about themselves, and to view themselves as special individuals. Children are encouraged to excel in competitive endeavors and to strive to stand out from the crowd. They are told that "the squeaky wheel gets the grease" and that "you have to stand up for yourself." Thus, Markus and Kitayama argue that *American culture fosters an independent view of the self.* American youngsters learn to define themselves in terms of their personal attributes, abilities, accom-

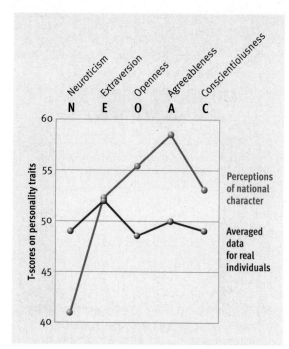

Figure 12.16

An example of inaccurate perceptions of national character. Terracciano et al. (2005) found that perceptions of national character (the prototype or typical personality for a particular culture) are largely inaccurate. The data shown here for one culture—Canadians—illustrates this inaccuracy. Mean scores on the Big Five traits for a sample of real individuals from Canada are graphed here in red. Averaged perceptions of national character for Canadians are graphed here in blue. The discrepancy between perception and reality is obvious. Terracciano and colleagues found similar disparities between views of national character and actual trait scores for a majority of the cultures they studied. (Adapted from McCrae & Terracciano, 2006)

plishments, and possessions. Their unique strengths and achievements become the basis for their sense of self-worth. Hence, they are prone to emphasize their uniqueness.

Most of us take this mentality for granted. Indeed, Markus and Kitayama maintain that "most of what psychologists currently know about human nature is based on one particular view—the so-called Western view of the individual as an independent, self-contained, autonomous entity" (1991, p. 224). However, they marshal convincing evidence that this view is *not* universal. They argue that in Asian cultures such as Japan and China, socialization practices foster a more *interdependent view of the self,* which emphasizes the fundamental connectedness of people to each other (see **Figure 12.17**). In these cultures, parents teach their children that they can rely on family and friends, that they should be modest about their personal accomplishments so they don't diminish others' achievements, and that they should view themselves as part of a larger social matrix. Children are encouraged to fit in with

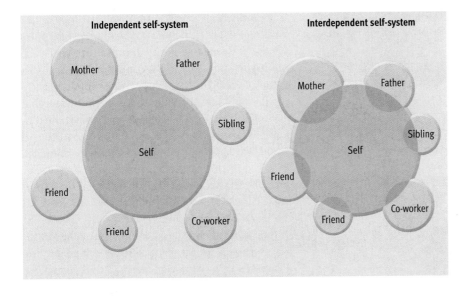

Figure 12.17

Culture and conceptions of self. According to Markus and Kitayama (1991), Western cultures foster an independent view of the self as a unique individual who is separate from others, as diagrammed on the left. In contrast, Asian cultures encourage an interdependent view of the self as part of an interconnected social matrix, as diagrammed on the right. The interdependent view leads people to define themselves in terms of their social relationships (for instance, as someone's daughter, employee, colleague, or neighbor).

SOURCE: Adapted from Markus, H. R., & Kitayama, S. (1991). Culture and the self: Implications for cognition, emotion, and motivation. *Psychological Review, 98*, 224–253. Copyright © 1991 by the American Psychological Association. Adapted by permission of the author.

others and to avoid standing out from the crowd. A popular adage in Japan reminds children that "the nail that stands out gets pounded down." Hence, Markus and Kitayama assert that Asian youngsters typically learn to define themselves in terms of the groups they belong to. Their harmonious relations with others and their pride in group achievements become the basis for their sense of self-worth. Because their self-esteem does not hinge so much on personal strengths, they are less likely to emphasize their uniqueness. Consistent with this analysis, Markus and Kitayama report that Asian subjects tend to view themselves as more similar to their peers than American subjects do.

REVIEW of Key Learning Goals

12.23 The basic trait structure of personality may be much the same across cultures, as the Big Five traits usually emerge in cross-cultural studies. However, some cultural variability has been seen when researchers compare average trait scores for various cultural groups.

12.24 Researchers have measured countries' national character by asking participants to describe the typical member of their culture on rating forms. However, averaged test data collected from real individuals show that these perceptions of national character tend to be inaccurate stereotypes.

12.25 Markus and Kitayama assert that American culture fosters an independent conception of self as a unique individual who is separate from others. In contrast, Asian cultures foster an interdependent view of the self, as part of an interconnected social matrix.

Reflecting on the Chapter's Themes

Our discussion of culture and personality obviously highlighted the text's theme that people's behavior is influenced by their cultural heritage. This chapter has also been ideally suited for embellishing two other unifying themes: psychology's theoretical diversity and the idea that psychology evolves in a sociohistorical context.

No other area of psychology is characterized by as much theoretical diversity as the study of personality, where there are literally dozens of insightful theories. Some of this diversity exists because different theories attempt to explain different facets of behavior. However, much of this theoretical diversity reflects genuine disagreements on basic questions about personality. Some of these disagreements are apparent on pages 520–521, which present an Illustrated Overview of the ideas of Freud, Skinner, Rogers, and Eysenck, as representatives of the psychodynamic, behavioral, humanistic, and biological approaches to personality.

The study of personality also highlights the sociohistorical context in which psychology evolves. Personality theories have left many marks on modern culture. The theories of Freud, Adler, and Skinner have had an enormous impact on childrearing practices. The ideas of Freud and Jung have found their way into literature (influencing the portrayal of fictional characters) and the visual arts. For example, Freud's theory helped inspire surrealism's interest in the world of dreams (see **Figure 12.18** on the next page). Maslow's hierarchy of needs and Skinner's affirmation of the value of positive reinforcement have influenced approaches to management in the world of business and industry.

Key Learning Goals

12.26 Identify the three unifying themes highlighted in this chapter.

 Cultural Heritage

Theoretical Diversity

 Sociohistorical Context

Figure 12.18

Freud and surrealism. The theories of Freud and Jung had considerable influence on the arts. For instance, their ideas about the unconscious guided the surrealists' explorations of the irrational world of dreams. Salvador Dali's 1936 painting *Soft Construction with Boiled Beans: Premonition of Civil War* is a bizarre image that symbolizes how a society can tear itself apart. Freud once commented, "I was tempted to consider the surrealists, which apparently have chosen me for their patron saint, as a bunch of complete nuts . . . [but] the young Spaniard [Dali], with the magnificent eyes of a fanatic and his undeniable technical mastery, has caused me to reconsider" (quoted in Gerard, 1968).

SOURCE: Salvador Dali, *Soft Construction with Boiled Beans: Premonitions of Civil War (1936)*. Photo by Graydon Wood, 1995, Philadelphia Museum of Art: The Louise and Walter Arensberg Collection. © 2009 Foundation Gala-Salvador Dali/VEGAP/Artists Rights Society (ARS), New York.

Sociohistorical forces also leave their imprint on psychology. This chapter provided many examples of how personal experiences, prevailing attitudes, and historical events have contributed to the evolution of ideas in psychology. For example, Freud's pessimistic view of human nature and his emphasis on the dark forces of aggression were shaped to some extent by his exposure to the hostilities of World War I and prevailing anti-Semitic sentiments. And Freud's emphasis on sexuality was surely influenced by the Victorian climate of sexual repression that existed in his youth. Adler's views also reflected the social context in which he grew up. His interest in inferiority feelings and compensation appear to have sprung from his own sickly childhood and the difficulties he had to overcome. In a similar vein, we saw that both Rogers and Maslow had to resist parental pressures in order to pursue their career interests. Their emphasis on the need to achieve personal fulfillment may have originated in these experiences.

Progress in the study of personality has also been influenced by developments in other areas of psychology. For instance, the enterprise of psychological testing originally emerged out of efforts to measure intelligence. Eventually, however, the principles of psychological testing were applied to the challenge of measuring personality. In the upcoming Personal Application we discuss the logic and limitations of personality tests.

REVIEW of Key Learning Goals

12.26 The study of personality illustrates how psychology is characterized by great theoretical diversity. It also demonstrates how ideas in psychology are shaped by sociohistorical forces and how cultural factors influence psychological processes.

PERSONAL APPLICATION

Understanding Personality Assessment

Key Learning Goals

12.27 Describe several prominent personality inventories, and evaluate the strengths and weaknesses of self-report inventories.

12.28 Describe two projective tests, and evaluate the strengths and weaknesses of projective testing.

12.29 Analyze the emerging role of the Internet in personality assessment.

Answer the following "true" or "false."

____ **1** Responses to personality tests are subject to unconscious distortion.

____ **2** The results of personality tests are often misunderstood.

____ **3** Personality test scores should be interpreted with caution.

____ **4** Personality tests serve many important functions.

If you answered "true" to all four questions, you earned a perfect score. Yes, personality tests are subject to distortion. Admittedly, test results are often misunderstood, and they should be interpreted cautiously. In spite of these problems, however, psychological tests can be quite useful.

Everyone engages in efforts to size up his or her own personality as well as that of others. When you think to yourself that "Mary Ann is shrewd and poised," or when you remark to a friend that "Carlos is timid and submissive," you're making personality assessments. In a sense, then, personality assessment is an ongoing part of daily life. Given the popular interest in personality assessment, it's not surprising that psychologists have devised formal measures of personality.

Personality tests can be helpful in (1) making clinical diagnoses of psychological disorders, (2) vocational counseling, (3) personnel selection in business and industry, and (4) measuring specific personality traits for research purposes. Personality tests can be divided into two broad categories: *self-report inventories* and *projective tests*. In this Personal Application, we'll discuss some representative tests from both categories and discuss their strengths and weaknesses.

Self-Report Inventories

Self-report inventories are personality tests that ask individuals to answer a series of questions about their characteristic behavior. The logic underlying this approach is simple: Who knows you better? Who has known you longer? Who has more access to your private feelings? We'll look at three examples of self-report scales, the MMPI, the 16PF, and the NEO Personality Inventory.

The MMPI

The most widely used self-report inventory is the Minnesota Multiphasic Personality Inventory (MMPI) (Butcher, 2005, 2006). The MMPI was originally designed to aid clinicians in the diagnosis of psychological disorders. It measures 10 personality traits that, when manifested to an extreme degree, are thought to be symptoms of disorders. Examples include traits such as paranoia, depression, and hysteria.

Are the MMPI clinical scales valid? That is, do they measure what they were designed to measure? Originally, it was assumed that the 10 clinical subscales would provide direct indexes of specific types of disorders. In other words, a high score on the depression scale would be indicative of depression, a high score on the paranoia scale would be indicative of a paranoid disorder, and so forth. However, research revealed that the relations between MMPI scores and various types of mental illness are much more complex than originally anticipated. People with most types of disorders show elevated scores on *several* MMPI subscales. This means that certain score *profiles* are indicative of specific disorders (see **Figure 12.19**). Thus, the interpretation of the MMPI is quite complicated. Nonetheless, the MMPI can be a helpful diagnostic tool for the clinician. The fact that the inventory has been translated into more than 115 languages is a testimonial to its usefulness (Adams & Culbertson, 2005).

The 16PF and NEO Personality Inventory

Raymond Cattell (1957, 1965) set out to identify and measure the *basic dimensions* of the *normal* personality. He started with a previously compiled list of 4504 personal-

ity traits. This massive list was reduced to 171 traits by weeding out terms that were virtually synonyms. Cattell then used factor analysis to identify clusters of closely related traits and the factors underlying them. Eventually, he reduced the list of 171 traits to 16 *source traits*. The Sixteen Personality Factor (16PF) Questionnaire (Cattell, Eber, & Tatsuoka, 1970; Cattell, 2007) is a 187–item scale that assesses these 16 basic dimensions of personality, which are listed in **Figure 12.20** on the next page.

As we noted in the main body of the chapter, some theorists believe that only five trait dimensions are required to provide a full description of personality. This view has led to the creation of a relatively new test—the NEO Personality Inventory. Developed by Paul Costa and Robert McCrae (1985, 1992), the NEO Inventory is designed to measure the Big Five traits: neuroticism, extraversion, openness to experience, agreeableness, and conscientiousness. The NEO inventory is widely used in research and clinical work, and updated revisions of the scale have been released (McCrae & Costa, 2004, 2007). An example of a NEO profile (averaged from many respondents) was shown in our discussion of culture and personality (see **Figure 12.16**).

Strengths and Weaknesses of Self-Report Inventories

To appreciate the strengths of self-report inventories, consider how else you might

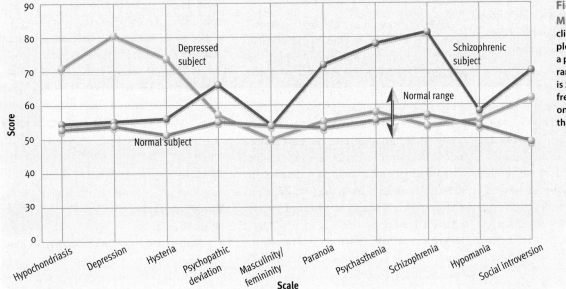

Figure 12.19

MMPI profiles. Scores on the 10 clinical scales of the MMPI are often plotted as shown here to create a profile for a client. The normal range for scores on each subscale is 50 to 65. People with disorders frequently exhibit elevated scores on several clinical scales rather than just one.

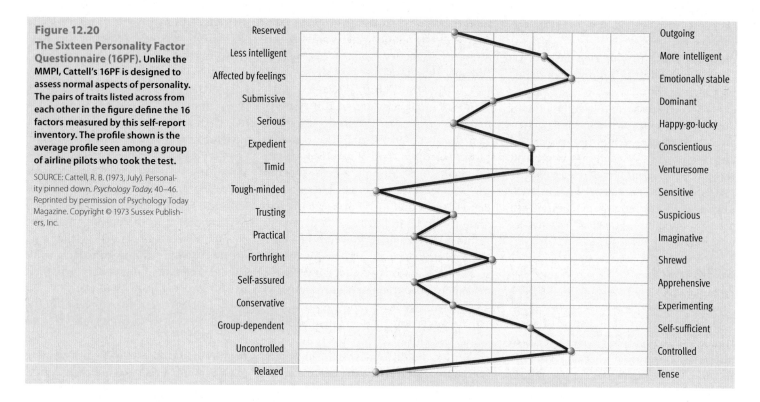

Figure 12.20

The Sixteen Personality Factor Questionnaire (16PF). Unlike the MMPI, Cattell's 16PF is designed to assess normal aspects of personality. The pairs of traits listed across from each other in the figure define the 16 factors measured by this self-report inventory. The profile shown is the average profile seen among a group of airline pilots who took the test.

SOURCE: Cattell, R. B. (1973, July). Personality pinned down. *Psychology Today*, 40–46. Reprinted by permission of Psychology Today Magazine. Copyright © 1973 Sussex Publishers, Inc.

Reserved		Outgoing
Less intelligent		More intelligent
Affected by feelings		Emotionally stable
Submissive		Dominant
Serious		Happy-go-lucky
Expedient		Conscientious
Timid		Venturesome
Tough-minded		Sensitive
Trusting		Suspicious
Practical		Imaginative
Forthright		Shrewd
Self-assured		Apprehensive
Conservative		Experimenting
Group-dependent		Self-sufficient
Uncontrolled		Controlled
Relaxed		Tense

inquire about an individual's personality. For instance, if you want to know how assertive someone is, why not just ask the person? Why administer an elaborate 50–item personality inventory that measures assertiveness? The advantage of the personality inventory is that it can provide a more objective and more precise estimate of the person's assertiveness, one that is better grounded in extensive comparative data based on information provided by many other respondents.

Of course, self-report inventories are only as accurate as the information that respondents provide. They are susceptible to several sources of error (Ben-Porath, 2003; Kline, 1995; Paulhus, 1991), including the following:

1. *Deliberate deception.* Some self-report inventories include many questions whose purpose is easy to figure out. This problem makes it possible for some respondents to intentionally fake particular personality traits (Rees & Metcalfe, 2003). Some studies suggest that deliberate faking is a serious problem when personality scales are used to evaluate job applicants (Birkeland et al., 2006), but other studies suggest that the problem is not all that significant (Hogan, Barrett, & Hogan, 2007).

2. *Social desirability bias.* Without realizing it, some people consistently respond to questions in ways that make them look good. The social desirability bias isn't a matter of deception so much as wishful thinking.

3. *Response sets.* A response set is a systematic tendency to respond to test items in a particular way that is unrelated to the content of the items. For instance, some people, called "yea-sayers," tend to agree with virtually every statement on a test. Other people, called "nay-sayers," tend to disagree with nearly every statement.

Test developers have devised a number of strategies to reduce the impact of deliberate deception, social desirability bias, and response sets (Berry, Wetter, & Baer, 1995; Lanyon & Goodstein, 1997). For instance, it's possible to insert a "lie scale" into a test to assess the likelihood that a respondent is engaging in deception. The best way to reduce the impact of social desirability bias is to identify items that are sensitive to this bias and drop them from the test. Problems with response sets can be reduced by systematically varying the way in which test items are worded. Although self-report inventories have some weaknesses, carefully constructed personality scales remain "an

indispensable tool for applied psychologists" (Hogan, 2005, p. 331).

Projective Tests

7a

Projective tests, which all take a rather indirect approach to the assessment of personality, are used extensively in clinical work. *Projective tests* **ask participants to respond to vague, ambiguous stimuli in ways that may reveal the subjects' needs, feelings, and personality traits.** The Rorschach test (Rorschach, 1921), for instance, consists of a series of ten inkblots. Respondents are asked to describe what they see in the blots. In the Thematic Apperception Test (TAT) (Murray, 1943), a series of pictures of simple scenes is presented to individuals who are asked to tell stories about what is happening in the scenes and what the characters are feeling. For instance, one TAT card shows a young boy contemplating a violin resting on a table in front of him (see **Figure 12.21** for another example).

The Projective Hypothesis

7a

The "projective hypothesis" is that ambiguous materials can serve as a blank screen onto which people project their character-

Figure 12.21

The Thematic Apperception Test (TAT). In taking the TAT, a respondent is asked to tell stories about scenes such as this one. The themes apparent in each story can be scored to provide insight about the respondent's personality.

SOURCE: Murray. H. A. (1971). *Thematic Apperception Test.* (CARD 12 F.) Cambridge, MA: Harvard University Press. Copyright © 1943 by The President and Fellows of Harvard College, Copyright © 1971 by Henry A. Murray. Reprinted by permission of the publisher.

istic concerns, conflicts, and desires (Frank, 1939). Thus, a competitive person who is shown the TAT card of the boy at the table with the violin might concoct a story about how the boy is contemplating an upcoming musical competition at which he hopes to excel. The same card shown to a person high in impulsiveness might elicit a story about how the boy is planning to sneak out the door to go dirt-bike riding with friends.

The scoring and interpretation of projective tests is very complicated. Rorschach responses may be analyzed in terms of content, originality, the feature of the inkblot that determined the response, and the amount of the inkblot used, among other criteria. In fact, six different systems exist for scoring the Rorschach (Adams & Culbertson, 2005). TAT stories are examined in terms of heroes, needs, themes, and outcomes.

Strengths and Weaknesses of Projective Tests

Proponents of projective tests assert that the tests have two unique strengths. First, they are not transparent to respondents. That is,

the subject doesn't know how the test provides information to the tester. Hence, it may be difficult for people to engage in intentional deception (Groth-Marnat, 1997). Second, the indirect approach used in these tests may make them especially sensitive to unconscious, latent features of personality.

Unfortunately, the scientific evidence on projective measures is unimpressive (Garb, Florio, & Grove, 1998; Hunsley, Lee, & Wood, 2003). In a thorough review of the relevant research, Lilienfeld, Wood, and Garb (2000) conclude that projective tests tend to be plagued by inconsistent scoring, low reliability, inadequate test norms, cultural bias, and poor validity estimates. They also assert that, contrary to advocates' claims, projective tests are susceptible to some types of intentional deception (primarily, faking poor mental health). Based on their analysis, Lilienfeld and his colleagues argue that projective tests should be referred to as projective "techniques" or "instruments" rather than tests because "most of these techniques as used in daily clinical practice do not fulfill the traditional criteria for psychological tests" (p. 29). In spite of these problems, projective tests continue to be used by many clinicians. Although the questionable scientific status of these techniques is a very real problem, their continued popularity suggests that they yield subjective information that many clinicians find useful (Viglione & Rivera, 2003).

Personality Testing on the Internet

The emergence of the Internet has had a considerable impact on the process of personality assessment. Self-report inventories are increasingly being administered over the Internet by researchers, clinicians, and companies (Naglieri et al., 2004). Most of the widely used personality scales are available in an online format. The advantages of online testing are substantial (Buchanan, 2007). Tests can be completed quickly, with reduced labor costs, and the data flow directly into interpretive software. Online testing also allows test administrators to collect additional data that would not be available from a traditional paper-and-pencil test. For instance, they can track answer

changing and how long respondents ponder specific questions. Online testing also allows clinicians to deliver assessment services to rural clients who do not have access to local psychologists (Barak & Buchanan, 2004). Given all these advantages, Buchanan (2007, p. 450) notes that "it is easy to imagine a future where virtually all testing is conducted online."

Are there any disadvantages to online personality assessment? Well, there are issues that merit concern, but they appear to be manageable. The item content of some tests is closely guarded, so security is an issue for some tests (Naglieri et al., 2004). And when personality tests are used for hiring purposes, verifying the identity of the respondent is important. The chief theoretical issue is whether tests delivered online yield results that are equivalent to what is found when the same tests are administered in a paper-and-pencil format. For the most part, research suggests that online tests are equivalent to their offline counterparts, but this issue should be checked empirically whenever a specific test is migrated to an online format (Buchanan, 2007; Epstein & Klinkenberg, 2001). Overall, though, the future of online personality testing appears bright. That said, consumers should remember that the Internet is utterly unregulated, so one can find an abundance of pop psychology tests online that have no scientific or empirical basis (Naglieri et al., 2004).

REVIEW of Key Learning Goals

12.27 Self-report inventories ask subjects to describe themselves. The MMPI is a widely used inventory that measures pathological aspects of personality. The 16PF assesses 16 dimensions of the normal personality. The NEO personality inventory measures the Big Five personality traits. Self-report inventories are vulnerable to certain sources of error, including deception, the social desirability bias, and response sets.

12.28 Projective tests assume that subjects' responses to ambiguous stimuli reveal something about their personality. In the Rorschach test, respondents describe what they see in 10 inkblots, whereas subjects formulate stories about simple scenes when they take the TAT. While the projective hypothesis seems plausible, projective tests' reliability and validity are disturbingly low.

12.29 Self-report inventories are increasingly being administered over the Internet. The advantages of online testing are substantial, although there are concerns about security and test equivalence.

Hindsight in Everyday Analyses of Personality

Key Learning Goals

12.30 Understand how hindsight bias affects everyday analyses and theoretical analyses of personality.

Consider the case of two close sisters who grew up together: Lorena and Christina. Lorena grew into a frugal adult who is careful about spending her money, only shops when there are sales, and saves every penny she can. In contrast, Christina became an extravagant spender who lives to shop and never saves any money. How do the sisters explain their striking personality differences? Lorena attributes her thrifty habits to the fact that her family was so poor when she was a child that she learned the value of being careful with money. Christina attributes her extravagant spending to the fact that her family was so poor that she learned to really enjoy any money that she might have. Now, it *is* possible that two sisters could react to essentially the same circumstances quite differently, but the more likely explanation is that both sisters have been influenced by the *hindsight bias*— **the tendency to mold one's interpretation of the past to fit how events actually turned out.** We saw how hindsight can distort memory in Chapter 7. Here, we will see how hindsight tends to make everyone feel

as if he or she is a personality expert and how it creates interpretive problems even for scientific theories of personality.

The Prevalence of Hindsight Bias

Hindsight bias is *ubiquitous,* which means that it occurs in a variety of settings, with all sorts of people (Blank, Musch, & Pohl, 2007; Sanna & Schwarz, 2006). Most of the time, people are not aware of the way their explanations are skewed by the fact that the outcome is already known. The experimental literature on hindsight bias offers a rich array of findings on how the knowledge of an outcome biases the way people think about its causes (Fischhoff, 2007; Guilbault et al., 2004). For example, when college students were told the results of hypothetical experiments, each group of students could "explain" why the studies turned out the way they did, even though different groups were given opposite results to explain (Slovic & Fischhoff, 1977). The students believed that the results of the studies were obvious when they were told what the experimenter found, but when they were given only the information that was available before the outcome was known, it was not obvious at all. This bias is also called the "I knew it all along" effect because that is the typical refrain of people when they have the luxury of hindsight. Indeed, after the fact, people often act as if events that would have been difficult to predict had in fact been virtually *inevitable.* Looking back at the disintegration of the Soviet Union and the end of the Cold War, for instance, many people today act as though these events were bound to happen, but in reality these landmark events were predicted by almost no one. It appears that outcome knowledge warps judgments in two ways (Erdfelder, Brandt, & Broder, 2007). First, knowing

the outcome of an event impairs one's recall of earlier expectations about the event. Second, outcome knowledge shapes how people reconstruct their thinking about the event.

Hindsight bias shows up in many contexts. For example, when a couple announces that they are splitting up, many people in their social circle will typically claim they "saw it coming." When a football team loses in a huge upset, you will hear many fans claim, "I knew they were overrated and vulnerable." When public authorities make a difficult decision that leads to a disastrous outcome—such as officials' decision not to evacuate New Orleans in preparation for Hurricane Katrina until relatively late—many of the pundits in the press are quick to criticize, often asserting that only incompetent fools could have failed to foresee the catastrophe. Interestingly, people are not much kinder to themselves when they make ill-fated decisions. When individuals make tough calls that lead to negative results—such as buying a car that turns out to be a lemon, or investing in a stock that plummets—they often say things like, "Why did I ignore the obvious warning signs?" or "How could I be such an idiot?"

Hindsight and Personality

Hindsight bias appears to be pervasive in everyday analyses of personality. Think about it: If you attempt to explain why you are so suspicious, why your mother is so domineering, or why your best friend is so insecure, the starting point in each case will be the personality outcome. It would probably be impossible to reconstruct the past without being swayed by your knowledge of these outcomes. Thus, hindsight makes everybody an expert on personality, as we can all come up with plausible explanations for the personality traits of people we know well. Perhaps this is why Judith Harris (1998) ignited a firestorm of protest when she wrote a widely read book arguing that parents have relatively little effect

When public officials make tough decisions that backfire, critics are often quick to argue that the officials should have shown greater foresight. This type of hindsight bias has been apparent in discussions of whether New Orleans mayor Ray Nagin (at left) and other state and federal officials should have been more proactive in evacuating New Orleans when Hurricane Katrina loomed as a threat.

© AP Images/Dennis Cook

on their children's personalities beyond the genetic material that they supply.

In her book *The Nurture Assumption,* Harris summarizes behavioral genetics research and other evidence suggesting that family environment has surprisingly little impact on children's personality (see p. 515). As discussed in the main body of the chapter, there is room for debate on this complex issue (Kagan, 1998; Tavris, 1998), but our chief interest here is that Harris made a cogent, compelling argument in her book that attracted extensive coverage in the press, which generated an avalanche of commentary from angry parents who argued that *parents do matter.* For example, *Newsweek* magazine received 350 letters, mostly from parents who provided examples of how they thought they influenced their children's personalities. However, parents' retrospective analyses of their children's personality development have to be treated with great skepticism, as they are likely to be distorted by hindsight bias (not to mention the selective recall frequently seen in anecdotal reports).

Unfortunately, hindsight bias is so prevalent it also presents a problem for scientific theories of personality. For example, the spectre of hindsight bias has been raised in many critiques of psychoanalytic theory (Torrey, 1992). Freudian theory was originally built mainly on a foundation of case studies of patients in therapy. Obviously, Freudian therapists who knew what their patients' adult personalities were like probably went looking for the types of childhood experiences hypothesized by Freud (oral fixations, punitive toilet training, Oedipal conflicts, and so forth) in their efforts to explain their patients' personalities.

Another problem with hindsight bias is that once researchers know an outcome, more often than not they can fashion some plausible explanation for it. For instance, Torrey (1992) describes a study inspired by

Freudian theory that examined breast-size preferences among men. The original hypothesis was that men who scored higher in dependence—thought to be a sign of oral fixation—would manifest a stronger preference for women with large breasts. When the actual results of the study showed just the opposite—that dependence was associated with a preference for smaller breasts—the finding was attributed to reaction formation on the part of the men. Instead of failing to support Freudian theory, the unexpected findings were simply reinterpreted in a way that was consistent with Freudian theory.

Hindsight bias also presents thorny problems for evolutionary theorists, who generally work backward from known outcomes to reason out how adaptive pressures in humans' ancestral past may have led to those outcomes (Cornell, 1997). Consider, for instance, evolutionary theorists' assertion that the Big Five traits are found to be fundamental dimensions of personality around the world because those specific traits have had major adaptive implications over the course of human history (Buss, 1995; Nettle, 2006). Their explanation makes sense, but what would have happened if some *other traits* had shown up in the Big Five? Would the evolutionary view have been weakened if dominance, or paranoia, or high sensation seeking had turned up in the Big Five? Probably not. With the luxury of hindsight, evolutionary theorists surely could have constructed plausible explanations for how these traits promoted reproductive success in the distant past. Thus, hindsight bias is a fundamental feature of human cognition, and the scientific enterprise is not immune to this problem.

Other Implications of "20/20 Hindsight"

Our discussion of hindsight has focused on its implications for thinking about per-

sonality, but there is ample evidence that hindsight can bias thinking in all sorts of domains. For example, consider the practice of obtaining second opinions on medical diagnoses. The doctor providing the second opinion usually is aware of the first physician's diagnosis, which creates a hindsight bias (Arkes et al., 1981). Second opinions would probably be more valuable if the doctors rendering them were not aware of previous diagnoses. Hindsight also has the potential to distort legal decisions in many types of cases where jurors evaluate defendants' responsibility for known outcomes, such as a failed surgery (Harley, 2007). For example, in trials involving allegations of negligence, jurors' natural tendency to think "how could they have failed to foresee this problem?" may exaggerate the appearance of negligence (LaBine & LaBine, 1996).

Hindsight bias is very powerful. The next time you hear of an unfortunate outcome to a decision made by a public official, carefully examine the way news reporters describe the decision. You will probably find that they believe that the disastrous outcome should have been obvious, because they can clearly see what went wrong after the fact. Similarly, if you find yourself thinking "Only a fool would have failed to anticipate this disaster" or "I would have foreseen this problem," take a deep breath and try to review the decision *using only information that was known at the time the decision was being made.* Sometimes good decisions, based on the best available information, can have terrible outcomes. Unfortunately, the clarity of "20/20 hindsight" makes it difficult for people to learn from their own and others' mistakes.

Table 12.3 Critical Thinking Skill Discussed in This Application

Skill	Description
Recognizing the bias in hindsight analysis	The critical thinker understands that knowing the outcome of events biases one's recall and interpretation of the events.

REVIEW of Key Learning Goals

12.30 Hindsight bias often leads people to assert that "I knew it all along" in discussing outcomes that they did not actually predict. Thanks to hindsight, people can almost always come up with plausible-sounding explanations for known personality traits. Psychoanalytic and evolutionary theories of personality have also been accused of falling victim to hindsight bias.

Key Ideas

The Nature of Personality

▌ The concept of personality explains the consistency in people's behavior over time and situations while also explaining their distinctiveness. The five-factor model has become the dominant conception of personality structure. The Big Five traits are predictive of everyday behavior, as well as important life outcomes.

Psychodynamic Perspectives

▌ Freud's psychoanalytic theory emphasizes the importance of the unconscious. Freud described personality structure in terms of three components—the id, ego, and superego—which are routinely involved in an ongoing series of internal conflicts.

▌ Freud theorized that conflicts centering on sex and aggression are especially likely to lead to anxiety. According to Freud, anxiety and other unpleasant emotions such as guilt are often warded off with defense mechanisms.

▌ Freud described a series of five stages of development: oral, anal, phallic, latency, and genital. Certain experiences during these stages can have lasting effects on adult personality.

▌ Jung's most innovative and controversial concept was the collective unconscious. Adler's individual psychology emphasizes how people strive for superiority to compensate for their feelings of inferiority.

▌ Overall, psychodynamic theories have produced many groundbreaking insights about the unconscious, the role of internal conflict, and the importance of early childhood experiences in personality development. However, psychodynamic theories have been criticized for their poor testability, their inadequate base of empirical evidence, and their male-centered views.

Behavioral Perspectives

▌ Behavioral theories view personality as a collection of response tendencies tied to specific stimulus situations. They assume that personality development is a lifelong process in which response tendencies are shaped and reshaped by learning, especially operant conditioning.

▌ Bandura's social cognitive theory focuses on how cognitive factors such as expectancies and self-efficacy regulate learned behavior. His concept of observational learning accounts for the acquisition of responses from models. Mischel has questioned the degree to which people display cross-situational consistency in behavior.

▌ Behavioral approaches to personality are based on rigorous research. They have provided ample insights into how environmental factors and learning mold personality. The behaviorists have been criticized for their fragmented analysis of personality, radical behaviorism's dehumanizing view of human nature, and the modern dilution of the behavioral approach.

Humanistic Perspectives

▌ Humanistic theories are phenomenological and take an optimistic view of human potential. Rogers focused on the self-concept as the critical aspect of personality. Maslow theorized that psychological health depends on fulfilling one's need for self-actualization.

▌ Humanistic theories deserve credit for highlighting the importance of subjective views of oneself and for helping to lay the foundation for positive psychology. Humanistic theories lack a firm base of research, are difficult to put to an empirical test, and may be overly optimistic about human nature.

Biological Perspectives

▌ Contemporary biological theories stress the genetic origins of personality. Eysenck suggests that heredity influences individual differences in physiological functioning that affect how easily people acquire conditioned responses. Research on the personality resemblance of twins provides impressive evidence that genetic factors shape personality.

▌ Evolutionary theorists argue that the major dimensions of personality reflect humans' adaptive landscape. The biological approach has demonstrated that personality is partly heritable, but it has been criticized for its narrow focus on heritability and because it offers no systematic model of how physiology shapes personality.

A Contemporary Empirical Approach: Terror Management Theory

▌ Terror management theory proposes that self-esteem and belief in a cultural worldview shield people from the profound anxiety associated with their mortality.

Consistent with this analysis, increasing mortality salience leads people to make efforts to bolster their self-esteem and defend their worldviews. These defensive reactions are automatic and subconscious.

Culture and Personality

▌ Research suggests that the basic trait structure of personality may be much the same across cultures, as the Big Five traits usually emerge in cross-cultural studies. However, there are cultural variations in the mean level of some personality traits.

▌ Perceptions of national character appear to be inaccurate stereotypes. Markus and Kitayama assert that American culture fosters an independent conception of self, whereas Asian cultures foster an interdependent view of the self.

Reflecting on the Chapter's Themes

▌ The study of personality illustrates how psychology is characterized by great theoretical diversity. It also demonstrates how ideas in psychology are shaped by sociohistorical forces and how cultural factors influence psychological processes.

PERSONAL APPLICATION Understanding Personality Assessment

▌ Personality assessment is useful in clinical diagnosis, counseling, personnel selection, and research. Self-report measures, such as the MMPI, 16PF, and NEO Inventory, ask subjects to describe themselves. Self-report inventories are vulnerable to certain sources of error, including deception, the social desirability bias, and response sets.

▌ Projective tests, such as the Rorschach and TAT, assume that subjects' responses to ambiguous stimuli reveal something about their personality. While the projective hypothesis seems plausible, projective tests' reliability and validity are disturbingly low. Personality assessments are increasingly being administered over the Internet.

CRITICAL THINKING APPLICATION Hindsight in Everyday Analyses of Personality

▌ Hindsight bias often leads people to assert that "I knew it all along" in discussing outcomes that they did not actually predict. Thanks to hindsight, people can almost always come up with plausible-sounding explanations for known personality traits.

Key Terms

Archetypes (p. 499)
Behaviorism (p. 502)
Collective unconscious (p. 499)
Compensation (p. 500)
Conscious (p. 494)
Defense mechanisms (p. 496)
Displacement (p. 496)
Ego (p. 494)
Factor analysis (p. 491)
Fixation (p. 498)
Hierarchy of needs (p. 510)
Hindsight bias (p. 528)
Humanism (p. 508)
Id (p. 494)
Identification (p. 496)
Incongruence (p. 509)
Model (p. 506)
Need for self-actualization (p. 511)
Observational learning (p. 506)
Oedipal complex (p. 499)
Personal unconscious (p. 499)
Personality (p. 491)
Personality trait (p. 491)
Phenomenological approach (p. 509)
Pleasure principle (p. 494)
Preconscious (p. 494)
Projection (p. 496)
Projective tests (p. 526)

Psychodynamic theories (p. 493)
Psychosexual stages (p. 498)
Rationalization (p. 496)
Reaction formation (p. 496)
Reality principle (p. 494)
Reciprocal determinism (p. 504)
Regression (p. 496)
Repression (p. 496)
Self-actualizing persons (p. 511)
Self-concept (p. 509)
Self-efficacy (p. 506)
Self-report inventories (p. 525)
Striving for superiority (p. 500)
Superego (p. 494)
Unconscious (p. 494)

Key People

Alfred Adler (pp. 500–501)
Albert Bandura (pp. 504, 506)
Hans Eysenck (pp. 513–514)
Sigmund Freud (pp. 493–499)
Carl Jung (pp. 499–500)
Abraham Maslow (pp. 510–512)
Robert McCrae & Paul Costa (pp. 491–492)
Walter Mischel (pp. 507–508)
Carl Rogers (pp. 509–510)
B. F. Skinner (pp. 502–504)

1. Harvey Hedonist has devoted his life to the search for physical pleasure and immediate need gratification. Freud would say that Harvey is dominated by:
   A. his ego.
   B. his superego.
   C. his id.
   D. Bacchus.

2. Furious at her boss for what she considers to be unjust criticism, Tyra turns around and takes out her anger on her subordinates. Tyra may be using the defense mechanism of:
   A. displacement.
   B. reaction formation.
   C. identification.
   D. replacement.

3. Freud believed that most personality disturbances are due to:
   A. the failure of parents to reinforce healthy behavior.
   B. a poor self-concept resulting from excessive parental demands.
   C. unconscious and unresolved sexual conflicts rooted in childhood experiences.
   D. the exposure of children to unhealthy role models.

4. According to Alfred Adler, the prime motivating force in a person's life is:
   A. physical gratification.
   B. existential anxiety.
   C. striving for superiority.
   D. the need for power.

5. Which of the following learning mechanisms does B. F. Skinner see as being the major means by which behavior is learned?
   A. classical conditioning
   B. operant conditioning
   C. observational learning
   D. insight learning

6. Always having been a good student, Irving is confident that he will do well in his psychology course. According to Bandura's social cognitive theory, Irving would be said to have:
   A. strong feelings of self-efficacy.
   B. a sense of superiority.
   C. strong feelings of self-esteem.
   D. strong defense mechanisms.

7. Which of the following approaches to personality is least deterministic?
   A. the humanistic approach
   B. the psychoanalytic approach
   C. Skinner's approach
   D. the behavioral approach

8. Which of the following did Carl Rogers believe fosters a congruent self-concept?
   A. conditional love
   B. appropriate role models
   C. immediate-need gratification
   D. unconditional love

9. The strongest support for the theory that personality is heavily influenced by genetics is provided by strong personality similarity between:
   A. identical twins reared together.
   B. identical twins reared apart.
   C. fraternal twins reared together.
   D. nontwins reared together.

10. Which of the following is the best way to regard heritability estimates?
    A. as reliable but not necessarily valid estimates
    B. as ballpark estimates of the influence of genetics
    C. as accurate estimates of the influence of genetics
    D. as relatively useless estimates of the influence of genetics

11. Research on terror management theory has shown that increased mortality salience leads to all of the following except:
    A. increased striving for self-esteem.
    B. more stereotypic thinking about minorities.
    C. more negative reactions to people who criticize one's country.
    D. reduced respect for cultural icons.

12. When English language personality scales have been translated and administered in other cultures:
    A. the trait structure of personality has turned out to be dramatically different.
    B. the usual Big Five traits have emerged from the factor analyses.
    C. the personality scales have proven useless.
    D. a seven-factor solution has usually emerged from the factor analyses.

13. In which of the following cultures is an independent view of the self most likely to be the norm?
    A. China
    B. Japan
    C. Africa
    D. United States

14. Which of the following is *not* a shortcoming of self-report personality inventories?
    A. The accuracy of the results is a function of the honesty of the respondent.
    B. Respondents may attempt to answer in a way that makes them look good.
    C. There is sometimes a problem with "yea-sayers" or "nay-sayers."
    D. They are objective measures that are easy to administer and score.

15. In *The Nurture Assumption,* Judith Harris argues that the evidence indicates that family environment has _____ on children's personalities.
    A. largely positive effects
    B. largely negative effects
    C. surprisingly little effect
    D. a powerful effect

Answers

1 C p. 494	6 A p. 506	11 B pp. 517–518
2 A p. 496	7 A pp. 508–509	12 B p. 519
3 C p. 499	8 D pp. 509–510	13 D pp. 522–523
4 C p. 500	9 B pp. 514–515	14 D p. 526
5 B pp. 503–504	10 B p. 516	15 C p. 529

PsykTrek

To view a demo: www.cengage.com/psychology/psyktrek
To order: www.cengage.com/psychology/weiten
Go to the PsykTrek website or CD-ROM for further study of the concepts in this chapter. Both online and on the CD-ROM, PsykTrek includes dozens of learning modules with videos, animations, and quizzes, as well as simulations of psychological phenomena and a multimedia glossary that includes word pronunciations.

CengageNow
www.cengage.com/tlc

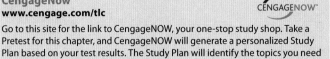

Go to this site for the link to CengageNOW, your one-stop study shop. Take a Pretest for this chapter, and CengageNOW will generate a personalized Study Plan based on your test results. The Study Plan will identify the topics you need to review and direct you to online resources to help you master those topics. You can then take a Posttest to help you determine the concepts you have mastered and what you still need to work on.

Companion Website
www.cengage.com/psychology/weiten

Go to this site to find online resources directly linked to your book, including a glossary, flash cards, drag-and-drop exercises, quizzes, and more!

13

STRESS, COPING, AND HEALTH

The Nature of Stress
Stress as an Everyday Event
Appraisal: Stress Lies in the Eye of the Beholder
Major Types of Stress

Responding to Stress
Emotional Responses
Physiological Responses
Behavioral Responses

The Effects of Stress on Psychological Functioning
Impaired Task Performance
Burnout
Psychological Problems and Disorders
Positive Effects

The Effects of Stress on Physical Health
Personality, Hostility, and Heart Disease
Emotional Reactions, Depression, and Heart Disease

FEATURED STUDY ▮ Is Depression a Risk Factor for Heart Disease?

Stress, Other Diseases, and Immune Functioning
Sizing Up the Link Between Stress and Illness

Factors Moderating the Impact of Stress
Social Support
Optimism and Conscientiousness

Health-Impairing Behavior
Smoking
Poor Nutritional Habits
Lack of Exercise
Alcohol and Drug Use
Behavior and AIDS
How Does Health-Impairing Behavior Develop?

Reactions to Illness
Deciding to Seek Treatment
Communicating with Health Providers
Adhering to Medical Advice

Reflecting on the Chapter's Themes

PERSONAL APPLICATION ▮ Improving Coping and Stress Management

Reappraisal: Ellis's Rational Thinking
Using Humor as a Stress Reducer
Releasing Pent-Up Emotions and Forgiving Others
Learning to Relax
Minimizing Physiological Vulnerability

CRITICAL THINKING APPLICATION ▮ Thinking Rationally About Health Statistics and Decisions

Evaluating Statistics on Health Risks
Thinking Systematically About Health Decisions

Recap

Practice Test

You're in your car headed home from school with a classmate. Traffic is barely moving. A radio report indicates that the traffic jam is only going to get worse. You groan audibly as you fiddle impatiently with the radio dial. Another motorist narrowly misses your fender trying to cut into your lane. Your pulse quickens as you shout insults at the unknown driver, who can't even hear you. You think about the term paper you have to work on tonight. Your stomach knots up as you recall all the crumpled drafts you tossed into the wastebasket last night. If you don't finish that paper soon, you won't be able to find any time to study for your math test, not to mention your biology quiz. Suddenly, you remember that you promised the person you're dating that the two of you would get together tonight. There's no way. Another fight looms on the horizon. Your classmate asks how you feel about the tuition increase that the college announced yesterday. You've been trying not to think about it. You're already in debt up to your ears. Your parents are bugging you about changing schools, but you don't want to leave your friends. Your heartbeat quickens as you contemplate the debate you're sure to have with your parents. You feel wired with tension as you realize that the stress in your life never seems to let up.

Many circumstances can create stress. It comes in all sorts of packages: big and small, pretty and ugly, simple and complex. All too often, the package comes as a surprise. In this chapter we'll try to sort out these packages. We'll discuss the nature of stress, how people cope with stress, and the potential effects of stress.

Our examination of the relationship between stress and physical illness will lead us into a broader discussion of the psychology of health. The way people in health professions think about physical illness has changed considerably in the past 30 years. The traditional view of physical illness as a purely biological phenomenon has given way to a biopsychosocial model of illness (Friedman & Adler, 2007). **The biopsychosocial model holds that physical illness is caused by a complex interaction of biological, psychological, and sociocultural factors.** This model does not suggest that biological factors are unimportant. It simply asserts that these factors operate in a psychosocial context that is also influential.

What has led to this shift in thinking? In part, it's a result of changing patterns of illness. Prior to the 20th century, the principal threats to health were *contagious diseases* caused by infectious agents—diseases such as smallpox, typhoid fever, diphtheria, yellow fever, malaria, cholera, tuberculosis, and polio. Today,

Figure 13.1

Changing patterns of illness. Historical trends in the death rates for various diseases reveal that contagious diseases (shown in blue) have declined as a threat to health. However, the death rates for stress-related chronic diseases (shown in red) have remained quite high. The pie chart (inset) shows the results of these trends: Three chronic diseases (heart disease, cancer, and stroke) account for about 55% of all deaths. Although these chronic diseases remain the chief threat to health in modern societies, it is interesting to note that deaths from heart disease have declined considerably since the 1980s. Many experts attribute much of this decline to improved health habits (Brannon & Feist, 2007), which demonstrates the important link between behavior and health. (Based on data from *National Vital Statistics Reports*, 2008, Volume 56, Number 10)

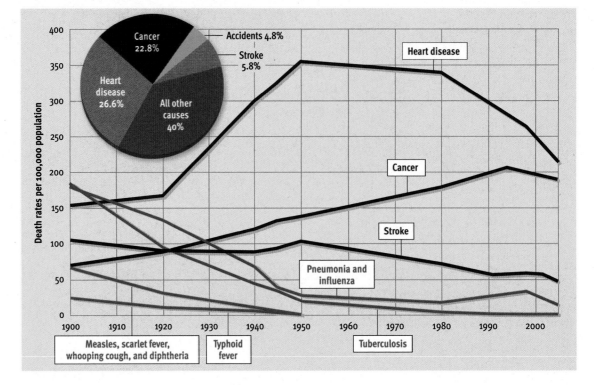

none of these diseases is among the leading killers in the United States. They were tamed by improvements in nutrition, public hygiene, sanitation, and medical treatment (Grob, 1983). Unfortunately, the void left by contagious diseases has been filled all too quickly by *chronic diseases* that develop gradually, such as heart disease, cancer, and stroke (see **Figure 13.1**). Psychosocial factors, such as stress and lifestyle, play a large role in the development of these chronic diseases. The growing recognition that psychological factors influence physical health eventually led to the emergence of a new specialty in psychology, called *health psychology* (Friedman & Adler, 2007). **Health psychology is concerned with how psychosocial factors relate to the promotion and maintenance of health and with the causation, prevention, and treatment of illness.** In the second half of this chapter, we'll explore this new domain of psychology. In the Personal Application, we'll focus on strategies for enhancing stress management, and in the Critical Thinking Application we'll discuss strategies for improving health-related decision making.

The Nature of Stress

Key Learning Goals

13.1 Evaluate the impact of minor stressors, and discuss the importance of people's appraisals of stress.

13.2 Distinguish between acute and chronic stressors and describe frustration as a form of stress.

13.3 Identify the three basic types of conflict and discuss which types are most troublesome.

13.4 Summarize evidence on life change and pressure as forms of stress.

The word *stress* has been used in different ways by different theorists. We'll define *stress* **as any circumstances that threaten or are perceived to threaten one's well-being and that thereby tax one's coping abilities.** The threat may be to immediate physical safety, long-range security, self-esteem, reputation, peace of mind, or many other things that one values. Stress is a complex concept, so let's explore a little further.

Stress as an Everyday Event

The word *stress* tends to spark images of overwhelming, traumatic crises. People may think of tornadoes, hurricanes, floods, and earthquakes. Undeniably, major disasters of this sort are extremely stressful events. Studies conducted in the aftermath of natural disasters typically find elevated rates of psychological problems and physical illness in the communities affected by these disasters (Stevens, Raphael, & Dobson, 2007; van Griensven et al., 2007; Weisler, Barbee, & Townsend, 2007). However, these unusual events are only a small part of what constitutes stress. Many everyday events, such as waiting in line, having car trouble, shopping for Christmas presents, misplacing your checkbook, and staring at bills you can't pay, are also stressful. Researchers have found that everyday problems and the minor nuisances of life are also important forms of stress (Almeida, 2005; Kohn, Lafreniere, & Gurevich, 1991).

You might guess that minor stresses would produce minor effects, but that isn't necessarily true. Richard Lazarus and his colleagues, who developed a scale to measure everyday hassles, have shown that routine hassles may have significant harmful effects on mental and physical health (Delongis, Folkman, & Lazarus, 1988). Other investigators, working with different types of samples and different measures of hassles, have also found that everyday hassles are predictive of impaired mental and physical health (Chang & Sanna, 2003; Sher, 2003). Why would minor hassles be so troublesome? The answer isn't entirely clear yet, but it may be because of the *cumulative* nature of stress (Seta, Seta, & McElroy, 2002). Stress adds up. Routine stresses at home, at school, and at work might be fairly benign individually, but collectively they could create great strain.

Appraisal: Stress Lies in the Eye of the Beholder

The experience of feeling stressed depends on what events one notices and how one chooses to appraise or interpret them (Lazarus, 1999; Semmer, McGrath, & Beehr, 2005). Events that are stressful for one person may evoke little or no stress response from another person (Steptoe, 2007). For example, many people find flying in an airplane somewhat stressful, but frequent fliers may not be bothered at all. Some people enjoy the excitement of going out on a date with someone new; others find the uncertainty terrifying.

Often, people aren't very objective in their appraisals of potentially stressful events. A study of hospitalized patients awaiting surgery showed only a slight correlation between the objective seriousness of a person's upcoming surgery and the amount of fear experienced by the patients (Janis, 1958). Clearly, some people are more prone than others to feel threatened by life's difficulties. A number of studies have shown that anxious, neurotic people report more stress than others (Cooper & Bright, 2001; Watson, David, & Suls, 1999), as do people who are relatively unhappy (Cacioppo et al., 2008). Thus, stress lies in the eye (actually, the mind) of the beholder. People's appraisals of stressful events are highly subjective.

Major Types of Stress

An enormous variety of events can be stressful for one person or another. To achieve a better understanding of stress, theorists have tried to analyze the nature of

stressful events and divide them into subtypes. One sensible distinction involves differentiating between *acute stressors and chronic stressors* (Dougall & Baum, 2001; Stowell, 2008). *Acute stressors are threatening events that have a relatively short duration and a clear endpoint.* Examples would include having an encounter with a belligerent drunk, dealing with the challenge of a major exam, or having your home threatened by severe flooding. *Chronic stressors are threatening events that have a relatively long duration and no readily apparent time limit.* Examples would include persistent financial strains produced by huge credit card debts, ongoing pressures from a hostile boss at work, or the demands of caring for a sick family member over a period of years.

None of the proposed schemes for classifying stressful events has turned out to be altogether satisfactory. Classifying stressful events into nonintersecting categories is virtually impossible. Although this problem presents conceptual headaches for researchers, it need not prevent us from describing four major types of stress: frustration, conflict, change, and pressure. As you read about each of them, you'll surely recognize some familiar adversaries.

Frustration

 11f

I had a wonderful relationship with a nice man for three months. One day when we planned to spend the entire day together, he called and said he wouldn't be meeting me and that he had decided to stop seeing me. I cried all morning. The grief was like losing someone through death. I still hurt, and I wonder if I'll ever get over him.

This scenario illustrates frustration. As psychologists use the term, *frustration occurs in any situation in which the pursuit of some goal is thwarted.* In essence, you experience frustration when you want something and you can't have it. Everyone has to deal with frustration virtually every day. Traffic jams and difficult daily commutes, for instance, are a routine source of frustration that can elicit anger and physical symptoms (Evans & Wener, 2006; Rasmussen, Knapp, & Garner, 2000), leading Schaefer (2005) to claim that "each added travel minute correlates with an increase in health problems" (p. 14). Fortunately, many frustrations are brief and insignificant. You may be quite upset when you go to a repair shop to pick up your ailing DVD player and find that it hasn't been fixed as promised. However, a week later you'll probably have your DVD player back, and the frustration will be forgotten.

Of course, some frustrations can be sources of significant stress. Failures and losses are two common kinds of frustration that are often highly stressful.

Richard Lazarus

"We developed the Hassle Scale because we think scales that measure major events miss the point. The constant, minor irritants may be much more important than the large, landmark changes."

web link 13.1

The Web's Stress Management & Emotional Wellness Page

Ernesto Randolfi (Montana State University) has gathered a comprehensive set of resources dealing with stress management. Topics covered include cognitive restructuring, relaxation techniques, and stress in the workplace and in college life.

Everyone fails in at least some of his or her endeavors. Some people make failure almost inevitable by setting unrealistically high goals for themselves. For example, many business executives tend to forget that for every newly appointed vice president in the business world, there are dozens of middle-level executives who don't get promoted. Losses can be especially frustrating, because people are deprived of something that they're accustomed to having. For example, few things are more frustrating than losing a dearly loved boyfriend, girlfriend, spouse, or parent.

Conflict

 11f

Should I or shouldn't I? I became engaged at Christmas. My fiance surprised me with a ring. I knew if I refused the ring he would be terribly hurt and our relationship would suffer. However, I don't really know whether or not I want to marry him. On the other hand, I don't want to lose him either.

Like frustration, conflict is an unavoidable feature of everyday life. The perplexing question "Should I or shouldn't I?" comes up countless times in everyone's life. *Conflict* **occurs when two or more incompatible motivations or behavioral impulses compete for expression.** Conflicts come

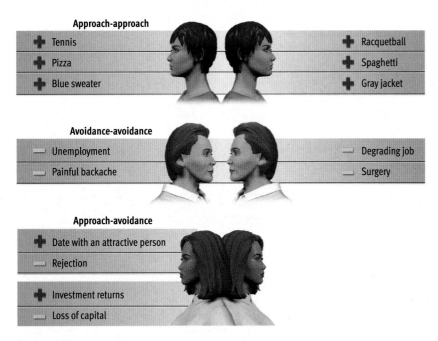

Figure 13.2

Types of conflict. Psychologists have identified three basic types of conflict. In approach-approach and avoidance-avoidance conflicts, a person is torn between two goals. In an approach-avoidance conflict, only one goal is under consideration, but it has both positive and negative aspects.

in three types, which were originally described by Kurt Lewin (1935) and investigated extensively by Neal Miller (1944, 1959). These three basic types of conflict—approach-approach, avoidance-avoidance, and approach-avoidance—are diagrammed in **Figure 13.2**.

In an *approach-approach conflict* **a choice must be made between two attractive goals.** The problem, of course, is that you can choose just one of the two goals. For example: You have a free afternoon; should you play tennis or racquetball? You can't afford both—should you buy the blue sweater or the gray jacket? Among the three kinds of conflict, the approach-approach type tends to be the least stressful. People don't usually stagger out of restaurants exhausted by the stress of choosing which of several appealing entrees to eat. Nonetheless, approach-approach conflicts over important issues may sometimes be troublesome. If you're torn between two appealing college majors or two attractive boyfriends, you may find the decision-making process quite stressful, since whichever alternative is not chosen represents a loss of sorts.

In an *avoidance-avoidance conflict* **a choice must be made between two unattractive goals.** Forced to choose between two repelling alternatives, you are, as they say, "caught between a rock and a hard place." For example, should you continue to collect unemployment checks, or should you take that degrading job at the car wash? Or suppose you have painful backaches. Should you submit to surgery that you dread, or should you continue to live with the back pain? Obviously, avoidance-avoidance conflicts are most unpleasant and highly stressful.

In an *approach-avoidance conflict* **a choice must be made about whether to pursue a single goal that has both attractive and unattractive aspects.** For instance, imagine that you're offered a career promotion that will mean a large increase in pay, but you'll have to move to a city where you don't want to live. Approach-avoidance conflicts are common and can be quite stressful. Any time you have to take a risk to pursue some desirable outcome, you're likely to find yourself in an approach-avoidance conflict. Approach-avoidance conflicts often produce *vacillation.* That is, you go back and forth, beset by indecision. You decide to go ahead, then you decide not to, then you decide to go ahead again. Humans are not unique in this respect. Many years ago, Neal Miller (1944) observed the same vacillation in his groundbreaking research with rats. He created approach-avoidance conflicts in hungry rats by alternately feeding and shocking them at one end of a runway

Identifying Types of Conflict

Check your understanding of the three basic types of conflict by identifying the type experienced in each of the following examples. The answers are in Appendix A.

Examples

_____ 1. John can't decide whether to take a demeaning job in a car wash or to go on welfare.

_____ 2. Desiree wants to apply to a highly selective law school, but she hates to risk the possibility of rejection.

_____ 3. Vanessa has been shopping for a new car and is torn between a nifty little sports car and a classy sedan, both of which she really likes.

Types of conflict

a. approach-approach

b. avoidance-avoidance

c. approach-avoidance

---

apparatus. Eventually, these rats tended to hover near the center of the runway, alternately approaching and retreating from the goal box at the end of the alley.

Change

After my divorce, I lived alone for four years. Six months ago I married a wonderful woman who has two children from her previous marriage. My biggest stress is suddenly having to adapt to living with three people instead of by myself. I was pretty set in my ways. I had certain routines. Now everything is chaos. I love my wife and I'm fond of the kids. They're not really doing anything wrong. But my house and my life just aren't the same, and I'm having trouble dealing with it all.

It has been proposed that life changes, such as a change in marital status, represent a key type of stress. *Life changes* **are any significant alterations in one's living circumstances that require readjustment.** The importance of life changes was first demonstrated by Thomas Holmes, Richard Rahe, and their colleagues in the 1960s (Holmes & Rahe, 1967; Rahe & Arthur, 1978). Theorizing that stress might make people more vulnerable to illness, they interviewed thousands of tuberculosis patients to find out what kinds of events had preceded the onset of their disease. Surprisingly, the most frequently cited events were not uniformly negative. There were plenty of aversive events, of course, but there were also many seemingly positive events, such as getting married, having a baby, and getting promoted.

Why would positive events, such as moving to a nicer home, produce stress? According to Holmes and Rahe, it's because they produce *change*. In their view, changes in personal relationships, changes

at work, changes in finances, and so forth can be stressful even when the changes are welcomed.

Based on this analysis, Holmes and Rahe (1967) developed the Social Readjustment Rating Scale (SRRS) to measure life change as a form of stress. The scale assigns numerical values to 43 major life events. These values are supposed to reflect the magnitude of the readjustment required by each change (see Table 13.1 on the next page). In using the scale, respondents are asked to indicate how often they experienced any of these 43 events during a certain time period (typically, the past year). The numbers associated with each event checked are then added. This total is an index of the amount of change-related stress the person has recently experienced.

The SRRS and similar scales based on it have been used in over 10,000 studies by researchers all over the world (Dohrenwend, 2006). Overall, these studies have shown that people with higher scores on the SRRS tend to be more vulnerable to many kinds of physical illness and to many types of psychological problems as well (Derogatis & Coons, 1993; Scully, Tosi, & Banning, 2000; Surtees & Wainwright, 2007). These results have attracted a great deal of attention, and the SRRS has been reprinted in many popular newspapers and magazines. The attendant publicity has led to the widespread conclusion that life change is inherently stressful.

More recently, however, experts have criticized the research on the connection between life events and health, citing problems with the methods used and raising questions about the meaning of the findings (Dohrenwend, 2006; Monroe, 2008; Wethington, 2007). At this point, it's a key interpretive issue that concerns us. Many critics have argued that the SRRS does not measure *change* exclusively. The main

Table 13.1 Social Readjustment Rating Scale

Life Event	Mean Value	Life Event	Mean Value
Death of a spouse	100	Change in responsibilities at work	29
Divorce	73	Son or daughter leaving home	29
Marital separation	65	Trouble with in-laws	29
Jail term	63	Outstanding personal achievement	28
Death of a close family member	63	Spouse begins or stops work	26
Personal injury or illness	53	Begin or end school	26
Marriage	50	Change in living conditions	25
Fired at work	47	Revision of personal habits	24
Marital reconciliation	45	Trouble with boss	23
Retirement	45	Change in work hours or conditions	20
Change in health of family member	44	Change in residence	20
Pregnancy	40	Change in school	20
Sex difficulties	39	Change in recreation	19
Gain of a new family member	39	Change in church activities	19
Business readjustment	39	Change in social activities	18
Change in financial state	38	Mortgage or loan for lesser purchase	
Death of a close friend	37	(car, TV, etc.)	17
Change to a different line of work	36	Change in sleeping habits	16
Change in number of arguments with		Change in number of family get-togethers	15
spouse	35	Change in eating habits	15
Mortgage or loan for major purchase		Vacation	13
(home, etc.)	31	Christmas	12
Foreclosure of mortgage or loan	30	Minor violations of the law	11

Source: Adapted from Holmes, T. H., & Rahe, R. (1967). The Social Readjustment Rating Scale. *Journal of Psychosomatic Research, 11,* 213–218. Copyright © 1967 by Elsevier Science Publishing Co. Reprinted by permission.

web link 13.2

Stress Management

University of Nebraska Professor Wesley E. Sime has posted outlines and notes of his lectures on the fundamentals of stress management and on other topics related to stress and its impact on health and performance.

problem is that the list of life changes on the SRRS is dominated by events that are clearly negative or undesirable (death of a spouse, being fired from a job, and so on). These negative events probably generate great frustration. Although there are some positive events on the scale, it turns out that negative life events cause most of the stress tapped by the SRRS (McLean & Link, 1994; Turner & Wheaton, 1995). Thus, it has become apparent that the SRRS assesses a wide range of stressful experiences, not just life change. At present, there's little reason to believe that change is inherently or inevitably stressful. Undoubtedly, some life changes may be quite challenging, but others may be quite benign.

Pressure

11f

My father questioned me at dinner about some things I didn't want to talk about. I know he doesn't want to hear my answers, at least not the truth. My father told me when I was little that I was his favorite because I was "pretty near perfect." I've spent my life trying to keep up that image, even though it's obviously not true. Recently, he has begun to realize this, and it's made our relationship very strained and painful.

At one time or another, most people have remarked that they're "under pressure." What does this term mean? **Pressure involves expectations or demands that one behave in a certain way.** You are under pressure to *perform* when you're expected to execute tasks and responsibilities quickly, effi-

ciently, and successfully. For example, salespeople are usually under pressure to move lots of merchandise. Professors at research institutions are often under pressure to publish in prestigious journals. Stand-up comedians are under intense pressure to make people laugh. Pressures to *conform* to others' expectations are also common in our lives. People in the business world are expected to dress in certain ways. Suburban homeowners are expected to keep their lawns well manicured. Teenagers are expected to adhere to their parents' values and rules.

Although widely discussed by the general public, the concept of pressure has received scant attention from researchers. However, Weiten (1988b, 1998) has devised a scale to measure pressure as a form of life stress. It assesses self-imposed pressure, pressure from work and school, and pressure from family relations, peer relations, and intimate relations. In research with this scale, a strong relationship has been found between pressure and a variety of psychological symptoms and problems. In fact, pressure has turned out to be more strongly related to measures of mental health than the SRRS and other established measures of stress (see **Figure 13.3**).

Recent research suggests that pressure related to academic pursuits may actually undermine academic performance and lead to problematic escape behaviors such as drinking (Kaplan, Liu, & Kaplan, 2005; Kiefer, Cronin, & Gawet, 2006). We tend to think of pressure as something imposed on us by outside forces. However, studies of high school and college students

Pressure comes in two varieties: pressure to perform and pressure to conform. For example, standup comedians are under intense pressure to make audiences laugh (pressure to perform), whereas corporate employees are often expected to dress in certain ways (pressure to conform).

find that *pressure is often self-imposed* (Kouzma & Kennedy, 2004; Misra & Castillo, 2004). For example, you might sign up for extra classes to get through school quickly. Or you might actively seek time-consuming leadership responsibilities to impress friends or to build your resume. People frequently put pressure on themselves to get good grades or to rapidly climb the corporate ladder. Actually, self-imposed stress is not unique to pressure. Research suggests that other forms of stress can also be self-generated (Roberts & Ciesla, 2007). One implication of this reality is that people might have more control over a substantial portion of the stress in their lives than they realize.

REVIEW of Key Learning Goals

13.1 Stress involves circumstances and experiences that are perceived as threatening. Stress is a common, everyday event, and even seemingly minor stressors, such as daily hassles, can be problematic. To a large degree, stress is subjective and lies in the eye of the beholder. People's appraisals of events determine what they find stressful.

13.2 Acute stressors have a short duration and clear endpoint, whereas chronic stressors have a relatively long duration. Major types of stress include frustration, conflict, change, and pressure. Frustration occurs when an obstacle prevents one from attaining some goal.

13.3 The three principal types of conflict are approach-approach, avoidance-avoidance, and approach-avoidance. The third type is especially stressful. Vacillation is a common response to approach-avoidance conflict.

13.4 A large number of studies with the SRRS suggest that life change is stressful. Although this may be true, it is now clear that the SRRS is a measure of general stress rather than just change-related stress. Two kinds of pressure (to perform and conform) also appear to be stressful.

Figure 13.3

Pressure and psychological symptoms. A comparison of pressure and life change as sources of stress suggests that pressure may be more strongly related to mental health than change is. In one study, Weiten (1988b) found a correlation of .59 between scores on the Pressure Inventory (PI) and symptoms of psychological distress. In the same sample, the correlation between SRRS scores and psychological symptoms was only .28.

concept check 13.2

Recognizing Sources of Stress

Check your understanding of the major sources of stress by indicating which type or types of stress are at work in each of the following examples. Bear in mind that the four basic types of stress are not mutually exclusive. There's some potential for overlap, so a specific experience might include both change and pressure, for instance. The answers are in Appendix A.

Examples

_____ 1. Marie is late for an appointment but is stuck in line at the bank.

_____ 2. Tamika decides that she won't be satisfied unless she gets straight A's this year.

_____ 3. Jose has just graduated from business school and has taken an exciting new job.

_____ 4. Morris has just been fired from his job and needs to find another.

Types of stress

a. frustration

b. conflict

c. change

d. pressure

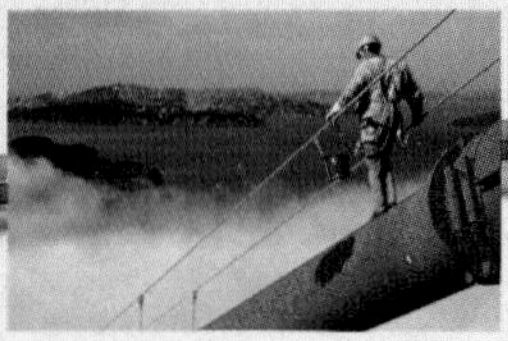

Key Learning Goals

13.5 Discuss the role of positive emotions in response to stress, and describe the effects of emotional arousal.

13.6 Describe the fight-or-flight response, Selye's general adaptation syndrome, and other physiological responses to stress.

13.7 Evaluate the adaptive value of giving up, aggression, and self-indulgence as coping responses.

13.8 Explain how defense mechanisms work, and clarify the nature of constructive coping.

Responding to Stress

People's response to stress is complex and multidimensional. Stress affects the individual at several levels. Consider again the chapter's opening scenario, in which you're driving home in heavy traffic and thinking about overdue papers, tuition increases, and parental pressures. Let's look at some of the reactions that were mentioned. When you groan in reaction to the traffic report, you're experiencing an *emotional response* to stress, in this case annoyance and anger. When your pulse quickens and your stomach knots up, you're exhibiting *physiological responses* to stress. When you shout insults at another driver, your verbal aggression is a *behavioral response* to the stress at hand. Thus, we can analyze a person's reactions to stress at three levels: (1) emotional responses, (2) physiological responses, and (3) behavioral responses. **Figure 13.4**, which diagrams these three levels of response, provides an overview of the stress process.

Emotional Responses 11g

When people are under stress, they often react emotionally. Studies that have tracked stress and mood on a daily basis have found intimate relationships between the two (Affleck et al., 1994; van Eck, Nicolson, & Berkhof, 1998).

Emotions Commonly Elicited 11g

No simple one-to-one connections have been found between certain types of stressful events and particular emotions. However, researchers *have* begun to uncover some strong links between specific *cognitive reactions to stress* (appraisals) and specific emotions (Smith & Lazarus, 1993). For example, self-blame tends to lead to guilt, helplessness to sadness, and so forth. Although many emotions can be evoked by stressful events, some are certainly more likely than others. Common responses to stress typically occur along three dimensions of emotion: (a) annoyance, anger, and rage, (b) apprehension, anxiety, and fear, and (c) dejection, sadness and grief (Lazarus, 1993).

Investigators have tended to focus heavily on the connection between stress and negative emotions, but research shows that positive emotions also occur during periods of stress (Folkman, 1997, 2008; Zautra et al., 2005). Although this finding seems counterintuitive, researchers have found that people experience a diverse array of pleasant emotions even while enduring dire circumstances. Consider, for example, a recent study that examined subjects' emotional functioning early in 2001 and again in the weeks following the 9/11 terrorist attacks in the United States (Fredrickson et al., 2003). Like most U.S. citizens, the participants reported many negative emotions in the aftermath of 9/11, including anger, sadness, and fear. However, within this "dense cloud of anguish" positive emotions also emerged. For example, people felt gratitude for the safety of their loved ones; many took stock and counted their blessings; and quite a few reported renewed love for their friends and family. Fredrickson et al. (2003) also found that the frequency of pleasant emotions correlated positively with a measure of subjects' resilience, whereas the frequency of unpleasant emotions correlated nega-

Figure 13.4
Overview of the stress process. A potentially stressful event, such as a major exam, elicits a subjective appraisal of how threatening the event is. If the event is viewed with alarm, the stress may trigger emotional, physiological, and behavioral reactions, as people's response to stress is multidimensional.

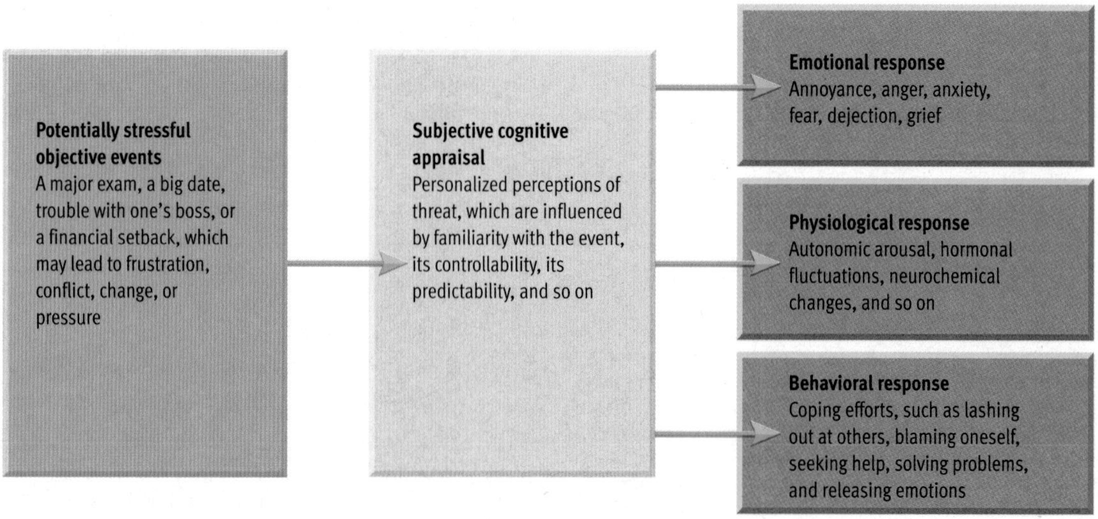
Potentially stressful objective events
A major exam, a big date, trouble with one's boss, or a financial setback, which may lead to frustration, conflict, change, or pressure
Subjective cognitive appraisal
Personalized perceptions of threat, which are influenced by familiarity with the event, its controllability, its predictability, and so on
Emotional response
Annoyance, anger, anxiety, fear, dejection, grief
Physiological response
Autonomic arousal, hormonal fluctuations, neurochemical changes, and so on
Behavioral response
Coping efforts, such as lashing out at others, blaming oneself, seeking help, solving problems, and releasing emotions

tively with resilience. Thus, contrary to common sense, positive emotions do *not* vanish during times of severe stress. Moreover, these positive emotions appear to play a key role in helping people bounce back from the difficulties associated with stress (Tugade & Fredrickson, 2004).

How do positive emotions promote resilience in the face of stress? Barbara Fredrickson's (2001, 2005, 2006) *broaden-and-build theory of positive emotions* can shed light on this question. First, positive emotions alter people's mindsets, broadening their scope of attention and increasing their creativity and flexibility in problem solving. Second, positive emotions can undo the lingering effects of negative emotions, and thus short-circuit the potentially damaging physiological responses to stress that we will discuss momentarily. Third, positive emotions can promote rewarding social interactions that help to build valuable social support, enhanced coping strategies, and other enduring personal resources.

Consistent with Fredrickson's model, recent research suggests that positive emotions widen people's scope of attention (Fredrickson & Branigan, 2005), promote healthy coping responses (Folkman, 2008), initiate upward spirals in emotional well-being (Burns et al., 2008), and facilitate flourishing mental health (Fredrickson & Losada, 2005). Studies have also found an association between positive emotion and lower levels of stress hormones (Steptoe et al., 2007) and reduced mortality in some populations (Pressman & Cohen, 2005).

One particularly interesting finding has been that a positive emotional style is associated with an enhanced immune response (Cohen & Pressman, 2006). For example, in a study by Sheldon Cohen and colleagues (2006), healthy volunteers were given nasal drops containing either a rhinovirus (cold virus) or flu virus and were carefully monitored for illness while living in quarantined conditions. The results showed that participants with a positive emotional style were less likely to develop an illness after exposure to either virus. Thus, it appears that the benefits of positive emotions may be more diverse and more far-reaching than widely appreciated.

Effects of Emotional Arousal   11g

Emotional responses are a natural and normal part of life. Even unpleasant emotions serve important purposes. Like physical pain, painful emotions can serve as warnings that one needs to take action. However, strong emotional arousal can also interfere with efforts to cope with stress. For example, there is evidence that high emotional arousal can interfere with attention and memory retrieval and can impair judgment and decision making (Janis, 1993; Lupien & Maheu, 2007; Mandler, 1993).

Although emotional arousal may hurt coping efforts, that isn't *necessarily* the case. The *inverted-U hypothesis* predicts that task performance should improve with increased emotional arousal—up to a point, after which further increases in arousal become disruptive and performance deteriorates (Anderson, 1990; Mandler, 1993). This idea is referred to as the inverted-U hypothesis because when performance is plotted as a function of arousal, the resulting graphs approximate an upside-down U (see **Figure 13.5**). In these graphs, the level of arousal at which performance peaks is characterized as the *optimal level of arousal* for a task.

This optimal level appears to depend in part on the complexity of the task at hand. The conventional wisdom is that *as tasks become more complex, the optimal level of arousal (for peak performance) tends to decrease*. This relationship is depicted in **Figure 13.5**. As you can see, a fairly high level of arousal should

Figure 13.5
Arousal and performance. Graphs of the relationship between emotional arousal and task performance tend to resemble an inverted U, as increased arousal is associated with improved performance up to a point, after which higher arousal leads to poorer performance. The optimal level of arousal for a task depends on the complexity of the task. On complex tasks, a relatively low level of arousal tends to be optimal. On simple tasks, however, performance may peak at a much higher level of arousal.

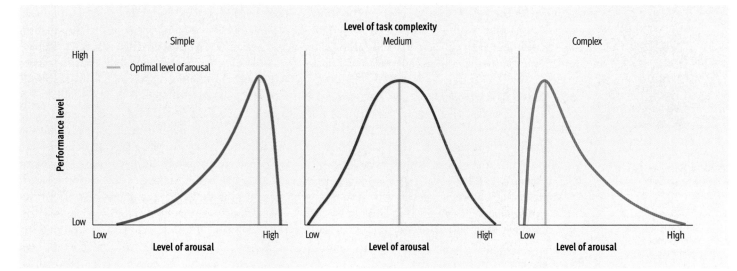

Hans Selye

"There are two main types of human beings: 'racehorses,' who thrive on stress and are only happy with a vigorous, fast-paced lifestyle; and 'turtles,' who in order to be happy require peace, quiet, and a generally tranquil environment."

be optimal on simple tasks that do not require complicated reasoning (such as driving 8 hours to help a friend in a crisis). However, performance should peak at a lower level of arousal on complex tasks (such as making a major decision in which you have to weigh many factors). Although doubts have been raised about the validity of the inverted-U hypothesis (Hancock & Ganey, 2003), it provides a plausible model of how emotional arousal could have either beneficial or disruptive effects on coping, depending on the nature of the stressful demands.

Physiological Responses

As we just discussed, stress frequently elicits strong emotional responses. Now we'll look at the important physiological changes that often accompany these responses.

The Fight-or-Flight Response

Walter Cannon (1932) was one of the first theorists to describe the fight-or-flight response. The *fight-or-flight response* is a physiological reaction to threat in which the autonomic nervous system mobilizes the organism for attacking (fight) or fleeing (flight) an enemy. As you may recall from Chapter 3, the *autonomic nervous system (ANS)* controls blood vessels, smooth muscles, and glands. The fight-or-flight response is mediated by the *sympathetic division* of the ANS (McCarty, 2007). In one experiment, Cannon studied the fight-or-flight response in cats by confronting them with dogs. Among other things, he noticed an immediate acceleration in their breathing and heart rate and a reduction in their digestive processes.

The physiological arousal associated with the fight-or-flight response is also seen in humans. In a sense, this automatic reaction is a "leftover" from humanity's evolutionary past. It's clearly an adaptive response in the animal kingdom, where the threat of predators often requires a swift response of fighting or fleeing. But in our modern world, the fight-or-flight response may be less adaptive for human functioning than it was thousands of generations ago (Nesse, Bhatnagar, & Young, 2007). Most human stresses can't be handled simply through fight or flight. Work pressures, marital problems, and financial difficulties require far more complex responses.

Shelley Taylor and her colleagues (Taylor 2002, 2006; Taylor et al., 2000) have questioned whether the fight-or-flight model applies equally well to both males and females. They note that in most species females have more responsibility for the care of young offspring than males do. Using an evolutionary perspective, they argue that this disparity may

make fighting and fleeing less adaptive for females, as both responses may endanger offspring and thus reduce the likelihood of an animal passing on its genes. Taylor et al. (2000) maintain that evolutionary processes have fostered more of a "tend and befriend" response in females. According to this analysis, in reacting to stress, females allocate more effort to the care of offspring and to seeking help and support. More research is needed to evaluate this provocative analysis. Although gender differences may exist in behavioral responses to stress, Taylor and her colleagues are quick to note that the "basic neuroendocrine core of stress responses" is largely the same for males and females.

The General Adaptation Syndrome

The concept of stress was identified and named by Hans Selye (1936, 1956, 1982). Selye was born in Vienna but spent his entire professional career at McGill University in Montreal. Beginning in the 1930s, Selye exposed laboratory animals to a diverse array of both physical and psychological stressors (heat, cold, pain, mild shock, restraint, and so on). The resulting patterns of physiological arousal seen in the animals were largely the same, regardless of the type of stress. Thus, Selye concluded that stress reactions are *nonspecific*. In other words, he maintained that the reactions do not vary according to the specific type of stress encountered. Initially, Selye wasn't sure what to call this nonspecific response to a variety of noxious agents. In the 1940s he decided to call it *stress*, and the word has been part of our vocabulary ever since (Russell, 2007).

Selye (1956, 1974) formulated an influential theory of stress reactions called the general adaptation syndrome. The *general adaptation syndrome is a model of the body's stress response, consisting of three stages: alarm, resistance, and exhaustion.* In the first stage of the general adaptation syndrome, an *alarm reaction* occurs when an organism first recognizes the existence of a threat. Physiological arousal occurs as the body musters its resources to combat the challenge. Selye's alarm reaction is essentially the fight-or-flight response originally described by Cannon.

However, Selye took his investigation of stress a few steps further by exposing laboratory animals to *prolonged* stress, similar to the chronic stress often endured by humans. As stress continues, the organism may progress to the second phase of the general adaptation syndrome, the *stage of resistance*. During this phase, physiological changes stabilize as coping efforts get under way. Typically, physiological arousal continues to be higher than normal, al-

though it may level off somewhat as the organism becomes accustomed to the threat.

If the stress continues over a substantial period of time, the organism may enter the third stage, the *stage of exhaustion.* According to Selye, the body's resources for fighting stress are limited. If the stress can't be overcome, the body's resources may be depleted. Eventually, he thought the organism would experience hormonal exhaustion, although we now know that the crux of the problem is that chronic overactivation of the stress response can have damaging physiological effects on a variety of organ systems (Sapolsky, 2007). These harmful physiological effects can lead to what Selye called "diseases of adaptation."

Brain-Body Pathways

Even in cases of moderate stress, you may notice that your heart has started beating faster, you've begun to breathe harder, and you're perspiring more than usual. How does all this bodily activity (and much more) happen? It appears that there are two major pathways along which the brain sends signals to the endocrine system in response to stress (Clow, 2001; Dallman, Bhatnagar, & Viau, 2007; Tsigos, Kyrou, & Chrousos, 2005). As we noted in Chapter 3, the *endocrine system* consists of glands located at various sites in the body that secrete chemicals called hormones. The *hypothalamus* is the brain structure that appears to initiate action along these two pathways.

The first pathway (see Figure 13.6) is routed through the autonomic nervous system. In response to stress, your hypothalamus activates the sympathetic division of the ANS. A key part of this activation involves stimulating the central part of the adrenal glands (the adrenal medulla) to release large amounts of *catecholamines* into the bloodstream. These hormones radiate throughout your body, producing the physiological changes seen in the fight-or-flight response. The net result of catecholamine elevation is that your body is mobilized for action (Lundberg, 2007). Heart rate and blood flow increase,

and more blood is pumped to your brain and muscles. Respiration and oxygen consumption speed up, which facilitates alertness. Digestive processes are inhibited to conserve your energy. The pupils of your eyes dilate, increasing visual sensitivity.

The second pathway involves more direct communication between the brain and the endocrine system (see Figure 13.6). The hypothalamus sends signals to the so-called master gland of the endocrine system, the pituitary. In turn, the pituitary se-

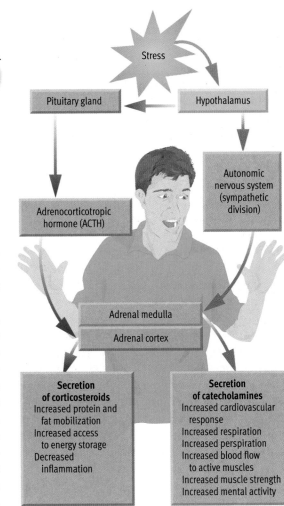

Figure 13.6
Brain-body pathways in stress. In times of stress, the brain sends signals along two pathways. The pathway through the autonomic nervous system controls the release of catecholamine hormones that help mobilize the body for action. The pathway through the pituitary gland and the endocrine system controls the release of corticosteroid hormones that increase energy and ward off tissue inflammation.

cretes a hormone (ACTH) that stimulates the outer part of the adrenal glands (the adrenal cortex) to release another important set of hormones—*corticosteroids*. These hormones stimulate the release of chemicals that help increase your energy and help inhibit tissue inflammation in case of injury (Miller, Chen, & Zhou, 2007; Munck, 2007).

An important new finding in research on stress and the brain is that stress can interfere with neurogenesis (Mirescu & Gould, 2006). As you may recall from Chapter 3, scientists have recently discovered that the adult brain is capable of **neurogenesis—the formation of new neurons**, primarily in key areas in the hippocampus. Neurogenesis appears to enhance learning and memory (see Chapter 7) and in Chapter 14 we will discuss evidence that suppressed neurogenesis may be a key cause of depression (Dranovsky & Hen, 2006). Thus, the capacity of stress to hinder neurogenesis may have important ramifications, which are currently the subject of intense research (Tanapat & Gould, 2006).

Behavioral Responses 11g

Although people respond to stress at several levels, it's clear that *behavior* is the crucial dimension of their reactions. Most behavioral responses to stress involve coping. *Coping* **refers to active efforts to master, reduce, or tolerate the demands created by stress.** Notice that this definition is neutral as to whether coping efforts are healthful or maladaptive. The popular use of the term often implies that coping is inherently healthful. When people say that someone "coped with her problems," the implication is that she handled them effectively.

In reality, however, coping responses may be adaptive or maladaptive (Folkman & Moskowitz, 2004; Kleinke, 2007). For example, if you were flunking a history course at midterm, you might cope with this stress by (1) increasing your study efforts, (2) seeking help from a tutor, (3) blaming your professor, or (4) giving up on the class without really trying. Clearly, the first two of these coping responses would be more adaptive than the last two. Thus, they may help or they may hurt, but coping tactics are the key determinant of whether stress leads to distress (Carver, 2007).

People cope with stress in an endless variety of ways (Folkman & Moskowitz, 2004). One review of coping research examined 100 scales intended to assess coping and found about 400 specific coping strategies (Skinner et al., 2003). Thus, in dealing with stress, people choose their coping strategies from a large and diverse menu of options.

That said, most individuals exhibit certain styles of coping that are fairly consistent across situations

(Carver & Scheier, 1994; Jang et al., 2007). Of course, an individual's coping strategies are also influenced by situational demands, and Cheng (2001, 2003) has argued that flexibility in coping is more desirable than consistently depending on the same strategy. According to Cheng and Cheung (2005), people who exhibit flexible coping differentiate among stressful events in terms of controllability and probable impact, allowing them to make better-informed decisions about how to handle stressful challenges.

Given the immense variety in coping strategies, we can only highlight a few of the more common patterns. In this section we'll focus most of our attention on styles of coping that tend to be less than ideal. We'll discuss a variety of more healthful coping strategies in the Personal Application on stress management.

Giving Up and Blaming Oneself 11g

When confronted with stress, people sometimes simply give up and withdraw from the battle. Some people routinely respond to stress with fatalism and resignation, passively accepting setbacks that might be dealt with effectively. This syndrome is referred to as *learned helplessness* (Seligman, 1974, 1992). *Learned helplessness* **is passive behavior produced by exposure to unavoidable aversive events.** Learned helplessness seems to occur when individuals come to believe that events are beyond their control. As you might guess, giving up generally has not been highly regarded as a method of coping. Consistent with this view, many studies suggest that learned helplessness can contribute to depression (Isaacowitz & Seligman, 2007).

Although giving up is clearly less than optimal in many contexts, new research suggests that when people struggle to pursue goals that turn out to be unattainable, it makes sense for them to cut their losses and disengage from the goal (Wrosch & Scheier, 2003). Recent studies have shown that people who are better able to disengage from unattainable goals report better health and exhibit lower levels of a key stress hormone (Wrosch et al., 2007). They also manifest lower levels of a protein marker associated with inflammation, which is thought to underlie many disease processes (Miller & Wrosch, 2007). Given the way people in our competitive culture tend to disparage the concept of "giving up," the authors note that it might be better to characterize this coping tactic as "goal adjustment."

Blaming oneself is another common response when people are confronted by stressful difficulties. The tendency to become highly self-critical in response to stress has been noted by a number of influential theorists. Albert Ellis (1973, 1987) calls this phenomenon "catastrophic thinking." According to Ellis, catastrophic thinking causes, aggravates, and perpetuates emotional reactions to stress that are often problematic (see the Personal Application for this chapter). In a similar vein, Aaron Beck (1976, 1987) argues that negative self-talk can contribute to the development of depressive disorders (see Chapter 15). Although there is something to be said for recognizing one's weaknesses and taking responsibility for one's failures, Ellis and Beck agree that excessive self-blame can be unhealthy.

Striking Out at Others

People often respond to stressful events by striking out at others with aggressive behavior. *Aggression is any behavior that is intended to hurt someone, either physically or verbally.* Many years ago, a team of psychologists (Dollard et al., 1939) proposed the *frustration-aggression hypothesis,* which held that aggression is always caused by frustration. Decades of research have supported this idea of a causal link between frustration and aggression (Berkowitz, 1989). However, this research has also shown that there isn't an inevitable, one-to-one correspondence between frustration and aggression.

Frequently people lash out aggressively at others who had nothing to do with their frustration, apparently because they can't vent their anger at the real source. For example, you'll probably suppress your anger rather than lash out verbally at your boss or at a police officer who's giving you a speeding ticket. Twenty minutes later, however, you might be verbally brutal to a sales clerk. As we discussed in Chapter 12, this diversion of anger to a substitute target was noticed long ago by Sigmund Freud, who called it *displacement.* Unfortunately, research suggests that when people are provoked, displaced aggression is a common response (Marcus-Newhall et al., 2000).

Freud theorized that behaving aggressively could get pent-up emotion out of one's system and thus be adaptive. He coined the term *catharsis* to refer

Lashing out at others with verbal aggression tends to be an ineffective coping tactic that often backfires, creating additional stress.

to this release of emotional tension. The Freudian notion that it is a good idea to vent anger has become widely disseminated and accepted in modern society. Books, magazines, and self-appointed experts routinely advise that it is healthy to "blow off steam" and thereby release and reduce anger. However, experimental research generally has *not* supported the catharsis hypothesis. Indeed, *most studies find just the opposite: Behaving in an aggressive manner tends to fuel more anger and aggression* (Bushman, 2002; Bushman, Baumeister, & Stack, 1999).

Indulging Oneself

Stress sometimes leads to reduced impulse control, or *self-indulgence* (Tice, Bratslavsky, & Baumeister, 2001). When troubled by stress, many people engage in excessive consumption—unwise patterns of eating, drinking, smoking, using drugs, spending money, and so forth. For example, I have a friend who copes with stress by making a beeline for the nearest shopping mall to indulge in a spending spree. It appears that my friend is not unusual. It makes sense that when things are going poorly in one area of their lives, people may try to compensate by pursuing substitute forms of

Albert Ellis

"People largely disturb themselves by thinking in a self-defeating, illogical, and unrealistic manner."

CATHY

satisfaction. After all, self-indulgent responses tend to be relatively easy to execute and highly pleasurable. Thus, it's not surprising that studies have linked stress to increases in eating (Barker, Williams, & Galambos, 2006), smoking (Kassel, Stroud, & Paronis, 2003), and consumption of alcohol and drugs (Goeders, 2004; Spada & Wells, 2006).

A new manifestation of this coping strategy that has attracted much attention recently is the tendency to immerse oneself in the online world of the Internet. Kimberly Young (1996, 1998) has described a syndrome called *Internet addiction,* **which consists of spending an inordinate amount of time on the Internet and inability to control online use.** People who exhibit this syndrome tend to feel anxious, depressed, or empty when they are not online (Kandell, 1998). Their Internet use is so excessive, it begins to interfere with their functioning at work, at school, or at home, which leads them to start concealing the extent of their dependence on the Internet. It is difficult to estimate the prevalence of Internet addiction, but the syndrome does *not* appear to be rare (Greenfield, 1999; Morahan-Martin & Schumacher, 2000). Although there is active debate about the wisdom of characterizing excessive Internet surfing as an *addiction* (Goldsmith & Shapira, 2006; Griffiths, 1999), it is clear that this new coping strategy is creating very real problems for at least a small portion of Internet users (Morahan-Martin, 2007).

Defensive Coping   10a, 11g

Many people exhibit consistent styles of defensive coping in response to stress (Vaillant, 1994). We noted in the previous chapter that Sigmund Freud originally developed the concept of the *defense mechanism.* Though rooted in the psychoanalytic tradition,

this concept has gained widespread acceptance from psychologists of most persuasions (Cramer, 2000). Building on Freud's initial insights, modern psychologists have broadened the scope of the concept and added to Freud's list of defense mechanisms.

***Defense mechanisms* are largely unconscious reactions that protect a person from unpleasant emotions such as anxiety and guilt.** Many specific defense mechanisms have been identified. For example, Laughlin (1979) lists 49 different defenses. We described 7 common defense mechanisms in our discussion of Freud's theory in the previous chapter. Table 13.2 introduces another 5 defenses that people use with some regularity: denial, fantasy, intellectualization, undoing, and overcompensation. Although widely discussed in the popular press, defense mechanisms are often misunderstood. To clear up some of the misconceptions, we'll use a question/answer format to elaborate on the nature of defense mechanisms.

What exactly do defense mechanisms defend against? Above all else, defense mechanisms shield the individual from the emotional discomfort that's so often elicited by stress. Their main purpose is to ward off unwelcome emotions or to reduce their intensity. Foremost among the emotions guarded against are anxiety, anger, guilt, and dejection.

How do they work? Through *self-deception.* Defense mechanisms accomplish their goals by distorting reality so that it doesn't appear so threatening. For example, suppose you're not doing well in school and you're in danger of flunking out. Initially you might use *denial* to block awareness of the possibility that you could flunk. This defense might temporarily fend off feelings of anxiety. If it becomes difficult to deny the obvious, you could resort to *fantasy.* You might daydream about how you'll sal-

Table 13.2 Additional Defense Mechanisms

Mechanism	Description	Example
Denial of reality	Protecting oneself from unpleasant reality by refusing to perceive or face it	A smoker concludes that the evidence linking cigarette use to health problems is scientifically worthless
Fantasy	Gratifying frustrated desires by imaginary achievements	A socially inept and inhibited young man imagines himself chosen by a group of women to provide them with sexual satisfaction
Intellectualization (isolation)	Cutting off emotion from hurtful situations or separating incompatible attitudes so that they appear unrelated	A prisoner on death row awaiting execution resists appeal on his behalf and coldly insists that the letter of the law be followed
Undoing	Atoning for or trying to magically dispel unacceptable desires or acts	A teenager who feels guilty about masturbation ritually touches door knobs a prescribed number of times following each occurrence of the act
Overcompensation	Covering up felt weakness by emphasizing some desirable characteristics, or making up for frustration in one area by overgratification in another	A dangerously overweight woman goes on eating binges when she feels neglected by her husband

Source: Adapted from Carson, R. C., Butcher, J. N., & Coleman, J. C. (1988). *Abnormal psychology and modern life.* Glenview, IL: Scott, Foresman. Copyright © 1988 by Scott, Foresman and Company. Adapted by permission of the publisher.

Note: See Table 12.1 for another list of defense mechanisms.

vage adequate grades by getting spectacular scores on the upcoming final exams, when the objective fact is that you're hopelessly behind in your studies. Thus, defense mechanisms work their magic by bending reality in self-serving ways.

Are they conscious or unconscious? Both. Freudian theory originally assumed that defenses operate entirely at an unconscious level. However, the concept of the defense mechanism has been broadened by other theorists to include maneuvers that people may be aware of. Thus, defense mechanisms may operate at varying levels of awareness, although they're largely unconscious (Cramer, 2001; Erdelyi, 2001).

Are they healthy? This is a complicated question. More often than not, the answer is "no." Generally, defensive coping is less than optimal. Avoidance strategies and wishful thinking rarely provide genuine solutions to personal problems (Bolger, 1990; Holahan & Moos, 1990). Although defensive behavior tends to be relatively unhealthful, Shelley Taylor and Jonathon Brown (1988, 1994) have reviewed several lines of evidence suggesting that "positive illusions" may be adaptive for mental health and well-being. First, they note that "normal" people tend to have overly favorable self-images. In contrast, depressed subjects exhibit less favorable—but more realistic—self-concepts. Second, normal subjects overestimate the degree to which they control chance events. In comparison, depressed subjects are less prone to this illusion of control. Third, normal individuals are more likely than depressed subjects to display unrealistic optimism in making projections about the fu-

ture. A variety of studies have provided support for the hypothesis that positive illusions can promote well-being (Reed et al., 1999; Taylor et al., 2003).

As you might guess, a variety of critics have expressed skepticism about the idea that illusions are adaptive (Asendorpf & Ostendorf, 1998; Colvin, Block, & Funder, 1995). Perhaps the best analysis of the issue comes from Roy Baumeister (1989), who theorizes that it's all a matter of degree and that there is an "optimal margin of illusion." According to Baumeister, extreme distortions of reality are maladaptive, but small illusions are often beneficial.

Constructive Coping 11g

Our discussion thus far has focused on coping strategies that usually are less than ideal. Of course, people also exhibit many healthful strategies for dealing with stress. The term **constructive coping refers to relatively healthful efforts that people make to deal with stressful events.** No strategy of coping can *guarantee* a successful outcome. The coping strategies that are likely to be effective will vary depending on the exact nature of the situation, and even the healthiest coping responses may turn out to be ineffective in some circumstances (Folkman & Moskowitz, 2004). Thus, the concept of constructive coping is simply meant to connote a healthful, positive approach, without promising success.

What makes certain coping strategies constructive? Frankly, it's a gray area in which psychologists' opinions vary to some extent. Nonetheless, a consensus

Shelley Taylor

"Rather than perceiving themselves, the world, and the future accurately, most people regard themselves, their circumstances, and the future as considerably more positive than is objectively likely.... These illusions are not merely characteristic of human thought; they appear actually to be adaptive, promoting rather than undermining good mental health."

---

concept check 13.3

Identifying More Defense Mechanisms

In the last chapter you checked your understanding of several defense mechanisms by identifying instances of them in a story. In this chapter, you've learned about five additional defense mechanisms that are sometimes used as ways of coping with stress (see **Table 13.2**). Check your understanding of these defense mechanisms by identifying them in the story below. Each example of a defense mechanism is underlined, with a number beneath it. Write the name of the defense mechanism exemplified in each case in the numbered spaces after the story. The answers are in Appendix A.

The guys at work have been trying to break it to me gently that they think my job's on the line because I've missed work too many days this year. I don't know how they came up with that idea; <u>I've got nothing to worry about.</u> Besides, every day I missed, <u>I always did a lot of cleaning up and other chores around here.</u> One of these days <u>the boss will finally recognize how really valuable I am to the company, and I'll be getting a big promotion.</u> Anyway, since the guys have been dropping these hints about my not missing any more days, <u>I've been trying really hard to make a good impression by saying "Hi" to everyone I see, especially the boss, and telling jokes.</u> You know, <u>it's really pretty interesting to observe how all these relationships unfold between guys who work together and the people who manage them.</u>

1. _____   4. _____

2. _____   5. _____

3. _____

about the nature of constructive coping has emerged from the sizable literature on stress management. Key themes in this literature include the following:

1. Constructive coping involves confronting problems directly. It is task relevant and action oriented. It entails a conscious effort to rationally evaluate your options so that you can try to solve your problems.

2. Constructive coping is based on reasonably realistic appraisals of your stress and coping resources. A little self-deception may sometimes be adaptive, but excessive self-deception and highly unrealistic negative thinking are not.

3. Constructive coping involves learning to recognize, and in some cases regulate, potentially disruptive emotional reactions to stress.

4. Constructive coping includes making efforts to ensure that your body is not especially vulnerable to the possibly damaging effects of stress.

These principles provide a rather general and abstract picture of constructive coping. We'll look at patterns of constructive coping in more detail in the Personal Application, which discusses various stress management strategies that people can use.

REVIEW of Key Points

13.5 Stress often triggers emotional reactions, such as anger, fear, and sadness. Fredrickson's broaden-and-build theory asserts that positive emotions broaden thinking and build coping resources. Evidence suggests that positive emotions foster enhanced immune responding and mental and physical health. Emotional arousal may interfere with coping. According to the inverted-U hypothesis, task performance improves with increased arousal up to a point and then declines. The optimal level of arousal on a task depends on the complexity of the task.

13.6 In the fight-or-flight response, the autonomic nervous system mobilizes the body for attack or fleeing. It may be less applicable to women than to men. Selye's general adaptation syndrome describes three stages of physiological reactions to stress: alarm, resistance, and exhaustion. Diseases of adaptation may appear during the stage of exhaustion. There are two

major pathways along which the brain sends signals to the endocrine system in response to stress, leading to the release of catecholamines and corticosteroids.

13.7 The behavioral response to stress takes the form of coping. Giving up is not a highly regarded approach to coping, but studies suggest that people who are able to disengage from unattainable goals exhibit better health. Aggression tends to fuel more anger and increase rather than decrease stress. Self-indulgence is another coping pattern that tends to be of limited value.

13.8 Defensive coping is quite common. Defense mechanisms protect against emotional distress through self-deception. Several lines of evidence suggest that positive illusions may be healthful, but there is some debate about the matter. Relatively healthful coping tactics are called constructive coping. Constructive coping is action-oriented and based on realistic appraisals of stress.

The Effects of Stress on Psychological Functioning

People struggle with many stresses every day. Most stresses come and go without leaving any enduring imprint. However, when stress is severe or when many stressful demands pile up, one's psychological functioning may be affected.

Research on the effects of stress has focused mainly on negative outcomes, so our coverage is slanted in that direction. However, it's important to emphasize that stress is not inherently bad. You would probably suffocate from boredom if you lived a stress-free existence. Stress makes life challenging and interesting. Along the way, though, stress can be harrowing, sometimes leading to impairments in performance, to burnout, and to other problems.

Impaired Task Performance

Stress often takes its toll on the ability to perform effectively on a task at hand. For instance, Roy Baumeis-

ter's work shows how pressure can interfere with performance. Baumeister's (1984) theory assumes that pressure to perform often makes people self-conscious and that this elevated self-consciousness disrupts their attention. He found support for his theory in a series of laboratory experiments in which he manipulated the pressure to perform on simple perceptual-motor tasks and found that many people tend to "choke" under pressure (Butler & Baumeister, 1998; Wallace, Baumeister, & Vohs, 2005). Pressure-induced performance decrements have also been found in studies of mathematical problem-solving and simple sports tasks (Beilock et al., 2002, 2004).

Other research suggests that Baumeister is on the right track in looking to *attention* to explain how stress impairs task performance. In a study of stress and decision making, Keinan (1987) found that stress disrupted two out of the three aspects of attention measured in the study. Stress increased subjects' tendency (1) to jump to a conclusion too quickly without considering all their options and (2) to do an unsystematic, poorly organized review of their available options. In a more recent study, Keinan and colleagues (1999) found that stress impaired performance on cognitive tasks. The results suggested that stress makes it harder for people to suppress competing thoughts. Research also suggests that stress can have detrimental effects on certain memory functions (Neupert et al., 2006; Shors, 2004), especially working memory (Beilock & Carr, 2005).

Burnout

Burnout is an overused buzzword that means different things to different people. Nonetheless, a few researchers have described burnout in a systematic way that has facilitated scientific study of the syndrome (Maslach, 2003; Maslach & Leiter, 2007). **Burnout involves physical and emotional exhaustion, cynicism, and a lowered sense of self-efficacy that can be brought on gradually by chronic work-related stress.** Exhaustion, which is central to burnout, includes chronic fatigue, weakness, and low energy. Cynicism is manifested in highly negative attitudes toward oneself, one's work, and life in general. Reduced self-efficacy involves declining feelings of competence at work that give way to feelings of hopelessness and helplessness.

What causes burnout? Factors in the workplace that appear to promote burnout include work overload, struggling with interpersonal conflicts at work, lack of control over work responsibilities and outcomes, and inadequate recognition for one's work (Maslach & Leiter, 2005; see **Figure 13.7**). As you might expect, burnout is associated with increased absenteeism and reduced productivity at work, as well as increased vulnerability to a variety of health problems (Maslach & Leiter, 2000). Burnout is a potential problem in a wide variety of occupations (Lee & Ashforth, 1996).

Psychological Problems and Disorders

On the basis of clinical impressions, psychologists have long suspected that chronic stress might contribute to many types of psychological problems and mental disorders. Since the late 1960s, advances in the measurement of stress have allowed researchers to verify these suspicions in empirical studies. When it comes to common psychological problems,

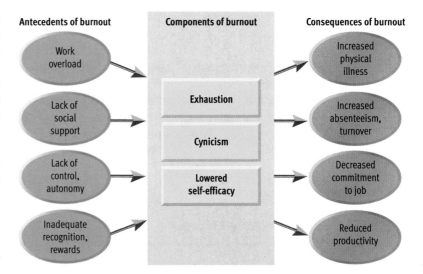

Figure 13.7

The antecedents, components, and consequences of burnout. Christina Maslach and Michael Leiter have developed a systematic model of burnout that specifies the antecedents, components, and consequences of this syndrome. The antecedents on the left in the diagram are the stressful features of the work environment that cause burnout. The syndrome itself consists of the three components shown in the center of the diagram. Some of the unfortunate results of burnout are listed on the right. (Based on Leiter & Maslach, 2001)

studies indicate that stress may contribute to poor academic performance (Akgun & Ciarrochi, 2003), insomnia and other sleep disturbances (Bernert et al., 2007; Kim & Dimsdale, 2007), sexual difficulties (Bodenmann et al., 2006), alcohol abuse (Sayette, 2007), and drug abuse (Goeders, 2004).

Above and beyond these everyday problems, research reveals that stress often contributes to the onset of full-fledged psychological disorders, including depression (Feliciano & Arean, 2007), schizophrenia (Walker, Mittal, & Tessner, 2008), and

Major disasters are just one of about a half-dozen types of calamitous events that can lead to posttraumatic stress disorder.

anxiety disorders (Beidel & Stipelman, 2007). In particular, stress plays a central role in the development of *posttraumatic stress disorder (PTSD),* which involves an enduring psychological disturbance attributable to the experience of a major traumatic event. We'll discuss these relations between stress and mental disorders in detail in Chapter 14. Of course, stress is only one of many factors that may contribute to psychological disorders. Nonetheless, it's sobering to realize that stress can have a dramatic impact on one's mental health.

Positive Effects

The effects of stress are not entirely negative. Recent years have brought increased interest in the positive aspects of the stress process, including favorable outcomes that follow in the wake of stress (Folkman & Moskowitz, 2000). To some extent, the new focus on the possible benefits of stress reflects a new emphasis on "positive psychology." As we noted in Chapters 1 and 10, some theorists have argued that the field of psychology has historically devoted too much attention to pathology and suffering (Seligman & Csikszentmihalyi, 2000). The advocates of positive psychology argue for increased research on well-being, hope, courage, perseverance, tolerance, and other human strengths and virtues (Peterson & Seligman, 2004). One of these strengths is *resilience* in the face of stress.

Research on resilience suggests that stress can promote personal growth or self-improvement (Calhoun & Tedeschi, 2006, 2008). For example, studies of people grappling with major health problems show that the majority of respondents report they derived benefits from their adversity (Tennen & Affleck, 1999). Stressful events sometimes force people to develop new skills, reevaluate priorities, learn new insights, and acquire new strengths. In other words, the adaptation process initiated by stress may lead to personal changes that are for the better. Confronting and conquering a stressful challenge may lead to improvements in specific coping abilities and to an enhanced self-concept. Moreover, even if people do not conquer stressors, they may be able to learn from their mistakes. Thus, researchers have begun to explore the growth potential of stressful events (Helgeson, Reynolds, & Tomich, 2006; Park & Fenster, 2004).

The predominant view has been that a substantial majority of people who are exposed to traumatic stress tend to suffer severe effects, with resilience being unusual, perhaps even rare. However, George Bonanno (2005) and his colleagues (Bonanno et al., 2002, 2005), who have studied the long-term effects of traumatic stressful events such as bereavement and exposure to combat and terrorism, have found that resilience is seen in as many as 35% to 55% of people (see **Figure 13.8**). Admittedly, a great many people do experience lasting ill effects from traumatic stress, but resilience is not the rare exception it was once believed to be.

Figure 13.8

Patterns of response to traumatic stress. Bonanno (2005) and colleagues have conducted a number of studies in which they have tracked the adjustment of people after exposure to severe, traumatic stress, such as bereavement. They have identified four patterns of response. Some people experience *chronic disruption* and others show *delayed disruption* of normal functioning, both of which show no abatement after two years. Others show a pattern of *recovery,* wherein initially severe symptoms gradually taper off. Finally, a fourth group exhibits *resilience,* in which relatively modest initial symptoms diminish fairly quickly. The surprising finding in this research is that resilience is the most common of the four patterns, suggesting that resilience is not as rare as previously assumed.

SOURCE: Bonanno, G. A. (2005). Resilience in the face of potential trauma. *Current Directions in Psychological Science, 14,* 135–138. Copyright © 2005 Blackwell Publishing. Reprinted by permission.

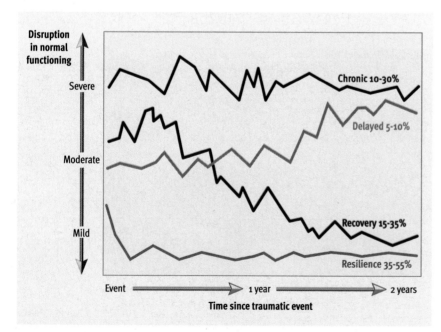

The Effects of Stress on Physical Health

The idea that stress can contribute to physical ailments is not entirely new. Evidence that stress can cause physical illness began to accumulate back in the 1930s. By the 1950s, the concept of *psychosomatic disease* was widely accepted. **Psychosomatic diseases were genuine physical ailments that were thought to be caused in part by stress and other psychological factors.** The classic psychosomatic illnesses were high blood pressure, peptic ulcers, asthma, skin disorders such as eczema and hives, and migraine and tension headaches (Kaplan, 1989; Rogers, Fricchione, & Reich, 1999). Please note, these diseases were not regarded as *imagined* physical ailments. The term *psychosomatic* has often been misused to refer to physical ailments that are "all in one's head," but that is an entirely different syndrome (see Chapter 14). Rather, psychosomatic diseases were viewed as *authentic* organic maladies that were heavily stress-related.

Since the 1970s, the concept of psychosomatic disease has gradually fallen into disuse because research has shown that stress can contribute to the development of a diverse array of other diseases previously believed to be purely physiological in origin (Dimsdale et al., 2005; Dougall & Baum, 2001). Thus, it has become apparent that there is nothing unique about the psychosomatic diseases that requires a special category. In this section we'll look at the evidence on the apparent link between stress and physical illness, beginning with heart disease, which is far and away the leading cause of death in North America.

Personality, Hostility, and Heart Disease

Heart disease accounts for about 27% of the deaths in the United States every year. *Coronary heart disease* involves a reduction in blood flow in the coronary arteries, which supply the heart with blood. This type of heart disease accounts for about 90% of heart-related deaths.

Atherosclerosis is the principal cause of coronary heart disease (Chrousos & Kaltsas, 2007). This condition is characterized by a gradual narrowing of the coronary arteries. A buildup of fatty deposits and other debris on the inner walls of the arteries is the usual cause of this narrowing. Atherosclerosis progresses slowly over a period of years. However, when

a narrowed coronary artery is blocked completely (by a blood clot, for instance), the abrupt interruption of blood flow can produce a heart attack. Atherosclerosis is more prevalent in men than women and tends to increase with age. Other established risk factors for atherosclerosis include smoking, lack of exercise, high cholesterol levels, and high blood pressure (Rippe, Angelopoulos, & Zukley, 2007). Contrary to public perception, cardiovascular diseases kill women just as much as men, but these diseases tend to emerge in women about 10 years later than in men (Stoney, 2003).

Recently, attention has shifted to the possibility that inflammation may contribute to atherosclerosis and elevated coronary risk (Miller & Blackwell, 2006). Evidence is mounting that inflammation plays a key role in the initiation and progression of atherosclerosis, as well as in the acute complications that trigger heart attacks (Nabi et al., 2008). Fortunately, researchers have found a marker for inflammation—levels of C-reactive protein (CRP) in the blood—that may help physicians estimate individuals' coronary risk more accurately than was previously possible (Kop & Weinstein, 2007; Ridker et al., 2005). Figure 13.9 on the next page shows how combined levels of CRP and cholesterol appear to be related to coronary risk.

Research on the relationship between *psychological* factors and heart attacks began in the 1960s and 1970s, when a pair of cardiologists, Meyer Friedman and Ray Rosenman (1974), discovered an apparent connection between coronary risk and a syndrome they called the *Type A personality*, which involves self-imposed stress and intense reactions to stress (Shaw & Dimsdale, 2007). **The *Type A personality* includes three elements: (1) a strong competitive orientation, (2) impatience and time urgency, and (3) anger and hostility.** Type A's are ambitious, hard-driving perfectionists who are exceedingly time-conscious. They routinely try to do several things at once. They fidget frantically over the briefest delays. Often they are highly competitive, achievement-oriented workaholics who drive themselves with many deadlines. They are easily irritated and are quick to anger. In contrast, **the *Type B personality* is marked by relatively relaxed, patient, easygoing, amicable behavior.** Type B's are less hurried, less competitive, and less easily angered than Type A's.

Key Learning Goals

13.11 Review the evidence linking personality factors to coronary heart disease.

13.12 Outline the evidence linking emotional reactions and depression to heart disease.

13.13 Discuss how stress affects immune functioning, and assess the link between stress and illness.

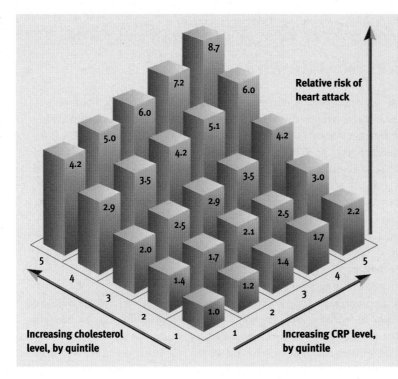

Figure 13.9

The relationship of cholesterol and inflammation to coronary risk. Levels of C-reactive protein (CRP) in the blood appear to be a useful index of the inflammation that contributes to atherosclerosis (Ridker, 2001). This graph shows how increasing CRP levels and increasing cholesterol levels combine to elevate cardiovascular risk (for a heart attack or stroke). The relative risks shown are for successive quintiles on each measure (each quintile represents one-fifth of the sample, ordered from those who scored lowest to those who scored highest). The relative risks are in relation to those who fall in the lowest quintile on both measures.

SOURCE: Ridker, P. M. (2001). High sensitivity C-reactive protein: Potential adjunct for global risk assessment in primary prevention of cardiovascular disease, *Circulation, 103,* 1813–1818. Copyright © 2001 American Heart Association. Adapted by permission of the publisher Lippincott Williams & Williams and the author.

Decades of research uncovered a tantalizingly modest correlation between Type A behavior and increased coronary risk. More often than not, studies found an association between Type A personality and an elevated incidence of heart disease, but the findings were not as strong or as consistent as expected (Baker, Suchday, & Krantz, 2007; Myrtek, 2007). However, more recently, researchers have found a stronger link between personality and coronary risk by focusing on a specific component of the Type A personality—*anger and hostility* (Boyle, Jackson, & Suarez, 2007; Powell & Williams, 2007). For example, in one study of almost 13,000 men and women who had no prior history of heart disease (Williams et al., 2000), investigators found an elevated incidence of heart attacks among participants who exhibited an angry temperament. The participants, who were followed for a median period of 4.5 years, were classified as being low (37.1%), moderate (55.2%), or high (7.7%) in anger. Among participants with normal blood pressure, the high-anger subjects experienced almost three times as many coronary events as the low-anger subjects (see Figure 13.10). Thus, anger/hostility appears to be the key toxic element in the Type A syndrome.

Emotional Reactions, Depression, and Heart Disease

Although work on personality risk factors has dominated research on how psychological functioning contributes to heart disease, recent studies suggest

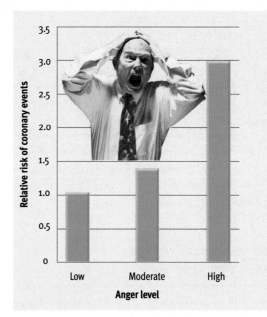

Figure 13.10

Anger and coronary risk. Working with a large sample of healthy men and women who were followed for a median of 4.5 years, Williams et al. (2000) found an association between anger and the likelihood of a coronary event. Among subjects who manifested normal blood pressure at the beginning of the study, a moderate anger level was associated with a 36% increase in coronary attacks and a high level of anger nearly tripled participants' risk for coronary disease. (Based on data in Williams et al., 2000)

that emotional reactions may also be critical. *One line of research has supported the hypothesis that transient mental stress and the resulting emotions that people experience can tax the heart.* Based on anecdotal evidence, cardiologists and laypersons have long voiced suspicions that strong emotional reactions might trigger heart attacks in individuals with coronary disease, but it has been difficult to document this connection. However, advances in cardiac monitoring have facilitated investigation of the issue.

As suspected, laboratory experiments have shown that brief periods of mental stress can trigger acute symptoms of heart disease (Baker, Suchday, & Krantz, 2007). Overall, the evidence suggests that mental stress can elicit cardiac symptoms in about 30%–70% of patients with coronary disease (Kop, Gottdiener, & Krantz, 2001). Moreover, research indicates that these patients have a higher risk for heart attack than the cardiology patients who do not exhibit symptoms in response to mental stress (Krantz et al., 2000). A recent study also demonstrated that mental stress can trigger temporary increases in the inflammation that is thought to contribute to cardiovascular risk (Kop et al., 2008). Subjects asked to perform stressful tasks in the laboratory showed elevated CRP levels, and these reactions were stronger in participants who had a history of coronary disease.

Another line of research has recently implicated depression as a risk factor for heart disease (Goldston & Baillie, 2008). *Depressive disorders,* which are characterized by persistent feelings of sadness and despair, are a fairly common form of mental illness (see Chapter 14). Elevated rates of depression have been found among patients suffering from heart disease, but most experts used to explain this correlation by asserting that being diagnosed with heart disease makes people depressed. Recent evidence, however, suggests that the causal relations may be just the opposite—*that the emotional dysfunction of depression may cause heart disease* (Frasure-Smith & Lesperance, 2005; Thomas, Kalaria, & O'Brien, 2004). This issue brings us to our Featured Study for this chapter, which examined the relationship between depression and cardiac health.

web link 13.7

Healthfinder
Through the Department of Health and Human Services, the U.S. government has opened an ambitious online gateway to consumer-oriented information about health in all its aspects. Annotated descriptions are available for all resources identified in no-cost searches of this database.

Is Depression a Risk Factor for Heart Disease?

FEATURED

STUDY

In the 1990s investigators began to suspect that depression might increase vulnerability to heart disease. A correlation between depression and coronary risk was reported in several studies, but given the profound importance of this issue, additional studies have been needed to replicate the finding in different types of samples and to get a more precise reading on the *degree* to which depression elevates coronary risk. Also, previous studies yielded conflicting results about whether depression elevates cardiac risk for healthy individuals or only among people who already have heart disease. Thus, the present study examined the impact of depression on cardiac mortality in people with and without preexisting coronary disease.

Method
Participants. The sample was made up of 2847 men and women between the ages of 55 and 85 who were participating in an ongoing study of aging based in Amsterdam. The subjects were a randomly selected sample of older persons drawn from 11 municipalities in the Netherlands. The mean age of the participants was 70.5, and 52% were female.

Procedure and measures. The study used a longitudinal design (see Chapter 11), which entailed following the participants' health and mortality over a period of four years. Subjects were carefully screened for the existence of cardiac disease at the beginning of the study. Depressed subjects were identified through a two-step process. First, all the participants completed a widely used 20-item self-report measure of depression. Those who scored above a standard cutoff on this scale were evaluated four weeks later with a diagnostic interview. Those who met the criteria for a diagnosis of depressive disorder (based on the interview)

were categorized as suffering from *major depression.* The remaining subjects who had scored above the cutoff on the screening scale but who did not meet the criteria for a full-fledged depressive disorder, were categorized as suffering from *minor depression.* The key dependent variable at the end of the study was the cardiac mortality rate among the subjects, which was based on tracking death certificates in the 11 municipalities where the participants resided.

Results
At the beginning of the study, 450 of the 2847 participants were found to have cardiac disease. Among these subjects, the cardiac mortality rate was elevated for those who had exhibited either minor or major depression (see **Figure 13.11a** on the next page). Similar trends were observed among the remaining 2397 subjects who were free of cardiac disease when the study was initiated (see **Figure 13.11b** on the next page). The risk trends for both groups remained largely the same even after statistical adjustments were made to control for confounding variables, such as age, sex, weight, and smoking history.

Discussion
The increased cardiac mortality rate associated with depression was fairly similar in subjects with and without preexisting cardiac disease. For both groups, major depression roughly tripled subjects' risk of cardiac death. The findings for subjects without preexisting cardiac disease were especially important. Given that these subjects' depressive disorders preceded their cardiac disease, one cannot argue that their heart disease caused their depression. It is far

SOURCE: Pennix, B. W. J. H., Beekman, A. T. F., Honig, A., Deeg, D. J. H., Schoevers, R. A., van Eijk, J. T. M., & van Tilburg, W. (2001). Depression and cardiac mortality: Results from a community-based longitudinal survey. *Archives of General Psychiatry, 58,* 221–227.

Figure 13.11

Depression and heart disease. These data show how minor and major depression were associated with elevated cardiac mortality rates both among participants with preexisting heart disease (a) and participants who were free of heart disease at the beginning of the study (b).

SOURCE: Pennix, B. W. J. H., Beekman, A. T. F., Honig, A., Deeg, D. J. H., Schoevers, R. A., van Eijk, J. T. M., & van Tilburg, W. (2001). Depression and cardiac mortality: Results from a community-based longitudinal survey. *Archives of General Psychiatry, 58,* 221–227. Copyright © 2001 by American Medical Association. Reprinted with permission.

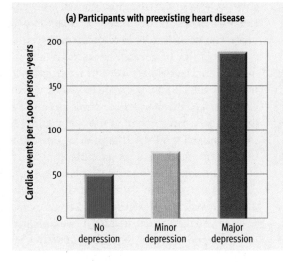

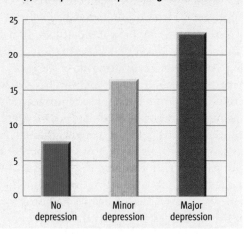

more likely that depression somehow contributed to the emergence of cardiac disease in these subjects.

Comment

This study is representative of a rich research tradition in health psychology in which various psychological factors (depression in this case) are examined in relation to health outcomes. These studies are crucial to our understanding of the determinants of wellness and disease. They illustrate the importance of correlational research, since predictors of disease generally cannot be studied using the experimental method.

The tripled cardiac risk observed in our Featured Study was partly a function of the older age group (over age 55) that was studied. Overall, when broader age ranges are examined, other studies have found that depression roughly doubles one's chances of developing heart disease (Lett et al., 2004; Herbst et al., 2007). Moreover, as suggested by the Featured Study, depression also appears to influence how heart disease progresses, as it is associated with a worse prognosis among cardiology patients (Glassman et al., 2003). Although the new emphasis is on how depression contributes to heart disease, experts caution that the relationship between the two conditions is surely bidirectional and that heart disease also increases vulnerability to depression (Sayers, 2004).

Stress, Other Diseases, and Immune Functioning

The development of questionnaires to measure life stress has allowed researchers to look for correlations between stress and a variety of diseases. These researchers have uncovered many connections between stress and illness. For example, Zautra and Smith (2001) found an association between life stress and the course of rheumatoid arthritis. Other studies have connected stress to the development of diabetes (Landel-Graham, Yount, & Rudnicki, 2003), herpes (Padgett & Sheridan, 2000), fibromy-algia (Wood, 2007), and flare-ups of irritable bowel syndrome (Blanchard & Keefer, 2003).

These are just a handful of representative examples of studies relating stress to physical diseases. Table 13.3 provides a longer list of health problems that have been linked to stress. Many of these stress-illness connections are based on tentative or inconsistent findings, but the sheer length and diversity of the list is remarkable. Why should stress increase the risk for so many kinds of illness? A partial answer may lie in the immune system.

The apparent link between stress and many types of illness raises the possibility that stress may undermine immune functioning. The *immune response* is **the body's defensive reaction to invasion by bacteria, viral agents, or other foreign substances.** The immune response works to protect the body from many forms of disease. Immune reactions are multifaceted, but they depend heavily on actions initiated by specialized white blood cells, called *lymphocytes.*

A wealth of studies indicate that experimentally induced stress can impair immune functioning *in animals* (Ader, 2001; Rose, 2007). That is, stressors such as crowding, shock, food restriction, and restraint reduce various aspects of immune reactivity in laboratory animals (Prolo & Chiappelli, 2007).

Studies by Janice Kiecolt-Glaser and her colleagues have related stress to suppressed immune activity *in humans* (Kiecolt-Glaser & Glaser, 1995). In one study,

Table 13.3 Health Problems That May Be Linked to Stress

Health Problem	Representative Evidence
AIDS	Stetler et al. (2005)
Appendicitis	Creed (1989)
Asthma	Lehrer et al. (2002)
Cancer	Dalton & Johansen (2005)
Chronic back pain	Lampe et al. (1998)
Common cold	Cohen (2005)
Complications of pregnancy	Dunkel-Schetter et al. (2001)
Heart disease	Theorell (2005)
Diabetes	Landel-Graham, Yount, & Rudnicki (2003)
Epileptic seizures	Kelly & Schramke (2000)
Hemophilia	Buxton et al. (1981)
Herpes virus	Padgett & Sheridan (2000)
Hyptertension	O'Callahan, Andrews, & Krantz (2003)
Hyperthyroidism	Yang, Liu, & Zang (2000)
Inflammatory bowel disease	Searle & Bennett (2001)
Migraine headaches	Ramadan (2000)
Multiple sclerosis	Mitsonis et al. (2006)
Periodontal disease	Marcenes & Sheiham (1992)
Premenstrual distress	Stanton et al. (2002)
Rheumatoid arthritis	Keefe et al. (2002)
Skin disorders	Arnold (2000)
Stroke	Harmsen et al. (1990)
Ulcers	Levenstein (2002)
Vaginal infections	Williams & Deffenbacher (1983)

medical students provided researchers with blood samples so that their immune response could be assessed (Kiecolt-Glaser et al., 1984). The students provided the baseline sample a month before final exams and contributed the "high-stress" sample on the first day of their finals. The subjects also responded to the SRRS as a measure of recent stress. Reduced levels of immune activity were found during the extremely stressful finals week. Reduced immune activity was also correlated with higher scores on the SRRS. In another study, investigators exposed quarantined volunteers to respiratory viruses that cause the common cold and found that those under high stress were more likely to be infected by the viruses (Cohen, Tyrell, & Smith, 1993). In a thorough review of 30 years of research on stress and immunity, Segerstrom and Miller (2004) conclude that chronic stress can reduce both *cellular immune responses* (which attack intracellular pathogens, such as viruses) and *humoral immune responses* (which attack extracellular pathogens, such as bacteria).

Although research in recent decades has mainly focused on the link between stress and immunosuppression, recent studies have shown that there are other important connections between immune function and vulnerability to illness. When the immune system responds to infection or injury it may release proinflammatory cytokines, proteins that "orchestrate a number of the immune activities that play a role in killing the pathogen and repairing damaged tissue" (Kemeny, 2007, p. 94). These crucial proteins may also trigger fever, reduced appetite, and decreased activity, which can conserve energy and promote recovery (Marshall, 2007). But exposure to long-term stress can sometimes foster persistent overproduction of proinflammatory cytokines, which can promote chronic inflammation (Robles, Glaser, & Kiecolt-Glaser, 2005). Scientists have only begun to fully appreciate the potential ramifications of this chronic inflammation in recent years. As we noted earlier, inflammation has recently been recognized as a major factor in the development of heart disease. But that's not all. Research has also demonstrated that chronic inflammation contributes to a diverse array of diseases, including arthritis, osteoporosis, respiratory diseases, diabetes, Alzheimer's disease, and some types of cancer (Feuerstein et al., 2007). Thus, chronic inflammation resulting from immune system dysregulation may be another key mechanism underlying the association between stress and wide variety of diseases.

Sizing Up the Link Between Stress and Illness

A wealth of evidence shows that stress is related to physical health, and converging lines of evidence suggest that stress contributes to the *causation* of illness (Cohen, Janicki-Deverts, & Miller, 2007). But we have to put this intriguing finding in perspective. The vast majority of the relevant research is correlational, so it can't demonstrate *conclusively* that stress causes illness (Smith & Gallo, 2001). Subjects' elevated levels of stress and illness could both be due to a third variable, perhaps some aspect of personality (see Figure 13.12 on the next page). For instance, some evidence suggests that neuroticism may make people overly prone to interpret events as stressful and overly prone to interpret unpleasant sensations as symptoms of illness, thus inflating the correlation between stress and illness (Turner & Wheaton, 1995).

Figure 13.12

Figure 13.12
The stress-illness correlation. One or more aspects of personality, physiology, or memory could play the role of a postulated third variable in the relationship between high stress and high incidence of illness. For example, neuroticism may lead some subjects to view more events as stressful and to remember more illness, thus inflating the apparent correlation between stress and illness.

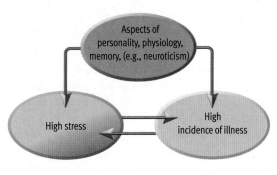

In spite of methodological problems favoring inflated correlations, the research in this area consistently indicates that the *strength* of the relationship between stress and health is *modest*. The correlations typically fall in the .20s and .30s (Cohen, Kessler, & Gordon, 1995). Clearly, stress is not an irresistible force that produces inevitable effects on health. Actually, this fact should come as no surprise, as stress is but one factor operating in a complex network of biopsychosocial determinants of health. Other key factors include one's genetic endowment, exposure to infectious agents and environmental toxins, nutrition, exercise, alcohol and drug use, smoking, use of medical care, and cooperation with medical advice. Furthermore, some people handle stress better than others, which is the matter we turn to next.

REVIEW of Key Points

13.11 The Type A personality has been implicated as a contributing cause of coronary heart disease, but the evidence has been equivocal. Recent research suggests that hostility may be the most toxic element of the Type A syndrome.

13.12 Transient, stress-induced emotional reactions can elicit cardiac symptoms. Although depression can be a result of heart disease, research also suggests that depression can increase one's risk for cardiovascular disease. Our Featured Study found that depression was a predictor of increased cardiac mortality.

13.13 Stress appears to play a role in a host of diseases, perhaps because it can temporarily suppress the effectiveness of the immune system. Exposure to long-term stress can also promote chronic inflammation. Although there's little doubt that stress can contribute to the development of physical illness, the link between stress and illness is modest. Stress is only one factor in a complex network of biopsychosocial variables that shape health.

Factors Moderating the Impact of Stress

Key Learning Goals

13.14 Understand how social support moderates the impact of stress.

13.15 Identify two personality factors related to stress resistance and health.

Some people seem to be able to withstand the ravages of stress better than others (Holohan & Moos, 1994). Why? Because a number of *moderator variables* can lessen the impact of stress on physical and mental health. We'll look at three key moderator variables—social support, optimism, and conscientiousness—to shed light on individual differences in how well people tolerate stress.

Social Support

Friends may be good for your health! This startling conclusion emerges from studies on social support as a moderator of stress. *Social support* **refers to various types of aid and emotional sustenance provided by members of one's social networks.** Many studies have found positive correlations between high social support and greater immune functioning (Uchino, Uno, & Holt-Lunstad, 1999). In contrast, the opposite of social support—loneliness and social isolation—was found to predict reduced immune responding in a recent study of college students (Pressman et al., 2005). In recent decades, a vast number of studies have found evidence that social support is favorably related to physical health (Taylor, 2007; Uchino, 2004), including all-important coronary health (Rutledge et al., 2004). The favorable effects of social support are strong enough to have an impact on participants' mortality! For example, one study followed patients for a mean period of 4.5 years following a nonfatal heart attack and found that higher levels of perceived social support were associated with reduced mortality among patients who did not manifest depression (Lett et al., 2007). Similarly, an Australian study that tracked 1477 participants aged 70 and over for ten years found that people with richer friendship networks lived longer (Giles et al., 2005).

Social support seems to be good medicine for the mind as well as the body, as most studies also find an association between social support and mental health (Davis, Morris, & Kraus, 1998). It appears that social support serves as a protective buffer during times of high stress, reducing the negative impact of stressful events, and that social support has its own positive effects on health, which may be apparent even when people aren't under great stress (Wills & Fegan, 2001).

Of course, social *bonds* are not equivalent to social *support*. Indeed, some people in one's social circles may be a source of more *stress* than *support* (Vinokur & van Ryn, 1993). Friends and family can be argumentative, put one under pressure, make one feel guilty, break promises, and so forth. Research suggests that social conflicts can increase susceptibility to illness (Cohen, 2004). For example, a recent study of older adults assessed the degree to which the participants had stable, consistent negative exchanges with people in their social networks (Newsom, et al., 2008). The study found that higher levels of negative interactions were predictive of lower self-rated health and of having a higher number of troublesome health conditions.

Optimism and Conscientiousness

Defining *optimism* as a **general tendency to expect good outcomes,** Michael Scheier and Charles Carver (1985) found a correlation between optimism and relatively good physical health in a sample of college students. Another study found optimism to be associated with more effective immune functioning (Segerstrom et al., 1998). Other studies have found that optimism helps people deal more effectively with a diagnosis of breast cancer (Carver et al., 2005) and with a death or onset of illness in one's immediate family (Kivimaki et al. 2005). Why is optimism beneficial to health? Research suggests that optimists cope with stress in more adaptive ways than pessimists (Aspinwall, Richter, & Hoffman, 2001; Nes & Segerstrom, 2006). Optimists are more likely to engage in action-oriented, problem-focused coping. They are more willing than pessimists to seek social support, and they are more likely to emphasize the positive in their appraisals of stressful events. In comparison, pessimists are more likely to deal with stress by giving up or engaging in denial or wishful thinking.

In a related line of research, Christopher Peterson and Martin Seligman have studied how people explain bad events (personal setbacks, mishaps, disappointments, and such). They have identified a *pessimistic explanatory style,* in which people tend to blame setbacks on their own personal shortcomings, versus an *optimistic explanatory style,* which leads people to attribute setbacks to temporary situational factors. In two retrospective studies of people born many decades ago, they found an association between an optimistic explanatory style and relatively good health (Peterson, Seligman, & Vaillant, 1988) and increased longevity (Peterson et al., 1998). Many other studies have linked this optimistic explanatory style to superior physical health (Peterson & Bossio, 2001), as well as higher academic achievement, increased job productivity, enhanced athletic performance, and higher marital satisfaction (Gillham et al., 2001).

Optimism versus pessimism is not the only dimension of personality that has been examined as a possible moderator of physical health. Howard

In times of stress, seeking support from one's friends is a very sensible and helpful coping strategy.

Friedman and his colleagues have found evidence that *conscientiousness,* one of the Big Five personality traits discussed in Chapter 12, may have an impact on physical health (Friedman et al., 1993; Martin, Friedman, & Schwartz, 2007). They have related personality measures to longevity in the gifted individuals first studied by Lewis Terman (see Chapter 9), who have been followed closely by researchers since 1921. Data were available on six personality traits, which were measured when the subjects were children. The one trait that predicted greater longevity was conscientiousness. Why does conscientiousness promote longevity? According to Friedman (2007), several considerations may contribute. For example, conscientious people may tend to gravitate to healthy environments, and they may show less reactivity to stress. But the key consideration appears to be that conscientiousness fosters better health habits. People who are high in conscientiousness are less likely than others to exhibit unhealthy habits, such as excessive drinking, drug abuse, dangerous driving, smoking, overeating, and risky sexual practices (Bogg & Roberts, 2004; Roberts, Walton, & Bogg, 2005).

Individual differences among people in social support, optimism, and conscientiousness explain why stress doesn't have the same impact on everyone. Differences in lifestyle may play an even larger role in determining health. We'll examine some critical aspects of lifestyle in the next section.

Martin Seligman

"The concept of explanatory style brings hope into the laboratory, where scientists can dissect it in order to understand how it works."

> **REVIEW of Key Points**
>
> **13.14** There are individual differences in how much stress people can tolerate without experiencing ill effects. Social support is a key moderator of the relationship between stress and both physical and mental health. Studies have even found that social support is related to mortality. Social support buffers the effects of stress and has its own positive effects on health.
>
> **13.15** Optimism is associated with relatively good physical health. Optimism may lead to more effective coping with stress, whereas pessimism has been related to passive coping and poor health practices. A study of Terman's sample of gifted children suggests that conscientiousness is associated with greater longevity. Conscientiousness appears to be related to better health habits.

Key Learning Goals

13.16 Explain the negative impact of smoking on health.

13.17 Discuss how poor nutrition and lack of exercise are related to physical health.

13.18 Clarify the relationship between behavioral factors and AIDS.

13.19 Understand how health-impairing lifestyles develop.

Health-Impairing Behavior

Some people seem determined to dig an early grave for themselves. They do precisely those things that are bad for their health. For example, some people drink heavily even though they know that they're damaging their liver. Others eat all the wrong foods even though they know that they're increasing their risk of a second heart attack. Behavior that's downright *self-destructive* is surprisingly common. In this section we'll discuss how health is affected by smoking, nutrition, exercise, and drug use, and we'll look at behavioral factors in AIDS. We'll also discuss *why* people develop health-impairing lifestyles.

Smoking

The percentage of people who smoke has declined noticeably since the mid-1960s (see **Figure 13.13**). Nonetheless, about 24% of adult men and 18% of adult women in the United States continue to smoke regularly. Unfortunately, these figures are slightly higher (28% for both sexes) among college students (Rigotti, Lee, & Wechsler, 2000). Moreover, smoking is even more common in many other societies.

The evidence clearly shows that smokers face a much greater risk of premature death than nonsmokers. For example, the average smoker has an estimated life expectancy *13–14 years shorter* than that of a similar nonsmoker (Schmitz & Delaune, 2005). The overall risk is positively correlated with the number of cigarettes smoked and their tar and nicotine content. Cigar smoking, which has increased dramatically in recent years, elevates health risks almost as much as cigarette smoking (Baker et al., 2000).

Why are mortality rates higher for smokers? Smoking increases the likelihood of developing a surprisingly large range of diseases (Schmitz & Delaune, 2005; Woloshin, Schwartz, & Welch, 2002). Lung cancer and heart disease kill the largest number of smokers. However, smokers also have an elevated risk for oral, bladder, and kidney cancer, as well as cancers of the larynx, esophagus, and pancreas; for arteriosclerosis, hypertension, stroke, and other cardiovascular diseases; and for bronchitis, emphysema, and other pulmonary diseases. Most smokers know about the risks associated with tobacco use, but they tend to underestimate the actual risks as applied to themselves (Ayanian & Cleary, 1999). They also tend to overestimate the likelihood that they can quit smoking when they decide to (Weinstein, Slovic, & Gibson, 2004).

Studies show that if people can give up smoking, their health risks decline reasonably quickly (Kenfield et al., 2008; Williams et al., 2002; see **Figure 13.14**). Evidence suggests that most smokers would like to quit but are reluctant to give up a major source of pleasure, and they worry about craving cigarettes, gaining weight, becoming anxious and irritable, and feeling less able to cope with stress (Grunberg, Faraday, & Rahman, 2001).

Unfortunately, it's difficult to give up cigarettes. People who enroll in formal smoking cessation programs are only slightly more successful than people who try to quit on their own (Swan, Hudmon, Khroyan, 2003). Long-term success rates are in the vicinity of only 25%, and some studies report even lower figures. For example, in one study of self-quitters, after six months only 3% had maintained complete abstinence from smoking (Hughes et al., 1992). Nonetheless, the fact that there are nearly 40 million ex-smokers in the United States indicates that it is possible to quit smoking successfully. Interestingly, many people fail several or more times before they eventually succeed. Evidence suggests that the readiness to give up smoking builds gradually as people cycle through periods of abstinence and relapse (Prochaska, 1994; Prochaska et al., 2004).

Poor Nutritional Habits

Evidence is accumulating that patterns of nutrition influence susceptibility to a variety of diseases and health problems. For example, in a study of over 42,000 women, investigators found an association

Figure 13.13

The prevalence of smoking in the United States. This graph shows how the percentage of U.S. adults who smoke has declined steadily since the mid-1960s. Although considerable progress has been made, smoking still accounts for a huge number of premature deaths each year. (Based on data from the Centers for Disease Control and Prevention)

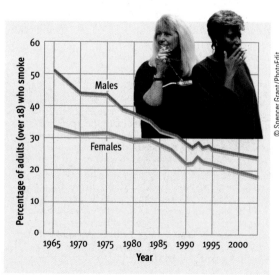

© Spencer Grant/PhotoEdit

between a measure of overall diet quality and mortality. Women who reported poorer quality diets had elevated mortality rates (Kant et al., 2000). What are the specific links between diet and health? In addition to the problems associated with obesity, which we discussed in Chapter 10, other possible connections between eating patterns and health include the following:

1. Heavy consumption of foods that elevate serum cholesterol level (eggs, cheeses, butter, shellfish, sausage, and the like) appears to increase the risk of cardiovascular disease (Stamler et al., 2000; see Figure 13.15). Eating habits are only one of several factors that influence serum cholesterol level, but they do make an important contribution.

2. Vulnerability to cardiovascular diseases may also be influenced by other dietary factors. For example, low-fiber diets may increase the likelihood of coronary disease (Timm & Slavin, 2008), and high intake of red and processed meats, sweets, potatoes, and refined grains is associated with increased cardiovascular risk (Hu & Willett, 2002). Recent research indicates that the omega 3 fatty acids found in fish and fish oils offer some protection against coronary disease (Din, Newby, & Flapan, 2004) and are also associated with reduced risk for arthritis, autoimmune diseases, and some types of cancer (Umhau & Dauphinais, 2007).

3. High salt intake is a contributing factor in the development of high blood pressure, referred to medically as hypertension (Havas, Dickinson, & Wilson, 2007). Many people only worry about the salt that they add at the table, but in the typical American diet that accounts for only 6% of salt intake (77% comes from processed and restaurant foods).

4. High caffeine consumption may elevate one's risk for hypertension (James, 2004) and for coronary disease (Happonen, Voutilainen, & Salonen, 2004), although the negative effects of caffeine appear relatively modest.

5. High-fat diets have been implicated as possible contributors to cardiovascular disease (Melanson, 2007) and to some forms of cancer, especially prostate cancer (Rose, 1997), colon and rectal cancer (Shike, 1999), and breast cancer (Wynder et al., 1997). Some studies also suggest that high-fiber diets may reduce one's risk for breast cancer, colon cancer, and diabetes (Timm & Slavin, 2008).

Of course, nutritional habits interact with other factors—genetics, exercise, environment, and so on—to determine whether one develops a particular disease. Nonetheless, the examples just described indicate that eating habits can influence one's physical health.

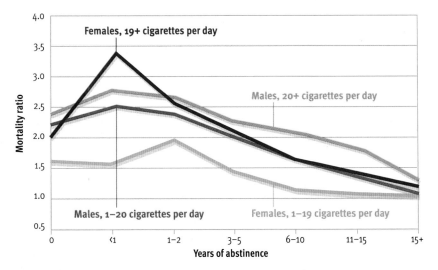

Lack of Exercise

Considerable evidence links lack of exercise to poor health. Research indicates that regular exercise is associated with increased longevity. For example, a recent study of over 15,000 men found that those who were high in fitness had a 70% reduction in mortality compared to those who were low in fitness (Kokkinos et al., 2008). Exercise provides similar benefits for women (Mora et al., 2007). Why would exercise help people live longer? For one thing, an appropriate exercise program can enhance cardiovascular fitness and thereby reduce susceptibility to deadly cardiovascular problems (Zoeller, 2007). Second, exercise may indirectly reduce one's risk for a variety of obesity-related health problems, such as diabetes and respiratory difficulties (Corsica & Perri, 2003). Third, recent studies suggest that exercise can help

Figure 13.14

Quitting smoking and health risk. Research suggests that various types of health risks associated with smoking decline gradually after people give up tobacco. The data shown here, from the 1990 U.S. Surgeon General's report on smoking, illustrate the overall effects on mortality rates. (Based on data from U.S. Department of Health and Human Services, 1990)

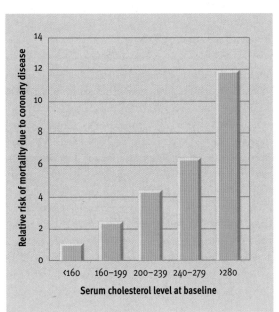

Figure 13.15

The link between cholesterol and coronary risk. In a review of several major studies, Stamler et al. (2000) summarize crucial evidence on the association between cholesterol levels and the prevalence of cardiovascular disease. This graph is based on a sample of over 11,000 men who were ages 18 to 39 at the beginning of the study (1967–1973) when their serum cholesterol level was measured. The data shown here depict participants' relative risk for coronary heart disease during the ensuing 25 years, as a function of their initial cholesterol level.

web link 13.8

Exercise and Sport Psychology

For anyone wondering about how psychological science deals with sports and athletics, this site, maintained by Division 47 of the American Psychological Association, is an excellent starting point, especially for those looking for career information.

diminish chronic inflammation, which is thought to contribute to quite a variety of diseases (Flynn, McFarlin, & Markofski, 2007). Fourth, exercise can serve as a buffer that reduces the potentially damaging physical effects of stress (Plante, Caputo, & Chizmar, 2000). This buffering effect may occur because people high in fitness show less physiological reactivity to stress than those who are less fit (Forcier et al., 2006). If these payoffs weren't enough to get people hustling to the gym, recent studies have turned up a new, unexpected benefit of exercise—it can facilitate the generation of new brain cells (Cotman, Berchtold, & Christie, 2007; Pereira et al., 2007). As noted earlier in the chapter (see p. 544), *neurogenesis* appears to be an important process that can be suppressed by stress. The finding that this neurodevelopmental process can be promoted by simple exercise may turn out to have profound implications.

Alcohol and Drug Use

Recreational drug use is another common health-impairing habit. The risks associated with the use of various drugs were discussed in detail in Chapter 5. Unlike smoking, poor eating habits, and inactivity, drugs can kill directly and immediately when they are taken in an overdose or when they impair the user enough to cause an accident. In the long run, various recreational drugs may also elevate one's risk for infectious diseases; respiratory, pulmonary, and cardiovascular diseases; liver disease; gastrointestinal problems; cancer; neurological disorders; and pregnancy complications (see Chapter 5). Ironically, the greatest physical damage in the population as a whole is caused by alcohol, the one recreational drug that's legal.

Behavior and AIDS

Some of the most problematic links between behavior and health may be those related to AIDS. AIDS stands for *acquired immune deficiency syndrome, a disorder in which the immune system is gradually weakened and eventually disabled by the human immunodeficiency virus (HIV).* Being infected with the HIV virus is *not* equivalent to having AIDS, which is the final stage of the HIV infection process, typically manifested years after the original infection (Carey & Vanable, 2003). With the onset of AIDS, one is left virtually defenseless against a variety of opportunistic infectious agents. AIDS inflicts its harm indirectly by opening the door to other diseases. The symptoms of AIDS vary widely,

web link 13.9

Centers for Disease Control and Prevention (CDC)

The CDC is the federal agency charged with monitoring and responding to serious threats to the nation's health as well as taking steps to prevent illness. This site's "Health Information from A to Z" offers the public in-depth medical explanations of many health problems, both common (flu, allergies, etc.) and less common (fetal alcohol syndrome, meningitis, etc.).

depending on the specific constellation of diseases that one develops (Cunningham & Selwyn, 2005). Unfortunately, the worldwide prevalence of this deadly disease continues to increase at an alarming rate, especially in certain regions of Africa (UNAIDS, 2006).

Prior to 1996–1997, the average length of survival for people after the onset of the AIDS syndrome was about 18 to 24 months. Encouraging advances in the treatment of AIDS with drug regimens referred to as *highly active antiretroviral therapy (HAART)* hold out promise for *substantially* longer survival (Anthony & Bell, 2008; Hammer et al., 2006). But these drugs have been rushed into service, and their long-term efficacy is yet to be determined. Medical experts are concerned that the general public has gotten the impression that these treatments have transformed AIDS from a fatal disease to a manageable one, which may be a premature conclusion. HIV strains are evolving, and many have developed resistance to the currently available antiretroviral drugs. Moreover, some patients do not respond well to the new drugs, and many patients who are responsive have difficulty sticking to drug regimens that often have adverse side effects (Beusterien et al., 2008; Hammer et al., 2006).

Transmission

The HIV virus is transmitted through person-to-person contact involving the exchange of bodily fluids, primarily semen and blood. The two principal modes of transmission in the United States have been sexual contact and the sharing of needles by intravenous (IV) drug users. In the United States, sexual transmission has occurred primarily among gay and bisexual men, but heterosexual transmission has increased in recent years (Centers for Disease Control, 2006). In the world as a whole, infection through heterosexual relations has been much more common from the beginning. In heterosexual relations, male-to-female transmission is estimated to be about eight times more likely than female-to-male transmission (Ickovics, Thayaparan, & Ethier, 2001). The HIV virus can be found in the tears and saliva of infected individuals, but the concentrations are low, and there is no evidence that the infection can be spread through casual contact. Even most forms of noncasual contact, including kissing, hugging, and sharing food with infected individuals, appear safe.

Misconceptions

Misconceptions about AIDS are widespread. Ironically, the people who hold these misconceptions fall into two polarized camps. On the one hand, a great many people have unrealistic fears that AIDS can be readily transmitted through casual contact with infected individuals. These people worry unnecessarily about contracting AIDS from a handshake, a sneeze, or an eating utensil, and they tend to be paranoid about interacting with homosexuals, thus fueling discrimination against gays.

On the other hand, many young heterosexuals who are sexually active with a variety of partners foolishly downplay their risk for HIV, naively assuming that they are safe as long as they avoid IV drug use and sexual relations with gay or bisexual men. They greatly underestimate the probability that their sexual partners previously may have used IV drugs or had unprotected sex with an infected individual. Also, because AIDS is usually accompanied by discernible symptoms, many young people believe that prospective sexual partners who carry the HIV virus will exhibit telltale signs of illness, but that is generally not the case. In reality, many HIV carriers do not know themselves that they are HIV-positive. In a recent study that screened over 5000 men for HIV, 77% of those who tested HIV-positive were previously unaware of their infection (MacKellar et al., 2005). In sum, many myths about AIDS persist, in spite of extensive efforts to educate the public about this complex and controversial disease. Figure 13.16 contains a short quiz to test your knowledge of the facts about AIDS.

Prevention

The behavioral changes that minimize the risk of developing AIDS are fairly straightforward, although making the changes is often much easier said than done. In all groups, the more sexual partners a person has, the higher the risk that one will be exposed to the HIV virus. Thus, people can reduce their risk by having sexual contacts with fewer partners and by using condoms to control the exchange of semen. It is also important to curtail certain sexual practices (in particular, anal sex) that increase the probability of semen/blood mixing. The 1980s and early 1990s saw considerable progress toward wider use of safe sex practices, but new cohorts of young people appear to be much less concerned about the risk of HIV infection than the generation that witnessed the original emergence of AIDS (Jaffe, Valdiserri, & De Cock, 2007). In particular, experts are concerned that recent advances in treatment may lead to more casual attitudes about risky sexual practices, a development that would not bode well for public health efforts to slow the spread of AIDS (Kalichman et al., 2007; van Kesteren, Hospers, & Kok, 2007).

AIDS Risk Knowledge Test

Answer the following "true" or "false."

T	F	1.	The AIDS virus cannot be spread through kissing.
T	F	2.	A person can get the AIDS virus by sharing kitchens and bathrooms with someone who has AIDS.
T	F	3.	Men can give the AIDS virus to women.
T	F	4.	The AIDS virus attacks the body's ability to fight off diseases.
T	F	5.	You can get the AIDS virus by someone sneezing, like a cold or the flu.
T	F	6.	You can get AIDS by touching a person with AIDS.
T	F	7.	Women can give the AIDS virus to men.
T	F	8.	A person who got the AIDS virus from shooting up drugs cannot give the virus to someone by having sex.
T	F	9.	A pregnant woman can give the AIDS virus to her unborn baby.
T	F	10.	Most types of birth control also protect against getting the AIDS virus.
T	F	11.	Condoms make intercourse completely safe.
T	F	12.	Oral sex is safe if partners "do not swallow."
T	F	13.	A person must have many different sexual partners to be at risk for AIDS.
T	F	14.	It is more important to take precautions against AIDS in large cities than in small cities.
T	F	15.	A positive result on the AIDS virus antibody test often occurs for people who do not even have the virus.
T	F	16.	Only receptive (passive) anal intercourse transmits the AIDS virus.
T	F	17.	Donating blood carries no AIDS risk for the donor.
T	F	18.	Most people who have the AIDS virus look quite ill.

Answers: 1.T 2.F 3.T 4.T 5.F 6.F 7.T 8.F 9.T 10.F 11.F 12.F 13.F 14.F 15.F 16.F 17.T 18.F

How Does Health-Impairing Behavior Develop?

It may seem puzzling that people behave in self-destructive ways. How does this happen? Several factors are involved. First, many health-impairing habits creep up on people slowly. For instance, drug use may grow imperceptibly over years, or exercise habits may decline ever so gradually. Second, many health-impairing habits involve activities that are quite pleasant at the time. Actions such as eating favorite foods, smoking cigarettes, or getting "high" are potent reinforcing events. Third, the risks associated with most health-impairing habits are chronic diseases such as cancer that usually lie 10, 20, or 30 years down the road. It's relatively easy to ignore risks that lie in the distant future.

Finally, people have a curious tendency to underestimate the risks that accompany their own health-impairing behaviors while viewing the risks associated with others' self-destructive behaviors much more accurately (Weinstein, 2003; Weinstein & Klein, 1996). Many people are well aware of the dangers associated with certain habits, but when it's time to apply this information to themselves, they often discount it. They figure, for instance, that smoking will lead to cancer or a heart attack in *someone else.*

So far, we've seen that physical health may be affected by stress and by aspects of lifestyle. Next, we'll look at the importance of how people react to physical symptoms, health problems, and health care efforts.

Figure 13.16

A quiz on knowledge of AIDS. Because misconceptions about AIDS abound, it may be wise to take this brief quiz to test your knowledge of AIDS. The answers are shown at the bottom of the figure.

SOURCE: Adapted from Kalichman, S. C. (1995). *Understanding AIDS: A guide for mental health professionals.* Washington, DC: American Psychological Association. Copyright © 1995 American Psychological Association. Reprinted by permission of the publisher and author.

REVIEW of Key Points

13.16 Smokers have much higher mortality rates than non-smokers because they are more vulnerable to a host of diseases. Health risks decline reasonably quickly for people who give up smoking, but quitting is difficult and relapse rates are high.

13.17 Poor nutritional habits have been linked to heart disease, hypertension, and cancer, among other things. Regular exercise can reduce one's risk for cardiovascular diseases, diminish chronic inflammation, and buffer the effects of stress. Recent research also indicates that exercise can facilitate neurogenesis.

13.18 Aspects of behavior influence one's risk of AIDS, which is transmitted through person-to-person contact involving the exchange of bodily fluids, primarily semen and blood. Misconceptions about AIDS are common, and the people who hold these misconceptions tend to fall into polarized camps, either overestimating or underestimating their risk of infection.

13.19 Health-impairing habits tend to develop gradually and often involve pleasant activities. The risks may be easy to ignore because they lie in the distant future and because people tend to underestimate risks that apply to them personally.

Key Learning Goals

13.20 Discuss individual differences in the willingness to seek medical treatment.

13.21 Describe some barriers to effective patient-provider communication and ways to overcome these problems.

13.22 Review the extent to which people tend to adhere to medical advice.

Reactions to Illness

Some people respond to physical symptoms and illnesses by ignoring warning signs of developing diseases, while others engage in active coping efforts to conquer their diseases. Let's examine the decision to seek medical treatment, communication with health providers, and compliance with medical advice.

Deciding to Seek Treatment

Have you ever experienced nausea, diarrhea, stiffness, headaches, cramps, chest pains, or sinus problems? Of course you have; we all experience some of these problems periodically. However, whether someone views these sensations as *symptoms* is a matter of individual interpretation. When two persons experience the same unpleasant sensations, one may shrug them off as a nuisance while the other may rush to a physician (Martin & Leventhal, 2004). Studies suggest that people who are relatively high in anxiety and neuroticism tend to report more symptoms of illness than others do (Petrie & Pennebaker, 2004). Those who are extremely attentive to bodily sensations and health concerns also report more symptoms than the average person (Barsky, 1988).

Variations in the perceived seriousness and disruptiveness of symptoms help explain the differences among people in their readiness to seek medical treatment (Cameron, Leventhal, & Leventhal, 1993). The biggest problem in regard to treatment seeking is the tendency of many people to delay the pursuit of needed professional consultation. Delays can be critical, because early diagnosis and quick intervention may facilitate more effective treatment of many health problems (Petrie & Pennebaker, 2004). Unfortunately, procrastination is the norm even when people are faced with a medical emergency, such as a heart attack (Martin & Leventhal, 2004). Why do people dawdle in the midst of a crisis?

Robin DiMatteo (1991), a leading expert on patient behavior, mentions a number of reasons, noting that people delay because they often (a) misinterpret and downplay the significance of their symptoms, (b) fret about looking silly if the problem turns out to be nothing, (c) worry about "bothering" their physician, (d) are reluctant to disrupt their plans (to go out to dinner, see a movie, and so forth), and (e) waste time on trivial matters (such as taking a shower, gathering personal items, or packing clothes) before going to a hospital emergency room.

Communicating with Health Providers

A large portion of medical patients leave their doctors' offices not understanding what they have been told and what they are supposed to do (Johnson & Carlson, 2004). This situation is unfortunate, because good communication is a crucial requirement for sound medical decisions, informed choices about treatment, and appropriate follow-through by patients (Buckman, 2002; Gambone, Reiter, & DiMatteo, 1994).

There are many barriers to effective provider-patient communication (DiMatteo, 1997; Marteau & Weinman, 2004). Economic realities dictate that medical visits are generally quite brief, allowing little time for discussion. Many providers use too much medical jargon and overestimate their patients' understanding of technical terms. Patients who are upset and worried about their illness may simply forget to report some symptoms or to ask questions they meant to ask. Other patients are evasive about their real concerns because they fear a serious diagnosis. Many patients are reluctant to challenge doctors' authority and are too passive in their interactions with providers.

Communication between health care providers and patients tends to be far from optimal, for a variety of reasons.

What can you do to improve your communication with health care providers? The key is to not be a passive consumer of medical services (Ferguson, 1993; Kane, 1991). Arrive at a medical visit on time, with your questions and concerns prepared in advance. Try to be accurate and candid in replying to your doctor's questions. If you don't understand something the doctor says, don't be embarrassed about asking for clarification. If you have doubts about the suitability or feasibility of your doctor's recommendations, don't be afraid to voice them.

Adhering to Medical Advice

Many patients fail to adhere to the instructions they receive from physicians and other health care professionals. The evidence suggests that noncompliance with medical advice may occur 30% of the time when short-term treatments are prescribed for acute conditions and 50% of the time when long-term treatments are needed for chronic illness (Johnson & Carlson, 2004). Nonadherence takes many forms. Patients may fail to begin a treatment regimen, stop the regimen early, reduce or increase the levels of treatment that were prescribed, or be inconsistent and unreliable in following treatment procedures (Dunbar-Jacob & Schlenk, 2001). Nonadherence is a major problem in our medical care system that has been linked to increased sickness, treatment failures,

and higher mortality (Christensen & Johnson, 2002; DiMatteo et al., 2002). Moreover, nonadherence wastes expensive medical visits and medications and increases hospital admissions, leading to enormous economic costs. DiMatteo (2004b) speculates that in the United States alone, nonadherence may be a $300 billion a year drain on the health care system.

Concern about nonadherence does not mean that patients should passively accept all professional advice from medical personnel. However, when patients have doubts about a prescribed treatment, they should speak up and ask questions. Passive resistance can backfire. For instance, if a physician sees no improvement in a patient who falsely insists that he has been taking his medicine, the physician may abandon an accurate diagnosis in favor of an inaccurate one. The inaccurate diagnosis could then lead to inappropriate treatments that might be harmful to the patient.

Why don't people comply with the advice that they've sought out from highly regarded health care professionals? Physicians tend to attribute noncompliance to patients' personal characteristics, but research indicates that personality traits and demographic factors are surprisingly unrelated to adherence rates (DiMatteo, 2004b; Marteau & Weinman, 2004). One factor that *is* related to adherence is patients' *social support*. Adherence is improved when patients have family members, friends, or co-workers who remind them and help them to comply with treatment requirements (DiMatteo, 2004a). Several

Robin DiMatteo

"A person will not carry out a health behavior if significant barriers stand in the way, or if the steps interfere with favorite or necessary activities."

other considerations can adversely influence the likelihood of adherence (Dunbar-Jacob & Schlenk, 2001; Johnson & Carlson, 2004):

1. *Frequently, noncompliance is a result of the patient's failure to understand the instructions as given.* Highly trained professionals often forget that what seems obvious and simple to them may be obscure and complicated to many of their patients.

2. *Another key factor is how aversive or difficult the instructions are.* If the prescribed regimen is unpleasant, compliance will tend to decrease. And the more that following instructions interferes with routine behavior, the less probable it is that the patient will cooperate successfully.

3. *If a patient has a negative attitude toward a physician, the probability of noncompliance will increase.* When patients are unhappy with their interactions with the doctor, they're more likely to ignore the medical advice provided.

In response to the noncompliance problem, researchers have investigated many methods of increasing patients' adherence to medical advice. Interventions have included simplifying instructions, providing more rationale for instructions, reducing the complexity of treatment regimens, helping patients with emotional distress that undermines adherence, and training patients in the use of behavior modification strategies. All of these interventions can improve adherence, although their effects tend to be modest (Christensen & Johnson, 2002; Roter et al., 1998).

REVIEW of Key Points

13.20 People high in anxiety or neuroticism report more symptoms of illness than others. The biggest problem in regard to treatment seeking is the tendency of many people to delay the pursuit of needed treatment.

13.21 There are many barriers to effective communication between patients and health care providers, such as brief visits, overdependence on medical jargon, and patients' evasiveness

and forgetfulness. The key for patients in improving communication is to not be a passive consumer of medical services.

13.22 Noncompliance with medical advice is a major problem, which may occur 30% of the time in the context of short-term treatments and 50% of the time in long-term treatments. The likelihood of nonadherence is greater when instructions are difficult to understand, when recommendations are difficult to follow, and when patients are unhappy with their doctor.

Reflecting on the Chapter's Themes

Key Learning Goals

13.23 Identify the two unifying themes highlighted in this chapter.

Multifactorial Causation

Subjectivity of Experience

Which of our themes were prominent in this chapter? As you probably noticed, our discussion of stress and health illustrated multifactorial causation and the subjectivity of experience. As we noted in Chapter 1, people tend to think simplistically, in terms of single causes. In recent years, the highly publicized research linking stress to health has led many people to point automatically to stress as an explanation for illness. In reality, stress has only a modest impact on physical health. Stress can increase the risk for illness, but health is governed by a dense network of factors. Important factors include inherited vulnerabilities, physiological reactivity, exposure to infectious agents, health-impairing habits, reactions to symptoms, treatment-seeking behavior, compliance with medical advice, personality, and social support. In other words, stress is but one actor on a crowded stage. This should be apparent in **Figure 13.17**, which shows the multitude of biopsychosocial factors that jointly influence physical health. It illustrates multifactorial causation in all its complexity.

The subjectivity of experience was demonstrated by the frequently repeated point that stress lies in the eye of the beholder. The same job promotion may be stressful for one person and invigorating for another. One person's pressure is another's challenge. When it comes to stress, objective reality is not nearly as important as subjective perceptions. More than anything else, the impact of stressful events seems to depend on how people view them. The critical importance of individual stress appraisals will continue to be apparent in the Personal Application on coping and stress management. Many stress management strategies depend on altering one's appraisals of events.

REVIEW of Key Points

13.23 Two of our integrative themes were prominent in this chapter. First, we saw that behavior and health are influenced by multiple causes. Second, we saw that experience is highly subjective, as stress lies in the eye of the beholder.

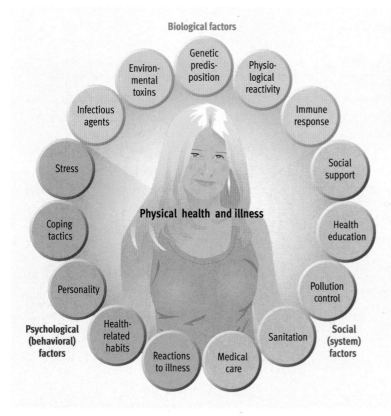

Biological factors

- Environmental toxins
- Genetic predisposition
- Physiological reactivity
- Immune response
- Infectious agents
- Social support
- Stress
- Health education
- Coping tactics
- Pollution control
- Personality
- Health-related habits
- Reactions to illness
- Medical care
- Sanitation
- Social (system) factors

Physical health and illness

Psychological (behavioral) factors

Figure 13.17

Biopsychosocial factors in health. Physical health can be influenced by a remarkably diverse set of variables, including biological, psychological, and social factors. The host of factors that affect health provide an excellent example of multifactorial causation.

Improving Coping and Stress Management

Answer the following "true" or "false."

____ **1** The key to managing stress is to avoid or circumvent it.

____ **2** It's best to suppress emotional reactions to stress.

____ **3** Laughing at one's problems is immature.

Courses and books on stress management have multiplied at a furious pace in the last couple of decades. They summarize experts' advice on how to cope with stress more effectively. How do these experts feel about the three statements above? As you'll see in this Application, most would agree that all three are false.

The key to managing stress does *not* lie in avoiding it. Stress is an inevitable element in the fabric of modern life. As Hans Selye (1973) noted, "Contrary to public opinion, we must not—and indeed can't—avoid stress" (p. 693). Thus, most stress management programs encourage people

to confront stress rather than sidestep it. Doing so requires training people to engage in action-oriented, rational, reality-based *constructive coping.* Fortunately, research suggests that stress management training can be beneficial in reducing the potential negative effects of stress (Evers et al., 2006; Storch et al., 2007).

As we noted earlier, some coping tactics are more healthful than others. In this Application, we'll examine a variety of constructive coping tactics, beginning with Albert Ellis's ideas about changing one's appraisals of stressful events.

Reappraisal: Ellis's Rational Thinking

Albert Ellis is a prominent theorist who believes that people can short-circuit their emotional reactions to stress by altering their appraisals of stressful events. Ellis's insights about stress appraisal are the foun-

PERSONAL

APPLICATION

Key Learning Goals

13.24 Summarize Albert Ellis's ideas about controlling one's emotions.

13.25 Analyze the adaptive value of humor, releasing pent-up emotions, and forgiving others.

13.26 Assess the adaptive value of relaxation and increasing one's fitness.

dation for a widely used system of therapy, called *rational-emotive behavior therapy* (Ellis, 1977, 1987), and several popular books on effective coping (Ellis, 1985, 1999, 2001).

Ellis maintains that *you feel the way you think.* He argues that problematic emotional reactions are caused by negative self-talk, which he calls catastrophic thinking. *Catastrophic thinking* involves unrealistically pessimistic appraisals of stress that exaggerate the magnitude of one's problems. According to Ellis, people unwittingly believe that stressful events cause their emotional turmoil, but he maintains that emotional reactions to personal setbacks are

Figure 13.18

Albert Ellis's A-B-C model of emotional reactions. Although most people attribute their negative emotional reactions directly to negative events that they experience, Ellis argues that events themselves do *not* cause emotional distress; rather, distress is caused by the way people *think* about negative events. According to Ellis, the key to managing stress is to change one's appraisal of stressful events.

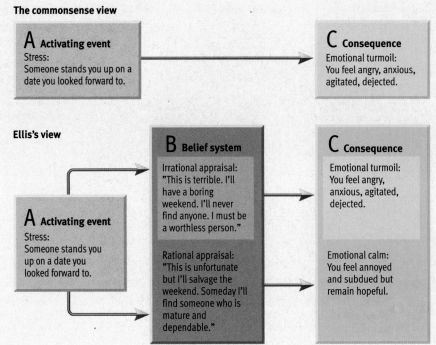

The commonsense view

A Activating event
Stress:
Someone stands you up on a date you looked forward to.

C Consequence
Emotional turmoil:
You feel angry, anxious, agitated, dejected.

Ellis's view

A Activating event
Stress:
Someone stands you up on a date you looked forward to.

B Belief system
Irrational appraisal:
"This is terrible. I'll have a boring weekend. I'll never find anyone. I must be a worthless person."

Rational appraisal:
"This is unfortunate but I'll salvage the weekend. Someday I'll find someone who is mature and dependable."

C Consequence
Emotional turmoil:
You feel angry, anxious, agitated, dejected.

Emotional calm:
You feel annoyed and subdued but remain hopeful.

actually caused by overly negative appraisals of stressful events (see **Figure 13.18**).

Ellis theorizes that unrealistic appraisals of stress are derived from irrational assumptions that people hold. He maintains that if you scrutinize your catastrophic thinking, you'll find that your reasoning is based on a logically indefensible premise, such as "I must have approval from everyone" or "I must perform well in all endeavors." These faulty assumptions, which people often hold unconsciously, generate catastrophic thinking and emotional turmoil. How can you reduce your unrealistic appraisals of stress? Ellis asserts that you must learn (1) how to detect catastrophic thinking and (2) how to dispute the irrational assumptions that cause it.

Using Humor as a Stress Reducer

A number of years ago, the Chicago area experienced its worst flooding in about a century. Thousands of people saw their homes wrecked when two rivers spilled over their banks. As the waters receded, the flood victims returning to their homes were subjected to the inevitable TV interviews. A remarkable number of victims, surrounded by the ruins of their homes, *joked* about their misfortune. When the going gets tough, it may pay to laugh about it. In a study of coping styles, McCrae (1984) found that 40% of his subjects used humor to deal with stress.

Empirical evidence showing that humor moderates the impact of stress has been accumulating over the last 25 years (Abel, 1998; Lefcourt, 2001). How does humor help to reduce the effects of stress and promote wellness? Several explanations have been proposed (see **Figure 13.19**). One possibility

People often turn to humor to help themselves cope during difficult times, as this photo taken in the aftermath of Hurricane Katrina illustrates. Research suggests that humor can help to reduce the negative impact of stressful events.

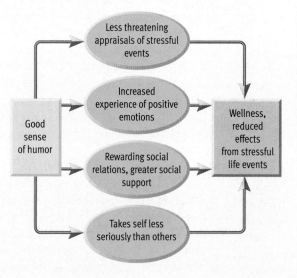

Figure 13.19

Possible explanations for the link between humor and wellness. Research suggests that a good sense of humor buffers the effects of stress and promotes wellness. Four hypothesized explanations for the link between humor and wellness are outlined in the middle column of this diagram. As you can see, humor may have a variety of beneficial effects.

Although there's no guarantee of it, you can sometimes reduce your physiological arousal by *expressing* your emotions. Evidence is accumulating that writing or talking about life's difficulties can be valuable in dealing with stress (Lyubomirsky, Sousa, & Dickerhoof, 2006; Smyth & Pennebaker, 1999). For example, in one study of college students, half the subjects were asked to write three essays about their difficulties in adjusting to college. The other half wrote three essays about superficial topics. The subjects who wrote about their personal problems enjoyed better health in the following months than the other subjects did (Pennebaker, Colder, & Sharp, 1990). Subsequent studies have replicated this finding and shown that emotional disclosure is associated with better immune functioning (Slatcher & Pennebaker, 2005; Smyth & Pennebaker, 2001). So, if you can find a good listener, you may be able to discharge problematic emotions by letting your secret fears, misgivings, and suspicions spill out in a candid conversation.

People tend to experience hostility and other negative emotions when they feel "wronged"—that is, when they believe that

is that humor affects appraisals of stressful events (Abel, 2002). Jokes can help people to put a less threatening spin on their trials and tribulations. Another possibility is that humor increases the experience of positive emotions (Martin, 2002), which can help people bounce back from stressful events (Tugade & Fredrickson, 2004). Another hypothesis is that a good sense of humor facilitates rewarding social interactions, which promote social support, which is known to buffer the effects of stress (Martin, 2002). Finally, Lefcourt and colleagues (1995) argue that high-humor people may benefit from not taking themselves as seriously as low-humor people do. As they put it, "If persons do not regard themselves too seriously and do not have an inflated sense of self-importance, then defeats, embarrassments, and even tragedies should have less pervasive emotional consequences for them" (p. 375).

Releasing Pent-Up Emotions and Forgiving Others

As we discussed in the main body of the chapter, stress often leads to emotional arousal. When this happens, there's merit in the commonsense notion that you should try to release the emotions welling up inside. Why? Because the physiological arousal that accompanies emotions can become problematic. For example, research suggests that people who inhibit the expression of anger and other emotions are

somewhat more likely than other people to have elevated blood pressure (Jorgensen et al., 1996). Moreover, research suggests that efforts to actively suppress emotions result in increased stress and autonomic arousal (Butler et al., 2003; Gross, 2001) and, ultimately, the experience of more negative emotions and fewer positive emotions (John & Gross, 2007).

In September 1994, Reg and Maggie Green were vacationing in Italy when their seven-year-old son Nicholas was shot and killed during a highway robbery. In an act of forgiveness that stunned Europe, the Greens chose to donate their son's organs, which went to seven Italians. The Greens, shown here five years after the incident, have weathered their horrific loss better than most, perhaps in part because of their willingness to forgive.

© Acey Harper/Time Life Pictures/Getty Images

the actions of another person were harmful, immoral, or unjust. People's natural inclination in such situations is either to seek revenge or to avoid further contact with the offender (McCullough, 2001). *Forgiving* someone involves counteracting these natural tendencies and releasing the person from further liability for his or her transgression. Research suggests that forgiving is associated with better adjustment and well-being (McCullough & Witvliet, 2002; Worthington & Scherer, 2004), including enhanced mood and reduced physical symptoms (Bono, McCullough, & Root, 2008). For example, in one study of divorced or permanently separated women reported by McCullough (2001), the extent to which the women had forgiven their former husbands was positively related to several measures of well-being and inversely related to measures of anxiety and depression. Research also shows that vengefulness is correlated with more rumination and negative emotion and with lower life satisfaction (McCullough et al., 2001). Taken together, these findings suggest that it may be healthful for people to learn to forgive others more readily.

Learning to Relax

Relaxation is a valuable stress management technique that can soothe emotional turmoil and reduce problematic physiological arousal (McGuigan & Lehrer, 2007; Smith, 2007). The value of relaxation became apparent to Herbert Benson (1975; Benson & Klipper, 1988) as a result of his research on meditation. Benson, a Harvard Medical School cardiologist, believes that relaxation is the key to the beneficial effects of meditation. According to Benson, the elaborate religious rituals and beliefs associated with meditation are irrelevant to its effects. After "demystifying" meditation, Benson set out to devise a simple, nonreligious procedure that could provide similar benefits. He calls his procedure the *relaxation response*. Although there are several other worthwhile approaches to relaxation training, we'll examine Benson's procedure, as its simplicity makes it especially useful. From his study of a variety of relaxation techniques, Benson concluded that four factors promote effective relaxation:

1. *A quiet environment.* It's easiest to induce the relaxation response in a distraction-free environment. After you become experienced with the relaxation response, you may be able to practice it in a crowded subway. Initially, however, you should practice it in a quiet, calm place.

2. *A mental device.* To shift attention inward and keep it there, you need to focus your attention on a constant stimulus, such as a sound or word recited repetitively.

3. *A passive attitude.* It's important not to get upset when your attention strays to distracting thoughts. You must realize that such distractions are inevitable. Whenever your mind wanders from your attentional focus, calmly redirect attention to your mental device.

4. *A comfortable position.* Reasonable body comfort is essential to avoid a major source of potential distraction. Simply sitting up straight generally works well. Lying down is too conducive to sleep.

Benson's simple relaxation procedure is described in **Figure 13.20**. For full benefit, it should be practiced daily.

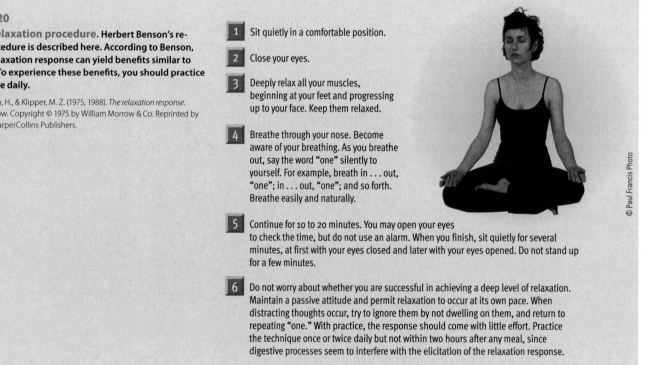

Figure 13.20

Benson's relaxation procedure. Herbert Benson's relaxation procedure is described here. According to Benson, his simple relaxation response can yield benefits similar to meditation. To experience these benefits, you should practice the procedure daily.

SOURCE: Benson, H., & Klipper, M. Z. (1975, 1988). *The relaxation response.* New York: Morrow. Copyright © 1975 by William Morrow & Co. Reprinted by permission of HarperCollins Publishers.

1   Sit quietly in a comfortable position.

2   Close your eyes.

3   Deeply relax all your muscles, beginning at your feet and progressing up to your face. Keep them relaxed.

4   Breathe through your nose. Become aware of your breathing. As you breathe out, say the word "one" silently to yourself. For example, breath in . . . out, "one"; in . . . out, "one"; and so forth. Breathe easily and naturally.

5   Continue for 10 to 20 minutes. You may open your eyes to check the time, but do not use an alarm. When you finish, sit quietly for several minutes, at first with your eyes closed and later with your eyes opened. Do not stand up for a few minutes.

6   Do not worry about whether you are successful in achieving a deep level of relaxation. Maintain a passive attitude and permit relaxation to occur at its own pace. When distracting thoughts occur, try to ignore them by not dwelling on them, and return to repeating "one." With practice, the response should come with little effort. Practice the technique once or twice daily but not within two hours after any meal, since digestive processes seem to interfere with the elicitation of the relaxation response.

© Paul Francis Photo

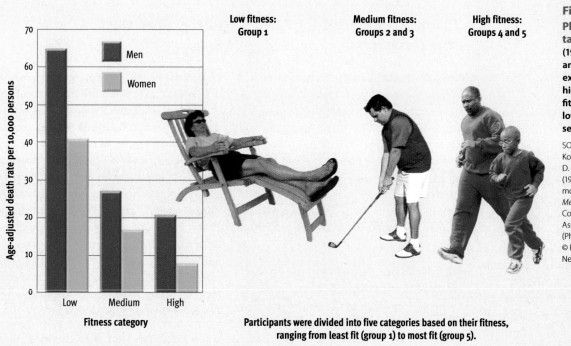

Figure 13.21

Figure 13.21

Physical fitness and mortality. Blair and colleagues (1989) studied death rates among men and women who exhibited low, medium, or high fitness. As you can see, fitness was associated with lower mortality rates in both sexes.

SOURCE: Adapted from Blair, S. N., Kohl, W. H., Paffenbarger, R. S., Clark, D. G., Cooper, K. H., & Gibbons, L. W. (1989). Physical fitness and all-cause mortality. *Journal of the American Medical Association, 262,* 2395–2401. Copyright © 1989 American Medical Association. Reprinted by permission. (Photos: left, © C. H. Wooley; middle, © Paul Francis Photo; right, © Michael Newman/PhotoEdit)

Low fitness:
Group 1

Medium fitness:
Groups 2 and 3

High fitness:
Groups 4 and 5

Participants were divided into five categories based on their fitness, ranging from least fit (group 1) to most fit (group 5).

Minimizing Physiological Vulnerability

Your body is intimately involved in your response to stress, and the wear and tear of stress can be injurious to your health. To combat this potential problem, it helps to keep your body in relatively sound shape. It's a good idea to consume a nutritionally balanced diet, get adequate sleep, and engage in at least a moderate amount of exercise. It's also a good idea to learn how to control overeating and the use of tobacco, alcohol, and other drugs. Good health habits will not make you immune to the ravages of stress. However, poor health habits generally will increase your vulnerability to stress-related diseases. We've discussed sleep patterns, drug use, and eating habits in other chapters, so the coverage here will focus exclusively on exercise.

The potential benefits of regular exercise are substantial. Fortunately, evidence indicates that you don't have to be a dedicated athlete to benefit from exercise. Even a mod-

erate amount of exercise—such as taking a brisk, half-hour walk each day—can reduce your risk of disease (Richardson et al., 2004; see **Figure 13.21**). Successful participation in an exercise program can also lead to improvements in your mood and ability to deal with stress (Hays, 1999; Plante, 1999b).

Embarking on an exercise program is difficult for many people. Exercise is time-consuming, and if you're out of shape, your initial attempts may be discouraging. People who do not get enough exercise cite lack of time, lack of convenience, and lack of enjoyment as their reasons (Jackicic & Gallagher, 2002). To circumvent these problems, it is wise to heed the following advice (Greenberg, 2002; Jackicic & Gallagher, 2002; Phillips, Kiernan, & King, 2001):

1. Select an activity that you find enjoyable.
2. Increase your participation gradually.
3. Exercise regularly without overdoing it.
4. Reinforce yourself for your efforts.

If you choose a competitive sport (such as tennis), try to avoid falling into the competition trap. If you become obsessed with winning, you'll put yourself under pressure and *add* to the stress in your life.

REVIEW of Key Points

13.24 Ellis emphasizes the importance of reappraising stressful events to detect and dispute catastrophic thinking. According to Ellis, emotional distress is often attributable to irrational assumptions that underlie one's thinking.

13.25 Humor may be useful in efforts to redefine stressful situations. In some cases, releasing pent-up emotions may pay off. Talking the anger out may help drain off negative emotions and foster better health. Stress can also be reduced by learning to be more forgiving toward others.

13.26 Relaxation techniques, such as Benson's relaxation response, can reduce the wear and tear of stress. Physical vulnerability may also be reduced by striving to increase one's fitness through healthy eating, sleeping, and exercise.

Key Learning Goals

13.27 Understand important considerations
in evaluating health statistics and making health
decisions.

Thinking Rationally About Health Statistics and Decisions

With so many conflicting claims about the best ways to prevent or treat diseases, how can anyone ever decide what to do? It seems that every day a report in the media claims that yesterday's health news was wrong. The inconsistency of health news is only part of the problem. We are also overwhelmed by health-related statistics. As mathematics pundit John Allen Paulos (1995, p. 133) puts it, "Health statistics may be bad for our mental health. Inundated by too many of them, we tend to ignore them completely, to accept them blithely, to disbelieve them closemindedly, or simply to misinterpret their significance."

Making personal decisions about health-related issues may not be easy, but it is particularly important to try to think rationally and systematically about such issues. In this Application, we will discuss a few insights that can help you to think critically about statistics on health risks, then we'll briefly outline a systematic approach to thinking through health decisions.

Evaluating Statistics on Health Risks

News reports seem to suggest that there are links between virtually everything people do, touch, and consume and some type of physical illness. For example, media have reported that coffee consumption is related to hypertension, that sleep loss is related to mortality, and that a high-fat diet is related to heart disease. It's enough to send even the most subdued person into a panic. Fortunately, your evaluation of data on health risks can become more sophisticated by considering the following.

Correlation Is No Assurance of Causation. It is not easy to conduct experiments on health risks, so the vast majority

of studies linking lifestyle and demographic factors to diseases are correlational studies. Hence, it pays to remember that no causal link may exist between two variables that happen to be correlated. Thus, when you hear that a factor is related to some disease, try to dig a little deeper and find out *why* scientists think this factor is associated with the disease. The suspected causal factor may be something very different from what was measured.

Statistical Significance Is Not Equivalent to Practical Significance. Reports on health statistics often emphasize that the investigators uncovered "statistically significant" findings. Statistically significant findings are results that are not likely to be due to chance fluctuations (see Chapter 2). Statistical significance is a useful concept, but it can sometimes be misleading (Matthey, 1998). Medical studies are often based on rather large samples, because such samples tend to yield more reliable conclusions than small samples. However, when a large sample is used, weak relationships and small differences between groups can turn out to

be statistically significant, and these small differences may not have much practical importance. For example, in one study of sodium (salt) intake and cardiovascular disease, which used a sample of over 14,000 participants, He et al. (1999) found a statistically significant link between high sodium intake and the prevalence of hypertension among normal-weight subjects. However, this statistically significant difference was not particularly large. The prevalence of hypertension among subjects with the lowest sodium intake was 19.1% compared to 21.8% for subjects with the highest sodium intake—not exactly a difference worthy of panic.

Base Rates Should Be Considered in Evaluating Probabilities. In evaluating whether a possible risk factor is associated with some disease, people often fail to consider the base rates of these events and draw far-reaching conclusions based on what may be a matter of sheer coincidence. For example, Paulos (1995) discusses how a handful of cases in which cell phone users developed brain cancer led to unfounded allegations that cell phones cause brain cancer.

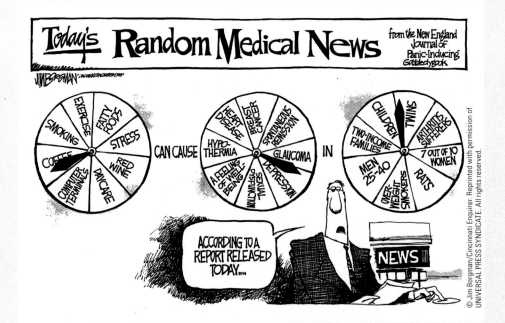

Brain cancer is a rare disease, striking only about 6 out of 100,000 Americans per year. But given that many millions of Americans use cell phones, one would expect to find thousands upon thousands of new cases of brain cancer annually among cell phone users. Given the small number of reported cases, Paulos playfully concludes that cell phones must prevent brain cancer.

It is also useful to consider base rates in evaluating percentage increases in diseases. If the base rate of a disease is relatively low, a small increase can sound quite large if it is reported as a percentage. For example, in the He et al. (1999) study, the prevalence of diabetes among subjects with the lowest sodium intake was 2.1% compared to 3.8% for subjects with the highest sodium intake. Based on this small but statistically significant difference, one could say (the investigators did not) that high sodium intake was associated with a 81% increase ([3.8 − 2.1] ÷ 2.1) in the prevalence of diabetes, which would be technically accurate, but an exaggerated way of portraying the results.

Thinking Systematically About Health Decisions

Health decisions are oriented toward the future, which means that there are always uncertainties. And such decisions usually involve weighing potential risks and ben-

efits. None of these variables is unique to health decisions—uncertainty, risks, and benefits play prominent roles in economic and political decisions as well as in personal decisions. To illustrate, let's apply some basic principles of quantitative reasoning to a treatment decision involving whether to prescribe Ritalin for a boy who has been diagnosed with attention deficit disorder (ADD). Keep in mind that the general principles applied in this example can be used for a wide variety of decisions.

Seek Information to Reduce Uncertainty. Gather information and check it carefully for accuracy, completeness, and the presence or absence of conflicting information. For example, is the diagnosis of ADD correct? Look for conflicting information that does not fit with this diagnosis. For example, if the child can sit and read for a long period of time, maybe the problem is an undetected hearing loss that makes him appear to be hyperactive in some situations. As you consider the additional information, begin quantifying the degree of uncertainty or its "flip side," your degree of confidence that the diagnosis is correct. If you decide that you are not confident about the diagnosis, you may be trying to solve the wrong problem.

Make Risk-Benefit Assessments. What are the risks and benefits of Ritalin? How

likely is this child to benefit from Ritalin, and just how much improvement can be expected? If the child is 8 years old and unable to read and is miserable in school and at home, any treatment that could reduce his problems deserves serious consideration. As in the first step, the quantification is at an approximate level.

List Alternative Courses of Action. What are the alternatives to Ritalin? How well do they work? What are the risks associated with the alternatives, including the risk of falling further behind in school? Consider the pros and cons of each alternative. A special diet that sometimes works might be a good first step, along with the decision to start drug therapy if the child does not show improvement over some time period. What are the relative success rates for various types of treatment for children like the one being considered? To answer these questions, you will need to use probability estimates in your decision making.

As you can see from this example, many parts of the problem have been quantified (confidence in the diagnosis, likelihood of improvement, probability of negative outcomes, and so forth). Precise probability values were not used because the actual numbers often are not known. Some of the quantified values reflect value judgments, others reflect likelihoods, and others assess the degree of uncertainty. If you are thinking that the quantification of many unknowns in decision making is a lot of work, you are right. But, it is work worth doing. Whenever important decisions must be made about health, the ability to think with numbers will help you reach a better decision. And yes, that assertion is a virtual certainty.

Table 13.4 Critical Thinking Skills Discussed in This Application

Skill	Description
Understanding the limitations of correlational evidence	The critical thinker understands that a correlation between two variables does not demonstrate that there is a causal link between the variables.
Understanding the limitations of statistical significance	The critical thinker understands that weak relationships can be statistically significant when large samples are used in research.
Utilizing base rates in making predictions and evaluating probabilities	The critical thinker appreciates that the initial proportion of some group or event needs to be considered in weighing probabilities.
Seeking information to reduce uncertainty	The critical thinker understands that gathering more information can often decrease uncertainty, and reduced uncertainty can facilitate better decisions.
Making risk-benefit assessments	The critical thinker is aware that most decisions have risks and benefits that need to be weighed carefully.
Generating and evaluating alternative courses of action	In problem solving and decision making, the critical thinker knows the value of generating as many alternatives as possible and assessing their advantages and disadvantages.

Key Ideas

The Nature of Stress

▌ Stress is a common, everyday event, and even seemingly minor stressors or hassles can be problematic. To a large degree, stress lies in the eye of the beholder, as appraisals of stress are highly subjective.

▌ Major types of stress include frustration, conflict, change, and pressure. Frustration occurs when an obstacle prevents one from attaining some goal. The three principal types of conflict are approach-approach, avoidance-avoidance, and approach-avoidance.

▌ A large number of studies with the SRRS suggest that change is stressful. Although this may be true, it is now clear that the SRRS is a measure of general stress rather than just change-related stress. Two kinds of pressure (to perform and conform) also appear to be stressful.

Responding to Stress

▌ Emotional reactions to stress typically include anger, fear, and sadness, although positive emotions may also occur and may promote resilience. Emotional arousal may interfere with coping. The optimal level of arousal on a task depends on the complexity of the task.

▌ Physiological arousal in response to stress was originally called the fight-or-flight response by Cannon. The fight-or-flight response may be less applicable to women than men. Selye's general adaptation syndrome describes three stages in physiological reactions to stress: alarm, resistance, and exhaustion.

▌ There are two major pathways along which the brain sends signals to the endocrine system in response to stress. Actions along these paths release two sets of hormones, catecholamines and corticosteroids, into the bloodstream. Stress may suppress the process of neurogenesis.

▌ Some coping responses are less than optimal. They include giving up, blaming oneself, and striking out at others with acts of aggression. Indulging oneself is another coping pattern that tends to be of limited value. Defense mechanisms protect against emotional distress through self-deception. Small positive illusions about oneself may sometimes be adaptive.

The Effects of Stress on Psychological Functioning

▌ Common negative effects of stress in terms of psychological functioning include impaired task performance, burnout, and a variety of other psychological problems and disorders. Stress may also have positive effects, stimulating personal growth and the acquisition of new strengths. Resilience may be more common than assumed.

The Effects of Stress on Physical Health

▌ The Type A personality has been implicated as a contributing cause of coronary heart disease, but hostility may be the toxic element of the Type A syndrome. Transient emotional reactions to stressful events and depression have also been identified as cardiovascular risk factors.

▌ Stress may play a role in a variety of diseases because it can temporarily suppress the effectiveness of the immune system and promote inflammation. Although there's little doubt that stress can contribute to the development of physical illness, the link between stress and illness is modest.

Factors Moderating the Impact of Stress

▌ Social support is a key moderator of the relationship between stress and illness; it is associated with better mental and physical health and with reduced mortality. Optimism may lead to more effective coping strategies, and conscientiousness may promote better health habits.

Health-Impairing Behavior

▌ People display many forms of health-impairing behavior. Smokers have much higher mortality rates than nonsmokers because they are more vulnerable to a host of diseases.

▌ Poor nutritional habits have been linked to heart disease, hypertension, and cancer, among other things. Lack of exercise elevates one's risk for cardiovascular diseases, whereas regular exercise is associated with a host of benefits. Alcohol and drug use carry the immediate risk of overdose and elevate the long-term risk of many diseases.

▌ Aspects of behavior also influence one's risk of AIDS. Misconceptions about AIDS are common, and the people who hold these misconceptions tend to fall into polarized camps, either overestimating or underestimating their risk of infection. Health-impairing habits tend to develop gradually and often involve pleasant activities.

Reactions to Illness

▌ Ignoring physical symptoms may result in the delay of needed medical treatment. There are many barriers to effective communication between patients and health care providers. Noncompliance with medical advice is a major problem.

Reflecting on the Chapter's Themes

▌ Two of our integrative themes were prominent in this chapter. First, we saw that behavior and health are influenced by multiple causes. Second, we saw that experience is highly subjective, as stress lies in the eye of the beholder.

PERSONAL APPLICATION Improving Coping and Stress Management

▌ Action-oriented, realistic, constructive coping can be helpful in managing the stress of daily life. Ellis emphasizes the importance of reappraising stressful events to detect and dispute catastrophic thinking. Humor may be useful in efforts to redefine stressful situations.

▌ In some cases, it may pay to release pent-up emotions by expressing them. Forgiving others' transgressions can also reduce stress. Relaxation techniques, such as Benson's relaxation response, can be helpful in stress management. Regular exercise can help make one less vulnerable to the ravages of stress.

CRITICAL THINKING APPLICATION Thinking Rationally About Health Statistics and Decisions

▌ Evaluations of statistics on health risks can be enhanced by remembering that correlation is no assurance of causation, that statistical significance is not equivalent to practical significance, and that base rates need to be considered in assessing probabilities. In trying to think systematically about health decisions, one should seek information to reduce uncertainty, make risk-benefit assessments, and consider alternative courses of action.

Key Terms

Acquired immune deficiency
  syndrome (AIDS) (p. 560)
Acute stressors (p. 535)
Aggression (p. 545)
Approach-approach conflict
  (p. 536)
Approach-avoidance conflict
  (p. 536)
Avoidance-avoidance conflict
  (p. 536)
Biopsychosocial model (p. 533)
Burnout (p. 549)
Catastrophic thinking (p. 565)
Catharsis (p. 545)
Chronic stressors (p. 535)
Conflict (p. 536)
Constructive coping (p. 547)
Coping (p. 544)
Defense mechanisms (p. 546)
Fight-or-flight response (p. 542)
Frustration (p. 535)
General adaptation syndrome
  (p. 542)
Health psychology (p. 534)
Immune response (p. 554)
Internet addiction (p. 546)
Learned helplessness (p. 544)
Life changes (p. 537)
Neurogenesis (p. 544)
Optimism (p. 557)
Pressure (p. 538)
Psychosomatic diseases (p. 551)
Social support (p. 556)
Stress (p. 534)
Type A personality (p. 551)
Type B personality (p. 551)

Key People

Walter Cannon (p. 542)
Robin DiMatteo (pp. 562–563)
Albert Ellis (pp. 545, 565–566)
Meyer Friedmpan and Ray
  Rosenman (p. 551)
Thomas Holmes and Richard
  Rahe (pp. 537–538)
Janice Kiecolt-Glaser (pp. 554–555)
Richard Lazarus (p. 535)
Martin Seligman (p. 557)
Hans Selye (pp. 542–543)
Shelley Taylor (pp. 542, 547)

1. It is the weekend before a major psychology exam on Monday, and Janine is experiencing total panic even though she is thoroughly prepared and aced the previous two psychology exams. Janine's panic illustrates that:
   A. high arousal is optimal on complex tasks.
   B. the appraisal of stress is quite objective.
   C. the appraisal of stress is highly subjective.
   D. her adrenal cortex is malfunctioning.

2. The four principal types of stress are:
   A. frustration, conflict, pressure, and anxiety.
   B. frustration, anger, pressure, and change.
   C. anger, anxiety, depression, and annoyance.
   D. frustration, conflict, pressure, and change.

3. When your boss tells you that a complicated report that you have not yet begun to write must be on her desk by this afternoon, you may experience:
   A. burnout.　　　　　　　C. a double bind.
   B. pressure.　　　　　　　D. catharsis.

4. You want to ask someone for a date, but you are afraid to risk rejection. You are experiencing:
   A. an approach-avoidance conflict.
   B. an avoidance-avoidance conflict.
   C. frustration.
   D. self-imposed pressure.

5. Research suggests that a high level of arousal may be most optimal for the performance of a task when:
   A. the task is complex.
   B. the task is simple.
   C. the rewards are high.
   D. an audience is present.

6. The alarm stage of Hans Selye's general adaptation syndrome is essentially the same as:
   A. the fight-or-flight response.
   B. constructive coping.
   C. catharsis.
   D. secondary appraisal.

7. The brain structure responsible for initiating action along the two major pathways through which the brain sends signals to the endocrine system is the:
   A. hypothalamus.　　　　C. corpus callosum.
   B. thalamus.　　　　　　D. medulla.

8. You have been doing poorly in your psychology class and are in danger of flunking. Which of the following qualifies as a defense mechanism in response to this situation?
   A. You seek the aid of a tutor.
   B. You decide to withdraw from the class and take it another time.
   C. You deny the reality that you are hopelessly behind in the class, convinced that you will somehow ace the final without seeking help.
   D. You consult with the instructor to see what you can do to pass the class.

9. Physical and emotional exhaustion, cynicism, and lowered self-efficacy attributable to chronic work-related stress is referred to as:
   A. learned helplessness.
   B. burnout.
   C. fallout.
   D. posttraumatic stress disorder.

10. Which personality trait seems to be most strongly related to increased coronary risk?
    A. Type B personality
    B. perfectionism
    C. competitiveness
    D. hostility

11. Many students develop colds and other minor ailments during final exams. This probably happens because:
    A. stress is associated with the release of corticosteroid hormones.
    B. stress is associated with the release of catecholamine hormones.
    C. burnout causes colds.
    D. stress can suppress immune functioning.

12. Research has found that optimists are more likely than pessimists to:
    A. take their time in confronting problems.
    B. identify the negatives before they identify the positives.
    C. engage in action-oriented, problem-focused coping.
    D. blame others for their personal problems.

13. Which of the following has *not* been found to be a mode of transmission for the HIV virus?
    A. sexual contact among homosexual men
    B. the sharing of needles by intravenous drug users
    C. sexual contact among heterosexuals
    D. sharing food

14. According to Albert Ellis, problematic emotional reactions are caused by:
    A the fight-or-flight response.
    B. catharsis.
    C. catastrophic thinking.
    D. excessive reliance on defense mechanisms.

15. In evaluating health statistics, it is useful to:
    A. remember that statistical significance is equivalent to practical significance.
    B. remember that correlation is a reliable indicator of causation.
    C. consider base rates in thinking about probabilities.
    D. do all of the above.

Answers

1 C p. 535	6 A p. 542	11 D pp. 554–555
2 D pp. 535–538	7 A p. 543	12 C p. 557
3 B p. 538	8 C p. 546	13 D pp. 560–561
4 A p. 536	9 B p. 549	14 C pp. 565–566
5 B pp. 541–542	10 D pp. 551–552	15 C pp. 570–571

PsykTrek

To view a demo: www.cengage.com/psychology/psyktrek
To order: www.cengage.com/psychology/weiten
Go to the PsykTrek website or CD-ROM for further study of the concepts in this chapter. Both online and on the CD-ROM, PsykTrek includes dozens of learning modules with videos, animations, and quizzes, as well as simulations of psychological phenomena and a multimedia glossary that includes word pronunciations.

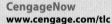

CengageNow

www.cengage.com/tlc

Go to this site for the link to CengageNOW, your one-stop study shop. Take a Pretest for this chapter, and CengageNOW will generate a personalized Study Plan based on your test results. The Study Plan will identify the topics you need to review and direct you to online resources to help you master those topics. You can then take a Posttest to help you determine the concepts you have mastered and what you still need to work on.

Companion Website

www.cengage.com/psychology/weiten

Go to this site to find online resources directly linked to your book, including a glossary, flash cards, drag-and-drop exercises, quizzes, and more!

14

PSYCHOLOGICAL
DISORDERS

Abnormal Behavior: Myths, Realities, and Controversies
The Medical Model Applied to Abnormal Behavior
Criteria of Abnormal Behavior
Stereotypes of Psychological Disorders
Psychodiagnosis: The Classification of Disorders
The Prevalence of Psychological Disorders

Anxiety Disorders
Generalized Anxiety Disorder
Phobic Disorder
Panic Disorder and Agoraphobia
Obsessive-Compulsive Disorder
Posttraumatic Stress Disorder
Etiology of Anxiety Disorders

Somatoform Disorders
Subtypes and Symptoms
Etiology of Somatoform Disorders

Dissociative Disorders
Dissociative Amnesia and Fugue
Dissociative Identity Disorder
Etiology of Dissociative Disorders

Mood Disorders
Major Depressive Disorder
Bipolar Disorder
Mood Disorders and Suicide
Etiology of Mood Disorders

FEATURED STUDY ▌ **Does Negative Thinking *Cause* Depression?**

Schizophrenic Disorders
General Symptoms
Subtypes, Course, and Outcome
Etiology of Schizophrenia

Personality Disorders
Diagnostic Problems
Antisocial Personality Disorder

Psychological Disorders and the Law
Insanity
Involuntary Commitment

Illustrated Overview of Three Categories of Psychological Disorders

Culture and Pathology
Are Equivalent Disorders Found Around the World?
Are Symptom Patterns Culturally Invariant?

Reflecting on the Chapter's Themes

PERSONAL APPLICATION ▌ **Understanding Eating Disorders**
Description
History and Prevalence
Etiology of Eating Disorders

CRITICAL THINKING APPLICATION ▌ **Working with Probabilities in Thinking About Mental Illness**

Recap

Practice Test

"The government of the United States was overthrown more than a year ago! I'm the president of the United States of America and Bob Dylan is vice president!" So said Ed, the author of a prominent book on journalism, who was speaking to a college journalism class, as a guest lecturer. Ed also informed the class that he had killed both John and Robert Kennedy, as well as Charles de Gaulle, the former president of France. He went on to tell the class that all rock music songs were written about him, that he was the greatest karate expert in the universe, and that he had been fighting "space wars" for 2000 years. The students in the class were mystified by Ed's bizarre, disjointed "lecture," but they assumed that he was putting on a show that would eventually lead to a sensible conclusion. However, their perplexed but expectant calm was shattered when Ed pulled a hatchet from the props he had brought with him and hurled the hatchet at the class! Fortunately, he didn't hit anyone, as the hatchet sailed over the students' heads. At that point,

the professor for the class realized that Ed's irrational behavior was not a pretense. The professor evacuated the class quickly while Ed continued to rant and rave about his presidential administration, space wars, vampires, his romances with female rock stars, and his personal harem of 38 "chicks." (Adapted from Pearce, 1974)

Clearly Ed's behavior was abnormal. Even *he* recognized that when he agreed later to be admitted to a mental hospital, signing himself in as the "President of the United States of America." What causes such abnormal behavior? Does Ed have a mental illness, or does he just behave strangely? What is the basis for judging behavior as normal versus abnormal? Are people who have psychological disorders dangerous? How common are such disorders? Can they be cured? These are just a few of the questions that we will address in this chapter as we discuss psychological disorders and their complex causes.

Abnormal Behavior: Myths, Realities, and Controversies

Key Learning Goals

14.1 Evaluate the medical model, and identify the most commonly used criteria of abnormality.

14.2 List three stereotypes of people with psychological disorders.

14.3 Outline the history and structure of the DSM diagnostic system.

14.4 Discuss estimates of the prevalence of psychological disorders.

Misconceptions about abnormal behavior are common. We therefore need to clear up some preliminary issues before we describe the various types of disorders. In this section, we will discuss (1) the medical model of abnormal behavior, (2) the criteria of abnormal behavior, (3) stereotypes regarding psychological disorders, (4) the classification of psychological disorders, and (5) the prevalence of such disorders.

The Medical Model Applied to Abnormal Behavior

In Ed's case, there's no question that his behavior was abnormal. But does it make sense to view his unusual and irrational behavior as an illness? This is a controversial question. **The *medical model* proposes that it is useful to think of abnormal behavior as a disease.** This point of view is the basis for many of the terms used to refer to abnormal behavior, including mental *illness*, psychological *disorder*, and psycho*pathology* (*pathology* refers to manifestations of disease). The medical model gradually became the dominant way of thinking about abnormal behavior during the 18th and 19th centuries, and its influence remains strong today.

The medical model clearly represented progress over earlier models of abnormal behavior. Prior to the 18th century, most conceptions of abnormal behavior were based on superstition. People who behaved strangely were thought to be possessed by demons, to be witches in league with the devil, or to be victims of God's punishment. Their disorders were "treated" with chants, rituals, exorcisms, and such. If the people's behavior was seen as threatening, they were candidates for chains, dungeons, torture, and death (see Figure 14.1).

The rise of the medical model brought improvements in the treatment of those who exhibited abnormal behavior. As victims of an illness, they were viewed with more sympathy and less hatred and fear. Although living conditions in early asylums were deplorable, gradual progress was made toward more humane care of the mentally ill. It took time, but ineffectual approaches to treatment eventually gave way to scientific investigation of the causes and cures of psychological disorders.

However, in recent decades, some critics have suggested that the medical model may have outlived its usefulness (Boyle, 2007; Kiesler, 1999). A particularly vocal critic has been Thomas Szasz (1974, 1990). He asserts that "strictly speaking, disease or illness can affect only the body; hence there can be no mental illness. . . . Minds can be 'sick' only in the sense that jokes are 'sick' or economies are 'sick'" (1974, p. 267). He further argues that abnormal behavior usually involves a deviation from social norms rather than an illness. He contends that such deviations are "problems in living" rather than medical problems. According to Szasz, the medical model's disease analogy converts moral and social questions about what is acceptable behavior into medical questions.

Although Szasz's criticism of the medical model has some merit, we'll take the position that the disease analogy continues to be useful, although one

Figure 14.1

Historical conceptions of mental illness. In the Middle Ages people who behaved strangely were sometimes thought to be in league with the devil. The top drawing depicts some of the cruel methods used to extract confessions from suspected witches and warlocks. Some psychological disorders were also thought to be caused by demonic possession. The bottom illustration depicts an exorcism.

SOURCE: (Right) Culver Pictures, Inc. (Below) *St. Catherine of Siena Exorcising a Possessed Woman*, c. 1500–1510. Girolamo Di Benvenuto. Denver Art Museum Collection, Gift of Samuel H. Kress Foundation Collection, 1967.171 © 2001 Denver Art Museum.

should remember that it is *only* an analogy. Medical concepts such as *diagnosis, etiology,* and *prognosis* have proven valuable in the treatment and study of abnormality. ***Diagnosis involves distinguishing one illness from another. Etiology refers to the apparent causation and developmental history of an illness. A*** *prognosis* **is a forecast about the probable course of an illness.** These medically based concepts have widely shared meanings that permit clinicians, researchers, and the public to communicate more effectively in their discussions of abnormal behavior.

Criteria of Abnormal Behavior

If your next-door neighbor scrubs his front porch twice a day and spends virtually all his time cleaning and recleaning his house, is he normal? If your sister-in-law goes to one physician after another seeking treatment for physical ailments that appear imaginary, is she psychologically healthy? How are we to judge what's normal and what's abnormal? More important, who's to do the judging?

These are complex questions. In a sense, *all* people make judgments about normality in that they all express opinions about others' (and perhaps their own) mental health. Of course, formal diagnoses of psychological disorders are made by mental health professionals. In making these diagnoses, clinicians rely on a variety of criteria, the foremost of which are the following:

1. *Deviance.* As Szasz has pointed out, people are often said to have a disorder because their behavior deviates from what their society considers acceptable. What constitutes normality varies somewhat from one culture to another, but all cultures have such norms. When people violate these standards and expectations, they may be labeled mentally ill. For example, *transvestic fetishism* is a sexual disorder in which a man achieves sexual arousal by dressing in women's clothing. This behavior is regarded as disordered because a man who wears a dress, brassiere, and nylons is deviating from our culture's norms.

2. *Maladaptive behavior.* In many cases, people are judged to have a psychological disorder because their everyday adaptive behavior is impaired. This is the key criterion in the diagnosis of substance use (drug) disorders. In and of itself, alcohol and drug use is not all that unusual or deviant. However, when the use of cocaine, for instance, begins to interfere with a person's social or occupational functioning, a substance use disorder exists. In such cases, it is the maladaptive quality of the behavior that makes it disordered.

3. *Personal distress.* Frequently, the diagnosis of a psychological disorder is based on an individual's report of great personal distress. This is usually the criterion met by people who are troubled by depression or anxiety disorders. Depressed people, for instance, may or may not exhibit deviant or maladaptive behavior. Such people are usually labeled as having a disorder when they describe their subjective pain and suffering to friends, relatives, and mental health professionals.

Although two or three criteria may apply in a particular case, people are often viewed as disordered when only one criterion is met. As you may have already noticed, diagnoses of psychological disorders involve *value judgments* about what represents normal or abnormal behavior (Sadler, 2005; Widiger & Sankis, 2000). The criteria of mental illness are not nearly as value-free as the criteria of physical illness. In evaluating physical diseases, people can usually agree that a malfunctioning heart or kidney is pathological, regardless of their personal values. However, judgments about mental illness reflect prevailing cultural values, social trends, and political forces, as well as scientific knowledge (Kutchins & Kirk, 1997; Mechanic, 1999).

Antonyms such as *normal* versus *abnormal* and *mental health* versus *mental illness* imply that people can be divided neatly into two distinct groups: those who are normal and those who are not. In reality, it is often difficult to draw a line that clearly separates normality from abnormality. On occasion, everybody acts in deviant ways, everyone displays some maladaptive behavior, and everyone experiences personal

Courtesy of Thomas Szasz

Thomas Szasz
"Minds can be 'sick' only in the sense that jokes are 'sick' or economies are 'sick.'"

web link 14.1

MentalHelp.Net

This is arguably the premier site to explore all aspects of mental health, including psychological disorders and treatment, professional issues, and information for consumers. It is a great starting point, with links to more than 8000 resources.

This man clearly exhibits a certain type of deviance, but does that mean that he has a psychological disorder? The critieria of mental illness are more subjective and complicated than most people realize, and to some extent, judgments of mental health represent value judgments.

distress. People are judged to have psychological disorders only when their behavior becomes *extremely* deviant, maladaptive, or distressing. Thus, normality and abnormality exist on a continuum. It's a matter of degree, not an either-or proposition (see Figure 14.2).

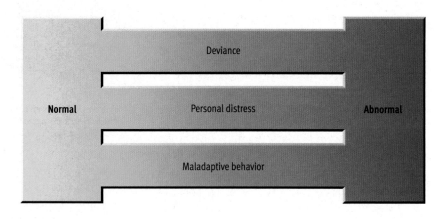

Figure 14.2

Normality and abnormality as a continuum. No sharp boundary exists between normal and abnormal behavior. Behavior is normal or abnormal in degree, depending on the extent to which one's behavior is deviant, personally distressing, or maladaptive.

---

concept check 14.1

Applying the Criteria of Abnormal Behavior

Check your understanding of the criteria of abnormal behavior by identifying the criteria met by each of the examples below and checking them off in the table provided. Keep in mind that a specific behavior may meet more than one criterion. The answers are in Appendix A.

Behavioral examples

1. Alan's performance at work has suffered because he has been drinking alcohol to excess. Several co-workers have suggested that he seek help for his problem, but he thinks that they're getting alarmed over nothing. "I just enjoy a good time once in a while," he says.

2. Monica has gone away to college and feels lonely, sad, and dejected. Her grades are fine, and she gets along okay with the other students in the dormitory, but inside she's choked with gloom, hopelessness, and despair.

3. Boris believes that he's Napoleon reborn. He believes that he is destined to lead the U.S. military forces into a great battle to recover California from space aliens.

4. Natasha panics with anxiety whenever she leaves her home. Her problem escalated gradually until she was absent from work so often that she was fired. She hasn't been out of her house in nine months and is deeply troubled by her problem.

Criteria met by each example

	Maladaptive behavior	Deviance	Personal distress
1. Alan	____	____	____
2. Monica	____	____	____
3. Boris	____	____	____
4. Natasha	____	____	____

Stereotypes of Psychological Disorders

We've seen that mental illnesses are not diseases in a strict sense and that judgments of mental health are not value-free. However, still other myths about abnormal behavior need to be exposed as such. Let's examine three stereotypes about psychological disorders that are largely inaccurate:

1. *Psychological disorders are incurable.* Admittedly, there are mentally ill people for whom treatment is largely a failure. However, they are greatly outnumbered by people who do get better, either spontaneously or through formal treatment (Lambert & Ogles, 2004). The vast majority of people who are diagnosed as mentally ill eventually improve and lead normal, productive lives. Even the most severe psychological disorders can be treated successfully.

2. *People with psychological disorders are often violent and dangerous.* Only a modest association has been found between mental illness and violence-prone tendencies (Monahan, 1997; Tardiff, 1999). This stereotype exists because incidents of violence involving the mentally ill tend to command media attention. For example, our opening case history, which described Ed's breakdown and the episode with the hatchet, was written up in a national news magazine. People such as John Hinckley, Jr., whose mental illness led him to attempt an assassination of President Ronald Reagan in 1981, and Seung-Hui Cho, whose mental disorder led him to massacre 32 fellow students at Virginia Tech University, receive enormous publicity. However, these individuals are not representative of the immense number of people who have struggled with psychological disorders.

3. *People with psychological disorders behave in bizarre ways and are very different from normal people.* This is true only in a small minority of cases, usually involving relatively severe disorders. As noted earlier, the line between normal and abnormal behavior can be difficult to draw. At first glance, people with psychological disorders are usually indistinguishable from those without disorders. A classic study by David Rosenhan (1973) showed that even mental health professionals may have difficulty distinguishing normality from abnormality. To study diagnostic accuracy, Rosenhan arranged for a number of normal people to seek admission to mental hospitals. These "pseudopatients" arrived at the hospitals complaining of one false symptom—hearing voices. Except for this single symptom, they acted as they normally would and gave accurate information when interviewed about their personal histories. *All* the pseudopatients were admitted, and the average length of their hospi-

talization was 19 days! As you might imagine, Rosenhan's study evoked quite a controversy about our diagnostic system for mental illness. Let's take a look at how this diagnostic system has evolved.

Psychodiagnosis: The Classification of Disorders

Lumping all psychological disorders together would make it extremely difficult to understand them better. A sound taxonomy of mental disorders can facilitate empirical research and enhance communication among scientists and clinicians (First, 2003; Zimmerman & Spitzer, 2005). Thus, a great deal of effort has been invested in devising an elaborate system for classifying psychological disorders (see Figure 14.3 on the next page).

Guidelines for psychodiagnosis were extremely vague and informal prior to 1952 when the American Psychiatric Association unveiled its *Diagnostic and Statistical Manual of Mental Disorders* (Nathan & Langenbucher, 2003). This classification scheme described about 100 disorders. Revisions intended to improve the system were incorporated into the second edition (DSM-II) published in 1968, but the diagnostic guidelines were still pretty sketchy. However, the third edition (DSM-III), published in 1980, represented a major advance, as the diagnostic criteria were made much more explicit, concrete, and detailed to facilitate more consistent diagnoses across clinicians (Blacker & Tsuang, 1999). The current, fourth edition (DSM-IV), which was released in 1994, and revised slightly in 2000, made use of intervening research to refine the criteria introduced in DSM-III. Each revision of the DSM system has expanded the list of disorders covered. The current version describes about three times as many types of psychological disorders as DSM-I (Houts, 2002).

The publication of DSM-III in 1980 introduced a new multiaxial system of classification, which asks for judgments about individuals on five separate dimensions, or "axes." Figure 14.3 provides an overview of the axes. The diagnoses of disorders are made on Axes I and II. Clinicians record most types of disorders on Axis I. They use Axis II to list long-running personality disorders or mental retardation. People may receive diagnoses on both Axes I and II. The remaining axes are used to record supplemental information. A patient's physical disorders are listed on Axis III (General Medical Conditions). On Axis IV (Psychosocial and Environmental Problems), the clinician makes notations regarding the types of stress experienced by the individual in the past year. On Axis V (Global Assessment of Functioning), estimates are made of the individual's cur-

rent level of adaptive functioning (in social and occupational behavior, viewed as a whole) and of the individual's highest level of functioning in the past year. Figure 14.4 on page 581 shows an example of a multiaxial evaluation. Most theorists agree that the multiaxial system is a step in the right direction because it recognizes the importance of information besides a traditional diagnostic label.

Work is currently underway to formulate the next edition (DSM-V) of the diagnostic system (e.g., Banzato, 2004; Spitzer, First, & Wakefield, 2007; Widiger & Simonsen, 2005), which is tentatively scheduled for publication in 2011. Clinical researchers are collecting data, holding conferences, and formulating arguments about whether various syndromes should be added, eliminated, redefined, or renamed. Should complicated grief reactions become a standard diagnostic option (Lichtenthal, Cruess, & Prigerson, 2004)? Should the diagnostic system use the term drug *dependence* or drug *addiction* (O'Brien, Volkow, & Li, 2006)? Should pathological gambling be lumped with impulse-control disorders or addictive disorders (Potenza, 2006)? Should the category of somatoform disorders (see pp. 586–588) be eliminated (Fava et al., 2007)? Should Internet addiction be added to the official list of disorders (Sandoz, 2004)? Vigorous debates about issues such as these will occupy clinical researchers in the upcoming years, and DSM-V may look somewhat different from its predecessors.

The Prevalence of Psychological Disorders

How common are psychological disorders? What percentage of the population is afflicted with mental illness? Is it 10%? Perhaps 25%? Could the figure range as high as 40% or 50%?

Such estimates fall in the domain of *epidemiology—the study of the distribution of mental or physical disorders in a population.* The 1980s and 1990s brought major advances in psychiatric epidemiology, as a number of large-scale investigations provided a huge, new database on the distribution of mental disorders (Murphy, Tohen, & Tsuang, 1999). In epidemiology, *prevalence* **refers to the percentage of a population that exhibit a disorder during a specified time period.** In the case of mental disorders, the most interesting data are the estimates of *lifetime prevalence,* the percentage of people who endure a specific disorder at any time in their lives.

Studies published in the 1980s and early 1990s found psychological disorders in roughly *one-third* of the population (Regier & Kaelber, 1995; Robins, Locke, & Regier, 1991). Subsequent research, which focused on a somewhat younger sample (ages 18–54 instead

David Rosenhan

"How many people, one wonders, are sane but not recognized as such in our psychiatric institutions?"

web link 14.2

National Alliance for the Mentally Ill (NAMI)

NAMI describes itself as "a grassroots, self-help support and advocacy organization of families and friends of people with serious mental illness, and those persons themselves." Its online site responds to their needs with extensive and current information about schizophrenia, bipolar disorder, and other severe disorders.

Figure 14.3

Overview of the DSM diagnostic system. Published by the American Psychiatric Association, the *Diagnostic and Statistical Manual of Mental Disorders* is the formal classification system used in the diagnosis of psychological disorders. It is a *multiaxial* system, which means that information is recorded on the five axes described here.

SOURCE: Adapted with permission from the *Diagnostic and Statistical Manual of Mental Disorders, 4th ed. (DSM–TR)*. Copyright © 2000 American Psychiatric Association.

Axis I
Clinical Syndromes

1. **Disorders usually first diagnosed in infancy, childhood, or adolescence**
   This category includes disorders that arise before adolescence, such as attention deficit disorders, autism, enuresis, and stuttering.

2. **Organic mental disorders**
   These disorders are temporary or permanent dysfunctions of brain tissue caused by diseases or chemicals. Examples are delirium, dementia, and amnesia.

3. **Substance-related disorders**
   This category refers to the maladaptive use of drugs and alcohol. This category requires an abnormal pattern of use, as with alcohol abuse and cocaine dependence.

4. **Schizophrenia and other psychotic disorders**
   The schizophrenias are characterized by psychotic symptoms (for example, grossly disorganized behavior, delusions, and hallucinations) and by over six months of behavioral deterioration. This category also includes delusional disorder and schizoaffective disorder.

5. **Mood disorders**
   The cardinal feature is emotional disturbance. These disorders include major depression, bipolar disorder, dysthymic disorder, and cyclothymic disorder.

6. **Anxiety disorders**
   These disorders are characterized by physiological signs of anxiety (for example, palpitations) and subjective feelings of tension, apprehension, or fear. Anxiety may be acute and focused (panic disorder) or continual and diffuse (generalized anxiety disorder).

7. **Somatoform disorders**
   These disorders are dominated by somatic symptoms that resemble physical illnesses. These symptoms cannot be fully accounted for by organic damage. This category includes somatization and conversion disorders and hypochondriasis.

8. **Dissociative disorders**
   These disorders all feature a sudden, temporary alteration or dysfunction of memory, consciousness, and identity, as in dissociative amnesia and dissociative identity disorder.

9. **Sexual and gender-identity disorders**
   There are three basic types of disorders in this category: gender identity disorders (discomfort with identity as male or female), paraphilias (preference for unusual acts to achieve sexual arousal), and sexual dysfunctions (impairments in sexual functioning).

10. **Eating Disorders**
    Eating disorders are severe disturbances in eating behavior characterized by preoccupation with weight concerns and unhealthy efforts to control weight. Examples include anorexia nervosa and bulimia nervosa.

Axis II
Personality Disorders or Mental Retardation

Personality disorders are longstanding patterns of extreme, inflexible personality traits that are deviant or maladaptive and lead to impaired functioning or subjective distress. *Mental retardation* refers to subnormal general mental ability accompanied by deficiencies in adaptive skills, originating before age 18.

Axis III
General Medical Conditions

Physical disorders or conditions are recorded on this axis. Examples include diabetes, arthritis, and hemophilia.

Axis IV
Psychosocial and Environmental Problems

Axis IV is for reporting psychosocial and environmental problems that may affect the diagnosis, treatment, and prognosis of mental disorders (Axes I and II). A psychosocial or environmental problem may be a negative life event, an environmental difficulty or deficiency, a familial or other interpersonal stress, an inadequacy of social support or personal resources, or another problem that describes the context in which a person's difficulties have developed.

Axis V
Global Assessment of Functioning (GAF) Scale

Code	Symptoms
100	Superior functioning in a wide range of activities
90	Absent or minimal symptoms, good functioning in all areas
80	Symptoms transient and expectable reactions to psychosocial stressors
70	Some mild symptoms or some difficulty in social, occupational, or school functioning, but generally functioning pretty well
60	Moderate symptoms or difficulty in social, occupational, or school functioning
50	Serious symptoms or impairment in social, occupational, or school functioning
40	Some impairment in reality testing or communication or major impairment in family relations, judgment, thinking, or mood
30	Behavior considerably influenced by delusions or hallucinations, serious impairment in communication or judgment, or inability to function in almost all areas
20	Some danger of hurting self or others, occasional failure to maintain minimal personal hygiene, or gross impairment in communication
10	Persistent danger of severely hurting self or others
1	

of over age 18), suggested that about 44% of the adult population will struggle with some sort of psychological disorder at some point in their lives (Kessler & Zhao, 1999; Regier & Burke, 2000). The most recent large-scale epidemiological study estimated the lifetime risk of a psychiatric disorder to be 51% (Kessler et al., 2005a). Obviously, all these figures are *estimates* that depend to some extent on the sampling methods and assessment techniques used (Wakefield, 1999b). The progressively higher estimates in recent years have begun to generate some controversy in the field. Some experts believe that recent estimates are

A DSM multiaxial evaluation (patient 49-year-old male)	
Axis I	Major depressive disorder Cocaine abuse
Axis II	Borderline personality disorder (provisional, rule out dependent personality disorder)
Axis III	Hypertension
Axis IV	Psychosocial stressors: recent divorce, permitted to see his children only infrequently, job is in jeopardy
Axis V	Current global assessment of functioning (GAF): 46

Figure 14.4

Example of a multiaxial evaluation. A multiaxial evaluation for a depressed man with a cocaine problem might look like this.

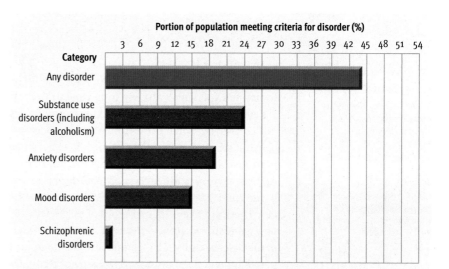

Figure 14.5

Lifetime prevalence of psychological disorders. The estimated percentage of people who have, at any time in their life, suffered from one of four types of psychological disorders or from a disorder of any kind (top bar) is shown here. Prevalence estimates vary somewhat from one study to the next, depending on the exact methods used in sampling and assessment. The estimates shown here are based on pooling data from Wave 1 and 2 of the Epidemiological Catchment Area studies and the National Comorbidity Study, as summarized by Regier and Burke (2000) and Dew, Bromet, and Switzer (2000). These studies, which collectively evaluated over 28,000 subjects, provide the best data to date on the prevalence of mental illness in the United States.

implausibly high and that they may trivialize psychiatric diagnoses (Wakefield & Spitzer, 2002). The debate centers on where to draw the line between normal difficulties in functioning and full-fledged mental illness—that is, when symptoms qualify as a disease (Regier, Narrow, & Rae, 2004).

In any event, whether one goes with conservative or liberal estimates, the prevalence of psychological disorders is quite a bit higher than most people assume. The data that yielded the 44% estimate of total lifetime prevalence are summarized in Figure 14.5, which shows prevalence estimates for the most common classes of disorders. As you can see, the most common types of psychological disorders are (1) substance (alcohol and drug) use disorders, (2) anxiety disorders, and (3) mood disorders.

The high prevalence of psychological disorders means that the economic costs of mental illness in modern societies are enormous. The annual cost of treating psychiatric illness in the United States was estimated to be about $150 billion in a 2003 report (New Freedom Commission on Mental Health, 2003). Another study estimated that more than 1.3 billion days of role performance (being able to go to work, function as a homemaker, and so forth) are lost each year in the U.S. to mental disorders (Merikangas et al., 2007). To put this exorbitant number in perspective, psychological disorders cause about three times as many disability days as cardiovascular diseases and vastly more than cancer. And there is no way to put a price on the extraordinary anguish suffered by the families of the mentally ill. Thus, the socioeconomic costs of psychological disorders are staggering.

We are now ready to start examining the specific types of psychological disorders. Obviously, we cannot cover all of the disorders listed in DSM-IV. However, we will introduce most of the major categories

of disorders to give you an overview of the many forms abnormal behavior takes (see Chapter 5 for a discussion of substance abuse). In discussing each set of disorders, we will begin with brief descriptions of the specific syndromes or subtypes that fall in the category. Then we'll focus on the *etiology* of the disorders in that category.

web link 14.3

Mental Health: A Report of the Surgeon General

In late 1999, the Surgeon General issued the first comprehensive survey of the state of mental health in the United States. This report has provided a crucial foundation of statistics and other information for understanding the needs for mental health care in the 21st century.

REVIEW of Key Points

14.1 The medical model assumes that it is useful to view abnormal behavior as a disease. This view has been criticized on the grounds that it turns questions about deviance into medical questions, but the model has proven useful. Three criteria are used in deciding whether people suffer from psychological disorders: deviance, personal distress, and maladaptive behavior. Judgments about abnormality reflect cultural values. Often it is difficult to clearly draw a line between normality and abnormality.

14.2 Contrary to popular stereotypes, people with psychological disorders are not particularly bizarre or dangerous, and even the most severe disorders are treatable. Research by David Rosenhan showed that pseudopatients were routinely admitted to mental hospitals, where staff were unable to detect the patients' normalcy. His study showed that the distinction between normality and abnormality is not clear-cut.

14.3 Originally introduced in 1952, the DSM is the official psychodiagnostic classification system in the United States. Since DSM-III, the system has asked for information about patients on five axes, or dimensions. The current version is DSM-IV, but work is under way on DSM-V.

14.4 It is difficult to obtain good data on the prevalence of psychological disorders. Nonetheless, it is clear that they are more common than widely believed. Recent studies suggest that 44% of the population will struggle with a disorder over the course of their lives. The most common types of disorders are substance use, anxiety, and mood disorders.

Anxiety Disorders

SIM 9

Everyone experiences anxiety from time to time. It is a natural and common reaction to many of life's difficulties. For some people, however, anxiety becomes a chronic problem. These people experience high levels of anxiety with disturbing regularity. *Anxiety disorders are a class of disorders marked by feelings of excessive apprehension and anxiety.* There are five principal types of anxiety disorders: generalized anxiety disorder, phobic disorder, panic disorder, obsessive-compulsive disorder, and posttraumatic stress disorder. They are not mutually exclusive, as many people who develop one anxiety syndrome often suffer from another at some point in their lives (Merikangas, 2005). Studies suggest that anxiety disorders are quite common, occurring in roughly 19% of the population (Dew, Bromet, & Switzer, 2000; Regier & Burke, 2000).

Generalized Anxiety Disorder

11a

Generalized anxiety disorder is marked by a chronic, high level of anxiety that is not tied to any specific threat. People with this disorder worry constantly about yesterday's mistakes and tomorrow's problems. They worry about minor matters related to family, finances, work, and personal illness. They hope that their worrying will help to ward off negative events (Beidel & Stipelman, 2007), but they nonetheless worry about how much they worry (Barlow et al., 2003). They often dread making decisions and brood over them endlessly. Their anxiety is commonly accompanied by physical symptoms, such as trembling, muscle tension, diarrhea, dizziness, faintness, sweating, and heart palpitations. Generalized anxiety disorder tends to have a gradual onset, has a lifetime prevalence of about 5%, and is seen more frequently in females than males (Brown, 1999; Merikangas, 2005).

Phobic Disorder

11a

In a phobic disorder, an individual's troublesome anxiety has a specific focus. *A phobic disorder is marked by a persistent and irrational fear of an object or situation that presents no realistic danger.* Although mild phobias are extremely common, people are said to have a phobic disorder only when their fears seriously interfere with their everyday behavior. Phobic reactions tend to be accompanied by physical symptoms of anxiety, such as trembling and palpitations (Rapee & Barlow, 2001). The following case provides an example of a phobic disorder:

Hilda is 32 years of age and has a rather unusual fear. She is terrified of snow. She cannot go outside in the snow. She cannot even stand to see snow or hear about it on the weather report. Her phobia severely constricts her day-to-day behavior. Probing in therapy revealed that her phobia was caused by a traumatic experience at age 11. Playing at a ski lodge, she was buried briefly by a small avalanche of snow. She had no recollection of this experience until it was recovered in therapy. (Adapted from Laughlin, 1967, p. 227)

As Hilda's unusual snow phobia illustrates, people can develop phobic responses to virtually anything. Nonetheless, certain types of phobias are more common than others. Particularly common are acrophobia (fear of heights), claustrophobia (fear of small, enclosed places), brontophobia (fear of storms), hydrophobia (fear of water), and various animal and insect phobias (Antony & McCabe, 2003). People troubled by phobias typically realize that their fears are irrational, but they still are unable to calm themselves when confronted by a phobic object. Among many of them, even *imagining* a phobic object or situation can trigger great anxiety (Thorpe & Salkovskis, 1995).

Panic Disorder and Agoraphobia

11a

A *panic disorder is characterized by recurrent attacks of overwhelming anxiety that usually occur suddenly and unexpectedly.* These paralyzing panic attacks are accompanied by physical symptoms of anxiety. After a number of panic attacks, victims often become apprehensive, wondering when their next panic will occur. Their concern about exhibiting panic in public may escalate to the point where they are afraid to leave home. This creates a condition called *agoraphobia,* which is a common complication of panic disorders.

Agoraphobia is a fear of going out to public places (its literal meaning is "fear of the marketplace or open places"). Because of this fear, some people become prisoners confined to their homes, although many will venture out if accompanied by a trusted companion (Hollander & Simeon, 2003). As its name

Key Learning Goals

14.5 Identify five anxiety disorders and the symptoms associated with each.

14.6 Discuss the role of biological factors and conditioning in the etiology of anxiety disorders.

14.7 Explain how cognitive factors and stress can contribute to the development of anxiety disorders.

suggests, agoraphobia has traditionally been viewed as a phobic disorder. However, more recent evidence suggests that agoraphobia is mainly a complication of panic disorder. About two-thirds of people who are diagnosed with panic disorder are female (Horwath & Weissman, 2000). The onset of panic disorder typically occurs during late adolescence or early adulthood (Pine & McClure, 2005).

Obsessive-Compulsive Disorder

PSYK TREK
11a

Obsessions are *thoughts* that repeatedly intrude on one's consciousness in a distressing way. Compulsions are *actions* that one feels forced to carry out. Thus, an *obsessive-compulsive disorder* (OCD) is marked by persistent, uncontrollable intrusions of unwanted thoughts (obsessions) and urges to engage in senseless rituals (compulsions). To illustrate, let's examine the bizarre behavior of a man once reputed to be the wealthiest person in the world:

The famous industrialist Howard Hughes was obsessed with the possibility of being contaminated by germs. This led him to devise extraordinary rituals to minimize the possibility of such contamination. He would spend hours methodically cleaning a single telephone. He once wrote a three-page memo instructing assistants on exactly how to open cans of fruit for him. The following is just a small portion of the instructions that Hughes provided for a driver who delivered films to his bungalow. "Get out of the car on the traffic side. Do not at any time be on the side of the car between the car and the curb. . . . Carry only one can of film at a time. Step over

the gutter opposite the place where the sidewalk dead-ends into the curb from a point as far out into the center of the road as possible. Do not ever walk on the grass at all, also do not step into the gutter at all. Walk to the bungalow keeping as near to the center of the sidewalk as possible." (Adapted from Barlett & Steele, 1979, pp. 227–237)

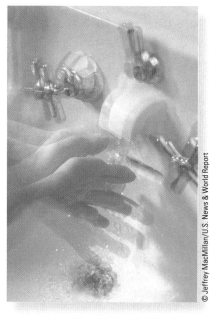

Repetitive handwashing is an example of a common compulsive behavior.

Obsessions often center on inflicting harm on others, personal failures, suicide, or sexual acts. People troubled by obsessions may feel that they have lost control of their mind. Compulsions usually involve stereotyped rituals that temporarily relieve anxiety. Common examples include constant handwashing; repetitive cleaning of things that are already clean; endless rechecking of locks, faucets, and such; and excessive arranging, counting, and hoarding of things (Pato, Eisen, & Phillips, 2003). Specific types of obsessions tend to be associated with specific types of compulsions. For example, obsessions about contamination tend to be paired with cleaning compulsions, and obsessions about symmetry tend to be paired with ordering and arranging compulsions (Leckman et al., 1997).

Although many of us can be compulsive at times, full-fledged obsessive-compulsive disorders occur in roughly 2.5% of the population (Turner et al., 2001). The typical age of onset for OCD is late adolescence,

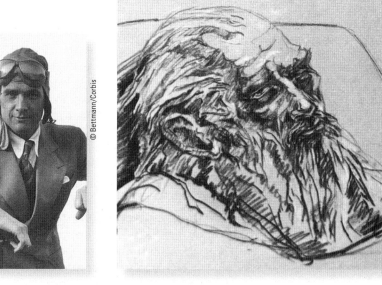

As a young man (shown in the photo), Howard Hughes was a handsome, dashing daredevil pilot and movie producer who appeared to be reasonably well adjusted. However, as the years went by, his behavior gradually became more and more maladaptive, as obsessions and compulsions came to dominate his life. In his later years (shown in the drawing), he spent most of his time in darkened rooms, naked, unkempt, and dirty, following bizarre rituals to alleviate his anxieties. (The drawing was done by an NBC artist and was based on descriptions from men who had seen Hughes.)

with most cases (75%) emerging before the age of 30 (Kessler et al., 2005a). OCD can be a particularly severe disorder, as it is often associated with serious social and occupational impairments (Torres et al., 2006).

Posttraumatic Stress Disorder

Posttraumatic stress disorder (PTSD) involves enduring psychological disturbance attributed to the experience of a major traumatic event. PTSD was first recognized as a disorder in the 1970s in the aftermath of the Vietnam war, when a great many veterans were traumatized by their combat experiences. Research eventually showed that PTSD can be caused by a variety of traumatic events besides harrowing war experiences. For example, PTSD is often seen after a rape or assault, a severe automobile accident, a natural disaster, or the witnessing of someone's death (Koren, Arnon, & Klein, 1999; Stein et al., 1997; Vernberg et al., 1996). Unfortunately, traumatic experiences such as these appear to be much more common than widely assumed. Research suggests that 7%–8% of people have suffered from PTSD at some point in their lives, with prevalence higher among women (10%) than men (5%) (Ozer et al., 2003). Currently, there is great concern about the number of military returnees from the Afghanistan and Iraq wars who will develop PTSD (Friedman, 2006). Similar to the experiences of Vietnam veterans, the preliminary data suggest that these troops are showing greatly elevated rates of PTSD (Hoge et al., 2007). Common symptoms in PTSD include reexperiencing the traumatic event in the form of nightmares and flashbacks, emotional numbing, alienation, problems in social relations, an increased sense of vulnerability, and elevated arousal, anxiety, anger, and guilt (Flannery, 1999; Shalev, 2001).

A variety of factors are predictors of individuals' risk for PTSD (McNally, 1999; Keane, Marshall, & Taft, 2006; Norris et al., 2001). As you might expect, increased vulnerability is associated with greater personal injuries and losses, greater intensity of exposure to the traumatic event, and more exposure to the grotesque aftermath of the event. One key predictor of vulnerability that emerged in a recent review of the relevant research is the *intensity of one's reaction at the time of the traumatic event* (Ozer et al., 2003). Individuals who have especially intense emotional reactions during or immediately after the traumatic event go on to show elevated vulnerability to PTSD. Vulnerability seems to be greatest among people whose reactions are so intense that they report dissociative experiences (a sense that things are not real, that time is stretching out, that one is watching oneself in a movie).

Etiology of Anxiety Disorders

11a

Like most psychological disorders, anxiety disorders develop out of complicated interactions among a variety of biological and psychological factors.

Biological Factors

11a

In studies that assess the impact of heredity on psychological disorders, investigators look at *concordance rates*. A *concordance rate* indicates the percentage of twin pairs or other pairs of relatives who exhibit the same disorder. If relatives who share more genetic similarity show higher concordance rates than relatives who share less genetic overlap, this finding supports the genetic hypothesis. The results of both *twin studies* (see Figure 14.6) and *family studies* (see Chapter 3 for discussions of both methods) suggest that there is a moderate genetic predisposition to anxiety disorders (Hettema, Neale, & Kendler, 2001; McMahon & Kassem, 2005). These findings are consistent with the idea that inherited differences in temperament might make some people more vulnerable than others to anxiety disorders. As we discussed in Chapter 11, Jerome Kagan and his colleagues (1992) have found that about 15%–20% of infants display an *inhibited temperament,* characterized by shyness, timidity, and wariness, which appears to have a strong genetic basis. Research suggests that this temperament is a risk factor for the development of anxiety disorders (Coles, Schofield, & Pietrefesa, 2006).

Another line of research suggests that *anxiety sensitivity* may make people vulnerable to anxiety disorders (McWilliams et al., 2007; Reiss, 1991; Schmidt, Zvolensky, & Maner, 2006). According to this notion, some people are highly sensitive to the internal physiological symptoms of anxiety and are prone to overreact with fear when they experience these symptoms. Anxiety sensitivity may fuel an inflationary spiral in which anxiety breeds more anxiety, which eventually spins out of control in the form of an anxiety disorder.

Recent evidence suggests that a link may exist between anxiety disorders and neurochemical activity in the brain. As you learned in Chapter 3, *neurotransmitters* are chemicals that carry signals from one neuron to another. Therapeutic drugs (such as Valium) that reduce excessive anxiety appear to alter neurotransmitter activity at GABA synapses. This finding and other lines of evidence suggest that disturbances in the neural circuits using GABA may play a role in some types of anxiety disorders (Skolnick, 2003). Abnormalities in neural circuits using serotonin have been implicated in PTSD and panic and obsessive-compulsive disorders (Stein & Hugo, 2004). Thus, scientists are beginning to unravel the neurochemical bases for anxiety disorders.

Conditioning and Learning   11a

Many anxiety responses may be *acquired through classical conditioning and maintained through operant conditioning* (see Chapter 6). According to Mowrer (1947), an originally neutral stimulus (the snow in Hilda's case, for instance) may be paired with a frightening event (the avalanche) so that it becomes a conditioned stimulus eliciting anxiety (see Figure 14.7a). Once a fear is acquired through classical conditioning, the person may start avoiding the anxiety-producing stimulus. The avoidance response is negatively reinforced because it is followed by a reduction in anxiety. This process involves operant conditioning (see Figure 14.7b). Thus, separate conditioning processes may create and then sustain specific anxiety responses (Levis, 1989). Consistent with this view, studies find that a substantial portion of people suffering from phobias can identify a traumatic conditioning experience that probably contributed to their anxiety disorder (Antony & McCabe, 2003; Mineka & Zinbarg, 2006).

The tendency to develop phobias of certain types of objects and situations may be explained by Martin Seligman's (1971) concept of *preparedness*. He suggests that people are biologically prepared by their evolutionary history to acquire some fears much more easily than others. His theory would explain why people develop phobias of ancient sources of threat (such as snakes and spiders) much more readily than modern sources of threat (such as electrical outlets or hot irons). As we noted in Chapter 6, Arne Öhman and Susan Mineka (2001) have updated the notion of preparedness, which they call an *evolved module for fear learning*. They maintain that this evolved module is automatically activated by stimuli related to past survival threats in evolutionary history and that it is relatively resistant to intentional efforts to suppress the resulting fears. Consistent with this view, phobic stimuli associated with evolutionary threats tend to produce more rapid conditioning of fears and stronger fear responses (Mineka & Öhman, 2002).

Critics note a number of problems with conditioning models of phobias (Rachman, 1990). For instance, many people with phobias cannot recall or identify a traumatic conditioning experience that led to their phobia. Conversely, many people endure extremely traumatic experiences that should create

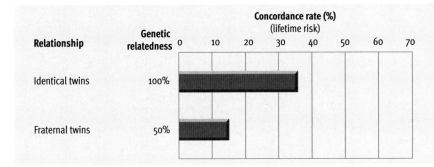

a phobia but do not. To provide better explanations for these complexities, conditioning models of anxiety disorders are currently being revised to include a larger role for cognitive factors (de Jong & Merckelbach, 2000), much like conditioning theories in general, as we saw in Chapter 6.

Cognitive Factors   11a

Cognitive theorists maintain that certain styles of thinking make some people particularly vulnerable to anxiety disorders (Craske & Waters, 2005). According to these theorists, some people are more likely to suffer from problems with anxiety because they tend to (a) misinterpret harmless situations as threatening, (b) focus excessive attention on perceived threats, and (c) selectively recall information that seems threatening (Beck, 1997; McNally, 1994, 1996). In one intriguing test of the cognitive view, anxious and nonanxious subjects were asked to read 32 sentences that could be interpreted in either a threatening or a nonthreatening manner (Eysenck et al., 1991). For instance, one such sentence was "The doctor examined little Emma's growth," which could mean that the doctor checked her height or the growth of a tumor. As Figure 14.8 on the next page shows, the anxious participants interpreted the sentences in a threatening way more often than the

Figure 14.6

Twin studies of anxiety disorders. The concordance rate for anxiety disorders in identical twins is higher than that for fraternal twins, who share less genetic overlap. These results suggest that there is a genetic predisposition to anxiety disorders. (Data based on Noyes et al., 1987; Slater & Shields, 1969; Torgersen, 1979, 1983)

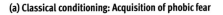

(a) Classical conditioning: Acquisition of phobic fear

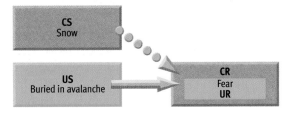

(b) Operant conditioning: Maintenance of phobic fear
(negative reinforcement)

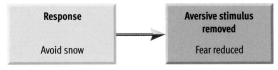

Figure 14.7

Conditioning as an explanation for phobias. (a) Many phobias appear to be acquired through classical conditioning when a neutral stimulus is paired with an anxiety-arousing stimulus. (b) Once acquired, a phobia may be maintained through operant conditioning. Avoidance of the phobic stimulus reduces anxiety, resulting in negative reinforcement.

Figure 14.8

Cognitive factors in anxiety disorders. Eysenck and his colleagues (1991) compared how subjects with anxiety problems and nonanxious subjects tended to interpret sentences that could be viewed as threatening or nonthreatening. Consistent with cognitive models of anxiety disorders, anxious subjects were more likely to interpret the sentences in a threatening light.

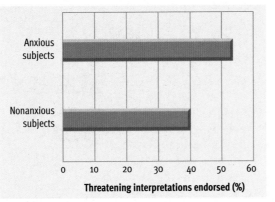

Figure 14.9

Stress and panic disorder. Faravelli and Pallanti (1989) assessed the amount of stress experienced during the 12 months before the onset of panic disorder in a group of 64 patients with this disorder and in a control group drawn from hospital employees and their friends. As you can see, a dramatic increase occurred in stress in the month prior to the onset of the patients' panic disorders. These data suggest that stress may contribute to the development of panic disorders.

SOURCE: Adapted from Faravelli, C., & Pallanti, S. (1989). Recent life events and panic disorders. *American Journal of Psychiatry, 146,* 622–626. Copyright © 1989 by the American Psychiatric Association.

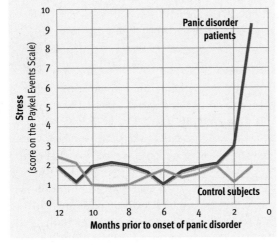

in every corner of their lives (Aikens & Craske, 2001; Riskind, 2005).

Stress

Finally, studies have supported the long-held suspicion that anxiety disorders can be stress-related (Beidel & Stipelman, 2007; Sandin et al., 2004). For instance, Faravelli and Pallanti (1989) found that patients with panic disorder had experienced a dramatic increase in stress in the month prior to the onset of their disorder (see **Figure 14.9**). In another study, Brown et al. (1998) found an association between stress and the development of social phobia. Thus, there is reason to believe that high stress often helps to precipitate the onset of anxiety disorders.

REVIEW of Key Points

14.5 Generalized anxiety disorder is marked by chronic, high anxiety, whereas phobic disorder involves irrational fears of specific objects or situations. Panic disorder is marked by recurrent panic attacks and agoraphobia. Obsessive-compulsive disorder is dominated by intrusions of unwanted thoughts and urges, whereas posttraumatic stress disorder consists of disturbance due to the experience of a major traumatic event.

14.6 Twin studies suggest that there is a weak genetic predisposition to anxiety disorders. These disorders may be more likely in people who are especially sensitive to the physiological symptoms of anxiety. Abnormalities in neurotransmitter activity at GABA synapses or serotonin synapses may also play a role. Many anxiety responses, especially phobias, may be caused by classical conditioning and maintained by operant conditioning, with preparedness influencing which phobias condition most readily.

14.7 Cognitive theorists maintain that certain styles of thinking—especially a tendency to overinterpret harmless situations as threatening—make some people more vulnerable to anxiety disorders. Stress may also predispose people to anxiety disorders.

nonanxious participants did. Thus, consistent with our theme that human experience is highly subjective, the cognitive view holds that some people are prone to anxiety disorders because they see threat

Key Learning Goals

14.8 Distinguish among three somatoform disorders.

14.9 Analyze how personality, cognitive factors, and the sick role contribute to somatoform disorders.

Somatoform Disorders

Chances are, you have met people who always seem to be complaining about aches, pains, and physical maladies of doubtful authenticity. You may have thought to yourself, "It's all in his head" and concluded that the person exhibited a "psychosomatic" condition. However, as we discussed in Chapter 13, the term *psychosomatic* has been widely misused. *Psychosomatic diseases* involve *genuine* physical ailments caused in part by psychological factors, especially reactions to stress. These diseases, which include mal-

adies such as ulcers, asthma, and high blood pressure, are not imagined ailments. They are recorded on the DSM axis for physical problems (Axis III). When physical illness appears *largely* psychological in origin, we are dealing with somatoform disorders, which are recorded on Axis I. **Somatoform disorders are physical ailments that cannot be fully explained by organic conditions and are largely due to psychological factors.** Although their symptoms are more imaginary than real, victims of somatoform disorders are *not* simply faking illness. Deliberate feigning of illness for personal gain is another matter altogether, called *malingering.*

People with somatoform disorders typically seek treatment from physicians practicing neurology, internal medicine, or family medicine, instead of from psychologists or psychiatrists. Making accurate diagnoses of somatoform disorders can be difficult, because the causes of physical ailments are sometimes hard to identify. In some cases, somatoform disorders are misdiagnosed when a genuine organic cause for a person's physical symptoms goes undetected in spite of extensive medical examinations and tests (Yutzy, 2003). Diagnostic ambiguities such as these have led some theorists to argue that the category of somatoform disorders should be eliminated in DSM-V (Mayou et al., 2005), but other theorists have expressed vigorous disagreement (Rief, Henningsen, & Hiller, 2006).

Subtypes and Symptoms

We will discuss three specific types of somatoform disorders: somatization disorder, conversion disorder, and hypochondriasis. Diagnostic difficulties make it hard to obtain sound data on the prevalence of somatoform disorders (Bouman, Eifert, & Lejuez, 1999).

Somatization Disorder

Individuals with somatization disorder are often said to "cling to ill health." **A *somatization disorder* is marked by a history of diverse physical complaints that appear to be psychological in origin.** Somatization disorder occurs mostly in women (Guggenheim, 2000) and often coexists with depression and anxiety disorders (Gureje et al., 1997). Victims report an endless succession of minor physical ailments that seem to wax and wane in response to the stress in their lives (Servan-Schreiber, Kolb, & Tabas, 1999). They usually have a long and complicated history of medical treatment from many doctors. The distinguishing feature of this disorder is the diversity of the victims' physical complaints. Over the years, they report a mixed bag of cardiovascular, gastrointestinal, pulmonary, neurological, and genitourinary symptoms. The unlikely nature of such a smorgasbord of symptoms occurring together often alerts a physician to the possible psychological basis for the patient's problems. However, somatization patients are typically very resistant to the suggestion that their symptoms might be the result of psychological distress (Hollifield, 2005).

Conversion Disorder

Conversion disorder is characterized by a significant loss of physical function (with no apparent organic basis), usually in a single organ system. Common symptoms include partial or complete loss of vision, partial or complete loss of hearing, partial paralysis, severe laryngitis or mutism, and loss of feeling or function in limbs. People with conversion disorder are usually troubled by more severe ailments than people with somatization disorder. In some cases of conversion disorder, telltale clues reveal the psychological origins of the illness because the patient's symptoms are not consistent with medical knowledge about their apparent disease. For instance, the loss of feeling in one hand that is seen in "glove anesthesia" is inconsistent with the known facts of neurological organization (see Figure 14.10). Conversion disorders tend to have an acute onset triggered by stress (Kirmayer & Looper, 2007).

Hypochondriasis

Hypochondriacs constantly monitor their physical condition, looking for signs of illness. Any tiny alteration from their physical norm leads them to conclude that they have contracted a disease. *Hypochondriasis* (more widely known as hypochondria) is characterized by excessive preoccupation with health concerns and incessant worry about developing physical illnesses. When hypochondriacs are assured by their physician that they do not have any real illness, they often are skeptical and disbelieving (Starcevic, 2001). They frequently assume that the physician must be incompetent, and they go shopping for another doctor. Hypochondriacs don't subjectively suffer from physical distress so much as they *overinterpret* every conceivable sign of illness. Hypochondria frequently appears alongside other

Figure 14.10
Glove anesthesia. In conversion disorders, the physical complaints are sometimes inconsistent with the known facts of physiology. For instance, given the patterns of nerve distribution in the arm shown in (a), it is impossible that a loss of feeling in the hand exclusively, as shown in (b), has a physical cause, indicating that the patient's problem is psychological in origin.

"Assuming I am a hypochondriac, couldn't that condition be brought on by a brain tumor?"

psychological disorders, especially anxiety disorders and depression (Iezzi, Duckworth, & Adams, 2001). For example, Howard Hughes's obsessive-compulsive disorder was coupled with profound hypochondria.

Etiology of Somatoform Disorders

Inherited aspects of physiological functioning, such as an elevated sensitivity to bodily sensations, may predispose some people to somatoform disorders (Kirmayer & Looper, 2007), but genetic factors do *not* appear to make much of a contribution to the development of these disorders (Hollifield, 2005). The available evidence suggests that these disorders are largely a function of personality and learning.

Personality Factors

People with certain types of personality traits seem to develop somatoform disorders more readily than others. The prime candidates appear to be people with *histrionic* personality characteristics (Nemiah, 1985; Slavney, 1990). The histrionic personality tends to be self-centered, suggestible, excitable, highly emotional, and overly dramatic. The personality trait of *neuroticism* also seems to elevate individuals' susceptibility to somatoform disorders (Noyes et al., 2005). In addition, research suggests

web link 14.6

National Institute of Mental Health: For the Public

A wealth of information on psychological disorders is available at this subpage of the National Institute of Mental Health's massive website. Visitors will find detailed online booklets on generalized anxiety disorder, obsessive-compulsive disorder, panic disorder, depression, bipolar disorder, and other psychological disorders. Brief fact sheets, dense technical reports, and many other resources can also be found here.

that the pathological care-seeking behavior seen in these disorders may be caused by *insecure attachment styles* (see Chapter 11) that are rooted in early experiences with caregivers (Noyes et al., 2003).

Cognitive Factors

In recent years, theorists have devoted increased attention to how cognitive peculiarities might contribute to somatoform disorders. For example, Barsky (2001) asserts that some people focus excessive attention on their internal physiological processes and amplify normal bodily sensations into symptoms of distress, which lead them to pursue unnecessary medical treatment. Recent evidence suggests that people with somatoform disorders tend to draw catastrophic conclusions about minor bodily complaints (Salkovskis & Warwick, 2001). They also seem to apply a faulty standard of good health, equating health with a complete absence of symptoms and discomfort, which is unrealistic (Barsky et al., 1993; Rief, Hiller, & Margraf, 1998).

The Sick Role

Another consideration is that some people grow fond of the role associated with being sick (Hotopf, 2004; Pilowsky, 1993). Their complaints of physical symptoms may be reinforced by indirect benefits derived from their illness (Schwartz, Slater, & Birchler, 1994). What benefits might be derived from physical illness? One payoff is that becoming ill is a superb way to avoid having to confront life's challenges. Many people with somatoform disorders are avoiding facing up to marital problems, career frustrations, family responsibilities, and the like. After all, when you're sick, others cannot place great demands on you. Another benefit is that physical problems can provide a convenient excuse when people fail, or worry about failing, in endeavors that are critical to their self-esteem (Organista & Miranda, 1991). Attention from others is another payoff that may reinforce complaints of physical illness. When people become ill, they command the attention of family, friends, co-workers, neighbors, and doctors.

---

concept check 14.2

Distinguishing Anxiety and Somatoform Disorders

Check your understanding of the nature of anxiety and somatoform disorders by making preliminary diagnoses for the cases described below. Read each case summary and write your tentative diagnosis in the space provided. The answers are in Appendix A.

1. Malcolm religiously follows an exact schedule every day. His showering and grooming ritual takes two hours. He follows the same path in walking to his classes every day, and he always sits in the same seat in each class. He can't study until his apartment is arranged perfectly. Although he tries not to, he thinks constantly about flunking out of school. Both his grades and his social life are suffering from his rigid routines.

   Preliminary diagnosis: _____

2. Jane has been unemployed for the last eight years because of poor health. She has suffered through a bizarre series of illnesses of mysterious origin. Troubles with devastating headaches were followed by months of chronic back pain. Then she developed respiratory problems, frequently gasping for breath. Her current problem is stomach pain. Physicians have been unable to find any physical basis for her maladies.

   Preliminary diagnosis: _____

3. Nathan owns a small restaurant that's in deep financial trouble. He dreads facing the possibility that his restaurant will fail. One day, he suddenly loses all feeling in his right arm and the ability to control the arm. He's hospitalized for his condition, but physicians can't find any organic cause for his arm trouble.

   Preliminary diagnosis: _____

Dissociative Disorders

Dissociative disorders are probably the most controversial set of disorders in the diagnostic system, sparking heated debate among normally subdued researchers and clinicians (Loewenstein & Putnam 2005). *Dissociative disorders* **are a class of disorders in which people lose contact with portions of their consciousness or memory, resulting in disruptions in their sense of identity.** We'll describe three dissociative syndromes—dissociative amnesia, dissociative fugue, and dissociative identity disorder—all of which appear to be relatively uncommon, although good data on the prevalence of these disorders are scarce (Kihlstrom, 2005b).

Dissociative Amnesia and Fugue

Dissociative amnesia and fugue are overlapping disorders characterized by serious memory deficits. *Dissociative amnesia* **is a sudden loss of memory for important personal information that is too extensive to be due to normal forgetting.** Memory losses may occur for a single traumatic event (such as an automobile accident or home fire) or for an extended period of time surrounding the event. Cases of amnesia have been observed after people have experienced disasters, accidents, combat stress, physical abuse, and rape, or after they have witnessed the violent death of a parent, among other things (Arrigo & Pezdek, 1997; Cardena & Gleaves, 2007). **In** *dissociative fugue,* **people lose their memory for their entire lives along with their sense of personal identity.** These people forget their name, their family, where they live, and where they work! Despite this wholesale forgetting, they remember matters unrelated to their identity, such as how to drive a car and how to do math.

Dissociative Identity Disorder

Dissociative identity disorder (DID) **involves the coexistence in one person of two or more largely complete, and usually very different, personalities.** The name for this disorder used to be *multiple personality disorder,* which still enjoys informal use. In dissociative identity disorder, the divergences in behavior go far beyond those that people normally display in adapting to different roles in life. People with "multiple personalities" feel that they have more than one identity. Each personality has his or her own name, memories, traits, and physical mannerisms. Although rare, this "Dr. Jekyll and Mr.

Hyde" syndrome is frequently portrayed in novels, television shows, and movies, such as the *Three Faces of Eve,* a classic 1957 film starring Joanne Woodward, and the satirical film *Me, Myself, and Irene,* a 2000 release starring Jim Carrey. In popular media portrayals, the syndrome is often mistakenly called *schizophrenia.* As you will see later, schizophrenic disorders are entirely different.

In dissociative identity disorder, the various personalities generally report that they are unaware of each other (Eich et al., 1997), although doubts have been raised about the accuracy of this assertion (Allen & Iacono, 2001). The alternate personalities commonly display traits that are quite foreign to the original personality. For instance, a shy, inhibited person might develop a flamboyant, extraverted alternate personality. Transitions between identities often occur suddenly. The disparities between identities can be bizarre, as different personalities may assert that they are different in age, race, gender, and sexual orientation (Kluft, 1996). Dissociative identity disorder rarely occurs in isolation. Most DID patients also have a history of anxiety, mood, or personality disorders (Ross, 1999).

Starting in the 1970s, a dramatic increase was seen in the diagnosis of multiple-personality disorder (Kihlstrom, 2001, 2005b). Only 79 well-documented cases had accumulated up through 1970, but by the late-1990s about 40,000 cases were estimated to have been reported (Lilienfeld & Lynn, 2003). Some theorists believe that these disorders used to be underdiagnosed—that is, they often went undetected (Maldonado & Spiegel, 2003a). However, other theorists argue that a handful of clinicians have begun overdiagnosing the condition and that some clinicians even *encourage and contribute* to the emergence of DID (McHugh, 1995; Powell & Gee, 1999). Consistent with this view, a survey of all the psychiatrists in Switzerland found that 90% of them had never seen a case of dissociative identity disorder, whereas three of the psychiatrists had each seen more than 20 DID patients (Modestin, 1992). The data from this study suggest that 6 psychiatrists (out of 655 surveyed) accounted for two-thirds of the dissociative identity disorder diagnoses in Switzerland.

Etiology of Dissociative Disorders

Psychogenic amnesia and fugue are usually attributed to excessive stress. However, relatively little is known

Key Learning Goals
14.10 Distinguish among three dissociative disorders.
14.11 Discuss the etiology of dissociative identity disorder.

about why this extreme reaction to stress occurs in a tiny minority of people but not in the vast majority who are subjected to similar stress. Some theorists speculate that certain personality traits—fantasy proneness and a tendency to become intensely absorbed in personal experiences—may make some people more susceptible to dissociative disorders, but adequate evidence is lacking on this line of thought (Kihlstrom, Glisky, & Angiulo, 1994).

The causes of dissociative identity disorders are particularly obscure. Some skeptical theorists, such as Nicholas Spanos (1994, 1996) and others (Gee, Allen, & Powell, 2003; Lilienfeld et al., 1999), believe that people with multiple personalities are engaging in intentional role playing to use mental illness as a face-saving excuse for their personal failings. Spanos also argues that a small minority of therapists help create multiple personalities in their patients by subtly encouraging the emergence of alternate personalities. According to Spanos, dissociative identity disorder is a creation of modern North American culture, much as demonic possession was a creation of early Christianity. To bolster his argument, he discusses how multiple-personality patients' symptom presentations seem to have been influenced by popular media. For example, the typical patient with dissociative identity disorder used to report having two or three personalities, but since the publication of *Sybil* (Schreiber, 1973) and other books describing patients with many personalities, the average number of alternate personalities has climbed to about 15.

Despite these concerns, some clinicians are convinced that DID is an authentic disorder (Cardena &

Gleaves, 2007). They argue that there is no incentive for either patients or therapists to manufacture cases of multiple personalities, which are often greeted with skepticism and outright hostility. They maintain that most cases of dissociative identity disorder are rooted in severe emotional trauma that occurred during childhood (Draijer & Langeland, 1999). A substantial majority of people with dissociative identity disorder report a childhood history of rejection from parents and physical and sexual abuse (Scroppo et al., 1998; Foote et al., 2006). In the final analysis, little is known about the causes of dissociative identity disorder, which remains a controversial diagnosis (Barry-Walsh, 2005). In one survey of American psychiatrists, only one-quarter of the respondents indicated that they felt there was solid evidence for the scientific validity of the DID diagnosis (Pope et al., 1999). Consistent with this finding, a more recent study found that scientific interest in DID has dwindled since the mid-1990s (Pope et al., 2006).

Mood Disorders

SIM9 PSYKTREK

What did Abraham Lincoln, Leo Tolstoy, Marilyn Monroe, Vincent Van Gogh, Ernest Hemingway, Winston Churchill, Virginia Wolff, Janis Joplin, Irving Berlin, Kurt Cobain, Francis Ford Coppola, Carrie Fisher, Ted Turner, Sting, Mike Wallace, Larry Flynt, Jane Pauley, and Ben Stiller have in common? Yes, they all achieved great prominence, albeit in different ways at different times. But, more pertinent to our interest, they all suffered from severe mood disorders. Although mood disorders can be terribly debilitating, people with mood disorders may still achieve greatness, because such disorders tend to be *episodic*. In other words, mood disturbances often come and go, interspersed among periods of normality.

Emotional fluctuations are natural, but some people are subject to extreme and sustained distortions of mood. *Mood disorders* **are a class of disorders marked by emotional disturbances of varied kinds that may spill over to disrupt physical, perceptual, social, and thought processes.** There are two basic types of mood disorders: unipolar and bipolar (see **Figure 14.11**). People with *unipolar disorder* experience emotional extremes at just one end of the mood continuum, as they are troubled only by *depression*. People with *bipolar disorder* are vulnerable to emotional extremes at both ends of the mood continuum, going through periods of both *depression* and *mania* (excitement and elation).

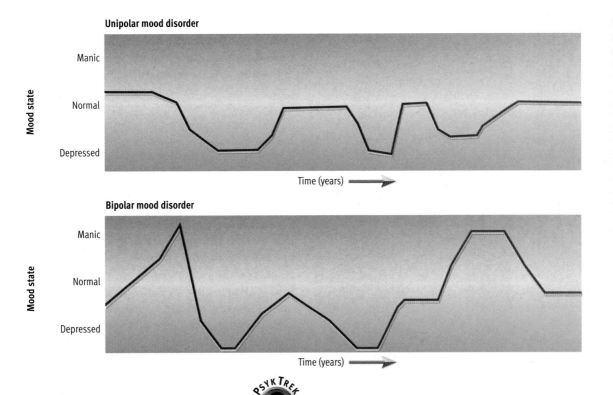

Unipolar mood disorder

Bipolar mood disorder

Figure 14.11
Episodic patterns in mood disorders. Time-limited episodes of emotional disturbance come and go unpredictably in mood disorders. People with unipolar disorders suffer from bouts of depression only, whereas people with bipolar disorders experience both manic and depressive episodes. The time between episodes of disturbance varies greatly with the individual and the type of disorder.

Major Depressive Disorder   11b

The line between normal dejection and unhappiness and abnormal depression can be difficult to draw (Kendler & Gardner, 1998). Ultimately, it requires a subjective judgment. Crucial considerations in this judgment include the duration of the depression and its disruptive effects. When a depression significantly impairs everyday adaptive behavior for more than a few weeks, there is reason for concern.

In *major depressive disorder* **people show persistent feelings of sadness and despair and a loss of interest in previous sources of pleasure.** Negative emotions form the heart of the depressive syndrome, but many other symptoms may also appear. The most common symptoms of major depression are summarized and compared with the symptoms of mania in Table 14.1. Depressed people often give up activities that they used to find enjoyable. For example, a depressed person might quit going bowling or might give up a favorite hobby such as photography. Alterations in appetite and sleep patterns are common. People with depression often lack energy. They tend to move sluggishly and talk slowly. Anxiety, irritability, and brooding are commonly observed. Self-esteem tends to sink as the depressed person begins to feel worthless. Depression plunges people into feelings of hopelessness, dejection, and boundless guilt. To make matters worse, people who suffer from depression often exhibit other disorders as well. Coexisting anxiety disorders and substance use disorders are particularly frequent (Boland & Keller, 2002).

The onset of depression can occur at any point in the life span, but a substantial majority of cases emerge before age 40 (Hammen, 2003). Depression occurs in children as well as adolescents and adults (Gruenberg & Goldstein, 2003). The vast majority (75%–95%) of people who suffer from depression experience more than one episode over the course of their lifetime (Dubovsky, Davies, & Dubovsky, 2003). In one longitudinal study, after recovery from a first episode of depression, the cumulative probability of recurrence was 25% after 1 year, 42% after two years, and 60% after 5 years (Solomon et al., 2000). The average number of depressive episodes is 5 to 6, and the average length of these episodes is about six months (Akiskal, 2005). The severity of depressive disorders varies considerably. When people display relatively mild symptoms of depression, they're

Table 14.1 Comparisons of Common Symptoms in Manic and Depressive Episodes

Characteristics	Manic Episode	Depressive Episode
Emotional	Elated, euphoric, very sociable, impatient at any hindrance	Gloomy, hopeless, socially withdrawn, irritable
Cognitive	Characterized by racing thoughts, flight of ideas, desire for action, and impulsive behavior; talkative, self-confident; experiencing delusions of grandeur	Characterized by slowness of thought processes, obsessive worrying, inability to make decisions, negative self-image, self-blame and delusions of guilt and disease
Motor	Hyperactive, tireless, requiring less sleep than usual, showing increased sex drive and fluctuating appetite	Less active, tired, experiencing difficulty in sleeping, showing decreased sex drive and decreased appetite

Source: Sarason, I. G., & Sarason, B. G. (1987). *Abnormal psychology: The problem of maladaptive behavior.* Upper Saddle River, NJ: Prentice-Hall. © 1987 Prentice-Hall, Inc. Reprinted by permission.

Mood disorders are common and have affected many successful, well-known people, such as Sheryl Crow and Harrison Ford.

given a diagnosis of *dysthymic disorder,* **which consists of chronic depression that is insufficient in severity to justify diagnosis of a major depressive episode.**

How common are depressive disorders? Well, estimates of the prevalence of depression vary quite a bit from one study to another because of the previously mentioned difficulty in drawing a line between normal dejection and abnormal depression. That said, depression is clearly a common disorder. The pooled data from the large-scale studies cited in **Figure 14.5** yielded a lifetime prevalence estimate of 13%–14%. A recent study of a nationally representative sample of over 9000 adults estimated that the lifetime prevalence of depressive disorder was 16.2% (Kessler et al., 2003a). That estimate suggests that over 30 million people in the United States have suffered or will suffer from depression!

Research indicates that the prevalence of depression is about twice as high in women as it is in men (Rihmer & Angst, 2005). The many possible explanations for this gender gap are the subject of considerable debate. The gap does *not* appear to be attributable to differences in genetic makeup (Kessler et al., 2003a). A small portion of the disparity may be the result of women's elevated vulnerability to depression at certain points in their reproductive life cycle (Kornstein & Sloan, 2006). Obviously, only women have to worry abut the phenomena of postpartum and postmenopausal depression. Susan Nolen-Hoeksema (2001) argues that women experience more depression than men because they are far more likely to be victims of sexual abuse and somewhat more likely to endure poverty, sexual harassment, role constraints, and excessive pressure to be thin and attractive. In other words, she attributes the higher prevalence

of depression among women to their experience of greater stress and adversity. Nolen-Hoeksema also believes that women have a greater tendency than men to *ruminate* about setbacks and problems. Evidence suggests that this tendency to dwell on one's difficulties elevates vulnerability to depression, as we will discuss momentarily.

Bipolar Disorder

11b

***Bipolar disorder* (formerly known as *manic-depressive disorder*) is characterized by the experience of one or more manic episodes as well as periods of depression.** One manic episode is sufficient to qualify for this diagnosis. The symptoms seen in manic periods generally are the opposite of those seen in depression (see **Table 14.1** for a comparison). In a manic episode, a person's mood becomes elevated to the point of euphoria. Self-esteem skyrockets as the person bubbles over with optimism, energy, and extravagant plans. He or she becomes hyperactive and may go for days without sleep. The individual talks rapidly and shifts topics wildly, as his or her mind races at breakneck speed. Judgment is often impaired. Some people in manic periods gamble impulsively, spend money frantically, or become sexually reckless. Like depressive disorders, bipolar disorders vary considerably in severity. People are given a diagnosis of *cyclothymic disorder* **when they exhibit chronic but relatively mild symptoms of bipolar disturbance.**

You may be thinking that the euphoria in manic episodes sounds appealing. If so, you are not entirely wrong. In their milder forms, manic states can seem attractive. The increases in energy, self-esteem, and optimism can be deceptively seductive. Because of the increase in energy, many bipolar patients report temporary surges of productivity and creativity (Goodwin & Jamison, 1990).

Although manic episodes may have some positive aspects, these periods often have a paradoxical negative undercurrent of irritability and depression (Dilsaver et al., 1999). Moreover, mild manic episodes usually escalate to higher levels that become scary and disturbing. Impaired judgment leads many victims to do things that they greatly regret later, as you'll see in the following case history:

Robert, a dentist, awoke one morning with the idea that he was the most gifted dental surgeon in his tristate area. He decided that he should try to provide services to as many people as possible, so that more people could benefit from his talents. Thus, he decided to remodel his two-chair dental office, installing 20 booths so that he could simultaneously attend to 20 patients. That same day he

web link 14.7

Dr. Ivan's Depression Central

Some might suggest psychiatrist Ivan Goldberg's site would be better titled "Everything You Ever Wanted to Know About Depression." He offers a great depth of resources regarding mood disorders.

"Those? Oh, just a few souvenirs from my bipolar-disorder days."

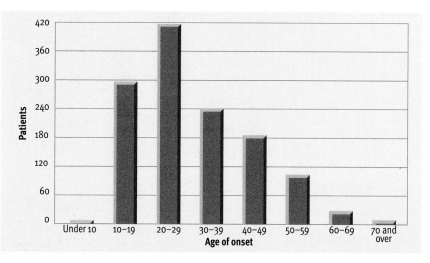

Figure 14.12

Age of onset for bipolar mood disorder. The onset of bipolar disorder typically occurs in adolescence or early adulthood. The data graphed here, which were combined from 10 studies, show the distribution of age of onset for 1304 bipolar patients. As you can see, bipolar disorder emerges most frequently during the 20s decade.

SOURCE: Goodwin, F. K., & Jamison, K. R. (1990). *Manic-depressive illness* (p. 132). New York: Oxford University Press. Copyright © 1990 Oxford University Press., Inc. Reprinted by permission.

drew up plans for this arrangement, telephoned a number of remodelers, and invited bids for the work. Later that day, impatient to get rolling on his remodeling, he rolled up his sleeves, got himself a sledgehammer, and began to knock down the walls in his office. Annoyed when that didn't go so well, he smashed his dental tools, washbasins, and X-ray equipment. Later, Robert's wife became concerned about his behavior and summoned two of her adult daughters for assistance. The daughters responded quickly, arriving at the family home with their husbands. In the ensuing discussion, Robert—after bragging about his sexual prowess—made advances toward his daughters. He had to be subdued by their husbands. (Adapted from Kleinmuntz, 1980, p. 309)

Although not rare, bipolar disorders are much less common than unipolar disorders. Bipolar disorder affects about 1%–2.5% of the population (Dubovsky et al., 2003). Unlike depressive disorder, bipolar disorder is seen equally often in males and females (Rihmer & Angst, 2005). As Figure 14.12 shows, the onset of bipolar disorder is age-related, with the age of 25 being the median age of onset (Miklowitz & Johnson, 2007). The mood swings in bipolar disorder can be patterned in many ways. About 20% of bipolar patients exhibit a *rapid-cycling pattern,* which means they go through four or more manic or depressive episodes within a year.

Mood Disorders and Suicide

A tragic, heartbreaking problem associated with mood disorders is suicide, which is the eleventh leading cause of death in the United States, accounting for about 30,000 deaths annually. Official statistics may underestimate the scope of the problem, as many suicides are disguised as accidents, either by the suicidal person or by the survivors who try to cover up afterward. Moreover, experts estimate

that suicide attempts may outnumber completed suicides by a ratio of as much as 20 to 1 (Sudak, 2005). Anyone can commit suicide, but some groups are at higher risk than others (Carroll-Ghosh, Victor, & Bourgeois, 2003). Evidence suggests that women *attempt* suicide three times more often than men. But men are more likely to actually kill themselves in an attempt, so they *complete* four times as many suicides as women. In regard to age, completed suicides peak in the over-75 age bracket.

With the luxury of hindsight, it is recognized that about 90% of the people who complete suicide suffer from some type of psychological disorder, although in some cases this disorder may not be readily apparent beforehand (Dawkins, Golden, & Fawcett, 2003). As you might expect, suicide rates are highest for people with mood disorders, who account for about 60% of completed suicides (Mann & Currier, 2006). Both bipolar disorder and depression are associated with dramatic elevations in suicide rates. Studies suggest that the lifetime risk of completed suicide is about 15%–20% in people with bipolar disorder and about 10% in those who have grappled with depression (Sudak, 2005). Smaller elevations in suicide rates are seen among people who suffer from schizophrenia, alcoholism, and substance abuse (Mann & Currier, 2006). Unfortunately, there is no foolproof way to prevent suicidal persons from taking their own life, but some useful tips are compiled in Figure 14.13 (on the next page).

Etiology of Mood Disorders 11b

Quite a bit is known about the etiology of mood disorders, although the puzzle certainly hasn't been assembled completely. There appear to be a number of routes into these disorders, involving intricate interactions among psychological and biological factors.

Figure 14.13
Preventing suicide. As Sudak (2005) notes, "it is not possible to prevent all suicides or to totally and absolutely protect a given patient from suicide. What is possible is to reduce the likelihood of suicide" (p. 2449). Hence, the advice summarized here may prove useful if you ever have to help someone through a suicidal crisis. (Based on American Association of Suicidology, 2007; American Foundation for Suicide Prevention, 2007; Fremouw et al., 1990; Rosenthal, 1988; Shneidman, Farberow, & Litman, 1994)

Suicide Prevention Tips

1. *Take suicidal talk seriously.* When people talk about suicide in vague generalities, it's easy to dismiss it as idle talk and let it go. However, people who talk about suicide are a high-risk group, and their veiled threats should not be ignored. The first step in suicide prevention is to directly ask such people if they're contemplating suicide.

2. *Provide empathy and social support.* It is important to show the suicidal person that you care. People often contemplate suicide because they see the world around them as indifferent and uncaring. Thus, you must demonstrate to the suicidal person that you are genuinely concerned. Suicide threats are often a last-ditch cry for help. It is therefore imperative that you offer to help.

3. *Identify and clarify the crucial problem.* The suicidal person is often confused and feels lost in a sea of frustration and problems. It is a good idea to try to help sort through this confusion. Encourage the person to try to identify the crucial problem. Once it is isolated, the problem may not seem quite so overwhelming.

4. *Do not promise to keep someone's suicidal ideation secret.* If you really feel like someone's life is in danger, don't agree to keep his or her suicidal plans secret to preserve your friendship.

5. *In an acute crisis, do not leave a suicidal person alone.* Stay with the person until additional help is available. Try to remove any guns, drugs, sharp objects, and so forth that might provide an available means to commit suicide.

6. *Encourage professional consultation.* Most mental health professionals have some experience in dealing with suicidal crises. Many cities have suicide prevention centers with 24-hour hotlines. These centers are staffed with people who have been specially trained to deal with suicidal problems. It is important to try to get a suicidal person to seek professional assistance.

Genetic Vulnerability 11b

Twin studies suggest that genetic factors are involved in mood disorders (Berrettini, 2006; Kelsoe, 2005). Concordance rates average around 65% for identical twins but only 14% for fraternal twins, who share less genetic similarity (see Figure 14.14). Thus, evidence suggests that heredity can create a *predisposition* to mood disorders. Environmental factors probably determine whether this predisposition is converted into an actual disorder. The influence of genetic factors appears to be stronger for bipolar disorders than for unipolar disorders (Kieseppa et al., 2004). Some promising results have been reported in *genetic mapping* studies that have attempted to pinpoint the specific genes that shape vulnerabil-

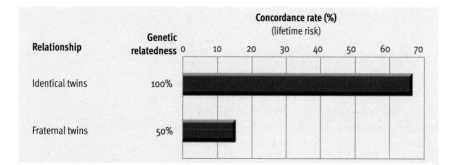

ity to mood disorders (Caspi et al., 2003; Holmans et al., 2007). However, results have been disturbingly inconsistent, and scientists do *not* appear to be on the verge of unraveling the genetic code for mood disorders, which probably depend on subtle variations in constellations of many genes (Kendler, 2005a, 2005b; Merikangas & Risch, 2003).

Neurochemical and Neuroanatomical Factors 11b

Heredity may influence susceptibility to mood disorders by creating a predisposition toward certain types of neurochemical abnormalities in the brain. Correlations have been found between mood disorders and abnormal levels of two neurotransmitters in the brain: norepinephrine and serotonin (Sher & Mann, 2003), although other neurotransmitter disturbances may also contribute (Thase, Jindal, & Howland, 2002). The details remain elusive, but low levels of serotonin appear to be a crucial factor underlying most forms of depression (Flores et al., 2004). A variety of drug therapies are fairly effective in the treatment of severe mood disorders. Most of these drugs are known to affect the availability (in the brain) of the neurotransmitters that have been related to mood disorders (Dubovsky et al., 2003). Since this effect is unlikely to be a coincidence, it bolsters the plausibility of the idea that neurochemical changes produce mood disturbances. That said, after 40 years of enormous research effort, the neurochemical bases of mood disorders remain more mysterious than scientists would like (Delgado & Moreno, 2006).

Studies have also found some interesting correlations between mood disorders and a variety of structural abnormalities in the brain (Flores et al., 2004). Perhaps the best documented correlation is the association between depression and *reduced hippocampal volume* (Campbell et al., 2004; Videbech, 2006). The *hippocampus,* which is known to play a major role in memory consolidation (see Chapter 7), tends to be about 8%–10% smaller in depressed subjects than in normal subjects (Videbech & Ravnkilde, 2004). A fascinating new theory of the biological bases of depression may be able to account for this finding. The springboard for this theory is the recent discovery that the human brain continues to generate new neurons in adulthood, especially in the hippocampal formation (Gage, 2002). As noted elsewhere (see Chapters 3, 7, and 13), this process is called *neurogenesis.* Recent evidence suggests that depression occurs when major life stress causes neurochemical reactions that suppress neurogenesis, resulting in reduced hippocampal volume (Jacobs, 2004; Warner-Schmidt & Duman, 2006). According to this view, it is the suppression of neurogenesis that is the central cause of depression and antidepressant drugs are successful because they promote neurogenesis (Duman & Montaggia, 2006). A great deal of additional research will be required to fully test this innovative new model of the biological bases of depressive disorders.

Cognitive Factors

11b

A variety of theories emphasize how cognitive factors contribute to depressive disorders (Christensen, Carney, & Segal, 2006). We will discuss Aaron Beck's (1976, 1987) influential cognitive theory of depression in Chapter 15, where his approach to therapy is described. In this section, we'll examine Martin Seligman's *learned helplessness model* of depression. Based largely on animal research, Seligman (1974) proposed that depression is caused by *learned helplessness*—passive "giving up" behavior produced by exposure to unavoidable aversive events (such as uncontrollable shock in the laboratory). He originally considered learned helplessness to be a product of conditioning but eventually revised his theory, giving it a cognitive slant. The reformulated theory of learned helplessness asserts that the roots of depression lie in how people explain the setbacks and other negative events that they experience (Abramson, Seligman, & Teasdale, 1978). According to Seligman (1990), people who exhibit a *pessimistic explanatory style* are especially vulnerable to depression. These people tend to attribute their setbacks to their personal flaws instead of situational factors, and they tend to draw global, far-reaching conclusions about their personal inadequacies based on these setbacks.

In accord with this line of thinking, Susan Nolen-Hoeksema (1991, 2000) has found that depressed people who *ruminate* about their depression remain depressed longer than those who try to distract themselves. People who respond to depression with rumination repetitively focus their attention on their depressing feelings, thinking constantly about how sad, lethargic, and unmotivated they are. According to Nolen-Hoeksema (1995), excessive rumination tends to extend and amplify individuals' episodes of depression. As we noted earlier, she believes that women are more likely to ruminate than men and that this disparity may be one of the primary reasons why depression is more prevalent in women.

In sum, cognitive models of depression maintain that negative thinking is what leads to depression in many people. The principal problem with cognitive theories is their difficulty in separating cause from effect (Feliciano & Arean, 2007). Does negative thinking cause depression? Or does depression cause negative thinking (see **Figure 14.15**)? A *clear* demonstration of a causal link between negative thinking and depression is not possible because it would require manipulating people's cognitive style (which is not easy to change) in sufficient degree to produce full-fledged depressive disorders (which would not be ethical). However, the research reported in our Featured Study provided impressive evidence consistent with a causal link between negative thinking and vulnerability to depression.

Courtesy of Susan Nolen-Hoeksema

Susan Nolen-Hoeksema

"By adolescence, girls appear to be more likely than boys to respond to stress and distress with rumination—focusing inward on feelings of distress and personal concerns rather than taking action to relieve their distress."

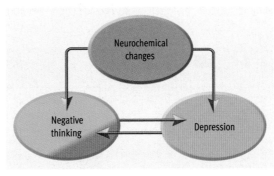

Figure 14.15

Interpreting the correlation between negative thinking and depression. Cognitive theories of depression assume that consistent patterns of negative thinking cause depression. Although these theories are highly plausible, depression could cause negative thoughts, or both could be caused by a third factor, such as neurochemical changes in the brain.

Does Negative Thinking Cause Depression?

This article describes a series of studies conducted at Temple University and at the University of Wisconsin, collectively referred to as the Temple-Wisconsin Cognitive Vulnerability to Depression Project. Although the article reports on many facets of the project, we will focus on the study intended to test the hypothesis that a negative cognitive style is predictive of elevated vulnerability to depression.

Method

Participants. Over 5,000 first-year students at the two universities responded to two measures of negative thinking. Students who scored in the highest quartile on both mea-

sures were characterized as having a *high risk* for depression, while those who scored in the lowest quartile on both measures were characterized as having a *low risk* for depression. Randomly selected subsets of these two groups were invited for additional screening to eliminate anyone who was *currently* depressed or suffering from any other major psychological disorder. People who had *previously* suffered from depression or other disorders were not eliminated. The final sample consisted of 173 students in the high-risk group and 176 students in the low-risk group.

Follow-up assessments. Self-report measures and structured interviews were used to evaluate the mental health

SOURCE: Alloy, L. B., Abramson, L. Y., Whitehouse, W. G., Hogan, M. E., Tashman, N. A., Steinberg, D. L., Rose, D. T., & Donovan, P. (1999). Depressogenic cognitive styles: Predictive validity, information processing and personality characteristics, and developmental origins. *Behavioral Research and Therapy, 37,* 503–531.

FEATURED

STUDY

of the participants every 6 weeks for the first two years and then every 16 weeks for an additional three years. The assessments were conducted by interviewers who were blind regarding the subjects' risk group status. The present report summarized the follow-up data for the first two and one-half years of the study. The results were given separately for those who did and did not have a prior history of depression.

Results

The data for students who had no prior history of depression showed dramatic differences between the high-risk and low-risk groups in vulnerability to depression. During the relatively brief 2.5-year period, a major depressive disorder emerged in 17% of the high-risk students in comparison to only 1% of the low-risk students. The high-risk subjects also displayed a much greater incidence of minor depressive episodes, as you can see in the left panel of **Figure 14.16**. The right panel of **Figure 14.16** shows the comparisons for participants who had a prior history of depression (but were not depressed or suffering from any other disorder at the beginning of the study). The data show that high-risk subjects were more vulnerable to a recurrence of both major and minor depression during the 2.5-year follow-up.

Discussion

The high-risk participants, who exhibited a negative cognitive style, were consistently found to have an elevated likelihood of developing depressive disorders. Hence, the authors conclude that their results provide strong support for the cognitive vulnerability hypothesis, which asserts that negative thinking makes people more vulnerable to depression.

Comment

Previous studies of the correlation between negative thinking and depression used *retrospective designs,* which look backward in time from known outcomes. For example, investigators might compare depressed subjects versus nondepressed subjects on some measure of negative thinking. What makes the design retrospective is that the researchers already know which people experienced the outcome of depression. Retrospective designs can yield useful information, but they don't provide much insight about causation. Why? Because if you find an association between depression and negative thinking you can't determine whether the negative thinking preceded the depression or the depression preceded the negative thinking. The present study used a *prospective design* which moves forward in time, testing hypotheses about future outcomes. Prospective studies are much more difficult and time-consuming to conduct, but they can provide more insight about causation because they can show that one event (in this instance, the development of a negative cognitive style) preceded another (the occurrence of depression). The data are still correlational, so they cannot definitively establish a causal link, but they provide much stronger evidence in favor of causation than retrospective data. Thus, the research by Alloy and her colleagues provides the best evidence to date in support of the hypothesis that negative thinking contributes to the causation of depressive disorders.

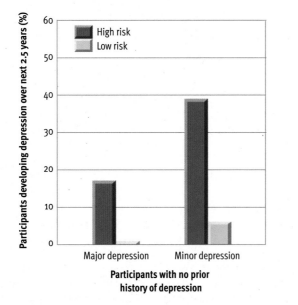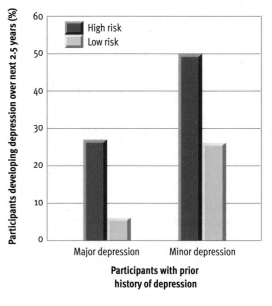

Figure 14.16

Negative thinking and prediction of depression. Alloy and colleagues (1999) measured the cognitive styles of first-year college students and characterized the students as high risk or low risk for depression. These graphs show the percentage of these students who experienced major or minor episodes of depression over the next 2.5 years. As you can see, the high-risk students who exhibited a negative thinking style proved to be much more vulnerable to depression.

Interpersonal Roots   11b

Behavioral approaches to understanding depression emphasize how inadequate social skills put people on the road to depressive disorders (see Figure 14.17; Coyne, 1999). According to this notion, depression-prone people lack the social finesse needed to acquire many important kinds of reinforcers, such as good friends, top jobs, and desirable spouses. This paucity of reinforcers could understandably lead to negative emotions and depression. Consistent with this theory, researchers have found correlations between poor social skills and depression (Petty, Sachs-Ericsson, & Joiner, 2004).

Another interpersonal factor is that depressed people tend to be depressing (Joiner & Katz, 1999). Individuals suffering from depression often are irritable and pessimistic. They complain a lot and aren't particularly enjoyable companions. They also alienate people by constantly asking for reassurances about their relationships and their worth (Burns et al., 2006). As a consequence, depressed people tend to court rejection from those around them (Joiner & Metalsky, 1995). Depressed people thus have fewer sources of social support than nondepressed people, which may aggravate and deepen their depression (Potthoff, Holahan, & Joiner, 1995). Moreover, recent evidence suggests that lack of social support may make a larger contribution to depression in women than in men (Kendler, Myers, & Prescott, 2005). To compound these problems, evidence indicates that depressed people may gravitate to partners who view them unfavorably and hence reinforce their negative views of themselves (Joiner, 2002).

Precipitating Stress   11b

Mood disorders sometimes appear mysteriously in people who are leading benign, nonstressful lives. For this reason, experts used to believe that mood

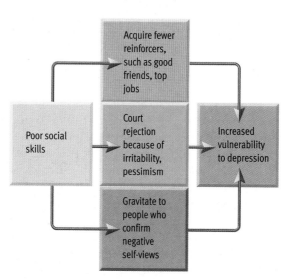

Figure 14.17

Interpersonal factors in depression. Behavioral theories about the etiology of depression emphasize how inadequate social skills may contribute to the development of the disorder through several mechanisms, as diagrammed here.

disorders are not influenced much by stress. However, advances in the measurement of personal stress have altered this picture. The evidence available today suggests a moderately strong link between stress and the onset of mood disorders (Hammen, 2005; Kendler, Kuhn, & Prescott, 2004). Stress also appears to affect how people with mood disorders respond to treatment and whether they experience a relapse of their disorder (Monroe & Hadjiyannakis, 2002).

Of course, many people endure great stress without getting depressed. The impact of stress varies, in part, because people vary in their degree of *vulnerability* to mood disorders (Lewinsohn, Joiner, & Rohde, 2001). Similar interactions between stress and vulnerability probably influence the development of many kinds of disorders, including those that are next on our agenda—the schizophrenic disorders.

REVIEW of Key Points

14.12 Major depression is marked by profound sadness, slowed thought processes, and loss of interest in previous sources of pleasure. Bipolar disorder involves the experience of both manic episodes and periods of depression. Manic episodes are characterized by inflated self-esteem, high energy, grandiose plans, and racing thoughts. Depression is extremely common, whereas the lifetime prevalence of bipolar disorder is about 1%–2.5%. Both types of mood disorders are associated with greatly elevated rates of suicide.

14.13 Evidence indicates that people vary in their genetic vulnerability to mood disorders. These disorders are accompanied by changes in neurochemical activity in the brain. Abnormalities at norepinephrine and serotonin synapses appear par-

ticularly critical. Reduced hippocampal volume and suppressed neurogenesis are also associated with depression.

14.14 Cognitive models posit that negative thinking contributes to depression. A pessimistic explanatory style has been implicated, as has a tendency to ruminate about one's problems. The Featured Study reported impressive evidence in support of the idea that negative thinking can contribute to the causation of depression.

14.15 Interpersonal inadequacies may contribute to depressive disorders. Poor social skills may lead to a paucity of life's reinforcers and frequent rejection. Mood disorders may also be precipitated by high stress, especially in those who are particularly vulnerable to mood disorders.

Key Learning Goals

14.16 Review the general characteristics of schizophrenia.

14.17 Outline the classification of schizophrenic subtypes and the course of schizophrenia.

14.18 Explain how genetic vulnerability and neurochemical factors can contribute to schizophrenia.

14.19 Analyze the role of structural abnormalities in the brain and neurodevelopmental processes in the etiology of schizophrenia.

14.20 Summarize how family dynamics and stress may be related to the development of schizophrenia.

Schizophrenic Disorders   SIM9

Literally, *schizophrenia* means "split mind." However, when Eugen Bleuler coined the term in 1911 he was referring to the fragmentation of thought processes seen in the disorder—not to a "split personality." Unfortunately, writers in the popular media often assume that the split-mind notion, and thus schizophrenia, refers to the rare syndrome in which a person manifests two or more personalities. As you have already learned, this syndrome is actually called *dissociative identity disorder* or *multiple-personality disorder.* Schizophrenia is a much more common, and altogether different, type of disorder.

Schizophrenic disorders are a class of disorders marked by delusions, hallucinations, disorganized speech, and deterioration of adaptive behavior. People with schizophrenic disorders often display some of the same symptoms seen in people with severe mood disorders; however, disturbed *thought* lies at the core of schizophrenic disorders, whereas disturbed *emotion* lies at the core of mood disorders.

How common is schizophrenia? Prevalence estimates suggest that about 1% of the population may suffer from schizophrenic disorders (Lauriello, Bustillo, & Keith, 2005). That may not sound like much, but it means that in the United States alone there may be several million people troubled by schizophrenic disturbances. Moreover, schizophrenia is an extremely costly illness for society, because it is a severe, debilitating disorder that tends to have an early onset and often requires lengthy hospital care (Buchanan & Carpenter, 2000). Because of these considerations, the financial impact of schizophrenia is estimated to exceed the costs of all types of cancers combined (Buchanan & Carpenter, 2005).

General Symptoms   11c

There are a number of distinct schizophrenic syndromes, but they share some general characteristics that we will examine before looking at the subtypes. Many of these characteristics are apparent in the following case history (adapted from Sheehan, 1982).

Sylvia was first given a diagnosis of schizophrenia at age 15. She has been in and out of many types of psychiatric facilities since then. She has never been able to hold a job for any length of time. During severe flare-ups of her disorder, her personal hygiene deteriorates. She rarely washes, she wears clothes that neither fit nor match, she smears makeup on heavily but randomly, and she slops food all over herself.

Sylvia occasionally hears voices talking to her. She tends to be argumentative, aggressive, and emotionally volatile. Over the years, she has been involved in innumerable fights with fellow patients, psychiatric staff members, and strangers. Her thoughts can be highly irrational, as is apparent from the following quote, which was recorded while she was a patient in a psychiatric facility called Creedmoor:

"Mick Jagger wants to marry me. If I have Mick Jagger, I don't have to covet Geraldo Rivera. Mick Jagger is St. Nicholas and the Maharishi is Santa Claus. I want to form a gospel rock group called the Thorn Oil, but Geraldo wants me to be the music critic on Eyewitness News, so what can I do? Got to listen to my boyfriend. Teddy Kennedy cured me of my ugliness. I'm pregnant with the son of God. I'm going to marry David Berkowitz and get it over with. Creedmoor is the headquarters of the American Nazi Party. They're eating the patients here. Archie Bunker wants me to play his niece on his TV show. I work for Epic Records. I'm Joan of Arc. I'm Florence Nightingale. The door between the ward and the porch is the dividing line between New York and California. Divorce isn't a piece of paper, it's a feeling. Forget about Zip Codes. I need shock treatments. The body is run by electricity. My wiring is all faulty." (Sheehan, 1982, pp. 104–105)

Sylvia's case clearly shows that schizophrenic thinking can be bizarre and that schizophrenia can be a severe and debilitating disorder. Although no single symptom is inevitably present, the following symptoms are commonly seen in schizophrenia (Ho, Black, & Andreasen, 2003; Lindenmayer & Khan, 2006).

Delusions and Irrational Thought

Cognitive deficits and disturbed thought processes are the central, defining feature of schizophrenic disorders (Barch, 2003; Heinrichs, 2005). Various kinds of delusions are common. **Delusions** are false beliefs that are maintained even though they clearly are out of touch with reality. For example, one patient's delusion that he was a tiger (with a deformed body) persisted for more than 15 years (Kulick, Pope, & Keck, 1990). More typically, affected persons believe that their private thoughts are being broadcast to other people, that thoughts are being injected into their mind against their will, or that their thoughts are being controlled by some external force (Maher, 2001). In *delusions of grandeur,* people maintain that they are famous or important.

Sylvia expressed an endless array of grandiose delusions, such as thinking that Mick Jagger wanted to marry her, that she had dictated the hobbit stories to J. R. R. Tolkien, and that she was going to win the Nobel prize for medicine.

Another characteristic of schizophrenia is that the person's train of thought deteriorates. Thinking becomes chaotic rather than logical and linear. The person experiences a "loosening of associations," as he or she shifts topics in disjointed ways. The quotation from Sylvia illustrates this symptom dramatically. The entire quote involves a wild flight of ideas, but at one point (beginning with the sentence "Creedmoor is the headquarters . . .") she rattles off ten consecutive sentences that have no apparent connection to each other.

Deterioration of Adaptive Behavior

Schizophrenia usually involves a noticeable deterioration in the quality of the person's routine functioning in work, social relations, and personal care. Friends will often make remarks such as "Hal just isn't himself anymore." This deterioration is readily apparent in Sylvia's inability to get along with others or to function in the work world. It's also apparent in her neglect of personal hygiene.

Hallucinations

A variety of perceptual distortions may occur with schizophrenia, the most common being auditory hallucinations, which are reported by about 75% of patients (Combs & Mueser, 2007). *Hallucinations are sensory perceptions that occur in the absence of a real, external stimulus or are gross distortions of perceptual input.* People with schizophrenia frequently report that they hear voices of nonexistent or absent people talking to them. Sylvia, for instance, said she heard messages from Paul McCartney. These voices often provide an insulting, running commentary on the person's behavior ("You're an idiot for shaking his hand"). They may be argumentative ("You don't need a bath"), and they may issue commands ("Prepare your home for visitors from outer space").

Disturbed Emotion

Normal emotional tone can be disrupted in schizophrenia in a variety of ways. Although it may not be an accurate indicator of their underlying emotional experience (Kring, 1999), some victims show little emotional responsiveness, a symptom referred to as "blunted or flat affect." Others show inappropriate emotional responses that don't jibe with the situation or with what they are saying. For instance, a schizophrenic patient might cry over a silly cartoon

and then laugh about a news story describing a child's tragic death. People with schizophrenia may also become emotionally volatile. This pattern was displayed by Sylvia, who often overreacted emotionally in erratic, unpredictable ways.

Subtypes, Course, and Outcome 11c

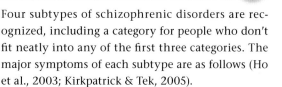

Four subtypes of schizophrenic disorders are recognized, including a category for people who don't fit neatly into any of the first three categories. The major symptoms of each subtype are as follows (Ho et al., 2003; Kirkpatrick & Tek, 2005).

Paranoid Type

As its name implies, *paranoid schizophrenia* is dominated by delusions of persecution, along with delusions of grandeur. In this common form of schizophrenia, people come to believe that they have many enemies who want to harass and oppress them. They may become suspicious of friends and relatives, or they may attribute the persecution to mysterious, unknown persons. They are convinced that they are being watched and manipulated in malicious ways. To make sense of this persecution, they often develop delusions of grandeur. They believe that they must be enormously important people, frequently seeing themselves as great inventors or as famous religious or political leaders. For example, in the case described at the beginning of the chapter, Ed's belief that he was president of the United States was a delusion of grandeur.

Catatonic Type

Catatonic schizophrenia is marked by striking motor disturbances, ranging from muscular rigidity to random motor activity. Some patients go into an extreme form of withdrawal known as a catatonic stupor. They may remain virtually motionless and seem oblivious to the environment around them for long periods of time. Others go into a state of catatonic excitement. They become hyperactive and incoherent. Some alternate between these dramatic extremes. The catatonic subtype is not particularly common, and its prevalence seems to be declining.

Disorganized Type

In *disorganized schizophrenia,* a particularly severe deterioration of adaptive behavior is seen. Prominent symptoms include emotional indifference, frequent incoherence, and virtually complete social withdrawal. Aimless babbling and giggling are common. Delusions often center on bodily functions ("My brain is melting out my ears").

web link 14.8

Doctor's Guide to the Internet: Schizophrenia

Produced by a communications and medical education consulting company, the free Doctor's Guide site is updated frequently to provide a current overview of the state of research on schizophrenic disorders. A more detailed set of resources for physicians parallels this site, which is intended primarily for patients and their families.

Undifferentiated Type

People who are clearly schizophrenic but who cannot be placed into any of the three previous categories are said to have *undifferentiated schizophrenia,* which is marked by idiosyncratic mixtures of schizophrenic symptoms. The undifferentiated subtype is fairly common.

Positive Versus Negative Symptoms

Many theorists have raised doubts about the value of dividing schizophrenic disorders into the four subtypes just described (Sanislow & Carson, 2001). Critics note that the catatonic subtype is disappearing and that undifferentiated cases aren't so much a subtype as a hodgepodge of "leftovers." Critics also point out that there aren't meaningful differences between the subtypes in etiology, prognosis, or response to treatment. The absence of such differences casts doubt on the value of the current classification scheme.

Because of such problems, Nancy Andreasen (1990) and others (Carpenter, 1992; McGlashan & Fenton, 1992) have proposed an alternative approach to subtyping. This new scheme divides schizophrenic disorders into just two categories based on the predominance of negative versus posi-

Nancy Andreasen

"Schizophrenia disfigures the emotional and cognitive faculties of its victims, and sometimes nearly destroys them."

tive symptoms. *Negative symptoms* involve behavioral deficits, such as flattened emotions, social withdrawal, apathy, impaired attention, and poverty of speech. *Positive symptoms* involve behavioral excesses or peculiarities, such as hallucinations, delusions, bizarre behavior, and wild flights of ideas.

Theorists advocating this scheme hoped to find consistent differences between the two subtypes in etiology, prognosis, and response to treatment, and some progress along these lines *has* been made. For example, a predominance of positive symptoms is associated with better adjustment prior to the onset of schizophrenia and greater responsiveness to treatment (Combs & Mueser, 2007; Galderisi et al., 2002). However, the assumption that patients can be placed into discrete categories based on this scheme now seems untenable. Most patients exhibit both types of symptoms and vary only in the *degree* to which positive or negative symptoms dominate (Black & Andreasen, 1999). Although it seems fair to say that the distinction between positive and negative symptoms is enhancing our understanding of schizophrenia, it has not yielded a classification scheme that can replace the traditional subtypes of schizophrenia.

Course and Outcome

Schizophrenic disorders usually emerge during adolescence or early adulthood, with 75% of cases manifesting by the age of 30 (Perkins, Miller-Anderson, & Lieberman, 2006). Those who develop schizophrenia usually have a long history of peculiar behavior and cognitive and social deficits, although most do not manifest a full-fledged psychological disorder during childhood (Walker et al., 2004). The emergence of schizophrenia may be sudden, but it is usually insidious and gradual. Once the disorder clearly emerges, its course is variable, but patients tend to fall into three broad groups. Some patients, presumably those with milder disorders, are treated successfully and enjoy a full recovery. Other patients experience a partial recovery and they can return to independent living for a time. However, they experience regular relapses over the remainder of their lives. Finally, a third group of patients endure chronic illness marked by relentless deterioration and extensive hospitalization. Estimates of the percentage of patients falling in each category vary. Overall, the preponderance of studies have suggested that only about 20 percent of schizophrenic patients enjoy a full recovery (Perkins et al., 2006; Robinson et al., 2004). However, to some extent, this low recovery rate may reflect the poor to mediocre quality of mental health care available for severe disorders in many countries (see Chapter 15). When

---

concept check 14.3

Distinguishing Schizophrenic and Mood Disorders

Check your understanding of the nature of schizophrenic and mood disorders by making preliminary diagnoses for the cases described below. Read each case summary and write your tentative diagnosis in the space provided. The answers are in Appendix A.

1. Max hasn't slept in four days. He's determined to write the "great American novel" before his class reunion, which is a few months away. He expounds eloquently on his novel to anyone who will listen, talking at such a rapid pace that no one can get a word in edgewise. He feels like he's wired with energy and is supremely confident about the novel, even though he's only written 10 to 20 pages. Last week, he charged $5000 worth of new computer equipment and software, which is supposed to help him write his book.

   Preliminary diagnosis: _____

2. Eduardo maintains that he invented the atomic bomb, even though he was born after its invention. He says he invented it to punish homosexuals, Nazis, and short people. It's short people that he's really afraid of. He's sure that all the short people on TV are talking about him. He thinks that short people are conspiring to make him look like a Republican. Eduardo frequently gets in arguments with people and is emotionally volatile. His grooming is poor, but he says it's okay because he's the secretary of state.

   Preliminary diagnosis: _____

3. Margaret has hardly gotten out of bed for weeks, although she's troubled by insomnia. She doesn't feel like eating and has absolutely no energy. She feels dejected, discouraged, spiritless, and apathetic. Friends stop by to try to cheer her up, but she tells them not to waste their time on "pond scum."

   Preliminary diagnosis: _____

comprehensive, well-coordinated, quality care is initiated promptly, higher recovery rates in the vicinity of 50% have been found (Hopper et al., 2007; Liberman & Kopelowicz, 2005). Thus, the outlook for schizophrenia may not need to be as pervasively negative as it has been.

Etiology of Schizophrenia 11c

You can probably identify, at least to some extent, with people who suffer from mood disorders, somatoform disorders, and anxiety disorders. You can probably imagine events that could unfold that might leave you struggling with depression, grappling with anxiety, or worrying about your physical health. But what could possibly have led Ed to believe that he had been fighting space wars and vampires? What could account for Sylvia's thinking that she was Joan of Arc or that she had dictated the hobbit novels to Tolkien? As mystifying as these delusions may seem, you'll see that the etiology of schizophrenic disorders is not all that different from the etiology of other psychological disorders. We'll begin our discussion by examining the matter of genetic vulnerability.

Genetic Vulnerability 11c

Evidence is plentiful that hereditary factors play a role in the development of schizophrenic disorders (Sullivan et al., 2006; Tsuang, Glatt, & Faraone, 2003). For instance, in twin studies, concordance rates average around 48% for identical twins, in comparison to about 17% for fraternal twins (Gottesman, 1991, 2001). Studies also indicate that a child born to two schizophrenic parents has about a 46% probability of developing a schizophrenic disorder (as compared to the probability in the general population of about 1%). These and other findings that demonstrate the genetic roots of schizophrenia are summarized in Figure 14.18. Overall, the picture is similar to that seen for mood disorders. Several converging lines of evidence indicate that some people inherit a polygenically transmitted *vulnerability* to schizophrenia (Riley & Kendler, 2005; Schneider & Deldin, 2001). Although some theorists suspect that genetic factors may account for as much as two-thirds of the variability in susceptibility to schizophrenia, genetic mapping studies have made little progress in identifying the specific genes at work (Crow, 2007; Walker & Tessner, 2008).

Neurochemical Factors 11c

Like mood disorders, schizophrenic disorders appear to be accompanied by changes in the activity of one

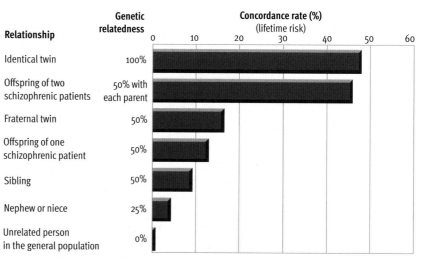

or more neurotransmitters in the brain (Patel, Pinals, & Breier, 2003). The *dopamine hypothesis* asserts that excess dopamine activity is the neurochemical basis for schizophrenia, as presented in Figure 14.19 on the next page. This hypothesis makes sense because most of the drugs that are useful in the treatment of schizophrenia are known to dampen dopamine activity in the brain (Javitt & Laruelle, 2006; Tamminga & Carlsson, 2003). However, the evidence linking schizophrenia to high dopamine levels is riddled with inconsistencies, complexities, and interpretive problems (Abi-Dargham, 2004). Researchers are currently exploring how interactions between the dopamine and serotonin neurotransmitter systems may contribute to schizophrenia (Patel et al., 2003).

Recent research has suggested that marijuana use during adolescence may help precipitate schizophrenia in young people who have a genetic vulnerability to the disorder (Compton, Goulding, & Walker, 2007; Degenhardt & Hall, 2006). This unexpected finding has generated considerable debate about whether and how cannabis might contribute to the emergence of schizophrenia (Castle, 2008; DeLisi, 2008). The current thinking is that the key chemical ingredient in marijuana (THC) may amplify neurotransmitter activity in dopamine circuits (Degenhardt & Hall, 2006; Di Forti et al., 2007). The data on this issue are still preliminary, and more research will be needed to fully understand the association between marijuana use and schizophrenia.

Structural Abnormalities in the Brain 11c

For decades, studies have suggested that individuals with schizophrenia exhibit a variety of deficits in attention, perception, and information processing (Gold & Green, 2005; Keefe & Eesley, 2006). Impairments in working (short-term) memory are

Figure 14.18

Genetic vulnerability to schizophrenic disorders. Relatives of schizophrenic patients have an elevated risk for schizophrenia. This risk is greater among closer relatives. Although environment also plays a role in the etiology of schizophrenia, the concordance rates shown here suggest that there must be a genetic vulnerability to the disorder. These concordance estimates are based on pooled data from 40 studies conducted between 1920 and 1987. (Data from Gottesman, 1991)

Figure 14.19

The dopamine hypothesis as an explanation for schizophrenia. Decades of research have implicated overactivity at dopamine synapses as a key cause of schizophrenic disorders. However, the evidence on the exact mechanisms underlying this overactivity, which is summarized in this graphic, is complex and open to debate. Recent hypotheses about the neurochemical bases of schizophrenia go beyond the simple assumption that dopamine activity is increased. For example, one theory posits that schizophrenia may be accompanied by decreased dopamine activity in one area of the brain (the prefrontal cortex) and increased activity or dysregulation in other areas of the brain (Egan & Hyde, 2000). Moreover, abnormalities in other neurotransmitter systems may also contribute to schizophrenia.

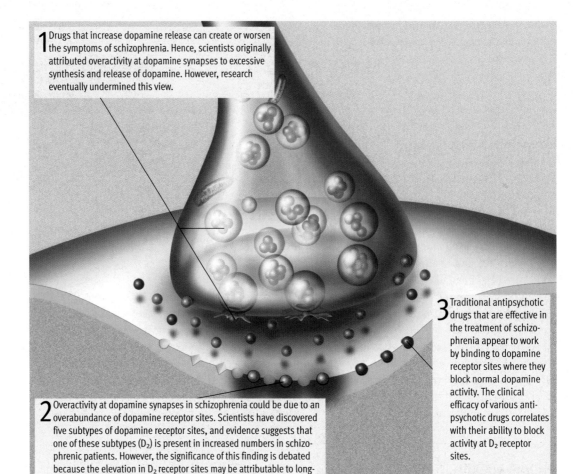

1 Drugs that increase dopamine release can create or worsen the symptoms of schizophrenia. Hence, scientists originally attributed overactivity at dopamine synapses to excessive synthesis and release of dopamine. However, research eventually undermined this view.

2 Overactivity at dopamine synapses in schizophrenia could be due to an overabundance of dopamine receptor sites. Scientists have discovered five subtypes of dopamine receptor sites, and evidence suggests that one of these subtypes (D_2) is present in increased numbers in schizophrenic patients. However, the significance of this finding is debated because the elevation in D_2 receptor sites may be attributable to long-term treatment with antipsychotic drugs.

3 Traditional antipsychotic drugs that are effective in the treatment of schizophrenia appear to work by binding to dopamine receptor sites where they block normal dopamine activity. The clinical efficacy of various antipsychotic drugs correlates with their ability to block activity at D_2 receptor sites.

especially prominent (Silver et al., 2003). These cognitive deficits suggest that schizophrenic disorders may be caused by neurological defects. Until recent decades this theory was based more on speculation than on actual research. Now, however, advances in brain-imaging technology have yielded mountains of intriguing data. The most reliable finding is that CT scans and MRI scans (see Chapter 3) suggest an association between enlarged brain ventricles (the hollow, fluid-filled cavities in the brain depicted in **Figure 14.20**) and schizophrenic disturbance (Belger & Dichter, 2006). Enlarged ventricles are assumed to reflect the degeneration of nearby brain tissue. The significance of enlarged ventricles is hotly debated, however. This structural deterioration (or failure to develop) could be a *consequence* of schizophrenia, or it could be a contributing *cause* of the illness.

Brain-imaging studies have also uncovered structural and metabolic abnormalities in the frontal lobes of individuals with schizophrenia. Although the research results are not entirely consistent, schizophrenia appears to be associated with smaller size and reduced metabolic activity in areas of the prefrontal

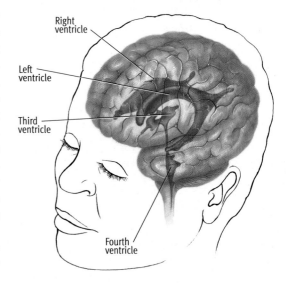

Right ventricle

Left ventricle

Third ventricle

Fourth ventricle

Figure 14.20

Schizophrenia and the ventricles of the brain. Cerebrospinal fluid (CSF) circulates around the brain and spinal cord. The hollow cavities in the brain filled with CSF are called ventricles. The four ventricles in the human brain are depicted here. Recent studies with CT scans and MRI scans suggest that an association exists between enlarged ventricles in the brain and the occurrence of schizophrenic disturbance.

cortex (Fowles, 2003). Scientists are also intrigued by the fact that a major dopamine pathway runs through the area in the prefrontal cortex where metabolic abnormalities have been found. A connection may exist between the abnormal dopamine activity implicated in schizophrenia and the dysfunctional metabolic activity seen in this area of the prefrontal cortex (Conklin & Iacono, 2002). Although the research on the prefrontal cortex is intriguing, Ho, Black, and Andreasen (2003) caution that the neural correlates of schizophrenia are complex and that the disease is not likely to be caused by "a single abnormality in a single region of the brain" (p. 408).

The Neurodevelopmental Hypothesis

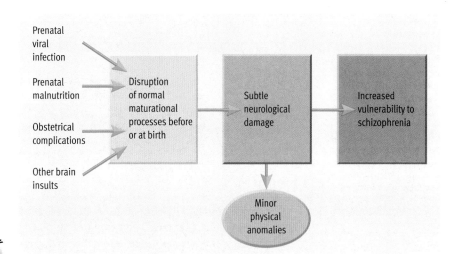

Several relatively new lines of evidence have led to the emergence of the *neurodevelopmental hypothesis* of schizophrenia, which asserts that schizophrenia is caused in part by various disruptions in the normal maturational processes of the brain before or at birth (Brown, 1999). According to this hypothesis, insults to the brain during sensitive phases of prenatal development or during birth can cause subtle neurological damage that elevates individuals' vulnerability to schizophrenia years later in adolescence and early adulthood (see **Figure 14.21**). What are the sources of these early insults to the brain? Thus far, research has mostly focused on viral infections or malnutrition during prenatal development and obstetrical complications during the birth process.

The evidence on viral infections has been building since Sarnoff Mednick and his colleagues (1988) discovered an elevated incidence of schizophrenia among individuals who were in their second trimester of prenatal development during a 1957 influenza epidemic in Finland. Several subsequent studies in other locations have also found a link between exposure to influenza during the second trimester and increased prevalence of schizophrenia (Brown et al., 2004). Another study, which investigated the possible impact of prenatal malnutrition, found an elevated incidence of schizophrenia in a cohort of people who were prenatally exposed to a severe famine in 1944–45 resulting from a Nazi blockade of food deliveries in the Netherlands during World War II (Susser et al., 1996). A recent study looked at a new source of disruption during prenatal development: severe maternal stress. The study found an elevated prevalence of schizophrenia among the offspring of women who suffered severe stress during their pregnancy (Khashan et al., 2008). Other research has shown that schizophrenic patients are more likely than control subjects to have a history of obstetrical complications (Kelly et al., 2004; Murray & Bramon, 2005). Finally, research suggests that minor physical anomalies (slight anatomical defects of the head, hands, feet, and face) that would be consistent with prenatal neurological damage are more common among people with schizophrenia than among others (McNeil, Canton-Graae, & Ismail, 2000; Schiffman et al., 2002). Collectively, these diverse studies argue for a relationship between early neurological trauma and a predisposition to schizophrenia (Mednick et al., 1998).

Expressed Emotion

Studies of expressed emotion have primarily focused on how this element of family dynamics influences the *course* of schizophrenic illness, after the onset of the disorder (Leff & Vaughn, 1985). *Expressed emotion (EE) is the degree to which a relative of a patient displays highly critical or emotionally overinvolved attitudes toward the patient.* Audiotaped interviews of relatives' communication are carefully evaluated for critical comments, hostility toward the patient, and excessive emotional involvement (overprotective, overconcerned attitudes) (Hooley, 2004).

Studies show that a family's expressed emotion is a good predictor of the course of a schizophrenic patient's illness (Hooley, 2007). After release from a hospital, people with schizophrenia who return to a family high in expressed emotion show relapse rates about three times that of patients who return to a family low in expressed emotion (see **Figure 14.22** on the next page; Hooley & Hiller, 1998). Part of the problem for patients returning to homes high in expressed emotion is that their families are probably sources of more *stress* than of *social support*

Figure 14.21

The neurodevelopmental hypothesis of schizophrenia. Recent findings have suggested that insults to the brain sustained during prenatal development or at birth may disrupt crucial maturational processes in the brain, resulting in subtle neurological damage that gradually becomes apparent as youngsters develop. This neurological damage is believed to increase both vulnerability to schizophrenia and the incidence of minor physical anomalies (slight anatomical defects of the head, face, hands, and feet).

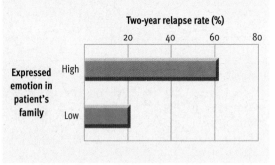

(Cutting & Docherty, 2000). Although the effects of expressed emotion have been explored primarily with schizophrenic patients, accumulating evidence suggests that high levels of expressed emotion also foster higher relapse rates for patients suffering from mood and anxiety disorders (Hooley, 2004, 2007).

Precipitating Stress

11c

Most theories of schizophrenia assume that stress plays a key role in triggering schizophrenic disorders (Walker & Tessner, 2008). According to this notion, various biological and psychological factors influence individuals' *vulnerability* to schizophrenia. High stress may then serve to precipitate a schizophrenic disorder in someone who is vulnerable. Research indicates that high stress can also trigger relapses in patients who have made progress toward recovery (Walker, Mittal, & Tessner, 2008).

Schizophrenia is the last of the major, Axis I diagnostic categories that we will consider. We'll com-

plete our overview of various types of abnormal behavior with a brief look at the personality disorders. These disorders are recorded on Axis II in the DSM classification system.

REVIEW of Key Points

14.16 Disturbed, irrational thought processes, including delusions, are the defining feature of schizophrenic disorders. Schizophrenia is also characterized by deterioration of everyday adaptive behavior, auditory hallucinations, and disturbed emotion.

14.17 Schizophrenic disorders are classified as paranoid, catatonic, disorganized, or undifferentiated. A classification scheme based on the predominance of positive versus negative symptoms has been proposed, but has not supplanted the traditional classification system. Schizophrenic disorders usually emerge during adolescence or young adulthood. The course of the disorder tends to involve chronic deterioration for many patients, but with prompt, effective care recovery is possible.

14.18 Twin studies and other research show that some people inherit a genetic vulnerability to schizophrenia. The dopamine hypothesis asserts that excess dopamine activity is the neurochemcial basis for schizophrenia. The dopamine hypothesis may explain why recent research has uncovered a link between marijuana use and vulnerability to schizophrenia.

14.19 Structural abnormalities in the brain, such as enlarged ventricles, are associated with schizophrenia, but their causal significance is unclear. The neurodevelopmental hypothesis of schizophrenia asserts that schizophrenia is attributable to disruptions in the normal maturational processes of the brain before or at birth that are caused by prenatal viral infections, obstetrical complications, and other insults to the brain.

14.20 Patients who come from homes high in expressed emotion have elevated relapse rates, suggesting that unhealthy family dynamics play a role in schizophrenia. High stress may also contribute to the onset of schizophrenia.

Personality Disorders

Key Learning Goals

14.21 Discuss the nature of personality disorders and problems with the diagnosis of such disorders.

14.22 Describe the antisocial personality disorder, and discuss its etiology.

We have seen repeatedly that it is often difficult to draw that imaginary line between healthy and disordered behavior. This is especially true in the case of personality disorders, most of which are milder disturbances in comparison to most of the Axis I disorders. *Personality disorders* **are a class of disorders marked by extreme, inflexible personality traits that cause subjective distress or impaired social and occupational functioning.** Essentially, people with these disorders display certain personality traits to an excessive degree and in rigid ways that undermine their adjustment. Personality disorders usually emerge during late childhood or adoles-

cence and often continue throughout adulthood. It is difficult to estimate the prevalence of these subtle disorders, but it is clear that they are common (Mattia & Zimmerman, 2001).

DSM-IV lists ten personality disorders, which are grouped into three related clusters: anxious-fearful, odd-eccentric, and dramatic-impulsive. These disorders are described briefly in Table 14.2. If you examine this table, you will find a diverse collection of maladaptive personality syndromes. You may also notice that some personality disorders essentially are milder versions of more severe Axis I disorders. For example, obsessive compulsive personality dis-

Table 14.2 Personality Disorders

Cluster	Disorder	Description	% Male/% Female
Anxious/fearful	Avoidant personality disorder	Excessively sensitive to potential rejection, humiliation, or shame; socially withdrawn in spite of desire for acceptance from others	50/50
	Dependent personality disorder	Excessively lacking in self-reliance and self-esteem; passively allowing others to make all decisions; constantly subordinating own needs to others' needs	31/69
	Obsessive-compulsive personality disorder	Preoccupied with organization, rules, schedules, lists, trivial details; extremely conventional, serious, and formal; unable to express warm emotions	50/50
Odd/eccentric	Schizoid personality disorder	Defective in capacity for forming social relationships; showing absence of warm, tender feelings for others	78/22
	Schizotypal personality disorder	Showing social deficits and oddities of thinking, perception, and communication that resemble schizophrenia	55/45
	Paranoid personality disorder	Showing pervasive and unwarranted suspiciousness and mistrust of people; overly sensitive; prone to jealousy	67/33
Dramatic/impulsive	Histrionic personality disorder	Overly dramatic; tending to exaggerated expressions of emotion; egocentric, seeking attention	15/85
	Narcissistic personality disorder	Grandiosely self-important; preoccupied with success fantasies; expecting special treatment; lacking interpersonal empathy	70/30
	Borderline personality disorder	Unstable in self-image, mood, and interpersonal relationships; impulsive and unpredictable	38/62
	Antisocial personality disorder	Chronically violating the rights of others; failing to accept social norms, to form attachments to others, or to sustain consistent work behavior; exploitive and reckless	82/18

Source: Estimated gender ratios from Millon (1981).

order is a milder version of obsessive-compulsive disorder, and the schizoid and schizotypal personality disorders are milder cousins of schizophrenic disorders. Some personality disorders are more common in men and some in women, as the figures in the far right column of the table indicate.

Diagnostic Problems

Many critics have argued that the personality disorders overlap too much with Axis I disorders and with each other (Clark, 2007). The extent of this problem was documented in a study by Leslie Morey (1988). Morey reviewed the cases of 291 patients who had received a specific personality disorder diagnosis to see how many could have met the criteria for any of the other personality disorders. Morey found massive overlap among the diagnoses. For example, among patients with a diagnosis of histrionic personality disorder, 56% also qualified for a borderline disorder, 54% for a narcissistic disorder, 32% for an avoidant disorder, and 30% for a dependent disorder. Clearly, there are fundamental problems with Axis II as a classification system (Tyrer et al., 2007; Widiger, 2007). The overlap among the personality disorders makes it extremely difficult to achieve reliable diagnoses. Doubts have also been raised about the decision to place personality disorders on a sepa-

rate axis, as there does not appear to be any fundamental distinction between personality disorders and Axis I disorders (Krueger, 2005).

In light of these problems, a variety of theorists have questioned the wisdom of the current *categorical approach* to describing personality disorders, which assumes (incorrectly, they argue) that people can reliably be placed in discontinuous (nonoverlapping) diagnostic categories (Verheul, 2005; Widiger & Trull, 2007). These theorists argue instead for a *dimensional approach,* which would describe personality disorders in terms of how people score on a limited number of continuous personality dimensions. The practical logistics of using a dimensional approach to describe personality disorders are formidable, and experts note that the categorical approach better reflects how clinicians think about pathology (Phillips, Yen, & Gunderson, 2003). In any event, vigorous debate about the classification of personality disorders is likely to continue as researchers grapple with how to move from DSM-IV to DSM-V.

The difficulties involved in the diagnosis of personality disorders have clearly hindered research on their etiology and prognosis. The only personality disorder that has a long history of extensive research is the antisocial personality disorder, which we examine next.

Antisocial Personality Disorder

Antisocial personality disorder has a misleading name. The antisocial designation does *not* mean that people with this disorder shun social interaction. In fact, rather than shrinking from social interaction, many such individuals are sociable, friendly, and superficially charming. People with this disorder are *antisocial* in that they choose to *reject widely accepted social norms* regarding moral principles and behavior.

Description

People with antisocial personalities chronically violate the rights of others. They often use their social charm to cultivate others' liking or loyalty for purposes of exploitation. The *antisocial personality disorder* is marked by impulsive, callous, manipulative, aggressive, and irresponsible behavior that reflects a failure to accept social norms. Since they haven't accepted the social norms they violate, people with antisocial personalities rarely feel guilty about their transgressions. Essentially, they lack an adequate conscience. The antisocial personality disorder occurs much more frequently among males than females. Studies suggest that it is a moderately common disorder, seen in roughly 3%–6% of males and about 1% of females (Widiger & Mullins, 2003).

Many people with antisocial personalities get involved in illegal activities. Moreover, antisocial personalities tend to begin their criminal careers at an early age, to commit offenses at a relatively high rate, and to be versatile offenders who get involved in many types of criminal activity (Douglas, Vincent, & Edens, 2006; Hare, 2006; Porter & Porter, 2007). However, many people with antisocial personalities keep their exploitive, amoral behavior channeled within the boundaries of the law. Such people may even enjoy high status in our society (Babiak & Hare, 2006; Hall & Benning, 2006). In other words, the concept of the antisocial personality disorder can apply to cut-throat business executives, scheming politicians, unprincipled lawyers, and money-hungry evangelists, as well as to con artists, drug dealers, thugs, burglars, and petty thieves.

People with antisocial personalities exhibit quite a variety of maladaptive traits (Hare, 2006; Hare & Neumann, 2008). Among other things, they rarely experience genuine affection for others. However, they may be skilled at faking affection so they can exploit people. Sexually, they are predatory and promiscuous. They also tend to be irresponsible and impulsive. They can tolerate little frustration, and they pursue immediate gratification. These charac-teristics make them unreliable employees, unfaithful spouses, inattentive parents, and undependable friends. Many people with antisocial personalities have a checkered history of divorce, child abuse, and job instability. The picture does tend to improve as those with antisocial personalities become middle-aged. One study that followed antisocial men into their 50s found substantial improvement in 58% of the subjects (Black, 2001).

Etiology

Many theorists believe that biological factors contribute to the development of antisocial personality disorders. Various lines of evidence suggest a genetic predisposition toward these disorders (Moffitt, 2005; Waldman & Rhee, 2006). A review of twin studies found an average concordance rate of 67% for identical twins in comparison to 31% for fraternal twins (Black, 2001). These findings are consistent with a fairly strong genetic vulnerability to the disorder. Many observers have noted that people with antisocial personalities lack the inhibitions that most of us have about violating moral standards. Their lack of inhibitions prompted Hans Eysenck (1982) to theorize that such people might inherit relatively sluggish autonomic nervous systems, leading to slow acquisition of inhibitions through classical conditioning. The notion that antisocial personalities exhibit underarousal has received some support (Raine, 1997), but the findings have been inconsistent (Blackburn, 2006), and some studies have suggested the opposite—that *overarousal* may promote antisocial behavior (Hart, Eisenberg, & Valiente, 2007). Part of the problem in this area of research may be that arousal can be quantified in a great many different ways.

Efforts to relate psychological factors to antisocial behavior have emphasized inadequate socialization in dysfunctional family systems (Farrington, 2006; Sutker & Allain, 2001). It's easy to envision how antisocial traits could be fostered in homes where parents make haphazard or halfhearted efforts to socialize their children to be respectful, truthful, responsible, unselfish, and so forth. Consistent with this idea, studies find that individuals with antisocial personalities tend to come from homes where discipline is erratic or ineffective or where they experience physical abuse and neglect (Luntz & Widom, 1994; Widom, 1997). Such people are also more likely to emerge from families where one or both parents exhibit antisocial traits (Black, 2001). These parents presumably model exploitive, amoral behaviors, which their children acquire through observational learning.

Psychological Disorders and the Law

Societies use laws to enforce their norms regarding appropriate behavior. Given this function, the law in our society has something to say about many issues related to abnormal behavior. In this section we examine the concepts of insanity and involuntary commitment.

Insanity

Insanity is *not* a diagnosis; it's a legal concept. *Insanity* **is a legal status indicating that a person cannot be held responsible for his or her actions because of mental illness.** Why is this an issue in the courtroom? Because criminal acts must be intentional. The law reasons that people who are "out of their mind" may not be able to appreciate the significance of what they're doing. The insanity defense is used in criminal trials by defendants who admit that they committed the crime but claim that they lacked intent.

No simple relationship exists between specific diagnoses of mental disorders and court findings of insanity. The vast majority of people with diagnosed psychological disorders would *not* qualify as insane. The people most likely to qualify are those troubled by severe disturbances that display delusional behavior. The courts apply various rules in making judgments about a defendant's sanity, depending on the jurisdiction (Simon, 2003). According to one widely used rule, called the *M'naghten rule, insanity exists when a mental disorder makes a person unable to distinguish right from wrong.* As you can imagine, evaluating insanity as defined in the M'naghten rule can be difficult for judges and jurors, not to mention the psychologists and psychiatrists who are called into court as expert witnesses.

Although highly publicized and controversial, the insanity defense is actually used less frequently and less successfully than widely believed (see Figure 14.23). One study found that the general public

estimates that the insanity defense is used in 37% of felony cases, when in fact it is used in less than 1% (Silver, Cirincione, & Steadman, 1994). Another study of over 60,000 indictments in Baltimore found that only 190 defendants (0.31%) pleaded insanity, and of these, only 8 were successful (Janofsky et al., 1996).

Involuntary Commitment

The issue of insanity surfaces only in *criminal* proceedings. Far more people are affected by *civil* proceedings relating to involuntary commitment. In *involuntary commitment* **people are hospitalized in psychiatric facilities against their will.** What are the grounds for such a dramatic action? They vary some from state to state. Generally, people are subject to involuntary commitment when mental health professionals and legal authorities believe that a mental disorder makes them (1) dangerous to themselves (usually suicidal), (2) dangerous to others (potentially violent), or (3) in need of treatment (applied in cases of severe disorientation). In emergency situations psychologists and psychiatrists can authorize *temporary* commitment, usually for 24 to 72 hours. Orders for long-term involuntary commitment are

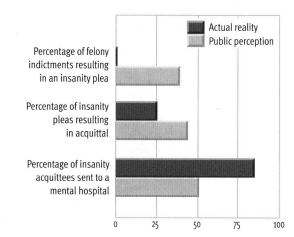

Figure 14.23

The insanity defense: Public perceptions and actual realities. Silver, Cirincione, and Steadman (1994) collected data on the general public's beliefs about the insanity defense and the realities of how often it is used and how often it is successful (based on a large-scale survey of insanity pleas in eight states). Because of highly selective media coverage, dramatic disparities are seen between public perceptions and actual realities, as the insanity defense is used less frequently and less successfully than widely assumed.

AXIS I CATEGORY

SUBTYPES

PREVALENCE/ WELL-KNOWN VICTIM

ANXIETY DISORDERS

Edvard Munch's *The Scream* expresses overwhelming feelings of anxiety.

National Gallery, Oslo, Norway. SCALA/Art Resource/NY; © 2009 The Munch Museum/The Munch–Ellingsen Group/Artists Rights Society (ARS), NY.

Generalized anxiety disorder: Chronic, high level of anxiety not tied to any specific threat

Phobic disorder: Persistent, irrational fear of object or situation that presents no real danger

Panic disorder: Recurrent attacks of overwhelming anxiety that occur suddenly and unexpectedly

Obsessive-compulsive disorder: Persistent, uncontrollable intrusions of unwanted thoughts and urges to engage in senseless rituals

Posttraumatic stress disorder: Enduring psychological disturbance attributable to the experience of a major traumatic event

0 2 4 6 8 10 12 14 16 18 20

19%

Prevalence

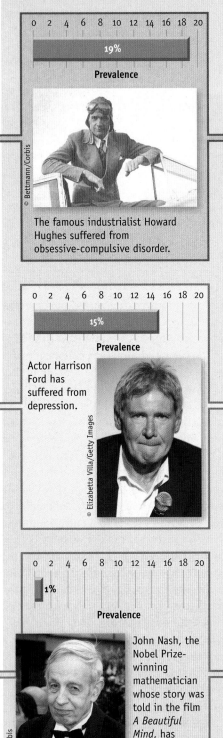

The famous industrialist Howard Hughes suffered from obsessive-compulsive disorder.

© Bettmann/Corbis

MOOD DISORDERS

Musee d'Orsay, Paris. © Erich Lessing/ Art Resource, NY.

Vincent Van Gogh's *Portrait of Dr. Gachet* captures the profound dejection experienced in depressive disorders.

Major depressive disorder: Two or more major depressive episodes marked by feelings of sadness, worthlessness, despair

Bipolar disorder: One or more manic episodes marked by inflated self-esteem, grandiosity, and elevated mood and energy, usually accompanied by major depressive episodes

0 2 4 6 8 10 12 14 16 18 20

15%

Prevalence

Actor Harrison Ford has suffered from depression.

© Elizabetta Villa/Getty Images

SCHIZOPHRENIC DISORDERS

The perceptual distortions seen in schizophrenia probably contributed to the bizarre imagery apparent in this portrait of a cat painted by Louis Wain.

© Derek Bayes/ Aspect Picture Library

Paranoid schizophrenia: Delusions of persecution and delusions of grandeur; frequent auditory hallucinations

Catatonic schizophrenia: Motor disturbances ranging from immobility to excessive, purposeless activity

Disorganized schizophrenia: Flat or inappropriate emotions; disorganized speech and adaptive behavior

Undifferentiated schizophrenia: Idiosyncratic mixtures of schizophrenic symptoms that cannot be placed into above three categories

0 2 4 6 8 10 12 14 16 18 20

1%

Prevalence

John Nash, the Nobel Prize-winning mathematician whose story was told in the film *A Beautiful Mind*, has struggled with schizophrenia.

© Reuters/Corbis

ETIOLOGY: BIOLOGICAL FACTORS

Genetic vulnerability: Twin studies and other evidence suggest a mild genetic predisposition to anxiety disorders.

Concordance rate (%)

Identical twins

Fraternal twins

Anxiety sensitivity: Oversensitivity to physical symptoms of anxiety may lead to overreactions to feelings of anxiety, so anxiety breeds anxiety.

Neurochemical bases: Disturbances in neural circuits releasing GABA may contribute to some disorders; abnormalities at serotonin synapses have been implicated in panic and obsessive-compulsive disorders.

Genetic vulnerability: Twin studies and other evidence suggest a genetic predisposition to mood disorders.

Concordance rate (%)

Identical twins

Fraternal twins

Suppressed neurogenesis: Disruption of neurogenesis may lead to reduced volume in the hippocampus and to depression.

Neurochemical bases: Disturbances in neural circuits releasing norepinephrine may contribute to some mood disorders; abnormalities at serotonin synapses have also been implicated as a factor in depression.

Genetic vulnerability: Twin studies and other evidence suggest a genetic predisposition to schizophrenic disorders.

Concordance rate (%)

Identical twins

Fraternal twins

Neurochemical bases: Overactivity in neural circuits releasing dopamine is associated with schizophrenia; but abnormalities in other neurotransmitter systems may also contribute.

Structural abnormalities in brain: Enlarged brain ventricles are associated with schizophrenia, but they may be an effect rather than a cause of the disorder.

ETIOLOGY: PSYCHOLOGICAL FACTORS

Learning: Many anxiety responses may be acquired through classical conditioning or observational learning; phobic responses may be maintained by operant reinforcement.

CS Snow

US Buried in avalanche

CR Fear UR

Stress: High stress may help to precipitate the onset of anxiety disorders.

Anxious subjects

Nonanxious subjects

Threatening interpretations endorsed (%)

Cognition: People who misinterpret harmless situations as threatening and who focus excessive attention on perceived threats are more vulnerable to anxiety disorders.

Acquire fewer reinforcers, such as good friends, top jobs

Court rejection because of irritability, pessimism

Poor social skills

Increased vulnerability to depression

Gravitate to people who confirm negative self-views

Interpersonal roots: Behavioral theories emphasize how inadequate social skills can result in a paucity of reinforcers and other effects that make people vulnerable to depression.

Stress: High stress can act as precipitating factor that triggers depression or bipolar disorder.

Cognition: Negative thinking can contribute to the development of depression; rumination may extend and amplify depression.

Negative thinking → Depression

Expressed emotion: A family's expressed emotion is a good predictor of the course of a schizophrenic patient's illness.

Two-year relapse rate (%)

Expressed emotion in patient's family

High

Low

Stress: High stress can precipitate schizophrenic disorder in people who are vulnerable to schizophrenia.

Disruption of normal maturational processes before or at birth → Subtle neurological damage → Increased vulnerability to schizophrenia

The neurodevelopmental hypothesis: Insults to the brain sustained during prenatal development or at birth may disrupt maturational processes in the brain resulting in elevated vulnerability to schizophrenia.

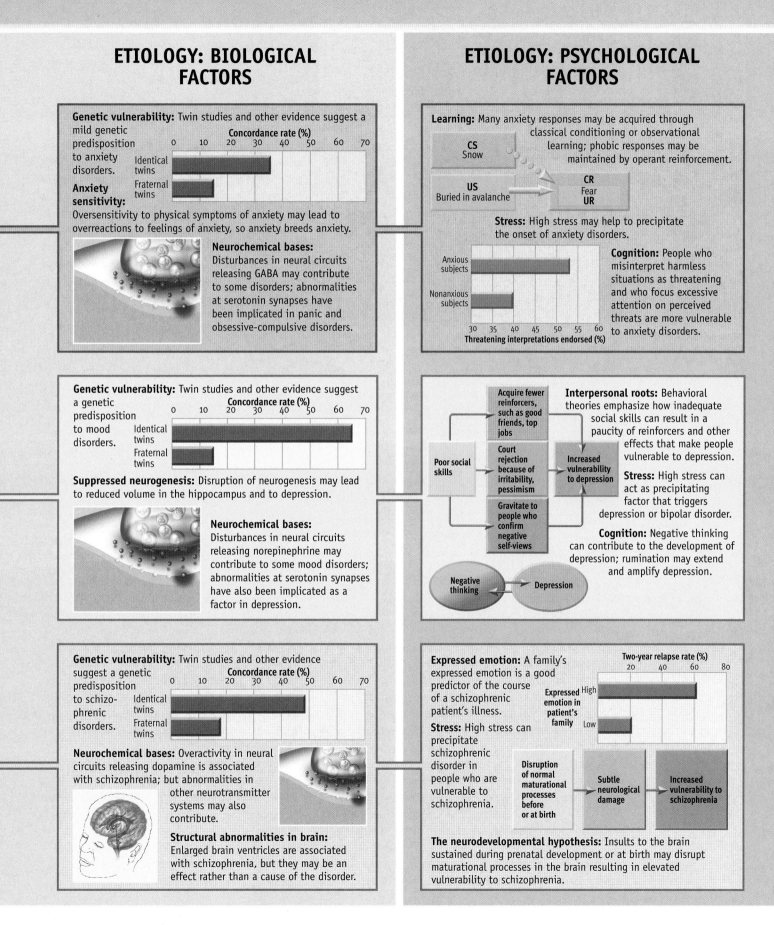

usually set up for renewable six-month periods and can be issued by a court only after a formal hearing. Mental health professionals provide extensive input in these hearings, but the courts make the final decisions (Simon, 2005).

Most involuntary commitments occur because people appear to be *dangerous* to themselves or others. The difficulty, however, is in predicting dangerousness. Studies suggest that clinicians' short-term predictions about which patients are likely to become violent are only moderately accurate and that their long-term predictions of violent behavior are largely inaccurate (Simon, 2003; Stone, 1999). This inaccuracy in predicting dangerousness is unfortunate, because involuntary commitment involves the *detention* of people for what they *might* do in the future. Such detention goes against the grain of the American legal principle that people are *innocent until proven guilty*. The inherent difficulty in predicting dangerousness makes involuntary commitment a complex and controversial issue.

Seung-Hui Cho, who gunned down 32 people at Virginia Tech in April of 2007, had a history of mental illness and showed many signs of psychological deterioration in the months leading up to the massacre. Given his struggles with psychological disturbance, many people were baffled about why he had not been subjected to involuntary commitment. But commitment proceedings based on his overt, known behavior prior to the murders (a couple of stalking incidents and some angry, violent class essays) probably would have failed. What most people do not understand is that laws in the United States generally set the bar very high for involuntary commitment. Why? Because predictions of dangerousness are not very accurate and because our legal system is reluctant to incarcerate people for what they might *do. Unfortunately, our conservative approach to involuntary commitment sometimes has tragic consequences.*

Culture and Pathology

Key Learning Goals

14.24 Compare the relativistic versus pancultural view of psychological disorders.

14.25 Assess the extent of cultural variability in the existence and presentation of mental disorders.

The legal rules governing insanity and involuntary commitment obviously are culture-specific. And we noted earlier that judgments of normality and abnormality are influenced by cultural norms and values. In light of these realities, would it be reasonable to infer that psychological disorders are culturally variable phenomena? Social scientists are sharply divided on the answer to this question. Some embrace a *relativistic view* of psychological disorders, whereas others subscribe to a *universalistic or pancultural view* (Tanaka-Matsumi, 2001). Theorists who embrace the *relativistic view* argue that the criteria of mental illness vary greatly across cultures and that there are no universal standards of normality and abnormality. According to the relativists, the DSM diagnostic system reflects an ethnocentric, Western, white, urban, middle- and upper-class cultural orientation

that has limited relevance in other cultural contexts. In contrast, those who subscribe to the *pancultural view* argue that the criteria of mental illness are much the same around the world and that basic standards of normality and abnormality are universal across cultures. Theorists who accept the pancultural view of psychopathology typically maintain that Western diagnostic concepts have validity and utility in other cultural contexts.

The debate about culture and pathology basically boils down to two specific issues: (1) Are the psychological disorders seen in Western societies found throughout the world? (2) Are the symptom patterns of mental disorders invariant across cultures? Let's briefly examine the evidence on these questions and then reconsider the relativistic and pancultural views of psychological disorders.

Are Equivalent Disorders Found Around the World?

Most investigators agree that the principal categories of serious psychological disturbance—schizophrenia, depression, and bipolar illness—are identifiable in all cultures (Tsai et al., 2001). Most behaviors that are regarded as clearly abnormal in Western culture are also viewed as abnormal in other cultures. People who are delusional, hallucinatory, disoriented, or incoherent are thought to be disturbed in all societies, although there are cultural disparities in exactly what is considered delusional or hallucinatory.

Cultural variations are more apparent in the recognition of less severe forms of psychological disturbance (Mezzich, Lewis-Fernandez, & Ruiperez, 2003). Additional research is needed, but relatively mild types of pathology that do not disrupt behavior in obvious ways appear to go unrecognized in many societies. Thus, syndromes such as generalized anxiety disorder, hypochondria, and narcissistic personality disorder, which are firmly established as diagnostic entities in the DSM, are viewed in some cultures as "run of the mill" difficulties and peculiarities rather than as full-fledged disorders.

Finally, researchers have discovered a small number of *culture-bound disorders* that further illustrate the diversity of abnormal behavior around the world (Griffith, Gonzalez, & Blue, 2003; Trujillo, 2005). **Culture-bound disorders are abnormal syndromes found only in a few cultural groups.** For example, *koro,* an obsessive fear that one's penis will withdraw into one's abdomen, is seen only among Chinese males in Malaya and several other regions of southern Asia. *Windigo,* which involves an intense craving for human flesh and fear that one will turn into a cannibal, is seen only among Algonquin Indian cultures. And until fairly recently, the eating disorder *anorexia nervosa,* discussed in this chapter's Personal Application, was largely seen only in affluent Western cultures.

Are Symptom Patterns Culturally Invariant?

Do the major types of psychological disorders manifest themselves in the same way around the world?

It depends to some extent on the disorder. The more a disorder has a strong biological component, the more it tends to be expressed in similar ways across varied cultures (Marsella & Yamada, 2007). Thus, the constellations of symptoms associated with schizophrenia and bipolar illness are largely the same across widely disparate societies (Draguns, 1980, 1990). However, even in severe, heavily biological disorders, cultural variations in symptom patterns are also seen (Mezzich et al., 2003). For example, delusions are a common symptom of schizophrenia in all cultures, but the specific delusions that people report are tied to their cultural heritage (Brislin, 1993). In technologically advanced societies, schizophrenic patients report that thoughts are being inserted into their minds through transmissions from electric lines, satellites, or microwave ovens. Victims of schizophrenia in less technological societies experience the same phenomenon but blame sorcerers or demons. Of the major disorders, symptom patterns are probably most variable for depression. For example, profound feelings of guilt and self-deprecation lie at the core of depression in Western cultures but are far less central to depression in many other societies. In non-Western cultures, depression tends to be expressed in terms of somatic symptoms, such as complaints of fatigue, headaches, and backaches, more than psychological symptoms, such as dejection and low self-esteem (Tsai et al., 2001; Young, 1997). These differences presumably occur because people learn to express symptoms of psychological distress in ways that are acceptable in their culture.

So, what can we conclude about the validity of the relativistic versus pancultural views of psychological disorders? Both views appear to have some merit. As we have seen in other areas of research, psychopathology is characterized by both cultural variance and invariance. Investigators have identified some universal standards of normality and abnormality and found considerable similarity across cultures in the syndromes that are regarded as pathological and in their patterns of symptoms. However, researchers have also discovered many cultural variations in the recognition, definition, and symptoms of various psychological disorders. Given this extensive variability, the relativists' concerns about the ethnocentric nature of the DSM diagnostic system seem well founded.

REVIEW of Key Points

14.24 Theorists who embrace a relativistic view of psychological disorders argue that there are no universal standards of normality and abnormality. Those who subscribe to the pancultural view argue that the criteria of mental illness are much the same around the world.

14.25 The principal categories of psychological disturbance are identifiable in all cultures. However, milder disorders may go unrecognized in some societies, and culture-bound disorders further illustrate the diversity of abnormal behavior around the world. The symptoms associated with specific disorders are largely the same across different cultures, but cultural variations are seen in the details of how these symptoms are expressed.

Key Learning Goals

14.26 Identify the four unifying themes highlighted in this chapter.

Multifactorial Causation

Heredity and Environment

Sociohistorical Context

Cultural Heritage

Reflecting on the Chapter's Themes

Our examination of abnormal behavior and its roots has highlighted four of our organizing themes: multifactorial causation, the interplay of heredity and environment, the sociohistorical context in which psychology evolves, and the influence of culture on psychological phenomena.

We can safely assert that every disorder described in this chapter has multiple causes. The development of mental disorders involves an interplay among a variety of psychological, biological, and social factors. We also saw that most psychological disorders depend on an interaction of genetics and experience. This interaction shows up most clearly in the *stress-vulnerability models* for mood disorders and schizophrenic disorders (see Figure 14.24). *Vulnerability* to these disorders seems to depend primarily on heredity, whereas stress is largely a function of environment. According to stress-vulnerability theories, disorders emerge when high vulnerability intersects with high stress. A high biological vulner-

ability may not be converted into a disorder if a person's stress is low. Similarly, high stress may not lead to a disorder if vulnerability is low. Thus, the impact of heredity depends on the environment, and the effect of environment depends on heredity.

This chapter also demonstrated that psychology evolves in a sociohistorical context. We saw that modern conceptions of normality and abnormality are largely shaped by empirical research, but social trends, economic necessities, and political realities also play a role. Finally, our discussion of psychological disorders showed once again that psychological phenomena are shaped to some degree by cultural parameters. Although some standards of normality and abnormality transcend cultural boundaries, cultural norms influence many aspects of psychopathology. Indeed, the influence of culture will be apparent in our upcoming Personal Application on eating disorders. These disorders are largely a creation of modern, affluent, Western culture.

REVIEW of Key Points

14.26 This chapter highlighted four of our unifying themes, showing that behavior is governed by multiple causes, that heredity and environment jointly influence mental disorders, that psychology evolves in a sociohistorical context, and that pathology is characterized by both cultural variance and invariance.

Figure 14.24
The stress-vulnerability model of schizophrenia. Multifactorial causation is readily apparent in current theories about the etiology of schizophrenic disorders. A variety of biological factors and personal history factors influence one's vulnerability to the disorder, which interacts with the amount of stress one experiences. Schizophrenic disorders appear to result from an intersection of high stress and high vulnerability.

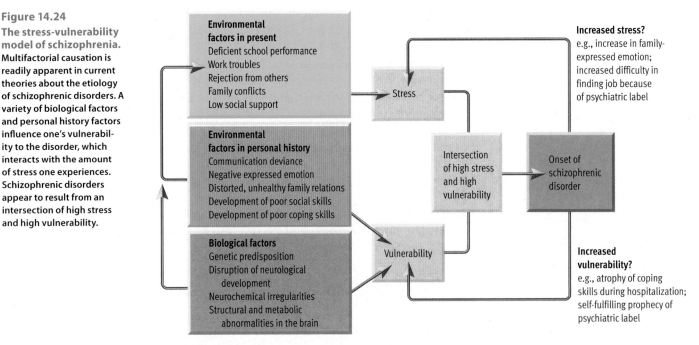

Understanding Eating Disorders

Answer the following "true" or "false."

____ **1** Although they have only attracted attention in recent years, eating disorders have a long history and have always been fairly common.

____ **2** People with anorexia nervosa are much more likely to recognize that their eating behavior is pathological than people suffering from bulimia nervosa are.

____ **3** The prevalence of eating disorders is twice as high in women as it is in men.

____ **4** The binge-and-purge syndrome seen in bulimia nervosa is not common in anorexia nervosa.

All of the above statements are false, as you will see in this Personal Application. The psychological disorders that we discussed in the main body of the chapter have largely been recognized for centuries, and most of them are found in one form or another in all cultures and societies. Eating disorders present a sharp contrast to this picture; they have only been recognized relatively recently and have largely been confined to affluent, Westernized cultures (G. F. M. Russell, 1995; Szmukler & Patton, 1995). In spite of these fascinating differences, eating disorders have much in common with traditional forms of pathology.

Description

Although most people don't seem to take eating disorders as seriously as other types of psychological disorders, you will see that they are dangerous and debilitating (Thompson, Roehrig, & Kinder, 2007). No psychological disorder is associated with a greater elevation in mortality (Striegel-Moore & Bulik, 2007). *Eating disorders are severe disturbances in eating behavior characterized by preoccupation with weight and unhealthy efforts to control weight.* In DSM-IV, two sometimes overlapping syndromes are recognized: *anorexia nervosa* and *bulimia nervosa*. A third syndrome, called *binge-eating disorder,* is described in the appendix of DSM-IV as a potential new disorder, pending further study. We will devote our attention in this Application to the two established eating disorders, but we will briefly outline the symptoms of this new disorder as well.

Anorexia Nervosa

Anorexia nervosa **involves intense fear of gaining weight, disturbed body image, refusal to maintain normal weight, and use of dangerous measures to lose weight.** Two subtypes have been observed (Herzog & Delinski, 2001). In *restricting type anorexia nervosa,* people drastically reduce their intake of food, sometimes literally starving themselves. In *binge-eating/purging type anorexia nervosa,* individuals attempt to lose weight by forcing themselves to vomit after meals, by misusing laxatives and diuretics, and by engaging in excessive exercise.

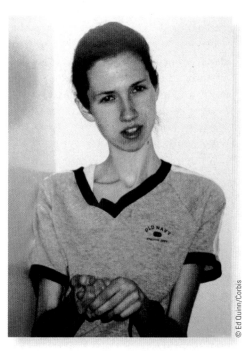

Eating disorders have become distressingly common among young women in Western cultures. No matter how frail they become, people suffering from anorexia insist that they are too fat.

PERSONAL

APPLICATION

Key Learning Goals

14.27 Describe the subtypes, history, and prevalence of eating disorders.

14.28 Outline how genetic factors, personality, culture, family dynamics, and disturbed thinking contribute to eating disorders.

People with both types suffer from disturbed body image. No matter how frail and emaciated they become, they insist that they are too fat. Their morbid fear of obesity means that they are never satisfied with their weight. If they gain a pound or two, they panic. The only thing that makes them happy is to lose more weight. The common result is a relentless decline in body weight; people entering treatment for anorexia nervosa are typically 25%–30% below their normal weight (Hsu, 1990). Because of their disturbed body image, people suffering from anorexia generally do *not* appreciate the maladaptive quality of their behavior and rarely seek treatment on their own. They are typically coaxed or coerced into treatment by friends or family members who are alarmed by their appearance.

Anorexia nervosa eventually leads to a cascade of medical problems, including *amenorrhea* (a loss of menstrual cycles in women), gastrointestinal problems, low blood pressure, *osteoporosis* (a loss of bone density), and metabolic disturbances that can lead to cardiac arrest or circulatory collapse (Pomeroy & Mitchell, 2002; Walsh, 2003). Anorexia is a serious illness that leads to death in 5%–10% of patients (Steinhausen, 2002).

Bulimia Nervosa

Bulimia nervosa **involves habitually engaging in out-of-control overeating followed by unhealthy compensatory efforts, such as self-induced vomiting, fasting, abuse of laxatives and diuretics, and excessive exercise.** The eating binges are usually carried out in secret and are followed by intense guilt and concern about gaining weight. These feelings motivate ill-advised strategies to undo the effects of the overeating. However, vomiting prevents the absorption of only about half of recently consumed food, and laxatives and diuretics have negligible impact on caloric intake, so people suffering from bulimia nervosa typically maintain a reasonably normal weight (Beumont, 2002; Kaye et al., 1993). Medical problems associated with bulimia nervosa include cardiac arrythmias, dental problems, metabolic deficiencies, and gastrointestinal problems (Halmi, 2002, 2003). Bulimia often coexists with other psychological disturbances, including depression, anxiety disorders, and substance abuse (Hudson et al., 2007).

Obviously, bulimia nervosa shares many features with anorexia nervosa, such as a morbid fear of becoming obese, preoccupation with food, and rigid, maladaptive approaches to controlling weight that are grounded in naive all-or-none thinking. The close relationship between the disorders is demonstrated by the fact that many patients who initially develop one syndrome cross over to display the other syndrome (Tozzi et al., 2005). However, the two syndromes also differ in crucial ways. First and foremost, bulimia is a much less life-threatening condition. Second, although their appearance is usually more "normal" than that seen in anorexia, people with bulimia are much more likely to recognize that their eating behavior is pathological and are more likely to cooperate with treatment (Striegel-Moore, Silberstein, & Rodin, 1993; Guarda et al., 2007).

Binge-Eating Disorder

A surprising number of people who exhibit disordered eating do not fit neatly into the anorexia or bulimia categories, which is why a third category has been proposed. *Binge-eating disorder* involves distress-inducing eating binges that are not accompanied by the purging, fasting, and excessive exercise seen in bulimia. Obviously, this syndrome resembles bulimia, but it is a less severe disorder. Still, this disorder creates great distress, as people tend to be disgusted by their bodies and distraught about their overeating. People with binge-eating disorder are frequently overweight. Their excessive eating is often triggered by stress

(Gluck, 2006). Research suggests that this comparatively mild syndrome may be more common than anorexia or bulimia (Hudson et al., 2007). Given the research that has been compiled since DSM-IV was released in 1994, it appears likely that binge-eating disorder will be recognized as an independent disorder in the forthcoming DSM-V (Striegel-Moore & Franko, 2008).

History and Prevalence

Historians have been able to track down descriptions of anorexia nervosa that date back centuries, so the disorder is *not* entirely new, but anorexia nervosa did not become a common affliction until the middle part of the 20th century (Vandereycken, 2002). Although binging and purging have a long history in some cultures, they were not part of pathological efforts to control weight, and bulimia nervosa appears to be a new syndrome that emerged gradually in the middle of the 20th century and was first recognized in the 1970s (G. F. M. Russell, 1997; Vandereycken, 2002).

Both disorders are a product of modern, affluent, Western culture, where food is generally plentiful and the desirability of being thin is widely endorsed. Until recently, these disorders were not seen outside of Western cultures (Hoek, 2002). However, advances in communication have exported Western culture to far-flung corners of the globe, and eating disorders have started showing up in many non-Western societies, especially affluent Asian countries (Becker & Fay, 2006; Lee & Katzman, 2002).

A huge gender gap is seen in the likelihood of developing eating disorders. About 90%–95% of individuals with eating disorders are female (Thompson & Kinder, 2003). This staggering discrepancy appears to be a result of cultural pressures rather than biological factors (Smolak & Murnen, 2001). Western standards of attractiveness emphasize slenderness more for females than for males, and women generally experience greater pressure to be physically attractive than men do (Strahan et al., 2008). Eating disorders mostly afflict *young* women. The typical age of onset is 14 to 18 for anorexia and 15 to 21 for bulimia (see Figure 14.25).

How common are eating disorders in Western societies? Studies of young women suggest that about 1% develop anorexia nervosa and about 2%–3% develop bulimia nervosa (Anderson & Yager, 2005). However, prevalence rates appear to be trending higher in more recent studies (Thompson et al., 2007). In some respects, these figures may only scratch the surface of the problem. Evidence suggests that as many as 20% of female college students may struggle with transient bulimic symptoms (Anderson & Yager, 2005). And recent community surveys suggest that there may be more undiagnosed eating disorders among men than generally appreciated (Hudson et al., 2007).

Etiology of Eating Disorders

Like other types of psychological disorders, eating disorders are caused by multiple determinants that work interactively. Let's take a brief look at some of the factors that contribute to the development of anorexia nervosa and bulimia nervosa.

Genetic Vulnerability

The evidence is not nearly as strong or complete as for many other types of psychopathology (such as anxiety, mood, and schizophrenic disorders), but some people may inherit a genetic vulnerability to eating disorders (Slof-Op't Landt et al., 2005). Studies show that relatives of patients with eating disorders have elevated rates of anorexia nervosa and bulimia nervosa (Bulik, 2004). Twin studies suggest that a genetic predisposition may be at work (Steiger, Bruce, & Israel, 2003).

Personality Factors

Certain personality traits may increase vulnerability to eating disorders. There are innumerable exceptions, but victims of anorexia nervosa tend to be obsessive, rigid, and emotionally restrained, whereas victims of bulimia nervosa tend to be impulsive, overly sensitive, and low in self-esteem (Anderluh et al., 2003; Wonderlich, 2002). Recent research also suggests that perfectionism is a risk factor for anorexia (Bulik et al., 2003; Halmi et al., 2000).

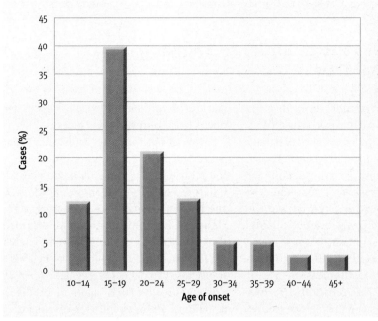

Figure 14.25

Age of onset for anorexia nervosa. Eating disorders tend to emerge during adolescence, as these data for anorexia nervosa show. This graph shows how age of onset was distributed in a sample of 166 female patients from Minnesota. As you can see, over half the patients experienced the onset of their illness before the age of 20, with vulnerability clearly peaking between the ages of 15 and 19. (Adapted from Lucas, et al., 1991)

Cultural Values

The contribution of cultural values to the increased prevalence of eating disorders can hardly be overestimated (Anderson-Fye & Becker, 2004; Striegel-Moore & Bulik, 2007). In Western society, young women are socialized to believe that they must be attractive, and to be attractive they must be as thin as the actresses and fashion models that dominate the media (Levine & Harrison, 2004). Thanks to this cultural milieu, many young women are dissatisfied with their weight, as the societal ideals promoted by the media are unattainable for most of them (Thompson & Stice, 2001). Unfortunately, in a portion of these women, the pressure to be thin, in combination with genetic vulnerability, family pathology, and other factors, leads to unhealthful efforts to control weight.

The Role of the Family

Quite a number of theorists emphasize how family dynamics can contribute to the development of anorexia and bulimia in young women (Haworth-Hoeppner, 2000). The principal issue appears to be that some mothers contribute to eating disorders simply by endorsing society's message that "you can never be too thin" and by modeling unhealthy dieting behaviors of their own (Francis & Birch, 2005). In conjunction with media pressures, this role modeling leads many daughters to internalize the idea that the thinner you are, the more attractive you are.

Cognitive Factors

Many theorists emphasize the role of disturbed thinking in the etiology of eating disorders (Williamson et al., 2001). For example, anorexic patients' typical belief that they are fat when they are really wasting away is a dramatic illustration of how thinking goes awry. Patients with eating disorders display rigid, all-or-none thinking and many maladaptive beliefs, such as "I must be thin to be accepted"; "If I am not in complete control, I will lose all control"; and "If I gain one pound, I'll go on to gain enormous weight." Additional research is needed to determine whether distorted thinking is a *cause* or merely a *symptom* of eating disorders.

REVIEW of Key Points

14.27 The principal eating disorders are anorexia nervosa and bulimia nervosa, with binge-eating disorder a proposed third syndrome. Anorexia and bulimia both lead to a cascade of medical problems, but anorexia is more dangerous. Both disorders are largely a product of affluent, Westernized culture that weren't recognized until the 20th century. Females account for 90%–95% of eating disorders. Among young women, about 1% develop anorexia nervosa and about 2%–3% develop bulimia nervosa, typically between the age of 15 to 20.

14.28 There appears to be a genetic vulnerability to eating disorders. Certain personality traits increase the vulnerability to eating disorders. Cultural pressures on young women to be thin clearly help to foster eating disorders. Families that endorse the idea that you can never be too thin can help to promote eating disorders. Rigid, disturbed thinking can also contribute to the development of these disorders.

Key Learning Goals

14.29 Understand how mental heuristics can distort estimates of cumulative and conjunctive probabilities.

Working with Probabilities in Thinking About Mental Illness

As you read about the various types of psychological disorders, did you think to yourself that you or someone you know was being described? On the one hand, there is no reason to be alarmed. The tendency to see yourself and your friends in descriptions of pathology is a common one, sometimes called the *medical students' disease* because beginning medical students often erroneously believe that they or their friends have whatever diseases they are currently learning about. On the other hand, realistically speaking, it *is* quite likely that you know *many* people with psychological disorders because—as you learned in the main body of the chapter—the likelihood of anyone having at least one DSM disorder is estimated to be about 44% (consult **Figure 14.5** on p. 581).

This estimate strikes most people as surprisingly high. Why is this so? One reason is that when people think about psychological disorders they tend to think of severe disorders, such as bipolar disorder or schizophrenia, which are relatively infrequent, rather than "run of the mill" disturbances, such as anxiety and depressive disorders, which are much more common. When it comes to mental illness, people tend to think of patients in straightjackets or of obviously disturbed homeless people who do not reflect the broad and diverse population of people who suffer from psychological disorders. In other words, their *prototypes* or "best examples" of mental illness consist of severe disorders that are infrequent, so they underestimate the prevalence of mental disorders. This distortion illustrates the influence of the *representativeness heuristic,* **which is basing the estimated probability of an event on how similar it is to the typical prototype of that event** (see Chapter 8).

Do you still find it hard to believe that the overall prevalence of psychological disorders is about 44%? Another reason this number seems surprisingly high is that

many people do not understand that the probability of having *at least one* disorder is much higher than the probability of having the most prevalent disorder by itself. For example, the probability of having a substance use disorder, the single most common type of disorder, is approximately 24%, but the probability of having a substance use disorder *or* an anxiety disorder *or* a mood disorder *or* a schizophrenic disorder jumps to 44%. These "or" relationships represent *cumulative probabilities.* Yet another consideration that makes the prevalence figures seem high is that many people confuse different types of *prevalence rates.* The 44% estimate is for *lifetime prevalence,* which means it is the probability of having *any* disorder *at least once* at any time in one's lifetime. The lifetime prevalence rate is another example of "or" relationships. It is a value that takes into account the probability of having a psychological disorder in childhood *or* adolescence *or* adulthood *or* old age. *Point prevalence rates,* which estimate the percentage of people manifesting various disorders *at a particular point in time,* are much lower

Highly publicized insanity trials, such as that of John Hinckley, Jr., who tried to assassinate President Reagan, lead the public to greatly overestimate how often the insanity defense is used, illustrating the impact of the availability heuristic.

because many psychological disorders last only a few months to a few years.

What about "and" relationships—that is, relationships in which we want to know the probability of someone having condition A *and* condition B? For example, given the lifetime prevalence estimates (from **Figure 14.5**) for each category of disorder, which are shown in the parentheses, what is the probability of someone having a substance use disorder (24% prevalence) *and* an anxiety disorder (19%) *and* a mood disorder (15%) *and* a schizophrenic disorder (1%) during his or her lifetime? Such "and" relationships represent *conjunctive probabilities.* Stop and think: what must be true about the probability of having all four types of disorders? Will this probability be less than 24%, between 24% and 44%, or over 44%? You may be surprised to learn that this figure is probably well under 1%. You can't have all four disorders unless you have the least frequent disorder (schizophrenia), which has a prevalence of 1%, so the answer *must* be 1% or less. Moreover, of all of the people with schizophrenia, only a tiny subset of them are likely to have all three of the other disorders, so the answer is probably well under 1% (see **Figure 14.26**). If this type of question strikes you as contrived, think again. Epidemiologists have devoted an enormous amount of research to the estimation of *comorbidity*—**the coexistence of two or more disorders**—because it greatly complicates treatment issues.

These are two examples of using statistical probabilities as a critical thinking tool. Let's apply this type of thinking to another problem dealing with physical health. Here is a problem used in a study by Tversky and Kahneman (1983, p. 308) that many physicians got wrong:

A health survey was conducted in a sample of adult males in British Columbia, of all ages and occupations. Please give your best estimate of the following values:

What percentage of the men surveyed have had one or more heart attacks? _____

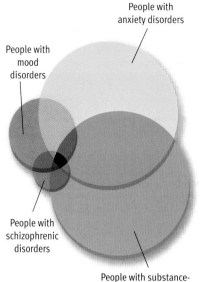

People with anxiety disorders

People with mood disorders

People with schizophrenic disorders

People with substance-related disorders

Figure 14.26

Conjunctive probabilities. The probability of someone having all four disorders depicted here cannot be greater than the probability of the least common condition by itself, which is 1% for schizophrenia. The intersection of all four disorders (shown in black) has to be a subset of schizophrenic disorders and is probably well under 1%. Efforts to think about probabilities can sometimes be facilitated by creating diagrams that show the relationships and overlap among various events.

What percentage of the men surveyed both are over 55 years old and have had one or more heart attacks? _____

Fill in the blanks above with your best guesses. Of course, you probably have only a very general idea about the prevalence of heart attacks, but go ahead and fill in the blanks anyway.

The actual values are not as important in this example as the relative values are. Over 65% of the physicians who participated in the experiment by Tversky and Kahneman gave a higher percentage value for the second question than for the first. What is wrong with their answers? The second question is asking about the conjunctive probability of two events. Hope-fully, you see why this figure *must* be less than the probability of either one of these events occurring alone. Of all of the men in the survey who had had a heart attack, only some of them are also over 55, so the second number must be smaller than the first. As we saw in Chapter 8, this common error in thinking is called the *conjunction fallacy*. **The *conjunction fallacy* occurs when people estimate that the odds of two uncertain events happening together are greater than the odds of either event happening alone.**

Why did so many physicians get this problem wrong? They were vulnerable to the conjunction fallacy because they were influenced by the *representativeness heuristic*, or the power of prototypes. When phy-sicians think "heart attack," they tend to envision a man over the age of 55. Hence, the second scenario fit so well with their prototype of a heart attack victim, they carelessly overestimated its probability.

Let's consider some additional examples of erroneous reasoning about probabilities involving how people think about psycho-logical disorders. Toward the beginning of the chapter, we discussed the fact that many people tend to stereotypically assume that mentally ill people are likely to be vio-lent. Near the end of the chapter, we noted that people tend to wildly overestimate (37-fold in one study) how often the insanity defense is used in criminal trials. These examples reflect the influence of the *avail-ability heuristic*, **which is basing the esti-mated probability of an event on the ease with which relevant instances come to mind.** Because of the availability heuristic, people tend to overestimate the probability of dramatic events that receive heavy media coverage, even when these events are rare, because examples of the events are easy to retrieve from memory. Violent acts by for-mer psychiatric patients tend to get lots of attention in the press. And because of the *hindsight bias,* journalists tend to question why authorities couldn't foresee and pre-vent the violence (see the Critical Thinking Application for Chapter 12), so the mental illness angle tends to be emphasized. In a similar vein, press coverage is usually in-tense when a defendant in a murder trial mounts an insanity defense.

In sum, the various types of statistics that come up in thinking about psycho-logical disorders demonstrate that we are constantly working with probabilities, even though we may not realize it. Criti-cal thinking requires a good understanding of the laws of probability because there are very few certainties in life.

Table 14.3 Critical Thinking Skills Discussed in This Application

Skill	Description
Understanding the limitations of the representativeness heuristic	The critical thinker understands that focusing on prototypes can lead to inaccurate probability estimates.
Understanding cumulative probabilities	The critical thinker understands that the probability of at least one of several events occurring is additive, and increases with time and the number of events.
Understanding conjunctive probabilities	The critical thinker appreciates that the probability of two uncertain events happening together is less than the probability of either event happening alone.
Understanding the limitations of the availability heuristic	The critical thinker understands that the ease with which examples come to mind may not be an accurate guide to the probability of an event.

REVIEW of Key Points

14.29 Probability estimates can be distorted by the representativeness heuristic and the availability heuristic. Cumulative probabilities are additive, whereas conjunctive probabilities are always less than the likelihood of any one of the events happening alone.

Key Ideas

Abnormal Behavior: Myths, Realities, and Controversies

▌ The medical model assumes that it is useful to view abnormal behavior as a disease. This view has been criticized on the grounds that it turns ethical questions about deviance into medical questions.

▌ Three criteria are used in deciding whether people suffer from psychological disorders: deviance, personal distress, and maladaptive behavior. People with psychological disorders are not particularly bizarre or dangerous, and even the most severe disorders are potentially curable.

▌ DSM-IV is the official psychodiagnostic classification system in the United States. This system asks for information about patients on five axes, or dimensions. Psychological disorders are more common than widely believed and the socioeconomic costs of mental illness are enormous.

Anxiety Disorders

▌ The anxiety disorders include generalized anxiety disorder, phobic disorder, panic disorder, obsessive-compulsive disorder, and posttraumatic stress disorder. Heredity, oversensitivity to the physiological symptoms of anxiety, and abnormalities in GABA or serotonin activity may contribute to these disorders.

▌ Many anxiety responses, especially phobias, may be caused by classical conditioning and then maintained by operant conditioning. Cognitive theorists hold that a tendency to overinterpret harmless situations as threatening may make some people vulnerable to anxiety disorders. Stress may also trigger anxiety disorders.

Somatoform Disorders

▌ Somatoform disorders include somatization disorder, conversion disorder, and hypochondriasis. These disorders often emerge in people with histrionic personalities and in people who focus excess attention on their internal physiological processes.

Dissociative Disorders

▌ Dissociative disorders include dissociative amnesia and fugue and dissociative identity disorder (DID). These disorders are uncommon and their causes are not well understood. Dissociative identity disorder is a controversial diagnosis.

Mood Disorders

▌ The principal mood disorders are major depressive disorder and bipolar disorder. Mood disorders are episodic. Depression is more common in females than males. Mood disorders are associated with dramatic elevations in suicide rates.

▌ Evidence indicates that people vary in their genetic vulnerability to mood disorders. These disorders are accompanied by changes in neurochemical activity in the brain. Depression is associated with reduced hippocampal volume and suppressed neurogenesis. Cognitive models posit that negative thinking contributes to depression. Depression is often rooted in interpersonal inadequacies and stress.

Schizophrenic Disorders

▌ Schizophrenic disorders are characterized by deterioration of adaptive behavior, delusions, hallucinations, and disturbed mood. Recognized subtypes are paranoid, catatonic, disorganized, and undifferentiated schizophrenia. Research has linked schizophrenia to genetic vulnerability, changes in neurotransmitter activity, and structural abnormalities in the brain.

▌ The neurodevelopmental hypothesis asserts that schizophrenia is attributable to disruptions in the normal maturational processes of the brain before or at birth that are caused by prenatal or obstetrical insults to the brain. Precipitating stress and high expressed emotion in families may also modulate the course of schizophrenia.

Personality Disorders

▌ Ten personality disorders, grouped into three clusters, are allocated to Axis II in the DSM. The antisocial personality disorder involves manipulative, impulsive, exploitive, aggressive behavior. Research on the etiology of this disorder has implicated genetic vulnerability, autonomic reactivity, inadequate socialization, and observational learning.

Psychological Disorders and the Law

▌ Insanity is a legal concept applied to people who cannot be held responsible for their actions because of mental illness. When people appear to be dangerous to themselves or others, courts may rule that they are subject to involuntary commitment in a hospital.

Culture and Pathology

▌ The principal categories of psychological disturbance are identifiable in all cultures, but milder disorders may go unrecognized in some societies. The symptoms associated with specific disorders are largely the same across different cultures, but some variability is seen.

Reflecting on the Chapter's Themes

▌ This chapter highlighted four of our unifying themes, showing that behavior is governed by multiple causes, that heredity and environment jointly influence mental disorders, that psychology evolves in a sociohistorical context, and that pathology is characterized by both cultural variance and invariance.

PERSONAL APPLICATION Understanding Eating Disorders

▌ The principal eating disorders are anorexia nervosa and bulimia nervosa. Binge-eating disorder has been proposed as a third diagnosis. Eating disorders appear to be largely a product of modern, affluent, Westernized culture. Females account for 90%–95% of eating disorders.

▌ There appears to be a genetic vulnerability to eating disorders. Cultural pressures on young women to be thin clearly help foster eating disorders. Unhealthful family dynamics and disturbed thinking can also contribute.

CRITICAL THINKING APPLICATION Working with Probabilities in Thinking About Mental Illness

▌ Probability estimates can be distorted by the representativeness heuristic and the availability heuristic. Cumulative probabilities are additive, whereas conjunctive probabilities are always less than the likelihood of any one of the events happening alone.

Key Terms

Agoraphobia (p. 582)
Anorexia nervosa (p. 613)
Antisocial personality disorder (p. 606)
Anxiety disorders (p. 582)
Availability heuristic (p. 617)
Binge-eating disorder (p. 614)
Bipolar disorder (p. 592)
Bulimia nervosa (p. 613)
Catatonic schizophrenia (p. 599)
Comorbidity (p. 616)
Concordance rate (p. 584)
Conjunction fallacy (p. 617)
Conversion disorder (p. 587)
Culture-bound disorders (p. 611)
Cyclothymic disorder (p. 592)
Delusions (p. 598)
Diagnosis (p. 577)
Disorganized schizophrenia (p. 599)
Dissociative amnesia (p. 589)
Dissociative disorders (p. 589)
Dissociative fugue (p. 589)
Dissociative identity disorder (DID) (p. 589)
Dysthymic disorder (p. 592)
Eating disorders (p. 613)
Epidemiology (p. 579)
Etiology (p. 577)
Expressed emotion (EE) (p. 603)
Generalized anxiety disorder (p. 582)
Hallucinations (p. 599)
Hypochondriasis (p. 587)
Insanity (p. 607)

Involuntary commitment (p. 607)
Major depressive disorder (p. 591)
Manic-depressive disorder (p. 592)
Medical model (p. 576)
Mood disorders (p. 590)
Multiple-personality disorder (p. 589)
Negative symptoms (p. 600)
Obsessive-compulsive disorder (OCD) (p. 583)
Panic disorder (p. 582)
Paranoid schizophrenia (p. 599)
Personality disorders (p. 604)
Phobic disorder (p. 582)
Positive symptoms (p. 600)
Posttraumatic stress disorder (PTSD) (p. 584)
Prevalence (p. 579)
Prognosis (p. 577)
Representativeness heuristic (p. 616)
Schizophrenic disorders (p. 598)
Somatization disorder (p. 587)
Somatoform disorders (p. 586)
Undifferentiated schizophrenia (p. 600)

Key People

Nancy Andreasen (p. 600)
Susan Nolen-Hoeksema (pp. 592, 595)
David Rosenhan (pp. 578–579)
Martin Seligman (pp. 585, 595)
Thomas Szasz (pp. 576–577)

1. According to Thomas Szasz, abnormal behavior usually involves:
   A. behavior that is statistically unusual.
   B. behavior that deviates from social norms.
   C. a disease of the mind.
   D. biological imbalance.

2. Although Sue is plagued by a high level of dread, worry, and anxiety, she still manages to meet her daily responsibilities. Sue's behavior:
   A. should not be considered abnormal, since her adaptive functioning is not impaired.
   B. should not be considered abnormal, since everyone sometimes experiences worry and anxiety.
   C. can still be considered abnormal, since she feels great personal distress.
   D. involves both a and b.

3. The fact that people acquire phobias of ancient sources of threat (such as snakes) much more readily than modern sources of threat (such as electrical outlets) can best be explained by:
   A. classical conditioning.
   B. operant conditioning.
   C. observational learning.
   D. preparedness or an evolved module for fear learning.

4. Which of the following statements about dissociative identity disorder is true?
   A. The original personality is always aware of the alternate personalities.
   B. The alternate personalities are usually unaware of the original personality.
   C. The personalities are typically all quite similar to one another.
   D. Starting in the 1970s, a dramatic increase occurred in the diagnosis of dissociative identity disorder.

5. People with unipolar disorders experience _____; people with bipolar disorders are vulnerable to _____.
   A. alternating periods of depression and mania; mania only
   B. depression only; alternating periods of depression and mania
   C. mania only; alternating periods of depression and mania
   D. alternating periods of depression and mania; depression and mania simultaneously

6. A concordance rate indicates:
   A. the percentage of relatives who exhibit the same disorder.
   B. the percentage of people with a given disorder who are currently receiving treatment.
   C. the prevalence of a given disorder in the general population.
   D. the rate of cure for a given disorder.

7. People who consistently exhibit _____ thinking are more vulnerable to depression than others.
   A. overly optimistic
   B. negative, pessimistic
   C. delusional
   D. dysthymic

8. Mary believes that while she sleeps at night, space creatures are attacking her and invading her uterus, where they will multiply until they are ready to take over the world. Mary would most likely be diagnosed as _____ schizophrenic.
   A. paranoid
   B. catatonic
   C. disorganized
   D. undifferentiated

9. As an alternative to the current classification scheme, it has been proposed that schizophrenic disorders be divided into just two categories based on:
   A. whether the prognosis is favorable or unfavorable.
   B. whether the disorder is mild or severe.
   C. the predominance of thought disturbances.
   D. the predominance of negative versus positive symptoms.

10. Most of the drugs that are useful in the treatment of schizophrenia are known to dampen _____ activity in the brain, suggesting that increases in the activity of this neurotransmitter may contribute to the development of the disorder.
    A. norepinephrine
    B. serotonin
    C. acetylcholine
    D. dopamine

11. The main problem with the current classification scheme for personality disorders is that:
    A. it falsely implies that nearly everyone has at least one personality disorder.
    B. the criteria for diagnosis are so detailed and specific that even extremely disturbed people fail to meet them.
    C. the categories often overlap, making diagnosis unreliable.
    D. it contains too few categories to be useful.

12. The diagnosis of antisocial personality disorder would apply to an individual who:
    A. withdraws from social interaction due to an intense fear of rejection.
    B. withdraws from social interaction due to a lack of interest.
    C. is emotionally cold and suspicious of everyone.
    D. is callous, impulsive, and manipulative.

13. Involuntary commitment to a psychiatric facility:
    A. can occur only after a mentally ill individual has been convicted of a violent crime.
    B. usually occurs because people appear to be a danger to themselves or others.
    C. no longer occurs under modern civil law.
    D. will be a lifelong commitment, even if the individual is no longer mentally ill.

14. Those who embrace a relativistic view of psychological disorders would agree that:
    A. the criteria of mental illness vary considerably across cultures.
    B. there are universal standards of normality and abnormality.
    C. Western diagnostic concepts have validity and utility in other cultural contexts.
    D. both b and c are true.

15. About _____ of patients with eating disorders are female.
    A. 40%
    B. 50%–60%
    C. 75%
    D. 90%–95%

Answers

1 B p. 576	6 A p. 584	11 C p. 605
2 C p. 577	7 B p. 595	12 D p. 606
3 D p. 585	8 A pp. 599–600	13 B pp. 607, 610
4 D p. 589	9 D p. 600	14 A p. 610
5 B pp. 590–592	10 D pp. 601–602	15 D p. 614

PsykTrek

To view a demo: www.cengage.com/psychology/psyktrek
To order: www.cengage.com/psychology/weiten
Go to the PsykTrek website or CD-ROM for further study of the concepts in this chapter. Both online and on the CD-ROM, PsykTrek includes dozens of learning modules with videos, animations, and quizzes, as well as simulations of psychological phenomena and a multimedia glossary that includes word pronunciations.

CengageNow

www.cengage.com/tlc

Go to this site for the link to CengageNOW, your one-stop study shop. Take a Pretest for this chapter, and CengageNOW will generate a personalized Study Plan based on your test results. The Study Plan will identify the topics you need to review and direct you to online resources to help you master those topics. You can then take a Posttest to help you determine the concepts you have mastered and what you still need to work on.

Companion Website

www.cengage.com/psychology/weiten

Go to this site to find online resources directly linked to your book, including a glossary, flash cards, drag-and-drop exercises, quizzes, and more!

15

TREATMENT OF PSYCHOLOGICAL DISORDERS

The Elements of the Treatment Process
Treatments: How Many Types Are There?
Clients: Who Seeks Therapy?
Therapists: Who Provides Professional Treatment?

Insight Therapies
Psychoanalysis
Client-Centered Therapy
Therapies Inspired by Positive Psychology
Group Therapy
How Effective Are Insight Therapies?
How Do Insight Therapies Work?

Behavior Therapies
Systematic Desensitization
Aversion Therapy
Social Skills Training
Cognitive-Behavioral Treatments
How Effective Are Behavior Therapies?

Biomedical Therapies
Treatment with Drugs
Electroconvulsive Therapy (ECT)
New Brain Stimulation Techniques

Current Trends and Issues in Treatment
Grappling with the Constraints of Managed Care
Blending Approaches to Treatment

Illustrated Overview of Five Major Approaches to Treatment

FEATURED STUDY ▌ Combining Insight Therapy and Medication

Increasing Multicultural Sensitivity in Treatment

Institutional Treatment in Transition
Disenchantment with Mental Hospitals
Deinstitutionalization
Mental Illness, the Revolving Door, and Homelessness

Reflecting on the Chapter's Themes

PERSONAL APPLICATION ▌ Looking for a Therapist
Where Do You Find Therapeutic Services?
Is the Therapist's Profession or Sex Important?
Is Treatment Always Expensive?
Is the Therapist's Theoretical Approach Important?
What Should You Look for in a Prospective Therapist?
What Is Therapy Like?

CRITICAL THINKING APPLICATION ▌ From Crisis to Wellness—But Was It the Therapy?

Recap

Practice Test

What do you picture when you hear the term *psychotherapy?* Unless you've had some personal exposure to therapy, your image of it has likely been shaped by depictions you've seen on television or in the movies. A good example is the 1999 film *Analyze This,* a comedy starring Billy Crystal as psychiatrist Ben Sobol and Robert De Niro as Paul Vitti, a mob boss who is suffering from "panic attacks." Complications ensue when Vitti—a man no one says "no" to—demands that Dr. Sobol cure him of his problem before his rivals in crime turn his "weakness" against him.

With his glasses and beard, Billy Crystal's Dr. Sobol resembles many people's picture of a therapist. Like many movie therapists, Dr. Sobol practices "talk therapy." He listens attentively as his patients talk about what is troubling them. Occasionally he offers comments that reflect their thoughts and feelings back to them or that offer some illuminating insight into their problems. We can get a feeling for his approach from a funny scene in which the uneducated Vitti turns Dr. Sobol's techniques on him:

Vitti: Hey, let's see how you like it. Let's talk about your father.

Dr. Sobol: Let's not.
Vitti: What kind of work does your father do?
Dr. Sobol: It's not important.
Vitti: You paused.

The popular film Analyze This derived much of its humor from common misconceptions about the process of psychotherapy.

Warner Bros./Shooting Star

Dr. Sobol: I did not.

Vitti: You just paused. That means you had a feeling, like a thought. . . .

Dr. Sobol: You know, we're running out of time. Let's not waste it talking about my problems.

Vitti: Your father's a problem?

Dr. Sobol: No!

Vitti: That's what you just said.

Dr. Sobol: I did not!

Vitti: Now you're upset.

Dr. Sobol (getting upset): I am not upset!

Vitti: Yes you are.

Dr. Sobol: Will you stop it!

Vitti: You know what, I'm getting good at this.

As in this scene, the film derives much of its humor from popular conceptions—and misconceptions—about therapy. The technique that Vitti makes fun of does resemble one type of therapeutic process. Like Vitti, many people do associate needing therapy with a shameful weakness. Further, therapy is often of considerable benefit in assisting people to make significant changes in their lives—even if those changes are not as dramatic as Vitti's giving up his life of crime at the end of the movie. On the other hand, the film's comic exaggerations also highlight some misconceptions about therapy, including the following:

• Vitti is driven to see a "shrink" because he feels like he's "falling apart." In fact, therapists help people with all kinds of problems. People need not have severe symptoms of mental illness to benefit from therapy.

• Dr. Sobol is a psychiatrist, but most therapists are not. And although Dr. Sobol quotes Freud and the film's plot turns on interpreting a dream (in this case, it's the psychiatrist's dream!), many therapists make little or no use of Freudian techniques.

• Dr. Sobol relies on "talk therapy" to produce insights that will help his patients overcome their troubles. In reality, this approach is only one of the many techniques used by therapists.

• Dr. Sobol "cures" Vitti by getting him to acknowledge a traumatic event in his childhood (the death of his father) that is at the root of his problems. But only rarely does therapy produce a single dramatic insight that results in wholesale change for the client.

In this chapter, we'll take a down-to-earth look at *psychotherapy,* using the term in its broadest sense, to refer to all the diverse approaches used in the treatment of mental disorders and psychological problems. We'll start by discussing some general questions about the provision of treatment. After considering these issues, we'll examine the goals, techniques, and effectiveness of some of the more widely used approaches to therapy and discuss recent trends and issues in treatment. In the Personal Application, we'll look at practical questions related to finding and choosing a therapist and getting the most out of therapy. And in the Critical Thinking Application we'll address problems involved in determining whether therapy actually helps.

The Elements of the Treatment Process

Key Learning Goals

15.1 Identify the three major categories of therapy, and discuss patterns of treatment seeking.

15.2 Distinguish the various types of mental health professionals involved in the provision of therapy.

Sigmund Freud is widely credited with launching modern psychotherapy. Ironically, the landmark case that inspired Freud was actually treated by one of his colleagues, Josef Breuer. Around 1880, Breuer began to treat a young woman referred to as Anna O (which was a pseudonym—her real name was Bertha Pappenheim). Anna exhibited a variety of physical maladies, including headaches, coughing, and a loss of feeling and movement in her right arm. Much to his surprise, Breuer discovered that Anna's physical symptoms cleared up when he encouraged her to talk about emotionally charged experiences from her past.

When Breuer and Freud discussed the case, they speculated that talking things through had enabled Anna to drain off bottled-up emotions that had caused her symptoms. Breuer found the intense emotional exchange in this treatment not to his liking, so he didn't follow through on his discovery. However, Freud applied Breuer's insight to other patients, and his successes led him to develop a systematic treatment procedure, which he called *psychoanalysis.* Anna O called her treatment "the talking cure." However, as you'll see, psychotherapy isn't always curative, and many modern treatments place little emphasis on talking.

Freud's breakthrough ushered in a century of progress for psychotherapy. Psychoanalysis spawned many offspring as Freud's followers developed their own systems of treatment. Since then, approaches to treatment have steadily grown more numerous, more diverse, and more effective. Today, people can choose from a bewildering array of therapies.

Treatments: How Many Types Are There?

In their efforts to help people, psychotherapists use many treatment methods. These methods include discussion, advice, emotional support, persuasion, conditioning procedures, relaxation training, role playing, drug therapy, biofeedback, and group therapy. No one knows exactly how many distinct types of psychotherapy there are. One expert (Kazdin, 1994) estimates that there may be over 400 approaches to treatment. Fortunately, we can impose some order on this chaos. As varied as therapists' procedures are, approaches to treatment can be classified into three major categories:

1. *Insight therapies.* Insight therapy is "talk therapy" in the tradition of Freud's psychoanalysis. In insight therapies, clients engage in complex verbal interactions with their therapists. The goal in these discussions is to pursue increased insight regarding the nature of the client's difficulties and to sort through possible solutions. Insight therapy can be conducted with an individual or with a group. Broadly speaking, family therapy and marital therapy fall into this category.

2. *Behavior therapies.* Behavior therapies are based on the principles of learning, which were introduced in Chapter 6. Instead of emphasizing personal insights, behavior therapists make direct efforts to alter problematic responses (phobias, for instance) and maladaptive habits (drug use, for instance). Behavior therapists work on changing clients' overt behaviors. They use different procedures for different kinds of problems.

3. *Biomedical therapies.* Biomedical approaches to therapy involve interventions into a person's biological functioning. The most widely used procedures are drug therapy and electroconvulsive (shock) therapy. As the term bio*medical* suggests, these treatments have traditionally been provided only by physicians with a medical degree (usually psychiatrists). This situation is changing, however, as psychologists have been campaigning for prescription privileges (Norfleet, 2002; Welsh, 2003). To date psychologists have obtained prescription authority in two states (New Mexico and Louisiana), and they have made legislative progress toward this goal in many other states (Long, 2005). Although some psychologists have argued against pursuing the right to prescribe medication (Heiby, 2002; Robiner et al., 2003), the movement is gathering momentum and seems likely to prevail.

Clients: Who Seeks Therapy?

In the therapeutic triad (therapists, treatments, clients), the greatest diversity is seen among the clients. According to the 1999 Surgeon General's report on mental health (U.S. Department of Health and Human Services, 1999) about 15% of the U.S. population use mental health services in a given year. These people bring to therapy the full range of human problems: anxiety, depression, unsatisfactory interpersonal relations, troublesome habits, poor self-control, low self-esteem, marital conflicts, self-doubt, a sense of emptiness, and feelings of personal stagnation. The two most common presenting problems are excessive anxiety and depression (Narrow et al., 1993).

Interestingly, people often delay for many years before finally seeking treatment for their psychological problems (Kessler, Olfson, & Berglund, 1998). One recent large-scale study (Wang, Berglund et al., 2005) found that the median delay in seeking treatment was 6 years for bipolar disorder and for drug dependence, 8 years for depression, 9 years for generalized anxiety disorder, and 10 years for panic disorder! Figure 15.1 summarizes data from the same study on the percentage of people with various disorders who seek treatment within the first year after the onset of the disorder. As you can see, the figures are surprisingly low for most disorders.

A client in treatment does *not* necessarily have an identifiable psychological disorder. Some people seek professional help for everyday problems (career decisions, for instance) or vague feelings of discontent

The case of Anna O, whose real name was Bertha Pappenheim, provided the inspiration for Sigmund Freud's invention of psychoanalysis.

Figure 15.1

Treatment seeking for various disorders. In a study of the extent to which people seek treatment for psychological disorders, Wang et al. (2005) found that only a minority of people promptly pursue treatment for their disorder. The data summarized here show the percentage of people who obtain professional treatment within the first year after the onset of various disorders. The percentages vary depending on the disorder, but all the figures are surprisingly low.

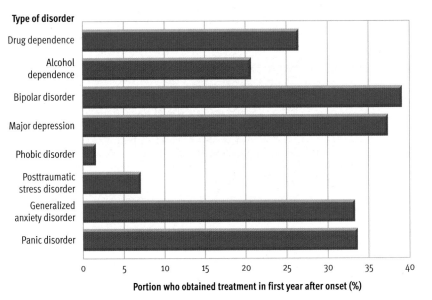

Portion who obtained treatment in first year after onset (%)

(Strupp, 1996). One surprising finding in recent research has been that only about half of the people who use mental health services in a given year meet the criteria for a full-fledged mental disorder (Kessler et al., 2005b).

People vary considerably in their willingness to seek psychotherapy. One study found that even among people who perceive a need for professional assistance, only 59% actually seek professional help (Mojtabai, Olfson, & Mechanic, 2002). As you can see in **Figure 15.2**, women are more likely than men to receive therapy. Treatment is also more likely when people have medical insurance and when they have more education (Olfson et al., 2002; Wang,

Lane et al., 2005). *Unfortunately, it appears that many people who need therapy don't receive it* (Kessler et al., 2005b). As **Figure 15.3** shows, only a portion of the people who need treatment get it. People who could benefit from therapy do not seek it for a variety of reasons. Lack of health insurance and cost concerns appear to be major barriers to obtaining needed care for many people. According to the Surgeon General's report, the biggest roadblock is the "stigma surrounding the receipt of mental health treatment." Unfortunately, many people equate seeking therapy with admitting personal weakness.

Therapists: Who Provides Professional Treatment?

People troubled by personal problems often solicit help from their friends, relatives, and clergy. These sources of assistance may provide excellent advice, but their counsel does not qualify as therapy. Therapy refers to *professional* treatment by someone with special training. However, a common source of confusion about psychotherapy is the variety of "helping professions" available to offer assistance (Murstein & Fontaine, 1993). Psychology and psychiatry are the principal professions involved in the provision of psychotherapy. However, therapy is increasingly provided by clinical social workers, psychiatric nurses, counselors, and marriage and family therapists. Let's look at the various mental health professions.

Psychologists

Two types of psychologists may provide therapy. *Clinical psychologists* and *counseling psychologists* specialize in the diagnosis and treatment of psychological disorders and everyday behavioral problems. Clinical psychologists' training emphasizes the treatment of full-fledged disorders. In contrast, counseling psychologists' training is slanted toward the treatment of everyday adjustment problems. In practice, however, quite a bit of overlap occurs between clinical and counseling psychologists in training, skills, and the clientele that they serve.

Both types of psychologists must earn a doctoral degree (Ph.D., Psy.D., or Ed.D.). A doctorate in psychology requires about five to seven years of training beyond a bachelor's degree. The process of gaining admission to a Ph.D. program in clinical psychology is highly competitive (about as difficult as getting into medical school). Psychologists receive most of their training in universities or independent professional schools. They then serve a one-year internship in a clinical setting, such as a hospital, usually followed by one or two years of postdoctoral fellowship training.

Figure 15.2

Therapy utilization rates. Olfson and colleagues (2002) gathered data on the use of non-hospital outpatient mental health services in the United States in relation to various demographic variables. In regard to marital status, utilization rates are particularly high among those who are divorced or separated. The use of therapy is greater among those who have more education; in terms of age, utilization peaks in the 35–44 age bracket. Females are more likely to pursue therapy than males are, but utilization rates are extremely low among ethnic minorities.

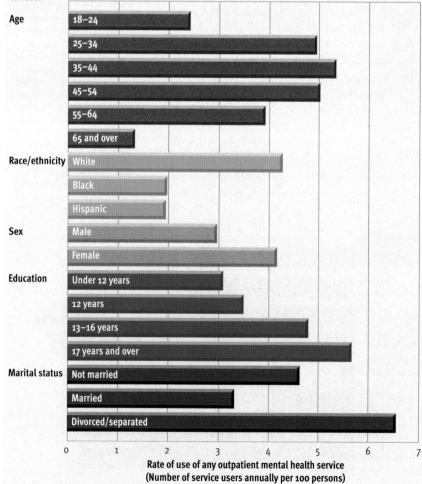

In providing therapy, psychologists use either insight or behavioral approaches. In comparison to psychiatrists, they are more likely to use behavioral techniques and less likely to use psychoanalytic methods. Clinical and counseling psychologists do psychological testing as well as psychotherapy, and many also conduct research.

Psychiatrists

Psychiatrists are physicians who specialize in the diagnosis and treatment of psychological disorders. Many psychiatrists also treat everyday behavioral problems. However, in comparison to psychologists, psychiatrists devote more time to relatively severe disorders (schizophrenia, mood disorders) and less time to everyday marital, family, job, and school problems.

Psychiatrists have an M.D. degree. Their graduate training requires four years of coursework in medical school and a four-year apprenticeship in a residency at a hospital. Their psychotherapy training occurs during their residency, since the required coursework in medical school is essentially the same for everyone, whether they are going into surgery, pediatrics, or psychiatry. In their provision of therapy, psychiatrists increasingly emphasize drug therapies (Olfson et al., 2002). In comparison to psychologists, psychiatrists are more likely to use psychoanalysis and less likely to use group therapies or behavior therapies. That said, contemporary psychiatrists primarily depend on medication as their principal mode of treatment.

Other Mental Health Professionals

Several other mental health professions also provide psychotherapy services, and some of these professions are growing rapidly. In hospitals and other institutions, *clinical social workers* and *psychiatric nurses* often work as part of a treatment team with a psychologist or psychiatrist. Psychiatric nurses, who may have a bachelor's or master's degree in their field, play a large role in hospital inpatient treatment. Clinical social workers generally have a master's degree and typically work with patients and their families to ease the patient's integration back into the community. Although social workers and psychiatric nurses have traditionally worked in institutional settings, they increasingly provide a wide range of therapeutic services as independent practitioners.

Many kinds of *counselors* also provide therapeutic services. Counselors are usually found working in schools, colleges, and assorted human service agencies (youth centers, geriatric centers, family planning centers, and so forth). Counselors typically have a master's degree. They often specialize

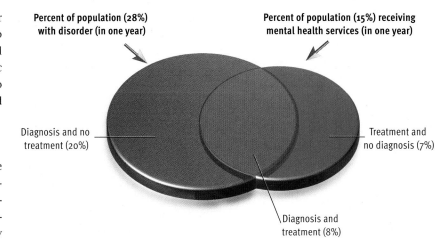

Percent of population (28%) with disorder (in one year)

Percent of population (15%) receiving mental health services (in one year)

Diagnosis and no treatment (20%)

Treatment and no diagnosis (7%)

Diagnosis and treatment (8%)

Figure 15.3

Psychological disorders and professional treatment. Not everyone who has a psychological disorder receives professional treatment, and not everyone who seeks treatment has a clear disorder. This graph, from the Surgeon General's report on mental health, shows that 15% of the U.S. adult population receive mental health treatment each year. Almost half of these people (7%) do not receive a psychiatric diagnosis, although some of them probably have milder disorders that are not assessed in epidemiological research. This graph also shows that over two-thirds of the people who *do* have disorders do *not* receive professional treatment. (Data from *Mental Health: A Report of the Surgeon General,* U.S. Public Health Service, 1999)

in particular types of problems, such as vocational counseling, marital counseling, rehabilitation counseling, and drug counseling.

Although there are clear differences among the helping professions in education and training, their roles in the treatment process overlap considerably. In this chapter, we will refer to psychologists or psychiatrists as needed, but otherwise we'll use the terms *clinician, therapist,* and *provider* to refer to mental health professionals of all kinds, regardless of their professional degree.

Now that we have discussed the basic elements in psychotherapy, we can examine specific approaches to treatment in terms of their goals, procedures, and effectiveness. We'll begin with some representative insight therapies.

web link 15.1

Online Dictionary of Mental Health

This thematically arranged "dictionary" at the University of Sheffield (UK) Medical School comprises diverse links related to many forms of psychotherapy, the treatment of psychological disorders, and general issues of mental health.

REVIEW of Key Points

15.1 Approaches to treatment are diverse, but they can be grouped into three categories: insight therapies, behavior therapies, and biomedical therapies. Clients bring a wide variety of problems to therapy and do not necessarily have a disorder. People vary in their willingness to seek treatment. Many people delay seeking treatment, and many who need therapy do not receive it.

15.2 Therapists come from a variety of professional backgrounds. Clinical and counseling psychologists, psychiatrists, clinical social workers, psychiatric nurses, and counselors are the principal providers of therapeutic services. Each of these professions shows different preferences for approaches to treatment. Psychologists typically practice insight or behavior therapy. Psychiatrists rely more heavily on drug therapies.

Insight Therapies

Key Learning Goals

15.3 Explain the logic of psychoanalysis and the techniques by which analysts probe the unconscious.

15.4 Clarify the nature of resistance and transference in psychoanalysis.

15.5 Understand the role of therapeutic climate and therapeutic process in client-centered therapy.

15.6 Discuss new approaches to insight therapy inspired by the positive psychology movement.

15.7 Articulate how group therapy is generally conducted, and identify some advantages of this approach.

15.8 Assess the efficacy of insight therapies and the role of common factors in therapy.

There are many schools of thought about how to do insight therapy. Therapists with various theoretical orientations use different methods to pursue different kinds of insights. However, what these varied approaches have in common is that *insight therapies* **involve verbal interactions intended to enhance clients' self-knowledge and thus promote healthful changes in personality and behavior.**

Although there may be hundreds of insight therapies, the leading eight or ten approaches appear to account for the lion's share of treatment. In this section, we'll delve into psychoanalysis, related psychodynamic approaches, client-centered therapy, and new approaches fostered by the positive psychology movement. We'll also discuss how insight therapy can be done with groups as well as individuals.

Psychoanalysis

After the case of Anna O, Sigmund Freud worked as a psychotherapist for almost 50 years in Vienna. Through a painstaking process of trial and error, he developed innovative techniques for the treatment of psychological disorders and distress. His system of *psychoanalysis* came to dominate psychiatry for many decades. Although this dominance has eroded in recent years, a diverse collection of psychoanalytic approaches to therapy continue to evolve and to remain influential today (Gabbard, 2005; McWilliams & Weinberger, 2003; Ursano & Silberman, 2003).

Psychoanalysis **is an insight therapy that emphasizes the recovery of unconscious conflicts, motives, and defenses through techniques such as free association and transference.** To appreciate the logic of psychoanalysis, we have to look at Freud's thinking about the roots of mental disorders. Freud mostly treated anxiety-dominated disturbances, such as phobic, panic, obsessive-compulsive, and conversion disorders, which were then called *neuroses.*

Freud believed that neurotic problems are caused by unconscious conflicts left over from early childhood. As explained in Chapter 12, he thought that these inner conflicts involve battles among the id, ego, and superego, usually over sexual and aggressive impulses. He theorized that people depend on defense mechanisms to avoid confronting these conflicts, which remain hidden in the depths of the unconscious (see **Figure 15.4**). However, he noted that defensive maneuvers often lead to self-defeating be-

havior. Furthermore, he asserted that defenses tend to be only partially successful in alleviating anxiety, guilt, and other distressing emotions. With this model in mind, let's take a look at the therapeutic procedures used in psychoanalysis.

Probing the Unconscious

Given Freud's assumptions, we can see that the logic of psychoanalysis is quite simple. The analyst attempts to probe the murky depths of the unconscious to discover the unresolved conflicts causing the client's neurotic behavior. In a sense, the analyst functions as a "psychological detective." In this effort to explore the unconscious, the therapist relies on two techniques: free association and dream analysis.

In *free association* clients spontaneously express their thoughts and feelings exactly as they occur, with as little censorship as possible. In free associating, clients expound on anything that comes to mind, regardless of how trivial, silly, or embarrassing it might be. Gradually, most clients begin to let everything pour out without conscious censorship. The analyst studies these free associations for clues about what is going on in the client's unconscious.

In *dream analysis* the therapist interprets the symbolic meaning of the client's dreams. Freud saw dreams as the "royal road to the unconscious," the most direct means of access to patients' innermost conflicts, wishes, and impulses. Clients are encouraged and trained to remember their dreams, which they describe in therapy. The therapist then analyzes the symbolism in these dreams to interpret their meaning.

To better illustrate these matters, let's look at an actual case treated through psychoanalysis (adapted from Greenson, 1967, pp. 40–41). Mr. N was troubled by an unsatisfactory marriage. He claimed to love his wife, but he preferred sexual relations with prostitutes. Mr. N reported that his parents also endured lifelong marital difficulties. His childhood conflicts about their relationship appeared to be related to his problems. Both dream analysis and free association can be seen in the following description of a session in Mr. N's treatment:

Mr. N reported a fragment of a dream. All that he could remember is that he was waiting for a red traffic light to change when he felt that someone had bumped into

Sigmund Freud

"The news that reaches your consciousness is incomplete and often not to be relied on."

him from behind. . . . The associations led to Mr. N's love of cars, especially sports cars. He loved the sensation, in particular, of whizzing by those fat, old expensive cars. . . .

His father always hinted that he had been a great athlete, but he never substantiated it. . . . Mr. N doubted whether his father could really perform. His father would flirt with a waitress in a cafe or make sexual remarks about women passing by, but he seemed to be showing off. If he were really sexual, he wouldn't resort to that.

As is characteristic of free association, Mr. N's train of thought meandered about with little direction. Nonetheless, clues about his unconscious conflicts are apparent. What did Mr. N's therapist extract from this session? The therapist saw sexual overtones in the dream fragment, where Mr. N was bumped from behind. The therapist also inferred that Mr. N had a competitive orientation toward his father, based on the free association about whizzing by fat, old expensive cars. As you can see, analysts must *interpret* their clients' dreams and free associations. This is a critical process throughout psychoanalysis.

Interpretation   11d

Interpretation **refers to the therapist's attempts to explain the inner significance of the client's thoughts, feelings, memories, and behaviors.** Contrary to popular belief, analysts do not interpret everything, and they generally don't try to dazzle clients with startling revelations. Instead, analysts move forward inch by inch, offering interpretations that should be just out of the client's own reach (Samberg & Marcus, 2005). Mr. N's therapist eventually offered the following interpretations to his client:

I said to Mr. N near the end of the hour that I felt he was struggling with his feelings about his father's sexual life. He seemed to be saying that his father was sexually not a very potent man. . . . He also recalls that he once found a packet of condoms under his father's pillow when he was an adolescent and he thought, "My father must be going to prostitutes." I then intervened and pointed out that the condoms under his father's pillow seemed to indicate more obviously that his father used the condoms with his mother, who slept in the same bed. However, Mr. N wanted to believe his wish-fulfilling fantasy: mother doesn't want sex with father and father is not very potent. The patient was silent and the hour ended.

As you may have already guessed, the therapist concluded that Mr. N's difficulties were rooted in an Oedipal complex (see Chapter 12). The man had

unresolved sexual feelings toward his mother and hostile feelings about his father. These unconscious conflicts, rooted in Mr. N's childhood, were distorting his intimate relations as an adult.

Resistance   11d

How would you expect Mr. N to respond to the therapist's suggestion that he was in competition with his father for the sexual attention of his mother? Obviously, most clients would have great difficulty accepting such an interpretation. Freud fully expected clients to display some resistance to therapeutic efforts. *Resistance* **refers to largely unconscious defensive maneuvers intended to hinder the progress of therapy.** Resistance is assumed to be an inevitable part of the psychoanalytic process (Samberg & Marcus, 2005). Why would clients try to resist the helping process? Because they don't want to face up to the painful, disturbing conflicts that they have buried in their unconscious. Although they have sought help, they are reluctant to confront their real problems.

Resistance can take many forms. Clients may show up late for their sessions, may merely pretend to engage in free association, or may express hostility toward their therapist. For instance, Mr. N's therapist noted that after the session just described, "The next day he [Mr. N] began by telling me that he was furious with me . . ." Analysts use a variety of strategies to deal with their clients' resistance. Often, a key consideration is the handling of transference, which we consider next.

Figure 15.4

Freud's view of the roots of disorders. According to Freud, unconscious conflicts among the id, ego, and superego sometimes lead to anxiety. This discomfort may lead to pathological reliance on defensive behavior.

web link 15.2

The American Psychoanalytic Association

The website for this professional organization provides a great deal of useful information about psychoanalytic approaches to treatment. The resources include news releases, background information on psychoanalysis, an engine for literature searches, and a bookstore.

In psychoanalysis, the therapist encourages the client to reveal thoughts, feelings, dreams, and memories, which can then be interpreted in relation to the client's current problems.

Intrapsychic conflict (between id, ego, and superego) → Anxiety → Reliance on defense mechanisms

Transference 11d

Transference occurs when clients unconsciously start relating to their therapist in ways that mimic critical relationships in their lives. Thus, a client might start relating to a therapist as if the therapist were an overprotective mother, a rejecting brother, or a passive spouse. In a sense, the client *transfers* conflicting feelings about important people onto the therapist. For instance, in his treatment, Mr. N transferred some of the competitive hostility he felt toward his father onto his analyst.

Psychoanalysts often encourage transference so that clients can reenact relations with crucial people in the context of therapy. These reenactments can help bring repressed feelings and conflicts to the surface, allowing the client to work through them. The therapist's handling of transference is complicated and difficult, because transference may arouse confusing, highly charged emotions in the client.

Undergoing psychoanalysis is not easy. It can be a slow, painful process of self-examination that routinely requires three to five years of hard work. It tends to be a lengthy process because patients need time to gradually work through their problems and genuinely accept unnerving revelations (Williams, 2005). Ultimately, if resistance and transference can be handled effectively, the therapist's interpretations should lead the client to profound insights. For instance, Mr. N eventually admitted, "The old boy is probably right, it does tickle me to imagine that my mother preferred me and I could beat out my father. Later, I wondered whether this had something to do with my own screwed-up sex life with my wife." According to Freud, once clients recognize the unconscious sources of conflicts, they can resolve these conflicts and discard their neurotic defenses.

Modern Psychodynamic Therapies

Though still available, classical psychoanalysis as done by Freud is not widely practiced anymore (Kay & Kay, 2003). Freud's psychoanalytic method was geared to a particular kind of clientele that he was seeing in Vienna many years ago. As his followers fanned out across Europe and America, many found it necessary to adapt psychoanalysis to different cultures, changing times, and new kinds of patients (Karasu, 2005). Thus, many variations on Freud's original approach to psychoanalysis have developed over the years. These descendants of psychoanalysis, which continue to emphasize exploration of the unconscious, are collectively known as *psychodynamic approaches* to therapy.

Some of these adaptations, such as those made by Carl Jung (1917) and Alfred Adler (1927), were sweeping revisions based on fundamental differences in theory. Other variations, such as those devised by Melanie Klein (1948) and Heinz Kohut (1971), made substantial changes in theory while retaining certain central ideas. Still other revisions (Alexander, 1954; Stekel, 1950) simply involved efforts to modernize and streamline psychoanalytic techniques.

As a result, today we have a rich diversity of psychodynamic approaches to therapy (Magnavita, 2008). Recent reviews of these treatments suggest that interpretation, resistance, and transference continue to play key roles in therapeutic effects (Luborsky & Barrett, 2006). For example, evidence suggests that the amount of resistance manifested in psychodynamic therapy predicts the outcome of therapy. People who exhibit more resistance are less likely to experience a positive outcome and more likely to drop out of therapy (Luborsky & Barrett, 2006). Recent research also suggests that psychodynamic approaches can be helpful in the treatment of a diverse array of disorders, including panic disorder, borderline personality disorder, and substance abuse (Gibbons, Crits-Christoph, & Hearon, 2008).

Client-Centered Therapy 11d

You may have heard of people going into therapy to "find themselves" or to "get in touch with their real feelings." These now-popular phrases emerged out of the human potential movement, which was stimulated in part by the work of Carl Rogers (1951, 1986). Using a humanistic perspective, Rogers devised *client-centered therapy* (also known as *person-centered therapy*) in the 1940s and 1950s.

Client-centered therapy **is an insight therapy that emphasizes providing a supportive emotional climate for clients, who play a major role in determining the pace and direction of their therapy.** You may wonder why the troubled, untrained client is put in charge of the pace and direction of the therapy. Rogers (1961) provides a compelling justification:

It is the client who knows what hurts, what directions to go, what problems are crucial, what experiences have been deeply buried. It began to occur to me that unless I had a need to demonstrate my own cleverness and learning, I would do better to rely upon the client for the direction of movement in the process. (pp. 11–12)

Rogers's theory about the principal causes of neurotic anxieties is quite different from the Freudian explanation. As discussed in Chapter 12, Rogers maintains that most personal distress is due to inconsistency, or "incongruence," between a person's self-concept and reality (see **Figure 15.5**). Accord-

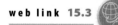

web link 15.3

Psychoanalytic Electronic Publishing

This site houses a remarkable archive of psychoanalytic literature, including full-text versions of 26 academic journals concerned with psychoanalysis, 56 classic books on psychoanalysis, and *The Complete Psychological Works of Sigmund Freud*. A search engine allows users to track down information on specific topics.

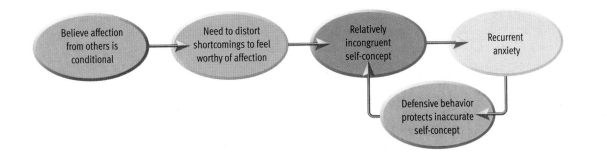

ing to his theory, incongruence makes people feel threatened by realistic feedback about themselves from others. For example, if you inaccurately viewed yourself as a hard-working, dependable person, you would feel threatened by contradictory feedback from friends or co-workers. According to Rogers, anxiety about such feedback often leads to reliance on defense mechanisms, to distortions of reality, and to stifled personal growth. Excessive incongruence is thought to be rooted in clients' overdependence on others for approval and acceptance.

Given Rogers's theory, client-centered therapists stalk insights that are quite different from the repressed conflicts that psychoanalysts go after. Client-centered therapists help clients to realize that they do not have to worry constantly about pleasing others and winning acceptance. They encourage clients to respect their own feelings and values. They help people restructure their self-concept to correspond better to reality. Ultimately, they try to foster self-acceptance and personal growth.

Therapeutic Climate 11d

According to Rogers, the *process* of therapy is not as important as the emotional *climate* in which the therapy takes place. He believes that it is critical for the therapist to provide a warm, supportive, accepting climate, which creates a safe environment in which clients can confront their shortcomings without feeling threatened. The lack of threat should reduce clients' defensive tendencies and thus help them open up. To create this atmosphere of emotional support, client-centered therapists must provide three conditions:

1. *Genuineness.* The therapist must be genuine with the client, communicating honestly and spontaneously. The therapist should not be phony or defensive.

2. *Unconditional positive regard.* The therapist must also show complete, nonjudgmental acceptance of the client as a person. The therapist should provide warmth and caring for the client, with no strings attached. This does not mean that the therapist must approve of everything that the client says or does.

A therapist can disapprove of a particular behavior while continuing to value the client as a human being.

3. *Empathy.* Finally, the therapist must provide accurate empathy for the client. This means that the therapist must understand the client's world from the client's point of view. Furthermore, the therapist must be articulate enough to communicate this understanding to the client.

Rogers firmly believed that a supportive emotional climate is the critical force promoting healthy changes in therapy. More recently, however, some client-centered therapists have begun to place more emphasis on the therapeutic process (Rice & Greenberg, 1992).

Therapeutic Process 11d

In client-centered therapy, the client and therapist work together as equals. The therapist provides relatively little guidance and keeps interpretation and advice to a minimum. So, just what does the client-centered therapist do, besides creating a supportive climate? Primarily, the therapist provides feedback to help clients sort out their feelings. The therapist's key task is *clarification*. Client-centered therapists try

Carl Rogers
"To my mind, empathy is in itself a healing agent."

Client-centered therapists emphasize the importance of a supportive emotional climate in therapy. They also work to clarify, rather than interpret, the feelings expressed by their patients.

to function like a human mirror, reflecting statements back to their clients, but with enhanced clarity. They help clients become more aware of their true feelings by highlighting themes that may be obscure in the clients' rambling discourse.

By working with clients to clarify their feelings, client-centered therapists hope to gradually build toward more far-reaching insights. In particular, they try to help clients better understand their interpersonal relationships and become more comfortable with their genuine selves. Obviously, these are ambitious goals. Client-centered therapy resembles psychoanalysis in that both seek to achieve a major reconstruction of a client's personality.

Therapies Inspired by Positive Psychology

The growth of the positive psychology movement has begun to inspire new approaches to insight therapy (Duckworth, Steen, & Seligman, 2005). As noted in Chapters 1 and 10, *positive psychology* uses theory and research to better understand the positive, adaptive, creative, and fulfilling aspects of human existence. The advocates of positive psychology maintain that the field has historically focused far too heavily on pathology, weakness, and suffering (and how to heal these conditions) rather than health and resilience (Seligman, 2003; Seligman & Csikszentmihalyi, 2000). They argue for increased research on contentment, well-being, human strengths, and positive emotions.

This philosophical approach has led to new therapeutic interventions. For example, *well-being therapy,* developed by Giovanni Fava and his colleagues (Fava, 1999; Ruini & Fava, 2004), seeks to enhance clients' self-acceptance, purpose in life, autonomy, and personal growth. It has been used successfully in the treatment of mood disorders and anxiety disorders (Fava et al., 2005).

Another new approach is *positive psychotherapy,* developed by Martin Seligman and colleagues (Seligman, Rashid, & Parks, 2006). Thus far, positive psychotherapy has been used mainly in the treatment of depression. This approach attempts to get clients to recognize their strengths, appreciate their blessings, savor positive experiences, forgive those who have wronged them, and find meaning in their lives. Preliminary research suggests that positive psychotherapy can be an effective treatment for depression. For example, in one study it was compared to treatment as usual (whatever the therapist would normally do) and treatment as usual with medication. The data shown in **Figure 15.6** compare mean depres-

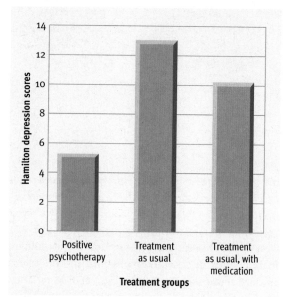

Figure 15.6

Positive psychotherapy for depression. In a study of the efficacy of positive psychotherapy, it was compared to treatment as usual (clinicians delivered whatever treatment they deemed appropriate) and to treatment as usual combined with antidepressant medication. At the end of 12 weeks of treatment, symptoms of depression were measured with the widely-used Hamilton Rating Scale for Depression. The mean depression scores for each group are graphed here. As you can see, the positive psychotherapy group showed less depression than the other two treatment groups, suggesting that positive psychotherapy can be an effective intervention for depression.

SOURCE: Adapted from Seligman, M. E. P., Rashid, T., & Parks, A. C. (2006). Positive psychotherapy. *American Psychologist, 61,* 774–788. (Figure 2, p. 784).

sion scores at the end of the study for participants in these three conditions (Seligman et al., 2006). As you can see, the lowest depression scores were observed in the group that received positive psychotherapy. These innovative interventions spurred by the positive psychology movement are in their infancy, but the early findings seem promising, and it will be interesting to see what the future holds.

Group Therapy

Although it dates back to the early part of the 20th century, group therapy came of age during World War II and its aftermath in the 1950s (Rosenbaum, Lakin, & Roback, 1992). During this period, the expanding demand for therapeutic services forced clinicians to use group techniques (Scheidlinger, 1993). *Group therapy* is the simultaneous psychological treatment of several clients in a group. Most major insight therapies have been adapted for use with groups. Because of economic pressures in mental health care, the use of group therapy appears likely to grow in future years (Burlingame & McClendon,

2008). Although group therapy can be conducted in a variety of ways, we will provide a general overview of the process as it usually unfolds with outpatient populations (see Alonso, Alonso, & Piper, 2003; Vinogradov, Cox, & Yalom, 2003; Wong, 2005).

Participants' Roles

A therapy group typically consists of 4–12 people, with 6–8 participants regarded as an ideal number (Vinogradov et al., 2003). The therapist usually screens the participants, excluding persons who seem likely to be disruptive. Some theorists maintain that judicious selection of participants is crucial to effective group treatment (Salvendy, 1993). There is some debate about whether it is better for the group to be homogeneous—made up of people who are similar in age, sex, and psychological problem. Practical necessities usually dictate that groups are at least somewhat diversified.

In group therapy, participants essentially function as therapists for one another (Stone, 2003). Group members describe their problems, trade viewpoints, share experiences, and discuss coping strategies. Most important, they provide acceptance and emotional support for each other. In this supportive atmosphere, group members work at peeling away the social masks that cover their insecurities. Once their problems are exposed, members work at correcting them. As members come to value one another's opinions, they work hard to display healthy changes to win the group's approval.

In group treatment, the therapist's responsibilities include selecting participants, setting goals for the group, initiating and maintaining the therapeutic process, and protecting clients from harm (Vinogradov et al., 2003). The therapist often plays a relatively subtle role in group therapy, staying in the background and focusing mainly on promoting group cohesiveness (although this strategy will vary depending on the nature of the group). The therapist models supportive behaviors for the participants and tries to promote a healthy climate. He or she always retains a special status, but the therapist and clients are usually on much more equal footing in group therapy than in individual therapy. The leader in group therapy expresses emotions, shares feelings, and copes with challenges from group members (Burlingame & McClendon, 2008).

Advantages of the Group Experience

Group therapies obviously save time and money, which can be critical in understaffed mental hospitals and other institutional settings (Vinogradov et al., 2003). Therapists in private practice usually

© John Greim/Photo Researchers, Inc.

charge less for group than individual therapy, making therapy affordable for more people. However, group therapy is *not* just a less costly substitute for individual therapy. For many types of patients and problems, group therapy can be just as effective as individual treatment (Knauss, 2005; Stone, 2003). Moreover, group therapy has unique strengths of its own. For example, in group therapy participants often come to realize that their misery is not unique. They are reassured to learn that many other people have similar or even worse problems. Another advantage is that group therapy provides an opportunity for participants to work on their social skills in a safe environment. Yet another plus is that certain types of problems and clients respond especially well to the social support that group therapy can provide.

Group treatments have proven particularly helpful when members share similar problems, such as alcoholism, overeating, or having been sexually abused as a child. Many approaches to insight therapy that were originally designed for individuals—such as client-centered therapy—have been adapted for treatment of groups.

concept check 15.1

Understanding Therapists' Conceptions of Disorders

Check your understanding of the three approaches to insight therapy covered in the text by matching each approach with the appropriate explanation of the typical origins of clients' psychological disorders. The answers are in Appendix A.

Theorized causes of disorders

_____ 1. Problems rooted in inadequate attention paid to one's strengths, blessings, and positive experiences

_____ 2. Problems rooted in unconscious conflicts left over from childhood

_____ 3. Problems rooted in inaccurate self-concept and excessive concern about pleasing others

Therapy

a. Psychoanalysis

b. Client-centered therapy

c. Positive psychotherapy

Whether insight therapies are conducted on a group or an individual basis, clients usually invest considerable time, effort, and money. Are these therapies worth the investment? Let's examine the evidence on their effectiveness.

How Effective Are Insight Therapies?

Evaluating the effectiveness of any approach to treatment is a complex challenge (Hill & Lambert, 2004; Kendall, Holmbeck, & Verduin, 2004). For one thing, psychological disorders (like many physical illnesses) sometimes run their course and clear up on their own. A *spontaneous remission* is a recovery from a disorder that occurs without formal treatment. Thus, if a client experiences a recovery after treatment, one cannot automatically assume that the recovery was due to the treatment (see the Critical Thinking Application).

Evaluating the effectiveness of treatment is especially complicated for insight therapies (Aveline, Strauss, & Stiles, 2005). If you were to undergo insight therapy, how would you judge its efficacy? By how you felt? By looking at your behavior? By asking your therapist? By consulting your friends and family? What would you be looking for? Various schools of thought pursue entirely different goals. And clients' ratings of their progress are likely to be slanted toward a favorable evaluation because they want to justify their effort, their heartache, their expense, and their time. Even evaluations by professional therapists can be highly subjective (Luborsky et al., 1999). Moreover, people enter therapy with diverse problems of varied severity, creating huge confounds in efforts to assess the effectiveness of therapeutic interventions.

Despite these difficulties, thousands of outcome studies have been conducted to evaluate the effectiveness of insight therapy. These studies have examined a broad range of clinical problems and used diverse methods to assess therapeutic outcomes, including scores on psychological tests and ratings by family members, as well as therapists' and clients' ratings. These studies consistently indicate that insight therapy *is* superior to no treatment or to placebo treatment and that the effects of therapy are reasonably durable (Kopta et al., 1999; Lambert & Archer, 2006). And when insight therapies are compared head-to-head against drug therapies, they usually show roughly equal efficacy (Arkowitz & Lilienfeld, 2007; Pinquart, Duberstein, & Lyness, 2006). Studies generally find the greatest improvement early in treatment (the first 13–18 weekly sessions), with further gains gradually diminishing over time (Lambert, Bergin, & Garfield, 2004). Overall, about 50% of patients show a clinically meaningful recovery within about 20 sessions, and another 25% of patients achieve this goal after about 45 sessions (Lambert & Ogles, 2004; see Figure 15.7). Of course, these broad generalizations mask considerable variability in outcome, but the general trends are encouraging.

How Do Insight Therapies Work?

Although there is considerable evidence that insight therapy tends to produce positive effects for a sizable majority of clients, vigorous debate continues about the *mechanisms of action* underlying these positive effects (Kazdin, 2007). The advocates of various therapies tend to attribute the benefits of therapy to the particular methods and procedures used by each specific approach (Chambless & Hollon, 1998). In essence, they argue that different therapies achieve similar benefits through different processes. An alternative view espoused by many theorists is that the diverse approaches to therapy share certain *common factors* and that these common factors account for much of the improvement experienced by clients (Frank & Frank, 1991). Evidence supporting the common factors view has mounted in recent years (Ahn & Wampold, 2001; Sparks, Duncan, & Miller, 2008).

What are the common denominators that lie at the core of diverse approaches to therapy? The models proposed to answer to this question vary consid-

INSIDE WOODY ALLEN

erably, but the most widely cited common factors include (1) the development of a therapeutic alliance with a professional helper, (2) the provision of emotional support and empathic understanding by the therapist, (3) the cultivation of hope and positive expectations in the client, (4) the provision of a rationale for the client's problems and a plausible method for reducing them, and (5) the opportunity to express feelings, confront problems, gain new insights, and learn new patterns of behavior (Grencavage & Norcross, 1990; Weinberger, 1995). How important are these factors in therapy? Some theorists argue that common factors account for virtually *all* of the progress that clients make in therapy (Wampold, 2001). It seems more likely that the benefits of therapy represent the combined effects of common factors and specific procedures (Beutler & Harwood, 2002). Either way, it is clear that common factors play a significant role in insight therapy.

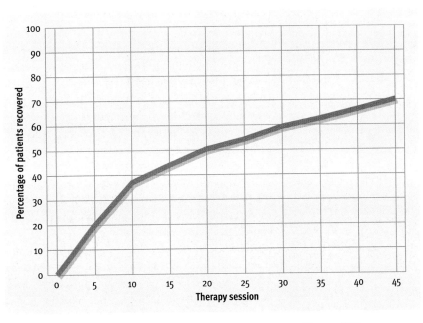

Figure 15.7

Recovery as a function of number of therapy sessions. Based on a national sample of over 6000 patients, Lambert, Hansen, and Finch (2001) mapped out the relationship between recovery and the duration of treatment. These data show that about half of the patients had experienced a clinically significant recovery after 20 weekly sessions of therapy. After 45 sessions of therapy, about 70% had recovered.

SOURCE: Adapted from Lambert, M. J., Hansen, N. B., & Finch, A. E. (2001). Patient-focused research: Using patient outcome data to enhance treatment effects. *Journal of Consulting and Clinical Psychology, 69,* 159–172. Copyright © 2001 by the American Psychological Association. Used by permission of the authors.

REVIEW of Key Points

15.3 Freudian approaches to therapy assume that neuroses originate from unresolved conflicts lurking in the unconscious. Therefore, in psychoanalysis free association (discussing whatever comes to mind with no censorship) and dream analysis are used to explore the unconscious.

15.4 When an analyst's probing hits sensitive areas, resistance, which involves unconscious defensive maneuvers to hinder progress, can be expected. The transference relationship may be used to overcome this resistance so that the client can handle interpretations that lead to insight.

15.5 Rogers's client-centered therapy assumes that neurotic anxieties are derived from incongruence between a person's self-concept and reality. Accordingly, the client-centered therapist emphasizes trying to provide a supportive climate marked by genuineness, unconditional positive regard, and empathy. The process of client-centered therapy depends on clarification of the client's feelings to promote self-acceptance.

15.6 The growth of the positive psychology movement has begun to inspire new approaches to insight therapy, such as

well-being therapy. Positive psychotherapy attempts to get clients to recognize their strengths, appreciate their blessings, savor positive experiences, and find meaning in their lives.

15.7 Participants in group therapy essentially act as therapists for one another, exchanging insights and emotional support. The therapist sets goals for the group and works to maintain a supportive climate. Group therapy is less expensive and has some advantages in comparison to individual therapy. People see that their problems are not unique, and they can work on social skills in a safe environment.

15.8 Evaluating the effectiveness of any approach to therapy is complex and difficult. Nonetheless, the weight of modern evidence suggests that insight therapies are superior to no treatment or to placebo treatment. Studies generally find the greatest improvement early in treatment. Much of the improvement seen in clients in therapy may be attributable to the operation of common factors, such as the development of a therapeutic alliance, the provision of emotional support, and the cultivation of hope.

Behavior Therapies

Behavior therapy is different from insight therapy in that behavior therapists make no attempt to help clients achieve grand insights about themselves. Why not? Because behavior therapists believe that such insights aren't necessary to produce constructive change. For example, consider a client troubled by compulsive gambling. The behavior therapist doesn't care whether this behavior is rooted in unconscious conflicts or parental rejection. What the

client needs is to get rid of the maladaptive behavior. Consequently, the therapist simply designs a program to eliminate the compulsive gambling.

The crux of the difference between insight therapy and behavior therapy is this: Insight therapists treat pathological symptoms as signs of an underlying problem, whereas behavior therapists think that the symptoms *are* the problem. Thus, *behavior therapies* involve the application of learning

Key Learning Goals

15.9 Describe the goals and procedures of systematic desensitization.

15.10 Outline the goals and techniques of aversion therapy and social skills training.

15.11 Articulate the logic, goals, and techniques of cognitive therapy.

15.12 Evaluate the efficacy of behavior therapies.

principles to direct efforts to change clients' maladaptive behaviors.

Behaviorism has been an influential school of thought in psychology since the 1920s. Nevertheless, behaviorists devoted little attention to clinical issues until the 1950s, when behavior therapy emerged out of three independent lines of research fostered by B. F. Skinner and his colleagues (Skinner, Solomon, & Lindsley, 1953) in the United States; by Hans Eysenck (1959) and his colleagues in Britain; and by Joseph Wolpe (1958) and his colleagues in South Africa (Glass & Arnkoff, 1992). Since then, there has been an explosion of interest in behavioral approaches to psychotherapy.

Behavior therapies are based on certain assumptions (Berkowitz, 2003). *First, it is assumed that behavior is a product of learning.* No matter how self-defeating or pathological a client's behavior might be, the behaviorist believes that it is the result of past learning and conditioning. *Second, it is assumed that what has been learned can be unlearned.* The same learning principles that explain how the maladaptive behavior was acquired can be used to get rid of it. Thus, behavior therapists attempt to change clients' behavior by applying the principles of classical conditioning, operant conditioning, and observational learning.

Systematic Desensitization

 PSYK TREK 11e

Devised by Joseph Wolpe (1958), systematic desensitization revolutionized psychotherapy by giving therapists their first useful alternative to traditional "talk therapy" (Fishman & Franks, 1992). *Systematic desensitization* is a behavior therapy used to reduce phobic clients' anxiety responses through counterconditioning. The treatment assumes that most anxiety responses are acquired through classical conditioning (as we discussed in Chapter 14). According to this model, a harmless stimulus (for instance, a bridge) may be paired with a fear-arousing event (lightning striking it) so that it becomes a conditioned stimulus eliciting anxiety. The goal of systematic desensitization is to weaken the association between the conditioned stimulus (the bridge) and the conditioned response of anxiety (see Figure 15.8). Systematic desensitization involves three steps.

In the first step, the therapist helps the client build an anxiety hierarchy. The hierarchy is a list of anxiety-arousing stimuli related to the specific source of anxiety, such as flying, academic tests, or snakes. The client ranks the stimuli from the least anxiety arousing to the most anxiety arousing. This ordered

Joseph Wolpe

"Neurotic anxiety is nothing but a conditioned response."

Courtesy of Joseph Wolpe

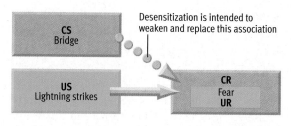

Figure 15.8

The logic underlying systematic desensitization. Behaviorists argue that many phobic responses are acquired through classical conditioning, as in the example diagrammed here. Systematic desensitization targets the conditioned associations between phobic stimuli and fear responses.

list of stimuli is the *anxiety hierarchy.* An example of an anxiety hierarchy for one woman's fear of heights is shown in Figure 15.9.

The second step involves training the client in deep muscle relaxation. This second phase may begin during early sessions while the therapist and client are still constructing the anxiety hierarchy. Various therapists use different relaxation training procedures. Whatever procedures are used, the client must learn to engage in deep, thorough relaxation on command from the therapist.

In the third step, the client tries to work through the hierarchy, learning to remain relaxed while imagining each stimulus. Starting with the least anxiety-arousing stimulus, the client imagines the situation as vividly as possible while relaxing. If the client experiences strong anxiety, he or she drops the imaginary scene and concentrates on relaxation. The client keeps repeating this process until he or she can imagine a scene with little or no anxiety. Once a particular scene is conquered, the client moves on to the next stimulus situation in the anxiety hierarchy. Gradually, over a number of therapy sessions, the client progresses through the hierarchy, unlearning troublesome anxiety responses.

As clients conquer *imagined* phobic stimuli, they may be encouraged to confront the *real* stimuli. Although desensitization to imagined stimuli *can* be effective by itself, contemporary behavior therapists usually follow it up with direct exposures to the real anxiety-arousing stimuli (Emmelkamp, 2004). Indeed, behavioral interventions emphasizing direct exposures to anxiety-arousing situations have become behavior therapists' treatment of choice for phobic and other anxiety disorders. Usually, these real-life confrontations prove harmless, and individuals' anxiety responses decline.

According to Wolpe (1958, 1990), the principle at work in systematic desensitization is simple. Anxi-

Systematic desensitization is a behavioral treatment for phobias. Early studies of the procedure's efficacy often used people who had snake phobias as research subjects because people with snake phobias were relatively easy to find. This research showed that systematic desensitization is generally an effective treatment.

An Anxiety Hierarchy for Systematic Desensitization	
Degree of fear	
5	I'm standing on the balcony of the top floor of an apartment tower.
10	I'm standing on a stepladder in the kitchen to change a light bulb.
15	I'm walking on a ridge. The edge is hidden by shrubs and treetops.
20	I'm sitting on the slope of a mountain, looking out over the horizon.
25	I'm crossing a bridge 6 feet above a creek. The bridge consists of an 18-inch-wide board with a handrail on one side.
30	I'm riding a ski lift 8 feet above the ground.
35	I'm crossing a shallow, wide creek on an 18-inch-wide board, 3 feet above water level.
40	I'm climbing a ladder outside the house to reach a second-story window.
45	I'm pulling myself up a 30-degree wet, slippery slope on a steel cable.
50	I'm scrambling up a rock, 8 feet high.
55	I'm walking 10 feet on a resilient, 18-inch-wide board, which spans an 8-foot-deep gulch.
60	I'm walking on a wide plateau, 2 feet from the edge of a cliff.
65	I'm skiing an intermediate hill. The snow is packed.
70	I'm walking over a railway trestle.
75	I'm walking on the side of an embankment. The path slopes to the outside.
80	I'm riding a chair lift 15 feet above the ground.
85	I'm walking up a long, steep slope.
90	I'm walking up (or down) a 15-degree slope on a 3-foot-wide trail. On one side of the trail the terrain drops down sharply; on the other side is a steep upward slope.
95	I'm walking on a 3-foot-wide ridge. The slopes on both sides are long and more than 25 degrees steep.
100	I'm walking on a 3-foot-wide ridge. The trail slopes on one side. The drop on either side of the trail is more than 25 degrees.

ety and relaxation are incompatible responses. The trick is to recondition people so that the conditioned stimulus elicits relaxation instead of anxiety. This is *counterconditioning*—an attempt to reverse the process of classical conditioning by associating the crucial stimulus with a new conditioned response. Although Wolpe's explanation of how systematic desensitization works has been questioned, the technique's effectiveness in eliminating specific anxieties has been well documented (Spiegler & Guevremont, 2003).

Aversion Therapy 11e

Aversion therapy is far and away the most controversial of the behavior therapies. It's not something that you would sign up for unless you were pretty desperate. Psychologists usually suggest it only as a treatment of last resort, after other interventions have failed. What's so terrible about aversion therapy? The client has to endure decidedly unpleasant stimuli, such as shocks or drug-induced nausea.

Aversion therapy is a behavior therapy in which an aversive stimulus is paired with a stimulus that elicits an undesirable response. For example, alcoholics have had an *emetic drug* (one that causes nausea and vomiting) paired with their favorite drinks during therapy sessions (Landabaso et al., 1999). By pairing the drug with alcohol, the therapist hopes to create a conditioned aversion to alcohol (see Figure 15.10).

Aversion therapy takes advantage of the automatic nature of responses produced through classical conditioning. Admittedly, alcoholics treated with aversion therapy know that they won't be given an emetic outside of their therapy sessions. However, their reflex response to the stimulus of alcohol may

Figure 15.9

Example of an anxiety hierarchy. Systematic desensitization requires the construction of an anxiety hierarchy like the one shown here, which was developed for a woman who had a fear of heights but wanted to go hiking in the mountains.

SOURCE: Rudestam, K. E. (1980). *Methods of self-change: An ABC primer*. Belmont, CA: Wadsworth. Copyright © 1980 by Wadsworth Publishing. Reprinted by permission of the author.

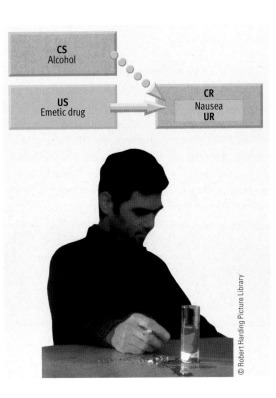

Figure 15.10

Aversion therapy. Aversion therapy uses classical conditioning to create an aversion to a stimulus that has elicited problematic behavior. For example, in the treatment of drinking problems, alcohol may be paired with a nausea-inducing drug to create an aversion to drinking.

be changed so they respond to it with nausea and distaste (remember the power of conditioned taste aversions described in Chapter 6?). Obviously, this response should make it much easier to resist the urge to drink.

Aversion therapy is not a widely used technique, and when it is used it is usually only one element in a larger treatment program. Troublesome behaviors treated successfully with aversion therapy have included drug and alcohol abuse, sexual deviance, gambling, shoplifting, stuttering, cigarette smoking, and overeating (Bordnick et al., 2004; Emmelkamp, 1994; Grossman & Ruiz, 2004; Maletzky, 2002).

Social Skills Training

Many psychological problems grow out of interpersonal difficulties. Behavior therapists point out that people are not born with social finesse—they acquire social skills through learning. Unfortunately, some people have not learned how to be friendly, how to make conversation, how to express anger appropriately, and so forth. Social ineptitude can contribute to anxiety, feelings of inferiority, and various kinds of disorders. In light of these findings, therapists are increasingly using social skills training in efforts to improve clients' social abilities. This approach to therapy has yielded promising results in the treatment of social anxiety (Herbert et al., 2005), autism (Scattone, 2007), attention deficit disorder (Monastra, 2008) and schizophrenia (Granholm et al., 2008).

Social skills training **is a behavior therapy designed to improve interpersonal skills that emphasizes modeling, behavioral rehearsal, and shaping.** This type of behavior therapy can be conducted with individual clients or in groups. Social skills training depends on the principles of operant conditioning and observational learning. With *modeling,* the client is encouraged to watch socially skilled friends and colleagues in order to acquire appropriate responses (eye contact, active listening, and so on) through observation. In *behavioral rehearsal,* the client tries to practice social techniques in structured role-playing exercises. The therapist provides corrective feedback and uses approval to reinforce progress. Eventually, of course, clients try their newly acquired skills in real-world interactions. Usually, they are given specific homework assignments. *Shaping* is used in that clients are gradually asked to handle more complicated and delicate social situations. For example, a nonassertive client may begin by working on making requests

of friends. Only much later will he be asked to tackle standing up to his boss at work.

Cognitive-Behavioral Treatments

In Chapter 14, we learned that cognitive factors play a key role in the development of many anxiety and mood disorders. Citing the importance of such findings, in the 1970s behavior therapists started to focus more attention on their clients' cognitions (Arnkoff & Glass, 1992; Hollon & Beck, 2004). *Cognitive-behavioral treatments* **use varied combinations of verbal interventions and behavior modification techniques to help clients change maladaptive patterns of thinking.** Some of these treatments, such as Albert Ellis's (1973) *rational-emotive behavior therapy* and Aaron Beck's (1976) *cognitive therapy,* emerged out of an insight therapy tradition, whereas other treatments, such as the systems developed by Donald Meichenbaum (1977) and Michael Mahoney (1974), emerged from the behavioral tradition. Here we will focus on Beck's cognitive therapy as an example of a cognitive-behavioral treatment (see Chapter 13 for a discussion of some of Ellis's ideas).

Cognitive therapy **uses specific strategies to correct habitual thinking errors that underlie various types of disorders.** In recent years cognitive therapy has been applied fruitfully to a wide range of disorders (Grant, Young, & DeRubeis, 2005; Hollon, Stewart, & Strunk, 2006), but it was originally devised as a treatment for depression. According to cognitive therapists, depression is caused by "errors" in thinking (see Figure 15.11). They assert that depression-prone people tend to (1) blame their setbacks on personal inadequacies without considering

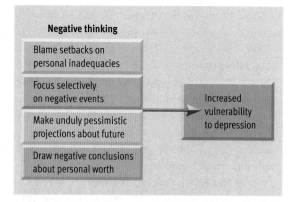

Negative thinking

- Blame setbacks on personal inadequacies
- Focus selectively on negative events
- Make unduly pessimistic projections about future
- Draw negative conclusions about personal worth

→ Increased vulnerability to depression

Figure 15.11

Beck's view of the roots of disorders. Beck's theory initially focused on the causes of depression, although it was gradually broadened to explain other disorders. According to Beck, depression is caused by the types of negative thinking shown here.

Aaron Beck

"Most people are barely aware of the automatic thoughts which precede unpleasant feelings or automatic inhibitions."

circumstantial explanations, (2) focus selectively on negative events while ignoring positive events, (3) make unduly pessimistic projections about the future, and (4) draw negative conclusions about their worth as a person based on insignificant events. For instance, imagine that you got a low grade on a minor quiz in a class. If you made the kinds of errors in thinking just described, you might blame the grade on your woeful stupidity, dismiss comments from a classmate that it was an unfair test, gloomily predict that you will surely flunk the course, and conclude that you are not genuine college material.

The goal of cognitive therapy is to change clients' negative thoughts and maladaptive beliefs (Kellogg & Young, 2008). To begin, clients are taught to detect their automatic negative thoughts. These are self-defeating statements that people are prone to make when analyzing problems. Examples might include "I'm just not smart enough," "No one really likes me," or "It's all my fault." Clients are then trained to subject these automatic thoughts to reality testing. The therapist helps them to see how unrealistically negative the thoughts are.

Cognitive therapy uses a variety of behavioral techniques, such as modeling, systematic monitoring of one's behavior, and behavioral rehearsal (Wright, Beck, & Thase, 2003), Cognitive therapists often give their clients "homework assignments" that focus on changing clients' overt behaviors. Clients may be instructed to engage in overt responses on their own, outside of the clinician's office. For example, one shy, insecure young man in cognitive therapy was told to go to a singles bar and engage three different women in conversations for up to five minutes each (Rush, 1984). He was instructed to record his thoughts before and after each of the conversations. This assignment elicited various maladaptive patterns of thought that gave the young man and his therapist plenty to work on in subsequent sessions.

How Effective Are Behavior Therapies?

Behavior therapists have historically placed more emphasis on the importance of measuring therapeutic outcomes than insight therapists have. Thus, there is ample evidence attesting to the effectiveness of behavior therapy (Jacob & Pelham, 2005). Of course, behavior therapies are not well suited to the treatment of some types of problems (vague feelings of discontent, for instance). Furthermore, it's misleading to make global statements about the

concept check 15.2

Understanding Therapists' Goals

Check your understanding of therapists' goals by matching various therapies with the appropriate description. The answers are in Appendix A.

Principal therapeutic goals

_____ 1. Elimination of maladaptive behaviors or symptoms

_____ 2. Acceptance of genuine self, personal growth

_____ 3. Recovery of unconscious conflicts, character reconstruction

_____ 4. Detection and reduction of negative thinking

Therapy

a. Psychoanalysis

b. Client-centered therapy

c. Cognitive therapy

d. Behavior therapy

effectiveness of behavior therapies, because they include many types of procedures designed for very different purposes. For example, the value of systematic desensitization for phobias has no bearing on the value of aversion therapy for sexual deviance. For our purposes, it is sufficient to note that there is favorable evidence on the efficacy of most of the widely used behavioral interventions (Zinbarg & Griffith, 2008). Behavior therapies can make important contributions to the treatment of phobias, obsessive-compulsive disorders, sexual dysfunction, schizophrenia, drug-related problems, eating disorders, psychosomatic disorders, hyperactivity, autism, and mental retardation (Berkowitz, 2003; Emmelkamp, 2004).

web link 15.5

The Beck Institute of Cognitive Therapy and Research

This site offers a diverse array of materials relating to Aaron Beck's cognitive therapy. Resources include newsletters, a referral system, a bookstore, recommended readings for clients, and questions and answers abut cognitive therapy.

REVIEW of Key Points

15.9 Behavior therapies use the principles of learning in direct efforts to change specific aspects of behavior. Wolpe's systematic desensitization is a treatment designed to relieve phobias. It involves the construction of an anxiety hierarchy, relaxation training, and step-by-step movement through the hierarchy, pairing relaxation with each phobic stimulus.

15.10 In aversion therapy, a stimulus associated with an unwanted response is paired with an unpleasant stimulus in an effort to eliminate the maladaptive response. Social skills training can improve clients' interpersonal skills through shaping, modeling, and behavioral rehearsal.

15.11 Cognitive-behavioral treatments concentrate on changing the way clients think about events in their lives. Cognitive therapists reeducate clients to detect and challenge automatic negative thoughts that cause depression and anxiety. Cognitive therapy also depends on modeling, behavioral rehearsal, and homework assignments.

15.12 Behavior therapists have historically placed more emphasis on the importance of measuring therapeutic outcomes than insight therapists have. There is ample evidence that behavior therapies are effective in the treatment of a wide variety of disorders.

Key Learning Goals

15.13 Summarize the therapeutic actions and side effects of antianxiety and antipsychotic drugs.

15.14 Summarize the therapeutic actions and side effects of antidepressant and mood stabilizing drugs.

15.15 Evaluate the overall efficacy of drug treatments and controversies surrounding pharmaceutical research.

15.16 Describe electroconvulsive therapy and assess its therapeutic effects and risks.

15.17 Describe the therapeutic use of transcranial magnetic stimulation and direct brain stimulation.

Biomedical Therapies

In the 1950s, a French surgeon looking for a drug that would reduce patients' autonomic response to surgical stress noticed that chlorpromazine produced a mild sedation. Based on this observation, Delay and Deniker (1952) decided to give chlorpromazine to hospitalized schizophrenic patients. They wanted to see whether the drug would have calming effects. Their experiment was a dramatic success. Chlorpromazine became the first effective antipsychotic drug, and a revolution in psychiatry was begun. Hundreds of thousands of severely disturbed patients who had appeared doomed to spend the remainder of their lives in mental hospitals were gradually sent home, thanks to the therapeutic effects of antipsychotic drugs. Today, biomedical therapies such as drug treatment lie at the core of psychiatric practice.

Biomedical therapies **are physiological interventions intended to reduce symptoms associated with psychological disorders.** These therapies assume that psychological disorders are caused, at least in part, by biological malfunctions. As we discussed in the previous chapter, this assumption clearly has merit for many disorders, especially the more severe ones. We will discuss the two standard biomedical approaches to psychotherapy, drug therapy and electroconvulsive (shock) therapy, and then delve into some experimental, new treatments involving brain stimulation.

Treatment with Drugs 11e

Psychopharmacotherapy **is the treatment of mental disorders with medication.** We will refer to this kind of treatment more simply as *drug therapy.* The four main categories of therapeutic drugs for psychological problems are (1) antianxiety drugs, (2) antipsychotic drugs, (3) antidepressant drugs, and (4) mood-stabilizing drugs.

Antianxiety Drugs 11e

Many people routinely pop pills to relieve anxiety. The drugs involved in this common coping strategy are *antianxiety drugs,* **which relieve tension, apprehension, and nervousness.** The most popular of these drugs are Valium and Xanax. These are the trade names (the proprietary names that pharmaceutical companies use in marketing drugs) for diazepam and alprazolam, respectively.

Valium, Xanax, and other drugs in the *benzodiazepine* family are often called *tranquilizers.* These drugs exert their effects almost immediately, and they can be fairly effective in alleviating feelings of anxiety (Dubovsky, 2005). However, their effects are measured in hours, so their impact is relatively short-lived. Antianxiety drugs are routinely prescribed for people with anxiety disorders, but they are also given to millions of people who simply suffer from chronic nervous tension.

All the drugs used to treat psychological problems have potentially troublesome side effects that show up in some patients but not others. The antianxiety drugs are no exception. The most common side effects of Valium and Xanax are listed in Table 15.1. Some of these side effects—such as drowsiness, depression, nausea, and confusion—present serious problems for some patients. These drugs also have potential for abuse, drug dependence, and overdose, although these risks have probably been exaggerated in the press (Ballenger, 2000; Silberman, 1998). Another drawback is that patients who have been on antianxiety drugs for a while often experience withdrawal symptoms when their drug treatment is stopped (Raj & Sheehan, 2004).

Antipsychotic Drugs 11e

Antipsychotic drugs are used primarily in the treatment of schizophrenia. They are also given to people with severe mood disorders who become delusional.

Table 15.1 Side Effects of Xanax and Valium

Side Effects	Patients Experiencing Side Effects (%)	
	Xanax	Valium
Drowsiness	36.0	49.4
Lightheadedness	18.6	24.0
Dry mouth	14.9	13.0
Depression	11.9	17.0
Nausea, vomiting	9.3	10.0
Constipation	9.3	11.3
Insomnia	9.0	6.7
Confusion	9.3	14.1
Diarrhea	8.5	10.5
Tachycardia, palpitations	8.1	7.2
Nasal congestion	8.1	7.2
Blurred vision	7.0	9.1

Source: Evans, R. L. (1981). New drug evaluations: Alprazolam. *Drug Intelligence and Clinical Pharmacy, 15,* 633–637. Copyright © 1981 by Harvey Whitney Books Company. Reprinted by permission.

The trade (and generic) names of some classic drugs in this category are Thorazine (chlorpromazine), Mellaril (thioridazine), and Haldol (haloperidol). *Antipsychotic drugs* **are used to gradually reduce psychotic symptoms, including hyperactivity, mental confusion, hallucinations, and delusions.** The traditional antipsychotics appear to decrease activity at certain subtypes of dopamine synapses, although the exact relationship between their neurochemical effects and their clinical effects remains obscure (Egan & Hyde, 2000; Miyamoto et al., 2003).

Studies suggest that antipsychotics reduce psychotic symptoms in about 70% of patients, albeit in varied degrees (Kane & Marder, 2005). When antipsychotic drugs are effective, they work their magic gradually, as shown in **Figure 15.12**. Patients usually begin to respond within one to three weeks, but considerable variability in responsiveness is seen (Emsley, Rabinowitz, & Medori, 2006). Further improvement may occur for several months. Many schizophrenic patients are placed on antipsychotics indefinitely, because these drugs can reduce the likelihood of a relapse into an active schizophrenic episode (Marder & van Kammen, 2005).

Antipsychotic drugs undeniably make a huge contribution to the treatment of severe mental disorders, but they are not without problems. They have many unpleasant side effects (Cohen, 1997; Wilkaitis, Mulvihill, & Nasrallah, 2004). Drowsiness, constipation, and cotton mouth are common. The drugs may also produce effects that resemble the symptoms of Parkinson's disease, including muscle tremors, muscular rigidity, and impaired motor coordination. After being released from a hospital, many schizophrenic patients discontinue their drug regimen because of the disagreeable side effects. Unfortunately, a relapse eventually occurs in most patients after they stop taking antipsychotic medication (Gitlin et al., 2001). In addition to minor side effects, antipsychotics may cause a severe and lasting problem called *tardive dyskinesia,* which is seen in about 20% of patients who receive long-term treatment with traditional antipsychotics (Miyamoto et al., 2003). *Tardive dyskinesia* **is a neurological disorder marked by involuntary writhing and ticlike movements of the mouth, tongue, face, hands, or feet.** Once this debilitating syndrome emerges, there is no cure, although spontaneous remission sometimes occurs after the discontinuation of antipsychotic medication (Pi & Simpson, 2000).

Psychiatrists are currently enthusiastic about a new class of antipsychotic agents called *atypical antipsychotic drugs* (such as clozapine, olanzapine, and quetiapine). These drugs are roughly as effective as traditional antipsychotics (Fleischhacker, 2002), and they can help some patients who do not respond to conventional antipsychotic medications (Volavka et al., 2002). Moreover, the atypical antipsychotics produce fewer unpleasant side effects and carry less risk for tardive dyskinesia (Correll, Leucht, & Kane, 2004; Lieberman et al., 2003). Of course, like all powerful drugs, they carry some risks, as they appear to increase patients' vulnerability to diabetes and cardiovascular problems (Meltzer et al., 2002).

Although they are much more expensive than traditional antipsychotics, the atypical antipsychotics have become the first line of defense in the treatment of schizophrenia (van Kammen & Marder, 2005). However, recent research has generated some controversy regarding this trend. These studies have found that the newer antipsychotics aren't any more effective than the older medications in reducing symptoms and that the side effects of the newer drugs are only marginally less troublesome than the side effects of the older drugs (Lieberman et al., 2005; Stroup, Kraus, & Marder, 2006). These findings raise vexing, complicated questions about the cost effectiveness of psychiatrists' reliance on the newer medications (Lieberman, 2006; Rosenheck, 2006).

Antidepressant Drugs

11e

As their name suggests, *antidepressant drugs* **gradually elevate mood and help bring people out of a depression.** Prior to 1987, there were two principal classes of antidepressants: *tricyclics* (such as Elavil) and *MAO inhibitors* (such as Nardil). These two sets of drugs affect neurochemical activity in different ways

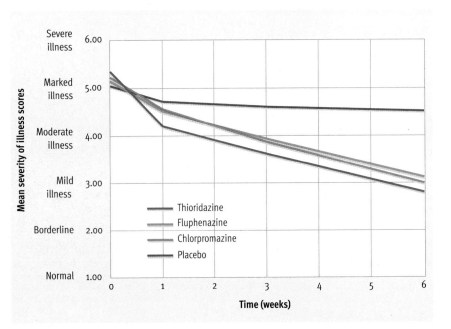

Figure 15.12
The time course of antipsychotic drug effects.
Antipsychotic drugs reduce psychotic symptoms gradually, over a span of weeks, as graphed here. In contrast, patients given placebo medication show little improvement.

SOURCE: Cole, J. O., Goldberg, S. C., & Davis, J. M. (1966). Drugs in the treatment of psychosis. In P. Solomon (Ed.), *Psychiatric drugs.* New York: Grune & Stratton. From data in the NIMH-PSC Collaborative Study I. Reprinted by permission of J. M. Davis.

Figure 15.13
Antidepressant drugs' mechanisms of action. The four types of antidepressant drugs have somewhat different, albeit overlapping, effects on neurotransmitter activity. Tricyclics and MAO inhibitors have effects at a much greater variety of synapses, which presumably explains why they have more side effects. The more recently developed SSRIs and SNRIs zero in on more specific synaptic targets.

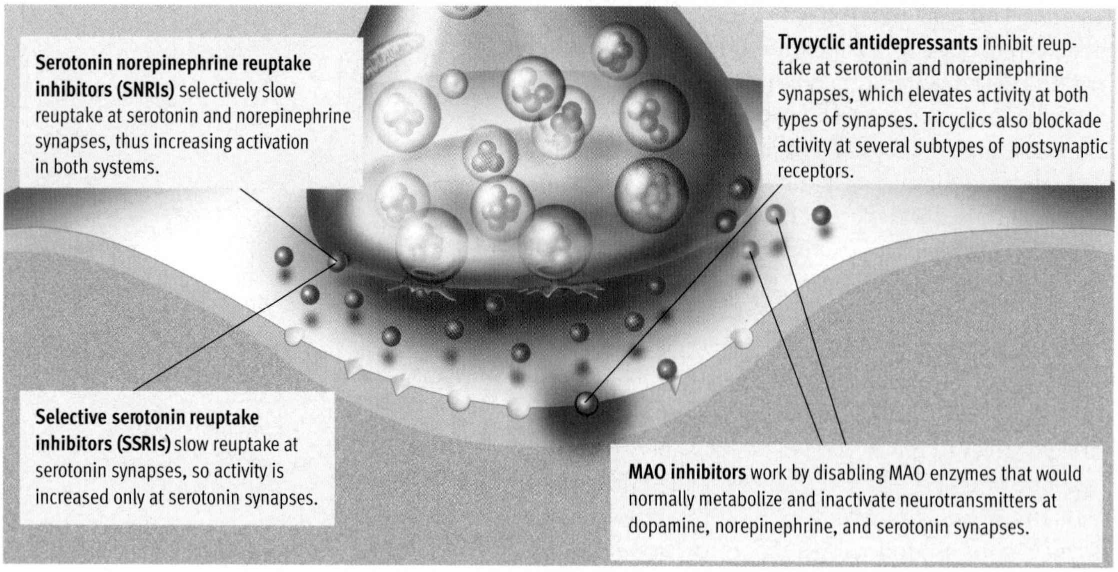

Serotonin norepinephrine reuptake inhibitors (SNRIs) selectively slow reuptake at serotonin and norepinephrine synapses, thus increasing activation in both systems.

Trycyclic antidepressants inhibit reuptake at serotonin and norepinephrine synapses, which elevates activity at both types of synapses. Tricyclics also blockade activity at several subtypes of postsynaptic receptors.

Selective serotonin reuptake inhibitors (SSRIs) slow reuptake at serotonin synapses, so activity is increased only at serotonin synapses.

MAO inhibitors work by disabling MAO enzymes that would normally metabolize and inactivate neurotransmitters at dopamine, norepinephrine, and serotonin synapses.

(see Figure 15.13) and tend to work with different patients. Overall, they are beneficial for about two-thirds of depressed patients (Gitlin, 2002), although only about one-third of treated patients experience a *complete resolution* of their symptoms (Shulman, 2001). The tricyclics have fewer problems with side effects and complications than the MAO inhibitors (Potter et al., 2006). Like antipsychotic drugs, antidepressants exert their effects gradually over a period of weeks.

Today, psychiatrists are more likely to prescribe a newer class of antidepressants, called *selective serotonin reuptake inhibitors (SSRIs),* which slow the reuptake process at serotonin synapses, thus increasing serotonin activation. The drugs in this class, which include Prozac (fluoxetine), Paxil (paroxetine), and Zoloft (sertraline), seem to yield therapeutic gains similar to the tricyclics in the treatment of depression (Shelton & Lester, 2006) while producing fewer unpleasant or dangerous side effects (Kelsey, 2005). SSRIs have also proven valuable in the treatment of obsessive-compulsive disorders, panic disorders, and other anxiety disorders (Rivas-Vazquez, 2001). However, there is some doubt about how effective the SSRIs (and other antidepressants) are in relieving episodes of depression among patients suffering from bipolar disorder (Thase, 2005). Bipolar patients do not seem to respond as well as those who suffer from depression only. And in some cases antidepressants appear to foster a switch back into a manic episode (Altshuler et al., 2006).

A major concern in recent years has been evidence from a number of studies that SSRIs may increase the risk for suicide, primarily among adolescents and young adults (Healy & Whitaker, 2003; Holden, 2004). The challenge of collecting definitive data on this issue is much more daunting than one might guess, in part because suicide rates are already elevated among people who exhibit the disorders for which SSRIs are prescribed (Rihmer, 2003; Wessely & Kerwin, 2004). Some researchers have collected data that suggest that suicide rates have *declined* slightly because of widespread prescription of SSRIs (Baldessarini et al., 2007; Gibbons et al., 2006), while others have found no association between SSRIs and suicide (Lapiere, 2003; Simon et al., 2006).

Overall, however, when antidepressants are compared to placebo treatment, the data suggest that antidepressants lead to a slight elevation in the risk of suicidal behavior, from roughly 2% to 4% (Bridge et al., 2007; Dubicka, Hadley, & Roberts, 2006; Hammad, Laughren, & Racoosin, 2006). The increased suicide risk appears to mainly be a problem among a small minority of children and adolescents in the first month after starting antidepressants, especially during the first nine days (Jick, Kaye, & Jick, 2004). Thus, patients starting on SSRIs should be carefully monitored by their physicians and families (Culpepper et al., 2004). Regulatory warnings from the U.S. Food and Drug Administration (FDA) have led to a decline in the prescription of SSRIs among adolescents (Nemeroff et al., 2007). This trend has prompted concern that increases in suicide may occur among untreated individuals. This concern seems legitimate in that suicide risk clearly peaks in the month prior to people beginning treatment for depression, whether that treatment involves SSRIs or psychotherapy (see Figure 15.14; Simon & Savarino, 2007). This pattern presumably occurs because the escalating agony of depression finally prompts people to seek treatment, but it also suggests that getting treatment with drugs or therapy reduces suicidal risk. In the final analysis, this is a complex issue, but the one thing experts

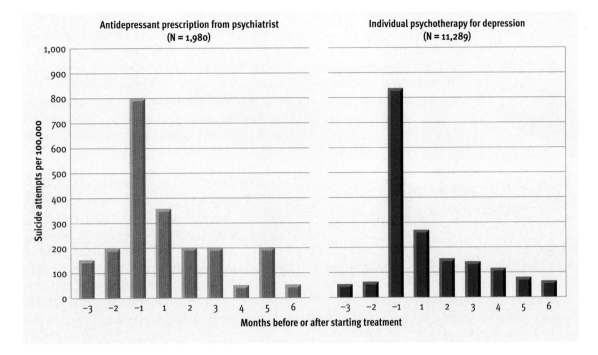

Antidepressant prescription from psychiatrist
(N = 1,980)

Individual psychotherapy for depression
(N = 11,289)

Months before or after starting treatment

Suicide attempts per 100,000

Figure 15.14
Probability of a suicide attempt in relation to the initiation of treatment. Examining medical records for thousands of patients, Simon and Savarino (2007) were able to gather information on the likelihood of a suicide attempt in the months before and after commencing treatment for depression. They compared patients who were put on an antidepressant medication against those who started in some form of insight or behavioral therapy. The data shown here, for young patients under the age of 25, indicate that suicide risk is highest in the month prior to treatment and next highest in the month after treatment is begun for both groups. These findings suggest that elevated suicide rates are not unique to starting on antidepressants and that getting treatment (whether it is medication or psychotherapy) reduces the risk of suicide.

SOURCE: Adapted from Simon, G. E., & Savarino, J. (2007). Suicide attempts among patients starting depression treatments with medications or psychotherapy. *American Journal of Psychiatry, 164*, 1029–1034 (Figure 2, p. 1032). Copyright © 2007 by the American Psychiatric Association. Adapted by permission of the American Psychiatric Association.

seem to agree on is that adolescents starting on SSRIs should be monitored closely.

The newest class of antidepressants consists of medications that inhibit reuptake at both serotonin and norepinephrine synapses, referred to as SNRIs. The first two drugs in this category are venlafaxine (Effexor) and duloxetine (Celexa). These drugs appear to produce slightly stronger antidepressant effects than the SSRIs (Thase & Denko, 2008). However, targeting two neurotransmitter systems also leads to a broader range of side effects, including troublesome elevations in blood pressure (Thase & Sloan, 2006).

Mood Stabilizers

Mood stabilizers **are drugs used to control mood swings in patients with bipolar mood disorders.** For many years, lithium was the only effective drug in this category. Lithium has proven valuable in preventing *future* episodes of both mania and depression in patients with bipolar illness (Geddes et al., 2004). Lithium can also be used in efforts to bring patients with bipolar illness out of *current* manic or depressive episodes (Keck & McElroy, 2006). However, antipsychotics and antidepressants are more commonly used for these purposes. On the negative side of the ledger, lithium does have some dangerous side effects if its use isn't managed skillfully (Jefferson & Greist, 2005). Lithium levels in the patient's blood must be monitored carefully, because high concentrations can be toxic and even fatal. Kidney and thyroid gland complications are the other major problems associated with lithium therapy.

In recent years a number of alternatives to lithium have been developed. The most popular of these newer mood stabilizers is an anticonvulsant agent called *valproate,* which has become more widely used than lithium in the treatment of bipolar disorders (Thase & Denko, 2008). Valproate appears to be roughly as effective as lithium in efforts to treat current manic episodes and to prevent future affective disturbances (Moseman et al., 2003). The advantage provided by valproate is that it has fewer side effects than lithium and is better tolerated by patients (Bowden, 2004).

How Effective Are Drug Therapies?

Drug therapies can produce clear therapeutic gains for many kinds of patients. What's especially impressive is that they can be effective with disorders that otherwise defy therapeutic endeavors. Nonetheless, drug therapies are controversial. Critics of drug therapy have raised a number of issues (Breggin & Cohen, 2007; Healy, 2004; Lickey & Gordon, 1991; Whitaker, 2002). First, some critics argue that drug therapies are not as effective as advertised and that they often produce superficial, short-lived curative effects. For example, Valium does not really solve problems with anxiety; it merely provides temporary relief from an unpleasant symptom. Moreover, relapse rates are substantial when drug regimens are discontinued. Second, critics charge that many drugs are overprescribed and many patients overmedicated. According to these critics, a number of physicians routinely hand out prescriptions without giving adequate consideration to more complicated and

web link 15.6

Dr. Bob's Psychopharmacology Tips

Psychopharmacology is the use of medication to treat psychological disorders. Physician and pharmacology specialist Robert Hsiang (University of Chicago) provides both broad and specific references about the interface of drugs and the human mind, including a searchable archive of professional information.

"I medicate first and ask questions later."

difficult interventions. Third, some critics charge that the damaging side effects of therapeutic drugs are underestimated by psychiatrists and that these side effects are often worse than the illnesses that the drugs are supposed to cure. Citing problems such as tardive dyskinesia, lithium toxicity, and addiction to antianxiety agents, these critics argue that the risks of therapeutic drugs aren't worth the benefits.

Critics maintain that the negative effects of psychiatric drugs are not fully appreciated because the pharmaceutical industry has managed to gain undue influence over the research enterprise as it relates to drug testing (Angell, 2000, 2004; Healy, 2004; Weber, 2006). Today, most researchers who investigate the benefits and risks of medications and write treatment guidelines have lucrative financial arrangements with the pharmaceutical industry (Bodenheimer, 2000; Choudhry, Stelfox, & Detsky, 2002; Lurie et al., 2006). Their studies are funded by drug companies, and they often receive substantial consulting fees. These financial arrangements have become so common, the prestigious *New England Journal of Medicine* had to relax its conflict-of-interest rules because it had difficulty finding expert reviewers who did not have financial ties to the drug industry (Drazen & Curfman, 2002). Unfortunately, these financial ties appear to undermine the objectivity required in scientific research, as studies funded by drug companies are far less likely to report unfavorable results than nonprofit-funded studies (Bekelman, Li, & Gross, 2003; Perlis et al., 2005; Rennie & Luft, 2000). Consistent with this finding, when specific antipsychotic drugs are pitted against each other in clinical trials, the sponsoring company's drug is reported to be superior to the other drugs in 90% of studies (Heres et al., 2006). Industry-financed drug trials also tend to be much too brief to detect the long-term risks associated with new drugs, and when unfavorable results emerge, the data are often withheld from publication (Antonuccio, Danton, &

McClanahan, 2003). Also, research designs are often slanted in a multitude of ways so as to exaggerate the positive effects and minimize the negative effects of the drugs under scrutiny (Carpenter, 2002; Chopra, 2003; Moncrieff, 2001). The conflicts of interest that appear to be pervasive in contemporary drug research raise grave concerns that require attention from researchers, universities, and federal agencies.

Obviously, drug therapies have stirred up some debate. However, this controversy pales in comparison to the furious debates inspired by electroconvulsive (shock) therapy (ECT). ECT is so controversial that the residents of Berkeley, California, voted in 1982 to outlaw ECT in their city. However, in subsequent lawsuits, the courts ruled that scientific questions cannot be settled through a vote, and they overturned the law. What makes ECT so controversial? You'll see in the next section.

Electroconvulsive Therapy (ECT)

In the 1930s, a Hungarian psychiatrist named Ladislas von Meduna speculated that epilepsy and schizophrenia could not coexist in the same body. On the basis of this observation, which turned out to be inaccurate, von Meduna theorized that it might be useful to induce epileptic-like seizures in schizophrenic patients. Initially, a drug was used to trigger these seizures. However, by 1938 a pair of Italian psychiatrists (Cerletti & Bini, 1938) demonstrated that it was safer to elicit the seizures with electric shock. Thus, modern electroconvulsive therapy was born.

Electroconvulsive therapy (ECT) is a biomedical treatment in which electric shock is used to produce a cortical seizure accompanied by convulsions. In ECT, electrodes are attached to the skull over the temporal lobes of the brain (see the photo on the facing page). A light anesthesia is induced, and the patient is given a variety of drugs to minimize the likelihood of complications. An electric current is then applied either to the right side or to both sides of the brain for about a second. Unilateral shock delivered to the right hemisphere is the preferred method of treatment today (Abrams, 2000). The current triggers a brief (about 30 seconds) convulsive seizure. The patient normally awakens in an hour or two and manifests some confusion, disorientation, and nausea, which usually clear up in a matter of hours. People typically receive between 6 and 12 treatments over a period of a month or so (Glass, 2001).

The clinical use of ECT peaked in the 1940s and 1950s, before effective drug therapies were widely

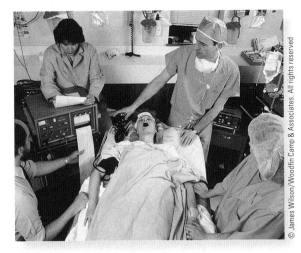
This patient is being prepared for electroconvulsive therapy. The mouthpiece keeps the patient from biting her tongue during the electrically induced seizures.

available. ECT has long been controversial, and its use did decline in the 1960s and 1970s. Nonetheless, the use of ECT has seen a resurgence in recent decades. Although only about 8% of psychiatrists administer ECT, it is not a rare form of treatment (Hermann et al., 1998). Some critics argue that ECT is overused because it is a lucrative procedure that boosts psychiatrists' income while consuming relatively little of their time in comparison to insight therapy (Frank, 1990). Conversely, some ECT advocates argue that ECT is underutilized because the public harbors many misconceptions about its effects and risks (McDonald et al., 2004). Although ECT is used in the treatment of a variety of disorders, in recent decades it has primarily been recommended for the treatment of depression.

Effectiveness of ECT

The evidence on the therapeutic efficacy of ECT is open to varied interpretations. Proponents maintain that it is a remarkably effective treatment for major depression (Prudic, 2005; Rudorfer, Henry, & Sackeim, 2003). Moreover, they note that many patients who do not benefit from antidepressant medication improve in response to ECT (Nobler & Sackeim, 2006). However, opponents argue that the available studies are flawed and inconclusive and that ECT is probably no more effective than a placebo (Rose et al., 2003). Overall, there does seem to be enough favorable evidence to justify *conservative* use of ECT in treating severe mood disorders in patients who have not responded to medication (Carney & Geddes, 2003; Metzger, 1999). Unfortunately, relapse rates after ECT are distressingly high. Over 50% of patients relapse within 6 to 12 months, although re-

lapse rates can be reduced by giving ECT patients antidepressant drugs (Sackeim et al., 2001).

Curiously, to the extent that ECT may be effective, no one is sure why. The discarded theories about how ECT works could fill several books. Many ECT advocates theorize that the treatment must affect neurotransmitter activity in the brain. However, the evidence supporting this view is fragmentary, inconsistent, and inconclusive (Abrams, 1992; Kapur & Mann, 1993). ECT opponents have a radically different, albeit equally unproven, explanation for why ECT might *appear* to be effective: They maintain that some patients find ECT so aversive that they muster all their willpower to climb out of their depression to avoid further ECT treatments.

Risks Associated with ECT

Even ECT proponents acknowledge that memory losses, impaired attention, and other cognitive deficits are common short-term side effects of electroconvulsive therapy (Lisanby et al., 2000; Sackeim et al., 2007). However, ECT proponents assert that these deficits are mild and usually disappear within a month or two (Glass, 2001). An American Psychiatric Association (2001) task force concluded that there is no objective evidence that ECT causes structural damage in the brain or that it has any lasting negative effects on the ability to learn and remember information. In contrast, ECT critics maintain that ECT-induced cognitive deficits are often significant and sometimes permanent (Breggin, 1991; Rose et al., 2003), although their evidence seems to be largely anecdotal. Given the concerns about the risks of ECT and the doubts about its efficacy, it appears that the use of ECT will remain controversial for some time to come.

concept check 15.3

Understanding Biomedical Therapies

Check your understanding of biomedical therapies by matching each treatment with its chief use. The answers are in Appendix A.

Treatment

_____ 1. Antianxiety drugs

_____ 2. Antipsychotic drugs

_____ 3. Antidepressant drugs

_____ 4. Mood stabilizers

_____ 5. Electroconvulsive therapy (ECT)

Chief purpose

a. To reduce psychotic symptoms

b. To bring a major depression to an end

c. To suppress tension, nervousness, and apprehension

d. To prevent future episodes of mania or depression in bipolar disorders

New Brain Stimulation Techniques

Scientists are always on the lookout for new methods of treating psychological disorders that might exhibit greater efficacy or fewer complications than ECT and drug treatments. Some new approaches to treatment involving stimulation of the brain are being explored with promising results, although they remain highly experimental at this time.

One new approach is *transcranial magnetic stimulation,* which was discussed in Chapter 3 as a method for studying brain function. **Transcranial magnetic stimulation (TMS) is a technique that permits scientists to temporarily enhance or depress activity in a specific area of the brain.** In TMS, a magnetic coil mounted on a small paddle is held over specific areas of the head to increase or decrease activity in discrete regions of the cortex (Nahas et al., 2007). Neuroscientists are mostly experimenting with TMS as a treatment for depression. Thus far, treatments delivered to the right and left prefrontal cortex show promise in reducing depressive symptoms (Nobler & Sackeim, 2006; O'Reardon et al., 2007). TMS generally is well tolerated, with minimal side effects. But a great deal of additional research will be necessary before the therapeutic value of TMS can be determined.

The other new approach to treatment is *deep brain stimulation.* In *deep brain stimulation (DBS)* a thin electrode is surgically implanted in the brain and connected to an implanted pulse generator so that various electrical currents can be delivered to brain tissue adjacent to the electrode (George, 2003; see Figure 15.15). DBS has proven valuable in the treatment of the motor disturbances associated with Parkinson's disease, tardive dyskinesia, and some seizure disorders (Halpern et al., 2007; Wider et al., 2008). Researchers are currently explor-

ing whether DBS may have value in the treatment of depression or obsessive-compulsive disorder (George et al., 2006; Hardesty & Sackeim, 2007). Obviously, this highly invasive procedure requiring brain surgery will never be a frontline therapy for mental disorders, but scientists hope that it may prove valuable for highly treatment-resistant patients who do not benefit from conventional therapies (Kuehn, 2007).

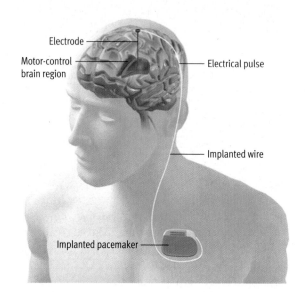

Figure 15.15

Deep brain stimulation. Deep brain stimulation requires a surgical procedure in which a thin electrode (about the width of a human hair) is inserted into deep areas of the brain. The electrode is connected to a pulse generator implanted under the skin of the chest. The placement of the electrode and the type of current generated depend on what condition is being treated. The electrode shown here was implanted in a motor area of the brain to treat the tremors associated with Parkinson's disease. Researchers are experimenting with other electrode placements in efforts to treat depression and obsessive-compulsive disorder.

SOURCE: Adapted from George, M. S. (2003). Stimulating the brain. *Scientific American, 289*(3), 67–73 (p. 70). © Bryan Christie Design.

REVIEW of Key Points

15.13 Antianxiety drugs exert their effects quickly and are fairly effective in reducing feelings of anxiety, but their impact is short-lived. They produce some nuisance side effects, and there can be complications involving abuse, dependence, and overdose. Antipsychotic drugs are used primarily in the treatment of schizophrenia. They reduce psychotic symptoms in about 70% of patients. Traditional antipsychotics can have a variety of serious side effects, which have been reduced in the newer, atypical antipsychotics.

15.14 Antidepressants are used to bring people out of episodes of depression. SSRIs are the dominant type used today, with SNRIs representing a new option. Side effects tend to be manageable, although there are concerns that antidepressants may increase suicide risk slightly. Mood stabilizers, such as lithium and valproate, are used to prevent the recurrence of episodes of disturbance in people with bipolar mood disorders.

15.15 Drug therapies can be quite effective, but they have their drawbacks. All of the drugs produce side effects, some

of which can be very troublesome. Some critics maintain that drugs' curative effects are superficial and that some drugs are overprescribed. Disturbing questions have been raised about the scientific impartiality of contemporary research on therapeutic drugs.

15.16 Electroconvulsive therapy (ECT) is used to trigger a cortical seizure that is believed to have therapeutic value for mood disorders, especially depression. Evidence about the effectiveness of ECT is contradictory but seems sufficient to justify conservative use of the procedure. Cognitive deficits are the principal risk, with much debate about how severe and enduring these deficits tend to be.

15.17 Transcranial magnetic stimulation is a new technique that permits scientists to temporarily enhance or depress activity in a specific area of the cortex. It may have value in the treatment of depression. In deep brain stimulation a thin electrode is surgically implanted so that electrical currents can be delivered to selected areas of the brain. It may have value in the treatment of depression or obsessive-compulsive disorder.

Current Trends and Issues in Treatment

The controversy about ECT is only one of many contentious issues and shifting trends in the world of mental health care. In this section, we will discuss the impact of managed care on psychotherapy, the continuing trend toward blending various approaches to therapy, and efforts to respond more effectively to increasing cultural diversity in Western societies.

Grappling with the Constraints of Managed Care

The 1990s brought a dramatic shift in how people in the United States pay for their health care. Alarmed by skyrocketing health care costs, huge numbers of employers and individuals moved from traditional fee-for-service arrangements to managed care health plans (Hogan & Morrison, 2003; Kiesler, 2000). In the *fee-for-service* system, hospitals, physicians, psychologists, and other providers charged fees for whatever health care services were needed, and most of these fees were reimbursed by private insurance or the government (through Medicaid, Medicare, and other programs). In *managed care systems* people enroll in prepaid plans with small co-payments for services, typically run by health maintenance organizations (HMOs), which agree to provide ongoing health care for a specific sum of money. Managed care usually involves a tradeoff: Consumers pay lower prices for their care, but they give up much of their freedom to choose their providers and to obtain whatever treatments they believe necessary. If an HMO's treatment expenses become excessive, it won't turn a profit, so HMOs have strong incentives to hold treatment costs down. The HMOs originally promised individuals and employers that they would be able to hold costs down without having a negative impact on the quality of care, by negotiating lower fees from providers, reducing inefficiency, and cracking down on medically unnecessary services. However, critics charge that managed care systems have squeezed all the savings they can out of the "fat" that existed in the old system and that they have responded to continued inflation in their costs by rationing care and limiting access to medically *necessary* services (Duckworth & Borus, 1999; Giles & Marafiote, 1998; Sanchez & Turner, 2003).

The possibility that managed care is having a negative effect on the quality of treatment is a source of concern throughout the health care professions, but the issue is especially sensitive in the domain of mental health care (Bursztajn & Brodsky, 2002; Campbell, 2000; Rosenberg & DeMaso, 2008). Critics maintain that mental health care has suffered particularly severe cuts in services because the question of what is "medically necessary" can be more subjective than in other treatment specialties (such as cardiology) and because patients who are denied psychotherapy services are relatively unlikely to complain (Duckworth & Borus, 1999). For example, a business executive who is trying to hide his depression or cocaine addiction from his employer will be reluctant to complain to his employer if therapeutic services are denied.

According to critics, the restriction of mental health services sometimes involves outright denial of treatment, but it often takes more subtle forms, such as underdiagnosing conditions, failing to make needed referrals to mental health specialists, and arbitrarily limiting the length of treatment (Miller, 1996). Long-term therapy is becoming a thing of the past unless patients can pay for it out of pocket, and the goal of treatment has been reduced to reestablishing a reasonable level of functioning (Zatzick, 1999). Many managed care systems hold down costs by rerouting patients from highly trained providers, such as psychiatrists and psychologists, to less-well-trained providers, such as masters-level counselors, who may not be adequately prepared to handle serious psychological disorders (Seligman & Levant, 1998). Cost containment is also achieved by requiring physicians to prescribe older antidepressant and antipsychotic drugs instead of the newer and much more expensive SSRIs and atypical antipsychotics (Docherty, 1999).

Unfortunately, there are no simple solutions to these problems on the horizon. Restraining the rapid growth of health care costs without compromising the quality of care, consumers' freedom of choice, and providers' autonomy is an enormously complex and daunting challenge. At this juncture, it is difficult to predict what the future holds. However, it is clear that economic realities have ushered in an era of transition for the treatment of psychological disorders and problems (Huey et al., 2005).

Blending Approaches to Treatment

In this chapter we have reviewed many approaches to treatment. However, there is no rule that a client

Key Learning Goals

15.18 Articulate the concerns that have been expressed about the impact of managed care on the treatment of psychological disorders.

15.19 Discuss the merits of blending approaches to therapy, including the Featured Study on combining insight therapy and medication.

15.20 Analyze the barriers that lead to underutilization of mental health services by ethnic minorities and possible solutions to the problem.

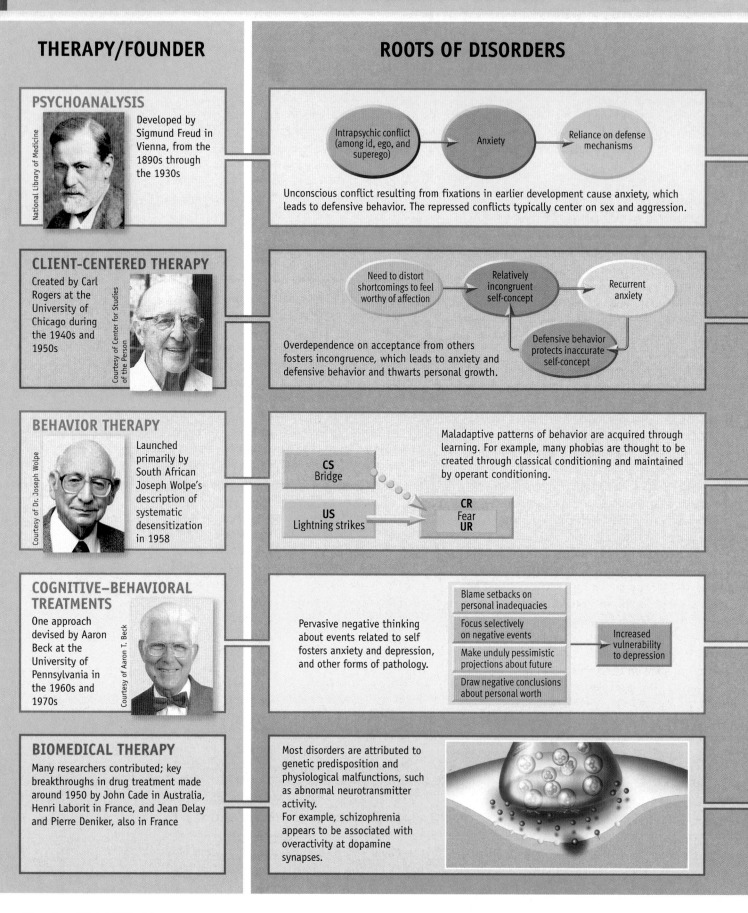

THERAPY/FOUNDER

ROOTS OF DISORDERS

PSYCHOANALYSIS

National Library of Medicine

Developed by Sigmund Freud in Vienna, from the 1890s through the 1930s

Intrapsychic conflict (among id, ego, and superego) → Anxiety → Reliance on defense mechanisms

Unconscious conflict resulting from fixations in earlier development cause anxiety, which leads to defensive behavior. The repressed conflicts typically center on sex and aggression.

CLIENT-CENTERED THERAPY

Created by Carl Rogers at the University of Chicago during the 1940s and 1950s

Courtesy of Center for Studies of the Person

Need to distort shortcomings to feel worthy of affection → Relatively incongruent self-concept → Recurrent anxiety

Defensive behavior protects inaccurate self-concept

Overdependence on acceptance from others fosters incongruence, which leads to anxiety and defensive behavior and thwarts personal growth.

BEHAVIOR THERAPY

Courtesy of Dr. Joseph Wolpe

Launched primarily by South African Joseph Wolpe's description of systematic desensitization in 1958

Maladaptive patterns of behavior are acquired through learning. For example, many phobias are thought to be created through classical conditioning and maintained by operant conditioning.

CS
Bridge

US
Lightning strikes

CR
Fear
UR

COGNITIVE–BEHAVIORAL TREATMENTS

One approach devised by Aaron Beck at the University of Pennsylvania in the 1960s and 1970s

Courtesy of Aaron T. Beck

Pervasive negative thinking about events related to self fosters anxiety and depression, and other forms of pathology.

Blame setbacks on personal inadequacies

Focus selectively on negative events

Make unduly pessimistic projections about future

Draw negative conclusions about personal worth

→ Increased vulnerability to depression

BIOMEDICAL THERAPY

Many researchers contributed; key breakthroughs in drug treatment made around 1950 by John Cade in Australia, Henri Laborit in France, and Jean Delay and Pierre Deniker, also in France

Most disorders are attributed to genetic predisposition and physiological malfunctions, such as abnormal neurotransmitter activity.
For example, schizophrenia appears to be associated with overactivity at dopamine synapses.

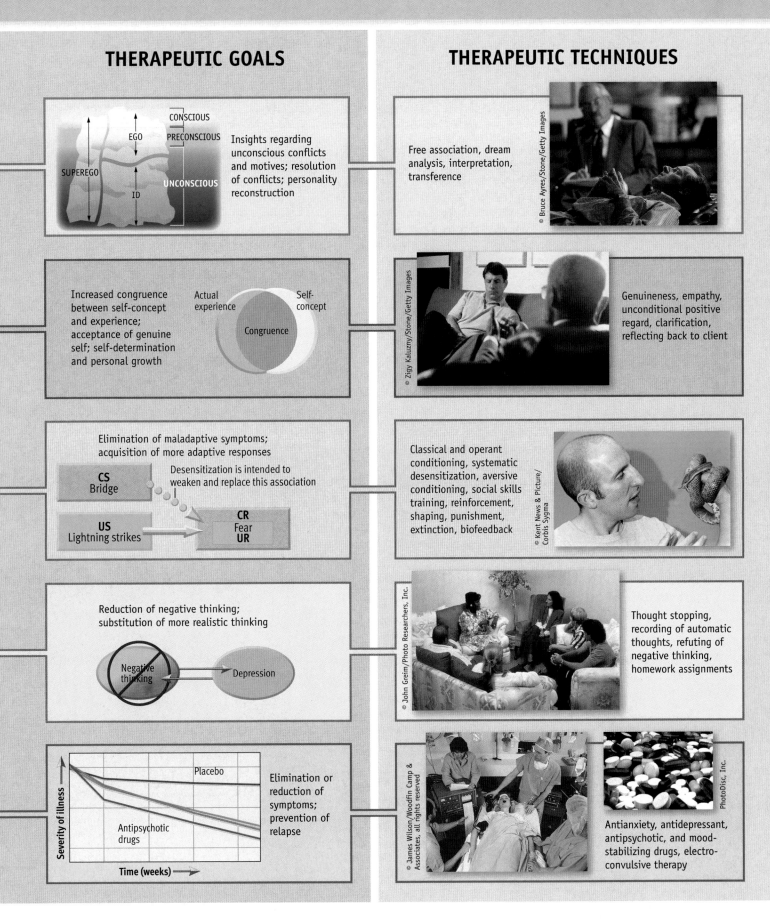

THERAPEUTIC GOALS

THERAPEUTIC TECHNIQUES

CONSCIOUS
PRECONSCIOUS
EGO
SUPEREGO
ID
UNCONSCIOUS

Insights regarding unconscious conflicts and motives; resolution of conflicts; personality reconstruction

Free association, dream analysis, interpretation, transference

© Bruce Ayres/Stone/Getty Images

Increased congruence between self-concept and experience; acceptance of genuine self; self-determination and personal growth

Actual experience | Self-concept
Congruence

Genuineness, empathy, unconditional positive regard, clarification, reflecting back to client

© Zigy Kaluzny/Stone/Getty Images

Elimination of maladaptive symptoms; acquisition of more adaptive responses

CS Bridge

Desensitization is intended to weaken and replace this association

US Lightning strikes

CR Fear UR

Classical and operant conditioning, systematic desensitization, aversive conditioning, social skills training, reinforcement, shaping, punishment, extinction, biofeedback

© Kent News & Picture/Corbis Sygma

Reduction of negative thinking; substitution of more realistic thinking

Negative thinking → Depression

Thought stopping, recording of automatic thoughts, refuting of negative thinking, homework assignments

© John Greim/Photo Researchers, Inc.

Placebo

Antipsychotic drugs

Severity of illness

Time (weeks)

Elimination or reduction of symptoms; prevention of relapse

Antianxiety, antidepressant, antipsychotic, and mood-stabilizing drugs, electro-convulsive therapy

© James Wilson/Woodfin Camp & Associates, all rights reserved

PhotoDisc, Inc.

must be treated with just one approach. Often, a clinician will use several techniques in working with a client. For example, a depressed person might receive cognitive therapy, social skills training, and antidepressant medication. Multiple approaches are particularly likely when a treatment team provides therapy. Studies suggest that combining approaches to treatment has merit (Glass, 2004; Riba & Miller, 2003), as you will see in our Featured Study for this chapter.

SOURCE: Reynolds, C. F., III, Frank, E., Perel, J. M., Imber, S. D., Cornes, C., Miller, M. D., Mazumdar, S., Houck, P. R., Dew, M. A., Stack, J. A., Pollock, B. G., & Kupfer, D. J. (1999). Nortriptyline and interpersonal psychotherapy as maintenance therapies for recurrent major depression: A randomized controlled trial in patients older than 50 years. *Journal of the American Medical Association, 28,* 39–45.

FEATURED STUDY

Combining Insight Therapy and Medication

Depression is common in older people and contributes to physical health problems, chronic disability, and increased mortality among the elderly. Geriatric depression is also a highly recurrent problem. After successful treatment of depression, elderly patients tend to relapse more quickly and more frequently than younger clients. The purpose of this study was to determine whether a combination of insight therapy and antidepressant medication could reduce the recurrence of depression in an elderly population.

Method

Participants. The participants were 107 elderly patients diagnosed with recurrent, unipolar, major depression. The mean age of the patients at the beginning of the study was 67.6. The subjects had all been successfully treated for a recent episode of depression and had remained stable for four months.

Treatments. The medication employed in the study was *nortriptyline,* a tricyclic antidepressant that appears to be relatively effective and well tolerated in elderly populations. The insight therapy was *interpersonal psychotherapy (IPT),* an approach to therapy that emphasizes the social roots of depression and focuses on how improved social relations can protect against depression (Klerman & Weissman, 1993). Clients learn how social isolation and unsatisfying interpersonal relationships can provoke depression and how confidants and supportive interactions can decrease vulnerability to depression.

Design. The subjects were randomly assigned to one of four maintenance treatment conditions: (1) monthly interpersonal therapy and medication, (2) medication alone, (3) monthly interpersonal therapy and placebo medication, and (4) placebo medication alone. A *double-blind* procedure was employed, so the clinicians who provided the treatments did not know which subjects were getting genuine medication as opposed to placebo pills. Patients remained in maintenance treatment for three years or until a recurrence of a major depressive episode.

Results

The relapse rates for the four treatment conditions are shown in **Figure 15.16**. The relapse rate for the combination of interpersonal therapy and medication was significantly less than that for either medication alone or interpersonal therapy alone (with placebo medication). The prophylactic value of the combined therapy proved most valuable to patients over 70 years of age and in the first year of the study, during which most relapses occurred.

Discussion

The authors conclude that "the continuation of combined medication and psychotherapy may represent the best long-term treatment strategy for preserving recovery in elderly patients with recurrent major depression" (p. 44). They speculate that the combined treatment may be "best-suited for dealing with both the biological and psychosocial substrates of old-age depression" (p. 45). How-

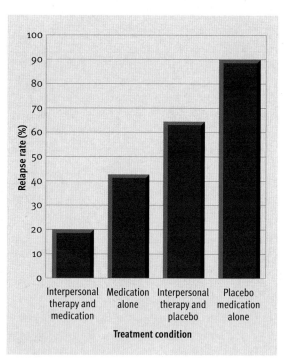

Figure 15.16

Relapse rates in the Reynolds et al. (1999) study. Following up over a period of three years, Reynolds et al. (1999) compared the preventive value of (1) monthly interpersonal therapy and medication, (2) medication alone, (3) monthly interpersonal therapy and placebo medication, and (4) placebo medication alone in a sample of elderly patients prone to recurrent depression. The combined treatment of insight therapy and medication yielded the lowest relapse rates and thus proved superior to either insight therapy or drug therapy alone.

ever, they acknowledge the need for further research and recommend additional studies with newer antidepressant drugs (the SSRIs) that are increasingly popular.

Comment

This study was featured because it illustrated how to conduct a well-controlled experimental evaluation of the efficacy of therapeutic interventions. It also highlighted the value of combining approaches to treatment, which is a laudable trend in the treatment of psychological disorders. The fact that the study was published in the highly prestigious *Journal of the American Medical Association* also demonstrates how prominent and important research on therapeutic efficacy has become in the era of managed care.

The value of multiple approaches to treatment may explain why a significant trend seems to have crept into the field of psychotherapy: a movement away from strong loyalty to individual schools of thought and a corresponding move toward integrating various approaches to therapy (Castonguay et al., 2003; D. A. Smith, 1999). Most clinicians used to depend exclusively on one system of therapy while rejecting the utility of all others. This era of fragmentation may be drawing to a close. One survey of psychologists' theoretical orientations, which is summarized in **Figure 15.17**, found that 36% of the respondents described themselves as *eclectic* in approach (Norcross, Hedges, & Castle, 2002).

Eclecticism **in the practice of therapy involves drawing ideas from two or more systems of therapy instead of committing to just one system.** Therapists can be eclectic in a number of ways (Arkowitz, 1992; Feixas & Botella, 2004; Goin, 2005). Two common approaches are theoretical integration and technical eclecticism. In *theoretical integration,* two or more systems of therapy are combined or blended to take advantage of the strengths of each. Paul Wachtel's (1977, 1991) efforts to blend psychodynamic and behavioral therapies is a prominent example. *Technical eclecticism* involves borrowing ideas, insights, and techniques from a variety of sources while tailoring one's intervention strategy to the unique needs of each client. Advocates of technical eclecticism, such as Arnold Lazarus (1992, 1995, 2008), maintain that therapists should ask themselves, "What is the best approach for this specific client, problem, and situation?" and then adjust their strategy accordingly.

Increasing Multicultural Sensitivity in Treatment

Modern psychotherapy emerged during the second half of the 19th century in Europe and America, spawned in part by a cultural milieu that viewed the self as an independent, reflective, rational being, capable of self-improvement (Cushman, 1992). Psychological disorders were assumed to have natural causes like physical diseases and to be amenable to medical treatments derived from scientific research. But the individualized, medicalized institution of modern psychotherapy reflects Western cultural values that are far from universal (Sue & Sue, 1999). In many nonindustrialized societies, psychological disorders are attributed to supernatural forces (possession, witchcraft, angry gods, and so forth), and victims seek help from priests, shamans, and folk healers, rather than doctors (Wittkower & Warnes, 1984). Thus, efforts to export Western psychotherapies to non-Western cultures have met with mixed success. Indeed, the highly culture-bound origins of modern therapies have raised questions about their applicability to ethnic minorities *within* Western culture (Miranda et al., 2005).

Research on how cultural factors influence the process and outcome of psychotherapy has burgeoned in recent years, motivated in part by the need to improve mental health services for ethnic minority groups in American society (Lee & Ramirez, 2000; Worthington, Soth-McNett, & Moreno, 2007). The data are ambiguous for a couple of ethnic groups, but studies suggest that American minority groups generally underutilize therapeutic services (Bender

web link 15.7

Psych Central

The work of John Grohol, Psych Central is a superb source for learning about all aspects of mental health, including psychological disorders and treatment, professional issues, and information for mental health care consumers. Almost 2000 annotated listings to information sources are offered here.

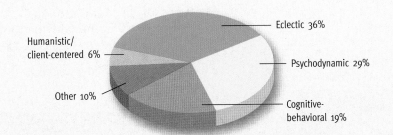

Figure 15.17

The leading approaches to therapy among psychologists. These data, from a survey of 531 psychologists who belong to the American Psychological Association's Division of Psychotherapy, provide some indication of how common an eclectic approach to therapy has become. The findings suggest that the most widely used approaches to therapy are eclectic, psychodynamic, and cognitive-behavioral treatments. (Based on data from Norcross, Hedges, & Castle, 2002)

et al., 2007; Olfson et al., 2002; Richardson, et al., 2003). Why? A variety of barriers appear to contribute to this problem (Snowden & Yamada, 2005; Zane et al., 2004; U.S. Department of Health and Human Services, 1999). One major consideration is that many members of minority groups have a history of frustrating interactions with American bureaucracies and are distrustful of large, intimidating institutions, such as hospitals and community mental health centers. Another issue is that most hospitals and mental health agencies are not adequately staffed with therapists who speak the languages used by minority groups in their service areas. Yet another problem is that the vast majority of therapists have been trained almost exclusively in the treatment of white middle-class Americans and are not familiar with the cultural backgrounds and unique characteristics of various ethnic groups. This culture gap often leads to misunderstandings and ill-advised treatment strategies.

Ethnicity aside, those who are poor are less likely than others to gain access to psychotherapy (Smith, 2005). This problem affects ethnic minorities disproportionately because many minority groups suffer from elevated rates of joblessness and poverty. And some critics argue that many middle-class therapists don't feel comfortable with impoverished clients and tend to distance themselves from the poor (Lott, 2002; Smith, 2005). Although this social class bias surely is not limited to therapists, it creates another huge barrier to equal access for those who already have to grapple with countless problems associated with poverty.

What can be done to improve mental health services for American minority groups? Researchers in this area have offered a variety of suggestions (Hong, Garcia, & Soriano, 2000; Miranda et al., 2005; Pedersen, 1994; Yamamoto et al., 1993). Discussions of possible solutions usually begin with the need to recruit and train more ethnic minority therapists. Studies show that ethnic minorities are more likely to go to mental health facilities that are staffed by a higher proportion of people who share their ethnic background (Snowden & Hu, 1996; Sue, Zane, & Young, 1994). Individual therapists have been urged to work harder at building a vigorous *therapeutic alliance* (a strong supportive bond) with their ethnic clients. A strong therapeutic alliance is associated with better therapeutic outcomes regardless of ethnicity, but some studies suggest that it is especially crucial for minority clients (Bender et al., 2007; Comas-Diaz, 2006). Finally, most authorities urge further investigation of how traditional approaches to therapy can be modified and tailored to be more compatible with specific cultural groups' attitudes, values, norms, and traditions (Hwang, 2006). A recent review of 76 studies that examined the effects of culturally adapted interventions found clear evidence that this tailoring process tends to yield positive effects (Griner & Smith, 2006). The benefits are particularly prominent when a treatment is tailored to a single, specific cultural group rather than a mixture of several or more cultural groups.

REVIEW of Key Points

15.18 In managed care systems, consumers usually pay lower prices but give up some of their freedom to obtain whatever treatments they believe necessary. Many clinicians and their clients believe that managed care has restricted access to mental health care and undermined its quality, as long-term therapy has become a thing of the past.

15.19 Combinations of insight, behavioral, and biomedical therapies are often used fruitfully in the treatment of psychological disorders. For example, the Featured Study showed how the tandem of interpersonal therapy and antidepressant medication could be valuable in preventing additional depressive episodes in an elderly population. Many modern therapists are eclectic, using specific ideas, techniques, and strategies gleaned from a number of theoretical approaches.

15.20 Because of cultural, language, and access barriers, therapeutic services are underutilized by most ethnic minorities in America. More culturally responsive approaches to treatment will require more minority therapists, more effort to build strong therapeutic alliances, and additional investigation of how traditional therapies can be tailored to be more compatible with specific ethnic groups' cultural heritage.

Institutional Treatment in Transition

Key Learning Goals

15.21 Explain why people grew disenchanted with mental hospitals.

15.22 Assess the effects of the deinstitutionalization movement.

Traditionally, much of the treatment of mental illness has been carried out in institutional settings, primarily in mental hospitals. A *mental hospital* is a medical institution specializing in providing inpatient care for psychological disorders. In the United States, a national network of state-funded mental hospitals started to emerge in the 1840s through the efforts of Dorothea Dix and other reformers (see **Figure 15.18**). Prior to these reforms, the mentally ill who were poor were housed in jails

Figure 15.18

Dorothea Dix and the advent of mental hospitals in America. During the 19th century, Dorothea Dix (inset) campaigned tirelessly to obtain funds for building mental hospitals. Many of these hospitals, such as the New York State Lunatic Asylum, were extremely large facilities. Although public mental hospitals improved the care of the mentally ill, they had a variety of shortcomings, which eventually prompted the deinstitutionalization movement.

SOURCE: National Library of Medicine; (inset) Detail of painting of Dorothea Dix in Harrisburg State Hospital, photo by Ken Smith/LLR Collection.

and poorhouses or were left to wander the countryside. Today, mental hospitals continue to play an important role in the delivery of mental health services. However, since World War II, institutional care for mental illness has undergone a series of major transitions—and the dust hasn't settled yet. Let's look at how institutional care has evolved in recent decades.

Disenchantment with Mental Hospitals

By the 1950s, it had become apparent that public mental hospitals were not fulfilling their goals very well (Mechanic, 1980; Menninger, 2005). Experts began to realize that hospitalization often *contributed* to the development of pathology instead of curing it. What were the causes of these unexpected negative effects? Part of the problem was that the facilities were usually underfunded (Bloom, 1984). The lack of adequate funding meant that the facilities were overcrowded and understaffed. Hospital personnel were undertrained and overworked, making them hard-pressed to deliver minimal custodial care. Despite gallant efforts at treatment, the demoralizing conditions made most public mental hospitals decidedly nontherapeutic (Scull, 1990). These problems were aggravated by the fact that state mental hospi-

tals served large geographic regions but were rarely placed near major population centers. As a result, most patients were uprooted from their community and isolated from their social support networks.

Disenchantment with the public mental hospital system inspired the *community mental health movement* that emerged in the 1960s (Duckworth & Borus, 1999; Huey, Ford, & Cole, 2005). The community mental health movement emphasizes (1) local, community-based care, (2) reduced dependence on hospitalization, and (3) the prevention of psychological disorders. Community mental health centers were intended to supplement mental hospitals with decentralized and more accessible services, but they have had their own funding struggles (Dixon & Goldman, 2004).

Deinstitutionalization

Mental hospitals continue to care for many people troubled by chronic mental illness, but their role in patient care has diminished. Since the 1960s, a policy of deinstitutionalization has been followed in the United States, as well as most other Western countries (Fakhoury & Priebe, 2002). *Deinstitutionalization* refers to transferring the treatment of mental illness from inpatient institutions to community-based facilities that emphasize outpatient

care. This shift in responsibility was made possible by two developments: (1) the emergence of effective drug therapies for severe disorders and (2) the deployment of community mental health centers to coordinate local care (Goff & Gudeman, 1999).

The exodus of patients from mental hospitals has been dramatic. The average inpatient population in state and county mental hospitals had dropped from a peak of nearly 550,000 in the mid-1950s to around 70,000 by 2000, as shown in **Figure 15.19**. This trend does not mean that hospitalization for mental illness has become a thing of the past. A great many people are still hospitalized, but the shift has been toward placing them in local general hospitals for brief periods instead of distant psychiatric hospitals for long periods (Kiesler, 1992). In keeping with the philosophy of deinstitutionalization, these local facilities try to get patients stabilized and back into the community as swiftly as possible.

How has deinstitutionalization worked out? It gets mixed reviews. On the positive side, many people have benefited by avoiding disruptive and unnecessary hospitalization. Ample evidence suggests that alternatives to hospitalization can be as effective as and less costly than inpatient care (McGrew et al., 1999; Reinharz, Lesage, & Contandriopoulos, 2000). Moreover, follow-up studies of discharged patients reveal that a substantial majority prefer the greater freedom provided by community-based treatment (Leff, 2006).

Nonetheless, some unanticipated problems have arisen (Elpers, 2000; Munk-Jorgensen, 1999; Talbott, 2004). Many patients suffering from chronic psychological disorders had nowhere to go when they were released. They had no families, friends, or homes to return to. Many had no work skills and were poorly prepared to live on their own. These people were supposed to be absorbed by "halfway houses," sheltered workshops, and other types of intermediate care facilities. Unfortunately, many communities

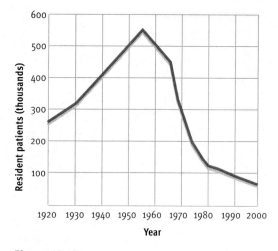

Figure 15.19

Declining inpatient population at state and county mental hospitals. The inpatient population in public mental hospitals has declined dramatically since the late 1950s, as a result of deinstitutionalization and the development of effective antipsychotic medication. (Data from the National Institute of Mental Health)

were never able to fund and build the planned facilities (Hogan & Morrison, 2003; Lamb, 1998). Thus, deinstitutionalization left two major problems in its wake: a "revolving door" population of people who flow in and out of psychiatric facilities, and a sizable population of homeless mentally ill people.

Mental Illness, the Revolving Door, and Homelessness

Although the proportion of hospital days attributable to mental illness has dwindled, admission rates for psychiatric hospitals have actually climbed. What has happened? Deinstitutionalization and drug therapy have created a revolving door through which many mentally ill people pass again and again (Castro et al., 2007; Geller, 1992; Langdon et al., 2001).

DOONESBURY

Most of the people caught in the mental health system's revolving door suffer from chronic, severe disorders (usually schizophrenia) that often require hospitalization (Haywood et al., 1995). However, they respond to drug therapies in the hospital. Once they're stabilized through drug therapy, they no longer qualify for expensive hospital treatment according to the new standards created by deinstitutionalization and managed care. Thus, they're sent back out the door, into communities that often aren't prepared to provide adequate outpatient care. Because they lack appropriate care and support, their condition deteriorates and they soon require readmission to a hospital, where the cycle begins once again. Over two-thirds of all psychiatric inpatient admissions involve rehospitalizing a former patient. Moreover, 40% to 50% of patients are readmitted within a year of their release (Bridge & Barbe, 2004).

Deinstitutionalization has also been blamed for the growing population of homeless people. Studies have consistently found elevated rates of mental illness among the homeless. Taken as a whole, the evidence suggests that roughly one-third of homeless people suffer from severe mental illness (schizophrenic and mood disorders), that another one-third or more are struggling with alcohol and drug problems, that many qualify for multiple diagnoses, and that the prevalence of mental illness among the homeless may be increasing (Bassuk et al., 1998; Folsom et al., 2005; Haugland et al., 1997; North et al., 2004). In essence, homeless shelters have become a *de facto* element of America's mental health care system (Callicutt, 2006).

The popular media routinely equate homelessness with mental illness, and it is widely assumed that deinstitutionalization is largely responsible for the rapid growth of homelessness in America. Although deinstitutionalization has probably *contributed* to the growth of homelessness, many experts in this area maintain that it is an oversimplification to blame the problem of homelessness chiefly on deinstitutionalization (Main, 1998; Sullivan, Burnam, & Koegel, 2000).

In light of the revolving door problem and homelessness among the mentally ill, what can we conclude about deinstitutionalization? It appears to be a worthwhile idea that has been poorly executed (Lamb, 1998). Overall, the policy has probably been a benefit to countless people with milder disorders but a cruel trick on many others with severe, chronic disorders. Ultimately, it's clear that our society is not providing adequate care for a sizable segment of the mentally ill population (Appelbaum, 2002; Elpers, 2000; Gittelman, 2005; Torrey, 1996). That's not a new development. Inadequate care for mental illness has always been the norm. Societies always struggle with the problem of what to do with the mentally ill and how to pay for their care (Duckworth & Borus, 1999).

Reflecting on the Chapter's Themes

In our discussion of psychotherapy, one of our unifying themes—the value of theoretical diversity—was particularly prominent, and one other theme—the importance of culture—surfaced briefly. Let's discuss the latter theme first. The approaches to treatment described in this chapter are products of modern, white, middle-class, Western culture. Some of these therapies have proven useful in some other cultures, but many have turned out to be irrelevant or counterproductive when used with different cultural groups, including ethnic minorities in Western society. Thus, we have seen once again that cultural factors influence psychological processes and that Western psychology cannot assume that its theories and practices have universal applicability.

As for theoretical diversity, its value can be illustrated with a rhetorical question: Can you imagine what the state of modern psychotherapy would be if everyone in psychology and psychiatry had simply accepted Freud's theories about the nature and

Key Learning Goals

15.23 Identify the two unifying themes highlighted in this chapter.

Cultural Heritage

Theoretical Diversity

treatment of psychological disorders? If not for theoretical diversity, psychotherapy might still be in the dark ages. Psychoanalysis can be a useful method of therapy, but it would be a tragic state of affairs if that were the *only* treatment available. Multitudes of people have benefited from alternative approaches to treatment that emerged out of tensions between psychoanalytic theory and other theoretical perspectives. People have diverse problems, rooted in varied origins, that call for the pursuit of different therapeutic goals. Thus, it's fortunate that people can choose from a diverse array of approaches to treatment. The illustrated overview on pages 646–647 summarizes and compares some of the approaches that we've discussed in this chapter. This summary chart shows that the major approaches to treatment

each have their own vision of the nature of human discontent and the ideal remedy.

Of course, diversity can be confusing. The range and variety of available treatments in modern psychotherapy leaves many people puzzled about their options. Thus, in the Personal Application we'll sort through the practical issues involved in selecting a therapist.

REVIEW of Key Points

15.23 Our discussion of psychotherapy highlighted the value of theoretical diversity. Conflicting theoretical orientations have generated varied approaches to treatment. Our coverage of therapy also showed once again that cultural factors shape psychological processes.

PERSONAL APPLICATION

Looking for a Therapist

Key Learning Goals

15.24 Discuss where to seek therapy and the potential importance of a therapist's sex and professional background.

15.25 Evaluate the importance of a therapist's theoretical approach.

15.26 Summarize what one should look for in a prospective therapist and what one should expect out of therapy.

Answer the following "true" or "false."

_____ **1** Psychotherapy is an art as well as a science.

_____ **2** Psychotherapy can be harmful or damaging to a client.

_____ **3** Psychotherapy does not have to be expensive.

_____ **4** The type of professional degree that a therapist holds is relatively unimportant.

All of these statements are true. Do any of them surprise you? If so, you're in good company. Many people know relatively little about the practicalities of selecting a therapist.

The task of finding an appropriate therapist is complex. Should you see a psychologist or psychiatrist? Should you opt for indi-

vidual therapy or group therapy? Should you see a client-centered therapist or a behavior therapist? The unfortunate part of this situation is that people seeking psychotherapy often feel overwhelmed by personal difficulties. The last thing they need is to be confronted by yet another complex problem.

Nonetheless, the importance of finding a good therapist cannot be overestimated. Treatment can sometimes have harmful rather than helpful effects. We have already discussed how drug therapies and ECT can sometimes be damaging, but problems are not limited to these interventions. Talking about your problems with a therapist may sound harmless, but studies indicate that insight therapies can also backfire (Lambert & Ogles, 2004; Lilienfeld, 2007). Although a great many talented therapists are available, psychotherapy, like any other profession, has incompetent practitioners as well. Therefore, you should shop for a skilled therapist, just as you would for a good attorney or a good mechanic.

In this application, we'll go over some information that should be helpful if you ever have to look for a therapist for yourself or for a friend or family member (based on

Beutler, Bongar, & Shurkin, 2001; Ehrenberg & Ehrenberg, 1994; Pittman, 1994).

Where Do You Find Therapeutic Services?

Psychotherapy can be found in a variety of settings. Contrary to general belief, most therapists are not in private practice. Many work in institutional settings such as community mental health centers, hospitals, and human service agencies. The principal sources of therapeutic services are described in Table 15.2. The exact configuration of therapeutic services available will vary from one community to another. To find out what your community has to offer, it is a good idea to consult your friends, your local phone book, or your local community mental health center.

Is the Therapist's Profession or Sex Important?

Psychotherapists may be trained in psychology, psychiatry, social work, counseling, psychiatric nursing, or marriage and family therapy. Researchers have *not* found any re-

John Steinhelber, Ph.D.
Betsy V. Hand, R.N., M.S.
John E. Johnson D.D.S., Inc.
John F. Herschleb, D.D.S., Inc.

Vitkoff Chiropractic
Jeffrey Felix, M.A., M.F.C.C.
Scott Thompson, D.D.S.

←FIRST FLOOR REAR

David G. Levine, M.D.
Edwyne Nazarian,M.D.

Robin Gayle, Ph.D., M.F.C.C.

SECOND FLOOR

Otto Vanoni, Ph.D.
Julia Gombos, M.F.C.C.
Maggie Tuteur, M.F.C.C.
Anthony Piccione, Ph.D.
Donald Nadler, Ph.D.
Carol Freeburg, M.A., M.F.C.C.
Lawrence B. Katz, Ph.D.
Beth Becker, Ph.D.
Life After Breakfast
Warren R. Westerhoff, D.D.S.
Jeanette R. Margolin M.D., Inc.
Alva J. Ackley M.S.
Louis M. Flohr, M.D.

Max Boveri, M.S.
Jane Cunningham, M.F.C.C.
Psychological Health Center
Robert W. Lutz, Ph.D.
Ann Rivo, Ph.D.
Perry Grey, Ph.D.
Tony Sabatasso, Ph.D.
Charles R. Billings, Ph.D.
Barbara Rose Billings, D.C.H.
Penny Wright, M.S., M.F.C.
Patricia Grasso, Ph.D.
De Lima, Associates
Madeline Sheron, C.H.T.

© Tom McCarthy/SKA

Finding the right therapist is no easy task. You need to take into account the therapist's training and orientation, fees charged, and personality. An initial visit should give you a good idea of what a particular therapist is like.

liable associations between therapists' professional background and therapeutic efficacy (Beutler et al., 2004), probably because many talented therapists can be found in all of these professions. Thus, the kind of degree that a therapist holds doesn't need to be a crucial consideration in your selection process.

Whether a therapist's sex is important depends on your attitude (Nadelson, Notman, & McCarthy, 2005). If *you* feel that the therapist's sex is important, then for you it is. The therapeutic relationship must be characterized by trust and rapport. Feeling uncomfortable with a therapist of one sex or the other could inhibit the therapeutic process. Thus, you should feel free to look for a male or female therapist if you prefer to do so. This point is probably most relevant to female clients whose troubles may be related to sexism in our society (Kaplan, 1985). It is entirely reasonable for women to seek a therapist with a feminist perspective if that would make them feel more comfortable.

Speaking of sex, you should be aware that sexual exploitation is an occasional problem in the context of therapy. Studies indicate that a small minority of therapists take advantage of their clients sexually (Pope, Keith-Spiegel, & Tabachnick, 1986). These incidents almost always involve a male therapist making advances to a female client. The available evidence indicates that these sexual liaisons are usually harmful to clients (Gabbard, 1994; Williams, 1992). There are absolutely no situations in which therapist-client sexual relations are an ethical therapeutic practice. If a therapist makes sexual advances, a client should terminate treatment.

Is Treatment Always Expensive?

Psychotherapy does not have to be prohibitively expensive. Private practitioners tend to be the most expensive, charging between $75 and $140 per (50-minute) hour. These fees may seem high, but they are in line with those of similar professionals, such as dentists and attorneys. Community mental health centers and social service agencies are usually supported by tax dollars. As a result they can charge lower fees than most therapists in private practice. Many of these organizations use a sliding scale, so that clients are charged according to how much they can afford to pay. Thus, most communities have inexpensive opportunities for psychotherapy. Moreover, most health insurance plans and HMOs provide coverage for at least some forms of mental health care.

Is the Therapist's Theoretical Approach Important?

Logically, you might expect that the diverse approaches to therapy ought to vary

Table 15.2 Principal Sources of Therapeutic Services

Source	Comments
Private practitioners	Self-employed therapists are listed in the Yellow Pages under their professional category, such as psychologists or psychiatrists. Private practitioners tend to be relatively expensive, but they also tend to be highly experienced therapists.
Community mental health centers	Community mental health centers have salaried psychologists, psychiatrists, and social workers on staff. The centers provide a variety of services and often have staff available on weekends and at night to deal with emergencies.
Hospitals	Several kinds of hospitals provide therapeutic services. There are both public and private mental hospitals that specialize in the care of people with psychological disorders. Many general hospitals have a psychiatric ward, and those that do not usually have psychiatrists and psychologists on staff and on call. Although hospitals tend to concentrate on in-patient treatment, many provide outpatient therapy as well.
Human service agencies	Various social service agencies employ therapists to provide short-term counseling. Depending on your community, you may find agencies that deal with family problems, juvenile problems, drug problems, and so forth.
Schools and workplaces	Most high schools and colleges have counseling centers where students can get help with personal problems. Similarly, some large businesses offer in-house counseling to their employees.

in their effectiveness. For the most part, this is *not* what researchers find, however. After reviewing many studies of therapeutic efficacy, Jerome Frank (1961) and Lester Luborsky and his colleagues (1975) both quote the dodo bird who has just judged a race in *Alice in Wonderland:* "*Everybody* has won, and *all* must have prizes." Improvement rates for various theoretical orientations usually come out pretty close in most studies (Lambert & Bergin, 2004; Luborsky et al., 2002; Wampold, 2001; see **Figure 15.20**).

However, these findings are a little misleading, as the estimates of overall effectiveness have been averaged across many types of patients and many types of problems. Most experts seem to think that *for certain types of problems, some approaches to therapy are more effective than others* (Beutler, 2002; Crits-Christoph, 1997; Norcross, 1995). For example, Martin Seligman (1995) asserts that panic disorders respond best to cognitive therapy, that specific phobias are most amenable to treatment with systematic desensitization, and that obsessive-compulsive disorders are best treated with behavior therapy or medication. Thus, for a specific type of problem, a therapist's theoretical approach *may* make a difference.

It is also important to point out that the finding that different approaches to therapy are roughly equal in overall efficacy does not mean that all *therapists* are created equal. Some therapists unquestionably

© Ilan Rosen/Alamy

Therapy is both a science and an art. It is scientific in that practitioners are guided in their work by a huge body of empirical research. It is an art in that therapists often have to be creative in adapting their treatment procedures to individual patients and their idiosyncrasies.

are more effective than others. However, these variations in effectiveness appear to depend on individual therapists' personal skills rather than on their theoretical orientation (Beutler et al., 2004). Good, bad, and mediocre therapists are found within each school of thought.

The key point is that effective therapy requires skill and creativity. Arnold Lazarus,

who devised multimodal therapy, emphasizes that therapists "straddle the fence between science and art." Therapy is scientific in that interventions are based on extensive theory and empirical research (Forsyth & Strong, 1986). Ultimately, though, each client is a unique human being, and the therapist has to creatively fashion a treatment program that will help that individual.

Figure 15.20

Estimates of the effectiveness of various approaches to psychotherapy. Smith and Glass (1977) reviewed nearly 400 studies in which clients who were treated with a specific type of therapy were compared with a control group made up of individuals with similar problems who went untreated. The bars indicate the percentile rank (on outcome measures) attained by the average client treated with each type of therapy when compared to control subjects. The higher the percentile, the more effective the therapy was. As you can see, the various approaches were fairly similar in their overall effectiveness.

SOURCE: Adapted from Smith, M. L., & Glass, G. V. (1977). Meta-analysis of psychotherapy outcome series. *American Psychologist, 32,* 752–760. Copyright © 1977 by the American Psychological Association. Adapted by permission of the author.

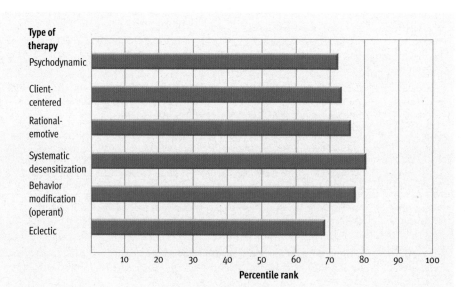

What Should You Look For in a Prospective Therapist?

Some clients are timid about asking prospective therapists questions about their training, approach, fees, and so forth. However, these are reasonable questions, and the vast majority of therapists will be most accommodating in providing answers. Usually, you can ask your preliminary questions over the phone. If things seem promising, you may decide to make an appointment for an interview (for which you will probably have to pay). In this interview, the therapist will gather more information to determine the likelihood of helping you, given his or her training and approach to treatment. At the same time, you should be making a similar judgment about whether *you* believe the therapist can help you with your problems.

What should you look for? First, you should look for personal warmth and sincere concern. Try to judge whether you will be able to talk to this person in a candid, nondefensive way. Second, look for empathy and understanding. Is the person capable of appreciating your point of view? Third, look for self-confidence. Self-assured therapists will communicate a sense of competence without trying to intimidate you with jargon or boasting needlessly about what they can do for you. When all is said and done, you should *like* your therapist. Otherwise, it will be difficult to establish the needed rapport.

What Is Therapy Like?

It is important to have realistic expectations about therapy, or you may be unnecessarily disappointed. Some people expect miracles. They expect to turn their life around quickly with little effort. Others expect their therapist to run their lives for them. These are unrealistic expectations.

Therapy is usually a slow process. Your problems are not likely to melt away quickly. Moreover, therapy is hard work, and your therapist is only a facilitator. Ultimately, *you* have to confront the challenge of changing your behavior, your feelings, or your personality. This process may not be pleasant. You may have to face up to some painful truths about yourself. As Ehrenberg and Ehrenberg (1986) point out, "Psychotherapy takes time, effort, and courage."

REVIEW of Key Points

15.24 Therapeutic services are available in many settings, and such services need not be expensive. Both excellent and mediocre therapists can be found in all of the mental health professions. Thus, therapists' personal skills are more important than their professional degree. Whether a therapist's sex is important depends on the client's attitude.

15.25 The various theoretical approaches to therapy appear to be fairly similar in overall effectiveness. However, for certain types of problems, some approaches are probably more effective than others, and all therapists are not created equal.

15.26 In selecting a therapist, warmth, empathy, confidence, and likability are desirable traits. It is important to have realistic expectations about therapy. Therapy tends to be a slow, challenging process requiring hard work.

From Crisis to Wellness—But Was It the Therapy?

Key Learning Goals

15.27 Understand how placebo effects and regression toward the mean can complicate the evaluation of therapy.

It often happens this way. Problems seem to go from bad to worse—the trigger could be severe pressures at work, an acrimonious fight with your spouse, or a child's unruly behavior spiraling out of control. At some point, you recognize that it might be prudent to seek professional assistance from a therapist, but where do you turn? If you are like most people, you will probably hesitate before actively seeking professional help. People hesitate because therapy carries a stigma, because the task of finding a therapist is daunting, and because they hope that their psychological problems will clear up on their own—which *does* happen with some regularity. When people finally decide to pursue mental health care, it is often because they feel like they have reached rock bottom in terms of their functioning and they have no choice. Motivated by their crisis, they enter into treatment, looking for a ray of hope. Will therapy help them feel better?

It may surprise you to learn that the answer *generally* would be "yes," even if professional treatment itself were utterly worthless and totally ineffectual. There are two major reasons that people entering therapy are likely to get better, regardless of whether their treatment is effective. You can probably guess one of these reasons, which has been mentioned repeatedly in the chapter: the power of the *placebo*. **Placebo effects occur when people's expectations lead them to experience some change even though they receive a fake treatment** (like getting a sugar pill instead of a real drug). Clients generally enter therapy with expectations that it will have positive effects, and as we have emphasized throughout this text, *people have a remarkable tendency to see what they expect to see.* Because of this factor, studies of the efficacy of medical drugs always include a placebo condition in which subjects are given fake medication (see Chapter 2). Researchers are often quite surprised

by just how much the placebo subjects improve (Fisher & Greenberg, 1997; Walsh et al., 2002). Placebo effects can be powerful and should be taken into consideration whenever efforts are made to evaluate the efficacy of some approach to treatment.

The other factor at work is the main focus in this Application. It is an interesting statistical phenomenon that we have not discussed previously: *regression toward the mean.* **Regression toward the mean occurs when people who score extremely high or low on some trait are measured a second time and their new scores fall closer to the mean (average).** Regression effects work in both directions: On the second measurement high scorers tend to fall back toward the mean and low scorers tend to creep upward toward the mean. For example, let's say we wanted to evaluate the effectiveness of a one-day coaching program intended to improve performance on the SAT test. We reason that coaching is most likely to help students who have performed poorly on the test, so we recruit a sample of high school students who have previously scored in the bottom 20% on the SAT. Thanks to regression toward the mean, most of these students will score higher if they take the SAT a second time, so our coaching program may *look* effective even if it has no value. By the way, if we set out to see whether our coaching program could increase the performance of high scorers, regression effects would be working *against* us. If we recruited a sample of students who had scored in the upper 20% on the SAT, their scores would

tend to move downward when tested a second time, which could cancel out most or all of the beneficial effects of the coaching program. The processes underlying regression toward the mean are complex matters of probability, but they can be approximated by a simple principle: If you are near the bottom, there's almost nowhere to go but up, and if you are near the top, there's almost nowhere to go but down.

What does all of this have to do with the effects of professional treatment for psychological problems and disorders? Well, chance variations in the ups and downs of life occur for all of us. But recall that most people enter psychotherapy during a time of severe crisis, when they are at a really low point in their lives. If you measure the

Placebo effects and regression toward the mean are two prominent factors that make it difficult to evaluate the efficacy of various approaches to therapy.

mental health of a group of people entering therapy, they will mostly get relatively low scores. If you measure their mental health again a few months later, chances are that most of them will score higher—with or without therapy—because of regression toward the mean. This is not a matter of idle speculation. Studies of untreated subjects demonstrate that poor scores on measures of mental health regress toward the mean when participants are assessed a second time (Flett, Vredenburg, & Krames, 1995; Hsu, 1995).

Does the fact that most people will get better even without therapy mean that there is no sound evidence that psychotherapy works? No, regression effects, along with placebo effects, do create major headaches for researchers evaluating the efficacy of various therapies, but these problems *can* be circumvented. Control groups, random assignment, placebo conditions, and statistical adjustments can be used to control for regression and placebo effects, as well as for other threats to validity. As discussed in the main body of the chapter, researchers have accumulated rigorous evidence that most approaches to therapy have demonstrated efficacy. However, our discussion of placebo and regression effects shows you some of the factors that make this type of research far more complicated and challenging than might be anticipated.

Recognizing how regression toward the mean can occur in a variety of contexts is an important critical thinking skill, so let's look at some additional examples. Think about an outstanding young pro baseball player who has a fabulous first season and is named "Rookie of the Year." What sort of performance would you predict for this athlete for the next year? Before you make

Placebo effects and regression toward the mean can help explain why phony, worthless treatments can have sincere supporters who really believe that the bogus interventions are effective.

© Tony Freeman/PhotoEdit

your prediction, think about regression toward the mean. Statistically speaking, our Rookie of the Year is likely to perform well above average the next year, but not as well as he did in his first year. If you are a sports fan, you may recognize this pattern as the "sophomore slump." Many sports columnists have written about the sophomore slump, which they typically blame on the athlete's personality or motivation ("He got lazy,'" "He got cocky," "The money and fame went to his head," and so forth). A simple appeal to regression toward the mean could explain this sort of outcome, with no need to denigrate the personality or motivation of the athlete. Of course, sometimes the Rookie of the

Year performs even better during his second year. Thus, our baseball example can be used to emphasize an important point. Regression toward the mean is not an inevitability. It is a statistical tendency that predicts what will happen far more often than not, but it is merely a matter of probability—which means it is a much more reliable principle when applied to groups (say, the top ten rookies in a specific year) rather than to individuals.

Let's return to the world of therapy for one last thought about the significance of both regression and placebo effects. Over the years, a host of quacks, charlatans, con artists, herbalists, and faith healers have marketed and sold an endless array of worthless treatments for both psychological problems and physical maladies. In many instances, people who have been treated with these phony therapies have expressed satisfaction or even praise and gratitude. For instance, you may have heard someone sincerely rave about some herbal remedy or psychic advice that you were pretty sure was really worthless. If so, you were probably puzzled by their glowing testimonials. Well, you now have two highly plausible explanations for why people can honestly believe that they have derived great benefit from harebrained, bogus treatments: placebo effects and regression effects. The people who provide testimonials for worthless treatments may have experienced *genuine* improvements in their conditions, but those improvements were probably the result of placebo effects and regression toward the mean. Placebo and regression effects add to the many reasons that you should always be skeptical about anecdotal evidence. And they help explain why charlatans can be so successful and why unsound, ineffective treatments can have sincere proponents.

Table 15.3 Critical Thinking Skills Discussed in This Application

Skill	Description
Recognizing situations in which placebo effects might occur	The critical thinker understands that if people have expectations that a treatment will produce a certain effect, they may experience that effect even if the treatment was fake or ineffectual.
Recognizing situations in which regression toward the mean may occur	The critical thinker understands that when people are selected for their extremely high or low scores on some trait, their subsequent scores will probably fall closer to the mean.
Recognizing the limitations of anecdotal evidence	The critical thinker is wary of anecdotal evidence, which consists of personal stories used to support one's assertions. Anecdotal evidence tends to be unrepresentative, inaccurate, and unreliable.

Key Ideas

The Elements of the Treatment Process

▌ Approaches to treatment are diverse, but they can be grouped into three categories: insight therapies, behavior therapies, and biomedical therapies.

▌ Therapists come from a variety of professional backgrounds. Clinical and counseling psychologists, psychiatrists, clinical social workers, psychiatric nurses, counselors, and marriage and family therapists are key providers of therapeutic services.

Insight Therapies

▌ Insight therapies involve verbal interactions intended to enhance self-knowledge. In psychoanalysis, free association and dream analysis are used to explore the unconscious. When an analyst's probing hits sensitive areas, resistance can be expected.

▌ The transference relationship may be used to overcome this resistance so that the client can handle interpretations that lead to insight. Classical psychoanalysis is not widely practiced anymore, but Freud's legacy lives on in a rich diversity of modern psychodynamic therapies.

▌ The client-centered therapist tries to provide a supportive climate in which clients can restructure their self-concept. The process of therapy emphasizes clarification of the client's feelings and self-acceptance. Positive psychotherapy attempts to get clients to recognize their strengths, appreciate their blessings, savor positive experiences, and to find meaning in their lives.

▌ Most theoretical approaches to insight therapy have been adapted for use with groups. Evaluating the effectiveness of any approach to treatment is complex and difficult. Nonetheless, the weight of the evidence suggests that insight therapies are superior to no treatment or placebo treatment. Studies suggest that common factors make a significant contribution to the benefits of various therapies.

Behavior Therapies

▌ Behavior therapies use the principles of learning in direct efforts to change specific aspects of behavior. Wolpe's systematic desensitization is a counterconditioning treatment for phobias. In aversion therapy, a stimulus associated with an unwanted response is paired with an unpleasant stimulus in an effort to eliminate the maladaptive response.

▌ Social skills training can improve clients' interpersonal skills through shaping, modeling, and behavioral rehearsal. Beck's cognitive therapy concentrates on changing the way clients think about events in their lives. There is ample evidence that behavior therapies are effective in the treatment of a wide variety of disorders.

Biomedical Therapies

▌ Biomedical therapies are physiological interventions for psychological problems. Antianxiety drugs are used to relieve excessive apprehension. Antipsychotic drugs are used primarily in the treatment of schizophrenia. Antidepressants are used to bring people out of episodes of depression. Bipolar mood disorders are treated with lithium and other mood stabilizers.

▌ Drug therapies can be quite effective, but they have their drawbacks. All of the drugs produce problematic side effects. The adverse effects of psychiatric drugs may be underestimated because pharmaceutical research is not as impartial as it should be.

▌ Electroconvulsive therapy (ECT) is used to trigger a cortical seizure that is believed to have therapeutic value for mood disorders, especially depression. Evidence about the effectiveness and risks of ECT is contradictory. Transcranial magnetic stimulation may have value in the treatment of depression, and deep brain stimulation is being investigated as a treatment for depression and obsessive-compulsive disorder.

Current Trends and Issues in Treatment

▌ Many clinicians and their clients believe that managed care has restricted access to mental health care and undermined its quality. Combinations of insight, behavioral, and biomedical therapies are often used fruitfully in the treatment of psychological disorders. Many modern therapists are eclectic, using specific ideas, techniques, and strategies gleaned from a number of theoretical approaches.

▌ Because of cultural, language, and access barriers, therapeutic services are underutilized by ethnic minorities in America. However, the crux of the problem is the failure of institutions to provide culturally sensitive and responsive forms of treatment for ethnic minorities.

Institutional Treatment in Transition

▌ Disenchantment with the negative effects of mental hospitals led to the advent of more localized community mental health centers and a policy of deinstitutionalization. Long-term hospitalization for mental disorders is largely a thing of the past.

▌ Unfortunately, deinstitutionalization has left some unanticipated problems in its wake, such as the revolving door problem and increased homelessness. However, many theorists believe that homelessness is primarily an economic problem.

Reflecting on the Chapter's Themes

▌ Our discussion of psychotherapy highlighted the value of theoretical diversity. Conflicting theoretical orientations have generated varied approaches to treatment. Our coverage of therapy also showed once again that cultural factors shape psychological processes.

PERSONAL APPLICATION Looking for a Therapist

▌ Therapeutic services are available in many settings, and such services need not be expensive. Excellent therapists and mediocre therapists can be found in all of the mental health professions, using the full range of therapeutic approaches.

▌ In selecting a therapist, you should look for warmth, empathy, confidence, and likability, and it is reasonable to insist on a therapist of one sex or the other. Therapy is often a difficult, gradual process that usually requires hard work.

CRITICAL THINKING APPLICATION From Crisis to Wellness—But Was It the Therapy?

▌ People entering therapy are likely to get better even if their treatment is ineffective, because of placebo effects and regression toward the mean.

▌ Regression toward the mean occurs when people selected for their extremely high or low scores on some trait are measured a second time and their new scores fall closer to the mean. Regression and placebo effects may also help explain why people can often be deceived by phony, ineffectual treatments.

Key Terms

Antianxiety drugs (p. 638)
Antidepressant drugs (p. 639)
Antipsychotic drugs (p. 639)
Aversion therapy (p. 635)
Behavior therapies (pp. 633–634)
Biomedical therapies (p. 638)
Client-centered therapy (p. 628)
Clinical psychologists (p. 624)
Cognitive-behavioral treatments (p. 636)
Cognitive therapy (p. 636)
Counseling psychologists (p. 624)
Deep brain stimulation (DBS) (p. 644)
Deinstitutionalization (pp. 651–652)
Dream analysis (p. 626)
Eclecticism (p. 649)
Electroconvulsive therapy (ECT) (p. 642)
Free association (p. 626)
Group therapy (p. 630)
Insight therapies (p. 626)
Interpretation (p. 627)
Mental hospital (p. 650)
Mood stabilizers (p. 641)
Placebo effects (p. 658)
Positive psychology (p. 630)
Psychiatrists (p. 625)
Psychoanalysis (p. 626)
Psychopharmacotherapy (p. 638)
Regression toward the mean (p. 658)
Resistance (p. 627)
Social skills training (p. 636)
Spontaneous remission (p. 632)
Systematic desensitization (p. 634)
Tardive dyskinesia (p. 639)
Transcranial magnetic stimulation (TMS) (p. 644)
Transference (p. 628)

Key People

Aaron Beck (pp. 636–637)
Dorothea Dix (pp. 650–651)
Sigmund Freud (pp. 626–628)
Carl Rogers (pp. 628–630)
Joseph Wolpe (pp. 634–635)

1. After undergoing psychoanalysis for several months, Karen has suddenly started "forgetting" to attend her therapy sessions. Karen's behavior is most likely a form of:
   A. resistance.   C. insight.
   B. transference.   D. catharsis.

2. Because Suzanne has an unconscious sexual attraction to her father, she behaves seductively toward her therapist. Suzanne's behavior is most likely a form of:
   A. resistance.
   B. transference.
   C. misinterpretation.
   D. an unconscious defense mechanism.

3. The key task of the client-centered therapist is:
   A. interpretation of the client's thoughts, feelings, memories, and behaviors.
   B. clarification of the client's feelings.
   C. confrontation of the client's irrational thoughts.
   D. modification of the client's problematic behaviors.

4. The goal of behavior therapy is to:
   A. identify the early childhood unconscious conflicts that are the source of the client's symptoms.
   B. achieve major personality reconstruction.
   C. alter the frequency of specific problematic responses by using conditioning techniques.
   D. alter the client's brain chemistry by prescribing specific drugs.

5. A therapist openly challenges a client's statement that she is a failure as a woman because her boyfriend left her, insisting that she justify it with evidence. Which type of therapy is probably being used?
   A. psychodynamic therapy   C. behavior therapy
   B. client-centered therapy   D. cognitive therapy

6. Collectively, numerous studies of therapeutic outcome suggest that:
   A. insight therapy is superior to no treatment or placebo treatment.
   B. individual insight therapy is effective, but group therapy is not.
   C. group therapy is effective, but individual insight therapy is not.
   D. insight therapy is only effective if patients are in therapy for at least two years.

7. Systematic desensitization is particularly effective for the treatment of _____ disorders.
   A. generalized anxiety   C. obsessive-compulsive
   B. panic   D. phobic

8. Linda's therapist has her practice active listening skills in structured role-playing exercises. Later, Linda is gradually asked to practice these skills with family members, friends, and finally, her boss. Linda is undergoing:
   A. systematic desensitization.   C. a token economy procedure.
   B. biofeedback.   D. social skills training.

9. After being released from a hospital, many schizophrenic patients stop taking their antipsychotic medication because:
   A. their mental impairment causes them to forget.
   B. of the unpleasant side effects.
   C. most schizophrenics don't believe they are ill.
   D. of all of the above.

10. Selective serotonin reuptake inhibitors (SSRIs) can be effective in the treatment of _____ disorders.
    A. depressive   C. obsessive-compulsive
    B. schizophrenic   D. both a and c

11. Modern psychotherapy:
    A. was spawned by a cultural milieu that viewed the self as an independent, rational being.
    B. embraces universal cultural values.
    C. has been successfully exported to many non-Western cultures.
    D. involves both b and c.

12. The community mental health movement emphasizes:
    A. segregation of the mentally ill from the general population.
    B. increased dependence on long-term inpatient care.
    C. local care and the prevention of psychological disorders.
    D. all of the above.

13. Many people repeatedly go in and out of mental hospitals. Typically, such people are released because _____; they are eventually readmitted because _____.
    A. they have been stabilized through drug therapy; their condition deteriorates once again because of inadequate outpatient care
    B. they run out of funds to pay for hospitalization; they once again can afford it
    C. they have been cured of their disorder; they develop another disorder
    D. they no longer want to be hospitalized; they voluntarily recommit themselves

14. The type of professional training a therapist has:
    A. is the most important indicator of his or her competence.
    B. should be the major consideration in choosing a therapist.
    C. is not all that important, since talented therapists can be found in all of the mental health professions.
    D. involves both a and b.

15. Which of the following could be explained by regression toward the mean?
    A. You get an average bowling score in one game and a superb score in the next game.
    B. You get an average bowling score in one game and a very low score in the next game.
    C. You get an average bowling score in one game and another average score in the next game.
    D. You get a terrible bowling score in one game and an average score in the next game.

Answers

1 A p. 627	6 A p. 632	11 A p. 649
2 B p. 628	7 D pp. 634–635	12 C p. 651
3 B pp. 629–630	8 D p. 636	13 A pp. 652–653
4 C pp. 633–634	9 B p. 639	14 C pp. 654–655
5 D pp. 636–637	10 D p. 640	15 D pp. 658–659

PsykTrek

To view a demo: www.cengage.com/psychology/psyktrek
To order: www.cengage.com/psychology/weiten

Go to the PsykTrek website or CD-ROM for further study of the concepts in this chapter. Both online and on the CD-ROM, PsykTrek includes dozens of learning modules with videos, animations, and quizzes, as well as simulations of psychological phenomena and a multimedia glossary that includes word pronunciations.

CengageNow

www.cengage.com/tlc

Go to this site for the link to CengageNOW, your one-stop study shop. Take a Pretest for this chapter, and CengageNOW will generate a personalized Study Plan based on your test results. The Study Plan will identify the topics you need to review and direct you to online resources to help you master those topics. You can then take a Posttest to help you determine the concepts you have mastered and what you still need to work on.

Companion Website

www.cengage.com/psychology/weiten

Go to this site to find online resources directly linked to your book, including a glossary, flash cards, drag-and-drop exercises, quizzes, and more!

16 SOCIAL BEHAVIOR

Person Perception: Forming Impressions of Others
Effects of Physical Appearance
Stereotypes
Subjectivity in Person Perception
An Evolutionary Perspective on Bias in Person Perception

Attribution Processes: Explaining Behavior
Internal Versus External Attributions
Attributions for Success and Failure
Bias in Attribution
Culture and Attributional Tendencies

Close Relationships: Liking and Loving
Key Factors in Attraction
Perspectives on the Mystery of Love
Culture and Close Relationships
The Internet and Close Relationships
An Evolutionary Perspective on Attraction

Attitudes: Making Social Judgments
Components and Dimensions of Attitudes
Attitudes and Behavior
Trying to Change Attitudes: Factors in Persuasion
Theories of Attitude Formation and Change

Conformity and Obedience: Yielding to Others
Conformity
Obedience

FEATURED STUDY ❚ "I Was Just Following Orders"
Cultural Variations in Conformity and Obedience
The Power of the Situation: The Stanford Prison Simulation

Behavior in Groups: Joining with Others
Behavior Alone and in Groups: The Case of the Bystander Effect
Group Productivity and Social Loafing
Decision Making in Groups

Reflecting on the Chapter's Themes

PERSONAL APPLICATION ❚ **Understanding Prejudice**
Stereotyping and Subjectivity in Person Perception
Biases in Attribution
Forming and Preserving Prejudicial Attitudes
Competition Between Groups
Dividing the World into Ingroups and Outgroups
Threats to Social Identity

CRITICAL THINKING APPLICATION ❚ **Whom Can You Trust?**
Analyzing Credibility and Influence Tactics
Evaluating Credibility
Recognizing Social Influence Strategies

Recap

Practice Test

When Muffy, "the quintessential yuppie," met Jake, "the ultimate working-class stiff," her friends got very nervous.

Muffy is a 28-year-old stockbroker and a self-described "snob" with a group of about ten close women friends. Snobs all. They're graduates of fancy business schools. All consultants, investment bankers, and CPAs. All "cute, bright, fun to be with, and really intelligent," according to Muffy. They're all committed to their high-powered careers, but they all expect to marry someday, too.

Unfortunately, most of them don't date much. In fact, they spend a good deal of time "lamenting the dearth of 'good men'" Well, lucky Muffy actually met one of those "good men." Jake is a salesman. He comes from a working-class neighborhood. His clothes come from Sears.

He wasn't like the usual men Muffy dated. He treats Muffy the way she's always dreamed of being treated. He listens; he cares; he remembers. "He makes me feel safe and more cherished than any man I've ever known," she says.

So she decided to bring him to a little party of about 30 of her closest friends. . . .

Perhaps it was only Jake's nerves that caused him to commit some truly unforgivable faux pas that night. His sins were legion. Where do we start? First of all, he asked for a beer when everyone else was drinking white wine. He wore a worn turtleneck while everyone else had just removed the Polo tags from their clothing. He smoked. . . .

"The next day at least half of the people who had been at the party called to give me their impressions. They all said that they felt they just had to let me know that they thought Jake 'lacked polish' or 'seemed loud' or 'might not be a suitable match,'" Muffy says.

Now, you may think that Muffy's friends are simply very sensitive, demanding people. But you'd be wrong. Actually, they've been quite accepting of some of the other men that Muffy has brought to their little parties. Winston, for example, was a great favorite.

"He got drunk, ignored me, and asked for other women's phone numbers right in front of me. But he was six-foot-four, the classic preppie, with blond hair, horn-rimmed glasses, and Ralph Lauren clothes."

So now Muffy is confused. "Jake is the first guy I've been out with in a long time that I've really liked. I was excited about him and my friends knew that. I was surprised by their reaction. I'll admit there's some validity in all their comments, but it's hard to express how violent it was. It made me think about what these women really want in a man. Whatever they say, what they really *want is someone they can take to a business dinner. They want someone who comes with a tux. Like a Ken doll."*

Muffy may have come to a crossroads in her young life. It's clear that there's no way she can bring Jake among her friends for a while.

"I don't want their reaction to muddy my feelings until I get them sorted out," she says.

(Excerpt from *Tales from the Front* by Cheryl Lavin and Laura Kavesh, Copyright © 1988 by Cheryl Lavin and Laura Kavesh. Used by permission of Doubleday, a division of Random House, Inc.)

The preceding account is a real story, taken from a book about contemporary intimate relationships (Lavin & Kavesh, 1988, pp. 118–121). Muffy is on the horns of a difficult dilemma. Romantic relationships are important to most people, but so are friendships, and Muffy may have to choose between the two. Muffy's story illustrates the significance of social relations in people's lives. It also foreshadows each of the topics that we'll cover in this chapter, as we look at behavior in its social context.

Social psychology is the branch of psychology concerned with the way individuals' thoughts, feelings, and behaviors are influenced by others. Our coverage of social psychology will focus on six broad topics highlighted in Muffy's story:

• *Person perception.* The crux of Muffy's problem is that Jake didn't make a very good impression on her friends, primarily because her friends have preconceived views of "working-class stiffs." To what extent do people's expectations color their impressions of others?

• *Attribution processes.* Muffy is struggling to understand her friends' rejection of Jake. When she implies that it is due to their snotty elitism, she's engaging in attribution, making an inference about the causes of her friends' behavior. How do people use attributions to explain social behavior?

• *Interpersonal attraction.* Jake and Muffy are different in many important ways—is it true that opposites attract? Why does Jake's lack of similarity to Muffy's friends lead to such disdain?

• *Attitudes.* Muffy's girlfriends have negative attitudes about working-class men. How are attitudes formed? What leads to attitude change? How do attitudes affect people's behavior?

• *Conformity and obedience.* Muffy's friends discourage her from dating Jake, putting her under pressure to conform to their values. What factors influence conformity? Can people be coaxed into doing things that contradict their values?

• *Behavior in groups.* Muffy belongs to a tight-knit group of friends who think along similar lines. Do people behave differently when they are in groups as opposed to when they are alone? Why do people in groups often think alike?

Social psychologists study how people are affected by the actual, imagined, or implied presence of others. Their interest is not limited to individuals' interactions with others, as people can engage in social behavior even when they're alone. For instance, if you were driving by yourself on a deserted highway and tossed your trash out your car window, your littering would be a social action. It would defy social norms, reflect your socialization and attitudes, and have repercussions (albeit, small) for other people in your society. Social psychologists often study individual behavior in a social context. This interest in understanding individual behavior should be readily apparent in our first section, on person perception.

Key Learning Goals

16.1 Understand how aspects of physical appearance may influence impressions of others.

16.2 Clarify how stereotyping and other factors contribute to subjectivity in person perception.

16.3 Articulate the evolutionary perspective on bias in person perception.

Person Perception: Forming Impressions of Others

Can you remember the first meeting of your introductory psychology class? What impression did your professor make on you that day? Did your instructor appear to be confident? Easygoing? Pompous? Open-minded? Cynical? Friendly? Were your first impressions supported or undermined by subsequent observations? When you interact with people, you're constantly engaged in *person perception,* **the process of forming impressions of others.** People show considerable ingenuity in piecing together clues about others' characteristics. However, impressions are often inaccurate because of the many biases and fallacies that occur in person perception. In this section we consider some of the factors that influence, and often distort, people's perceptions of others.

Effects of Physical Appearance

SIM10

"You shouldn't judge a book by its cover." People know better than to let physical attractiveness determine their perceptions of others' personal qualities.

"Beauty is life's E-Z Pass."

Or do they? One recent study showed that good-looking people grab our attention almost immediately and hold on to our attention longer than less attractive individuals do (Maner et al., 2007). And a number of studies have demonstrated that judgments of others' personality are often swayed by their appearance, especially their physical attractiveness. People tend to ascribe desirable personality characteristics to those who are good looking, seeing them as more sociable, friendly, poised, warm, and well adjusted than those who are less attractive (Eagly et al., 1991; van Leeuwen & Macrae, 2004). In reality, research findings suggest that little correlation exists between attractiveness and personality traits (Feingold, 1992). Why do we inaccurately assume that a connection exists between good looks and personality? One reason is that extremely attractive people are vastly overrepresented in the entertainment media, where they are mostly portrayed in a highly favorable light (Smith, McIntosh, & Bazzini, 1999).

You might guess that physical attractiveness would influence perceptions of competence less than perceptions of personality, but the data suggest otherwise. A thorough review of the relevant research found that people have a surprisingly strong tendency to view good-looking individuals as more competent than less attractive individuals (Langlois et al., 2000). This bias literally pays off for good-looking people, as they tend to secure better jobs and earn higher salaries than less attractive individuals (Collins & Zebrowitz, 1995; Senior et al., 2007). For example, research on attorneys whose law school class photos were evaluated by independent raters found that physical attractiveness boosted their actual income by 10%–12% (Engemann & Owyang, 2005). Fortunately, not all trait inferences are influenced by physical attractiveness. For instance, good looks seem to have relatively little impact on perceptions of honesty and integrity (Eagly et al., 1991).

Judgments of people's faces seem to be particularly important, as recent evidence suggests that these judgments are associated with significant outcomes in the real world. For example, one study found that perceptions of competence based solely on facial appearance predicted the outcomes of U.S. congressional elections surprisingly well (Todorov et al., 2005). Naive participants rated the competence of political candidates from all over the country based on brief exposures to head shots. The candidates who were viewed as more competent ended up winning 72% of Senate races and 67% of House races. In another study, participants rated the competence/power of 100 chief executive officers (CEOs) of large companies based on their facial appearance (Rule & Ambady, 2008). These ratings correlated .34 with the corporate profits of the CEOs' companies. Thus, perceptions of personality based on facial features are associated with objective measures of successful performance in important arenas of life.

Moreover, studies indicate that social perceptions based on facial appearance are formed in the blink of an eye. You might guess that people would need 20–30 seconds to size someone up, but a recent, compelling study demonstrated that it only takes a tenth of a second to draw inferences about individuals based on facial features. Willis and Todorov (2006) asked subjects to assess traits such as competence, trustworthiness, and aggressiveness based on brief exposures (1/10 of a second, half a second, or one second) to facial photographs. They compared these assessments to judgments of the same photos made by other participants who were given no time constraints and found that the instant judgments were highly correlated with the leisurely judgments. Thus, first impressions based on faces can occur almost instantly.

Stereotypes

Stereotypes can have a dramatic effect on the process of person perception. **Stereotypes are widely held beliefs that people have certain characteristics because of their membership in a particular group.** The most common stereotypes in our society are those based on sex, age, and membership in ethnic or occupational groups. People who subscribe

DILBERT

to traditional *gender stereotypes* tend to assume that women are emotional, submissive, illogical, and passive, while men are unemotional, dominant, logical, and aggressive. *Age stereotypes* suggest that elderly people are slow, feeble, rigid, forgetful, and asexual. Notions that Jews are mercenary, Germans are methodical, and Italians are passionate are examples of common *ethnic stereotypes. Occupational stereotypes* suggest that lawyers are manipulative, accountants are conforming, artists are moody, and so forth.

Stereotyping is a normal cognitive process that is usually automatic and that saves on the time and effort required to get a handle on people individually (Devine & Monteith, 1999; Operario & Fiske, 2001). Stereotypes save energy by simplifying our social world. However, this conservation of energy often comes at some cost in terms of accuracy (Wigboldus, Dijksterhuis, & Knippenberg, 2003). Stereotypes tend to be broad overgeneralizations that ignore the diversity within social groups and foster inaccurate perceptions of people (Hilton & von Hippel, 1996). Obviously, not all males, Jews, and lawyers behave alike. Most people who subscribe to stereotypes realize that not all members of a group are identical. For instance, they may admit that some men aren't competitive, some Jews aren't mercenary, and some lawyers aren't manipulative. However, they may still tend to assume that males, Jews, and lawyers are *more likely* than others to have these characteristics. Even if stereotypes mean only that people think in terms of slanted *probabilities,* their expectations may lead them to misperceive individuals with whom they interact. As we've noted in previous chapters, perception is subjective, and people often see what they expect to see.

Subjectivity in Person Perception

Stereotypes create biases in person perception that often lead to confirmation of people's expectations

about others. If someone's behavior is ambiguous, people are likely to interpret what they see in a way that's consistent with their expectations (Olson, Roese, & Zanna, 1996). Thus, after dealing with a pushy female customer, a salesman who holds traditional gender stereotypes might characterize the woman as "emotional." In contrast, he might characterize a male who exhibits the same pushy behavior as "aggressive."

People not only see what they expect to see, they also tend to overestimate how often they see it (Johnson & Mullen, 1994; Shavitt et al., 1999). *Illusory correlation* occurs when people estimate that they have encountered more confirmations of an association between social traits than they have actually seen. People also tend to underestimate the number of disconfirmations they have encountered, as illustrated by statements like "I've never met an honest lawyer." One recent study showed that it takes only one instance of unusual or memorable behavior on the part of someone from an unfamiliar group to create an illusory correlation between that behavior and that group (Risen, Gilovich, & Dunning, 2007). Thus, illusory correlations routinely make contributions to stereotypes of various groups.

Memory processes can contribute to confirmatory biases in person perception in a variety of ways. Often, individuals selectively recall facts that fit with their stereotypes (Fiske, 1998; Quinn, Macrae, & Bodenhausen, 2003). Evidence for such a tendency was found in a study by Cohen (1981). In this experiment, participants watched a videotape of a woman, described as either a waitress or a librarian, who engaged in a variety of activities, including listening to classical music, drinking beer, and watching TV. When asked to recall what the woman did during the filmed sequence, participants tended to remember activities consistent with their stereotypes of waitresses and librarians. For instance, subjects who thought the woman was a waitress tended to recall her beer drink-

web link 16.1

Social Psychology Network

Wesleyan University social psychologist Scott Plous offers a broad collection of resources related to all aspects of social (and general) psychology as well as information about careers and graduate study in this field.

ing, while subjects who thought she was a librarian tended to recall her listening to classical music.

An Evolutionary Perspective on Bias in Person Perception

Why is the process of person perception riddled with bias? Evolutionary psychologists argue that many of the biases seen in social perception were adaptive in humans' ancestral environment (Krebs & Denton, 1997). For example, they argue that person perception is swayed by physical attractiveness because attractiveness was associated with reproductive potential in women and with health, vigor, and the accumulation of material resources in men.

What about the human tendency to automatically categorize others? Evolutionary theorists attribute this behavior to our distant ancestors' need to quickly separate friend from foe. They assert that humans are programmed by evolution to immediately classify people as members of an *ingroup*—a **group that one belongs to and identifies with,** or as members of an *outgroup*—a **group that one does not belong to or identify with.** This crucial categorization is thought to structure subsequent perceptions. As Krebs and Denton (1997) put it, "It is as though the act of classifying others as ingroup or outgroup members activates two quite different brain circuits" (p. 27). In-group members tend to be viewed in a favorable light, whereas outgroup members tend to be viewed in terms of various negative stereotypes. According to Krebs and Denton, these negative stereotypes ("They are inferior; they are all alike; they will exploit us") move outgroups out of our domain of empathy, so we feel justified in not liking them or discriminating against them.

Thus, evolutionary psychologists ascribe much of the bias in person perception to cognitive mechanisms that have been shaped by natural selection. Their speculation is thought provoking, but empirical work is needed to test their hypotheses.

> **REVIEW of Key Learning Goals**
>
> **16.1** People's perceptions of a person can be distorted by his or her physical appearance. People tend to attribute desirable characteristics, such as intelligence, competence, warmth, and friendliness, to those who are good looking. Perceptions of competence based on facial appearance are particularly important. Social perceptions based on facial features can be formed in the blink of an eye.
>
> **16.2** Stereotypes are widely held beliefs that others will have certain characteristics because of their membership in a specific group. Gender, age, ethnic, and occupational stereotypes are common. In interacting with others, stereotypes may lead people to see what they expect to see. People also tend to overestimate how often their expectations are confirmed, a phenomenon called the illusory correlation effect.
>
> **16.3** Evolutionary psychologists argue that many biases in person perception were adaptive in humans' ancestral past. The human tendency to automatically categorize others may reflect the primitive need to quickly separate friend from foe.

Attribution Processes: Explaining Behavior

It's Friday evening and you're sitting around at home feeling bored. You call a few friends to see whether they'd like to go out. They all say that they'd love to go, but they have other commitments and can't. Their commitments sound vague, and you feel that their reasons for not going out with you are rather flimsy. How do you explain these rejections? Do your friends really have commitments? Are they worn out by school and work? When they said that they'd love to go, were they being sincere? Or do they find you boring? Could they be right? Are you boring? These questions illustrate a process that people engage in routinely: the explanation of behavior. *Attributions* play a key role in these explanatory efforts, and they have significant effects on social relations.

What are attributions? *Attributions* **are inferences that people draw about the causes of events,** others' behavior, and their own behavior. If you conclude that a friend turned down your invitation because she's overworked, you have made an attribution about the cause of her behavior (and, implicitly, have rejected other possible explanations). If you conclude that you're stuck at home with nothing to do because you failed to plan ahead, you've made an attribution about the cause of an event (being stuck at home). If you conclude that you failed to plan ahead because you're a procrastinator, you've made an attribution about the cause of your own behavior. People make attributions mainly because they have a strong need to understand their experiences. They want to make sense out of their own behavior, others' actions, and the events in their lives. In this section, we'll take a look at some of the patterns seen when people make attributions.

Key Learning Goals

16.4 Explain what attributions are, and distinguish between internal and external attributions.

16.5 Summarize Weiner's theory of attributions for success and failure.

16.6 Identify several types of bias in patterns of attribution.

16.7 Describe cultural variations in attributional tendencies.

Fritz Heider

"Often the momentary situation which, at least in part, determines the behavior of a person is disregarded and the behavior is taken as a manifestation of personal characteristics."

Internal Versus External Attributions

12a

Fritz Heider (1958) was the first to describe how people make attributions. He asserted that people tend to locate the cause of behavior either *within a person*, attributing it to personal factors, or *outside a person*, attributing it to environmental factors.

Elaborating on Heider's insight, various theorists have agreed that explanations of behavior and events can be categorized as internal or external attributions (Jones & Davis, 1965; Kelley, 1967; Weiner, 1974). *Internal attributions* ascribe the causes of behavior to personal dispositions, traits, abilities, and feelings. *External attributions* ascribe the causes of behavior to situational demands and environmental constraints. For example, if a friend's business fails, you might attribute it to his or her lack of business acumen (an internal, personal factor) or to negative trends in the nation's economic climate (an external, situational explanation). Parents who find out that their teenage son has just banged up the car may blame it on his carelessness (a personal disposition) or on slippery road conditions (a situational factor).

Internal and external attributions can have a tremendous impact on everyday interpersonal interactions. Blaming a friend's business failure on poor business acumen as opposed to a poor economy will have a great impact on how you view your friend.

Likewise, if parents attribute their son's automobile accident to slippery road conditions, they're likely to deal with the event very differently than if they attribute it to his carelessness.

Attributions for Success and Failure

12a

Some psychologists have sought to discover additional dimensions of attributional thinking besides the internal-external dimension. After studying the attributions that people make in explaining success and failure, Bernard Weiner (1980, 1986, 1994) concluded that people often focus on the *stability* of the causes underlying behavior. According to Weiner, the stable-unstable dimension in attribution cuts across the internal-external dimension, creating four types of attributions for success and failure, as shown in Figure 16.1.

Let's apply Weiner's model to a concrete event. Imagine that you're contemplating why you failed to get a job that you wanted. You might attribute your setback to internal factors that are stable (lack of ability) or unstable (inadequate effort to put together an eye-catching résumé). Or you might attribute your setback to external factors that are stable (too much outstanding competition) or unstable (bad luck). If you got the job, your explanations for your success would fall into the same four categories: internal-stable (your excellent ability), internal-unstable (your hard work to assemble a superb résumé), external-stable (lack of top-flight competition), and external-unstable (good luck).

Bias in Attribution

12a

Attributions are only inferences. Your attributions may not be the correct explanations for events. Paradoxical as it may seem, people often arrive at inaccurate explanations even when they contemplate the causes of *their own behavior*. Attributions ultimately represent *guesswork* about the causes of events, and these guesses tend to be slanted in certain directions. Let's look at the principal biases seen in attribution.

Actor-Observer Bias

12a

Your view of your own behavior can be quite different from the view of someone else observing you. When an actor and an observer draw inferences about the causes of the actor's behavior, they often make different attributions. A common form of bias seen in observers is the *fundamental attribution error,* which refers to observers' bias in favor of

---

concept check 16.1

Analyzing Attributions

Check your understanding of attribution processes by analyzing possible explanations for an athletic team's success. Imagine that the women's track team at your school has just won a regional championship that qualifies it for the national tournament. Around the campus, you hear people attribute the team's success to a variety of factors. Examine the attributions shown below and place each of them in one of the cells of Weiner's model of attribution (just record the letter inside the cell). The answers are in Appendix A.

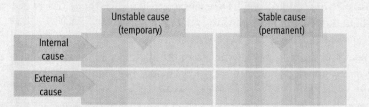

	Unstable cause (temporary)	Stable cause (permanent)
Internal cause		
External cause		

a. "They won only because the best two athletes on Central State's team were out with injuries—talk about good fortune!"

b. "They won because they have some of the best talent in the country."

c. "Anybody could win this region; the competition is far below average in comparison to the rest of the country."

d. "They won because they put in a great deal of last-minute effort and practice, and they were incredibly fired up for the regional tourney after last year's near-miss."

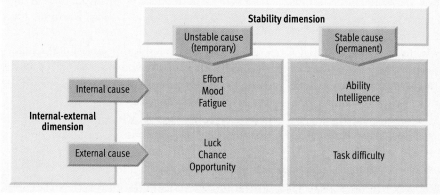

Stability dimension

Figure 16.1

Weiner's model of attributions for success and failure. Weiner's model assumes that people's explanations for success and failure emphasize internal versus external causes and stable versus unstable causes. Examples of causal factors that fit into each of the four cells in Weiner's model are shown in the diagram.

SOURCE: Weiner, B., Friese, I., Kukla, A., Reed, L., & Rosenbaum, R. M. (1972). Perceiving the causes of success and failure. In E. E. Jones, D. E. Kanouse, H. H. Kelley, R. E. Nisbett, S. Valins, & B. Weiner (Eds.), *Perceiving the causes of behavior.* Morristown, NJ: General Learning Press. Used by permission of Bernard Weiner.

internal attributions in explaining others' behavior. Of course, in many instances, an internal attribution may not be an "error." However, observers have a curious tendency to overestimate the likelihood that an actor's behavior reflects personal qualities rather than situational factors (Krull, 2001). Why? One reason is that situational pressures may not be readily apparent to an observer. As Gilbert and Malone (1995) put it, "When one tries to point to a situation, one often stabs empty air" (p. 25). It is not that people assume that situational factors have little impact on behavior (Gawronski, 2004). Rather, it's that attributing others' behavior to their dispositions is a relatively effortless, almost automatic process, whereas explaining people's behavior in terms of situational factors requires more thought and effort (see **Figure 16.2**; Krull & Erickson, 1995). Another factor favoring internal attributions is that many people feel that few situations are so coercive that they negate all freedom of choice (Forsyth, 2004).

To illustrate the gap that often exists between actors' and observers' attributions, imagine that you're visiting your bank and you fly into a rage over a mistake made on your account. Observers who witness your rage are likely to make an internal attribution and infer that you are surly, temperamental, and quarrelsome. They may be right, but if asked, you'd probably attribute your rage to the frustrating situation. Perhaps you're normally a calm, easygoing person, but today you've been in line for 20 minutes, you just straightened out a similar error by the same bank last week, and you're being treated rudely by the teller. Observers are often unaware of historical and situational considerations such as these, so they tend to make internal attributions for another's behavior (Gilbert, 1998).

In contrast, the circumstances that have influenced an actor's behavior tend to be more apparent to the actor. Hence, actors are more likely than observers to locate the cause of their behavior in the situa-

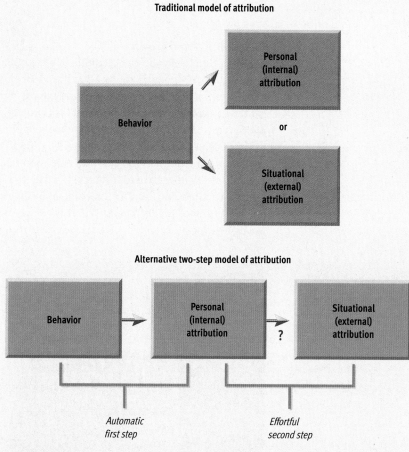

Figure 16.2

An alternative view of the fundamental attribution error. According to Gilbert (1989) and others, the nature of attribution processes favors the *fundamental attribution error.* Traditional models of attribution assume that internal and external attributions are an either-or proposition requiring equal amounts of effort. In contrast, Gilbert maintains that people tend to automatically make internal attributions with little effort, and then they *may* expend additional effort to adjust for the influence of situational factors, which can lead to an external attribution. Thus, external attributions for others' behavior require more thought and effort, which makes them less common than personal attributions.

tion. In general, then, *actors favor external attributions for their behavior, whereas observers are more likely to explain the same behavior with internal attributions* (Jones & Nisbett, 1971; Krueger, Ham, & Linford, 1996).

That said, a recent study identified an interesting variable that appears to reduce observers' tendency to explain actors' behavior with internal attributions. That variable is whether the observers have experienced the same situation themselves (Balcetis & Dunning, 2008). Dealing with a specific situation gives people an opportunity to learn about the power of external forces in that situation. This knowledge makes them less likely to commit the fundamental attribution error in interpreting the behavior of others in the same situation. For example, people who have been tricked by a con artist, or who have suffered through a foreclosure, generally will be less likely to make internal attributions in explaining why others have experienced a similar fate.

Defensive Attribution 12a

In attempting to explain the calamities and setbacks that befall other people, an observer's tendency to make internal attributions may become even stronger than normal. Let's say that a friend gets mugged and severely beaten. You may attribute the mugging to your friend's carelessness or stupidity ("He should have known better than to be in that neighborhood at that time") rather than to bad luck. Why? Because if you attribute your friend's misfortune to bad luck, you have to face the ugly reality that it could just as easily happen to you. To avoid such disturbing thoughts, people often attribute mishaps to victims' negligence (Idisis, Ben-David, & Ben-Nachum, 2007; Salminen, 1992; Thornton, 1992).

Defensive attribution **is a tendency to blame victims for their misfortune, so that one feels less likely to be victimized in a similar way.** *Hindsight bias* probably contributes to this tendency, but blaming victims also helps people maintain their belief that they live in a just world, where they're unlikely to experience similar troubles (Lerner & Goldberg, 1999). The bias toward making defensive attributions can have unfortunate consequences. Blaming victims for their setbacks causes them to be seen in a negative light, and undesirable traits are unfairly attributed to them. Thus, it is assumed that burglary victims must be careless, that people who get fired must be incompetent, that poor people must be lazy, that rape victims must be seductive ("She probably asked for it"), and so on. As you can see, defensive attribution can lead to unwarranted derogation of victims of misfortune.

Self-Serving Bias 12a

The self-serving bias in attribution comes into play when people attempt to explain success and failure. This bias may either strengthen or weaken one's normal attributional tendencies, depending on whether one is trying to explain positive or negative

A common example of defensive attribution is the tendency to blame the homeless for their plight.

© Mark Peterson/Corbis

outcomes (Mezulis et al., 2004; Shepperd, Malone, & Sweeny, 2008). The *self-serving bias* is the tendency to attribute one's successes to personal factors and one's failures to situational factors. Interestingly, this bias grows stronger as time passes after an event, so that people tend to take progressively more credit for their successes and less responsibility for their failures (Burger, 1986). *In explaining failure, the usual actor-observer biases are apparent.* Actors tend to blame failures on unfavorable situational factors, while observers are more likely to attribute the same failures to the actors' personal shortcomings. *In explaining success, the usual actor-observer differences are reversed to some degree.* Actors make internal attributions to take credit for their accomplishments, whereas observers are more likely to assume that the actor benefited from favorable situational factors.

Culture and Attributional Tendencies

Do the patterns of attribution observed in subjects from Western societies transcend culture? More research is needed, but the preliminary evidence suggests not. Some interesting cultural disparities have emerged in research on attribution processes.

According to Harry Triandis (1989, 1994, 2001), cultural differences in *individualism* versus *collectivism* influence attributional tendencies as well as other aspects of social behavior. As noted in Chapter 12, *individualism* involves putting personal goals ahead of group goals and defining one's identity in terms of personal attributes rather than group memberships. In contrast, *collectivism* involves putting group goals ahead of personal goals and defining one's identity in terms of the groups one belongs to (such as one's family, tribe, work group, social class, and so on). In comparison to individualistic cultures, collectivist cultures place a higher priority on shared values and resources, cooperation, mutual interdependence, and concern for how one's actions will affect other group members. In childrearing, collectivist cultures emphasize the importance of obedience, reliability, and proper behavior, whereas individualistic cultures emphasize the development of independence, self-esteem, and self-reliance.

A variety of factors influence whether societies cherish individualism as opposed to collectivism. Among other things, increases in a culture's affluence, education, urbanization, and social mobility tend to foster more individualism (Triandis, 1994). Many contemporary societies are in transition, but generally speaking, North American and Western European cultures tend to be individualistic, whereas Asian, African, and Latin American cultures

Hofstede's rankings of national cultures' individualism		
Individualistic cultures	**Intermediate cultures**	**Collectivist cultures**
1. United States	19. Israel	37. Hong Kong
2. Australia	20. Spain	38. Chile
3. Great Britain	21. India	40. Singapore
4. Canada	22. Argentina	40. Thailand
4. Netherlands	22. Japan	40. West Africa region
6. New Zealand	24. Iran	42. El Salvador
7. Italy	25. Jamaica	43. South Korea
8. Belgium	26. Arab region	44. Taiwan
9. Denmark	26. Brazil	45. Peru
10. France	28. Turkey	46. Costa Rica
11. Sweden	29. Uruguay	47. Indonesia
12. Ireland	30. Greece	47. Pakistan
13. Norway	31. Philippines	49. Colombia
14. Switzerland	32. Mexico	50. Venezuela
15. West Germany	34. East Africa region	51. Panama
16. South Africa	34. Portugal	52. Ecuador
17. Finland	34. Yugoslavia	53. Guatemala
18. Austria	36. Malaysia	

tend to be collectivistic (Hofstede, 1980, 1983, 2001) (see Figure 16.3).

How does individualism versus collectivism relate to patterns of attribution? The evidence suggests that collectivist cultures may promote different attributional biases than individualistic cultures. For example, people from collectivist societies appear to be less prone to the *fundamental attribution error* than those from individualistic societies (Choi, Nisbett, & Norenzayan, 1999; Triandis, 2001). In Western cultures, people are viewed as autonomous individuals who are responsible for their actions. Endorsing beliefs such as "You can do anything you put your mind to" or "You have no one to blame but yourself," Westerners typically explain behavior in terms of people's personality traits and unique abilities. In contrast, collectivists, who value interdependence and obedience, are more likely to assume that one's behavior reflects adherence to group norms.

Research suggests that Asians view events in the context of webs of interdependent social relationships. This holistic perception of the world leads them to make more complex causal attributions than Westerners. This way of thinking also tends to make Asians more aware of the sometimes indirect and distant consequences of events, what one might refer to as unexpected *ripple effects* (Maddux & Yuki, 2006). For example, when asked about the consequences of a specific event, such as being laid off or being in an car accident, Asian subjects estimate that far more people will be affected than Western participants do.

Although the *self-serving bias* has been documented in a variety of cultures, it is particularly prevalent in individualistic, Western societies, where

Figure 16.3

Individualism versus collectivism around the world. Hofstede (1980, 1983, 2001) used survey data from over 100,000 employees of a large, multinational corporation to estimate the emphasis on individualism versus collectivism in 50 nations and 3 regions. His large, diverse international sample remains unequaled to date. In the figure, cultures are ranked in terms of how strongly they embraced the values of individualism. As you can see, Hofstede's estimates suggest that North American and Western European nations tend to be relatively individualistic, whereas more collectivism is found in Asian, African, and Latin American countries.

SOURCE: Adapted from Hofstede, G. (2001). *Culture's consequences* (2nd Ed., p. 215). Thousand Oaks, CA: Sage. Copyright © 2001 Sage Publications. Adapted by permission of Dr. Geert Hofstede.

Recognizing Bias in Social Cognition

Check your understanding of bias in social cognition by identifying various types of errors that are common in person perception and attribution. Imagine that you're a nonvoting student member of a college committee at Southwest State University that is hiring a new political science professor. As you listen to the committee's discussion, you hear examples of (a) the illusory correlation effect, (b) stereotyping, (c) the fundamental attribution error, and (d) defensive attribution. Indicate which of these is at work in the excerpts from committee members' deliberations below. The answers are in Appendix A.

_____ 1. "I absolutely won't consider the fellow who arrived 30 minutes late for his interview. Anybody who can't make a job interview on time is either irresponsible or hopelessly disorganized. I don't care what he says about the airline messing up his reservations."

_____ 2. "You know, I was very, very impressed with the young female applicant, and I would love to hire her, but every time we add a young woman to the faculty in liberal arts, she gets pregnant within the first year." The committee chairperson, who has heard this line from this professor before replies, "You always say that, so I finally did a systematic check of what's happened in the past. Of the last 14 women hired in liberal arts, only one has become pregnant within a year."

_____ 3. "The first one I want to rule out is the guy who's been practicing law for the last ten years. Although he has an excellent background in political science, I just don't trust lawyers. They're all ambitious, power-hungry, manipulative cutthroats. He'll be a divisive force in the department."

_____ 4. "I say we forget about the two candidates who lost their faculty slots in the massive financial crisis at Western Polytechnic last year. I know it sounds cruel, but they brought it on themselves with their fiscal irresponsibility over at Western. Thank goodness we'll never let anything like that happen around here. As far as I'm concerned, if these guys couldn't see that crisis coming, they must be pretty dense."

an emphasis on competition and high self-esteem motivates people to try to impress others, as well as themselves (Mezulis et al., 2004). In contrast, Japanese subjects exhibit a *self-effacing bias* in explaining success (Akimoto & Sanbonmatsu, 1999; Markus & Kitayama, 1991), as they tend to attribute their successes to help they receive from others or to the ease of the task, while downplaying the importance of their ability. When they fail, Japanese subjects tend to be more self-critical than subjects from individualistic cultures (Heine & Renshaw, 2002).

REVIEW of Key Learning Goals

16.4 Attributions are inferences about the causes of events and behavior. Individuals make attributions to understand their social world. Attributions can be classified as internal or external. Internal attributions ascribe behavior to personal dispositions and traits, whereas external attributions locate the cause of behavior in the environment.

16.5 Weiner's model proposes that attributions for success and failure should be analyzed in terms of the stability of causes, as well as along the internal-external dimension, yielding four possible types of attributions: internal-stable, internal-unstable, external-stable, and external-unstable.

16.6 Observers favor internal attributions to explain another's behavior, which is called the fundamental attribution error, while actors favor external attributions to explain their own behavior. In defensive attribution, people unfairly blame victims for their misfortune (with internal attributions) to reduce their own feelings of vulnerability. The self-serving bias is the tendency to attribute one's good outcomes to personal factors and one's bad outcomes to situational factors.

16.7 Cultures vary in their emphasis on individualism as opposed to collectivism, and these differences appear to influence attributional tendencies. The fundamental attribution error and the self-serving bias in attribution may be more prevalent in Western cultures that are high in individualism.

Close Relationships: Liking and Loving

Key Learning Goals

16.8 Evaluate the role of physical attractiveness and similarity in attraction.

16.9 Clarify the role of reciprocity and romantic ideals in attraction.

16.10 Distinguish between passionate love and companionate love and between intimacy and commitment.

16.11 Outline the evidence on love as a form of attachment.

16.12 Discuss cultural variations in close relationships and how the Internet has affected romantic relationships.

16.13 Understand evolutionary analyses of mating preferences and tactics.

"I just don't know what she sees in him. She could do so much better for herself. I suppose he's a nice guy, but they're just not right for each other." Can't you imagine Muffy's friends making these comments in discussing her relationship with Jake? You've probably heard similar remarks on many occasions. These comments illustrate people's interest in analyzing the dynamics of attraction. *Interpersonal attraction* refers to positive feelings toward another. Social psychologists use this term broadly to encompass a variety of experiences, including liking, friendship, admiration, lust, and love. In this section, we'll analyze key factors that influence attraction and examine some theoretical perspectives on the mystery of love.

Key Factors in Attraction

Many factors influence who is attracted to whom. Here we'll discuss factors that promote the development of liking, friendship, and love. Although these are different types of attraction, the interpersonal dynamics at work in each are largely similar.

Physical Attractiveness

It is often said that "beauty is only skin deep," but the empirical evidence suggests that most people don't really believe that homily (Fitness, Fletcher, & Overall, 2003). The importance of physical attractiveness was demonstrated in a study in which unacquainted men and women were sent off on a "get-acquainted" date (Sprecher & Duck, 1994). The investigators were mainly interested in how communication might affect the process of attraction, but to put this factor in context they also measured subjects' perceptions of their date's physical attractiveness and similarity to themselves. They found that the quality of communication during the date did have some effect on females' interest in friendship, but the key determinant of romantic attraction for both sexes was the physical attractiveness of the other person. Consistent with this finding, research has shown, as one might expect, that attractive people of both sexes enjoy greater mating success than their less attractive peers (Rhodes, Simmons, & Peters, 2005). Many other studies have demonstrated the singular prominence of physical attractiveness in the initial stage of dating and have shown that it continues to influence the course of commitment as relationships evolve (McNulty, Neff, & Karney, 2008; Patzer, 2006). In the realm of romance, being physically attractive appears to be more important for females' desirability (Gottschall, 2007; Regan, 2003). For example, in a study of college students (Speed & Gangestad, 1997), the correlation between romantic popularity (assessed by peer ratings) and physical attractiveness was higher for females (.76) than for males (.47).

Although people prefer physically attractive partners in romantic relationships, they may consider their own level of attractiveness in pursuing dates. What people want in a partner may be different from what they are willing to settle for (Regan, 1998). The *matching hypothesis* **proposes that males and females of approximately equal physical attractiveness are likely to select each other as partners.** The matching hypothesis is supported by evidence that married couples tend to be very similar in level of physical attractiveness (Feingold, 1988b). Interestingly, people expect that individuals who are similar in attractiveness will be more satisfied as couples and less likely to break up (Garcia & Khersonsky, 1996), although a recent study of actual married couples failed to support this notion (McNulty et al., 2008).

Similarity Effects

Is it true that "birds of a feather flock together," or do "opposites attract"? Research provides far more support for the former than the latter. Married and dating couples tend to be similar in age, race, religion, social class, education, intelligence, physical attractiveness, values, and attitudes (Kalmijn, 1998; Watson et al., 2004). Similarity is also seen among friends. For instance, adult friends tend to be relatively similar in terms of income, education, occu-

According to the matching hypothesis, males and females who are similar in physical attractiveness are likely to be drawn together. This type of matching may also influence the formation of friendships.

pational status, ethnicity, and religion (Blieszner & Adams, 1992). Among romantic couples, similarity in *personality* appears to be modest (Luo & Klohnen, 2005). However, some couples are more similar in personality than others, and this convergence in personality does correlate moderately with relationship satisfaction (Gonzaga, Campos, & Bradbury, 2007).

The most obvious explanation for these correlations is that similarity causes attraction. Laboratory experiments on *attitude similarity,* conducted by Donn Byrne and his colleagues, suggest that similarity *does* cause attraction (Byrne, 1997; Byrne, Clore, & Smeaton, 1986). However, research also suggests that attraction can foster similarity (Anderson, Keltner, & John, 2003). For example, Davis and Rusbult (2001) found that dating partners gradually modify their attitudes in ways that make them more congruent, a phenomenon they called *attitude alignment.* Moreover, people in stable, satisfying intimate relationships tend to subjectively overestimate how similar they and their partners are (Murray et al.,

"It would never work out between us, Tom—we're from two totally different tiers of the upper middle class."

2002). Wanting to believe that they have found a kindred spirit, they tend to assume that their partners are mirrors of themselves.

Reciprocity Effects

People often attempt to gain others' liking by showering them with praise and flattery. However, we've all heard that "flattery will get you nowhere." However, the evidence suggests that flattery will indeed get you somewhere, with some people, some of the time. In interpersonal attraction, *reciprocity* involves liking those who show that they like you. In general, research indicates that we tend to like those who show that they like us and that we tend to see others as liking us more if we like them. Thus, it appears that liking breeds liking and loving promotes loving (Sprecher, 1998).

Romantic Ideals

In the realm of romance, people want their partner to measure up to their ideals. These ideals spell out the personal qualities that one hopes to find in a partner, such as warmth, good looks, loyalty, high status, a sense of humor, and so forth. According to Simpson, Fletcher, and Campbell (2001), people routinely evaluate how close their intimate partners come to matching these ideal standards, and these evaluations influence how relationships progress. Consistent with this theory, research shows that the more closely individuals' perceptions of their partners match their ideals, the more satisfied they tend to be with their relationship—both in the early stages of dating (Fletcher, Simpson, & Thomas, 2000) and in stable, long-term relationships (Fletcher, Simpson, & Thomas, 1999). Moreover, the size of the discrepancy between ideals and perceptions predicts how much partners try to influence each other's behavior and whether a relationship will continue or dissolve (Fletcher et al., 2000; Overall, Fletcher, & Simpson, 2006).

Of course, these evaluations of how one's partner compares to one's ideals are subjective, leaving room for distortion. When people are highly invested in a relationship, they can reduce the discrepancy between their ideals and their perceptions either by lowering their standards or by making charitable evaluations of their partners. Research suggests that the latter strategy is more common. For example, in a study of 180 couples, Murray, Holmes, and Griffin (1996) found that most participants viewed their partners more favorably than the partners viewed themselves. Individuals' perceptions of their romantic partners seemed to reflect their ideals for a partner more than reality. As Boyes and Fletcher (2007) put it, "entrusting one's happiness to another person seems to require a leap of faith and the need to see one's partner through rose-colored glasses" (p. 286). Interestingly, research suggests that people are happier in their relationship when they idealize their partners and when their partners idealize them. This line of research suggests that small, positive illusions about one's partner may foster happier and more resilient romantic relationships (Miller, Niehuis, & Huston, 2006; Murray, 2001).

Perspectives on the Mystery of Love

Love has proven to be an elusive subject. It's difficult to define and study because there are many types of love (Berscheid, 2006). Nonetheless, psychologists have begun to make some progress in their study of love. Let's look at their theories and research.

Passionate and Companionate Love

12b

Two early pioneers in research on love, Elaine Hatfield (formerly Walster) and Ellen Berscheid (Berscheid, 1988; Berscheid & Walster, 1978; Hatfield & Rapson, 1993), have proposed that romantic relationships are characterized by two kinds of love: passionate love and companionate love. **Passionate love** is a complete absorption in another that includes tender sexual feelings and the agony and ecstasy of intense emotion. Passionate love has its ups and downs, as it is associated with large swings in positive and negative emotions (Reis & Aron, 2008). **Companionate love** is warm, trusting, tolerant affection for another whose life is deeply intertwined with one's own. Passionate and companionate love *may* coexist, but they don't necessarily go hand in hand. Research suggests that, as a general rule, companionate love is more strongly related to relationship satisfaction than passionate love (Fehr, 2001).

The distinction between passionate and companionate love has been further refined by Robert Sternberg (1988a, 2006), who suggests that love has three facets rather than just two. He subdivides companionate love into intimacy and commitment. **Intimacy** refers to warmth, closeness, and sharing in a relationship. **Commitment** is an intent to maintain a relationship in spite of the difficulties and costs that may arise. Sternberg has mapped out the probable relations between the passage of time and the three components of love, as shown in **Figure 16.4**. Like Hatfield and Berscheid, he suspects that passion reaches its zenith in the early phases of love and then erodes. He believes that intimacy and commitment increase with time, although at different rates.

Research suggests that passionate love is a powerful motivational force that produces profound

Ellen Berscheid

"The emotion of romantic love seems to be distressingly fragile. As a 16th-century sage poignantly observed, 'the history of a love affair is the drama of its fight against time.'"

Elaine Hatfield

"Passionate love is like any other form of excitement. By its very nature, excitement involves a continuous interplay between elation and despair, thrills and terror."

changes in people's thinking, emotion, and behavior (Reis & Aron, 2008). Interestingly, brain-imaging research indicates that when people think about someone they are passionately in love with, these thoughts light up the dopamine circuits in the brain that are known to be activated by cocaine and other addictive drugs (Aron, Fisher, & Mashek, 2005). Perhaps that explains why passionate love sometimes resembles an addiction. Although passionate love is the glamorous face of love, commitment appears to be the crucial facet of love that is predictive of relationship stability. For example, declining commitment is associated with an increased likelihood of infidelity in dating relationships (Drigotas, Safstrom, & Gentilia, 1999). A study of dating couples who were followed for four years, found that participants' feelings of commitment were more predictive of whether they broke up than their ratings of their overall love (Sprecher, 1999). Interestingly, the participants who broke up indicated that their love had remained reasonably stable, but their commitment and satisfaction had declined.

Love as Attachment

12b

In another groundbreaking analysis of love, Cindy Hazan and Phillip Shaver (1987) looked not at the components of love but at similarities between love and *attachment relationships* in infancy. We noted in our chapter on human development (Chapter 11) that infant-caretaker bonding, or attachment,

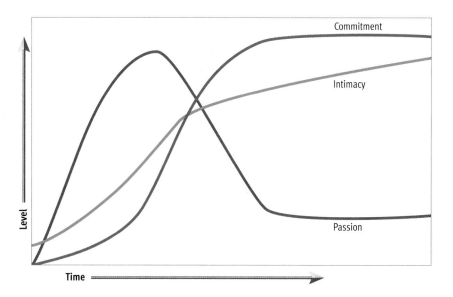

Figure 16.4
Sternberg's view of love over time. In his theory of love, Robert Sternberg (1988a) hypothesizes that the various elements of love progress in different ways over the course of time. According to Sternberg, passion peaks early in a relationship, whereas intimacy and commitment typically continue to build gradually. (Graphs adapted from Trotter, 1986)

emerges in the first year of life. Early attachments vary in quality, and *most* infants tend to fall into one of three groups, which depend in part on parents' caregiving styles (Ainsworth et al., 1978). A majority of infants develop a *secure attachment*. However, some are very anxious when separated from their caretaker, a syndrome called *anxious-ambivalent attachment*. A third group of infants, characterized by *avoidant attachment,* never bond very well with their caretaker (see Figure 16.5).

According to Hazan and Shaver, romantic love is an attachment process, and people's intimate relationships in adulthood follow the same form as their

Figure 16.5
Infant attachment and romantic relationships. According to Hazan and Shaver (1987), people's romantic relationships in adulthood are similar in form to their attachment patterns in infancy, which are determined in part by parental caregiving styles. The theorized relations between parental styles, attachment patterns, and intimate relations are outlined here. (Data for parental caregiving styles and adult attachment styles based on Hazan and Shaver, 1986, 1987; infant attachment patterns adapted from Shaffer, 1985)

Parents' caregiving style	Infant attachment	Adult attachment style
Warm/responsive She/he was generally warm and responsive; she/he was good at knowing when to be supportive and when to let me operate on my own; our relationship was almost always comfortable, and I have no major reservations or complaints about it.	**Secure attachment** An infant-caregiver bond in which the child welcomes contact with a close companion and uses this person as a secure base from which to explore the environment	**Secure** I find it relatively easy to get close to others and am comfortable depending on them and having them depend on me. I don't often worry about being abandoned or about someone getting too close to me.
Cold/rejecting She/he was fairly cold and distant, or rejecting, not very responsive; I wasn't her/his highest priority, her/his concerns were often elsewhere; it's possible that she/he would just as soon not have had me.	**Avoidant attachment** An insecure infant-caregiver bond, characterized by little separation protest and a tendency of the child to avoid or ignore the caregiver	**Avoidant** I am somewhat uncomfortable being close to others; I find it difficult to trust them, difficult to allow myself to depend on them. I am nervous when anyone gets too close, and often love partners want me to be more intimate than I feel comfortable being.
Ambivalent/inconsistent She/he was noticeably inconsistent in her/his reactions to me, sometimes warm and sometimes not; she/he had her/his own agenda, which sometimes got in the way of her/his receptiveness and responsiveness to my needs; she/he definitely loved me but didn't always show it in the best way.	**Anxious/ambivalent attachment** An insecure infant-caregiver bond, characterized by strong separation protest and a tendency of the child to resist contact initiated by the caregiver, particularly after a separation	**Anxious/ambivalent** I find that others are reluctant to get as close as I would like. I often worry that my partner doesn't really love me or won't want to stay with me. I want to merge completely with another person, and this desire sometimes scares people away.

attachments in infancy. According to their theory, a person who had an anxious-ambivalent attachment in infancy will tend to have romantic relations marked by anxiety and ambivalence in adulthood. In other words, people relive their early bonding experiences with their parents in their adult romantic relationships.

Hazan and Shaver's (1987) initial survey study provided striking support for their theory. They found that adults' love relationships could be sorted into groups that paralleled the three patterns of attachment seen in infants. *Secure adults* (56% of the subjects) found it relatively easy to get close to others, described their love relations as trusting, rarely worried about being abandoned, and reported the fewest divorces. *Anxious-ambivalent adults* (20% of the subjects) reported a preoccupation with love accompanied by expectations of rejection and described their love relations as volatile and marked by jealousy. *Avoidant adults* (24% of the subjects) found it difficult to get close to others and described their love relations as lacking intimacy and trust. Research eventually showed that attachment patterns are reasonably stable over time (Fraley, 2002) and that people's working models of attachment are carried forward from one relationship to the next (Brumbaugh & Fraley, 2006), supporting the notion that individuals' infant attachment experiences shape their intimate relations in adulthood.

After years of research on adult attachment, many theorists now believe that attachment is best conceptualized in terms of where people fall on two continuous dimensions: attachment anxiety and attachment avoidance (Fraley & Shaver, 2000; Mikulincer, 2006). *Attachment anxiety* reflects how much people worry that their partners will not be available when needed. This vigilance about abandonment stems, in part, from their doubts about their lovability. *Attachment avoidance* reflects the degree to which people feel uncomfortable with closeness and intimacy and therefore tend to maintain emotional distance from their partners.

Although this new approach was intended to restructure thinking about attachment in terms of continuous dimensions, it is also compatible with the original emphasis on attachment style subtypes. But it yields one additional subtype, as people who score high or low on the two dimensions can be divided into four attachment styles. As explained in **Figure 16.6**, this scheme yields a *secure* subtype, a *preoccupied* subtype that is essentially equivalent to the original anxious-ambivalent subtype, and two variations on avoidant attachment: *avoidant-dismissing* and *avoidant-fearful*. Currently, some researchers measure attachment style in terms of the original

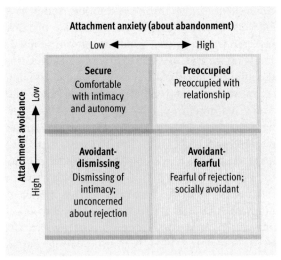

Figure 16.6

Attachment styles and their underlying dimensions. Attachment styles can be viewed in terms of where people fall along two continuous dimensions that range from low to high: attachment avoidance and attachment anxiety (about abandonment). This system yields four attachment styles, which are described in the four cells shown here. (Adapted from Brennan, Clark, & Shaver, 1998; Fraley & Shaver, 2000)

three subtypes, whereas others measure attachment in terms of the two dimensions that can generate four subtypes.

Research on the correlates of adult attachment styles has grown exponentially since the mid-1990s. Consistent with the original theory, research has shown that securely attached individuals have more committed, satisfying, interdependent, well-adjusted, and longer-lasting relationships compared to people with anxious-ambivalent or avoidant attachment styles (Feeney, 1999). Moreover, studies have shown that people with different attachment styles are predisposed to think, feel, and behave differently in their relationships (Collins & Allard, 2001). For example, anxious-ambivalent people tend to report more intense emotional highs and lows in their romantic relationships. They also report having more conflicts with their partners, that these conflicts are especially stressful, and that these conflicts often have a negative impact on how they feel about their relationship (Campbell et al., 2005). In a similar vein, attachment anxiety promotes *excessive reassurance seeking*—the tendency to persistently ask for assurances from partners that one is worthy of love (Shaver, Schachner & Mikulincer, 2005).

Attachment style also appears to be intimately related to people's patterns of sexual interaction. People with secure attachment tend to be more comfortable with their sexuality, more motivated to show love for their partner during sex, more open to sexual exploration, more likely to have sex in the context of committed relationships, and less accepting of casual sex (Cooper et al., 2006; Shaver & Mikulincer, 2006). In contrast, people high in attachment anxiety tend to have sex to reduce their feelings of insecurity and are more likely to consent to unwanted sexual acts and less likely to practice safe sex (Cooper et al., 2006; Schachner & Shaver, 2004). People high in avoidant attachment tend to engage in more casual sex in an effort to impress their peers, and they are more likely to use sex to manipulate their partners (Schachner & Shaver, 2004; Shaver & Mikulincer, 2006).

Reactions to romantic breakups also tend to vary depending on attachment style. People who are high in attachment anxiety have much more difficulty than others in dealing with the dissolution of romantic relationships. They report greater emotional and physical distress, greater preoccupation with the former partner, more attempts to regain the lost partner, more angry and vengeful behavior, and more maladaptive coping responses, such as using alcohol and drugs to cope with the loss (Davis, Shaver, & Vernon, 2003).

Studies have further suggested that attachment patterns may have far-reaching repercussions that extend into many aspects of people's lives besides their romantic relationships. For instance, people with secure attachments tend to have high self-esteem and to be relatively well adjusted. In contrast, people with avoidant or anxious-ambivalent attachments tend to be overrepresented in groups suffering from depression, eating disorders, and other types of psychopathology (Crowell, Fraley, & Shaver, 1999). Attachment security promotes compassionate feelings and values and more helping behavior when people are in need (Mikulincer & Shaver, 2005). Researchers have also found correlations between attachment styles and gender roles (Schwartz, Waldo, & Higgins, 2004), religious beliefs (Kirkpatrick, 2005), health habits (Huntsinger & Luecken, 2004), reactions to stressful events (Powers et al., 2006), styles of coping with stress (Howard & Medway, 2004), vulnerability to burnout (Pines, 2004), and leadership qualities (Davidovitz et al. 2007). Thus, Hazan and Shaver's innovative ideas about the long-term effects of infant attachment experiences have triggered an avalanche of thought-provoking research.

Culture and Close Relationships

Relatively little cross-cultural research has been conducted on the dynamics of close relationships. The limited evidence suggests both similarities and differences between cultures in romantic relationships (Hendrick & Hendrick, 2000; Schmitt, 2005). For the most part, similarities have been seen when research has focused on what people look for in prospective mates. As we discussed in Chapter 10, David Buss (1989, 1994a) has collected data on mate preferences in 37 divergent cultures and found that people all over the world value mutual attraction, kindness, intelligence, emotional stability, dependability, and good health in a mate. Buss also found that gender differences in mating priorities are nearly universal, with males placing more emphasis on physical attractiveness and females putting a higher priority on social status and financial resources.

Cultures vary, however, in their emphasis on love—especially passionate love—as a prerequisite for marriage. Although romantic love appears to be found in all cultures (Buss, 2006), passionate love as the basis for marriage is an 18th-century invention of Western culture (Stone, 1977). As Hatfield and Rapson (1993) note, "Marriage-for-love represents an ultimate expression of individualism" (p. 2). In contrast, marriages arranged by families and other go-betweens remain common in cultures high in collectivism, including India, Japan, and China (Hatfield, Rapson, & Martel, 2007). This practice is declining in some societies as a result of Westernization, but in collectivist societies people contemplating marriage still tend to think in terms of "What will my parents and other people say?" rather than "What does my heart say?" (Triandis, 1994). Although romantic love is routinely seen in collectivist societies (Lieberman & Hatfield, 2006), subjects from societies high in individualism tend to report that romantic love is more important for marriage than subjects from collectivist cultures do (Dion & Dion, 2006; Levine et al., 1995).

Marriages based on romantic love are the norm in Western cultures, whereas arranged marriages prevail in collectivist cultures.

The Internet and Close Relationships

In recent years the Internet has dramatically expanded opportunities for people to meet and develop close relationships through social networking services (Myspace, Friendster), online dating services, e-mail, chat rooms, and news groups. Some critics worry that this trend will undermine face-to-face interactions and that many people will be lured into dangerous liaisons by unscrupulous people. But research to date generally paints a positive picture of the Internet's impact on people's connections with one another (Whitty, 2008). For example, the Internet offers a wealth of opportunities to interact for those who suffer from physical infirmities or social anxieties (McKenna & Bargh, 2000). Also, Internet groups provide a safer venue than real life for individuals with stigmatized identities (for example, gay people) to interact and receive support.

One survey based on a nationally representative sample of American adults reported that 31% knew someone who had used a dating website and 11% had visited such a site to meet people (Madden & Lenhart, 2006). Among those who used online dating sites, a majority (52%) reported "mostly positive" experiences, although a considerable portion (29%) had "mostly negative" experiences. This report also asked the Internet users who said they were single and looking for a romantic partner to identify how they used the Internet for dating. You can see their responses in **Figure 16.7**.

Although critics are concerned that Internet relationships are superficial, research suggests that virtual relationships are just as intimate as face-to-face ones and are sometimes even closer (Bargh, McKenna, & Fitzsimons, 2002). Moreover, many virtual relationships evolve into face-to-face interactions (Boase & Wellman, 2006). Researchers find that romantic relationships that begin on the Internet seem to be just as stable over two years as traditional relationships ((McKenna, Green, & Gleason, 2002).

The differences between Internet and face-to-face communication may undermine some established principles of relationship development (Bargh & McKenna, 2004). For example, good looks and physical proximity are powerful factors in initial attraction in the real world. On the Internet, where people often form relationships sight-unseen, these factors may be less influential. Online, where people rely on self-disclosure to develop relationships, similarity of interests and values assumes more power than it does in face-to-face relationships. Because the Internet can foster anonymity, people often take greater risks in self-disclosure (Johnson & Paine, 2007). Thus, feelings of intimacy can develop more quickly. But instant intimacy can create uncomfortable feelings if a face-to-face meeting ensues—that is, meeting with a stranger who knows "too much" about you (Hamilton, 1999). Of course, face-to-face meetings can also go smoothly.

Anonymity also allows people to construct a virtual identity. Obviously, this can be a problem if one person adopts a fictional persona and an-

Figure 16.7
Dating-related activities online. Researchers asked Internet users who were single and looking for a romantic partner how they used the Internet (including e-mail and instant messaging) for dating (Madden & Lenhart, 2006). Flirting and going to an online dating website were most frequently mentioned. Most respondents engaged in three or fewer of these activities.

Adapted from Madden, M. & Lenhart, A. (2006). *Online dating.* Retrieved April 29, 2007 from http://www.pewinternet.org/pdfs/PIP_Online_Dating.pdf. (Dating-Related Activities Online table, p. 5). Reprinted by permission of Pew Internet & American Life Project. Washington, D.C.

Dating-Related Activities Online	
Online Activities	**Single and Looking Internet Users (%)**
Flirt with someone	40
Go to an online dating website	37
Ask someone out on a date	28
Find a place offline, like a nightclub or singles event, where you might meet someone to date	27
Been introduced to a potential date by a third party using e-mail or instant messaging	21
Participate in an online group where you hope to meet people to date	19
Search for information about someone you dated in the past	18
Maintain a long-distance relationship	18
Search for information about someone you are currently dating or are about to meet for a first date	17
Break up with someone you are dating	9

other assumes that it is authentic and begins to take the relationship seriously. A related concern is the truthfulness of online daters. In one survey, 25% of online daters admitted to using deception (Brym & Lenton, 2001). Yet, a whopping 86% of participants at one online dating site felt that others misrepresented their physical appearance (Gibbs, Ellison, & Heino, 2006). Admittedly, creating an accurate online representation of oneself can be a complex process: People want to put their best self forward to attract potential dates, but they also need to present themselves authentically if they expect to eventually meet face to face (Gibbs, et al., 2006). One study found that online daters dealt with this tension by constructing profiles that reflected their "ideal self" rather than their "actual self" (Ellison, Heino, & Gibbs, 2006). The most common factors that online daters misrepresent are age, appearance, and marital status (Brym & Lenton, 2001).

An Evolutionary Perspective on Attraction

Evolutionary psychologists have a great deal to say about heterosexual attraction. For example, they assert that physical appearance is an influential determinant of attraction because certain aspects of good looks can be indicators of sound health, good genes, and high fertility, all of which can contribute to reproductive potential (Soler et al., 2003; Sugiyama, 2005). Consistent with this analysis, recent research has found that some standards of attractiveness are more consistent across cultures than previously believed (Sugiyama, 2005). For example, *facial symmetry* seems to be a key element of attractiveness in highly diverse cultures (Fink & Penton-Voak, 2002). Facial symmetry is thought to be valued because a variety of environmental insults and developmental abnormalities are associated with physical asymmetries, which may serve as markers of relatively poor genes or health (Fink et al., 2006). Another facet of appearance that may transcend culture is *women's waist-to-hip ratio*. Around the world, men seem to prefer women with a moderately low waist-to-hip ratio, which appears to be a meaningful correlate of females' reproductive potential (Hughes & Gallup, 2003; Sugiyama, 2005), as it signals that a woman is healthy, young, and not pregnant.

The most thoroughly documented findings on the evolutionary bases of heterosexual attraction are those on gender differences in humans' mating preferences. Consistent with the notion that humans are programmed by evolution to behave in ways that enhance their reproductive fitness, evidence indicates that men generally are more interested than women in seeking youthfulness and physical attractiveness in their mates because these traits should be associated with greater reproductive potential (see Chapter 10). On the other hand, research shows that women place a greater premium on prospective mates' ambition, social status, and financial potential because these traits should be associated with the ability to invest material resources in children (Li et al., 2002; Shackelford, Schmitt, & Buss, 2005). The degree to which these trends transcend history and culture was driven home by a study that examined the mate preferences apparent in 658 traditional folktales drawn from the ancient oral traditions of 48 different cultures (Gottschall et al., 2004). The analyses showed that the characters in these extremely old and diverse stories showed the same gender differences seen in contemporary research: Male characters tended to place a greater emphasis on potential mates' physical attractiveness, while female characters showed more interest in potential mates' wealth and social status.

There are some qualifications to these trends, but even these caveats make evolutionary sense. For example, when women are asked what they prefer in a *short-term partner* (for casual sex) they value physical attractiveness just as much as men (Li & Kenrick, 2006). And very attractive women, aware of their own high mate value, want it all—they want prospective male partners to exhibit excellent economic potential *and* physical attractiveness (Buss & Shackelford, 2008). Women's menstrual cycles also influence their mating preferences. When women are in mid-cycle approaching ovulation—that is, when they are most fertile—their preferences shift to favor men who exhibit masculine facial and bodily features, attractiveness, and dominance (Gangestad, Thornhill, & Garver-Apgar, 2005; Gangestad et al., 2007; Little et al., 2007). Men seem to recognize this shift, as they rate masculine males as more threatening when their partners are in the fertile portion of their menstrual cycle (Burriss & Little, 2006). Interestingly, although ovulation is far from obvious in human females, strippers earn more tip money per night when they are in their most fertile period (Miller, Tybur, & Jordan, 2007). Researchers aren't sure whether male patrons are "detecting" the strippers' heightened fertility or whether the ovulating dancers come on to the customers more because they are more sexually motivated.

The tactics used by people in pursuing their romantic relationships may include efforts at deception. Research shows that many men and women would be willing to lie about their personality, income, past relationships, and career skills to impress

ONE SECOND BEFORE THE BLIND DATE

BIZARRO © by Dan Piraro. Reprinted by permission of King Features Syndicate

do (Keenan et al., 1997). Perhaps this is the reason women tend to underestimate the strength of men's relationship commitment (Haselton & Buss, 2000). Men do not appear to show a similar bias, but they do show a tendency to overestimate women's sexual interest. These cognitive biases seem to be designed to reduce the probability that ancestral women would consent to sex and then be abandoned and to minimize the likelihood that ancestral men would overlook sexual opportunities (Buss, 2001).

Deception lies at the heart of *mate poaching,* a phenomenon that has recently attracted the interest of evolutionary psychologists. Mate poaching occurs when someone tries to attract another person who is already in a relationship. Although it presents some extra challenges and risks, this strategy is not rare, as 50%–60% of the undergraduate subjects in one study reported that they had attempted to poach someone (Schmitt & Buss, 2001). Mate poaching has probably occurred throughout history and is universally seen across cultures, although its prevalence varies some from one culture to another (Schmitt et al., 2003). Men are somewhat more likely than women to make poaching attempts, but the gap is modest and poaching by women is common (Schmitt et al., 2003). The tactics used in poaching efforts overlap considerably with the normal tactics of attraction, except the tactics are more likely to be executed in a disguised and secretive manner. Poaching is a two-way street, as people often try to entice others into poaching them by expressing boredom about their current relationship, complaining about their partner, or asking for "advice" about their relationship (Schmitt & Shackelford, 2003).

a prospective date who was attractive (Rowatt, Cunningham, & Druen, 1999). Consistent with evolutionary theory, women report that they are most upset when men exaggerate their social status, their financial resources, or the depth of their romantic commitment to the woman, whereas men are most upset when women conceal a history of "promiscuity" (Haselton et al., 2005). Females anticipate more deception from prospective dates than males

REVIEW of Key Learning Goals

16.8 People tend to like and love others who are physically attractive. The matching hypothesis asserts that people who are similar in physical attractiveness are more likely to be drawn together than those who are not. Byrne's research suggests that similarity causes attraction, although attitude alignment may also be at work.

16.9 Reciprocity involves liking those who show that they like you. In intimate relationships, how well a partner matches up with one's romantic ideals tends to influence the progress of the relationship. But comparisons to one's ideals are subjective, and romantic partners often idealize each other.

16.10 Berscheid and Hatfield distinguished between passionate love (complete absorption with sexual feelings) and companionate love (trusting, tolerant entwinement). Sternberg built on their distinction by dividing companionate love into intimacy (warmth, closeness, and sharing) and commitment (intent to maintain a relationship).

16.11 Hazan and Shaver's theory suggests that love relationships in adulthood mimic attachment patterns in infancy. People tend to fall into three attachment subtypes (secure, avoidant, or anxious-ambivalent) in their romantic relationships, although attachment style can also be viewed in terms of how people score on two dimensions (attachment anxiety and avoidance). Those who are secure tend to have more committed, satisfying relationships. People high in attachment anxiety tend to have sex to reduce their insecurity and tend to have more difficulty than others with romantic breakups. Attachment style is related to many aspects of behavior.

16.12 The characteristics that people seek in prospective mates and gender differences in mating priorities are much the same around the world. However, cultures vary considerably in their emphasis on passionate love as a prerequisite for marriage. Although critics are concerned that Internet relationships are superficial and open to deception, Internet-initiated relationships appear to be just as intimate and stable as relationships forged offline.

16.13 According to evolutionary psychologists, certain aspects of good looks, such as facial symmetry and waist-to-hip ratio in women, influence attraction because they are indicators of reproductive fitness. Consistent with evolutionary theory, men tend to seek youthfulness and attractiveness in their mates, whereas women emphasize prospective mates' financial potential and willingness to invest material resources in children. People's courtship tactics may include deception. Females anticipate more deception than males do. Mate poaching is common and appears to be universal across cultures.

Attitudes: Making Social Judgments

Key Learning Goals

16.14 Analyze the structure (components and dimensions) of attitudes and the link between attitudes and behavior.

16.15 Summarize how source, message, and receiver factors influence the process of persuasion.

16.16 Clarify how learning processes and cognitive dissonance can contribute to attitude formation and change.

16.17 Relate self-perception theory and the elaboration likelihood model to attitude change.

In our chapter-opening story, Muffy's friends exhibited decidedly negative attitudes about working-class men. Their behavior reveals a basic feature of attitudes: they're evaluative. Social psychology's interest in attitudes has a much longer history than its interest in attraction. Indeed, in its early days social psychology was defined as the study of attitudes. In this section we'll discuss the nature of attitudes, efforts to change attitudes through persuasion, and theories of attitude change.

What are attitudes? *Attitudes* are positive or negative evaluations of objects of thought. "Objects of thought" may include social issues (capital punishment or gun control, for example), groups (liberals, farmers), institutions (the Lutheran church, the Supreme Court), consumer products (yogurt, computers), and people (the president, your next-door neighbor).

Components and Dimensions of Attitudes

Social psychologists have traditionally viewed attitudes as being made up of three components: a cognitive component, an affective component, and a behavioral component. However, it gradually became apparent that many attitudes do not include all three components (Fazio & Olson, 2003), so it is

more accurate to say that *attitudes may include up to three components*. The *cognitive component* of an attitude is made up of the beliefs that people hold about the object of an attitude. The *affective component* of an attitude consists of the *emotional feelings* stimulated by an object of thought. The *behavioral component* of an attitude consists of *predispositions to act* in certain ways toward an attitude object. Figure 16.8 provides concrete examples of how someone's attitude about gun control might be divided into its components.

Attitudes also vary along several crucial dimensions, including their *strength, accessibility,* and *ambivalence* (Olson & Maio, 2003). Definitions of *attitude strength* differ, but strong attitudes are generally seen as ones that are firmly held (resistant to change), that are durable over time, and that have a powerful impact on behavior (Petty, Wheeler, & Tormala, 2003). The *accessibility* of an attitude refers to how often one thinks about it and how quickly it comes to mind. Highly accessible attitudes are quickly and readily available (Fabrigar, MacDonald, & Wegener, 2005). Attitude accessibility is correlated with attitude strength, as highly accessible attitudes *tend* to be strong, but the concepts are distinct and there is no one-to-one correspondence. *Ambivalent attitudes* are conflicted evaluations that include both positive and negative feelings about an object of thought (Fabrigar et al., 2005). Like attitude

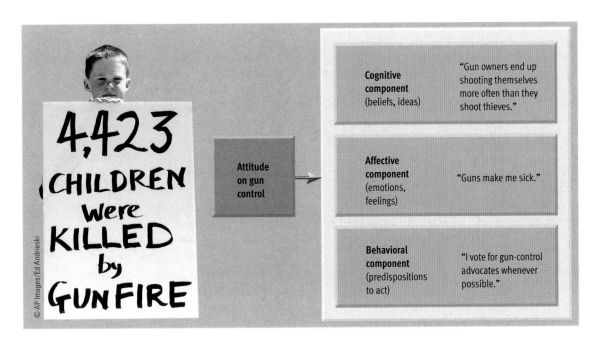

Figure 16.8

The possible components of attitudes. Attitudes may include cognitive, affective, and behavioral components, as illustrated here for a hypothetical person's attitude about gun control.

strength, attitude ambivalence has been measured in various ways (Priester & Petty, 2001). Generally speaking, ambivalence increases as the ratio of positive to negative evaluations gets closer to being equal. When ambivalence is high, an attitude tends to be less predictive of behavior and more pliable in the face of persuasion (Crano & Prislin, 2006).

Attitudes and Behavior

In the early 1930s, when prejudice against Asians was common in the United States, Richard LaPiere journeyed across the country with a Chinese couple. He was more than a little surprised when they weren't turned away from any of the restaurants they visited in their travels—184 restaurants in all. About six months after his trip, LaPiere surveyed the same restaurants and asked whether they would serve Chinese customers. Roughly half of the restaurants replied to the survey, and over 90% of them indicated that they would not seat Chinese patrons. Thus, LaPiere (1934) found that people who voice prejudicial attitudes may not behave in discriminatory ways. Since then, theorists have often asked: Why don't attitudes predict behavior better?

Admittedly, LaPiere's study had a fundamental flaw that you may already have detected. The person who seated LaPiere and his Chinese friends may not have been the same person who responded to the mail survey sent later. Nonetheless, numerous follow-up studies, using more sophisticated methods, have repeatedly shown that attitudes are mediocre predictors of people's behavior (Ajzen & Fishbein, 2005; Kraus, 1995). That's not to say that attitudes are irrelevant or meaningless. When Wallace and his colleagues (2005) reviewed 797 attitude-behavior studies, they found that the average correlation between attitudes and behavior was .41. That figure is high enough to justify Eagly's (1992) conclusion that researchers have identified "many conditions under which attitudes are substantial predictors of behavior" (p. 697). But on the whole, social psychologists have been surprised by how often a favorable attitude toward a candidate or product does not translate into a vote or a purchase.

Why aren't attitude-behavior relations more consistent? One consideration is that until recently researchers failed to take variations in *attitude strength, accessibility, and ambivalence* into account. Accumulating evidence indicates that these factors influence the connection between attitudes and behavior, but they have generally been left uncontrolled in decades of research on attitudes (Cooke & Sheeran, 2004; Olson & Maio, 2003). Research suggests that strong attitudes that are highly accessible and have been stable over time tend to be more predictive of behavior (Glasman & Albarracin, 2006). Another consideration is that attitudes are often measured in a *general, global* way that isn't likely to predict *specific* behaviors (Bohner & Schwarz, 2001). Although you may express favorable feelings about protecting civil liberties (a very general, abstract concept), you may not be willing to give $100 to the American Civil Liberties Union (a very specific action).

Finally, inconsistent relations between attitudes and behavior are seen because behavior depends on situational constraints—especially your subjective perceptions of how people expect you to behave (Ajzen & Fishbein, 2000, 2005). The review of research cited earlier (Wallace et al., 2005), which found that attitudes correlate .41 with behavior on average, also noted that when social pressures are high, this correlation diminishes to .30. Thus, attitudes interact with situational constraints to shape people's behavior. For instance, you may be strongly opposed to marijuana use but may not say anything when friends start passing a joint around at a party because you don't want to turn the party into an argument. However, in another situation governed by different norms, such as a class discussion, you may speak out forcefully against marijuana use. If so, you may be trying to change others' attitudes, the process we'll discuss next.

Trying to Change Attitudes: Factors in Persuasion

The fact that attitudes aren't always good predictors of a person's behavior doesn't stop others from trying to change those attitudes. Indeed, every day you're bombarded by efforts to alter your attitudes. To illustrate, let's trace the events of an imaginary morning. You may not even be out of bed before you start hearing radio advertisements intended to influence your attitudes about specific mouthwashes, computers, athletic shoes, and cell phones. If you check the news on your computer, you find not only more ads but quotes from government officials and special interest groups, carefully crafted to shape your opinions. When you arrive at school, you encounter a group passing out leaflets that urge you to repent your sins and join them in worship. In class, your economics professor champions the wisdom of free markets in international trade. At lunch, the person you've been dating argues about the merits of an "open relationship." Your discussion is interrupted by someone who wants both of you to sign a petition. "Doesn't it ever let up?" you wonder. When it comes to persuasion, the answer is "no." As Anthony Pratkanis and Elliot Aronson (2000) put it, we live in the "age of propaganda." In light of this reality, let's examine some of the factors that determine whether persuasion works.

The process of persuasion includes four basic elements: source, receiver, message, and channel (see Figure 16.9). The *source* is the person who sends a communication, and the *receiver* is the person to whom the message is sent. Thus, if you watch a presidential news conference on TV, the president is the source, and you and millions of other viewers are the receivers. The *message* is the information transmitted by the source, and the *channel* is the medium through which the message is sent. Although the research on communication channels is interesting, we'll confine our discussion to source, message, and receiver variables.

Source Factors

Occasional exceptions to the general rule are seen, but persuasion tends to be more successful when the source has high *credibility* (Pornpitakpan, 2004). What gives a person credibility? Either expertise or trustworthiness. *Expertise* tends to be more influential when an argument is ambiguous or when the receiver is not motivated to pay close attention to the argument (Chaiken & Maheswaran, 1994; Reimer, Mata, & Stoecklin, 2004). People try to convey their expertise by mentioning their degrees, their training, and their experience or by showing an impressive grasp of the issue at hand.

Expertise is a plus, but *trustworthiness* can be even more important. Many people tend to accept messages from trustworthy sources with little scrutiny (Priester & Petty, 1995, 2003). If you were told that your state needs to reduce corporate taxes to stimulate its economy, would you be more likely to believe it from the president of a huge corporation in your state or from an economics professor from out of state? Probably the latter. Trustworthiness is undermined when a source, such as the corporation president, appears to have something to gain. In contrast, trustworthiness is enhanced when people appear to argue against their own interests (Hunt, Smith, & Kernan, 1985). This effect explains why salespeople often make remarks like, "Frankly, my snowblower isn't the best. They have a better brand down the street. Of course, you'll have to spend quite a bit more . . ."

Likability also increases the effectiveness of a persuasive source (Johnson, Maio, & Smith-McLallen, 2005), and some of the factors at work in attraction therefore have an impact on persuasion. Thus, the favorable effect of *physical attractiveness* on likability can make persuasion more effective (Reinhard, Messner, & Sporer, 2006). People also respond better to sources who are *similar* to them in ways that are relevant to the issue at hand (Hilmert, Kulik, & Christenfeld, 2006).

Message Factors

If you were going to give a speech to a local community group advocating a reduction in state taxes on corporations, you'd probably wrestle with a number of questions about how to structure your message. Should you look at both sides of the issue, or should you present just your side? Should you deliver a low-key, logical speech? Or should you try to strike fear into the hearts of your listeners? These questions are concerned with message factors in persuasion.

Let's assume that you're aware that there are two sides to the taxation issue. On the one hand, you're convinced that lower corporate taxes will bring new companies to your state and stimulate economic growth. On the other hand, you realize that reduced tax revenues may hurt the quality of education and roads in your state (but you think the benefits will outweigh the costs). Should you present a *one-sided argument* that ignores the possible problems for education and road quality? Or should you present a *two-sided argument* that acknowledges concern about education and road quality and then downplays the probable magnitude of these problems? The optimal strategy depends on a variety of considerations, but overall, two-sided arguments tend to be more effective (Petty & Wegener, 1998). Just mentioning that

web link 16.3

Influence at Work

This site offers an intriguing set of materials that explore a wide variety of social influence phenomena, including persuasion, propaganda, brainwashing, and the tactics that cults use in recruiting. The site is maintained by Kelton Rhodes and Robert Cialdini, perhaps the world's leading authority on social influence strategies.

Figure 16.9
Overview of the persuasion process. The process of persuasion essentially boils down to *who* (the source) communicates *what* (the message) *by what means* (the channel) *to whom* (the receiver). Thus, four sets of variables influence the process of persuasion: source, message, channel, and receiver factors. The diagram lists some of the more important factors in each category (including some that are not discussed in the text due to space limitations). (Adapted from Lippa, 1994)

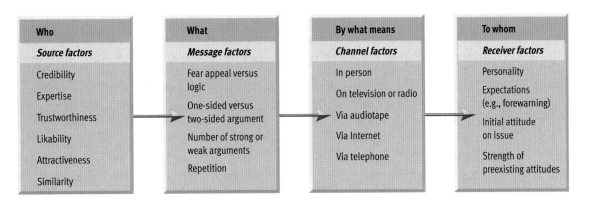

Who	What	By what means	To whom
Source factors	**Message factors**	**Channel factors**	**Receiver factors**
Credibility	Fear appeal versus logic	In person	Personality
Expertise	One-sided versus two-sided argument	On television or radio	Expectations (e.g., forewarning)
Trustworthiness	Number of strong or weak arguments	Via audiotape	Initial attitude on issue
Likability	Repetition	Via Internet	Strength of preexisting attitudes
Attractiveness		Via telephone	
Similarity			

there are two sides to an issue can increase your credibility with an audience.

Frequent repetition of a message also seems to be an effective strategy. The *validity effect* refers to the finding that simply repeating a statement causes it to be perceived as more valid or true. It doesn't matter whether the statement is true, false, or clearly just an opinion; if you repeat something often enough, some people come to believe it (Boehm, 1994; Weaver et al., 2007).

Persuasive messages frequently attempt to arouse fear. Opponents of nuclear power scare us with visions of meltdowns. Antismoking campaigns emphasize the threat of cancer, and deodorant ads highlight the risk of embarrassment. You could follow their lead and argue that if corporate taxes aren't reduced, your state will be headed toward economic ruin and massive unemployment. *Do appeals to fear work?* Yes—if they are successful in arousing fear. Research reveals that many messages intended to induce fear fail to do so. However, studies involving a wide range of issues (nuclear policy, auto safety, dental hygiene, and so on) have shown that messages that are effective in arousing fear tend to increase persuasion (Ruiter, Abraham, & Kok, 2001). Fear appeals are most likely to work when your listeners view the dire consequences that you describe as exceedingly unpleasant, fairly probable if they don't take your advice, and avoidable if they do (Das, de Wit, & Stroebe, 2003).

Receiver Factors

What about the receiver of the persuasive message? Are some people easier to persuade than others? Undoubtedly, but researchers have not found any personality traits that are reliably associated with susceptibility to persuasion (Petty & Wegener, 1998). Other factors, such as forewarning a receiver about a persuasive effort, generally seem to be more influential than the receiver's personality. An old saying suggests that "to be forewarned is to be forearmed." The value of *forewarning* applies to targets of persuasive efforts (Wood & Quinn, 2003). When you shop for a new TV, you *expect* salespeople to work at persuading you, and to some extent this forewarning reduces the impact of their arguments. Considerations that stimulate counterarguing in the receiver tend to increase resistance to persuasion (Jain, Buchanan, & Maheswaran, 2000).

Furthermore, studies show that *stronger attitudes are more resistant to change* (Eagly & Chaiken, 1998; Miller & Peterson, 2004). Strong attitudes may be tougher to alter because they tend to be embedded in networks of beliefs and values that might also require change (Erber, Hodges, & Wilson, 1995).

Finally, *resistance can promote resistance*. That is, when people successfully resist persuasive efforts to change specific attitudes, they often become more certain about those attitudes (Tormala & Petty, 2002, 2004).

Our review of source, message, and receiver variables has shown that attempting to change attitudes through persuasion involves a complex interplay of factors—and we haven't even looked beneath the surface yet. How do people acquire attitudes in the first place? What dynamic processes within people produce attitude change? We turn to these theoretical issues next.

Theories of Attitude Formation and Change

12c

Many theories have been proposed to explain the mechanisms at work in attitude change, whether or not it occurs in response to persuasion. We'll look at four theoretical perspectives: learning theory, dissonance theory, self-perception theory, and the elaboration likelihood model.

Learning Theory

12c

We've seen repeatedly that *learning theory* can help explain a wide range of phenomena, from conditioned fears to the acquisition of sex roles to the development of personality traits. Now we can add attitude formation and change to our list.

The affective, or emotional, component in an attitude can be created through a special subtype of *classical conditioning,* called evaluative conditioning (Olson & Fazio, 2001, 2002). As we discussed in Chapter 6, *evaluative conditioning* consists of efforts to transfer the emotion attached to a US to a new CS (Kruglanski & Stroebe, 2005; Schimmack & Crites, 2005). Advertisers routinely try to take advantage of evaluative conditioning by pairing their products with stimuli that elicit pleasant emotional responses, such as extremely attractive models, highly likable spokespersons, and cherished events, such as the Olympics (Till & Priluck, 2000). This conditioning process is diagrammed in **Figure 16.10**.

Operant conditioning may come into play when you openly express an attitude, such as "I believe that husbands should do more housework." Some people may endorse your view, while others may jump down your throat. Agreement from other people generally functions as a reinforcer, strengthening your tendency to express a specific attitude (Bohner & Schwarz, 2001). Disagreement often functions as a form of punishment, which may gradually weaken your commitment to your viewpoint.

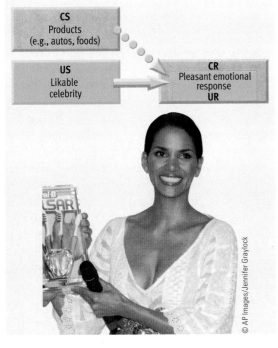

CS
Products
(e.g., autos, foods)

US
Likable
celebrity

CR
Pleasant emotional
response
UR

© AP Images/Jennifer Graylock

Figure 16.10

Classical conditioning of attitudes in advertising. Advertisers routinely pair their products with likable celebrities in the hope that their products will come to elicit pleasant emotional responses. As discussed in Chapter 6, this special type of classical conditioning is called *evaluative conditioning.* See the Critical Thinking Application in Chapter 6 for a more in-depth discussion of this practice.

concept check 16.3

Understanding Attitudes and Persuasion

Check your understanding of the possible components of attitudes and the elements of persuasion by analyzing hypothetical political strategies. Imagine you're working on a political campaign and you're invited to join the candidate's inner circle in strategy sessions, as staff members prepare the candidate for upcoming campaign stops. During the meetings, you hear various strategies discussed. For each strategy below, indicate which component of voters' attitudes (cognitive, affective, or behavioral) is being targeted for change, and indicate which element in persuasion (source, message, or receiver factors) is being manipulated. The answers are in Appendix A.

1. "You need to convince this crowd that your program for regulating nursing homes is sound. Whatever you do, don't acknowledge the two weaknesses in the program that we've been playing down. I don't care if you're asked point blank. Just slide by the question and keep harping on the program's advantages."

   _____

2. "You haven't been smiling enough lately, especially when the TV cameras are rolling. Remember, you can have the best ideas in the world, but if you don't seem likable, you're not gonna get elected. By the way, I think I've lined up some photo opportunities that should help us create an image of sincerity and compassion."

   _____

3. "This crowd is already behind you. You don't have to alter their opinions on any issue. Get right to work convincing them to contribute to the campaign. I want them lining up to give money."

   _____

Another person's attitudes may rub off on you through *observational learning* (Oskamp, 1991). If you hear your uncle say, "Republicans are nothing but puppets of big business" and your mother heartily agrees, your exposure to your uncle's attitude and your mother's reinforcement of your uncle may influence your attitude toward the Republican party. Studies show that parents and their children tend to have similar political attitudes (Sears, 1975) and that college students living in residence halls tend to show some convergence in attitudes (Cullum & Harton, 2007). Observational learning may account for much of this similarity. The opinions of teachers, coaches, co-workers, talk-show hosts, rock stars, and so forth are also likely to sway people's attitudes through observational learning.

Dissonance Theory

PSYK TREK 12c

Leon Festinger's *dissonance theory* assumes that inconsistency among attitudes propels people in the direction of attitude change. Dissonance theory burst into prominence in 1959 when Festinger and J. Merrill Carlsmith published a famous study of counterattitudinal behavior. Let's look at their findings and at how dissonance theory explains them.

Festinger and Carlsmith (1959) had male college students come to a laboratory, where they worked on excruciatingly dull tasks such as turning pegs repeatedly. When a subject's hour was over, the experimenter confided that some participants' motivation was being manipulated by telling them that the task was interesting and enjoyable before they started it. Then, after a moment's hesitation, the experimenter asked if the subject could help him out of a jam. His usual helper was delayed and he needed someone to testify to the next "subject" (really an accomplice) that the experimental task was interesting. He offered to pay the subject if he would tell the person in the adjoining waiting room that the task was enjoyable and involving.

This entire scenario was enacted to coax participants into doing something that was inconsistent with their true feelings—that is, to engage in *counterattitudinal behavior.* Some participants received a token payment of $1 for their effort, while others received a more substantial payment of $20 (an amount equivalent to about $80–$90 today, in light of inflation). Later, a second experimenter inquired about the subjects' true feelings regarding the dull

Courtesy of Professor Jerry Suls

Leon Festinger

"Cognitive dissonance is a motivating state of affairs. Just as hunger impels a person to eat, so does dissonance impel a person to change his opinions or his behavior."

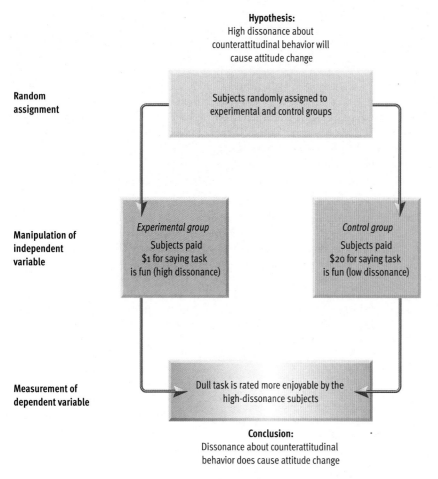

Hypothesis:
High dissonance about
counterattitudinal behavior will
cause attitude change

Random assignment

Subjects randomly assigned to
experimental and control groups

Manipulation of independent variable

Experimental group
Subjects paid
$1 for saying task
is fun (high dissonance)

Control group
Subjects paid
$20 for saying task
is fun (low dissonance)

Measurement of dependent variable

Dull task is rated more enjoyable by the
high-dissonance subjects

Conclusion:
Dissonance about counterattitudinal
behavior does cause attitude change

Figure 16.11
Design of the Festinger and Carlsmith (1959) study. The sequence of events in this landmark study of counterattitudinal behavior and attitude change is outlined here. The diagram omits a third condition (no dissonance), in which subjects were not induced to lie. The results in the nondissonance condition were similar to those found in the low-dissonance condition.

experimental task. Figure 16.11 summarizes the design of the Festinger and Carlsmith study.

Who do you think rated the task more favorably—the subjects who were paid $1 or those who were paid $20? Both common sense and learning theory would predict that the subjects who received the greater reward ($20) should come to like the task more. In reality, however, the subjects who were paid $1 exhibited more favorable attitude change— just as Festinger and Carlsmith had predicted. Why? Dissonance theory provides an explanation.

According to Festinger (1957), *cognitive dissonance* **exists when related cognitions are inconsistent—that is, when they contradict each other.** Cognitive dissonance is thought to create an unpleasant state of tension that motivates people to reduce their dissonance—usually by altering their cognitions. In the study by Festinger and Carlsmith, the subjects' contradictory cognitions were "The task is boring" and "I told someone the task was enjoyable." The subjects who were paid $20 for lying had an obvious reason for behaving inconsistently with their true attitudes, so these subjects experienced little dissonance. In contrast, the subjects paid $1 had no readily apparent justification for their lie and experienced high dissonance. To re-

duce it, they tended to persuade themselves that the task was more enjoyable than they had originally thought. Thus, dissonance theory sheds light on why people sometimes come to believe their own lies.

Cognitive dissonance is also at work when people turn attitudinal somersaults to justify efforts that haven't panned out, a syndrome called *effort justification.* Aronson and Mills (1959) studied effort justification by putting college women through a "severe initiation" before they could qualify to participate in what promised to be an interesting discussion of sexuality. In the initiation, the women had to read obscene passages out loud to a male experimenter. After all that, the highly touted discussion of sexuality turned out to be a boring, taped lecture on reproduction in lower animals. Subjects in the severe initiation condition experienced highly dissonant cognitions ("I went through a lot to get here" and "This discussion is terrible"). How did they reduce their dissonance? Apparently by changing their attitude about the discussion, since they rated it more favorably than subjects in two control conditions. Effort justification may be at work in many facets of everyday life. For example, people who wait in line for an hour or more to get into an exclusive restaurant often praise the restaurant afterward even if they have been served a mediocre meal.

Dissonance theory has been tested in hundreds of studies with mixed, but largely favorable, results. The dynamics of dissonance appear to underlie many important types of attitude changes (Draycott & Dabbs, 1998; Keller & Block, 1999; Petty et al., 2003). Research has largely supported Festinger's claim that dissonance involves genuine psychological discomfort and even physiological arousal (Visser & Cooper, 2003; Devine et al., 1999). However, dissonance effects are not among the most reliable phenomena in social psychology. Researchers have had difficulty specifying the conditions under which dissonance will occur, and it has become apparent that people can reduce their dissonance in quite a variety of ways besides changing their attitudes (Olson & Stone, 2005; Visser & Cooper, 2003).

Self-Perception Theory   12c

After taking a close look at studies of counterattitudinal behavior, Daryl Bem (1967) concluded that self-perception, rather than dissonance, explains why people sometimes come to believe their own lies. According to Bem's *self-perception theory,* people often *infer* their attitudes from their behavior. Thus, Bem argued that in the study by Festinger and Carlsmith (1959), the subjects paid $1 probably thought to themselves, "A dollar isn't enough money to get me to lie, so I must have found the task enjoyable."

This thinking isn't much different from what dissonance theory would predict. Both theories suggest that people often think, "If I said it, it must be true." But the two theories propose that similar patterns of thought unfold for entirely different reasons. According to dissonance theory, subjects think along these lines because they're struggling to reduce tension caused by inconsistency among their cognitions. According to self-perception theory, subjects are engaged in normal attributional efforts to better understand their own behavior. Bem originally believed that most findings explained by dissonance were really due to self-perception. However, studies eventually showed that self-perception is at work primarily when subjects do not have well-defined attitudes regarding the issue at hand (Olson & Roese, 1995). Although self-perception theory did not replace dissonance theory, Bem's work demonstrated that attitudes are sometimes inferred from one's own behavior (Olson & Stone, 2005; see **Figure 16.12**).

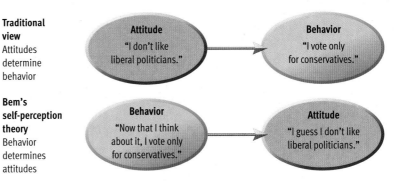

Elaboration Likelihood Model   12c

The *elaboration likelihood model* of attitude change, originally proposed by Richard Petty and John Cacioppo (1986), asserts that there are two basic "routes" to persuasion (Petty & Brinol, 2008; Petty & Wegener, 1999). The *central route* is taken when people carefully ponder the content and logic of persuasive messages. The *peripheral route* is taken when persuasion depends on nonmessage factors, such as the attractiveness and credibility of the source, or on conditioned emotional responses (see **Figure 16.13**). For example, a politician who campaigns by delivering carefully researched speeches that thoughtfully analyze complex issues is following the central route to persuasion. In contrast, a politician who depends on marching bands, flag waving, celebrity endorsements, and emotional slogans is following the peripheral route.

Both routes can lead to persuasion. However, according to the elaboration likelihood model, the durability of attitude change depends on the extent to which people elaborate on (think about) the contents of persuasive communications. Studies suggest that the central route to persuasion leads to more enduring attitude change than the peripheral route and that attitudes changed through central processes predict behavior better than attitudes changed through peripheral processes (Kruglanski & Stroebe, 2005; Petty & Wegener, 1998).

REVIEW of Key Learning Goals

16.14 Attitudes may be made up of cognitive, affective, and behavioral components. Attitudes vary along the dimensions of strength, accessibility, and ambivalence. Attitudes and behavior aren't as consistent as one might assume, for a variety of reasons, including the need to consider situational pressures.

16.15 A source of persuasion who is credible, expert, trustworthy, likable, and physically attractive tends to be relatively effective in stimulating attitude change. Although there are some situational limitations, two-sided arguments and fear arousal are effective elements in persuasive messages. Repetition of a message is also helpful. Persuasion is more difficult when a receiver is forewarned and when strong attitudes are targeted.

16.16 Attitudes may be shaped through classical conditioning, operant conditioning, and observational learning. Festinger's dissonance theory asserts that inconsistent attitudes cause tension and that people alter their attitudes to reduce cognitive dissonance. Dissonance theory has been used to explain attitude change following counterattitudinal behavior and efforts that haven't panned out.

16.17 Self-perception theory proposes that people sometimes infer their attitudes from their behavior. The elaboration likelihood model holds that the central route to persuasion, which depends on the logic of persuasive messages, tends to yield longer-lasting attitude change than the peripheral route, which depends on nonmessage factors.

Figure 16.12
Bem's self-perception theory. The traditional view is that attitudes determine behavior. However, Bem stood conventional logic on its head when he proposed that behavior often determines (or causes people to draw inferences about) their attitudes. Subsequent research on attribution has shown that sometimes people *do* infer their attitudes from their behavior.

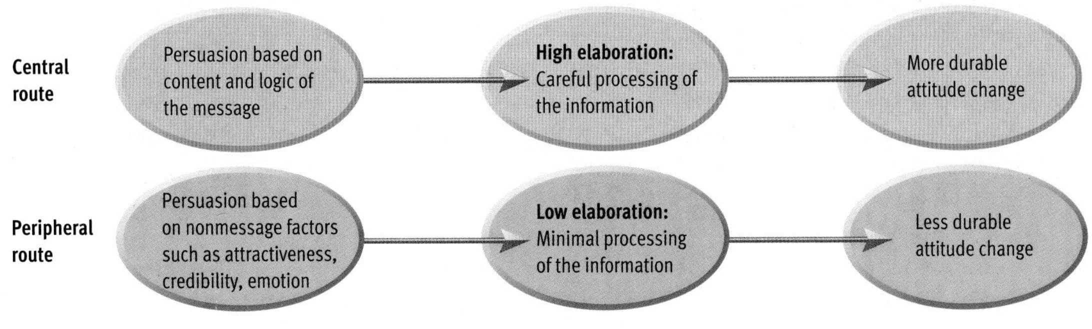

Figure 16.13
The elaboration likelihood model. According to the elaboration likelihood model (Petty & Cacioppo, 1986), the central route to persuasion leads to more elaboration of message content and more enduring attitude change than the peripheral route to persuasion.

Conformity and Obedience: Yielding to Others

Key Learning Goals

16.18 Review Asch's work on conformity.

16.19 Describe the Featured Study by Milgram on obedience to authority, and assess the ensuing controversy.

16.20 Discuss cultural variations in conformity and obedience.

16.21 Describe the Stanford Prison Simulation and its implications.

A number of years ago, the area that I lived in experienced a severe flood that required the mobilization of the National Guard and various emergency services. At the height of the crisis, a young man arrived at the scene of the flood, announced that he was from an obscure state agency that no one had ever heard of, and proceeded to take control of the emergency. City work crews, the fire department, local police, municipal officials, and the National Guard followed his orders with dispatch for several days, evacuating entire neighborhoods—until an official thought to check and found out that the man was just someone who had walked in off the street. The imposter, who had had small armies at his beck and call for several days, had no training in emergency services, just a history of unemployment and psychological problems.

After news of the hoax spread, people criticized red-faced local officials for their compliance with the imposter's orders. However, many of the critics probably would have cooperated in much the same way if they had been in the officials' shoes. For most people, willingness to obey someone in authority is the rule, not the exception. In this section, we'll analyze the dynamics of social influence at work in conformity and obedience.

Conformity

12e

If you keep a well-manicured lawn, are you exhibiting conformity? According to social psychologists, it depends on whether your behavior is the result of group pressure. *Conformity* **occurs when people yield to real or imagined social pressure.** For example, if you maintain a well-groomed lawn only to avoid complaints from your neighbors, you're conforming to social pressure. However, if you maintain a nice lawn because you genuinely prefer a nice lawn, that's *not* conformity.

In the 1950s, Solomon Asch (1951, 1955, 1956) devised a clever procedure that reduced ambiguity about whether subjects were conforming, allowing him to investigate the variables that govern conformity. Let's re-create one of Asch's (1955) classic experiments, which have become the most widely replicated studies in the history of social psychology (Markus, Kitayama, & Heiman, 1996). The participants are male undergraduates recruited for a study of visual perception. A group of seven subjects are shown a large card with a vertical line on it and

are then asked to indicate which of three lines on a second card matches the original "standard line" in length (see Figure 16.14). All seven subjects are given a turn at the task, and they announce their choice to the group. The subject in the sixth chair doesn't know it, but everyone else in the group is an accomplice of the experimenter, and they're about to make him wonder whether he has taken leave of his senses.

The accomplices give accurate responses on the first two trials. On the third trial, line number 2 clearly is the correct response, but the first five "subjects" all say that line number 3 matches the standard line. The genuine subject is bewildered and can't believe his ears. Over the course of the next 15 trials, the accomplices all give the same incorrect response on 11 of them. How does the real subject respond? The line judgments are easy and unambiguous. So, if the participant consistently agrees with the accomplices, he isn't making honest mistakes—he's conforming.

Averaging across all 50 participants, Asch (1955) found that the young men conformed on 37% of the trials. The subjects varied considerably in their tendency to conform, however. Of the 50 participants, 13 never caved in to the group, while 14 conformed on more than half the trials. One could argue that the results show that people confronting a unanimous majority generally tend to *resist* the pressure to conform, but given how clear and easy the line judgments were, most social scientists viewed the findings as a dramatic demonstration of humans' propensity to conform (Levine, 1999).

Solomon Asch

"That we have found the tendency to conformity in our society so strong that reasonably intelligent and well-meaning young people are willing to call white black is a matter of concern."

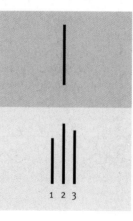

Figure 16.14

Stimuli used in Asch's conformity studies. Subjects were asked to match a standard line (top) with one of three other lines displayed on another card (bottom). The task was easy—until experimental accomplices started responding with obviously incorrect answers, creating a situation in which Asch evaluated subjects' conformity.

SOURCE: Adapted from Asch, S. (1955). Opinion and social pressure. *Scientific American, 193* (5), 31–35. Based on illustrations by Sara Love. Copyright © 1955 by Scientific American, Inc. All rights reserved.

In subsequent studies, Asch (1956) found that *group size* and *group unanimity* are key determinants of conformity. To examine the impact of group size, Asch repeated his procedure with groups that included from 1 to 15 accomplices. Little conformity was seen when a subject was pitted against just one person, but conformity increased as group size went up to 4, and then leveled off (see Figure 16.15). Thus, Asch reasoned that as groups grow larger, conformity increases—up to a point, a conclusion that has been echoed by other researchers (Cialdini & Trost, 1998).

However, group size made little difference if just one accomplice "broke" with the others, wrecking their unanimous agreement. The presence of another dissenter lowered conformity to about one-quarter of its peak, even when the dissenter made *inaccurate* judgments that happened to conflict with the majority view. Apparently, the participants just needed to hear someone else question the accuracy of the group's perplexing responses. The importance of unanimity in fostering conformity has been replicated in subsequent research (Nemeth & Chiles, 1988).

Obedience

12e

Obedience is a form of compliance that occurs when people follow direct commands, usually from someone in a position of authority. To a surprising extent, when an authority figure says, "Jump!" many people simply ask, "How high?"

Milgram's Studies

12e

Stanley Milgram wanted to study this tendency to obey authority figures. Like many other people after World War II, he was troubled by how readily the citizens of Germany had followed the orders of dic-

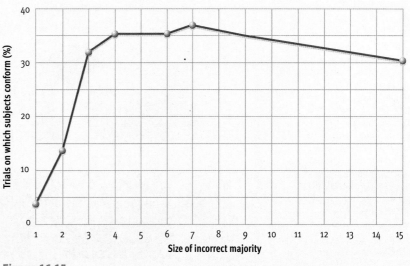

Figure 16.15

Conformity and group size. This graph shows the percentage of trials on which participants conformed as a function of group size in Asch's research. Asch found that conformity became more frequent as group size increased up to about four, and then the amount of conformity leveled off.

SOURCE: Adapted from Asch, S. (1955). Opinion and social pressure. *Scientific American, 193* (5), 31–35. Based on illustrations by Sara Love. Copyright © 1955 by Scientific American, Inc. All rights reserved.

tator Adolf Hitler, even when the orders required morally repugnant actions, such as the slaughter of millions of Jews. Milgram, who had worked with Solomon Asch, set out to design a standard laboratory procedure for the study of obedience, much like Asch's procedure for studying conformity. The clever experiment that Milgram devised became one of the most famous and controversial studies in the annals of psychology. It has been hailed as a "monumental contribution" to science and condemned as "dangerous, dehumanizing, and unethical research" (Ross, 1988). Because of its importance, it's our Featured Study for this chapter.

FEATURED STUDY

"I Was Just Following Orders"

"I was just following orders." That was the essence of Adolf Eichmann's defense when he was tried for his war crimes, which included masterminding the Nazis' attempted extermination of European Jews. Milgram wanted to determine the extent to which people are willing to follow authorities' orders. In particular, he wanted to identify the factors that lead people to follow commands that violate their ethics, such as commands to harm an innocent stranger.

Method

The participants were a diverse collection of 40 men from the local community, recruited through advertisements to participate in a study at Yale University. When a subject arrived at the lab, he met the experimenter and another sub-

ject, a likable, 47-year-old accountant, who was actually an accomplice of the experimenter. The "subjects" were told that the study would concern the effects of punishment on learning. They drew slips of paper from a hat to get their assignments, but the drawing was fixed so that the real subject always became the "teacher" and the accomplice the "learner."

The participant then watched as the learner was strapped into an electrified chair through which a shock could be delivered to the learner whenever he made a mistake on the task (left photo in Figure 16.16 on the next page). The subject was told that the shocks would be painful but "would not cause tissue damage," and he was then taken to an adjoining room that housed the shock

SOURCE: Milgram, S. (1963). Behavioral study of obedience. *Journal of Abnormal and Social Psychology, 67,* 371–378.

Figure 16.16

Milgram's experiment on obedience. The photo on the left shows the "learner" being connected to the shock generator during one of Milgram's experimental sessions. The photo on the right shows the fake shock generator used in the study. The surprising results of the Milgram (1963) study are summarized in the bar graph. Although subjects frequently protested, the vast majority (65%) delivered the entire series of shocks to the learner.

SOURCE: Photos copyright © 1965 by Stanley Milgram. From the film *Obedience*, distributed by The Pennsylvania State University. Reprinted by permission of Alexandra Milgram.

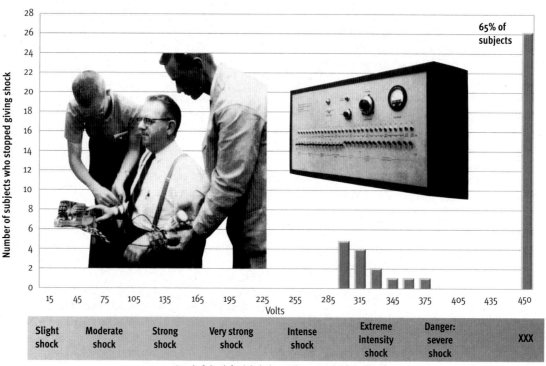

Stanley Milgram

"The essence of obedience is that a person comes to view himself as the instrument for carrying out another person's wishes, and he therefore no longer regards himself as responsible for his actions."

generator that he would control in his role as the teacher. This elaborate apparatus (right photo in **Figure 16.16**) had 30 switches designed to administer shocks varying from 15 to 450 volts, with labels ranging from "Slight shock" to "Danger: severe shock" and "XXX." Although the apparatus looked and sounded realistic, it was a fake, and the learner was never shocked.

As the "learning experiment" proceeded, the accomplice made many mistakes that necessitated shocks from the teacher, who was instructed to increase the shock level after each wrong answer. At "300 volts," the learner began to pound on the wall between the two rooms in protest and soon stopped responding to the teacher's questions. At this point, participants ordinarily turned to the experimenter for guidance. The experimenter, a 31-year-old male in a gray lab coat, firmly indicated that no response was the same as a wrong answer and that the teacher should continue to give stronger and stronger shocks to the now silent learner. If the participant expressed unwillingness to continue, the experimenter responded sternly with one of four pre-arranged prods, such as, "It is absolutely essential that you continue."

When a participant refused to obey the experimenter, the session came to an end. The dependent variable was the maximum shock the participant was willing to administer before refusing to cooperate. After each session, the true purpose of the study was explained to the subject, who was reassured that the shock was fake and the learner was unharmed.

Results

No participant stopped cooperating before the learner reached the point of pounding on the wall, but 5 quit at that point. As the graph in **Figure 16.16** shows, only 14 out of 40 subjects defied the experimenter before the full series of shocks was completed. Thus, 26 of the 40 subjects (65%) administered all 30 levels of shock. Although they tended to obey the experimenter, many participants voiced and displayed considerable distress about harming the learner. The horrified subjects groaned, bit their lips, stuttered, trembled, and broke into a sweat, but they continued administering the shocks.

Discussion

Based on these results, Milgram concluded that obedience to authority is even more common than he or others had anticipated. Before the study was conducted, Milgram had described it to 40 psychiatrists and had asked them to predict how much shock subjects would be willing to administer to their innocent victims. Most of the psychiatrists had predicted that fewer than 1% of the subjects would continue to the end of the series of shocks!

In interpreting his results, Milgram argued that strong pressure from an authority figure can make decent people do indecent things to others. Applying this insight to Nazi war crimes and other travesties, Milgram asserted that some sinister actions may not be due to actors' evil character so much as to situational pressures that can lead normal people to engage in acts of treachery and violence. Thus, he arrived at the disturbing conclusion that given the right circumstances, anyone might obey orders to inflict harm on innocent strangers.

Comment

In itself, obedience is not necessarily bad or wrong. Social groups of any size depend on obedience to function smoothly. Life would be chaotic if orders from police, parents, physicians, bosses, generals, and presidents were routinely ignored. However, Milgram's study suggests that many people are overly willing to submit to the orders of someone in command.

If you're like most people, you're probably confident that you wouldn't follow an experimenter's demands to inflict harm on a helpless victim. But the empirical findings indicate that you're probably wrong. After many replications, the results are deplorable, but clear: Most people can be coerced into engaging in actions that violate their morals and values. This finding is disheartening, but it sharpens our understanding of moral atrocities, such as the Nazi persecutions of Jews.

After his initial demonstration, Milgram (1974) tried about 20 variations on his experimental procedure, looking for factors that influence participants' obedience. In one variation, Milgram moved the study away from Yale's campus to see if the prestige of the university was contributing to the subjects' obedience. When the study was run in a seedy office building by the "Research Associates of Bridgeport," only a small decrease in obedience was observed (48% of the subjects gave all the shocks).

In another version of the study, Milgram borrowed a trick from Asch's conformity experiments and set up teams of three teachers that included two more accomplices. When they drew lots, the real subject was always selected to run the shock apparatus in consultation with his fellow teachers. When both accomplices accepted the experimenter's orders to continue shocking the learner, the pressure increased obedience a bit. However, if an accomplice defied the experimenter and supported the subject's objections, obedience declined dramatically (only 10% of the subjects gave all the shocks), just as conformity had dropped rapidly when dissent surfaced in Asch's conformity studies. Dissent from another "teacher" turned out to be one of the few variations that reduced participants' obedience appreciably. As a whole, Milgram was surprised at how high subjects' obedience remained as he changed various aspects of his experiment.

The Ensuing Controversy

PSYK TREK 12e

Milgram's study evoked a controversy that continues through today. Some critics argued that Milgram's results couldn't be generalized to apply to the real world (Baumrind, 1964; Orne & Holland, 1968). They maintained that participants went along only because they knew it was an experiment and "everything must be okay." Or they argued that subjects who agree to participate in a scientific study *expect to obey* orders from an experimenter. Milgram (1964, 1968) replied by arguing that if subjects had thought "everything must be okay," they wouldn't have experienced the enormous distress that they clearly showed.

As for the idea that research participants expect to follow an experimenter's commands, Milgram pointed out that so do real-world soldiers and bureaucrats who are accused of villainous acts performed in obedience to authority. "I reject Baumrind's argument that the observed obedience doesn't count because it occurred where it is appropriate," said Milgram (1964). "That is precisely why it *does* count." Overall, the evidence supports the generalizability of Milgram's results, which were consistently replicated for many years, in diverse settings, with a variety of subjects and procedural variations (Blass, 1999; Miller, 1986).

Critics also questioned the ethics of Milgram's procedure (Baumrind, 1964; Kelman, 1967). They noted that without prior consent, subjects were exposed to extensive deception that could undermine their trust in people and to severe stress that could leave emotional scars. Moreover, most participants also had to confront the disturbing fact that they caved in to the experimenter's commands to inflict harm on an innocent victim.

Milgram's defenders argued that the brief distress experienced by his participants was a small price to pay for the insights that emerged from his obedience studies. Looking back, however, many psychologists seem to share the critics' concerns about the ethical implications of Milgram's work. His procedure is questionable by contemporary standards of research ethics, and no exact replications of his obedience study have been conducted in the United States since the mid-1970s (Blass, 1991)—a bizarre epitaph for what may be psychology's best-known experiment.

Cultural Variations in Conformity and Obedience

Are conformity and obedience unique to American culture? By no means. The Asch and Milgram experiments have been repeated in many societies, where they have yielded results roughly similar to those seen in the United States. Thus, the phenomena of conformity and obedience seem to transcend culture.

The replications of Milgram's obedience study have largely been limited to industrialized nations similar to the United States. Comparisons of the

web link 16.4

Stanley Milgram
This site provides a wealth of accurate information about the work of Stanley Milgram, arguably one of the most controversial and creative social psychologists in the field's history. The site is maintained by Thomas Blass, a psychology professor at the University of Maryland (Baltimore County), who has published many articles and books on the life and work of Milgram.

results of these studies must be made with caution because the composition of the samples and the experimental procedures have varied somewhat. But many of the studies have reported even higher obedience rates than those seen in Milgram's American samples. For example, obedience rates of over 80% have been reported for samples from Italy, Germany, Austria, Spain, and Holland (Smith & Bond, 1994). Thus, the surprisingly high level of obedience observed by Milgram does not appear to be peculiar to the United States.

The Asch experiment has been repeated in a more diverse range of societies than the Milgram experiment. Like many other cultural differences in social behavior, variations in conformity appear to be related to the degree of *individualism versus collectivism* seen in a society. Various theorists have argued that collectivistic cultures, which emphasize respect for group norms, cooperation, and harmony, probably encourage more conformity than individualistic cultures (Schwartz, 1990) and have a more positive view of conformity (Kim & Markus, 1999). As Matsumoto (1994) puts it, "To conform in American culture is to be weak or deficient somehow. But this is not true in other cultures. Many cultures foster more collective, group-oriented values, and concepts of conformity, obedience, and compliance enjoy much higher status" (p. 162). Consistent with this analysis, studies *have* found higher levels of conformity in collectivistic cultures than in individualistic cultures (Bond & Smith, 1996; Smith, 2001).

The Power of the Situation: The Stanford Prison Simulation

The research of Asch and Milgram provided dramatic demonstrations of the potent influence that situational factors can have on social behavior. The power of the situation was underscored once again, about a decade after Milgram's obedience research, in another landmark study conducted by Philip Zimbardo, who, ironically, was a high school classmate of Milgram's. Zimbardo and his colleagues designed the Stanford Prison Simulation to investigate why prisons tend to become abusive, degrading, violent environments (Haney, Banks, & Zimbardo, 1973; Zimbardo, Haney, & Banks, 1973). Like Milgram, Zimbardo wanted to see how much the power of the situation would shape the behavior of normal, average subjects.

The participants were college students recruited for a study of prison life through a newspaper ad. After giving 70 volunteers an extensive battery of tests and interviews, the researchers chose 24 students who appeared to be physically healthy and psychologically stable to be the subjects. A coin flip determined which of them would be "guards" and which would be "prisoners" in a simulated prison setup at Stanford University. The prisoners were "arrested" at their homes, handcuffed, and transported to a mock prison on the Stanford campus. Upon arrival, they were ordered to strip, sprayed with a delousing agent, given prison uniforms (smocks), assigned numbers as their identities, and locked up in iron-barred cells. The subjects assigned to be guards were given khaki uniforms, billy clubs, whistles, and reflective sunglasses. They were told that they could run their prison in whatever way they wanted except that they were not allowed to use physical punishment.

What happened? In short order, confrontations occurred between the guards and prisoners, and the guards quickly devised a variety of sometimes cruel strategies to maintain total control over their prisoners. Meals, blankets, and bathroom privileges were selectively denied to some prisoners to achieve control. The prisoners were taunted, humiliated, called demeaning names, and forced to beg for opportunities to go to the bathroom. Pointless, petty rules were strictly enforced and difficult prisoners were punished with hard labor (doing pushups and jumping jacks, cleaning toilets with their bare hands). The guards harassed the prisoners by waking them up in the middle of the night to assemble and count off. And the guards creatively turned a 2-foot by 2-foot closet into a "hole" for solitary confinement of rebellious prisoners. Although there was some variation among the guards, collectively they became mean, malicious, and abusive in fulfilling their responsibilities. How did the prisoners react? A few showed signs of emotional disturbance and had to be released early, but they mostly became listless, apathetic, and demoralized. The study was designed to run two weeks, but Zimbardo decided that he needed to end it prematurely after just six days because he was concerned about the rapidly escalating abuse and degradation of the prisoners. The subjects were debriefed, offered counseling, and sent home.

How did Zimbardo and his colleagues explain the stunning transformations of their subjects? First, they attributed the participants' behavior to the enormous influence of social roles. **Social roles are widely shared expectations about how people in certain positions are supposed to behave.** We have role expectations for salespeople, waiters, ministers, medical patients, students, bus drivers, tourists, flight attendants, and, of course, prison guards and prisoners. The participants had a rough idea of what it meant to act like a guard or a prisoner and they were gradually consumed by their roles (Haney & Zimbardo, 1998). Second, the researchers attributed

Philip Zimbardo

"But in the end, I called off the experiment not because of the horror I saw out there in the prison yard, but because of the horror of realizing that I could have easily traded places with the most brutal guard or become the weakest prisoner full of hatred at being so powerless."

Courtesy of Philip Zimbardo

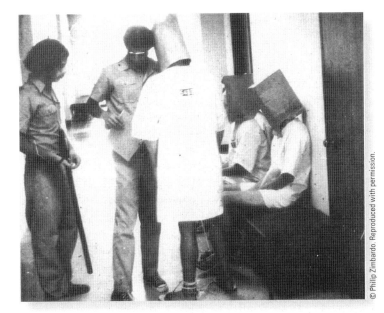

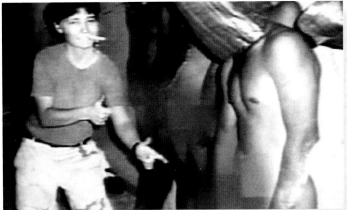

The recent Abu Ghraib prison scandal in Iraq has sparked renewed interest in the Stanford Prison Simulation. Some of the photos taken of the abuse at Abu Ghraib (right) are stunningly similar to photos from the Stanford study (left). For instance, in both cases, the guards "dehumanized" their prisoners by placing bags over their heads.

their subjects' behavior to the compelling power of situational factors. Before the study began, the tests and interviews showed no measureable differences in personality or character between those randomly assigned to be guards versus prisoners. The stark differences in their behavior had to be due to the radically different situations that they found themselves in. As Haney and Zimbardo (1998, p. 719) put it, the study "demonstrated the power of situations to overwhelm people and elicit from them unexpectedly cruel, yet 'situationally appropriate' behavior." As a result, Zimbardo, like Milgram before him, concluded that situational pressures can lead normal, decent people to behave in sinister, repugnant ways.

The results of the Stanford Prison Simulation were eye-opening, to say the least. Within a short time, subjects with no obvious character flaws became tyrannical, sadistic, brutal guards. If this transformation can occur so swiftly in a make-believe prison, one can only imagine how the much stronger situational forces in real prisons readily promote abusive behavior. Although the Stanford Prison Simulation was conducted over 30 years ago, renewed interest in the study was sparked by the Abu Ghraib prison scandal in Iraq in 2004. American military personnel with little or no experience in running prisons were found to have engaged in "sadistic, blatant, and wanton criminal abuses" of their Iraqi prisoners (Hersh, 2004). Some of the photos taken of the abuse at Abu Ghraib are eerily reminiscent of photos from the Stanford simulation. The U.S. government blamed these horrific abuses on "a few bad apples" who were presumed to be pathological or morally deficient, writing off the incident as an aberration. Yet the evidence from the Stanford Prison Simulation clearly suggests otherwise. Phil Zimbardo (2004,

2007) argues, and has testified as an expert witness, that it is far more likely that situational pressures led normal, average Americans to commit morally reprehensible abuses. This explanation does *not* absolve the brutal guards of responsibility for their behavior. However, Zimbardo emphasizes that making scapegoats out of a handful of guards does not solve the real problem, which lies in the system. He maintains that abuses in prisons are more likely than not and can only be reduced if authorities provide extensive training and strong supervision for guards, enact explicit sanctions for abuses, and maintain clear accountability in the chain of command.

web link 16.5

Stanford Prison Experiment

The Stanford Prison Simulation is one of psychology's most renowned studies. At this site, Phil Zimbardo provides a fascinating slide show explaining the study in depth. The site also includes discussion questions, reflections on the study 30 years after it was conducted, and links to a host of related materials. The links include recent writings by Zimbardo that analyze the Abu Ghraib prison scandal.

REVIEW of Key Learning Goals

16.18 Asch found that subjects often conform to the group, even when the group reports inaccurate judgments on a simple line-judging task. Conformity becomes more likely as group size increases, up to a group size of four, then levels off. If a small group isn't unanimous, conformity declines rapidly.

16.19 In Milgram's landmark study of obedience to authority, adult men drawn from the community showed a remarkable tendency, despite their misgivings, to follow orders to shock an innocent stranger. Milgram concluded that situational pressures can make decent people do indecent things. Critics asserted that Milgram's results were not generalizable to the real world and that his methods were unethical. The generalizability of Milgram's findings has stood the test of time, but his work also helped to stimulate stricter ethical standards for research.

16.20 The Asch and Milgram experiments have been replicated in many cultures. These replications have uncovered modest cultural variations in the propensity to conform or to obey an authority figure.

16.21 The Stanford Prison Simulation, in which normal, healthy students were randomly assigned to be prisoners or guards, demonstrated that social roles and other situational pressures can exert tremendous influence over social behavior. Like Milgram, Zimbardo showed that situational forces can lead normal people to exhibit surprisingly callous, abusive behavior.

Behavior in Groups: Joining with Others

Key Learning Goals

16.22 Clarify the nature of groups and the bystander effect.

16.23 Evaluate evidence on group productivity, including social loafing.

16.24 Explain group polarization, groupthink, and the favorable effects of groups on decision making.

Social psychologists study groups as well as individuals, but exactly what is a group? Are all the divorced fathers living in Baltimore a group? Are three strangers moving skyward in an elevator a group? What if the elevator gets stuck? How about four students from your psychology class who study together regularly? A jury deciding a trial? The Boston Celtics? The U.S. Congress? Some of these collections of people are groups and others aren't. Let's examine the concept of a group to find out which of these collections qualify.

In social psychologists' eyes, a *group* consists of two or more individuals who interact and are interdependent. The divorced fathers in Baltimore aren't likely to qualify on either count. Strangers sharing an elevator might interact briefly, but they're not interdependent. However, if the elevator got stuck and they had to deal with an emergency together, they could suddenly become a group. Your psychology classmates who study together are a group, as they interact and depend on each other to achieve shared goals. So do the members of a jury, a sports team such as the Celtics, and a large organization such as the U.S. Congress. Historically, most groups have interacted on a face-to-face basis, but advances in telecommunications are changing that reality. In the era of the Internet, people can interact, become interdependent, and develop a group identity without ever meeting in person (Bargh & McKenna, 2004; McKenna & Bargh, 1998).

Groups vary in many ways. Obviously, a study group, the Celtics, and Congress are very different in terms of size, purpose, formality, longevity, similarity of members, and diversity of activities. Can anything meaningful be said about groups if they're so diverse? Yes. In spite of their immense variability, groups share certain features that affect their functioning. Among other things, most groups have *roles* that allocate special responsibilities to some members, *norms* about suitable behavior, a *communication structure* that reflects who talks to whom, and a *power structure* that determines which members wield the most influence (Forsyth, 2006).

Thus, when people join together in a group, they create a social organism with unique characteristics and dynamics that can take on a life of its own. One of social psychology's enduring insights is that in a given situation you may behave quite differently when you're in a group than when you're alone. To illustrate this point, let's look at some interesting research on helping behavior.

Behavior Alone and in Groups: The Case of the Bystander Effect

Imagine that you have a precarious medical condition and that you must go through life worrying about whether someone will leap forward to provide help if the need ever arises. Wouldn't you feel more secure when around larger groups? After all, there's "safety in numbers." Logically, as group size increases, the probability of having a "good Samaritan" on the scene increases. Or does it?

We've seen before that human behavior isn't necessarily logical. When it comes to helping behavior, many studies have uncovered an apparent paradox called the *bystander effect:* **People are less likely to provide needed help when they are in groups than when they are alone.** Evidence that your probability of getting help *declines* as group size increases was first described by John Darley and Bibb Latané (1968), who were conducting research on the determinants of helping behavior. In the Darley and Latané study, students in individual cubicles connected by an intercom participated in discussion groups of three sizes. (The separate cubicles allowed the researchers to examine each individual's behavior in a group context, a technique that minimizes confounded variables in individual-group comparisons.) Early in the discussion, a student who was an experimental accomplice hesitantly mentioned that he was prone to seizures. Later in the discussion, the same accomplice feigned a severe seizure and cried out for help. Although a majority of subjects sought assistance for the student, the tendency to seek help *declined* with increasing group size.

Similar trends have been seen in many other experiments, in which over 6000 subjects have had opportunities to respond to apparent emergencies, including fires, asthma attacks, faintings, crashes, and flat tires, as well as less pressing needs to answer a door or to pick up objects dropped by a stranger (Latané & Nida, 1981). Many of the experiments have been highly realistic studies conducted in subways, stores, and shopping malls, and many have compared individuals against groups in face-to-face interaction. Pooling the results of this research, Latané and Nida (1981) estimated that subjects who were alone provided help 75% of the time, whereas subjects in the presence of others provided help only 53% of the time. They concluded that the only significant limiting condition on the bystander effect is that it is less likely to occur when the need for help is unambiguous. For example, the bystander effect is less likely when someone is in obvious physical danger (Fischer et al., 2006).

What accounts for the bystander effect? A number of factors may be at work. Bystander effects are most likely in ambiguous situations because people look around to see whether others think there's an emergency. If everyone hesitates, their inaction suggests that there's no real need for help. The *diffusion of responsibility* that occurs in a group is also important. If you're by yourself when you encounter someone in need of help, the responsibility to provide help rests squarely on your shoulders. However, if other people are present, the responsibility is divided among you, and you may all say to yourselves, "Someone else will help." A reduced sense of responsibility may contribute to other aspects of behavior in groups, as we'll see in the next section.

Group Productivity and Social Loafing

Have you ever driven through a road construction project—at a snail's pace, of course—and become irritated because so many workers seem to be just standing around? Maybe the irony of the posted sign "Your tax dollars at work" made you imagine that they were all dawdling. And then again, perhaps not. Individuals' productivity often *does* decline in larger groups (Karau & Williams, 1993). This fact is unfortunate, as many important tasks can only be accomplished in groups. Group productivity is crucial to committees, sports teams, firefighting crews, sororities, study groups, symphonies, and work teams of all kinds, from the morning crew in a little diner to the board of directors of a Fortune 500 company.

Two factors appear to contribute to reduced individual productivity in larger groups. One factor is *reduced efficiency* resulting from the *loss of coordination* among workers' efforts. As you put more people on a yearbook staff, for instance, you'll probably create more and more duplication of effort and increase how often group members end up working at cross purposes.

The second factor contributing to low productivity in groups involves *effort* rather than efficiency. *Social loafing* is a reduction in effort by individuals when they work in groups as compared to when they work by themselves. To investigate social loafing, Latané and his colleagues (1979) measured the sound output produced by subjects who were asked to cheer or clap as loud as they could. So they couldn't see or hear other group members, subjects were told that the study concerned the importance of sensory feedback and were asked to don blindfolds and put on headphones through which loud noise was played. This maneuver permitted a simple deception: Subjects were *led to believe* that they were working alone or in a group of two or six, when in fact *individual* output was actually measured.

When participants *thought* that they were working in larger groups, their individual output declined. Since lack of coordination could not affect individual output, the subjects' decreased sound production had to be due to reduced effort. Latané and his colleagues also had the same subjects clap and shout in genuine groups of two and six and found an additional decrease in production that was attributed to loss of coordination. Figure 16.17 on the next page shows how social loafing and loss of coordination combined to reduce productivity as group size increased.

The social-loafing effect has been replicated in numerous studies in which subjects have worked on a variety of tasks, including cheering, pumping air, swimming in a relay race, solving mazes, evaluating editorials, and brainstorming for new ideas (Karau & Williams, 1995; Levine & Moreland, 1998). Social loafing and the bystander effect appear to share a common cause: diffusion of responsibility in groups (Comer, 1995; Latané, 1981). As group size increases, the responsibility for getting a job done is divided among more people, and many group members ease up because their individual contribution is less recognizable. Thus, social loafing occurs in situations where individuals can "hide in the crowd" (Karau & Williams, 1993).

Social loafing is *not* inevitable. For example, people with high achievement motivation are less likely to exhibit social loafing than others (Hart et al., 2004). People who score high on the personality traits of agreeableness and conscientiousness are also less prone to social loafing (Klehe & Anderson, 2007). Social loafing is less likely when individuals' personal contributions to productivity are readily identifiable (Hoigaard & Ingvaldsen, 2006) and when group norms encour-

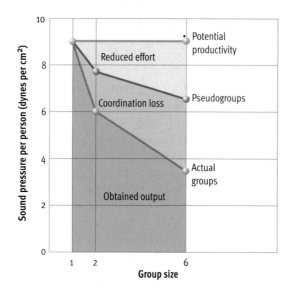

Figure 16.17

The effect of loss of coordination and social loafing on group productivity. The amount of sound produced per person declined noticeably when people worked in actual groups of two or six (orange line). This decrease in productivity reflects both loss of coordination and social loafing. Sound per person also declined when subjects merely thought they were working in groups of two or six (purple line). This smaller decrease in productivity is due to social loafing.

SOURCE: Adapted from Latané, B., Williams, K., & Harkins, S. (1979). Many hands make light the work: The causes and consequences of social loafing. *Journal of Personality and Social Psychology, 37,* 822–832. Copyright © 1979 by the American Psychological Association. Adapted by permission of the author.

age productivity and personal involvement (Hoigaard, Safvenbom, & Tonnessen, 2006). And social loafing is reduced when people work in smaller and more cohesive groups (Liden et al., 2004). Cultural factors may also influence the likelihood of social loafing. Studies with subjects from Japan, China, and Taiwan suggest that social loafing may be less prevalent in collectivistic cultures, which place a high priority on meeting group goals and contributing to one's ingroups (Karau & Williams, 1995; Smith, 2001).

Decision Making in Groups

Productivity is not the only issue that commonly concerns groups. When people join together in groups, they often have to make decisions about what the group will do and how it will use its resources. Whether it's your study group deciding what type of pizza to order, a jury deciding on a verdict, or Congress deciding on whether to pass a bill, groups make decisions.

Evaluating decision making is often more complicated than evaluating productivity. In many cases, the "right" decision may not be readily apparent. Who can say whether your study group ordered the right pizza or whether Congress passed the right bills? Nonetheless, social psychologists have discovered some interesting tendencies in group decision making.

Group Polarization

Who leans toward more cautious decisions: individuals or groups? Common sense suggests that groups will work out compromises that cancel out members' extreme views. Hence, the collective wisdom of the group should yield relatively conservative choices. Is common sense correct? To investigate this question, Stoner (1961) asked individual subjects to give their recommendations on tough decisions and then asked the same subjects to engage in group discussion to arrive at joint recommendations. When Stoner compared individuals' average recommendation against their group decision generated through

---

concept check 16.4

Scrutinizing Common Sense

Check your understanding of the implications of research in social psychology by indicating whether the common-sense assertions listed below have been supported by empirical findings. Do the trends in research summarized in this chapter indicate that the following statements are true or false? The answers are in Appendix A.

_____ 1. Generally, in forming their impressions of others, people don't judge a book by its cover.

_____ 2. When it comes to attraction, birds of a feather flock together.

_____ 3. In the realm of love, opposites attract.

_____ 4. If you're the target of persuasion, to be forewarned is to be forearmed.

_____ 5. When you need help, there's safety in numbers.

discussion, he found that groups arrived at *riskier* decisions than individuals did. Stoner's finding was replicated in other studies (Pruitt, 1971), and the phenomenon acquired the name *risky shift*.

However, investigators eventually determined that groups can shift either way, toward risk or caution, depending on which way the group is leaning to begin with (Friedkin, 1999). A shift toward a more extreme position, an effect called *polarization,* is often the result of group discussion (Tindale, Kameda, & Hinsz, 2003). Thus, **group polarization occurs when group discussion strengthens a group's dominant point of view and produces a shift toward a more extreme decision in that direction** (see Figure 16.18). Group polarization does *not* involve widening the gap between factions in a group, as its name might suggest. In fact, group polarization can contribute to consensus in a group, as we'll see in our discussion of groupthink.

Groupthink

In contrast to group polarization, which is a normal process in group dynamics, groupthink is more like a "disease" that can infect decision making in groups.

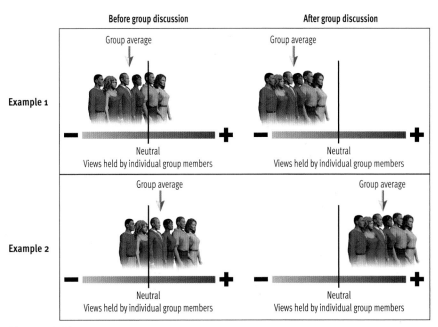

Figure 16.18

Group polarization. Two examples of group polarization are diagrammed here. The positions of the people on the horizontal scales reflect their positive or negative attitudes regarding an idea before and after group discussion. In the first example (top) a group starts out mildly opposed to an idea, but after discussion sentiment against the idea is stronger. In the second example (bottom), a group starts out with a favorable disposition toward an idea, and this disposition is strengthened by group discussion.

Many types of groups have to arrive at collective decisions. The social dynamics of group decisions are complicated, and a variety of factors can undermine effective decision making.

Groupthink occurs when members of a cohesive group emphasize concurrence at the expense of critical thinking in arriving at a decision. As you might imagine, groupthink doesn't produce very effective decision making. Indeed, groupthink can lead to major blunders that may look incomprehensible after the fact. Irving Janis (1972) first described groupthink in his effort to explain how President John F. Kennedy and his advisers could have miscalculated so badly in deciding to invade Cuba at the Bay of Pigs in 1961. The attempted invasion failed miserably and, in retrospect, seemed remarkably ill-conceived.

Applying his many years of research and theory on group dynamics to the Bay of Pigs fiasco, Janis developed a model of groupthink. When groups get caught up in groupthink, members suspend their critical judgment and the group starts censoring dissent as the pressure to conform increases. Soon, everyone begins to think alike. Moreover, "mind guards" try to shield the group from information that contradicts the group's view.

If the group's view is challenged from outside, victims of groupthink tend to think in simplistic "us versus them" terms. Members begin to overestimate the ingroup's unanimity, and they begin to view the outgroup as the enemy. Groupthink also promotes incomplete gathering of information. Like individuals, groups often display a confirmation bias, as they tend to seek and focus on information that supports their initial views (Schulz-Hardt et al., 2000).

What causes groupthink? According to Janis, a key precondition is high group cohesiveness. *Group cohesiveness* refers to the strength of the liking relationships linking group members to each other and to the group itself. Members of cohesive groups are close-knit, are committed, have "team spirit," and are loyal to the group. Cohesiveness itself isn't bad. It can facilitate group productivity (Mullen & Copper, 1994) and help groups achieve great things. But Janis maintains that the danger of groupthink is greater when groups are highly cohesive. Groupthink is also more likely when a group

works in relative isolation, when the group's power structure is dominated by a strong, directive leader, and when the group is under stress to make a major decision. Under these conditions, group discussions can easily lead to group polarization, strengthening the group's dominant view.

A relatively small number of experiments have been conducted to test Janis's theory, because the antecedent conditions thought to foster groupthink—such as high decision stress, strong group cohesiveness, and dominating leadership—are difficult to create effectively in laboratory settings (Aldag & Fuller, 1993). The studies that have been conducted have yielded mixed results in that high cohesiveness and strong leadership do not *necessarily* produce groupthink (Baron, 2005; Kerr & Tindale, 2004). Thus, the evidence on groupthink consists mostly of retrospective case studies of major decision-making fiascos (Eaton, 2001). In light of this situation, Janis's model of groupthink should probably be characterized as an innovative, sophisticated, intuitively appealing theory that needs to be subjected to much more empirical study.

Favorable Effects in Groups

After reading about group polarization and groupthink you may be thinking that decision making in groups is fundamentally flawed, but groups have their advantages as well as their disadvantages. For example, Forsyth (2006) notes that investment groups are superior to individuals in picking stocks, that groups exhibit greater accuracy than individuals on person perception tasks, and that teams of physicians generate better diagnoses than individual physicians. Research also shows that teams of students outperform individual students on academic tests (Zimbardo, Butler, & Wolfe, 2003). And studies have demonstrated that groups are better than individuals at solving complicated logic problems (Laughlin et al., 2003, 2006). So, although group decision making can go awry, groups are nonetheless superior to individuals on many types of tasks.

REVIEW of Key Learning Goals

16.22 A group consists of two or more people who interact and are interdependent. People are more likely to help someone in need when they are alone than when a group is present. This phenomenon, called the bystander effect, occurs primarily because a group creates diffusion of responsibility.

16.23 Individuals' productivity often declines in larger groups because of loss of coordination and because of social loafing. Social loafing seems to be due mostly to diffusion of re-

sponsibility and may be less prevalent in certain circumstances and in collectivist cultures.

16.24 Group polarization occurs when discussion leads a group to shift toward a more extreme decision in the direction the group was already leaning. In groupthink, a cohesive group suspends critical judgment in a misguided effort to promote agreement in decision making. Nonetheless, groups are superior to individuals on many types of decision making tasks

Reflecting on the Chapter's Themes

Our discussion of social psychology has provided a final embellishment on three of our seven unifying themes. One of these is the value of psychology's commitment to empiricism—that is, its reliance on systematic observation through research to arrive at conclusions. The second theme that stands out is the importance of cultural factors in shaping behavior, and the third is the extent to which people's experience of the world is highly subjective. Let's consider the virtues of empiricism first.

It's easy to question the need to do scientific research on social behavior, because studies in social psychology often seem to verify common sense. While most people wouldn't presume to devise their own theory of color vision, question the significance of REM sleep, or quibble about the principal causes of schizophrenia, everyone has beliefs about the nature of love, how to persuade others, and people's willingness to help in times of need. Thus, when studies demonstrate that credibility enhances persuasion, or that good looks facilitate attraction, it's tempting to conclude that social psychologists go to great lengths to document the obvious, and some critics say, "Why bother?"

You saw why in this chapter. Research in social psychology has repeatedly shown that the predictions of logic and common sense are often wrong. Consider just a few examples. Even psychiatric experts failed to predict the remarkable obedience to authority uncovered in Milgram's research. The bystander effect in helping behavior violates cold-blooded mathematical logic. Dissonance research has shown that after a severe initiation, the bigger

the letdown, the more favorable people's feelings are. These principles defy common sense. Thus, research on social behavior provides dramatic illustrations of why psychologists put their faith in empiricism.

Our coverage of social psychology also demonstrated once again that, cross-culturally, behavior is characterized by both variance and invariance. Thus, we saw substantial cultural differences in patterns of attribution, the role of romantic love in marriage, attitudes about conformity, the tendency to obey authority figures, and the likelihood of social loafing. Although basic social phenomena such as stereotyping, attraction, obedience, and conformity probably occur all over the world, cross-cultural studies of social behavior show that research findings based on American samples may not generalize precisely to other cultures.

Research in social psychology is also uniquely suited for making the point that people's view of the world is highly personal and subjective. In this chapter we saw how physical appearance can color perception of a person's ability or personality, how stereotypes can lead people to see what they expect to see in their interactions with others, how pressure to conform can make people begin to doubt their senses, and how groupthink can lead group members down a perilous path of shared illusions.

The subjectivity of social perception will surface once again in our Applications for the chapter. The Personal Application focuses on prejudice, a practical problem that social psychologists have shown great interest in, whereas the Critical Thinking Application examines aspects of social influence.

Key Learning Goals
16.25 Identify the three unifying themes highlighted in this chapter.

Empiricism

Cultural Heritage

Subjectivity of Experience

REVIEW of Key Learning Goals

16.25 Our study of social psychology highlighted three of the text's unifying themes: the value of empiricism, the cultural limits of research based on American samples, and the subjectivity of perception.

Understanding Prejudice

Answer the following "true" or "false."

____ **1** Prejudice and discrimination amount to the same thing.

____ **2** Stereotypes are always negative or unflattering.

____ **3** Ethnic and racial groups are the only widespread targets of prejudice in modern society.

____ **4** People see members of their own in-group as being more alike than the members of outgroups.

Key Learning Goals

16.26 Relate person perception processes and attributional bias to prejudice.

16.27 Relate principles of attitude formation and intergroup competition to prejudice.

16.28 Relate ingroups, outgroups, and threats to social identity to prejudice.

James Byrd Jr., a 49-year-old black man, was walking home from a family gathering in the summer of 1998 when he was offered a ride by three white men, one of whom he knew. Shortly thereafter, pieces of Byrd's savagely beaten body were found strewn along a rural road in Texas. Apparently, he had been beaten, then shackled by his ankles to the back of the truck and dragged to death over 2 miles of road. Police say that Byrd was targeted simply because he was black. Thankfully, such tragic events are relatively rare in the United States. Nonetheless, they remind us that prejudice and discrimination still exist.

Prejudice is a major social problem. It harms victims' self-concepts, suppresses their potential, creates enormous stress in their lives, and promotes tension and strife between groups (Dion, 2003). The first step toward reducing prejudice is to understand its roots. Hence, in this Application, we'll try to achieve a better understanding of why prejudice is so common. Along the way, you'll learn the answers to the true-false questions on the previous page.

Prejudice and discrimination are closely related concepts, and the terms have become nearly interchangeable in popular use. Social scientists, however, prefer to define their terms precisely, so let's clarify the concepts. *Prejudice* is a negative attitude held toward members of a group. Like many other attitudes, prejudice can include three components (see Figure 16.19): beliefs ("Indians are mostly alcoholics"), emotions ("I despise Jews"), and behavioral dispositions ("I wouldn't hire a Mexican"). Racial prejudice receives the lion's share of publicity, but prejudice is *not* limited to ethnic groups. Women, homosexuals, the aged, the disabled, and the mentally ill are also targets of widespread prejudice. Thus, many people hold prejudicial attitudes toward one group or another, and many have been victims of prejudice.

Prejudice may lead to *discrimination*, which involves behaving differently, usually unfairly, toward the members of a group. Prejudice and discrimination tend to go hand in hand, but as LaPiere's (1934) pioneering study of discrimination in restaurant seating showed (see p. 682), attitudes and behavior do not necessarily correspond

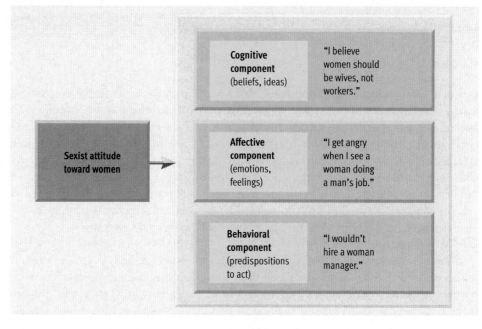

Figure 16.19

The three potential components of prejudice as an attitude. Attitudes can consist of up to three components. The tricomponent model of attitudes, applied to prejudice against women, would view sexism as negative beliefs about women (cognitive component) that lead to a feeling of dislike (affective component), which in turn leads to a readiness to discriminate against women (behavioral component).

(Hogg & Abrams, 2003; see Figure 16.20). In our discussion, we'll concentrate primarily on the attitude of prejudice. Let's begin by looking at processes in person perception that promote prejudice.

Stereotyping and Subjectivity in Person Perception 12d

Perhaps no factor plays a larger role in prejudice than *stereotypes*. That's not to say

that stereotypes are inevitably negative. For instance, it's hardly insulting to assert that Americans are ambitious or that the Japanese are industrious. Unfortunately, many people do subscribe to derogatory stereotypes of various ethnic groups. Although studies suggest that negative racial stereotypes have diminished over the last 50 years, they're not a thing of the past (Madon et al., 2001; Mellor, 2003). Not surprisingly, white Americans tend to think more progress has occurred toward racial equality

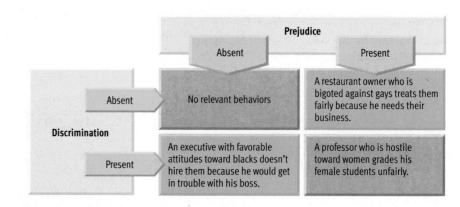

Figure 16.20

Relationship between prejudice and discrimination. As these examples show, prejudice can exist without discrimination and discrimination without prejudice. In the green cells, there is a disparity between attitude and behavior.

than black Americans do (Eibach & Keegan, 2006). According to a variety of investigators, modern racism has merely become more subtle (Devine, Plant, & Blair, 2001; Dovidio & Gaertner, 2000, 2008). Many people carefully avoid overt expressions of prejudicial attitudes but covertly continue to harbor negative views of racial minorities. These people endorse racial equality as an abstract principle but often oppose concrete programs intended to promote equality, on the grounds that discrimination is no longer a problem (Wright & Taylor, 2003). Studies suggest that modern sexism has become subtle in much the same way as racism (Swim & Campbell, 2001).

Research indicates that prejudicial stereotypes are so pervasive and insidious they often operate automatically (Amodio et al., 2004; Fiske, 2000), even in people who truly renounce prejudice. Thus, a man who rejects prejudice against homosexuals may still feel uncomfortable sitting next to a gay male on a bus, even though he regards his reaction as inappropriate.

Unfortunately, stereotypes are highly resistant to change. When people encounter members of a group that they view with prejudice who deviate from the stereotype of that group, they often find ways to discount this evidence. For example, people who are high in prejudice tend to attribute minorities' stereotype-consistent behavior to internal factors (the person), whereas they attribute stereotype-inconsistent behavior to external factors (the situation). This pattern of thinking allows people to preserve their stereotypes (Sherman et al., 2005).

Stereotypes also persist because the *subjectivity* of person perception makes it likely that people will see what they expect to see when they actually come into contact with groups that they view with prejudice (Dunning & Sherman, 1997). For example, Dun-can (1976) had white subjects watch and evaluate interaction on a TV monitor that was supposedly live (it was actually a videotape) and varied the race of a person who gets into an argument and gives another person a slight shove. The shove was coded as "violent behavior" by 73% of the subjects when the actor was black but by only 13% of the subjects when the actor was white. As we've noted before, people's perceptions are highly subjective. Because of stereotypes, even "violence" may lie in the eye of the beholder.

Memory biases are also tilted in favor of confirming people's prejudices (Ybarra, Stephan, & Schaberg, 2000). For example, if a man believes that "women are not cut out for leadership roles," he may dwell with delight on his female supervisor's mistakes and quickly forget about her achievements. Thus, the *illusory correlation effect* can contribute to the maintenance of prejudicial stereotypes (Berndsen et al., 2002).

Members of many types of groups are victims of prejudice. Besides racial minorities, others that have been stereotyped and discriminated against include gays and lesbians, women, the homeless, and those who are overweight.

© UPI Photo/Terry Schmitt/Landov

Biases in Attribution

12d

Attribution processes can also help perpetuate stereotypes and prejudice (Maass, 1999). Research taking its cue from Weiner's (1980) model of attribution has shown that people often make *biased attributions for success and failure*. For example, men and women don't get equal credit for their successes (Swim & Sanna, 1996). Observers often discount a woman's success by attributing it to good luck, sheer effort, or the ease of the task (except on traditional feminine tasks). In comparison, a man's success is more likely to be attributed to his outstanding ability (see Figure 16.21). For example, one recent study found that when a man and woman collaborate on a stereotypically "male" task, both male and female observers downplay the woman's contribution (Heilman & Haynes, 2005). These biased patterns of attribution help sustain the stereotype that men are more competent than women.

Recall that the *fundamental attribution error* is a bias toward explaining events by pointing to the actor's personal characteristics as causes (internal attributions). Research suggests that people are particularly likely to make this error when evaluating targets of prejudice (Hewstone, 1990). Thus, when people take note of ethnic neighborhoods dominated by crime and poverty, the personal qualities of the residents are blamed for these problems, whereas other explanations emphasizing situational factors (job discrimination, poor police service, and so on) are downplayed or ignored. The old saying "They should be able to pull themselves up by their bootstraps" is a blanket dismissal of how situational factors may make it especially difficult for minorities to achieve upward mobility.

Defensive attribution, which involves unjustly blaming victims of misfortune for their adversity, can also contribute to prejudice. A prominent example in recent years has been the assertion by some people that homosexuals brought the AIDS crisis on themselves and so deserve their fate (Anderson, 1992). By blaming AIDS on gays' alleged character flaws, heterosexuals may be unknowingly seeking to reassure themselves that they're immune to a similar fate.

Forming and Preserving Prejudicial Attitudes

12d

If prejudice is an attitude, where does it come from? Many prejudices appear to be handed down as a legacy from parents (Ponterotto & Pedersen, 1993). Prejudicial attitudes can be found in children as young as ages 4 or 5 (Aboud & Amato, 2001). Research suggests that parents' racial attitudes often influence their children's racial attitudes (Sinclair, Dunn, & Lowery, 2004). This transmission of prejudice across generations presumably depends to some extent on *observational learning*. For example, if a young boy hears his father ridicule homosexuals, his exposure to his father's attitude is likely to affect his attitude about gays. If the young boy then goes to school and makes disparaging remarks about gays that are reinforced by approval from peers, his prejudice will be strengthened through *operant conditioning*. Of course, prejudicial attitudes are not acquired only through direct experience. Stereotypic portrayals of various groups in the media can also foster prejudicial attitudes (Williams & Giles, 1998; Mastro, Behm-Morawitz, Kopacz, 2008).

Competition Between Groups

One of the oldest and simplest explanations for prejudice is that competition between groups can fuel animosity. If two groups compete for scarce resources, such as good jobs and affordable housing, one group's gain is the other's loss. *Realistic group conflict theory* asserts that intergroup hostility and prejudice are a natural outgrowth of fierce competition between groups.

A classic study at Robbers' Cave State Park in Oklahoma provided support for this theory many years ago (Sherif et al., 1961). The subjects were 11-year-old white boys attending a three-week summer camp at the park, who did not know that the camp counselors were actually researchers (their parents knew). The boys were randomly assigned to one of two groups. During the first week, the boys got to know the other members of their own group through typical camp activities and developed a group identity, choosing to call themselves the Rattlers and the Eagles. In the second week, the Rattlers and Eagles were put into a series of competitive situations, such as a football game, a treasure hunt, and a tug of war, with trophies and other prizes at stake. As predicted by realistic group conflict theory, hostile feelings quickly erupted between the two groups, as food fights broke out in the mess hall, cabins were ransacked, and group flags were burned.

If competition between innocent groups of children pursuing trivial prizes can foster hostility, you can imagine what is likely to happen when adults from very different

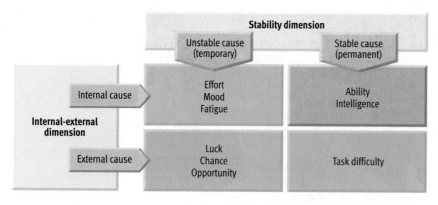

Figure 16.21

Bias in the attributions used to explain success and failure by men and women. Attributions about the two sexes often differ. For example, men's successes tend to be attributed to their ability and intelligence (blue cell), whereas women's successes tend to be attributed to hard work, good luck, or low task difficulty (green cells). These attributional biases help to perpetuate the belief that men are more competent than women.

backgrounds battle for genuinely important resources. Research has repeatedly shown that conflict over scarce resources can fuel prejudice and discrimination (Bourhis & Gagnon, 2001). Even the mere *perception* of competition can breed prejudice (Zarate et al., 2004).

Dividing the World into Ingroups and Outgroups 12d

As noted in the main body of the chapter, when people join together in groups, they sometimes divide the social world into "us versus them," or *ingroups versus outgroups*. As you might anticipate, people tend to evaluate outgroup members less favorably than ingroup members (Krueger, 1996; Reynolds, Turner, & Haslam, 2000). People also tend to think simplistically about outgroups. They tend to see diversity among the members of their own group but to overestimate the homogeneity of the outgroup (Boldry, Gaertner, & Quinn, 2007). At a simple, concrete level, the essence of this process is captured by the statement "They all look alike." The illusion of homogeneity in the outgroup makes it easier to sustain stereotypic beliefs about its members (Rothbart, 2001). This point disposes of our last unanswered question from the list that opened the Application. Just in case you missed one of the answers, the statements were all false.

Threats to Social Identity

According to the *social identity perspective,* self-esteem depends on both one's *personal* identity and one's *social* identity (Tajfel & Turner, 1979; Turner et al., 1987). *Social identity* refers to the pride individuals derive from their membership in various groups, such as ethnic groups, religious denominations, occupational groups, neighborhoods,

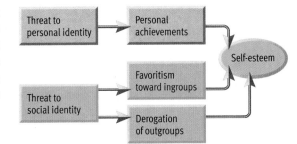

Figure 16.22

Threats to social identity and prejudice. According to Tajfel (1982) and Turner (1987), individuals have both a personal identity (based on a unique sense of self) and a social identity (based on group memberships). When social identity is threatened, people are motivated to restore self-esteem by either showing favoritism to ingroup members or derogating members of outgroups. These tactics contribute to prejudice and discrimination. (Adapted from Brehm & Kassin, 1993)

country clubs, and so forth. The theory further proposes that self-esteem can be undermined by either threats to personal identity (you didn't get called for that job interview) or social identity (your football team loses a big game). Threats to both personal and social identity may motivate efforts to restore self-esteem, but threats to social identity are more likely to provoke responses that foster prejudice and discrimination.

When social identity is threatened, individuals may react in two key ways to bolster it (see **Figure 16.22**). One common response is to show *ingroup favoritism*—for example, tapping an ingroup member for a job opening or rating the performance of an ingroup member higher than that of an outgroup member (Capozza & Brown, 2000). A second common reaction is to engage in *outgroup derogation*—in other words, to "trash" outgroups that are perceived as threatening. Outgroup derogation is more likely when people identify especially strongly with the threatened ingroup (Levin et al, 2003; Schmitt & Maes, 2002). When people derogate an outgroup, they tend to feel superior as a result, and this feeling helps affirm their self-worth (Fein & Spencer, 1997). These unfortunate reactions are *not* inevitable, but threats to social identity represent yet another dynamic process that can foster prejudice (Turner & Reynolds, 2001).

Our discussion has shown that a plethora of processes conspire to create and maintain personal prejudices against a di-

verse array of outgroups. Most of the factors at work reflect normal, routine processes in social behavior. Thus, it is understandable that most people—whether privileged or underprivileged, minority members or majority members—probably harbor some prejudicial attitudes. Our analysis of the causes of prejudice may have permitted you to identify prejudices of your own or their sources. Perhaps it's wishful thinking on my part, but an enhanced awareness of your personal prejudices may help you become a little more tolerant of the endless diversity seen in human behavior. If so, that alone would mean that my efforts in writing this book have been amply rewarded.

Key Learning Goals

16.29 Identify useful criteria for evaluating credibility, and recognize standard social influence strategies.

Whom Can You Trust? Analyzing Credibility and Influence Tactics

You can run, but you cannot hide. This statement aptly sums up the situation that exists when it comes to persuasion and social influence. There is no way to successfully evade the constant, pervasive, omnipresent efforts of others to shape your attitudes and behavior. In this Application we will address two topics that can enhance your resistance to manipulation. First, we will outline some ideas that can be useful in evaluating the credibility of a persuasive source. Second, we will describe some widely used social influence strategies that it pays to know about.

Evaluating Credibility

The salesperson at your local health food store swears that a specific herb combination improves memory and helps people stay healthy. A popular singer touts a psychic hotline, where the operators can "really help" with the important questions in life. Speakers at a "historical society" meeting claim that the Holocaust never happened. These are just a few real-life examples of the pervasive attempts to persuade the public to believe something. In these examples, the "something" people are expected to believe runs counter to the conventional or scientific view, but who is to say who is right? After all, people are entitled to their own opinions, aren't they?

Yes, people *are* entitled to their own opinions, but that does not mean that all opinions are equally valid. Some opinions are just plain wrong, and others are highly dubious. Every person is not equally believable. In deciding what to believe, it is important to carefully examine the evidence presented and the logic of the argument that supports the conclusion (see the Critical Thinking Application for Chapter 10). You also need to decide *whom* to believe,

a task that requires assessing the *credibility* of the source of the information. Following are a few questions that can provide guidance in this decision-making process.

Does the source have a vested interest in the issue at hand? If the source is likely to benefit in some way from convincing you of something, you need to take a skeptical attitude. In the examples provided here, it is easy to see how the sales clerk and popular singer will benefit if you buy the products they are selling, but what about the so-called historical society? How would members benefit by convincing large numbers of people that the Holocaust never happened? Like the sales clerk and singer, they are also selling something, in this case a particular view of history that they hope will influence future events in certain ways. Someone does *not* have to have a financial gain at stake to have a vested interest in an issue. Of course, the fact that these sources have a vested interest does not necessarily mean that the information they are providing is false or that their arguments are invalid. But a source's credibility does need to be evaluated with extra caution when the person or group has something to gain.

What are the source's credentials? Does the person have any special training, an advanced degree, or any other basis for claiming special knowledge about the topic? The usual training for a sales clerk or singer does not include how to assess research results in medical journals or claims of psychic powers. The Holocaust deniers are more difficult to evaluate. Some of them have studied history and written books on the topic, but the books are mostly self-published and few of these "experts" hold positions at reputable universities where scholars are subject to peer evaluation. That's *not* to say that legitimate credentials ensure a source's credibility. A number of popular diets that are widely regarded by nutritional experts as worthless, if not hazardous, have been created and marketed by genuine physicians (Drewnowski, 1995; Dwyer, 1995). Of

course, these physicians have a *vested interest* in the diets, as they have made millions of dollars from them.

Is the information grossly inconsistent with the conventional view on the issue? Just being different from the mainstream view certainly does *not* make a conclusion wrong. But claims that vary radically from most other information on a subject should raise a red flag that leads to careful scrutiny. Bear in mind that charlatans and hucksters are often successful because they typically try to persuade people to believe things that they want to believe. Wouldn't it be great if we could effortlessly enhance our memory, foretell the future, eat all we want and still lose weight, and earn hundreds of dollars per hour working at home? And wouldn't it be nice if the Holocaust never happened? It pays to be wary of wishful thinking.

What was the method of analysis used in reaching the conclusion? The purveyors of miracle cures and psychic advice inevitably rely on anecdotal evidence. But you have already learned about the perils and unreliability of anecdotal evidence (see Chapter 2). One method frequently used by charlatans is to undermine the credibility of conventional information by focusing on trivial inconsistencies. This is one of the many strategies used by the people who argue that the Holocaust never occurred. They question the credibility of thousands of historical documents, photographs, and artifacts, and the testimony of countless people, by highlighting small inconsistencies among historical records relating to trivial matters, such as the number of people transported to a concentration camp in a specific week, or the number of bodies that could be disposed of in a single day (Shermer, 1997). Some inconsistencies are exactly what one should expect based on piecing together multiple accounts from sources working with different portions of incomplete information. But the strategy of focusing on trivial inconsistencies is a standard method for raising doubts about credible information. For example, this strategy was used brilliantly by the defense attorneys in the O. J. Simpson murder trial.

Recognizing Social Influence Strategies

It pays to understand social influence strategies because advertisers, salespeople, and fundraisers—not to mention your friends and neighbors—frequently rely on them to manipulate your behavior. Let's look at four basic strategies: the foot-in-the-door technique, misuse of the reciprocity norm, the lowball technique, and feigned scarcity.

Door-to-door salespeople have long recognized the importance of gaining a *little* cooperation from sales targets (getting a "foot in the door") before hitting them with the real sales pitch. **The *foot-in-the-door technique* involves getting people to agree to a small request to increase the chances that they will agree to a larger request later.** This technique is widely used in all walks of life. For example, groups seeking donations often ask people to simply sign a petition first.

In an early study of the foot-in-the-door technique (Freedman & Fraser, 1966), the large request involved asking homemakers whether a team of six men doing consumer research could come into their home to classify *all* their household products. Only 22% of the control subjects agreed to this outlandish request. However, when the same request was made three days after a small request (to answer a few questions about soap preferences), 53% of the participants agreed to the large request. Why does the foot-in-the-door technique work? According to Burger (1999), quite a variety of processes contribute to its effectiveness, including people's tendency to try to behave

consistently (with their initial response) and their reluctance to renege on their sense of commitment to the person who made the initial request.

Most of us have been socialized to believe in the *reciprocity norm*—the rule that we should pay back in kind what we receive from others. Robert Cialdini (2007) has written extensively about how the reciprocity norm is used in social influence efforts. For example, groups seeking donations routinely send address labels, key rings, and other small gifts with their pleas. Salespeople using the reciprocity principle distribute free samples to prospective customers. When they return a few days later, most of the customers feel obligated to buy some of their products. The reciprocity rule is meant to promote fair exchanges in social interactions. However, when people manipulate the reciprocity norm, they usually give something of minimal value in the hopes of getting far more in return (Howard, 1995).

The lowball technique is even more deceptive. The name for this technique derives from a common practice in automobile sales, in which a customer is offered a terrific bargain on a car. The bargain price gets the customer to commit to buying the car. Soon after this commitment is made, however, the dealer starts revealing some hidden costs. Typically, the customer learns that options assumed to be included in the original price are actually going to cost extra, or that a promised low loan rate has "fallen through" leading to a higher car payment. Once they have committed to buying a car, most customers are unlikely to cancel the deal. Thus, **the *lowball technique* involves getting someone to commit to an attractive proposition before its hidden costs are revealed.** Car dealers aren't the only ones who use this

Advertisers often try to artificially create scarcity to make their products seem more desirable.

© Tony Freeman/PhotoEdit

technique. For instance, a friend might ask whether you want to spend a week with him at his charming backwoods cabin. After you accept this seemingly generous proposition, he may add, "Of course there's some work for us to do. We need to repair the pier, paint the exterior, and . . ." Lowballing is a surprisingly effective strategy (Cialdini & Trost, 1998; Gueguen, Pascual, & Dagot, 2002).

A number of years ago, Jack Brehm (1966) demonstrated that telling people they can't have something only makes them want it more. This phenomenon helps explain why companies often try to create the impression that their products are in scarce supply. Scarcity threatens your freedom to choose a product, thus creating an increased desire for the scarce commodity. Advertisers frequently feign scarcity to drive up the demand for products. Thus, we constantly see ads that scream "limited supply available," "for a limited time only," "while they last," and "time is running out." Like genuine scarcity, feigned scarcity *can* enhance the desirability of a commodity (Highhouse et al., 1998; Lynn, 1992).

Table 16.1 Critical Thinking Skills Discussed in This Application

Skill	Description
Judging the credibility of an information source	The critical thinker understands that credibility and bias are central to determining the quality of information and looks at factors such as vested interests, credentials, and appropriate expertise.
Recognizing social influence strategies	The critical thinker is aware of manipulative tactics such as the foot-in-the-door and lowball techniques, misuse of the reciprocity norm, and feigned scarcity.

Key Ideas

Person Perception: Forming Impressions of Others

▌ People tend to attribute desirable characteristics to those who are good looking. Perceptions of competence based on facial appearance, which can be made in an instant, are particularly important.

▌ Stereotypes are beliefs that lead people to expect that others will have certain characteristics because of their membership in a specific group. In interacting with others, stereotypes may lead people to see what they expect to see and to overestimate how often they see it.

Attribution Processes: Explaining Behavior

▌ Internal attributions ascribe behavior to personal traits, whereas external attributions locate the cause of behavior in the environment. Weiner's model proposes that attributions for success and failure be analyzed in terms of the stability of causes as well as along the internal-external dimension.

▌ Observers favor internal attributions to explain another's behavior (the fundamental attribution error), while actors favor external attributions to explain their own behavior. Cultures vary in their emphasis on individualism as opposed to collectivism, and these differences appear to influence attributional tendencies.

Close Relationships: Liking and Loving

▌ People tend to like and love others who are similar, who reciprocate expressions of affection, and who are physically attractive. In intimate relationships, romantic ideals influence the progress of relationships.

▌ Berscheid and Hatfield distinguished between passionate and companionate love. Sternberg built on their distinction by dividing companionate love into intimacy and commitment. Hazan and Shaver's theory suggests that love relationships in adulthood mimic attachment patterns in infancy. People tend to fall into three subtypes (secure, avoidant, or anxious-ambivalent) in their romantic relationships. Attachment style is related to many aspects of behavior.

▌ The characteristics that people seek in prospective mates are much the same around the world. However, cultures vary considerably in their emphasis on passionate love as a prerequisite for marriage. Although critics are concerned that Internet relationships are superficial and open to deception, Internet-initiated relationships appear to be just as intimate and stable as relationships forged offline.

▌ According to evolutionary psychologists, certain aspects of good looks influence attraction because they are indicators of reproductive fitness. Consistent with evolutionary theory, gender differences in mating preferences appear to transcend culture. People's courtship tactics may include deception. Mate poaching is common and appears to be universal across cultures.

Attitudes: Making Social Judgments

▌ Attitudes may be made up of cognitive, affective, and behavioral components. Attitudes vary in strength, accessibility, and ambivalence. Attitudes and behavior aren't as consistent as one might assume.

▌ A source of persuasion who is credible, expert, trustworthy, likable, and physically attractive tends to be relatively effective. Two-sided arguments, repetition, and fear arousal are effective elements in persuasive messages.

▌ Attitudes may be shaped through classical conditioning, operant conditioning, and observational learning. Festinger's dissonance theory asserts that inconsistent attitudes cause tension and that people alter their attitudes to reduce cognitive dissonance.

▌ Self-perception theory asserts that people may infer their attitudes from their behavior. The elaboration likelihood model holds that the central route to persuasion tends to yield longer-lasting attitude change than the peripheral route.

Conformity and Obedience: Yielding to Others

▌ Asch found that conformity becomes more likely as group size increases, up to a group size of four, and then levels off. If a small group isn't unanimous, conformity declines rapidly.

▌ In Milgram's study of obedience, subjects showed a remarkable tendency to follow orders to shock an innocent stranger. The generalizability of Milgram's findings has stood the test of time, but his work also helped to stimulate stricter ethical standards for research.

▌ The Asch and Milgram experiments have been replicated in many cultures. These replications have uncovered modest cultural variations in the propensity to conform or to obey an authority figure.

▌ The Stanford Prison Simulation demonstrated that social roles and other situational pressures can exert tremendous influence over social behavior. Like Milgram, Zimbardo showed that situational forces can lead normal people to exhibit surprisingly callous, abusive behavior.

Behavior in Groups: Joining with Others

▌ The bystander effect occurs primarily because a group creates diffusion of responsibility. Individuals' productivity often declines in larger groups because of loss of coordination and because of social loafing.

▌ Group polarization occurs when discussion leads a group to shift toward a more extreme decision in the direction the group was already leaning. In groupthink, a cohesive group suspends critical judgment in a misguided effort to promote agreement in decision making. Nonetheless, groups are superior to individuals on many types of decision-making tasks.

Reflecting on the Chapter's Themes

▌ Our study of social psychology illustrated the value of empiricism, the cultural limits of research based on American samples, and the subjectivity of perception.

PERSONAL APPLICATION Understanding Prejudice

▌ Prejudice is supported by selectivity and memory biases in person perception and stereotyping. Stereotypes are highly resistant to change. Attributional biases, such as the tendency to assume that others' behavior reflects their dispositions, can contribute to prejudice.

▌ Negative attitudes about groups are often acquired through observational learning and strengthened through operant conditioning. Realistic group conflict theory proposes that competition between groups fosters prejudice. The propensity to see outgroups as homogenous serves to strengthen prejudice. Threats to social identity can lead to ingroup favoritism and outgroup derogation.

CRITICAL THINKING APPLICATION Whom Can You Trust? Analyzing Credibility and Influence Tactics

▌ Useful criteria in judging credibility include whether a source has vested interests or appropriate credentials. One should also consider the method of analysis used in reaching conclusions and why information might not coincide with conventional wisdom.

▌ To resist manipulative efforts, it helps to be aware of social influence tactics, such as the foot-in-the-door technique, misuse of the reciprocity norm, the lowball technique, and feigned scarcity.

Key Terms

Attitudes (p. 681)
Attributions (p. 667)
Bystander effect (p. 694)
Channel (p. 683)
Cognitive dissonance (p. 686)
Collectivism (p. 671)
Commitment (p. 674)
Companionate love (p. 674)
Conformity (p. 688)
Defensive attribution (p. 670)
Discrimination (p. 700)
External attributions (p. 668)
Foot-in-the-door technique (p. 705)
Fundamental attribution error
 (pp. 668–669)
Group (p. 684)
Group cohesiveness (p. 698)
Group polarization (p. 697)
Groupthink (p. 698)
Illusory correlation (p. 666)
Individualism (p. 671)
Ingroup (p. 667)
Internal attributions (p. 668)
Interpersonal attraction (p. 672)
Intimacy (p. 674)
Lowball technique (p. 705)
Matching hypothesis (p. 673)
Message (p. 683)

Obedience (p. 689)
Outgroup (p. 667)
Passionate love (p. 674)
Person perception (p. 664)
Prejudice (p. 700)
Receiver (p. 683)
Reciprocity (p. 674)
Reciprocity norm (p. 705)
Self-serving bias (p. 671)
Social loafing (p. 695)
Social psychology (p. 664)
Social roles (p. 692)
Source (p. 683)
Stereotypes (p. 665)

Key People

Solomon Asch (pp. 688–689)
Ellen Berscheid (p. 674)
Leon Festinger (pp. 685–686)
Elaine Hatfield (p. 674)
Cindy Hazan and Philip Shaver
 (pp. 675–676)
Fritz Heider (p. 668)
Irving Janis (p. 698)
Stanley Milgram (pp. 689–691)
Bernard Weiner (pp. 668–669)
Philip Zimbardo (pp. 692–693)

1. Stereotypes:
   A. are often automatic products of normal cognitive processes.
   B. are widely held beliefs that people have certain characteristics because of their membership in a particular group.
   C. equivalent to prejudice.
   D. both a and b.

2. You believe that short men have a tendency to be insecure. The concept of illusory correlation implies that you will:
   A. overestimate how often short men are insecure.
   B. underestimate how often short men are insecure.
   C. overestimate the frequency of short men in the population.
   D. falsely assume that shortness in men causes insecurity.

3. A father suggests that his son's low marks in school are due to the child's laziness. The father has made a (an) _____ attribution.
   A. external   C. situational
   B. internal   D. high consensus

4. Bob explains his failing grade on a term paper by saying that he really didn't work very hard at it. According to Weiner's model, Bob is making an _____ attribution about his failure.
   A. internal-stable   C. external-stable
   B. internal-unstable   D. external-unstable

5. The fundamental attribution error refers to the tendency of:
   A. observers to favor external attributions in explaining the behavior of others.
   B. observers to favor internal attributions in explaining the behavior of others.
   C. actors to favor external attributions in explaining the behavior of others.
   D. actors to favor situational attributions in explaining their own behavior.

6. According to Hazan and Shaver (1987):
   A. romantic relationships in adulthood follow the same form as attachment relationships in infancy.
   B. those who had ambivalent attachments in infancy are doomed never to fall in love as adults.
   C. those who had avoidant attachments in infancy often overcompensate by becoming excessively intimate in their adult love relationships.
   D. all of the above are the case.

7. Cross-cultural similarities are most likely to be found in which of the following areas?
   A. what people look for in prospective mates
   B. the overall value of romantic love
   C. passionate love as a prerequisite for marriage
   D. the tradition of prearranged marriages

8. Cognitive dissonance theory predicts that after people engage in counterattitudinal behavior, they will:
   A. convince themselves they really didn't perform the behavior.
   B. change their attitude to make it more consistent with their behavior.
   C. change their attitude to make it less consistent with their behavior.
   D. do nothing.

9. "I always choose romance novels rather than biographies. I guess I must like romance novels better." This thought process illustrates the premise of _____ theory.
   A. cognitive dissonance   C. evolutionary
   B. learning   D. self-perception

10. The elaboration likelihood model of attitude change suggests that:
    A. the peripheral route results in more enduring attitude change.
    B. the central route results in more enduring attitude change.
    C. only the central route to persuasion can be effective.
    D. only the peripheral route to persuasion can be effective.

11. The results of Milgram's (1963) study imply that:
    A. in the real world, most people will refuse to follow orders to inflict harm on a stranger.
    B. many people will obey an authority figure even if innocent people get hurt.
    C. most people are willing to give obviously wrong answers when ordered to do so.
    D. most people stick to their own judgment, even when group members unanimously disagree.

12. According to Latané (1981), social loafing is due to:
    A. social norms that stress the importance of positive interactions among group members.
    B. duplication of effort among group members.
    C. diffusion of responsibility in groups.
    D. a bias toward making internal attributions about the behavior of others.

13. Groupthink occurs when members of a cohesive group:
    A. are initially unanimous about an issue.
    B. stress the importance of caution in group decision making.
    C. emphasize concurrence at the expense of critical thinking in arriving at a decision.
    D. shift toward a less extreme position after group discussion.

14. Discrimination:
    A. refers to a negative attitude toward members of a group.
    B. refers to unfair behavior toward the members of a group.
    C. is the same thing as prejudice.
    D. is all of the above.

15. The foot-in-the-door technique involves asking people to agree to a _____ request first to increase the likelihood that they will comply with a _____ request later.
    A. large; small   C. large; large
    B. small; large   D. large; larger

Answers

1 D pp. 665–666	6 A pp. 675–676	11 B p. 690
2 A p. 666	7 A p. 677	12 C p. 695
3 B p. 668	8 B pp. 685–686	13 C p. 698
4 B pp. 668–669	9 D pp. 686–687	14 B p. 700
5 B pp. 668–669	10 B p. 687	15 B p. 705

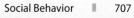

Answers to Concept Checks

Chapter 1

Concept Check 1.1

1. c. Sigmund Freud (1905, pp. 77–78), arguing that it is possible to probe into the unconscious depths of the mind.

2. a. Wilhelm Wundt (1874/1904, p. v), campaigning for a new, independent science of psychology.

3. b. William James (1890), commenting negatively on the structuralists' efforts to break consciousness into its elements and his view of consciousness as a continuously flowing stream.

Concept Check 1.2

1. b. B. F. Skinner (1971, p. 17), explaining why he believes that freedom is an illusion.

2. c. Carl Rogers (1961, p. 27), commenting on others' assertion that he had an overly optimistic (Pollyannaish) view of human potential and discussing humans' basic drive toward personal growth.

3. a. John B. Watson (1930, p. 103), dismissing the importance of genetic inheritance while arguing that traits are shaped entirely by experience.

Concept Check 1.3

a. 2. Psychology is theoretically diverse.

b. 6. Heredity and environment jointly influence behavior.

c. 4. Behavior is determined by multiple causes.

d. 7. Our experience of the world is highly subjective.

Chapter 2

Concept Check 2.1

1. IV: Film violence (present versus absent)

   DV: Heart rate and blood pressure (there are two DVs)

2. IV: Courtesy training (training versus no training)

   DV: Number of customer complaints

3. IV: Stimulus complexity (high versus low) and stimulus contrast (high versus low) (there are two IVs)

   DV: Length of time spent staring at the stimuli

4. IV: Group size (large versus small)

   DV: Conformity

Concept Check 2.2

1. d. Survey. You would distribute a survey to obtain information on subjects' social class, education, and attitudes about nuclear disarmament.

2. c. Case study. Using a case study approach, you could interview people with anxiety disorders, interview their parents, and examine their school records to look for similarities in childhood experiences. As a second choice, you might have people with anxiety disorders fill out a survey about their childhood experiences.

3. b. Naturalistic observation. To answer this question properly, you would want to observe baboons in their natural environment, without interference.

4. a. Experiment. To demonstrate a causal relationship, you would have to conduct an experiment. You would manipulate the presence or absence of food-related cues in controlled circumstances where subjects had an opportunity to eat some food, and monitor the amount eaten.

Concept Check 2.3

1. b and e. The other three conclusions all equate correlation with causation.

2. a. Negative. As age increases, more people tend to have visual problems and acuity tends to decrease.

   b. Positive. Studies show that highly educated people tend to earn higher incomes and that people with less education tend to earn lower incomes.

   c. Negative. As shyness increases, the size of one's friendship network should decrease. However, research suggests that this inverse association may be weaker than widely believed.

Concept Check 2.4

Methodological flaw	Study 1	Study 2
Sampling bias	✓	✓
Placebo effects	✓	
Confounding of variables	✓	
Distortions in self-report data		✓
Experimenter bias	✓	

Explanations for Study 1. Sensory deprivation is an unusual kind of experience that may intrigue certain potential subjects, who may be more adventurous or more willing to take risks than the population at large. Using the first 80 students who sign up for this study may not yield a sample that is representative of the population. Assigning the first 40 subjects who sign up to the experimental group may confound these extraneous variables with the treatment (students who sign up most quickly may be the most adventurous). In announcing that he will be examining the *detrimental* effects of sensory deprivation, the experimenter has created expectations in the subjects. These expectations could lead to placebo effects. The experimenter has also revealed that he has a bias about the outcome of the study. Since he supervises the treatments, he knows which subjects are in the experimental and control groups, thus aggravating potential problems with experimenter bias. For example, he might unintentionally give the control group subjects better instructions on how to do the pursuit-rotor task and thereby slant the study in favor of finding support for his hypothesis.

Explanations for Study 2. Sampling bias is a problem because the researcher has sampled only subjects from a low-income, inner-city neighborhood. A sample obtained in this way is not likely to be representative of the population at large. People are sensitive about the issue of racial prejudice, so distortions in self-report data are also likely. Many subjects may be swayed by social desirability bias and rate themselves as less prejudiced than they really are.

Chapter 3

Concept Check 3.1

1. d. Dendrite
2. f. Myelin
3. b. Neuron
4. e. Axon
5. a. Glia
6. g. Terminal button
7. h. Synapse

Concept Check 3.2

1. d. Serotonin
2. b. and d. Serotonin and norepinephrine
3. e. Endorphins
4. c. Dopamine
5. a. Acetylcholine

Concept Check 3.3

1. Left hemisphere damage, probably to Wernicke's area
2. Deficit in dopamine synthesis in an area of the midbrain
3. Degeneration of myelin sheaths surrounding axons
4. Disturbance in dopamine activity, possibly associated with enlarged ventricles in the brain

Please note that neuropsychological assessment is not as simple as this introductory exercise may suggest. There are many possible causes of most disorders, and we discussed only a handful of leading causes for each.

Concept Check 3.4

1. Closer relatives; more distant relatives
2. Identical twins; fraternal twins
3. Biological parents; adoptive parents
4. Genetic overlap or closeness; trait similarity

Chapter 4

Concept Check 4.1

Dimension	Rods	Cones
Physical shape	Elongated	Stubby
Number in the retina	125 million	5–6.4 million
Area of the retina in which they are dominant receptor	Periphery	Center/fovea
Critical to color vision	No	Yes
Critical to peripheral vision	Yes	No
Sensitivity to dim light	Strong	Weak
Speed of dark adaptation	Slow	Rapid

Concept Check 4.2

✓ 1. Interposition. The arches in front cut off part of the corridor behind them.

✓ 2. Height in plane. The back of the corridor is higher on the horizontal plane than the front of the corridor is.

✓ 3. Texture gradient. The more distant portions of the hallway are painted in less detail than the closer portions are.

✓ 4. Relative size. The arches in the distance are smaller than those in the foreground.

✓ 5. Light and shadow. Light shining in from the crossing corridor (it's coming from the left) contrasts with shadow elsewhere.

✓ 6. Linear perspective. The lines of the corridor converge in the distance.

Concept Check 4.3

Dimension	Vision	Hearing
1. Stimulus	Light waves	Sound waves
2. Elements of stimulus and related perceptions	Wavelength/hue Amplitude/brightness Purity/saturation	Frequency/pitch Amplitude/loudness Purity/timbre
3. Receptors	Rods and cones	Hair cells
4. Location of receptors	Retina	Basilar membrane
5. Main location of processing in brain	Occipital lobe, visual cortex	Temporal lobe, auditory cortex
6. Spatial aspect of perception	Depth perception	Auditory localization

Concept Check 4.4

Dimension	Taste	Smell	Touch
1. Stimulus	Soluble chemicals in saliva	Volatile chemicals in air	Mechanical, thermal, and chemical energy due to external contact
2. Receptors	Clusters of taste cells	Olfactory cilia (hairlike structures)	Many (at least 6) types
3. Location of receptors	Taste buds on tongue	Upper area of nasal passages	Skin
4. Basic elements of perception	Sweet, sour, salty, bitter	No satisfactory classification scheme	Pressure, hot, cold, pain

Chapter 5

Concept Check 5.1

Characteristic	REM sleep	NREM sleep
1. Type of EEG activity	"Wide awake" brain waves, mostly beta	Varied, lots of delta waves
2. Eye movements	Rapid, lateral	Slow or absent
3. Dreaming	Frequent, vivid	Less frequent
4. Depth (difficulty in awakening)	Varied, generally difficult to awaken	Varied, generally easier to awaken
5. Percentage of total sleep (in adults)	About 20%–25%	About 75%–80%
6. Increases or decreases (as percentage of sleep) during childhood	Percent decreases	Percent increases
7. Timing in sleep (dominates early or late)	Dominates late in cycle	Dominates early in cycle

Concept Check 5.2

1. Beta. Video games require alert information processing, which is associated with beta waves.

2. Alpha. Meditation involves relaxation, which is associated with alpha waves, and studies show increased alpha in meditators.

3. Theta. In stage 1 sleep, theta waves tend to be prevalent.

4. Delta. Sleepwalking usually occurs in deep NREM sleep, which is dominated by delta activity.

5. Beta. Nightmares are dreams, so you're probably in REM sleep, which paradoxically produces "wide awake" beta waves.

Concept Check 5.3

1. c. Stimulants.

2. d. Hallucinogens.

3. b. Sedatives.

4. f. Alcohol.

5. a. Narcotics.

6. e. Cannabis.

Chapter 6

Concept Check 6.1

1. CS: Fire in fireplace
   US: Pain from burn   CR/UR: Fear

2. CS: Brake lights in rain
   US: Car accident   CR/UR: Tensing up

3. CS: Sight of cat
   US: Cat dander   CR/UR: Wheezing

Concept Check 6.2

1. FR. Each sale is a response and every third response earns reinforcement.

2. VI. A varied amount of time elapses before the response of doing yardwork can earn reinforcement.

3. VR. Reinforcement occurs after a varied number of unreinforced casts (time is irrelevant; the more casts Martha makes, the more reinforcers she will receive).

4. CR. The designated response (reading a book) is reinforced (with a gold star) every time.

5. FI. A fixed time interval (three years) has to elapse before Skip can earn a salary increase (the reinforcer).

Concept Check 6.3

1. Punishment.

2. Positive reinforcement.

3. Punishment.

4. Negative reinforcement (for Audrey); the dog is positively reinforced for its whining.

5. Negative reinforcement.

6. Extinction. When Sharma's co-workers start to ignore her complaints, they are trying to extinguish the behavior (which had been positively reinforced when it won sympathy).

Concept Check 6.4

1. Classical conditioning. Midori's blue windbreaker is a CS eliciting excitement in her dog.

2. Operant conditioning. Playing new songs leads to negative consequences (punishment), which weaken the tendency to play new songs. Playing old songs leads to positive reinforcement, which gradually strengthens the tendency to play old songs.

3. Classical conditioning. The song was paired with the passion of new love so that it became a CS eliciting emotional, romantic feelings.

4. Both. Ralph's workplace is paired with criticism so that his workplace becomes a CS eliciting anxiety. Calling in sick is operant behavior that is strengthened through negative reinforcement (because it reduces anxiety).

Chapter 7

Concept Check 7.1

Feature	Sensory memory	Short-term memory	Long-term memory
Encoding format	Copy of input	Largely phonemic	Largely semantic
Storage capacity	Limited	Small (7±2 chunks)	No known limit
Storage duration	About 1/4 second	Up to 20 seconds	Minutes to years

Concept Check 7.2

1. Ineffective encoding due to lack of attention

2. Retrieval failure due to motivated forgetting

3. Proactive interference (previous learning of Justin Timberlake's name interferes with new learning)

4. Retroactive interference (new learning of sociology interferes with older learning of history)

Concept Check 7.3

1. a. Declarative memory
2. c. Long-term memory
3. a. Sensory memory
4. f. Episodic memory
5. e. Nondeclarative memory
6. g. Semantic memory
7. i. Prospective memory
8. b. Short-term memory

Chapter 8

Concept Check 8.1

1. 1. One-word utterance in which the word is overextended to refer to a similar object.
2. 4. Words are combined into a sentence, but the rule for past tense is overregularized.
3. 3. Telegraphic sentence.
4. 5. Words are combined into a sentence, and past tense is used correctly.
5. 2. One-word utterance without overextension.
6. 6. "Longer" sentence with metaphor.

Concept Check 8.2

1. Functional fixedness
2. Forming subgoals
3. Insight
4. Searching for analogies
5. Arrangement problem

Concept Check 8.3

1. Elimination by aspects
2. Availability heuristic
3. Shift to additive strategy

Chapter 9

Concept Check 9.1

1. Test-retest reliability
2. Criterion-related validity
3. Content validity

Concept Check 9.2

1. H. Given that the identical twins were reared apart, their greater similarity in comparison to fraternals reared together can only be due to heredity. This comparison is probably the most important piece of evidence supporting the genetic determination of IQ.

2. E. We tend to associate identical twins with evidence supporting heredity, but in this comparison

genetic similarity is held constant since both sets of twins are identical. The only logical explanation for the greater similarity in identicals reared together is the effect of their being reared together (environment).

3. E. This comparison is similar to the previous one. Genetic similarity is held constant and a shared environment produces greater similarity than being reared apart.

4. B. This is nothing more than a quantification of Galton's original observation that intelligence runs in families. Since families share both genes and environment, either or both could be responsible for the observed correlation.

5. B. The similarity of adopted children to their biological parents can only be due to shared genes, and the similarity of adopted children to their foster parents can only be due to shared environment, so these correlations show the influence of both heredity and environment.

Concept Check 9.3

1. b. Gardner
2. a. Galton
3. c. Jensen
4. d. Scarr
5. e. Sternberg

Chapter 10

Concept Check 10.1

1. I. Early studies indicated that lesioning the ventromedial nucleus of the hypothalamus leads to overeating (although it is an oversimplification to characterize the VMH as the brain's "stop eating" center).

2. I. According to Mayer, hunger increases when the amount of glucose in the blood decreases.

3. I or ?. Food cues generally trigger hunger and eating, but reactions vary among individuals.

4. D. Food preferences are mostly learned, and we tend to like what we are accustomed to eating. Most people will not be eager to eat a strange-looking food.

5. I. People tend to eat more when a variety of foods are available.

6. I. Reactions vary, but stress generally tends to increase eating.

Concept Check 10.2

1. d. Fear of failure
2. c. Incentive value of success
3. b. Perceived probability of success
4. a. Need for achievement

Concept Check 10.3

2. James-Lange theory
3. Schachter's two-factor theory
4. Evolutionary theories

Chapter 11

Concept Check 11.1

	Event	Stage	Organism	Time span
1.	Uterine implantation	Germinal	Zygote	0–2 weeks
2.	Muscle and bone begin to form	Fetal	Fetus	2 months to birth
3.	Vital organs and body systems begin to form	Embryonic	Embryo	2 weeks to 2 months

Concept Check 11.2

1. b. Animism is characteristic of the preoperational period.
2. c. Mastery of hierarchical classification occurs during the concrete operational period.
3. a. Lack of object permanence is characteristic of the sensorimotor period.

Concept Check 11.3

1. c. Commitment to personal ethics is characteristic of postconventional reasoning.
2. b. Concern about approval of others is characteristic of conventional reasoning.
3. a. Emphasis on positive or negative consequences is characteristic of preconventional reasoning.

Chapter 12

Concept Check 12.1

1. Regression
2. Projection
3. Reaction formation
4. Repression
5. Rationalization

Concept Check 12.2

1. Bandura's observational learning. Sarah imitates a role model from television.
2. Maslow's need for self-actualization. Yolanda is striving to realize her fullest potential.
3. Freud's Oedipal complex. Vladimir shows preference for his opposite-sex parent and emotional distance from his same-sex parent.

Concept Check 12.3

1. Maslow (1971, p. 36), commenting on the need for self-actualization.
2. Eysenck (1977, pp. 407–408), commenting on the biological roots of personality.
3. Freud (in Malcolm, 1980), commenting on the repression of sexuality.

Chapter 13

Concept Check 13.1

1. b. A choice between two unattractive options
2. c. Weighing the positive and negative aspects of a single goal
3. a. A choice between two attractive options

Concept Check 13.2

1. a. Frustration due to delay
2. d. Pressure to perform
3. c. Change associated with leaving school and taking a new job
4. a. Frustration due to loss of job

   c. Change in life circumstances

   d. Pressure to perform (in quickly obtaining new job)

Concept Check 13.3

1. Denial of reality
2. Undoing
3. Fantasy
4. Overcompensation
5. Intellectualization

Chapter 14

Concept Check 14.1

		Deviance	Maladaptive behavior	Personal distress
1.	Alan		✓	
2.	Monica			✓
3.	Boris	✓		
4.	Natasha	✓	✓	✓

Concept Check 14.2

1. Obsessive-compulsive disorder (key symptoms: frequent rituals, ruminations about school)
2. Somatization disorder (key symptoms: history of physical complaints involving many different organ systems)
3. Conversion disorder (key symptoms: loss of function in single organ system)

Concept Check 14.3

1. Bipolar disorder, manic episode (key symptoms: extravagant plans, hyperactivity, reckless spending)
2. Paranoid schizophrenia (key symptoms: delusions of persecution and grandeur, along with deterioration of adaptive behavior)
3. Major depression (key symptoms: feelings of despair, low self-esteem, lack of energy)

Chapter 15

Concept Check 15.1

1. c   2. a   3. b

Concept Check 15.2

1. d   2. b   3. a   4. c

Concept Check 15.3

1. c   2. a   3. b   4. d   5. b

Chapter 16

Concept Check 16.1

	Unstable	Stable
Internal	d	b
External	a	c

Concept Check 16.2

1. c. Fundamental attribution error (assuming that arriving late reflects personal qualities)

2. a. Illusory correlation effect (overestimating how often one has seen confirmations of the assertion that young, female professors get pregnant soon after being hired)

3. b. Stereotyping (assuming that all lawyers have certain traits)

4. d. Defensive attribution (derogating the victims of misfortune to minimize the apparent likelihood of a similar mishap)

Concept Check 16.3

1. Target: Cognitive component of attitudes (beliefs about program for regulating nursing homes)

   Persuasion: Message factor (advice to use one-sided instead of two-sided arguments)

2. Target: Affective component of attitudes (feelings about candidate)

   Persuasion: Source factor (advice on appearing likable, sincere, and compassionate)

3. Target: Behavioral component of attitudes (making contributions)

   Persuasion: Receiver factor (considering audience's initial position regarding the candidate)

Concept Check 16.4

1. False   2. True   3. False   4. True   5. False

Statistical Methods

Empiricism depends on observation; precise observation depends on measurement; and measurement requires numbers. Thus, scientists routinely analyze numerical data to arrive at their conclusions. Over 3000 empirical studies are cited in this text, and all but a few of the simplest ones required a statistical analysis. *Statistics* is the use of mathematics to organize, summarize, and interpret numerical data. We discussed statistics briefly in Chapter 2, but in this Appendix we take a closer look.

To illustrate statistics in action, let's assume that we want to test a hypothesis that has generated quite an argument in your psychology class. The hypothesis is that college students who watch a great deal of television aren't as bright as those who watch TV infrequently. For the fun of it, your class decides to conduct a correlational study of itself, collecting survey and psychological test data. Your classmates all agree to respond to a short survey on their TV viewing habits. Because everyone at your school has had to take the SAT, the class decides to use scores on the SAT Critical Reading subtest as an index of how bright students are. All of them agree to allow the records office at the college to furnish their SAT scores to the professor, who replaces each student's name with a subject number (to protect students' right to privacy). Let's see how we could use statistics to analyze the data collected in our pilot study (a small, preliminary investigation).

Graphing Data

 1c

After collecting our data, our next step is to organize the data to get a quick overview of our numerical re-

sults. Let's assume that there are 20 students in your class, and when they estimate how many hours they spend per day watching TV, the results are as follows:

3	2	0	3	1
3	4	0	5	1
2	3	4	5	2
4	5	3	4	6

One of the simpler things that we can do to organize data is to create a *frequency distribution—an orderly arrangement of scores indicating the frequency of each score or group of scores.* Figure B.1(a) shows a frequency distribution for our data on TV viewing. The column on the left lists the possible scores (estimated hours of TV viewing) in order, and the column on the right lists the number of subjects with each score. Graphs can provide an even better overview of the data. One approach is to portray the data in a *histogram, which is a bar graph that presents data from a frequency distribution.* Such a histogram, summarizing our TV viewing data, is presented in Figure B.1(b).

Another widely used method of portraying data graphically is the *frequency polygon—a line figure used to present data from a frequency distribution.* Figures B.1(c) and B.1(d) show how our TV viewing data can be converted from a histogram to a frequency polygon. In both the bar graph and the line figure, the horizontal axis lists the possible scores and the vertical axis is used to indicate the frequency of each score. This use of the axes is nearly universal for frequency polygons, although sometimes it is reversed in histograms (the vertical axis lists possible scores, so the bars become horizontal).

Figure B.1
Graphing data. (a) Our raw data are tallied into a frequency distribution. **(b)** The same data are portrayed in a bar graph called a histogram. **(c)** A frequency polygon is plotted over the histogram. **(d)** The resultant frequency polygon is shown by itself.

Score	Tallies	Frequency
6	I	1
5	III	3
4	IIII	4
3	THH	5
2	III	3
1	II	2
0	II	2

(a) Frequency distribution

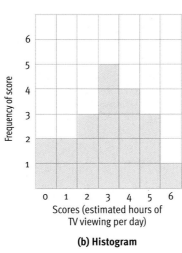

(b) Histogram

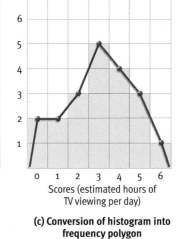

(c) Conversion of histogram into frequency polygon

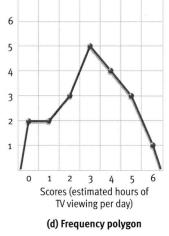

(d) Frequency polygon

Figure B.2
Measures of central tendency. Although the mean, median, and mode sometimes yield different results, they usually converge, as in the case of our TV viewing data.

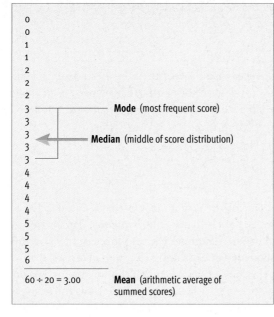

```
0
0
1
1
2
2
2
3  ──────────  Mode (most frequent score)
3
3  ──────────  Median (middle of score distribution)
3  ◄────────
3
4
4
4
4
5
5
5
6
─────────────
60 ÷ 20 = 3.00    Mean (arithmetic average of
                   summed scores)
```

Our graphs improve on the jumbled collection of scores that we started with, but *descriptive statistics*, which are used to organize and summarize data, provide some additional advantages. Let's see what the three measures of central tendency tell us about our data.

Measuring Central Tendency

1c

In examining a set of data, it's routine to ask "What is a typical score in the distribution?" For instance, in this case we might compare the average amount of TV watching in our sample to national estimates, to determine whether our subjects appear to be representative of the population. The three measures of central tendency—the median, the mean, and the mode—give us indications regarding the typical score in a data set. As explained in Chapter 2, the

median is the score that falls in the center of a distribution, the *mean* is the arithmetic average of the scores, and the *mode* is the score that occurs most frequently.

All three measures of central tendency are calculated for our TV viewing data in **Figure B.2**. As you can see, in this set of data, the mean, median, and mode all turn out to be the same score, which is 3. Although our example in Chapter 2 emphasized that the mean, median, and mode can yield different estimates of central tendency, the correspondence among them seen in our TV viewing data is quite common. Lack of agreement usually occurs when a few extreme scores pull the mean away from the center of the distribution, as shown in **Figure B.3**. The curves plotted in **Figure B.3** are simply "smoothed out" frequency polygons based on data from many subjects. They show that when a distribution is symmetric, the measures of central tendency fall together, but this is not true in skewed or unbalanced distributions.

Figure B.3(b) shows a *negatively skewed distribution,* in which most scores pile up at the high end of the scale (the negative skew refers to the direction in which the curve's "tail" points). A *positively skewed distribution,* in which scores pile up at the low end of the scale, is shown in **Figure B.3(c)**. In both types of skewed distributions, a few extreme scores at one end pull the mean, and to a lesser degree the median, away from the mode. In these situations, the mean may be misleading and the median usually provides the best index of central tendency.

In any case, the measures of central tendency for our TV viewing data are reassuring, since they all agree and they fall reasonably close to national estimates regarding how much young adults watch TV (Nielsen Media Research, 1998). Given the small size of our group, this agreement with national norms doesn't prove that our sample is rep-

Figure B.3
Measures of central tendency in skewed distributions. In a symmetrical distribution (a), the three measures of central tendency converge. However, in a negatively skewed distribution (b) or in a positively skewed distribution (c), the mean, median, and mode are pulled apart as shown here. Typically, in these situations the median provides the best index of central tendency.

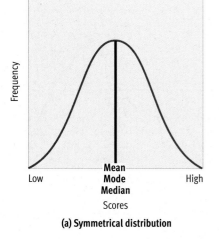

(a) Symmetrical distribution

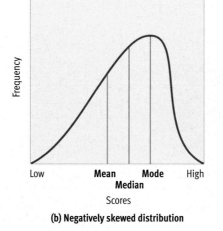

(b) Negatively skewed distribution

(c) Positively skewed distribution

resentative of the population, but at least there's no obvious reason to believe that it is unrepresentative.

Measuring Variability 1c

Of course, the subjects in our sample did not report identical TV viewing habits. Virtually all data sets are characterized by some variability. *Variability* **refers to how much the scores tend to vary or depart from the mean score.** For example, the distribution of golf scores for a mediocre, erratic golfer would be characterized by high variability, while scores for an equally mediocre but consistent golfer would show less variability.

The *standard deviation* **is an index of the amount of variability in a set of data.** It reflects the dispersion of scores in a distribution. This principle is portrayed graphically in **Figure B.4**, where the two distributions of golf scores have the same mean but the upper one has less variability because the scores are "bunched up" in the center (for the consistent golfer). The distribution in **Figure B.4(b)**

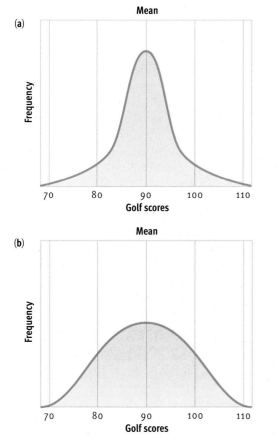

Figure B.4
The standard deviation and dispersion of data. Although both these distributions of golf scores have the same mean, their standard deviations will be different. In (a) the scores are bunched together and there is less variability than in (b), yielding a lower standard deviation for the data in distribution (a).

is characterized by more variability, as the erratic golfer's scores are more spread out. This distribution will yield a higher standard deviation than the distribution in **Figure B.4(a)**.

The formula for calculating the standard deviation is shown in **Figure B.5**, where d stands for each score's deviation from the mean and Σ stands for summation. A step-by-step application of this formula to our TV viewing data, shown in **Figure B.5**, reveals that the standard deviation for our TV viewing data is 1.64. The standard deviation has a variety of uses. One of these uses will surface in the next section, where we discuss the normal distribution.

The Normal Distribution 7c

The hypothesis in our study is that brighter students watch less TV than relatively dull students. To test this hypothesis, we're going to correlate TV viewing with SAT scores. But to make effective use of the SAT data, we need to understand what SAT scores mean, which brings us to the normal distribution.

The *normal distribution* **is a symmetric, bell-shaped curve that represents the pattern in which many human characteristics are dispersed in the**

TV viewing score (X)	Deviation from mean (d)	Deviation squared (d^2)
0	−3	9
0	−3	9
1	−2	4
1	−2	4
2	−1	1
2	−1	1
2	−1	1
3	0	0
3	0	0
3	0	0
3	0	0
3	0	0
4	+1	1
4	+1	1
4	+1	1
4	+1	1
5	+2	4
5	+2	4
5	+2	4
6	+3	9

$N = 20$

$\Sigma X = 60$ $\Sigma d^2 = 54$

$$\text{Mean} = \frac{\Sigma X}{N} = \frac{60}{20} = 3.0$$

$$\text{Standard deviation} = \sqrt{\frac{\Sigma d^2}{N}} = \sqrt{\frac{54}{20}}$$

$$= \sqrt{2.70} = 1.64$$

Figure B.5
Steps in calculating the standard deviation. (1) Add the scores (ΣX) and divide by the number of scores (N) to calculate the mean (which comes out to 3.0 in this case). (2) Calculate each score's deviation from the mean by subtracting the mean from each score (the results are shown in the second column). (3) Square these deviations from the mean and total the results to obtain (Σd^2) as shown in the third column. (4) Insert the numbers for N and Σd^2 into the formula for the standard deviation and compute the results.

population. A great many physical qualities (for example, height, nose length, and running speed) and psychological traits (intelligence, spatial reasoning ability, introversion) are distributed in a manner that closely resembles this bell-shaped curve. When a trait is normally distributed, most scores fall near the center of the distribution (the mean), and the number of scores gradually declines as one moves away from the center in either direction. The normal distribution is not a law of nature. It's a mathematical function, or theoretical curve, that approximates the way nature seems to operate.

The normal distribution is the bedrock of the scoring system for most psychological tests, including the SAT. As we discuss in Chapter 9, psychological tests are relative measures; they assess how people score on a trait in comparison to other people. The normal distribution gives us a precise way to measure how people stack up in comparison to each other. The scores under the normal curve are dispersed in a fixed pattern, with the standard deviation serving as the unit of measurement, as shown in **Figure B.6**. About 68% of the scores in the distribution fall within plus or minus 1 standard deviation of the mean, while 95% of the scores fall within plus or minus 2 standard deviations of the mean. Given this fixed pattern, if you know the mean and standard deviation of a normally distributed trait, you can tell where any score falls in the distribution for the trait.

Although you may not have realized it, you probably have taken many tests in which the scoring system is based on the normal distribution. On the SAT, for instance, raw scores (the number of items correct on each subtest) are converted into standard scores that indicate where you fall in the normal distribution for the trait measured. In this conversion, the mean is set arbitrarily at 500 and the standard deviation at 100, as shown in **Figure B.7**. Therefore, a score of 400 on the SAT Critical Reading subtest means that you scored 1 standard deviation below the mean, while an SAT score of 600 indicates that you scored 1 standard deviation above the mean. Thus, SAT scores tell you how many standard deviations above or below the mean your score was. This system also provides the metric for IQ scales and many other types of psychological tests (see Chapter 9).

Test scores that place examinees in the normal distribution can always be converted to percentile scores, which are a little easier to interpret. A *percentile score* indicates the percentage of people who score at or below the score you obtained. For example, if you score at the 60th percentile, 60% of the people who take the test score the same or below you, while the remaining 40% score above you. There are tables available that permit us to convert any stan-

Figure B.6

The normal distribution. Many characteristics are distributed in a pattern represented by this bell-shaped curve (each dot represents a case). The horizontal axis shows how far above or below the mean a score is (measured in plus or minus standard deviations). The vertical axis shows the number of cases obtaining each score. In a normal distribution, most cases fall near the center of the distribution, so that 68.26% of the cases fall within plus or minus 1 standard deviation of the mean. The number of cases gradually declines as one moves away from the mean in either direction, so that only 13.59% of the cases fall between 1 and 2 standard deviations above or below the mean, and even fewer cases (2.14%) fall between 2 and 3 standard deviations above or below the mean.

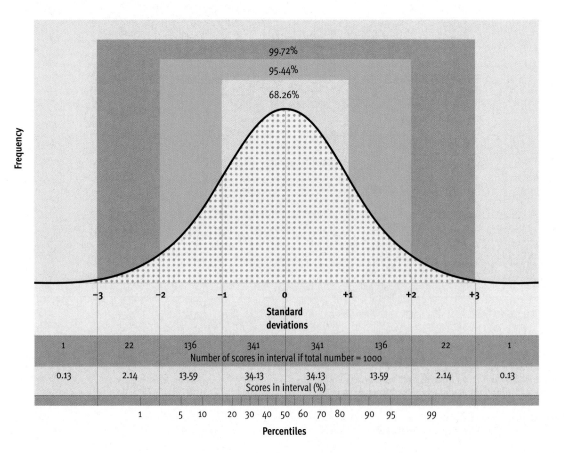

dard deviation placement in a normal distribution into a precise percentile score. Figure B.6 gives some percentile conversions for the normal curve.

Of course, not all distributions are normal. As we saw in Figure B.3, some distributions are skewed in one direction or the other. As an example, consider what would happen if a classroom exam were much too easy or much too hard. If the test were too easy, scores would be bunched up at the high end of the scale, as in Figure B.3(b). If the test were too hard, scores would be bunched up at the low end, as in Figure B.3(c).

Measuring Correlation

 1d

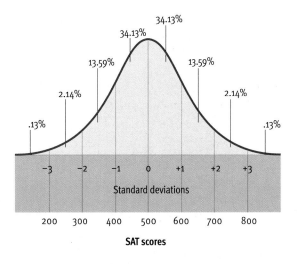

Figure B.7
The normal distribution and SAT scores. The normal distribution is the basis for the scoring system on many standardized tests. For example, on the SAT, the mean is set at 500 and the standard deviation at 100. Hence, an SAT score tells you how many standard deviations above or below the mean you scored. For example, a score of 700 means you scored 2 standard deviations above the mean.

To determine whether TV viewing is related to SAT scores, we have to compute a *correlation coefficient*—a numerical index of the degree of relationship between two variables. As discussed in Chapter 2, a *positive* correlation means that two variables—say X and Y—co-vary in the *same* direction. This means that high scores on variable X are associated with high scores on variable Y and that low scores on X are associated with low scores on Y. A *negative* correlation indicates that two variables co-vary in the *opposite* direction. This means that people who score high on variable X tend to score low on variable Y, whereas those who score low on X tend to score high on Y. In our study, we hypothesized that as TV viewing increases, SAT scores will decrease, so we should expect a negative correlation between TV viewing and SAT scores.

The *magnitude* of a correlation coefficient indicates the *strength* of the association between two variables. This coefficient can vary between 0 and ± 1.00. The coefficient is usually represented by the letter r (for example, $r = .45$). A coefficient near 0 tells us that there is no relationship between two variables. A coefficient of $+1.00$ or -1.00 indicates that there is a perfect, one-to-one correspondence between two variables. A perfect correlation is found only rarely when working with real data. The closer the coefficient is to either -1.00 or $+1.00$, the stronger the relationship is.

The direction and strength of correlations can be illustrated graphically in scatter diagrams (see Figure B.8). A *scatter diagram* is a graph in which **paired X and Y scores for each subject are plotted as single points.** Figure B.8 shows scatter diagrams for positive correlations in the upper half and for negative correlations in the bottom half. A perfect positive correlation and a perfect negative correlation are shown on the far left. When a correlation is perfect, the data points in the scatter diagram fall exactly in a straight line. However, positive and negative correlations yield lines slanted in the opposite direction because the lines map out opposite types of associations. Moving to the right in Figure B.8, you can see what happens when the magnitude of a

Figure B.8
Scatter diagrams of positive and negative correlations. Scatter diagrams plot paired X and Y scores as single points. Score plots slanted in the opposite direction result from positive (top row) as opposed to negative (bottom row) correlations. Moving across both rows (to the right), you can see that progressively weaker correlations result in more and more scattered plots of data points.

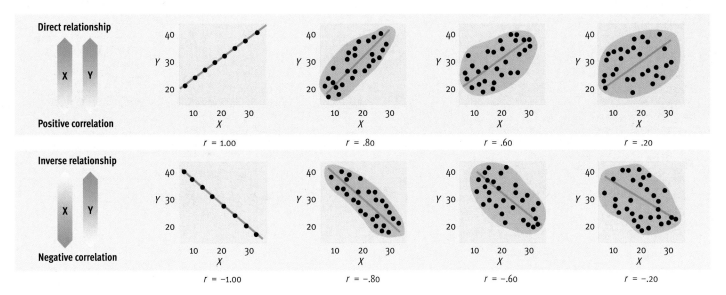

Scatter diagram of the correlation between TV viewing and SAT scores. Our hypothetical data relating TV viewing to SAT scores are plotted in this scatter diagram. Compare it to the scatter diagrams seen in Figure B.8 and see whether you can estimate the correlation between TV viewing and SAT scores in our data (see the text for the answer).

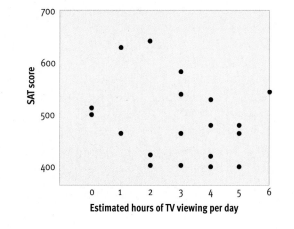

correlation decreases. The data points scatter farther and farther from the straight line that would represent a perfect relationship.

What about our data relating TV viewing to SAT scores? Figure B.9 shows a scatter diagram of these data. Having just learned about scatter diagrams, perhaps you can estimate the magnitude of the correlation between TV viewing and SAT scores. The scat-

ter diagram of our data looks a lot like the one seen in the bottom right corner of Figure B.8, suggesting that the correlation will be in the vicinity of −.20.

The formula for computing the most widely used measure of correlation—the Pearson product-moment correlation—is shown in Figure B.10, along with the calculations for our data on TV viewing and SAT scores. The data yield a correlation of $r = -.24$. This coefficient of correlation reveals that we have found a weak inverse association between TV viewing and performance on the SAT. Among our participants, as TV viewing increases, SAT scores decrease, but the trend isn't very strong. We can get a better idea of how strong this correlation is by examining its predictive power.

Correlation and Prediction   1d

As the magnitude of a correlation increases (gets closer to either −1.00 or +1.00), our ability to predict one variable based on knowledge of the other variable steadily increases. This relationship between the

Figure B.10

Computing a correlation coefficient. The calculations required to compute the Pearson product-moment coefficient of correlation are shown here. The formula looks intimidating, but it's just a matter of filling in the figures taken from the sums of the columns shown above the formula.

Subject number	TV viewing score (X)	X²	SAT score (Y)	Y²	XY
1	0	0	500	250,000	0
2	0	0	515	265,225	0
3	1	1	450	202,500	450
4	1	1	650	422,500	650
5	2	4	400	160,000	800
6	2	4	675	455,625	1350
7	2	4	425	180,625	850
8	3	9	400	160,000	1200
9	3	9	450	202,500	1350
10	3	9	500	250,000	1500
11	3	9	550	302,500	1650
12	3	9	600	360,000	1800
13	4	16	400	160,000	1600
14	4	16	425	180,625	1700
15	4	16	475	225,625	1900
16	4	16	525	275,625	2100
17	5	25	400	160,000	2000
18	5	25	450	202,500	2250
19	5	25	475	225,625	2375
20	6	36	550	302,500	3300
$N = 20$	$\Sigma X = 60$	$\Sigma X^2 = 234$	$\Sigma Y = 9815$	$\Sigma Y^2 = 4{,}943{,}975$	$\Sigma XY = 28{,}825$

Formula for Pearson product-moment correlation coefficient

$$r = \frac{(N)\Sigma XY - (\Sigma X)(\Sigma Y)}{\sqrt{[(N)\Sigma X^2 - (\Sigma X)^2][(N)\Sigma Y^2 - (\Sigma Y)^2]}}$$

$$= \frac{(20)(28{,}825) - (60)(9815)}{\sqrt{[(20)(234) - (60)^2][(20)(4{,}943{,}975) - (9815)^2]}}$$

$$= \frac{-12{,}400}{\sqrt{[1080][2{,}545{,}275]}}$$

$$= -.237$$

magnitude of a correlation and predictability can be quantified precisely. All we have to do is square the correlation coefficient (multiply it by itself) and this gives us the *coefficient of determination,* **the percentage of variation in one variable that can be predicted based on the other variable.** Thus, a correlation of .70 yields a coefficient of determination of .49 (.70 × .70 = .49), indicating that variable *X* can account for 49% of the variation in variable *Y.* Figure B.11 shows how the coefficient of determination goes up as the magnitude of a correlation increases.

Unfortunately, a correlation of .24 doesn't give us much predictive power. We can account only for a little over 6% of the variation in variable *Y.* So, if we tried to predict individuals' SAT scores based on how much TV they watched, our predictions wouldn't be very accurate. Although a low correlation doesn't have much practical, predictive utility, it may still have theoretical value. Just knowing that there is a relationship between two variables can be theoretically interesting. However, we haven't yet addressed the question of whether our observed correlation is strong enough to support our hypothesis that there is a relationship between TV viewing and SAT scores. To make this judgment, we have to turn to *inferential statistics* and the process of hypothesis testing.

Hypothesis Testing

Inferential statistics go beyond the mere description of data. *Inferential statistics* **are used to interpret data and draw conclusions.** They permit researchers to decide whether their data support their hypotheses.

In Chapter 2, we showed how inferential statistics can be used to evaluate the results of an experiment;

the same process can be applied to correlational data. In our study of TV viewing we hypothesized that we would find an inverse relationship between amount of TV watched and SAT scores. Sure enough, that's what we found. However, we have to ask ourselves a critical question: Is this observed correlation large enough to support our hypothesis, or might a correlation of this size have occurred by chance?

We have to ask a similar question nearly every time we conduct a study. Why? Because we are working only with a sample. In research, we observe a limited *sample* (in this case, 20 participants) to draw conclusions about a much larger *population* (college students in general). There's always a possibility that if we drew a different sample from the population, the results might be different. Perhaps our results are unique to our sample and not generalizable to the larger population. If we were able to collect data on the entire population, we would not have to wrestle with this problem, but our dependence on a sample necessitates the use of inferential statistics to precisely evaluate the likelihood that our results are due to chance factors in sampling. Thus, inferential statistics are the key to making the inferential leap from the sample to the population (see Figure B.12 on the next page).

Although it may seem backward, in hypothesis testing we formally test the *null hypothesis.* As applied to correlational data, the *null hypothesis* is **the assumption that there is no true relationship between the variables observed.** In our study, the null hypothesis is that there is no genuine association between TV viewing and SAT scores. We want to determine whether our results will permit us to *reject* the null hypothesis and thus conclude that our *research hypothesis* (that there *is* a relationship between

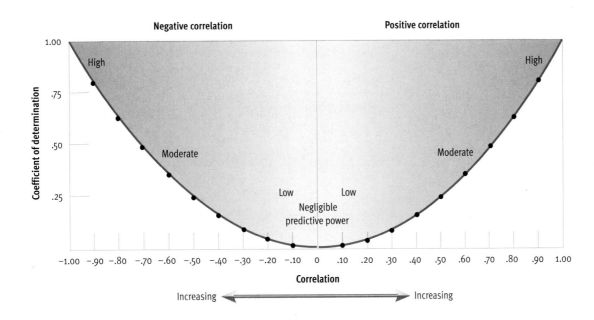

Figure B.11
Correlation and the coefficient of determination. The coefficient of determination is an index of a correlation's predictive power. As you can see, whether positive or negative, stronger correlations yield greater predictive power.

Figure B.12

The relationship between the population and the sample. In research, we are usually interested in a broad population, but we can observe only a small sample from the population. After making observations of our sample, we draw inferences about the population, based on the sample. This inferential process works well as long as the sample is reasonably representative of the population.

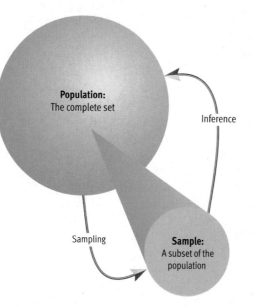

the variables) has been supported. Why do we directly test the null hypothesis instead of the research hypothesis? Because our probability calculations depend on assumptions tied to the null hypothesis. Specifically, we compute the probability of obtaining the results that we have observed if the null hypothesis is indeed true. The calculation of this probability hinges on a number of factors. A key factor is the amount of variability in the data, which is why the standard deviation is an important statistic.

Statistical Significance

When we reject the null hypothesis, we conclude that we have found *statistically significant* results. *Statistical significance* is said to exist when the probability that the observed findings are due to chance is very low, usually less than 5 chances in 100. This means that if the null hypothesis is correct and we conduct our study 100 times, drawing a new sample from the population each time, we will get results such as those observed only 5 times out of 100. If our calculations allow us to reject the null hypothesis, we conclude that our results support our research hypothesis. Thus, statistically significant results typically are findings that *support* a research hypothesis.

The requirement that there be less than 5 chances in 100 that research results are due to chance is the *minimum* requirement for statistical significance.

When this requirement is met, we say the results are significant at the .05 level. If researchers calculate that there is less than 1 chance in 100 that their results are due to chance factors in sampling, the results are significant at the .01 level. If there is less than a 1 in 1000 chance that findings are attributable to sampling error, the results are significant at the .001 level. Thus, there are several levels of significance that you may see cited in scientific articles.

Because we are only dealing in matters of probability, there is always the possibility that our decision to accept or reject the null hypothesis is wrong. The various significance levels indicate the probability of erroneously rejecting the null hypothesis (and inaccurately accepting the research hypothesis). At the .05 level of significance, there are 5 chances in 100 that we have made a mistake when we conclude that our results support our hypothesis, and at the .01 level of significance the chance of an erroneous conclusion is 1 in 100. Although researchers hold the probability of this type of error quite low, the probability is never zero. This is one of the reasons that competently executed studies of the same question can yield contradictory findings. The differences may be due to chance variations in sampling that can't be prevented.

What do we find when we evaluate our data linking TV viewing to students' SAT scores? The calculations indicate that, given our sample size and the variability in our data, the probability of obtaining a correlation of $-.24$ by chance is greater than 20%. That's not a high probability, but it's *not* low enough to reject the null hypothesis. Thus, our findings are not strong enough to allow us to conclude that we have supported our hypothesis.

Statistics and Empiricism

In summary, conclusions based on empirical research are a matter of probability, and there's always a possibility that the conclusions are wrong. However, two major strengths of the empirical approach are its precision and its intolerance of error. Scientists can give you precise estimates of the likelihood that their conclusions are wrong, and because they're intolerant of error, they hold this probability extremely low. It's their reliance on statistics that allows them to accomplish these goals.

Industrial/Organizational Psychology

by Kathy A. Hanisch (Iowa State University)

You have applied for a job, submitted your résumé and taken a series of tests. You have been interviewed by your potential supervisor and given a tour of the company. You now find yourself sitting across from the co-owners, who have just offered you a position. They tell you that their organization is a great place to work. As evidence, they tell you that no one has quit their job in the last five years and that employees are rarely absent. They also tell you that they have flexible policies. You can work whatever hours you like and take vacation whenever you want. And if you decide to work for them, you will have access to spending cash as well as keys to the company.

You try to maintain your composure. You had heard interesting things about this company but didn't really believe them. Finally, the co-owners ask you what you are worth, indicating they will pay you whatever you wish. Now you're really dumbfounded and wonder what the catch is but sit quietly while they talk about other issues. Does this sound too good to be true? Wouldn't this be ideal?

Almost this exact scenario played out in an organization owned and managed by an Oakland appliance dealer in the 1970s. His name was Arthur Friedman, and he had decided to change how he ran his business. Friedman, as reported in the *Washington Post* (Koughan, 1975), announced at one of his staff meetings that employees could work the hours they wanted, be paid what they thought they were worth, take vacation time and time off from work whenever they wanted, and help themselves to petty cash if they were in need of spending money. New employees would be allowed to set their own wages too. As you might imagine, the employees weren't sure how to take this news. It was reported that no one said anything during the meeting when Friedman first described his plan (Koughan, 1975).

When asked why he was changing his business practices, Friedman replied, "I always said that if you give people what they want, you get what you want. You have to be willing to lose, to stick your neck out. I finally decided that the time had come to practice what I preached" (Koughan, 1975). In the final analysis, Friedman's experiment worked. The organization was profitable. Friedman signed union contracts without reading them (the employees didn't need a union with him in charge). Employees didn't quit, they didn't steal from the company, and they were rarely absent. Net profits increased, and the company was a success. The employees realized that to make the organization work and remain in business, they had to be reasonable in their requests and behavior (Koughan, 1975).

A more recent company with some extra benefits for employees is Google, headquartered in Mountain View, California (the heart of Silicon Valley). In 2007, *Fortune* magazine rated it the number one company to work for. Included among its many perks are free gourmet meals, snack rooms, free haircuts, gyms, massages, subsidized exercise classes, classes to learn another language, child care, on-site doctors for free employee checkups, a pet-friendly facility, and a traveling library for book checkout. In addition, Google offers free shuttlebus transportation to work or, if the employee drives, free on-site car washes and oil changes. When an employee has a baby, Google provides up to $500 reimbursement for takeout food to ease the transition home. If an employee refers a friend to work at Google and the friend is hired, the referring employee gets a cash bonus. Google even provides washers and dryers so employees can do their laundry at work for free (the detergent is provided, too!). In addition to all these benefits, Google rewards innovation, both high-tech and otherwise, and allow employees such as engineers to spend some of their time at work on independent projects.

Google provides many employee perks, including free meals and haircuts, exercise classes, game rooms, child care, and on-site doctors. Would you want to work for Google?

Organizations such as Google and Friedman's company are interesting in the way they deal with their employees and in the ways such treatment affects their employees' behaviors. Psychologists who study people's behavior at work are called *industrial and organizational psychologists*. **Industrial and organizational (I/O) psychology is the branch of psychology concerned with human behavior in the work environment.** I/O psychologists assist organizations in important areas such as motivating employees, alleviating job stress, hiring the best workers, and combating safety problems. Work is an important avenue of study for psychology because of its link to the health of the American economy, as well as people's feelings of self-worth and well-being. I/O psychologists study employee selection, performance appraisal, training, job design, communication, work stress, motivation, leadership, groups and teams, organizational culture, human factors, job attitudes, well-being, and work behavior. This appendix will introduce you to the field of I/O psychology.

The Role of Work in People's Lives

You have learned about work since you were a small child. You may have asked where your mother was going when she took you to day care or why your father left the house before 8 A.M. and did not return until after 5 P.M. You likely "played" at different jobs by dressing up as an astronaut, firefighter, teacher,

chef, or construction worker. As you got older, other sources of information about work may have come from your friends, other family members, school, and the media. In high school, more education and a part-time job may have given you additional details about the meaning of work. As you pursue a college degree, you may receive information about the work and jobs available in your chosen field through classes, internships, or other job experiences.

Work is an important part of life for most people. We often ask people we meet what they "do," which translates into "What is your job and for whom do you work?" Many people identify with their work because they spend so much of their waking lives at work. Work is important because it provides many of the things people need and value. Work for pay provides the money necessary to satisfy people's basic needs for food, shelter, and security (health care, retirement income), while the "leftover" money provides discretionary funds to use as one sees fit. These funds can go toward a round of golf, an iPod, or a fancy place to live; can go to support charities or attend athletic or fine art performances; or to save money for college. Essentially, money, typically from work, provides people with a standard of living that depends on their income and how they choose to spend it. And work provides much more: a source of social interactions and friendships, independence, a sense of accomplishment, satisfaction, a reason to get up in the morning, happiness, a sense of identity, recognition, and varied amounts of prestige (see **Figure C.1**).

Although most researchers and practitioners agree that money and recognition are nearly universal motivators (Clark, 2003), what is valued or sought from work varies from person to person. For example, the prestige of a job may not be important to you but might be important to your best friend. Perhaps you want your work to provide you with a sense of accomplishment or a source of social interactions, while your friend simply sees it as a way to pay the bills. It is important to understand what you want from your work as well as what a job can provide.

From an employer's perspective, it is useful to determine what employees want because satisfied employees will be more likely than dissatisfied employees to work diligently to meet organizational goals. Part of a supervisor's job is to determine what employees value, because those values can be used to motivate employees to perform well in their jobs.

Types of Jobs

There are many types of work, in many types of jobs, in many organizational settings. These settings in-

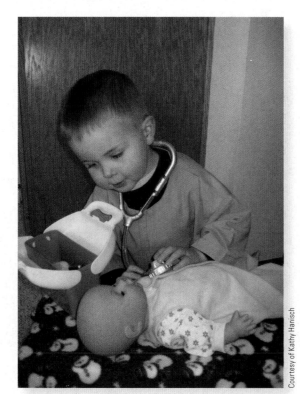

The Doctor is In! Socialization about the nature and importance of work begins very early in life.

Courtesy of Kathy Hanisch

clude multinational conglomerates; public and private companies; nonprofits; federal, state, and local government organizations; and home businesses.

People in the United States work a variety of schedules, from extended workweeks (45+ hours) to standard workweeks (35–44 hours) to part-time workweeks (less than 35 hours). Some workers, such as police officers, medical personnel, and factory workers, have work shifts other than the typical 8 A.M. to 5 P.M. Others are offered flexible working schedules that best fit their lives as long as they work the required number of hours and accomplish their work. Telecommuting is becoming more and more popular, because of advances in communication technologies. Regardless of the type of job or your work schedule, it is likely that you will spend most of your waking hours in some type of employment for many years. Many people spend their weekends working, too. Because work is critical to who you are and what you do, studying the psychological principles and some of the topics examined by I/O psychologists will provide you with information that may be useful to you in your future careers. Before focusing on the specific aspects of getting and keeping a job, let's briefly explore the subfields of I/O psychology and possible career paths in this area.

Subfields and Other Aspects of I/O Psychology

I/O psychology is made up of three specialty areas. I/O psychology consists primarily of the two areas that define its name: (1) *industrial (I) psychology,* and (2) *organizational (O) psychology.* The third area is known as *human factors* or *human engineering psychology. Industrial psychology* (also known as *personnel psychology*) deals with the how-to side of I/O psychology, including how to select individuals for the right positions, how to evaluate their job performance, how to train them, and how to compensate them. This is the oldest of the three subfields. The broad areas of job analysis, job evaluation, test validation, employee selection (including interviewing), employee training, legal issues including employment discrimination in the organization, and performance evaluation are included in this subfield. *Organizational psychology* is concerned with how employees are integrated into the work environment from both emotional and social perspectives. Some of the areas covered include job satisfaction, job stress, work motivation, leadership, organizational culture, teamwork, and organizational development. Although not included in the field's name, human factors psychology is also an important specialization within I/O psychology.

Jobs with the Highest and Lowest Prestige		
	Job description	Percent rating job as high prestige
Highest prestige	Firefighter	63%
	Doctor	58%
	Nurse	55%
	Scientist	54%
	Teacher	52%*
Lowest prestige	Stockbroker	11%
	Business executive	11%
	Real estate broker/agent	6%

*The prestige ratings for teachers rose from 29% in 1977 to 52% in 2006, the only job surveyed to show a positive change in prestige over 29 years.

SOURCE: www.harrisinteractive.com

Figure C.1

Variations in job prestige. Among other things, jobs vary in the prestige that they convey. This chart lists a few examples of jobs that possess either high prestige or low prestige, based on a 2006 survey.

Human factors (or *human engineering*) *psychology* examines the ways in which work, systems, and system features can be designed or changed to most effectively correspond with the capabilities and limitations of individuals, often with a focus on the human body. Examples of issues in this area include redesigning machines to be easier on the systemic aspects of the body, changing the positions of controls on machines to reduce the number of accidents, modifying displays so that the user can quickly determine the information presented, and making the job more interesting by increasing the types of skills needed to perform the work. All three areas—industrial psychology, organizational psychology, and human factors psychology—are interrelated when addressing problems or issues in the world of business and industry.

Most I/O psychologists have graduate degrees that typically require an additional two to five years of school beyond the bachelor's degree. I/O psychologists obtain jobs primarily in four work settings: industry, academia, consulting firms, and government, with the largest percentage in industry and academia. Figure C.2 on the next page provides examples of typical job postings for I/O psychologists taken from recent recruitment ads for each of the four areas.

In the United States, a fairly recent advance of relevance to the I/O field is the development of the *Occupational Information Network (O*NET).* The O*NET is a comprehensive, detailed, and flexible set of job descriptors based on an extensive research program (Peterson et al., 1999), which can be accessed via the Internet. O*NET can be used to find details about occupations (for example, tasks, knowledge, skills, work activities, wages, employment outlook) or to select preferred work activities or interests and locate corresponding occupations. It is a helpful starting point for individuals seeking details about the types of occupations that may interest them as well as the salary and occupational outlook for various

Academic position	Industry position	Consulting position	Government position
The Department of Psychological Sciences at Purdue University is excited to invite applicants to apply for a tenure track position in Industrial/Organizational Psychology at the beginning or advanced Assistant Professor level beginning in the Fall. For this position the successful candidate will have a strong publication history, the beginnings of a strong research program with the likelihood of future funding, as well as a record of teaching excellence.	GEICO, a Berkshire Hathaway company and the fastest growing auto insurer in the country, is seeking a senior manager to lead our Selection Systems group in its corporate headquarters in Chevy Chase, Maryland (just outside of Washington, DC). The position reports directly to the Corporate Vice President of Staff Development.	AutoZone, a Fortune 500 company is seeking an experienced, innovative Organization Development Consultant at our Memphis Store Support Center. This position will be responsible for improving and executing core Organization Development processes (e.g., performance management, talent and succession planning, and employee development) and for performance improvement consulting with business leaders to drive solutions to business issues in an environment of substantial growth and rapid change.	Immediate opening for a psychologist (YA-180-02) at the Center for Army Leadership, Fort Leavenworth, KS. Applicants should be prepared to conduct research using principles, theories and findings from leadership, organizational behavior, experimental psychology, and social psychology, and to conduct training to enhance leaders' performance and combat readiness. Immediate research areas include cross-cultural influence, leadership development, and competency measurement.

Figure C.2
Recruitment advertisements for I/O psychologists. Abbreviated versions of recent ads for positions available for individuals with I/O psychology degrees are shown here. The industry position prefers an individual with a master's degree, whereas the other three positions require or prefer a Ph.D.

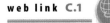

web link C.1

Occupational Information Network (O*NET)

This site provides occupational information for various occupations and contains information on job descriptions, salaries, and occupational outlook.

web link C.2

Society for Industrial and Organizational Psychology (SIOP)

The Society for Industrial and Organizational Psychology (SIOP) is the leading professional organization for I/O psychologists. Although primarily intended for society members, its website provides a variety of resources for students and teachers who are interested in this specialty area. Included among the resources are excellent discussions of employment testing, legal aspects, and ways I/O psychologists can contribute to organizational excellence.

occupations. It is also useful to employers who need to develop thorough job descriptions for their organizations. Although there have been some concerns about its coverage and information, O*NET is viewed as a major achievement in occupational information (Sackett & Laczo, 2003). Information continues to be updated and added to the O*NET. According to O*NET, the projected growth for I/O psychologists of 21% for 2006–2016 is much faster than average.

The Society for Industrial and Organizational Psychology (SIOP) is the primary professional organization for I/O psychologists. There are approximately 6000 members, including individuals from academia, industry, consulting positions, and the government. The SIOP website is a great resource for information about graduate school, jobs, and articles in I/O psychology.

Selecting Employees

One of the most important tasks for any business enterprise is to select talented, motivated employees who will work hard to help the organization meet its goals. As you will see in this section, the task of employee selection is complicated and must be handled with sensitivity and fairness.

The Hiring Process

In the early 1900s, when someone needed a job he or she would hang around the outside of a company and wait to see whether the company needed workers. Many times the people who worked for the company told their friends or relatives about possible job openings, prompting them to apply for work. This often meant that individuals hired for the available jobs were similar to those working there (such as white males). Industrial and organizational psychologists first became involved in the process of selecting employees when the United States government needed help selecting and placing officers and soldiers in World War I (Aamodt, 2007). They used

mental ability tests to determine who would become officers and who would be assigned to the infantry.

The process many employers use now to hire employees is very detailed, typically consisting of five components: job analysis, testing, legal issues, recruitment, and the selection decision.

Job Analysis

Job analysis is a method for breaking a job into its constituent parts. It is a process used to identify the most important parts of the job. I/O psychologists have helped devise effective strategies for determining three basic aspects of any job: (1) What tasks and behaviors are essential to the job? (2) What knowledge, skills, and abilities are needed to perform the job? and (3) What are the conditions (such as stress, safety, and temperature) under which the job is performed? A job analysis can be conducted in many ways. An analyst may interview current employees, have them complete questionnaires, observe people in the job, or talk to people knowledgeable about the job (Gael, 1988).

I/O psychologists continue to research effective job analysis techniques. Current research suggests that worker-oriented methods are best for employee selection (Aamodt, 2007) because of their focus on the worker as opposed to the tasks. One worker-oriented method is the Critical Incident Technique (CIT), which uses critical incidents or behaviors that discriminate between excellent and poor behavior for someone performing the job (Flanagan, 1954). For example, excellent behavior for a university professor might involve lecturing about relevant material beyond what is covered in the textbook (Aamodt, 2007).

The information from a job analysis is used in many types of personnel functions. including employee selection, performance appraisal, training, and human resources planning. Within the hiring process, job analysis is used to write job descriptions; to determine what tests might be used to assess the relevant knowledge, skills, and abilities of job applicants; and to assist in meeting legal requirements that affect the selection process.

Testing and Other Employee Selection Procedures

The next step in personnel selection is assessing whether job candidates have the attributes required for specific jobs that are available. Employers use quite a variety of employee selection tools, including individual and panel interviews, standardized paper-and-pencil tests of abilities and knowledge, assessments of personality traits, such as conscientiousness, and honesty tests. In addition, work samples, in which applicants do a replica of the work they will be asked to do on the job, can be useful. Reference checks, Internet searches, and drug testing are also used to help find top-flight employees. Selection procedures that are properly developed and carefully used are vital to the success of organizations.

Psychological testing has long played an important role in employee selection efforts. As noted in Chapter 9, a *psychological test* **is a standardized measure of a sample of a person's behavior.** Employers can purchase tests from commercial test publishers or can develop special tests to meet their own needs. Early on in the process of using a test, it behooves organizations to assess the *reliability* and *validity* of the test, as discussed in Chapter 9. *Reliability* **refers to the measurement consistency of a test (or of other kinds of measurement techniques).** Reliable tests yield consistent results over the course of multiple testings. *Validity* **refers to the ability of a test to measure what it was designed to measure.** Evidence regarding validity is crucial when tests are used for employee selection purposes. When an organization purchases a commercial test for use, the information about reliability and validity is normally provided by the test publisher.

Once a suitable test has been found or developed, the next step is to administer it to job candidates and decide which of them has the greatest probability of being successful on the job. Justifying the use of psychological tests in hiring people depends on collecting data that demonstrates a relationship between test scores and performance on the job. In a simple scenario the scores achieved on a test by job applicants are compared to their job performance ratings or evaluations some time after being hired (such as six months or one year). These comparisons can be used to calculate a correlation coefficient that will indicate how strong the relation is between the test scores and job performance. The ideal relationship would be a strong positive correlation that would in-

dicate that as tests score improve, job performance ratings improve and, alternatively, as tests score decrease, job performance decreases. A graph illustrating this type of relationship is shown in Figure C.3.

Personality testing appears quite frequently in employers' selection processes. One type of personality test being used by many organizations is the integrity test. *Integrity tests* **are standardized measures used to assess attitudes and experiences related to honesty and trustworthiness.** Employers want to be able to use these tests to help them choose applicants who are dependable, honest, and trustworthy. Research indicates that integrity tests are reliable and scores are related to theft, absenteeism, and performance (Aamodt, 2007). Use of these tests in hiring has also led to a reduction in compensation claims (Sturman & Sherwyn, 2007).

Although standardized mental ability and personality tests are commonly used in personnel selection, the most widely used device remains the interview. Nearly all organizations use some type of employee interview in their selection process (Salgado, Viswesvaran, & Ones, 2003). There are two broad types of interviews: unstructured and structured (see Figure C.4 on the next page). *Unstructured interviews* are informal: Job candidates are asked different questions with no scoring key, and there is no method for assigning scores to applicants. Although many employers rely heavily on this type of interview, research suggests that it is highly subjective and does not provide very reliable or useful information in the selection of employees (Aamodt, 2007). *Structured interviews* are more like standardized tests. The same questions are asked of all candidates by a trained interviewer and are based on attributes

Figure C.3
A hypothetical example of the relationship between test scores and job performance. When a standardized test is used to select the most promising job candidates, the expectation is that higher scores on the test will be associated with better performance on the job. The relationship won't be perfect, but when employers look at the relationship between test scores and subsequent performance ratings, the findings should resemble the hypothetical data shown here. These data would yield a very strong positive correlation between test scores and job performance, indicating the test is a good predictor of job performance.

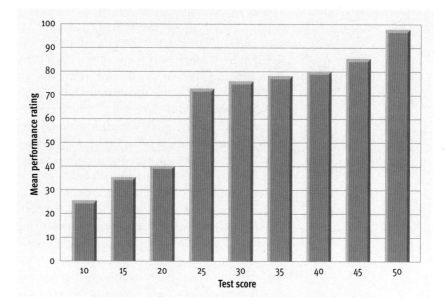

Figure C.4
Structured versus unstructured interviews. Structured interviews can yield very different kinds of information than unstructured interviews. These examples of typical interview questions can give you some idea of how the two types of interviews differ.

necessary for success on the job in question (based on the job analysis). There are clear guidelines for judging the adequacy of the answers given, and the scores assigned to an applicant have known relationships to the attributes being measured. Structured interviews can be constructed to be reliable and valid (McDaniel et al., 1994). In addition, they hold the promise of supplying useful information *not* supplied by psychological testing (about characteristics such as oral comprehension, communication and listening skills, and motivation).

Legal Issues

One of the most important pieces of legislation regarding employment, and specifically the hiring of employees, is Title VII of the Civil Rights Act of 1964 (Equal Employment Opportunity Commission, 2002). Title VII "prohibits discrimination based on race, color, religion, sex, and national origin," referred to in some quarters as the "Big 5." Providing protection based on the Big 5 helps ensure that all applicants have an equal opportunity for employment. Exceptions to this provision include matters of national security, employers with seniority systems in place, and *bona fide occupational qualifications (BFOQs)*. BFOQs permit organizations to discriminate in hiring persons in a protected class if the qualification is determined to be reasonably necessary to the operation of the business. For example, women can be discriminated against when hiring someone to model men's swimwear, and vice versa. It is reasonably necessary to the marketing and selling of swimwear that organizations hire men to model male swimwear and women to model female swimwear; sex is a thus a BFOQ in this case. It is not

reasonably necessary, however, that a secretary in a church who does secretarial work and not church or religious work be the same religion as the church that employs him or her; religion could not be used as a BFOQ in this case.

It is important for employers to abide by laws that protect people against discrimination, as the costs of litigation can be very high, in terms of both financial costs and the organization's reputation. This situation applies to discrimination based not only on the Big 5, covered under the Civil Rights Act, but also on age (Age Discrimination in Employment Act) and disability (Americans with Disabilities Act). Employment law in the United States is meant to protect and provide equal opportunities for all individuals.

There are differences among countries with regard to fair employment practices, laws, and what is considered discriminatory in the employment setting. The United States has several acts that prohibit discrimination based on a number of group characteristics. Other countries allow what would be considered discrimination in the United States. For instance, the advertisement shown in **Figure C.5** for a position in Thailand would not be legal in the United States. It specifies that the applicant must be male, which would be illegal under Title VII. It also specifies an age range of 26–28, which would be il-

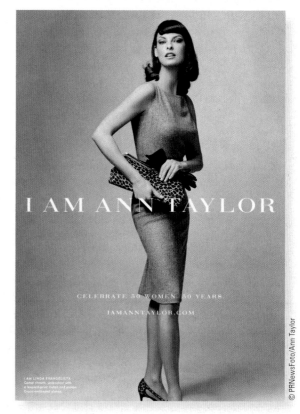

What would happen to this advertisement if the model were male? Sex is a BFOQ in this case.

legal in most states. U.S. federal law prohibits age discrimination once a person reaches the age of 40 (Age Discrimination in Employment Act). It is likely that females and those older than 28 and perhaps even younger than 26 could perform just as well in the job of sales engineer.

Nondiscriminatory hiring practices attempt to guarantee fair treatment for any person looking for a job. In the United States, organizations with several employees (typically 15) are required to abide by the employment laws. Equal opportunity laws make the job market a more level playing field in the United States than in many countries.

Recruitment

Recruitment is the process organizations use to identify potential employees for a job. Depending on the job, an organization may recruit from inside the company or seek someone outside the organization. Openings may be advertised on the company's website or on a site for specific types of jobs. In addition, websites such as monster.com, hotjobs.com, and careerbuilder.com link potential employees and employers in a variety of jobs and locations. Other recruitment sources include newspapers, radio and television advertisements, trade magazines, professional publications, and employee referrals.

Research indicates that employees recruited through *inside sources,* such as employee referrals, tend to hold their jobs longer and to exhibit better job performance than those recruited through *outside sources,* such as advertisements, employment agencies, and recruiters (Zottoli & Wanous, 2000). Studies have supported the idea that those recruited using inside sources receive more accurate information about the job (a realistic job preview) than those recruited through external sources (Conrad & Ashworth, 1986; McManus & Baratta, 1992). Research also shows that employees who stay with the organization longer typically were referred by successful employees rather than unsuccessful employees (Aamodt & Rupert, 1990).

A survey of the 50 best small and medium organizations to work for in the United States found that 92% use employee referrals. The survey also found that more than 30 percent of all hires were referred by a current employee (Pomeroy, 2005). Because of the effectiveness of employee referrals, some companies provide rewards to employees who recommend an applicant who is hired. These rewards can include cash, vacations, and raffles for prizes such as televisions and free maid service for a year (Stewart et al., 1990). Typically, the new employee must work for the organization a set period of time for the referring employee to receive the award (Stewart et al., 1990).

☐ **Sales Engineer**

Post Date :	Friday, September 05, 2008	Location :	Srinakarin Road
Salary :	20-25,000		
Business Type :	Trading : equipment & machinery		

Qualifications:
- Male, age 26-28 years old
- Degree in Mechanical, Electrical Engineering or related field
- At least 2 years experience in sales function for equipment or machinery
- Knowledge in technical support and troubleshooting
- Human relations, service-minded and good negotiation skills
- Good command of English and PC skill
- Own car with driving license

Job description:
- All daily sales activities of company in terms of visiting customers, meetings for requirements and coordinating with customers & concerned parties, etc.

SOURCE: http://www.pasona.co.th/en/hotjob.aspx

Google rewards employees with a $2,000 bonus if their referral accepts Google's offer and remains employed for at least 60 days (Google, 2008).

After applicants have submitted either a résumé or an application, someone from the organization such as the human resources manager or supervisor will determine which applicants should be considered further. In that process, he or she may make telephone inquiries of previous employers or other references and conduct criminal background checks to alleviate potential legal problems as well as to hire appropriate personnel. Reference checks can help organizations avoid costly errors when hiring employees. For instance, one company unknowingly hired someone who had just gotten out of jail and was on parole in another state (and was not supposed to leave the state). Upon finding out about the parole violation, the hiring company also found out that the new employee had been in jail for stealing from his previous employer. These types of hiring mistakes can often be avoided by conducting reference and background checks on job applicants.

Internet searches focusing on job applicants' background are becoming more common because of advances in technology and the ease with which employers can learn about potential employees before hiring them. Employers are searching social networking sites such as MySpace and Facebook to learn about job applicants. On these sites, recruiters and companies have found promising candidates reporting on their drug use, sexual exploits, and drinking, along with suggestive photographs (Finder, 2006). As you might guess, these indiscretions are considered "red flags" by employers. Companies generally assume that these applicants are lacking in good judgment and typically remove them from their selection process (Finder, 2006). Information that students thought would only be viewed by their peers is making its way into the public arena at all

Figure C.5

Culture and employment laws. The laws governing fairness and equal opportunity in hiring vary from one country to another. This advertisement for a position in Thailand would not be legal in the United States because the unnecessary specifications regarding applicants' gender and age would violate the Civil Rights Act and the Age Discrimination in Employment Act.

web link C.3

Equal Employment Opportunity Commission

The EEOC enforces federal laws related to prohibiting employment discrimination. Employees can file employment discrimination complaints with the EEOC, which then decides whether to help individuals deal with a particular violation of federal law.

Based on this photo, would you hire this job candidate? Employers are increasingly searching social networking web sites to gather information on prospective employees. In light of this reality, students may want to exercise more discretion about what they post online.

©Louis Quail/Corbis

levels, with future employers and relatives viewing the information without the students' knowledge.

Making the Hiring Decision

When selecting employees, employers are looking for a good match between the employee and the organization. They would like to match the requirements for excellent job performance with the person's own knowledge, skills, abilities, personality, and motivation. They attempt to accomplish this by using the various selection tools discussed earlier.

Researchers have posited two factors that determine an employee's performance in a job: the "can-do" and the "will-do" factors (Schmitt et al., 2003). *Can-do factors* suggest what employees are capable of doing on the job if they are working to the best of their ability. *Will-do factors* suggest the time and effort employees are willing to exert for the organization. Personality factors such as conscientiousness and need for achievement as well as integrity have been classified as important will-do factors in performance (Schmitt et al., 2003). A person's can-do and will-do factors may change as he or she moves from organization to organization. Once a person is selected, the important process of being accepted and socialized into the organization at all levels begins.

Socializing Employees: Culture, Groups, and Leadership

When you report for your first day of work in an organization, you will need to learn many things in order to be successful in your job. *Organizational socialization* refers to the process by which new members are absorbed into the culture of an organization (Jablin, 1982). Organizational socialization consists of people learning how the organization operates by using information provided by management, co-workers, observation, and company handbooks or memos.

Nowadays, electronic communication is an important part of how workers are socialized (Flanagin & Waldeck, 2004). Employees communicate through e-mail, company websites, chat groups, and blogs. Job applicants may also use these resources to learn about an organization before submitting their applications. Consulting business websites is an excellent way for job applicants to assess whether there might be a good fit between them and an organization.

Supervisors and co-workers are also important sources of socialization information. *Mentoring* is a form of training in which a current and often long-term employee (the mentor) is paired with a new employee to aid his or her growth and development within the organization. The mentor's role is to help the new employee adapt to the job by assisting with advice or resources. The mentor may provide information about how the organization works and about career advancement opportunities. Good mentoring helps new employees become successful on the job and learn the formal and informal rules of the organization (Aamodt, 2007).

Research indicates that both mentors and those they mentor often benefit from the relationship. For example, in one study of health care employees, it was found that those who were mentored reported higher salaries, greater promotion rates, and more positive career success than those who did not receive mentoring (Allen, Lentz, & Day, 2006). Employees who have been mentored experience more effective socialization and better compensation, advancement, career satisfaction, job satisfaction, job involvement, and organizational commitment than those with no mentoring (Greenhaus, 2003).

Organizational Culture and Climate

Organizational culture refers to the shared assumptions, beliefs, values, and customs of the people in an organization. These cognitions then influence the *organizational climate,* which consists of employees' shared perceptions about specific aspects of the workplace environment. Because culture and climate generally operate in concert, our discussion will refer to these elements collectively as *culture* (Ostroff, Kinicki, & Tamkins, 2003). Organizational culture is important because it lets employees know what is expected of them and affects how they think and behave. Culture is often shaped by the founders of the organization, but it may be modified over time by other influential leaders and by the successes and failures of the organization.

There have been several case studies of organizations that have successfully changed their culture. Remember Arthur Friedman from the beginning of this appendix? He allowed his employees to set their own wages and decide the hours they worked; he also required employees to belong to the union. After Friedman made these changes, employee grumbling stopped. The organizational culture changed, resulting in better morale, increased productivity, and longer employee tenure. No one wanted to quit working in a culture where the employees got to make their own decisions that affected the organization's bottom line. Finding an organizational culture that fits your working style is likely to have consequences for your morale, performance, and tenure in the organization.

Work Teams

Work teams and the leadership of an organization tend to have great influence on the culture of an organization. Groups have been studied by social psychologists for more than 75 years (e.g., Hare, 1962; McGrath, 1966). Research has focused on group dynamics topics such as individual versus group problem solving (Hill, 1982; Paulus, 2000) and the effects of participation in decision making on members' satisfaction and performance (Likert, 1967; Sagie, 1997). Industrial and organizational psychologists have focused on studying groups or teams in organizations. The use of teams or groups in organizations has been increasing in recent years because work is now being increasingly organized around team-based structures instead of individual jobs (Lawler, Mohrman, & Ledford, 1995).

Many college courses have assignments that require students to work in groups, and students are graded as a group instead of as individuals. Do you like to work on projects in a group? Do you put in as much effort as you would if you were completing the assignment alone? Among other benefits, students working in groups gain insights into group dynamics, develop their interpersonal skills, and are exposed to other viewpoints (Mello, 1993). Students with less experience with group assignments and grading tend to support group grading; older students are less satisfied with a group experience than younger students; and students who work part-time view the group grading experience as more positive than do those who work full-time (Barfield, 2003). The odds are good that you will find yourself in groups in college classrooms that will prepare you for the almost inevitable work teams in your future.

Work teams, or *work groups,* **can be defined as two or more employees who have common goals, pursue tasks that are interdependent, interact socially, and work within specific requirements and rules** (Kozlowski & Bell, 2003). Just as an organization can have its own culture, groups or teams exhibit subcultures that may encourage or discourage certain types of work-related behaviors and attitudes. These subcultures then form the basis for the socialization of new group or team members.

"I don't know how it started, either. All I know is that it's part of our corporate culture."

Virtual work teams are becoming more commonplace in the workforce because of the desire to involve employees with specific talents on projects and because of the globalization of many businesses. Virtual work teams can continue to function when members work from home, are away traveling, or are otherwise outside of the traditional office (Wiesenfeld, Raghuram, & Garud, 2001). Virtual work teams typically meet using some type of electronic technology. For example, they may communicate by e-mail or teleconferencing. Virtual work teams have a number of advantages. They can provide a way for groups to collaborate more effectively and less expensively, they often reduce office space requirements if individuals

Virtual work teams, where team members interact using teleconferencing and email to get their work accomplished, have become more commonplace in the last decade because of advances in technology.

can work from home, and they permit more flexibility for employees dealing with personal problems or long commutes.

Although most organizations provide formal means of socializing new employees, the dynamics and norms of a work team may have informal but substantial effects on employees' socialization (Anderson & Thomas, 1996). Of course, the outcomes of informal and formal socialization processes may be different. Work teams may have appointed leaders or they may be self-managing. When teams fail, the failure is often linked to the team leader. Team leaders may be too autocratic, wielding too much power or influence. As a result, the team does not realize the autonomy and control it needs to be successful (Stewart & Manz, 1995). Self-managing teams tend to show better productivity, an increase in work quality, improved quality of life for employees, decreased absenteeism, and decreased turnover (Cohen & Ledford, 1994).

Developing a work team may mean successfully integrating new employees into the team as well as helping with the transition of individuals into and out of the team, depending on the team's function. Team leaders are critical to the success of work teams' newcomers. Establishing and maintaining conditions wherein the team can perform well is also an important role for the team leader.

Leadership

Former U.S. President Dwight D. Eisenhower once said, "Leadership is the art of getting someone else to do something you want done because he wants to do it." As his remark suggests, *leadership* **involves influencing and motivating people to pursue organizational goals.**

Oprah Winfrey is a modern-day charismatic, transformational leader. She is probably best known as the host of the Oprah Winfrey Show. *In addition, she has built a multi-faceted entertainment empire and started multiple charity groups, donating millions of dollars across the globe.*

UNA·USA

The Waldorf-Astoria

Leadership has received a lot of research attention in industrial and organizational psychology. Many theories exist, and most have been helpful in understanding what makes a good leader and how to improve leadership style.

Personality plays a key role in many leadership theories. Certainly, it is important in determining whether or not a leader will be successful. Kirkpatrick and Locke's (1991) review suggests that drive, honesty and integrity, self-confidence, cognitive abilities, and knowledge are associated with successful leaders. Leaders with poor cognitive abilities and social skills and those who are indecisive, low in self-confidence and self-esteem, dishonest, and lacking in ambition tend to be less successful (Kaplan, Drath, & Kofodimos, 1991).

Arthur Friedman's integrity likely made him a successful leader. He decided to give employees what he would want, providing them with the capability to make major decisions that could either make or break the organization. In his case, he created a self-managing group that had no need for external assistance from unions or other entities. As a result, Friedman demonstrated the transformational leadership approach (Bass, 1990). *Transformational leadership* **is characterized by high ethical standards, inspirational motivation, intellectual stimulation, and individual consideration**—all clearly evident in Arthur Friedman's leadership style.

Leaders today must contend with information-based team environments requiring the capacity for sifting through large amounts of information coming from computer networks (Avolio, Kahai, & Dodge, 2000). The widely varying working environments that result from global competition also require leaders to be adaptable (Mann, 1959), capable of handling stress (Goleman, 1998), knowledgeable about competitors and products (Kirpatrick & Locke, 1991), and able to solve complex problems quickly (Zaccaro et al., 2000).

Training and Human Factors

Employers hope that the applicants they choose for positions in their organization will be great workers who are dependable and have good attitudes. However, sometimes a poor fit between the employee and the job indicates that some type of change may be needed in the employee, the job, or some specific aspect of the job. Trying to change the employee to better fit the job or work that needs to be done involves *training*, while changing the job to better fit the employee is a *human factors issue*. Both of these areas are of importance to organizations, and both types of changes can help organizations maximize job performance.

The premise behind training is that it will lead to learning that will in turn lead to an improvement in job performance. Important questions to address before conducting training include (1) What are the goals of the training program? (2) Who needs the training and for what purpose? and (3) What should the content of the training program be? The goals of the training program will likely come from the training department or human resources department. Whatever the specific goals are for the organization, support from top management is critical for training to be a success. Deciding who needs training is relatively simple if an effective performance evaluation system is in place in the organization. Accurate and valid performance evaluation procedures can provide valuable information on who needs additional training.

Many types of training are available, including both on-the-job and off-the-job programs. On-the-job training includes job rotation, mentoring (discussed earlier), and apprenticeships, while off-the-job training is the typical lecture or taped presentation. All of these can be effective under the right circumstances, so the training needs to be tailored to the employees who would benefit the most. Some of the important issues with regard to training include setting specific, concrete, and obtainable goals, and motivating employees to attend the training and transfer it to their jobs (Aamodt, 2007). It is vital that the training program be evaluated to determine whether it is effective in changing behavior or improving performance and whether the cost is worth the results. All organizations must engage in some type of training for their employees, from orientation meetings to sessions on how to use a new software package or new machine.

As noted earlier, *human factors psychology* examines the ways in which work, systems, and system features can be designed to most effectively correspond with the capabilities and limitations of workers. In other words, human factors is concerned with changing the system, in this case the work, the work environment, or the job itself, so that employees' interactions with the system are better from a psychological, emotional, or physical standpoint. An important subfield of human factors work is *ergonomics,* which focuses on the capabilities and limitations of the human body. For example, if the desk chair that a computer programmer is using causes her back problems because the seat height can't be adjusted, she can be given a new chair with adjustable seat height. Or if a receptionist is not motivated because his work lacks variety, the work could be en-

Human factors psychology plays an important role in the design of all sorts of equipment, ranging from consumer products to industrial machines.

Courtesy of NIOSH Pittsburgh Research Laboratory

riched or changed so that more skills could be used in the job. Human factors focuses on changing the system to better fit the employee using the system. This may be a critical issue if problems are found with employees' behaviors and attitudes in an organization. Redesigning a job or equipment can sometimes be the key to enhancing performance.

Attitudes and Behaviors at Work

One of the most important factors influencing whether people will be motivated to do a good job hinges on their attitudes at work. The causes and consequences of work attitudes have been extensively researched. Some of the determinants of work attitudes include job security issues, the type of work (e.g, interesting or boring), and pay and promotion issues. Job attitudes can influence many important outcomes in the world of work, such as whether employees volunteer for projects or help out co-workers, whether employees are frequently tardy or absent, and whether they think about quitting or early retirement.

Attitudes at Work

Attitudes at work include commitment to the organization and satisfaction with such job aspects as the work itself, pay and benefits, supervision, co-workers, promotion opportunities, working conditions, and job security. In general, you can be satisfied or dissatisfied with the tasks and conditions at work, the people in your work environment, and the rewards you get from work. Employee satisfaction is important because it has been shown to be related to employee behaviors at work (Hanisch, 1995). Job satisfaction and organizational commitment are two of the most commonly studied work attitudes.

Job satisfaction consists of the positive or negative emotions associated with a job (Thurstone,

1931). In other words, job satisfaction reflects how much employees like or dislike their work. Some of the ways organizations can create satisfied employees include offering flexible working hours, professional growth opportunities, interesting work (Hackman & Oldham, 1976), autonomy, job security, a good supervisor, good benefits, competitive pay, and opportunities for promotion (Cranny, Smith, & Stone, 1992). What makes one worker satisfied may not make another worker satisfied. For some people, interesting work is paramount. Others place higher emphasis on having co-workers they like. Still others feel that the pay and benefits they receive are most important. Just as in the hiring process, a match between what you want and what the organization can provide will result in a more successful outcome for both parties.

Some organizations take the emotional temperature of their employees by periodically administering questionnaires. These questionnaires typically ask workers to rate their levels of satisfaction on the basic factors that contribute to job satisfaction. An example of a measure of job satisfaction can be seen in Figure C.6. Organizations go to the trouble of gathering this information because they believe (and research supports) that job satisfaction is related to employee withdrawal behaviors such as absenteeism and turnover (Hanisch, 1995).

A recent survey found that listening to music at work leads to higher levels of reported employee satisfaction. About one-third of those participating in a Spherion Workplace Snapshot survey conducted by Harris Interactive in 2006 reported they listened to an iPod, MP3 player, or other personal music device while working (Spherion, 2006). More than three-fourths of the participants reported that listening to music improved their job satisfaction and productivity at work. Allowing workers to listen to music may become more and more popular in jobs where music does not interfere with co-workers, safety, or job performance. Having happy workers contributes to an organization's success.

Employee commitment to an organization is related to employee retention within the organization. According to Meyer and Allen (1991) there are three types of organizational commitment: affective, normative, and continuance. *Affective commitment* consists of an employee's emotional attachment to the organization, which makes the employee want to stay in the organization. *Normative commitment* is

Figure C.6
The Work on Present Job Scale. One measure often used to assess employee work attitudes and specific facets of job satisfaction is the Job Descriptive Index (JDI) originally published by Smith, Kendall, and Hulin (1969). This index, which has been improved based on years of research (Balzer et al., 1997; Hanisch, 1992), measures five facets of job satisfaction. The five subscales assess satisfaction with: the work itself, supervisors, co-workers, present pay, and opportunities for promotion. The most frequently used subscale is the one shown here, which measures satisfaction with the work itself.

Work on Present Job Scale

Think of the work you do at present. How well does each of the following words or phrases describe your job? In the blank beside each word or phrase below, write:

Y for "Yes" if it describes your work
N for "No" if it does NOT describe it
? if you cannot decide

_____ 1. Fascinating
_____ 2. Routine
_____ 3. Satisfying
_____ 4. Boring
_____ 5. Good
_____ 6. Creative
_____ 7. Respected
_____ 8. Uncomfortable
_____ 9. Pleasant
_____ 10. Useful
_____ 11. Tiring
_____ 12. Healthful
_____ 13. Challenging
_____ 14. Too much to do
_____ 15. Frustrating
_____ 16. Simple
_____ 17. Repetitive
_____ 18. Gives sense of accomplishment

Scoring Key:

1. Y=3, N=0, ?=1	7. Y=3, N=0, ?=1	13. Y=3, N=0, ?=1
2. Y=0, N=3, ?=1	8. Y=0, N=3, ?=1	14. Y=0, N=3, ?=1
3. Y=3, N=0, ?=1	9. Y=3, N=0, ?=1	15. Y=0, N=3, ?=1
4. Y=0, N=3, ?=1	10. Y=3, N=0, ?=1	16. Y=0, N=3, ?=1
5. Y=3, N=0, ?=1	11. Y=0, N=3, ?=1	17. Y=0, N=3, ?=1
6. Y=3, N=0, ?=1	12. Y=3, N=0, ?=1	18. Y=3, N=0, ?=1

To interpret your score on the this scale, 27 is considered the neutral value (Balzer, et al., 1997). Values considerably higher would be evaluated as very satisfied, values considerably lower would be evaluated as very dissatisfied with the work on your present job.

Employees report that their job satisfaction and productivity increase if they are allowed privileges such as listening to music while they work.

based on feelings of obligation to the organization. *Continuance commitment* results when an employee remains with a company because of the high cost of losing organizational membership, including monetary (pension benefits) and social (friendships) costs. Meyer and Herscovitch (2001) argue that employees have an organizational commitment profile at any given time in their job, with high or low values on each of the three types of commitment. In other words, an employee may have high scores on normative and continuance commitment but be lower on affective commitment. Depending on the profile, the employee may engage in different behaviors, such as quitting or helping out the organization.

Students may experience these different types of commitment to their college. A student acting under affective commitment would feel an emotional attachment to the school because she really likes it, including her classes, the football team, and the town. The student wants to stay in that school because of her attachment to it. Normative commitment might be evidenced by a student whose parents attended that college and who feels obligated to do the same thing regardless of whether it is the best school for him. Staying at a college because one's friends are there and one has already paid for two years of college would typify acting under continuance commitment.

One of the key factors in organizational commitment is job satisfaction. People who are satisfied with their job tend to be more committed to their organization than those who are less satisfied (Mueller et al., 1994). Other determinants of organizational commitment include trust in one's supervisor and human resources practices that are supportive of employees (Arthur, 1994). The organizational commitment of Arthur Friedman's employees was very high, as evidenced by a complete lack of turnover in five years.

Behaviors at Work

Employers want their employees to engage in behaviors that will make them successful in the job be-

"Employee morale is at an all-time high. We must be paying them too much."

cause employee success helps the organization meet its goals, including earning profits and fulfilling its mission. Employees have control over two aspects of their work—their time and their effort (Naylor, Pritchard, & Ilgen, 1980). Employees arriving at work on time instead of being late or absent is important to performance and productivity. Positive behaviors generally help an organization meet its goals, whereas negative behaviors make it harder to reach those goals.

Organizational citizenship behaviors (OCBs) are often described as extra-role behaviors because they are not specifically required by the job and are not usually evaluated during performance reviews. These behaviors go beyond what is formally expected by the organization (Smith, Organ, & Near, 1983). Examples include staying late to finish a project, mentoring a new employee, volunteering for work, and helping a co-worker. Some reasons why people engage in organizational citizenship behaviors are job satisfaction, high job autonomy, a positive organizational culture, high agreeableness (as a personality dimension; Witt et al., 2002), and high conscientiousness (Borman et al., 2001). Often, however, males who engage in OCBs are viewed positively, whereas females are viewed as just doing their jobs (Heilman & Chen, 2005; Kidder & Parks, 2001)—a difference that may result in gender disparities in performance ratings. OCBs have positive consequences for the organization and for employees in their day-to-day interactions with others in the organization.

You may engage in prosocial behaviors that are analogous to OCBs at your university—for instance, by helping a student in a class by tutoring him or allowing him to study with you. You may also exhibit these types of behaviors in your personal life by donating blood or being a Big Brother or Sister to a boy or girl who needs a positive role model. Altruism and prosocial behaviors are closely linked; they likely carry over into the work environment.

In contrast to OCBs, some unhappy employees cause problems for organizations because they engage in behaviors that researchers refer to as *organizational withdrawal* (Hanisch, Hulin, & Roznowski, 1998) and counterproductive behaviors (Sackett & DeVore, 2003). Organizational withdrawal consists of behaviors employees use to avoid their work (work withdrawal) or their job (job withdrawal) (Hanisch, 1995; Hanisch & Hulin, 1990, 1991). Examples of work withdrawal include being absent from work, leaving work early, arriving to work late, missing meetings, and using work equipment for personal use without permission. Examples of job withdrawal are quitting one's job, transferring to another department within an organization, and retiring.

College students may be familiar with withdrawal behaviors when it comes to certain college courses. Some classes may fail to keep your attention, and you may find yourself taking a nap in class or reading the newspaper. You may even look for legitimate reasons not to attend class, such as offering to fill in for another employee at work or deciding to attend an optional session for another class.

Counterproductive behaviors, although similar in some ways to withdrawal behaviors, are defined as "any intentional behavior on the part of an organizational member viewed by the organization as contrary to its legitimate interests" (Sackett & DeVore, 2003). An example of a counterproductive behavior would be an intentional violation of safety procedures that puts the employee and the organization at risk. Other examples of counterproductive behavior are theft, destruction of property, unsafe behavior, poor attendance, drug use, and inappropriate physical actions such as attacking a co-worker.

Relations Between Attitudes and Behaviors

Organizational citizenship behaviors are positively related to job satisfaction and organizational commitment. In other words, employees with good attitudes who feel committed to their organization are more likely to do positive things to assist the organization (LePine, Erez, & Johnson, 2002). Research indicates that those employees who demonstrate organizational citizenship behaviors are less likely to engage in counterproductive behaviors (Dalal, 2006). Researchers have found strong links between job satisfaction and specific withdrawal or counterproductive behaviors such as absenteeism (Hackett, 1989), and even stronger links with job withdrawal (Hanisch & Hulin, 1990).

Counterproductive behaviors may sometimes be an outcome of high job stress. In such cases, the counterproductive behaviors often represent dysfunctional coping mechanisms (Lennings, 1997). For example, an employee experiencing stress from having too much work to do might respond by being absent from work or by sabotaging work equipment.

Many years of research indicate a link between employees' attitudes and their behaviors at work. Sometimes the most revealing information about employees occurs when unforeseen circumstances arise and they then have to choose how to behave without concern for what a supervisor, co-workers, or their work team might think. An interesting study along these lines was conducted by Smith (1977) when he took advantage of inclement weather to study the relationship between job attitudes and job behaviors.

Smith compared functional work groups in Chicago, where a terrible snowstorm had occurred, to work groups in New York where the weather was fine. All employees worked for the same organization, and they had completed an organization-wide survey assessing work attitudes a few months earlier. Examining both organizational sites provided a comparison not typically available and allowed the researcher to examine the relationship between work attitudes and attendance under difficult circumstances. The comparison was done to determine which employees would opt to attend work the day after the storm in Chicago.

Correlational results indicated a positive relationship between work attitudes and attendance for the employees headquartered in Chicago; those reporting higher satisfaction were more likely than those with lower satisfaction to attend work. It was up to the discretion of the individuals in the Chicago sample whether to attend work the day after the storm; the correlational results suggest that those work groups with more positive attitudes made a greater effort to attend work that day than those with less positive attitudes. Interestingly, the relationship between work attitudes and attendance was not significant for the groups based in New York, where weather-related challenges were not an issue (see Figure C.7).

Employers need to evaluate their work environment and fringe benefit packages and make modi-

Correlations between job satisfaction and attendance in different weather conditions		
Job Satisfaction Scale	**Chicago**	**New York**
	(following severe storm)	(normal weather conditions)
Supervision	.54*	.12
Amount of work	.36*	.01
Kind of work	.37*	.06
Financial rewards	.46*	.11
Career future	.60*	.14
Company Identification	.42*	.02

* Statistically significant

Figure C.7

An example of the link between work attitudes and work behavior. Smith (1977) had an interesting opportunity to explore the link between job satisfaction and work behavior when a nasty snowstorm in Chicago made it difficult for employees to get to work. These data show the correlation between satisfaction with various aspects of work and the likelihood of job attendance following the severe storm. The correlations for similar workers in New York, where weather was not a problem that day, provide a control condition. As you can see, satisfied employees were much more likely to brave the elements and show up for work, illustrating the importance of work attitudes.

fications where necessary to ensure that they have employees who are satisfied and committed. Art Friedman made modifications in the work environment of his organization that resulted in high satisfaction and commitment among his employees. To help with the commute to and from work, Google added a free shuttle service that many employees say is the best fringe benefit, given the traffic in Silicon Valley (Helft, 2007). Employees need to learn how to seek out satisfying work and perks that will result in a sense of commitment to the organization. Satisfaction and commitment facilitate OCBs and decrease withdrawal and counterproductive behaviors. Together, the right employee attitudes and behaviors will lead to successful organizational functioning.

Integration of the Field

I/O psychologists grapple with issues related to the world of work from both the employee and employer perspectives. Moreover, the three subfields of I/O psychology are highly interrelated. I/O psychologists often have expertise in more than one subfield because in dealing with many organizational problems or concerns, information from two or more of the subfields may be necessary to effectively address the issue. For example, I was asked to be a consultant on a project for a large utility company because several instances of employee "near-misses" had occurred in a short time frame. In other words, employees had almost been severely hurt or killed as a result of accidents on the job. To address such a problem, I met with the safety and training directors to obtain a clear understanding of the equipment being used in the field (a human factors topic) as well as the types of training implemented to ensure a safe environment, including safety training (an industrial psychology topic). I also met with the personnel director to ascertain how employees were selected for the various positions in question regarding the safety violations (an industrial psychology topic). Finally, I administered an attitude survey to try to better understand employees' attitudes toward their work, the organizational climate for safety, and behaviors with a specific focus on withdrawal, counterproductive, and safety behaviors (an organizational psychology topic). Any one or a combination of two or three of these issues could have been causing the safety problems. The results of my investigation indicated there

were problems with safety attitudes and training as well as with work attitudes in general. A specific finding from my research was that even though the employees were encouraged to engage in safe behaviors by management, they were simultaneously being told to work faster, with greater emphasis being placed (albeit unknowingly) on working faster. Employees also had suggestions for ways to improve the equipment they used to be more effective in their jobs. An integration and understanding of the many areas that could impinge on organizational issues or problems aids in finding an appropriate solution to them.

Conclusion

In this appendix a consistent theme has been that appropriate matches between people's characteristics and their jobs are important for both employees and employers. A good match can help ensure that you enjoy and are successful in the job, while at the same time ensuring that the organization is a success in terms of its bottom line regarding performance and costs. The first type of match that is important is the correspondence between your knowledge, skills, ability, and personality, and the needs of the job you are applying for. This match is important because you don't want to be bored if the job doesn't use your skills or overstressed if the job requires an ability you do not have. Just as it is important for an organization to hire the right person, it is important for you to find the right employer and the right position for your talents. Another crucial match is between an employer's organizational climate and your preferred organizational culture (friendly versus aloof, supportive versus competitive). Again, those who run the organization desire a good match so that you will be a productive employee; your satisfaction and commitment to the organization will be higher within a culture that fits your personality. Finally, the reason these matches are important is that an organization must be profitable, and that requires dedicated and effective employees. Happy, productive employees will likely lead to a profitable venture for both employees and those who manage or own organizations. I/O psychologists have been critical in facilitating these matches for mutually beneficial relations between employees and employers for many decades, and they will continue to play a vital role in these matching processes in the future.

Careers and Areas in Psychology

by Margaret A. Lloyd (Georgia Southern University)

web link D.1

Marky Lloyd's Careers in Psychology Page

Professor Marky Lloyd, the author of this appendix, has put together a wide variety of helpful resources for those who want to learn about entry-level jobs for psychology majors as well as those jobs requiring a master's or doctoral degree. The information and tips on getting into graduate school are especially helpful.

web link D.2

***Occupational Outlook Handbook (OOH)* Online**

Every two years the Bureau of Labor Statistics publishes the *OOH*, now available via the Internet. This essential occupational guide provides information about every occupation in the United States, including descriptions of the nature of each job and its working conditions, educational requirements, future employment and earnings prospects, and places to find additional information. The site also provides information about job and workforce trends.

Perhaps you have already heard the disheartening claim, "You can't get a job with a bachelor's degree in psychology." Is there any truth to this assertion? If by "job," you mean working as a professional psychologist, then the saying is true. Psychologists must have a doctoral degree in psychology because the nature of their work requires more extensive education and training than can be gained at the undergraduate level. But it simply is *not* true that you can't get a good entry-level job with a psychology degree.

In the following pages, we will briefly explore the kinds of entry-level jobs that are available to psychology majors as well as some occupations that require graduate degrees. I will also share some pointers to help you compete effectively in the job market and to enhance your chances of getting into graduate school.

Entry-Level Career Options for Psychology Majors

It would be easy to spot entry-level jobs if you could look in the want ads under the heading "psychologist," but as already noted, that tactic won't work. Because the connection between the psychology major (and other liberal arts majors) and relevant entry-level jobs is not as obvious as it is in applied majors (nursing and accounting, for example), identifying relevant entry-level jobs requires some detective work.

Thanks to the Internet, it has become easier to identify job titles of interest. A number of websites have search engines that allow you to locate specific occupations and learn about the relevant skills, educational requirements, salaries, and other useful points (see Web Links D.2, D.3, and D.4).

Because most psychology majors would like jobs in which they can help other people, *counseling* is a popular career option. If you think about it, though, there are many other ways to help people. For example, managers help employees to do their best, child welfare agents help children in trouble, and probation officers help juvenile offenders stay on the right track. Also, in doing your detective work, you should be aware that occupations requiring essentially the same skills are often listed under a variety of titles. Don't overlook a viable option because the title is unfamiliar. Figure D.1 will give you an idea of the wide range of job options open to psychology majors.

Once you have identified some occupations of interest, compare them on the critical factors of current job openings, salary, and future employment outlook. An excellent resource for this information is the *Occupational Outlook Handbook* (see Web Link D.2). This step is essential if you want to make *informed* occupational choices.

The average starting salary for psychology (and other liberal arts) majors tends to be lower than for most applied majors. In 2007-2008, it was around $30,000 (National Association of Colleges and Employers, 2008). Jobs in business and research com-

Figure D.1
Entry-level positions open to psychology majors. **A bachelor's degree in psychology can prepare students for a diverse array of entry-level jobs in a variety of occupational areas. The jobs listed here are merely a handful of examples of the entry-level positions for which psychology majors qualify.**

Potential Jobs for Psychology Majors with a Bachelor's Degree

Business area	Health and human services areas
customer relations	behavioral analyst
employment interviewer	case worker
human resources recruiter	child welfare agent
insurance agent	director of volunteer services
loan officer	drug counselor
management trainee	family services worker
marketing representative	hospital patient service representative
realtor	nursing home administrator
sales representative	rehabilitation advisor
store manager	residential youth counselor
Law and corrections areas	**Other areas**
case manager	affirmative action officer
corrections officer	college admissions representative
court officer	newspaper reporter
EPA investigator	research assistant
probation/parole officer	technical writer

mand higher salaries than those in human services (counseling and social work, for example). If you are like most students, however, your job decision will not be based on money alone. A recent survey regarding what college graduates seek when choosing an employer found that "a high starting salary" was ranked surprisingly low, whereas "enjoying what I do" earned the top ranking (National Association of Colleges and Employers, 2005). Thus, salary is just one of many factors that you should consider in pursuing a job.

Keys to Success in the Entry-Level Job Market

There are three keys to a successful job search. First, you need to have accurate information about the knowledge, skills, and values required for occupations that interest you. You may be surprised to learn that these skills and values are not as job-specific as most people assume. Surveys of employers reveal that a relatively small set of skills and values are considered essential for success in wide variety of occupations (see Figure D.2). You don't have to be a genius to figure out the second key to success: You need to acquire these skills that are prized by employers. The third key to a successful job search is to assemble convincing documentation for prospective employers that you possess these skills and values.

Developing Valuable Skills

To help you acquire these highly rated work skills, you have three excellent skill-building vehicles available: college courses, relevant work experience, and extracurricular activities. Obviously, the earlier in your college career you start your "skills development project," the more time you have to hone your skills.

College courses. Within the constraints of curriculum requirements, choose courses to help you develop occupationally relevant knowledge and skills. Make thoughtful choices across all areas of the curriculum: general education courses, psychology courses, and general electives. The content of courses is an obvious and important aspect of education. Your coursework also provides learning opportunities that are less obvious. In addition to teaching course content, college courses provide numerous opportunities to learn a remarkable variety of skills that can give you a competitive edge in the job market. For example, your courses can help you improve your critical thinking skills, acquire insights into your behavior and that of others, enhance your interpersonal skills, clarify your values, acquaint you with ethical principles, improve your communication abilities, increase your computer sophistication and information literacy, and bolster your self-management skills (setting and completing goals, managing your time, coping with stress). The

web link D.3

The Riley Guide: Employment Opportunities and Job Resources on the Internet

This site, developed by the well-regarded career expert Margaret F. Dikel, complements her excellent book, the *Guide to Internet Job Searching*. Her website contains hundreds of annotated links regarding almost any topic related to employment and careers.

web link D.4

CollegeGrad.com

This website bills itself as "The #1 entry-level job site." Key sections include Preparation (explore careers, résumés, cover letters, and internship preparation), Find the Job (advice, posting résumés, and searching for internships and jobs), and Offers (salary, negotiating, and new job advice). To find jobs in counseling, look under the Community and Social Services category.

General Work Skills and Personal Values Employers Seek

Work skills

- **Communication skills.** Almost always rated first, communication skills include being able to write and speak effectively. A third, often overlooked, communication skill is effective listening, including being sensitive enough to hear and relate to the emotions behind another's words.

- **Adaptability/flexibility.** Employers value workers who can adapt to changing conditions and work assignments (learn new skills), deal with ambiguity, and appreciate that there are usually several legitimate perspectives on an issue.

- **Analytical/research skills.** These important skills involve critical thinking; extracting key ideas from written material, graphs, and tables; and solving problems and answering questions.

- **Computer skills.** Employers want workers who are competent in using word-processing, spreadsheet, and database management programs, as well as the Internet and e-mail.

- **Social and teamwork skills.** Today's workers need to interact effectively in one-on-one settings and on teams. They must also be able to work well with co-workers from diverse cultures and backgrounds.

- **Self-management skills.** These critical skills include having self-confidence, being able to work with little supervision, being able to set manageable goals and complete them on time, and being able to manage time effectively. Emotional maturity is also important, especially the ability to cope with undesirable behavior in others and to refrain from petty behavior.

Personal values

- **Integrity/honesty.** Employers greatly value ethical behavior in their employees.

- **Dependability and loyalty.** Workers who come to the workplace prepared to work, who arrive on time, and who show up every day are prized. Employers also value personal and company loyalty in their employees.

- **Positive attitude and motivation/energy.** Valued employees are those who have a "can-do" attitude, bring energy to their work, and are willing to learn new skills and information.

Figure D.2

Qualities employers value in employees. Employers widely agree on the general work skills and values they desire in employees. To be competitive in the job market, workers must have the qualities listed here and document them in cover letters, résumés, and interviews. (Based on Appleby, 2000; Hansen & Hansen, 2003; Landrum & Harrold, 2003)

psychology major can definitely help you develop the general skills and values that employers seek. Figure D.3 lists ten learning goals that a psychology major should support, based on the consensus of a national task force. If you compare this list with the list of employers' preferred skills and values in Figure D.2, you will see that there is a close match.

Relevant work experience (internships, paid work, and volunteer activities). If you must work while attending school, look for a job that will help you develop useful skills. For example, if you want to be a probation officer, seek out volunteer opportunities to work with adolescents. Many colleges have Volunteer Services offices that match students' interests with community needs. Another excellent resource on how to obtain real-world experience is a short paperback, *Getting from College to Career: 90 Things to Do Before You Join the Real World* (Pollak, 2007). The author, a recent college graduate, offers useful and specific advice on how to shape your college experience to give you a "jump start" on your career.

Extracurricular activities. Involvement in campus clubs and student activities can also help you develop work-related abilities—especially leadership and interpersonal skills. Be careful not to overload yourself with work, volunteering, and extracurricular activities to the detriment of your grades. Good grades are important in obtaining your first job and getting good recommendations from faculty members, and they are *essential* to qualify for graduate school.

Documenting Your Skills

Once you acquire the skills and values employers want, you must be able to document this fact to prospective employers. You do so by preparing résumés and cover letters that showcase your skills. The job interview is another key aspect of this process. Even if you have a bundle of talents, you can easily falter at these critical points. There is a lot to know in developing a competitive résumé, a compelling cover letter, and good interviewing skills. You can learn the essentials at your Career Services office.

Next Steps

It is critical that you start the job search process early—the spring term of your senior year is too late. Attend career fairs, where job recruiters come to your college campus, to learn about job options and what recruiters are looking for. When you are clear about the occupational titles you want to pursue, visit your Career Services office. The staff can get you started off right on your job search.

Career Options at the Master's Level

After working several years in an entry-level position, you may want more challenges, a higher salary, or greater independence. One way to move up the career ladder is to return to school. Alternatively, you may want to attend graduate school directly upon graduation. If you want to extend your knowledge and skills, but do not want to invest the time, effort, and money required for a doctoral degree, then a master's degree may be just the ticket for you. Because counseling is a popular career option among psychology majors, we will focus on three master's-level career options in the mental health area. There are also master's-level careers in other areas of psychology, such as industrial/organizational psychology. An undergraduate major in psychology is excellent preparation for all these career paths.

Clinical Psychology

Clinical psychologists diagnose and treat people with psychological problems and administer psychological tests. Although most programs in clinical

---

Learning Goals for the Psychology Major

Knowledge, skills, and values consistent with the science and application of psychology

Goal 1. Knowledge base of psychology. Students should show familiarity with the major concepts, theoretical perspectives, empirical findings, and historical trends in psychology.

Goal 2. Research methods in psychology. Students should understand and apply basic research methods in psychology, including research design, data analysis, and interpretation.

Goal 3. Critical thinking skills in psychology. Students should respect and use critical and creative thinking, skeptical inquiry, and, when possible, the scientific approach to solve problems related to behavior and mental processes.

Goal 4. Application of psychology. Students should understand and apply psychological principles to personal, social, and organizational issues.

Goal 5. Values in psychology. Students should be able to weigh evidence, tolerate ambiguity, act ethically, and reflect other values that are the underpinnings of psychology as a discipline.

Knowledge, skills, and values consistent with liberal arts education that are further developed in psychology

Goal 6. Information and technological literacy. Students should demonstrate information competence and the ability to use computers and other technology for many purposes.

Goal 7. Communication skills. Students should be able to communicate effectively in a variety of formats.

Goal 8. Sociocultural and international awareness. Students should recognize, understand, and respect the complexity of sociocultural and international diversity.

Goal 9. Personal development. Students should develop insight into their own and others' behavior and mental processes and apply effective strategies for self-management and self-improvement.

Goal 10. Career planning and development. Students should emerge from the major with realistic ideas about how to implement their psychological knowledge, skills, and values in occupational pursuits in a variety of settings.

Figure D.3

Knowledge, skills, and values supported by the psychology major. Ten learning goals for the undergraduate psychology major have been outlined by a national task force (American Psychological Association, 2007). The first five goals include knowledge, skills, and values developed specifically in the psychology major. The remaining goals consist of knowledge, skills, and values developed in the liberal arts (general education) curriculum and that psychology further advances.

SOURCE: American Psychological Association. (2007). *APA guidelines for the undergraduate psychology major.* Washington, DC: Author. Retrieved May 1, 2008, from http://www.apa.org/ed/psymajor_guideline.pdf.

psychology are offered at the doctoral level, there are terminal master's degree programs in clinical psychology and some other subfields. Clinical master's programs typically teach students how to administer selected psychological tests as well as the basics of psychological diagnosis and psychotherapy. Students in these programs receive either an M.A. (Master of Arts) or an M.S. (Master of Science) degree. Upon graduation, they either seek employment or apply to doctoral programs.

Some states license individuals with master's degrees in clinical psychology, but many do not. A license is a quality-control credential that gives individuals legal authority to work independently—that is, without the supervision of a doctoral-level professional. Individuals with a master's degree in clinical psychology may qualify for licenses such as "psychological associate," "professional counselor," or "marriage and family therapist." Note that they are not licensed as "psychologists"—this title is reserved for those with doctoral degrees. Whether licensed or not, these individuals are qualified to work in supervised settings such as community mental health centers.

Clinical Social Work

Unlike social workers or case workers, *clinical social workers* diagnose and treat psychological problems. Clinical social workers are educated in departments or colleges of social work (not psychology departments). The degree that they earn is the M.S.W. (Master of Social Work). They do not do psychological testing, so you should consider majoring in psychology or education if you want to do assessment. They work in community mental health centers, counseling centers, hospitals, and schools. Importantly, all 50 states license clinical social workers at the master's level. This fact makes clinical social work an attractive career option. For more information, see Web Link D.7.

Agency Counseling

Agency counselors provide various types of counseling assistance to clients and may administer a limited number of psychological tests (occupational interest tests, for example). Thus, the work is somewhat like that done by those with a master's degree in clinical psychology. Counselors are educated in departments of education; they receive the M.Ed. (Master of Education) degree. Most people assume that a degree in education requires one to work in a school setting. Agency counseling (sometimes called "community counseling") is an important exception. If you want to counsel but do not want to work in a school setting, consider this option. Graduates typically work in community mental health centers.

They may have a private practice if they obtain a license (typically as a "professional counselor" or "marriage and family therapist").

Career Options at the Doctoral Level

Doctoral-level education and training will give you access to occupations that offer more options and independence as well as higher salaries, compared to those at the master's level. An important consideration is whether you want to emphasize teaching and research or applied work.

Teaching and Research Versus Applied Work

If you want to teach in a university setting, you will probably also be expected to conduct research. If you want to focus solely on teaching, consider a job at a two-year college, as research is not usually required in these institutions. If you are solely interested in doing research, think about working for government agencies (for example, the Centers for Disease Control) or private organizations (for example, the Educational Testing Service). To work in a university psychology department, you will need a Ph.D. (Doctor of Philosophy) in psychology—not a degree in another field such as education or social work. As discussed in Chapter 1, the major research subfields in psychology include cognitive psychology, developmental psychology, educational psychology, experimental psychology, health psychology, personality psychology, physiological psychology, psychometrics, and social psychology. We will discuss some career options in these areas shortly.

In certain subfields, psychologists are qualified to apply their knowledge by offering professional services to the public. These applied areas of specialization include clinical psychology, counseling psychology, industrial/organizational psychology, school psychology, clinical neuropsychology, and forensic psychology. The required degree for most of these areas is typically the Ph.D. (Doctor of Philosophy). The Psy.D. (Doctor of Psychology) is also appropriate in clinical and counseling psychology, and the Ed.D. (Doctor of Education) is awarded in counseling psychology. We will examine career options in these applied areas shortly.

Before looking at the various specialty areas, let's touch on the differences between the Ph.D. and Psy.D. degrees, as students often have questions about this issue. The Ph.D. degree is the terminal (highest) degree offered in all liberal arts and scientific disciplines (psychology, history, physics, and so forth). Thus, the vast majority of college and university professors have the Ph.D. degree. The Psy.D.

web link D.5

Salary.com

This helpful site allows you to determine salary ranges for numerous occupations at different experience levels and in different geographical areas and to compare these to national averages. You can probably get all the information you need for free, but you can also pay (a lot) for a customized report.

web link D.6

CBcampus.com

This site, powered by CareerBuilder.com, is geared to college students seeking their first job. Check out the section on internships, where you can search by city, state, or internship category.

web link D.7

National Association of Social Workers

The National Association of Social Workers site contains a Student Center subpage (listed under Resources) that describes what social workers do, provides salary information, and answers questions about education, licensing, and credentialing.

degree is awarded *only* in psychology and *only* in the professional areas of clinical and counseling psychology—not in other applied areas such as school psychology or industrial/organizational psychology, nor in any of the research subfields (experimental, developmental, or social psychology, for example). The primary difference between the two degrees is the emphasis on research. The Ph.D. degree prepares clinical and counseling psychologists to be both researchers and practitioners. In contrast, Psy.D. programs focus exclusively on preparing clinicians and counselors to be practitioners, although they also strive to make their students highly sophisticated consumers of psychological research. The crux of the difference is that Ph.D. students are required to conduct research to earn their degree, whereas Psy.D. students are not. This means that Ph.D. students typically take a number of courses in research design and statistics and devote much of their time to research projects. Psy.D. programs, on the other hand, tend to require students to spend more time in "hands-on" clinical training.

Another distinction concerns the types of institutions in which the programs are housed. Ph.D. programs in psychology are housed in traditional university psychology departments (as are a few Psy.D. programs), whereas most Psy.D. programs are housed in private, independent, professional schools of psychology. One practical repercussion of this difference is that university-based Ph.D. programs tend to benefit from research grants that permit them to offer many of their students tuition waivers and financial stipends that can greatly reduce the financial cost of graduate training. Lacking this source of revenue, Psy.D. programs are generally able to provide far less financial aid and thus tend to be more expensive than Ph.D. programs. Both types of doctoral programs have their advantages and disadvantages. Ultimately, the choice between pursuing a Ph.D versus a Psy.D. typically hinges on how interested students are in working on original research.

Career Options in Research Areas

To give you a fuller understanding of the breadth of psychology as a field of study, we'll briefly examine the nine major research areas in the discipline and some selected career options in these areas. Psychologists in these subfields are most likely to work in academic settings, where they teach undergraduate and/or graduate students and conduct research in their areas of interest. Faculty members who teach undergraduates typically do more teaching and less research than faculty who teach graduate students. Most faculty members in psychology do some research, although expectations for research vary depending on the nature of the college.

Cognitive psychology. The field of cognitive psychology is concerned with thinking and mental activity—how people (and animals) acquire, process, retrieve, and apply information. Cognitive psychologists also focus on language, problem solving, concept formation, mental imagery, reasoning, decision making, and creativity. Examples of research topics in the field include the effects of encoding strategies on memory retention, the influence of bilingualism on language development, and the factors that people weigh in making risky decisions. Chapters 7 and 8 in this text provide extensive coverage of cognitive psychology topics. Most cognitive psychologists teach and conduct research in academic settings, but they can also use their expertise in business, government, and military settings (which, typically, pay better than academia). For example, some work in computer programming and artificial intelligence. Others may work in management science, applying their knowledge of problem solving and decision making.

Developmental psychology. Developmental psychologists study how individuals develop physically, intellectually, socially, and emotionally over the lifespan ("from womb to tomb," as some say). Some developmental psychologists focus on just one period of life (for example, childhood or later adulthood), while others study development across the entire lifespan. In a field so broad, the research questions are practically limitless. Examples of research topics include the psychological and social effects of shyness in childhood, conformity to peer pressure in adolescence, and the effects of a spouse's death on the surviving partner. Developmental psychology topics are covered primarily in Chapter 11 of this text, although language development is discussed in Chapter 8, and personality development in Chapter 12. As for career options, developmental psychologists usually teach and conduct research in academic settings. Some serve as consultants to day-care centers, schools, or social service agencies. Others consult with toy and media companies to ensure that toys, games, television programs, and other media products match the cognitive, social, and physical skills of different-aged children.

Experimental psychology. The term *experimental psychology* refers to a diverse hodgepodge of topics that made up the core of psychology in the first half-century of its existence, including sensation, perception, learning, motivation, and emotion. Re-

web link D.8

APA Online

The American Psychological Association website has two especially useful links for students. Under the Students menu, the Divisions link enables you to access the individual webpages of the many subfields of psychology. The link to the Students page will help you find information about undergraduate psychology honoraries, getting into graduate school, and related topics.

searchers in these areas frequently study animals instead of humans. Although psychologists in all research areas conduct experiments, the name for this area reflects its *heavy* reliance on experimentation and its relatively infrequent use of correlational methods. Examples of research topics include how background factors influence object recognition, how variations in reinforcement patterns affect the acquisition of responses, and how external food cues regulate eating behavior. Chapters 4, 6, and 10 in this text provide many examples of research in experimental psychology. The vast majority of experimental psychologists work in academic settings or research laboratories, although their expertise occasionally leads them into applied fields. For example, experts in perception sometimes work in human engineering (see Appendix C).

Physiological psychology. This domain of research, also known as *biopsychology* and *behavioral neuroscience,* explores how behavior is influenced by genetic, neural, and hormonal functioning. Examples of topics include how the hypothalamus contributes to the regulation of eating behavior, how various drugs produce changes in synaptic transmission, and how the pineal gland regulates biological rhythms. Chapter 3 in the text is devoted exclusively to physiological topics, but biopsychology is so basic it shows up in virtually every chapter of the book, for example in discussions of the biological bases of pain perception (Chapter 4), sleep (5), constraints on learning (6) memory (7), language (8), intelligence (9), emotion (10), aging (11), personality (12), stress responses (13), psychological disorders (14), and drug treatments for mental disorders (15). Most biopsychologists are employed in academia or research centers, but there are applied specialties, such as *clinical neuropsychology,* which you will read about momentarily.

Personality psychology. This subfield is concerned with understanding and describing people's enduring behavior patterns and the psychological processes that underlie them (personality traits, for example). Personality psychology also focuses on how personality develops and the factors that shape it (heredity and parenting, for example). Some personality psychologists develop psychological tests and other techniques by which to study and evaluate aspects of personality (interests, creativity, and so forth). Examples of research topics include the behavioral correlates of personality traits, such as extraversion or conscientiousness, the impact of self-efficacy on sports performance, and whether culture influences

personality structure. Personality topics are mostly covered in Chapter 12 of this text. Career options for personality psychologists include teaching and conducting research in university settings and working for companies that develop personality tests.

Psychometrics. This area of research is concerned with the precise measurement of behavior and mental processes. Psychologists in this field design psychological tests to measure various aspects of personality, intelligence, and specific abilities. In their work, psychometricians are concerned about ensuring that psychological tests are reliable, valid, and used fairly, among other things. Psychometrics also includes the development of statistical procedures and computer programs to execute these procedures. Examples of research topics include exploring cultural variations in average scores on tests of mental abilities, analyzing the causes of generational changes in measured intelligence, and investigating the relationship between IQ scores and vocational success. Psychometric topics are examined mainly in Chapter 9 of this text but also are considered in the Chapter 12 application on personality testing. Measurement psychologists typically work in academic settings or for companies that develop psychological tests.

Educational psychology. Educational psychologists study the intertwined processes of teaching and learning, including a wide range of relevant factors such as motivation, abilities, learning styles, classroom diversity, curriculum design, instructional methods, and achievement testing. Educational psychologists attempt to understand how students learn and then develop materials and strategies to enhance the teaching process. Examples of research topics include comparing strategies and techniques for teaching reading, analyzing the effects of verbal praise on student motivation, and exploring the effects of mainstreaming on children with various types of disabilities. Educational psychology topics mainly appear in Chapter 9 of this text. Most educational psychologists are trained in departments or colleges of education, as opposed to departments of psychology. They are usually employed in academic settings.

Health psychology. Health psychologists are concerned with the role of psychological factors in the promotion and maintenance of good health, the prevention and treatment of illness, and the formulation of health policy. They study important societal health concerns such as teenage pregnancy, substance abuse, poor nutrition, and sedentary lifestyles. Examples of research topics include how to enhance the effectiveness of smoking cessation programs, how stress modulates immune system responding, and how to increase adherence to medical advice. Health psychology is covered primarily in Chapter 13 of this text. Health psychologists typically teach and conduct research in universities or medical schools. That said, a fair number of health psychologists are also involved in applied work. They frequently treat patients in hospitals, rehabilitation centers, or other health care settings. For example, they may assist patients with stress management, relaxation training, pain management, or medication compliance. Health psychology may eventually become a distinct applied specialty, but at present most health psychologists in professional practice first obtain degrees in clinical or counseling psychology and then do postdoctoral training in applications of health psychology (Kuther & Morgan, 2007).

Social psychology. Social psychologists study how other people influence our beliefs, feelings, and behaviors. Some general topics of interest to social psychologists are attitude formation and change, conformity, helping behavior, aggression, prejudice, and interpersonal attraction. Examples of more specific research topics include how physical appearance sways perceptions of personality and competence, how attachment styles influence romantic relationships, how fear appeals work in persuasion, and how culture is related to social loafing. Social psychology is mainly covered in Chapter 16, but the social roots and contexts of behavior surface throughout the book. Examples of social psychology topics in other chapters include the effects of expectations on social perceptions (Chapter 1), the effect of anxiety on the need to be with others (2), the influence of social models on aggressive behavior (6), the sociocultural bases of mating preferences (10), the socialization of gender roles (11), social cognitive approaches to personality (12), the influence of social support on physical health (13), and the relationship between attributional style and depression (14). Most social psychologists work in academic settings, but the applied nature of the subfield also lends itself to work outside academia. For example, some social psychologists consult or work for federal agencies or for businesses that conduct research in marketing and product development.

Career Options in Applied Areas

As noted in Chapter 1, psychology is also made up of various applied subfields. Applied psychology has grown rapidly since World War II sparked a revolution in the training of clinical psychologists. Indeed, today psychologists working in applied fields outnumber those who focus mainly on research by a sizable margin. We will look at six applied areas of specialization: clinical psychology, counseling psychology, clinical neuropsychology, school psychology, forensic psychology, and industrial/organizational psychology.

Clinical psychology. Clinical psychologists assess, diagnose, and treat people with psychological problems and disorders. They may act as therapists for people experiencing normal psychological crises (grief, for example) or for individuals suffering from severe, chronic disorders (bipolar disorder and schizophrenia, for example). Some clinical psychologists are generalists who work with a wide variety of populations, while others work with specific groups such as children, the elderly, or those with specific disorders (for example, schizophrenia). They may work with individuals or groups. Clinical psychologists are educated in university-based psychology departments or professional schools of psychology. Clinical psychologists can work in a diverse array of settings: academia, hospitals and medical centers, community mental health centers, or private practice. The nature of their work can also be wide ranging: administering and interpreting psychological tests, providing psychotherapy, teaching, conducting research, consulting, and serving in administrative capacities. Clinical psychology is the largest applied area in the field by far, as about two-thirds of applied psychologists are found in this specialty (see Chapter 1). Issues related to clinical psychology are mostly discussed in Chapters 14 and 15 of this text.

Counseling psychology. Counseling psychologists do many of the same things that clinical psychologists do. However, counseling psychologists *tend* to focus more on persons with normal adjustment problems rather than on those suffering from severe psychological disorders. Also, the testing they do is usually for career counseling rather than for diagnosing serious psychological disorders. Like clinical psychologists, some counseling psychologists are generalists who work with a wide variety of problems and populations, whereas others specialize in family, marital, or career counseling. Counseling psychology programs are offered in psychology departments, in professional schools of psychology, and in colleges or departments of education. Counseling psychologists are employed in private practice, colleges and universities (in the classroom or in counseling centers), community mental health centers, government agencies, and corporations (providing testing and therapy or serving in administrative roles). Issues related to counseling psychology are mostly discussed in Chapters 14 and 15 of this text.

Clinical neuropsychology.   As its name suggests, this relatively new specialization combines clinical psychology (assessment and psychotherapy) and behavioral neuroscience (the study of the neural bases of behavior). Clinical neuropsychologists assess and treat individuals with central nervous system dysfunctions such as traumatic brain injury, stroke, dementia, and seizure disorders. Clinical neuropsychologists must first obtain a doctoral degree in clinical psychology. Because of the specialized nature of their work, they must also complete additional training in clinical neuropsychology during a year-long internship or additional postdoctoral study (Kuther & Morgan, 2007). Clinical neuropsychologists work in a variety of settings, including universities, hospitals, medical centers, and private practice. Topics related to clinical neuropsychology mostly surface in Chapter 3.

School psychology.   School psychologists strive to promote the cognitive, emotional, and social development of children in educational settings. They deal with such issues as study skills, time management, family problems, and alcohol and drug problems. School psychologists use psychological tests to assess students' psychoeducational abilities and to understand the nature of their problems. They also counsel students and their parents and often serve as consultants to parents, teachers, and school administrators. School psychologists are typically trained in departments or colleges of education (versus departments of psychology). Many school psychologists have Ph.D. or Ed.D. degrees; others obtain the Ed.S. (education specialist), a degree between a master's and doctoral degree. Most school psychologists work in public school systems, often traveling among schools. Other employment settings include community mental health centers, criminal justice settings, hospitals, and private practice. Some topics related to school psychology can be found in Chapter 9.

Forensic psychology.   In forensic psychology, psychological principles are applied to the legal system. Thus forensic psychologists are concerned with child custody decisions and involuntary commitment, among other issues. Increasingly, forensic psychologists play a role in personal injury, medical malpractice, and worker's compensation litigation. Forensic psychologists often serve as expert witnesses in criminal trials and may, occasionally, help develop criminal profiles. Most forensic psychologists are trained as clinical or counseling psychologists. Some forensic psychologists have both doctoral and law degrees. Forensic psychologists may also be involved in developing public policies involving the law and mental health issues. Forensic psychologists work in a variety of settings, including prisons, jails, community mental health centers, and agencies that provide court-related services. Issues related to forensic psychology are discussed briefly in Chapter 14.

Industrial/organizational psychology.   Industrial/organizational (I/O) psychology is concerned with the application of psychological principles in the workplace. I/O psychologists are mainly interested in selecting employees, improving organizational effectiveness and the quality of work life, and designing work environments to match people's capacities and limitations. Most I/O psychologists are employed in business and government settings. Many head up or work in human resources departments, guiding personnel selection, employee training and development, and performance evaluation. I/O psychologists may also recommend organizational structures, policies, and procedures that will enhance organizational effectiveness. Others serve as consultants to business and industry. I/O psychologists who are interested in human factors work to help companies design machines and consumer products that mesh with human information processing capacities and response propensities. Some I/O psychologists teach and conduct research in psychology or business departments. Unlike the other professional areas of psychology, I/O psychology is not a mental health specialty requiring licensure, but it is an important, growing, and widely practiced area of applied psychology. Industrial/organizational psychology is covered in some depth in Appendix C.

Gaining Admission to Graduate School

The most important requirements for admission to graduate school are high scores on the Graduate Record Exam (GRE), excellent grades, glowing faculty recommendations, and research experience. For the record, it is much harder to gain admission to a doctoral program than a master's program. Common *minimum* scores required on the GRE verbal and quantitative sections for doctoral programs are around 550 to 600 (on each test); for master's programs, they hover around 500. The *minimum* cumulative grade-point average for admission to doctoral programs is typically around 3.2; for a master's program, it is around 3.0. On average, admitted students tend to have GPAs that are quite a bit higher than these minimum figures. Gaining admission to Ph.D. programs in clinical psychology is roughly as competitive and challenging as gaining admission to medical school. Of course, requirements vary among programs within the two levels. Departments with excellent reputations usually have more stringent requirements.

Early Preparation

Early in your college career you may not know whether you will want to try to gain admission to graduate school. To keep this educational door open until you are sure that you want to close it, keep the following points in mind.

1. *Begin early to develop the knowledge and skills graduate programs seek.* As with the job search, you need to begin early to develop the qualities listed in **Figure D.2**, as they are also important to success in graduate school. In addition, you must hone your verbal, quantitative, and critical thinking skills to a very high degree and be able to demonstrate that you have these skills through your GRE scores, grades, and letters of recommendation. Demonstrating that you have research experience is also important. An excellent way to start is to volunteer to help faculty members with their research. Also note that graduate schools place much less emphasis on extracurricular activities than employers do.

2. *Keep your grades up.* Performing well in all of your classes will help you to learn the information and develop the thinking skills that will permit you to score high on the GRE. It is especially important to do well in your Research Methods and Statistics courses. Good grades will also make you eligible for membership in Psi Chi, the national honor society in psychology.

3. *Position yourself to obtain strong letters of recommendation from three faculty members.* Graduate schools want recommendations only from faculty members. (For employers, recommendations from supervisors and clergy are also acceptable.) Try to take some smaller courses that may enable your professors to get to know you and to become familiar with your work. Otherwise, it will be difficult for them to write good letters of recommendation for you.

Next Steps

You need to prepare your applications for graduate school during the fall term of your senior year. Thus, in your junior year, you should begin identifying the subfield (clinical or social, for instance) in which you want to specialize, as well as schools that interest you. The graduate school application process is complicated and involves dealing with information and issues that are unfamiliar to virtually all students. Thus, it is essential to identify a knowledgeable faculty member in the psychology department at your school to advise you about the admissions process. Although Careers Services' staff members are experts on career issues, they are far less knowledgeable about graduate school admissions. For details about the process of applying to graduate programs in psychology, see Web Link D.1.

Critical Thinking About Internet Research Sources: What Students Need to Know

by Vincent W. Hevern (LeMoyne College)

Is the earth a globe or flat as a pancake? Was Copernicus right that the sun stands at the center of the solar system or does it circle the earth? Did Neil Armstrong really set foot on the lunar surface in 1969 or did NASA stage all those moon landings at a secret movie lot somewhere in the American desert? Probably 99.9999% of people know that the earth is round, Copernicus was right, and Armstrong really walked on the moon. But, type these four words—"flat earth Charles Johnson"—into Google, Yahoo, or another Internet search engine and you'll discover what the other 0.0001% believe. The late Mr. Johnson claimed that he could prove the earth was flat, Copernicus lied, and NASA has tricked us all for decades. So, who's right? After all, information supporting the "Flat Earth" hypothesis can be found on the Internet. Isn't that enough to justify you becoming a "Flat Earther" yourself?

I am starting out with this silly example to highlight a serious problem that students and teachers face in the 21st century: it is easy to find a lot of terrible as well as excellent information online. And, when students (and some teachers, too) don't critically judge their information sources, the overall quality of their research slips (Brown, Freeman, & Williamson, 2000). We live at a time when the amount and availability of information is growing exponentially. But our use of all that data is often handicapped, as it seems harder and harder to figure out where to find, and how to evaluate, research sources. So, whether you are exploring psychology as your major or just because it is an interesting subject, you need to learn how to think critically about Internet-based sources of information in psychology (and every other subject). When you finish school, you may find yourself working in business or for a governmental agency or even in another academic setting. Wherever your future takes you, your skills at finding and evaluating information online will be important and valued. I hope that some of the suggestions in this essay will help you learn to be a better researcher online.

Two Fundamental Facts about Research

No matter how large the Internet grows, libraries will continue to be the foundation for good research.

Yet, as Jenson (2004) argues, "many students are convinced that they can and should do all of their library work in their pajamas and slippers from the relative comfort of their dorm rooms or apartments" (p. 111). If that's your belief, frankly you will not become a better researcher, whether online or off. Colleges continue to spend hundreds of thousands to millions of dollars every year on their libraries because libraries remain the principal repositories of sound, scholarly information. That money also pays for librarians who have special skills and knowledge that permit them to help students and faculty with their research. So, the most basic rule of informational literacy states that *you need to know what is in your school's library*. And, to do so, you should consult the professional reference librarians there to help you. Because the best materials for research in cyberspace are often rooted in print-based library resources, you should learn the basics of the library to enhance your sophistication online.

The second fundamental fact can be summed up by the phrase, "No pain, no gain." It takes time and real effort to develop the skills necessary to be effective in seeking scholarly information. Just as you wouldn't think of playing a varsity sport unless you had trained for it over many months or years, *your ability to conduct research requires regular practice*. In fact, studies usually find that hard work and practice—more so than talent or genius—are what distinguishes experts from other people (van Gelder, 2005). A corollary to the need for practice is the notion that *good research itself takes time*. Very few students can gather the sources needed for an important report in just a few hours or overnight. Assembling the data, weighing the arguments, synthesizing the best materials, and preparing a report in your own words requires dedicated time and attention. That said, the process of research does get easier with experience.

Criteria for Quality on the Net

So, what are the standards or criteria by which you can judge the quality of a webpage or resource? What can you do to increase the chances that the material you take from the Internet is worth your effort? In recent years, information specialists have explored how to answer these questions. Their studies have come to slightly different conclusions, but there is substantial agreement about what characteristics are associated with quality on the web. The rest of this essay synthesizes their work and my own experience from over a decade of helping students and teachers use the Net (see **Figure E.1** for an overview). If I had to reduce this advice to its simplest terms, the most important key to finding quality resources online will always be the *active exercise of judgment and critical thinking.*

Let's discuss the process of finding sources first. *It is important to understand the difference between online databases and Internet search engines.* Although it is simple and painless to type a phrase into Google or Yahoo! or another Internet search engine, these engines should not normally be the first or only mechanism you use to find resources. It is a better idea to go to the indexes your school's library provides. These indexes can often be accessed through a library's webpage. By subscribing to various online databases (such as PsycINFO and full-text digital journal archives such as PsycARTICLES), your library has already pointed out the most direct path to finding quality materials. If you do use an Internet search engine, try the more specialized ones such as Google Scholar <http://scholar.google.com/> or Scirus <www.scirus.com/>. And remember, it may be prudent to ask your school's reference librarian for suggestions as you develop your own research competence.

It is also critical that you understand the difference between print-based and web-based sources. Online databases such as PsycINFO will give you *abstracts* (brief summaries) of articles from professional journals. The articles themselves may be found in any of three places: in digital archives online, on the shelves of your school's library, or via interlibrary loan from another school. Every school has different levels of access or availability for different journals. Thus, print-based sources, particularly journal articles, may require you to recover them in person rather than online. On the other hand, Internet search engines will generally lead you to sources at different websites. The materials at these sites may appear directly on your web browser, or you may need to download the documents to your personal computer.

Once you have found such sources, how do you evaluate if they are worthwhile? The comments that follow suggest what you should think about.

Identity and Qualifications of the Authors

The Internet is a kind of worldwide democracy. Just about anyone—qualified or not—can construct a webpage and put what they want to say online. With so few restrictions on Internet publishing, the range and quality of online resources is bound to vary from invaluable to completely worthless. So, researchers who turn to the Net need to ask two related questions: *Who has written this material?* and *What are their qualifications for so doing?* These are probably the two most important guides to the quality of online resources.

Sometimes you will find no clues to the identity of the author of a particular webpage or resource— no name, no organizational affiliation, nothing that reveals the authorship of the material. If this is the case, you should be skeptical about relying on this

Figure E.1
Evaluating online resources. The questions listed here, which draw heavily on the work of Alexander and Tate (1999), can help you to evaluate the quality and reliability of resource materials found on the Internet.

Questions to Ask in Evaluating Materials on the Internet

1. Identity and qualifications of the author(s)
- Who is the author of the material? Is the author identified or anonymous?
- What is the author's academic or professional background and experience?
- Is the author writing within or outside his/her area of expertise and skill?
- If the material is the product of a group (a committee, governmental agency, or the like), what is that group's qualifications or expertise regarding this subject?

2. Publisher or sponsor of the website
- Is the material self-published by the author or is there some recognized organization (university, medical center, government agency, nonprofit foundation, and so forth) that sponsors the website for the material?
- Does the site's sponsor or publisher have a positive reputation?

3. Balance, objectivity, and independence
- Does the material or website strive for balance and objectivity rather than use extreme, inflammatory, or highly subjective language or opinions?
- Is more than one point of view evident at the site?
- If the material takes a strong stand on one side of a controversial issue, does the author or site acknowledge there may be another side to the matter?
- Is the website sponsored by any commercial or political organization that advocates for a particular point of view?
- Does the author have any financial or commercial interest that might conflict with a fair or objective presentation of the topic?
- Is the material drawn from a site that sells a product or solicits customers for a service?

4. Quality of online presentation
- Is the site well organized or designed so that browsers can easily visit and retrieve information?
- Does the site or online material show care in its preparation, such as proper spelling and good grammar in all posted materials?
- Does the site work effectively, so that the links to subpages and external sites are accurate and helpful?
- How recently has the site been updated? Does the site show evidence that someone regularly attends to it with corrections, new materials, and so forth?

5. Other cues to quality
- Does the material contain clear and useful references to other scholarship from journals, professional books, and recognized research studies?
- Have supporting references in the material been published in recent years, or do they include mostly out-of-date, or possibly obsolete sources?
- Have any editors or external reviewers judged the quality of the material at the site?

information. It's hard to defend the quality of a work when "Anonymous" is the author.

Suppose one or more authors are listed by name. The next task is to discover the *qualifications* of these authors. Do they have some type of expertise to justify writing the online material or constructing the online site? You should look for a statement of an author's academic credentials (such as an advanced degree like a Ph.D. or an M.D.) or appropriate work experience (such as "director of personnel" at a company or "senior researcher" at a laboratory). You may be able to read through a résumé at a personal webpage showing the author's qualifications. You should also try to determine whether the author has published on a similar topic in reputable, peer-reviewed journals or belongs to professional or scholarly organizations concerned with the subject.

There are other cautions to keep in mind. Some authors may be qualified to comment on one topic but go beyond their expertise into other domains of knowledge—for example, a physician commenting on economics or a biologist on educational methods. Researchers need to be cautious with writers who move too far away from their fields of specialization. Another consideration is whether authors may have a financial stake or commercial interest in the issue that might compromise their objectivity.

Finally, suppose the "author" of a web-based publication has an institutional identity such as a professional association, a governmental agency, a research center, or a nonprofit organization. How should qualifications be weighed in such a case? Certainly the overall reputation of the institutional author should be recognized. For example, a consensus statement on a treatment approach produced by the National Institute of Mental Health or a report on the employment characteristics of psychologists issued by the American Psychological Association would both be rated positively as reference sources. You may also check whether a broad corporate board of editors or advisors is associated with an institutional voice on the Net. However, beware of fancy-sounding "Institutes" or "Commissions" or "Associations" that may be the product of a single person or handful of individuals and serve only to artificially embellish the opinions of their creators.

Publisher or Sponsor of the Website

Book authors traditionally use print publishers to promote and distribute their writings. In turn, publishers place their reputations on the line by issuing new books. Discerning readers rely on a publisher's overall standing when they consider whether to acquire new works. Especially in academic publishing, readers know that an editorial and review process precedes publication and that such efforts seek to ensure a high level of quality for the published material. Indeed, the essence of academic scholarship lies in a willingness to submit research to pre-publication critiques by knowledgeable colleagues. Occasionally, though, an author circumvents the editorial and peer review process and pays to have his or her book set in print directly. This practice is called "vanity publishing" and is usually looked down upon by other scholars.

In a practice reminiscent of vanity publishing, many web authors post materials online directly through commercial or free Internet service providers. Because these writings have not been edited or evaluated prior to their publication, you need to be cautious in judging their quality. This is not to disparage all self-published resources on the web. Clearly, experts have posted some valuable resources online without peer review. But, in the absence of a clear process of scholarly peer review, you must look for other indicators of quality. For this reason, the overall qualifications of an author as an expert may be crucial in determining whether to use a resource published without peer review.

Websites that are sponsored by academic institutions, government agencies, and nonprofit or scholarly organizations have URLs that end with the designation *.edu, .gov,* or *.org* rather than *.com* or *.net.* Such sites would be expected to offer some assurance of higher quality for data posted there. A particular clue to quality at corporate sites may be a copyright notice by a sponsoring organization rather than a single individual. Often located at the bottom of a webpage, this notice may signal that the organization is willing to put its reputation behind the resource. For example, there are many online health information centers that range in quality from dismal to superb. At one excellent site, The Virtual Hospital <www.uihealthcare.com/vh>, it is significant to find the notice on its title page, "Copyright © 2006 The University of Iowa."

Balance, Objectivity, and Independence

At the checkout line in a supermarket, shoppers often face a set of tabloid newspapers with outrageous headlines and the promise of lurid stories inside. Many people pick up a copy of their favorite tabloid as entertainment, something to be read purely for relaxation and enjoyment but not as an objective or reliable source of reporting about the world. Although tabloid papers are an extreme example, other sources of information should arouse similar suspicions because of their subjective, unbalanced, and biased style of presentation. In similar fashion, Internet resources should be evaluated for their apparent balance and objectivity. Certainly, the presence of language, graphic images, or opinions that are extreme, inflammatory, or highly subjective suggests that the material should be treated with some skepticism. The more extreme, vulgar, or intemperate the manner of presentation, the less likely that the resource is reliable and trustworthy.

A more difficult case arises from material found on sites clearly advocating a particular point of view, such as those for a lobbying group, political movement, or professional advocacy or commercial trade association. Researchers should expect that resources available at these sites will support the point of view of the group. This fact does not necessarily disqualify the importance of materials found there. The sponsoring organizations may provide valuable information for visitors to their sites. Greater reliance can probably be given to resources found on a site that acknowledges there is more than one side to a controversial issue or, even, that the topic is controversial in the first place. Some sites even offer links to the opposing side of a disputed topic. This openness should inspire confidence by users of the site because it suggests a sense of fairness.

A frequent challenge to researchers of psychological topics arises from commercial sites that stand to make money or gain new customers on the basis of what they post online. These sites may be businesses (with a *.com* address) or may be allied with the professional office or practice of individuals such as psychotherapists or physicians. Sometimes these sites offer a "Resource Center" or similar area that is filled with articles relating to the product or service of the site's sponsor. These articles may include scientific-sounding titles and come from magazines, journals, or books that seem to be similarly professional. Most evaluators warn researchers to be careful when using materials from any site that has a direct financial motivation in sharing information. Finding quality in online materials is always a judgment call, and the more you know about a topic from other sources, the better you can make that call at commercial sites.

Quality of Online Presentation and Other Cues

Another important index of quality is the care with which websites and materials have been organized and maintained. You should consider how easily you can use a website. Do the hypertext links within the site work or do they point to empty or missing pages? Can visitors easily find the information they are looking for? Is there evidence that the design of the site was carefully considered and executed? Similarly, the actual text of materials retrieved from the Net should be free from gross errors. Poor grammar and improper spelling usually signal that something is amiss. Reputable scholars are fanatical about eliminating sloppiness or careless mistakes in what they write. They believe any such errors would suggest a parallel sloppiness in their thinking. Thus, the presence of mechanical and stylistic mistakes at a website or in a document should raise doubts about how reputable the actual content of a resource may be. Finally, more credibility can be assigned to materials retrieved from sites that are frequently updated and carefully corrected. You should look for clear dates on pages containing important information. Ideally, one date will indicate when the page was first posted online and another when it was last changed or revised.

When I use the Net for research purposes, I use at least two further cues to evaluate the quality of the material or sites I find. First, in articles or papers online, I look at the references used by the author and consider whether they include scholarly materials from journals, professional books, or other recognized research sources. These sources should go well beyond the author's own previous writings. Second, I examine the dates of the supporting references. How recent are they? Do they include sources published in the last several years? Or, do they include only older and possibly out-of-date materials? The more up-to-date the references, the more I tend to trust the source.

A Final Note of Advice

I hope the suggestions summarized here make it clear that any researcher must actively exercise judgment and critical thinking skills in evaluating online resources. Such skills are enormously enhanced when the researcher chooses a balanced overall research strategy. It is one thing to seek a quick fact or a simple definition through a website; it is another to rely on the Internet as the *sole* data source for a major paper or research project. Yet for many people, the Internet is an easily "surfable" medium, one that can quickly lead to information of varying levels of quality. The very ease of conducting research online often seduces student researchers to skip more difficult, but crucially important, steps offline.

The most important strategy a student can bring to any research project is to develop an overall perspective or a broad vantage point regarding the topic of the project. This situation is unlikely to happen unless the investigator uses sources of different types—scholarly books, journal and magazine articles, and printed research reports—*in addition to* materials retrieved from the Internet. It is both easy to understand, but embarrassing in the long run, when a student hands in a paper with only Internet-based sources and later discovers in a professor's grading that the Net provided a biased or slanted view of the topic. Without the counterbalance of non-Net sources, a student risks seriously misjudging how psychologists, physicians, and other research scientists actually approach an issue. So, my final suggestion about research is a simple rule of thumb: The longer and more important the research project or paper, the broader the kinds of references you should use to answer the research question.

For Further Reference and Reading

Students who wish to further enhance their ability to evaluate Internet materials and sites should consider these outstanding online resources:

Beck, S. (1997). Evaluation criteria. [Online] The good, the bad, and the ugly: Or, why it's a good idea to evaluate web sources. Available at the New Mexico State University Library website: http://lib.nmsu.edu/instruction/eval.html

Kirk, E. E. (1996). Evaluating information found on the Internet. [Online] Available at the Sheridan Libraries of the Johns Hopkins University website: http://www.library.jhu.edu/researchhelp/general/evaluating/

U.C. Berkeley Teaching Library Internet Workshops. (2005). Evaluating webpages: Techniques to apply and questions to ask. [Online] Available at the University of California at Berkeley Library website: http://www.lib.berkeley.edu/TeachingLib/Guides/Internet/Evaluate.html

GLOSSARY

A

Absolute refractory period The minimum length of time after an action potential during which another action potential cannot begin.

Absolute threshold The minimum amount of stimulation that an organism can detect for a specific type of sensory input.

Achievement motive The need to master difficult challenges, to outperform others, and to meet high standards of excellence.

Achievement tests Tests that gauge a person's mastery and knowledge of various subjects.

Acquired immune deficiency syndrome (AIDS) A disorder in which the immune system is gradually weakened and eventually disabled by the human immunodeficiency virus (HIV).

Acquisition The formation of a new conditioned response tendency.

Action potential A brief change in a neuron's electrical charge.

Acute stressors Threatening events that have a relatively short duration and a clear endpoint.

Adaptation An inherited characteristic that increased in a population (through natural selection) because it helped solve a problem of survival or reproduction during the time it emerged.

Additive color mixing Formation of colors by superimposing lights, putting more light in the mixture than exists in any one light by itself.

Adoption studies Research studies that assess hereditary influence by examining the resemblance between adopted children and both their biological and their adoptive parents.

Affective forecasting A person's efforts to predict his or her emotional reactions to future events.

Afferent nerve fibers Axons that carry information inward to the central nervous system from the periphery of the body.

Afterimage A visual image that persists after a stimulus is removed.

Age of viability The age at which a baby can survive in the event of a premature birth.

Aggression Any behavior that is intended to hurt someone, either physically or verbally.

Agonist A chemical that mimics the action of a neurotransmitter.

Agoraphobia A fear of going out to public places.

Alcohol A variety of beverages containing ethyl alcohol.

Algorithm A methodical, step-by-step procedure for trying all possible alternatives in searching for a solution to a problem.

Amnesia A significant memory loss that is too extensive to be due to normal forgetting. See also *Anterograde amnesia, Retrograde amnesia.*

Androgens The principal class of gonadal hormones in males.

Anecdotal evidence Personal stories about specific incidents and experiences.

Animism The belief that all things are living.

Anorexia nervosa Eating disorder characterized by intense fear of gaining weight, disturbed body image, refusal to maintain normal weight, and dangerous measures to lose weight.

Antagonist A chemical that opposes the action of a neurotransmitter.

Anterograde amnesia Loss of memories for events that occur after a head injury.

Antianxiety drugs Medications that relieve tension, apprehension, and nervousness.

Antidepressant drugs Medications that gradually elevate mood and help bring people out of a depression.

Antipsychotic drugs Medications used to gradually reduce psychotic symptoms, including hyperactivity, mental confusion, hallucinations, and delusions.

Antisocial personality disorder A type of personality disorder marked by impulsive, callous, manipulative, aggressive, and irresponsible behavior that reflects a failure to accept social norms.

Anxiety disorders A class of disorders marked by feelings of excessive apprehension and anxiety.

Applied psychology The branch of psychology concerned with everyday, practical problems.

Approach-approach conflict A conflict situation in which a choice must be made between two attractive goals.

Approach-avoidance conflict A conflict situation in which a choice must be made about whether to pursue a single goal that has both attractive and unattractive aspects.

Aptitude tests Psychological tests used to assess talent for specific types of mental ability.

Archetypes According to Jung, emotionally charged images and thought forms that have universal meaning.

Argument One or more premises used to provide support for a conclusion.

Ascending reticular activating system (ARAS) The afferent fibers running through the reticular formation that influence physiological arousal.

Assumptions Premises for which no proof or evidence is offered.

Attachment A close, emotional bond of affection between infants and their caregivers.

Attention Focusing awareness on a narrowed range of stimuli or events.

Attitudes Orientations that locate objects of thought on dimensions of judgment.

Attributions Inferences that people draw about the causes of events, others' behavior, and their own behavior.

Auditory localization Locating the source of a sound in space.

Autonomic nervous system (ANS) The system of nerves that connect to the heart, blood vessels, smooth muscles, and glands.

Availability heuristic Basing the estimated probability of an event on the ease with which relevant instances come to mind.

Aversion therapy A behavior therapy in which an aversive stimulus is paired with a stimulus that elicits an undesirable response.

Avoidance-avoidance conflict A conflict situation in which a choice must be made between two unattractive goals.

Avoidance learning Learning that has occurred when an organism engages in a response that prevents aversive stimulation from occurring.

Axon A long, thin fiber that transmits signals away from the neuron cell body to other neurons, or to muscles or glands.

B

Basilar membrane A structure that runs the length of the cochlea in the inner ear and holds the auditory receptors, called hair cells.

Behavior Any overt (observable) response or activity by an organism.

Behavior modification A systematic approach to changing behavior through the application of the principles of conditioning.

Behavior therapies Application of the principles of learning to direct efforts to change clients' maladaptive behaviors.

Behavioral contract A written agreement outlining a promise to adhere to the contingencies of a behavior modification program.

Behaviorism A theoretical orientation based on the premise that scientific psychology should study only observable behavior.

Bilingualism The acquisition of two languages that use different speech sounds, vocabularies, and grammatical rules.

Binge-eating disorder Distress-induced eating binges that are not accompanied by the purging, fasting, and excessive exercise seen in bulimia.

Binocular depth cues Clues about distance based on the differing views of the two eyes.

Biological rhythms Periodic fluctuations in physiological functioning.

Biomedical therapies Physiological interventions intended to reduce symptoms associated with psychological disorders.

Biopsychosocial model A model of illness that holds that physical illness is caused by a complex interaction of biological, psychological, and sociocultural factors.

Bipolar disorder (formerly known as manic-depressive disorder) Mood disorder marked by the experience of both depressed and manic periods.

Bisexuals Persons who seek emotional-sexual relationships with members of either sex.

Body mass index (BMI) Weight (in kilograms) divided by height (in meters) squared (kg/m^2).

Bottom-up processing In form perception, progression from individual elements to the whole.

Bulimia nervosa Eating disorder characterized by habitually engaging in out-of-control overeating followed by unhealthy compensatory efforts, such as self-induced vomiting, fasting, abuse of laxatives and diuretics, and excessive exercise.

Burnout Physical, mental, and emotional exhaustion that is attributable to work-related stress.

Bystander effect A paradoxical social phenomenon in which people are less likely to provide needed help when they are in groups than when they are alone.

C

Cannabis The hemp plant from which marijuana, hashish, and THC are derived.

Case study An in-depth investigation of an individual subject.

Catastrophic thinking Unrealistically pessimistic appraisals of stress that exaggerate the magnitude of one's problems.

Catatonic schizophrenia A type of schizophrenia marked by striking motor disturbances, ranging from muscular rigidity to random motor activity.

Catharsis The release of emotional tension.

Central nervous system (CNS) The brain and the spinal cord.

Centration The tendency to focus on just one feature of a problem, neglecting other important aspects.

Cephalocaudal trend The head-to-foot direction of motor development.

Cerebral cortex The convoluted outer layer of the cerebrum.

Cerebral hemispheres The right and left halves of the cerebrum.

Cerebrospinal fluid (CSF) A solution that fills the hollow cavities (ventricles) of the brain and circulates around the brain and spinal cord.

Channel The medium through which a message is sent.

Chromosomes Threadlike strands of DNA (deoxyribonucleic acid) molecules that carry genetic information.

Chronic stressors Threatening events that have a relatively long duration and no readily apparent time limit.

Chunk A group of familiar stimuli stored as a single unit.

Circadian rhythms The 24-hour biological cycles found in humans and many other species.

Classical conditioning A type of learning in which a neutral stimulus acquires the ability to evoke a response that was originally evoked by another stimulus.

Client-centered therapy An insight therapy that emphasizes providing a supportive emotional climate for clients, who play a major role in determining the pace and direction of their therapy.

Clinical psychologists Psychologists who specialize in the diagnosis and treatment of psychological disorders and everyday behavioral problems.

Clinical psychology The branch of psychology concerned with the diagnosis and treatment of psychological problems and disorders.

Cochlea The fluid-filled, coiled tunnel in the inner ear that contains the receptors for hearing.

Coefficient of determination The percentage of variation in one variable that can be predicted based on the other variable.

Cognition The mental processes involved in acquiring knowledge.

Cognitive-behavioral treatments A varied combination of verbal interventions and behavioral modification techniques used to help clients change maladaptive patterns of thinking.

Cognitive development Transitions in youngsters' patterns of thinking, including reasoning, remembering, and problem solving.

Cognitive dissonance A psychological state that exists when related cognitions are inconsistent.

Cognitive therapy An insight therapy that emphasizes recognizing and changing negative thoughts and maladaptive beliefs.

Cohort effects Differences between age groups that are attributable to the groups growing up in different time periods.

Collective unconscious According to Jung, a storehouse of latent memory traces inherited from people's ancestral past.

Collectivism Putting group goals ahead of personal goals and defining one's identity in terms of the groups one belongs to.

Color blindness Deficiency in the ability to distinguish among colors.

Commitment An intent to maintain a relationship in spite of the difficulties and costs that may arise.

Comorbidity The coexistence of two or more disorders.

Companionate love Warm, trusting, tolerant affection for another whose life is deeply intertwined with one's own.

Compensation According to Adler, efforts to overcome imagined or real inferiorities by developing one's abilities.

Complementary colors Pairs of colors that produce gray tones when added together.

Conceptual hierarchy A multilevel classification system based on common properties among items.

Concordance rate The percentage of twin pairs or other pairs of relatives that exhibit the same disorder.

Conditioned reinforcers. See *Secondary reinforcers*.

Conditioned response (CR) A learned reaction to a conditioned stimulus that occurs because of previous conditioning.

Conditioned stimulus (CS) A previously neutral stimulus that has, through conditioning, acquired the capacity to evoke a conditioned response.

Cones Specialized visual receptors that play a key role in daylight vision and color vision.

Confirmation bias The tendency to seek information that supports one's decisions and beliefs while ignoring disconfirming information.

Conflict A state that occurs when two or more incompatible motivations or behavioral impulses compete for expression.

Conformity The tendency for people to yield to real or imagined social pressure.

Confounding of variables A condition that exists whenever two variables are linked together in a way that makes it difficult to sort out their independent effects.

Conjunction fallacy An error that occurs when people estimate that the odds of two uncertain events happening together are greater than the odds of either event happening alone.

Connectionist models. See *parallel distributed processing (PDP) models*.

Conscious Whatever one is aware of at a particular point in time.

Conservation Piaget's term for the awareness that physical quantities remain constant in spite of changes in their shape or appearance.

Consolidation A hypothetical process involving the gradual conversion of information into durable memory codes stored in long-term memory.

Construct validity The extent to which there is evidence that a test measures a particular hypothetical construct.

Constructive coping Relatively healthful efforts that people make to deal with stressful events.

Content validity The degree to which the content of a test is representative of the domain it's supposed to cover.

Continuous reinforcement Reinforcing every instance of a designated response.

Control group Subjects in a study who do not receive the special treatment given to the experimental group.

Convergence A cue to depth that involves sensing the eyes converging toward each other as they focus on closer objects.

Convergent thinking Narrowing down a list of alternatives to converge on a single correct answer.

Conversion disorder A somatoform disorder characterized by a significant loss of physical function (with no apparent organic basis), usually in a single organ system.

Coping Active efforts to master, reduce, or tolerate the demands created by stress.

Corpus callosum The structure that connects the two cerebral hemispheres.

Correlation The extent to which two variables are related to each other.

Correlation coefficient A numerical index of the degree of relationship between two variables.

Counseling psychologists Psychologists who specialize in the treatment of everyday adjustment problems.

Creativity The generation of ideas that are original, novel, and useful.

Criterion-related validity Test validity that is estimated by correlating subjects' scores on a test with their scores on an independent criterion (another measure) of the trait assessed by the test.

Critical period A limited time span in the development of an organism when it is optimal for certain capacities to emerge because the organism is especially responsive to certain experiences.

Critical thinking The use of cognitive skills and strategies that increase the probability of a desired outcome.

Cross-sectional design A research design in which investigators compare groups of subjects of differing age who are observed at a single point in time.

Culture The widely shared customs, beliefs, values, norms, institutions, and other products of a community that are transmitted socially across generations.

Crystallized intelligence The ability to apply acquired knowledge and skills in problem solving.

Culture-bound disorders Abnormal syndromes found only in a few cultural groups.

Cumulative recorder A graphic record of reinforcement and responding in a Skinner box as a function of time.

Cyclothymic disorder Exhibiting chronic but relatively mild symptoms of bipolar disturbance.

D

Dark adaptation The process in which the eyes become more sensitive to light in low illumination.

Data collection techniques Procedures for making empirical observations and measurements.

Decay theory The idea that forgetting occurs because memory traces fade with time.

Decision making The process of evaluating alternatives and making choices among them.

Declarative memory system Memory for factual information.

Deep brain stimulation (DBS) A treatment approach that involves a thin electrode being surgically implanted in the brain and connected to an implanted pulse generator so that various electrical currents can be delivered to brain tissue adjacent to the electrode.

Defense mechanisms Largely unconscious reactions that protect a person from unpleasant emotions such as anxiety and guilt.

Defensive attribution The tendency to blame victims for their misfortune, so that one feels less likely to be victimized in a similar way.

Deinstitutionalization Transferring the treatment of mental illness from inpatient institutions to community-based facilities that emphasize outpatient care.

Delusions False beliefs that are maintained even though they are clearly out of touch with reality.

Dementia An abnormal condition marked by multiple cognitive defects that include memory impairment.

Dendrites Branchlike parts of a neuron that are specialized to receive information.

Dependent variable In an experiment, the variable that is thought to be affected by the manipulation of the independent variable.

Depth perception Interpretation of visual cues that indicate how near or far away objects are.

Descriptive statistics Statistics that are used to organize and summarize data.

Development The sequence of age-related changes that occur as a person progresses from conception to death.

Developmental norms The average age at which individuals display various behaviors and abilities.

Deviation IQ scores Scores that locate subjects precisely within the normal distribution, using the standard deviation as the unit of measurement.

Diagnosis Distinguishing one illness from another.

Discrimination Behaving differently, usually unfairly, toward the members of a group.

Discriminative stimuli Cues that influence operant behavior by indicating the probable consequences (reinforcement or nonreinforcement) of a response.

Disorganized schizophrenia A type of schizophrenia in which particularly severe deterioration of adaptive behavior is seen.

Displacement Diverting emotional feelings (usually anger) from their original source to a substitute target.

Display rules Cultural norms that regulate the appropriate expressions of emotions.

Dissociation A splitting off of mental processes into two separate, simultaneous streams of awareness.

Dissociative amnesia A sudden loss of memory for important personal information that is too extensive to be due to normal forgetting.

Dissociative disorders A class of disorders in which people lose contact with portions of their consciousness or memory, resulting in disruptions in their sense of identity.

Dissociative fugue A disorder in which people lose their memory for their entire lives along with their sense of personal identity.

Dissociative identity disorder (DID) A type of dissociative disorder characterized by the coexistence in one person of two or more largely complete, and usually very different, personalities. Also called multiple-personality disorder.

Distal stimuli Stimuli that lie in the distance (that is, in the world outside the body).

Divergent thinking Trying to expand the range of alternatives by generating many possible solutions.

Dominant gene A gene that is expressed when paired genes are heterozygous (different).

Double-blind procedure A research strategy in which neither subjects nor experimenters know which subjects are in the experimental or control groups.

Dream analysis A psychoanalytic technique in which the therapist interprets the symbolic meaning of the client's dreams.

Drive An internal state of tension that motivates an organism to engage in activities that should reduce the tension.

Dual-coding theory Paivio's theory that memory is enhanced by forming semantic and visual codes, since either can lead to recall.

Dysthymic disorder A chronic depression that is insufficient in severity to merit diagnosis of a major depressive episode.

E

Eating disorders Severe disturbances in eating behavior characterized by preoccupation with weight concerns and unhealthy efforts to control weight.

Eclecticism In psychotherapy, drawing ideas from two or more systems of therapy instead of committing to just one system.

Efferent nerve fibers Axons that carry information outward from the central nervous system to the periphery of the body.

Ego According to Freud, the decision-making component of personality that operates according to the reality principle.

Egocentrism A limited ability to share another person's viewpoint.

Elaboration Linking a stimulus to other information at the time of encoding.

Electrical stimulation of the brain (ESB) Sending a weak electric current into a brain structure to stimulate (activate) it.

Electroconvulsive therapy (ECT) A biomedical treatment in which electric shock is used to produce a cortical seizure accompanied by convulsions.

Electroencephalograph (EEG) A device that monitors the electrical activity of the brain over time by means of recording electrodes attached to the surface of the scalp.

Electromyograph (EMG) A device that records muscular activity and tension.

Electrooculograph (EOG) A device that records eye movements.

Elicit To draw out or bring forth.

Embryonic stage The second stage of prenatal development, lasting from two weeks until the end of the second month.

Emit To send forth.

Emotion A subjective conscious experience (the cognitive component) accompanied by bodily arousal (the physiological component) and by characteristic overt expressions (the behavioral component).

Emotional intelligence (EI) The ability to perceive and express emotion, assimilate emotion in thought, understand and reason with emotion, and regulate emotion.

Empiricism The premise that knowledge should be acquired through observation.

Encoding Forming a memory code.

Encoding specificity principle The idea that the value of a retrieval cue depends on how well it corresponds to the memory code.

Endocrine system A group of glands that secrete chemicals into the bloodstream that help control bodily functioning.

Endorphins The entire family of internally produced chemicals that resemble opiates in structure and effects.

Epidemiology The study of the distribution of mental or physical disorders in a population.

Episodic memory system Chronological, or temporally dated, recollections of personal experiences.

Escape learning A type of learning in which an organism acquires a response that decreases or ends some aversive stimulation.

Estrogens The principal class of gonadal hormones in females.

Ethnocentrism The tendency to view one's own group as superior to others and as the standard for judging the worth of foreign ways.

Etiology The apparent causation and developmental history of an illness.

Evaluative conditioning Efforts to transfer the emotion attached to a UCS to a new CS.

Evolutionary psychology Theoretical perspective that examines behavioral processes in terms of their adaptive value for a species over the course of many generations.

Experiment A research method in which the investigator manipulates a variable under carefully controlled conditions and observes whether any changes occur in a second variable as a result.

Experimental group The subjects in a study who receive some special treatment in regard to the independent variable.

Experimenter bias A phenomenon that occurs when a researcher's expectations or preferences about the outcome of a study influence the results obtained.

Expressed emotion (EE) The degree to which a relative of a patient displays highly critical or emotionally overinvolved attitudes toward the patient.

External attributions Ascribing the causes of behavior to situational demands and environmental constraints.

Extinction The gradual weakening and disappearance of a conditioned response tendency.

Extraneous variables Any variables other than the independent variable that seem likely to influence the dependent variable in a specific study.

F

Factor analysis Statistical analysis of correlations among many variables to identify closely related clusters of variables.

Family studies Scientific studies in which researchers assess hereditary influence by examining blood relatives to see how much they resemble each other on a specific trait.

Farsightedness A vision deficiency in which distant objects are seen clearly but close objects appear blurry.

Fast mapping The process by which children map a word onto an underlying concept after only one exposure to the word.

Feature analysis The process of detecting specific elements in visual input and assembling them into a more complex form.

Feature detectors Neurons that respond selectively to very specific features of more complex stimuli.

Fetal alcohol syndrome A collection of congenital (inborn) problems associated with excessive alcohol use during pregnancy.

Fetal stage The third stage of prenatal development, lasting from two months through birth.

Fight-or-flight response A physiological reaction to threat in which the autonomic nervous system mobilizes the organism for attacking (fight) or fleeing (flight) an enemy.

Fitness The reproductive success (number of descendants) of an individual organism relative to the average reproductive success of the population.

Fixation According to Freud, failure to move forward from one psychosexual stage to another as expected.

Fixed-interval (FI) schedule A reinforcement schedule in which the reinforcer is given for the first response that occurs after a fixed time interval has elapsed.

Fixed-ratio (FR) schedule A reinforcement schedule in which the reinforcer is given after a fixed number of nonreinforced responses.

Flashbulb memories Unusually vivid and detailed recollections of momentous events.

Fluid intelligence Basic reasoning ability, memory capacity, and speed of information processing.

Foot-in-the-door technique Getting people to agree to a small request to increase the chances that they will agree to a larger request later.

Forebrain The largest and most complicated region of the brain, encompassing a variety of structures, including the thalamus, hypothalamus, limbic system, and cerebrum.

Forgetting curve A graph showing retention and forgetting over time.

Fovea A tiny spot in the center of the retina that contains only cones; visual acuity is greatest at this spot.

Framing How issues are posed or how choices are structured.

Fraternal twins Twins that result when two eggs are fertilized simultaneously by different sperm cells, forming two separate zygotes. Also called *dizygotic twins*.

Free association A psychoanalytic technique in which clients spontaneously express their thoughts and feelings exactly as they occur, with as little censorship as possible.

Frequency distribution An orderly arrangement of scores indicating the frequency of each score or group of scores.

Frequency polygon A line figure used to present data from a frequency distribution.

Frequency theory The theory that perception of pitch corresponds to the rate, or frequency, at which the entire basilar membrane vibrates.

Frustration The feeling that people experience in any situation in which their pursuit of some goal is thwarted.

Functional fixedness The tendency to perceive an item only in terms of its most common use.

Functionalism A school of psychology based on the belief that psychology should investigate the function or purpose of consciousness, rather than its structure.

Fundamental attribution error Observers' bias in favor of internal attributions in explaining others' behavior.

G

Galvanic skin response (GSR) An increase in the electrical conductivity of the skin that occurs when sweat glands increase their activity.

Gambler's fallacy The belief that the odds of a chance event increase if the event hasn't occurred recently.

Gate-control theory The idea that incoming pain sensations must pass through a "gate" in the spinal cord that can be closed, thus blocking pain signals.

Gender Culturally constructed distinctions between masculinity and femininity.

Gender differences Actual disparities between the sexes in typical behavior or average ability.

Gender roles Expectations about what is appropriate behavior for each sex.

Gender stereotypes Widely held beliefs about males' and females' abilities, personality traits, and behavior.

General adaptation syndrome Selye's model of the body's stress response, consisting of three stages: alarm, resistance, and exhaustion.

Generalized anxiety disorder A psychological disorder marked by a chronic, high level of anxiety that is not tied to any specific threat.

Genes DNA segments that serve as the key functional units in hereditary transmission.

Genetic mapping The process of determining the location and chemical sequence of specific genes on specific chromosomes.

Genotype A person's genetic makeup.

Germinal stage The first phase of prenatal development, encompassing the first two weeks after conception.

Glia Cells found throughout the nervous system that provide various types of support for neurons.

Glucose A simple sugar that is an important source of energy.

Glucostats Neurons sensitive to glucose in the surrounding fluid.

Group Two or more individuals who interact and are interdependent.

Group cohesiveness The strength of the liking relationships linking group members to each other and to the group itself.

Group polarization A phenomenon that occurs when group discussion strengthens a group's dominant point of view and produces a shift toward a more extreme decision in that direction.

Group therapy The simultaneous treatment of several clients in a group.

Groupthink A process in which members of a cohesive group emphasize concurrence at the expense of critical thinking in arriving at a decision.

Gustatory system The sensory system for taste.

H

Hallucinations Sensory perceptions that occur in the absence of a real, external stimulus, or gross distortions of perceptual input.

Hallucinogens A diverse group of drugs that have powerful effects on mental and emotional functioning, marked most prominently by distortions in sensory and perceptual experience.

Health psychology The subfield of psychology concerned with how psychosocial factors relate to the promotion and maintenance of health and with the causation, prevention, and treatment of illness.

Hedonic adaptation An effect that occurs when the mental scale that people use to judge the pleasantness-unpleasantness of their experiences shifts so that their neutral point, or baseline for comparison, changes.

Heritability ratio An estimate of the proportion of trait variability in a population that is determined by variations in genetic inheritance.

Heterosexuals Persons who seek emotional-sexual relationships with members of the other sex.

Heterozygous condition The situation that occurs when two genes in a specific pair are different.

Heuristic A strategy, guiding principle, or rule of thumb used in solving problems or making decisions.

Hierarchy of needs Maslow's systematic arrangement of needs according to priority, which assumes that basic needs must be met before less basic needs are aroused.

Higher-order conditioning A type of conditioning in which a conditioned stimulus functions as if it were an unconditioned stimulus.

Hill-climbing heuristic Problem-solving approach that entails selecting the alternative at each choice point that appears to lead most directly to one's goal.

Hindbrain The part of the brain that includes the cerebellum and two structures found in the lower part of the brainstem: the medulla and the pons.

Hindsight bias The tendency to mold one's interpretation of the past to fit how events actually turned out.

Histogram A bar graph that presents data from a frequency distribution.

Homeostatsis A state of physiological equilibrium or stability.

Homosexuals Persons who seek emotional-sexual relationships with members of the same sex.

Homozygous condition The situation that occurs when two genes in a specific pair are the same.

Hormones The chemical substances released by the endocrine glands.

Human factors (human engineering) psychology Area of psychology that examines the ways in which work, work systems, and system features can be designed or changed to most effectively correspond with the capabilities and limitations of human beings, often with a focus on the human body.

Humanism A theoretical orientation that emphasizes the unique qualities of humans, especially their freedom and their potential for personal growth.

Hypnosis A systematic procedure that typically produces a heightened state of suggestibility.

Hypochondriasis A somatoform disorder characterized by excessive preoccupation with health concerns and incessant worry about developing physical illnesses.

Hypothalamus A structure found near the base of the forebrain that is involved in the regulation of basic biological needs.

Hypothesis A tentative statement about the relationship between two or more variables.

I

Id According to Freud, the primitive, instinctive component of personality that operates according to the pleasure principle.

Identical twins Twins that emerge from one zygote that splits for unknown reasons. Also called *monozygotic twins*.

Identification Bolstering self-esteem by forming an imaginary or real alliance with some person or group.

Illusory correlation A misperception that occurs when people estimate that they have encountered more confirmations of an association between social traits than they have actually seen.

Immune response The body's defensive reaction to invasion by bacteria, viral agents, or other foreign substances.

Impossible figures Objects that can be represented in two-dimensional pictures but cannot exist in three-dimensional space.

Inattentional blindness Failure to see visible objects or events because one's attention is focused elsewhere.

Incentive An external goal that has the capacity to motivate behavior.

Inclusive fitness The sum of an individual's own reproductive success plus the effects the organism has on the reproductive success of related others.

Incongruence The degree of disparity between one's self-concept and one's actual experience.

Independent variable In an experiment, a condition or event that an experimenter varies in order to see its impact on another variable.

Individualism Putting personal goals ahead of group goals and defining one's identity in terms of personal attributes rather than group memberships.

Industrial and organizational (I/O) psychology The branch of psychology concerned with human behavior in the work environment.

Industrial psychology Subfield of I/O psychology that deals with the how-to side, including how to select individuals for the right positions, how to evaluate their job performance, how to train them, and how to compensate them.

Inferential statistics Statistics that are used to interpret data and draw conclusions.

Ingroup The group that people belong to and identify with.

Insanity A legal status indicating that a person cannot be held responsible for his or her actions because of mental illness.

Insight In problem solving, the sudden discovery of the correct solution following incorrect attempts based primarily on trial and error.

Insight therapies Psychotherapy methods characterized by verbal interactions intended to enhance clients' self-knowledge and thus promote healthful changes in personality and behavior.

Insomnia Chronic problems in getting adequate sleep.

Instinctive drift The tendency for an animal's innate responses to interfere with conditioning processes.

Integrity tests Standardized measures used to assess attitudes and experience related to honesty and trustworthiness.

Intellectual disability Subnormal general mental ability accompanied by deficiencies in everyday living skills originating prior to age 18.

Intelligence quotient (IQ) A child's mental age divided by chronological age, multiplied by 100.

Intelligence tests Psychological tests that measure general mental ability.

Interference theory The idea that people forget information because of competition from other material.

Intermittent reinforcement A reinforcement schedule in which a designated response is reinforced only some of the time.

Internal attributions Ascribing the causes of behavior to personal dispositions, traits, abilities, and feelings.

Internet addiction Spending an inordinate amount of time on the Internet and being unable to control online use.

Internet-mediated research Studies in which data collection occurs over the web.

Interpersonal attraction Positive feelings toward another.

Interpretation In psychoanalysis, the therapist's attempts to explain the inner significance of the client's thoughts, feelings, memories, and behaviors.

Intimacy Warmth, closeness, and sharing in a relationship.

Introspection Careful, systematic observation of one's own conscious experience.

Involuntary commitment A civil proceeding in which people are hospitalized in psychiatric facilities against their will.

Irreversibility The inability to envision reversing an action.

J

Job satisfaction The positive or negative emotions associated with a job.

Journal A periodical that publishes technical and scholarly material, usually in a narrowly defined area of inquiry.

Just noticeable difference (JND) The smallest difference in the amount of stimulation that a specific sense can detect.

L

Language A set of symbols that convey meaning, and rules for combining those symbols, that can be used to generate an infinite variety of messages.

Language acquisition device (LAD) An innate mechanism or process that facilitates the learning of language.

Latent content According to Freud, the hidden or disguised meaning of the events in a dream.

Latent learning Learning that is not apparent from behavior when it first occurs.

Lateral antagonism A process in the retina that occurs when neural activity in a cell opposes activity in surrounding cells.

Law of effect The principle that if a response in the presence of a stimulus leads to satisfying effects, the association between the stimulus and the response is strengthened.

Leadership The ability to influence and motivate people to pursue organizational goals.

Learned helplessness Passive behavior produced by exposure to unavoidable aversive events.

Learning A relatively durable change in behavior or knowledge that is due to experience.

Lens The transparent eye structure that focuses the light rays falling on the retina.

Lesioning Destroying a piece of the brain.

Levels-of-processing theory The theory holding that deeper levels of mental processing result in longer-lasting memory codes.

Lie detector. See *Polygraph*.

Life changes Any noticeable alterations in one's living circumstances that require readjustment.

Light adaptation The process whereby the eyes become less sensitive to light in high illumination.

Limbic system A densely connected network of structures roughly located along the border between the cerebral cortex and deeper subcortical areas.

Linguistic relativity The theory that one's language determines the nature of one's thought.

Link method Forming a mental image of items to be remembered in a way that links them together.

Long-term memory (LTM) An unlimited capacity store that can hold information over lengthy periods of time.

Long-term potentiation (LTP) A long-lasting increase in neural excitability in synapses along a specific neural pathway.

Longitudinal design A research design in which investigators observe one group of subjects repeatedly over a period of time.

Lowball technique Getting someone to commit to an attractive proposition before revealing the hidden costs.

Lucid dreams Dreams in which people can think clearly about the circumstances of waking life and the fact that they are dreaming, yet they remain asleep in the midst of a vivid dream.

M

Major depressive disorder Mood disorder characterized by persistent feelings of sadness and despair and a loss of interest in previous sources of pleasure.

Manic-depressive disorder See *Bipolar disorder*.

Manifest content According to Freud, the plot of a dream at a surface level.

Matching hypothesis The idea that males and females of approximately equal physical attractiveness are likely to select each other as partners.

Maturation Development that reflects the gradual unfolding of one's genetic blueprint.

MDMA A compound drug related to both amphetamines and hallucinogens, especially mescaline; commonly called "ecstasy."

Mean The arithmetic average of the scores in a distribution.

Mean length of utterance (MLU) The average length of children's spoken statements (measured in phonemes).

Median The score that falls exactly in the center of a distribution of scores.

Medical model The view that it is useful to think of abnormal behavior as a disease.

Meditation A family of mental exercises in which a conscious attempt is made to focus attention in a nonanalytical way.

Menarche The first occurrence of menstruation.

Mental age In intelligence testing, a score that indicates that a child displays the mental ability typical of a child of that chronological (actual) age.

Mental hospital A medical institution specializing in providing inpatient care for psychological disorders.

Mental retardation See *Intellectual disability*.

Mental set Persisting in using problem-solving strategies that have worked in the past.

Mentoring A form of on-the-job training in which a current and often long-term employee (the mentor) is paired with a new employee to aid his or her growth and development within the organization.

Message The information transmitted by a source.

Metalinguistic awareness The ability to reflect on the use of language.

Method of loci A mnemonic device that involves taking an imaginary walk along a familiar path where images of items to be remembered are associated with certain locations.

Midbrain The segment of the brain stem that lies between the hindbrain and the forebrain.

Mirror neurons Neurons that are activated by performing an action or by seeing another monkey or person perform the same action.

Misinformation effect Phenomenon that occurs when participants' recall of an event they witnessed is altered by introducing misleading postevent information.

Mnemonic devices Strategies for enhancing memory.

Mode The score that occurs most frequently in a distribution.

Model A person whose behavior is observed by another.

Monocular depth cues Clues about distance based on the image from either eye alone.

Mood disorders A class of disorders marked by emotional disturbances of varied kinds that may spill over to disrupt physical, perceptual, social, and thought processes.

Mood stabilizers Drugs used to control mood swings in patients with bipolar mood disorders.

Morphemes The smallest units of meaning in a language.

Motion parallax Cue to depth that involves images of objects at different distances moving across the retina at different rates.

Motivated forgetting Purposeful suppression of memories.

Motivation Goal-directed behavior.

Motor development The progression of muscular coordination required for physical activities.

Multiple-personality disorder See *Dissociative identity disorder*.

N

Narcolepsy A disease marked by sudden and irresistible onsets of sleep during normal waking periods.

Narcotics Drugs derived from opium that are capable of relieving pain.

Natural selection Principle stating that heritable characteristics that provide a survival reproductive advantage are more likely than alternative characteristics to be passed on to subsequent generations and thus come to be "selected" over time.

Naturalistic observation A descriptive research method in which the researcher engages in careful, usually prolonged, observation of behavior without intervening directly with the subjects.

Nearsightedness A vision deficiency in which close objects are seen clearly but distant objects appear blurry.

Need for self-actualization The need to fulfill one's potential.

Negative reinforcement The strengthening of a response because it is followed by the removal of an aversive (unpleasant) stimulus.

Negative symptoms Schizophrenic symptoms that involve behavioral deficits, such as flattened emotions, social withdrawal, apathy, impaired attention, and poverty of speech.

Negatively skewed distribution A distribution in which most scores pile up at the high end of the scale.

Nerves Bundles of neuron fibers (axons) that are routed together in the peripheral nervous system.

Neurogenesis The formation of new neurons in the brain.

Neurons Individual cells in the nervous system that receive, integrate, and transmit information.

Neurotransmitters Chemicals that transmit information from one neuron to another.

Night terrors Abrupt awakenings from NREM sleep accompanied by intense autonomic arousal and feelings of panic.

Nightmares Anxiety-arousing dreams that lead to awakening, usually from REM sleep.

Non-REM (NREM) sleep Sleep stages 1 through 4, which are marked by an absence of rapid eye movements, relatively little dreaming, and varied EEG activity.

Nondeclarative memory system Memory for actions, skills, and operations.

Nonsense syllables Consonant-vowel-consonant arrangements that do not correspond to words.

Normal distribution A symmetric, bell-shaped curve that represents the pattern in which many characteristics are dispersed in the population.

Null hypothesis In inferential statistics, the assumption that there is no true relationship between the variables being observed.

O

Obedience A form of compliance that occurs when people follow direct commands, usually from someone in a position of authority.

Obesity The condition of being overweight.

Object permanence Recognizing that objects continue to exist even when they are no longer visible.

Observational learning A type of learning that occurs when an organism's responding is influenced by the observation of others, who are called models.

Obsessive-compulsive disorder (OCD) A type of anxiety disorder marked by persistent, uncontrollable intrusions of unwanted thoughts (obsessions) and urges to engage in senseless rituals (compulsions).

Oedipal complex According to Freud, children's manifestation of erotically tinged desires for their opposite-sex parent, accompanied by feelings of hostility toward their same-sex parent.

Olfactory system The sensory system for smell.

Operant chamber. See *Skinner box*.

Operant conditioning A form of learning in which voluntary responses come to be controlled by their consequences.

Operational definition A definition that describes the actions or operations that will be made to measure or control a variable.

Opiates. See *Narcotics*.

Opponent process theory The theory that color perception depends on receptors that make antagonistic responses to three pairs of colors.

Optic chiasm The point at which the optic nerves from the inside half of each eye cross over and then project to the opposite half of the brain.

Optic disk A hole in the retina where the optic nerve fibers exit the eye.

Optical illusion See *Visual illusion*.

Optimism A general tendency to expect good outcomes.

Organizational culture The shared assumptions, beliefs, values, and customs of the people in an organization.

Organizational psychology Area of psychology concerned with how employees are integrated into the work environment, both emotionally and socially.

Organizational socialization The process by which new members are absorbed into the culture of an organization.

Outgroup People who are not part of the ingroup.

Overextension Using a word incorrectly to describe a wider set of objects or actions than it is meant to.

Overlearning Continued rehearsal of material after one first appears to have mastered it.

Overregularization In children, incorrect generalization of grammatical rules to irregular cases where they do not apply.

P

Panic disorder A type of anxiety disorder characterized by recurrent attacks of overwhelming anxiety that usually occur suddenly and unexpectedly.

Parallel distributed processing (PDP) models Models of memory that assume cognitive processes depend on patterns of activation in highly interconnected computational networks that resemble neural networks. Also called *connectionist models*.

Parallel processing Simultaneously extracting different kinds of information from the same input.

Paranoid schizophrenia A type of schizophrenia that is dominated by delusions of persecution along with delusions of grandeur.

Parasympathetic division The branch of the autonomic nervous system that generally conserves bodily resources.

Parental investment What each sex invests—in terms of time, energy, survival risk, and forgone opportunities—to produce and nurture offspring.

Partial reinforcement. See *Intermittent reinforcement*.

Participants See *Subjects*.

Passionate love A complete absorption in another that includes tender sexual feelings and the agony and ecstasy of intense emotion.

Pavlovian conditioning. See *Classical conditioning*.

Percentile score A figure that indicates the percentage of people who score below the score one has obtained.

Perception The selection, organization, and interpretation of sensory input.

Perceptual asymmetries Left-right imbalances between the cerebral hemispheres in the speed of visual or auditory processing.

Perceptual constancy A tendency to experience a stable perception in the face of continually changing sensory input.

Perceptual hypothesis An inference about which distal stimuli could be responsible for the proximal stimuli sensed.

Perceptual set A readiness to perceive a stimulus in a particular way.

Peripheral nervous system All those nerves that lie outside the brain and spinal cord.

Person perception The process of forming impressions of others.

Personal unconscious According to Jung, the level of awareness that houses material that is not within one's conscious awareness because it has been repressed or forgotten.

Personality An individual's unique constellation of consistent behavioral traits.

Personality disorders A class of psychological disorders marked by extreme, inflexible personality traits that cause subjective distress or impaired social and occupational functioning.

Personality tests Psychological tests that measure various aspects of personality, including motives, interests, values, and attitudes.

Personality trait A durable disposition to behave in a particular way in a variety of situations.

Personnel psychology See *Industrial psychology*.

Phenomenological approach The assumption that one must appreciate individuals' personal, subjective experiences to truly understand their behavior.

Phenotype The ways in which a person's genotype is manifested in observable characteristics.

Phi phenomenon The illusion of movement created by presenting visual stimuli in rapid succession.

Phobias Irrational fears of specific objects or situations.

Phobic disorder A type of anxiety disorder marked by a persistent and irrational fear of an object or situation that presents no realistic danger.

Phonemes The smallest units of sound in a spoken language.

Physical dependence The condition that exists when a person must continue to take a drug to avoid withdrawal illness.

Pictorial depth cues Clues about distance that can be given in a flat picture.

Pituitary gland The "master gland" of the endocrine system; it releases a great variety of hormones that fan out through the body, stimulating actions in the other endocrine glands.

Place theory The idea that perception of pitch corresponds to the vibration of different portions, or places, along the basilar membrane.

Placebo effects The fact that subjects' expectations can lead them to experience some change even though they receive an empty, fake, or ineffectual treatment.

Placenta A structure that allows oxygen and nutrients to pass into the fetus from the mother's bloodstream and bodily wastes to pass out to the mother.

Pleasure principle According to Freud, the principle upon which the id operates, demanding immediate gratification of its urges.

Polygenic traits Characteristics that are influenced by more than one pair of genes.

Polygraph A device that records autonomic fluctuations while a subject is questioned, in an effort to determine whether the subject is telling the truth.

Population The larger collection of animals or people from which a sample is drawn and that researchers want to generalize about.

Positive psychology An approach to psychology that uses theory and research to better understand the positive, adaptive, creative, and fulfilling aspects of human existence.

Positive reinforcement Reinforcement that occurs when a response is strengthened because it is followed by the presentation of a rewarding stimulus.

Positive symptoms Schizophrenic symptoms that involve behavioral excesses or peculiarities, such as hallucinations, delusions, bizarre behavior, and wild flights of ideas.

Positively skewed distribution A distribution in which scores pile up at the low end of the scale.

Postsynaptic potential (PSP) A voltage change at the receptor site on a postsynaptic cell membrane.

Posttraumatic stress disorder (PTSD) Disturbed behavior that is attributed to a major stressful event but that emerges after the stress is over.

Preconscious According to Freud, the level of awareness that contains material just beneath the surface of conscious awareness that can easily be retrieved.

Prejudice A negative attitude held toward members of a group.

Premises The reasons presented to persuade someone that a conclusion is true or probably true.

Prenatal period The period from conception to birth, usually encompassing nine months of pregnancy.

Preparedness Species-specific predispositions to be conditioned in certain ways and not others.

Pressure Expectations or demands that one behave in a certain way.

Prevalence The percentage of a population that exhibits a disorder during a specified time period.

Primary reinforcers Events that are inherently reinforcing because they satisfy biological needs.

Primary sex characteristics The sexual structures necessary for reproduction.

Proactive interference A memory problem that occurs when previously learned information interferes with the retention of new information.

Problem solving Active efforts to discover what must be done to achieve a goal that is not readily available.

Problem space The set of possible pathways to a solution considered by the problem solver.

Prognosis A forecast about the probable course of an illness.

Projection Attributing one's own thoughts, feelings, or motives to another.

Projective tests Psychological tests that ask subjects to respond to vague, ambiguous stimuli in ways that may reveal the subjects' needs, feelings, and personality traits.

Prospective memory The ability to remember to perform actions in the future.

Proximal stimuli The stimulus energies that impinge directly on sensory receptors.

Proximodistal trend The center-outward direction of motor development.

Psychiatrists Physicians who specialize in the diagnosis and treatment of psychological disorders.

Psychiatry A branch of medicine concerned with the diagnosis and treatment of psychological problems and disorders.

Psychoactive drugs Chemical substances that modify mental, emotional, or behavioral functioning.

Psychoanalysis An insight therapy that emphasizes the recovery of unconscious conflicts, motives, and defenses through techniques such as free association and transference.

Psychoanalytic theory A theory developed by Freud that attempts to explain personality, motivation, and mental disorders by focusing on unconscious determinants of behavior.

Psychodynamic theories All the diverse theories descended from the work of Sigmund Freud that focus on unconscious mental forces.

Psychological dependence The condition that exists when a person must continue to take a drug in order to satisfy intense mental and emotional craving for the drug.

Psychological test A standardized measure of a sample of a person's behavior.

Psychology The science that studies behavior and the physiological and cognitive processes that underlie it, and the profession that applies the accumulated knowledge of this science to practical problems.

Psychopharmacotherapy The treatment of mental disorders with medication.

Psychophysics The study of how physical stimuli are translated into psychological experience.

Psychosexual stages According to Freud, developmental periods with a characteristic sexual focus that leave their mark on adult personality.

Psychosomatic diseases Physical ailments with a genuine organic basis that are caused in part by psychological factors, especially emotional distress.

Puberty The period of early adolescence marked by rapid physical growth and the development of sexual (reproductive) maturity.

Pubescence The two-year span preceding puberty during which the changes leading to physical and sexual maturity take place.

Punishment An event that follows a response that weakens or suppresses the tendency to make that response.

Pupil The opening in the center of the iris that helps regulate the amount of light passing into the rear chamber of the eye.

R

Random assignment The constitution of groups in a study such that all subjects have an equal chance of being assigned to any group or condition.

Rationalization Creating false but plausible excuses to justify unacceptable behavior.

Reaction formation Behaving in a way that's exactly the opposite of one's true feelings.

Reaction range Genetically determined limits on IQ or other traits.

Reactivity Alteration of a subject's behavior as a result of the presence of an observer.

Reality monitoring The process of deciding whether memories are based on external sources (our perceptions of actual events) or internal sources (our thoughts and imaginations).

Reality principle According to Freud, the principle on which the ego operates, which seeks to delay gratification of the id's urges until appropriate outlets and situations can be found.

Recall A memory test that requires subjects to reproduce information on their own without any cues.

Receiver The person to whom a message is sent.

Receptive field of a visual cell The retinal area that, when stimulated, affects the firing of that cell.

Recessive gene A gene whose influence is masked when paired genes are different (heterozygous).

Reciprocal determinism The assumption that internal mental events, external environmental events, and overt behavior all influence each other.

Reciprocity Liking those who show that they like you.

Reciprocity norm The rule that people should pay back in kind what they receive from others.

Recognition A memory test that requires subjects to select previously learned information from an array of options.

Refractory period A time following orgasm during which males are largely unresponsive to further stimulation.

Regression A reversion to immature patterns of behavior.

Regression toward the mean Effect that occurs when people who score extremely high or low on some trait are measured a second time and their new score falls closer to the mean (average).

Rehearsal The process of repetitively verbalizing or thinking about information to be stored in memory.

Reification Giving an abstract concept a name and then treating it as though it were a concrete, tangible object.

Reinforcement An event following a response that strengthens the tendency to make that response.

Reinforcement contingencies The circumstances or rules that determine whether responses lead to the presentation of reinforcers.

Relearning A memory test that requires a subject to memorize information a second time to determine how much time or effort is saved by having learned it before.

Reliability The measurement consistency of a test (or of other kinds of measurement techniques).

REM sleep A deep stage of sleep marked by rapid eye movements, high-frequency brain waves, and dreaming.

Renewal effect Phenomenon that occurs if a response is extinguished in a different environment than it was acquired; the extinguished response will reappear if the animal is returned to the original environment where acquisition took place.

Replication The repetition of a study to see whether the earlier results are duplicated.

Representativeness heuristic Basing the estimated probability of an event on how similar it is to the typical prototype of that event.

Repression Keeping distressing thoughts and feelings buried in the unconscious.

Research methods Differing approaches to the manipulation and control of variables in empirical studies.

Resistance Largely unconscious defensive maneuvers a client uses to hinder the progress of therapy.

Resistance to extinction In operant conditioning, the phenomenon that occurs when an organism continues to make a response after delivery of the reinforcer for it has been terminated.

Response set A tendency to respond to questions in a particular way that is unrelated to the content of the questions.

Respondent conditioning. See *Classical conditioning.*

Resting potential The stable, negative charge of a neuron when it is inactive.

Retention The proportion of material retained (remembered).

Retina The neural tissue lining the inside back surface of the eye; it absorbs light, processes images, and sends visual information to the brain.

Retinal disparity A cue to the depth based on the fact that objects within 25 feet project images to slightly different locations on the left and right retinas, so the right and left eyes see slightly different views of the object.

Retrieval Recovering information from memory stores.

Retroactive interference A memory problem that occurs when new information impairs the retention of previously learned information.

Retrograde amnesia Loss of memories for events that occurred prior to a head injury.

Retrospective memory The ability to remember events from the past or previously learned information.

Reuptake A process in which neurotransmitters are sponged up from the synaptic cleft by the presynaptic membrane.

Reversible figure A drawing that is compatible with two different interpretations that can shift back and forth.

Risky decision making Making choices under conditions of uncertainty.

Rods Specialized visual receptors that play a key role in night vision and peripheral vision.

S

Sample The collection of subjects selected for observation in an empirical study.

Sampling bias A problem that occurs when a sample is not representative of the population from which it is drawn.

Scatter diagram A graph in which paired X and Y scores for each subject are plotted as single points.

Schedule of reinforcement A specific presentation of reinforcers over time.

Schema An organized cluster of knowledge about a particular object or sequence of events.

Schizophrenic disorders A class of psychological disorders marked by disturbances in thought that spill over to affect perceptual, social, and emotional processes.

Secondary (conditioned) reinforcers Stimulus events that acquire reinforcing qualities by being associated with primary reinforcers.

Secondary sex characteristics Physical features that are associated with gender but that are not directly involved in reproduction.

Sedatives Sleep-inducing drugs that tend to decrease central nervous system activation and behavioral activity.

Self-actualizing persons People with exceptionally healthy personalities, marked by continued personal growth.

Self-concept A collection of beliefs about one's own nature, unique qualities, and typical behavior.

Self-efficacy One's belief about one's ability to perform behaviors that should lead to expected outcomes.

Self-esteem A person's overall assessment of her or his personal adequacy or worth.

Self-referent encoding Deciding how or whether information is personally relevant.

Self-report inventories Personality tests that ask individuals to answer a series of questions about their characteristic behavior.

Self-serving bias The tendency to attribute one's successes to personal factors and one's failures to situational factors.

Semantic memory system General knowledge that is not tied to the time when the information was learned.

Semantic network Concepts joined together by links that show how the concepts are related.

Semantics The area of language concerned with understanding the meaning of words and word combinations.

Sensation The stimulation of sense organs.

Sensory adaptation A gradual decline in sensitivity to prolonged stimulation.

Sensory memory The preservation of information in its original sensory form for a brief time, usually only a fraction of a second.

Separation anxiety Emotional distress seen in many infants when they are separated from people with whom they have formed an attachment.

Serial-position effect In memory tests, the fact that subjects show better recall for items at the beginning and end of a list than for items in the middle.

Set-point theory The idea that the body monitors fat-cell levels to keep them (and weight) fairly stable.

Settling-point theory The idea that weight tends to drift around a level at which the constellation of factors that determine food consumption and energy expenditure achieve an equilibrium.

Sex The biologically based categories of male and female.

Sexual orientation A person's preference for emotional and sexual relationships with individuals of the same sex, the other sex, or either sex.

Shaping The reinforcement of closer and closer approximations of a desired response.

Short-term memory (STM) A limited-capacity store that can maintain unrehearsed information for about 20 to 30 seconds.

Signal-detection theory A psychophysiological theory proposing that the detection of stimuli involves decision processes as well as sensory processes, which are influenced by a variety of factors besides the physical intensity of a stimulus.

Skinner box A small enclosure in which an animal can make a specific response that is systematically recorded while the consequences of the response are controlled.

Sleep apnea A sleep disorder characterized by frequent reflexive gasping for air that awakens a person and disrupts sleep.

Slow-wave sleep (SWS) Sleep stages 3 and 4, during which low-frequency delta waves become prominent in EEG recordings.

Social comparison theory The idea that people compare themselves with others to understand and evaluate their own behavior.

Social desirability bias A tendency to give socially approved answers to questions about oneself.

Social loafing A reduction in effort by individuals when they work in groups as compared to when they work by themselves.

Social psychology The branch of psychology concerned with the way individuals' thoughts, feelings, and behaviors are influenced by others.

Social roles Widely shared expectations about how people in certain positions are supposed to behave.

Social skills training A behavior therapy designed to improve interpersonal skills that emphasizes shaping, modeling, and behavioral rehearsal.

Social support Various types of aid and succor provided by members of one's social networks.

Socialization The acquisition of the norms, roles, and behaviors expected of people in a particular society.

Soma The cell body of a neuron; it contains the nucleus and much of the chemical machinery common to most cells.

Somatic nervous system The system of nerves that connect to voluntary skeletal muscles and to sensory receptors.

Somatization disorder A type of somatoform disorder marked by a history of diverse physical complaints that appear to be psychological in origin.

Somatoform disorders A class of psychological disorders involving physical ailments with no authentic organic basis that are due to psychological factors.

Somnambulism (sleepwalking) Arising and wandering about while remaining asleep.

Source The person who sends a communication.

Source monitoring The process of making attributions about the origins of memories.

Source-monitoring error An error that occurs when a memory derived from one source is misattributed to another source.

Spermarche The first occurrence of ejaculation.

Split-brain surgery A procedure in which the bundle of fibers that connects the cerebral hemispheres (the corpus callosum) is cut to reduce the severity of epileptic seizures.

Spontaneous recovery In classical conditioning, the reappearance of an extinguished response after a period of nonexposure to the conditioned stimulus.

Spontaneous remission Recovery from a disorder without formal treatment.

SQ3R A study system designed to promote effective reading by means of five steps: survey, question, read, recite, and review.

Stage A developmental period during which characteristic patterns of behavior are exhibited and certain capacities become established.

Standard deviation An index of the amount of variability in a set of data.

Standardization The uniform procedures used in the administration and scoring of a test.

Statistical significance The condition that exists when the probability that the observed findings are due to chance is very low.

Statistics The use of mathematics to organize, summarize, and interpret numerical data. See also *Descriptive statistics, Inferential statistics.*

Stereotypes Widely held beliefs that people have certain characteristics because of their membership in a particular group.

Stimulants Drugs that tend to increase central nervous system activation and behavioral activity.

Stimulus discrimination The phenomenon that occurs when an organism that has learned a response to a specific stimulus does not respond in the same way to stimuli that are similar to the original stimulus.

Stimulus generalization The phenomenon that occurs when an organism that has learned a response to a specific stimulus responds in the same way to new stimuli that are similar to the original stimulus.

Storage Maintaining encoded information in memory over time.

Stress Any circumstances that threaten or are perceived to threaten one's well-being and that thereby tax one's coping abilities.

Striving for superiority According to Adler, the universal drive to adapt, improve oneself, and master life's challenges.

Structuralism A school of psychology based on the notion that the task of psychology is to analyze consciousness into its basic elements and to investigate how these elements are related.

Subjective contours The perception of contours where none actually exist.

Subjective well-being Individuals' perceptions of their overall happiness and life satisfaction.

Subjects The persons or animals whose behavior is systematically observed in a study.

Subliminal perception The registration of sensory input without conscious awareness.

Subtractive color mixing Formation of colors by removing some wavelengths of light, leaving less light than was originally there.

Superego According to Freud, the moral component of personality that incorporates social standards about what represents right and wrong.

Survey A descriptive research method in which researchers use questionnaires or interviews to gather information about specific aspects of subjects' behavior.

Sympathetic division The branch of the autonomic nervous system that mobilizes the body's resources for emergencies.

Synapse A junction where information is transmitted from one neuron to the next.

Synaptic cleft A microscopic gap between the terminal button of a neuron and the cell membrane of another neuron.

Syntax A system of rules that specify how words can be combined into phrases and sentences.

Systematic desensitization A behavior therapy used to reduce clients' anxiety responses through counterconditioning.

T

Tactile system The sensory system for touch.

Tardive dyskinesia A neurological disorder marked by chronic tremors and involuntary spastic movements.

Teams See *Work teams.*

Telegraphic speech Speech that consists mainly of content words; articles, prepositions, and other less critical words are omitted.

Temperament An individual's characteristic mood, activity level, and emotional reactivity.

Terminal buttons Small knobs at the end of axons that secrete chemicals called neurotransmitters.

Test norms Standards that provide information about where a score on a psychological test ranks in relation to other scores on that test.

Testosterone A male sex hormone produced by the testes; women secrete smaller amounts of testosterone from the adrenal cortex and ovary.

Testwiseness The ability to use the characteristics and format of a cognitive test to maximize one's score.

Theory A system of interrelated ideas that is used to explain a set of observations.

Theory of bounded rationality Simon's assertion that people tend to use simple strategies in decision making that focus on only a few facets of available options and often result in "irrational" decisions that are less than optimal.

Tip-of-the-tongue phenomenon A temporary inability to remember something accompanied by a feeling that it's just out of reach.

Token economy A system for doling out symbolic reinforcers that are exchanged later for a variety of genuine reinforcers.

Tolerance A progressive decrease in a person's responsiveness to a drug.

Top-down processing In form perception, a progression from the whole to the elements.

Transcranial magnetic stimulation (TMS) A technique that permits scientists to temporarily enhance or depress activity in a specific area of the brain.

Transfer-appropriate processing The situation that occurs when the initial processing of information is similar to the type of processing required by the subsequent measures of attention.

Transference In therapy, the phenomenon that occurs when clients start relating to their therapists in ways that mimic critical relationships in their lives.

Transformational leadership Leadership characterized by high ethical standards, inspirational motivation, intellectual stimulation, and individual consideration.

Trial In classical conditioning, any presentation of a stimulus or pair of stimuli.

Trial and error Trying possible solutions sequentially and discarding those that are in error until one works.

Trichromatic theory The theory of color vision holding that the human eye has three types of receptors with differing sensitivities to different wavelengths.

Twin studies A research design in which hereditary influence is assessed by comparing the resemblance of identical twins and fraternal twins with respect to a trait.

Type A personality Personality characterized by (1) a strong competitive orientation, (2) impatience and time urgency, and (3) anger and hostility.

Type B personality Personality characterized by relatively relaxed, patient, easygoing, amicable behavior.

U

Unconditioned response (UR) An unlearned reaction to an unconditioned stimulus that occurs without previous conditioning.

Unconditioned stimulus (US) A stimulus that evokes an unconditioned response without previous conditioning.

Unconscious According to Freud, thoughts, memories, and desires that are well below the surface of conscious awareness but that nonetheless exert great influence on behavior.

Underextensions Errors that occur when a child incorrectly uses a word to describe a narrower set of objects or actions than it is meant to.

Undifferentiated schizophrenia A type of schizophrenia marked by idiosyncratic mixtures of schizophrenic symptoms.

V

Validity The ability of a test to measure what it was designed to measure.

Variability The extent to which the scores in a data set tend to vary from each other and from the mean.

Variable-interval (VI) schedule A reinforcement schedule in which the reinforcer is given for the first response after a variable time interval has elapsed.

Variable-ratio (VR) schedule A reinforcement schedule in which the reinforcer is given after a variable number of nonreinforced responses.

Variables Any measurable conditions, events, characteristics, or behaviors that are controlled or observed in a study.

Vasocongestion Engorgement of blood vessels.

Visual illusion An apparently inexplicable discrepancy between the appearance of a visual stimulus and its physical reality.

Volley principle The theory holding that groups of auditory nerve fibers fire neural impulses in rapid succession, creating volleys of impulses.

W

Work teams Two or more employees who have common goals, pursue tasks that are interdependent, interact socially, and work within specific requirements and rules.

Z

Zone of proximal development (ZPD) The gap between what a learner can accomplish alone and what he or she can achieve with guidance from more skilled partners.

Zygote A one-celled organism formed by the union of a sperm and an egg.

REFERENCES

Aamodt, M. G. (2007). *Industrial/organizational psychology: An applied approach.* Belmont, CA: Wadsworth.

Aamodt, M. G., & Rupert, G. T. (1990). Employee referral programs: Do successful employees refer better applicants than unsuccessful employees? *Proceedings of the Annual Meeting of the International Personnel Management Association Assessment Council,* San Diego, CA.

Abdel-Khalek, A. M. (2006). Happiness, health, and religiosity: Significant relations. *Mental Health, 9*(1), 85–97.

Abel, M. H. (1998). Interaction of humor and gender in moderating relationships between stress and outcomes. *Journal of Psychology, 132,* 267–276.

Abel, M. H. (2002). Humor, stress, and coping strategies. *Humor: International Journal of Humor Research, 15,* 365–381.

Abi-Dargham, A. (2004). Do we still believe in the dopamine hypothesis? New data bring new evidence. *International Journal of Neuropsychopharmacology, 7*(Supplement 1), S1–S5.

Aboud, F. E., & Amato, M. (2001). Developmental and socialization influences on intergroup bias. In R. Brown & S. L. Gaertner (Eds.), *Blackwell handbook of social psychology: Intergroup processes.* Malden, MA: Blackwell.

Abraham, W. C. (2006). Memory maintenance. *Current Directions in Psychological Science, 15*(1), 5–8.

Abramowitz, A. J., & O'Leary, S. G. (1990). Effectiveness of delayed punishment in an applied setting. *Behavior Therapy, 21,* 231–239.

Abrams, R. (1992). *Electroconvulsive therapy.* New York: Oxford University Press.

Abrams, R. (2000). Electroconvulsive therapy requires higher dosage levels: Food and Drug Administration action is required. *General Psychiatry, 57,* 445–446.

Abrams, R. L., Klinger, M. R., & Greenwald, A. G. (2002). Subliminal words activate semantic categories (not automated motor responses). *Psychonomic Bulletin & Review, 9*(1), 100–106.

Abramson, L. Y., Alloy, L. B., Hankin, B. L., Haeffel, G. J., MacCoon, D. G., & Gibb, B. E. (2002). Cognitive vulnerability-stress models of depression in a self-regulatory and psychobiological context. In I. H. Gotlib & C. L. Hammen (Eds.), *Handbook of depression.* New York: Guilford.

Abramson, L. Y., Seligman, M. E. P., & Teasdale, J. (1978). Learned helplessness in humans: Critique and reformulation. *Journal of Abnormal Psychology, 87,* 32–48.

Accornero, V. H., Amado, A. J., Morrow, C. E., Xue, L., Anthony, J. C., & Bandstra, E. S. (2007). Impact of prenatal cocaine exposure on attention and response inhibition as assessed by continuous performance tests. *Journal of Developmental & Behavioral Pediatrics, 28,* 195–205.

Acker, M. M., & O'Leary, S. G. (1996). Inconsistency of mothers' feedback and toddlers' misbehavior and negative affect. *Journal of Abnormal Child Psychology, 24,* 703–714.

Ackerman, P. L., & Beier, M. E. (2005). Knowledge and intelligence. In O. Wilhelm & R. W. Engle (Eds.), *Handbook of understanding and measuring intelligence.* Thousand Oaks, CA: Sage.

Adam, T. C., & Epel, E. (2007). Stress, eating and the reward system. *Physiology and Behavior, 91,* 449–458.

Adamopoulos, J., & Lonner, W. J. (2001). Culture and psychology at a crossroad: Historical perspective and theoretical analysis. In D. Matsumoto (Ed.), *The handbook of culture and psychology.* New York: Oxford University Press.

Adams, J. L. (1980). *Conceptual blockbusting.* San Francisco: W. H. Freeman.

Adams, R. L., & Culbertson, J. L. (2005). Personality assessment: Adults and children. In B. J. Sadock & V. A. Sadock (Eds.), *Kaplan & Sadock's comprehensive textbook of psychiatry.* Philadelphia: Lippincott Williams & Wilkins.

Ader, R. (2001). Psychoneuroimmunology. *Current Directions in Psychological Science, 10*(3), 94–98.

Ader, R. (2003). Conditioned immunomodulation: Research needs and directions. *Brain, Behavior, and Immunity, 17*(1), S51–S57.

Ader, R., & Cohen, N. (1984). Behavior and the immune system. In W. D. Gentry (Ed.), *Handbook of behavioral medicine.* New York: Guilford.

Ader, R., & Cohen, N. (1993). Psychoneuroimmunology: Conditioning and stress. *Annual Review of Psychology, 44,* 53–85.

Adler, A. (1917). *Study of organ inferiority and its psychical compensation.* New York: Nervous and Mental Diseases Publishing Co.

Adler, A. (1927). *Practice and theory of individual psychology.* New York: Harcourt, Brace & World.

Adler, L. L. (Ed.). (1993). *International handbook on gender roles.* Westport, CT: Greenwood.

Adolph, K. E., & Berger, S. E. (2005). Physical and motor development. In M. H. Bornstein & M. E. Lamb (Eds.), *Developmental science: An advanced textbook.* Mahwah, NJ: Erlbaum.

Affleck, G., Tennen, H., Urrows, S., & Higgins, P. (1994). Person and contextual features of daily stress reactivity: Individual differences in relations of undesirable daily events with mood disturbance and chronic pain intensity. *Journal of Personality and Social Psychology, 66,* 329–340.

Agnoli, F., & Krantz, D. H. (1989). Suppressing natural heuristics by formal instruction: The case of the conjunction fallacy. *Cognitive Psychology, 21,* 515–550.

Ahima, R. S., & Osei, S. Y. (2004). Leptin signaling. *Physiology & Behavior, 81,* 223–241.

Ahn, H., & Wampold, B. E. (2001). Where oh where are the specific ingredients? A meta-analysis of component studies in counseling and psychotherapy. *Journal of Counseling Psychology, 48,* 251–257.

Aikins, D. E., & Craske, M. G. (2001). Cognitive theories of generalized anxiety disorder. *Psychiatric Clinics of North America, 24*(1), 57–74.

Ainsworth, M. D. S. (1979). Attachment as related to mother-infant interaction. In J. S. Rosenblatt, R. A. Hinde, C. Beer, & M. Busnel (Eds.), *Advances in the study of behavior* (Vol. 9). New York: Academic Press.

Ainsworth, M. D. S., Blehar, M. C., Waters, E., & Wall, S. (1978). *Patterns of attachment: A psychological study of the strange situation.* Hillsdale, NJ: Erlbaum.

Ajzen, I., & Fishbein, M. (2000). Attitudes and the attitude-behavior relation: Reasoned and automatic processes. In W. Stroebe & M. Hewstone (Eds.), *European review of social psychology* (Vol. 11). Chichester, UK: Wiley.

Ajzen, I., & Fishbein, M. (2005). The influence of attitudes on behavior. In D. Albarracin, B. T. Johnson, & M. P. Zanna (Eds.), *The handbook of attitudes.* Mahwah, NJ: Erlbaum.

Akarian, A. V., Bushnell, M. C., Treede, R.-D., & Zubieta, J.-K. (2005). Human brain mechanisms of pain perception and regulation in health and disease. *European Journal of Pain, 9,* 463–484.

Akerstedt, T., Hume, K., Minors, D., & Waterhouse, J. (1997). Good sleep—its timing and physiological sleep characteristics. *Journal of Sleep Research, 6,* 221–229.

Akgun, S., & Ciarrochi, J. (2003). Learned resourcefulness moderates the relationship between academic stress and academic performance. *Educational Psychology, 23,* 287–294.

Akimoto, S. A., & Sanbonmatsu, D. M. (1999). Differences in self-effacing behavior between European and Japanese Americans: Effect on competence evaluations. *Journal of Cross-Cultural Psychology, 30,* 159–177.

Akiskal, H. S. (2005). Mood disorders: Clinical features. In B. J. Sadock & V. A. Sadock (Eds.), *Kaplan & Sadock's comprehensive textbook of psychiatry.* Philadelphia: Lippincott Williams & Wilkins.

Albert, M. S., & Killiany, R. J. (2001). Age-related cognitive change and brain-behavior relationships. In J. E. Birren & K. W. Schaie (Eds.), *Handbook of the psychology of aging* (5th ed., pp. 160–184). San Diego, CA: Academic Press.

Albert, M. S., & Moss, M. B. (2002). Neuropsychological approaches to preclinical identification of Alzheimer's disease. In L. R. Squire & D. L. Schacter (Eds.), *Neuropsychology of memory.* New York: Guilford.

Alcock, J. (1998). *Animal behavior: An evolutionary approach.* Sunderland, MA: Sinauer Associates.

Alcock, J. (2005). *Animal behavior.* Sunderland, MA: Sinauer Associates.

Aldag, R. J., & Fuller, S. R. (1993). Beyond fiasco: A reappraisal of the groupthink phenomenon and a new model of group decision processes. *Psychological Bulletin, 113,* 533–552.

Aldington, S., Harwood, M., Cox, B., Weatherall, M., Beckert, L., Hansell, A., et al. (2008). Cannabis use and risk of lung cancer: A case-control study. *European Respiratory Journal, 31,* 280–286.

Aldington, S., Williams, M., Nowitz, M., Weatherall, M., Pritchard, A., McNaughton, A., et al. (2007). Effects of cannabis on pulmonary structure, function and symptoms. *Thorax, 62,* 1058–1063.

Aldrich, M. S. (2000). Cardinal manifestations of sleep disorders. In M. H. Kryger, T. Roth & W. C. Dement (Eds), *Principles and practice of sleep medicine.* Philadelphia: Saunders.

Aldwin, C. M., & Gilmer, D. F. (2004). *Health, illness, and optimal aging: Biological and psychosocial perspectives.* Thousand Oaks, CA: Sage Publications.

Alexander, C. N., Davies, J. L., Dixon, C. A., Dillbeck, M. C., Druker, S. M., Oetzel, R. M., Muehlman, J. M., & Orme-Johnson, D. W. (1990). Growth of higher states of consciousness: The Vedic psychology of human development. In C. N. Alexander & E. J. Langer (Eds.), *Higher stages of human development: Perspectives on adult growth*. New York: Oxford University Press.

Alexander, C. N., Robinson, P., Orme-Johnson, D. W., Schneider, R. H., et al. (1994). The effects of transcendental meditation compared with other methods of relaxation and meditation in reducing risk factors, morbidity, and mortality. *Homeostasis in Health & Disease, 35,* 243–263.

Alexander, F. (1954). Psychoanalysis and psychotherapy. *Journal of the American Psychoanalytic Association, 2,* 722–733.

Alexander, J., & Tate, M. (1999). *Web wisdom: How to evaluate and create information quality on the web.* Mahwah, NJ: Erlbaum.

Alexander, M. G., & Fisher, T. D. (2003). Truth and consequences: Using the bogus pipeline to examine sex differences in self-reported sexuality. *Journal of Sex Research, 40*(1), 27–35.

Allan, R. W. (1998). Operant-respondent interactions. In W. O'Donohue (Ed.), *Learning and behavior therapy*. Boston: Allyn & Bacon.

Allen, J. J. B., & Iacono, W. G. (2001). Assessing the validity of amnesia in dissociative identity disorder: A dilemma for the DSM and the courts. *Psychology, Public Policy, and Law, 7,* 311–344.

Allen, M. J., Noel, R., Degan, J., Halpern, D. F., & Crawford, C. (2000). *Goals and objectives for the undergraduate psychology major: Recommendations from a meeting of the California State University psychology faculty.* Distributed by the Office of Teaching Resources in Psychology, Society for the Teaching of Psychology: Available at http://www.lemoyne.edu/OTRP/otrpresources/otrpoutcomes.html.

Allen, M., Emmers, T., Gebhardt, L., & Giery, M. A. (1995). Exposure to pornography and acceptance of rape myths. *Journal of Communication, 45,* 5–26.

Allen, T. D., Lentz, E., & Day, R. (2006). Career success outcomes associated with mentoring others: A comparison of mentors and nonmentors. *Journal of Career Development, 32,* 272–285.

Allgood, W. P., Risko, V. J., Alvarez, M. C., & Fairbanks, M. M. (2000). Factors that influence study. In R. F. Flippo & D. C. Caverly (Eds.), *Handbook of college reading and study strategy research.* Mahwah, NJ: Erlbaum.

Allison, D. B., Heshka, S., Neale, M. C., Lykken, D. T., & Heymsfield, S. B. (1994). A genetic analysis of relative weight among 4,020 twin pairs, with an emphasis on sex effects. *Health Psychology, 13,* 362–365.

Alloy, L. B., Abramson, L. Y., Whitehouse, W. G., Hogan, M. E., Tashman, N. A., Steinberg, D. L., Rose, D. T., & Donovan, P. (1999). Depressogenic cognitive styles: Predictive validity, information processing and personality characteristics, and developmental origins. *Behavioral Research and Therapy, 37,* 503–531.

Allport, G. W. (1937). *Personality: A psychological interpretation.* New York: Holt.

Almeida, D. M. (2005). Resilience and vulnerability to daily stressors assessed via diary methods. *Current Directions in Psychological Science, 14*(2), 64–68.

Alonso, A., Alonso, S., & Piper, W. (2003). Group psychotherapy. In G. Stricker & T. A. Widiger (Eds.), *Handbook of psychology, Vol. 8: Clinical psychology.* New York: Wiley.

Altman, I. (1990). Centripetal and centrifugal trends in psychology. In L. Brickman & H. Ellis (Eds.), *Preparing psychologists for the 21st century: Proceedings of the National Conference on Graduate Education in Psychology.* Hillsdale, NJ: Erlbaum.

Altmann, E. M., & Gray, W. D. (2002). Forgetting to remember: The functional relationship of decay and interference. *Psychological Science, 13*(1), 27–33.

Altshuler, L. L., Suppes, T., Black, D. O., Nolen, W. A., Leverich, G., Keck, P. E., Jr., et al. (2006). Lower switch rate in depressed patients with Bipolar II than Bipolar I disorder treated adjunctively with second-generation antidepressants. *American Journal of Psychiatry, 163,* 313–315.

Amabile, T. M. (1996). *Creativity in context.* Boulder, CO: Westview.

Amabile, T. M. (2001). Beyond talent: John Irving and the passionate craft of creativity. *American Psychologist, 56,* 333–336.

Amato, P. R. (2001). The consequences of divorce for adults and children. In R. M. Milardo (Ed.), *Understanding families into the new millenium: A decade in review.* Minneapolis: National Council on Family Relations.

Amato, P. R. (2003). Reconciling divergent perspectives: Judith Wallerstein, quantitative family research and children of divorce. *Family Relations: Interdisciplinary Journal of Applied Family Studies, 52,* 332–339.

Amedi, A., Floel, A., Knecht, S., Zohary, E., & Cohen, L. G. (2004). Transcranial magnetic stimulation of the occipital pole interferes with verbal processing in blind subjects. *Nature Neuroscience, 7,* 1266–1270.

American Association of Suicidology. (2007). *Understanding and helping the suicidal individual.* Retrieved April 12, 2007 from http://www.suicidology.org/associations/1045/files/Understanding.pdf.

American Foundation for Suicide Prevention. (2007). *When you fear someone may take their own life.* Retrieved April 12, 2007 from http://www.afsp.org/index.cfm?page_id=F2F25092-7E90-9BD4-C4658F1D2B5D19A0

American Psychiatric Association Task Force on Electroconvulsive Therapy. (2001). *The practice of electroconvulsive therapy: Recommendations for treatment* (2nd ed.). Washington, DC: American Psychiatric Association.

American Psychiatric Association. (1952). *Diagnostic and statistical manual of mental disorders.* Washington, DC: Author.

American Psychiatric Association. (1968). *Diagnostic and statistical manual of mental disorders* (2nd ed.). Washington, DC: Author.

American Psychiatric Association. (1980). *Diagnostic and statistical manual of mental disorders* (3rd ed.). Washington, DC: Author.

American Psychiatric Association. (1987). *Diagnostic and statistical manual of mental disorders* (3rd ed., rev.). Washington, DC: Author.

American Psychiatric Association. (1994). *Diagnostic and statistical manual of mental disorders* (4th ed.). Washington, DC: Author.

American Psychiatric Association. (2000). *Diagnostic and statistical manual of mental disorders* (4th ed. Text revision). Washington, DC: Author.

American Psychological Association. (1984). *Behavioral research with animals.* Washington, DC: Author.

American Psychological Association. (2002). Ethical principles of psychologists and code of conduct. *American Psychologist, 57,* 1060–1073.

American Psychological Association. (2007). *APA guidelines for the undergraduate psychology major.* Washington, DC: American Psychological Association.

Ammaniti, M., Speranza, A. M., & Fedele, S. (2005). Attachment in infancy and in early and late childhood: A longitudinal study. In K. A. Kerns, & R. A. Richardson (Eds.), *Attachment in middle childhood.* New York: Guilford.

Amodio, D. M., Harmon-Jones, E., Devine, P. G., Curtin, J. J., Hartley, S. L., & Covert, A. E. (2004). Neural signals for the detection of unintentional race bias. *Psychological Science, 15*(2), 88–93.

Anand, B. K., & Brobeck, J. R. (1951). Hypothalamic control of food intake in rats and cats. *Yale Journal of Biology and Medicine, 24,* 123–140.

Anderluh, M. B., Tchanturia, K., & Rabe-Hesketh. (2003). Childhood obsessive-compulsive personality traits in adult women with eating disorders: Defining a broader eating disorder phenotype. *American Journal of Psychiatry, 160,* 242–247.

Anderson, A. E., & Yager, J. (2005). Eating disorders. In B. J. Sadock & V. A. Sadock (Eds.), *Kaplan & Sadock's comprehensive textbook of psychiatry.* Philadelphia: Lippincott Williams & Wilkins.

Anderson, B. (2003). Brain imaging and g. In H. Nyborg (Ed.), *The scientific study of general intelligence: Tribute to Arthur R. Jensen.* Oxford, UK: Pergamon.

Anderson, B. F. (1980). *The complete thinker.* Englewood Cliffs, NJ: Prentice-Hall.

Anderson, C., Keltner, D., & John, O. P. (2003). Emotional convergence between people over time. *Journal of Personality and Social Psychology, 84,* 1054–1068.

Anderson, C. A. (2004). An update on the effects of playing violent video games. *Journal of Adolescence, 27*(1), 113–122.

Anderson, C. A., Berkowitz, L., Donnerstein, E., Huesman, L. R., Johnson, J. D., Linz, D., Malamuth, N. M. , & Wartella, E. (2003). The influence of media violence on youth. *Psychological Science in the Public Interest, 4*(3), 81–110.

Anderson, E. A., Kohler, J. K., & Letiecq, B. L. (2002). Low-income fathers and "Responsible Fatherhood" programs: A qualitative investigation of participants' experiences. *Family Relations, 51,* 148–155.

Anderson, K. J. (1990). Arousal and the inverted-U hypothesis: A critique of Neiss's "reconceptualizing arousal." *Psychological Bulletin, 107,* 96–100.

Anderson, M. C., & Neely, J. H. (1996). Interference and inhibition in memory retrieval. In E. L. Bjork & R. A. Bjork (Eds.), *Memory.* San Diego: Academic Press.

Anderson, N., & Thomas, H. D. C. (1996). Work group socialization. In M. A. West (Ed.), *Handbook of work group psychology* (pp. 423–450). Chichester, UK: Wiley.

Anderson, S. E., Dallal, G. E., & Must, A. (2003). Relative weight and race influence average age at menarche: Results from two nationally representative surveys of U.S. girls studied 25 years apart. *Pediatrics, 111,* 844–850.

Anderson, V. N. (1992). For whom is this world just? Sexual orientation and AIDS. *Journal of Applied Social Psychology, 22*(3), 248–259.

Anderson-Fye, E. P., & Becker, A. E. (2004). Sociocultural aspects of eating disorders and obesity. In J. K. Thompson (Ed.), *Handbook of eating disorders and obesity.* New York: Wiley.

Andreasen, N. C. (1987). Creativity and mental illness: Prevalence rates in writers and their first-degree relatives. *American Journal of Psychiatry, 144,* 1288–1292.

Andreasen, N. C. (1990). Positive and negative symptoms: Historical and conceptual aspects. In N. C. Andreasen (Ed.), *Modern problems of pharmacopsychiatry: Positive and negative symptoms and syndromes.* Basel: Karger.

Andreasen, N. C. (1996). Creativity and mental illness: A conceptual and historical overview. In J. J. Schildkraut & A. Otero (Eds.), *Depression and the spiritual in modern art: Homage to Miro.* New York: Wiley.

Andreasen, N. C. (2001). *Brave new brain: Conquering mental illness in the era of the human genome.* New York: Oxford University Press.

Andreasen, N. C. (2005). *The creating brain: The neuroscience of genius.* New York: Dana Press.

Andrews, B. (2001). Recovered memories in therapy: Clinicians' beliefs and practices. In G. M. Davies & T. Dalgleish (Eds.), *Recovered memories: Seeking the middle ground.* Chichester, England: Wiley.

Angell, M. (2000). Is academic medicine for sale? *New England Journal of Medicine, 342,* 1516–1518.

Angell, M. (2004). *The truth about the drug companies: How they deceive us and what to do about it.* New York: Random House.

Anglin, J. M. (1993). Vocabulary development: A morphological analysis. *Monographs of the Society for Research in Child Development, 58.*

Annemiek, V. (2004). Residual effects of hypnotics: Epidemiology and clinical implications. *CNS Drugs, 18,* 297–328.

Anthony, I. C., & Bell, J. E. (2008). The neuropathology of HIV/AIDS. *International Review of Psychiatry, 20*(1), 15–24.

Antonuccio, D. O., Danton, W. G., & McClanahan, T. M. (2003). Psychology in the prescription era: Building a firewall between marketing and science. *American Psychologist, 58,* 1028–1043.

Antony, M. M., & McCabe, R. E. (2003). Anxiety disorders: Social and specific phobias. In A. Tasman, J. Kay, & J. A. Lieberman (Eds.), *Psychiatry.* New York: Wiley.

Antrobus, J. (1993). Characteristics of dreams. In M. A. Carskadon (Ed.), *Encyclopedia of sleep and dreaming.* New York: Macmillan.

Antrobus, J. (2000). Theories of dreaming. In M. H. Kryger, T. Roth & W. C. Dement (Eds.), *Principles and practice of sleep medicine.* Philadelphia: Saunders.

Apkarian, A. V., Bushnell, M. C., Treede, R., & Zubieta, J. (2005). Human brain mechanisms of pain perception and regulation in health and disease. *European Journal of Pain, 9,* 463–484.

Appelbaum, P. S. (2002). Responses to the presidential debate—The systematic defunding of psychiatric care: A crisis at our doorstep. *American Journal of Psychiatry, 159,* 1638–1640.

Appleby, D. (2000). Job skills valued by employers who interview psychology majors. *Eye on Psi Chi, 4*(3), 17.

Appleton, K. M., Gentry, R. C., & Shepherd, R. (2006). Evidence of a role for conditioning in the development of liking for flavours in humans in everyday life. *Physiology & Behavior, 87,* 478–486.

Aquilino, W. S. (2006). Family relationships and support systems in emerging adulthood. In J. J. Arnett & J. L. Tanner (Eds.), *Emerging adults in America: Coming of age in the 21st century.* Washington, DC: American Psychological Association.

Archer, J. (1996). Sex differences in social behavior: Are the social role and evolutionary explanations compatible? *American Psychologist, 51,* 909–917.

Archer, J. (2005). Are women or men the more aggressive sex? In S. Fein, G. R. Goethals, & M. J. Sansdtrom (Eds.), *Gender and aggression: Interdisciplinary perspectives.* Mahwah, NJ: Erlbaum.

Archer, J. (2006). Testosterone and human aggression: An evaluation of the challenge hypothesis. *Neuroscience and Biobehavioral Reviews, 30,* 319–345.

Archibald, A. B., Graber, J. A., & Brooks–Gunn, J. (2003). Pubertal processes and physiological growth in adolescence. In G. R. Adams & M. D. Berzonsky (Eds.), *Blackwell handbook of adolescence.* Malden, MA: Blackwell Publishing.

Arendt, J., & Skene, D. J. (2005). Melatonin as a chronobiotic. *Sleep Medicine Review, 9*(1), 25–39.

Arendt, J., Stone, B., & Skene, D. J. (2005). Sleep disruption in jet lag and other circadian rhythm-related disorders. In M. H. Kryger, T. Roth, & W. C. Dement (Eds.). *Principles and practice of sleep medicine.* Philadelphia: Elsevier Saunders.

Argyle, M. (1987). *The psychology of happiness.* London: Methuen.

Argyle, M. (1999). Causes and correlates of happiness. In D. Kahneman, E. Diener & N. Schwarz (Eds.), *Well-being: The foundations of hedonic psychology.* New York: Russell Sage Foundation.

Argyle, M. (2001). *The psychology of happiness.* New York: Routledge.

Arien, M. (2003). Inattentional blindness: Looking without seeing. *Current Directions in Psychological Science, 12*(5), 180–184.

Arkes, H. R., Wortmann, R. L., Saville, P. D., & Harkness, A. R. (1981). Hindsight bias among physicians weighing the likelihood of diagnoses. *Journal of Applied Psychology, 66,* 252–254.

Arkowitz, H. (1992). Integrative theories of therapy. In D. K. Freedheim (Ed.), *History of psychotherapy: A century of change.* Washington, DC: American Psychological Association.

Arkowitz, H., & Lilienfeld, S. O. (2007). The best medicine? How drugs stack up against talk therapy for the treatment of depression. *Scientific American Mind, 18*(5), 80–83.

Armbruster, B. B. (2000). Taking notes from lectures. In R. F. Flippo & D. C. Caverly (Eds.), *Handbook of college reading and study strategy research.* Mahwah, NJ: Erlbaum.

Arndt, J., Cook, A., & Routledge, C. (2004). The blueprint of terror management: Understanding the cognitive architecture of psychological defense against the awareness of death. In J. Greenberg, S. L. Koole, & T. Pyszczynski (Eds.), *Handbook of experimental existential psychology.* New York: Guilford.

Arndt, J., Goldenberg, J. L., Greenberg, J., Pyszczynski, T., & Solomon, S. (2000). Death can be hazardous to your health: Adaptive and ironic consequences of defenses against the terror of death. In P. R. Duberstein & J. M. Masling (Eds.), *Psychodynamic perspectives on sickness and health.* Washington, DC: American Psychological Association.

Arnett, J. J. (1999). Adolescent storm and stress, reconsidered. *American Psychologist, 54,* 317–326.

Arnett, J. J. (2000). Emerging adulthood: A theory of development from the late teens through the twenties. *American Psychologist, 55,* 469–480.

Arnett, J. J. (2001). Conceptions of the transition to adulthood: Perspectives from adolescence to midlife. *Journal of Adult Development, 8,* 133–143.

Arnett. J. J. (2004). *Emerging adulthood: The winding road from the late teens through the twenties.* New York: Oxford University Press.

Arnett, J. J. (2006). Emerging adulthood: Understanding the new way of coming of age. In J. J. Arnett & J. L. Tanner (Eds.), *Emerging adults in America: Coming of age in the 21st century.* Washington, DC: American Psychological Association.

Arnkoff, D. B., & Glass, C. R. (1992). Cognitive therapy and psychotherapy. In D. K. Freedheim (Ed.), *History of psychotherapy: A century of change.* Washington, DC: American Psychological Association.

Arnold, L. M. (2000). Psychocutaneous disorders. In B. J. Sadock & V. A. Sadock (Eds.), *Kaplan and Sadock's comprehensive textbook of psychiatry* (7th ed., pp. 1818–1827). Philadelphia: Lippincott Williams & Wilkins.

Aron, A., Fisher, H., & Mashek, D. J. (2005). Reward, motivation, and emotion systems associated with early–stage intense romantic love. *Journal of Neurophysiology, 94*(1), 327–337.

Aronson, E., & Mills, J. (1959). The effect of severity of initiation on liking for a group. *Journal of Abnormal and Social Psychology, 59,* 177–181.

Arrigo, J. M., & Pezdek, K. (1997). Lessons from the study of psychogenic amnesia. *Current Directions in Psychological Science, 6,* 148–152.

Arthur, J. B. (1994). Effects of human resource systems on manufacturing performance and turnover. *Academy of Management Journal, 37,* 670–687.

Asch, S. E. (1951). Effects of group pressure on the modification and distortion of judgments. In H. Guetzkow (Ed.), *Groups, leadership, and men.* Pittsburgh: Carnegie Press.

Asch, S. E. (1955). Opinions and social pressures. *Scientific American, 193*(5), 31–35.

Asch, S. E. (1956). Studies of independence and conformity: A minority of one against a unanimous majority. *Psychological Monographs, 70*(9, Whole No. 416).

Asendorpf, J. B., & Ostendorf, F. (1998). Is self-enhancement healthy? Conceptual, psychometric, and empirical analysis. *Journal of Personality and Social Psychology, 74,* 955–966.

Ashford, J. W., & Mortimer, J. A. (2002). Non-familial Alzheimer's disease is mainly due to genetic factors. *Journal of Alzheimer's Disease, 4,* 169–177.

Ashton, M. C., Lee, K., & Goldberg, L. R. (2004). A hierarchical analysis of 1,710 English personality-descriptive adjectives. *Journal of Personality and Social Psychology, 87,* 707–721.

Aspinwall, L. G., Richter, L., & Hoffman R. R., III. (2001). Understanding how optimism works: An examination of optimists' adaptive moderation of belief and behavior. In E. C. Chang (Ed.), *Optimism and pessimism: Implications for theory, research, and practice* (pp. 217–238). Washington, DC: American Psychological Association.

Assefi, S. L., & Garry, M. (2003). Absolut® memory distortions: Alcohol placebos influence the misinformation effect. *Psychological Science, 14*(1), 77–80.

Atkinson, J. W. (1974). The mainsprings of achievement-oriented activity. In J. W. Atkinson & J. O. Raynor (Eds.), *Motivation and achievement.* New York: Wiley.

Atkinson, J. W. (1981). Studying personality in the context of an advanced motivational psychology. *American Psychologist, 36,* 117–128.

Atkinson, J. W. (1992). Motivational determinants of thematic apperception. In C. P. Smith (Ed.), *Motivation and personality: Handbook of thematic content analysis.* New York: Cambridge University Press.

Atkinson, J. W., & Litwin, G. H. (1960). Achievement motive and test anxiety conceived as motive to approach success and to avoid failure. *Journal of Abnormal and Social Psychology, 60,* 52–63.

Atkinson, R. C., & Shiffrin, R. M. (1968). Human memory: A proposed system and its control processes. In K. W. Spence & J. T. Spence (Eds.), *The psychology of learning and motivation* (Vol. 2). New York: Academic Press.

Atkinson, R. C., & Shiffrin, R. M. (1971). The control of short-term memory. *Scientific American, 225,* 82–90.

Ator, N. A. (2005). Conducting behavioral research: Methodological and laboratory animal welfare issues. In C. K. Akins, S. Panicker, & C. L. Cunningham (Eds.), *Laboratory animals in research and teaching: Ethics, care and methods.* Washington, DC: American Psychological Association.

Aucoin, K. J., Frick, P. J., & Bodin, S. D. (2006). Corporal punishment and child adjustment. *Journal of Applied Developmental Psychology, 27,* 527–541.

Aveline, M., Strauss, B., & Stiles, W. B. (2005). Psychotherapy research. In G. O. Gabbard, J. S. Beck, & J. Holmes (Eds.), *Oxford textbook of psychotherapy.* New York: Oxford University Press.

Averill, J. A. (1980). A constructivist view of emotion. In R. Plutchik & H. Kellerman (Eds.), *Emotion: Theory, research, and experience: Vol. 1. Theories of emotion.* New York: Academic Press.

Avolio, B. J., Kahai, S. S., & Dodge, G. (2000). E-leading in organizations and its implications for theory, research and practice. *Leadership Quarterly, 11,* 615–670.

Axel, R. (1995, April). The molecular logic of smell. *Scientific American, 273,* 154–159.

Ayanian, J. Z., & Cleary, P. D. (1999). Perceived risks of heart disease and cancer among cigarette smokers. *Journal of the American Medical Association, 281,* 1019–1021.

Ayas, N. T., White, D. P., Manson, J. E., Stampfer, M. J., Speizer, F. E., Malhotra, A., et al. (2003). A prospective study of sleep duration and coronary heart disease in women. *Archives of Internal Medicine, 163,* 205–209.

Baars, B. J. (1986). *The cognitive revolution in psychology.* New York: Guilford.

Babiak, P., & Hare, R. D. (2006). *Snakes in suits: When psychopaths go to work.* New York: Regan Books/Harper Colllins Publishers.

Baddeley, A. D. (1986). *Working memory.* New York: Oxford University Press.

Baddeley, A. D. (1992). Working memory. *Science, 255,* 556–559.

Baddeley, A. D. (2001). Is working memory still working? *American Psychologist, 56,* 851–864.

Baddeley, A. D. (2003). Working memory: Looking back and looking forward. *Nature Reviews Neuroscience, 4,* 829–839.

Baddeley, A. D. (2007). *Working memory, thought, and action.* New York: Oxford University Press.

Baddeley, A. D., & Hitch, G. (1974). Working memory. In G. H. Bower (Ed.), *The psychology of learning and motivation* (Vol. 8). New York: Academic Press.

Baenninger, R. (1997). On yawning and its functions. *Psychonomic Bulletin & Review, 4,* 198–207.

Baer, R. A. (2003). Mindfulness training as a clinical intervention: A conceptual and empirical review. *Clinical Psychology: Science and Practice, 10,* 125–143.

Bahrick, H. P. (2000). Long-term maintenance of knowledge. In E. Tulving & F. I. M. Craik (Eds.), *The Oxford handbook of memory* (pp. 347–362). New York: Oxford University Press.

Bailey, C. H., & Kandel, E. R. (2004). Synaptic growth and the persistence of long–term memory: A molecular perspective. In M. S. Gazzaniga (Ed.),

The cognitive neurosciences. Cambridge, MA: MIT Press.

Bailey, J. M. (2003). Biological perspectives on sexual orientation. In L. D. Garnets & D. C. Kimmel (Eds.), *Psychological perspectives on lesbian, gay, and bisexual experiences.* New York: Columbia University Press.

Bailey, J. M., Dunne, M. P., & Martin, N. G. (2000). Genetic and environmental influences on sexual orientation and its correlates in an Australian twin sample. *Journal of Personality and Social Psychology, 78,* 524–536.

Bailey, J. M., & Pillard, R. C. (1991). A genetic study of male homosexual orientation. *Archives of General Psychology, 48,* 1089–1097.

Bailey, J. M., Pillard, R. C., Neale, M. C. I., & Agyei, Y. (1993). Heritable factors influence sexual orientation in women. *Archives of General Psychiatry, 50,* 217–223.

Bailey, J. M., & Zucker, K. J. (1995). Childhood sex-typed behavior and sexual orientation: A conceptual analysis and quantitative review. *Developmental Psychology, 31,* 43–55.

Baillargeon, R. (2002). The acquisition of physical knowledge in infancy: A summary in eight lessons. In U. Goswami (Ed.), *Blackwell handbook of childhood cognitive development.* Malden, MA: Blackwell Publishing.

Baillargeon, R. (2004). Infants' physical world. *Current Directions in Psychological Science, 13*(3), 89–94.

Baillargeon, R. (2008). Innate ideas revisited: For a principle of persistence in infants' physical reasoning. *Perspectives on Psychological Science, 3*(1), 2–13.

Bain, J. (2007). The many faces of testosterone. *Clinical Interventions in Aging, 2,* 567–576.

Bains, J. S., & Oliet, S. H. R. (2007). Glia: They make your memories stick! *Trends in Neuroscience, 30,* 417–424.

Baker, F., Ainsworth, S. R., Dye, J. T., Crammer, C., Thun, M. J., Hoffmann, D., Repace, J. L., Henningfield, J. E., Slade, J., Pinney, J., Shanks, T., Burns, D. M., Connolly, G. N., & Shopland, D. R. (2000). Health risks associated with cigar smoking. *Journal of the American Medical Association, 284,* 735–740.

Baker, G. J., Suchday, S., & Krantz, D. S. (2007). Heart disease/attack. In G. Fink (Ed.), *Encyclopedia of stress.* San Diego: Elsevier.

Baker, T. B., Japuntich, S. J., Hogle, J. M., McCarthy, D. E., & Curtin, J. J. (2006). Pharmacologic and behavioral withdrawal from addictive drugs. *Current Directions in Psychological Science, 15,* 232–236.

Baker, T. B., Piper, M. E., McCarthey, D. E., Majeskie, M. R., & Fiore, M. C. (2004). Addiction motivation reformulated: An affective processing model of negative reinforcement. *Psychological Review, 111,* 33–51.

Balcetis, E., & Dunning, D. A. (2006). See what you want to see: Motivational influences on visual perception. *Journal of Personality and Social Psychology, 91,* 612–625.

Balcetis, E., & Dunning, D. A. (2008). A mile in moccasins: How situational experience diminishes dispositionism in social inference. *Personality and Social Psychology Bulletin, 34*(1), 102–114.

Baldessarini, R. J., Tondo, L., Strombom, I. M., Dominguez, S., Fawcett, J., Licinio, J., Oquendo, M. A., Tollefson, G. D., Valuck, R. J., & Tohen, M. (2007). Ecological studies of antidepressant treatment and suicidal risks. *Harvard Review of Psychiatry, 15,* 133–145.

Baldwin, E. (1993). The case for animal research in psychology. *Journal of Social Issues, 49*(1), 121–131.

Baldwin, W. (2000). Information no one else knows: The value of self-report. In A. A. Stone, J. S. Turkkan, C. A. Bachrach, J. B. Jobe, H. S. Kurtzman & V. Cain (Eds.), *The science of self-report: Implications for research and practice.* Mahwah, NJ: Erlbaum.

Ball, H. L., Hooker, E., & Kelly, P. J. (2000). Parent-infant co-sleeping: Father's roles and perspectives. *Infant and Child Development, 9*(2), 67–74.

Ballenger, J. C. (2000). Benzodiazepine receptor agonists and antagonists. In B. J. Sadock & V. A. Sadock (Eds.), *Kaplan and Sadock's comprehensive textbook of psychiatry.* Philadelphia: Lippincott/ Williams & Wilkins.

Balsam, P. D. (1988). Selection, representation, and equivalence of controlling stimuli. In R. C. Atkinson, R. J. Herrnstein, G. Lindzey, & R. D. Luce (Eds.), *Stevens' handbook of experimental psychology.* New York: Wiley.

Baltes, P. B., Staudinger, U. M., & Lindenberger, U. (1999). Lifespan psychology: Theory and application to intellectual functioning. *Annual Review of Psychology, 50,* 471–507.

Balzer, W. L., Kihm, J. A., Smith, P. C., Irwin, J. L., Bachiochi, P. D., Robie, C., et al. (1997). *Users' manual for the job descriptive index (JDI, 1997 revision) and the job in general scales.* Bowling Green, OH: Bowling Green State University.

Bandura, A. (1977). *Social learning theory.* Englewood Cliffs, NJ: Prentice-Hall.

Bandura, A. (1986). *Social foundations of thought and action: A social-cognitive theory.* Englewood Cliffs, NJ: Prentice-Hall.

Bandura, A. (1993). Perceived self-efficacy in cognitive development and functioning. *Educational Psychologist, 28*(2), 117–148.

Bandura, A. (1995). Exercise of personal and collective efficacy in changing societies. In A. Bandura (Ed.), *Self-efficacy in changing societies.* New York: Cambridge University Press.

Bandura, A. (1999a). Social cognitive theory of personality. In L. A. Pervin, & O. P. John (Eds.), *Handbook of personality: Theory and research.* New York: Guilford.

Bandura, A. (1999b). A sociocognitive analysis of substance abuse: An agentic perspective. *Psychological Science, 10*(3), 214–217.

Bandura, A. (2001). Social cognitive theory: An agentic perspective. *Annual Review of Psychology, 52,* 1–26.

Bandura, A. (2004). Health promotion by social cognitive means. *Health Education & Behavior, 31,* 143–164.

Bandura, A. (2006). Toward a psychology of human agency. *Perspectives on Psychological Science, 1,* 164–180.

Bandura, A., Ross, D., & Ross, S. A. (1963a). Imitation of film-mediated aggressive models. *Journal of Abnormal and Social Psychology, 66,* 3–11.

Bandura, A., Ross, D., & Ross, S. A. (1963b). Vicarious reinforcement and imitative learning. *Journal of Abnormal and Social Psychology, 63,* 601–607.

Banich, M. T. (2003). Interaction between the hemispheres and its implications for the processing capacity of the brain. In K. Hugdahl & R. J. Davidson (Eds.), *The asymmetrical brain.* Cambridge, MA: MIT Press.

Banich, M. T., & Heller, W. (1998). Evolving perspectives on lateralization of function. *Current Directions in Psychological Science, 7,* 1.

Banks, A., & Gartell, N. K. (1995). Hormones and sexual orientation: A questionable link. *Journal of Homosexuality, 28,* 247–268.

Banks, S., & Dinges, D. F. (2007). Behavioral and physiological consequences of sleep restriction. *Journal of Clinical Sleep Medicine, 3*(5), 519–528.

Banks, W. A., & Watkins, L. R. (2006). Mediation of chronic pain: Not by neurons alone. *Pain, 124,* 1–2.

Banks, W. P., & Krajicek, D. (1991). Perception. *Annual Review of Psychology, 42,* 305–331.

Banyard, V. L., & Williams, L. M. (1999). Memories for child sexual abuse and mental health functioning: Findings on a sample of women and implications for future research. In L. M. Williams & V. L. Banyard (Eds.), *Trauma & memory.* Thousand Oaks, CA: Sage.

Banyard, V. L., Plante, E. G., Cohn, E. S., Moorhead, C., Ward, S., & Walsh, W. (2005). Revisiting unwanted sexual experiences on campus: A 12-year follow-up. *Violence Against Women, 11,* 426–446.

Banzato, C. E. M. (2004). Classification in psychiatry: The move towards ICD-11 and DSM-V. *Current Opinion in Psychiatry, 17,* 497–501.

Barak, A., & Buchanan, T. (2004). Internet-based psychological testing and assessment. In R. Krause, G. Stricker & J. Zack (Eds.), *Online counseling: A handbook for mental health professionals.* San Diego: Elsevier Academic Press.

Baral, B. D., & Das, J. P. (2004). Intelligence: What is indigenous to India and what is shared? In R. J. Sternberg (Ed.), *International handbook of intelligence.* New York: Cambridge University Press.

Barba, G. D., Parlato, V., Jobert, A., Samson, Y., & Pappata, S. (1998). Cortical networks implicated in semantic and episodic memory: Common or unique. *Cortex, 34,* 547–561.

Barber, B. K. (1994). Cultural, family, and personal contexts of parent-adolescent conflict. *Journal of Marriage and the Family, 56,* 375–386.

Barber, T. X. (1969). *Hypnosis: A scientific approach.* New York: Van Nostrand Reinhold.

Barber, T. X. (1979). Suggested ("hypnotic") behavior: The trance paradigm versus an alternative paradigm. In E. Fromm & R. E. Shor (Eds.), *Hypnosis: Developments in research and new perspectives.* New York: Aldine.

Barber, T. X. (1986). Realities of stage hypnosis. In B. Zilbergeld, M. G. Edelstien, & D. L. Araoz (Eds.), *Hypnosis: Questions and answers.* New York: Norton.

Barch, D. M. (2003). Cognition in schizophrenia: Does working memory work? *Current Directions in Psychological Science, 12*(4), 146–150.

Bard, P. (1934). On emotional experience after decortication with some remarks on theoretical views. *Psychological Review, 41,* 309–329.

Barfield, R. L. (2003). Students' perceptions of and satisfaction with group grades and the group experience in the college classroom. *Assessment and Evaluation in Higher Education, 28*(4).

Bargh, J. A., & McKenna, K. Y. A. (2002). Can you see the real me? Activation and expression of the "true self" on the Internet. *Journal of Social Issues, 58*(1), 33–48.

Bargh, J. A., & McKenna, K. Y. A. (2004). The Internet and social life. *Annual Review of Psychology, 55,* 573–590.

Bargh, J. A., McKenna, K. Y. A., & Fitzsimons, G. M. (2002). Can you see the real me? Activation and expression of the "true self" on the Internet. *Journal of Social Issues, 58,* 33–48.

Barker, E. T., Williams, R. L., & Galambos, N. L. (2006). Daily spillover to and from binge eating in first-year university females. *Eating Disorders: The Journal of Treatment and Prevention, 14,* 229–242.

Barlett, D. L., & Steele, J. B. (1979). *Empire: The life, legend and madness of Howard Hughes.* New York: Norton.

Barlow, D. H., Pincus, D. B., Heinrichs, N., & Choate, M. L. (2003). Anxiety disorders. In G. Stricker & T. A. Widiger (Eds.), *Handbook of psychology, Vol. 8: Clinical psychology.* New York: Wiley.

Barnes, V. A., Treiber, F., & Davis, H. (2001). The impact of Transcendental Meditation on cardiovascular function at rest and during acute stress in adolescents with high normal blood pressure. *Journal of Psychosomatic Research, 51,* 597–605.

Barnett, S. W. (2004). Does Head Start have lasting cognitive effects? The myth of fade-out. In E. Zigler & S. J. Styfco (Eds.), *The Head Start debates.* Baltimore: Paul H. Brooks Publishing.

Barnier, A. J. (2002). Posthypnotic amnesia for autobiographical episodes: A laboratory model of functional amnesia. *Psychological Science, 13,* 232–237.

Barnier, A. J., McConkey, K. M., & Wright, J. (2004). Posthypnotic amnesia for autobiographical episodes: Influencing memory accessibility and quality. *International Journal of Clinical and Experimental Hypnosis, 52,* 260–279.

Baron, A., & Galizio, M. (2005). Positive and negative reinforcement: Should the distinction be preserved? *Behavior Analyst, 28*(2), 85–98.

Baron, R. S. (2005). So right it's wrong: Groupthink and the ubiquitous nature of polarized group decision making. In M. P. Zanna (Ed.), *Advances in experimental social psychology.* San Diego: Elsevier Academic Press.

Barrett, D. (1988–1989). Dreams of death. *Omega, 19*(2), 95–101.

Barrett, L. F. (2006). Are emotions natural kinds? *Perspectives on Psychological Science, 1*(1), 28–58.

Barrett, L. F., Mesquita, B., Ochsner, K. N., & Gross, J. J. (2007). The experience of emotion. *Annual Review of Psychology, 58,* 373–403.

Barron, F. (1963). *Creativity and psychological health.* Princeton, NY: Van Nostrand.

Barry, L. J. (2004). Depression: The brain finally gets into the act. *Current Directions in Psychological Science, 13*(3), 104–106.

Barry-Walsh, J. (2005). Dissociative identity disorder. *Australian & New Zealand Journal of Psychiatry, 39*(1-2), 109–110.

Barsky, A. J. (1988). The paradox of health. *New England Journal of Medicine, 318,* 414–418.

Barsky, A. J. (2001). Somatosensory amplification and hypochondriasis. In V. Starcevic & D. R. Lipsitt (Eds.), *Hypochondriasis: Modern perspectives on an ancient malady.* New York: Oxford University Press.

Barsky, A. J., Coeytaux, R. R., Sarnie, M. K., & Cleary, P. D. (1993). Hypochondriacal patients' beliefs about good health. *American Journal of Psychiatry, 150,* 1085–1090.

Bartels, M., Rietveld, M. J. H., Van Baal, G. C. M., & Boomsma, D. I. (2002). Genetic and environmental influences on the development of intelligence. *Behavior Genetics, 32*(4), 237–249.

Bartlett, F. C. (1932). *Remembering: A study in experimental and social psychology.* New York: Macmillan.

Bartoshuk, L. M. (1993a). Genetic and pathological taste variation: What can we learn from animal models and human disease? In D. Chadwick, J. Marsh, & J. Goode (Eds.), *The molecular basis of smell and taste transduction.* New York: Wiley.

Bartoshuk, L. M. (1993b). The biological basis of food perception and acceptance. *Food Quality and Preference, 4,* 21–32.

Bartoshuk, L. M. (2000). Comparing sensory experiences across individuals: Recent psychophysical advances illuminate genetic variation in taste perception. *Chemical Senses, 25,* 447–460.

Bartoshuk, L. M., Duffy, V. B., & Miller, I. J. (1994). PTC/PROP taste: Anatomy, psychophysics, and sex effects. *Physiology & Behavior, 56,* 1165–1171.

Basbaum, A. I., & Jessel, T. M. (2000). The perception of pain. In E. R. Kandel, J. H. Schwartz, & T. M. Jessell (Eds.), *Principles of neural science.* New York: McGraw-Hill.

Basow, S. A. (1992). *Gender: Stereotypes and roles.* Pacific Grove, CA: Brooks/Cole.

Bass, B. M. (1990). *Bass and Stogdill's handbook of leadership: Theory research, and managerial applications.* New York: Free Press.

Bass, B. M. (1990, Winter). From transactional to transformational leadership: Learning to share the vision. *Organizational Dynamics,* pp. 19–31.

Bass, B. M. (1995). Theory of transformational leadership redux. *Leadership Quarterly, 6.*

Bassok, M. (2003). Analogical transfer in problem solving. In J. E. Davidson & R. J. Sternberg (Eds.), *The psychology of problem solving.* New York: Cambridge University Press.

Basson, M. D., Bartoshuk, L. M., Dichello, S. Z., Panzini, L., Weiffenbach, J. M., & Duffy, V. B. (2005). Association between 6-n-propylthiouracil (PROP) bitterness and colonic neoplasms. *Digestive Diseases Sciences, 50,* 483–489.

Bassuk, E. L., Buckner, J. C., Perloff, J. N., & Bassuk, S. S. (1998). Prevalence of mental health and substance use disorders among homeless and low-income housed mothers. *American Journal of Psychiatry, 155,* 1561–1564.

Bates, E. (1999). Plasticity, localization, and language development. In S. H. Broman & J. M. Fletcher (Eds.), *The changing nervous system: Neurobehavioral consequences of early brain disorders* (pp. 214–247). New York: Oxford University Press.

Bates, E., Devescovi, A., & Wulfeck, B. (2001). Psycholinguistics: A cross-language perspective. *Annual Review of Psychology, 52,* 369–396.

Baudry, M., & Lynch, G. (2001). Remembrance of arguments past: How well is the glutamate receptor hypothesis of LTP holding up after 20 years? *Neurobiology of Learning and Memory, 76,* 284–297.

Bauer, M. S. (2003). Mood disorders: Bipolar (manic-depressive) disorders. In A. Tasman, J. Kay, & J. A. Lieberman (Eds.), *Psychiatry.* New York: Wiley.

Baumeister, R. F. (1984). Choking under pressure: Self-consciousness and paradoxical effects of incentives on skillful performance. *Journal of Personality and Social Psychology, 46,* 610–620.

Baumeister, R. F. (1989). The optimal margin of illusion. *Journal of Social and Clinical Psychology, 8,* 176–189.

Baumeister, R. F. (2000). Gender differences in erotic plasticity: The female sex drive as socially flexible and responsive. *Psychological Bulletin, 126,* 347–374.

Baumeister, R. F. (2004). Gender and erotic plasticity: Sociocultural influences on the sex drive. *Sexual and Relationship Therapy, 19,* 133–139.

Baumeister, R. F., Bratslavsky, E., Finkenauer, C., & Vohs, K. D. (2001a). Bad is stronger than good. *Review of General Psychology, 5,* 323–370.

Baumeister, R. F., Catanese, K. R., & Vohs, K. D. (2001b). Is there a gender difference in strength of sex drive? Theoretical views, conceptual distinctions and a review of relevant evidence. *Personality and Social Psychology Review, 5,* 242–273.

Baumeister, R. F., DeWall, N. C., Ciarocco, N. J., & Twenge, J. M. (2005). Social exclusion impairs self-regulation. *Journal of Personality and Social Psychology, 88,* 589–604.

Baumeister, R. F., & Leary, M. R. (1995). The need to belong: Desire for interpersonal attachments as a fundamental human motivation. *Psychological Bulletin, 117,* 497–529.

Baumeister, R. F., & Twenge, J. M. (2002). Cultural suppression of female sexuality. *Review of General Psychology, 6,* 166–203.

Baumrind, D. (1964). Some thoughts on the ethics of reading Milgram's "Behavioral study of obedience." *American Psychologist, 19,* 421–423.

Baumrind, D. (1985). Research using intentional deception: Ethical issues revisited. *American Psychologist, 40,* 165–174.

Baumrind, D., Larzelere, R. E., & Cowan, P. A. (2002). Ordinary physical punishment: Is it harmful? Comment on Gershoff. *Psychological Bulletin, 128,* 580–589.

Bauserman, R. (1996). Sexual aggression and pornography: A review of correlational research. *Basic and Applied Social Psychology, 18,* 405–427.

Baylis, G. C., & Driver, J. (1995). One-sided edge assignment in vision: 1. Figure-ground segmentation and attention to objects. *Current Directions in Psychological Science, 4,* 140–146.

Beck, A. T. (1976). *Cognitive therapy and the emotional disorders.* New York: International Universities Press.

Beck, A. T. (1987). Cognitive therapy. In J. K. Zeig (Ed.), *The evolution of psychotherapy.* New York: Brunner/Mazel.

Beck, A. T. (1997). Cognitive therapy: Reflections. In J. K. Zeig (Ed.), *The evolution of psychotherapy: The third conference.* New York: Brunner/Mazel.

Beck, E., Burnet, K. L., & Vosper, J. (2006). Birth-order effects on facets of extraversion. *Personality and Individual Differences, 40,* 953–959.

Becker, A., & Fay, K. (2006). Sociocultural issues and eating disorders. In S. Wonderlich, J. Mitchell, M. de Zwaan, & H. Steiger (Eds.), *Annual review of eating disorders.* Oxon, England: Radcliffe.

Becker, S., & Wojtowicz, J. M. (2007). A model of hippocampal neurogenesis in memory and mood disorders. *Trends in Cognitive Sciences, 11*(2), 70–76.

Beckers, T., Miller, R. R., DeHouwer, J., & Urushihara, K. (2006). Reasoning rats: Forward blocking in Pavlovian animal conditioning is sensitive to constraints of causal inference. *Journal of Experimental Psychology: General, 135,* 92–102.

Becskei, C., Lutz, T. A., & Riediger, T. (2008). Glucose reverses fasting-induced activation in the arcuate nucleus of mice. *Neuroreport: For Rapid Communication of Neuroscience Research, 19*(1), 105–109.

Beeman, M. J., & Chiarello, C. (1998). Complementary right and left hemisphere language comprehension. *Current Directions in Psychological Science, 7,* 2–7.

Beer, J. M., Arnold, R. D., & Loehlin, J. C. (1998). Genetic and environmental influences on MMPI Factor Scales: Joint model fitting to twin and adoption data. *Journal of Personality and Social Psychology, 74,* 818–827.

Beer, J. S., Shimamura, A. P., & Knight, R. T. (2004). Frontal lobe contributions to executive control of cognitive and social behavior. In M. S. Gazzaniga (Ed.), *The cognitive neurosciences.* Cambridge, MA: MIT Press.

Beidel, D. C., & Stipelman, B. (2007). Anxiety disorders. In M. Hersen, S. M. Turner, & D. C. Beidel (Eds.), *Adult psychopathology and diagnosis.* New York: Wiley.

Beilin, H. (1992). Piaget's enduring contribution to developmental psychology. *Developmental Psychology, 28,* 191–204.

Beilock, S. L., & Carr, T. H. (2005). When high-powered people fail: Working memory and "choking under pressure" in math. *Psychological Science, 16,* 101–105.

Beilock, S. L., Carr, T. H., MacMahon, C., & Starkes, J. L. (2002). When paying attention becomes counterproductive: Impact of divided versus skill-focused attention on novice and experienced performance of sensorimotor skills. *Journal of Experimental Psychology: Applied, 8*(1), 6–16.

Beilock, S. L., Kulp, C. A., Holt, L. E., & Carr, T. H. (2004). More on the fragility of performance: Choking under pressure in mathematical problem solving. *Journal of Experimental Psychology: General, 133,* 584–600.

Bekelman, J. E., Li, Y., & Gross, C. P. (2003). Scope and impact of financial conflicts of interest in biomedical research. *Journal of the American Medical Association, 289,* 454–465.

Békésy, G. von. (1947). The variation of phase along the basilar membrane with sinusoidal vibrations. *Journal of the Acoustical Society of America, 19,* 452–460.

Belger, A., & Dichter, G. (2006). Structural and functional neuroanatomy. In J. A. Lieberman, T. S. Stroup, & D. O. Perkins (Eds.), *Textbook of schizophrenia.* Washington, DC: American Psychiatric Publishing.

Bell, A. P., Weinberg, M. S., & Hammersmith, S. K. (1981). *Sexual preference: Its development in men and women.* Bloomington: Indiana University Press.

Beller, M., & Gafni, N. (1996). The 1991 international assessment of educational progress in mathematics and sciences: The gender differences perspective. *Journal of Educational Psychology, 88,* 365–377.

Bellinger, D. C., & Adams, H. F. (2001). Environmental pollutant exposures and children's cognitive abilities. In R. J. Sternberg & E. L. Grigorenko (Eds.), *Environmental effects on cognitive abilities.* Mahwah, NJ: Erlbaum.

Bellis, M. A., Downing, J., & Ashton, J. R. (2006). Adults at 12? Trends in puberty and their public health consequences. *Journal of Epidemiology and Community Health, 60,* 910–911.

Belsky, J. (1988). The "effects" of infant day care reconsidered. *Early Childhood Research Quarterly, 3,* 235–272.

Belsky, J. (1992). Consequences of child care for children's development: A deconstructionist view. In A. Booth (Ed.), *Child care in the 1990s.* Hillsdale, NJ: Erlbaum.

Belsky, J. (1999). Modern evolutionary theory and patterns of attachment. In J. Cassidy & P. R. Shaver (Eds.), *Handbook of attachment: Theory, research and clinical applications.* New York: Guilford.

Belsky, J. (2006). Early child care and early child development: Major findings of the NICHD study of early child care. *European Journal of Developmental Psychology, 3*(1), 95–110.

Belsky, J. (2007). Experience in childhood and the development of reproductive strategies. *Acta Psychologica Sinica, 39,* 454–468.

Belsky, J., & Kelly, J. (1994). *The transition to parenthood.* New York: Dell.

Belsky, J., Vandell, D. L., Burchinal, M., Clarke-Stewart, K. A., McCartney, K., Owen, M. T., et al. (2007). Are there long-term effects of early child care? *Child Development, 78,* 681–701.

Bem, D. J. (1967). Self-perception: An alternative interpretation of cognitive dissonance phenomena. *Psychological Review, 74,* 183–200.

Bem, D. J. (1996). Exotic becomes erotic: A developmental theory of sexual orientation. *Psychological Review, 103,* 320–335.

Bem, D. J. (1998). Is EBE theory supported by the evidence? Is it androcentric? A reply to Peplau et al. *Psychological Review, 105,* 395–398.

Bem, D. J. (2000). Exotic becomes erotic: Interpreting the biological correlates of sexual orientation. *Archives of Sexual Behavior, 29,* 531–548.

Bem, S. L. (1985). Androgyny and gender schema theory: A conceptual and empirical integration. In T. B. Sonderegger (Ed.), *Nebraska symposium on motivation, 1984: Psychology and gender* (Vol. 32). Lincoln: University of Nebraska Press.

Benbow, C. P., & Stanley, J. C. (1983). *Academic precocity: Aspects of its development.* Baltimore: Johns Hopkins University Press.

Benbow, C. P., & Stanley, J. C. (1996). Inequity in equity: How "equity" can lead to inequality for high-potential students. *Psychology, Public Policy, and Law, 2,* 249–292.

Benca, R. M. (2001). Consequences of insomnia and its therapies. *Journal of Clinical Psychiatry, 62*(suppl 10), 33–38.

Bender, D. S., Skodol, A. E., Dyck, I. R., Markowitz, J. C., Shea, M. T., Yen, S., et al. (2007). Ethnicity and mental health treatment utilization by patients with personality disorders. *Journal of Consulting and Clinical Psychology, 75,* 992–999.

Benedict, R. (1934). *Patterns of culture.* Boston: Houghton Mifflin.

Benjamin, L. T., Jr. (2000). The psychology laboratory at the turn of the 20th century. *American Psychologist, 55,* 318–321.

Benjamin, L. T., Jr., & Baker, D. B. (2004). *From seance to science: A history of the profession of psychology in America.* Belmont, CA: Wadsworth.

Benjamin, L. T., Jr., Cavell, T. A., & Shallenberger, W. R., III. (1984). Staying with initial answers on objective tests: Is it a myth? *Teaching of Psychology, 11,* 133–141.

Benjamin, L. T., Jr., DeLeon, P. H., Freedheim, D. K., & VandenBos, G. R. (2003). Psychology as a profession. In D. K. Freedheim (Ed.), *Handbook of psychology, Vol. 1: History of psychology.* New York: Wiley.

Benjamin, L. T., Jr., & VandenBos, G. R. (2006). The window on psychology's literature: A history of psychological abstracts. *American Psychologist, 61,* 941–954.

Ben-Porath, Y. S. (2003). Assessing personality and psychopathology with self-report inventories. In J. R. Graham & J. A. Naglieri (Eds.), *Handbook of psychology, Volume 10: Assessment psychology.* New York: Wiley.

Benson, H. (1975). *The relaxation response.* New York: Morrow.

Benson, H., & Klipper, M. Z. (1988). *The relaxation response.* New York: Avon.

Benton, D. (2004). Role of parents in the determination of the food preferences of children and the development of obesity. *International Journal of Obesity, 28,* 858–869.

Berenbaum, S. A., & Snyder, E. (1995). Early hormonal influences on childhood sex-typed activity and playmate preferences: Implications for the development of sexual orientation. *Developmental Psychology, 31,* 31–42.

Berghmans, R. L. P. (2007). Misleading research participants: Moral aspects of deception in psychological research. *Netherlands Journal of Psychology, 63*(1), 14–20.

Berkowitz, L. (1989). Frustration-aggression hypothesis: Examination and reformulation. *Psychological Bulletin, 106,* 59–73.

Berkowitz, R. I. (2003). Behavior therapies. In R. E. Hales & S. C. Yudofsky (Eds.), *Textbook of Clinical Psychiatry.* Washington, DC: American Psychiatric Publishing.

Berlin, B., & Kay, P. (1969). *Basic color terms: Their universality and evolution.* Berkeley, CA: University of California Press.

Berliner, L., & Briere, J. (1999). Trauma, memory, and clinical practice. In L. M. Williams & V. L. Banyard (Eds.), *Trauma & memory.* Thousand Oaks, CA: Sage Publications.

Berman, R. F. (1991). Electrical brain stimulation used to study mechanisms and models of memory. In J. L. Martinez Jr. & R. P. Kesner (Eds.), *Learning and memory: A biological view.* San Diego: Academic Press.

Berndsen, M., Spears, R., van der Plight, J., & McGarty, C. (2002). Illusory correlation and stereotype formation: Making sense of group differences and cognitive biases. In C. McGarty, V. Y. Yzerbyt, & R. Spears (Eds.), *Stereotypes as explanations: The formation of meaningful beliefs about social groups.* New York: Cambridge University Press.

Bernert, R. A., Merrill, K. A., Braithwaite, S. R., Van Orden, K. A., & Joiner, T. E., Jr. (2007). Family life stress and insomnia symptoms in a prospective evaluation of young adults. *Journal of Family Psychology, 21*(1), 58–66.

Bernhard, F., & Penton-Voak, I. (2002). Evolutionary psychology of facial attractiveness. *Current Directions in Psychological Science, 11*(5), 154–158.

Berrettini, W. (2006). Genetics of bipolar and unipolar disorders. In D. J. Stein, D. J. Kupfer, & A. F. Schatzberg (Eds.), *Textbook of mood disorders.* Washington, DC: American Psychiatric Publishing.

Berridge, K. C. (2003). Comparing the emotional brains of humans and other animals. In R. J. Davidson, K. R. Scherer, & H. H. Goldsmith (Eds.), *Handbook of affective sciences.* New York: Oxford University Press.

Berridge, K. C. (2004). Motivation concepts in behavioral neuroscience. *Physiology and Behavior, 81*(2), 179–209.

Berry, D. T. R., Wetter, M. W., & Baer, R. A. (1995). Assessment of malingering. In J. N. Butcher (Ed.), *Clinical personality assessment: Practical approaches.* New York: Oxford University Press.

Berry, J. W. (1994). Cross-cultural variations in intelligence. In R. J. Sternberg (Ed.), *Encyclopedia of human intelligence.* New York: Macmillan.

Berry, J. W., Poortinga, Y., Segall, M., & Dasen, P. (1992). *Cross-cultural psychology.* New York: Cambridge University Press.

Bersani, H. (2007). President's address 2007: The past is prologue: "MR," go gentle into that good night. *Intellectual and Developmental Disabilities, 45,* 399–404.

Berscheid, E. (1988). Some comments on love's anatomy: Or, whatever happened to old-fashioned lust? In R. J. Sternberg & M. L. Barnes (Eds.), *The psychology of love.* New Haven: Yale University Press.

Berscheid, E. (2006). Searching for the meaning of "love." In R. J. Sternberg & K. Weis (Eds.), *The new psychology of love.* New Haven, CT: Yale University Press.

Berscheid, E., & Reis, H. T. (1998). Attraction and close relationships. In D. T. Gilbert, S. T. Fiske, & G. Lindzey (Eds.), *The handbook of social psychology.* New York: McGraw-Hill.

Berscheid, E., & Walster, E. (1978). *Interpersonal attraction.* Reading, MA: Addison-Wesley.

Bertenthal, B. I., & Clifton, R. K. (1998). Perception and action. In W. Damon (Ed.), *Handbook of child psychology (Vol. 2): Cognition, perception, and language.* New York: Wiley.

Berthoud, H. R., & Morrison, C. (2008). The brain, appetite, and obesity. *Annual Review of Psychology, 59,* 55–92.

Bertram, G. (2004). Theory-based bias correction in dispositional inference: The fundamental attribution error is dead, long live the correspondence bias. In W. Stroeb & M. Hewstone (Eds.), *European review of social psychology.* Hove, England: Psychology Press/Taylor & Francis.

Bertrand, R. M., & Lachman, M. E. (2003). Personality development in adulthood and old age. In R. M. Lerner, M. A. Easterbrooks, & J. Mistry (Eds.), *Handbook of psychology, Vol. 6: Developmental psychology.* New York: Wiley.

Berzonsky, M., & Adams, G. (1999). Commentary: Reevaluating the identity status paradigm: Still useful after 35 years. *Developmental Review, 19,* 557–590.

Beumont, P. J. V. (2002). Clinical presentation of anorexia nervosa and bulimia nervosa. In C. G. Fairburn & K. D. Brownell (Eds.), *Eating disorders and obesity: A comprehensive handbook.* New York: Guilford.

Beusterien, K. M., Davis, E. A., Flood, R., Howard, K., & Jordan, J. (2008). HIV patient insight on adhering to medication: A qualitative analysis. *AIDS Care, 20,* 251–259.

Beutler, L. E. (2002). The dodo bird is extinct. *Clinical Psychology: Science & Practice, 9*(1), 30–34.

Beutler, L. E., & Harwood, T. M. (2002). What is and can be attributed to the therapeutic relationship? *Journal of Contemporary Psychotherapy, 32*(1), 25–33.

Beutler, L. E., Bongar, B., & Shurkin, J. N. (2001). *A consumers guide to psychotherapy.* New York: Oxford University Press.

Beutler, L. E., Malik, M., Alimohamed, S., Harwood, T. M., Talebi, H., Noble, S., & Wong, E. (2004). Therapist variables. In M. J. Lambert (Ed.), *Bergin and Garfield's handbook of psychotherapy and behavior change.* New York: Wiley.

Beutler, L. E., Rocco, F., Moleiro, C. M., & Talebi, H. (2001). Resistance. *Psychotherapy: Theory, Research, Practice, Training, 38,* 431–436.

Bi, G. Q., & Poo, M.-M. (2001). Synaptic modification by correlated activity: Hebb's postulate revisited. *Annual Review of Neuroscience, 24,* 139–166.

Bialystok, E. (2001). *Bilingualism in development: Language, literacy, and cognition.* Cambridge, UK: Cambridge University Press.

Bialystok, E. (2005). Consequences of bilingualism for cognitive development. In J. F. Kroll & A. M. B. de Groot (Eds.), *Handbook of bilingualism: Psycholinguistic approaches.* New York: Oxford University Press.

Bialystok, E. (2007). Cognitive effects of bilingualism: How linguistic experience leads to cognitive change. *International Journal of Bilingual Education and Bilingualism, 10,* 210–223.

Bianchi, S., Milkie, M. A., Sayer, L. C., & Robinson, J. P. (2000). Is anyone doing the housework? Trends in the gender division of household labor. *Social Forces, 79*(1), 191–228.

Biederman, I., Hilton, H. J., & Hummel, J. E. (1991). Pattern goodness and pattern recognition. In G. R. Lockhead & J. R. Pomerantz (Eds.), *The perception of structure.* Washington, DC: American Psychological Association.

Biehl, M., Matsumoto, D., Ekman, P., Hearn, V., Heider, K., Kudoh, T., & Ton, V. (1997). Matsumoto and Ekman's Japanese and Caucasian Facial Expressions of Emotion (JACFEE): Reliability data and cross-national differences. *Journal of Nonverbal Behavior, 21,* 3–21.

Biermann, T., Estel, D., Sperling, W., Bleich, S., Kornhuber, J., & Reulbach, U. (2005). Influence of lunar phases on suicide: The end of a myth? A population-based study. *Chronobiology International, 22,* 1137–1143.

Bigler, E. D., Blatter, D. D., Anderson, C. V., Johnson, S. C., Gale, S. D., Hopkins, R. O., & Burnett, B. (1997). Hippocampal volume in normal aging and traumatic brain injury. *American Journal of Neuroradiology, 18,* 11–23.

Binet, A. (1911). Nouvelle recherches sur la mesure du niveau intellectuel chez les enfants d'école. *L'Année Psychologique, 17,* 145–201.

Binet, A., & Simon, T. (1905). Méthodes nouvelles pour le diagnostic du niveau intellectuel des anormaux. *L'Année Psychologique, 11,* 191–244.

Binet, A., & Simon, T. (1908). Le développement de l'intelligence chez les enfants. *L'Année Psychologique, 14,* 1–94.

Birch, L. L., & Fisher, J. A. (1996). The role of experience in the development of children's eating behavior. In E. D. Capaldi (Ed.), *Why we eat what we eat: The psychology of eating* (pp. 113–143). Washington, DC: American Psychological Association.

Birkeland, S. A., Manson, T. M., Kisamore, J. L., Brannick, M. T., & Smith, M. A. (2006). A metaanalytic investigation of job applicant faking on personality measures. *International Journal of Selection and Assessment, 14,* 317–335.

Birnbaum, M. H. (2004a). Base rates in Bayesian inference. In F. P. Rudiger (Ed.), *Cognitive illusions.* New York: Psychology Press.

Birnbaum, M. H. (2004b). Human research and data collection via the Internet. *Annual Review of Psychology, 55,* 803–832.

Birney, D. P., Citron-Pousty, J. H., Lutz, D. J., & Sternberg, R. J. (2005). The development of cognitive and intellectual abilities. In M. H. Bornstein & M. E. Lamb (Eds.), *Developmental science: An advanced textbook.* Mahwah, NJ: Erlbaum.

Bishop, S. R. (2002). What do we really know about mindfulness-based stress reduction? *Psychosomatic Medicine, 64*(1), 71–83.

Björntorp, P. (2002). Definition and classification of obesity. In C. G. Fairburn & K. D. Brownell (Eds.), *Eating disorders and obesity: A comprehensive handbook* (pp. 377–381). New York: Guilford.

Black, D. W. (2001). Antisocial personality disorder: The forgotten patients of psychiatry. *Primary Psychiatry, 8*(1), 30–81.

Black, D. W., & Andreasen, N. C. (1999). Schizophrenia, schizophreniform disorder, and delusional (paranoid) disorders. In R. E. Hales, S. C. Yudofsky, & J. A. Talbott (Eds.), *American Psychiatric Press textbook of psychiatry* (3rd ed.). Washington, DC: American Psychiatric Press.

Blackburn, R. (2006). Other theoretical models of psychopathy. In C. J. Patrick (Ed.), *Handbook of Psychopathy.* New York: Guilford.

Blacker, D., & Tsuang, M. T. (1999). Classification and DSM-IV. In A. M. Nicholi (Ed.), *The Harvard guide to psychiatry.* Cambridge, MA: Harvard University Press.

Blacker, L. (1999). The launching phase of the life cycle. In B. Carter & M. McGoldrick (Eds.), *The expanded family life cycle: Individual, family, and social perspectives* (3rd ed., pp. 287–306). Boston: Allyn & Bacon.

Blagrove, M. (1992). Dreams as a reflection of our waking concerns and abilities: A critique of the problem-solving paradigm in dream research. *Dreaming, 2,* 205–220.

Blagrove, M. (1996). Problems with the cognitive psychological modeling of dreaming. *Journal of Mind and Behavior, 17,* 99–134.

Blagrove, M., Farmer, L., & Williams, E. (2004). The relationship of nightmare frequency and nightmare distress to well-being. *Journal of Sleep Research, 12*(2), 129–136.

Blair, S. N., Kohl, H. W., Paffenbarger, R. S., Clark, D. G., Cooper, K. H., & Gibbons, L. W. (1989). Physical fitness and all-cause mortality: A prospective study of healthy men and women. *Journal of the American Medical Association, 262,* 2395–2401.

Blakeslee, T. R. (1980). *The right brain.* Garden City, NY: Doubleday/Anchor.

Blanchard, E. B., & Keefer, L. (2003). Irritable bowel syndrome. In A. M. Nezu, C. M. Nezu, & P. A. Geller (Eds.), *Handbook of psychology, Vol. 9: Health psychology.* New York: Wiley.

Blanchard, R., Zucker, K. J., Bradley, S. J., & Hume, C. S. (1995). Birth order and siblings sex ratio in homosexual male adolescents and probably prehomosexual feminine boys. *Developmental Psychology, 31,* 22–30.

Blanco, C., Laje, G., Olfson, M., Marcus, S. C., & Pincus, H. A. (2002). Trends in the treatment of bipolar disorder by outpatient psychiatrists. *American Journal of Psychiatry, 159,* 1005–1010.

Blank, H., Musch, J., & Pohl, R. F. (2007). Hindsight bias: On being wise after the event. *Social Cognition, 25*(1), 1–9.

Blankenhorn, D. (1995). *Fatherless America: Confronting our most urgent social problem.* New York: Basic Books.

Blass, T. (1991). Understanding behavior in the Milgram obedience experiment: The role of personality, situations, and their interactions. *Journal of Personality and Social Psychology, 60,* 398–413.

Blass, T. (1999). The Milgram Paradigm after 35 years: Some things we now know about obedience to authority. *Journal of Applied Social Psychology, 29,* 955–978.

Bleuler, E. (1911). *Dementia praecox or the group F schizophrenias.* New York: International Universities Press.

Blieszner, R., & Adams, R. G. (1992). *Adult friendship.* Newbury Park, CA: Sage.

Bliwise, D. L. (2005). Normal aging. In M. H. Kryger, T. Roth, & W. C. Dement (Eds.), *Principles and practice of sleep medicine.* Philadelphia: Elsevier Saunders.

Block, J. (1995). A contrarian view of the five-factor approach to personality description. *Psychological Bulletin, 117,* 187–215.

Block, J. R., & Yuker, H. E. (1992). *Can you believe your eyes?: Over 250 illusions and other visual oddities.* New York: Brunner/Mazel.

Block, N. (2002). How heritability misleads us about race. In J. Fish (Ed.), *Race and intelligence: Separating science from myth.* Mahwah, NJ: Erlbaum.

Bloom, B. L. (1984). *Community mental health: A general introduction.* Pacific Grove, CA: Brooks/Cole.

Bloom, B. S. (Ed.). (1985). *Developing talent in young people.* New York: Ballantine.

Bloom, F. E. (1995). Cellular mechanisms active in emotion. In M. S. Gazzaniga (Ed), *The cognitive neurosciences.* Cambridge, MA: MIT Press.

Bloomfield, H. H., & Kory, R. B. (1976). *Happiness: The TM program, psychiatry, and enlightenment.* New York: Simon & Schuster.

Blum, R., & Rinehart, P. (2000). *Reducing the risk: Connections that make a difference in the lives of youth.* Minneapolis: University of Minnesota, Division of General Pediatrics and Adolescent Health.

Boakes, R. A. (2003). The impact of Pavlov on the psychology of learning in English-speaking countries. *The Spanish Journal of Psychology, 6*(2), 93–98.

Boase, J., & Wellman, B. (2006). Personal relationships: On and off the Internet. In A. L. Vangelisti & D. Perlman (Eds.), *The Cambridge handbook of personal relationships.* New York: Cambridge University Press.

Bochner, S., & Jones, J. (2003). *Child language development: Learning to talk.* London: Whurr Publishers.

Bock, P. K. (2000). Culture and personality revisited. *American Behavioral Scientist, 44,* 32–40.

Bodenheimer, T. (2000). Uneasy alliance: Clinical investigators and the pharmaceutical industry. *New England Journal of Medicine, 342,* 1539–1544.

Bodenmann, G., Ledermann, T., Blattner, D., & Galluzzo, C. (2006). Associations among everyday stress, critical life events, and sexual problems. *Journal of Nervous and Mental Disease, 194,* 494–501.

Boehm, L. E. (1994). The validity effect: A search for mediating variables. *Personality and Social Psychology Bulletin, 20,* 285–293.

Bogen, J. E. (1985). The dual brain: Some historical and methodological aspects. In D. F. Benson & E. Zaidel (Eds.), *The dual brain: Hemispheric specialization in humans.* New York: Guilford.

Bogen, J. E. (1990). Partial hemispheric independence with the neocommissures intact. In C. Trevarthen (Ed.), *Brain circuits and functions of the mind. Essays in honor of Roger W. Sperry.* Cambridge, MA: Cambridge University Press.

Bogen, J. E. (2000). Split-brain basics: Relevance for the concept of one's other mind. *Journal of the American Academy of Psychoanalysis & Dynamic Psychiatry, 28,* 341–369.

Bogg, T., & Roberts, B. W. (2004). Conscientiousness and health-related behaviors: A meta-analysis of the leading behavioral contributors to mortality. *Psychological Bulletin, 130,* 887–919.

Boggild, H., & Knutsson, A. (1999). Shift work, risk factors and cardiovascular disease. *Scandinavian Journal of Work, Environment & Health, 25*(2), 85–99.

Bohannon, J. N., III, & Bonvillian, J. D. (2001). Theoretical approaches to language acquisition. In J. B. Gleason (Ed.), *The development of language* (5th ed., pp. 254–314). Boston: Allyn & Bacon.

Bohner, G., & Schwarz, N. (2001). Attitudes, persuasion, and behavior. In A. Tesser & N. Schwarz (Eds.), *Blackwell handbook of social psychology: Intraindividual processes.* Malden, MA: Blackwell.

Bohner, G., Siebler, F., & Schmelcher, J. (2006). Social norms and the likelihood of raping: Perceived rape myth acceptance of others affects men's rape proclivity. *Personality and Social Psychology Bulletin, 32,* 286–297.

Boland, R. J., & Keller, M. B. (2002). Course and outcome of depression. In I. H. Gotlib & C. L. Hammen (Eds.), *Handbook of depression.* New York: Guilford.

Boldry, J. G., Gaertner, L., & Quinn, J. (2007). Measuring the measures: A meta-analytic investigation of the measures of outgroup homogeneity. *Group Processes & Intergroup Relations, 10,,* 157–178.

Bolger, N. (1990). Coping as a personality process: A prospective study. *Journal of Personality and Social Psychology, 59,* 525–537.

Bolla, K. I., Brown, K., Eldreth, D. , Tate, K., & Cadet, J. L. (2002). Dose-related neurocognitive effects of marijuana use. *Neurology, 59,* 1337–1343.

Bolles, R. C. (1975). *Theory of motivation.* New York: Harper & Row.

Bolling, M. Y., Terry, C. M., & Kohlenberg, R. J. (2006). Behavioral theories. In J. C. Thomas & D. L. Segal (Eds.), *Comprehensive handbook of personality and psychopathology.* New York: Wiley.

Boly, M., Faymonville, M.-E., Vogt, B. A., Maquet, P., & Laureys, S. (2007). Hypnotic regulation of consciousness and the pain neuromatrix. In G. A. Jamieson (Ed.), *Hypnosis and conscious states: The cognitive neuroscience perspective.* New York: Oxford University Press.

Bonanno, G. A. (2005). Resilience in the face of potential trauma. *Current Directions in Psychological Science, 14*(3), 135–138.

Bonanno, G. A., Field, N. P., Kovacevic, A., & Kaltman, S. (2002). Self-enhancement as a buffer against extreme adversity: Civil war in Bosnia and traumatic loss in the United States. *Personality and Social Psychology Bulletin, 28,* 184–196.

Bonanno, G. A., Moskowitz, J. T., Papa, A., & Folkman, S. (2005). Resilience to loss in bereaved spouses, bereaved parents, and bereaved gay men. *Journal of Personality and Social Psychology, 88,* 827–843.

Bond, R., & Smith, P. B. (1996). Culture and conformity: A meta-analysis of studies using Asch's line judgment task. *Psychological Bulletin, 119,* 111–137.

Bonnet, M. H. (2000). Sleep deprivation. In M. H. Kryger, T. Roth, & W. C. Dement (Eds.), *Principles and practice of sleep medicine.* Philadelphia: Saunders.

Bonnet, M. H. (2005). Acute sleep deprivation. In M. H. Kryger, T. Roth, & W. C. Dement (Eds.), *Principles and practice of sleep medicine.* Philadelphia: Elsevier Saunders.

Bono, G., McCullough, M. E., & Root, L. M. (2008). Forgiveness, feeling connected to others, and well-being: Two longitudinal studies. *Personality and Social Psychology Bulletin, 34,* 182–195.

Booth, C. L., Clarke-Stewart, K. A., Vandell, D. L., McCartney, K., & Owen, M. T. (2002). Child-care usage and mother-infant "quality time." *Journal of Marriage and Family, 64,* 16–26.

Bootzin, R. R., Manber, R., Loewy, D. H., Kuo, T. F., & Franzen, P. L. (2001). Sleep disorders. In P. B. Sutker & H. E. Adams (Eds.), *Comprehensive handbook of psychopathology.* New York: Kluwer Academic/Plenum.

Borbely, A. A. (1986). *Secrets of sleep.* New York: Basic Books.

Borbely, A. A., & Achermann, P. (2005). Sleep homeostasis and models of sleep regulation. In M. H. Kryger, T. Roth, & W. C. Dement (Eds.), *Principles and practice of sleep medicine.* Philadelphia: Elsevier Saunders.

Bordnick, P. S., Elkins, R. L., Orr, T. E., Walters, P., & Thyer, B. A. (2004). Evaluating the relative effectiveness of three aversion therapies designed to reduce craving among cocaine abusers. *Behavioral Interventions, 19*(1), 1–24.

Borgida, E., & Nisbett, R. E. (1977). The differential impact of abstract vs. concrete information on decisions. *Journal of Applied Social Psychology, 7,* 258–271.

Boring, E. G. (1966). A note on the origin of the word *psychology. Journal of the History of the Behavioral Sciences, 2,* 167.

Borman, W. C., Penner, L. A., Allen, T. D., & Motowidlo, S. J. (2001). Personality predictors of citizenship performance. *International Journal of Selection and Assessment, 9,* 52–69.

Bornstein, R. F. (2003). Psychodynamic models of personality. In T. Millon & M. J. Lerner (Eds.), *Handbook of psychology, Vol. 5: Personality and social psychology.* New York: Wiley.

Boroditsky, L. (2001). Does language shape thought? Mandarin and English speakers' conceptions of time. *Cognitive Psychology, 43*(1), 1–22.

Bosma, H., van Boxtel, M. P. J., Ponds, R. W. H. M., Houx, P. J., Burdorf, A., & Jolles, J. (2002). Mental work demands protect against cognitive impairment: MAAS prospective cohort study. *Experimental Aging Research, 29*(1), 33–45.

Bosson, J. K., & Swann, W. B. (2001). The paradox of the sincere chameleon: Strategic self-verification in close relationships. In J. H. Harvey & A. Wenzel (Eds.), *Close romantic relationships: Maintenance and enhancement.* Mahwah, N.J.: Erlbaum.

Bost, K. K., Cox, M. J., Burchinal, M. R., & Payne, C. (2002). Structural and supporting changes in couples' family and friendship networks across the transition to parenthood. *Journal of Marriage and the Family, 64,* 517–531.

Both, S., Spiering, M., Everaerd, W. , & Laan, E. (2004). Sexual behavior and responsiveness to sexual stimuli following laboratory-induced sexual arousal. *Journal of Sex Research, 41,* 242–258.

Bouchard, C. (2002). Genetic influences on body weight. In C. G. Fairburn & K. D. Brownell (Eds.), *Eating disorders and obesity: A comprehensive handbook* (pp. 16–21). New York: Guilford.

Bouchard, T. J., Jr. (1997). IQ similarity in twins reared apart: Findings and responses to critics. In R. J. Sternberg, & E. L. Grigorenko (Eds.), *Intelligence, heredity, and environment.* New York: Cambridge University Press.

Bouchard, T. J., Jr. (1998). Genetic and environmental influences on adult intelligence and special mental abilities. *Human Biology, 70,* 257–279.

Bouchard, T. J., Jr. (2004). Genetic influence on human psychological traits: A survey. *Current Directions in Psychological Science, 13*(4), 148–151.

Bouchard, T. J., Jr., Lykken, D. T., McGue, M., Segal, N. L., & Tellegen, A. (1990). Sources of human psychological differences: The Minnesota study of twins reared apart. *Science, 250,* 223–228.

Boudreaux, E., Carmack, C. L., Scarinci, I. C., & Brantley, P. J. (1998). Predicting smoking stage of change among a sample of low socioeconomic status, primary care outpatients: Replication and extension using decisional balance and self-efficacy theories. *International Journal of Behavioral Medicine, 5,* 148–165.

Bouman, T. K., Eifert, G. H., & Lejeuz, C. W. (1999). Somatoform disorders. In T. Millon, P. H. Blaney, & R. D. Davis (Eds.), *Oxford textbook of psychopathology* (pp. 444–465). New York: Oxford University Press.

Bourgeois, J. A., Seaman, J. S., & Servis, M. E. (2003). Delirium, dementia, and amnestic disorders. In R. E. Hales & S. C. Yudofsky (Eds.), *Textbook of clinical Psychiatry.* Washington, DC: American Psychiatric Publishing.

Bourhis, R. Y., & Gagnon, A. (2001). Social orientations in the minimal group paradigm. In R. Brown & S. L. Gaertner (Eds.), *Blackwell handbook of social psychology: Intergroup processes.* Malden, MA: Blackwell Publishing.

Bousfield, W. A. (1953). The occurrence of clustering in the recall of randomly arranged associates. *Journal of General Psychology, 49,* 229–240.

Bouton, M. E. (2000). A learning theory perspective on lapse, relapse, and the maintenance of behavior change. *Health Psychology, 19*(1), 57–63.

Bouton, M. E. (2002). Context, ambiguity, and unlearning: Sources of relapse after behavioral extinction. *Biological Psychiatry, 52,* 976–986.

Bouton, M. E. (2004). Context and behavioral processes in extinction. *Learning & Memory, 11,* 485–494.

Bowd, A. D., & Shapiro, K. J. (1993). The case against laboratory animal research in psychology. *Journal of Social Issues, 49*(1), 133–142.

Bowden, C. L. (2004). Valproate. In A. F. Schatzberg & C. B. Nemeroff (Eds.), *Textbook of psychopharmacology.* Washington, DC: American Psychiatric Publishing.

Bower, G. H. (1970). Organizational factors in memory. *Cognitive Psychology, 1,* 18–46.

Bower, G. H. (2000). A brief history of memory research. In E. Tulving & F. I. M. Craik (Eds.), *The Oxford handbook of memory* (pp. 3–32). New York: Oxford University Press.

Bower, G. H., & Clark, M. C. (1969). Narrative stories as mediators of serial learning. *Psychonomic Science, 14,* 181–182.

Bower, G. H., Clark, M. C., Lesgold, A. M., & Winzenz, D. (1969). Hierarchical retrieval schemes in recall of categorized word lists. *Journal of Verbal Learning and Verbal Behavior, 8,* 323–343.

Bower, G. H., & Springston, F. (1970). Pauses as recoding points in letter series. *Journal of Experimental Psychology, 83,* 421–430.

Bowlby, J. (1969). *Attachment and loss: Vol. 1. Attachment.* New York: Basic Books.

Bowlby, J. (1973). *Attachment and loss: Vol. 2. Separation, anxiety and anger.* New York: Basic Books.

Bowlby, J. (1980). *Attachment and loss: Vol. 3. Sadness and depression.* New York: Basic Books.

Boyes, A. D., & Fletcher, G. J. O. (2007). Metaperceptions of bias in intimate relationships. *Journal of Personality and Social Psychology, 92,* 286–306.

Boyle, M. (2007). The problem with diagnosis. *The Psychologist, 20,* 290–292.

Boyle, S. H., Jackson, W. G., & Suarez, E. C. (2007). Hostility, anger, and depression predict increases in C3 over a 10-year period. *Brain, Behavior, and Immunity, 21,* 816–823.

Boynton, R. M. (1990). Human color perception. In K. N. Leibovic (Ed.), *Science of vision.* New York: Springer-Verlag.

Bradshaw, J. L. (1981). In two minds. *Behavioral and Brain Sciences, 4,* 101–102.

Bradshaw, J. L. (1989). *Hemispheric specialization and psychological function.* New York: Wiley.

Brainerd, C. J. (1996). Piaget: A centennial celebration. *Psychological Science, 7,* 191–195.

Brainerd, C. J., & Reyna, V. F. (2005). *The science of false memory.* New York: Oxford University Press.

Branaman, T. F., & Gallagher, S. N. (2005). Polygraph testing in sex offender treatment: A review of limitations. *American Journal of Forensic Psychology, 23*(1), 45–64.

Brand, C. R., Constales, D., & Kane, H. (2003). Why ignore the *g* factor? Historical considerations. In H. Nyborg (Ed.), *The scientific study of general intelligence: Tribute to Arthur R. Jensen.* Amsterdam: Pergamon.

Brannon, L., & Feist, J. (2007). *Health psychology: An introduction to behavior and health.* Belmont, CA: Wadsworth.

Bransford, J. D., & Stein, B. S. (1993). *The IDEAL problem solver.* New York: W. H. Freeman.

Branson, R. (2005). *Losing my virginity: The autobiography.* London: Virgin.

Branson, R. (2006). *Screw it, let's do it: Lessons in life.* London: Virgin.

Brase, G. L. (2006). Cues of parental investment as a factor in attractiveness. *Evolution and Human Behavior, 27,* 145–157.

Brase, G. L., Cosmides, L., & Tooby, J. (1998). Individuation, counting, and statistical inference: The role of frequency and whole-object representations in judgment under certainty. *Journal of Experimental Psychology: General, 127,* 3–21.

Braun, K. A., Ellis, R., & Loftus, E. F. (2002). Make my memory: How advertising can change our memories of the past. *Psychology and Marketing, 19,* 1–23.

Bredart, S., Lampinen, J. M., & Defeldre, A. C. (2003). Phenomenal characteristics of cryptomnesia. *Memory, 11*(1), 1–11.

Bredt, B. M., Higuera-Alhino, D., Hebert, S. J., McCune, J. M., & Abrams, D. I. (2002). Short-term effects of cannabinoids on immune phenotype and function in HIV-1-infected patients. *Journal of Clinical Pharmacology, 42,* 90S–96S.

Breedlove, S. M. (1994). Sexual differentiation of the human nervous system. *Annual Review of Psychology, 45,* 389–418.

Breggin, P. R. (1991). *Toxic psychiatry.* New York: St. Martin's Press.

Breggin, P. R., & Cohen, D. (2007). *Your drug may be your problem: How and why to stop taking psychiatric medications.* New York: Da Capo Lifelong Books.

Brehm, J. W. (1966). *A theory of psychological reactance.* New York: Academic Press.

Brehm, S. S., & Kassin, S. M. (1993). *Social psychology.* Boston: Houghton Mifflin.

Breland, K., & Breland, M. (1961). The misbehavior of organisms. *American Psychologist, 16,* 681–684.

Breland, K., & Breland, M. (1966). *Animal behavior.* New York: Macmillan.

Brennan, K. A., Clark, C. L., & Shaver, P. R. (1998). Self-report measurement of adult attachment: An integrative overview. In J. A. Simpson & W. S. Rholes (Eds.), *Attachment theory and close relationships.* (pp. 46–76). New York: Guilford.

Brennen, T., Vikan, A., & Dybdahl, R. (2007). Are tip-of-the-tongue states universal? Evidence from the speakers of an unwritten language. *Memory, 15,* 167–176.

Breslau, N., Roth, T., Rosenthal, L., & Andreski, P. (1996). Sleep disturbance and psychiatric disorders: A longitudinal epidemiological study of young adults. *Biological Psychiatry, 39,* 411–418.

Breugelmans, S. M., & Poortinga, Y. H. (2006). Emotion without a word: Shame and guilt among Rarámuri Indians and rural Javanese. *Journal of Personality and Social Psychology, 91*(6), 1111–1122.

Breugelmans, S. M., Poortinga, Y. H., Ambadar, Z., Setiadi, B., Vaca, J. B., Widiyanto, P., et al. (2005). Body sensations associated with emotions in Raramuri Indians, rural Javanese, and three student samples. *Emotion, 5,* 166–174.

Brewer, W. F. (2000). Bartlett, functionalism, and modern schema theories. *Journal of Mind and Behavior, 21,* 37–44.

Brewer, W. F., & Treyens, J. C. (1981). Role of schemata in memory for places. *Cognitive Psychology, 13,* 207–230.

Brewin, C. R. (2003). *Posttraumatic stress disorder: Malady or myth.* New Haven: Yale University Press.

Brewin, C. R. (2004). Commentary on McNally "Is traumatic amnesia nothing but psychiatric folklore?" *Cognitive Behaviour Therapy, 33*(2), 102–104.

Brewin, C. R. (2007). Autobiographical memory for trauma: Update on four controversies. *Memory, 15,* 227–248.

Brewster, K. L., & Padavic, I. (2000). Change in gender-ideology, 1977–1996: The contributions of intracohort change and population turnover. *Journal of Marriage and the Family, 62,* 477–487.

Brickman, P., Coates, D., & Janoff-Bulman, R. (1978). Lottery winners and accident victims: Is happiness relative? *Journal of Personality and Social Psychology, 36,* 917–927.

Bridge, J. A., & Barbe, R. P. (2004). Reducing hospital readmission in depression and schizophrenia: Current evidence. *Current Opinion in Psychiatry, 17,* 505–511.

Bridge, J. A., Iyengar, S., Salary, C. B., Barbe, R. P., Birmaher, B., Pincus, H. A., et al. (2007). Clinical response and risk for reported suicidal ideation and suicide attempts in pediatric antidepressant treatment: A meta-analysis of randomized controlled trials. *Journal of the American Medical Association, 297,* 1683–1969.

Briere, J., & Conte, J. R. (1993). Self-reported amnesia for abuse in adults molested as children. *Journal of Traumatic Stress, 6*(1), 21–31.

Bringmann, W. G., & Balk, M. M. (1992). Another look at Wilhelm Wundt's publication record. *History of Psychology Newsletter, 24*(3/4), 50–66.

Brislin, R. (1993). *Understanding culture's influence on behavior.* Fort Worth: Harcourt Brace College Publishers.

Brislin, R. (2000). *Understanding culture's influence on behavior.* Belmont, CA: Wadsworth.

Broadbent, D. E. (1958). *Perception and communication.* New York: Pergamon Press.

Brobeck, J. R., Tepperman, T., & Long, C. N. (1943). Experimental hypothalamic hyperphagia in the albino rat. *Yale Journal of Biology and Medicine, 15,* 831–853.

Bröder, A. (1998). Deception can be acceptable. *American Psychologist, 53,* 805–806.

Brody, N. (1992). *Intelligence.* San Diego: Academic Press.

Brody, N. (2000). History of theories and measurements of intelligence. In R. J. Sternberg (Ed.), *Handbook of intelligence* (pp. 16–33). New York: Cambridge University Press.

Brody, N. (2003). Jensen's genetic interpretation of racial differences in intelligence: Critical evaluation. In H. Nyborg (Ed.), *The scientific study of general intelligence: Tribute to Arthur R. Jensen.* Oxford, UK: Pergamon.

Brody, N. (2005). To *g* or not to *g*—that is the question. In O. Wilhelm & R. W. Engle (Eds.), *Handbook of understanding and measuring intelligence.* Thousand Oaks, CA: Sage Publications.

Bronstein, P., & Quina, K. (1988). Perspectives on gender balance and cultural diversity in the teaching of psychology. In P. Bronstein & K. Quina (Eds.), *Teaching a psychology of people: Resources for gender and sociocultural awareness.* Washington, DC: American Psychological Association.

Broughton, R. (1994). Important underemphasized aspects of sleep onset. In R. D. Ogilvie & J. R. Harsh (Eds.), *Sleep onset: Normal and abnormal processes.* Washington, DC: American Psychological Association.

Brown, A. S. (1991). A review of the tip-of-the-tongue experience. *Psychological Bulletin, 109,* 204–223.

Brown, A. S. (1999). New perspectives on the neurodevelopmental hypothesis of schizophrenia. *Psychiatric Annals, 29*(3), 128–130.

Brown, A. S., Begg, M. D., Gravenstein, S., Schaefer, C. S., Wyatt, R. J., Bresnahan, M., Babulas, V. P., & Susser, E. S. (2004). Serologic evidence of prenatal influenza in the etiology of schizophrenia. *Archives of General Psychiatry, 61,* 774–780.

Brown, D., Scheflin, A. W., & Hammond, D. C. (1998). *Memory, trauma treatment, and the law.* New York: Norton.

Brown, D., Scheflin, A. W., & Whitfield, C. L. (1999). Recovered memories: The current weight of the evidence in science and in the courts. *Journal of Psychiatry & Law, 27,* 5–156.

Brown, E. J., Juster, H. R., Heimberg, R. G., & Winning, C. D. (1998). Stressful life events and personality styles: Relation to impairment and treatment outcome in patients with social phobia. *Journal of Anxiety Disorders, 12,* 233–251.

Brown, H. D., & Kosslyn, S. M. (1993). Cerebral lateralization. *Current Opinion in Neurobiology, 3,* 183–186.

Brown, M. (1974). Some determinants of persistence and initiation of achievement-related activities. In J. W. Atkinson & J. O. Raynor (Eds.), *Motivation and achievement.* Washington, DC: Halsted.

Brown, M. (1998). *Richard Branson: The inside story.* London: Headline.

Brown, M. N., Freeman, K. E., & Williamson, C. L. (2000). The importance of critical thinking for student use of the Internet. *College Student Journal, 34,* 391–398.

Brown, R., & McNeill, D. (1966). The "tip-of-the-tongue" phenomenon. *Journal of Verbal Learning and Verbal Behavior, 5*(4), 325–337.

Brown, R. D., & Cothern, C. M. (2002). Individual differences in faking integrity tests. *Psychological Reports, 91,* 691–702.

Brown, R. D., Goldstein, E., & Bjorklund, D. F. (2000). The history and zeitgeist of the repressed–false-memory debate: Scientific and sociological perspectives on suggestibility and childhood memory. In D. F. Bjorklund (Ed.), *False-memory creation in children and adults* (pp. 1–30). Mahwah, NJ: Erlbaum.

Brown, R. T. (1989). Creativity: What are we to measure? In J. A. Glover, R. R. Ronning, & C. R. Reynolds (Eds.), *Handbook of creativity.* New York: Plenum.

Brown, S. C., & Craik, F. I. M. (2000). Encoding and retrieval of information. In E. Tulving & F. I. M. Craik (Eds.), *The Oxford handbook of memory* (pp. 93–108). New York: Oxford University Press.

Brown, T. T., & Dobs, A. S. (2002). Endocrine effects of marijuana. *Journal of Clinical Pharmacology, 42,* 97S–102S.

Brown, W. D. (2006). Insomnia: Prevalence and daytime consequences. In T. Lee-Chiong (Ed.), *Sleep: A comprehensive handbook.* Hoboken, NJ: Wiley-Liss.

Brownell, K. D. (2002). The environment and obesity. In C. G. Fairburn & K. D. Brownell (Eds.), *Eating disorders and obesity: A comprehensive handbook* (pp. 433–438). New York: Guilford.

Bruce, D., Dolan, A., & Phillips-Grant, K. (2000). On the transition from childhood amnesia to the recall of personal memories. *Psychological Science, 11,* 360–364.

Bruer, J. T. (1999). *The myth of the first three years: A new understanding of early brain development and life-long learning.* New York: Free Press.

Bruer, J. T. (2002). Avoiding the pediatrician's error: How neuroscientists can help educators (and themselves). *Nature Neuroscience, 5,* 1031–1033.

Bruer, J. T., & Greenough, W. T. (2001). The subtle science of how experience affects the brain. In D. B. Bailey Jr., J. T. Bruer, F. J. Symons, & J. W. Lichtman (Eds.), *Critical thinking about critical periods.* Baltimore, MD: Paul H. Brookes Publishing.

Bruggerman, E. L., & Hart, K. J. (1996). Cheating, lying, and moral reasoning by religious and secular high school students. *Journal of Educational Research, 89,* 340–344.

Brumbaugh, C. C., & Fraley, R. C. (2006). Transference and attachment: How do attachment patterns get carried forward from one relationship to the next? *Personality and Social Psychology Bulletin, 32,* 552–560.

Bryden, M. P. (1982). *Laterality: Functional asymmetry in the intact brain.* New York: Academic Press.

Brym, R., & Lenton, R. (2001). *Love online: A report on digital dating in Canada.* Retrieved from http://www.chass.utoronto.ca/brym/pubs.htm.

Buccino, G., & Riggio, L. (2006). The role of the mirror neuron system in motor learning. *Kinesiology, 38*(1), 5–15.

Buchanan, R. W., & Carpenter, W. T. (2000). Schizophrenia: Introduction and overview. In B. J. Sadock & V. A. Sadock (Eds.), *Kaplan and Sadock's comprehensive textbook of psychiatry* (7th ed., Vol. 1). Philadelphia: Lippincott/Williams & Wilkins.

Buchanan, R. W., & Carpenter, W. T. (2005). Concept of schizophrenia. In B. J. Sadock & V. A. Sadock (Eds.), *Kaplan & Sadock's comprehensive textbook of psychiatry.* Philadelphia: Lippincott Williams & Wilkins.

Buchanan, T. (2000). Potential of the Internet for personality research. In M. H. Birnbaum (Ed.), *Psychological experiments on the Internet.* San Diego: Academic Press.

Buchanan, T. (2007). Personality testing on the Internet: What we know, and what we do not. In A. N. Joinson, K. Y. A. McKenna, T. Postmes, & U-D. Reips (Eds.), *The Oxford handbook of Internet psychology.* New York: Oxford University Press.

Buck, L. B. (2000). Smell and taste: The chemical senses. In E. R. Kandel, J. H. Schwartz, & T. M. Jessell (Eds.), *Principles of neural science*. New York: McGraw-Hill.

Buck, L. B. (2004). Olfactory receptors and coding in mammals. *Nutrition Reviews, 62*, S184–S188.

Buckman, R. (2002). Communications and emotions: Skills and effort are key. *British Medical Journal, 325*, 672.

Budiansky, S. (2004). Human and animal intelligence: The gap is a chasm. *Cerebrum, 6*(2), 85–95.

Bufe, B., Breslin, P. A. S., Kuhn, C., Reed, D. R., Tharp, C. D., Slack, J. P., Kim, U., Drayna, D., & Meyerhof, W. (2005). The molecular basis of individual differences in phenylthiocarbamide and propylthiouracil bitterness perception. *Current Biology, 15*, 322–327.

Bühler, C., & Allen, M. (1972). *Introduction to humanistic psychology*. Pacific Grove, CA: Brooks/Cole.

Bulcroft, R., & Teachman, J. (2004). Ambiguous constructions: Development of a childless or child-free life course. In M. Coleman & L. H. Ganong (Eds.), *Handbook of contemporary families: Considering the past, contemplating the future*. Thousand Oaks, CA: Sage.

Bulik, C. M. (2004). Genetic and biological risk factors. In J. K. Thompson (Ed.), *Handbook of eating disorders and obesity*. New York: Wiley.

Bulik, C. M., Tozzi, F., Anderson, C., Mazzeo, S. E., Aggen, S., & Sullivan, P. F. (2003). The relation between eating disorders and components of perfectionism. *American Journal of Psychiatry, 160*, 366–368.

Bull, D. L. (1999). A verified case of recovered memories of sexual abuse. *American Journal of Psychotherapy, 53*, 221–224.

Burger, J. M. (1999). The foot-in-the-door compliance procedure: A multiple process analysis review. *Personality and Social Psychology Review, 3*, 303–325.

Burger, J. M. (2008). *Personality*. Belmont, CA: Wadsworth.

Burgess, A. (2007). On the contribution of neurophysiology to hypnosis research: Current state and future directions. In G. A. Jamieson (Ed.), *Hypnosis and conscious states: The cognitive neuroscience perspective*. New York: Oxford University Press.

Burke, D. M., & Shafto, M. A. (2004). Aging and language production. *Current Directions in Psychological Science, 13*(1), 21–24.

Burlingame, G. M., & McClendon, D. T. (2008). Group therapy. In J. L. Lebow (Ed.), *Twenty-first century psychotherapies: Contemporary approaches to theory and practice*. New York: Wiley.

Burns, A. B., Brown, J. S., Plant, E. A., Sachs-Ericsson, N., & Joiner, T. E. Jr. (2006). On the specific depressotypic nature of excessive reassurance-seeking. *Personality and Individual Differences, 40*, 135–145.

Burns, A. B., Brown, J. S., Sachs-Ericsson, N., Plant, E. A., Curtis, J. T., Fredrickson, B. L., et al. (2008). Upward spirals of positive emotion and coping: Replication, extension, and initial exploration of neurochemical substrates. *Personality and Individual Differences, 44*, 360–370.

Burns, B. D., & Corpus, B. (2004). Randomness and inductions from streaks: "Gambler's fallacy" versus "hot hand." *Psychonomic Bulletin & Review, 11*(1), 179–184.

Burriss, R. P., & Little, A. C. (2006). Effects of partner conception risk phase on male perception of dominance in faces. *Evolution and Human Behavior, 27*, 297–305.

Bursztajn, H. J., & Brodsky, A. (2002). Managed health care: Complications, liability risk, and clinical remedies. *Primary Psychiatry, 9*(4), 37–41.

Burtt, H. E. (1929). *Psychology and industrial efficiency*. New York: Appleton.

Bushman, B. J. (2002). Does venting anger feed or extinguish the flame? Catharsis, rumination, distraction, anger, and aggressive responding. *Personality and Social Psychology Bulletin, 28*, 724–731.

Bushman, B. J., & Anderson, C. A. (2001). Media violence and the American public: Scientific facts versus media misinformation. *American Psychologist, 56*, 477–489.

Bushman, B. J., Baumeister, R. F., & Stack, A. D. (1999). Catharsis, aggression, and persuasive influence: Self-fulfilling or self-defeating prophecies? *Journal of Personality and Social Psychology, 76*, 367–376.

Bushman, B. J., & Huesmann, L. R. (2001). Effects of televised violence on aggression. In D. G. Singer & J. L. Singer (Eds.), *Handbook of children and the media*. Thousand Oaks, CA: Sage.

Buss, D. M. (1985). Human mate selection. *American Scientist, 73*, 47–51.

Buss, D. M. (1988). The evolution of human intrasexual competition: Tactics of mate attraction. *Journal of Personality and Social Psychology, 54*, 616–628.

Buss, D. M. (1989). Sex differences in human mate preferences: Evolutionary hypotheses tested in 37 cultures. *Behavioral and Brain Sciences, 12*, 1–49.

Buss, D. M. (1991). Evolutionary personality psychology. *Annual Review of Psychology, 42*, 459–491.

Buss, D. M. (1994a). *The evolution of desire: Strategies of human mating*. New York: Basic Books.

Buss, D. M. (1994b). Mate preferences in 37 cultures. In W. J. Lonner & R. S. Malpass (Eds.), *Psychology and culture*. Boston: Allyn & Bacon.

Buss, D. M. (1995). Evolutionary psychology: A new paradigm for psychological science. *Psychological Inquiry, 6*, 1–30.

Buss, D. M. (1996). The evolutionary psychology of human social strategies. In E. T. Higgins & A. W. Kruglanski (Eds.), *Social psychology: Handbook of basic principles*. New York: Guilford.

Buss, D. M. (1997). Evolutionary foundation of personality. In R. Hogan, J. Johnson, & S. Briggs (Eds.), *Handbook of personality psychology*. San Diego: Academic Press.

Buss, D. M. (1998). The psychology of human mate selection: Exploring the complexity of the strategic repertoire. In C. Crawford, & D. L. Krebs (Eds.), *Handbook of evolutionary psychology: Ideas, issues, and applications*. Mahwah, NJ: Erlbaum.

Buss, D. M. (1999). *Evolutionary psychology: The new science of the mind*. Boston: Allyn & Bacon.

Buss, D. M. (2001). Cognitive biases and emotional wisdom in the evolution of conflict between the sexes. *Current Directions in Psychological Science, 10*, 219–223.

Buss, D. M., & Kenrick, D. T. (1998). Evolutionary social psychology. In D. T. Gilbert, S. T. Fiske, & G. Lindzey (Eds.), *The handbook of social psychology*. New York: McGraw-Hill.

Buss, D. M., & Reeve, H. K. (2003). Evolutionary psychology and developmental dynamics: Comment on Lickliter and Honeycutt (2003). *Psychological Bulletin, 129*, 848–853.

Buss, D. M., & Schmitt, D. P. (1993). Sexual strategies theory: A contextual evolutionary analysis of human mating. *Psychological Review, 100*, 204–232.

Buss, D. M., & Shackelford, T. K. (2008). Attractive women want it all: Good genes, economic invest-ment, parenting proclivities, and emotional commitment. *Evolutionary Psychology, 6*(1), 134–146.

Bussey, K., & Bandura, A. (1984). Influence of gender constancy and social power on sex-linked modeling. *Journal of Personality and Social Psychology, 47*, 1292–1302.

Bussey, K., & Bandura, A. (1999). Social cognitive theory of gender development and differentiation. *Psychological Review, 106*, 676–713.

Bussey, K., & Bandura, A. (2004). Social cognitive theory of gender development and functioning. In A. H. Eagly, A. E. Beall, & R. J. Sternberg (Eds.), *The psychology of gender*. New York: Guilford.

Buster, J. E., & Carson, S. A. (2002). Endocrinology and diagnosis of pregnancy. In S. G. Gabbe, J. R. Niebyl, & J. L. Simpson (Eds.), *Obstetrics: Normal and problem pregnancies*. New York: Churchill Livingstone.

Butcher, J. N. (2005). *A beginner's guide to the MMPI-2*. Washington, DC: American Psychological Association.

Butcher, J. N. (2006). *MMPI-2: A practitioner's guide*. Washington, DC: American Psychological Association.

Butcher, L. M., Meaburn, E., Dale, P. S., Sham, P., Schalkwyk, L. C., Craig, I. W., & Plomin, R. (2005). Association analysis of mild mental impairment using DNA pooling to screen 432 brain expressed single-nucleotide polymorphisms. *Molecular Psychiatry, 10*, 384–392.

Butler, E. A., Egloff, B., Wilhelm, F. H., Smith, N. C., Erickson, E. A., & Gross, J. J. (2003). The social consequences of expressive suppression. *Emotion, 3*(1), 48–67.

Butler, J. L., & Baumeister, R. F. (1998). The trouble with friendly faces: Skilled performance with a supportive audience. *Journal of Personality and Social Psychology, 75*, 1213–1230.

Button, T. M. M., Maughan, B., & McGuffin, P. (2007). The relationship of maternal smoking to psychological problems in the offspring. *Early Human Development, 83*, 727–732.

Buxton, M. N., Arkey, Y., Lagos, J., Deposito, F., Lowenthal, F., & Simring, S. (1981). Stress and platelet aggregation in hemophiliac children and their family members. *Research Communications in Psychology, Psychiatry and Behavior, 6*(1), 21–48.

Byrne, D. (1997). An overview (and underview) of research and theory within the attraction paradigm. *Journal of Social and Personal Relationships, 14*, 417–431.

Byrne, D., Clore, G. L., & Smeaton, G. (1986). The attraction hypothesis: Do similar attitudes affect anything? *Journal of Personality and Social Psychology, 51*, 1167–1170.

Cabeza, R., & Nyberg, L. (2000). Imaging cognition II: An empirical review of 275 PET and fMRI studies. *Journal of Cognitive Neuroscience, 12*, 1–47.

Cabral, G. A., & Petit, D. A. D. (1998). Drugs and immunity: Cannabinoids and their role in decreased resistance to infectious disease. *Journal of Neuroimmunology, 83*, 116–123.

Cabýoglu, M. T., Ergene, N., & Tan, U. (2006). The mechanism of acupuncture and clinical applications. *International Journal of Neuroscience, 116*(2), 115–125.

Cacioppo, J. T., & Berntson, G. G. (1999). The affect system: Architecture and operating characteristics. *Current Directions in Psychological Science, 8*, 133–137.

Cacioppo, J. T., & Gardner, W. L. (1999). Emotion. *Annual Review of Psychology, 50*, 191–214.

Cacioppo, J. T., Hawkley, L. C., Kalil, A., Hughes, M. E., Waite, L., & Thisted, R. A. (2008). Happiness and the invisible threads of social connection: The Chicago health, aging, and social relations study. In M. Eid & R. J. Larsen (Eds.), *The science of subjective well-being*. New York: Guilford.

Cacioppo, J. T., Klein, D. J., Berntson, G. G., & Hatfield, E. (1993). The psychophysiology of emotions. In M. Lewis & J. M. Haviland (Eds.), *Handbook of emotions*. New York: Guilford.

Cadinu, M., Maass, A., Rosabianca, A., & Kiesner, J. (2005). Why do women underperform under stereotype threat? Evidence for the role of negative thinking. *Psychological Science, 16*, 572–578.

Cahill, L. (2006). Why sex matters for neuroscience. *Nature Reviews Neuroscience, 7*, 477–484.

Cahn, B. R., & Polich, J. (2006). Meditation states and traits: EEG, ERP, and neuroimaging studies. *Psychological Bulletin, 132*, 180–211.

Cain, C. K., Blouin, A. M., & Barad, M. (2003). Temporarily massed CS presentations generate more fear extinction than spaced presentations. *Journal of Experimental Psychology: Animal Behavior Processes, 29*(4), 323–333.

Cain, W. S. (1988). Olfaction. In R. C. Atkinson, R. J. Herrnstein, G. Lindzey, & R. D. Luce (Eds.), *Stevens' handbook of experimental psychology: Perception and motivation* (Vol. 1). New York: Wiley.

Caine, E. D., & Lyness, J. M. (2000). Delirium, dementia, and amnestic and other cognitive disorders. In B. J. Sadock & V. A. Sadock (Eds.), *Kaplan and Sadock's comprehensive textbook of psychiatry*. Philadelphia: Lippincott/Williams & Wilkins.

Calhoun, L. G., & Tedeschi, R. G. (2006). The foundations of posttraumatic growth: An expanded framework. In L. G. Calhoun & R. G. Tedeschi (Eds.), *Handbook of posttraumatic growth: Research & practice*. Mahwah, NJ: Erlbaum.

Calhoun, L. G., & Tedeschi, R. G. (2008). The paradox of struggling with trauma: Guidelines for practice and directions for research. In S. Joseph & P. A. Linley (Eds.), *Trauma, recovery, and growth: Positive psychological perspectives on posttraumatic stress*. Hoboken, NJ: Wiley.

Callahan, C. M. (2000). Intelligence and giftedness. In R. J. Sternberg (Ed.), *Handbook of intelligence* (pp. 159–175). New York: Cambridge University Press.

Callicutt, J. W. (2006). Homeless shelters: An uneasy component of the de facto mental health system. In J. Rosenberg & S. Rosenberg (Eds.), *Community mental health: Challenges for the 21st century*. New York: Routledge.

Calvert, C. (1997). Hate speech and its harms: A communication theory perspective. *Journal of Communication, 47*, 4–19.

Camaioni, L. (2001). Early language. In G. Bremner & A. Fogel (Eds.), *Blackwell handbook of infant development*. Malden, MA: Blackwell.

Camerer, C. (2005). Three cheers—psychological, theoretical, empirical—for loss aversion. *Journal of Marketing Research, 42*(2), 129–133.

Cameron, L., Leventhal, E. A., & Leventhal, H. (1993). Symptom representations and affect as determinants of care seeking in a community-dwelling, adult sample population. *Health Psychology, 12*, 171–179.

Cami, J., & Farre, M. (2003). Mechanisms of disease: Drug addiction. *New England Journal of Medicine, 349*, 975–986.

Campbell, A. (2005). Aggression. In D. M. Buss (Ed.), *The handbook of evolutionary psychology*. New York: Wiley.

Campbell, J. (1971). *Hero with a thousand faces*. New York: Harcourt Brace Jovanovich.

Campbell, K. B. (2000). Introduction to the special section: Information processing during sleep onset and sleep. *Canadian Journal of Experimental Psychology, 54*(4), 209–218.

Campbell, L., Simpson, J. A., Boldry, J., & Kashy, D. A. (2005). Perceptions of conflict and support in romantic relationships: The role of attachment anxiety. *Journal of Personality and Social Psychology, 88*, 510–531.

Campbell, R., & Sais, E. (1995). Accelerated metalinguistic (phonological) awareness in bilingual children. *British Journal of Developmental Psychology, 13*, 61–68.

Campbell, R., & Wasco, S. M. (2005). Understanding rape and sexual assault: 20 years of progress and future decisions. *Journal of Interpersonal Violence, 20*(1), 127–131.

Campbell, R. J. (2000). Managed care. In B. J. Sadock & V. A. Sadock (Eds.), *Kaplan and Sadock's comprehensive textbook of psychiatry* (7th ed., Vol. 2). Philadelphia: Lippincott/Williams & Wilkins.

Campbell, S., Marriott, M., Nahmias, C., & MacQueen, G. M. (2004). Lower hippocampal volume in patients suffering from depression: A meta-analysis. *American Journal of Psychiatry, 161*, 598–607.

Campfield, L. A. (2002). Leptin and body weight regulation. In C. G. Fairburn & K. D. Brownell (Eds.), *Eating disorders and obesity: A comprehensive handbook* (pp. 32–36). New York: Guilford.

Campos, P. (2004). *The obesity myth: Why America's obsession with weight is hazardous to your health*. New York: Gotham Books.

Cannon, W. B. (1927). The James-Lange theory of emotions: A critical examination and an alternate theory. *American Journal of Psychology, 39*, 106–124.

Cannon, W. B. (1929). *Bodily changes in pain, hunger, fear and rage*. New York: Appleton.

Cannon, W. B. (1932). *The wisdom of the body*. New York: Norton.

Cannon, W. B., & Washburn, A. L. (1912). An explanation of hunger. *American Journal of Physiology, 29*, 444–454.

Canter, P. H. (2003). The therapeutic effects of meditation. *British Medical Journal, 326*, 1049–1050.

Cao, Y., Vikingstad, E. M., Huttenlocher, P. R., Towle, V. L., & Levin, D. N. (1994). Functional magnetic resonance imaging studies of the reorganization of the human head sensorimotor area after unilateral brain injury. *Proceeding of the National Academy of Sciences of the United States of America, 91*, 9612–9616.

Capaldi, E. D., & VandenBos, G. R. (1991). Taste, food exposure, and eating behavior. *Hospital and Community Psychiatry, 42*(8), 787–789.

Capozza, D., & Brown, R. (2000). *Social identity processes: Trends in theory and research*. London: Sage.

Cardeña, E., & Gleaves, D. H. (2007). Dissociative disorders. In M. Hersen, S. M. Turner, & D. C. Beidel (Eds.), *Adult psychopathology and diagnosis*. New York: Wiley.

Carey, M. P., & Vanable, P. A. (2003). AIDS/HIV. In A. M. Nezu, C. M. Nezu, & P. A. Geller (Eds.), *Handbook of psychology, Vol. 9: Health psychology*. New York: Wiley.

Carli, L. L. (1999). Cognitive, reconstruction, hindsight, and reactions to victims and perpetrators. *Personality & Social Psychology Bulletin, 25*, 966–979.

Carlo, G. (2006). Care-based and altruistically based morality. In M. Killen & J. G. Smetana (Eds.), *Handbook of moral development*. Mahwah, NJ: Erlbaum.

Carlson, K. A., Meloy, M. G., & Russo, J. E. (2006). Leader-driven primacy: Using attribute order to affect consumer choice. *Journal of Consumer Research, 32*, 513–518.

Carlson, M. J. (2006). Family structure, father involvement, and adolescent behavioral outcomes. *Journal of Marriage and Family, 68*, 137–154.

Carnagey, N. L., & Anderson, C. A. (2004). Violent video game exposure and aggression: A literature review. *Minerva Psichiatrica, 45*, 1–18.

Carnagey, N. L., Anderson, C. A., & Bartholow, B. D. (2007). Media violence and social neuroscience: New questions and new opportunities. *Current Directions in Psychological Science, 16*, 178–182.

Carnagey, N. L., Anderson, C. A., & Bushman, B. J. (2007). The effect of video game violence on physiological desensitization. *Journal of Experimental Social Psychology, 43*, 489–496.

Carney, S., & Geddes, J. (2003). Electroconvulsive therapy. *British Medical Journal, 326*, 1343–1344.

Carpenter, W. T. (1992). The negative symptom challenge. *Archives of General Psychiatry, 49*, 236–237.

Carpenter, W. T. (2002). From clinical trial to prescription. *Archives of General Psychology, 59*, 282–285.

Carroll, J. B. (1993). *Human cognitive abilities: A survey of factor-analytic studies*. Cambridge: Cambridge University Press.

Carroll, J. B. (1996). A three-stratum theory of intelligence: Spearman's contribution. In I. Dennis & P. Tapsfield (Eds.), *Human abilities: Their nature and measurement*. Mahwah, NJ: Erlbaum.

Carroll, J. M., & Russell, J. A. (1997). Facial expressions in Hollywood's portrayal of emotion. *Journal of Personality and Social Psychology, 72*, 164–176.

Carroll, M. E., & Overmier, J. B. (2001). *Animal research and human health*. Washington, DC: American Psychological Association.

Carroll-Ghosh, T., Victor, B. S., & Bourgeois, J. A. (2003). Suicide. In R. E. Hales & S. C. Yudofsky (Eds.), *Textbook of clinical psychiatry* (pp. 1457–1484). Washington, DC: American Psychiatric Publishing.

Carskadon, M. A., & Dement, W. C. (2005). Normal human sleep: An overview. In M. H. Kryger, T. Roth, & W. C. Dement (Eds.), *Principles and practice of sleep medicine*. Philadelphia: Elsevier Saunders.

Carskadon, M. A., & Rechtschaffen, A. (2005). Monitoring and staging human sleep. In M. H. Kryger, T. Roth, & W. C. Dement (Eds.), *Principles and practice of sleep medicine*. Philadelphia: Elsevier Saunders.

Carter, P. J., & Russell, K. (2001). *Workout for a balanced brain: Exercises, puzzles & games to sharpen both sides of your brain*. Readers Digest Association.

Carter, R. (1998). *Mapping the mind*. Berkeley: University of California Press.

Cartwright, R. D. (1977). *Night life: Explorations in dreaming*. Englewood Cliffs, NJ: Prentice-Hall.

Cartwright, R. D. (1991). Dreams that work: The relation of dream incorporation to adaptation to stressful events. *Dreaming, 1*, 3–9.

Cartwright, R. D. (2004). The role of sleep in changing our minds: A psychologist's discussion of papers on memory reactivation and consolidation in sleep. *Learning & Memory, 11,* 660–663.

Cartwright, R. D. (2006). Sleepwalking. In T. Lee-Chiong (Ed.), *Sleep: A comprehensive handbook.* Hoboken, NJ: Wiley-Liss.

Cartwright, R. D., & Lamberg, L. (1992). *Crisis dreaming.* New York: HarperCollins.

Cartwright-Finch, U., & Lavie, N. (2007). The role of perceptual load in inattentional blindness. *Cognition, 102,* 321–340.

Carver, C. S. (2007). Stress, coping, and health. In H. S. Friedman & R. C. Silver (Eds.), *Foundations of health psychology.* New York: Oxford University Press.

Carver, C. S., & Scheier, M. F. (1994). Situational coping and coping dispositions in a stressful transaction. *Journal of Personality and Social Psychology, 66,* 184–195.

Carver, C. S., Smith, R. G., Antoni, M. H., Petronis, V. M., Weiss, S., & Derhagopian, R. P. (2005). Optimistic personality and psychosocial well-being during treatment predict psychosocial well-being among long-term survivors of breast cancer. *Health Psychology, 24,* 508–516.

Casanova, C., Merabet, L., Desautels, A., & Minville, K. (2001). Higher-order motion processing in the pulvinar. *Progress in Brain Research, 134,* 71–82.

Caspi, A., Harrington, H., Milne, B., Amell, J. W., Theodore, R. F., & Moffitt, T. E. (2003). Children's behavioral styles at age 3 are linked to their adult personality traits at age 26. *Journal of Personality, 71*(4), 495–513.

Caspi, A., & Herbener, E. S. (1990). Continuity and change: Assortative marriage and the consistency of personality in adulthood. *Journal of Personality and Social Psychology, 58*(2), 250–258.

Caspi, A., & Moffitt, T. E. (2006). Gene-environment interactions in psychiatry: Joining forces with neuroscience. *Nature Reviews Neuroscience, 7,* 583–590.

Caspi, A., Roberts, B. W., & Shiner, R. L. (2005). Personality development: Stability and change. *Annual Review of Psychology, 56,* 453–484.

Caspi, A., Sugden, K., Moffitt, T. E., Taylor, A., Craig, I. W., Harrington, H., McClay, J., Mill, J., Martin, J., Braithwaite, A., & Poulton, R. (2003). Influence of life stress on depression: Moderation by a polymorphism in the 5-HTT gene. *Science, 301,* 386–389.

Caspi, O., & Burleson, K. O. (2005). Methodological challenges in meditation research. *Advances in Mind-Body Medicine, 21*(1), 4–11.

Cassel, R. N. (2000). Third force psychology and person-centered theory: From ego-status to ego-ideal. *Psychology: A Journal of Human Behavior, 37*(3), 44–48.

Cassidy, J. (1999). The nature of the child's ties. In J. Cassidy & P. R. Shaver (Eds.), *Handbook of attachment: Theory, research, and clinical applications.* New York: Guilford.

Castle, D. (2008). Drawing conclusions about cannabis and psychosis. *Psychological Medicine, 38*(3), 459–460.

Castonguay, L. G., Reid, J. J., Jr., Halperin, G. S., & Goldfried, M. R. (2003). Psychotherapy integration. In G. Stricker & T. A. Widiger (Eds.), *Handbook of psychology, Vol. 8: Clinical psychology.* New York: Wiley.

Castro, B., Bahadori, S., Tortelli, L., Ailam, N., & Skurnik, N. (2007). Revolving door syndrome. *Annales Médico-Psychologiques, 165,* 276–281.

Catania, A. C. (1992). Reinforcement. In L. R. Squire (Ed.), *Encyclopedia of learning and memory.* New York: Macmillan.

Catania, A. C., & Laties, V. G. (1999). Pavlov and Skinner: Two lives in science (an introduction to B. F. Skinner's "Some responses to the stimulus 'Pavlov'"). *Journal of the Experimental Analysis of Behavior, 72,* 455–461.

Catrambone, R. (1998). The subgoal learning model: Creating better examples so that students can solve novel problems. *Journal of Experimental Psychology: General, 127,* 355–376.

Cattell, H. E. P. (2004). The Sixteen Personality Factor (16PF) Questionnaire. In M. J. Hilsenroth & D. L. Segal (Eds.), *Comprehensive handbook of psychological assessment: Vol. 2. Personality.* Hoboken, NJ: Wiley.

Cattell, R. B. (1950). *Personality: A systematic, theoretical and factual study.* New York: McGraw-Hill.

Cattell, R. B. (1957). *Personality and motivation: Structure and measurement.* New York: Harcourt, Brace & World.

Cattell, R. B. (1965). *The scientific analysis of personality.* Baltimore: Penguin.

Cattell, R. B. (1966). *The scientific analysis of personality.* Chicago: Aldine.

Cattell, R. B. (1990). Advances in Cattellian personality theory. In L. A. Pervin (Ed.), *Handbook of personality: Theory and research.* New York: Guilford.

Cattell, R. B., Eber, H. W., & Tatsuoka, M. M. (1970). *Handbook of the Sixteen Personality Factor Questionnaire (16PF).* Champaign, IL: Institute for Personality and Ability Testing.

Catz, S. L., & Kelly, J. A. (2001). Living with HIV disease. In A. Baum, T. A. Revenson, & J. E. Singer (Eds.), *Handbook of health psychology* (pp. 841–850). Mahwah, NJ: Erlbaum.

Cavanaugh, J. C. (1993). *Adult development and aging* (2nd ed.). Pacific Grove, CA: Brooks/Cole.

Caverly, D. C., Orlando, V. P., & Mullen, J. L. (2000). Textbook study reading. In R. F. Flippo & D. C. Caverly (Eds.), *Handbook of college reading and study strategy research.* Mahwah, NJ: Erlbaum.

Ceci, S. J., Rosenblum, T., de Bruyn, E., & Lee, D. Y. (1997). A bio-ecological model of intellectual development: Moving beyond *h2*. In R. J. Sternberg & E. L. Grigorenko (Eds.), *Intelligence, heredity, and environment.* New York: Cambridge University Press.

Centers for Disease Control. (2006). *Sexually transmitted diseases.* Retrieved from http://www.cdc.gov/std.

Cepeda, N. J., Pashler, H., Vul, E., Wixted, J. T., & Roher, D. (2006). Distributed practice in verbal recall tasks: A review and quantitative synthesis. *Psychological Bulletin, 132,* 354–380.

Cerletti, U., & Bini, L. (1938). Un nuevo metodo di shockterapie "L'elettro-shock". *Boll. Acad. Med. Roma, 64,* 136–138.

Chaiken, S., & Maheswaran, D. (1994). Heuristic processing can bias systematic processing: Effects of source credibility, argument ambiguity, and task importance on attitude judgment. *Journal of Personality and Social Psychology, 66,* 460–473.

Chambless, D. L., & Hollon, S. D. (1998). Defining empirically supported therapies. *Journal of Consulting & Clinical Psychology, 66,* 7–18.

Chan, J. W. C., & Vernon, P. E. (1988). Individual differences among the peoples of China. In S. H. Irvine & J. W. Berry (Eds.), *Human abilities in cultural context.* New York: Cambridge University Press.

Chance, P. (1999). Thorndike's puzzle boxes and the origins of the experimental analysis of behavior. *Journal of the Experimental Analysis of Behavior, 72,* 433–440.

Chance, P. (2001, September/October). The brain goes to school: Why neuroscience research is going to the head of the class. *Psychology Today,* p. 72.

Chandler, C. C., & Fisher, R. P. (1996). Retrieval processes and witness memory. In E. L. Bjork & R. A. Bjork (Eds.), *Memory.* San Diego: Academic Press.

Chang, E. C., & Sanna, I. J. (2003). Experience of life hassles and psychological adjustment among adolescents: Does it make a difference if one is optimistic or pessimistic? *Personality and Individual Differences, 34,* 867–879.

Chapman, P. D. (1988). *Schools as sorters: Lewis M. Terman, applied psychology, and the intelligence testing movement.* New York: New York University Press.

Chemers, M. M., Hu, L., & Garcia, B. F. (2001). Academic self-efficacy and first-year college student performance and adjustment. *Journal of Educational Psychology, 93*(1), 55–64.

Cheng, C. (2001). Assessing coping flexibility in real-life and laboratory settings: A multimethod approach. *Journal of Personality and Social Psychology, 80,* 814–833.

Cheng, C. (2003). Cognitive and motivational processes underlying coping flexibility: A dual-process model. *Journal of Personality and Social Psychology, 84,* 425–438.

Cheng, C., & Cheung, M. W. L. (2005). Cognitive processes underlying coping flexibility: Differentiation and integration. *Journal of Personality, 73,* 859–886.

Cherrier, M. M., Matsumoto, A. M., Amory, J. K., Johnson, M., Craft, S., Peskinf, E. R., & Raskind, M. A. (2007). Characterization of verbal and spatial memory changes from moderate to supraphysiological increases in serum testosterone in healthy older men. *Psychoneuroendocrinology, 32*(1), 72–79.

Chess, S., & Thomas, A. (1996). *Temperament: Theory and practice.* New York: Brunner/Mazel.

Chiroro, P., Bohner, G., Viki, G. T., & Jarvis, C. I. (2004). Rape myth acceptance and rape proclivity: Expected dominance versus expected arousal as mediators in acquaintance–rape situations. *Journal of Interpersonal Violence, 19,* 427–441.

Chiu, C. Y., Leung, A. K. Y., & Kwan, L. (2007). Language, cognition, and culture: Beyond the Whorfian hypothesis. In S. Kitayama & D. Cohen (Eds.), *Handbook of cultural psychology* (pp. 668–690). New York: Guilford.

Choi, I., Nisbett, R. E., & Norenzayan, A. (1999). Causal attribution across cultures: Variation and universality. *Psychological Bulletin, 125,* 47–63.

Chomsky, N. (1957). *Syntactic structures.* The Hague: Mouton.

Chomsky, N. (1959). A review of B. F. Skinner's "Verbal Behavior." *Language, 35,* 26–58.

Chomsky, N. (1965). *Aspects of theory of syntax.* Cambridge, MA: MIT Press.

Chomsky, N. (1975). *Reflections on language.* New York: Pantheon.

Chomsky, N. (1986). *Knowledge of language: Its nature, origins, and use.* New York: Praeger.

Chomsky, N. (2006). *Language and mind* (3rd ed.). New York: Cambridge University Press.

Chopra, S. S. (2003). Industry funding of clinical trials: Benefit of bias? *Journal of the American Medical Association, 290,* 113–114.

Choudhry, N. K., Stelfox, H. T., & Detsky, A. S. (2002). Relationships between authors of clinical practice guidelines and the pharmaceutical industry. *Journal of the American Medical Association, 287(5),* 612–617.

Christensen, A. J., & Johnson, J. A. (2002). Patient adherence with medical treatment regimens: An interactive approach. *Current Directions in Psychological Science, 11(3),* 94–97.

Christensen, B. K., Carney, C. E., & Segal, Z. V. (2006). Cognitive processing models of depression. In D. J. Stein, D. J. Kupfer, & A. F. Schatzberg (Eds.), *Textbook of mood disorders.* Washington, DC: American Psychiatric Publishing.

Christensen, B. T., & Schunn, C. D. (2007). The relationship of analogical distance to analogical function and preinventive structure: The case of engineering design. *Memory & Cognition, 35(1),* 29–38.

Christensen, C. C. (2005). Preferences for descriptors of hypnosis: A brief communication. *International Journal of Clinical and Experimental Hypnosis, 53,* 281–289.

Christensen, L. (1988). Deception in psychological research: When is its use justified? *Personality and Social Psychology Bulletin, 14,* 664–675.

Christoph, R. T., Schoenfeld, G. A., & Tansky, J. W. (1998). Overcoming barriers to training utilizing technology: The influence of self-efficacy factors on multimedia-based training receptiveness. *Human Resource Development Quarterly, 9,* 25–38.

Chronicle, E. P., MacGregor, J. N., & Ormerod, T. C. (2004). What makes an insight problem? The roles of heuristics, goal conception, and solution recording in knowledge-lean problems. *Journal of Experimental Psychology: Learning, Memory, and Cognition, 30(1),* 14–27.

Chrousos, G. P., & Kaltsas, G. (2007). Stress and cardiovascular disease. In G. Fink (Ed.), *Encyclopedia of stress.* San Diego: Elsevier.

Chudler, E. H. (2007). The power of the full moon. Running on empty? In S. Della Sala (Ed.), *Tall tales about the mind & brain: Separating fact from fiction* (pp. 401–410). New York: Oxford University Press.

Chun, M. M., & Wolfe, J. M. (2001). Visual attention. In E. B. Goldstein (Ed.), *Blackwell handbook of perception.* Malden, MA: Blackwell.

Cialdini, R. B. (2001). *Influence: Science and practice.* Boston: Allyn & Bacon.

Cialdini, R. B. (2001). *Influence: Science and practice.* New York: HarperCollins.

Cialdini, R. B., & Trost, M. R. (1998). Social influence: Social norms, conformity, and compliance. In D. T. Gilbert, S. T. Fiske, & G. Lindzey (Eds.), *The handbook of social psychology.* New York: McGraw-Hill.

Cianciolo, A. T., & Sternberg, R. J. (2004). *Intelligence: A brief history.* Malden, MA: Blackwell Publishing.

Ciarrochi, J., Dean, F. P., & Anderson, S. (2002). Emotional intelligence moderates the relationship between stress and mental health. *Personality & Individual Differences, 32,* 197–209.

Cicero, T. J., Inciardi, J. A., & Surratt, H. (2007). Trends in the use and abuse of branded and generic extended release oxycodone and fentanyl products in the United States. *Drug and Alcohol Dependence, 91(2–3),* 115–120.

Clark, L. A. (2007). Assessment and diagnosis of personality disorder: Perennial issues and an emerging reconceptualization. *Annual Review of Psychology, 58,* 227–257.

Clark, L. A., & Watson, D. (2003). Constructing validity: Basic issues in objective scale development. In A. E. Kazdin (Ed.), *Methodological issues & strategies in clinical research* (pp. 207–231). Washington, DC: American Psychological Association.

Clark, R. D., & Hatfield, E. (1989). Gender differences in receptivity to sexual offers. *Journal of Psychology & Human Sexuality, 2(1),* 39–55.

Clark, R. E. (2003). Fostering the work motivation of individuals and teams. *Performance Improvement, 42(3),* 21–29.

Clark, R. E. (2004). The classical origins of Pavlov's conditioning. *Integrative Physiological & Behavioral Science, 39,* 279–294.

Clarke-Stewart, K. A., & Allhusen, V. (2002). Nonparental caregiving. In M. Bornstein (Ed.), *Handbook of parenting.* Mahwah, NJ: Erlbaum.

Clayton, T., & Craig, P. (2001). *Diana: Story of a princess.* New York: Pocket Books.

Clifasefi, S. L., Takarangi, M. K., & Bergman, J. S. (2006). Blind drunk: The effects of alcohol on inattentional blindness. *Applied Cognitive Psychology, 20,* 697–704.

Cloninger, C. R., Adolfsson, R., & Svrakic, D. (1996). Mapping genes for human personality. *Nature Genetics, 12,* 3–4.

Clow, A. (2001). The physiology of stress. In F. Jones & J. Bright (Eds.), *Stress: Myth, theory, and research.* Harlow, UK: Pearson, Education.

Coates, T. J., & Collins, C. (1998). Preventing HIV infection. *Scientific American, 279(1),* 96–97.

Coderre, T. J., Mogil, J. S., & Bushnell, M. C. (2003). The biological psychology of pain. In M. Gallagher & R. J. Nelson (Eds.), *Handbook of psychology, Vol. 3: Biological psychology.* New York: Wiley.

Coenen, A. (1998). Neuronal phenomena associated with vigilance and consciousness: From cellular mechanisms to electroencephalographic patterns. *Consciousness & Cognition: An International Journal, 7,* 42–53.

Cohen, C. E. (1981). Person categories and social perception: Testing some boundaries of the processing effects of prior knowledge. *Journal of Personality and Social Psychology, 40,* 441–452.

Cohen, D. (1997). A critique of the use of neuroleptic drugs in psychiatry. In S. Fisher & R. P. Greenberg (Eds.), *From placebo to panacea: Putting psychiatric drugs to the test.* New York: Wiley.

Cohen, D. B. (1999). *Stranger in the nest: Do parents really shape their child's personality, intelligence, or character?* New York: Wiley.

Cohen, F., Solomon, S., Maxfield, M., Pyszczynski, T., & Greenberg, J. (2004). Fatal attraction: The effects of mortality salience on evaluations of charismatic, task-oriented, and relationship-oriented leaders. *Psychological Science, 15,* 846–851.

Cohen, L. B., & Cashon, C. H. (2003). Infant perception and cognition. In R. M. Lerner, M. A. Easterbrooks, & J. Mistry (Eds.), *Handbook of psychology, Vol. 6: Developmental psychology.* New York: Wiley.

Cohen, M. N. (2002). An anthropologist looks at "race" and IQ testing. In J. M. Fish (Ed.), *Race and intelligence: Separating science from myth* (pp. 201–224). Mahwah, NJ: Erlbaum.

Cohen, S. (2004). Social relationships and health. *American Psychologist, 59,* 676–684.

Cohen, S. (2005). Pittsburgh common cold studies: Psychosocial predictors of susceptibility to respiratory infectious illness. *International Journal of Behavioral Medicine, 12(3),* 123–131.

Cohen, S., Alper, C. M., Doyle, W. J., Treanor, J. J., & Turner, R. B. (2006). Positive emotional style predicts resistance to illness after experimental exposure to Rhinovirus or Influenza A virus. *Psychosomatic Medicine, 68,* 809–815.

Cohen, S., Janicki-Deverts, D., & Miller, G. E. (2007). Psychological stress and disease. *Journal of the American Medical Association, 298,* 1685–1687.

Cohen, S., Kessler, R. C., & Gordon, L. U. (1995). Strategies for measuring stress in studies of psychiatric and physical disorders. In S. Cohen, R. C. Kessler, & L. U. Gordon (Eds.), *Measuring stress: A guide for health and social scientists* (pp. 3–28). New York: Oxford University Press.

Cohen, S., & Pressman, S. D. (2006). Positive affect and health. *Current Directions in Psychological Science, 15(3),* 122–125.

Cohen, S., Tyrrell, D. A. J., & Smith, A. P. (1993). Negative life events, perceived stress, negative affect, and susceptibility to the common cold. *Journal of Personality and Social Psychology, 64,* 131–140.

Cohen, S. G., & Ledford, G. E., Jr. (1994). The effectiveness of self-managing teams: A quasi-experiment. *Human Relations, 47,* 13–43.

Colby, A., & Kohlberg, L. (1987). *The measurement of moral judgment* (Vols. 1–2). New York: Cambridge University Press.

Coles, M. E., Schofield, C. A., & Pietrefesa, A. S. (2006). Behavioral inhibition and obsessive-compulsive disorder. *Journal of Anxiety Disorders, 20,* 1118–1132.

Coles, R. (1970). *Erik H. Erikson: The growth of his work.* Boston: Little, Brown.

Colflesh, G. J. H., & Conway, A. R. A. (2007). Individual differences in working memory capacity and divided attention in dichotic listening. *Psychonomic Bulletin & Review, 14,* 699–703.

Collins, A. M., & Loftus, E. F. (1975). A spreading activation theory of semantic processing. *Psychological Review, 82,* 407–428.

Collins, F. S., Green, E. D., Guttmacher, A. E., & Guyer, M. S. (2006). A vision for the future of genomics research: A blueprint for the genomic era. In H. T. Tavani (Ed.), *Ethics, computing, and genomics* (pp. 287–315). Boston: Jones and Bartlett.

Collins, M. A., & Zebrowitz, L. A. (1995). The contributions of appearance to occupational outcomes in civilian and military settings. *Journal of Applied Social Psychology, 25,* 129–163.

Collins, N. L., & Allard, L. M. (2001). Cognitive representations of attachment: The content and function of working models. In G. J. O. Fletcher & M. S. Clark (Eds.), *Blackwell handbook of social psychology: Interpersonal processes.* Malden, MA: Blackwell.

Collins, W. A., & Laursen, B. (2006). Parent-adolescent relationships. In P. Noller & J. A. Feeney (Eds.), *Close relationships: Functions, forms and processes.* Hove, England: Psychology Press.

Collins, W. A., Maccoby, E. E., Steinberg, L., Hetherington, E. M., & Bornstein, M. H. (2000). Contemporary research in parenting: The case for nature and nurture. *American Psychologist, 55,* 218–232.

Collop, N. A. (2006). Polysomnography. In T. Lee-Chiong (Ed.), *Sleep: A comprehensive handbook.* Hoboken, NJ: Wiley-Liss.

Coltrane, S. (2001). Research on household labor: Modeling and measuring the social embeddedness of routine family work. In R. M. Milardo (Ed.), *Understanding families into the new millennium: A decade in review* (pp. 427–452). Minneapolis, MN: National Council on Family Relations.

Colvin, C. R., Block, J., & Funder, D. C. (1995). Overly positive self-evaluations and personality: Negative implications for mental health. *Journal of Personality and Social Psychology, 68,* 1152–1162.

Colwill, R. M. (1993). An associative analysis of instrumental learning. *Current Directions in Psychological Science, 2*(4), 111–116.

Comas-Diaz, L. (2006). Cultural variation in the therapeutic relationship. In C. D. Goodheart, A. E. Kazdin, & R. J. Sternberg (Eds.), *Evidence-based psychotherapy: Where practice and research meet.* Washington, DC: American Psychological Association.

Combs, D. R., & Mueser, K. T. (2007). Schizophrenia. In M. Hersen, S. M. Turner, & D. C. Beidel (Eds.), *Adult psychopathology and diagnosis.* New York: Wiley.

Comer, D. R. (1995). A model of social loafing in real work groups. *Human Relations, 48,* 647–667.

Compas, B. E. (2004). Processes of risk and resilience during adolescence: Linking contexts and individuals. In R. M. Lerner & L. Steinberg (Eds.), *Handbook of adolescent psychology.* New York: Wiley.

Compton, D. M., Dietrich, K. L., & Smith, J. S. (1995). Animal rights activism and animal welfare concerns in the academic setting: Levels of activism and perceived importance of research with animals. *Psychological Reports, 76,* 23–31.

Compton, M. T., Goulding, S. M., & Walker, E. F. (2007). Cannabis use, first-episode psychosis, and schizotypy: A summary and synthesis of recent literature. *Current Psychiatry Reviews, 3,* 161–171.

Compton, W. M., Thomas, Y. F., Conway, K. P., & Colliver, J. D. (2005). Developments in the epidemiology of drug use and drug use disorders. *American Journal of Psychiatry, 162,* 1494–1502.

Conger, J., & Kanungo, R. N. (1994). Charismatic leadership in organizations: Perceived behavioral attributes and their measurement. *Journal of Organizational Behavior, 15,* 439–452.

Conklin, H. M., & Iacono, W. G. (2002). Schizophrenia: A neurodevelopmental perspective. *Current Directions in Psychological Science, 11,* 33–37.

Connolly, T., & Zeelenberg, M. (2002). Regret in decision making. *Current Directions in Psychological Science, 11*(6), 212–216.

Conrad, M. A., & Ashworth, S. D. (1986). *Recruiting source effectiveness: A meta-analysis and reexamination of two rival hypotheses.* Paper presented at the First Annual Meeting of the Society for Industrial and Organizational Psychology, Chicago, IL.

Conte, J. M., & Dean, M. A. (2006). Can emotional intelligence be measured? In K. R. Murphy (Ed.), *A critique of emotional intelligence: What are the problems and how can they be fixed?* (pp. 59–78). Mahwah, NJ: Erlbaum.

Conway, A. R. A., Kane, M. J., & Engle, R. W. (2003). Working memory capacity and its relation to general intelligence. *Trends in Cognitive Sciences, 7,* 547–552.

Conway, L. C., & Schaller, M. (2002). On the verifiability of evolutionary psychological theories: An analysis of the psychology of scientific persuasion. *Personality and Social Psychology Review, 6,* 152–166.

Cooke, L. (2007). The importance of exposure for healthy eating in childhood: A review. *Journal of Human Nutrition and Dietetics, 20,* 294–301.

Cooke, R., & Sheeran, P. (2004). Moderation of cognition-intention and cognition-behaviour relations: A meta-analysis of properties of variables from the theory of planned behaviour. *British Journal of Social Psychology, 43,* 159–186.

Cooper, C. L., & Dewe, P. (2007). Stress: A brief history from the 1950s to Richard Lazarus. In A. Monat, R. S. Lazarus, & G. Reevy (Eds.), *The Praeger handbook on stress and coping.* Westport, CT: Praeger.

Cooper, E. (1991). A critique of six measures for assessing creativity. *Journal of Creative Behavior, 25*(3), 194–204.

Cooper, J., & Cooper, G. (2002). Subliminal motivation: A story revisited. *Journal of Applied Psychology, 32,* 2213–2227.

Cooper, L., & Bright, J. (2001). Individual differences in reactions to stress. In F. Jones & J. Bright (Eds.), *Stress: Myth, theory and research.* Harlow, UK: Pearson Education.

Cooper, M. L., Pioli, M., Levitt, A. , Talley, A. E., Micheas, L., & Collins, N. L. (2006). Attachment styles, sex motives, and sexual behavior: Evidence for gender-specific expressions of attachment dynamics. In M. Mikulincer & G. S. Goodman (Eds.), *Dynamics of romantic love: Attachment, caregiving, and sex.* New York: Guilford.

Cooper, Z. (1995). The development and maintenance of eating disorders. In K. D. Brownell & C. G. Fairburn (Eds.), *Eating disorders and obesity: A comprehensive handbook.* New York: Guilford.

Cope, M. B., Fernandez, J. R., & Allison, D. B. (2004). Genetic and biological risk factors. In J. K. Thompson (Ed.), *Handbook of eating disorders and obesity.* New York: Wiley.

Corballis, M. C. (1991). *The lopsided ape.* New York: Oxford University Press.

Corballis, M. C. (1999). Are we in our right minds? In S. D. Sala (Ed.), *Mind myths: Exploring popular assumptions about the mind and brain* (pp. 25–41). New York: Wiley.

Corballis, P. M. (2003). Visuospatial processing and the right-hemisphere interpreter. *Brain & Cognition, 53*(2), 171–176.

Coren, S. (1992). *The left-hander syndrome: The causes and consequences of left-handedness.* New York: Free Press.

Coren, S. (1996). *Sleep thieves: An eye-opening exploration into the science and mysteries of sleep.* New York: Free Press.

Coren, S., & Aks, D. J. (1990). Moon illusion in pictures: A multimechanism approach. *Journal of Experimental Psychology: Human Perception and Performance, 16,* 365–380.

Coren, S., & Girgus, J. S. (1978). *Seeing is deceiving: The psychology of visual illusions.* Hillsdale, NJ: Erlbaum.

Corkin, S. (1984). Lasting consequences of bilateral medial temporal lobectomy: Clinical course and experimental findings in H. M. *Seminars in Neurology, 4,* 249–259.

Corkin, S. (2002). What's new with the amnesic patient H. M.? *Nature Reviews Neuroscience, 3,* 153–159.

Cornell, D. G. (1997). Post hoc explanation is not prediction. *American Psychologist, 52,* 1380.

Correll, C. U., Leucht, S., & Kane, J. M. (2004). Lower risk for tardive dyskinesia associated with second-generation antipsychotics: A systematic review of 1-year studies. *American Journal of Psychiatry, 161,* 414–425.

Corsica, J. A., & Perri, M. G. (2003). Obesity. In A. M. Nezu, C. M. Nezu, & P. A. Geller (Eds.), *Handbook of psychology, Vol. 9: Health psychology.* New York: Wiley.

Corson, D. (2000). Emancipatory leadership. *International Journal of Leadership in Education, 3*(2), 93–120.

Cosmides, L., & Tooby, J. (1989). Evolutionary psychology and the generation of culture. Part II. Case study: A computational theory of social exchange. *Ethology and Sociobiology, 10,* 51–97.

Cosmides, L., & Tooby, J. (1994). Beyond intuition and instinct blindness: Toward an evolutionarily rigorous cognitive science. *Cognition, 50,* 41–77.

Cosmides, L., & Tooby, J. (1996). Are humans good intuitive statisticians after all? Rethinking some conclusions from the literature on judgment under uncertainty. *Cognition, 58,* 1–73.

Costa, P. T., Jr., & McCrae, R. R. (1985). *NEO Personality Inventory.* Odessa, FL: Psychological Assessment Resources.

Costa, P. T., Jr., & McCrae, R. R. (1992). *Revised NEO Personality Inventory: NEO PI and NEO Five-Factor Inventory* (Professional Manual). Odessa, FL: Psychological Assessment Resources.

Costa, P. T., Jr., & McCrae, R. R. (1994). Set like plaster? Evidence for the stability of adult personality. In T. F. Heatherton & J. L. Weinberger (Eds.), *Can personality change?* Washington, DC: American Psychological Association.

Costa, P. T., Jr., & McCrae, R. R. (1997). Longitudinal stability of adult personality. In R. Hogan, J. Johnson, & S. Briggs (Eds.), *Handbook of personality psychology.* San Diego: Academic Press.

Côté, J. E. (2006). Emerging adulthood as an institutionalized moratorium: Risks and benefits to identity formation. In J. J. Arnett & J. L. Tanner (Eds.), *Emerging adults in America: Coming of age in the 21st century.* Washington, DC: American Psychological Association.

Cotman, C. W., Berchtold, N. C., & Christie, L.-A. (2007). Exercise builds brain health: Key roles of growth factor cascades and inflammation. *Trends in Neurosciences, 30,* 464–472.

Cotter, A., & Potter, J. E. (2006). Mother to child transmission. In J. Beal, J. J. Orrick, & K. Alfonso (Eds.), *HIV/AIDS: Primary care guide* (pp. 503–515). Norwalk, CT: Crown House.

Courage, M. L., & Howe, M. L. (2002). From infant to child: The dynamics of cognitive change in the second year of life. *Psychological Bulletin, 128*(2), 250–277.

Coutts, A. (2000). Nutrition and the life cycle. 1: Maternal nutrition and pregnancy. *British Journal of Nursing, 9,* 1133–1138.

Cowan, N. (1988). Evolving conceptions of memory storage, selective attention, and their mutual constraints within the human information-processing system. *Psychological Bulletin, 104,* 163–191.

Cowan, N. (1999). An embedded-processes model of working memory. In A. Miyake & P. Shah (Eds.), *Models of working memory: Mechanisms of active maintenance and executive control.* New York: Cambridge University Press.

Cowan, N. (2001). The magical number 4 in short-term memory: A reconsideration of mental storage capacity. *Behavioral & Brain Sciences, 14*(1), 87–185.

Cowan, N. (2005). *Working memory capacity.* New York: Psychology Press.

Cowart, B. J. (2005). Taste, our body's gustatory gatekeeper. *Cerebrum, 7*(2), 7–22.

Cowart, B. J., & Rawson, N. E. (2001). Olfaction. In E. B. Goldstein (Ed.), *Blackwell handbook of perception.* Malden, MA: Blackwell.

Cowey, A. (1994). Cortical visual areas and the neurobiology of higher visual processes. In M. J. Farah & G. Ratcliff (Eds.), *The neuropsychology of high-level vision: Collected tutorial essays.* Hillsdale, NJ: Erlbaum.

Cox, D., Meyers, E., & Sinha, P. (2004). Contextually evoked object-specific responses in human visual cortex. *Science, 304,* 115–117.

Cox, M. J., Paley, B., Burchinal, M., & Payne, C. (1999). Marital perceptions and interactions across the transition to parenthood. *Journal of Marriage and the Family, 61,* 611–625.

Coyne, J. C. (1999). Thinking interactionally about depression: A radical restatement. In T. E. Joiner & J. V. Coyne (Eds.), *Interpersonal processes in depression* (pp. 369–392). Washington, DC: American Psychological Association.

Craig, J. C., & Rollman, G. B. (1999). Somesthesis. *Annual Review of Psychology, 50,* 305–331.

Craik, F. I. M. (2001). Effects of dividing attention on encoding and retrieval processes. In H. L. Roediger III, J. S. Nairne, I. Neath, & A. M. Surprenant (Eds.), *The nature of remembering: Essays in honor of Robert G. Crowder* (pp. 55–68). Washington, DC: American Psychological Association.

Craik, F. I. M. (2002). Levels of processing: Past, present . . . and future? *Memory, 10*(5–6), 305–318.

Craik, F. I. M., & Kester, J. D. (2000). Divided attention and memory: Impairment of processing or consolidation? In E. Tulving (Ed.), *Memory, consciousness, and the brain: The Tallinn conference* (pp. 38–51). Philadelphia: Psychology Press.

Craik, F. I. M., & Lockhart, R. S. (1972). Levels of processing: A framework for memory research. *Journal of Verbal Learning and Verbal Behavior, 11,* 671–684.

Craik, F. I. M., & Tulving, E. (1975). Depth of processing and the retention of words in episodic memory. *Journal of Experimental Psychology: General, 104,* 268–294.

Cramer, P. (2000). Defense mechanisms in psychology today: Further processes for adaptation. *American Psychologist, 55*(6), 637–646.

Cramer, P. (2001). The unconscious status of defense mechanisms. *American Psychologist, 56,* 762–763.

Cramond, B. (2004). Can we, should we, need we agree on a definition of giftedness? *Roeper Review, 27*(1), 15–16.

Cranny, C. J., Smith, P. C., & Stone, E. F. (1992). *Job satisfaction: How people feel about their jobs and how it affects their performance.* New York: Lexington Books.

Crano, W. D., & Prislin, R. (2006). Attitudes and persuasion. *Annual Review of Psychology, 57,* 345–374.

Craske, M. G., & Waters, A. M. (2005). Panic disorders, phobias, and generalized anxiety disorder. *Annual Review of Clinical Psychology, 1,* 197–225.

Cravens, H. (1992). A scientific project locked in time: The Terman Genetic Studies of Genius, 1920s–1950s. *American Psychologist, 47,* 183–189.

Crawford, M., & Popp, D. (2003). Sexual double standards: A review and methodological critique of two decades of research. *Journal of Sex Research, 40*(1), 13–26.

Creed, F. (1989). Appendectomy. In G. W. Brown & T. O. Harris (Eds.), *Life events and illness.* New York: Guilford.

Creusere, M. A. (1999). Theories of adults' understanding and use of irony and sarcasm: Applications to and evidence from research with children. *Developmental Review, 19,* 213–262.

Crews, F. (2006). *Follies of the wise: Dissenting essays.* Emeryville, CA: Shoemaker Hoard.

Crits-Christoph, P. (1997). Limitations of the dodo bird verdict and the role of clinical trials in psychotherapy research: Comment on Wampold et al (1997). *Psychological Bulletin, 122,* 216–220.

Crockett, H. (1962). The achievement motive and differential occupational mobility in the United States. *American Sociological Review, 27,* 191–204.

Croizet, J., Despres, G., Gauzins, M. E., Huguet, P., Leyens, J., & Meot, A. (2004). Stereotype threat undermines intellectual performance by triggering a disruptive mental load. *Personality and Social Psychology Bulletin, 30,* 721–731.

Cronbach, L. J. (1992). *Acceleration among the Terman males: Correlates in midlife and after.* Paper presented at the Symposium in Honor of Julian Stanley, San Francisco.

Cronk, L., & Gerkey, D. (2007). Kinship and descent. In R. I. M. Dunbar, & L. Barrett (Eds.), *Oxford handbook of evolutionary psychology* (pp. 463–478). New York: Oxford University Press.

Cropley, A. J. (2000). Defining and measuring creativity: Are creativity tests worth using? *Roeper Review, 23,* 72–79.

Cross, S. E., & Markus, H. R. (1993). Gender in thought, belief, and action: A cognitive approach. In A. E. Beall & R. J. Sternberg (Eds.), *The psychology of gender.* New York: Guilford.

Cross, S. E., & Markus, H. R. (1999). The cultural constitution of personality. In L. A. Pervin & O. P. John (Eds.), *Handbook of personality: Theory and research.* New York: Guilford.

Crow, T. J. (2007). How and why genetic linkage has not solved the problem of psychosis: Review and hypothesis. *American Journal of Psychiatry, 164,* 13–21.

Crowder, R. G. (1993). Short-term memory: Where do we stand? *Memory & Cognition, 21,* 142–45.

Crowell, J. A., Fraley, R. C., & Shaver, P. R. (1999). Measurement of individual differences in adolescent and adult attachment. In J. Cassidy & P. R. Shaver (Eds.), *Handbook of attachment: Theory, research, and clinical applications.* New York: Guilford.

Crowley, K., Callanan, M. A., Tenenbaum, H. R., & Allen, E. (2001). Parents explain more often to boys than to girls during shared scientific thinking. *Psychological Science, 12,* 258–261.

Cruz, C., della Rocco, P., & Hackworth, C. (2000). Effects of quick rotating schedules on the health and adjustment of air traffic controllers. *Aviation, Space, & Environmental Medicine, 71,* 400–407.

Csikszentmihalyi, M. (1994). Creativity. In R. J. Sternberg (Ed.), *Encyclopedia of human intelligence.* New York: Macmillan.

Csikszentmihalyi, M. (1999). Implications of a systems perspective for the study of creativity. In R. J. Sternberg (Ed.), *Handbook of creativity.* New York: Cambridge University Press.

Csikszentmihalyi, M. (2000). The contribution of flow to positive psychology. In J. E. Gillham (Ed.), *The science of optimism and hope: Research essays in honor of Martin E. P. Seligman.* Philadelphia: Templeton Foundation Press.

Cuban, L. (2004). Assessing the 20-year impact of multiple intelligences on schooling. *Teachers College Record, 106*(1), 140–146.

Culham, J. C. (2006). Functional neuroimaging: Experimental design and analysis. In R. Cabeza & A. Kingstone (Eds.), *Handbook of functional neuroimaging of cognition* (pp. 53–82). Cambridge, MA: MIT Press.

Cullum, J., & Harton, H. C. (2007). Cultural evolution: Interpersonal influence, issue importance, and the development of shared attitudes in college residence halls. *Personality and Social Psychology Bulletin, 33,* 1327–1339.

Culpepper, L., Davidson, J. R. T., Dietrich, A. J., Goodman, W. K., Kroenke, K., & Schwenk, T. L. (2004). Suicidality as a possible effect of antidepressant treatment. *Journal of Clinical Psychiatry, 65,* 742–749.

Cummings, D. E. (2006). Ghrelin and the short- and long-term regulation of appetite and body weight. *Physiology & Behavior, 89,* 71–84.

Cummins, D. (2005). Dominance, status, and social hierarchies. In D. M. Buss (Ed.), *The handbook of evolutionary psychology.* New York: Wiley.

Cunningham, C. O., & Selwyn, P. A. (2005). HIV-related medical complications and treatment. In J. H. Lowinson, P. Ruiz, R. B. Millman, & J. G. Langrod (Eds.), *Substance abuse: A comprehensive textbook.* Philadelphia: Lippincott/Williams & Williams.

Cunningham, M. (2001). The influence of parental attitudes and behaviors on children's attitudes toward gender and household labor in early adulthood. *Journal of Marriage and the Family, 63,* 111–122.

Cushman, P. (1992). Psychotherapy to 1992: A historically situated interpretation. In D. K. Freedheim (Ed.), *History of psychotherapy: A century of change.* Washington, DC: American Psychological Association.

Cutting, L. P., & Docherty, N. M. (2000). Schizophrenia outpatients' perceptions of their parents: Is expressed emotion a factor? *Journal of Abnormal Psychology, 109,* 266–272.

Czeisler, C. A., Buxton, O. M., & Khalsa, S. (2005). The human circadian timing system and sleep-wake regulation. In M. H. Kryger, T. Roth, & W. C. Dement (Eds.), *Principles and practice of sleep medicine.* Philadelphia: Elsevier Saunders.

Czeisler, C. A., Cajochen, C., & Turek, F. W. (2000). Melatonin in the regulation of sleep and circadian rhythms. In M. H. Kryger, T. Roth, & W. C. Dement (Eds.), *Principles and practice of sleep medicine.* Philadelphia: Saunders.

Dahl, R. (2003). Beyond raging hormones: The tinderbox in the teenage brain. *Cerebrum, 5*(3), 7–22.

Daiek, D. B., & Anter, N. M. (2004). *Critical reading for college and beyond.* New York: McGraw Hill.

Dalal, R. (2006). A meta-analysis of the relationship between organizational citizenship behavior and counterproductive work behavior. *Journal of Applied Psychology, 90,* 1241–1255.

Dallman, M. F., Bhatnagar, S., & Viau, V. (2007). Hypothalamic-pituitary-adrenal axis. In G. Fink (Ed.), *Encyclopedia of stress.* San Diego: Elsevier.

Dalton, S. O., & Johansen, C. (2005). Stress and cancer: The critical research. In C. L. Cooper (Ed.), *Handbook of stress medicine and health.* Boca Raton, FL: CRC Press.

Daly, M., & Wilson, M. (1985). Child abuse and other risks of not living with both parents. *Ethology and Sociobiology, 6,* 197–210.

Daly, M., & Wilson, M. (1988). *Homicide.* Hawthorne, NY: Aldine.

Dan, B. A., & Gleason, J. B. (2001). Semantic development: Learning the meanings of words. In J. B. Gleason (Ed.), *The development of language* (5th ed., pp. 125–161). Boston: Allyn & Bacon.

D'Andrade, R. G. (1961). Anthropological studies of dreams. In F. Hsu (Ed.), *Psychological anthropology: Approaches to culture and personality.* Homewood, IL: Dorsey Press.

Daniels, H. (2005). Introduction. In H. Daniels (Ed.), *An introduction to Vygotsky.* New York: Routledge.

Danner, D. D., Snowdon, D. A., & Friesen, W. V. (2001). Positive emotions in early life and longevity: Findings from the nun study. *Journal of Personality & Social Psychology, 80,* 804–813.

Danziger, K. (1990). *Constructing the subject: Historical origins of psychological research.* Cambridge, England: Cambridge University Press.

Dapretto, M., & Bjork, E. (2000). The development of word retrieval abilities in the second year and its relation to early vocabulary growth. *Child Development, 71,* 635–648.

Dapretto, M., Davies, M. S., Pfeifer, J. H., Scott, A. A., Sigman, M., Bookheimer, S. Y., & Iacoboni, M. (2006). Understanding emotions in others: Mirror neuron dysfunction in children with autism spectrum disorders. *Nature Neuroscience, 9*(1), 28–30.

Darley, J. M., & Latané, B. (1968). Bystander intervention in emergencies: Diffusion of responsibility. *Journal of Personality and Social Psychology, 8,* 377–383.

Darwin, C. (1859). *On the origin of species.* London: Murray.

Darwin, C. (1871). *Descent of man.* London: Murray.

Darwin, C. (1872). *The expression of emotions in man and animals.* New York: Philosophical Library.

Das, H. H. J., & de Wit, J. B. F. (2003). Fear appeals motivate acceptance of action recommendations: Evidence for a positive bias in the processing of persuasive messages. *Personality and Social Psychology Bulletin, 29,* 650–664.

Das, H. H. J., de Wit, J. B. F., & Stroebe, W. (2005). Fear appeals motivate acceptance of action recommendations: Evidence for a positive bias in the processing of persuasive messages. *Personality and Social Psychology Bulletin, 29,* 650–664.

Dasen, P. R. (1994). Culture and cognitive development from a Piagetian perspective. In W. J. Lonner & R. Malpass (Eds.), *Psychology and culture.* Boston: Allyn & Bacon.

Davenport, J. L., & Potter, M. C. (2004). Scene consistency in object and background perception. *Psychological Science, 15,* 559–564.

Davidoff, J. (2001). Language and perceptual categorization. *Trends in Cognitive Sciences, 5,* 382–387.

Davidoff, J. (2004). Coloured thinking. *Psychologist, 17,* 570–572.

Davidovitz, R., Mikulincer, M., Shaver, P. R., Izsak, R., & Popper, M. (2007). Leaders as attachment figures: Leaders' attachment orientations predict leadership-related mental representations and followers' performance and mental health. *Journal of Personality and Social Psychology, 93,* 632–650.

Davidson, J. E. (2003). Insights about insightful problem solving. In J. E. Davidson & R. J. Sternberg (Eds.), *The psychology of problem solving.* New York: Cambridge University Press.

Davidson, L. (2000). Philosophical foundations of humanistic psychology. *The Humanistic Psychologist, 28*(1–3), 7–31.

Davidson, R. J., Fox, A., & Kalin, N. H. (2007). Neural bases of emotion regulation in nonhuman primates and humans. In J. J. Gross (Ed.), *Handbook of emotion regulation* (pp. 47–68). New York: Guilford.

Davidson, R. J., Kabat-Zinn, J., Schumacher, J., Rosenkranz, M., Muller, D., Santorelli, S. F., Urbanowski, F., Harrington, A., Bonus, K., & Sheridan, J. F. (2003a). Alterations in brain and immune function produced by mindfulness meditation. *Psychosomatic Medicine, 65,* 564–570.

Davidson, R. J., Pizzagalli, D., Nitschke, J. B., & Kalin, N. H. (2003b). Parsing the subcomponents of emotion and disorders of emotion: Perspectives from affective neuroscience. In R. J. Davidson, K. R. Scherer, & H. H. Goldsmith (Eds.), *Handbook of affective sciences.* New York: Oxford University Press.

Davies, I. R. L. (1998). A study of colour in three languages: A test of linguistic relativity hypothesis. *British Journal of Psychology, 89,* 433–452.

Davis, A. S., & Dean, R. S. (2005). Lateralization of cerebral functions and hemispheric specialization: Linking behavior, structure, and neuroimaging. In R. C. D'Amato, E. Fletcher-Janzen, & C. R. Reynolds (Eds.), *Handbook of school neuropsychology* (pp. 120–141). Hoboken, NJ: Wiley.

Davis, D., & Loftus, E. F. (2007). Internal and external sources of misinformation in adult witness memory. In M. P. Toglia, J. D. Read, D. F. Ross, & R. C. L. Lindsay (Eds.), *Handbook of eyewitness psychology: Volume 1. Memory for events.* Mahwah, NJ: Erlbaum.

Davis, D., Shaver, P. R., & Vernon, M. L. (2003). Physical, emotional, and behavioral reactions to breaking up: The roles of gender, age, emotional involvement, and attachment style. *Personality and Social Psychology Bulletin, 29,* 871–884.

Davis, J. L., & Rusbult, C. E. (2001). Attitude alignment in close relationships. *Journal of Personality and Social Psychology, 81*(1), 65–84.

Davis, M. H., Morris, M. M., & Kraus, L. A. (1998). Relationship-specific and global perceptions of social support: Associations with well-being and attachment. *Journal of Personality and Social Psychology, 74,* 468–481.

Davis, O. S. P., Arden, R., & Plomin, R. (2008). *g* in middle childhood: Moderate genetic and shared environmental influence using diverse measures of general cognitive ability at 7, 9 and 10 years in a large population sample of twins. *Intelligence, 36,* 68–80.

Dawkins, K., Golden, R. N., & Fawcett, J. A. (2003). Therapeutic management of the suicidal patient. In A. Tasman, J. Kay, & J. A. Lieberman (Eds.), *Psychiatry* (pp. 2112–2135). New York: Wiley.

Dawson, W. A. (1993). Aboriginal dreaming. In M. A. Carskadon (Ed.), *Encyclopedia of sleep and dreaming.* New York: Macmillan.

Day, R. H. (1965). Inappropriate constancy explanation of spatial distortions. *Nature, 207,* 891–893.

Deary, I. J. (2000). Simple information processing and intelligence. In R. J. Sternberg (Ed.), *Handbook of intelligence* (pp. 267–284). New York: Cambridge University Press.

Deary, I. J. (2003). Reaction time and psychometric intelligence: Jensen's contributions. In H. Nyborg (Ed.), *The scientific study of general intelligence: Tribute to Arthur R. Jensen.* Oxford, UK: Pergamon.

Deary, I. J., Caryl, P. G., & Gibson, G. J. (1993). Nonstationarity and the measurement of psychological response in a visual inspection time task. *Perception, 22,* 1245–1256.

Deary, I. J., & Stough, C. (1996). Intelligence and inspection time: Achievements, prospects, and problems. *American Psychologist, 51,* 599–608.

Deary, I. J., Strand, S., Smith, P., & Fernandes, C. (2007). Intelligence and educational achievement. *Intelligence, 35,* 13–21.

Deary, I. J., Whiteman, M. C., Starr, J. M., Whalley, L. J., & Fox, H. C. (2004). The impact of childhood intelligence on later life: Following up the Scottish mental surveys of 1932 and 1947. *Journal of Personality and Social Psychology, 86,* 130–147.

de Bruin, W. B., Parker, A. M., & Fischhoff, B. (2007). Individual differences in adult decision-making competence. *Journal of Personality and Social Psychology, 92,* 938–956.

de Castro, J. M. (2000). Eating behavior: Lessons from the real world of humans. *Nutrition, 16,* 800–813.

DeCarvalho, R. J. (1991). *The founders of humanistic psychology.* New York: Praeger.

Deecher, D., Andree, T. H., Sloan, D., & Schechter, L. E. (2008). From menarche to menopause: Exploring the underlying biology of depression in women experiencing hormonal changes. *Psychoneuroendocrinology, 33*(1), 3–17.

Deese, J. (1959). On the prediction of occurrence of particular verbal intrusions in immediate recall. *Journal of Experimental Psychology, 58,* 17–22.

Defeyter, M. A., & German, T. P. (2003). Acquiring an understanding of design: Evidence from children's insight problem solving. *Cognition, 89*(2), 133–155.

DeFrain, J., & Olson, D. H. (1999). Contemporary family patterns and relationships. In M. B. Sussman, S. K. Steinmetz, & G. W. Peterson (Eds.), *Handbook of marriage and the family* (pp. 309–326). New York: Plenum.

Degenhardt, L., & Hall, W. (2006). Is cannabis use a contributory cause of psychosis? *Canadian Journal of Psychiatry, 51,* 556–565.

Dehaene, S., Changeux, J.-P., Naccache, L., Sackur, J., & Sergent, C. (2006). Conscious, preconscious, and subliminal processing: A testable taxonomy. *Trends in Cognitive Sciences, 10,* 204–211.

de Houwer, A. (1995). Bilingual language acquisition. In P. Fletcher & B. MacWhinney (Eds.), *The handbook of child language.* Oxford, OH: Basil Blackwell.

de Houwer, J. (2001). Contingency awareness and evaluative conditioning: When will it be enough? *Consciousness & Cognition: An International Journal, 10,* 550–558.

de Houwer, J., Hendrickx, H., & Baeyens, F. (1997). Evaluative learning with "subliminally" presented stimuli. *Consciousness & Cognition: An International Journal, 6,* 87–107.

de Jong, P. J., & Merckelbach, H. (2000). Phobia-relevant illusory correlations: The role of phobic responsivity. *Journal of Abnormal Psychology, 109,* 597–601.

de Koninck, J. (2000). Waking experiences and dreaming. In M. H. Kryger, T. Roth, & W. C. Dement (Eds.), *Principles and practice of sleep medicine.* Philadelphia: Saunders.

Delay, J., & Deniker, P. (1952). *Trente-huit cas de psychoses traitées par la cure prolongée et continue de 4560 RP.* Paris: Masson et Cie.

Delgado, P. L., & Moreno, F. A. (2006). Neurochemistry of mood disorders. In D. J. Stein, D. J. Kupfer, & A. F. Schatzberg (Eds.), *Textbook of mood disorders* (pp. 101–116). Washington, DC: American Psychiatric Publishing.

Delis, D. C., & Lucas, J. A. (1996). Memory. In B. S. Fogel, R. B. Schiffer, & S. M. Rao (Eds.), *Neuropsychiatry.* Baltimore: Williams & Wilkins.

DeLisi, L. E. (2008). The effect of cannabis on the brain: Can it cause brain anomalies that lead to increased risk for schizophrenia? *Current Opinion in Psychiatry, 21,* 140–150.

DelMonte, M. M. (2000). Retrieved memories of childhood sexual abuse. *British Journal of Medical Psychology, 73,* 1–13.

DeLong, M. R. (2000). The basal ganglia. In E. R. Kandel, J. H. Schwartz, & T. M. Jessell (Eds.),

Principles of neural science (pp. 853–872). New York: McGraw-Hill.

DeLongis, A., Folkman, S., & Lazarus, R. S. (1988). The impact of daily stress on health and mood: Psychological and social resources as mediators. *Journal of Personality and Social Psychology, 54,* 486–495.

Dement, W. C. (1978). *Some must watch while some must sleep.* New York: Norton.

Dement, W. C. (1992). *The sleepwatchers.* Stanford, CA: Stanford Alumni Association.

Dement, W. C. (2000). History of sleep physiology and medicine. In M. H. Kryger, T. Roth, & W. C. Dement (Eds.), *Principles and practice of sleep medicine.* Philadelphia: Saunders.

Dement, W. C. (2003). Knocking on Kleitman's door: The view from 50 years later. *Sleep Medicine Reviews, 7*(4), 289–292.

Dement, W. C. (2005). History of sleep psychology. In M. H. Kryger, T. Roth, & W. C. Dement (Eds.), *Principles and practice of sleep medicine.* Philadelphia: Elsevier Saunders.

Dement, W. C., & Vaughan, C. (1999). *The promise of sleep.* New York: Delacorte Press.

Dement, W. C., & Wolpert, E. (1958). The relation of eye movements, bodily motility, and external stimuli to dream content. *Journal of Experimental Psychology, 53,* 543–553.

Dempster, F. N. (1996). Distributing and managing the conditions of encoding and practice. In E. L. Bjork & R. A. Bjork (Eds.), *Memory.* San Diego: Academic Press.

De Neys, W. (2006). Dual processing in reasoning: Two systems but one reasoner. *Psychological Science, 17,* 428–433.

Denison, D. R. (1996). What IS the difference between organizational culture and organizational climate? A native's point of view on a decade of paradigm wars. *Academy of Management Review, 21,* 619–654.

Dennerstein, L., Dudley, E., & Guthrie, J. (2002). Empty nest or revolving door? A prospective study of women's quality of life in midlife during the phase of children leaving and re-entering the home. *Psychological Medicine, 32,* 545–550.

Dennis, C., & Ross, L. (2005). Relationships among infant sleep patterns, maternal fatigue, and development of depressive symptomatology. *Birth, 32,* 187–193.

Dennis, W. (1966). Age and creative productivity. *Journal of Gerontology, 21*(1), 1–8.

Derevensky, J. L., & Gupta, R. (2004). Preface. In J. L. Derevensky, & R. Gupta (Eds.), *Gambling problems in youth: Theoretical and applied perspectives* (pp. xxi–xxiv). New York: Kluwer/Plenum.

Derogatis, L. R., & Coons, H. L. (1993). Self-report measures of stress. In L. Goldberger & S. Breznitz (Eds.), *Handbook of stress: Theoretical and clinical aspects* (2nd ed.). New York: Free Press.

Des Jarlais, D. C., Hagan, H., & Friedman, S. R. (2005). Epidemiology and emerging public health perspectives. In J. H. Lowinson, P. Ruiz, R. B. Millman, & J. G. Langrod (Eds.), *Substance abuse: A comprehensive textbook.* Philadelphia: Lippincott/Williams & Wilkins.

de St. Aubin, E., McAdams, D. P., & Kim, T. (2004). *The generative society: Caring for future generations.* Washington, DC: American Psychological Association.

Detterman, L. T., Gabriel, L. T., & Ruthsatz, J. M. (2000). Intelligence and mental retardation. In R. J. Sternberg (Ed.), *Handbook of intelligence* (pp. 141–158). New York: Cambridge University Press.

Deutsch, J. A. (1990). Food intake: Gastric factors. In E. M. Stricker (Ed), *Handbook of behavioral neurobiology, Vol. 10: Neurobiology of food and fluid intake.* New York: Plenum.

DeValois, R. L., & Jacobs, G. H. (1984). Neural mechanisms of color vision. In I. Darian-Smith (Ed.), *The nervous system* (Vol. 3). Baltimore: Williams & Wilkins.

de Villiers, J. G., & de Villiers, P. A. (1999). Language development. In M. H. Bornstein & M. E. Lamb (Eds.), *Developmental psychology: An advanced textbook* (pp. 313–373). Mahwah, NJ: Erlbaum.

De Villiers, P. (1977). Choice in concurrent schedules and a quantitative formulation of the law of effect. In W. K. Honig & J. E. R. Staddon (Eds.), *Handbook of operant behavior.* Englewood Cliffs, NJ: Prentice-Hall.

Devine, P. G., & Baker, S. M. (1991). Measurements of racial stereotypes subtyping. *Personality and Social Psychology Bulletin, 17,* 44–50.

Devine, P. G., & Monteith, M. J. (1999). Automaticity and control in stereotyping. In S. Chaiken & Y. Trope (Eds.), *Dual-process theories in social psychology.* New York: Guilford.

Devine, P. G., Plant, E. A., & Blair, I. V. (2001). Classic and contemporary analysis of racial prejudice. In R. Brown & S. L. Gaertner (Eds.), *Blackwell handbook of social psychology: Intergroup processes.* Malden, MA: Blackwell.

Devine, P. G., Tauer, J. M., Barron, K. E., Elliot, A. J., & Vance, K. M. (1999). Moving beyond attitude change in the study of dissonance-related processes. In E. Harmon-Jones & J. Mills (Eds.), *Cognitive dissonance: Progress on a pivotal theory in social psychology.* Washington, DC: American Psychological Association.

Devlin, B., Fienberg, S. E., Resnick, D. P., & Roeder, K. (2002). Intelligence and success: Is it all in the genes? In J. M. Fish (Ed.), *Race and intelligence: Separating science from myth* (pp. 355–368). Mahwah, NJ: Erlbaum.

DeVries, R. (2000). Vygotsky, Piaget, and education: A reciprocal assimilation of theories and educational practices. *New Ideas in Psychology, 18*(2–3), 187–213.

Dew, M. A., Bromet, E. J., & Switzer, G. E. (2000). Epidemiology. In M. Hersen & A. S. Bellack (Eds.), *Psychopathology in adulthood.* Boston: Allyn & Bacon.

De Waal, F. (2001). *The ape and the sushi master: Cultural reflections of a primatologist.* New York: Basic Books.

de Wijk, R. A., Schab, F. R., & Cain, W. S. (1995). Odor identification. In F. R. Schab & R. G. Crowder (Eds.), *Memory for odors.* Mahwah, NJ: Erlbaum.

Deyoub, P. L. (1984). Hypnotic stimulation of antisocial behavior: A case report. *International Journal of Clinical and Experimental Hypnosis, 32*(3), 301–306.

Diamond, L. M. (2003). Was it a phase? Young women's relinquishment of lesbian/bisexual identities over a 5-year period. *Journal of Personality and Social Psychology, 84,* 352–364.

Diamond, L. M. (2007). The evolution of plasticity in female-female desire. *Journal of Psychology & Human Sexuality, 18,* 245–274.

Di Chiara, G. (1999). Drug addiction as a dopamine-dependent associative learning disorder. *European Journal of Pharmacology, 375,* 13–30.

Dick, D. M., & Rose, R. J. (2002). Behavior genetics: What's new? What's next? *Current Directions in Psychological Science, 11*(2), 70–74.

Dickens, W. T., & Flynn, J. R. (2001). Heritability estimates versus large environmental effects: The IQ paradox resolved. *Psychological Review, 108,* 346–369.

Dickens, W. T., & Flynn, J. R. (2006). Black Americans reduce the racial IQ gap: Evidence from standardization samples. *Psychological Science, 17,* 913–920.

Diekman, A. B., & Murnen, S. K. (2004). Learning to be little women and little men: The inequitable gender equality of nonsexist children's literature. *Sex Roles, 50,* 373–385.

Diener, E. (1984). Subjective well-being. *Psychological Bulletin, 93,* 542–575.

Diener, E., & Diener, C. (1996). Most people are happy. *Psyhological Science, 7,* 181–185.

Diener, E., & Diener, M. (1995). Cross-cultural correlates of life satisfaction and self-esteem. *Journal of Personality and Social Psychology, 68,* 653–663.

Diener, E., Gohm, C. L., Suh, E., & Oishi, S. (2000). Similarity of the relations between marital status and subjective well-being across cultures. *Journal of Cross-Cultural Psychology, 31,* 419–436.

Diener, E., & Lucas, R. E. (1999). Personality and subjective well-being. In D. Kahneman, E. Diener, & N. Schwarz (Eds.), *Well-being: The foundations of hedonic psychology.* New York: Russell Sage Foundation.

Diener, E., Lucas, R. E., & Scollon, C. N. (2006). Beyond the hedonic treadmill: Revising the adaptation theory of well-being. *American Psychologist, 61,* 305–314.

Diener, E., & Oishi, S. (2005). The nonobvious social psychology of happiness. *Psychological Inquiry, 16*(4), 162–167.

Diener, E., Sandvik, E., Seidlitz, L., & Diener, M. (1993). The relationship between income and subjective well-being. Relative or absolute? *Social Indicators Research, 28,* 195–223.

Diener, E., & Seligman, M. E. P. (2002). Very happy people. *Psychological Science, 13,* 81–84.

Diener, E., & Seligman, M. E. P. (2004). Beyond money: Toward an economy of well-being. *Psychological Science in the Public Interest, 5*(1), 1–31.

Diener, E., Wolsic, B., & Fujita, F. (1995). Physical attractiveness and subjective well-being. *Journal of Personality and Social Psychology, 69,* 120–129.

Dietrich, E. (1999). Algorithm. In R. A. Wilson & F. C. Keil (Eds.), *The MIT encyclopedia of the cognitive sciences.* Cambridge, MA: MIT Press.

Di Forti, M., Morrison, P. D., Butt, A., & Murray, R. M. (2007). Cannabis use and psychiatric and cognitive disorders: The chicken or the egg? *Current Opinion in Psychiatry, 20,* 228–234.

Dijksterhuis, A. (2004a). I like myself but I don't know why: Enhancing implicit self-esteem by subliminal evaluative conditioning. *Journal of Personality and Social Psychology, 86,* 345–355.

Dijksterhuis, A. (2004b). Think different: The merits of unconscious thought in preference development and decision making. *Journal of Personality and Social Psychology, 87,* 586–598.

Dijksterhuis, A., Bos, M. W., Nordgren, L. F., & van Baaren, R. B. (2006). On making the right choice: The deliberation-without-attention effect. *Science, 311,* 1005–1007.

Dijksterhuis, A., & Nordgren, L. F. (2006). A theory of unconscious thought. *Perspectives on Psychological Science, 1*(2), 95–109.

Dijksterhuis, A., & van Olden, Z. (2006). On the benefits of thinking unconsciously: Unconscious thought can increase post-choice satisfaction. *Journal of Experimental Social Psychology, 42,* 627–631.

Dillbeck, M. C., & Orme-Johnson, D. W. (1987). Physiological differences between transcendental meditation and rest. *American Psychologist, 42,* 879–881.

Di Lorenzo, P. M., & Youngentob, S. L. (2003). Olfaction and taste. In M. Gallagher & R. J. Nelson (Eds.), *Handbook of psychology, Vol. 3: Biological psychology.* New York: Wiley.

Dilsaver, S. C., Chen, Y. R., Shoaib, A. M., & Swann, A. C. (1999). Phenomenology of mania: Evidence for distinct depressed, dysphoric, and euphoric presentations. *American Journal of Psychiatry, 156,* 426–430.

Di Marzo, V., & Matias, I. (2005). Endocannabinoid control of food intake and energy balance. *Nature Neuroscience, 8,* 585–569.

DiMatteo, M. R. (1991). *The psychology of health, illness, and medical care: An individual perspective.* Pacific Grove, CA: Brooks/Cole.

DiMatteo, M. R. (1997). Health behaviors and care decisions: An overview of professional-patient communication. In D. S. Gochman (Ed.), *Handbook of health behavior research II: Provider determinants.* New York: Plenum.

DiMatteo, M. R. (2004a). Social support and patient adherence to medical treatment: A meta-analysis. *Health Psychology, 23,* 207–218.

DiMatteo, M. R. (2004b). Variations in patients' adherence to medical recommendations: A quantitative review of 50 years of research. *Medical Care, 42,* 200–209.

DiMatteo, M. R., Giordani, P. J., Lepper, H. S., & Croghan, T. W. (2002). Patient adherence and medical treatment outcomes: A meta-analysis. *Medical Care, 40,* 794–811.

Dimsdale, J. E., Irwin, M., Keefe, F. J., & Stein, M. B. (2005). Stress and anxiety. In B. J. Sadock & V. A. Sadock (Eds.), *Kaplan & Sadock's comprehensive textbook of psychiatry.* Philadelphia: Lippincott/ Williams & Wilkins.

Din, J. N., Newby, D. E., & Flapan, A. D. (2004). Omega 3 fatty acids and cardiovascular disease— fishing for a natural treatment. *British Medical Journal, 328,* 30–35.

Dinehart, M. E., Hayes, J. E., Bartoshuk, L. M., Lanier, S. L., & Duffy, V. B. (2006). Bitter taste markers explain variability in vegetable sweetness, bitterness, and intake. *Physiology & Behavior, 87,* 304–313.

Dinges, D. F. (1993). Napping. In M. A. Carskadon (Ed.), *Encyclopedia of sleep and dreaming.* New York: Macmillan.

Dinges, D. F., Rogers, N. L., & Baynard, M. D. (2005). Chronic sleep deprivation. In M. H. Kryger, T. Roth, & W. C. Dement (Eds.), *Principles and practice of sleep medicine.* Philadelphia: Elsevier Saunders.

Dinsmoor, J. A. (1992). Setting the record straight: The social views of B. F. Skinner. *American Psychologist, 47,* 1454–1463.

Dinsmoor, J. A. (1998). Punishment. In W. O'Donohue (Ed.), *Learning and behavior therapy.* Boston: Allyn & Bacon.

Dinsmoor, J. A. (2004). The etymology of basic concepts in the experimental analysis of behavior. *Journal of the Experimental Analysis of Behavior, 82,* 311–316.

Dion, K. K., & Dion, K. L. (2006). Individualism, collectivism, and the psychology of love. In R. J. Sternberg & K. Weis (Eds.), *The new psychology of love.* New Haven, CT: Yale University Press.

Dion, K. L. (2003). Prejudice, racism, and discrimination. In T. Millon & M. J. Lerner (Eds.), *Handbook of psychology, Vol. 5: Personality and social psychology.* New York: Wiley.

DiPietro, J. A. (2004). The role of prenatal maternal stress in child development. *Current Directions in Psychological Science, 13*(2), 71–74.

Dissell, R. (2005, December 14). Student from Ohio robbed bank to feed gambling habit, lawyer says. *Cleveland Plain Dealer,* pp. 24–31.

Dixon, L., & Goldman, H. (2004). Forty years of progress in community mental health: The role of evidence-based practices. *Administration & Policy in Mental Health, 31*(5), 381–392.

Dixon, R. A., & Cohen, A. (2003). Cognitive development in adulthood. In R. M. Lerner, M. A. Easterbrooks, & J. Mistry (Eds.), *Handbook of psychology, Vol. 6: Developmental psychology.* New York: Wiley.

Dobbs, D. (2005). Fact or phrenology. *Scientific American Mind, 16*(1), 224–231.

Dobbs, D. (2006). A revealing reflection. *Scientific American Mind, 17*(2), 22–28.

Dobzhansky, T. (1937). *Genetics and the origin of species.* New York; Columbia University Press.

Docherty, J. P. (1999). Cost of treating mental illness from a managed care perspective. *Journal of Clinical Psychiatry, 60,* 49–53.

Doerr, P., Pirke, K. M., Kockott, G., & Dittmor, F. (1976). Further studies on sex hormones in male homosexuals. *Archives of General Psychiatry, 33,* 611–614.

Doghramji, P. P. (2001). Detection of insomnia in primary care. *Journal of Clinical Psychiatry, 62*(suppl 10), 18–26.

Dohrenwend, B. P. (2006). Inventorying stressful life events as risk factors for psychopathology: Toward resolution of the problem of intracategory variability. *Psychological Bulletin, 132,* 477–495.

Dolan, M., Anderson, I. M., & Deakin, J. F. W. (2001). Relationship between 5-HT function and impulsivity and aggression in male offenders with personality disorders. *British Journal of Psychiatry, 178,* 352–359.

Dollard, J., & Miller, N. E. (1950). *Personality and psychotherapy: An analysis in terms of learning, thinking and culture.* New York: McGraw-Hill.

Dollard, J., Doob, L. W., Miller, N. E., Mowrer, O. H., & Sears, R. R. (1939). *Frustration and aggression.* New Haven: Yale University Press.

Domhoff, G. W. (2001). A new neurocognitive theory of dreams. *Dreaming, 11,* 13–33.

Domhoff, G. W. (2005a). The content of dreams: Methodologic and theoretical implications. In M. H. Kryger, T. Roth, & W. C. Dement (Eds.), *Principles and practice of sleep medicine.* Philadelphia: Elsevier Saunders.

Domhoff, G. W. (2005b). Refocusing the neurocognitive approach to dreams: A critique of the Hobson versus Solms debate. *Dreaming, 15*(1), 3–20.

Domhoff, G. W. (2007). Realistic simulation and bizarreness in dream content: Past findings and suggestions for future research. In D. Barrett & P. McNamara (Eds.), *The new science of dreaming: Content, recall, and personality correlates.* Westport, CT: Praeger.

Dominowski, R. L., & Bourne, L. E., Jr. (1994). History of research on thinking and problem solving. In R. J. Sternberg (Ed.), *Thinking and problem solving.* San Diego: Academic Press.

Domjan, M. (1992). Adult learning and mate choice: Possibilities and experimental evidence. *American Zoologist, 32,* 48–61.

Domjan, M. (1994). Formulation of a behavior system for sexual conditioning. *Psychonomic Bulletin & Review, 1,* 421–428.

Domjan, M. (2005). Pavlovian conditioning: A functional perspective. *Annual Review of Psychology, 56,* 179–206.

Domjan, M., Blesbois, E., & Williams, J. (1998). The adaptive significance of sexual conditioning: Pavlovian control of sperm release. *Psychological Science, 9,* 411–415.

Domjan, M., Cusato, B., & Krause, M. (2004). Learning with arbitrary versus ecological conditioned stimuli: Evidence from sexual conditioning. *Psychonomic Bulletin & Review, 11,* 232–246.

Domjan, M., & Purdy, J. E. (1995). Animal research in psychology: More than meets the eye of the general psychology student. *American Psychologist, 50,* 496–503.

Donahoe, J. W., & Vegas, R. (2004). Pavlovian conditioning: The CS-UR relation. *Journal of Experimental Psychology: Animal Behavior Processes, 30*(1), 17–33.

Donn, L. (1988). *Freud and Jung: Years of friendship, years of loss.* New York: Scribner's.

Donnerstein, E., Linz, D., & Penrod, S. (1987). *The question of pornography: Research findings and policy implications.* New York: Free Press.

Donnerstein, E., & Malamuth, N. (1997). Pornography: Its consequences on the observer. In L. B. Schlesinger & E. Revitch (Eds.), *Sexual dynamics of anti-social behavior.* Springfield, IL: Charles C. Thomas.

Dorner, G. (1988). Neuroendocrine response to estrogen and brain differentiation. *Archives of Sexual Behavior, 17*(1), 57–75.

Dorrian, J., & Dinges, D. F. (2006). Sleep deprivation and its effects on cognitive performance. In T. Lee-Chiong (Ed.), *Sleep: A comprehensive handbook.* Hoboken, NJ: Wiley-Liss.

Doty, R. L. (1991). Olfactory system. In T. V. Getchell, R. L. Doty, L. M. Bartoshuk, & J. B. Snow, Jr. (Eds.), *Smell and taste in health and disease.* New York: Raven.

Doty, R. L. (2001). Olfaction. *Annual Review of Psychology, 52,* 423–452.

Dougall, A. L., & Baum, A. (2001). Stress, health, and illness. In A. Baum, T. A. Revenson & J. E. Singer (Eds.), *Handbook of health psychology* (pp. 321–338). Mahwah, NJ: Erlbaum.

Douglas, K. S., Vincent, G. M., & Edens, J. F. (2006). Risk for criminal recidivism: The role of psychopathy. In C. J. Patrick (Ed.), *Handbook of psychopathy.* New York: Guilford.

Douzenis, A., Tsirka, Z., Vassilopoulou, C., & Christodoulou, G. N. (2004). The role of serotonin in neurobiology of aggression. *Psychiatriki, 15*(2), 169–179.

Dovidio, J. F., & Gaertner, S. L. (2000). Aversive racism and selection decisions: 1989 and 1999. *Psychological Science, 11,* 315–319.

Dovidio, J. F., & Gaertner, S. L. (2008). New directions in aversive racism research: Persistence and pervasiveness. In C. Willis-Esqueda (Ed.), *Motivational aspects of prejudice and racism.* New York: Springer Science + Business Media.

Dowling, K. W. (2005). The effect of lunar phases on domestic violence incident rates. *The Forensic Examiner, 14*(4), 13–18.

Downing, P. E., Chan, A. W. Y., Peelen, M. V., Dodds, C. M., & Kanwisher, N. (2006). Domain specificity in visual cortex. *Cerebral Cortex, 16,* 1453–1461.

Draganski, B., Gaser, C., Busch, V., Schuierer, G., Bogdahn, U., & May, A. (2004). Changes in grey matter induced by training. *Nature, 427,* 311–312.

Draguns, J. G. (1980). Psychological disorders of clinical severity. In H. C. Triandis & J. Draguns (Eds.), *Handbook of cross-cultural psychology* (Vol. 6). Boston: Allyn & Bacon.

Draguns, J. G. (1990). Applications of cross-cultural psychology in the field of mental health. In R. Brislin (Ed.), *Applied cross-cultural psychology.* Newbury Park, CA: Sage.

Draijer, N., & Langeland, W. (1999). Childhood trauma and perceived parental dysfunction in the etiology of dissociative symptoms in psychiatric inpatients. *American Journal of Psychiatry, 156,* 379–385.

Dranovsky, A., & Hen, R. (2006). Hippocampal neurogenesis: Regulation by stress and antidepressants. *Biological Psychiatry, 59,* 1136–1143.

Draycott, S., & Dabbs, A. (1998). Cognitive dissonance 1: An overview of the literature and its integration into theory and practice of clinical psychology. *British Journal of Clinical Psychology, 37,* 341–353.

Drazen, J. M., & Curfman, G. D. (2002). Financial associations of authors. *New England Journal of Medicine, 346,* 1901–1902.

Drewnowski, A. (1995). Standards for the treatment of obesity. In K. D. Brownell, & C. G. Fairburn (Eds.), *Eating disorders and obesity: A comprehensive handbook.* New York: Guilford.

Drigotas, S. M., Safstrom, C. A., & Gentilia, T. (1999). An investment model prediction of dating infidelity. *Journal of Personality and Social Psychology, 77,* 509–524.

Driskell, J. E., Willis, R. P., & Copper, C. (1992). Effect of overlearning on retention. *Journal of Applied Psychology, 77*(5), 615–622.

D'Souza, D. C. (2007). Cannabinoids and psychosis. *International Review of Neurobiology, 78,* 289–326.

Dubicka, B., Hadley, S., & Roberts, C. (2006). Suicidal behaviour in youths with depression treated with new-generation antidepressants—Meta-analysis. *British Journal of Psychiatry, 189,* 393–398.

Dubovsky, S. (2005). Benzodiazepine receptor agonists and antagonists. In B. J. Sadock & V. A. Sadock (Eds.), *Kaplan and Sadock's comprehensive textbook of psychiatry* (pp. 2781–2790). Philadelphia: Lippincott Williams & Wilkins.

Dubovsky, S. L., Davies, R., & Dubovsky, A. N. (2003). Mood disorders. In R. E. Hales & S. C. Yudofsky (Eds.), *Textbook of clinical psychiatry.* Washington, DC: American Psychiatric Publishing.

Duckworth, A. L., & Seligman, M. E. P. (2005). Self-discipline outdoes IQ in predicting academic performance of adolescents. *Psychological Science, 16,* 939–944.

Duckworth, A. L., Steen, T. A., & Seligman, M. E. P. (2005). Positive psychology in clinical practice. *Annual Review of Clinical Psychology, 1*(1), 629–651.

Duckworth, K., & Borus, J. F. (1999). Population-based psychiatry in the public sector and managed care. In A. M. Nicholi (Ed.), *The Harvard guide to psychiatry.* Cambridge, MA: Harvard University Press.

Dudai, Y. (2004). The neurobiology of consolidation, or, how stable is the engram? *Annual Review of Psychology, 55,* 51–86.

Duff, P. (2002). Maternal and perinatal infection. In S. G. Gabbe, J. R. Niebyl, & J. L. Simpson (Eds.), *Obstetrics: Normal and problem pregnancies.* New York: Churchill Livingstone.

Duffy, V. B. (2004). Associations between oral sensation, dietary behaviors and risk of cardiovascular disease (CVD). *Appetite, 43*(1), 5–9.

Duffy, V. B., Lucchina, L. A., & Bartoshuk, L. M. (2004). Genetic variation in taste: Potential biomarker for cardiovascular disease risk? In J. Prescott & B. J. Tepper (Eds.), *Genetic variations in taste sensitivity: Measurement, significance and implications* (pp. 195–228). New York: Dekker.

Duffy, V. B., & Peterson, J. M., Bartoshuk, L. M. (2004). Associations between taste genetics, oral sensations and alcohol intake. *Physiology & Behavior, 82,* 435–445.

Duman, R. S., & Monteggia, L. M. (2006). A neurotrophic model for stress-related mood disorders. *Biological Psychiatry, 59,* 1116–1127.

Dunbar, K., & Blanchette, I. (2001). The in vivo/in vitro approach to cognition: The case of analogy. *Trends in Cognitive Sciences, 5,* 334–339.

Dunbar, R. (1996). *Grooming, gossip, and the evolution of language.* Cambridge, MA: Harvard University Press.

Dunbar-Jacob, J., & Schlenk, E. (2001). Patient adherence to treatment regimen. In A. Baum, T. A. Revenson, & J. E. Singer (Eds.), *Handbook of health psychology* (pp. 571–580). Mahwah, NJ: Erlbaum.

Duncan, B. L. (1976). Differential social perception and attribution of intergroup violence: Testing the lower limits of stereotyping of blacks. *Journal of Personality and Social Psychology, 34,* 590–598.

Dunkel-Schetter, C., Gurung, R. A. R., Lobel, M., & Wadhwa, P. D. (2001). Stress processes in pregnancy and birth: Psychological, biological, and sociocultural influences. In A. Baum, T. A. Revenson, & J. E. Singer (Eds.), *Handbook of health psychology* (pp. 495–518). Mahwah, NJ: Erlbaum.

Dunning, D., & Sherman, D. A. (1997). Stereotypes and tacit inference. *Journal of Personality and Social Psychology, 73,* 459–471.

Durlach, N. I., & Colburn, H. S. (1978). Binaural phenomenon. In E. C. Carterette & M. P. Friedman (Eds.), *Handbook of perception* (Vol. 4). New York: Academic Press.

Durmer, J. S., & Dinges, D. F. (2005). Neurocognitive consequences of sleep deprivation. *Seminars in Neurology, 25,* 117–129.

Durrant, R., & Ellis, B. J. (2003). Evolutionary psychology. In M. Gallagher & R. J. Nelson (Eds.), *Handbook of psychology, Vol. 3: Biological psychology.* New York: Wiley.

Durston, S., Hulshoff, P., Hilleke, E., Casey, B. J., Giedd, J. N., Buitelaar, J. K., & van Engeland, H. (2001). Anatomical MRI of the developing human brain: What have we learned? *Journal of the American Academy of Child and Adolescent Psychiatry , 40,* 1012–1020.

Dwyer, J. (1995). Popular diets. In K. D. Brownell & C. G. Fairburn (Eds.), *Eating disorders and obesity.* New York: Guilford.

Eagle, M. N., & Wolitzky, D. L. (1992). Psychoanalytic theories of psychotherapy. In D. K. Freedheim (Ed.), *History of psychotherapy: A century of change.* Washington, DC: American Psychological Association.

Eagly, A. H. (1992). Uneven progress: Social psychology and the study of attitudes. *Journal of Personality and Social Psychology, 63,* 693–710.

Eagly, A. H. (1995). The science and politics of comparing women and men. *American Psychologist, 50,* 145–158.

Eagly, A. H., Ashmore, R. D., Makhijani, M. G., & Longo, L. C. (1991). What is beautiful is good, but . . . : A meta-analytic review of research on the physical attractiveness stereotype. *Psychological Bulletin, 110,* 109–128.

Eagly, A. H., & Chaiken, S. (1998). Attitude structure and function. In D. T. Gilbert, S. T. Fiske, & G. Lindzey (Eds.), *The handbook of social psychology.* New York: McGraw-Hill.

Eagly, A. H., & Wood, W. (1999). The origins of sex differences in human behavior: Evolved dispositions versus social roles. *American Psychologist, 54,* 408–423.

Eaker, E. D., Sullivan, L. M., Kelly-Hayes, M., D'Agostino, R. B., & Benjamin, E. J. (2004). Anger and hostility predict the development of atrial fibrillation in men in the Framingham Offspring Study. *Circulation, 109,* 1267–1271.

Easterlin, B. L., & Cardena, E. (1999). Cognitive and emotional differences between short- and long-term Vipassana meditators. *Imagination, Cognition and Personality, 18*(1), 68–81.

Eastman, R. (2004). The EEG in psychiatry. *South African Psychiatry Review, 7*(2), 29.

Eaton, J. (2001). Management communication: The threat of groupthink. *Corporate Communications, 6,* 183–192.

Ebbinghaus, H. (1885/1964). *Memory: A contribution to experimental psychology* (H. A. Ruger & E. R. Bussemius, Trans.). New York: Dover. (Original work published 1885)

Eby, L. T., Casper, W. J., Lockwood, A., Bordeaux, C., & Brinley, A. (2005). Work and family research in IO/OBL: Content analysis and review of the literature (1980–2002). *Journal of Vocational Behavior, 66*(1), 124–197.

Edinger, J. D., & Means, M. K. (2005). Overview of insomnia: Definitions, epidemiology, differential diagnosis, and assessment. In M. H. Kryger, T. Roth, & W. C. Dement (Eds.), *Principles and practice of sleep medicine.* Philadelphia: Elsevier Saunders.

Edlin, G., & Golanty, E. (1992). *Health and wellness: A holistic approach.* Boston: Jones and Bartlett.

Edwards, A. (1999). *Ever after: Diana and the life she led.* New York: St. Martin's Press.

Edwards, D. J. A. (2007). Collaborative versus adversarial stances in scientific discourse: Implications for the role of systematic case studies in the development of evidence-based practice in psychotherapy. *Pragmatic Case Studies in Psychotherapy, 3*(1), 6–34.

Efron, R. (1990). *The decline and fall of hemispheric specialization.* Hillsdale, NJ: Erlbaum.

Egan, J. P. (1975). *Signal detection theory and ROC-analysis.* New York: Academic Press.

Egan, M. F., & Hyde, T. M. (2000). Schizophrenia: Neurobiology. In B. J. Sadock & V. A. Sadock (Eds.), *Kaplan and Sadock's comprehensive textbook of psychiatry* (7th ed., Vol. 1, pp. 1129–1146). Philadelphia: Lippincott/Williams & Wilkins.

Ehrenberg, O., & Ehrenberg, M. (1986). *The psychotherapy maze.* Northvale, NJ: Aronson.

Ehrenberg, O., & Ehrenberg, M. (1994). *The psychotherapy maze: A consumer's guide to getting in and out of therapy.* Northvale, NJ: Jason Aronson.

Eibach, R. P., & Keegan, T. (2006). Free at last? Social dominance, loss aversion, and white and black Americans' differing assessments of racial progress. *Journal of Personality and Social Psychology, 90,* 453–467.

Eich, E., Macaulay, D., Loewenstein, R. J., & Dihle, P. H. (1997). Memory, amnesia, and dissociative identity disorder. *Psychological Science, 8,* 417–422.

Eichenbaum, H. (1997). Declarative memory: Insights from cognitive neurobiology. *Annual Review of Psychology, 48,* 547–572.

Eichenbaum, H. (2003). Memory systems. In M. Gallagher & R. J. Nelson (Eds.), *Handbook of psychology, Vol. 3: Biological psychology.* New York: Wiley.

Eichenbaum, H. (2004). An information processing framework for memory representation by the hippocampus. In M. S. Gazzaniga (Ed.), *The cognitive neurosciences.* Cambridge, MA: MIT Press.

Eid, M., & Diener, E. (2001). Norms for experiencing emotions in different cultures: Inter- and intranational differences. *Journal of Personality and Social Psychology, 81,* 869–885.

Einstein, G. O., & McDaniel, M. A. (1996). Remembering to do things: Remembering a forgotten topic. In D. J. Herrmann, C. McEvoy, C. Hertzog, P. Hertel, & M. K. Johnson (Eds.), *Basic and applied memory research: Practical applications* (Vol. 2). Mahwah, NJ: Erlbaum.

Einstein, G. O., & McDaniel, M. A. (2004). *Memory fitness: A guide for successful aging.* New Haven, CT: Yale University Press.

Einstein, G. O., & McDaniel, M. A. (2005). Prospective memory: Multiple retrieval processes. *Current Directions in Psychological Science, 14,* 286–290.

Einstein, G. O., McDaniel, M. A., Williford, C. L., Pagan, J. L., & Dismukes, R. K. (2003). Forgetting of intentions in demanding situations is rapid. *Journal of Experimental Psychology: Applied, 9*(3), 147–162.

Eisenberg, N., Spinrad, T., & Sadovsky, A. (2006). Empathy-related responding in children. In M. Killen & J. G. Smetana (Eds.), *Handbook of moral development.* Mahwah, NJ: Erlbaum.

Eisner, E. W. (2004). Multiple intelligences. *Teachers College Record, 106*(1), 31–39.

Ekman, P. (1992). Facial expressions of emotion: New findings, new questions. *Psychological Science, 3,* 34–38.

Ekman, P. (1993). Facial expression and emotion. *American Psychologist, 48,* 384–392.

Ekman, P., & Friesen, W. V. (1975). *Unmasking the face.* Englewood Cliffs, NJ: Prentice-Hall.

Ekman, P., & Friesen, W. V. (1984). *Unmasking the face.* Palo Alto: Consulting Psychologists Press.

Elbert, T., Pantev, C., Weinbruch, C., Rockstroh, B., & Taub, E. (1995). Increased cortical representation of the fingers of the left hand in string players. *Science, 270,* 305–307.

Elfenbein, H. A., & Ambady, N. (2002). On the universality and cultural specificity of emotion recognition: A meta-analysis. *Psychological Bulletin, 128*(2), 203–235.

Elfenbein, H. A., & Ambady, N. (2003). Universals and cultural differences in recognizing emotions of a different cultural group. *Current Directions in Psychological Science, 12*(5), 159–164.

Ellis, A. (1973). *Humanistic psychotherapy: The rational-emotive approach.* New York: Julian Press.

Ellis, A. (1977). *Reason and emotion in psychotherapy.* Seacaucus, NJ: Lyle Stuart.

Ellis, A. (1985). *How to live with and without anger.* New York: Citadel Press.

Ellis, A. (1987). The evolution of rational-emotive therapy (RET) and cognitive behavior therapy (CBT). In J. K. Zeig (Ed.), *The evolution of psychotherapy.* New York: Brunner/Mazel.

Ellis, A. (1999). *How to make yourself happy and remarkably less disturbable.* Atascadero, CA: Impact Publishers.

Ellis, A. (2001). *Feeling better, getting better, staying better: Profound self-help therapy for your emotions.* Atascadero, CA: Impact Publishers.

Ellis, B. J. (2004). Timing of pubertal maturation in girls: An integrated life history approach. *Psychological Bulletin, 130,* 920–958.

Ellison, N., Heino, R., & Gibbs, J. (2006). Managing impressions online: Self-presentation processes in the online dating environment. *Journal of Computer-Mediated Communication, 11,* 415–441.

Ellsworth, P. C., & Scherer, K. R. (2003). Appraisal processes in emotion. In R. J. Davidson, K. R. Scherer, & H. H. Goldsmith (Ed.), *Handbook of affective sciences.* New York: Oxford University Press.

Ellsworth, P. C., Scherer, K. R., & Keltner, D. (2003). Appraisal processes in emotion. In R. J. Davidson, K. R. Scherer, & H. H. Goldsmith (Eds.), *Handbook of affective sciences.* New York: Oxford University Press.

Elman, J. L. (1999). The emergence of language: A conspiracy theory. In B. MacWhinney (Ed.), *The emergence of language* (pp. 1–28). Mahwah, NJ: Erlbaum .

Elpers, J. R. (2000). Public psychiatry. In B. J. Sadock & V. A. Sadock (Eds.), *Kaplan and Sadock's comprehensive textbook of psychiatry* (7th ed., Vol. 2). Philadelphia: Lippincott/Williams & Wilkins.

Emavardhana, T., & Tori, C. D. (1997). Changes in self-concept, ego defense mechanisms, and religiosity following seven-day Vipassana meditation retreats. *Journal for the Scientific Study of Religion, 36,* 194–206.

Emmelkamp, P. M. G. (1994). Behavior therapy with adults. In A. E. Bergin & S. L. Garfield (Eds.), *Handbook of psychotherapy and behavior change* (4th ed.). New York: Wiley.

Emmelkamp, P. M. G. (2004). In M. J. Lambert (Ed.), *Bergin and Garfield's handbook of psychotherapy and behavior change.* New York: Wiley.

Emsley, R., Rabinowitz, J., & Medori, R. (2006). Time course for antipsychotic treatment response in first-episode schizophrenia. *American Journal of Psychiatry, 163,* 743–745.

Engemann, K. M., & Owyang, M. T. (2005, April). So much for that merit raise: The link between wages and appearance. *The Regional Economist,* pp. 10–11.

Engle, R. W. (2001). What is working memory capacity? In H. L. Roediger III, J. S. Nairne, I. Neath, & A. M. Surprenant (Eds.), *The nature of remembering: Essays in honor of Robert G. Crowder.* Washington, DC: American Psychological Association.

Enns, J. T. (2004). *The thinking eye, the seeing brain: Explorations in visual cognition.* New York: Norton.

Epley, N., & Gilovich, T. (2006). The anchoring-and-adjustment heuristic: Why the adjustments are insufficient. *Psychological Science, 17,* 311–318.

Epley, N., & Huff, C. (1998). Suspicion, affective response, and educational benefit as a result of deception in psychology research. *Personality and Social Psychology Bulletin, 24,* 759–768.

Epstein, J., & Kinkenberg, W. D. (2001). From Eliza to Internet: A brief history of computerized assessment. *Computers in Human Behavior, 17,* 295–314.

Epstein, R. (2007). Smooth thinking about sexuality: "Gay" and "straight" are misleading terms. *Scientific American Mind, 18*(5), 14.

Epstein, S., Donovan, S., & Denes-Raj, V. (1999). The missing link in the paradox of the Linda conjunction problem: Beyond knowing and thinking of the conjunction rule, the intrinsic appeal of heuristic processing. *Personality and Social Psychology Bulletin, 25,* 204–214.

Epstein, S. P. (1980). The stability of confusion: A reply to Mischel and Peake. *Psychological Review, 90,* 179–184.

Epstein, S. P. (1986). Does aggregation produce spuriously high estimates of behavior stability? *Journal of Personality and Social Psychology, 50,* 1199–1210.

Equal Employment Opportunity Commission. (2002). *Federal laws prohibiting job discrimination: Questions and answers.* Washington, DC: Equal Employment Opportunity Commission.

Erber, M. W., Hodges, S. D., & Wilson, T. D. (1995). Attitude strength, attitude stability, and the effects of analyzing reasons. In R. E. Petty & J. A. Krosnick (Eds.), *Attitude strength: Antecedents and consequences.* Mahwah, NJ: Erlbaum.

Erdelyi, M. H. (2001). Defense processes can be conscious or unconscious. *American Psychologist, 56,* 761–762.

Erdfelder, E., Brandt, M., & Bröder, A. (2007). Recollection biases in hindsight judgments. *Social Cognition, 25,* 114–131.

Erickson, R. P., DiLorenzo, P. M., & Woodbury, M. A. (1994). Classification of taste responses in brain stem: Membership in fuzzy sets. *Journal of Neurophysiology, 71,* 2139–2150.

Ericsson, K. A., Roring, R. W., & Nandagopal, K. (2007). Giftedness and evidence for reproducibly superior performance: An account based on the expert performance framework. *High Ability Studies, 18*(1), 3–56.

Erikson, E. (1963). *Childhood and society.* New York: Norton.

Erikson, E. (1968). *Identity: Youth and crisis.* New York: Norton.

Ernst, C., & Angst, J. (1983). Birth order: Its influence on personality. *Behavioral and Brain Sciences, 10*(1), 55.

Ess, C. (2007). Internet research ethics. In A. N. Joinson, K. Y. A. McKenna, T. Postmes, & U-D. Reips (Eds.), *The Oxford handbook of Internet psychology* (pp. 487–502). New York: Oxford University Press.

Esterson, A. (1993). *Seductive mirage: An exploration of the work of Sigmund Freud.* Chicago: Open Court.

Esterson, A. (2001). The mythologizing of psychoanalytic history: Deception and self-deception in Freud's accounts of the seduction theory episode. *History of Psychiatry, 7,* 329–352.

Estes, R. E., Coston, M. L., & Fournet, G. P. (1990). *Rankings of the most notable psychologists by department chairpersons.* Unpublished manuscript.

Estes, W. K. (1999). Models of human memory: A 30-year retrospective. In C. Izawa (Ed.), *On human memory: Evolution, progress, and reflections on the 30th anniversary of the Atkinson-Shiffrin model.* Mahwah, NJ: Erlbaum.

Evans, F. J. (1990). Behavioral responses during sleep. In R. R. Bootzin, J. F. Kihlstrom, & D. L. Schacter (Eds.), *Sleep and cognition.* Washington, DC: American Psychological Association.

Evans, G. W. (2004). The environment of childhood poverty. *American Psychologist, 59*(2), 77–92.

Evans, G. W., & Wener, R. E. (2006). Rail commuting duration and passenger stress. *Health Psychology, 25,* 408–412.

Evers, K. E., Prochaska, J. O., Johnson, J. L., Mauriello, J. M., Padula, J. A., & Prochaska, J. M. (2006). A randomized clinical trial of a population- and transtheoretical model-based stress-management intervention. *Health Psychology, 25,* 521–529.

Eysenck, H. J. (1959). Learning theory and behaviour therapy. *Journal of Mental Science, 195,* 61–75.

Eysenck, H. J. (1967). *The biological basis of personality.* Springfield, IL: Charles C. Thomas.

Eysenck, H. J. (1977). *Crime and personality.* London: Routledge & Kegan Paul.

Eysenck, H. J. (1982). *Personality, genetics and behavior: Selected papers.* New York: Praeger.

Eysenck, H. J. (1989). Discrimination reaction time and "g": A reply to Humphreys. *Intelligence, 13*(4), 325–326.

Eysenck, H. J. (1990a). Biological dimensions of personality. In L. A. Pervin (Ed.), *Handbook of personality: Theory and research.* New York: Guilford.

Eysenck, H. J. (1990b). *Decline and fall of the Freudian empire.* Washington, DC: Scott-Townsend.

Eysenck, H. J., & Kamin, L. (1981). *The intelligence controversy.* New York: Wiley.

Eysenck, M. W., Mogg, K., May, J., Richards, A., & Mathews, A. (1991). Bias in interpretation of ambiguous sentences related to threat in anxiety. *Journal of Abnormal Psychology, 100,* 144–150.

Fabes, R. A., Carlo, G., Kupanoff, K., & Laible, D. (1999). Early adolescence and prosocial/moral behavior I: The role of individual processes. *Journal of Early Adolescence, 19,* 5–16.

Fabrigar, L. R., MacDonald, T. K., & Wegener, D. T. (2005). The structure of attitudes. In D. Albarracin, B. T. Johnson, & M. P. Zanna (Eds.), *The handbook of attitudes.* Mahwah, NJ: Erlbaum.

Fagan, J. F., & Holland, C. R. (2002). Equal opportunity and racial differences in IQ. *Intelligence, 30,* 361–387.

Fagan, J. F., & Holland, C. R. (2007). Racial equality in intelligence: Predictions from a theory of intelligence as processing. *Intelligence, 35,* 319–334.

Fagot, B. I., Hagan, R., Leinbach, M. D., & Kronsberg, S. (1985). Differential reactions to assertive and communicative acts of toddler boys and girls. *Child Development, 56,* 1499–1505.

Fakhoury, W., & Priebe, S. (2002). The process of deinstitutionalization: An international overview. *Current Opinion in Psychiatry, 15*(2), 187–192.

Falls, W. A. (1998). Extinction: A review of therapy and the evidence suggesting that memories are not erased with nonreinforcement. In W. O'Donohue (Ed.), *Learning and behavior therapy.* Boston: Allyn & Bacon.

Fancher, R. E. (1979). *Pioneers of psychology.* New York: Norton.

Fancher, R. E. (2000). Snapshot of Freud in America, 1899–1999. *American Psychologist, 55,* 1025–1028.

Fancher, R. E. (2005). Galton: "Hereditary talent and character". *General Psychologist, 40*(2), 13–14.

Faraday, A. (1974). *The dream game.* New York: Harper & Row.

Faravelli, C., & Pallanti, S. (1989). Recent life events and panic disorders. *American Journal of Psychiatry, 146,* 622–626.

Farrington, D. P. (2006). Family background and psychopathy. In C. J. Patrick (Ed.), *Handbook of Psychopathy.* New York: Guilford.

Fausto-Sterling, A. (1992). *Myths of gender.* New York: Basic Books.

Fava, G. A. (1999). Well-being therapy: Conceptual and technical issues. *Psychotherapy and Psychosomatics, 68*(4), 171–179.

Fava, G. A., Fabbri, S., Sirri, L., & Wise, T. N. (2007). Psychological factors affecting medical condition: A new proposal for DSM-V. *Psychosomatics: Journal of Consultation Liaison Psychiatry, 42*(2), 103–111.

Fava, G. A., Ruini, C., Rafanelli, C., Finos, L., Salmaso, L., Mangelli, L., et al. (2005). Well-being therapy of generalized anxiety disorder. *Psychotherapy and Psychosomatics, 74*(1), 26–30.

Fazio, R. H., & Olson, M. A. (2003). Attitudes: Foundations, functions, and consequences. In M. A. Hogg & J. Cooper (Eds.), *The Sage handbook of social psychology.* Thousand Oaks, CA: Sage.

Feeney, D. M. (1987). Human rights and animal welfare. *American Psychologist, 42,* 593–599.

Feeney, J. A. (1999). Adult romantic attachment and couple relationships. In J. Cassidy & P. R. Shaver (Eds.), *Handbook of attachment: Theory, research, and clinical applications.* New York: Guilford.

Fehr, B. (2001). The status of theory and research on love and commitment. In G. J. O. Fletcher & M. S. Clark (Eds.), *Blackwell handbook of social psychology: Interpersonal processes.* Malden, MA: Blackwell Publishing.

Fein, S., & Spencer, S. J. (1997). Prejudice as self-image maintenance: Affirming the self through derogating others. *Journal of Personality and Social Psychology, 73,* 31–44.

Feingold, A. (1988a). Cognitive gender differences are disappearing. *American Psychologist, 43,* 95–103.

Feingold, A. (1988b). Matching for attractiveness in romantic partners and same-sex friends: A meta-analysis and theoretical critique. *Psychological Bulletin, 104,* 226–235.

Feingold, A. (1992). Good-looking people are not what we think. *Psychological Bulletin, 111,* 304–341.

Feist, G. J. (1998). A meta-analysis of personality in scientific and artistic creativity. *Personality and Social Psychology Review, 2,* 290–309.

Feist, G. J. (2004). The evolved fluid specificity of human creativity talent. In R. J. Sternberg, E. L. Grigorenko, & J. L. Singer (Eds.), *Creativity: From potential to realization.* Washington, DC: American Psychological Association.

Feixas, G., & Botella, L. (2004). Psychotherapy integration: Reflections and contributions from a constructivist epistemology. *Journal of Psychotherapy Integration, 14*(2), 192–222.

Fekken, G. C. (2000). Reliability. In A. E. Kazdin (Ed.), *Encyclopedia of psychology* (pp. 30–34). Washington, DC: American Psychological Association.

Feldman, D. H. (1988). Creativity: Dreams, insights, and transformations. In R. J. Sternberg (Ed.), *The nature of creativity: Contemporary psychological perspectives.* Cambridge: Cambridge University Press.

Feldman, D. H. (1999). The development of creativity. In R. J. Sternberg (Ed.), *Handbook of creativity.* New York: Cambridge University Press.

Feldman, D. H. (2003). Cognitive development in childhood. In R. M. Lerner, M. A. Easterbrooks, & J. Mistry (Eds.), *Handbook of psychology, Vol. 6: Developmental psychology.* New York: Wiley.

Feliciano, L., & Areán. (2007). Mood disorders: Depressive disorders. In M. Hersen, S. M. Turner, & D. C. Beidel (Eds.), *Adult psychopathology and diagnosis.* New York: Wiley.

Fenwick, P. (1987). Meditation and the EEG. In M. A. West (Ed.), *The psychology of meditation.* Oxford: Clarendon Press.

Ferguson, M. J., & Bargh, J. A. (2004). Liking is for doing: The effects of goal pursuit on automatic evaluation. *Journal of Personality and Social Psychology, 87,* 557–572.

Ferguson, T. (1993). Working with your doctor. In D. Goleman & J. Gurin (Eds.), *Mind-body medicine: How to use your mind for better health.* Yonkers, NY: Consumer Reports Books.

Ferster, C. S., & Skinner, B. F. (1957). *Schedules of reinforcement.* New York: Appleton-Century-Crofts.

Festinger, L. (1957). *A theory of cognitive dissonance.* Stanford, CA: Stanford University Press.

Festinger, L., & Carlsmith, J. M. (1959). Cognitive consequences of forced compliance. *Journal of Abnormal and Social Psychology, 58,* 203–210.

Feuerstein, G. Z., Ruffolo, R. R., Coughlin, C., Wang, J., & Miller, D. (2007). Inflammation. In G. Fink (Ed.), *Encyclopedia of stress.* San Diego: Elsevier.

Fiedler, K., Schmid, J., & Stahl, T. (2002). What is the current truth about polygraph lie detection? *Basic & Applied Social Psychology, 24,* 313–324.

Fields, R. D. (2004). The other half of the brain. *Scientific American, 290*(4), 54–61.

Fields, R. D., & Stevens-Graham, B. (2002). New insights into neuron-glia communication. *Science, 298,* 556–562.

Fifer, W. P., Monk, C. E., & Grose-Fifer, J. (2001). Prenatal development and risk. In G. Bremner & A. Fogel (Eds.), *Blackwell handbook of infant development* (pp. 505–542). Malden, MA: Blackwell.

Figueredo, A. J., Sefcek, J. A., Vasquez, G., Brumbach, B. H., King, J. E., & Jacobs, W. J. (2005). Evolutionary personality psychology. In D. M. Buss (Ed.), *The handbook of evolutionary psychology.* New York: Wiley.

Filaire, F., Maso, F., Sagnol, M., Ferrand, C., & Lac, G. (2001). Anxiety, hormonal responses, and coping during a judo competition. *Aggressive Behavior, 27,* 55–63.

Finder, A. (2006, June 11). For some, online persona undermines a resume. *New York Times.*

Fink, B., & Penton-Voak, I. (2002). Evolutionary psychology of facial attractiveness. *Current Directions in Psychological Science, 11*(5), 154–158.

Fink, B., Neave, N., Manning, J. T., & Grammer, K. (2006). Facial symmetry and judgments of attractiveness, health and personality. *Personality and Individual Differences, 41,* 1253–1262.

Finnegan, L. P., & Kandall, S. R. (1997). Maternal and neonatal effects of alcohol and drugs. In J. H. Lowinson, P. Ruiz, R. B. Millman, & J. G. Langrod (Eds.), *Substance abuse: A comprehensive textbook.* Baltimore: Williams & Wilkins.

Firestein, S. (2001). How the olfactory system makes sense of scents. *Nature, 413,* 211–218.

First, M. B. (2003). Psychiatric classification. In A. Tasman, J. Kay, & J. A. Lieberman (Eds.), *Psychiatry.* New York: Wiley.

Fischer, K. W., & Hencke, R. W. (1996). Infants' construction of actions in context: Piaget's contribution to research on early development. *Psychological Science, 7,* 204–210.

Fischer, P., Greitemeyer, T., Pollozek, F., & Frey, D. (2006). The unresponsive bystander: Are bystanders more responsive in dangerous emergencies? *European Journal of Social Psychology, 36,* 267–278.

Fischhoff, B. (1982). Debiasing. In D. Kahneman, P. Slovic, & A. Tversky (Eds.), *Judgment under uncertainty: Heuristics and biases.* Cambridge, MA: Cambridge University Press.

Fischhoff, B. (1988). Judgment and decision making. In R. J. Sternberg & E. E. Smith (Eds.), *The psychology of human thought.* Cambridge: Cambridge University Press.

Fischhoff, B. (1999). Judgment heuristics. In R. A. Wilson & F. C. Keil (Eds.), *The MIT encyclopedia of the cognitive sciences*. Cambridge, MA: MIT Press.

Fischhoff, B. (2007). An early history of hindsight research. *Social Cognition, 25*(1), 10–13.

Fisher, B. S., Daigle, L. E., Cullen, F. T., & Turner, M. G. (2003). Reporting sexual victimization to the police and others: Results from a national-level study of college women. *Criminal Justice & Behavior, 30*(1), 6–38.

Fisher, C., & Fyrberg, D. (1994). College students weigh the costs and benefits of deceptive research. *American Psychologist, 49*, 417–427.

Fisher, S., & Greenberg, R. P. (1985). *The scientific credibility of Freud's theories and therapy*. New York: Columbia University Press.

Fisher, S., & Greenberg, R. P. (1996). *Freud scientifically reappraised: Testing the theories and therapy*. New York: Wiley.

Fisher, S., & Greenberg, R. P. (1997). The curse of the placebo: Fanciful pursuit of a pure biological therapy. In S. Fisher & R. P. Greenberg (Eds.), *From placebo to panacea: Putting psychiatric drugs to the test*. New York: Wiley.

Fishman, D. B. (2007). Seeking an equal place at the therapy research table: An introduction to a series on the pragmatic case study method. *Pragmatic Case Studies in Psychotherapy, 3*(1), 1–5.

Fishman, D. B., & Franks, C. M. (1992). Evolution and differentiation within behavior therapy: A theoretical epistemological review. In D. K. Freedheim (Ed.), *History of psychotherapy: A century of change*. Washington, DC: American Psychological Association.

Fisk, J. E. (2004). Conjunction fallacy. In F. P. Rudiger (Ed.), *Cognitive illusions*. New York: Psychology Press.

Fiske, S. T. (1998). Stereotyping, prejudice, and discrimination. In D. T. Gilbert, S. T. Fiske, & G. Lindzey (Eds.), *The handbook of social psychology*. New York: McGraw-Hill.

Fiske, S. T. (2000). Stereotyping, prejudice, and discrimination at the seam between the centuries: Evolution, culture, mind and brain. *European Journal of Social Psychology, 30*, 299–322.

Fiske, S. T. (2004). Mind the gap: In praise of informal sources of formal theory. *Personality and Social Psychology Review, 8*(2), 132–137.

Fitness, J., Fletcher, G., & Overall, N. (2003). Interpersonal attraction and intimate relationships. In M. A. Hogg & J. Cooper (Eds.), *The Sage handbook of social psychology*. Thousand Oaks, CA: Sage.

Flanagan, J. C. (1954). The critical incident technique. *Psychological Bulletin, 51*, 327–358.

Flanagin, A. J., & Waldeck, J. H. (2004). Technology use and organizational newcomer socialization. *Journal of Business Communication, 41*, 137–165.

Flannery, R. B., Jr. (1999). Psychological trauma and posttraumatic stress disorder: A review. *International Journal of Mental Health, 1*, 135–140.

Flavell, J. H. (1996). Piaget's legacy. *Psychological Science, 7*, 200–203.

Fleeson, W. (2004). Moving personality beyond the person-situation debate: The challenge and the opportunity of within-person variability. *Current Directions in Psychological Science, 13*(2), 83–87.

Fleeson, W., Malanos, A. B., & Achille, N. M. (2002). An intraindividual process approach to the relationship between extraversion and positive affect: Is acting extraverted as "good" as being extraverted? *Journal of Personality and Social Psychology, 83*, 1409–1422.

Flegal, K. M., Graubard, B. I., Williamson, D. F., & Gail, M. H. (2005). Excess deaths associated with underweight, overweight, and obesity. *Journal of the American Medical Association, 293*, 1861–1861.

Flegal, K. M., Graubard, B. I., Williamson, D. F., & Gail, M. H. (2007). Cause-specific excess deaths associated with underweight, overweight, and obesity. *Journal of the American Medical Association, 298*, 2028–2037.

Fleischhacker, W. W. (2002). Second-generation antipsychotics. *Psychopharmacology, 162*(1), 90–91.

Fletcher, G. J. O., Simpson, J. A., & Thomas, G. (2000). Ideals, perceptions, and evaluations in early relationship development. *Journal of Personality and Social Psychology, 79*, 933–940.

Fletcher, G. J. O., Simpson, J. A., Thomas, G., & Giles, L. (1999). Ideals in intimate relationships. *Journal of Personality and Social Psychology, 76*, 72–89.

Flett, G. L., Vredenburg, K., & Krames, L. (1995). The stability of depressive symptoms in college students: An empirical demonstration of regression to the mean. *Journal of Psychopathology & Behavioral Assessment, 17*, 403–415.

Flippo, R. F. (2000). *Testwise: Strategies for success in taking tests*. Torrance, CA: Good Apple.

Flippo, R. F., Becker, M. J., & Wark, D. M. (2000). Preparing for and taking tests. In R. F. Flippo & D. C. Caverly (Eds.), *Handbook of college reading and study strategy research*. Mahwah, NJ: Erlbaum.

Flores, B. H., Musselman, D. L., DeBattista, C., Garlow, S. J., Schatzberg, A. F., & Nemeroff, C. B. (2004). Biology of mood disorders. In A. F. Schatzberg & C. B. Nemeroff (Eds.), *Textbook of psychopharmacology*. Washington, DC: American Psychiatric Publishing.

Floyd, J. A., Janisse, J. J., Jenuwine, E. S., & Ager, J. W. (2007). Changes in REM-sleep percentage over the adult lifespan. *Sleep, 30*, 829–836.

Flynn, F. J. (2005). Having an open mind: The impact of openness to experience on interracial attitudes and impression formation. *Journal of Personality and Social Psychology , 88*, 816–826.

Flynn, J. R. (1987). Massive IQ gains in 14 nations: What IQ tests really measure. *Psychological Bulletin, 101*, 171–191.

Flynn, J. R. (1999). Searching for justice: The discovery of IQ gains over time. *American Psychologist, 54*, 5–20.

Flynn, J. R. (2000). The hidden history of IQ and special education: Can the problems be solved? *Psychology, Public Policy, & Law, 6*(1), 191–198.

Flynn, J. R. (2003). Movies about intelligence: The limitations of *g*. *Current Directions in Psychological Science, 12*(3), 95–99.

Flynn, J. R. (2007). *What is intelligence? Beyond the Flynn effect*. New York: Cambridge University Press.

Flynn, M. G., McFarlin, B. K., & Markofski, M. M. (2007). The anti-inflammatory actions of exercise training. *American Journal of Lifestyle Medicine, 1*, 220–235.

Fodor, E. M., & Carver, R. A. (2000). Achievement and power motives, performance feedback, and creativity. *Journal of Research in Personality, 34*, 380–396.

Fogassi, L., & Ferrari, P. F. (2007). Mirror neurons and the evolution of embodied language. *Current Directions in Psychological Science, 16*(3), 136–141.

Fogg, N. P., Harrington, P. E., & Harrington, T. F. (2004). *College majors handbook*. Indianapolis: JIST Works.

Foldvary-Schaefer, N. (2006). *Getting a good night's sleep*. Cleveland: Cleveland Clinic Press.

Folkman, S. (1997). Positive psychological states and coping with severe stress. *Social Science and Medicine, 45*, 1207–1221.

Folkman, S. (2008). The case for positive emotions in the stress process. *Anxiety, Stress & Coping: An International Journal, 21*(1), 3–14.

Folkman, S., & Moskowitz, J. T. (2000). Positive affect and the other side of coping. *American Psychologist, 55*, 647–654.

Folkman, S., & Moskowitz, J. T. (2004). Coping: Pitfalls and promise. *Annual Review of Psychology, 55*, 745–774.

Folsom, D. P., Hawthorne, W., Lindamer, L., Gilmer, T., Bailey, A., Golsham, S., Garcia, P., Unutzer, J., Hough, R., & Jeste, D. V. (2005). Prevalence and risk factors for homelessness and utilization of mental health services among 10,340 patients with serious mental illness in a large public mental health system. *American Journal Psychiatry, 162*, 370–376.

Fontaine, K. R., Redden, D. T., Wang, C., Westfall, A. O., & Allison, D. B. (2003). Years of life lost due to obesity. *Journal of the American Medical Association, 289*, 187–193.

Foote, B., Smolin, Y., Kaplan M., Legatt, M. E., & Lipschitz, D. (2006). Prevalence of dissociative disorders in psychiatric outpatients. *American Journal of Psychiatry, 163*, 623–629.

Forcier, K., Stroud, L. R., Papandonatos, G. D., Hitsman, B., Reiches, M., Krishnamoorthy, J., et al. (2006). Links between physical fitness and cardiovascular reactivity and recovery to psychological stressors: A meta-analysis. *Health Psychology, 25*, 723–739.

Formicelli, L. (2001, March-April). Baby blues. *Psychology Today*, p. 24.

Forsén, T., Eriksson, J., Tuomilehto, J., Reunanen, A., Osmond, C., & Barker, D. (2000). The fetal and childhood growth of persons who develop type 2 diabetes. *Annals of Internal Medicine, 133*, 176–182.

Forsyth, D. R. (2004). Inferences about actions performed in constraining contexts: Correspondence bias or correspondent inference? *Current Psychology: Developmental, Learning, Personality, Social , 23*(1), 41–51.

Forsyth, D. R. (2006). *Group dynamics*. Wadsworth: Belmont, CA.

Forsyth, D. R., & Strong, S. R. (1986). The scientific study of counseling and psychotherapy: A unificationist view. *American Psychologist, 41*, 113–119.

Foschi, R., & Cicciola, E. (2006). Politics and naturalism in the 20th century psychology of Alfred Binet. *History of Psychology, 9*, 267–289.

Foster, R. G. (2004). Are we trying to banish biological time? *Cerebrum, 6*, 7–26.

Foster, R. G., & Kreitzman, L. (2004). *Rhythms of life: The biological clocks that control the daily lives of every living thing*. New Haven, CT: Yale University Press.

Foulkes, D. (1985). *Dreaming: A cognitive-psychological analysis*. Hillsdale, NJ: Erlbaum.

Foulkes, D. (1996). Dream research: 1953–1993. *Sleep, 19*, 609–624.

Fowers, B. J., & Davidov, B. J. (2006). The virtue of multiculturalism: Personal transformation, character, and openness to the other. *American Psychologist, 61*, 581–594.

Fowles, D. C. (2003). Schizophrenia spectrum disorders. In G. Stricker & T. A. Widiger (Eds.), *Handbook of psychology, Vol. 8: Clinical psychology*. New York: Wiley.

Fox, G. L., Bruce, C., & Combs-Orme, T. (2000). Parenting expectations and concerns of fathers and mothers of newborn infants. *Family Relations, 49*(2), 123–131.

Fozard, J. L., & Gordon-Salant, S. (2001). Changes in vision and hearing with aging. In J. E. Birren & K. W. Schaie (Eds.), *Handbook of the psychology of aging* (5th ed., pp. 240–265). San Diego, CA: Academic Press.

Fraley, R. C. (2002). Attachment stability from infancy to adulthood: Meta-analysis and dynamic modeling of developmental mechanisms. *Personality and Social Psychology Review, 6,* 123–151.

Fraley, R. C., & Shaver, P. R. (2000). Adult romantic attachment: Theoretical developments, emerging controversies, and unanswered questions. *Review of General Psychology, 4,* 132–154.

Francis, L. A., & Birch, L. L. (2005). Maternal influences on daughters' restrained eating behavior. *Health Psychology, 24,* 548–554.

Frank, J. D. (1961). *Persuasion and healing.* Baltimore: Johns Hopkins University Press.

Frank, J. D., & Frank, J. B. (1991). *Persuasion and healing: A comparison study of psychotherapy.* Baltimore: Johns Hopkins University Press.

Frank, L. K. (1939). Projective methods for the study of personality. *Journal of Psychology, 8,* 343–389.

Frank, L. R. (1990). Electroshock: Death, brain damage, memory loss, and brainwashing. *The Journal of Mind and Behavior, 11*(3/4), 489–512.

Frank, M. G. (2006). The function of sleep. In T. Lee-Chiong (Ed.), *Sleep: A comprehensive handbook.* Hoboken, NJ: Wiley-Liss.

Frankland, P. W., & Bontempi, B. (2005). The organization of recent and remote memories. *Nature Reviews Neuroscience, 6*(2), 119–130.

Frasure-Smith, N., & Lesperance, F. (2005). Depression and coronary heart disease: Complex synergism of mind, body, and environment. *Current Directions in Psychological Science, 14*(1), 39–43.

Frazer, A., Daws, L. C., Duncan, G. E., & Morilak, D. A. (2003). Basic mechanisms of neurotransmitter action. In A. Tasman, J. Kay, & J. A. Lieberman (Eds.), *Psychiatry.* New York: Wiley.

Frederick, S., & Loewenstein, G. (1999). Hedonic adaptation. In D. Kahneman, E. Diener, & N. Schwarz (Eds.), *Well-being: The foundations of hedonic psychology.* New York: Russell Sage Foundation.

Fredrickson, B. L. (1998). What good are positive emotions? *Review of General Psychology, 2,* 300–319.

Fredrickson, B. L. (2001). The role of positive emotions in positive psychology: The broaden-and-build theory of positive emotions. *American Psychologist, 56,* 218–226.

Fredrickson, B. L. (2002). Positive emotions. In C. R. Snyder & S. J. Lopez (Eds.), *Handbook of positive psychology* (pp. 120–134). New York: Oxford University Press.

Fredrickson, B. L. (2005). The broaden-and-build theory of positive emotions. In F. A. Huppert, N. Baylis, & B. Keverne (Eds.), *The science of well-being* (pp. 217–238). New York: Oxford University Press.

Fredrickson, B. L. (2006). The broaden-and-build theory of positive emotions. In M. Csikszentmihalyi, & I. S. Csikszentmihalyi (Eds.), *A life worth living: Contributions to positive psychology.* New York: Oxford University Press.

Fredrickson, B. L., & Branigan, C. (2001). Positive emotions. In T. J. Mayne & G. A. Bonanno (Eds.), *Emotions: Current issues and future directions* (pp. 123–151). New York: Guilford.

Fredrickson, B. L., & Branigan, C. (2005). Positive emotions broaden the scope of attention and thought-action repertoires. *Cognition and Emotion, 19,*313–332.

Fredrickson, B. L., & Losada, M. F. (2005). Positive affect and the complex dynamics of human flourishing. *American Psychologist, 60,* 678–686.

Fredrickson, B. L., Tugade, M. M., Waugh, C. E., & Larkin, G. R. (2003). What good are positive emotions in crises? A prospective study of resilience and emotions following the terrorist attacks on the United States on September 11, 2001. *Journal of Personality and Social Psychology, 84,* 365–376.

Freed, J., & Parsons, L. (1998). *Right-brained children in a left-brained world: Unlocking the potential of your ADD child.* New York: Simon & Schuster.

Freedman, J. L., & Fraser, S. C. (1966). Compliance without pressure: The foot-in-the-door technique. *Journal of Personality and Social Psychology, 4,* 195–202.

Freeman, J. (2005). Permission to be gifted: How conceptions of giftedness can change lives. In R. J. Sternberg & J. E. Davidson (Eds.), *Conceptions of giftedness.* New York: Cambridge University Press.

Freese, J., Powell, B., & Steelman, L. C. (1999). Rebel without a cause or effect: Birth order and social attitudes. *American Sociological Review, 64,* 207–231.

Fremouw, W. J., de Perczel, M., & Ellis, T. E. (1990). *Suicide risk: Assessment and response guidelines.* New York: Pergamon.

French, S. A., Harnack, L., & Jeffrey, R. W. (2000). Fast food restaurant use among women in the Pound of Prevention study: Dietary, behavioral and demographic correlates. *International Journal of Obesity, 24,* 1353–1359.

Freud, S. (1900/1953). *The interpretation of dreams.* In J. Strachey (Ed.), *The standard edition of the complete psychological works of Sigmund Freud* (Vols. 4 and 5). London: Hogarth.

Freud, S. (1901/1960). *The psychopathology of everyday life.* In J. Strachey (Ed.), *The standard edition of the complete psychological works of Sigmund Freud* (Vol. 6). London: Hogarth.

Freud, S. (1905/1953). *Fragment of an analysis of a case of hysteria.* In J. Strachey (Ed.), *The standard edition of the complete psychological works of Sigmund Freud* (Vol. 7). London: Hogarth.

Freud, S. (1915/1959). Instincts and their vicissitudes. In E. Jones (Ed.), *The collected papers of Sigmund Freud* (Vol. 4). New York: Basic Books.

Freud, S. (1924). *A general introduction to psychoanalysis.* New York: Boni & Liveright.

Freud, S. (1933/1964). *New introductory lectures on psychoanalysis.* In J. Strachey (Ed.), *The standard edition of the complete psychological works of Sigmund Freud* (Vol. 22). London: Hogarth.

Freud, S. (1940). An outline of psychoanalysis. *International Journal of Psychoanalysis, 21,* 27–84.

Frey, B. S., & Stutzer, A. (2002). What can economists learn from happiness research? *Journal of Economic Literature, 40,* 402–435.

Freyd, J. J. (1996). *Betrayal trauma: The logic of forgetting childhood abuse.* Cambridge, MA: Harvard University Press.

Freyd, J. J. (2001). Memory and dimensions of trauma: Terror may be "all-too-well remembered" and betrayal buried. In J. R. Conte (Ed.), *Critical issues in child sexual abuse: Historical, legal, and psychological perspectives.* Thousand Oaks, CA: Sage.

Freyd, J. J., DePrince, A. P., & Gleaves, D. H. (2007). The state of betrayal trauma theory: Reply to McNally—Conceptual issues and future directions. *Memory, 15,* 295–311.

Friedkin, N. E. (1999). Choice shift and group polarization. *American Sociological Review, 64,* 856–875.

Friedman, H. S. (2007). Personality, disease, and self-healing. In H. S. Friedman & R. C. Silver (Eds.), *Foundations of health psychology.* New York: Oxford University Press.

Friedman, H. S., & Adler, N. E. (2007). The history and background of health psychology. In H. S. Friedman & R. C. Silver (Eds.), *Foundations of health psychology.* New York: Oxford University Press.

Friedman, H. S., Tucker, J. S., Tomlinson-Keasey, C., Schwartz, J. E., Wingard, D. L., & Criqui, M. H. (1993). Does childhood personality predict longevity? *Journal of Personality and Social Psychology, 65,* 176–185.

Friedman, M. J. (2006). Posttraumatic stress disorder among military returnees from Afghanistan and Iraq. *American Journal of Psychiatry, 163,* 586–593.

Friedman, M., & Rosenman, R. F. (1974). *Type A behavior and your heart.* New York: Knopf.

Frijda, N. H. (1999). Emotions and hedonic experience. In D. Kahneman, E. Diener, & N. Schwarz (Eds.), *Well-being: The foundations of hedonic psychology.* New York: Russell Sage Foundation.

Frishman, L. J. (2001). Basic visual processes. In E. B. Goldstein (Ed.), *Blackwell handbook of perception.* Malden, MA: Blackwell.

Friston, K. J. (2003). Characterizing functional asymmetries with brain mapping. In K. Hugdahl & R. J. Davidson (Eds.), *The asymmetrical brain* (pp. 161–186). Cambridge, MA: MIT Press.

Fritz, C., & Sonnentag, S. (2005). Recovery, health, and job performance: Effects of weekend experiences. *Journal of Occupational Health Psychology, 10*(3), 187–199.

Fromm, E. (1979). The nature of hypnosis and other altered states of consciousness: An ego-psychological theory. In E. Fromm & R. E. Shor (Eds.), *Hypnosis: Developments in research and new perspectives.* New York: Aldine.

Fromm, E. (1992). An ego-psychological theory of hypnosis. In E. Fromm & M. R. Nash (Eds.), *Contemporary hypnosis research.* New York: Guilford.

Frumkes, T. E. (1990). Classical and modern psychophysical studies of dark and light adaptation and their relationship to underlying retinal function. In K. N. Leibovic (Ed.), *Science of vision.* New York: Springer-Verlag.

Fuchs, A. H., & Milar, K. S. (2003). Psychology as a science. In D. K. Freedheim (Ed.), *Handbook of psychology, Vol. 1: History of psychology.* New York: Wiley.

Funder, D. C. (2001). Personality. *Annual Review of Psychology, 52,* 197–221.

Furnham, A., & Mak, T. (1999). Sex-role stereotyping in television commercials: A review and comparison of fourteen studies done on five continents over 25 years. *Sex Roles, 41,* 413–437.

Furumoto, L. (1980). Mary Whiton Calkins (1863–1930). *Psychology of Women Quarterly, 5,* 55–68.

Furumoto, L., & Scarborough, E. (1986). Placing women in the history of psychology: The first American women psychologists. *American Psychologist, 41,* 35–42.

Gabbard, G. O. (1994). Reconsidering the American Psychological Association's policy on sex with former patients: Is it justifiable? *Professional Psychology: Research and Practice, 25,* 329–335.

Gabbard, G. O. (2005). Major modalities: Psychoanalytic/psychodynamic. In G. O. Gabbard, J. S.

Beck, & J. Holmes (Eds.), *Oxford textbook of psychotherapy*. New York: Oxford University Press.

Gaddis, C. (1999, August 8). A Boggs life. *Tampa Tribune*. Retrieved at http://rays.tbo.com/rays/MGBWZ4RSL3E.html.

Gael, S. A. (1988). *The job analysis handbook for business, industry, and government*. New York: Wiley.

Gaeth, G. J., & Shanteau, J. (2000). Reducing the influence of irrelevant information on experienced decision makers. In T. Connolly, H. R. Arkes, & K. R. Hammond (Eds.), *Judgment and decision making: An interdisciplinary reader* (2nd ed., pp. 305–323). New York: Cambridge University Press.

Gage, F. H. (2002). Neurogenesis in the adult brain. *Journal of Neuroscience, 22*, 612–613.

Gais, S., & Born, J. (2004). Declarative memory consolidation: Mechanisms acting during human sleep. *Learning & Memory, 11*, 679–685.

Galambos, N. L. (2004). Gender and gender role development in adolescence. In R. M. Lerner & L. Steinberg (Eds.), *Handbook of adolescent psychology*. New York: Wiley.

Galanter, E. (1962). Contemporary psychophysics. In R. Brown (Ed.), *New directions in psychology*. New York: Holt, Rinehart & Winston.

Galati, D., Scherer, K. R., & Ricci-Bitti, P. E. (1997). Voluntary facial expression of emotion: Comparing congenitally blind with normally sighted encoders. *Journal of Personality and Social Psychology, 73*, 1363–1379.

Galderisi, S., Maj, M., Mucci, A., Cassano, G. B., Invernizzi, G., Rossi, A., Vita, A., Dell'Osso, L., Daneluzzo, E., & Pini, S. (2002). Historical, psychopathological, neurological, and neuropsychological, aspects of deficit schizophrenia: A multicenter study. *American Journal of Psychiatry, 159*, 983–990.

Gallagher, R. M., & Rosenthal, L. J. (2007, Summer). A multidisciplinary approach to the management of chronic pain. *Practical Neuroscience for Primary Care Physicians*, pp. 14–16.

Gallese, V., Fadiga, L., Fogassi, L., & Rizzolatti, G. (1996). Action recognition in the premotor cortex. *Brain, 119*, 593–609.

Gallistel, C. R. (2000). The replacement of general-purpose learning models with adaptively specialized learning modules. In M. S. Gazzaniga (Ed.), *The new cognitive neurosciences* (2nd ed., pp. 1179–1192). Cambridge, MA: MIT Press.

Gallup, A. C., & Gallup Jr., G. G. (2007). Yawning as a brain cooling mechanism: Nasal breathing and forehead cooling diminish the incidence of contagious yawning. *Evolutionary Psychology, 5*, 92–101.

Galton, F. (1869). *Hereditary genius: An inquiry into its laws and consequences*. New York: Appleton.

Gambone, J. C., Reiter, R. C., & DiMatteo, M. R. (1994). *The PREPARED provider: A guide for improved patient communication*. Beaverton, OR: Mosybl Great Performance.

Gangestad, S. W., Garver-Apgar, C. E., Simpson, J. A., & Cousins, A. J. (2007). Changes in women's mate preferences across the ovulatory cycle. *Journal of Personality and Social Psychology, 92*, 151–163.

Gangestad, S. W., Thornhill, R., & Garver-Apgar, C. E. (2005). Adaptations to ovulation: Implications for sexual and social behavior. *Current Directions in Psychological Science, 14*, 312–316.

Gangwisch, J. E., Heymsfield, S. B., Boden–Albala, B., et al. (2006). Short sleep duration as a risk factor for hypertension: Analyses of the first National Health and Nutrition Examination Survey. *Hypertension, 5*, 833–839.

Gantt, W. H. (1975, April 25). Unpublished lecture, Ohio State University. Cited in D. Hothersall, (1984), *History of psychology*. New York: Random House.

Garb, H. N., Florio, C. M., & Grove, W. M. (1998). The validity of the Rorschach and the Minnesota Multiphasic Personality Inventory: Results form meta-analysis. *Psychological Science, 9*, 402–404.

Garcia, J. (1989). Food for Tolman: Cognition and cathexis in concert. In T. Archer & L. G. Nilsson (Eds.), *Aversion, avoidance, and anxiety: Perspectives on aversively motivated behavior*. Hillsdale, NJ: Erlbaum.

Garcia, J., Clarke, J. C., & Hankins, W. G. (1973). Natural responses to scheduled rewards. In P. P. G. Bateson & P. Klopfer (Eds.), *Perspectives in ethology*. New York: Plenum.

Garcia, J., & Koelling, R. A. (1966). Learning with prolonged delay of reinforcement. *Psychonomic Science, 5*, 121–122.

Garcia, J., & Rusiniak, K. W. (1980). What the nose learns from the mouth. In D. Muller-Schwarze & R. M. Silverstein (Eds.), *Chemical signals*. New York: Plenum.

Garcia, S. D., & Khersonsky, D. (1996). "They make a lovely couple": Perceptions of couple attractiveness. *Journal of Social Behavior and Personality, 11*, 667–682.

Gardner, E. P., & Kandel, E. R. (2000). Touch. In E. R. Kandel, J. H. Schwartz, & T. M. Jessell (Eds.), *Principles of neural science*. New York: McGraw-Hill.

Gardner, H. (1983). *Frames of mind: The theory of multiple intelligences*. New York: Basic Books.

Gardner, H. (1985). *The mind's new science: A history of the cognitive revolution*. New York: Basic Books.

Gardner, H. (1993). *Multiple intelligences: The theory in practice*. New York: Basic Books.

Gardner, H. (1998). A multiplicity of intelligences. *Scientific American Presents Exploring Intelligence, 9*, 18–23.

Gardner, H. (1999). *Intelligence reframed: Multiple intelligences for the 21st century*. New York: Basic Books.

Gardner, H. (2004). Audiences for the theory of multiple intelligences. *Teachers College Record, 106*(1), 212–220.

Gardner, H. (2006). *Multiple intelligences: New horizons*. New York: Basic Books.

Gardner, M., & Steinberg, L. (2005). Peer influence on risk-taking, risk preference, and risky decision-making in adolescence and adulthood: An experimental study. *Developmental Psychology, 41*, 625–635.

Gardner, R. A., & Gardner, B. T. (1969). Teaching sign language to a chimpanzee. *Science, 165*, 664–672.

Gardos, P. S., & Mosher, D. L. (1999). Gender differences in reactions to viewing pornographic vignettes: Essential or interpretive? *Journal of Psychology & Human Sexuality, 11*, 65–83.

Garland, A. F., & Zigler, E. (1999). Emotional and behavioral problems among highly intellectually gifted youth. *Roeper Review, 22*, 41–44.

Garnett, N. (2005). Laws, regulations, and guidelines. In C. K. Akins, S. Panicker, & C. L. Cunningham (Eds.), *Laboratory animals in research and teaching: Ethics, care and methods*. Washington, DC: American Psychological Association.

Garry, M., & Gerrie, M. P. (2005). When photographs create false memories. *Current Directions in Psychological Science, 14*, 321–325.

Gaschler, K. (2006, February/March). One person, one neuron? *Scientific American Mind*, pp. 76–80.

Gauthier, I., & Curby, K. M. (2005). A perceptual traffic jam on highway N170: Interference between face and car expertise. *Current Directions in Psychological Science, 14*(1), 30–33.

Gauthier, I., Tarr, M. J., Anderson, A. W., Skudlarski, P., & Gore, J. C. (1999). Activation of the middle fusiform "face area" increases with expertise in recognizing novel objects. *Nature Neuroscience, 2*, 568–573.

Gawronski, B. (2004). Theory-based bias correction in dispositional inference: The fundamental attribution error is dead, long live the correspondence bias. In W. Stroebe & M. Hewstone (Eds.). *European review of social psychology* (Vol. 15). Hove, England: Psychology Press/Taylor & Francis.

Gazzaniga, M. S. (1970). *The bisected brain*. New York: Appleton-Century-Crofts.

Gazzaniga, M. S. (2000). Cerebral specialization and interhemispheric communication. *Brain, 123*, 1293–1326.

Gazzaniga, M. S. (2005). Forty-five years of split-brain research and still going strong. *Nature Reviews Neuroscience, 6*, 653–659.

Gazzaniga, M. S., Bogen, J. E., & Sperry, R. W. (1965). Observations on visual perception after disconnection of the cerebral hemispheres in man. *Brain, 88*, 221–236.

Geddes, J. R., Burgess, S., Hawton, K., Jamison, K., & Goodwin, G. M. (2004). Long-term lithium therapy for bipolar disorder: Systematic review and meta-analysis of randomized controlled trials. *American Journal of Psychiatry, 161*, 217–222.

Gee, T., Allen, K., & Powell, R. A. (2003). Questioning premorbid dissociative symptomatology in dissociative identity disorder. *Professional Psychology: Research & Practice, 34*(1), 114–116.

Geer, J. H., & Janssen, E. (2000). The sexual response system. In J. T. Cacioppo, L. G. Tassinary, & G. Bernston (Eds.), *Handbook of psychophysiology*. New York: Cambridge University Press.

Geier, A. B., Rozin, P., & Doros, G. (2006). Unit bias: A new heuristic that helps explain the effect of portion size on food intake. *Psychological Science, 17*, 521–525.

Geiger, M. A. (1997). An examination of the relationship between answer changing, testwiseness and examination performance. *Journal of Experimental Education, 66*, 49–60.

Geller, J. L. (1992). A historical perspective on the role of state hospitals viewed from the era of the "revolving door." *American Journal of Psychiatry, 149*, 1526–1533.

Gelman, R., & Williams, E. M. (1998). Enabling constraints for cognitive development and learning: Domain-specificity and epigenesis. In W. Damon (Ed.), *Handbook of child psychology (Vol. 2): Cognition, perception, and language*. New York: Wiley.

Gennari, S. P., Sloman, S. A., Malt, B. C., & Fitch, W. T. (2002). Motion events in language and cognition. *Cognition, 83*(1), 49–79.

Gentile, D. A., & Anderson, C. A. (2006). Violent video games: The effects on youth, and public policy implications. In N. Dowd, D. G. Singer, & R. F. Wilson (Eds.), *Handbook of children, culture, and violence* (pp. 225–246). Thousand Oaks, CA: Sage.

Gentner, D. (1988). Metaphor as structure mapping: The relational shift. *Child Development, 59*, 47–59.

George, J. M. (2000). Emotions and leadership: The role of emotional intelligence. *Human Relations, 53*, 1027–1055.

George, M. S. (2003, September). Stimulating the brain. *Scientific American, 289*(3), 66–93.

George, M. S., Bohning, D. E., Lorberbaum, J. P., Nahas, Z., Anderson, B., Borckardt, J. J., et al. (2007). Overview of transcranial magnetic stimulation: History, mechanisms, physics, and safety. In M. S. George & R. H. Belmaker (Eds.), *Transcranial magnetic stimulation in clinical psychiatry*. Washington, DC: American Psychiatric Publishing.

George, M. S., Nahas, Z., Bohning, D. E., Kozel, F. A., Anderson, B., Mu, C., et al. (2006). Vagus nerve stimulation and deep brain stimulation. In D. J. Stein, D. J. Kupfer, & A. F. Schatzberg (Eds.), *Textbook of mood disorders*. Washington, DC: American Psychiatric Publishing.

Gerard, M. (Ed.). (1968). *Dali*. Paris: Draeger.

Gergen, K. J., Gulerce, A., Lock, A., & Misra, G. (1996). Psychological science in cultural context. *American Psychologist, 51*, 496–503.

Gershkoff-Stowe, L., & Hahn, E. R. (2007). Fast mapping skills in the developing lexicon. *Journal of Speech, Language, and Hearing Research, 50*, 682–696.

Gershoff, E. T. (2002). Parental corporal punishment and associated child behaviors and experiences: A meta-analytic and theoretical review. *Psychological Bulletin, 128*, 539–579.

Geschwind, N., & Galaburda, A. M. (1987). *Cerebral lateralization: Biological mechanisms, associations, and pathology*. Cambridge, MA: MIT Press.

Getzel, E. E., & Wehman, P. (2005). *Going to college: Expanding opportunities with disabilities*. Baltimore: Brookes.

Ghez, C., & Thach, W. T. (2000). The cerebellum. In E. R. Kandel, J. H. Schwartz & T. M. Jessell (Eds.), *Principles of neural science* (pp. 832–852). New York: McGraw-Hill.

Gibbons, M. B. C., Crits-Christoph, P., & Hearon, B. (2008). The empirical status of psychodynamic therapies. *Annual Review of Clinical Psychology, 4*, 93–108.

Gibbons, R. D., Hur, K., Bhaumik, D. K., & Mann, J. J. (2006). The relationship between antidepressant prescription rates and rate of early adolescent suicide. *American Journal of Psychiatry, 163*, 1898–1904.

Gibbs, J., Ellison, N. B., & Heino, R. D. (2006). Self-presentation in online personals: The role of anticipated future interaction, self-disclosure, and perceived success in Internet dating. *Communication Research, 33*, 152–177.

Gibbs, W. W. (2005). Obesity: An overblown epidemic? *Scientific American, 292*(6), 70–77.

Gibson, C. B., & Cohen, S. G. (2003). *Virtual teams that work: Creating conditions for virtual team effectiveness*. San Francisco: Jossey-Bass.

Giedd, J. N. (2008). The teen brain: Insights from neuroimaging. *Journal of Adolescent Health, 42*, 335–343.

Gigerenzer, G. (1997). Ecological intelligence: An adaption for frequencies. *Psychologische Beitraege, 39*, 107–125.

Gigerenzer, G. (2000). *Adaptive thinking: Rationality in the real world*. New York: Oxford University Press.

Gigerenzer, G. (2004). Fast and frugal heuristics: The tools of bounded rationality. In D. J. Koehler & N. Harvey (Eds.), *Blackwell handbook of judgment and decision making*. Malden, MA: Blackwell Publishing.

Gigerenzer, G. (2008). Why heuristics work. *Perspective on Psychological Science, 3*(1), 20–29.

Gigerenzer, G., & Hoffrage, U. (1999). Overcoming difficulties in Bayesian reasoning: A reply to Lewis and Keren (1999) and Mellers and McGraw (1999). *Psychological Review, 106*, 425–430.

Gigerenzer, G., & Todd, P. M. (1999). Fast and frugal heuristics: The adaptive toolbox. In G. Gigerenzer, P. M. Todd, & ABC Research Group (Eds.), *Simple heuristics that make us smart* (pp. 3–36). New York: Oxford University Press.

Gilbert, A. N., & Firestein, S. (2002). Dollars and scents: Commercial opportunities in olfaction and taste. *Nature Neuroscience, 5*, 1043–1045.

Gilbert, D. T. (1989). Thinking lightly about others: Automatic components of the social inference process. In J. S. Uleman & J. A. Bargh (Eds.), *Unintended thought: Limits of awareness, intention, and control*. New York: Guilford.

Gilbert, D. T. (1998). Speeding with Ned: A personal view of the correspondence bias. In J. M. Darley & J. Cooper (Ed.), *Attribution and social interaction: The legacy of Edward E. Jones*. Washington, DC: American Psychological Association.

Gilbert, D. T. (2006). *Stumbling on happiness*. New York: Alfred A. Knopf.

Gilbert, D. T., Driver-Linn, E., & Wilson, T. D. (2002). The trouble with Vronsky: Impact bias in the forecasting of future affective states. In L. F. Barrett & S. P (Eds.), *The wisdom in feeling: Psychological processes in emotional intelligence* (pp. 114–143). New York: Guilford.

Gilbert, D. T., & Malone, P. S. (1995). The correspondence bias. *Psychological Bulletin, 117*, 21–38.

Gilbert, D. T., Morewedge, C. K., Risen, J. L., & Wilson, T. D. (2004). Looking forward to looking backward: The misprediction of regret. *Psychological Science, 15*, 346–350.

Giles, L. C., Glonek, G. F. V., Luszcz, M. A., & Andrews, G. R. (2005). Effect of social networks on 10-year survival in very old Australians: The Australian longitudinal study of aging. *Journal of Epidemiology & Community Health, 59*, 574–579.

Giles, T. R., & Marafiote, R. A. (1998). Managed care and the practitioner: A call for unity. *Clinical Psychology: Science & Practice, 5*, 41–50.

Gilgen, A. R. (1982). *American psychology since World War II: A profile of the discipline*. Westport, CT: Greenwood Press.

Gillham, J. E., Shatté, A. J., Reivich, K. J., & Seligman, M. E. P. (2001). Optimism, pessimism, and explanatory style. In E. C. Chang (Ed.), *Optimism & pessimism: Implications for theory, research, and practice* (pp. 53–76). Washington, DC: American Psychological Association.

Giordano, G. (2005). *How testing came to dominate American schools: The history of educational assessment*. New York: Peter Lang.

Gitlin, M. (2002). Pharmacological treatment of depression. In I. H. Gotlib & C. L. Hammen (Eds.), *Handbook of depression*. New York: Guilford.

Gitlin, M., Nuechterlein, K., Subotnik, K. L., Ventura, J., Mintz, J., Fogelson, D. L., Bartzokis, G., & Aravagiri, M. (2001). Clinical outcome following neuroleptic discontinuation in patients with remitted recent-onset schizophrenia. *American Journal of Psychiatry, 158*, 1835–1842.

Gittelman, M. (2005). The neglected disaster. *International Journal of Mental Health, 34*(2), 9–21.

Gladue, B. A. (1994). The biopsychology of sexual orientation. *Current Directions in Psychological Science, 3*, 150–154.

Gladwell, M. (2005). *Blink: The power of thinking without thinking*. New York: Little, Brown.

Glaser, J., & Kahn, K. (2005). Prejudice, discrimination, and the Internet. In Y. Amichai-Hamburger (Ed.), *The social net: Understanding human behavior in cyberspace* (pp. 247–276). New York: Oxford University Press.

Glasman, L. R., & Albarracín, D. (2006). Forming attitudes that predict future behavior: A meta-analysis of the attitude-behavior relation. *Psychological Bulletin, 132*, 778–822.

Glass, C. R., & Arnkoff, D. B. (1992). Behavior therapy. In D. K. Freedheim (Ed.), *History of psychotherapy: A century of change*. Washington, DC: American Psychological Association.

Glass, R. M. (2001). Electroconvulsive therapy. *Journal of the American Medical Association, 285*, 1346–1348.

Glass, R. M. (2004). Treatment of adolescents with major depression: Contributions of a major trial. *Journal of the American Medical Association, 292*, 861–863.

Glasser, R. (1991). Intelligence as an expression of acquired knowledge. In H. A. H. Rowe (Ed.), *Intelligence: Reconceptualization and measurement*. Hillsdale, NJ: Erlbaum.

Glassman, A., Shapiro, P. A., Ford, D. E., Culpepper, L., Finkel, M. S., Swenson, J. R., Bigger, J. T., Rollman, B. L., & Wise, T. N. (2003). Cardiovascular health and depression. *Journal of Psychiatric Practice, 9*, 409–421.

Glassner, B. (1999). *The culture of fear: Why Americans are afraid of the wrong things*. New York: Perseus Books Group.

Gleaves, D. H. (1994). On "The reality of repressed memories." *American Psychologist, 49*, 440–441.

Gleaves, D. H., Smith, S. M., Butler, L. D., & Spiegel, D. (2004). False and recovered memories in the laboratory and clinic: A review of experimental and clinical evidence. *Clinical Psychology: Science & Practice, 11*(1), 3–28.

Gleitman, L., & Newport, E. (1996). *The invention of language by children*. Cambridge, MA: MIT Press.

Gleitman, L., & Papafragou, A. (2005). Language and thought. In K. J. Holyoak & R. G. Morrison (Eds.), *The Cambridge handbook of thinking and reasoning*. New York: Cambridge University Press.

Gluck, M. E. (2006). Stress response and binge eating disorder. *Appetite, 46*(1), 26–30.

Goeders, N. E. (2004). Stress, motivation, and drug addiction. *Current Directions in Psychological Science, 13*(1), 33–35.

Goff, D. C., & Gudeman, J. E. (1999). The person with chronic mental illness. In A.M. Nicholi (Ed.), *The Harvard guide to psychiatry*. Cambridge, MA: Harvard University Press.

Gogtay, N., Giedd, J. N., Lusk, L., Hayashi, K. M., Rapoport, J. L., Thompson, P. M., et al. (2004). Dynamic mapping of human cortical development during childhood through early adulthood. *Proceedings of the National Academy of Sciences, 101*, 8174–8179.

Goin, M. K. (2005). A current perspective on the psychotherapies. *Psychiatric Services, 56*(3), 255–257.

Gold, J. M., & Green, M. F. (2005). Schizophrenia: Cognition. In B. J. Sadock & V. A. Sadock (Eds.), *Kaplan & Sadock's comprehensive textbook of psychiatry* (pp. 1436–1447). Philadelphia: Lippincott Williams & Wilkins.

Gold, M. S., & Jacobs, W. S. (2005). Cocaine and crack: Clinical aspects. In J. H. Lowinson, P. Ruiz, R. B. Millman, & J. G. Langrod (Eds.), *Substance abuse: A comprehensive textbook*. Philadelphia: Lippincott Williams & Wilkins.

Goldbenberg, J. L. (2005). The body stripped down: An existential account of the threat posed by the physical body. *Current Directions in Psychological Science, 14,* 224–228.

Goldberg, M. E., & Hudspeth, A. J. (2000). The vestibular system. In E. R. Kandel, J. H. Schwartz, & T. M. Jessell (Eds.), *Principles of neural science.* New York: McGraw-Hill.

Goldenberg, H. (1983). *Contemporary clinical psychology.* Pacific Grove, CA: Brooks/Cole.

Goldenberg, J. L., Cox, C. R., Pyszczynski, T., Greenberg, J., & Solomon, S. (2002). Understanding human ambivalence about sex: The effects of stripping sex of meaning. *Journal of Sex Research, 39,* 310–320.

Goldenberg, J. L., Pyszczynski, T., McCoy, S. K., Greenberg, J., & Solomon, S. (1999). Death, sex, love and neuroticism: Why is sex such a problem? *Journal of Personality and Social Psychology, 77,* 1173–1187.

Goldfield, B. A., & Reznick, J. S. (1990). Early lexical acquisition: Rate, content, and the vocabulary spurt. *Journal of Child Language, 17,* 171–183.

Goldsmith, T. D., & Shapira, N. A. (2006). Problematic Internet use. In E. Hollander & D. J. Stein (Eds.), *Clinical manual of impulse-control disorders* (pp. 291–308). Washington, DC: American Psychiatric Publishing.

Goldstein, D. G., & Gigerenzer, G. (2002). Models of ecological rationality: The recognition heuristic. *Psychological Review, 109,* 75–90.

Goldstein, E. B. (1996). *Sensation and perception* (4th ed.). Pacific Grove, CA: Brooks/Cole.

Goldstein, E. B. (2001). Pictorial perception and art. In E. B. Goldstein (Ed.), *Blackwell handbook of perception.* Malden, MA: Blackwell.

Goldstein, E. B. (2008). *Cognitive psychology: Connecting mind, research, and everyday experience.* Belmont, CA: Wadsworth.

Goldstein, H. W., Zedeck, S., & Goldstein, I. L. (2002). g: Is this your final answer? *Human Performance, 15,* 123–142.

Goldstein, W. M., & Hogarth, R. M. (1997). Judgement and decision research: Some historical context. In W. M. Goldstein, & R. M. Hogarth (Eds.), *Research on judgement and decision making.* New York: Cambridge University Press.

Goldston, K., & Baillie, A. J. (2008). Depression and coronary heart disease: A review of the epidemiological evidence, explanatory mechanisms and management approaches. *Clinical Psychology Review, 28,* 288–306.

Goleman, D. (1995). *Emotional intelligence.* New York: Bantam Books.

Goleman, D. (1998). *Working with emotional intelligence.* New York: Bantam Books.

Gonzaga, G. C., Campos, B., & Bradbury, T. (2007). Similarity, convergence, and relationship satisfaction in dating and married couples. *Journal of Personality and Social Psychology, 93,* 34–48.

Gonzalez-Bono, E., Salvador, A., Serrano, M. A., & Ricarte, J. (1999). Testosterone, cortisol and mood in a sports team competition. *Hormones and Behavior, 35,* 55–62.

Goodall, J. (1986). Social rejection, exclusion, and shunning among the Gombe chimpanzees. *Ethology & Sociobiology, 7,* 227–236.

Goodall, J. (1990). *Through a window: My thirty years with the chimpanzees of Gombe.* Boston, MA: Houghton, Mifflin.

Goodenough, D. R. (1991). Dream recall: History and current status of the field. In S. J. Ellman & J. S. Antrobus (Eds.), *The mind in sleep: Psychology and psychophysiology* (2nd ed.). New York: Wiley.

Goodwin, C. J. (1991). Misportraying Pavlov's apparatus. *American Journal of Psychology, 104*(1), 135–141.

Goodwin, F. K., & Jamison, K. R. (1990). *Manic-depressive illness.* New York: Oxford University Press.

Goodwin, R. D., & Friedman, H. S. (2006). Health status and the five-factor personality traits in a nationally representative sample. *Journal of Health Psychology, 11,* 643–654.

Goodwin, R. D., Jacobi, F., Bittner, A., & Wittchen, H.-U. (2006). Epidemiology of mood disorders. In D. J. Stein, D. J. Kupfer, & A. F. Schatzberg (Eds.), *Textbook of mood disorders* (pp. 33–54). Washington, DC: American Psychiatric Publishing.

Google. (2008). Google jobs. Retrieved from http://www.google.com/support/jobs/bin/static .py?page=benefits.html.

Gooley, J. J., & Saper, C. B. (2005). Anatomy of the mammalian circadian system. In M. H. Kryger, T. Roth, & W. C. Dement (Eds.), *Principles and practice of sleep medicine.* Philadelphia: Elsevier Saunders.

Gopnik, A., Meltzoff, A. N., & Kuhl, P. K. (1999). *The scientist in the crib: Minds, brains, and how children learn.* New York: Morrow.

Gordon, H. W. (1990). The neurobiological basis of hemisphericity. In C. Trevarthen (Ed.), *Brain circuits and functions of the mind. Essays in honor of Roger W. Sperry.* Cambridge, MA: Cambridge University Press.

Gordon, J., & Abramov, I. (2001). Color vision. In E. B. Goldstein (Ed.), *Blackwell handbook of perception.* Malden, MA: Blackwell.

Göritz, A. S. (2006). Cash lotteries as incentives in online panels. *Social Science Computer Review, 24,* 445–459.

Göritz, A. S. (2007). Using online panels in psychological research. In A. N. Joinson, K. Y. A. McKenna, T. Postmes, & U–D. Reips (Eds.), *The Oxford handbook of Internet psychology* (pp. 473–486). New York: Oxford University Press.

Gorner, P. (2006, May 10). Daddy material? It takes just one look. *Chicago Tribune.*

Gorski, R. A. (2000). Sexual differentiation of the nervous system. In E. R. Kandel, J. H. Schwartz, & T. M. Jessell (Eds.), *Principles of Neural Science.* New York: McGraw-Hill.

Gosling, S. D., Ko, S. J., Mannarelli, T., & Morris, M. E. (2002). A room with a cue: Personality judgments based on offices and bedrooms. *Journal of Personality and Social Psychology, 82,* 379–398.

Goswami, U. (2006). Neuroscience and education: From research to practice? *Nature Reviews Neuroscience, 7*(5), 2–7.

Gottesman, I. I. (1991). *Schizophrenia genesis: The origins of madness.* New York: W. H. Freeman.

Gottesman, I. I. (2001). Psychopathology through a life span–genetic prism. *American Psychologist, 56,* 867–878.

Gottesman, I. I., & Hanson, D. R. (2005). Human development: Biological and genetic processes. *Annual Review of Psychology, 56,* 263–86.

Gottesman, I. I., & Moldin, S. O. (1998). Genotypes, genes, genesis, and pathogenesis in schizophrenia. In M. F. Lenzenweger & R. H. Dworkin (Eds.), *Origins and development of schizophrenia: Advances in experimental psychopathology.* Washington, DC: American Psychological Association.

Gottfredson, L. S. (2002). Where and why g matters: Not a mystery. *Human Performance, 15,* 25–46.

Gottfredson, L. S. (2003a). Dissecting practical intelligence theory: Its claims and evidence. *Intelligence, 31,* 343–397.

Gottfredson, L. S. (2003b). *G,* jobs and life. In H. Nyborg (Ed.), *The scientific study of general intelligence: Tribute to Arthur R. Jensen.* Oxford, UK: Pergamon.

Gottfredson, L. S. (2004). Intelligence: Is it the epidemiologists' elusive "fundamental cause" of social class inequalities in health? *Journal of Personality & Social Psychology, 86,* 174–199.

Gottfredson, L. S. (2005). What if the hereditarian hypothesis is true? *Psychology, Public Policy, and the Law, 11*(2), 311–319.

Gottfredson, L. S., & Deary, I. J. (2004). Intelligence predicts health and longevity, but why? *Current Directions in Psychological Science, 13*(1), 1–4.

Gottlieb, D. J., Punjabi, N. M., Newman, A. B., Resnick, H. E., Redline, S., Baldwin, C. M., & Nieto, F. J. (2005). Association of sleep time with diabetes mellitus and impaired glucose tolerance. *Archives of Internal Medicine, 8,* 863–867.

Gottschall, J. (2007). Greater emphasis on female attractiveness in *Homo sapiens:* A revised solution to an old evolutionary riddle. *Evolutionary Psychology, 5*(1), 347–357.

Gottschall, J., Martin, J., Quish, H., & Rea, J. (2004). Sex differences in mate choice criteria are reflected in folktales from around the world and in historical European literature. *Evolution and Human Behavior, 25,* 102–112.

Gould, E. (2004). Stress, deprivation, and adult neurogenesis. In M. S. Gazzaniga (Ed.), *The cognitive neurosciences* (pp. 139–148). Cambridge, MA: MIT Press.

Gould, E., & Gross, C. G. (2002). Neurogenesis in adult mammals: Some progress and problems. *Journal of Neuroscience, 22,* 619–623.

Gould, R. L. (1975, February). Adult life stages: Growth toward self-tolerance. *Psychology Today,* pp. 74–78.

Gould, S. J. (1993). The sexual politics of classification. *Natural History,* 20–29.

Gould, S. J., & Eldredge, N. (1977). Punctuated equilibria: The tempo and mode of evolution reconsidered. *Paleobiology, 3,* 115–151.

Goulven, J., & Tzourio-Mazoyer, N. (2004). Hemispheric specialization for language. *Brain Research Reviews, 44*(1), 1–12.

Gouras, P. (1991). Color vision. In E. R. Kandel, J. H. Schwartz, & T. M. Jessell (Eds.), *Principles of neural science* (3rd ed.). New York: Elsevier Saunders.

Gourevitch, M. N., & Arnsten, J. H. (2005). Medical complications of drug use. In J. H. Lowinson, P. Ruiz, R. B. Millman, & J. G. Langrod (Eds.), *Substance abuse: A comprehensive textbook.* Philadelphia: Lippincott/Williams & Wilkins.

Gouzoulis-Mayfrank, E., Daumann, J., Tuchtenhagen, F., Pelz, S., Becker, S., Kunert, H. J., Fimm, B., & Sass, H. (2000). Impaired cognition in drug free users of recreational ecstasy (MDMA). *Journal of Neurology, Neurosurgery, & Psychiatry, 68,* 719–725.

Grady, D. (2006). Management of menopausal symptoms. *New England Journal of Medicine, 355,* 2338–2347.

Graf, P., & Uttl, B. (2001). Prospective memory: A new focus for research. *Consciousness & Cognition: An International Journal, 10,* 437–450.

Granberg, G., & Holmberg, S. (1991). Self-reported turnout and voter validation. *American Journal of Political Science, 35,* 448–459.

Granholm, E., McQuaid, J. R., Link, P. C., Fish, S., Patterson, T., & Jeste, D. V. (2008). Neuropsychological predictors of functional outcome in cognitive behavioral social skills training for older people with schizophrenia. *Schizophrenia Research, 100*,133–143.

Granic, I., Dishion, T. J., & Hollenstein, T. (2003). The family ecology of adolescence: A dynamic systems perspective on normative development. In G. R. Adams & M. D. Berzonsky (Eds.), *Blackwell handbook of adolescence*. Malden, MA: Blackwell Publishing.

Grant, P., Young, P. R., & DeRubeis. (2005). Cognitive and behavioral therapies. In G. O. Gabbard, J. S. Beck, & J. Holmes (Eds.), *Oxford textbook of psychotherapy*. New York: Oxford University Press.

Grantham-McGregor, S., Ani, C., & Fernald, L. (2001). The role of nutrition in intellectual development. In R. J. Sternberg & E. L. Grigorenko (Eds.), *Environmental effects on cognitive abilities* (pp. 119–156). Mahwah, NJ: Erlbaum.

Grau, R., Salanova, M., & Peiro, J. M. (2001). Moderator effects of self-efficacy on occupational stress. *Psychology in Spain, 5*(1), 63–74.

Gray, J. R. (2004). Integration of emotion and cognitive control. *Current Directions in Psychological Science, 13*(2), 46–48.

Graziano, W. G., & Eisenberg, N. H. (1997). Agreeableness: A dimension of personality. In R. Hogan, J. Johnson, & S. Briggs (Eds.), *Handbook of personality psychology*. San Diego: Academic Press.

Green, J. P. (1999). Hypnosis, context effects, and recall of early autobiographical memories. *International Journal of Clinical & Experimental Hypnosis, 47*, 284–300.

Greenberg, B. D. (2007). Transcranial magnetic stimulation in anxiety disorders. In M. S. George & R. H. Belmaker (Eds.), *Transcranial magnetic stimulation in clinical psychiatry*. Washington, DC: American Psychiatric Publishing.

Greenberg, D. L. (2004). President Bush's false "flashbulb" memory of 9/11/01. *Applied Cognitive Psychology, 18*, 363–370.

Greenberg, J., Pyszczynski, T., Solomon, S., Rosenblatt, A., Veeder, M., & Kirkland, S. (1990). Evidence for terror management theory II: The effects of mortality salience on reactions to those who threaten or bolster the cultural worldview. *Journal of Personality and Social Psychology, 58*, 308–318.

Greenberg, J. S. (2002). *Comprehensive stress management: Health and human performance*. New York: McGraw-Hill.

Greene, R. L. (1992a). *Human memory: Paradigms and paradoxes*. Hillsdale, NJ: Erlbaum.

Greene, R. L. (1992b). Repetition and learning. In L. R. Squire (Ed.), *Encyclopedia of learning and memory*. New York: Macmillian.

Greenfield, D. N. (1999). Psychological characteristics of compulsive Internet use: A preliminary analysis. *CyberPsychology and Behavior, 2*, 403–412.

Greenhaus, J. H. (2003). Career dynamics. In W. C. Borman, D. R. Ilgen, & R. J. Klimoski (Eds.), *Handbook of psychology*, vol. 12: *Industrial and organizational psychology* (pp. 519–540). New York: Wiley.

Greeno, C. G., & Wing, R. R. (1994). Stress-induced eating. *Psychological Bulletin, 115*, 444–464.

Greeno, J. G. (1978). Nature of problem-solving abilities. In W. K. Estes (Ed.), Handbook of learning and cognitive processes (Vol. 5). Hillsdale, NJ: Erlbaum.

Greenough, W. T. (1975). Experiential modification of the developing brain. *American Scientist, 63*, 37–46.

Greenough, W. T., & Volkmar, F. R. (1973). Pattern of dendritic branching in occipital cortex of rats reared in complex environments. *Experimental Neurology, 40*, 491–504.

Greenson, R. R. (1967). *The technique and practice of psychoanalysis* (Vol. 1). New York: International Universities Press.

Greenwald, A. G. (1992). New look 3: Unconscious cognition reclaimed. *American Psychologist, 47*, 766–779.

Gregory, R. J. (1996). *Psychological testing: History, principles, and applications* (2nd ed.). Boston: Allyn & Bacon.

Gregory, R. L. (1973). *Eye and brain*. New York: McGraw-Hill.

Gregory, R. L. (1978). *Eye and brain* (2nd ed.). New York: McGraw-Hill.

Grencavage, L. M., & Norcross, J. C. (1990). Where are the commonalities among the therapeutic factors? *Professional Psychology: Research and Practice, 21*, 372–378.

Griffith, E. E., Gonzales, C. A., & Blue, H. C. (2003). Introduction to cultural psychiatry. In R. E. Hales & S. C. Yudofsky (Eds.), *Textbook of clinical psychiatry*. Washington, DC: American Psychiatric Publishing.

Griffiths, M. (1999). Internet addiction: Fact or fiction? *Psychologist, 12*, 246–250.

Grigorenko, E. L. (2000). Heritability and intelligence. In R. J. Sternberg (Ed.), *Handbook of intelligence* (pp. 53–91). New York: Cambridge University Press.

Grigorenko, E. L., & Sternberg, R. J. (2001). Analytical, creative, and practical intelligence as predictors of self-reported adaptive functioning: A case study in Russia. *Intelligence, 29*, 57–73.

Grigorenko, E. L., & Sternberg, R. J. (2003). The nature-nurture issue. In A. Slater & G. Bremner (Eds.), *An introduction to development psychology*. Malden, MA: Blackwell Publishers.

Grill, H. J. (2006). Distributed neural control of energy balance: Contributions from hindbrain and hypothalamus. *Obesity, 14*(Suppl5), 216S–221S.

Griner, D., & Smith, T. B. (2006). Culturally adapted mental health intervention: A meta-analytic review. *Psychotherapy: Theory, Research, Practice, Training, 43*, 531–548.

Grinspoon, L., Bakalar, J. B., & Russo, E. (2005). Marihuana: Clinical aspects. In J. H. Lowinson, P. Ruiz, R. B. Millman, & J. G. Langrod (Eds.), *Substance abuse: A comprehensive textbook*. Philadelphia: Lippincott/Williams & Wilkins.

Grob, C. S., & Poland, R. E. (2005). MDMA. In J. H. Lowinson, P. Ruiz, R. B. Millman, & J. G. Langrod (Eds.), *Substance abuse: A comprehensive textbook*. Philadelphia: Lippincott/Williams & Wilkins.

Grob, G. N. (1983). Disease and environment in American history. In D. Mechanic (Ed.), *Handbook of health, health care, and the health professions*. New York: Free Press.

Gronholm, P., Juha, O., Vorobyev, V. , & Laine, M. (2005). Naming of newly learned objects: A PET activation study. *Cognitive Brain Research, 25*, 359–371.

Gross, C. G. (2000). Neurogenesis in the adult brain: Death of a dogma. *Nature Reviews Neuroscience, 1*, 67–73.

Gross, J. J. (2001). Emotion regulation in adulthood: Timing is everything. *Current Directions in Psychological Science, 10*, 214–219.

Grossbaum, M. F., & Bates, G. W. (2002). Correlates of psychological well-being at midlife: The role of generativity, agency and communion, and narrative themes. *International Journal of Behavioral Development, 26*(2), 120–127.

Grossman, J. B., & Ruiz, P. (2004). Shall we make a leap-of-faith to disulfiram (Antabuse)? *Addictive Disorders & Their Treatment, 3*(3), 129–132.

Grossman, P., Niemann, L., Schmidt, S., & Walach, H. (2004). Mindfulness-based stress reduction and health benefits: A meta-analysis. *Journal of Psychosomatic Research, 57*, 35–43.

Grossman, R. P., & Till, B. D. (1998). The persistence of classically conditioned brand attitudes. *Journal of Advertising, 27*, 23–31.

Grossman, S. P., Dacey, D., Halaris, A. E., Collier, T., & Routtenberg, A. (1978). Aphagia and adipsia after preferential destruction of nerve cell bodies in hypothalamus. *Science, 202*, 537–539.

Grossmann, K. E., & Grossmann, K. (1990). The wider concept of attachment in cross-cultural research. *Human Development, 33*, 31–47.

Groth-Marnat, G. (1997). *Handbook of psychological assessment*. New York: Wiley.

Grubin, D., & Madsen, L. (2005). Lie detection and the polygraph: A historical review. *Journal of Forensic Psychiatry & Psychology, 16*, 357–369.

Gruenberg, A. M., & Goldstein, R. D. (2003). Mood disorders: Depression. In A. Tasman, J. Kay, & J. A. Lieberman (Eds.), *Psychiatry*. New York: Wiley.

Grunberg, N. E., Faraday, M. M., & Rahman, M. A. (2001). The psychobiology of nicotine self-administration. In A. Baum, T. A. Revenson, & J. E. Singer (Eds.), *Handbook of health psychology* (pp. 249–262). Mahwah, NJ: Erlbaum.

Grusec, J. E. (2006). The development of moral behavior and conscience from a socialization perspective. In M. Killen & J. G. Smetana (Eds.), *Handbook of moral development*. Mahwah, NJ: Erlbaum.

Guarda, A. S., Pinto, A. M., Coughlin, J. W., Hussain, S., Haug, N. A., & Heinberg, L. J. (2007). Perceived coercion and change in perceived need for admission in patients hospitalized for eating disorders. *American Journal of Psychiatry, 164*, 108–114.

Gudjonsson, G. H. (2001). Recovered memories: Effects upon the family and community. In G. M. Davies & T. Dalgleish (Eds.), *Recovered memories: Seeking the middle ground*. Chichester, England: Wiley.

Guéguen, N., Pascual, A., & Dagot, L. (2002). Lowball and compliance to a request: An application in a field setting. *Psychological Reports, 91*, 81–84.

Guenther, K. (1988). Mood and memory. In G. M. Davies & D. M. Thomson (Eds.), *Memory in context: Context in memory*. New York: Wiley.

Guerini, I., Thomson, A. D., & Gurling, H. D. (2007). The importance of alcohol misuse, malnutrition, and genetic susceptibility on brain growth and plasticity. *Neuroscience & Biobehavioral Reviews, 31*, 212–220.

Guggenheim, F. G. (2000). Somatoform disorders. In B. J. Sadock & V. A. Sadock (Eds.), *Kaplan and Sadock's comprehensive textbook of psychiatry* (7th ed., Vol. 1, pp. 1504–1532). Philadelphia: Lippincott/Williams & Wilkins.

Guilbault, R. L., Bryant, F. B., Brockway, J. H., & Posavac, E. J. (2004). A meta analysis of research on hindsight bias. *Basic and Applied Social Psychology, 26*, 103–117.

Guilford, J. P. (1959). Three faces of intellect. *American Psychologist, 14*, 469–479.

Guilleminault, C., & Bassiri, A. (2005). Clinical features and evaluation of obstructive sleep apnea-hyponea syndrome and upper airway resistance syndrome. In M. H. Kryger, T. Roth, & W. C. Dement (Eds.). *Principles and practice of sleep medicine*. Philadelphia: Elsevier Saunders.

Guilleminault, C., & Fromherz, S. (2005). Narcolepsy: Diagnosis and management. In M. H. Kryger, T. Roth, & W. C. Dement (Eds.). *Principles and practice of sleep medicine.* Philadelphia: Elsevier Saunders.

Gunn, D. V., Warm, J. S., Dember, W. N., & Temple, J. N. (2000). Subjective organization and the visibility of illusory contours. *American Journal of Psychology, 113,* 553–568.

Gunn, S. R., & Gunn, W. S. (2006). Are we in the dark about sleepwalking's dangers? *Cerebrum,* 1–12.

Gureje, O., Simon, G. E., Ustun, T. B., & Goldberg, D. P. (1997). Somatization in cross-cultural perspective: A world health organization study in primary care. *American Journal of Psychiatry, 154,* 989–995.

Gusnard, D. A., & Raichle, M. E. (2004). Functional imaging, neurophysiology, and the resting state of the human brain. In M. S. Gazzaniga (Ed.), *The cognitive neurosciences* (pp. 1267–1280). Cambridge, MA: MIT Press.

Guyton, A. C. (1991). *Textbook of medical physiology.* Philadelphia: Saunders.

Güzeldere, G., Flanagan, O., & Hardcastle, V. G. (2000). The nature and function of consciousness: Lessons from blindsight. In M. S. Gazzaniga (Ed.), *The new cognitive neurosciences.* Cambridge, MA: The MIT Press.

Haas, L. (1999). Families and work. In M. B. Sussman, S. K. Steinmetz, & G. W. Peterson (Eds.), *Handbook of marriage and the family* (pp. 571–612). New York: Plenum.

Hackett, R. D. (1989). Work attitudes and employee absenteeism: A synthesis of the literature. *Journal of Occupational Psychology, 62,* 235–248.

Hackman, J. R., & Oldham, G. R. (1976). Motivation through the design of work: A test of a theory. *Organizational Behavior and Human Performance, 16,* 250–279.

Hadaway, C. K., Marler, P. L., & Chaves, M. (1993). What the polls don't show: A closer look at U.S. church attendance. *American Sociological Review, 58,* 741–752.

Hadjistavropoulos, H., Dash, H., Hadjistavropoulos, T., & Sullivan, T. (2007). Recurrent pain among university students: Contributions of self-efficacy and perfectionism to the pain experience. *Personality and Individual Differences, 42,* 1081–1091.

Hagen, E. H. (2005). Controversial issues in evolutionary psychology. In D. M. Buss (Ed.), *The handbook of evolutionary psychology* (pp. 145–176). New York: Wiley.

Hagen, J. D., & DeVries, H. M. (2004). Marital satisfaction at the empty-nest phase of the family life cycle: A longitudinal study. *Marriage & Family: A Christian Journal, 7*(1), 83–98.

Hagerty, M. R. (2000). Social comparisons of income in one's community: Evidence from national surveys of income and happiness. *Journal of Personality and Social Psychology, 78,* 764–771.

Haggbloom, S. J., Warnick, R., Warnick, J. E., Jones, V. K., Yarbrough, G. L., Russell, T. M., Borecky, C. M., McGahhey, R., Powell III, J. L., Beavers, J., & Monte, E. (2002). The 100 most eminent psychologists of the 20th century. *Review of General Psychology, 6,* 139–152.

Hahn, P. Y., Olson, L. J., & Somers, V. K. (2006). Cardiovascular complications of obstructive sleep apnea. In T. Lee-Chiong (Ed.), *Sleep: A comprehensive handbook.* Hoboken, NJ: Wiley-Liss.

Hakuta, K. (1986). *Mirror of language.* New York: Basic Books.

Hakuta, K. (2000). Bilingualism. In A. E. Kazdin (Ed.), *Encyclopedia of psychology* (pp. 410–414). Washington, DC: American Psychological Association.

Haladyna, T. M. (2006). Roles and importance of validity studies in test development. In S. M. Downing & T. M. Haladyna (Eds.), *Handbook of test development* (pp. 739–755). Mahwah, NJ: Erlbaum.

Hales, D. (1987). *How to sleep like a baby.* New York: Ballantine.

Halford, J. C. G., & Blundell, J. E. (2000). Separate systems for serotonin and leptin in appetite control. *Annals of Medicine, 32,* 222–232.

Halford, J. C. G., Gillespie, J., Brown, V., Pontin, E. E., & Dovey, T. M. (2004). Effect of television advertisements for foods on food consumption in children. *Appetite, 42*(2), 221–225.

Hall, C. C. I. (1997). Cultural malpractice: The growing obsolescence of psychology with the changing U.S. population. *American Psychologist, 52,* 642–651.

Hall, C. S. (1966). *The meaning of dreams.* New York: McGraw-Hill.

Hall, C. S. (1979). The meaning of dreams. In D. Goleman & R. J. Davidson (Eds.), *Consciousness: Brain, states of awareness, and mysticism.* New York: Harper & Row.

Hall, E. (1987). *Growing and changing: What the experts say.* New York: Random House.

Hall, G. S. (1904). *Adolescence.* New York: Appleton.

Hall, J. A., Carter, J. D., & Horgan, T. G. (2000). Gender differences in the nonverbal communication of emotion. In A. Fischer (Ed.), *Gender and emotion.* Cambridge, UK: Cambridge University Press.

Hall, J. A., & Mast, M. S. (2008). Are women always more interpersonally sensitive than men? Impact of goals and content domain. *Personality and Social Psychology Bulletin, 34,* 144–155.

Hall, J. R., & Benning, S. D. (2006). The "successful" psychopath: Adaptive and subclinical manifestations of psychopathy in the general population. In C. J. Patrick (Ed.), *Handbook of Psychopathy.* New York: Guilford.

Halmi, K. A. (2002). Physiology of anorexia nervosa and bulimia nervosa. In C. G. Fairburn & K. D. Brownell (Eds.), *Eating disorders and obesity: A comprehensive handbook.* New York: Guilford.

Halmi, K. A. (2003). Eating disorders: Anorexia nervosa, bulimia nervosa, and obesity. In R. E. Hales & S. C. Yudofsky (Eds.), *Textbook of Clinical Psychiatry.* Washington, DC: American Psychiatric Publishing.

Halmi, K. A., Sunday, S. R., Strober, M., Kaplan, A., Woodside, D. B., Fichter, M., Treasure, J., Berrettini, W. H., & Kaye, W. H. (2000). Perfectionism in anorexia nervosa: Variation by clinical subtype, obsessionality, and pathological eating behavior. *American Journal of Psychiatry, 157,* 1799–1805.

Halonen, J. S., Appleby, D. C., Brewer, C. L., Buskist, W., Gillem, A. R., Halpern, D., Hill, G. W., Lloyd, M. A. Rudmann, J. L. & Whitlow, V. M. (2002). *Undergraduate psychology major learning goals and outcomes: A report.* Retrieved August 10, 2005, from www.apa.org/ed/pcue/taskforcereport2.pdf.

Halpern, C., Hurtig, H., Jaggi, J., Grossman, M., Won, M., & Baltuch, G. (2007). Deep brain stimulation in neurologic disorders. *Parkinsonism & Related Disorders, 13*(1), 1–16.

Halpern, D. F. (1984). *Thought and knowledge: An introduction to critical thinking.* Hillsdale, NJ: Erlbaum.

Halpern, D. F. (1992). *Sex differences in cognitive abilities.* Hillsdale, NJ: Erlbaum.

Halpern, D. F. (1996). *Thought and knowledge: An introduction to critical thinking.* Mahwah, NJ: Erlbaum.

Halpern, D. F. (1997). Sex differences in intelligence: Implications for education. *American Psychologist, 52,* 1091–1102.

Halpern, D. F. (1998). Teaching critical thinking for transfer across domains: Dispositions, skills, structure training, and metacognitive monitoring. *American Psychologist, 53,* 449–455.

Halpern, D. F. (2000). *Sex differences in cognitive abilities.* Mahwah, NJ: Erlbaum.

Halpern, D. F. (2003). *Thought and knowledge: An introduction to critical thinking.* Mahwah, NJ: Erlbaum.

Halpern, D. F. (2004). A cognitive-process taxonomy for sex differences in cognitive abilities. *Current Directions in Psychological Science, 13*(4), 135–139.

Halpern, D. F. (2007). The nature and nurture of critical thinking. In R. J. Sternberg, H. L. Roediger III, & D. F. Halpern (Eds.), *Critical thinking in psychology* (pp. 1–14). New York: Cambridge University Press.

Halpern, D. F., Benbow, C. P., Geary, D. C., Gur, R. C., Hyde, J. S., & Gernsbacher, M. A. (2007). The science of sex differences in science and mathematics. *Psychological Science in the Public Interest, 8,* 1–51.

Hamann, S. B., Herman, R. A., Nolan, C. L., & Wallen, K. (2004). Men and women differ in amygdala response to visual sexual stimuli. *Nature Neuroscience, 7,* 411–416.

Hamill, R., Wilson T. D., & Nisbett, R. E. (1980). Insensitivity to sample bias: Generalizing from atypical cases. *Journal of Personality and Social Psychology, 39,* 578–589.

Hamilton, A. (1999). You've got mail! *Time,* p. 83.

Hamilton, W. D. (1964). The evolution of social behavior. *Journal of Theoretical Biology, 7,* 1–52.

Hamilton, W. D., & Zuk, M. (1982). Heritable true fitness and bright birds: A role for parasites. *Science, 218,* 384–387.

Hammad, T. A., Laughren, T., & Racoosin, J. (2006). Suicidality in pediatric patients treated with antidepressant drugs. *Archives of General Psychiatry, 63,* 332–339.

Hammen, C. (2003). Mood disorders. In G. Stricker & T. A. Widiger (Eds.), *Handbook of psychology, Vol. 8: Clinical psychology.* New York: Wiley.

Hammen, C. (2005). Stress and depression. *Annual Review of Clinical Psychology, 1,* 293–319.

Hammer, S. M., Saag, M. S., Schechter, M., Montaner, J. S. G., Schooley, R. T., Jacobsen, D. M., et al. (2006). Treatment for adult HIV infection: 2006 recommendations of the international AIDS society-USA panel. *Journal of the American Medical Association, 296,* 827–843.

Hampel, S. (2005). Reliability. In J. Miles & P. Gilbert (Eds.), *A handbook of research methods for clinical and health psychology* (pp. 193–204). New York: Oxford University Press.

Hampson, E., & Moffat, S. D. (2004). The psychobiology of gender: Cognitive effects of reproductive hormones in the adult nervous system. In A. H. Eagly, A. E. Beall, & R. J. Sternberg (Eds.), *The psychology of gender.* New York: Guilford.

Hampson, E., van Anders, S. M., & Mullin, L. I. (2006). A female advantage in the recognition of emotional facial expressions: Test of an evolutionary hypothesis. *Evolution and Human Behavior, 27,* 401–416.

Hampton, T. (2004). Fetal environment may have profound long-term consequences for health. *Journal of the American Medical Association, 292,* 1285–1286.

Han, K. F. G. C. (2000). Construct validity. In A. E. Kazdin (Ed.), *Encyclopedia of psychology* (pp. 281–283). Washington, DC: American Psychological Association.

Hancock, P. A., & Ganey, H. C. N. (2003). From the inverted-U to the extended-U: The evolution of a law of psychology. *Journal of Human Performance in Extreme Environments, 7*(1), 5–14.

Haneda, K., Nomura, M., Iidaka, T., & Ohira, H. (2003). Interaction of prime and target in the sub-liminal affective priming effect. *Perceptual & Motor Skills, 96,* 695–702.

Haney, C., Banks, W. C., & Zimbardo, P. G. (1973). Interpersonal dynamics in a simulated prison. *International Journal of Criminology and Penology, 1,* 69–97.

Haney, C., & Zimbardo, P. G. (1998). The past and future of U.S. prison policy: Twenty-five years after the Stanford Prison Experiment. *American Psychologist, 53,* 709–727.

Hanisch, K. A. (1992). The Job Descriptive Index revisited: Questions about the question mark. *Journal of Applied Psychology, 77,* 377–382.

Hanisch, K. A. (1995). Behavioral families and multiple causes: Matching the complexity of responses to the complexity of antecedents. *Current Directions in Psychological Science, 4,* 156–162.

Hanisch, K. A., & Hulin, C. L. (1990). Job attitudes and organizational withdrawal: An examination of retirement and other voluntary withdrawal behaviors. *Journal of Vocational Behavior, 37*(1), 60–78.

Hanisch, K. A., & Hulin, C. L. (1991). General attitudes and organizational withdrawal: An evaluation of a causal model. *Journal of Vocational Behavior, 39,* 110–128.

Hanisch, K. A., Hulin, C. L., & Roznowski, M. A. (1998). The importance of individuals' repertoires of behaviors: The scientific appropriateness of studying multiple behaviors and general attitudes. *Journal of Organizational Behavior, 19,* 463–480.

Hannigan, J. H., & Armant, D. R. (2000). Alcohol in pregnancy and neonatal outcome. *Seminars in Neonatology, 5,* 243–254.

Hansen, R. S., & Hansen, K. (2003). What do employers really want? Top skills and values employers seek from job seekers. *Quintzine, 4*(23). Retrieved August 8, 2005 from http://www.quintcareers.com/job_skills_values.html.

Happonen, P., Voutilainen, S., & Salonen, J. T. (2004). Coffee drinking is dose-dependently related to the risk of acute coronary events in middle-aged men. *Journal of Nutrition, 134,* 2381–2386.

Hardcastle, V. G., & Stewart, C. M. (2002). What do brain data really show? *Philosophy of Science, 69*(3), 72–83.

Hardesty, D. E., & Sackeim, H. A. (2007). Deep brain stimulation in movement and psychiatric disorders. *Biological Psychiatry, 31,* 831–835.

Hare, A. P. (1962). *Handbook of small group research.* New York: Free Press.

Hare, R. D. (2006). Psychopathy: A clinical and forensic overview. *Psychiatric Clinics of North America, 29,* 709–724.

Hare, R. D., & Neumann, C. S. (2008). Psychopathy as a clinical and empirical construct. *Annual Review of Clinical Psychology, 4,* 217–246.

Harley, E. M. (2007). Hindsight bias in legal decision making. *Social Cognition, 25,* 48–63.

Harley, T. A. (2008). *The psychology of language: From data to theory.* New York: Psychology Press.

Harlow, H. F. (1958). The nature of love. *American Psychologist, 13,* 673–685.

Harlow, H. F. (1959). Love in infant monkeys. *Scientific American, 200*(6), 68–74.

Harmsen, P., Rosengren, A., Tsipogianni, A., & Wilhelmsen, L. (1990). Risk factors for stroke in middle-aged men in Goteborg, Sweden. *Stroke, 21,* 23–29.

Haroutunian, V., & Davis, K. L. (2003). Psychiatric pathophysiology. In A. Tasman, J. Kay, & J. A. Lieberman (Eds.), *Psychiatry.* New York: Wiley.

Harrington, M. E., & Mistlberger, R. E. (2000). Anatomy and physiology of the mammalian circadian system. In M. H. Kryger, T. Roth, & W. C. Dement (Eds.), *Principles and practice of sleep medicine.* Philadelphia: Saunders.

Harris, E., & Capellini, I. (2007). Phylogeny of sleep and dreams. In D. Barrett & P. McNamara (Eds.), *The new science of dreaming.* Westport, CT: Praeger.

Harris, J. E. (1984). Remembering to do things: A forgotten topic. In J. E. Harris & P. E. Morris (Eds.), *Everyday memory, actions, and absent-mindedness.* New York: Academic Press.

Harris, J. R. (1998). *The nurture assumption: Why children turn out the way they do.* New York: Free Press.

Harris, J. R. (2000). Context-specific learning, personality, and birth order. *Current Directions in Psychological Science, 9*(5), 174–177.

Hart, D., Eisenberg, N., & Valiente, C. (2007). Personality change at the intersection of autonomic arousal and stress. *Psychological Science, 18,* 492–497.

Hart, J. W., Karau, S. J., Stasson, M. F., & Kerr, N. A. (2004). Achievement motivation, expected co-worker performance, and collective task motivation: Working hard or hardly working? *Journal of Applied Social Psychology, 34,* 984–1000.

Hartley, A. (2006). Changing role of the speed of processing construct in the cognitive psychology of human aging. In J. E. Birren & K. W. Schaie (Eds.), *Handbook of the psychology of aging.* San Diego: Academic Press.

Harvey, M. H. (1999). Memory research and clinical practice: A critique of three paradigms and a framework for psychotherapy with trauma survivors. In L. M. Williams & V. L. Banyard (Eds.), *Trauma & memory.* Thousand Oaks, CA: Sage .

Haselton, M. G., & Buss, D. M. (2000). Error management theory: A new perspective on biases in cross-sex mind reading. *Journal of Personality and Social Psychology, 78,* 81–91.

Haselton, M. G., Buss, D. M., Oubaid, V., & Angleitner, A. (2005). Sex, lies, and strategic interference: The psychology of deception between the sexes. *Personality and Social Psychology Bulletin, 31,* 3–23.

Hashimoto, K., Shimizu, E., & Iyo, M. (2005). Dysfunction of glia-neuron communication in pathophysiology of schizophrenia. *Current Psychiatry Reviews, 1,* 151–163.

Haslam, N. (1997). Evidence that male sexual orientation is a matter of degree. *Journal of Personality and Social Psychology, 73,* 862–870.

Haslam, S. A. (2007). I think, therefore I err? *Scientific American Mind, 18*(2), 16–17.

Hastorf, A., & Cantril, H. (1954). They saw a game: A case study. *Journal of Abnormal and Social Psychology, 49,* 129–134.

Hatfield, E., & Rapson, R. L. (1993). *Love, sex, and intimacy: Their psychology, biology, and history.* New York: HarperCollins.

Hatfield, E., Rapson, R. L., & Martel, L. D. (2007). Passionate love. In S. Kitayama & D. Cohen (Eds.), *Handbook of cultural psychology.* New York: Guilford.

Haugland, G., Siegel, C., Hopper, K., & Alexander, M. J. (1997). Mental illness among homeless individuals in a suburban county. *Psychiatric Services, 48,* 504–509.

Hauri, P. J. (2002). Psychological and psychiatric issues in the etiopathogenesis of insomnia. *Journal of Clinical Psychiatry, 4*(suppl 1), 17–20.

Hauser, M., & Carey, S. (1998). Building a cognitive creature from a set of primitives: Evolutionary and developmental insights. In D. D. Cummins & C. Allen (Eds.), *The evolution of mind.* New York: Oxford University Press.

Havas, S., Dickinson, B. D., & Wilson, M. (2007). The urgent need to reduce sodium consumption. *Journal of the American Medical Association, 298,* 1439–1441.

Haworth-Hoeppner, S. (2000). The critical shapes of body image: The role of culture and family in the production of eating disorders. *Journal of Marriage and the Family, 62,* 212–227.

Hayne, H. (2007). Verbal recall of preverbal memories: Implications for the clinic and the courtroom. In M. Garry & H. Hayne (Eds.), *Do justice and let the sky fall: Elizabeth F. Lotus and her contributions to science, law, and academic freedom.* Mahwah, NJ: Erlbaum.

Hays, K. F. (1999). *Working it out: Using exercise in psychotherapy.* Washington, DC: American Psychological Association.

Haywood, T. W., Kravitz, H. M., Grossman, L. S., Cavanaugh, J. L., Jr., Davis, J. M., & Lewis, D. A. (1995). Predicting the "revolving door" phenomenon among patients with schizophrenic, schizoaffective, and affective disorders. *American Journal of Psychiatry, 152,* 861–956.

Hazan, C., & Shaver, P. (1986). *Parental caregiving style questionnaire.* Unpublished questionnaire.

Hazan, C., & Shaver, P. (1987). Romantic love conceptualized as an attachment process. *Journal of Personality and Social Psychology, 52,* 511–524.

He, J., Ogden, L. G., Vupputuri, S., Bazzano, L. A., Loria, C., & Whelton, P. K. (1999). Dietary sodium intake and subsequent risk of cardiovascular disease in overweight adults. *Journal of the American Medical Association, 282,* 2027–2034.

Healy, D. (2004). *Let them eat Prozac: The unhealthy relationship between the pharmaceutical industry and depression.* New York: NYU Press.

Healy, D., & Whitaker, C. (2003). Antidepressants and suicide: Risk-benefit conundrums. *Journal of Psychiatry & Neuroscience, 28*(5), 28.

Healy, M. D., & Ellis, B. J. (2007). Birth order, conscientiousness, and openness to experience tests of the family-niche model of personality using a within-family methodology. *Evolution and Human Behavior, 28,* 55–59.

Heaps, C. M., & Nash, M. (2001). Comparing recollective experience in true and false autobiographical memories. *Journal of Experimental Psychology: Learning, Memory, and Cognition, 27,* 920–930.

Hearst, E. (1988). Fundamentals of learning and conditioning. In R. C. Atkinson, R. J. Herrnstein, G. Lindzey, & R. D. Luce (Eds.), *Stevens' handbook of experimental psychology.* New York: Wiley.

Heatherton, T. F., Striepe, M., & Wittenberg, L. (1998). Emotional distress and disinhibited eating:

The role of self. *Personality and Social Psychology Bulletin, 24,* 301–313.

Heaton, T. B., Jacobson, C. K., & Holland, K. (1999). Persistence and change in decisions to remain childless. *Journal of Marriage and the Family, 61,* 531–539.

Hedegaard, M. (2005). The zone of proximal development as basis for instruction. In H. Daniels (Ed.), *An introduction to Vygotsky.* New York: Routledge.

Heiby, E. M. (2002). It is time for a moratorium on legislation enabling prescription privileges for psychologists. *Clinical Psychology: Science & Practice, 9*(3), 256–258.

Heider, F. (1958). *The psychology of interpersonal relations.* New York: Wiley.

Heilman, M. E., & Chen, J. J. (2005). Same behavior, different consequences: Reactions to men's and women's altruistic citizenship behaviors. *Journal of Applied Psychology, 90,* 431–441.

Heilman, M. E., & Haynes, M. C. (2005). No credit where credit is due: Attributional rationalization of women's success in male-female teams. *Journal of Applied Psychology, 90,* 905–916.

Heine, S. J., & Norenzayan, A. (2006). Toward a psychological science for a cultural species. *Perspectives on Psychological Sciences, 1,* 251–269.

Heine, S. J., & Renshaw, K. (2002). Interjudge agreement, self-enhancement, and liking: Cross-cultural divergences. *Personality and Social Psychology Bulletin, 28*(5), 578–587.

Heinrichs, R. W. (2005). The primacy of cognition in schizophrenia. *American Psychologist, 60,* 229–242.

Helft, M. (2007, March 10). Google's buses help its workers beat the rush. *New York Times.*

Helgeson, V. S., Reynolds, K. A., & Tomich, P. L. (2006). A meta-analytic review of benefit finding and growth. *Journal of Consulting and Clinical Psychology, 74,* 797–816.

Hellige, J. B. (1990). Hemispheric asymmetry. *Annual Review of Psychology, 41,* 55–80.

Hellige, J. B. (1993a). Unity of thought and action: Varieties of interaction between left and right cerebral hemispheres. *Current Directions in Psychological Science, 2*(1), 21–25.

Hellige, J. B. (1993b). *Hemispheric asymmetry: What's right and what's left.* Cambridge, MA: Harvard University Press.

Helmholtz, H. von. (1852). On the theory of compound colors. *Philosophical Magazine, 4,* 519–534.

Helmholtz, H. von. (1863). *On the sensations of tone as a physiological basis for the theory of music* (A. J. Ellis, Trans.). New York: Dover.

Helms, J. E. (1992). Why is there no study of cultural equivalence in standard cognitive ability testing? *American Psychologist, 47,* 1083–1101.

Helms, J. E. (2006). Fairness is not validity or cultural bias in racial-group assessment: A quantitative perspective. *American Psychologist, 61,* 845–859.

Helms, J. E., Jernigan, M., & Mascher, J. (2005). The meaning of race in psychology and how to change it: A methodological review. *American Psychologist, 60*(1), 27–36.

Helson, R., Jones, C., & Kwan, V. S. Y. (2002). Personality change over 40 years of adulthood: Hierarchical linear modeling analyses of two longitudinal studies. *Journal of Personality & Social Psychology, 83,* 752–766.

Hempel, S. (2005). Reliability. In J. Miles & P. Gilbert (Eds.), *A handbook of research methods for clinical and health psychology* (pp. 193–204). New York: Oxford University Press.

Henderson, K. E., & Brownell, K. D. (2004). The toxic environment and obesity: Contribution and cure. In J. K. Thompson (Ed.), *Handbook of eating disorders and obesity.* New York: Wiley.

Hendrick, S. S., & Hendrick, C. (2000). Romantic love. In S. S. Hendrick & C. Hendrick (Eds.), *Close relationships.* Thousand Oaks, CA: Sage.

Henriksson, M. M., Aro, H. M., Marttunen, M. J., Heikkinen, M. E., Isometsa, E. T., Kuoppasalmi, K. I., & Lonnqvist, J. K. (1993). Mental disorders and comorbidity of suicide. *American Journal of Psychiatry, 150,* 935–940.

Henry, K. R. (1984). Cochlear damage resulting from exposure to four different octave bands of noise at three different ages. *Behavioral Neuroscience, 1,* 107–117.

Henry, P. J., Sternberg, R. J., & Grigorenko, E. L. (2005). Capturing successful intelligence through measures of analytic, creative, and practical skills. In O. Wilhelm & R. W. Engle (Eds.), *Handbook of understanding and measuring intelligence.* Thousand Oaks, CA: Sage.

Hepper, P. (2003). *Prenatal psychological and behavioural development.* Thousand Oaks, CA: Sage.

Herbert, J. D., Gaudiano, B. A., Rheingold, A. A., Myers, V. H., Dalrymple, K., & Nolan, E. M. (2005). Social skills training augments the effectiveness of cognitive behavioral group therapy for social anxiety disorder. *Behavior Therapy, 36,* 125–138.

Herbst, S., Pietrzak, R. H., Wagner, J., White, W. B., & Petry, N. M. (2007). Lifetime major depression is associated with coronary heart disease in older adults: Results from the national epidemiologic survey on alcohol and related conditions. *Psychosomatic Medicine, 69,* 729–734.

Herek, G. M. (1996). Heterosexism and homophobia. In R. P. Cabaj & T. S. Stein (Eds.), *Textbook of homosexuality and mental health.* Washington, DC: American Psychiatric Press.

Herek, G. M. (2000). The psychology of sexual prejudice. *Current Directions in Psychological Science, 9,* 19–22.

Heres, S., Davis, J., Maino, K., Jetzinger, E., Kissling, W., & Leucht, S. (2006). Why olanzapine beats risperidone, risperidone beats quetiapine, and quetiapine beats olanzapine: An exploratory analysis of head-to-head comparison studies of second-generation antipsychotics. *American Journal of Psychiatry, 163,* 185–194.

Hering, E. (1878). *Zür lehre vom lichtsinne.* Vienna: Gerold.

Herman, L. M., Kuczaj, S. A., & Holder, M. D. (1993). Responses to anomalous gestural sequences by a language-trained dolphin: Evidence for processing of semantic relations and syntactic information. *Journal of Experimental Psychology: General, 122,* 184–194.

Herman-Giddens, M. E. (2006). Recent data on pubertal milestones in United States children: The secular trend towards earlier development. *International Journal of Andrology, 29,* 241.

Hermann, R. C., Ettner, S. L., Dorwart, R. A., Hoover, C. W., & Yeung, E. (1998). Characteristics of psychiatrists who perform ECT. *American Journal of Psychiatry, 155,* 889–894.

Hermans, D., Craske, M. G., Mineks, S., & Lovibond, P. F. (2006). Extinction in human fear conditioning. *Biological Psychiatry, 60,* 361–368.

Hermans, H. J. M., & Kempen, H. J. G. (1998). Moving cultures: The perilous problems of cultural dichotomies in a globalizing society. *American Psychologist, 53,* 1111–1120.

Hernandez, A. E., & Li, P. (2007). Age of acquisition: Its neural and computational mechanisms. *Psychological Bulletin, 133,* 638–650.

Herrmann, D., Raybeck, D., & Gruneberg, M. (2002). *Improving memory and study skills: Advances in theory and practice.* Ashland, OH: Hogrefe & Huber.

Herrnstein, R. J., & Murray, C. (1994). *The bell curve: Intelligence and class structure in American life.* New York: Free Press.

Hersh, S. M. (2004, May 10). Torture at Abu Ghraib. *New Yorker, 80*(17), 54–67.

Hertwig, R., Barron, G., Weber, E. U., & Erev, I. (2004). Decisions from experience and the effect of rare events in risky choice. *Psychological Science, 15,* 534–539.

Hertwig, R., & Gigerenzer, G. (1999). The "conjunction fallacy" revisited: How intelligent inferences look like reasoning errors. *Journal of Behavioral Decision Making, 12,* 275–306.

Hertwig, R., & Todd, P. M. (2002). Heuristics. In V. S. Ramachandran (Ed.), *Encyclopedia of the human brain* (pp. 449–460). San Diego: Academic Press.

Herz, R. S., & Schooler, J. W. (2002). A naturalistic study of autobiographical memories evoked by olfactory and visual cues: Testing the Proustian hypothesis. *American Journal of Psychology, 115,* 21–32.

Herzberg, F. (1966). *Work and the nature of man.* Cleveland: World Publishing.

Herzog, D. B., & Delinski, S. S. (2001). Classification of eating disorders. In R. H. Striegel-Moore & L. Smolak (Eds.), *Eating disorders* (pp. 31–50). Washington, DC: American Psychological Association.

Herzog, H. A. (2005). Dealing with the animal research controversy. In C. K. Akins, S. Panicker, & C. L. Cunningham (Eds.), *Laboratory animals in research and teaching: Ethics, care and methods.* Washington, DC: American Psychological Association.

Hetherington, E. M. (1999). Should we stay together for the sake of the children? In E. M. Hetherington (Ed.), *Coping with divorce, single parenting, and remarriage.* Mahwah, NJ: Erlbaum.

Hetherington, E. M. (2003). Intimate pathways: Changing patterns in close personal relationships across time. *Family Relations: Interdisciplinary Journal of Applied Family Studies, 52,* 318–331.

Hetherington, M. M., & Rolls, B. J. (1996). Sensory-specific satiety: Theoretical frameworks and central characteristics. In E. D. Capaldi (Ed.), *Why we eat what we eat: The psychology of eating* (267–290). Washington, DC: American Psychological Association.

Hettema, J. M., Annas, P., Neale, M. C., Kendler, K. S., & Fredrikson, M. (2003). A twin study of the genetics of fear conditioning. *Archives of General Psychiatry, 6,* 402–707.

Hettema, J. M., Neale, M. C., & Kendler, K. S. (2001). A review and meta-analysis of the genetic epidemiology of anxiety disorders. *American Journal of Psychiatry, 158,* 1568–1578.

Hettich, P. I. (1998). *Learning skills for college and career.* Pacific Grove, CA: Brooks/Cole.

Hewson, C. (2003). Conducting research on the Internet. *The Psychologist, 16,* 290–293.

Hewson, C. (2007). Gathering data on the Internet: Qualitative approaches and possibilities for mixed methods and research. In A. N. Joinson, K. Y. A. McKenna, T. Postmes, & U-D. Reips (Eds.), *The Oxford handbook of Internet psychology* (pp. 405–428). New York: Oxford University Press.

Hewstone, M. (1990). The "ultimate attribution error"? A review of the literature on intergroup causal attribution. *European Journal of Social Psychology, 20,* 311–335.

Hicks, J. L., Marsh, R. L., & Cook, G. I. (2005). Task interference in time-based, event-based, and dual intention prospective memory conditions. *Memory and Language, 53,* 430–444.

Higgins, E. T. (2004). Making a theory useful: Lessons handed down. *Personality and Social Psychology Review, 8*(2), 138–145.

Highhouse, S., Beadle, D., Gallo, A., & Miller, L. (1998). Get 'em while they last! Effects of scarcity information in job advertisements. *Journal of Applied Social Psychology, 28,* 779–795.

Hilgard, E. R. (1965). *Hypnotic susceptibility.* New York: Harcourt, Brace & World.

Hilgard, E. R. (1986). *Divided consciousness: Multiple controls in human thought and action.* New York: Wiley.

Hilgard, E. R. (1987). *Psychology in America: A historical survey.* San Diego: Harcourt Brace Jovanovich.

Hilgard, E. R. (1989). The early years of intelligence measurement. In R. L. Linn (Ed.), *Intelligence: Measurement, theory, and public policy.* Urbana: University of Illinois Press.

Hilgard, E. R. (1992). Dissociation and theories of hypnosis. In E. Fromm & M. R. Nash (Eds.), *Contemporary hypnosis research.* New York: Guilford.

Hilgetag, C. C. (2004). Learning from switched-off brains. *Scientific American Mind, 14*(1), 8–9.

Hill, C. E., & Lambert, M. J. (2004). Methodological issues in studying psychotherapy processes and outcomes. In M. J. Lambert (Ed.), *Bergin and Garfield's handbook of psychotherapy and behavior change.* New York: Wiley.

Hill, G. W. (1982). Group versus individual performance: Are N+1 heads better than one? *Psychological Bulletin, 91,* 517–539.

Hill, J. O., & Peters, J. C. (1998). Environmental contributions to the obesity epidemic. *Science, 280,* 1371–1374.

Hilliard, A. G., III. (1984). IQ testing as the emperor's new clothes: A critique of Jensen's *Bias in Mental Testing.* In C. R. Reynolds & R. T. Brown (Eds.), *Perspectives on bias in mental testing.* New York: Plenum.

Hilmert, C. J., Kulik, J. A., & Christenfeld, N. J. S. (2006). Positive and negative opinion modeling: The influence of another's similarity and dissimilarity. *Journal of Personality and Social Psychology, 90,* 440–452.

Hilton, J. L., & von Hippel, W. (1996). Stereotypes. *Annual Review of Psychology, 47,* 237–271.

Hines, M. (2004). Androgen, estrogen, and gender: Contributions of the early hormone environment to gender-related behavior. In A. H. Eagly, A. E. Beall, & R. J. Sternberg (Eds.), *The psychology of gender.* New York: Guilford.

Hingson, R., & Sleet, D. A. (2006). Modifying alcohol use to reduce motor vehicle injury. In A. C. Gielen, D. A. Sleet, & R. J. DiClemente (Eds.), *Injury and violence prevention: Behavioral science theories, methods, and applications.* San Francisco: Jossey-Bass.

Hirsh, I. J., & Watson, C. S. (1996). Auditory psychophysics and perception. *Annual Review of Psychology, 47,* 461–484.

Hirt, E. R., McDonald, H. E., & Markman, K. D. (1998). Expectancy effects in reconstructive memory: When the past is just what we expected. In S. J. Lynn & K. M. McConkey (Eds.), *Truth in memory.* New York: Guilford.

Ho, B., Black, D. W., & Andreasen, N. C. (2003). Schizophrenia and other psychotic disorders. In R. E. Hales & S. C. Yudofsky (Eds.), *Textbook of clini-cal psychiatry.* Washington, DC: American Psychiatric Publishing.

Hobson, J. A. (1988). *The dreaming brain.* New York: Basic Books.

Hobson, J. A. (2007). Current understanding of cellular models of REM expression. In D. Barrett & P. McNamara (Eds.), *The new science of dreaming.* Westport, CT: Praeger.

Hobson, J. A., & McCarley, R. W. (1977). The brain as a dream state generator: An activation-synthesis hypothesis of the dream process. *American Journal of Psychiatry, 134,* 1335–1348.

Hobson, J. A., Pace-Schott, E. F., & Stickgold, R. (2000). Dreaming and the brain: Toward a cognitive neuroscience of conscious states. *Behavioral and Brain Sciences, 23,* 793–842; 904–1018; 1083–1121.

Hocevar, D., & Bachelor, P. (1989). A taxonomy and critique of measurements used in the study of creativity. In J. A. Glover, R. R. Ronning, & C. R. Reynolds (Eds.), *Handbook of creativity.* New York: Plenum.

Hochberg, J. (1988). Visual perception. In R. C. Atkinson, R. J. Herrnstein, G. Lindzey, & R. D. Luce (Eds.), *Stevens' handbook of experimental psychology* (2nd ed., Vol. 1). New York: Wiley.

Hodapp, R. M. (1994). Cultural-familial mental retardation. In R. J. Sternberg (Ed.), *Encyclopedia of human intelligence.* New York: Macmillan.

Hodgkin, A. L., & Huxley, A. F. (1952). Currents carried by sodium and potassium ions through the membrane of the giant axon of Loligo. *Journal of Physiology, 116,* 449–472.

Hoek, H. W. (2002). Distribution of eating disorders. In C. G. Fairburn & K. D. Brownell (Eds.), *Eating disorders and obesity: A comprehensive handbook.* New York: Guilford.

Hofbauer, R. K., Rainville, P., Duncan, G. H., & Bushnell, M. C. (2001). Cortical representation of the sensory dimension of pain. *Journal of Neurophysiology, 86,* 402–411.

Hoff, E. (2001). *Language development.* Belmont, CA: Wadsworth.

Hoff, E. (2005). *Language development.* Belmont, CA: Wadsworth.

Hoffman, E. (1994). *The drive for self: Alfred Adler and the founding of individual psychology.* Reading, MA: Addison-Wesley.

Hoffman, R. E. (2007). Transcranial magnetic stimulation studies of schizophrenia. In M. S. George & R. H. Belmaker (Eds.), *Transcranial magnetic stimulation in clinical psychiatry.* Washington, DC: American Psychiatric Publishing.

Hoffstein, V. (2005). Snoring and upper airway resistance. In M. H. Kryger, T. Roth, & W. C. Dement (Eds.), *Principles and practice of sleep medicine.* Philadelphia: Elsevier Saunders.

Hofstede, G. (1980). *Culture's consequences: International differences in work-related values.* Beverly Hills, CA: Sage.

Hofstede, G. (1983). Dimensions of national cultures in fifty countries and three regions. In J. Deregowski, S. Dziurawiec, & R. Annis (Eds.), *Explications in cross-cultural psychology.* Lisse: Swets and Zeitlinger.

Hofstede, G. (2001). *Culture's consequences: Comparing values, behaviors, institutions, and organizations across nations.* Thousand Oaks, CA: Sage.

Hogan, J., Barrett, P., & Hogan, R. (2007). Personality measurement, faking, and employment selection. *Journal of Applied Psychology, 92,* 1270–1285.

Hogan, M. F., & Morrison, A. K. (2003). Organization and financing of mental health care. In A. Tasman, J. Kay, & J. A. Lieberman (Eds.), *Psychiatry.* New York: Wiley.

Hogan, R. (2005). In defense of personality measurement: New wine for old whiners. *Human Performance, 18,* 331–341.

Hogan, R., & Kaiser, R. B. (2005). What we know about leadership. *Review of General Psychology, 9*(2), 169–180.

Hogan, R., & Stokes, L. W. (2006). Business susceptibility to consulting fads: The case of emotional intelligence. In K. R. Murphy (Ed.), *A critique of emotional intelligence: What are the problems and how can they be fixed?* (pp. 263–280). Mahwah, NJ: Erlbaum.

Hoge, C. W., Terhakopian, A., Castro, C. A., Messer, S. C., & Engel, C. C. (2007). Association of posttraumatic stress disorder with somatic symptoms, health care visits, and absenteeism among Iraq War veterans. *American Journal of Psychiatry, 164,* 150–153.

Hogg, M. A., & Abrams, D. (2003). Intergroup behavior and social identity. In M. A. Hogg & J. Cooper (Eds.), *The Sage handbook of social psychology.* Thousand Oaks, CA: Sage.

Hoigaard, R., & Ingvaldsen, R. P. (2006). Social loafing in interactive groups: The effects of identifiability on effort and individual performance in floorball. *Athletic Insight: Online Journal of Sport Psychology, 8*(2).

Hoigaard, R., Säfvenbom, R., & Tonnessen, F. E. (2006). The relationship between group cohesion, group norms, and perceived social loafing in soccer teams. *Small Group Research, 37,* 217–232.

Holahan, C. J., & Moos, R. H. (1990). Life stressors, resistance factors, and improved psychological functioning: An extension of the stress resistance paradigm. *Journal of Personality and Social Psychology, 58,* 909–917.

Holahan, C. J., & Moos, R. H. (1994). Life stressors and mental health: Advances in conceptualizing stress resistance. In W. R. Avison & J. H. Gotlib (Eds.), *Stress and mental health: Contemporary issues and prospects for the future.* New York: Plenum.

Holahan, C., & Sears, R. (1995). *The gifted group in later maturity.* Stanford, CA: Stanford University Press.

Holden, C. (1986, October). The rational optimist. *Psychology Today,* pp. 55–60.

Holden, C. (2004). FDA weighs suicide risk in children on antidepressants. *Science, 303,* 745.

Holden, G. W. (2002). Perspectives on the effects of corporal punishment: Comment on Gershoff. *Psychological Bulletin, 128,* 590–595.

Holland, R. W., Hendriks, M., & Aarts, H. (2005). Smells like clean spirit: Nonconscious effects of scent on cognition and behavior. *Psychological Science, 16,* 689–693.

Hollander, E., & Samons, D. M. (2003). Male menopauses: An unexplored area of men's health. *Psychiatric Annals, 33,* 497–500.

Hollander, E., & Simeon, D. (2003). Anxiety disorders. In R. E. Hales & S. C. Yudofsky (Eds.), *Textbook of clinical psychiatry.* Washington, DC: American Psychiatric Publishing.

Hollands, C. (1989). Trivial and questionable research on animals. In G. Langley (Ed.), *Animal experimentation: The consensus changes.* New York: Chapman & Hall.

Hollifield, M. A. (2005). Somatoform disorders. In B. J. Sadock & V. A. Sadock (Eds.), *Kaplan & Sadock's comprehensive textbook of psychiatry* (pp. 1800–1828). Philadelphia: Lippincott Williams & Wilkins.

Hollingworth, L. S. (1914). *Functional periodicity: An experimental study of the mental and motor abilities of women during menstruation.* New York: Teachers College, Columbia University.

Hollingworth, L. S. (1916). Sex differences in mental tests. *Psychological Bulletin, 13*, 377–383.

Hollis, J. H., & Henry, C. J. K. (2007). Sensory-specific satiety and flavor amplification of foods. *Journal of Sensory Studies, 22*, 367–376.

Hollis, K. L. (1997). Contemporary research on Pavlovian conditioning: A "new" functional analysis. *American Psychologist, 52*, 956–965.

Hollon, S. D., & Beck, A. T. (2004). Cognitive and cognitive behavioral therapies. In M. J. Lambert (Ed.), *Bergin and Garfields handbook of psychotherapy and behavior change.* New York: Wiley.

Hollon, S. D., Stewart, M. O., & Strunk, D. (2006). Enduring effects for cognitive behavior therapy in the treatment of depression and anxiety. *Annual Review of Psychology, 57*, 285–315.

Holmans, P., Weissman, M. M., Zubenko, G. S., Scheftner, W. A., Crowe, R. R., & DePaulo, J. R. et al. (2007). Genetics of recurrent early-onset major depression (GenRED): Final genome scan report. *American Journal of Psychiatry, 164*, 248–258.

Holmes, D. (1995). The evidence for repression: An examination of sixty years of research. In J. Singer (Ed.), *Repression and dissociation: Implications for personality, theory, psychopathology, and health* (pp. 85–102). Chicago: University of Chicago Press.

Holmes, D. S. (1987). The influence of meditation versus rest on physiological arousal: A second examination. In M. A. West (Ed.), *The psychology of meditation.* Oxford: Clarendon Press.

Holmes, T. H., & Rahe, R. H. (1967). The Social Readjustment Rating Scale. *Journal of Psychosomatic Research, 11*, 213–218.

Holtgraves, T. (2004). Social desirability and self-reports: Testing models of socially desirable responding. *Personality and Social Psychology Bulletin, 30*, 161–172.

Holyoak, K. J. (1995). Problem solving. In E. E. Smith & D. N. Osherson (Eds.), *Thinking* (2nd ed.). Cambridge, MA: MIT Press.

Holyoak, K. J. (2005). Analogy. In K. J. Holyoak & R. G. Morrison (Eds.), *The Cambridge handbook of thinking and reasoning.* New York: Cambridge University Press.

Hong, G. K., Garcia, M., & Soriano, M. (2000). Responding to the challenge: Preparing mental health professionals for the new millennium. In I. Cuellar & F. A. Paniagua (Eds.), *Handbook of multicultural mental health: Assessment and treatment of diverse populations.* San Diego: Academic Press.

Honig, W. K., & Alsop, B. (1992). Operant behavior. In L. R. Squire (Ed.), *Encyclopedia of learning and memory.* New York: Macmillan.

Hooley, J. M. (2004). Do psychiatric patients do better clinically if they live with certain kinds of families? *Current Directions in Psychological Science, 13*(5), 202–205.

Hooley, J. M. (2007). Expressed emotion and relapse of psychopathology. *Annual Review of Clinical Psychology, 3*, 329–352.

Hooley, J. M., & Hiller, J. B. (1998). Expressed emotion and the pathogenesis of relapse in schizophrenia. In M. F. Lenzenweger & R. H. Dworkin (Eds.), *Origins and development of schizophrenia: Advances in experimental psychopathology.* Washington DC: American Psychological Association.

Hooper, J., & Teresi, D. (1986). *The 3-pound universe—The brain.* New York: Laurel.

Hopcroft, R. L. (2006). Sex, status, and reproductive success in the contemporary United States. *Evolution and Human Behavior, 27*, 104–120.

Hopko, D. R., Crittendon, J. A., Grant, E., & Wilson, S. A. (2005). The impact of anxiety on performance IQ. *Anxiety, Stress, & Coping: An International Journal, 18*(1), 17–35.

Hopper, K., Harrison, G., Janca, A., & Satorius, N. (2007). *Recovery from schizophrenia: An international perspective—A report from the WHO Collaborative Project, the international study of schizophrenia.* New York: Oxford University Press.

Horn, J. L. (2002). Selections of evidence, misleading assumptions, and oversimplifications: The political message of *The Bell Curve.* In J. M. Fish (Ed.), *Race and intelligence: Separating science from myth* (pp. 297–326). Mahwah, NJ: Erlbaum.

Horn, J. L., & Hofer, S. M. (1992). Major abilities and development in the adult period. In R. J. Sternberg & C. A. Berg (Eds.), *Intellectual development.* Cambridge: Cambridge University Press.

Horn, J., Nelson, C. E., & Brannick, M. T. (2004). Integrity, conscientiousness, and honesty. *Psychological Reports, 95*(1), 27–38.

Horowitz, F. D. (1992). John B. Watson's legacy: Learning and environment. *Developmental Psychology, 28*, 360–367.

Horrey, W. J., & Wickens, C. D. (2006). Examining the impact of cell phone on driving using meta-analytic techniques. *Human Factors, 48*, 196–205.

Horwath, E., & Weissman, M. M. (2000). Anxiety disorders: Epidemiology. In B. J. Sadock & V. A. Sadock (Eds.), *Kaplan and Sadock's comprehensive textbook of psychiatry* (7th ed., Vol. 1, pp. 1441–1449). Philadelphia: Lippincott/Williams & Wilkins.

Hossain, J. L., & Shapiro, C. M. (1999). Considerations and possible consequences of shift work. *Journal of Psychosomatic Research, 47*, 293–296.

Hotopf, M. (2004). Preventing somatization. *Psychological Medicine, 34*(2), 195–198.

Houston, D. M., Santelmann, L. M., & Jusczyk, P. W. (2004). English-learning infants' segmentation of trisyllabic words from fluent speech. *Language and Cognitive Processes, 19*(1), 97–136.

Houts, A. C. (2002). Discovery, invention, and the expansion of the modern *Diagnostic and Statistical Manuals of Mental Disorders.* In L. E. Beutler & M. L. Malik (Eds.), *Rethinking the DSM.* Washington, DC: American Psychological Association.

Howard, A., Pion, G. M., Gottfredson, G. D., Flattau, P. E., Oskamp, S., Pfafflin, S. M., Bray, D. W., & Burstein, A. G. (1986). The changing face of American psychology: A report from the committee on employment and human resources. *American Psychologist, 41*, 1311–1327.

Howard, D. J. (1995). "Chaining" the use of influence strategies for producing compliance behavior. *Journal of Social Behavior and Personality, 10*, 169–185.

Howard, M. S., & Medway, F. J. (2004). Adolescents' attachment and coping with stress. *Psychology in Schools, 41*, 391–402.

Howe, M. J. A. (1999). *The psychology of high abilities.* New York: New York University Press.

Hoyer, W. J., & Verhaeghen, P. (2006). Memory aging. In J. E. Birren & K. W. Schaie (Eds.), *Handbook of the psychology of aging.* San Diego: Academic Press.

Hrdy, S. B. (1997). Raising Darwin's consciousness: Female sexuality and the prehominid origins of patriarchy. *Human Nature: An Interdisciplinary Biosocial Perspective, 8*, 1–49.

Hsee, C. K., & Hastie, R. (2006). Decision and experience: Why don't we choose what makes us happy? *Trends in Cognitive Science, 10*, 31–37.

Hsee, C. K., & Zhang, J. (2004). Distinction bias: Misprediction and mischoice due to joint evaluation. *Journal of Personality and Social Psychology, 86*, 680–695.

Hsee, C. K., Zhang, J., & Chen, J. (2004). Internal and substantive inconsistencies in decision making. In D. J. Koehler & N. Harvey (Eds.), *Blackwell handbook of judgment and decision making.* Malden, MA: Blackwell Publishing.

Hsu, L. K. G. (1990). *Eating disorders.* New York: Guilford.

Hsu, L. M. (1995). Regression toward the mean associated with measurement error and identification of improvement and deterioration in psychotheray. *Journal of Consulting & Clinical Psychology, 63*, 141–144.

Hu, F. B., & Willett, W. C. (2002). Optimal diets for prevention of coronary heart disease. *Journal of the American Medical Association, 288*, 2569–2578.

Hu, Y., Zhang, R., & Li, W. (2005). Relationships among jealousy, self-esteem and self-efficacy. *Chinese Journal of Clinical Psychology, 13*, 165–166, 172.

Hua, J. Y., & Smith, S. J. (2004). Neural activity and the dynamics of central nervous system development. *Nature Neuroscience, 7,*, 327–332.

Hubel, D. H., & Wiesel, T. N. (1962). Receptive fields, binocular interaction and functional architecture in the cat's visual cortex. *Journal of Physiology, 160*, 106–154.

Hubel, D. H., & Wiesel, T. N. (1963). Receptive fields of cells in striate cortex of very young visually inexperienced kittens. *Journal of Neurophysiology, 26*, 994–1002.

Hubel, D. H., & Wiesel, T. N. (1979). Brain mechanisms of vision. In Scientific American (Eds.), *The brain.* San Francisco: W. H. Freeman.

Hubel, D. H., & Wiesel, T. N. (1998). Early exploration of the visual cortex. *Neuron, 20*, 401–412.

Hublin, C. G. M., & Partinen, M. M. (2002). The extent and impact of insomnia as a public health problem. *Journal of Clinical Psychiatry, 4*(suppl 1), 8–12.

Hudson, J. I., Hiripi, E., Pope Jr., Harrison, G., & Kessler, R. C. (2007). The prevalence and correlates of eating disorders in the national comorbidity survey replication. *Biological Psychiatry, 61*, 348–358.

Hudson, W. (1960). Pictorial depth perception in sub-cultural groups in Africa. *Journal of Social Psychology, 52*, 183–208.

Hudson, W. (1967). The study of the problem of pictorial perception among unacculturated groups. *International Journal of Psychology, 2*, 89–107.

Hudspeth, A. J. (2000). Sensory transduction in the ear. In E. R. Kandel, J. H. Schwartz, & T. M. Jessell (Eds.), *Principles of neural science.* New York: McGraw-Hill.

Hudziak, J., & Waterman, G. S. (2005). Buspirone. In B. J. Sadock & V. A. Sadock (Eds.), *Kaplan and Sadock's comprehensive textbook of psychiatry* (pp. 2797–2801). Philadelphia: Lippincott Williams & Wilkins.

Huesmann, L. R. (1986). Psychological processes promoting the relation between exposure to media violence and aggressive behavior by the viewer. *Journal of Social Issues, 42*, 125–139.

Huesmann, L. R., & Miller, L. S. (1994). Long-term effects of repeated exposure to media violence in childhood. In L. R. Huesmann (Ed.), *Aggressive behavior: Current perspectives.* New York: Plenum Press.

Huesmann, L. R., Moise-Titus, J., Podolski, C. L., & Eron, L. D. (2003). Longitudinal relations between children's exposure to TV violence and their aggressive and violent behavior in young adulthood: 1977–1992. *Developmental Psychology, 39,* 201–221.

Huettel, S. A., Mack, P. B., McCarthy, G., Hua, J. Y., & Smith, S. J. (2002). Perceiving patterns in random series: Dynamic processing of sequence in prefrontal cortex. *Nature Neuroscience, 5,* 485–490.

Huey, E. D., Krueger, F., & Grafman, J. (2006). Representations in the human prefrontal cortex. *Current Directions in Psychological Science, 15,* 167–171.

Huey, L. Y., Cole, S., Trestman, R. L., & Tinsley, J. A. (2005). Health care reform. In B. J. Sadock & V. A. Sadock (Eds.), *Kaplan & Sadock's comprehensive textbook of psychiatry.* Philadelphia: Lippincott Williams & Wilkins.

Huey, L. Y., Ford, J. D., & Cole, R. F. (2005). Public and community psychiatry. In B. J. Sadock & V. A. Sadock (Eds.), *Kaplan & Sadock's comprehensive textbook of psychiatry.* Philadelphia: Lippincott Williams & Wilkins.

Hughes, J. R., Gulliver, S. B., Fenwick, J. W., Valliere, W. A., Cruser, K., Pepper, S., Shea, P., Solomon, L. J., & Flynn, B. S. (1992). Smoking cessation among self-quitters. *Health Psychology, 11,* 331–334.

Hughes, J., Smith, T. W., Kosterlitz, H. W., Fothergill, L. A., Morgan, B. A., & Morris, H. R. (1975). Identification of two related pentapeptides from the brain with the potent opiate agonist activity. *Nature, 258,* 577–579.

Hughes, S. M., & Gallup, G. G. (2003). Sex differences in morphological predictors of sexual behavior. *Evolution and Human Behavior, 24,* 173–178.

Hull, C. L. (1943). *Principles of behavior.* New York: Appleton.

Hultsch, D. F., Hertzog, C., Small, B. J., & Dixon, R. A. (1999). Use it or lose it: Engaged lifestyles as a buffer of cognitive decline in aging. *Psychology and Aging, 14,,* 245–263.

Hunsley, J., Lee, C. M., & Wood, J. M. (2003). Controversial and questionable assessment techniques. In S. O. Lilienfield, S. J. Lynn, & J. M. Lohr (Eds.), *Science and pseudoscience in clinical psychology.* New York: Guilford.

Hunt, E. (1994). Problem solving. In R. J. Sternberg (Ed.), *Thinking and problem solving.* San Diego: Academic Press.

Hunt, E. (2001). Multiple views of multiple intelligence [Review of the book *Intelligence reframed: Multiple intelligence in the 21st century*]. *Contemporary Psychology, 46,* 5–7.

Hunt, H. (1989). *The multiplicity of dreams: Memory, imagination and consciousness.* New Haven: Yale University Press.

Hunt, J. M., Smith, M. F., & Kernan, J. B. (1985). The effects of expectancy disconfirmation and argument strength on message processing level: An application to personal selling. In E. C. Hirschman & M. B. Holbrook (Eds.), *Advances in consumer research* (Vol. 12). Provo, UT: Association for Consumer Research.

Hunt, S. P., & Mantyh, P. W. (2001). The molecular dynamics of pain control. *Nature Reviews Neuroscience, 2,* 83–91.

Hunter, J. E., & Schmidt, F. L. (2000). Racial and gender bias in ability and achievement tests: Resolving the apparent paradox. *Psychology, Public Policy, and Law, 6,* 151–158.

Huntsinger, E. T., & Luecken, L. J. (2004). Attachment relationships and health behavior: The mediational role of self-esteem. *Psychology & Health, 19,* 515–526.

Hurvich, L. M. (1981). *Color vision.* Sunderland, MA: Sinnauer Associates.

Huston, A. C., Donnerstein, E., Fairchild, H., Feshbach, N. D., Katz, P. A., & Murray, J. P. (1992). *Big world, small screen: The role of television in American society.* Lincoln: University of Nebraska Press.

Huttenlocher, P. R. (2002). *Neural plasticity: The effects of environment on the development of the cerebral cortex.* Cambridge, MA: Harvard University Press.

Hwang, W. C. (2006). The psychotherapy adaptation and modification framework: Application to Asian Americans. *American Psychologist, 61,* 702–715.

Hybels, C. F., & Blazer, D. G. I. (2005). Epidemiology of psychiatric disorders. In B. J. Sadock & V. A. Sadock (Eds.), *Kaplan & Sadock's comprehensive textbook of psychiatry.* Philadelphia: Lippincott Williams & Wilkins.

Hyde, J. S. (2005a). The gender similarities hypothesis. *American Psychologist, 60,* 581–892.

Hyde, J. S. (2005b). The genetics of sexual orientation. In J. S. Hyde (Ed.), *Biological substrates of human sexuality* (pp. 9–20). Washington, DC: American Psychological Association.

Hyde, M., Roehrs, T., & Roth, T. (2006). Drugs of abuse and sleep. In T. Lee–Chiong (Ed.), *Sleep: A comprehensive handbook.* Hoboken, NJ: Wiley-Liss.

Hyman, I. E., Jr., Husband, T. H., & Billings, J. F. (1995). False memories of childhood experiences. *Applied Cognitive Psychology, 9,* 181–197.

Hyman, I. E., Jr., & Kleinknecht, E. E. (1999). False childhood memories: Research, theory, and applications. In L. M. Williams, & V. L. Banyard (Eds.), *Trauma & memory.* Thousand Oaks, CA: Sage.

Iacoboni, M., & Dapretto, M. (2006). The mirror neuron system and the consequences of its dysfunction. *Nature Reviews Neuroscience, 7,* 942–951.

Iacono, W. G., & Lykken, D. T. (1997). The validity of the lie detector: Two surveys of scientific opinion. *Journal of Applied Psychology, 82,* 426–433.

Iacono, W. G., & Patrick, C. J. (1999). Polygraph ("lie detector") testing: The state of the art. In A. K. Hess & I. B. Weiner (Eds.), *The handbook of forensic psychology* (pp. 440–473). New York: Wiley.

Iams, J. D. (2002). Preterm birth. In S. G. Gabbe, J. R. Niebyl, & J. L. Simpson (Eds.), *Obstetrics: Normal and problem pregnancies.* New York: Churchill Livingstone.

Ickovics, J. R., Thayaparan, B., & Ethier, K. A. (2001). Women and AIDS: A contextual analysis. In A. Baum, T. A. Revenson, & J. E. Singer (Eds.), *Handbook of health psychology* (pp. 817–840). Mahwah, NJ: Erlbaum.

Idisis, Y., Ben-David, S., & Ben-Nachum, E. (2007). Attribution of blame to rape victims among therapists and non-therapists. *Behavioral Sciences & the Law, 25*(1), 103–120.

Iezzi, T., Duckworth, M. P., & Adams, H. E. (2001). Somatoform and factitious disorders. In P. B. Sutker & H. E. Adams (Eds.), *Comprehensive handbook of psychopathology* (3rd ed., pp. 211–258). New York: Kluwer Academic/Plenum Publishers.

Infante, J. R., Torres-Avisbal, M., Pinel, P., Vallejo. J. A., Peran, F., Gonzalez, F., Contreras, P., Pacheco, C., Roldan, A., & Latre, J. M. (2001). Catecholamine levels in practitioners of the transcendental meditation technique. *Physiology & Behavior, 72*(1-2), 141–146.

Innocenti, G. M. (1994). Some new trends in the study of the corpus callosum. *Behavioral and Brain Research, 64,* 1–8.

Irvine, S. H., & Berry, J. W. (1988). *Human abilities in cultural context.* New York: Cambridge University Press.

Irwin, M. R., Wang, M., Campomayor, C. O., Collado-Hidalgo, A., & Cole, S. (2006). Sleep deprivation and activation of morning levels of cellular and genomic markers of inflammation. *Archives of Internal Medicine, 166,* 1756–1762.

Isaacowitz, D. M., & Seligman, M. E. P. (2007). Learned helplessness. In G. Fink (Ed.), *Encyclopedia of stress.* San Diego: Elsevier.

Isometsa, E. T., Heikkinen, M. E., Marttunen, M. J., Henriksson, M. M., Aro, H. M., & Lonnqvist, J. K. (1995). The last appointment before suicide: Is suicide intent communicated? *American Journal of Psychiatry, 152,* 919–922.

Iversen, S., Iversen, L., & Saper, C. B. (2000). The autonomic nervous system and the hypothalamus. In E. R. Kandel, J. H. Schwartz, & T. M. Jessell (Eds.), *Principles of neural science* (pp. 960–981). New York: McGraw-Hill.

Iwata, B. A. (2006). On the distinction between positive and negative reinforcement. *Behavior Analyst, 29*(1), 121–123.

Iwawaki, S., & Vernon, P. E. (1988). Japanese abilities and achievements. In S. H. Irvine & J. W. Berry (Eds.), *Human abilities in cultural context.* New York: Cambridge University Press.

Izard, C. E. (1984). Emotion-cognition relationships and human development. In C. E. Izard, J. Kagan, & R. B. Zajonc (Eds.), *Emotions, cognition and behavior.* Cambridge, England: Cambridge University Press.

Izard, C. E. (1990). Facial expressions and the regulation of emotions. *Journal of Personality and Social Psychology, 58,* 487–498.

Izard, C. E. (1991). *The psychology of emotions.* New York: Plenum.

Izard, C. E. (1994). Innate and universal facial expressions: Evidence from developmental and cross-cultural research. *Psychological Bulletin, 115,* 288–299.

Izard, C. E. (2007). Basic emotions, natural kinds, emotion schemas, and a new paradigm. *Perspectives on Psychological Science, 2,* 260–280.

Izard, C. E., & Saxton, P. M. (1988). Emotions. In R. C. Atkinson, R. J. Herrnstein, G. Lindzey, & R. D. Luce (Eds.), *Stevens' handbook of experimental psychology* (Vol. 1). New York: Wiley.

Jablin, F. M. (1982). Organizational communication: An assimilation approach. In M. E. Rolff & C. R. Berger (Eds.), *Social cognition and communication* (pp. 255–286). Beverly Hills, CA: Sage.

Jackicic, J., & Gallagher, K. I. (2002). Physical activity considerations for management of body weight. In D. H. Bessesen & R. Kushner (2002), *Evaluation and management of obesity.* Philadelphia: Hanley & Belfus.

Jacob, R. G., & Pelham, W. (2000). Behavior therapy. In B. J. Sadock & V. A. Sadock (Eds.), *Kaplan and Sadock's comprehensive textbook of psychiatry* (7th ed., Vol. 1, pp. 2080–2127). Philadelphia: Lippincott/ Williams & Wilkins.

Jacob, R. G., & Pelham, W. (2005). Behavior therapy. In B. J. Sadock & V. A. Sadock (Eds.), *Kaplan and Sadock's comprehensive textbook of psychiatry* (pp. 2498–2547). Philadelphia: Lippincott Williams & Wilkins.

Jacob, S., McClintock, M. K., Zelano, B., & Ober, C. (2002). Paternally inherited HLA alleles are associated with women's choice of male odor. *Nature Genetics, 30,* 175–179.

Jacobs, B. L. (2004). Depression: The brain finally gets into the act. *Current Directions in Psychological Science, 13*(3), 103–106.

Jacobs, D. F. (2004). Youth gambling in North America: Long-term trends and future prospects. In J. L. Derevensky & R. Grupta (Eds.), *Gambling problems in youth: Theoretical and applied perspectives* (pp. 1–24). New York: Kluwer/Plenum.

Jacobs, H. S. (2001). Idea of male menopause is not useful. *Medical Crossfire, 3,* 52–55.

Jacobson, E. (1938). *Progressive relaxation.* Chicago: University of Chicago Press.

Jacoby, L. L., Hessels, S., & Bopp, K. (2001). Proactive and retroactive effects in memory performance: Dissociating recollection and accessibility bias. In H. L. Roediger, J. S. Nairne, I. Neath, & A. M. Surprenant (Eds.), *The nature of remembering: Essays in honor of Robert G. Crowder* (pp. 35–54). Washington, DC: American Psychological Association.

Jaffe, H. W., Valdiserri, R. O., & De Cock, K. M. (2007). The reemerging HIV/AIDS epidemic in men who have sex with men. *Journal of the American Medical Association, 298,* 2412–2414.

Jager, G., de Win, M. M. L., van der Tweel, I., Schilt, T., Kahn, R. S., van den Brink, W., et al. (2008). Assessment of cognitive brain function in ecstasy users and contributions of other drugs of abuse: Results from an fMRI study. *Neuropsychopharmacology, 33*(2), 247–258.

Jain, S. P., Buchanan, B., & Maheswaran, D. (2000). Comparative versus noncomparative advertising. *Journal of Consumer Psychology, 9,* 201–211.

James, J. E. (2004). Critical review of dietary caffeine and blood pressure: A relationship that should be taken more seriously. *Psychosomatic Medicine, 66*(1), 63–71.

James, W. (1884). What is emotion? *Mind, 19,* 188–205.

James, W. (1890). *The principles of psychology.* New York: Holt.

James, W. (1902). *The varieties of religious experience.* New York: Modern Library.

James, W. H. (2005). Biological and psychosocial determinants of male and female human sexual orientation. *Journal of Biosocial Science, 37,* 555–567.

Jamison, K. R. (1988). Manic-depressive illness and accomplishment: Creativity, leadership, and social class. In F. K. Goodwin & K. R. Jamison (Eds.), *Manic-depressive illness.* Oxford, England: Oxford University Press.

Jang, K. L., Thordarson, D. S., Stein, M. B., Cohan, S. L., & Taylor, S. (2007). Coping styles and personality: A biometric analysis. *Anxiety, Stress & Coping: An International Journal, 20*(1), 17–24.

Janig, W. (2003). The autonomic nervous system and its coordination by the brain. In R. J. Davidson, K. R. Scherer, & H. H. Goldsmith (Eds.), *Handbook of affective sciences.* New York: Oxford University Press.

Janis, I. L. (1958). *Psychological stress.* New York: Wiley.

Janis, I. L. (1972). *Victims of groupthink.* Boston: Houghton Mifflin.

Janis, I. L. (1993). Decision making under stress. In L. Goldberger & S. Breznitz (Eds.), *Handbook of stress: Theoretical and clinical aspects* (2nd ed.). New York: Free Press.

Janis, I. L., & Mann, L. (1977). *Decision making: A psychological analysis of conflict, choice, and commitment.* New York: Free Press.

Janofsky, J. S., Dunn, M. H., Roskes, E. J., Briskin, J. K., & Rudolph, M. S. L. (1996). Insanity defense pleas in Baltimore city: An analysis of outcome. *American Journal of Psychiatry, 153,* 1464–1468.

Janowsky, J. S. (2006). Thinking with your gonads: Testosterone and cognition. *Trends in Cognitive Sciences, 10*(2), 77–82.

Janssen, E., Carpenter, D., & Graham, C. A. (2003). Selecting films for sex research: Gender differences in erotic film preference. *Archives of Sexual Behavior, 32,* 243–251.

Jaroff, L. (1993, November 29). Lies of the mind. *Time,* pp. 52–59.

Javitt, D. C., & Laruelle, M. (2006). Neurochemical theories. In J. A. Lieberman, T. S. Stroup, & D. O. Perkins (Eds.), *Textbook of schizophrenia* (pp. 85–116). Washington, DC: American Psychiatric Publishing.

Jefferson, J. W., & Greist, J. H. (2000). Lithium. In B. J. Sadock & V. A. Sadock (Eds.), *Kaplan and Sadock's comprehensive textbook of psychiatry* (7th ed., Vol. 1, pp. 2377–2389). Philadelphia: Lippincott/Williams & Wilkins.

Jefferson, J. W., & Greist, J. H. (2005). Lithium. In B. J. Sadock & V. A. Sadock (Eds.), *Kaplan and Sadock's comprehensive textbook of psychiatry* (pp. 2839–2850). Philadelphia: Lippincott Williams & Wilkins.

Jeffrey, R. W., Epstein, L. H., Wilson, G. T., Drewnowski, A., Stunkard, A. J., Wing, R. R., & Hill, D. R. (2000). Long-term maintenance of weight loss: Current status. *Health Psychology, 19*(1), 5–16.

Jensen, A. R. (1969). How much can we boost IQ and scholastic achievement? *Harvard Educational Review, 39,* 1–23.

Jensen, A. R. (1980). *Bias in mental testing.* New York: Free Press.

Jensen, A. R. (1982). Reaction time and psychometric *g.* In H. J. Eysenck (Ed.), *A model for intelligence.* New York: Springer-Verlag.

Jensen, A. R. (1987). Process differences and individual difference in some cognitive tasks. *Intelligence, 11,* 107–136.

Jensen, A. R. (1992). The importance of intraindividual variation in reaction time. *Personality and Individual Differences, 13,* 869–881.

Jensen, A. R. (1993). Why is reaction time correlated with psychometric *g*? *Current Directions in Psychological Science, 2*(2), 53–56.

Jensen, A. R. (1998). *The g factor: The science of mental ability.* Westport, CT: Praeger.

Jensen, E. (2000). *Brain-based learning.* San Diego: Brain Store.

Jensen, E. (2006). *Enriching the brain.* San Francisco: Jossey-Bass.

Jensen-Campbell, L. A., & Graziano, W. G. (2001). Agreeableness as a moderator of interpersonal conflict. *Journal of Personality, 69,* 323–362.

Jenson, J. D. (2004). It's the information age, so where's the information? *College Teaching, 52*(3), 107–112.

Jessell, T. M., & Kelly, D. D. (1991). Pain and analgesia. In E. R. Kandel, J. H. Schwartz, & T. M. Jessell (Eds.), *Principles of neural science* (3rd ed.). New York: Elsevier.

Jewell, L. N. (1998). *Contemporary industrial/organizational psychology.* Belmont, CA: Wadsworth.

Jick, H., Kaye, J. A., & Jick, S. S. (2004). Antidepressants and the risk of suicidal behaviors. *Journal of the American Medical Association, 292,* 338–343.

John, O. P., & Gross, J. J. (2007). Individual differences in emotion regulation. In J. J. Gross (Ed.), *Handbook of emotion regulation.* New York: Guilford.

John, O. P., & Srivastava, S. (1999). The big five trait taxonomy: History, measurement, and theoretical perspectives. In L. A. Pervin & O. P. John (Eds.), *Handbook of personality: Theory and research.* New York: Guilford.

Johnson, A. (2003). Procedural memory and skill acquisition. In A. F. Healy & R. W. Proctor (Eds.), *Handbook of psychology, Vol. 4: Experimental psychology.* New York: Wiley.

Johnson, B. A., & Ait-Daoud, N. (2005). Alcohol: Clinical aspects. In J. H. Lowinson, P. Ruiz, R. B. Millman, & J. G. Langrod (Eds.), *Substance abuse: A comprehensive textbook.* Philadelphia: Lippincott/Williams & Wilkins.

Johnson, B. T., Maio, G. R., & Smith-McLallen, A. (2005). Communication and attitude change: Causes, processes, and effects. In D. Albarracin, B. T. Johnson, & M. P. Zanna (Eds.), *The handbook of attitudes.* Mahwah, NJ: Erlbaum.

Johnson, C., & Mullen, B. (1994). Evidence for the accessibility of paired distinctiveness in distinctiveness-based illusory correlation in stereotyping. *Personality and Social Psychology Bulletin, 20,* 65–70.

Johnson, D. (1990). Animal rights and human lives: Time for scientists to right the balance. *Psychological Science, 1,* 213–214.

Johnson, E. O., & Breslau, N. (2006). Is the association of smoking and depression a recent phenomenon? *Nicotine & Tobacco Research, 8,* 257–262.

Johnson, M. E., & Dowling-Guyer, S. (1996). Effects of inclusive vs. exclusive language on evaluations of the counselor. *Sex Roles, 34,* 407–418.

Johnson, M. K. (1996). Fact, fantasy, and public policy. In D. J. Herrmann, C. McEvoy, C. Hertzog, P. Hertel, & M. K. Johnson (Eds.), *Basic and applied memory research: Theory in context* (Vol. 1). Mahwah, NJ: Erlbaum.

Johnson, M. K. (2006). Memory and reality. *American Psychologist, 61,* 760–771.

Johnson, M. K., Hashtroudi, S., & Lindsay, D. S. (1993). Source monitoring. *Psychological Bulletin, 114,* 3–28.

Johnson, M. K., Kahan, T. L., & Raye, C. L. (1984). Dreams and reality monitoring. *Journal of Experimental Psychology: General, 113,* 329–344.

Johnson, S. B., & Carlson, D. N. (2004). Medical regimen adherence: Concepts assessment, and interventions. In J. M. Raczynski & L. C. Leviton (Eds.), *Handbook of clinical health psychology: Vol 2. Disorders of behavior and health.* Washington, DC: American Psychological Association.

Johnson, W., & Krueger, R. F. (2006). How money buys happiness: Genetic and environmental processes linking finances and life satisfaction. *Journal of Personality and Social Psychology, 90,* 680–691.

Johnston, J. C., & McClelland, J. L. (1974). Perception of letters in words: Seek not and ye shall find. *Science, 184,* 1192–1194.

Joiner, T. E. (2002). Depression in its interpersonal context. In I. H. Gotlib & C. L. Hammen (Eds.), *Handbook of depression.* New York: Guilford.

Joiner, T. E., & Katz, J. (1999). Contagion of depressive symptoms and mood: Meta-analytic review and explanations from cognitive, behavioral, and interpersonal viewpoints. *Clinical Psychology: Science and Practice, 6,* 149–164.

Joiner, T. E., & Metalsky, G. I. (1995). A prospective test of an integrative interpersonal theory of depression: A naturalistic study of college students. *Journal of Personality and Social Psychology, 69,* 778–788.

Joinson, A. N., & Paine, C. B. (2007). Self-disclosure, privacy and the Internet. In A. N. Joinson, K. Y. A. McKenna, T. Postmes, & U.-D. Reips (Eds.), *The Oxford handbook of Internet psychology.* New York: Oxford University Press.

Jonathan, K. (2004). The truth about lying. *Nature, 428,* 692–694.

Jones, B. E. (2000). Basic mechanisms of sleep-wake states. In M. H. Kryger, T. Roth, & W. C. Dement (Eds.), *Principles and practice of sleep medicine.* Philadelphia: Elsevier Saunders.

Jones, B. E. (2005). Basic mechanisms in sleep-wake states. In M. H. Kryger, T. Roth, & W. C. Dement (Eds.). *Principles and practice of sleep medicine.* Philadelphia: Elsevier Saunders.

Jones, E. E., & Davis, K. E. (1965). From acts to dispositions: The attribution process in person perception. In L. Berkowitz (Ed.), *Advances in experimental social psychology* (Vol. 2). New York: Academic Press.

Jones, E. E., & Nisbett, R. E. (1971). The actor and the observer: Divergent perceptions of the causes of behavior. In E. E. Jones, D. E. Kanouse, H. H. Kelley, R. E. Nisbett, S. Valins, & B. Weiner (Eds.), *Attribution: Perceiving the causes of behavior.* Morristown, NJ: General Learning Press.

Jones, F., & Bright, J. (2007). Stress: Health and illness. In A. Monat, R. S. Lazarus, & G. Reevy (Eds.), *The Praeger handbook on stress and coping.* Westport, CT: Praeger.

Jones, G. V. (1990). Misremembering a common object: When left is not right. *Memory & Cognition, 18*(2), 174–182.

Jones, L. V. (2000). Thurstone, L. L. In A. E. Kazdin (Ed.), *Encyclopedia of psychology* (pp. 83–84). Washington, DC: American Psychological Association.

Jonides, J., Lacey, S. C., & Nee, D. E. (2005). Process of working memory in mind and brain. *Current Directions in Psychological Science, 14*(1), 2–5.

Jonides, J., Lewis, R. L., Nee, D. E., Lustig, C. A., Berman, M. G., & Moore, K. S. (2008). The mind and brain of short-term memory. *Annual Review of Psychology, 59,* 193–224.

Jordan, P. J., Ashton-James, C. E., & Ashkanasy, N. M. (2006). Evaluating the claims: Emotional intelligence in the workplace. In K. R. Murphy (Ed.), *A critique of emotional intelligence: What are the problems and how can they be fixed?* (pp. 189–210). Mahwah, NJ: Erlbaum.

Jorgensen, R. S., Johnson, B. T., Kolodziej, M. E., & Schreer, G. E. (1996). Elevated blood pressure and personality: A meta-analytic review. *Psychological Bulletin, 120,* 293–320.

Josse, G., & Tzourio-Mazoyer, N. (2004). Hemispheric specialization for language. *Brain Research Reviews, 44,* 1–12.

Judge, T. A., & Cable, D. M. (2004). The effect of physical height on workplace success and income: Preliminary test of a theoretical model. *Journal of Applied Psychology, 89,* 428–441.

Judge, T. A., & Klinger, R. (2008). Job satisfaction: Subjective well-being at work. In M. Eid & R. J. Larsen (Eds.), *The science of subjective well-being* (pp. 393–413). New York: Guilford.

Judge, T. A., Thoresen, C. J., Bono, J. E., & Patton, G. K. (2001). The job satisfaction–job performance relationship: A qualitative and quantitative review. *Psychological Bulletin, 127,* 376–407.

Julien, R. M., Advokat, C. D., & Comaty, J. E. (2008). *A primer of drug action: A comprehensive guide to the actions, uses, and side effects of psychoactive drugs.* New York: Worth.

Jung, C. G. (1917/1953). *On the psychology of the unconscious.* In H. Read, M. Fordham, & G. Adler (Eds.), *Collected works of C. G. Jung* (Vol. 7). Princeton, NJ: Princeton University Press.

Jung, C. G. (1921/1960). *Psychological types.* In H. Read, M. Fordham, & G. Adler (Eds.), *Collected works of C. G. Jung* (Vol. 6). Princeton, NJ: Princeton University Press.

Jung, C. G. (1933). *Modern man in search of a soul.* New York: Harcourt, Brace & World.

Kaas, J. H. (2000). The reorganization of sensory and motor maps after injury in adult mammals. In M. S. Gazzaniga (Ed.), *The new cognitive neurosciences.* Cambridge, MA: The MIT Press.

Kabat-Zinn, J. (2003). Mindfulness-based stress reduction (MBSR). *Constructivism in the Human Sciences , 8,* 73–107.

Kagan, J. (1998, November/December). A parent's influence is peerless. *Harvard Education Letter.*

Kagan, J. (2004). New insights into temperament. *Cerebrum, 6*(1), 51–66.

Kagan, J., & Fox, A. (2006). Biology, culture, and temperamental biases. In N. Eisenberg, W. Damon, & R. M. Lerner (Eds.), *Handbook of child psychology: Social, emotional, and personality development* (pp. 167–225). Hoboken, NJ: Wiley.

Kagan, J., Reznik, J. S., & Snidman, N. (1999). Biological basis of childhood shyness. In A. Slater & D. Muir (Eds.), *The Blackwell reader in developmental psychology* (pp. 65–78). Malden, MA: Blackwell.

Kagan, J., & Snidman, N. (1991). Temperamental factors in human development. *American Psychologist, 46,* 856–862.

Kagan, J., & Snidman, N. (1999). Early childhood predictors of adult anxiety disorders. *Biological Psychiatry, 46,* 1536–1541.

Kagan, J., Snidman, N., & Arcus, D. M. (1992). Initial reactions to unfamiliarity. *Current Directions in Psychological Science, 1*(6), 171–174.

Kahan, T. L. (2001). Consciousness in dreaming: A metacognitive approach. In K. Bulkeley (Ed.), *Dreams: A reader on religious, cultural, and psychological dimensions of dreaming* (pp. 333–360). New York: Palgrave Macmillan.

Kahan, T. L., & Johnson, M. K. (1992). Self-effects in memory for person information. *Social Cognition, 10*(1), 30–50.

Kahan, T. L., & LaBerge, S. (1994). Lucid dreaming as metacognition: Implications for cognitive science. *Consciousness and Cognition, 3,* 246–264.

Kahan, T. L., & LaBerge, S. (1996). Cognition and metacognition in dreaming and waking: Comparisons of first- and third-person ratings. *Dreaming, 6,* 235–249.

Kahan, T., Mohsen, R., Tandez, J., & McDonald, J. (1999). Discriminating memories for actual and imagined taste experiences: A reality monitoring approach. *American Journal of Psychology, 112,* 97–112.

Kahane, H. (1992). *Logic and contemporary rhetoric: The use of reason in everyday life.* Belmont, CA: Wadsworth.

Kahn, D. (2007). Metacognition, recognition, and reflection while dreaming. In D. Barrett & P. McNamara (Eds.), *The new science of dreaming.* Westport, CT: Praeger.

Kahneman, D. (1991). Judgment and decision making: A personal view. *Psychological Science, 2,* 142–145.

Kahneman, D. (1999). Objective happiness. In D. Kahneman, E. Diener, & N. Schwarz (Eds.), *Well-being: The foundations of hedonic psychology.* New York: Russell Sage Foundation.

Kahneman, D. (2003). A perspective on judgment and choice: Mapping bounded rationality. *American Psychologist, 58,* 697–720.

Kahneman, D., & Frederick, S. (2005). A model of heuristic judgment. In K. J. Holyoak & R. G. Morrison (Eds.), *The Cambridge handbook of thinking and reasoning.* New York: Cambridge University Press.

Kahneman, D., Krueger, A. B., Schkade, D., Schwarz, N., & Stone, A. A. (2006). Would you be happier if you were richer? A focusing illusion. *Science, 312,* 1908–1910.

Kahneman, D., & Tversky, A. (1979). Prospect theory: An analysis of decision under risk. *Econometrica, 47,* 263–292.

Kahneman, D., & Tversky, A. (1982). Subjective probability: A judgment of representativeness. In D. Kahneman, P. Slovic, & A. Tversky (Eds.), *Judgment under uncertainty: Heuristics and biases.* Cambridge: Cambridge University Press.

Kahneman, D., & Tversky, A. (1984). Choices, values, and frames. *American Psychologist, 39,* 341–350.

Kahneman, D., & Tversky, A. (2000). *Choices, values, and frames.* New York: Cambridge University Press.

Kako, E. (1999). Elements of syntax in the systems of three language-trained animals. *Animal Learning and Behavior, 27,* 1–14.

Kales, J. D., Kales, A., Bixler, E. O., Soldatos, C. R., Cadieux, R. J., Kashurba, G. J., & Vela-Bueno, A. (1984). Biopsychobehavioral correlates of insomnia: V. Clinical characteristics and behavioral correlates. *American Journal of Psychiatry, 141,* 1371–1376.

Kalichman, S. C., Eaton, L., Cain, D., Cherry, C., Fuhrel, A., Kaufman, M., & Pope, H. (2007). Changes in HIV treatment beliefs and sexual risk behaviors among gay and bisexual men, 1997–2005. *Health Psychology, 26,* 650–656.

Kalivas, P. W., & Volkow, N. D. (2005). The neural basis of addiction: A pathology of motivation and choice. *American Journal of Psychiatry, 162,* 1403–1413.

Kalmijn, M. (1998). Intermarriage and homogamy: Causes, patterns, trends. *Annual Review of Sociology, 24,* 395–421.

Kamin, L. J. (1974). *The science and politics of IQ.* Hillsdale, NJ: Erlbaum.

Kanaya, T., Scullin, M. H., & Ceci, S. J. (2003). The Flynn effect and U.S. policies: The impact of rising IQ scores on American society via mental retardation diagnoses. *American Psychologist, 58*(10), 778–790.

Kanazawa, S. (2006). Mind the gap . . . in intelligence: Reexamining the relationship between inequality and health. *British Journal of Health Psychology, 11,* 623–642.

Kandel, E. R. (2000). Nerve cells and behavior. In E. R. Kandel, J. H. Schwartz, & T. M. Jessell (Eds.), *Principles of neural science* (pp. 19–35). New York: McGraw-Hill.

Kandel, E. R. (2001). The molecular biology of memory storage: A dialogue between genes and synapses. *Science, 294,* 1030–1038.

Kandel, E. R., & Jessell, T. M. (1991). Touch. In E. R. Kandel, J. H. Schwartz, & T. M. Jessell (Eds.),

Principles of neural science (3rd ed.). New York: Elsevier Saunders.

Kandel, E. R., & Siegelbaum, S. A. (2000). Synaptic integration. In E. R. Kandel, J. H. Schwartz & T. M. Jessell (Eds.), *Principles of neural science* (pp. 207–228). New York: McGraw-Hill.

Kandell, J. J. (1998). Internet addiction on campus: The vulnerability of college students. *CyberPsychology and Behavior, 1*(1), 11–17.

Kane, J. (1991). *Be sick well: A healthy approach to chronic illness.* Oakland, CA: New Harbinger Publications.

Kane, J. M., & Marder, S. R. (2005). Schizophrenia: Somatic treatment. In B. J. Sadock & V. A. Sadock (Eds.), *Kaplan and Sadock's comprehensive textbook of psychiatry* (pp. 1467–1475). Philadelphia: Lippincott Williams & Wilkins.

Kane, M. (2006). Content-related validity evidence in test development. In S. M. Downing & T. M. Haladyna (Eds.), *Handbook of test development* (pp. 131–153). Mahwah, NJ: Erlbaum.

Kane, M. J., Brown, L. H., McVay, J. C., Silivia, P. J., Myin-Germeys, I., & Kwapil, T. R. (2007). For whom the mind wanders, and when: An experience-sampling study of working memory and executive control in daily life. *Psychological Science, 18*, 614–621.

Kane, M. J., & Engle, R. W. (2002). The role of prefrontal cortex in working-memory capacity, executive attention, and general fluid intelligence: An individual-differences perspective. *Psychonomic Bulletin & Review, 9*, 637–671.

Kant, A. K., Schatzkin, A., Graubard, B. I., & Shairer, C. (2000). A prospective study of diet quality and mortality in women. *Journal of the American Medical Association, 283*, 2109–2115.

Kaplan, A. G. (1985). Female or male therapists for women patients: New formulations. *Psychiatry, 48*, 111–121.

Kaplan, D. S., Liu, R. X., & Kaplan, H. B. (2005). School-related stress in early adolescence and academic performance three years later: The conditional influence of self-expectation. *Social Psychology of Education, 8*, 3–17.

Kaplan, H., & Dove, H. (1987). Infant development among the Ache of Eastern Paraguay. *Developmental Psychology, 23*, 190–198.

Kaplan, H. I. (1989). History of psychosomatic medicine. In H. I. Kaplan & B. J. Sadock (Eds.), *Comprehensive textbook of psychiatry* (5th ed.). Baltimore: Williams & Wilkins.

Kaplan, J. T., & Iacoboni, M. (2006). Getting a grip on other minds: Mirror neurons, intention understanding, and cognitive empathy. *Social Neuroscience, 1*, 175–183.

Kaplan, R. E., Drath, W. H., Kofodimos, J. R. (1991). *Beyond ambition: How driven managers can lead better and live better.* San Francisco: Jossey-Bass.

Kaplan, R. M., & Saccuzzo, D. P. (2005). *Psychological testing: Principles, applications, and issues.* Belmont, CA: Wadsworth.

Kapur, S., & Mann, J. J. (1993). Antidepressant action and the neurobiologic effects of ECT: Human studies. In C. E. Coffey (Ed.), *The clinical science of electroconvulsive therapy.* Washington, DC: American Psychiatric Press.

Karasu, T. B. (2005). Psychoanalysis and psychoanalytic psychotherapy. In B. J. Sadock & V. A. Sadock (Eds.), *Kaplan and Sadock's comprehensive textbook of psychiatry* (pp. 2472–2497). Philadelphia: Lippincott Williams & Wilkins.

Karau, S. J., & Williams, K. D. (1993). Social loafing: A meta-analytic review and theoretical integration. *Journal of Personality and Social Psychology, 65*, 681–706.

Karau, S. J., & Williams, K. D. (1995). Social loafing: Research findings, implications, and future directions. *Current Directions in Psychological Science, 4*, 134–140.

Kardiner, A., & Linton, R. (1945). *The individual and his society.* New York: Columbia University Press.

Karremans, J. C., Stroebe, W., & Claus, J. (2006). Beyond Vicary's fantasies: The impact of subliminal priming and brand choice. *Journal of Experimental Social Psychology, 42*, 792–798.

Kass, S. J., Cole, K. S., & Stanny, C. J. (2007). Effects of distraction and experience on situation awareness and simulated driving. *Transportation Research Part F: Traffic Psychology and Behaviour, 10*, 321–329.

Kassel, J. D., Stroud, L. R., & Paronis, C. A. (2003). Smoking, stress, and negative affect: Correlation, causation, and context across stages of smoking. *Psychological Bulletin, 129*, 270–304.

Kasser, T. (2002). *The high prices of materialism.* Cambridge, MA: MIT Press.

Kasser, T., Ryan, R. M., Couchman, C. E., & Sheldon, K. M. (2004). Materialistic values: Their causes and consequences. In T. Kasser & A. D. Kanner (Eds.), *Psychology and consumer culture: The struggle for a good life in a materialistic world.* Washington, DC: American Psychological Association.

Kasser, T., & Sharma, Y. S. (1999). Reproductive freedom, educational equality, and females' preference for resource-acquisition characteristics in mates. *Psychological Science, 10*, 374–377.

Kassin, S. M., Tubb, V. A., Hosch, H. M., & Memon, A. (2001). On the "general acceptance" of eyewitness testimony research: A new survey of the experts. *American Psychologist, 56*, 405–416.

Katigbak, M. S., Church, A. T., Guanzon-Lapena, M. A., Carlota, A. J. & del Pilar, G. H. (2002). Are indigenous personality dimensions culture specific? Philippine inventories and the five-factor model. *Journal of Personality and Social Psychology, 82*, 89–101.

Katz, A. N., Blasko, D. G., & Kazmerski, V. A. (2004). Saying what you don't mean: Social influences on sarcastic language processing. *Current Directions in Psychological Science, 13*(5), 186–189.

Katzell, R. A., & Austin, J. T. (1992). From then until now: The development of industrial and organizational psychology in the United States. *Journal of Applied Psychology, 77*, 803–835.

Kaufman, A. S. (2000). Tests of intelligence. In R. J. Sternberg (Ed.), *Handbook of intelligence* (pp. 445–476). New York: Cambridge University Press.

Kaufman, G., & Taniguchi, H. (2006). Gender and marital happiness in later life. *Journal of Family Issues, 27*, 735–757.

Kaufman, J. C. (2001). The Sylvia Plath effect: Mental illness in eminent creative writers. *Journal of Creative Behavior, 35*(1), 37–50.

Kaufman, J. C. (2005). The door that leads into madness: Eastern European poets and mental illness. *Creativity Research Journal, 17*(1), 99–103.

Kaufman, J. C., & Baer, J. (2002). Could Steven Spielberg manage the Yankees?: Creative thinking in different domains. *Korean Journal of Thinking & Problem Solving, 12*(2), 5–14.

Kaufman, J. C., & Baer, J. (2004). Hawking's haiku, Madonna's math: Why it is hard to be creative in every room of the house. In R. J. Sternberg, E. L. Grigorenko, & J. L. Singer (Eds.), *Creativity: From potential to realization.* Washington, DC: American Psychological Association.

Kaufman, L., & Rock, I. (1962). The moon illusion I. *Science, 136*, 953–961.

Kavesh, L., & Lavin, C. (1988). *Tales from the front.* New York: Doubleday.

Kay, J., & Kay, R. I. (2003). Individual psychoanalytic psychotherapy. In A. Tasman, J. Kay, & J. A. Lieberman (Eds.), *Psychiatry.* New York: Wiley.

Kaye, W. H., Bailer, U. F., Frank, G. K., Wagner, A., & Henry, S. E. (2005). Brain imaging of serotonin after recovery from anorexia and bulimia nervosa. *Physiology and Behavior, 86*, 15–17.

Kaye, W. H., Weltzin, T. E., Hsu, L. K. G., McConaha, C. W., & Bolton, B. (1993). Amount of calories retained after binge eating and vomiting. *American Journal of Psychiatry, 150*, 969–971.

Kayser, C. (2007). Listening with your eyes. *Scientific American Mind, 18*(2), 24–29.

Kazdin, A. (1994). Methodology, design, and evaluation in psychotherapy research. In A. E. Bergin & S. L. Garfield (Eds.), *Handbook of psychotherapy and behavior change* (4th ed.). New York: Wiley.

Kazdin, A. (2001). *Behavior modification in applied settings.* Belmont: Wadsworth.

Kazdin, A. (2007). Mediators and mechanisms of change in psychotherapy research. *Annual Review of Clinical Psychology, 3*, 1–27.

Kazdin, A., & Benjet, C. (2003). Spanking children: Evidence and issues. *Current Directions in Psychological Science, 12*(3), 99–103.

Keane, T. M., Marshall, A. D., & Taft, C. T. (2006). Posttraumatic stress disorder: Etiology, epidemiology, and treatment outcome. *Annual Review of Clinical Psychology, 2*, 161–197.

Keating, D. P. (2004). Cognitive and brain development. In R. M. Lerner & L. Steinberg (Eds.), *Handbook of adolescent psychology.* New York: Wiley.

Keating, D. P., & Stanley, I. C. (1972). Extreme measures for the exceptionally gifted in mathematics and science. *Educational Researcher, 1*, 3–7.

Keck, P. E. Jr., & McElroy, S. L. (2006). Lithium and mood stabilizers. In D. J. Stein, D. J. Kupfer, & A. F. Schatzberg (Eds.), *Textbook of mood disorders* (pp. 281–290). Washington, DC: American Psychiatric Publishing.

Keefauver, S. P., & Guilleminault, C. (1994). Sleep terrors and sleepwalking. In M. H. Kryger, T. Roth, & W. C. Dement (Eds.), *Principles and practice of sleep medicine* (2nd ed.). Philadelphia: Saunders.

Keefe, F. J., Smith, S. J., Buffington, A. L. H., Gibson, J., Studts, J. L., & Caldwell, D. S. (2002). Recent advances and future directions in the biopsychosocial assessment and treatment of arthritis. *Journal of Consulting & Clinical Psychology, 70*, 640–655.

Keefe, R. S. E., & Eesley, C. E. (2006). Neurocognitive impairments. In J. A. Lieberman, T. S. Stroup, & D. O. Perkins (Eds.), *Textbook of schizophrenia* (pp. 245–260). Washington, DC: American Psychiatric Publishing.

Keenan, J. P., Gallup, G. G. Jr., Goulet, N., & Kulkarni, M. (1997). Attributions of deception in human mating strategies. *Journal of Social Behavior and Personality, 12*, 45–52.

Keesey, R. E. (1993). Physiological regulation of body energy: Implications for obesity. In A. J. Stunkard & T. A. Wadden (Eds.), *Obesity theory and therapy.* New York: Raven.

Keesey, R. E. (1995). A set point model of body weight regulation. In K. D. Brownell & C. G. Fairburn (Eds.), *Eating disorders and obesity: A comprehensive handbook*. New York: Guilford.

Keesey, R. E., & Powley, T. L. (1975). Hypothalamic regulation of body weight. *American Scientist, 63,* 558–565.

Kehoe, E. J., & Macrae, M. (1998). Classical conditioning. In W. O'Donohue (Ed.), *Learning and behavior therapy*. Boston: Allyn & Bacon.

Keinan, G. (1987). Decision making under stress: Scanning of alternatives under controllable and uncontrollable threats. *Journal of Personality and Social Psychology, 52,* 639–644.

Keinan, G., Friedland, N., Kahneman, D., & Roth, D. (1999). The effect of stress on the suppression of erroneous competing responses. *Anxiety, Stress & Coping: An International Journal, 12,* 455–476.

Keller, H. E., & Lee, S. (2003). Ethical issues surrounding human participants research using the Internet. *Ethics & Behavior, 13*(3), 211–219.

Keller, P. A., & Block, L. G. (1999). The effect of affect-based dissonance versus cognition-based dissonance on motivated reasoning and health-related persuasion. *Journal of Experimental Psychology: Applied, 5,* 302–313.

Kelley, H. H. (1950). The warm-cold variable in first impressions of persons. *Journal of Personality, 18,* 431–439.

Kelley, H. H. (1967). Attributional theory in social psychology. *Nebraska Symposium on Motivation, 15,* 192–241.

Kellogg, S. H., & Young, J. E. (2008). Cognitive Therapy. In J. L. Lebow (Ed.), *Twenty-first century psychotherapies: Contemporary approaches to theory and practice*. New York: Wiley.

Kelly, B. D., Feeney, L., O'Callaghan, E., Browne, R., Byrne, M., Mulryan, N., Scully, A., Morris, M., Kinsella, A., Takei, N., McNeil, T., Walsh, D., & Larkin, C. (2004). Obstetric adversity and age at first presentation with schizophrenia: Evidence of a dose-response relationship. *American Journal of Psychiatry, 161,* 920–922.

Kelly, K. M., & Schramke, C. J. (2000). Epilepsy. In G. Fink (Ed.), *Encyclopedia of stress* (pp. 66–70). San Diego: Academic Press.

Kelly, S. J., Day, N., & Streissguth, A. P. (2000). Effects of prenatal alcohol exposure on social behavior in humans and other species. *Neurotoxicology & Teratology, 22,* 143–149.

Kelman, H. C. (1967). Human use of human subjects: The problem of deception in social psychological experiments. *Psychological Bulletin, 67,* 1–11.

Kelman, H. C. (1982). Ethical issues in different social science methods. In T. L. Beauchamp, R. R. Faden, R. J. Wallace, Jr., & L. Walters (Eds.), *Ethical issues in social science research*. Baltimore: Johns Hopkins University Press.

Kelsey, J. E. (2005). Selective serotonin reuptake inhibitors. In B. J. Sadock & V. A. Sadock (Eds.), *Kaplan and Sadock's comprehensive textbook of psychiatry* (pp. 2887–2913). Philadelphia: Lippincott Williams & Wilkins.

Kelsoe, J. (2005). Mood disorders: Genetics. In B. J. Sadock & V. A. Sadock (Eds.), *Kaplan & Sadock's comprehensive textbook of psychiatry* (pp. 1582–1593). Philadelphia: Lippincott Williams & Wilkins.

Kelsoe, J. R. (2004). Genomics and the human genome project: Implications for psychiatry. *International Review of Psychiatry, 16*(4), 294–300.

Keltner, D., Ekman, P., Gonzaga, G. C., & Beer, J. (2003). Facial expression of emotion. In R. J. Davidson, K. R. Scherer, & H. H. Goldsmith (Eds.), *Handbook of affective sciences*. New York: Oxford University Press.

Kemeny, M. E. (2007). Psychoneuroimmunology. In H. S. Friedman & R. C. Silver (Eds.), *Foundations of health psychology*. New York: Oxford University Press.

Kendall, P. C., Holmbeck, G., & Verduin, T. (2004). Methodology, design, and evaluation in psychotherapy research. In M. J. Lambert (Ed.), *Bergin and Garfield's handbook of psychotherapy and behavior change*. New York: Wiley.

Kendler, K. S. (2005a). "A gene for . . . ?": The nature of gene action in psychiatric disorders. *American Journal of Psychiatry, 162,* 1243–1252.

Kendler, K. S. (2005b). Psychiatric genetics: A methodologic critique. *American Journal of Psychiatry, 162,* 3–11.

Kendler, K. S., & Gardner, C. O., Jr. (1998). Boundaries of major depression: An evaluation of DSM-IV criteria. *American Journal of Psychiatry, 155,* 172–177.

Kendler, K. S., & Greenspan, R. J. (2006). The nature of genetic influences on behavior: Lessons from "simpler" organisms. *American Journal of Psychiatry, 163,* 1683–1694.

Kendler, K. S., Kuhn, J., & Prescott, C. A. (2004). The interrelationship of neuroticism, sex, and stressful life events in the prediction of episodes of major depression. *American Journal of Psychiatry, 161,* 631–636.

Kendler, K. S., Myers, J., & Prescott, C. A. (2005). Sex differences in the relationship between social support and risk for major depression: A longitudinal study of opposite-sex twin pairs. *American Journal of Psychiatry, 162,* 250–256.

Kendler, K. S., Thornton, L. M., Gilman, S. E., & Kessler, R. C. (2000). Sexual orientation in a U.S. national sample of twin and nontwin sibling pairs. *American Journal of Psychiatry, 157,* 1843–1846.

Kenfield, S. A., Stampfer, M. J., Rosner, B. A., & Colditz, G. A. (2008). Smoking and smoking cessation in relation to mortality in women. *Journal of the American Medical Association, 299,* 2037–2047.

Kennedy, T. E., Hawkins, R. D., & Kandel, E. R. (1992). Molecular interrelationships between short- and long-term memory. In L. R. Squire & N. Butters (Eds.), *Neuropsychology of Memory* (2nd ed.). New York: Wiley.

Kenrick, D. T., & Funder, D. C. (1991). The person-situation debate: Do personality traits really exist? In N. J. Derlega, B. A. Winstead, & W. H. Jones (Eds.), *Personality: Contemporary theory and research*. Chicago: Nelson-Hall.

Kenrick, D. T., & Gutierres, S. E. (1980). Contrast effects and judgments of physical attractiveness: When beauty becomes a social problem. *Journal of Personality and Social Psychology, 38,* 131–140.

Kenrick, D. T., Trost, M. R., & Sundie, J. M. (2004). Sex roles as adaptations: An evolutionary perspective on gender differences and similarities. In A. H. Eagly, A. E. Beall, & R. J. Sternberg (Eds.), *The psychology of gender*. New York: Guilford.

Keren, G. (1990). Cognitive aids and debiasing methods: Can cognitive pills cure cognitive ills? In J. P. Caverni, J. M. Fabre, & M. Gonzalez (Eds.), *Cognitive biases*. Amsterdam: North-Holland.

Kermer, D. A., Driver-Linn, E., Wilson, T. D., & Gilbert, D. T. (2006). Loss aversion is an affective forecasting error. *Psychological Science, 17,* 649–653.

Kerns, K. A., Abraham, M. M., Schlegelmilch, A., & Morgan, T. A. (2007). Mother-child attachment in later middle-childhood: Assessment approaches and associations with mood and emotion. *Attachment & Human Development, 9*(1), 33–53.

Kerr, N. L., & Tindale, R. S. (2004). Group performance and decision making. *Annual Review of Psychology, 55,* 623–55.

Kershaw, T. C., & Ohlsson, S. (2004). Multiple causes of difficulty in insight: The case of the nine-dot problem. *Journal of Experimental Psychology: Learning, Memory, and Cognition, 30,* 3–13.

Kesner, R. P. (1998). Neural mediation of memory for time: Role of the hippocampus and medial prefrontal cortex. *Pscyhonomic Bulletin & Review, 5,* 585–596.

Kessen, W. (1996). American psychology just before Piaget. *Psychological Science, 7,* 196–199.

Kessler, R. C., Berglund, P., Demler, O., Jin, R., Koretz, D., Merikangas, K. R., Rush, A. J., Walters, E. E., & Wang, P. S. (2003a). The epidemiology of major depressive disorder: Results from the national comorbidity survey replication (NCS-R). *Journal of the American Medical Association, 189,* 3095–3105.

Kessler, R. C., Berglund, P., Demler, O., Jin, R., & Walters, E. E. (2005a). Lifetime prevalence and age-of-onset distributions of DSM-IV disorders in the national comorbidity survey replication. *Archives of General Psychiatry, 62,* 593–602.

Kessler, R. C., Demier, O., Frank, R. G., Olfson, M., Pincus, H. A., Walters, E. E., Wang, P., Wells, K. B., & Zaslavsky, A. M. (2005b). Prevalence and treatment of mental disorders: 1990–2003. *New England Journal of Medicine, 352,* 2515–2523.

Kessler, R. C., Merikangas, K. R., Berglund, P., Eaton, W. W., Koretz, D. S., & Walters, E. E. (2003b). Mild disorders should not be eliminated from the DSM-V. *Archives of General Psychiatry 60,* 1117–1122.

Kessler, R. C., Olfson, M., & Berglund, P. A. (1998). Patterns and predictors of treatment contact after first onset of psychiatric disorders. *American Journal of Psychiatry, 155,* 62–69.

Kessler, R. C., & Zhao, S. (1999). The prevalence of mental illness. In A. V. Horvitz & T. L. Scheid (Eds.), *A handbook for the study of mental health: Social contexts, theories, and systems*. New York: Cambridge University Press.

Key, W. B. (1973). *Subliminal seduction*. Englewood Cliffs, NJ: Prentice-Hall.

Key, W. B. (1976). *Media sexploitation*. Englewood Cliffs, NJ: Prentice-Hall.

Key, W. B. (1980). *The clam-plate orgy and other subliminal techniques for manipulating your behavior*. Englewood Cliffs, NJ: Prentice-Hall.

Key, W. B. (1992). *Subliminal adventures in erotic art*. Boston: Branden Books.

Khashan, A. S., Abel, K. M., McNamee, R., Pedersen, M. G., Webb, R. T., Baker, P. N., et al. (2008). Higher risk of offspring schizophrenia following antenatal maternal exposure to severe adverse life events. *Archives of General Psychiatry, 65,* 146–152.

Kidder, D. L., & Parks, J. M. (2001). The good soldier: Who is s(he)? *Journal of Organizational Behavior, 22,* 939–959

Kiecolt-Glaser, J. K., Garner, W., Speicher, C., Penn, G. M., Holliday, J., & Glaser, R. (1984). Psychosocial modifiers of immunocompetence in medical students. *Psychosomatic Medicine, 46*(1), 7–14.

Kiecolt-Glaser, J. K., & Glaser, R. (1995). Measurement of immune response. In S. Cohen, R. C. Kessler, & L. U. Gordon (Eds.), *Measuring stress: A guide for health and social scientists*. New York: Oxford University Press.

Kieffer, K. M., Cronin, C., & Gawet, D. L. (2006). Test and study worry and emotionality in the prediction of college students' reason for drinking: An exploratory investigation. *Journal of Alcohol and Drug Addiction, 50,* 57–81.

Kieseppa, T., Partonen, T., Huakka, J., Kaprio, J., & Lonnqvist, J. (2004). High concordance of bipolar 1 disorder in a nationwide sample of twins. *American Journal of Psychiatry, 161,* 1814–1821.

Kiesler, C. A. (1992). U.S. mental health policy: Doomed to fail. *American Psychologist, 47,* 1077–1082.

Kiesler, C. A. (2000). The next wave of change for psychology and mental health services in the health care revolution. *American Psychologist, 55,* 481–487.

Kiesler, D. J. (1999). *Beyond the disease model of mental disorders.* New York: Praeger Publishers.

Kihlstrom, J. F. (2001). Dissociative disorders. In P. B. Sutker & H. E. Adams (Eds.), *Comprehensive handbook of psychopathology* (3rd ed., pp. 259–276). New York: Kluwer Academic/Plenum Publishers.

Kihlstrom, J. F. (2002). No need for repression. *Trends in Cognitive Sciences, 6*(12), 502.

Kihlstrom, J. F. (2004). An unbalanced balancing act: Blocked, recovered, and false memories in the laboratory and clinic. *Clinical Psychology: Science & Practice, 11*(1), 34–41.

Kihlstrom, J. F. (2005a). Dissociative disorders. *Annual Review of Clinical Psychology, 1,* 227–253.

Kihlstrom, J. F. (2005b). Is hypnosis an altered state of consciousness or what? *Contemporary Hypnosis, 22,* 34–38.

Kihlstrom, J. F. (2007). Consciousness in hypnosis. In P. D. Zelazo, M. Moscovitch, & E. Thompson (Eds.), *The Cambridge handbook of consciousness.* New York: Cambridge University Press.

Kihlstrom, J. F., Barnhardt, T. M., & Tataryn, D. J. (1992). Implicit perception. In R. F. Bornstein & T. S. Pittman (Eds.), *Perception without awareness: Cognitive, clinical, and social perspectives.* New York: Guilford.

Kihlstrom, J. F., & Cork, R. C. (2007). Consciousness and anesthesia. In M. Velmans & S. Schneider (Eds.), *The Blackwell companion to consciousness.* Malden, MA: Blackwell Publishing.

Kihlstrom, J. F., Glisky, M. L., & Angiulo, M. J. (1994). Dissociative tendencies and dissociative disorders. *Journal of Abnormal Psychology, 103,* 117–124.

Killeen, P. R. (1981). Learning as causal inference. In M. L. Commons & J. A. Nevin (Eds.), *Quantitative analyses of behavior: Vol. 1. Discriminative properties of reinforcement schedules.* Cambridge, MA: Ballinger.

Kim, E.-J., & Dimsdale, J. E. (2007). The effect of psychological stress on sleep: A review of polysomnographic evidence. *Behavioral Sleep Medicine, 5,* 256–278.

Kim, H., & Markus, H. R. (1999). Deviance or uniqueness, harmony or conformity? A cultural analysis. *Journal of Personality and Social Psychology, 77,* 785–800.

Kim, K. H. (2005). Can only intelligent people be creative? *Journal of Secondary Gifted Education, 16,* 57–66.

Kimmel, A. J. (1996). *Ethical issues in behavioral research: A survey.* Cambridge, MA: Blackwell.

Kimmel, M. S., & Linders, A. (1996). Does censorship make a difference? An aggregate empirical analysis of pornography and rape. *Journal of Psychology and Human Sexuality, 8,* 1–20.

Kimura, D. (1973). The asymmetry of the human brain. *Scientific American, 228,* 70–78.

Kimura, D., & Hampson, E. (1993). Neural and hormonal mechanisms mediating sex differences in cognition. In P. A. Vernon (Ed.), *Biological approaches to the study of human intelligence.* Norwood, NJ: Ablex.

King, A. C., Oman, R. F., Brassington, G. S., Bliwise, D. L., & Haskell, W. L. (1997). Moderate-intensity exercise and self-rated quality of sleep in older adults: A randomized controlled trial. *Journal of the American Medical Association, 277,* 32–37.

King, B. H., Hodapp, R. M., & Dykens, E. M. (2005). Mental retardation. In B. J. Sadock & V. A. Sadock (Eds.), *Kaplan & Sadock's comprehensive textbook of psychiatry* (pp. 3076–3106). Philadelphia: Lippincott Williams & Wilkins.

King, B. M. (2006). The rise, fall, and resurrection of the ventromedial hypothalamus in the regulation of feeding behavior and body weight. *Physiology & Behavior, 87,* 221–244.

King, G. R., & Ellinwood Jr., E. H. (2005). Amphetamines and other stimulants. In J. H. Lowinson, P. Ruiz, R. B. Millman, & J. G. Langrod (Eds.), *Substance abuse: A comprehensive textbook.* Philadelphia: Lippincott/Williams & Wilkins.

Kinnunen, T., Haukkala, A., Korhonen, T., Quiles, Z. N., Spiro, A. I., & Garvey, A. J. (2006). Depression and smoking across 25 years of the normative aging study. *International Journal of Psychiatry in Medicine, 36,* 413–426.

Kinsbourne, M. (1980). If sex differences in brain lateralization exist, they have yet to be discovered. *Behavioral and Brain Sciences, 3,* 241–242.

Kinsbourne, M. (1997). What qualifies a representation for a role in consciousness? In J. D. Cohen & J. W. Schooler (Eds.), *Scientific approaches to consciousness.* Mahwah, NJ: Erlbaum.

Kinsey, A. C., Pomeroy, W. B., & Martin, C. E. (1948). *Sexual behavior in the human male.* Philadelphia: Saunders.

Kinsey, A. C., Pomeroy, W. B., Martin, C. E., & Gebhard, P. H. (1953). *Sexual behavior in the human female.* Philadelphia: Saunders.

Kirby, S. (2007). The evolution of language. In R. I. M. Dunbar & L. Barrett (Eds.), *Oxford handbook of evolutionary psychology.* New York: Oxford University Press.

Kirkpatrick, B., & Tek, C. (2005). Schizophrenia: Clinical features and psychopathology concepts. In B. J. Sadock & S. V. (Eds.), *Kaplan & Sadock's comprehensive textbook of psychiatry* (pp. 1416–1435). Philadelphia: Lippincott Williams & Wilkins.

Kirkpatrick, L. A. (2005). *Attachment, evolution, and the psychology of religion.* New York: Guilford.

Kirkpatrick, S. A., & Locke, E. A. (1991). Leadership: Do traits matter? *Academy of Management Executive, 5,* 48–60.

Kirmayer, L. J., & Looper, K. J. (2007). Somatoform disorders. In M. Hersen, S. M. Turner, & D. C. Beidel (Eds.), *Adult psychopathology and diagnosis.* New York: Wiley.

Kirsch, I. (1997). Response expectancy theory and application: A decennial review. *Applied and Preventive Psychology, 6,* 69–79.

Kirsch, I. (2000). The response set theory of hypnosis. *American Journal of Clinical Hypnosis, 42,* 274–292.

Kirsch, I. (2004). Altered states in hypnosis: The debate goes on. *American Journal of Clinical Hypnosis, 13*(1). pages?

Kirsch, I., & Lynn, S. J. (1998a). Dissociation theories of hypnosis. *Psychological Bulletin, 123,* 100–115.

Kirsch, I., & Lynn, S. J. (1998b). Social-cognitive alternatives to dissociation theories of hypnotic involuntariness. *Review of General Psychology, 2,* 66–80.

Kirsch, I., Mazzoni, G., & Montgomery, G. H. (2007). Remembrance of hypnosis past. *American Journal of Clinical Hypnosis, 49,* 171–178.

Kirschenbaum, H., & Jourdan, A. (2005). The current status of Carl Rogers and the person-centered approach. *Psychotherapy: Theory, Research, Practice, Training, 42,* 37–51.

Kitayama, S., Duffy, S., Kawamura, T., & Larsen, J. T. (2003). Perceiving an object and its context in different cultures: A cultural look at new look. *Psychological Science, 14*(3), 201–206.

Kitayama, S., Mesquita, B., & Karasawa, M. (2006). Cultural affordances and emotional experience: Socially engaging and disengaging emotions in Japan and the United States. *Journal of Personality and Social Psychology, 91,* 890–903.

Kitchens, A. (1991). Left brain/right brain theory: Implications for developmental math instruction. *Review of Research in Developmental Education, 8,* 20–23.

Kittler, P. G., & Sucher, K. P. (2008). *Food and culture.* Belmont, CA: Wadsworth.

Kivimäki, M., Vahtera, J., Elovainio, M., Helenius, H., Singh-Manoux, A., & Pentti, J. (2005). Optimism and pessimism as predictors of change in health after death or onset of severe illness in family. *Health Psychology, 24,* 413–421.

Klapper, D., Ebling, C., & Temme, J. (2005). Another look at loss aversion in brand choice data: Can we characterize the loss-averse consumer? *International Journal of Research in Marketing, 22,* 239–254.

Klehe, U.-C., & Anderson, N. (2007). The moderating influence of personality and culture on social loafing in typical versus maximum performance situations. *International Journal of Selection and Assessment, 15,* 250–262.

Klein, M. (1948). *Contributions to psychoanalysis.* London: Hogarth.

Klein, P. D. (1997). Multiplying the problems of intelligence by eight: A critique of Gardner's theory. *Canadian Journal of Education, 22,* 377–394.

Klein, T. W., Friedman, H., & Specter, S. (1998). Marijuana, immunity and infection. *Journal of Neuroimmunology, 83,* 102–115.

Kleinke, C. L. (2007). What does it mean to cope? In A. Monat, R. S. Lazarus, & G. Reevy (Eds.), *The Praeger handbook on stress and coping.* Westport, CT: Praeger.

Kleinke, C. L., Peterson, T. R., & Rutledge, T. R. (1998). Effects of self-generated facial expressions on mood. *Journal of Personality and Social Psychology, 74,* 272–279.

Kleinmuntz, B. (1980). *Essentials of abnormal psychology.* San Francisco: Harper & Row.

Klerman, E. B., Davis, J. B., Duffy, J. F., Dijk, D., & Kronauer, R. E. (2004). Older people awaken more frequently but fall back asleep at the same rate as younger people. *Sleep: Journal of Sleep & Sleep Disorders Research, 27,* 793–798.

Klerman, G. L., & **Weissman**, M. M. E. (1993). *New applications of interpersonal therapy*. Washington, DC: American Psychiatric Press.

Kliegel, M., **Zimprich**, D., & **Rott**, C. (2004). Life-long intellectual activities mediate the predictive effect of early education on cognitive impairment in centenarians: A retrospective study. *Aging & Mental Health, 8*, 430–437.

Klimoski, R. J., & **Zukin**, L. B. (2003). Psychological assessment in industrial/organizational settings. In J. R. Graham & J. A. Naglieri (Eds.), *Handbook of psychology, Vol. 10: Assessment psychology*. New York: Wiley.

Kline, P. (1991). *Intelligence: The psychometric view*. New York: Routledge, Chapman, & Hall.

Kline, P. (1995). A critical review of the measurement of personality and intelligence. In D. H. Saklofske & M. Zeidner (Eds.), *International handbook of personality and intelligence*. New York: Plenum.

Klosch, G., & **Kraft**, U. Sweet dreams are made of this. *Scientific American Mind, 16*(2), 38–45.

Kluckhohn, C., & **Murray**, H. A. (1948). *Personality in nature, society and culture*. New York: Knopf.

Kluft, R. P. (1996). Dissociative identity disorder. In L. K. Michelson & W. J. Ray (Eds.), *Handbook of dissociation: Theoretical, empirical, and clinical perspectives*. New York: Plenum.

Kluft, R. P. (1999). True lies, false truths, and naturalistic raw data: Applying clinical research findings to the false memory debate. In L. M. Williams & V. L. Banyard (Eds.), *Trauma & memory*. Thousand Oaks, CA: Sage.

Klump, K. L., & **Culbert**, K. M. (2007). Molecular genetic studies of eating disorders: Current status and future directions. *Current Directions in Psychological Science, 16*, 37–41.

Knauss, W. (2005). Group psychotherapy. In G. O. Gabbard, J. S. Beck, & J. Holmes (Eds.), *Oxford textbook of psychotherapy*. New York: Oxford University Press.

Knecht, S., **Drager**, B., **Floel**, A., **Lohmann**, H., **Breitenstein**, C., **Henningsen**, H., & **Ringelstein**, E. B. (2001). Behavioural relevance of atypical language lateralization in healthy subjects. *Brain, 124*, 1657–1665.

Knecht, S., **Fioel**, A., **Drager**, B., **Breitenstein**, C., **Sommer**, J., **Henningsen**, H., **Ringelstein**, E. B., & **Pascual-Leone**, A. (2002). Degree of language lateralization determines susceptibility to unilateral brain lesions. *Nature Neuroscience, 5*, 695–699.

Knight, J. (2004). The truth about lying. *Nature, 428*, 692–694.

Kochanska, G. (2001). Emotional development in children with different attachment histories: The first three years. *Child Development, 72*, 474–490.

Koehler, J. J. (1996). The base rate fallacy reconsidered: Descriptive, normative, and methodological challenges. *Behavioral Brain Sciences, 19*, 1–53.

Kohatsu, N. D., **Tsai**, R., **Young**, T., **VanGilder**, R., **Burmeister**, L. F., **Stromquist**, A. M., et al. (2006). Sleep duration and body mass index in a rural population. *Archives of Internal Medicine, 166*, 1701–1705.

Kohlberg, L. (1963). The development of children's orientations toward a moral order: I. Sequence in the development of moral thought. *Vita Humana, 6*, 11–33.

Kohlberg, L. (1969). Stage and sequence: The cognitive-developmental approach to socialization. In D. A. Goslin (Ed.), *Handbook of socialization theory and research*. Chicago: Rand McNally.

Kohlberg, L. (1976). Moral stages and moralization: Cognitive-developmental approach. In T. Lickona (Ed.), *Moral development and behavior: Theory, research and social issues*. New York: Holt, Rinehart & Winston.

Kohlberg, L. (1984). *Essays on moral development: Vol. 2. The psychology of moral development*. San Francisco: Harper & Row.

Kohn, P. M., **Lafreniere**, K., & **Gurevich**, M. (1991). Hassles, health, and personality. *Journal of Personality and Social Psychology, 61*, 478–482.

Kohut, H. (1971). *Analysis of the self*. New York: International Universities Press.

Kokkinos, P., **Myers**, J., **Kokkinos**, J. P., **Pittaras**, A., **Narayan**, P., **Manolis**, A., et al. (2007). Exercise capacity and mortality in black and white men. *Circulation , 117*, 614–622.

Kolb, B., **Gibb**, R., & **Robinson**, T. E. (2003). Brain plasticity and behavior. *Current Directions in Psychological Science, 12*, 1–5.

Koob, G. F., & **Le Moal**, M. (2006). *Neurobiology of addiction*. San Diego: Academic Press.

Koocher, G. P., & **Rey-Casserly**, C. M. (2003). Ethical issues in psychological assessment. In J. R. Graham & J. A. Naglieri (Eds.), *Handbook of psychology, Vol. 10: Assessment psychology*. New York: Wiley.

Kop, W. J., **Gottdiener**, J. S., & **Krantz**, D. S. (2001). Stress and silent ischemia. In A. Baum, T. A. Revenson, & J. E. Singer (Eds.), *Handbook of health psychology* (pp. 669–682). Mahwah, NJ: Erlbaum.

Kop, W. J., & **Weinstein**, A. A. (2007). C-reactive protein. In G. Fink (Ed.), *Encyclopedia of stress*. San Diego: Elsevier.

Kop, W. J., **Weissman**, N. J., **Zhu**, J., **Bonsall**, R. W., **Doyle**, M., **Stretch**, M. R., **Glaes**, S. B., **Krantz**, D. S., **Gottdiener**, J. S., & **Tracy**, R. P. (2008). Effect of acute mental stress and exercise on inflammatory markers in patients with coronary artery disease and healthy controls. *American Journal of Cardiology, 101*, 767–773.

Kopta, S. M., **Lueger**, R. J., **Saunders**, S. M., & **Howard**, K. I. (1999). Individual psychotherapy outcome and process research: Challenges leading to greater turmoil or a positive transition? *Annual Review of Psychology, 50*, 441–69.

Koren, D., **Arnon**, I., & **Klein**, E. (1999). Acute stress response and posttraumatic stress disorder in traffic accident victims: A one-year prospective, follow-up study. *American Journal of Psychiatry, 156*, 367–373.

Koriat, A., & **Bjork**, R. A. (2005). Illusions of competence in monitoring one's knowledge during study. *Journal of Experimental Psychology: Learning, Memory, and Cognition, 31*(2), 187–194.

Koriat, A., **Goldsmith**, M., & **Pansky**, A. (2000). Toward a psychology of memory accuracy. *Annual Review of Psychology, 51*, 481–537.

Koriat, A., **Lichtenstein**, S., & **Fischhoff**, B. (1980). Reasons for confidence. *Journal of Experimental Psychology, 6*, 107–118.

Korn, J. H. (1997). *Illusions of reality: A history of deception in social psychology*. Albany: State University of New York Press.

Kornhaber, M. L. (2004). Multiple intelligences: From the ivory tower to the dusty classroom—But why? *Teachers College Record, 106*(1), 57–76.

Kornstein, S. G., & **Sloan**, D. M. E. (2006). Depression and gender. In D. J. Stein, D. J. Kupfer, & A. F. Schatzberg (Eds.), *Textbook of mood disorders*. Washington, DC: American Psychiatric Publishing.

Koropeckyj-Cox, T., & **Pendell**, G. (2007). The gender gap in attitudes about childlessness in the United States. *Journal of Marriage and Family, 69*, 899–915.

Koss, M. P. (1993). Rape: Scope, impact, interventions, and public policy responses. *American Psychologist, 48*, 1062–1069.

Koss, M. P., **Gidycz**, C. A., & **Wisniewski**, N. (1988). The scope of rape: Incidence and prevalence of sexual aggression and victimization in a national sample of higher education students. *Journal of Consulting and Clinical Psychology, 55*, 162–170.

Kostreva, M., **McNelis**, E., & **Clemens**, E. (2002). Using a circadian rhythms model to evaluate shift schedules. *Ergonomics, 45*, 739–763.

Kotaro, S. (2007). The moon illusion: Kaufman and Rock's (1962) apparent-distance theory reconsidered. *Japanese Psychological Research, 49*(1), 57–67.

Kotovsky, K., **Hayes**, J. R., & **Simon**, H. A. (1985). Why are some problems hard? Evidence from Tower of Hanoi. *Cognitive Psychology, 17*, 248–294.

Kotulak, R. (1996). *Inside the brain: Revolutionary discoveries of how the mind works*. Kansas City, MO: Andrews McMeel.

Koughan, M. (1975, February 23). Arthur Friedman's outrage: Employees decide their pay. *Washington Post*.

Koukounas, E., & **McCabe**, M. (1997). Sexual and emotional variables influencing sexual response to erotica. *Behaviour Research and Therapy, 35*, 221–230.

Kouzma, N. M., & **Kennedy**, G. A. (2004). Self-reported sources of stress in senior high school students. *Psychological Reports, 94*, 314–316.

Kozlowski, S. W., & **Bell**, B. S. (2003). Work groups and teams in organizations. In W. C. Borman, D. R. Ilgen, & R. J. Klimoski (Eds.), *Handbook of psychology, vol. 12: Industrial and organizational psychology* (pp. 333–375). New York: Wiley.

Kozorovitskiy, Y., & **Gould**, E. (2007). Adult neurogenesis and regeneration in the brain. In Y. Sern (Ed.), *Cognitive reserve: Theory and applications*. Philadelphia: Taylor and Francis.

Kozulin, A. (2005). The concept of activity in Soviet psychology: Vygotsky, his disciples and critics. In H. Daniels (Ed.), *An introduction to Vygotsky*. New York: Routledge.

Kracke, W. (1991). Myths in dreams, thought in images: An Amazonian contribution to the psycho-analytic theory of primary process. In B. Tedlock (Ed.), *Dreaming: Anthropological and psychological interpretations*. Santa Fe, NM: School of American Research Press.

Krakauer, J. (1998). *Into thin air: A personal account of the Mount Everest disaster*. New York: Villard.

Kramer, M. (1994). The scientific study of dreaming. In M. H. Kryger, T. Roth, & W. C. Dement (Eds.), *Principles and practice of sleep medicine* (2nd ed.). Philadelphia: Saunders.

Kramer, P. D. (2006). *Freud: Inventor of the modern mind*. New York: HarperCollins.

Krantz, D. S., **Sheps**, D. S., **Carney**, R. M., & **Natelson**, B. H. (2000). Effects of mental stress in patients with coronary artery disease. *Journal of the American Medical Association, 283*, 1800–1802.

Kraus, S. J. (1995). Attitudes and the prediction of behavior: A meta-analysis of the empirical literature. *Personality and Social Psychology Bulletin, 21*, 58–75.

Krebs, D. L., & **Denton**, K. (1997). Social illusions and self-deception: The evolution of biases in person perception. In J. A. Simpson & D. T. Kenrick (Eds.), *Evolutionary social psychology*. Mahwah, NJ: Erlbaum.

Kribbs, N. B. (1993). Siesta. In M. A. Carskadon (Ed.), *Encyclopedia of sleep and dreaming.* New York: Macmillan.

Kring, A. M. (1999). Emotion in schizophrenia: Old mystery, new understanding. *Current Directions in Psychological Science, 8,* 160–163.

Krishnan, K. R. R., & Hamilton, M. A. (1997). Obesity. *Primary Psychiatry, 5,* 49–53.

Kristeller, J. L., Baer, R. A., & Quillian-Wolever, R. (2006). Mindfulness-based approaches to eating disorders. In R. A. Baer (Ed.), *Mindfulness-based treatment approaches: Clinician's guide to evidence base and applications* (pp. 75–91). San Diego: Elsevier.

Kroger, J. (2003). Identity development during adolescence. In G. R. Adams & M. D. Berzonsky (Eds.), *Blackwell handbook of adolescence.* Malden, MA: Blackwell Publishing.

Krojgaard, P. (2005). Continuity and discontinuity in developmental psychology. *Psyke & Logos, 26*(2), 377–394.

Krosnick, J. A. (1999). Survey research. *Annual Review Psychology, 50,* 537–567.

Krosnick, J. A., & Fabrigar, L. R. (1998). *Designing good questionnaires: Insights from psychology.* New York: Oxford University Press.

Krueger, J. (1996). Personal beliefs and cultural stereotypes about racial characteristics. *Journal of Personality and Social Psychology, 71,* 536–548.

Krueger, J., Ham, J. J., & Linford, K. M. (1996). Perceptions of behavioral consistency: Are people aware of the actor-observer effect? *Psychological Science, 7,* 259–264.

Krueger, R. F. (2005). Continuity of axes I and II: Toward a unified model of personality, personality disorders, and clinical disorders. *Journal of Personality Disorders, 19,* 233–261.

Krueger, R. F., & Kling, C. (2000). Validity. In A. E. Kazdin (Ed.), *Encyclopedia of psychology* (pp. 149–153). Washington, DC: American Psychological Association.

Krueger, W. C. F. (1929). The effect of overlearning on retention. *Journal of Experimental Psychology, 12,* 71–78.

Kruglanski, A. W., & Stroebe, W. (2005). The influence of beliefs and goals on attitudes: Issues of structure, function, and dynamics. In D. Albarracin, B. T. Johnson, & M. P. Zanna (Eds.), *The handbook of attitudes.* Mahwah, NJ: Erlbaum.

Krull, D. S. (2001). On partitioning the fundamental attribution error: Dispositionalism and the correspondence bias. In G. B. Moskowitz (Ed.), *Cognitive social psychology: The Princeton Symposium on the legacy and future of social cognition.* Mahwah, NJ: Erlbaum.

Krull, D. S., & Erickson, D. J. (1995). Inferential hopscotch: How people draw social inferences from behavior. *Current Directions in Psychological Science, 4,* 35–38.

Kryger, M. H. (1993). Snoring. In M. A. Carskadon (Ed.), *Encyclopedia of sleep and dreaming.* New York: Macmillan.

Kryger, M. H., Roth, T., & Dement, W. C. (2005). *Principles and practice of sleep medicine.* Philadelphia: Elsevier Saunders.

Kubovy, M., Epstein, W., & Gepshtein, S. (2003). Foundations of visual perception. In A. F. Healy & R. W. Proctor (Eds.), *Handbook of psychology.* New York: Wiley.

Kuehn, B. M. (2007). Scientists probe deep brain stimulation: Some promise for brain injury, psychiatric illness. *Journal of the American Medical Association, 298,* 2249–2207.

Kuhl, B. A., Dudukovic, N. M., Kahn, I., & Wagner, A. D. (2007). Decreased demands on cognitive control reveal the neural processing benefits of forgetting. *Nature Neuroscience, 10,* 908–914.

Kuhn, D. (2006). Do cognitive changes accompany developments in the adolescent brain? *Perspectives on Psychological Science, 1*(1), 59–67.

Kulick, A. R., Pope, H. G., & Keck, P. E. (1990). Lycanthropy and self-identification. *Journal of Nervous & Mental Disease, 178*(2), 134–137.

Kumar, V. M. (2004). Body temperature and sleep: Are they controlled by the same mechanism? *Sleep & Biological Rhythms, 2*(2), 103–125.

Kung, S., & Mrazek, D. A. (2005). Psychiatric emergency department visits on full-moon nights. *Psychiatric Services, 56,* 221–222.

Kuo, Y. T., Parkinson, J. R. C., Chaudhri, O. B., Herlihy, A. H., So, P. W., Dhillo, W. S., et al. (2007). The temporal sequence of gut peptide-CNS interactions tracked in vivo by magnetic resonance imaging. *Journal of Neuroscience, 27,* 12341–12348.

Kupfermann, I., Kandel, E. R., & Iversen, S. (2000). Motivational and addictive states. In E. R. Kandel, J. H. Schwartz, & T. M. Jessell (Eds.), *Principles of neural science.* New York: McGraw-Hill.

Kurtz, K. J., & Loewenstein, J. (2007). Converging on a new role for analogy in problem solving and retrieval: When two problems are better than one. *Memory & Cognition, 35,* 334–342.

Kutchins, H., & Kirk, S. A. (1997). *Making us crazy: DSM—The psychiatric Bible and the creation of mental disorders.* New York: Free Press.

Kutchinsky, B. (1991). Pornography and rape: Theory and practice? Evidence from crime data in four countries where pornography is easily available. *International Journal of Law and Psychiatry, 14,* 47–64.

Kuther, T., & Morgan, R.D. (2007). *Careers in psychology: Opportunities in a changing world.* Belmont, CA: Wadsworth.

LaBar, K. S., & LeDoux, J. E. (2003). Emotional learning circuits in animals and humans. In R. J. Davidson, K. R. Scherer, & H. H. Goldsmith (Eds.), *Handbook of affective sciences.* New York: Oxford University Press.

LaBerge, S. (1990). Lucid dreaming: Psychophysiological studies of consciousness during REM sleep. In R. R. Bootzin, J. F. Kihlstrom, & D. L. Schacter (Eds.), *Sleep and cognition.* Washington, DC: American Psychological Association.

LaBerge, S. (2007). Lucid dreaming. In D. Barrett & P. McNamara (Eds.), *The new science of dreaming: Content, recall, and personality correlates.* Westport, CT: Praeger.

LaBine, S. J., & LaBine, G. (1996). Determinations of negligence and the hindsight bias. *Law & Human Behavior, 20,* 501–516.

Labouvie-Vief, G. (2006). Emerging structures of adult thought. In J. J. Arnett & J. L. Tanner (Eds.), *Emerging adults in America: Coming of age in the 21st century.* Washington, DC: American Psychological Association.

Lachman, S. J. (1996). Processes in perception: Psychological transformations of highly structured stimulus material. *Perceptual and Motor Skills, 83,* 411–418.

Lachter, J., Forster, K. I., & Ruthruff, E. (2004). Forty-five years after Broadbent (1958): Still no identification without attention. *Psychological Review, 111,* 880–913.

La Cerra, P., & Kurzban, R. (1995). The structure of scientific revolutions and the nature of the adapted mind. *Psychological Inquiry, 6,* 62–65.

Lader, M. H. (2002). Managing dependence and withdrawal with newer hypnotic medications in the treatment of insomnia. *Journal of Clinical Psychiatry, 4*(suppl 1), 33–37.

Laditka, S. B., Laditka, J. N., & Probst, J. C. (2006). Racial and ethnic disparities in potentially avoidable delivery complications among pregnant Medicaid beneficiaries in South Carolina. *Maternal & Child Health Journal, 10,* 339–350.

Laitinen, J., Ek, E., & Sovio, U. (2002). Stress-related eating and drinking behavior and body mass index and predictors of this behavior. *Preventive Medicine: An International Journal Devoted to Practice & Theory, 34,* 29–39.

Lakein, A. (1996). *How to get control of your time and your life.* New York: New American Library.

Lam, L. T., & Kirby, S. L. (2002). Is emotional intelligence an advantage? An exploration of the impact of emotional and general intelligence on individual performance. *Journal of Social Psychology, 142,* 133–143.

Lamb, H. R. (1998). Deinstitutionalization at the beginning of the new millennium. *Harvard Review of Psychiatry, 6,* 1–10.

Lamb, M. E., Hwang, C. P., Ketterlinus, R. D., & Fracasso, M. P. (1999). Parent-child relationships: Development in the context of the family. In M. H. Bornstein & M. E. Lamb (Eds.), *Developmental psychology and advanced textbook.* Mahwah, NJ: Erlbaum.

Lamb, M. E., Ketterlinus, R. D., & Fracasso, M. P. (1992). Parent-child relationships. In M. H. Bornstein & M. E. Lamb (Eds.), *Developmental psychology: An advanced textbook* (3rd ed.). Hillsdale, NJ: Erlbaum.

Lambert, M. J., & Archer, A. (2006). Research findings on the effects of psychotherapy and their implications for practice. In C. D. Goodheart, A. E. Kazdin, & R. J. Sternberg (Eds.), *Evidence-based psychotherapy: Where practice and research meet* (pp. 111–130). Washington, DC: American Psychological Association.

Lambert, M. J., & Bergin, A. E. (1992). Achievements and limitations of psychotherapy research. In D. K. Freedheim (Ed.), *History of psychotherapy: A century of change.* Washington, DC: American Psychological Association.

Lambert, M. J., Bergin, A. E., & Garfield, S. L. (2004). Introduction and historical overview. In M. J. Lambert (Ed.), *Bergin and Garfield's handbook of psychotherapy and behavior change.* New York: Wiley.

Lambert, M. J., & Ogles, B. M. (2004). The efficacy and effectiveness of psychotherapy. In M. J. Lambert (Ed.), *Bergin and Garfield's handbook of psychotherapy and behavior change.* New York: Wiley.

Lampe, A., Soellner, W., Krismer, M., Rumpold, G., Kantner-Rumplmair, W., Ogon, M., & Rathner, G. (1998). The impact of stressful life events on exacerbation of chronic low-back pain. *Journal of Psychosomatic Research, 44,* 555–563.

Lampinen, J. M., Neuschatz, J. S., & Payne, D. G. (1999). Source attributions and false memories: A test of the demand characteristics account. *Psychonomic Bulletin & Review, 6,* 130–135.

Lampl, M., Veldhuis, J. D., & Johnson, M. L. (1992). Saltation and stasis: A model of human growth. *Science, 258,* 801–803.

Landabaso, M. A., Iraurgi, I., Sanz, J., Calle, R., Ruiz de Apodaka, J., Jimenez-Lerma, J. M., & Gutierrez-Fraile, M. (1999). Naltrexone in the treatment of alcoholism. Two-year follow up results. *European Journal of Psychiatry, 13*, 97–105.

Landau, M. J., Goldenberg, J. L., Greenberg, J., Gillath, O., Solomon, S., Cox, C., et al. (2006). The siren's call: Terror management and the threat of men's sexual attraction to women. *Personality and Social Psychology, 90*, 129–146.

Landel-Graham, J., Yount, S. E., & Rudnicki, S. R. (2003). Diabetes mellitus. In A. M. Nezu, C. M. Nezu, & P. A. Geller (Eds.). *Handbook of psychology, Vol. 9: Health psychology*. New York: Wiley.

Landrum, R. E., & Harrold, R. (2003). What employers want from psychology graduates. *Teaching of Psychology, 30*(2), 131–133.

Landsberger, H. A. (1958). *Hawthorne revisited: Management and the worker, its critics and developments in human relations in industry*. Ithaca: New York State School of Industrial and Labor Relations.

Landy, F. J. (1988). The early years of I/O: "Dr. Mayo." *The Industrial and Organizational Psychologist, 25*, 53–55.

Landy, F. J., Quick, J. C., & Kasl, S. (1994). Work, stress, and well-being. *International Journal of Stress and Management, 1*, 33–73.

Laney, C., & Loftus, E. F. (2005). Traumatic memories are not necessarily accurate memories. *The Canadian Journal of Psychiatry, 50*, 823–828.

Lang, P. J. (1995). The emotion probe: Studies of motivation and attention. *American Psychologist, 50*, 372–385.

Langdon, P. E., Yagueez, L., Brown, J., & Hope, A. (2001). Who walks through the "revolving door" of a British psychiatric hospital? *Journal of Mental Health (UK), 10*, 525–533.

Lange, C. (1885). One leuds beveegelser. In K. Dunlap (Ed.), *The emotions*. Baltimore: Williams & Wilkins.

Langevin, R., & Curnoe, S. (2004). The use of pornography during the commission of sexual offenses. *International Journal of Offender Therapy & Comparative Criminology, 48*, 572–586.

Langlois, J. H., Kalakanis, L., Rubenstein, A. J., Larson, A., Hallam, M., & Smoot, M. (2000). Maxims or myths of beauty? A meta-analytic and theoretical review. *Psychological Bulletin, 126*, 390–423.

Lanyon, R. I., & Goodstein, L. D. (1997). *Personality assessment*. New York: Wiley.

LaPiere, R. T. (1934). Attitude and actions. *Social Forces, 13*, 230–237.

Lapierre, Y. D. (2003). Suicidality with selective serotonin reuptake inhibitors: Valid claim? *Journal of Psychiatry & Neuroscience, 28*, 340–347.

Lapsley, D. K. (2006). Moral stage theory. In M. Killen & J. G. Smetana (Eds.), *Handbook of moral development*. Mahwah, NJ: Erlbaum.

Lareau, A. (2003). *Unequal childhoods: Class, race, and family life*. Berkeley: University of California Press.

Larsen, J. T., McGraw, A. P., Mellers, B. A., & Cacioppo, J. T. (2004). The agony of victory and thrill of defeat: Mixed emotional reactions to disappointing wins and relieving losses. *Psychological Science, 15*, 325–330.

Larsen, R. J., & Prizmic, Z. (2008). Regulation of emotional well-being: Overcoming the hedonic treadmill. In M. Eid & R. J. Larsen (Eds.), *The science of subjective well-being* (pp. 258–289). New York: Guilford.

Larson, R., & Wilson, S. (2004). Adolescence across place and time: Globalization and the changing pathways to adulthood. In R. M. Lerner & L. Steinberg (Eds.), *Handbook of adolescent psychology*. New York: Wiley.

Larzelere, R. E., Schneider, W. N., Larson, D. B., & Pike, P. L. (1996). The effects of discipline responses in delaying toddler misbehavior recurrences. *Child and Family Behavior Therapy, 18*, 35–37.

Latané, B. (1981). The psychology of social impact. *American Psychologist, 36*, 343–356.

Latané, B., & Nida, S. A. (1981). Ten years of research on group size and helping. *Psychological Bulletin, 89*, 308–324.

Latané, B., Williams, K., & Harkins, S. (1979). Many hands make light the work: The causes and consequences of social loafing. *Journal of Personality and Social Psychology, 37*, 822–832.

La Torre, M. A. (2007). Positive psychology: Is there too much of a push? *Perspectives in Psychiatric Care, 43*, 151–153.

Lattal, K. A. (1992). B. F. Skinner and psychology [Introduction to the Special Issue]. *American Psychologist, 27*, 1269–1272.

Latz, S., Wolf, A. W., & Lozoff, B. (1999). Cosleeping in context: Sleep practices and problems in young children in Japan and United States. *Archives of Pediatrics & Adolescent Medicine, 153*, 339–346.

Lauderdale, D. S., Knutson, K. L., Yan, L. L., Rathouz, P. J., Hulley, S. B., Sidney, S., et al. (2006). Objectively measured sleep characteristics among early-aged adults the CARDIA study. *American Journal of Epidemiology, 164*, 5–16.

Laughlin, H. (1967). *The neuroses*. Washington, DC: Butterworth.

Laughlin, H. (1979). *The ego and its defenses*. New York: Aronson.

Laughlin, P. R., Hatch, E. C., Silver, J. S., & Boh, L. (2006). Groups perform better than the best individuals on letters-to-numbers problems: Effects of group size. *Journal of Personality and Social Psychology, 90*, 644–651.

Laughlin, P. R., Zander, M. L., Knievel, E. M., & Tan, T. K. (2003). Groups perform better than the best individuals on letters-to-numbers problems: Informative equations and effective strategies. *Journal of Personality and Social Psychology, 85*, 684–694.

Laumann, E. O., Gagnon, J. H., Michael, R. T., & Michaels, S. (1994). *The social organization of sexuality: Sexual practices in the United States*. Chicago: University of Chicago Press.

Lauriello, J., Bustillo, J. R., & Keith, J. (2005). Schizophrenia: Scope of the problem. In B. J. Sadock & V. A. Sadock (Eds.), *Kaplan & Sadock's comprehensive textbook of psychiatry* (pp. 1345–1353). Philadelphia: Lippincott Williams & Wilkins.

Laursen, B., Coy, K. C., & Collins, W. A. (1998). Reconsidering changes in parent-child conflict across adolescence: A meta-analysis. *Child Development, 69*, 817–832.

Lavie, N. (2005). Distracted and confused? Selective attention under load. *Trends in Cognitive Sciences, 9*(2), 75–82.

Lavie, N. (2007). Attention and consciousness. In M. Velmans & S. Schneider (Eds.), *The Blackwell companion to consciousness* (pp. 489–503). Malden, MA: Blackwell Publishing.

Lawler, E. E., Mohrman, S. A., & Ledford, G. E. (1995). *Creating high-performance organizations: Practices and results of employee involvement and total quality management in Fortune 1000 companies*. San Francisco: Jossey-Bass.

Lawless, H. T. (2001). Taste. In E. B. Goldstein (Ed.), *Blackwell handbook of perception*. Malden, MA: Blackwell.

Lazarus, A. A. (1992). Multimodal therapy: Technical eclecticism with minimal integration. In J. C. Norcross & M. R. Goldfried (Eds.), *Handbook of psychotherapy integration*. New York: Basic Books.

Lazarus, A. A. (1995). Different types of eclecticism and integration: Let's be aware of the dangers. *Journal of Psychotherapy Integration, 5*, 27–39.

Lazarus, A. A. (2008). Technical eclecticism and multimodal therapy. In J. L. Lebow (Ed.), *Twenty-first century psychotherapies: Contemporary approaches to theory and practice*. New York: Wiley.

Lazarus, R. S. (1993). Why we should think of stress as a subset of emotion. In L. Goldberger & S. Breznitz (Eds.), *Handbook of stress: Theoretical and clinical aspects* (2nd ed.). New York: Free Press.

Lazarus, R. S. (1999). *Stress and emotion: A new synthesis*. New York: Springer Publishing Company.

Lazarus, R. S. (2003). Does the positive psychology movement have legs? *Psychological Inquiry, 14*(2), 93–109.

Leary, D. E. (2003). A profound and radical change: How William James inspired the reshaping of American psychology. In R. J. Sternberg (Ed.), *The anatomy of impact: What makes the great works of psychology great* (pp. 19–42). Washington, DC: American Psychological Association.

Leavitt, F. (1995). *Drugs and behavior* (3rd ed.). Thousand Oaks, CA: Sage.

Leavitt, F. (2001). Iatrogenic recovered memories: Examining the empirical evidence. *American Journal of Forensic Psychology, 19*(2), 21–32.

LeBoeuf, M. (1980, February). Managing time means managing yourself. *Business Horizons*, 41–46.

LeBoeuf, R. A., & Shafir, E. B. (2005). Decision making. In K. J. Holyoak & R. G. Morrison (Eds.), *The Cambridge handbook of thinking and reasoning*. New York: Cambridge University Press.

Leckman, J. F., Grice, D. E., Boardman, J., Zhang, H., Vitale, A., Bondi, C., Alsobrook, J., Peterson, B. S., Cohen, D. J., Rasmussen, S. A., Goodman, W. K., McDougle, C. J., & Pauls, D. (1997). Symptoms of obsessive-compulsive disorder. *American Journal of Psychiatry, 154*, 911–917.

LeDoux, J. E. (1993). Emotional networks in the brain. In M. Lewis & J. M. Haviland (Eds.), *Handbook of emotions*. New York: Guilford.

LeDoux, J. E. (1994). Emotion, memory and the brain. *Scientific American, 270*, 50–57.

LeDoux, J. E. (1995). Emotion: Clues from the brain. *Annual Review of Psychology, 46*, 209–235.

LeDoux, J. E. (1996). *The emotional brain*. New York: Simon & Schuster.

LeDoux, J. E. (2000). Emotion circuits in the brain. *Annual Review of Neuroscience, 23*, 155–184.

Lee, R. M., & Ramirez, M. (2000). The history, current status, and future of multicultural psychotherapy. In I. Cuellar & F. A. Paniagua (Eds.), *Handbook of multicultural mental health: Assessment and treatment of diverse populations*. San Diego: Academic Press.

Lee, R. T., & Ashforth, B. E. (1996). A meta-analytic examination of the correlates of the three dimensions of job burnout. *Journal of Applied Psychology, 81*, 123–133.

Lee, S., & Katzman, M. A. (2002). Cross-cultural perspectives on eating disorders. In C. G. Fairburn & K. D. Brownell (Eds.), *Eating disorders and obesity: A comprehensive handbook*. New York: Guilford.

Lee, Y., Gaskins, D., Anand, A., & Shekhar, A. (2007). Glia mechanisms in mood regulation: A novel model of mood disorders. *Psychopharmacology, 191*, 55–65.

Lee-Chiong, T., & Sateia, M. (2006). Pharmacologic therapy of insomnia. In T. Lee-Chiong (Ed.), *Sleep: A comprehensive handbook*. Hoboken, NJ: Wiley-Liss.

Leeper, R. W. (1935). A study of a neglected portion of the field of learning: The development of sensory organization. *Journal of Genetic Psychology, 46*, 41–75.

Lefcourt, H. M. (2001). The humor solution. In C. R. Snyder (Ed.), *Coping with stress: Effective people and processes* (pp. 68–92). New York: Oxford University Press.

Lefcourt, H. M., Davidson, K., Shepherd, R., Phillips, M., Prkachin, K., & Mills, D. (1995). Perspective-taking humor: Accounting for stress moderation. *Journal of Social and Clinical Psychology, 14*, 373–391.

Leff, J. (2006). Whose life is it anyway? Quality of life for long-stay patients discharged from psychiatric hospitals. In H. Katschnig, H. Freeman, & N. Sartorius (Eds.), *Quality of life in mental disorders*. New York: Wiley.

Leff, J., & Vaughn, C. (1985). *Expressed emotion in families*. New York: Guilford.

Legault, E., & Laurence, J.-R. (2007). Recovered memories of childhood sexual abuse: Social worker, psychologist, and psychiatrist reports of beliefs, practices, and cases. *Australian Journal of Clinical & Experimental Hypnosis, 35*, 111–133.

Lehman, D. R., Chiu, C., & Schaller, M. (2004). Psychology and culture. *Annual Review of Psychology, 55*, 689–714.

Lehrer, P., Feldman, J., Giardino, N., Song, H., & Schmaling, K. (2002). Psychological aspects of asthma. *Journal of Consulting & Clinical Psychology, 70*, 691–711.

Leibovic, K. N. (1990). Vertebrate photoreceptors. In K. N. Leibovic (Ed.), *Science of vision*. New York: Springer-Verlag.

Leighton, J. P., & Sternberg, R. J. (2003). Reasoning and problem solving. In A. F. Healy & R. W. Proctor (Eds.), *Handbook of psychology, Vol. 4: Experimental psychology*. New York: Wiley.

Leiter, M. P., & Maslach, C. (2001). Burnout and health. In A. Baum, T. A. Revenson, & J. E. Singer (Eds.), *Handbook of health psychology* (pp. 415–426). Mahwah, NJ: Erlbaum.

LeMagnen, J. (1981). The metabolic basis of dual periodicity of feeding in rats. *Behavioral and Brain Sciences, 4*, 561–607.

Lemery, K. S., Goldsmith, H. H., Klinnert, M. D., & Mrazek, D. A. (1999). Developmental models of infant and childhood temperament. *Developmental Psychology, 35*, 189–204.

Lenert, L., & Skoczen, S. (2002). The Internet as a research tool: Worth the price of admission? *Annals of Behavioral Medicine, 24*, 251–256.

Lennie, P. (2000). Color vision. In E. R. Kandel, J. H. Schwartz, & T. M. Jessell (Eds.), *Principles of neural science*. New York: McGraw-Hill.

Lennings, C. J. (1997). Police and occupationally related violence: A review. *Policing: An International Journal of Police Strategies and Management, 20*, 555–566.

Leo, J. (1987, January). Exploring the traits of twins. *Time*, p. 63.

Leopold, D. A., Wilke, M., Maier, A., & Logothetis, N. K. (2002). Stable perception of visually ambiguous patterns. *Nature Neuroscience, 5*, 605–609.

LePine, J. A., Erez, A., & Johnston, D. E. (2002). The nature and dimensionality of organizational citizenship behavior: A critical review and a meta-analysis. *Journal of Applied Psychology, 87*, 52–65.

Lepine, R., Barrouillet, P., & Camos, V. (2005). What makes working memory spans so predictive of high-level cognition? *Psychonomic Bulletin & Review, 12*(1), 165–170.

Lerman, H. (1986). *A mote in Freud's eye: From psychoanalysis to the psychology of women*. New York: Springer.

Lerner, J. S., Small, D. A., & Loewenstein, G. (2004). Heart strings and purse strings: Carryover effects of emotions on economic decisions. *Psychological Science, 15*, 337–341.

Lerner, M. J., & Goldberg, J. H. (1999). When do decent people blame victims? The differing effects of the explicit/rational and implicit/experiential cognitive systems. In S. Chaiken & Y. Trope (Eds.), *Dual-process theories in social psychology*. New York: Guilford.

Leslie, A. M. (1994). ToMM, ToBy, and agency: Core architecture and domain specificity in cognition and culture. In L. A. Hirschfeld & S. A. Gelman (Eds.), *Mapping the mind: Domain specificity in cognition and culture*. New York: Cambridge University Press.

Lett, H. S., Blumenthal, J. A., Babyak, M. A., Catellier, D. J., Carney, R. M., Berkman, L. F., et al. (2007). Social support and prognosis in patients at increased psychosocial risk recovering from myocardial infarction. *Health Psychology, 26*, 418–427.

Lett, H. S., Blumenthal, J. A., Babyak, M. A., Sherwood, A., Strauman, T., Robbins, C., & Newman, M. F. (2004). Depression as a risk factor for coronary artery disease: Evidence, mechanisms, and treatment. *Psychosomatic Medicine, 66*, 305–315.

Leuner, B., Gould, E., & Shors, T. J. (2006). Is there a link between adult neurogenesis and learning? *Hippocampus, 16*, 216–224.

LeVay, S. (1996). *Queer science: The use and abuse of research into homosexuality*. Cambridge, MA: MIT Press.

Levenson, R. W. (1992). Autonomic nervous system differences among emotions. *Psychological Science, 3*, 23–27.

Levenson, R. W. (2003). Autonomic specificity and emotion. In R. J. Davidson, K. R. Scherer, & H. H. Goldsmith (Eds.), *Handbook of affective sciences*. New York: Oxford University Press.

Levenstein, S. (2002). Psychosocial factors in peptic ulcer and inflammatory bowel disease. *Journal of Consulting & Clinical Psychology, 70*, 739–750.

Leventhal, H., & Tomarken, A. J. (1986). Emotion: Today's problems. *Annual Review of Psychology, 37*, 565–610.

Levesque, M. J., Nave, C. S., & Lowe, C. A. (2006). Toward an understanding of gender differences in inferring sexual interest. *Psychology of Women Quarterly, 30*, 150–158.

Levin, S., Henry, P. J., Pratto, F., & Sidanius, J. (2003). Social dominance and social identity in Lebanon: Implications for support of violence against the West. *Group Processes and Intergroup Relations, 6*, 353–368.

Levine, B., Turner, G. R., Tisserand, D., Hevenor, S. J., Graham, S. J., & McIntosh, A. R. (2004). The functional neuroanatomy of episodic and semantic autobiographical remembering: A prospective functional MRI study. *Journal of Cognitive Neuroscience, 16*, 1633–1646.

Levine, J. M. (1999). Solomon Asch's legacy for group research. *Personality and Social Psychology Review, 3*, 358–364.

Levine, J. M., & Moreland, R. L. (1998). Small groups. In D. T. Gilbert, S. T. Fiske, & G. Lindzey (Eds.), *The handbook of social psychology*. New York: McGraw-Hill.

Levine, M. P., & Harrison, K. (2004). Media's role in the perpetuation and prevention of negative body image and disordered eating. In J. K. Thompson (Ed.), *Handbook of eating disorders and obesity*. New York: Wiley.

Levine, M. W. (2001). Principles of neural processing. In E. B. Goldstein (Ed.), *Blackwell handbook of perception*. Malden, MA: Blackwell.

LeVine, R. (2001). Culture and personality studies, 1918–1960. *Journal of Personality, 69*, 803–818.

Levine, R., & Norenzayan, A. (1999). The pace of life in 31 countries. *Journal of Cross-Cultural Psychology, 30*, 178–205.

Levine, R., Sata, S., Hashimoto, T., & Verma, J. (1995). Love and marriage in eleven cultures. *Journal of Cross-Cultural Psychology, 26*, 554–571.

Levinthal, C. F. (2008). *Drugs, behavior, and modern society*. Boston: Pearson.

Levis, D. J. (1989). The case for a return to a two-factor theory of avoidance: The failure of non-fear interpretations. In S. B. Klein & R. R. Bowrer (Eds.), *Contemporary learning theories: Pavlovian conditioning and the status of traditional learning theory*. Hillsdale NJ: Erlbaum.

Levis, D. J., & Brewer, K. E. (2001). The neurotic paradox: Attempts by two-factor fear theory and alternative avoidance models to resolve the issues associated with sustained avoidance responding in extinction. In R. R. Mowrer & S. B. Klein (Eds.), *Handbook of contemporary learning theories* (pp. 561–597). Mahwah, NJ: Erlbaum.

Levy, G. D., Taylor, M. G., & Gelman, S. A. (1995). Traditional and evaluative aspects of flexibility in gender roles, social conventions, moral rules, and physical laws. *Child Development, 66*, 515–531.

Levy, J. (1985, May). Right brain, left brain: Fact or fiction. *Psychology Today*, 38–44.

Levy, J., Trevarthen, C., & Sperry, R. W. (1972). Perception of bilateral chimeric figures following hemispheric disconnection. *Brain, 95*, 61–78.

Lewandowsky, S., Duncan, M., & Brown, G. D. A. (2004). Time does not cause forgetting in short-term serial recall. *Psychonomic Bulletin & Review, 11*(5), 771–790.

Lewin, K. (1935). *A dynamic theory of personality*. New York: McGraw-Hill.

Lewinsohn, P. M., Joiner, T. E., Jr., & Rohde, P. (2001). Evaluation of cognitive diathesis-stress models in predicting major depressive disorder in adolescents. *Journal of Abnormal Psychology, 110*, 203–215.

Lewis, C., & Lamb, M. E. (2003). Fathers' influences on children's development: The evidence from two-parent families. *European Journal of Psychology of Education, 18*, 211–228.

Li, N. P., Bailey, J. M., Kenrick, D. T., & Linsenmeier, J. A. W. (2002). The necessities and luxuries of mate preferences: Testing the tradeoffs. *Journal of Personality and Social Psychology, 82*, 947–955.

Li, N. P., & Kenrick, D. T. (2006). Sex similarities and differences in preferences for short-term mates: What, whether, and why. *Journal of Personality and Social Psychology, 90*, 468–489.

Li, S. C., Lindenberger, U., Hommel, B., Aschersleben, G., Prinz, W., & Baltes, P. B. (2004). Transformations in the couplings among intellectual abilities and constituent cognitive processes across the life span. *Psychological Science, 15*, 155–163.

Li, W., Moallem, I., Paller, K. A., & Gottfried, J. A. (2007). Subliminal smells can guide social preferences. *Psychological Science, 18,* 1044–1049.

Liberman, R. P., & Kopelowicz, A. (2005). Recovery from schizophrenia: A concept in search of research. *Psychiatric Services, 56,* 735–742.

Liberman, R. P., Kopelowicz, A., Ventura, J., & Gutkind, D. (2002). Operational criteria and factors related to recovery from schizophrenia. *International Review of Psychiatry, 14*(4), 256–272.

Lichten, W., & Simon, E. W. (2007). Defining mental retardation: A matter of life or death. *Intellectual and Developmental Disabilities, 45,* 335–346.

Lichtenstein, S., Fischhoff, B., & Phillips, L. (1982). Calibration of probabilities: The state of the art to 1980. In D. Kahneman, P. Slovic, & A. Tversky (Eds.), *Judgment under uncertainty: Heuristics and biases.* Cambridge, England: Cambridge University Press.

Lichtenthal, W. G., Cruess, D. G., & Prigerson, H. G. (2004). A case for establishing complicated grief as a distinct mental disorder in DSM-V. *Clinical Psychology Review, 24,* 637–662.

Lickey, M. E., & Gordon, B. (1991). *Medicine and mental illness: The use of drugs in psychiatry.* New York: W. H. Freeman.

Lickliter, R., & Honeycutt, H. (2003). Developmental dynamics: Toward a biologically plausible evolutionary psychology. *Psychological Bulletin, 129,* 819–835.

Liden, R. C., Wayne, S. J., Jaworski, R. A., & Bennett, N. (2004). Social loafing: A field investigation. *Journal of Management, 30,* 285–304.

Lieberman, D., & Hatfield, E. (2006). Passionate love: Cross-cultural and evolutionary perspectives. In R. J. Sternberg & K. Weis (Eds.), *The new psychology of love.* New Haven, CT: Yale University Press.

Lieberman, J. A. (2006). Comparative effectiveness of antipsychotic drugs. *Archives of General Psychiatry, 63,* 1069–1072.

Lieberman, J. A., Stoup, T. S., McEvoy, J. P., Swartz, M. S., Rosenheck, R. A., & Perkins, D. O. et al. (2005). Effectiveness of antipsychotic drugs in patients with chronic schizophrenia. *New England Journal of Medicine, 353,* 1209–1223.

Lieberman, J. A., Tollefson, G., Tohen, M., Green, A. I., Gur, R. E., Kahn, R., McEvoy, J., Perkins, D., Sharma, T., Zipursky, R., Wei, H., Hamer, R. M., & HGDH Group Study. (2003). Comparative efficacy and safety of atypical and conventional antipsychotic drugs in first-episode psychosis: A randomized double-blind trial of olazapine versus haloperidol. *American Journal of Psychiatry, 160,* 1396–1404.

Liebert, R. M., & Liebert, L. L. (1998). *Liebert & Spiegler's personality strategies and issues.* Pacific Grove: Brooks/Cole.

Lien, M.-C., Ruthruff, E., & Johnston, J. C. (2006). Attentional limitations in doing two tasks at once. *Current Directions in Psychological Science, 15,* 89–93.

Likert, R. (1967). *The human organization: Its management and value.* New York: McGraw-Hill.

Lilienfeld, S. O. (2007). Psychological treatments that cause harm. *Perspectives on Psychological Science, 2,* 53–70.

Lilienfeld, S. O., & Lynn, S. J. (2003). Dissociative identity disorder: Multiple personalities, multiple controversies. In S. O. Lilienfeld, S. J. Lynn, & J. M. Lohr (Eds.), *Science and pseudoscience in clinical psychology.* New York: Guilford.

Lilienfeld, S. O., Lynn, S. J., Kirsch, I., Chaves, J. F., Sarbin, T. R., Ganaway, G. K., & Powell, R. A. (1999). Dissociative identity disorder and the sociocognitive model: Recalling the lessons of the past. *Psychological Bulletin, 125,* 507–523.

Lilienfeld, S. O., Wood, J. M., & Garb, H. N. (2000). The scientific status of projective tests. *Psychological Science in the Public Interest, 1*(2), 27–66.

Lin, S. W., & Anthnelli, R. M. (2005). Genetic factors in the risk for substance use disorders. In J. H. Lowinson, P. Ruiz, R. B. Millman, & J. G. Langrod (Eds.), *Substance abuse: A comprehensive textbook.* Philadelphia: Lippincott/Williams & Wilkins.

Linde, J. A., Rothman, A. J., Baldwin, A. S., & Jeffery, R. W. (2006). The impact of self-efficacy on behavior change and weight change among overweight participants in a weight-loss trial. *Health Psychology, 25,* 282–291.

Lindenmayer, J. P., & Khan, A. (2006). Psychopathology. In J. A. Lieberman, T. S. Stroup, & D. O. Perkins (Eds.), *Textbook of schizophrenia* (pp. 187–222). Washington, DC: American Psychiatric Publishing.

Lindgren, H. C. (1969). *The psychology of college success: A dynamic approach.* New York: Wiley.

Lindsay, M., & Lester, D. (2004). *Suicide by cop: Committing suicide by provoking police to shoot you (death, value and meaning).* Amityville, NY: Baywood Publishing.

Lindsay, P. H., & Norman, D. A. (1977). *Human information processing.* New York: Academic Press.

Lindsay, S. D., Allen, B. P., Chan, J. C. K., & Dahl, L. C. (2004). Eyewitness suggestibility and source similarity: Intrusions of details from one event into memory reports of another event. *Journal of Memory & Language, 50*(1), 96–111.

Lindsay, S. D., & Read, J. D. (1994). Psychotherapy and memories of childhood sexual abuse: A cognitive perspective. *Applied Cognitive Psychology, 8,* 281–338.

Lindsay, S. D., & Read, J. D. (2001). The recovered memories controversy: Where do we go from here? In G. M. Davies & T. Dalgleish (Eds.), *Recovered memories: Seeking the middle ground.* Chichester, England: Wiley.

Lipert, J., Bauder, H., Miltner, W. H. R., Taub, E., & Weiller, C. (2000). Treatment-induced cortical reorganization after stroke in humans. *Stroke, 31,* 1210–1216.

Lippa, R. A. (1994). *Introduction to social psychology.* Pacific Grove, CA: Brooks/Cole.

Lippa, R. A., Martin, L. R., & Friedman, H. S. (2000). Gender-related individual differences and mortality in the Terman longitudinal study: Is masculinity hazardous to your health? *Personality and Social Psychology Bulletin, 26,* 1560–1570.

Lipton, J. S., & Spelke, E. S. (2004). Discrimination of large and small numerosities by human infants. *Infancy, 5,* 271–290.

Lisanby, S. H., Maddox, J. H., Prudic, J., Devanand, D. P., & Sackeim, H. A. (2000). The effects of electroconvulsive therapy on memory of autobiographical and public events. *General Psychiatry, 57,* 581–590.

Little, A. C., & Mannion, H. (2006). Viewing attractive or unattractive same-sex individuals changes self-rated attractiveness and face preferences in women. *Animal Behaviour, 72,* 981–987.

Little, A. C., Jones, B. C., & Burriss, R. P. (2007). Preferences for masculinity in male bodies change across the menstrual cycle. *Hormones and Behavior, 51,* 633–639.

Livesley, W. J., Jang, K. L., & Vernon, P. A. (2003). Genetic basis of personality structure. In T. Millon & M. J. Lerner (Eds.), *Handbook of psychology, Vol. 5: Personality and social psychology.* New York: Wiley.

Lizarraga, M. L. S., & Ganuza, J. M. G. (2003). Improvement of mental rotation in girls and boys. *Sex Roles, 40,* 277–286.

Lledo, P.-M., Alonso, M., & Grubb, M. S. (2006). Adult neurogenesis and functional plasticity in neural circuits. *Nature Reviews Neuroscience, 7,* 179–193.

Locke, E. A. (1968). Toward a theory of task motivation and incentives. *Organizational Behavior and Human Performance, 3,* 157–189.

Locke, E. A. (1970). Job satisfaction and job performance. *Organizational Behavior and Human Performance, 5,* 484–500.

Locke, E. A. (1976). The nature and causes of job satisfaction. In M. D. Dunnette (Ed.), *The handbook of industrial and organizational psychology.* Chicago: Rand McNally.

Lockhart, R. S. (1992). Measurement of memory. In L. R. Squire (Ed.), *Encyclopedia of learning and memory.* New York: Macmillan.

Lockhart, R. S. (2000). Methods of memory research. In E. Tulving & F. I. M. Craik (Eds.), *The Oxford handbook of memory* (pp. 45–58). New York: Oxford University Press.

Lockhart, R. S. (2002). Levels of processing, transfer-appropriate processing and the concept of robust encoding. *Memory, 10,* 397–403.

Lockhart, R. S., & Craik, F. I. (1990). Levels of processing: A retrospective commentary on a framework for memory research. *Canadian Journal of Psychology, 44*(1), 87–112.

Locurto, C. (1990). The malleability of IQ as judged from adoption studies. *Intelligence, 14,* 275–292.

Loehlin, J. C. (1992). *Genes and environment in personality development.* Newbury Park, CA: Sage.

Loehlin, J. C. (1994). Behavior genetics. In R. J. Sternberg (Ed.), *Encyclopedia of human intelligence.* New York: Macmillan.

Loehlin, J. C. (2000). Group differences in intelligence. In R. J. Sternberg (Ed.), *Handbook of intelligence* (pp. 176–195). New York: Cambridge University Press.

Loehlin, J. C., Horn, J. M., & Willerman, L. (1997). Heredity, environment, and IQ in the Texas Adoption Project. In R. J. Sternberg & E. L. Grigorenko (Eds.), *Intelligence, heredity, and environment.* New York: Cambridge University Press.

Loewenstein, G. (2007). Affect regulation and affective forecasting. In J. J. Gross (Ed.), *Handbook of emotion regulation.* New York: Guilford.

Loewenstein, G., & Schkade, D. (1999). Wouldn't it be nice? Predicting future feelings. In D. Kahneman, E. Diener, & N. Schwartz (Eds.), *Well-being: The foundations of hedonic psychology.* New York: Sage.

Loewenstein, R. L., & Putnam, F. W. (2005). Dissociative disorders. In B. J. Sadock & V. A. Sadock (Eds.), *Kaplan & Sadock's comprehensive textbook of psychiatry* (pp. 1844–1901). Philadelphia: Lippincott Williams & Wilkins.

Loftus, E. F. (1979). *Eyewitness testimony.* Cambridge, MA: Harvard University Press.

Loftus, E. F. (1992). When a lie becomes memory's truth: Memory distortion after exposure to misinformation. *Current Directions in Psychological Science, 1,* 121–123.

Loftus, E. F. (1993). Psychologist in the eyewitness world. *American Psychologist, 48,* 550–552.

Loftus, E. F. (1994). The repressed memory controversy. *American Psychologist, 49,* 443–445.

Loftus, E. F. (2000). Remembering what never happened. In E. Tulving (Ed.), *Memory, consciousness, and the brain: The Tallinn conference* (pp. 106–118). Philadelphia: Psychology Press.

Loftus, E. F. (2004). Memories of things unseen. *Current Directions in Psychological Science, 13*(4), 145–147.

Loftus, E. F. (2005). Planting misinformation in the human mind: A 30-year investigation of the malleability of memory. *Learning & Memory, 12,* 361–366.

Loftus, E. F., & Bernstein, D. M. (2005). Rich false memories: The royal road to success. In A. F. Healy (Ed.), *Experimental cognitive psychology and its applications*. Washington, DC: American Psychological Association.

Loftus, E. F., & Cahill, L. (2007). Memory distortion: From misinformation to rich false memory. In J. S. Nairne (Ed.), *The foundations of remembering: Essays in honor of Henry L. Roediger III.* New York: Psychology Press.

Loftus, E. F., & Davis, D. (2006). Recovered memories. *Annual Review of Clinical Psychology, 2,* 469–498.

Loftus, E. F., Garry, M., & Feldman, J. (1998). Forgetting sexual trauma: What does it mean when 38% forget? In R. A. Baker (Ed.), *Child sexual abuse and false memory syndrome*. Amherst, NY: Prometheus Books.

Loftus, E. F., & Mazzoni, G. A. L. (1998). Using imagination and personalized suggestion to change people. *Behavior Therapy, 29,* 691–706.

Loftus, E. F., & Palmer, J. C. (1974). Reconstruction of automobile destruction: An example of the interaction between language and memory. *Journal of Verbal Learning and Verbal Behavior, 13,* 585–589.

Logue, A. W. (1991). *The psychology of eating and drinking* (2nd ed.). New York: W. H. Freeman.

Lohman, D. F. (1989). Human intelligence: An introduction to advances in theory and research. *Review of Educational Research, 59*(4), 333–373.

Lohmann, R. I. (2007). Dreams and ethnography. In D. Barrett & P. McNamara (Eds.), *The new science of dreaming*. Westport, CT: Praeger.

Long, J. E., Jr. (2005). Power to prescribe: The debate over prescription privileges for psychologists and the legal issues implicated. *Law & Psychology, 29,* 243–260.

Longman, D. G., & Atkinson, R. H. (2005). *College learning and study skills*. Belmont, CA: Wadsworth.

Lopes, P. N., Brackett, M. A., Nezlek, J. B., Schutz, A., Sellin, I., & Salovey, P. (2004). Emotional intelligence and social interaction. *Personality and Social Psychology Bulletin, 30,* 1018–1034.

Lott, B. (1987). *Women's lives*. Pacific Grove, CA: Brooks/Cole.

Lott, B. (2002). Cognitive and behavioral distancing from the poor. *American Psychologist, 57,* 100–110.

Lowden, A., Akerstedt, T., & Wibom, R. (2004). Suppression of sleepiness and melatonin by bright light exposure during breaks in night work. *Journal of Sleep Research, 12*(1), 37–43.

Lowinson, J. H., Ruiz, P., Millman, R. B., & Langrod, J. G. (2005). *Substance abuse: A comprehensive textbook*. Philadelphia: Lippincott/Williams & Wilkins.

Lubart, T. I. (2003). In search of creative intelligence. In R. J. Sternberg, J. Lautrey, & T. I. Lubart (Eds.), *Models of intelligence: International perspectives*. Washington, DC: American Psychological Association.

Lubinski, D., & Benbow, C. P. (2006). Study of mathematically precocious youth after 35 years: Uncovering antecedents for the development of math-science expertise. *Perspectives on Psychological Science, 1,* 316–345.

Luborsky, L., & Barrett, M. S. (2006). The history and empirical status of key psychoanalytic concepts. *Annual Review Clinical Psychology, 2,* 1–19.

Luborsky, L., Diguer, L., Seligman, D. A., Rosenthal, R., Krause, E. D., Johnson, S., Halperin, G., Bishop, M., Berman, J. S., & Schweizer, E. (1999). The researcher's own therapy allegiance: A "wild card" in comparisons of treatment efficacy. *Clinical Psychology: Science & Practice, 6*(1), 95–106.

Luborsky, L., Rosenthal, R., Diguer, L., Andrusyna, T. P., Berman, J. S., Levitt, J. T., Seligman, D. A., & Krause, E. D. (2002). The dodo bird verdict is alive and well—mostly. *Clinical Psychology: Science & Practice, 9,* 2–12.

Luborsky, L., Singer, B., & Luborsky, L. (1975). Comparative studies of psychotherapies: Is it true that everyone has won and all must have prizes? *Archives of General Psychiatry, 32,* 995–1008.

Lucas, R. E. (2007). Adaptation and the set-point model of subjective well-being: Does happiness change after major life events? *Current Directions in Psychological Science, 16,* 75–79.

Lucas, R. E. (2008). Personality and subjective well-being. In M. Eid & R. J. Larsen (Eds.), *The science of subjective well-being* (pp. 171–194). New York: Guilford.

Lucas, R. E., Clark, A. E., Georgellis, Y., & Diener, E. (2003). Reexamining adaptation and set point model of happiness: Reactions to changes in marital status. *Journal of Personality and Social Psychology, 84,* 527–539.

Lucas, R. E., Clark, A. E., Georgellis, Y., & Diener, E. (2004). Unemployment alters the set point for life satisfaction. *Psychological Science, 15*(1), 8–13.

Luchins, A. S. (1942). Mechanization in problem solving. *Psychological Monographs, 54* (6, Whole No. 248).

Ludwig, A. M. (1994). Mental illness and creative activity in female writers. *American Journal of Psychiatry, 151,* 1650–1656.

Ludwig, A. M. (1995). *The price of greatness: Resolving the creativity and madness controversy*. New York: Guilford.

Ludwig, A. M. (1998). Method and madness in the arts and sciences. *Creativity Research Journal, 11,* 93–101.

Lugaresi, E., Cirignotta, F., Montagna, P., & Sforza, E. (1994). Snoring: Pathogenic, clinical, and therapeutic aspects. In M. H. Kryger, T. Roth, & W. C. Dement (Eds.), *Principles and practice of sleep medicine* (2nd ed.). Philadelphia: Saunders.

Luh, C. W. (1922). The conditions of retention. *Psychological Monographs, 31.*

Lund, O. C. H., Tamnes, C. K., Moestue, C., Buss, D. M., & Vollrath, M. (2007). Tactics of hierarchy negotiation. *Journal of Research in Personality, 41,* 25–44.

Lundberg, U. (2000). Catecholamines. In G. Fink (Ed.), *Encyclopedia of stress* (Vol. 1, pp. 408–413). San Diego: Academic Press.

Lundberg, U. (2007). Catecholamines. In G. Fink (Ed.), *Encyclopedia of stress*. San Diego: Elsevier.

Luntz, B. K., & Widom, C. S. (1994). Antisocial personality disorder in abused and neglected children grown up. *Journal of Psychiatry, 151,* 670–674.

Luo, S., & Klohen, E. C. (2005). Assortative mating and marital quality in newlyweds: A couple-centered approach. *Journal of Personality and Social Psychology, 88,* 304–326.

Lupien, S. J., & Maheu, F. S. (2007). Memory and stress. In G. Fink (Ed.), *Encyclopedia of stress*. San Diego: Elsevier.

Lurie, P., Almeida, C. M., Stine, N. , Stine, A. R., & Wolfe, S. M. (2006). Financial conflict of interest disclosure and voting patterns at food and drug administration drug advisory committee meetings. *Journal of the American Medical Association, 295,* 1921–1928.

Lutz, A., Dunne, J. D., & Davidson, R. J. (2007). Meditation and the neuroscience of consciousness: An introduction. In P. D. Zelazo, M. Moscovitch, & E. Thompson (Eds.), *The Cambridge handbook of consciousness* (pp. 499–551). New York: Cambridge University Press.

Lutz, C. (1987). Goals, events and understanding in Ifaluk emotion theory. In N. Quinn & D. Holland (Eds.), *Cultural models in language and thought*. Cambridge, England: Cambridge University Press.

Lutz, W. (1989). *Doublespeak*. New York: Harper Perennial.

Lykken, D. T. (1998). *A tremor in the blood: Uses and abuses of the lie detector*. New York: Plenum Press.

Lykken, D. T. (1999). *Happiness: The nature and nurture of joy and contentment*. New York: St. Martin's.

Lykken, D. T., McGue, M., Tellegen, A., & Bouchard, T. J., Jr. (1992). Emergenesis: Genetic traits that may not run in families. *American Psychologist, 47,* 1565–1577.

Lykken, D. T., & Tellegen, A. (1996). Happiness is a stochastic phenomenon. *Psychological Science, 7,* 186–189.

Lynch, G., & Gall, C. M. (2006). Ampakines and the threefold path to cognitive enhancement. *Trends in Neurosciences, 29,* 554–562.

Lynch, M. A. (2004). Long-term potentiation and memory. *Psychological Review, 84,* 87–136.

Lynch, S. K., Turkheimer, E., D'Onofrio, B. M., Mendle, J., Emery, R. E., Slutske, W. S., et al. (2006). A genetically informed study of the association between harsh punishment and offspring behavioral problems. *Journal of Family Psychology, 20,* 190–198.

Lynn, M. (1992). Scarcity's enhancement of desirability: The role of naive economic theories. *Basic & Applied Social Psychology, 13,* 67–78.

Lynn, S. J., Kirsch, I., Barabasz, A., Cardena, E., & Patterson, D. (2000). Hypnosis as an empirically supported clinical intervention: The state of the evidence and a look to the future. *International Journal of Clinical & Experimental Hypnosis, 48,* 239–259.

Lynn, S. J., Kirsch, I., Knox, J., Fassler, O., & Lilienfeld, S. O. (2007). Hypnotic regulation of consciousness and the pain neuromatrix. In G. A. Jamieson (Ed.), *Hypnosis and conscious states: The cognitive neuroscience perspective* (pp. 145–166). New York: Oxford University Press.

Lynn, S. J., Lock, T., Loftus, E. F. , Krackow, E., & Lilienfeld, S. O. (2003). The remembrance of things past: Problematic memory recovery techniques in psychotherapy. In S. O. Lilienfeld, S. J. Lynn, & J. M. Lohr (Eds.), *Science and pseudoscience in clinical psychology*. New York: Guilford.

Lynn, S. J., Neuschatz, J., & Fite, R. (2002). Hypnosis and memory: Implications for the courtroom and psychotherapy. In M. L. Eisen (Ed.), *Memory and suggestibility in the forensic interview*. Mahwah, NJ: Erlbaum.

Lynne, S. D., Graber, J. A., Nichols, T. R., & Brooks-Gunn, J., & Botwin, G. J. (2007). Links between pubertal timing, peer influences, and externalizing behaviors among urban students followed through middle school. *Journal of Adolescent Health, 40*(2).

Lyons-Ruth, K., & Jacobvitz, D. (1999). Attachment disorganization: Unresolved loss, relational violence, and lapses in behavioral and attentional strategies. In J. Cassidy & P. R. Shaver (Eds.), *Handbook of attachment: Theory, research, and clinical applications*. New York: Guilford.

Lytton, H. (1997). Physical punishment is a problem, whether conduct disorder is endogenous or not. *Psychological Inquiry, 8*, 211–214.

Lyubomirsky, S., Sheldon, K. M., & Schkade, D. (2005). Pursuing happiness: The architecture of sustainable change. *Review of General Psychology, 9*, 111–131.

Lyubomirsky, S., Sousa, L., & Dickerhoof, R. (2006). The costs and benefits of writing, talking, and thinking about life's triumphs and defeats. *Journal of Personality and Social Psychology, 90*, 692–708.

Lyubomirsky, S., Tkach, C., & DiMatteo, R. M. (2006). What are the differences between happiness and self-esteem? *Social Indicators Research, 78*, 363–404.

Maas, J. B. (1998). *Power sleep*. New York: Harper Perennial.

Maass, A. (1999). Linguistic intergroup bias: Stereotype perpetuation through language. *Advances in Experimental Social Psychology, 31*, 79–121.

Maccoby, E. E. (2000). Parenting and its effects on children: On reading and misreading behavior genetics. *Annual Review of Psychology, 51*, 1–27.

MacCoun, R. J. (1998). Biases in the interpretation and use of research results. *Annual Review Psychology, 49*, 259–287.

MacGregor, J. N., Ormerod, T. C., & Chronicle, E. P. (2001). Information-processing and insight: A process model of performance on the nine-dot and related problems. *Journal of Experimental Psychology: Learning, Memory, and Cognition, 27*, 176–201.

Macht, M., & Simons, G. (2000). Emotions and eating in everyday life. *Appetite, 35*, 65–71.

Mack, A. (2003). Inattentional blindness: Looking without seeing. *Current Directions in Psychological Science, 12*(5), 180–184.

Mack, A. H., Franklin Jr., J. E., & Frances, R. J. (2003). Substance use disorders. In R. E. Hales & S. C. Yudofsky (Eds.), *Textbook of clinical psychiatry*. Washington, DC: American Psychiatric Publishing.

MacKellar, D. A., Valleroy, L. A., Secura, G. M., Behel, S., Bingham, T., Celentano, D. D., Koblin, B. A., LaLota, M., McFarland, W., Shehan, D., Thiede, H., Torian, L. V., & Janssen, R. S., & Young Men's Survey Study Group. (2005). Unrecognized HIV infection, risk behaviors, and perceptions of risk among young men who have sex with men: Opportunities for advancing HIV prevention in the third decade of HIV/AIDS. *Journal of Acquired Immune Deficiency Syndromes, 38*, 603–614.

Mackintosh, N. J. (1998). *IQ and human intelligence*. Oxford: Oxford University Press.

Maclean, A. W., Davies, D. R. T., & Thiele, K. (2003). The hazards and prevention of driving while sleepy. *Sleep Medicine Reviews,7*, 507–521.

MacLean, P. D. (1954). Studies on limbic system ("viosceal brain") and their bearing on psychosomatic problems. In E. D. Wittkower & R. A. Cleghorn (Eds.), *Recent developments in psychosomatic medicine*. Philadelphia: Lippincott.

MacLean, P. D. (1993). Cerebral evolution of emotion. In M. Lewis & J. M. Haviland (Eds.), *Handbook of emotions*. New York: Guilford.

MacMillan, H. L., Fleming, J. E., Streiner, D. L., Lin, E., Boyle, M. H., Jamieson, E., Duku, E. K., Walsh, C. A., Wong, M. Y. Y., & Beardslee, W. R. (2001). Childhood abuse and lifetime psychopathology in a community sample. *American Journal of Psychiatry, 158*, 1878–1883.

MacMillan, H. L., Fleming, J. E., Trocme, N., Boyle, M. H., Wong, M., Racine, Y. A., Beardslee, W. R., & Offord, D. R. (1997). Prevalence of child physical and sexual abuse in the community: Results from the Ontario health supplement. *Journal of the American Medical Association, 278*, 131–135.

MacWhinney, B. (1998). Models of the emergence of language. *Annual Review of Psychology, 49*, 199–227.

MacWhinney, B. (1999). The emergence of language from embodiment. In B. MacWhinney (Ed.), *The emergence of language* (pp. 213–256). Mahwah, NJ: Erlbaum.

MacWhinney, B. (2001). Emergentist approaches to language. In J. Bybee & P. Hooper (Eds.), *Frequency and the emergence of linguistic structure*. Amsterdam: John Benjamins Publishing.

MacWhinney, B. (2004). A multiple process solution to the logical problem of language acquisition. *Journal of Child Language, 31*, 883–914.

Madden, M., & Lenhart, A. (2006). *Online dating*. Retrieved from http://www.pewInternet.org/pdfs/PIP_Online_Dating.pdf.

Maddux, W. W., & Yuki, M. (2006). The "ripple effect": Cultural differences in perceptions of the consequences of events. *Personality and Social Psychology Bulletin, 32*, 669–683.

Madon, S., Guyll, M., Aboufadel, K., Montiel, E., Smith, A., Palumbo, P., & Jussim, L. (2001). Ethnic and national stereotypes: The Princeton trilogy revisited and revised. *Personality and Social Psychology Bulletin, 27*, 996–1010.

Madsen, K. B. (1968). *Theories of motivation*. Copenhagen: Munksgaard.

Madsen, K. B. (1973). Theories of motivation. In B. B. Wolman (Ed.), *Handbook of general psychology*. Englewood Cliffs, NJ: Prentice-Hall.

Magnavita, J. J. (2008). Psychoanalytic psychotherapy. In J. L. Lebow (Ed.), *Twenty-first century psychotherapies: Contemporary approaches to theory and practice*. New York: Wiley.

Magnusson, D., & Stattin, H. (1998). Person-context interaction theories. In W. Damon (Ed.), *Handbook of child psychology (Vol. 1): Theoretical models of human development*. New York: Wiley.

Maguire, W., Weisstein, N., & Klymenko, V. (1990). From visual structure to perceptual function. In K. N. Leibovic (Ed.), *Science of vision*. New York: Springer-Verlag.

Maher, B. A. (2001). Delusions. In P. B. Sutker & H. E. Adams (Eds.), *Comprehensive handbook of psychopathology* (3rd ed., pp. 309–370). New York: Kluwer Academic/Plenum Publishers.

Mahoney, M. J. (1974). *Cognition and behavior modification*. Cambridge, MA: Ballinger.

Mahowald, M. W. (1993). Sleepwalking. In M. A. Carskadon (Ed.), *Encyclopedia of sleep and dreaming*. New York: Macmillan.

Mahowald, M. W., & Schenck, C. H. (2005). Insights from studying human sleep disorders. *Nature, 437*, 1279–1285.

Maier, N. (1930). Reasoning in humans. I. On direction. *Journal of Comparative Psychology, 10*, 15–43.

Main, M., & Solomon, J. (1986). Discovery of a new, insecure–disorganized/disoriented attachment pattern. In T. B. Brazelton & M. W. Yogman (Eds.), *Affective development in infancy*. Norwood, NJ: Ablex.

Main, M., & Solomon, J. (1990). Procedures for identifying infants as disorganized/disoriented during the Ainsworth strange situation. In M. T. Greenberg, D. Ciccehetti, & E. M. Cummings (Eds.), *Attachment in the preschool years: Theory, research, and intervention*. Chicago: University of Chicago Press.

Main, T. (1998). How to think about homelessness: Balancing structural and individual causes. *Journal of Social Distress & the Homeless, 7*, 41–54.

Malamuth, N. M., Addison, T., & Koss, M. (2000). Pornography and sexual aggression: Are there reliable effects and can we understand them? *Annual Review of Sex Research, 11*, 26–91.

Maldonado, J. R., & Spiegel, D. (2003a). Dissociative disorders. In R. E. Hales & S. C. Yudofsky (Eds.), *Textbook of clinical psychiatry*. Washington, DC: American Psychiatric Publishing.

Maldonado, J. R., & Spiegel, D. (2003b). Hypnosis. In R. E. Hales & S. C. Yudofsky (Eds.), *Textbook of clinical psychiatry*. Washington, DC: American Psychiatric Publishing.

Maletzky, B. M. (2002). The paraphilias: Research and treatment. In P. E. Nathan & J. M. Gorman (Eds.), *A guide to treatments that work*. London: Oxford University Press.

Malnic, B., Hirono, J., Sata, T., & Buck, L. B. (1999). Combinatorial receptor codes for odors. *Cell, 96*, 713–723.

Maltzman, I. (1994). Why alcoholism is a disease. *Journal of Psychoactive Drugs, 26*, 13–31.

Mandler, G. (1984). *Mind and body*. New York: Norton.

Mandler, G. (1993). Thought, memory, and learning: Effects of emotional stress. In L. Goldberger & S. Breznitz (Eds.), *Handbook of stress: Theoretical and clinical aspects* (2nd ed.). New York: Free Press.

Mandler, G. (2002). Origins of the cognitive revolution. *Journal of the History of the Behavioral Sciences, 38*, 339–353.

Maner, J. K., Gailliot, M. T., Rouby, D. A., & Miller, S. L. (2007). Can't take my eyes off you: Attentional adhesion to mates and rivals. *Journal of Personality and Social Psychology, 93*, 389–401.

Mann, R. D. (1959). A review of the relationships between personality and performance in small groups. *Psychological Bulletin, 56*, 241–270.

Mann, J. J., & Currier, D. (2006). Understanding and preventing suicide. In D. J. Stein, D. J. Kupfer, & A. F. Schatzberg (Eds.), *Textbook of mood disorders* (pp. 485–496). Washington, DC: American Psychiatric Publishing.

Mann, T., Tomiyama, A. J., Westling, E., Lew, A. M., Samuels, B., & Chatman, J. (2007). Medicare's search for effective obesity treatments. *American Psychologist, 62*, 220–233.

Manson, J. E., Skerrett, P. J., & Willett, W. C. (2002). Epidemiology of health risks associated with obesity. In C. G. Fairburn & K. D. Brownell (Eds.), *Eating disorders and obesity: A comprehensive handbook* (pp. 422–428). New York: Guilford.

Mantovani, A., & Lisanby, S. H. (2007). Transcranial magnetic stimulation in major depression. In M. S. George & R. H. Belmaker (Eds.), *Transcranial magnetic stimulation in clinical psychiatry* (pp. 113–152). Washington, DC: American Psychiatric Publishing.

Maratsos, M. P. (2007). Commentary. *Monographs of the Society for Research in Child Development, 72*, 121–126.

Marcelino, A. S., Adam, A. S., Couronne, T., Koester, E. P., & Sieffermann, J. M. (2001). Internal and external determinants of eating initiation in humans. *Appetite, 36,* 9–14.

Marcenes, W. G., & Sheiham, A. (1992). The relationship between work stress and oral health status. *Social Science and Medicine, 35,* 1511.

Marcia, J. E. (1966). Development and validation of ego identity status. *Journal of Personality and Social Psychology, 3,* 551–558.

Marcia, J. E. (1980). Identity in adolescence. In J. Adelson (Ed.), *Handbook of adolescent psychology.* New York: Wiley.

Marcia, J. E. (1994). The empirical study of ego identity. In H. A. Bosma, T. L. G. Graafsma, H. D. Grotevant, & D. J. de Levita (Eds.), *Identity and development: An interdisciplinary approach.* Thousand Oaks, CA: Sage.

Marcus, G. F. (1996). Why do children say "breaked"? *Current Directions in Psychological Science, 5,* 81–85.

Marcus-Newhall, A., Pedersen, W. C., Carlson, M., & Miller, N. (2000). Displaced aggression is alive and well: A meta-analytic review. *Journal of Personality and Social Psychology, 78,* 670–689.

Marder, S. R., & van Kammen, D. P. (2005). Dopamine receptor antagonists (typical antipsychotics). In B. J. Sadock & V. A. Sadock (Eds.), *Kaplan and Sadock's comprehensive textbook of psychiatry* (pp. 2817–2838). Philadelphia: Lippincott Williams & Wilkins.

Maris, R. W., Berman, A. L., & Silverman, M. M. (2000). *Comprehensive textbook of suicidology.* New York: Guilford.

Mark, V. (1996). Conflicting communicative behavior in a split-brain patient: Support for dual consciousness. In S. R. Hameroff, A. W. Kaszniak, & A. C. Scott (Eds.), *Toward a science of consciousness. The first Tucson discussions and debates.* Cambridge, MA: MIT Press.

Markman, E. M., Wasow, J. L., & Hansen, M. B. (2003). Use of the mutual exclusivity assumption by young word learners. *Cognitive Psycology, 47,* 241–275.

Markowitsch, H. J. (2000). Neuroanatomy of memory. In E. Tulving & F. I. M. Craik (Eds.), *The Oxford handbook of memory* (pp. 465–484). New York: Oxford University Press.

Marks, G. A. (2006). The neurobiology of sleep. In T. Lee-Chiong (Ed.), *Sleep: A comprehensive handbook.* Hoboken, NJ: Wiley-Liss.

Marks, I. M. (2004). The Nobel prize award in physiology to Ivan Petrovich Pavlov. *Australian and New Zealand Journal of Psychiatry, 38*(9), 674–677.

Markus, H. R., & Hamedani, M. G. (2007). Sociocultural psychology: The dynamic interdependence among self systems and social systems. In S. Kitayama & D. Cohen (Eds.), *Handbook of cultural psychology* (pp. 3–39). New York: Guilford.

Markus, H. R., & Kitayama, S. (1991). Culture and the self: Implications for cognition, emotion, and motivation. *Psychological Review, 98,* 224–253.

Markus, H. R., & Kitayama, S. (1994). The cultural construction of self and emotion: Implications for social behavior. In S. Kitayama & H. R. Markus (Eds.), *Emotions and culture: Empirical studies of mutual influence.* Washington, DC: American Psychological Association.

Markus, H. R., & Kitayama, S. (2003). Culture, self, and the reality of the social. *Psychological Inquiry, 14*(3–4), 277–283.

Markus, H. R., Kitayama, S., & Heiman, R. J. (1996). Culture and "basic" psychological principles. In E. T. Higgins, & A. W. Kruglanski (Eds.), *Social psychology: Handbook of basic principles.* New York: Guilford.

Marschark, M. (1992). Coding processes: Imagery. In L. R. Squire (Ed.), *Encyclopedia of learning and memory.* New York: Macmillan.

Marsella, A. J., & Yamada, A. M. (2007). Culture and psychopathology: Foundations, issues, and directions. In S. Kitayama & D. Cohen (Eds.), *Handbook of cultural psychology.* New York: Guilford.

Marsh, E. J. (2007). Retelling is not the same as recalling: Implications for memory. *Current Directions in Psychological Science, 16*(1), 16–20.

Marsh, E. J., Meade, M. L., & Roediger, H. L. (2003). Learning facts from fiction. *Journal of Memory & Language, 49,* 519–536.

Marsh, E. J., & Tversky, B. (2004). Spinning the stories of our lives. *Applied Cognitive Psychology, 18,* 491–503.

Marshall, G. D. (2007). Cytokines. In G. Fink (Ed.), *Encyclopedia of stress.* San Diego: Elsevier.

Marshall, N. L. (2004). The quality of early child care and children's development. *Current Directions in Psychological Science, 13*(4), 165–168.

Marteau, T. M., & Weinman, J. (2004). Communicating about health threats and treatments. In S. Sutton, A. Baum, & M. Johnston (Ed), *The Sage handbook of health psychology.* Thousand Oaks, CA: Sage.

Martin, C. L., & Ruble, D. (2004). Children's search for gender cues: Cognitive perspectives on gender development. *Current Directions in Psychological Science, 13*(2), 67–70.

Martin, J. H. (1991). The collective electrical behavior of cortical neurons: The electroencephalogram and the mechanisms of epilepsy. In E. R. Kandel, J. H. Schwartz, & T. M. Jessell (Eds.), *Principles of neural science* (3rd ed.). New York: Elsevier Saunders.

Martin, J. N., & Fox, N. A. (2006). Temperament. In K. McCartney & D. Phillips (Eds.), *Blackwell handbook of early childhood development* (pp. 126–146). Malden, MA: Blackwell Publishing.

Martin, L. (1986). "Eskimo words for snow": A case study in the genesis and decay of an anthropological example. *American Psychologist, 88,* 418–423.

Martin, L. R., Friedman, H. S., & Schwartz, J. E. (2007). Personality and mortality risk across the life span: The importance of conscientiousness as a biopsychosocial attribute. *Health Psychology, 26,* 428–436.

Martin, R., & Leventhal, H. (2004). Symptom perception and health care–seeking behavior. In J. M. Raczynski & L. C. Leviton (Eds.), *Handbook of clinical health psychology, Vol. 2: Disorders of behavior and health.* Washington, DC: American Psychological Association.

Martin, R. A. (2002). IS laughter the best medicine? Humor, laughter, and physical health. *Current Directions in Psychological Science, 11*(6), 216–220.

Maslach, C. (2003). Job burnout: New directions in research and intervention. *Current Directions in Psychological Science, 12,* 189–192.

Maslach, C., & Leiter, M. P. (2000). Burnout. In G. Fink (Ed.), *Encyclopedia of stress* (Vol. 1, pp. 358–362). San Diego: Academic Press.

Maslach, C., & Leiter, M. P. (2005). Stress and burnout: The critical research. In C. L. Cooper (Ed.), *Handbook of stress medicine and health.* Boca Raton, FL: CRC Press.

Maslach, C., & Leiter, M. P. (2007). Burnout. In G. Fink (Ed.), *Encyclopedia of stress.* San Diego: Elsevier.

Maslen, R. J. C., Theakston, A. L., Lieven, E. V. M., & Tomasello, M. (2004). A dense corpus study of past tense and plural overregularization in English. *Journal of Speech, Language, & Hearing Research, 47,* 1319–1333.

Maslow, A. H. (1954). *Motivation and personality.* New York: Harper & Row.

Maslow, A. H. (1968). *Toward a psychology of being.* New York: Van Nostrand.

Maslow, A. H. (1970). *Motivation and personality.* New York: Harper & Row.

Massaro, D. W., & Loftus, G. R. (1996). Sensory and perceptual storage: Data and theory. In E. L. Bjork & R. A. Bjork (Eds.), *Memory.* San Diego: Academic Press.

Massen, C., & Vaterrodt-Plünnecke, B. (2006). The role of proactive interference in mnemonic techniques. *Memory, 14,* 189–196.

Masters, W. H., & Johnson, V. E. (1966). *Human sexual response.* Boston: Little, Brown.

Masters, W. H., & Johnson, V. E. (1970). *Human sexual inadequacy.* Boston: Little, Brown.

Mastro, D. E., Behm-Morawitz, E., & Kopacz, M. A. (2008). Exposure to television portrayals of Latinos: The implications of aversive racism and social identity theory. *Human Communication Research, 34,* 1–27.

Masuda, T., & Nisbett, R. E. (2001). Attending holistically versus analytically: Comparing the context sensitivity of Japanese and Americans. *Journal of Personality and Social Psychology, 81,* 922–934.

Mathy, R. M., Schillace, M., Coleman, S. M., & Berquist, B. E. (2002). Methodological rigor with Internet samples: New ways to reach underrepresented populations. *Cyber-Psychology and Behavior, 5,* 253–266.

Matlin, M. W. (2008). *The psychology of women.* Belmont, CA: Wadsworth.

Matsumoto, D. (1994). *People: Psychology from a cultural perspective.* Pacific Grove, CA: Brooks/Cole.

Matsumoto, D. (2001). Culture and emotion. In D. Matsumoto (Ed.), *The handbook of culture and psychology* (pp. 171–194). New York: Oxford University Press.

Matsumoto, D. (2003). Cross-cultural research. In S. F. Davis (Ed.), *Handbook of research methods in experimental psychology.* Malden, MA: Blackwell Publishers.

Matsumoto, D., & Juang, L. (2008). *Culture and psychology.* Belmont, CA: Wadsworth.

Matsumoto, D., Nezlek, J. B., & Koopmann, B. (2007). Evidence for universality in phenomenological emotion response system coherence. *Emotion, 7,* 57–67.

Matsumoto, D., & Willingham, B. (2006). The thrill of victory and the agony of defeat: Spontaneous expressions of medal winners of the 2004 Athens Olympic games. *Journal of Personality and Social Psychology, 91,* 568–581.

Matsumoto, D., & Yoo, S. (2006). Toward a new generation of cross-cultural research. *Perspectives on Psychological Science, 1,* 234–250.

Matthews, G., Emo, A. K., Roberts, R. D., & Zeidner, M. (2006). What is this thing called emotional intelligence? In K. R. Murphy (Ed.), *A critique of emotional intelligence: What are the problems and how can they be fixed?* (pp. 3–36). Mahwah, NJ: Erlbaum.

Matthey, S. (1998). P.<05—But it is clinically *significant?*: Practical examples for clinicians. *Behaviour Change, 15,* 140–146.

Mattia, J. I., & Zimmerman, M. (2001). Epidemiology. In W. J. Livesley (Ed.), *Handbook of personality disorders: Theory, research, and treatment.* New York: Guilford.

Matusov, E., & Hayes, R. (2000). Sociocultural critique of Piaget and Vygotsky. *New Ideas in Psychology, 18*(2–3), 215–239.

Mauro, R., Sato, K., & Tucker, J. (1992). The role of appraisal in human emotions: A cross-cultural study. *Journal of Personality and Social Psychology, 62,* 301–317.

Mayer, J. (1955). Regulation of energy intake and the body weight: The glucostatic theory and the lipostatic hypothesis. *Annals of the New York Academy of Science, 63,* 15–43.

Mayer, J. (1968). *Overweight: Causes and control.* Englewood Cliffs, NJ: Prentice-Hall.

Mayer, J. D., Perkins, D. M., Caruso, D. R., & Salovey, P. (2001). Emotional intelligence and giftedness. *Roeper Review, 23,* 131–137.

Mayer, J. D., Salovey, P., & Caruso, D. (2002). *Mayer-Salovey-Caruso Emotional Intelligence Test (MSCEIT): User's manual.* Toronto: Multi-Health Systems.

Mayou, R., Kirmayer, L. J., Simon, G., Kroenke, K., & Sharpe, M. (2005). Somatoform disorders: Time for a new approach in DSM-V. *American Journal of Psychiatry, 162,* 847–855.

Mays, V. M., Rubin, J., Sabourin, M., & Walker, L. (1996). Moving toward a global psychology: Changing theories and practice to meet the needs of a changing world. *American Psychologist, 51,* 485–487.

Mazzoni, G., & Lynn, S. J. (2007). Using hypnosis in eyewitness memory: Past and current issues. In M. P. Toglia, J. D. Read, D. F. Ross, & R. C. L. Lindsay (Eds.), *Handbook of eyewitness psychology: Volume 1. Memory for events.* Mahwah, NJ: Erlbaum.

McAnarney, E. R. (2008). Adolescent brain development: Forging new links? *Journal of Adolescent Health, 42*(4), 321–323.

McBride-Chang, C., & Jacklin, C. N. (1993). Early play arousal, sex-typed play, and activity level as precursors to later rough-and-tumble play. *Early Education & Development, 4,* 99–108.

McBurney, D. H. (1996). *How to think like a psychologist: Critical thinking in psychology.* Upper Saddle River, NJ: Prentice-Hall.

McBurney, D. H., Zapp, D. J., & Streeter. S. A. (2005). Preferred number of sexual partners: Tails of distributions and tales of mating systems. *Evolution and Human Behavior, 26,* 271–278.

McCarley, R. W. (1994). Dreams and the biology of sleep. In M. H. Kryger, T. Roth, & W. C. Dement (Eds.), *Principles and practice of sleep medicine* (2nd ed.). Philadelphia: Saunders.

McCarty, R. (2007). Fight-or-flight response. In G. Fink (Ed.), *Encyclopedia of stress.* San Diego: Elsevier.

McCauley, M. E., Eskes, G., & Moscovitch, M. (1996). The effect of imagery on explicit and implicit tests of memory in young and old people: A double dissociation. *Canadian Journal of Experimental Psychology, 50,* 34–41.

McClelland, D. C. (1975). *Power: The inner experience.* New York: Irvington.

McClelland, D. C. (1985). How motives, skills and values determine what people do. *American Psychologist, 40,* 812–825.

McClelland, D. C. (1987). Characteristics of successful entrepreneurs. *Journal of Creative Behavior, 3,* 219–233.

McClelland, D. C., Atkinson, J. W., Clark, R. A., & Lowell, E. L. (1953). *The achievement motive.* New York: Appleton-Century-Crofts.

McClelland, D. C., & Boyatzis, R. E. (1982). The leadership motive pattern and long-term success in management. *Journal of Applied Psychology, 67,* 737–743.

McClelland, D. C., & Koestner, R. (1992). The achievement motive. In C. P. Smith (Ed.), *Motivation and personality: Handbook of thematic content analysis.* New York: Cambridge University Press.

McClelland, J. L. (1992). Parallel-distributed processing models of memory. In L. R. Squire (Ed.), *Encyclopedia of learning and memory.* New York: Macmillan.

McClelland, J. L. (2000). Connectionist models of memory. In E. Tulving & F. I. M. Craik (Eds.), *The Oxford handbook of memory* (pp. 583–596). New York: Oxford University Press.

McClelland, J. L., & Rogers, T. T. (2003). The parallel distributed processing approach to semantic cognition. *Nature Reviews Neuroscience, 4,* 310–322.

McClelland, J. L., & Rumelhart, D. E. (1985). Distributed memory and the representation of general and specific information. *Journal of Experimental Psychology: General, 114,* 159–188.

McConkey, K. M. (1992). The effects of hypnotic procedures on remembering: The experimental findings and their implications for forensic hypnosis. In E. Fromm & M. R. Nash (Eds.), *Contemporary hypnosis research.* New York: Guilford.

McConnell, J. V. (1962). Memory transfer through cannibalism in planarians. *Journal of Neuropsychiatry, 3*(Suppl. 1), 542–548.

McConnell, J. V., Cutler, R. L., & McNeil, E. B. (1958). Subliminal stimulation: An overview. *American Psychologist, 13,* 229–242.

McCord, J. (2005). Unintended consequences of punishment. In M. Donnelly & M. A. Straus (Eds.), *Corporal punishment of children in theoretical perspective* (pp. 165–169). New Haven, CT: Yale University Press.

McCrae, R. R. (1984). Situational determinants of coping responses: Loss, threat and challenge. *Journal of Personality and Social Psychology, 46,* 919–928.

McCrae, R. R. (1996). Social consequences of experimental openness. *Psychological Bulletin, 120,* 323–337.

McCrae, R. R. (2005). Personality structure. In V. A. Derlega, B. A. Winstead, & W. H. Jones (Eds.), *Personality: Contemporary theory and research.* Belmont, CA: Wadsworth.

McCrae, R. R., & Costa, P. T., Jr. (1985). Updating Norman's "adequate taxonomy": Intelligence and personality dimensions in natural language and in questionnaires. *Journal of Personality and Social Psychology, 49,* 710–721.

McCrae, R. R., & Costa, P. T., Jr. (1987). Validation of the five-factor model of personality across instruments and observers. *Journal of Personality and Social Psychology, 52,* 81–90.

McCrae, R. R., & Costa, P. T., Jr. (1997). Personality trait structure as a human universal. *American Psychologist, 52,* 509–516.

McCrae, R. R., & Costa, P. T., Jr. (1999). A five-factor theory of personality. In L. A. Pervin & O. P. John (Eds.), *Handbook of personality: Theory and research.* New York: Guilford.

McCrae, R. R., & Costa, P. T., Jr. (2003). *Personality in adulthood: A five-factor theory perspective.* New York: Guilford.

McCrae, R. R., & Costa, P. T., Jr. (2004). A contemplated revision of the NEO five-factor inventory. *Personality and Individual Differences, 36,* 587–596.

McCrae, R. R., & Costa, P. T., Jr. (2007). Brief versions of the NEO-PI-3. *Journal of Individual Differences, 28,* 116–128.

McCrae, R. R., & Terracciano, A. (2006). National character and personality. *Current Directions in Psychological Science, 15,* 156–161.

McCrae, R. R., & Terracciano, A., & Personality Profiles of Cultures Project. (2005a). Personality profiles of cultures: Aggregate personality traits. *Journal of Personality and Social Psychology, 89,* 407–425.

McCrae, R. R., Terracciano, A., & 78 members of the Personality Profiles of Cultures Project. (2005b). Universal features of personality traits from the observer's perspective: Data from 50 cultures. *Journal of Personality and Social Psychology, 88,* 547–561.

McCrink, K., & Wynn, K. (2004). Large-number addition and subtraction by 9-month-old infants. *Psychological Science, 15,* 776–781.

McCrory, C., & Cooper, C. (2007). Overlap between visual inspection time tasks and general intelligence. *Learning and Individual Differences, 17,* 187–192.

McCullough, M. E. (2001). Forgiving. In C. R. Snyder (Ed.), *Coping with stress: Effective people and processes* (pp. 93–113). New York: Oxford University Press.

McCullough, M. E., Bellah, C. G., Kilpatrick, S. D., & Johnson, J. L. (2001). Vengefulness: Relationships with forgiveness, rumination, well-being, and the Big Five. *Personality and Social Psychology Bulletin, 27,* 601–610.

McCullough, M. E., & Witvliet, C. V. (2002). The psychology of forgiveness. In C. R. Synder & S. J. Lopez (Eds.), *Handbook of positive psychology.* New York: Oxford University Press.

McDaniel, M. A. (2005). Big-brained people are smarter: A meta-analysis of the relationship between *in vivo* brain volume and intelligence. *Intelligence, 33,* 337–346.

McDaniel, M. A., & Einstein, G. O. (1986). Bizarre imagery as an effective memory aid: The importance of distinctiveness. *Journal of Experimental Psychology: Learning, Memory & Cognition, 12,* 54–65.

McDaniel, M. A., & Einstein, G. O. (2007). *Prospective memory: An overview and synthesis of an emerging field.* Thousand Oaks, CA: Sage.

McDaniel, M. A., Einstein, G. O., Stout, A. C., & Morgan, Z. (2003). Aging and maintaining intentions over delays: Do it or lose it. *Psychology and Aging, 18,* 823–835.

McDaniel, M. A., Waddill, P. J., & Shakesby, P. S. (1996). Study strategies, interest, and learning from text: The application of material-appropriate processing. In D. J. Herrmann, C. McEvoy, C. Hertzog, P. Hertel, & M. K. Johnson (Eds.), *Basic and applied memory research: Theory in context* (Vol. 1). Mahwah, NJ: Erlbaum.

McDaniel, M. A., Whetzel, D. L., Schmidt, F. L., & Maurer, S. D. (1994). The validity of employment interviews: A comprehensive review and meta-analysis. *Journal of Applied Psychology, 79,* 599–616.

McDermott, K. B. (2007). Inducing false memories through associated lists: A window onto everyday false memories? In J. S. Nairne (Ed.), *The foundations of remembering: Essays in honor of Henry L. Roediger III.* New York: Psychology Press.

McDonald, C., & Murphy, K. C. (2003). The new genetics of schizophrenia. *Psychiatric Clinics of North America, 26*(1), 41–63.

McDonald, R. V., & Siegel, S. (2004). Intraadministration associations and withdrawal symptoms: Morphine-elicited morphine withdrawal. *Experimental & Clinical Psychopharmacology, 12*(1), 3–11.

McDonald, W. M., Thompson, T. R., McCall W. V., & Zormuski, C. F. (2004). Electroconvulsive therapy. In A. F. Schatzberg & C. B. Nemeroff (Eds.), *Textbook of psychopharmacology.* Washington, DC: American Psychiatric Publishing.

McEwen, B. S. (2004). How sex and stress hormones regulate the structural and functional plasticity of hippocampus. In M. S. Gazzaniga (Ed.), *The cognitive neurosciences* (pp. 171–182). Cambridge, MA: MIT Press.

McFarland, L. A. (2005). The career column: I-O psychologists in the Department of Homeland Security. *The Industrial-Organizational Psychologist, 42*(3), 49–54.

McGaugh, J. L. (2002). The amygdala regulates memory consolidation. In L. R. Squire & D. L. Schacter (Eds.), *Neuropsychology of memory.* New York: Guilford.

McGaugh, J. L. (2004). The amygdala modulates the consolidation of memories of emotionally arousing experiences. *Annual Review of Neuroscience, 27,* 1–28.

McGaugh, J. L., & Roozendaal, B. (2002). Role of adrenal stress hormones in forming lasting memories in the brain. *Current Opinions in Neurobiology, 12,* 205–210.

McGeoch, J. A., & McDonald, W. T. (1931). Meaningful relation and retroactive inhibition. *American Journal of Psychology, 43,* 579–588.

McGlashan, T. H., & Fenton, W. S. (1992). The positive-negative distinction in schizophrenia: Review of natural history validators. *Archives of General Psychiatry, 49,* 63–72.

McGrath, J. E. (1966). *Small group research.* New York: Holt, Rinehart, & Winston.

McGraw, K. O., Tew, M. D., & Williams, J. E. (2000). The integrity of web-delivered experiments: Can you trust the data? *Psychological Science, 11,* 502–506.

McGregor, H. A., Lieberman, J. D., Greenberg, J., Solomon, S., Arndt, J., Simon, L., & Pyszczynski, T. (1998). Terror management and aggression: Evidence that mortality salience motivates aggression against worldview-threatening others. *Journal of Personality and Social Psychology, 74,* 590–605.

McGrew, J. H., Wright, E. R., Pescosolido, B. A., & McDonel, E. C. (1999). The closing of Central State Hospital: Long-term outcomes for persons with severe mental illness. *Journal of Behavioral Health Services & Research, 26,* 246–261.

McGue, M., Bouchard, T. J., Jr., Iacono, W. G., & Lykken, D. T. (1993). Behavioral genetics of cognitive ability: A life-span perspective. In R. Plomin & G. E. McClearn (Eds.), *Nature, nurture and psychology.* Washington, DC: American Psychological Association.

McGuigan, F. J., & Lehrer, P. M. (2007). Progressive relaxation: Origins, principles, and clinical applications. In P. M. Lehrer, R. L. Woolfolk, & W. E. Sime (Eds.), *Principles and practice of stress management.* New York: Guilford.

McHale, S. M., Crouter, A. C., & Whiteman, S. D. (2003). The family contexts of gender development in childhood and adolescence. *Social Development, 12,* 125–148.

McHugh, P. R. (1995). Dissociative identity disorder as a socially constructed artifact. *Journal of Practical Psychiatry and Behavioral Health, 1,* 158–166.

McHugh, P. R., Lief, H. I., Freyd, P. P., & Fetkewicz, J. M. (2004). From refusal to reconciliation: Family relationships after an accusation based on recovered memories. *Journal of Nervous and Mental Disease, 192,* 525–531.

McKean, K. (1985, June). Decisions, decisions. *Discover,* pp. 22–31.

McKelvie, P., & Low, J. (2002). Listening to Mozart does not improve children's spatial ability: Final curtains for the Mozart effect. *British Journal of Development Psychology, 20,* 241–258.

McKenna, J. J. (1993). Co-sleeping. In M. A. Carskadon (Ed.), *Encyclopedia of sleep and dreaming.* New York: Macmillan.

McKenna, K. Y. A., & Bargh, J. A. (1998). Coming out in the age of the Internet: Identity "demarginalization" through virtual group participation. *Journal of Personality and Social Psychology, 75,* 681–694.

McKenna, K. Y. A., & Bargh, J. A. (2000). Plan 9 from cyberspace: The implications of the Internet for personality and social psychology. *Personality and Social Psychology Review, 4,* 57–75.

McKenna, K. Y. A., Green, A., & Gleason, M. (2002). Relationship formation on the Internet: What's the big attraction? *Journal of Social Issues, 58,* 9–31.

McKenna, K., & Seidman, G. (2005). You, me, and we: Interpersonal processes in electronic groups. In Y. Amichai-Hamburger (Ed.), *The social net: Understanding human behavior in cyberspace* (pp. 191–218). New York: Oxford University Press.

McLay, R. N., Daylo, A. A., & Hammer, P. S. (2006). No effect of lunar cycle on psychiatric admissions or emergency evaluations. *Military Medicine, 171,* 1239–1242.

McLean, D. E., & Link, B. G. (1994). Unraveling complexity: Strategies to refine concepts, measures, and research designs in the study of life events and mental health. In W. R. Avison & I. H. Gotlib (Eds.), *Stress and mental health: Contemporary issues and prospects for the future.* New York: Plenum.

McLellan, A. T., Lewis, D. C., O'Brien, C. P., & Kleber, H. D. (2000). Drug dependence, a chronic mental illness: Implications for treatment, insurance, and outcome evaluation. *Journal of the American Medical Association, 284,* 1689–1695.

McLoughlin, K., & Paquet, M. (2005, December 14). Gambling led Hogan to robbery, lawyer says. *Lehigh University's The Brown and White.* Retrieved March 21, 2006 from http://www.bw.lehigh.edu/story .asp?ID=19313.

McLoyd, V. C. (1998). Socioeconomic disadvantage and child development. *American Psychologist, 53,* 185–204.

McMahon, F. J., & Kassem, L. (2005). Anxiety disorders: Genetics. In B. J. Sadock & V. A. Sadock (Eds.), *Kaplan & Sadock's comprehensive textbook of psychiatry* (pp. 1759–1761). Philadelphia: Lippincott Williams & Wilkins.

McManus, M. A., & Baratta, J. E. (1992). *The relationship of recruiting source to performance and survival.* Paper presented at the annual meeting of the Society for Industrial and Organizational Psychology, Montreal, Canada.

McNally, R. J. (1994). Cognitive bias in panic disorder. *Current Directions in Psychological Science, 3,* 129–132.

McNally, R. J. (1996). *Panic disorder: A critical analysis.* New York: Guilford.

McNally, R. J. (1999). Posttraumatic stress disorder. In T. Millon, P. H. Blaney, & R. D. Davis (Eds.), *Oxford textbook of psychopathology* (pp. 144–165). New York: Oxford University Press.

McNally, R. J. (2003). *Remembering trauma.* Cambridge, MA: Belknap Press/Harvard University Press.

McNally, R. J. (2004). Is traumatic amnesia nothing but psychiatric folklore? *Cognitive Behaviour Therapy, 33*(2), 97–101.

McNally, R. J. (2007). Betrayal trauma theory: A critical appraisal. *Memory, 15,* 280–294.

McNamara, P., Nunn, C., Barton, R., Harris, E., & Capellini, I. (2007). Phylogeny of sleep and dreams. In D. Barrett & P. McNamara (Eds.), *The new science of dreaming.* Westport, CT: Praeger.

McNeil, T. F., Cantor-Graae, E., & Ismail, B. (2000). Obstetrics complications and congenital malformation in schizophrenia. *Brain Research Reviews, 31,* 166–178.

McNulty, J. K., Neff, L. A., & Karney, B. R. (2008). Beyond initial attraction: Physical attractiveness in newlywed marriage. *Journal of Family Psychology, 22*(4), 135–143.

McWhorter, K. T. (2007). *College reading & study skills.* New York: Pearson Longman.

McWilliams, L. A., Becker, E. S., Margraf, J., Clara, I. P., & Vriends, N. (2007). Anxiety disorders specificity of anxiety sensitivity in a community sample of young women. *Personality and Individual Differences, 42,* 345–354.

McWilliams, N., & Weinberger, J. (2003). Psychodynamic psychotherapy. In G. Stricker & T. A. Widiger (Eds.), *Handbook of psychology: Clinical Psychology.* New York: Wiley.

Mechanic, D. (1980). *Mental health and social policy.* Englewood Cliffs, NJ: Prentice-Hall.

Mechanic, D. (1999). Mental health and mental illness. In A. V. Horvitz & T. L. Scheid (Eds.), *A handbook for the study of mental health: Social contexts, theories, and systems.* New York: Cambridge University Press.

Mednick, S. A., Machon, R. A., Huttunen, M. O., & Bonett, D. (1988). Adult schizophrenia following prenatal exposure to an influenza epidemic. *Archives of General Psychiatry, 45,* 189–192.

Mednick, S. A., & Mednick, M. T. (1967). *Examiner's manual, Remote Associates Test.* Boston: Houghton Mifflin.

Mednick, S. A., Watson, J. B., Huttunen, M., Cannon, T. D., Katila, H., Machon, R., et al. (1998). A two-hit working model of the etiology of schizophrenia. In M. F. Lenzenweger & R. H. Dworkin (Eds.), *Origins and developmental psychopathology.* Washington. DC: American Psychological Association.

Mehra, R., Moore, B. A., Crothers, K., Tetrault, J., & Fiellin, D. A. (2006). The association between marijuana smoking and lung cancer: A systematic review. *Archives of Internal Medicine, 166,* 1359–1367.

Meichenbaum, D. H. (1977). *Cognitive-behavior modification.* New York: Plenum.

Meilman, P. W. (1979). Cross-sectional age changes in ego identity status during adolescence. *Developmental Psychology, 15,* 230–231.

Meiser, T., & Klauer, K. C. (1999). Working memory and changing-state hypothesis. *Journal of Experimental Psychology: Learning, Memory, & Cognition, 25,* 1272–1299.

Meister, B. (2007). Neurotransmitters in key neurons of the hypothalamus that regulate feeding behavior and body weight. *Physiology & Behavior, 92,* 263–271.

Melanson, K. J. (2007). Dietary factors in reducing risk of cardiovascular diseases. *American Journal of Lifestyle Medicine, 1*(1), 24–28.

Mellers, B., Hertwig, R., & Kahneman, D. (2001). Do frequency representations eliminate conjunction effects? An exercise in adversarial collaboration. *Psychological Science, 12,* 269–275.

Mello, J. A. (1993). Improving individual member accountability in small group settings. *Journal of Management Education, 17,* 253–259.

Mellor, D. (2003). Contemporary racism in Australia: The experiences of Aborigines. *Personality and Social Psychology Bulletin, 29,* 474–486.

Meltzer, H. Y., Davidson, M., Glassman, A. H., & Vieweg, V. R. (2002). Assessing cardiovascular risks versus clinical benefits of atypical antipsychotic drug treatment. *Journal of Clinical Psychiatry, 63*(9), 25–29.

Melzack, R., & Wall, P. D. (1965). Pain mechanisms: A new theory. *Science, 150,* 971–979.

Melzack, R., & Wall, P. D. (1982). *The challenge of pain.* New York: Basic Books.

Mendelson, W. B. (2001). Neurotransmitters and sleep. *Journal of Clinical Psychiatry, 62*(suppl 10), 5–8.

Mendelson, W. B. (2005). Hypnotic medications: Mechanisms of action and pharmacologic effects. In M. H. Kryger, T. Roth, & W. C. Dement (Eds.). *Principles and practice of sleep medicine.* Philadelphia: Elsevier Saunders.

Mennella, J. A., & Beauchamp, G. K. (1996). The early development of human flavor preferences. In E. D. Capaldi (Ed.), *Why we eat what we eat: The psychology of eating* (pp. 83–112). Washington, DC: American Psychological Association.

Menninger, W. W. (2005). Role of the psychiatric hospital in the treatment of mental illness. In B. J. Sadock & V. A. Sadock (Eds.), *Kaplan & Sadock's comprehensive textbook of psychiatry.* Philadelphia: Lippincott Williams & Wilkins.

Mentzer, R. L. (1982). Response biases in multiple-choice test item files. *Educational and Psychological Measurement, 42,* 437–448.

Merikangas, K. R. (2005). Anxiety disorders: Epidemiology. In B. J. Sadock & V. A. Sadock (Eds.), *Kaplan & Sadock's comprehensive textbook of psychiatry* (pp. 1720–1727). Philadelphia: Lippincott Williams & Wilkins.

Merikangas, K. R., Ames, M., Cui, L., Stang, P. E., Ustun, T. B., Von Korff, M., et al. (2007). The impact of comorbidity of mental and physical conditions on role disability in the U.S. adult household population. *Archive of General Psychiatry, 64,* 1180–1188.

Merikangas, K. R., & Risch, N. (2003). Will the genomics revolution revolutionize psychiatry? *American Journal of Psychiatry, 160,* 625–635.

Merikle, P. M. (2000). Subliminal perception. In A. E. Kazdin (Ed.), *Encyclopedia of Psychology* (pp. 497–499). New York: Oxford University Press.

Merikle, P. M. (2007). Preconscious processing. In M. Velmans & S. Schneider (Eds.), *The Blackwell companion to consciousness.* Malden, MA: Blackwell Publishing.

Mesquita, B. (2003). Emotions as dynamic cultural phenomena. In R. J. Davidson, K. R. Scherer, & H. H. Goldsmith (Eds.), *Handbook of affective sciences.* New York: Oxford University Press.

Mesquita, B., & Leu, J. (2007). The cultural psychology of emotion. In S. Kitayama & D. Cohen (Eds.), *Handbook of cultural psychology* (pp. 734–759). New York: Guilford.

Messer, S. B., & McWilliams, N. (2003). The impact of Sigmund Freud and the interpretation of dreams. In R. J. Sternberg (Ed.), *The anatomy of impact: What makes the great works of psychology great* (pp. 71–88). Washington, DC: American Psychological Association.

Metzger, E. D. (1999). Electroconvulsive therapy. In A. M. Nicholi (Ed.), *The Harvard guide to psychiatry.* Cambridge, MA: Harvard University Press.

Meyer, D. E., & Schvaneveldt, R. W. (1976). Meaning, memory structure, and mental processes. *Science, 192,* 27–33.

Meyer, R. E. (1996). The disease called addiction: Emerging evidence in a 200-year debate. *The Lancet, 347,* 162–166.

Meyer, R. G. (1992). *Practical clinical hypnosis: Techniques and applications.* New York: Lexington Books.

Meyer, J. P., & Allen, N. J. (1991). A three-component conceptualization of organizational commitment. *Human Resource Management Review, 1,* 61–89.

Meyer, J. P., & Herscovitch, L. (2001). Commitment in the workplace: Toward a general model. *Human Resource Management Review, 11,* 299–326.

Meyer-Bahlburg, H. F. L., Ehrhardt, A. A., Rosen, L. R., Gruen, R. S., Veridiano, N. P., Vann, F. H., & Neuwalder, H. F. (1995). Prenatal estrogens and the development of homosexual orientation. *Developmental Psychology, 31,* 12–21.

Mezulis, A. H., Abramson, L. Y., Hyde, J. S., & Hankin, B. L. (2004). Is there a universal positivity bias in attributions? A meta-analytic review of individual, developmental and cultural differences in the self-serving attributional bias. *Psychological Bulletin, 130,* 711–747.

Mezzich, J. E., Lewis-Fernandez, R., & Ruiperez, M. A. (2003). The cultural framework of psychiatric disorders. In A. Tasman, J. Kay, & J. A. Lieberman (Eds.), *Psychiatry.* New York: Wiley.

Michaels, S. (1996). The prevalance of homosexuality in the United States. In R. P. Cabaj & T. S. Stein (Eds.), *Textbook of homosexuality and mental health.* Washington, DC: American Psychiatric Press.

Mignot, E. (2005). Narcolepsy: Diagnosis and management. In M. H. Kryger, T. Roth, & W. C. Dement (Eds.), *Principles and practice of sleep medicine.* Philadelphia: Elsevier Saunders.

Miklowitz, D. J., & Johnson, S. L. (2007). Bipolar disorders. In M. Hersen, S. M. Turner, & D. C. Beidel (Eds.), *Adult psychopathology and diagnosis.* New York: Wiley.

Mikulincer, M. (2006). Attachment, caregiving, and sex within romantic relationships: A behavioral systems perspective. In M. Mikulincer & G. S. Goodman (Eds.), *Dynamics of romantic love: Attachment, caregiving, and sex.* New York: Guilford.

Mikulincer, M., & Shaver, P. R. (2005). Attachment security, compassion, and altruism. *Current Directions in Psychological Science, 14*(1), 34–38.

Mikulincer, M., & Shaver, P. R. (2007). *Attachment in adulthood: Structure, dynamics, and change.* New York: Guilford.

Milar, K. S. (2000). The first generation of women psychologists and the psychology of women. *American Psychologist, 55,* 616–619.

Milgram, S. (1963). Behavioral study of obedience. *Journal of Abnormal and Social Psychology, 67,* 371–378.

Milgram, S. (1964). Issues in the study of obedience. *American Psychologist, 19,* 848–852.

Milgram, S. (1968). Reply to the critics. *International Journal of Psychiatry, 6,* 294–295.

Milgram, S. (1974). *Obedience to authority.* New York: Harper & Row.

Miller, A. G. (1986). *The obedience experiments: A case study of controversy in social science.* New York: Praeger.

Miller, E. K., & Cohen, J. D. (2001). An integrative theory of prefrontal cortex fuction. *Annual Review of Neuroscience, 24,* 167–202.

Miller, G., Tybur, J. M., & Jordan, B. D. (2007). Ovulatory cycle effects on tip earnings by lap dancers: Economic evidence for human estrus? *Evolution and Human Behavior, 28,* 375–381.

Miller, G. A. (1956). The magical number seven, plus or minus two: Some limits on our capacity for processing information. *Psychological Review, 63,* 81–97.

Miller, G. A. (2003). The cognitive revolution: A historical perspective. *Trends in Cognitive Sciences, 7*(3), 141–144.

Miller, G. E., & Blackwell, E. (2006). Turning up the heat: Inflammation as a mechanism linking chronic stress, depression, and heart disease. *Current Directions in Psychological Science, 15,* 269–272.

Miller, G. E., Chen, E., & Zhou, E. S. (2007). If it goes up, must it come down? Chronic stress and the hypothalamic-pituitary-adrenocortical axis in humans. *Psychological Bulletin, 133,* 25–45.

Miller, G. E., & Wrosch, C. (2007). You've gotta know when to fold 'em: Goal disengagement and systemic inflammation in adolescence. *Psychological Science, 18,* 773–777.

Miller, I. J. (1996). Managed care is harmful to outpatient mental health services: A call for accountability. *Professional Psychology: Research and Practice, 27,* 349–363.

Miller, I. J., & Reedy, F. E. Jr. (1990). Variations in human taste-bud density and taste intensity perception. *Physiological Behavior, 47,* 1213–1219.

Miller, J. G. (2006). Insights into moral development from cultural psychology. In M. Killen & J. G. Smetana (Eds.), *Handbook of moral development.* Mahwah, NJ: Erlbaum.

Miller, J. M., & Peterson, D. A. M. (2004). Theoretical and empirical implications of attitude strength. *Journal of Politics, 66,* 847–867.

Miller, N. E. (1941). The frustration-aggression hypothesis. *Psychological Review, 48,* 337–342.

Miller, N. E. (1944). Experimental studies of conflict. In J. M. Hunt (Ed.), *Personality and the behavior disorders* (Vol. 1). New York: Ronald.

Miller, N. E. (1959). Liberalization of basic S-R concepts: Extension to conflict behavior, motivation, and social learning. In S. Koch (Ed.), *Psychology: A study of a science* (Vol. 2). New York: McGraw-Hill.

Miller, N. E. (1985). The value of behavioral research on animals. *American Psychologist, 40,* 423–440.

Miller, P. J., Niehuis, S., & Huston, T. L. (2006). Positive illusions in marital relationships: A 13-year longitudinal study. *Personality and Social Psychology Bulletin, 32,* 1579–1594.

Miller, R. R., & Grace, R. C. (2003). Conditioning and learning. In A. F. Healy & R. W. Proctor (Eds.), *Handbook of psychology, Vol. 4: Experimental psychology.* New York: Wiley.

Millman, J., Bishop, C. H., & Ebel, R. (1965). An analysis of test-wiseness. *Educational and Psychological Measurement, 25,* 707–726.

Millon, T. (1981). *Disorders of personality: DSM-III, axis II.* New York: Wiley.

Millstone, E. (1989). Methods and practices of animal experimentation. In G. Langley (Ed.), *Animal experimentation: The consensus changes*. New York: Chapman & Hall.

Milner, B., Corkin, S., & Teuber, H. (1968). Further analysis of the hippocampal amnesic syndrome: 14-year follow-up study of H. M. *Neuropsychologia, 6,* 215–234.

Mineka, S., & Öhman, A. (2002). Phobias and preparedness: The selective, automatic and encapsulated nature of fear. *Biological Psychiatry, 52,* 927–937.

Mineka, S., & Zinbarg, R. E. (2006). A contemporary learning theory perspective on the etiology of anxiety disorders: It's not what you thought it was. *American Psychologist, 61,* 10–26.

Minton, H. L. (2000). Lewis Madison Terman. In A. E. Kazdin (Ed.), *Encyclopedia of psychology* (pp. 37–39). Washington, DC: American Psychological Association.

Miranda, J., Bernal, G., Lau, A., Kohn, L., Hwang, W., & LaFromboise, T. (2005). State of the science on psychosocial interventions for ethnic minorities. *Annual Review of Clinical Psychology, 1,* 113–42.

Mirescu, C., & Gould, E. (2006). Stress and adult neurogenesis. *Hippocampus, 16,* 233–238.

Mischel, W. (1961). Delay of gratification, need for achievement, and acquiescence in another culture. *Journal of Abnormal and Social Psychology, 62,* 543–552.

Mischel, W. (1973). Toward a cognitive social learning conceptualization of personality. *Psychological Review, 80,* 252–283.

Mischel, W. (1984). Convergences and challenges in the search for consistency. *American Psychologist, 39,* 351–364.

Misra, R., & Castillo, L. G. (2004). Academic stress among college students: Comparison of American and international students. *International Journal of Stress Management, 11,* 132–148.

Mitchell, K. J., & Johnson, M. K. (2000). Source monitoring: Attributing mental experiences. In E. Tulving & F. I. M. Craik (Eds.), *The Oxford handbook of memory* (pp. 179–196). New York: Oxford University Press.

Mitsonis, C., Zervas, I., Potagas, K., Mandellos, D., Koutsis, G., & Sfagos, K. (2006). The role of stress in multiple sclerosis: Three case reports and review of the literature. *Psychiatriki, 17,* 325–342.

Miyamoto, S., Lieberman, J. A., Fleishhacker, W. W., Aoba, A., & Marder, S. R. (2003). Antipsychotic drugs. In A. Tasman, J. Kay, & J. A. Lieberman (Eds.), *Psychiatry*. New York: Wiley.

Miyamoto, Y., Nisbett, R. E., & Masuda, T. (2006). Culture and the physical environment: Holistic versus analytic perceptual affordances. *Psychological Science, 17,* 113–119.

Mobeley, W. H., Horner, S. O., & Hollingsworth, A. T. (1978). An evaluation of precursors of hospital employee turnover. *Journal of Applied Psychology, 63,* 408–414.

Modestin, J. (1992). Multiple personality disorder in Switzerland. *American Journal of Psychiatry, 149,* 88–92.

Moe, A., & De Bini, R. (2004). Studying passages with the loci method: Are subject-generated more effective than experimenter-supplied loci pathways? *Journal of Mental Imagery, 28*(3–4), 75–86.

Moffitt, T. E. (2005). The new look of behavioral genetics in developmental psychopathology: Gene-environment interplay in antisocial behaviors. *Psychological Bulletin, 131,* 533–554.

Moghaddam, F. M., Taylor, D. M., & Wright, S. C. (1993). *Social psychology in cross-cultural perspective*. New York: W. H. Freeman.

Mojtabai, R., Olfson, M., & Mechanic, D. (2002). Perceived need and help-seeking in adults with mood, anxiety, or substance use disorder. *Archives of General Psychiatry, 59*(1), 77–84.

Mokdad, A. H., Ford, E. S., Bowman, B. A., Dietz, W. H., Vinicor, F., Bales, V. S., & Marks, J. S. (2003). Prevalence of obesity, diabetes, and obesity-related health risk factors, 2001. *Journal of the American Medical Association, 289,* 76–79.

Monaghan, T., & Anderson, R. (1986). *Pizza tiger*. New York: Random House.

Monahan, J. (1997). Major mental disorders and violence to others. In D. M. Stoff, J. Breiling, & J. D. Maser (Eds.), *Handbook of antisocial behavior*. New York: Wiley.

Monahan, J. L., Murphy, S. T., & Zajonc, R. B. (2000). Subliminal mere exposure: Specific, general, and diffuse effects. *Psychological Science, 11,* 462–466.

Monastra, V. J. (2008). Social skills training for children and teens with ADHD: The neuroeducational life skills program. In V. J. Monastra (Ed.), *Unlocking the potential of patients with ADHD: A model for clinical practice*. Washington, DC: American Psychological Association.

Moncrieff, J. (2001). Are antidepressants overrated? A review of methodological problems in antidepressant trials. *Journal of Nervous and Mental Disorders, 189,* 288–295.

Monk, T. H. (2000). Shift work. In M. H. Kryger, T. Roth, & W. C. Dement (Eds.), *Principles and practice of sleep medicine*. Philadelphia: Saunders.

Monk, T. H. (2005). Shift work: Basic principles. In M. H. Kryger, T. Roth, & W. C. Dement (Eds.). *Principles and practice of sleep medicine*. Philadelphia: Elsevier Saunders.

Monk, T. H. (2006). Jet lag. In T. Lee-Chiong (Ed.), *Sleep: A comprehensive handbook*. Hoboken, NJ: Wiley-Liss.

Monroe, S. M. (2008). Modern approaches to conceptualizing and measuring human life stress. *Annual Review of Clinical Psychology, 4,* 33–52.

Monroe, S. M., & Hadjiyannakis, K. (2002). The social environment and depression: Focusing on severe life stress. In I. H. Gotlib & C. L. Hammen (Eds.), *Handbook of depression*. New York: Guilford.

Moore, B. C. J. (2001). Basic auditory processes. In E. B. Goldstein (Ed.), *Blackwell handbook of perception*. Malden, MA: Blackwell.

Moore, J. (2005). Some historical and conceptual background to the development of B. F. Skinner's "Radical Behaviorism." *Journal of Mind and Behavior, 26,* 65–94.

Moore, K. L., & Persaud, T. V. N. (2003). *Before we are born*. Philadelphia: Saunders.

Moore, R. Y. (2006). Biological rythms and sleep. In T. Lee-Chiong (Ed.), *Sleep: A comprehensive handbook*. Hoboken, NJ: Wiley-Liss.

Mora, S., Cook, N., Buring, J. E., Ridker, P. M., & Lee, I. M. (2007). Physical activity and reduced risk of cardiovascular events: Potential mediating mechanisms. *Circulation, 116,* 2110–2118.

Morahan-Martin, J. (2007). Internet use and abuse and psychological problems. In A. N. Joinson, K. Y. A. McKenna, T. Postmes, & U.-D. Reips (Eds.), *The Oxford handbook of Internet psychology*. New York: Guilford.

Morahan-Martin, J., & Schumacher, P. (2000). Incidence and correlates of pathological Internet use among college students. *Computers in Human Behavior, 16*(1), 13–29.

Moran, T. H. (2004). Gut peptides in the control of food intake: 30 years of ideas. *Physiology & Behavior, 82,* 175–180.

Morey, L. C. (1988). Personality disorders in DSM-III and DSM-III-R: Convergence, coverage, and internal consistency. *American Journal of Psychiatry, 145,* 573–577.

Morgan, H. (1996). An analysis of Gardner's theory of multiple intelligence. *Roeper Review, 18,* 263–269.

Morgan, M. J. (2000). Ecstacy (MDMA): A review of its possible persistent psychological effects. *Psychopharmacology, 152,* 230–248.

Moriarity, J. L., Boatman, D., Krauss, G. L., Storm, P. B., & Lenz, F. A. (2001). Human "memories" can be evoked by stimulation of the lateral temporal cortex after ipsilateral medical temporal lobe resection. *Journal of Neurology, Neurosurgery & Psychiatry, 71,* 549–551.

Morin, C. M. (2002). Contributions of cognitive-behavioral approaches to the clinical management of insomnia. *Journal of Clinical Psychiatry, 4* (suppl 1), 21–26.

Morin, C. M. (2005). Psychological and behavioral treatments for primary insomnia. In M. H. Kryger, T. Roth, & W. C. Dement (Eds.), *Principles and practice of sleep medicine*. Philadelphia: Elsevier Saunders.

Morley, J. E., & Perry, H. M. I. (2003). Andropause: An old concept in new clothing. *Clinics in Geriatric Medicine, 19,* 507–528.

Morokoff, P. J., Quina, K., Harlow, L. L., Whitmire, L., Grimley, D. M., Gibson, P. R., & Burkholder, G. J. (1997). Sexual assertivenes scale (SAS) for women: Development and validation. *Journal of Personality and Social Psychology, 73,* 790–804.

Morris, C. D., Bransford, J. D., & Franks, J. J. (1977). Levels of processing versus transfer-appropriate processing. *Journal of Verbal Learning and Verbal Behavior, 16,* 519–533.

Morrison, A. R. (2003). The brain on night shift. *Cerebrum, 5*(3), 23–36.

Morton, A. (1998). *Diana: Her true story. The commemorative edition*. New York: Pocket Books.

Moruzzi, G. (1964). Reticular influences on the EEG. *Electroencephalography and Clinical Neurophysiology, 16,* 2–17.

Moseman, S. E., Freeman, M. P., Misiazek, J., & Gelenberg, A. J. (2003). Mood stabilizers. In A. Tasman, J. Kay, & J. A. Lieberman (Eds.), *Psychiatry*. New York: Wiley.

Mosher, D., & Maclan, P. (1994). College men and women respond to X-rated videos intended for male or female audiences: Gender and sexual scripts. *Journal of Sex Research, 31,* 99–113.

Moss, P. (1994). Validity. In R. J. Sternberg (Ed.), *Encyclopedia of human intelligence*. New York: Macmillan.

Most, S. B., Scholl, B. J., Clifford, E. R., & Simons, D. J. (2005). What you see is what you set: Sustained inattentional blindness and the capture of awareness. *Psychological Review, 112,*217–242.

Most, S. B., Simons, D. J., Scholl, B. J., Jimenez, R., Clifford, E., & Chabris, C. F. (2001). How not to be seen: The contribution of similarity and selective ignoring to sustained inattentional blindness. *Psychological Science, 12*(1), 9–17.

Motivala, S. J., & Irwin, M. R. (2007). Sleep and immunity: Cytokine pathways linking sleep and health outcomes. *Current Directions in Psychological Science, 16,* 21–25.

Mowrer, O. H. (1947). On the dual nature of learning: A reinterpretation of "conditioning" and "problem-solving." *Harvard Educational Review, 17,* 102–150.

Mrdjenovic, G., & Levitsky, D. A. (2005). Children eat what they are served: The imprecise regulation of energy intake. *Appetite, 44,* 273–282.

Mroczek, D. K., & Almeida, D. M. (2004). The effect of daily stress, personality, and age on daily negative effect. *Journal of Personality, 72,* 355–378.

Mullen, B., & Copper, C. (1994). The relation between group cohesiveness and performance: An integration. *Psychological Bulletin, 115,* 210–227.

Muller, M., Aleman, A., Grobbee, D. E., de Haan, E. H., & van der Schouw, Y. T. (2005). Endogenous sex hormone levels and cognitive function in aging men: Is there an optimal level? *Neurology, 64,* 866–871.

Mulligan, N. W. (1998). The role of attention during encoding in implicit and explicit memory. *Journal of Experimental Psychology: Learning, Memory, & Cognition, 24,* 27–47.

Mulvaney, M. K., & Mebert, C. J. (2007). Parental corporal punishment predicts behavior problems in early childhood. *Journal of Family Psychology, 21,* 389–397.

Munck, A. (2007). Corticosteroids and stress. In G. Fink (Ed.), *Encyclopedia of stress.* San Diego: Elsevier.

Munk-Jorgensen, P. (1999). Has deinstitutionalization gone too far? *European Archives of Psychiatry & Clinical Neuroscience, 249*(3), 136–143.

Münzberg, H., & Myers, M. G. Jr. (2005). Molecular and anatomical determinants of central leptin resistance. *Nature Neuroscience, 8,* 566–570.

Murdock, B. (2001). Analysis of the serial position curve. In H. L. Roediger III, J. S. Nairne, I. Neath, & A. M. Surprenant (Eds.), *The nature of remembering: Essays in honor of Robert G. Crowder* (pp. 151–170). Washington, DC: American Psychological Association.

Muris, P. (2002). Relationships between self-efficacy and symptoms of anxiety disorders and depression in a normal adolescent sample. *Personality and Individual Differences, 32,* 337–348.

Muris, P., & Merckelbach, H. (2001). The etiology of childhood specific phobia: A multifactorial model. In M. W. Vasey, & M. R. Dadds (Eds.), *The developmental psychopathology of anxiety.* (pp. 355–385). New York: Oxford University Press.

Murphy, J. M., Tohen, M., & Tsuang, M. T. (1999). Psychiatric epidemiology. In A. M. Nicholi (Ed.), *The Harvard guide to psychiatry.* Cambridge, MA: Harvard University Press.

Murphy, K. R. (2002). Can conflicting perspectives on the role of *g* in personnel selection be resolved? *Human Performance, 15,* 173–186.

Murphy, K. R., & Cleveland, J. N. (1995). *Understanding performance appraisal: Social, organizational, and goal-based perspectives.* Thousand Oaks, CA: Sage.

Murphy K. R., & Sideman, L. (2006a). The fadification of emotional intelligence. In K. R. Murphy (Ed.), *A critique of emotional intelligence: What are the problems and how can they be fixed?* (pp. 283–300). Mahwah, NJ: Erlbaum.

Murphy K. R., & Sideman, L. (2006b). The two EIs. In K. R. Murphy (Ed.), *A critique of emotional intelligence: What are the problems and how can they be fixed?* (pp. 37–58). Mahwah, NJ: Erlbaum.

Murray, E. A. (2007). The amygdala, reward and emotion. *Trends in Cognitive Sciences, 11,* 489–497.

Murray, H. A. (1938). *Explorations in personality.* New York: Oxford University Press.

Murray, H. A. (1943). *Thematic Apperception Test Manual.* Cambridge, MA: Harvard University Press.

Murray, J. B. (1995). Evidence for acupuncture's analgesic effectiveness and proposals for the physiological mechanisms involved. *Journal of Psychology, 129,* 443–461.

Murray, M. M., Foxe, D. M., Javitt, D. C., & Foxe, J. J. (2004). Setting boundaries: Brain dynamics of modal and amodal illusory shape completion in humans. *Journal of Neuroscience, 24,* 6898–6903.

Murray, R. M., & Bramon, E. (2005). Developmental model of schizophrenia. In B. J. Sadock & V. A. Sadock (Eds.), *Kaplan & Sadock's comprehensive textbook of psychiatry* (pp. 1381–1395). Philadelphia: Lippincott Williams & Wilkins.

Murray, R. M., Morrison, P. D., Henquet, C., & Di Forti, M. (2007). Cannabis, the mind and society: The hash realities. *Nature Reviews: Neuroscience, 8,* 885–895.

Murray, S. L. (2001). Seeking a sense of conviction: Motivated cognition in close relationships. In G. J. O. Fletcher & M. S. Clark (Eds.), *Blackwell handbook of social psychology: Interpersonal processes.* Malden, MA: Blackwell.

Murray, S. L., & Holmes, J. G. (1999). The (mental) ties that bind: Cognitive structures that predict relationship resilience. *Journal of Personality and Social Psychology, 77,* 1228–1244.

Murray, S. L., Holmes, J. G., Bellavia, G., Griffin, D. W., & Dolderman, D. (2002). Kindred spirits? The benefits of egocentrism in close relationships. *Journal of Personality and Social Psychology, 82,* 563–581.

Murstein, B. I., & Fontaine, P. A. (1993). The public's knowledge about psychologists and other mental health professionals. *American Psychologist, 48,* 839–845.

Mustanski, B. S., Chivers, M. L., & Bailey, J. M. (2002). A critical review of recent biological research on human sexual orientation. *Annual Review of Sex Research, 12,* 89–140.

Myers, D. G. (1992). *The pursuit of happiness: Who is happy—and why.* New York: Morrow.

Myers, D. G. (1999). Close relationships and quality of life. In D. Kahneman, E. Diener, & N. Schwarz (Eds.), *Well-being: The foundations of hedonic psychology.* New York: Russell Sage Foundation.

Myers, D. G. (2001). Do we fear the right things? *American Psychological Society Observer, 14*(10), 3.

Myers, D. G. (2002). *Intuition: Its powers and perils.* New Haven, CT: Yale University Press.

Myers, D. G. (2008). Religion and human flourishing. In M. Eid & R. J. Larsen (Eds.), *The science of subjective well-being* (pp. 323–346). New York: Guilford.

Myers, D. G., & Diener, E. (1995). Who is happy? *Psychological Science, 6,* 10–19.

Mynatt, C. R., Doherty, M. E., & Tweney, R. D. (1978). Consequences of confirmation and disconfirmation in a simulated research environment. *Quarterly Journal of Experimental Psychology, 30,* 395–406.

Myrtek, M. (2007). Type A behavior and hostility as independent risk factors for coronary heart disease. In J. Jordan, B. Bardé, & A. M. Zeiher (Eds.), *Contributions toward evidence-based psychocardiology: A systematic review of the literature.* Washington, DC: American Psychological Association.

Nabi, H., Singh-Manoux, A., Shipley, M., Gimeno, D., Marmot, M. G., & Kivimaki, M. (2008). Do psychological factors affect inflammation and incident coronary heart disease? The Whitehall II study. *Arteriosclerosis, Thrombosis, and Vascular Biology, 24.* page numbers?1398-1406.

Nadelson, C. C., Notman, M. T., & McCarthy, M. K. (2005). Gender issues in psychotherapy. In G. O. Gabbard, J. S. Beck, & J. Holmes (Eds.), *Oxford textbook of psychotherapy.* New York: Oxford University Press.

Naglieri, J. A., Drasgow, F., Schmit, M., Handler, L., Prifitera, A., Margolis, A., et al. (2004). Psychological testing on the Internet: New problems, old issues. *American Psychologist, 59,* 150–162.

Nahas, Z., George, M. S., Lorberbaum, J. P., Risch, S. C., & Spicer, K. M. (1998). SPECT and PET in neuropsychiatry. *Primary Psychiatry, 5,* 52–59.

Nahas, Z., Kozel, F. A., Molnar, C., Ramsey, D., Holt, R., Ricci, R., et al. (2007). Methods of administering transcranial magnetic stimulation. In M. S. George & R. H. Belmaker (Eds.), *Transcranial magnetic stimulation in clinical psychiatry* (pp. 39–58). Washington, DC: American Psychiatric Publishing.

Nairne, J. S. (1996). Short-term/working memory. In E. L. Bjork & R. A. Bjork (Eds.), *Memory.* San Diego: Academic Press.

Nairne, J. S. (2001). A functional analysis of primary memory. In H. L. I. Roediger III, J. S. Nairne, I. Neath, & A. M. Surprenant (Eds.), *The nature of remembering: Essays in honor of Robert G. Crowder* (pp. 283–296). Washington, DC: American Psychological Association.

Nairne, J. S. (2002). Remembering over the short-term: The case against the standard model. *Annual Review of Psychology, 53,* 53–81.

Nairne, J. S. (2003). Sensory and working memory. In A. F. Healy & R. W. Proctor (Eds.), *Handbook of psychology, Vol. 4: Experimental psychology.* New York: Wiley.

Naish, P. L. N. (2006). Time to explain the nature of hypnosis? *Contemporary Hypnosis, 23,*, 33–46.

Nakajima, S., & Patterson, R. L. (1997). The involvement of dopamine D2 receptors, but not D3 or D4 receptors, in the rewarding effect of brain stimulation in the rat. *Brain Research, 760,* 74–79.

Narrow, W. E., Regier, D. A., Rae, D. S., Manderscheid, R. W., & Locke, B. Z. (1993). Use of services by persons with mental and addictive disorders: Findings from the National Institute of Mental Health Epidemiologic Catchment Area Program. *Archives of General Psychiatry, 50,* 95–107.

Narumoto, J., Okada, T., Sadato, N., Fukui, K., & Yonekura, Y. (2001). Attention to emotion modulates fMRI activity in human right superior temporal sulcus. *Cognitive Brain Research, 12,* 225–231.

Nash, M. R. (2001, July). The truth and hype of hypnosis. *Scientific American, 285,* 36–43.

Näslund, E., & Hellström, P. M. (2007). Appetite signaling: From gut peptides and enteric nerves to brain. *Physiology & Behavior, 92,* 256–262.

Nathan, P. E., & Langenbucher, J. (2003). Diagnosis and classification. In G. Stricker & T. A. Widiger (Eds.), *Handbook of psychology: Clinical psychology.* New York: Wiley.

National Association of Colleges and Employers. (2005). *Summer 2005 salary survey.* Retrieved August 8, 2005, from http://www.naceweb.org/pubs/salsur/salary_by_degree_and_job_function.asp.

National Association of Colleges and Employers. (2008, Spring). *Salary survey: A study of 2007–2008 beginning offers.* Bethlehem, PA: National Association of Colleges and Employers.

Naylor, J. C., Pritchard, R. D., & Ilgen, D. R. (1980). *A theory of behavior in organizations*. New York: Academic Press.

Neisser, U. (1967). *Cognitive psychology*. New York: Appleton-Century-Crofts.

Neisser, U. (1998). Introduction: Rising test scores and what they mean. In U. Neisser (Ed.), *The rising curve: Long-term gains in IQ and related measures*. Washington, DC: American Psychological Association.

Neisser, U., & Harsch, N. (1992). Phantom flashbulbs: False recollections of hearing the news about *Challenger*. In E. Winograd & U. Neisser (Eds.), *Affect and accuracy in recall: Studies of "flashbulb" memories*. New York: Cambridge University Press.

Neisser, U., Boodoo, G., Bouchard, T. J., Jr., Boykin, A. W., Brody, N., Ceci, S. J., Halpern, D. F., Loehlin, J. C., Perloff, R., Sternberg, R. J., & Urbina, S. (1996). Intelligence: Knowns and unknowns. *American Psychologist, 51,* 77–101.

Nelson, C. (2001). The magical number 4 in short-term memory: A reconsideration of mental storage capacity. *Behavioral & Brain Sciences, 24*(1), 87–185.

Nelson, C. A., Bloom, F. E., Cameron, J. L., Amaral, D., Dahl, R. E., & Pine, D. (2002). An integrative, multidisciplinary approach to the study of brain-behavior relations in the context of typical and atypical development. *Development and Psychopathology, 14,* 499–520.

Nemeroff, C. B., Kalali, A., Keller, M. B., Charney, D. S., Lenderts, S. E., Cascade, E. F., et al. (2007). Impact of publicity concerning pediatric suicidality data on physician practice patterns in the United States. *Archives of General Psychiatry, 64,* 466–472.

Nemes, I. (1992). The relationship between pornography and sex crimes. *Journal of Psychiatry and Law, 20,* 459–481.

Nemeth, C., & Chiles, C. (1988). Modelling courage: The role of dissent in fostering independence. *European Journal of Social Psychology, 18,* 275–280.

Nemiah, J. C. (1985). Somatoform disorders. In H. I. Kaplan & B. J. Sadock (Eds.), *Comprehensive textbook of psychiatry* (4th ed.). Baltimore: Williams & Wilkins.

Nes, L. S., & Segerstrom, S. C. (2006). Dispositional optimism and coping: A meta-analytic review. *Personality and Social Psychology Review, 10,* 235–251.

Nesse, R. M., Bhatnagar, S., & Young, E. A. (2007). Evolutionary origins and functions of the stress response. In G. Fink (Ed.), *Encyclopedia of stress*. San Diego: Elsevier.

Nesse, R. M., & Young, E. A. (2000). Evolutionary origins and functions of the stress response. In G. Fink (Ed.), *Encyclopedia of stress* (Vol. 2, pp. 79–83). San Diego: Academic Press.

Nestler, E. J., & Malenka, R. C. (2004). The addicted brain. *Scientific American, 290*(3), 78–85.

Nettelbeck, T. (2003). Inspection time and *g*. In H. Nyborg (Ed.), *The scientific study of general intelligence: Tribute to Arthur R. Jensen*. Oxford, UK: Pergamon.

Nettle, D. (2001). *Strong imagination, madness, creativity, and human nature*. New York: Oxford University Press.

Nettle, D. (2006). The evolution of personality variation in humans and other animals. *American Psychologist, 61,* 622–631.

Neugroschl, J. A., Kolevzon, A., Samuels, S. C., & Marin, D. B. (2005). Dementia. In B. J. Sadock & V. A. Sadock (Eds.), *Kaplan & Sadock's comprehensive textbook of psychiatry* (pp. 1068–1092). Philadelphia: Lippincott Williams & Wilkins.

Neupert, S. D., Almeida, D. M., Mroczek, D. K., & Spiro, A. (2006). Daily stressors and memory failures in a naturalistic setting: Findings from the VA normative aging study. *Psychology and Aging, 21,* 424–429.

Neuschatz, J. S., Lampinen, J. M., Preston, E. L., Hawkins, E. R., & Toglia, M. P. (2002). The effect of memory schemata on memory and the phenomenological experience of naturalistic situations. *Applied Cognitive Psychology, 16,* 687–708.

Neuschatz, J. S., Lampinen, J. M., Toglia, M. P., Payne, D. G., & Cisneros, E. P. (2007). False memory research: History, theory, and applied implications. In M. P. Toglia, J. D. Read, D. F. Ross, & R. C. L. Lindsay (Eds.), *Handbook of eyewitness psychology: Volume 1. Memory for events*. Mahwah, NJ: Erlbaum.

New Freedom Commission on Mental Health. (2003). *Achieving the promise: Transforming mental health care in America*. Rockville, MD: DHHS Pub. No. SMA-03-3831.

Newcombe, N., & Huttenlocher, J. (1992). Children's early ability to solve perspective-taking problems. *Developmental Psychology, 28,* 635–643.

Newell, A., Shaw, J. C., & Simon, H. A. (1958). Elements of a theory of human problem solving. *Psychological Review, 65,* 151–166.

Newell, A., & Simon, H. A. (1972). *Human problem solving*. Englewood Cliffs, NJ: Prentice-Hall.

Newsom, J. T., Mahan, T. L., Rook, K. S., & Krause, N. (2008). Stable negative social exchanges and health. *Health Psychology, 27,* 78–86.

Niccols, A. (2007). Fetal alcohol syndrome and the developing socio-emotional brain. *Brain and Cognition, 65,* 135–142.

NICHD Early Child Care Research Network. (1997). The effects of infant child care on infant-mother attachment security: Results of the NICHD study of early child care. *Child Development, 68,* 860–879.

NICHD Early Child Care Research Network. (2003). Early child care and mother-child interaction from 36 months through first grade. *Infant Behavior and Development, 26,* 345–370.

NICHD Early Child Care Research Network. (2006). Child-care effect sizes for the NICHD study of early child care and youth development. *American Psychologist, 61,* 99–116.

Nickerson, C., Schwarz, N., Diener, E., & Kahneman, D. (2003). Zeroing in on the dark side of the American dream: A closer look at the negative consequences of the goal for financial success. *Psychological Science, 14,* 531–536.

Nickerson, R. S., & Adams, M. J. (1979). Long-term memory for a common object. *Cognitive Psychology, 11,* 287–307.

Nicoladis, E., & Genesee, F. (1997). Language development in preschool bilingual children. *Journal of Speech-Language Pathology & Audiology, 21,* 258–270.

Niebyl, J. R. (2002). Drugs in pregnancy and lactation. In S. G. Gabbe, J. R. Niebyl, & J. L. Simpson (Eds.), *Obstetrics: Normal and problem pregnancies*. New York: Churchill Livingstone.

Nielsen, T. A., & Stenstrom, P. (2005). What are the memory sources of dreaming? *Nature, 437,* 1286–1289.

Nielsen, T. A., & Zadra, A. (2000). Dreaming disorders. In M. H. Kryger, T. Roth, & W. C. Dement (Eds.), *Principles and practice of sleep medicine*. Philadelphia: Saunders.

Nielsen, T. A., Zadra, A. L., Simard, V., Saucier, S., Stenstrom, P., Smith, C., & Kuiken, D. (2003). The typical dreams of Canadian university students. *Dreaming, 13*(4), 211–235.

Nievar, M. A., & Becker, B. J. (2008). Sensitivity as a privileged predictor of attachment: A second perspective on De Wolff and Van IJzendoorn's meta-analysis. *Social Development, 17,* 102–114.

Nikelly, A. G. (1994). Alcoholism: Social as well as psycho-medical problem—The missing "big picture." *Journal of Alcohol & Drug Education, 39,* 1–12.

Nisbett, R. E. (Ed.). (1993). *Rules for reasoning*. Hillsdale, NJ: Erlbaum.

Nisbett, R. E. (2005). Heredity, environment, and race differences in IQ: A commentary on Rushton and Jensen. *Psychology, Public Policy, and the Law, 11,* 302–310.

Nisbett, R. E., & Miyamoto, Y. (2005). The influence of culture: Holistic versus analytic perception. *Trends in Cognitive Sciences, 9,* 467–473.

Nisbett, R. E., Peng, K., Choi, I., & Norenzayan, A. (2001). Culture and systems of thought: Holistic versus analytic cognition. *Psychological Review, 108,* 291–310.

Nist, S. L., & Holschuh, J. L. (2000). Comprehension strategies at the college level. In R. F. Flippo & D. C. Caverly (Eds.), *Handbook of college reading and study strategy research*. Mahwah, NJ: Erlbaum.

Nithianantharajah, J., & Hannan, A. J. (2006). Enriched environments, experience–dependent plasticity and disorders of the nervous system. *Nature Reviews Neuroscience, 7,* 697–709.

Noble, K. G., McCandliss, B. D., & Farah, M. J. (2007). Socioeconomic gradients predict individual differences in neurocognitive abilities. *Developmental Science, 10,* 464–480.

Nobler, M. S., & Sackeim, H. A. (2006). Electroconvulsive therapy and transcranial magnetic stimulation. In D. J. Stein, D. J. Kupfer, & A. F. Schatzberg (Eds.), *Textbook of mood disorders*. Washington, DC: American Psychiatric Publishing.

Noftle, E. E., & Robins, R. W. (2007). Personality predictors of academic outcomes: Big Five correlates of GPA and SAT scores. *Journal of Personality and Social Psychology, 93,* 116–130.

Nolen-Hoeksema, S. (1991). Responses to depression and their effects on the duration of depressive episodes. *Journal of Abnormal Psychology, 100,* 569–582.

Nolen-Hoeksema, S. (1995). Gender differences in coping with depression across the lifespan. *Depression, 3,* 81–90.

Nolen-Hoeksema, S. (2000). The role of rumination in depressive disorders and mixed anxiety/depressive symptoms. *Journal of Abnormal Psychology, 109,* 504–511.

Nolen-Hoeksema, S. (2001). Gender differences in depression. *Current Directions in Psychological Science, 10,* 173–176.

Nomaguchi, K. M., & Milkie, M. A. (2003). Costs and rewards of children: The effects of becoming a parent on adults' lives. *Journal of Marriage and the Family, 65,* 356–374.

Norcross, J. C. (1995). Dispelling the dodo bird verdict and the exclusivity myth in psychotherapy. *Psychotherapy, 32,* 500–504.

Norcross, J. C., Hedges, M., & Castle, P. H. (2002). Psychologists conducting psychotherapy in 2001: A study of the Division 29 membership. *Psychotherapy: Theory, Research, Practice, Training, 39,* 97–102.

Norenzayan, A., & Heine, S. J. (2005). Psychological universals: What are they and how can we know? *Psychological Bulletin, 131,* 763–784.

Norfleet, M. A. (2002). Responding to society's needs: Prescription privileges for psychologists. *Journal of Clinical Psychology, 58,* 599–610.

Norman, D. A. (1988). *The psychology of everyday things.* New York: Basic Books.

Norman, D. A. (2002). *The design of everyday things.* New York: Basic Books.

Norris, F. H., with Byrne, C. M., Diaz, E., & Kaniasty, K. (2001). *Risk factors for adverse outcomes in natural and human-caused disasters: A review of the empirical literature.* Retrieved November 21, 2001 from U.S. Department of Veterans Affairs National Center for PTSD Website: http://www.ncptsd.org/facts/disasters/fs_riskfactors.html.

North, C. S., Eyrich, K. M., Pollio, D. E., & Spitznagel, E. L. (2004). Are rates of psychiatric disorders in the homeless population changing? *American Journal of Public Health, 94*(1), 103–108.

Norton, C. (2005). Animal experiments—A cardinal sin? *The Psychologist, 18*(2), 69.

Novemsky, N., & Kahneman, D. (2005). The boundaries of loss aversion. *Journal of Marketing Research, 42,* 119–128.

Novick, L. R., & Bassok, M. (2005). Problem solving. In K. J. Holyoak & R. G. Morrison (Eds.), *The Cambridge handbook of thinking and reasoning.* New York: Cambridge University Press.

Noyes, R., Jr., Clarkson, C., Crowe, R. R., Yates, W. R., & McChesney, C. M. (1987). A family study of generalized anxiety disorder. *American Journal of Psychiatry, 144,* 1019–1024.

Noyes, R., Jr., Stuart, S. P., Lanbehn, D. R., Happel, R., Longley, S. L., Muller, B. A., & Yagla, S. J. (2003). Test of an interpersonal model of hypochondriasis. *Psychosomatic Medicine, 65,* 292–300.

Noyes, R., Jr., Watson, D. B., Letuchy, E. M., Longley, S. L., Black, D. W., Carney, C. P., & Doebbeling, B. N. (2005). Relationship between hypochondriacal concerns and personality dimensions and traits in a military population. *Journal of Nervous and Mental Disease, 193*(2), 110–118.

Nucci, L. P. (2002). The development of moral reasoning. In U. Goswami (Eds.), *Blackwell handbook of childhood cognitive development.* Malden, MA: Blackwell.

Nunnally, J. C., & Bernstein, I. H. (1994). *Psychometric theory.* New York: McGraw-Hill.

Nyberg, L., Forkstam, C., Petersson, K. M., Cabeza, R., & Ingvar, M. (2002). Brain imaging of human memory systems: Between-systems similarities and within-system differences. *Cognitive Brain Research, 13,* 287–292.

Oakes, M. E., & Slotterback, C. S. (2000). Self-reported measures of appetite in relation to verbal cues about many foods. *Current Psychology: Developmental, Learning, Personality, Social, 19,* 137–142.

Oberauer, K., Süß, H.-M., Wilhelm, O., & Sander, N. (2007). Individual differences in working memory capacity and reasoning ability. In A. R. A. Conway, C. Jarrold, M. J. Kane, A. Miyake, & J. N. Towse (Eds.), *Variation in working memory* (pp. 49–75). New York: Oxford University Press.

O'Brien, C. P., Volkow, N., & Li, T.-K. (2006). What's in a word? Addiction versus dependence in DSM-V. *American Journal of Psychiatry, 163,* 764–765.

O'Callahan, M., Andrews, A. M., & Krantz, D. S. (2003). Coronary heart disease and hypertension. In A. M. Nezu, C. M. Nezu, & P. A. Geller (Eds.), *Handbook of psychology, Vol. 9: Health psychology.* New York: Wiley.

Ochse, R. (1990). *Before the gates of excellence: The determinants of creative genius.* Cambridge, England: Cambridge University Press.

O'Connor, D. B., Jones, F., Ferguson, E., Conner, M., & McMillan, B. (2008). Effects of daily hassles and eating style on eating behavior. *Health Psychology, 27,* S20–S31.

O'Donohue, W. (1998). Conditioning and third-generation behavior therapy. In W. O'Donohue (Ed.), *Learning and behavior therapy.* Boston: Allyn & Bacon.

Ogden, C. L., Carroll, M. D., Curtin, L. R., McDowell, M. A., Tabak, C. J., & Flegal, K. M. (2006). Prevalence of overweight and obesity in the United States, 1999–2004. *Journal of the American Medical Association, 195,* 1549–1555.

Ohayon, M. M., Carskadon, M. A., Guilleminault, C., & Vitiello, M. V. (2004). Meta-analysis of quantitative sleep parameters from childhood to old age in healthy individuals: Developing normative sleep values across the human lifespan. *Sleep: Journal of Sleep & Sleep Disorders Research, 27,* 1255–1273.

Ohayon, M. M., & Guilleminault, C. (2006). Epidemiology of sleep disorders. In T. Lee-Chiong (Ed.), *Sleep: A comprehensive handbook.* Hoboken, NJ: Wiley-Liss.

Öhman, A. (1979). Fear relevance, autonomic conditioning, and phobias: A laboratory model. In P-O Sjödén, S. Bates & W. S. Dockens III (Eds.), *Trends in behavior therapy* (pp. 107–134). New York: Academic Press.

Öhman, A., Dimberg, U., & Öst, L.-G. (1985). Animal and social phobias: Biological constraints on learned fear responses. In S. Reiss, & R. R. Bootzin (Eds.), *Theoretical issues in behavior therapy* (pp. 123–178). New York: Academic Press.

Öhman, A., & Mineka, S. (2001). Fears, phobias, and preparedness: Toward an evolved module of fear and fear learning. *Psychological Review, 108,* 483–522.

Öhman, A., & Mineka, S. (2003). The malicious serpent: Snakes as a prototypical stimulus for an evolved module of fear. *Current Directions in Psychological Science, 12,* 5–9.

Öhman, A., & Wiens, S. (2003). On the automaticity of autonomic responses in emotion: An evolutionary perspective. In R. J. Davidson, K. R. Scherer, & H. H. Goldsmith (Eds.), *Handbook of affective sciences.* New York: Oxford University Press.

Okami, P., & Shackelford, T. K. (2001). Human sex differences in sexual psychology and behavior. *Annual Review of Sex Research, 12,* 186–241.

Olds, J. (1956). Pleasure centers in the brain. *Scientific American, 193,* 105–116.

Olds, J., & Milner, P. (1954). Positive reinforcement produced by electrical stimulation of the septal area and other regions of the rat brain. *Journal of Comparative and Physiological Psychology, 47,* 419–427.

Olds, M. E., & Fobes, J. L. (1981). The central basis of motivation: Intracranial self-stimulation studies. *Annual Review of Psychology, 32,* 523–574.

O'Leary, K. D., Kent, R. N., & Kanowitz, J. (1975). Shaping data collection congruent with experimental hypotheses. *Journal of Applied Behavior Analysis, 8,* 43–51.

Olfson, M., Marcus, S. C., Druss, B. , & Pincus, H. A. (2002). National trends in the use of outpatient psychotherapy. *American Journal of Psychiatry, 159,* 1914–1920.

Olfson, M., Shaffer, D., Marcus, S. C., & Greenberg, T. (2003). Relationship between antidepressant medication treatment and suicide in adolescents. *Archives of General Psychiatry, 60,* 978–982.

Olio, K. (1994). Truth in memory. *American Psychologist, 49,* 442–443.

Oliver, J. E. (2006). *Fat politics: The real story behind America's obesity epidemic.* New York: Oxford University Press.

Oliveri, M., Turriziani, P., Carlesimo, G. A., Koch, G., Tomaiuolo, F., Panella, M., & Caltagirone, C. (2001). Parieto-frontal interactions in visual-object and visual-spatial working memory: Evidence from transcranial magnetic stimulation, *Cortex , 11,* 606–618.

Oller, K., & Pearson, B. Z. (2002). Assessing the effects of bilingualism: D. K. D. Oller & R. E. Eilers (Eds.), *Language and literacy in bilingual children.* Clevedon, UK: Multilingual Matters.

Olson, E. J., & Park, J. G. (2006). Snoring. In T. Lee-Chiong (Ed.), *Sleep: A comprehensive handbook.* Hoboken, NJ: Wiley-Liss.

Olson, J. M., & Maio, G. R. (2003). Persuasion and attitude change. In T. Millon & M. J. Lerner (Eds.), *Handbook of psychology, Vol. 5: Personality and social psychology.* New York: Wiley.

Olson, J. M., & Roese, N. J. (1995). The perceived funniness of humorous stimuli. *Personality and Social Psychology Bulletin, 21,* 908–913.

Olson, J. M., Roese, N. J., & Zanna, M. P. (1996). Expectancies. In E. T. Higgins & A. W. Kruglanski (Eds.), *Social psychology: Handbook of basic principles.* New York: Guilford.

Olson, J. M., & Stone, J. (2005). The influence of behavior on attitudes. In D. Albarracin, B. T. Johnson, & M. P. Zanna (Eds.), *The handbook of attitudes.* Mahwah, NJ: Erlbaum.

Olson, M. A., & Fazio, R. H. (2001). Implicit attitude formation through classical conditioning. *Psychological Science, 12,* 413–417.

Olson, M. A., & Fazio, R. H. (2002). Implicit acquisition and manifestation of classically conditioned attitudes. *Social Cognition, 20*(2), 89–104.

Olszewski-Kubilius, P. (2003). Gifted education programs and procedures. In W. M. Reynolds & G. E. Miller (Eds.), *Handbook of psychology, Vol. 7: Educational psychology.* New York: Wiley.

Ondeck, D. M. (2003). Impact of culture on pain. *Home Health Care Management & Practice, 15,* 255–257.

Ones, D. S., Viswesvaran, C., & Dilchert, S. (2005). Cognitive ability in selection decisions. In O. Wilhelm & R. W. Engle (Eds.), *Handbook of understanding and measuring intelligence.* Thousand Oaks, CA: Sage.

Operario, D., & Fiske, S. T. (2001). Stereotypes: Content, structures, processes, and context. In R. Brown & S. L. Gaertner (Eds.), *Blackwell handbook of social psychology: Interpersonal processes.* Malden, MA: Blackwell.

O'Reardon, J. P., Solvason, H. B., Janicak, P. G., Sampson, S., Isenberg, K. E., Nahas, Z., et al. (2007). Efficacy and safety of transcranial magnetic stimulation in the acute treatment of major depression: A multisite randomized controlled trial. *Biological Psychiatry, 62,* 1208–1216.

Organista, P. B., & Miranda, J. (1991). Psychosomatic symptoms in medical outpatients: An investigation of self-handicapping theory. *Health Psychology, 10,* 427–431.

Orme-Johnson, D. W., Schneider, R. H., Son, Y. D., Nidich, S., & Cho, Z.-H. (2006). Neuroimaging of meditation's effect on brain reactivity to pain. *Neuroreport: For Rapid Communication of Neuroscience Research, 17,* 1359–1363.

Orne, M. T. (1951). The mechanisms of hypnotic age regression: An experimental study. *Journal of Abnormal and Social Psychology, 46,* 213–225.

Orne, M. T., & Holland, C. C. (1968). On the ecological validity of laboratory deceptions. *International Journal of Psychiatry, 6,* 282–293.

Ornstein, R. E. (1977). *The psychology of consciousness.* New York: Harcourt Brace Jovanovich.

Ornstein, R. E. (1997). *The right mind: Making sense of the hemispheres.* San Diego: Harcourt.

Ornstein, R. E., & Dewan, T. (1991). *The evolution of consciousness: Of Darwin, Freud, and cranial fire—The origins of the way we think.* New York: Prentice-Hall.

Ortigue, S., Bianchi-Demicheli, F., de C. Hamilton, A. F., & Grafton, S. T. (2007). The neural basis of love as a subliminal prime: An event-related functional magnetic resonance imaging study. *Journal of Cognitive Neuroscience, 19,* 1218–1230.

Ortigue, S., Grafton, S. T., & Bianchi-Demicheli, F. (2007). Correlation between insula activation and self-reported quality of orgasm in women. *NeuroImage, 37,* 551–560.

Ortmann, A., & Hertwig, R. (1997). Is deception acceptable? *American Psychologist, 52,* 746–747.

Oskamp, S. (1991). *Attitudes and opinions.* Englewood Cliffs, NJ: Prentice-Hall.

Osrin, D., & de L Costello, A. M. (2000). Maternal nutrition and fetal growth: Practical issues in international health. *Seminars in Neonatology, 5,* 209–219.

Ost, J. (2006). Recovered memories. In T. Williamson (Ed.), *Investigative interviewing: Rights, research, regulation* (pp. 259–291). Devon, United Kingdom: Willan Publishing.

Ostovich, J. M., & Sabini, J. (2004). How are sociosexuality, sex drive, and lifetime number of sexual partners related? *Personality and Social Psychology Bulletin, 30,* 1255–1266.

Ostroff, C., Kinicki, A. J., & Tamkins, M. M. (2003). Organizational culture and climate. In W. C. Borman, D. R. Ilgen, & R. J. Klimoski (Eds.), *Handbook of psychology,* vol. 12: *Industrial and organizational psychology.* New York: Wiley.

Oswald, L. M., Wong, D. F., McCaul, M., Zhou, Y., Kuwabara, H., Choi, L., Brasic, J., & Wand, G. S. (2005). Relationships among ventral striatal dopamine release, cortisol secretion, and subjective responses to amphetamine. *Neuropsychopharmacology, 30,* 821–832.

Otsuka, Y., & Osaka, N. (2005). Working memory in the elderly: Role of prefrontal cortex. *Japanese Psychological Review, 48,* 518–529.

Outz, J. L. (2002). The role of cognitive ability tests in employment selection. *Human Performance, 15,* 161–171.

Overall, N. C., Fletcher, G. J. O., & Simpson, J.A. (2006). Regulation processes in intimate relationships: The role of ideal standards. *Journal of Personality and Social Psychology, 91,* 662–685.

Oyster, C. W. (1999). *The human eye: Structure and function.* Sunderland, MA: Sinauer.

Ozer, D. J., & Benet-Martínez, V. (2006). Personality and the prediction of consequential outcomes. *Annual Review of Psychology, 57,* 401–421.

Ozer, D. J., & Reise, S. P. (1994). Personality assessment. *Annual Review of Psychology, 45,* 357–388.

Ozer, E. J., Best, S. R., Lipsey, T. L., & Weiss, D. S. (2003). Predictors of posttraumatic stress disorder and symptoms in adults: A meta-analysis. *Psychological Bulletin, 129,* 52–73.

Ozgen, E. (2004). Language, learning, and color perception. *Current Directions in Psychological Science, 13*(3), 95–98.

Pace-Schott, E. F. (2005). The neurobiology of dreaming. In M. H. Kryger, T. Roth, & W. C. Dement (Eds.). *Principles and practice of sleep medicine.* Philadelphia: Elsevier Saunders.

Padgett, D. A., & Sheridan, J. F. (2000). Herpes viruses. In G. Fink (Ed.), *Encyclopedia of stress* (pp. 357–363). San Diego: Academic Press.

Pagel, J. F., Blagrove, M., Levin, R., States, B., Stickgold, B., & White, S. (2001). Definitions of dream: A paradigm for comparing field-descriptive specific studies of dream. *Dreaming: Journal of the Association for the Study of Dreams, 11,* 195–202.

Paivio, A. (1969). Mental imagery in associative learning and memory. *Psychological Review, 76,* 241–263.

Paivio, A. (1986). *Mental representations: A dual-coding approach.* New York: Oxford University Press.

Paivio, A. (2007). *Mind and its evolution: A dual-coding theoretical approach.* Mahwah, NJ: Erlbaum.

Paivio, A., Khan, M., & Begg, I. (2000). Concreteness of relational effects on recall of adjective-noun pairs. *Canadian Journal of Experimental Psychology, 54*(3), 149–160.

Paivio, A., Smythe, P. E., & Yuille, J. C. (1968). Imagery versus meaningfulness of nouns in paired-associate learning. *Canadian Journal of Psychology, 22,* 427–441.

Palladino, J. J., & Carducci, B. J. (1984). Students' knowledge of sleep and dreams. *Teaching of Psychology, 11,* 189–191.

Palmer, S. E. (2003). Visual perception of objects. In A. F. Healy & R. W. Proctor (Eds.), *Handbook of psychology, Vol. 4: Experimental psychology.* New York: Wiley.

Palmer, S. E., Rosch, E., & Chase, P. (1981). Canonical perspective and the perception of objects. In J. Long & A. Baddeley (Eds.), *Attention and Performance.* Hillsdale, NJ: Erlbaum.

Palmeri, T. J., & Gauthier, I. (2004). Visual object understanding. *Nature Reviews Neuroscience, 5,* 291–303.

Panksepp, J. (1991). Affective neuroscience: A conceptual framework for the neurobiological study of emotions. In K. T. Strongman (Ed.), *International review of studies on emotion.* Chichester, England: Wiley.

Paris, J. (1999). *Genetics and psychopathology: Predisposition-stress interactions.* Washington, DC: American Psychiatric Press.

Park, C. L., & Fenster, J. R. (2004). Stress-related growth: Predictors of occurrence and correlates with psychological adjustment. *Journal of Social and Clinical Psychology, 23,* 195–215.

Parke, R. D. (2002). Punishment revisited—Science, values, and the right question: Comment on Gershoff. *Psychological Bulletin, 128,* 596–601.

Parke, R. D. (2004). Development in the family. *Annual Review of Psychology, 55,* 365–99.

Parker, A. M., & Fischhoff, B. (2005). Decision-making competence: External validation through an individual-differences approach. *Journal of Behavioral Decision Making, 18,* 1–27.

Parrot, A. C. (2000). Human research on MDMA (3,4-Methylene-dioxymethamphetamine) neurotoxicity: Cognitive and behavioral indices of change. *Neuropsychobiology, 42*(1), 17–24.

Partinen, M., & Hublin, C. (2005). Epidemiology of sleep disorders. In M. H. Kryger, T. Roth, & W. C.

Dement (Eds.). *Principles and practice of sleep medicine.* Philadelphia: Elsevier Saunders.

Pashler, H., & Carrier, M. (1996). Structures, processes, and the flow of information. In E. L. Bjork & R. A. Bjork (Eds.), *Memory.* San Diego: Academic Press.

Pashler, H., Johnston, J. C., & Ruthruff, E. (2001). Attention and performance. *Annual Review of Psychology, 52,* 629–651.

Pasternak, T., Bisley, J. W., & Calkins, D. (2003). Visual processing in the primate brain. In M. Gallagher & R. J. Nelson (Eds.), *Handbook of psychology: Biological psychology* (pp. 139–186). New York: Wiley.

Patel, J. K., Pinals, D. A., & Breier, A. (2003). Schizophrenia and other psychoses. In A. Tasman, J. Kay, & J. A. Lieberman (Eds.), *Psychiatry.* New York: Wiley.

Patel, S. R., Ayas, N. T., Malhotra, M. R., White, D. P., Schernhammer, E. S., Speizer, F. E., et al. (2004). A prospective study of sleep duration and mortality risk in women. *Sleep: Journal of Sleep and Sleep Disorders Research, 27,* 440–444.

Patel, S. R., Malhotra, A., Gottlieb, D. J., White, P., & Hu, F. B. (2006). Correlates of long sleep deprivation. *Sleep: Journal of Sleep and Sleep Disorders Research, 29,* 881–889.

Pato, M. T., Eisen, J. L., & Phillips, K. A. (2003). Obsessive-compulsive disorder. In A. Tasman, J. Kay, & J. A. Lieberman (Eds.), *Psychiatry.* New York: Wiley.

Patrick, H., Nicklas, T. A., Hughes, S. O., & Morales, M. (2005). The benefits of authoritative feeding style: Caregiver feeding styles and children's food consumption patterns. *Appetite, 44,* 243–249.

Patterson, D. R. (2004). Treating pain with hypnosis. *Current Directions in Psychological Science, 13*(6), 252–255.

Patterson, D. R., & Jensen, M. P. (2003). Hypnosis and clinical pain. *Psychological Bulletin, 129,* 495–521.

Patzer, G. L. (2006). *The power and paradox of physical attractiveness.* Boca Raton, FL: Brown Walker Press.

Pauk, W. (1990). *How to study in college.* Boston: Houghton Mifflin.

Paul, E. F., & Paul, J. (2001). *Why animal experimentation matters: The use of animals in medical research.* New Brunswick, NJ: Transaction Publishers.

Paulhus, D. L., Fridhandler, B., & Hayes, S. (1997). Psychological defense: Contemporary theory and research. In R. Hogan, J. Johnson, & S. Briggs (Eds.), *Handbook of personality psychology.* San Diego: Academic Press.

Paulhus, D. L., Trapnell, P. D., & Chen, D. (1999). Birth order effects on personality and achievement within families. *Psychological Science, 10,* 482–488.

Paulos, J. A. (1995). *A mathematician reads the newspaper.* New York: Doubleday.

Paulus, P. B. (2000). Groups, teams, and creativity: The creative potential of idea-generating groups. *Applied Psychology: An International Review, 49,,* 237–262.

Paunonen, S. V. (1998). Hierarchical organization of personality and prediction of behavior. *Journal of Personality and Social Psychology, 74,* 538–556.

Paunonen, S. V. (2003). Big Five factors of personality and replicated predictions of behavior. *Journal of Personality and Social Psychology, 84,* 411–424.

Paunonen, S. V., & Ashton, M. C. (1998). The structured assessment of personality across cultures. *Journal of Cross-Cultural Psychology, 29,* 150–170.

Paunonen, S. V., & Jackson, D. N. (2000). What is beyond the Big Five? Plenty! *Journal of Personality, 68,*, 821–835.

Pavlov, I. P. (1906). The scientific investigation of psychical faculties or processes in the higher animals. *Science, 24,* 613–619.

Pavlov, I. P. (1927). *Conditioned reflexes* (G. V. Anrep, Trans.). London: Oxford University Press.

Payne, D. G., & Blackwell, J. M. (1998). Truth in memory: Caveat emptor. In S. J. Lynn & K. M. McConkey (Eds.), *Truth in memory.* New York: Guilford.

Payne, J. W., & Bettman, J. R. (2004). Walking with the scarecrow: The information-processing approach to decision research. In D. J. Koehler & N. Harvey (Ed.), *Blackwell handbook of judgment and decision making.* Malden, MA: Blackwell.

Pearce, L. (1974). Duck! It's the new journalism. *New Times, 2*(10), 40–41.

Pearson, S. E., & Pollack, R. H. (1997). Female response to sexually explicit films. *Journal of Psychology and Human Sexuality, 9,* 73–88.

Pedersen, P. (1994). A culture-centered approach to counseling. In W. J. Lonner & R. Malpass (Eds.), *Psychology and culture.* Boston: Allyn & Bacon.

Peele, S. (1989). *Diseasing of America: Addiction treatment out of control.* Lexington, MA: Lexington Books.

Peele, S. (2000). What addiction is and is not: The impact of mistaken notions of addiction. *Addiction Research, 8,* 599–607.

Peladeau, N., Forget, J., & Gagne, F. (2003). Effect of paced and unpaced practice on skill application and retention: How much is enough? *American Educational Research Journal, 40,* 769–801.

Pelayo, R., & Lopes, M. C. (2006). Narcolepsy. In T. Lee-Chiong (Ed.), *Sleep: A comprehensive handbook.* Hoboken, NJ: Wiley-Liss.

Pellegrino, J. E., & Pellegrino, L. (2008). Fetal alcohol syndrome and related disorders. In P. J. Accardo (Eds.), *Capture and Accardo's neurodevelopment disabilities in infancy and childhood: Neurodevelopmental diagnosis and treatment* (pp. 269–284). Baltimore, MD: Paul H. Brookes Publishing.

Peltier, M. E. (1999). Healthcare environments using environmental aroma technology. *The Aroma-Chology Review, 8*(2), 2–3, 12.

Penfield, W., & Perot, P. (1963). The brain's record of auditory and visual experience. *Brain, 86,* 595–696.

Penn, D. C., & Povinelli, D. J. (2007). Causal cognition in human and nonhuman animals: A comparative, critical review. *Annual Review of Psychology, 58,* 97–118.

Pennebaker, J. W., Colder, M., & Sharp, L. K. (1990). Accelerating the coping process. *Journal of Personality and Social Psychology, 58,* 528–537.

Pennix, B. W. J. H., Beekman, A. T. F., Honig, A., Deeg, D. J. H., Schoevers, R. A., van Eijk, J. T. M., & van Tilburg, W. (2001). Depression and cardiac mortality: Results from a community-based longitudinal survey. *Archives of General Psychiatry, 58,* 221–227.

Peplau, L. A. (2003). Human sexuality: How do men and women differ? *Current Directions in Psychological Science, 12*(2), 37–40.

Peplau, L. A., Fingerhut, A., & Beals, K. P. (2004). Sexuality in the relationships of lesbians and gay men. In J. H. Harvey, A. Wenzel, & S. Sprecher (Eds.), *The handbook of sexuality in close relationships.* Mahwah, NJ: Erlbaum.

Pepperberg, I. M. (1993). Cognition and communication in an African Grey parrot (*Psittacus erithacus*): Studies on a nonhuman, nonprimate, nonmammalian subject. In H. L. Roitblat, L. H. Herman, & P. E. Nachtigall (Eds.), *Language and communication: Comparative perspectives.* Hillsdale, NJ: Erlbaum.

Pepperberg, I. M. (2002). Cognitive and communicative abilities of grey parrots. *Current Directions in Psychological Science, 11*(3), 83–87.

Pereira, A. C., Huddleston, D. E., Brickman, A. M., Sosunov, A. A., Hen, R., McKhann, G. M., et al. (2007). An in vivo correlate of exercise-induced neurogenesis in the adult dentate gyrus. *Proceedings of the National Academy of Sciences, 104,* 5638–5643.

Perkins, D. F., & Borden, L. M. (2003). Positive behaviors, problem behaviors, and resiliency in adolescence. In R. M. Lerner, M. A. Easterbrooks, & J. Mistry (Eds.), *Handbook of psychology: Developmental psychology.* New York: Wiley.

Perkins, D. O., Miller-Anderson, L., & Lieberman, J. A. (2006). Natural history and predictors of clinical course. In J. A. Lieberman, T. S. Stroup, & D. O. Perkins (Eds.), *Textbook of schizophrenia* (pp. 289–302). Washington, DC: American Psychiatric Publishing.

Perlis, R. H., Perlis, C. S., Wu, Y. , Hwang, C., Joseph, M., & Nierenberg, A. A. (2005). Industry sponsorship and financial conflict of interest in the reporting of clinical trials in psychiatry. *American Journal of Psychiatry, 162,* 1957–1960.

Perone, M., Galizio, M., & Baron, A. (1988). The relevance of animal-based principles in the laboratory study of human operant conditioning. In G. Davey & C. Cullen (Eds.), *Human operant conditioning and behavior modification.* New York: Wiley.

Perrin, F., Maquet, P., Peigneux, P. , Ruby, P., Degueldre, C., Balteau, E., & Del Fiore, G. (2005). Neural mechanisms involved in the detection of our first name: A combined ERPs and PET study. *Neuropsychologia, 43,* 12–19.

Perry, C., Nadon, R., & Button, J. (1992). The measurement of hypnotic ability. In E. Fromm & M. R. Nash (Eds.), *Contemporary hypnosis research.* New York: Guilford.

Perry, D. G., Kusel, S. J., & Perry, L. C. (1988). Victims of peer aggression. *Developmental Psychology, 24,* 807–814.

Person, E. S. (1990). The influence of values in psychoanalysis: The case of female psychology. In C. Zanardi (Ed.), *Essential papers in psychoanalysis.* New York: New York University Press.

Pert, C. B. (2002). The wisdom of the receptors: Neuropeptides, the emotions, and bodymind. *Advances in Mind-Body Medicine, 18*(1), 30–35.

Pert, C. B., & Snyder, S. H. (1973). Opiate receptor: Demonstration in the nervous tissue. *Science, 179,* 1011–1014.

Perugini, E. M., Kirsch, I., Allen, S. T., Coldwell, E., Meredith, J. M., Montgomery, G. H., & Sheehan, J. (1998). Surreptitious observation of response to hypnotically suggested hallucinations: A test of the compliance hypothesis. *International Journal of Clinical & Experimental Hypnosis, 46,* 191–203.

Pervin, L. A., & John, O. P. (2001). *Personality: Theory and research.* New York: Wiley.

Petersen, A. C., Compas, B. E., Brooks-Gunn, J., Stemmler, M., Ey, S., & Grant, K. E. (1993). Depression in adolescence. *American Psychologist, 48,* 155–168.

Peterson, C. (2000). The future of optimism. *American Psychologist, 55*(1), 44–55.

Peterson, C. (2006). *A primer in positive psychology.* New York: Oxford University Press.

Peterson, C., & Bossio, L. M. (2001). Optimism and physical well-being. In E. C. Chang (Ed.), *Optimism and pessimism: Implications for theory, research, and practice* (pp. 127–146). Washington, DC: American Psychological Association.

Peterson, C., & Seligman, M. E. P. (2004). *Character strengths and virtues: A handbook and classification.* Washington, DC: American Psychological Association.

Peterson, C., Seligman, M. E. P., & Vaillant, G. E. (1988). Pessimistic explanatory style is a risk factor for physical illness: A thirty-five-year longitudinal study. *Journal of Personality and Social Psychology, 55,* 23–27.

Peterson, C., Seligman, M. E. P., Yurko, K. H., Martin, L. R., & Friedman, H. S. (1998). Catastrophizing and untimely death. *Psychological Science, 9,* 127–130.

Peterson, L. R., & Peterson, M. J. (1959). Short-term retention of individual verbal items. *Journal of Experimental Psychology, 58,* 193–198.

Peterson, N. G., Mumford, M. D., Borman, W. C., Jeanneret, P. R., & Fleishmann, E. A. (1999). *An occupational information system for the 21st century: The development of O*NET.* Washington, DC: American Psychological Association.

Petrie, K. J., & Pennebaker, J. W. (2004). Health-related cognitions. In S. Sutton, A. Baum, & M. Johnston (Eds.), *The Sage handbook of health psychology.* Thousand Oaks, CA: Sage.

Petrie, M. (1994). Improved growth and survival of offspring of peacocks with more elaborate trains. *Nature, 371,* 585–586.

Petrill, S. A. (2005). Behavioral genetics and intelligence. In O. Wilhelm & R. W. Engle (Eds.), *Handbook of understanding and measuring intelligence.* Thousand Oaks, CA: Sage.

Petry, N. M. (2005). *Pathological gambling: Etiology, comorbidity, and treatment.* Washington, DC: American Psychological Association.

Petty, R. E., & Briñol, P. (2008). Persuasion: From single to multiple to metacognitive processes. *Perspectives on Psychological Science, 3,* 137–147.

Petty, R. E., & Cacioppo, J. T. (1986). *Communication and persuasion: Central and peripheral routes to attitude change.* New York: Springer-Verlag.

Petty, R. E., & Wegener, D. T. (1998). Attitude change: Multiple roles for persuasion variables. In D. T. Gilbert, S. T. Fiske, & G. Lindzey (Eds.), *The handbook of social psychology.* New York: McGraw-Hill.

Petty, R. E., & Wegener, D. T. (1999). The elaboration likelihood model: Current status and controversies. In S. Chaiken & Y. Trope (Eds.), *Dual-process theories in social psychology.* New York: Guilford.

Petty, R. E., Wheeler, S. C., & Tormala, Z. L. (2003). Persuasion and attitude change. In T. Millon & M. J. Lerner (Eds.), *Handbook of psychology, Vol. 5: Personality and social psychology.* New York: Wiley.

Petty, S. C., Sachs-Ericsson, N., & Joiner, T. E., Jr. (2004). Interpersonal functioning deficits: Temporary or stable characteristics of depressed individuals. *Journal of Affective Disorders, 81,* 115–122.

Pezdek, K. (2003). Event memory and autobiographical memory for the events of September 11, 2001. *Applied Cognitive Psychology, 17,* 1033–1045.

Pezdek, K., & Lam, S. (2007). What research paradigms have cognitive psychologists used to study "false memory," and what are the implications of these choices? *Consciousness and Cognition: An International Journal, 16*(1), 2–17.

Pfau, M., Kenski, H. C., Nitz, M., & Sorenson, J. (1990). Efficacy of inoculation strategies in promoting resistance to political attack messages: Application to direct mail. *Communication Monographs, 57,* 25–43.

Pfaus, J. G., Kippin, T. E., & Centeno, S. (2001). Conditioning and sexual behavior: A review. *Hormones & Behavior, 40,* 291–321.

Phelps, E. A. (2005). The interaction of emotion and cognition: The relation between the human amygdala and cognitive awareness. In R. R. Hassin, J. S. Uleman, & J. A. Bargh (Eds.), *The new unconcious: Oxford series in social cognition and social neuroscience* (pp. 61–76). New York: Oxford University Press.

Phelps, E. A. (2006). Emotion and cognition: Insights from studies of the human amygdala. *Annual Review of Psychology, 57,* 27–53.

Phillips, B., & Kryger, M. H. (2005). Management of obstructive sleep apnea-hypopnea syndrome. In M. H. Kryger, T. Roth, & W. C. Dement (Eds.), *Principles and practice of sleep medicine.* Philadelphia: Saunders.

Phillips, D., McCartney, K., & Sussman, A. (2006). Child care and early development. In K. McCartney & D. Phillips (Eds.), *Blackwell handbook of early childhood development* (pp. 471–489). Malden, MA: Blackwell Publishing.

Phillips, K. A., Yen, S., & Gunderson, J. G. (2003). Personality disorders. In R. E. Hales & S. C. Yudofsky (Eds.), *Textbook of clinical psychiatry.* Washington, DC: American Psychiatric Publishing.

Phillips, W. T., Kiernan, M., & King, A. C. (2001). The effects of physical activity on physical and psychological health. In A. Baum, T. A. Revenson, & J. E. Singer (Eds.), *Handbook of health psychology* (pp. 627–660). Mahwah, NJ: Erlbaum.

Pi, E. H., & Simpson, G. M. (2000). Medication-induced movement disorders. In B. J. Sadock & V. A. Sadock (Eds.), *Kaplan and Sadock's comprehensive textbook of psychiatry* (7th ed., Vol. 2). Philadelphia: Lippincott/Williams & Wilkins.

Piaget, J. (1929). *The child's conception of the world.* New York: Harcourt, Brace.

Piaget, J. (1932). *The moral judgment of the child.* Glencoe, IL: Free Press.

Piaget, J. (1952). *The origins of intelligence in children.* New York: International Universities Press.

Piaget, J. (1954). *The construction of reality in the child.* New York: Basic Books.

Piaget, J. (1983). Piaget's theory. In P. H. Mussen (Ed.), *Handbook of child psychology* (Vol. 1). New York: Wiley.

Pickles, J. O. (1988). *An introduction to the physiology of hearing* (2nd ed.). London: Academic Press.

Pierce, R. C., & Kumaresan, V. (2006). The mesolimbic dopamine system: The final common pathway for the reinforcing effect of drugs of abuse? *Neuroscience Biobehavioral Reviews, 30,* 215–238.

Pilling, M., & Davies, I. R. L. (2004). Linguistic relativism and colour cognition. *British Journal of Psychology, 95,* 429–455.

Pilowsky, I. (1993). Aspects of abnormal illness behaviour. *Psychotherapy and Psychosomatics, 60,* 62–74.

Pine, D. S., & McClure, E. B. (2005). Anxiety disorders: Genetics. In B. J. Sadock & V. A. Sadock (Eds.), *Kaplan & Sadock's comprehensive textbook of psychiatry* (pp. 1768–1779). Philadelphia: Lippincott Williams & Wilkins.

Pinel, J. P. J., Assanand, S., & Lehman, D. R. (2000). Hunger, eating, and ill health. *American Psychologist, 55,* 1105–1116.

Pines, A. M. (2004). Adult attachment styles and their relationship to burnout: A preliminary, cross-cultural investigation. *Work & Stress, 18*(1), 66–80.

Pink, D. H. (2005). *A whole new mind: Why right-brainers will rule the future.* New York: Penguin.

Pinker, S., & Bloom, P. (1992). Natural language and natural selection. In J. H. Barkow, L. Cosmides, & J. Tooby (Eds.), *The adapted mind: Evolutionary psychology and the generation of culture.* New York: Oxford University Press.

Pinker, S., & Jackendoff, R. (2005). The faculty of language: What's special about it? *Cognition, 95,* 201–236.

Pinker, S. (1994). *Language is to us as flying is to geese.* New York: Morrow.

Pinker, S. (2004). Language as an adaptation to the cognitive niche. In D. T. Kenrick & C. L. Luce (Eds.), *The functional mind: Readings in evolutionary psychology.* Essex, England: Pearson Education Limited.

Pinquart, M., Duberstein, P. R., & Lyness, J. M. (2006). Treatments for later-life depressive conditions: A meta-analytic comparison of pharmacotherapy and psychotherapy. *American Journal of Psychiatry, 163,* 1493–1501.

Pinyerd, B., & Zipf, W. B. (2005). Puberty—Timing is everything! *Journal of Pediatric Nursing, 20,* 75–82.

Piomelli, D. (2004). The endogenous cannabinoid system and the treatment of marijuana dependence. *Neuropharmacology, 47,* 359–367.

Pi-Sunyer, F. X. (2002). Medical complications of obesity in adults. In C. G. Fairburn & K. D. Brownell (Eds.), *Eating disorders and obesity: A comprehensive handbook* (pp. 467–472). New York: Guilford.

Pittenger, D. J. (2003). Internet research: An opportunity to revisit classic ethical problems in behavioral research. *Ethics & Behavior, 13*(1), 45–60.

Pittman, F., III. (1994, January/February). A buyer's guide to psychotherapy. *Psychology Today,* 50–53, 74–81.

Pizzagalli, D., Shackman, A. J., & Davidson, R. J. (2003). The functional neuroimaging of human emotion: Asymmetric contributions of cortical and subcortical circuitry. In K. Hugdahl & R. J. Davidson (Eds.), *The asymmetrical brain.* Cambridge, MA: MIT Press.

Plante, T. G. (1999a). *Contemporary clinical psychology.* New York: Wiley.

Plante, T. G. (1999b). Could the perception of fitness account for many of the mental and physical health benefits of exercise? *Advances in Mind-Body Medicine, 15,* 291–295.

Plante, T. G., Caputo, D., & Chizmar, L. (2000). Perceived fitness and responses to laboratory-induced stress. *International Journal of Stress Management, 7*(1), 61–73.

Plassmann, H., O'Doherty, J., Shiv, B., & Rangel. (2008). Marketing actions can modulate neural representations of experienced pleasantness. *Proceedings of the National Academy of Science, 105,* 1050–1054.

Platek, S. M., Mohamed, F. B., & Gallup, G. G. Jr. (2005). Contagious yawning and the brain. *Cognitive Brain Research, 23,* 448–452.

Pliner, P., & Mann, N. (2004). Influence of social norms and palatability on amount consumed and food choice. *Appetite, 42,* 227–237.

Plomin, R. (1993). Nature and nurture: Perspective and prospective. In R. Plomin & G. E. McClearn (Eds.), *Nature, nurture and psychology.* Washington, DC: American Psychological Association.

Plomin, R. (2003). General cognitive ability. In R. Plomin & J. C. DeFries (Eds.), *Behavioral genetics in the postgenomic era.* Washinton, DC: American Psychological Association.

Plomin, R. (2004). Genetics and developmental psychology. *Merrill-Palmer Quarterly, 50,* 341–352.

Plomin, R., DeFries, J. C., McClearn, G. E., & McGuffin, P. (2001). *Behavioral genetics.* New York: Freeman.

Plomin, R., DeFries, J. C., McClearn, G. E., & McGuffin, P. (2008). *Behavioral genetics.* New York: Worth.

Plomin, R., Kennedy, J. K. J., & Craig, I. W. (2006). The quest for quantitative, trait loci associated with intelligence. *Intelligence, 34,* 513–526.

Plomin, R., & McGuffin, P. (2003). Psychopathology in the postgenomic era. *Annual Review of Psychology, 54,* 205–228.

Plomin, R., & Spinath, F. M. (2004). Intelligence: Genetics, genes, and genomics. *Journal of Personality & Social Psychology, 86,* 112–129.

Plotkin, H. (1998). *Evolution in mind: An introduction to evolutionary psychology.* Cambridge, MA: Harvard University Press.

Plotkin, H. (2004). *Evolutionary thought in psychology: A brief history.* Malden, MA: Blackwell.

Plous, S. (1991). An attitude survey of animal rights activists. *Psychological Science, 2,* 194–196.

Plucker, J. A., & Renzulli, J. S. (1999). Psychometric approaches to the study of human creativity. In R. J. Sternberg (Ed.), *Handbook of creativity.* New York: Cambridge University Press.

Plutchik, R. (1980, February). A language for the emotions. *Psychology Today,* pp. 68–78.

Plutchik, R. (1984). Emotions: A general psycho-evolutionary theory. In K. R. Scherer & P. Ekman (Eds.), *Approaches to emotion.* Hillsdale, NJ: Erlbaum.

Plutchik, R. (1993). Emotions and their vicissitudes: Emotions and psychopathology. In M. Lewis & J. M. Haviland (Eds.), *Handbook of emotions.* New York: Guilford.

Pohl, R. F. (2004). Effects of labeling. In F. P. Rudiger (Ed.), *Cognitive illusions.* New York: Psychology Press.

Poldrack, R. A., & Willingham, D. T. (2006). Functional neuroimaging of skill learning. In R. Cabeza & A. Kingstone (Eds.), *Handbook of functional neuroimaging of cognition* (pp. 113–148). Cambridge, MA: MIT Press.

Polger, T. (2007). Rethinking the evolution of consciousness. In M. Velmans & S. Schneider (Eds.), *The Blackwell companion to consciousness.* Malden, MA: Blackwell Publishing.

Policastro, E., & Gardner, H. (1999). From case studies to robust generalizations: An approach to the study of creativity. In R. J. Sternberg (Ed.), *Handbook of creativity.* New York: Cambridge University Press.

Pollak, L. (2007). *Getting from college to career: 90 things to do before you join the real world.* New York: Collins Business.

Pomerantz, E. M., Ng, F. F. Y., & Wang, Q. (2004). Gender socialization: A parent X child model. In A. H. Eagly, A. E. Beall, & R. J. Sternberg (Eds.), *The psychology of gender.* New York: Guilford.

Pomeroy, A. (2005). 50 best small and medium places to work: Money talks. *HR Magazine, 50*(7), 44–65.

Pomeroy, C., & Mitchell, J. E. (2002). Medical complications of anorexia nervosa and bulimia nervosa. In C. G. Fairburn & K. D. Brownell (Eds.), *Eating disorders and obesity: A comprehensive handbook.* New York: Guilford.

Ponterotto, J. G., & Pedersen, P. B. (1993). *Preventing prejudice: A guide for counselors and educators.* Newbury Park, CA: Sage.

Pope, H. G., Barry, S., Bodkin, A., & Hudson, J. I. (2006). Tracking scientific interest in the dissociative disorders: A study of scientific publication output 1984–2003. *Psychotherapy and Psychosomatics, 75,* 19–24.

Pope, H. G., Gruber, A. J., Hudson, J. I., Huestis, M. A., & Yurgelun-Todd, D. (2001). Neuropsychological performance in long-term cannabis users. *Archives of General Psychiatry, 58,* 909–915.

Pope, H. G., Gruber, A. J., & Yurgelun-Todd, D. (2001). Residual neuropsychologic effects of cannabis. *Current Psychiatry Report, 3,* 507–512.

Pope, H. G., & Hudson, J. I. (1998). Can memories of childhood sexual abuse be repressed? In R. A. Baker (Ed.), *Child sexual abuse and false memory syndrome.* Amherst, NY: Prometheus Books.

Pope, H. G., Oliva, P. S., Hudson, J. I., Bodkin, J. A., & Gruber, A. J. (1999). Attitudes toward DSM-IV dissociative disorders diagnoses among board-certified American psychiatrists. *American Journal of Psychiatry, 156,* 321–323.

Pope, K. S., Keith-Spiegel, P., & Tabachnick, B. G. (1986). Sexual attraction to clients. *American Psychologist, 41,* 147–158.

Popenoe, D. (1996). *Life without father.* New York: Pressler Press.

Popper, C. W., & Steingard, R. J. (1994). Disorders usually first diagnosed in infancy, childhood, or adolescence. In R. E. Hales, S. C. Yudofsky, & J. A. Talbott (Eds.), *The American Psychiatric Press textbook of psychiatry.* Washington, DC: American Psychiatric Press.

Popper, C. W., Gammon, G. D., West, S. A., & Bailey, C. E. (2003). Disorders usually first diagnosed in infancy, childhood, and adolescence. In Robert E. Hales & Stuart C. Yudofsky (Eds.), *Textbook of clinical psychiatry.* Washington, DC: American Psychiatric Publishing.

Pornpitakpan, C. (2004). The persuasiveness of source credibility: A critical review of five decades' evidence. *Journal of Applied Social Psychology, 34,* 243–281.

Porter, L. W., & Lawler, E. E. (1968). *Managerial attitudes and performance.* Homewood, IL: Dorsey Press.

Porter, S., & Porter, S. (2007). Psychopathy and violent crime. In H. Hervé, & J. C. Yuille (Eds.), *The psychopath: Theory, research, and practice.* Mahwah, NJ: Erlbaum.

Porter, S., Yuille, J. C., & Lehman, D. R. (1999). The nature of real, implanted, and fabricated memories for emotional childhood events: Implications for the recovered memory debate. *Law and Human Behavior, 23,* 517–537.

Posada, G., Kaloustian, G., Richmond, K., & Moreno, A. J. (2007). Maternal secure base support and preschoolers' secure base behavior in natural environments. *Attachment & Human Development, 9,* 393–411.

Posner, M. I., & DiGirolamo, G. J. (2000). Attention in cognitive neuroscience: An overview. In M. S. Gazzaniga (Ed.), *The new cognitive neurosciences* (2nd ed., pp. 623–632). Cambridge, MA: MIT Press.

Post, F. (1996). Verbal creativity, depression and alcoholism: An investigation of one hundred American and British writers. *British Journal of Psychiatry, 168,* 545–555.

Posthuma, D., & de Geus, E. J. C. (2006). Progress in the molecular–genetic study of intelligence. *Current Directions in Psychological Science, 15*(4), 151–155.

Posthuma, D., Luciano, M., de Geus, E. J. C., Wright, M. J., Slagboom, P. E., Montgomery, G. W., et al. (2005). A genome-wide scan for intelligence identifies quantitative trait loci on 2q and 6p. *American Journal of Human Genetics, 77,* 318–326.

Postman, L. (1985). Human learning and memory. In G. A. Kimble & K. Schlesinger (Eds.), *Topics in the history of psychology.* Hillsdale, NJ: Erlbaum.

Postmes, T., Spears, R., & Cihangir, S. (2001). Quality of decision making and group norms. *Journal of Personality and Social Psychology, 80,* 918–930.

Potenza, M. N. (2006). Should addictive disorders include non-substance-related conditions? *Addiction, 101*(Suppl 1), 142–151.

Potter, W. Z., Padich, R. A., Rudorfer, M. V., & Krishnan, K. R. R. (2006). Tricyclics, tetracyclics, and monoamine oxidase inhibitors. In D. J. Stein, D. J. Kupfer, & A. F. Schatzberg (Eds.), *Textbook of mood disorders* (pp. 251–262). Washington, DC: American Psychiatric Publishing.

Potthoff, J. G., Holahan, C. J., & Joiner, T. E., Jr. (1995). Reassurance-seeking, stress generation, and depressive symptoms: An integrative model. *Journal of Personality and Social Psychology, 68,* 664–670.

Poulin-Dubois, D., & Graham, S. A. (2007). Cognitive processes in early word learning. In E. Hoff & M. Shatz (Eds.), *Blackwell handbook of language development* (pp. 191–212). Malden, MA: Blackwell.

Powell, L. H., & Williams, K. (2007). Hostility. In G. Fink (Ed.), *Encyclopedia of stress.* San Diego: Elsevier.

Powell, R. A., & Boer, D. P. (1995). Did Freud misinterpret reported memories of sexual abuse as fantasies? *Psychological Reports, 77,* 563–570.

Powell, R. A., & Gee, T. L. (1999). The effects of hypnosis on dissociative identity disorder: A re-examination of the evidence. *Canadian Journal of Psychiatry, 44,* 914–916.

Powell, R. A., Symbaluk, D. G., & MacDonald, S. E. (2002). *Introduction to learning and behavior.* Belmont, CA: Wadsworth.

Powers, S. I., Pietromonaco, P. R., Gunlicks, M., & Sayer, A. (2006). Dating couples' attachment styles and patterns of cortisol reactivity and recovery in response to a relationship conflict. *Journal of Personality and Social Psychology, 90,* 613–628.

Pratkanis, A. R., & Aronson, E. (2000). *Age of propaganda: The everyday use and abuse of persuasion.* New York: Freeman.

Preckel, F., Holling, H., & Wiese, M. (2006). Relationship of intelligence and creativity in gifted and non-gifted students: An investigation of threshold theory. *Personality and Individual Differences, 40,* 159–170.

Premack, D. (1985). "Gavagai!" or the future history of the animal language controversy. *Cognition, 19,* 207–296.

Prentky, R. (1989). Creativity and psychopathology: Gambling at the seat of madness. In J. A. Glover, R. R. Ronning, & C. R. Reynolds (Eds.), *Handbook of creativity.* New York: Plenum.

Pressman, S. D., & Cohen, S. (2005). Does positive affect influence health? *Psychological Bulletin, 131,* 925–971.

Pressman, S. D., Cohen, S., Miller, G. E., Barkin, A., Rabin, B. S., & Treanor, J. J. (2005). Loneliness, social network size, and immune response to influenza vaccination in college freshman. *Health Psychology, 24,* 297–306.

Pretz, J. E., Naples, A. J., & Sternberg, R. J. (2003). Recognizing, defining, and representing problems. In J. E. Davidson & R. J. Sternberg (Eds.), *The psychology of problem solving.* New York: Cambridge University Press.

Priester, J. R., & Petty, R. E. (1995). Source attributions and persuasion; Perceived honesty as a determinant of message scrutiny. *Personality and Social Psychology Bulletin, 21,* 637–654.

Priester, J. R., & Petty, R. E. (2001). Extending the bases of subjective attitudinal ambivalence: Interpersonal and intrapersonal antecedents of evaluative tension. *Journal of Personality and Social Psychology, 80,* 19–34.

Priester, J. R., & Petty, R. E. (2003). The influence of spokesperson trustworthiness on message elaboration, attitude strength, and advertising. *Journal of Consumer Psychology, 13,* 408–421.

Prifitera, A. (1994). Wechsler scales of intelligence. In R. J. Sternberg (Ed.), *Encyclopedia of human intelligence.* New York: Macmillan.

Prochaska, J. O. (1994). Strong and weak principles for progressing from precontemplation to action on the basis of twelve problem behaviors. *Health Psychology, 13,* 47–51.

Prochaska, J. O., Velicer, W. F., Prochaska, J. M., & Johnson, J. L. (2004). Size, consistency, and stability of stage effects for smoking cessation. *Addictive Behaviors, 29,* 207–213.

Proffitt, D. R. (2006a). Distance perception. *Current Directions in Psychological Science, 15,* 131–135.

Proffitt, D. R. (2006b). Embodied perception and the economy of action. *Perspectives on Psychological Science, 1,* 110–122.

Proffitt, D. R., Bhalla, M., Gossweiler, R., & Midgett, J. (1995). Perceiving geographical slant. *Psychonomic Bulletin & Review, 2,* 409–428.

Proffitt, D. R., & Caudek, C. (2003). Depth perception and the perception of events. In A. F. Healy & R. W. Proctor (Eds.), *Handbook of psychology, Vol. 4: Experimental psychology.* New York: Wiley.

Proffitt, D. R., Stefanucci, J., Banton, T., & Epstein, W. (2003). The role of effort in perceiving distance. *Psychological Science, 14,* 106–112.

Prolo, P., & Chiappelli, F. (2007). Immune suppression. In G. Fink (Ed.), *Encyclopedia of stress.* San Diego: Elsevier.

Pronin, E., Gilovich, T., & Ross, L. (2004). Objectivity in the eye of the beholder: Divergent perceptions of bias in self versus others. *Psychological Review, 111,* 781–799.

Pronin, E., Lin, D. Y., & Ross L. (2002). The bias blind spot: Perceptions of bias in self versus others. *Personality and Social Psychology Bulletin, 28,* 369–381.

Provine, R. R. (2005). Yawning. *American Scientist, 93,* 532–539.

Prudic, J. (2005). Electroconvulsive therapy. In B. J. Sadock & V. A. Sadock (Eds.), *Kaplan and Sadock's comprehensive textbook of psychiatry* (pp. 2968–2982). Philadelphia: Lippincott Williams & Wilkins.

Pruitt, D. G. (1971). Choice shifts in group discussion: An introductory review. *Journal of Personality and Social Psychology, 20,* 339–360.

Pucetti, R. (1981). The case for mental duality: Evidence from split brain data and other considerations. *Behavioral and Brain Sciences, 4,* 93–123.

Puente, A. E. (1990). Psychological assessment of minority group members. In G. Goldstein & M. Hersen (Eds.), *Handbook of psychological assessment.* New York: Pergamon Press.

Pullum, G. K. (1991). *The Great Eskimo vocabulary hoax.* Chicago: University of Chicago Press.

Pyszczynski, T., Greenberg, J., & Solomon, S. (1999). A dual-process model of defense against conscious and unconscious death-related thoughts: An extension of terror management theory. *Psychological Review, 106,* 835–845.

Pyszczynski, T., Greenberg, J., Solomon, S., Arndt, J., & Schimel, J. (2004). Why do people need self-esteem? A theoretical and empirical review. *Psychological Bulletin, 130,* 435–468.

Pyszczynski, T., Solomon, S., & Greenberg, J. (2003). *In the wake of 9/11: The psychology of terror.* Washington, DC: American Psychological Association.

Quinn, K. A., Macrae, C. N., & Bodenhausen, G. V. (2003). Stereotyping and impression formation: How categorical thinking shapes person perception. In M. A. Hogg & J. Cooper (Eds.), *The Sage handbook of social psychology.* Thousand Oaks, CA: Sage.

Quirk, G. J. (2007). Prefrontal-amygdala interactions in the regulation of fear. In J. J. Gross (Ed.), *Handbook of emotion regulation* (pp. 27–46). New York: Guilford.

Quiroga, R. Q., Reddy, L., Kreiman, G., Koch, C., & Fried, I. (2005). Invariant visual representation by single neurons in the human brain. *Nature, 435,* 1102–1107.

Quitkin, F. M. (1999). Placebos, drug effects, and study design: A clinician's guide. *American Journal of Psychiatry, 156,* 829–836.

Rabins, P. V., Lyketsos, C. G., & Steele, C. D. (1999). *Practical dementia care.* New York: Oxford University Press.

Rachman, S. J. (1990). *Fear and courage.* New York: W. H. Freeman.

Rachman, S. J. (1992). Behavior therapy. In L. R. Squire (Ed.), *Encyclopedia of learning and memory.* New York: Macmillan.

Rafal, R. (2001). Virtual neurology. *Nature Neuroscience, 4,* 862–864.

Rahe, R. H., & Arthur, R. H. (1978). Life change and illness studies. *Journal of Human Stress, 4*(1), 3–15.

Raichle, M. E. (2006). Functional neuroimaging: A historical and physiological perspective. In R. Cabeza & A. Kingstone (Eds.), *Handbook of functional neuroimaging of cognition* (pp. 3–20). Cambridge, MA: MIT Press.

Raine, A. (1997). Antisocial behavior and psychophysiology: A biosocial perspective and a prefrontal dysfunction hypothesis. In D. M. Stoff, J. Breiling, & J. D. Maser (Eds.), *Handbook of antisocial behavior.* New York: Wiley.

Rains, G. D. (2002). *Principles of human neuropsychology.* New York: McGraw-Hill.

Raitt, F. E., & Zeedyk, M. S. (2003). False memory syndrome: Undermining the credibility of complaintants in sexual offenses. *International Journal of Law & Psychiatry, 26,* 453–471.

Raj, A., & Sheehan, D. (2004). Benzodiazepines. In A. F. Schatzberg & C. B. Nemeroff (Eds.), *Textbook of psychopharmacology.* Washington, DC: American Psychiatric Publishing.

Rakic, P., Bourgeois, J. P., & Goldman-Rakic, P. S. (1994). Synaptic development of the cerebral cortex: Implications for learning, memory, and mental illness. *Progress in brain research.*

Rama, A. N., Cho, S. C., & Kushida, C. A. (2006). Normal human sleep. In T. Lee-Chiong (Ed.), *Sleep: A comprehensive handbook.* Hoboken, NJ: Wiley-Liss.

Ramadan, N. M. (2000). Migraine. In G. Fink (Ed.), *Encyclopedia of stress* (pp. 757–770). San Diego: Academic Press.

Ramaekers, J. G., Berghaus, G., van Laar, M., & Drummer, O. H. (2004). Dose-related risk of motor vehicle crashes after cannabis use. *Drug and Alcohol Dependence, 73,* 109–119.

Ramey, C. T., & Ramey, S. L. (2004). Early educational interventions and intelligence. In E. Zigler & S. J. Styfco (Eds.), *The Head Start debate.* Baltimore: Paul H. Brookes Publishing.

Ramey, S. L. (1999). Head Start and preschool education: Toward continued improvement. *American Psychologist, 54,* 344–346.

Ramin, M. (2005). Perceived reasons for loss of housing and continued homelessness among homeless persons with mental illness. *Psychiatric Services, 56*(2), 172–178.

Ramsay, D. S., Seeley, R. J., Bolles, R. C., & Woods, S. C. (1996). Ingestive homeostasis: The primacy of learning. In E. D. Capaldi (Ed.), *Why we eat what we eat: The psychology of eating* (pp. 11–29). Washington, DC: American Psychological Association.

Ranganath, C., & Blumenfeld, R. S. (2005). Doubts about double dissociations between short- and long-term memory. *Trends in Cognitive Sciences, 9,* 374–380.

Ranganathan, M., & D'Souza, D. C. (2006). The acute effects of cannabinoids on memory in humans: A review. *Psychopharmacology, 188,* 425–444.

Ranson, K. E., & Urichuk, L. J. (2008). The effect of parent-child attachment relationships on child biopsychosocial outcomes: A review. *Early Child Development and Care, 178,* 129–152.

Rapee, R. M., & Barlow, D. H. (2001). Generalized anxiety disorders, panic disorders, and phobias. In P. B. Sutker & H. E. Adams (Eds.), *Comprehensive handbook of psychopathology* (3rd ed., pp. 131–154). New York: Kluwer Academic/Plenum Publishers.

Rasmussen, C., Knapp, T. J., & Garner, L. (2000). Driving-induced stress in urban college students. *Perceptual & Motor Skills, 90,* 437–443.

Rasmussen, T., & Milner, B. (1977). The role of early left brain injury in determining lateralization of cerebral speech functions. *Annals of the New York Academy of Sciences, 299,* 355–369.

Ratner, N. B., Gleason, J. B., & Narasimhan, B. (1998). An introduction to psycholinguistics: What do language users know? In J. B. Gleason & N. B. Ratner (Eds.), *Psycholinguistics* (2nd ed., pp. 1–40). Fort Worth, TX: Harcourt College Publishers.

Rauscher, F. H., Shaw, G. L., & Ky, K. N. (1993). Music and spatial task performance. *Nature, 365,* 611.

Rauscher, F. H., Shaw, G. L., & Ky, K. N. (1995). Listening to Mozart enhances spatial-temporal reasoning: Towards a neurophysiological basis. *Neuroscience Letters, 185,* 44–47.

Ray, W. J., & Oathes, D. (2003). Brain imaging techniques. *International Journal of Clinical and Experimental Hypnosis, 51,* 97–104.

Raynor, H. A., & Epstein, L. H. (2001). Dietary variety, energy regulation, and obesity. *Psychological Bulletin, 127,* 325–341.

Raynor, H. A., Niemeier, H. M., & Wing, R. R. (2006). Effect of limiting snack food variety on long-term sensory-specific satiety monotony during obesity treatment. *Eating Disorders, 7,* 1–14.

Raynor, J. O., & Entin, E. E. (1982). Future orientation and achievement motivation. In J. O. Raynor & E. E. Entin (Eds.), *Motivation, career striving, and aging.* New York: Hemisphere.

Read, C. R. (1991). Achievement and career choices: Comparisons of males and females. *Roeper Review, 13,* 188–193.

Reber, R. (2004). Availability. In F. P. Rudiger (Ed.), *Cognitive illusions.* New York: Psychology Press.

Recht, L. D., Lew, R. A., & Schwartz, W. J. (1995). Baseball teams beaten by jet lag. *Nature, 377,* 583.

Rechtschaffen, A. (1994). Sleep onset: Conceptual issues. In R. D. Ogilvie & J. R. Harsh (Eds.), *Sleep onset: Normal and abnormal processes.* Washington, DC: American Psychological Association.

Reed, G. M., Kemeny, M. E., Taylor, S. E., & Visscher, B. R. (1999). Negative HIV-specific expectancies and AIDS-related bereavement as predictors of symptom onset in asymptomatic HIV-positive gay men. *Health Psychology, 18,* 354–363.

Reed, J. G., & Baxter, P. M. (2003). *Library use: A handbook for psychology.* Washington, DC: American Psychological Association.

Rees, C. J., & Metcalfe, B. (2003). The faking of personality questionnaire results: Who's kidding whom? *Journal of Managerial Psychology, 18*(2), 156–165.

Reeve, C. L., & Hakel, M. D. (2002). Asking the right questions about g. *Human Performance, 15,* 47–74.

Refinetti, R. (2006). *Circadian physiology.* Boca Raton, FL: Taylor & Francis.

Regan, P. C. (1998). What if you can't get what you want? Willingness to compromise ideal mate selection standards as a function of sex, mate value, and relationship context. *Personality and Social Psychology Bulletin, 24,* 1294–1303.

Regan, P. C. (2003). *The mating game: A primer on love, sex, and marriage.* Thousand Oaks, CA: Sage.

Regan, T. (1997). The rights of humans and other animals. *Ethics & Behavior, 7*(2), 103–111.

Regier, D. A., & Burke, J. D. (2000). Epidemiology. In B. J. Sadock & V. A. Sadock (Eds.), *Kaplan and Sadock's comprehensive textbook of psychiatry.* Philadelphia: Lippincott/Williams & Wilkins.

Regier, D. A., & Kaelber, C. T. (1995). The Epidemiologic Catchment Area (ECA) program: Studying the prevalence and incidence of psychopathology. In M. T. Tsuang, M. Tohen, & G. E. P. Zahner (Eds.), *Textbook in psychiatric epidemiology.* New York: Wiley.

Regier, D. A., Narrow, W. E., & Rae, D. S. (2004). For DSM-V, It's the "disorder threshold," stupid. *Archives of General Psychiatry, 61,* 1051.

Reibel, D. K., Greeson, J. M., Brainard, G. C., & Rosenzweig, S. (2001). Mindfulness-based stress reduction and health-related quality of life in a heterogeneous patient population. *General Hospital Psychiatry, 23*(4), 183–192.

Reichert, T. (2003). The prevalence of sexual imagery in ads targeted to young adults. *Journal of Consumer Affairs, 37,* 403–412.

Reichert, T., Heckler, S. E., & Jackson, S. (2001). The effects of sexual social marketing appeals on cognitive processing and persuasion. *Journal of Advertising, 30*(1), 13–27.

Reichert, T., & Lambiase, J. (2003). How to get "kissably close": Examining how advertisers appeal to consumers' sexual needs and desires. *Sexuality & Culture: An Interdisciplinary Quarterly, 7*(3), 120–136.

Reimer, T., Mata, R., & Stoecklin, M. (2004). The use of heuristics in persuasion: Deriving cues on source expertise from argument quality. *Current Research in Social Psychology, 10*(6).pages?

Reinhard, M. A., Messner, M., & Sporer, S. L. (2006). Explicit persuasive intent and its impact on success at persuasion—The determining roles of attractiveness and likeableness. *Journal of Consumer Psychology, 16*, 249–259.

Reinharz, D., Lesage, A. D., & Contandriopoulos, A. P. (2000). Cost-effectiveness analysis of psychiatric deinstitutionalization. *Canadian Journal of Psychiatry, 45*, 533–538.

Reips, U.-D. (2000). The web experiment method: Advantages, disadvantages, and solutions. In M. H. Birnbaum (Ed.), *Psychological experiments on the Internet*. San Diego: Academic Press.

Reips, U.-D. (2007). The methodology of Internet-based experiments. In A. N. Joinson, K. Y. A. McKenna, T. Postmes, & U-D. Reips (Eds.), *The Oxford handbook of Internet psychology* (pp. 373–390). New York: Oxford University Press.

Reis, H. T., & Aron, A. (2008). Love: What is it, why does it matter, and how does it operate? *Perspectives on Psychological Science, 3*, 80–86.

Reisner, A. D. (1998). Repressed memories: True and false. In R. A. Baker (Ed.), *Child sexual abuse and false memory syndrome*. Amherst, NY: Prometheus Books.

Reiss, S. (1991). Expectancy model of fear, anxiety and panic. *Clinical Psychology Review, 11*, 141–154.

Rennie, D., & Luft, H. S. (2000). Making them transparent, making them credible. *Journal of the American Medical Association, 283*, 2516–2521.

Renzulli, J. S. (1986). The three-ring conception of giftedness: A developmental model for creative productivity. In R. J. Sternberg & J. E. Davidson (Eds.), *Conceptions of giftedness*. Cambridge: Cambridge University Press.

Renzulli, J. S. (1999). What is this thing called giftedness, and how do we develop it? A twenty-five year perspective. *Journal for the Education of the Gifted, 23*, 3–54.

Renzulli, J. S. (2002). Emerging conceptions of giftedness: Building a bridge to the new century. *Exceptionality, 10*, 67–75.

Renzulli, J. S. (2005). The three-ring conception of giftedness: A developmental model for promoting creative productivity. In R. J. Sternberg & J. E. Davidson (Eds.), *Conceptions of giftedness*. New York: Cambridge University Press.

Repetto, M., & Gold, M. S. (2005). Cocaine and crack: Neurobiology. In J. H. Lowinson, P. Ruiz, R. B. Millman, & J. G. Langrod (Eds.), *Substance abuse: A comprehensive textbook*. Philadelphia: Lippincott/Williams & Wilkins.

Rescorla, R. A. (1978). Some implications of a cognitive perspective on Pavlovian conditioning. In S. H. Hulse, H. Fowler, & W. K. Honig (Eds.), *Cognitive processes in animal behavior*. Hillsdale, NJ: Erlbaum.

Rescorla, R. A. (1980). *Pavlovian second-order conditioning*. Hillsdale, NJ: Erlbaum.

Rescorla, R. A., & Wagner, A. R. (1972). A theory of Pavlovian conditioning: Variations in the effectiveness of reinforcement and nonreinforcement. In A. H. Black & W. F. Prokasky (Eds.), *Classical conditioning: II. Current research and theory*. New York: Appleton-Century-Crofts.

Rest, J. R. (1986). *Moral development: Advances in research and theory*. New York: Praeger.

Reuter-Lorenz, P. A., & Miller, A. C. (1998). The cognitive neuroscience of human laterality: Lessons from the bisected brain. *Current Directions in Psychological Science, 7*, 15–20.

Reynolds, A. J., Temple, J. T., Robertson, D. L., & Mann, E. A. (2001). Long-term effects of an early childhood intervention on educational achievement and juvenile arrest: A 15-year follow-up of low-income children in public schools. *Journal of the American Medical Association, 285*, 2339–2346.

Reynolds, C. F., III, Frank, E., Perel, J. M., Imber, S. D., Cornes, C., Miller, M. D., Mazumdar, S., Houck, P. R., Dew, M. A., Stack, J. A., Pollock, B. G., & Kupfer, D. J. (1999). Nortriptyline and interpersonal psychotherapy as maintenance therapies for recurrent major depression: A randomized controlled trial in patients older than 50 years. *Journal of the American Medical Association, 28*, 39–45.

Reynolds, C. R. (2000). Why is psychometric research on bias in mental testing so often ignored? *Psychology, Public Policy, and Law, 6*, 144–150.

Reynolds, C. R., & Ramsay, M. C. (2003). Bias in psychological assessment: An empirical review and recommendations. In J. R. Graham & J. A. Naglieri (Eds.), *Handbook of psychology, Vol. 10: Assessment psychology*. New York: Wiley.

Reynolds, K. J., Turner, J. C., & Haslam, S. A. (2000). When are we better than them and they worse than us? A closer look at social discrimination in positive and negative domains. *Journal of Personality and Social Psychology, 78*, 64–80.

Rhodes, G., Simmons, L. W., & Peters, M. (2005). Attractiveness and sexual behavior: Does attractiveness enhance mating success? *Evolution and Human Behavior, 26*, 186–201.

Riba, M. B., & Miller, R. R. (2003). Combined therapies: Psychotherapy and pharmacotherapy. In A. Tasman, J. Kay, & J. A. Lieberman (Eds.), *Psychiatry*. New York: Wiley.

Rice, L. N., & Greenberg, L. S. (1992). Humanistic approaches to psychotherapy. In D. K. Freedheim (Ed.), *History of psychotherapy: A century of change*. Washington, DC: American Psychological Association.

Richardson, C. R., Kriska, A. M., Lantz, P. M., & Hayword, R. A. (2004). Physical activity and mortality across cardiovascular disease risk groups. *Medicine and Science in Sports and Exercise, 36*, 1923–1929.

Richardson, G. S. (2006). Shift work sleep disorder. In T. Lee-Chiong (Ed.), *Sleep: A comprehensive handbook*. Hoboken, NJ: Wiley-Liss.

Richardson, J., Anderson, T., Flaherty, J., & Bell, C. (2003). The quality of mental health care for African Americans. *Culture, Medicine and Psychiatry, 27*, 487–498.

Richert, E. S. (1997). Excellence with equity in identification and programming. In N. Colangelo, & G. A. Davis (Eds.), *Handbook of gifted education*. Boston: Allyn & Bacon.

Ridker, P. M. (2001). High-sensitivity C-reactive protein: Potential adjunct for global risk assessment in the primary prevention of cardiovascular disease. *Circulation, 103*, 1813–1818.

Ridker, P. M., Cannon, C. P., Morrow, D., Rifai, N., Rose, L. M., McCabe, C. H., Pfeffer, M. A., & Braunwald, E. (2005). C-reactive protein levels and outcomes after statin therapy. *New England Journal of Medicine, 6*(352), 20–28.

Rieber, R. W. (1998). The assimilation of psychoanalysis in America: From popularization to vulgarization. In R. W. Rieber & K. D. Salzinger (Eds.), *Psychology: Theoretical-historical perspectives*. Washington, DC: American Psychological Association.

Rief, W., Henningsen, P., & Hiller, W. (2006). Classification of somatoform disorders. *American Journal of Psychiatry, 163*, 746–747.

Rief, W., Hiller, W., & Margraf, J. (1998). Cognitive aspects of hypochondriasis and the somatization syndrome. *Journal of Abnormal Psychology, 107*, 587–595.

Rieskamp, J., & Hoffrage, U. (1999). When do people use simple heuristics, and how can we tell? In G. Gigerenzer, P. M. Todd, & ABC Research Group (Eds.), *Simple heuristics that make us smart* (pp. 141–168). New York: Oxford University Press.

Riggio, H. R., & Halpern, D. F. (2006). Understanding human thought: Educating students as critical thinkers. In W. Buskist & S. F. Davis (Eds.), *Handbook of the teaching of psychology* (pp. 78–84). Malden, MA: Blackwell Publishing.

Rigotti, N. A., Lee, J. E., & Wechsler, H. (2000). U.S. college students' use of tobacco products: Results of a national survey. *Journal of the American Medical Association, 284*, 699–705.

Rihmer, Z. (2003). Do SSRIs increase the risk of suicide among depressives even if they are only taking placebo? *Psychotherapy & Psychosomatics, 72*, 357–358.

Rihmer, Z., & Angst, J. (2005). Mood disorders: Epidemiology. In B. J. Sadock & V. A. Sadock (Eds.), *Kaplan & Sadock's comprehensive textbook of psychiatry* (pp. 1575–1581). Philadelphia: Lippincott Williams & Wilkins.

Riis, J., Loewenstein, G., Baron, J. , Jepson, C., Fagerlin, A., & Ubel, P. A. (2005). Ignorance of hedonic adaptation to hemodialysis: A study using ecological momentary assessment. *Journal of Experimental Psychology: General, 134*(1), 3–9.

Riley, B. P., & Kendler, K. S. (2005). Schizophrenia: Genetics. In B. J. Sadock & V. A. Sadock (Eds.), *Kaplan & Sadock's comprehensive textbook of psychiatry* (pp. 1354–1370). Philadelphia: Lippincott Williams & Wilkins.

Rilling, M. (1996). The mystery of the vanished citations: James McConnell's forgotten 1960s quest for planarian learning, a biochemical engram, and celebrity. *American Psychologist, 51*, 589–598.

Rilling, M. (2000a). How the challenge of explaining learning influenced the origins and development of John B. Watson's behaviorism. *American Journal of Psychology, 113*, 275–301.

Rilling, M. (2000b). John Watson's paradoxical struggle to explain Freud. *American Psychologist, 55*, 301–312.

Rimal R. N. (2001). Longitudinal influences of knowledge and self-efficacy on exercise behavior: Tests of a mutual reinforcement model. *Journal of Health Psychology, 6*, 31–46.

Rippe, J. M., Angelopoulous, T. J., & Zukley, L. (2007). The rationale for intervention to reduce the risk of coronary heart disease. *American Journal of Lifestyle Medicine, 1*, 10–19.

Risch, N., & Merikangas, K. R. (2003). Will the genomics revolution revolutionize psychiatry? *American Journal of Psychiatry, 160*, 625–635.

Risen, J., & Gilovich, T. (2007). Informal logical fallacies. In R. J. Sternberg, H. L. Roediger III, & D. F. Halpern (Eds.), *Critical thinking in psychology*. New York: Cambridge University Press.

Risen, J., Gilovich, T., & Dunning, D. (2007). One-shot illusory correlations and stereotype formation. *Personality and Social Psychology Bulletin, 33*, 1492–1502.

Riskind, J. H. (2005). Cognitive mechanisms in generalized anxiety disorder: A second generation of theoretical perspectives. *Cognitive Therapy & Research, 29*(1), 1–5.

Ritter, R. C. (2004). Gastrointestinal mechanisms of satiation for food. *Physiology & Behavior, 81,* 249–273.

Rivas-Vazquez, R. A. (2001). Antidepressants as first-line agents in the current pharmacotherapy of anxiety disorders. *Professional Psychology: Research & Practice, 32*(1), 101–104.

Rizzolatti, G. (2005). The mirror neuron system and imitation. In S. Hurley, & N. Chater (Eds.), *Perspectives on imitation: From neuroscience to social science: Vol. 1. Mechanisms of imitation and imitation in animals* (pp. 55–76). Cambridge, MA: MIT Press.

Rizzolatti, G., & Craighero, L. (2004). The mirror-neuron system. *Annual Review of Neuroscience, 27,* 169–192.

Roazen, P. (1976). *Erik H. Erikson: The power and limits of a vision.* New York: Free Press.

Roberson, D., Davidoff, J., Davies, I. R. L., & Shapiro, L. R. (2005). Color categories: Evidence for the cultural relativity hypothesis. *Cognitive Psychology, 50,* 378–411.

Roberson, D., Davidoff, J., & Shapiro, L. (2002). Squaring the circle: The cultural relativity of good shape. *Journal of Cognition & Culture, 2*(1), 29–51.

Roberson, D., Davies, I., & Davidoff, J. (2000). Color categories are not universal: Replications and new evidence from a stone-age culture. *Journal of Experimental Psychology: General, 129,* 369–398.

Roberts, B. W., Caspi, A., & Moffitt, T. (2003). Work experiences and personality development in young adulthood. *Journal of Personality and Social Psychology, 84,* 582–593.

Roberts, B. W., & DelVecchio, W. F. (2000). The rank-order consistency of personality traits from childhood to old age: A quantitative review of longitudinal studies. *Psychological Bulletin, 126,* 3–25.

Roberts, B. W., Kuncel, N. R., Shiner, R., Caspi, A., & Goldberg, L. R. (2007). The power of personality: The comparative validity of personality traits, socioeconomic status, and cognitive ability for predicting important life outcomes. *Perspectives on Psychological Science, 2,* 313–345.

Roberts, B. W., & Mroczek, D. (2008). Personality trait change in adulthood. *Current Directions in Psychological Science, 17,* 31–35.

Roberts, B. W., & Pomerantz, E. M. (2004). On traits, situations, and their integration: A developmental perspective. *Personality and Social Psychology Review, 8,* 402–416.

Roberts, B. W., & Wood, D. (2006). Personality development in the context of the Neo-socioanalytic model of personality. In D. Mroczek & T. Little (Eds.), *Handbook of personality development* (pp. 11–39). Mahwah, NJ: Erlbaum.

Roberts, B. W., Walton, K. E., & Bogg, T. (2005). Conscientiousness and health across the life course. *Review of General Psychology, 9*(2), 156–168.

Roberts, B. W., Walton, K., & Viechtbauer, W. (2006). Patterns of mean-level change in personality traits across the life course: A meta-analysis of longitudinal studies. *Psychological Bulletin, 132,* 1–25.

Roberts, J. E., & Ciesla, J. A. (2007). Stress generation. In G. Fink (Ed.), *Encyclopedia of stress.* San Diego: Elsevier.

Roberts, R. D., Markham, P. M., Matthews, G., & Zeidner, M. (2005). Assessing intelligence: Past, present, and future. In O. Wilhelm & R. W. Engle (Eds.), *Handbook of understanding and measuring intelligence.* Thousand Oaks, CA: Sage.

Robertson, S. I. (2001). *Problem solving.* East Sussex, England: Psychology Press.

Robiner, W. N., Bearman, D. L., Berman, M., Grove, W. M., Colon, E., Armstrong, J., Mareck, S., & Tanenbaum, R. L. (2003). Prescriptive authority for psychologists: Despite deficits in education and knowledge. *Journal of Clinical Psychology in Medical Settings, 10*(3), 211–212.

Robins, L. N., Locke, B. Z., & Regier, D. A. (1991). An overview of psychiatric disorders in America. In L. N. Robins & D. A. Regier (Eds.), *Psychiatric disorders in America: The epidemiologic catchment area study.* New York: Free Press.

Robins, R. W., Gosling, S. D., & Craik, K. H. (1999). An empirical analysis of trends in psychology. *American Psychologist, 54,* 117–128.

Robinson, A., & Clinkenbeard, P. R. (1998). Giftedness: An exceptionality examined. *Annual Review of Psychology, 49,* 117–139.

Robinson, D. G., Woerner, M. G., McMeniman, M., Mendelowitz, A., & Bilder, R. M. (2004). Symptomatic and functional recovery from a first episode of schizophrenia or schizoaffective disorder. *American Journal of Psychiatry, 161,* 473–479.

Robinson, F. P. (1970). *Effective study* (4th ed.). New York: Harper & Row.

Robles, T. F., Glaser, R., & Kiecolt-Glaser, J. K. (2005). Out of balance: A new look at chronic stress, depression, and immunity. *Current Directions in Psychological Science, 14,* 111–115.

Rockey, D. L. Jr., Beason, K. R., Howington, E. B., Rockey, C. M., & Gilbert, J. D. (2005). Gambling by Greek-affiliated college students: An association between affiliation and gambling. *Journal of College Student Development, 46,* 75–87.

Rodgers, J. E. (1982). The malleable memory of eyewitnesses. *Science Digest, 3,* 32–35.

Rodieck, R. W. (1998). *The first steps in seeing.* Sunderland, MA: Sinauer.

Roediger, H. L., III. (1980). Memory metaphors in cognitive psychology. *Memory & Cognition, 8,* 231–246.

Roediger, H. L., III. (2000). Why retrieval is the key process in understanding human memory. In E. Tulving (Ed.), *Memory, consciousness, and the brain: The Tallinn conference* (pp. 52–75). Philadelphia: Psychology Press.

Roediger, H. L., III, & Gallo, D. A. (2001). Levels of processing: Some unanswered questions. In M. Naveh-Benjamin, M. Moscovitch, & H. L. Roediger III (Eds.), *Perspectives on human memory and cognitive aging: Essays in honor of Fergus Craik.* New York: Psychology Press.

Roediger, H. L., III, Gallo, D. A., & Geraci, L. (2002). Processing approaches to cognition: The impetus from the levels-of-processing framework. *Memory, 10,* 319–332.

Roediger, H. L., III, & Guynn, M. J. (1996). Retrieval processes. In E. L. Bjork & R. A. Bjork (Eds.), *Memory.* San Diego: Academic Press.

Roediger, H. L., III, & Karpicke, J. D. (2006a). Test-enhanced learning: Taking memory tests improves long-term retention. *Psychological Science, 17,* 249–255.

Roediger, H. L., III, & Karpicke, J. D. (2006b). The power of testing memory: Basic research and implications for educational practice. *Perspectives on Psychological Science, 1*(3), 181–210.

Roediger, H. L., III, & McDermott, K. B. (1995). Creating false memories: Remembering words not presented in lists. *Journal of Experimental Psychology: Learning, Memory, and Cognition, 21,* 803–814.

Roediger, H. L., III, & McDermott, K. B. (2000). Tricks of memory. *Current Directions in Psychological Science, 9,* 123–127.

Roediger, H. L., III, Wheeler, M. A., & Rajaram, S. (1993). Remembering, knowing, and reconstructing the past. In D. L. Medin (Ed.), *The psychology of learning and motivation: Advances in research and theory.* San Diego: Academic Press.

Roehrs, T., & Roth, T. (2000). Hypnotics: Efficacy and adverse effects. In M. H. Kryger, T. Roth, & W. C. Dement (Eds.), *Principles and practice of sleep medicine.* Philadelphia: Saunders.

Roehrs, T., & Roth, T. (2004). "Hypnotic" prescription patterns in a large managed-care population. *Sleep Medicine, 5,* 463–466.

Roehrs, T., Carskadon, M. A., Dement, W. C., & Roth, T. (2005). Daytime sleepiness and alertness. In M. H. Kryger, T. Roth, & W. C. Dement (Eds.). *Principles and practice of sleep medicine.* Philadelphia: Elsevier Saunders.

Roehrs, T., Zorick, F. J., & Roth, T. (2000). Transient and short-term insomnias. In M. H. Kryger, T. Roth, & W. C. Dement (Eds.), *Principles and practice of sleep medicine.* Philadelphia: Saunders.

Roethlisberger, F. J., & Dickson, W. J. (1939). *Management and the worker.* Cambridge, MA: Harvard University Press.

Rogers, C. R. (1951). *Client-centered therapy: Its current practice, implications, and theory.* Boston: Houghton Mifflin.

Rogers, C. R. (1961). *On becoming a person: A therapist's view of psychotherapy.* Boston: Houghton Mifflin.

Rogers, C. R. (1980). *A way of being.* Boston: Houghton Mifflin.

Rogers, C. R. (1986). Client-centered therapy. In I. L. Kutash & A. Wolf (Eds.), *Psychotherapist's casebook.* San Francisco: Jossey-Bass.

Rogers, M. P., Fricchione, G., & Reich, P. (1999). Psychosomatic medicine and consultation-liaison psychiatry. In A. M. Nicholi (Ed.), *The Harvard guide to psychiatry* (3rd ed., pp. 362–389). Cambridge, MA: Harvard University Press.

Rogers, N. L., & Dinges, D. F. (2002). Shiftwork, circadian disruption, and consequences. *Primary Psychiatry, 9*(8), 50.

Rogers, P. (1998). The cognitive psychology of lottery gambling: A theoretical review. *Journal of Gambling Studies, 14,* 111–134.

Rogers, T. B., Kuiper, N. A., & Kirker, W. S. (1977). Self-reference and the encoding of personal information. *Journal of Personality and Social Psychology, 35,* 677–688.

Rogers, W. T., & Yang, P. (1996). Test-wiseness: Its nature and application. *European Journal of Psychological Assessment, 12,* 247–259.

Rogoff, B. (1998). Cognition as a collaborative process. In D. Kuhn & R. S. Siegler (Eds.), *Handbook of child psychology, Vol. 2: Cognition perception, and language.* New York: Wiley.

Rogoff, B. (2003). *The cultural nature of human development.* New York: Oxford University Press.

Rohde, P. A., Atzwanger, K., Butovskayad, M., Lampert, A., Mysterud, I., Sanchez-Andres, A., & Sulloway, F. J. (2003). Perceived parental favoritism, closeness to kin and the rebel of the family: The effects of birth order and sex. *Evolution & Human Behavior, 24*(4), 261–276.

Rohner, R. P., & Veneziano, R. A. (2001). The importance of father love: History and contemporary evidence. *Review of General Psychology, 5,* 382–405.

Rohrer, D., & Taylor, K. (2006). The effects of overlearning and distributed practice on the retention of mathematics knowledge. *Applied Cognitive Psychology, 20,* 1209–1224.

Rohrer, D., Taylor, K., Pashler, H., Wixted, J. T., & Capeda, N. J. (2005). The effect of overlearning on long-term retention. *Applied Cognitive Psychology, 19,* 361–374.

Rolls, E. T. (1990). A theory of emotion, and its application to understanding the neural basis of emotion. *Cognitive and Emotion, 4,* 161–190.

Rolls, E. T., & Tovee, M. T. (1995). Sparseness of the neuronal representation of stimuli in the primate temporal visual cortex. *Journal of Neurophysiology, 73,* 713–726.

Romanski, L. M., Chafee, M. V., & Goldman-Rakic, P. S. (2004). Domain specificity in cognitive systems. In M. S. Gazzaniga (Ed.), *The cognitive neurosciences.* Cambridge, MA: MIT Press.

Roney, J. R., Hanson, K. N., Durante, K. M., & Maestripieri, D. (2006). Reading men's faces: Women's mate attractiveness judgments track men's testosterone and interest in infants. *Proceedings of the Royal Society, 273,* 2169–2175.

Rorden, C., & Karnath, H.-O. (2004). Using human brain lesions to infer function: A relic from a past era in the fMRI age? *Nature Reviews Neuroscience, 5,* 813–819.

Rorden, C., Karnath, H.-O., & Bonilha, L. (2007). Improving lesion-symptom mapping. *Journal of Cognitive Neuroscience, 19,* 1081–1088.

Rorschach, H. (1921). *Psychodiagnostik.* Berne: Birchen.

Rorschach, H. (1942). *Psychodiagnostics: A diagnostic test based on perception.* Berne: Huber.

Rosch, E. H. (1973). Natural categories. *Cognitive Psychology, 4,* 328–350.

Rose, D. P. (1997). Dietary fatty acids and cancer. *American Journal of Clinical Nutrition, 66,* 998S–1003S.

Rose, D., Wykes, T., Leese, M., Bindman, J., & Fleischmann, P. (2003). Patient's perspectives on electroconvulsive therapy: Systematic review. *British Medical Journal, 326,* 1363–1365.

Rose, H., & Rose, S. E. (2000). *Alas, poor Darwin: Arguments against evolutionary psychology.* New York: Harmony Books.

Rose, N. R. (2007). Neuroimmunomodulation. In G. Fink (Ed.), *Encyclopedia of stress.* San Diego: Elsevier.

Roseboom, T., de Rooij, S., & Painter, R. (2006). The Dutch famine and its long-term consequences for adult health. *Early Human Development, 82,* 485–491.

Rosenbaum, M., Lakin, M., & Roback, H. B. (1992). Psychotherapy in groups. In D. K. Freedheim (Ed.), *History of psychotherapy: A century of change.* Washington, DC: American Psychological Association.

Rosenberg, E., & DeMaso, D. R. (2008). A doubtful guest: Managed care and mental health. *Child and Adolescent Psychiatric Clinics of North America, 17,* 53–66.

Rosenblatt, A., Greenberg, J., Solomon, S., Pyszczynski, T., & Lyon, D. (1989). Evidence for terror management theory: I. The effect of mortality salience on reactions to those who violate or uphold cultural values. *Journal of Personality and Social Psychology, 57,* 681–690.

Rosenblum, G. D., & Lewis, M. (2003). Emotional development in adolescence. In G. R. Adams &

M. D. Berzonsky (Eds.), *Blackwell handbook of adolescence.* Malden, MA: Blackwell Publishing.

Rosenhan, D. L. (1973). On being sane in insane places. *Science, 179,* 250–258.

Rosenheck, R. A. (2006). Outcomes, costs, and policy caution. *Archives of General Psychiatry, 63,* 1074–1076.

Rosenthal, H. (1988). *Not with my life I don't: Preventing suicide and that of others.* Muncie, IN: Accelerated Development.

Rosenthal, L. (2006). Physiologic processes during sleep. In T. Lee-Chiong (Ed.), *Sleep: A comprehensive handbook.* Hoboken, NJ: Wiley-Liss.

Rosenthal, R. (1976). *Experimenter effects in behavioral research.* New York: Halsted.

Rosenthal, R. (1994). Interpersonal expectancy effects: A 30–year perspective. *Current Directions in Psychological Science, 3,* 176–179.

Rosenthal, R. (2002). Experimenter and clinical effects in scientific inquiry and clinical practice. *Prevention & Treatment, 5*(38), no pagination specified.

Rosenthal, R., & Fode, K. L. (1963). Three experiments in experimenter bias. *Psychological Reports, 12,* 491–511.

Rosenweig, E. S., Barnes, C. A., & McNaughton, B. L. (2002). Making room for new memories. *Nature Neuroscience, 5,* 6–8.

Rosenzweig, M. R., & Bennet, E. L. (1996). Psychobiology of plasticity: Effects of training and experience on brain and behavior. *Behavioural Brain Research, 78*(5), 57–65.

Rosenzweig, M. R., Krech, D., & Bennett, E. L. (1961). Heredity, environment, brain biochemistry, and learning. In *Current trends in psychological theory.* Pittsburgh: University of Pittsburgh Press.

Rosenzweig, M., Krech, D., Bennett, E. L., & Diamond, M. (1962). Effects of environmental complexity and training on brain chemistry and anatomy: A replication and extension. *Journal of Comparative and Physiological Psychology, 55,* 429–437.

Rosenzweig, S. (1985). Freud and experimental psychology: The emergence of idiodynamics. In S. Koch & D. E. Leary (Eds.), *A century of psychology as a science.* New York: McGraw-Hill.

Rosler, F. (2005). From single-channel recordings to brain-mapping devices: The impact of electro-encephalography on experimental psychology. *History of Psychology, 8*(1), 95–117.

Ross, B. (1991). William James: Spoiled child of American psychology. In G. A. Kimble, M. Wertheimer, & C. White (Eds.), *Portraits of pioneers in psychology.* Hillsdale, NJ: Erlbaum.

Ross, C. A. (1999). Dissociative disorders. In T. Millon, P. H. Blaney, & R. D. Davis (Eds.), *Oxford textbook of psychopathology* (pp. 466–484). New York: Oxford University Press.

Ross, L. D. (1988). The obedience experiments: A case study of controversy. *Contemporary Psychology, 33,* 101–104.

Roter, D. L., Hall, J. A., Merisca, R., Nordstrom, B., Cretin, D., & Svarstad, B. (1998). Effectiveness of interventions to promote patient compliance. *Medical Care, 36,* 1138–1161.

Roth, T., & Drake, C. (2004). Evolution of insomnia: Current status and future direction. *Sleep Medicine, 5*(Supplemental 1), S23–S30.

Rothbart, M. (2001). Category dynamics and the modification of outgroup stereotypes. In R. Brown & S. L. Gaertner (Eds.), *Blackwell handbook of social psychology: Intergroup processes.* Malden, MA: Blackwell.

Rothbart, M. K. (2007). Temperament, development, and personality. *Current Directions in Psychological Science, 16,* 207–212.

Rothbart, M. K., & Bates, J. E. (2006). Temperament. In N. Eisenberg, W. Damon, & R. M. Lerner (Eds.), *Handbook of child psychology: Social, emotional, and personality development* (pp. 99–166). Hoboken, NJ: Wiley.

Rotter, J. B. (1982). *The development and application of social learning theory.* New York: Praeger.

Rotter, J. B., & Rafferty, J. E. (1950). *Manual: The Rotter incomplete sentence blank.* New York: Psychological Corporation.

Rouiller, E. M. (1997). Functional organization of the auditory pathways. In G. Ehret & R. Romand (Eds.), *The central auditory system.* Oxford, England: Oxford University Press.

Routh, D. K., & Reisman, J. M. (2003). Clinical psychology. In D. K. Freedheim (Ed.), *Handbook of psychology, Vol. 1: History of psychology.* New York: Wiley.

Rowatt, W. C., Cunningham, M. R., & Druen, P. B. (1999). Lying to get a date: The effect of facial physical attractiveness on the willingness to deceive prospective dating partners. *Journal of Social & Personal Relationships, 16,* 209–223.

Rowe, D. (1994). *The limits of family influence: Genes, experience, and behavior.* New York: Guilford.

Rowe, D., & van den Oord, E. J. C. G. (2005). Genetic and environmental influences. In V. A. Derlega, B. A. Winstead, & W. H. Jones (Eds.), *Personality: Contemporary theory and research.* Belmont, CA: Wadsworth.

Rowe, S. M., & Wertsch, J. V. (2002). Vygotsky's model of cognitive development. In U. Goswami (Ed.), *Blackwell handbook of childhood cognitive development.* Malden, MA: Blackwell.

Rozee, P. D., & Koss, M. P. (2001). Rape: A century of resistance. *Psychology of Women Quarterly, 25* (4), 295–311.

Rozin, P. (1990). The importance of social factors in understanding the acquisition of food habits. In E. D. Capaldi & T. L. Powley (Eds.), *Taste, experience, and feeding.* Washington, DC: American Psychological Association.

Rozin, P. (1996). Towards a psychology of food and eating: From motivation to module to model to marker, morality, meaning, and metaphor. *Current Directions in Psychological Science, 5,* 18–24.

Rozin, P. (2003). Introduction: Evolutionary and cultural perspectives on affect. In R. J. Davidson, K. R. Scherer, & H. H. Goldsmith (Eds.), *Handbook of affective sciences.* New York: Oxford University Press.

Rozin, P. (2007). Food and eating. In S. Kitayama & D. Cohen (Eds.), *Handbook of cultural psychology* (pp. 391–416). New York: Guilford.

Rozin, P., Dow, S., Moscovitch, M., & Rajaram, S. (1998). What causes humans to begin and end a meal? A role for memory for what has been eaten, as evidenced by a study of multiple meal eating in amnesic patients. *Psychological Science, 9,* 392–396.

Rozin, P., Kabnick, K., Pete, E., Fischler, C., & Shields, C. (2003). The ecology of eating: Smaller portion sizes in France than in the United States help explain the French paradox. *Psychological Science, 14,* 450–454.

Rozin, P., & Royzman, E. (2001). Negativity bias, negativity dominance, and contagion. *Personality & Social Psychology Review, 5,* 296–320.

Ruble, D. N., & Martin, C. L. (1998). Gender development. In W. Damon (Ed.), *Handbook of child* psychology (Vol. 3): Social, emotional, and personality development. New York: Wiley.

Ruble, T. L. (1983). Sex stereotypes: Issues of change in the 70s. *Sex Roles, 9,* 397–402.

Rudorfer, M. V., Henry, M. E., & Sackheim, H. A. (2003). Electroconvulsive therapy. In A. Tasman, J. Kay, & J. A. Lieberman (Eds.), *Psychiatry.* New York: Wiley.

Ruini, C., & Fava, G. A. (2004). Clinical application of well-being therapy. In P. A. Linley & S. Joseph (Eds.), *Positive psychology in practice.* Hoboken, NJ: Wiley.

Ruiter, R. A., Abraham, C., & Kok, G. (2001). Scary warnings and rational precautions: A review of the psychology of fear appeals. *Psychology & Health, 16,* 613–630.

Rule, N. O., & Ambady, N. (2008). The face of success: Inferences from chief executive officers' appearance predict company profits. *Psychological Science, 19,* 109–111.

Runco, M. A. (2004). Divergent thinking, creativity, and giftedness. In R. J. Sternberg (Ed.), *Definitions and conceptions of giftedness* (pp. 47–62). Thousand Oaks, CA: Corwin Press.

Runyan, J. D., & Dash, P. K. (2005). Distinct prefrontal molecular mechanisms for information storage lasting seconds versus minutes. *Learning & Memory, 12*(3), 232–238.

Runyan, W. M. (2006). Psychobiography and the psychology of science: Understanding relations between the life and work of individual psychologists. *Review of General Psychology, 10,,* 147–162.

Rupp, H. A., & Wallen, K. (2007). Relationship between testosterone and interest in sexual stimuli: The effect of experience. *Hormones and Behavior, 52,* 581–589.

Ruscio, J. (2006). *Clear thinking with psychology: Separating sense from nonsense.* Belmont, CA: Wadsworth.

Rush, A. J. (1984). Cognitive therapy. In T. B. Karasu (Ed.), *The psychiatric therapies.* Washington, DC: American Psychiatric Press.

Rush, A. J., & Beck, A. T. (2000). Cognitive therapy. In B. J. Sadock & V. A. Sadock (Eds.), *Kaplan and Sadock's comprehensive textbook of psychiatry* (7th ed., Vol. 1, pp. 2167–2177). Philadelphia: Lippincott/ Williams & Wilkins.

Rushton, J. P. (2003). Race differences in *g* and the "Jensen effect." In H. Nyborg (Ed.), *The scientific study of general intelligence: Tribute to Arthur R. Jensen.* Oxford, UK: Pergamon.

Rushton, J. P., & Ankney, C. D. (2007). The evolution of brain size and intelligence. In S. M. Platek, J. P. Keenan, & T. K. Shackleford (Eds.), *Evolutionary cognitive neuroscience.* Cambridge: MIT Press.

Rushton, J. P., & Jensen, A. R. (2005). Thirty years of research on race differences in cognitive ability. *Psychology, Public Policy, and Law, 11,* 235–294.

Russell, G. F. M. (1995). Anorexia nervosa through time. In G. Szmukler, C. Dare, & J. Treasure (Eds.), *Handbook of eating disorders: Theory, treatment, and research.* New York: Wiley.

Russell, G. F. M. (1997). The history of bulimia nervosa. In D. M. Garner, & P. E. Garfinkel (Eds.), *Handbook of treatment for eating disorders.* New York: Guilford.

Russell, J. A. (1991). Culture and the categorization of emotions. *Psychological Bulletin, 110,* 426–450.

Russell, J. A. (1994). Is there universal recognition of emotion from facial expression? A review of the cross-cultural studies. *Psychological Bulletin, 115,* 102–141.

Russell, J. A. (1995). Facial expressions of emotion: What lies beyond minimal universality? *Psychological Bulletin, 118,* 379–391.

Russell, J. A. (2007). Stress milestones. *Stress: The International Journal on the Biology of Stress, 10*(1), 1–2.

Russo, J. E., Carlson, K. A., & Meloy, M. G. (2006). Choosing an inferior alternative. *Psychological Science, 17,* 899–904.

Russo, N. F., & Denmark, F. L. (1987). Contributions of women to psychology. *Annual Review of Psychology, 38,* 279–298.

Rutherford, A. (2000). Radical behaviorism and psychology's public: B. F. Skinner in the popular press, 1934–1990. *History of Psychology, 3,* 371–395.

Rutherford, W. (1886). A new theory of hearing. *Journal of Anatomy and Physiology, 21,* 166–168.

Rutledge, T., Reis, S. E., Olson, M., Owens, J., Kelsey, S. F., Pepine, C. J., Mankad, S., Rogers, W. J., Merz, C. N. B., Sopko, G., Cornell, C. E., Sharaf, B., & Matthews, K. A. (2004). Social networks are associated with lower mortality rates among women with suspected coronary disease: The National Heart, Lung, and Blood Institute– sponsored women's ischemia syndrome evaluation study. *Psychosomatic Medicine, 66,* 882–888.

Rutter, M. (2006). *Genes and behavior: Nature-nurture interplay explained.* Maiden, MA: Blackwell Publishing.

Rutter, M. (2007). Gene-environment interdependence. *Developmental Science, 10,* 12–18.

Ryckeley, R. (2005, May). Don't send in the clowns. *The Citizen.*

Ryder, R. D. (2006). Speciesism in the laboratory. In P. Singer (Ed.), *In defense of animals: The second wave* (pp. 87–103). Malden, MA: Blackwell Publishing.

Sack, A. T., Hubl, D., Prvulovic, D. , Formisano, E., Jandl, M., Zanella, F. E., Maurer, K., Goebel, R., Dierks, T., & Linden, D. E. J. (2002). The experimental combination of r TMS and fMRI reveals the functional relevance of parietal cortex for visuo-spatial functions. *Cognitive Brain Resarch., 13,* 85–93.

Sack, A. T., & Linden, D. E. J. (2003). Combining transcranial magnetic stimulation and functional imaging in cognitive brain research: Possibilities and limitations. *Brain Research Reviews, 43*(1), 41–56.

Sackeim, H. A., Haskett, R. F., Mulsant, B. H., Thase, M. E., Mann, J. J., Pettinati, H. M., Greenberg, R. M., Crowe, R. R., Cooper, T. B., & Prudic, J. (2001). Continuation pharmacotherapy in the prevention of relapse following electroconvulsive therapy: A randomized controlled trial. *Journal of the American Medical Association, 285,* 1299–1307.

Sackeim, H. A., Prudic, J., Fuller, R., Keilp, J., Lavori, P. W., & Olfson, M. (2007). The cognitive effects of electroconvulsive therapy in community settings. *Neuropsychopharmacology, 32,* 244–254.

Sackett, P. R., & DeVore, C. J. (2001). Counterproductive behaviors at work. In In N. Anderson, D. S. Ones, H. K. Sinangil, & C. Viswesvaran (Eds.), *Handbook of industrial, work and organizational psychology* (pp. 145–165). Thousand Oaks, CA: Sage.

Sackett, P. R., & Laczo, R. M. (2003). Job and work analysis. In W. C. Borman, D. R. Ilgen, & R. J. Klimoski (Eds.), *Handbook of psychology*, vol. 12: *Industrial and organizational psychology* (pp. 21–37). New York: Wiley.

Sacks, O. (1987). *The man who mistook his wife for a hat.* New York: Harper & Row.

Sadker, M., & Sadker, D. (1994). *Failing at fairness: How America's schools cheat girls.* New York: Scribners.

Sadler, J. Z. (2005). *Values and psychiatric diagnosis.* New York: Oxford University Press.

Sagie, A. (1997). Leader direction and employee participation in decision making: Contradictory or compatible practices? *Applied Psychology: An International Review, 46*(4), 387–452.

Saks, A. M. (2006). Multiple predictions and criteria of job search success. *Journal of Vocational Behavior, 68,* 400–415.

Sala, J. B., & Courtney, S. M. (2007). Binding of what and where during working memory maintenance. *Cortex, 43,* 5–21.

Salgado, J. F., Viswesvaran, C., & Ones, D. (2003). Predictors used for personnel selection: An overview of constructs, methods and techniques. In N. Anderson, D. S. Ones, H. K. Sinangil, & C. Viswesvaran (Eds.), *Handbook of industrial, work and organizational psychology* (pp. 166–199). Thousand Oaks, CA: Sage.

Salminen, S. (1992). Defensive attribution hypothesis and serious occupational accidents. *Psychological Reports, 70,* 1195–1199.

Salmon, P., Sephton, S., Weissbecker, I., Hoover, K., Ulmer, C., & Studts, J. L. (2004). Mindfulness mediation in clinical practice. *Cognitive and Behavioral Practice, 11,* 434–446.

Salovey, P., & Grewal, D. (2005). The science of emotional intelligence. *Current Directions in Psychological Science, 14,* 281–285.

Salovey, P., & Mayer, J. D. (1990). Emotional intelligence. *Imagination, Cognition, and Personality, 9,* 185–211.

Salovey, P., Mayer, J. D., & Caruso, D. (2002). The positive psychology of emotional intelligence. In C. R. Synder & J. Lopez (Eds.), *Handbook of positive psychology.* New York: Oxford University Press.

Salthouse, T. A. (1996). The processing-speed theory of adult age differences in cognition. *Psychological Review, 103,* 403–428.

Salthouse, T. A. (2000). Aging and measures of processing speed. *Biological Psychology, 54,* 35–54.

Salthouse, T. A. (2003). Memory aging from 18–80. *Alzheimer Disease & Associated Disorders, 17*(3), 162–167.

Salthouse, T. A. (2004). What and when of cognitive aging. *Current Directions in Psychological Science, 13*(4), 140–144.

Salthouse, T. A. (2005). Time as a factor in the development and decline of mental processes. In A.-N. Perret-Clermont (Ed.), *Thinking time: A multidisciplinary perspective on time.* Ashland, OH: Hogrefe & Huber Publishers.

Salthouse, T. A. (2006). Mental exercise and mental aging. *Perspectives on Psychological Science, 1,* 68–87.

Salvendy, J. T. (1993). Selection and preparation of patients and organization of the group. In H. I. Kaplan & B. J. Sadock (Eds.), *Comprehensive group psychotherapy.* Baltimore: Williams & Wilkins.

Samberg, E., & Marcus, E. R. (2005). Process, resistance, and interpretation. In E. S. Person, A. M. Cooper, & G. O. Gabbard (Eds.), *Textbook of psychoanalysis* (pp. 229–240). Washington, DC: American Psychiatric Publishing.

Sanchez, D. T., Kiefer, A. K., & Ybarra, O. (2006). Sexual submissiveness in women: Costs for sexual autonomy and arousal. *Personality and Social Psychology Bulletin, 32,* 512–524.

Sanchez, I. M., & Turner, S. M. (2003). Practicing psychology in the era of managed care: Implications for practice and training. *American Psychologist, 58*(2), 116–129.

Sanders, M. H., & Givelber, R. J. (2006). Overview of obstructive sleep apnea in adults. In T. Lee-Chiong (Ed.), *Sleep: A comprehensive handbook*. Hoboken, NJ: Wiley-Liss.

Sandin, B., Chorot, P., Santed, M. A., & Valiente, R. M. (2004). Differences in negative life events between patients with anxiety disorders, depression and hypochondriasis. *Anxiety, Stress & Coping: An International Journal*, 17(1), 37–47.

Sandoz, J. (2004). Internet addiction. *Annals of the American Psychotherapy Association*, 7, 34.

Sanger, D. J. (2004). The pharmacology and mechanisms of action of new generation, nonbenzodiazepine hypnotic agents. *CNS Drugs*, 18(Suppl1), 9–15.

Sanislow, C. A., & Carson, R. C. (2001). Schizophrenia: A critical examination. In P. B. Sutker & H. E. Adams (Eds.), *Comprehensive handbook of psychopathology* (3rd ed., pp. 403–444). New York: Kluwer Academic/Plenum.

Sanna, L. J., & Schwarz, N. (2006). Metacognitive experiences and human judgment: The case of hindsight bias and its debiasing. *Current Directions in Psychological Science*, 15, 172–176.

Sanson, A., Hemphill, S. A., & Smart, D. (2002). Temperament and social development. In P. K. Smith & C. H. Hart (Eds.), *Blackwell handbook of childhood social development*. Malden, MA: Blackwell.

Saper, C. B. (2000). Brain stem, reflexive behavior, and the cranial nerves. In E. R. Kandel, J. H. Schwartz, & T. M. Jessell (Eds.), *Principles of neural science* (pp. 873–888). New York: McGraw-Hill.

Saper, C. B., Scammell, T. E., & Lu, J. (2005). Hypothalamic regulation of sleep and circadian rhythms. *Nature*, 437, 1257–1263.

Sapolsky, R. M. (2007). Stress, stress-related disease, and emotion regulation. In J. J. Gross (Ed.), *Handbook of emotion regulation*. New York: Guilford.

Sarason, I. G., & Sarason, B. G. (1987). *Abnormal psychology: The problem of maladaptive behavior*. Englewood Cliffs, NJ: Prentice-Hall.

Sato, T., Namiki, H., Ando, J., & Hatano, G. (2004). Japanese conception of and research on intelligence. In R. J. Sternberg (Ed.), *International handbook of intelligence* (pp. 302–324). New York: Cambridge University Press.

Sauter, S. L., Murphy, L. R., & Hurrell, J. J. (1990). Prevention of work-related psychological disorders: A national strategy proposed by the National Institute for Occupational Safety and Health. *American Psychologist*, 45, 1146–1158.

Savage-Rumbaugh, S. (1991). Language learning in the bonobo: How and why they learn. In N. A. Krasnegor, D. M. Rumbaugh, & R. L. Schiefelbusch/ M. Studdert-Kennedy (Eds.), *Biological and behavioral determinants of language development*. Hillsdale, N.J.: Erlbaum.

Savage-Rumbaugh, S., Rumbaugh, D. M., & Fields, W. M. (2006). Language as a window on rationality. In S. Hurley & M. Nudds (Eds.), *Rational animals?* (pp. 513–552). New York: Oxford University Press.

Savage-Rumbaugh, S., Shanker, S. G., & Taylor, T. J. (1998). *Apes, language, and the human mind*. New York: Oxford University Press.

Savin-Williams, R. C. (2006). Who's gay? Does it matter? *Current Directions in Psychological Science*, 15, 40–44.

Savitsky, K., Epley, N., & Gilovich, T. (2001). Do others judge us as harshly as we think? Overestimating the impact of our failures, shortcomings, and mishaps. *Journal of Personality and Social Psychology*, 81, 44–56.

Saxe, L. (1994). Detection of deception: Polygraph and integrity tests. *Current Directions in Psychological Science*, 3, 69–73.

Sayer, L. C. (2005). Gender, time, and inequality: Trends in women's and men's paid work, unpaid work, and free time. *Social Forces*, 84, 285–303.

Sayers, S. L. (2004). Depression and heart disease: The interrelationship between these two common disorders is complex and requires careful diagnostic and treatment methods. *Psychiatric Annals*, 34(4), 282–288.

Sayette, M. A. (2007). Alcohol and stress: Social and psychological aspects. In G. Fink (Ed.), *Encyclopedia of stress*. San Diego: Elsevier.

Scarr, S. (1991). *Theoretical issues in investigating intellectual plasticity*. S. E. Brauth, W. S. Hall, & R. Dooling (Eds.), *Plasticity of development*. Cambridge, MA: MIT Press.

Scarr, S., & Weinberg, R. A. (1977). Intellectual similarities within families of both adopted and biological children. *Intelligence*, 32, 170–190.

Scarr, S., & Weinberg, R. A. (1983). The Minnesota adoption studies: Genetic differences and malleability. *Child Development*, 54, 260–267.

Scattone, D. (2007). Social skills interventions for children with autism. *Psychology in the Schools*, 44, 717–726.

Schachner, D. A., & Shaver, P. R. (2004). Attachment dimensions and sexual motives. *Personal Relationships*, 11(2), 179–195.

Schachter, S. (1959). *The psychology of affiliation*. Stanford, CA: Stanford University Press.

Schachter, S. (1964). The interaction of cognitive and physiological determinants of emotional state. In L. Berkowitz (Ed.), *Advances in experimental social psychology* (Vol. 1). New York: Academic Press.

Schachter, S., & Singer, J. E. (1962). Cognitive, social and physiological determinants of emotional state. *Psychological Review*, 69, 379–399.

Schachter, S., & Singer, J. E. (1979). Comments on the Maslach and Marshall-Zimbardo experiments. *Journal of Personality and Social Psychology*, 37, 989–995.

Schacter, D. L. (1996). *Searching for memory: The brain, the mind, and the past*. New York: Basic Books.

Schacter, D. L. (1999). The seven sins of memory: Insights from psychology and cognitive neuroscience. *American Psychologist*, 54, 182–203.

Schacter, D. L. (2001). *The seven sins of memory: How the mind forgets and remembers*. Boston: Houghton Mifflin.

Schacter, D. L., Wagner, A. D., & Buckner, R. L. (2000). Memory systems of 1999. In E. Tulving & F. I. M. Craik (Eds.), *Oxford handbook of memory*. New York: Oxford University Press.

Schaefer, A. (2005). Commuting takes its toll. *Scientific American Mind*, 16(3), 14–15.

Schaeffer, N. C. (2000). Asking questions about threatening topics: A selective overview. In A. A. Stone, J. S. Turkkan, C. A. Bachrach, J. B. Jobe, H. S. Kurtzman, & V. Cain (Eds.), *The science of self-report: Implications for research and practice*. Mahwah, NJ: Erlbaum.

Schafe, G. E., & Ledoux, J. E. (2004). The neural basis of fear. In M. S. Gazzaniga (Ed.), *The cognitive neurosciences* (pp. 987–1003). Cambridge, MA: MIT Press.

Schafe, G. E., Doyère, V., & LeDoux, J. E. (2005). Tracking the fear engram: The lateral amygdala is an essential locus of fear memory storage. *Journal of Neuroscience*, 25, 10010–10015.

Schaie, K. W. (1990). Intellectual development in adulthood. In J. E. Birren & K. W. Schaie (Eds.), *Handbook of the psychology of aging* (3rd ed.). San Diego: Academic Press.

Schaie, K. W. (1994). The course of adult intellectual development. *American Psychologist*, 49, 304–313.

Schaie, K. W. (1996). *Adult intellectual development: The Seattle longitudinal study*. New York: Cambridge University Press.

Schaie, K. W. (2005). *Developmental influences on adult intelligence: The Seattle longitudinal study*. New York: Oxford University Press.

Schalock, R. L., Luckasson, R. A., Shogren, K. A., Borthwick-Duffy, S., Bradley, V., Buntinx, W. H. E., et al. (2007). The renaming of mental retardation: Understanding the change to the term intellectual disability. *Intellectual and Developmental Disabilities*, 45, 116–124.

Scheer, F. A., Cajochen, C., Turek, F. W., & Czeisler, C. A. (2005). Melatonin in the regulation of sleep and circadian rhythms. In M. H. Kryger, T. Roth, & W. C. Dement (Eds.). *Principles and practice of sleep medicine*. Philadelphia: Elsevier Saunders.

Scheidlinger, S. (1993). History of group psychotherapy. In H. I. Kaplan & B. J. Sadock (Eds.), *Comprehensive group psychotherapy*. Baltimore: Williams & Wilkins.

Scheier, M. F., & Carver, C. S. (1985). Optimism, coping and health: Assessment and implications of generalized expectancies. *Health Psychology*, 4, 219–247.

Scherer, K. R., & Wallbott, H. G. (1994). Evidence for universality and cultural variation of differential emotion response patterning. *Journal of Personality and Social Psychology*, 66, 310–328.

Schieber, F. (2006). Vision and aging. In J. E. Birren & K. W. Schaie (Eds.), *Handbook of the psychology of aging*. San Diego: Academic Press.

Schiff, M., & Lewontin, R. (1986). *Education and class: The irrelevance of IQ genetic studies*. Oxford: Clarendon Press.

Schiffman, J., Ekstrom, M., LaBrie, J., Schulsinger, F., Sorenson, H., & Mednick, S. (2002). Minor physical anomalies and schizophrenia spectrum disorders: A prospective investigation. *American Journal of Psychiatry*, 159, 238–243.

Schiffman, S. S., Graham, B. G., Sattely-Miller, E. A., & Warwick, Z. S. (1998). Orosensory perception of dietary fat. *Current Directions in Psychological Science*, 7, 137–143.

Schilt, T., de Win, M. M. L., Koeter, M., Jager, G., Korf, D. J., van den Brink, W., & Schmand, B. (2007). Cognition in novice Ecstasy users with minimal exposure to other drugs: A prospective cohort study. *Archives of General Psychiatry*, 64, 728–736.

Schimel, J., Simon, L., Greenberg, J., Pyszczynski, T., Solomon, S., Waxmonsky, J., & Arndt, J. (1999). Stereotypes and terror management: Evidence that mortality salience enhances stereotypic thinking and preference. *Journal of Personality and Social Psychology*, 77, 905–926.

Schimmack, U., & Crites, S. L. (2005). The structure of affect. In D. Albarracin, B. T. Johnson, & M. P. Zanna (Eds.), *The handbook of attitudes*. Mahwah, NJ: Erlbaum.

Schlegel, A., & Barry, H., III. (1991). *Adolescence: An anthropological inquiry*. New York: Free Press.

Schmidt, F. L. (2002). The role of general cognitive ability and job performance: Why there cannot be a debate. *Human Performance*, 15, 187–210.

Schmidt, F. L., & Hunter, J. (2004). General mental ability in the world of work: Occupational attainment and job performance. *Journal of Personality and Social Psychology, 86,* 162–173.

Schmidt, N. B., Zvolensky, M. J., & Maner, J. K. (2006). Anxiety sensitivity: Prospective prediction of panic attacks and Axis I pathology. *Journal of Psychiatric Research, 40,* 691–699.

Schmit, M. J. (2006). EI in the business world. In K. R. Murphy (Ed.), *A critique of emotional intelligence: What are the problems and how can they be fixed?* (pp. 211–234). Mahwah, NJ: Erlbaum.

Schmithorst, V. J., Wilke, M., Dardzinski, B. J., & Holland, S. K. (2002). Correlation of white matter diffusivity and anisotropy with age during childhood and adolescence: A cross-sectional diffusion-tensor MR imaging study. *Radiology, 222,* 212–218.

Schmitt, D. P. (2005). Fundamentals of human mating strategies. In D. M. Buss (Ed.), *The handbook of evolutionary psychology.* New York: Wiley.

Schmitt, D. P., & Buss, D. M. (2001). Human mate poaching: Tactics and temptations for infiltrating existing mateships. *Journal of Personality and Social Psychology, 80,* 894–917.

Schmitt, D. P., & Shackelford, T. K. (2003). Nifty ways to leave your lover: The tactics people use to entice and disguise the process of human mate poaching. *Personality and Social Psychology Bulletin, 29,* 1018–1035.

Schmitt, D. P., & International Sexuality Description Project. (2003). Universal sex differences in the desire for sexual variety: Tests from 52 nations, 6 continents, and 13 islands. *Journal of Personality and Social Psychology, 85,* 85–104.

Schmitt, D. P., & 121 members of the International Sexuality Description Project. (2004). Patterns and universals of mate poaching across 53 nations: The effects of sex, culture, and personality on romantically attracting another person's partner. *Journal of Personality and Social Psychology, 86,* 560–584.

Schmitt, M. T., & Maes, J. (2002). Stereotypic ingroup bias as self-defense against relative deprivation: Evidence from a longitudinal study of the German unification process. *European Journal of Social Psychology, 32,* 309–326.

Schmitt, N., Cortina, J. M., Ingerick, M. J., & Wiechmann, D. (2003). Personnel selection and employee performance. In W. C. Borman, D. R. Ilgen, & R. J. Klimoski (Eds.), *Handbook of psychology,* vol. 12: *Industrial and organizational psychology* (pp. 77–105). New York: Wiley.

Schmitz, J. M., & DeLaune, K. A. (2005). Nicotine. In J. H. Lowinson, P. Ruiz, R. B. Millman, & J. G. Langrod (Eds.), *Substance abuse: A comprehensive textbook.* Philadelphia: Lippincott/Williams & Williams.

Schmolck, H., Buffalo, E. A., & Squire, L. R. (2000). Memory distortions develop over time: Recollections of the O. J. Simpson trial verdict after 15 and 32 months. *Psychological Science, 11,* 39–45.

Schneewind, K. A. (1995). Impact of family processes on control beliefs. In A. Bandura (Ed.), *Self-efficacy in changing societies.* New York: Cambridge University Press.

Schneider, F., & Deldin, P. J. (2001). Genetics and schizophrenia. In P. B. Sutker & H. E. Adams (Eds.), *Comprehensive handbook of psychopathology* (3rd ed., pp. 371–402). New York: Kluwer Academic/Plenum.

Scholey, A. B., Parrott, A. C., Buchanan, T., Heffernan, T. M., Ling, J., & Rodgers, J. (2004). Increased intensity of Ecstasy and polydrug usage in the more experienced recreational Ecstasy/MDMA users: A WWW study. *Addictive Behaviors, 29,* 743–752.

Scholz, J., & Woolf, C. J. (2002). Can we conquer pain? *Nature Neuroscience, Supplement 5,* 1062–1067.

Schooler, C. (2007). Use it—and keep it, longer, probably: A reply to Salthouse. *Perspectives on Psychological Science, 2,* 24–29.

Schooler, J. W., & Fiore, S. M. (1997). Consciousness and the limits of language: You can't always say what you think or think what you say. In J. D. Cohen & J. W. Schooler (Eds.), *Scientific approaches to consciousness.* Mahwah, NJ: Erlbaum.

Schrag, R. D. A., Styfco, S. J., & Zigler, E. (2004). Familiar concept, new name: Social competence. In E. Zigler & S. J. Styfco (Eds.), *The Head Start debate.* Baltimore: Paul H. Brookes Publishing.

Schramm, D. G., Marshall, J. P., Harris, V. W., & Lee, T. R. (2005). After "I do": The newlywed transition. *Marriage and Family Review, 38,* 45–67.

Schredl, M. (2007). Gender differences in dreaming. In D. Barrett & P. McNamara (Eds.), *The new science of dreaming: Content, recall, and personality correlates.* Westport, CT: Praeger.

Schredl, M., & Piel, E. (2005). Gender differences in dreaming: Are they stable over time? *Personality and Individual Differences, 39,* 309–316.

Schreiber, F. R. (1973). *Sybil.* New York: Warner.

Schuit, A. J., Feskens, E. J., Launer, L. J., & Kromhaut, D. (2001). Physical activity and cognitive decline, the role of the apolipoprotein e4 allele. *Medicine and Science in Sports and Exercise, 33,* 772–777.

Schultheiss, O. C., Wirth, M., Torges, C. M., Pang, J. S., Villacorta, M. A., & Welsh, K. M. (2005). Effects of implicit power motivation on men's and women's implicit learning and testosterone changes after social victory or defeat. *Journal of Personality and Social Psychology, 88,* 174–188.

Schultz, J. H., & Luthe, W. (1959). *Autogenic training.* New York: Grune & Stratton.

Schulz-Hardt, S., Frey, D., Luethgens, C., & Moscovici, S. (2000). Biased information search in group decision making. *Journal of Personality & Social Psychology, 78,* 655–669.

Schuman, H., & Kalton, G. (1985). Survey methods. In G. Lindzey & E. Aronson (Eds.), *Handbook of social psychology* (3rd ed.). New York: Random House.

Schusterman, R. J., & Gisiner, R. (1988). Artificial language comprehension in dolphins and sea lions: The essential cognitive skills. *Psychological Record, 38,* 311–348.

Schwartz, B. (2004). *The paradox of choice: Why more is less.* New York: Ecco.

Schwartz, B. L. (1999). Sparkling at the end of the tongue: The etiology of tip-of-the-tongue phenomenology. *Psychonomic Bulletin & Review, 6,* 379–393.

Schwartz, B. L. (2002). *Tip-of-the-tongue states: Phenomenology, mechanism, and lexical retrieval.* Mahwah, NJ: Erlbaum.

Schwartz, B. L., Travis, D. M., Castro, A. M., & Smith, S. M. (2000). The phenomenology of real and illusory tip-of-the-tongue states. *Memory & Cognition, 28,* 18–27.

Schwartz, G. L., & Azzara, A. V. (2004). Sensory neurobiological analysis of neuropeptide modulation of meal size. *Physiology & Behavior , 82,* 81–87.

Schwartz, J. H. (2000). Neurotransmitters. In E. R. Kandel, J. H. Schwartz, & T. M. Jessell (Eds.), *Principles of neural science.* New York: McGraw-Hill.

Schwartz, J. H., & Westbrook, G. L. (2000). The cytology of neurons. In E. R. Kandel, J. H. Schwartz, & T. M. Jessell (Eds.), *Principles of neural science* (pp. 67–104). New York: McGraw-Hill.

Schwartz, J. P., Waldo, M., & Higgins, A. J. (2004). Attachment styles: Relationship to masculine gender role conflict in college men. *Psychology of Men & Masculinity, 5*(2), 143–146.

Schwartz, L., Slater, M. A., & Birchler, G. R. (1994). Interpersonal stress and pain behaviors in patients with chronic pain. *Journal of Consulting and Clinical Psychology, 62,* 861–864.

Schwartz, M. W., Peskind, E., Raskind, M., Nicolson, M., Moore, J., Morawiecki, A., Boyko, E. J., & Porte, D. J. (1996). Cerebrospinal fluid leptin levels: Relationship to plasma levels and to adiposity in humans. *Nature Medicine, 2,* 589–593.

Schwartz, M. W., Woods, S. C., Porte, D., Seeley, R. J., & Baskin, D. G. (2000). Central nervous system control of food intake. *Nature, 404,* 661–671.

Schwartz, S. H. (1990). Individualism-collectivism: Critique and proposed refinements. *Journal of Cross-Cultural Psychology, 21,* 139–157.

Schwarz, N. (1999). Self-reports: How the questions shape the answers. *American Psychologist, 54,* 93–105.

Schwarz, N., & Strack, F. (1999). Reports of subjective well-being: Judgmental processes and their methodological implications. In D. Kahneman, E. Diener, & N. Schwarz (Eds.), *Well-being: The foundations of hedonic psychology.* New York: Russell Sage Foundation.

Scoboria, A., Mazzoni, G., Kirsch, I., & Milling, L. S. (2002). Immediate and persisting effects of misleading questions and hypnosis on memory reports. *Journal of Experimental Psychology: Applied, 8*(1), 26–32.

Scott, T. R. (1990). The effect of physiological need on taste. In E. D. Capaldi & T. L. Powley (Eds.), *Taste, experience, and feeding.* Washington, DC: American Psychological Association.

Scott, V., McDade, D. M., & Luckman, S. M. (2007). Rapid changes in the sensitivity of arcuate nucleus neurons to central ghrelin in relation to feeding status. *Physiology & Behavior, 90,* 180–185.

Scoville, W. B., & Milner, B. (1957). Loss of recent memory after bilateral hippocampal lesions. *Journal of Neurology, Neurosurgery & Psychiatry, 20,* 11–21.

Scroppo, J. C., Drob, S. L., Weinberger, J. L., & Eagle, P. (1998). Identifying dissociative identity disorder: A self-report and projective study. *Journal of Abnormal Psychology, 107,* 272–284.

Scull, A. (1990). Deinstitutionalization: Cycles of despair. *The Journal of Mind and Behavior, 11*(3/4), 301–312.

Scully, J. A., Tosi, H., & Banning, K. (2000). Life event checklists: Revisiting the social readjustment rating scale after 30 years. *Educational & Psychological Measurement, 60,* 864–876.

Seabrook, R., Brown, G. D. A., & Solity, J. E. (2005). Distributed and massed practice: From laboratory to classroom. *Applied Cognitive Psychology, 19*(1), 107–122.

Searle, A., & Bennett, P. (2001). Psychological factors and inflammatory bowel disease: A review of a decade of literature. *Psychology, Health and Medicine, 6,* 121–135.

Searleman, A. (1996). Personality variables and prospective memory performance. In D. J. Herrmann, C. McEvoy, C. Hertzog, P. Hertel, & M. K. Johnson (Eds.), *Basic and applied memory research: Practical applications* (Vol. 2). Mahwah, NJ: Erlbaum.

Searleman, A., & Herrmann, D. (1994). *Memory from a broader perspective.* New York: McGraw-Hill.

Sears, D. O. (1975). Political socialization. In F. I. Greenstein & N. W. Polsby (Eds.), *Handbook of political science* (Vol. 2). Reading, MA: Addison-Wesley.

Sears, D. O. (1986). College sophomores in the laboratory: Influences of a narrow database on social psychology's view of human nature. *Journal of Personality and Social Psychology, 51*, 515–530.

Seeley, R. J., & Schwartz, M. W. (1997). Regulation of energy balance: Peripheral endocrine signals and hypothalamic neuropeptides. *Current Directions in Psychological Science, 6*, 39–44.

Segall, M. H., Campbell, D. T., Herskovits, M. J. (1966). *The influence of culture on visual perception.* Indianapolis: Bobbs-Merrill.

Segall, M. H., Dasen, P. R., Berry, J. W., & Poortinga, Y. H. (1990). *Human behavior in global perspective: An introduction to cross-cultural psychology.* New York: Pergamon Press.

Segall, M. H., Lonner, W. J., & Berry, J. W. (1998). Cross-cultural psychology as a scholarly discipline: On the flowering of culture in behavioral research. *American Psychologist, 53*, 1101–1110.

Segerstrom, S. C., & Miller, G. E. (2004). Psychological stress and the human immune system: A meta-analytic study of 30 years of inquiry. *Psychological Bulletin, 130*, 601–630.

Segerstrom, S. C., Taylor, S. E., Kemeny, M. E., & Fahey, J. L. (1998). Optimism is associated with mood, coping and immune change in response to stress. *Journal of Personality and Social Psychology, 74*, 1646–1655.

Seifer, R. (2001). Socioeconomic status, multiple risks, and development of intelligence. In R. J. Sternberg & E. L. Grigorenko (Eds.), *Environmental effects on cognitive abilities* (pp. 59–82). Mahwah, NJ: Erlbaum.

Self, D. W. (1997). Neurobiological adaptations to drug use. *Hospital Practice, April*, 5–9.

Seligman, M. E. P. (1971). Phobias and preparedness. *Behavior Therapy, 2*, 307–321.

Seligman, M. E. P. (1974). Depression and learned helplessness. In R. J. Friedman & M. M. Katz (Eds.), *The psychology of depression: Contemporary theory and research.* New York: Wiley.

Seligman, M. E. P. (1990). *Learned optimism.* New York: Pocket Books.

Seligman, M. E. P. (1992). *Helplessness: On depression, development, and death.* New York: Freeman.

Seligman, M. E. P. (1995). The effectiveness of psychotherapy. *American Psychologist, 50*, 965–974.

Seligman, M. E. P. (2002). Positive psychology, positive prevention, and positive therapy. In C. R. Snyder & S. J. Lopez (Eds.), *Handbook of positive psychology* (pp. 3–11). New York: Oxford University Press.

Seligman, M. E. P. (2003). The past and future of positive psychology. In C. L. M. Keyes & J. Haidt (Eds.), *Flourishing: Positive psychology and the life well-lived.* Washington, DC: American Psychological Association.

Seligman, M. E. P., & Csikszentmihalyi, M. (2000). Positive psychology: An introduction. *American Psychologist, 55*, 5–14.

Seligman, M. E. P., & Hager, J. L. (1972, August). Biological boundaries of learning (The sauce béarnaise syndrome). *Psychology Today*, pp. 59–61, 84–87.

Seligman, M. E. P., & Levant, R. F. (1998). Managed care policies rely on inadequate science. *Professional Psychology: Research and Practice, 29*, 211–212.

Seligman, M. E. P., Rashid, T., & Parks, A. C. (2006). Positive psychotherapy. *American Psychologist, 61*, 774–788.

Selye, H. (1936). A syndrome produced by diverse nocuous agents. *Nature, 138*, 32.

Selye, H. (1956). *The stress of life.* New York: McGraw-Hill.

Selye, H. (1973). The evolution of the stress concept. *American Scientist, 61*(6), 672–699.

Selye, H. (1974). *Stress without distress.* New York: Lippincott.

Selye, H. (1982). History and present status of the stress concept. In L. Goldberger & S. Breznitz (Eds.), *Handbook of stress: Theoretical and clinical aspects.* New York: Free Press.

Semmer, N. K., McGrath, J. E., & Beehr, T. A. (2005). Conceptual issues in research on stress and health. In C. L. Cooper (Ed.), *Handbook of stress medicine and health.* Boca Raton, FL: CRC Press.

Senior, C., Thomson, K., Badger, J., & Butler, M. J. R. (2008). Interviewing strategies in the face of beauty: A psychophysiological investigation into the job negotiation process. *Annals of the New York Academy of Sciences, 1118*, 142–162.

Seroczynski, A. D., Jacquez, F. M., & Cole, D. A. (2003). Depression and suicide during adolescence. In G. R. Adams & M. D. Berzonsky (Eds.), *Blackwell handbook of adolescence.* Malden, MA: Blackwell.

Serpell, R. (2000). Intelligence and culture. In R. J. Sternberg (Ed.), *Handbook of intelligence.* Cambridge, UK: Cambridge University Press.

Servan-Schreiber, D., Kolb, R., & Tabas, G. (1999). The somatizing patient. *Primary Care, 26*, 225–242.

Seta, J. J., Seta, C. E., & McElroy, T. (2002). Strategies for reducing the stress of negative life experiences: An average/summation analysis. *Personality and Social Psychology Bulletin, 28*, 1574–1585.

Seto, M. C., Maric, A., & Barbaree, H. E. (2001). The role of pornography in the etiology of sexual aggression. *Aggression & Violent Behavior, 6*, 35–53.

Shackelford, T. K., Schmitt, D. P., & Buss, D. M. (2005). Universal dimensions of human mate preferences. *Personality & Individual Differences, 39*, 447–458.

Shaffer, D. R. (1985). *Developmental psychology: Theory, research, and applications.* Pacific Grove, CA: Brooks/Cole.

Shafir, E., & LeBoeuf, R. A. (2002). Rationality. *Annual Review of Psychology, 53*, 491–517.

Shafir, E., & LeBoeuf, R. A. (2004). Context and conflict in multiattribute choice. In D. J. Koehler & N. Harvey (Ed), *Blackwell handbook of judgment and decision making.* Malden, MA: Blackwell.

Shalev, A. Y. (2001). Posttraumatic stress disorder. *Primary Psychiatry, 8*(10), 41–46.

Shalitin, S., & Phillip, M. (2003). Role of obesity and leptin in the pubertal process and pubertal growth—A review. *International Journal of Obesity, 27*, 869–874.

Shamay-Tsoory, S. G., Tomer, R., & Aharon-Peretz, J. (2005). The neuroanatomical basis of understanding sarcasm and its relationship to social cognition. *Neuropsychology, 19*, 288–300.

Shank, R. P., Smith-Swintosky, V. L., & Twyman, R. E. (2000). Amino acid neurotransmitters. In B. J. Sadock & V. A. Sadock (Eds), *Comprehensive textbook of psychiatry* (Vol. 1). New York: Lippincott/Williams & Wilkins.

Shapiro, A. F., Gottman, J. M., & Carrère. (2000). The baby and marriage: Identifying factors that buffer against decline in marital satisfaction after the first baby arrives. *Journal of Family Psychology, 14*, 59–70.

Shapiro, D. H., Jr. (1984). Overview: Clinical and physiological comparison of meditation with other self-control strategies. In D. H. Shapiro, Jr., & R. N. Walsh (Eds.), *Meditation: Classic and contemporary perspectives.* New York: Aldine.

Shapiro, D. H., Jr. (1987). Implications of psychotherapy research for the study of meditation. In M. A. West (Ed.), *The psychology of meditation.* Oxford: Clarendon Press.

Shapiro, J. R., & Neuberg, S. L. (2007). From stereotype threat to stereotype threats: Implications of a multi-threat framework for causes, moderators, mediators, consequences, and interventions. *Personality & Social Psychology Review, 11*, 107–130.

Shapiro, S. L., Schwartz, G. E. R., & Santerre, C. (2002). Meditation and positive psychology. In C. R. Snyder & S. J. Lopez (Eds.), *Handbook of positive psychology.* New York: Oxford University Press.

Sharpe, D., Adair, J. G., & Roese, N. J. (1992). Twenty years of deception research: A decline in subjects' trust? *Personality and Social Psychology Bulletin, 18*, 585–590.

Sharps, M. J., & Wertheimer, M. (2000). Gestalt perspectives on cognitive science and on experimental psychology. *Review of General Psychology, 4*, 315–336.

Shatz, C. J. (1992, September). The developing brain. *Scientific American*, 60–67.

Shaver, P. R., & Mikulincer, M. (2006). A behavioral systems approach to romantic love relationships: Attachment, caregiving, and sex. In R. J. Sternberg & K. Weis (Eds.), *The new psychology of love.* New Haven, CT: Yale University Press.

Shaver, P. R., Schachner, D. A., & Mikulincer, M. (2005). Attachment style, excessive reassurance seeking, relationship processes, and depression. *Personality and Social Psychology Bulletin, 31*(3), 343–359.

Shavitt, S., Sanbonmatsu, D. M., Smittipatana, S., & Posavac, S. S. (1999). Broadening the conditions for illusory correlation formation: Implications for judging minority groups. *Basic & Applied Social Psychology, 21*, 263–279.

Shaw, J. S. I., McClure, K. A., & Dykstra, J. A. (2007). Eyewitness confidence from the witnessed event through trial. In M. P. Toglia, J. D. Read, D. F. Ross, & R. C. L. Lindsay (Eds.), *Handbook of eyewitness psychology: Volume 1. Memory for events.* Mahwah, NJ: Erlbaum.

Shaw, W. S., & Dimsdale, J. E. (2007). Type A personality, type B personality. In G. Fink (Ed.), *Encyclopedia of stress.* San Diego: Elsevier.

Shea, A. K., & Steiner, M. (2008). Cigarette smoking during pregnancy. *Nicotine & Tobacco Research, 10*, 267–278.

Shear, J., & Jevning, R. (1999). Pure consciousness: Scientific exploration of meditation techniques. *Journal of Consciousness Studies, 6*, 189–209.

Shearer, B. (2004). Multiple intelligences theory after 20 years. *Teachers College Record, 106*(1), 2–16.

Sheehan, S. (1982). *Is there no place on earth for me?* Boston: Houghton Mifflin.

Sheldon, C. (2004). Social relationships and health. *American Psychologist, 59*, 676–684.

Sheldon, K. M., & Kasser, T. (2001). Goals, congruence, and positive well-being: New empirical support for humanistic theories. *Journal of Humanistic Psychology, 41*(1), 30–50.

Shelton, R. C., & Lester, N. (2006). Selective serotonin reuptake inhibitors and newer antidepressants. In D. J. Stein, D. J. Kupfer, & A. F. Schatzberg (Eds.), *Textbook of mood disorders* (pp. 263–280). Washington, DC: American Psychiatric Publishing.

Shepard, R. N. (1990). *Mind sights*. New York: W. H. Freeman.

Shepperd, J. A., & McNulty, J. K. (2002). The affective consequences of expected and unexpected outcomes. *Psychological Science, 13*, 85–88.

Shepperd, J., Malone, W., & Sweeny, K. (2008). Exploring causes of the self-serving bias. *Social and Personality Psychology Compass, 2*, 895–908.

Sher, L. (2003). Daily hassles, cortisol, and depression. *Australia and New Zealand Journal of Psychiatry, 37*, 383–384.

Sher, L., & Mann, J. J. (2003). Psychiatric pathophysiology: Mood disorders. In A. Tasman, J. Kay, & J. A. Lieberman (Eds.), *Psychiatry*. New York: Wiley.

Sherif, M., Harvey, O., White, B., Hood, W., & Sherif, C. (1961). *Intergroup conflict and cooperation: The Robber's Cave experiment*. Norman: University of Oklahoma, Institute of Group Behavior.

Sherman, D. K., Nelson, L. D., & Ross, L. D. (2003). Naive realism and affirmative action: Adversaries are more similar than they think. *Basic and Applied Social Psychology, 25*, 275–289.

Sherman, J. W., Stroessner, S. J., Conrey, F. R., & Azam, O. A. (2005). Prejudice and stereotype maintenance processes: Attention, attribution, and individuation. *Journal of Personality and Social Psychology, 89*, 607–622.

Sherman, M., & Key, C. B. (1932). The intelligence of isolated mountain children. *Child Development, 3*, 279–290.

Sherman, P. W. (1981). Kinship, demography, and Belding's ground squirrel nepotism. *Behavioral Ecology and Sociobiology, 8*, 251–259.

Shermer, M. (1997). *Why people believe weird things: Pseudoscience, superstition, and other confusions of our time*. New York: W. H. Freeman.

Shermer, M. (2004, March). None so blind. *Scientific American*, p. 42.

Sherry, D. F. (1992). Evolution and learning. In L. R. Squire (Ed.), *Encyclopedia of learning and memory*. New York: Macmillan.

Shettleworth, S. J. (1998). *Cognition, evolution, and behavior*. New York: Oxford University Press.

Shike, M. (1999). Diet and lifestyle in the prevention of colorectal cancer: An overview. *American Journal of Medicine, 106*(1A), 11S–15S, 50S–51S.

Shimamura, A. P., Berry, J. M., Mangels, J. A., Rusting, C. L., & Jurica, P. J. (1995). Memory and cognitive abilities in university professors: Evidence for successful aging. *Psychological Science, 6*, 271–277.

Shimp, T. A., Stuart, E. W., & Engle, R. W. (1991). A program of classical conditioning experiments testing variations in the conditioned stimulus and context. *Journal of Consumer Research, 18*, 1–12.

Shneidman, E. S., Farberow, N. L., & Litman, R. E. (1994). *The psychology of suicide: A clinician's guide to evaluation and treatment*. Northvale, NJ: J. Aronson.

Shobe, K. K., & Schooler, J. W. (2001). Discovering fact and fiction: Case-based analyses of authentic and fabricated discovered memories of abuse. In G. M. Davies & T. Dalgleish (Eds.), *Recovered memories: Seeking the middle ground*. Chichester, England: Wiley.

Shors, T. J. (2004). Learning during stressful times. *Learning and Memory, 11*(2), 137–144.

Shulman, R. B. (2001). Response versus remission in the treatment of depression: Understanding residual symptoms. *Primary Psychiatry, 8*(5), 28–30, 34.

Siebert, A., & Karr, M. (2003). *The adult student's guide to survival & success*. Portland, OR: Practical Psychology Press.

Sieck, W. R. (2005). The recalcitrance of overconfidence and its contribution to decision aid neglect. *Journal of Behavioral Decision Making, 18*(1), 29–53.

Sieck, W. R., & Arkes, H. R. (2005). The recalcitrance of overconfidence and its contribution to decision aid neglect. *Journal of Behavioral Decision Making, 18*(1), 29–53.

Siegel, J. M. (2004). The neurotransmitters of sleep. *Journal of Clinical Psychiatry, 65*(Suppl16), 4–7.

Siegel, J. M. (2005a). Clues to the functions of mammalian sleep. *Nature, 437*, 1264–1271.

Siegel, J. M. (2005b). REM sleep. In M. H. Kryger, T. Roth, & W. C. Dement (Eds.). *Principles and practice of sleep medicine*. Philadelphia: Elsevier Saunders.

Siegel, S. (2001). Pavlovian conditioning and drug overdose: When tolerance fails. *Addiction Research & Theory, 9*, 503–513.

Siegel, S. (2005). Drug tolerance, drug addiction, and drug anticipation. *Current Directions in Psychological Science, 14*, 296–300.

Siegel, S., Baptista, M. A. S., Kim, J. A., McDonald, R. V., & Weise-Kelly, L. (2000). Pavlovian psychopharmacology: The associative basis of tolerance. *Experimental and Clinical Psychopharmacology, 8*, 276–293.

Siegel, S., & Ramos, B. C. (2002). Applying laboratory research: Drug anticipation and the treatment of drug addiction. *Experimental and Clinical Psychopharmacology, 10*, 162–183.

Siegler, R. S. (1992). The other Alfred Binet. *Developmental Psychology, 28*, 179–190.

Siegler, R. S. (1994). Cognitive variability: A key to understanding cognitive development. *Current Directions in Psychological Science, 3*(1), 1–5.

Siegler, R. S., & Alibali, M. W. (2005). *Children's thinking*. Upper Saddle River, NJ: Prentice-Hall.

Sigel, I. E. (2004). Head Start—Revisiting a historical psychoeducational intervention: A revisionist perspective. In E. Zigler & S. J. Styfco (Eds.), *The Head Start debate*. Baltimore: Paul H. Brookes Publishing.

Signorielli, N. (2001). Television's gender role images and contribution to stereotyping: Past present future. In D. G. Singer & J. L. Singer (Eds.), *Handbook of children and the media*. Thousand Oaks, CA: Sage.

Signorielli, N., McLeod, D., & Healy, E. (1994). Gender stereotypes in MTV commercials: The beat goes on. *Journal of Broadcasting & Electronic Media, 38*, 91–101.

Silber, L. (2004). *Organizing from the right side of the brain: A creative approach to getting organized*. New York: St. Martin's Press.

Silberman, E. K. (1998). Psychiatrists' and internists' beliefs. *Primary Psychiatry, 5*, 65–71.

Silver, E., Cirincion, C., & Steadman, H. J. (1994). Demythologizing inaccurate perceptions of the insanity defense. *Law & Human Behavior, 18*, 63–70.

Silver, H., Feldman, P., Bilker, W., & Gur, R. C. (2003). Working memory deficit as a core neuropsychological dysfunction in schizophrenia. *American Journal of Psychiatry, 160*, 1809–1816.

Silverman, I., & Choi, J. (2005). Locating places. In D. M. Buss (Ed.), *The handbook of evolutionary psychology*. New York: Wiley.

Silverman, I., Choi, J., Mackewn, A., Fisher, M., Moro, J., & Olshansky, E. (2000). Evolved mechanisms underlying wayfinding: Further studies on the hunter-gatherer theory of spatial sex differences. *Evolution and Human Behavior, 21*, 201–213.

Silverman, I., & Eals, M. (1992). Sex differences in spatial ability: Evolutionary theory and data. In J. Barkow, L. Cosmides, & J. Tooby (Eds.), *The adapted mind*. New York: Oxford University Press.

Silverman, I., & Phillips, K. (1998). The evolutionary psychology of spatial sex differences. In C. Crawford & D. L. Krebs (Eds.), *Handbook of evolutionary psychology: Ideas, issues, and applications*. Mahwah, NJ: Erlbaum.

Silverstein, L. B., & Auerbach, C. F. (1999). Deconstructing the essential father. *American Psychologist, 54*, 397–407.

Silvia, P. J. (2008). Another look at creativity and intelligence: Exploring higher-order models and probable confounds. *Personality and Individual Differences, 44*, 1012–1021.

Simon, G. E., & Savarino, J. (2007). Suicide attempts among patients starting depression treatment with medications or psychotherapy. *American Journal of Psychiatry, 164*, 1029–1034.

Simon, G. E., Savarino, J., Operskalski, B., & Wang, P. S. (2006). Suicide risk during antidepressant treatment. *American Journal of Psychiatry, 163*, 41–47.

Simon, H. A. (1974). How big is a chunk? *Science, 183*, 482–488.

Simon, H. A. (1992). Alternative representations for cognition: Search and reasoning. In H. L. Pick, Jr., P. Van Den Broek, & D. C. Knill (Eds.), *Cognition: Conceptual and methodological issues*. Washington, DC: American Psychological Association.

Simon, H. A., & Reed, S. K. (1976). Modeling strategy shifts in a problem-solving task. *Cognitive Psychology, 8*, 86–97.

Simon, R. I. (2003). The law and psychiatry. In R. E. Hales & S. C. Yudofsky (Eds.), *Textbook of clinical psychiatry*. Washington, DC: American Psychiatric Publishing.

Simon, R. I. (2005). Clinical-legal issues in psychiatry. In B. J. Sadock & V. A. Sadock (Eds.), *Kaplan & Sadock's comprehensive textbook of psychiatry*. Philadelphia: Lippincott Williams & Wilkins.

Simon, T. (1997). Reconceptualizing the origins of number knowledge: A "non-numerical" account. *Cognitive Development, 12*, 349–372.

Simons, D. K., & Chabris, C. F. (1999). Gorillas in our midst: Sustained inattentional blindness for dynamic events. *Perception, 28*, 1059–1074.

Simonton, D. K. (1990). Creativity and wisdom in aging. In J. E. Birren & K. W. Schaie (Eds.), *Handbook of the psychology of aging*. San Diego: Academic Press.

Simonton, D. K. (1997). Creative productivity: A predictive and explanatory model of career trajectories and landmarks. *Psychological Review, 104*, 66–89.

Simonton, D. K. (1999a). Creativity and genius. In L. A. Pervin & O. John (Eds.), *Handbook of personality theory and research*. New York: Guilford.

Simonton, D. K. (1999b). Talent and its development: An emergenic and epigenetic model. *Psychological Review, 106*, 435–457.

Simonton, D. K. (2001). Totally made, not at all born [Review of the book *The psychology of high abilities*]. *Contemporary Psychology, 46*, 176–179.

Simonton, D. K. (2003). Francis Galton's hereditary genius: Its place in the history and psychology of science. In R. J. Sternberg (Ed.), *The anatomy of* impact: What makes the great works of psychology great (pp. 3–18). Washington, DC: American Psychological Association.

Simonton, D. K. (2004). Creativity in science: Chance, logic, genius, and Zeitgeist. New York: Cambridge University Press.

Simonton, D. K. (2005). Genetics of giftedness: The implications of an emergenic-epigenetic model. In R. J. Sternberg & J. E. Davidson (Eds.), Conceptions of giftedness. New York: Cambridge University Press.

Simpson, J. A., Fletcher, G. J. O., & Campbell, L. (2001). The structure and function of ideal standards in close relationships. In G. J. O. Fletcher & M. S. Clark (Eds.), Blackwell handbook of social psychology: Interpersonal processes. Malden, MA: Blackwell.

Simpson, J. L. (2002). Fetal wastage. In S. G. Gabbe, J. R. Niebyl, & J. L. Simpson (Eds.), Obstetrics: Normal and problem pregnancies. New York: Churchill Livingstone.

Simpson, J. L., & Niebyl, J. R. (2002). Occupational and environmental perspectives on birth defects. In S. G. Gabbe, J. R. Niebyl & J. L. Simpson (Eds.), Obstetrics: Normal and problem pregnancies. New York: Churchill Livingstone.

Sinclair, D. (1981). Mechanisms of cutaneous stimulation. Oxford, England: Oxford University Press.

Sinclair, R. C., Hoffman, C., Mark, M. M., Martin, L. L., & Pickering, T. L. (1994). Construct accessibility and the misattribution of arousal: Schachter and Singer revisited. Psychological Science, 5, 15–19.

Sinclair, S., Dunn, R., & Lowery, B. S. (2005). The relationship between parental racial attitudes and children's implicit prejudice. Journal of Experimental Social Psychology, 41, 283–289.

Singer, L. T., Minnes, S., Short, E., Arendt, R., Farkas, K., Lewis, B., Klein, N., Russ, S., Min, M. O., & Kirchner, H. L. (2004). Cognitive outcomes of preschool children with prenatal cocaine exposure. Journal of the American Medical Association, 291, 2448–2456.

Singer, W. (2007). Large-scale temporal coordination of cortical activity as a prerequisite for conscious experience. In M. Velmans & S. Schneider (Eds.), The Blackwell companion to consciousness. Malden, MA: Blackwell Publishing.

Sinha, D. (1983). Human assessment in the Indian context. In S. H. Irvine & J. W. Berry (Eds.), Human assessment and cultural factors. New York: Plenum.

Sivertsen, B., Omvik, S., Pallesen, S., Bjorvatn, B., Havik, O. E., Kvale, G., et al. (2006). Cognitive behavioral therapy vs. Zopiclone for treatment of chronic primary insomnia in older adults: A randomized controlled trial. Journal of the American Medical Association, 295, 2851–2858.

SJB. (2006, March 6). Overcoming problem gambling [Why?]. Message posted to http://www.gamcare.org.uk/forum/index.php?tid=7193.

Skinner, A. E. G. (2001). Recovered memories of abuse: Effects on the individual. In G. M. Davies, & T. Dalgleish (Eds.), Recovered memories: Seeking the middle ground. Chichester, England: Wiley & Sons.

Skinner, B. F. (1938). The behavior of organisms. New York: Appleton-Century-Crofts.

Skinner, B. F. (1953). Science and human behavior. New York: Macmillan.

Skinner, B. F. (1957). Verbal behavior. New York: Appleton-Century-Crofts.

Skinner, B. F. (1967). Autobiography. In E. G. Boring & G. Lindzey (Eds.), A history of psychology in autobiography (Vol. 5). New York: Appleton-Century-Crofts.

Skinner, B. F. (1969). Contingencies of reinforcement. New York: Appleton-Century-Crofts.

Skinner, B. F. (1971). Beyond freedom and dignity. New York: Knopf.

Skinner, B. F. (1974). About behaviorism. New York: Knopf.

Skinner, B. F. (1984). Selection by consequences. Behavioral and Brain Sciences, 7(4), 477–510.

Skinner, B. F., Solomon, H. C., & Lindsley, O. R. (1953). Studies in behavior therapy: Status report I. Waltham, MA: Unpublished report, Metropolitan State Hospital.

Skinner, E. A., Edge, K., Altman, J., & Sherwood, H. (2003). Searching for the structure of coping: A review and critique of category systems for classifying ways of coping. Psychological Bulletin, 129, 216–269.

Skinner, N. F. (2003). Birth order effects in dominance: Failure to support Sulloway's view. Psychological Reports, 92, 387–388.

Skitka, L., & Sargis, E. (2005). Social psychological research and the Internet: The promise and peril of a new methodological frontier. In Y. Amichai-Hamburger (Ed.), The social net: Understanding human behavior in cyberspace (pp. 1–26). New York: Oxford University Press.

Skitka, L., & Sargis, E. G. (2006). The Internet as psychological laboratory. Annual Review of Psychology, 57, 529–555.

Skolnick, P. (2003). Psychiatric pathophysiology: Anxiety disorders. In A. Tasman, J. Kay, & J. A. Lieberman (Eds.), Psychiatry. New York: Wiley.

Skurnik, I., Yoon, C., Park, D. C., & Schwarz, N. (2005). How warnings about false claims become recommendations. Journal of Consumer Research, 31, 713–724.

Slamecka, N. J. (1985). Ebbinghaus: Some associations. Journal of Experimental Psychology: Learning, Memory and Cognition, 11, 414–435.

Slamecka, N. J. (1992). Forgetting. In L. R. Squire (Ed.), Encyclopedia of learning and memory. New York: Macmillan.

Slatcher, R. B., & Pennebaker, J. W. (2005). Emotional processing of traumatic events. In C. L. Cooper (Ed.), Handbook of stress medicine and health. Boca Raton, FL: CRC Press.

Slater, E., & Shields, J. (1969). Genetical aspects of anxiety. In M. H. Lader (Ed.), Studies of anxiety. Ashford, England: Headley Brothers.

Slaughter, M. (1990). The vertebrate retina. In K. N. Leibovic (Ed.), Science of vision. New York: Springer-Verlag.

Slavney, P. R. (1990). Perspectives on hysteria. Baltimore: Johns Hopkins University Press.

Sligh, A. C., Conners, F. A., & Roskos-Ewoldsen, B. (2005). Relation of creativity to fluid and crystallized intelligence. Journal of Creative Behavior, 39, 123–136.

Slobin, D. I. (1985). A cross-linguistic study of language acquisition. Hillsdale, NJ: Erlbaum.

Slobin, D. I. (1992). The crosslinguistic study of language acquisition. Hillsdale, NJ: Erlbaum.

Slof-Op't Landt, M. C. T., van Furth, E. F., Meulenbelt, I., Slagboom, P. E., Bartels, M., & Boomsma, D. I., et al. (2005). Eating disorders: From twin studies to candidate genes and beyond. Twin Research and Human Genetics, 8, 467–482.

Slovic, P. (1990). Choice. In D. N. Osherson & E. E. Smith (Eds.), Thinking: An invitation to cognitive science (Vol. 3). Cambridge, MA: MIT Press.

Slovic, P., & Fischhoff, B. (1977). On the psychology of experimental surprises. Journal of Experimental Psychology: Human Perception and Performance, 3, 544–551.

Slovic, P., Fischhoff, B., & Lichtenstein, S. (1982). Facts versus fears: Understanding perceived risk. In D. Kahneman, P. Slovic, & A. Tversky (Eds.), Judgment under uncertainty: Heuristics and biases. Cambridge, England: Cambridge University Press.

Slovic, P., Lichtenstein, S., & Fischhoff, B. (1988). Decision making. In R. C. Atkinson, R. J. Herrnstein, G. Lindzey, & R. D. Luce (Eds.), Stevens' handbook of experimental psychology (Vol. 2). New York: Wiley.

Small, G. W. (2005). Alzheimer's disease and other dementias. In B. J. Sadock & V. A. Sadock (Eds.), Kaplan & Sadock's comprehensive textbook of psychiatry. Philadelphia: Lippincott Williams & Wilkins.

Smedley, S. R., & Eisner, T. (1996). Sodium: A male moth's gift to its offspring. Proceedings of the National Academy of Sciences, 93, 809–813.

Smetana, J. G., Campione, B. N., & Metzger, A. (2006). Adolescent development in interpersonal and societal contexts. Annual Review of Psychology, 57, 255–284.

Smith, B. D. (2005). Breaking through college reading. New York: Pearson Longman.

Smith, C. A., & Lazarus, R. S. (1993). Appraisal components, core relational themes, and the emotions. Cognition and Emotion, 7, 233–269.

Smith, C. A., Organ, D. W., & Near, J. P. (1983). Organizational citizenship behavior: Its nature and antecedents. Journal of Applied Psychology, 68, 653–663.

Smith, C. P. (1992). Reliability issues. In C. P. Smith (Ed.), Motivation and personality: Handbook of thematic content analysis. New York: Cambridge University Press.

Smith, D. A. (1999). The end of theoretical orientations? Applied & Preventative Psychology, 8, 269–280.

Smith, D. M., Langa, K. M., Kabeto, M. U., & Ubel, P. A. (2005). Health, wealth, and happiness: Financial resources buffer subjective well-being after the onset of a disability. Psychological Science, 16, 663–666.

Smith, D. V., & Margolskee, R. F. (2006). Making sense of taste. Scientific American, 16(3), 84–92.

Smith, E. E. (2000). Neural bases of human working memory. Current Directions in Psychological Science, 9, 45–49.

Smith, F. J. (1977). Work attitudes as a predictor of attendance on a specific day. Journal of Applied Psychology, 62, 16–19.

Smith, F. J., & Campfield, L. A. (1993). Meal initiation occurs after experimental induction of transient declines in blood glucose. American Journal of Physiology, 265, 1423–1429.

Smith, G. T., Spillane, N. S., & Annus, A. M. (2006). Implications of an emerging integration of universal and culturally specific psychologies. Perspectives on Psychological Science, 1, 211–233.

Smith, J. C. (1975). Meditation and psychotherapy: A review of the literature. Psychological Bulletin, 32, 553–564.

Smith, J. C. (2007). The psychology of relaxation. In P. M. Lehrer, R. L. Woolfolk, & W. E. Sime (Eds.), Principles and practice of stress management. New York: Guilford.

Smith, L. (2005). Psychotherapy, classism, and the poor: Conspicuous by their absence. American Psychologist, 60, 687–696.

Smith, M. J. (2003). Testosterone treatment algorithms in psychiatry. *Psychiatric Annals, 33,* 511–516.

Smith, M. L., & Glass, G. V. (1977). Meta-analysis of psychotherapy outcome studies. *American Psychologist, 32,* 752–760.

Smith, M. T., Perlis, M. L., Park, A., Smith, M. S., Pennington, J., Giles, D. E., & Buysse, D. J. (2002). Comparative meta-analysis of pharmacotherapy and behavior therapy for persistent insomnia. *American Journal of Psychiatry, 159,* 5–11.

Smith, P. B. (2001). Cross-cultural studies of social influence. In D. Matsumoto (Ed.), *The handbook of culture and psychology.* New York: Oxford University Press.

Smith, P. B., & Bond, M. H. (1994). *Social psychology across cultures: Analysis and perspectives.* Boston: Allyn & Bacon.

Smith, P. C., Kendall, L. M., & Hulin, C. L. (1969). *The measurement of satisfaction in work and retirement.* Chicago: Rand McNally.

Smith, S. (1988). Environmental context-dependent memory. In G. M. Davies & D. M. Thomson (Eds.), *Memory in context: Context in memory.* New York: Wiley.

Smith, S. B. (2000). *Diana in search of herself: Portrait of a troubled princess.* New York: Signet.

Smith, S. M. (1995). Getting into and out of mental ruts: A theory of fixation, incubation, and insight. In R. J. Sternberg & J. E. Davidson (Eds.), *The nature of insight* (pp. 229–251). Cambridge, MA: MIT Press.

Smith, S. M., & Gleaves, D. H. (2007). Recovered memories. In M. P. Toglia, J. D. Read, D. F. Ross, & R. C. L. Lindsay (Eds.), *Handbook of eyewitness psychology: Volume 1. Memory for events.* Mahwah, NJ: Erlbaum.

Smith, S. M., McIntosh, W. D., & Bazzini, D. G. (1999). Are the beautiful good in Hollywood? An investigation of the beauty-and-goodness stereotype on film. *Basic & Applied Social Psychology, 21,* 69–80.

Smith, T. W., & Gallo, L. C. (2001). Personality traits as risk factors for physical illness. In A. Baum, T. A. Revenson, & J. E. Singer (Eds.), *Handbook of health psychology* (pp. 139–174). Mahwah, NJ: Erlbaum.

Smith, T. W., Pope, M. K., Sanders, J. D., Allred, K. D., & O'Keefe, J. L. (1988). Cynical hostility at home and work: Psychosocial vulnerability across domains. *Journal of Research in Personality, 22,* 525–548.

Smith, W. P., Compton, W. C., & West, W. B. (1995). Meditation as an adjunct to a happiness enhancement program. *Journal of Clinical Psychology, 51,* 269–273.

Smolak, L., & Murnen, S. K. (2001). Gender and eating problems. In R. H. Striegel-Moore & L. Smolak (Eds.), *Eating disorders: Innovative directions in research and practice* (pp. 91–110). Washington, DC: American Psychological Association.

Smyth, J. M., & Pennebaker, J. W. (1999). Sharing one's story: Translating emotional experiences into words as a coping tool. In C. R. Snyder (Ed.), *Coping: The psychology of what works.* New York: Oxford University Press.

Smyth, J. M., & Pennebaker, J. W. (2001). What are the health effects of disclosure? In A. Baum, T. A. Revenson & J. E. Singer (Eds.), *Handbook of health psychology* (pp. 339–348). Mahwah, NJ: Erlbaum.

Snedecor, S. M., Pomerleau, C. S., Mehringer, A. M., Ninowski, R., & Pomerleau, O. F. (2006). Differences in smoking-related variables based on phenylthiocabamide "taster" status. *Addictive Behaviors, 31,* 2309–2312.

Snodgrass, M., Bernat, E., & Shevrin, H. (2004). Unconscious perception: A model-based approach to method and evidence. *Perception & Psychophysics, 66,* 846–867.

Snow, C. E. (1998). Bilingualism and second language acquisition . In J. B. Gleason & N. B. Ratner (Eds.), *Psycholinguistics.* Fort Worth, TX: Harcourt College Publishers.

Snow, R. E. (1986). Individual differences in the design of educational programs. *American Psychologist, 41,* 1029–1039.

Snowden, L. R., & Hu, T. W. (1996). Outpatient service use in minority-serving mental health programs. *Administration and Policy in Mental Health, 24,* 149–159.

Snowden, L. R., & Yamada, A. (2005). Cultural differences in access to care. *Annual Review of Clinical Psychology, 1,* 143–166.

Snowdon, D. (2001). *Aging with grace: What the Nun Study teaches us about leading longer, healthier, and more meaningful lives.* New York: Bantam Books.

Snyder, A. (1989). *Relationship excellence: Right brain relationship skills for left brain personalities.* Seattle: Gresham Publishing.

Snyder, S. H. (2002). Forty years of neurotransmitters: A personal account. *Archives of General Psychiatry, 59,* 983–994.

Snyder, S. H., & Ferris, C. D. (2000). Novel neurotransmitters and their neuropsychiatric relevance. *American Journal of Psychiatry, 157,* 1738–1751.

Sohlberg, S., & Birgegard, A. (2003). Persistent complex subliminal activation effects: First experimental observations. *Journal of Personality and Social Psychology, 85,* 302–316.

Sokol, R. J., Janisse, J. J., Louis, J. M., Bailey, B. N., Ager, J., Jacobson, S. W., & Jacobson, J. L. (2007). Extreme prematurity: An alcohol-related birth effect. *Alcoholism: Clinical and Experimental Research, 31,* 1031–1037.

Solberg, E. C., Diener, E., Wirtz, D., Lucas, R. E., & Oishi, S. (2002). Wanting, having, and satisfaction: Examining the role of desire discrepancies in satisfaction with income. *Journal of Personality and Social Psychology, 83,* 725–734.

Soldatos, C. R., Allaert, F. A., Ohta, T., & Dikeos, D. G. (2005). How do individuals sleep around the world? Results from a single-day survey in ten countries. *Sleep Medicine, 6,* 5–13.

Soler, C., Nunez, M., Gutierrez, R., Nunez, J., Medina, P., Sancho, M., Alvarez, J., & Nunez, A. (2003). Facial attractiveness in men provides clues to semen quality. *Evolution and Human Behavior, 24,* 199–207.

Solinas, M., Justinova, Z., Goldberg, S. R., & Tanda, G. (2006). Anandamide administration alone and after inhibition of fatty acid amide hydrolase (FAAH) increases dopamine levels in the nucleus accumbens shell in rats. *Journal of Neurochemistry, 98,* 408–419.

Solinas, M., Panlilio, L. V., Antoniou, K., Pappas, L. A., & Goldberg, S. R. (2003). The cannabinoid CB1 antagonist N-piperidinyl-5-(4-chlorophenyl)-1-(2,4-dichlorophenyl)-4-methylpyrazole-3-carboxamide (SR-141716A) differentially alters the reinforcing effects of heroin under continuous reinforcement, fixed ratio, and progressive ratio schedules of drug self-administration in rats. *Journal of Pharmacology and Experimental Therapeutics, 306,* 93–102.

Soll, J. B., & Klayman, J. (2004). Overconfidence in interval estimates. *Journal of Experimental Psychology: Learning, Memory, & Cognition, 30,* 299–314.

Solms, M. (2000a). Freudian dream theory today. *Psychologist, 13,* 618–619.

Solms, M. (2000b). Dreaming and REM sleep are controlled by different brain mechanisms. *Behavioral and Brain Sciences, 23,* 843–850.

Solms, M. (2004). Freud returns. *Scientific American, 290*(5), 83–88.

Solomon, D. A., Keller, M. B., Leon, A. C., Mueller, T. I., Shea, M. T., Warshaw, M., Maser, J. D., Coryell, W., & Endicott, J. (1997). Recovery from major depression: A 10-year prospective follow-up across multiple episodes. *Archives of General Psychiatry, 54,* 1001–1006.

Solomon, S., Greenberg, J., & Pyszczynski, T. (1991). A terror management theory of social behavior: The psychological functions of self-esteem and cultural worldviews. In M. Zanna (Ed.), *Advances in experimental social psychology* (Vol. 24). Orlando, FL: Academic Press.

Solomon, S., Greenberg, J., & Pyszczynski, T. (2004a). Lethal consumption: Death-denying materialism. In T. Kasser, & A. D. Kanner (Eds.), *Psychology and consumer culture: The struggle for a good life in a materialistic society.* Washington, DC: American Psychological Association.

Solomon, S., Greenberg, J., & Pyszczynski, T. (2004b). The cultural animal: Twenty years of terror management. In J. Greenberg, S. L. Koole, & T. Pyszczynski (Eds.), *Handbook of experimental existential psychology.* New York: Guilford.

Solomon, S. G., & Lennie, P. (2007). The machinery of colour vision. *Nature Reviews Neuroscience, 8,* 276–286.

Solowij, N., Stephens, R. S., Roffman, R. A., Babor, T., Kadden, R., Miller, M., Christiansen. K., McRee, B., & Vendetti, J. (2002). Cognitive functioning of long-term heavy cannabis users seeking treatment. *Journal of the American Medical Association, 287,* 1123–1131.

Solso, R. L. (1994). *Cognition and the visual arts.* Cambridge, MA: MIT Press.

Sommer, B. (1987). *Not another diet book: A right-brain program for successful weight management.* Alameda, CA: Hunter House.

Song, A. W., Huettel, S. A., & McCarthy, G. (2006). Functional neuroimaging: Basic principles of functional MRI. In R. Cabeza & A. Kingstone (Eds.), *Handbook of functional neuroimaging of cognition* (pp. 21–52). Cambridge, MA: MIT Press.

Song, S., Sjostrom, P. J., Reigl, M. , Nelson, S., & Chklovskii, D. B. (2005). Highly nonrandom features of synaptic connectivity in local cortical circuits. *PLoS Biol, 3*(3), 1–13.

Sousa, D. A. (2000). *How the brain learns: A classroom teacher's guide.* Thousand Oaks, CA: Corwin Press.

Spada, M. M., & Wells, A. (2006). Metacognitions about alcohol use in problem drinkers. *Clinical Psychology & Psychotherapy, 13,* 138–143.

Spangler, W. D. (1992). Validity of questionnaire and TAT measures of need for achievement: Two meta-analyses. *Psychological Bulletin, 112,* 140–154.

Spanos, N. P. (1986). Hypnotic behavior: A social-psychological interpretation of amnesia, analgesia, and "trance logic." *Behavioral & Brain Sciences, 9*(3), 449–467.

Spanos, N. P. (1991). A sociocognitive approach to hypnosis. In S. J. Lynn & J. W. Rhue (Eds.), *Theories of hypnosis: Current models and perspectives* (pp. 324–361). New York: Guilford.

Spanos, N. P. (1994). Multiple identity enactments and multiple personality disorder: A sociocognitive perspective. *Psychological Bulletin, 116,* 143–165.

Spanos, N. P. (1996). *Multiple identities and false memories.* Washington, DC: American Psychological Association.

Sparks, J. A., Duncan, B. L., & Miller, S. D. (2008). Common factors in psychotherapy. In J. L. Lebow (Ed.), *Twenty-first century psychotherapies: Contemporary approaches to theory and practice.* New York: Wiley.

Spear, P. (2000). The adolescent brain and age-related behavioral manifestations. *Neuroscience and Biobehavioral Reviews, 24,* 417–463.

Spearman, C. (1904). "General intelligence" objectively determined and measured. *American Journal of Psychology, 15,* 202–293.

Spearman, C. (1927). *The abilities of man, their nature and measurement.* London: Macmillan.

Speed, A., & Gangestad, S. W. (1997). Romantic popularity and mate preferences: A peer-nomination study. *Personality and Social Psychology Bulletin, 23,* 928–936.

Spelke, E. S., & Kinzler, K. D. (2007). Core knowledge. *Developmental Science, 10*(1), 89–96.

Spelke, E. S., & Newport, E. L. (1998). Nativism, empiricism, and the development of knowledge. In W. Damon (Ed.), *Handbook of child psychology (Vol. 1): Theoretical models of human development.* New York: Wiley.

Spence, I., Wong, P., Rusan, M., & Rastegar, N. (2006). How color enhances visual memory for natural scenes. *Psychological Science, 14*(1), 1–6.

Sperling, G. (1960). The information available in brief visual presentations. *Psychological Monographs, 74*(11, Whole No. 498).

Sperry, R. W. (1982). Some effects of disconnecting the cerebral hemispheres. *Science, 217,* 1223–1226, 1250.

Spherion. (2006, September 18). Spherion survey: Workers say listening to music while working improves job satisfaction, productivity. Retrieved from http://www.spherion.com/press/releases/2006/IPod_at_Work_Snapshot.jsp.

Spiegel, D. (1995). Hypnosis, dissociation, and trauma: Hidden and overt observers. In J. L. Singer (Ed.), *Repression and dissociation: Implications for personality theory, psychopathology, and health.* Chicago: University of Chicago Press.

Spiegel, D. (2003a). Hypnosis and traumatic dissociation: Therapeutic opportunities. *Journal of Trauma & Dissociation, 4*(3), 73–90.

Spiegel, D. (2003b). Negative and positive visual hypnotic hallucinations: Attending inside and out. *International Journal of Clinical & Experimental Hypnosis, 51*(2), 130–146.

Spiegel, D. (2007). Commentary: Reversing amnesia about hypnosis. *American Journal of Clinical Hypnosis, 49*(3), 181–182.

Spiegel, D., Cutcomb, S., Ren, C., & Pribram, K. (1985). Hypnotic hallucination alters evoked potentials. *Journal of Abnormal Psychology, 94,* 249–255.

Spiegel, H., Greenleaf, M., & Spiegel, D. (2005). Hypnosis. In B. J. Sadock & V. A. Sadock (Eds.), *Kaplan & Sadock's comprehensive textbook of psychiatry.* Philadelphia: Lippincott WIlliams & Wilkins.

Spiegel, K., Tasali, E., Penev, P., et al. (2004). Sleep curtailment in healthy young men is associated with decreased leptin levels, elevated ghrelin levels and increased hunger and appetite. *Annals of Internal Medicine, 141,* 846–850.

Spiegler, M. D., & Guevremont, D. C. (2003). *Contemporary behavior therapy.* Belmont, CA: Wadsworth.

Spitzer, R. L., First, M. B., & Wakefield, J. C. (2007). Saving PTSD from itself in DSM-V. *Journal of Anxiety Disorders, 21*(2), 233–241.

Sprecher, S. (1998). Insiders' perspectives on reasons for attraction to a close other. *Social Psychology Quarterly, 61,* 287–300.

Sprecher, S. (1999). "I love you more today than yesterday": Romantic partners' perceptions of changes in love and related affect over time. *Journal of Personality and Social Psychology, 76,* 46–53.

Sprecher, S., & Duck, S. (1994). Sweet talk: The importance of perceived communication for romantic and friendship attraction experienced during a get-acquainted date. *Personality and Social Psychology Bulletin, 20,* 391–400.

Sprenger, M. (2001). *Becoming a "wiz" at brain-based teaching: From translation to application.* Thousand Oaks, CA: Corwin Press.

Springer, S. P., & Deutsch, G. (1998). *Left brain, right brain.* New York: W. H. Freeman.

Squire, L. R. (1987). *Memory and brain.* New York: Oxford University Press.

Squire, L. R. (2004). Memory systems of the brain: A brief history and current perspective. *Neurobiology of Learning & Memory, 82*(3), 171–177.

Squire, L. R., Clark, R. E., & Bayley, P. J. (2004). Medial temporal lobe function and memory. In M. S. Gazzaniga (Ed.), *The cognitive neurosciences* (pp. 691–708). Cambridge, MA: MIT Press.

Squire, L. R., Knowlton, B., & Musen, G. (1993). The structure and organization of memory. *Annual Review of Psychology, 44,* 453–495.

Staats, A. W., & Staats, C. K. (1963). *Complex human behavior.* New York: Holt, Rinehart & Winston.

Stajkovic, A. D., & Luthans, F. (1998). Self-efficacy and work-related performance: A meta-analysis. *Psychological Bulletin, 124,* 240–261.

Stamler, J., Daviglus, M. L., Garside, D. B., Dyer, A. R., Greenland, P., & Neaton, J. D. (2000). Relationship of baseline serum cholesterol levels in three large cohorts of younger men to long-term coronary, cardiovascular, and all-cause mortality and to longevity. *Journal of the American Medical Association, 284,* 311–318.

Stanovich, K. E. (1999). *Who is rational? Studies of individual differences in reasoning.* Mahwah, NJ: Erlbaum.

Stanovich, K. E. (2003). The fundamental computational biases of human cognition: Heuristics that (sometimes) impair decision making and problem solving. In J. E. Davidson & R. J. Sternberg (Eds.), *The psychology of problem solving.* New York: Cambridge University Press.

Stanovich, K. E. (2004). *How to think straight about psychology.* Boston: Allyn & Bacon.

Stanovich, K. E., & West, R. F. (2002). Individual differences in reasoning: Implications for the rationality debate. In T. Gilovich, D. Griffin, & D. Kahneman (Eds.), *Heuristics and biases.* New York: Cambridge University Press.

Stanton, A. L., Lobel, M., Sears, S., & DeLuca, R. S. (2002). Psychosocial aspects of selected issues in women's reproductive health: Current status and future directions. *Journal of Consulting & Clinical Psychology, 70,* 751–770.

Starcevic, V. (2001). Clinical features and diagnosis of hypochondriasis. In V. Starcevic & D. R. Lipsitt (Eds.), *Hypochondriasis: Modern perspectives on an ancient malady.* New York: Oxford University Press.

Stasser, G., Vaughan, S. I., & Stewart, D. D. (2000). Pooling unshared information: The benefits of knowing how access to information is distributed among group members. *Organizational Behavior and Human Decision Processes, 82,* 102–116.

Steel, P. (2007). The nature of procrastination: A meta-analytic and theoretical review of quintessential self-regulatory failure. *Psychological Bulletin, 133,* 65–94.

Steele, C. M. (1992, April). Race and the schooling of black Americans. *Atlantic Monthly,* pp. 68–78.

Steele, C. M. (1997). A threat in the air: How stereotypes shape intellectual identity and performance. *American Psychologist, 52,* 613–629.

Steele, C. M., & Aronson, J. (1995). Stereotype threat and the intellectual test performance of African Americans. *Journal of Personality and Social Psychology, 69,* 797–811.

Steele, K. M. (2003). Do rats show a Mozart effect? *Music Perception, 21,* 251–265.

Steiger, H., & Seguin, J. R. (1999). Eating disorders: Anorexia nervosa and bulimia nervosa. In T. Millon, P. H. Blaney, & R. D. Davis (Eds.), *Oxford textbook of psychopathology* (pp. 365–389). New York: Oxford University Press.

Steiger, H., Bruce, K. R., & Israel, M. (2003). Eating disorders. In G. Stricker & T. A. Widiger (Eds.), *Handbook of psychology, Vol. 8: Clinical psychology.* New York: Wiley.

Steiger, H., Gauvin, L., Engelberg, M. J., Kin, N. M. K. N. Y., Israel, M., Wonderlich, S. A., et al. (2005). Mood- and restraint-based antecedents to binge episodes in bulimia nervosa: Possible influences of the serotonin system. *Psychological Medicine, 35,* 1553–1562.

Stein, B. E., & Meredith, M. A. (1993). *Vision, touch, and audition: Making sense of it all.* Cambridge, MA: MIT Press.

Stein, B. E., Wallace, M. T., & Stanford, T. R. (2000). Merging sensory signals in the brain: The development of multisensory integration in the superior colliculus. In M. S. Gazzaniga (Ed.), *The new cognitive neurosciences.* Cambridge, MA: The MIT Press.

Stein, B. E., Wallace, M. T., & Stanford, T. R. (2001). Brain mechanisms for synthesizing information from different sensory modalities. In E. B. Goldstein (Ed.), *Blackwell handbook of perception.* Malden, MA: Blackwell.

Stein, D. J., & Hugo, F. J. (2004). Neuropsychiatric aspects of anxiety disorders. In S. C. Yudofsky & R. E. Hales (Eds.), *Essentials of neuropsychiatry and clinical neurosciences.* Washington, DC: American Psychiatric Publishing.

Stein, M. B., Walker, J. R., Hazen, A. L., & Forde, D. R. (1997). Full and partial posttraumatic stress disorder: Findings from a community survey. *American Journal of Psychiatry, 154,* 1114–1119.

Steinberg, L. (2001). We know some things: Adolescent-parent relationships in retrospect and prospect. *Journal of Research on Adolescence, 11,* 1–20.

Steinberg, L. (2007). Risk taking in adolescence: New perspectives from brain and behavioral science. *Perspectives on Psychological Science, 16,* 55–59.

Steinberg, L., & Levine, A. (1997). *You and your adolescent: A parents' guide for ages 10 to 20.* New York: Harper Perennial.

Steinberg, L., & Morris, A. S. (2001). Adolescent development. *Annual Review of Psychology, 52,* 83–110.

Steinhausen, H. (2002). The outcome of anorexia nervosa in the 20th century. *American Journal of Psychiatry, 159,* 1284–1293.

Steinmetz, J. E. (1998). The localization of a simple type of learning and memory: The cerebellum and classical eyeblink conditioning. *Current Directions in Psychological Science, 7,* 72–77.

Stekel, W. (1950). *Techniques of analytical psychotherapy.* New York: Liveright.

Stellar, E. (1954). The physiology of motivation. *Psychological Review, 61,* 5–22.

Stemberger, R. T., Turner, S. M., Beidel, D. C., & Calhoun, K. S. (1995). Social phobia: An analysis of possible developmental factors. *Journal of Abnormal Psychology, 104,* 526–531.

Stemler, S. E., Grigorenko, E. L., Jarvin, L., & Sternberg, R. J. (2006). Using the theory of successful intelligence as a basis for augmenting AP exams in psychology and statistics. *Contemporary Educational Psychology, 31,* 344–376.

Stepanski, E. J. (2006). Causes of insomnia. In T. Lee-Chiong (Ed.), *Sleep: A comprehensive handbook.* Hoboken, NJ: Wiley-Liss.

Stepanski, E. J., & Wyatt, J. K. (2003). Use of sleep hygiene in the treatment of insomnia. *Sleep Medicine Reviews, 7*(3), 215–225.

Stephens, R. S. (1999). Cannabis and hallucinogens. In B. S. McCrady & E. E. Epstein (Eds.), *Addictions: A comprehensive guidebook.* New York: Oxford University Press.

Steptoe, A. (2007). Stress effects: Overview. In G. Fink (Ed.), *Encyclopedia of stress.* San Diego: Elsevier.

Steptoe, A., Gibson, E. L., Hamer, M., & Wardle, J. (2007). Neuroendocrine and cardiovascular correlates of positive affect measured by ecological momentary assessment and by questionnaire. *Psychoneuroendocrinology, 32,* 56–64.

Steriade, M. (2005). Brain electrical activity and sensory processing during waking and sleep states. In M. H. Kryger, T. Roth, & W. C. Dement (Eds.). *Principles and practice of sleep medicine.* Philadelphia: Elsevier Saunders.

Stern, W. (1914). *The psychological method of testing intelligence.* Baltimore: Warwick & York.

Sternberg, R. J. (1985). *Beyond IQ: A triarchic theory of human intelligence.* New York: Cambridge University Press.

Sternberg, R. J. (1986). *Intelligence applied: Understanding and increasing your intellectual skills.* New York: Harcourt Brace Jovanovich.

Sternberg, R. J. (1988a). A three-facet model of creativity. In R. J. Sternberg (Ed.), *The nature of creativity: Contemporary psychological perspectives.* Cambridge, England: Cambridge University Press.

Sternberg, R. J. (1988b). *The triarchic mind: A new theory of human intelligence.* New York: Viking.

Sternberg, R. J. (1991). Theory-based testing of intellectual abilities: Rationale for the triarchic abilities test. In H. A. H. Rowe (Ed.), *Intelligence: Reconceptualization and measurement.* Hillsdale, NJ: Erlbaum.

Sternberg, R. J. (1998). How intelligent is intelligence testing? *Scientific American Presents Exploring Intelligence, 9,* 12–17.

Sternberg, R. J. (1999). The theory of successful intelligence. *Review of General Psychology, 3,* 292–316.

Sternberg, R. J. (2000a). Creativity is a decision. In A. L. Costa (Ed.), *Teaching for intelligence II* (pp. 85–106). Arlington Heights, IL: Skylight Training.

Sternberg, R. J. (2000b). Successful intelligence: A unified view of giftedness. In C. F. M. van Lieshout & P. G. Heymans (Eds.), *Developing talent across the life span* (pp. 43–65). Philadelphia: Psychology Press.

Sternberg, R. J. (2003a). Construct validity of the theory of successful intelligence. In R. J. Sternberg, J. Lautrey, & T. I. Lubart (Eds.), *Models of intelligence: International perspectives.* Washington, DC: American Psychological Association.

Sternberg, R. J. (2003b). My house is a very, very, very fine house—But it is not the only house. In H. Nyborg (Ed.), *The scientific study of general intelligence: Tribute to Arthur R. Jensen.* Oxford, UK: Pergamon.

Sternberg, R. J. (2004). Culture and intelligence. *American Psychologist, 59,* 325–338.

Sternberg, R. J. (2005a). There are no public policy implications: A reply to Rushton and Jensen. *Psychology, Public Policy, and the Law, 11,* 295–301.

Sternberg, R. J. (2005b). The triarchic theory of successful intelligence. In D. P. Flanagan & P. L. Harrison (Eds.), *Contemporary intellectual assessment: Theories, tests and issues* (pp. 103–119). New York: Guillford Press.

Sternberg, R. J. (2005c). The WICS model of giftedness. In R. J. Sternberg & J. E. Davidson (Eds.), *Conceptions of giftedness.* New York: Cambridge University Press.

Sternberg, R. J. (2006). A duplex theory of love. In R. J. Sternberg & K. Weis (Eds.), *The new psychology of love.* New Haven, CT: Yale University Press.

Sternberg, R. J. (2007). Intelligence and culture. In S. Kitayama & D. Cohen (Eds.), *Handbook of cultural psychology* (pp. 547–568). New York: Guilford.

Sternberg, R. J., Castejon, J. L., Prieto, M. D., Hautamaeki, J., & Grigorenko, E. L. (2001). Confirmatory factor analysis of the Sternberg Triarchic Abilities Test in three international samples: An empirical test of the triarchic theory of intelligence. *European Journal of Psychological Assessment, 17,* 1–16.

Sternberg, R. J., Conway, B. E., Ketron, J. L., & Bernstein, M. (1981). People's conceptions of intelligence. *Journal of Personality and Social Psychology, 41,* 37–55.

Sternberg, R. J., Grigorenko, E. L., Ferrari, M., & Clinkenbeard, P. (1999). A triarchic analysis of an aptitude interaction. *European Journal of Psychological Assessment, 15,* 1–11.

Sternberg, R. J., Grigorenko, E. L., & Kidd, K. K. (2005). Intelligence, race, and genetics. *American Psychologist, 60,* 45–69.

Sternberg, R. J., & Hedlund, J. (2002). Practical intelligence, g, and work psychology. *Human Performance, 15,* 143–160.

Sternberg, R. J., & Jarvin, L. (2003). Alfred Binet's contributions as a paradigm for impact in psychology. In R. J. Sternberg (Ed.), *The anatomy of impact: What makes the great works of psychology great* (pp. 89–107). Washington, DC: American Psychological Association.

Sternberg, R. J., & O'Hara, L. A. (1999). Creativity and intelligence. In R. J. Sternberg (Ed.), *Handbook of creativity.* New York: Cambridge University Press.

Sternberg, R. J., & the Rainbow Project Collaborators. (2006). The Rainbow Project: Enhancing the SAT through assessments of analytical, practical, and creative skills. *Intelligence, 34,* 321–350.

Stetler, C., Murali, R., Chen, E., & Miller, G. E. (2005). Stress, immunity, and disease. In C. L. Cooper (Ed.), *Handbook of stress medicine and health.* Boca Raton, FL: CRC Press.

Steven, M. S., & Blakemore, C. (2004). Cortical plasticity in the adult human brain. In M. S. Gazzaniga (Ed.), *The cognitive neurosciences* (pp. 1243–1254). Cambridge, MA: MIT Press.

Stevens, G., Raphael, B., & Dobson, M. (2007). Effects of public disasters and mass violence. In G. Fink (Ed.), *Encyclopedia of stress.* San Diego: Elsevier.

Stevens, S. S. (1955). The measurement of loudness. *Journal of the Acoustical Society of America, 27,* 815–819.

Stewart, A., Ostrove, J. M., & Helson, R. (2001). Middle aging in women: Patterns of personality change from the 30s to the 50s. *Journal of Adult Development, 8*(1), 23–37.

Stewart, G. L., & Manz, C. C. (1995). Leadership for self-managing work teams: A typology and integrative model. *Human Relations, 48,* 347–370.

Stewart, R., Ellenburg, G., Hicks, L., Kremen, M., & Daniel, M. (1990). Employee references as a recruitment source. *Applied H.R.M. Research, 1*(1), 1–3.

Stewart, W. H., Jr., & Roth, P. L. (2007). A meta-analysis of achievement motivation differences between entrepreneurs and managers. *Journal of Small Business Management, 45,* 401–421.

Stewart-Williams, S. (2004). The placebo puzzle: Putting the pieces together. *Health Psychology, 23,* 198–206.

Stickgold, R. (2001). Toward a cognitive neuroscience of sleep. *Sleep Medicine Reviews, 5,* 417–421.

Stickgold, R. (2005). Why we dream. In M. H. Kryger, T. Roth, & W. C. Dement (Eds.). *Principles and practice of sleep medicine.* Philadelphia: Elsevier Saunders.

Stickgold, R., & Walker, M. P. (2004). To sleep, perchance to gain creative insight. *Trends in Cognitive Sciences, 8*(5), 191–192.

Stickgold, R., & Walker, M. P. (2005). Memory consolidation and reconsolidation: What is the role of sleep? *Trends in Neurosciences, 28*(8), 408–415.

Stoddard, G. (1943). *The meaning of intelligence.* New York: Macmillan.

Stone, A. A. (1999). Psychiatry and the law. In A. M. Nicholi (Ed.), *The Harvard guide to psychiatry.* Cambridge, MA: Harvard University Press.

Stone, J., & Olson, J. M. (2005). The influence of attitudes on behavior. In D. Albarracin, B. T. Johnson, & M. P. Zanna (Eds.), *The handbook of attitudes.* Mahwah, NJ: Erlbaum.

Stone, L. (1977). *The family, sex and marriage in England 1500–1800.* New York: Harper & Row.

Stone, W. N. (2003). Group psychotherapy. In A. Tasman, J. Kay, & J. A. Lieberman (Eds.), *Psychiatry.* New York: Wiley.

Stoner, J. A. F. (1961). *A comparison of individual and group decisions involving risk.* Unpublished master's thesis, Massachusetts Institute of Technology.

Stoney, C. M. (2003). Gender and cardiovascular disease: A psychobiological and integrative approach. *Current Directions in Psychological Science, 12*(4), 129–133.

Stoohs, R. A., Blum, H. C., Haselhorst, M., Duchna, H. W., Guilleminault, C., & Dement, W. C. (1998). Normative data on snoring: A comparison between younger and older adults. *European Respiratory Journal, 11,* 451–457.

Stoolmiller, M. (1999). Implications of the restricted range of family environments for estimates of heritability and nonshared environment in behavior-genetic adoption studies. *Psychological Bulletin, 125,* 392–409.

Storch, M., Gaab, J., Küttel, Y., Stüssi, A.-C., & Fend, H. (2007). Psychoneuroendocrine effects of resource-activating stress management training. *Health Psychology, 26*(4), 456–463.

Stowell, J. R. (2008). Stress and stressors. In S. F. Davis & W. Buskist (Eds.), *21st century psychology: A reference handbook.* Thousand Oaks, CA: Sage.

Strager, S. (2003). What men watch when they watch pornography. *Sexuality & Culture: An Interdisciplinary Quarterly, 7*(1), 50–61.

Strahan, E. J., Lafrance, A., Wilson, A. E., Ethier, N., Spencer, S. J., & Zanna, M. P. (2008). Victoria's dirty secret: How sociocultural norms influence adolescent girls and women. *Personality and Social Psychology Bulletin, 34*(2), 288–301.

Strange, D., Clifasefi, S., & Garry, M. (2007). False memories. In M. Garry & H. Hayne (Eds.), *Do justice and let the sky fall: Elizabeth F. Lotus and her contributions to science, law, and academic freedom.* Mahwah, NJ: Erlbaum.

Straus, M. A. (2000). Corporal punishment and primary prevention of physical abuse. *Child Abuse & Neglect, 24,* 1109–1114.

Straus, M. A., & Stewart, J. H. (1999). Corporal punishment by American parents: National data on prevalence, chronicity, severity, and duration, in relation to child family characteristics. *Clinical Child & Family Psychology Review, 2*(2), 55–70.

Strayer, D. L., & Drews, F. A. (2007). Cell-phone-induced driver distraction. *Current Directions in Psychological Science, 16,* 128–131.

Strayer, D. L., Drews, F. A., & Crouch, D. J. (2006). A comparison of the cell phone driver and the drunk driver. *Human Factors, 48,* 381–391.

Strayer, D. L., & Johnston, W. A. (2001). Driven to distraction: Dual-task studies of simulated driving and conversing on a cellular telephone. *Psychological Science, 12,* 462–466.

Streissguth, A. (2007). Offspring effects of prenatal alcohol exposure from birth to 25 years: The Seattle prospective longitudinal study. *Journal of Clinical Psychology in Medical Settings, 14,* 81–101.

Streissguth, A. P., Bookstein, F. L., Barr, H. M., Sampson, P. D., O'Malley, K., & Young, J. K. (2004). Risk factors for adverse life outcomes in fetal alcohol syndrome and fetal alcohol effects. *Journal of Developmental & Behavioral Pediatrics, 25,* 228–238.

Streit, W. J. (2005). Microglia and neuroprotection: Implications for Alzheimer's disease. *Brain Research Reviews, 48,* 234–239.

Strenze, T. (2007). Intelligence and socioeconomic success: A meta-analytic review of longitudinal research. *Intelligence, 35,* 401–426.

Striegel-Moore, R. H., & Bulik, C. M. (2007). Risk factors for eating disorders. *American Psychologist, 62,* 181–198.

Striegel-Moore, R. H., & Franko, D. L. (2008). Should binge eating disorder be included in the DSM-V? A critical review of the state of the evidence. *Annual Review of Clinical Psychology, 4,* 305–324.

Striegel-Moore, R. H., Silberstein, L. R., & Rodin, J. (1993). The social self in bulimia nervosa: Public self-consciousness, social anxiety, and perceived fraudulence. *Journal of Abnormal Psychology, 102.*

Strollo, P. J. Jr., Atwood, C. W. Jr., & Sanders, M. H. (2007). Medical therapy for obstructive sleep apnea-hypopnea syndrome. In M. H. Kryger, T. Roth, & W. C. Dement (Eds.), *Principles and practice of sleep medicine.* Philadelphia: Saunders.

Stroup, T. S., Kraus, J. E., & Marder, S. R. (2006). Pharmacotherapies. In J. A. Lieberman, T. S. Stroup, & D. O. Perkins (Eds.), *Textbook of schizophrenia* (pp. 303–326). Washington, DC: American Psychiatric Publishing.

Strupp, H. H. (1996). The tripartite model and the *Consumer Reports* study. *American Psychologist, 51,* 1017–1024.

Stubbe, J. H., Posthuma, D., Boomsma, D. I., & de Geus, E. J. C. (2005). Heritability of life satisfaction in adults: A twin study. *Psychological Medicine, 35,* 1581–1588.

Stunkard, A. J., Harris, J. R., Pederson, N. L., & McClearn, G. E. (1990). The body-mass index of twins who have been reared apart. *New England Journal of Medicine, 322,* 1483–1487.

Stunkard, A. J., Sorensen, T., Hanis, C., Teasdale, T. W., Chakraborty, R., Schull, W. J., & Schulsinger, F. (1986). An adoption study of human obesity. *New England Journal of Medicine, 314,* 193–198.

Sturman, M. C., & Sherwyn, D. (2007). The truth about integrity tests: The validity and utility of integrity testing for the hospital industry. *The Center for Hospitality Research, 7*(15).

Sudak, H. S. (2005). Suicide. In B. J. Sadock & V. A. Sadock (Eds.), *Kaplan & Sadock's comprehensive textbook of psychiatry.* Philadelphia: Lippincott WIlliams & Wilkins.

Sue, D. W., & Sue, D. (1999). *Counseling the culturally different: Theory and practice.* New York: Wiley.

Sue, S. (2003). In defense of cultural competency in psychotherapy and treatment. *American Psychologist, 58,* 964–970.

Sue, S., Zane, N., & Young, K. (1994). Research on psychotherapy with culturally diverse populations. In A. E. Bergin & S. L. Garfield (Eds.), *Handbook of psychotherapy and behavior change* (4th ed.). New York: Wiley.

Sufka, K. J., & Price, D. D. (2002). Gate control theory reconsidered. *Brain & Mind, 3,* 277–290.

Sugarman, J. (2007). Practical rationality and the questionable promise of positive psychology. *Journal of Humanistic Psychology, 47,* 175–197.

Sugiyama, L. S. (2005). Physical attractiveness in adaptionist perspective. In D. M. Buss (Ed.), *The handbook of evolutionary psychology.* New York: Wiley.

Sullivan, G. M., & Coplan, J. D. (2000). Anxiety disorders: Biochemical aspects. In B. J. Sadock & V. A. Sadock (Eds.), *Kaplan and Sadock's comprehensive textbook of psychiatry,* (7th ed., Vol. 1). Philadelphia: Lippincott/Williams & Wilkins.

Sullivan, G., Burnam, A., & Koegel, P. (2000). Pathways to homelessness among the mentally ill. *Social Psychiatry & Psychiatric Epidemiology, 35,* 444–450.

Sullivan, P. F., Owen, M. J., O'Donovan, M. C., & Freedman, R. (2006). Genetics. In J. A. Lieberman, T. S. Stroup, & D. O. Perkins (Eds.), *Textbook of schizophrenia* (pp. 39–54). Washington, DC: American Psychiatric Publishing.

Sulloway, F. J. (1995). Birth order and evolutionary psychology: A meta-analytic overview. *Psychological Inquiry, 6,* 75–80.

Sulloway, F. J. (1996). *Born to rebel: Birth order, family dynamics, and creative lives.* New York: Pantheon Books.

Sulloway, F. J. (2007). Birth order. In C. A. Salmon & T. K. Shackelford (Eds.), *Family relationships: An evolutionary perspective.* New York: Oxford University Press.

Super, C. M. (1976). Environmental effects on motor development: A case of African infant pre-cocity. *Developmental Medicine and Child Neurology, 18,* 561–567.

Surtees, P., & Wainwright, N. (2007). Life events and health. In G. Fink (Ed.), *Encyclopedia of stress.* San Diego: Elsevier.

Susman, E. J., Dorn, L. D., & Schiefelbein, V. L. (2003). Puberty, sexuality, and health. In R. M. Lerner, M. A. Easterbrooks, & J. Mistry (Eds.), *Handbook of psychology, Vol. 6: Developmental psychology.* New York: Wiley.

Susman, E. J., & Rogol, A. (2004). Puberty and psychological development. In R. M. Lerner & L. Steinberg (Eds.), *Handbook of adolescent psychology.* New York: Wiley.

Susser, E. B., Brown, A., & Matte, T. D. (1999). Prenatal factors and adult mental and physical health. *Canadian Journal of Psychiatry, 44,* 326–334.

Susser, E. B., Neugebauer, R., Hoek, H. W., Brown, A. S., Lin, S., Labovitz, D., & Gorman, J. M. (1996). Schizophrenia after prenatal famine: Further evidence. *Archives of General Psychiatry, 53,* 25–31.

Sutker, P. B., & Allain, A. N. (2001). Antisocial personality disorder. In P. B. Sutker & H. E. Adams (Eds.), *Comprehensive handbook of psychopathology.* New York: Kluwer Academic/Plenum.

Suzuki, K. (2007). The moon illusion: Kaufman and Rock's (1962) apparent-distance theory reconsidered. *Japanese Psychological Research, 49,* 57–67.

Swan, G. E., Hudmon, K. S., & Kroyan, T. V. (2003). Tobacco dependence. In A. M. Nezu, C. M. Nezu, & P. A. Geller (Eds.), *Handbook of psychology, Vol. 9: Health psychology.* New York: Wiley.

Swets, J. A., Tanner, W. P., & Birdsall, T. G. (1961). Decision processes in perception. *Psychological Review, 68,* 301–340.

Swim, J. K., & Campbell, B. (2001). Sexism: Attitudes, beliefs, and behaviors. In R. Brown & S. L. Gaertner (Eds.), *Blackwell handbook of social psychology: Intergroup processes.* Malden, MA: Blackwell.

Swim, J. K., & Sanna, L. J. (1996). He's skilled, she's lucky: A meta-analysis of observers' attributions for women's and men's successes and failures. *Personality and Social Psychology Bulletin, 22,* 507–519.

Symons, C. S., & Johnson, B. T. (1997). The self-reference effect in memory: A meta-analysis. *Psychological Bulletin, 121,* 371–394.

Szasz, T. (1974). *The myth of mental illness.* New York: Harper & Row.

Szasz, T. (1990). Law and psychiatry: The problems that will not go away. *The Journal of Mind and Behavior, 11*(3/4), 557–564.

Szegedy-Maszak, M. (2005, August 8). In gambling's grip. *Los Angeles Times.*

Szmukler, G. I., & Patton, G. (1995). Sociocultural models of eating disorders. In G. Szmukler, C. Dare, & J. Treasure (Eds.), *Handbook of eating disorders: Theory, treatment, and research.* New York: Wiley.

Szymanski, L. S., & Wilska, M. (2003). Childhood disorders: Mental retardation. In A. Tasman, J. Kay, & J. A. Lieberman (Eds.), *Psychiatry.* New York: Wiley.

Taglialatela, J. P., Russell, J. L., Schaeffer, J. A., & Hopkins, W. D. (2008). Communicative, signaling activates "Broca's" homolog in chimpanzees. *Current Biology, 18,* 1–6.

Tajfel, H. (1982). *Social identity and intergroup reflections.* London: Cambridge University Press.

Tajfel, H., & Turner, J. C. (1979). An integrative theory of intergroup conflict. In W. G. Austin & S. Worchel (Eds.), *The social psychology of intergroup relations.* Monterey, CA: Brooks/Cole.

Takahashi, M., & Kaida, K. (2006). Napping. In T. Lee–Chiong (Ed.), *Sleep: A comprehensive handbook*. Hoboken, NJ: Wiley-Liss.

Takahashi, T., Murata, T., Hamada, T., Omori, M., Kosaka, H., Kikuchi, M., Yoshida, H., & Wada, Y. (2005). Changes in EEG and autonomic nervous activity during meditation and their association with personality traits. *International Journal of Psychophysiology, 55*(2), 199–207.

Talarico, J. M., & Rubin, D. C. (2003). Confidence, not consistency, characterizes flashbulb memories. *Psychological Science, 14*, 455–461.

Talarico, J. M., & Rubin, D. C. (2007). Flashbulb memories are special after all; in phenomenology, not accuracy. *Applied Cognitive Psychology, 21*, 557–578.

Talbott, J. A. (2004). Deinstitutionalization: Avoiding the disasters of the past. *Psychiatric Services, 55*, 1112–1115.

Talwar, S. K., Xu, S., Hawley, E. S., Weiss, S. A., Moxon, K. A., & Chapin, J. K. (2002). Behavioural neuroscience: Rat navigation guided by remote control. *Nature, 417*, 37–38.

Tamakoshi, A., Ohno, Y., & JACC Study Group. (2004). Self-reported sleep duration as a predictor of all-cause mortality: Results from JACC study, Japan. *Sleep: A Journal of Sleep and Sleep Disorders Research, 27*, 51–54.

Tamminga, C. A., & Carlsson A. (2003). Psychiatric pathophysiology: Schizophrenia. In A. Tasman, J. Kay, & J. A. Lieberman (Eds.), *Psychiatry*. New York: Wiley.

Tanaka, J., Weiskopf, D., & Williams, P. (2001). The role of color in high-level vision. *Trends in Cognitive Sciences, 5*, 211–215.

Tanaka-Matsumi, J. (2001). Abnormal psychology and culture. In D. Matsumoto (Ed.), *The handbook of culture & psychology*. New York: Oxford University Press.

Tanapat, P., & Gould, E. (2007). Neurogenesis. In G. Fink (Ed.), *Encyclopedia of stress*. San Diego: Elsevier.

Tangney, J. P., Stuewig, J., & Mashek, D. J. (2007). Moral emotions and moral behavior. *Annual Review of Psychology, 58*, 345–372.

Tanner, J. L. (2006). Recentering during emerging adulthood: A critical turning point in life span human development. In J. J. Arnett & J. L. Tanner (Eds.), *Emerging adults in America: Coming of age in the 21st century*. Washington, DC: American Psychological Association.

Tardiff, K. (1999). Violence. In R. E. Hales, S. C. Yudofsky, & J. A. Talbott (Eds.), *American Psychiatric Press textbook of psychiatry*. Washington, DC: American Psychiatric Press.

Tart, C. T. (1988). From spontaneous event to lucidity: A review of attempts to consciously control nocturnal dreaming. In J. Gackenbach & S. LaBerge (Eds.), *Conscious mind, sleeping brain: Perspectives on lucid dreaming*. New York: Plenum.

Tashkin, D. P., Baldwin, G. C., Sarafian, T., Dubinett, S., & Roth, M. D. (2002). Respiratory and immunologic consequences of marijuana smoking. *Journal of Clinical Pharmacology, 42*, 71S–81S.

Tavris, C. (1998, September 13). Peer pressure (Review of *The Nurture Assumption*). *The New York Times Book Review, 103*, p. 14.

Taylor, E. (1999). An intellectual renaissance of humanistic psychology. *Journal of Humanistic Psychology, 39*, 7–25.

Taylor, E. (2001). Positive psychology and humanistic psychology: A reply to Seligman. *Journal of Humanistic Psychology, 41*(1), 13–29.

Taylor, F. W. (1911). *The principles of scientific management*. New York: Harper & Row.

Taylor, I., & Taylor, M. M. (1990). *Psycholinguistics: Learning and using language*. Englewood Cliffs, NJ: Prentice-Hall.

Taylor, J. H., & Walker, L. J. (1997). Moral climate and the development of moral reasoning: The effects of dyadic discussions between young offenders. *Journal of Moral Education, 26*, 21–43.

Taylor, S. (2004). Amnesia, folklore and folks: Recovered memories in clinical practice. *Cognitive Behaviour Therapy, 33*(2), 105–108.

Taylor, S. E. (2002). *The tending instinct: How nurturing is essential to who we are and how we live*. New York: Holt.

Taylor, S. E. (2006). Tend and befriend: Biobehavioral bases of affiliation under stress. *Current Directions in Psychological Science, 15*, 273–277.

Taylor, S. E. (2007). Social support. In H. S. Friedman & R. C. Silver (Eds.), *Foundations of health psychology*. New York: Oxford University Press.

Taylor, S. E., & Brown, J. D. (1988). Illusion and well-being: A social psychological perspective on mental health. *Psychological Bulletin, 103*, 193–210.

Taylor, S. E., & Brown, J. D. (1994). Positive illusions and well-being revisited: Separating fact from fiction. *Psychological Bulletin, 116*, 21–27.

Taylor, S. E., Klein, L. C., Lewis, B. P., Gruenewald, T. L., Gurung, R. A. R., & Updegraff, J. A. (2000). Biobehavioral responses to stress in females: Tend and befriend, not fight or flight. *Psychological Review, 107*, 411–429.

Taylor, S. E., Lerner, J. S., Sherman, D. K., Sage, R. M., & McDowell, N. K. (2003). Are self-enhancing cognitions associated with healthy or unhealthy biological profiles? *Journal of Personality and Social Psychology, 85*, 605–615.

Tedlock, L. B. (1992). Zuni and Quiche dream sharing and interpreting. In B. Tedlock (Ed.), *Dreaming: Anthropological and psychological interpretations*. Santa Fe, NM: School of American Research Press.

Teigen, K. H. (2004). Judgments by representativeness. In F. P. Rudiger (Ed.), *Cognitive illusions*. New York: Psychology Press.

Tellegen, A., Lykken, D. T., Bouchard, T. J., Jr., Wilcox, K. J., Segal, N. L., & Rich, S. (1988). Personality similarity in twins reared apart and together. *Journal of Personality and Social Psychology, 54*, 1031–1039.

Temple, J. L., Giacomelli, A. M., Roemmich, J. N., & Epstein, L. H. (2008). Dietary variety impairs habituation in children. *Health Psychology, 27*, S10–S19.

Tennen, H., & Affleck, G. (1999). Finding benefits in adversity. In C. R. Snyder (Ed.), *Coping: The psychology of what works*. New York: Oxford University Press.

Tenopyr, M. L. (2002). Theory versus reality: Evaluation of *g* in the workplace. *Human Performance, 15*, 107–122.

Tepper, B. J., & Nurse, R. J. (1997). Fat perception is related to PROP taster status. *Physiology & Behavior, 61*, 949–954.

Terman, L. M. (1916). *The measurement of intelligence*. Boston: Houghton Mifflin.

Terman, L. M. (1925). *Genetic studies of genius: Vol. 1. Mental and physical traits of a thousand gifted children*. Stanford, CA: Stanford University Press.

Terman, L. M., & Oden, M. H. (1959). *Genetic studies of genius: Vol. 5. The gifted group at mid-life*. Stanford, CA: Stanford University Press.

Terr, L. (1994). *Unchained memories*. New York: Basic Books.

Terracciano, A., Abdel-Khalak, A. M., Adam, N., Adamovova, L., Ahn, C. K., Ahn, H. N., et al. (2005). National character does not reflect mean personality trait levels in 49 cultures. *Science, 310*, 96–100.

Terrace, H. S. (1986). *Nim: A chimpanzee who learned sign language*. New York: Columbia University Press.

Tessier-Lavigne, M. (2000). Visual processing by the retina. In E. R. Kandel, J. H. Schwartz, & T. M. Jessell (Eds.), *Principles of neural science*. New York: McGraw-Hill.

Tett, R. P., & Burnett, D. D. (2003). A personality trait–based interactionist model of job performance. *Journal of Applied Psychology, 88*, 500.

Teuber, M. (1974). Sources of ambiguity in the prints of Maurits C. Escher. *Scientific American, 231*, 90–104.

Thase, M. E. (2005). Bipolar depression: Issues in diagnosis and treatment. *Harvard Review of Psychiatry, 13*, 257–271.

Thase, M. E., & Denko, T. (2008). Pharmacotherapy of mood disorders. *Annual Review of Clinical Psychology, 4*, 53–91.

Thase, M. E., Jindal, R., & Howland, R. H. (2002). Biological aspects of depression. In I. H. Gotlib & C. L. Hammen (Eds.), *Handbook of depression*. New York: Guilford.

Thase, M. E., & Sloan D. M. E. (2006). Venlafaxine. In A. F. Schatzberg & C. B. Nemeroff (Eds.), *Essentials of clinical psychopharmacology*. Washington, DC: American Psychological Association.

Thayer, A., & Lynn, S. J. (2006). Guided imagery and recovered memory therapy: Considerations and cautions. *Journal of Forensic Psychology Practice, 6*, 63–73.

Thayer, R. E. (1996). *The origin of everyday moods*. New York: Oxford University Press.

Thelen, E. (1995). Motor development: A new synthesis. *American Psychologist, 50*, 79–95.

Theorell, T. (2005). Stress and prevention of cardiovascular disease. In C. L. Cooper (Ed.), *Handbook of stress medicine and health*. Boca Raton, FL: CRC Press.

Thomas, A., & Chess, S. (1977). *Temperament and development*. New York: Brunner/Mazel.

Thomas, A., & Chess, S. (1989). Temperament and personality. In G. A. Kohnstamm, J. E. Bates, & M. K. Rothbart (Eds.), *Temperament in childhood*. New York: Wiley.

Thomas, A., Chess, S., & Birch, H. G. (1970). The origin of personality. *Scientific American, 223*(2), 102–109.

Thomas, A. J., Kalaria, R. N., & O'Brien, J. T. (2004). Depression and vascular disease: What is the relationship? *Journal of Affective Disorders, 79*(1–3), 81–95.

Thomas, D. R. (1992). Discrimination and generalization. In L. R. Squire (Ed.), *Encyclopedia of learning and memory*. New York: Macmillan.

Thomas, R. M. (2005). *Comparing theories of child development*. Belmont, CA: Wadsworth.

Thompson, J. K., & Kinder, B. (2003). Eating disorders. In M. Hersen, & S. Turner (Eds.), *Handbook of adult psychopathology*. New York: Plenum Press.

Thompson, J. K., & Stice, E. (2001). Thin-ideal internalization: Mounting evidence for a new risk factor for body-image disturbance and eating pathology. *Current Directions in Psychological Science, 10*(5), 181–183.

Thompson, J. K., Roehrig, M., & Kinder, B. N. (2007). Eating disorders. In M. Hersen, S. M. Turner, & D. C. Beidel (Eds.), *Adult psychopathology and diagnosis*. New York: Wiley.

Thompson, R. A. (1998). Early socio-personality development. In N. Eisènberg (Ed.), *Handbook of child psychology: Social, emotional, and personality* (pp. 25–104). New York: Wiley.

Thompson, R. A. (2000). The legacy of early attachments. *Child Development, 71*, 145–152.

Thompson, R. A., Easterbrooks, M. A., & Padilla-Walker, L. M. (2003). Social and emotional development in infancy. In R. M. Lerner, M. A. Easterbrooks, & J. Mistry (Eds.), *Handbook of psychology, Vol. 6: Developmental psychology*. New York: Wiley.

Thompson, R. A., & Goodvin, R. (2005). The individual child: Temperament, emotion, self, and personality. In M. H. Bornstein & M. E. Lamb (Eds.), *Developmental science: An advanced textbook* (pp. 391–428). Mahwah, NJ: Erlbaum.

Thompson, R. A., & Nelson, C. A. (2001). Developmental science and the media: Early brain development. *American Psychologist, 56*, 5–15.

Thompson, R. F. (1989). A model system approach to memory. In P. R. Solomon, G. R. Goethals, C. M. Kelley, & B. R. Stephens (Eds.), *Memory: Interdisciplinary approaches*. New York: Springer-Verlag.

Thompson, R. F. (1992). Memory. *Current Opinion in Neurobiology, 2*, 203–208.

Thompson, R. F. (2005). In search of memory traces. *Annual Review of Psychology, 56*, 1–23.

Thompson, R. F., & Zola, S. M. (2003). In D. K. Freedheim (Ed.), *Handbook of psychology* (Vol. 2): New York: Wiley.

Thorndike, E. L. (1913). *Educational psychology: The psychology of learning* (Vol. 2). New York: Teachers College.

Thorne, B. M., & Henley, T. B. (1997). *Connections in the history and systems of psychology*. Boston: Houghton Mifflin.

Thornhill, R. (1976). Sexual selection and nuptial feeding behavior in *Bittacus apicalis* (Insecta: Mecoptera). *American Naturalist, 110*, 529–548.

Thornton, B. (1992). Repression and its mediating influence on the defensive attribution of responsibility. *Journal of Research in Personality, 26*, 44–57.

Thornton, B., & Maurice, J. K. (199). Physical attractiveness contrast effect and the moderating influence of self-consciousness. *Sex Roles, 40*, 379–392.

Thornton, B., & Moore, S. (1993). Physical attractiveness contrast effect: Implications for self-esteem and evaluations of the social self. *Personality and Social Psychology Bulletin, 19*, 474–480.

Thorpe, S. J., & Salkozskis, P. M. (1995). Phobia beliefs: Do cognitive factors play a role in specific phobias? *Behavioral Research and Therapy, 33*, 805–816.

Thorpy, M., & Yager, J. (2001). *Sleeping well: The sourcebook for sleep and sleep disorders*. New York: Checkmark Books.

Thurstone, L. L. (1931). The measurement of social attitudes. *Journal of Abnormal and Social Psychology, 26*, 249–269.

Thurstone, L. L. (1931). Multiple factor analysis. *Psychological Review, 38*, 406–427.

Thurstone, L. L. (1938). *Primary mental abilities*. Chicago: University of Chicago Press.

Thurstone, L. L. (1955). *The differential growth of mental abilities*. Chapel Hill: University of North Carolina.

Tice, D. M., Bratslavsky, E., & Baumeister, R. F. (2001). Emotional distress regulation takes precedence over impulse control: If you feel bad, do it! *Journal of Personality and Social Psychology, 80*, 53–67.

Till, B. D., & Priluck, R. L. (2000). Stimulus generalization in classical conditioning: An initial investigation and extension. *Psychology and Marketing, 17*, 55–72.

Timm, D. A., & Slavin, J. L. (2008). Dietary fiber and the relationship to chronic diseases. *American Journal of Lifestyle Medicine, 2,*, 233–240.

Tindale, R. S., Kameda, T., & Hinsz, V. B. (2003). Group decision making. In M. A. Hogg & J. Cooper (Eds.), *The Sage handbook of social psychology*. Thousand Oaks, CA: Sage.

Titsworth, B. S., & Kiewra, K. A. (2004). Spoken organizational lecture cues and student notetaking as facilitators of student learning. *Contemporary Educational Psychology, 29*, 447–461.

Todd, J. T., & Morris, E. K. (1992). Case histories in the great power of steady misrepresentation. *American Psychologist, 47*, 1441–1453.

Todd, P. M., & Gigerenzer, G. (2000). Precis of simple heuristics that make us smart. *Behavioral & Brain Sciences, 23*, 727–780.

Todd, P. M., & Gigerenzer, G. (2007). Environments that make us smart: Ecological rationality. *Current Directions in Psychological Science, 16*, 167–171.

Todorov, A., Mandisodza, A. N., Goren, A., & Hall, C. C. (2005). Inferences of competence from faces predict election outcomes. *Science, 308*, 1623–1626.

Toga, A. W., Thompson, P. M., & Sowell, E. R. (2006). Mapping brain maturation. *Trends in Neurosciences, 29*, 148–159.

Tolman, D. L., & Diamond, L. M. (2001). Desegregating sexuality research: Cultural and biological perspectives on gender and desire. *Annual Review of Sex Research, 12*, 33–74.

Tolman, E. C. (1922). A new formula for behaviorism. *Psychological Review, 29*, 44–53.

Tolman, E. C. (1932). *Purposive behavior in animals and men*. New York: Appleton-Century-Crofts.

Tolman, E. C. (1938). The determiners of behavior at a choice point. *Psychological Review, 45*, 1–41.

Tolman, E. C. (1948). Cognitive maps in rats and men. *Psychological Review, 55*, 189–208.

Tolman, E. C., & Honzik, C. H. (1930). Introduction and removal of reward, and maze performance in rats. *University of California Publications in Psychology, 4*, 257–275.

Tom, S. M., Fox, C. R., Trepel, C., & Poldrack, R. A. (2007). The neural basis of loss aversion in decision making under risk. *Science, 315*, 515–518.

Tomkins, S. S. (1980). Affect as amplification: Some modifications in theory. In R. Plutchik & H. Kellerman (Eds.), *Emotion: Theory, research and experience* (Vol. 1). New York: Academic Press.

Tomkins, S. S. (1991). *Affect, imagery, consciousness: 3. Anger and fear*. New York: Springer-Verlag.

Tooby, J., & Cosmides, L. (1989). Evolutionary psychology and the generation of culture: Part 1. Theoretical considerations. *Ethology and Sociobiology, 10*, 29–49.

Tooby, J., & Cosmides, L. (2005). Conceptual foundations of evolutionary psychology. In D. M. Buss (Ed.), *The handbook of evolutionary psychology*. New York: Wiley.

Torgersen, S. (1979). The nature and origin of common phobic fears. *British Journal of Psychiatry, 119*, 343–351.

Torgersen, S. (1983). Genetic factors in anxiety disorders. *Archives of General Psychiatry, 40*, 1085–1089.

Tormala, Z. L., & Petty, R. E. (2002). What doesn't kill me makes me stronger: The effects of resisting persuasion on attitude certainty. *Journal of Personality and Social Psychology, 83*, 1298–1313.

Tormala, Z. L., & Petty, R. E. (2004). Resistance to persuasion and attitude certainty: The moderating role of elaboration. *Personality and Social Psychology Bulletin, 30*, 1446–1457.

Torrance, E. P. (1962). *Guiding creative talent*. Englewood Cliffs, NJ: Prentice-Hall.

Torres, A. R., Prince, M. J., Bebbington, P. E., Bhugra, D., Brugha, T. S., & Farrell, M. et al. (2006). Obsessive-compulsive disorder: Prevalence, comorbidity, impact, and help-seeking in the British national psychiatric morbidity survey of 2000. *American Journal of Psychiatry, 163*, 1978–1985.

Torrey, E. F. (1992). *Freudian fraud: The malignant effect of Freud's theory on American thought and culture*. New York: Harper Perennial.

Torrey, E. F. (1996). *Out of the shadows*. New York: Wiley.

Tourangeau, R. (2004). Survey research and societal change. *Annual Review of Psychology, 55*, 775–801.

Tourangeau, R., & Yan, T. (2007). Sensitive questions in surveys. *Psychological Bulletin, 133*, 859–883.

Tov, W., & Diener, E. (2007). Culture and subjective well-being. In S. Kitayama & D. Cohen (Eds.), *Handbook of cultural psychology* (pp. 691–713). New York: Guilford.

Tower, R. B., & Krasner, M. (2006). Marital closeness, autonomy, mastery, and depressive symptoms in a U.S. Internet sample. *Personal Relationships, 13*, 429–449.

Toyota, H., & Kikuchi, Y. (2004). Self-generated elaboration and spacing effects on incidental memory. *Perceptual and Motor Skills, 99*, 1193–1200.

Toyota, H., & Kikuchi, Y. (2005). Encoding richness of self-generated elaboration and spacing effects on incidental memory. *Perceptual and Motor Skills, 101*, 621–627.

Tozzi, F., Thornton, L. M., Klump, K. L., Fichter, M. M., Halmi, K. A., Kaplan, A. S., Strober, M., Woodside, D. B., Crow, S., Mitchell, J., Rotondo, A., Mauri, M., Cassano, G., Keel, P., Plotnicov, K. H., Pollice, C., Lilenfeld, L. R., Berrettini, W. H., Bulik, C. M., & Kaye, W. H. (2005). Symptom fluctuation in eating disorders: Correlates of diagnostic crossover. *American Journal of Psychiatry, 162*, 732–740.

Tracy, J. L., & Robins, R. W. (2008). The automaticity of emotion recognition. *Emotion, 8*, 81–95.

Travis, F. (2001). Autonomic and EEG patterns distinguish transcending from other experiences during Transcendental Meditation practice. *International Journal of Psychophysiology, 42*, 1–9.

Travis, F., & Pearson, C. (2000). Pure consciousness: Distinct phenomenological and physiological correlates of "consciousness itself." *International Journal of Neuroscience, 100*(1-4), 77–89.

Triandis, H. C. (1989). Self and social behavior in differing cultural contexts. *Psychological Review, 96*, 269–289.

Triandis, H. C. (1994). *Culture and social behavior*. New York: McGraw-Hill.

Triandis, H. C. (2001). Individualism and collectivism: Past, present, and future. In D. Matsumoto

(Ed.), *The handbook of culture and psychology.* New York: Oxford University Press.

Triandis, H. C. (2007). Culture and psychology: A history of the study of their relationship. In S. Kitayama & D. Cohen (Eds.), *Handbook of cultural psychology* (pp. 59–76). New York: Guilford.

Trick, L., & Pylyshyn, Z. (1994). Why are small and large numbers enumerated differently? A limited-capacity preattentive stage in vision. *Psychological Review, 101,* 80–102.

Trivers, R. L. (1971). The evolution of reciprocal altruism. *Quarterly Review of Biology, 46,* 35–57.

Trivers, R. L. (1972). Parental investment and sexual selection. In B. Campbell (Ed.), *Sexual selection and the descent of man.* Chicago: Aldine.

Trotter, R. J. (1986, September). The three faces of love. *Psychology Today,* pp. 46–54.

Trujillo, M. (2005). Culture-bound syndromes. In B. J. Sadock & V. A. Sadock (Eds.), *Kaplan & Sadock's comprehensive textbook of psychiatry.* Philadelphia: Lippincott Williams & Wilkins.

Tsai, J. L., Butcher, J. N., Muñoz, R. F., & Vitousek, K. (2001). Culture, ethnicity, and psychopathology. In P. B. Sutker & H. E. Adams (Eds.), *Comprehensive handbook of psychopathology.* New York: Kluwer Academic/Plenum.

Tseng, W. S. (1997). Overview: Culture and psychopathology. In W. S. Tseng & J. Streltzer (Eds.), *Culture and psychopathology: A guide to clinical assessment.* New York: Brunner/Mazel.

Tsigos, C., Kyrou, I., & Chrousos, G. P. (2005). Stress, endocrine manifestations and diseases. In C. L. Cooper (Ed.), *Handbook of stress medicine and health.* Boca Raton, FL: CRC Press.

Tsuang, M. T., Glatt, S. J., & Faraone, S. V. (2003). Genetics and genomics in schizophrenia. *Primary Psychiatry, 10*(3), 37–40, 50.

Tucker, A. M., Dinges, D. F., & Van Dongen, H. P. A. (2007). Trait interindividual differences in the sleep physiology of healthy young adults. *Journal of Sleep Research, 16,* 170–180.

Tuckey, M. R., & Brewer, N. (2003). The influence of schemas, stimulus ambiguity, and interview schedule on eyewitness memory over time. *Journal of Experimental Psychology: Applied, 9,* 101–118.

Tugade, M. M., & Fredrickson, B. L. (2004). Resilient individuals use positive emotions to bounce back from negative emotional experiences. *Journal of Personality and Social Psychology, 86,* 320–333.

Tulving, E. (1985). How many memory systems are there? *American Psychologist, 40,* 385–398.

Tulving, E. (1986). What kind of a hypothesis is the distinction between episodic and semantic memory? *Journal of Experimental Psychology: Learning, Memory and Cognition, 12,* 307–311.

Tulving, E. (1987). Multiple memory systems and consciousness. *Human Neurobiology, 6*(2), 67–80.

Tulving, E. (1993). What is episodic memory? *Current Directions in Psychological Science, 2*(3), 67–70.

Tulving, E. (2001). Origin of autonoesis in episodic memory. In H. L. Roediger III, J. S. Nairne, I. Neath, & A. M. Surprenant (Eds.), *The nature of remembering: Essays in honor of Robert G. Crowder* (pp. 17–34). Washington, DC: American Psychological Association.

Tulving, E. (2002). Episodic memory: From mind to brain. *Annual Review of Psychology, 53,* 1–25.

Tulving, E., & Thomson, D. M. (1973). Encoding specificity and retrieval processes in episodic memory. *Psychological Review, 80,* 352–373.

Tunnell, K. D. (2005). The Oxycontin epidemic and crime panic in rural Kentucky. *Contemporary Drug Problems, 32,* 225–258.

Turek, F. W., & Gillette, M. U. (2004). Melatonin, sleep, and circadian rhythms: Rationale for development of specific melatonin agonists. *Sleep Medicine, 5,* 523–532.

Turk, D. C., & Okifuji, A. (2003). Pain management. In A. M. Nezu, C. M. Nezu, & P. A. Geller (Eds.), *Handbook of psychology, Vol. 9: Health psychology.* New York: Wiley.

Turkheimer, E. (1994). Socioeconomic status and intelligence. In R. J. Sternberg (Ed.), *Encyclopedia of human intelligence.* New York: Macmillan.

Turkheimer, E., Haley, A., Waldron, M., D'Onofrio, B., & Gottesman, I. I. (2003). Socioeconomic status modifies heritability of IQ in young children. *Psychological Science, 14,* 623–628.

Turkheimer, E., & Waldron, M. (2000). Nonshared environment: A theoretical, methodological, and quantitative review. *Psychological Bulletin, 126,* 78–108.

Turkkan, J. S. (1989). Classical conditioning: The new hegemony. *Behavioral and Brain Sciences, 12,* 121–179.

Turner, J. C., & Reynolds, K. J. (2001). The social identity perspective in intergroup relations: Theories, themes, and controversies. In R. Brown & S. L. Gaertner (Eds.), *Blackwell handbook of social psychology: Intergroup processes.* Malden, MA: Blackwell.

Turner, J. G., Hogg, M. A., Oakes, P. J., Reicher, S. D., & Wetherell, M. S. (1987). *Rediscovering the social group: A self-categorization theory.* Oxford, UK: Basil Blackwell.

Turner, J. R., & Wheaton, B. (1995). Checklist measurement of stressful life events. In S. Cohen, R. C. Kessler, & L. U. Gordon (Eds.), *Measuring stress: A guide for health and social scientists.* New York: Oxford University Press.

Turner, S. M., DeMers, S. T., Fox, H. R., & Reed, G. M. (2001). APA's guidelines for test user qualifications: An executive summary. *American Psychologist, 56,* 1099–1113.

Tversky, A. (1972). Elimination by aspects: A theory of choice. *Psychological Review, 79,* 281–299.

Tversky, A., & Kahneman, D. (1973). Availability: A heuristic for judging frequency and probability. *Cognitive Psychology, 5,* 207–232.

Tversky, A., & Kahneman, D. (1974). Judgments under uncertainty: Heuristics and biases. *Science, 185,* 1124–1131.

Tversky, A., & Kahneman, D. (1982). Judgment under uncertainty: Heuristics and biases. In D. Kahneman, P. Slovic, & A. Tversky (Eds.), *Judgment under uncertainty: Heuristics and biases.* New York: Cambridge University Press.

Tversky, A., & Kahneman, D. (1983). Extensional versus intuitive reasoning: The conjunction fallacy in probability judgment. *Psychological Review, 90,* 283–315.

Tversky, A., & Kahneman, D. (1988). Rational choice and the framing of decisions. In D. E. Bell, H. Raiffa, & A. Tversky (Eds.), *Decision making: Descriptive, normative, and prescriptive interactions.* New York: Cambridge University Press.

Tversky, A., & Kahneman, D. (1991). Loss aversion in riskless choice: A reference-dependent model. *Quarterly Journal of Economics, 106,* 1039–1061.

Twenge, J. M., Campbell, W. K., & Foster, C. A. (2003). Parenthood and marital satisfaction: A meta-analytic review. *Journal of Marriage and the Family, 65,* 574–583.

Tyrer, P., Coombs, N., Ibrahimi, F., Mathilakath, A., Bajaj, P., Ranger, M., et al. (2007). Critical developments in the assessment of personality disorder. *British Journal of Psychiatry, 90,* 51–59.

Uchino, B. N. (2004). *Social support and physical health outcomes: Understanding the health consequences of our relationships.* New Haven, CT: University Press.

Uchino, B. N., Uno, D., & Holt-Lunstad, J. (1999). Social support, physiological processes, and health. *Current Directions in Psychological Science, 8,* 145–148.

Ulrich, R. E. (1991). Animal rights, animal wrongs and the question of balance. *Psychological Science, 2,* 197–201.

Umbel, V. M., Pearson, B. Z., Fernandez, S. C., & Oller, D. K. (1992). Measuring bilingual children's receptive vocabularies. *Child Development, 63,* 1012–1020.

Umhau, J. C., & Dauphinais, K. M. (2007). Omega-3 polyunsaturated fatty acids and health. In L. L'Abate (Ed.), *Low-cost approaches to promote physical and mental health: Theory, research, and practice.* New York: Springer Science + Business Media.

UNAIDS. (2005). *AIDS epidemic.* Retrieved from http://www.unaids.org/Epi2005/doc/EPIupdate2005_html_en/epi05_03_

Underwood, B. J. (1961). Ten years of massed practice on distributed practice. *Psychological Review, 68,* 229–247.

Ungerleider, L. G., & Haxby, J. V. (1994). "What" and "where" in the human brain. *Current Opinion in Neurobiology, 4,* 157–165.

Ursano, R. J., & Silberman, E. K. (1999). Psychoanalysis, psychoanalytic psychotherapy, and supportive psychotherapy. In R. E. Hales, S. C. Yudofsky, & J. A. Talbott (Eds.), *American Psychiatric Press textbook of psychiatry.* Washington, DC: American Psychiatric Press.

Ursano, R. J., & Silberman, E. K. (2003). Psychoanalysis, psychoanalytic psychotherapy, and supportive psychotherapy. In R. E. Hales & S. C. Yudofsky (Eds.), *Textbook of clinical psychiatry.* Washington, DC: American Psychiatric Publishing.

Ursin, R. (2002). Serotonin and sleep. *Sleep Medicine Reviews, 6*(1), 55–67.

U.S. Department of Health and Human Services. (1990). *The health benefits of smoking cessation: A report of the surgeon general.* Washington, DC: U.S. Government Printing Office.

U.S. Department of Health and Human Services. (1999). *Mental health: A report of the Surgeon General.* Washington, DC: U.S. Government Printing Office.

Uttal, W. R. (2001). *The new phrenology: The limits of localizing cognitive processes in the brain.* Cambridge, MA: MIT Press.

Uttal, W. R. (2002). Precis of *The New Phrenology: The limits of localizing cognitive processes in the brain. Brain and Mind, 3,* 221–228.

Vaillant, G. E. (1994). Ego mechanisms of defense and personality psychopathology. *Journal of Abnormal Psychology, 103,* 44–50.

Valenstein, E. S. (1973). *Brain control.* New York: Wiley.

Van Blerkom, D. L. (2006). *College study skills: Becoming a strategic learner.* Belmont, CA: Wadsworth.

Van Boven, L. (2005). Experientialism, materialism, and the pursuit of happiness. *Review of General Psychology, 9,* 132–142.

Van de Castle, R. L. (1993). Content of dreams. In M. A. Carskadon (Ed.), *Encyclopedia of sleep and dreaming.* New York: Macmillan.

Van de Castle, R. L. (1994). *Our dreaming mind*. New York: Ballantine Books.

van den Boom, D. (1994). The influence of temperament and mothering on attachment and exploration: An experimental manipulation of sensitive responsiveness among lower-class mothers and irritable infants. *Child Development, 65*, 1457–1477.

van den Boom, D. (2001). First attachments: Theory and research. In G. Bremner & A. Fogel (Eds.), *Blackwell handbook of infant development* (pp. 296–325). Malden, MA: Blackwell Publishing.

Vandereycken, W. (2002). History of anorexia nervosa and bulimia nervosa. In C. G. Fairburn, & K. D. Brownell (Eds.), *Eating disorders and obesity*. New York: Guilford.

van der Post, L. (1975). *Jung and the story of our time*. New York: Vintage Books.

Van Dongen, H. P. A., & Dinges, D. F. (2005). Circadian rhythms in sleepiness, alertness, and performance. In M. H. Kryger, T. Roth, & W. C. Dement (Eds.), *Principles and practice of sleep medicine*. Philadelphia: Elsevier Saunders.

Van Dongen, H. P. A., Baynard, M. D., Maislin, G., & Dinges, D. F. (2004). Systematic interindividual differences in neurobehavioral impairment from sleep loss: Evidence of trait-like differential vulnerability. *Sleep: Journal of Sleep & Sleep Disorders Research, 27*, 423–433.

Van Dongen, H. P. A., Maislin, G., Mullington, J. M., & Dinges, D. F. (2003). The cumulative cost of additional wakefulness: Dose-response effects on neurobehavioral functions and sleep physiology from chronic sleep restriction and total sleep deprivation. *Sleep: Journal of Sleep & Sleep Disorders Research, 26*, 117–126.

van Eck, M., Nicolson, N. A., & Berkhof, J. (1998). Effects of stressful daily events on mood states: Relationship to global perceived stress. *Journal of Personality and Social Psychology, 75*, 1572–1585.

Van Gelder, T. (2005). Teaching critical thinking: Some lessons from cognitive science. *College Teaching, 53*(1), 41–46.

van Griensven, F., Chakkraband, M. L. S., Thienkrua, W., Pengjuntr, W., Cardozo, B. L., & Tantipiwatanaskul, P. et al. (2007). Mental health problems among adults in tsunami-affected areas in Southern Thailand. *Journal of the American Medical Association, 296*, 537–548.

Van Hoesen, G. W., Morecraft, R. J., & Semendeferi, K. (1996). Functional neuroanatomy of the limbic system and prefrontal cortex. In B. S. Fogel, R. B. Schiffer, & S. M. Rao (Eds), *Neuropsychiatry*. Baltimore: Williams & Wilkins.

van Ijzendoorn, M. H., & Bakermans-Kranenburg, M. J. (2004). Maternal sensitivity and infant temperament in the formation of attachment. In G. Bremner & A. Slater (Eds.), *Theories of infant development* (pp. 233–257). Malden, MA: Blackwell Publishing.

van Ijzendoorn, M. H., & Juffer, F. (2005). Adoption is a successful natural intervention enhancing adopted children's IQ and school performance. *Current Directions in Psychological Science, 14*, 326–330.

van Ijezendoorn, M. H., & Kroonenberg, P. M. (1988). Cross-cultural patterns of attachment: A meta-analysis of the strange situation. *Child Development, 59*, 147–156.

van Ijzendoorn, M. H., & Sagi, A. (1999). Cross-cultural patterns of attachment: Universal and contextual dimensions. In J. Cassidy & P. R. Shaver (Eds.), *Handbook of attachment: Theory, research, and clinical applications*. New York: Guilford.

van Kammen, D. P., & Marder, S. R. (2005). Serotonin-dopamine antagonists (atypical or second-generation antipsychotics). In B. J. Sadock & V. A. Sadock (Eds.), *Kaplan and Sadock's comprehensive textbook of psychiatry* (pp. 2914–2937). Philadelphia: Lippincott Williams & Wilkins.

van Kesteren, N. M. C., Hospers, H. J., & Kok, G. (2007). Sexual risk behavior among HIV-positive men who have sex with men: A literature review. *Patient Education and Counseling, 65*, 5–20.

van Leeuwen, M. L., & Macrae, C. N. (2004). Is beautiful always good? Implicit benefits of facial attractiveness. *Social Cognition, 22*, 637–649.

Van Praag, H., Zhao, X., & Gage, F. H. (2004). Neurogenesis in the adult mammalian brain. In M. S. Gazzaniga (Ed.), *The cognitive neurosciences* (3rd ed.) (pp. 127–137). Cambridge, MA: MIT Press.

Vase, L. R., Riley, I. J., & Price, D. (2002). A comparison of placebo effects in clinical analgesic trials versus studies of placebo analgesia. *Pain, 99*, 443–452.

Vecera, S. P., & Palmer, S. E. (2006). Grounding the figure: Surface attachment influences figure-ground organization. *Psychonomic Bulletin & Review, 13*, 563–569.

Veenhoven, R. (1993). *Happiness in nations*. Rotterdam, Netherlands: Risbo.

Vega, V., & Malamuth, N. M. (2007). Predicting sexual aggression: The role of pornography in the context of general and specific risk factors. *Aggressive Behavior, 33*, 104–117.

Verdone, P. (1993). Psychophysiology of dreaming. In M. A. Carskadon (Ed.), *Encyclopedia of dreaming*. New York: Macmillan.

Verheul, R. (2005). Clinical utility for dimensional models of personality pathology. *Journal of Personality Disorders, 19*, 283–302.

Vermeeren, A. (2004). Residual effects of hypnotics: Epidemiology and clinical implications. *CNS Drugs, 18*(5), 297–328.

Vernberg, E. M., La Greca, A. M., Silverman, W. K., & Prinstein, M. J. (1996). Prediction of posttraumatic stress symptoms in children after Hurricane Andrew. *Journal of Abnormal Psychology, 105*, 237–248.

Vernon, P. A., Wickett, J. C., Bazana, G. P., & Stelmack, R. M. (2000). The neuropsychology and psychophysiology of human intelligence. In R. J. Sternberg (Ed.), *Handbook of intelligence*. Cambridge, UK: Cambridge University Press.

Victoroff, J. (2005). Central nervous system changes with normal aging. In B. J. Sadock & V. A. Sadock (Eds.), *Kaplan & Sadock's comprehensive textbook of psychiatry*. Philadelphia: Lippincott Williams & Wilkins.

Videbech, P. (2006). Hippocampus and unipolar depression. *Directions in Psychiatry, 26*, 183–194.

Videbech, P., & Ravnkilde, B. (2004). Hippocampal volume and depression: A meta-analysis of MRI studies. *American Journal of Psychiatry, 161*, 1957–1966.

Vierck, C. (1978). Somatosensory system. In R. B. Masterston (Ed.), *Handbook of sensory neurobiology*. New York: Plenum.

Viglione, D. J., & Rivera, B. (2003). Assessing personality and psychopathology with projective methods. In J. R. Graham & J. A. Naglieri (Eds.), *Handbook of psychology, Vol. 10: Assessment psychology*. New York: Wiley.

Villarreal, D. M., Do, V., Haddad, E., & Derrick, B. E. (2002). NMDA receptor antagonists sustain LTP and spatial memory: Active processes mediate LTP decay. *Nature Neuroscience, 5*, 48–52.

Vinogradov, S., Cox. P. D., & Yalom, I. D. (2003). Group therapy. In R. E. Hales & S. C. Yudofsky (Eds.), *Textbook of clinical psychiatry*. Washington, DC: American Psychiatric Publishing.

Vinokur, A. D., & van Ryn, M. (1993). Social support and undermining in close relationships: Their independent effects on the mental health of unemployed persons. *Journal of Personality and Social Psychology, 65*, 350–359.

Visser, P. S., & Cooper, J. (2003). Attitude change. In M. A. Hogg & J. Cooper (Eds.), *The Sage handbook of social psychology*. Thousand Oaks, CA: Sage.

Viteles, M. (1932). *Industrial psychology*. New York: Norton.

Vokey, J. R., & Read, J. D. (1985). Subliminal messages: Between the devil and the media. *American Psychologist, 40*, 1231–1239.

Volavka, J., Czobor, P., Sheitman, B., Lindenmayer, J. P., Citrome, L., McEvoy, J. P., Cooper, T. B. , Chakos, M., & Lieberman, J. A. (2002). Clozapine, olanzapine, risperidone, haloperidol in the treatment of patients with chronic schizophrenia and schizoaffective disorder. *American Journal of Psychiatry, 159*, 255–262.

Volkow, N. D., Fowler, J. S., & Wang, G. J. (2004). The addicted human brain viewed in the light of imaging studies: Brain circuits and treatment strategies. *Neuropharmacology, 47*, 3–13.

Volkow, N. D., Fowler, J. S., Wang, G. J., & Swanson, J. M. (2004). Dopamine in drug abuse and addiction: Results from imaging studies and treatment implications. *Molecular Psychiatry, 9*, 557–569.

von Károlyi, C., & Winner, E. (2005). Extreme giftedness. In R. J. Sternberg & J. E. Davidson (Eds.), *Conceptions of giftedness*. New York: Cambridge University Press.

Voyer, D. (1996). On the magnitude of laterality effects and sex differences in functional lateralities. *Laterality, 1*, 51–83.

Voyer, D., Nolan, C., & Voyer, S. (2000). The relation between experience and spatial performance in men and women. *Sex Roles, 43*, 891–915.

Vroom, V. H. (1964). *Work and motivation*. New York: Wiley.

Vygotsky, L. S. (1934/1962). *Thought and language*. E. Hanfmann, & G. Vakar (Trans). Cambridge, MA: MIT Press.

Vygotsky, L. S. (1934/1986). *Thought and language*. A. Kozulin (Trans). Cambridge, MA: MIT Press.

Vyse, S. A. (2000). *Believing in magic: The psychology of superstition*. New York: Oxford University Press.

Vythilingam, M., Shen, J., Drevets, W. C., & Innis, R. B. (2005). Nuclear magnetic resonance imaging: Basic principles and recent findings in neuropsychiatric disorders. In B. J. Sadock & V. A. Sadock (Eds.), *Kaplan & Sadock's comprehensive textbook of psychiatry*. Philadelphia: Lippincott Williams & Wilkins.

Wachtel, P. L. (1977). *Psychoanalysis and behavior therapy: Toward an integration*. New York: Basic Books.

Wachtel, P. L. (1991). From eclecticism to synthesis: Toward a more seamless psychotherapeutic integration. *Journal of Psychotherapy Integration, 1*, 43–54.

Wagner, H. (1989). The physiological differentiation of emotions. In H. Wagner & A. Manstead (Eds), *Handbook of social psychophysiology*. New York: Wiley.

Wagner, U., Gais, H., Haider, H., Verleger, R., & Born, J. (2004). Sleep inspires insight. *Nature, 427,* 352–355.

Wakefield, J. C. (1999a). Evolutionary versus prototype analyses of the concept of disorder. *Journal of Abnormal Psychology, 108,* 374–399.

Wakefield, J. C. (1999b). The measurement of mental disorder. In A. V. Horvitz & T. L. Scheid (Eds.), *A handbook for the study of mental health: Social contexts, theories, and systems.* New York: Cambridge University Press.

Wakefield, J. C., & Spitzer, R. L. (2002). Lowered estimates—But of what? *Archives of General Psychiatry, 59*(2), 129–130.

Wald, G. (1964). The receptors of human color vision. *Science, 145,* 1007–1017.

Wald, M., Miner, M., & Seftel, A. D. (2008). Male menopause: Fact or fiction? *American Journal of Lifestyle Medicine, 2,* 132.

Waldman, I. D., & Rhee, S. H. (2006). Genetic and environmental influences on psychopathy and antisocial behavior. In C. J. Patrick (Ed.), *Handbook of Psychopathy.* New York: Guilford.

Waldrop, D., Lightsey, O. R., Ethington, C. A., Woemmel, C. A., & Coke, A. L. (2001). Self-efficacy, optimism, health competence, and recovery from orthopedic surgery. *Journal of Counseling Psychology, 48,* 233–238.

Walker, E., Kestler, L., Bollini, A., & Hochman, K. M. (2004). Schizophrenia: Etiology and course. *Annual Review of Psychology, 55,* 401–430.

Walker, E., Mittal, V., & Tessner, K. (2008). Stress and the hypothalamic pituitary adrenal axis in the developmental course of schizophrenia. *Annual Review of Clinical Psychology, 4,* 189–216.

Walker, E., & Tessner, K. (2008). Schizophrenia. *Perspectives on Psychological Science, 3,* 30–37.

Walker, I., & Hulme, C. (1999). Concrete words are easier to recall than abstract words: Evidence for a semantic contribution to short-term serial recall. *Journal of Experimental Psychology: Learning, Memory, & Cognition, 25,* 1256–1271.

Walker, L. J. (1988). The development of moral reasoning. In R. Vasta (Ed.), *Annals of child development* (Vol. 5). Greenwich, CT: JAI Press.

Walker, L. J. (1989). A longitudinal study of moral reasoning. *Child Development, 60,* 157–166.

Walker, L. J. (2007). Progress and prospects in the psychology of moral development. In G. W. Ladd (Ed.), *Appraising the human developmental sciences: Essays in honor of Merrill-Palmer Quarterly* (pp. 226–237). Detroit: Wayne State University Press.

Walker, L. J., & Taylor, J. H. (1991). Strange transitions in moral reasoning: A longitudinal study of developmental processes. *Developmental Psychology, 27,* 330–337.

Walker, M. P., Brakefield, T., Morgan, A., Hobson, J. A., & Stickgold, R. (2002). Practice with sleep makes perfect: Sleep dependent motor skill learning. *Neuron, 35,* 205–211.

Walker, M. P., & Stickgold, R. (2004). Sleep-dependent learning and memory consolidation. *Neuron, 44,* 121–133.

Walker, M. P., & Stickgold, R. (2006). Sleep, memory, and plasticity. *Annual Review of Psychology, 57,* 139–166.

Wallace, B., & Fisher, L. E. (1999). *Consciousness and behavior.* Boston: Allyn & Bacon.

Wallace, D. S., Paulson, R. M., Lord, C. G., & Bond, C. F. Jr. (2005). Which behaviors do attitudes predict? Meta-analyzing the effects of social pressure and perceived difficulty. *Review of General Psychology, 9,* 214–227.

Wallace, H. M., Baumeister, R. F., & Vohs, K. D. (2005). Audience support and choking under pressure: A home disadvantage? *Journal of Sports Sciences, 23,* 429–438.

Wallace, R. K., & Benson, H. (1972). The physiology of meditation. *Scientific American, 226,* 84–90.

Wallbott, H. G., & Scherer, K. R. (1988). How universal and specific is emotional experience? Evidence from 27 countries. In K. R. Scherer (Ed.), *Facets of emotions.* Hillsdale, NJ: Erlbaum.

Wallman, J. (1992). *Aping language.* Cambridge, England: Cambridge University Press.

Walraven, J., Enroth-Cugell, C., Hood, D. C., MacLeod, D. I. A., & Schnapf, J. L. (1990). The control of visual sensitivity: Receptoral and post-receptoral processes. In L. Spillmann & J. S. Werner (Eds.), *Visual perception: The neurophysiological foundations.* San Diego: Academic Press.

Walsh, B. T. (2003). Eating disorders. In A. Tasman, J. Kay, & J. A. Lieberman (Eds.), *Psychiatry.* New York: Wiley.

Walsh, B. T., Seidman, S. N., Sysko, R., & Gould, M. (2002). Placebo response studies of major depression: Variable, substantial and growing. *Journal of the American Medical Association, 287,* 1840–1847.

Walsh, J. K., Dement, W. C., & Dinges, D. F. (2005). Sleep medicine, public policy, and public health. In M. H. Kryger, T. Roth, & W. C. Dement (Eds.). *Principles and practice of sleep medicine.* Philadelphia: Elsevier Saunders.

Walsh, R., & Shapiro, S. L. (2006). The meeting of meditative disciplines and Western psychology: A mutually enriching dialogue. *American Psychologist, 61,* 227–239.

Walter, C. A. (2000). The psychological meaning of menopause: Women's experiences. *Journal of Women and Aging, 12*(3–4), 117–131.

Walther, E., & Grigoriadis, S. (2003). Why sad people like shoes better: The influence of mood on the evaluative conditioning of consumer attitudes. *Psychology & Marketing, 10,* 755–775.

Walther, E., Nagengast, B., & Trasselli, C. (2005). Evaluative conditioning in social psychology: Facts and speculations. *Cognition and Emotion, 19*(2), 175–196.

Walton, K. G., Fields, J. Z., Levitsky, D. K., Harris, D. A., Pugh, N. D., & Schneider, R. H. (2004). Lowering cortisol and CVD risk in postmenopausal women: A pilot study using Transcendental Meditation program. In R. Yehuda, & B. McEwen (Eds.), *Biobehavioral stress response: Protective and damaging effects* (pp. 211–215). New York: Annals of the New York Academy of Sciences.

Walton, M. E., Devlin, J. T., & Rushworth, M. F. S. (2004). Interactions between decision making and performance monitoring within prefrontal cortex. *Nature Neuroscience, 7,* 1259–1265.

Wampold, B. E. (2001). *The great psychotherapy debate.* Mahwah, NJ: Erlbaum.

Wang, P. S., Berglund, P., Olfson, M., Pincus, H. A., Wells, K. B., & Kessler, R. C. (2005). Failure and delay in initial treatment contact after first onset of mental disorders in the National Comorbidity Survey Replication. *Archives of General Psychiatry, 62,* 603–613.

Wang, P. S., Lane, M., Olfson, M., Pincus, H. A., Wells, K. B., & Kessler, R. C. (2005). Twelve-month use of mental health services in the United States: Results from the National Comorbidity Survey Replication. *Archives of General Psychiatry, 62,* 629–640.

Wang, S., Baillargeon, R., & Paterson, S. (2005). Detecting continuity violations in infancy: A new account and new evidence from covering and tube events. *Cognition, 95,* 129–173.

Wangensteen, O. H., & Carlson, A. J. (1931). Hunger sensation after total gastrectomy. *Proceedings of the Society for Experimental Biology, 28,* 545–547.

Warner-Schmidt, J. L., & Duman, R. S. (2006). Hippocampal neurogenesis: Opposing effects of stress and antidepressant treatment. *Hippocampus, 16,* 239–249.

Warr, P. (1999). Well-being and the workplace. In D. Kahneman, E. Diener, & N. Schwarz (Eds.), *Well-being: The foundations of hedonic psychology.* New York: Russell Sage Foundation.

Warwick, D. P. (1975, February). Social scientists ought to stop lying. *Psychology Today,* pp. 38, 40, 105–106.

Wasserman, J. D., & Bracken, B. A. (2003). Psychometric characteristics of assessment procedures. In J. R. Graham & J. A. Naglieri (Eds.), *Handbook of psychology, Vol. 10: Assessment psychology.* New York: Wiley.

Waterhouse, L. (2006). Multiple intelligences, the Mozart effect, and emotional intelligence: A critical review. *Educational Psychologist, 41,* 207–225.

Watkins, L. R. (2007). Immune and glial regulation of pain. *Brain, Behavior, and Immunity, 21,* 519–521.

Watkins, L. R., & Maier, S. F. (2002). Beyond neurons: Evidence that immune and glial cells contribute to pathological pain states. *Physiological Reviews, 82,* 981–1011.

Watkins, L. R., & Maier, S. F. (2003). When good pain turns bad. *Current Directions in Psychological Science, 12,* 232–236.

Watkins, L. R., Hutchinson, M. R., Ledeboer, A., Wieseler-Frank, J., Milligan, E. D., & Maier, S. F. (2007). Glia as the "bad guys": Implications for improving clinical pain control and the clinical utility of opioids. *Brain, Behavior, and Immunity, 21,* 131–146.

Watkins, M. J. (2002). Limits and province of levels of processing: Considerations of a construct. *Memory, 10,* 339–343.

Watson, D. L., & Tharp, R. G. (2007). *Self-directed behavior: Self-modification for personal adjustment.* Belmont, CA: Wadsworth.

Watson, D., & Clark, L. A. (1997). Extraversion and its positive emotional core. In R. Hogan, J. Johnson, & S. Briggs (Eds.), *Handbook of personality psychology.* San Diego: Academic Press.

Watson, D., David, J. P., & Suls, J. (1999). Personality, affectivity, and coping. In C. R. Snyder (Ed.), *Coping: The psychology of what works.* New York: Oxford University Press.

Watson, D., Klohen, E. C., Casillas, A., Nus Simms, E., Haig, J., & Berry, D. S. (2004). Match makers and deal breakers: Analyses of assortative mating in newlywed couples. *Journal of Personality, 72,* 1029–1068.

Watson, J. B. (1913). Psychology as the behaviorist views it. *Psychological Review, 20,* 158–177.

Watson, J. B. (1919). *Psychology from the standpoint of a behaviorist.* Philadelphia: Lippincott.

Watson, J. B. (1924). *Behaviorism.* New York: Norton.

Watson, J. B. (1925). *Behaviorism.* New York: Norton.

Watson, J. B. (1930). *Behaviorism.* New York: Norton.

Watson, J. B., & Rayner, R. (1920). Conditioned emotional reactions. *Journal of Experimental Psychology, 3,* 1–14.

Waugh, N. C., & Norman, D. A. (1965). Primary memory. *Psychological Review, 72,* 89–104.

Waxman, S. R. (2002). Early word-learning and conceptual development: Everything had a name and each name gave birth to a new thought. In U. Goswami (Ed.), *Blackwell handbook of childhood cognitive development* (pp. 102–126). Malden, MA: Blackwell.

Weatherall, A. (1992). Gender and languages: Research in progress. *Feminism & Psychology, 2,* 177–181.

Weaver, C. A., & Krug, K. S. (2004). Consolidation-like effects in flashbulb memories: Evidence from September 11, 2001. *American Journal of Psychology, 117,* 517–530.

Weaver, K., Garcia, S. M., Schwarz, N., & Miller, D. T. (2007). Inferring the popularity of an opinion from its familiarity: A repetitive voice can sound like a chorus. *Journal of Personality and Social Psychology, 92,* 821–833.

Webb, W. B. (1992a). Developmental aspects and a behavioral model of human sleep. In C. Stampi (Ed.), *Why we nap: Evolution, chronobiology, and functions of polyphasic and ultrashort sleep.* Boston: Birkhaeuser.

Webb, W. B. (1992b). *Sleep: The gentle tyrant.* Bolton, MA: Anker.

Webb, W. B., & Dinges, D. F. (1989). Cultural perspectives on napping and the siesta. In D. F. Dinges & R. J. Broughton (Eds.), *Sleep and alertness: Chronobiological, behavioral, and medical aspects of napping.* New York: Raven.

Weber, L. J. (2006). *Profits before people?* Bloomington, IN: Indiana University Press.

Wechsler, D. (1939). *The measurement of adult intelligence.* Baltimore: Williams & Wilkins.

Wechsler, D. (1949). *Wechsler intelligence scale for children.* New York: Psychological Corporation.

Wechsler, D. (1955). *Manual, Wechsler adult intelligence scale.* New York: Psychological Corporation.

Wechsler, D. (1967). *Manual for the Wechsler preschool and primary scale of intelligence.* New York: Psychological Corporation.

Wechsler, D. (1981). *Manual for the Wechsler adult intelligence scale—revised.* New York: Psychological Corporation.

Wechsler, D. (1991). *WISC-III manual.* San Antonio: Psychological Corporation.

Wechsler, D. (1997). *Wechsler Adult Intelligence Scale-Third Edition (WAIS–III).* San Antonio, TX: Psychological Corporation.

Wechsler, D. (2003). *Wechsler Intelligence Scale for Children—Fourth Edition (WISC IV).* San Antonio, TX: Psychological Corporation.

Wechsler, H., Lee J. E., Kuo, M., Seibring, M., Nelson, T. F., & Lee, H. (2002). Trends in college binge drinking during a period of increased prevention efforts. *Journal of American College Health, 50*(5), 203–217.

Wegner, D. M. (1997). Why the mind wanders. In J. D. Cohen & J. W. Schooler (Eds.), *Scientific approaches to consciousness.* Mahwah, NJ: Erlbaum.

Weinberg, R. A. (1989). Intelligence and IQ: Landmark issues and great debates. *American Psychologist, 44,* 98–104.

Weinberger, J. (1995). Common factors aren't so common: The common factors dilemma. *Clinical Psychology: Science and Practice, 2,* 45–69.

Weiner, B. (Ed.) (1974). *Achievement motivation and attribution theory.* Morristown, NJ: General Learning Press.

Weiner, B. (1980). *Human motivation.* New York: Holt, Rinehart & Winston.

Weiner, B. (1986). *An attributional theory of motivation and emotion.* New York: Springer-Verlag.

Weiner, B. (1994). Integrating social and personal theories of achievement striving. *Review of Educational Research, 64,* 557–573.

Weinfield, N. S., Sroufe, L. A., Egeland, B., & Carlson, E. A. (1999). The nature of individual differences in infant–caregiver attachment. In J. Cassidy & P. R. Shaver (Eds.), *Handbook of attachment: Theory, research, and clinical applications.* New York: Guilford.

Weinger, M. B., & Ancoli-Israel, S. (2002). Sleep deprivation and clinical performance. *Journal of the American Medical Association, 287,* 955–957.

Weinstein, L. N., Schwartz, D. G., & Arkin, A. M. (1991). Qualitative aspects of sleep mentation. In S. J. Ellman & J. S. Antrobus (Eds.), *The mind in sleep: Psychology and psychophysiology* (2nd ed.). New York: Wiley.

Weinstein, N. D. (1984). Why it won't happen to me: Perceptions of risk factors and susceptibility. *Health Psychology, 3,* 431–458.

Weinstein, N. D. (2003). Exploring the links between risk perceptions and preventative health behavior. In J. Suls & K. A. Wallston (Eds.), *Social psychological foundations of health and illness.* Malden, MA: Blackwell.

Weinstein, N. D., & Klein, W. M. (1995). Resistance of personal risk perceptions to debiasing interventions. *Health Psychology, 14,* 132–140.

Weinstein, N. D., & Klein, W. M. (1996). Unrealistic optimism: Present and future. *Journal of Social and Clinical Psychology, 15,* 1–8.

Weinstein, N. D., Slovic, P., & Gibson, G. (2004). Accuracy and optimism in smokers' beliefs about quitting. *Nicotine & Tobacco Research, 6,* 375–380.

Weisberg, R. W. (1986). *Creativity: Genius and other myths.* New York: W. H. Freeman.

Weisberg, R. W. (1993). *Creativity: Beyond the myth of genius.* New York: W. H. Freeman.

Weisberg, R. W. (1999). Creativity and knowledge: A challenge to theories. In R. J. Sternberg (Ed.), *Handbook of creativity.* New York: Cambridge University Press.

Weisberg, R. W. (2006). *Creativity: Understanding innovation in problem solving, science, invention, and the arts.* New York: Wiley.

Weise-Kelly, L., & Siegel, S. (2001). Self-administration cues as signals: Drug self-administration and tolerance. *Journal of Experimental Psychology: Animal Behavior Processes, 27,* 125–136.

Weisler, R. H., Barbee, J. G., & Townsend, M. H. (2007). Mental health and recovery in the Gulf Coast after Hurricanes Katrina and Rita. *Journal of the American Medical Association, 296,* 585–588.

Weiss, A., Bates, T. C., & Luciano, M. (2008). Happiness is a personal(ity) thing. *Psychological Science, 19,* 205–210.

Weissman, D. H., & Banich, M. T. (2000). The cerebral hemispheres cooperate to perform complex but not simple tasks. *Neuropsychology, 14,* 41–59.

Weiten, W. (1984). Violation of selected item-construction principles in educational measurement. *Journal of Experimental Education, 51,* 46–50.

Weiten, W. (1988a). Objective features of introductory psychology textbooks as related to professors' impressions. *Teaching of Psychology, 15,* 10–16.

Weiten, W. (1988b). Pressure as a form of stress and its relationship to psychological symptomatology. *Journal of Social and Clinical Psychology, 6*(1), 127–139.

Weiten, W. (1998). Pressure, major life events, and psychological symptoms. *Journal of Social Behavior and Personality, 13,* 51–68.

Weiten, W. (2002). Wiring the introductory psychology course: How should we harness the Internet? In S. F. Davis & B. Buskist (Eds.), *The teaching of psychology: Essays in honor of Wilbert J. McKeachie and Charles L. Brewer.* Mahwah, NJ: Erlbaum.

Weiten, W., & Diamond, S. S. (1979). A critical review of the jury-simulation paradigm: The case of defendant characteristics. *Law and Human Behavior, 3,* 71–93.

Weiten, W., Guadagno, R. E., & Beck, C. A. (1996). Students' perceptions of textbook pedagogical aids. *Teaching of Psychology, 23,* 105–107.

Weiten, W., & Wight, R. D. (1992). Portraits of a discipline: An examination of introductory psychology textbooks in America. In A. E. Puente, J. R. Matthews, & C. L. Brewer (Eds.), *Teaching psychology in America: A history.* Washington, DC: American Psychological Association.

Wells, C. G. (1991). *Right-brain sex: How to reach the heights of sensual pleasure by releasing the erotic power of your mind.* New York: Avon.

Wells, G. L., & Bradfield, A. L. (1998). "Good, you identified the suspect": Feedback to eyewitnesses distorts their reports of the witnessing experience. *Journal of Applied Psychology, 83,* 360–376.

Wells, G. L., Memon, A., & Penrod, S. D. (2006). Eyewitness evidence: Improving its probative value. *Psychological Science in the Public Interest, 7,* 45–75.

Wells, G. L., & Olson, E. A. (2003). Eyewitness testimony. *Annual Review of Psychology, 54,* 277–295.

Wells, G. L., Olson, E. A., & Charman, S. D. (2002). The confidence of eyewitnesses in their identifications from lineups. *Current Directions in Psychological Science, 11*(5), 151–154.

Wells, K., Klap, R., Koike, A., & Sherbourne, C. (2001). Ethnic disparities in unmet need for alcoholism, drug abuse, and mental health care. *American Journal of Psychiatry, 158,* 2027–2032.

Welsh, C. H., & Fugit, R. V. (2006). Medications that can cause insomnia. In T. Lee-Chiong (Ed.), *Sleep: A comprehensive handbook.* Hoboken, NJ: Wiley-Liss.

Welsh, R. S. (2003). Prescription privileges: Pro or con. *Clinical Psychology: Science & Practice, 10,* 371–372.

Werker, J. F., & Desjardins, R. N. (1995). Listening to speech in the 1st year of life: Experiential influences on phoneme perception. *Current Directions in Psychological Science, 4,* 76–81.

Werker, J. F., & Tees, R. C. (1999). Influences on infant speech processing: Toward a new synthesis. *Annual Review of Psychology, 50,* 509–535.

Wertheimer, M. (1912). Experiment-elle studien über das sehen von bewegung. *Zeitschrift für Psychologie, 60,* 312–378.

Wertsch, J. V., & Tulviste, P. (2005). L. S. Vygotsky and contemporary developmental psychology. In H. Daniels (Ed.), *An introduction to Vygotsky.* New York: Routledge.

Wertz, F. J. (1998). The role of the humanistic movement in the history of psychology. *Journal of Humanistic Psychology, 38,* 42–70.

Wessely, S., & Kerwin, R. (2004). Suicide risk and the SSRIs. *Journal of the American Medical Association, 292,* 379–381.

Wesson, D. R., Smith, D. E., Ling, W., & Seymour, R. B. (2005). Sedative-hypnotics. In M. H. Kryger, T. Roth, & W. C. Dement (Eds.). *Principles and practice of sleep medicine.* Philadelphia: Elsevier Saunders.

West, D. S., Harvey-Berino, J., & Raczynski, J. M. (2004). Behavioral aspects of obesity, dietary intake, and chronic disease. In J. M. Raczynski & L. C. Leviton (Eds.), *Handbook of clinical health psychology: Vol. 2. Disorders of behavior and health.* Washington, DC: American Psychological Association.

West, R. F., & Stanovich, K. E. (1997). The domain specificity and generality of overconfidence: Individual differences in performance estimation bias. *Psychonomic Bulletin & Review, 4,* 387–392.

Westbrook, G. L. (2000). Seizures and epilepsy. In E. R. Kandel, J. H. Schwartz, & T. M. Jessell (Eds.), *Principles of neural science.* New York: McGraw-Hill.

Westen, D. (1998). The scientific legacy of Sigmund Freud: Toward a psychodynamically informed psychological science. *Psychological Bulletin, 124,* 333–371.

Westen, D., & Gabbard, G. O. (1999). Psychoanalytic approaches to personality. In L. A. Pervin & O. P. John (Eds.), *Handbook of personality: Theory and research.* New York: Guilford.

Wethington, E. (2007). Life events scale. In G. Fink (Ed.), *Encyclopedia of stress.* San Diego: Elsevier.

Wever, E. G., & Bray, C. W. (1937). The perception of low tones and the resonance-volley theory. *Journal of Psychology, 3,* 101–114.

Wexler, B. E., Gottschalk, C. H., Fulbright, R. K., Prohovnik, I., Lacadie, C. M., Rounsaville, B. J., & Gore, J. C. (2001). Functional magnetic resonance imaging of cocaine craving. *American Journal of Psychiatry, 158,* 86–95.

Whitaker, R. (2002). *Mad in America: Bad science, bad medicine, and the enduring mistreatment of the mentally ill.* New York: Perseus.

Whitbourne, S. K., Zuschlag, M. K., Elliot, L. B., & Waterman, A. S. (1992). Psychosocial development in adulthood: A 22-year sequential study. *Journal of Personality and Social Psychology, 63,* 260–271.

White, S. H. (2000). Conceptual foundations of IQ testing. *Psychology, Public Policy, and Law, 6,* 33–43.

Whitfield, C. L. (1995). *Memory and abuse: Remembering and healing the effects of trauma.* Deerfield Beach, FL: Health Communications.

Whitty, M. T. (2008). Liberating or debilitating? An examination of romantic relationships, sexual relationships and friendships on the net. *Computers in Human Behavior, 24,* 1837–1850.

Whorf, B. L. (1956). Science and linguistics. In J. B. Carroll (Ed.), *Language, thought and reality: Selected writings of Benjamin Lee Whorf.* Cambridge, MA: MIT Press.

Widiger, T. A. (2007). Current controversies in nosology and diagnosis of personality disorders. *Psychiatric Annals, 37,* 93–99.

Widiger, T. A., & Mullins, S. (2003). Personality disorders. In A. Tasman, J. Kay, & J. A. Lieberman (Eds.), *Psychiatry.* New York: Wiley.

Widiger, T. A., & Sankis, L. M. (2000). Adult psychopathology: Issues and controversies. *Annual Review of Psychology, 51,* 377–404.

Widiger, T. A., & Simonsen, E. (2005). Introduction to the special section: The American Psychiatric Association's research agenda for the DSM-V. *Journal of Personality Disorders, 19,* 103–109.

Widiger, T. A., & Trull, T. J. (2007). Plate tectonics in the classification of personality disorder: Shifting to a dimensional model. *American Psychologist, 62,* 71–83.

Widom, C. S. (1997). Child abuse, neglect, and witnessing violence. In D. M. Stoff, J. Breiling, & J. D. Maser (Eds.), *Handbook of antisocial behavior.* New York: Wiley.

Wiederman, M. W. (1993). Evolved gender differences in mate preferences: Evidence from personal advertisements. *Ethology and Sociobiology, 14,* 331–352.

Wiese, A. M., & Garcia, E. E. (2006). Educational policy in the United States regarding bilinguals in early childhood education. In B. Spodek & O. N. Saracho (Eds.), *Handbook of research on the education of young children.* Mahwah, NJ: Erlbaum.

Wiesel, T. N., & Hubel, D. H. (1963). Single-cell responses in striate cortex of kittens deprived of vision in one eye. *Journal of Neurophysiology, 26,* 1003–1017.

Wiesel, T. N., & Hubel, D. H. (1965). Extent of recovery from the effects of visual deprivation in kittens. *Journal of Neurophysiology, 28,* 1060–1072.

Wiesenfeld, B., Raghuram, S., & Garud, R. (2001). Organizational identification among virtual workers: The role of need for affiliation and work-based social support. *Journal of Management, 27,* 213–229.

Wigboldus, D. H. J., Dijksterhuis, A., & van Knippenberg, A. (2003). When stereotypes get in the way: Stereotypes obstruct stereotype-inconsistent trait inferences. *Journal of Personality and Social Psychology, 84,* 470–484.

Wiggs, C. L., Weisberg, J., & Martin, A. (1999). Neural correlates of semantic and episodic memory retrieval. *Neuropsychologia, 37,* 103–118.

Wilder, C., Pollo, C., Bloch, J., Burkhard, P. R., & Vingerhoets, F. J. G. (2008). Long-term outcome of 50 consecutive Parkinson's disease patients treated with subthalamic deep brain stimulation. *Parkinsonism & Related Disorders, 14,* 114–119.

Wilding, J., & Valentine, E. (1996). Memory expertise. In D. J. Herrmann, C. McEvoy, C. Hertzog, P. Hertel, & M. K. Johnson (Eds.), *Basic and applied memory research: Theory in context* (Vol. 1). Mahwah, NJ: Erlbaum.

Wiley, E. W., Bialystok, E., & Hakuta, K. (2005). New approaches to using census data to test the critical-period hypothesis for second-language acquisition. *Psychological Science, 16,* 341–343.

Wilkaitis, J., Mulvhill, T., & Nasrallah, H. A. (2004). Classic antipsychotic medications. In A. F. Schatzberg & C. B. Nemeroff (Eds.), *Textbook of psychopharmacology.* Washington, DC: American Psychiatric Publishing.

Willford, J. A., Leech, S. L., & Day, N. L. (2006). Moderate prenatal alcohol exposure and cognitive status of children at age 10. *Alcoholism: Clinical and Experimental Research, 30,* 1051–1059.

William, B. F. (2000). Bartlett's concept of the schema and its impact on theories of knowledge representation in contemporary cognitive psychology. In A. Saito (Ed.), *Bartlett, culture and cognition.* Philadelphia: Psychology Press.

Williams, A., & Giles, H. (1998). Communication of ageism. In M. C. Hecht (Ed.), *Communicating prejudice* (pp. 136–160). Thousand Oaks, CA: Sage.

Williams, B. A. (1988). Reinforcement, choice, and response strength. In R. C. Atkinson, R. J. Herrnstein, G. Lindzey, & R. D. Luce (Eds.), *Stevens' handbook of experimental psychology.* New York: Wiley.

Williams, C. D. (1959). The elimination of tantrum behavior by extinction procedures. *Journal of Abnormal and Social Psychology, 59,* 269.

Williams, C. G., Gagne, M., Ryan, R. M., & Deci, E. L. (2002). Facilitating autonomous motivation for smoking cessation. *Health Psychology, 21,* 40–50.

Williams, G. C. (1966). *Adaptation and natural selection.* Princeton, NJ: Princeton University Press.

Williams, J. E., Paton, C. C., Siegler, I. C., Eigenbrodt, M. L., Neito, F. J., & Tyroler, H. A. (2000). Anger proneness predicts coronary heart disease risk. *Circulation, 101,* 2034–2039.

Williams, L. M. (1994). Recall of childhood trauma: A prospective study of women's memories of child sexual abuse. *Journal of Consulting and Clinical Psychology, 62,* 1167–1176.

Williams, M. H. (1992). Exploitation and inference: Mapping the damage from therapist-patient sexual involvement. *American Psychologist, 47,* 412–421.

Williams, N. A., & Deffenbacher, J. L. (1983). Life stress and chronic yeast infections. *Journal of Human Stress, 9*(1), 26–31.

Williams, P. (2005). What is psychoanalysis? What is a psychoanalyst? In E. S. Person, A. M. Cooper, & G. O. Gabbard (Eds.), *Textbook of psychoanalysis.* Washington, DC: American Psychiatric Publishing.

Williams, R., & Stockmyer, J. (1987). *Unleashing the right side of the brain: The LARC creativity program.* New York: Viking Penguin.

Williams, R. E., Kaliani, L., DiBenedetti, D. B., Zhou, X., Fehnel, S. E., & Clark, R. V. (2007). Healthcare seeking and treatment for menopausal symptoms in the United States. *Maturitas, 58,* 348–358.

Williams, R. L., & Eggert, A. (2002). Notetaking predictors of test performance. *Teaching of Psychology, 29*(3), 234–237.

Williams, W. M., & Ceci, S. J. (1997). Are Americans becoming more or less alike?: Trends in race, class, and ability differences in intelligence. *American Psychologist, 52,* 1226–1235.

Williamson, D. A., Zucker, N. L., Martin, C. K., & Smeets, M. A. M. (2001). Etiology and management of eating disorders. In P. B. Sutker & H. E. Adams (Eds.), *Comprehensive handbook of psychopathology.* New York: Kluwer Academic/Plenum.

Willis, J., & Todorov, A. (2006). First impressions: Making up your mind after a 100-ms exposure to a face. *Psychological Science, 17,* 592–598.

Willis, W. D. (1985). *The pain system. The neural basis of nociceptive transmission in the mammalian nervous system.* Basel: Karger.

Willoughby, T., Motz, M., & Wood, E. (1997). The impact of interest and strategy use on memory performance for child, adolescent, and adult learners. *Alberta Journal of Educational Research, 43,* 127–141.

Wills, T. A., & Fegan, M. (2001). Social networks and social support. In A. Baum, T. A. Revenson, & J. E. Singer (Eds.), *Handbook of health psychology* (pp. 209–234). Mahwah, NJ: Erlbaum.

Wilsnack, S. C., Wonderlich, S. A., Kristjanson, A. F., Vogeltanz-Holm, N. D., & Wilsnack, R. W. (2002). Self-reports of forgetting and remembering childhood sexual abuse in a nationally representative sample of U.S. women. *Child Abuse and Neglect, 26*(2), 139–147.

Wilson, R. S., & Bennett, D. A. (2003). Cognitive activity and risk of Alzheimer's disease. *Current Directions in Psychological Science, 12*(3), 87–91.

Wilson, T. D., & Gilbert, D. T. (2005). Affective forecasting: Knowing what to want. *Current Directions in Psychological Science, 14,* 131–134.

Windholz, G. (1997). Ivan P. Pavlov: An overview of his life and psychological work. *American Psychologist, 52,* 941–946.

Wing, R. R., & Polley, B. A. (2001). Obesity. In A. Baum, T. A. Revenson, & J. E. Singer (Eds.), *Handbook of health psychology*. Mahwah, NJ: Erlbaum.

Wingfield, A., Tun, P. A., & McCoy, S. L. (2005). Hearing loss in older adulthood: What it is and how it interacts with cognitive performance. *Current Directions in Psychological Science, 14,* 144–148.

Winick, C., & Evans, J. T. (1996). The relationship between nonenforcement of state pornography laws and rates of sex crime arrests. *Archives of Sexual Behavior, 25,* 439–453.

Winick, C., & Norman, R. L. (2005). Epidemiology. In J. H. Lowinson, P. Ruiz, R. B. Millman, & J. G. Langrod (Eds.), *Substance abuse: A comprehensive textbook*. Philadelphia: Lippincott/Williams & Wilkins.

Winkielman, P., & Berridge, K. C. (2004). Unconscious emotion. *Current Directions in Psychological Science, 13*(3), 120–123.

Winn, P. (1995). The lateral hypothalmus and motivated behavior: An old syndrome reassessed and a new perspective gained. *Current Directions in Psychological Science, 4,* 182–187.

Winner, E. (1997). Exceptionally high intelligence and schooling. *American Psychologist, 52,* 1070–1081.

Winner, E. (1998). Uncommon talents: Gifted children, prodigies, and savants. *Scientific American Presents Exploring Intelligence, 9,* 32–37.

Winner, E. (2000). The origins and ends of giftedness. *American Psychologist, 55,* 159–169.

Winner, E. (2003). Creativity and talent. In M. H. Bornstein & L. Davidson (Eds.), *Well-being: Positive development across the life course*. Mahwah, NJ: Erlbaum.

Winsler, A. (2003). Introduction to special issue: Vygotskian perspectives in early childhood education. *Early Education & Development, 14*(3), 253–269.

Winters, K. C., Arthur, N., Leitten, W., & Botzet, A. (2004). Gambling and drug abuse in adolescence. In J. L. Derevensky & R. Grupta (Eds.), *Gambling problems in youth: Theoretical and applied perspectives*. New York: Kluwer/Plenum.

Winzelberg, A. J., & Luskin, F. M. (1999). The effect of a meditation training in stress levels in secondary school teachers. *Stress Medicine, 15,* 69–77.

Wise, M. G., Gray, K. F., & Seltzer, B. (1999). Delirium, dementia, and amnestic disorders. In R. E. Hales, S. C. Yudofsky, & J. A. Talbott (Eds.), *The American Psychiatric Press textbook of psychiatry* (3rd ed., pp. 317–362). Washington, DC: American Psychiatric Press.

Wise, R. A. (1999). Animal models of addiction. In D. S. Charney, E. J. Nestler, & B. S. Bunney (Eds.), *Neurobiology of mental illness*. New York: Oxford University Press.

Wise, R. A. (2002). Brain reward circuitry: Insights from unsensed incentives. *Neuron, 36,* 229–240.

Wise, R. J. S., & Price, C. J. (2006). Functional neuroimaging of language. In R. Cabeza & A. Kingstone (Eds.), *Handbook of functional neuroimaging of cognition*. Cambridge, MA: MIT Press.

Witt, J. K., Proffitt, D. R., & Epstein, W. (2004). Perceiving distance: A role of effort and intent. *Perception, 33,* 577–590.

Witt, L. A., Kacmar, M., Carlson, D. S., & Zivnuska, S. (2002). Interactive effects of personality and organizational politics on contextual performance. *Journal of Organizational Behavior, 23,* 911–926.

Wittkower, E. D., & Warnes, H. (1984). Cultural aspects of psychotherapy. In J. E. Mezzich & C. E. Berganza (Eds.), *Culture and psychopathology*. New York: Columbia University Press.

Wolford, G., Miller, M. B., & Gazzaniga, M. S. (2004). Split decisions. In M. S. Gazzaniga (Ed.), *The cognitive neurosciences*. Cambridge, MA: MIT Press.

Wolitzky, D. L. (2006). Psychodynamic theories. In J. C. Thomas, & D. L. Segal (Eds.), *Comprehensive handbook of personality and psychopathology*. New York: Wiley.

Woloshin, S., Schwartz, L. M., & Welch, H. G. (2002). Risk charts: Putting cancer in context. *Journal of the National Cancer Institute, 94,* 799–804.

Wolpe, J. (1958). *Psychotherapy by reciprocal inhibition*. Stanford, CA: Stanford University Press.

Wolpe, J. (1990). *The practice of behavior therapy*. Elmsford, NY: Pergamon.

Wonder, J. (1992). *Whole brain thinking: Working both sides of the brain to achieve peak job performance*. New York: Morrow.

Wonderlich, S. A. (2002). Personality and eating disorders. In C. G. Fairburn & K. D. Brownell (Eds.), *Eating disorders and obesity: A comprehensive handbook*. New York: Guilford.

Wong, L. A. (2006). *Essential study skills*. Boston: Houghton Mifflin.

Wong, N. (2005). Group psychotherapy and combined individual and group psychotherapy. In B. J. Sadock & V. A. Sadock (Eds.), *Kaplan and Sadock's comprehensive textbook of psychiatry*. Philadelphia: Lippincott Williams & Wilkins.

Wong, P. T. P. (2006). Existential and humanistic theories. In J. C. Thomas & D. L. Segal (Eds.), *Comprehensive handbook of personality and psychopathology*. New York: Wiley.

Wood, E., Desmarais, S., & Gugula, S. (2002). The impact of parenting experience on gender stereotyped toy play of children. *Sex Roles, 47*(1–2), 39–49.

Wood, F., Ebert, V., & Kinsbourne, M. (1982). The episodic-semantic memory distinction in memory and amnesia: Clinical and experimental observations. In L. Cermak (Ed.), *Human memory and amnesia*. Hillsdale, NJ: Erlbaum.

Wood, J. N., & Spelke, E. S. (2005). Chronometric studies of numerical cognition in five-month-old infants. *Cognition, 97,* 23–39.

Wood, N. L., & Cowan, N. (1995). The cocktail party phenomenon revisited: Attention and memory in the classic selective listening procedure of Cherry (1953). *Journal of Experimental Psychology: Learning, Memory, & Cognition, 21,* 255–260.

Wood, P. B. (2007). Fibromyalgia. In G. Fink (Ed.), *Encyclopedia of stress*. San Diego: Elsevier.

Wood, W., & Quinn, J. M. (2003). Forewarned and forearmed? Two meta-analytic syntheses of forewarnings of influence appeals. *Psychological Bulletin, 129,* 119–138.

Woodcock, R. W. (1994). Norms. In R. J. Sternberg (Ed.), *Encyclopedia of human intelligence*. New York: Macmillan.

Woodhead, M. (1999). When psychology informs public policy: The case. In E. Zigler & S. J. Styfco (Eds.), *The Head Start debate*. Baltimore: Paul H. Brookes Publishing.

Wop, W. J., Weissman, N. J., Zhu, J. , Bonsall, R. W., Doyle, M., Stretch, M. R., et al. (2008). Effects of acute mental stress and exercise on inflammatory markers in patients with coronary artery disease and healthy controls. *American Journal of Cardiology, 101,* 767–773.

Worthen, J. B., & Wade, C. E. (1999). Direction of travel and visiting team athletic performance: Support for a circadian dysrhythmia hypothesis. *Journal of Sport Behavior, 22,* 279–287.

Worthington, E. L., Jr., & Scherer, M. (2004). Forgiveness is an emotion-focused coping strategy that can reduce health risks and promote health resilience: Theory, review, and hypotheses. *Psychology and Health, 19,* 385–405.

Worthington, R. L., Soth-McNett, A. M., & Moreno, M. V. (2007). Multicultural counseling competencies research: A 20-year content analysis. *Journal of Counseling Psychology, 54,* 351–361.

Wright, J. H., Beck, A. T., & Thase, M. E. (2003). Cognitive therapy. In R. E. Hales & S. C. Yudofsky (Eds.), *Textbook of clinical psychiatry*. Washington, DC: American Psychiatric Publishing.

Wright, S. C., & Taylor, D. M. (2003). The social psychology of cultural diversity: Social stereotyping, prejudice, and discrimination. In M. A. Hogg & J. Cooper (Eds.), *The Sage handbook of social psychology*. Thousand Oaks, CA: Sage.

Wrosch, C., Miller, G. E., Scheier, M. F., & de Pontet, S. B. (2007). Giving up on unattainable goals: Benefits for health? *Personality and Social Psychology Bulletin, 33,* 251–265.

Wrosch, C., & Scheier, M. F. (2003). Personality and quality of life: The importance of optimism and goal adjustment. *Quality of Life Research: An International Journal of Quality of Life Aspects of Treatment, Care & Rehabilitation, 12,* 59–72.

Wundt, W. (1874/1904). *Principles of physiological psychology*. Leipzig: Engelmann.

Wurtz, R. H., & Kandel, E. R. (2000). Central visual pathways. In E. R. Kandel, J. H. Schwartz, & T. M. Jessell (Eds.), *Principles of neural science*. New York: McGraw-Hill.

Wynder, E. L., Cohen, L. A., Muscat, J. E., Winters, B., Dwyer, J. T., & Blackburn, G. (1997). Breast cancer: Weighing the evidence for a promoting role of dietary fat. *Journal of the National Cancer Institute, 89,* 766–775.

Wynn, K. (1992). Addition and subtraction by human infants. *Nature, 358,* 749–750.

Wynn, K. (1996). Infants' individuation and enumeration of sequential actions. *Psychological Science, 7,* 164–169.

Wynn, K. (1998). An evolved capacity for number. In D. D. Cummins & C. Allen (Eds.), *The evolution of mind*. New York: Oxford University Press.

Wynne, C. D. L. (2004). *Do animals think?* Princeton, NJ: Princeton University Press.

Yamamoto, J., Silva, J. A., Justice, L. R., Chang, C. Y., & Leong, G. B. (1993). Cross-cultural psychotherapy. In A. C. Gaw (Ed.), *Culture, ethnicity, and mental illness*. Washington, DC: American Psychiatric Press.

Yang, H., Liu, T., & Zang, D. (2000). A study of stressful life events before the onset of hypothyroidism. *Chinese Mental Health Journal, 14,* 201–202.

Yates, F. A. (1966). *The art of memory*. London: Routledge & Kegan Paul.

Ybarra, O., Stephan, W. G., & Schaberg, L. (2000). Misanthropic memory for the behavior of group members. *Personality and Social Psychology Bulletin, 26,* 1515–1525.

Yeomans, M. R., Tepper, B. J., Rietzschel, J., & Prescott, J. (2007). Human hedonic responses to sweetness: Role of taste genetics and anatomy. *Physiology & Behavior, 91,* 264–273.

Yerkes, R. M. (1921). *Memories of the National Academy of Sciences: Psychological examining in the United States Army* (Vol. 15). Washington, DC: U.S. Government Printing Office.

Yerkes, R. M., & Morgulis, S. (1909). The method of Pavlov in animal psychology. *Psychological Bulletin, 6,* 257–273.

Yost, W. A. (2000). *Fundamentals of hearing: An introduction.* San Diego: Academic Press.

Yost, W. A. (2001). Auditory, localization, and scene perception. In E. B. Goldstein (Ed.), *Blackwell handbook of perception.* Malden, MA: Blackwell.

Yost, W. A. (2003). Audition. In A. F. Healy & R. W. Proctor (Eds.), *Handbook of psychology, Vol. 4: Experimental psychology.* New York: Wiley.

Young, D. M. (1997). Depression. In W. S. Tseng & J. Streltzer (Eds.), *Culture and psychopathology: A guide to clinical assessment.* New York: Brunner/Mazel.

Young, K. S. (1996, August). *Internet addiction: The emergence of a new clinical disorder.* Paper presented at the meeting of the American Psychological Association: Toronto, Ontario, Canada.

Young, K. S. (1998). *Caught in the net: How to recognize the signs of Internet addiction—and a winning strategy for recovery.* New York: Wiley.

Yudofsky, S. C. (1999). Parkinson's disease, depression, and electrical stimulation of the brain. *New England Journal of Medicine, 340,* 1500–1502.

Yutzy, S. H. (2003). Somatoform disorders. In R. E. Hales & S. C. Yudofsky (Eds.), *Textbook of clinical psychiatry.* Washington, DC: American Psychiatric Publishing.

Zaccaro, S. J., Mumford, M. D., Connelly, M., Marks, M., & Gilbert, J. A. (2000). Assessment of leader abilities. *Leadership Quarterly, 11,* 37–64.

Zacks, R. T., Hasher, L., & Li, K. Z. H. (2000). Human memory. In F. I. M. Craik & T. A. Salthouse (Eds.), *Handbook of aging and cognition.* Mahwah, NJ: Erlbaum.

Zagorsky, J. L. (2007). Do you have to be smart to be rich? The impact of IQ on wealth, income and financial distress. *Intelligence, 35,* 489–501.

Zajonc, R. B. (1980). Feeling and thinking: Preferences need no inferences. *American Psychologist, 35,* 151–175.

Zane, N., Hall, G. C. N., Sue, S., Young, K., & Nunez, J. (2004). Research on psychotherapy with culturally diverse populations. In M. J. Lambert (Ed.), *Bergin and Garfield's handbook of psychotherapy and behavior change.* New York: Wiley.

Zaragoza, M. S., Belli, R. F., & Payment, K. E. (2007). Misinformation effects and the suggestibility of eyewitness memory. In M. Garry & H. Hayne (Eds.), *Do justice and let the sky fall: Elizabeth F. Lotus and her contributions to science, law, and academic freedom.* Mahwah, NJ: Erlbaum.

Zarate, M. A., Garcia, B., Garza, A. A., & Hitlan, R. T. (2004). Cultural threat and perceived realistic group conflict as dual predictors of prejudice. *Journal of Experimental Social Psychology, 40,* 99–105.

Zarcone, V. P., Jr. (2000). Sleep hygiene. In M. H. Kryger, T. Roth, & W. C. Dement (Eds.), *Principles and practice of sleep medicine.* Philadelphia: Saunders.

Zatzick, D. F. (1999). Managed care and psychiatry. In R. E. Hales, S. C. Yudofsky, & J. A. Talbott (Eds.), *American Psychiatric Press textbook of psychiatry.* Washington, DC: American Psychiatric Press.

Zatzick, D. F., & Dimsdale, J. E. (1990). Cultural variations in response to painful stimuli. *Psychosomatic Medicine, 52*(5), 544–557.

Zautra, A. J., Affleck, G. G., Tennen, H., Reich, J. W., & Davis, M. C. (2005). Dynamic approaches to emotions and stress in everyday life: Bolger and Zuckerman reloaded with positive as well as negative affects. *Journal of Personality, 73,* 1–28.

Zautra, A. J., & Smith, B. W. (2001). Depression and reactivity to stress in older women with rheumatoid arthritis and osteoarthritis. *Psychosomatic Medicine, 63,* 687–696.

Zechmeister, E. B., & Nyberg, S. E. (1982). *Human memory: An introduction to research and theory.* Pacific Grove, CA: Brooks/Cole.

Zeiler, M. (1977). Schedules of reinforcement: The controlling variables. In W. K. Honig & J. E. R. Staddon (Eds.), *Handbook of operant behavior.* Englewood Cliffs, NJ: Prentice-Hall.

Zellner, D. A. (1991). How foods get to be liked: Some general mechanisms and some special cases. In R. C. Bolles (Ed.), *The hedonics of taste.* Hillsdale, NJ: Erlbaum.

Zenhausen, R. (1978). Imagery, cerebral dominance and style of thinking: A unified field model. *Bulletin of the Psychonomic Society, 12,* 381–384.

Zentall, T. R. (2003). Imitation by animals: How do they do it? *Current Directions in Psychological Science, 12*(3), 91–95.

Zepelin, H., Siegel, J. M., & Tobler, I. (2005). Mammalian sleep. In M. H. Kryger, T. Roth, & W. C. Dement (Eds.). *Principles and practice of sleep medicine.* Philadelphia: Elsevier Saunders.

Zhao, X., & Gage, F. H. (2004). Neurogenesis in the adult mammalian brain. In M. S. Gazzaniga (Ed.), *The cognitive neurosciences.* Cambridge, MA: MIT Press.

Zhou, J., & George, J. M. (2003). Awakening employee creativity: The role of leader emotional intelligence. *Leadership Quarterly, 14,* 545–568.

Zillmann, D., & Bryant, J. (1984). Effects of massive exposure to pornography. In N. M. Malamuth & E. Donnerstein (Eds.), *Pornography and sexual aggression.* New York: Academic Press.

Zillmann, D., & Bryant, J. (1988). Pornography's impact on sexual satisfaction. *Journal of Applied Social Psychology, 18,* 438–453.

Zillmer, E. A., Spiers, M. V., & Culbertson, W. C. (2008). *Principles of neuropsychology.* Belmont, CA: Wadsworth.

Zimbardo, P. G. (2004, May 9). Power turns good soldiers into "bad apples." *Boston Globe.* Retrieved from http://www.boston.com/news/globe/editorial_opinion/oped/articles/2004/05/09.

Zimbardo, P. G. (2007). *The Lucifer effect: Understanding how good people turn evil.* New York: Random House.

Zimbardo, P. G., Butler, L. D., & Wolfe, V. A. (2003). Cooperative college examinations: More gain, less pain when students share information and grades. *Journal of Experimental Education, 71,* 101–125.

Zimbardo, P. G., Haney, C., & Banks, W. C. (1973, April 8). The mind is a formidable jailer: A Pirandellian prison. *New York Times Magazine,* Section 6, p. 36.

Zimmerman, B. J. (1995). Self-efficacy and educational development. In A. Bandura (Ed.), *Self-efficacy in changing societies.* New York: Cambridge University Press.

Zimmerman, I. L., & Woo-Sam, J. M. (1984). Intellectual assessment of children. In G. Goldstein & M. Hersen (Eds.), *Handbook of psychological assessment.* New York: Pergamon Press.

Zimmerman, M., & Spitzer, R. L. (2005). Psychiatric classification. In B. J. Sadock & V. A. Sadock (Eds.), *Kaplan & Sadock's comprehensive textbook of psychiatry.* Philadelphia: Lippincott Williams & Wilkins.

Zinbarg, R. E., & Griffith, J. W. (2008). Behavior Therapy. In J. L. Lebow (Ed.), *Twenty-first century psychotherapies: Contemporary approaches to theory and practice.* New York: Wiley.

Zoeller, R. F. Jr. (2007). Physical activity and fitness in the prevention of coronary heart disease and associated risk factors. *American Journal of Lifestyle Medicine, 1,* 29–33.

Zohar, D., & Luria, G. (2005). A multilevel model of safety climate: Cross-level relationships between organization and group level climates. *Journal of Applied Psychology, 90,* 616–628.

Zola, S. M., & Squire, L. R. (2000). The medial temporal lobe and the hippocampus. In E. Tulving & F. I. M. Craik (Eds.), *The Oxford handbook of memory* (pp. 485–500). New York: Oxford University Press.

Zorick, F. J., & Walsh, J. K. (2000). Evaluation and management of insomnia: An overview. In M. H. Kryger, T. Roth, & W. C. Dement (Eds.), *Principles and practice of sleep medicine.* Philadelphia: Saunders.

Zottoli, M .A., & Wanous, J. P. (2000). Recruitment source research: Current status and future directions. *Human Resource Management Review, 10,* 435–451.

Zrenner, E., Abramov, I., Akita, M., Cowey, A., Livingstone, M., & Valberg, A. (1990). Color perception: Retina to cortex. In L. Spillman & J. S. Werner (Eds.), *Visual perception: The neurophysiological foundations.* San Diego: Academic Press.

Zubieta, J., Smith, Y. R., Bueller, J. A., Xu, Y., Kilbourn, M. R., Jewett, D. M., Meyer, C. R., Loeppe, R. A., & Stohler, C. S. (2001). Regional mu opioid receptor regulation of sensory and affective dimensions of pain. *Science, 293,* 311–315.

Zull, J. E. (2002). *The art of changing the brain: Enriching teaching by exploring the biology of learning.* Sterling, VA: Stylus.

Zurbriggen, E. L., & Sturman, T. S. (2002). Linking motives and emotions: A test of McClelland's hypothesis. *Personality & Social Psychology Bulletin, 28,* 521–535.

Zwislocki, J. J. (1981). Sound analysis in the ear: A history of discoveries. *American Scientist, 69,* 184–192.

NAME INDEX

A

Aamodt, M. G., A-18, A-19, A-21, A-22, A-25
Aarts, H., 168
Abdel-Khalek, A. M., 431
Abel, M. H., 566, 567
Abi-Dargham, A., 601
Aboud, F. E., 702
Abraham, C., 684
Abraham, W. C., 303
Abramov, I., 145
Abramowitz, A. J., 253
Abrams, D., 700
Abrams, R., 642, 643
Abrams, R. L., 132
Abramson, L. Y., 595
Accornero, V. H., 444
Achemann, P., 199
Achille, N. M., 492
Acker, M. M., 253
Ackerman, P. L., 381
Acton, G. S., 515
Adair, J. G., 67
Adam, T. C., 88
Adamopoulos, J., 15
Adams, G., 467
Adams, H. E., 588
Adams, H. F., 380
Adams, J. L., 331
Adams, M. J., 275
Adams, R. G., 673
Adams, R. L., 525, 527
Addison, T., 414
Ader, R., 236, 554
Adler, A., 7, 11., 500–501, 524, 628
Adler, L. L., 35
Adler, N. E., 533, 534
Adolph, K. E., 443, 445
Advocat, C. D., 214
Affleck, G., 540, 550
Agnoli, F., 346
Aharon-Peretz, J., 323
Ahima, R. S., 401
Ahn, H., 632
Aikens, D. E., 586
Ainsworth, M. D. S., 449–450, 675
Ait-Daoud, N., 219, 226
Ajzen, I., 682
Akerstedt, T., 189, 190
Akgun, S., 549
Akimoto, S. A., 672
Akiskal, H. S., 591
Aks, D. J., 159
Albarracin, D., 682
Albert, M. S., 304, 472
Alcock, J., 118, 119
Aldag, R. I., 698
Aldington, S., 220
Aldrich, M. S., 203
Aldwin, C. M., 471
Alexander, C. N., 61, 213
Alexander, F., 628
Alexander, J., A-40
Alexander, M. G., 409
Alibali, M. W., 320
Allain, A. N., 606
Allan, R. W., 234, 241
Allard, L. M., 676
Allen, J. J. B., 589, 590
Allen, M., 11, 413

Allen, N. J., A-26
Allen, T. D., A-22
Allgood, W. P., 29
Allison, D. B, 404
Alloy, L. B., 595–596
Almeida, D. M., 492, 535
Alonso, A., 631
Alonso, M., 104
Alonso, S., 631
Alsop, B., 246
Altman, I., 24
Altmann, E. M., 296
Altshuler, L. L., 640
Amabile, T. M., 388, 389
Amato, M., 702
Amato, P. R., 485
Ambady, N., 424, 665
Amedi, A., 104
Ames, A., 158
Ammaniti, M., 450
Amodio, D. M., 701
Anand, B. K., 399
Ancoli-Israel, S., 198
Anderluh, M. B., 614
Anderson, A. E., 614
Anderson, B., 383
Anderson, C., 673
Anderson, C. A., 261, 262, 263
Anderson, E. A., 485
Anderson, I. M., 86
Anderson, K. J., 541
Anderson, M. C., 296
Anderson, N., 695, A-24
Anderson, S., 386
Anderson, V. N., 702
Anderson-Fye, E. P., 615
Andreasen, N. C., 95, 113, 372, 389, 598, 600, 603
Andrews, A. M., 555
Andrews, B., 298
Angell, M., 642
Angelopoulos, T. J., 551
Angiulo, M. J., 590
Anglin, J. M., 321
Angst, J., 501, 592, 593
Ani, C., 380
Ankney, C. D., 383
Annus , A. M., 14
Anter, N. M., 31
Anthenelli, R. M., 226
Anthony, I. C., 560
Antonuccio, D. O., 642
Antony, M. M., 232, 235, 582, 585
Antrobus, J., 204
Apkarian,A. V., 88
Appelbaum, P. S., 653
Appleton, K. M., 402
Aquilino, W. S., 468
Archer, A., 632
Archer, J., 109, 480, 481
Archibald, A. B., 463, 464
Arcus, D. M., 448
Arden, R., 373
Arean, P. A., 549, 595
Arendt, J., 189, 190
Argyle, M., 431, 432, 433
Arkes, H. R., 348, 529
Arkin, A. M., 225
Arkowitz, H., 632, 649

Armant, D. R., 444
Armbruster, B. B., 31
Arndt, J., 518
Arnett, J., 466, 467–468
Arnkoff, D. B., 634, 636
Arnold, L. M., 555
Arnold, R. D., 515
Arnon, I., 584
Arnsten, J. H., 219
Aron, A., 674, 675
Aronson, E., 682–683, 686
Aronson, J., 380–381
Arrigo, J. M., 589
Arthur, J. B., A-27
Arthur, R. H., 537
Asch, S., 688–689
Asendorpf, J. B., 547
Aserinsky, E., 185–186
Ashford, J. W., 473
Ashforth, B. E., 549
Ashkanasy, N. M., 386
Ashton, J. R., 464
Ashton, M. C., 492, 519
Ashton-James, C. E., 386
Ashworth, S. D., A-21
Aspinwall, L. G., 557
Assanand, S., 404
Assefi, S. L., 60, 216
Atkinson, J., 418–419
Atkinson, R. C., 280, 281
Atkinson, R. H., 31
Ator, N. A., 68
Atwood, C. W., Jr., 202
Aucoin, K. J., 253
Auerbach, C. F., 484
Aveline, M., 632
Averill, J. A., 420
Avolio, B. J,, A-24
Axel, R., 168
Ayanian, J. Z., 558
Ayas, N. T., 200
Azzara, A. V., 401

B

Baars, B. J., 318
Babiak, P., 606
Bachelor, P., 388
Baddely, A., 283–284
Baenninger, R., 223
Baer, J., 388
Baer, R. A., 213, 526
Baeyens, F., 133
Bahrick, H. P., 294
Bailey, C. H., 302
Bailey, J. M., 415, 416
Baillargeon, R., 456, 458
Baillie, A. J., 553
Bain, J., 472
Bains, J. S., 81
Bakalar, J. B., 220
Baker, D. B., 13
Baker, F., 558
Baker, G. J., 552, 553
Baker, T. B., 218, 250
Bakermans-Kranenburg, M. J., 450
Bakketeig, L. S., 444
Balcetis, E., 147, 670
Baldessarini, R. J., 640
Baldwin, E., 68

Baldwin, W., 61
Balk, M. M., 4
Ball, H. L., 196
Ballenger, J. C., 201, 638
Balsam, P. D., 240
Baltes, P. B., 473
Bandura, A., 10, 259–262, 264, 482, 483, 504–507
Banich, M. T., 121, 122
Banks, A., 150, 415
Banks, S., 223
Banks, W. A., 81
Banks, W. C., 692
Banning, K., 537
Banyard, V. L., 298, 413
Banzato, C. E. M., 579
Barak, A., 527
Baral, B. D., 369
Baratta, J. E., A-21
Barba, G. D., 306
Barbaree, H. E., 413
Barbe, R. P., 653
Barbee, J. G., 534
Barber, T. X., 210
Barch, D. M., 598
Bard, P., 427
Barfield, R. L., A-23
Bargh, J. A., 65, 420, 678, 694
Barker, E. T., 546
Barlett, D. L., 583
Barlow, D. H., 582
Barnes, C. A., 303
Barnes, V. A., 213
Barnett, S. W., 390, 391
Barnhardt, T. M., 133
Barnier, A. J., 210, 291
Baron, A., 250
Baron, R. S., 698
Barrett, D., 225
Barrett, L. F., 419
Barrett, M. S., 8, 628
Barrett, P., 526
Barron, F., 389
Barrouillet, P. 284
Barry, H., III, 463
Barry-Walsh, J., 590
Barsky, A. J., 562, 588, 588
Bartels, M., 373
Bartholow, B. D., 263
Bartlett, F., 291
Bartoshuk, L. M., 166, 167
Basbaum, A. I., 88, 174
Basow, S. A., 481
Bass, B. M., A-24
Bassok, M., 332, 334, 335
Basson, M. O., 167
Bassuk, E. L., 653
Bates, E., 320, 321, 326
Bates, J. E., 448
Baudry, M., 88
Baum, A., 535, 551
Baumeister, R. F., 398, 403, 408, 409, 412, 416, 420, 480, 545, 547, 548
Baumrind, D., 66, 253, 691
Bauserman, R., 413
Baxter, P. M., 70
Bayley, P. J., 100, 304
Baylis, G. C., 149
Baynard, M. D., 198

Bazzini, D. G., 665
Beauchamp, G. K., 402
Beck, A. T., 585., 636–637, 646–647
Beck, A., 545, 595
Beck, E., 501
Beck, S., A-43
Becker, A., 614, 615
Becker, M. J., 31
Becker, R. J., 450
Becker, S., 303
Beckers, T., 259
Becskei, C., 399
Beehr, T. A., 535
Beeman, M. J., 122
Beer, J. M., 515
Beer, J. S., 104
Begg, I., 279
Behm-Morawitz, E., 702
Beidel, D. C., 550, 582, 586
Beier, M. E., 381
Beilin, H., 456
Beilock, S. L., 548, 549
Bekelman, J. E., 642
Békésy, G. von, 163
Belger, A., 602
Bell, A. P., 415
Bell, B. S., A-23
Bell, J. E., 560
Beller, M., 481
Belli, R. F., 292
Bellinger, D. C., 380
Bellis, M. A., 464
Belsky, J., 451, 464, 471
Bem, D. J., 415, 416, 686–687
Bem, S. L., 482
Benbow, C. P., 373
Benca, R. M., 200
Ben-David, S., 670
Bender, D. S., 649, 650
Benet-Martinez, V., 492
Benjamin, L. T., Jr., 4, 12, 13, 32, 72
Benjet, C., 253
Ben-Nachum, E., 670
Bennet, D. A., 473
Bennett, E. L., 383
Bennett, P., 555
Benning, S. D., 606
Ben-Porath, Y. S., 526
Benson, H., 224, 568
Benton, D., 402
Berchtold, N. C., 560
Berenbaum, S. A., 416
Berger, H., 92
Berger, S. E., 443, 445
Berghmans, R. L. D., 66
Bergin, A. E., 632, 656
Berglund, P. A., 623
Bergman, J. S., 147
Berkhof, J., 540
Berkowitz, L., 545
Berkowitz, R. I., 634, 637
Berlin, B., 327
Berliner, L., 301
Berman, A. L., 466
Berman, R. F., 93
Bernat, E., 132
Berndsen, M., 701
Bernert, R. A., 549
Bernstein, D. M., 300
Bernstein, I. H., 358
Berntson, G. G., 420
Berrettini, W. H., 594
Berridge, K. C., 397, 420, 422, 423

Berry, D. T. R., 526
Berry, J. W., 15, 154, 368
Bersani, H., 369
Berscheid, E., 674
Bertenthal, B. I., 445
Berthoud, H. R., 401
Bertrand, R. M., 469
Berzonsky, M., 467
Bettman, J. R., 338
Beumont, P. J. V., 614
Beusterien, K. M., 560
Beutler, L. E., 633, 654, 655, 656
Bhalla, M., 155
Bhatnagar, S., 542, 543
Bi, G. Q., 303
Bialystok, E., 324
Bianchi-Demicheli, F., 407
Bianci, S., 470
Biederman, H. J., 150
Biehl, M., 424
Biermann, T., 75
Bigler, E. D., 482
Billings, J. F., 300
Binet, A, 20, 361
Bini, L., 642
Birch, H. G., 447
Birch, L. L., 402, 615
Birchler, G. R., 588
Birdsall, T. G., 131
Birgegard, A., 132
Birnbaum, M. H., 65, 342
Birney, D. P., 456, 457
Bishop, C. H., 32
Bishop, S. R., 213
Bisley, J. W., 140
Bjork, E., 321
Bjork, R. A., 308, 313
Bjorklund, D. F., 299
Bjorntorp, P., 403
Black, D. W., 113, 598, 600, 603, 606
Blackburn, R., 606
Blacker, D., 579
Blacker, L., 471
Blackwell, E., 551
Blackwell, J. M., 286
Blagrove, M., 202
Blair, I. V., 701
Blair, S. N., 569
Blakemore, C., 104
Blakeslee, T. R., 122
Blanchard, E. B., 554
Blanchard, R., 415
Blanchette, L., 334
Blank, H., 528
Blankenhorn, 484, 485
Blasgrove, M., 207
Blasko, D. S., 323
Blass, T., 691
Blazer, D. G. I., 472
Blesbois, E., 236
Bleuler, E., 598
Blieszner, R., 673
Bliwise, D. L., 193
Block, J., 492, 547
Block, L. G., 686
Block, N., 379
Bloom, B. L., 651
Bloom, B. S., 372
Bloom, P., 325
Bloomenfeld, R. S., 287
Bloomfield, H. H., 212
Blue, H. C., 611
Blum, R., 466

Blundell, J. E., 399
Boakes, R. A., 234
Boase, J., 678
Bochner, S., 322
Bock, P. R., 519
Bodenhausen, G. V., 666
Bodenheimer, T., 642
Bodenmann, G., 549
Bodin, S. D., 253
Boehm, L. E., 684
Boer, D. P., 502
Boeree, C. G., 504
Bogen, J. E., 14, 106, 121, 122
Bogg, T., 557
Boggild, H., 190
Bohannon, J. N., III, 326
Bohner, G., 413, 682, 684
Boland, R. J., 591
Boldry, J. G., 703
Bolger, N., 547
Bolla, K. I., 220
Bolles, R. C., 397
Bolling, M. V., 503
Boly, M., 210
Bonanno, G., 550
Bond, R., 692
Bongar, B., 654
Bonhila, L., 93
Bonnet, M. H., 197, 199
Bono, G., 568
Bontempi, B., 304
Bonvillian, J. D., 326
Bootzin, R. R., 202
Bopp, K., 296
Borbely, A. A., 199
Borden, L. M., 466
Bordnick, P. S., 636
Borgida, E., 74
Borgman, W. C., A-27
Born, J., 199
Bornstein, R. F., 501
Boroditsky, 328
Borus, J. F., 645, 651, 652
Bos, M. W., 339
Bosma, H., 474
Bossio, L. M., 557
Bost, K. K., 471
Botella, L., 649
Both, S., 413
Bouchard, C, 404
Bouchard, T. J., Jr., 374, 375, 376
Boudreaux, E., 506
Bouman, T. K., 587
Bourgeois, J. A., 86, 472, 593
Bourgeois, J. P., 125
Bourhis, R. Y., 703
Bourne, L. E., Jr., 330
Bousfield, W. A., 287
Bouton, M. E., 239
Bowd, A. D., 67
Bowden, C. L., 641
Bower, G. H., 283, 288, 296, 310, 311
Bowlby, J., 449
Boyatzis, R. E., 418
Boyle, M., 576
Boyle, S. H., 552
Boynton, R. M., 143
Bracken, B. A., 357, 359
Bradfield, A. L., 313
Bradshaw, J. L., 108, 122, 123
Braid, J., 208

Brainerd, C. J., 299, 456
Bramon, E., 603
Branaman, T. F., 422
Brand, C. R., 363
Brandt, M., 528
Branigan, C., 420, 541
Brannon, L., 534
Bransford, J. D., 297
Brase, G. L., 344, 411
Bratslavsky, E., 403, 420, 545
Braun, K. A., 292
Bray, C. W., 164
Bredart, S., 293
Bredt, B. M., 220
Breedlove, S. M., 415, 416
Breggin, P. R., 641, 643
Brehm, J., 705
Brehm, S. S., 703
Breier, A., 601
Breland, K., 245
Breland, M., 245
Brennen, T., 290
Bresalu, N., 58, 200, 201
Bretherton, I., 450
Breuer, J., 622
Breugelmans, S. M., 425
Brewer, K. E., 251
Brewer, W. F., 288
Brewin, C. R., 298, 301
Brewster, K. L., 470
Brickman, P., 432
Bridge, J. A., 640, 653
Briere, J., 298, 301
Bright, J., 535
Brill, A., 7
Bringmann, W. G., 4
Brinol, P., 687
Brislin, R., 15, 26, 611
Broadbent, D. E., 280
Brobeck, J. R., 399
Broca, P., 105
Bröder, A., 66, 528
Brodsky, A., 645
Brody, N., 361, 378, 380
Bromet, E. J., 582
Bronstein, P., 15
Brooks-Dunn, J., 463
Broughton, R., 192
Brown, A., 290, 443
Brown, A. S., 582, 603
Brown, D., 301
Brown, E. J., 586
Brown, G. D. A., 283, 309
Brown, H. D., 122
Brown, J., 547
Brown, M., 418, 489, 490
Brown, M. N., A-39
Brown, R., 290, 703
Brown, R. D., 299
Brown, R. T., 388
Brown, S. C., 296
Brown, T. T., 220
Brown, W. D., 201
Brownell, K. D., 403, 405
Bruce, C., 471
Bruce, D., 301
Bruce, K. R., 614
Bruer, J. T., 124, 125
Bruggerman, E. L., 461
Brumbaugh, C. C., 676
Bryant, J., 413
Bryden, M. P., 108
Brym, R., 679
Buccino, G., 103

Buchanan, B., 684
Buchanan, R. W., 598
Buchanan, T., 65, 527
Buck, L. B., 166
Buckman, R., 562
Buckner, R. L., 306
Budiansky, S., 324
Bufe, B., 167
Buffalo, E. A., 285
Bühler, C., 11
Bulcroft, R., 470
Bulik, C. M., 613, 614
Bull, D. L., 298
Burger, J. M., 512, 671, 705
Burgess, A., 210
Burke, D. M., 290
Burke, J. D., 580, 582
Burleson, K. O., 213
Burlingame, G. M., 630, 631
Burnam, A., 653
Burnet, K. L., 501
Burns, A. B., 597
Burns, B. D., 346
Burriss, R. P., 679
Bursztajn, H. J., 645
Bushman, B. J., 261, 263, 545
Bushnell, M. C., 170
Busis, N., 84, 87
Buss, D. M., 11, 16, 398, 408, 409,
    410, 411, 412, 481, 515–516, 529,
    677, 679, 680
Bussey, K., 482, 483
Buster, J. E., 441
Bustillo, J. R., 598
Butcher, J. N., 525, 546
Butcher, L. M., 377
Butler, E. A., 567
Butler, J. L., 548
Butler, L. D., 698
Button, J., 209
Button, T. M. M., 444
Buxton, M. N., 555
Buxton, O. M., 189
Byrne, D., 673

C

Cabeza, R., 97
Cable, D., 53, 57, 71
Cabral, G. A., 220
Cabyoglu, M. T., 174
Cacioppo, J. T., 419, 420, 421, 535,
    687
Cade, J., 646
Cadinu, M., 381
Cahill, L., 299, 481
Cahn, B. R., 187, 212
Cain, W. S., 168
Caine, E. D., 472
Cajochen, C., 190
Calhoun, L. G., 550
Calkins, D., 140
Calkins, M. W., 6
Callahan, C. M., 371, 372
Callicutt, J. W., 653
Calvert, C., 350
Camaioni, L., 321
Camerer, C., 349
Cameron, L., 562
Cami, J., 218, 226
Camos, V., 284
Campbell, A., 481
Campbell, B., 701
Campbell, J., 499

Campbell, K. B., 187
Campbell, L., 674, 676
Campbell, R., 324, 413
Campbell, S., 594
Campbell, W. K., 471
Campell, D. T., 159
Campfield, L. A., 400, 401
Campione-Barr, B. N., 471
Campos, P., 404
Campos, B., 673
Cannon, W., 90, 396, 399, 427, 542
Canter, P. H., 61, 213
Canton-Graae, E., 603
Cantril, H., 26–27
Cao, Y., 104
Capaldi, E. D., 166
Capozza, D., 703
Caputo, D., 560
Cardena, E., 213, 589, 590
Carducci, B. J., 222
Carey, M. P., 560
Carey, S., 458, 460
Carli, L. L., 313
Carlo, G., 462
Carlsmith, J. M., 685–686
Carlson, A. J., 399
Carlson, D. N., 562, 563, 564
Carlson, K. A., 348
Carlson, M. J., 485
Carlsson, A., 87, 601
Carnagey, N. L., 263
Carney, C. V., 595
Carney, S., 643
Carpenter, D., 413
Carpenter, W. T., 598, 600, 642
Carr, T. H., 549
Carrére, 471
Carrier, M., 280
Carroll, J. B., 363
Carroll, J. M., 423
Carroll, M. E., 68
Carroll-Ghosh, T., 593
Carskadon, M. A., 191, 223
Carson, R. C., 546, 600
Carson, S. A., 441
Carter, J. D., 480
Carter, P. J., 122
Carter, R., 85
Cartwright, R. D., 203, 207
Cartwright-Finch, U., 147
Caruso, D., 386
Carver, C. S., 544, 557
Carver, R. A., 418
Casanova, C., 140
Caspi, A., 115, 448, 469, 492, 594
Caspi, O., 213
Cassel, R. N., 508
Cassidy, J., 448
Castillo, L. G., 539
Castle, D., 601
Castle, P. H., 649
Castonguay, L. G., 649
Castro, B., 652
Catanese, K. R., 408
Catania, A. C., 242, 243
Catrambone, R., 332
Cattell, J. M., 6
Cattell, R. B., 491, 525, 526
Caudek, C., 152
Cavanaugh, J. C., 472
Cavell, T. A., 32
Caverly, D. C., 30, 31
Ceci, S. J., 369, 375, 380
Centeno, S., 236

Cepeda, N. J., 309, 310
Cerletti, U., 642
Chabris, C. F., 147
Chaiken, S., 683, 684
Chambless, D. L., 632
Chan, J. W. C., 368
Chance, P., 124, 241
Chandler, C. C., 291
Chang, E. C., 535
Chapman, P. D., 362
Charman, S. D., 313
Chaves, M., 61
Cheit, R., 301
Chemers, M. M., 506
Chen, E., 544
Chen, J., 339
Chen, J. J., A-27
Cheng, C., 544
Cherrier, M. M., 109
Chess, S., 446–447, 448
Cheung, M. W., L., 544
Chiapelli, F., 554
Chiarello, C., 122
Chiles, C., 689
Chiroro, P., 413
Chiu, C., 15
Chiu, C. Y., 327
Chivers, M. L., 416
Chizmar, L., 560
Cho, S. C., 192
Choi, I., 671
Choi, J., 35, 481
Chomsky, N., 11, 14, 318, 325, 326
Chopra, S. S., 642
Choudhry, N. K., 642
Christenfeld, N. J. S., 683
Christensen, A. J., 563, 564
Christensen, B. A., 595
Christensen, B. T., 334
Christensen, C. C., 210
Christensen, L., 66
Christie, L. A., 560
Christoph, R. T., 506
Chronicle, E. P., 332, 333
Chrousos, G. P., 543, 551
Chudler, E. H., 75
Chun, M. M., 147
Cialdini, R. B., 180, 271, 689, 705
Cianciolo, A. T., 363, 381
Ciarrochi, J., 386, 549
Cicero, T. J., 214
Ciciola, E., 361
Ciesla, J. A., 539
Cilfasefi, S., 299
Cirincione, C., 607
Clark, K., 21
Clark, L. A., 359, 492
Clark, M. C., 310, 311
Clark, R. E., 100, 232, 304, 409, 605,
    A-16
Clarke, J. C., 255
Claus, J., 133
Clayton, T., 439, 440
Cleary, P. D., 558
Clemens, E., 191
Clifasefi, S. L., 147
Clifton, R. K., 445
Clinkenbeard, P. R., 371
Clore, G. L., 673
Clow, A., 109, 543
Coates, D., 432
Coderre, T. J., 170
Coenen, A., 99
Cohen, A., 473, 474

Cohen, C. E., 666
Cohen, D., 639, 641
Cohen, D. B., 515
Cohen, F., 518
Cohen, J. D., 104
Cohen, M. N., 381
Cohen, N., 236
Cohen, S., 541, 555, 556, 557
Cohen, S. G., A-24
Colburn, H. S., 165
Colby, A., 460
Cole, D. A., 466
Cole, K. S., 278
Cole, R. F., 651
Coleman, J. C., 546
Coles, M. E., 584
Coles, R., 467
Colflesh, G. J. H., 284
Collins, A. M., 289
Collins, F. S., 115
Collins, M. A., 665
Collins, N. L., 676
Collins, W. A., 471
Collins, W. R., 515
Collop, N. A., 191
Colvin, C. R., 547
Colwill, R. M., 246
Comas-Diaz, L., 650
Comaty, J. E., 214
Combs, D. R., 599, 600
Combs-Orme, T., 471
Comer, D. R., 695
Compas, B. E., 465
Compton, D. M., 68
Compton, M. T., 601
Compton, W. C., 214
Conklin, H. M., 603
Conners, B., 389
Connolly, T., 349
Conrad, M. A., A-21
Constales, D., 363
Contandriopoulos, A. P., 652
Conte, J. M., 386
Conte, J. R., 298
Conway, A. R. A., 284
Conway, L. C., 16
Cook, A., 518
Cook, G. I., 307
Cooke, L., 402
Coons, H. L., 537
Cooper, C. 382
Cooper, E., 388
Cooper, G., 133
Cooper, J., 133, 686
Cooper, L., 535
Cooper, M., L., 677
Cope, M. B, 404
Coplan, J. D., 86
Copper, C., 308., 698
Corballis, M. C., 121, 122, 123
Corballis, P. M., 108
Coren, S., 123, 158, 159
Cork, R. C., 187
Corkin, S., 304
Cornell, D. G., 481, 529
Corpus, B., 346
Correll, C. U., 639
Corsica, J. A., 403, 559
Cosmides, L., 11, 16, 344, 346, 398
Costa, P. T., Jr., 469, 491–492, 525
Coston, M. L., 10
Coté, J. E., 468
Cotman, C. W., 560
Cotter, A., 444

Courage, M. L., 457
Courtney, S. M., 103
Coutts, A., 443
Cowan, N., 277, 283, 287
Cowan, P. A., 253
Cowart, B. J., 166, 168
Cowey, A., 142
Cox, D., 142
Cox, M. J., 471
Cox, P. D., 631
Coy, K. C., 471
Coyne, J. C., 597
Craig, I. W., 115, 377
Craig, J. C., 174
Craig, P., 440
Craighero, L., 103
Craik, F. I. M., 278, 279, 296, 309
Craik, K. H., 14, 15
Cramer, P., 546, 547
Cramond, B., 371
Cranny, C. J., A-26
Crano, W. D., 682
Craske, M. G., 585, 586
Cravens, H., 373
Crawford, M., 409
Creed, F., 555
Creusere, M. A., 322
Crews, F., 501
Crites, S. L., 684
Crits-Cristoph, P., 628, 656
Crockett, H., 418
Croizet, J., 381
Cronbach, L. J., 371
Cronin, C., 538
Cronk, L., 118
Cropley, A. J., 388
Cross, S. E., 482
Crouch, D. J., 278
Crouter, A. C., 483
Crow, T. J., 601
Crowder, R. G., 287, 295
Crowell, J. A., 677
Crowley, K., 483
Cruess, D. G., 579
Cruz, C., 190
Csikszentmihalyi, M., 16, 369, 420, 550, 630
Cuban, L., 385
Culbert, K. M., 86
Culbertson, J. L., 527
Culbertson, W. C., 89
Culham, J. C., 97
Culpepper, L., 640
Cummings, D. E., 401
Cummins, D., 481
Cunningham, C. O., 560
Cunningham, M., 483
Cunningham, M. R., 680
Curby, K. M., 142
Curfman, G. D., 642
Curnoe, S., 413
Currer, D., 593
Cusato, B., 256
Cushman, P., 649
Cutler, R. L., 132
Cutting, L. P., 604
Czeisler, C. A., 189, 190

D

Dabbs, A., 686
Dagot, L., 705
Dahl, R. 465
Daiek, D. B., 31
Dalal, R., A-28
Dallman, M. F., 543

Dalton, S. O., 555
Daly, M., 11, 16
Dan, B. A., 321
D'Andrade, R. G., 206
Daniels, H., 457
Danner, D. D., 473
Danton, W. G., 642
Danziger, K., 24
Dapretto, M., 103, 321
Darley, J., 694
Darwin, C., 5, 15–16, 116, 427
Das, E. H. H., 684
Das, J. P., 369
Dasen, P. R., 457
Dash, P. K., 304
Dauphinais, K. M., 559
Davenport, J. L., 152, 153
David, J. P., 535
Davidoff, J., 327, 328
Davidov, B. J., 15
Davidowitz, R., 677
Davidson, J. E., 333
Davidson, L., 11
Davidson, R. J., 108, 212, 213, 423
Davies, D. R. T., 198
Davies, I. R. L., 327
Davies, R., 591
Davis, A. S., 121
Davis, D., 299, 312, 677
Davis, H., 213
Davis, J. L., 673
Davis, K. L., 472
Davis, M. N., 556
Davis, O. S. P., 373
Davis, R., 10, 668
Davis, S. F., 10
Dawkins, K., 593
Dawson, W. A., 206
Day, N. L., 444
Day, R., A-22
Day, R. H., 157
Daylo, A. A., 75
Deakin, J. F. W., 86
Dean, F. P., 386
Dean, M. A., 386
Dean, R. S., 121
Deary, I. J., 366, 382, 383
De Beni, R., 311
de Bruin, W. B., 346
DeCarvalho, R. J., 508
de Castro, J. M., 401, 381
De Cock, K. M., 561
Deecher, D., 472
Deese, J., 300
Defeldre, A. C., 293
Defeyter, M. A., 330
Deffenbacher, J. L., 555
DeFrain, J., 470
Degenhardt, L., 220, 601
de Geus, E. J., C., 377
Dehaene, S., 133
de Houwer, A., 323
De Houwer, J., 132, 133
de Jong, P. J., 585
De Koninck, J., 204, 205
Delaune, K. A., 558
Delay, J., 638, 646
del Costello, A. M., 421
Deldin, P. J., 601
Delgado, P. L., 86, 594
Delinsky, S. S., 613
Delis, D. C., 304, 305
DeLisi, L. E., 601
della Rocca, P., 190
DelMonte, M. M., 298
DeLong, M. R., 86, 99

Delongis, A., 535
Delprato, D. J., 10
DelVecchio, W. F., 469
DeMaso, D. R., 646
Dement, W. C., 185, 186, 191, 192, 193, 197, 202, 205, 223
Dempster, F. N., 309
Denes-Raj, V., 343
De Neys, W., 345
Deniker, P., 638, 646
Denko, T., 641
Denmark, F. L., 6
Dennerstein, L., 471
Dennis, C., 471
Dennis, W., 474
Denton, K., 667
DePrince, A. P., 299
Derevensky, J. L., 3
Derogitis, L. R., 537
DeRubeis, R. J., 636
Descartes, R., 6
Des Jarlais, D. C., 219
Desmarais, S., 483
de St. Aubin, E., 469
Detsky, A. S., 642
Detterman, L. T., 370
Deutsch, G., 108, 122, 123, 481
Deutsch, J. A., 400
De Valois, R. L., 146
Devescovi, A., 320
Devine, P. G., 666, 686, 701
de Villiers, J. G., 322
de Villiers, P. A., 249, 322
Devlin, B., 378
Devlin, J. T., 103
DeVore, C. J., A-27, A-28
DeVries, H. M., 471
DeVries, R., 457
Dew, M. A., 582
De Waal, F, 231
Dewan, T., 187
Dewey, J., 6
de wijk, R. A., 168
de Wit, J. B. F., 684
Deyoub, P. L., 210
Diamond, L. M., 416
Diamond, S. S., 50
Di Chara, G., 218
Dichter, G., 602
Dick, D., 116
Dickens, W. T., 375, 376, 378, 379
Dickerhoof, R., 567
Dickinson, B. D., 559
Diekman, A. B., 483
Diener, E., 425, 430, 431, 433
Diener, M., 430
Dietrich, E., 332
Dietrich, K. L., 68
Di Forti, M, 220, 601
DiGirolamo, M. E., 277
Dijksterhuis, A., 132, 339–340, 666
Dikel, M. F., A-31
Dilchert, S., 368
Dillbeck, M. C., 212
Di Lorenzo, P. M., 166, 167
Dilsaver, S. C., 592
Di Marzo, V., 400
Di Matteo, R., 432, 562, 563
Dimberg, U., 255
Dimsdale, J. E., 170, 549, 551
Din, J. N., 559
Dinehart, M. E., 167
Dinges, D. F., 188, 190, 191, 193, 196, 197, 198, 199, 223
Dinsmoor, J. A., 251, 9, 10

Dion, K. K., 677
Dion, K. L., 677, 700
DiPietro, J. A., 444
Dishion, T. J., 466
Dissell, R., 1
Dixon, L., 651
Dixon, R. A., 473, 474
Dobbs, D., 97, 103
Dobs, A. S., 220
Dobson, M., 534
Dobzhansky, T., 118
Docherty, J. P., 645
Docherty, N. M., 604
Dodge, G., A-24
Doerr, P., 415
Doghramji, P. P., 199
Doherty, M. E., 313
Dolan, A., 301
Dolan, M., 86
Dollard, J., 502, 545
Domhoff, G. W., 204, 205, 206, 207
Dominowski, R. L., 330
Domjan, M., 68, 236, 256
Donahoe, J. W., 241
Donnerstein, E., 413
Donovan, S., 343
Dorn, L. D., 110, 464
Dorner, G., 415
Doros, G., 401
Dorrian, J., 197
Doty, R. L., 168
Dougall, A. L., 535, 551
Douglas, K. S., 606
Douzenis, A., 86
Dove, H., 446
Dovidio, J.. F., 701
Dowling, K. W., 75
Dowling-Guyer, S., 350
Downing, J., 464
Downing, P. E., 142
Doyere, V., 304
Draganski, B., 104
Draguns, J. G., 611
Draijer, N., 590
Drake, C., 201
Dranovsky, A., 544
Drath, W. H., A-24
Draycott, S., 686
Drazen, J. M., 642
Drewnowski, A., 704
Drews, F. A., 147, 278
Drigotas, S. M., 675
Driskell, J. E., 308
Driver, J., 149
Driver-Linn, E., 349
Druen, P. B., 680
D'Souza, D. C., 220
Duberstein, P. R., 632
Dubicka, B., 640
Dubovsky, A. N., 591
Dubovsky, S. L., 591, 593, 594
Duck, S., 673
Duckworth, A. L., 366, 630
Duckworth, K., 645, 651, 652
Duckworth, M. P., 588
Dudai, Y., 100, 304
Dudley, E., 471
Duff, P., 444
Duffy, V. B., 167
Duman, R. S., 594, 595
Dunbar, K., 334
Dunbar, R., 325
Dunbar-Jacob, J., 563, 563, 564
Duncan, B. L., 632, 701
Duncan, M., 283

Dunkel-Schetter, C., 555
Dunn, R., 702
Dunne, J. D., 212
Dunne, M. P., 416
Dunning, D., 147, 666, 670, 701
Durante, K. M., 411
Durlach, N. L., 165
Durmer, J. S., 198, 199
Durrant, R., 397
Durston, S., 464
Dwyer, J., 704
Dybdahl, R., 290
Dykens, E. M., 369
Dykstra, J. A., 313

E

Eagly, A. H., 412, 480, 481, 665, 682, 684
Eals, M., 35
Easterbrooks, M. A., 448
Easterlin, B. L., 213
Eastman, R., 92
Eaton, J., 698
Ebbinghaus, H., 294, 295
Ebel, K., 32
Eber, H. W., 525
Ebert, V., 306
Ebling, C., 349
Edens, J. F., 606
Edinger, J. D., 200
Edwards, A., 439
Edwards, D. G. A., 53
Eesley, C. E., 601
Efron, R., 122
Egan, J. P., 131
Egan, M. F., 639
Eggert, A., 31
Ehrenberg, M., 654, 657
Ehrenberg, O., 654, 657
Eibach, R. P., 700
Eich, E., 589
Eichenbaum, H., 304, 305
Eid, M., 425
Eifert, G. H., 587
Einstein, G. O., 306, 307, 310
Eisen, J. L., 583
Eisenberg, N., 462, 606
Eisner, E. W., 385
Eisner, T., 119
Ek, E., 403
Ekman, P., 423–424, 425
Elbert, T., 104
Eldredge, N., 117
Elfenbein, H. A., 424
Ellinwood, E. H., Jr., 87
Ellis, A., 545, 565–566, 636
Ellis, B. J., 397, 464, 501
Ellis, R., 292
Ellison, N. B., 679
Ellsworth, P. C., 420
Elman, J. L., 326
Elpers, J. R., 652, 653
Emavardhana, T., 213
Emmelkamp, P. M. G., 634, 636, 637
Emsley, R., 639
Engemann, K. M., 665
Engle, R. W., 104, 271, 284
Enns, J. T., 152
Entin, E. E., 418
Epel, E., 88
Epley, N., 66, 348
Epstein, J., 527
Epstein, L. H., 401
Epstein, R., 414
Epstein, S., 343

Epstein, S. P., 507
Epstein, W., 132, 155
Erber, M. W., 684
Erdelyi, M. H., 547
Erdfelder, E., 528
Erez, A., A-28
Ergene, N., 174
Erickson, D. J., 669
Erickson, R. P., 166
Ericsson, K. A., 372
Erikson, E., 21, 451–452, 466–467, 469
Ernst, C., 501
Eskes, G., 279
Ess, C., 68
Esterson, A., 502
Estes, R. E., 10
Estes, W. K., 280
Ethier, K. A., 560
Evans, F. J., 187
Evans, G. W., 379, 535
Evans, J. T., 413
Evans, R. L., 638
Evers, K. E., 565
Eysenck, H. J., 379, 382, 513–514, 520, 606, 634
Eysenck, H. L., 585, 586

F

Fabes, R. A., 461
Fabrigar, L. R., 61, 681
Fagan, J. F., 381
Fagot, B. L., 483
Fakhoury, W., 651
Fancher, R. E., 7, 233, 361
Faraday, A., 225
Faraday, M. M., 558
Farah, M. J., 379
Faraone, S. V., 601
Faravelli, C., 586
Farmer, L., 202
Farre, M., 218, 226
Farrington, D. P., 606
Fausto-Sterling, A., 481
Fava, G. A., 579, 630
Fawcett, J. A., 593
Fay, K., 614
Fazio, R. H., 270, 681, 684
Fechner, G., 130–131
Fedele, S., 450
Feeney, D. M., 68
Feeney, J. A., 676
Fegan, M., 556
Fehr, B., 674
Fein, S., 703
Feingold, A., 665
Feist, G. J., 388, 389
Feist, J., 534
Feixas, G., 649
Fekken, G. C., 358
Feldman, D. H., 388, 389, 456, 457, 458
Feldman, J., 299
Feliciano, L., 549, 595
Fenster, J. R., 550
Fenton, W. S., 600
Fenwick, P., 212
Ferenczi, S., 7
Ferguson, M. J., 420
Ferguson, T., 563
Fernald, L., 380
Fernandez, J. R, 404
Ferrari, P. F., 103
Ferris, C. D., 85
Ferster, C. S., 247

Festinger, L., 685–686
Feuerstein, G. Z., 555
Fiedler, K., 422
Fields, R. D., 81, 174
Fields, W. M., 324
Fifer, W. P., 443
Figueredo, A. J., 515
Filaire, F., 109
Finch, A. E., 633
Finder, A., A-21
Fink, B., 679
Finkenauer, C., 420
Finnegan, L. P., 421
Fiore, S. M., 186
Firestein, S., 168
First, M. B., 579
Fischer, K. W., 456
Fischer, P., 695
Fischhoff, B., 313, 332, 341, 346, 347, 348, 528
Fishbein, M., 682
Fisher, B. S., 413
Fisher, H., 675
Fisher, J. A., 402
Fisher, L. E., 187
Fisher, R. P., 291
Fisher, S., 206, 502, 658
Fisher, T. D., 409
Fishman, D. B., 634
Fisk, J. E., 343
Fiske, S. T., 41, 666, 701
Fite, R., 291
Fitness, J., 672
Fitzsimons, G. M., 678
Flanagan, J. C., A-18
Flanagan, O., 187
Flanagin, A. J., A-22
Flannery, R. B., Jr., 584
Flapan, A. D., 559
Flavell, J. H., 456
Fleeson, W., 492, 507
Flegal, K. M., 403, 404
Fleischhacker, W. W., 639
Fletcher, G., 672, 674
Flett, G. L., 659
Flippo, R. F., 31, 32, 33
Flores, B. H., 594, 594
Florio, C. M., 527
Floyd, J., 193
Flynn, F. J., 492
Flynn, J. R., 369, 373, 375, 376, 378, 379
Flynn, M. G., 560
Fobes, J. L., 101
Fode, K. L., 66
Fodor, E. M., 418
Fogassi, L., 103
Foldvary-Schaefer, N., 223
Folkman, S., 535, 540, 541, 544, 547, 550
Folsom, D. P., 653
Fontaine, K. R., 403
Fontaine, P. A., 624
Foote, B., 590
Forcier, K., 560
Ford, J. D., 651
Forget, J., 309
Formicelli, L., 471
Forsén, T., 443
Forster, K. L., 277
Forsyth, D. R., 656, 669, 694, 696, 698
Foschi, R., 361
Foster, C. A., 471
Foster, R. G., 188, 189
Foulkes, D., 207, 225

Fournet, G. P., 10
Fowers, B. J., 15
Fowler, J. S., 218
Fowles, D. C., 603
Fox, A., 423, 450
Fox, G. L., 471
Fox, N. A., 446, 448
Fozard, J. L., 472
Fracasso, M. P., 449
Fraley, R. C., 450, 676, 677
Frances, R. J., 219
Francis, G., 281
Francis, L. A., 615
Frank, J., 656
Frank, J. B., 632
Frank, J. D., 632
Frank, L. K., 527
Frank, L. R., 643
Frank, M. G., 197
Frankland, P. W., 304
Franklin, J. E., Jr., 219
Franko, D. L., 614
Franks, C. M., 634
Franks, J. J., 297
Fraser, S. C., 705
Frasure-Smith, N., 553
Frazer, A., 88
Frederick, S., 345, 433
Frederickson, B. L., 16, 420, 540, 541, 567
Freed, J., 122
Freedman, J. L., 705
Freeman, J., 371
Freeman, K. E., A-39
Freese, J., 501
French, S. A, 405
Freud, A., 467
Freud, S., 7, 10, 11, 21, 24, 177, 186–187, 205, 206, 297–298, 396, 493–499, 520, 523, 524, 545, 546, 622, 626–628, 646–647
Frey, B. S., 430
Freyd, J. J., 298, 299
Fricchione, G., 551
Frick, P. J., 253
Fridhandler, B., 496
Friedkin, N. E., 697
Friedman, H., 220
Friedman, H. S., 371, 492, 533, 534, 557
Friedman, M., 551
Friedman, M. J., 584
Friedman, S. R., 219
Friesen, W., 423–424, 473
Frijda, N. H., 425, 426
Frishman, L. J., 138
Friston, K. J., 108
Fromherz, S., 202
Fromm, E., 211
Frumkes, T. E., 138
Fuchs, A. H., 4
Fugit, R. V., 201
Fujita, F., 431
Fuller, S. R., 698
Funder, D. C., 507, 516, 547
Furnham, A., 483
Furumoto, L., 6

G

Gabbard, G. O., 501, 502, 655, 626
Gabriel, L. T., 370
Gaddis, C., 231
Gael, S. A., A-18
Gaertner, L., 703
Gaertner, S. L., 701

Gaeth, C. J., 330
Gafni, N., 481
Gage, F. H., 104
Gagne, F., 309
Gagnon, A., 703
Gais, S., 199
Galaburda, A. M., 482
Galambos, N. L., 483, 546
Galanter, E., 131
Galati, B., 423
Galderisi, S., 600
Galizio, M., 249, 250
Gall, C. M., 303
Gallagher, K. I., 569
Gallagher, R. M., 170
Gallagher, S. N., 422
Gallese, V., 102
Gallo, D. A., 278, 279
Gallo, L. C., 555
Gallup, A., 223
Gallup, G. G., 223, 679
Galton, F., 26, 361
Gambone, J. C., 562
Ganey, H. N. C., 542
Gangestad, S. W., 673, 679
Gangwisch, J. E., 200
Gantt, W. H., 233
Ganuza, J. M. G., 35
Garb, H. N., 527
Garcia, B. F., 506
Garcia, E., 323
Garcia, J., 255
Garcia, M., 650
Garcia, S. D., 673
Gardner, B. T., 324
Gardner, C. O., Jr., 591
Gardner, E. P., 170
Gardner, H., 14, 318, 363, 385, 388
Gardner, M., 465
Gardner, R. A., 324
Gardner, W. L., 419
Gardos, P., 412
Garfield, S. L., 632
Garland, A. F., 371
Garner, L., 535
Garnett, N., 68
Garry, M., 60, 216, 299, 300
Gartrell, N. K., 415
Garud, R., A-23
Gaschler, K., 142
Gauthier, I., 142–143
Gaver-Apgar, C. E., 679
Gawet, D. L., 538
Gawronski, B., 669
Gazzaniga, M. S., 14, 106, 108
Geddes, J. R., 641, 643
Gee, T. L., 589, 590
Geer, J. H., 412
Geier, A. B., 401
Geiger, M. A., 31
Geller, J. L., 652
Gelman, R., 460
Gelman, S. A., 482
Genesee, F., 323
Gennari, S. P., 328
Gentilia, T., 675
Gentner, D., 322
Gentry, R. C., 402
George, J. M., 472
George, M. S., 93, 644
Gepshtein, S., 132
Geraci, L., 279
Gerard, M., 524
Gergen, K. J., 14
German, T. P., 330
Gerrie, M. P., 300

Gershkoff-Stowe, L., 321
Gershoff, E. T., 252–253
Gersky, D., 118
Geschwind, N., 482
Getzel, E. E., 370
Ghez, C., 99
Gibb, R., 104
Gibbons, M. B. C., 628
Gibbons, R. D., 640
Gibbs, J., 679
Gibbs, W. W., 404
Gibson, G., 559
Gidycz, C. A., 413
Giedd, J. N., 464
Gigerenzer, G., 343, 344
Gilbert, A. N., 168
Gilbert, D. T., 349, 433, 669
Giles, H., 702
Giles, L. C., 556
Giles, T. R., 645
Gilgen, A. R., 10, 242
Gillette, M. U., 202
Gillham, J. E., 557
Gilmer, D. F., 471
Gilovich, T., 27, 343, 348, 666
Giordano, G., 355
Girgus, J. S., 158
Gistner, R., 324
Gitlin, M., 639, 640
Gittelman, M., 653
Givelber, R. J., 202
Gladue, B. A., 416
Gladwell, M., 340
Glaser, J., 65
Glaser, R., 554, 555
Glasman, L. R., 682
Glass, C. R., 634, 636
Glass, G. V., 656
Glass, R. M., 642, 643, 648
Glassman, A., 554
Glassner, B., 347
Glatt, S. J., 601
Gleason, J. B., 319, 321
Gleason, M., 678
Gleaves, D. H., 299, 300, 589, 590
Gleitman, L. R., 326, 327
Glisky, M. L., 590
Gluck, M. E., 614
Goeders, N. E., 546, 549
Goff, D. C., 652
Gogtay, N., 465
Goin, M. K., 649
Gold, J. M., 601
Gold, M. S., 87, 219
Gold, S., 219
Goldberg, I., 591
Goldberg, J. H., 670
Goldberg, L. R., 492
Golden, R. N., 593
Goldenberg, H., 12, 13
Goldenberg, J. L., 518
Goldman, R., 651
Goldman-Rakic, P. S., 125
Goldsmith, M., 288
Goldsmith, T. D., 546
Goldstein, D. G., 344
Goldstein, E., 164, 299, 278
Goldstein, H. W., 368
Goldstein, I. L., 368
Goldstein, R. D., 591
Goldstein, W. M., 337, 343, 346
Goldston, K., 553
Goleman, D., 385, A-24
Gonzaga, G. C., 673
Gonzalez, C. A., 611
Gonzalez-Bono, E., 109

Goodall, J., 52
Goodenough, D. R., 224
Goodstein, L. D., 526
Goodvin, R., 448
Goodwin, C. J., 233
Goodwin, F. K., 592
Goodwin, R. D., 492
Gooley, J. J., 189
Gordon, B., 641
Gordon, H. W., 123
Gordon, J., 145
Gordon, J. U., 556
Gordon-Salant, S., 472
Goritz, A. S., 64
Gorski, R. A., 110
Gosling, S. D., 14, 15, 505–506
Gossweller, R., 155
Goswami, U., 124
Gottdiener, J. S., 553
Gottesman, I. I., 113, 601
Gottfredson, L. S., 367, 368, 383, 384
Gottlieb, D. J., 200
Gottman, J. M., 471
Gottschall, J., 673, 679
Gould, E., 104, 125, 303, 544
Gould, R., 469
Gould, S. J., 16, 117
Goulding, S. M., 601
Gouras, P., 145
Gourevitch, M. N., 219
Gouzoulis-Mayfrank, E., 221
Graber, J. A., 463
Grace, R. C., 238
Grady, D., 472
Graf, P., 306
Grafman, J., 103
Grafton, S., 407
Graham, C. A., 413
Graham, S. A., 321
Granberg, G., 61
Granholm, E., 636
Granic, I., 466
Grant, P., 636
Grantham-McGregor, S., 380
Grau, R., 507
Gray, J. R., 420
Gray, K. F., 472
Gray, W. D., 296
Graziano, W. G., 15, 492
Green, A., 678
Green, J. P., 211
Green, M. F., 601
Greenberg, B. D., 94
Greenberg, D. L., 286
Greenberg, J. L., 517–519
Greenberg, J. S., 569
Greenberg, L. S., 629
Greenberg, R. P., 206, 502, 658
Greene, R. L., 295, 308
Greenfield, D., 53
Greenfield, D. N., 546
Greenhaus, J. H., A-22
Greenleaf, M., 209
Greeno, C. G., 403
Greeno, J., 328, 329
Greenough, W. T., 124, 125
Greenson, R. R., 626
Greenspan, R. J., 112
Greenwald, A. G., 132
Gregory, R. J., 57
Gregory, R. L., 151, 157
Greist, J. H., 641
Grencavage, L. M., 633
Grewel, D., 386
Griffin, D. W., 674

Griffith, E. E., 611
Griffith, J. W., 637
Griffiths, M., 546
Grigoradis, S., 271
Grigorenko, E. L., 26, 115, 373, 375, 376, 378, 384, 516
Grill, H. J., 399
Griner, D., 650
Grinspoon, L., 220
Grob, C. S., 221
Grob, G. N., 534
Gronholm, P., 95
Grose-Fifer, J., 443
Gross, C. G., 104
Gross, C. P., 642
Gross, J. J., 567
Grossman, J. B., 636
Grossman, P., 213
Grossman, R. P., 271
Grossman, S. P., 99
Grossmann, K., 451
Grossmann, K. E., 451
Groth-Marnat, G., 527
Grove, W. M., 527
Grubb, M. S., 104
Gruber, A. J., 220
Grubin, D., 421
Gruenberg, A. M., 591
Grunberg, N. E., 558
Gruneberg, M., 308
Grusec, J. E., 462
Guarda, A. S., 614
Gudeman, J. E., 652
Gudjonsson, G. H., 298
Gueguen, N., 705
Guenther, K., 298
Guerrini, I., 443
Guevremont, D. C., 635
Guggenheim, P. G., 587
Gugula, S., 483
Guilbault, R. L., 312, 528
Guilford, J. P., 388
Guilleminault, C., 201, 202, 203
Gunderson, J. G., 605
Gunn, D. V., 148
Gunn, S. R., 203
Gunn, W. S., 203
Gupta, R., 3
Gureje, O., 587
Gurevich, M., 535
Gurling, H. D., 443
Gusnard, D. A., 96
Guthrie, J., 471
Gutierres, S. E., 181
Guynn, M. J., 297
Guzeldere, G., 187

H

Haas, L., 470
Hackett, R. D., A-28
Hackman, J. R., A-26
Hackworth, C., 190
Hadaway, C. K., 61
Hadjistavropoulos, H., 506
Hadjiyannakis, K., 597
Hadley, S., 640
Hagan, H., 219
Hagen, E., 410
Hagen, E. H., 16
Hagen, J. D., 471
Hager, J. L., 254
Haggbloom, S. J., 10
Hahn, E. R., 321
Hahn, P. Y., 202
Hakel, M. D., 375

Hakuta, K., 323
Haladyna, T. M., 358
Hales, D., 224
Halford, J. C. G., 399, 402
Hall, C. C. I., 15
Hall, C. S., 204, 225
Hall, E., 456
Hall, G. S., 4–5, 7, 10, 20, 466
Hall, J. A., 480
Hall, J. R., 606
Hall, W., 220, 601
Halmi, K. A., 614
Halpern, C., 644
Halpern, D. F., 34, 35, 335, 347, 350, 434, 435, 480, 481, 482
Ham, J. J., 669
Hamann, S., 96–97
Hamedani, M. G., 15, 25, 26
Hamilton, A., 678
Hamilton, W. D., 16, 118, 119
Hammad, T. A., 640
Hammen, C., 591, 597
Hammer, P. S., 75
Hammer, S. M., 560
Hammerstein, S. K., 415
Hammill, R., 74
Hammond, D. C., 301
Hampson, E., 480, 482
Hampton, T., 443
Han, K. F. G. C., 359
Hancock, P. A., 542
Haneda, K., 132
Haney, C., 692, 693
Hanisch, K. A., A-15, A-25 A-26, A-27, A-28
Hankins, W. G., 255
Hannan, A. J., 124
Hannigan, J. H., 444
Hansen, M. B., 321, 633
Hanson, D. R., 115
Hanson, K. N., 411
Happonen, P., 559
Hardcastle, V. G., 97, 187
Hardesty, D. E., 644
Hare, A. P., A-23
Hare, R. D., 606
Harley, E. M., 529
Harley, T. A., 322
Harlow, H., 449
Harmsen, P., 555
Harnack, L, 405
Haroutunian, V., 472
Harrington, M. E., 189
Harris, J., 528–529
Harris, J. E., 306
Harris, J. R., 501, 515
Harrison, K., 615
Harsch, N., 285
Hart, D., 606
Hart, J. W., 695
Hart, K. J., 461
Hartley, A., 474
Harvey, M. H., 301
Harwood, T. M., 633
Haselton, M. G., 680
Hasher, L., 284
Hashimoto, K., 81
Hashtroudi, S., 292
Haslam, N., 414
Haslam, S. A., 340, 703
Hastie, R., 433
Hatch, T., 385
Hatfield, E., 409, 674, 677
Haughland, G., 653
Hauri, P. J., 201

Hauser, M., 458, 460
Havas, S., 559
Hawkins, R. D., 302
Haworth-Hoeppner, S., 615
Haxby, T. V., 142
Hayes, J. R., 333
Hayes, R., 457
Hayes, S., 496
Hayne, H., 301
Haynes, M. C., 702
Hays, K. F., 569
Haywood, T. W., 653
Hazan, C., 675–676
He, J., 570, 571
Healy, D., 640, 641, 642
Healy, E., 483
Healy, M. D., 501
Heaps, C. M., 300
Hearon, B., 628
Hearst, E., 238
Heatherton, T. F., 403
Heaton, T. B., 471
Heckler, S. E., 271
Hedegaard, M., 457
Hedges, M., 649
Hedlund, J., 368
Heiby, E. M., 623
Heider, F., 668
Heilman, M. E., 702, A-27
Heiman, R. J., 688
Heine, S. J., 14, 15, 672
Heino, R. D., 679
Heinrichs, R. W., 598
Helft, M., A-29
Helgeson, V. S., 550
Heller, W., 121
Hellige, J. B., 122, 123, 481
Hellstrom, P. M., 399, 401
Helmholtz, H. von, 144, 163, 164
Helms, J. E., 381
Helson, R., 469
Hempel, S., 357
Hemphill, S. A., 448
Hen, R., 544
Hencke, R. W., 456
Henderson, K. E, 405
Hendrick, C., 677
Hendrick, S. S., 677
Hendrickx, H., 133
Hendriks, M., 168
Henley, T. B., 5
Hennigsen, P., 587
Henriksson, M. M., 52
Henry, J. K., 401
Henry, K. R., 161
Henry, M. E., 643
Henry, P. J., 384
Hepper, P., 442
Herbener, E. S., 469
Herbert, J. D., 636
Herbst, S., 554
Herek, G. M., 415
Heres, S., 642
Herman, L. M., 324
Herman, R. A., 96–97
Herman-Giddens, M. E., 464
Hermann, R. C., 643
Hermanns, D., 239
Hermans, H. J. M., 15
Herrmann, D., 308, 310
Herrnstein, R. J., 367, 373, 378, 390
Herscovitch, L., A-27
Hersh, S. M., 693
Herskovits, M. J., 159
Hertwig, R., 66, 332, 344, 347
Herz, R. S., 168

Herzog, D. B., 613
Herzog, H. A., 68
Hessels, S., 296
Hetherington, E. M., 485
Hetherington, M. M., 401
Hettema, J. M., 235., 584
Hettich, P. I., 29
Hevern, V. W., A-39
Hewson, C., 65
Hewstone, M., 702
Hicks, J. L., 306
Higgins, A. J., 451, 677
Higgins, E. T., 41
Highhouse, S., 705
Hilgard, E. R., 5, 24, 209, 211, 257, 361
Hilgard, J., 209
Hilgetag, C. C., 94
Hill, G. W., A-23
Hill, J. O, 405
Hill, M. J., 632
Hiller, J. B., 603
Hiller, W., 587, 588
Hilliard, A. G., III, 381
Hillmert, C. J., 683
Hilton, H. J., 150
Hilton, J. L., 666
Hines, M., 481
Hingson, R., 219
Hinsz, V. B., 697
Hirsh, I. J., 161
Hirt, E. R., 292
Hitch, G., 283
Ho, B., 113, 598, 599, 603
Hobson, J. A., 207, 224
Hocevar, D., 388
Hochberg, J., 151, 152
Hodapp, R. M., 369, 370
Hodges, S. D., 684
Hodgkin, A., 81–82
Hoek, H. W., 614
Hofbauer, R. K., 211
Hofer, S. M., 473
Hoff, E., 319, 321, 322, 323
Hoffman, E., 501
Hoffman, R. E., 94
Hoffman, R. R., III, 557
Hoffrage, U., 344
Hoffstein, L., 223
Hofstede, G., 671
Hogan, J., 526
Hogan, M. F., 645, 652
Hogan, R., 386, 526
Hogarth, R. M., 337, 343, 346
Hoge, C. W., 584
Hogg, M. A., 700
Hoigaard, R., 695
Holahan, C. J., 371, 547, 556, 597
Holden, C., 318, 640
Holden, G. W., 253
Holder, M. D., 324
Holland, C. C., 691
Holland, C. R., 381
Holland, K., 471
Holland, R. W., 168
Hollander, E., 472, 582
Hollands, C., 67
Hollenstein, T., 466
Hollifield, M. A., 587, 588
Holling, H., 389
Hollingworth, L. S., 6, 20
Hollis, J. H., 401
Hollis, K. L., 256
Hollon, S. D., 632, 636
Holmans, P., 594
Holmbeck, G., 632

Holmberg, S., 61
Holmes, D. S., 212, 298
Holmes, J. G., 674
Holmes, T. H., 537, 538
Holschuh, J. L., 31
Holtgraves, T., 61
Holt-Lunstad, J., 556
Holyoak, K. J., 332, 333
Honeycutt, H., 16
Hong, G. K., 650
Honig, W. K., 246
Honzik, C. H., 257
Hooker, E., 196
Hooley, J. M., 603, 604
Hooper, J., 121, 123
Hopcroft, R. L., 411
Hopko, D. R., 364
Hopper, C., 289
Hopper, K., 601
Horgan, T. G., 480
Horn, J. L., 378, 473
Horn, J. M., 375
Hornstein, G. A., 7
Horowitz, F. D., 9
Horrey, W. J., 278
Horwath, E., 583
Hospers, H. J., 561
Hossain, J. L., 190
Hotopf, M., 588
Houston, D. M., 320
Houts, A. C., 555
Howard, A., 17
Howard, D. J., 705
Howard, M. S., 677
Howe, M. J. A., 372
Howe, M. L., 457
Howland, R. H., 594
Hoyer, W. J., 473, 474
Hrdy, S. B., 412
Hsee, C. K., 339, 433
Hsiang, R., 641
Hsu, L. K. G., 613
Hsu, L. M., 626
Hu, F. B., 559
Hu, L., 506
Hu, T. W., 650
Hu, Y., 506
Hua, J. Y., 85
Hubel, D., 11, 14, ,101, 124, 141–142
Hublin, C. G. M., 200, 201, 202
Hudman, K. S., 558
Hudson, J. I., 299, 614
Hudson, W., 154
Hudspeth, A. J., 163
Huesmann, L. R., 263
Huettel, S. A., 95, 103
Huey, E. D., 103, 104
Huey, L. Y., 645, 651
Huff, C., 66
Hughes, J., 88
Hughes, J. R., 558
Hughes, S. M., 679
Hugo, F. J., 585
Huitt, B., 366
Hulin, C., A-27, A-28
Hull, C., 21, 396
Hulme, C., 287
Hultsch, D. F., 474
Hummel, J. E., 150
Hunsley, J., 527
Hunt, E., 332, 385
Hunt, H., 206
Hunt, J. M., 683
Hunt, S. P., 170
Hunter, J., 367, 368, 381

Huntsinger, E. T., 677
Hurvich, L. M., 146
Husband, T. H., 300
Huston, A. C., 261
Huston, T. L., 674
Huttenlocher, J., 456
Huttenlocher, P. R., 85, 125
Huxley, A., 81–82
Hwang, W. C., 650
Hybels, C. F., 472
Hyde, J. S., 416, 480
Hyde, M., 223
Hyde, T. M., 639
Hyman, I. A., 252
Hyman, I. E., Jr., 300

I

Iacoboni, M., 103
Iacono, W. G., 421, 589, 603
Iams, J. D., 443
Ickovics, J. R., 560
Idsis, Y., 670
Iezzi, T., 588
Ilgen, D. R., A-27
Inciardi, J. A., 214
Infante, J. R., 213
Ingvaldsen, R. P., 695
Innocenti, G. M., 482
Irvine, S. H., 368
Irwin, M. R., 200
Isaacowitz, D. M., 544
Ismail, B., 603
Isometsa, E. T., 52
Israel, M., 614
Iversen, L., 99
Iversen, S., 99
Iwata, B. A., 250
Iyo. M., 81
Izard, C. E., 419, 422, 423, 424, 427,
    428

J

Jablin, F. M., A-22
Jackendoff, R., 325
Jackicic, J., 569
Jacklin, C., 21, 483
Jackson, D. N., 492
Jackson, S., 271
Jackson, W. E., 552
Jacob, R. G., 637
Jacob, S., 168
Jacobs, B. L., 594
Jacobs, D. F., 1, 2
Jacobs, G. H., 146
Jacobs, H. S., 472
Jacobs, W. S., 219
Jacobson, C. K., 471
Jacobson, E., 224
Jacobson, G., 444
Jacovitz, D., 450
Jacoby, L. L., 296
Jacquez, F. M., 466
Jaffe, H. W., 561
Jager, G., 221
Jain, S. P., 684
James, J. E., 559
James, W., 4, 5–6, 10, 20, 186,
    426–427
James, W. H., 416
Jamison, K. R., 389, 592
Jang, K. L., 514, 544
Janicki-Deverts, D., 555
Janig, W., 421, 427

Janis, I. L., 535, 541, 698
Janoff-Bulman, R., 432
Janofsky, J. S., 607
Janowsky, J. S., 110
Janssen, E., 412, 413
Jarvin, L., 361
Javitt, D. C., 87, 88, 601
Jefferson, J. W., 641
Jeffrey, R. W., 405
Jensen, A. R., 363, 373, 375,
    378–379, 382, 390
Jensen, E., 124
Jensen, M. P., 210
Jensen-Campbell, A., 492
Jenson, J. D., A-39
Jessell, T. M., 88, 170, 174
Jevning, R., 212
Jick, H., 640
Jick, S. S., 640
Jindal, K., 594
Johansen, C., 555
John, O. P., 492, 508, 567, 673
Johnson, A., 305
Johnson, A. N., 678
Johnson, B. A., 219, 226
Johnson, B. T., 280, 683
Johnson, C., 666
Johnson, D., 68
Johnson, D. E., A-28
Johnson, E. O., 58, 430, 431
Johnson, J. A., 563, 564
Johnson, M. E., 350
Johnson, M. K., 280, 292, 293
Johnson, M. L., 445
Johnson, S. B., 562, 563, 564
Johnson, S. L., 593
Johnson, V., 406–407
Johnston, J. C., 148, 278
Joiner, T. E., Jr., 597
Jones, B. E., 86, 197
Jones, C., 469
Jones, E. E., 7, 668, 669
Jones, J., 322
Jones, L. V., 363
Jonides, J., 284, 287
Jordan, B. D., 679
Jordan, P. J., 386
Jorgensen, R. S., 567
Josse, G., 122
Jourdan, A., 12
Juang, L., 25
Judge, T. A., 53, 57, 71, 432
Juffer, F., 376
Julien, R. M., 214, 216
Jung, C., 7, 11, 499–500, 628, 523
Jusczyk, P. W., 320

K

Kaas, J. H., 104
Kabat-Zinn, J., 213
Kaelber, C. T., 579
Kagan, J., 448, 529, 584
Kahai, S. S., A-24
Kahan, T. L., 204, 280, 293
Kahane, H., 350
Kahn, K., 65
Kahneman, D, 337, 341–342, 343,
    344, 345, 346, 348, 349, 430, 433,
    616, 617
Kaida, K., 223
Kaiser, P., 138
Kako, E., 324
Kalaria, R. N., 553
Kales, J. D., 224, 225

Kalichman, S. C., 561
Kalin, N. H., 423
Kalivas, P. W., 218
Kalmijn, M., 673
Kalton, G., 61
Kaltsas, G., 551
Kameda, T., 697
Kamin, L., 379, 382
Kanaya, T., 369
Kanazawa, S., 373
Kandall, S. R., 421
Kandel, E. R., 82, 84, 85, 89, 99, 140,
    170, 302
Kandell, J. J., 546
Kane, H., 363
Kane, J., 563
Kane, J. M., 186, 639
Kanowitz, J., 61
Kant, A. K., 559
Kaplan, A. G., 655
Kaplan, D. S., 538
Kaplan, H., 446
Kaplan, H. B., 538
Kaplan, H. I., 551
Kaplan, R. E., A-24
Kaplan, S. T., 103
Kapur, S., 643
Karasawa, M., 425
Karasu, T. B., 628
Karau, S. J., 695, 696
Kardiner, A., 519
Karnath, H.O., 93, 97
Karney, B. R., 673
Karpicke, J. D., 308
Karr, M., 28
Karremans, J. C., 133
Kass, S. J., 278
Kassel, J. D., 546
Kassem, L., 584
Kasser, T., 412, 430, 512
Kassin, S. M., 312, 703
Katigbak, M. S., 519
Katz, A. N., 323
Katz, J., 597
Katzman, M. A., 614
Kaufman, A. S., 361, 363, 364
Kaufman, G., 470
Kaufman, J. C., 388, 389
Kaufman, L., 159
Kavesh, L., 664
Kay, J., 628
Kay, P., 327
Kay, R. L., 628
Kaye, J. A., 640
Kaye, W. H., 86, 614
Kayser, C., 174
Kazdin, A., 253, 267, 632, 623
Kazmerski, V. A., 323
Keane, T. M., 584
Keating, D. P., 373, 465
Keck, P. E., 598, 641
Keefauver, S. P., 203
Keefe, F. J., 555
Keefe, R. S. E., 601
Keefer, L., 554
Keegan, T., 700
Keenan, J. P., 680
Keesey, R. E., 99, 405
Kehoe, E. J., 237
Keinan, G., 548, 549
Keith, J., 598
Keith-Spiegel, P., 655
Keller, H. E., 68

Keller, M. B., 591
Keller, P. A., 686
Kelley, B. D., 603
Kelley, H. H., 27, 668
Kellogg, S. H., 637
Kelly, J., 471
Kelly, J. P., 174
Kelly, K. M., 555
Kelly, P. J., 196
Kelly, S. J., 444
Kelman, H. C., 66, 691
Kelsey, J. E., 640
Kelsoe, J., 594
Kelsoe, J. R., 115
Keltner, D., 423, 424, 673
Kemeny, M. E., 555
Kempen, H. J. G., 15
Kendall, P. C., 632
Kendler, K. S., 112, 584, 591, 594,
    597, 601
Kenfield, S. A., 559
Kennedy, G. A., 539
Kennedy, J. K. J., 115, 377
Kennedy, T. E., 302
Kenrick, D. T., 181, 480, 481, 507,
    679
Kent, R. N., 61
Keren, G., 346
Kermer, D. A., 350
Kernan, J. B., 683
Kerns, K. A., 450
Kerr, N. L., 698
Kershaw, T. C., 332
Kerwin, R., 640
Kesner, R. P., 103
Kessen, W., 453
Kessler, R. C., 556, 580, 584, 592,
    623, 624
Kester, J. D., 278
Ketterlinus, R. D., 449
Key, C. B., 376
Key, W. B., 132
Khalsa, S., 189
Khan, A., 598
Khan, M., 279
Khashan, A. S., 603
Khersonsky, D., 673
Khroyan, T. V., 558
Kidd, K. K., 373, 516
Kidder, D. L., A-27
Kiecolt-Glaser, J., 554–555
Kiefer, A. K., 407
Kieffer, K. M., 538
Kiehle, U.-C., 695
Kiernan, M., 568
Kieseppa, T., 594
Kiesler, C. A., 576, 645, 652
Kiewra, K. A., 31
Kihlstrom, J. F., 133, 209, 210,
    211–212, 298, 299, 589, 590
Kikuchi, Y., 279
Killiany, R. J., 472
Kim, A., 692
Kim, E.-J., 549
Kim, K. H., 389
Kim, T., 469
Kimmel, A. J., 67
Kimmel, M. S., 413
Kimura, D., 122, 482
Kinder, B. N., 613, 614
King, A. C., 223, 568
King, B. H., 369, 370
King, B. M., 399
King, G. R., 87
Kinicki, A. J., A-22

Kinnunen, T., 58
Kinsbourne, M., 187, 306, 482
Kinsey, A., 414
Kinzler, K. D., 460
Kippin, T. E., 236
Kirby, S., 325
Kirk, E. E., A-43
Kirk, S. A., 577
Kirker, W. S., 280
Kirkpatrick, B., 599
Kirkpatrick, L. A., 451, 677
Kirkpatrick, S. A., A-24
Kirmayer, L. J., 587, 588
Kirsch, I., 210, 212
Kirschenbaum, H., 12
Kitayama, S., 336, 425, 522, 523, 672, 688
Kitchens, A., 122
Kivimaki, M., 557
Klapper, D., 349
Klauer, K. C., 287
Klayman, J., 348
Klein, E., 584
Klein, M., 628
Klein, P. D., 385
Klein, T. W., 220
Klein, W. M., 342, 561
Kleinke, C. L., 423, 544
Kleinknecht, E. E., 300
Kleinmurtz, B., 593
Kleitman, N., 185–186
Klerman, E. B., 193
Klerman, G. L., 648
Kliegel, M., 474
Kline, P., 366, 526
Kling, C., 359
Klingenberg, W. D., 527
Klinger, M. R., 132
Klinger, R., 432
Klipper, M. Z., 224, 568
Klohnen, E. C., 673
Klosch, G., 224
Kluckhohn, C., 519
Kluft, R. P., 301, 589
Klump, K. L., 86
Klymenko, V., 142
Knapp, T. J., 535
Knauss, W., 631
Knecht, S., 94, 123
Knight, J., 421
Knight, R. T., 104
Knippenberg, A., 666
Knowlton, B., 305
Knutsson, A., 190
Ko, S., J., 505
Kochanska, G., 450
Koegel, P., 653
Koehler, J. J., 342
Koelling, R. A., 255
Koester, J., 82
Koestner, R., 418
Kofodimos, J. R., A-24
Kohatsu, N. D., 200
Kohlberg, L., 460–462
Kohlenberg, R. J., 503
Kohler, J. K., 485
Kohn, P. M., 535
Kohut, H., 628
Kok, G., 561 , 684
Kokkinos, P., 559
Kolb, B., 104
Kolb, R., 587
Koob, G. F., 101, 218
Koocher, G. P., 355
Koopman, B., 425

Kop, W. J., 551, 553
Kopacz, M., 702
Kopelwicz, A., 601
Kopta, S. M., 632
Koren, D., 584
Koriat, A., 288, 308, 313
Korn, J. H., 10, 66
Kornhaber, M. L., 385
Kornstein, S. G., 592
Koropeckyj-Cox, T., 470
Kory, R. B., 212
Koss, M. P., 413, 414
Kosslyn, S. M., 122
Kostreva, M., 191
Kotovsky, K., 333
Kotulak, R., 124
Koughan, M., A-15
Koukounas, E., 412
Kouzma, N. M., 539
Kozlowski, S. W., A-23
Kozorovitskiy, Y., 104
Kozulin, A., 457
Kracke, W., 206
Kraft, U., 224
Krajicek, N. K., 150
Krakauer, J., 395–396
Kramer, M., 205
Kramer, P. D., 501
Krames, L., 659
Krantz, D. H., 346
Krantz, D. S., 552, 553, 555
Krantz, J., 150
Krasner, M., 64
Kraus, J. E., 639
Kraus, L. A., 556
Kraus, S. J., 682
Krause, M., 256
Krebs, D. L., 667
Kreitzman, L., 188
Kribbs, N. B., 196
Kring, A. M., 599
Kristeller, J. L., 213
Kroger, J., 467
Krojgaard, P., 457
Krosnick, J. A., 54, 61
Krueger, F., 103
Krueger, J., 669, 703
Krueger, R. F., 359, 430, 431, 605
Krueger, W. C. F., 309
Krug, K. S., 285
Kruglanski, A. W., 684, 687
Krull, D. S., 669
Kryger, M. H., 202, 223
Kubovsky, M. 132
Kuczaj, S. A., 324
Kuehn, B. M., 644
Kuhn, D., 465
Kuhn, J., 597
Kulich, A. R., 598
Kulik, J. A., 683
Kumar, V. M., 189
Kumaresan, V., 218
Kung, S., 75
Kuo, Y, T., 401
Kuper, N. A., 280
Kupferman, L., 99
Kurtz, K. J., 334
Kurzban, R., 15
Kusel, S. J., 211
Kushida, C. A., 192
Kutchins, H. 577
Kuther, T., A-36, A-37
Kwan, L., 327
Kwan, V. S. Y., 469

Ky, K. N., 125
Kyrou, I., 543

L

LaBar, K. S., 422
LaBerge, S., 204, 225
LaBine, G., 529
LaBine, S. J., 529
Laborit, H., 646
Labouvie-Vief, G., 468
La Cerra, P., 15
Lacey, S. E., 284
Lachman, M. E., 469
Lachter, J., 277
Laczo, R. M., A-18
Lader, M. H., 201
Lafreniere, K., 535
Laitinen, J., 403
Lakein, A., 28
Lakin, M., 630
Lam, S., 301
Lamb, H. R., 449, 652, 653
Lamb, M. E., 485
Lamberg, L., 207
Lambert, M. J., 578, 632, 609, 632, 633, 654, 656
Lambiase, J., 270
Lampe, A., 555
Lampi, M., 445
Lampinen, J. M., 293
Landabaso, M. A., 635
Landau, M. J., 518
Landel-Graham, J., 554, 555
Landrigan, D., 158
Lane, D. M., 57
Lane, M., 624
Laney, C., 299
Lang, P. J., 420
Langdon, P. E., 652
Lange, C., 426–427
Langeland, W., 590
Langenbucher, J., 579
Langevin, R., 413
Langlois, J. H., 665
Lanyon, R. I., 526
Lapiere, Y. D., 640
LaPierre, R. T., 682, 700
Lapsley, D. K., 461
Lareau, A., 379
Larsen, J. T., 420
Larsen, R. J., 433
Larson, R., 463
Laruelle, M., 87, 88, 601
Larzelere, R. E., 253
Latané, B., 694, 695
Laties, V. G., 242
La Torre, M. A., 16
Lattal, K. A., 242
Latz, S., 196
Lauderdale, D. S., 200
Laughlin, H., 546, 582
Laughlin, P. R., 698
Laughren, T., 640
Laumann, E. O., 407
Laurence, J.-R., 298
Lauriello, J., 598
Laursen, B., 471
Lavie, N., 147, 277
Lavin, C., 664
Lawler, E. E., A-23
Lawler, J., 320
Lawless, H. T., 167
Lazarus, A. A., 420, 649, 656
Lazarus, R. S., 17, 535, 540

Leary, M. R., 398
Leavitt, F., 214, 216, 301
LeBoeuf, M., 30
LeBoeuf, R. A., 338, 339, 343, 344
Leckman, J. F., 583
Ledford, G. E., A-23
LeDoux, J. E., 100, 304 , 419, 420, 422, 427
Lee, C. M., 527
Lee, J. E., 558
Lee, K., 492
Lee, R. M., 649
Lee, R. T., 549
Lee, S., 68, 614
Lee, Y., 81
Lee-Chiong, T., 201
Leech, S. L., 444
Leeper, R. W., 152
Lefcourt, H. M., 566, 567
Leff, J., 603, 604, 652
Legault, E., 298
Lehman, D. R., 15, 300, 404
Lehrer, P., 555, 568
Leibovic, K. N., 137
Leighton, J. P., 331
Leiter, M., 549
Lejuez, C. W., 587
LeMagnen, J., 400
Le Moal, M., 101, 218
Lenert., L., 64, 65
Lenhart, A., 678
Lennie, P., 145
Lennings, C. J., A-28
Lenton, R., 679
Lentz, E., A-22
Leo, J., 513
Leopold, D. A., 152
LePine, J. A., A-28
Lepine, R., 284
Lerman, H., 502
Lerner, J. S., 339
Lerner, M. J., 670
Lesage, A. D., 652
Leslie, E. M., 460
Lesperance, F., 553
Lester, D., 1
Lester, N., 640
Letiecq, B.-L., 485
Lett, H,. S., 554, 556
Leucht, S., 639
Leuner, B., 104, 303
Leung, A. K. Y., 327
Levant, R. F., 645
LeVay, S., 414
Levenson, R. W., 423, 427
Levenstein, S., 555
Leventhal, E. A., 562
Leventhal, H., 427, 562
Levesque, M. J., 408
Levin, L., 703
Levine, A., 466
Levine, B., 306
Levine, J. M., 688, 695
Levine, M. P., 615
Levine, M. W., 142
Levine, R., 677
LeVine, R. A., 519
Levine, R. V., 51–52, 54, 57
Levinthal, C. F., 214
Levis, D. J., 251, 585
Levitsky, D. A., 401
Levy, G. D., 482
Levy, J., 106, 123
Lew, R. A., 190
Lewandowsky, S., 283

Lewin, K., 10, 536
Lewinsohn, P. M., 597
Lewis, C., 485
Lewis, M., 466
Lewis-Fernandez, R., 611
Lewontin, R., 376
Li, K. Z. H., 284
Li, N. P., 679
Li, S. C., 473
Li, T.-K., 579
Li, W., 168, 506
Li, Y., 642
Liberman, R. P., 601
Lichten, W., 369, 370
Lichtenstein, B., 341, 347, 348
Lichtenstein, S., 313
Lichtenthal, W. G., 579
Lickey, M. E., 641
Lickliter, R., 16
Liden, R. C., 696
Lieberman, J. A., 600, 639, 677
Liebert, L. L., 508
Liebert, R. M., 508
Lien, M.C., 278
Likert, R., A-23
Lilienfeld, S. O., 527, 589, 590, 632, 654
Lin, D. Y., 27
Lin, S. W., 226
Linde, J. A., 506
Linden, D. E. J., 93
Lindenberger, U., 473
Lindenmeyer, J. P., 598
Linders, A., 413
Lindren, H. C., 31
Lindsay, M., 1
Lindsay, P. H., 148
Lindsay, S. D., 292, 293, 299, 301
Lindsley, O. R., 634
Linford, K. M., 669
Link, B. G., 538
Linton, R., 519
Linz, D., 413
Lipert, J., 104
Lippa, R. A., 371
Lipton, J. S., 458
Lisanby, S. H., 94, 643
Little, A. C., 181, 679
Litwin, G. H., 418
Liu, R. X., 538
Liu, T., 555
Livesley, W. J., 514
Lizarraga, M. L. S., 35
Lledo, R. M., 104
Lloyd, M., 22, A-30
Locke, B. Z., 579
Locke, E. A., A-24
Lockhart, R. S., 278, 294, 295, 297
Locurto, C., 375
Loehlin, J. C., 375, 378, 515
Loewenstein, G., 339, 341, 433
Loewenstein, R. J., 589
Loftus, E. F., 75, 289, 291–292, 299, 300, 301, 312
Loftus, G. R., 281
Logue, A. W., 118
Lohmann, R. L., 206
Long, C. N., 399
Long, J. E., Jr., 623
Longman, D. G., 31
Lonner, W. J., 15
Looper, K. J., 587, 588
Lopes, M. C., 202
Lopes, P. N., 386
Losada, M. F., 541
Lott, B., 379, 407, 650

Low, J., 125
Lowden, A., 178
Lowe, C. A., 408
Lowenstein, J., 334
Lowery, B. S., 702
Lowinson, J. H., 214
Lozoff, B., 196
Lu, J., 196
Lubinski, D., 373
Luborsky, L., 8, 628, 632, 656
Lucas, J. A., 304, 305
Lucas, R. E., 432, 433
Lucchina, L. A., 167
Luchins, A., 330–331
Luckman, S. M., 399
Ludwig, A, M., 389, 372
Luecken, L. J., 677
Lugaresi, E., 223
Luh, C. W., 295
Lund, O. C. H., 492
Lundberg, U., 543
Lundberg, U., 543
Luntz, B. K., 606
Luo, S., 673
Lupien, S. J., 541
Lurie, P., 642
Luthans, F., 507
Luthe, W., 224
Lutz, A., 212
Lutz, T. A., 399
Lutz, W., 350, 425
Lykken, D. T., 421, 422, 431, 513
Lynch, G., 88, 303
Lynch, M. A., 253
Lyness, J. M., 472, 632
Lynn, M., 705
Lynn, S. J., 208, 210, 291, 299, 300, 589, 590
Lynne, S. D., 464
Lyons-Ruth, K., 450
Lytton, H., 252
Lyubomirsky, S., 432, 567

M

Maas, J. B., 223
Maass, A., 702
Maccoby, E. E., 21, 515
MacCoun, R. J., 59, 61
MacDonald, K., 529
MacDonald, S. E., 253
MacDonald, T. K., 681
MacGregor, J. N., 331, 332
Macht, M., 403
MacIan, P., 412–413
Mack, A., 147, 219, 226
MacKellar, D. A., 561
Mackintosh, N. J., 366
MacLean, A. W., 198
MacLean, P., 100, 422
MacMillan, H. L., 298, 299
Macrae, C. N., 665, 666
Macrae, M., 237
MacWhinney, B., 321, 326
Madden, M., 678
Maddux, W. W., 671
Madon, S., 700
Madsen, K. B., 398
Madsen, L., 421
Maes, J., 703
Maestripieri, D., 411
Magnavita, J. J., 628
Magnusson, D., 447
Maguire, W., 142, 148
Maher, B. A., 598
Maheswaran, D., 683, 684
Maheu, F. S., 541

Mahoney, M., 636
Mahowald, M. W., 201, 203
Maier, N. R. F., 331
Maier, S. F., 174
Main, M., 450
Main, T., 653
Maio, G. R., 681, 683
Maislin, G., 197
Mak, T., 483
Malamuth, N., 413, 414
Malanos, A. B., 492
Maldonado, J. R., 208, 589
Malenka, R. C., 87, 218, 423
Maletzky, B. M., 636
Malnick, B., 168
Malone, P. S., 669
Malone, W., 671
Malthus, T., 116
Maltzman, I., 226
Mander, S. R., 639
Mandler, G., 13, 541
Maner, J. K., 584, 665
Mann, J. J., 593, 594, 643
Mann, N., 401
Mann, R. D., A-24
Mann, T., 405
Mannarelli, T., 505
Mannion, H., 181
Manson, J. E., 403
Mantavani, A., 94
Mantyh, P. W., 170
Manz, C. C., A-24
Maragiote, R. A., 645
Maratsos, M. P., 457
Marcelino, A. S., 402
Marcenes, W. G., 555
Marcia, J., 467
Marcus, E. R., 627
Marcus, G. F., 322
Marcus-Newhall, A., 545
Marder, S. R., 639
Margolskee, R. F., 167
Margraf, J., 588
Maric, A., 413
Maris, R. W., 466
Mark, V., 122
Markman, E. M., 321
Markman, K. D., 292
Markofski, M. M., 560
Markowitsch, H., J., 304
Marks, G. A., 196
Marks, I. M., 234
Markus, H. R., 15, 25, 26, 482, 522, 523, 672, 688, 692
Marler, P. L., 61
Marschark, M., 279
Marsella, A. J., 611
Marsh, E. J., 292, 293
Marsh, R. L., 306
Marshall, A. D., 584
Marshall, G. P., 555
Marteau, T. M., 562, 563
Martel, L. D., 677
Martin, A., 306
Martin, C. L., 482, 483
Martin, J. H., 92
Martin, J. N., 446, 448
Martin, L., 327
Martin, L. R., 371, 492, 557
Martin, N. G., 416
Martin, R. A., 567
Martin, R., 562
Mashek, D. J., 462, 675
Maslach, C., 549
Maslen, R. J. C., 322
Maslow, A., 11, 21, 510–512, 523

Massaro, D. W., 281
Massen, C., 311
Mast, M. S., 480
Masters, W., 406–407
Mastro, D., E., 702
Masuda, T., 336
Mata, R., 683
Mathy, R. M., 65
Matias, I., 400
Matlin, M. W., 482
Matsumoto, D., 15, 25, 424, 425, 692
Matte, T. D., 443
Matthews, G., 386
Matthey, S., 570
Mattia, J. I., 604
Matusov, E., 457
Maughan, B., 444
Maurice, J. K., 181
Mauro, R., 425
Mayer, J., 400
Mayer, J. D., 385, 386
Mayou, R., 587
Mays, V. M., 15
Mazzoni, G., 210, 291, 301
McAdams, D. P., 469
McAnarney, A. R., 464
McBride-Chang, C., 483
McBurney, D. H., 89, 408
McCabe, M., 412
McCabe, R. E., 232, 235, 582, 585
McCandless, B. D., 379
McCarley, R. W., 192, 207
McCarthy, G., 95
McCarthy, M. K., 655
McCartney, K., 451
McCarty, R., 542
McCauley, M. E., 279
McClanahan, T. M., 642
McClelland, D. C., 397, 417, 418
McClelland, J. L., 148, 289–290
McClendon, G. T., 630, 631
McClure, E. B., 583
McClure, K., 313
McConkey, K. M., 211, 291
McConnell, J. V., 132, 302
McCord, J., 252
McCoy, S. L., 472
McCrae, R. R., 469, 491–492, 519, 522, 525, 566
McCready, D., 159
McCrink, K., 458–459
McCrory, C., 382
McCullough, M. E., 568
McDade, D. M., 399
McDaniel, M. A., 306, 307, 310, 383, A-20
McDermott, K. M., 300, 301
McDonald, C., 115
McDonald, E. H., 292
McDonald, R. V., 237
McDonald, W. M., 643
McDonald, W. T., 296, 297
McElroy, S. L., 641
McElroy, T., 535
McEwen, B. S., 109
McFarlin, B. K., 560
McGaugh, J. L., 304
McGeoch, J. A., 296, 297
McGlashan, T. H., 600
McGrath, J. E., 535, A-23
McGraw, K. O., 65
McGregor, H. A., 518
McGrew, J. H., 652
McGue, M., 374
McGuffin, P., 115, 444

McGuigan, F. J., 568
McHale, S. M., 483
McHugh, P. R., 298, 589
McIntosh, W. E., 665
McKean, K., 343, 348
McKelvie, P., 125
McKenna, J. J., 195
McKenna, K. Y. A., 65, 694, 678
McLay, R. N., 75
McLean, D. E., 538
McLellan, A. T., 226
McLeod, D., 483
McLouglin, K., 1
McLoyd, V. C., 379, 485
McMahon, F. J., 584
McManus, M. A., A-21
McNally, R. J., 299, 584, 585
McNamara, P., 204
McNaughton, B. L., 303
McNeil, E. B., 132
McNeil, T. F., 603
McNeilis, E., 191
McNeill, D., 290
McNulty, J. K., 49–50, 433, 673
McWhorter, K. T., 31
McWilliams, L. A., 584
McWilliams, N., 7, 626
Meade, M. L., 293
Means, M. K., 200
Mebert, C. J., 253
Mechanic, D., 577, 624, 651
Mednick, S., 603
Medori, R., 639
Medway, E. J., 677
Mehra, R., 220
Meichenbaum, D., 636
Meiser, T., 287
Meister, B., 399
Melanson, K. J., 559
Mellers, B. A., 49, 344
Mello, J. A., A-23
Mellor, D., 700
Meloy, M. G., 348
Meltzer, H. Y., 639
Melzack, R., 170, 171
Memon, A., 312
Mendel, G., 117
Mendelson, W. B., 197, 201
Mennella, J. A., 402
Menninger, W. W., 651
Mentzer, R. L., 32
Merckelbach, H., 235, 585
Meredith, M. A., 140
Merikangas, K. R., 594
Merikle, P. M., 132, 133, 187
Mesquita, B., 425
Messer, S. B., 7
Messner, M., 683
Metalsky, G. I., 597
Metcalfe, B., 526
Metzger, A., 471
Metzger, E. D., 643
Meyer, D. E., 289
Meyer, J. P., A-26, A-27
Meyer, R. E., 226
Meyer, R. G., 208, 291
Meyer-Bahlburg, H. F. L., 416
Meyers, E., 142
Mezulis, A. H., 671, 672
Mezzich, J. E., 611
Michaels, S., 415
Midgett, J., 155
Miklowitz, D. J., 593
Mikulincer, M., 451, 676, 677
Milar, K. S., 4
Milgram, S., 21, 689–691

Milkie, M. A., 471
Miller, A. C., 108, 123
Miller, A. G., 691
Miller, E. K., 104
Miller, G., 283, 318
Miller, G. A., 14
Miller, G. E., 109, 544, 551, 555
Miller, G. M., 679
Miller, I. J., 167
Miller, J. G., 462
Miller, J. M., 684
Miller, L. S., 263
Miller, M. B., 106
Miller, N., 502, 536
Miller, N. E., 68
Miller, P. J., 674
Miller, R. R., 238, 645, 648
Miller, S. D., 632
Miller-Anderson, L., 600
Millman, J., 32
Millon, T., 605
Mills, J., 686
Millstone, E., 67
Milner, B., 122, 304
Milner, P., 100
Mineka, S., 235, 255, 256, 260, 585
Miner, M., 472
Minton, H. L., 361
Miranda, J., 588, 649, 650
Mirescu, C., 544
Misra, R., 539
Mistlberger, R. E., 189
Mitchell, J. E., 613
Mitchell, K. J., 292
Mitsonis, C., 555
Mittal, V., 549, 604
Miyamoto, S., 639
Miyamoto, Y., 336
Modestin, J., 589
Moe, A., 311
Moffat, S. D., 481
Moffitt, T., 115, 492, 606
Moghaddam, F. M., 26
Mogil, J. S., 170
Mohammed, F. B., 223
Mohrman, S. A., A-23
Mojtabai, R., 624
Mokdad, A. H., 403
Moldin, S. O., 113
Monahan, J., 578
Monahan, J. L., 132
Monastra, V. J., 636
Moncrieff, J., 642
Monk, C. E., 443
Monk, T. H., 190
Monroe, S. M., 537, 597
Monteggia, L. M., 595
Monteith, M. J., 666
Montgomery, G. H., 210
Moore, B. C. J., 162
Moore, J., 9
Moore, K. L., 442, 443
Moore, R. Y., 188
Moore, S., 181
Moos, R. H., 547, 556
Mora, S., 559
Morahan-Martin, J., 546
Moran, T. H., 401
Morecraft, R. J., 100
Moreland, R. L., 695
Moreno, F. A., 86, 594
Moreno, M. V., 649
Morey, L. C., 605
Morgan, H., 385
Morgan, M. J., 221

Morgan, R. D., A-36, A-37
Moriarty, J. L., 93
Morin, C. M., 202
Morley, J. E., 472
Morokoff, P. J., 408
Morris, A. S., 464
Morris, C. D., 297
Morris, E. K., 9
Morris, M. E., 505
Morris, M. M., 556
Morrison, A. K., 645, 652
Morrison, A. R., 193
Morrison, C., 401
Mortimer, J. A., 473
Morton, A., 439
Moruzzi, G., 196
Moscovitch, M., 279
Moseman, S. E., 641
Mosher, D. L., 412
Moskowitz, J. T., 544, 550
Moss, M. B., 304
Most, S. B., 147
Motivala, S. J., 200
Motz, M., 279
Mowrer, O. H., 251, 585
Mrazek, D. A., 75
Mrdjenovic, G., 401
Mroczek, D., 469, 492
Mueller, C. W., A-27
Mueser, K. T., 599, 600
Mullen, B., 666, 698
Mullen, J. L., 30, 31
Muller, M., 109
Mulligan, N. W., 277
Mullin, L. I., 480
Mullington, J. M., 197
Mullins, S., 606
Mulvaney, M. K., 253
Mulvihill, T., 639
Munck, A., 544
Munholland, K. A., 450
Munk-Jorgensen, P., 652
Munzber, H., 401
Murdock, B., 309
Muris, P., 235
Muris, P., 506
Murnen, S. K., 483, 614
Murphy, J. M., 579
Murphy, K. C., 115
Murphy, K. R., 368, 386
Murphy, S. T., 132
Murray, C., 367, 373, 378, 390
Murray, E. A., 422
Murray, H. A., 398, 519, 526, 527
Murray, M. A., 148
Murray, R. M., 220, 603
Murray, S. L., 673, 674
Murstein, B. I., 624
Musch, J., 528
Musen, G., 305
Mustanski, B. S., 416
Myers, D. G., 340, 430, 431, 432
Myers, J., 597
Myers, M. G., Jr., 401
Mynatt, C. R., 313
Myrtek, M., 552

N

Nabi, H., 551
Nadelson, C. C., 655
Nadon, R., 209
Nagengast, B., 270
Naglieri, J. A., 527
Nahas, Z., 93, 644
Nairne, J. S., 281, 283, 287

Naish, P. I., N., 211
Nakajima, S., 101
Nandagopal, K., 372
Naples, A. J., 335
Narasimhan, B., 319
Narrow, W. E., 581, 623
Nash, M., 209, 300
Naslund, E., 399, 401
Nasrallah, H. A., 639
Nathan, P. E., 579
Nave, C. S., 408
Naylor, J. C., A-27
Neale, M. C., 584
Near, J. P., A-27
Nee, D. E., 284
Neely, J. H., 296
Neese, R. M., 542
Neff, L. A., 673
Neisser, U., 14, 285, 376, 381, 390
Nelson, C. A., 124, 125, 465
Nelson, L. D., 41–43
Nemeroff, C., 640
Nemes, I., 413
Nemeth, C., 689
Nemiah, J. C., 588
Nes, L. S., 557
Nestler, E. J., 87, 218, 423
Nettelback, T., 382
Nettle, D., 389, 516, 529
Neuberg, S. L., 381
Neugebauer, R., 579
Neugroschl, J. A., 86, 472
Neumann, C. S., 606
Neupert, S. D., 549
Neuschatz, J. S., 288, 291, 293, 300
Newby, D. E., 559
Newcombe, N., 456
Newell, A., 14, 318, 332
Newport, E., 326
Newport, E. L., 458, 460
Newsom, J. T., 557
Nezlek, J. B., 425
Ng, F. F. Y., 483
Niccols, A., 444
Nicholson, N. A., 540
Nickerson, C., 430
Nickerson, R. S., 275, 348
Nicoladis, E., 323
Nida, S. A., 695
Niebyl, J. R., 442, 444
Niehuis, S., 674
Nielsen, T. A., 202, 204, 205
Niemeier, H. M., 401
Nievar, M. A., 450
Nikelly, A. G., 226
Nisbett, R. E., 34, 74, 336, 378, 669, 671
Nist, S. L., 31
Nithianatharajah, J., 124
Noble, K. G., 379
Nobler, M. S., 643, 644
Noftle, E. E., 492
Nolan, C., 35, 96–97
Nolen-Hoeksema, S., 592, 595
Nomaguchi, K. M., 471
Norcross, J. C., 633, 649, 656
Nordgren, L. F., 339
Norenzayan, A., 14, 15, 51–52, 54, 57, 671
Norfleet, M. A., 623
Norman, D. A., 148, 280
Norman, R. L., 214
Norris, F. H., 584
North, C. S., 653
Norton, C., 67
Notman, M. T., 655

Novemsky, N., 349
Novick, L. R., 332, 335
Noyes, R., Jr., 588
Nucci, L. P., 462
Nunnally, J. C., 358
Nurse, R. J., 167
Nyberg, L., 97
Nyberg, S. E., 28

O

Oakes, M. E., 402
Oathes, D., 187
Oberauer, K., 284
O'Brien, C. P., 579
O'Brien, J. T., 553
O'Callahan, M., 555
Ochse, R., 368
Oden, M. H., 371
O'Donahue, W., 267
Ogden, C. L., 403
Ogles, B, M., 578, 632, 654
O'Hara, L. A., 368
Ohayon, M. M., 193, 201
Ohlsson, S., 332
Öhman, A., 255, 256, 260, 420, 585
Oishi, S., 433
Okami, P., 40
Okifiji, A., 170
Oldham, G. R., A-26
Olds, J., 11, 14, 100
Olds, M. E., 101
O'Leary, K. D., 61
O'Leary, S. G., 253
Olfson, M., 623, 624, 625, 650
Oliet, S. H. R., 81
Olio, K., 301
Oliver, J. E., 404
Oliveri, M., 94
Oller, K., 323
Olson, D. H., 470
Olson, E. A., 313
Olson, E. J., 223
Olson, J. M., 666, 686, 687
Olson, L. J., 202
Olson, M. A., 270, 681, 684
Olszewski-Kubilius, P., 371
Omerod, T. C., 332
Ondeck, D. M., 170
Ones, D., 368, A-19
Operario, D., 666
O'Reardon, S. P., 644
Organ, D. W., A-27
Organista, P. B., 588
Orlando, V. P., 30, 31
Orme-Johnson, D. W., 212, 213
Orne, M. T., 211, 691
Ornstein, R. E., 121, 122, 187
Ortigue, S., 133, 407
Ortmann, A., 66
Osaka, N., 284
Osei, S. Y., 401
Oskamp, S., 685
Osrin, D., 421
Ost, J., 299
Öst, L. G., 255
Ostendorf, F., 547
Ostovich, J. M., 408
Ostroff, C., A-22
Ostrove, J. M., 469
Oswald, L. M., 95
Otsuka, Y., 284
Outtz, J. L., 368
Overall, N., 672, 674
Overmier, J. B., 68
Owyang, M. T., 665

Oyster, C. W., 137
Ozer, D. J., 492
Ozer, E. J., 584
Ozgen, E., 327

P

Pace-Schott, E. F., 192, 207
Pacquet, M., 1
Padavic, I., 470
Padgett, D. A., 554, 555
Padilla-Walker, L. M., 448
Pagel, J. F., 204
Paine, C. B., 678
Painter, R., 443
Paivio, A., 279, 280, 311
Palladino, J. J., 222
Pallanti, S., 586
Palmer, J. C., 292
Palmer, S. E., 149
Palmeri, T. J., 142
Panksepp, J., 427
Pansky, A., 288
Papafragou, A., 327
Paris, J., 115
Park, C. L., 550
Park, J. G., 223
Parke, R. D., 253, 471
Parker, A. M., 346
Parks, A. C., 630
Parks, J. M., A-27
Paronis, C. A., 546
Parrott, A. C., 221
Parsons, L., 122
Partinen, M. M., 200, 201, 202
Pascual, A., 705
Pashler, H., 278, 280
Pasternak, T., 140, 142
Paterson, S., 456
Pato, M. T., 583
Patrick, C. J., 421
Patrick, H., 166
Patterson, D. R., 210
Patterson, R. L., 101
Patton, G., 613
Patzer, G. L., 673
Pauk, W., 33
Paul, E. F., 68
Paul, J., 68
Paulhus, D. L., 496, 526
Paulos, J. A., 570
Paulus, P. B., A-23
Paunonen, S. V., 492, 519
Pavlov, I., 9, 11, 20, 232–234, 238, 264
Payment, K. E., 292
Payne, D. G., 286, 293
Payne, J. W., 338
Pearce, L., 575
Pearson, B. Z., 323
Pearson, C., 212
Pearson, S. E., 413
Pedersen, P., 650
Pedersen, P. B., 702
Peele, S., 226
Peiro, J. M., 507
Peladeau, N., 309
Pelayo, R., 202
Pelham, W. H., 637
Pellegrino, J. E., 444
Pellegrino, L., 444
Peltier. M. E., 168
Pendell, G., 470
Penfield, W., 284–285, 302

Penn, D. C., 259
Pennebaker, J. W., 562, 567
Pennix, B. W., 530–531
Penrod, S. D., 312, 413
Penton-Voak, I., 679
Peplau, L. A., 408
Pepperberg, I. M., 324
Pereira, A. C., 560
Perkins, D. F., 466
Perkins, D. O., 600
Perlis, R. H., 642
Perone, M., 249
Perot, P., 302
Perri, M. G., 403, 559
Perrin, F., 95
Perry, C., 209
Perry, D. G., 211
Perry, H. M. I., 472
Perry, L. C., 211
Persaud, T. V. N., 442, 443
Person, E. S., 502
Pert, C., 88, 174
Perugini, E. M., 211
Pervin, L. A., 508
Peters, J. C., 405
Peters, M., 673
Petersen, A. C., 466
Peterson, C., 16, 550, 557
Peterson, D. A. M., 684
Peterson, J. M., 167
Peterson, M. J., 282
Peterson, R., 281, 282
Peterson, T. R., 423
Petit, D. A. D., 220
Petrie, K. J., 562
Petrie, M., 119
Petrill, S. A., 375, 376, 377
Petry, N. M., 2, 3
Petty, R. E., 681, 682, 683, 684, 687
Petty, S. C., 597
Pezdek, K., 285, 301, 589
Pfau, M., 271
Pfaus, J. G., 236
Phelps, E. A., 100, 304, 421
Phillips, B., 202
Phillips, D., 451
Phillips, K., 35
Phillips, K. A., 583, 605
Phillips, L., 313, 348
Phillips, W. T., 568
Phillips-Grant, K., 301
Pi, E. H., 639
Pi-Sunyer, F. X., 403
Pickles, J. O., 163
Piel, E., 204
Pierce, R. C., 218
Pietrefesa, A. S., 584
Pillard, R. C., 415, 416
Pilling, M., 327
Pilowsky, I., 588
Pinals, D. A., 601
Pine, D. S., 583
Pinel, J. P. J., 404, 405
Pines, A. M., 677
Pink, D. H., 121
Pinker, S., 325
Pinquart, M., 632
Pinyerd, B., 464
Piomelli, D., 218
Piper, W., 631
Pittenger, O. J., 68
Pittman, E., III, 654
Pizzagalli, D., 108
Plant, E. A., 701
Plante, T. G., 560, 569

Plassmann, H., 339
Platek, S. M., 223
Pliner, P., 401
Plomin, R., 26, 114, 115, 373, 374, 375, 377, 514
Plotkin, H., 16
Plous, S., 67, 666
Plucker, J., 363, 388
Plutchik, R., 427, 428
Pohl, R. F., 350, 528
Poland, R. E., 221
Poldrack, R. A., 95
Polger, T., 187
Policastro, E., 388
Polich, J., 187, 212
Pollack, R. H., 413
Pollak, L., A-32
Polley, B. A, 404
Pomerantz, E. M., 483, 507
Pomeroy, A., A-21
Pomeroy, C., 613
Ponterotto, J. G., 702
Poo M.-M., 303
Poortinga, Y. H., 425
Pope, H. G., 220, 299, 590, 598
Pope, K. S., 655
Popenoe, D., 484, 485
Popp, D., 409
Popper, C. W., 370, 371
Pornpitakpan, C., 683
Porter, S., 300, 606
Posada, G., 450
Posner, M. I., 277
Post, F., 389
Posthuma, D., 377
Postman, L., 294
Potenza, M. N., 579
Potter, J. E., 444
Potter, M. C., 152, 153
Potter, W. Z., 640
Potthoff, J. G., 597
Poulin-Dubois, D., 321
Powell, B., 501
Powell, L. H., 552
Powell, R. A., 253, 502, 589, 590
Powers, S. I., 677
Powley, T. L., 99
Pratkanis, A., 682–683
Preckel, F., 389
Premack, D., 325
Prentky, R., 389
Prescott, C. A., 597
Pressman, S. D., 541, 556
Pretz, J. E., 335
Price C. J., 95
Price, D., 170, 174
Priebe, S., 651
Priester, J. R., 682, 683
Prifitera, A., 362
Prigerson, H. G., 579
Priluck, R. L., 236, 270, 684
Prislin, R., 682
Pritchard, R. D., A-27
Prizmic, Z., 433
Prochaska, J. O., 558
Proffitt, D. R., 152, 155–156
Prolo, P., 554
Pronin, E., 27
Provine, R. R., 223
Prudic, J., 643
Pruitt, D. G., 697
Pucetti, R., 121
Pullman, G. K., 327
Purdy, J. E., 68
Putnam, F. W., 589

Pylyshyn, Z., 458
Pysyczynski, T. A., 517–519

Q

Quillian-Wolever, R., 213
Quina, K., 15
Quinn, J., 703
Quinn, J. M., 684
Quinn, K. A., 666
Quirk, G. J., 423
Quiroga, R. Q., 142
Quitkin, F. M., 60

R

Rabinowitz, J., 639
Rachman, S. J., 267, 585
Racoosin, J., 640
Rae, D. S., 581
Rafal, R., 93
Raghuram, S., A-23
Rahe, R. A., 537, 538
Rahman, M. A., 558
Raichle, M. E., 94, 96
Raine, A., 584
Rains, G. D., 104
Raitt, F. E., 301
Raj, A., 638
Rajaram, S., 291
Rakic, P., 125
Rama, A. N., 192, 193
Ramadan, N. M., 555
Ramaekers, J. G., 220
Ramey, C. T., 391
Ramey, S. L., 391
Ramirez, M., 649
Ramos, B. C., 237
Ramsay, D. S., 401
Ramsay, M. C., 381
Randolfi, E., 535
Ranganath, C., 287
Ranson, K. E., 450
Rapee, R. M., 582
Raphael, B., 534
Rapson, R. L., 674, 677
Rashid, T., 630
Rasmussen, C., 535
Rasmussen, T., 122
Ratner, N. B., 319
Rauscher, F. H., 125
Ravnkilde, B., 594
Rawson, N. E., 168
Ray, W. J., 187
Ray-Casserly, C. M., 355
Raybeck, D., 308
Raye, C. L., 293
Raynor, H. A., 401
Raynor, J. O., 418
Raynor, R., 239–240
Read, J. D., 132, 299, 301
Reber, R., 347
Recht, L. D., 190
Rechtschaffen, A., 191, 192
Reed, G. M., 547
Reed, J. G., 70
Reed, S. K., 332
Reedy, F. E., Jr., 167
Rees, C. J., 526
Reeve, C. L., 375
Reeve, H. K., 16
Refinetti, R., 188
Regan, P. C., 673
Regan, T., 67
Regier, D. A., 579, 580, 582
Reibel, D. K., 61, 213

Reich, P., 551
Reichert, T., 270, 271
Reimer, T., 683
Reinhard, M. A., 683
Reinharz, D., 652
Reips, U.D., 65
Reis, H. T., 674, 675
Reise, S. P., 492
Reisman, J. M., 13
Reisner, A. D., 298
Reiss, S., 584
Reiter, R. C., 562
Rennie, D., 642
Renshaw, K., 672
Renzulli, J., 372, 388
Repetto, M., 87, 219
Rescorla, R., 240, 257–258
Rest, J. R., 461
Reuter-Lorenz, P. A., 108, 123
Revelle, W., 510
Reyna, V. F., 299
Reynolds, A. J., 391
Reynolds, C. F., III, 648–649
Reynolds, C. R., 381
Reynolds, K. A., 550
Reynolds, K. J., 703
Reznick, J. S., 448
Rhee, S. H., 606
Rhodes, G., 673
Rhodes, K., 683
Riba, M. B., 648
Ricci-Bitti, P. E., 423
Rice, L. N., 629
Richardson, C. B., 569
Richardson, G. S., 189, 190
Richardson, J., 650
Richert, E. S., 372
Richter, L., 557
Ridker, D. M., 551, 552
Rieber, R. W., 7
Riediger, T., 399
Rief, W., 587, 588
Rieskamp, J., 344
Riggio, H. R., 34
Riggo, L., 103
Rigotti, N. A., 558
Rihmer, Z., 592, 593, 640
Riis, J., 431
Riley, B. P., 601
Riley, I. J., 170
Rilling, M., 8, 9, 302
Rimal, R. N., 506
Rinehart, P., 466
Rippe, J. M., 551
Risch, N., 594
Risen, J., 343, 666
Riskind, J. H., 586
Ritter, R. C., 400
Rivas-Vazquez, R. A., 640
Rivera, B., 527
Rizzolatti, G., 103
Roazen, P., 467
Roback, H. B., 630
Roberson, D., 327, 328
Roberts, B. W., 469, 492, 507, 557
Roberts, C., 640
Roberts, J. E., 539
Roberts, R. D., 361
Robertson, S. I., 333
Robiner, W. N., 623
Robins, L. N., 579
Robins, R. W., 14, 15, 423, 492
Robinson, A., 371
Robinson, D. G., 600
Robinson, F. P., 29–30

Robinson, T. E., 104
Robles, T. F., 555
Rock, I., 159
Rockey, D. L., 3
Rodgers, J. E., 312
Rodieck, R. W., 137
Rodin, J., 614
Roediger, H. L., III, 278, 279, 281, 290, 291, 293, 297, 300, 301, 308
Roehrig, M., 613
Roehrs, T., 198, 201, 223
Roese, N. J., 67, 666, 687
Rogers, C. R., 10, 11, 21, 509–510, 520, 628–630, 646–647
Rogers, N. L., 190, 191, 198
Rogers, P. M., 551
Rogers, T. B., 280
Rogers, T. T., 289
Rogers, W. T., 31
Rogoff, B., 457, 458
Rogol, A., 463
Rohde, P., 501, 597
Rohner, R. P., 485
Rohrer, D., 309
Rollman, G. B., 174
Rolls, B. J., 401
Rolls, E. T., 142, 427
Roney, J. R., 411–412
Root, L. M., 568
Rorden, C., 93, 97
Roring, R. W., 372
Rorschach, H., 526
Rosch, E. H., 327
Rose, D., 643
Rose, D. P., 559
Rose, H., 16
Rose, N. R., 554
Rose, R., 116
Rose, S. E., 16
Roseboom, T., 443
Rosenbaum, M., 630
Rosenberg, E., 646
Rosenblum, G. D., 466
Rosenhack, R. A., 639
Rosenhan, D., 578–579
Rosenman, R., 551
Rosenthal, L., 191
Rosenthal, L. T., 170
Rosenthal, R., 61, 64
Rosenzweig, M., 124, 125, 383
Rosenzweig, S., 8
Rosenzwig, E. S., 303
Roskos-Ewoldsen, F. A., 389
Rosler, F., 92
Ross, C. A., 589
Ross, D., 261–262
Ross, L., 27, 471
Ross, L. D., 41–43, 689
Ross, S., 261–262
Roter, D. L., 564
Roth, P. L., 416
Roth, T., 201, 202, 223
Rothbart, M., 703
Rothbart, M. K., 448
Rott, R., 474
Rotter, J., 504
Rouiller, E. M., 163
Routh, D. K., 13
Routledge, C., 518
Rowatt, W. C., 680
Rowe, D. C., 514, 515
Rowe, S. M., 457
Royzman, E., 420
Rozee, P. D., 413
Rozin, P., 166, 401, 402, 420
Roznowski, M. A., A-27

Rubin, D. G., 285–286
Ruble, D., 482, 483
Ruble, T. L., 480
Rudnicki, S. R., 554, 555
Rudorfer, M. V., 643
Ruini, C., 630
Ruiperez, M. A., 611
Ruiter, R. A., 684
Ruiz, P., 636
Rule, N. O., 665
Rumbaugh, D. M., 324
Rumelhart, D. E., 289
Runco, M. A., 388
Runyan, J. D., 304
Runyan, W. M., 24
Rupert, G. T., A-21
Rusbult, C. E., 673
Ruscio, J., 74
Rush, A. J., 637
Rushton, J. P., 373, 378, 383
Rushworth, M. F. S., 103
Rusiniak, K. W., 255
Russell, G. F. M., 613, 614
Russell, J. A., 423, 424, 425, 542
Russell, K., 122
Russo, E., 220
Russo, J. E., 348
Russo, N. F., 6
Rutherford, A., 10
Rutherford, W., 163
Ruthruff, E., 277, 278
Ruthsatz, J. M., 370
Rutledge, T., 556
Rutledge, T. R., 423
Rutter, M., 115
Ryckeley, R., 231
Ryder, R. D., 67

S

Sabini, J., 408
Sachs-Ericsson, N., 597
Sack, A. T., 93, 94, 97
Sackeim, H. A., 643, 644
Sackett, P. R., A-18, A-27, A-28
Sacks, O., 129, 130
Sadker, D., 483
Sadker, M., 483
Sadler, J. Z., 577
Sadovsky, A., 462
Safstrom, C. A., 675
Safvenbom, R., 696
Sagi, A., 451
Sagie, A., A-23
Sais, E., 324
Saks, A. M., 506
Sala, J. B., 103
Salanova, M., 507
Salgado, J. F., A-19
Salkovskis, P. M., 582, 588
Salmon, P., 213
Salonen, J. T., 559
Salovey, P., 385, 386
Salthouse, T. A., 473, 474
Salvendy, J. T., 631
Samberg, E., 627
Samons, D. M., 472
Sanbonmatsu, D. M., 672
Sanchez, D. T., 407
Sanchez, I. M., 645
Sanders, M. H., 202
Sandin, B., 586
Sandoz, J., 579
Sanger, D. J., 201
Sanislow, C. A., 600
Sankis, L. M., 577

Sanna, L. J., 535, 702
Sanson, A., 448
Santelmann, L. M., 320
Santerre, C., 213
Saper, C. B., 99, 189, 196
Sapolsky, R. M., 543
Sarason, B. G., 591
Sarason, I. G., 591
Sargis, E. G., 54, 65
Sateia, M., 201
Sato, K., 425
Sato, T., 369
Savage-Rumbaugh, S., 324
Savarino, J., 640, 641
Savin-Williams, R. C., 414
Saxton, P. M., 422
Sayer, L. C., 470
Sayers, S. L., 554
Sayette, M. A., 549
Scammel, T. E., 196
Scarborough, E., 6
Scarr, S., 376
Scattone, D., 636
Schab, F. R., 168
Schaberg, L., 701
Schachner, D. A., 676, 677
Schachter, S., 45–46, 47, 66, 427
Schacter, D. L., 75, 306, 312
Schaefer, A., 535
Schaeffer, N. C., 61
Schafe, G. E., 100, 304
Schaie, K. W., 473
Schaller, M., 15, 16
Schalock, R. L., 369
Scheflin, A. W., 301
Scheidlinger, S., 630
Scheier, M. F., 544, 557
Schenck, C. H., 201
Scherer, K. R., 420, 423, 424, 425
Scherer, M., 568
Schieber, F., 472
Schiefelbein, V. L., 110, 464
Schiff, M., 376
Schiffman, J., 402, 603
Schilt, T., 221
Schimel, J., 518
Schimmack, U., 684
Schkade D., 341, 432
Schlegel, A., 463
Schlenk, E., 563, 564
Schmelcher, J., 413
Schmid, J., 422
Schmidt, F. L., 367, 368, 381
Schmidt, N. B., 584
Schmit , M. J., 386
Schmithorst, V. J., 464
Schmitt, D. P., 409, 410, 481, 677, 679, 680
Schmitt, M., A-22
Schmitt, M. T., 703
Schmitz, J. M., 558
Schmolck, H., 285
Schneider, F., 601
Schoenfeld, G. A., 506
Schofield, C. A., 584
Scholey, A. B., 221
Scholz, J., 170
Schooler, C., 474
Schooler, J. W., 168, 186, 298, 299
Schrag, R. D., 391
Schramke, C. J., 555
Schramm, D. G., 470
Schredl, M., 204
Schreiber, F. R., 590
Schuitt, A. J., 473
Schultheiss, O. C., 109

Schultz, J. H., 224
Schulz-Hardt, S., 698
Schumacher, P., 546
Schuman, H., 61
Schunn, C. D., 334
Schusterman, R. J., 324
Schvaneveldt, R. W., 289
Schwartz, B., 337–338
Schwartz, B. L., 290
Schwartz, D. G., 225
Schwartz, G. E. R., 213
Schwartz, G. L., 401
Schwartz, J. E., 492
Schwartz, J. H., 81, 85
Schwartz, J. P., 451, 677
Schwartz, L., 588
Schwartz, L. M., 558
Schwartz, M. W., 399, 401
Schwartz, S. H., 692
Schwartz, W. J., 190
Schwarz, N., 61, 433, 682, 684
Scoboria, A., 211
Scollon, C. N., 433
Scott, T. R., 166
Scott, V., 399, 400
Scoville, W. B., 304
Scroppo, J. C., 590
Scull, A., 651
Scullin, M. H., 369
Scully, J. A., 537
Seabrook, R., 309
Seaman, J. S., 86, 472
Searle, A., 555
Searleman, A., 306, 308
Sears, D. O., 60, 685
Sears, R., 371
Seeley, R. J., 399
Seftel, A. D., 472
Segal, C. E., 595
Segall, M. H., 15, 159, 174
Segerstrom, S. C., 109, 555, 557
Seidman, G., 65
Seifer, R., 379, 380
Self, D. W., 218
Seligman, M. E. P., 16, 254, 255, 366, 420, 430, 544, 550, 557, 585, 595, 630, 645, 656
Seltzer, B., 472
Selwyn, P. A., 560
Selye, H., 21, 90, 542–543, 565
Semendeferi, K., 100
Semmer, N. K., 535
Senior, C., 665
Serocynski, A. D., 466
Serpell, R., 369
Servan-Schreiber, D., 587
Servis, M. E., 86, 472
Seta, E. E., 535
Seta, J. J., 535
Seto, M. C., 413
Shackelford, T. K., 408, 410, 679, 680
Shackman, A. J., 108
Shafir, E., 338, 339, 343, 344
Shafto, M. A., 290
Shakesby, P. S., 310
Shalev, A. Y., 584
Shalitin, S., 463
Shallenberger, W. R., III, 32
Shamay-Tsoory, S. G., 323
Shank, R. P., 87
Shanker, S. G., 324
Shanteau, J., 330
Shapira, N. A., 546
Shapiro, A. F., 471
Shapiro, C. M., 190

Shapiro, D. H., Jr., 61, 212
Shapiro, J. R., 381
Shapiro, K. J., 67
Shapiro, L., 328
Shapiro, S. L., 212, 213
Sharma, Y. S., 412
Sharp, D., 67
Sharps, M. J., 151
Shatz, C. J., 125
Shaver, P. R., 451, 675–676, 677
Shavitt, S., 666
Shaw, G. L., 125
Shaw, J. C., 14
Shaw, J. S. L., 313
Shaw, W., 551
Shea, A. K., 444
Shear, J., 212
Shearer, B., 385
Sheehan, D., 638
Sheehan, P. W., 291
Sheehan, S., 598
Sheiham, A., 555
Sheldon, K. M., 432, 512
Shelton, R. C., 640
Shepard, R., 158, 159
Shepherd, R., 402
Shepperd, J., 671
Shepperd, J. A., 49–50, 433
Sher, L., 535, 594
Sheridan, J. F., 554, 555
Sherif, M., 703
Sherman, D. A., 701
Sherman, D. K., 41–43
Sherman, M., 376
Sherman, P. W., 118
Shermer, M., 147, 704
Sherry, D. F., 256
Sherwyn, D., A-19
Shettleworth, S. J., 256
Shevrin, H., 132
Shiffrin, R. M., 280, 281
Shike, M., 559
Shimamura, A. P., 104
Shimizu, E., 81
Shimp, T. A., 271
Shiner, R. L., 469
Shobe, K. K., 298, 299
Shors, T. J., 104, 303, 549
Shulman, R. B., 640
Shurkin, J. N., 654
Sideman, L., 386
Siebert, A., 28
Siebler, F., 413
Sieck, W. R., 348
Siegel, J. M., 87, 196, 197
Siegel, S., 236, 237
Siegelbaum, J. A., 82, 85
Siegler, R. S., 320, 361, 456
Sigel, I. E., 391
Signorielli, N., 483
Silber, L., 123
Silberman, E. K., 626, 638
Silberstein, L. R., 614
Silver, E., 607
Silver, H., 602
Silverman, I., 35, 481
Silverman, M. M., 466
Silverstein, L. B., 484
Silvia, P. J., 389
Sime, W. E., 538
Simeon, D., 582
Simmons, L. W., 673
Simon, E. W., 369, 370
Simon, G. E., 640, 641
Simon, H. A., 14, 283, 318, 332, 333, 337

Simon, R. I., 607, 610
Simon, T., 361, 458
Simons, D. K., 147
Simons, G., 403
Simonsen, E., 579
Simonton, D. K., 361, 372, 389, 474
Simpson, G. M., 639
Simpson, J. A., 674
Simpson, J. L., 441, 442
Sinclair, D., 169
Sinclair, R. C., 427
Sinclair, S., 702
Singer, J. E., 427
Singer, L. T., 444
Singer, W., 187
Sinha, D., 368
Sinha, P., 142
Sivertsen, B., 201, 202
Skene, D. J., 189, 190
Skerrett, P. J., 403
Skinner, B. F., 9–10, 11, 21, 241, 242–243, 247, 264, 325, 326, 397, 502–504, 520, 523, 634
Skinner, E. A., 544
Skinner, N. F., 298, 501
Skitka, L. J., 54, 65
Skoczen, S., 64, 65
Skolnick, P., 87, 584–585
Slamecka, N. J., 294, 296
Slatcher, R. B., 567
Slater, M. A., 588
Slaughter, M., 139
Slavin, J. L., 559
Slavney, P. R., 588
Sleet, D. A., 219
Sligh, A. C., 389
Sloan, D. M. E., 592, 641
Slobin, D. I., 322, 326
Slof-Op't Landt, M. C. T., 614
Slotterback, C. S., 402
Slovic, P., 338, 341, 347, 528, 559
Small, D. A., 339
Small, G. W., 472
Smart, D., 448
Smeaton, G., 673
Smedley, S. R., 119
Smetana, J. G., 471
Smith, A. P., 555
Smith, B. D., 32
Smith, B. W., 554
Smith, C., 417
Smith, C. A., 540, A-27
Smith, D. A., 649
Smith, D. M., 431
Smith, D. V., 167
Smith, E., 304
Smith, F. J., 400, A-28
Smith, G. T., 14
Smith, J. C., 568
Smith, J. S., 68
Smith, L., 650
Smith, M. F., 683
Smith, M. J., 472
Smith, M. L., 656
Smith, M. T., 202
Smith, P. B., 692
Smith, P. C., A-26
Smith, S., 291
Smith, S. B., 440
Smith, S. J., 85
Smith, S. M., 331, 665
Smith, T. B., 650
Smith, T. W., 555
Smith-McLallen, A., 683
Smith-Swintosky, V. L., 87
Smolak, L., 614

Smyth, J. M., 567
Smythe, P. E., 279, 280
Snedecor, S. M., 167
Snidman, N., 448
Snodgrass, M., 132
Snow, C. E., 323
Snow, R. E., 388
Snowden, L. R., 650
Snowdon, D. A., 473
Snyder, A., 123
Snyder, E., 416
Snyder, S. H., 85, 88
Sohlberg, S., 132
Sokol, R. J., 444
Solberg, E. C., 430
Soldatos, C. R., 192, 193, 196
Soler, C., 679
Solinas, M., 218
Solity, J. E., 309
Soll, J. B., 348
Solms, M., 207
Solomon, D. A., 591
Solomon, H. C., 634
Solomon, J., 450
Solomon, S. G., 145, 517–519
Solowij, N., 220
Solso, R. L., 176
Somers, U. K., 202
Sommer, B., 123
Song, A. W., 95
Song, S., 85
Soriano, M., 650
Soth-McNett, A. M., 649
Sousa, D. A., 124
Sousa, L., 567
Sovio, U., 403
Sowell, E. R., 465
Spada, M. M., 546
Spangler, W. D., 417
Spanos, N. P., 210, 299, 590
Sparks, J. A., 632
Spearman, C., 362–363
Specter, S., 220
Speed, A., 673
Spelke, E. S., 458, 460
Spence, L., 143
Spencer, S. J., 703
Speranza, A. M., 450
Sperling, G., 281, 282
Sperry, R., 11, 14, 21, 106, 107
Spiegel, D., 208, 209, 211, 210, 589
Spiegel, H., 209
Spiegel, K., 200
Spiegler, M. D., 635
Spiers, M. V., 89
Spillane, N. S., 14
Spinath, F. M., 374, 375
Spinrad, T., 462
Spitzer, R. L., 579, 581
Sporer, S. L., 683
Sprecher, S., 673, 674, 675
Sprenger, M., 124
Springer, S. P., 108, 122, 123, 481
Springston, F., 283
Squire, L. R., 100, 285, 304, 305
Srivastava, S., 492
Staats, A. W., 326
Staats, C. K., 326
Stack, A. D., 545
Stahl, T., 422
Stajkovic, A. D., 507
Stamler, J., 559
Stanford, T. R., 99, 174
Stanley, J., 373
Stanny, C. J., 278
Stanovich, K. E., 74, 345, 346, 348

Stanton, A. L., 555
Starcevic, V., 587
Stattin, H., 447
Staudinger, U. M., 473
Steadman, H. J., 607
Steel, P., 506
Steele, C. M., 380–381
Steele, J. B., 583
Steele, K. M., 125
Steelman, L. C., 501
Steen, T. A., 630
Steiger, H., 614
Steiger, K. M., 86
Stein, B. E., 99, 140, 174
Stein, D. J., 585
Stein, M. B., 584
Steinberg, L., 464, 465, 466, 471
Steiner, M., 444
Steingard, R. J., 371
Steinhausen, H., 613
Steinmetz, J. E., 303
Stekel, W., 628
Stelfox, H. T., 642
Stellar, E., 399
Stemler, S. E., 384
Stenstrom, P., 204
Stepanski, E. J., 201, 223
Stephan, W. G., 701
Stephens, R. S., 218
Steptoe, A., 535, 541
Steriade, M., 196
Sternberg, R. J., 26, 328, 330, 331,
    334, 335, 361, 362, 367, 368, 369,
    373, 375, 376, 378, 381, 383–384,
    389, 516, 674–675
Stetler, C., 555
Steven, M. S., 104
Stevens, G., 534
Stevens, S. S., 161
Stevens-Graham, B., 81
Stewart, A. J., 469
Stewart, C. M., 97
Stewart, G. L., A-24
Stewart, J. H., 252
Stewart, M. O., 636
Stewart, R., A-21
Stewart, W. H., 418
Stewart-Williams, S., 60, 170
Stice, E., 615
Stickgold, R., 199, 207, 304
Stiles, W. B., 632
Stipelman, B., 550, 582, 586
Stockmyer, J., 122
Stoddard, G., 376
Stoecklin, M., 683
Stokes, L. W., 386
Stone, A. A., 610
Stone, B., 189
Stone, E. F., A-26
Stone, J., 686, 687
Stone, L., 677
Stone, W. N., 631
Stoner, J. A. F., 696
Stoney, C. M., 551
Stoohs, R. A., 223
Stoolmiller, M., 515
Storch, M., 565
Stough, C., 382
Stowell, J. R., 535
Strack, F., 433
Strager, S., 412
Strahan, E. J., 614
Strange, D., 299
Straus, M. A., 252
Strauss, B., 632
Strayer, D. L., 147, 278

Streeter, S. A., 409
Streissguth, A. P., 444
Streit, W. J., 81
Strenze, T., 367
Striegel-Moore, R. H., 613, 614, 615
Striepe, M., 403
Stroebe, W., 133, 684, 687
Strollo, P. J., Jr., 202
Strong, S. R., 656
Stroud, L. R., 546
Stroup, T. S., 639
Strunk, D., 636
Strupp, H. H., 624
Stuart, E. W., 271
Stuewig, J., 462
Stunkard, A. J, 404
Sturman, M. C., A-19
Sturman, T. S., 419
Styfco, S. J., 391
Suarez, G. C., 552
Suchday, S., 552, 553
Sudak, H. S., 466, 593
Sue, D. W., 649, 650
Sue, S., 15
Sufka, K. J., 174
Sugarman, J., 16
Sugiyama, L. S., 679
Sullivan, G., 653
Sullivan, G. M., 86
Sullivan, P. F., 601
Sulloway, F., 501
Suls, J., 535
Sundie, J. M., 480
Super, C. M., 446
Surratt, H., 214
Surtees, P., 537
Susman, E. J., 110, 463, 464
Susser, E., 443, 603
Sussman, A., 451
Sutker, P. D., 606
Suzuki, K., 159
Swan, G. E., 558
Sweeny, K., 671
Swets, J. A., 131
Swim, J. K., 701, 702
Switzer, G. E., 582
Symbaluk, D. G., 253
Symons, C. S., 280
Szasz, T. S., 576–577
Szegedy-Maszak, M., 3
Szmanski, L. S., 370
Szmukler, G. L., 613

T

Tabachnick, B. G., 655
Tabas, G., 587
Taft, C. T., 584
Taglialatela, J. P., 324
Tajfel, H., 703
Takahashi, M., 223
Takahashi, T., 92
Takarangi, M. K., 147
Talarico, J. M., 285–286
Talbott, J. A., 652
Talwar, S., 246
Tamakoshi, A., 200, 223
Tamkins, M. M., A-22
Tamminga, C. A., 87, 601
Tan, U., 174
Tanaka, J., 143
Tanaka-Matsumi, J., 610
Tanapat, P., 544
Tangney, J. P., 462
Taniguchi, H., 470
Tanner, J. L., 468

Tanner, W. P., 131
Tansky, J. W., 506
Tardiff, K., 578
Tart, C. T., 206
Tashkin, D. P., 220
Tataryn, D. J., 133
Tate, M., A-40
Tatsuoka, M. M., 525
Tavris, C., 529
Taylor, D. M., 26, 701
Taylor, E., 12, 512
Taylor, J. H., 461, 462
Taylor, K., 309
Taylor, L., 324
Taylor, M. G., 482
Taylor, M. M., 324
Taylor, S., 301, 519, 547, 556
Taylor, T. J., 324
Teachman, J. D., 470
Teasdale, J. D., 595
Tedeshi, R. G., 550
Tedlock, L. B., 206
Tees, R. C., 320
Tek, C., 599
Tellegen, A., 432, 514
Temme, J., 349
Temple, J. L., 401
Tennen, H., 550
Tepper, B. J., 167
Tepperman, T., 399
Teresi, D., 121, 123
Terman, L., 21, 361–362, 371, 557
Terr, L., 298
Terracciano, A., 522
Terrace, H., 324
Terry, C. M., 503
Tessier-Lavigne, M., 139
Tessner, K., 549, 601, 604
Teuber, H., 304
Teuber, M., 177
Tew, M. D., 65
Thach, W. T., 99
Tharp, R. G., 267
Thase, M. E., 594, 637, 640, 641
Thayaparan, B., 560
Thayer, A., 299
Thayer, R. E., 403, 420
Thelen, E., 445
Theorell, T., 555
Thiele, K., 198
Thomas, A., 446–447, 448
Thomas, A. J., 553
Thomas, D. R., 239, 240
Thomas, G., 674
Thomas, H. D. C., A-24
Thomas, R. M., 453, 457
Thompson, J. K., 613, 614, 615
Thompson, P. M., 465
Thompson, R. A., 124, 125, 448,
    450
Thompson, R. F., 14, 303
Thomson, A. D., 443
Thomson, D. M., 297
Thorndike, E. L., 10, 241–242
Thorne, B. M., 5
Thornhill, R., 119, 679
Thornton, B., 181
Thorpe, S. J., 582
Thorpy, M. J., 202, 223
Thurstone, L. L., 363, A-25
Tice, D. M., 403, 545
Tiegen, K. H., 342
Till, B. D., 236, 270, 271, 684
Timm, D. A., 559
Tindale, R. S., 697, 698
Titchener, E., 5

Titsworth, B. S., 31
Tkach, C., 432
Tobler, I., 197
Todd, J. T., 9
Todd, P. M., 332, 344
Todorov, A., 665
Toga, A. W., 465
Tohen, M., 579
Tolman, D. L., 416
Tolman, E. C., 257, 261
Tom, S., 95
Tomarken, A. J., 427
Tomer, R., 323
Tomich, P. L., 550
Tomkins, S. S., 423, 427, 428
Tonnessen, F. E., 696
Tooby, J., 11, 16, 344, 346, 398
Tori, C. D., 213
Tormala, Z. L., 681, 684
Torrance, E. P., 389
Torres, A. R., 584
Torrey, E. F., 501, 529, 653
Tosi, H., 537
Tourangeau, R., 53, 61
Tov, W., 430
Tovee, M. T., 142
Tower, R. B., 64
Townsend, M. H., 534
Toyota, H., 279
Tozzi, F., 614
Tracy, J. L., 423
Trasselli, C., 270
Trasti, N., 444
Travis, F., 212
Treiber, F., 213
Trevarthen, C., 106
Treyens, J. C., 288
Triandis, H. C., 25, 671, 677
Trick, L., 458
Trivers, R. L., 16, 408
Trost, M. R., 480, 689, 705
Trujillo, M., 611
Trull, T. J., 605
Tsai, J. L., 611
Tsigos, C., 543
Tsuang, M. T., 579, 601
Tucker, A. M., 193
Tucker, J., 425
Tuckey, M. R., 288
Tugade, M. M., 541, 567
Tulving, E., 278, 296, 297,
    305–306, 309
Tulviste, P., 457
Tun, P. A., 472
Tunnell, K. D., 214
Turek, F. W., 190, 202
Turk, D. C., 170
Turkheimer, E., 378, 380, 515
Turkkan, J. S., 241
Turner, J. C., 703
Turner, J. R., 538, 555
Turner, S. M., 583, 645
Tversky, A., 292, 338, 341–342, 343,
    346, 348, 349, 616, 617
Tweney, R. D., 313
Twenge, J. M., 412, 471
Twyman, R. E., 87
Tybur, J. M., 679
Tyrell, D. A., 555
Tyrer, P., 605
Tzourio-Mazoyer, N., 122

U

Uchino, B., 556
Ulrich, R. E., 67

Umbel, V. M., 323
Umhau, J. C., 559
Underwood, B. J., 28
Ungerleider, L. G., 142
Uno, D., 556
Urichuk, L. J., 450
Ursano, R. J., 626
Ursin, R., 196
Uttal, W. R., 96
Uttl, B., 306

V

Vaillant, G. E., 496, 546, 557
Valdiserri, R. O., 561
Valenstein, E. S., 399
Valentine, E., 308
Valiente, C., 606
Valkow, N., 579
Vanable, F. A., 560
van Anders, S. M., 480
van Baaren, R. B., 339
Van Blerkom, S. L., 31, 32
Van Boven, L., 430
Van de Castle, R., 204
van den Boom, D., 450
VandenBos, G. R., 72, 166
van den Oord, E. J. C. G., 514, 515
Vandereycken, W., 614
van der Post, L., 499
Van Dongen, H. P. A., 188, 193,
    197–198
van Eck, M., 540
van Gelder, T., A-39
van Griensven, F., 534
Van Hoesen, G. W., 100
van IJzendoorn, M. H., 376, 450,
    451
van Kammen, D. P., 639
van Kesteren, N. M. C., 561
van Leeuwen, M. L., 665
van Olden, Z., 682
Van Praag, H., 104
van Ryn, M., 556
Vase, L., 170
Vaughn, C., 223, 603, 604
Vega, V., 413
Vegas, R., 241
Veldhuis, J. D., 445
Veneziano, R. A., 485
Verdone, P., 204
Verduin, T., 632
Verhaeghen, P., 473, 474
Verheul, R., 605
Vermeeren, A., 201
Vernberg, E. M., 584
Vernon, M. L., 677
Vernon, P., 514
Vernon, P. A., 383
Vernon, P. E., 368
Viau, V., 543
Victor, B. S., 593
Victoroff, J., 472
Videbech, P., 594
Viechtbauer, W., 469
Viglione, D. J., 527
Vikan, A., 290
Villarreal, D. M., 303
Vincent, G. M., 606
Vinogradov, S., 631
Vinokur, A. D., 556
Visser, P. S., 686
Viswesvaran, C., 368, A-19
Vohs, K. D., 408, 548
Vokey, J. R., 132
Volkmar, F. R., 124

Volkow, N. D., 218
Volvaka, J., 639
von Hippel, W., 666
von Karolyi, C., 371
von Meduna, L., 642
Vosper, J., 501
Voutilainen, S., 559
Voyer, D., 35, 481
Voyer, S., 35
Vredenburg, K., 659
Vterrodt-Plunnecke, B., 311
Vygotsky, L., 457
Vyse, S. A., 231
Vythilingamm, M., 95

W

Wachtel, P., 649
Wadden, T. A., 403
Waddill, P. J., 310
Wade, C. E., 190
Wagner, A. D., 306
Wagner, A. R., 257
Wagner, H., 427
Wagner, U., 199
Wainright, N., 537
Wakefield, J. C., 579, 580, 581
Walbott, H. G., 424, 425
Wald, G., 145
Wald, M., 472
Waldeck, J. H., A-22
Waldman, I. D., 606
Waldo, M., 451, 677
Waldron, M., 515
Waldrop, D., 506
Walker, E., 549, 600, 601 604
Walker, L., 287
Walker, L. J., 461, 462
Walker, M. P., 199, 207, 304
Wall, P., 170, 171
Wallace, B., 187
Wallace, D. S., 682
Wallace, H. M., 548
Wallace, M. T., 99, 174
Wallen, K., 96–97
Wallman, J., 324
Walraven, J., 138
Walsh, B. T., 613, 658
Walsh, J. K., 197, 201
Walsh, R., 212, 213
Walster, E., 674
Walter, C. A., 472
Walther, E., 270, 271
Walton, K., 469
Walton, K. E., 557
Walton, K. G., 213
Walton, M. E., 103
Wampold, B. E., 632, 633, 656
Wang, G. C., 218
Wang, P. S., 623, 624
Wang, Q., 483
Wang, S., 456
Wangensteen, O. H., 399
Wanous, J. P., A-21
Wark, D. M., 31
Warner-Schmidt, J. L., 594
Warnes, H., 649
Warwick, D. P., 67
Warwick, H. M. C., 588
Wasco, S. M., 413
Washburn, A. L., 399
Washburn, M. F., 6, 20
Wasow, J. L., 321
Wasserman, J. D., 357, 359
Waterhouse, L., 385
Waters, A. M., 585

Watkins, L. R., 81, 174
Watkins, M. J., 278
Watson, C. S., 161
Watson, D., 359, 492, 535, 673
Watson, D. L., 267
Watson, J. B., 8–9, 10, 11, 20, 26,
    239–240, 502
Waugh, N. C., 280
Waxman, S. R., 321
Weatherall, A., 350
Weaver, C. A., 285
Weaver, K., 684
Webb, W. B., 193, 196, 223
Weber, J. L., 642
Wechsler, D., 362, 364, 365
Wechsler, H., 216, 558
Wegener, D. T., 681, 683, 684, 687
Wegner, D. M., 186, 205
Wehman, P., 370
Weinberg, M. S., 415
Weinberg, R. A., 376
Weinberger, J., 626, 633
Weiner, B., 668, 669, 702
Weinfield, N. S., 450
Weinger, M. B., 198
Weinman, J., 562, 563
Weinstein, A. A., 551
Weinstein, L. M., 225
Weinstein, N. D., 342, 559, 561
Weisberg, J., 306
Weisberg, R., 388, 389
Weisler, R. H., 534
Weissman, D. H., 122
Weissman, M. M., 583, 648
Weisstein, N., 142
Weiten, W., 5, 32, 50, 64, 538, 539
Welch, H. G., 558
Wellman, B., 678
Wells, A., 546
Wells, C. G., 123
Wells, G. L., 312, 313
Welsh, B. T., 623
Welsh, C. H., 201
Wender, R. E., 535
Weriskopf, D., 143
Werker, J. F., 320
Wertheimer, M., 149, 151
Wertsch, J. V., 457
Wertz, F. J., 12
Wessely, S., 640
Wesson, D. R., 201
West, D. S., 403
West, R. F., 345, 348
Westbrook, G. L., 81, 92
Westen, D., 8, 501, 502
Wethington, E., 537
Wetter, M. W., 526
Wever, E. G., 164
Wexler, B. E., 95
Wheaton, B., 538, 555
Wheeler, M. A., 291
Wheeler, S. C., 681
Whitaker, C., 640, 641
Whitbourne, S. K., 469
White, S. H., 362
Whiteman, S. D., 483
Whitfield, C. L., 298
Whitty, M. T., 678
Whorf, B. L., 327
Wibom, R., 178
Wickens, C. D., 278
Widiger, T. A., 577, 579, 605, 606
Widom, C. S., 606
Wiederman, M. W., 411
Wiens, S., 420
Wiese, A. M., 323

Wiese, M., 389
Wiese-Kelly, L., 237
Wiesel, T., 11, 14, 101, 124, 141–142
Wiesenfeld, B., A-23
Wigboldus, D. H. J., 666
Wiggs, C. L., 306
Wight, W., 5
Wilder, C., 644
Wilding, J., 308
Wilkaitis, J., 639
Willerman, L., 375
Willett, W. C., 403, 559
Willford, J. A., 444
Williams, A., 702
Williams, C. D., 558
Williams, E., 202
Williams, E. M., 460
Williams, G. C., 16
Williams, J., 236
Williams, J. E., 65, 552
Williams, K., 552
Williams, K. D., 695, 696
Williams, L. M., 298
Williams, M. H., 655
Williams, N. A., 555
Williams, P., 143, 628
Williams, R., 122
Williams, R. E., 472
Williams, R. L., 31, 546
Williams, W. M., 248, 380
Williamson, C. L., A-39
Williamson, D. A., 615
Willingham, B., 425
Willingham, D. T., 95
Willis, J., 665
Willis, R. P., 308
Willis, W. D., 170
Willoughby, T., 279
Wills, T. A., 556
Willshire, D., 607
Wilska, M., 370
Wilsnack, S. C., 298, 301
Wilson, M., 11, 16, 559
Wilson, R. S., 473
Wilson, S., 463
Wilson, T. D., 74, 349, 433, 684
Windholz, G., 234

Wing, R. R., 401, 403, 404
Wingfield, A., 472
Winick, C., 214, 413
Winkielman, P., 420
Winn, P., 399
Winner, E., 371–372
Winsler, A., 458
Winters, K. C., 2
Wise, M. G., 472
Wise, R. A., 87, 101
Wise, R. J. S., 95
Wisniewski, N., 413
Witt, J. K., 155
Witt, L.A., A-27
Wittenberg, L., 403
Wittkower, E. D., 649
Witviliet, C. J., 568
Wojtowicz, J. M., 303
Wolf, A. W., 196
Wolfe, J. M., 147
Wolfe, V. A., 698
Wolford, G., 106, 122
Wolitzky, D. L., 502
Woloshin, S., 558
Wolpe, J., 634–635, 646–647
Wolpert, E., 205
Wolsic, B., 431
Wonder, J., 122
Wonderlich, S. A., 614
Wong, L. A., 28, 33, 509, 512
Wong, N., 631
Wood, D., 469
Wood, E., 279, 483
Wood, F., 306
Wood, J. M., 527
Wood, J. N., 458
Wood, N. L., 277
Wood, P. B., 554
Wood, W., 412, 481, 684
Woodbury, M. A., 166
Woodcock, R. W., 357
Woodhead, M., 391
Woolf, C. J., 170
Woo-Sam, J. M., 365
Worthen, J. B., 190
Worthington, E. L., Jr., 568
Worthington, R. L., 649

Wright, J. H., 637
Wright, S. C., 26, 701
Wrosch, C., 544
Wulfeck, B., 320
Wundt, W., 4, 5, 10, 20
Wurtz, R. H., 140
Wyatt, J. K., 223
Wynder, E. L., 559
Wynn, K., 458–459
Wynne, C. D. L., 324

Y

Yager, J., 223, 614
Yalom, I. D., 631
Yamada, A., 611, 650
Yamamoto, J., 650
Yan, T., 61
Yang, H., 555
Yang, P., 31
Yates, F. A., 308
Ybarra O., 407, 701
Yen, S., 605
Yeomans, M. R., 167
Yoo, S., 15, 25
Yost, W. A., 164, 165, 472
Young, D. M., 611
Young, E. A., 542
Young, J. E., 637
Young, K., 546, 650
Young, P. R., 636
Young, T., 144
Youngentob, S. L., 166, 167
Yount, S. E., 554, 555
Yudofsky, S. C., 93
Yuille, J. C., 279, 280, 300
Yuki, M., 671
Yurgelun-Todd, D., 220
Yutzy, S. H., 587

Z

Zaccaro, S. J., A-24
Zacks, R. T., 284
Zadra, A., 202
Zagorsky, J. L., 367
Zajonc, R. B., 132, 420

Zane, N., 650
Zang, D., 555
Zanna, M. P., 666
Zapp, D. J., 409
Zaragoza, M. S., 292
Zarate, M. A., 703
Zarcone, V. P., Jr., 223
Zatzick, D. F., 170, 645
Zautra, A. J., 540, 554
Zebrowski, L. A., 665
Zechmeister, E. B., 28
Zedeck, S., 368
Zeedyk, M. S., 301
Zeelenberg, M., 349
Zeiler, M., 248
Zellner, D. A., 166
Zenhausen, R., 121
Zentall, T. R., 260
Zepelin, H., 197
Zhang, J., 339
Zhang, R., 506
Zhao, S., 580
Zhao, X., 104
Zhou, E. S., 544
Zigler, E., 371, 391
Zillman, D., 413
Zillmer, E. A., 89, 104
Zimbardo, P. G., 692–693, 698
Zimmerman, B. J., 506
Zimmerman, I. L., 365
Zimmerman, M., 579, 604
Zimprich, D., 474
Zinbarg, R., 235, 585, 637
Zipf, W. B., 464
Zoeller, R. F., Jr., 559
Zola, S. M., 14, 304
Zorick, F. J., 201
Zottoli, M. A., A-21
Zrenner, E., 146
Zubieta, J., 174
Zuck, M., 119
Zucker, K. J., 415
Zukley, L., 551
Zull, J. E., 124
Zurbriggen, E. L., 419
Zvolensky, M. J., 584
Zwislocki, J. J., 164

A

abnormal behavior
  criteria of, 577–578
  culture and, 610
  medical model of, 576–577
  misconceptions about, 576
  see also psychological disorders
aborigines, 206
absolute refractory period, 82
absolute threshold, 131, 161
abstract thinking, 456
abstracts, of journal articles, 70, 73, A-40
Abu Ghraib, 693
academic performance, 308
  improving, 28–33
  pressure and, 538–539
  SAT scores and, 57
  self-efficacy and, 506
  stress and, 549
accidents
  drug use and, 219, 220
  inattentional blindness and, 147
  sleep deprivation and, 198–199
accommodation, visual, 135, 137, 153
acetylcholine (ACh), 85, 87
Ache (Paraguay), 446
achievement, IQ and, 371
achievement motive, 417–419, 695
achievement tests, 357
acquired immune deficiency syndrome. *See* AIDS
acquisition
  in classical conditioning, 237–238, 239, 247
  in observational learning, 260–261
  in operant conditioning, 245–246, 247
acronyms, 310
acrophobia, 582
acrostics, 310
ACTH, 543, 544
action potential, 82–83
activation-synthesis model, of dreams, 207
actor-observer bias, 668–669
acupuncture, 174
acute stressors, 535
adaptation
  behavioral, 118–119, 134
  dark and light, 138
  evolutionary, 117, 118
  hedonic, 433
  sensory, 133–134
addition-subtraction abilities, 458–459
additive color mixing, 143, 144
additive strategy, 338
A-delta fibers, 170, 171
adolescence, 463–468, 478
  cognitive development in, 456
  conflict with parents in, 466, 471
  eating disorders in, 614, 615
  Freud's view of, 499
  personality development in, 466–467, 478
  physiological changes in, 463–465, 478
  search for identity in, 466–467

sleep patterns in, 194
  suicide in, 466
  turmoil in, 466
adoption studies, 114–115
  of homosexuality, 415
  of intelligence, 374–375, 376
adrenal glands, 90, 109, 543, 544
adrenocorticotropic hormone (ACTH), 543, 544
adulthood, 468–474, 477–479
  adjusting to marriage in, 470
  adjusting to parenthood in, 471
  emerging, 467–468, 478
  personality development in, 468–469, 477–479
advertising, 682
  classical conditioning in, 236, 270, 684, 685
  political, 271
  subliminal, 132
  techniques in, 705
affective forecasting, 433
afferent nerve fibers, 90
affiliation motive, 45, 46–47, 398, 418
affirmative action, 42
African Americans
  IQ scores of, 377–378, 380
  mental health services utilization by, 624
  test anxiety and, 380–381
afterimage, 134, 281
age
  happiness and, 431
  mental health services utilization and, 624
age discrimination, A-21
age of viability, 443
age stereotypes, 666
agency counselors, A-33
aggression, 545–546
  in children, 253, 259, 261–262
  cultural worldviews and, 518
  evolutionary perspective on, 15
  Freud's view of, 495
  gender differences in, 480, 481
  media violence and, 263
  research approaches to, 62
  serotonin and, 86
  testosterone and, 109
aggressive pornography, 413
aging, 471–474, 479
  memory and, 307
  sleep cycle and, 193
agonist chemicals, 86
agoraphobia, 582–583
agreeableness, 469, 491, 492, 515, 516, 522
aha myth, 388
AIDS, 219, 472, 560–562
  misconceptions about, 561–562
  prenatal exposure to, 444
  prevalence of, 560
  prevention of, 562
  transmission of, 561
  treatment for, 560
alarm reaction, 542
Albers, Josef, 180, 181
alcohol, 215, 216, 219
  health effects of, 219, 560

health risks of, 226, 227
  insomnia and, 201
  prenatal development and, 444
  stress and, 549
alcohol dependence, treatment seeking for, 623
alcoholism
  as disease, 226–227
  treatment for, 635–636
alertness, 190
algorithms, 332
Ali, Muhammed, 87
all-or-none law, 82–83
alpha waves, 188, 212
alprazolam, 638
alternative explanations, 35
alternatives, evaluating, 337–339, 571
Alzheimer's disease, 81, 86, 304, 472–473
amacrine cells, 137
Ambien, 201, 203
ambiguous figures, 147, 151
ambivalence, in attitudes, 681–682
amenorrhea, 613
American Association on Intellectual and Developmental Disabilities (AAIDD), 349
American Institute of Stress, 542
American Psychiatric Association, 579, 580
American Psychoanalytic Association, 627
American Psychological Association (APA)
  founding of, 4–5
  ethical principles of, 68, 69
  membership in, 17, 18
  website for, 18, A-34
  women in, 6
American Sign Language (ASL), 324
American Speech-Language-Hearing Association, 182
Ames room, 158
amino acids, as neurotransmitters, 87
amnesia
  dissociative, 589
  organic, 303–304
  posthypnotic, 210
amphetamines, 214, 215, 217, 218
  brain function and, 95
  neurotransmitters and, 87
amplitude
  of brain waves, 187
  of light waves, 134, 135, 143
  of sound waves, 161
amygdala, 96, 98, 100, 218, 303, 422, 423
anagrams, 329
anal stage, 498
analogies
  in problem solving, 333–334
  weak, 435
analogy problems, 329
analytic cognitive style, 336
analytical intelligence, 384
analytical psychology, 499–500
Anaylze This, 621–622
androgens, 415–416, 481

anecdotal evidence, 73–74, 704
anesthesia
  awareness under, 187
  hypnosis for, 210
anger, 496, 540, 545, 551, 552
  managing, 567–568
animal magnetism, 208
Animal Mind, The (Washburn), 6
animal research, 9–10
  criticisms of, 508
  ethics of, 67–68
animal rights activists, 67–68
Animal Welfare Information Center, 68
animals
  decision making by, 343, 344
  language learning in, 324
  naturalistic observation of, 52
  training of, 9, 246
animism, 455
Anna O, 622, 623
annoyance, 540
anonymity, of online dating, 678–679
anorexia, nervosa, 611, 613–615
answer changing, on tests, 32, 33
antagonist chemicals, 86
antecedents, 268
  control of, 269
anterograde amnesia, 304
antianxiety drugs, 584, 638
antibodies, 236
anticipatory name calling, 351
antidepressant drugs, 594, 639–641, 648
antipsychotic drugs, 601, 602, 638–639
antisocial personality disorder, 605, 606
anxiety, 540, 546
  affiliation need and, 45, 46–47
  attachment, 676, 677
  buffering of, 518
  buffers against, 518
  about death, 517–518, 519
  Freud's view of, 495–496
  illness symptoms and, 562
  insomnia and, 201, 224
  Rogers's view of, 510, 628–629
  separation, 449
  subjectivity of, 535
  testing and, 380–381
anxiety disorders, 582–586, 608–609
  biological factors in, 584–585
  classical conditioning of, 634–635
  cognitive factors in, 585–586
  conditioning of, 585
  drug therapy for, 638
  etiology of, 584–586, 609
  GABA and, 87
  lifetime prevalence of, 581
  prevalence of, 584, 608
  stress and, 586
  treatment for, 634–635, 636–637
  types of, 582–584, 608
anxiety hierarchy, 634–635
anxiety sensitivity, 584
anxious-ambivalent attachment, 449–450, 675, 676

anxious/fearful personality disorders, 605
appeal to ignorance, 390
appeals to fear, 684
appearance, person perception and, 664–665
application, as goal of scientific approach, 40
applied psychology, 12–13, 19, 22, A-33
appraisal, of stressful events, 535, 565–566
appraisals, cognitive, 420, 422, 425
apprehension, 540
approach-approach conflict, 536
approach-avoidance conflict, 536
aptitude tests, 356–357
Arapesh, 206
archetypes, 499–500
archival records, as data source, 43
Archives of the History of American Psychology (AHAP), 14
arcuate nucleus, 399, 401
arguments
  components of, 434–435
  evaluating, 435
  one-sided versus two-sided, 683
Aristotle, 280
arithmetic, infants and, 458–460
Army General Classification Test, 13
arousability, 514
arousal
  emotional, 541–542, 567
  optimal level of, 541–542
  physiological, 421–422
arrangement, problems of, 328–329
art, perceptual principles and, 175–179
arthritis, stress and, 554
articles, journal, 70–73
artists, mental illness and, 389
ascending reticular activating system (ARAS), 196
assertiveness, 522
Association for Behavioral anad Cognitive Therapies, 636
Association for Psychological Science (APS), 13, 18
associations, learned, 233, 234
assumptions, 434
astrocysts, 174
asylums, 576, 651
atherosclerosis, 551, 552
attachment
  culture and, 451
  in infants, 448–451
  love and, 675–677
  patterns of, 449–450
  reinforcement theory of, 449
  theories of, 449
attachment styles, 675–676
attention
  deliberation without, 340
  divided, 278
  marijuana use and, 220
  memory encoding and, 277–278
  observational learning and, 260
  pain perception and, 159
  positive emotions and, 541
  selective, 147, 307
  stress and, 548–549
  in working memory, 284
attention filter, 277
attitude alignment, 673
attitudes, 633, 681–687
  accessibility of, 681

ambivalent, 681–682
behavior and, 682
changing, 682–684
classical conditioning of, 684
components of, 681, 682
conditioning of, 270
defined, 681
dimensions of, 681–682
existing, 684
formation of, 684, 702
observational learning of, 685
operant conditioning of, 684
prejudiced, 699–703
sexual, 413
similarity in, 673
strength of, 681, 682
subliminal influences on, 133
work and, A-25–A-26, A-28–A-29
attraction. See interpersonal attraction
attractiveness
  cultural standards for, 679
  eating disorders and, 614, 615
  happiness and, 431
  impressions and, 665
  mate preferences and, 410, 411
  persuasion and, 683
attribution processes, 664, 667–672
attributions, 667
  bias in, 668–671, 702
  culture and, 671–672
  defensive, 670
  external, 668, 669, 670
  internal, 668, 669, 670
  stable-unstable dimension of, 668, 669
  for success and failure, 668, 669
atypical antipsychotic drugs, 639
auditory cortex, 102, 163
auditory hallucinations, 599
auditory localization, 164–165
auditory nerves, 164
auditory processing, in brain, 102, 106
auditory system, 160–165, 172–173
authority, obedience to, 689–692
autism, 103
autogenic training attention, 224
autonomic arousal, 421–422
autonomic nervous system (ANS), 90, 91, 99, 109, 421, 542
autonomic specificity, 427
autonomy versus shame and doubt, 452
availability heuristic, 341–342, 347, 617
averages, 55
aversion therapy, 635–636
aversive stimulus, 249–250, 251
avoidance-avoidance conflict, 536
avoidance behavior, 268
avoidance learning, 250–251
avoidance response, 585
avoidant attachment, 450, 675, 676
awareness, levels of, 186–187, 494
axons, 80, 81
  from eye to brain, 137, 138
  squid, 82

B

babbling, 320, 321
babies. See infancy
bachelor's degree, in psychology, A-30

background checks, on job applicants, A-21
balance, 99
Bantu, 154–155
barbiturates, 214
barn swallow, 119
Barnes, Carolyn, 377
base rates, 570–571
  ignoring, 342–343
baseball teams, jet lag and, 190
baseline data, 267
basilar membrane, 162–163
Bay of Pigs, 698
Beck Institute of Cognitive Therapy and Research, 637
bedtime
  ideal, 189
  regular, 224
behavior
  cultural factors in, 25–26
  defined, 8
  evolution of, 118–119
  multifactorial causation of, 24–25
  observable, 9
behavior modification, 29, 267–269, 636, 656
Behavior of Organisms, The (Skinner), 242
behavior therapies, 623, 633–637, 646–647, 656
  aversion therapy, 635–636
  cognitive therapy, 636–637, 646–647
  effectiveness of, 637
  social skills training, 636
  systematic desensitization, 634–635, 646–647
behavioral contract, 269
behavioral disengagement, 544–545
behavioral genetics, 110, 514–515, 516
behavioral maneuvers, 118–119
behavioral neuroscience, A-35
behavioral perspective, 20
  on attachment, 449
  evaluation of, 508
  on personality, 502–508, 520–521
behavioral residue, 505
behavioral traits, evolution of, 118
behaviorism, 8–9, 11, 502, 634
  criticism of, 10
  defined, 8
  history of, 8–10
  radical, 508
beliefs, 681, 700
Bell Curve, The (Herrnstein & Murray), 378, 379
Bellini, Gentile and Giovanni, 176
bell-shaped curve, 361, 364, 366, A-9–A-10, A-11
Belvedere (Escher), 179
Benoit, Chris, 110
benzodiazepines, 201, 638
beta waves, 188
Beyond Freedom and Dignity (Skinner), 10
bias
  in attributions, 668–671n, 702
  confirmation, 347, 698
  experimenter, 61, 64, 70
  in person perception, 666, 667
  sampling, 59–60, 65, 74
  self-effacing, 672
  self-serving, 670–671
  social desirability, 61, 526
Big Five traits, 491–492, 501

cross-cultural studies of, 519
evolutionary perspective on, 519
health and, 557
heritability of, 515
measurement of, 525
bilingualism, 323–324
Binet-Simon intelligence scale, 361, 368
binge drinking, 216
binge eating/purging, 613
binge-eating disorder, 614
binocular cues, to depth perception, 152–153
biological constraints, on conditioning, 254–256
biological drives, 498
biological motives, 398
biological perspective, 11, 14
  on attachment, 449
  evaluation of, 516
  on personality, 513–516, 520–521
biological rhythms, 188–191
biomedical therapies, 623, 638–644, 646–647
biopsychology, A-35
biopsychosocial model, 533–534
bipolar cells, 137
bipolar disorder, 590, 591, 592–593, 611
  drug therapy for, 640, 641
  treatment seeking for, 623
bird and train problem, 335
birth defects, 442
birth order, 501
birth weight, 443
bisexuals, 414, 561
blaming, of victims, 670, 702
blind spot, 137
blindness, inattentional, 147
blood, glucose levels in, 400
blood flow, in brain, 95
blood pressure, 213, 551, 559, 570
blood type, 112
Bobo doll, 261
body image, disturbed, 613
body language, 423
body mass index (BMI), 403, 404
body temperature, 189, 396–397
body weight, See weight
Boggs, Wade, 231, 232
bona fide occupational qualifications (BFOQs), A-20
bonobo pygmy chimpanzees, 324
botox, 86
bottom-up processing, 148, 149, 159
bounded rationality, theory of, 337
brain
  in adolescence, 464–465
  blood flow in, 95
  deterioration of, 472
  development of, 124
  drug effects on, 218–219
  electrical recordings of, 92
  electrical stimulation of, 93
  lesioning of, 92–93
  lobes of, 101–102
  number of neurons in, 89
  percentage "in use," 89
  plasticity of, 104
  structure of, 97–105
  study of, 92–97
  ventricles of, 90, 91602
  visual pathways in, 140, 141
  weight of, 91, 472
brain activity, consciousness and, 187–188

brain-based learning, 124
brain damage, 92–93, 104
brain-imaging procedures, 94–97, 602
brain organization, gender differences in, 481
brain size, intelligence and, 383
brain surgery, 93, 644
brain waves, 92, 187–188
"brainedness," 121
brainstem, 97, 98, 99, 170
Branson, Richard, 489–490
breast size, men's preferences for, 529
breeding, selective, 113
brightness, of colors, 134, 135, 143, 144
broaden-and-build theory, 541
Broca's area, 105, 324
brontophobia, 582
Bryant, Kobe, 418
bulimia nervosa, 613–614
burnout, 549
business negotiations, classical conditioning in, 270–271
Byrd, James, Jr., 700
bystander effect, 694–695

C

C fibers, 170, 171
caffeine, 214, 224, 559–559
calcium intake, 559
Cambridge, Center for Behavioral Studies, 250
cancer, 534
  cell phones and, 571
  diet and, 559
  marijuana and, 220
  smoking and, 558
candle problem, 335
cannabinoid receptors, 218
cannabinoids, endogenous, 400
cannabis, 215, 216
Cannon-Bard theory, 426, 427
cardiovascular disease, 551
career success, 418
careers, in psychology, A-30–A-38
caregivers, attachment to, 448
caregiving styles, 675
case studies, 52–53, 54, 62–63, 73–74, 502
catastrophic thinking, 545, 565–566, 588
catatonic schizophrenia, 599
catecholamines, 543, 544
catharsis, 545
causation
  correlational research and, 51, 54, 56, 570
  experimental research and, 50
  see also multifactorial causation
Cavalin, Moshe Kai, 372
CBcampus.com, A-33
CCK, 401
Celexa, 641
cell membrane, of neuron, 82, 83
cell phones, 571
  attention and, 147
  driving and, 278
cells
  in brain, 104
  genetic material in, 110–111
  in nervous system, 80–81
  in retina, 137–139
cellular immune responses, 555

center-surround arrangement, 139, 170
Centers for Disease Control and Prevention, 561
central nervous system, 89, 90–91
  see also brain; spinal cord
central tendency, measures of, 55, A-8
centration, 454
cephalocaudal trend, 445
cerebellum, 97, 98, 99, 286, 303
cerebral cortex, 98, 101–102
cerebral hemispheres, 101, 105, 106, 481
cerebral laterality, 105–108
cerebral specialization, 120–123, 481–482
cerebrospinal fluid (CSF), 90, 91, 602
cerebrum, 98, 101–104
chance, research results and, 59, A-14
change, as source of stress, 537–538
channel factors, in persuasion, 683
Charles, Prince, 439–440
chemical senses, 165–168, 172–173
child abuse
  multiple personality and, 590
  repressed memories of, 298–302
childlessness, 470–471
childrearing, 515
  cultural differences in, 671
children
  aggression in, 259, 261–262
  bilingual, 323–324
  cognitive development in, 453–456, 476–477
  deciding whether to have, 470
  effect of father absence on, 484–485
  environmental deprivation and, 379
  food preferences in, 402, 167
  fostering independence in, 522
  gender-role socialization of, 482–483
  imitation of models by, 506
  language development in, 320–323
  media violence and, 261–263, 266
  moral development in, 460–462
  motor development in, 445–446, 476, 477
  nightmares in, 202
  parental love for, 509, 510
  personality development in, 451–453, 476–477, 498–499
  physical punishment of, 252–253
Chimpanzee and Human Communication Institute, 324
chimpanzees, 324
  Goodall's study of, 52
China, 369, 522
chlamydia, 444
chlorpromazine, 638, 639
Cho, Seung-Hui, 578, 610
choices
  conflict and, 536
  factors in, 337–339
cholesterol, 551, 559
chromosomes, 110, 111, 440
chronic diseases, 534
chronic stressors, 535
chunks, in short-term memory, 283
cicada, 188
cichlid fish, 119
cigarettes, 270, 558

cigars, 558
cingulate cortex, 423
cingulate gyrus, 100
circadian rhythms, 188–191
circular reactions, 454
circular reasoning, 227, 435
Civil Rights Act of 1964, A-20
clarification, in client-centered therapy, 629–630
Clark University, 7
class attendance, grades and, 31
classical conditioning, 232–241
  acquisition in, 238, 247
  in advertising, 270
  of anxiety, 585, 634–635
  of attitudes, 684
  aversion therapy and, 635–636
  avoidance learning and, 250–251
  basic processes in, 237–240
  in business negotiations, 270–271
  discrimination in, 240, 247
  of drug effects, 237
  of emotions, 235–236
  in everyday life, 234–235
  extinction in, 238, 247
  of food preferences, 402
  generalization in, 239–240, 247
  observational learning and, 259
  overview of, 264–265
  Pavlov's formulation of, 233–234
  of physiological responses, 236
  in politics, 271
  relation to operant conditioning, 241
  signal relations in, 258
  spontaneous recovery in, 238–239
  terminology and procedures for, 234
classical music, for infants, 124, 125
claustrophobia, 582
client-centered therapy, 628–630, 646–647
  effectiveness of, 656
climate, organizational, A-22
clinical neuropsychology, 19, 22
  careers in, A-37
clinical psychologists, 53, 624
clinical psychology, 12, 19, 22, A-32–A-33
  careers in, A-36
clinical social workers, 625, A-33
closure, as Gestalt principle, 150
Clouser, Ronald, 312
clozapine, 639
clustering, 287
CNS depressants, 215, 219, 223
CNS stimulants, 215
cocaine, 214, 215, 217, 218, 219
  brain activity and, 95
  neurotransmitters and, 87
  prenatal development and, 443–444
cochlea, 162, 163
cocktail party phenomenon, 277
coefficient of determination, A-13
cognition, 13–14, 318
cognitive abilities
  aging and, 473–474
  gender differences in, 35, 480
Cognitive Abilities Test, 363
cognitive appraisal, of stressful events, 540
cognitive-behavioral therapy, 636–637, 646–647
cognitive development, 453–460, 476–479

moral development and, 460
Piaget's stage theory of, 453–456, 476–477
sociocultural theory of, 457
cognitive dissonance, 686
cognitive functioning,
  marijuana use and, 220
  sleep deprivation and, 198
cognitive load, 277–278
cognitive maps, 257
cognitive perspective, 11, 13–14, 318
  on conditioning, 256–259
  on emotions, 420
  on intelligence, 383–384
cognitive processes, 14
cognitive psychology, 18, 19
  careers in, A-34
cognitive style, 123
  culture and, 336
  depression and, 596
cognitive tasks, hemispheres and, 121, 122
cognitive therapy, 636–637, 646–647, 656
cognitive vulnerability, 596
cohort effects, 447
collective unconscious, 499
collectivism, 671, 695
  conformity and, 692
  marriage and, 677
college admissions tests, 57
college students
  alcohol and, 216
  date rape among, 413
  gambling by, 1–2
  as research subjects, 60
  sleep deprivation in, 197–198
colleges, psychology laboratories at, 4
color blindness, 144–145
color circle, 145
color mixing, 143–144
color solid, 144
color vision, 134–135, 138, 143–146
colors, naming of, 327
Columbia space shuttle, 528
commitment, 467
  employee, A-26–A-27
  in romantic relationships, 674–645
  psychiatric, 607, 610
committees, ethics, 67
common sense, versus scientific approach, 44–45
communication, 318
  in animals, 324
  on dates, 673
  in groups, 694
  with health providers, 562–563
  nonverbal, 423
  persuasive, 682–684
communities, positive, 16
community counseling, A-33
community mental health centers, 655
community mental health movement, 651
comorbidity, 616
companionate love, 674
comparative evaluations, 339
comparitors, 180–181
compensation, 500–501
compensatory CRs, 237
competition
  between groups, 702–703
  individualism and, 672

competitiveness, 522
complementary colors, 144, 145
compliance
  with authority, 689–692
  with group, 689
  with medical advice, 563–564
compulsions, 583
conception, 440
concepts, semantic networks of, 289
conceptual hierarchy, 287–288
conclusions, 434
concordance rate
  for antisocial personality disorder, 606
  for anxiety disorders, 584
  for mood disorders, 594
  for schizophrenia, 601
concrete operational period, 454, 455–456
conditionability, 514
conditioned reflex, 9, 305
conditioned reinforcers, 244
conditioned response (CR), 234, 235, 236, 237, 239, 585, 634, 635, 684, 685
conditioned responses, compensatory, 237
conditioned stimulus (CS), 234, 235, 236, 237, 238, 239, 251, 585, 634, 635, 684, 685
  ecologically relevant, 256
  predictive value of, 258
conditioning, 232
  biological constraints on, 254–256
  cognitive processes in, 256–259
  contingencies and, 258
  evaluative, 270, 684
  personality and, 503–504
  rapid, 256
  see also classical conditioning; operant conditioning
cones, 137–138, 145
confidence intervals, 348
confirmation bias, 347, 666, 698
conflict(s)
  between groups, 702
  dreaming about, 204
  internal, 495
  parent-adolescent, 466, 471
  as source of stress, 536
  types of, 536
  unconscious, 626–627
conformity, 633, 688–689, 688–689
conformity pressure, 538–539
confounding of variables, 47
congruence, 509, 510, 628
conjunction fallacy, 343, 617
conjunctive probabilities, 616, 617
connectionist models, of memory, 289–290
connotation, 320
conscience, 462
  lack of, 606
conscientiousness, 469, 491, 492, 515, 516, 557
conscious, 494
consciousness
  altered states of, 209, 211
  altering with drugs, 214–221
  contents of, 186
  defined, 186
  divided, 211
  evolutionary roots of, 187
  stream of, 6, 121, 122, 186
  study of, 4, 5, 6, 186
  unity of, 121

conservation, 454–455
consistency, cross-situational, 490, 507
consolidation, of memory, 199, 304
constancies, perceptual, 157, 159
constraint, 492
constraints, unnecessary, 331–332
construct validity, 359, 360
constructive coping, 547–548, 565–569
contact comfort, 449
contagious diseases, 533–534
content validity, 359, 360
context
  perceptual hypotheses and, 152
  for personality development, 501
context cues, 291
contingencies
  conditioning and, 258
  reinforcement, 261, 268–269
continuity, as Gestalt principle, 150
contradictory evidence, 35, 391
contrast effects, 180–181
control, as goal of scientific approach, 40
control group, 46
conventional level, 460, 461
convergence, of eyes, 153
convergent thinking, 389
conversion disorder, 587
cooperativeness, 522
coping, 544–545
  constructive, 547–548, 565–569
  defensive, 546–547
  healthy, 541
  problem-focused, 557
cornea, 135, 136
Cornell University, 6
coronary arteries, 551
corporal punishment, 252–253
corpus callosum, 98, 101, 106, 482
correlation, 56–58, A-11–A-12
  causation and, 57–58, 484–485, 570
  invention of concept, 361
  positive and negative, 56, 57
  prediction and, 57, A-12–A-13
  reliability and, 358
  strength of, 57, A-11
correlation coefficient, 56, 57, A-11
  calculating, A-12
  in test reliability, 358
correlational research, 51–54
corticosteroids, 543, 544
co-sleeping, 195–196
counseling, careers in, A-30, A-33
counseling psychology, 19, 22
  careers in, A-36
counselors, 625
counterarguments, 434, 684
counterattitudinal behavior, 685–686
counterconditioning, 635
counterproductive behaviors, A-28
courtship behavior, 119–119
crack cocaine, 215, 219
cramming, for exams, 28, 309
C-reactive protein, 551, 552, 553
creative intelligence, 384
creativity, 387–389
  eminence and, 372
credibility
  of online sources, A-40–A-42
  of source, 683
  evaluating, 704–705
cricket, 119

criminal activity, antisocial personality disorder and, 606
criterion-related validity, 359, 360
Critical Incident Technique (CIT), A-18
critical periods, 124, 125
critical thinking, defined, 34
cross-cultural research, 15
  on close relationships, 677
  on emotion, 423–425
  on mate preferences, 410
  on motor development, 446
  on personality, 519, 522–523
  on social behavior, 699
cross-sectional designs, 447
cross-situational consistency, 507
crossing over, of chromosomes, 111
Crow, Sheryl, 592
cryptamnesia, 293
crystal meth, 215
Crystal, Billy, 621
crystallized intelligence, 473
CT (computerized tomography) scans, 94–95
Cuba, 698
Cubism, 176, 177
cues, to depth perception, 152–154
cultural bias, on IQ tests, 381–382
cultural differences
  in attachment patterns, 451
  in attributional processes, 671–672
  in close relationships, 677
  in depth perception, 154–155
  in dreaming, 206
  in intelligence testing, 368–369
  in IQ scores, 377–382
  in motor development, 446
  in perception, 175
  in perception of visual illusions, 159–160
  in psychological disorders, 610–611
  in sleep patterns, 193, 195–196
cultural diversity, psychology and, 14–15
cultural influences, on behavior, 25–26
cultural worldviews, 517–519
culture
  archetypes and, 500
  cognitive development and, 457
  cognitive style and, 336
  conformity and, 691–692
  defined, 25
  eating disorders and, 615
  emotions and, 423–425
  employment laws and, A-20–A-21
  food preferences and, 402
  gender differences and, 481
  language and, 327–328
  mate preferences and, 410
  obedience and, 691–692
  organizational, A-22–A-23
  pace of life and, 51–52
  personality and, 519, 522–523
  problem solving and, 336
  psychotherapy and, 649
  social loafing and, 695
  taste preferences and, 166, 167
culture-bound disorders, 611
cumulative deprivation hypothesis, 375–376
cumulative probabilities, 616
cumulative recorder, 243, 244
curare, 86
curriculum reform, 122

custody decisions, 73
customs, culture and, 26
cyberspace, 391
cyclothymic disorder, 592
cynicism, 549
cystic fibrosis, 115

D

daily cycles, 189
Dalai Lama, 367
Dali, Salvador, 177, 204524
Dalmane, 201
dark adaptation, 138
data, graphing of, A-7–A-8
data analysis, 43–44
data collection, 43, A-7
  using Internet, 65
databases, online, A-40
date rape, 413
dating, 673, 674
  online, 678–679
  tactics in, 679
day care, attachment and, 451
day residue, 205
death, inevitability of, 517
death anxiety, 517–518, 519
decay, of memory traces, 282, 287, 296
decentration, 455
deception
  in personality testing, 526
  in research, 66–67, 691
  in romantic relationships, 680
decibels (dB), 161
decision affect theory, 49
decision making, 337–345
  evidence-based, 74
  evolutionary perspective on, 343–344, 346
  fast, 344–345
  in groups, 696–698
  health-related, 571
  intuitive, 339–340
  mistakes in, 337
  postchoice satisfaction with, 340
  prefrontal cortex and, 103
  risky, 341, 346, 697
  in signal detection, 131–132
  stress and, 548–549
  uncertainty in, 341
  unconscious, 340
declarative memory system, 305
deep brain stimulation (DBS), 644
deep sleep, 188
Deese-Roediger-McDermott paradigm, 300
defense mechanisms, 495–496, 497, 510, 546–547, 626, 629
defensive attribution, 670, 702
definitions
  operational, 42
  power of, 226–227
DeGeneres, Ellen, 416
deinstitutionalization, 651–652
dejection, 540
deliberation, careful, 339–340
deliberation without attention effect, 340
delta waves, 188
delusions, 598–599, 611
  of grandeur, 598–599
  of persecution, 599
dementia, 472
Demerol, 215
demonic possession, 576

dendrites, 80, 81
dendritic branching, 104
dendritic trees, 80
denial, 546
DeNiro, Robert, 621
denotation, 320
dentate gyrus, 303, 304
dependent variables, 46, 48
depression, 590
  brain stimulation for, 644
  creativity and, 389
  death anxiety and, 518
  drug therapy for, 639–641
  electroconvulsive therapy for,
    642–643
  geriatric, 648
  heart disease and, 552–554
  insomnia and, 201
  marital adjustment and, 65
  menopause and, 472
  neurotransmitters and, 86
  positive psychotherapy for, 630
  postpartum, 471
  self-blame and, 544–545
  smoking and, 58
  stress and, 549
  suppressed neurogenesis and, 544
  treatment for, 636–637
depressive disorder(s), 591–592
  biological factors in, 594–595
  blended therapy for, 648
  cognitive factors in, 595–596
  culture and, 611
  drug therapy for, 638–639
  etiology of, 593–597, 609
  gender differences in, 592
  genetic vulnerability to, 594
  interpersonal roots of, 597
  neuroochemical factors in,
    594–595
  onset of, 591
  prevalence of, 592
  stress and, 597
  symptoms of, 591
  treatment seeking for, 623
deprivation, environmental,
  375–376
depth cues, in paintings, 176
depth perception, 152–153
description, as goal of scientific
  approach, 40, 41
descriptive/correlational research,
  51–54
descriptive statistics, 55–58,
  A-8–A-13
desensitization, systematic,
  634–635, 646–647
detectability, of stimuli, 132
determinism, 503
  reciprocal, 504
development
  in adolescence, 463–468, 478
  in adulthood, 468–474, 478–479
  in childhood, 445–462, 476–477
  cognitive, 453–460, 476–479
  continuity as characteristic of,
    440
  defined, 440
  emotional, 448–451
  moral, 460–462
  motor, 445–446
  personality, 446–448, 451–453,
    466–467, 476–479
  physical, 445–446, 463–465,
    476–479
  prenatal, 440–444

sexual, 463–464
  transition as characteristic of, 440
developmental norms, 445, 446
developmental psychology, 18, 19
  careers in, A-34
deviance, as criterion for abnormality, 577
deviation IQ scores, 364
diabetes, 554, 571
diagnosis, 577
Diagnostic and Statistical Manual
  of Mental Disorders (DSM), 579,
  580, 581
diazepam, 638
dichromats, 144–145
diet, quality of, 558–559
dietary restraint, 405
dieting, 403
Differential Aptitude Tests, 357
difficult children, 448
diffusion of responsibility, 695
digestive system, hunger and,
  400–401
disabilities, animal research and, 68
disability, intellectual 369–371
disagreements, perceptions in, 42
disasters, stress and, 550
discipline, parental, 252
disclosure, emotional, 567
disconfirming evidence, 313
discrimination
  in classical conditioning, 240, 247
  in operant conditioning, 246, 247
discrimination (social)
  in hiring, A-20
  against homosexuals, 416
  prejudice and, 700
discriminative stimuli, 246
disease(s)
  biopsychosocial model of, 533–534
  chronic, 534
  prenatal development and, 444
  psychosomatic, 551
  see also illness
disinhibition, 606
  with hypnosis, 210
disorganized-disoriented attachment, 450
disorganized schizophrenia, 599
displacement, 496, 497, 545
display rules, 424
dissociation, in hypnosis, 209, 211
dissociative amnesia, 589
dissociative disorders, 589–590
dissociative identity disorder (DID),
  589, 590, 598
dissonance theory, 685–686
distal stimuli, 151
distributed practice, 309
distribution
  normal, A-9–A-10, A-11
  skewed, A-8
divergent thinking, 388–389
division of labor, 470, 481
divorce, 484, 485, 568
  happiness and, 432
  personality traits and, 492
Dix, Dorothea, 650, 651
dizygotic twins, 113, 114
DNA, 111
  manipulating, 115
doctoral degree, in psychology,
  A-33–A-37
dolphins, 193
dominant gene, 112
door-in-the-face technique, 180

dopamine, 86, 87, 101, 218, 639
dopamine circuits, 95, 99
dopamine hypothesis, 86–87, 601,
  602, 603
double-blind procedure, 64, 648
Doublespeak (Lutz), 350
doubt, 453
Down syndrome, 370
"downers," 215
Doyle, Arthur Conan, 317
dramatic/impulsive personality
  disorders, 605
dream analysis, 500, 626
dream interpretation, 301
dreaming, 204–208
  REM and, 186, 192
  theories of, 206–208
dreams, 204–208
  common questions about,
    224–225
  common themes in, 205
  content of, 204, 205, 206
  culture and, 206
  interpretation of, 225
  links with waking life, 204–205
  recall for, 224–225
  shocking, 225
  symbolism in, 225
drinking
  on college campuses, 216
  stress and, 546
drive reduction, 397
drives, 99, 396–397
driving, cell phone use and, 278
drowsiness, 198
drudge theory, 372
drug companies, 642
drug dependence, 217, 218
  treatment seeking for, 623
drug therapy
  deinstitutionalization and, 652
  effectiveness of, 641–642
  for psychological disorders, 623,
    638–644, 646–647
drug use
  during pregnancy, 443–444
  health effects of, 560
  insomnia and, 201
  stress and, 546, 549
drugs, psychoactive, 214–221
drunk driving, test for, 99
DSM-IV, 579, 580, 581, 605
DSM-V, 579
dual-coding theory, 279
dual-process theories, of decision
  making, 345
Duchamp, Marcel, 177, 178
duloxetine, 641
dysthymic disorder, 591

E

ear
  auditory localization and, 164
  sensory processing in, 162–163
eardrum, 162
earlobes, detached, 111
early maturation, 465
easy children, 447–448
eating behavior
  biological factors in, 399–401
  with eating disorders, 613–614
  environmental cues to, 401–402
  obesity and, 404–405
  observational learning and, 402
  in rats, 118

regulation of, 99
  serotonin and, 86
  stress and, 403, 546
eating disorders, 580, 587–589
eating habits
  poor, 558–559
  sleep and, 224
eclecticism, 649, 656
ecologically relevant conditioned
  stimuli, 2256
ecstasy, 216, 220–221
educational psychology, 18, 19
  careers in, A-35
EEG patterns, 92
efferent nerve fibers, 90
Effexor, 641
efficiency, in groups, 695
effort justification, 686
egg cell, 111, 440
ego, 493, 494, 495, 496, 626
egocentrism, 455
Eichman, Adolf, 689
Eisenhower, Dwight D., A-24
ejaculation, 407, 464
elaboration, in encoding, 279
elaboration likelihood model, 687
Elavil, 639
election campaign ads, 271
electrical stimulation of the brain
  (ESB), 93, 100
electroconvulsive therapy (ECT),
  642–643
electrodes, 92, 93, 187, 643, 644
electroencephalograph (EEG), 92,
  187–188
electromyograph (EMG), 191
electrooculograph (EOG), 191
elicited responses, 234
elimination by aspects, 338
embryonic stage, 441–442
emergentist theories, 326
emetic drugs, 635
eminence
  contributions to, 372
  mental disorders and, 389
emotion(s), 419–425
  attitudes and, 681, 700
  autonomic nervous system and, 90
  behavioral component of, 423
    Cannon-Bard theory of, 427
  categorization of, 424
  cognitive component of, 420
  conditioning of, 235–236,
    239–240, 270, 684
  control of, 420
  culture and, 423–425
  defined, 419–520
  Ellis's model of, 565–566
  evolutionary perspective on,
    427–428
  expected outcomes and, 49–50
  expressed, 603
  facial expressions for, 423, 424
  fundamental, 423
  heart disease and, 552–554
  in schizophrenia, 599
  innate, 427–428
  James-Lange theory of, 426
  language and, 350
  limbic system and, 100
  manipulation of, 270, 271
  moral, 462
  motivation and, 419
  negative, 349, 403, 420, 424, 497,
    540, 591
  neural circuits for, 422–423

physiological component of, 421–423

Plutchik's model of, 428

positive, 16, 420, 540

primary, 428

release of, 545, 567

situational cues for, 427

socially disengaging, 424

socially engaging, 424

stress and, 540–541

suppressing, 424, 567

theories of, 426–428

two-factor theory of, 427

words for, 424

emotional arousal, 541–542, 567

emotional development, 448–451

emotional intelligence, 385–386

emotionality, positive, 432

empathy, 522

mirror neurons and, 103

of therapist, 629, 633

empirical approach, in psychology, 39–40

empiricism, 23, 39, 69–70, 120

in social psychology, 699

statistics and, A-7, A-14

employees

commitment of, A-27–A-28

job satisfaction of, A-25–A-26

selection of, A-18–A-22

socializing, A-22–A-24

training of, A-24–A-25

withdrawal of, A-27–A-28

work attitudes of, A-25–A-27, A-28

in work teams, A-23–A-24

employers, qualities sought in job applicants, A-31

empty nest, 471

encoding, 276, 277–280

enriching, 279–280, 310–311

ineffective, 296

self-referent, 280

encoding specificity principle, 297

endocannabinoids, 218

endocrine system, 99, 108–109, 421, 543

endorphins, 87, 88, 174, 218

English tit-mouse, 260

environment

heredity and, 26, 115–116, 120, 376–377, 387, 475

intelligence and, 375–376

work, A-25

environmental enrichment, 124, 125, 376

environmental fragrancing, 168

environmental tobacco smoke, 558

Epidemiological Catchment Area studies, 581

epidemiology, 579

epilepsy, surgery for, 107

episodic memory system, 305–306, 473

Equal Employment Opportunity Commission, A-21

equilibrium, 397, 99

erection, 406

ergonomics, A-25

erotic materials, 412–413

ESB, memory triggers and, 284, 285

escape learning, 250, 251

Escher, M. C., 177–178

Eskimos, 327, 424

essay exams, 33, 295

ethics

APA standards for, 68, 69

in research, 66–69, 691

ethnic differences, in IQ scores, 377–382

ethnic groups, mental health services utilization by, 624

ethnic stereotypes, 666, 700–701

ethnocentrism, 15

etiology, 577

euphoria, in bipolar disorders, 592

evaluative conditioning, 270, 684

event-based tasks, 306

evidence

anecdotal, 73–74

disconfirming, 313

lack of, 390

evolutionary biology, 16

evolutionary perspective, 11, 15–16, 116–119

on cognitive abilities, 460

on color vision, 143

on conditioned taste aversion, 256

on consciousness, 187

criticism of, 16, 412

Darwin's, 116–117

on emotion, 427–428

evaluating, 34–35

on fight-or-flight response, 542

on flaws in decision making, 343–344, 346

on gender differences, 481

on gender differences in taste sensitivity, 167

hindsight bias and, 529

on human sexual behavior, 407–412

on interpersonal attraction, 679–680

on language, 324–325

on learning, 256

on motivation, 397–398

on obesity, 404

on person perception, 667

on personality, 515

on sleep, 197

evolutionary theory, 5–6

exams, preparing for, 32–33, 309–310

excitatory PSPs, 84, 85

excitement phase, of sexual response cycle, 406, 407

exercise, 569

aging and, 473

lack of, 404–405, 551, 559–560

self-efficacy and, 506

sleep and, 223

exhaustion stage, 543

exhaustion, 549

exorcism, 577

expectations

conforming to, 538–539

in conducting research, 61

drug effects and, 216

happiness and, 433

for marital roles, 470

for outcomes, 49–50

pain perception and, 159

perception and, 27, 152

person perception and, 666

role, 692

schema-based, 288

expected value, 341

experience

brain structure and, 104

perception and, 152

subjectivity of, 70

experimental approach, methodological problems with, 61

experimental group, 46

experimental psychology, 18, 19

careers in, A-34–A-35

experimental research, 45–50

advantages of, 50, 63

disadvantages of, 50, 63

elements of, 45–46, 48, 62

experimenter bias, 61, 64, 70

experiments, 45, 62

design for, 47–48

using Internet, 64

expertise, of sources, 683

explanations, alternative, 35, 391, 485

expressed emotion, 603

external attributions, 668, 669, 670

extinction

in classical conditioning, 238, 247

in operant conditioning, 246, 247

resistance to, 246, 251

extraneous variables, 47

extrapolation, 124–125

extraversion, 114, 359, 360, 432, 469, 491, 492, 514, 515, 416, 522

eye, structure of, 135–177

eyeblink response, 303

eyewitnesses

fallibility of, 312–313

recall of, 291, 292

F

faces, recognition of, 142–143

facial-feedback hypothesis, 423, 424

facial expressions, 423, 424

facial symmetry, 679

factor analysis, 362–363, 491, 519, 525

failure

attributions for, 668, 669

fear of, 380, 588

frustration and, 535–536

faith, happiness and, 431

fallacies, logical, 390, 435, 485

false dichotomy, 435, 485

false memory syndrome, 298–302

False Memory Syndrome Foundation, 298

family

antisocial personality and, 606

eating disorders and, 615

schizophrenia and, 603

social support from, 556

as source of gender-role socialization, 483

family environment, personality and, 515

family studies, 113

of anxiety disorders, 584

of intelligence, 373–374

fantasy, as defense mechanism, 546, 547

farsightedness, 136, 137, 472

fast mapping, 321

fat cells, 401, 405, 463

fatalism, 545

father absence, 484–485

fatigue, 200, 549

fatty foods, 559

taste preferences for, 118, 402

fear appeals, 684

fear(s), 426, 540

amygdala and, 100

conditioned, 235, 239–240, 251, 255–256, 585, 634–635

irrational, 232, 582

learned, 304

neural circuits for, 422, 423

subjectivity of, 535

feature analysis, 148–149

feature detectors, 141–142, 148, 149, 170

feelings

attitudes and, 681

subjective, 420

see also emotion(s)

femininity, 475

fetal alcohol syndrome, 444

fetal stage, 441, 442–443

fetishes, 236

fiber, dietary, 559, 559

fibromyalgia, 554

fight-or-flight response, 90, 109, 117, 421, 426, 542

figure and ground, 149

finches, house, 119

findings, reporting, 70

Finland, 52

first-borns, 501

fitness

cardiovascular, 559

inclusive, 118

reproductive, 117, 118

fixation, 498, 529

fixed-interval schedules of reinforcement, 248, 249

fixed-ratio schedules of reinforcement, 248, 249

flashbulb memories, 285–286

flattery, 674

flatworms, 302

flavor, perception of, 167

fluid intelligence , 473

fluoxetine, 640

fluphenazine, 639

Flynn effect, 376, 379

fMRI scans, 108

food

incentive value of, 401, 402

palatability of, 401

preoccupation with, 614

food preferences, 166, 167, 402

foot-in-the-door technique, 705

Ford, Harrison, 592

Fore (New Guinea), 424

forebrain, 98, 99

forensic psychology, 19, 22

careers in, A-37

foreplay, 406

forewarning, 271, 684

forgetting, 276, 294–302

aging and, 473

causes of, 295–297

in dissociative amnesia, 589

of dreams, 224

measures of, 294–295

motivated, 297–298, 496

forgetting curve, 294, 295

forgiving, 567, 568

formal operational period, 454, 456

forms, perception of, 146–152

fovea, 136, 138

Fox, Michael J., 87

framing, of questions, 348–349

Francesco, S., 176

fraternal twins, 113, 114

free association, 626, 627

free-basing, 215

free will, 10, 503

frequency

of brain waves, 187

of sound waves, 161

frequency distribution, A-7
frequency polygon, A-7
frequency theory, of hearing, 163
Freudian slips, 7, 494
Friedman, Arthur, A-15, A-24
friends, 556, 672, 673
frontal lobe, 102, 105, 307, 602–603
frustration, 498, 535
frustration-aggression hypothesis, 545
functional fixedness, 330
functional magnetic resonance imaging (fMRI), 95
functionalism, 5–6
fundamental attribution error, 668–669, 670, 702
Futurism, 177

G

g (general mental ability), 363, 366
GABA (gamma-aminobutyric acid), 87, 88, 196, 218, 399, 584
galvanic skin response (GSR), 421
gambler's fallacy, 346
gambling, 247, 248, 341
  by college students, 1–2
ganglion cells, 137, 138, 139, 146
gate-control theory, 171, 174
gay rights, 417
gender, 475
gender differences, 475, 480–483
  in aggression, 480, 481
  biological origins of, 480–482
  in brain organization, 481
  in cognitive abilities, 35, 480
  in depressive disorder, 592
  in dream content, 204
  in eating disorders, 614
  environmental origins of, 482–483
  evolutionary perspective on, 35
  in fight-or-flight response, 542
  in generalized anxiety disorder, 582
  in identifying odors, 168
  in job performance ratings, A27
  in mate preferences, 410–411, 677
  in motivation, 398
  nature versus nurture in, 480
  in orgasm, 407
  in panic disorders, 583
  in response to erotic materials, 413
  in seeking psychotherapy, 597
  in sexual activity, 408–409
  in sexual arousal, 96
  in sexual orientation, 416
  in social behavior, 480
  in somatization disorder, 587
  in spatial ability, 35
  in suicide attempts, 593
  in taste sensitivity, 167
  in visual-spatial ability, 458
gender-role socialization, 482–483
gender roles, 470, 482
gender stereotypes, 380, 475, 480, 666, 701
gene pool, 117, 118
general adaptation syndrome, 542–543
generalization
  in classical conditioning, 239–240, 247
  in operant conditioning, 246, 247
  from samples, 60
generalization gradients, 240

generalized anxiety disorder, 582, 623
generational gains, in IQ, 376, 379
generativity versus self-absorption, 469
genes, 111, 440
genetic mapping, 115, 377, 594
genetic predisposition/vulnerability
  to alcoholism, 226
  to antisocial personality disorder, 606
  to anxiety disorders, 584
  to eating disorders, 614
  to mood disorders, 594
  to schizophrenia, 115, 601
  to obesity, 404
genetic relatedness, 112, 374
  homosexuality and, 415, 416
  obesity and, 404
genetics
  of intelligence, 374
  of taste buds, 166–167
  principles of, 110–112
  see also heredity
genital stage, 499
genius, 371
  inheritance of, 361
genotypes, 112
genuineness, of therapist, 629
geographic slant, perception of, 155–157
germinal stage, 441
Gestalt principles, 149–150
  in paintings, 1765
Getting from College to Career (Pollack), A-32
ghrelin, 399, 400, 401
giftedness, 366, 371–373
glands, endocrine, 108–109
glia, 81, 174
Global Assessment of Functioning (GAF) Scale, 580
glocuse, 400
glove anesthesia, 587
glucostatic theory, 400
glutamate, 87, 88, 218, 601
goal adjustment, 544
Goddard, Henry, 382
gonadotropins, 110
gonads, 110
gonorrhea, 444
Google, A-15, A-21, A-29
Google Scholar, A-40
grades
  class attendance and, 31
  conscientiousness and, 492
  IQ and, 366
Graduate Record Exam (GRE), 380
graduate school, A-37–A-38
grammar, 322
grandmother cell, 142
graphs, of data, A-7–A-8
grasshoppers, camouflage by, 119
gratification
  delayed, 418
  excessive, 498
gray matter, 465
Greebles, 142–143
Green, Reg and Maggie, 567
grief, 540
group cohesiveness, 698
group differences, 480
group intelligence tests, 363
group norms, 671, 692, 693
group polarization, 696–697
group size

conformity and, 689
  helping behavior and, 694
  productivity and, 695
group therapy, 630–631
groups, 633, 694–698, 694–698
  communication in, 694
  conflict between, 702
  decision making in, 696
  identification with, 522, 671
  productivity in, 695–696
  work teams as, A-23–A-24
groupthink, 697–698
growth, personal, 511
growth spurt, adolescent, 463
growth trends, in children, 445, 446
guilt, 453, 494, 496, 546
gustatory system, 165–168, 172–173

H

H. M., 304
hair cells, for hearing, 162–163
Halcion, 201
Haldol, 639
halfway houses, 652
hallucinations, 599
  under hypnosis, 210
Hallucinogenic Toreador, The (Dali), 178
hallucinogens, 215, 216
haloperidol, 639
Hamilton Rating Scale for Depression, 630
handedness, 122, 123
handwashing, compulsive, 584
hangingfly, black-tipped, 119
happiness, 429–433
  measurement of, 430
  moderately good predictors of, 431
  of nations, 430
  strong predictors of, 431–432
  unimportant determinants of, 430–431
haptic measures, 156
Harvard Group Scale of Hypnotic Susceptibility, 209
Harvard University, 6
hashish, 215
hassles, everyday, 535
Head Start programs, 390–391
health
  biopsychosocial factors in, 564
  effects of stress on, 551–556
  happiness and, 431
  personality traits and, 492
  sleep loss and, 199–200
health care, managed, 645
health care providers, 562–563
health-impairing habits, 342–343, 558–561
health maintenance organizations (HMOs), 645
health providers, communicating with, 562–563
health psychology, 18, 19, 534
  careers in, A-35–A-36
health-related habits, intelligence and, 383
health risks
  of alcohol, 226, 227
  of drug use, 217, 219–220, 219–220
  of obesity, 404
hearing, 160–165, 172–173
  absolute threshold for, 131
  aging and, 471–472

prenatal development of, 442
  theories of, 163–164
hearing damage, 161
hearsay evidence, 74
heart attack, 551, 552, 553
heart disease, 534, 551–552, 570
  depression and, 552–554
  diet and, 559
  personality and, 551–552
  smoking and, 558
Heche, Anne, 416
hedonic adaptation, 433
hedonic treadmill, 433
height, success and, 53
height in plane, 153, 154
helping behavior, 694
helplessness, learned, 545, 595
hemispheric specialization, 105–108, 120–123, 323
Hereditary Genius (Galton), 341
heredity
  environment and, 26, 115–116, 120, 376–377, 387, 475
  evolutionary perspective on, 117–118
  homosexuality and, 415–416
  intelligence and, 361
  mental retardation and, 370
  mood disorders and, 594
  obesity and, 404
  personality and, 514–515
  principles of, 110–116
  schizophrenia and, 601
heritability ratios, 375, 391
heritability
  of intelligence, 378–379
  of personality traits, 515, 516
Hermann grid, 139
heroin addiction, 237
heroin, 214, 215, 443
herpes, 444
hertz, 161
heterosexuals, 414
heterozygous condition, 111
heuristics, 332
  fast and frugal, 344–345
  in judging probabilities, 341–342
hidden observer, 211
hierarchical classification, 456
hierarchy of needs, 510–511
higher-order conditioning, 240
highly active antiretroviral therapy (HAART), 560
highway hypnosis, 211
hill-climbing heuristic, 333
hills, steepness of, 156–157
Hinckley, John, Jr., 578
hindbrain, 97–98
hindsight bias, 312–313, 336, 528, 617
Hinkley, John, Jr., 616
hippocampus, 98, 100, 104, 142, 143, 303, 304, 472, 594
hiring process, A-18–A-22
  legal issues in, A-20–A-21
Hispanic Americans
  IQ scores of, 377–378, 380
  mental health services utilization by, 624
histogram, A-7
histrionic personality, 588
hobbits and orcs problem, 329, 330
Hogan, Greg, 1
holistic cognitive style, 336
Holmes, Sherlock, 317

Holocaust, occurrence of, 704
homelessness, 653, 670
homeostasis, 396–397
homophobia, 497
homosexuality, 414–416, 496
  biological theories of, 415–416
  discrimination and, 416
  environmental theories of, 415
  prevalence of, 414–415
homosexuals, AIDS and, 561
homozygous condition, 111
honesty-humility, 492
hopelessness, 591
hormones, 99, 108–109
  in adolescence, 463
  aging and, 472
  emotions and, 421, 422
  homosexuality and, 415, 416
  hunger and, 401
  memory and, 303
  in prenatal development, 481
  stress and, 543
hospitalization, for psychological
  disorders, 650–651
hostility, 551, 552
  managing, 567–568
household chores, 470, 483
How to Sleep Like a Baby (Hales),
  224
hucksters, 704
hue, of colors, 134, 135, 143, 144
Hughes, Howard, 583
Human Behavior and Evolution
  Society, 117
human engineering psychology,
  A-17
human factors, A-25
human factors psychology, A-17
human genome, 377
Human Genome Project, 115
human immunodeficiency virus
  (HIV), 444, 560
human nature, optimistic view of,
  11, 509, 512–513
human services agencies, 655
humanism, 10–11, 508
humanistic perspective, 10–11
  evaluation of, 512–513
  Maslow's, 510–511
  on personality, 508–512, 520–521
  Rogers's, 509–510
humor, as stress reducer, 566–567
humoral immune responses, 555
hunger
  biological factors in, 399–401
  brain regulation of, 399–400
  digestive regulation of, 400–401
  environmental factors in, 401–403
  hormonal regulation of, 401
  regulation of, 99
hunting-and-gathering societies,
  35, 398, 481
Huntington's disease, 115, 472
hydrocephaly, 370
hydrophobia, 582
hypnic jerks, 192
hypnosis, 208–212
  as altered state, 211
  for eyewitness recall, 291
  memory and, 210, 300–301
  misconceptions about, 209
  as role playing, 210, 212
  susceptibility to, 209
  theories of, 210–211
hypnotic induction, 208–209
hypochondriasis, 587–588

hypothalamus, 98, 99, 100, 543, 544
  endocrine system and, 109
  in regulation of eating behavior,
    399–400, 401
  sexual motivation and, 96
hypotheses, 40
  formulating, 41–42
  null, A-13
  perceptual, 151–152, 160
  testing, A-13–A-14

I

"I have a friend who" syndrome, 74
I/O psychology. *See* industrial and
  organizational (I/O) psychology
id, 493, 494, 495, 496, 626
ideas, creative, 388
identical twins, 113, 114, 374, 513,
  514
identification, 496–497
identity, social, 703
identity achievement, 467
identity diffusion, 467
identity foreclosure, 467
identity moratorium, 467
identity statuses, 467
identity versus confusion, 467
Ifaluk, 424
ignorance, appeal to, 390
illness, 533–534
  correlates of, 570
  hypochondriasis and, 588
  life changes and, 537–538
  psychosomatic, 551, 586
  reactions to, 562–564
  stress and, 551–556
  see also disease
illusions
  positive, 547
  visual, 157–160
illusory correlation, 666, 701
imagery, encoding and, 279, 280
imitation
  in language learning, 326
  of models, 261, 262, 482, 506
  mirror neurons and, 103
immigrants, mental abilities of, 382
immune functioning
  classical conditioning of, 236, 237
  emotional disclosure and, 567
  marijuana and, 220
  optimism and, 557
  prenatal, 444
  sleep duration and, 200
  social support and, 556
  stress and, 554–555
immune response, 554–555
  enhanced, 541
  meditation and, 213
immunosuppression, 236, 237
impossible figures, 158–159, 178,
  179
impotence, marijuana and, 220
impression formation, 664–667
Impressionist paintings, 176, 177
improbable, overestimating, 347
*Improving Memory and Study
  Skills* (Hermann, Raybeck, &
  Gruneberg), 308
impulsiveness, 606
inattentional blindness, 147
incentive theories, 397
incentives, 418
inclines, 155–157
inclusive fitness, 118

income
  happiness and, 430
  height and, 53
incongruence, 509, 510, 628
Incurably Ill for Animal Research,
  The, 68
independent variables, 46, 48
independent view of self, 522
India, 26, 369
individual differences
  in achievement motivation, 417
  in cognitive development, 456
  in stress modulation, 557
  in taste sensitivity, 167
  measurement of, 356
  stage theories and, 453
individualism, 671
  conformity and, 692
  marriage and, 677
inducing structure, problems of,
  328
industrial and organizational (I/O)
  psychology, 19, 22, A-15–A-29
  careers in, A-37
  subfields of, A-17–A-18, A-29
industry versus inferiority, 453
infant mortality, 444
infant-caregiver attachment, 675
infants
  attachment in, 448–451
  cognitive abilities of, 454, 457–460
  cognitive development in,
    453–456
  language learning in, 320–321
  mathematical abilities of, 458–460
  motor development in, 445–446
  neural development in, 124
  personality development in,
    451–453
  sleep cycle of, 193, 194
  temperament in, 446–448
infectious diseases, 533–534
  prenatal development and, 444
inferences, drawing, 344
inferential statistics, 58–59,
  A-13–A-14
inferiority, 453
inferiority complex, 501
inflammation
  disengagement and, 544
  exercise and, 560
  heart disease and, 551, 552, 553,
    555
inflammatory responses, 200
information
  for decision making, 338
  on Internet, A-39–A-43
  irrelevant, 330
  organization of, in memory,
    287–290
  predecisional distortion of, 348
  retention of, 294–295
  storage of, 260, 280–290
information processing
  model for, 276, 280, 281
  in nervous system, 80–88
  in retina, 138–139
  in visual cortex, 140–143, 146
infrared spectrum, 135
ingroup favoritism, 703
ingroups, 667, 703
inhibited temperament, 448, 584
inhibitions, 514
  loss of, 210
inhibitory PSPs, 84, 85
initiative versus guilt, 453

inkblot test, 527
innate talents, 372
inner ear, 162
insanity, defense, 607
insecure attachment, 588
insight, 332, 388
insight therapies, 623, 626–633
  client-centered, 628–630, 646–647
  effectiveness of, 632, 656
  group, 630–631
  mechanisms of, 632–633
  psychoanalysis, 626–628, 646–647
insomnia, 201–202, 224
inspection time, 382, 383
institutions, positive, 16
instrumental learning, 241
insulin, 109, 401
integrity tests, A-19
integrity versus despair, 469
intellectual disability, 369–371
intellectualization, 546
intelligence
  biological indexes of, 382
  brain size and, 383
  cognitive perspective on, 383–384
  components of, 367
  creativity and, 389
  crystallized, 473
  emotional, 385–386
  extremes of, 369–373
  fluid, 473
  happiness and, 431
  heredity and, 114, 361, 373–375
  heredity and environment in, 390
  inspection time and, 382–383
  longevity and, 383
  normal distribution of, 364, 366
  reification of, 391
  synaptic density and, 125
  testing perspective n, 383
  triarchic theory of, 384
  types of, 384–386
intelligence quotient (IQ), 361–362
intelligence tests (testing), 355,
  356–357
  cultural bias on, 381–382
  in employment hiring, 368
  group, 363
  in other cultures, 368–369
  history of, 361–363
  questions on, 364
  reliability of, 345–346
  Stanford-Binet, 361–362
  validity of, 366–367
  WAIS, 362, 365
  what they measure, 364
  see also IQ scores
interactionist theories, 326–327
interdependent view of self, 522
interference
  as cause of forgetting, 296, 297
  with long-term memory,
    282–283, 287
  minimizing, 309
  within short-term memory,
    282–283
internal attributions, 668, 669, 670
Internet
  dating via, 678–679
  psychological research and, 64–65
  research sources on, A-39–A-43
Internet addiction, 546
interpersonal attraction, 664,
  672–680
  evolutionary perspective on,
    679–680

interpersonal attraction (continued)
key factors in, 672–674
physical attractiveness and, 672–673
interpersonal psychotherapy (IP), 648
interpersonal skills, 636
interposition, 153, 154
interpretation
of dreams, 225, 301
in psychoanalysis, 627, 628
interval schedules of reinforcement, 248, 249
interviewing, of job applicants, A-19–A-20
interviews, as data collection method, 43
intimacy, 674, 675
intimacy versus isolation, 469
intimate relationships, 673, 674–676
intravenous (IV) drug use, 219, 561
introspection, 5, 318, 514
inverted-U hypothesis, 541–542
involuntary commitment, 607, 610
ions, 82
Iowa Tests of Basic Skills, 355
Iowa Writers Workshop, 389
IQ scores
cultural differences in, 377–382
deviation, 364, 366
generational gains in, 376
of gifted, 371
intellectual disability and, 369
job performance and, 368
meaning of, 364
reaction range for, 376–377
school performance and, 367
vocational success and, 368
IQ tests. See intelligence tests
iris, 136, 137
irony, 322
irrational thought, 598–599
irreversibility, 455
irritable bowel syndrome, 554

J

James-Lange theory, 426
Japan (Japanese), 196, 336, 368 424, 522
jet lag, 189–190
Jews, in Nazi Germany, 271
job, falling asleep on, 198
job analysis, A-18–A-19
job applicants
background checks on, A-21
interviewing of, A-19–A-20
testing of, A-19–A-20
job attitudes, A-25–A-26
job descriptions, A-17–A-18
job openings, A-21
job performance, A27
IQ scores and, 368
test scores and, A-19
job satisfaction, 432, A-25–A-26, A27
job search, A-30–A-32
job withdrawal, A27–A-28
jobs
prestige of, A-17
types of, A-16–A-17
Jobs, Steve, 367
Johns Hopkins University, 4
journals, psychology, 4, 17, 44, 70–73, A-40
juggling, brain and, 104

juries, studies of, 50
justice noticeable different (JND), 131

K

Kaluli (New Guinea), 424
Kanzi, 324
Kennedy, John F., 698
Kinetic Art, 178
Kipsigis (Kenya), 446
knowledge
from scientific research, 45
representation in memory, 287–290
tacit, 384
koro, 611
Krakauer, John, 395–396
Kung San, 446

L

labeling
as explanation, 227
effects of, 350, 351
mental retardation and, 369
laboratory research, 50
language, 318–328
adaptive value of, 325
ambiguities in, 322
animal use of, 324
brain centers for, 105
culture and, 327–328
defined, 318
evolutionary perspective on, 324–325
manipulative, 350
mirror neurons and, 103
second, 323–324
structure of, 319–320
thought and, 327
language acquisition device (LAD), 326
language development, 320–324, 457
bilingualism and, 324
theories of, 325–327
latency stage, 499
latent content, of dreams, 206
latent learning, 257
lateral antagonism, 139
lateral geniculate nucleus (LGN), 140, 141, 146
lateral hypothalamus (LH), 399, 400
law, psychological disorders and, 607, 610
law of effect, 241–242
L-dopa, 86
leadership, of teams, A-24
learned helplessness, 545, 595
learning
of attitudes, 684
brain-based, 124
defined, 231
evolutionary perspective on, 256
of gender roles, 482
interference with, 296, 297
of language, 320–323
of maladaptive behavior, 634
observational, 259–263, 264–265, 266
personality and, 504
programmed, 266
studying and, 28
see also classical conditioning; operant conditioning
learning aids, 30–31

lectures, getting more from, 31
legal issues, in hiring, A-20–A-21
lens, 135, 136
leptin, 401, 463
leptin resistance, 401
Les Promenades d'Euclide (Magritte), 179
lesbians, 416
see also homosexuality
lesioning, of brain, 92–93
levels-of-processing theory, 278–279
liberalism, 492
libraries, research using, A-39
Library Use: A Handbook for Psychology (Reed & Baxter), 70
lie detector, 421–422
lie scale, on personality tests, 526
life changes, 537–538
life expectancy, smoking and, 558
life span. See development
lifestyle, health and, 558–561
lifetime prevalence, 581
light, as stimulus for vision, 134, 135, 143
light adaptation, 138
light and shadow, as depth cue, 153, 154
likeability, of sources, 683
liking, 672, 673–674
lily pond problem, 333
limbic system, 99–100, 422
linear perspective, 153, 154
linguistic relativity, 327–328, 350
link method, 310
listening, active, 31
lithium, 641
Little Albert, 239–240
Littledean Hall, 390
localization, of sounds, 164–165
longevity
exercise and, 559
intelligence and, 383
optimism and, 557
longitudinal designs, 446–447
long-term depression (LTD), 303
long-term memory (LTM), 284–286
organization of, 287–290
permanence of, 284–285
relation to short-term memory, 286–287
long-term potentiation (LTP), 88, 303
loss
frustration and, 535–536
posttraumatic stress disorder and, 584
loss aversion, 349
loudness, 161
love, 674–677
as attachment, 675–677
components of, 674–675
happiness and, 431
marriage and, 677
unconditional, 509–510
lowball technique, 705
LSD, 215
lucid dreams, 225
Lunesta, 201
lung cancer, 220, 558
lymphocytes, 555

M

M'Naghten rule, 607
macaques, 231
"The Magical Number Seven" (Miller), 283

magnetic field, for brain study, 93–94
magnocellular channel, 140
Magritte, René, 178, 179
major depressive disorder. See depressive disorder
maladaptive behavior, as criterion for abnormality, 577
malingering, 587
malnutrition, 379
during prenatal development, 443, 603
managed care, 645
mandalas, 500
manic-depressive disorder, 592–593
manic episodes, 591, 592
drug treatment for, 641
manifest content, of dreams, 206
mantra, 212
MAO inhibitors, 639
Mapping the Mind (Carter), 84
marijuana, 215, 219–220, 601
marital satisfaction, parenthood and, 471
marital status
happiness and, 431–432
mental health services utilization and, 624
marriage, 470
arranged, 677
cultural differences in, 677
Marston, William, 421
masculinity, 475
women's judgments of, 411–412
massed practice, 309
master's degree, in psychology, A-32–A-33
matching hypothesis, 673
matchstick problem, 332, 334
mate poaching, 680
materialism, 518
mathematical ability
gender differences in, 480
in infants, 458–460
mating preferences
gender differences in, 410–411, 679–680
parental investment and, 408, 411
mating strategies, in animals, 119
maturation, 445, 446
language learning and, 326
sexual, 463–464
Mayer-Salovey-Caruso Emotional Intelligence Test, 386
maze running, 257
MDMA, 216, 220–221
Me, Myself, and Irene, 589
mean, 55, A-8
regression toward, 658, 659
mean length of utterance (MLU), 322
meaning, memory encoding and, 278, 294, 310
measurement, as goal of scientific approach, 40
media
portrayal of women in, 615
as source of gender-role socialization, 483
as source of prejudicial attitudes, 702
violence in, 261–263, 266
medial forebrain bundle, 101, 218
medial temporal lobe, 305, 307
medial temporal lobe memory system, 304

median, 55, A-8
medical advice, adhering to, 563–564
medical diagnoses, hindsight bias and, 529
medical model, of abnormal behavior, 576–577
medical services, using, 563
medical statistics, 570
medical students' disease, 616
medical treatment, seeking, 562
meditation, 60, 92, 212–213, 568
medulla, 97, 98
Meissner corpuscle, 169
melatonin, 189, 190, 201
Mellaril, 639
memorization, 308
Memory Fitness (Einstein & McDaniel), 308
memory
  aging and, 473
  biological basis of, 302–304
  brain areas for, 303, 304
  connectionist model of, 289–290
  consolidation of, 199 304
  distortions in, 282
  for dreams, 224–225
  ESB studies of, 284, 285
  false, 298–302
  glutamate and, 88
  hypnosis and, 210, 300–301
  imperfection of, 301
  improving, 308–311
  information processing approach to, 276, 280, 281
  levels-of-processing theory, 278–279
  limbic system and, 100
  loss of, 303–304, 589
  marijuana use and, 220
  prefrontal cortex and, 103
  reconstructive nature of, 291–292, 312
  for routine tasks, 307
  sensory, 280–281, 282
  short-term, 281–284
  for skills, 305
  stereotypes and, 666, 701
  stress and, 549
memory systems, 305–307
memory trace, 282, 302
  decay of, 296
  latent, 499
menarche, 464
meninges, 90
meningitis, 90
menopause, 472
mental abilities, primary, 363
mental ability tests, 356–357, 361
mental age, calculation of, 361, 362
mental health care, 645
mental health services, utilization of, 624, 650
mental hospitals, 650–651
  commitment to, 607, 610
  inpatient population of, 652
  revolving door situation with, 652–653
mental illness. *See* psychological disorders
mental retardation, 366, 369–371, 391, 444, 580
mental rotation, 35
mental sets, 330–331
mental speed, 382, 474, 458
mentoring, A-22

mere exposure effects, 132
Merkel receptors, 169
mescaline, 215
Mesmer, Franz Anton, 208
mesmerism, 208
mesolimbic dopamine pathway, 218, 423
message factors, in persuasion, 683–684
messages, subliminal, 132–133
metalinguistic awareness, 320, 322
metaphors, 322
methadone, 215
methamphetamine, 215
method of loci, 308, 310–311
Michelle Remembers (Smith & Pazder), 590
microelectrodes, 82
microglia, 174
midbrain, 98, 99, 171, 174, 196
Miller, Zell, 124
Mind Tools, 291
Minnesota Multiphasic Personality Inventory (MMPI), 525
minorities
  mental health services for, 649
  socioeconomic disadvantage of, 379–380
  stereotyping of, 518
mirror neurons, 102–103
miscarriage, 442
misinformation effect, 291–292, 299, 312
MMPI, 525
mnemonic devices, 308, 310–311
modal personality, 519
mode, 55, A-8
models (modeling), 259, 482, 506, 636, 637
molecular genetics, 115, 377
monamine neurotransmitters, 86–87
Monet, Claude, 177
money, happiness and, 430
monocular cues to depth perception, 153–154
monozygotic twins, 113, 114
Monroe, Marilyn, 501
mood disorders, 590–597, 608–609
  biological factors in, 594–595
  cognitive factors in, 595–596
  creativity and, 389
  culture and, 611
  drug therapy for, 638–639
  electroconvulsive therapy for, 642–643
  etiology of, 593–597, 609
  glia and, 81
  among homeless, 653
  interpersonal roots of, 597
  lifetime prevalence of, 581
  prevalence of, 592, 593, 608
  stress and, 594
  treatment of, 594, 636–637
  types of, 590–593, 608
  vulnerability to, 612
mood stabilizers, 641
mood swings, 591, 592–593
moon illusion, 159
moral behavior, moral reasoning and, 461
moral development
  Freud's view of, 494
  Kohlberg's stage theory of, 460–462
morphemes, 320

morphine, 88, 174, 214, 215
mortality
  awareness of, 517, 519
  personality traits and, 492
  sleep duration and, 200
mortality rates, 347, 534
  depression and, 553
  exercise and, 569
  sleep length and, 223
  smoking and, 558
mortality salience, 518
mother-infant attachment, 448–451
moths, 119
motion, illusion of, 149
motion parallax, 153
motivated forgetting, 297, 496
motivation
  achievement, 417–419
  Adler's view of, 500
  defined, 396
  drive theories of, 396–397
  eminence and, 372
  emotion and, 419
  evolutionary theories of, 397–398
  incentive theories of, 397
  observational learning and, 260
  of hunger and eating, 399–405
  sexual, 406–409
  for work, A-16
motives, 396, 398
motor cortex, 102, 103
motor development, 445–446
motor neurons, 85
motor skills, mirror neurons and, 103
Mount Everest, 395–396
movement
  coordination of, 99
  motor cortex and, 102, 103
Mozart effect, 125
MRI (magnetic resonance imaging), 95, 383
Müller-Lyer illusion, 157, 158
multiaxial system, 579, 580, 581
multicultural sensitivity, in psychotherapy, 649–650
multifactorial causation, 24–25, 64, 120, 216, 429, 519
multimodal therapy, 656
multiple personality disorder, 589, 590
multiple sclerosis, 80–81
multiple-choice tests, 32–33, 295
multitasking, 278
muscles
  nerves and, 90
  neurotransmitters and, 86
muscular dystrophy, 115
music
  for babies, 124, 125
  for workers, A-26
musicians, brain organization of, 104
mutations, 111
myelin, 464–465
myelin sheath, 80, 81

N

naive realism, 42
name calling, 351
names, remembering, 277
napping, 196, 223
narcolepsy, 202
narcotics, 214, 215, 216, 217, 443
Nardil, 639

narrative methods, 310, 311
NASA, 528
National Alliance for the Mentally Ill, 579
National Association of Social Workers, A-33
National Center for PTSD, 585
national character, 519, 522
National Comorbidity Study, 581
National Institute for Mental Health, 588
National Institute of Child Health and Human Development, 451
National Institute on Alcohol Abuse and Alcoholism, 219
National Institute on Drug Abuse, 219
National Sleep Foundation, 199
National Television Violence Study, 262
nations, subjective well-being of, 430
Native Americans, IQ scores of, 377
nativist theories, 326, 459–460
natural selection, 5–6, 15–16, 116, 117, 118, 397–398, 481
  of cognitive abilities, 460
  face recognition and, 142
  language and, 325
  of personality traits, 515
  sensory adaptation and, 134
naturalistic observation, 51–52, 62, 65
nature versus nurture, 8–9, 26
  in gender differences, 480
  in intelligence, 361, 373–381
  in language acquisition, 325–326
  in learning, 266
  see also environment; heredity
Nazi Germany, 271, 689
nearsightedness, 136, 137
Necker cube, 152, 178
need for achievement, 417–419
need for self-actualization, 511
need for affiliation, 418
needs
  biological, 398
  gratification of, 498
  Maslow's hierarchy of, 510–512
negative correlation, 56, 57, A-11
negative emotionality, 492
negative reinforcement, 249–250, 251, 268
negative self-talk, 545, 565–566
negative symptoms, of schizophrenia, 600
negative thinking, 595–596, 636
negligence lawsuits, 529
NEO Personality Inventory, 525
nerve endings, 170
nerves, 89–90
nervous system
  autonomic, 90
  cells in, 80–81
  information processing in, 80–88
  organization of, 89–91
  peripheral, 89–90
neural circuits, for memory, 303
neural impulse, 81–83
neural networks, 84–85
neural reorganization, 104
neurodevelopmental hypothesis, 603–604
neurogenesis, 104, 109, 303, 544
  exercise and, 560
  suppression of, 594–595

neurons, 80–81
  aging and, 472
  creation of new, 104
  as feature detectors, 141, 142
  mirror, 102–103
  motor, 85
  myelination of, 464–465
  number of in brain, 89
  resting potential of, 82
neuropeptide Y, 399
Neuropsychology Central, 81
neuroscientists, 92
neuroses, 626
neuroticism, 469, 491, 492, 514, 515, 516, 555, 562, 588
neurotransmitters, 84, 85–88
  anxiety disorders and, 584–585
  hormones and, 108–109
  in hunger, 399–400
  memory and, 303
  monamine, 86–87
  mood disorders and, 594
  psychoactive drug action and, 217–218
  regulating sleep and waking, 196–197
  in schizophrenia, 601, 602
  see also specific neurotransmitters
New England Journal of Medicine, 642
newborns
  sleep cycle of, 193, 194
  taste preferences in, 166
nicotine, 214, 86
night terrors, 202, 203
night vision, 138
nightmares, 202, 203
nine-dot problem, 331–332, 334
noise, signal detection and, 132
nominal fallacy, 227
non sequitur, 435
nondeclarative memory system, 305
non-REM (NREM) sleep, 193, 194
nonsense syllables, 294
nonverbal behavior, 423
norepinephrine (NE), 86, 87, 108, 217, 218, 594, 640, 641
normal distribution, 362, 364, 366, A-9–A-10, A-11
normality, versus abnormality, 577–578
norms, situational, 682
nortriptyline, 648
nose, smell and, 168
note taking, during lectures, 31
nucleus accumbens, 218
Nude Descending a Staircase
  (Duchamp), 178
null hypothesis, A-13
Nun Study, 473
Nurture Assumption, The
  (Harris), 529
nutrition
  poor, 558–559
  prenatal development and, 443

O

obedience, 633, 689–693, 689–692
obesity, 200, 403
  exercise and, 559
  fear of, 613
  hormones and, 401
Obesity Society, 404
object permanence, 454, 456
object recognition, background
  consistency and, 152

observation
  direct, 43
  naturalistic, 51–52, 62
  precise, A-7
observational learning, 259–263, 264–265, 266
  of attitudes, 685
  eating behavior and, 402
  of fears, 585
  of gender roles, 482
  overview of, 264–265
  personality and, 506
  of prejudice, 702
  of social skills, 636
observers, biases of, 668–669
obsessions, 583
obsessive-compulsive disorder, 583–584
  brain stimulation for, 644
  prevalence of, 584
  drug therapy for, 640
  neurotransmitters and, 86
  therapy for, 656
obsessive-compulsive personality
  disorder, 604–605
occipital lobe, 101–102, 140, 141
occupational attainment, IQ scores
  and, 368
Occupational Information Network
  (O*NET), A-17–A-18
Occupational Outlook Handbook,
  A-30
occupational psychology, A-17
occupational stereotypes, 666
occupations, A-17
octopus, 79
odd/eccentric personality disorders, 605
odors
  adaptation to, 133
  types of, 168
  see also smell
Oedipal complex, 498–499, 627
olanzapine, 639
olfactory bulb, 100, 104, 168
olfactory cilia, 168
olfactory system, 168, 172–173
omega 3 fatty acids, 559
online dating, 678–679
online resources, evaluating,
  A-39–A-43
on-the-job training, A-25
openness to experience, 469, 491, 492, 515, 516
operant chamber, 243
operant conditioning, 241–253
  acquisition in, 245–246, 247
  of anxiety responses, 585
  of attitudes, 684
  basic processes in, 244–246
  discrimination in, 246, 247
  extinction in, 246, 247
  of gender roles, 482
  generalization in, 246, 247
  observational learning and, 259
  overview of, 264–265
  personality and, 503, 504
  of prejudice, 702
  relation to classical conditioning,
  241
  shaping in, 245–246
  Skinner's conception of, 242
  terminology and procedures for,
  243–244
operational definitions, 42
operations, mental, 455

opiates, 101, 215, 216
opinions, 704
opponent process theory, of color
  vision, 145
optic chiasm, 140, 141
optic disk, 136, 137, 138
optic nerve, 136, 137, 138, 139, 140, 141
optical illusions, 157–160, 178, 179
optimal level of arousal, 541–542
optimism, 432, 547
  stress reduction and, 557
optimistic explanatory style, 557
options, choosing among, 337–339
oral stage, 498
orders, obeying, 689–692
orexins, 399
organizational citizenship behaviors (OCBs), A27–A-28
organizational commitment,
  A-27–A-28
organizational culture, A-22–A-23
organizational socialization,
  A-22–A-24
organizational withdrawal, A27–A-28
orgasm phase, of sexual response
  cycle, 406–407
Origin of Species (Darwin), 116
ossicles, of ear, 162
osteoporosis, 559, 613
Otis-Lennon School Ability Test,
  363
outcomes
  expected, 49–50
  reinforcement and, 258–259
outgroup derogation, 703
outgroups, 667, 703
outlining, 310
oval window, 162
ovaries, 464
overcompensation, 501, 546
overconfidence, 313
overconfidence effect, 348
overdose, drug, 217, 219, 237
overeating, 269, 402, 404, 613
overextension, 322
overextrapolations, 125
overlearning, 308–309
overregularization, 322
owls, 100

P

pace of life, culture and, 51–52
Pacinian corpuscle, 169
Pagano, Bernard, 312
pain
  chronic, 81, 174
  endorphins and, 88
  glia and, 81
  perception of, 170–171, 174
  tolerance for, 170
paintings, perceptual principles
  and, 175–179
palatability, of food, 401
Panbanisha, 324
pancultural view, of psychological
  disorders, 610, 611
panic attacks, 582
panic disorder, 582–583, 586
  drug therapy for, 640
  psychotherapy for, 656
  treatment seeking for, 623
Pappenheim, Bertha, 623
parallel distributed processing
  (PDP), 289–290

parallel processing
  of auditory input, 163
  in visual cortex, 140
paralysis
  in conversion disorder, 587
  from spinal cord damage, 91
paranoid schizophrenia, 599
parasympathetic division, of autonomic nervous system, 90, 91, 421
paraventricular nucleus (PVN), 399, 400, 401
parental investment theory, 408, 411
parent-child attachment, 448–451
parenthood, 431, 471
parents
  caregiving styles of, 675
  children's personality and, 515, 529
  conflict with adolescents, 466, 471
  disciplinary procedures of,
  252–253
  as source of prejudicial attitudes,
  702
  unconditional love from, 509, 510
parietal lobe, 102, 170
Parkinsonism, 86, 87, 99, 472, 644
paroxetine, 640
participants, in research, 43, 66–67
parvocellular channel, 140
passion, 674, 675
passionate love, 674, 677
patriotism, 518
patterns, perception of, 146–152
Pavlovian conditioning, 233–234
Paxil, 640
PDP models, 304
peacocks, 119
peak experiences, 512
Pearson product-moment correlation, A-12
peer review process, 44
peers, risk taking and, 465
penis, 406
penis envy, 499, 502
pennies, 275
People for the Ethical Treatment of
  Animals (PETA), 68
percentile scores, 357, 361,
  A-10–A-11
perception
  auditory, 163–164
  defined, 130
  of depth, 152–153
  of forms and patterns, 146–152
  of geographic slant, 155–157
  Gestalt principles of, 149–150
  of pain, 170–171, 174
  person, 664–667
  psychophysics of, 130–134
  study of, 5
  subjectivity of, 26–27, 146, 160,
  175, 222, 666–667, 699
  subliminal, 132–133
  of taste, 167
  without awareness, 133
perceptual asymmetries, 108, 122
perceptual constancies, 157, 159
perceptual hypotheses, 151–152,
  160
perceptual motor tasks, 305
perceptual set, 147
perfectionism, 614
performance
  individual vs. group, 695

of learned response, 261
see also academic performance
performance pressure, 538–539
Pergament, Moshe, 1
periaqueductal gray (PAG), 174
peripheral nervous system, 89–90
peripheral vision, 138
persecution, delusions of, 599
person-centered theory, of personality, 509–510, 520–521
person-centered therapy, 12, 628
person-situation controversy, 506–507
person perception, 664–667
   evolutionary perspective on, 667
   expectations and, 27
   subjectivity in, 666–667
personal ads, 411
personal distress, as criterion for abnormality, 577
personal unconscious, 499
personality
   Adler's theory of, 500–501
   attractiveness and, 665
   behavioral perspectives on, 502–508, 520–521
   biological perspectives on, 513–516, 520–521
   compliance with medical advice and, 563
   consistency of, 490
   culture and, 519, 522–523
   distinctiveness of, 490
   five-factor model of, 491–492
   Freud's psychoanalytic theory of, 493–499, 520–521
   genetic basis for, 514–515
   happiness and, 432
   health and, 557
   healthy, 511
   heart disease and, 551–552
   heredity and, 114
   hindsight and, 528–529
   humanistic perspectives on, 508–512, 520–521
   hypnotic susceptibility and, 209
   in infants, 446–448
   Jung's theory of, 499–500
   leadership and A-24
   Maslow's view of, 510–512
   nature of, 490–493
   observational learning and, 506
   persuasability and, 684
   psychodynamic perspectives on, 493–502, 520–521
   Rogers's person-centered theory of, 509–510, 520–521
   of rooms, 505–506
   somatoform disorders and, 588
   stability of, 468–469
personality development, 446–448, 451–453, 466–467, 476–479
   Freud's stages of, 498–499, 521
   Rogers's view of, 509–510, 520–521
   Skinner's view of, 503–504, 521
personality disorders, 580, 604–606
   diagnostic problems with, 605
   types of, 605
personality psychology, 18, 19
   careers in, A-35
personality structure
   Eysenck's view of, 513–514, 521
   Freud's view of, 493–494, 521
   Rogers's view of, 509, 521
   Skinner's view of, 503, 521
personality tests, 357, 524–527

for job applicants, A-19
   projective, 417, 418
personality traits, 491
   basic, 491–492, 513–514
   creativity and, 389
   culture and, 519
   eating disorders and, 614
   evolution and, 515–516
   heritability of, 515
   testing of, 357, 525, 526
personnel psychology, A-17
persuasion, 682–684
   central route to, 687
   classical conditioning and, 270–271
   peripheral route to, 687
   resistance to, 684
   susceptibility to, 684
   techniques of, 180, 704–705
pessimistic explanatory style, 557, 595
PET (positron emission tomography) scans, 95
Ph.D., in psychology, A-33–A-34
phallic stage, 498
pharmaceutical industry, 642
phenomenological approach, 509
phenotypes, 112
phenylketonuria, 370
phi phenomenon, 149
phobias, 232, 582
   conditioning of, 251, 585
   preparedness and, 255–256
   therapy for, 656
   treatment for, 634–635
phobic disorder, 582, 623
phonemes, 319–320
phonemic encoding, 278, 279, 281, 287, 297
phonological loop, 283
physical appearance, person perception and, 664–665
physical attractiveness, judgments of, 181
physical dependence, on drugs, 201, 217, 218
physical fitness, 559, 569
physiological arousal, 90, 213, 421–422
physiological psychology, 18, 19
   careers in, A-35
physiological recording, as data collection method, 43
physiology, psychology and, 3–4
Picasso, Pablo, 176, 177
pictorial depth cues, 153–154
pineal gland, 189
pinna, 162
pitch, 161, 163
pituitary gland, 98, 100, 109, 543, 544
place theory, of hearing, 163
placebo, 60
placebo effects, 60–61, 70, 170, 658, 659
placenta, 441
plagiarism, 293
plateau phase, of sexual response cycle, 406, 407
Plato, 280
play, aggressive, 261
pleasure centers, in brain, 100–101, 218
pleasure principle, 494
poets, mental illness and, 389
Poggendorff illusion, 157

point prevalence rates, 616
pointillism, 176, 177
political agenda, 485
political debates, 42
political views, 518
politics, classical conditioning and, 271
polygenic traits, 112, 115
polygraph, 421–422
pons, 196, 207, 224, 97, 98
Ponzo illusion, 157, 158
population, for research, 60, A-13, A-14
pornography, 412–413
positive correlation, 56, 57, A-11
positive emotionality, 432, 492
positive illusions, 547
positive psychology, 550, 630
positive psychology movement, 16–17, 420, 512
positive psychotherapy, 630
positive symptoms, of schizophrenia, 600
postconventional level, 461
posthypnotic suggestion, 210
postpartum depression, 471
postsynaptic neuron, 83, 84, 217
postsynaptic potential (PSP), 84
posttraumatic stress disorder (PTSD), 550, 584, 623
potassium ions, 82
poverty, 485
   happiness and, 430
   homelessness and, 653
   use of mental health services and, 650
Power Sleep (Maas), 223
practical intelligence, 367, 384
practice, in learning, 308
Pragnanz, 150
preconscious, 494
preconventional level, 460–461
predators, avoiding, 118–119
predecisional distortion, of information, 348
prediction, as goal of scientific approach, 40
predictions, confidence in, 348
preferences, classical conditioning of, 270
preferences, making choices about, 337–339
prefrontal cortex, 103–104, 218, 303, 304, 422–423, 465, 603, 644
pregnancy, 440–444
   drinking during, 444
   illness during, 444, 603
   nutrition during, 443
   stress during, 444
prejudice, 699–703
   cultural worldviews and, 518
   defined, 700
   learning, 702
premises, 434
prenatal development, 440–444
   antisocial behavior and, 584
   environmental factors in, 443–444
   hormones in, 110, 416, 481
   maternal drug use and, 443
   maternal illness and, 444, 603
   maternal nutrition and, 443–444
   schizophrenia and, 603
preoperational period, 454–455, 456
preparedness, 255–256, 585
prescriptions, drug, 623, 642

pressure
   choking under, 525
   sense of, 169–170
   as source of stress, 538–539
presynaptic neuron, 83, 84
prevalence
   lifetime, 616–617
   of psychological disorders, 579–581
primary auditory cortex, 102
primary colors, 144
primary motor cortex, 102, 103
primary-process thinking, 494
primary sex characteristics, 464
primary somatosensory cortex, 102
primary visual cortex, 102, 140, 141
Princess Diana, 439–440
Principles of Psychology (James), 5
Priscilla the Fastidious Pig, 246
prison guards, 692–693
private speech, 458
proactive interference, 296, 297
probabilities
   evaluating, 570–571
   judging, 341–342, 346
   in prevalence of psychological disorders, 616–617
   reasoning about, 616–617
probability, research results and, 59, A-14
problem solving, 328–336
   aging and, 473, 474
   approaches to, 332–335
   barriers to, 330–331
   in childhood, 455–456
   culture and, 336
   in groups, 698
problem-solving view, of dreams, 207
problem space, 332
problems
   confronting, 548
   representation of, 334–335
   types of, 328, 329
"problems in living," 577
procedural memory, 474
procrastination, 562
productivity
   aging and, 474
   creativity and, 389
   group, 695–696
prognosis, 577
progressive relaxation, 224
projection, 496, 497
projective tests, 417, 526–527
propaganda, 271
prosocial behavior, 462, A-27
prospective design, 596
prospective memory, 306
protein synthesis, 303
prototypes, 616, 617
provider-patient communications, 562–563
proximal stimuli, 151
proximity, as Gestalt principle, 149, 150
proximodistal trend, 445
Prozac, 640
psilocybin, 215
psyche, 3
psychiatric nurses, 625
psychiatrists, 623, 625
psychiatry, 22
psychic reflexes, 233
PsychINFO, 71–72, A-40
PsychINFO Direct, 45

psychoactive drugs, 214–221
  dependence on, 217, 218–219
  effects of, 216
  medical uses of, 215
  neurochemical action of, 217–218
  principal types of, 214–216
  side effects of, 215
  sleep and, 223
psychoanalysis, 7, 493, 626–628,
  646–647
psychoanalytic theory, 7–8, 10, 11,
  14, 493–499, 529
psychodynamic theories,
  493–502, 520–521
  Adler's, 500–501
  evaluation of, 501–502
  Freud's, 493–499
  Jung's, 499–500
psychodynamic therapies, 628, 656
Psychological Abstracts, 72
psychological autopsies, 52
psychological dependence, on
  drugs, 217, 218
psychological disorders
  classification of, 579, 580, 581
  creativity and, 389
  culture and, 610–611
  legal aspects of, 607, 610
  medical model of, 576–577
  prevalence of, 616
  recovery from, 632
  stereotypes of, 578
  stress and, 549
  suicide and, 52–53
  testing for, 525
  treatment of, 622–659
  see also specific disorders
Psychological Screening Inventory,
  359, 360
psychological tests (testing), 24,
  355, 524–527
  achievement, 357
  aptitude, 357
  of creativity, 389–390
  as data collection method, 43
  of job applicants, A-19–A-20
  key concepts in, 356–360
  normal distribution on, A-10
  projective, 417
  reliability of, 357
  standardization of, 357
  types of, 356–357
  validity of, 358–359, 360
  see also intelligence tests, personal-
    ity tests
psychologists, 624
  settings for, 18, 19, A-33
psychology major, A-30, A-32
psychology, applied, 12–13, 19, 22,
  A-33, A-36–A-37
psychology
  careers in, A-30
  clinical, 12
  college major in, 18
  defined, 17
  early history of, 3–12
  empiricism in, 23, 39–40
  ethics in, 66–69
  first formal laboratory for, 4
  origin of word, 3
  positive, 16
  as practical, 2
  as profession, 12–13, 18–19, 21
  professional specialties in, 19, 22
  research areas in, 18–19
  schools of, 11, 14

as a science, 4
  scientific approach in, 40–45
  sociohistorical context for, 24
  subfields of, A-33–A-37
  theoretical diversity in, 23–24
  as way of thinking, 2–3
psychometrics, 18, 19
  careers in, A-35
psychopathology, 576
psychopharmacotherapy, 638–644
psychophysics, 120–124
psychosexual stages, 497–499
psychosocial crises, 452
psychosomatic diseases, 551, 586
psychotherapy, 621–659
  behavioral approaches to, 633–
    637, 646–647
  benefits of, 632
  blending approaches to, 645,
    648–650
  careers in, A-36
  client-centered, 628–630, 646–647
  clients for, 623–624
  cognitive-behavioral approaches
    to, 636–637, 646–647
  common denominators in, 632–633
  cost of, 655
  eclecticism in, 649
  effectiveness of, 632, 637, 656–627,
    658–659
  elements of, 622–625
  group, 630–631
  multicultural sensitivity in,
    649–650
  placebo effects in, 658
  positive, 630
  practitioners of, 624–625
  process of, 657
  psychoanalytic approach to,
    626–628, 646–647
  psychodynamic approaches to, 628
  quack, 659
  settings for, 654
  stigma associated with, 624
  types of, 623
  utilization rates for, 623, 624
  willingness to seek, 624
  see also specific therapies;
    therapists
psychoticism, 514
PTC (phenylthiocarbamide), 167
puberty, 110, 464, 499
  timing of, 464
pubescence, 463
PubMed, 45
pulmonary diseases, 558
pulsatile hormone release, 109
punctuality, 26
punishment, 251–253
  aggression in children and, 259
  in behavior modification pro-
    grams, 269
  physical, 252–253
  toilet training and, 498
pupil, 136, 137
purity
  of light, 134, 135, 143
  of sound waves, 161, 162
Pys.D degree, A-33–A-34

Q

quail, 236
Queer Resources Directory, 415
questionnaires
  as data collection method, 43

problems with, 61
questions
  framing of, 348–349
  on IQ tests, 364
  multiple choice, 32–33
quetiapine, 639
Quichua (Ecuador), 425

R

racial prejudice, 700
racial stereotypes, 700–701
racism, modern, 701
radical behaviorism, 508
radio-controlled rodents, 246
rage, 540
random assignment, 47
rape
  aggressive pornography and, 413
  alcohol and, 216
rapid eye movements, 185, 192–193
Raramuri Indians, 425
ratio schedules of reinforcement,
  248, 249
rational-emotive behavior therapy,
  565, 636, 656
rationality, standards of, 343
rationalization, 496, 497
reaction formation, 496, 497, 529
reaction range, 376–377
reaction time, intelligence and, 382
reactivity, 52
reading, improving, 29–30
Reagan, Ronald, 578, 616
realistic group conflict theory, 702
reality monitoring, 293
reality principle, 494
reasoning
  circular, 227, 435
  errors in, 344
  fallacies in, 390, 435
  in health decisions, 571
  irrational, 566
  moral, 460–462
  prefrontal cortex and, 103
  reinforcement and, 258
reassurance seeking, 676
recall
  ESB-induced, 284, 285
  eyewitness, 291
  measures of retention, 294
receiver factors, in persuasion, 683,
  684
receptive field
  of cells in visual cortex, 141–143
  of retinal cells, 139
  of skin cells, 170
receptor sites, 83, 84, 85, 86, 217,
  601, 602
receptors
  for hearing, 162–163
  for smell, 168
  sensory, 173
  for taste, 166
  for touch, 169
  visual, 137–138
recessive gene, 112
reciprocal determinism, 504
reciprocity effects, 674
reciprocity norm, 271, 705
recognition heuristic, 344
recognition measures of retention,
  295
reconstructive memory, 291–292, 312
recordkeeping, for self-
  modification program, 268

recovered memories controversy,
  298–302
Recovered Memory Project, 301
recreational drugs, 214–221
recruiting, job, A-21–A-22
reflex learning, 302
reflex responses, 635
reflexes, conditioned, 234, 305
reflexive communication, 320
refractory period
  in male sexual response, 407
  of neuron, 82
regression, 211, 496
regression toward the mean, 658, 659
regret, anticipated, 349
rehearsal, 308
  behavioral, 636, 637
  in short-term memory, 281, 283
reification, 391
reinforcement
  in behavior modification pro-
    grams, 269
  continuous, 247
  defined, 242, 243
  of gender roles, 482
  intermittent, 247–248
  in language learning, 326
  negative, 249–250, 251, 269
  personality development and,
    503–504
  positive, 249, 250, 269
  response-outcome relations and,
    258–259
  schedules of, 246–249
reinforcement contingencies, 243,
  261, 268–269
reinforcers
  primary vs. secondary, 244
  for self-modification programs,
    269
relationships, close, 672–680
relative size in plane, 153, 154
relativistic view, of psychological
  disorders, 610, 611
relativity, of perception, 180
relaxation
  meditation and, 212, 213
  systematic, 224
relaxation response, 568
relaxation training, 634–635
relearning measures of retention,
  295
reliability
  of IQ tests, 364–365
  of psychological tests, 357, A-19
reliability coefficients, 358
religion, happiness and, 431
religious faith, 518
REM sleep, 192–193, 194, 224
  deprivation of, 199
  dreaming and, 204
remedies, quack, 659
"Remembering to Do Things: A
  Forgotten Topic," 306
Renaissance artists, 176
renewal effect, 239
replication, of research, 59
representativeness heuristic, 342,
  616, 617
repression, 297–298, 496, 497
  of child abuse memories, 298–302
repressive coping style, 497
reproductive fitness, 256, 408, 481,
  679
reproductive success, 15, 117, 119,
  398

research
  deception in, 66–67, 691
  ethics in, 691
  ethnocentrism in, 15
  evaluating, 59–61, 64
  Internet-mediated, 64–65,
    A-39–A-43
  longitudinal vs. cross-sectional,
    446–447
  replication of, 59
  see also correlational research;
    experimental research
research areas, career options in,
  A-34–A-36
research design, prospective vs.
  retrospective, 596
research findings, reporting, 44
research laboratories, for psychology, 4
research methods, 45, 120
  choosing, 42–43
  for studying heredity, 112–115
  see also specific methods
resignation, 545
resilience, 527, 540–541
resistance
  to persuasion, 684
  in psychoanalysis, 627, 628
resistance to extinction, 246
resistance stage, 542
resistant attachment, 450
resolution phase, of sexual response
  cycle, 407
response-outcome (R-O) associations, 246
response-outcome relations,
  258–259
response patterns, reinforcement
  schedules and, 248–249
response rate, operant, 244
response sets, 526
response tendencies, 503, 504
responses
  conditioned, 234, 235, 236, 237,
    239
  operant, 243
  performance vs. acquisition of, 261
  unconditioned, 234, 235, 236, 237,
    239
responsibility, diffusion of, 695
resting potential, 82
Restoril, 201
résumé, A-32
retention, 294–295
  improving, 308
  visual imagery and, 279, 280
reticular formation, 98, 99, 196
retina, 135, 136, 137–139, 145–146
retinal disparity, 153
retrieval, 276, 290–293
retrieval cues, 290
retrieval failure, 296–297
retroactive interference, 296, 297
retrograde amnesia, 303–304
retrospective designs, 596
retrospective memory, 306
reuptake, 84, 217, 640, 641
reversibility, 455
reversible figures, 146, 147, 151–152
revolving door, for mental hospitals, 652–653
reward pathway, in brain, 218
rewards. *See* reinforcement
rhymes, for memorization, 310
rhythms, biological, 188–191
Riley Guide, A-31

risk-benefit assessments, 571
risks
  health, 570
  underestimating, 561
risky behavior, in adolescence, 465
risky decision making, 341, 346
risky shift, 697
rituals, 231
RNA transfer studies, 302
Robber's Cave study, 702
roborats, 246
rods, 137–138
role expectations, in marriage, 470
role models, 259, 482, 506
role playing
  hypnosis as, 210, 212
  of social skills, 636
roles
  in groups, 694
  social, 692
romantic ideals, 674
romantic relationships, 674–677
  break-up of, 677
  culture and, 677
  deception in, 680
  evolutionary perspective on, 680
  happiness and, 431
  idealization of partner in, 674
  love in, 674–675
rooms, personality of, 505–506
Rorschach test, 527
Ruffini cylinder, 169
rules of thumb, 332
rumination, 592, 595
Rutherford, Tom, 299

S

sadness, 540
safe sex, 561
salary, for careers in psychology,
  A-30, A-31
salary.com, A-33
salivation response, in dogs, 233
salt, preferences for, 402
salt intake, 559, 570, 571
sample, from population, A-13, A-14
sampling, of behavior, 356
sampling bias, 59–60, 65, 74
sarcasm, 322
SAT scores, 57, 373, A-10, A-11
satin bowerbird, 119
saturation, of colors, 134, 135, 143,
  144
sauce béarnaise syndrome, 254
savings scores, 295
scarcity, feigned, 705
scare tactics, 214
scatter diagrams, A-11, A-12
schedule, for studying, 28–29
schedules of reinforcement, 246–249
schemas, 288
schizophrenic disorders, 598–604,
  608–609
  biological factors in, 576–579, 583
  brain abnormalities and, 95, 578,
    583
  culture and, 611
  dopamine and, 86–87
  drug therapy for, 638
  emergence of, 600
  etiology of, 601–604, 609
  expressed emotion and, 579, 583
  among homeless, 653
  genetic vulnerability to, 115, 576,
    583

glia and, 81
glutamate and, 88
heredity and, 113
lifetime prevalence of, 581
marijuana use and, 220
multiple causation of, 120
neurodevelopmental hypothesis
  of, 578–579, 583
prenatal malnutrition and, 443
prevalence of, 598
prognosis for, 600
relapse in, 604
stress and, 549, 579, 583
stress-vulnerability model of, 612
subtypes of, 599–600, 608
symptoms of, 598
school performance, IQ scores and,
  366
school psychology, 19, 22
  careers in, A-37
schools
  bilingualism in, 323
  hemispheric specialization and,
    122, 123
  as source of gender-role socializa-
    tion, 483
scientific approach
  advantages of, 44–45
  goals of, 40–45
  in psychology, 40–45
  steps in, 41–44
scientific method, 8, 23
Scirus, A-40
scorpion fly, 119
Screw It, Let's Do It (Branson), 490
sea slug, 302
search engines, A-40
second-hand smoke, 558
secondary-process thinking, 494
secondary sex characteristics, 110,
  463
secure attachment, 449–450, 675,
  676, 677
sedatives, 201, 214, 215, 216
  prenatal development and, 443
selective attention, 277
selective breeding, 113
selective serotonin reuptake inhibitors (SSRIs), 640
self-actualization, 511
self-actualizing persons, 511–512
self-blame, 540, 544–545
self-concept
  culture and, 522
  Rogers's view of, 509, 628–629
  stress and, 550
self-confidence, 522
self-deception, 496, 546–547
self-destructive behavior, 558
self-discipline, school performance
  and, 366
self-disclosure, online dating and,
  678
self-effacing bias, 672
self-efficacy, 506–507, 549
self-enhancement, 522
self-esteem
  attachment styles and, 677
  collectivism and, 672
  depression and, 591
  happiness and, 432
  height and, 53
  individualism and, 672
  social identity and, 703
  terror management theory of, 517,
    518

self-indulgence, 545–546
self-modification program, 267–269
self-perception theory, 686–687
self-preservation, 517
self-referent encoding, 280
self-report data, 61, 74
self-report inventories, 525–526
self-sacrifice, 118
self-serving bias, 670–671
self-socialization, 482
self-stimulation, of brain pleasure
  centers, 100
self-testing, 308
self-worth, 522
semantic encoding, 278, 279
semantic memory system, 305, 306,
  474
semantic networks, 289
semantic priming, 132
semantic processing, 297
semantic slanting, 350
semantics, 320
senility, 472
sensation(s)
  brain integration of, 99
  defined, 130
  memory for, 281
  psychophysics of, 130–134
  study of, 5
senses, absolute thresholds for, 131
sensorimotor period, 454
sensory adaptation, 133–134
  to smells, 168
  to touch, 170
sensory integration, 174
sensory memory, 280–281, 282, 287
sensory receptors, 90
sensory-specific satiety, 401
sentences, in English language, 319
separation anxiety, 449
September 11 terrorist attacks, 518
  emotions associated with, 540
  flashbulb memories for, 285–286
serial-position effect, 309
serial processing, 290
serotonin, 86, 87, 174, 196, 217, 218,
  399, 585, 594, 601, 640, 641
sertraline, 640
set-point theory, 405
settling-point theory, 405
Seurat, Georges, 176, 177
sex cells, 111
sex crimes, 413
sex drive, 408
  Freud's view of, 495, 497–498
sex research, 406
sex, 475
sexism, 700, 701
  in psychoanalytic theory, 502
sexual abuse, repressed memories
  of, 298–302
sexual activity, casual, 408
sexual appeals, in advertising, 270,
  271
sexual arousal
  brain function and, 96
  classical conditioning of, 236
sexual development, 463–464
sexual disorders, 577, 580
sexual fantasies, 408
sexual motivation
  evolutionary perspective on,
    407–412
  gender differences in, 408–409
sexual orientation, 414–417
sexual partners, number of, 408–409

sexual problems, stress and, 549
sexual response cycle, 406–396
sexual urges, Freud's view of, 7
sexually transmitted diseases, 444
shame, 453
shaping
  in operant conditioning, 245–246
  of social skills, 636
Shelley, Mary, 204
shift work, 190–191
short-term memory (STM), 281–284
  capacity of, 283
  durability of, 281–282
  as part of long-term memory,
    286–287
  as working memory, 283–284
shuttle box, 250
siblings,
  heredity and, 112, 113
  personality differences in, 515
  see also genetic relatedness; twins
sick role, 588
SIECUS, 408
siesta cultures, 196
sight. See vision
signal-detection theory, 131–132
signal relations, 257–258
similarity
  attraction and, 673
  as Gestalt principle, 150
  of persuasive sources, 683
simplicity, as Gestalt principle, 150
Simpson, O. J., 705
singlehood, 470
Siriono, 206
situational specificity, 507
six-coin problem, 333, 334
Sixteen Personality Factor (16PF)
    Questionnaire, 525, 526
size constancy, 159
skepticism, 23, 45, 69
skewed distributions, A-8
skills
  memory for, 305
  motor, 446
skin, receptors in, 169
Skinner box, 243, 244, 250
slant, geographic, 155–157
sleep apnea, 202
sleep deprivation, 197–200
  health and, 199–200
  selective, 199
sleep disorders, 200–202, 223–224,
    549
sleep laboratories, 191
sleep restriction, 197–198
sleep spindles, 192
sleep, 191–203
  age trends in, 193, 194
  amount of, 196
  awareness during, 187
  brain centers for, 99
  common questions about,
    222–224
  culture and, 193, 195–196
  duration of, 200
  evolutionary bases of, 197
  need for, 222–223
  neural bases of, 196
  onset of, 192
  quality of, 189, 190
  rapid eye movements in, 185
  serotonin and, 86
  stages of, 191–196
sleeping pills, 201
SleepNet, 192

SleepQuest, 193
sleepwalking, 203
slippery slope, 435, 485
slips of the tongue, 7, 494
slot machines, 249
slow-to-warm-up children, 447–448
slow-wave sleep (SWS), 192, 193
  deprivation of, 199
smell
  absolute threshold for, 131
  sense of, 168, 172–173
smoking, 86, 558
  behavior modification for, 269
  depression and, 58
  during pregnancy, 444
  heart disease and, 551
  prevalence of, 558
  quitting, 558, 559
  self-efficacy and, 506
  stress and, 546
snoring, 202, 223
social activity, happiness and, 431
social bonds, 556–557
social cognitive theory, 504–507,
    508
social desirability bias, 61, 65, 74,
    526
social identity, 703
social influence, 688–693
  strategies of, 705
social intelligence, 367
social learning theory, 504, 506
social loafing, 695–696
social mobility, 418
social motives, 398
social networking, 678
social norms, 494, 495
  deviation from, 577
social phobias, 586
social psychology, 18, 19, 664
  careers in, A-36
Social Readjustment Rating Scale
    (SRRS), 537–538
social roles, 692
social skills,
  group therapy for, 632
  poor, 597
social skills training, 636
social support
  adherence to medical advice and,
    563
  in group therapy, 631
  lack of, 597
  providing, 556
  stress and, 556–557, 567
social workers, 625, A-33
socialization, 522
  cultural differences in, 671
  gender-role, 482–483
  organizational, A-22–A-24
Society for Industrial and Organiza-
    tional Psychology (SIOP), A-18
Society for Judgment and Decision
    Making, 338
Society for Neuroscience, 104
sociocultural theory, 457
socioeconomic status
  achievement motive and, 418
  father absence and, 485
  IQ scores and, 378, 379–380
  mental retardation and, 350,
    370–371
sociohistorical context, 24, 429, 523
sodium ions, 82
Soft Construction with Boiled Beans
    (Dali), 524

soma, of neuron, 80, 81
somatic nervous system, 90
somatization disorder, 587, 588
somatoform disorders, 586–588
somatosensory cortex, 102, 104,
    170, 171
somnambulism, 203
Sonata, 201
sound, 160–161
  localization of, 164–165
source factors, in persuasion, 683,
    704
source monitoring, 292–293
source-monitoring error, 293, 312
Spain, 196
spanking, 252–253
spatial ability, gender differences
    in, 35
special education programs, 373
specialization, in psychology, 19, 22
species, evolution of, 116–117
spectrum, of light, 134, 135, 143,
    144
speech, brain centers for, 105, 122,
    123
Spencer, Diana, 439
sperm, 111, 440
sperm release, classical condition-
    ing of, 236
spermarche, 464
Spherion Workplace Snapshot,
    A-26
spinal cord, 90–91, 98, 174
split-brain research, 106–107, 122
split personality, 598
Spokane Research Library, A-25
spokespeople, advertising, 684
spontaneous recovery, in classical
    conditioning, 238–239
spontaneous remission, 632
sports, competitive, 569
sports teams, travel effects on, 190
spreading activation, in semantic
    networks, 289
SQ3R, 29–31
stage theories, 452, 476–479
  Erikson's, 452–453, 466
  Freud's, 497–499
  Kohlberg's, 460–462
  Piaget's, 453–456
standard deviation (SD), 55–56, 59,
    364, 366, A-8, A-10
standardization, of tests, 336, 355,
    357
Stanford-Binet Intelligence Scale,
    361–362
Stanford Hypnotic Susceptibility
    Scale (SHSS), 209
Stanford Prison Simulation,
    692–693
statistical significance, 59, 570, A-14
statistics, 43–44, 55, A-7
  descriptive, 55–58, A-8–A-13
  empiricism and, A-14
  health-related, 570–571
  inferential, 58–59, A-13–A-14
  probabilities and, 616–617
stereotaxic instrument, 93
stereotype vulnerability, 380–381
stereotypes, 518, 665–666, 667, 703
  gender, 475, 480
  prejudice and, 700–701
steroid abuse, 110
Stevenson, Robert Louis, 204
stimulants, 87, 101, 214, 215, 216,
    224

stimulus, 130
  aversive, 249–250, 251
  for color vision, 143
  conditioned, 234, 235, 236, 237,
    238, 239, 251, 258
  discriminative, 246
  distal, 151
  for hearing, 160–161
  neutral, 233–234
  proximal, 151
  subliminal, 132–133
  for touch, 168
  unconditioned, 234, 235, 236, 237,
    238, 239, 254, 255
stimulus contiguity, 238
stimulus control, 246
stimulus discrimination, 240, 247
stimulus generalization, 239–240,
    247
stimulus intensity, 131
stimulus-response (S-R) psychol-
    ogy, 9
stomach contractions, hunger and,
    399, 400
storage, memory, 276, 280–290
strategies
  decision making, 337–339,
    344–345
  problem solving, 332–335
stream of consciousness, 6, 121,
    122, 186
Streep, Meryl, 367
stress
  autonomic arousal and, 90
  behavioral response to, 544–546
  brain-body pathways in, 543
  burnout and, 549
  chronic, 542
  coining of term, 542
  coping with, 565–569
  defined, 534
  depression and, 594
  dissociative disorders and, 590
  eating behavior and, 403
  emotional responses to, 540–542
  as everyday effect, 534–535
  exercise and, 560
  factors moderating, 556–557
  illness and, 555
  immune functioning and,
    554–555
  as inevitable, 565
  insomnia and, 201
  meditation and, 213
  mood disorders and, 597
  physiological responses to,
    542–543
  psychological functioning and,
    525–527
  relaxation and, 568
  resistance to, self-efficacy and, 506
  schizophrenia and, 604
  self-generated, 539
  task performance and, 548–549
  traumatic, 550
  types of, 535–539
stress hormones, 109
stress management, 565–569
stress-vulnerability models, 612
stressful events, appraisal of, 535,
    565–566
string problem, 329
stroke, 534
structural encoding, 278, 279
structuralism, 5
study habits, 28–29, 309–310

subgoals, in problem solving, 332–333
subjective contours, 148–149
subjective utility, 341
subjective well-being, 429–433
subjectivity
  of experience, 70, 216, 307, 564
  of perception, 26–27, 146, 160, 175, 222, 666–667
  of person perception, 699
subjects
  deception of, 66–67
  in experiments, 46
  in Internet-mediated research, 65
  random assignment of, 47
  research, 5, 15, 43, 60
subliminal odors, 168
subliminal perception, 132–133
substance abuse treatment, 506
substance use disorders, 580, 581
subtractive color mixing, 143–144
success
  attributions for, 668, 669, 670
  height and, 53
  incentive value of, 418
sudden infant death syndrome, 444
suggestibility, 208, 210
  of eyewitnesses, 292
suggestion, power of, 298
suicide rates, 445, 466
suicide
  by cop, 1
  case studies of, 52–53
  mood disorders and, 593
  SSRIs and, 640–641
Sunday Afternoon on the Island of La Grande Jatte (Seurat), 176, 177
superego, 493, 494, 495, 496, 626
superior colliculus, 140, 141
superiority, striving for, 500–501
superstition, 231, 232
supertasters, 167
suprachiasmatic nucleus (SCN), 189
Surgeon General's Report, 581
Surrealism, 177, 524
surrogate mothers, 449
survey research, 43, 53–54, 61, 62–63
  using Internet, 64–65
susceptibility, to persuasion, 684
Sybil (Schreiber), 590
symbolism, in dreams, 225, 626
symbols
  archetypes and, 499–500
  language as, 318
sympathetic division
sympathetic division, of autonomic nervous system, 90, 91, 421, 542
sympathy, sick role and, 588
symptoms, interpretation of, 562
synaptic cleft, 217, 218
synapse(s), 81, 83–85
  action of neurotransmitters at, 85
  density of, 125
  dopamine, 601, 602
  drug effects at, 217–218, 640
  formation of, 124, 125
  for memory, 302, 303
  new, 104
  number of, in brain, 89
  in visual cells, 139
synaptic cleft, 83, 84
synaptic pruning, 85, 125, 465
synaptic vesicles, 83, 84
syntax, 320
systematic desensitization, 634–635, 646–647, 656

T

tactile stimulation, 169–170
Tahiti, 424
talent, development of, 372
tardive dyskinesia, 639
task performance
  achievement motivation and, 418
  arousal and, 541–542
  stress and, 548–549
tasks, habitual, 306
taste
  absolute threshold for, 131
  sense of, 165–168
taste aversion, conditioned, 254–255
taste buds, 166
taste preferences, 118, 166, 167, 402
taste sensitivity, 167
tastes, primary, 166
teachers, as source of gender-role socialization, 483
teaching psychology, A-33
teams, work, A-23–A-24
teleconferencing, A-23
telegraphic speech, 322
television
  as optical illusion, 159
  as source of gender-role socialization, 483
temperament
  heart disease and, 552
  inhibited, 584
  in infants, 446–448
temperature regulation, 396–397
temperature, body, 189
Temple-Wisconsin Cognitive Vulnerability to Depression Project, 595–596
temporal lobe, 102, 105, 142, 163, 284
"tend and befriend" response, 542
terminal buttons, 81, 83, 84
terror management theory, 517–519
terrorist attacks, probability of, 347
terrycloth mothers, 449
test anxiety, 380–381
test norms, 337, 357
test-retest reliability, 357–358
test taking, strategies for, 31–33
testes, 464
testimonials, for remedies, 659
testimony, eyewitness, 312–313
testing, 24
  of employees, A-19
  see also psychological tests (testing)
testing effect, 308, 309
testing perspective, on intelligence, 383
testosterone, 109, 220, 472
testosterone levels, masculinity and, 412
testosterone supplements, 472
testwiseness, 31
textbooks, studying, 30–31, 310
texture gradient, 153, 154
Thailand, A-20
thalamus, 98, 99
  auditory processing and, 163
  emotions and, 422, 423
  sense of touch and, 170, 171
  vision and, 140, 141
THC, 215, 218, 601
Thematic Apperception Test (TAT), 417, 418, 526, 527
theoretical diversity, 23–24, 175, 222, 307–308, 523, 653–654

theories, 22, 41
  behaviorial, 8–10, 11, 20
  biological, 11, 14
  cognitive, 11, 13–14
  constructing, 41
  evolutionary, 11, 15–16
  functionalism, 5–6
  humanistic, 10–11
  psychoanalytic, 7, 11, 20
  structuralism, 5
therapist(s)
  approach of, 655–656
  in behavior therapy, 634–635
  in client-centered therapy, 629
  dissociative identity disorder and, 590
  finding, 654–657
  in group therapy, 630–631
  minority patients and, 649–650
  professional background of, 654–655
  questions for, 657
  recovered memories controversy and, 298–302
  sexual exploitation by, 655
  types of, 624–625
therapy. *See* psychotherapy
theta waves, 188, 212
thinking
  abstract, 456
  catastrophic, 565–566, 588
  convergent, 389
  critical, 34
  divergent, 388–389
  eating disorders and, 615
  intuitive, 345
  irrational, 636
  modes of, 121
  negative, 595–596, 636
  see also decision making; problem solving
thioridazine, 639
Thorazine, 639
Thought and Language (Vygotsky), 457
thought
  distorted, 615
  disturbed, 598
  language and, 327, 350
threats
  implied, 351
  interpretation of, 585
Three Faces of Eve, 589
threshold, 131
timbre, 161, 162
time-based tasks, 307
time management, 29, 30
time zones, jet lag and, 189–190
tip-of-the-tongue phenomenon, 275–276, 290
toilet training, 452, 498
tolerance, drug, 216, 217, 236–237
tongue, 166
top-down processing, 148, 149
touch
  absolute threshold for, 131
  adaptation to, 134
  sense of, 169–171, 172–173, 174
tower of Hanoi problem, 332–333
toxic environment, for eating, 405
toys, gender roles and, 483
traffic accidents
  drug use and, 219
  sleep deprivation and, 198–199
traits. See personality traits
tranquilizers, 638

transcendental meditation (TM), 212
transcranial magnetic stimulation (TMS), 93–94, 644
transfer-appropriate processing, 297, 308
transference, in psychoanalysis, 628
transformation, problems of, 329
transformational leadership, A-24
transvestic fetishism, 577
traumatic events, 584
  multiple personality and, 590
  repressed memories of, 298–302
treatment, seeking, 562
trial and error, 332
trials, in classical conditioning, 234
triarchic theory of intelligence, 384
trichromatic theory, of color vision, 144–145
tricyclics, 639, 648
trust versus mistrust, 452
trustworthiness, of sources, 683
truth, lie detector and, 421–422
Tukoer-Ter-Ur (Vasarely), 178, 179
turkeys, wild, 119
Tuskegee Syphilis Study, 66
20/20 hindsight, 529
twin studies, 113–114, 513
  of antisocial personality disorder, 606
  of anxiety disorders, 584, 585
  of homosexuality, 415–416
  of intelligence, 374
  of mood disorders, 594
  of obesity, 404
  of schizophrenia, 601
twins, 112
two-factor theory, of emotion, 426, 427
Type A personality, 551
Type B personality, 551

U

ultraviolet spectrum, 135
uncertainty
  decision making and, 417
  reducing, 571
unconditional positive regard, 629
unconditioned response (UR), 234, 235, 236, 237, 239, 585, 634, 635, 684, 685
unconditioned stimulus (US), 234, 235, 236, 237, 238, 239, 254, 255, 585, 634, 635, 684, 685
unconscious, 186
  Freud's view of, 7, 297, 494–495, 547, 626
  Jung's view of, 499–500
underextension, 322
understanding, as goal of scientific approach, 40, 41
undifferentiated schizophrenia, 600
undoing, 546
unemployment, 432
uninhibited temperament, 448
unipolar disorder. *See* depressive disorder
universalistic view, of psychological disorders, 610
universities, psychology laboratories at, 4
University of Leipzig, 4
University of Minnesota Center for Twin and Adoption Research, 513
upside-down T, 157

V

vacillation, 536
vagus nerve, 400
validity
  of IQ tests, 366–367
  of psychological tests, 358–359, 360, A-19
validity effect, 684
Valium, 584, 638
valproate, 641
value, expected, 341
variability, in data, 55–56, 59, A-8
variable-interval schedules of reinforcement, 248, 249
variable-ratio schedules of reinforcement, 248, 249
variables, 40, 45–46
  confounding of, 47
  correlations between, 56–57, A-11
  extraneous, 47
Vasarely, Victor, 178, 179
vasocongestion, 406
vengefulness, 568
venlafaxine, 641
ventricles, of brain, 90, 91, 95, 602
ventromedial nucleus of the hypothalamus (VMH), 399, 400
Verbal Behavior (Skinner), 326
verbal intelligence, 367
verbal material, brain hemispheres and, 121
verbal skills, gender differences in, 480
verifiability, of scientific claims, 8
Veterans Administration (VA), 13
viability, age of, 443
victims, blaming of, 670, 702
video games, 263
Vienna Psychoanalytic Society, 500

violence
  against women, 413
  in media, 261–263, 266
  mental illness and, 578
violent crime, alcohol and, 216
Violin and Grapes (Picasso), 176, 177
Virgin companies, 489
Virtual Hospital, A-41
virtual teams, A-23–A-24
Visible Human Project, 93
vision
  absolute threshold for, 131
  aging and, 471–472
  color, 138, 143–146
  night, 138
  perceptual constancies in, 157
  peripheral, 138
  stimulus for, 134, 135
Vision Science, 135
visual acuity, 138
visual agnosia, 130
visual cortex, 102, 140–143
visual fields, 106–107, 141
visual illusions, 157–160, 178, 179
visual imagery, encoding and, 279, 280
visual priming, 132
visual processing, in brain, 102
visual system, 134–160, 172–173
visual-spatial ability, 35
  gender differences in, 480
visuospatial sketchpad, 283
vocabulary, children's, 321
vocabulary spurt, 320, 321
vocalizations, of infants, 321
vocational success, IQ scores and, 367–368
volley principle, 164
voltage, in neuron, 82
vomiting, 614
von Meduna, Ladislas, 642

W

waist-to-hip ratio, 679
walking speed, 51
Washoe, 324
water jar problem, 329, 330, 334
Waterfall (Escher), 177, 179
wavelength,
  of light waves, 134, 135, 143, 145
  of sound waves, 161
wealth, happiness and, 430
websites, research using, A-39–A-43
Wechsler Adult Intelligence Scale (WAIS), 362, 365
weight, 403–404
  aging and, 471
  loss of, 613
  preoccupation with, 613
well-being, subjective, 429–433
well-being therapy, 630
Wellesley College, 6
Wernicke's area, 105
what and where pathways, 142
white blood cells, 555
Whole Child, The, 444
Whorfian hypothesis, 327
windigo, 611
wine tasting, 165, 168
  comparative evaluations and, 339
Winfrey, Oprah, A-24
wish fulfillment, dreams as, 206, 207
withdrawal, job, A27–A-28
withdrawal illness, 218, 638
women
  in history of psychology, 6
  portrayal of in media, 615
  violence against, 413
  see also gender differences
Woodhouse's toad, 119

words
  children's first, 321
  emotionally laden, 350–351
  meaning of, 320
work
  happiness and, 432
  nighttime, 198
  role of, A-16
work attendance, A-28–A-29
Work on Present Job Scale, A-26
work shifts, 190–191, A-17
work teams, A-23–A-24
workaholics, 551
working backward, in problem solving, 333
working memory, 103, 283–284, 304, 473–474
workplace, A-25
  burnout in, 549
World War II, 12–13, 24
World Wide Web, 64
worldviews, cultural, 517–518
worrying, 582
writers, mental illness and, 389

XYZ

X rays, of brain, 94–95
Xanax, 638
Yale University, 689
yawning, 223
Yoruba (Nigeria), 424
Zollner illusion, 157
Zoloft, 640
zone of proximal development (ZPD), 457–458
Zulu, 160
zygote, 111, 440, 441

CREDITS

Photo Credits

This page constitutes an extension of the copyright page. We have made every effort to trace the ownership of all copyrighted material and to secure permission from copyright holders. In the event of any question arising as to the use of any material, we will be pleased to make the necessary corrections in future printings. Thanks are due to the following authors, publishers, and agents for permission to use the material indicated.

Contents xiv © ML Sinibaldi/ Corbis; xxiv: © Fred Derwai/Hemis/ Corbis; xxv: © Patrick Byrd /Science Faction /Getty Images; xxvii: © DAJ/ Getty Images; xxviii: © Jean-Pierre Lescourret/Corbis;. xxix: © Massimo Borchi/Atlantide Phototravel/Corbis; xxx: © Keren Su/Corbis; xxxi: © Joe Viesti/Viesti Associates; xxxii: © Richard Berenholtz/Corbis; xxxiii: © Adam Woolfitt/Robert Harding Picture Library Ltd / Alamy; xxxiv: © Royalty Free/Masterfile; xxxv: © Rich Reid/National Geographic Image Collection; xxxvi: © Roger Ressmeyer/ Corbis; xxxvii: © Jens Lucking/ Stone/ Getty Images; xxviii: © Richard T. Nowitz/National Geographic/Getty Images; xxxix: © Jose Fuste Raga/ Corbis

Chapter 1. 1 (and repeats pp 3, 12, 17, 23): © ML Sinibaldi/Corbis 2: left, © AP Images/Jeff Blake 2: right, © Michael Newman/PhotoEdit 5: Archives of the History of American Psychology, University of Akron, Akron, Ohio 6: (all), Archives of the History of American Psychology, University of Akron, Akron, Ohio 7: Courtesy of the Clark University Archives 10: Copyright © 1971 Time Inc. Reprinted by permission/ via Getty Images 13: (both), Archives of the History of American Psychology, University of Akron, Akron, Ohio 16: © Michael & Patricia Fogden/Corbis 18: © White Packert/Iconica/Getty Images 20: (Pavlov lab) Bettmann Corbis 20: (Hollingworth) (Washburn) (Wundt & others) Archives of the History of American Psychology, University of Akron, Akron, Ohio 20: (airplane) Stock Montage, Inc. 20: (intelligence test) Bettmann Corbis 20: (telephone) Antman Archives/The Image Works 20: Compliments of Clark University, Worcester, Massachusetts 21: (Atomic bomb) Photo12/ The Image Works 21: (Erikson) AP Images/Associated Press 21: (Kahneman) Courtesy of Daniel Kahneman 21: (Kenneth Clark) © Bettmann Corbis 21: (Loftus) Courtesy of Elizabeth Loftus 21: (Maccoby) Chuck Painter/Stanford News Service

21: (Seligman) Courtesy of Martin E. P. Seligman 21: (Shuttle liftoff) NASA 21: (Vietnam) AP Images/Associated Press 25: © Julian Abram Wainwright 26: © AP Images/Associated Press 27: Preferred Stock and Gazelle Technologies 29: © Anderson Ross/ Digital Vision/Getty Images 33: inset, © Rob Gage/Taxi/Getty Images.

Chapter 2. 38 (and repeats pp 40, 45, 51, 55, 59, 64, 66, 69): © Fred Derwai/Hemis/Corbis 52: © Michael Nichols/National Geographic Image Collection 53: right, Figure 2.10: photo © David Buffinton/ Photodisc Green/Getty Imges 60: © StudioDL/Corbis/Photolibrary 61: Courtesy of Robert Rosenthal 62: (pedestrians) © Rob Crandall/Alamy 62: (therapy) photo © David Buffinton/Photodisc Green/Getty Imges 62: © Studio DL/Corbis/Photolibrary 63: (Goodall and chimp) © Michael Nichols/National Geographic Image Collection/ 67: © 2005 Foundation for Biomedical Research 67: right, © William West/AFP/Getty Images 68: Courtesy of Neal Miller 75: © Jacob Taposchaner/ Photographer's Choice/ Getty Images.

Chapter 3. 78 (and repeats pp 80, 89, 92, 97, 105, 108, 110, 116, 120): © Patrick Byrd /Science Faction/ Getty Images 86: © Digital Vision/ Getty Images 87: © 2002 Associated Press /AP Images 88: top, Courtesy of Candice Pert 88: bottom, Courtesy of Solomon Snyder 92: inset, Figure 3.10: photo © Science Photo Library/ Photo Researchers, Inc. 94: bottom left, Figure 3.13a: photo © Henrik Sorensen/ Photonica/Getty Images 94: top right, Figure 3.13c: photo: © Dan McCoy/Rainbow 95: right, Figure 3.15: photo Courtesy and by permission of Dr. Jack Belliveau, Chief, NMR, MGH 95: left, Figure 3.15: photo © ISM- Sovereign/PhotoTake 95: top, © Wellcome Dept of Cognitive Neurology/Science Photo Library/Photo Researchers, Inc. 100: © John Netherton/Oxford Scientific Films /Photolibrary 101: left, Figure 3.18: photo Wadsworth Collection 107: Photo by Bob Paz/Caltech, Courtesy of Roger Sperry 108: Courtesy of Michael S. Gazzaniga 110: © Kevin Mazur/WireImage/Getty Images 111: left, Figure 3.26: photos (both): © Laura Dwight 114: bottom, Figure 3.29: photo © Mary Kate Denny/Photo Edit 114: top, Figure 3.29: photo © Marina Jefferson/Taxi-Getty Images 115: Photo courtesy of Tara McKearney 116: © Bettmann/Corbis 117: © John Dominis/Time Life Pictures/ Getty Images 119: Courtesy of John Alcock 121: © Plush Studios/Blend Images

Chapter 4. 128 (and repeats pp 130,134, 146, 160, 165, 169. 175) © DAJ/Getty Images 129: © Steve Cole/ Photodisc Green/Getty Images 131: Archives of the History of American Psychology, University of Akron, Akron, Ohio 132: inset, © Fernado Serna/Corbis 134: © 2008 Publiphoto/ Photo Researchers, Inc. 136: right, Craig McClain 141: Courtesy of David Hubel 143: left, Figure 4.17: photo © Steve Granitz/ WireImage/ Getty Images 144: Figure 4.18: Courtesy of BASF 149: top right, Archives of the History of American Psychology # The University of Akron 149: left, © Tony Freeman/PhotoEdit 154: Figure 4.36 (road) © Royalty Free/Corbis 154: Figure 4.36: (balloons) © Jose Fuste Raga/zefa/Corbis 154: Figure 4.36 (cracked mud) © Jean-Marc Truchet/ Getty Imges 154: Figure 4.36: (crater) U.S. Department of Energy 154: Figure 4.36: (glassware) © Ron Fehling/ Masterfile 154: Figure 4.36: (swan) © Chris George/Alamy 155: Vincent van Gogh, *A Corridor in the Asylum* (1889), Black chalk and gouache on pink Ingres paper. H. 25-5/8 in. W. 19-5/16/2 in. (65.1 x 49.1.cm.): The Metropolitan Museum of Art, Bequest of Abby Aldrich Rockefeller, 1948.(48.190.2) Photograph © 1998 The Metropolitan Museum of Art. 156: Courtesy of Dennis R. Proffitt, University of Virginia 158: inset, Figure 4.44: photo © Wayne Weiten 159: © N. R. Rowan/ The Image Works 160: © Alan Evrard/ Robert Harding/Getty Images 161: inset, Figure 4.48: photo © Betts Anderson Loman/PhotoEdit 164: Stock Montage, Inc. 165: © Commercial Eye/ Stone/Getty Images 167: center right, Courtesy of Linda Bartoshuk 167: left, Figure 4.53: photo © Malcolm S. Kirk 167: right, Figure 4.53: photo © Danielle Pelligrini/Science Source/Photo Researchers, Inc. 167: center, Figure 4.53: photo © Guy Mary-Rousseliere/ Catholic Mission, Northwest, Canada 172: (massage) © IS713/ Image Source Pink / Alamy 172: (sipping wine) © Lisa Woollett/Photofusion Picture Library / Alamy 172: (sunrise) © John White Photos / Alamy 172: (trumpet player) © Photodisc/Getty Images 172: (woman and flowers) © Blend Images/ Jamie Grill 174: © AP Images/Luca Bruno 176: Figure 4.57: *Maestro della cattura di Cristo, Cattura di Cristo,* parte centrale, Assisi, S. Francisco, Scala/Art Resource, New York 176: Figure 4.58: *Brera Predica di S. Marco Pinaocteca,* by Gentile and Giovanni Belini in Egitto. Scala/Art Resource, New York 177: Figure 4.59: (top -both) Georges Seurat, French, 1859-1891, *Sunday Afternoon on the Island of La Grande Jatte - 1884,* 1884–86, (and detail) Oil on canvas, 81-3/4 x 121-1/4 in. (207.5 x 308.1 cm),

Helen Birch Bartlett Memorial Collection, 1926.224, The Art Institute of Chicago. Photography © The Art Institute of Chicago. (The Art Institute web page: http://www.artic.edu/aic/; Image not for download.) 177: Figure 4.60: Pablo Picasso, *Violin and Grapes, Céret and Sorgues,* spring-summer 1912. Oil on canvas, 20 x 24" (50.6 x 61 cm), collection, The Museum of Modern Art, New York, Mrs. David M. Levy Bequest (32.1960). Digital image © The Museum of Modern Art/Licensed by SCALA/ Art Resource, New York. © 2009 Estate of Pablo Picasso/ Artists Rights Society (ARS), New York. Reproduction, including downloading is prohibited by copyright laws and international conventions without the express written permission of Artists Rights Society (ARS), New York. 178: left, Figure 4.61: Duchamp, Marcel, 1912, *Nude Descending a Staircase, No. 2.* oil on canvas, 58" x 35". Philadelphia Museum of Art: Louise and Walter Arensburg Collection, # 1950- 134-69. Reproduced by permission. © 2009 Artists Rights Society (ARS), New York / ADAGP, Paris /Succession Marcel Duchamp. 178: Figure 4.62: Salvador Dali, *The Slave Market with the Disappearing Bust of Voltaire,* (1940), Oil on canvas, 18-1/4 x 25-3/8 inches. Collection of The Salvador Dali Museum, St. Petersburg, Fl. Copyright © 2006 The Salvador Dali Museum, Inc. © 2009 Salvador Dali, Gala-Salvador Dali Foundation/Artists Rights Society (ARS), New York. 179: Figure 4.63: M.C. Escher's *Waterval 1961.* © 2008 The M.C. Escher Company-Holland. All rights reserved. www.mcescher. com 179: Figure 4.64: M.C. Escher's *Belvedere, 1958.* © 2008 The M.C. Escher Company-Holland. All rights reserved. www.mcescher.com 179: Figure 4.65: Vasarely, Victor (1908-1997) *Tukoer-Ter-Ur, 1989.* Acrylic on canvas, 220 x 220 cm. Private Collection, Monaco. © Erich Lessing / Art Resource, NY. Copyright © 2009 Artists Rights Society (ARS), New York/ADAGP, Paris. 179: Figure 4.66: Magritte, Rene, *Les Promenades d'Euclide,* The Minneapolis Institute of Arts, The William Hood Dunwoody Fund. Copyright © 2009 Charly Herscovic, Brussels / Artists Rights Society (ARS) New York.

Chapter 5. 184 (and repeats pp 186, 187, 191, 204, 208, 212, 214, 222): © Jean-Pierre Lescourret/Corbis 188: © Gary Meszaros 2008/ Photo Researchers, Inc. 191: © Christian Voulagaropoulos /ISM/PhotoTake 193: © Steve Bloom Images/Alamy 194: right, © Larry Dale Gordon/The Image Bank /Getty Images 194: left, © Mark Hall/Taxi/Getty Images - 197: Courtesy of William Dement 198: ©

Press, Copyright © 1943 by The President and Fellows of Harvard College, © 1971 by Henry A. Murray **528:** © AP Images/Dennis Cook.

Chapter 13. 532 (and repeats pp 534, 540, 548, 551, 556, 558, 562, 564): © Roger Ressmeyer/Corbis **535:** Courtesy of Richard S. Lazarus **539:** left, © Ethan Miller/Getty Images for Comedy Central **539:** right, © George Doyle/Stockbyte/ Getty Images **542:** © Bettmann/Corbis **545:** right, Courtesy of Albert Ellis Institute **545:** top, © Paul Thomas/The Image Bank/ Getty Images **547:** Courtesy of Shelley Taylor **549:** © Associated Press/ AP Images **552:** inset, Figure 13.10: photo Digital Vision/Getty Images **557:** Courtesy of Martin E. P. Seligman **557:** top, © Jon Feingersh/Corbis **558:** inset, Figure 13.13: photo © Spencer Grant./Photo Edit **563:** right, Courtesy of University of California, Riverside **563:** top, © Adamsmith/ SuperStock/Alamy **566:** bottom, © Radhika Chalasani/Getty Images **567:** © Acey Harper/Time Life Pictures/ Getty Images **568:** inset, Figure 13.20: photo © Paul Francis Photo **569:** inset, Figure 13.20: photo (center) © Paul Francis Photo **569:** inset, Figure 13.21: photo (left) © C. H. Wooley **569:** inset, Figure 13.21: photo (right) © Michael Newman/PhotoEdit.

Chapter 14. 574 (and repeats pp 576, 582, 586, 589, 590, 598, 604, 607, 610, 612 : © Jens Lucking / Stone/ Getty Images **576:** bottom, Figure 14.1: : "St. Catherine of Siena Exorcising a Possessed Woman," c.1500-1510. Girolamo Di Benvenuto. Denver Art Museum Collection, Gift of Samuel H. Kress Foundation Collection, 1961.171 © Denver Art Museum 2003. All rights reserved. **576:** top, Figure 14.1: Culver Pictures, Inc. **577:** top, Courtesy of Thomas Szasz **577:** bottom, © AP Images/John Miller **579:** Stanford University News Service **583:** bottom right, © AP Images/Associated Press **583:** bottom left, © Bettmann/Corbis **583:** top, © Jeffrey MacMillan/*U.S. News & World Report* **592:** right, © Elisabetta Villa/Getty Images **592:** left, © Tim Mosenfelder/Getty Images **595:** Courtesy of Susan Nolen-Hoeksema **600:** Courtesy of Nancy Andreasen. M.D. **608:** center right, (Ford) © Elisabetta Villa/Getty Images **608:** top right, (Hughes) © Bettmann/Corbis **608:** bottom right, (Nash) © Reuters/ Corbis **608:** top left, Munch, Edvard: **The Scream.** National Gallery, Oslo, Norway. SCALA/ Art Resource/NY; © 2009 The Munch Museum/The Munch-Ellingsen Group/Artists Rights Society (ARS), NY. Reproduction including downloading is prohibited by copyright laws and international conventions without the express written permission of Artists Rights Society (ARS), New York. **608:** center left, van Gogh, Vincent: **Portrait of Dr.**

Gachet. Musee d'Orsay, Paris. © Erich Lessing/Art Resource, NY **608:** bottom left, © Derek Bayes/Aspect Picture Library **610:** © AP Images/ Richard Drew **613:** © Ed Quinn/Corbis **616:** © Trippett/Sipa Press.

Chapter 15. 620 (and repeats pp 622, 626, 633, 638, 645, 650, 653): © Richard T. Nowitz/National Geographic/Getty Images **621:** Warner Bros./Shooting Star **623:** Mary Evans/ Sigmund Freud Copyrights **626:** National Library of Medicine **627:** © Bruce Ayres/Stone/Getty Images **629:** center, Courtesy of Carl Rodgers Memorial Library **629:** bottom, © Zigy Kaluzny/Stone/Getty Images **631:** © John Greim / Photo Researchers, Inc. **634:** Courtesy of Dr. Joseph Wolpe **635:** inset, Figure 15.10: photo © Robert Harding Picture Library **635:** top left, © Kent News & Picture/Corbis Sygma **636:** Courtesy of Aaron T. Beck **643:** © James Wilson/Woodfin Camp & Associates, all rights reserved **646:** (Beck) Courtesy of Aaron T. Beck **646:** (Freud) National Library of Medicine **646:** (Rogers) Courtesy Center for Studies of the Person **646:** (Wolpe) Courtesy of Dr. Joseph Wolpe **647:** (2nd down) © Zigy Kaluzny/ Stone/Getty Images **647:** (3rd down) © Kent News & Picture/Corbis Sygma **647:** (top) © Bruce Ayres/Stone/Getty Images **647:** bottom right, © James Wilson/Woodfin Camp & Associates, all rights reserved **647:** © John Greim / Photo Researchers, Inc. **647:** bottom right, © PhotoDisc, Inc. **651:** right, Figure 15.18: (Asylum) National Library of Medicine **651:** inset, Figure 15.18: (Dix) Detail of painting of Dorothea Dix in Harrisburg State Hospital, photo by Ken Smith/LLR Collection **655:** © Tom McCarthy/ SKA **656:** © Ilan Rosen /Alamy **658:** © Janine Wiedel Photolibrary / Alamy **659:** © Tony reeman/PhotoEdit.

Chapter 16. 662 (and repeats pp 664, 667, 672, 681, 688, 694, 699): © Jose Fuste Raga/Corbis **668:** spencer Research Library, University of Kansas Libraries **670:** © Mark Peterson/ Corbis **673:** © Thomas Barwick/ Photolibrary **674:** bottom, Courtesy of Elaine Hatfield **674:** top, Courtesy of Ellen Berscheid **677:** © DPA/The Image Works **681:** inset, Figure 16.9 photo: © AP Images/Ed Andrieski **685:** Courtesy of Prof. Jerry Suls **685:** inset, Figure 16.10 photo: © 2005 AP Images/Jennifer Graylock **688:** Courtesy of University of Pennsylvania, University Communications **690:** inset, Figure 16.16 Photos copyright © 1965 by Stanley Milgram. From the film *Obedience*, distributed by The Pennsylvania State University. Reprinted by permission of Alexandra Milgram **690:** Photo by Eric Kroll, courtesy of the Alexandra Milgram **692:** Courtesy of Philip Zimbardo **693:** left, From A Simulation Study of the Psychology of

Imprisonment Conducted at Stanford University, 1971. Copyright © Philip Zimbardo. Reproduced with permission. **693:** right, © AFP /Getty Images **697:** © Joseph Pobereskin/ Stone/ Getty Images **701:** © UPI Photo/Terry Schmitt /Landov **705:** © Tony Freeman/Photo Edit.

Appendix C: **A-15:** © AP Images/ John Cogill **A-16:** Courtesy of Kathy Hanisch **A-20:** PRNewsFoto/Ann Taylor **A-22:** © Louis Quail/Corbis **A-23:** © AP Images/Tony Avelar **A-24:** © Peter Kramer/Getty Images **A-25:** Courtesy of NIOSH Pittsburgh Research Lab **A-26:** © Christopher Robbins/Digital Vision/Photolibrary.

Text Credits

Chapter 1. **10:** Figure 1.3: Adapted from (left) Korn, J. H., Davis, R., & Davis, S. F. (1991) "Historians' and chairpersons' judgments of eminence among psychologists," [with data from "Rankings of the most notable psychologists by Department Chairpersons," by R. E. Estes, M. L. Coston & G. P. Fournet, 1990, unpublished manuscript], *American Psychologist, 46* (7), 789–792. Copyright © 1991 by the American Psychological Association; (right) Haggbloom, S. J. et al., 2002, The 100 most eminent psychologists of the 20th century, *Review of General Psychology, 6,* 139–152. Copyright © by the Educational Publishing Foundation. **14:** Figure 1.4: Adapted from Robins, E. W., Gosling, S. D., & Craik, K. H. (1999) "An empirical analysis of trends in psychology," *American Psychologist, 54* (2), 117–128. Copyright © 1999 by the American Psychological Association. Adapted by permission of the author. **27:** Figure 1.10: Description from H. H. Kelley (1950) "The warm-cold variable in first impressions of persons," *Journal of Personality, 8,* 431–439. Copyright © 1950 by the Ecological Society of America. Reprinted by permission. **30:** Figure 1.12: From questionnaire "Managing time means managing yourself," by LeBoeuf, 1980, p. 45. *Business Horizons Magazine,* 1980, 23 (1) February, Table 3. Copyright © 1980 by the Board of Trustees at of Indiana University, Kelley School of Business. Reprinted with permission from Elsevier. **31:** Figure 1.13: Data from H.C. Lindgren, 1969, *The Psychology of College Success A Dynamic Approach.* John Wiley & Sons. Adapted by permission of H.C. Lindgren. **32:** Cartoon DOONESBURY © 2007 by G. B. Trudeau. Dist. by UNIVERSAL PRESS SYNDICATE. Reprinted with permission. All rights reserved. **34:** Cartoon NON SEQUITUR © 2004 by Wiley Miller. Dist. by UNIVERSAL PRESS SYNDICATE. Reprinted with permission. All rights reserved. **35:** Figure 1.16: From Form AA, 1962, Identical Blocks, by R. E. Stafford and H. Gullikson.

Chapter 2. **42:** Cartoon © 2004 by Sidney Harris/Science Cartoons Plus, com. **43:** Figure 2.3 From Sherman, D. K., Nelson, L. D., & Ross, L. D., (2003), "Naive realism and affirmative action: Adversaries are more similar than they think," *Basic and Applied Social Psychology, 25,* 275–289. Copyright © 2003 Lawrence Erlbaum Associates, Inc. Reprinted by permission. **51:** Table 2.2: Adapted from Levine, R. V., and Norenzayan, A., "The pace of life in 31 countries," 1999, *Journal of Cross-Cultural Psychology, 30* (2), 178–205. Copyright © 1999 Sage Publications. Reprinted by permission. **53:** Figure 2.9: From Greenfeld, D. (1985). *The Psychotic Patient: Medication and Psychotherapy,* New York: The Free Press. Copyright © 1985 by David Greenfeld. Reprinted by permission of the author. **54:** Cartoon © 2004 by Sidney Harris/ Science Cartoons Plus, com. **71:** Figure 2.18: Sample record reprinted with permission of the American Psychological Association, publisher of the PsycINFO® database. Copyright © 1887–present, American Psychological Association. All rights reserved. For more information contact psycinfo. apa.org. **72:** Figure 2.19: Sample record reprinted with permission of the American Psychological Association, publisher of the PsycINFO® database. Copyright © 1887–present, American Psychological Association. All rights reserved. For more information contact psycinfo.apa.org. **74:** Cartoon DILBERT: © Scott Adams/Dist. by United Feature Syndicate, Inc.

Chapter 3. **85:** Figure 3.5: Data based on Huttenlocher, P. R. (1994). Synaptogenesis in human cerebral cortex. In G. Dawson & K. W. Fischer (Eds.), *Human Behavior and the Developing Brain.* New York: Guilford Press. Graphic adapted from Kolb, B. & Whishaw, I. Q. (2001). *An introduction to Brain and Behavior.* New York: Worth Publishers. **90:** Figure 3.7: Based on Nairne, J. S. (2000), *Psychology: The Adaptive Mind.* Belmont, CA: Wadsworth © 2000 Wadsworth. Reprinted by permission. **92:** Figure 3.10: EEG read-out from "Current concepts: The sleep disorders," by P. Hauri, 1982, The Upjohn Company, Kalamazoo, Michigan. Reprinted by permission. **94:** © Bryan Christie Design **107:** bottom, Cartoon © 1988. Used by permission of John L. Hart FLP, and Creators Syndicate, Inc. **113:** Cartoon © The New Yorker Collection 2003 Leo Cullum from the cartoonbank. com. All rights reserved. **113:** Figure 3.28: Based on *Schizophrenia Genesis: The Origins of Madness,* by I.I. Gottesman, 1991. Copyright © 1991 W. H. Freeman Company. **114:** Figure 3.29 (left) Adapted from Kalat, J. W., *Introduction to Psychology, 4th edition,* p. 78 © 1996 Wadsworth. Reprinted by permission. **119:** Table 3.2 Adapted from *Animal Behavior* by John Alcock,

Chapter 8. 319: Figure 8.1: Figure from Clarke-Stewart, A., Friedman, S., & Koch, J. (1985) *Child Development: A Topical Approach,* p. 417. Copyright © 1985 by John Wiley & Sons, Inc. Reprinted by permission of John Wiley & Sons, Inc. 319: Table 8.1: From Hoff, E., *Language Development, 2nd edition.* © 2001 Wadsworth. Reprinted by permission. 321: Figure 8.2: Adapted from Goldfield, B. A., & Resnick, J. S. (1990) "Early lexical acquisition: Rate, content, and the vocabulary spurt," *Journal of Child Language, 17,* 171–183. Copyright © 1990 by Cambridge University Press. 321: Figure 8.3: From Anglin, J. M. (1993) "Vocabulary development: A morphological analysis," *Child Development, 58,* Serial 238. Copyright © 1993 The Society for Research in Child Development, Inc. Reprinted by permission. 325: Cartoon: FRANK & ERNEST © 2007 Bob Thaves/Dist by Newspaper Enterprise Association, Inc. 331: DILBERT: © 2003 Scott Adams/Dist. by United Feature Syndication, Inc. 331: Figure 8.8: Based on Luchins, A. S. (1942) "Mechanization in problem solving," *Psychological Monographs, 54 (Whole No. 248).* 331: Figure 8.9: From *Conceptual Blockbusting: A Guide to Better Ideas,* by James L. Adams, pp. 17–18. Copyright © 1980 by James L. Adams. Reprinted by permission of W. H. Freeman 332: Figure 8.10: From Kendler, Howard H. (1974) *Basic Psychology, 3rd Edition,* pp. 403, 404. Copyright © 1974 The Benjamin-Cummings Publishing Co. Adapted by permission of Howard H. Kendler. 333: Cartoon CALVIN & HOBBES © by Bill Watterson. Dist. by UNIVERSAL PRESS SYNDICATE. Reprinted with permission. All rights reserved. 334: Figure 8.13: Based on by Luchins, A. S. (1942), "Mechanization in problem solving," *Psychological Monographs, 54* (Whole No. 248). 334: Figure 8.14: From *Conceptual Blockbusting: A Guide to Better Ideas,* by James L. Adams, pp. 17–18. Copyright © 1980 by James L. Adams. Reprinted by permission of W. H. Freeman 334: Figure 8.15: From Kendler, Howard H. (1974) *Basic Psychology 3rd Edition,* pp. 403, 404. Copyright © 1974 The Benjamin-Cummings Publishing Co. Adapted by permission of Howard H. Kendler. 340: Figure 8-19 From Dijksterhuis, A., Bos, N. W., Nordgren, L. F., & van Baaren, R. B., (2006), "On making the right choice: The deliberation-without-attention effect," *Science, 311* (5763), 1005–1007. Copyright © 2006 the American Society for the Study of Science. Reprinted by permission from the AAAS. 340: Figure 8.20 From Dijksterhuis, A., Bos, N. W., Nordgren, L. F., & van Baaren, R. B., (2006), "On making the right choice: The deliberation-without-attention effect," *Science, 311* (5763), 1005–1007. Copyright © 2006 the American Society for the Study of Science. Reprinted by permission. 343: Cartoon © 2005 Steve Kelley. The Times-Picayune. Reprinted with permisson.

Chapter 9. 362: Cartoon © 2005 by Sidney Harris/Science CartoonPlus. com 367: Figure 9.8: Adapted from Sternberg, R. J., Conway, B. E., Keton, J. L. & Bernstein, M. (1981), "People's conceptions of intelligence," *Journal of Personality and Social Psychology, 41 (1),* p.45. Copyright © 1981 by the American Psychological Association. Adapted by permission of the publisher and author. 368: Cartoon © 2004 by Sidney Harris/Science Cartoons Plus. com. 372: Figure 9.12: Adapted from Renzulli, J. S., (1986) "The three-ring conception of giftedness: A developmental model for creative productivity " In R.J. Sternberg and J.E. Davidson (Eds.), *Conceptions of Giftedness,* pp. 53–92. Cambridge University Press. 376: Figure 9.15: Adapted from J. Horgan, "Get smart, take a test," *Scientific American, 273 (5),* pg. 14. Copyright © 1995 by Scientific American, Inc. Adapted by permission of the author. 378: Cartoon © The New Yorker Collection 1994 Charles Barsotti from the cartoonbank.com. All rights reserved. 381: Figure 9.18: Adapted from Steele, C. M., & Aronson, J. (1995) "Stereotype threat and the intellectual test performance of African Americans," *Journal of Personality and Social Psychology, 69,* 797–811. Copyright © 1995 American Psychological Association. Adapted by permission of the author. 383: Figure 9.19: Graph adapted from Deary, I. J., Caryl P. G., & Gibson, G. J. (1993), "Nonstationarity and the measurement of psychophysical response in a visual inspection time task," *Perception, 22,* p. 1250. Copyright © 1993 by Pion Ltd. Adapted by permission. 385: Table 9.3: Adapted from Gardner, H., & Hatch, T., (1989) "Multiple intelligences go to school: Educational implications of the theory of multiple intelligences," *Educational Researcher, 18 (8),* 4–10. American Educational Research Association. Additional data from Gardner, 1998.

Chapter 10. 402: Cartoon CATHY © 2008 by Cathy Guisewite. Dist. by UNIVERSAL PRESS SYNDICATE. Reprinted with permission. All rights reserved. 405: Cartoon CATHY © by Cathy Guisewite. Dist. by UNIVERSAL PRESS SYNDICATE. Reprinted with permission. All rights reserved. 407: Figure 10.6: Data based on Masters, W. H., & Johnson, V. E., 1966, *Human Sexual Response.* Little Brown and Company. 409: Figure 10.10: From Schmitt, D. P., and 118 Members of the International Sexuality Descript Project (2003), "Universal sex differences in the desire for sexual variety: Tests from 52 nations, 6 continents, and 13 islands," *Journal of Personality and Social Psychology, 85,* 85–104. Copyright © 2003 by the American Psychological Association. Reprinted by permission of the author. 410: Cartoon Bizarro © 2001 Dan Piraro. Reprinted by permission of King Features Syndicate. 414: Figure 10.15 From Epstein, R. (2007) "Smooth thinking about sexuality," *Scientific American Mind, 18 (5)* October/November, p. 14. Copyright © 2007 by Robert Epstein. Reprinted by permission of the author. 418: Figure 10.18: Descriptions reprinted by permission of Dr. David McClelland. 428: Figure 10.26: Based on art in "A language for emotions," by R. Plutchik, 1980, *Psychology Today, 13 (9),* 68–78. Reprinted with permission from Psychology Today Magazine. Copyright © 1980 (Sussex Publishers, Inc.) 431: Cartoon © The New Yorker Collection 1987 Mischa Richter from the cartoonbank.com. All rights reserved. 432: Figure 10.29: Reproduced from "Marital status and Happiness," by David G. Myers. In *Well-Being, The Foundations of Hedonic Psychology,* edited by Daniel Kahneman, Ed Diener, and Norbert Schwarz . Copyright © 1999 Russell Sage Foundation, 112 East 64th Street, New York, NY 10021. Reprinted with permission. 434: Figure 10.31: From Halpern, D. F. (2003) *Thought & Knowledge: An Introduction to Critical Thinking,* p. 199, figure 5.1. Copyright © 2003 Lawrence Erlbaum Associates. Reprinted by permission of Lawrence Erlbaum Associates and the author.

Chapter 11. 443: Figure 11.2: Figure adapted from Moore, K. L., & Persaud, T. V. N (2008) *Before We Are Born: Essentials of Embryology and Birth Defects.* Copyright © 2008, 1998 Elsevier Science (USA). All rights reserved. Reprinted by permission of Elsevier Science. 450: Figure 11.5: Adapted from Shaver, P. R., & Hazan, C., "Attachment" (1994). In A. Weber and J. H. Harvey (Eds.), *Perspectives on close relationships.* Copyright © 1994 by Allyn and Bacon. Reprinted by permission. 458: Figure 11.12: From Wynn, K. "Addition and subtraction by human infants," (1992), *Nature, 358,* 749–750. Copyright © 1992 Macmillan Magazines, Ltd. Reprinted with permission from Nature and the author. 462: Cartoon NON SEQUITUR © 2002 by Wiley Miller. Dist. by UNIVERSAL PRESS SYNDICATE. Reprinted with permission. All rights reserved. 465: Cartoon ZITS by Scott and Borgman. © 2008 by ZITS Partnership, King Features Syndicate, Inc. Reprinted by permission. 465: Figure 11.18 Adapted from Steinberg, L., (2007), "Risk taking in adolescence: New perspectives from brain and behavioral science," *Current Directions in Psychological Science, 16,* 55–59. Copyright © 2007 Blackwell Publishing 467: Figure 11.20: Adapted from "Identity in adolescence," by J. E. Marcia, 1980. In J. Adelson (Ed.), *Handbook of Adolescent Psychology,* pp. 159–210. Copyright © 1980 by John Wiley & Sons, Inc. Adapted by permission of John Wiley & Sons, Inc. 468: Figure 11.21: From Arnett, J. J. (2006), "Emerging adulthood: Understanding the new way of coming of age. In J. J. Arnett & J. L. Tanner (Eds.), *Emerging adults in America: Coming of Age in the 21st Century.* Copyright © 2006 by the American Psychological Association. Reprinted by permission of the author. 469: Figure 11.22 From Roberts, B. W. & Mroczek, D., (2008), "Personality trait change in adulthood," *Current Directions in Psychological Science, 17,* 31–35.–59. Copyright © 2008 Blackwell Publishing. Reprinted by permission. 473: Figure 11.25: From Schaie, K. W. (1990) "Intellectual development in adulthood," In J. E. Birren and K. W. Schaie (Eds.), *Handbook of the Psychology of Aging, 3rd ed.* pp. 291–309. Copyright © 1990 Elsevier Science (USA), reproduced with permission from the publisher. 480: Table 11.1: Adapted from Ruble, T. L. (1983) "Sex stereotypes: Issues of change in the 70s," *Sex Roles, 9,* 397–402. Copyright © 1983 Plenum Publishing Group. Adapted by permission. With kind permission of Springer Science and Business Media.

Chapter 12. 491: Figure 12.1: Adapted from McCrae R. R., and Costa, P. T. (1986), "Clinical assessment can benefit from recent advances in personality psychology," *American Psychologist, 41,* 1001–1003. 496: bottom, Cartoon © 2004 by Sidney Harris/Science Cartoons Plus, com. 511: Figure 12.12: Adapted from Potkay, C. R., & Allen, B. P. (1986), *Personality Theory, Research and Application,* p. 246. Brooks/Cole Publishing Company. Copyright © 1986 by C. R. Potkay & Bem Allen. Adapted by permission of the author. 512: bottom, Cartoon © PEANUTS reprinted by permission of United Feature Syndicate, Inc. 514: Figure 12.13: From Eysenck, H. J. (1976) *The Biological Basis of Personality, 1st Ed.,* p. 36. Courtesy of Charles C. Thomas, Publisher, Springfield, Illinois. Reprinted by permission of the publisher. 523: Figure 12.17: Adapted from Markus, H. R., & Kitayama, S. (1991) "Culture and the self: Implications for cognition, emotion, and motivation," *Psychological Review, 98,* 224–253. Copyright © 1991 by the American Psychological Association. Adapted by permission of the author. 526: Figure 12.20: From R. B. Cattell in "Personality pinned down," *Psychology Today (July) 1973,* 40–46. Reprinted by permission from Psychology Today Magazine. Copyright © 1973 (Sussex Publishers,Inc.).

Chapter 13. 538: Table 13.1: Reprinted with permission from *Journal of Psychosomatic Research, 11,* 213–218, by T. H. Holmes and R. Rahe in "The Social Readjustment Rating Scale,"

Integrated Coverage of Evolutionary Psychology

Emergence of evolutionary psychology as a major theory, pp. 15–16

Evolutionary basis of gender differences in spatial skills, pp. 34–35

Overview of Darwin's original theory and key concepts, pp. 116–117

Further refinements to evolutionary theory, including inclusive fitness, pp. 117–118

Evolutionary bases of selected animal behaviors, pp. 118–119

Evolutionary significance of sensory adaptation, p. 134

Evolutionary significance of color vision, p. 143

Evolution and perception of geographical slant, pp. 156

Evolution and gender differences in taste sensitivity, p. 167

Evolutionary roots of consciousness, p. 187

Evolutionary bases of sleep, p. 197

Evolution and classical conditioning of sexual arousal, p. 236

Evolutionary significance of conditioned taste aversion, p. 255

Evolution, preparedness, and an evolved module for fear learning, pp. 255–256

Evolution and species-specific learning propensities, p. 256

Evolutionary significance of ecologically relevant conditioned stimuli, p. 256

Language in evolutionary context, p. 325

Evolutionary analysis of error and bias in decision making, pp. 343–344

Evolutionary basis of fast and frugal heuristics in decision making, p. 344

Evolutionary approach to motivation, pp. 397–398

Evolutionary explanation of increasing prevalence of obesity, p. 404

Implications of parental investment theory for human sexual behavior, p. 408

Evolution and gender differences in sexual activity, pp. 408–409

Evolutionary basis of mating priorities, pp. 410–411

Evolution and women's instant judgments of men's mate potential, pp. 411–412

Critique of evolutionary analyses of human sexual behavior, p. 412

Evolutionary theories of emotion, pp. 427–428

Evolutionary perspective on innate cognitive abilities, p. 460

Evolutionary approach to explaining gender differences in human abilities, p. 481

Evolutionary basis of Big-Five personality traits, pp. 515–516

Problem of hindsight in evolutionary analyses of personality, p. 529

Evolutionary basis of fight-or-flight response, p. 542

Evolution, preparedness, and phobias, p. 585

Evolutionary explanations of bias in person perception, p. 667

Evolutionary analyses of how aspects of physical appearance influence reproductive fitness, p. 679

Evolutionary basis of mate-attraction tactics, p. 679

Evolutionary basis of gender differences in the perception of sexual interest and relationship commitment, p. 680

Evolutionary analysis of mate poaching, p. 680

Integrated Coverage of Cultural Factors

Increased interest in cultural diversity, pp. 14–15

Introduction of theme: Behavior is shaped by cultural heritage, pp. 25–26

Cultural variations in the pace of life, pp. 51–52

Culture and depth perception, p. 154

Cultural variations in susceptibility to illusions, pp. 159–160

Cultural variations in taste preferences, p. 166

Cultural variations in pain tolerance, p. 170

Culture and napping and cosleeping, pp. 193, 195–196

Cultural variance and invariance in patterns of sleep, pp. 193, 195

Cultural variations in the significance of dreams, p. 206

Cultural similarities in the pace of language development, p. 326

Effects of bilingualism, pp. 323–324

Linguistic relativity hypothesis, pp. 327–328

Cultural variations in cognitive style, p. 336

IQ testing in non-Western cultures, pp. 368–369

Cultural and ethnic differences in IQ scores, pp. 377–382

Stereotype vulnerability and ethnic differences in IQ scores, pp. 380–381

Cultural bias in IQ testing, pp. 381–382

Culture and food preferences, p. 402

Cross-cultural similarity of mating preferences, pp. 410–411

Cultural similarities in expressive aspects of emotions, pp. 423–424

Cultural variations in categories of emotions, display rules, p. 425

Culture and motor development, p. 446

Culture and patterns of attachment, p. 451

Cross-cultural validity of Piaget's theory, p. 457

Cross-cultural validity of Kohlberg's theory, p. 462

Culture and the transition to adolescence, p. 463

(continues on following page)

(Cultural Factors continued)

Culture and modal personality, p. 519

Cross-cultural validity of the Big Five trait model, p. 519

Culture and independent versus interdependent views of self, p. 522

Culture and the concept of normality, p. 577

Relativistic versus pancultural view of psychological disorders, p. 610–611

Culture-bound disorders, p. 611

Culture and symptom patterns, p. 611

Cultural variations in existence of eating disorders, p. 614

Contribution of Western cultural values to eating disorders, p. 615

Western cultural roots of psychotherapy, p. 649

Barriers to the use of therapy by ethnic minorities, p. 650

Culture, collectivism, and individualism, p. 671

Culture and attributional bias, pp. 671–672

Cultural variations in romantic relationships, p. 677

Gender differences in mate preferences in relation to culture and history, p. 679

Cultural variations in conformity and obedience, pp. 691–692

Culture and social loafing, p. 696

Ethnic stereotypes and modern racism, pp. 700–701

Contribution of attribution bias to ethnic stereotypes, p. 702

Learning of ethnic stereotypes, p. 702

Outgroup homogeneity and ethnic stereotypes, p. 703

Realistic group conflict theory as an explanation for racial prejudice, pp. 702–703

Social identity perspective as a model of racial prejudice, p. 703

Integrated Coverage of Issues Related to Gender

Important women in the history of psychology, p. 6

Alternative explanations for gender differences in spatial skills, p. 35

Underrepresentation of females in research samples, p. 60

Possible neural bases for gender differences in responsiveness to visual sexual stimuli, p. 96

Association between sex and color blindness, p. 144

Gender gap among super-tasters, p. 167

Gender differences in dream content, p. 204

Frequency of childhood sexual abuse among men and women, p. 299

Steele's analysis of stereotype vulnerability in women, pp. 380–381

Gender and the heritability of weight, p. 404

Physiology of human sexual response in males and females, pp. 406–407

Sex differences in parental investment, p. 408

Gender differences in number of sexual partners, uncommitted sex, pp. 408–409

Reliance on self-report data may exaggerate gender differences in sexual motivation, p. 409

Gender differences in mating priorities, pp. 410–411

Gender differences in responsiveness to erotic materials, pp. 412–413

Possible link between aggressive pornography and sexual coercion by males, p. 413

Nature and prevalence of date rape, pp. 413–414

Prevalence of homosexuality among males and females, p. 415

Genetic influences on homosexuality in males and females, p. 415

Childhood masculinity and femininity in relation to development of homosexuality, p. 415

Possible link between prenatal exposure to hormone (DES) and lesbian sexual orientation, p. 416

Gender and the plasticity of sexual orientation, p. 416

Development of secondary sex characteristics in males and females, p. 463

Effects of early and late maturation in males and females, p. 464

Gender gap in marital role expectations, p. 470

Postpartum stress in women, p. 471

Mothers' adjustment to the empty nest, p. 471

Effects of menopause, p. 472

Nature of gender stereotypes, p. 480

Gender differences in cognitive abilities, p. 480

Gender differences in social behavior and personality, p. 480

Evolutionary explanations for gender differences, p. 481

Contribution of hormones to gender differences, p. 481

Brain organization and gender differences, pp. 481–482

Environmental processes contributing to gender differences, pp. 482–483

Sources of gender-role socialization, p. 483

Possible social ramifications of father absence, p. 484

Controversy regarding the effects of father absence, pp. 484–485

Concerns about possible sexist bias in Freudian theory, p. 502

Gender and the fight-or-flight response, p. 542

AIDS transmission in males and females, p. 560

Gender gap in the prevalence of panic disorder, p. 583

Gender gap in the prevalence of somatization disorder, p. 587

Gender gap in the prevalence of major depression, p. 592

Gender, depression, and rumination, p. 595

Gender disparities in various personality disorders, p. 605

Gender gap in the prevalence of antisocial personality disorder, p. 606

Gender gap in the prevalence of eating disorders, p. 614